PROSE
OF THE
BRITISH ROMANTIC MOVEMENT

PROSE

OF THE

BRITISH ROMANTIC MOVEMENT

EDITED BY

John R. Nabholtz

LOYOLA UNIVERSITY, CHICAGO

Macmillan Publishing Co., Inc.

NEW YORK

Collier Macmillan Limited

LONDON

MACMILLAN PUBLISHING CO., INC.
866 Third Avenue, New York, New York 10022

COLLIER-MACMILLAN CANADA, LTD., Toronto, Ontario

Library of Congress Cataloging in Publication Data

Nabholtz, John R.   comp.
    Prose of the British romantic movement.

    Bibliography: p. 815.
    1. English prose literature—19th century.
    2. English poetry—19th century—History and criticism.
    I. Title.
    PR1302.N3   828'.08   72-88811
    ISBN 0-02-385840-0

Printing: 1 2 3 4 5 6 7 8   Year: 4 5 6 7 8 9 0

ACKNOWLEDGMENTS

The editor makes grateful acknowledgment to the publishers and editors for permission to reprint the following selections:

BLAKE: *There is no Natural Religion* [first and second series]; *All Religions are One*; "To the Deists" and "To the Christians" from *Jerusalem*; Annotations to Reynolds' *Discourses* I, III, VI, VII; *A Descriptive Catalogue of Pictures*; A Vision of the Last Judgment; Annotations to *Poems by William Wordsworth* and *The Excursion*; Letters to Dr. Trusler (23 August 1799); William Hayley (6 May 1800); Thomas Butts (10 January 1802); Thomas Butts (25 April 1803); George Cumberland (12 April 1827). All from *The Complete Writings of William Blake*, edited by Geoffrey Keynes. Copyright © 1966 by Oxford University Press. Reprinted by permission of Oxford University Press.

COLERIDGE: *Essays on the Principles of Genial Criticism*, from *Biographia Literaria by S. T. Coleridge*, edited by J. Shawcross. Copyright 1907 by Oxford University Press. Reprinted by permission of The Clarendon Press, Oxford.

SOUTHEY: Passage from letter of Robert Southey to John Rickman (14 January 1820), from *New Letters of Robert Southey*, edited by Kenneth Curry. Copyright © 1965 by Columbia University Press, Ltd. Reprinted by permission of Columbia University Press.

LAMB: Footnote material to the essays: "On the Tragedies of Shakspeare," "Preface. By a Friend of the Late Elia," "The South-Sea House," "Oxford in the Vacation," "New Year's Eve," "Dream-Children," "On the Artificial Comedy of the Last Century," "Old China," "Blakesmoor in H——shire," "Stage Illusion," "Sanity of True Genius," "Barrenness of the Imaginative Faculty," from *Charles Lamb: Selected Essays*, edited by John R. Nabholtz. Copyright © 1967 by Meredith Publishing Company. Reprinted by permission of Appleton-Century-Crofts, Educational Division/Meredith Corporation.

HAZLITT: From the introduction by John R. Nabholtz to *An Essay on the Principles of Human Action* (*1805*) by William Hazlitt, 1969. Reprinted by permission of Scholars' Facsimiles and Reprints.

Footnote material to the essays: "On Gusto," "On Genius and Common Sense," "The Same Subject Continued," "On Going a Journey," "On Familiar Style," "Bentham," "Mr. Coleridge," "A Farewell to Essay Writing," from *William Hazlitt: Selected Essays*, edited by John R. Nabholtz. Copyright © 1970 by Meredith Corporation. Reprinted by permission of Appleton-Century-Crofts, Educational Division/Meredith Corporation.

DE QUINCEY: Material from *Thomas De Quincey, Literary Critic: His Method and Achievement* by John E. Jordan, University of California Press Publications in English Studies, Volume 4. Originally published by the University of California Press, 1952; reprinted by permission of the Regents of the University of California.

PEACOCK: *The Four Ages of Poetry*, from *Peacock's Four Ages of Poetry, Shelley's Defence of Poetry, Browning's Essay on Shelley*, edited by H. F. B. Brett-Smith, Percy Reprints Number 3, second edition, 1923. Copyright 1921 by Basil Blackwell Publishers. Reprinted by permission of Basil Blackwell Publishers.

BYRON: Selections from "Detached Thoughts" in *The Works of Lord Byron: Letters and Journals*, Volume V, edited by Rowland E. Prothero, 1922. Reprinted by permission of John Murray (Publishers) Ltd.

SHELLEY: *The Necessity of Atheism; A Refutation of Deism;* "Essay on Life"; "Essay on Love"; *A Philosophical View of Reform; A Defence of Poetry*, from *The Complete Works of Percy Bysshe Shelley*, the Julian Edition, edited by Roger Ingpen and Walter E. Peck, 10 volumes. Copyright 1927–1930 by Ernest Benn Limited. Reprinted by permission of Ernest Benn Limited.

KEATS: Letters to B. R. Haydon (10, 11 May 1817): Benjamin Bailey (22 November 1817); George and Tom Keats (21, 27 [?]

[iv]

1817); John Taylor (30 January 1818); J. H. Reynolds (3 February 1818); J. H. Reynolds (19 February 1818); John Taylor (27 February 1818); Benjamin Bailey (13 March 1818); J. H. Reynolds (3 May 1818); Tom Keats (25–27 June 1818); Richard Woodhouse (28 October 1818); George and Georgiana Keats (14 February–3 May 1819); Fanny Brawne (8 July 1819); Charles Brown (23 September 1819); Fanny Brawne (13 October 1819); John Taylor (17 November 1819); Georgiana Keats (13–28 January 1820); James Rice (14, 16 February 1820); Fanny Brawne (February [?] 1820); Fanny Brawne (August [?] 1820); Percy Bysshe Shelley (16 August 1820); Charles Brown (1 November 1820); Charles Brown (30 November 1820). Reprinted by permission of the publishers from Hyder Edward Rollins, editor, *The Letters of John Keats*, Volumes I and II, Cambridge, Mass.: Harvard University Press. Copyright 1958, by the President and Fellows of Harvard College.

Letters to Fanny Brawne: (1 July 1819), (25 July 1819), (February [?] 1820), and (5 July [?] 1820), from *The Letters of John Keats*, edited by Maurice Buxton Forman, fourth edition, 1952. Published by Oxford University Press.

Letters to John Taylor: (30 January 1818), (27 February 1818), and (17 November 1819). Reprinted by permission of the Pierpont Morgan Library.

Letter to Fanny Brawne (8 July 1819). Reprinted by permission of the Historical Society of Pennsylvania.

Letter to Fanny Brawne (13 October 1819). Reprinted by permission of the Library, Haverford College.

Letter to Georgiana Wylie Keats (13–28 January 1820). Reprinted by permission of the Library, The University of Texas at Austin.

Letter to Fanny Brawne (August [?] 1820). Reprinted by permission of The New York Public Library.

LOEB CLASSICAL LIBRARY: Passages from the following volumes of the Loeb Classical Library are reprinted with the permission of the Harvard University Press: *Aristophanes*, with an English translation by Benjamin Beckley Rogers, 1937; *Catullus, Tibullus and Pervigilium Veneris*, 1912; *Cicero. De Oratore, together with De Fato*, with an English translation by H. Rackham, 1942; *Euripides*, with an English translation by Arthur S. Way; *Hesiod. The Homeric Hymns and Homerica*, with an English translation by Hugh G. Evelyn-White, 1914; *Ovid*, with an English translation by A. L. Wheeler; *The Odes of Pindar*, with an English translation by Sir John Sandys, 1915; *Petronius*, with an English translation by Michael Heseltine, 1930; *Pliny. Letters*, with an English translation by William Melmoth, revised by W. M. L. Hutchinson, 1915; *Pliny. Letters and Panegyricus*, with an English translation by Betty Radice, 1969; *Pliny. Natural History*, with an English translation by H. Rackham, 1938; *Plotinus*, with an English translation by A. H. Armstrong, 1966; *Plutarch's Moralia*, with an English translation by Harold Cherniss and William C. Helmbold, 1957; *Seneca. Moral Essays*, with an English translation by John W. Basore; *Suetonius*, with an English translation by J. C. Rolfe; *Tacitus. The Annals*, with an English translation by John Jackson; *Virgil*, with an English translation by H. Rushton Fairclough, 1932.

PREFACE

THE present collection seeks to fulfil three purposes: (1) to bring together a full and representative selection of the prose writings of the major figures of English Romanticism; (2) to reproduce the writings, wherever possible, from original texts (usually the final text the author is known to have supervised in his lifetime),* silently correcting obvious misprints but retaining the original spelling and punctuation except in the few cases where such retention might confuse the modern reader; (3) to provide by way of headnotes and annotations such information or interpretative commentary as may be helpful to the student. My hope is that this collection will make apparent the richness and variety, in both form and content, of English Romantic prose, ranging from personal letters and political editorials to the most carefully crafted "modes of impassioned prose" and complex speculations on philosophy and religion. The prose of English Romanticism is more than a necessary supplement to the study of the poetry of the period; it is a challenging and rewarding discipline of its own. In these terms, I have tried to present works complete or in long excerpts, so that the reader can follow the total context and structure of subject and argument.

In preparing this collection, I have received assistance and encouragement from many sources, which are here gratefully acknowledged: at Macmillan Publishing Co., Inc., to Mr. Scott Bridge, who originally proposed the idea of a new anthology of English Romantic Prose; to Mr. D. Anthony English, editor of the College and Professional Division, who has offered help and counsel in the preparation of the manuscript; and particularly, to my production editor, Miss Frances Long, whose good judgment in problem solving and unfailing cooperation have made my final labors much easier than I had any right to expect; at Loyola University, to John Gerrietts, Chairman of the Department of English, who with characteristic generosity provided funds for the reproduction of material; to James Barry, Assistant Chairman, who arranged relief from some of my teaching duties when the tasks of completing this collection became burdensome; to Stanley Clayes of the Department of English, who offered shrewd advice at a difficult moment; to Edwin Menes of the Classics Department, who helped invaluably in tracking down elusive classical quotations and in translating Greek and Latin passages; to the Inter-library Loan Service of the Cudahy Memorial Library, for locating texts in other collections.

The annotations and headnotes to the texts are indebted to the work of previous editors and scholars. To the following I am especially obliged (specific titles are indicated in the separate Author Bibliographies): for BLAKE, G. E. Bentley, Jr.,

* At the end of each selection will be found, to the right, the date of publication of the text here followed. The appearance of an additional date to the left indicates the *initial* publication of the selection in the author's lifetime, if different from the date of the text here followed.

Harold Bloom, David V. Erdman, Geoffrey Keynes; for WORDSWORTH, Ernest De Sélincourt, Mary Moorman; for COLERIDGE, Kathleen Coburn, Earl Leslie Griggs, Peter Mann, Lewis Patton, Barbara Rooke; for SOUTHEY, Kenneth Curry, Jack Simmons; for LANDOR, R. H. Super; for HAZLITT, P. P. Howe; for LEIGH HUNT, A. S. Cook, L. H. and C. W. Houtchens, Louis Landré; for DE QUINCEY, H. A. Eaton, John E. Jordan, David Masson; for PEACOCK, H. F. B. Brett-Smith; for BYRON, Leslie Marchand, Rowland E. Prothero; for SHELLEY, Kenneth Neill Cameron, David Lee Clark, N. I. White; for KEATS, Hyder Rollins, Walter Jackson Bate; for THE REVIEWERS, Walter Graham, John O. Hayden, Hill Shine, and Helen Chadwick Shine.

J. R. N.

CONTENTS

ROBERT SOUTHEY
1774–1843

WALTER SAVAGE LANDOR
1775–1846

CONTENTS

William Blake

1757–1827

• OUTLINE OF EVENTS

1757   Born November 28, in London, third of the six children of James Blake (*c.* 1723–1784), hosier, and Catherine (Harmitage) (*c.* 1722–1792). At age four has vision of God looking at him through the window; at ages nine to eleven has vision of a "tree filled with angels, bright angelic wings bespangling every bough like stars."

1767   Is sent to drawing school.

1769   Begins to write the poems that appear in *Poetical Sketches* of 1783.

1772–79   Is apprenticed to the engraver James Basire; first engraving (Joseph of Arimathea) dates from 1773. By 1778, completes the poems that appear in *Poetical Sketches*. Does drawings of the monuments at Westminster Abbey; 1779, studies at the Royal Academy.

1780   Becomes acquainted with various artists: Thomas Stothard, George Cumberland, Henry Fuseli, and the sculptor John Flaxman.

1782   Marries Catherine Boucher (1762–1831).

1783   *Poetical Sketches* published with aid of John Flaxman.

1784   Opens print shop with James Parker, fellow-apprentice at Basire's.

1787   Death of brother Robert occasions vision of eternity. Through the bookseller Joseph Johnson, who has been employing him as an engraver of book illustrations, Blake associates with the political radicals Tom Paine, William Godwin, Mary Wollstonecraft, and Joseph Priestley.

1788   "Illuminated Printing" of the series of aphorisms *There is No Natural Religion* and *All Religions are One*. Becomes interested in the doctrines of Swedenborg.

1789   *Songs of Innocence* and *The Book of Thel* in illuminated printing.

1793   *Visions of the Daughters of Albion* and *America, a Prophecy* in illuminated printing.

1794   *Songs of Innocence and of Experience Shewing the Two Contrary States of the Human Soul, Europe* and *The First Book of Urizen* in illuminated printing.

1795   *The Book of Los, The Song of Los* and *The Book of Ahania* in illuminated printing. Probably begins composition of the major symbolic poem *Vala or The Four Zoas*.

1797   Edition of Young's *Night Thoughts* with engravings by Blake published. Comes under the patronage of his friend Thomas Butts.

1800–03   Lives at Felpham, Sussex, in association with the poet William Hayley. Makes illustrations for an edition of Cowper prepared by Hayley. Begins to prepare the symbolic poem *Milton*.

1804   Brought to trial and acquitted on charge of high treason for assault and "seditious words" against a soldier. Begins to compose the prophetic poem *Jerusalem*.

1808   Edition of Blair's *The Grave* with engravings from designs by Blake published, and hostilely reviewed by Robert Hunt in *The Examiner*.

1809   In May, major exhibition of Blake's pictures opens in his brother James's shop in London and is attacked by *The Examiner*.

1810–17 Period of obscurity.

1818   Finds friend and patron in the artist John Linnell, through whom he meets other artists and obtains commissions.

1822   Dramatic poem *The Ghost of Abel* is etched.

1826   *Illustrations of the Book of Job* issued.

1827   August 12, dies in London.

SELECTED BIBLIOGRAPHY

BIOGRAPHY

BENTLEY, G. E., JR., *Blake Records*, Oxford: Clarendon Press, 1969.

GILCHRIST, ALEXANDER, *Life of William Blake*, "*Pictor Ignotus*," 2 vols., London: Macmillan and Company, 1863.

WILSON, MONA, *The Life of William Blake*, new edition, edited by Geoffrey Keynes, London: Oxford University Press, 1971. [First published 1927.]

WRIGHT, THOMAS, *The Life of William Blake*, 2 vols., Olney, England: T. Wright, 1929.

EDITIONS

ERDMAN, DAVID V. (ed.), *The Poetry and Prose of William Blake*, Garden City, New York: Doubleday and Company, 1965. [Commentaries on the texts by Harold Bloom.]

KEYNES, GEOFFREY (ed.), *The Complete Writings of William Blake*, Oxford Standard Authors, London: Oxford University Press, 1966.

SCHOLARSHIP AND CRITICISM

DAMON, SAMUEL FOSTER, *William Blake, His Philosophy and Symbols*, London: Constable and Company, 1924.

———, *A Blake Dictionary; The Ideas and Symbols of William Blake*, Providence: Brown University Press, 1965.

ERDMAN, DAVID V., *Blake, Prophet Against Empire; a Poet's Interpretation of the History of His Own Times*, Princeton: Princeton University Press, 1954.

FRYE, NORTHROP, *Fearful Symmetry: A Study of William Blake*, Princeton: Princeton University Press, 1947.

HAGSTRUM, JEAN H., *William Blake: Poet and Painter*, Chicago: University of Chicago Press, 1964.

MURRY, J. MIDDLETON, *William Blake*, London: Jonathan Cape, 1933.

SAURAT, DENIS, *Blake and Modern Thought*, London: Constable and Company, 1929.

SWINBURNE, ALGERNON CHARLES, *William Blake, A Critical Study*, London: J. C. Hotten, 1868. [Reprinted in modern edition by Hugh J. Luke, Lincoln, Neb.: University of Nebraska Press, 1970.]

YEATS, WILLIAM BUTLER, *Ideas of Good and Evil*, London: A. H. Bullen, 1903.

THREE TRACTATES

The two series of "There Is No Natural Religion" and a third tractate "All Religions Are One" are a summary of many of Blake's key beliefs. The two series against "Natural Religion" (the Deistic beliefs based on reason and experience rather than revelation) exalt the primacy of the poetic and imaginative faculty as the instrument of true knowledge and religion over the testimony of sensible knowledge and the "ratio," the man-made abstraction of sensible knowledge by which scientific study is conducted. On the difficult V–VII propositions of the second series, Harold Bloom has written: "The possessed are bounded, and 'the bounded is loathed by its possessor.' More! is a mistaken cry, for only the unbounded infinite can satisfy a fully human desire. To see the infinite in all things is to see God because it is to see as God sees, which Blake believes is the only way to see God. But to see as God sees, man must himself be infinite, a state to be attained only by the individual utterly possessed by the Poetic Character" (The Poetry and Prose of William Blake, edited by David V. Erdman [Garden City, New York: Doubleday and Company, 1965], p. 807). In the third tractate, Blake describes "the Poetical Character" as both the generative source of the human form and as "the True Man," the spokesman through all cultures and tongues of the one true religion. For further discussion, see J. Middleton Murry, William Blake (London: Jonathan Cape, 1933), pp. 13–29.

The texts of the three tractates, as of all of Blake's prose in this anthology, are reprinted from Geoffrey Keynes's edition of The Complete Writings of William Blake, *Oxford Standard Authors, London: Oxford University Press, 1966.*

Three Tractates

THERE IS NO NATURAL RELIGION

[FIRST SERIES]

Etched about 1788

The Argument. Man has no notion of moral fitness but from Education. Naturally he is only a natural organ subject to Sense.

I. Man cannot naturally Percieve but through his natural or bodily organs.

II. Man by his reasoning power can only compare & judge of what he has already perciev'd.

III. From a perception of only 3 senses or 3 elements none could deduce a fourth or fifth.

IV. None could have other than natural or organic thoughts if he had none but organic perceptions.

V. Man's desires are limited by his perceptions, none can desire what he has not perciev'd.

VI. The desires & perceptions of man, untaught by any thing but organs of sense, must be limited to objects of sense.

Conclusion. If it were not for the Poetic or Prophetic character the Philosophic & Experimental would soon be at the ratio of all things, & stand still, unable to do other than repeat the same dull round over again.

THERE IS NO NATURAL RELIGION

[SECOND SERIES]

Etched about 1788

I. Man's perceptions are not bounded by organs of perception; he percieves more than sense (tho' ever so acute) can discover.

II. Reason, or the ratio of all we have already known, is not the same that it shall be when we know more.

III. [*This proposition has been lost.*]

IV. The bounded is loathed by its possessor. The same dull round, even of a universe, would soon become a mill with complicated wheels.

V. If the many become the same as the few when possess'd, More! More! is the cry of a mistaken soul; less than All cannot satisfy Man.

VI. If any could desire what he is incapable of possessing, despair must be his eternal lot.

VII. The desire of Man being Infinite, the possession is Infinite & himself Infinite.

Application. He who sees the Infinite in all things, sees God. He who sees the Ratio only, sees himself only.

Therefore God becomes as we are, that we may be as he is.

ALL RELIGIONS are ONE

Etched about 1788

The Voice of one crying in the Wilderness

The Argument. As the true method of knowledge is experiment, the true faculty of knowing must be the faculty which experiences. This faculty I treat of.

PRINCIPLE 1st. That the Poetic Genius is the true Man, and that the body or outward form of Man is derived from the Poetic Genius. Likewise that the forms of all things are derived from their Genius, which by the Ancients was call'd an Angel & Spirit & Demon.

PRINCIPLE 2d. As all men are alike in outward form, So (and with the same infinite variety) all are alike in the Poetic Genius.

PRINCIPLE 3d. No man can think, write, or speak from his heart, but he must intend truth. Thus all sects of Philosophy are from the Poetic Genius adapted to the weaknesses of every individual.

PRINCIPLE 4th. As none by travelling over known lands can find out the unknown, So from already acquired knowledge Man could not acquire more: therefore an universal Poetic Genius exists.

PRINCIPLE 5th. The Religions of all Nations are derived from each Nation's different reception of the Poetic Genius, which is every where call'd the Spirit of Prophecy.

PRINCIPLE 6th. The Jewish & Christian Testaments are An original derivation from the Poetic Genius; this is necessary from the confined nature of bodily sensation.

PRINCIPLE 7th. As all men are alike (tho' infinitely various), So all Religions &, as all similars, have one source.

The true Man is the source, he being the Poetic Genius.

[1788]   [1966]

────

JERUSALEM

Blake began his major prophetic poem Jerusalem *in 1804, but it was probably not completed before 1815. The addresses "To the Deists" and "To the Christians" occur at the start of Chapters 3 and 4. Harold Bloom explains that in the first of these Blake is referring to "a Church of England that had covertly assimilated many Deist attitudes." "Primarily, he means Rahab, the Eternal State Religion, the organized violence carried out in the names of Jesus and Jehovah. Blake's defense of 'a Monk or a Methodist' here certainly does not mean that he was in full sympathy with either figure, but only that he was resolved to defend Enthusiasm or even superstition against every 'enlightened' attack, for Enthusiasm was an analogy of his own imaginative stance"* (Erdman edition, p. 855).

────

F R O M

JERUSALEM

Rahab is an Eternal State.	To the Deists	The Spiritual States of the Soul are all Eternal. Distinguish between the Man & his present State.

He never can be a Friend to the Human Race who is the Preacher of Natural Morality or Natural Religion; he is a flatterer who means to betray, to perpetuate Tyrant Pride & the Laws of that Babylon which he Foresees shall shortly be destroyed, with the Spiritual and not the Natural Sword. He is in the State named Rahab, which State must be put off before he can be the Friend of Man.

You, O Deists, profess yourselves the Enemies of Christianity, and you are so: you are also the Enemies of the Human Race & of Universal Nature. Man is born a Spectre or Satan & is altogether an Evil, & requires a New Selfhood continually, & must continually be changed into his direct Contrary. But your Greek Philosophy (which is a remnant of Druidism) teaches that Man is Righteous in his Vegetated Spectre: an Opinion of fatal & accursed consequence to Man, as the Ancients saw plainly by Revelation, to the intire abrogation of Experimental Theory; and many believed what they saw and Prophecied of Jesus.

Man must & will have Some Religion: if he has not the Religion of Jesus, he will have the Religion of Satan & will erect the Synagogue of Satan, calling the Prince of this World, God, and destroying all who do not worship Satan under the Name of God. Will any one say, "Where are those who worship Satan under the Name of God?" Where are they? Listen! Every Religion that Preaches Vengeance for Sin is the Religion of the Enemy & Avenger and not of the Forgiver of Sin, and their God is Satan, Named by the Divine Name. Your Religion, O Deists! Deism, is the Worship of the God of this World by the means of what you call Natural Religion and Natural Philosophy, and of Natural Morality or Self-Righteousness, the Selfish Virtues of the Natural Heart. This was the Religion of the Pharisees who murder'd Jesus. Deism is the same & ends in the same.

Voltaire, Rousseau, Gibbon, Hume, charge the Spiritually Religious with Hypocrisy; but how a Monk, or a Methodist either, can be a Hypocrite, I cannot concieve. We are Men of like passions with others & pretend not to be holier than others; therefore, when a Religious Man falls into Sin, he ought not to be call'd a Hypocrite; this title is more properly to be given to a Player who falls into Sin, whose profession is Virtue & Morality & the making Men Self-Righteous. Foote in calling Whitefield,[1] Hypocrite, was himself one; for Whitefield pretended not to be holier than others, but confessed his Sins before all the World. Voltaire! Rousseau! You cannot escape my charge that you are Pharisees & Hypocrites, for you are constantly talking of the Virtues of the Human Heart and particularly of your own, that you may accuse others, & especially the Religious, whose errors you, by this display of pretended Virtue, chiefly design to expose. Rousseau thought Men Good by Nature: he found them Evil & found no friend. Friendship cannot exist without Forgiveness of Sins continually. The Book written by Rousseau call'd his

───

[1] George Whitefield (1714–1770), evangelical preacher and leading Methodist. Samuel Foote (1720–1777), the actor and dramatist, had ridiculed Whitefield in his play *The Minor* (1760).

Confessions, is an apology & cloke for his sin & not a confession.

But you also charge the poor Monks & Religious with being the causes of War, while you acquit & flatter the Alexanders & Caesars, the Lewis's & Fredericks, who alone are its causes & its actors. But the Religion of Jesus, Forgiveness of Sin, can never be the cause of a War nor of a single Martyrdom.

Those who Martyr others or who cause War are Deists, but never can be Forgivers of Sin. The Glory of Christianity is To Conquer by Forgiveness. All the Destruction, therefore, in Christian Europe has arisen from Deism, which is Natural Religion.

To the Christians

| Devils are False Religions. | I give you the end of a golden string, Only wind it into a ball, |
| "Saul, Saul, "Why persecutest thou me?" | It will lead you in at Heaven's gate Built in Jerusalem's wall. |

We are told to abstain from fleshly desires that we may lose no time from the Work of the Lord: Every moment lost is a moment that cannot be redeemed; every pleasure that intermingles with the duty of our station is a folly unredeemable, & is planted like the seed of a wild flower among our wheat: All the tortures of repentance are tortures of self-reproach on account of our leaving the Divine Harvest to the Enemy, the struggles of intanglement with incoherent roots. I know of no other Christianity and of no other Gospel than the liberty both of body & mind to exercise the Divine Arts of Imagination, Imagination, the real & eternal World of which this Vegetable Universe is but a faint shadow, & in which we shall live in our Eternal or Imaginative Bodies when these Vegetable Mortal Bodies are no more. The Apostles knew of no other Gospel. What were all their spiritual gifts? What is the Divine Spirit? is the Holy Ghost any other than an Intellectual Fountain? What is the Harvest of the Gospel & its Labours? What is that Talent which it is a curse to hide? What are the Treasures of Heaven which we are to lay up for ourselves, are they any other than Mental Studies & Performances? What are all the Gifts of the Gospel, are they not all Mental Gifts? Is God a Spirit who must be worshipped in Spirit & in Truth, and are not the Gifts of the Spirit Every-thing to Man? O ye Religious, discountenance every one among you who shall pretend to despise Art & Science! I call upon you in the Name of Jesus! What is the Life of Man but Art & Science? is it Meat & Drink? is not the Body more than Raiment? What is Mortality but the things relating to the Body which Dies? What is Immortality but the things relating to the Spirit which Lives Eternally? What is the Joy of Heaven but Improvement in the things of the Spirit? What are the Pains of Hell but Ignorance, Bodily Lust, Idleness & devastation of the things of the Spirit? Answer this to yourselves, & expel from among you those who pretend to despise the labours of Art & Science, which alone are the labours of the Gospel. Is not this plain & manifest to the thought? Can you think at all & not pronounce heartily That to Labour in Knowledge is to Build up Jerusalem, and to Despise Knowledge is to Despise Jerusalem & her Builders. And remember: He who despises & mocks a Mental Gift in another, calling it pride & selfishness & sin, mocks Jesus the giver of every Mental Gift, which always appear to the ignorance-loving Hypocrite as Sins; but that which is a Sin in the sight of cruel Man is not so in the sight of our kind God. Let every Christian, as much as in him lies, engage himself openly & publicly before all the World in some Mental pursuit for the Building up of Jerusalem.

[1966]

ANNOTATIONS TO SIR JOSHUA REYNOLDS

Blake's annotations were written in a copy of the first volume of The Works of Sir Joshua Reynolds, Knight . . . and An Account of the Life and Writings of the Author, *by Edmund Malone, second edition, 1798. Although the usually accepted date is 1808, David Erdman suggests that the annotations could have been written any time between 1798 and 1809. Blake's comments are here printed in larger type; the remarks by Reynolds are printed in smaller type.*

Among the romantic prose writers, Blake was not alone in his objection to the aesthetic theories of the high priest of late eighteenth-century English art. Hazlitt repeatedly attacked Reynolds' notion of "general nature" and his slighting of the "particular." See his two essays "On Certain Inconsistencies in Sir Joshua Reynolds' Discourses," which appeared in the first volume of Table Talk *(1821).*

FROM

ANNOTATIONS TO *THE WORKS OF SIR JOSHUA REYNOLDS*

DISCOURSE I

Page 2.

I consider Reynolds's Discourses to the Royal Academy as the Simulations of the Hypocrite who smiles particularly where he means to Betray. His Praise of Rafael is like the Hysteric Smile of Revenge. His Softness & Candour, the hidden trap & the poisoned feast. He praises Michel Angelo for Qualities which Michel Angelo abhorr'd, & He blames Rafael for the only Qualities which Rafael Valued. Whether Reynolds knew what he was doing is nothing to me: the Mischief is just the same whether a Man does it Ignorantly or Knowingly. I always consider'd True Art & True Artists to be particularly Insulted & Degraded by the Reputation of these Discourses, As much as they were Degraded by the Reputation of Reynolds's Paintings, & that Such Artists as Reynolds are at all times Hired by the Satans for the Depression of Art—A Pretence of Art, To destroy Art.

Page 3.

The Neglect of Fuseli's Milton [1] in a Country pretending to the Encouragement of Art is a Sufficient Apology for My Vigorous Indignation, if indeed the Neglect of My own Powers had not been. Ought not the Employers of Fools to be Execrated in future Ages? They Will and Shall! Foolish Men, your own real Greatness depends on your Encouragement of the Arts, & your Fall will depend on [your *del.*] their Neglect & Depression. What you Fear is your true Interest. Leo X [2] was advised not to Encourage the Arts; he was too Wise to take this Advice.

Page 4.

The Rich Men of England form themselves into a Society to Sell & Not to Buy Pictures. The Artist who does not throw his Contempt on such Trading Exhibitions, does not know either his own Interest or his Duty.

When Nations grow Old, The Arts grow Cold
And Commerce settles on every Tree,
And the Poor & the Old can live upon Gold,
For all are Born Poor, Aged Sixty three.

Page 5.

Reynolds's Opinion was that Genius May be Taught & that all Pretence to Inspiration is a Lie & a Deceit, to say the least of it. For if it is a Deceit, the whole Bible is Madness. This Opinion originates in the Greeks' Calling the Muses Daughters of Memory.

---

[1] A Swiss-born artist and early friend and encourager of Blake, Henry Fuseli (1741–1825) opened a London gallery in 1799 to show forty pictures inspired by the works of Milton. The exhibition proved a failure and closed in two months. A second exhibition of the paintings the following year also failed.

[2] Leo X was pope from 1513 to 1521 and a great patron of art and learning in the Renaissance. He employed both Raphael and Michelangelo.

The Enquiry in England is not whether a Man has Talents & Genius, But whether he is Passive & Polite & a Virtuous Ass & obedient to Noblemen's Opinions in Art & Science. If he is, he is a Good Man. If Not, he must be Starved.

Page 7.

After so much has been done by His Majesty. . . .
; Farthings!

Page 9.

Raffaelle, it is true, had not the advantage of studying in an Academy; but all Rome, and the works of Michael Angelo in particular, were to him an Academy. On the sight of the Capella Sistina, he immediately from a dry, Gothick, and even insipid manner, which attends to the minute accidental discriminations of particular and individual objects, assumed that grand style of painting which improves partial representation by the general and invariable ideas of nature.

Minute Discrimination is Not Accidental. All Sublimity is founded on Minute Discrimination.
I do not believe that Rafael taught Mich. Angelo, or that Mich. Angelo taught Rafael, any more than I believe that the Rose teaches the Lilly how to grow, or the Apple tree teaches the Pear tree how to bear Fruit. I do not believe the tales of Anecdote writers when they militate against Individual Character.

Page 11.

I would chiefly recommend that an implicit obedience to the Rules of Art, as established by the practice of the great Masters should be exacted from the young Students. That those models, which have passed through the approbation of ages, should be considered by them as perfect and infallible guides; as subjects for their imitation, not their criticism.

Imitation is Criticism.

Page 13.

A facility in composing—a lively, and what is called a masterly handling of the chalk or pencil are . . . captivating qualities to young minds.

I consider The Following sentence is Supremely Insolent for the following Reasons:—Why this Sentence should be begun by the Words "A Facility in Composing" I cannot tell, unless it was to cast a stigma upon Real Facility in Composition by Assimilating it with a Pretence to, & Imitation of, Facility in Execution; or are we to understand him to mean that Facility in Composing is a Frivolous pursuit? A Facility in Composing is the Greatest Power of Art, & Belongs to None but the Greatest Artists and the Most Minutely Discriminating & Determinate.

Page 14.

By this useless industry they are excluded from all power of advancing in real excellence. Whilst boys, they are arrived at their utmost perfection; . . . and make the mechanical felicity the chief excellence of the art, which is only an ornament.

Mechanical Excellence is the Only Vehicle of Genius.

This seems to me to be one of the most dangerous sources of corruption . . . which has actually infected all foreign Academies. The directors . . . praised their dispatch at the expence of their correctness.

This is all False & Self-Contradictory.

But young men have not only this frivolous ambition of being thought masters of execution, inciting them on one hand, but also their natural sloth tempting them on the other.

Execution is the Chariot of Genius.

Page 15.
They wish to find some shorter path to excellence, . . . They must therefore be told again and again, that labour is the only price of solid fame, . . .

This is All Self-Contradictory, Truth & Falsehood Jumbled Together.

When we read the lives of the most eminent Painters, every page informs us that no part of their time was spent in dissipation . . . They pursued their studies . . .

The Lives of Painters say that Rafael Died of Dissipation. Idleness is one Thing & Dissipation Another. He who has Nothing to Dissipate Cannot Dissipate; the Weak Man may be Virtuous Enough, but will Never be an Artist.

Painters are noted for being Dissipated & Wild.

Page 16.
When they [the old masters] conceived a subject, they first made a variety of sketches, then a finished drawing of the whole; after that a more correct drawing of every separate part—heads, hands, feet, and pieces of drapery; they then painted the picture, *and after all re-touched it from life.*

This is False.

The Students instead of vying with each other which shall have the readiest hand, should be taught to contend who shall have the purest and most correct outline.

Excellent!

Page 17.
The error I mean is, that the students never draw exactly from the living models which they have before them. They make a drawing rather of what they think the figure ought to be, than of what it appears. I have thought this the obstacle that has stopped the progress of many young men . . . I very much doubt whether a habit of drawing correctly what we see, will not give a proportionable power of drawing correctly what we imagine.

This is Admirably Said. Why does he not always allow as much?

Page 18.
He who endeavours to copy nicely the figure before him, not only

acquires a habit of exactness and precision, but is continually advancing in his knowledge of the human figure.

Excellent!

Page 22.

The Labour'd Works of Journeymen employ'd by Correggio, Titian, Veronese & all the Venetians, ought not to be shewn to the Young Artist as the Works of original Conception any more than the Engravings of Strange, Bartollozzi, or Wollett.[3] They are Works of Manual Labour.

[3] Sir Robert Strange (1721–1792), Francesco Bartolozzi (1727–1815), and William Woollett (1735–1785) were leading late eighteenth-century engravers.

DISCOURSE III

Page 50.

A work of Genius is a Work "Not to be obtain'd by the "Invocation of Memory & her Syren Daughters, but "by Devout prayer to that Eternal Spirit, who can "enrich with all utterance & knowledge & sends out "his Seraphim with the hallowed fire of his Altar to "touch & purify the lips of whom he pleases."
MILTON.

The following [Lecture *del.*] Discourse is particularly Interesting to Block heads, as it Endeavours to prove That there is No such thing as Inspiration & that any Man of a plain Understanding may by Thieving from Others become a Mich. Angelo.

Page 58.
The wish of the genuine painter must be more extensive: instead of endeavouring to amuse mankind with the minute neatness of his imitations, he must endeavour to improve them by the grandeur of his ideas.

Without Minute Neatness of Execution The Sublime cannot Exist! Grandeur of Ideas is founded on Precision of Ideas.

Page 54.
The Moderns are not less convinced than the Ancients of this superior power existing in the art; nor less sensible of its effects.

I wish that this was True.

Page 55.
Such is the warmth with which both the Ancients and Moderns speak of this divine principle of the art;

And such is the Coldness with which Reynolds speaks! And such is his Enmity.

but, as I have formerly observed, enthusiastick admiration seldom promotes knowledge.

Enthusiastic Admiration is the first Principle of

Knowledge & its last. Now he begins to Degrade, to Deny & to Mock.

Though a student by such praise may have his attention roused ... *He examines* his own mind, and perceives there nothing of that divine inspiration, with which, he is told, so many others have been favoured.

The Man who on Examining his own Mind finds nothing of Inspiration ought not to dare to be an Artist; he is a Fool & a Cunning Knave suited to the Purposes of Evil Demons.

Page 56.

He never travelled to heaven to gather new ideas; and he finds himself possessed of no other qualifications than what mere common observation and a plain understanding can confer.

The Man who never in his Mind & Thoughts travel'd to Heaven Is No Artist.

Artists who are above a plain Understanding are Mock'd & Destroy'd by this President of Fools.

But on this, as upon many other occasions, we ought to distinguish how much is to be given to enthusiasm, and how much to reason ... taking care ... not to lose in terms of vague admiration, that solidity and truth of principle, upon which alone we can reason, and may be enabled to practise.

It is Evident that Reynolds Wish'd none but Fools to be in the Arts & in order to this, he calls all others Vague Enthusiasts or Madmen. What has Reasoning to do with the Art of Painting?

Page 57.

... most people err, not so much from want of capacity to find their object, as from not knowing what object to pursue.

The Man who does not know what Object to Pursue is an Idiot.

This great ideal perfection and beauty are not to be sought in the heavens, but upon the earth.

A Lie!

They are about us, and upon every side of us.

A Lie!

But the power of discovering what is deformed in nature, or in other words, what is particular and uncommon, can be acquired only by experience;

A Lie!

Page 58.

and the whole beauty of the art consists, in my opinion, in being able to get above all singular forms, local customs, particularities, and details of every kind.

A Folly! Singular & Particular Detail is the Foundation of the Sublime.

All the objects which are exhibited to our view by nature, upon close examination will be found to have their blemishes and defects. The most beautiful forms have something about them like weakness, minuteness, or imperfection.

Minuteness is their whole Beauty.

This long laborious comparison should be the first study of the painter, who aims at the greatest style ... he corrects nature by herself ... This idea of the perfect state of nature, which the Artist calls the Ideal Beauty, is the great leading principle by which works of genius are conducted.

Knowledge of Ideal Beauty is Not to be Acquired. It is Born with us. Innate Ideas are in Every Man, Born with him; they are truly Himself. The Man who says that we have No Innate Ideas must be a Fool & Knave, Having No Con-Science or Innate Science.

Page 60.

Thus it is from a reiterated experience and a close comparison of the objects in nature, that an artist becomes possessed of the idea of that central form ... from which every deviation is deformity.

One Central Form composed of all other Forms being Granted, it does not therefore follow that all other Forms are Deformity.

All Forms are Perfect in the Poet's Mind, but these are not Abstracted nor Compounded from Nature, but are from Imagination.

Page 61.

Even the great Bacon treats with ridicule the idea of confining proportion to rules, or of producing beauty by selection.

The Great Bacon—he is Call'd: I call him the Little Bacon—says that Every thing must be done by Experiment; his first principle is Unbelief, and yet here he says that Art must be produc'd Without such Method. He is Like Sr Joshua, full of Self-Contradiction & Knavery.

There is a rule, obtained out of general nature, to contradict which is to fall into deformity.

What is General Nature? is there Such a Thing? what is General Knowledge? is there such a Thing? Strictly Speaking All Knowledge is Particular.

Page 62.

To the principle I have laid down, that the idea of beauty in each species of beings is an invariable one, it may be objected, that in every particular species there are various central forms, which are separate and distinct from each other, and yet are each undeniably beautiful.

Here he loses sight of a Central Form & Gets into Many Central Forms.

Page 63.

It is true, indeed, that these figures are each perfect in their kind, though of different characters and proportions; but still none of them is the representation of an individual, but of a class.

Every Class is Individual.

Thus, though the forms of childhood and age differ exceedingly, there is a common form in childhood, and a common form in age, which is the more perfect, as it is more remote from all peculiarities.

There is no End to the Follies of this Man. Childhood & Age are Equally belonging to Every Class.

. . . though the most perfect forms of each of the general divisions of the human figure are ideal . . . yet the highest perfection of the human figure is not to be found in any one of them. It is not in the Hercules, nor in the Gladiator, nor in the Apollo.

Here he comes again to his Central Form.

Page 64.

There is, likewise, a kind of symmetry, or proportion, which may properly be said to belong to deformity. A figure lean or corpulent, tall or short, though deviating from beauty, may still have a certain union of the various parts.

The Symmetry of Deformity is a Pretty Foolery. Can any Man who Thinks Talk so ? Leanness or Fatness is not Deformity, but Reynolds thought Character Itself Extravagance & Deformity. Age & Youth are not Classes, but [Situations *del.*] Properties of Each Class; so are Leanness & Fatness.

Page 65.

When the Artist has by diligent attention acquired a clear and distinct idea of beauty and symmetry; when he has reduced the variety of nature to the abstract idea . . .

What Folly!

Page 67.

. . . the painter . . . must divest himself of all prejudices in favour of his age or country; he must disregard all local and temporary ornaments, and look only on those general habits, which are every where and always the same . . .

Generalizing in Every thing, the Man would soon be a Fool, but a Cunning Fool.

Page 71.

Albert Durer, as Vasari has justly remarked, would, probably, have been one of the first painters of his age . . . had he been initiated into those great principles of the art, which were so well understood and practised by his contemporaries in Italy.

What does this mean, "*Would have been*" *one of the first Painters of his Age*? Albert Durer *Is*, Not would have been. Besides, let them look at Gothic Figures & Gothic Buildings & not talk of Dark Ages or of any Age. Ages are all Equal. But Genius is Always Above The Age.

Page 74.

I should be sorry, if what is here recommended, should be at all understood to countenance a careless or indetermined manner of painting. For though the painter is to overlook the accidental discriminations of nature, he is to exhibit distinctly, and with precision, the general forms of things.

Here he is for Determinate & yet for Indeterminate. Distinct General Form Cannot Exist. Distinctness is Particular, Not General.

Page 75.

A firm and determined outline is one of the characteristics of the great style in painting; and let me add, that he who possesses the knowledge of the exact form which every part of nature ought to have, will be fond of expressing that knowledge with correctness and precision in all his works.

A Noble Sentence!

Here is a Sentence, Which overthrows all his Book.

To conclude; I have endeavoured to reduce the idea of beauty to general principles.

[Sir Joshua proves *del.*] that Bacon's Philosophy makes both Statesmen & Artists Fools & Knaves.

DISCOURSE VI

Page 144.

Imitation.—Genius begins where rules end.—Invention;—Acquired by being conversant with the inventions of others.—The true method of imitating . . .

When a Man talks of Acquiring Invention & of learning how to produce Original Conception, he must expect to be call'd a Fool by Men of Understanding; but such a Hired Knave cares not for the Few. His Eye is on the Many, or, rather, on the Money.

Page 147.

Those who have undertaken to write on our art, and have represented it as a kind of inspiration . . . seem to insure a much more favourable disposition from their readers . . . than he who attempts to examine, coldly, whether there are any means by which this art may be acquired . . .

Bacon's Philosophy has Destroy'd [*word cut away*] Art & Science. The Man who says that the Genius is not born, but Taught—Is a Knave.

O Reader, behold the Philosopher's Grave!
He was born quite a Fool, but he died quite a Knave.

Page 149.

. . . to owe nothing to another, is the praise which men . . . bestow sometimes upon others; and sometimes on themselves; and their imaginary dignity is naturally heightened by a supercilious censure of . . . the servile imitator.

How ridiculous it would be to see the Sheep Endeavouring to walk like the Dog, or the Ox striving to trot like the Horse; just as Ridiculous it is to see One Man Striving to Imitate Another. Man varies from Man more than Animal from Animal of different Species.

Page 152.

But the truth is, that the degree of excellence which proclaims

Genius is different, in different times and different places; and
what shews it to be so is, that mankind have often changed their
opinion upon this matter.

Never, Never!

Page 153.

These excellencies were, heretofore, considered merely as the
effects of genius; and justly, if genius is not taken for inspiration,
but as the effect of close observation and experience.

Damn'd Fool!

Page 154.

He who first made any of these observations . . . had that merit,
but probably no one went very far at once . . . others worked
more and improved further . . .

If Art was Progressive We should have had Mich.
Angelos & Rafaels to Succeed & to Improve upon each
other. But it is not so. Genius dies with its Possessor &
comes not again till Another is Born with It.

Page 155.

It must of necessity be, that even works of Genius, like every other
effect, as they must have their cause, must likewise have their
rules.

Identities or Things are Neither Cause nor Effect.
They are Eternal.

Page 157.

. . . our minds should be habituated to the contemplation of
excellence . . . we should to the last moment of our lives continue
a settled intercourse with all the true examples of grandeur. Their
inventions are not only the food of our infancy, but the substance
which supplies the fullest maturity of our vigour.

Reynolds Thinks that Man Learns all that he knows.
I say on the Contrary that Man Brings All that he has
or can have Into the World with him. Man is Born Like
a Garden ready Planted & Sown. This World is too
poor to produce one Seed.

The mind is but a barren soil; a soil which is soon exhausted, and
will produce no crop, . . .

The mind that could have produced this Sentence must
have been a Pitiful, a Pitiable Imbecillity. I always
thought that the Human Mind was the most Prolific of
All Things & Inexhaustible. I certainly do Thank God
that I am not like Reynolds.

Page 158.

. . . or only one, unless it be continually fertilized and enriched
with foreign matter.

Nonsense!

Page 159.

It is vain for painters or poets to endeavour to invent without
materials on which the mind may work. . . . Nothing can come of
nothing.

Is the Mind Nothing?

. . . we are certain that Michael Angelo, and Raffaelle, were
equally possessed of all the knowledge in the art which had been
discovered in the works of their predecessors.

If so they knew all that Titian & Correggio knew.
Correggio was two years older than Mich. Angelo.
Correggio born 1472, Mich. Angelo born 1474.

Page 161.

. . . it is not to be understood, that I advise any endeavour to copy
the exact peculiar colour and complexion of another man's
mind. . . . His model may be excellent but the copy will be
ridiculous.

Why then Imitate at all?

Page 163.

Art in its perfection is not ostentatious; it lies hid, and works
its effect, itself unseen. It is the proper study and labour of an
artist to uncover and find out the latent cause of conspicuous
beauties . . .

This is a Very Clever Sentence; who wrote it, God
knows.

Page 165.

Peculiar marks, I hold to be, generally, if not always, defects; . . .

Peculiar Marks are the Only Merit.

Peculiarities in the works of art, are like those in the human
figure . . . they are always so many blemishes;

Infernal Falshood!

Page 166.

Even the great name of Michael Angelo may be used, to keep in
countenance a deficiency or rather neglect of colouring, and every
other ornamental part of the art.

No Man who can see Michael Angelo can say that he
wants either Colouring or Ornamental parts of Art in
the highest degree, for he has Every Thing of Both.

Page 167.

. . . there is no defect that may not be excused, if it is a sufficient
excuse that it can be imputed to considerable artists; . . .

He who Admires Rafael Must admire Rafael's Execution. He who does not admire Rafael's Execution Cannot Admire Rafael.

Page 172.

. . . want of strength of parts. In this certainly men are not
equal . . .

A Confession!

Page 176.

In order to encourage you to imitation, to the utmost extent, let
me add, that the very finished artists in the inferior branches of
the art, will contribute to furnish the mind and give hints . . .

This Sentence is to Introduce another in Condemnation & Contempt of Alb. Durer.

The works of Albert Durer, Lucas Van Leyden, the numerous inventions of Tobias Stimmer, and Jost Ammon, afford a rich mass of genuine materials . . .

A Polish'd Villain who Robs & Murders!

Page 178.

The greatest style, if that style is confined to small figures, . . . would receive an additional grace by the elegance and precision of pencil so admirable in the works of Teniers . . .

What does Precision of Pencil mean? If it does not mean Outline, it means Nothing.

Page 179.

Jan Steen seems to be one of the most diligent and accurate observers . . . if [he] . . . had been blessed with Michael Angelo and Raffaelle for his masters . . . he now would have ranged with the great pillars and supporters of our Art.

Jan Steen was a Boor, & neither Rafael nor Mich. Ang. could have made him any better.

Page 180.

Men who although thus bound down by the almost invincible powers of early habits have still exerted extraordinary abilities . . . and have . . . given . . . great force and energy to their works . . .

He who can be bound down is No Genius. Genius cannot be Bound; it may be Render'd Indignant & Outrageous.

   "Opression makes the Wise Man Mad."

           SOLOMON.

DISCOURSE VII

Page 188.

The Purpose of the following discourse is to Prove That Taste & Genius are not of Heavenly Origin & that all who have supposed that they Are so, are to be Consider'd as Weak headed Fanatics.
The Obligations Reynolds has laid on Bad Artists of all Classes will at all times make them his Admirers, but most especially for this discourse, in which it is proved that the Stupid are born with Faculties Equal to other Men, Only they have not Cultivated them because they thought it not worth the trouble.

Page 194.

We will allow a poet to express his meaning, when his meaning is not well known to himself, with a certain degree of obscurity, as it is one source of the sublime.

Obscurity is Neither the Source of the Sublime nor of any Thing Else.

But when, in plain prose, we gravely talk of courting the muse in shady bowers; waiting the call and inspiration of Genius . . .; of attending to times and seasons when the imagination shoots with greatest vigour, . . . sagaciously observing how much the wild

freedom and liberty of imagination is cramped by attention to established rules . . . we at best entertain notions not only groundless but pernicious.

The Ancients & the wisest of the Moderns were of the opinion that Reynolds condemns & laughs at.

Page 195.

. . . scarce a poet is to be found . . . who . . . continued practising his profession to the very last, whose latter works are not as replete with the fire of imagination, as those which were produced in his more youthful days.

As Replete, but Not More Replete.

To understand literally these metaphors or ideas expressed in poetical language, seems to be equally absurd as to conclude . . .

The Ancients did not mean to Impose when they affirm'd their belief in Vision & Revelation. Plato was in Earnest: Milton was in Earnest. They believ'd that God did Visit Man Really & Truly & not as Reynolds pretends.

Page 196.

. . . that because painters sometimes represent poets writing from the dictates of a little winged boy or genius, that this same genius really did inform him in a whisper what he was to write; and that he is himself but a mere machine, unconscious of the operations of his own mind.

How very Anxious Reynolds is to Disprove & Contemn Spiritual Perception!

Page 197.

It is supposed . . . that under the name of genius great works are produced, and under the name of taste an exact judgement given, without our knowing why . . .

Who Ever said this?

One can scarce state these opinions without exposing their absurdity . . .

He states Absurdities in Company with Truths & calls both Absurd.

Page 198.

. . . I am persuaded, that even among those few who may be called thinkers, the prevalent opinion allows less than it ought to the powers of reason . . .

The Artifice of the Epicurean Philosophers is to Call all other Opinions Unsolid & Unsubstantial than those which are derived from Earth.

We often appear to differ in Sentiments from each other, merely from the inaccuracy of terms.

It is not in Terms that Reynolds & I disagree. Two Contrary Opinions can never by any Language be made alike. I say, Taste & Genius are Not Teachable or Acquirable, but are born with us. Reynolds says the Contrary.

Page 199.

We apply the term TASTE to that act of the mind by which we like or dislike, whatever be the subject. . . . We are obliged to take words as we find them; all we can do is to distinguish the THINGS to which they are applied.

This is False; the Fault is not in Words, but in Things. Locke's Opinions of Words & their Fallaciousness are Artful Opinions & Fallacious also.

Page 200.

It is the very same taste which relishes a demonstration in geometry, that is pleased with the resemblance of a picture to an original, and touched with the harmony of musick.

Demonstration, Similitude & Harmony are Objects of Reasoning. Invention, Identity & Melody are Objects of Intuition.

Page 201.

Colouring is true . . . from brightness, from softness, from harmony, from resemblance; because these agree with their object, NATURE, and therefore are true; as true as mathematical demonstration; . . .

God forbid that Truth should be Confined to Mathematical Demonstration!

But beside real, there is also apparent truth, or opinion, or prejudice. With regard to real truth, when it is known, the taste which conforms to it, is, and must be, uniform.

He who does not Know Truth at Sight is unworthy of Her Notice.

In proportion as these prejudices are known to be generally diffused . . . the taste which conforms to them approaches nearer to certainty, . . .

Here is a great deal to do to Prove that All Truth is Prejudice, for All that is Valuable in Knowledge is Superior to Demonstrative Science, such as is Weighed or Measured.

Page 202.

As these prejudices become more narrow, . . . this secondary taste becomes more and more fantastical; . . .

And so he thinks he has proved that Genius & Inspiration are All a Hum.

Having laid down these positions, I shall proceed with less method . . .

He calls the Above proceeding with Method!

We will take it for granted, that reason is something invariable and fixed in the nature of things; . . .

Reason, or A Ratio of All we have Known, is not the Same it shall be when we know More; he therefore takes a Falshood for granted to set out with.

Page 203.

. . . we will conclude, that whatever goes under the name of

taste, which we can fairly bring under the dominion of reason must be considered as equally exempt from change.

Now this is Supreme Fooling.

The arts would lie open for ever to caprice and casualty, if those who are to judge of their excellencies had no settled principles by which they are to regulate their decisions, . . .

He may as well say that if Man does not lay down settled Principles, The Sun will not rise in a Morning.

Page 204.

My notion of nature comprehends not only the forms which nature produces, but also the nature and internal fabrick and organization . . . of the human mind and imagination.

Here is a Plain Confession that he Thinks Mind & Imagination not to be above the Mortal & Perishing Nature. Such is the End of Epicurean or Newtonian Philosophy; it is Atheism.

Page 208.

This [Poussin's Perseus and Medusa's head] is undoubtedly a subject of great bustle and tumult, and that the first effect of the picture may correspond to the subject, every principle of composition is violated; . . . I remember turning from it with disgust . . .

Reynolds's Eye could not bear Characteristic Colouring or Light & Shade.

This conduct of Poussin I hold to be entirely improper to imitate. A picture should please at first sight, and appear to invite the spectator's attention; . . .

Please Whom? Some Men cannot see a Picture except in a Dark Corner.

Page 209.

No one can deny, that violent passions will naturally emit harsh and disagreeable tones: . . .

Violent Passions Emit the Real, Good & Perfect Tones.

Page 214.

If it be objected that Rubens judged ill at first in thinking it necessary to make his work so very ornamental, this puts the question upon new ground.

Here it is call'd Ornamental that the Roman & Bolognian Schools may be Insinuated not to be Ornamental.

Page 215.

Nobody will dispute but some of the best of the Roman or Bolognian schools would have produced a more learned and more noble work.

Learned & Noble is Ornamental.

This leads us to another important province of taste, that of weighing the value of the different classes of the art, . . .

A Fool's Balance is no Criterion because, tho' it goes

down on the heaviest side, we ought to look what he puts into it.

Page 232.
If an European, when he has cut off his beard, . . . or bound up his own natural hair in regular hard knots, as unlike nature as he can possibly make it; . . . meets a Cherokee Indian, who has . . . laid on with equal care and attention his yellow and red oker . . .; whoever of these two despises the other for this attention to the fashion of his country . . . is the barbarian.

Excellent!

Page 242.
In the midst of the highest flights of fancy or imagination, reason ought to preside from first to last, . . .

If this is True, it is a devilish Foolish Thing to be an Artist.

[1966]

A DESCRIPTIVE CATALOGUE OF PICTURES

An exhibition of Blake's paintings was held at his brother's shop in London from May through the early fall of 1809. It did not prove a success, although it attracted a number of important visitors, Charles Lamb among them. Robert Hunt wrote a hostile review of the exhibition, which began: "If beside the stupid and mad-brained political project of their rulers, the sane part of the people of England required fresh proof of the alarming increase of the effects of insanity, they will be too well convinced from its having spread into the hitherto sober region of Art" (Examiner, September 17, 1809). The "Descriptive Catalogue" issued by Blake for the show is of interest, not only for his defense and explanation of his art, but also for the comments on Chaucer, which are insightful literary criticism.

A
DESCRIPTIVE CATALOGUE
OF
PICTURES,
Poetical and Historical Inventions,

PAINTED BY
WILLIAM BLAKE
IN
WATER COLOURS,
BEING THE ANCIENT METHOD OF
FRESCO PAINTING RESTORED:
AND
DRAWINGS,
FOR PUBLIC INSPECTION,
AND FOR
Sale by Private Contract,

LONDON: Printed by D. N. SHURY, 7, Berwick-Street, Soho, for J. Blake, 28, Broad-Street, Golden-Square. 1809.

CONDITIONS OF SALE

I. *One third of the price to be paid at the time of Purchase, and the remainder on Delivery.*

II. *The Pictures and Drawings to remain in the Exhibition till its close, which will be on the 29th of September 1809; and the Picture of the Canterbury Pilgrims, which is to be engraved, will be Sold only on condition of its remaining in the Artist's hands twelve months, when it will be delivered to the Buyer.*

PREFACE

The eye that can prefer the Colouring of Titian and Rubens to that of Michael Angelo and Rafael, ought to be modest and to doubt its own powers. Connoisseurs talk as if Rafael and Michael Angelo had never seen the colouring of Titian or Correggio: They ought to know that Correggio was born two years before Michael Angelo, and Titian but four years after. Both Rafael and Michael Angelo knew the Venetian, and contemned and rejected all he did with the utmost disdain, as that which is fabricated for the purpose to destroy art.

Mr. B. appeals to the Public, from the judgment of those narrow blinking eyes, that have too long governed art in a dark corner. The eyes of stupid cunning never will be pleased with the work any more than with the look of self-devoting genius. The quarrel of the Florentine with the Venetian is not because he does not understand Drawing, but because he does not understand Colouring. How should he? he who does not know how to draw a hand or a foot, know how to colour it?

Colouring does not depend on where the Colours are put, but on where the lights and darks are put, and all depends on Form or Outline, on where that is put; where that is wrong, the Colouring never can be right; and it is always wrong in Titian and Correggio, Rubens and Rembrandt. Till we get rid of Titian and Correggio, Rubens and Rembrandt, We never shall equal Rafael and Albert Durer, Michael Angelo, and Julio Romano.

INDEX TO THE CATALOGUE.

DESCRIPTIVE CATALOGUE
&c. &c.

NUMBER I.

The spiritual form of Nelson guiding Leviathan, in whose wreathings are infolded the Nations of the Earth.

Clearness and precision have been the chief objects in painting these Pictures. Clear colours unmudded by oil, and firm and determinate lineaments unbroken by shadows, which ought to display and not to hide form, as is the practice of the latter schools of Italy and Flanders.

NUMBER II, ITS COMPANION.

The Spiritual form of Pitt, guiding Behemoth; he is that Angel who, pleased to perform the Almighty's orders, rides on the whirlwind, directing the storms of war: He is ordering the Reaper to reap the Vine of the Earth, and the Plowman to plow up the Cities and Towers.

This Picture also is a proof of the power of colours unsullied with oil or with any cloggy vehicle. Oil has falsely been supposed to give strength to colours: but a little consideration must shew the fallacy of this opinion. Oil will not drink or absorb colour enough to stand the test of very little time and of the air. It deadens every colour it is mixed with, at its first mixture, and in a little time becomes a yellow mask over all that it touches. Let the works of modern Artists since Rubens' time witness the villany of some one of that time, who first brought oil Painting into general opinion and practice: since which we have never had a Picture painted, that could shew itself by the side of an earlier production. Whether Rubens or Vandyke, or both, were guilty of this villany, is to be enquired in another work on Painting, and who first forged the silly story and known falshood, about John of Bruges inventing oil colours: in the meantime let it be observed, that before Vandyke's time, and in his time all the genuine Pictures are on Plaster or Whiting grounds and none since.

The two pictures of Nelson and Pitt are compositions of a mythological cast, similar to those Apotheoses of Persian, Hindoo, and Egyptian Antiquity, which are still preserved on rude monuments, being copies from some stupendous originals now lost or perhaps buried till some happier age. The Artist having been taken in vision into the ancient republics, monarchies, and patriarchates of Asia, has seen those wonderful originals called in the Sacred Scriptures the Cherubim, which were sculptured and painted on walls of Temples, Towers, Cities, Palaces, and erected in the highly cultivated states of Egypt, Moab, Edom, Aram, among the Rivers of Paradise, being originals from which the Greeks and Hetrurians copied Hercules Farnese, Venus of Medicis, Apollo Belvidere, and all the grand works of ancient art. They were executed in a very superior style to those justly admired copies, being with their accompaniments terrific and grand in the highest degree. The Artist has endeavoured to emulate the grandeur of those seen in his vision, and to apply it to modern Heroes, on a smaller scale.

No man can believe that either Homer's Mythology, or Ovid's, were the production of Greece or of Latium; neither will any one believe, that the Greek statues, as they are called, were the invention of Greek Artists; perhaps the Torso is the only original work remaining; all the rest are evidently copies, though fine ones, from greater works of the Asiatic Patriarchs. The Greek Muses are daughters of Mnemosyne, or Memory, and not of Inspiration or Imagination, therefore not authors of such sublime conceptions. Those wonderful originals seen in my visions, were some of them one hundred feet in height; some were painted as pictures, and some carved as basso relievos, and some as groupes of statues, all containing mythological and recondite meaning, where more is meant than meets the eye. The Artist wishes it was now the fashion to make such monuments, and then he should not doubt of having a national commission to execute these two Pictures on a scale that is suitable to the grandeur of the nation, who is the parent of his heroes, in high finished fresco, where the colours would be as pure and as permanent as precious stones, though the figures were one hundred feet in height.

All Frescoes are as high finished as miniatures or enamels, and they are known to be unchangeable; but oil, being a body itself, will drink or absorb very little colour, and changing yellow, and at length brown, destroys every colour it is mixed with, especially every delicate colour. It turns every permanent white to a yellow and brown putty, and has compelled the use of that destroyer of colour, white lead; which, when its protecting oil is evaporated, will become lead again. This is an awful thing to say to oil Painters; they may call it madness, but it is true. All the genuine old little pictures, called Cabinet Pictures, are in fresco and not in oil. Oil was not used, except by blundering ignorance, till after Vandyke's time, but the art of fresco painting being lost, oil became a fetter to genius, and a dungeon to art. But one convincing proof among many others, that these assertions are true is, that real gold and silver cannot be used with oil, as they are in all the old pictures and in Mr. B.'s frescos.

NUMBER III.

Sir Jeffery Chaucer and the nine and twenty Pilgrims on their journey to Canterbury.

The time chosen is early morning, before sunrise, when the jolly company are just quitting the Tabarde Inn. The Knight and Squire with the Squire's Yeoman lead the Procession; next follow the youthful

Abbess, her nun and three priests; her greyhounds attend her—

"Of small hounds had she, that she fed
"With roast flesh, milk and wastel bread."

Next follow the Friar and Monk; then the Tapiser, the Pardoner, and the Somner and Manciple. After these "Our Host," who occupies the center of the cavalcade, directs them to the Knight as the person who would be likely to commence their task of each telling a tale in their order. After the Host follows the Shipman, the Haberdasher, the Dyer, the Franklin, the Physician, the Plowman, the Lawyer, the poor Parson, the Merchant, the Wife of Bath, the Miller, the Cook, the Oxford Scholar, Chaucer himself, and the Reeve comes as Chaucer has described:

"And ever he rode hinderest of the rout."

These last are issuing from the gateway of the Inn; the Cook and the Wife of Bath are both taking their morning's draught of comfort. Spectators stand at the gateway of the Inn, and are composed of an old Man, a Woman, and Children.

The Landscape is an eastward view of the country, from the Tabarde Inn, in Southwark, as it may be supposed to have appeared in Chaucer's time, interspersed with cottages and villages; the first beams of the Sun are seen above the horizon; some buildings and spires indicate the situation of the great City; the Inn is a gothic building, which Thynne in his Glossary [1] says was the lodging of the Abbot of Hyde, by Winchester. On the Inn is inscribed its title, and a proper advantage is taken of this circumstance to describe the subject of the Picture. The words written over the gateway of the Inn are as follow: "The Tabarde Inn, by Henry Baillie, the lodgynge-house for Pilgrims, who journey to Saint Thomas's Shrine at Canterbury."

The characters of Chaucer's Pilgrims are the characters which compose all ages and nations: as one age falls, another rises, different to mortal sight, but to immortals only the same; for we see the same characters repeated again and again, in animals, vegetables, minerals, and in men; nothing new occurs in identical existence; Accident ever varies, Substance can never suffer change nor decay.

Of Chaucer's characters, as described in his Canterbury Tales, some of the names or titles are altered by time, but the characters themselves for ever remain unaltered, and consequently they are the physiognomies or lineaments of universal human life, beyond which Nature never steps. Names alter, things never alter. I

---

[1] William Thynne (d. 1546) prepared the collected edition of Chaucer's works of 1532.

have known multitudes of those who would have been monks in the age of monkery, who in this deistical age are deists. As Newton numbered the stars, and as Linneus numbered the plants, so Chaucer numbered the classes of men.

The Painter has consequently varied the heads and forms of his personages into all Nature's varieties; the Horses he has also varied to accord to their Riders; the costume is correct according to authentic monuments.

The Knight and Squire with the Squire's Yeoman lead the procession, as Chaucer has also placed them first in his prologue. The Knight is a true Hero, a good, great, and wise man; his whole length portrait on horseback, as written by Chaucer, cannot be surpassed. He has spent his life in the field; has ever been a conqueror, and is that species of character which in every age stands as the guardian of man against the oppressor. His son is like him with the germ of perhaps greater perfection still, as he blends literature and the arts with his warlike studies. Their dress and their horses are of the first rate, without ostentation, and with all the true grandeur that unaffected simplicity when in high rank always displays. The Squire's Yeoman is also a great character, a man perfectly knowing in his profession:

"And in his hand he bare a mighty bow."

Chaucer describes here a mighty man; one who in war is the worthy attendant on noble heroes.

The Prioress follows these with her female chaplain:

"Another Nonne also with her had she,
"That was her Chaplaine, and Priests three."

This Lady is described also as of the first rank, rich and honoured. She has certain peculiarities and little delicate affectations, not unbecoming in her, being accompanied with what is truly grand and really polite; her person and face Chaucer has described with minuteness; it is very elegant, and was the beauty of our ancestors, till after Elizabeth's time, when voluptuousness and folly began to be accounted beautiful.

Her companion and her three priests were no doubt all perfectly delineated in those parts of Chaucer's work which are now lost; we ought to suppose them suitable attendants on rank and fashion.

The Monk follows these with the Friar. The Painter has also grouped with these the Pardoner and the Sompnour and the Manciple, and has here also introduced one of the rich citizens of London: Characters likely to ride in company, all being above the common rank in life or attendants on those who were so.

For the Monk is described by Chaucer, as a man of the first rank in society, noble, rich, and expensively

attended; he is a leader of the age, with certain humorous accompaniments in his character, that do not degrade, but render him an object of dignified mirth, but also with other accompaniments not so respectable.

The Friar is a character also of a mixed kind:

"A friar there was, a wanton and a merry."

but in his office he is said to be a "full solemn man": eloquent, amorous, witty, and satyrical; young, handsome, and rich; he is a complete rogue, with constitutional gaiety enough to make him a master of all the pleasures of the world.

"His neck was white as the flour de lis,
"Thereto strong he was as a champioun."

It is necessary here to speak of Chaucer's own character, that I may set certain mistaken critics right in their conception of the humour and fun that occurs on the journey. Chaucer is himself the great poetical observer of men, who in every age is born to record and eternize its acts. This he does as a master, as a father, and superior, who looks down on their little follies from the Emperor to the Miller; sometimes with severity, oftener with joke and sport.

Accordingly Chaucer has made his Monk a great tragedian, one who studied poetical art. So much so, that the generous Knight is, in the compassionate dictates of his soul, compelled to cry out:

"'Ho,' quoth the Knyght,—'good Sir, no more of this;
"'That ye have said is right ynough I wis;
"'And mokell more, for little heaviness
"'Is right enough for much folk, as I guesse.
"'I say, for me, it is a great disease,
"'Whereas men have been in wealth and ease,
"'To heare of their sudden fall, alas,
"'And the contrary is joy and solas.'"

The Monk's definition of tragedy in the proem to his tale is worth repeating:

"Tragedie is to tell a certain story,
"As old books us maken memory,
"Of hem that stood in great prosperity,
"And be fallen out of high degree,
"Into miserie, and ended wretchedly."

Though a man of luxury, pride and pleasure, he is a master of art and learning, though affecting to despise it. Those who can think that the proud Huntsman and Noble Housekeeper, Chaucer's Monk, is intended for a buffoon or burlesque character, know little of Chaucer.

For the Host who follows this group, and holds the center of the cavalcade, is a first rate character, and his jokes are no trifles; they are always, though uttered with audacity, and equally free with the Lord and the Peasant, they are always substantially and weightily expressive of knowledge and experience; Henry Baillie, the keeper of the greatest Inn of the greatest City; for such was the Tabarde Inn in Southwark, near London: our Host was also a leader of the age.

By way of illustration, I instance Shakspeare's Witches in Macbeth. Those who dress them for the stage, consider them as wretched old women, and not as Shakspeare intended, the Goddesses of Destiny; this shews how Chaucer has been misunderstood in his sublime work. Shakspeare's Fairies also are the rulers of the vegetable world, and so are Chaucer's; let them be so considered, and then the poet will be understood, and not else.

But I have omitted to speak of a very prominent character, the Pardoner, the Age's Knave, who always commands and domineers over the high and low vulgar. This man is sent in every age for a rod and scourge, and for a blight, for a trial of men, to divide the classes of men; he is in the most holy sanctuary, and he is suffered by Providence for wise ends, and has also his great use, and his grand leading destiny.

His companion, the Sompnour, is also a Devil of the first magnitude, grand, terrific, rich and honoured in the rank of which he holds the destiny. The uses to Society are perhaps equal of the Devil and of the Angel, their sublimity, who can dispute.

> "In daunger had he at his own gise,
> "The young girls of his diocese,
> "And he knew well their counsel, &c."

The principal figure in the next groupe is the Good Parson; an Apostle, a real Messenger of Heaven, sent in every age for its light and its warmth. This man is beloved and venerated by all, and neglected by all: He serves all, and is served by none; he is, according to Christ's definition, the greatest of his age. Yet he is a Poor Parson of a town. Read Chaucer's description of the Good Parson, and bow the head and the knee to him, who, in every age, sends us such a burning and a shining light. Search, O ye rich and powerful, for these men and obey their counsel, then shall the golden age return: But alas! you will not easily distinguish him from the Friar or the Pardoner; they, also, are "full solemn men," and their counsel you will continue to follow.

I have placed by his side the Sergeant at Lawe, who appears delighted to ride in his company, and between him and his brother, the Plowman; as I wish men of Law would always ride with them, and take their counsel, especially in all difficult points. Chaucer's

Lawyer is a character of great venerableness, a Judge, and a real master of the jurisprudence of his age.

The Doctor of Physic is in this groupe, and the Franklin, the voluptuous country gentleman, contrasted with the Physician, and on his other hand, with two Citizens of London. Chaucer's characters live age after age. Every age is a Canterbury Pilgrimage; we all pass on, each sustaining one or other of these characters; nor can a child be born, who is not one of these characters of Chaucer. The Doctor of Physic is described as the first of his profession; perfect, learned, completely Master and Doctor in his art. Thus the reader will observe, that Chaucer makes every one of his characters perfect in his kind; every one is an Antique Statue; the image of a class, and not of an imperfect individual.

This groupe also would furnish substantial matter, on which volumes might be written. The Franklin is one who keeps open table, who is the genius of eating and drinking, the Bacchus; as the Doctor of Physic is the Esculapius, the Host is the Silenus, the Squire is the Apollo, the Miller is the Hercules, &c. Chaucer's characters are a description of the eternal Principles that exist in all ages. The Franklin is voluptuousness itself, most nobly pourtrayed:

> "It snewed in his house of meat and drink."

The Plowman is simplicity itself, with wisdom and strength for its stamina. Chaucer has divided the ancient character of Hercules between his Miller and his Plowman. Benevolence is the plowman's great characteristic; he is thin with excessive labour, and not with old age, as some have supposed:

> "He would thresh, and thereto dike and delve
> "For Christe's sake, for every poore wight,
> "Withouten hire, if it lay in his might."

Visions of these eternal principles or characters of human life appear to poets, in all ages; the Grecian gods were the ancient Cherubim of Phoenicia; but the Greeks, and since them the Moderns, have neglected to subdue the gods of Priam. These gods are visions of the eternal attributes, or divine names, which, when erected into gods, become destructive to humanity. They ought to be the servants, and not the masters of man, or of society. They ought to be made to sacrifice to Man, and not man compelled to sacrifice to them; for when separated from man or humanity, who is Jesus the Saviour, the vine of eternity, they are thieves and rebels, they are destroyers.

The Plowman of Chaucer is Hercules in his supreme eternal state, divested of his spectrous shadow; which is the Miller, a terrible fellow, such as exists in all times and places for the trial of men, to astonish every neighbourhood with brutal strength and courage, to get rich and powerful to curb the pride of Man.

The Reeve and the Manciple are two characters of the most consummate worldly wisdom. The Shipman, or Sailor, is a similar genius of Ulyssean art; but with the highest courage superadded.

The Citizens and their Cook are each leaders of a class. Chaucer has been somehow made to number four citizens, which would make his whole company, himself included, thirty-one. But he says there was but nine and twenty in his company:

"Full nine and twenty in a company."

The Webbe, or Weaver, and the Tapiser, or Tapestry Weaver, appear to me to be the same person; but this is only an opinion, for full nine and twenty may signify one more or less. But I dare say that Chaucer wrote "A Webbe Dyer," that is, a Cloth Dyer:

"A Webbe Dyer, and a Tapiser."

The Merchant cannot be one of the Three Citizens, as his dress is different, and his character is more marked, whereas Chaucer says of his rich citizens:

"All were yclothed in o liverie."

The characters of Women Chaucer has divided into two classes, the Lady Prioress and the Wife of Bath. Are not these leaders of the ages of men? The lady prioress, in some ages, predominates, and in some the wife of Bath, in whose character Chaucer has been equally minute and exact, because she is also a scourge and a blight. I shall say no more of her, nor expose what Chaucer has left hidden; let the young reader study what he has said of her: it is useful as a scarecrow. There are of such characters born too many for the peace of the world.

I come at length to the Clerk of Oxenford. This character varies from that of Chaucer, as the contemplative philosopher varies from the poetical genius. There are always these two classes of learned sages, the poetical and the philosophical. The painter has put them side by side, as if the youthful clerk had put himself under the tuition of the mature poet. Let the Philosopher always be the servant and scholar of inspiration and all will be happy.

Such are the characters that compose this Picture, which was painted in self-defence against the insolent and envious imputation of unfitness for finished and scientific art; and this imputation, most artfully and industriously endeavoured to be propagated among the public by ignorant hirelings. The painter courts comparison with his competitors, who, having received

fourteen hundred guineas and more, from the profits of his designs in that well-known work, Designs for Blair's Grave,[2] have left him to shift for himself, while others, more obedient to an employer's opinions and directions, are employed, at a great expence, to produce works, in succession to his, by which they acquired public patronage. This has hitherto been his lot—to get patronage for others and then to be left and neglected, and his work, which gained that patronage, cried down as eccentricity and madness; as unfinished and neglected by the artist's violent temper; he is sure the works now exhibited will give the lie to such aspersions.

Those who say that men are led by interest are knaves. A knavish character will often say, 'of what interest is it to me to do so and so?' I answer, 'of none at all, but the contrary, as you well know. It is of malice and envy that you have done this; hence I am aware of you, because I know that you act, not from interest, but from malice, even to your own destruction.' It is therefore become a duty which Mr. B. owes to the Public, who have always recognized him, and patronized him, however hidden by artifices, that he should not suffer such things to be done, or be hindered from the public Exhibition of his finished productions by any calumnies in future.

The character and expression in this picture could never have been produced with Rubens' light and shadow, or with Rembrandt's, or anything Venetian or Flemish. The Venetian and Flemish practice is broken lines, broken masses, and broken colours. Mr. B.'s practice is unbroken lines, unbroken masses, and unbroken colours. Their art is to lose form; his art is to find form, and to keep it. His arts are opposite to theirs in all things.

As there is a class of men whose whole delight is the destruction of men, so there is a class of artists, whose whole art and science is fabricated for the purpose of destroying art. Who these are is soon known: "by their works ye shall know them." All who endeavour to raise up a style against Rafael, Mich. Angelo, and the Antique; those who separate Painting from Drawing; who look if a picture is well Drawn, and, if it is, immediately cry out, that it cannot be well Coloured—those are the men.

But to shew the stupidity of this class of men

<hr />

[2] In 1805, the engraver Robert Hartley Cromek had commissioned from Blake a set of drawings, which were to be engraved as illustrations for an edition of Blair's poem *The Grave*. Blake was also to prepare the engravings and thereby receive considerable financial reward from the publication. However, Cromek purchased only twelve of Blake's twenty drawings (for the modest sum of £20) and turned the job of engraving over to the rival engraver Schiavonetti.

nothing need be done but to examine my rival's prospectus.[3]

The two first characters in Chaucer, the Knight and the Squire, he has put among his rabble; and indeed his prospectus calls the Squire the fop of Chaucer's age. Now hear Chaucer:

"Of his Stature, he was of even length,
"And wonderly deliver, and of great strength;
"And he had be sometime in Chivauchy,
"In Flanders, in Artois, and in Picardy,
"And borne him well, as of so litele space."

Was this a fop?

"Well could he sit a horse, and faire ride,
"He could songs make, and eke well indite
"Just, and eke dance, pourtray, and well write."

Was this a fop?

"Curteis he was, and meek, and serviceable;
"And kerft before his fader at the table"

Was this a fop?

It is the same with all his characters; he has done all by chance, or perhaps his fortune,—money, money. According to his prospectus he has Three Monks; these he cannot find in Chaucer, who has only One Monk, and that no vulgar character, as he has endeavoured to make him. When men cannot read they should not pretend to paint. To be sure Chaucer is a little difficult to him who has only blundered over novels, and catchpenny trifles of booksellers. Yet a little pains ought to be taken even by the ignorant and weak. He has put The Reeve, a vulgar fellow, between his Knight and Squire, as if he was resolved to go contrary in everything to Chaucer, who says of the Reeve:

"And ever he rode hinderest of the rout."

In this manner he has jumbled his dumb dollies together and is praised by his equals for it; for both himself and his friend are equally masters of Chaucer's language. They both think that the Wife of Bath is a young, beautiful, blooming damsel, and H——[4] says, that she is the Fair Wife of Bath, and that the Spring appears in her Cheeks. Now hear what Chaucer has made her say of herself, who is no modest one:

"But Lord when it remembereth me
"Upon my youth and on my jollity
"It tickleth me about the heart root,
"Unto this day it doth my heart boot,
"That I have had my world as in my time;
"But age, alas, that all will envenime
"Hath bireft my beauty and my pith
"Let go; farewell: the Devil go therewith,
"The flower is gone; there is no more to tell
"The bran, as best I can, I now mote sell;
"And yet to be right merry will I fond,—
"Now forth to tell of my fourth husband."

She has had four husbands, a fit subject for this painter; yet the painter ought to be very much offended with his friend H——, who has called his "a common scene," "and very ordinary forms," which is the truest part of all, for it is so, and very wretchedly so indeed. What merit can there be in a picture of which such words are spoken with truth?

But the prospectus says that the Painter has represented Chaucer himself as a knave, who thrusts himself among honest people, to make game of and laugh at them; though I must do justice to the painter, and say that he has made him look more like a fool than a knave. But it appears in all the writings of Chaucer, and particularly in his Canterbury Tales, that he was very devout, and paid respect to true enthusiastic superstition. He has laughed at his knaves and fools, as I do now. But he has respected his True Pilgrims, who are a majority of his company, and are not thrown together in the random manner that Mr. S——[5] has done. Chaucer has no where called the Plowman old, worn out with age and labour, as the prospectus has represented him, and says that the picture has done so too. He is worn down with labour, but not with age. How spots of brown and yellow, smeared about at random, can be either young or old, I cannot see. It may be an old man; it may be a young one; it may be any thing that a prospectus pleases. But I know that where there are no lineaments there can be no character. And what connoisseurs call touch, I know by experience, must be the destruction of all character and expression, as it is of every lineament.

The scene of Mr. S——'s Picture is by Dulwich Hills, which was not the way to Canterbury; but perhaps the painter thought he would give them a ride round about, because they were a burlesque set of scare-crows, not worth any man's respect or care.

---

[3] Refers to the engravings, sponsored and publicized by Cromek, of Thomas Stothard's painting of "Chaucer's Procession to Canterbury." The exact details of the controversy are not clear, but Blake believed that Cromek had gotten the idea of an engraving of the Canterbury Tales from Blake's own preparation of a drawing on the subject.

[4] John Hoppner (1758–1810), popular portrait painter, who wrote a praiseful letter about Stothard's painting in the journal *The Artist* in 1807, which was quoted by Cromek in his prospectus for the engraving.

---

[5] Thomas Stothard (1755–1834), painter and book illustrator.

But the painter's thoughts being always upon gold, he has introduced a character that Chaucer has not; namely, a Goldsmith; for so the prospectus tells us. Why he has introduced a Goldsmith, and what is the wit of it, the prospectus does not explain. But it takes care to mention the reserve and modesty of the Painter; this makes a good epigram enough:

> "The fox, the owl, the spider, and the mole,
> "By sweet reserve and modesty get fat."

But the prospectus tells us, that the painter has introduced a Sea Captain; Chaucer has a Ship-man a Sailor, a Trading Master of a Vessel, called by courtesy Captain, as every master of a boat is; but this does not make him a Sea Captain. Chaucer has purposely omitted such a personage, as it only exists in certain periods: it is the soldier by sea. He who would be a Soldier in inland nations is a sea captain in commercial nations.

All is misconceived, and its mis-execution is equal to its misconception. I have no objection to Rubens and Rembrandt being employed, or even to their living in a palace; but it shall not be at the expence of Rafael and Michael Angelo living in a cottage, and in contempt and derision. I have been scorned long enough by these fellows, who owe to me all that they have; it shall be so no longer.

> "I found them blind, I taught them how to see;
> "And, now, they know me not, nor yet themselves."

NUMBER IV.

The Bard, from Gray.

> "On a rock, whose haughty brow
> "Frown'd o'er old Conway's foaming flood,
> "Robed in the sable garb of woe,
> "With haggard eyes the Poet stood;
> "Loose his beard, and hoary hair
> "Stream'd like a meteor to the troubled air.
>
> "Weave the warp, and weave the woof,
> "The winding sheet of Edward's race."

Weaving the winding sheet of Edward's race by means of sounds of spiritual music and its accompanying expressions of articulate speech, is a bold, and daring, and most masterly conception, that the public have embraced and approved with avidity. Poetry consists in these conceptions; and shall Painting be confined to the sordid drudgery of fac-simile representations of merely mortal and perishing substances, and not be as poetry and music are, elevated into its own proper sphere of invention and visionary conception? No, it shall not be so! Painting, as well as poetry and

music, exists and exults in immortal thoughts. If Mr. B.'s Canterbury Pilgrims had been done by any other power than that of the poetic visionary, it would have been as dull as his adversary's.

The Spirits of the murdered bards assist in weaving the deadly woof:

> "With me in dreadful harmony they join
> "And weave, with bloody hands, the tissue of thy line."

The connoisseurs and artists who have made objections to Mr. B.'s mode of representing spirits with real bodies, would do well to consider that the Venus, the Minerva, the Jupiter, the Apollo, which they admire in Greek statues are all of them representations of spiritual existences, of Gods immortal, to the mortal perishing organ of sight; and yet they are embodied and organized in solid marble. Mr. B. requires the same latitude, and all is well. The Prophets describe what they saw in Vision as real and existing men, whom they saw with their imaginative and immortal organs; the Apostles the same; the clearer the organ the more distinct the object. A Spirit and a Vision are not, as the modern philosophy supposes, a cloudy vapour, or a nothing: they are organized and minutely articulated beyond all that the mortal and perishing nature can produce. He who does not imagine in stronger and better lineaments, and in stronger and better light than his perishing and mortal eye can see, does not imagine at all. The painter of this work asserts that all his imaginations appear to him infinitely more perfect and more minutely organized than any thing seen by his mortal eye. Spirits are organized men. Moderns wish to draw figures without lines, and with great and heavy shadows; are not shadows more unmeaning than lines, and more heavy? O who can doubt this!

King Edward and his Queen Elenor are prostrated, with their horses, at the foot of a rock on which the Bard stands; prostrated by the terrors of his harp on the margin of the river Conway, whose waves bear up a corse of a slaughtered bard at the foot of the rock. The armies of Edward are seen winding among the mountains.

> "He wound with toilsome march his long array."

Mortimer and Gloucester lie spell bound behind their king.

The execution of this picture is also in Water Colours, or Fresco.

NUMBER V.

The Ancient Britons

In the last Battle of King Arthur, only Three Britons escaped; these were the Strongest Man, the Beautifullest Man, and the Ugliest Man; these three marched through the field un-

subdued, as Gods, and the Sun of Britain set, but shall arise again with tenfold splendor when Arthur shall awake from sleep, and resume his dominion over earth and ocean.

The three general classes of men who are represented by the most Beautiful, the most Strong, and the most Ugly, could not be represented by any historical facts but those of our own country, the Ancient Britons, without violating costume. The Britons (say historians) were naked civilized men, learned, studious, abstruse in thought and contemplation; naked, simple, plain in their acts and manners; wiser than after-ages. They were overwhelmed by brutal arms, all but a small remnant; Strength, Beauty, and Ugliness escaped the wreck, and remain for ever unsubdued, age after age.

The British Antiquities are now in the Artist's hands; all his visionary contemplations, relating to his own country and its ancient glory, when it was, as it again shall be, the source of learning and inspiration. Arthur was a name for the constellation Arcturus, or Boötes, the keeper of the North Pole. And all the fables of Arthur and his round table; of the warlike naked Britons; of Merlin; of Arthur's conquest of the whole world; of his death, or sleep, and promise to return again; of the Druid monuments or temples; of the pavement of Watling-street; of London stone; of the caverns in Cornwall, Wales, Derbyshire, and Scotland; of the Giants of Ireland and Britain; of the elemental beings called by us by the general name of fairies; and of these three who escaped, namely Beauty, Strength, and Ugliness. Mr. B. has in his hands poems of the highest antiquity. Adam was a Druid, and Noah; also Abraham was called to succeed the Druidical age, which began to turn allegoric and mental signification into corporeal command, whereby human sacrifice would have depopulated the earth. All these things are written in Eden. The artist is an inhabitant of that happy country; and if every thing goes on as it has begun, the world of vegetation and generation may expect to be opened again to Heaven, through Eden, as it was in the beginning.

The Strong Man represents the human sublime. The Beautiful Man represents the human pathetic, which was in the wars of Eden divided into male and female. The Ugly Man represents the human reason. They were originally one man, who was fourfold; he was self-divided, and his real humanity slain on the stems of generation, and the form of the fourth was like the Son of God. How he became divided is a subject of great sublimity and pathos. The Artist has written it under inspiration, and will, if God please, publish it; it is voluminous, and contains the ancient history of Britain, and the world of Satan and of Adam.

In the mean time he has painted this Picture, which supposes that in the reign of that British Prince, who lived in the fifth century, there were remains of those naked Heroes in the Welch Mountains; they are there now, Gray saw them in the person of his bard on Snowdon; there they dwell in naked simplicity; happy is he who can see and converse with them above the shadows of generation and death. The giant Albion, was Patriarch of the Atlantic; he is the Atlas of the Greeks, one of those the Greeks called Titans. The stories of Arthur are the acts of Albion, applied to a Prince of the fifth century, who conquered Europe, and held the Empire of the world in the dark age, which the Romans never again recovered. In this Picture, believing with Milton the ancient British History, Mr. B. has done as all the ancients did, and as all the moderns who are worthy of fame, given the historical fact in its poetical vigour so as it always happens, and not in that dull way that some Historians pretend, who, being weakly organized themselves, cannot see either miracle or prodigy; all is to them a dull round of probabilities and possibilities; but the history of all times and places is nothing else but improbabilities and impossibilities; what we should say was impossible if we did not see it always before our eyes.

The antiquities of every Nation under Heaven, is no less sacred than that of the Jews. They are the same thing, as Jacob Bryant[6] and all antiquaries have proved. How other antiquities came to be neglected and disbelieved, while those of the Jews are collected and arranged, is an enquiry worthy both of the Antiquarian and the Divine. All had originally one language, and one religion: this was the religion of Jesus, the everlasting Gospel. Antiquity preaches the Gospel of Jesus. The reasoning historian, turner and twister of causes and consequences, such as Hume, Gibbon, and Voltaire, cannot with all their artifice turn or twist one fact or disarrange self evident action and reality. Reasons and opinions concerning acts are not history. Acts themselves alone are history, and these are neither the exclusive property of Hume, Gibbon, nor Voltaire, Echard, Rapin, Plutarch, nor Herodotus. Tell me the Acts, O historian, and leave me to reason upon them as I please; away with your reasoning and your rubbish! All that is not action is not worth reading. Tell me the What; I do not want you to tell me the Why, and the How; I can find that out myself, as well as you can, and I will not be fooled by you into opinions, that you please to impose, to disbelieve what you think improbable or impossible. His opinions, who does not see spiritual agency, is not worth any man's reading; he

---

[6] Jacob Bryant (1715–1804), author of *Analysis of Ancient Mythology* (1774–1776).

who rejects a fact because it is improbable, must reject all History and retain doubts only.

It has been said to the Artist, "take the Apollo for the model of your beautiful Man, and the Hercules for your strong Man, and the Dancing Fawn for your Ugly Man." Now he comes to his trial. He knows that what he does is not inferior to the grandest Antiques. Superior they cannot be, for human power cannot go beyond either what he does, or what they have done; it is the gift of God, it is inspiration and vision. He had resolved to emulate those precious remains of antiquity; he has done so and the result you behold; his ideas of strength and beauty have not been greatly different. Poetry as it exists now on earth, in the various remains of ancient authors, Music as it exists in old tunes or melodies, Painting and Sculpture as it exists in the remains of Antiquity and in the works of more modern genius, is Inspiration, and cannot be surpassed; it is perfect and eternal. Milton, Shakspeare, Michael Angelo, Rafael, the finest specimens of Ancient Sculpture and Painting and Architecture, Gothic, Grecian, Hindoo and Egyptian, are the extent of the human mind. The human mind cannot go beyond the gift of God, the Holy Ghost. To suppose that Art can go beyond the finest specimens of Art that are now in the world, is not knowing what Art is; it is being blind to the gifts of the spirit.

It will be necessary for the Painter to say something concerning his ideas of Beauty, Strength and Ugliness.

The Beauty that is annexed and appended to folly, is a lamentable accident and error of the mortal and perishing life; it does but seldom happen; but with this unnatural mixture the sublime Artist can have nothing to do; it is fit for the burlesque. The Beauty proper for sublime art is lineaments, or forms and features that are capable of being the receptacles of intellect; accordingly the Painter has given in his beautiful man, his own idea of intellectual Beauty. The face and limbs that deviates or alters least, from infancy to old age, is the face and limbs of greatest Beauty and perfection.

The Ugly, likewise, when accompanied and annexed to imbecility and disease, is a subject for burlesque and not for historical grandeur; the Artist has imagined his Ugly man, one approaching to the beast in features and form, his forehead small, without frontals; his jaws large; his nose high on the ridge, and narrow; his chest, and the stamina of his make, comparatively little, and his joints and his extremities large; his eyes, with scarce any whites, narrow and cunning, and every thing tending toward what is truly Ugly, the incapability of intellect.

The Artist has considered his strong Man as a receptacle of Wisdom, a sublime energizer; his features and limbs do not spindle out into length without strength, nor are they too large and unwieldy for his brain and bosom. Strength consists in accumulation of power to the principal seat, and from thence a regular gradation and subordination; strength is compactness, not extent nor bulk.

The strong Man acts from conscious superiority, and marches on in fearless dependance on the divine decrees, raging with the inspirations of a prophetic mind. The Beautiful Man acts from duty and anxious solicitude for the fates of those for whom he combats. The Ugly Man acts from love of carnage, and delight in the savage barbarities of war, rushing with sportive precipitation into the very teeth of the affrighted enemy.

The Roman Soldiers rolled together in a heap before them: "Like the rolling thing before the whirlwind"; each shew a different character, and a different expression of fear, or revenge, or envy, or blank horror, or amazement, or devout wonder and unresisting awe.

The dead and the dying, Britons naked, mingled with armed Romans, strew the field beneath. Among these the last of the Bards who were capable of attending warlike deeds, is seen falling, outstretched among the dead and the dying, singing to his harp in the pains of death.

Distant among the mountains are Druid Temples, similar to Stone Henge. The Sun sets behind the mountains, bloody with the day of battle.

The flush of health in flesh exposed to the open air, nourished by the spirits of forests and floods in that ancient happy period, which history has recorded, cannot be like the sickly daubs of Titian or Rubens. Where will the copier of nature, as it now is, find a civilized man, who has been accustomed to go naked? Imagination only can furnish us with colouring appropriate, such as is found in the Frescos of Rafael and Michael Angelo: the disposition of forms always directs colouring in works of true art. As to a modern Man, stripped from his load of cloathing, he is like a dead corpse. Hence Rubens, Titian, Correggio and all of that class, are like leather and chalk; their men are like leather, and their women like chalk, for the disposition of their forms will not admit of grand colouring; in Mr. B.'s Britons the blood is seen to circulate in their limbs; he defies competition in colouring.

NUMBER VI.

A Spirit vaulting from a cloud to turn and wind a fiery Pegasus.—Shakspeare. The Horse of Intellect is leaping from the cliffs of Memory and Reasoning; it is a barren Rock: it is also called the Barren Waste of Locke and Newton.

This Picture was done many years ago, and was one of the first Mr. B. ever did in Fresco; fortunately, or rather, providentially, he left it unblotted and un-blurred, although molested continually by blotting and blurring demons; but he was also compelled to leave it unfinished, for reasons that will be shewn in the following.

NUMBER VII.

The Goats, an experiment Picture.

The subject is taken from the Missionary Voyage, and varied from the literal fact for the sake of pic-turesque scenery. The savage girls had dressed them-selves with vine leaves, and some goats on board the missionary ship stripped them off presently. This Picture was painted at intervals, for experiment with the colours, and is laboured to a superabundant black-ness; it has, however, that about it, which may be worthy the attention of the Artist and Connoisseur for reasons that follow.

NUMBER VIII.

The Spiritual Preceptor, an experiment Picture.

The subject is taken from the Visions of Emanuel Swedenborg, Universal Theology, No. 623. The Learned, who strive to ascend into Heaven by means of learning, appear to Children like dead horses, when repelled by the celestial spheres. The works of this visionary are well worthy the attention of Painters and Poets; they are foundations for grand things; the reason they have not been more attended to is because corporeal demons have gained a predominance; who the leaders of these are, will be shewn below. Un-worthy Men who gain fame among Men, continue to govern mankind after death, and in their spiritual bodies oppose the spirits of those who worthily are famous; and, as Swedenborg observes, by entering into disease and excrement, drunkenness and con-cupiscence, they possess themselves of the bodies of mortal men, and shut the doors of mind and of thought by placing Learning above Inspiration. O Artist! you may disbelieve all this, but it shall be at your own peril.

NUMBER IX.

Satan calling up his Legions, from Milton's Paradise Lost; a composition for a more perfect Picture afterward executed for a Lady of high rank. An experiment Picture.

This Picture was likewise painted at intervals, for experiment on colours without any oily vehicle; it may be worthy of attention, not only on account of its composition, but of the great labour which has been bestowed on it, that is, three or four times as much as would have finished a more perfect Picture; the labour

has destroyed the lineaments; it was with difficulty brought back again to a certain effect, which it had at first, when all the lineaments were perfect.

These Pictures, among numerous others painted for experiment, were the result of temptations and per-turbations, labouring to destroy Imaginative power, by means of that infernal machine called Chiaro Oscuro, in the hands of Venetian and Flemish Demons, whose enmity to the Painter himself, and to all Artists who study in the Florentine and Roman Schools, may be removed by an exhibition and exposure of their vile tricks. They cause that every thing in art shall become a Machine. They cause that the execution shall be all blocked up with brown shadows. They put the original Artist in fear and doubt of his own original conception. The spirit of Titian was particularly active in raising doubts concerning the possibility of executing without a model, and when once he had raised the doubt, it became easy for him to snatch away the vision time after time, for, when the Artist took his pencil to execute his ideas, his power of imagination weakened so much and darkened, that memory of nature, and of Pictures of the various schools possessed his mind, instead of appropriate execution resulting from the inventions; like walking in another man's style, or speaking, or looking in another man's style and manner, unappropriate and repugnant to your own individual character; tormenting the true Artist, till he leaves the Florentine, and adopts the Venetian practice, or does as Mr. B. has done, has the courage to suffer poverty and disgrace, till he ultimately conquers.

Rubens is a most outrageous demon, and by infusing the remembrances of his Pictures and style of execu-tion, hinders all power of individual thought: so that the man who is possessed by this demon loses all admiration of any other Artist but Rubens and those who were his imitators and journeymen; he causes to the Florentine and Roman Artist fear to execute; and though the original conception was all fire and animation, he loads it with hellish brownness, and blocks up all its gates of light except one, and that one he closes with iron bars, till the victim is obliged to give up the Florentine and Roman practice, and adopt the Venetian and Flemish.

Correggio is a soft and effeminate, and consequently a most cruel demon, whose whole delight is to cause endless labour to whoever suffers him to enter his mind. The story that is told in all Lives of the Painters about Correggio being poor and but badly paid for his Pictures is altogether false; he was a petty Prince in Italy, and employed numerous Journeymen in manu-facturing (as Rubens and Titian did) the Pictures that go under his name. The manual labour in these Pictures of Correggio is immense, and was paid for originally at the immense prices that those who keep manufactories of art always charge to their employers, while they themselves pay their journeymen little enough. But though Correggio was not poor, he will make any true artist so who permits him to enter his mind, and take possession of his affections; he infuses a love of soft and even tints without boundaries, and of endless reflected lights that confuse one another, and hinder all correct drawing from appearing to be correct; for if one of Rafael or Michael Angelo's figures was to be traced, and Correggio's reflections and refractions to be added to it, there would soon be an end of proportion and strength, and it would be weak, and pappy, and lumbering, and thick headed, like his own works; but then it would have softness and evenness by a twelve-month's labour, where a month would with judgment have finished it better and higher; and the poor wretch who executed it, would be the Correggio that the life writers have written of: a drudge and a miserable man, compelled to softness by poverty. I say again, O Artist, you may disbelieve all this, but it shall be at your own peril.

Note. These experiment Pictures have been bruized and knocked about without mercy, to try all experiments.

NUMBER X.
The Bramins.—A Drawing.

The subject is, Mr. Wilkin [7] translating the Geeta; an ideal design, suggested by the first publication of that part of the Hindoo Scriptures translated by Mr. Wilkin. I understand that my Costume is incorrect, but in this I plead the authority of the ancients, who often deviated from the Habits to preserve the Manners, as in the instance of Laocoön, who, though a priest, is represented naked.

NUMBER XI.
The Body of Abel found by Adam and Eve; Cain, who was about to bury it, fleeing from the face of his Parents—A Drawing.

NUMBER XII.
The Soldiers casting lots for Christ's Garment.—A Drawing.

NUMBER XIII.
Jacob's Ladder.—A Drawing.

---

[7] Sir Charles Wilkins (c. 1749–1836), described by the *Dictionary of National Biography* as "the first Englishman to gain a thorough grasp of Sanskrit." Wilkins' translation of the *Bhagavad-gita* was published in 1785.

NUMBER XIV.
The Angels hovering over the Body of Jesus in the Sepulchre.— A Drawing.

The above four drawings the Artist wishes were in Fresco on an enlarged scale to ornament the altars of churches, and to make England, like Italy, respected by respectable men of other countries on account of Art. It is not the want of Genius that can hereafter be laid to our charge; the Artist who has done these Pictures and Drawings will take care of that; let those who govern the Nation take care of the other. The times require that every one should speak out boldly; England expects that every man should do his duty, in Arts, as well as in Arms, or in the Senate.

NUMBER XV.
Ruth.—A Drawing.

This Design is taken from the most pathetic passage in the Book of Ruth, where Naomi, having taken leave of her daughters in law with intent to return to her own country, Ruth cannot leave her, but says, "Whither "thou goest I will go; and where thou lodgest I will "lodge; thy people shall be my people, and thy God my "God; where thou diest I will die, and there will I be "buried; God do so to me and more also, if ought but "death part thee and me."

The distinction that is made in modern times between a Painting and a Drawing proceeds from ignorance of art. The merit of a Picture is the same as the merit of a Drawing. The dawber dawbs his Drawings; he who draws his Drawings draws his Pictures. There is no difference between Rafael's Cartoons and his Frescos, or Pictures, except that the Frescos, or Pictures, are more finished. When Mr. B. formerly painted in oil colours his Pictures were shewn to certain painters and connoisseurs, who said that they were very admirable Drawings on canvass, but not Pictures; but they said the same of Rafael's Pictures. Mr. B. thought this the greatest of compliments, though it was meant otherwise. If losing and obliterating the outline constitutes a Picture, Mr. B. will never be so foolish as to do one. Such art of losing the outlines is the art of Venice and Flanders; it loses all character, and leaves what some people call expression; but this is a false notion of expression; expression cannot exist without character as its stamina; and neither character nor expression can exist without firm and determinate outline. Fresco Painting is susceptible of higher finishing than Drawing on Paper, or than any other method of Painting. But he must have a strange organization of sight who does not prefer a Drawing on Paper to a

Dawbing in Oil by the same master, supposing both to be done with equal care.

The great and golden rule of art, as well as of life, is this: That the more distinct, sharp, and wirey the bounding line, the more perfect the work of art; and the less keen and sharp, the greater is the evidence of weak imitation, plagiarism, and bungling. Great inventors, in all ages, knew this: Protogenes and Apelles knew each other by this line. Rafael and Michael Angelo and Albert Dürer are known by this and this alone. The want of this determinate and bounding form evidences the want of idea in the artist's mind, and the pretence of the plagiary in all its branches. How do we distinguish the oak from the beech, the horse from the ox, but by the bounding outline? How do we distinguish one face or countenance from another, but by the bounding line and its infinite inflexions and movements? What is it that builds a house and plants a garden, but the definite and determinate? What is it that distinguishes honesty from knavery, but the hard and wiry line of rectitude and certainty in the actions and intentions? Leave out this line, and you leave out life itself; all is chaos again, and the line of the almighty must be drawn out upon it before man or beast can exist. Talk no more then of Correggio, or Rembrandt, or any other of those plagiaries of Venice or Flanders. They were but the lame imitators of lines drawn by their predecessors, and their works prove themselves contemptible, dis-arranged imitations, and blundering, misapplied copies.

NUMBER XVI.

The Penance of Jane Shore in St. Paul's Church.—A Drawing.

This Drawing was done above Thirty Years ago, and proves to the Author, and he thinks will prove to any discerning eye, that the productions of our youth and of our maturer age are equal in all essential points. If a man is master of his profession, he cannot be ignorant that he is so; and if he is not employed by those who pretend to encourage art, he will employ himself, and laugh in secret at the pretences of the ignorant, while he has every night dropped into his shoe, as soon as he puts it off, and puts out the candle, and gets into bed, a reward for the labours of the day, such that the world cannot give, and patience and time await to give him all that the world can give.

FINIS

[1809]   [1966]

A VISION OF THE LAST JUDGMENT

In 1807, at the instigation of his friend Ozias Humphry, Blake undertook to paint the Last Judgment for the Countess of Egremont. A much larger treatment of the same subject in fresco (measuring seven feet by five and containing a thousand figures) was to be included in an exhibition that Blake apparently intended to hold in 1810. For the catalogue of the proposed exhibition Blake wrote the following account of "A Vision of the Last Judgment," which survives in the rough state of his notebook. (Page references are to the leaves of the notebook.) The fresco itself has disappeared.

A VISION OF THE LAST JUDGMENT

P. 70.

For the Year 1810
Additions to Blake's Catalogue of Pictures &c

The Last Judgment [will be] when all those are Cast away who trouble Religion with Questions concerning Good & Evil or Eating of the Tree of those Knowledges or Reasonings which hinder the Vision of God, turning all into a Consuming Fire. When Imagination, Art & Science & all Intellectual Gifts, all the Gifts of the Holy Ghost, are [despis'd *del.*] look'd upon as of no use & only Contention remains to Man, then the Last Judgment begins, & its Vision is seen by the [Imaginative Eye *del.*] of Every one according to the situation he holds.

P. 68.

The Last Judgment is not Fable or Allegory, but Vision. Fable or Allegory are a totally distinct & inferior kind of Poetry. Vision or Imagination is a Representation of what Eternally Exists, Really & Unchangeably. Fable or Allegory is Form'd by the daughters of Memory. Imagination is surrounded by the daughters of Inspiration, who in the aggregate are call'd Jerusalem. Fable is Allegory, but what Critics call The Fable, is Vision itself. The Hebrew Bible & the Gospel of Jesus are not Allegory, but Eternal Vision or Imagination of All that Exists. Note here that Fable or Allegory is seldom without some Vision. Pilgrim's Progress is full of it, the Greek Poets the same; but [Fable & Allegory *del.*] Allegory & Vision [& Visions of Imagination *del.*] ought to be known as Two Distinct Things, & so call'd for the Sake of Eternal Life. Plato has made Socrates say that Poets & Prophets do not know or Understand what they write or Utter; this is a most Pernicious Falshood. If they do not, pray is an inferior kind to be call'd Knowing? Plato confutes himself.

Pp. 68–69.

The Last Judgment is one of these Stupendous Visions. I have represented it as I saw it; to different People it appears differently as everything else does; for tho' on Earth things seem Permanent, they are less permanent than a Shadow, as we all know too well.

The Nature of Visionary Fancy, or Imagination, is very little Known, & the Eternal nature & permanence of its ever Existent Images is consider'd as less permanent than the things of Vegetative & Generative Nature; yet the Oak dies as well as the Lettuce, but Its Eternal Image & Individuality never dies, but renews by its seed; just [as *del.*] so the Imaginative Image returns [according to *del.*] by the seed of Contemplative Thought; the Writings of the Prophets illustrate these conceptions of the Visionary Fancy by their various sublime & Divine Images as seen in the Worlds of Vision.

Pp. 71–72.

The Learned m . . . or Heroes; this is an . . . & not Spiritual . . . while the Bible . . . of Virtue & Vice . . . as they are Ex . . . is the Real Di . . . Things. The . . . when they Assert that Jupiter usurped the Throne of his Father, Saturn, & brought on an Iron Age & Begat on Mnemosyne, or Memory, The Greek Muses, which are not Inspiration as the Bible is. Reality was Forgot, & the Vanities of Time & Space only Remember'd & call'd Reality. Such is the Mighty difference between Allegoric Fable & Spiritual Mystery. Let it here be Noted that the Greek Fables originated in Spiritual Mystery & Real Visions, which are lost & clouded in Fable & Allegory, [which *del.*] while the Hebrew Bible & the Greek Gospel are Genuine, Preserv'd by the Saviour's Mercy. The Nature of my Work is Visionary or Imaginative; it is an Endeavour to Restore what the Ancients call'd the Golden Age.

Pp. 69–70.

This world of Imagination is the world of Eternity; it is the divine bosom into which we shall all go after the death of the Vegetated body. This World of Imagination is Infinite & Eternal, whereas the world of Generation, or Vegetation, is Finite & [for a small moment *del.*] Temporal. There Exist in that Eternal World the Permanent Realities of Every Thing which we see reflected in this Vegetable Glass of Nature. All Things are comprehended in their Eternal Forms in the divine body of the Saviour, the True Vine of Eternity, The Human Imagination, who appear'd to Me as Coming to Judgment among his Saints & throwing off the Temporal that the Eternal might be Establish'd; around him were seen the Images of Existences according to [their Aggregate . . . *del.*] a

certain order Suited to my Imaginative Eye [In the following order *del.*] as follows.

Query, the Above ought to follow the description. Here follows the description of the Picture:

P. 76.

Jesus seated between the Two Pillars, Jachin & Boaz, with the Word of divine Revelation on his knees, & on each side the four & twenty Elders sitting in judgment; the Heavens opening around him by unfolding the clouds around his throne. The Old H[eave]n & O[ld] Earth are passing away & the N[ew] H[eaven] & N[ew] Earth descending [as on a Scroll *del.*]. The Just arise on his right & the wicked on his Left hand. A sea of fire issues from before the throne. Adam & Eve appear first, before the [throne *del.*] Judgment seat in humiliation. Abel surrounded by Innocents, & Cain, with the flint in his hand with which he slew his brother, falling with the head downward. From the Cloud on which Eve stands, Satan is seen falling headlong wound round by the tail of the serpent whose bulk, nail'd to the Cross round which he wreathes, is falling into the Abyss. Sin is also represented as a female bound in one of the Serpent's folds, surrounded by her fiends. Death is Chain'd to the Cross, & Time falls together with death, dragged down by [an Angel *del.*] a demon crown'd with Laurel; another demon with a Key has the charge of Sin & is dragging her down by the hair; beside them a [scaled *del.*] figure is seen, scaled with iron scales from head to feet [with *del.*], precipitating himself into the Abyss with the Sword & Balances: he is Og, King of Bashan.

On the Right, Beneath the Cloud on which Abel Kneels, is Abraham with Sarah & Isaac, also Hagar & Ishmael. Abel kneels on a bloody Cloud &c. (*to come in here as two leaves forward*).

P. 80.

Abel kneels on a bloody cloud descriptive of those Churches before the flood, that they were fill'd with blood & fire & vapour of smoke; even till Abraham's time the vapor & heat was not extinguish'd; these States Exist now. Man Passes on, but States remain for Ever; he passes thro' them like a traveller who may as well suppose that the places he has passed thro' exist no more, as a Man may suppose that the States he has pass'd thro' Exist no more. Every thing is Eternal.

P. 79.

In Eternity one Thing never Changes into another Thing. Each Identity is Eternal: consequently Apuleius's Golden Ass & Ovid's Metamorphosis & others of the like kind are Fable; yet they contain

Vision in a sublime degree, being derived from real Vision in More ancient Writings. Lot's Wife being Changed into [a] Pillar of Salt alludes to the Mortal Body being render'd a Permanent Statue, but not Changed or Transformed into Another Identity while it retains its own Individuality. A Man can never become Ass nor Horse; some are born with shapes of Men, who may be both, but Eternal Identity is one thing & Corporeal Vegetation is another thing. Changing Water into Wine by Jesus & into Blood by Moses relates to Vegetable Nature also.

Pp. 76–77.

[Beneath] Ishmael is Mahomed, & on the left, beneath the falling figure of Cain, is Moses casting his tables of stone into the deeps. It ought to be understood that the Persons, Moses & Abraham, are not here meant, but the States Signified by those Names, the Individuals being representatives or Visions of those States as they were reveal'd to Mortal Man in the Series of Divine Revelations as they are written in the Bible; these various States I have seen in my Imagination; when distant they appear as One Man, but as you approach they appear Multitudes of Nations. Abraham hovers above his posterity, which appear as Multitudes of Children ascending from the Earth, surrounded by Stars, as it was said: 'As the Stars of Heaven for Multitude.' Jacob & [their *del.*] his Twelve Sons hover beneath the feet of Abraham & recieve their children from the Earth. I have seen, when at a distance, Multitudes of Men in Harmony appear like a single Infant, sometimes in the Arms of a Female; this represented the Church.

But to proceed with the description of those on the Left hand—beneath the Cloud on which Moses kneels is two figures, a Male & Female, chain'd together by the feet; they represent those who perish'd by the flood; beneath them a multitude of their associates are seen falling headlong; by the side of them is a Mighty fiend with a Book in his hand, which is Shut; he represents the person nam'd in Isaiah, xxii c. & 20 v., Eliakim, the Son of Hilkiah: he drags Satan down headlong: he is crown'd with oak [& has *del.*]; by the side of the Scaled figure representing Og, King of Bashan, is a Figure with a Basket, emptying out the vanities of Riches & Worldly Honours: he is Araunah, the Jebusite, master of the threshing floor; above him are two figures, elevated on a Cloud, representing the Pharisees who plead their own Righteousness before the throne; they are weighed down by two fiends. Beneath the Man with the Basket are three fiery fiends with grey beards & scourges of fire: they represent Cruel Laws; they scourge a groupe of figures down into the deeps; beneath them are various figures in

attitudes of contention representing various States of Misery, which, alas, every one on Earth is liable to enter into, & against which we should all watch. The Ladies will be pleas'd to see that I have represented the Furies by Three Men & not by three Women. It is not because I think the Ancients wrong, but they will be pleas'd to remember that mine is Vision & not Fable. The Spectator may suppose them Clergymen in the Pulpit, scourging Sin instead of Forgiving it.

The Earth beneath these falling Groupes of figures is rocky & burning, and seems as if convuls'd by Earthquakes; a Great City on fire is seen in the distance; the armies are fleeing upon the Mountains. On the foreground, hell is opened & many figures are descending into it down stone steps & beside a Gate beneath a rock where sin & death are to be closed Eternally [howling & lamenting *del.*] by that Fiend who carries the key [& drags *del.*] in one hand & drags them down with the other. On the rock & above the Gate a fiend with wings urges [them *del.*] the wicked onwards with fiery darts; he [represents the Assyrian *del.*] is Hazael, the Syrian, who drives abroad all those who rebell against their Saviour; beneath the steps [is] Babylon, represented by a King crowned, Grasping his Sword & his Sceptre: he is just awaken'd out of his Grave; around him are other Kingdoms arising to Judgment, represented in this Picture [as in the Prophets *del.*] as Single Personages according to the descriptions in the Prophets. The Figure dragging up a Woman by her hair represents the Inquisition, as do those contending on the sides of the Pit, & in Particular the Man strangling two women represents a Cruel Church.

P. 78.

Two persons, one in Purple, the other in Scarlet, are descending [into Hell *del.*] down the steps into the Pit; these are Caiphas & Pilate—Two States where all those reside who Calumniate & Murder under Pretence of Holiness & Justice. Caiphas has a Blue Flame like a Miter on his head. Pilate has bloody hands that never can be cleansed; the Females behind them represent the Females belonging to such States, who are under perpetual terrors & vain dreams, plots & secret deceit. Those figures that descend into the Flames before Caiphas & Pilate are Judas & those of his Class. Achitophel is also here with the cord in his hand.

Pp. 80–81.

Between the Figures of Adam & Eve appears a fiery Gulph descending from the sea of fire Before the throne; in this Cataract Four Angels descend headlong with four trumpets to awake the dead; beneath these is the Seat of the Harlot, nam'd Mystery in the Revelations. She is [bound *del.*] siezed by Two Beings each with three heads; [representing *del.*] they Represent Vegetative Existence; as it is written in Revelations, they strip her naked & burn her with fire; it represents the Eternal Consummation of Vegetable Life & Death with its Lusts. The wreathed Torches in their hands represents Eternal Fire which is the fire of Generation or Vegetation; it is an Eternal Consummation. Those who are blessed with Imaginative Vision see This Eternal Female & tremble at what others fear not, while they despise & laugh at what others fear. Her Kings & Councellors & Warriors descend in Flames, Lamenting & looking upon her in astonishment & Terror, & Hell is open'd beneath her Seat on the Left hand. Beneath her feet is a flaming Cavern in which is seen the Great Red Dragon with seven heads & ten Horns [who *del.*]; he has Satan's book of Accusations lying on the Rock open before him; he is bound in chains by Two strong demons; they are Gog & Magog, who have been compell'd to subdue their Master (Ezekiel, xxxviii c, 8 v.) with their Hammer & Tongs, about to new-Create the Seven-Headed Kingdoms. The Graves beneath are open'd, & the dead awake & obey the call of the Trumpet; those on the Right hand awake in joy, those on the Left in Horror; beneath the Dragon's Cavern a Skeleton begins to Animate, starting into life at the Trumpet's sound, while the Wicked contend with each other on the brink of perdition. On the Right a Youthful couple are awaked by their Children; an Aged patriarch is awaked by his aged wife—He is Albion, our Ancestor, patriarch of the Atlantic Continent, whose History Preceded that of the Hebrews & in whose Sleep, or Chaos, Creation began; [his Emanation or Wife is Jerusalem, who is about to be reciev'd like the Bride of the . . . *del.*]; at their head the Aged Woman is Brittannica, the Wife of Albion: Jerusalem is their daughter. Little infants creep out of the [mould *del.*] flowery mould into the Green fields of the blessed who in various joyful companies embrace & ascend to meet Eternity.

The Persons who ascend to Meet the Lord, coming in the Clouds with power & great Glory, are representations of those States described in the Bible under the Names of the Fathers before & after the Flood. Noah is seen in the Midst of these, Canopied by a Rainbow, on his right hand Shem & on his Left Japhet; these three Persons represent Poetry, Painting & Music, the three Powers in Man of conversing with Paradise, which the flood did not Sweep away. Above Noah is the Church Universal, represented by a Woman Surrounded by Infants. There is such a State in Eternity: it is composed of the Innocent civilized Heathen & the Uncivilized Savage, who, having not the Law, do by Nature the things contain'd in the Law.

This State appears like a Female crown'd with stars, driven into the Wilderness; she has the Moon under her feet. The Aged Figure with Wings, having a writing tablet & taking account of the numbers who arise, is That Angel of the Divine Presence mention'd in Exodus, xiv c., 19 v. & in other Places; this Angel is frequently call'd by the Name of Jehovah Elohim, The "I am" of the Oaks of Albion.

Around Noah & beneath him are various figures Risen into the Air; among these are Three Females, representing those who are not of the dead but of those found alive at the Last Judgment; they appear to be innocently gay & thoughtless, not being among the condemn'd because ignorant of crime in the midst of a corrupted Age; the Virgin Mary was of this Class. A Mother Meets her numerous Family in the Arms of their Father; these are representations of the Greek Learned & Wise, as also of those of other Nations, such as Egypt & Babylon, in which were multitudes who shall meet the Lord coming in the Clouds.

The Children of Abraham, or Hebrew Church, are represented as a Stream of [Light *del.*] Figures, on which are seen Stars somewhat like the Milky way; they ascend from the Earth where Figures kneel Embracing above the Graves, & Represent Religion, or Civilized Life such as it is in the Christian Church, who are the Offspring of the Hebrew.

Pp. 82–84.

Just above the graves & above the spot where the Infants creep out of the Ground stand two, a Man & Woman; these are the Primitive Christians. The two Figures in purifying flames by the side of the dragon's cavern represents the Latter state of the Church when on the verge of Perdition, yet protected by a Flaming Sword. Multitudes are seen ascending from the Green fields of the blessed in which a Gothic Church is representative of true Art, Call'd Gothic in All Ages by those who follow'd the Fashion, as that is call'd which is without Shape or Fashion. On the right hand of Noah a Woman with Children Represents the State Call'd Laban the Syrian; it is the Remains of Civilization in the State from whence Abraham was taken. Also On the right hand of Noah A Female descends to meet her Lover or Husband, representative of that Love, call'd Friendship, which Looks for no other heaven than their Beloved & in him sees all reflected as in a Glass of Eternal Diamond.

On the right hand of these rise the diffident & Humble, & on their left a solitary Woman with her infant: these are caught up by three aged Men who appear as suddenly emerging from the blue sky for their help. These three Aged Men represent divine Providence as oppos'd to, & distinct from, divine vengeance, represented by three Aged men on the side of the Picture among the Wicked, with scourges of fire.

If the Spectator could Enter into these Images in his Imagination, approaching them on the Fiery Chariot of his Contemplative Thought, if he could Enter into Noah's Rainbow or into his bosom, or could make a Friend & Companion of one of these Images of wonder, which always intreats him to leave mortal things (as he must know), then would he arise from his Grave, then would he meet the Lord in the Air & then he would be happy. General Knowledge is Remote Knowledge; it is in Particulars that Wisdom consists & Happiness too. Both in Art & in Life, General Masses are as Much Art as a Pasteboard Man is Human. Every Man has Eyes, Nose & Mouth; this Every Idiot knows, but he who enters into & discriminates most minutely the Manners & Intentions, the [Expression del.] Characters in all their branches, is the alone Wise or Sensible Man, & on this discrimination All Art is founded. I intreat, then, that the Spectator will attend to the Hands & Feet, to the Lineaments of the Countenances; they are all descriptive of Character, & not a line is drawn without intention, & that most discriminate & particular. As Poetry admits not a Letter that is Insignificant, so Painting admits not a Grain of Sand or a Blade of Grass Insignificant—much less an Insignificant Blur or Mark.

Above the Head of Noah is Seth; this State call'd Seth is Male & Female in a higher state of Happiness & wisdom than Noah, being nearer the State of Innocence; beneath the feet of Seth two figures represent the two Seasons of Spring & Autumn, while beneath the feet of Noah Four Seasons represent [our present changes of Extremes del.] the Changed State made by the flood.

By the side of Seth is Elijah; he comprehends all the Prophetic Characters; he is seen on his fiery Chariot, bowing before the throne of the Saviour; in like manner The figures of Seth & his wife comprehends the Fathers before the flood & their Generations; when seen remote they appear as One Man; a little below Seth on his right are Two Figures, a Male & Female, with numerous Children; these represent those who were not in the Line of the Church & yet were Saved from among the Antediluvians who Perished; between Seth & these a female figure [with the back turn'd del.] represents the Solitary State of those who, previous to the Flood, walked with God.

All these arise toward the opening Cloud before the Throne, led onward by triumphant Groupes of Infants, & the Morning Stars sing together. Between Seth & Elijah three Female Figures crown'd with Garlands Represent Learning & Science, which accompanied Adam out of Eden.

The Cloud that opens, rolling apart before the throne & before the New Heaven & the New Earth, is Composed of Various Groupes of Figures, particularly the Four Living Creatures mention'd in Revelations as Surrounding the Throne; these I suppose to have the chief agency in removing the [former del.] old heavens & the old Earth to make way for the New Heaven & the New Earth, to descend from the throne of God & of the Lamb; that Living Creature on the Left of the Throne Gives to the Seven Angels the Seven Vials of the wrath of God, with which they, hovering over the deeps beneath, pour out upon the wicked their Plagues; the Other Living Creatures are descending with a Shout & with the Sound of the Trumpet, directing the Combats in the upper Elements; in the two Corners of the Picture [where . . . Apollyon del.], on the Left hand Apollyon is foiled before the Sword of Michael, & on the Right the Two Witnesses are subduing their Enemies.

[Around the Throne Heaven is Opened del.] On the Cloud are open'd the Books of Remembrance of Life & of Death: before that of Life, on the Right, some figures bow in humiliation; before that of Death, on the Left, the Pharisees are pleading their own Righteousness; the one shines with beams of Light, the other utters Lightnings & tempests.

A Last Judgment is Necessary because Fools flourish. Nations Flourish under Wise Rulers & are depress'd under foolish Rulers; it is the same with Individuals as Nations; works of Art can only be produc'd in Perfection where the Man is either in Affluence or is Above the Care of it. Poverty is the Fool's Rod, which at last is turn'd on his own back; this is A Last Judgment—when Men of Real Art Govern & Pretenders Fall. Some People & not a few Artists have asserted that the Painter of this Picture would not have done so well if he had been properly Encourag'd. Let those who think so, reflect on the State of Nations under Poverty & their incapability of Art; tho' Art is Above Either, the Argument is better for Affluence than Poverty; & tho' he would not have been a greater Artist, yet he would have produc'd Greater works of Art in proportion to his means. A Last Judgment is not for the purpose of making Bad Men better, but for the Purpose of hindering them from opressing the Good with Poverty & Pain by means of Such Vile Arguments & Insinuations.

Around the Throne Heaven is open'd & the Nature of Eternal Things Display'd, All Springing from the Divine Humanity. All beams from him [& (Because del.) as he himself has said, All dwells in him del.]. He is the Bread & the Wine; he is the Water of Life; accordingly on Each Side of the opening Heaven appears an Apostle; [one del.] that on the Right Represents

Baptism, [& the Other *del.*] that on the Left Represents the Lord's Supper. All Life consists of these Two, Throwing off Error & Knaves from our company continually & Recieving Truth or Wise Men into our Company continually. He who is out of the Church & opposes it is no less an Agent of Religion than he who is in it; to be an Error & to be Cast out is a part of God's design. No man can Embrace True Art till he has Explor'd & cast out False Art (such is the Nature of Mortal Things), or he will be himself Cast out by those who have Already Embraced True Art. Thus My Picture is a History of Art & Science, the Foundation of Society, [all *del.*] Which is Humanity itself. What are all the Gifts of the Spirit but Mental Gifts? Whenever any Individual Rejects Error & Embraces Truth, a Last Judgment passes upon that Individual.

P. 85.

Over the Head of the Saviour & Redeemer The Holy Spirit, like a Dove, is surrounded by a blue Heaven in which are the two Cherubim that bow'd over the Ark, for here the temple is open'd in Heaven & the Ark of the Covenant is as a Dove of Peace. The Curtains are drawn apart, Christ having rent the Veil. The Candlestick & the Table of Shew-bread appear on Each side; a Glorification of Angels with Harps surround the Dove.

The Temple stands on the Mount of God; from it flows on each side the River of Life, on whose banks Grows the tree of Life, among whose branches temples & Pinnacles, tents & pavilions, Gardens & Groves, display Paradise with its Inhabitants walking up & down in Conversations concerning Mental Delights. Here they are &c. (*as three leaves on*).

Pp. 90-91.

Here they are no longer talking of what is Good & Evil, or of what is Right or Wrong, & puzzling themselves in Satan's [Maze *del.*] Labyrinth, But are Conversing with Eternal Realities as they Exist in the Human Imagination. We are in a World of Generation & death, & this world we must cast off if we would be Painters such as Rafael, Mich. Angelo & the Ancient Sculptors; if we do not cast off this world we shall be only Venetian Painters, who will be cast off & Lost from Art.

P. 85.

Jesus is surrounded by Beams of Glory in which are seen all around him Infants emanating from him; these represent the Eternal Births of Intellect from the divine Humanity. A Rainbow surrounds the throne & the Glory, in which youthful Nuptials recieve the infants in their hands. In Eternity Woman is the Emanation of Man; she has No Will of her own. There is no such thing in Eternity as a Female Will, & Queens [of England *del.*].

On the Side next Baptism are seen those call'd in the Bible Nursing Fathers & Nursing Mothers; [they have Crowns; the Spectator may suppose them to be the Good . . . *del.*] they represent Education. On the Side next the Lord's Supper The Holy Family, consisting of Mary, Joseph, John the Baptist, Zacharias & Elizabeth, recieving the Bread & Wine, among other Spirits of the Just made perfect. [Just *del.*] beneath these a Cloud of Women & Children are taken up, fleeing from the rolling Cloud which separates the Wicked from the Seats of Bliss. These represent those who, tho' willing, were too weak to Reject Error without the Assistance & Countenance of those Already in the Truth; for a Man Can only Reject Error by the Advice of a Friend or by the Immediate Inspiration of God; it is for this Reason among many others that I have put the Lord's Supper on the Left hand of the [Picture *del.*] Throne, for it appears so at the Last Judgment, for a Protection.

Pp. 91-92.

Many suppose that before [Adam *del.*] the Creation All was Solitude & Chaos. This is the most pernicious Idea that can enter the Mind, as it takes away all sublimity from the Bible & Limits All Existence to Creation & to Chaos, To the Time & Space fixed by the Corporeal Vegetative Eye, & leaves the Man who entertains such an Idea the habitation of Unbelieving demons. Eternity Exists, and All things in Eternity, Independent of Creation which was an act of Mercy. I have represented those who are in Eternity by some in a Cloud within the Rainbow that Surrounds the Throne; they merely appear as in a Cloud when any thing of Creation, Redemption or Judgment are the Subjects of Contemplation, tho' their Whole Contemplation is concerning these things; the Reason they so appear is The Humiliation of the Reason & doubting Self-hood, & the Giving all up to Inspiration. By this it will be seen that I do not consider either the Just or the Wicked to be in a Supreme State, but to be every one of them States of the Sleep [of *del.*] which the Soul may fall into in its deadly dreams of Good & Evil when it leaves Paradise [with *del.*] following the Serpent.

P. 91 (sideways).

The Greeks represent Chronos or Time as a very Aged Man; this is Fable, but the Real Vision of Time is in Eternal Youth. I have, however, somewhat accomodated my Figure of Time to the common opinion, as I myself am also infected with it & my Visions also infected, & I see Time Aged, alas, too much so.

Allegories are things that Relate to Moral Virtues. Moral Virtues do not Exist; they are Allegories & dissimulations. But Time & Space are Real Beings, a Male & a Female. Time is a Man, Space is a Woman, & her Masculine Portion is Death.

Pp. 86, 90.

The Combats of Good & Evil [& of Truth & Error which are the same thing *del.*] is Eating of the Tree of Knowledge. The Combats of Truth & Error is Eating of the Tree of Life; these are not only Universal, but Particular. Each are Personified. There is not an Error but it has a Man for its [Actor *del.*] Agent, that is, it is a Man. There is not a Truth but it has also a Man. Good & Evil are Qualities in Every Man, whether a Good or Evil Man. These are Enemies & destroy one another by every Means in their power, both of deceit & of open Violence. The deist & the Christian are but the Results of these Opposing Natures. Many are deists who would in certain Circumstances have been Christians in outward appearance. Voltaire was one of this number; he was as intolerant as an Inquisitor. Manners make the Man, not Habits. It is the same in Art: by their Works ye shall know them; the Knave who is Converted to [Christianity *del.*] Deism & the Knave who is Converted to Christianity is still a Knave, but he himself will not know it, tho' Every body else does. Christ comes, as he came at first, to deliver those who were bound under the Knave, not to deliver the Knave. He Comes to deliver Man, the Accused, & not Satan, the Accuser. We do not find any where that Satan is Accused of Sin; he is only accused of Unbelief & thereby drawing Man into Sin that he may accuse him. Such is the Last Judgment—a deliverance from Satan's Accusation. Satan thinks that Sin is displeasing to God; he ought to know that Nothing is displeasing to God but Unbelief & Eating of the Tree of Knowledge of Good & Evil.

P. 87.

Men are admitted into Heaven not because they have curbed & govern'd their Passions or have No Passions, but because they have Cultivated their Understandings. The Treasures of Heaven are not Negations of Passion, but Realities of Intellect, from which all the Passions Emanate Uncurbed in their Eternal Glory. The Fool shall not enter into Heaven let him be ever so Holy. Holiness is not The Price of Enterance into Heaven. Those who are cast out are All Those who, having no Passions of their own because No Intellect, Have spent their lives in Curbing & Governing other People's by the Various arts of Poverty & Cruelty of all kinds. Wo, Wo, Wo to you Hypocrites. Even Murder, the Courts of Justice, more merciful than the Church, are compell'd to allow is not done in Passion, but in Cool Blooded design & Intention.

The Modern Church Crucifies Christ with the Head Downwards.

Pp. 92-95.

Many Persons, such as Paine & Voltaire, with some of the Ancient Greeks, say: "we will not converse concerning Good & Evil; we will live in Paradise & Liberty." You may do so in Spirit, but not in the Mortal Body as you pretend, till after the Last Judgment; for in Paradise they have no Corporeal & Mortal Body—that originated with the Fall & was call'd Death & cannot be removed but by a Last Judgment; while we are in the world of Mortality we Must Suffer. The Whole Creation Groans to be deliver'd; there will always be as many Hypocrites born as Honest Men, & they will always have superior Power in Mortal Things. You cannot have Liberty in this World without what you call Moral Virtue, & you cannot have Moral Virtue without the Slavery of [half *del.*] that half of the Human Race who hate what you call Moral Virtue.

The Nature of Hatred & Envy & of All the Mischiefs in the World are here depicted. No one Envies or Hates one of his Own Party; even the devils love one another in their Way; they torment one another for other reasons than Hate or Envy; these are only employ'd against the Just. Neither can Seth Envy Noah, or Elijah Envy Abraham, but they may both of them Envy the Success of Satan or of Og or Molech. The Horse never Envies the Peacock, nor the Sheep the Goat, but they Envy a Rival in Life & Existence whose ways & means exceed their own, let him be of what Class of Animals he will; a dog will envy a Cat who is pamper'd at [his *del.*] the expense of his comfort, as I have often seen. The Bible never tells us that devils torment one another thro' Envy; it is thro' this that [makes *del.*] they torment the Just—but for what do they torment one another? I answer: For the Coercive Laws of Hell, Moral Hypocrisy. They torment a Hypocrite when he is discover'd; they punish a Failure in the tormentor who has suffer'd the Subject of his torture to Escape. In Hell all is Self Righteousness; there is no such thing there as Forgiveness of Sin; he who does Forgive Sin is Crucified as an Abettor of Criminals, & he who performs Works of Mercy in Any shape whatever is punish'd &, if possible, destroy'd, not thro' envy or Hatred or Malice, but thro' Self Righteousness that thinks it does God service, which God is Satan. They do not Envy one another: They contemn & despise one another: Forgiveness of Sin is only at the Judgment Seat of Jesus the Saviour, where the Accuser is cast out, not because he Sins, but because he torments the Just & makes them do what he condemns as Sin & what he knows is opposite to their own Identity.

It is not because Angels are Holier than Men or Devils that makes them Angels, but because they do not Expect Holiness from one another; but from God only.

The Player is a liar when he says: "Angels are hap-"pier than Men because they are better." Angels are happier than Men & Devils because they are not always Prying after Good & Evil in one another & eating the Tree of Knowledge for Satan's Gratification.

Thinking as I do that the Creator of this World is a very Cruel Being, & being a Worshipper of Christ, I cannot help saying: "the Son, O how unlike the "Father!" First God Almighty comes with a Thump on the Head. Then Jesus Christ comes with a balm to heal it.

The Last Judgment is an Overwhelming of Bad Art & Science. Mental Things are alone Real; what is call'd Corporeal, Nobody Knows of its Dwelling Place: it is in Fallacy, & its Existence an Imposture. Where is the Existence Out of Mind or Thought? Where is it but in the Mind of a Fool? Some People flatter themselves that there will be No Last Judgment & that Bad Art will be adopted & mixed with Good Art, That Error or Experiment will make a Part of Truth, & they Boast that it is its Foundation; these People flatter themselves: I will not Flatter them. Error is Created. Truth is Eternal. Error, or Creation, will be Burned up, & then, & not till Then, Truth or Eternity will appear. It is Burnt up the Moment Men cease to behold it. I assert for My Self that I do not behold the outward Creation & that to me it is hindrance & not Action; it is as the Dirt upon my feet, No part of Me. "What," it will be Question'd, "When the Sun rises, do you not see a round disk of fire somewhat like a Guinea?" O no, no, I see an Innumerable company of the Heavenly host crying 'Holy, Holy, Holy is the Lord God Almighty.' I question not my Corporeal or Vegetative Eye any more than I would Question a Window concerning a Sight. I look thro' it & not with it.

[1966]

ANNOTATIONS TO WORDSWORTH

Blake's annotations to Wordsworth's Poems *of 1815 and* The Excursion *(1814) were written in 1826. The comments of Blake are printed in larger type; the passages from Wordsworth in smaller type. The annotations to* The Excursion *are all on the verses "from the conclusion of the first book of* The Recluse," *which were quoted by Wordsworth in the preface to his poem of 1814.*

ANNOTATIONS TO
"POEMS"
BY WILLIAM WORDSWORTH
VOL. I, LONDON, MDCCCXV

Page viii.

The powers requisite for the production of poetry are, first, those of observation and description . . . 2dly, Sensibility.

One Power alone makes a Poet: Imagination, The Divine Vision.

Page 1.

[*Sub-title*]: "Poems Referring to the Period of Childhood."

I see in Wordsworth the Natural Man rising up against the Spiritual Man Continually, & then he is No Poet but a Heathen Philosopher at Enmity against all true Poetry or Inspiration.

Page 3.

And I could wish my days to be
Bound each to each by natural piety.

There is no such Thing as Natural Piety Because The Natural Man is at Enmity with God.

Page 43.

"To H.C. Six Years Old."

This is all in the highest degree Imaginative & equal to any Poet, but not Superior. I cannot think that Real Poets have any competition. None are greatest in the Kingdom of Heaven; it is so in Poetry.

Page 44.

"Influence of Natural Objects
"In calling forth and strengthening the Imagination
"in Boyhood and early Youth."

Natural Objects always did & now do weaken, deaden & obliterate Imagination in Me. Wordsworth must know that what he Writes Valuable is Not to be found in Nature. Read Michael Angelo's Sonnet, vol. 2, p. 179:

[Heaven-born, the Soul a heaven-ward course must hold;
Beyond the visible world She soars to seek,
(For what delights the sense is false and weak)
Ideal Form, the universal mould.]

Page 341.

"Essay, Supplementary to the Preface."

I do not know who wrote these Prefaces: they are very mischievous & direct contrary to Wordsworth's own Practise.

Pages 364-5.

In Macpherson's work it is exactly the reverse; every thing (that is not stolen) is in this manner defined, insulated, dislocated, deadened,—yet nothing distinct . . . Yet, much as these pretended treasures of antiquity have been admired, they have been wholly uninfluential upon the literature of the country . . . no Author in the least distinguished, has ventured formally to imitate them—except the Boy, Chatterton, on their first appearance.

I believe both Macpherson & Chatterton, that what they say is Ancient Is so.

I own myself an admirer of Ossian equally with any other Poet whatever, Rowley & Chatterton also.

Pages 314–5.

Is it the result of the whole that, in the opinion of the Writer, the judgment of the People is not to be respected ? The thought is most injurious; . . . to the People . . . his devout respect, his reverence, is due. He . . . takes leave of his Readers by assuring them—that if he were not persuaded that the Contents of these Volumes, and the Work to which they are subsidiary, evinced something of the "Vision and the Faculty divine," . . . he would not, if a wish could do it, save them from immediate destruction.

It appears to me as if the last Paragraph beginning "Is it the result" Was writ by another hand & mind from the rest of these Prefaces. Perhaps they are the opinions of a Portrait or Landscape painter. Imagination is the Divine Vision not of The World, or of Man, nor from Man as he is a Natural Man, but only as he is a Spiritual Man. Imagination has nothing to do with Memory.

Pages xii–xiii.

> How exquisitely the individual Mind
> (And the progressive powers perhaps no less
> Of the whole species) to the external World
> Is fitted :—& how exquisitely, too,
> Theme this but little heard of among Men,
> The external World is fitted to the Mind.

You shall not bring me down to believe such fitting & fitted. I know better & please your Lordship.

> Such grateful haunts foregoing, if I oft
> Must turn elsewhere—to travel near the tribes
> And fellowships of Men, & see ill sights
> Of madding passions mutually inflamed;
> Must hear *Humanity in fields & groves*
> *Pipe solitary anguish;* or must hang
> Brooding above the fierce confederate storm
> Of Sorrow, barricadoed evermore
> With the walls of cities; may these sounds
> Have their authentic comment,—that, even these
> Hearing, I be not downcast or forlorn!

Does not this Fit, & is it not Fitting most Exquisitely too, but to what ?—not to Mind, but to the Vile Body only & to its Laws of Good & Evil & its Enmities against Mind.

[1966]

LETTERS

ANNOTATIONS TO "THE EXCURSION, BEING A PORTION OF THE RECLUSE, A POEM" BY WILLIAM WORDSWORTH, LONDON, MDCCCXIV

> All strength—all terror, single or in bands,
> That ever was put forth in personal form;
> Jehovah—with his thunder, and the choir
> Of shouting Angels, and the empyreal thrones,
> I pass them, unalarmed . . .

Solomon, when he Married Pharaoah's daughter & became a Convert to the Heathen Mythology, Talked exactly in this way of Jehovah as a Very inferior object of Man's Contemplation; he also passed him by unalarm'd & was permitted. Jehovah dropped a tear & follow'd him by his Spirit into the Abstract Void; it is called the Divine Mercy. Satan dwells in it, but Mercy does not dwell in him; he knows not to Forgive.

LETTER TO DR. TRUSLER

Dr. John Trusler (1735–1820) was a clergyman and author, whom Blake had met earlier in the summer of 1799. He commissioned a painting of "Malevolence," but rejected Blake's design for it, declaring: "Your Fancy . . . seems to be in the other world, or the World of Spirits, which accords not with my Intentions, which, whilst living in This World, Wish to follow the Nature of it." Blake's letter of August 23 was written in reply to Trusler's objection.

TO DR. TRUSLER

Revd Sir,

I really am sorry that you are fall'n out with the Spiritual World, Especially if I should have to answer for it. I feel very sorry that your Ideas & Mine on Moral Painting differ so much as to have made you angry with my method of Study. If I am wrong, I am wrong in good company. I had hoped your plan comprehended All Species of this Art, & Expecially that you would not regret that Species which gives Existence to Every other, namely, Visions of Eternity. You say that I want somebody to Elucidate my Ideas. But you ought to know that What is Grand is necessarily obscure to Weak men. That which can be made Explicit to the

Idiot is not worth my care. The wisest of the Ancients consider'd what is not too Explicit as the fittest for Instruction, because it rouzes the faculties to act. I name Moses, Solomon, Esop, Homer, Plato.

But as you have favor'd me with your remarks on my Design, permit me in return to defend it against a mistaken one, which is, That I have supposed Malevolence without a Cause. Is not Merit in one a Cause of Envy in another, & Serenity & Happiness & Beauty a Cause of Malevolence? But Want of Money & the Distress of A Thief can never be alledged as the Cause of his Thieving, for many honest people endure greater hardships with Fortitude. We must therefore seek the Cause elsewhere than in want of Money, for that is the Miser's passion, not the Thief's.

I have therefore proved your Reasonings Ill proportion'd, which you can never prove my figures to be; they are those of Michael Angelo, Rafael & the Antique, & of the best living Models. I percieve that your Eye is perverted by Caricature Prints, which ought not to abound so much as they do. Fun I love, but too much Fun is of all things the most loathsom. Mirth is better than Fun, & Happiness is better than Mirth. I feel that a Man may be happy in This World. And I know that This World Is a World of imagination & Vision. I see Every thing I paint In This World, but Every body does not see alike. To the Eyes of a Miser a Guinea is more beautiful than the Sun, & a bag worn with the use of Money has more beautiful proportions than a Vine filled with Grapes. The tree which moves some to tears of joy is in the Eyes of others only a Green thing that stands in the way. Some See Nature all Ridicule & Deformity, & by these I shall not regulate my proportions; & Some Scarce see Nature at all. But to the Eyes of the Man of Imagination, Nature is Imagination itself. As a man is, So he Sees. As the Eye is formed, such are its Powers. You certainly Mistake, when you say that the Visions of Fancy are not to be found in This World. To Me This World is all One continued Vision of Fancy or Imagination, & I feel Flatter'd when I am told so. What is it sets Homer, Virgil & Milton in so high a rank of Art? Why is the Bible more Entertaining & Instructive than any other book? Is it not because they are addressed to the Imagination, which is Spiritual Sensation, & but mediately to the Understanding or Reason? Such is True Painting, and such was alone valued by the Greeks & the best modern Artists. Consider what Lord Bacon says: "Sense sends over to Imagination before Reason have judged, & Reason sends over to Imagination before the Decree can be acted." See Advancem^t of Learning, Part 2, P. 47 of first Edition.

But I am happy to find a Great Majority of Fellow Mortals who can Elucidate My Visions, & Particularly they have been Elucidated by Children, who have taken a greater delight in contemplating my Pictures than I even hoped. Neither Youth nor Childhood is Folly or Incapacity. Some Children are Fools & so are some Old Men. But There is a vast Majority on the side of Imagination or Spiritual Sensation.

To Engrave after another Painter is infinitely more laborious than to Engrave one's own Inventions. And of the size you require my price has been Thirty Guineas, & I cannot afford to do it for less. I had Twelve for the Head I sent you as a Specimen; but after my own designs I could do at least Six times the quantity of labour in the same time, which will account for the difference of price as also that Chalk Engraving is at least six times as laborious as Aqua tinta. I have no objection to Engraving after another Artist. Engraving is the profession I was apprenticed to, & should never have attempted to live by any thing else, If orders had not come in for my Designs & Paintings, which I have the pleasure to tell you are Increasing Every Day. Thus If I am a Painter it is not to be attributed to Seeking after. But I am contented whether I live by Painting or Engraving.

I am, Revd Sir, your very obedient servant,

William Blake

13 Hercules Buildings
Lambeth
August 23. 1799

LETTER TO WILLIAM HAYLEY

William Hayley (1745–1820) was a poet (principal work, The Triumphs of Temper [1781]) and the author of lives of Milton, Cowper, and the painter George Romney. He is now best known for his friendship and patronage of Blake.

TO WILLIAM HAYLEY

Dear Sir,

I am very sorry for your immense loss,[1] which is a repetition of what all feel in this valley of misery & happiness mixed. I send the Shadow of the departed Angel[2]: hope the likeness is improved. The lip I have again lessened as you advised & done a good many other softenings to the whole. I know that our deceased friends are more really with us than when they were apparent to our mortal part. Thirteen years ago I lost a brother[3] & with his spirit I converse daily & hourly in

[1] Refers to death of Hayley's son Thomas on May 2.
[2] An engraving of a medallion of his son Thomas to be included in Hayley's *Essay on Sculpture* (1800).
[3] Robert Blake, who died in 1787.

the Spirit & See him in my remembrance in the regions of my Imagination. I hear his advice & even now write from his Dictate. Forgive me for Expressing to you my Enthusiasm which I wish all to partake of Since it is to me a Source of Immortal Joy: even in this world by it I am the companion of Angels. May you continue to be so more & more & to be more & more perswaded that every Mortal loss is an Immortal Gain. The Ruins of Time builds Mansions in Eternity.—I have also sent A Proof of Pericles[4] for your Remarks, thanking you for the Kindness with which you Express them & feeling heartily your Grief with a brother's Sympathy.

I remain, Dear Sir, Your humble Servant

William Blake

Lambeth. May 6. 1800

LETTERS TO THOMAS BUTTS

Thomas Butts (1757–1845), chief clerk in the office of the Commissary General of the Musters, was a friend of Blake from 1793 and a generous collector of his works.

TO THOMAS BUTTS

Felpham Jan.y 10. 1802

Dear Sir,

Your very kind & affectionate Letter & the many kind things you have said in it, call'd upon me for an immediate answer; but it found My Wife & Myself so Ill, & My wife so very ill, that till now I have not been able to do this duty. The Ague & Rheumatism have been almost her constant Enemies, which she has combated in vain ever since we have been here; & her sickness is always my sorrow, of course. But what you tell me about your sight afflicted me not a little, & that about your health, in another part of your letter, makes me intreat you to take due care of both; it is a part of our duty to God & man to take due care of his Gifts; & tho' we ought not [to] think *more* highly of ourselves, yet we ought to think *As* highly of ourselves as immortals ought to think.

When I came down here, I was more sanguine than I am at present; but it was because I was ignorant of many things which have since occurred, & chiefly the unhealthiness of the place. Yet I do not repent of coming on a thousand accounts; & M.r H., I doubt not, will do ultimately all that both he & I wish—that is, to lift me out of difficulty; but this is no easy matter to a man who, having Spiritual Enemies of such formidable magnitude, cannot expect to want natural hidden ones.

⁴ An engraving of Pericles for Hayley's *Essay on Sculpture.*

Your approbation of my pictures is a Multitude to Me, & I doubt not that all your kind wishes in my behalf shall in due time be fulfilled. Your kind offer of pecuniary assistance I can only thank you for at present, because I have enough to serve my present purpose here; our expenses are small, & our income, from our incessant labour, fully adequate to [it *del.*] them at present. I am now engaged in Engraving 6 small plates for a New Edition of M.r Hayley's Triumphs of Temper, from drawings by Maria Flaxman, sister to my friend the Sculptor, and it seems that other things will follow in course, if I do but Copy these well; but Patience! if Great things do not turn out, it is because such things depend on the Spiritual & not on the Natural World; & if it was fit for me, I doubt not that I should be Employ'd in Greater things; & when it is proper, my Talents shall be properly exercised in Public, as I hope they are now in private; for, till then, I leave no stone unturn'd & no path unexplor'd that tends to improvement in my beloved Arts. One thing of real consequence I have accomplish'd by coming into the country, which is to me consolation enough: namely, I have recollected all my scatter'd thoughts on Art & resumed my primitive & original ways of Execution in both painting & engraving, which in the confusion of London I had very much lost & obliterated from my mind. But whatever becomes of my labours, I would rather that they should be preserv'd in your Green House (not, as you mistakenly call it, dung hill) than in the cold gallery of fashion.—The Sun may yet shine, & then they will be brought into open air.

But you have so generously & openly desired that I will divide my griefs with you, that I cannot hide what it is now become my duty to explain.—My unhappiness has arisen from a source which, if explor'd too narrowly, might hurt my pecuniary circumstances, As my dependence is on Engraving at present, & particularly on the Engravings I have in hand for M.r H.: & I find on all hands great objections to my doing any thing but the meer drudgery of business, & intimations that if I do not confine myself to this, I shall not live; this has always pursu'd me. You will understand by this the source of all my uneasiness. This from Johnson & Fuseli brought me down here, & this from M.r H. will bring me back again; for that I cannot live without doing my duty to lay up treasures in heaven is Certain & Determined, & to this I have long made up my mind, & why this should be made an objection to Me, while Drunkenness, Lewdness, Gluttony & even Idleness itself, does not hurt other men, let Satan himself Explain. The Thing I have most at Heart—more than life, or all that seems to make life comfortable without— Is the Interest of True Religion & Science, & whenever any thing appears to affect that Interest (Especially if I myself omit any duty to my [self *del.*] Station as a Soldier of Christ), It gives me the greatest of torments. I am not ashamed, afraid, or averse to tell you what Ought to be Told: That I am under the direction of Messengers from Heaven, Daily & Nightly; but the nature of such things is not, as some suppose, without trouble or care. Temptations are on the right hand & left; behind, the sea of time & space roars & follows swiftly; he who keeps not right onward is lost, & if our footsteps slide in clay, how can we do otherwise than fear & tremble? but I should not have troubled You with this account of my spiritual state, unless it had been necessary in explaining the actual cause of my uneasiness, into which you are so kind as to Enquire; for I never obtrude such things on others unless question'd, & then I never disguise the truth.—But if we fear to do the dictates of our Angels, & tremble at the Tasks set before us; if we refuse to do Spiritual Acts because of Natural Fears of Natural Desires! Who can describe the dismal torments of such a state!—I too well remember the Threats I heard!—If you, who are organised by Divine Providence for Spiritual communion, Refuse, & bury your Talent in the Earth, even tho' you should want Natural Bread, Sorrow & Desperation pursues you thro' life, & after death shame & confusion of face to eternity. Every one in Eternity will leave you, aghast at the Man who was crown'd with glory & honour by his brethren, & betray'd their cause to their enemies. You will be call'd the base Judas who betray'd his Friend!—Such words would make any stout man tremble, & how then could I be at ease? But I am now no longer in That State, & now go on again with my Task, Fearless, and tho' my path is difficult, I have no fear of stumbling while I keep it.

My wife desires her kindest Love to Mrs Butts, & I have permitted her to send it to you also; we often wish that we could unite again in Society, & hope that the time is not distant when we shall do so, being determin'd not to remain another winter here, but to return to London.

I hear a voice you cannot hear, that says I must not
    stay,
I see a hand you cannot see, that beckons me away.[1]

Naked we came here, naked of Natural things, & naked we shall return; but while cloth'd with the Divine Mercy, we are richly cloth'd in Spiritual & suffer all the rest gladly. Pray give my Love to Mrs Butts & your family.
I am, Yours Sincerely,

                                   William Blake

P.S. Your Obliging proposal of Exhibiting my two Pictures likewise calls for my thanks; I will finish the other, & then we shall judge of the matter with certainty.

TO THOMAS BUTTS

*   *   *   *   *

Accept of my thanks for your kind & heartening Letter. You have Faith in the Endeavours of Me, your weak brother & fellow Disciple; how great must be your faith in our Divine Master! You are to me a Lesson of Humility, while you Exalt me by such distinguishing commendations. I know that you see certain merits in me, which, by God's Grace, shall be made fully apparent & perfect in Eternity; in the mean time I must not bury the Talents in the Earth, but do my endeavour to live to the Glory of our Lord & Saviour; & I am also grateful to the kind hand that endeavours to lift me out of despondency, even if it lifts me too high.

And now, My Dear Sir, Congratulate me on my return to London, with the full approbation of Mr Hayley & with Promise—But, Alas!

Now I may say to you, what perhaps I should not dare to say to any one else: That I can alone carry on my visionary studies in London unannoy'd, & that I may converse with my friends in Eternity, See Visions, Dream Dreams & prophecy & speak Parables unobserv'd & at liberty from the Doubts of other Mortals; perhaps Doubts proceeding from Kindness, but Doubts are always pernicious, Especially when we Doubt our Friends. Christ is very decided on this Point: "He who is Not With Me is Against Me." There is no Medium or Middle state; & if a Man is the Enemy of my Spiritual Life while he pretends to be the Friend of my Corporeal, he is a Real Enemy—but the Man may be the friend of my Spiritual Life while he seems the Enemy of my Corporeal, but Not Vice Versa.

What is very pleasant, Every one who hears of my going to London again Applauds it as the only course for the interest of all concern'd in My Works, Observing that I ought not to be away from the opportunities London affords of seeing fine Pictures, and the various improvements in Works of Art going on in London.

But none can know the Spiritual Acts of my three years' Slumber on the banks of the Ocean, unless he has seen them in the Spirit, or unless he should read My long Poem[1] descriptive of those Acts; for I have in

---

these three years composed an immense number of verses on One Grand Theme, Similar to Homer's Iliad or Milton's Paradise Lost, the Persons & Machinery intirely new to the Inhabitants of Earth (some of the Persons Excepted). I have written this Poem from immediate Dictation, twelve or sometimes twenty or thirty lines at a time, without Premeditation & even against my Will; the Time it has taken in writing was thus render'd Non Existent, & an immense Poem Exists which seems to be the Labour of a long Life, all produc'd without Labour or Study. I mention this to shew you what I think the Grand Reason of my being brought down here.

I have a thousand & ten thousand things to say to you. My heart is full of futurity. I percieve that the sore travel which has been given me these three years leads to Glory & Honour. I rejoice & I tremble: "I am fearfully & wonderfully made." I had been reading the cxxxix Psalm a little before your Letter arrived. I take your advice. I see the face of my Heavenly Father; he lays his Hand upon my Head & gives a blessing to all my works; why should I be troubled? why should my heart & flesh cry out? I will go on in the Strength of the Lord; through Hell will I sing forth his Praises, that the Dragons of the Deep may praise him, & that those who dwell in darkness & in the Sea coasts may be gather'd into his Kingdom. Excuse my, perhaps, too great Enthusiasm. Please to accept of & give our Loves to Mrs Butts & your amiable Family, & believe me to be,

> Ever Yours Affectionately,
> Will Blake

Felpham
 April 25. 1803

LETTER TO GEORGE CUMBERLAND

George Cumberland (1754–1848), an early and close friend of Blake, was an amateur painter and etcher, and the author of several books, including A Poem on the Landscapes of Great Britain *(1793) and* Thoughts on Outline, Sculpture, and the System That Guided the Ancient Artists . . . *(1796) (with engravings by Blake).*

TO GEORGE CUMBERLAND

Dear Cumberland,

I have been very near the Gates of Death & have returned very weak & an Old Man feeble & tottering, but not in Spirit & Life, not in The Real Man The Imagination which Liveth for Ever. In that I am stronger & stronger as this Foolish Body decays. I thank you for the Pains you have taken with Poor Job. [1] I know too well that a great majority of Englishmen are fond of The Indefinite which they Measure by Newton's Doctrine of the Fluxions of an Atom, A Thing that does not Exist. These are Politicians & think that Republican Art is Inimical to their Atom. For a Line or Lineament is not formed by Chance: a Line is a Line in its Minutest Subdivisions: Strait or Crooked It is Itself & Not Intermeasurable with or by any Thing Else. Such is Job, but since the French Revolution Englishmen are all Intermeasurable One by Another, Certainly a happy state of Agreement to which I for One do not Agree. God keep me from the Divinity of Yes & No too, The Yea Nay Creeping Jesus, from supposing Up & Down to be the same Thing as all Experimentalists must suppose.

You are desirous I know to dispose of some of my Works & to make them Pleasin[g]. I am obliged to you & to all who do so. But having none remaining of all that I had Printed I cannot Print more Except at a great loss, for at the time I printed those things I had a whole House to range in: now I am shut up in a Corner therefore am forced to ask a Price for them that I scarce expect to get from a Stranger. I am now Printing a Set of the Songs of Innocence & Experience for a Friend at Ten Guineas which I cannot do under Six Months consistent with my other Work, so that I have little hope of doing any more of such things. The Last Work I produced is a Poem Entitled Jerusalem the Emanation of the Giant Albion, but find that to Print it will Cost my Time the amount of Twenty Guineas. One I have Finish'd. It contains 100 Plates but it is not likely that I shall get a Customer for it.

As you wish me to send you a list with the Prices of these things they are as follows

	£	s	d
America	6.	6.	0
Europe	6.	6.	0
Visions &c	5.	5.	0
Thel	3.	3.	0
Songs of Inn. & Exp.	10.	10.	0
Urizen	6.	6.	0

The Little Card [2] I will do as soon as Possible but when you Consider that I have been reduced to a Skeleton from which I am slowly recovering you will I hope have Patience with me.

[1] Blake's *Illustrations of the Book of Job* (1826).
[2] Blake's final engraving was for a message card for Cumberland.

Flaxman [3] is Gone & we must All soon follow, every one to his Own Eternal House, Leaving the Delusive Goddess Nature & her Laws to get into Freedom from all Law of the Members into The Mind, in which every one is King & Priest in his own House. God send it so on Earth as it is in Heaven.

I am, Dear Sir, Yours Affectionately

William Blake

12 April 1827
N 3 Fountain Court Strand

[1966]

◇◇◇◇◇◇◇◇◇◇◇◇◇◇◇◇◇◇◇◇◇◇◇◇◇◇◇◇◇◇◇◇◇

[3] John Flaxman (1755–1826) was a leading sculptor and an early encourager of Blake. He had died in December 1826.

William Wordsworth

===

1770–1850

===

OUTLINE OF EVENTS

1770   Born April 7, at Cockermouth, Cumberland. Father, John Wordsworth (b. 1741), attorney in the service of the leading landowner and political power of the area Sir James Lowther; mother, Ann (Cookson) (b. 1748); brothers, Richard (b. 1768), John (b. 1772), Christopher (b. 1774); sister Dorothy (b. 1771).

1778   Mother dies.

1779–87 Attends Hawkshead Grammar School.

1783   Father dies. Wordsworth children are left in the care of their uncles Richard Wordsworth and Christopher Cookson.

1787   Enters St. John's College, Cambridge.

1790   Summer, walking-tour of France and Switzerland.

1791   January, graduates from Cambridge; unsettled on career. November, goes to France (remaining until December 1792), and lives in Orleans and Blois; becomes supporter of the Revolution; falls in love with Annette Vallon of Blois, who gives birth to their child Anne-Caroline, December 15, 1792.

1793   Lives in London, where his poems *An Evening Walk* and *Descriptive Sketches* are brought out by the radical publisher Joseph Johnson. Summer, walking tour to Salisbury Plain, Isle of Wight, Wye Valley, and Wales; composes *A Letter to the Bishop of Llandaff*.

1795   Receives legacy from friend Raisley Calvert. Becomes associated in London with William Godwin and other political radicals. Summer, visits Bristol, where he first meets Coleridge, and settles with Dorothy at Racedown, Dorsetshire.

1797   Summer, moves with Dorothy to Alfoxden, Somersetshire, to be near Coleridge at Nether Stowey.

1798   *Lyrical Ballads* composed and published. September, sails to Germany with Coleridge and Dorothy and settles at Goslar.

1799   Spring, returns to England. December, settles at Dove Cottage, Grasmere, with Dorothy.

1800   Prepares second edition of *Lyrical Ballads* with "Preface," which appears in January 1801.

1802   August, meets Annette and daughter at Calais. October 4, marries Mary Hutchinson.

1805   February, death of brother John, sea-captain, in shipwreck. May, completes first version of *Prelude*.

1807   *Poems in Two Volumes* published.

1809–10 Important period of prose publication: May, 1809, *Convention Of Cintra* published; Dec. 1809–Feb. 1810, contributes "Reply to a Letter of Mathetes" and "Essay on Epitaphs"

[39]

to Coleridge's *The Friend; Guide to the Lakes* first published as introduction to Wilkinson's *Select Views* (1810).

1813   Takes up permanent residence at Rydal Mount. Receives political appointment from Tory government as Distributor of Stamps [collector of duties on legal documents, publications and licences] for Westmorland.

1814   *Excursion* published.

1815   First collected edition of poems published with "Preface" and "Essay, Supplementary."

1816   *Letter to a Friend of Robert Burns* published.

1818   *Two Addresses to the Freeholders of Westmorland* published in support of the Lowther family in their parliamentary contest with the radical reformer Henry Brougham.

1819   *Peter Bell* published.

1820   *River Duddon* volume of poems published, with new text of *Guide to the Lakes*.

1822   *Ecclesiastical Sketches* and first independent edition of *Guide to the Lakes* published.

1835   *Yarrow Revisited and other Poems* (with prose "Postscript" on politics and religion) published.

1843   Is appointed poet-laureate on death of Southey.

1845   *Kendal and Windermere Railway: Two Letters Reprinted from the Morning Post* published in opposition to a proposed extension of railroads into the Lake District.

1850   Dies, April 23. July, *The Prelude* published.

SELECTED BIBLIOGRAPHY

BIOGRAPHY

MOORMAN, MARY, *William Wordsworth: A Biography. The Early Years 1770–1803*, Oxford: Clarendon Press, 1957.

————, *William Wordsworth: A Biography. The Later Years 1803–1850*. Oxford: Clarendon Press, 1965.

REED, MARK L., *Wordsworth: The Chronology of the Early Years 1770–1799*, Cambridge, Mass.: Harvard University Press, 1967.

EDITIONS OF WORDSWORTH'S PROSE

DE SÉLINCOURT, ERNEST (ed.), *Wordsworth's Guide to the Lakes. Fifth Edition (1835)*, London: Henry Frowde, 1906.

GROSART, ALEXANDER B. (ed.), *The Prose Works of William Wordsworth*, 3 vols., London: Edward Moxon, 1876.

KNIGHT, WILLIAM A. (ed.), *The Prose Works of William Wordsworth*, 2 vols., London: Macmillan and Co., 1896.

OWEN, W. J. B., "Wordsworth's Preface to the *Lyrical Ballads*," *Anglistica*, IX (1957).

PEACOCK, MARKHAM L., JR., *The Critical Opinions of William Wordsworth*, Baltimore: The Johns Hopkins Press, 1950.

ZALL, PAUL M. (ed.), *Literary Criticism of William Wordsworth*, Regents Critics Series, Lincoln, Nebraska: University of Nebraska Press, 1966.

WORDSWORTH'S LITERARY CRITICISM

ABRAMS, M. H., *The Mirror and the Lamp: Romantic Theory and the Critical Tradition*, New York: Oxford University Press, 1953.

BARSTOW, MARJORIE L., *Wordsworth's Theory of Poetic Diction*, Yale Studies in English, LVII, New Haven: Yale University Press, 1917.

HEFFERNAN, JAMES A. W., *Wordsworth's Theory of Poetry: The Transforming Imagination*, Ithaca, New York: Cornell University Press, 1969.

OWEN, W. J. B., *Wordsworth as Critic*, Toronto: University of Toronto Press, 1969.

PARRISH, STEPHEN M., "Wordsworth and Coleridge on Meter," *Journal of English and Germanic Philology*, LIX (1960), 41–49.

WELLEK, RENÉ, *The History of Modern Criticism: 1750–1950*, II (*The Romantic Age*), New Haven: Yale University Press, 1955.

WORDSWORTH'S POLITICS AND POLITICAL WRITING

BRINTON, C. C., *The Political Ideas of the English Romanticists*, London: Oxford University Press, 1926.

COBBAN, ALFRED, *Edmund Burke and the Revolt against the Eighteenth Century*, London: George Allen and Unwin Ltd., 1929.

DICEY, A. V., *The Statesmanship of Wordsworth*, Oxford: Clarendon Press, 1917.

FINK, ZERA S., "Wordsworth and the English Republican Tradition," *Journal of English and Germanic Philology*, XLVII (1948), 107–26.

GRIERSON, HERBERT J. C., *Milton and Wordsworth: Poets and Prophets, A Study of their Reactions to Political Events*, New York: Macmillan Publishing Co., Inc., 1937.

ROBERTS, C. W., "The Influence of Godwin on Wordsworth's Letter to the Bishop of Llandaff," *Studies in Philology*, XXIX (1932), 588–606.

TODD, F. M., *Politics and the Poet: A Study of Wordsworth*, London: Methuen and Co., 1957.

WOODRING, CARL, *Politics in English Romantic Poetry*, Cambridge, Mass.: Harvard University Press, 1970.

A LETTER TO THE BISHOP OF LLANDAFF

Richard Watson (1737–1816), Anglican theologian and writer, had become Bishop of Llandaff [Wales] in 1782, and had won for himself the title of "levelling prelate" and "bishop of the Dissenters" for the independence of his political opinions from the policies of the Tory government which had appointed him. At the start of the French Revolution, Watson had given his "hearty approbation" to the goals of the revolutionists; however, the subsequent course of events, particularly the "murder" of Louis XVI on January 21, 1793, had led him to publish soon after that event Strictures on the French Revolution as an appendix to one of his sermons. Strictures was a defense of the established form and conduct of the British government and a repudiation of republican principles: "Now a republic is a form of government which, of all others, I most dislike . . . because of all forms of government, scarcely excepting the most despotic, I think a republic the most oppressive to the bulk of the people: they are deceived in it with the show of liberty; but they live in it under the most odious of all tyrannies, the tyranny of their equals."

Wordsworth's "Letter" was written in 1793, but was never published before its inclusion in Alexander B. Grosart's edition of The Prose Works of William Wordsworth (1876). Grosart's text is here followed. A new text, based on the study of the original manuscripts in the Wordsworth Library at Grasmere, is to appear in the forthcoming edition of Wordsworth's prose, prepared by W. J. B. Owen and Jane W. Smyser.

A comparison of the "Letter" of 1793 with the Convention of Cintra *treatise of 1809 reveals the changes in Wordsworth's political beliefs. In 1793, the "republican" Wordsworth views power in the hands of the few and hereditary distinctions and privileges as violations of the political rights of the individual and sources of corruption of his moral nature. Sixteen years later, Wordsworth espouses the traditional beliefs and hereditary institutions of a nation, including the "superstitions" of the Spanish religion and the "delusive" devotion of the people for their monarch; such beliefs and institutions, he argues, provide identity, dignity, and moral strength for a people. Tom Paine and abstract rights have given place to Edmund Burke and "organic" nationalism.*

It should be noted that the "Letter" of 1793, despite its vigorous republicanism, calls for reform rather than violent revolution. In June 1794, Wordsworth had written to his friend William Mathews: "I recoil from the bare idea of a revolution; yet, if our conduct with reference both to foreign and domestic policy continues such as it has been for the last two years how is that dreadful event to be averted? Aware of the difficulty of this it seems to me that a writer who has the welfare of mankind at heart should call forth his best exertions to convince the people that they can only be preserved from a convulsion by economy in the administration of the public purse and a gradual and constant reform of those abuses which, if left to themselves, may grow to such a height as to render, even a Revolution desirable."

FROM

A LETTER TO THE BISHOP OF LLANDAFF

ON THE

EXTRAORDINARY AVOWAL OF HIS
POLITICAL PRINCIPLES,
CONTAINED IN THE
APPENDIX TO HIS LATE SERMON:
BY A REPUBLICAN

*   *   *   *   *

Your Lordship will scarcely question that much of human misery, that the great evils which desolate States, proceed from the governors having an interest distinct from that of the governed. It should seem a natural deduction, that whatever has a tendency to identify the two must also in the same degree promote the general welfare. As the magnitude of almost all States prevents the possibility of their enjoying a pure democracy, philosophers—from a wish, as far as is in their power, to make the governors and the governed one—will turn their thoughts to the system of universal representation, and will annex an equal importance to the suffrage of every individual. Jealous of giving up no more of the authority of the people than is necessary, they will be solicitous of finding out some method by which the office of their delegates may be confined as much as is practicable to the proposing and deliberating upon laws rather than to enacting them; reserving to the people the power of finally inscribing them in the national code. Unless this is attended to, as soon as a people has chosen representatives it no longer has a political existence, except as it is understood to retain the privilege of annihilating the trust when it shall think proper, and of resuming its original power. Sensible that at the moment of election an interest distinct from that of the general body is created, an enlightened legislator will endeavour by every possible method to diminish the operation of such interest. The first and most natural mode that presents itself is that of shortening the regular duration of this trust, in order that the man who has betrayed it may soon be superseded by a more worthy successor. But this is not enough; aware of the possibility of imposition, and of the natural tendency of power to corrupt the heart of man, a sensible Republican will think it essential that the office of legislator be not intrusted to the same man for a succession of years. He will also be induced to this wise restraint by the grand principle of identification; he will be more sure of the virtue of the legislator by knowing that, in the capacity of private citizen, tomorrow he must either smart under the oppression or bless the justice of the law which he has enacted to-day.

Perhaps in the very outset of this inquiry the principle on which I proceed will be questioned, and I shall be told that the people are not the proper judges of their own welfare. But because under every government of modern times, till the foundation of the American Republic, the bulk of mankind have appeared incapable of discerning their true interests, no conclusion can be drawn against my principle. At this moment have we not daily the strongest proofs of the success with which, in what you call the best of all monarchical governments, the popular mind may be debauched? Left to the quiet exercise of their own judgment, do you think that the people would have thought it necessary to set fire to the house of the philosophic Priestley,[1] and to hunt down his life like that of a traitor or a parricide? that, deprived almost of the necessaries of existence by the burden of their taxes, they would cry out, as with one voice, for a war from which not a single ray of consolation can visit them to compensate for the additional keenness with which they are about to smart under the scourge of labour, of cold, and of hunger?

Appearing, as I do, the advocate of Republicanism, let me not be misunderstood. I am well aware, from the abuse of the executive power in States, that there is not a single European nation but what affords a melancholy proof that if, at this moment, the original authority of the people should be restored, all that could be expected from such restoration would in the beginning be but a change of tyranny. Considering the nature of a Republic in reference to the present condition of Europe, your Lordship stops here; but a philosopher will extend his views much farther: having dried up the source from which flows the corruption of the public opinion, he will be sensible that the stream will go on gradually refining itself. I must add also, that the coercive power is of necessity so strong in all the old governments, that a people could not at first make an abuse of that liberty which a legitimate Republic supposes. The animal just released from its stall will exhaust the overflow of its spirits in a round of wanton vagaries; but it will soon return to itself, and enjoy its freedom in moderate and regular delight.

But, to resume the subject of universal representation, I ought to have mentioned before, that in the choice of its representatives a people will not immorally hold out wealth as a criterion of integrity, nor lay down as a fundamental rule, that to be qualified for the trying duties of legislation a citizen should be possessed of a

---

[1] Joseph Priestley (1733–1804) was the famous scientist, philosopher, and leading political and religious dissenter. His espousal of the cause of the Revolution had led a mob, possibly encouraged by civil and religious authorities, to destroy his house and laboratory in Birmingham on July 14, 1791.

certain fixed property. Virtues, talents, and acquirements are all that it will look for.

Having destroyed every external object of delusion, let us now see what makes the supposition necessary that the people will mislead themselves. Your Lordship respects 'peasants and mechanics when they intrude not themselves into concerns for which their education has not fitted them.'

Setting aside the idea of a peasant or mechanic being a legislator, what vast education is requisite to enable him to judge amongst his neighbours which is most qualified by his industry and integrity to be intrusted with the care of the interests of himself and of his fellow-citizens? But leaving this ground, as governments formed on such a plan proceed in a plain and open manner, their administration would require much less of what is usually called talents and experience, that is, of disciplined treachery and hoary Machiavelism; and at the same time, as it would no longer be their interest to keep the mass of the nation in ignorance, a moderate portion of useful knowledge would be universally disseminated. If your Lordship has travelled in the democratic cantons of Switzerland,[2] you must have seen the herdsman with the staff in one hand and the book in the other. In the constituent Assembly of France was found a peasant whose sagacity was as distinguished as his integrity, whose blunt honesty overawed and baffled the refinements of hypocritical patriots. The people of Paris followed him with acclamations, and the name of Père Gérard[3] will long be mentioned with admiration and respect through the eighty-three departments.

From these hints, if pursued further, might be demonstrated the expediency of the whole people 'intruding themselves' on the office of legislation, and the wisdom of putting into force what they may claim as a right. But government is divided into two parts—the legislative and executive. The executive power you would lodge in the hands of an individual. Before we inquire into the propriety of this measure, it will be necessary to state the proper objects of the executive power in governments where the principle of universal representation is admitted. With regard to that portion of this power which is exerted in the application of the laws, it may be observed that much of it would be superseded. As laws, being but the expression of the general will, would be enacted only from an almost

universal conviction of their utility, any resistance to such laws, any desire of eluding them, must proceed from a few refractory individuals. As far, then, as relates to the internal administration of the country, a Republic has a manifest advantage over a Monarchy, inasmuch as less force is requisite to compel obedience to its laws. . . .

. . . [W]ith regard to the other branches of the executive government, which relate rather to original measures than to administering the law, it may be observed that the power exercised in conducting them is distinguished by almost imperceptible shades from the legislative, and that all such as admit of open discussion and of the delay attendant on public deliberations are properly the province of the representative assembly. If this observation be duly attended to, it will appear that this part of the executive power will be extremely circumscribed, will be stripped almost entirely of a deliberative capacity, and will be reduced to a mere hand or instrument. As a Republican government would leave this power to a select body destitute of the means of corruption, and whom the people, continually contributing, could at all times bring to account or dismiss, will it not necessarily ensue that a body so selected and supported would perform their simple functions with greater efficacy and fidelity than the complicated concerns of royalty can be expected to meet with in the councils of princes; of men who from their wealth and interest have forced themselves into trust; and of statesmen, whose constant object is to exalt themselves by laying pitfalls for their colleagues and for their country.

I shall pursue this subject no further; but adopting your Lordship's method of argument, instead of continuing to demonstrate the superiority of a Republican executive government, I will repeat some of the objections which have been often made to monarchy, and have not been answered.

My first objections to regal government is its instability, proceeding from a variety of causes. Where monarchy is found in its greatest intensity, as in Morocco and Turkey, this observation is illustrated in a very pointed manner, and indeed is more or less striking as governments are more or less despotic. The reason is obvious: as the monarch is the chooser of his ministers, and as his own passions and caprice are in general the sole guides of his conduct, these ministers, instead of pursuing directly the one grand object of national welfare, will make it their chief study to vary their measures according to his humours. But a minister *may* be refractory: his successor will naturally run headlong into plans totally the reverse of the former system; for if he treads in the same path, he is well aware that a similar fate will attend him. This observa-

---

2 Wordsworth visited the cantons during his continental walking tour of 1790. His poetic record of that trip *Descriptive Sketches* (1793) voices "democratic" principles similar to those found in the "Letter."

3 Michel Gérard (1737–1815), a popular and widely admired figure, was an early Jacobin and a peasant representative from Brittany to the French National Assembly.

tion will apply to each succession of kings, who, from vanity and a desire of distinction, will in general studiously avoid any step which may lead to a suspicion that they are so spiritless as to imitate their predecessor. That a similar instability is not incident to Republics is evident from their very constitution.

As from the nature of monarchy, particularly of hereditary monarchy, there must always be a vast disproportion between the duties to be performed and the powers that are to perform them; and as the measures of government, far from gaining additional vigour, are, on the contrary, enfeebled by being intrusted to one hand, what arguments can be used for allowing to the will of a single being a weight which, as history shows, will subvert that of the whole body politic? And this brings me to my grand objection to monarchy, which is drawn from THE ETERNAL NATURE OF MAN. The office of king is a trial to which human virtue is not equal. Pure and universal representation, by which alone liberty can be secured, cannot, I think, exist together with monarchy. It seems madness to expect a manifestation of the *general* will, at the same time that we allow to a *particular* will that weight which it must obtain in all governments that can with any propriety be called monarchical. They must war with each other till one of them is extinguished. It was so in France and
* * *

I shall not pursue this topic further, but, as you are a teacher of purity of morals, I cannot but remind you of that atmosphere of corruption without which it should seem that courts cannot exist.[4]

*   *   *   *   *

Thus far we have considered inequalities inseparable from civil society. But other arbitrary distinctions exist among mankind, either from choice or usurpation. I allude to titles, to stars, ribbons, and garters, and other badges of fictitious superiority. Your Lordship will not question the grand principle on which this inquiry set out; I look upon it, then, as my duty to try the propriety of these distinctions by that criterion, and think it will be no difficult task to prove that these separations among mankind are absurd, impolitic, and immoral. Considering hereditary nobility as a reward for services rendered to the State—and it is to my charity that you owe the permission of taking up the question on this ground—what services can a man render to the State adequate to such a compensation that the making of laws, upon which the happiness of millions is to

depend, shall be lodged in him and his posterity, however depraved may be their principles, however contemptible their understandings?

But here I may be accused of sophistry; I ought to subtract every idea of power from such distinction, though from the weakness of mankind it is impossible to disconnect them. What services, then, can a man render to society to compensate for the outrage done to the dignity of our nature when we bind ourselves to address him and his posterity with humiliating circumlocutions, calling him most noble, most honourable, most high, most august, serene, excellent, eminent, and so forth; when it is more than probable that such unnatural flattery will but generate vices which ought to consign him to neglect and solitude, or make him the perpetual object of the finger of scorn? And does not experience justify the observation, that where titles—a thing very rare—have been conferred as the rewards of merit, those to whom they have descended, far from being thereby animated to imitate their ancestor, have presumed upon that lustre which they supposed thrown round them, and, prodigally relying on such resources, lavished what alone was their own, their personal reputation?

It would be happy if this delusion were confined to themselves; but, alas, the world is weak enough to grant the indulgence which they assume. Vice, which is forgiven in one character, will soon cease to meet with sternness of rebuke when found in others. Even at first she will entreat pardon with confidence, assured that ere long she will be charitably supposed to stand in no need of it.

But let me ask you seriously, from the mode in which these distinctions are originally conferred, is it not almost necessary that, far from being the rewards of services rendered to the State, they should usually be the recompense of an industrious sacrifice of the general welfare to the particular aggrandisement of that power by which they are bestowed? Let us even alter their source, and consider them as proceeding from the Nation itself, and deprived of that hereditary quality; even here I should proscribe them, and for the most evident reason—that a man's past services are no sufficient security for his future character; he who to-day merits the civic wreath may to-morrow deserve the Tarpeian rock. Besides, where respect is not perverted, where the world is not taught to reverence men without regarding their conduct, the esteem of mankind will have a very different value, and, when a proper independence is secured, will be regarded as a sufficient recompense for services however important, and will be a much surer guarantee of the continuance of such virtues as may deserve it.

I have another strong objection to nobility, which is

---

4 Omitted here are four paragraphs in which Wordsworth discusses the "inevitable inequalities" of civil society in terms of power and wealth, which he wishes curbed by the reform or abolition of their "hereditary" possession.

that it has a necessary tendency to dishonour labour, a prejudice which extends far beyond its own circle; that it binds down whole ranks of men to idleness, while it gives the enjoyment of a reward which exceeds the hopes of the most active exertions of human industry. The languid tedium of this noble repose must be dissipated, and gaming, with the tricking manœuvres of the horse-race, afford occupation to hours which it would be happy for mankind had they been totally unemployed.

Reflecting on the corruption of the public manners, does your Lordship shudder at the prostitution which miserably deluges our streets? You may find the cause in our aristocratical prejudices. Are you disgusted with the hypocrisy and sycophancy of our intercourse in private life? You may find the cause in the necessity of dissimulation which we have established by regulations which oblige us to address as our superiors, indeed as our masters, men whom we cannot but internally despise. Do you lament that such large portions of mankind should stoop to occupations unworthy the dignity of their nature? You may find in the pride and luxury thought necessary to nobility how such servile arts are encouraged. Besides, where the most honourable of the Land do not blush to accept such offices as groom of the bedchamber, master of the hounds, lords in waiting, captain of the honourable band of gentlemen-pensioners, is it astonishing that the bulk of the people should not ask of an occupation, what is it? but what may be gained by it?

If the long equestrian train of equipage should make your Lordship sigh for the poor who are pining in hunger, you will find that little is thought of snatching the bread from their mouths to eke out the 'necessary splendour' of nobility.

I have not time to pursue this subject further, but am so strongly impressed with the baleful influence of aristocracy and nobility upon human happiness and virtue, that if, as I am persuaded, monarchy cannot exist without such supporters, I think that reason sufficient for the preference I have given to the Republican system.

* * * * *

I congratulate your Lordship upon your enthusiastic fondness for the judicial proceedings of this country. I am happy to find you have passed through life without having your fleece torn from your back in the thorny labyrinth of litigation. But you have not lived always in colleges, and must have passed by some victims, whom it cannot be supposed, without a reflection on your heart, that you have forgotten. Here I am reminded of what I have said on the subject of representation—to be qualified for the office of

legislation you should have felt like the bulk of mankind; their sorrows should be familiar to you, of which, if you are ignorant, how can you redress them? As a member of the assembly which, from a confidence in its experience, sagacity, and wisdom, the constitution has invested with the supreme appellant jurisdiction to determine the most doubtful points of an intricate jurisprudence, your Lordship cannot, I presume, be ignorant of the consuming expense of our never-ending process, the verbosity of unintelligible statutes, and the perpetual contrariety in our judicial decisions . . . .[5]

As a teacher of religion, your Lordship cannot be ignorant of a class of breaches of duty which may be denominated faults of omission. You profess to give your opinions upon the present turbulent crisis, expressing a wish that they may have some effect in tranquillising the minds of the people. Whence comes it, then, that the two grand causes of this working of the popular mind are passed over in silence? Your Lordship's conduct may bring to mind the story of a company of strolling comedians, who gave out the play of *Hamlet* as the performance of the evening. The audience were not a little surprised to be told, on the drawing up of the curtain, that from circumstances of particular convenience it was hoped they would dispense with the omission of the character of— Hamlet! But to be serious—for the subject is serious in the extreme—from your silence respecting the general call for a PARLIAMENTARY REFORM, supported by your assertion that we at present enjoy as great a portion of liberty and equality as is consistent with civil society, what can be supposed but that you are a determined enemy to the redress of what the people of England call and feel to be grievances?

From your omitting to speak upon the war, and your general disapprobation of French measures and French principles, expressed particularly at this moment, we are necessarily led also to conclude that you have no wish to dispel an infatuation which is now giving up to the sword so large a portion of the poor, and consigning the rest to the more slow and more painful consumption of want. I could excuse your silence on this point, as it would ill become an English bishop at the close of the eighteenth century to make the pulpit the vehicle of exhortations which would have disgraced the incen-

<hr>

5 Most readers have seen in this paragraph a reference to the Wordsworth family's long and unsuccessful attempt to obtain payment from James Lowther, Earl of Lonsdale, of a large debt owed to Wordsworth's father, who had served as "law-agent" to the politically powerful Lord. From 1787 through 1791, legal action against Lord Lonsdale continued, at great expense to the Wordsworths; finally, in August 1791, judgment was obtained in favor of the plaintiffs. However, further delays and obstructions from Lord Lonsdale's counsel resulted in abandonment of their prosecution of the suit. It was not finally settled until 1802.

diary of the Crusades, the hermit Peter. But you have deprived yourself of the plea of decorum by giving no opinion on the REFORM OF THE LEGISLATURE. As undoubtedly you have some secret reason for the reservation of your sentiments on this latter head, I cannot but apply the same reason to the former. Upon what principle is your conduct to be explained? In some parts of England it is quaintly said, when a drunken man is seen reeling towards his home, that he has business on both sides of the road. Observing your Lordship's tortuous path, the spectators will be far from insinuating that you have partaken of Mr. Burke's intoxicating bowl;[6] they will content themselves, shaking their heads as you stagger along, with remarking that you have business on both sides of the road. . . .

[1876]

―――――

PREFACE TO LYRICAL BALLADS

Lyrical Ballads was published in 1798 in one volume. In 1801 [title-page dated 1800], an expanded second edition in two volumes appeared with the "Preface" setting forth the supposed principles on which the poems were composed. In the third edition of 1802, Wordsworth reprinted the "Preface," considerably expanding it with a section largely devoted to a discussion of the character of a poet. (The addition begins after "I answer that . . .", p. 50, and continues through "for, as it may be proper to remind the Reader," p. 53.) The 1802 text, which is here reprinted, remained the basic text thereafter through the final edition of Wordsworth's poems in 1849–1850. See Wordsworth's Preface to Lyrical Ballads, ed. W. J. B. Owen, Anglistica, IX (1957), for an extended discussion of the significance of the changes in the text between 1800 and 1802 and an analysis of the major themes of the argument. Chapter V of M. H. Abrams' The Mirror and the Lamp (New York: Oxford University Press, 1953) has an illuminating discussion of the relationship between the premises of Wordsworth's "Preface" and eighteenth-century thought.

The "Preface to Lyrical Ballads" was to prove a highly controversial document. As Coleridge indicates in Biographia Literaria, much of the violent critical objection to the poems of Wordsworth was in effect based on opposition to the tenets of the "Preface"; one of the major goals of the Biographia was precisely to demonstrate how Wordsworth's true distinction and genius as a poet lay in his deviation from the principles of the "Preface."

◇◇◇◇◇◇◇◇◇◇◇◇◇◇◇◇◇◇◇◇◇◇◇◇◇◇◇◇◇◇◇◇

6 Refers to Edmund Burke's *Reflections On the Revolution in France* (1790), an influential and brilliantly written attack on the principles and conduct of the Revolution. The work was interpreted by Burke's own Whig party and by political dissenters as a flagrant and self-serving abandonment of the political ideals which had earlier led him to defend the American Revolution. In the introductory paragraphs omitted here, Wordsworth had indicated that one reason for preparing his "Letter" had been that the authority and respect Watson commanded for his previous independent stand might cause many to become similarly "intoxicated" with the reactionary political opinions voiced in *Strictures.*

PREFACE TO
LYRICAL BALLADS,
WITH PASTORAL AND OTHER POEMS

THE FIRST Volume of these Poems has already been submitted to general perusal. It was published, as an experiment, which, I hoped, might be of some use to ascertain, how far, by fitting to metrical arrangement a selection of the real language of men in a state of vivid sensation, that sort of pleasure and that quantity of pleasure may be imparted, which a Poet may rationally endeavour to impart.

I had formed no very inaccurate estimate of the probable effect of those Poems: I flattered myself that they who should be pleased with them would read them with more than common pleasure: and, on the other hand, I was well aware, that by those who should dislike them they would be read with more than common dislike. The result has differed from my expectation in this only, that I have pleased a greater number, than I ventured to hope I should please.

For the sake of variety, and from a consciousness of my own weakness, I was induced to request the assistance of a Friend, who furnished me with the Poems of the ANCIENT MARINER, the FOSTER-MOTHER'S TALE, the NIGHTINGALE, and the Poem entitled LOVE. I should not, however, have requested this assistance, had I not believed that the Poems of my Friend would in a great measure have the same tendency as my own, and that, though there would be found a difference, there would be found no discordance in the colours of our style; as our opinions on the subject of poetry do almost entirely coincide.

Several of my Friends are anxious for the success of these Poems from a belief, that, if the views with which they were composed were indeed realized, a class of Poetry would be produced, well adapted to interest mankind permanently, and not unimportant in the multiplicity, and in the quality of its moral relations: and on this account they have advised me to prefix a systematic defence of the theory, upon which the poems were written. But I was unwilling to undertake the task, because I knew that on this occasion the Reader would look coldly upon my arguments, since I might be suspected of having been principally influenced by the selfish and foolish hope of *reasoning* him into an approbation of these particular Poems: and I was still more unwilling to undertake the task, because, adequately to display my opinions, and fully to enforce my arguments, would require a space wholly disproportionate to the nature of a preface. For to treat the subject with the clearness and coherence, of which I believe it susceptible, it would be necessary to give a full account of the present state of the public taste in this country, and to determine how far this taste is healthy or depraved; which, again, could not be determined, without pointing out, in what manner language and the human mind act and re-act on each other, and without retracing the revolutions, not of literature alone, but likewise of society itself. I have therefore altogether declined to enter regularly upon this defence; yet I am sensible, that there would be some impropriety in abruptly obtruding upon the Public, without a few words of introduction, Poems so materially different from those, upon which general approbation is at present bestowed.

It is supposed, that by the act of writing in verse an Author makes a formal engagement that he will gratify certain known habits of association; that he not only thus apprizes the Reader that certain classes of ideas and expressions will be found in his book, but that others will be carefully excluded. This exponent or symbol held forth by metrical language must in different æras of literature have excited very different expectations: for example, in the age of Catullus, Terence and Lucretius and that of Statius or Claudian;[1] and in our own country, in the age of Shakespeare and Beaumont and Fletcher, and that of Donne and Cowley, or Dryden, or Pope. I will not take upon me to determine the exact import of the promise which by the act of writing in verse an Author, in the present day, makes to his Reader; but I am certain, it will appear to many persons that I have not fulfilled the terms of an engagement thus voluntarily contracted. They who have been accustomed to the gaudiness and inane phraseology of many modern writers, if they persist in reading this book to its conclusion, will, no doubt, frequently have to struggle with feelings of strangeness and aukwardness: they will look round for poetry, and will be induced to inquire by what species of courtesy these attempts can be permitted to assume that title. I hope therefore the Reader will not censure me, if I attempt to state what I have proposed to myself to perform; and also, (as far as the limits of a preface will permit) to explain some of the chief reasons which have determined me in the choice of my purpose: that at least he may be spared any unpleasant feeling of disappointment, and that I myself may be protected from the most dishonorable accusation which can be brought against an Author, namely, that of an indolence which prevents him from endeavouring to ascertain what is his duty, or, when his duty is ascertained, prevents him from performing it.

The principal object, then, which I proposed to myself in these Poems was to chuse incidents and situations from common life, and to relate or describe them, throughout, as far as was possible, in a selection of language really used by men; and, at the same time, to throw over them a certain colouring of imagination, whereby ordinary things should be presented to the mind in an unusual way; and, further, and above all, to make these incidents and situations interesting by tracing in them, truly though not ostentatiously, the primary laws of our nature: chiefly, as far as regards the manner in which we associate ideas in a state of excitement. Low and rustic life was generally chosen, because in that condition, the essential passions of the heart find a better soil in which they can attain their maturity, are less under restraint, and speak a plainer and more emphatic language; because in that condition of life our elementary feelings co-exist in a state of greater simplicity, and, consequently, may be more accurately contemplated, and more forcibly communicated; because the manners of rural life germinate from those elementary feelings; and, from the necessary character of rural occupations, are more easily comprehended; and are more durable; and lastly, because in that condition the passions of men are incorporated with the beautiful and permanent forms of nature. The language, too, of these men is adopted (purified indeed from what appear to be its real defects, from all lasting and rational causes of dislike or disgust) because such men hourly communicate with the best objects from which the best part of language is originally derived; and because, from their rank in society and the sameness and narrow circle of their intercourse, being less under the influence of social vanity they convey their feelings and notions in simple and unelaborated expressions. Accordingly, such a language, arising out of repeated experience and regular feelings, is a more permanent, and a far more philosophical language, than that which is frequently substituted for it by Poets, who think that they are conferring honour upon themselves and their art, in proportion as they separate themselves from the sympathies of men, and indulge in arbitrary and capricious habits of expression, in order to furnish food for fickle tastes, and fickle appetites, of their own creation.*

I cannot, however, be insensible of the present outcry against the triviality and meanness both of thought and language, which some of my contemporaries have occasionally introduced into their

---

[1] Wordsworth distinguishes between early and Golden Age Roman poets (Catullus, Terence, Lucretius), who flourished in the first and second centuries B.C., and Silver Age or later poets (Statius, c. A.D. 45–96, and Claudian, c. A.D. 370–c. 404).

* It is worth while here to observe that the affecting parts of Chaucer are almost always expressed in language pure and universally intelligible even to this day.

metrical compositions; and I acknowledge, that this defect, where it exists, is more dishonorable to the Writer's own character than false refinement or arbitrary innovation, though I should contend at the same time that it is far less pernicious in the sum of its consequences. From such verses the Poems in these volumes will be found distinguished at least by one mark of difference, that each of them has a worthy *purpose*. Not that I mean to say, that I always began to write with a distinct purpose formally conceived; but I believe that my habits of meditation have so formed my feelings, as that my descriptions of such objects as strongly excite those feelings, will be found to carry along with them a *purpose*. If in this opinion I am mistaken, I can have little right to the name of a Poet. For all good poetry is the spontaneous overflow of powerful feelings: but though this be true, Poems to which any value can be attached, were never produced on any variety of subjects but by a man, who being possessed of more than usual organic sensibility, had also thought long and deeply. For our continued influxes of feeling are modified and directed by our thoughts, which are indeed the representatives of all our past feelings; and, as by contemplating the relation of these general representatives to each other we discover what is really important to men, so, by the repetition and continuance of this act, our feelings will be connected with important subjects, till at length, if we be originally possessed of much sensibility, such habits of mind will be produced, that, by obeying blindly and mechanically the impulses of those habits, we shall describe objects, and utter sentiments, of such a nature and in such connection with each other, that the understanding of the being to whom we address ourselves, if he be in a healthful state of association, must necessarily be in some degree enlightened, and his affections ameliorated.

I have said that each of these poems has a purpose. I have also informed my Reader what this purpose will be found principally to be: namely to illustrate the manner in which our feelings and ideas are associated in a state of excitement. But, speaking in language somewhat more appropriate, it is to follow the fluxes and refluxes of the mind when agitated by the great and simple affections of our nature. This object I have endeavoured in these short essays to attain by various means; by tracing the maternal passion through many of its more subtile windings, as in the poems of the IDIOT BOY and the MAD MOTHER; by accompanying the last struggles of a human being, at the approach of death, cleaving in solitude to life and society, as in the Poem of the FORSAKEN INDIAN; by shewing, as in the Stanzas entitled WE ARE SEVEN, the perplexity and obscurity which in childhood attend our notion of death, or rather our utter inability to admit that notion; or by displaying the strength of fraternal, or to speak more philosophically, of moral attachment when early associated with the great and beautiful objects of nature, as in THE BROTHERS; or, as in the Incident of SIMON LEE, by placing my Reader in the way of receiving from ordinary moral sensations another and more salutary impression than we are accustomed to receive from them. It has also been part of my general purpose to attempt to sketch characters under the influence of less impassioned feelings, as in the TWO APRIL MORNINGS, THE FOUNTAIN, THE OLD MAN TRAVELLING, THE TWO THIEVES, &c. characters of which the elements are simple, belonging rather to nature than to manners, such as exist now, and will probably always exist, and which from their constitution may be distinctly and profitably contemplated. I will not abuse the indulgence of my Reader by dwelling longer upon this subject; but it is proper that I should mention one other circumstance which distinguishes these Poems from the popular Poetry of the day; it is this, that the feeling therein developed gives importance to the action and situation, and not the action and situation to the feeling. My meaning will be rendered perfectly intelligible by referring my Reader to the Poems entitled POOR SUSAN and the CHILDLESS FATHER, particularly to the last Stanza of the latter Poem.

I will not suffer a sense of false modesty to prevent me from asserting, that I point my Reader's attention to this mark of distinction, far less for the sake of these particular Poems than from the general importance of the subject. The subject is indeed important! For the human mind is capable of being excited without the application of gross and violent stimulants; and he must have a very faint perception of its beauty and dignity who does not know this, and who does not further know, that one being is elevated above another, in proportion as he possesses this capability. It has therefore appeared to me, that to endeavour to produce or enlarge this capability is one of the best services in which, at any period, a Writer can be engaged; but this service, excellent at all times, is especially so at the present day. For a multitude of causes, unknown to former times, are now acting with a combined force to blunt the discriminating powers of the mind, and unfitting it for all voluntary exertion to reduce it to a state of almost savage torpor. The most effective of these causes are the great national events which are daily taking place, and the encreasing accumulation of men in cities, where the uniformity of their occupations produces a craving for extraordinary incident, which the rapid communication of intelligence hourly gratifies. To this tendency of life and manners the literature and theatrical exhibitions of the country have conformed themselves. The invaluable works of our elder writers, I had almost said the works of Shakespear and Milton, are driven into neglect by frantic novels, sickly and stupid German Tragedies,[2] and deluges of idle and extravagant stories in verse.—When I think upon this degrading thirst after outrageous stimulation, I am almost ashamed to have spoken of the feeble effort with which I have endeavoured to counteract it; and, reflecting upon the magnitude of the general evil, I should be oppressed with no dishonorable melancholy, had I not a deep impression of certain inherent and indestructible qualities of the human mind, and likewise of certain powers in the great and permanent objects that act upon it which are equally inherent and indestructible; and did I not further add to this impression a belief, that the time is approaching when the evil will be systematically opposed, by men of greater powers, and with far more distinguished success.

Having dwelt thus long on the subjects and aim of these Poems, I shall request the Reader's permission to apprize him of a few circumstances relating to their *style*, in order, among other reasons, that I may not be censured for not having performed what I never attempted. The Reader will find that personifications of abstract ideas rarely occur in these volumes; and, I hope, are utterly rejected as an ordinary device to elevate the style, and raise it above prose. I have proposed to myself to imitate, and, as far as is possible, to adopt the very language of men; and assuredly such personifications do not make any natural or regular part of that language. They are, indeed, a figure of speech occasionally prompted by passion, and I have made use of them as such; but I have endeavoured utterly to reject them as a mechanical device of style, or as a family language which Writers in metre seem to lay claim to by prescription. I have wished to keep my Reader in the company of flesh and blood, persuaded that by so doing I shall interest him. I am, however, well aware that others who pursue a different track may interest him likewise; I do not interfere with their claim, I only wish to prefer a different claim of my own. There will also be found in these volumes little of what is usually called poetic diction; I have taken as much pains to avoid it as others ordinarily take to produce it; this I have done for the reason already alleged, to bring my language near to the language of

men, and further, because the pleasure which I have proposed to myself to impart is of a kind very different from that which is supposed by many persons to be the proper object of poetry. I do not know how without being culpably particular I can give my Reader a more exact notion of the style in which I wished these poems to be written than by informing him that I have at all times endeavoured to look steadily at my subject, consequently, I hope that there is in these Poems little falsehood of description, and that my ideas are expressed in language fitted to their respective importance. Something I must have gained by this practice, as it is friendly to one property of all good poetry, namely, good sense; but it has necessarily cut me off from a large portion of phrases and figures of speech which from father to son have long been regarded as the common inheritance of Poets. I have also thought it expedient to restrict myself still further, having abstained from the use of many expressions, in themselves proper and beautiful, but which have been foolishly repeated by bad Poets, till such feelings of disgust are connected with them as it is scarcely possible by any art of association to overpower.

If in a Poem there should be found a series of lines, or even a single line, in which the language, though naturally arranged and according to the strict laws of metre, does not differ from that of prose, there is a numerous class of critics, who, when they stumble upon these prosaisms as they call them, imagine that they have made a notable discovery, and exult over the Poet as over a man ignorant of his own profession. Now these men would establish a canon of criticism which the Reader will conclude he must utterly reject, if he wishes to be pleased with these volumes. And it would be a most easy task to prove to him, that not only the language of a large portion of every good poem, even of the most elevated character, must necessarily, except with reference to the metre, in no respect differ from that of good prose, but likewise that some of the most interesting parts of the best poems will be found to be strictly the language of prose, when prose is well written. The truth of this assertion might be demonstrated by innumerable passages from almost all the poetical writings, even of Milton himself. I have not space for much quotation; but, to illustrate the subject in a general manner, I will here adduce a short composition of Gray, who was at the head of those who by their reasonings have attempted to widen the space of separation betwixt Prose and Metrical composition, and was more than any other man curiously elaborate in the structure of his own poetic diction.

In vain to me the smiling mornings shine,
And reddening Phoebus lifts his golden fire:

---

2 From the 1780's, translations of dramas by Goethe, Schiller, August von Kotzebue, and other German writers had enjoyed a considerable vogue in England. In particular, Wordsworth may be referring to the sentimental and melodramatic works of Kotzebue, which achieved great popularity in both published translations and stage productions in the years 1798–1800.

The birds in vain their amorous descant join,
Or cheerful fields resume their green attire:
These ears alas! for other notes repine;
A different object do these eyes require;
My lonely anguish melts no heart but mine;
And in my breast the imperfect joys expire;
Yet morning smiles the busy race to cheer,
And new-born pleasure brings to happier men;
The fields to all their wonted tribute bear;
To warm their little loves the birds complain.
I fruitless mourn to him that cannot hear
And weep the more because I weep in vain.[3]

It will easily be perceived that the only part of this Sonnet which is of any value is the lines printed in Italics: it is equally obvious, that, except in the rhyme, and in the use of the single word "fruitless" for fruitlessly, which is so far a defect, the language of these lines does in no respect differ from that of prose.

By the foregoing quotation I have shown that the language of Prose may yet be well adapted to Poetry; and I have previously asserted that a large portion of the language of every good poem can in no respect differ from that of good Prose. I will go further. I do not doubt that it may be safely affirmed, that there neither is, nor can be, any essential difference between the language of prose and metrical composition. We are fond of tracing the resemblance between Poetry and Painting, and, accordingly, we call them Sisters: but where shall we find bonds of connection sufficiently strict to typify the affinity betwixt metrical and prose composition? They both speak by and to the same organs; the bodies in which both of them are clothed may be said to be of the same substance, their affections are kindred and almost identical, not necessarily differing even in degree; Poetry* sheds no tears "such as Angels weep,"[4] but natural and human tears; she can boast of no celestial Ichor that distinguishes her vital juices from those of prose; the same human blood circulates through the veins of them both.

If it be affirmed that rhyme and metrical arrangement of themselves constitute a distinction which

* I have used the word "Poetry" (though against my own judgment) as opposed to the word Prose, and synonymous with metrical composition. But much confusion has been introduced into criticism by this contradistinction of Poetry and Prose, instead of the more philosophical one of Poetry and Matter of fact, or Science. The only strict antithesis to Prose is Metre; nor is this, in truth, a *strict* antithesis; because lines and passages of metre so naturally occur in writing prose, that it would be scarcely possible to avoid them, even were it desirable.

[3] "Sonnet [On the Death of Richard West]," first published in 1775.
[4] *Paradise Lost,* I, 620.

overturns what I have been saying on the strict affinity of metrical language with that of prose, and paves the way for other artificial distinctions which the mind voluntarily admits, I answer that the language of such Poetry as I am recommending is, as far as is possible, a selection of the language really spoken by men; that this selection, wherever it is made with true taste and feeling, will of itself form a distinction far greater than would at first be imagined, and will entirely separate the composition from the vulgarity and meanness of ordinary life; and, if metre be super-added thereto, I believe that a dissimilitude will be produced altogether sufficient for the gratification of a rational mind. What other distinction would we have? Whence is it to come? And where is it to exist? Not, surely, where the Poet speaks through the mouths of his characters: it cannot be necessary here, either for elevation of style, or any of its supposed ornaments; for, if the Poet's subject be judiciously chosen, it will naturally, and upon fit occasion, lead him to passions the language of which, if selected truly and judiciously, must necessarily be dignified and variegated, and alive with metaphors and figures. I forbear to speak of an incongruity which would shock the intelligent Reader, should the Poet interweave any foreign splendour of his own with that which the passion naturally suggests: it is sufficient to say that such addition is unnecessary. And, surely, it is more probable that those passages, which with propriety abound with metaphors and figures, will have their due effect, if, upon other occasions where the passions are of a milder character, the style also be subdued and temperate.

But, as the pleasure which I hope to give by the Poems I now present to the Reader must depend entirely on just notions upon this subject, and, as it is in itself of the highest importance to our taste and moral feelings, I cannot content myself with these detached remarks. And if, in what I am about to say, it shall appear to some that my labour is unnecessary, and that I am like a man fighting a battle without enemies, I would remind such persons, that, whatever may be the language outwardly holden by men, a practical faith in the opinions which I am wishing to establish is almost unknown. If my conclusions are admitted, and carried as far as they must be carried if admitted at all, our judgments concerning the works of the greatest Poets both ancient and modern will be far different from what they are at present, both when we praise, and when we censure: and our moral feelings influencing, and influenced by these judgments will, I believe, be corrected and purified.

Taking up the subject, then, upon general grounds, I ask what is meant by the word Poet? What is a Poet?

To whom does he address himself? And what language is to be expected from him? He is a man speaking to men: a man, it is true, endued with more lively sensibility, more enthusiasm and tenderness, who has a greater knowledge of human nature, and a more comprehensive soul, than are supposed to be common among mankind; a man pleased with his own passions and volitions, and who rejoices more than other men in the spirit of life that is in him; delighting to contemplate similar volitions and passions as manifested in the goings-on of the Universe, and habitually impelled to create them where he does not find them. To these qualities he has added a disposition to be affected more than other men by absent things as if they were present; an ability of conjuring up in himself passions, which are indeed far from being the same as those produced by real events, yet (especially in those parts of the general sympathy which are pleasing and delightful) do more nearly resemble the passions produced by real events, than any thing which, from the motions of their own minds merely, other men are accustomed to feel in themselves; whence, and from practice, he has acquired a greater readiness and power in expressing what he thinks and feels, and especially those thoughts and feelings which, by his own choice, or from the structure of his own mind, arise in him without immediate external excitement.

But, whatever portion of this faculty we may suppose even the greatest Poet to possess, there cannot be a doubt but that the language which it will suggest to him, must, in liveliness and truth, fall far short of that which is uttered by men in real life, under the actual pressure of those passions, certain shadows of which the Poet thus produces, or feels to be produced, in himself. However exalted a notion we would wish to cherish of the character of a Poet, it is obvious, that, while he describes and imitates passions, his situation is altogether slavish and mechanical, compared with the freedom and power of real and substantial action and suffering. So that it will be the wish of the Poet to bring his feelings near to those of the persons whose feelings he describes, nay, for short spaces of time perhaps, to let himself slip into an entire delusion, and even confound and identify his own feelings with theirs; modifying only the language which is thus suggested to him, by a consideration that he describes for a particular purpose, that of giving pleasure. Here, then, he will apply the principle on which I have so much insisted, namely, that of selection; on this he will depend for removing what would otherwise be painful or disgusting in the passion; he will feel that there is no necessity to trick out or to elevate nature: and, the more industriously he applies this principle, the deeper will be his faith that no words, which his fancy or imagination can suggest, will be to be compared with those which are the emanations of reality and truth.

But it may be said by those who do not object to the general spirit of these remarks, that, as it is impossible for the Poet to produce upon all occasions language as exquisitely fitted for the passion as that which the real passion itself suggests, it is proper that he should consider himself as in the situation of a translator, who deems himself justified when he substitutes excellences of another kind for those which are unattainable by him; and endeavours occasionally to surpass his original, in order to make some amends for the general inferiority to which he feels that he must submit. But this would be to encourage idleness and unmanly despair. Further, it is the language of men who speak of what they do not understand; who talk of Poetry as of a matter of amusement and idle pleasure; who will converse with us as gravely about a *taste* for Poetry, as they express it, as if it were a thing as indifferent as a taste for Rope-dancing, or Frontiniac [5] or Sherry. Aristotle, I have been told, hath said, that Poetry is the most philosophic of all writing: [6] it is so: its object is truth, not individual and local, but general, and operative; not standing upon external testimony, but carried alive into the heart by passion; truth which is its own testimony, which gives strength and divinity to the tribunal to which it appeals, and receives them from the same tribunal. Poetry is the image of man and nature. The obstacles which stand in the way of the fidelity of the Biographer and Historian, and of their consequent utility, are incalculably greater than those which are to be encountered by the Poet who has an adequate notion of the dignity of his art. The Poet writes under one restriction only, namely, that of the necessity of giving immediate pleasure to a human Being possessed of that information which may be expected from him, not as a lawyer, a physician, a mariner, an astronomer or a natural philosopher, but as a Man. Except this one restriction, there is no object standing between the Poet and the image of things; between this, and the Biographer and Historian there are a thousand.

Nor let this necessity of producing immediate pleasure be considered as a degradation of the Poet's art. It is far otherwise. It is an acknowledgment of the beauty of the universe, an acknowledgment the more sincere because it is not formal, but indirect; it is a task light and easy to him who looks at the world in the spirit of love: further, it is a homage paid to the native

---

5 An elegant French wine.
6 In his *Poetics*, section IX, Aristotle asserts that poetry is more philosophical than history because it deals with the universal (" what may happen ") rather than the particular (" what has happened ").

and naked dignity of man, to the grand elementary principle of pleasure, by which he knows, and feels, and lives, and moves. We have no sympathy but what is propagated by pleasure: I would not be misunderstood; but wherever we sympathize with pain it will be found that the sympathy is produced and carried on by subtle combinations with pleasure. We have no knowledge, that is, no general principles drawn from the contemplation of particular facts, but what has been built up by pleasure, and exists in us by pleasure alone. The Man of Science, the Chemist and Mathematician, whatever difficulties and disgusts they may have had to struggle with, know and feel this. However painful may be the objects with which the Anatomist's knowledge is connected, he feels that his knowledge is pleasure; and where he has no pleasure he has no knowledge. What then does the Poet? He considers man and the objects that surround him as acting and re-acting upon each other, so as to produce an infinite complexity of pain and pleasure; he considers man in his own nature and in his ordinary life as contemplating this with a certain quantity of immediate knowledge, with certain convictions, intuitions, and deductions which by habit become of the nature of intuitions; he considers him as looking upon this complex scene of ideas and sensations, and finding every where objects that immediately excite in him sympathies which, from the necessities of his nature, are accompanied by an overbalance of enjoyment.

To this knowledge which all men carry about with them, and to these sympathies in which without any other discipline than that of our daily life we are fitted to take delight, the Poet principally directs his attention. He considers man and nature as essentially adapted to each other, and the mind of man as naturally the mirror of the fairest and most interesting qualities of nature. And thus the Poet, prompted by this feeling of pleasure which accompanies him through the whole course of his studies, converses with general nature with affections akin to those, which, through labour and length of time, the Man of Science has raised up in himself, by conversing with those particular parts of nature which are the objects of his studies. The knowledge both of the Poet and the Man of Science is pleasure; but the knowledge of the one cleaves to us as a necessary part of our existence, our natural and unalienable inheritance; the other is a personal and individual acquisition, slow to come to us, and by no habitual and direct sympathy connecting us with our fellow-beings. The Man of Science seeks truth as a remote and unknown benefactor; he cherishes and loves it in his solitude: the Poet, singing a song in which all human beings join with him, rejoices in the presence of truth as our visible friend and hourly companion.

Poetry is the breath and finer spirit of all knowledge; it is the impassioned expression which is in the countenance of all Science. Emphatically may it be said of the Poet, as Shakespeare hath said of man, "that he looks before and after." [7] He is the rock of defence of human nature; an upholder and preserver, carrying every where with him relationship and love. In spite of difference of soil and climate, of language and manners, of laws and customs, in spite of things silently gone out of mind and things violently destroyed, the Poet binds together by passion and knowledge the vast empire of human society, as it is spread over the whole earth, and over all time. The objects of the Poet's thoughts are every where; though the eyes and senses of man are, it is true, his favorite guides, yet he will follow wheresoever he can find an atmosphere of sensation in which to move his wings. Poetry is the first and last of all knowledge—it is as immortal as the heart of man. If the labours of men of Science should ever create any material revolution, direct or indirect, in our condition, and in the impressions which we habitually receive, the Poet will sleep then no more than at present, but he will be ready to follow the steps of the man of Science, not only in those general indirect effects, but he will be at his side, carrying sensation into the midst of the objects of the Science itself. The remotest discoveries of the Chemist, the Botanist, or Mineralogist, will be as proper objects of the Poet's art as any upon which it can be employed, if the time should ever come when these things shall be familiar to us, and the relations under which they are contemplated by the followers of these respective Sciences shall be manifestly and palpably material to us as enjoying and suffering beings. If the time should ever come when what is now called Science, thus familiarized to men, shall be ready to put on, as it were, a form of flesh and blood, the Poet will lend his divine spirit to aid the transfiguration, and will welcome the Being thus produced, as a dear and genuine inmate of the household of man.—It is not, then, to be supposed that any one, who holds that sublime notion of Poetry which I have attempted to convey, will break in upon the sanctity and truth of his pictures by transitory and accidental ornaments, and endeavour to excite admiration of himself by arts, the necessity of which must manifestly depend upon the assumed meanness of his subject.

What I have thus far said applies to Poetry in general; but especially to those parts of composition where the Poet speaks through the mouths of his characters; and upon this point it appears to have such weight that I will conclude, there are few persons, of

[7] See *Hamlet*, IV, iv, 37.

good sense, who would not allow that the dramatic parts of composition are defective, in proportion as they deviate from the real language of nature, and are coloured by a diction of the Poet's own, either peculiar to him as an individual Poet, or belonging simply to Poets in general, to a body of men who, from the circumstance of their compositions being in metre, it is expected will employ a particular language.

It is not, then, in the dramatic parts of composition that we look for this distinction of language; but still it may be proper and necessary where the Poet speaks to us in his own person and character. To this I answer by referring my Reader to the description which I have before given of a Poet. Among the qualities which I have enumerated as principally conducing to form a Poet, is implied nothing differing in kind from other men, but only in degree. The sum of what I have there said is, that the Poet is chiefly distinguished from other men by a greater promptness to think and feel without immediate external excitement, and a greater power in expressing such thoughts and feelings as are produced in him in that manner. But these passions and thoughts and feelings are the general passions and thoughts and feelings of men. And with what are they connected? Undoubtedly with our moral sentiments and animal sensations, and with the causes which excite these; with the operations of the elements and the appearances of the visible universe; with storm and sun-shine, with the revolutions of the seasons, with cold and heat, with loss of friends and kindred, with injuries and resentments, gratitude and hope, with fear and sorrow. These, and the like, are the sensations and objects which the Poet describes, as they are the sensations of other men, and the objects which interest them. The Poet thinks and feels in the spirit of the passions of men. How, then, can his language differ in any material degree from that of all other men who feel vividly and see clearly? It might be *proved* that it is impossible. But supposing that this were not the case, the Poet might then be allowed to use a peculiar language, when expressing his feelings for his own gratification, or that of men like himself. But Poets do not write for Poets alone, but for men. Unless therefore we are advocates for that admiration which depends upon ignorance, and that pleasure which arises from hearing what we do not understand, the Poet must descend from this supposed height, and, in order to excite rational sympathy, he must express himself as other men express themselves. To this it may be added, that while he is only selecting from the real language of men, or, which amounts to the same thing, composing accurately in the spirit of such selection, he is treading upon safe ground, and we know what we are to expect from him. Our feelings are the same with respect to

metre; for, as it may be proper to remind the Reader, the distinction of metre is regular and uniform, and not like that which is produced by what is usually called poetic diction, arbitrary, and subject to infinite caprices upon which no calculation whatever can be made. In the one case, the Reader is utterly at the mercy of the Poet respecting what imagery or diction he may choose to connect with the passion, whereas, in the other, the metre obeys certain laws, to which the Poet and Reader both willingly submit because they are certain, and because no interference is made by them with the passion but such as the concurring testimony of ages has shown to heighten and improve the pleasure which co-exists with it.

It will now be proper to answer an obvious question, namely, why, professing these opinions, have I written in verse? To this, in addition to such answer as is included in what I have already said, I reply in the first place, because, however I may have restricted myself, there is still left open to me what confessedly constitutes the most valuable object of all writing whether in prose or verse, the great and universal passions of men, the most general and interesting of their occupations, and the entire world of nature, from which I am at liberty to supply myself with endless combinations of forms and imagery. Now, supposing for a moment that whatever is interesting in these objects may be as vividly described in prose, why am I to be condemned, if to such description I have endeavoured to superadd the charm which, by the consent of all nations, is acknowledged to exist in metrical language? To this, by such as are unconvinced by what I have already said, it may be answered, that a very small part of the pleasure given by Poetry depends upon the metre, and that it is injudicious to write in metre, unless it be accompanied with the other artificial distinctions of style with which metre is usually accompanied, and that by such deviation more will be lost from the shock which will be thereby given to the Reader's associations, than will be counterbalanced by any pleasure which he can derive from the general power of numbers. In answer to those who still contend for the necessity of accompanying metre with certain appropriate colours of style in order to the accomplishment of its appropriate end, and who also, in my opinion, greatly under-rate the power of metre in itself, it might perhaps, as far as relates to these Poems, have been almost sufficient to observe, that poems are extant, written upon more humble subjects, and in a more naked and simple style than I have aimed at, which poems have continued to give pleasure from generation to generation. Now, if nakedness and simplicity be a defect, the fact here mentioned affords a strong presumption that poems somewhat less naked and simple are capable of affording pleasure at the present day; and, what I wished *chiefly* to attempt, at present, was to justify myself for having written under the impression of this belief.

But I might point out various causes why, when the style is manly, and the subject of some importance, words metrically arranged will long continue to impart such a pleasure to mankind as he who is sensible of the extent of that pleasure will be desirous to impart. The end of Poetry is to produce excitement in co-existence with an over-balance of pleasure. Now, by the supposition, excitement is an unusual and irregular state of the mind; ideas and feelings do not in that state succeed each other in accustomed order. But, if the words by which this excitement is produced are in themselves powerful, or the images and feelings have an undue proportion of pain connected with them, there is some danger that the excitement may be carried beyond its proper bounds. Now the co-presence of something regular, something to which the mind has been accustomed in various moods and in a less excited state, cannot but have great efficacy in tempering and restraining the passion by an intertexture of ordinary feeling, and of feeling not strictly and necessarily connected with the passion. This is unquestionably true, and hence, though the opinion will at first appear paradoxical, from the tendency of metre to divest language in a certain degree of its reality, and thus to throw a sort of half consciousness of unsubstantial existence over the whole composition, there can be little doubt but that more pathetic situations and sentiments, that is, those which have a greater proportion of pain connected with them, may be endured in metrical composition, especially in rhyme, than in prose. The metre of the old Ballads is very artless; yet they contain many passages which would illustrate this opinion, and, I hope, if the following Poems be attentively perused, similar instances will be found in them. This opinion may be further illustrated by appealing to the Reader's own experience of the reluctance with which he comes to the re-perusal of the distressful parts of Clarissa Harlowe, or the Gamester.[8] While Shakespeare's writings, in the most pathetic scenes, never act upon us as pathetic beyond the bounds of pleasure—an effect which, in a much greater degree than might at first be imagined, is to be ascribed to small, but continual and regular impulses of pleasurable surprise from the metrical arrangement.—On the other hand (what it must be allowed will much more frequently happen) if the Poet's words should be incommensurate with the passion, and inadequate to raise the Reader to

a height of desirable excitement, then, (unless the Poet's choice of his metre has been grossly injudicious) in the feelings of pleasure which the Reader has been accustomed to connect with metre in general, and in the feeling, whether chearful or melancholy, which he has been accustomed to connect with that particular movement of metre, there will be found something which will greatly contribute to impart passion to the words, and to effect the complex end which the Poet proposes to himself.

If I had undertaken a systematic defence of the theory upon which these poems are written, it would have been my duty to develope the various causes upon which the pleasure received from metrical language depends. Among the chief of these causes is to be reckoned a principle which must be well known to those who have made any of the Arts the object of accurate reflection; I mean the pleasure which the mind derives from the perception of similitude in dissimilitude. This principle is the great spring of the activity of our minds, and their chief feeder. From this principle the direction of the sexual appetite, and all the passions connected with it take their origin: it is the life of our ordinary conversation; and upon the accuracy with which similitude in dissimilitude, and dissimilitude in similitude are perceived, depend our taste and our moral feelings. It would not have been a useless employment to have applied this principle to the consideration of metre, and to have shewn that metre is hence enabled to afford much pleasure, and to have pointed out in what manner that pleasure is produced. But my limits will not permit me to enter upon this subject, and I must content myself with a general summary.

I have said that Poetry is the spontaneous overflow of powerful feelings: it takes its origin from emotion recollected in tranquillity: the emotion is contemplated till by a species of reaction the tranquillity gradually disappears, and an emotion, kindred to that which was before the subject of contemplation, is gradually produced, and does itself actually exist in the mind. In this mood successful composition generally begins, and in a mood similar to this it is carried on; but the emotion, of whatever kind and in whatever degree, from various causes is qualified by various pleasures, so that in describing any passions whatsoever, which are voluntarily described, the mind will upon the whole be in a state of enjoyment. Now, if Nature be thus cautious in preserving in a state of enjoyment a being thus employed, the Poet ought to profit by the lesson thus held forth to him, and ought especially to take care, that whatever passions he communicates to his Reader, those passions, if his Reader's mind be sound and vigorous, should always be accompanied with an

---

[8] *Clarissa Harlowe*, sentimental novel by Richardson, published 1747–1748. *Gamester*, popular domestic tragedy of 1753, by Edward Moore.

overbalance of pleasure. Now the music of harmonious metrical language, the sense of difficulty overcome, and the blind association of pleasure which has been previously received from works of rhyme or metre of the same or similar construction, an indistinct perception perpetually renewed of language closely resembling that of real life, and yet, in the circumstance of metre, differing from it so widely, all these imperceptibly make up a complex feeling of delight, which is of the most important use in tempering the painful feeling which will always be found intermingled with powerful descriptions of the deeper passions. This effect is always produced in pathetic and impassioned poetry; while, in lighter compositions, the ease and gracefulness with which the Poet manages his numbers are themselves confessedly a principal source of the gratification of the Reader. I might perhaps include all which it is *necessary* to say upon this subject by affirming, what few persons will deny, that, of two descriptions, either of passions, manners, or characters, each of them equally well executed, the one in prose and the other in verse, the verse will be read a hundred times where the prose is read once. We see that Pope by the power of verse alone, has contrived to render the plainest common sense interesting, and even frequently to invest it with the appearance of passion. In consequence of these convictions I related in metre the Tale of GOODY BLAKE and HARRY GILL, which is one of the rudest of this collection. I wished to draw attention to the truth that the power of the human imagination is sufficient to produce such changes even in our physical nature as might almost appear miraculous.[9] The truth is an important one; the fact (for it is a *fact*) is a valuable illustration of it. And I have the satisfaction of knowing that it has been communicated to many hundreds of people who would never have heard of it, had it not been narrated as a Ballad, and in a more impressive metre than is usual in Ballads.

Having thus explained a few of the reasons why I have written in verse, and why I have chosen subjects from common life, and endeavoured to bring my language near to the real language of men, if I have been too minute in pleading my own cause, I have at the same time been treating a subject of general interest; and it is for this reason that I request the Reader's permission to add a few words with reference solely to these particular poems, and to some defects which will probably be found in them. I am sensible that my associations must have sometimes been particular instead of general, and that, consequently, giving to things a false importance, sometimes from diseased impulses I may have written upon unworthy subjects; but I am less apprehensive on this account, than that my language may frequently have suffered from those arbitrary connections of feelings and ideas with particular words and phrases, from which no man can altogether protect himself. Hence I have no doubt, that, in some instances, feelings even of the ludicrous may be given to my Readers by expressions which appeared to me tender and pathetic. Such faulty expressions, were I convinced they were faulty at present, and that they must necessarily continue to be so, I would willingly take all reasonable pains to correct. But it is dangerous to make these alterations on the simple authority of a few individuals, or even of certain classes of men; for where the understanding of an Author is not convinced, or his feelings altered, this cannot be done without great injury to himself: for his own feelings are his stay and support, and, if he sets them aside in one instance, he may be induced to repeat this act till his mind loses all confidence in itself, and becomes utterly debilitated. To this it may be added, that the Reader ought never to forget that he is himself exposed to the same errors as the Poet, and perhaps in a much greater degree: for there can be no presumption in saying, that it is not probable he will be so well acquainted with the various stages of meaning through which words have passed, or with the fickleness or stability of the relations of particular ideas to each other; and above all, since he is so much less interested in the subject, he may decide lightly and carelessly.

Long as I have detained my Reader, I hope he will permit me to caution him against a mode of false criticism which has been applied to Poetry in which the language closely resembles that of life and nature. Such verses have been triumphed over in parodies of which Dr. Johnson's stanza is a fair specimen.

> " I put my hat upon my head,
>   And walk'd into the Strand,
>   And there I met another man
>   Whose hat was in his hand." [10]

Immediately under these lines I will place one of the most justly admired stanzas of the "*Babes* in the Wood."

---

[9] Through the force of his guilty conscience, the "cold-hearted" farmer Harry Gill is forever afflicted with a chill, for cruelly apprehending a poor woman who had gathered wood from his property in the depths of winter.

[10] Johnson's stanza, first published in 1785, was intended as a parody of the "simplicity" of Bishop Percy's imitation ballad *The Hermit of Warkworth* (1771). See "Essay, Supplementary to the Preface" (1815), footnote 27, p. 84.

"These pretty Babes with hand in hand
　　Went wandering up and down;
But never more they saw the Man
　　Approaching from the Town." [11]

In both these stanzas the words, and the order of the words, in no respect differ from the most unimpassioned conversation. There are words in both, for example, "the Strand," and "the Town," connected with none but the most familiar ideas; yet the one stanza we admit as admirable, and the other as a fair example of the superlatively contemptible. Whence arises this difference? Not from the metre, not from the language, not from the order of the words; but the *matter* expressed in Dr. Johnson's stanza is contemptible. The proper method of treating trivial and simple verses to which Dr. Johnson's stanza would be a fair parallelism is not to say, this is a bad kind of poetry, or this is not poetry; but this wants sense; it is neither interesting in itself, nor can *lead* to any thing interesting; the images neither originate in that sane state of feeling which arises out of thought, nor can excite thought or feeling in the Reader. This is the only sensible manner of dealing with such verses. Why trouble yourself about the species till you have previously decided upon the genus? Why take pains to prove that an Ape is not a Newton when it is self-evident that he is not a man?

I have one request to make of my Reader, which is, that in judging these Poems he would decide by his own feelings genuinely, and not by reflection upon what will probably be the judgment of others. How common is it to hear a person say, "I myself do not object to this style of composition or this or that expression, but to such and such classes of people it will appear mean or ludicrous." This mode of criticism, so destructive of all sound unadulterated judgment, is almost universal: I have therefore to request, that the Reader would abide independently by his own feelings, and that if he finds himself affected he would not suffer such conjectures to interfere with his pleasure.

If an Author by any single composition has impressed us with respect for his talents, it is useful to consider this as affording a presumption, that, on other occasions where we have been displeased, he nevertheless may not have written ill or absurdly; and, further, to give him so much credit for this one composition as may induce us to review what has displeased us with more care than we should otherwise have bestowed upon it. This is not only an act of justice, but, in our decisions upon poetry especially, may

conduce in a high degree to the improvement of our own taste: for an *accurate* taste in poetry, and in all the other arts, as Sir Joshua Reynolds has observed, [12] is an *acquired* talent, which can only be produced by thought and a long continued intercourse with the best models of composition. This is mentioned, not with so ridiculous a purpose as to prevent the most inexperienced Reader from judging for himself, (I have already said that I wish him to judge for himself;) but merely to temper the rashness of decision, and to suggest, that, if Poetry be a subject on which much time has not been bestowed, the judgment may be erroneous; and that in many cases it necessarily will be so.

I know that nothing would have so effectually contributed to further the end which I have in view as to have shewn of what kind the pleasure is, and how that pleasure is produced, which is confessedly produced by metrical composition essentially different from that which I have here endeavoured to recommend: for the Reader will say that he has been pleased by such composition; and what can I do more for him? The power of any art is limited; and he will suspect, that, if I propose to furnish him with new friends, it is only upon condition of his abandoning his old friends. Besides, as I have said, the Reader is himself conscious of the pleasure which he has received from such composition, composition to which he has peculiarly attached the endearing name of Poetry; and all men feel an habitual gratitude, and something of an honorable bigotry for the objects which have long continued to please them: we not only wish to be pleased, but to be pleased in that particular way in which we have been accustomed to be pleased. There is a host of arguments in these feelings; and I should be the less able to combat them successfully, as I am willing to allow, that, in order entirely to enjoy the Poetry which I am recommending, it would be necessary to give up much of what is ordinarily enjoyed. But, would my limits have permitted me to point out how this pleasure is produced, I might have removed many obstacles, and assisted my Reader in perceiving that the powers of language are not so limited as he may suppose; and that it is possible that poetry may give other enjoyments, of a purer, more lasting, and more exquisite nature. This part of my subject I have not altogether neglected; but it has been less my present aim to prove, that the interest excited by some other kinds of poetry is less vivid, and less worthy of the nobler powers of the mind, than to offer reasons for presuming, that, if the object which I have proposed to myself were adequately attained, a species of poetry would be produced, which is genuine poetry; in its nature well

---

[11] From the ballad more usually known as "The Children in the Wood." See Lamb's "Dream Children," footnote 1.

[12] See Reynolds's *Discourses* VII and XV.

adapted to interest mankind permanently, and likewise important in the multiplicity and quality of its moral relations.

From what has been said, and from a perusal of the Poems, the Reader will be able clearly to perceive the object which I have proposed to myself: he will determine how far I have attained this object; and, what is a much more important question, whether it be worth attaining; and upon the decision of these two questions will rest my claim to the approbation of the public.

[1800]   [1802]

APPENDIX
[TO THE PREFACE OF 1802][1]

As PERHAPS I have no right to expect from a Reader of an introduction to a volume of Poems that attentive perusal without which it is impossible, imperfectly as I have been compelled to express my meaning, that what I have said in the Preface should throughout be fully understood, I am the more anxious to give an exact notion of the sense in which I use the phrase *poetic diction*; and for this purpose I will here add a few words concerning the origin of the phraseology which I have condemned under that name.—The earliest Poets of all nations generally wrote from passion excited by real events; they wrote naturally, and as men: feeling powerfully as they did, their language was daring, and figurative. In succeeding times, Poets, and men ambitious of the fame of Poets, perceiving the influence of such language, and desirous of producing the same effect, without having the same animating passion, set themselves to a mechanical adoption of those figures of speech, and made use of them, sometimes with propriety, but much more frequently applied them to feelings and ideas with which they had no natural connection whatsoever. A language was thus insensibly produced, differing materially from the real language of men in *any situation*. The Reader or Hearer of this distorted language found himself in a perturbed and unusual state of mind: when affected by the genuine language of passion he had been in a perturbed and unusual state of mind also: in both cases he was willing that his common judgment and understanding should be laid asleep, and he had no instinctive and infallible perception of the true to make him reject the false; the one served as a passport for the other. The agitation and confusion of mind were in both cases delightful, and no wonder if he confounded the one with the other, and

believed them both to be produced by the same, or similar causes. Besides, the Poet spake to him in the character of a man to be looked up to, a man of genius and authority. Thus, and from a variety of other causes, this distorted language was received with admiration; and Poets, it is probable, who had before contented themselves for the most part with misapplying only expressions which at first had been dictated by real passion, carried the abuse still further, and introduced phrases composed apparently in the spirit of the original figurative language of passion, yet altogether of their own invention, and distinguished by various degrees of wanton deviation from good sense and nature.

It is indeed true that the language of the earliest Poets was felt to differ materially from ordinary language, because it was the language of extraordinary occasions; but it was really spoken by men, language which the Poet himself had uttered when he had been affected by the events which he described, or which he had heard uttered by those around him. To this language it is probable that metre of some sort or other was early superadded. This separated the genuine language of Poetry still further from common life, so that whoever read or heard the poems of these earliest Poets felt himself moved in a way in which he had not been accustomed to be moved in real life, and by causes manifestly different from those which acted upon him in real life. This was the great temptation to all the corruptions which have followed: under the protection of this feeling succeeding Poets constructed a phraseology which had one thing, it is true, in common with the genuine language of poetry, namely, that it was not heard in ordinary conversation; that it was unusual. But the first Poets, as I have said, spake a language which though unusual, was still the language of men. This circumstance, however, was disregarded by their successors; they found that they could please by easier means: they became proud of a language which they themselves had invented, and which was uttered only by themselves; and, with the spirit of a fraternity, they arrogated it to themselves as their own. In process of time metre became a symbol or promise of this unusual language, and whoever took upon him to write in metre, according as he possessed more or less of true poetic genius, introduced less or more of this adulterated phraseology into his compositions, and the true and the false became so inseparably interwoven that the taste of men was gradually perverted; and this language was received as a natural language; and, at length, by the influence of books upon men, did to a certain degree really become so. Abuses of this kind were imported from one nation to another, and with the progress of refinement this diction became daily

---

[1] See Preface, page 53.—"by what is usually called poetic diction."

more and more corrupt, thrusting out of sight the plain humanities of nature by a motley masquerade of tricks, quaintnesses, hieroglyphics, and enigmas.

It would be highly interesting to point out the causes of the pleasure given by this extravagant and absurd language; but this is not the place; it depends upon a great variety of causes, but upon none perhaps more than its influence in impressing a notion of the peculiarity and exaltation of the Poet's character, and in flattering the Reader's self-love by bringing him nearer to a sympathy with that character; an effect which is accomplished by unsettling ordinary habits of thinking, and thus assisting the Reader to approach to that perturbed and dizzy state of mind in which if he does not find himself, he imagines that he is *balked* of a peculiar enjoyment which poetry can, and ought to bestow.

The sonnet which I have quoted from Gray, in the Preface, except the lines printed in Italics, consists of little else but this diction, though not of the worst kind; and indeed, if I may be permitted to say so, it is far too common in the best writers, both antient and modern. Perhaps I can in no way, by positive example, more easily give my Reader a notion of what I mean by the phrase *poetic diction* than by referring him to a comparison between the metrical paraphrases which we have of passages in the old and new Testament, and those passages as they exist in our common Translation. See Pope's "Messiah" throughout, Prior's "Did sweeter sounds adorn my flowing tongue," [2] &c. &c. "Though I speak with the tongues of men and of angels," &c. &c. See 1st Corinthians, chapter xiiith. By way of immediate example, take the following of Dr. Johnson:

"Turn on the prudent Ant thy heedless eyes,
    Observe her labours, Sluggard, and be wise;
No stern command, no monitory voice,
Prescribes her duties, or directs her choice;
Yet, timely provident she hastes away
To snatch the blessings of a plenteous day;
When fruitful Summer loads the teeming plain,
She crops the harvest and she stores the grain.
How long shall sloth usurp thy useless hours,
Unnerve thy vigour, and enchain thy powers?
While artful shades thy downy couch enclose,
And soft solicitation courts repose,
Amidst the drowsy charms of dull delight,
Year chases year with unremitted flight,
Till want now following, fraudulent and slow,
Shall spring to seize thee, like an ambushed foe." [3]

From this hubbub of words pass to the original. "Go to the Ant, thou Sluggard, consider her ways, and be wise: which having no guide, overseer, or ruler, provideth her meat in the summer, and gathereth her food in the harvest. How long wilt thou sleep, O Sluggard? when wilt thou arise out of thy sleep? Yet a little sleep, a little slumber, a little folding of the hands to sleep. So shall thy poverty come as one that travaileth, and thy want as an armed man." Proverbs, chap. 6th.

One more quotation and I have done. It is from Cowper's verses supposed to be written by Alexander Selkirk:

"Religion! what treasure untold
    Resides in that heavenly word!
More precious than silver and gold,
    Or all that this earth can afford.
But the sound of the church-going bell
    These valleys and rocks never heard
Ne'er sighed at the sound of a knell,
    Or smiled when a sabbath appeared.
Ye winds, that have made me your sport,
    Convey to this desolate shore
Some cordial endearing report
    Of a land I must visit no more.
My Friends, do they now and then send
    A wish or a thought after me?
O tell me I yet have a friend
    Though a friend I am never to see." [4]

I have quoted this passage as an instance of three different styles of composition. The first four lines are poorly expressed; some Critics would call the language prosaic; the fact is, it would be bad prose, so bad, that it is scarcely worse in metre. The epithet "church-going" applied to a bell, and that by so chaste a writer as Cowper, is an instance of the strange abuses which Poets have introduced into their language till they and their Readers take them as matters of course, if they do not single them out expressly as objects of admiration. The two lines "Ne'er sigh'd at the sound," &c. are, in my opinion, an instance of the language of passion wrested from its proper use, and, from the mere circumstance of the composition being in metre, applied upon an occasion that does not justify such violent expressions, and I should condemn the passage, though perhaps few Readers will agree with me, as vicious poetic diction. The last stanza is throughout admirably expressed: it would be equally good whether in prose or verse, except that the Reader has an exquisite

---

[2] Pope's "Messiah," published in 1712, paraphrases in verse a number of passages from *Isaiah*. "Did sweeter sounds adorn my flowing tongue" is the opening line of Matthew Prior's poem "Charity. A Paraphrase on the Thirteenth Chapter of the First Epistle to the Corinthians" (1704).

[3] "The Ant," first published in 1766.

[4] Ll. 25–40 of William Cowper's "Verses Supposed to be Written by Alexander Selkirk" (1782). Alexander Selkirk was a Scottish seaman, whose abandonment and adventures on the Juan Fernandez Islands of the South Pacific were the inspiration for Defoe's *Robinson Crusoe*.

pleasure in seeing such natural language so naturally connected with metre. The beauty of this stanza tempts me here to add a sentiment which ought to be the pervading spirit of a system, detached parts of which have been imperfectly explained in the Preface, namely, that in proportion as ideas and feelings are valuable, whether the composition be in prose or in verse, they require and exact one and the same language.

[1802]

THE CONVENTION OF CINTRA

In the fall of 1807, French military forces, with the permission of a subservient Spanish government, had entered Spain and proceeded to conquer Britain's traditional ally Portugal. Under the pretext of supporting the army in Portugal, massive French forces subsequently occupied Spain, forced the monarchy of the Bourbon Charles IV and his son Ferdinand VII to abdicate (May 1808), and placed Napoleon's brother Joseph on the Spanish throne. Beginning with the famous May 2 ("dos de mayo") uprising of the citizens of Madrid, which was savagely suppressed by the French authorities, cities throughout Spain spontaneously rose in revolt, formed their own Juntas, and began military operations against the occupying army. On August 1, 1808, British forces under Sir Arthur Wellesley (later Lord Wellington) landed in Portugal and defeated the forces of the French General Junot at Vimiera on August 21. Nine days later, the Convention of Cintra was held, presumably to formalize the French defeat. To the consternation of the British public, who had seen the victory in Portugal as the opportunity for a major reversal of Napoleon's conquests and his continued threats to England, the British authorities granted General Junot the most lenient terms of surrender, including transportation of the defeated forces back to France with all the plunder of their Portuguese occupation; moreover, the legitimate Portuguese authorities were not consulted in drawing up the Convention.

Wordsworth's indignation at this course of events led him to "ease his heart in a pamphlet," which he began to write in November 1808. The work was not published until late May 1809, by which time interest in the events had largely subsided. Although it did not produce the effect Wordsworth had hoped (not quite half the 500 copies were sold in the next year, and many of the remaining copies "were disposed of by the publishers as waste paper"), the Convention of Cintra remains the most eloquent statement of Wordsworth's mature political ideals, and one of the major statements in English literature of the centrality of moral principle to national policy.

The following text is that of the first edition, second issue. On the complicated history of the composition and publication of the work, see: J. E. Wells, "The Story of Wordsworth's 'Cintra,'" Studies in Philology, XVIII (1921), 15–76; Mary Moorman, William Wordsworth a Biography: The Later Years 1803–1850 (London: Oxford University Press, 1965), pp. 136–45; John E. Jordan, De Quincey to Wordsworth. A Biography of a Relationship (Berkeley-Los Angeles: University of California Press, 1962), pp. 63–85. Gordon Kent Thomas' Wordsworth's Dirge and Promise: Napoleon, Wellington, and the Convention of Cintra (Lincoln, Neb.: University of Nebraska Press, 1971) is a comprehensive study of the historical background, composition, and political ideas of the treatise.

FROM

CONCERNING THE

RELATIONS

OF

Great Britain, Spain, and Portugal

TO EACH OTHER,

AND TO THE COMMON ENEMY,

AT THIS

CRISIS;

AND SPECIFICALLY AS

AFFECTED BY THE

CONVENTION OF CINTRA:

THE WHOLE

BROUGHT TO THE TEST OF THOSE

PRINCIPLES,

BY WHICH ALONE THE

INDEPENDENCE AND FREEDOM

OF

NATIONS

CAN BE

PRESERVED OR RECOVERED.

THE CONVENTION, recently concluded by the Generals at the head of the British army in Portugal, is one of the most important events of our time. It would be deemed so in France, if the Ruler of that country could dare to make it public with those merely of its known bearings and dependences with which the English people are acquainted; it has been deemed so in Spain and Portugal as far as the people of those countries have been permitted to gain, or have gained, a knowledge of it; and what this nation has felt and still feels upon the subject is sufficiently manifest. Wherever the tidings were communicated, they carried agitation along with them—a conflict of sensations in which, though sorrow was predominant, yet, through force of scorn, impatience, hope, and indignation, and through the universal participation in passions so complex, and the sense of power which this necessarily included—the whole partook of the energy and activity of congratulation and joy. Not a street, not a public room, not a fire-side in the island which was not disturbed as by a local or private trouble; men of all estates, conditions, and tempers were affected apparently in equal degrees. Yet was the event by none received as an open and measurable affliction: it had indeed features bold and intelligible to every one; but there was an under-expression which was strange, dark, and mysterious—and, accordingly as different notions prevailed, or the object was looked at in different points of view, we were astonished like men who are overwhelmed without forewarning—fearful like men who feel themselves to be helpless, and indignant and angry like men who are betrayed. In a word, it would not be too much to say that the tidings of this event did not spread with the commotion of a storm which sweeps visibly over our heads, but like an earthquake which rocks the ground under our feet.

How was it possible that it could be otherwise? For that army had been sent upon a service which appealed so strongly to all that was human in the heart of this nation—that there was scarcely a gallant father of a family who had not his moments of regret that he was not a soldier by profession, which might have made it his duty to accompany it; every high-minded youth grieved that his first impulses, which would have sent him upon the same errand, were not to be yielded to, and that after-thought did not sanction and confirm the instantaneous dictates or the reiterated persuasions of an heroic spirit. The army took its departure with prayers and blessings which were as widely spread as they were fervent and intense. For it was not doubted that, on this occasion, every person of which it was composed, from the General to the private soldier, would carry both into his conflicts with the enemy in the field, and into his relations of peaceful intercourse with the inhabitants, not only the virtues which might be expected from him as a soldier, but the antipathies and sympathies, the loves and hatreds of a citizen—of a human being—acting, in a manner hitherto unprecedented under the obligation of his human and social nature. If the conduct of the rapacious and merciless adversary rendered it neither easy nor wise—made it, I might say, impossible to give way to that unqualified admiration of courage and skill, made it impossible in relation to him to be exalted by those triumphs of the courteous affections, and to be purified by those refinements of civility which do, more than any thing, reconcile a man of thoughtful mind and humane dispositions to the horrors of ordinary war; it was felt that for such loss the benign and accomplished soldier would upon this mission be abundantly recompensed by the enthusiasm of fraternal love with which his Ally, the oppressed people whom he was going to aid in rescuing themselves, would receive him; and that this, and the virtues which he would witness in them, would furnish his heart with never-failing and far nobler objects of complacency and admiration. The discipline

of the army was well known; and as a machine, or a vital organized body, the Nation was assured that it could not but be formidable; but thus to the standing excellence of mechanic or organic power seemed to be superadded, at this time, and for this service, the force of *inspiration:* could any thing therefore be looked for, but a glorious result? The army proved its prowess in the field; and what has been the result is attested, and long will be attested, by the downcast looks—the silence—the passionate exclamations—the sighs and shame of every man who is worthy to breathe the air or to look upon the green-fields of Liberty in this blessed and high-favoured Island which we inhabit.

If I were speaking of things however weighty, that were long past and dwindled in the memory, I should scarcely venture to use this language; but the feelings are of yesterday—they are of to-day; the flower, a melancholy flower it is! is still in blow, nor will, I trust, its leaves be shed through months that are to come: for I repeat that the heart of the nation is in this struggle. This just and necessary war, as we have been accustomed to hear it styled from the beginning of the contest in the year 1793, had, some time before the Treaty of Amiens, viz. after the subjugation of Switzerland,[1] and not till then, begun to be regarded by the body of the people, as indeed both just and necessary; and this justice and necessity were by none more clearly perceived, or more feelingly bewailed, than by those who had most eagerly opposed the war in its commencement, and who continued most bitterly to regret that this nation had ever borne a part in it. Their conduct was herein consistent: they proved that they kept their eyes steadily fixed upon principles; for, though there was a shifting or transfer of hostility in their minds as far as regarded persons, they only combated the same enemy opposed to them under a different shape; and that enemy was the spirit of selfish tyranny and lawless ambition. This spirit, the class of persons of whom I have been speaking, (and I would now be understood, as associating them with an immense majority of the people of Great Britain, whose affections, notwithstanding all the delusions which had

<hr />

[1] As J. C. Maxwell points out ("Wordsworth and the Subjugation of Switzerland," *Modern Language Review*, LXV [1970], 16–18), this statement is neither clear nor historically accurate. The Treaty of Amiens was signed in March 1802, ending temporarily the hostilities between England and France. Although the French had invaded Switzerland in 1798 before the Treaty, the initial invasion did not affect the feelings of the British people (or of Wordsworth) as the statement indicates. The popular belief that the war was "just and necessary" was the result of later events, one of which was Napoleon's invasion of Switzerland *during* the Peace of Amiens, in October 1802. From the perspective of 1808–1809, Wordsworth apparently traced back to 1798 a national hostility to Napoleon and the French Revolution that in fact was only beginning to develop *after* the Treaty of Amiens.

been practised upon them, were, in the former part of the contest, for a long time on the side of their nominal enemies,) this spirit, when it became undeniably embodied in the French government, they wished, in spite of all dangers, should be opposed by war; because peace was not to be procured without submission, which could not but be followed by a communion, of which the word of greeting would be, on the one part, insult,—and, on the other, degradation. The people now wished for war, as their rulers had done before, because open war between nations is a defined and effectual partition, and the sword, in the hands of the good and the virtuous, is the most intelligible symbol of abhorrence. It was in order to be preserved from spirit-breaking submissions—from the guilt of seeming to approve that which they had not the power to prevent, and out of a consciousness of the danger that such guilt would otherwise actually steal upon them, and that thus, by evil communications and participations, would be weakened and finally destroyed, those moral sensibilities and energies, by virtue of which alone, their liberties, and even their lives, could be preserved,—that the people of Great Britain determined to encounter all perils which could follow in the train of open resistance.—There were some, and those deservedly of high character in the country, who exerted their utmost influence to counteract this resolution; nor did they give to it so gentle a name as want of prudence, but they boldly termed it blindness and obstinacy. Let them be judged with charity! But there are promptings of wisdom from the penetralia of human nature, which a people can hear, though the wisest of their practical Statesmen be deaf towards them. This authentic voice, the people of England had heard and obeyed: and, in opposition to French tyranny growing daily more insatiate and implacable, they ranged themselves zealously under their Government; though they neither forgot nor forgave its transgressions, in having first involved them in a war with a people then struggling for its own liberties under a twofold infliction—confounded by inbred faction, and beleagured by a cruel and imperious external foe.[2] But these remembrances did not vent themselves in reproaches, nor hinder us from being reconciled to our Rulers, when a change or rather a revolution in circumstances had imposed new duties: and, in defiance of local and personal clamour, it may be safely said, that the nation united heart and hand with the Government in its resolve to meet the worst, rather than stoop its head to receive that which, it was felt, would not be the garland but the yoke of peace. Yet it was an afflicting

alternative; and it is not to be denied, that the effort, if it had the determination, wanted the cheerfulness of duty. Our condition savoured too much of a grinding constraint—too much of the vassalage of necessity;—it had too much of fear, and therefore of selfishness, not to be contemplated in the main with rueful emotion. We desponded though we did not despair. In fact a deliberate and preparatory fortitude—a sedate and stern melancholy, which had no sunshine and was exhilarated only by the lightnings of indignation—this was the highest and best state of moral feeling to which the most noble-minded among us could attain.

But, from the moment of the rising of the people of the Pyrenean peninsula, there was a mighty change; we were instantaneously animated; and, from that moment, the contest assumed the dignity, which it is not in the power of any thing but hope to bestow: and, if I may dare to transfer language, prompted by a revelation of the state of being that admits not of decay or change, to the concerns and interests of our transitory planet, from that moment "this corruptible put on incorruption, and this mortal put on immortality."[3] This sudden elevation was on no account more welcome—was by nothing more endeared, than by the returning sense which accompanied it of inward liberty and choice, which gratified our moral yearnings, inasmuch as it would give henceforward to our actions as a people, an origination and direction unquestionably moral—as it was free—as it was manifestly in sympathy with the species—as it admitted therefore of fluctuations of generous feeling—of approbation and of complacency. We are intellectualized also in proportion; we looked backward upon the records of the human race with pride, and, instead of being afraid, we delighted to look forward into futurity. It was imagined that this newborn spirit of resistance, rising from the most sacred feelings of the human heart, would diffuse itself through many countries; and not merely for the distant future, but for the present, hopes were entertained as bold as they were disinterested and generous.

Never, indeed, was the fellowship of our sentient nature more intimately felt—never was the irresistible power of justice more gloriously displayed than when the British and Spanish Nations, with an impulse like that of two ancient heroes throwing down their weapons and reconciled in the field, cast off at once their aversions and enmities, and mutually embraced each other—to solemnize this conversion of love, not by the festivities of peace, but by combating side by side through danger and under affliction in the devotedness of perfect brotherhood. This was a con-

---

[2] The "external foe" refers to the Prussian and Austrian monarchies, which had sought to restore Louis XVI to the throne.

[3] I Corinthians, xv, 53.

junction which excited hope as fervent as it was rational. On the one side was a nation which brought with it sanction and authority, inasmuch as it had tried and approved the blessings for which the other had risen to contend: the one was a people which, by the help of the surrounding ocean and its own virtues, had preserved to itself through ages its liberty, pure and inviolated by a foreign invader; the other a high-minded nation, which a tyrant, presuming on its decrepitude, had, through the real decrepitude of its Government, perfidiously enslaved. What could be more delightful than to think of an intercourse beginning in this manner? On the part of the Spaniards their love towards us was enthusiasm and adoration; the faults of our national character were hidden from them by a veil of splendour; they saw nothing around us but glory and light; and, on our side, we estimated *their* character with partial and indulgent fondness;—thinking on their past greatness; not as the undermined foundation of a magnificent building, but as the root of a majestic tree recovered from a long disease, and beginning again to flourish with promise of wider branches and a deeper shade than it had boasted in the fulness of its strength. If in the sensations with which the Spaniards prostrated themselves before the religion of their country we did not keep pace with them—if even their loyalty was such as, from our mixed constitution of government and from other causes, we could not thoroughly sympathize with,—and if, lastly, their devotion to the person of their Sovereign appeared to us to have too much of the alloy of delusion,—in all these things we judged them gently: and, taught by the reverses of the French revolution, we looked upon these dispositions as more human—more social—and therefore as wiser, and of better omen, than if they had stood forth the zealots of abstract principles, drawn out of the laboratory of unfeeling philosophists. Finally, in this reverence for the past and present, we found an earnest that they were prepared to contend to the death for as much liberty as their habits and their knowledge enabled them to receive. To assist them and their neighbours the Portuguese in the attainment of this end, we sent to them in love and in friendship a powerful army to aid—to invigorate—and to chastise: —they landed; and the first proof they afforded of their being worthy to be sent on such a service—the first pledge of amity given by them was the victory of Vimiera; the second pledge (and this was from the hand of their Generals,) was the Convention of Cintra.

The reader will by this time have perceived, what thoughts were uppermost in my mind, when I began with asserting, that this Convention is among the most important events of our times:—an assertion, which was made deliberately, and after due allowance for that infirmity which inclines us to magnify things present and passing, at the expence of those which are past. It is my aim to prove, wherein the real importance of this event lies: and, as a necessary preparative for forming a right judgment upon it, I have already given a representation of the sentiments, with which the people of Great Britain and those of Spain looked upon each other. I have indeed spoken rather of the Spaniards than of the Portuguese; but what has been said, will be understood as applying in the main to the whole Peninsula. The wrongs of the two nations have been equal, and their cause is the same: they must stand or fall together. What their wrongs have been, in what degree they considered themselves united, and what their hopes and resolutions were, we have learned from public Papers issued by themselves and by their enemies. These were read by the people of this Country, at the time when they were severally published, with due impression.—Pity, that those impressions could not have been as faithfully retained as they were at first received deeply! Doubtless, there is not a man in these Islands, who is not convinced that the cause of Spain is the most righteous cause in which, since the opposition of the Greek Republics to the Persian Invader at Thermopylæ and Marathon, sword ever was drawn! But this is not enough. We are actors in the struggle; and, in order that we may have steady PRINCIPLES to controul and direct us, (without which we may do much harm, and can do no good,) we ought to make it a duty to revive in the memory those words and facts, which first carried the conviction to our hearts: that, as far as it is possible, we may see as we then saw, and feel as we then felt.[4]

*   *   *   *   *

In following the stream of these thoughts, I have not wandered from my course: I have drawn out to open day the truth from its recesses in the minds of my countrymen.—Something more perhaps may have been done: a shape hath perhaps been given to that which was before a stirring spirit. I have shewn in what manner it was their wish that the struggle with the adversary of all that is good should be maintained—by pure passions and high actions. They forbid that their noble aim should be frustrated by measuring against each other things which are incommensurate—mechanic against moral power—body against soul. They will not suffer, without expressing their sorrow,

---

[4] In a long section here omitted, Wordsworth reviews French injustices and cruelties to the Spanish people; argues the essentially moral basis of the Spanish response; and indicts the signers of the Convention and the British government that approved it for their "*moral* depravity."

that purblind calculation should wither the purest hopes in the face of all-seeing justice. These are times of strong appeal—of deep-searching visitation; when the best abstractions of the prudential understanding give way, and are included and absorbed in a supreme comprehensiveness of intellect and passion; which is the perfection and the very being of humanity.

How base! how puny! how inefficient for all good purposes are the tools and implements of policy, compared with these mighty engines of Nature!—There is no middle course: two masters cannot be served:—Justice must either be enthroned above might, and the moral law take place of the edicts of selfish passion; or the heart of the people, which alone can sustain the efforts of the people, will languish: their desires will not spread beyond the plough and the loom, the field and the fireside: the sword will appear to them an emblem of no promise; an instrument of no hope; an object of indifference, of disgust, or fear. Was there ever—since the earliest actions of men which have been transmitted by affectionate tradition or recorded by faithful history, or sung to the impassioned harp of poetry—was there ever a people who presented themselves to the reason and the imagination, as under more holy influences than the dwellers upon the Southern Peninsula; as rouzed more instantaneously from a deadly sleep to a more hopeful wakefulness; as a mass fluctuating with one motion under the breath of a mightier wind; as breaking themselves up, and settling into several bodies, in more harmonious order; as reunited and embattled under a standard which was reared to the sun with more authentic assurance of final victory?—The superstition (I do not dread the word), which prevailed in these nations, may have checked many of my countrymen who would otherwise have exultingly accompanied me in the challenge which, under the shape of a question, I have been confidently uttering; as I know that this stain (so the same persons termed it) did, from the beginning, discourage their hopes for the cause. Short-sighted despondency! Whatever mixture of superstition there might be in the religious faith or devotional practices of the Spaniards; this must have necessarily been transmuted by that triumphant power, wherever that power was felt, which grows out of intense moral suffering—from the moment in which it coalesces with fervent hope. The chains of bigotry, which enthralled the mind, must have been turned into armour to defend and weapons to annoy. Wherever the heaving and effort of freedom was spread, purification must have followed it. And the types and ancient instruments of error, where emancipated men shewed their foreheads to the day, must have become a language and a ceremony of imagination; expressing, consecrating, and invigorat-

ing, the most pure deductions of Reason and the holiest feelings of universal Nature.

When the Boy of Saragossa [5] (as we have been told), too immature in growth and unconfirmed in strength to be admitted by his Fellow-citizens into their ranks, too tender of age for them to bear the sight of him in arms—when this Boy, forgetful or unmindful of the restrictions which had been put upon him, rushed into the field where his Countrymen were engaged in battle, and, fighting with the sinew and courage of an unripe Hero, won a standard from the enemy, and bore his acquisition to the Church, and laid it with his own hands upon the Altar of the Virgin;—surely there was not less to be hoped for his Country from this act, than if the banner, taken from his grasp, had, without any such intermediation, been hung up in the place of worship—a direct offering to the incorporeal and supreme Being. Surely there is here an object which the most meditative and most elevated minds may contemplate with absolute delight; a well-adapted outlet for the dearest sentiments; an organ by which they may act; a function by which they may be sustained.—Who does not recognise in this presentation a visible affinity with deliverance, with patriotism, with hatred of oppression, and with human means put forth to the height for accomplishing, under divine countenance, the worthiest ends?

Such is the burst and growth of power and virtue which may rise out of excessive national afflictions from tyranny and oppression;—such is the hallowing influence, and thus mighty is the sway, of the spirit of moral justice in the heart of the individual and over the wide world of humanity. Even the very faith in present miraculous interposition, which is so dire a weakness and cause of weakness in tranquil times when the listless Being turns to it as a cheap and ready substitute upon every occasion, where the man sleeps, and the Saint, or the image of the Saint, is to perform his work, and to give effect to his wishes;—even this infirm faith, in a state of incitement from extreme passion sanctioned by a paramount sense of moral justice; having for its object a power which is no longer sole nor principal, but secondary and ministerial; a power added to a power; a breeze which springs up unthought-of to assist the strenuous oarsman;—even this faith is subjugated in order to be exalted; and—instead of operating as a temptation to relax or to be remiss, as an encouragement to indolence or cowardice; instead of being a false stay, a necessary and definite depend-

---

[5] Saragossa had set the standard of heroic defiance for the Spanish people in their opposition to Napoleon by enduring two extended sieges: June–August 1808, ending in a French defeat; December 1808–February 1809, ending in a Spanish defeat.

ence which may fail—it passes into a habit of obscure and infinite confidence of the mind in its own energies, in the cause from its own sanctity, and in the ever-present invisible aid or momentary conspicuous approbation of the supreme Disposer of things.

Let the fire, which is never wholly to be extinguished, break out afresh: let but the human creature be rouzed; whether he have lain heedless and torpid in religious or civil slavery—have languished under a thraldom, domestic or foreign, or under both these alternately—or have drifted about a helpless member of a clan of disjointed and feeble barbarians; let him rise and act;—and his domineering imagination, by which from childhood he has been betrayed, and the debasing affections, which it has imposed upon him, will from that moment participate the dignity of the newly ennobled being whom they will now acknowledge for their master; and will further him in his progress, whatever be the object at which he aims. Still more inevitable and momentous are the results, when the individual knows that the fire, which is reanimated in him, is not less lively in the breasts of his associates; and sees the signs and testimonies of his own power, incorporated with those of a growing multitude and not to be distinguished from them, accompany him wherever he moves.—Hence those marvellous achievements which were performed by the first enthusiastic followers of Mohammed; and by other conquerors, who with their armies have swept large portions of the earth like a transitory wind, or have founded new religions or empires.—But, if the object contended for be worthy and truly great (as, in the instance of the Spaniards, we have seen that it is); if cruelties have been committed upon an ancient and venerable people, which "shake the human frame with horror;" if not alone the life which is sustained by the bread of the mouth, but that—without which there is no life—the life in the soul, has been directly and mortally warred against; if reason has had abominations to endure in her inmost sanctuary;—then does intense passion, consecrated by a sudden revelation of justice, give birth to those higher and better wonders which I have described; and exhibit true miracles to the eyes of men, and the noblest which can be seen. It may be added that,—as this union brings back to the right road the faculty of imagination, where it is prone to err, and has gone farthest astray; as it corrects those qualities which (being in their essence indifferent), and cleanses those affections which (not being inherent in the constitution of man, nor necessarily determined to their object) are more immediately dependent upon the imagination, and which may have received from it a thorough taint of dishonour;—so the domestic loves and sanctities which are in their nature less liable to be

stained,—so these, wherever they have flowed with a pure and placid stream, do instantly, under the same influence, put forth their strength as in a flood; and, without being sullied or polluted, pursue—exultingly and with song—a course which leads the contemplative reason to the ocean of eternal love.

I feel that I have been speaking in a strain which it is difficult to harmonize with the petty irritations, the doubts and fears, and the familiar (and therefore frequently undignified) exterior of present and passing events. But the theme is justice: and my voice is raised for mankind; for us who are alive, and for all posterity: —justice and passion; clear-sighted aspiring justice, and passion sacred as vehement. These, like twin-born Deities delighting in each other's presence, have wrought marvels in the inward mind through the whole region of the Pyrenëan Peninsula. I have shewn by what process these united powers sublimated the objects of outward sense in such rites—practices—and ordinances of Religion—as deviate from simplicity and wholesome piety; how they converted them to instruments of nobler use; and raised them to a conformity with things truly divine. The same reasoning might have been carried into the customs of civil life and their accompanying imagery, wherever these also were inconsistent with the dignity of man; and like effects of exaltation and purification have been shewn.

*　　*　　*　　*　　*

Deeming myself justified then in what has been said,—I will continue to lay open (and, in some degree, to account for) those privations in the materials of judgment, and those delusions of opinion, and infirmities of mind, to which practical Statesmen, and particularly such as are high in office, are more than other men subject;—as containing an answer to that question, so interesting at this juncture,—How far is it in our power to make amends for the harm done?

After the view of things which has been taken,—we may confidently affirm that nothing, but a knowledge of human nature directing the operations of our government, can give it a right to an intimate association with a cause which is that of human nature. I say, an intimate association founded on the right of thorough knowledge;—to contradistinguish this best mode of exertion from another which might found *its* right upon a vast and commanding military power put forth with manifestation of sincere intentions to benefit our allies—from a conviction merely of policy that their liberty, independence, and honour, are our genuine gain;—to distinguish the pure brotherly connection from this other (in its appearance at least more magisterial) which such a power, guided by such intention uniformly displayed, might authorize. But of the former connection (which supposes the main military effort to be made, even at present, by the people of the Peninsula on whom the moral interest more closely presses), and of the knowledge which it demands, I have hitherto spoken—and have further to speak.

It is plain *à priori* that the minds of Statesmen and Courtiers are unfavourable to the growth of this knowledge. For they are in a situation exclusive and artificial; which has the further disadvantage, that it does not separate men from men by collateral partitions which leave, along with difference, a sense of equality—that they, who are divided, are yet upon the same level; but by a degree of superiority which can scarcely fail to be accompanied with more or less of pride. This situation therefore must be eminently unfavourable for the reception and establishment of that knowledge which is founded not upon things but upon sensations;—sensations which are general, and under general influences (and this it is which makes them what they are, and gives them their importance);—not upon things which may be *brought;* but upon sensations which must be *met.* Passing by the kindred and usually accompanying influence of birth in a certain rank—and, where education has been pre-defined from childhood for the express purpose of future political power, the tendency of such education to warp (and therefore weaken) the intellect;—we may join at once, with the privation which I have been noticing, a delusion equally common. It is this: that practical Statesmen assume too much credit to themselves for their ability to see into the motives and manage the selfish passions of their immediate agents and dependants; and for the skill with which they baffle or resist the aims of their opponents. A promptness in looking through the most superficial part of the characters of those men—who, by the very circumstance of their contending ambitiously for the rewards and honours of government, are separated from the mass of the society to which they belong—is mistaken for a knowledge of human kind. Hence, where higher knowledge is a prime requisite, they not only are unfurnished; but, being unconscious that they are so, they look down contemptuously upon those who endeavour to supply (in some degree) their want.—The instincts of natural and social man; the deeper emotions; the simpler feelings; the spacious range of the disinterested imagination; the pride in country for country's sake, when to serve has not been a formal profession—and the mind is therefore left in a state of dignity only to be surpassed by having served nobly and generously; the instantaneous accomplishment in which they start up who, upon a searching call, stir for the land which they love—not from personal motives, but for a reward which is undefined and cannot be missed; the solemn fraternity which a great Nation composes—gathered together, in a stormy season, under the shade of ancestral feeling; the delicacy of moral honour which pervades the minds of a people, when despair has been suddenly thrown off and expectations are lofty; the apprehensiveness to a touch unkindly or irreverent, where sympathy is at once exacted as a tribute and welcomed as a gift; the power of injustice and inordinate calamity to transmute, to invigorate, and to govern—to sweep away the barriers of opinion—to reduce under submission passions purely evil—to exalt the nature of indifferent qualities, and to render them fit companions for the absolute virtues with which they are summoned to associate—to consecrate passions which, if not bad in themselves, are of such temper that, in the calm of ordinary life, they are rightly deemed so—to correct and embody these passions—and, without weakening them (nay, with tenfold addition to their strength), to make them worthy of taking their place as the advanced guard of hope, when a sublime movement of deliverance is to be originated;—these arrangements and resources of nature, these ways and means of society, have so little connection with those others upon which a ruling minister of a long-established government is accustomed to depend; these—elements as it were of a universe, functions of a living body—are so opposite, in their mode of action, to the formal machine which it has been his pride to manage;—that he has but a faint perception of their immediate efficacy; knows not the facility with which they assimilate with other powers; nor the property by which such of them—as, from necessity of nature, must change or pass away—will, under wise and fearless management, surely generate lawful successors to fill their place when their appropriate work is performed. Nay, of the majority of men, who are usually found in high stations under old governments, it may without injustice be said; that, when they look about them in times (alas! too rare) which present the glorious product of such agency to their eyes, they have not a right to say—with a dejected man in the midst of the woods, the rivers, the mountains, the sunshine, and shadows of some transcendant landscape—

"I see, not feel, how beautiful they are."[6]

These spectators neither see nor feel. And it is from the blindness and insensibility of these, and the train whom they draw along with them, that the throes of nations have been so ill recompensed by the births which have followed; and that revolutions, after passing from crime to crime and from sorrow to

[6] Coleridge's "Dejection: an Ode," l. 38.

sorrow, have often ended in throwing back such heavy reproaches of delusiveness upon their first promises.

I am satisfied that no enlightened Patriot will impute to me a wish to disparage the characters of men high in authority, or to detract from the estimation which is fairly due to them. My purpose is to guard against unreasonable expectations. That specific knowledge,— the paramount importance of which, in the present condition of Europe, I am insisting upon,—they, who usually fill places of high trust in old governments, neither do—nor, for the most part, can—possess: nor is it necessary, for the administration of affairs in ordinary circumstances, that they should.—The progress of their own country, and of the other nations of the world, in civilization, in true refinement, in science, in religion, in morals, and in all the real wealth of humanity, might indeed be quicker, and might correspond more happily with the wishes of the benevolent,—if Governors better understood the rudiments of nature as studied in the walks of common life; if they were men who had themselves felt every strong emotion "inspired by nature and by fortune taught;" and could calculate upon the force of the grander passions. Yet, at the same time, there is temptation in this. To know may seduce; and to have been agitated may compel. Arduous cares are attractive for their own sakes. Great talents are naturally driven towards hazard and difficulty; as it is there that they are most sure to find their exercise, and their evidence, and joy in anticipated triumph—the liveliest of all sensations. Moreover; magnificent desires, when least under the bias of personal feeling, dispose the mind— more than itself is conscious of—to regard commotion with complacency, and to watch the aggravations of distress with welcoming; from an immoderate confidence that, when the appointed day shall come, it will be in the power of intellect to relieve. There is danger in being a zealot in any cause—not excepting that of humanity. Nor is it to be forgotten that the incapacity and ignorance of the regular agents of long-established governments do not prevent some progress in the dearest concerns of men; and that society may owe to these very deficiencies, and to the tame and unenterprizing course which they necessitate, much security and tranquil enjoyment.

Nor, in the other hand, (for reasons which may be added to those already given) is it so desirable as might at first sight be imagined, much less is it desirable as an absolute good, that men of comprehensive sensibility and tutored genius—either for the interests of mankind or for their own—should, in ordinary times, have vested in them political power. The Empire, which they hold, is more independent: its constituent parts are sustained by a stricter connection: the dominion is purer and of higher origin; as mind is more excellent than body—the search of truth an employment more inherently dignified than the application of force—the determinations of nature more venerable than the accidents of human institution. Chance and disorder, vexation and disappointment, malignity and perverseness within or without the mind, are a sad exchange for the steady and genial processes of reason. Moreover; worldly distinctions and offices of command do not lie in the path—nor are they any part of the appropriate retinue—of Philosophy and Virtue. Nothing, but a strong spirit of love, can counteract the consciousness of pre-eminence which ever attends pre-eminent intellectual power with correspondent attainments: and this spirit of love is best encouraged by humility and simplicity in mind, manners, and conduct of life; virtues, to which wisdom leads. But,—though these be virtues in a Man, a Citizen, or a Sage,—they cannot be recommended to the especial culture of the Political or Military Functionary; and still less of the Civil Magistrate. Him, in the exercise of his functions, it will often become to carry himself highly and with state; in order that evil may be suppressed, and authority respected by those who have not understanding. The power also of office, whether the duties be discharged well or ill, will ensure a never-failing supply of flattery and praise: and of these—a man (becoming at once double-dealer and dupe) may, without impeachment of his modesty, receive as much as his weakness inclines him to; under the shew that the homage is not offered up to himself, but to that portion of the public dignity which is lodged in his person. But, whatever may be the cause, the fact is certain—that there is an unconquerable tendency in all power, save that of knowledge acting by and through knowledge, to injure the mind of him who exercises that power; so much so, that best natures cannot escape the evil of such alliance. Nor is it less certain that things of soundest quality, issuing through a medium to which they have only an arbitrary relation, are vitiated: and it is inevitable that there should be a reäscent of unkindly influence to the heart of him from whom the gift, thus unfairly dealt with, proceeded.——In illustration of these remarks, as connected with the management of States, we need only refer to the Empire of China—where superior endowments of mind and acquisitions of learning are the sole acknowledged title to offices of great trust; and yet in no country is the government more bigotted or intolerant, or society less progressive.

To prevent misconception; and to silence (at least to throw discredit upon) the clamours of ignorance;—I have thought proper thus, in some sort, to strike a balance between the claims of men of routine—and men of original and accomplished minds—to the management of State affairs in ordinary circumstances. But ours is not an age of this character: and,—after having seen such a long series of misconduct, so many unjustifiable attempts made and sometimes carried into effect, good endeavours frustrated, disinterested wishes thwarted, and benevolent hopes disappointed, —it is reasonable that we should endeavour to ascertain to what cause these evils are to be ascribed. I have directed the attention of the Reader to one primary cause: and can he doubt of its existence, and of the operation which I have attributed to it?

In the course of the last thirty years we have seen two wars waged against Liberty—the American war, and the war against the French People in the early stages of their Revolution. In the latter instance the Emigrants and the Continental Powers and the British did, in all their expectations and in every movement of their efforts, manifest a common ignorance—originating in the same source. And, for what more especially belongs to ourselves at this time, we may affirm—that the same presumptuous irreverence of the principles of justice, and blank insensibility to the affections of human nature, which determined the conduct of our government in those two wars *against* liberty, have continued to accompany its exertions in the present struggle *for* liberty,—and have rendered them fruitless. The British government deems (no doubt), on its own part, that its intentions are good. It must not deceive itself: nor must we deceive ourselves. Intentions—thoroughly good—could not mingle with the unblessed actions which we have witnessed. A disinterested and pure intention is a light that guides as well as cheers, and renders desperate lapses impossible.

Our duty is—our aim ought to be—to employ the true means of liberty and virtue for the ends of liberty and virtue. In such policy, thoroughly understood, there is fitness and concord and rational subordination; it deserves a higher name—organization, health, and grandeur. Contrast, in a single instance, the two processes; and the qualifications which they require. The ministers of that period found it an easy task to hire a band of Hessians, and to send it across the Atlantic, that they might assist *in bringing the Americans* (according to the phrase then prevalent) *to reason*. The force, with which these troops would attack, was gross,—tangible, —and might be calculated; but the spirit of resistance, which their presence would create, was subtle— ethereal—mighty—and incalculable. Accordingly, from the moment when these foreigners landed—men who had no interest, no business, in the quarrel, but what the wages of their master bound him to, and he imposed upon his miserable slaves;—nay, from the first rumour of their destination, the success of the

British was (as hath since been affirmed by judicious Americans) impossible.

The British government of the present day have been seduced, as we have seen, by the same common-place facilities on the one side; and have been equally blind on the other. A physical auxiliar force of thirty-five thousand men is to be added to the army of Spain: but the moral energy, which thereby *might* be taken away from the principal, is overlooked or slighted; the material being too fine for their calculation. What does it avail to graft a bough upon a tree; if this be done so ignorantly and rashly that the trunk, which can alone supply the sap by which the whole must flourish, receives a deadly wound? Palpable effects of the Convention of Cintra, and self-contradicting consequences even in the matter especially aimed at, may be seen in the necessity which it entailed of leaving 8,000 British troops to protect Portuguese traitors from punishment by the laws of their country. A still more serious and fatal contradiction lies in this—that the English army was made an instrument of injustice, and was dishonoured, in order that it might be hurried forward to uphold a cause which could have no life but by justice and honour. The nation knows how that army languished in the heart of Spain: that it accomplished nothing except its retreat, is sure: what great service it might have performed, if it had moved from a different impulse, we have shewn.

It surely then behoves those who are in authority— to look to the state of their own minds. There is indeed an inherent impossibility that they should be equal to the arduous duties which have devolved upon them: but it is not unreasonable to hope that something higher might be aimed at; and that the People might see, upon great occasions,—in the practice of its Rulers—a more adequate reflection of its own wisdom and virtue. Our Rulers, I repeat, must begin with their own minds. This is a precept of immediate urgency; and, if attended to, might be productive of immediate good.

* * * * *

There are multitudes by whom, I know, these sentiments will not be languidly received at this day; and sure I am—that, a hundred and fifty years ago, they would have been ardently welcomed by all. But, in many parts of Europe (and especially in our own country), men have been pressing forward, for some time, in a path which has betrayed by its fruitfulness; furnishing them constant employment for picking up things about their feet, when thoughts were perishing in their minds. While Mechanic Arts, Manufactures, Agriculture, Commerce, and all those products of knowledge which are confined to gross—definite—and tangible objects, have, with the aid of Experimental Philosophy, been every day putting on more brilliant colours; the splendour of the Imagination has been fading: Sensibility, which was formerly a generous nursling of rude Nature, has been chased from its ancient range in the wide domain of patriotism and religion with the weapons of derision by a shadow calling itself Good Sense: calculations of presumptuous Expediency—groping its way among partial and temporary consequences—have been substituted for the dictates of paramount and infallible Conscience, the supreme embracer of consequences: lifeless and circumspect Decencies have banished the graceful negligence and unsuspicious dignity of Virtue.

The progress of these arts also, by furnishing such attractive stores of outward accommodation, has misled the higher orders of society in their more disinterested exertions for the service of the lower. Animal comforts have been rejoiced over, as if they were the end of being. A neater and more fertile garden; a greener field; implements and utensils more apt; a dwelling more commodious and better furnished; —let these be attained, say the actively benevolent, and we are sure not only of being in the right road, but of having successfully terminated our journey. Now a country may advance, for some time, in this course with apparent profit: these accommodations, by zealous encouragement, may be attained: and still the Peasant or Artisan, their master, be a slave in mind; a slave rendered even more abject by the very tenure under which these possessions are held: and—if they veil from us this fact, or reconcile us to it—they are worse than worthless. The springs of emotion may be relaxed or destroyed within him; he may have little thought of the past, and less interest in the future.— The great end and difficulty of life for men of all classes, and especially difficult for those who live by manual labour, is a union of peace with innocent and laudable animation. Not by bread alone is the life of Man sustained; not by raiment alone is he warmed;— but by the genial and vernal inmate of the breast, which at once pushes forth and cherishes; by self-support and self-sufficing endeavours; by anticipations, apprehensions, and active remembrances; by elasticity under insult, and firm resistance to injury; by joy, and by love; by pride which his imagination gathers in from afar; by patience, because life wants not promises; by admiration; by gratitude which—debasing him not when his fellow-being is its object—habitually expands itself, for his elevation, in complacency towards his Creator.

Now, to the existence of these blessings, national independence is indispensible; and many of them it will itself produce and maintain. For it is some consola-

tion to those who look back upon the history of the world to know—that, even without civil liberty, society may possess—diffused through its inner recesses in the minds even of its humblest members— something of dignified enjoyment. But, without national independence, this is impossible. The difference, between inbred oppression and that which is from without, is *essential;* inasmuch as the former does not exclude, from the minds of a people, the feeling of being self-governed; does not imply (as the latter does, when patiently submitted to) an abandonment of the first duty imposed by the faculty of reason. In reality: where this feeling has no place, a people are not a society, but a herd; man being indeed distinguished among them from the brute; but only to his disgrace. I am aware that there are too many who think that, to the bulk of the community, this independence is of no value; that it is a refinement with which they feel they have no concern; inasmuch as, under the best frame of Government, there is an inevitable dependence of the poor upon the rich—of the many upon the few—so unrelenting and imperious as to reduce this other, by comparison, into a force which has small influence, and is entitled to no regard. Superadd civil liberty to national independence; and this position is overthrown at once: for there is no more certain mark of a sound frame of polity than this; that, in all individual instances (and it is upon these generalized that this position is laid down), the dependence is in reality far more strict on the side of the wealthy; and the labouring man leans less upon others than any man in the community.—But the case before us is of a country not internally free, yet supposed capable of repelling an external enemy who attempts its subjugation. If a country have put on chains of its own forging; in the name of virtue, let it be conscious that to itself it is accountable: let it not have cause to look beyond its own limits for reproof: and,—in the name of humanity,—if it be self-depressed, let it have its pride and some hope within itself. The poorest Peasant, in an unsubdued land, feels this pride. I do not appeal to the example of Britain or of Switzerland, for the one is free, and the other lately was free (and, I trust, will ere long be so again): but talk with the Swede; and you will see the joy he finds in these sensations. With him animal courage (the substitute for many and the friend of all the manly virtues) has space to move in; and is at once elevated by his imagination, and softened by his affections: it is invigorated also; for the whole courage of his Country is in his breast.

In fact: the Peasant, and he who lives by the fair reward of his manual labour, has ordinarily a larger proportion of his gratifications dependent upon these thoughts—than, for the most part, men in other classes have. For he is in his person attached, by stronger roots, to the soil of which he is the growth: his intellectual notices are generally confined within narrower bounds: in him no partial or antipatriotic interests counteract the force of those nobler sympathies and antipathies which he has in right of his Country; and lastly the belt or girdle of his mind has never been stretched to utter relaxation by false philosophy, under a conceit of making it sit more easily and gracefully. These sensations are a social inheritance to him: more important, as he is precluded from luxurious—and those which are usually called refined—enjoyments.

Love and admiration must push themselves out towards some quarter: otherwise the moral man is killed. Collaterally they advance with great vigour to a certain extent—and they are checked: in that direction, limits hard to pass are perpetually encountered: but upwards and downwards, to ancestry and to posterity, they meet with gladsome help and no obstacles; the tract is interminable.—Perdition to the Tyrant who would wantonly cut off an independent Nation from its inheritance in past ages; turning the tombs and burial-places of the Forefathers into dreaded objects of sorrow, or of shame and reproach, for the Children! Look upon Scotland and Wales: though, by the union of these with England under the same Government (which was effected without conquest in one instance), ferocious and desolating wars, and more injurious intrigues, and sapping and disgraceful corruptions, have been prevented; and tranquillity, security, and prosperity, and a thousand interchanges of amity, not otherwise attainable, have followed;—yet the flashing eye, and the agitated voice, and all the tender recollections, with which the names of Prince Llewellin and William Wallace[7] are to this day pronounced by the fire-side and on the public road, attest that these substantial blessings have not been purchased without the relinquishment of something most salutary to the moral nature of Man: else the remembrances would not cleave so faithfully to their abiding-place in the human heart. But, if these affections be of general interest, they are of especial interest to Spain; whose history, written and traditional, is pre-eminently stored with the sustaining food of such affections: and in no country are they more justly and generally prized, or more feelingly cherished.

In the conduct of this argument I am not speaking *to* the humbler ranks of society: it is unnecessary: *they*

trust in nature, and are safe. The People of Madrid, and Corunna, and Ferrol,[8] resisted to the last; from an impulse which, in their hearts, was its own justification. The failure was with those who stood higher in the scale. In fact; the universal rising of the Peninsula, under the pressure and in the face of the most tremendous military power which ever existed, is evidence which cannot be too much insisted upon; and is decisive upon this subject, as involving a question of virtue and moral sentiment. All ranks were penetrated with one feeling: instantaneous and universal was the acknowledgement. If there have been since individual fallings-off; those have been caused by that kind of after-thoughts which are the bastard offspring of selfishness. The matter was brought home to Spain; and no Spaniard has offended herein with a still conscience.—It is to the worldlings of our own country, and to those who think without carrying their thoughts far enough, that I address myself. Let them know, there is no true wisdom without imagination; no genuine sense;—that the man, who in this age feels no regret for the ruined honour of other Nations, must be poor in sympathy for the honour of his own Country; and that, if he be wanting here towards that which circumscribes the whole, he neither has—nor can have—a social regard for the lesser communities which Country includes. Contract the circle, and bring him to his family; such a man cannot protect *that* with dignified love. Reduce his thoughts to his own person; he may defend himself,—what *he* deems his honour; but it is the *action* of a brave man from the impulse of the brute, or the motive of a coward.

*   *   *   *   *

[1809]

PREFACE TO POEMS (1815)

Poems by William Wordsworth was published in 1815 in two volumes and was the first collected edition of the poet's work. It was here that Wordsworth first arranged his poems in groups or classes on the basis of the three-fold division: "the powers of mind predominant in the production of them" (Fancy, Imagination, etc.); "the mould in which they are cast" (sonnets, epitaphs, inscriptions); "the subjects to which they relate" (childhood, old age, etc.). It was to the first of these classifications, and especially to the discussion of Fancy and Imagination, that Wordsworth devotes most of the "Preface." Wordsworth's definition of these two faculties was to provoke Coleridge's famous analysis and definition in Biographia Literaria. See Chapters IV, XII–XIII.

For an extended treatment of the "Preface" and the Poems of 1815 as well as the wider significance of Fancy and Imagination

---

7 Llewelyn Ap Gruffydd (d. 1282), the first recognized Prince of Wales, met his death in battle against the armies of Edward I, thus ending Welsh independence. William Wallace (*c.* 1272-1305) was a Scotch patriot and symbol of resistance to English authority, who was captured and executed by Edward I.

8 Madrid surrendered to French forces under the personal command of Napoleon on December 4, 1808. La Corunna and El Ferrol, seaports on Spain's Atlantic coast, fell to the French in January 1809.

in Wordsworth's thought, see James Scoggins' Imagination and Fancy: Complementary Modes in the Poetry of Wordsworth (Lincoln, Neb.: University of Nebraska Press, 1966).

PREFACE TO *POEMS*

THE OBSERVATIONS prefixed to that portion of these Volumes, which was published many years ago, under the title of "Lyrical Ballads," have so little of a special application to the greater part, perhaps, of this collection, as subsequently enlarged and diversified, that they could not with any propriety stand as an Introduction to it. Not deeming it, however, expedient to suppress that exposition, slight and imperfect as it is, of the feelings which had determined the choice of the subjects, and the principles which had regulated the composition of those Pieces, I have transferred it to the end of the second Volume, to be attended to, or not, at the pleasure of the Reader.

In the Preface to that part of "The Recluse," lately published under the title of "The Excursion," I have alluded to a meditated arrangement of my minor Poems, which should assist the attentive Reader in perceiving their connection with each other, and also their subordination to that Work. I shall here say a few words explanatory of this arrangement, as carried into effect in the present Volumes.

The powers requisite for the production of poetry are, first, those of observation and description, i.e. the ability to observe with accuracy things as they are in themselves, and with fidelity to describe them, unmodified by any passion or feeling existing in the mind of the Describer: whether the things depicted be actually present to the senses, or have a place only in the memory. This power, though indispensable to a Poet, is one which he employs only in submission to necessity, and never for a continuance of time; as its exercise supposes all the higher qualities of the mind to be passive, and in a state of subjection to external objects, much in the same way as the Translator or Engraver ought to be to his Original. 2dly, Sensibility, —which, the more exquisite it is, the wider will be the range of a Poet's perceptions; and the more will he be incited to observe objects, both as they exist in themselves and as re-acted upon by his own mind. (The distinction between poetic and human sensibility has been marked in the character of the Poet delineated in the original preface, before-mentioned.)[1] 3rdly, Reflection,—which makes the Poet acquainted with the value of actions, images, thoughts, and feelings;

and assists the sensibility in perceiving their connection with each other. 4thly, Imagination and Fancy,—to modify, to create, and to associate. 5thly, Invention,— by which characters are composed out of materials supplied by observation; whether of the Poet's own heart and mind, or of external life and nature; and such incidents and situations produced as are most impressive to the imagination, and most fitted to do justice to the characters, sentiments, and passions, which the Poet undertakes to illustrate. And, lastly, Judgment,— to decide how and where, and in what degree, each of these faculties ought to be exerted; so that the less shall not be sacrificed to the greater; nor the greater, slighting the less, arrogate, to its own injury, more than its due. By judgment, also, is determined what are the laws and appropriate graces of every species of composition.

The materials of Poetry, by these powers collected and produced, are cast, by means of various moulds, into divers forms. The moulds may be enumerated, and the forms specified, in the following order. 1st, the Narrative,—including the Epopoeia,[2] the Historic Poem, the Tale, the Romance, the Mock-heroic, and, if the spirit of Homer will tolerate such neighbourhood, that dear production of our days, the metrical Novel. Of this Class, the distinguishing mark, is, that the Narrator, however liberally his speaking agents be introduced, is himself the source from which every thing primarily flows. Epic Poets, in order that their mode of composition may accord with the elevation of their subject, represent themselves as *singing* from the inspiration of the Muse, Arma virum que *cano*;[3] but this is a fiction, in modern times, of slight value: The Iliad or the Paradise Lost would gain little in our estimation by being chaunted. The other poets who belong to this class are commonly content to *tell* their tale;—so that of the whole it may be affirmed that they neither require nor reject the accompaniment of music.

2ndly, The Dramatic,—consisting of Tragedy, Historic Drama, Comedy, and Masque; in which the poet does not appear at all in his own person, and where the whole action is carried on by speech and dialogue of the agents; music being admitted only incidentally and rarely. The Opera may be placed here, in as much as it proceeds by dialogue; though depending, to the degree that it does, upon music, it has a strong claim to be ranked with the Lyrical. The characteristic and impassioned Epistle, of which Ovid and Pope have given examples,[4] considered as a species of mono-

---

[1] See "Preface to *Lyrical Ballads*" (1802), pp. 50–51.

[2] The Epic.
[3] "Arms and the man I sing," the opening words of the *Aeneid*.
[4] See Pope's *Eloisa to Abelard*, modelled on Ovid's *Heroides*, the classic example of the Heroic Epistle.

drama, may, without impropriety, be placed in this class.

3rdly, The Lyrical,—containing the Hymn, the Ode, the Elegy, the Song, and the Ballad; in all which, for the production of their *full* effect, an accompaniment of music is indispensable.

4thly, The Idyllium,—descriptive chiefly either of the processes and appearances of external nature, as the "Seasons" of Thomson; or of characters, manners, and sentiments, as are Shenstone's School-mistress, The Cotter's Saturday Night of Burns, The Twa Dogs of the same Author; or of these in conjunction with the appearances of Nature, as most of the pieces of Theocritus, the Allegro and Penseroso of Milton, Beattie's Minstrel, Goldsmith's "Deserted Village." The Epitaph, the Inscription, the Sonnet, most of the epistles of poets writing in their own persons, and all loco-descriptive poetry, belong to this class.

5thly, Didactic,—the principal object of which is direct instruction; as the Poem of Lucretius, the Georgics of Virgil, "the Fleece" of Dyer, Mason's "English Garden," 5 &c.

And, lastly, philosophical satire, like that of Horace and Juvenal; personal and occasional Satire rarely comprehending sufficient of the general in the individual to be dignified with the name of Poetry.

Out of the three last classes has been constructed a composite species, of which Young's Night Thoughts and Cowper's Task are excellent examples.

It is deducible from the above, that poems, apparently miscellaneous, may with propriety be arranged either with reference to the powers of mind *predominant* in the production of them; or to the mould in which they are cast; or, lastly, to the subjects to which they relate. From each of these considerations, the following Poems have been divided into classes; which, that the work may more obviously correspond with the course of human life, for the sake of exhibiting in it the three requisites of a legitimate whole, a beginning, a middle, and an end, have been also arranged, as far as it was possible, according to an order of time, commencing with Childhood, and terminating with Old Age, Death, and Immortality. My guiding wish was, that the small pieces of which these volumes consist, thus discriminated, might be regarded under a two-fold view; as composing an entire work within themselves, and as adjuncts to the philosophical Poem, "The Recluse." This arrangement has long presented itself habitually to my own mind. Nevertheless, I should have preferred to scatter

the contents of these volumes at random, if I had been persuaded that, by the plan adopted, any thing material would be taken from the natural effect of the pieces, individually, on the mind of the unreflecting Reader. I trust there is a sufficient variety in each class to prevent this; while, for him who reads with reflection, the arrangement will serve as a commentary unostentatiously directing his attention to my purposes, both particular and general. But, as I wish to guard against the possibility of misleading by this classification, it is proper first to remind the Reader, that certain poems are placed according to the powers of mind, in the Author's conception, predominant in the production of them; *predominant*, which implies the exertion of other faculties in less degree. Where there is more imagination than fancy in a poem it is placed under the head of imagination, and vice versâ. Both the above Classes might without impropriety have been enlarged from that consisting of "Poems founded on the Affections"; as might this latter from those, and from the class "Proceeding from Sentiment and Reflection." The most striking characteristics of each piece, mutual illustration, variety, and proportion, have governed me throughout.

It may be proper in this place to state, that the Extracts 6 in the 2nd Class entitled "Juvenile Pieces," are in many places altered from the printed copy, chiefly by omission and compression. The slight alterations of another kind were for the most part made not long after the publication of the Poems from which the Extracts are taken. These Extracts seem to have a title to be placed here as they were the productions of youth, and represent implicitly some of the features of a youthful mind, at a time when images of nature supplied to it the place of thought, sentiment, and almost of action; or, as it will be found expressed, of a state of mind when

> "the sounding cataract
> Haunted me like a passion: the tall rock,
> The mountain, and the deep and gloomy wood,
> Their colours and their forms were then to me
> An appetite, a feeling and a love,
> That had no need of a remoter charm,
> By thought supplied, or any interest
> Unborrowed from the eye"—7

I will own that I was much at a loss what to select of these descriptions; and perhaps it would have been better either to have reprinted the whole, or suppressed what I have given.

---

5 *The Fleece* (1757) was an extended poetic treatment of sheep care and the wool trade by John Dyer. *The English Garden* (1783) consisted of four books on landscape gardening by William Mason.

6 From Wordsworth's first published poems *An Evening Walk* and *Descriptive Sketches*, 1793.
7 "Tintern Abbey," ll. 76–83.

None of the other Classes, except those of Fancy and Imagination, require any particular notice. But a remark of general application may be made. All Poets, except the dramatic, have been in the practice of feigning that their works were composed to the music of the harp or lyre: with what degree of affectation this has been done in modern times, I leave to the judicious to determine. For my own part, I have not been disposed to violate probability so far, or to make such a large demand upon the Reader's charity. Some of these pieces are essentially lyrical; and, therefore, cannot have their due force without a supposed musical accompaniment; but, in much the greatest part, as a substitute for the classic lyre or romantic harp, I require nothing more than an animated or impassioned recitation, adapted to the subject. Poems, however humble in their kind, if they be good in that kind, cannot read themselves: the law of long syllable and short must not be so inflexible—the letter of metre must not be so impassive to the spirit of versification—as to deprive the Reader of a voluntary power to modulate, in subordination to the sense, the music of the poem;—in the same manner as his mind is left at liberty, and even summoned, to act upon its thoughts and images. But, though the accompaniment of a musical instrument be frequently dispensed with, the true Poet does not therefore abandon his privilege distinct from that of the mere Proseman;

"He murmurs near the running brooks
A music sweeter than their own." [8]

I come now to the consideration of the words Fancy and Imagination, as employed in the classification of the following Poems. "A man," says an intelligent Author, has "imagination," in proportion as he can distinctly copy in idea the impressions of sense: it is the faculty which *images* within the mind the phenomena of sensation. A man has fancy in proportion as he can call up, connect, or associate, at pleasure, those internal images (φαυταζειν is to cause to appear) so as to complete ideal representations of absent objects. Imagination is the power of depicting, and fancy of evoking and combining. The imagination is formed by patient observation; the fancy by a voluntary activity in shifting the scenery of the mind. The more accurate the imagination, the more safely may a painter, or a poet, undertake a delineation, or a description, without the presence of the objects to be characterized. The more versatile the fancy, the more original and striking

will be the decorations produced.—*British Synonyms discriminated, by W. Taylor.*[9]

Is not this as if a man should undertake to supply an account of a building, and be so intent upon what he had discovered of the foundation as to conclude his task without once looking up at the superstructure? Here, as in other instances throughout the volume, the judicious Author's mind is enthralled by Etymology; he takes up the original word as his guide, his conductor, his escort, and too often does not perceive how soon he becomes its prisoner, without liberty to tread in any path but that to which it confines him. It is not easy to find out how imagination, thus explained, differs from distinct remembrance of images; or fancy from quick and vivid recollection of them: each is nothing more than a mode of memory. If the two words bear the above meaning, and no other, what term is left to designate that Faculty of which the Poet is "all compact";[10] he whose eye glances from earth to heaven, whose spiritual attributes body-forth what his pen is prompt in turning to shape; or what is left to characterise fancy, as insinuating herself into the heart of objects with creative activity?—Imagination, in the sense of the word as giving title to a Class of the following Poems, has no reference to images that are merely a faithful copy, existing in the mind, of absent external objects; but is a word of higher import, denoting operations of the mind upon those objects, and processes of creation or of composition, governed by certain fixed laws. I proceed to illustrate my meaning by instances. A parrot *hangs* from the wires of his cage by his beak or by his claws; or a monkey from the bough of a tree by his paws or his tail. Each creature does so literally and actually. In the first Eclogue of Virgil, the Shepherd, thinking of the time when he is to take leave of his Farm, thus addresses his Goats;

"Non ego vos posthac viridi projectus in antro
Dumosa *pendere* procul de rupe videbo." [11]

—"half way up
Hangs one who gathers samphire,"

is the well-known expression of Shakespear, delineating an ordinary image upon the Cliffs of Dover. In these two instances is a slight exertion of the faculty

---

8 Wordsworth's "A Poet's Epitaph," ll. 39–40.

9 More accurately, *English Synonyms Discriminated* (1813), by William Taylor (1765–1836), best known as the translator and introducer of German literature into England.

10 *Midsummer Night's Dream*, V, i, 8.

11 "No more, stretched in some mossy grot, shall I watch you in the distance hanging from a bushy crag," ll. 75–76 (Fairclough translation, Loeb Classical Library). The next quotation is from *King Lear*, IV, vi, 14–15.

which I denominate imagination, in the use of one word: neither the goats nor the samphire-gatherer do literally hang, as does the parrot or the monkey; but, presenting to the senses something of such an appearance, the mind in its activity, for its own gratification, contemplates them as hanging.

"As when far off at Sea a Fleet descried
Hangs in the clouds, by equinoxial winds
Close sailing from Bengala or the Isles
Of Ternate or Tydore, whence Merchants bring
Their spicy drugs; they on the trading flood
Through the wide Ethiopian to the Cape
Ply, stemming nightly toward the Pole: so seem'd
Far off the flying Fiend." [12]

Here is the full strength of the imagination involved in the word, *hangs*, and exerted upon the whole image: First, the Fleet, an aggregate of many Ships, is represented as one mighty Person, whose track, we know and feel, is upon the waters; but, taking advantage of its appearance to the senses, the Poet dares to represent it as *hanging in the clouds*, both for the gratification of the mind in contemplating the image itself, and in reference to the motion and appearance of the sublime object to which it is compared.

From images of sight we will pass to those of sound:

"Over his own sweet voice the Stock-dove *broods*"; [13]

of the same bird,

"His voice was *buried* among trees,
Yet to be come at by the breeze";

"O, Cuckoo! shall I call thee *Bird*,
Or but a wandering *Voice*?"

The Stock-dove is said to *coo*, a sound well imitating the note of the bird; but, by the intervention of the metaphor *broods*, the affections are called in by the imagination to assist in marking the manner in which the Bird reiterates and prolongs her soft note, as if herself delighting to listen to it, and participating of a still and quiet satisfaction, like that which may be supposed inseparable from the continuous process of incubation. "His voice was buried among trees," a metaphor expressing the love of *seclusion* by which this Bird is marked; and characterising its note as not partaking of the shrill and the piercing, and therefore more easily deadened by the intervening shade; yet a note so peculiar, and withal so pleasing, that the breeze, gifted with that love of the sound which the Poet feels, penetrates the shade in which it is entombed, and conveys it to the ear of the listener.

Shall I call thee Bird
Or but a wandering Voice?

This concise interrogation characterises the seeming ubiquity of the voice of the Cuckoo, and dispossesses the creature almost of a corporeal existence; the imagination being tempted to this exertion of her power by a consciousness in the memory that the Cuckoo is almost perpetually heard throughout the season of Spring, but seldom becomes an object of sight.

Thus far of images independent of each other, and immediately endowed by the mind with properties that do not inhere in them, upon an incitement from properties and qualities the existence of which is inherent and obvious. These processes of imagination are carried on either by conferring additional properties upon an object, or abstracting from it some of those which it actually possesses, and thus enabling it to react upon the mind which hath performed the process, like a new existence.

I pass from the Imagination acting upon an individual image to a consideration of the same faculty employed upon images in a conjunction by which they modify each other. The Reader has already had a fine instance before him in the passage quoted from Virgil, where the apparently perilous situation of the Goat, hanging upon the shaggy precipice, is contrasted with that of the Shepherd, contemplating it from the seclusion of the Cavern in which he lies stretched at ease and in security. Take these images separately, and how unaffecting the picture compared with that produced by their being thus connected with, and opposed to, each other!

"As a huge Stone is sometimes seen to lie
Couched on the bald top of an eminence,
Wonder to all who do the same espy
By what means it could thither come, and whence;
So that it seems a thing endued with sense,
Like a Sea-beast crawled forth, which on a shelf
Of rock or sand reposeth, there to sun himself.
Such seemed this Man; not all alive or dead,
Nor all asleep, in his extreme old age.
Motionless as a cloud the old Man stood,
That heareth not the loud winds when they call,
And moveth altogether if it move at all." [14]

---

[12] *Paradise Lost*, II, 636–43.
[13] "Resolution and Independence," l. 5. The next two quotations are from "O Nightingale! Thou Surely Art," ll. 13–14; and "To the Cuckoo," ll. 3–4.

---

[14] "Resolution and Independence," ll. 57–65, 75–77.

In these images, the conferring, the abstracting, and the modifying powers of the Imagination, immediately and mediately acting, are all brought into conjunction. The Stone is endowed with something of the power of life to approximate it to the Sea-beast; and the Sea-beast stripped of some of its vital qualities to assimilate it to the stone; which intermediate image is thus treated for the purpose of bringing the original image, that of the stone, to a nearer resemblance to the figure and condition of the aged Man; who is divested of so much of the indications of life and motion as to bring him to the point where the two objects unite and coalesce in just comparison. After what has been said, the image of the Cloud need not be commented upon.

Thus far of an endowing or modifying power: but the Imagination also shapes and *creates*; and how? By innumerable processes; and in none does it more delight than in that of consolidating numbers into unity, and dissolving and separating unity into number,—alternations proceeding from, and governed by, a sublime consciousness of the soul in her own mighty and almost divine powers. Recur to the passage already cited from Milton. When the compact Fleet, as one Person, has been introduced "Sailing from Bengala," "They," i.e. the "Merchants," representing the Fleet resolved into a Multitude of Ships, "ply" their voyage towards the extremities of the earth: "So" (referring to the word "As" in the commencement) "seemed the flying Fiend"; the image of his Person acting to recombine the multitude of Ships into one body,—the point from which the comparison set out. "So seemed," and to whom seemed? To the heavenly Muse who dictates the poem, to the eye of the Poet's mind, and to that of the Reader, present at one moment in the wide Ethiopian, and the next in the solitudes, then first broken in upon, of the infernal regions!

Modo me Thebis, modo ponit Athenis.[15]

Here again this mighty Poet,—speaking of the Messiah going forth to expel from Heaven the rebellious Angels,

Attended by ten thousand, thousand Saints
He onward came: far off from his coming shone,—

the retinue of Saints, and the Person of the Messiah himself, lost almost and merged in the splendour of that indefinite abstraction, "His coming!"

As I do not mean here to treat this subject further than to throw some light upon the present Volumes, and especially upon one division of them, I shall spare myself and the Reader the trouble of considering the Imagination as it deals with thoughts and sentiments, as it regulates the composition of characters, and determines the course of actions: I will not consider it (more than I have already done by implication) as that power which, in the language of one of my most esteemed Friends, "draws all things to one, which makes things animate or inanimate, beings with their attributes, subjects with their accessaries, take one colour and serve to one effect."* The grand store-house of enthusiastic and meditative Imagination, of poetical, as contradistinguished from human and dramatic Imagination, is the prophetic and lyrical parts of the holy Scriptures, and the works of Milton, to which I cannot forbear to add those of Spenser. I select these writers in preference to those of ancient Greece and Rome because the anthropomorphitism of the Pagan religion subjected the minds of the greatest poets in those countries too much to the bondage of definite form; from which the Hebrews were preserved by their abhorrence of idolatry. This abhorrence was almost as strong in our great epic Poet, both from circumstances of his life, and from the constitution of his mind. However imbued the surface might be with classical literature, he was a Hebrew in soul; and all things tended in him towards the sublime. Spenser, of a gentler nature, maintained his freedom by aid of his allegorical spirit, at one time inciting him to create persons out of abstractions; and at another, by a superior effort of genius, to give the universality and permanence of abstractions to his human beings, by means of attributes and emblems that belong to the highest moral truths and the purest sensations,—of which his character of Una is a glorious example. Of the human and dramatic Imagination the works of Shakespear are an inexhaustible source.

"I tax not you, ye Elements, with unkindness,
I never gave you Kingdoms, called you Daughters."[17]

And if, bearing in mind the many Poets distinguished by this prime quality, whose names I omit to mention; yet justified by a recollection of the insults which the Ignorant, the Incapable, and the Presumptuous have heaped upon these and my other writings, I may be permitted to anticipate the judgment of posterity upon myself; I shall declare (censurable, I grant, if the notoriety of the fact above stated does not justify me) that I have given, in these unfavourable times, evidence of exertions of this faculty upon its worthiest objects, the external universe, the moral and religious senti-

---

[15] "He places me sometimes at Thebes, sometimes at Athens," said of an inspiring poet, in Horace, *Epistles*, II, i, 213. The next quotation is from *Paradise Lost*, VI, 767–68.

* Charles Lamb upon the genius of Hogarth.[16]

[16] See "On the Genius & Character of Hogarth," below.
[17] *King Lear*, III, ii, 16–17.

ments of Man, his natural affections, and his acquired passions; which have the same ennobling tendency as the productions of men, in this kind, worthy to be holden in undying remembrance.

I dismiss this subject with observing—that, in the series of Poems placed under the head of Imagination, I have begun with one of the earliest processes of Nature in the development of this faculty. Guided by one of my own primary consciousnesses, I have represented a commutation and transfer of internal feelings, co-operating with external accidents to plant, for immortality, images of sound and sight, in the celestial soil of the Imagination. The Boy, there introduced, is listening, with something of a feverish and restless anxiety, for the recurrence of the riotous sounds which he had previously excited; and, at the moment when the intenseness of his mind is beginning to remit, he is surprised into a perception of the solemn and tranquillizing images which the Poem describes.[18]—The Poems next in succession exhibit the faculty exerting itself upon various objects of the external universe; then follow others, where it is employed upon feelings, characters, and actions; and the Class is concluded with imaginative pictures of moral, political, and religious sentiments.

To the mode in which Fancy has already been characterized as the Power of evoking and combining, or, as my friend Mr. Coleridge has styled it, "the aggregative and associative Power,"[19] my objection is only that the definition is too general. To aggregate and to associate, to evoke and to combine, belong as well to the Imagination as to the Fancy; but either the materials evoked and combined are different; or they are brought together under a different law, and for a different purpose. Fancy does not require that the materials which she makes use of should be susceptible of change in their constitution, from her touch; and, where they admit of modification, it is enough for her purpose if it be slight, limited, and evanescent. Directly the reverse of these, are the desires and demands of the Imagination. She recoils from every thing but the plastic, the pliant, and the indefinite. She leaves it to Fancy to describe Queen Mab as coming,

"In shape no bigger than an agate stone
On the fore-finger of an Alderman."[20]

Having to speak of stature, she does not tell you that her gigantic Angel was as tall as Pompey's Pillar;[21] much less that he was twelve cubits, or twelve hundred cubits high; or that his dimensions equalled those of Teneriffe or Atlas;—because these, and if they were a million times as high, it would be the same, are bounded: The expression is, "His stature reached the sky!"[22] the illimitable firmament!—When the Imagination frames a comparison, if it does not strike on the first presentation, a sense of the truth of the likeness, from the moment that it is perceived, grows—and continues to grow—upon the mind; the resemblance depending less upon outline of form and feature than upon expression and effect, less upon casual and outstanding, than upon inherent and internal, properties: —moreover, the images invariably modify each other. —The law under which the processes of Fancy are carried on is as capricious as the accidents of things, and the effects are surprizing, playful, ludicrous, amusing, tender, or pathetic, as the objects happen to be appositely produced or fortunately combined. Fancy depends upon the rapidity and profusion with which she scatters her thoughts and images, trusting that their number, and the felicity with which they are linked together, will make amends for the want of individual value: or she prides herself upon the curious subtilty and the successful elaboration with which she can detect their lurking affinities. If she can win you over to her purpose, and impart to you her feelings, she cares not how unstable or transitory may be her influence, knowing that it will not be out of her power to resume it upon an apt occasion. But the Imagination is conscious of an indestructible dominion;—the Soul may fall away from it, not being able to sustain its grandeur, but, if once felt and acknowledged, by no act of any other faculty of the mind can it be relaxed, impaired, or diminished.—Fancy is given to quicken and to beguile the temporal part of our Nature, Imagination to incite and to support the eternal.—Yet is it not the less true that Fancy, as she is an active, is also, under her own laws and in her own spirit, a creative faculty. In what manner Fancy ambitiously aims at a rivalship with the Imagination, and Imagination stoops to work with the materials of Fancy, might be illustrated from the compositions of all eloquent writers, whether in prose or verse; and chiefly from those of our own Country. Scarcely a page of the im-

---

[18] Refers to "There was a Boy," first published in *Lyrical Ballads* (1800) and later incorporated into Book V of *The Prelude*.

[19] From entry 174 ("The Soul and its organs of Sense") in *Omniana* (1812), a collection of observations and short essays on various topics by Coleridge and Southey.

[20] *Romeo and Juliet*, I, iv, 55–56.

[21] A tall monument on the highest spot in Alexandria, Egypt, erected in honor of the Roman Emperor Diocletian. Teneriffe and Atlas, next mentioned, are proverbial expressions of great height: Teneriffe, a peak in the Canary Islands; Atlas, an African mountain range.

[22] See *Paradise Lost*, IV, 985–88.

passioned parts of Bishop Taylor's Works[23] can be opened that shall not afford examples.—Referring the Reader to those inestimable Volumes, I will content myself with placing a conceit (ascribed to Lord Chesterfield) in contrast with a passage from the Paradise Lost;

> "The dews of the evening most carefully shun,
>   They are the tears of the sky for the loss of the Sun."[24]

After the transgression of Adam, Milton, with other appearances of sympathizing Nature, thus marks the immediate consequence,

> "Sky lowered, and muttering thunder, some sad drops
>   Wept at completion of the mortal sin."

The associating link is the same in each instance;—dew or rain, not distinguishable from the liquid substance of tears, are employed as indications of sorrow. A flash of surprize is the effect in the former case, a flash of surprize and nothing more; for the nature of things does not sustain the combination. In the latter, the effects of the act, of which there is this immediate consequence and visible sign, are so momentous that the mind acknowledges the justice and reasonableness of the sympathy in Nature so manifested; and the sky weeps drops of water as if with human eyes, as "Earth had, before, trembled from her entrails, and Nature given a second groan."[25]

Awe-stricken as I am by contemplating the operations of the mind of this truly divine Poet, I scarcely dare venture to add that "An address to an Infant,"[26] which the Reader will find under the Class of Fancy in the present Volumes, exhibits something of this communion and interchange of instruments and functions between the two powers; and is, accordingly, placed last in the class, as a preparation for that of Imagination which follows.

Finally, I will refer to Cotton's "Ode upon Winter,"[27] an admirable composition though stained with some peculiarities of the age in which he lived, for a general illustration of the characteristics of Fancy. The middle part of this ode contains a most lively description of the entrance of Winter, with his retinue, as "A palsied King," and yet a military Monarch,—advancing for conquest with his Army; the several bodies of which, and their arms and equipments, are described with a rapidity of detail, and a profusion of *fanciful* comparisons, which indicate on the part of the Poet extreme activity of intellect, and a correspondent hurry of delightful feeling. He retires from the Foe into his fortress, where

> "a magazine
> Of sovereign juice is cellared in.
> Liquor that will the siege maintain
> Should Phoebus ne'er return again."

Though myself a water-drinker, I cannot resist the pleasure of transcribing what follows, as an instance still more happy of Fancy employed in the treatment of feeling than, in its preceding passages, the Poem supplies of her management of forms.

> 'Tis that, that gives the Poet rage,
> And thaws the gelly'd blood of Age;
> Matures the Young, restores the Old,
> And makes the fainting Coward bold.
>
> It lays the careful head to rest,
> Calms palpitations in the breast,
> Renders our lives' misfortune sweet;
> *   *   *   *   *
>
> Then let the chill Sirocco blow,
> And gird us round with hills of snow,
> Or else go whistle to the shore,
> And make the hollow mountains roar.
>
> Whilst we together jovial sit
> Careless, and crown'd with mirth and wit;
> Where, though bleak winds confine us home,
> Our fancies round the world shall roam.
>
> We'll think of all the Friends we know,
> And drink to all worth drinking to;
> When having drunk all thine and mine,
> We rather shall want healths than wine.
>
> But where Friends fail us, we'll supply
> Our friendships with our charity;
> Men that remote in sorrows live,
> Shall by our lusty Brimmers thrive.
>
> We'll drink the Wanting into Wealth,
> And those that languish into health,
> The Afflicted into joy; th' Opprest
> Into security and rest.

---

[23] Refers to Jeremy Taylor (1613–1667), Anglican divine, whose *Holy Living* and *Holy Dying* (1650, 1651) and other religious works were models of English prose style and much admired by the Romantics.

[24] "Advice to a Lady in Autumn" (1748), by Philip Stanhope Earl of Chesterfield. The next quotation is from *Paradise Lost*, IX 1002–3.

[25] *Paradise Lost*, IX, 1000–1.

[26] Refers to "Address to my Infant Daughter, Dora."

[27] Charles Cotton (1630–1687) was a poet, translator of Montaigne's *Essays*, and contributor to Walton's *Complete Angler*. Wordsworth quotes ll. 153–96 from "Ode upon Winter," omitting, as the asterisks indicate, the "indelicate" line: "And Venus frolic in the sheet." Wordsworth became acquainted with the poem through Lamb, who was to quote another of Cotton's poems in "New Year's Eve," below.

The Worthy in disgrace shall find
Favour return again more kind,
And in restraint who stifled lie,
Shall taste the air of liberty.

The Brave shall triumph in success,
The Lovers shall have Mistresses,
Poor unregarded Virtue, praise,
And the neglected Poet, Bays.

Thus shall our healths do others good,
Whilst we ourselves do all we would;
For, freed from envy and from care,
What would we be but what we are?

It remains that I should express my regret at the necessity of separating my compositions from some beautiful Poems of Mr. Coleridge, with which they have been long associated in publication. The feelings, with which that joint publication was made, have been gratified; its end is answered, and the time is come when considerations of general propriety dictate the separation. Three short pieces (now first published) are the work of a Female Friend; [28] and the Reader, to whom they may be acceptable, is indebted to me for his pleasure; if any one regard them with dislike, or be disposed to condemn them, let the censure fall upon him, who, trusting in his own sense of their merit and their fitness for the place which they occupy, *extorted* them from the Authoress.

When I sate down to write this preface it was my intention to have made it more comprehensive; but as all that I deem necessary is expressed, I will here detain the reader no longer:—what I have further to remark shall be inserted, by way of interlude, at the close of this Volume.

[1815]

———

ESSAY, SUPPLEMENTARY TO THE PREFACE (1815)
The "Preface" and "Essay, Supplementary" of 1815 may be seen as Wordsworth's two-sided defense of his poems in this the first collected edition, and a guide to properly understanding them. The "Preface" explained the arrangement of the poems, and most importantly the operations of the "powers" of the creative mind involved in their production. The second essay "supplemented" the first by focusing on the reception of original works of genius by readers and critics.

———

◇◇◇◇◇◇◇◇◇◇◇◇◇◇◇◇◇◇◇◇◇◇◇◇◇◇◇◇◇◇◇

[28] To the 1815 edition, Dorothy Wordsworth contributed "Address to a Child, During a boisterous Winter Evening," "The Mother's Return," and "The Cottager to her Infant."

ESSAY,
Supplementary to the Preface

By this time, I trust that the judicious Reader, who has now first become acquainted with these poems, is persuaded that a very senseless outcry has been raised against them and their Author.—Casually, and very rarely only, do I see any periodical publication, except a daily newspaper; but I am not wholly unacquainted with the spirit in which my most active and perserving Adversaries have maintained their hostility; nor with the impudent falsehoods and base artifices to which they have had recourse. These, as implying a consciousness on their parts that attacks honestly and fairly conducted would be unavailing, could not but have been regarded by me with triumph; had they been accompanied with such display of talents and information as might give weight to the opinions of the Writers, whether favourable or unfavourable. But the ignorance of those who have chosen to stand forth as my enemies, as far as I am acquainted with their enmity, has unfortunately been still more gross than their disingenuousness, and their incompetence more flagrant than their malice. The effect in the eyes of the discerning is indeed ludicrous: yet, contemptible as such men are, in return for the forced compliment paid me by their long-continued notice (which, as I have appeared so rarely before the public, no one can say has been solicited) I entreat them to spare themselves. The lash, which they are aiming at my productions, does, in fact, only fall on phantoms of their own brain; which, I grant, I am innocently instrumental in raising.—By what fatality the orb of my genius (for genius none of them seem to deny me) acts upon these men like the moon upon a certain description of patients, it would be irksome to inquire; nor would it consist with the respect which I owe myself to take further notice of opponents whom I internally despise.

With the young, of both sexes, Poetry is, like love, a passion; but, for much the greater part of those who have been proud of its power over their minds, a necessity soon arises of breaking the pleasing bondage; or it relaxes of itself;—the thoughts being occupied in domestic cares, or the time engrossed by business. Poetry then becomes only an occasional recreation; while to those whose existence passes away in a course of fashionable pleasure it is a species of luxurious amusement.—In middle and declining age, a scattered number of serious persons resort to poetry, as to religion, for a protection against the pressure of trivial employments, and as a consolation for the afflictions of life. And lastly, there are many, who, having been enamoured of this art, in their youth, have found leisure, after youth was spent, to cultivate general literature; in which poetry has continued to be comprehended *as a study*.

Into the above Classes the Readers of poetry may be divided; Critics abound in them all; but from the last only can opinions be collected of absolute value, and worthy to be depended upon, as prophetic of the destiny of a new work. The young, who in nothing can escape delusion, are especially subject to it in their intercourse with poetry. The cause, not so obvious as the fact is unquestionable, is the same as that from which erroneous judgments in this art, in the minds of men of all ages, chiefly proceed; but upon Youth it operates with peculiar force. The appropriate business of poetry, (which, nevertheless, if genuine is as permanent as pure science) her appropriate employment, her privilege and her *duty*, is to treat of things not as they *are*, but as they *appear*; not as they exist in themselves, but as they *seem* to exist to the *senses* and to the *passions*. What a world of delusion does this acknowledged principle prepare for the inexperienced! what temptations to go astray are here held forth for those whose thoughts have been little disciplined by the understanding, and whose feelings revolt from the sway of reason! —When a juvenile Reader is in the height of his rapture with some vicious passage, should experience throw in doubts, or common-sense suggest suspicions, a lurking consciousness that the realities of the Muse are but shows, and that her liveliest excitements are raised by transient shocks of conflicting feeling and successive assemblages of contradictory thoughts—is ever at hand to justify extravagance, and to sanction absurdity. But, it may be asked, as these illusions are unavoidable, and no doubt eminently useful to the mind as a process, what good can be gained by making observations the tendency of which is to diminish the confidence of youth in its feelings, and thus to abridge its innocent and even profitable pleasures? The reproach implied in the question could not be warded off, if Youth were incapable of being delighted with what is truly excellent; or if these errors always terminated of themselves in due season. But, with the majority, though their force be abated, they continue through life. Moreover, the fire of youth is too vivacious an element to be extinguished or damped by a philosophical remark; and, while there is no danger that what has been said will be injurious or painful to the ardent and the confident, it may prove beneficial to those who, being enthusiastic, are, at the same time, modest and ingenuous. The intimation may unite with their own misgivings to regulate their sensibility, and to bring in, sooner than it would otherwise have arrived, a more discreet and sound judgment.

If it should excite wonder that men of ability, in later life, whose understandings have been rendered acute by practice in affairs, should be so easily and so far imposed upon when they happen to take up a new work in verse, this appears to be the cause;—that, having discontinued their attention to poetry, whatever progress may have been made in other departments of knowledge, they have not, as to this art, advanced in true discernment beyond the age of youth. If then a new poem falls in their way, whose attractions are of that kind which would have enraptured them during the heat of youth, the judgment not being improved to a degree that they shall be disgusted, they are dazzled; and prize and cherish the faults for having had power to make the present time vanish before them, and to throw the mind back, as by enchantment, into the happiest season of life. As they read, powers seem to be revived, passions are regenerated, and pleasures restored. The Book was probably taken up after an escape from the burthen of business, and with a wish to forget the world, and all its vexations and anxieties. Having obtained this wish, and so much more, it is natural that they should make report as they have felt.

If Men of mature age, through want of practice, be thus easily beguiled into admiration of absurdities, extravagances, and misplaced ornaments, thinking it proper that their understandings should enjoy a holiday, while they are unbending their minds with verse, it may be expected that such Readers will resemble their former selves also in strength of prejudice, and an inaptitude to be moved by the unostentatious beauties of a pure style. In the higher poetry, an enlightened Critic chiefly looks for a reflexion of the wisdom of the heart and the grandeur of the imagination. Wherever these appear, simplicity accompanies them; Magnificence herself, when legitimate, depending upon a simplicity of her own, to regulate her ornaments. But it is a well known property of human nature that our estimates are ever governed by comparisons, of which we are conscious with various degrees of distinctness. Is it not, then, inevitable (confining these observations to the effects of style merely) that an eye, accustomed to the glaring hues of diction by which such Readers are caught and excited, will for the most part be rather repelled than attracted by an original Work the coloring of which is disposed according to a pure and refined scheme of harmony? It is in the fine arts as in the affairs of life, no man can *serve* (i.e. obey with zeal and fidelity) two Masters.

As Poetry is most just to its own divine origin when it administers the comforts and breathes the spirit of religion, they who have learned to perceive this truth, and who betake themselves to reading verse for sacred purposes, must be preserved from numerous illusions to which the two Classes of Readers, whom we have been considering, are liable. But, as the mind grows serious from the weight of life, the range of its passions is contracted accordingly; and its sympathies become so exclusive that many species of high excellence wholly escape, or but languidly excite, its notice. Besides, Men who read from religious or moral inclinations, even when the subject is of that kind which they approve, are beset with misconceptions and mistakes peculiar to themselves. Attaching so much importance to the truths which interest them, they are prone to overrate the Authors by whom these truths are expressed and enforced. They come prepared to impart so much passion to the Poet's language, that they remain unconscious how little, in fact, they receive from it. And, on the other hand, religious faith is to him who holds it so momentous a thing, and error appears to be attended with such tremendous consequences, that, if opinions touching upon religion occur which the Reader condemns, he not only cannot sympathize with them however animated the expression, but there is, for the most part, an end put to all satisfaction and enjoyment. Love, if it before existed, is converted into dislike; and the heart of the Reader is set against the Author and his book.—To these excesses, they, who from their professions ought to be the most guarded against them, are perhaps the most liable; I mean those sects whose religion, being from the calculating understanding, is cold and formal. For when Christianity, the religion of humility, is founded upon the proudest quality of our nature, what can be expected but contradictions? Accordingly, believers of this cast are at one time contemptuous; at another, being troubled as they are and must be with inward misgivings, they are jealous and suspicious;—and at all seasons, they are under temptation to supply, by the heat with which they defend their tenets, the animation which is wanting to the constitution of the religion itself.

Faith was given to man that his affections, detached from the treasures of time, might be inclined to settle upon those of eternity:—the elevation of his nature, which this habit produces on earth, being to him a presumptive evidence of a future state of existence; and giving him a title to partake of its holiness. The religious man values what he sees chiefly as an "imperfect shadowing forth" of what he is incapable of seeing. The concerns of religion refer to indefinite objects, and are too weighty for the mind to support them without relieving itself by resting a great part of the burthen upon words and symbols. The commerce between Man and his Maker cannot be carried on but by a process where much is represented in little, and the infinite Being accommodates himself to a finite capacity. In all this may be perceived the affinities between religion and poetry;—between religion—making up the de-

ficiencies of reason by faith, and poetry—passionate for the instruction of reason; between religion—whose element is infinitude, and whose ultimate trust is the supreme of things, submitting herself to circumscription and reconciled to substitutions; and poetry—etherial and transcendant, yet incapable to sustain her existence without sensuous incarnation. In this community of nature may be perceived also the lurking incitements of kindred error;—so that we shall find no poetry has been more subject to distortion, than that species the argument and scope of which is religious; and no lovers of the art have gone further astray than the pious and the devout.

Whither then shall we turn for that union of qualifications which must necessarily exist before the decisions of a critic can be of absolute value? For a mind at once poetical and philosophical; for a critic whose affections are as free and kindly as the spirit of society, and whose understanding is severe as that of dispassionate government? Where are we to look for that initiatory composure of mind which no selfishness can disturb? For a natural sensibility that has been tutored into correctness without losing any thing of its quickness; and for active faculties capable of answering the demands which an Author of original imagination shall make upon them,—associated with a judgment that cannot be duped into admiration by aught that is unworthy of it?—Among those and those only, who, never having suffered their youthful love of poetry to remit much of its force, have applied, to the consideration of the laws of this art, the best power of their understandings. At the same time it must be observed —that, as this Class comprehends the only judgments which are trust-worthy, so does it include the most erroneous and perverse. For to be mis-taught is worse than to be untaught; and no perverseness equals that which is supported by system, no errors are so difficult to root out as those which the understanding has pledged its credit to uphold. In this Class are contained Censors, who, if they be pleased with what is good, are pleased with it only by imperfect glimpses, and upon false principles; who, should they generalize rightly to a certain point, are sure to suffer for it in the end;— who, if they stumble upon a sound rule, are fettered by misapplying it, or by straining it too far; being incapable of perceiving when it ought to yield to one of higher order. In it are found Critics too petulant to be passive to a genuine Poet, and too feeble to grapple with him; Men, who take upon them to report of the course which *he* holds whom they are utterly unable to accompany,—confounded if he turn quick upon the wing, dismayed if he soar steadily into "the region",— Men of palsied imaginations and indurated hearts; in whose minds all healthy action is languid,—who, therefore, feed as the many direct them, or with the many, are greedy after vicious provocatives;—Judges, whose censure is auspicious, and whose praise ominous! In this Class meet together the two extremes of best and worst.

The observations presented in the foregoing series, are of too ungracious a nature to have been made without reluctance; and were it only on this account I would invite the Reader to try them by the test of comprehensive experience. If the number of judges who can be confidently relied upon be in reality so small, it ought to follow that partial notice only, or neglect, perhaps long continued, or attention wholly inadequate to their merits—must have been the fate of most works in the higher departments of poetry; and that, on the other hand, numerous productions have blazed into popularity, and have passed away, leaving scarcely a trace behind them:—it will be, further, found that when Authors have at length raised themselves into general admiration and maintained their ground, errors and prejudices have prevailed concerning their genius and their works, which the few who are conscious of those errors and prejudices would deplore; if they were not recompensed by perceiving that there are select Spirits for whom it is ordained that their fame shall be in the world an existence like that of Virtue, which owes its being to the struggles it makes, and its vigour to the enemies whom it provokes;—a vivacious quality ever doomed to meet with opposition, and still triumphing over it; and, from the nature of its dominion, incapable of being brought to the sad conclusion of Alexander, when he wept that there were no more worlds for him to conquer.

Let us take a hasty retrospect of the poetical literature of this Country for the greater part of the last two Centuries, and see if the facts correspond with these inferences.

Who is there that can now endure to read the "Creation" of Dubartas?[1] Yet all Europe once resounded with his praise; he was caressed by Kings; and, when his Poem was translated into our language, the Faery Queen faded before it. The name of Spenser, whose genius is of a higher order than even that of Ariosto, is at this day scarcely known beyond the limits of the British Isles. And, if the value of his works is to be estimated from the attention now paid to them by his Countrymen, compared with that which they bestow on those of other writers, it must be pronounced small indeed.

"The laurel, meed of mighty Conquerors
  And Poets *sage*"—[2]

are his own words; but his wisdom has, in this particular, been his worst enemy; while, its opposite, whether in the shape of folly or madness, has been their best friend. But he was a great power; and bears a high name: the laurel has been awarded to him.

A Dramatic Author, if he write for the Stage, must adapt himself to the taste of the Audience, or they will not endure him; accordingly the mighty genius of Shakespeare was listened to. The People were delighted; but I am not sufficiently versed in Stage antiquities to determine whether they did not flock as eagerly to the representation of many pieces of contemporary Authors, wholly undeserving to appear upon the same boards. Had there been a formal contest for superiority among dramatic Writers, that Shakespeare, like his predecessors Sophocles and Euripides, would have often been subject to the mortification of seeing the prize adjudged to sorry competitors, becomes too probable when we reflect that the Admirers of Settle and Shadwell[3] were, in a later age, as numerous, and reckoned as respectable in point of talent as those of Dryden. At all events, that Shakespeare stooped to accommodate himself to the People, is sufficiently apparent; and one of the most striking proofs of his almost omr˙ potent genius, is, that he could turn to such glorious purpose those materials which the prepossessions of the age compelled him to make use of. Yet even this marvellous skill appears not to have been enough to prevent his rivals from having some advantage over him in public estimation; else how can we account for passages and scenes that exist in his works, unless upon a supposition that some of the grossest of them, a fact which in my own mind I have no doubt of, were foisted in by the Players, for the gratification of the many?

But that his Works, whatever might be their reception upon the stage, made little impression upon the ruling Intellects of the time, may be inferred from the fact that Lord Bacon, in his multifarious writings, no where either quotes or alludes to him.—* His dramatic

---

* The learned Hakewill (a 3rd edition of whose book bears date 1635) writing to refute the error "touching Nature's perpetual and universal decay," cites triumphantly the names of Ariosto, Tasso, Bartas, and Spenser, as instances that poetic genius had not degenerated; but he makes no mention of Shakespeare.[4]

---

[1] The epic of Guillaume Salluste Du Bartas (1544–1590) was translated into English as *Divine Weeks and Works* (1605); it was admired by Sidney, Spenser, and Milton, and enjoyed enormous popularity throughout the seventeenth century.

[2] *Faerie Queene*, I, i, 9.

[3] Elkanah Settle (1648–1724) was a mediocre playwright of historical tragedies and a deliberate rival to Dryden. Thomas Shadwell (c. 1642–1692), another of Dryden's literary and political opponents, was a prodigious writer of comedy and took the

excellence enabled him to resume possession of the stage after the Restoration; but Dryden tells us that in his time two of Beaumont's and Fletcher's Plays was acted for one of Shakespeare's.[5] And so faint and limited was the perception of the poetic beauties of his dramas in the time of Pope, that, in his Edition of the Plays, with a view of rendering to the general Reader a necessary service, he printed between inverted commas those passages which he thought most worthy of notice.

At this day, the French Critics have abated nothing of their aversion to this darling of our Nation: "the English with their Buffon de Shakespeare" is as familiar an expression among them as in the time of Voltaire. Baron Grimm[6] is the only French writer who seems to have perceived his infinite superiority to the first names of the French Theatre; an advantage which the Parisian Critic owed to his German blood and German education. The most enlightened Italians, though well acquainted with our language, are wholly incompetent to measure the proportions of Shakespeare. The Germans only, of foreign nations, are approaching towards a knowledge and feeling of what he is. In some respects they have acquired a superiority over the fellow-countrymen of the Poet; for among us it is a current, I might say, an established opinion that Shakespeare is justly praised when he is pronounced to be "a wild irregular genius, in whom great faults are compensated by great beauties." How long may it be before this misconception passes away, and it becomes universally acknowledged that the judgment of Shakespeare in the selection of his materials, and in the manner in which he has made them, heterogeneous as they often are, constitute a unity of their own, and contribute all to one great end, is not less admirable than his imagination, his invention, and his intuitive knowledge of human Nature!

There is extant a small Volume of miscellaneous Poems[7] in which Shakespeare expresses his own feelings in his own Person. It is not difficult to conceive that the Editor, George Stevens, should have been insensible to the beauties of one portion of that Volume,

the Sonnets; though there is not a part of the writings of this Poet where is found in an equal compass a greater number of exquisite feelings felicitously expressed. But, from regard to the Critic's own credit, he would not have ventured to talk of an* act of parliament not being strong enough to compel the perusal of these, or any production of Shakespeare, if he had not known that the people of England were ignorant of the treasures contained in those little pieces; and if he had not, moreover, shared the too common propensity of human nature to exult over a supposed fall into the mire of a genius whom he had been compelled to regard with admiration, as an inmate of the celestial regions,—"there sitting where he durst not soar."[9]

Nine years before the death of Shakespeare, Milton was born; and early in life he published several small poems, which, though on their first appearance they were praised by a few of the judicious, were afterwards neglected to that degree that Pope, in his youth, could pilfer from them without danger of detection.—Whether these poems are at this day justly appreciated I will not undertake to decide: nor would it imply a severe reflection upon the mass of Readers to suppose the contrary; seeing that a Man of the acknowledged genius of Voss, the German Poet, could suffer their spirit to evaporate; and could change their character, as is done in the translation made by him of the most popular of those pieces.[10] At all events it is certain that these Poems of Milton are now much read, and loudly praised; yet were they little heard of till more than 150 years after their publication; and of the Sonnets, Dr. Johnson, as appears from Boswell's Life of him,[11] was in the habit of thinking and speaking as contemptuously as Stevens wrote upon those of Shakespeare.

About the time when the Pindaric Odes of Cowley and his imitators, and the productions of that class of curious thinkers whom Dr. Johnson has strangely styled Metaphysical Poets,[12] were beginning to lose

* This flippant insensibility was publickly reprehended by Mr. Coleridge in a course of Lectures upon Poetry given by him at the Royal Institution. For the various merits of thought and language in Shakespeare's Sonnets see Numbers 27, 29, 30, 32, 33, 54, 64, 66, 68, 73, 76, 86, 91, 92, 97, 98, 105, 107, 108, 109, 111, 113, 114, 116, 117, 129, and many others.[8]

---

honor of poet laureate away from Dryden following the "Glorious Revolution" of 1788.

4 George Hakewill (1578–1649) was an Anglican divine and writer on moral and theological topics. Wordsworth refers to his most famous work *An Apologie or Declaration of the Power and Providence of God*, first published in 1627.

5 See Dryden's "Essay on Dramatic Poesy."

6 Friedrich Melchior, Baron de Grimm (1723–1807) was a Franco-German critic and diplomat, and a central figure in Parisian literary life.

7 George Steevens (1736–1800) brought out in 1766 an historically important edition of *Twenty of the Plays of Shakespeare*, including in its fourth volume the Sonnets.

8 Steevens' opinion of the sonnets is reported in Alexander Chambers' edition *The Works of the English Poets* (1810), volume V.

9 *Paradise Lost*, IV, 829.

10 J. H. Voss (1751–1826) was an eminent German poet and translator. His versions of Milton's *L'Allegro* and *Il Penseroso* appeared in 1789 and 1792 respectively.

11 See entry of June 13, 1784.

12 See Johnson's "Life of Cowley."

something of that extravagant admiration which they had excited, the Paradise Lost made its appearance. "Fit audience find though few,"[13] was the petition addressed by the Poet to his inspiring Muse. I have said elsewhere[14] that he gained more than he asked, this I believe to be true; but Dr. Johnson has fallen into a gross mistake when he attempts to prove, by the sale of the work, that Milton's Countrymen were "*just to it*" upon its first appearance.[15] Thirteen hundred Copies were sold in two years; an uncommon example, he asserts, of the prevalence of genius in opposition to so much recent enmity as Milton's public conduct had excited. But be it remembered that, if Milton's political and religious opinions, and the manner in which he announced them, had raised him many enemies, they had procured him numerous friends; who, as all personal danger was passed away at the time of publication, would be eager to procure the master-work of a Man whom they revered, and whom they would be proud of praising. The demand did not immediately increase; "for," says Dr. Johnson, "many more Readers" (he means Persons in the habit of reading poetry) "than were supplied at first the Nation did not afford." How careless must a writer be who can make this assertion in the face of so many existing title pages to belie it! Turning to my own shelves, I find the folio of Cowley, 7th Edition, 1681. A book near it is Flatman's Poems, 4th Edition, 1686; Waller, 5th Edition, same date. The Poems of Norris of Bemerton[16] not long after went, I believe, through nine Editions. What further demand there might be for these works I do not know, but I well remember, that 25 Years ago, the Bookseller's stalls in London swarmed with the folios of Cowley. This is not mentioned in disparagement of that able writer and amiable Man; but merely to shew— that, if Milton's work was not more read, it was not because readers did not exist at the time. Only 3000 copies of the Paradise Lost sold in 11 Years; and the Nation, says Dr. Johnson, had been satisfied from 1623 to 1664, that is 41 Years, with only two Editions of the Works of Shakespeare; which probably did not together make 1000 Copies; facts adduced by the critic to prove the "paucity of Readers."—There were Readers in multitudes; but their money went for other purposes, as their admiration was fixed elsewhere. We are authorized, then, to affirm that the reception of the

Paradise Lost, and the slow progress of its fame, are proofs as striking as can be desired that the positions which I am attempting to establish are not erroneous. —*How amusing to shape to one's self such a critique as a Wit of Charles's days, or a Lord of the Miscellanies, or trading Journalist, of King William's time, would have brought forth, if he had set his faculties industriously to work upon this Poem, every where impregnated with *original* excellence!

So strange indeed are the obliquities of admiration, that they whose opinions are much influenced by authority will often be tempted to think that there are no fixed principles† in human nature for this art to rest upon. I have been honoured by being permitted to peruse in MS. a tract composed between the period of the Revolution and the close of that Century. It is the Work of an English Peer of high accomplishments, its object to form the character and direct the studies of his Son. Perhaps no where does a more beautiful treatise of the kind exist. The good sense and wisdom of the thoughts, the delicacy of the feelings, and the charm of the style, are, throughout, equally conspicuous. Yet the Author, selecting among the Poets of his own Country those whom he deems most worthy of his son's perusal, particularizes only Lord Rochester, Sir John Denham, and Cowley. Writing about the same time, Shaftsbury, an Author at present unjustly depreciated, describes the English Muses as only yet lisping in their Cradles.[18]

The arts by which Pope, soon afterwards, contrived to procure to himself a more general and a higher reputation than perhaps any English Poet ever attained during his life-time, are known to the judicious. And as well known is it to them, that the undue exertion of these arts, is the cause why Pope has for some time held a rank in literature, to which, if he had not been seduced by an over-love of immediate popularity, and had confided more in his native genius, he never could have descended. He bewitched the nation by his melody, and dazzled it by his polished style, and was himself blinded by his own success. Having wandered

---

* Hughes is express upon this subject; in his dedication of Spenser's Works to Lord Somers he writes thus. "It was your Lordship's encouraging a beautiful Edition of Paradise Lost that first brought that incomparable Poem to be generally known and esteemed."[17]

† This opinion seems actually to have been entertained by Adam Smith, the worst critic, David Hume not excepted, that Scotland, a soil to which this sort of weed seems natural, has produced.

---

[17] John Hughes (1677–1720) was a minor poet and dramatist. His edition of Spenser appeared in 1715.

[18] Anthony Ashley Cooper (1671–1713) was Third Earl of Shaftesbury. Wordsworth refers to a remark in the third treatise of *Characteristics* (1711).

---

[13] *Paradise Lost*, VII, 31.

[14] In the Prospectus verses ("On Man, on Nature, and of Human Life"), ll. 23–24, published in the "Preface to *The Excursion*" (1814).

[15] See Johnson's "Life of Milton."

[16] Thomas Flatman (1637–1688). John Norris (1657–1711) was a religious philosopher of strongly Platonic tendencies, and author of the popular *A Collection of Miscellanies* (ninth edition, 1730).

from humanity in his Eclogues with boyish inexperience, the praise, which these compositions obtained, tempted him into a belief that nature was not to be trusted, at least in pastoral Poetry. To prove this by example, he put his friend Gay upon writing those Eclogues[19] which the Author intended to be burlesque. The Instigator of the work, and his Admirers, could perceive in them nothing but what was ridiculous. Nevertheless, though these Poems contain some odious and even detestable passages, the effect, as Dr. Johnson well observes, "of reality and truth became conspicuous even when the intention was to shew them grovelling and degrading." These Pastorals, ludicrous to those who prided themselves upon their refinement, in spite of those disgusting passages "became popular, and were read with delight as just representations of rural manners and occupations."

Something less than 60 years after the publication of the Paradise Lost appeared Thomson's Winter; which was speedily followed by his other Seasons. It is a work of inspiration; much of it is written from himself, and nobly from himself. How was it received? "It was no sooner read," says one of his contemporary Biographers,[20] "than universally admired: those only excepted who had not been used to feel, or to look for any thing in poetry, beyond a *point* of satirical or epigrammatic wit, a smart *antithesis* richly trimmed with rhyme, or the softness of an *elegiac* complaint. To such his manly classical spirit could not readily commend itself; till, after a more attentive perusal, they had got the better of their prejudices, and either acquired or affected a truer taste. A few others stood aloof, merely because they had long before fixed the articles of their poetical creed, and resigned themselves to an absolute despair of ever seeing any thing new and original. These were somewhat mortified to find their notions disturbed by the appearance of a poet, who seemed to owe nothing but to nature and his own genius. But, in a short time, the applause became unanimous; every one wondering how so many pictures, and pictures so familiar, should have moved them but faintly to what they felt in his descriptions. His digressions too, the overflowings of a tender benevolent heart, charmed the reader no less; leaving him in doubt, whether he should more admire the Poet or love the Man."

This case appears to bear strongly against us:—but we must distinguish between wonder and legitimate admiration. The subject of the work is the changes produced in the appearances of nature by the revolution of the year: and, by undertaking to write in verse, Thomson pledged himself to treat his subject as became a Poet. Now it is remarkable that, excepting a passage or two in the Windsor Forest of Pope, and some delightful pictures in the Poems of Lady Winchelsea,[21] the Poetry of the period intervening between the publication of the Paradise Lost and the Seasons does not contain a single new image of external nature; and scarcely presents a familiar one from which it can be inferred that the eye of the Poet had been steadily fixed upon his object, much less that his feelings had urged him to work upon it in the spirit of genuine imagination. To what a low state knowledge of the most obvious and important phenomena had sunk, is evident from the style in which Dryden has executed a description of Night in one of his Tragedies, and Pope his translation of the celebrated moon-light scene in the Iliad.[22] A blind man, in the habit of attending accurately to descriptions casually dropped from the lips of those around him, might easily depict these appearances with more truth. Dryden's lines are vague, bombastic, and senseless;* those of Pope, though he had Homer to guide him, are throughout false and contradictory. The verses of Dryden, once highly celebrated, are forgotten; those of Pope still retain their hold upon public estimation,—nay, there is not a passage of descriptive poetry, which at this day finds so many and such ardent admirers. Strange to think of an Enthusiast, as may have been the case with thousands, reciting those verses under the cope of a moon-light sky, without having his raptures in the least disturbed by a suspicion of their absurdity.—If these two distinguished Writers could habitually think that the visible universe was of so little consequence to a Poet, that it was scarcely necessary for him to cast his eyes upon it, we may be assured that those passages of

---

*   CORTES *alone, in a night-gown.*
All things are hush'd as Nature's self lay dead:
The mountains seem to nod their drowsy head:
The little Birds in dreams their songs repeat,
And sleeping Flowers beneath the Night-dew sweat:
Even Lust and Envy sleep; yet Love denies
Rest to my soul, and slumber to my eyes.

Dryden's Indian Emperor.[23]

---

[19] Refers to Gay's *The Shepherd's Week* (1714), written in part to discredit Ambrose Phillips' *Pastorals* (1709), which Pope had earlier satirized. Johnson's opinion of *The Shepherd's Week*, next mentioned, is found in his "Life of Gay."

[20] Patrick Murdoch, in "An Account of the Life and Writings of Mr. James Thomson" prefacing an edition of Thomson's works in 1788.

[21] Refers to Anne Finch, Countess of Winchelsea (1661–1720), whose *Miscellany Poems* (1713) contain a number of verses of natural description, among them "Nocturnal Reverie," much admired by Wordsworth.

[22] See VIII, 685–708 of Pope's translation (1715–1720).

[23] The passage occurs in III, ii, 1–7 of Dryden's heroic tragedy of 1665.

the elder Poets which faithfully and poetically describe the phenomena of nature, were not at that time holden in much estimation, and that there was little accurate attention paid to these appearances.

Wonder is the natural product of Ignorance; and as the soil was *in such good condition* at the time of the publication of the Seasons, the crop was doubtless abundant. Neither individuals nor nations become corrupt all at once, nor are they enlightened in a moment. Thomson was an inspired Poet, but he could not work miracles; in cases where the art of seeing had in some degree been learned, the teacher would further the proficiency of his pupils, but he could do little *more*, though so far does vanity assist men in acts of self-deception that many would often fancy they recognized a likeness when they knew nothing of the original. Having shewn that much of what his Biographer deemed genuine admiration must in fact have been blind wonderment,—how is the rest to be accounted for?—Thomson was fortunate in the very title of his Poem, which seemed to bring it home to the prepared sympathies of every one: in the next place, notwithstanding his high powers, he writes a vicious style; and his false ornaments are exactly of that kind which would be most likely to strike the undiscerning. He likewise abounds with sentimental common-places, that from the manner in which they were brought forward bore an imposing air of novelty. In any well-used Copy of the Seasons the Book generally opens of itself with the rhapsody on love, or with one of the stories, (perhaps Damon and Musidora);[24] these also are prominent in our Collections of Extracts; and are the parts of his Works which, after all, were probably most efficient in first recommending the Author to general notice. Pope, repaying praises which he had received, and wishing to extol him to the highest, only styles him "an elegant and philosophical Poet";[25] nor are we able to collect any unquestionable proofs that the true characteristics of Thomson's genius as an imaginative Poet were perceived, till the elder Warton, almost 40 Years after the publication of the Seasons, pointed them out by a note in his Essay on the life and writings of Pope. In the Castle of Indolence (of which Gray speaks so coldly) these characteristics were almost as conspicuously displayed, and in verse more harmonious and diction more pure. Yet that fine Poem was

neglected on its appearance, and is at this day the delight only of a Few!

When Thomson died, Collins breathed his regrets into an Elegiac Poem,[26] in which he pronounces a poetical curse upon *him* who should regard with insensibility the place where the Poet's remains were deposited. The Poems of the mourner himself have now passed through innumerable Editions, and are universally known; but if, when Collins died, the same kind of imprecation had been pronounced by a surviving admirer, small is the number whom it would not have comprehended. The notice which his poems attained during his life-time was so small, and of course the sale so insignificant, that not long before his death he deemed it right to repay to the Bookseller the sum which he had advanced for them, and threw the Edition into the fire.

Next in importance to the Seasons of Thomson, though at considerable distance from that work in order of time, come the Reliques of Ancient English Poetry; collected, new-modelled, and in many instances (if such a contradiction in terms may be used) composed, by the editor, Dr. Percy.[27] This Work did not steal silently into the world, as is evident from the number of legendary tales, which appeared not long after its publication; and which were modelled, as the Authors persuaded themselves, after the old Ballad. The Compilation was however ill-suited to the then existing taste of City society; and Dr. Johnson, mid the little senate to which he gave laws, was not sparing in his exertions to make it an object of contempt. The Critic triumphed, the legendary imitators were deservedly disregarded, and, as undeservedly, their ill-imitated models sank, in this Country, into temporary neglect; while Burger,[28] and other able Writers of Germany, were translating, or imitating, these Reliques, and composing, with the aid of inspiration thence derived, Poems, which are the delight of the German nation. Dr. Percy was so abashed by the ridicule flung upon his labours from the ignorance and insensibility of the Persons with whom he lived, that, though while he was writing under a mask he had not wanted resolution to follow his genius into the

---

[24] For the "rhapsody on love," see the concluding section of "Spring." For Damon and Musidora see "Summer," ll. 1269–1370.

[25] The remark is made in the "Testimonies of Authors" prefacing Pope's *Dunciad*. Joseph Warton's praise of Thomson is found in his *Essay on the Writings and Genius of Pope* (1756), pp. 41–50. Gray's opinion of *The Castle of Indolence* was given in a letter of June 5, 1748, published in William Mason's *Memoirs of the Life and Writing of Thomas Gray* (1775).

[26] Collins' *Ode Occasioned by the Death of Mr. Thomson* (1749).

[27] *Reliques of Ancient English Poetry* (1765) was an historically important collection of early ballads ("Chevy Chase," "Edward, Edward," "Sir Patrick Spens," among them) as well as some seventeenth- and eighteenth-century poems, prepared by Thomas Percy (1729–1811), who freely altered and "improved" the older texts. Johnson's "contempt" for *Reliques* is preserved in George Steevens' *Johnsoniana* (1785) in the same account that records the parody cited in the "Preface to *Lyrical Ballads*." See p. 55.

[28] Gottfried August Bürger (1747–1794) was a leading German ballad writer. Five of his poems are imitations or translations from Percy's collection.

regions of true simplicity and genuine pathos, (as is evinced by the exquisite ballad of Sir Cauline and by many other pieces) yet, when he appeared in his own person and character as a poetical writer, he adopted, as in the tale of the Hermit of Warkworth, a diction scarcely in any one of its features distinguishable from the vague, the glossy, and unfeeling language of his day. I mention this remarkable fact with regret, esteeming the genius of Dr. Percy in this kind of writing superior to that of any other man by whom, in modern times, it has been cultivated. That even Burger, (to whom Klopstock gave, in my hearing,[29] a commendation which he denied to Goethe and Schiller, pronouncing him to be a genuine Poet, and one of the few among the Germans whose works would last) had not the fine sensibility of Percy, might be shewn from many passages, in which he has deserted his original only to go astray. For example,

> Now daye was gone, and night was come,
> And all were fast asleepe,
> All, save the Ladye Emmeline,
> Who sate in her bowre to weepe:
>
> And soone shee heard her true Love's voice
> Low whispering at the walle,
> Awake, awake, my deare Ladye,
> 'Tis I thy true-love call.[30]

Which is thus tricked out and dilated,

> Als nun die Nacht Gebirg' und Thal
> Vermummt in Rabenschatten,
> Und Hochburgs Lampen über-all
> Schon ausgeflimmert hatten,
> Und alles tief entschlafen war;
> Doch nur das Fräulein immerdar,
> Voll Fieberangst, noch wachte,
> Und seinen Ritter dachte:
> Da horch! Ein süsser Liebeston
> Kam leis empor geflogen.
> "Ho, Trudchen, ho! Da bin ich schon!
> Frisch auf! Dich angezogen!"

But from humble ballads we must ascend to heroics. All hail Macpherson! hail to thee, Sire of Ossian! The Phantom was begotten by the snug embrace of an impudent Highlander upon a cloud of tradition—it travelled southward, where it was greeted with acclamation, and the thin Consistence took its course through Europe, upon the breath of popular applause. The Editor of the "Reliques" had indirectly preferred

a claim to the praise of invention by not concealing that his supplementary labours were considerable: how selfish his conduct contrasted with that of the disinterested Gael, who, like Lear, gives his kingdom away, and is content to become a pensioner upon his own issue for a beggarly pittance!—Open this far-famed Book!—I have done so at random, and the beginning of the "Epic Poem Temora,"[31] in 8 Books, presents itself. "The blue waves of Ullin roll in light. The green hills are covered with day. Trees shake their dusky heads in the breeze. Grey torrents pour their noisy streams. Two green hills with aged oaks surround a narrow plain. The blue course of a stream is there. On its banks stood Cairbar of Atha. His spear supports the king; the red eyes of his fear are sad. Cormac rises on his soul with all his ghastly wounds." Precious memorandums from the pocket-book of the blind Ossian!

If it be unbecoming, as I acknowledge that for the most part it is, to speak disrespectfully of Works that have enjoyed for a length of time a widely spread reputation, without at the same time producing irrefragable proofs of their unworthiness, let me be forgiven upon this occasion.—Having had the good fortune to be born and reared in a mountainous Country, from my very childhood I have felt the falsehood that pervades the volumes imposed upon the World under the name of Ossian. From what I saw with my own eyes, I knew that the imagery was spurious. In nature every thing is distinct, yet nothing defined into absolute independent singleness.[32] In Macpherson's work it is exactly the reverse; every thing (that is not stolen) is in this manner defined, insulated, dislocated, deadened, —yet nothing distinct. It will always be so when words are substituted for things. To say that the characters never could exist, that the manners are impossible, and that a dream has more substance than the whole state of society, as there depicted, is doing nothing more than pronouncing a censure which Macpherson defied; when, with the steeps of Morven before his eyes, he could talk so familiarly of his Car-borne heroes;—Of Morven, which, if one may judge from its appearance at the distance of a few miles,[33] contains scarcely an acre of ground sufficiently accommodating for a sledge to be trailed along its surface.—Mr. Malcolm Laing[34] has ably shewn that the diction of this pretended translation is a motley assembly from all

---

[29] At Hamburg in 1798, Wordsworth had met the leading German poet Friedrich Klopstock (1724–1803), author of the epic *Messias* modelled on *Paradise Lost*.

[30] "The Childe of Elle," ll. 53–60, in Percy's *Reliques*.

[31] Published 1763.

[32] Cf. *Guide to the Lakes*, Section Third, below, p. 104.

[33] Wordsworth visited Morven, the mountainous district in the northwest coastal area of Scotland, on tours in 1803 and 1814.

[34] Malcolm Laing's (1762–1818) *History of Scotland* (1800) had included an appendix on the "Supposed Authenticity of Ossian's Poems". In 1805, Laing had brought out an edition of the Ossianic poems, which extensively developed Macpherson's clever and constant borrowings from earlier writers.

quarters; but he is so fond of making out parallel passages as to call poor Macpherson to account for his very "*ands*" and his "*buts!*" and he has weakened his argument by conducting it as if he thought that every striking resemblance was a *conscious* plagiarism. It is enough that the coincidences are too remarkable for its being probable or possible that they could arise in different minds without communication between them. Now as the Translators of the Bible, Shakespeare, Milton, and Pope, could not be indebted to Macpherson, it follows that he must have owed his fine feathers to them; unless we are prepared gravely to assert, with Madame de Stael, that many of the characteristic beauties of our most celebrated English Poets, are derived from the ancient Fingallian;[35] in which case the modern translator would have been but giving back to Ossian his own.—It is consistent that Lucien Buonaparte,[36] who could censure Milton for having surrounded Satan in the infernal regions with courtly and regal splendour, should pronounce the modern Ossian to be the glory of Scotland;—a Country that has produced a Dunbar, a Buchanan,[37] a Thomson, and a Burns! These opinions are of ill omen for the Epic ambition of him who has given them to the world.

Yet, much as these pretended treasures of antiquity have been admired, they have been wholly uninfluential upon the literature of the Country. No succeeding Writer appears to have caught from them a ray of inspiration; no Author in the least distinguished, has ventured formally to imitate them—except the Boy, Chatterton, on their first appearance. He had perceived, from the successful trials which he himself had made in literary forgery, how few critics were able to distinguish between a real ancient medal and a counterfeit of modern manufacture; and he set himself to the work of filling a Magazine with *Saxon poems*,[38] —counterparts of those of Ossian, as like his as one of his misty stars is to another. This incapability to amalgamate with the literature of the Island, is, in my estimation, a decisive proof that the book is essentially unnatural; nor should I require any other to demonstrate it to be a forgery, audacious as worthless.

◇◇◇◇◇◇◇◇◇◇◇◇◇◇◇◇◇◇◇◇◇◇◇◇◇◇

35 Madame de Staël (1766–1817) was one of the leading intellectual figures of the time. Her observations on Fingal were presented in *De la Litterature dans ses rapports avec les Institutions Sociales* (1800).

36 Lucien Buonaparte (1775–1840) was the brother of Napoleon. Wordsworth refers to Lucien's notes to his epic poem *Charlesmagne, ou l'Église délivrée* (1814).

37 William Dunbar (*c.* 1460–*c.* 1520) was the Scotch Chaucerian poet. George Buchanan (1506–1582) was a Scotch historian, religious controversalist, and a distinguished Latin poet. See *Guide to the Lakes*, Section First, p. 97, where Wordsworth refers to one of Buchanan's poems.

38 In 1769–1770, Chatterton had published Ossianic imitations in the *Town and Country Magazine*.

—Contrast, in this respect, the effect of Macpherson's publication with the Reliques of Percy, so unassuming, so modest in their pretensions!—I have already stated how much Germany is indebted to this latter work; and for our own Country, its Poetry has been absolutely redeemed by it. I do not think that there is an able Writer in verse of the present day who would not be proud to acknowledge his obligations to the Reliques; I know that it is so with my friends; and, for myself, I am happy in this occasion to make a public avowal of my own.

Dr. Johnson, more fortunate in his contempt of the labours of Macpherson than those of his modest friend, was solicited not long after to furnish Prefaces biographical and critical for some of the most eminent English Poets.[39] The Booksellers took upon themselves to make the collection; they referred probably to the most popular miscellanies, and, unquestionably, to their Books of accounts; and decided upon the claim of Authors to be admitted into a body of the most Eminent, from the familiarity of their names with the readers of that day, and by the profits, which, from the sale of his works, each had brought and was bringing to the Trade. The Editor was allowed a limited exercise of discretion, and the Authors whom he recommended are scarcely to be mentioned without a smile. We open the volume of Prefatory Lives, and to our astonishment the *first* name we find ˙s that of Cowley!—What is become of the Morning-star of English Poetry? Where is the bright Elizabethan Constellation? Or, if Names are more acceptable than images, where is the ever-to-be-honoured Chaucer? where is Spenser? where Sydney? and lastly where he, whose rights as a Poet, contradistinguished from those which he is universally allowed to possess as a Dramatist, we have vindicated, where Shakespeare?—These, and a multitude of others not unworthy to be placed near them, their contemporaries and successors, we have *not*. But in their stead, we have (could better be expected when precedence was to be settled by an abstract of reputation at any given period made as in the case before us?) we have Roscommon, and Stepney, and Phillips, and Walsh, and Smith, and Duke, and King, and Spratt—Halifax, Granville, Sheffield, Congreve, Broome,[40]

◇◇◇◇◇◇◇◇◇◇◇◇◇◇◇◇◇◇◇◇◇◇◇◇◇◇

39 *The Lives of the English Poets* (1779–1781).

40 Wentworth Dillon, Earl of Roscommon (*c.* 1633–1685) was primarily a translator; George Stepney (1663–1707); Ambrose Phillips (*c.* 1675–1749); William Walsh (1663–1708) was an early encourager of Pope; Edmund Smith (1672–1710); Richard Duke (1658–1711); William King (1663–1712); Thomas Sprat (1635–1713) was author of the famous *History of the Royal Society* (1667); Charles Montague, Earl of Halifax (1661–1715); George Granville, Lord Lansdown (1667–1735); John Sheffield (1648–1721) was author of the popular verse *Essay on Poetry* (1682); William Congreve, the dramatist; William Broome (1689–1715).

and other reputed Magnates; Writers in metre utterly worthless and useless, except for occasions like the present, when their productions are referred to as evidence what a small quantity of brain is necessary to procure a considerable stock of admiration, provided the aspirant will accommodate himself to the likings and fashions of his day.

As I do not mean to bring down this retrospect to our own times, it may with propriety be closed at the era of this distinguished event. From the literature of other ages and countries, proofs equally cogent might have been adduced that the opinions announced in the former part of this Essay are founded upon truth. It was not an agreeable office, not a prudent undertaking, to declare them, but their importance seemed to render it a duty. It may still be asked, where lies the particular relation of what has been said to these Volumes?—The question will be easily answered by the discerning Reader who is old enough to remember the taste that was prevalent when some of these Poems were first published, 17 years ago;[41] who has also observed to what degree the Poetry of this Island has since that period been coloured by them; and who is further aware of the unremitting hostility with which, upon some principle or other, they have each and all been opposed. A sketch of my own notion of the constitution of Fame, has been given; and, as far as concerns myself, I have cause to be satisfied. The love, the admiration, the indifference, the slight, the aversion, and even the contempt, with which these Poems have been received, knowing, as I do, the source within my own mind, from which they have proceeded, and the labour and pains, which, when labour and pains appeared needful, have been bestowed upon them,—must all, if I think consistently, be received as pledges and tokens, bearing the same general impression though widely different in value;—they are all proofs that for the present time I have not laboured in vain; and afford assurances, more or less authentic, that the products of my industry will endure.

If there be one conclusion more forcibly pressed upon us than another by the review which has been given of the fortunes and fate of Poetical Works, it is this,—that every Author, as far as he is great and at the same time *original*, has had the task of *creating* the taste by which he is to be enjoyed: so has it been, so will it continue to be. This remark was long since made to me by the philosophical Friend for the separation of whose Poems from my own I have previously expressed my regret. The predecessors of an original Genius of a high order will have smoothed the way for all that he has in common with them;—and much he will have in common; but, for what is peculiarly his own, he will be called upon to clear and often to shape his own road:— he will be in the condition of Hannibal among the Alps.

And where lies the real difficulty of creating that taste by which a truly original Poet is to be relished? Is it in breaking the bonds of custom, in overcoming the prejudices of false refinement, and displacing the aversions of inexperience? Or, if he labour for an object which here and elsewhere I have proposed to myself, does it consist in divesting the Reader of the pride that induces him to dwell upon those points wherein Men differ from each other, to the exclusion of those in which all Men are alike, or the same; and in making him ashamed of the vanity that renders him insensible of the appropriate excellence which civil arrangements, less unjust than might appear, and Nature illimitable in her bounty, have conferred on Men who stand below him in the scale of society? Finally, does it lie in establishing that dominion over the spirits of Readers by which they are to be humbled and humanized, in order that they may be purified and exalted?

If these ends are to be attained by the mere communication of *knowledge*, it does *not* lie here.—TASTE, I would remind the Reader, like IMAGINATION, is a word which has been forced to extend its services far beyond the point to which philosophy would have confined them. It is a metaphor, taken from a *passive* sense of the human body, and transferred to things which are in their essence *not* passive,—to intellectual *acts* and *operations*. The word, imagination, has been overstrained, from impulses honourable to mankind, to meet the demands of the faculty which is perhaps the noblest of our nature. In the instance of taste, the process has been reversed; and from the prevalence of dispositions at once injurious and discreditable,— being no other than that selfishness which is the child of apathy,—which, as Nations decline in productive and creative power, makes them value themselves upon a presumed refinement of judging. Poverty of language is the primary cause of the use which we make of the word, imagination; but the word, Taste, has been stretched to the sense which it bears in modern Europe by habits of self-conceit, inducing that inversion in the order of things whereby a passive faculty is made paramount among the faculties conversant with the fine arts. Proportion and congruity, the requisite knowledge being supposed, are subjects upon which taste may be trusted; it is competent to this office;—for in its intercourse with these the mind is *passive*, and is affected painfully or pleasurably as by an instinct. But the profound and the exquisite in feeling, the lofty and universal in thought and imagination; or in ordinary language the pathetic and the sublime;—are neither of

---

[41] In *Lyrical Ballads* (1798).

them, accurately speaking, objects of a faculty which could ever without a sinking in the spirit of Nations have been designated by the metaphor—*Taste*. And why? Because without the exertion of a co-operating *power* in the mind of the Reader, there can be no adequate sympathy with either of these emotions: without this auxiliar impulse elevated or profound passion cannot exist.

Passion, it must be observed, is derived from a word which signifies, *suffering*;[42] but the connection which suffering has with effort, with exertion, and *action*, is immediate and inseparable. How strikingly is this property of human nature exhibited by the fact, that, in popular language, to be in a passion, is to be angry!—But,

> "Anger in hasty *words* or *blows*
> Itself discharges on its foes."

To be moved, then, by a passion, is to be excited, often to external, and always to internal, effort; whether for the continuance and strengthening of the passion, or for its suppression, accordingly as the course which it takes may be painful or pleasurable. If the latter, the soul must contribute to its support, or it never becomes vivid,—and soon languishes, and dies. And this brings us to the point. If every great Poet with whose writings men are familiar, in the highest exercise of his genius, before he can be thoroughly enjoyed, has to call forth and to communicate *power*, this service, in a still greater degree, falls upon an original Writer, at his first appearance in the world.—Of genius the only proof is, the act of doing well what is worthy to be done, and what was never done before: Of genius, in the fine arts, the only infallible sign is the widening the sphere of human sensibility, for the delight, honor, and benefit of human nature. Genius is the introduction of a new element into the intellectual universe: or, if that be not allowed, it is the application of powers to objects on which they had not before been exercised, or the employment of them in such a manner as to produce effects hitherto unknown. What is all this but an advance, or a conquest, made by the soul of the Poet? Is it to be supposed that the Reader can make progress of this kind, like an Indian Prince or General—stretched on his Palanquin,[43] and borne by his Slaves? No, he is invigorated and inspirited by his Leader, in order that he may exert himself, for he cannot proceed in quiescence, he cannot be carried like a dead weight. Therefore to create taste is to call forth and bestow power, of

which knowledge is the effect; and *there* lies the true difficulty.

As the pathetic participates of an *animal* sensation, it might seem—that, if the springs of this emotion were genuine, all men, possessed of competent knowledge of the facts and circumstances, would be instantaneously affected. And, doubtless, in the works of every true Poet will be found passages of that species of excellence, which is proved by effects immediate and universal. But there are emotions of the pathetic that are simple and direct, and others—that are complex and revolutionary; some—to which the heart yields with gentleness, others,—against which it struggles with pride: these varieties are infinite as the combinations of circumstance and the constitutions of character. Remember, also, that the medium through which, in poetry, the heart is to be affected—is language; a thing subject to endless fluctuations and arbitrary associations. The genius of the Poet melts these down for his purpose; but they retain their shape and quality to him who is not capable of exerting, within his own mind, a corresponding energy. There is also a meditative, as well as a human, pathos; an enthusiastic, as well as an ordinary, sorrow; a sadness that has its seat in the depths of reason, to which the mind cannot sink gently of itself—but to which it must descend by treading the steps of thought. And for the sublime,—if we consider what are the cares that occupy the passing day, and how remote is the practice and the course of life from the sources of sublimity, in the soul of Man, can it be wondered that there is little existing preparation for a Poet charged with a new mission to extend its kingdom, and to augment and spread its enjoyments?

Away, then, with the senseless iteration of the word, *popular*, applied to new works in Poetry, as if there were no test of excellence in this first of the fine arts but that all Men should run after its productions, as if urged by an appetite, or constrained by a spell!—The qualities of writing best fitted for eager reception are either such as startle the world into attention by their audacity and extravagance; or they are chiefly of a superficial kind, lying upon the surfaces of manners; or arising out of a selection and arrangement of incidents, by which the mind is kept upon the stretch of curiosity, and the fancy amused without the trouble of thought. But in every thing which is to send the soul into herself, to be admonished of her weakness or to be made conscious of her power;—wherever life and nature are described as operated upon by the creative or abstracting virtue of the imagination; wherever the instinctive wisdom of antiquity and her heroic passions uniting, in the heart of the Poet, with the meditative wisdom of later ages, have produced that accord of sublimated humanity, which is at once a history of the

---

[42] From the Latin verb *patior*. The next quotation is from Edmund Waller's "Of Love," ll. 1–2.

[43] An elegant box-like litter used to transport Eastern dignitaries.

remote past and a prophetic annunciation of the remotest future, *there*, the Poet must reconcile himself for a season to few and scattered hearers.—Grand thoughts, (and Shakespeare must often have sighed over this truth) as they are most naturally and most fitly conceived in solitude, so can they not be brought forth in the midst of plaudits without some violation of their sanctity. Go to a silent exhibition of the productions of the Sister Art, and be convinced that the qualities which dazzle at first sight, and kindle the admiration of the multitude, are essentially different from those by which permanent influence is secured. Let us not shrink from following up these principles as far as they will carry us, and conclude with observing—that there never has been a period, and perhaps never will be, in which vicious poetry, of some kind or other, has not excited more zealous admiration, and been far more generally read, than good; but this advantage attends the good, that the *individual*, as well as the species, survives from age to age: whereas, of the depraved, though the species be immortal the individual quickly *perishes*; the object of present admiration vanishes, being supplanted by some other as easily produced; which, though no better, brings with it at least the irritation of novelty,—with adaptation, more or less skilful, to the changing humours of the majority of those who are most at leisure to regard poetical works when they first solicit their attention.

Is it the result of the whole that, in the opinion of the Writer, the judgment of the People is not to be respected? The thought is most injurious; and could the charge be brought against him, he would repel it with indignation. The People have already been justified, and their eulogium pronounced by implication, when it was said, above—that, of *good* Poetry, the *individual*, as well as the species, *survives*. And how does it survive but through the People? what preserves it but their intellect and their wisdom?

> "—Past and future, are the wings
> On whose support, harmoniously conjoined,
> Moves the great Spirit of human knowledge—"
> *MS.*[44]

The voice that issues from this Spirit, is that Vox populi which the Deity inspires. Foolish must he be who can mistake for this a local acclamation, or a transitory outcry—transitory though it be for years, local though from a Nation. Still more lamentable is his error, who can believe that there is any thing of divine infallibility in the clamour of that small though loud portion of the community, ever governed by factitious influence,

which, under the name of the PUBLIC, passes itself, upon the unthinking, for the PEOPLE. Towards the Public, the Writer hopes that he feels as much deference as it is intitled to: but to the People, philosophically characterized, and to the embodied spirit of their knowledge, so far as it exists and moves, at the present, faithfully supported by its two wings, the past and the future, his devout respect, his reverence, is due. He offers it willingly and readily; and, this done, takes leave of his Readers, by assuring them—that, if he were not persuaded that the Contents of these Volumes, and the Work to which they are subsidiary, evinced something of the "Vision and the Faculty divine";[45] and that, both in words and things, they will operate in their degree, to extend the domain of sensibility for the delight, the honor, and the benefit of human nature, notwithstanding the many happy hours which he has employed in their composition, and the manifold comforts and enjoyments they have procured to him, he would not, if a wish could do it, save them from immediate destruction;—from becoming at this moment, to the world, as a thing that had never been.

[1815]

A GUIDE THROUGH THE DISTRICT OF THE LAKES

Wordsworth's Guide was first published anonymously in 1810 as the introductory text to Select Views in Cumberland, Westmoreland, and Lancashire, a set of engravings by Joseph Wilkinson. It appeared subsequently in 1820 as a part of the River Duddon volume of Wordsworth's poetry, and in independent editions of 1822, 1823, and 1835, undergoing considerable revision and expansion along the way. I follow the 1835 edition, omitting the introductory "Directions and Information for the Tourist" and the concluding chapter "Miscellaneous Observations."

Guide to the Lakes has obvious connections with the large body of eighteenth-century picturesque travel literature, but is distinctly Wordsworthian in its purpose and procedure. Previous accounts, such as William Gilpin's Observations of 1786, had largely been directed to the eye of the reader and had offered pictures of the surfaces of Westmorland and Cumberland mountains, valleys, and lakes. In the introductory "Directions and Information," Wordsworth announced his different emphasis: "In preparing this Manual, it was the author's principal wish to furnish a Guide or Companion for the Minds of Persons of Taste, and feeling for landscape. . ." Accordingly, he sought to penetrate beneath the surface appearances to those operations of nature and habits of human society lived in cooperation with nature which produced the visual appearances. If in his various "Prefaces" Wordsworth had sought to "create the taste" by which his works were to be enjoyed, in the Guide he similarly wished to provide the knowledge of and call out reverent dispositions toward, nature and man necessary for the true appreciation of the landscapes of his native District.

---

44 From the then unpublished *Prelude*, VI, 448–50.

45 *Excursion*, I, 79.

The structure of the Guide, *in its movement from nature's operations (Section First) to man's cooperation with nature (Section Second), parallels the movement of* The Prelude *and many of Wordsworth's most distinctive lyrics. For further discussion of the background and argument of the* Guide, *see my essay "Wordsworth's* Guide to the Lakes *and the Picturesque Tradition,"* Modern Philology, *LXI (1964), 288–97.*

F R O M

A

GUIDE

THROUGH THE

DISTRICT OF THE LAKES

IN THE

NORTH OF ENGLAND,

WITH A

DESCRIPTION OF THE SCENERY,

&c.

SECTION FIRST

VIEW OF THE COUNTRY AS FORMED BY NATURE

At Lucerne in Switzerland, is shewn a Model of the Alpine country which encompasses the Lake of the four Cantons. The Spectator ascends a little platform, and sees mountains, lakes, glaciers, rivers, woods, waterfalls, and vallies, with their cottages, and every other object contained in them, lying at his feet; all things being represented in their appropriate colours. It may be easily conceived that this exhibition affords an exquisite delight to the imagination, tempting it to wander at will from valley to valley, from mountain to mountain, through the deepest recesses of the Alps. But it supplies also a more substantial pleasure: for the sublime and beautiful region, with all its hidden treasures, and their bearings and relations to each other, is thereby comprehended and understood at once.

Something of this kind, without touching upon minute details and individualities which would only confuse and embarrass, will here be attempted, in respect to the Lakes in the north of England, and the vales and mountains enclosing and surrounding them. The delineation, if tolerably executed, will, in some instances, communicate to the traveller, who has already seen the objects, new information; and will assist in giving to his recollections a more orderly arrangement than his own opportunities of observing may have permitted him to make; while it will be still more useful to the future traveller, by directing his attention at once to distinctions in things which, without such previous aid, a length of time only could enable him to discover. It is hoped, also, that this Essay may become generally serviceable, by leading to habits of more exact and considerate observation than, as far as the writer knows, have hitherto been applied to local scenery.

To begin, then, with the main outlines of the country;—I know not how to give the reader a distinct image of these more readily, than by requesting him to place himself with me, in imagination, upon some given point; let it be the top of either of the mountains, Great Gavel, or Scawfell; or, rather, let us suppose our station to be a cloud hanging midway between those two mountains, at not more than half a mile's distance from the summit of each, and not many yards above their highest elevation; we shall then see stretched at our feet a number of vallies, not fewer than eight, diverging from the point, on which we are supposed to stand, like spokes from the nave of a wheel. First, we note, lying to the south-east, the vale of Langdale,* which will conduct the eye to the long lake of Winandermere, stretched nearly to the sea; or rather to the sands of the vast bay of Morcamb, serving here for the rim of this imaginary wheel;—let us trace it in a direction from the south-east towards the south, and we shall next fix our eyes upon the vale of Coniston, running up likewise from the sea, but not (as all the other vallies do) to the nave of the wheel, and therefore it may be not inaptly represented as a broken spoke sticking in the rim. Looking forth again, with an inclination towards the west, we see immediately at our feet the vale of Duddon, in which is no lake, but a copious stream winding among fields, rocks, and mountains, and terminating its course in the sands of Duddon. The fourth vale, next to be observed, viz. that of the Esk, is of the same general character as the last, yet beautifully discriminated from it by peculiar features. Its stream passes under the woody steep upon which stands Muncaster Castle, the ancient seat of the Penningtons, and after forming a short and narrow æstuary enters the sea below the small town of Ravenglass. Next, almost due west, look down into, and along the deep valley of Wastdale, with its little chapel and half a dozen neat dwellings scattered upon a plain of meadow and corn-ground intersected with stone walls apparently innumerable, like a large piece of lawless patchwork, or an array of mathematical figures, such as in the ancient schools of geometry might have been sportively and fantastically traced out upon sand. Beyond this little fertile plain lies, within a bed of steep

* Anciently spelt Langden, and so called by the old inhabitants to this day—*dean*, from which the latter part of the word is derived, being in many parts of England a name for a valley.

mountains, the long, narrow, stern, and desolate lake of Wastdale; and, beyond this, a dusky tract of level ground conducts the eye to the Irish Sea. The stream that issues from Wast-water is named the Irt, and falls into the æstuary of the river Esk. Next comes in view Ennerdale, with its lake of bold and somewhat savage shores. Its stream, the Ehen or Enna, flowing through a soft and fertile country, passes the town of Egremont, and the ruins of the castle,—then, seeming, like the other rivers, to break through the barrier of sand thrown up by the winds on this tempestuous coast, enters the Irish Sea. The vale of Buttermere, with the lake and village of that name, and Crummock-water, beyond, next present themselves. We will follow the main stream, the Coker, through the fertile and beautiful vale of Lorton, till it is lost in the Derwent, below the noble ruins of Cockermouth Castle. Lastly, Borrowdale, of which the vale of Keswick is only a continuation, stretching due north, brings us to a point nearly opposite to the vale of Winandermere with which we began. From this it will appear, that the image of a wheel, thus far exact, is little more than one half complete; but the deficiency on the eastern side may be supplied by the vales of Wytheburn, Ulswater, Hawswater, and the vale of Grasmere and Rydal; none of these, however, run up to the central point between Great Gavel and Scawfell. From this, hitherto our central point, take a flight of not more than four or five miles eastward to the ridge of Helvellyn, and you will look down upon Wytheburn and St. John's Vale, which are a branch of the vale of Keswick; upon Ulswater, stretching due east:—and not far beyond to the southeast (though from this point not visible) lie the vale and lake of Hawswater; and lastly, the vale of Grasmere, Rydal, and Ambleside, brings you back to Winandermere, thus completing, though on the eastern side in a somewhat irregular manner, the representative figure of the wheel.

Such, concisely given, is the general topographical view of the country of the Lakes in the north of England; and it may be observed, that, from the circumference to the centre, that is, from the sea or plain country to the mountain stations specified, there is—in the several ridges that enclose these vales, and divide them from each other, I mean in the forms and surfaces, first of the swelling grounds, next of the hills and rocks, and lastly of the mountains—an ascent of almost regular gradation, from elegance and richness, to their highest point of grandeur and sublimity. It follows therefore from this, first, that these rocks, hills, and mountains, must present themselves to view in stages rising above each other, the mountains clustering together towards the central point; and next, that an observer familiar with the several vales, must, from

their various position in relation to the sun, have had before his eyes every possible embellishment of beauty, dignity, and splendour, which light and shadow can bestow upon objects so diversified. For example, in the vale of Winandermere, if the spectator looks for gentle and lovely scenes, his eye is turned towards the south; if for the grand, towards the north: in the vale of Keswick, which (as hath been said) lies almost due north of this, it is directly the reverse. Hence, when the sun is setting in summer far to the north-west, it is seen, by the spectator from the shores or breast of Winandermere, resting among the summits of the loftiest mountains, some of which will perhaps be half or wholly hidden by clouds, or by the blaze of light which the orb diffuses around it; and the surface of the lake will reflect before the eye correspondent colours through every variety of beauty, and through all degrees of splendour. In the vale of Keswick, at the same period, the sun sets over the humbler regions of the landscape, and showers down upon *them* the radiance which at once veils and glorifies,—sending forth, meanwhile, broad streams of rosy, crimson, purple, or golden light, towards the grand mountains in the south and south-east, which, thus illuminated, with all their projections and cavities, and with an intermixture of solemn shadows, are seen distinctly through a cool and clear atmosphere. Of course, there is as marked a difference between the *noontide* appearance of these two opposite vales. The bedimming haze that overspreads the south, and the clear atmosphere and determined shadows of the clouds in the north, at the same time of the day, are each seen in these several vales, with a contrast as striking. The reader will easily conceive in what degree the intermediate vales partake of a kindred variety.

I do not indeed know any tract of country in which, within so narrow a compass, may be found an equal variety in the influences of light and shadow upon the sublime or beautiful features of landscape; and it is owing to the combined circumstances to which the reader's attention has been directed. From a point between Great Gavel and Scawfell, a shepherd would not require more than an hour to descend into any one of eight of the principal vales by which he would be surrounded; and all the others lie (with the exception of Hawswater) at but a small distance. Yet, though clustered together, every valley has its distinct and separate character; in some instances, as if they had been formed in studied contrast to each other, and in others with the united pleasing differences and resemblances of a sisterly rivalship. This concentration of interest gives to the country a decided superiority over the most attractive districts of Scotland and Wales, especially for the pedestrian traveller. In Scotland and

Wales are found, undoubtedly, individual scenes, which, in their several kinds, cannot be excelled. But, in Scotland, particularly, what long tracts of desolate country intervene! so that the traveller, when he reaches a spot deservedly of great celebrity, would find it difficult to determine how much of his pleasure is owing to excellence inherent in the landscape itself; and how much to an instantaneous recovery from an oppression left upon his spirits by the barrenness and desolation through which he has passed.

But to proceed with our survey;—and, first, of the MOUNTAINS. Their *forms* are endlessly diversified, sweeping easily or boldly in simple majesty, abrupt and precipitous, or soft and elegant. In magnitude and grandeur they are individually inferior to the most celebrated of those in some other parts of this island; but, in the combinations which they make, towering above each other, or lifting themselves in ridges like the waves of a tumultuous sea, and in the beauty and variety of their surfaces and colours, they are surpassed by none.

The general *surface* of the mountains is turf, rendered rich and green by the moisture of the climate. Sometimes the turf, as in the neighbourhood of Newlands, is little broken, the whole covering being soft and downy pasturage. In other places rocks predominate; the soil is laid bare by torrents and burstings of water from the sides of the mountains in heavy rains; and not unfrequently their perpendicular sides are seamed by ravines (forced also by rains and torrents) which, meeting in angular points, entrench and scar the surface with numerous figures like the letters W and Y.

In the ridge that divides Eskdale from Wastdale, granite is found; but the MOUNTAINS are for the most part composed of the stone by mineralogists termed schist, which, as you approach the plain country, gives place to lime-stone and free-stone; but schist being the substance of the mountains, the predominant *colour* of their *rocky* parts is bluish, or hoary grey—the general tint of the lichens with which the bare stone is encrusted. With this blue or grey colour is frequently intermixed a red tinge, proceeding from the iron that interveins the stone, and impregnates the soil. The iron is the principle of decomposition in these rocks; and hence, when they become pulverized, the elementary particles crumbling down, overspread in many places the steep and almost precipitous sides of the mountains with an intermixture of colours, like the compound hues of a dove's neck. When in the heat of advancing summer, the fresh green tint of the herbage has somewhat faded, it is again revived by the appearance of the fern profusely spread over the same ground: and, upon this plant, more than upon any thing else, do the

changes which the seasons make in the colouring of the mountains depend. About the first week in October, the rich green, which prevailed through the whole summer, is usually passed away. The brilliant and various colours of the fern are then in harmony with the autumnal woods; bright yellow or lemon colour, at the base of the mountains, melting gradually, through orange, to a dark russet brown towards the summits, where the plant, being more exposed to the weather, is in a more advanced state of decay. Neither heath nor furze are *generally* found upon the *sides* of these mountains, though in many places they are adorned by those plants, so beautiful when in flower. We may add, that the mountains are of height sufficient to have the surface towards the summit softened by distance, and to imbibe the finest aërial hues. In common also with other mountains, their apparent forms and colours are perpetually changed by the clouds and vapours which float round them: the effect indeed of mist or haze, in a country of this character, is like that of magic. I have seen six or seven ridges rising above each other, all created in a moment by the vapours upon the side of a mountain, which, in its ordinary appearance, shewed not a projecting point to furnish even a hint for such an operation.

I will take this opportunity of observing, that they who have studied the appearances of nature feel that the superiority, in point of visual interest, of mountainous over other countries—is more strikingly displayed in winter than in summer. This, as must be obvious, is partly owing to the *forms* of the mountains, which, of course, are not affected by the seasons; but also, in no small degree, to the greater variety that exists in their winter than their summer *colouring*. This variety is such, and so harmoniously preserved, that it leaves little cause of regret when the splendour of autumn is passed away. The oak-coppices, upon the sides of the mountains, retain russet leaves; the birch stands conspicuous with its silver stem and puce-coloured twigs; the hollies, with green leaves and scarlet berries, have come forth to view from among the deciduous trees, whose summer foliage had concealed them: the ivy is now plentifully apparent upon the stems and boughs of the trees, and upon the steep rocks. In place of the deep summer-green of the herbage and fern, many rich colours play into each other over the surface of the mountains; turf (the tints of which are interchangeably tawny-green, olive, and brown,) beds of withered fern, and grey rocks, being harmoniously blended together. The mosses and lichens are never so fresh and flourishing as in winter, if it be not a season of frost; and their minute beauties prodigally adorn the foreground. Wherever we turn, we find these productions of nature, to which winter is rather favourable than unkindly, scattered over the walls, banks of earth, rocks, and stones, and upon the trunks of trees, with the inter-mixture of several species of small fern, now green and fresh; and, to the observing passenger, their forms and colours are a source of inexhaustible admiration. Add to this the hoar-frost and snow, with all the varieties they create, and which volumes would not be sufficient to describe. I will content myself with one instance of the colouring produced by snow, which may not be uninteresting to painters. It is extracted from the memorandum-book of a friend;[1] and for its accuracy I can speak, having been an eye-witness of the appear-ance. "I observed," says he, "the beautiful effect of the drifted snow upon the mountains, and the perfect *tone* of colour. From the top of the mountains downwards a rich olive was produced by the powdery snow and the grass, which olive was warmed with a little brown, and in this way harmoniously combined, by insensible gradations, with the white. The drifting took away the monotony of snow; and the whole vale of Grasmere, seen from the terrace walk in Easedale, was as varied, perhaps more so, than even in the pomp of autumn. In the distance was Loughrigg-Fell, the basin-wall of the lake: this, from the summit downward, was a rich orange-olive; then the lake of a bright olive-green, nearly the same tint as the snow-powdered mountain tops and high slopes in Easedale; and lastly, the church, with its firs, forming the centre of the view. Next to the church came nine distinguishable hills, six of them with woody sides turned towards us, all of them oak-copses with their bright red leaves and snow-powdered twigs; these hills—so variously situated in relation to each other, and to the view in general, so variously powdered, some only enough to give the herbage a rich brown tint, one intensely white and lighting up all the others—were yet so placed, as in the most inobtrusive manner to harmonise by contrast with a perfect naked, snowless bleak summit in the far distance."

Having spoken of the forms, surface, and colour of the mountains, let us descend into the Vales. Though these have been represented under the general image of the spokes of a wheel, they are, for the most part, winding; the windings of many being abrupt and intricate. And, it may be observed, that, in one cir-cumstance, the general shape of them all has been determined by that primitive conformation through which so many became receptacles of lakes. For they are not formed, as are most of the celebrated Welsh vallies, by an approximation of the sloping bases of the opposite mountains towards each other, leaving

little more between than a channel for the passage of a hasty river; but the bottom of these vallies is mostly a spacious and gently declining area, apparently level as the floor of a temple, or the surface of a lake, and broken in many cases, by rocks and hills, which rise up like islands from the plain. In such of the vallies as make many windings, these level areas open upon the traveller in succession, divided from each other some-times by a mutual approximation of the hills, leaving only passage for a river, sometimes by correspondent windings, without such approximation; and some-times by a bold advance of one mountain towards that which is opposite it. It may here be observed with pro-priety that the several rocks and hills, which have been described as rising up like islands from the level area of the vale, have regulated the choice of the inhabi-tants in the situation of their dwellings. Where none of these are found, and the inclination of the ground is not sufficiently rapid easily to carry off the waters, (as in the higher part of Langdale, for instance,) the houses are not sprinkled over the middle of the vales, but confined to their sides, being placed merely so far up the mountain as to be protected from the floods. But where these rocks and hills have been scattered over the plain of the vale, (as in Grasmere, Donner-dale, Eskdale, &c.) the beauty which they give to the scene is much heightened by a single cottage, or cluster of cottages, that will be almost always found under them, or upon their sides; dryness and shelter having tempted the Dalesmen to fix their habitations there.

I shall now speak of the Lakes of this country. The form of the lake is most perfect when, like Derwent-water, and some of the smaller lakes, it least resembles that of a river;—I mean, when being looked at from any given point where the whole may be seen at once, the width of it bears such proportion to the length, that, however the outline may be diversified by far-receding bays, it never assumes the shape of a river, and is con-templated with that placid and quiet feeling which be-longs peculiarly to the lake—as a body of still water under the influence of no current; reflecting therefore the clouds, the light, and all the imagery of the sky and surrounding hills; expressing also and making visible the changes of the atmosphere, and motions of the lightest breeze, and subject to agitation only from the winds—

———— The visible scene
Would enter unawares into his mind
With all its solemn imagery, its rocks,
Its woods, and that uncertain heaven received
Into the bosom of the *steady* lake![2]

---

[1] An entry by Coleridge, dated January 5, 1804, in his "Note-book 16." See *The Notebooks of Samuel Taylor Coleridge*, ed. Kath-leen Coburn, I [text] (London, 1957), entry 1812.

[2] Wordsworth's "There was a Boy" (1800), ll. 21-25.

It must be noticed, as a favourable characteristic of the lakes of this country, that, though several of the largest, such as Winandermere, Ulswater, Hawswater, do, when the whole length of them is commanded from an elevated point, lose somewhat of the peculiar form of the lake, and assume the resemblance of a magnificent river; yet, as their shape is winding, (particularly that of Ulswater and Hawswater) when the view of the whole is obstructed by those barriers which determine the windings, and the spectator is confined to one reach, the appropriate feeling is revived; and one lake may thus in succession present to the eye the essential characteristic of many. But, though the forms of the large lakes have this advantage, it is nevertheless favourable to the beauty of the country that the largest of them are comparatively small; and that the same vale generally furnishes a succession of lakes, instead of being filled with one. The vales in North Wales, as hath been observed, are not formed for the reception of lakes; those of Switzerland, Scotland, and this part of the North of England, *are* so formed; but, in Switzerland and Scotland, the proportion of diffused water is often too great, as at the lake of Geneva for instance, and in most of the Scotch lakes. No doubt it sounds magnificent and flatters the imagination, to hear at a distance of expanses of water so many leagues in length and miles in width; and such ample room may be delightful to the fresh-water sailor, scudding with a lively breeze amid the rapidly-shifting scenery. But, who ever travelled along the banks of Loch-Lomond, variegated as the lower part is by islands, without feeling that a speedier termination of the long vista of blank water would be acceptable; and without wishing for an interposition of green meadows, trees, and cottages, and a sparkling stream to run by his side? In fact, a notion of grandeur, as connected with magnitude, has seduced persons of taste into a general mistake upon this subject. It is much more desirable, for the purposes of pleasure, that lakes should be numerous, and small or middle-sized, than large, not only for communication by walks and rides, but for variety, and for recurrence of similar appearances. To illustrate this by one instance:—How pleasing is it to have a ready and frequent opportunity of watching, at the outlet of a lake, the stream pushing its way among the rocks in lively contrast with the stillness from which it has escaped; and how amusing to compare its noisy and turbulent motions with the gentle playfulness of the breezes, that may be starting up or wandering here and there over the faintly-rippled surface of the broad water! I may add, as a general remark, that, in lakes of great width, the shores cannot be distinctly seen at the same time, and therefore contribute little to mutual illustration and ornament; and, if the opposite shores are out of sight of each other, like those of the American and Asiatic lakes, then unfortunately the traveller is reminded of a nobler object; he has the blankness of a sea-prospect without the grandeur and accompanying sense of power.

As the comparatively small size of the lakes in the North of England is favourable to the production of variegated landscape, their *boundary-line* also is for the most part gracefully or boldly indented. That uniformity which prevails in the primitive frame of the lower grounds among all chains or clusters of mountains where large bodies of still water are bedded, is broken by the *secondary* agents of nature, ever at work to supply the deficiencies of the mould in which things were originally cast. Using the word *deficiencies*, I do not speak with reference to those stronger emotions which a region of mountains is peculiarly fitted to excite. The bases of those huge barriers may run for a long space in straight lines, and these parallel to each other; the opposite sides of a profound vale may ascend as exact counterparts, or in mutual reflection, like the billows of a troubled sea; and the impression be, from its very simplicity, more awful and sublime. Sublimity is the result of Nature's first great dealings with the superficies of the earth; but the general tendency of her subsequent operations is towards the production of beauty; by a multiplicity of symmetrical parts uniting in a consistent whole. This is every where exemplified along the margins of these lakes. Masses of rock, that have been precipitated from the heights into the area of waters, lie in some places like stranded ships; or have acquired the compact structure of jutting piers; or project in little peninsulas crested with native wood. The smallest rivulet—one whose silent influx is scarcely noticeable in a season of dry weather—so faint is the dimple made by it on the surface of the smooth lake—will be found to have been not useless in shaping, by its deposits of gravel and soil in time of flood, a curve that would not otherwise have existed. But the more powerful brooks, encroaching upon the level of the lake, have, in course of time, given birth to ample promontories of sweeping outline that contrasts boldly with the longitudinal base of the steeps on the opposite shore; while their flat or gently-sloping surfaces never fail to introduce, into the midst of desolation and barrenness, the elements of fertility, even where the habitations of men may not have been raised. These alluvial promontories, however, threaten, in some places, to bisect the waters which they have long adorned; and, in course of ages, they will cause some of the lakes to dwindle into numerous and insignificant pools; which, in their turn, will finally be filled up. But, checking these intrusive calculations, let us rather be content with appearances as they are, and pursue in imagination the meandering shores, whether rugged steeps, admitting of no cultivation, descend into the water; or gently-sloping lawns and woods, or flat and fertile meadows stretch between the margin of the lake and the mountains. Among minuter recommendations will be noticed, especially along bays exposed to the setting-in of strong-winds, the curved rim of fine blue gravel, thrown up in course of time by the waves, half of it perhaps gleaming from under the water, and the corresponding half of a lighter hue; and in other parts bordering the lake, groves, if I may so call them, of reeds and bulrushes; or plots of water-lilies lifting up their large target-shaped leaves to the breeze, while the white flower is heaving upon the wave.

*   *   *   *   *

Having spoken of Lakes I must not omit to mention, as a kindred feature of this country, those bodies of still water called TARNS. In the economy of nature these are useful, as auxiliars to Lakes; for if the whole quantity of water which falls upon the mountains in time of storm were poured down upon the plains without intervention, in some quarters, of such receptacles, the habitable grounds would be much more subject than they are to inundation. But, as some of the collateral brooks spend their fury, finding a free course toward and also down the channel of the main stream of the vale before those that have to pass through the higher tarns and lakes have filled their several basins, a gradual distribution is effected; and the waters thus reserved, instead of uniting, to spread ravage and deformity, with those which meet with no such detention, contribute to support, for a length of time, the vigour of many streams without a fresh fall of rain. Tarns are found in some of the vales, and are numerous upon the mountains. A Tarn, in a *Vale*, implies, for the most part, that the bed of the vale is not happily formed; that the water of the brooks can neither wholly escape, nor diffuse itself over a large area. Accordingly, in such situations, Tarns are often surrounded by an unsightly tract of boggy ground; but this is not always the case, and in the cultivated parts of the country, when the shores of the Tarn are determined, it differs only from the Lake in being smaller, and in belonging mostly to a smaller valley, or circular recess. Of this class of miniature lakes, Loughrigg Tarn, near Grasmere, is the most beautiful example. It has a margin of green firm meadows, of rocks, and rocky woods, a few reeds here, a little company of water-lilies there, with beds of gravel or stone beyond; a tiny stream issuing neither briskly nor sluggishly out of it; but its feeding rills, from the shortness of their course, so small as to be scarcely visible. Five or six cottages are reflected in its peaceful bosom; rocky and barren steeps rise up above the hanging en-

closures; and the solemn pikes of Langdale overlook, from a distance, the low cultivated ridge of land that forms the northern boundary of this small, quiet, and fertile domain. The *mountain* Tarns can only be recommended to the notice of the inquisitive traveller who has time to spare. They are difficult of access and naked; yet some of them are, in their permanent forms, very grand; and there are accidents of things which would make the meanest of them interesting. At all events, one of these pools is an acceptable sight to the mountain wanderer; not merely as an incident that diversifies the prospect, but as forming in his mind a centre or conspicuous point to which objects, otherwise disconnected or insubordinated, may be referred. Some few have a varied outline, with bold heath-clad promontories; and, as they mostly lie at the foot of a steep precipice, the water, where the sun is not shining upon it, appears black and sullen; and, round the margin, huge stones and masses of rock are scattered; some defying conjecture as to the means by which they came thither; and others obviously fallen from on high—the contribution of ages! A not unpleasing sadness is induced by this perplexity, and these images of decay; while the prospect of a body of pure water unattended with groves and other cheerful rural images by which fresh water is usually accompanied, and unable to give furtherance to the meagre vegetation around it—excites a sense of some repulsive power strongly put forth, and thus deepens the melancholy natural to such scenes. Nor is the feeling of solitude often more forcibly or more solemnly impressed than by the side of one of these mountain pools: though desolate and forbidding, it seems a distinct place to repair to; yet where the visitants must be rare, and there can be no disturbance. Water-fowl flock hither; and the lonely Angler may here be seen; but the imagination, not content with this scanty allowance of society, is tempted to attribute a voluntary power to every change which takes place in such a spot, whether it be the breeze that wanders over the surface of the water, or the splendid lights of evening resting upon it in the midst of awful precipices.

"There, sometimes does a leaping fish
        Send through the tarn a lonely cheer;
        The crags repeat the raven's croak
        In symphony austere:
        Thither the rainbow comes, the cloud,
        And mists that spread the flying shroud,
        And sunbeams, and the sounding blast."[3]

It will be observed that this country is bounded on the south and east by the sea, which combines beauti-

---

3 Wordsworth's "Fidelity" (1807), ll. 25–31.

fully, from many elevated points, with the inland scenery; and, from the bay of Morcamb, the sloping shores and back-ground of distant mountains are seen, composing pictures equally distinguished for amenity and grandeur. But the æsturies on this coast are in a great measure bare at low water;* and there is no instance of the sea running far up among the mountains, and mingling with the Lakes, which are such in the strict and usual sense of the word, being of fresh water. Nor have the streams, from the shortness of their course, time to acquire that body of water necessary to confer upon them much majesty. In fact, the most considerable, while they continue in the mountain and lake-country, are rather large brooks than rivers. The water is perfectly pellucid, through which in many places are seen, to a great depth, their beds of rock, or of blue gravel, which give to the water itself an exquisitely cerulean colour: this is particularly striking in the rivers Derwent and Duddon, which may be compared, such and so various are their beauties, to any two rivers of equal length of course in any country. The number of the torrents and smaller brooks is infinite, with their water-falls and water-breaks; and they need not here be described. I will only observe that, as many, even of the smallest rills, have either found, or made for themselves, recesses in the sides of the mountains or in the vales, they have tempted the primitive inhabitants to settle near them for shelter; and hence, cottages so placed, by seeming to withdraw from the eye, are the more endeared to the feelings.

The WOODS consist chiefly of oak, ash, and birch, and here and there Wych-elm, with underwood of hazle, the white and black thorn, and hollies; in moist places alders and willows abound; and yews among the rocks. Formerly the whole country must have been covered with wood to a great height up the mountains; where native Scotch first† must have grown in great profusion, as they do in the northern part of Scotland to this day. But not one of these old inhabitants has existed, perhaps, for some hundreds of years; the beautiful traces, however, of the universal sylvan‡ ap-

pearance the country formerly had, yet survive in the native coppice-woods that have been protected by inclosures, and also in the forest-trees and hollies, which, though disappearing fast, are yet scattered both over the inclosed and uninclosed parts of the mountains. The same is expressed by the beauty and intricacy with which the fields and coppice-woods are often intermingled: the plough of the first settlers having followed naturally the veins of richer, dryer, or less stony soil; and thus it has shaped out an intermixture of wood and lawn, with a grace and wildness which it would have been impossible for the hand of studied art to produce. Other trees have been introduced within these last fifty years, such as beeches, larches, limes, &c. and plantations of firs, seldom with advantage, and often with great injury to the appearance of the country; but the sycamore (which I believe was brought into this island from Germany, not more than two hundred years ago) has long been the favourite of the cottagers; and, with the fir, has been chosen to screen their dwellings: and is sometimes found in the fields whither the winds or the waters may have carried its seeds.

*   *   *   *   *

It may now be proper to say a few words respecting climate, and "skiey influences," [4] in which this region, as far as the character of its landscapes is affected by them, may, upon the whole, be considered fortunate. The country is, indeed, subject to much bad weather, and it has been ascertained that twice as much rain falls here as in many parts of the island; but the number of black drizzling days, that blot out the face of things, is by no means *proportionally* great. Nor is a continuance of thick, flagging, damp air so common as in the West of England and Ireland. The rain here comes down heartily, and is frequently succeeded by clear, bright weather, when every brook is vocal, and every torrent sonorous; brooks and torrents, which are never muddy, even in the heaviest floods, except, after a drought, they happen to be defiled for a short time by waters that have swept along dusty roads, or have broken out into ploughed fields. Days of unsettled weather, with partial showers, are very frequent; but the showers, darkening, or brightening, as they fly from hill to hill, are not less grateful to the eye than finely interwoven passages of gay and sad music are touching to the ear. Vapours exhaling from the lakes and meadows after sun-rise, in a hot season, or, in moist weather, brooding upon the heights, or descending towards the vallies with inaudible motion, give a visionary character to everything around them; and are in themselves so beautiful, as to dispose us to enter into the feelings of those simple

---

* In fact there is not an instance of a harbour on the Cumberland side of the Solway frith that is not dry at low water; that of Ravenglass, at the mouth of the Esk, as a natural harbour is much the best. The Sea appears to have been retiring slowly for ages from this coast. From Whitehaven to St. Bees extends a track of level ground, about five miles in length, which formerly must have been under salt water, so as to have made an island of the high ground that stretches between it and the Sea.

† This species of fir is in character much superior to the American which has usurped its place. Where the fir is planted for ornament, let it be by all means of the aboriginal species, which can only be procured from the Scotch nurseries.

‡ A squirrel (so I have heard the old people of Wytheburn say) might have gone from their chapel to Keswick without alighting on the ground.

[4] *Measure for Measure*, III, i, 9.

nations (such as the Laplanders of this day) by whom they are taken for guardian deities of the mountains; or to sympathise with others who have fancied these delicate apparitions to be the spirits of their departed ancestors. Akin to these are fleecy clouds resting upon the hill-tops; they are not easily managed in picture, with their accompaniments of blue sky; but how glorious are they in nature! how pregnant with imagination for the poet! and the height of the Cumbrian mountains is sufficient to exhibit daily and hourly instances of those mysterious attachments. Such clouds, cleaving to their stations, or lifting up suddenly their glittering heads from behind rocky barriers, or hurrying out of sight with speed of the sharpest edge—will often tempt an inhabitant to congratulate himself on belonging to a country of mists and clouds and storms, and make him think of the blank sky of Egypt, and of the cerulean vacancy of Italy, as an unanimated and even a sad spectacle. The atmosphere, however, as in every country subject to much rain, is frequently unfavourable to landscape, especially when keen winds succeed the rain which are apt to produce coldness, spottiness, and an unmeaning or repulsive detail in the distance;—a sunless frost, under a canopy of leaden and shapeless clouds, is, as far as it allows things to be seen, equally disagreeable.

It has been said that in human life there are moments worth ages. In a more subdued tone of sympathy may we affirm, that in the climate of England there are, for the lover of nature, days which are worth whole months,—I might say—even years. One of these favoured days sometimes occurs in spring-time, when that soft air is breathing over the blossoms and new-born verdure, which inspired Buchanan with his beautiful Ode to the first of May;[5] the air, which, in the luxuriance of his fancy, he likens to that of the golden age,—to that which gives motion to the funereal cypresses on the banks of Lethe;—to the air which is to salute beatified spirits when expiatory fires shall have consumed the earth with all her habitations. But it is in autumn that days of such affecting influence most frequently intervene;—the atmosphere seems refined, and the sky rendered more crystalline, as the vivifying heat of the year abates; the lights and shadows are more delicate; the colouring is richer and more finely harmonized; and, in this season of stillness, the ear being unoccupied, or only gently excited, the sense of vision becomes more susceptible of its appropriate enjoyments. A resident in a country like this which we are treating of, will agree with me, that the presence of a lake is indispensable to exhibit in perfection the beauty of one of these days; and he must have experienced, while looking on the unruffled waters, that the imagination, by their aid, is carried into recesses of feeling otherwise impenetrable. The reason of this is, that the heavens are not only brought down into the bosom of the earth, but that the earth is mainly looked at, and thought of, through the medium of a purer element. The happiest time is when the equinoxial gales are departed; but their fury may probably be called to mind by the sight of a few shattered boughs, whose leaves do not differ in colour from the faded foliage of the stately oaks from which these relics of the storm depend: all else speaks of tranquillity;—not a breath of air, no restlessness of insects, and not a moving object perceptible—except the clouds gliding in the depths of the lake, or the traveller passing along, an inverted image, whose motion seems governed by the quiet of a time, to which its archetype, the living person, is, perhaps, insensible:—or it may happen, that the figure of one of the larger birds, a raven or a heron, is crossing silently among the reflected clouds, while the voice of the real bird, from the element aloft, gently awakens in the spectator the recollection of appetites and instincts, pursuits and occupations, that deform and agitate the world,—yet have no power to prevent nature from putting on an aspect capable of satisfying the most intense cravings for the tranquil, the lovely, and the perfect, to which man, the noblest of her creatures, is subject.

Thus far, of climate, as influencing the feelings through its effect on the objects of sense. We may add, that whatever has been said upon the advantages derived to these scenes from a changeable atmosphere, would apply, perhaps still more forcibly, to their appearance under the varied solemnities of night. Milton, it will be remembered, has given a *clouded* moon to Paradise itself.[6] In the night-season also, the narrowness of the vales, and comparative smallness of the lakes, are especially adapted to bring surrounding objects home to the eye and to the heart. The stars, taking their stations above the hill-tops, are contemplated from a spot like the Abyssinian recess of Rasselas,[7] with much more touching interest than they are likely to excite when looked at from an open country with ordinary undulations: and it must be obvious, that it is the *bays* only of large lakes that can present such contrasts of light and shadow as those of smaller dimensions display from every quarter. A deep contracted valley, with diffused waters, such a valley and plains level and wide as those of Chaldea, are the two ex-

---

5 See "Essay, Supplementary," footnote 37, p. 86. Wordsworth refers to Buchanan's poem "Calendae Majae."

6 See *Paradise Lost*, IV, 606–607.
7 See Chapter I of Johnson's *The History of Rasselas, Prince of Abyssinia* (1759).

tremes in which the beauty of the heavens and their connexion with the earth are most sensibly felt. Nor do the advantages I have been speaking of imply here an exclusion of the aerial effects of distance. These are insured by the height of the mountains, and are found, even in the narrowest vales, where they lengthen in perspective, or act (if the expression may be used) as telescopes for the open country.

The subject would bear to be enlarged upon: but I will conclude this section with a night-scene suggested by the Vale of Keswick. The Fragment is well known; but it gratifies me to insert it, as the Writer was one of the first who led the way to a worthy admiration of this country.

"Now sunk the sun, now twilight sunk, and night
Rode in her zenith; not a passing breeze
Sigh'd to the grove, which in the midnight air
Stood motionless, and in the peaceful floods
Inverted hung: for now the billows slept
Along the shore, nor heav'd the deep; but spread
A shining mirror to the moon's pale orb,
Which, dim and waning, o'er the shadowy cliffs,
The solemn woods, and spiry mountain tops,
Her glimmering faintness threw: now every eye,
Oppress'd with toil, was drown'd in deep repose,
Save that the unseen Shepherd in his watch,
Propp'd on his crook, stood listening by the fold,
And gaz'd the starry vault, and pendant moon;
Nor voice, nor sound, broke on the deep serene;
But the soft murmur of swift-gushing rills,
Forth issuing from the mountain's distant steep,
(Unheard till now, and now scarce heard) proclaim'd
All things at rest, and imag'd the still voice
Of quiet, whispering in the ear of night." *

* Dr. Brown, the author of this fragment, was from his infancy brought up in Cumberland, and should have remembered that the practice of folding sheep by night is unknown among these mountains, and that the image of the Shepherd upon the watch is out of its place, and belongs only to countries, with a warmer climate, that are subject to ravages from beasts of prey. It is pleasing to notice a dawn of imaginative feeling in these verses. Tickel, a man of no common genius, chose, for the subject of a Poem, Kensington Gardens, in preference to the Banks of the Derwent, within a mile or two of which he was born. But this was in the reign of Queen Anne, or George the first. Progress must have been made in the interval; though the traces of it, except in the works of Thomson and Dyer are not very obvious.[8]

8 Dr. John Brown (1715–1766), born at Rothbury, Northumberland, is best known for his *Estimate of the Manners and Principles of the Times* (1757), which Wordsworth mentions at the beginning of Section Third. His "Rhapsody, Written at the Lakes in Westmorland" was first published in 1776 and reprinted in the various editions of Thomas West's *Guide to the Lakes* (see Section Second, footnote 1). Thomas Tickell (1686–1740), born at Bridekirk, Cumberland, was a minor poet, friend of Addison, and the editor of his works. *Kensington Garden* was published in 1722.

SECTION SECOND

ASPECT OF THE COUNTRY, AS AFFECTED BY ITS INHABITANTS

HITHERTO I have chiefly spoken of the features by which nature has discriminated this country from others. I will now describe, in general terms, in what manner it is indebted to the hand of man. What I have to notice on this subject will emanate most easily and perspicuously from a description of the ancient and present inhabitants, their occupations, their condition of life, the distribution of landed property among them, and the tenure by which it is holden.

The reader will suffer me here to recall to his mind the shapes of the vallies, and their position with respect to each other, and the forms and substance of the intervening mountains. He will people the vallies with lakes and rivers: the coves and sides of the mountains with pools and torrents; and will bound half of the circle which we have contemplated by the sands of the sea, or by the sea itself. He will conceive that, from the point upon which he stood, he looks down upon this scene before the country had been penetrated by any inhabitants:—to vary his sensations, and to break in upon their stillness, he will form to himself an image of the tides visiting and revisiting the friths, the main sea dashing against the bolder shore, the rivers pursuing their course to be lost in the mighty mass of waters. He may see or hear in fancy the winds sweeping over the lakes, or piping with a loud voice among the mountain peaks; and, lastly, may think of the primeval woods shedding and renewing their leaves with no human eye to notice, or human heart to regret or welcome the change. "When the first settlers entered this region (says an animated writer)[1] they found it overspread with wood; forest trees, the fir, the oak, the ash, and the birch had skirted the fells, tufted the hills, and shaded the vallies, through centuries of silent solitude; the birds and beasts of prey reigned over the meeker species; and the *bellum inter omnia* maintained the balance of nature in the empire of beasts."

Such was the state and appearance of this region when the aboriginal colonists of the Celtic tribes were first driven or drawn towards it, and became joint tenants with the wolf, the boar, the wild bull, the red deer, and the leigh, a gigantic species of deer which has been long extinct; while the inaccessible crags were occupied by the falcon, the raven, and the eagle. The inner parts were too secluded, and of too little value, to

1 Thomas West (1720–1779), English Jesuit and antiquarian of the Lake District, was the author of a very popular *Guide to the Lakes* (1778) and *Antiquities of Furness* (1774), from which Wordsworth here quotes.

participate much of the benefit of Roman manners; and though these conquerors encouraged the Britons to the improvement of their lands in the plain country of Furness and Cumberland, they seem to have had little connexion with the mountains, except for military purposes, or in subservience to the profit they drew from the mines.

When the Romans retired from Great Britain, it is well known that these mountain-fastnesses furnished a protection to some unsubdued Britons, long after the more accessible and more fertile districts had been seized by the Saxon or Danish invader. A few, though distinct, traces of Roman forts or camps, as at Ambleside, and upon Dunmallet, and a few circles of rude stones attributed to the Druids,* are the only vestiges

* It is not improbable that these circles were once numerous, and that many of them may yet endure in a perfect state, under no very deep covering of soil. A friend of the Author, while making a trench in a level piece of ground, not far from the banks of the Emont, but in no connection with that river, met with some stones which seemed to him formally arranged; this excited his curiosity, and proceeding, he uncovered a perfect circle of stones, from two to three or four feet high, with a *sanctum sanctorum*— the whole a complete place of Druidical worship of small dimensions, having the same sort of relation to Stonehenge, Long Meg and her Daughters near the river Eden, and Karl Lofts near Shap (if this last be not Danish), that a rural chapel bears to a stately church, or to one of our noble cathedrals. This interesting little monument having passed, with the field in which it was found, into other hands, has been destroyed. It is much to be regretted, that the striking relic of antiquity at Shap has been in a great measure destroyed also.

The Daughters of Long Meg are placed not in an oblong, as the Stones of Shap, but in a perfect circle, eighty yards in diameter, and seventy-two in number, and from above three yards high, to less than so many feet: a little way out of the circle stands Long Meg herself—a single stone eighteen feet high.

When the Author first saw this monument, he came upon it by surprize, therefore might overrate its importance as an object; but he must say, that though it is not to be compared with Stonehenge, he has not seen any other remains of those dark ages, which can pretend to rival it in singularity and dignity of appearance.

> A weight of awe not easy to be borne
> Fell suddenly upon my spirit, cast
> From the dread bosom of the unknown past,
> When first I saw that sisterhood forlorn;—
> And Her, whose strength and stature seem to scorn
> The power of years—pre-eminent, and placed
> Apart, to overlook the circle vast.
> Speak, Giant-mother! tell it to the Morn,
> While she dispels the cumbrous shades of night;
> Let the Moon hear, emerging from a cloud,
> When, how, and wherefore, rose on British ground
> That wondrous Monument, whose mystic round
> Forth shadows, some have deemed, to mortal sight
> The inviolable God that tames the proud.[2]

———◇◇◇◇◇◇◇◇◇◇◇◇◇◇◇———

[2] "A friend of the Author" refers to Thomas Wilkinson, a beloved Quaker acquaintance of Wordsworth and Coleridge, and

that remain upon the surface of the country, of these ancient occupants; and, as the Saxons and Danes, who succeeded to the possession of the villages and hamlets which had been established by the Britons, seem at first to have confined themselves to the open country,—we may descend at once to times long posterior to the conquest by the Normans, when their feudal polity was regularly established. We may easily conceive that these narrow dales and mountain sides, choaked up as they must have been with wood, lying out of the way of communication with other parts of the Island, and upon the edge of a hostile kingdom, could have little attraction for the high-born and powerful; especially as the more open parts of the country furnished positions for castles and houses of defence, sufficient to repel any of those sudden attacks, which, in the then rude state of military knowledge, could be made upon them. Accordingly, the more retired regions (and to such I am now confining myself) must have been neglected or shunned even by the persons whose baronial or signorial rights extended over them, and left, doubtless, partly as a place of refuge for outlaws and robbers, and partly granted out for the more settled habitation of a few vassals following the employment of shepherds or woodlanders. Hence these lakes and inner vallies are unadorned by any remains of ancient grandeur, castles, or monastic edifices, which are only found upon the skirts of the country, as Furness Abbey, Calder Abbey, the Priory of Lannercost, Gleaston Castle,—long ago a residence of the Flemings,[3]—and the numerous ancient castles of the Cliffords, the Lucys, and the Dacres. On the southern side of these mountains, (especially in that part known by the name of Furness Fells, which is more remote from the borders,) the state of society would necessarily be more settled; though it also was fashioned, not a little, by its neighbourhood to a hostile kingdom. We will, therefore, give a sketch of the economy of the Abbots in the distribution of lands among their tenants, as similar plans were doubtless adopted by other Lords, and as the consequences have affected the face of the country materially to the present day, being, in fact, one of the principal causes which give it such a striking superiority, in beauty and interest, over all other parts of the island.

"When the Abbots of Furness," says an author before cited, "enfranchised their villains, and raised them

———◇◇◇◇◇◇◇◇◇◇◇◇◇◇◇———

landscape gardener in the Lake District. The sonnet here quoted, "The Monument Commonly called Long Meg and her Daughters, near the River Eden," was first published in the 1822 edition of the *Guide*.

[3] The Flemings were an ancient Lake District family. Rydal Mount, Wordsworth's residence after 1813, was the property of Lady Fleming.

to the dignity of customary tenants, the lands, which they had cultivated for their lord, were divided into whole tenements; each of which, besides the customary annual rent, was charged with the obligation of having in readiness a man completely armed for the king's service on the borders, or elsewhere; each of these whole tenements was again subdivided into four equal parts; each villain had one; and the party tenant contributed his share to the support of the man of arms, and of other burdens. These divisions were not properly distinguished; the land remained mixed; each tenant had a share through all the arable and meadow-land, and common of pasture over all the wastes. These sub-tenements were judged sufficient for the support of so many families; and no further division was permitted. These divisions and sub-divisions were convenient at the time for which they were calculated: the land, so parcelled out, was of necessity more attended to, and the industry greater, when more persons were to be supported by the produce of it. The frontier of the kingdom, within which Furness was considered, was in a constant state of attack and defence; more hands, therefore, were necessary to guard the coast, to repel an invasion from Scotland, or make reprisals on the hostile neighbour. The dividing the lands in such manner as has been shown, increased the number of inhabitants, and kept them at home till called for: and, the land being mixed, and the several tenants united in equipping the plough, the absence of the fourth man was no prejudice to the cultivation of his land, which was committed to the care of three.

"While the villains of Low Furness were thus distributed over the land, and employed in agriculture; those of High Furness were charged with the care of flocks and herds, to protect them from the wolves which lurked in the thickets, and in winter to browze them with the tender sprouts of hollies and ash. This custom was not till lately discontinued in High Furness; and holly-trees were carefully preserved for that purpose when all other wood was cleared off; large tracts of common being so covered with these trees, as to have the appearance of a forest of hollies. At the Shepherd's call, the flocks surrounded the holly-bush, and received the croppings at his hand, which they greedily nibbled up, bleating for more. The Abbots of Furness enfranchised these pastoral vassals, and permitted them to enclose *quillets* to their houses, for which they paid encroachment rent."—West's *Antiquities of Furness*.

However desirable, for the purposes of defence, a numerous population might be, it was not possible to make at once the same numerous allotments among the untilled vallies, and upon the sides of the mountains, as had been made in the cultivated plains. The enfran-

chised shepherd, or woodlander, having chosen there his place of residence, builds it of sods, or of the mountain-stone, and, with the permission of his lord, encloses, like Robinson Crusoe, a small croft or two immediately at his door for such animals as he wishes to protect. Others are happy to imitate his example, and avail themselves of the same privileges: and thus a population, mainly of Danish or Norse origin, as the dialect indicates, crept on towards the more secluded parts of the vallies. Chapels, daughters of some distant mother-church, are first erected in the more open and fertile vales, as those of Bowness and Grasmere, offsets of Kendal: which again, after a period, as the settled population increases, become mother-churches to smaller edifices, planted, at length, in almost every dale throughout the country. The enclosures, formed by the tenantry, are for a long time confined to the homesteads; and the arable and meadow land of the vales is possessed in common field; the several portions being marked out by stones, bushes, or trees: which portions, where the custom has survived, to this day are called *dales*, from the word *deylen*, to distribute; but, while the valley was thus lying open, enclosures seem to have taken place upon the sides of the mountains; because the land there was not intermixed, and was of little comparative value; and, therefore, small opposition would be made to its being appropriated by those to whose habitations it was contiguous. Hence the singular appearance which the sides of many of these mountains exhibit, intersected, as they are, almost to the summit, with stone walls. When first erected, these stone fences must have little disfigured the face of the country; as part of the lines would every where be hidden by the quantity of native wood then remaining; and the lines would also be broken (as they still are) by the rocks which interrupt and vary their course. In the meadows, and in those parts of the lower grounds where the soil has not been sufficiently drained, and could not afford a stable foundation, there, when the increasing value of land, and the inconvenience suffered from intermixed plots of ground in common field, had induced each inhabitant to enclose his own, they were compelled to make the fences of alders, willows, and other trees. These, where the native wood had disappeared, have frequently enriched the vallies with a sylvan appearance; while the intricate intermixture of property has given to the fences a graceful irregularity, which, where large properties are prevalent, and large capitals employed in agriculture, is unknown. This sylvan appearance is heightened by the number of ash-trees planted in rows along the quick fences, and along the walls, for the purpose of browzing the cattle at the approach of winter. The branches are lopped off and strewn upon the pastures; and when the cattle have stripped them of the leaves, they are used for repairing the hedges or for fuel.

We have thus seen a numerous body of Dalesmen creeping into possession of their home-steads, their little crofts, their mountain-enclosures; and, finally, the whole vale is visibly divided; except, perhaps, here and there some marshy ground, which, till fully drained, would not repay the trouble of enclosing. But these last partitions do not seem to have been general, till long after the pacification of the Borders, by the union of the two crowns:[4] when the cause, which had first determined the distribution of land into such small parcels, had not only ceased,—but likewise a general improvement had taken place in the country, with a correspondent rise in the value of its produce. From the time of the union, it is certain that this species of feudal population must rapidly have diminished. That it was formerly much more numerous than it is at present, is evident from the multitude of tenements (I do not mean houses, but small divisions of land) which belonged formerly each to a several proprietor, and for which separate fines are paid to the manorial lord at this day. These are often in the proportion of four to one of the present occupants. "Sir Launcelot Threlkeld, who lived in the reign of Henry VII., was wont to say, he had three noble houses, one for pleasure, Crosby, in Westmoreland, where he had a park full of deer; one for profit and warmth, wherein to reside in winter, namely, Yanwith, nigh Penrith; and the third, Threlkeld, (on the edge of the vale of Keswick), well stocked with tenants to go with him to the wars." But, as I have said, from the union of the two crowns, this numerous vassalage (their services not being wanted) would rapidly diminish; various tenements would be united in one possessor; and the aboriginal houses, probably little better than hovels, like the kraels[5] of savages, or the huts of the Highlanders of Scotland, would fall into decay, and the places of many be supplied by substantial and comfortable buildings, a majority of which remain to this day scattered over the vallies, and are often the only dwellings found in them.

From the time of the erection of these houses, till within the lasty sixty years, the state of society, though no doubt slowly and gradually improving, underwent no material change. Corn was grown in these vales (through which no carriage-road had yet been made) sufficient upon each estate to furnish bread for each family, and no more: notwithstanding the union of several tenements, the possessions of each inhabitant

still being small, in the same field was seen an inter-mixture of different crops; and the plough was interrupted by little rocks, mostly overgrown with wood, or by spongy places, which the tillers of the soil had neither leisure nor capital to convert into firm land. The storms and moisture of the climate induced them to sprinkle their upland property with outhouses of native stone, as places of shelter for their sheep, where, in tempestuous weather, food was distributed to them. Every family spun from its own flock the wool with which it was clothed; a weaver was here and there found among them; and the rest of their wants was supplied by the produce of the yarn, which they carded and spun in their own houses, and carried to market, either under their arms, or more frequently on pack-horses, a small train taking their way weekly down the valley or over the mountains to the most commodious town. They had, as I have said, their rural chapel, and of course their minister, in clothing or in manner of life, in no respect differing from themselves, except on the Sabbath-day; this was the sole distinguished individual among them; every thing else, person and possession, exhibited a perfect equality, a community of shepherds and agriculturists, proprietors, for the most part, of the lands which they occupied and cultivated.

While the process above detailed was going on, the native forest must have been every where receding; but trees were planted for the sustenance of the flocks in winter,—such was then the rude state of agriculture; and, for the same cause, it was necessary that care should be taken of some part of the growth of the native woods. Accordingly, in Queen Elizabeth's time, this was so strongly felt, that a petition was made to the Crown, praying, "that the Blomaries in High Furness might be abolished, on account of the quantity of wood which was consumed in them for the use of the mines, to the great detriment of the cattle." But this same cause, about a hundred years after, produced effects directly contrary to those which had been deprecated. The re-establishment, at that period, of furnaces upon a large scale, made it the interest of the people to convert the steeper and more stony of the enclosures, sprinkled over with remains of the native forest, into close woods, which, when cattle and sheep were excluded, rapidly sowed and thickened themselves. The reader's attention has been directed to the cause by which tufts of wood, pasturage, meadow, and arable land, with its various produce, are intricately inter-mingled in the same field; and he will now see, in like manner, how enclosures entirely of wood, and those of cultivated ground, are blended all over the country under a law of similar wildness.

An historic detail has thus been given of the manner in which the hand of man has acted upon the surface of

---

4 *De facto* union was achieved in 1603, when James VI of Scotland became James I of England. The official Act of Union occurred in 1707.

5 Poor huts, originally applied to primitive African villages.

the inner regions of this mountainous country, as incorporated with and subservient to the powers and processes of nature. We will now take a view of the same agency—acting, within narrower bounds, for the production of the few works of art and accommodations of life which, in so simple a state of society, could be necessary. These are merely habitations of man and coverts for beasts, roads and bridges, and places of worship.

And to begin with the COTTAGES. They are scattered over the vallies, and under the hill sides, and on the rocks; and, even to this day, in the more retired dales, without any intrusion of more assuming buildings;

> Cluster'd like stars some few, but single most,
> And lurking dimly in their shy retreats,
> Or glancing on each other cheerful looks,
> Like separated stars with clouds between.   MS.[6]

The dwelling-houses, and contiguous outhouses, are, in many instances, of the colour of the native rock, out of which they have been built; but, frequently the Dwelling or Fire-house, as it is ordinarily called, has been distinguished from the barn or byer[7] by roughcast and white wash, which, as the inhabitants are not hasty in renewing it, in a few years acquires, by the influence of weather, a tint at once sober and variegated. As these houses have been, from father to son, inhabited by persons engaged in the same occupations, yet necessarily with changes in their circumstances, they have received without incongruity additions and accommodations adapted to the needs of each successive occupant, who, being for the most part proprietor, was at liberty to follow his own fancy: so that these humble dwellings remind the contemplative spectator of a production of nature, and may (using a strong expression) rather be said to have grown than to have been erected;—to have risen, by an instinct of their own, out of the native rock—so little is there in them of formality, such is their wildness and beauty. Among the numerous recesses and projections in the walls and in the different stages of their roofs, are seen bold and harmonious effects of contrasted sunshine and shadow. It is a favourable circumstance, that the strong winds, which sweep down the vallies, induced the inhabitants, at a time when the materials for building were easily procured, to furnish many of these dwellings with substantial porches; and such as have not this defence, are seldom unprovided with a projection of two large slates over their thresholds. Nor will the singular beauty of the chimneys escape the eye of the attentive traveller.

Sometimes a low chimney, almost upon a level with the roof, is overlaid with a slate, supported upon four slender pillars, to prevent the wind from driving the smoke down the chimney. Others are of a quadrangular shape, rising one or two feet above the roof; which low square is often surmounted by a tall cylinder, giving to the cottage chimney the most beautiful shape in which it is ever seen. Nor will it be too fanciful or refined to remark, that there is a pleasing harmony between a tall chimney of this circular form, and the living column of smoke, ascending from it through the still air. These dwellings, mostly built, as has been said, of rough unhewn stone, are roofed with slates, which were rudely taken from the quarry before the present art of splitting them was understood, and are, therefore, rough and uneven in their surface, so that both the coverings and sides of the houses have furnished places of rest for the seeds of lichens, mosses, ferns, and flowers. Hence buildings, which in their very form call to mind the processes of nature, do thus, clothed in part with a vegetable garb, appear to be received into the bosom of the living principle of things, as it acts and exists among the woods and fields; and, by their colour and their shape, affectingly direct the thoughts to that tranquil course of nature and simplicity, along which the humble-minded inhabitants have, through so many generations, been led. Add the little garden with its shed for bee-hives, its small bed of pot-herbs, and its borders and patches of flowers for Sunday posies, with sometimes a choice few too much prized to be plucked; an orchard of proportioned size; a cheese-press, often supported by some tree near the door; a cluster of embowering sycamores for summer shade; with a tall fir, through which the winds sing when other trees are leafless; the little rill or household spout murmuring in all seasons;—combine these incidents and images together, and you have the representative idea of a mountain-cottage in this country so beautifully formed in itself, and so richly adorned by the hand of nature.

*   *   *   *   *

Thus has been given a faithful description, the minuteness of which the reader will pardon, of the face of this country as it was, and had been through centuries, till within the last sixty years. Towards the head of these Dales was found a perfect Republic of Shepherds and Agriculturists, among whom the plough of each man was confined to the maintenance of his own family, or to the occasional accommodation of his neighbour.* Two or three cows furnished each family

---

[6] "Home at Grasmere," ll. 122–25.
[7] Cow-house.

* One of the most pleasing characteristics of manners in secluded and thinly-peopled districts, is a sense of the degree in which human happiness and comfort are dependent on the contingency of neighbourhood. This is implied by the rhyming

with milk and cheese. The chapel was the only edifice that presided over these dwellings, the supreme head of this pure Commonwealth; the members of which existed in the midst of a powerful empire, like an ideal society or an organized community, whose constitution had been imposed and regulated by the mountains which protected it. Neither high-born nobleman, knight, nor esquire, was here; but many of these humble sons of the hills had a consciousness that the land, which they walked over and tilled, had for more than five hundred years been possessed by men of their name and blood; and venerable was the transition, when a curious traveller, descending from the heart of the mountains, had come to some ancient manorial residence in the more open parts of the Vales, which, through the rights attached to its proprietor, connected the almost visionary mountain republic he had been contemplating with the substantial frame of society as existing in the laws and constitution of a mighty empire.

SECTION THIRD

CHANGES, AND RULES OF TASTE FOR PREVENTING THEIR BAD EFFECTS

SUCH, as hath been said, was the appearance of things till within the last sixty years. A practice, denominated Ornamental Gardening, was at that time becoming prevalent over England. In union with an admiration of this art, and in some instances in opposition to it, had been generated a relish for select parts of natural scenery: and Travellers, instead of confining their observations to Towns, Manufactories, or Mines, began (a thing till then unheard of) to wander over the island in search of sequestered spots, distinguished as they might accidently have learned, for the sublimity or beauty of the forms of nature there to be seen.—Dr. Brown, the celebrated Author of the Estimate of the Manners and Principles of the Times, published a letter to a friend,[1] in which the attractions of the Vale

of Keswick were delineated with a powerful pencil, and the feeling of a genuine Enthusiast. Gray, the Poet, followed: he died soon after his forlorn and melancholy pilgrimage to the Vale of Keswick, and the record left behind him of what he had seen and felt in this journey, excited that pensive interest with which the human mind is ever disposed to listen to the farewell words of a man of genius. The journal of Gray[2] feelingly showed how the gloom of ill-health and low spirits had been irradiated by objects, which the Author's powers of mind enabled him to describe with distinctness and unaffected simplicity. Every reader of this journal must have been impressed with the words which conclude his notice of the Vale of Grasmere:—"Not a single red tile, no flaring gentleman's house or garden-wall, breaks in upon the repose of this little unsuspected paradise; but all is peace, rusticity, and happy poverty, in its neatest and most becoming attire."

What is here so justly said of Grasmere applied almost equally to all its sister Vales. It was well for the undisturbed pleasure of the Poet that he had no forebodings of the change which was soon to take place; and it might have been hoped that these words, indicating how much the charm of what *was*, depended upon what was *not*, would of themselves have preserved the ancient franchises of this and other kindred mountain retirements from trespass; or (shall I dare to say?) would have secured scenes so consecrated from profanation. The lakes had now become celebrated; visitors flocked hither from all parts of England; the fancies of some were smitten so deeply, that they became settlers; and the Islands of Derwentwater and Winandermere, as they offered the strongest temptation, were the first places seized upon, and were instantly defaced by the intrusion.

The venerable wood that had grown for centuries round the small house called St. Herbert's Hermitage, had indeed some years before been felled by its native proprietor, and the whole island planted anew with Scotch firs, left to spindle up by each other's side—a melancholy phalanx, defying the power of the winds, and disregarding the regret of the spectator, who might otherwise have cheated himself into a belief, that some of the decayed remains of those oaks, the place of which was in this manner usurped, had been planted by the Hermit's own hand. This sainted spot, however, suffered comparatively little injury. At the bidding of an alien improver, the Hind's Cottage, upon Vicar's

---

adage common here, "*Friends are far, when neighbours are nar*" (near). This mutual helpfulness is not confined to out-of-doors work; but is ready upon all occasions. Formerly, if a person became sick, especially the mistress of a family, it was usual for those of the neighbours who were more particularly connected with the party by amicable offices, to visit the house, carrying a present; this practice, which is by no means obsolete, is called *owning* the family, and is regarded as a pledge of a disposition to be otherwise serviceable in a time of disability and distress.

◇◇◇◇◇◇◇◇◇◇◇◇◇◇◇◇◇◇◇◇◇◇◇◇◇◇◇◇◇◇◇◇◇◇◇◇◇◇◇

[1] Brown's *Letter Describing the Vale and Lake of Keswick* was first published in 1767 and helped initiate the vogue of picturesque travel to the Lake District.

◇◇◇◇◇◇◇◇◇◇◇◇◇◇◇◇◇◇◇◇◇◇◇◇◇◇◇◇◇◇◇◇◇◇◇◇◇◇◇

[2] A record of the poet's visit to the Lake District in October 1769, less than two years before his death in 1771. The journal, in the form of a letter to his friend Dr. Wharton, was first published in William Mason's *Memoirs of the Life and Writings of Mr. Gray* (1775).

island, in the same lake, with its embowering sycamores and cattle-shed, disappeared from the corner where they stood; and right in the middle, and upon the precise point of the island's highest elevation, rose a tall square habitation, with four sides exposed, like an astronomer's observatory, or a warren-house reared upon an eminence for the detection of depredators, or like the temple of Œolus, where all the winds pay him obeisance. Round this novel structure, but at a respectful distance, platoons of firs were stationed, as if to protect their commander when weather and time should somewhat have shattered his strength. Within the narrow limits of this island were typified also the state and strength of a kingdom, and its religion as it had been, and was,—for neither was the druidical circle uncreated, nor the church of the present establishment; nor the stately pier, emblem of commerce and navigation; nor the fort to deal out thunder upon the approaching invader. The taste of a succeeding proprietor rectified the mistakes as far as was practicable, and has ridded the spot of its puerilities. The church, after having been docked of its steeple, is applied both ostensibly and really, to the purpose for which the body of the pile was actually erected, namely, a boat-house; the fort is demolished; and, without indignation on the part of the spirits of the ancient Druids who officiated at the circle upon the opposite hill, the mimic arrangement of stones, with its *sanctum sanctorum*, has been swept away.

The present instance has been singled out, extravagant as it is, because, unquestionably, this beautiful country has, in numerous other places, suffered from the same spirit, though not clothed exactly in the same form, nor active in an equal degree. It will be sufficient here to utter a regret for the changes that have been made upon the principal Island at Winandermere, and in its neighbourhood. What could be more unfortunate than the taste that suggested the paring of the shores, and surrounding with an embankment this spot of ground, the natural shape of which was so beautiful! An artificial appearance has thus been given to the whole, while infinite varieties of minute beauty have been destroyed. Could not the margin of this noble island be given back to nature? Winds and waves work with a careless and graceful hand: and, should they in some places carry away a portion of the soil, the trifling loss would be amply compensated by the additional spirit, dignity, and loveliness, which these agents and the other powers of nature would soon communicate to what was left behind. As to the larch-plantations upon the main shore,—they who remember the original appearance of the rocky steeps, scattered over with native hollies and ash-trees, will be prepared to agree

with what I shall have to say hereafter upon plantations* in general.

But, in truth, no one can now travel through the more frequented tracts, without being offended, at almost every turn, by an introduction of discordant objects, disturbing that peaceful harmony of form and colour, which had been through a long lapse of ages most happily preserved.

All gross transgressions of this kind originate, doubtless, in a feeling natural and honourable to the human mind, viz. the pleasure which it receives from distinct ideas, and from the perception of order, regularity, and contrivance. Now, unpractised minds receive these impressions only from objects that are divided from each other by strong lines of demarcation; hence the delight with which such minds are smitten by formality and harsh contrast. But I would beg of those who are eager to create the means of such gratification, first carefully to study what already exists; and they will find, in a country so lavishly gifted by nature, an abundant variety of forms marked out with a precision that will satisfy their desires. Moreover, a new habit of pleasure will be formed opposite to this, arising out of the perception of the fine gradations by which in nature one thing passes away into another, and the boundaries that constitute individuality disappear in one instance only to be revived elsewhere under a more alluring form. The hill of Dunmallet, at the foot of Ulswater, was once divided into different portions, by avenues of fir-trees, with a green and almost perpendicular lane descending down the steep hill through each avenue;—contrast this quaint appearance with the image of the same hill overgrown with self-planted wood,—each tree springing up in the situation best suited to its kind, and with that shape which the situation constrained or suffered it to take. What endless melting and playing into each other of forms and colours does the one offer to a mind at once attentive and active; and how insipid and lifeless, compared with it, appear those parts of the former exhibition with which a child, a peasant perhaps, or a citizen unfamiliar with natural imagery, would have been most delighted!

The disfigurement which this country has undergone has not, however, proceeded wholly from the common feelings of human nature which have been referred to as the primary sources of bad taste in rural imagery; another cause must be added, that has chiefly shown itself in its effect upon buildings. I mean a warping of the natural mind occasioned by a consciousness that, this country being an object of general admiration, every new house would be looked at and

---

* These are disappearing fast, under the management of the present Proprietor, and native wood is resuming its place.

commented upon either for approbation or censure. Hence all the deformity and ungracefulness that ever pursue the steps of constraint or affectation. Persons, who in Leicestershire or Northamptonshire would probably have built a modest dwelling like those of their sensible neighbours, have been turned out of their course; and, acting a part, no wonder if, having had little experience, they act it ill. The craving for prospect, also, which is immoderate, particularly in new settlers, has rendered it impossible that buildings, whatever might have been their architecture, should in most instances be ornamental to the landscape; rising as they do from the summits of naked hills in staring contrast to the snugness and privacy of the ancient houses.

No man is to be condemned for a desire to decorate his residence and possessions; feeling a disposition to applaud such an endeavour, I would show how the end may be best attained. The rule is simple; with respect to grounds—work, where you can, in the spirit of nature, with an invisible hand of art. Planting, and a removal of wood, may thus, and thus only, be carried on with good effect; and the like may be said of building, if Antiquity, who may be styled the co-partner and sister of Nature, be not denied the respect to which she is entitled. I have already spoken of the beautiful forms of the ancient mansions of this country, and of the happy manner in which they harmonise with the forms of nature. Why cannot such be taken as a model, and modern internal convenience be confined within their external grace and dignity? Expense to be avoided, or difficulties to be overcome, may prevent a close adherence to this model; still, however, it might be followed to a certain degree in the style of architecture and in the choice of situation, if the thirst for prospect were mitigated by those considerations of comfort, shelter, and convenience, which used to be chiefly sought after. But should an aversion to old fashions unfortunately exist, accompanied with a desire to transplant into the cold and stormy North, the elegancies of a villa formed upon a model taken from countries with a milder climate, I will adduce a passage from an English poet, the divine Spenser, which will show in what manner such a plan may be realised without injury to the native beauty of these scenes.

"Into that forest farre they thence him led,
Where was their dwelling in a pleasant glade
With MOUNTAINS round about environed,
And MIGHTY WOODS which did the valley shade,
And like a stately theatre it made,
Spreading itself into a spacious plaine;
And in the midst a little river plaide
Emongst the pumy stones which seem'd to 'plaine
With gentle murmure that his course they did restraine.

Beside the same a dainty place there lay,
Planted with mirtle trees and laurels green,
In which the birds sang many a lovely lay
Of God's high praise, and of their sweet loves teene,
As it an earthly paradise had beene;
In whose *enclosed shadow* there was pight
A fair pavillion, *scarcely to be seen*,
The which was all within most richly dight,
That greatest princes living it mote well delight."[3]

Houses or mansions suited to a mountainous region, should be "not obvious, not obtrusive, but retired;"[4] and the reasons for this rule, though they have been little adverted to, are evident. Mountainous countries, more frequently and forcibly than others, remind us of the power of the elements, as manifested in winds, snows, and torrents, and accordingly make the notion of exposure very unpleasing; while shelter and comfort are in proportion necessary and acceptable. Far-winding vallies difficult of access, and the feelings of simplicity habitually connected with mountain retirements, prompt us to turn from ostentation as a thing there eminently unnatural and out of place. A mansion, amid such scenes, can never have sufficient dignity or interest to become principal in the landscape, and to render the mountains, lakes, or torrents, by which it may be surrounded, a subordinate part of the view. It is, I grant, easy to conceive, that an ancient castellated building, hanging over a precipice or raised upon an island, or the peninsula of a lake, like that of Kilchurn Castle, upon Loch Awe, may not want, whether deserted or inhabited, sufficient majesty to preside for a moment in the spectator's thoughts over the high mountains among which it is embosomed; but its titles are from antiquity—a power readily submitted to upon occasion as the vicegerent of Nature: it is respected, as having owed its existence to the necessities of things, as a monument of security in times of disturbance and danger long passed away,—as a record of the pomp and violence of passion, and a symbol of the wisdom of law;—it bears a countenance of authority, which is not impaired by decay.

"Child of loud-throated war, the mountain-stream
Roars in thy hearing; but thy hour of rest
Is come, and thou art silent in thy age!"[5]

To such honours a modern edifice can lay no claim; and the puny efforts of elegance appear contemptible, when, in such situations, they are obtruded in rivalship

---

[3] *Faerie Queene*, III, v, 39–40.
[4] *Paradise Lost*, VIII, 504.
[5] Ll. 1–3 of Wordsworth's sonnet "Address to Kilchurn Castle, upon Loch Awe," first published complete in 1827.

with the sublimities of Nature. But, towards the verge of a district like this of which we are treating, where the mountains subside into hills of moderate elevation, or in an undulating or flat country, a gentleman's mansion may, with propriety, become a principal feature in the landscape; and, itself being a work of art, works and traces of artificial ornament may, without censure, be extended around it, as they will be referred to the common centre, the house; the right of which to impress within certain limits a character of obvious ornament will not be denied, where no commanding forms of nature dispute it, or set it aside. Now, to a want of the perception of this difference, and to the causes before assigned, may chiefly be attributed the disfigurement which the Country of the Lakes has undergone, from persons who may have built, demolished, and planted, with full confidence, that every change and addition was or would become an improvement.

*　　*　　*　　*　　*

The principle taken as our guide, viz. that the house should be so formed, and of such apparent size and colour, as to admit of its being gently incorporated with the works of nature, should also be applied to the management of the grounds and plantations, and is here more urgently needed; for it is from abuses in this department, far more even than from the introduction of exotics in architecture (if the phrase may be used), that this country has suffered. Larch and fir plantations have been spread, not merely with a view to profit, but in many instances for the sake of ornament. To those who plant for profit, and are thrusting every other tree out of the way, to make room for their favourite, the larch, I would utter first a regret, that they should have selected these lovely vales for their vegetable manufactory, when there is so much barren and irreclaimable land in the neighbouring moors, and in other parts of the island, which might have been had for this purpose at a far cheaper rate. And I will also beg leave to represent to them, that they ought not to be carried away by flattering promises from the speedy growth of this tree; because in rich soils and sheltered situations, the wood, though it thrives fast, is full of sap, and of little value; and is, likewise, very subject to ravage from the attacks of insects, and from blight. Accordingly, in Scotland, where planting is much better understood, and carried on upon an incomparably larger scale than among us, good soil and sheltered situations are appropriated to the oak, the ash, and other deciduous trees; and the larch is now generally confined to barren and exposed ground. There the plant, which is a hardy one, is of slower growth; much less liable to injury; and the timber is of better quality. But the circum-

stances of many permit, and their taste leads them, to plant with little regard to profit; and there are others, less wealthy, who have such a lively feeling of the native beauty of these scenes, that they are laudably not unwilling to make some sacrifices to heighten it. Both these classes of persons, I would entreat to enquire of themselves wherein that beauty which they admire consists. They would then see that, after the feeling has been gratified that prompts us to gather round our dwelling a few flowers and shrubs, which from the circumstance of their not being native, may, by their very looks, remind us that they owe their existence to our hands, and their prosperity to our care; they will see that, after this natural desire has been provided for, the course of all beyond has been predetermined by the spirit of the place. Before I proceed, I will remind those who are not satisfied with the restraint thus laid upon them, that they are liable to a charge of inconsistency, when they are so eager to change the face of that country, whose native attractions, by the act of erecting their habitations in it, they have so emphatically acknowledged. And surely there is not a single spot that would not have, if well managed, sufficient dignity to support itself, unaided by the productions of other climates, or by elaborate decorations which might be becoming elsewhere.

Having adverted to the feelings that justify the introduction of a few exotic plants, provided they be confined almost to the doors of the house, we may add that a transition should be contrived, without abruptness, from these foreigners to the rest of the shrubs, which ought to be of the kinds scattered by Nature, through the woods—holly, broom, wild-rose, elder, dogberry, white and black thorn, &c.—either these only, or such as are carefully selected in consequence of their being united in form, and harmonising in colour with them, especially with respect to colour, when the tints are most diversified, as in autumn and spring. The various sorts of fruit-and-blossom-bearing trees usually found in orchards, to which may be added those of the woods,—namely, the wilding, black cherry tree, and wild cluster-cherry (here called heck-berry)—may be happily admitted as an intermediate link between the shrubs and the forest trees; which last ought almost entirely to be such as are natives of the country. Of the birch, one of the most beautiful of the native trees, it may be noticed, that, in dry and rocky situations, it outstrips even the larch, which many persons are tempted to plant merely on account of the speed of its growth. The Scotch fir is less attractive during its youth than any other plant; but, when full-grown, if it has had room to spread out its arms, it becomes a noble tree; and, by those who are disinterested enough to plant for posterity, it may be placed along with the sycamore near the house; for, from their massiveness, both these trees unite well with buildings, and in some situations with rocks also; having, in their forms and apparent substances, the effect of something intermediate betwixt the immovableness and solidity of stone, and the spray and foliage of the lighter trees. If these general rules be just, what shall we say to whole acres of artificial shrubbery and exotic trees among rocks and dashing torrents, with their own wild wood in sight—where we have the whole contents of the nurseryman's catalogue jumbled together—colour at war with colour, and form with form?—among the most peaceful subjects of Nature's kingdom, everywhere discord, distraction, and bewilderment! But this deformity, bad as it is, is not so obtrusive as the small patches and large tracts of larch-plantations that are overrunning the hill sides. To justify our condemnation of these, let us again recur to Nature. The process by which she forms woods and forests, is as follows. Seeds are scattered indiscriminately by winds, brought by waters, and dropped by birds. They perish, or produce, according as the soil and situation upon which they fall are suited to them: and under the same dependence, the seedling or the sucker, if not cropped by animals, (which Nature is often careful to prevent by fencing it about with brambles or other prickly shrubs) thrives, and the tree grows, sometimes single, taking its own shape without constraint, but for the most part compelled to conform itself to some law imposed upon it by its neighbours. From low and sheltered places, vegetation travels upwards to the more exposed; and the young plants are protected, and to a certain degree fashioned, by those that have preceded them. The continuous mass of foliage which would be thus produced, is broken by rocks, or by glades or open places, where the browzing of animals has prevented the growth of wood. As vegetation ascends, the winds begin also to bear their part in moulding the forms of the trees; but, thus mutually protected, trees, though not of the hardiest kind, are enabled to climb high up the mountains. Gradually, however, by the quality of the ground, and by increasing exposure, a stop is put to their ascent; the hardy trees only are left: those also, by little and little, give way—and a wild and irregular boundary is established, graceful in its outline, and never contemplated without some feeling, more or less distinct, of the powers of Nature by which it is imposed.

Contrast the liberty that encourages, and the law that limits, this joint work of nature and time, with the disheartening necessities, restrictions, and disadvantages, under which the artificial planter must proceed, even he whom long observation and fine feeling have best qualified for his task. In the first place his trees, however well chosen and adapted to their several situations, must generally start all at the same time; and this necessity would of itself prevent that fine connection of parts, that sympathy and organization, if I may so express myself, which pervades the whole of a natural wood, and appears to the eye in its single trees, its masses of foliage, and their various colours, when they are held up to view on the side of a mountain; or when, spread over a valley, they are looked down upon from an eminence. It is therefore impossible, under any circumstances, for the artificial planter to rival the beauty of nature. But a moment's thought will show that, if ten thousand of this spiky tree, the larch, are stuck in at once upon the side of a hill, they can grow up into nothing but deformity; that, while they are suffered to stand, we shall look in vain for any of those appearances which are the chief sources of beauty in a natural wood.

It must be acknowledged that the larch, till it has outgrown the size of a shrub, shows, when looked at singly, some elegance in form and appearance, especially in spring, decorated, as it then is, by the pink tassels of its blossoms; but, as a tree, it is less than any other pleasing: its branches (for *boughs* it has none) have no variety in the youth of the tree, and little dignity, even when it attains its full growth; *leaves* it cannot be said to have, consequently neither affords shade nor shelter. In spring the larch becomes green long before the native trees; and its green is so peculiar and vivid, that finding nothing to harmonize with it, wherever it comes forth, a disagreeable speck is produced. In summer, when all other trees are in their pride, it is of a dingy lifeless hue; in autumn of a spiritless unvaried yellow, and in winter it is still more lamentably distinguished from every other deciduous tree of the forest, for they seem only to sleep, but the larch appears absolutely dead. If an attempt be made to mingle thickets, or a certain proportion of other forest-trees, with the larch, its horizontal branches intolerantly cut them down as with a scythe, or force them to spindle up to keep pace with it. The terminating spike renders it impossible that the several trees, where planted in numbers, should ever blend together so as to form a mass or masses of wood. Add thousands to tens of thousands, and the appearance is still the same—a collection of separate individual trees, obstinately presenting themselves as such; and which, from whatever point they are looked at, if but seen, may be counted upon the fingers. Sunshine or shadow, has little power to adorn the surface of such a wood; and the trees not carrying up their heads, the wind raises among them no majestic undulations. It is indeed true, that in countries where the larch is a native, and where, without interruption, it may sweep from valley to valley, and from hill to hill, a sublime image may be produced by such a forest, in the same manner as by one composed of any other single tree, to the spreading of which no limits can be assigned. For sublimity will never be wanting, where the sense of innumerable multitude is lost in, and alternates with, that of intense unity; and to the ready perception of this effect, similarity and almost identity of individual form and monotony of colour contribute. But this feeling is confined to the native immeasurable forest; no artificial plantation can give it.

The foregoing observations will, I hope, (as nothing has been condemned or recommended without a substantial reason) have some influence upon those who plant for ornament merely. To such as plant for profit, I have already spoken. Let me then entreat that the native deciduous trees may be left in complete possession of the lower ground; and that plantations of larch, if introduced at all, may be confined to the highest and most barren tracts. Interposition of rocks would there break the dreary uniformity of which we have been complaining; and the winds would take hold of the trees, and imprint upon their shapes a wildness congenial to their situation.

Having determined what kinds of trees must be wholly rejected, or at least very sparingly used, by those who are unwilling to disfigure the country; and having shown what kinds ought to be chosen; I should have given, if my limits had not already been overstepped, a few practical rules for the manner in which trees ought to be disposed in planting. But to this subject I should attach little importance, if I could succeed in banishing such trees as introduce deformity, and could prevail upon the proprietor to confine himself, either to those found in the native woods, or to such as accord with them. This is, indeed, the main point; for, much as these scenes have been injured by what has been taken from them—buildings, trees, and woods, either through negligence, necessity, avarice, or caprice—it is not the removals, but the harsh *additions* that have been made, which are the worst grievance—a standing and unavoidable annoyance. Often have I felt this distinction, with mingled satisfaction and regret; for, if no positive deformity or discordance be substituted or superinduced, such is the benignity of Nature, that, take away from her beauty after beauty, and ornament after ornament, her appearance cannot be marred—the scars, if any be left, will gradually disappear before a healing spirit; and what remains will still be soothing and pleasing.—

"Many hearts deplored
The fate of those old trees; and oft with pain
The traveller at this day will stop and gaze
On wrongs which nature scarcely seems to heed:

For sheltered places, bosoms, nooks, and bays,
And the pure mountains, and the gentle Tweed,
And the green silent pastures, yet remain." [6]

There are few ancient woods left in this part of England upon which such indiscriminate ravage as is here "deplored," could now be committed. But, out of the numerous copses, fine woods might in time be raised, probably without sacrifice of profit, by leaving, at the periodical fellings, a dur proportion of the healthiest trees to grow up into timber.—This plan has fortunately, in many instances, been adopted; and they, who have set the example, are entitled to the thanks of all persons of taste. As to the management of planting with reasonable attention to ornament, let the images of nature be your guide, and the whole secret lurks in a few words; thickets or underwoods—single trees—trees clustered or in groups—groves—unbroken woods, but with varied masses of foliage—glades—invisible or winding boundaries—in rocky districts, a seemly proportion of rock left wholly bare, and other parts half hidden—disagreeable objects concealed, and formal lines broken—trees climbing up to the horizon, and, in some places, ascending from its sharp edge, in which they are rooted, with the whole body of the tree appearing to stand in the clear sky—in other parts, woods surmounted by rocks utterly bare and naked, which add to the sense of height, as if vegetation could not thither be carried, and impress a feeling of duration, power of resistance, and security from change!

The author has been induced to speak thus at length, by a wish to preserve the native beauty of this delightful district, because still further changes in its appearance must inevitably follow, from the change of inhabitants and owners which is rapidly taking place.—About the same time that strangers began to be attracted to the country, and to feel a desire to settle in it, the difficulty, that would have stood in the way of their procuring situations was lessened by an unfortunate alteration in the circumstances of the native peasantry, proceeding from a cause which then began to operate, and is now felt in every house. The family of each man, whether *estatesman* or farmer, formerly had a two-fold support; first, the produce of his lands and flocks; and, secondly, the profit drawn from the employment of the women and children, as manufacturers; spinning their own wool in their own houses (work chiefly done in the winter season), and carrying it to market for sale. Hence, however numerous the children, the income of the family kept pace with its increase. But, by the invention and universal application of machinery, this

---

[6] Wordsworth's sonnet "Composed at —— Castle" (1807), ll. 8–14.

second resource has been cut off; the gains being so far reduced, as not to be sought after but by a few aged persons disabled from other employment. Doubtless, the invention of machinery has not been to these people a pure loss; for the profits arising from home-manufactures operated as a strong temptation to choose that mode of labour in neglect of husbandry. They also participate in the general benefit which the island has derived from the increased value of the produce of land, brought about by the establishment of manu-factories, and in the consequent quickening of agricul-tural industry. But this is far from making them amends; and now that home-manufactures are nearly done away, though the women and children might, at many seasons of the year, employ themselves with ad-vantage in the fields beyond what they are accustomed to do, yet still all possible exertion in this way cannot be rationally expected from persons whose agricultural knowledge is so confined, and, above all, where there must necessarily be so small a capital. The consequence, then, is—that proprietors and farmers being no longer able to maintain themselves upon small farms, several are united in one, and the buildings go to decay, or are destroyed; and that the lands of the *estatesmen* being mortgaged, and the owners constrained to part with them, they fall into the hands of wealthy purchasers, who in like manner unite and consolidate; and, if they wish to become residents, erect new mansions out of the ruins of the ancient cottages, whose little enclosures, with all the wild graces that grew out of them, dis-appear. The feudal tenure under which the estates are held has indeed done something towards checking this influx of new settlers; but so strong is the inclination, that these galling restraints are endured; and it is probable, that in a few years the country on the margin of the Lakes will fall almost entirely into the possession of gentry, either strangers or natives. It is then much to be wished, that a better taste should prevail among these new proprietors; and, as they cannot be expected to leave things to themselves, that skill and knowledge should prevent unnecessary deviations from that path of simplicity and beauty along which, without design and unconsciously, their humble predecessors have moved. In this wish the author will be joined by persons of pure taste throughout the whole island, who, by their visits (often repeated) to the Lakes in the North of England, testify that they deem the district a sort of national property, in which every man has a right and interest who has an eye to perceive and a heart to enjoy.

[1810]   [1835]

Samuel Taylor Coleridge

1772–1834

OUTLINE OF EVENTS

1772   Born October 21, at Ottery St. Mary, Devonshire, youngest of ten children of Rev. John Coleridge, vicar and schoolmaster, and Ann (Bowdon).

1781   Father dies.

1782–91   Attends Christ's Hospital, a London charity school, where he proves a brilliant and precocious student and forms friendship with fellow-student Charles Lamb.

1791   Enters Jesus College, Cambridge.

1793   Enlists in army as Silas Tomkyn Comberbache.

1794   April, returns to Cambridge. During summer, meets Robert Southey at Oxford, with whom he concocts plan for "pantisocracy" community in Pennsylvania. Becomes engaged to Sara Fricker. Returns to Cambridge in fall, but leaves in December without taking degree.

1795   In Bristol, delivers lectures on politics and religion. During summer, meets Wordsworth, quarrels with Southey, and abandons "pantisocracy." October 4, marries Sara Fricker. December, *Conciones ad Populum* published.

1796   March–May, conducts periodical *The Watchman*, which fails after ten issues. April, *Poems on Various Subjects* published. September, son Hartley born. December, moves to Nether Stowey, Somersetshire.

1797   Resides at Nether Stowey, where in summer close association with Wordsworth develops. Second edition of *Poems* published.

1798   January, meets Hazlitt and receives annuity from the Wedgwoods. May, son Berkeley born. September, sails with William and Dorothy Wordsworth to Germany, where he eventually settles at University of Göttingen. *Lyrical Ballads* published.

1799   July, returns to England. Fall, in Lake District with Wordsworths and meets Sara Hutchinson (sister to Wordsworth's future wife). November, accepts journalistic position on the London newspaper *Morning Post*.

1800   July, moves to Greta Hall, Keswick, to be near Wordsworth. September, son Derwent born.

1801   Serious illness and opium addiction.

1802   Period of marital dispute. *Dejection: an Ode* written April, published October 4, date of Wordsworth's marriage and anniversary of Coleridge's marriage. December, daughter Sara born.

1803   June, third edition of *Poems* published. August, tours Scotland with William and Dorothy Wordsworth.

1804   April, sails to Malta to recover health, and becomes private secretary to Alexander Ball, British High Commissioner.

1805   Becomes Public Secretary to the Government at Malta. Visits Sicily, Naples, and Rome.

1806   In Italy until June, when he sails for England. November, seeks separation from wife.

1807   Resides with Wordsworths at Coleorton, Leicestershire, estate of Sir George Beaumont. August, meets De Quincey. November, resides in London.

1808   January–June, delivers lectures on "The Principles of Poetry" at Royal Institution, London. September, moves to Grasmere and initiates plan for the periodical *The Friend*.

1809   June–March 1810, publishes *The Friend*. December–January 1810, contributes "Letters on the Spaniards" to London newspaper *Courier*.

1810   October, moves to London; angry estrangement from Wordsworth.

1811   April–September, contributes political journalism to *Courier*. November–January 1812, delivers "A Course of Lectures on Shakespear and Milton" for the London Philosophical Society.

1812   Delivers several series of literary lectures in London. Is reconciled with Wordsworth. June, reissues *The Friend*. November, publishes with Southey *Omniana*.

1813   January, *Remorse* presented with success at Drury Lane Theatre, London. October–November, lectures in Bristol on "The Characteristics of Shakespear."

1814   April, gives additional lectures in Bristol; August–September, publishes essays "On the Principles of Genial Criticism." Resides with the J. J. Morgans at Ashley (near Bristol) and throughout 1815 at Calne, Wiltshire.

1815   Begins composing *Biographia Literaria* and preparing edition of his poems.

1816   April, places himself under permanent care of Dr. James Gillman, Highgate, London. *Christabel*, *Kubla Kahn*, and *The Statesman's Manual* published.

1817   Second Lay Sermon *"Blessed are ye that Sow beside all Waters,"* *Biographia Literaria*, collection of poems *Sibylline Leaves*, and the dramatic poem *Zapolya* published.

1818   January–May, gives literary lectures for the Philosophical Society in London. November, publishes new edition of *The Friend*. December–March 1819, delivers two sets of lectures: on the history of philosophy and on literature.

1825   *Aids to Reflection* published.

1828   *Poetical Works* published in three volumes. Tours Netherlands and the Rhine with Wordsworth and his daughter Dora.

1830   *On the Constitution of the Church and State* published.

1834   Dies, July 25, Highgate.

SELECTED BIBLIOGRAPHY

BIOGRAPHY

CHAMBERS, E. K., *Samuel Taylor Coleridge. A Biographical Study*, Oxford: Clarendon Press, 1938.
HANSON, LAWRENCE, *The Life of S. T. Coleridge: The Early Years*, London: George Allen and Unwin, 1938.

EDITIONS OF COLERIDGE'S PROSE

COBURN, KATHLEEN (ed.), *Inquiring Spirit: A New Presentation of Coleridge from His Published and Unpublished Prose Writings*, London: Routledge and Kegan Paul, 1951.

——, *The Notebooks of Samuel Taylor Coleridge*, London: Routledge and Kegan Paul, 1957–. (Published thus far: Volume I [1794–1804], 1957; Volume II [1804–1808] 1962.)

——, *The Philosophical Lectures of Samuel Taylor Coleridge*, New York: Philosophical Library, 1949.

—— and BART WINER (eds.), *The Collected Works of Samuel Taylor Coleridge*, London: Routledge and Kegan Paul; Princeton: Princeton University Press, 1969– (Published thus far: Volume I, Lewis Patton and Peter Mann [eds.], *Lectures 1795 on Politics and Religion*, 1971; Volume II, Lewis Patton [ed.], *The Watchman*, 1970; Volume IV, Barbara Rooke [ed.], *The Friend*, 2 vols., 1969.)

RAYSOR, T. M. (ed.), *Coleridge's Miscellaneous Criticism*, Cambridge, Mass.: Harvard University Press, 1936.

——, *Coleridge's Shakespearean Criticism*, 2 vols., London: Constable and Company, 1930. [Revised edition, Everyman's Library, 1960.]

SHAWCROSS, J. (ed.), *Biographia Literaria*, 2 vols., London: Oxford University Press, 1907.

SHEDD, W. G. T. (ed.), *The Complete Works of Samuel Taylor Coleridge*, 7 vols., New York: Harper Brothers, 1853.

SNYDER, ALICE D. (ed.), *Coleridge on Logic and Learning: With Selections from the Unpublished Manuscripts*, New Haven: Yale University Press, 1929.

WATSON, GEORGE (ed.), *Biographia Literaria*, Everyman's Library, London: J. M. Dent and Sons Ltd., 1965.

COLERIDGE'S AESTHETICS, PHILOSOPHY AND RELIGION

ABRAMS, M. H., *The Mirror and the Lamp: Romantic Theory and the Critical Tradition*, New York: Oxford University Press, 1953.

APPLEYARD, J. A., *Coleridge's Philosophy of Literature: The Development of a Concept of Poetry 1791–1819*, Cambridge, Mass.: Harvard University Press, 1965.

BAKER, JAMES VOLANT, *The Sacred River: Coleridge's Theory of the Imagination*, Baton Rouge: Louisiana State University Press, 1957.

BARTH, J. ROBERT, *Coleridge and Christian Doctrine*, Cambridge, Mass.: Harvard University Press, 1969.

BATE, WALTER JACKSON, "Coleridge on the Function of Art," in *Perspectives on Criticism*, ed. Harry Levin, Cambridge, Mass.: Harvard University Press, 1950.

BOULGER, JAMES D., *Coleridge as Religious Thinker*, New Haven: Yale University Press, 1961.

FOGLE, R. H., *The Idea of Coleridge's Criticism*, Berkeley and Los Angeles: University of California Press, 1962.

HARRIS, WENDELL V., "The Shape of Coleridge's 'Public' System," *Modern Philology*, LXVIII (1970), 46–61.

JACKSON, J. R. DeJ., *Method and Imagination in Coleridge's Criticism*, London: Routledge and Kegan Paul, 1969.

McFARLAND, THOMAS, *Coleridge and the Pantheist Tradition*, Oxford: Clarendon Press, 1969.

McKENZIE, GORDON, *Organic Unity in Coleridge*, University of California Publications in English, Vol VII, No. 1, Berkeley: University of California Press, 1939.

MILLER, CRAIG W., "Coleridge's Concept of Nature," *Journal of the History of Ideas*, XXV (1964), 77–96.

MUIRHEAD, JOHN H., *Coleridge as Philosopher*, London: George Allen and Unwin Ltd., 1930.

RAINSBERRY, FREDERICK B., "Coleridge and the Paradox of the Poetic Imperative," *Journal of English Literary History*, XXI (1954), 114–45.

RAYSOR, THOMAS M., "Coleridge's Criticism of Wordsworth," *Publications of the Modern Language Association*, LIV (1939), 496–510.

RICHARDS, I. A., *Coleridge on Imagination*, Bloomington, Indiana: Indiana University Press, 1960. [First edition published 1934.]

SANDERS, C. R., *Coleridge and the Broad Church Movement*, Durham, N.C.: Duke University Press, 1942.

THORPE, CLARENCE D., "Coleridge as Aesthetician and Critic," *Journal of the History of Ideas*, V (1944), 387–414.

WILLEY, BASIL, *Nineteenth Century Studies: Coleridge to Matthew Arnold*, London: Chatto and Windus, 1949.

COLERIDGE'S POLITICS AND POLITICAL WRITINGS

BRINTON, CRANE, *The Political Ideas of the English Romanticists*, London: Oxford University Press, 1926.

CALLEO, DAVID P., *Coleridge and the Idea of the Modern State*, New Haven: Yale University Press, 1966.

COBBAN, ALFRED, *Edmund Burke and the Revolt Against the Eighteenth Century*, London: George Allen and Unwin Ltd., 1929.

COLMER, JOHN, *Coleridge: Critic of Society*, Oxford: Clarendon Press, 1959.

WOODRING, CARL, *Politics in the Poetry of Coleridge*, Madison: University of Wisconsin Press, 1961.

CONCIONES AD POPULUM

Conciones ad Populum ("*Addresses to the People*"), published in December 1795, consisted of two of the political lectures delivered by Coleridge at Bristol in late January or early February of that year. The "*Introductory Address*" had been published separately in February as A Moral and Political Lecture. The revised December text is here followed.

"*From all the facts . . . that have occurred as subjects of reflection within the sphere of my experience*," Coleridge declared in 1809, "*I have fully persuaded my own mind, that formerly MEN WERE WORSE THAN THEIR PRINCIPLES, but that at present THE PRINCIPLES ARE WORSE THAN THE MEN.*" The development of true principles for nineteenth-century man became the central impulse of Coleridge's intellectual life. His major work The Friend *was written "to aid in the formation of fixed principles in Politics, Morals, and Religion." Even the presentation of his disagreement with Wordsworth's poetical theory and practice in* Biographia Literaria *required a prior definition and "application of rules, deduced from philosophical principles." This constant attempt to train the minds of his readers to the knowledge of principles at the basis of right judgment and conduct informed the "Introductory Address" of 1795, the first of Coleridge's political publications. In addressing his audience of political dissenters in Bristol (with whose goals of reform he heartily agreed), Coleridge declared it his purpose to "evince the necessity of bottoming on fixed Principles, that so we may not be the unstable Patriots of Passion or Accident, nor hurried away by names of which we have not sifted the meaning, and by tenets of which we have not examined the consequences." It was to the absence of true principles for assessing the possibilities of reforming men's characters and institutions that Coleridge traced both the violence and terror of the French Revolution, and the ineffectiveness or excesses of reformers at home.*

The guiding theme of the "Address" is the call for the "illumination" of the minds of all segments of society as a necessary prior condition for the achievement or true enjoyment of freedom. This "illumination," Coleridge argues, must start with a select few cultivating in themselves and actively practicing "benevolent Christian affections," which by their example would gradually but inevitably *spread throughout society. Underlying this inevitability was Coleridge's belief at the time (and continuing for several years) in the "doctrine of philosophical necessity," which he had derived from the works of David Hartley and Joseph Priestley. This highly optimistic doctrine held that all experience, past, present and future, both in nature and in the mind, is held in a chain of cause and effect originating in the first cause, the benevolent will of God, and leading to the inevitable perfection and happiness of man. (See Coleridge's poem "Religious Musings," written 1794, published 1796.) In these terms, evil is not a permanent condition of man's nature but the effect of errors in judgment caused, in turn, by the circumstances surrounding him, such as grinding poverty in the poor or excessive wealth in the rich. By attempting to strengthen the intellect of others through the example of virtuous behavior and by gradually altering the circumstances that encourage a "Tyranny of Association", the true patriot can assist the inevitable progress.*

For a detailed discussion of the political lectures of 1795 and the philosophical influences at play in the "Introductory Address," see the edition by Lewis Patton and Peter Mann of Lectures 1795 on Politics and Religion, *Volume I (1971) of* The Collected Works of Samuel Taylor Coleridge, *ed. Kathleen Coburn and Bart Winer, 1969–.*

FROM

CONCIONES AD POPULUM

INTRODUCTORY ADDRESS

WHEN THE Wind is fair and the Planks of the Vessel sound, we may safely trust every thing to the management of professional Mariners: in a Tempest and on board a crazy Bark, all must contribute their Quota of Exertion. The Stripling is not exempted from it by his Youth, nor the Passenger by his In-experience. Even so, in the present agitations of the public mind, every one ought to consider his intellectual faculties as in a state of immediate requisition. All may benefit Society in some degree. The exigences of the Times do not permit us to stay for the maturest years, lest the opportunity be lost, while we are waiting for an increase of power.

Companies resembling the present will, from a variety of circumstances, consist *chiefly* of the zealous Advocates for Freedom. It will therefore be our endeavour, not so much to excite the torpid, as to regulate the feelings of the ardent: and above all, to evince the necessity of *bottoming* on fixed Principles, that so we may not be the unstable Patriots of Passion or Accident, nor hurried away by names of which we have not sifted the meaning, and by tenets of which we have not examined the consequences. The Times are trying; and in order to be prepared against their difficulties, we should have acquired a prompt facility of adverting in all our doubts to some grand and comprehensive Truth. In a deep and strong Soil must that Tree fix its Roots, the height of which, is to "reach to Heaven, and the Sight of it to the ends of all the Earth." [1]

The Example of France is indeed a "Warning to Britain." [2] A Nation wading to their Rights through Blood, and marking the track of Freedom by Devastation! Yet let us not embattle our Feelings against our Reason. Let us not indulge our malignant Passions under the mask of Humanity. Instead of railing with infuriate declamation against these excesses, we shall be more profitably employed in developing the sources of them. French Freedom is the Beacon, which while it guides to Equality, should shew us the Dangers that throng the road.

The Annals of the French Revolution have recorded in Letters of Blood, that the Knowledge of the Few cannot counteract the Ignorance of the Many; that the Light of Philosophy, when it is confined to a small Minority, points out the Possessors as the Victims, rather than the Illuminators, of the Multitude. The Patriots of France either hastened into the dangerous and gigantic Error of making certain Evil the means of contingent Good, or were sacrified by the Mob, with whose prejudices and ferocity their unbending Virtue forbade them to assimilate. Like Sampson, the People were strong—like Sampson, the People were blind. Those two massy Pillars of Oppression's Temple, the Monarchy and Aristocracy,

With horrible Convulsion to and fro
They tugg'd, they shook—till down they came and drew
The whole Roof after them with burst of Thunder
Upon the heads of all who sat beneath,
Lords, Ladies, Captains, Counsellors, and Priests,
Their choice Nobility!

Milton. Sam. Agon.[3]

There was not a Tyrant in Europe, who did not tremble on his Throne. Freedom herself heard the Crash aghast!—

The Girondists, who were the first republicans in power, were men of enlarged views and great literary attainments; but they seem to have been deficient in that vigour and daring activity, which circumstances made necessary. Men of genius are rarely either prompt in action or consistent in general conduct: their early habits have been those of contemplative indolence; and the day-dreams, with which they have been accustomed to amuse their solitude, adapt them for splendid speculation, not temperate and practicable counsels. Brissot, the leader of the Gironde party,[4] is entitled to the character of a virtuous man, and an eloquent speaker; but he was rather a sublime visionary, than a quick-eyed politician; and his excellences equally with his faults rendered him unfit for the helm, in the stormy hour of Revolution. Robespierre, who displaced him, possessed a glowing ardor that still remembered the *end*, and a cool ferocity that never either overlooked, or scrupled, the *means*. What that *end* was, is not known: that it was a wicked one, has by no means been proved. I rather think, that the distant prospect, to which he was travelling, appeared to him grand and beautiful; but that he fixed his eye on it with such intense eagerness as to neglect the foulness of the road. If however his first intentions were pure, his subsequent enormities yield us a melancholy proof, that it is not the character of the possessor which directs the power, but the power which shapes and depraves the character of the possessor. In Robespierre, its influence was assisted by the properties of his disposition.—Enthusiasm, even in the gentlest temper, will frequently generate sensations of an unkindly

---

3 Ll. 1649–1654.

4 The Girondists (named for the Gironde district of France from which many of its members came), a leading political group in the early stages of the Revolution, consisted largely of well-educated professional men. Under the leadership of Jacques Pierre Brissot (1754–1793), they had urged declarations of war against the external enemies of the Revolution as a means of consolidating the movement at home and arousing its supporters abroad. Following the execution of the King in January 1793, which the Girondists had opposed, and military defeats abroad, the Girondists faced mounting popular opposition led by their more radical revolutionary opponents the Montagnards under Robespierre. The Girondist leaders, including Brissot, were brought to trial in October 1793 and executed.

---

1 Daniel, iv, 11.
2 Refers to Arthur Young's *The Example of France, a Warning to Britain* (1793).

order. If we clearly perceive any one thing to be of vast and infinite importance to ourselves and all mankind, our first feelings impel us to turn with angry contempt from those, who doubt and oppose it. The ardor of undisciplined benevolence seduces us into malignity: and whenever our hearts are warm, and our objects great and excellent, intolerance is the sin that does most easily beset us. But this enthusiasm in Robespierre was blended with gloom, and suspiciousness, and inordinate vanity. His dark imagination was still brooding over supposed plots against freedom— to prevent tyranny he became a Tyrant—and having realized the evils which he suspected, a wild and dreadful Tyrant.—Those loud-tongued adulators, the mob, overpowered the lone-whispered denunciations of conscience—he despotized in all the pomp of Patriotism, and masqueraded on the bloody stage of Revolution, a Caligula [5] with the cap of Liberty on his head.

It has been affirmed, and I believe with truth, that the system of Terrorism [6] by suspending the struggles of contrariant Factions communicated an energy to the operations of the Republic, which had been hitherto unknown, and without which it could not have been preserved. The system depended for its existence on the general sense of its necessity, and when it had answered its end, it was soon destroyed by the same power that had given it birth—popular opinion. It must not however be disguised, that at *all* times, but more especially when the public feelings are wavy and tumultuous, artful Demagogues may create this opinion: and they, who are inclined to tolerate evil as the means of contingent good, should reflect, that if the excesses of terrorism gave to the Republic that efficiency and *repulsive* force which its circumstances made necessary, they likewise afforded to the hostile Courts the most powerful support, and excited that indignation and horror, which every where precipitated the subject into the designs of the ruler. Nor let it be forgotten, that these excesses perpetuated the war in La Vendee and made it more terrible, both by the accession of numerous partizans, who had fled from the persecution of Robespierre, and by inspiring the Chouans [7] with fresh fury, and an unsubmitting spirit of revenge and desperation.

Revolutions are sudden to the unthinking only. Political Disturbances happen not without their warning Harbingers. Strange Rumblings and confused Noises still precede these earthquakes and hurricanes of the moral World. The process of Revolution in France has been dreadful, and should incite us to examine with an anxious eye the motives and manners of those, whose conduct and opinions seem calculated to forward a similar event in our own country. The oppositionists to "things as they are," are divided into many and different classes. To delineate them with an unflattering accuracy may be a delicate, but it is a necessary Task, in order that we may enlighten, or at least beware of, the misguided Men who have enlisted under the banners of Liberty, from no principles or with bad ones: whether they be those, who

> admire they know not what,
> And know not whom, but as one leads the other: [8]

or whether those,

> Whose end is private Hate, not help to Freedom,
> Adverse and turbulent when she would lead
> To Virtue.

The majority of Democrats appear to me to have attained that portion of knowledge in politics, which Infidels possess in religion. I would by no means be supposed to imply, that the objections of both are equally unfounded, but that they both attribute to the system which they reject, all the evils existing under it; and that both contemplating truth and justice "in the nakedness of abstraction," [9] condemn constitutions and dispensations without having sufficiently examined the natures, circumstances, and capacities of their recipients.

The first Class among the professed Friends of Liberty is composed of Men, who unaccustomed to the labour of thorough investigation, and not particularly oppressed by the Burthen of State, are yet impelled by their feelings to disapprove of its grosser depravities, and prepared to give an indolent Vote in favour of Reform. Their sensibilities unbraced by the co-operation of fixed Principles, they offer no sacrifices to the divinity of active Virtue. Their political Opinions depend with weather-cock uncertainty on the winds of rumour, that blow from France. On the report of French victories they blaze into Republicanism, at a tale of French excesses they darken into Aristocrats; and seek for shelter among those despicable adherents to fraud and tyranny, who ironically style themselves

---

5 Tyrannical Roman emperor A.D. 37–41.

6 The Reign of Terror was instituted by Robespierre after the fall of the Girondists in 1793 and lasted until his execution on July 27, 1794.

7 La Vendee, an area of western France and a center of conservative and royalist support, rose in arms against the revolutionary government in 1793. Bitter fighting lasted throughout that year and into the next. Chouans were guerilla bands of Vendee peasants who joined with the royalists.

---

8 *Paradise Regained*, III, 52–53. For the next quotation, cf. *Sampson Agonistes*, ll. 1039–40, 1265–66.

9 From Burke's *Reflections on the Revolution in France*.

Constitutionalists.[10]—These *dough-baked Patriots* are not however useless. This oscillation of political opinion will retard the day of Revolution, and it will operate as a preventive to its excesses. Indecisiveness of character, though the effect of timidity, is almost always associated with benevolence.

Wilder features characterize the second class. Sufficiently possessed of natural sense to despise the Priest, and of natural feeling to hate the Oppressor, they listen only to the inflammatory harangues of some mad-headed Enthusiast, and imbibe from them Poison, not Food; Rage, not Liberty. Unillumined by Philosophy, and stimulated to a lust of revenge by aggravated wrongs, they would make the Altar of Freedom stream with blood, while the grass grew in the desolated halls of Justice. These men are the rude materials from which a detestable Minister[11] manufactures conspiracies. Among these men he sends a brood of sly political monsters, in the character of sanguinary Demagogues, and like Satan of old, "the Tempter ere the Accuser,"[12] ensnares a few into Treason, that he may alarm the whole into Slavery. He, who has dark purposes to serve, must use dark means—light would discover, reason would expose him: he must endeavour to shut out both—or if this prove impracticable, make them appear frightful by giving them frightful names: for farther than Names the Vulgar enquire not. Religion and Reason are but poor substitutes for "Church and Constitution;" and the sable-vested Instigators of the Birmingham riots[13] well knew, that a Syllogism could not disarm a drunken Incendiary of his Firebrand, or a Demonstration *helmet* a Philosopher's head against a Brickbat. But in the principles, which this Apostate has, by his emissaries, sown among a few blind zealots for Freedom, he has digged a pit into which he himself may perhaps be doomed to fall. We contemplate those principles with horror. Yet they possess a kind of wild Justice well calculated to spread them among the grossly ignorant. To unenlightened minds, there are terrible charms in the idea of Retribution, however savagely it be inculcated. The Groans of the Oppressors make fearful yet pleasant music to the ear of him, whose mind is darkness, and into whose soul the iron has entered.

This class, at present, is comparatively small—Yet soon to form an overwhelming majority, unless great and immediate efforts are used to lessen the intolerable grievances of our poorer brethren, and infuse into their sorely wounded hearts the healing qualities of knowledge. For can we wonder that men should want humanity, who want all the circumstances of life that humanize? Can we wonder that with the ignorance of Brutes they should unite their ferocity? peace and comfort be with these! But let us shudder to hear from Men of dissimilar opportunities sentiments of similar revengefulness. The purifying alchemy of Education may transmute the fierceness of an ignorant man into virtuous energy—but what remedy shall we apply to him, whom Plenty has not softened, whom Knowledge has not taught Benevolence? This is one among the many fatal effects which result from the want of fixed principles. Convinced that vice is error, we shall entertain sentiments of Pity for the vicious, not of Indignation—and even with respect to that bad Man, to whom we have before alluded, altho' we are now groaning beneath the burthen of his misconduct, we shall harbour no sentiments of Revenge; but rather *condole* with him that his chaotic Iniquities have exhibited such a complication of extravagance, inconsistency, and rashness as may *alarm* him with apprehensions of approaching lunacy!

There are a third class among the friends of Freedom, who possess not the wavering character of the first description, nor the ferocity last delineated. They pursue the interests of Freedom steadily, but with narrow and self-centering views: they anticipate with exultation the abolition of privileged orders, and of Acts that persecute by exclusion from the right of citizenship. They are prepared to join in digging up the rubbish of mouldering Establishments, and stripping off the tawdry pageantry of Governments. Whatever is above them they are most willing to drag down; but every proposed alteration, that would elevate the ranks of our poorer brethren, they regard with suspicious jealousy, as the dreams of the visionary; as if there were any thing in the superiority of Lord to Gentleman, so mortifying in the barrier, so fatal to happiness in the consequences, as the more real distinction of master and servant, of rich man and of poor. Wherein am I made worse by my ennobled neighbour? Do the childish titles of Aristocracy detract from my domestic comforts, or prevent my intellectual acquisitions? But those institutions of Society which should condemn me to the necessity of twelve hours daily toil, would make my *soul* a slave, and sink the *rational* being in the mere animal. It is a mockery of our fellow creatures' wrongs to call them equal in rights, when by the bitter compulsion of their wants we make them inferior to us in all that can

---

[10] The Constitutionalists were the conservative defenders of the established practices and traditions of British government. Both Burke and Bishop Watson (see Wordsworth's *Letter to the Bishop of Llandaff*) would be included in this designation. "Dough-baked Patriots" means imperfect or feeble patriots.

[11] Refers to William Pitt.

[12] *Paradise Lost*, IV, 10.

[13] See footnote 1, p. 42.

soften the heart, or dignify the understanding. Let us not say that this is the work of time—that it is impracticable at present, unless we each in our individual capacities do strenuously and perseveringly endeavour to diffuse among our domestics those comforts and that illumination which far beyond all political ordinances are the true equalizers of men.

We turn with pleasure to the contemplation of that small but glorious band, whom we may truly distinguish by the name of thinking and disinterested Patriots. These are the men who have encouraged the sympathetic passions till they have become irresistible habits, and made their duty a necessary part of their self-interest, by the long-continued cultivation of that moral taste which derives our most exquisite pleasures from the contemplation of possible perfection, and proportionate pain from the perception of existing *depravation*. Accustomed to regard all the affairs of man as a process, they never hurry and they never pause. Theirs is not that twilight of political knowledge which gives us just light enough to place one foot before the other; as they advance the scene still opens upon them, and they press right onward with a vast and various landscape of existence around them. Calmness and energy mark all their actions. Convinced that vice originates not in the man, but in the surrounding circumstances; not in the heart, but in the understanding; he is hopeless concerning no one—to correct a vice or generate a virtuous conduct he pollutes not his hands with the scourge of coercion; but by endeavouring to alter the circumstances would remove, or by strengthening the intellect, disarms, the temptation. The unhappy children of vice and folly, whose tempers are adverse to their own happiness as well as to the happiness of others, will at times awaken a natural pang; but he looks forward with gladdened heart to that glorious period when Justice shall have established the universal fraternity of Love. These soul-ennobling views bestow the virtues which they anticipate. He whose mind is habitually imprest with them soars above the present state of humanity, and may be justly said to dwell in the presence of the Most High.

——————would the forms
Of servile custom cramp the Patriot's power?
Would sordid policies, the barbarous growth
Of ignorance and rapine, bow him down
To tame pursuits, to Indolence and Fear?
Lo! he appeals to Nature, to the winds
And rolling waves, the sun's unwearied course,
The elements and seasons—all declare
For what the Eternal Maker has ordain'd
The powers of Man: we feel within ourselves
His energy divine: he tells the heart

He meant, he made us to behold and love
What he beholds and loves, the general orb
Of Life and Being—to be great like him,
Beneficent and active.

Akenside.[14]

Such is Joseph Gerald![15] Withering in the sickly and tainted gales of a prison, his healthful soul looks down from the citadel of his integrity on his impotent persecutors. I saw him in the foul and naked room of a jail—his cheek was sallow with confinement—his body was emaciated; yet his eye spoke the invincible purposes of his soul, and he still sounded with rapture the successes of Freemen, forgetful of his own lingering martyrdom! Such too were the illustrious Triumvirate* whom as a Greek Poet expresses it, it's not lawful for bad men even to praise. I will not say that I have abused your patience in thus indulging my feelings in strains of unheard gratitude to those who may seem to justify God in the creation of man. It is with pleasure that I am permitted to recite a yet unpublished tribute to their merit, the production of one[17] who has sacrificed all the energies of his heart and head, a splendid offering on the altar of Liberty.

TO THE EXILED PATRIOTS.

MARTYRS OF FREEDOM—ye who firmly good
  Stept forth the Champions in her glorious cause,
Ye who against Corruption nobly stood
  For Justice, Liberty, and equal Laws.

Ye who have urg'd the cause of man so well,
  Whilst proud Oppression's torrent swept along,
Ye who so firmly stood, so nobly fell,
  Accept one ardent Briton's grateful song.

For shall Oppression vainly think by Fear
  To quench the fearless energy of mind?
And glorying in your fall, exult it here
  As tho' no honest heart were left behind?

Thinks the proud Tyrant by the pliant law,
  The timid jury and the judge unjust,
To strike the soul of Liberty with awe,
  And scare the friends of freedom from their trust?

* MUIR, PALMER, and MARGAROT.[16]

———————————————————

[14] Mark Akenside's *The Pleasures of Imagination* (1744), III, 615–29.
[15] Joseph Gerrald (1763–1796), an agitator for political reform, was tried for sedition in March 1794, imprisoned in London for a year, and then sent to Botany Bay in May 1795.
[16] Thomas Muir (1765–1798), Thomas Fyshe Palmer (1747–1802), and Maurice Margarot were political reformers, who were tried for sedition and sent to Botany Bay in 1794.
[17] Referring to Robert Southey.

As easy might the Despot's empty pride
   The onward course of rushing ocean stay;
As easy might his jealous caution hide
   From mortal eyes the orb of general day.

For like that general orb's eternal flame
   Glows the mild force of Virtue's constant light;
Tho' clouded by Misfortune, still the same,
   For ever constant, and for ever bright.

Not till eternal chaos shall that light
   Before Oppression's fury fade away;
Not till the sun himself be lost in night;
   Not till the frame of Nature shall decay.

Go then secure, in steady virtue go,
   Nor heed the peril of the stormy seas,
Nor heed the felon's name, the outcast's woe;
   Contempt and pain, and sorrow and disease.

Tho' cankering cares corrode the sinking frame,
   Tho' sickness rankle in the sallow breast;
Tho' Death were quenching fast the vital flame,
   Think but for what ye suffer, and be blest.

So shall your great examples fire each soul,
   So in each free-born breast for ever dwell,
Till Man shall rise above the unjust controul,
   Stand where ye stood, and triumph where ye fell.

Yes! there are those who have loved Freedom with wise ardor, and propagated its principles with unshaken courage! For it was ordained at the foundation of the world, that there should always remain Pure Ones and uncorrupt, who should shine like Lights in Darkness, reconciling us to our own nature.

That general Illumination should precede Revolution, is a truth as obvious, as that the Vessel should be cleansed before we fill it with a pure Liquor. But the mode of diffusing it is not discoverable with equal facility. We certainly should never attempt to make Proselytes by appeals to the *selfish* feelings—and consequently, should plead *for* the Oppressed, not *to* them. The Author of an essay on political Justice [18] considers private Societies as the sphere of real utility —that (each one illuminating those immediately beneath him,) Truth by a gradual descent may at last reach the lowest order. But this is rather plausible than just or practicable. Society as at present constituted does not resemble a chain that ascends in a continuity of Links.—There are three ranks possessing an intercourse with each other: these are well comprized in the superscription of a Perfumer's advertisement, which I lately saw—"the Nobility, Gentry, and People of Dress." But alas! between the Parlour and the Kitchen, the Tap and the Coffee Room—there is a gulph that may not be passed. He would appear to me to have adopted the best as well as the most benevolent mode of diffusing Truth, who uniting the zeal of the Methodist with the views of the Philosopher, should be *personally* among the Poor, and teach them their *Duties* in order that he may render them susceptible of their *Rights*.

Yet by what means can the lower Classes be made to learn their Duties, and urged to practise them? The human Race may perhaps possess the capability of all excellence; and Truth, I doubt not, is omnipotent to a mind already disciplined for its reception; but assuredly the over-worked Labourer, skulking into an Ale-house, is not likely to exemplify the one, or prove the other. In that barbarous tumult of inimical Interests, which the present state of Society exhibits, *Religion* appears to offer the only means universally *efficient*. The perfectness of future Men is indeed a benevolent tenet, and may operate on a few Visionaries, whose studious habits supply them with employment, and seclude them from temptation. But a distant prospect, which we are never to reach, will seldom quicken our footsteps, however lovely it may appear; and a Blessing, which not ourselves but *posterity* are destined to enjoy, will scarcely influence the actions of *any*—still less of the ignorant, the prejudiced, and the selfish.

"Go, preach the GOSPEL to the Poor." [19] By its Simplicity it will meet their comprehension, by its Benevolence soften their affections, by its Precepts it will direct their conduct, by the vastness of its Motives ensure their obedience. The situation of the Poor is perilous: they are indeed both

"from within and from without
Unarm'd to all Temptations." [20]

Prudential reasonings will in general be powerless with them. For the incitements of this world are weak in proportion as we are wretched—

The World is not *my* Friend, nor the World's Law.
The World has got no Law to make *me* rich.

They too, who live *from Hand to Mouth*, will most

[18] Refers to Godwin's *Enquiry Concerning Political Justice* (1793).

[19] Luke, iv, 18.
[20] Cf. *Paradise Lost*, IV, 64–65. For the next quotation, cf. *Romeo and Juliet*, V, i, 72–73.

frequently become improvident. Possessing no *stock* of happiness they eagerly seize the gratifications of the moment, and snatch the froth from the wave as it passes by them. Nor is the desolate state of their families a restraining motive, unsoftened as they are by education, and benumbed into selfishness by the torpedo touch of extreme Want. Domestic affections depend on association. We love an object if, as often as we see or recollect it, an agreeable sensation arises in our minds. But alas! how should *he* glow with the charities of Father and Husband, who gaining scarcely more, than his own necessities demand, must have been accustomed to regard his wife and children, not as the Soothers of finished labour, but as Rivals for the insufficient meal! In a man so circumstanced the Tyranny of the *Present* can be overpowered only by the tenfold mightiness of the *Future*. Religion will cheer his gloom with her promises, and by habituating his mind to anticipate an infinitely great Revolution hereafter, may prepare it even for the sudden reception of a less degree of amelioration in this World.

But if we hope to instruct others, we should familiarize our own minds to some fixed and determinate principles of action. The World is a vast labyrinth, in which almost every one is running a different way, and almost every one manifesting hatred to those who do not run the same way. A few indeed stand motionless, and not seeking to lead themselves or others out of the maze laugh at the failures of their brethren. Yet with little reason: for more grossly than the most bewildered wanderer does *he* err, who never aims to go right. It is more honourable to the Head, as well as to the Heart, to be misled by our eagerness in the pursuit of Truth, than to be safe from blundering by contempt of it. The happiness of Mankind is the *end* of Virtue, and Truth is the Knowledge of the *means*; which he will never seriously attempt to discover, who has not habitually interested himself in the welfare of others. The searcher after Truth must love and be beloved; for general Benevolence is a necessary motive to constancy of pursuit; and this general Benevolence is begotten and rendered permanent by social and domestic affections. Let us beware of that proud Philosophy, which affects to inculcate Philanthropy while it denounces every home-born feeling, by which it is produced and nurtured. The paternal and filial duties discipline the Heart and prepare it for the love of all Mankind. The intensity of private attachments encourages, not prevents, universal Benevolence. The nearer we approach to the Sun, the more intense his heat: yet what corner of the system does he not cheer and vivify?

The Man who would find Truth, must likewise seek it with an humble and simple Heart, otherwise he will be precipitant and overlook it; or he will be prejudiced, and refuse to see it. *To emancipate itself from the Tyranny of Association*, is the most arduous effort of the mind, particularly in Religious and Political disquisitions. The asserter of the system has associated with it the preservation of Order, and public Virtue; the oppugner Imposture, and Wars, and Rapine. Hence, when they dispute, each trembles at the *consequences* of the other's opinions instead of attending to his train of arguments. Of this however we may be certain, whether we be Christians or Infidels, Aristocrats or Republicans, that our minds are in a state unsusceptible of Knowledge, when we feel an eagerness to detect the Falsehood of an Adversary's reasonings, not a sincere wish to discover if there be Truth in them;—when we examine an argument in order that we may answer it, instead of answering because we have examined it.

Our opponents are chiefly successful in confuting the Theory of Freedom by the practices of its Advocates: from our lives they draw the most forcible arguments against our doctrines. Nor have they adopted an unfair mode of reasoning. In a Science the evidence suffers neither diminution or increase from the actions of its professors; but the comparative wisdom of political systems depends necessarily on the manners and capacities of the recipients. Why should all things be thrown into confusion to acquire that liberty which a faction of sensualists and gamblers will neither be able or willing to preserve? "The simplicity of wants and of pleasures may be taken as the criterion of Patriotism. Would you prove to me your Patriotism? Let me penetrate into the interior of your House. What! I see your antichamber full of insolent Lackies; they give you still those vain Titles, which Liberty treads under foot, and you suffer it and you call yourself a Patriot! I penetrate a little further;—your Cielings are gilded—magnificent Vases adorn your Chimney-Pieces—I walk upon the richest Carpets—the most costly Wines, the most exquisite Dishes, cover your Table—a crowd of Servants surround it—you treat them with haughtiness;—No! you are not a Patriot. The most consummate pride reigns in your heart, the pride of Birth, of Riches, and of Talents. With this triple pride, a man never sincerely believes the doctrine of Equality: he may repeat its dogmas, but efficient Faith is not in him." *Preface to Brissot's Travels in America.*[21]

---

[21] Referring to Brissot's *Nouveau voyage dans les États-Unis de l'Amérique Septentrionale* (1791), which appeared in an English translation in 1792.

You reply to Brissot, that these luxuries are the employment of industry, and the best means of circulating your property. Be it so. Renounce then the proud pretensions of democracy; do not profess Tenets which it is impossible for you surrounded by all the symbols of superiority to wish realized. But you plead, it seems, for equalization of *Rights*, not of *Condition*. O mockery! All that can delight the poor man's senses or strengthen his understanding, you preclude; yet with generous condescension you would bid him exclaim "LIBERTY and EQUALITY!" because, forsooth, he should possess the same *Right* to an Hovel which you claim to a Palace. This the Laws have already given. And what more do *you* promise?

A system of fundamental Reform will scarcely be effected by massacres mechanized into Revolution. Yet rejected intreaty leads in its consequences to fierce coercion. And much as we deprecate the event, we have reason to conjecture that throughout all Europe it may not be far distant. The folly of the rulers of mankind grows daily more wild and ruinous: Oppression is grievous—the oppressed feel and are restless. Such things *may* happen. We cannot therefore inculcate on the minds of each other too often or with too great earnestness the necessity of cultivating benevolent affections. We should be cautious how we indulge the feelings even of virtuous indignation. Indignation is the handsome brother of Anger and Hatred. The Temple of Despotism, like that of Tescalipoca, the Mexican Deity, is built of human skulls, and cemented with human blood;[22]—let us beware that we be not transported into revenge while we are levelling the loathsome Pile; lest when we erect the edifice of Freedom we but vary the stile of Architecture, not change the materials. Let us not wantonly offend even the prejudices of our weaker brethren, nor by ill-timed and vehement declarations of opinion excite in them malignant feelings towards us. The energies of mind are wasted in these intemperate effusions. Those materials of projectile force, which now carelessly scattered explode with an offensive and useless noise, directed by wisdom and union might heave Rocks from their base,—or perhaps (dismissing the metaphor) might produce the desired effect without the convulsion.

For this "subdued sobriety" of temper a practical faith in the doctrine of philosophical necessity seems the only preparative. That vice is the effect of error and the offspring of surrounding circumstances, the object therefore of condolence not of anger, is a proposition easily understood, and as easily demonstrated. But to make it spread from the understanding to the affections, to call it into action, not only in the great exertions of Patriotism, but in the daily and hourly occurrences of social life, requires the most watchful attentions of the most energetic mind. It is not enough that we have once swallowed these Truths—we must feed on them, as insects on a leaf, till the whole heart be coloured by their qualities, and shew its food in every the minutest fibre.

Finally, in the Words of an Apostle, ·

Watch ye! Stand fast in the principles of which ye have been convinced! Quit yourselves like Men! Be strong! Yet let all things be done in the spirit of Love.[23]

[February 1795]   [December 1795]

POEMS, BY S. T. COLERIDGE, SECOND EDITION

The "Preface to the First Edition" and "Introduction to the Sonnets" are among the very earliest examples of Coleridge's literary criticism. (A review of Mrs. Radcliffe's The Mysteries of Udolpho *in the August 1794 issue of the* Critical Review *and three other reviews in the November 1796 issue have been attributed to Coleridge.) The "Preface" originally appeared in the first collection of Coleridge's verses* Poems on Various Subjects *(1796); the "Introduction" originally appeared in a collection of twenty-eight sonnets (by himself, Southey, Lamb, Bowles, and others) prepared by Coleridge in the same year. Both essays, with revisions, were published in the second edition of his verses entitled* Poems by S. T. Coleridge, *to which are now added* Poems *by Charles Lamb and Charles Lloyd (1797).*

The third paragraph of the "Introduction to the Sonnets" is of considerable critical importance. M. H. Abrams has written: "Even so early in his career Coleridge was an integral thinker for whom questions of poetic structure were inseparable from general philosophic issues, and he [interpreted Bowles'] device [of 'moral Sentiments, Affections, or Feelings . . . deduced from, and associated with, the scenery of Nature'] as the correlate of a mode of perception which unites the mind to its physical environment" ("Structure and Style in the Greater Romantic Lyric," From Sensibility to Romanticism, ed. Frederick W. Hilles and Harold Bloom [New York: Oxford University Press, 1965], p. 544). See Biographia Literaria, *Chapter I, for Coleridge's own discussion of the importance of Bowles in his poetic development.*

---

22 Coleridge had footnoted a similar passage in *The Friend* (1818): "To the best of my recollection, these were Mr. Southey's words in the year 1794." For further reference to Tescalipoca, an Aztec god, see Southey's *Madoc* (1805), II ("Madoc in Aztlan"), ii, 64–96. Southey began composing his epic in 1794.

23 I Corinthians, xvi, 13–14.

FROM

POEMS,

BY

S. T. COLERIDGE

SECOND EDITION

PREFACE

TO THE FIRST EDITION

COMPOSITIONS resembling those of the present volume are not unfrequently condemned for their querulous Egotism. But Egotism is to be condemned then only when it offends against Time and Place, as in an History or an Epic Poem. To censure it in a Monody or Sonnet is almost as absurd as to dislike a circle for being round. Why then write Sonnets or Monodies?[1] Because they give me pleasure when perhaps nothing else could. After the more violent emotions of Sorrow, the mind demands amusement, and can find it in employment alone; but full of its late sufferings, it can endure no employment not in some measure connected with them. Forcibly to turn away our attention to general subjects is a painful and most often an unavailing effort:

> But O! how grateful to a wounded heart
> The tale of Misery to impart—
> From others' eyes bid artless sorrows flow,
> And raise esteem upon the base of Woe!
>
> Shaw.[2]

The communicativeness of our Nature leads us to describe our own sorrows; in the endeavour to describe them, intellectual activity is exerted; and from intellectual activity there results a pleasure, which is gradually associated, and mingles as a corrective, with the painful subject of the description. "True!" (it may be answered) "but how are the PUBLIC interested in your Sorrows or your Description?" We are for ever attributing personal Unities to imaginary Aggregates. —What is the PUBLIC, but a term for a number of scattered Individuals? Of whom as many will be interested in these sorrows, as have experienced the same or similar.

> "Holy be the lay
> Which mourning soothes the mourner on his way."

If I would judge of others by myself, I should not hesitate to affirm, that the most interesting passages in our most interesting Poems are those, in which the Author developes his own feelings. The sweet voice of Cona* never sounds so sweetly, as when it speaks of itself; and I should almost suspect that man of an unkindly heart, who could read the opening of the third book of the Paradise Lost[4] without peculiar emotion. By a law of our Nature, he, who labours under a strong feeling, is impelled to seek for sympathy; but a Poet's feelings are all strong.—Quicquid amet valde amat.[5]—Akenside therefore speaks with philosophical accuracy, when he classes Love and Poetry, as producing the same effects:

> "Love and the wish of Poets when their tongue
> Would teach to others' bosoms, what so charms
> Their own."
>
> PLEASURES OF IMAGINATION.[6]

There is one species of Egotism which is truly disgusting; not that which leads us to communicate our feeling to others, but that which would reduce the feelings of others to an identity with our own. The Atheist, who exclaims, "pshaw!" when he glances his eye on the praises of Deity, is an Egotist: an old man, when he speaks contemptuously of Love-verses, is an Egotist: and the sleek Favorites of Fortune are Egotists, when they condemn all "melancholy, discontended" verses. Surely, it would be candid not merely to ask whether the poem pleases ourselves, but to consider whether or no there may not be others, to whom it is well-calculated to give an innocent pleasure.

I shall only add, that each of my readers will, I hope, remember, that these Poems on various subjects, which he reads at one time and under the influence of one set of feelings, were written at different times and prompted by very different feelings; and therefore that the supposed inferiority of one Poem to another may sometimes be owing to the temper of mind, in which he happens to peruse it.

* Ossian.[3]

---

[3] Cona was the Ossianic name of a river and district in northwestern Scotland, supposed site of the kingdom of Fingal, the hero of the poems of Ossian.

[4] Coleridge refers to the invocation to Book III, 1–55, in which Milton mourns his blindness and asks that "Celestial light/Shine inward . . . that I may see and tell/Of things invisible to mortal sight."

[5] Quicquid . . . amat: "Whatever he loves he loves strongly."

[6] I, 285–86, of the 1757 revised version of Mark Akenside's *Pleasures of Imagination*.

---

[1] Both the first and second editions had included Coleridge's "Monody on the Death of Chatterton," a selection of sonnets, and other reflective ("egotistic") verse "Effusions" and "Epistles," among them "The Eolian Harp."

[2] "An Evening Address to a Nightingale," by the minor poet Cuthbert Shaw (1739–1771).

INTRODUCTION TO THE SONNETS

THE COMPOSITION of the Sonnet has been regulated by Boileau in his Art of Poetry, and since Boileau, by William Preston, in the elegant preface to his Amatory Poems:[1] the rules, which they would establish, are founded on the practice of Petrarch. I have never yet been able to discover either sense, nature, or poetic fancy in Petrarch's poems; they appear to me all one cold glitter of heavy conceits and metaphysical abstractions. However, Petrarch, although not the inventor of the Sonnet, was the first who made it popular; and his countrymen have taken *his* poems as the model. Charlotte Smith and Bowles[2] are they who first made the Sonnet popular among the present English: I am justified therefore by analogy in deducing its laws from *their* compositions.

The Sonnet then is a small poem, in which some lonely feeling is developed. It is limited to a *particular* number of lines, in order that the reader's mind having expected the close at the place in which he finds it, may rest satisfied; and that so the poem may acquire, as it were, a *Totality*,—in plainer phrase, may become a *Whole*. It is confined to fourteen lines, because as some particular number is necessary, and that particular number must be a small one, it may as well be fourteen as any other number. When no reason can be adduced against a thing, Custom is a sufficient reason for it. Perhaps, if the Sonnet were comprized in less than fourteen lines, it would become a serious Epigram; if it extended to more, it would encroach on the province of the Elegy. Poems, in which no lonely feeling is developed, are not Sonnets because the Author has chosen to write them in fourteen lines: they should rather be entitled Odes, or Songs, or Inscriptions. The greater part of Warton's Sonnets are severe and masterly likenesses of the style of the Greek επιγραμματα.[3]

In a Sonnet then we require a developement of some lonely feeling, by whatever cause it may have been excited; but those Sonnets appear to me the most exquisite, in which moral Sentiments, Affections, or Feelings, are deduced from, and associated with, the scenery of Nature. Such compositions generate a habit of thought highly favourable to delicacy of character. They create a sweet and indissoluble union between the intellectual and the material world. Easily remembered from their briefness, and interesting alike to the eye and the affections, these are the poems which we can "lay up in our heart, and our soul," and repeat them "when we walk by the way, and when we lie down, and when we rise up."[4] Hence, the Sonnets of BOWLES derive their marked superiority over all other Sonnets; hence they domesticate with the heart, and become, as it were, a part of our identity.

Respecting the metre of a Sonnet, the Writer should consult his own convenience.—Rhymes, many or few, or no rhymes at all—whatever the chastity of his ear may prefer, whatever the rapid expression of his feelings will permit;—all these things are left at his own disposal. A sameness in the final sound of its words is the great and grevious defect of the Italian language. That rule therefore, which the Italians have established, of exactly *four* different sounds in the Sonnet, seems to have arisen from their wish to have *as many*, not from any dread of finding *more*. But surely it is ridiculous to make the *defect* of a foreign language a reason for our not availing ourselves of one of the marked excellencies of our own. "The Sonnet (says Preston) will ever be cultivated by those who write on tender pathetic subjects. It is peculiarly adapted to the state of a man violently agitated by a real passion, and wanting composure and vigor of mind to methodize his thought. It is fitted to express a momentary burst of passion," &c. Now, if there be one species of composition more difficult and artificial than another, it is an English Sonnet on the Italian Model. Adapted to the agitations of a real passion! Express momentary bursts of feeling in it! I should sooner expect to write pathetic *Axes* or *pour forth extempore Eggs and Altars*![5] But the best confutation of such idle rules is to be found in the Sonnets of those who have observed them, in their inverted sentences, their quaint phrases, and incongruous mixture of obsolete and spenserian words: and when, at last, the thing is toiled and ham-

---

[1] Nicolas Boileau-Despréaux (1636–1711) was a leading French neoclassical critic and poet. For his remarks on the sonnet, see *l'Art Poétique* (1674), II, 82–102. William Preston (1753–1807) was a minor poet and dramatist. Coleridge refers to, and later quotes from, the introductory comments to "Sonnets, Love Elegies, and Amatory Poems," in *The Poetical Works of William Preston* (1793), I, 268.

[2] Charlotte Smith (1749–1806) was a poet and popular novelist. Her *Elegiac Sonnets* (1784) enjoyed an enormous success. William Lisle Bowles (1762–1850) was the author of the very influential *Fourteen Sonnets written chiefly on Picturesque Spots during a Journey* published in 1789.

[3] Thomas Warton's *Poems* (1777) had included nine much-admired sonnets. In contrast to the personal voice and "lonely feeling" developed in the sonnets of Bowles and Coleridge, Warton's sonnets were more like "serious" Greek επιγραμματα ("epigrams"), that is, commemorative inscription-verses on historic places, personages, and works of art. See especially the

sonnets "Written at Stonehenge," "On King Arthur's Round Table at Wincester," and "Written in a Blank Leaf of Dugdale's Monasticon."

[4] See Deuteronomy, xi, 18–19.

[5] Refers to *Carmina Figurata*, poems artfully constructed in the shape of the objects they describe, such as George Herbert's "Altar" and "Easter Wings."

mered into fit shape, it is in general racked and tortured Prose rather than any thing resembling Poetry.

The Sonnet has been ever a favorite species of composition with me; but I am conscious that I have not succeeded in it. From a large number I have retained ten only, as not beneath mediocrity. Whatever more is said of them, ponamus lucro.[6]

[1796]   [1797]

PITT

Between 1799 and 1803, Coleridge attempted to support himself and his family by writing political articles for the London newspaper The Morning Post. *Of the more than sixty articles identified as Coleridge's or attributed to him, the most famous was the characterization of Pitt. Despite his personal and political differences with Coleridge, Hazlitt included this "masterly" essay in his* Political Essays *of 1819; and it remains today, in the works of Walter Jackson Bate, "one of the classics of political journalism." The essay on Pitt was to have been followed by one on Napoleon, which was never written.*

Coleridge's journalism was first brought together in Essays on his own Times, *prepared by his daughter Sara, in 1850. A new edition for* The Collected Works of Samuel Taylor Coleridge *is in preparation by David Erdman.*

PITT

PLUTARCH, in his comparative biography of Rome and Greece, has generally chosen for each pair of Lives the two contemporaries who most nearly resembled each other. His work would perhaps have been more interesting, if he had adopted the contrary arrangement, and selected those rather, who had attained to the possession of similar influence, or similar fame, by means, actions, and talents the most dissimilar. For power is the sole object of philosophical attention in man, as in inanimate nature; and in the one equally as in the other, we understand it more intimately, the more diverse the circumstances are with which we have observed it co-exist. In our days the two persons, who appear to have influenced the interests and actions of men the most deeply and the most diffusively, are beyond doubt the Chief Consul of France, and the Prime Minister of Great Britain: and in these two are presented to us similar situations, with the greatest dissimilitude of characters.

William Pitt was the younger son of Lord Chatham;[1] a fact of no ordinary importance in the solution of his character, of no mean significance in the heraldry of morals and intellect. His father's rank, fame, political connections, and parental ambition were his mould:—he was cast, rather than grew. A palpable election, a conscious predestination controlled the free agency, and transfigured the individuality of his mind; and that, which he *might have been*, was compelled into that, which he *was to be*. From his early childhood it was his father's custom to make him stand up on a chair, and declaim before a large company; by which exercise, practised so frequently, and continued for so many years, he acquired a premature and unnatural dexterity in the combination of words, which must of necessity have diverted his attention from present objects, obscured his impressions, and deadened his genuine feelings. Not the *thing* on which he was speaking, but the praises to be gained by the speech, were present to his intuition; hence he associated all the operations of his faculties with words, and his pleasures with the surprise excited by them.—But an inconceivably large portion of human knowledge and human power is involved in the science and management of *words*; and an education of words, though it destroys genius, will often create, and always foster, talent. The young Pitt was conspicuous far beyond his fellows, both at school and at college. He was always full grown: he had neither the promise nor the awkwardness of a growing intellect. Vanity, early satiated, formed and elevated itself into a love of power; and in losing this colloquial vanity, he lost one of the prime links that connect the individual with the species, too early for the affections, though not too early for the understanding. At college he was a severe student; his mind was founded and elemented in words and generalities, and these too formed all the super-structure. That revelry and that debauchery, which are so often fatal to the powers of intellect, would probably have been serviceable to him; they would have given him a closer communion with realities, they would have induced a greater presentness to present objects. But Mr. Pitt's conduct was correct, unimpressibly correct. His after-discipline in the special pleader's office, and at the bar, carried on the scheme of his education with unbroken uniformity, His first political connections were with the Reformers; but those who accuse him of sympathising or coalescing with their intemperate or visionary plans, misunderstand his character, and are ignorant of the historical facts. Imaginary situations in an imaginary state of things rise up in minds that possess a power and facility in combining images. —Mr. Pitt's ambition was conversant with old situations in the old state of things, which furnish nothing to the imagination, though much to the wishes. In his endeavours to realise his father's plan of reform, he

---

[6] ponamus lucro: "let us count as pure profit."
[1] William Pitt, first Earl of Chatham (1708–1778), was one of the leading statesmen and political figures of his time.

was probably as sincere as a being, who had derived so little knowledge from actual impressions, could be. But his sincerity had no living root of affection: while it was propped up by his love of praise and immediate power, so long it stood erect and no longer. He became a Member of the Parliament—supported the popular opinions, and in a few years, by the influence of the popular party was placed in that high and awful rank in which he now is. The fortunes of his country, we had almost said, the fates of the world, were placed in his wardship—we sink in prostration before the inscrutable dispensations of Providence, when we reflect in whose wardship the fates of the world were placed!

The influencer of his country and of his species was a young man, the creature of another's pre-determination, sheltered and weather-fended from all the elements of experience; a young man, whose feet had never wandered; whose very eye had never turned to the right or to the left; whose whole track had been as curveless as the motion of a fascinated reptile! It was a young man, whose heart was solitary, because he had existed always amid objects of futurity, and whose imagination too was unpopulous, because those objects of hope, to which his habitual wishes had transferred, and as it were *projected*, his existence, were all familiar and long-established objects!—A plant sown and reared in a hot-house, for whom the very air, that surrounded him, had been regulated by the thermometer of previous purpose; to whom the light of nature had penetrated only through glasses and covers; who had had the sun without the breeze; whom no storm had shaken; on whom no rain had pattered; on whom the dews of Heaven had not fallen!—A being, who had had no feelings connected with man or nature, no spontaneous impulses, no unbiassed and desultory studies, no genuine science, nothing that constitutes individuality in intellect, nothing that teaches brotherhood in affection! Such was the man—such, and so denaturalised the spirit, on whose wisdom and philanthropy the lives and living enjoyments of so many millions of human beings were made unavoidably dependent. From this time a real enlargement of mind became almost impossible. Pre-occupations, intrigue, the undue passion and anxiety, with which all facts must be surveyed; the crowd and confusion of those facts, none of them seen, but all communicated, and by that very circumstance, and by the necessity of perpetually classifying them, transmuted into words and generalities; pride; flattery; irritation; artificial power; these, and circumstances resembling these, necessarily render the heights of office barren heights, which command indeed a vast and extensive prospect, but attract so many clouds and vapours, that most often

all prospect is precluded. Still, however, Mr. Pitt's situation, however inauspicious for his real being, was favourable to his fame. He heaped period on period; persuaded himself and the nation, that extemporaneous arrangement of sentences was eloquence; and that eloquence implied wisdom. His father's struggles for freedom, and his own attempts, gave him an almost unexampled popularity; and his office necessarily associated with his name all the great events, that happened during his Administration. There were not however wanting men, who saw through this delusion; and refusing to attribute the industry, integrity, and enterprising spirit of our merchants, the agricultural improvements of our land-holders, the great inventions of our manufacturers, or the valour and skilfulness of our sailors to the merits of a Minister, they have continued to decide on his character from those acts and those merits, which belong to him, and to him alone. Judging him by this standard, they have been able to discover in him no one proof or symptom of a commanding genius. They have discovered him never controlling, never creating, events, but always yielding himself to them with rapid change, and sheltering from inconsistency by perpetual indefiniteness. In the Russian war,[2] they saw him abandoning meanly what he had planned weakly, and threatened insolently. In the debates on the Regency,[3] they detected the laxity of his constitutional principles, and received proofs that his eloquence consisted, not in the ready application of a general system to particular questions, but in the facility of arguing for or against any question by specious generalities, without reference to any system. In these debates, he combined what is most dangerous in democracy, with all that is most degrading in the old superstitions of Monarchy, and taught an inherency of the office in the person, in order to make the office itself a nullity, and the Premiership, with its accompanying majority, the sole and permanent power of the State. And now came the French Revolution. This was a new event; the old routine of reasoning, the common trade of politics, were to become obsolete. He appeared wholly unprepared for it. Half favouring, half condemning, ignorant of what he

---

[2] Referring to the Russian-Turkish War, 1787–1792. In 1791, Pitt sent Catherine the Great an ultimatum to return all of the captured Turkish territory except the Crimea. Lack of support for Pitt's action within his own government and the country at large caused him subsequently to reverse his position.

[3] The insanity of George III in November 1788 provoked heated debates between the opposition party, which demanded the immediate installation as Regent of their favorite, the Prince of Wales; and Pitt, who sought to delay the action by arguing, in a dramatic reversal of usual Tory philosophy, for the claims of the Commons against such a regency. The King's recovery in February 1789 ended the political dispute.

favoured, and why he condemned, he neither displayed the honest enthusiasm and fixed principle of Mr. Fox, nor the intimate acquaintance with the general nature of man, and the consequent *prescience* of Mr. Burke. After the declaration of war, long did he continue in the common cant of office, in declamation about the Scheld, and Holland, and all the vulgar causes of common contests! and when at least the immense genius of his new supporter had beat him out of these *words*, (words, signifying *places* and *dead objects*, and signifying nothing more) he adopted other words in their places, other generalities—Atheism and Jacobinism—phrases, which he learnt from Mr. Burke, but without learning the philosophical definitions and involved consequences, with which that great man accompanied those words. Since the death of Mr. Burke, the forms and the sentiments, and the tone of the French, have undergone many and important changes: how indeed is it possible, that it should be otherwise, while man is the creature of experience! But still Mr. Pitt proceeds in an endless repetition of the same *general phrases*. This is his element; deprive him of general and abstract phrases, and you reduce him to silence. But you cannot deprive him of them. Press him to specify an *individual* fact of advantage to be derived from a war—and he answers, SECURITY! Call upon him to particularise a crime, and he exclaims—JACOBINISM! Abstractions defined by abstractions! Generalities defined by generalities! As a Minister of Finance, he is still, as ever, the man of words, and abstractions! Figures, custom-house reports, imports and exports, commerce and revenue—all flourishing, all splendid! Never was such a prosperous country, as England, under his administration! Let it be objected, that the agriculture of the country is, by the overbalance of commerce, and by various and complex causes, in such a state, that the country hangs as a pensioner for bread on its neighbours, and a bad season uniformly threatens us with famine—this (it is replied) is owing to our PROSPERITY—all *prosperous* nations are in great distress for food!—Still PROSPERITY, still GENERAL PHRASES, unenforced by one *single image*, one *single fact* of real national amelioration, of any one comfort enjoyed, where it was not before enjoyed, of any one class of society becoming healthier, or wiser, or happier. These are *things*, these are realities; and these Mr. Pitt has neither the imagination to body forth, or the sensibility to feel for. Once indeed, in an evil hour, intriguing for popularity, he suffered himself to be persuaded to evince a talent, for the Real, the Individual: and he brought in his POOR BILL!! When we hear the Minister's talents for finance so loudly trumpeted, we turn involuntarily to his POOR BILL—to that acknowledged abortion—that unanswerable

evidence of his ignorance respecting all the fundamental relations and actions of property, and of the social union!

As his reasonings, even so is his eloquence. One character pervades his whole being. Words on words, finely arranged, and so dexterously consequent, that the whole bears the semblance of argument, and still keeps awake a sense of surprise—but when all is done, nothing remarkable has been said; no one philosophical remark, no one image, not even a pointed aphorism. Not a sentence of Mr. Pitt's has ever been quoted, or formed the favourite phrase of the day—a thing unexampled in any man of equal reputation. But while he speaks, the effect varies according to the character of his auditor. The man of no talent is swallowed up in surprise: and when the speech is ended, he remembers his feelings, but nothing distinct of that which produced them—(how opposite an effect to that of nature and genius, from whose works the idea still remains, when the feeling is passed away—remains to connect itself with other feelings, and combine with new impressions!) The mere man of talent hears him with admiration—the mere man of genius with contempt—the philosopher neither admires nor contemns, but listens to him with a deep and solemn interest, tracing in the effects of his eloquence the power of words and phrases, and that peculiar constitution of human affairs in their present state, which so eminently favours this power.

Such appears to us to be the Prime Minister of Great Britain, whether we consider him as a statesman, or as an orator. The same character betrays itself in his private life, the same coldness to realities, to images of realities, and to all whose excellence relates to reality. He has patronised no science, he has raised no man of genius from obscurity, he counts no one prime work of God among his friends. From the same source he has no attachment to female society, no fondness for children, no perceptions of beauty in natural scenery; but he is fond of convivial indulgencies, of that stimulation, which, keeping up the glow of self-importance and the sense of internal power, gives feelings without the mediation of ideas.

These are the elements of his mind; the accidents of his fortune, the circumstances that enabled such a mind to acquire and retain such a power, would form the subject of a philosophical history, and that too of no scanty size. We can scarcely furnish the chapter of contents to a work, which would comprise subjects so important and delicate, as the causes of the diffusion and intensity of secret influence; the machinery and state-intrigue of marriages; the overbalance of the commercial interest; the panic of property struck by the late Revolution; the short-sightedness of the careful; the carelessness of the far-sighted; and all those many and various events which have given to a decorous profession of religion, and a seemliness of private morals, such an unwonted weight in the attainment and preservation of public power. We are unable to determine whether it be more consolatory or humiliating to human nature, that so many complexities of event, situation, character, age, and country, should be necessary in order to the production of a Mr. PITT.

[March 19, 1800]

A COURSE OF LECTURES ON SHAKESPEAR
AND MILTON

Some of Coleridge's finest literary criticism was contained in the various series of lectures he delivered between 1808 and 1819. Unlike Hazlitt, Coleridge published none of his lecture series; and, with the exception of those for the London Philosophical Society in 1818 for which he wrote a fairly full text in advance, he delivered most of the literary lectures extemporaneously from only the most meager outline or notes. Fortunately, extensive reports of seven of the seventeen "Lectures on Shakespear and Milton" delivered in London between November 18, 1811, and January 27, 1812, survive from the shorthand accounts of J. P. Collier (1789–1883), parliamentary reporter, journalist, and a literary editor of considerable importance and controversy. Collier's transcriptions of these reports were first published in full in 1856 as Seven Lectures on Shakespeare and Milton. *The texts of the seventh, ninth, and twelfth lectures are here reproduced from the 1856 edition. The history and often-questioned authenticity of Collier's texts are discussed at length in R. A. Foakes's introduction to his edition* Coleridge on Shakespeare: The Text of the Lectures of 1811–1812 (London: Routledge and Kegan Paul, 1971).*

For a full account of Coleridge's various literary lectures, see Thomas Middleton Raysor's editions of* Coleridge's Shakespearean Criticism, *2 vols. (London: Constable and Co., 1930) [revised edition, Everyman's Library, 1960]; and* Coleridge's Miscellaneous Criticism *(Cambridge, Mass.: Harvard University Press, 1936).*

A COURSE OF
LECTURES
ON
SHAKESPEAR and MILTON,
IN ILLUSTRATION OF THE
PRINCIPLES OF POETRY

THE SEVENTH LECTURE
[*Romeo and Juliet*]
DECEMBER 9, 1811

IN A FORMER lecture I endeavoured to point out the union of the Poet and the Philosopher, or rather the warm embrace between them, in the "Venus and Adonis" and "Lucrece" of Shakespeare. From thence I passed on to "Love's Labours Lost," as the link between his character as a Poet, and his art as a Dramatist; and I shewed that, although in that work the former was still predominant, yet that the germs of his subsequent dramatic power were easily discernible.

I will now, as I promised in my last, proceed to "Romeo and Juliet," not because it is the earliest, or among the earliest of Shakespeare's works of that kind, but because in it are to be found specimens, in degree, of all the excellences which he afterwards displayed in his more perfect dramas, but differing from them in being less forcibly evidenced, and less happily combined: all the parts are more or less present, but they are not united with the same harmony.

There are, however, in "Romeo and Juliet" passages where the poet's whole excellence is evinced, so that nothing superior to them can be met with in the productions of his after years. The main distinction between this play and others is, as I said, that the parts are less happily combined, or to borrow a phrase from the painter, the whole work is less in keeping. Grand portions are produced: we have limbs of giant growth; but the production, as a whole, in which each part gives delight for itself, and the whole, consisting of these delightful parts, communicates the highest intellectual pleasure and satisfaction, is the result of the application of judgment and taste. These are not to be attained but by painful study, and to the sacrifice of the stronger pleasures derived from the dazzling light which a man of genius throws over every circumstance, and where we are chiefly struck by vivid and distinct images. Taste is an attainment after a poet has been disciplined by experience, and has added to genius that talent by which he knows what part of his genius he can make acceptable, and intelligible to the portion of mankind for which he writes.

In my mind it would be a hopeless symptom, as regards genius, if I found a young man with anything like perfect taste. In the earlier works of Shakespeare we have a profusion of double epithets,[1] and sometimes even the coarsest terms are employed, if they convey a more vivid image; but by degrees the associations are connected with the image they are designed to impress, and the poet descends from the ideal into the real world so far as to conjoin both—to give a sphere of active operations to the ideal, and to elevate and refine the real.

In "Romeo and Juliet" the principal characters may be divided into two classes: in one class passion—the passion of love—is drawn and drawn truly, as well as beautifully; but the persons are not individualised farther than as the actor appears on the stage.[2] It is a very just description and development of love, without giving, if I may so express myself, the philosophical history of it—without shewing how the man became acted upon by that particular passion, but leading it through all the incidents of the drama, and rendering it predominant.

Tybalt is, in himself, a common-place personage. And here allow me to remark upon a great distinction between Shakespeare, and all who have written in imitation of him. I know no character in his plays, (unless indeed Pistol[3] be an exception) which can be called the mere portrait of an individual: while the reader feels all the satisfaction arising from individuality, yet that very individual is a sort of class character, and this circumstance renders Shakespeare the poet of all ages.

Tybalt is a man abandoned to his passions—with all the pride of family, only because he thought it belonged to him as a member of that family, and valuing himself highly, simply because he does not care for death. This indifference to death is perhaps more common than any other feeling: men are apt to flatter themselves extravagantly, merely because they possess a quality which it is a disgrace not to have, but which a wise man never puts forward, but when it is necessary.

Jeremy Taylor in one part of his voluminous works, speaking of a great man, says that he was naturally a coward, as indeed most men are, knowing the value of life, but the power of his reason enabled him, when required, to conduct himself with uniform courage and hardihood. The good bishop, perhaps, had in his mind a story, told by one of the ancients, of a Philosopher and a Coxcomb, on board the same ship during a storm: the Coxcomb reviled the Philosopher for betraying marks of fear: "Why are you so frightened? I am not afraid of being drowned: I do not care a farthing for my life."—"You are perfectly right," said the Philosopher, "for your life is not worth a farthing."

Shakespeare never takes pains to make his characters win your esteem, but leaves it to the general command of the passions, and to poetic justice. It is most beautiful to observe, in "Romeo and Juliet," that the characters principally engaged in the incidents are preserved innocent from all that could lower them in our opinion, while the rest of the personages, deserving little interest in themselves, derive it from being instrumental in those situations in which the more important personages develope their thoughts and passions.

Look at Capulet—a worthy, noble-minded old man of high rank, with all the impatience that is likely to accompany it. It is delightful to see all the sensibilities of our nature so exquisitely called forth; as if the poet had the hundred arms of the polypus, and had thrown them out in all directions to catch the predominant feeling. We may see in Capulet the manner in which anger seizes hold of everything that comes in its way, in order to express itself, as in the lines where he reproves Tybalt for his fierceness of behaviour, which led him to wish to insult a Montague, and disturb the merriment.—

> "Go to, go to;
> You are a saucy boy. Is't so, indeed?
> This trick may chance to scath you;—I know what.
> You must contrary me! marry, 'tis time.—
> Well said, my hearts!—You are a princox: go:
> Be quiet or—More light, more light!—For shame!
> I'll make you quiet.—What! cheerly, my hearts!"
>
> *Act I., Scene 5.*[4]

The line

"This trick may chance to scath you;—I know what,"

was an allusion to the legacy Tybalt might expect; and

---

[1] See *Biographia Literaria*, Chapter I, in which Coleridge acknowledges that "a profusion of new coined double epithets" was characteristic of his own early poetry.

[2] Collier's account of the two classes of characters is not very clear. The first class would seem to embrace Tybalt, Capulet, and the Nurse; the second class, "Shakespeare's favourite" and more deeply developed characters, is illustrated by Mercutio. However, as Coleridge argued, even Shakespeare's treatment of the first class meant not merely the external noting of eccentric details of character, but a psychological penetration into and a becoming of the character observed, thus producing believable and universally recognizable representative or "class" characters.

[3] A bombastic associate of Falstaff in *Merry Wives of Windsor, Henry the Fourth*, Part II, and *Henry the Fifth*.

[4] Ll. 84–90.

then, seeing the lights burn dimly, Capulet turns his anger against the servants. Thus we see that no one passion is so predominant, but that it includes all the parts of the character, and the reader never has a mere abstract of a passion, as of wrath or ambition, but the whole man is presented to him—the one predominant passion acting, if I may so say, as the leader of the band to the rest.

It could not be expected that the poet should introduce such a character as Hamlet into every play; but even in those personages, which are subordinate to a hero so eminently philosophical, the passion is at least rendered instructive, and induces the reader to look with a keener eye, and a finer judgment into human nature.

Shakespeare has this advantage over all other dramatists—that he has availed himself of his psychological genius to develope all the minutiæ of the human heart: shewing us the thing that, to common observers, he seems solely intent upon, he makes visible what we should not otherwise have seen: just as, after looking at distant objects through a telescope, when we behold them subsequently with the naked eye, we see them with greater distinctness, and in more detail, than we should otherwise have done.

Mercutio is one of our poet's truly Shakespearian characters; for throughout his plays, but especially in those of the highest order, it is plain that the personages were drawn rather from meditation than from observation, or to speak correctly, more from observation, the child of meditation. It is comparatively easy for a man to go about the world, as if with a pocket-book in his hand, carefully noting down what he sees and hears: by practice he acquires considerable facility in representing what he has observed, himself frequently unconscious of its worth, or its bearings. This is entirely different from the observation of a mind, which, having formed a theory and a system upon its own nature, remarks all things that are examples of its truth, confirming it in that truth, and, above all, enabling it to convey the truths of philosophy, as mere effects derived from, what we may call, the outward watchings of life.

Hence it is that Shakespeare's favourite characters are full of such lively intellect. Mercutio is a man possessing all the elements of a poet: the whole world was, as it were, subject to his law of association. Whenever he wishes to impress anything, all things become his servants for the purpose: all things tell the same tale, and sound in unison. This faculty, moreover, is combined with the manners and feelings of a perfect gentleman, himself utterly unconscious of his powers. By his loss it was contrived that the whole catastrophe of the tragedy should be brought about: it endears him

to Romeo, and gives to the death of Mercutio an importance which it could not otherwise have acquired.

I say this in answer to an observation, I think by Dryden, (to which indeed Dr. Johnson has fully replied)[5] that Shakespeare having carried the part of Mercutio as far as he could, till his genius was exhausted, had killed him in the third Act, to get him out of the way. What shallow nonsense! As I have remarked, upon the death of Mercutio the whole catastrophe depends; it is produced by it. The scene in which it occurs serves to show how indifference to any subject but one, and aversion to activity on the part of Romeo, may be overcome and roused to the most resolute and determined conduct. Had not Mercutio been rendered so amiable and so interesting, we could not have felt so strongly the necessity for Romeo's interference, connecting it immediately, and passionately, with the future fortunes of the lover and his mistress.

But what am I to say of the Nurse? We have been told that her character is the mere fruit of observation—that it is like Swift's "Polite Conversation,"[6] certainly the most stupendous work of human memory, and of unceasingly active attention to what passes around us, upon record. The Nurse in "Romeo and Juliet" has sometimes been compared to a portrait by Gerard Dow,[7] in which every hair was so exquisitely painted, that it would bear the test of the microscope. Now, I appeal confidently to my hearers whether the closest observation of the manners of one or two old nurses would have enabled Shakespeare to draw this character of admirable generalisation? Surely not. Let any man conjure up in his mind all the qualities and peculiarities that can possibly belong to a nurse, and he will find them in Shakespeare's picture of the old woman: nothing is omitted. This effect is not produced by mere observation. The great prerogative of genius (and Shakespeare felt and availed himself of it) is now to swell itself to the dignity of a god, and now to subdue and keep dormant some part of that lofty nature, and to descend even to the lowest character—to become everything, in fact, but the vicious.

Thus, in the Nurse you have all the garrulity of old age, and all its fondness; for the affection of old age is one of the greatest consolations of humanity. I have

5 See "A Defense of the Epilogue" in Dryden's *The Conquest of Granada, the Second Part* (1672). Johnson's reply was made in a note on *Romeo and Juliet* in his edition of Shakespeare (1765).

6 Refers to *A Complete Collection of Genteel and Ingenious Conversation* (1738), Swift's satire on the false wit, pedantry, and emptiness of social discourse. The work consists of three dialogues constructed of "polite questions, answers, repartees, replies, and rejoiners [collected] with infinite labour, and close attention during the space of thirty-six years."

7 Gerard Dou (1613–1675) was a Dutch genre painter.

often thought what a melancholy world this would be without children, and what an inhuman world without the aged.

You have also in the Nurse the arrogance of ignorance, with the pride of meanness at being connected with a great family. You have the grossness, too, which that situation never removes, though it sometimes suspends it; and, arising from that grossness, the little low vices attendant upon it, which, indeed, in such minds are scarcely vices.—Romeo at one time was the most delightful and excellent young man, and the Nurse all willingness to assist him; but her disposition soon turns in favour of Paris, for whom she professes precisely the same admiration. How wonderfully are these low peculiarities contrasted with a young and pure mind, educated under different circumstances!

Another point ought to be mentioned as characteristic of the ignorance of the Nurse:—it is, that in all her recollections, she assists herself by the remembrance of visual circumstances. The great difference, in this respect, between the cultivated and the uncultivated mind is this—that the cultivated mind will be found to recal the past by certain regular trains of cause and effect; whereas, with the uncultivated mind, the past is recalled wholly by coincident images, or facts which happened at the same time.[8] This position is fully exemplified in the following passages put into the mouth of the Nurse:—

> "Even or odd, of all days in the year,
>   Come Lammas eve at night shall she be fourteen.
> Susan and she—God rest all Christian souls!—
> Were of an age.—Well, Susan is with God;
> She was too good for me. But, as I said,
> On Lammas eve at night shall she be fourteen;
> That shall she, marry: I remember it well.
> 'Tis since the earthquake now eleven years;
> And she was wean'd,—I never shall forget it,—
> Of all the days of the year, upon that day;
> For I had then laid wormwood to my dug,
> Sitting in the sun under the dove-house wall:
> My lord and you were then at Mantua.—
> Nay, I do bear a brain:—but, as I said,
> When it did taste the wormwood on the nipple
> Of my dug, and felt it bitter, pretty fool,
> To see it tetchy, and fall out with the dug!
> Shake, quoth the dove-house: 'twas no need, I trow,
> To bid me trudge.
> And since that time it is eleven years;
> For then she could stand alone."

Act I., Scene 3.[9]

She afterwards goes on with similar visual impressions, so true to the character.—More is here brought into one portrait than could have been ascertained by one man's mere observation, and without the introduction of a single incongruous point.

I honour, I love, the works of Fielding as much, or perhaps more, than those of any other writer of fiction of that kind: take Fielding in his characters of postillions, landlords, and landladies, waiters, or indeed, of any-body who had come before his eye, and nothing can be more true, more happy, or more humorous; but in all his chief personages, Tom Jones for instance, where Fielding was not directed by observation, where he could not assist himself by the close copying of what he saw, where it is necessary that something should take place, some words be spoken, or some object described, which he could not have witnessed, (his soliloquies for example, or the interview between the hero and Sophia Western before the reconciliation)[10] and I will venture to say, loving and honouring the man and his productions as I do, that nothing can be more forced and unnatural: the language is without vivacity or spirit, the whole matter is incongruous, and totally destitute of psychological truth.

On the other hand, look at Shakespeare: where can any character be produced that does not speak the language of nature? where does he not put into the mouths of his *dramatis personæ*, be they high or low, Kings or Constables, precisely what they must have said? Where, from observation, could he learn the language proper to Sovereigns, Queens, Noblemen or Generals? yet he invariably uses it.—Where, from observation, could he have learned such lines as these, which are put into the mouth of Othello, when he is talking to Iago of Brabantio?

> "Let him do his spite:
> My services, which I have done the signiory,
> Shall out-tongue his complaints. 'Tis yet to know,
> Which, when I know that boasting is an honour,
> I shall promulgate, I fetch my life and being
> From men of royal siege; and my demerits
> May speak, unbonneted, to as proud a fortune
> As this that I have reach'd: for know, Iago,
> But that I love the gentle Desdemona,
> I would not my unhoused free condition
> Put into circumscription and confine
> For the sea's worth."

Act I., Scene 2.[11]

I ask where was Shakespeare to observe such language as this? If he did observe it, it was with the in-

---

[8] See Essay IV ["On Method"] from Section the Second of *The Friend* (1818).
[9] Ll. 16–36.

[10] See *Tom Jones*, Book XVIII, Chapter xii.   [11] Ll. 17–28.

ward eye of meditation upon his own nature: for the time, he became Othello, and spoke as Othello, in such circumstances, must have spoken.

Another remark I may make upon "Romeo and Juliet" is, that in this tragedy the poet is not, as I have hinted, entirely blended with the dramatist,—at least, not in the degree to be afterwards noticed in "Lear," "Hamlet," "Othello," or "Macbeth." Capulet and Montague not unfrequently talk a language only belonging to the poet, and not so characteristic of, and peculiar to, the passions of persons in the situations in which they are placed—a mistake, or rather an indistinctness, which many of our later dramatists have carried through the whole of their productions.

When I read the song of Deborah,[12] I never think that she is a poet, although I think the song itself a sublime poem: it is as simple a dithyrambic production as exists in any language; but it is the proper and characteristic effusion of a woman highly elevated by triumph, by the natural hatred of oppressors, and resulting from a bitter sense of wrong: it is a song of exultation on deliverance from these evils, a deliverance accomplished by herself. When she exclaims, "The inhabitants of the villages ceased, they ceased in Israel, until that I, Deborah, arose, that I arose a mother in Israel," it is poetry in the highest sense: we have no reason, however, to suppose that if she had not been agitated by passion, and animated by victory, she would have been able so to express herself; or that if she had been placed in different circumstances, she would have used such language of truth and passion. We are to remember that Shakespeare, not placed under circumstances of excitement, and only wrought upon by his own vivid and vigorous imagination, writes a language that invariably, and intuitively becomes the condition and position of each character.

On the other hand, there is a language not descriptive of passion, not uttered under the influence of it, which is at the same time poetic, and shows a high and active fancy, as when Capulet says to Paris,—

"Such comfort as do lusty young men feel,
When well-apparell'd April on the heel
Of limping winter treads, even such delight
Among fresh female buds, shall you this night
Inherit at my house."

Act I., Scene 2.[13]

Here the poet may be said to speak, rather than the dramatist; and it would be easy to adduce other passages from this play, where Shakespeare, for a moment

forgetting the character, utters his own words in his own person.

In my mind, what have often been censured as Shakespeare's conceits are completely justifiable, as belonging to the state, age, or feeling of the individual. Sometimes, when they cannot be vindicated on these grounds, they may well be excused by the taste of his own and of the preceding age; as for instance, in Romeo's speech,

"Here's much to do with hate, but more with love:—
Why then, O brawling love! O loving hate!
O anything, of nothing first created!
O heavy lightness! serious vanity!
Misshapen chaos of well-seeming forms!
Feather of lead, bright smoke, cold fire, sick health!
Still-waking sleep, that is not what it is!"

Act I., Scene 1.[14]

I dare not pronounce such passages as these to be absolutely unnatural, not merely because I consider the author a much better judge than I can be, but because I can understand and allow for an effort of the mind, when it would describe what it cannot satisfy itself with the description of, to reconcile opposites and qualify contradictions, leaving a middle state of mind more strictly appropriate to the imagination than any other, when it is, as it were, hovering between images. As soon as it is fixed on one image, it becomes understanding; but while it is unfixed and wavering between them, attaching itself permanently to none, it is imagination. Such is the fine description of Death in Milton:—

"The other shape,
If shape it might be call'd, that shape had none
Distinguishable in member, joint, or limb,
Or substance might be call'd, that shadow seem'd,
For each seem'd either: black it stood as night;
Fierce as ten furies, terrible as hell,
And shook a dreadful dart: what seem'd his head
The likeness of a kingly crown had on."

Paradise Lost, Book II.[15]

The grandest efforts of poetry are where the imagination is called forth, not to produce a distinct form, but a strong working of the mind, still offering what is still repelled, and again creating what is again rejected; the result being what the poet wishes to impress, namely, the substitution of a sublime feeling of the unimaginable for a mere image. I have sometimes thought that the passage just read might be quoted as exhibiting the narrow limit of painting, as compared

---

[12] See Judges, v.   [13] Ll. 26–30.   [14] Ll. 182–88.   [15] Ll. 666–73.

with the boundless power of poetry: painting cannot go beyond a certain point; poetry rejects all control, all confinement. Yet we know that sundry painters have attempted pictures of the meeting between Satan and Death at the gates of Hell; and how was Death represented? Not as Milton has described him, but by the most defined thing that can be imagined—a skeleton, the dryest and hardest image that it is possible to discover; which, instead of keeping the mind in a state of activity, reduces it to the merest passivity,—an image, compared with which a square, a triangle, or any other mathematical figure, is a luxuriant fancy.

It is a general but mistaken notion that, because some forms of writing, and some combinations of thought, are not usual, they are not natural; but we are to recollect that the dramatist represents his characters in every situation of life and in every state of mind, and there is no form of language that may not be introduced with effect by a great and judicious poet, and yet be most strictly according to nature. Take punning, for instance, which may be the lowest, but at all events is the most harmless, kind of wit, because it never excites envy. A pun may be a necessary consequence of association: one man, attempting to prove something that was resisted by another, might, when agitated by strong feeling, employ a term used by his adversary with a directly contrary meaning to that for which that adversary had resorted to it: it might come into his mind as one way, and sometimes the best, of replying to that adversary. This form of speech is generally produced by a mixture of anger and contempt, and punning is a natural mode of expressing them.

It is my intention to pass over none of the important so-called conceits of Shakespeare, not a few of which are introduced into his later productions, with great propriety and effect. We are not to forget, that at the time he lived there was an attempt at, and an affectation of, quaintness and adornment, which emanated from the Court, and against which satire was directed by Shakespeare in the character of Osrick in Hamlet. Among the schoolmen of that age, and earlier, nothing was more common than the use of conceits: it began with the revival of letters, and the bias thus given was very generally felt and acknowledged.

I have in my possession a dictionary of phrases, in which the epithets applied to love, hate, jealousy, and such abstract terms, are arranged; and they consist almost entirely of words taken from Seneca [16] and his imitators, or from the schoolmen, showing perpetual antithesis, and describing the passions by the conjunction and combination of things absolutely irreconcileable. In treating the matter thus, I am aware that I am only palliating the practice in Shakespeare: he ought to have had nothing to do with merely temporary peculiarities: he wrote not for his own only, but for all ages, and so far I admit the use of some of his conceits to be a defect. They detract sometimes from his universality as to time, person, and situation.

If we were able to discover, and to point out the peculiar faults, as well as the peculiar beauties of Shakespeare, it would materially assist us in deciding what authority ought to be attached to certain portions of what are generally called his works. If we met with a play, or certain scenes of a play, in which we could trace neither his defects nor his excellences, we should have the strongest reason for believing that he had had no hand in it. In the case of scenes so circumstanced we might come to the conclusion that they were taken from the older plays, which, in some instances, he reformed or altered, or that they were inserted afterwards by some under-hand, in order to please the mob. If a drama by Shakespeare turned out to be too heavy for popular audiences, the clown might be called in to lighten the representation; and if it appeared that what was added was not in Shakespeare's manner, the conclusion would be inevitable, that it was not from Shakespeare's pen.

It remains for me to speak of the hero and heroine, of Romeo and Juliet themselves; and I shall do so with unaffected diffidence, not merely on account of the delicacy, but of the great importance of the subject. I feel that it is impossible to defend Shakespeare from the most cruel of all charges,—that he is an immoral writer—without entering fully into his mode of pourtraying female characters, and of displaying the passion of love. It seems to me, that he has done both with greater perfection than any other writer of the known world, perhaps with the single exception of Milton in his delineation of Eve.

When I have heard it said, or seen it stated, that Shakespeare wrote for man, but the gentle Fletcher for woman, [17] it has always given me something like acute pain, because to me it seems to do the greatest injustice to Shakespeare: when, too, I remember how much character is formed by what we read, I cannot look upon it as a light question, to be passed over as a mere amusement, like a game of cards or chess. I never have been able to tame down my mind to think poetry a sport, or an occupation for idle hours.

Perhaps there is no more sure criterion of refinement in moral character, of the purity of intellectual

---

[16] A famous first-century Stoic philosopher and dramatist.

[17] See Dryden's "Preface to *Troilus and Cressida*" (1679).

intention, and of the deep conviction and perfect sense of what our own nature really is in all its combinations, than the different definitions different men would give of love. I will not detain you by stating the various known definitions, some of which it may be better not to repeat: I will rather give you one of my own, which, I apprehend, is equally free from the extravagance of pretended Platonism (which, like other things which super-moralise, is sure to demoralise) and from its grosser opposite.

Consider myself and my fellow-men as a sort of link between heaven and earth, being composed of body and soul, with power to reason and to will, and with that perpetual aspiration which tells us that this is ours for a while, but it is not ourselves; considering man, I say, in this two-fold character, yet united in one person, I conceive that there can be no correct definition of love which does not correspond with our being, and with that subordination of one part to another which constitutes our perfection. I would say therefore that—

"Love is a desire of the whole being to be united to some thing, or some being, felt necessary to its completeness, by the most perfect means that nature permits, and reason dictates."

It is inevitable to every noble mind, whether man or woman, to feel itself, of itself, imperfect and insufficient, not as an animal only, but as a moral being. How wonderfully, then, has Providence contrived for us, by making that which is necessary to us a step in our exaltation to a higher and nobler state! The Creator has ordained that one should possess qualities which the other has not, and the union of both is the most complete ideal of human character. In everything the blending of the similar with the dissimilar is the secret of all pure delight. Who shall dare to stand alone, and vaunt himself, in himself, sufficient? In poetry it is the blending of passion with order that constitutes perfection: this is still more the case in morals, and more than all in the exclusive attachment of the sexes.

True it is, that the world and its business may be carried on without marriage; but it is so evident that Providence intended man (the only animal of all climates, and whose reason is pre-eminent over instinct) to be the master of the world, that marriage, or the knitting together of society by the tenderest, yet firmest ties, seems ordained to render him capable of maintaining his superiority over the brute creation. Man alone has been privileged to clothe himself, and to do all things so as to make him, as it were, a secondary creator of himself, and of his own happiness or misery: in this, as in all, the image of the Deity is impressed upon him.

Providence, then, has not left us to prudence only; for the power of calculation, which prudence implies, cannot have existed, but in a state which pre-supposes marriage. If God has done this, shall we suppose that he has given us no moral sense, no yearning, which is something more than animal, to secure that, without which man might form a herd, but could not be a society? The very idea seems to breathe absurdity.

From this union arise the paternal, filial, brotherly and sisterly relations of life; and every state is but a family magnified. All the operations of mind, in short, all that distinguishes us from brutes, originate in the more perfect state of domestic life.—One infallible criterion in forming an opinion of a man is the reverence in which he holds women. Plato has said, that in this way we rise from sensuality to affection, from affection to love, and from love to the pure intellectual delight by which we become worthy to conceive that infinite in ourselves, without which it is impossible for man to believe in a God. In a word, the grandest and most delightful of all promises has been expressed to us by this practical state—our marriage with the Redeemer of mankind.

I might safely appeal to every man who hears me, who in youth has been accustomed to abandon himself to his animal passions, whether when he first really fell in love, the earliest symptom was not a complete change in his manners, a contempt and a hatred of himself for having excused his conduct by asserting, that he acted according to the dictates of nature, that his vices were the inevitable consequences of youth, and that his passions at that period of life could not be conquered? The surest friend of chastity is love: it leads us, not to sink the mind in the body, but to draw up the body to the mind—the immortal part of our nature. See how contrasted in this respect are some portions of the works of writers, whom I need not name, with other portions of the same works: the ebullitions of comic humour have at times, by a lamentable confusion, been made the means of debasing our nature, while at other times, even in the same volume, we are happy to notice the utmost purity, such as the purity of love, which above all other qualities renders us most pure and lovely.

Love is not, like hunger, a mere selfish appetite: it is an associative quality. The hungry savage is nothing but an animal, thinking only of the satisfaction of his stomach: what is the first effect of love, but to associate the feeling with every object in nature? the trees whisper, the roses exhale their perfumes, the nightingales sing, nay the very skies smile in unison with the feeling of true and pure love. It gives to every object in nature a power of the heart, without which it would indeed be spiritless.

Shakespeare has described this passion in various states and stages, beginning, as was most natural, with love in the young. Does he open his play by making Romeo and Juliet in love at first sight—at the first glimpse, as any ordinary thinker would do? Certainly not: he knew what he was about, and how he was to accomplish what he was about: he was to develope the whole passion, and he commences with the first elements—that sense of imperfection, that yearning to combine itself with something lovely. Romeo became enamoured of the idea he had formed in his own mind, and then, as it were, christened the first real being of the contrary sex as endowed with the perfections he desired. He appears to be in love with Rosaline; but, in truth, he is in love only with his own idea. He felt that necessity of being beloved which no noble mind can be without. Then our poet, our poet who so well knew human nature, introduces Romeo to Juliet, and makes it not only a violent, but a permanent love—a point for which Shakespeare has been ridiculed by the ignorant and unthinking. Romeo is first represented in a state most susceptible of love, and then, seeing Juliet, he took and retained the infection.

This brings me to observe upon a characteristic of Shakespeare, which belongs to a man of profound thought and high genius. It has been too much the custom, when anything that happened in his dramas could not easily be explained by the few words the poet has employed, to pass it idly over, and to say that it is beyond our reach, and beyond the power of philosophy—a sort of terra incognita [18] for discoverers—a great ocean to be hereafter explored. Others have treated such passages as hints and glimpses of something now non-existent, as the sacred fragments of an ancient and ruined temple, all the portions of which are beautiful, although their particular relation to each other is unknown. Shakespeare knew the human mind, and its most minute and intimate workings, and he never introduces a word, or a thought, in vain or out of place: if we do not understand him, it is our own fault or the fault of copyists and typographers; but study, and the possession of some small stock of the knowledge by which he worked, will enable us often to detect and explain his meaning. He never wrote at random, or hit upon points of character and conduct by chance; and the smallest fragment of his mind not unfrequently gives a clue to a most perfect, regular, and consistent whole.

As I may not have another opportunity, the introduction of Friar Laurence into this tragedy enables me to remark upon the different manner in which Shake-

speare has treated the priestly character, as compared with other writers. In Beaumont and Fletcher priests are represented as a vulgar mockery; and, as in others of their dramatic personages, the errors of a few are mistaken for the demeanour of the many: but in Shakespeare they always carry with them our love and respect. He made no injurious abstracts: he took no copies from the worst parts of our nature; and, like the rest, his characters of priests are truly drawn from the general body.

It may strike some as singular, that throughout all his productions he has never introduced the passion of avarice. The truth is, that it belongs only to particular parts of our nature, and is prevalent only in particular states of society; hence it could not, and cannot, be permanent. The Miser of Molière and Plautus,[19] is now looked upon as a specics of madman, and avarice as a species of madness. Elwes,[20] of whom everybody has heard, was an individual influenced by an insane condition of mind; but, as a passion, avarice has disappeared. How admirably, then, did Shakespeare foresee, that if he drew such a character it could not be permanent! he drew characters which would always be natural, and therefore permanent, inasmuch as they were not dependent upon accidental circumstances.

There is not one of the plays of Shakespeare that is built upon anything but the best and surest foundation; the characters must be permanent—permanent while men continue men,—because they stand upon what is absolutely necessary to our existence. This cannot be said even of some of the most famous authors of antiquity. Take the capital tragedies of Orestes, or of the husband of Jocasta: great as was the genius of the writers, these dramas have an obvious fault, and the fault lies at the very root of the action. In Œdipus a man is represented oppressed by fate for a crime of which he was not morally guilty; and while we read we are obliged to say to ourselves, that in those days they considered actions without reference to the real guilt of the persons.

There is no character in Shakespeare in which envy is pourtrayed, with one solitary exception—Cassius, in "Julius Cæsar"; yet even there the vice is not hateful, inasmuch as it is counter-balanced by a number of excellent qualities and virtues. The poet leads the reader to suppose that it is rather something constitutional, something derived from his parents, something that he cannot avoid, and not something that he has himself acquired; thus throwing the blame from the will of man to some inevitable circumstance, and lead-

---

[18] terra incognita: "unknown land."

[19] Plautus' Latin comedy *Aulularia* ("The Pot of Gold") was the model for Molière's *l'Avare*.

[20] John Elwes (1714–1789) was a notorious and eccentric miser.

ing us to suppose that it is hardly to be looked upon as one of those passions that actually debase the mind.

Whenever love is described as of a serious nature, and much more when it is to lead to a tragical result, it depends upon a law of the mind, which, I believe, I shall hereafter be able to make intelligible, and which would not only justify Shakespeare, but show an analogy to all his other characters.

F R O M

THE NINTH LECTURE
[*The Tempest*]

DECEMBER 16, 1811

IT IS a known but unexplained phenomenon, that among the ancients statuary rose to such a degree of perfection, as almost to baffle the hope of imitating it, and to render the chance of excelling it absolutely impossible; yet painting, at the same period, notwithstanding the admiration bestowed upon it by Pliny [1] and others, has been proved to be an art of much later growth, as it was also of far inferior quality. I remember a man of high rank, equally admirable for his talents and his taste, pointing to a common sign-post, and saying that had Titian never lived, the richness of representation by colour, even there, would never have been attained. In that mechanical branch of painting, perspective, it has been shown that the Romans were very deficient. The excavations and consequent discoveries, at Herculaneum [2] and elsewhere, prove the Roman artists to have been guilty of such blunders, as to give plausibility to the assertions of those, who maintain that the ancients were wholly ignorant of perspective. However, that they knew something of it is established by Vitruvius in the introduction to his second book. [3]

Something of the same kind, as I endeavoured to explain in a previous lecture, was the case with the drama of the ancients, which has been imitated by the French, Italians, and by various writers in England since the Restoration. All that is there represented seems to be, as it were, upon one flat surface: the theme, if we may so call it in reference to music, admits of nothing more than the change of a single

note, and excludes that which is the true principle of life—the attaining of the same result by an infinite variety of means.

The plays of Shakespeare are in no respect imitations of the Greeks: they may be called analogies, because by very different means they arrive at the same end; whereas the French and Italian tragedies I have read, and the English ones on the same model, are mere copies, though they cannot be called likenesses, seeking the same effect by adopting the same means, but under most inappropriate and adverse circumstances.

I have thus been led to consider, that the ancient drama (meaning the works of Æschylus, Euripides, and Sophocles, for the rhetorical productions of the same class by the Romans are scarcely to be treated as original theatrical poems) might be contrasted with the Shakespearian drama.—I call it the Shakespearian drama to distinguish it, because I know of no other writer who has realized the same idea, although I am told by some, [4] that the Spanish poets, Lopez de Vega and Calderon, have been equally successful. The Shakespearian drama and the Greek drama may be compared to statuary and painting. In statuary, as in the Greek drama, the characters must be few, because the very essence of statuary is a high degree of abstraction, which prevents a great many figures being combined in the same effect. In a grand group of Niobe, or in any other ancient heroic subject, how disgusting even it would appear, if an old nurse were introduced. Not only the number of figures must be circumscribed, but nothing undignified must be placed in company with what is dignified: no one personage must be brought in that is not an abstraction: all the actors in the scene must not be presented at once to the eye; and the effect of multitude, if required, must be produced without the intermingling of anything discordant.

Compare this small group with a picture by Raphael or Titian, in which an immense number of figures may be introduced, a beggar, a cripple, a dog, or a cat; and by a less degree of labour, and a less degree of abstraction, an effect is produced equally harmonious to the mind, more true to nature with its varied colours, and, in all respects but one, superior to statuary. The man of taste feels satisfied, and to that which the reason conceives possible, a momentary reality is given by the aid of imagination.

I need not here repeat what I have said before, regarding the circumstances which permitted Shakespeare to make an alteration, not merely so suitable

---

[1] Pliny the Elder (A.D. 23–79) devoted Book XXXV of his *Natural History* to the subject of painting.

[2] Herculaneum, an ancient Italian city, near Pompeii, was destroyed by the eruption of Vesuvius in A.D. 79. Extensive excavations were begun in the eighteenth century.

[3] Vitruvius, a Roman architect and engineer of the first century B.C., was author of the influential treatise *De Architectura Libri Decem*.

---

[4] Refers to Lectures XII and XIV of Schlegel's *Lectures on Dramatic Art and Poetry*. See footnote 9.

to the age in which he lived, but, in fact, so necessitated by the condition of that age. I need not again remind you of the difference I pointed out between imitation and likeness, in reference to the attempt to give reality to representations on the stage. The distinction between imitation and likeness depends upon the admixture of circumstances of dissimilarity; an imitation is not a copy, precisely as likeness is not sameness, in that sense of the word "likeness" which implies difference conjoined with sameness. Shakespeare reflected manners in his plays, not by a cold formal copy, but by an imitation; that is to say, by an admixture of circumstances, not absolutely true in themselves, but true to the character and to the time represented.

It is fair to own that he had many advantages. The great of that day, instead of surrounding themselves by the *chevaux de frise*,[5] of what is now called high breeding, endeavoured to distinguish themselves by attainments, by energy of thought, and consequent powers of mind. The stage, indeed, had nothing but curtains for its scenes, but this fact compelled the actor, as well as the author, to appeal to the imaginations, and not to the senses of the audience: thus was obtained a power over space and time, which in an ancient theatre would have been absurd, because it would have been contradictory. The advantage is vastly in favour of our own early stage: the dramatic poet there relies upon the imagination, upon the reason, and upon the noblest powers of the human heart; he shakes off the iron bondage of space and time; he appeals to that which we most wish to be, when we are most worthy of being, while the ancient dramatist binds us down to the meanest part of our nature, and the chief compensation is a simple acquiescence of the mind in the position, that what is represented might possibly have occurred in the time and place required by the unities. It is a poor compliment to a poet to tell him, that he has only the qualifications of a historian.

In dramatic composition the observation of the unities of time and place so narrows the period of action, so impoverishes the sources of pleasure, that of all the Athenian dramas there is scarcely one in which the absurdity is not glaring, of aiming at an object, and utterly failing in the attainment of it: events are sometimes brought into a space in which it is impossible for them to have occurred, and in this way the grandest effort of the dramatist, that of making his play the mirror of life, is entirely defeated.

The limit allowed by the rules of the Greek stage was twenty-four hours; but, inasmuch as, even in this case, time must have become a subject of imagination, it was just as reasonable to allow twenty-four months, or even years. The mind is acted upon by such strong stimulants, that the period is indifferent; and when once the boundary of possibility is passed, no restriction can be assigned. In reading Shakespeare, we should first consider in which of his plays he means to appeal to the reason, and in which to the imagination, faculties which have no relation to time and place, excepting as in the one case they imply a succession of cause and effect, and in the other form a harmonious picture, so that the impulse given by the reason is carried on by the imagination.

We have often heard Shakespeare spoken of as a child of nature, and some of his modern imitators, without the genius to copy nature, by resorting to real incidents, and treating them in a certain way, have produced that stage-phenomenon which is neither tragic nor comic, nor tragi-comic, nor comi-tragic, but sentimental. This sort of writing depends upon some very affecting circumstances, and in its greatest excellence aspires no higher than the genius of an onion,—the power of drawing tears; while the author, acting the part of a ventriloquist, distributes his own insipidity among the characters, if characters they can be called, which have no marked and distinguishing features. I have seen dramas of this sort, some translated and some the growth of our own soil, so well acted, and so ill written, that if I could have been made for the time artificially deaf, I should have been pleased with that performance as a pantomime, which was intolerable as a play.

Shakespeare's characters, from Othello and Macbeth down to Dogberry[6] and the Grave-digger, may be termed ideal realities. They are not the things themselves, so much as abstracts of the things, which a great mind takes into itself, and there naturalises them to its own conception. Take Dogberry: are no important truths there conveyed, no admirable lessons taught, and no valuable allusions made to reigning follies, which the poet saw must for ever reign? He is not the creature of the day, to disappear with the day, but the representative and abstract of truth which must ever be true, and of humour which must ever be humorous.

The readers of Shakespeare may be divided into two classes:—

1. Those who read his works with feeling and understanding;

2. Those who, without affecting to criticise, merely feel, and may be said to be the recipients of the poet's power.

---

5 A defense or protective obstruction.

6 The ignorant but pretentious constable in *Much Ado about Nothing*.

Between the two no medium can be endured. The ordinary reader, who does not pretend to bring his understanding to bear upon the subject, often feels that some real trait of his own has been caught, that some nerve has been touched; and he knows that it has been touched by the vibration he experiences—a thrill, which tells us that, by becoming better acquainted with the poet, we have become better acquainted with ourselves.

In the plays of Shakespeare every man sees himself, without knowing that he does so: as in some of the phenomena of nature, in the mist of the mountain, the traveller beholds his own figure, but the glory round the head distinguishes it from a mere vulgar copy. In traversing the Brocken,[7] in the north of Germany, at sunrise, the brilliant beams are shot askance, and you see before you a being of gigantic proportions, and of such elevated dignity, that you only know it to be yourself by similarity of action. In the same way, near Messina, natural forms, at determined distances, are represented on an invisible mist, not as they really exist, but dressed in all the prismatic colours of the imagination.[8] So in Shakespeare: every form is true, everything has reality for its foundation; we can all recognize the truth, but we see it decorated with such hues of beauty, and magnified to such proportions of grandeur, that, while we know the figure, we know also how much it has been refined and exalted by the poet.

It is humiliating to reflect that, as it were, because heaven has given us the greatest poet, it has inflicted upon that poet the most incompetent critics: none of them seem to understand even his language, much less the principles upon which he wrote, and the peculiarities which distinguish him from all rivals. I will not now dwell upon this point, because it is my intention to devote a lecture more immediately to the prefaces of Pope and Johnson. Some of Shakespeare's contemporaries appear to have understood him, and imitated him in a way that does the original no small honour; but modern preface-writers and commentators, while they praise him as a great genius, when they come to publish notes upon his plays, treat him like a schoolboy; as if this great genius did not understand himself, was not aware of his own powers, and wrote without design or purpose. Nearly all they can do is to express

the most vulgar of all feelings, wonderment—wondering at what they term the irregularity of his genius, sometimes above all praise, and at other times, if they are to be trusted, below all contempt. They endeavour to reconcile the two opinions by asserting that he wrote for the mob; as if a man of real genius ever wrote for the mob. Shakespeare never consciously wrote what was below himself: careless he might be, and his better genius may not always have attended him; but I fearlessly say, that he never penned a line that he knew would degrade him. No man does anything equally well at all times; but because Shakespeare could not always be the greatest of poets, was he therefore to condescend to make himself the least?

Yesterday afternoon a friend left a book for me by a German critic,[9] of which I have only had time to read a small part; but what I did read I approved, and I should be disposed to applaud the work much more highly, were it not that in so doing I should, in a manner, applaud myself. The sentiments and opinions coincident with those to which I gave utterance in my lectures at the Royal Institution.[10] It is not a little wonderful, that so many ages have elapsed since the time of Shakespeare, and that it should remain for foreigners first to feel truly, and to appreciate justly, his mighty genius. The solution of this circumstance must be sought in the history of our nation: the English have become a busy commercial people, and they have unquestionably derived from this propensity many social and physical advantages: they have grown to be a mighty empire—one of the great nations of the world, whose moral superiority enables it to struggle successfully against him, who may be deemed the evil genius of our planet.[11]

On the other hand, the Germans, unable to distinguish themselves in action, have been driven to speculation: all their feelings have been forced back into the thinking and reasoning mind. To do, with them is impossible, but in determining what ought to be done, they perhaps exceed every people of the globe. Incapable of acting outwardly, they have acted internally: they first rationally recalled the ancient philosophy, and set their spirits to work with an energy of which England produces no parallel, since those truly heroic

---

[7] The Brocken is the highest mountain of the Hartz range and the source of many superstitions, including the optical illusion here referred to, the Spectre of the Brocken. Coleridge had ascended the Brocken in 1799.

[8] Refers to another famous optical illusion, the *Fata-Morgana*, occurring in the straits of Messina between Sicily and Italy. Under certain atmospheric conditions, the objects on the shore appear to exist in and move along the surface of the water.

[9] August Wilhelm von Schlegel (1767–1845) was a leading German Romantic critic and translator of Shakespeare. Coleridge refers to his *Ueber dramatische Kunst und Literratur. Vorlesungen*, Vols. I–II [part 1] (1809), II [part 2] (1811). The 1811 volume contained the lectures on Shakespeare. From the time of his lectures of 1811–1812 and continuing to the present, the extent of Coleridge's coincidence with or borrowings from Schlegel has been a matter of controversy and debate.

[10] A series of wide-ranging lectures on "the principles of poetry" delivered in London in 1808.

[11] Napoleon.

times, heroic in body and soul, the days of Elizabeth.

If all that has been written upon Shakespeare by Englishmen were burned, in the want of candles, merely to enable us to read one half of what our dramatist produced, we should be great gainers. Providence has given England the greatest man that ever put on and put off mortality, and has thrown a sop to the envy of other nations, by inflicting upon his native country the most incompetent critics. I say nothing here of the state in which his text has come down to us, farther than that it is evidently very imperfect: in many places his sense has been perverted, in others, if not entirely obscured, so blunderingly represented, as to afford us only a glimpse of what he meant, without the power of restoring his own expressions. But whether his dramas have been perfectly or imperfectly printed, it is quite clear that modern inquiry and speculative ingenuity in this kingdom have done nothing; or I might say, without a solecism, less than nothing (for some editors have multiplied corruptions) to retrieve the genuine language of the poet. His critics among us, during the whole of the last century, have neither understood nor appreciated him; for how could they appreciate what they could not understand?

*   *   *   *   *

It is a mistake to say that any of Shakespeare's characters strike us as portraits: they have the union of reason perceiving, of judgment recording, and of imagination diffusing over all a magic glory. While the poet registers what is past, he projects the future in a wonderful degree, and makes us feel, however slightly, and see, however dimly, that state of being in which there is neither past nor future, but all is permanent in the very energy of nature.

Although I have affirmed that all Shakespeare's characters are ideal, and the result of his own meditation, yet a just separation may be made of those in which the ideal is most prominent—where it is put forward more intensely—where we are made more conscious of the ideal, though in truth they possess no more nor less ideality; and of those which, though equally idealised, the delusion upon the mind is of their being real. The characters in the various plays may be separated into those where the real is disguised in the ideal, and those where the ideal is concealed from us by the real. The difference is made by the different powers of mind employed by the poet in the representation.

At present I shall only speak of dramas where the ideal is predominant; and chiefly for this reason—that those plays have been attacked with the greatest violence. The objections to them are not the growth of our own country, but of France—the judgment of

monkeys, by some wonderful phenomenon, put into the mouths of people shaped like men. These creatures have informed us that Shakespeare is a miraculous monster, in whom many heterogeneous components were thrown together, producing a discordant mass of genius—an irregular and ill-assorted structure of gigantic proportions.

Among the ideal plays, I will take "The Tempest," by way of example. Various others might be mentioned, but it is impossible to go through every drama, and what I remark on "The Tempest" will apply to all Shakespeare's productions of the same class.

In this play Shakespeare has especially appealed to the imagination, and he has constructed a plot well adapted to the purpose. According to his scheme, he did not appeal to any sensuous impression (the word "sensuous" is authorised by Milton)[12] of time and place, but to the imagination, and it is to be borne in mind, that of old, and as regards mere scenery, his works may be said to have been recited rather than acted—that is to say, description and narration supplied the place of visual exhibition: the audience was told to fancy that they saw what they only heard described; the painting was not in colours, but in words.

This is particularly to be noted in the first scene—a storm and its confusion on board the king's ship. The highest and the lowest characters are brought together, and with what excellence! Much of the genius of Shakespeare is displayed in these happy combinations—the highest and the lowest, the gayest and the saddest; he is not droll in one scene and melancholy in another, but often both the one and the other in the same scene. Laughter is made to swell the tear of sorrow, and to throw, as it were, a poetic light upon it, while the tear mingles tenderness with the laughter. Shakespeare has evinced the power, which above all other men he possessed, that of introducing the profoundest sentiments of wisdom, where they would be least expected, yet where they are most truly natural. One admirable secret of his art is, that separate speeches frequently do not appear to have been occasioned by those which preceded, and which are consequent upon each other, but to have arisen out of the peculiar character of the speaker.

Before I go further, I may take the opportunity of explaining what is meant by mechanic and organic regularity. In the former the copy must appear as if it had come out of the same mould with the original; in the latter there is a law which all the parts obey, conforming themselves to the outward symbols and mani-

---

[12] In his treatise "Of Education" (1644), Milton used the word "sensuous" to describe poetry.

festations of the essential principle. If we look to the growth of trees, for instance, we shall observe that trees of the same kind vary considerably, according to the circumstances of soil, air, or position; yet we are able to decide at once whether they are oaks, elms, or poplars.

So with Shakespeare's characters: he shows us the life and principle of each being with organic regularity. The Boatswain, in the first scene of "The Tempest," when the bonds of reverence are thrown off as a sense of danger impresses all, gives a loose to his feelings, and thus pours forth his vulgar mind to the old Counsellor:—

"Hence! What care these roarers for the name of King? To cabin: silence! trouble us not."

Gonzalo replies—"Good; yet remember whom thou hast aboard." To which the Boatswain answers—"None that I more love than myself. You are a counsellor: if you can command these elements to silence, and work the peace of the present, we will not hand a rope more; use your authority: if you cannot, give thanks that you have lived so long, and make yourself ready in your cabin for the mischance of the hour, if it so hap.—Cheerly, good hearts!—Out of our way, I say."[13]

An ordinary dramatist would, after this speech, have represented Gonzalo as moralising, or saying something connected with the Boatswain's language; for ordinary dramatists are not men of genius: they combine their ideas by association, or by logical affinity; but the vital writer, who makes men on the stage what they are in nature, in a moment transports himself into the very being of each personage, and, instead of cutting out artificial puppets, he brings before us the men themselves. Therefore, Gonzalo soliloquises,—"I have great comfort from this fellow: methinks, he hath no drowning mark upon him; his complexion is perfect gallows. Stand fast, good fate, to his hanging! make the rope of his destiny our cable, for our own doth little advantage. If he be not born to be hanged, our case is miserable."

In this part of the scene we see the true sailor with his contempt of danger, and the old counsellor with his high feeling, who, instead of condescending to notice the words just addressed to him, turns off, meditating with himself, and drawing some comfort to his own mind, by trifling with the ill expression of the boatswain's face, founding upon it a hope of safety.

Shakespeare had pre-determined to make the plot of this play such as to involve a certain number of low characters, and at the beginning he pitched the note of

the whole. The first scene was meant as a lively commencement of the story; the reader is prepared for something that is to be developed, and in the next scene he brings forward Prospero and Miranda. How is this done? By giving to his favourite character, Miranda, a sentence which at once expresses the violence and fury of the storm, such as it might appear to a witness on the land, and at the same time displays the tenderness of her feelings—the exquisite feelings of a female brought up in a desert, but with all the advantages of education, all that could be communicated by a wise and affectionate father. She possesses all the delicacy of innocence, yet with all the powers of her mind unweakened by the combats of life. Miranda exclaims:—

"O! I have suffered
With those that I saw suffer: a brave vessel,
Who had, no doubt, some noble creatures in her,
Dash'd all to pieces."[14]

The doubt here intimated could have occurred to no mind but to that of Miranda, who had been bred up in the island with her father and a monster only: she did not know, as others do, what sort of creatures were in a ship; others never would have introduced it as a conjecture. This shows, that while Shakespeare is displaying his vast excellence, he never fails to insert some touch or other, which is not merely characteristic of the particular person, but combines two things—the person, and the circumstances acting upon the person. She proceeds:—

"O! the cry did knock
Against my very heart. Poor souls! they perish'd.
Had I been any god of power, I would
Have sunk the sea within the earth, or e'er
It should the good ship so have swallow'd, and
The fraughting souls within her."

She still dwells upon that which was most wanting to the completeness of her nature—these fellow creatures from whom she appeared banished, with only one relict to keep them alive, not in her memory, but in her imagination.

Another proof of excellent judgment in the poet, for I am now principally adverting to that point, is to be found in the preparation of the reader for what is to follow. Prospero is introduced, first in his magic robe, which, with the assistance of his daughter, he lays aside, and we then know him to be a being possessed of supernatural powers. He then instructs Miranda in the story of their arrival in the island, and this is conducted in such a manner, that the reader never conjectures the

---

[13] In this and the next paragraph, Coleridge quotes from I, i, 17–36.

[14] This and the following quotation are from I, ii, 5–13.

technical use the poet has made of the relation, by informing the auditor of what it is necessary for him to know.

The next step is the warning by Prospero, that he means, for particular purposes, to lull his daughter to sleep; and here he exhibits the earliest and mildest proof of magical power. In ordinary and vulgar plays we should have had some person brought upon the stage, whom nobody knows or cares anything about, to let the audience into the secret. Prospero having cast a sleep upon his daughter, by that sleep stops the narrative at the very moment when it was necessary to break it off, in order to excite curiosity, and yet to give the memory and understanding sufficient to carry on the progress of the history uninterruptedly.

Here I cannot help noticing a fine touch of Shakespeare's knowledge of human nature, and generally of the great laws of the human mind: I mean Miranda's infant remembrance. Prospero asks her—

> "Canst thou remember
> A time before we came unto this cell?
> I do not think thou canst, for then thou wast not
> Out three years old."

Miranda answers,

> "Certainly, sir, I can."

Prospero inquires,

> "By what? by any other house or person?
> Of any thing the image tell me, that
> Hath kept with thy remembrance."

To which Miranda returns,

> "'Tis far off;
> And rather like a dream than an assurance
> That my remembrance warrants. Had I not
> Four or five women once, that tended me?"
> *Act I., Scene 2.*[15]

This is exquisite! In general, our remembrances of early life arise from vivid colours, especially if we have seen them in motion: for instance, persons when grown up will remember a bright green door, seen when they were quite young; but Miranda, who was somewhat older, recollected four or five women who tended her. She might know men from her father, and her remembrance of the past might be worn out by the present object, but women she only knew by herself, by the contemplation of her own figure in the fountain, and she recalled to her mind what had been. It was not, that she had seen such and such grandees, or such and such

peeresses, but she remembered to have seen something like the reflection of herself: it was not herself, and it brought back to her mind what she had seen most like herself.

In my opinion the picturesque power displayed by Shakespeare, of all the poets that ever lived, is only equalled, if equalled, by Milton and Dante. The presence of genius is not shown in elaborating a picture: we have had many specimens of this sort of work in modern poems, where all is so dutchified, if I may use the word, by the most minute touches, that the reader naturally asks why words, and not painting, are used? I know a young lady of much taste, who observed, that in reading recent versified accounts of voyages and travels, she, by a sort of instinct, cast her eyes on the opposite page, for coloured prints of what was so patiently and punctually described.

The power of poetry is, by a single word perhaps, to instil that energy into the mind, which compels the imagination to produce the picture. Prospero tells Miranda,

> "One midnight,
> Fated to the purpose, did Antonio open
> The gates of Milan; and i' the dead of darkness,
> The ministers for the purpose hurried thence
> Me, and thy crying self."

Here, by introducing a single happy epithet, "crying," in the last line, a complete picture is presented to the mind, and in the production of such pictures the power of genius consists.

In reference to preparation, it will be observed that the storm, and all that precedes the tale, as well as the tale itself, serve to develope completely the main character of the drama, as well as the design of Prospero. The manner in which the heroine is charmed asleep fits us for what follows, goes beyond our ordinary belief, and gradually leads us to the appearance and disclosure of a being of the most fanciful and delicate texture, like Prospero, preternaturally gifted.

In this way the entrance of Ariel, if not absolutely forethought by the reader, was foreshewn by the writer: in addition, we may remark, that the moral feeling called forth by the sweet words of Miranda,

> "Alack, what trouble
> Was I then to you!"

in which she considered only the sufferings and sorrows of her father, puts the reader in a frame of mind to exert his imagination in favour of an object so innocent and interesting. The poet makes him wish that, if supernatural agency were to be employed, it should be used for a being so young and lovely. "The wish is father to

---

[15] Ll. 38–47. Subsequently quoted are ll. 128–32 and 151–52.

the thought," [16] and Ariel is introduced. Here, what is called poetic faith is required and created, and our common notions of philosophy give way before it: this feeling may be said to be much stronger than historic faith, since for the exercise of poetic faith the mind is previously prepared. I make this remark, though somewhat digressive, in order to lead to a future subject of these lectures—the poems of Milton. When adverting to those, I shall have to explain farther the distinction between the two.

Many Scriptural poems have been written with so much of Scripture in them, that what is not Scripture appears to be not true, and like mingling lies with the most sacred revelations. Now Milton, on the other hand, has taken for his subject that one point of Scripture of which we have the mere fact recorded, and upon this he has most judiciously constructed his whole fable. So of Shakespeare's "King Lear": we have little historic evidence to guide or confine us, and the few facts handed down to us, and admirably employed by the poet, are sufficient, while we read, to put an end to all doubt as to the credibility of the story. It is idle to say that this or that incident is improbable, because history, as far as it goes, tells us that the fact was so and so. Four or five lines in the Bible include the whole that is said of Milton's story, and the Poet has calld up that poetic faith, that conviction of the mind, which is necessary to make that seem true, which otherwise might have been deemed almost fabulous.

But to return to "The Tempest," and to the wondrous creation of Ariel. If a doubt could ever be entertained whether Shakespeare was a great poet, acting upon laws arising out of his own nature, and not without law, as has sometimes been idly asserted, that doubt must be removed by the character of Ariel. The very first words uttered by this being introduce the spirit, not as an angel, above man; not a gnome, or a fiend, below man; but while the poet gives him the faculties and the advantages of reason, he divests him of all mortal character, not positively, it is true, but negatively. In air he lives, from air he derives his being, in air he acts; and all his colours and properties seem to have been obtained from the rainbow and the skies. There is nothing about Ariel that cannot be conceived to exist either at sun-rise or at sun-set: hence all that belongs to Ariel belongs to the delight the mind is capable of receiving from the most lovely external appearances. His answers to Prospero are directly to the question, and nothing beyond; or where he expatiates, which is not unfrequently, it is to himself and upon his own delights, or upon the unnatural situation in which he is

placed, though under a kindly power and to good ends.

Shakespeare has properly made Ariel's very first speech characteristic of him. After he has described the manner in which he had raised the storm and produced its harmless consequences, we find that Ariel is discontented—that he has been freed, it is true, from a cruel confinement, but still that he is bound to obey Prospero, and to execute any commands imposed upon him. We feel that such a state of bondage is almost unnatural to him, yet we see that it is delightful for him to be so employed.—It is as if we were to command one of the winds in a different direction to that which nature dictates, or one of the waves, now rising and now sinking, to recede before it bursts upon the shore: such is the feeling we experience, when we learn that a being like Ariel is commanded to fulfil any mortal behest.

When, however, Shakespeare contrasts the treatment of Ariel by Prospero with that of Sycorax, we are sensible that the liberated spirit ought to be grateful, and Ariel does feel and acknowledge the obligation; he immediately assumes the airy being, with a mind so elastically correspondent, that when once a feeling has passed from it, not a trace is left behind.

Is there anything in nature from which Shakespeare caught the idea of this delicate and delightful being, with such child-like simplicity, yet with such preternatural powers? He is neither born of heaven, nor of earth; but, as it were, between both, like a May-blossom kept suspended in air by the fanning breeze, which prevents it from falling to the ground, and only finally, and by compulsion, touching earth. This reluctance of the Sylph to be under the command even of Prospero is kept up through the whole play, and in the exercise of his admirable judgment Shakespeare has availed himself of it, in order to give Ariel an interest in the event, looking forward to that moment when he was to gain his last and only reward—simple and eternal liberty.

Another instance of admirable judgment and excellent preparation is to be found in the creature contrasted with Ariel—Caliban; who is described in such a manner by Prospero, as to lead us to expect the appearance of a foul, unnatural monster. He is not seen at once: his voice is heard; this is the preparation; he was too offensive to be seen first in all his deformity, and in nature we do not receive so much disgust from sound as from sight. After we have heard Caliban's voice he does not enter, until Ariel has entered like a water-nymph. All the strength of contrast is thus acquired without any of the shock of abruptness, or of that unpleasant sensation, which we experience when the object presented is in any way hateful to our vision.

The character of Caliban is wonderfully conceived: he is a sort of creature of the earth, as Ariel is a sort of

---

[16] *Henry the Fourth*, Part II, IV, v, 93.

creature of the air. He partakes of the qualities of the brute, but is distinguished from brutes in two ways:—by having mere understanding without moral reason; and by not possessing the instincts which pertain to absolute animals. Still, Caliban is in some respects a noble being: the poet has raised him far above contempt: he is a man in the sense of the imagination: all the images he uses are drawn from nature, and are highly poetical; they fit in with the images of Ariel. Caliban gives us images from the earth, Ariel images from the air. Caliban talks of the difficulty of finding fresh water, of the situation of morasses, and of other circumstances which even brute instinct, without reason, could comprehend. No mean figure is employed, no mean passion displayed, beyond animal passion, and repugnance to command.

The manner in which the lovers are introduced is equally wonderful, and it is the last point I shall now mention in reference to this, almost miraculous, drama. The same judgment is observable in every scene, still preparing, still inviting, and still gratifying, like a finished piece of music. I have omitted to notice one thing, and you must give me leave to advert to it before I proceed: I mean the conspiracy against the life of Alonzo. I want to shew you how well the poet prepares the feelings of the reader for this plot, which was to execute the most detestable of all crimes, and which, in another play, Shakespeare has called "the murder of sleep." [17]

Antonio and Sebastian at first had no such intention: it was suggested by the magical sleep cast on Alonzo and Gonzalo; but they are previously introduced scoffing and scorning at what was said by others, without regard to age or situation—without any sense of admiration for the excellent truths they heard delivered, but giving themselves up entirely to the malignant and unsocial feeling, which induced them to listen to everything that was said, not for the sake of profiting by the learning and experience of others, but of hearing something that might gratify vanity and self-love, by making them believe that the person speaking was inferior to themselves.

This, let me remark, is one of the grand characteristics of a villain; and it would not be so much a presentiment, as an anticipation of hell, for men to suppose that all mankind were as wicked as themselves, or might be so, if they were not too great fools. Pope, you are perhaps aware, objected to this conspiracy; but in my mind, if it could be omitted, the play would lose a charm which nothing could supply.

Many, indeed innumerable, beautiful passages might be quoted from this play, independently of the astonishing scheme of its construction. Every body will call to mind the grandeur of the language of Prospero in that divine speech, where he takes leave of his magic art; [18] and were I to indulge myself by repetitions of the kind, I should descend from the character of a lecturer to that of a mere reciter. Before I terminate, I may particularly recall one short passage, which has fallen under the very severe, but inconsiderate, censure of Pope and Arbuthnot, [19] who pronounce it a piece of the grossest bombast. Prospero thus addresses his daughter, directing her attention to Ferdinand:

"The fringed curtains of thine eye advance,
And say what thou seest yond."
Act I., Scene 2. [20]

Taking these words as a periphrase of—"Look what is coming yonder," it certainly may to some appear to border on the ridiculous, and to fall under the rule I formerly laid down,—that whatever, without injury, can be translated into a foreign language in simple terms, ought to be in simple terms in the original language; but it is to be borne in mind, that different modes of expression frequently arise from difference of situation and education: a blackguard would use very different words, to express the same thing, to those a gentleman would employ, yet both would be natural and proper; difference of feeling gives rise to difference of language: a gentleman speaks in polished terms, with due regard to his own rank and position, while a blackguard, a person little better than half a brute, speaks like half a brute, showing no respect for himself, nor for others.

But I am content to try the lines I have just quoted by the introduction to them; and then, I think, you will admit, that nothing could be more fit and appropriate than such language. How does Prospero introduce them? He has just told Miranda a wonderful story, which deeply affected her, and filled her with surprise and astonishment, and for his own purposes he afterwards lulls her to sleep. When she awakes, Shakespeare has made her wholly inattentive to the present, but wrapped up in the past. An actress, who understands the character of Miranda, would have her eyes cast down, and her eyelids almost covering them, while she was, as it were, living in her dream. At this moment Prospero sees Ferdinand, and wishes to point him out to his daughter, not only with great, but with scenic

---

[17] See *Macbeth*, II, ii, 36.

[18] V, i, 33–57.
[19] In *Peri Bathous or, Martinus Scriblerus His Treatise of the Art of Sinking in Poetry* (1727), chapter XII; the two lines are cited as an example of raising "what is Base and Low to a ridiculous Visibility."
[20] Ll. 408–409.

solemnity, he standing before her, and before the spectator, in the dignified character of a great magician. Something was to appear to Miranda on the sudden, and as unexpectedly as if the hero of a drama were to be on the stage at the instant when the curtain is elevated. It is under such circumstances that Prospero says, in a tone calculated at once to arouse his daughter's attention,

> "The fringed curtains of thine eye advance,
>   And say what thou seest yond."

Turning from the sight of Ferdinand to his thoughtful daughter, his attention was first struck by the downcast appearance of her eyes and eyelids; and, in my humble opinion, the solemnity of the phraseology assigned to Prospero is completely in character, recollecting his preternatural capacity, in which the most familiar objects in nature present themselves in a mysterious point of view. It is much easier to find fault with a writer by reference to former notions and experience, than to sit down and read him, recollecting his purpose, connecting one feeling with another, and judging of his words and phrases, in proportion as they convey the sentiments of the persons represented.

Of Miranda we may say, that she possesses in herself all the ideal beauties that could be imagined by the greatest poet of any age or country; but it is not my purpose now, so much to point out the high poetic powers of Shakespeare, as to illustrate his exquisite judgment, and it is solely with this design that I have noticed a passage with which, it seems to me, some critics, and those among the best, have been unreasonably dissatisfied. If Shakespeare be the wonder of the ignorant, he is, and ought to be, much more the wonder of the learned: not only from profundity of thought, but from his astonishing and intuitive knowledge of what man must be at all times, and under all circumstances, he is rather to be looked upon as a prophet than as a poet. Yet, with all these unbounded powers, with all this might and majesty of genius, he makes us feel as if he were unconscious of himself, and of his high destiny, disguising the half god in the simplicity of a child.

THE TWELFTH LECTURE
[*Richard II and Hamlet*]
JANUARY 2, 1812

IN THE last lecture I endeavoured to point out in Shakespeare those characters in which pride of intellect, without moral feeling, is supposed to be the ruling impulse, such as Iago, Richard III., and even Falstaff. In Richard III., ambition is, as it were, the channel in

which this impulse directs itself; the character is drawn with the greatest fulness and perfection; and the poet has not only given us that character, grown up and completed, but he has shown us its very source and generation. The inferiority of his person made the hero seek consolation and compensation in the superiority of his intellect; he thus endeavoured to counterbalance his deficiency. This striking feature is pourtrayed most admirably by Shakespeare, who represents Richard bringing forward his very defects and deformities as matters of boast. It was the same pride of intellect, or the assumption of it, that made John Wilkes [1] vaunt that, although he was so ugly, he only wanted, with any lady, ten minutes' start of the handsomest man in England. This certainly was a high compliment to himself; but a higher to the female sex, on the supposition that Wilkes possessed this superiority of intellect, and relied upon it for making a favourable impression, because ladies would know how to estimate his advantages.

I will now proceed to offer some remarks upon the tragedy of "Richard II.," on account of its not very apparent, but still intimate, connection with "Richard III." As, in the last, Shakespeare has painted a man where ambition is the channel in which the ruling impulse runs, so, in the first, he has given us a character, under the name of Bolingbroke, or Henry IV., where ambition itself, conjoined unquestionably with great talents, is the ruling impulse. In Richard III. the pride of intellect makes use of ambition as its means; in Bolingbroke the gratification of ambition is the end, and talents are the means.

One main object of these lectures is to point out the superiority of Shakespeare to other dramatists, and no superiority can be more striking, than that this wonderful poet could take two characters, which at first sight seem so much alike, and yet, when carefully and minutely examined, are so totally distinct.

The popularity of "Richard II." is owing, in a great measure, to the masterly delineation of the principal character; but were there no other ground for admiring it, it would deserve the highest applause, from the fact that it contains the most magnificent, and, at the same time, the truest eulogium of our native country that the English language can boast, or which can be produced from any other tongue, not excepting the proud claims of Greece and Rome. When I feel, that upon the morality of Britain depends the safety of Britain, and that her morality is supported and illustrated by our national feeling, I cannot read these grand lines without joy and

---

[1] John Wilkes (1727–1797) was one of the leading political controversialists of his time, lord mayor of London, and a notorious profligate.

triumph. Let it be remembered, that while this country is proudly pre-eminent in morals, her enemy has only maintained his station by superiority in mechanical appliances. Many of those who hear me will, no doubt, anticipate the passage I refer to, and it runs as follows:—

> "This royal throne of kings, this scepterd isle,
> This earth of majesty, this seat of Mars,
> This other Eden, demi-paradise;
> This fortress, built by nature for herself
> Against infection and the hand of war;
> This happy breed of men, this little world,
> This precious stone set in the silver sea,
> Which serves it in the office of a wall,
> Or as a moat defensive to a house,
> Against the envy of less happier lands;
> This blessed plot, this earth, this realm, this England,
> This nurse, this teeming womb of royal kings,
> Feared by their breed, and famous by their birth,
> Renowned for their deeds as far from home,
> For Christian service and true chivalry,
> As is the Sepulchre in stubborn Jewry
> Of the world's ransom, blessed Mary's son:
> This land of such dear souls, this dear, dear land,
> Dear for her reputation through the world,
> Is now leas'd out, I die pronouncing it,
> Like to a tenement, or pelting farm.
> England, bound in with the triumphant sea,
> Whose rocky shore beats back the envious siege
> Of watery Neptune, is now bound in with shame,
> With inky blots, and rotten parchment bonds."
> *Act II., Scene 1.*[2]

Every motive to patriotism, every cause producing it, is here collected, without one of those cold abstractions so frequently substituted by modern poets. If this passage were recited in a theatre with due energy and understanding, with a proper knowledge of the words, and a fit expression of their meaning, every man would retire from it secure in his country's freedom, if secure in his own constant virtue.

The principal personages in this tragedy are Richard II., Bolingbroke, and York. I will speak of the last first, although it is the least important; but the keeping of all is most admirable. York is a man of no strong powers of mind, but of earnest wishes to do right, contented in himself alone, if he have acted well: he points out to Richard the effects of his thoughtless extravagance, and the dangers by which he is encompassed, but having done so, he is satisfied; there is no after action on his part; he does nothing; he remains passive. When old Gaunt is dying, York takes care to give his own opinion to the King, and that done he retires, as it were, into himself.

It has been stated, from the first, that one of my purposes in these lectures is, to meet and refute popular objections to particular points in the works of our great dramatic poet; and I cannot help observing here upon the beauty, and true force of nature, with which conceits, as they are called, and sometimes even puns, are introduced. What has been the reigning fault of an age must, at one time or another, have referred to something beautiful in the human mind; and, however conceits may have been misapplied, however they may have been disadvantageously multiplied, we should recollect that there never was an abuse of anything, but it previously has had its use. Gaunt, on his death-bed, sends for the young King, and Richard, entering, insolently and unfeelingly says to him:

> "What, comfort, man! how is't with aged Gaunt?"
> *Act II., Scene 1.*[3]

and Gaunt replies:

> "O, how that name befits my composition!
> Old Gaunt, indeed; and gaunt is being old:
> Within me grief hath kept a tedious fast,
> And who abstains from meat, that is not gaunt?
> For sleeping England long time have I watched;
> Watching breeds leanness, leanness is all gaunt:
> The pleasure that some fathers feed upon
> Is my strict fast, I mean my children's looks;
> And therein fasting, thou hast made me gaunt.
> Gaunt am I for the grave, gaunt as a grave,
> Whose hollow womb inherits nought but bones."

Richard inquires,

> "Can sick men play so nicely with their names?"

To which Gaunt answers, giving the true justification of conceits:

> "No; misery makes sport to mock itself:
> Since thou dost seek to kill my name in me,
> I mock my name, great king, to flatter thee."

He that knows the state of the human mind in deep passion must know, that it approaches to that condition of madness, which is not absolute frenzy or delirium, but which models all things to one reigning idea; still it strays from the main subject of complaint, and still it returns to it, by a sort of irresistible impulse. Abruptness of thought, under such circumstances, is true to nature, and no man was more sensible of it than Shakespeare. In a modern poem a mad mother thus complains:

---

[2] Ll. 40–64.

[3] Ll. 72–87.

"The breeze I see is in yon tree:
         It comes to cool my babe and me."[4]

This is an instance of the abruptness of thought, so natural to the excitement and agony of grief; and if it be admired in images, can we say that it is unnatural in words, which are, as it were, a part of our life, of our very existence? In the Scriptures themselves these plays upon words are to be found, as well as in the best works of the ancients, and in the most delightful parts of Shakespeare; and because this additional grace, not well understood, has in some instances been converted into a deformity—because it has been forced into places, where it is evidently improper and unnatural, are we therefore to include the whole application of it in one general condemnation? When it seems objectionable, when it excites a feeling contrary to the situation, when it perhaps disgusts, it is our business to enquire whether the conceit has been rightly or wrongly used—whether it is in a right or in a wrong place?

In order to decide this point, it is obviously necessary to consider the state of mind, and the degree of passion, of the person using this play upon words. Resort to this grace may, in some cases, deserve censure, not because it is a play upon words, but because it is a play upon words in a wrong place, and at a wrong time. What is right in one state of mind is wrong in another, and much more depends upon that, than upon the conceit (so to call it) itself. I feel the importance of these remarks strongly, because the greater part of the abuse, I might say filth, thrown out and heaped upon Shakespeare, has originated in want of consideration. Dr. Johnson asserts that Shakespeare loses the world for a toy, and can no more withstand a pun, or a play upon words, than his Antony could resist Cleopatra.[5] Certain it is, that Shakespeare gained more admiration in his day, and long afterwards, by the use of speech in this way, than modern writers have acquired by the abandonment of the practice: the latter, in adhering to, what they have been pleased to call, the rules of art, have sacrificed nature.

Having said thus much on the, often falsely supposed, blemishes of our poet—blemishes which are said to prevail in "Richard II." especially,—I will now advert to the character of the King. He is represented as a man not deficient in immediate courage, which displays itself at his assassination; or in powers of mind, as appears by the foresight he exhibits throughout the play: still, he is weak, variable, and womanish, and possesses feelings, which, amiable in a female, are displaced in a man, and altogether unfit for a king. In

prosperity he is insolent and presumptuous, and in adversity, if we are to believe Dr. Johnson, he is humane and pious.[6] I cannot admit the latter epithet, because I perceive the utmost consistency of character in Richard: what he was at first, he is at last, excepting as far as he yields to circumstances: what he shewed himself at the commencement of the play, he shews himself at the end of it. Dr. Johnson assigns to him rather the virtue of a confessor than that of a king.

True it is, that he may be said to be overwhelmed by the earliest misfortune that befalls him; but, so far from his feelings or disposition being changed or subdued, the very first glimpse of the returning sunshine of hope reanimates his spirits, and exalts him to as strange and unbecoming a degree of elevation, as he was before sunk in mental depression: the mention of those in his misfortunes, who had contributed to his downfall, but who had before been his nearest friends and favourites, calls forth from him expressions of the bitterest hatred and revenge. Thus, where Richard asks:

"Where is the Earl of Wiltshire? Where is Bagot?
    What is become of Bushy? Where is Green?
    That they have let the dangerous enemy
    Measure our confines with such peaceful steps?
    If we prevail, their heads shall pay for it.
    I warrant they have made peace with Bolingbroke."
                              Act III., Scene 2.[7]

Scroop answers:

"Peace have they made with him, indeed, my lord."

Upon which Richard, without hearing more, breaks out:

"O villains! vipers, damn'd without redemption!
    Dogs, easily won to fawn on any man!
    Snakes, in my heart-blood warm'd, that sting my heart!
    Three Judases, each one thrice worse than Judas!
    Would they make peace? terrible hell make war
    Upon their spotted souls for this offence!"

Scroop observes upon this change, and tells the King how they had made their peace:

"Sweet love, I see, changing his property
    Turns to the sourest and most deadly hate.
    Again uncurse their souls: their peace is made
    With heads and not with hands: those whom you curse
    Have felt the worst of death's destroying wound,
    And lie full low, grav'd in the hollow ground."

Richard receiving at first an equivocal answer,—
"Peace have they made with him, indeed, my lord,"

---

4 Wordsworth's "Her Eyes are Wild" (1798), ll. 39–40.
5 See Johnson's "Preface to *Shakespeare*" (1765).

6 The opinion is expressed in a note to III, ii, 93, in Johnson's edition of Shakespeare.
7 Ll. 122–40.

—takes it in the worst sense: his promptness to suspect those who had been his friends turns his love to hate, and calls forth the most tremendous execrations.

From the beginning to the end of the play he pours out all the peculiarities and powers of his mind: he catches at new hope, and seeks new friends, is disappointed, despairs, and at length makes a merit of his resignation. He scatters himself into a multitude of images, and in conclusion endeavours to shelter himself from that which is around him by a cloud of his own thoughts. Throughout his whole career may be noticed the most rapid transitions—from the highest insolence to the lowest humility—from hope to despair, from the extravagance of love to the agonies of resentment, and from pretended resignation to the bitterest reproaches. The whole is joined with the utmost richness and copiousness of thought, and were there an actor capable of representing Richard, the part would delight us more than any other of Shakespeare's masterpieces,—with, perhaps, the single exception of King Lear. I know of no character drawn by our great poet with such unequalled skill as that of Richard II.

Next we come to Henry Bolingbroke, the rival of Richard II. He appears as a man of dauntless courage, and of ambition equal to that of Richard III.; but, as I have stated, the difference between the two is most admirably conceived and preserved. In Richard III. all that surrounds him is only dear as it feeds his inward sense of superiority: he is no vulgar tyrant—no Nero or Caligula: he had always an end in view, and vast fertility of means to accomplish that end. On the other hand, in Bolingbroke we find a man who in the outset has been sorely injured: then, we see him encouraged by the grievances of his country, and by the strange mismanagement of the government, yet at the same time scarcely daring to look at his own views, or to acknowledge them as designs. He comes home under the pretence of claiming his dukedom, and he professes that to be his object almost to the last; but, at the last, he avows his purpose to its full extent, of which he was himself unconscious in the earlier stages.

This is proved by so many passages, that I will only select one of them; and I take it the rather, because out of the many octavo volumes of text and notes, the page on which it occurs is, I believe, the only one left naked by the commentators. It is where Bolingbroke approaches the castle in which the unfortunate King has taken shelter: York is in Bolingbroke's company—the same York who is still contented with speaking the truth, but doing nothing for the sake of the truth,—drawing back after he has spoken, and becoming merely passive when he ought to display activity. Northumberland says,

> "The news is very fair and good, my lord:
> Richard not far from hence hath hid his head."
>
> *Act III., Scene 3.*[8]

York rebukes him thus:

> "It would beseem the Lord Northumberland
>   To say King Richard:—Alack, the heavy day,
>   When such a sacred king should hide his head!"

Northumberland replies:

> "Your grace mistakes me: only to be brief
>   Left I his title out."

To which York rejoins:

>   "The time hath been,
>   Would you have been so brief with him, he would
>   Have been so brief with you, to shorten you,
>   For taking so the head, your whole head's length."

Bolingbroke observes,

> "Mistake not, uncle, farther than you should;"

And York answers, with a play upon the words "take" and "mistake":

> "Take not, good cousin, farther than you should,
>   Lest you mistake. The heavens are o'er our heads."

Here, give me leave to remark in passing, that the play upon words is perfectly natural, and quite in character: the answer is in unison with the tone of passion, and seems connected with some phrase then in popular use. Bolingbroke tells York:

> "I know it, uncle, and oppose not myself
>   Against their will."

Just afterwards, Bolingbroke thus addresses himself to Northumberland:

>   "Noble lord,
>   Go to the rude ribs of that ancient castle;
>   Through brazen trumpet send the breath of parle
>   Into his ruin'd ears, and thus deliver."

Here, in the phrase "into his ruin'd ears," I have no doubt that Shakespeare purposely used the personal pronoun, "his," to shew, that although Bolingbroke was only speaking of the castle, his thoughts dwelt on the king. In Milton the pronoun, "her," is employed, in relation to "form," in a manner somewhat similar.[9] Bolingbroke had an equivocation in his mind, and was thinking of the king, while speaking of the castle. He

---

8 Ll. 5–60.
9 See *Paradise Lost*, IX, 457.

goes on to tell Northumberland what to say, beginning,

"Henry Bolingbroke,"

which is almost the only instance in which a name forms the whole line; Shakespeare meant it to convey Bolingbroke's opinion of his own importance:—

"Henry Bolingbroke
  On both his knees doth kiss King Richard's hand,
  And sends allegiance and true faith of heart
  To his most royal person; hither come
  Even at his feet to lay my arms and power,
  Provided that, my banishment repealed,
  And lands restor'd again, be freely granted.
  If not, I'll use th' advantage of my power,
  And lay the summer's dust with showers of blood,
  Rain'd from the wounds of slaughter'd Englishmen."

At this point Bolingbroke seems to have been checked by the eye of York, and thus proceeds in consequence:

"The which, how far off from the mind of Bolingbroke
  It is, such crimson tempest should bedrench
  The fresh green lap of fair King Richard's land,
  My stooping duty tenderly shall show."

He passes suddenly from insolence to humility, owing to the silent reproof he received from his uncle. This change of tone would not have taken place, had Bolingbroke been allowed to proceed according to the natural bent of his own mind, and the flow of the subject. Let me direct attention to the subsequent lines, for the same reason; they are part of the same speech:

"Let's march without the noise of threat'ning drum,
  That from the castle's tatter'd battlements
  Our fair appointments may be well perused.
  Methinks, King Richard and myself should meet
  With no less terror than the elements
  Of fire and water, when the thundering shock
  At meeting tears the cloudy cheeks of heaven."

Having proceeded thus far with exaggeration of his own importance, York again checks him, and Bolingbroke adds, in a very different strain,

"He be the fire, I'll be the yielding water:
  The rage be his, while on the earth I rain
  My waters; on the earth, and not on him."

I have thus adverted to the three great personages in this drama, Richard, Bolingbroke, and York; and of the whole play it may be asserted, that with the exception of some of the last scenes (though they have exquisite beauty) Shakespeare seems to have risen to the summit of excellence in the delineation and preservation of character.

We will now pass to "Hamlet," in order to obviate some of the general prejudices against the author, in reference to the character of the hero. Much has been objected to, which ought to have been praised, and many beauties of the highest kind have been neglected, because they are somewhat hidden.

The first question we should ask ourselves is—What did Shakespeare mean when he drew the character of Hamlet? He never wrote any thing without design, and what was his design when he sat down to produce this tragedy? My belief is, that he always regarded his story, before he began to write, much in the same light as a painter regards his canvas, before he begins to paint—as a mere vehicle for his thoughts—as the ground upon which he was to work. What then was the point to which Shakespeare directed himself in Hamlet? He intended to pourtray a person, in whose view the external world, and all its incidents and objects, were comparatively dim, and of no interest in themselves, and which began to interest only, when they were reflected in the mirror of his mind. Hamlet beheld external things in the same way that a man of vivid imagination, who shuts his eyes, sees what has previously made an impression on his organs.

The poet places him in the most stimulating circumstances that a human being can be placed in. He is the heir apparent of a throne; his father dies suspiciously; his mother excludes her son from his throne by marrying his uncle. This is not enough; but the Ghost of the murdered father is introduced, to assure the son that he was put to death by his own brother. What is the effect upon the son?—instant action and pursuit of revenge? No: endless reasoning and hesitating—constant urging and solicitation of the mind to act, and as constant an escape from action; ceaseless reproaches of himself for sloth and negligence, while the whole energy of his resolution evaporates in these reproaches. This, too, not from cowardice, for he is drawn as one of the bravest of his time—not from want of forethought or slowness of apprehension, for he sees through the very souls of all who surround him, but merely from that aversion to action, which prevails among such as have a world in themselves.

How admirable, too, is the judgment of the poet! Hamlet's own disordered fancy has not conjured up the spirit of his father; it has been seen by others: he is prepared by them to witness its re-appearance, and when he does see it, Hamlet is not brought forward as having long brooded on the subject. The moment before the Ghost enters, Hamlet speaks of other matters: he mentions the coldness of the night, and observes that he had not heard the clock strike, adding, in reference to the custom of drinking, that it is

"More honour'd in the breach than the observance."
Act I., Scene 4.[10]

Owing to the tranquil state of his mind, he indulges in some moral reflections. Afterwards, the Ghost suddenly enters.

> "*Hor.*   Look, my lord! it comes.
> *Ham.*   Angels and ministers of grace defend us!"

The same thing occurs in "Macbeth": in the dagger-scene, the moment before the hero sees it, he has his mind applied to some indifferent matters; "Go, tell thy mistress," &c.[11] Thus, in both cases, the preternatural appearance has all the effect of abruptness, and the reader is totally divested of the notion, that the figure is a vision of a highly wrought imagination.

Here Shakespeare adapts himself so admirably to the situation—in other words, so puts himself into it—that, though poetry, his language is the very language of nature. No terms, associated with such feelings, can occur to us so proper as those which he has employed, especially on the highest, the most august, and the most awful subjects that can interest a human being in this sentient world. That this is no mere fancy, I can undertake to establish from hundreds, I might say thousands, of passages. No character he has drawn, in the whole list of his plays, could so well and fitly express himself, as in the language Shakespeare has put into his mouth.

There is no indecision about Hamlet, as far as his own sense of duty is concerned; he knows well what he ought to do, and over and over again he makes up his mind to do it. The moment the players, and the two spies set upon him, have withdrawn, of whom he takes leave with a line so expressive of his contempt,

> "Ay so; good bye you.—Now I am alone,"

he breaks out into a delirium of rage against himself for neglecting to perform the solemn duty he had undertaken, and contrasts the factitious and artificial display of feeling by the player with his own apparent indifference;

> "What's Hecuba to him, or he to Hecuba,
>   That he should weep for her?"

Yet the player did weep for her, and was in an agony of grief at her sufferings, while Hamlet is unable to rouse himself to action, in order that he may perform the command of his father, who had come from the grave to incite him to revenge:—

> "This is most brave!
> That I, the son of a dear father murder'd,
> Prompted to my revenge by heaven and hell,
> Must, like a whore, unpack my heart with words,
> And fall a cursing like a very drab,
> A scullion."
> *Act II., Scene 2.*[12]

It is the same feeling, the same conviction of what is his duty, that makes Hamlet exclaim in a subsequent part of the tragedy:

> "How all occasions do inform against me,
>   And spur my dull revenge! What is a man,
>   If his chief good, and market of his time,
>   Be but to sleep and feed? A beast, no more.
>
> * * * * *
>
> ————————— I do not know
> Why yet I live to say—'this thing's to do,'
> Sith I have cause and will and strength and means
> To do't."
> *Act IV., Scene 4.*[13]

Yet with all this strong conviction of duty, and with all this resolution arising out of strong conviction, nothing is done. This admirable and consistent character, deeply acquainted with his own feelings, painting them with such wonderful power and accuracy, and firmly persuaded that a moment ought not to be lost in executing the solemn charge committed to him, still yields to the same retiring from reality, which is the result of having, what we express by the terms, a world within himself.

Such a mind as Hamlet's is near akin to madness. Dryden has somewhere said,

> "Great wit to madness nearly is allied,"[14]

and he was right; for he means by "wit" that greatness of genius, which led Hamlet to a perfect knowledge of his own character, which, with all strength of motive, was so weak as to be unable to carry into act his own most obvious duty.

With all this he has a sense of imperfectness, which becomes apparent when he is moralising on the skull in the churchyard. Something is wanting to his completeness—something is deficient which remains to be supplied, and he is therefore described as attached to Ophelia. His madness is assumed, when he finds that witnesses have been placed behind the arras to listen to what passes, and when the heroine has been thrown in his way as a decoy.

---

[10] L. 16. Next quoted are ll. 38–39.
[11] See *Macbeth*, II, i, 31–64.

[12] Ll. 575–615.
[13] Ll. 32–46.
[14] *Absalom and Achitophel*, l. 163.

Another objection has been taken by Dr. Johnson, and Shakespeare has been taxed very severely. I refer to the scene where Hamlet enters and finds his uncle praying, and refuses to take his life, excepting when he is in the height of his iniquity. To assail him at such a moment of confession and repentance, Hamlet declares,

"Why, this is hire and salary, not revenge."
                    Act III., Scene 3.[15]

He therefore forbears, and postpones his uncle's death, until he can catch him in some act

"That has no relish of salvation in't."

This conduct, and this sentiment, Dr. Johnson has pronounced to be so atrocious and horrible, as to be unfit to be put into the mouth of a human being.[16] The fact, however, is that Dr. Johnson did not understand the character of Hamlet, and censured accordingly: the determination to allow the guilty King to escape at such a moment is only part of the indecision and irresoluteness of the hero. Hamlet seizes hold of a pretext for not acting, when he might have acted so instantly and effectually: therefore, he again defers the revenge he was bound to seek, and declares his determination to accomplish it at some time,

"When he is drunk, asleep, or in his rage,
Or in th' incestuous pleasures of his bed."

This, allow me to impress upon you most emphatically, was merely the excuse Hamlet made to himself for not taking advantage of this particular and favourable moment for doing justice upon his guilty uncle, at the urgent instance of the spirit of his father.

Dr. Johnson farther states, that in the voyage to England, Shakespeare merely follows the novel as he found it, as if the poet had no other reason for adhering to his original; but Shakespeare never followed a novel, because he found such and such an incident in it, but because he saw that the story, as he read it, contributed to enforce, or to explain some great truth inherent in human nature. He never could lack invention to alter or improve a popular narrative; but he did not wantonly vary from it, when he knew that, as it was related, it would so well apply to his own great purpose. He saw at once how consistent it was with the character of Hamlet, that after still resolving, and still deferring, still determining to execute, and still postponing execution, he should finally, in the infirmity of his disposition, give himself up to his destiny, and hopelessly

place himself in the power, and at the mercy of his enemies.

Even after the scene with Osrick, we see Hamlet still indulging in reflection, and hardly thinking of the task he has just undertaken: he is all dispatch and resolution, as far as words and present intentions are concerned, but all hesitation and irresolution, when called upon to carry his words and intentions into effect; so that, resolving to do everything, he does nothing. He is full of purpose, but void of that quality of mind which accomplishes purpose.

Anything finer than this conception, and working out of a great character, is merely impossible. Shakespeare wished to impress upon us the truth, that action is the chief end of existence—that no faculties of intellect, however brilliant, can be considered valuable, or indeed otherwise than as misfortunes, if they withdraw us from, or render us repugnant to action, and lead us to think and think of doing, until the time has elapsed when we can do anything effectually. In enforcing this moral truth, Shakespeare has shown the fulness and force of his powers: all that is amiable and excellent in nature is combined in Hamlet, with the exception of one quality. He is a man living in meditation, called upon to act by every motive human and divine, but the great object of his life is defeated by continually resolving to do, yet doing nothing but resolve.

[1856]

---

[15] Ll. 79–92.
[16] See note to III, iii, 94, in Johnson's edition.

ESSAYS ON THE PRINCIPLES OF GENIAL CRITICISM

The Essays *were published in* Felix Farley's Bristol Journal *in August–September 1814, in connection with an exhibition of paintings by Washington Allston (1779–1843), an American painter whom Coleridge had met and admired in Rome in 1806. (Allston painted two portraits of Coleridge, the first done in Rome, the second in Bristol.) Originally intended to "serve poor Allston," who was in financial difficulties and had recently recovered from severe illness, the Essays instead became, in the words of J. A. Appleyard, "Coleridge's only venture into general aesthetics before the thirteenth lecture ['On Poesy and Art'] of 1818." The text of the* Essays *is here reproduced from J. Shawcross' edition of* Biographia Literaria *(London: Oxford University Press, 1907), II, 219–46. See Shawcross' notes (II, 304–15) and Appleyard's* Coleridge's Philosophy of Literature *(Cambridge, Mass.: Harvard University Press, 1965), pp. 156–68, for discussions of the many confusions and contradictions in the arguments of the* Essays.

FROM

ESSAYS

ON THE

PRINCIPLES

OF

GENIAL CRITICISM

CONCERNING THE FINE ARTS,

MORE ESPECIALLY THOSE OF

STATUARY AND PAINTING,

DEDUCED FROM THE

LAWS AND IMPULSES

WHICH GUIDE THE TRUE ARTIST

IN THE

PRODUCTION OF HIS WORKS

PRELIMINARY ESSAY

"Unus ergo idemque perpetuo Sol perseverans atque manens aliis atque aliis, aliter atque aliter dispositis, alius efficitur atque alius. Haud secus de hac solari arte varii varie sentiunt, diversi diversa dicunt: quot capita, tot sententiae—et tot voces. Hinc corvi crocitant, cuculi cuculant, lupi ululant, sues grundiunt, oves balant, hinniunt equi, mugiunt boves, rudunt asini. Turpe est, dixit Aristoteles, solicitum esse ad quemlibet interrogantem respondere. Boves bobus admugiant, equi equis adhinniant, asinis adrudant asini! Nostrum est hominibus aliquid circa hominum excellentissimorum inventiones pertentare."—JORDAN: BRUNUS *de Umbris Idearum.*[1]

[1] "Therefore one and the same sun, while constantly persevering and remaining, yet becomes one thing or another as some

IT WILL not appear complimentary to liken the Editors of Newspapers, in one respect, to galley-slaves; but the likeness is not the less apt on that account, and a simile is not expected *to go on all fours.* When storms blow high in the political atmosphere, the events of the day fill the sails, and the writer may draw in his oars, and let his brain rest; but when calm weather returns, then comes too "the tug of toil," hard work and little speed. Yet he not only sympathizes with the public joy, as a man and a citizen, but will seek to derive some advantages even for his editorial functions, from the cessation of battles and revolutions.[2] He cannot indeed hope to excite the same keen and promiscuous sensation as when he had to announce events, which by the mere bond of interest brought home the movements of monarchs and empires to every individual's counting-house and fire-side; but he consoles himself by the reflection, that these troublesome times occasioned thousands to acquire a habit, and almost a necessity, of reading, which it now becomes his object to retain by the gradual substitution of a milder stimulant, which though less intense is more permanent, and by its greater divergency no less than duration, even more pleasureable.—And how can he hail and celebrate the return of peace more worthily or more appropriately, than by exerting his best faculties to direct the taste and affections of his readers to the noblest works of peace? The tranquillity of nations per. .its our patriotism to repose. We are now allowed to think and feel as men, for all that may confer honor on human nature; not ignorant, meantime, that the greatness of a nation is by no distant links connected with the celebrity of its individual citizens—that whatever raises our country in the eyes of the civilized world, will make that country dearer and more venerable to its inhabitants, and thence actually more powerful, and more worthy of love and veneration. Add too (what in a great commercial city will not be deemed trifling or inappertinent) the certain reaction of the Fine Arts on the more immediate utilities of life. The transfusion of the fairest

objects are disposed some ways sometimes and other objects are disposed other ways at other times. Not unlike this solar manner, various men feel various ways, and different classes of being speak different things: there are as many opinions as heads—and as many voices. Hence crows caw, cuckoos cuckoo, wolves howl, pigs grunt, sheep bleat, horses neigh, cows low, and donkeys bray. Aristotle said it is shameful to be solicitous in answering everyone who asks a question. Cows low to cattle, horses neigh to horses, and donkeys bray to donkeys! It is our purpose to prove to men something about the inventions [discoveries, devisings] of most excellent men." The quotation runs together two passages spoken by "Philothimus" from the introductory "Dialogus praelib. Apologeticus" to *De Umbris Idearum* (1582) by Giordano Bruno (*c.* 1548–1600), the Italian Neoplatonic philosopher.

[2] In April 1814, Napoleon abdicated; in May, he was exiled to Elba.

forms of Greece and Rome into the articles of hourly domestic use by Mr. Wedgwood; the impulse given to our engravings by Boydell;[3] the superior beauty of our patterns in the cotton manufactory, of our furniture and musical instruments, hold as honorable a rank in our archives of trade, as in those of taste.

Regarded from these points of view, painting and statuary call on our attention with superior claims. All the fine arts are different species of poetry. The same spirit speaks to the mind through different senses by manifestations of itself, appropriate to each. They admit therefore of a natural division into poetry of language (poetry in the emphatic sense, because less subject to the accidents and limitations of time and space); poetry of the ear, or music; and poetry of the eye, which is again subdivided into plastic poetry, or statuary, and graphic poetry, or painting. The common essence of all consists in the excitement of emotion for the immediate purpose of pleasure through the medium of beauty; herein contra-distinguishing poetry from science, the immediate object and primary purpose of which is truth and possible utility. (The sciences indeed may and will give a high and pure pleasure; and the Fine Arts may lead to important truth, and be in various ways useful in the ordinary meaning of the word; but these are not the direct and characteristic ends, and we define things by their peculiar, not their common properties.)

Of the three sorts of poetry each possesses both exclusive and comparative advantages. The last (i.e. the plastic and graphic) is more permanent, and incomparably less dependent, than the second,[4] i.e. music; and though yielding in both these respects to the first, yet it regains its balance and equality of rank by the universality of its language. Michael Angelo and Raphael are for all beholders; Dante and Ariosto only for the readers of Italian. Hence though the title of these essays proposes, as their subject, the Fine Arts in general, which as far as the main principles are in question, will be realized in proportion to the writer's ability; yet the application and illustration of them will be confined to those of Painting and Statuary, and of these, chiefly to the former,

"Which, like a second and more lovely nature,
Turns the blank canvas to a magic mirror;

That makes the absent present, and to shadows
Gives light, depth, substance, bloom, yea, thought and
motion."[5]

To this disquisition two obstacles suggest themselves —that enough has been already written on the subject (this we may suppose an objection on the part of the reader) and the writer's own feeling concerning the grandeur and delicacy of the subject itself. As to the first, he would consider himself as having grossly failed in his duty to the public, if he had not carefully perused all the works on the Fine Arts known to him; and let it not be rashly attributed to self-conceit, if he dares avow his conviction that much remains to be done; a conviction indeed, which every author must entertain, who, whether from disqualifying ignorance or utter want of thought, does not act with the full consciousness of acting to no wise purpose. The works, that have hitherto appeared, have been either technical, or useful only to the Artist himself (if indeed useful at all) or employed in explaining by the laws of association the effects produced on the spectator by such and such impressions. In the latter, as in Alison,[6] &c., much has been said well and truly; but the principle itself is too vague for practical guidance.—Association in philosophy is like the term stimulus in medicine; explaining every thing, it explains nothing; and above all, leaves itself unexplained. It is an excellent charm to enable a man to talk *about* and *about* any thing he likes, and to make himself and his hearers as wise as before. Besides, the specific object of the present attempt is to enable the spectator to judge in the same spirit in which the Artist produced, or ought to have produced.

To the second objection, derived from the author's own feelings, he would find himself embarrassed in the attempt to answer, if the peculiar advantages of the subject itself did not aid him. His illustrations of his principles do not here depend on his own ingenuity— he writes for those, who can consult their own eyes and judgements. The various collections, as of

---

3 Josiah Wedgwood (1730–1795) was the founder of the celebrated Wedgwood pottery works. His sons Thomas (1771–1805) and Josiah (1769–1843) were early patrons of Coleridge. John Boydell (1719–1804) was an engraver and leading publisher of prints in England. He was notable for his employment of English engravers and for his commissioning of prints of paintings by contemporary English artists.

4 This is because the success of music depends upon the ability of the performer.

5 Lines written in 1814 in praise of Sir George Beaumont (1753–1827), a patron and friend of Wordsworth and Coleridge, and a landscape painter. The lines are from an appendage to Coleridge's play *Remorse*, II, ii, 42, first published in full in 1828.

6 Archibald Alison (1757–1839) was the author of *Essays on the Nature and Principles of Taste* (1790), an influential presentation of aesthetics in terms of associationist psychology. Coleridge frames his discussion of beauty in opposition to associationist aesthetics. Whereas Alison had argued that "no Forms or species of Forms, are in themselves originally beautiful; but . . . their Beauty in all cases arises from their being expressive to us of some pleasing or affecting Qualities," Coleridge argues for an authentic beauty residing in the composition of the object: in the relations of parts to whole, material to form, "multiety in unity." Thus, for Coleridge a work of art pleases because of our perception of this authentic beauty; for Alison, it is beautiful because it pleases.

Mr. Acraman (the father of the Fine Arts in this city*), of Mr. Davis, Mr. Gibbons, &c.; to which many of our readers either will have had, or may procure, access; and the admirable works exhibiting now by Allston; whose great picture, with his Hebe, landscape, and sea-piece,[8] would of themselves suffice to elucidate the fundamental doctrines of color, ideal form, and grouping; assist the reasoner in the same way as the diagrams aid the geometrician, but far more and more vividly. The writer therefore concludes this his preparatory Essay by two postulates, the only ones he deems necessary for his complete intelligibility: the first, that the reader would steadily look into his own mind to know whether the principles stated are ideally true; the second, to look at the works or parts of the works mentioned, as illustrating or exemplifying the principle, to judge whether or how far it has been realized.

ESSAY SECOND

In Mathematics the definitions, of necessity, precede not only the demonstrations, but likewise the postulates and axioms: they are the rock, which at once forms the foundation and supplies the materials of the edifice. Philosophy, on the contrary, concludes with the definition: it is the result, the compendium, the remembrancer of all the preceding facts and inferences.[1] Whenever, therefore, it appears in the front, it ought to be considered as a faint outline, which answers all its intended purposes, if only it circumscribe the subject, and direct the reader's anticipation toward the one road, on which he is to travel.

Examined from this point of view, the definition of poetry, in the preliminary Essay, as the regulative idea of all the Fine Arts, appears to me after many experimental applications of it to general illustrations and to

* Bristol.[7]

⟡⟡⟡⟡⟡⟡⟡⟡⟡⟡⟡⟡⟡⟡⟡⟡⟡⟡⟡⟡⟡⟡⟡⟡⟡⟡⟡⟡⟡⟡⟡⟡⟡

[7] John Acraman was a wealthy Bristol merchant. William Gibbons was an ironmonger, and mayor of Bristol in 1800.
[8] "Great picture" is a reference to "The Dead Man Revived by Touching the Bones of the Prophet Elisha" (now in the Pennsylvania Academy of Fine Arts, Philadelphia). "Hebe" was Allston's painting of the Greek goddess of youth. "The landscape" is a reference to "Diana and her Nymphs in the Chase. Swiss Landskip," painted in Rome in 1805, where Coleridge first saw and admired it. "The sea-piece" is probably "Rising of a Thunderstorm at Sea" (now in the Museum of Fine Arts, Boston).
[1] "The inspiration [for Coleridge's description of the differences between Mathematics and Philosophy] is Kantian and comes from the distinction between the mathematical method of synthesis where the objects of the mind are constructed by the mind, and the analytic method of natural philosophy where sense experience results in indistinct and confused notions which must be progressively clarified if they are to be useful" (Appleyard, p. 159). Shawcross points out in his notes the indebtedness to Kant throughout the *Essays*.

individual instances, liable to no just *logical* reversion, or complaint: "the excitement of emotion for the purpose of *immediate* pleasure, through the medium of beauty."—But like all previous statements in Philosophy (as distinguished from Mathematics) it has the inconvenience of presuming conceptions which do not perhaps consciously or distinctly exist. Thus, the former part of my definition might appear equally applicable to any object of our animal appetites, till by after-reasonings the attention has been directed to the full force of the word "*immediate*";[2] and till the mind, by being led to refer discriminatingly to its own experience, has become conscious that all objects of mere desire constitute an interest (i.e. aliquid quod est inter hoc et aliud, or that which is between the agent and his motive), and which is therefore valued only as the means to the end. To take a trivial but unexceptionable instance, the venison is agreeable because it gives pleasure; while the Apollo Belvedere is not beautiful because it pleases, but it pleases us because it is beautiful. The term, pleasure, is unfortunately so comprehensive, as frequently to become equivocal: and yet it is hard to discover a substitute. *Complacency*, which would indeed better express the intellectual nature of the enjoyment essentially involved in the sense of the beautiful, yet seems to preclude all emotion: and *delight*, on the other hand, conveys a comparative *degree* of pleasureable emotion, and is therefore unfit for a *general* definition, the object of which is to abstract the *kind*. For this reason, we added the words "through the medium of beauty." But here the same difficulty recurs from the promiscuous use of the term, Beauty. Many years ago, the writer, in company with an accidental party of travellers, was gazing on a cataract of great height, breadth, and impetuosity, the summit of which appeared to blend with the sky and clouds, while the lower part was hidden by rocks and trees; and on his observing, that it was, in the strictest sense of the word, a sublime object, a lady present assented with warmth to the remark, adding—"Yes! and it is not only sublime, but beautiful and absolutely pretty."[3]

And let not these distinctions be charged on the writer, as obscurity and needless subtlety; for it is in

⟡⟡⟡⟡⟡⟡⟡⟡⟡⟡⟡⟡⟡⟡⟡⟡⟡⟡⟡⟡⟡⟡⟡⟡⟡⟡⟡⟡⟡⟡⟡⟡⟡

[2] As Shawcross points out, "disinterested" would be a clearer word. In the case of the venison, "an object of mere desire" mentioned several lines later, the pleasure comes from the satisfaction of an "animal appetite;" the object is "agreeable," not in itself but only as "the means to the end" of that satisfaction. In aesthetic pleasure, on the other hand, the work of art (the statue Apollo Belvedere) is objectively beautiful; the pleasure comes from our perception of this objective beauty, without regard to its utility in satisfying an animal appetite.
[3] The incident is recorded in Dorothy Wordsworth's "Recollections of a Tour Made in Scotland A.D. 1803," entry for August 21.

the nature of all disquisitions on matters of taste, that the reasoner must appeal for his very premises to facts of feeling and of inner sense, which all men do not possess, and which many, who do possess and even act upon them, yet have never reflectively adverted to, have never made them objects of a full and distinct consciousness. The geometrician refers to certain figures in space, and to the power of describing certain lines, which are intuitive to all men, as men; and therefore his demonstrations are throughout *compulsory*. The moralist and the philosophic critic lay claim to no *positive*, but only to a *conditional* necessity. It is not necessary, that A or B should judge *at all* concerning poetry; but *if* he does, in order to a just taste, such and such faculties *must have* been developed in his mind. If a man, upon questioning his own experience, can detect no difference in *kind* between the enjoyment derived from the eating of turtle, and that from the perception of a new truth; if in *his* feelings a taste *for* Milton is essentially the same as the taste *of* mutton, he may still be a sensible and a valuable member of society; but it would be desecration to argue with him on the Fine Arts; and should he himself dispute on them, or even publish a book (and such books *have* been perpetrated within the memory of man) we can answer him only by silence, or a courteous waiving of the subject. To tell a blind man, declaiming concerning light and color, "you should wait till you have got eyes to see with," would indeed be telling the truth, but at the same time be acting a useless as well as an inhuman part. An English critic, who assumes and proceeds on the identity in kind of the pleasures derived from the palate and from the intellect, and who literally considers *taste* to mean one and the same thing, whether it be the taste of venison, or a taste for Virgil, and who, in strict consistence with his principles, passes sentence on Milton as a tiresome poet, because he finds nothing *amusing* in the Paradise Lost (i.e. damnat Musas, quia animum a musis non divertunt)—this tastemeter to the fashionable world gives a ludicrous portrait of an African belle, and concludes with a triumphant exclamation, "such is the ideal of beauty in Dahoma!"[4] Now it is curious, that a very intelligent traveller,

describing the low state of the human mind in this very country, gives as an instance, that in their whole language they have no word for beauty, or the beautiful; but say either it is nice, or it is good; doubtless, says he, because this very sense is as yet dormant, and the idea of beauty as little developed in their minds, as in that of an infant.—I give the substance of the meaning, not the words; as I quote both writers from memory.

There are few mental exertions more instructive, or which are capable of being rendered more entertaining, than the attempt to establish and exemplify the distinct meaning of terms, often confounded in common use, and considered as mere synonyms. Such are the words, Agreeable, Beautiful, Picturesque, Grand, Sublime: and to attach a distinct and separate sense to each of these, is a previous step of indispensable necessity to a writer, who would reason intelligibly, either to himself or to his readers, concerning the works of poetic genius, and the sources and the nature of the pleasure derived from them. But more especially on the essential difference of the beautiful and the agreeable, rests fundamentally the whole question, which assuredly must possess no vulgar or feeble interest for all who regard the dignity of their own nature: whether the noblest productions of human genius (such as the Iliad, the works of Shakspeare and Milton, the Pantheon, Raphael's Gallery, and Michael Angelo's Sistine Chapel, the Venus de Medici and the Apollo Belvedere, involving, of course, the human forms that approximate to them in actual life) delight us merely by chance, from accidents of local associations—in short, please us because they please us (in which case it would be impossible either to praise or to condemn any man's taste, however opposite to our own, and we could be no more justified in assigning a corruption or absence of just taste to a man, who should prefer Blackmore to Homer or Milton, or the Castle Spectre[5] to Othello, than to the same man for preferring a black-pudding to a sirloin of beef); or whether there exists in the constitution of the human soul a sense, and a regulative principle, which may indeed be stifled and latent in some, and be perverted and denaturalized in others, yet is nevertheless universal in a given state of intellectual and moral culture; which is independent of local and temporary circumstances, and dependent only on

---

[4] The critic is Richard Payne Knight (1750–1824), author of *An Analytical Inquiry into the Principles of Taste* (1805). Knight's strictures on *Paradise Lost* are found in Part II, chapter I, section xxviii; his "ludicrous portrait of an African belle" occurs in the Introduction, section 9. damnat Musas ... non divertunt: "he damns the Muses, because they do not divorce the mind from studies"; that is, such a critic as Knight equates the pleasures of taste with thoughtless relaxation, and therefore rejects the discipline and exertion of mind required for a taste for serious literature (the Muses). Coleridge is making an elaborate pun between the English word "amuses" and the Latin "*a musis*" (away from studies) and "*Musas*" (the Muses). For Knight, "a-musement" literally means being "away from the Muses."

[5] Richard Blackmore (d. 1729), physician to William III and Queen Anne, was the author of a number of grandiose literary productions, including the "heroic poems" *Prince Arthur* (1695) and *King Arthur* (1697), and *The Creation: a philosophical Poem demonstrating the Existence and Providence of God* (1712). *Castle Spectre* was a very popular melodrama by Matthew ("Monk") Lewis, first produced in 1797; the plot involves some elements superficially similar to *Othello*: a persecuted heroine, a revengeful African, in addition to ghosts and other cheaply sensational elements.

the degree in which the faculties of the mind are developed; and which, consequently, it is our duty to cultivate and improve, as soon as the sense of its actual existence dawns upon us.

The space allotted to these Essays obliges me to defer this attempt to the following week: and I will now conclude by requesting the candid reader not altogether to condemn this second Essay, without having considered, that the ground-works of an edifice cannot be as sightly as the superstructure, and that the philosopher, unlike the architect, must lay his foundations in sight; unlike the musician, must tune his instruments in the hearing of his audience. TASTE is the intermediate faculty which connects the active with the passive powers of our nature, the intellect with the senses; and its appointed function is to elevate the *images* of the latter, while it realizes the *ideas* of the former. We must therefore have learned what is peculiar to each, before we can understand that "Third something," which is formed by a harmony of both.

FROM

ESSAY THIRD

*   *   *   *   *

AGREEABLE.—We use this word in two senses; in the first for whatever agrees with our nature, for that which is congruous with the primary constitution of our senses. Thus green is naturally agreeable to the eye. In this sense the word expresses, at least involves, a pre-established harmony between the organs and their appointed objects. In the second sense, we convey by the word *agreeable*, that the thing has by force of habit (thence called a second nature) been made to agree with us; or that it has become agreeable to us by its recalling to our minds some one or more things that were dear and pleasing to us; or lastly, on account of some after pleasure or advantage, of which it has been the constant cause or occasion. Thus by force of custom men *make* the taste of tobacco, which was at first hateful to the palate, agreeable to them; thus too, as our Shakspeare observes,

> "Things base and vile, holding no quality,
> Love can transpose to form and dignity—" [1]

the crutch that had supported a revered parent, after the first anguish of regret, becomes agreeable to the affectionate child; and I once knew a very sensible and accomplished Dutch gentleman, who, spite of his own sense of the ludicrous nature of the feeling, was more

delighted by the first grand concert of frogs he heard in this country, than he had been by Catalina singing in the compositions of Cimarosa.[2] The last clause needs no illustrations, as it comprises all the objects that are agreeable to us, only because they are the means by which we gratify our smell, touch, palate, and mere bodily feeling.

The BEAUTIFUL, contemplated in its essentials, that is, in *kind* and not in *degree*, is that in which the *many*, still seen as many, becomes one. Take a familiar instance, one of a thousand. The frost on a window-pane has by accident crystallized into a striking resemblance of a tree or a seaweed. With what pleasure we trace the parts, and their relations to each other, and to the whole! Here is the stalk or trunk, and here the branches or sprays—sometimes even the buds or flowers. Nor will our pleasure be less, should the caprice of the crystallization represent some object disagreeable to us, provided only we can see or fancy the component parts each in relation to each, and all forming a whole. A lady would see an admirably painted tiger with pleasure, and at once pronounce it beautiful, —nay, an owl, a frog, or a toad, who would have shrieked or shuddered at the sight of the things themselves. So far is the Beautiful from depending wholly on association, that it is frequently produced by the mere removal of associations. Many a sincere convert to the beauty of various insects, as of the dragon-fly, the fangless snake, &c., has Natural History made, by exploding the terror or aversion that had been connected with them.

The most general definition of beauty, therefore, is —that I may fulfil my threat of plaguing my readers with hard words—Multëity in Unity. Now it will be always found, that whatever is the definition of the *kind*, independent of degree, becomes likewise the definition of the highest degree of that kind. An old coach-wheel lies in the coachmaker's yard, disfigured with tar and dirt (I purposely take the most trivial instances)—if I turn away my attention from these, and regard the *figure* abstractly, "still," I might say to my companion, "there is beauty in that wheel, and you yourself would not only admit, but would feel it, had you never seen a wheel before. See how the rays proceed from the centre to the circumferences, and how many different images are distinctly comprehended at one glance, as forming one whole, and each part in some harmonious relation to each and to all." But imagine the polished golden wheel of the chariot of the

---

[1] *Midsummer Night's Dream*, I, i, 232–33.

[2] Angelica Catalani (1780–1849) was one of the leading prima donnas of her time. Domenico Cimarosa (1749–1801) was an Italian composer of operas and other vocal works.

Sun, as the poets have described it: then the figure, and the real thing so figured, exactly coincide.[3] There is nothing heterogeneous, nothing to abstract from: by its perfect smoothness and circularity in width, each part is (if I may borrow a metaphor from a sister sense) as perfect a melody, as the whole is a complete harmony. This, we should say, is beautiful throughout. Of all "the many," which I actually see, each and all are really reconciled into unity: while the effulgence from the whole coincides with, and seems to represent, the effluence of delight from my own mind in the intuition of it.

It seems evident then, first, that beauty is harmony, and subsists only in composition, and secondly, that the first species of the Agreeable can alone be a component part of the beautiful, that namely which is naturally consonant with our senses by the pre-established harmony between nature and the human mind; and thirdly, that even of this species, those objects only can be admitted (according to rule the first) which belong to the eye and ear, because they alone are susceptible of distinction of parts.[4] Should an Englishman gazing on a mass of cloud rich with the rays of the rising sun exclaim, even without distinction of, or reference to its form, or its relation to other objects, how beautiful! I should have no quarrel with him. First, because by the law of association there is in all visual beholdings at least an indistinct subsumption of form and relation: and, secondly, because even in the coincidence between the sight and the object there is an approximation to the reduction of the many into one. But who, that heard a Frenchman call the flavor of a leg of mutton a beautiful taste, would not immediately recognize him for a Frenchman, even though there should be neither grimace or characteristic nasal twang? The result, then, of the whole is that the shapely (i.e. *formosus*) joined with the naturally agreeable, constitutes what, speaking accurately, we mean by the word beautiful (i.e. *pulcher*).

But we are conscious of faculties far superior to the highest impressions of sense; we have life and free-will.—What then will be the result, when the Beautiful, arising from regular form, is so modified by the perception of life and spontaneous action, as that the latter only shall be the object of our conscious *perception*, while the former merely acts, and yet does effec-

tively act, on our feelings? With pride and pleasure I reply by referring my reader to the group in Mr. Allston's grand picture of the "Dead Man reviving from the touch of the bones of the Prophet Elisha," beginning with the slave at the head of the reviving body, then proceeding to the daughter clasping her swooning mother; to the mother, the wife of the reviving man; then to the soldier behind who supports her; to the two figures eagerly conversing: and lastly, to the exquisitely graceful girl who is bending downward, and whose hand nearly touches the thumb of the slave! You will find, what you had not suspected, that you have here before you a circular group. But by what variety of life, motion, and passion is all the stiffness, that would result from an obvious regular figure, swallowed up, and the figure of the group as much concealed by the action and passion, as the skeleton, which gives the form of the human body, is hidden by the flesh and its endless outlines!

In Raphael's admirable Galatea[5] (the print of which is doubtless familiar to most of my readers) the circle is perceived at first sight; but with what multiplicity of rays and chords within the area of the circular group, with what elevations and depressions of the circumference, with what an endless variety and sportive wildness in the component figure, and in the junctions of the figures, is the balance, the perfect reconciliation, effected between these two conflicting principles of the FREE LIFE, and of the confining FORM! How entirely is the stiffness that would have resulted from the obvious regularity of the latter, *fused* and (if I may hazard so bold a metaphor) almost *volatilized* by the interpenetration and electrical flashes of the former.

But I shall recur to this consummate work for more specific illustrations hereafter: and have indeed in some measure offended already against the laws of method, by anticipating materials which rather belong to a more advanced stage of the disquisition. It is time to recapitulate, as briefly as possible, the arguments already advanced, and having summed up the result, to leave behind me this, the only portion of these essays, which, as far as the subject itself is concerned, will demand any *effort* of attention from a reflecting and intelligent reader. And let me be permitted to remind him, that the distinctions, which it is my object to prove and elucidate, have not merely a foundation in nature and the noblest faculties of the human mind, but are likewise the very ground-work, nay, an indispensable condition, of all *rational* enquiry concerning the Arts. For it is self-evident, that whatever may be judged of

---

[3] That is, both the matter and form are beautiful. In the case of the "old coach-wheel," although the form is beautiful in the relation of parts to whole, the material properties (tar and dirt) distract the observer from the perception of that beauty and require an abstraction of the form from matter.

[4] As Coleridge explains later in "Principle the Second," the senses of taste, smell, and feeling cannot make us aware of the relation of parts to whole; and the pleasure of aesthetic beauty depends on our perception of that relationship.

[5] "The Triumph of Galatea" is a famous mythological fresco in the Villa Farnesina in Rome.

differently by different persons, in the very same degree of moral and intellectual cultivation, extolled by one and condemned by another, without any error being assignable to either, can never be an object of general principles: and *vice versâ*, that whatever can be brought to the test of general principles presupposes a distinct origin from these pleasures and tastes, which, for the wisest purposes, are made to depend on local and transitory fashions, accidental associations, and the peculiarities of individual temperament: to all which the philosopher, equally with the well-bred man of the world, applies the old adage, *de gustibus non est disputandum*.[6] Be it, however, observed that "de gustibus" is by no means the same as "de gustu," nor will it escape the scholar's recollection, that taste, in its metaphorical use, was first adopted by the Romans, and unknown to the less luxurious Greeks, who designated this faculty, sometimes by the word αἴσθησις, and sometimes by φιλοκαλία[7]—"ἀνδρῶν τῶν καθ᾽ ἡμᾶς φιλοκαλώτατος γεγονώς—i.e. endowed by nature with the most exquisite taste of any man of our age," says Porphyry of his friend, Castricius.[8] Still, this metaphor, borrowed from the pregustatores[9] of the old Roman Banquets, is singularly happy and appropriate. In the palate, the perception of the object and its qualities is involved in the *sensation*, in the mental taste it is involved in the *sense*. We have a *sensation* of sweetness, in a healthy palate, from honey; a *sense* of beauty, in an uncorrupted taste, from the view of the rising or setting sun.

RECAPITULATION. *Principle the First.* That which has become, or which has been *made* agreeable to us, from causes not contained in its own nature, or in its original conformity to the human organs and faculties; that which is not pleasing for its own sake, but by connection or association with some other thing, separate or separable from it, is neither beautiful, nor capable of being a component part of Beauty: though it may greatly increase the sum of our pleasure, when it does not interfere with the beauty of the object, nay, even when it detracts from it. A moss-rose, with a sprig of myrtle and jasmine, is not more *beautiful* from having been plucked from the garden, or presented to us by the hand of the woman we love, but is abundantly more delightful. The total pleasure received from one of Mr.

Bird's[10] finest pictures may, without any impeachment of our taste, be the greater from his having introduced into it the portrait of one of our friends, or from our pride in him as our townsman, or from our knowledge of his personal qualities; but the amiable artist would rightly consider it a coarse compliment, were it affirmed, that the *beauty* of the piece, or its merit as a work of genius, was the more perfect on this account. I am conscious that I look with a stronger and more pleasureable emotion at Mr. Allston's large landscape, in the spirit of Swiss scenery, from its having been the occasion of my first acquaintance with him in Rome. This may or may not be a compliment to *him*; but the true compliment to the picture was made by a lady of high rank and cultivated taste, who declared, in my hearing, that she never stood before that landscape without seeming to feel the breeze blow out of it upon her. But the most striking instance is afforded by the portrait of a departed or absent friend or parent; which is endeared to us, and more delightful, from some awkward position of the limbs, which had defied the contrivances of art to render it picturesque, but which was the characteristic habit of the original.

Principle the Second.—That which is naturally agreeable and consonant to human nature, so that the exceptions may be attributed to disease or defect; that, the pleasure from which is contained in the immediate impression; cannot, indeed, with strict propriety, be called beautiful, exclusive of its relations, but one among the component parts of beauty, in whatever instance it is susceptible of existing as a part of a whole. This, of course, excludes the mere objects of the taste, smell, and feeling, though the sensation from these, especially from the latter when organized into touch, may secretly, and without our consciousness, enrich and vivify the perceptions and images of the eye and ear; which alone are true organs of sense, their sensations in a healthy or uninjured state being too faint to be noticed by the mind. We may, indeed, in common conversation, call purple a beautiful color, or the tone of a single note on an excellent piano-forte a beautiful tone; but if we were questioned, we should agree that a rich or delightful color; a rich, or sweet, or clear tone; would have been more appropriate—and this with less hesitation in the latter instance than in the former, because the single tone is more manifestly of the nature of a *sensation*, while color is the medium which seems to blend sensation and perception, so as to hide, as it were, the former in the latter; the direct opposite of which takes place in the lower senses of feeling, smell, and taste. (In strictness, there is even in these an

---

[6] de gustibus . . . disputandum: "There is no disputing about tastes."

[7] αἴσθησις: "sensation"; φιλοκαλία: "love for the beautiful."

[8] Porphyry (A.D. 233–c. 304) was a pupil and interpreter of Plotinus, and the author of a variety of works on philosophy, religion, morals, and history. The praiseful remark on Castricius occurs in Porphyry's *On the Life of Plotinus and the Order of his Books*, chapter 7.

[9] Persons of extremely sensitive and sophisticated palates.

[10] Edward Bird (1772–1819) was a Bristol painter of genre scenes.

ascending scale. The smell is less sensual and more sentient than mere feeling, the taste than the smell, and the eye than the ear: but between the ear and the taste exists the chasm or break, which divides the beautiful and the elements of beauty from the merely agreeable.) When I reflect on the manner in which smoothness, richness of sound, &c., enter into the formation of the beautiful, I am induced to suspect that they act negatively, rather than positively. Something there must be to realize the form, something in and by which the *forma informans*[11] reveals itself: and these, less than any that could be substituted, and in the least possible degree, distract the attention, in the least possible degree obscure the idea, of which they (composed into outline and surface) are the symbol. An illustrative hint may be taken from a pure crystal, as compared with an opaque, semi-opaque or clouded mass, on the one hand, and with a perfectly transparent body, such as the air, on the other. The crystal is lost in the light, which yet it contains, embodies, and gives a shape to; but which passes shapeless through the air, and, in the ruder body, is either quenched or dissipated.

Principle the Third. The safest definition, then, of Beauty, as well as the oldest, is that of Pythagoras: THE REDUCTION OF MANY TO ONE—or, as finely expressed by the sublime disciple of Ammonius,[12] τὸ ἄμερες ὄν, ἐν πολλοῖς φανταζόμενον, of which the following may be offered as both paraphrase and corollary. *The sense of beauty subsists in simultaneous intuition of the relation of parts, each to each, and of all to a whole: exciting an immediate and absolute complacency, without intervenence, therefore, of any interest, sensual or intellectual.* The BEAUTIFUL is thus at once distinguished both from the AGREEABLE, which is beneath it, and from the GOOD, which is above it: for both these have an interest necessarily attached to them: both act on the WILL, and excite a desire for the actual existence of the image or idea contemplated: while the sense of beauty rests gratified in the mere contemplation or intuition, regardless whether it be a fictitious Apollo, or a real Antinous.[13]

The Mystics meant the same, when they define beauty as the subjection of matter to spirit so as to be transformed into a symbol, in and through which the spirit reveals itself; and declare *that* the *most* beautiful, where the most obstacles to a full manifestation have been most perfectly overcome. I would that the readers, for whom alone I write (*intelligibilia enim, non intellectum adfero*)[14] had Raphael's Galatea, or his School of Athens,[15] before them! or that the Essay might be read by some imaginative student, warm from admiration of the King's College Chapel at Cambridge, or of the exterior and interior of York Cathedral! I deem the sneers of a host of petty critics, unalphabeted in the life and truth of things, and as devoid of sound learning as of intuitive taste, well and wisely hazarded for the prospect of communicating the pleasure, which to such minds the following passage of Plotinus will not fail to give—Plotinus, a name venerable even to religion with the great Cosmus, Lorenzo de Medici, Ficinus, Politian,[16] Leonardo da Vinci, and Michael Angelo, but now known only as a name to the majority even of our most learned Scholars!—Plotinus, difficult indeed, but under a rough and austere rind concealing fruit worthy of Paradise; and if obscure, "*at tenet umbra Deum!*"[17] Ὅταν οὖν καὶ ἡ αἴσθησις τὸ ἐν σώμασιν εἶδος ἴδη συνδησάμενον καὶ κρατῆσαν τῆς φύσεως τῆς ἐναντίας, καὶ μορφὴν ἐπ' ἄλλαις μορφαῖς ἐκπρεπῶς ἐποχουμένην, συνελοῦσα ἀθρόον αὐτὸ τὸ πολλαχῆ ἀνήνεγκέ τε καὶ εδωκε τῷ ἔνδον σύμφωνον καὶ συναρμόττον καὶ φίλον.[18] A divine passage, faintly represented in the following lines, written many years ago by the writer, though without reference to, or recollection of, the above.

"O lady! we *receive* but what we *give*,
  And in *our* life alone does nature live!
  Ours is her wedding-garment, ours her shroud!
  And would we aught behold of higher worth,
  Than that inanimate cold world allow'd
  To the poor, loveless, ever-anxious crowd:
  Ah! from the soul itself must issue forth
  A light, a glory, a fair luminous cloud,
      Enveloping the earth!

---

11 forma informans: "the informing form."

12 Ammonius was a third-century Alexandrian philosopher and founder of Neoplatonism. His "sublime disciple" was Plotinus. The Greek phrase from Plotinus' *Ennead* may be translated: "The one [undivided] conceived as it is issuing through diversity [multiplicity]."

13 Antinous (d. A.D. 122) was a page and favorite of the Emperor Hadrian, who commissioned statues in his honor.

14 intelligibilia ... adfero: "I bring forward intelligible things, but not the intellect [by which they are to be understood]."

15 "School of Athens" is one of the frescoes in Raphael's Vatican Gallery, depicting Plato, Aristotle, and other philosophers of ancient Greece.

16 Marsilio Ficino (1433–1499) was a philosopher and leader of the Platonic Academy at Florence, with which was associated also Angelo Ambrogini (Poliziano) (1454–1494), distinguished classical scholar, and a Latin and Italian poet of distinction.

17 at tenet umbra Deum: "yet the shadow holds God!"

18 Ὅταν οὖν καὶ ... συναρμόττον καὶ φίλον: "When sense-perception, then, sees the form in bodies binding and mastering the nature opposed to it, which is shapeless, and shape riding gloriously upon other shapes, it gathers into one that which appears dispersed and brings it back and takes it in, now without parts, to the soul's interior and presents it to that which is within as something in tune with it and fitting it and dear to it." *Ennead*, I, 6, iii (Armstrong translation, Loeb Classical Library, Harvard University Press).

And from the soul itself must there be sent
A sweet and powerful voice, of its own birth,
 Of all sweet sounds the life and element!
O pure of heart! thou need'st not ask of me,
What this strong music in the soul may be;
 What and wherein it doth subsist,
This light, this glory, this fair luminous mist,
 This beautiful, and beauty-making power!
Joy, O beloved! joy, that ne'er was given,
Save to the pure and in their purest hour,
Life of our life, the parent and the birth,
Which, wedding nature to us, gives in dower
 A new heaven and new earth,
Undreamt of by the sensual and the proud—
This is the strong voice, this the luminous cloud!
 Our inmost selves rejoice:
And thence flows all that glads or ear or sight,
All melodies the echoes of that voice,
All colors a suffusion from that light,
And its celestial tint of yellow-green:
And still I gaze—and with how blank an eye!
And those thin clouds above, in flakes and bars,
That give away their motion to the stars;
Those stars, that glide behind them or between,
Now sparkling, now bedimm'd, but always seen;
Yon crescent moon, that seems as if it grew
In its own starless, cloudless lake of blue—
I see them all, so excellently fair!
I see, not feel, how beautiful they are."
       S. T. C. MS. Poem.[19]

SCHOLIUM. We have sufficiently distinguished the beautiful from the agreeable, by the sure criterion, that, when we find an object agreeable, the *sensation* of pleasure always precedes the judgement, and is its determining cause. We *find* it agreeable. But when we declare an object beautiful, the contemplation or intuition of its beauty precedes the *feeling* of complacency, in order of nature at least: nay, in great depression of spirits may even exist without sensibly producing it.—

"A grief without a pang, void, dark, and drear!
 A stifled, drowsy, unimpassion'd grief,
  That finds no natural outlet, no relief
   In word, or sigh, or tear!
 O dearest lady! in this heartless mood,
 To other thoughts by yon sweet throstle woo'd!
 All this long eve, so balmy and serene,
 Have I been gazing at the western sky."

---

[19] "Dejection: an Ode," ll. 47–75, followed by ll. 29–38. In the SCHOLIUM [a comment or gloss], Coleridge quotes ll. 21–28.

Now the least reflection convinces us that our sensations, whether of pleasure or of pain, are the incommunicable parts of our nature; such as can be reduced to no universal rule; and in which therefore we have no right to expect that others should agree with us, or to blame them for disagreement. That the Greenlander prefers train oil[20] to olive oil, and even to wine, we explain at once by our knowledge of the climate and productions to which he has been habituated. Were the man as enlightened as Plato, his palate would still find that most agreeable to which it had been most accustomed. But when the Iroquois Sachem, after having been led to the most perfect specimens of architecture in Paris, said that he saw nothing so beautiful as the cook's shops, we attribute this without hesitation to savagery of intellect, and infer with certainty that the sense of the beautiful was either altogether dormant in his mind, or at best very imperfect. The Beautiful, therefore, not originating in the sensations, must belong to the intellect: and therefore we *declare* an object beautiful, and feel an inward right to *expect* that others should coincide with us. But we feel no right to *demand* it: and this leads us to that, which hitherto we have barely touched upon and which we shall now attempt to illustrate more fully, namely, to the distinction of the Beautiful from the Good.

Let us suppose Milton in company with some stern and prejudiced Puritan, contemplating the front of York Cathedral, and at length expressing his admiration of its beauty. We will suppose it too at that time of his life, when his religious opinions, feelings, and prejudices most nearly coincided with those of the rigid Anti-prelatists.[21]—P. Beauty; I am sure, it is not the beauty of holiness. M. True; but yet it is beautiful.—P. It delights not me. What is it good for? Is it of any use but to be stared at?—M. Perhaps not! but still it is beautiful.—P. But call to mind the pride and wanton vanity of those cruel shavelings, that wasted the labor and substance of so many thousand poor creatures in the erection of this haughty pile.—M. I do. But still it is very beautiful.—P. Think how many score of places of worship, incomparably better suited both for prayer and preaching, and how many faithful ministers might have been maintained, to the blessing of tens of thousands, to them and their children's children, with the treasures lavished on this worthless mass of stone and cement.—M. Too true! but nevertheless it is *very* beautiful.—P. And it is not merely useless; but it feeds

---

[20] Whale oil.
[21] The anti-prelatists were the group of radical Protestant reformers in the 1640's, who urged the abolition of the Anglican ecclesiastical hierarchy. In 1641–1642, Milton wrote a number of treatises in support of the anti-prelatist position, among them *The Reason of Church Government urg'd against Prelaty* (1642).

the pride of the prelates, and keeps alive the popish and carnal spirit among the people.—M. Even so! and I presume not to question the wisdom, nor detract from the pious zeal, of the first Reformers of Scotland, who for these reasons destroyed so many fabrics, scarce inferior in beauty to this now before our eyes. But I did not call it *good*, nor have I told thee, brother! that if this were levelled with the ground, and existed only in the works of the modeller or engraver, that I should desire to reconstruct it. The GOOD consists in the congruity of a thing with the laws of the reason and the nature of the will, and in its fitness to determine the latter to actualize the former: and it is always discursive. The Beautiful arises from the perceived harmony of an object, whether sight or sound, with the inborn and constitutive rules of the judgement and imagination: and it is always intuitive. As light to the eye, even such is beauty to the mind, which cannot but have complacency in whatever is perceived as pre-configured to its living faculties. Hence the Greeks called a beautiful object καλόν quasi καλοῦν, i.e. *calling on* the soul, which receives instantly, and welcomes it as something connatural. Πάλιν οὖν ἀναλαβόντες, λέγωμεν τί δῆτα ἐστὶ τὸ ἐν τοῖς σώμασι καλόν. Πρῶτον ἔστι μὲν γάρ τι καὶ βολῆ τῆ πρώτῃ αἰσθητὸν γινόμενον, καὶ ἡ ψυχὴ ὥσπερ συνεῖσα λέγει, καὶ ἐπιγνοῦσα ἀποδέχεται, καὶ οἷον συναρμόττεται. Πρὸς δὲ τὸ αἰσχρὸν προσβαλοῦσα ἀνίλλεται, καὶ ἀρνεῖται καὶ ἀνανεύει ἐπ' αὐτοῦ οὐ συμφωνοῦσα, καὶ ἀλλοτριουμένη.— PLOTIN: Ennead. I. Lib. 6.[22]

APPENDIX

"He, (Charles Brandon, Duke of Suffolk) knowing that learning hath no enemy but ignorance, did suspect always the want of it in those men who derided the habit of it in others, like the fox in the fable, who being, by mischance or degeneracy, without a tail, persuaded others to cut theirs off as a burden. But he liked well the philosopher's division of men into three ranks; some who knew good and were willing to teach others.— These he said, were like gods among men; others who though they knew not much, yet were willing to learn and thankful for instruction.—These, he said, were like men among beasts; and some who knew not truth or good, and yet despised and maligned such as would

teach them.—These he esteemed as beasts among men."—*Lloyd's State Worthies*, p. 33.[1]

THUS, then, let us at once sum up and exemplify the whole. Its ambrosial odour renders the rose more agreeable to us, but it is not by this addition, that nature wrests the palm of beauty from the flower-pieces of Van Huysun.[2] The patience strength, and laboriousness of the Ox and the Ass, invaluable as we rightly deem them, can yet by no influence of association, bribe us to compare them in charm of form, and disposition of colors, with the fierce and untamable Zebra. The rough Sheep-dog is almost indispensable to the civilization of the human race. He appears to possess not Valuableness only, but even Worth! His various moral qualities, which seem above the effects of mere Instinct devoid of Will, compel our respect and regard, and excite our gratitude *to* him, as well as *for* him. Yet neither his paramount utility, no, nor even his incorruptible fidelity and disinterested affection, enable us to equal him, in outward beauty, with the cruel and cowardly panther, or leopard, or tiger, the hate and horror of the flock and of the shepherd.

But may not the sense of Beauty originate in our perception of the fitness of the means to the end in and for the animal itself? Or may it not depend on a law of Proportion? No! The shell of the Oyster, rough and unshapely, is its habitation and strong hold, its defence and organ of locomotion: the pearl, the beautiful ornament of the beautiful, is its disease. How charming the Moss Rose with its luxuriancy of petals! That moss, that luxuriancy, are the effects of degeneracy, and unfit the flower for the multiplication of its kind. Disproportion indeed may in certain cases preclude the sense of Beauty, and will do so wherever it destroys or greatly disturbs the wholeness and simultaneousness of the impression. But still proportion is not the positive cause, or the universal and necessary condition of beauty, were it only that proportion implies the perception of the coincidence of quantities with a pre-established rule of measurement, and is therefore always accompanied with an act of discursive thought. We declare at first sight the Swan beautiful, as it floats on with its long arching neck and protruding breast, which uniting to their reflected image in the watery mirror, present to our delighted eye the stringless bow of dazzling silver, which the Poets and Painters assign to the God of Love. We ask not what proportion the

---

[22] Πάλιν . . καὶ ἀλλοτριουμένη: "So let us go back to the beginning and state what the primary beauty in bodies really is. It is something which we become aware of even at the first glance; the soul speaks of it as if it understood it, recognises and welcomes it and as it were adapts itself to it. But when it encounters the ugly it shrinks back and rejects it and turns away from it and is out of tune and alienated from it." (Armstrong translation, Loeb Classical Library, Harvard University Press.)

[1] David Lloyd's *State-Worthies: Or, the States-men and Favourites of England since the Reformation*. Coleridge quotes from the second edition, 1670.
[2] Jan Van Huysum (1682–1749) was a Dutch painter of fruit and flower pieces.

neck bears to the body;—through all the changes of graceful motion it brings itself into unity, as an harmonious part of an harmonious whole. The very word "part" imperfectly conveys what we see and feel; for the moment we look at it in division, the charm ceases. In this spirit the Lover describing the incidents of a walk on the river-banks by moonlight is made by the poet to exclaim:

> "The pairing swans have heard my tread,
>   And rustle from their reedy bed.
>   O beauteous birds! methinks ye measure
>   Your movements to some heavenly tune!
>   O beauteous birds! 'tis such a pleasure
>   To see you move beneath the moon,
>   I would it were your true delight
>   To rest by day and wake all night." 3

The long neck of the ostrich is in exact and evident proportion to the height of the animal, and is of manifest utility and necessity to the bird, as it stoops down to graze and still walks on. But not being harmonized with the body by plumage or color, it seems to run along the grass like a serpent before the headless tall body that still stalks after it, inspiring at once the sense of the Deformed and the Fantastic.

I here close my metaphysical Preliminaries, in which I have confined myself to the Beauty of the Senses, and by the Good have chiefly referred to the relatively good. Of the supersensual Beauty, the Beauty of Virtue and Holiness, and of its relation to the ABSOLUTELY GOOD, distinguishable, not separable (even such relation as that of color to the Light of Heaven, and as the Light itself bears to the Knowledge, which it awakens), I discourse not now, waiting for a loftier mood, a nobler subject, a more appropriate audience, warned from within and from without, that it is profanation to speak of these mysteries "τοῖς μηδέποτε φαντασθεῖσιν, ὡς καλὸν τὸ τῆς δικαιοσύνης καὶ σωφροσύνης πρόσωπον, καὶ ὡς οὔτε ἕσπερος οὔτε ἐῷος οὕτω καλά. Τὸν γὰρ ὁρῶντα πρὸς τὸ ὁρώμενον συγγενὲς καὶ ὅμοιον ποιησάμενον δεῖ ἐπιβάλλειν τῇ θέᾳ· οὐ γὰρ ἄν πώποτε εἶδεν ὀφθαλμὸς ἥλιον, ἡλιοειδὴς μὴ γεγενημένος, οὐδὲ τὸ καλὸν ἄν ἴδοι ψυχὴ μὴ γενομένη."4

[1814]   [1907]

⋄⋄⋄⋄⋄⋄⋄⋄⋄⋄⋄⋄⋄⋄⋄⋄⋄⋄⋄⋄⋄⋄⋄⋄⋄⋄⋄⋄⋄⋄⋄⋄

3 Coleridge's "Lewti" (1798), ll. 57–64.
4 This selection from Plotinus' *Ennead* (I, 6, iv and ix) was quoted again in the sixth chapter of *Biographia Literaria*, where Coleridge provided the following translation:

"To those to whose imagination it has never been presented, how beautiful is the countenance of justice and wisdom; and that neither the morning nor the evening star are so fair. For in order to direct the view aright, it behoves that the beholder

THE STATESMAN'S MANUAL

Published in December 1816, The Statesman's Manual *consisted of an essay proper of 63 pages developing the argument of the subtitle:* The Bible the Best Guide to Political Skill and Foresight; *and an "Appendix, containing Comments and Essays" totaling 67 pages. It was the first of three projected "Lay Sermons on the existing Distresses and Discontents" and was addressed to the "Higher Classes of Society." The second "Lay Sermon" entitled "Blessed are ye that Sow beside all Waters" was addressed to "the Higher and Middle Classes" and appeared in 1817. A third "Lay Sermon" addressed to "the Labouring Classes" was never written.*

Here reproduced are the central section of the essay, containing Coleridge's famous distinction between symbol and allegory, as well as a long section from "C," the second of the "Comments and Essays," one of the clearest presentations of the key concepts of Coleridge's philosophy. The discussion of Imagination and Reason and Understanding in The Statesman's Manual *is elaborated in other selections from Coleridge in this anthology: on Imagination, see* Biographia Literaria *(written and in the press before* The Statesman's Manual *was composed, although not finally published until 1817); on Reason and Understanding, see the selections from* The Friend *and* Aids to Reflection.

*The Understanding is the faculty that operates entirely in relation to the data of the senses and is the source of Reflection, Generalization, and Prudence: "... it combines these multifarious impressions [of the senses] into individual Notions, and by reducing these notions to Rules, according to the analogy of all its former notices, constitutes Experience" (*The Friend, *1818).*

The Reason is the "power" of the mind "by which we become possessed of principles" (as compared to Notions), the ultimate laws and sources of the life of things. It is an intuitive power, as compared to the discursive faculty of the Understanding. Only the Reason can furnish conviction about the "Necessity" or ultimate ground of being of any object, by penetrating to the creative I AM *(God) responsible for the life of the object.*

The Imagination mediates between and reconciles Reason and sense by presenting the fluctuating particulars of sense in terms of the permanence of their ultimate principles of being, thus producing symbols ("the translucence of the Eternal through and in the Temporal"). The events recorded by imagination in the Scriptures are in these terms "at once Portraits and Ideals." In contrast, an allegory, the product of the Understanding and its related artistic faculty the Fancy, loses both the particularity of the individual sensible object and the universality of the ultimate principle of life of that object; it presents a picture abstracted from the objects of the sense, and joins to it a notion of the Understanding, not the ultimate principles of its life.

⋄⋄⋄⋄⋄⋄⋄⋄⋄⋄⋄⋄⋄⋄⋄⋄⋄⋄⋄⋄⋄⋄⋄⋄⋄⋄⋄⋄⋄⋄⋄⋄

should have made himself congenerous and similar to the object beheld. Never could the eye have beheld the sun, had not its own essence been soliform," (i.e., *pre-configured to light by a similarity of essence with that of light*) "neither can a soul not beautiful attain to an intuition of beauty."

FROM

THE STATESMAN'S MANUAL;

OR

THE BIBLE THE BEST GUIDE

TO

Political Skill and Foresight:

A LAY SERMON,

ADDRESSED TO THE

HIGHER CLASSES OF SOCIETY,

WITH AN

APPENDIX,

CONTAINING COMMENTS AND ESSAYS

CONNECTED WITH THE

STUDY OF THE INSPIRED WRITINGS

* * * * *

But do you require some one or more particular passage from the Bible, that may at once illustrate and examplify its applicability to the changes and fortunes of empires? Of the numerous chapters that relate to the Jewish tribes, their enemies and allies, before and after their division into two kingdoms,[1] it would be more difficult to state a single one, from which some guiding light might *not* be struck. And in nothing is Scriptural history more strongly contrasted with the histories of highest note in the present age, than in its freedom from the hollowness of abstractions. While the latter present a shadow-fight of Things and Quantities, the former gives us the history of Men, and balances the important influence of individual Minds with the previous state of the national morals and manners, in which, as constituting a specific susceptibility, it presents to us the true cause both of the Influence itself, and of the Weal or Woe that were its Consequents. How should it be otherwise? The histories and political economy of the present and preceding century partake in the general contagion of its mechanic philosophy, and are the *product* of an unenlivened generalizing Understanding. In the Scriptures they are the living *educts* of the Imagination; of that reconciling and mediatory power, which incorporating the Reason in Images of the Sense, and organizing (as it were) the flux of the Senses by the permanence and self-circling energies of the Reason, gives birth to a

system of symbols, harmonious in themselves, and consubstantial with the truths, of which they are the *conductors*. These are the Wheels which Ezekiel beheld, when the hand of the Lord was upon him, and he saw visions of God as he sate among the captives by the river of Chebar. *Whithersoever the Spirit was to go, the wheels went, and thither was their spirit to go: for the spirit of the living creature was in the wheels also.*[2] The truths and the symbols that represent them move in conjunction and form the living chariot that bears up (for *us*) the throne of the Divine Humanity. Hence, by a derivative, indeed, but not a divided, influence, and though in a secondary yet in more than a metaphorical sense, the Sacred Book is worthily intitled *the* WORD OF GOD. Hence too, its contents present to us the stream of time continuous as Life and a symbol of Eternity, inasmuch as the Past and the Future are virtually contained in the Present. According therefore to our relative position on its banks the Sacred History becomes prophetic, and Sacred Prophecies historical, while the power and substance of both inhere in its Laws, its Promises, and its Comminations.[3] In the Scriptures therefore both Facts and Persons must of necessity have a two-fold significance, a past and a future, a temporary and a perpetual, a particular and a universal application. They must be at once Portraits and Ideals.

Eheu! paupertina philosophia in paupertinam religionem ducit:—A hunger-bitten and idea-less philosophy naturally produces a starveling and comfortless religion. It is among the miseries of the present age that it recognizes no medium between *Literal* and *Metaphorical*. Faith is either to be buried in the dead letter, or its name and honors usurped by a counterfeit product of the mechanical understanding, which in the blindness of self-complacency confounds SYMBOLS with ALLEGORIES. Now an Allegory is but a translation of abstract notions into a picture-language which is itself nothing but an abstraction from objects of the senses; the principal being more worthless even than its phantom proxy, both alike unsubstantial, and the former shapeless to boot. On the other hand a Symbol (ὁ ἔστιν ἀεὶ ταυτηγόρικον)[4] is characterized by a translucence of the Special in the Individual or of the General in the Especial or of the Universal in the General. Above all by the translucence of the Eternal through and in the Temporal. It always partakes of the Reality which it renders intelligible; and while it enunciates the whole, abides itself as a living part in that Unity, of which it is the representative. The

---

[1] See I Kings, xi–xiv. Following the decadent and tyrannical rule of Solomon, the kingdom of Israel was divided into two: a southern kingdom thereafter called Judah and with Jerusalem as its center under the rule of Solomon's son Rehoboam; a northern kingdom called Israel ruled by Jeroboam. The continual warfare between the two kingdoms is used later in the essay as a parallel with the disputes between England and Ireland.

[2] Ezekiel, i, 20.
[3] Threats of divine wrath.
[4] ὁ ἔστιν ἀεὶ ταυτηγόρικον: "that which always reveals itself."

other are but empty echoes which the fancy arbitrarily associates with apparitions of matter, less beautiful but less shadowy than the sloping orchard or hill-side pasture-field seen in the transparent lake below. Alas! for the flocks that are to be led forth to such pastures! *"It shall even be as when the hungry dreameth, and behold! he eateth; but he waketh and his soul is empty: or as when the thirsty dreameth, and behold he drinketh; but he awaketh and is faint!"* (ISAIAH XXIX. 8.) O! that we would seek for the bread which was given from heaven, that we should eat thereof and be strengthened! O that we would draw at the well at which the flocks of our forefathers had living water drawn for them, even that water which, instead of mocking the thirst of him to whom it is given, becomes a well within himself springing up to life everlasting!

When we reflect how large a part of our present knowledge and civilization is owing, directly or indirectly, to the Bible; when we are compelled to admit, as a fact of history, that the Bible has been the main Lever by which the moral and intellectual character of Europe has been raised to its present comparative height; we should be struck, me thinks, by the marked and prominent difference of this Book from the works which it is now the fashion to quote as guides and authorities in morals, politics and history. I will point out a few of the excellencies by which the one is distinguished, and shall leave it to your own judgment and recollection to perceive and apply the contrast to the productions of highest name in these latter days. In the Bible every agent appears and acts as a self-subsisting individual: each has a life of its own, and yet all are one life. The elements of necessity and free-will are reconciled in the higher power of an omnipresent Providence, that predestinates the whole in the moral freedom of the integral parts. Of this the Bible never suffers us to lose sight. The root is never detached from the ground. It is God everywhere: and all creatures conform to his decrees, the righteous by performance of the law, the disobedient by the sufferance of the penalty.

Suffer me to inform or remind you, that there is a threefold Necessity. There is a logical, and there is a mathematical, necessity; but the latter is always hypothetical, and both subsist *formally* only, not in any real object. Only by the intuition and immediate spiritual consciousness of the idea of God, as the One and Absolute, at once the Ground and the Cause, who alone containeth in himself the ground of his own nature, and therein of *all* natures, do we arrive at the third, which alone is a real *objective*, necessity. Here the immediate consciousness decides: the idea is its own evidence, and is insusceptible of all other. It is necessarily groundless and indemonstrable; because it

is itself the ground of all possible demonstration. The Reason has faith in itself, in its own relevations. Ο ΛΟΓΟΣ ΕΦΗ. IPSE DIXIT![5] So it is: for it is so! All the necessity of causal relations (which the mere understanding reduces, and must reduce to co-existence and regular succession* in the objects of which they are predicated, and to habit and association in the mind predicting) depends on, or rather inheres in, the idea of the Omnipresent and Absolute: for this it is, in which the Possible is one and the same with the Real and the Necessary. Herein the Bible differs from all the books of Greek philosophy, and in a two-fold manner. It doth not affirm a Divine Nature only, but a God: and not a God only, but the living God. Hence in the Scripture alone is the *Jus divinum*,[7] or direct Relation of the State and its Magistracy to the Supreme Being, taught as a vital and indispensable part of all moral and of all political wisdom, even as the Jewish alone was a true theocracy.

But I refer to the demand.[8] Were it my object to touch on the present state of public affairs in this kingdom, or on the prospective measures in agitation respecting our sister island,[9] I would direct your most serious meditations to the latter period of the reign of Solomon, and to the revolutions in the reign of Rehoboam, his successor. But I should tread on glowing embers. I will turn to a subject on which all men of reflection are at length in agreement—the causes of the revolution and fearful chastisement of France. We have learned to trace them back to the rising importance of the commercial and manufacturing class, and its incompatibility with the old feudal privileges and prescriptions; to the spirit of sensuality and ostentation, which from the court had spread through all the towns and cities of the empire; to the predominance of a presumptuous and irreligious philosophy; to the

---

* See Hume's Essays. The sophist evades, as Cicero long ago remarked, the better half of the predicament, which is not "praeire" but "*efficienter* praeire."[6]

<><><><><><><><><><><><><><><><><><><><><><><>

5 O . . . dixit!: "Reason has spoken. He has said it."
6 The reference is to Hume's *Philosophical Essays concerning Human Understanding* (1748), sections IV–VII. In *De Fato*, xv, 34, Cicero had answered the conception of causation in terms of "co-existence and regular succession" by declaring: "But a cause is that which makes the thing of which it is the cause come about—as a wound is the cause of death, failure to digest one's food of illness, fire of heat. Accordingly, 'cause' is not to be understood in such a way as to make what precedes a thing a cause of that thing, but what precedes it effectively . . ." (translation by H. Rackham, Loeb Classical Library, Harvard University Press).
7 Jus divinum: "divine justice or law."
8 To show the relevance of the Bible to political action.
9 The severe economic depression following Waterloo led to widespread unemployment and intensified the disorders and demands for political reform in Ireland. These demands were met by the garrisoning of 25,000 British troops in Ireland, the suspension of habeas corpus, and other coercive measures.

extreme over-rating of the knowledge and power given by the improvements of the arts and sciences, especially those of astronomy, mechanics, and a wonder-working chemistry; to an assumption of prophetic power, and the general conceit that states and governments might be and ought to be constructed as machines, every movement of which might be foreseen and taken into previous calculation; to the consequent multitude of plans and constitutions, of planners and constitution-makers, and the remorseless arrogance with which the authors and proselytes of every new proposal were ready to realize it, be the cost what it might in the established rights, or even in the lives, of men; in short, to restlessness, presumption, sensual indulgence, and the idolatrous reliance on false philosophy in the whole domestic, social, and political life of the stirring and effective part of the community: these all acting, at once and together, on a mass of materials supplied by the unfeeling extravagance and oppressions of the government, which "shewed no mercy, and very heavily laid its yoke."[10]

Turn then to the chapter from which the last words were cited, and read the following seven verses; and I am deceived if you will not be compelled to admit, that the Prophet Isaiah revealed the true philosophy of the French revolution more than two thousand years before it became a sad irrevocable truth of history. "And thou saidst, I shall be a lady for ever: so that thou didst not lay these things to thy heart, neither didst remember the latter end of it. Therefore, hear now this, thou that art given to pleasures, that dwellest carelessly, that sayest in thine heart, I am, and none else besides me! I shall not sit as a widow, neither shall I know the loss of children. But these two things shall come to thee in a moment, in one day; the loss of children, and widowhood; they shall come upon thee in their perfection, for the multitude of thy sorceries, and for the abundance of thine enchantments. For thou hast trusted in thy wickedness; thou hast said, there is no overseer. Thy wisdom and thy knowledge, it hath perverted thee; and thou hast said in thine heart, I am, and none else besides me. Therefore shall evil come upon thee, thou shalt not know* from whence it

riseth: and mischief shall fall upon thee, thou shalt not be able to put it of; and desolation shall come upon thee suddenly, which thou shalt not know. Stand now with thine enchantments, and with the multitude of thy sorceries, wherein thou hast laboured from thy youth; if so be thou shalt be able to profit, if so be thou mayest prevail. Thou art wearied in the multitude of thy counsels: let now the astrologers, the stargazers, the monthly prognosticators stand up, and save thee from these things that shall come upon thee."[12]

There is a grace that would enable us to take up vipers, and the evil thing shall not hurt us: a spiritual alchemy which can transmute poisons into a panacæa. We are counselled by our Lord himself to make unto ourselves friends of the Mammon of Unrighteousness:[13] and in this age of sharp contrasts and grotesque combinations it would be a wise method of sympathizing with the tone and spirit of the Times, if we elevated even our daily newspapers and political journals into COMMENTS ON THE BIBLE.

*   *   *   *   *

APPENDIX C

REASON and Religion differ only as a two-fold application of the same power. But if we are obliged to distinguish, we must *ideally* separate. In this sense I affirm, that Reason is the knowledge of the laws of the WHOLE considered as ONE: and as such it is contradistinguished from the Understanding, which concerns itself exclusively with the quantities, qualities, and relations of *particulars* in time and space. The UNDERSTANDING, therefore, is the science of phænomena, and their subsumption under distinct kinds and sorts, (*genus* and *species*). Its functions supply the rules and constitute the possibility of EXPERIENCE; but remain mere logical *forms*, except as far as *materials* are given by the senses or sensations. The REASON, on the other hand, is the science of the *universal*, having the ideas of ONENESS and ALLNESS as its two

---

* The Reader will scarcely fail to find in this verse a re-membrancer of the sudden setting-in of the frost, a fortnight before its usual time (in a country too, where the commencement of its two seasons is in general scarcely less regular than that of the wet and dry seasons between the tropics) which caused, and the desolation which accompanied, the flight from Moscow. The Russians baffled the *physical* forces of the imperial Jacobin, because they were inaccessible to his *imaginary* forces. The faith in St. Nicholas kept off at safe distance, the more

pernicious superstition of the Destinies of Napoleon the Great. The English in the Peninsula overcame the real, because they *set at defiance*, and had heard only to despise, the imaginary powers of the irresistible Emperor. Thank heaven, the heart of the country was sound at the *core.*[11]

11 On October 18, 1812, Napoleon abandoned Moscow and began the retreat of his forces. Within the next few weeks severe frost and snow decimated the French forces. St. Nicholas was the patron saint of Russia. "The English in the Peninsula" refers to the war against Napoleon in Spain and Portugal, 1808–1814.

12 Isaiah, xlvii, 7–13.
13 Luke, xvi, 9.

10 Isaiah, xlvii, 6.

elements or primary factors. In the language of the old schools,

$$Unity \quad + \quad Omn\ddot{e}ity$$
$$=$$
$$Totality.$$

The Reason first manifests itself in man by the *tendency* to the comprehension of all as one. We can neither rest in an infinite that is not at the same time a whole, nor in a whole that is not infinite. Hence the natural Man is always in a state either of resistance or of captivity to the understanding and the fancy, which cannot represent totality without limit: and he either loses the ONE in the striving after the INFINITE, (i.e., Atheism with or without polytheism) or the INFINITE in the striving after the ONE, (i.e., anthropomorphic monotheism).

The rational instinct, therefore, taken abstractedly and unbalanced, did *in itself*, ("ye shall be as gods!" Gen. iii. 5.) and in its consequences, (the lusts of the flesh, the eye, and the understanding, as in verse the sixth,) form the original temptation, through which man fell: and in all ages has continued to originate the same, even from Adam, in whom we all fell, to the atheists who deified the human reason in the person of a harlot during the earlier period of the French revolution.[1]

To this tendency, therefore, RELIGION, as the consideration of the Particular and Individual (in which respect it takes up and identifies with itself the excellence of the *Understanding*) but of the Individual, as it exists and has its being in the Universal (in which respect it is one with the pure *Reason*,)—to this tendency, I say, RELIGION assigns the due limits, and is the echo of the "voice of the *Lord* God walking in the garden."[2] Hence in all the ages and countries of civilization Religion has been the parent and fosterer of the Fine Arts, as of Poetry, Music, Painting, &c. the common essence of which consists in a similar union of the Universal and the Individual. In this union, moreover, is contained the true sense of the IDEAL. Under the old Law the altar, the curtains, the priestly vestments, and whatever else was to represent the BEAUTY OF HOLINESS, had an *ideal* character: and the Temple itself was a master-piece of Ideal Beauty.

There exists in the human being, at least in man fully developed, no mean symbol of Tri-unity, in Reason, Religion, and the Will. For each of the three, though a distinct agency, implies and demands the other two, and loses its own nature at the moment that from distinction it passes into division or separation. The perfect frame of a man is the perfect frame of a state: and in the light of this idea we must read Plato's REPUBLIC. For, if I judge rightly, this celebrated work is to "The History of the Town of Man-soul,"[3] what Plato was to John Bunyan.

The comprehension, impartiality, and far-sightedness of Reason, (the LEGISLATIVE of our nature) taken singly and exclusively, becomes mere visionariness in *intellect*, and indolence or hard-heartedness in *morals*. It is the science of cosmopolitism without country, of philanthropy without neighbourliness or consanguinity, in short, of all the impostures of that philosophy of the French revolution, which would sacrifice each to the shadowy idol of ALL. For Jacobinism is *monstrum hybridum*, made up in part of despotism, and in part of abstract reason misapplied to objects that belong entirely to experience and the understanding.[4] Its instincts and mode of action are in strict correspondence with its origin. In all places, Jacobinism betrays its mixt parentage and nature, by applying to the brute passions and physical force of the multitude (that is, to man as a mere animal,) in order to build up government and the frame of society on natural rights instead of social privileges, on the universals of abstract reason instead of positive institutions, the lights of specific experience, and the modifications of existing circumstances. RIGHT in its most proper sense is the creature of law and statute, and only in the technical language of the courts has it any substantial and independent sense. In morals, Right is a word without meaning except as the correlative of Duty.

From all this it follows, that Reason as the science of All as the Whole, must be interpenetrated by a Power,

---

[1] Refers to an incident in November 1793, when Notre Dame Cathedral was "consecrated" as the Temple of Reason with the installation of the Goddess of Reason impersonated by an opera girl.

[2] Genesis, iii, 8.

[3] Bunyan's allegory *The Holy War . . . or; the Losing and Taking Again of the Town of Mansoul* (1682).

[4] Coleridge explains this point at length in the essay "On the Grounds of Government as Laid Exclusively in the Pure Reason," which appeared in both the 1809–1810 and 1818 editions of *The Friend*. To Rousseau's argument that "there is an inalienable sovereignty inherent in every human being possessed of Reason," Coleridge replied that the degree of the development of that faculty in individual men varies widely, from "the judgment of a well-educated English lad, bred in a virtuous and enlightened family" to the ignorant superstitions of "a brutal Russian." "Nothing therefore, which subsists wholly in degrees . . . can be subjects of pure science, or determinable by mere Reason. For these things we must rely on our *Understandings*, enlightened by past experience and immediate observation, and determining our choice by comparisons of expediency." monstrum hybridum: "a hybrid monster."

that represents the concentration of All in Each—a Power that acts by a contraction of universal truths into individual duties, as the only form in which those truths can attain life and reality. Now this is RE-LIGION, which is the EXECUTIVE of our nature, and on this account the name of highest dignity, and the symbol of sovereignty.

Yet this again—yet even Religion itself, if ever in its too exclusive devotion to the *specific* and *individual* it neglects to interpose the contemplation of the *universal*, changes its being into Superstition, and becoming more and more earthly and servile, as more and more estranged from the one in all, goes wandering at length with its pack of amulets, bead-rolls, periapts, fetisches, and the like pedlary, on pilgrimages to Loretto, Mecca, or the temple of Jaggernaut,[5] arm in arm with sensuality on one side and self-torture on the other, followed by a motly group of friars, pardoners, faquirs, gamesters, flagellants, mountebanks, and harlots.

But neither can reason or religion exist or co-exist as reason and religion, except as far as they are actuated by the WILL (the platonic Θυμὸς,) which is the sustaining, coercive and ministerial power, the functions of which in the individual correspond to the officers of war and police in the ideal Republic of Plato. In its state of immanence (or indwelling) in reason and religion, the WILL appears indifferently, as wisdom or as love: two names of the same power, the former more intelligential, and latter more spiritual, the former more frequent in the Old, the latter in the New Testament. But in its utmost abstraction and consequent state of reprobation, the Will becomes satanic pride and rebellious self-idolatry in the relations of the spirit to itself, and remorseless despotism relatively to others; the more hopeless as the more obdurate by its subjugation of sensual impulses, by its superiority to toil and pleasure; in sort, by the fearful resolve to find in itself alone the one absolute motive of action, under which all other motives from within and from without must be either subordinated or crushed.

This is the character which Milton has so philosophically as well as sublimely embodied in the Satan of his Paradise Lost. Alas! too often has it been embodied in *real* life! Too often has it given a dark and savage grandeur to the historic page! And wherever it has appeared, under whatever circumstances of time and country, the same ingredients have gone to its

composition; and it has been identified by the same attributes. Hope in which there is no Chearfulness; Stedfastness within and immovable Resolve, with outward Restlessness and whirling Activity; Violence with Guile; Temerity with Cunning; and, as the result of all, Interminableness of Object with perfect Indifference of Means; these are the qualities that have constituted the COMMANDING GENIUS! these are the Marks, that have characterized the Masters of Mischief, the Liberticides, and mighty Hunters of Mankind, from NIMROD[6] to NAPOLEON. And from inattention to the possibility of such a character as well as from ignorance of its elements, even men of honest intentions too frequently become fascinated. Nay, whole nations have been so far duped by this want of insight and reflection as to regard with palliative admiration, instead of wonder and abhorrence, the Molocks[7] of human nature, who are indebted, for the far longer portion of their meteoric success, to their total want of principle, and who surpass the generality of their fellow creatures in one act of courage only, that of daring to say with their whole heart, "Evil, be thou my good!"—[8] All *system* so far is power; and a *systematic* criminal, self-consistent and entire in wickedness, who entrenches villainy within villainy, and barricadoes crime by crime, has removed a world of obstacles by the mere decision, that he will have no obstacles, but those of force and brute matter.

I have only to add a few sentences, in completion of this note, on the CONSCIENCE and on the UNDERSTANDING. The conscience is neither reason, religion, or will, but an *experience* (sui generis) of the coincidence of the human will with reason and religion. It might, perhaps, be called a *spiritual sensation*; but that there lurks a contradiction in the terms, and that it is often deceptive to give a common or generic name to that, which being unique, can have no fair analogy. Strictly speaking, therefore, the conscience is neither a sensation or a sense; but a testifying state, best described in the words of our liturgy, as THE PEACE OF GOD THAT PASSETH ALL UNDERSTANDING.[9]

Of this latter faculty considered in and of itself the peripatetic aphorism, nihil in intellectu quod non prius in sensu, is strictly true, as well as the legal maxim, de rebus non apparentibus et non existentibus eadem est

---

[5] Pilgrimage shrines of the Catholic, Moslem, and Hindu faiths, respectively. Loretto refers to "the Holy House of Loretto" in Italy, a shrine to the Virgin and the reputed original of the house at Nazareth. The temple of Jaggernaut in Puri, India, contained an image of the Hindu god Vishnu.

[6] "The mighty hunter before the Lord" mentioned in Genesis, x, 8–9.

[7] Moloch was a pagan god mentioned in the Old Testament, to whom children were sacrificed; a symbol of brutal and inhuman power.

[8] *Paradise Lost*, IV, 110.

[9] Philippians, iv, 7.

ratio.[10] The eye is not more inappropriate to sound, than the *mere* understanding to the modes and laws of spiritual existence. In this sense I have used the term; and in this sense I assert that "the understanding or experiential faculty, unirradiated by the reason and the spirit, has no appropriate object but the material world in relation to our worldly interests. The far-sighted prudence of man, and the more narrow but at the same time far less fallible cunning of the fox, are both no other than a nobler *substitute for salt, in order* that the hog may not putrefy before its destined hour!!" FRIEND, p. 80.[11]

It must not, however be overlooked, that this insulation of the understanding is our own act and deed. The man of healthful and undivided intellect uses his understanding in this state of abstraction only as a tool or organ: even as the arithmetician uses numbers, that is, as the means not the end of knowledge. Our Shakespear in agreement both with truth and the philosophy of his age names it "*discourse* of reason,"[12] as an instrumental faculty *belonging* to reason: and Milton opposes the discursive to the intuitive, as the lower to the higher,

"Differing but in degree, in *kind* the same!"

Of the *discursive* understanding, which forms for itself general notions and terms of classification for the purpose of comparing and arranging phænomena, the Characteristic is Clearness without Depth. It contemplates the unity of things in their *limits* only, and is consequently a knowledge of superficies without substance. So much so indeed, that it entangles itself in contradictions in the very effort of comprehending the *idea* of substance. The completing power which units clearness with depth, the plenitude of the sense with the comprehensibility of the understanding, is the IMAGINATION, impregnated with which the understanding itself becomes intuitive, and a living power. The REASON, (not the abstract reason, not the reason as the mere *organ* of science, or as the faculty of scientific principles and schemes a priori; but reason) as the integral *spirit* of the regenerated man, reason substantiated and vital, "one only, yet manifold, over-

seeing all, and going through all understanding; the breath of the power of God, and a pure influence from the glory of the Almighty; which remaining in itself regenerateth all other powers, and in all ages entering into holy souls maketh them friends of God and prophets;" (Wisdom of Solomon, c.vii.) the REASON without being either the SENSE, the UNDERSTANDING or the IMAGINATION contains all three within itself, even as the mind contains its thoughts, and is present in and through them all; or as the expression pervades the different features of an intelligent countenance. Each individual must bear witness of it to his own mind, even as he describes life and light: and with the silence of light it describes itself, and dwells in *us* only as far as we dwell in *it*. It cannot in strict language be called a faculty, much less a personal property, of any human mind! He, with whom it is present, can as little appropriate it, whether, totally or by partition, as he can claim ownership in the breathing air or make an inclosure in the cope of heaven.

The object of the preceding discourse was to recommend the Bible, as the end and center of our reading and meditation. I can truly affirm of myself, that my studies have been profitable and availing to me only so far, as I have endeavoured to use all my other knowledge as a glass enabling me to receive more light in a wider field of vision from the word of God. If you have accompanied me thus far, thoughtful reader! Let it not weary you if I digress for a few moments to another book, likewise a revelation of God—the great book of his servant Nature. That in its obvious sense and literal interpretation it declares the being and attributes of the Almighty Father, none but the *fool in heart* has ever dared gainsay. But it has been the music of gentle and pious minds in all ages, it is the *poetry* of all human nature, to read it likewise in a figurative sense, and to find therein correspondencies and symbols of the spiritual world.

I have at this moment before me, in the flowery meadow, on which my eye is now reposing, one of its most soothing chapters, in which there is no lamenting word, no one character of guilt or anguish. For never can I look and meditate on the vegetable creation without a feeling similar to that with which we gaze at a beautiful infant that has fed itself asleep at its mother's bosom, and smiles in its strange dream of obscure yet happy sensations. The same tender and genial pleasure takes possession of me, and this pleasure is checked and drawn inward by the like aching melancholy, by the same whispered remonstrance, and made restless by a similar impulse of aspiration. It seems as if the soul said to herself: from this state hast *thou* fallen! Such shouldst thou still become, thy Self all permeable to a holier power! thy Self at once hidden and glorified by

---

[10] nihil . . . sensu: "Nothing in the intellect which is not first in the senses." de rebus . . . ratio: "The rule in legal proceedings is the same concerning things which do not appear [to exist] and things which do not exist."

[11] The quotation is from *The Friend*, No. 5, September 14, 1809. With "substitute for salt . . . hour!" Coleridge is recalling an aphorism by the philosopher Chrysippus of Soli (280–207 B.C.), quoted in Cicero's *De Natura Deorum* (II, lxiv, 160): "Nature has given to the Hog a *soul* instead of *salt*, in order to keep it from putrifying."

[12] *Hamlet*, I, ii, 150. The next quotation comes from *Paradise Lost*, V, 490.

its own transparency, as the accidental and dividuous in this quiet and harmonious object is subjected to the life and light of nature which shines in it, even as the transmitted power, love and wisdom, of God over all fills, and shines through, nature! But what the plant *is*, by an act not its own and unconsciously—*that* must thou *make* thyself to *become*! must by prayer and by a watchful and unresisting spirit, *join* at least with the preventive and assisting grace to *make* thyself, in that light of conscience which inflameth not, and with that knowledge which puffeth not up.

But further, and with particular reference to that undivided Reason, neither merely speculative or merely practical, but both in one, which I have in this annotation endeavoured to contra-distinguish from the Understanding, I seem to myself to behold in the quiet objects, on which I am gazing, more than an arbitrary illustration, more than a mere *simile*, the work of my own Fancy! I feel an awe, as if there were before my eyes the same Power, as that of the REASON —the same Power in a lower dignity, and therefore a symbol established in the truth of things. I feel it alike, whether I contemplate a single tree or flower, or meditate on vegetation throughout the world, as one of the great organs of the life of nature. Lo!—with the rising sun it commences its outward life and enters into open communion with all the elements, at once assimilating them to itself and to each other. At the same moment it strikes its roots and unfolds its leaves, absorbs and respires, steams forth its cooling vapour and finer fragrance, and breathes a repairing spirit, at once the food and tone of the atmosphere, into the atmosphere that feeds *it*. Lo!—at the touch of light how it returns an air akin to light, and yet with the same pulse effectuates its own secret growth, still contracting to fix what expanding it had refined. Lo!—how upholding the ceaseless plastic motion of the parts in the profoundest rest of the whole it becomes the visible organismus of the whole *silent* or *elementary* life of nature and, therefore, in incorporating the one extreme becomes the symbol of the other; the natural symbol of that higher life of reason, in which the whole series (known to us in our present state of being) is perfected, in which, therefore, all the subordinate gradations recur, and are re-ordained "*in more abundant honor.*"[13] We had seen each in its own cast, and we now recognize them all as co-existing in the unity of a higher form, the Crown and Completion of the Earthly, and the Mediator of a new and heavenly series. Thus finally, the vegetable creation, in the simplicity and uniformity of its *internal* structure symbolizing the unity of nature,

while it represents the omniformity of her delegated functions in its *external* variety and manifoldness, becomes the record and chronicle of her ministerial acts, and inchases [14] the vast unfolded volume of the earth with the hieroglyphics of her history.

O!—if as the plant to the orient beam, we would but open out our minds to that holier light, which "being compared with light is found before it, more beautiful than the sun, and above all the order of stars," (Wisdom of Solomon, vii. 29.) ungenial, alien, and adverse to our very nature would appear the boastful wisdom which, beginning in France, gradually tampered with the taste and literature of all the most civilized nations of christendom, seducing the understanding from its natural allegiance, and therewith from all its own lawful claims, titles, and privileges. It was placed as a ward of honour in the courts of faith and reason; but it chose to dwell alone, and became an harlot by the way-side. The commercial spirit, and the ascendancy of the experimental philosophy which took place at the close of the fourteenth century, though both good and beneficial in their own kinds, combined to foster its corruption. Flattered and dazzled by the real or supposed discoveries, which it had made, the more the understanding was enriched, the more did it become debased; till science itself put on a selfish and sensual character, and *immediate utility*, in exclusive reference to the gratification of the wants and appetites of the animal, the vanities and caprices of the social, and the ambition of the political, man was imposed as the test of all intellectual powers and pursuits. *Worth* was degraded into a lazy synonyme of *value*; and value was exclusively attached to the interest of the senses. But though the growing alienation and self-sufficiency of the understanding was perceptible at an earlier period, yet it seems to have been about the middle of the last century, under the influence of Voltaire, D'Alembert, Diderot, say generally of the so-called Encyclopœdists, and alas!—of their crowned proselytes and disciples, Frederick, Joseph, and Catherine,[15] that the Human Understanding, and this too in its narrowest form, was tempted to throw off all show of reverence to the spiritual and even to the moral powers and impulses of the soul; and usurping the name of reason openly joined the banners of Antichrist, at once the pander and the prostitute of sensuality, and whether in the cabinet, laboratory, the dissecting room, or the brothel, alike busy in the schemes of vice and irreligion. Well and

---

[14] Embellishes or covers as with engraving.
[15] Frederick the Great (1712–1786), the Holy Roman Emperor Joseph II (1741–1790), and Catherine the Great all aspired to be "modern" political and social reformers, in the spirit of the French Enlightenment philosophers.

---

[13] Cf. *Paradise Lost*, V, 72–73, 315.

truly might it, thus personified in our fancy, have been addressed in the words of the evangelical prophet, which I have once before quoted. "Thou hast said, none is my overseer!—thy wisdom and thy knowledge, it hath perverted thee!—and thou hast said in thy heart, I am, and there is none besides me!" (Isaiah, xlvii. 10).

Prurient, bustling, and revolutionary, this French wisdom has never more than grazed the surfaces of knowledge. As political economy, in its zeal for the increase of food it habitually overlooked the qualities and even the sensations of those that were to feed on it. As ethical philosophy, it recognized no duties which it could not reduce into debtor and creditor accounts on the ledgers of self-love, where no coin was sterling which could not be rendered into *agreeable sensations*. And even in its height of self-complacency as chemical art, greatly am I deceived if it has not from the very beginning mistaken the products of destruction, cadavera rerum,[16] for the elements of composition: and most assuredly it has dearly purchased a few brilliant inventions at the loss of all communion with life and the spirit of nature. As the process, such the result! a heartless frivolity alternating with a sentimentality as heartless—an ignorant contempt of antiquity—a neglect of moral self-discipline—a deadening of the religious sense, even in the less reflecting forms of natural piety—a scornful reprobation of all consolations and secret refreshings from above—and as the caput mortuum[17] of human nature evaporated, a French nature of rapacity, levity, ferocity, and presumption.

Man of understanding, canst thou command the stone to lie, canst thou bid the flower bloom, where thou hast placed it in thy classification?—Canst thou persuade the living or the inanimate to stand separate even as thou hast separated them?—And do not far rather all things spread out before thee in glad confusion and heedless intermixture, even as a lightsome chaos on which the Spirit of God is moving?—Do not all press and swell under one attraction, and live together in promiscuous harmony, each joyous in its own kind, and in the immediate neighbourhood of Myriad others that in the system of thy understanding are distant as the Poles?—If to mint and to remember names delight thee, still arrange and classify and pore and pull to pieces, and peep into Death to look for Life, as monkeys put their hands behind a looking-glass! Yet consider, in the first sabbath which thou imposest on the busy discursion of thought, that all

this is at *best* little more than a technical memory: that like can only be known by like: that as Truth is the correlative of Being, so is the act of Being the great organ of Truth: that in natural no less than in moral science, quantum sumus, scimus.[18]

That, which we find in ourselves, is (gradu mutato)[19] the substance and the life of *all* our knowledge. Without this latent presence of the "I am," all modes of existence in the external world would flit before us as colored shadows, with no greater depth, root, or fixture, than the image of a rock hath in a gliding stream or the rain-bow on a fast-sailing rain-storm. The human mind is the compass, in which the laws and actuations of all outward essences are revealed as the dips and declinations. (The application of Geometry to the forces and movements of the material world is both proof and instance.) The fact therefore, that the mind of man in its own primary and constituent forms represents the laws of nature, is a mystery which of itself should suffice to make us religious: for it is a problem of which God is the only solution, God, the one before all, and of all, and through all!—True natural philosophy is comprized in the study of the science and language of *symbols*. The power delegated to nature is all in every part: and by a symbol I mean, not a metaphor or allegory or any other figure of speech or form of fancy, but an actual and essential part of that, the whole of which it represents. Thus our Lord speaks symbolically when he says that "the eye is the light of the body."[20] The genuine naturalist is a dramatic poet in his own line: and such as our myriad-minded Shakespear is, compared with the Racines and Metastasios, such and by a similar process of self-transformation would the man be, compared with the Doctors of the mechanic school, who should construct his physiology on the heaven-descended, Know Thyself.[21]

*   *   *   *   *

[1816]

[16] cadavera rerum: "the dead bodies of things."
[17] caput mortuum: "dead head," a term from alchemy, designating the worthless residue left after exhaustive distillation.

[18] quantum sumus, scimus: "We know as much as we are."
[19] gradu mutato: "in a corresponding degree."
[20] Matthew, vi, 22.
[21] Coleridge is comparing "Shakespear" and "the genuine naturalist" on the one hand, with "the Racines and Metastasios" and "the Doctors of the mechanic shool" on the other. From their consciousness of the vital principles that are the ground of their own life and individuality, both Shakespeare and "the genuine naturalist" are able to represent characters or natural objects both in their living particularity and as symbols of the laws or processes which generate and sustain them. Such dramatists as Racine and Metastasio conceived their highly stylized plots and characters in terms of the abstractions of "love" vs. "duty," "passion" vs. "reason;" and "the Doctors of the mechanic school," proceeding by the laws of the Understanding, can record only the formal properties and characteristics of objects divorced from their living reality. That the mind of man

BIOGRAPHIA LITERARIA

In part autobiography, in part philosophical speculation of such difficulty that Coleridge himself admits all but a few readers will be unable to comprehend it, in part aesthetic definitions and detailed literary analysis, Biographia Literaria *is a formidably complicated and apparently miscellaneous work. (Some of its digressive character was the result of the problems of composition and publication; see the discussion by Earl Leslie Griggs in his edition of* The Collected Letters of Samuel Taylor Coleridge, *III [Oxford: Clarendon Press, 1959], xlvii–lii.) Yet Coleridge's most famous and influential work is not without its order and controlling impulse. Wordsworth is a central concern and presence throughout. The entire second volume (Chapters XIV–XXIV) is Coleridge's attempt to define "the real poetic character" of Wordsworth through an analysis of his poetic theory and practice, climaxing in the tribute to the poet's "imaginative power" by which "he stands nearest of all modern writers to Shakespear and Milton . . ." The first volume, proceeding partly by an autobiographical account of the growth of Coleridge's literary taste up to the dramatic first encounters with Wordsworth's poetry (Chapters I and IV) and partly by metaphysical discussion (V–XII), is intended to provide "the rules, deduced from philosophic principles" necessary for the analysis of the second volume.*

The first volume closes with the famous and much debated definitions of Imagination (both Primary and Secondary, Primary being the spontaneous *power of human preception, Secondary being the* voluntary *power that produces art) and Fancy. Among the many discussions and explications of these terms, see: J. Shawcross' edition of* Biographia Literaria *(London: Oxford University Press, 1907), I, lxvi–lxviii, 272; I. A. Richards,* Coleridge on Imagination, *third edition (Bloomington, Indiana: Indiana University Press, 1960), pp. 57–99; Walter Jackson Bate, "Coleridge on the Function of Art," in* Perspectives on Criticism, *ed. Harry Levin (Cambridge, Mass.: Harvard University Press, 1950), pp. 145–48; M. H. Abrams,* The Mirror and the Lamp *(New York: Oxford University Press, 1953), pp. 118–20, 167–77, 282–83; James Volant Baker,* The Sacred River: Coleridge's Theory of Imagination *(Baton Rouge: Louisiana State University Press, 1957), pp. 114–29; J. A. Appleyard,* Coleridge's Philosophy of Literature *(Cambridge, Mass.: Harvard University Press, 1965), pp. 197–208.*

FROM

BIOGRAPHIA LITERARIA;
OR
Biographical Sketches
of my
Literary Life and Opinions

CHAPTER I

The motives of the present work—Reception of the Author's first publication—The discipline of his taste at school—The effect of contemporary writers on youthful minds—Bowles's sonnets—Comparison between the Poets before and since Mr. Pope.

Iᴛ ʜᴀs been my lot to have had my name introduced both in conversation, and in print, more frequently than I find it easy to explain, whether I consider the fewness, unimportance, and limited circulation of my writings, or the retirement and distance, in which I have lived, both from the literary and political world. Most often it has been connected with some charge, which I could not acknowledge, or some principle which I had never entertained. Nevertheless, had I had no other motive, or incitement, the reader would not have been troubled with this exculpation. What my additional purposes were, will be seen in the following pages. It will be found, that the least of what I have written concerns myself personally. I have used the narration chiefly for the purpose of giving a continuity to the work, in part for the sake of the miscellaneous reflections suggested to me by particular events, but still more as introductory to the statement of my principles in Politics, Religion, and Philosophy, and an application of the rules, deduced from philosophical principles, to poetry and criticism. But of the objects, which I proposed to myself, it was not the least important to effect, as far as possible, a settlement of the long continued controversy concerning the true nature of poetic diction: and at the same time to define with the utmost impartiality the real *poetic* character of the poet, by whose writings this controversy was first kindled, and has been since fuelled and fanned.

In 1794, when I had barely passed the verge of manhood, I published a small volume of juvenile poems.[1] They were received with a degree of favor, which, young as I was, I well know, was bestowed on them not

---

should be able to "represent" the laws of nature is, Coleridge admits, a "mystery," which is solved only by God, the infinite I AM, who coordinates both man and nature in one process of creative life, the projection of his own eternally generative being. This argument is developed further in the Eleventh Chapter of the Essays on Method in *The Friend.*

---

[1] Referring to the collection *Poems on Various Subjects* published in 1796.

so much for any positive merit, as because they were considered buds of hope, and promises of better works to come. The critics of that day, the most flattering, equally with the severest, concurred in objecting to them, obscurity, a general turgidness of diction, and a profusion of new coined double epithets.* The first is the fault which a writer is the least able to detect in his own compositions: and my mind was not then sufficiently disciplined to receive the authority of others, as a substitute for my own conviction. Satisfied that the thoughts, such as they were, could not have been expressed otherwise, or at least more perspicuously, I forgot to enquire, whether the thoughts themselves did not demand a degree of attention unsuitable to the nature and objects of poetry. This remark however applies chiefly, though not exclusively, to the *Religious Musings*. The remainder of the charge I admitted to its full extent, and not without sincere acknowledgments both to my private and public censors for their friendly admonitions. In the after editions, I pruned the double epithets with no sparing hand, and used my best efforts to tame the swell and glitter both of thought and diction; though in truth, these parasite plants of youthful poetry had insinuated themselves into my longer poems with such intricacy of union, that I was often obliged to omit disentangling the weed, from the fear of snapping the flower. From that period to the

* The authority of Milton and Shakspeare may be usefully pointed out to young authors. In the Comus, the earlier Poems of Milton there is a superfluity of double epithets; while in the Paradise Lost we find very few, in the Paradise Regained scarce any. The same remark holds almost equally true, of the Love's Labour Lost, Romeo and Juliet, Venus and Adonis, and Lucrece compared with the Lear, Macbeth, Othello, and Hamlet of our great Dramatist. The rule for the admission of double epithets seems to be this: either that they should be already denizens of our Language, such as blood-stained, terror-stricken self-applauding: or when a new epithet, or one found in books only, is hazarded, that it, at least, be one word, not two words made one by mere virtue of the printer's hyphen. A language which, like the English, is almost without cases, is indeed in its very genius unfitted for compounds. If a writer, every time a compounded word suggests itself to him, would seek for some other mode of expressing the same sense, the chances are always greatly in favor of his finding a better word. "Tanquam scopulum sic vites insolens verbum," is the wise advice of Caesar to the Roman Orators, and the precept applies with double force to the writers in our own language. But it must not be forgotten, that the same Caesar wrote a grammatical treatise for the purpose of reforming the ordinary language by bringing it to a greater accordance with the principles of Logic or universal Grammar.[2]

2 Tanquam ... verbum: Avoid a strange and unfamiliar word as you would a dangerous reef." The remark is recorded in *Noctes Atticae*, I, x, 4, a second-century miscellany of notes and anecdotes on various subjects of classical learning and history prepared by Aulus Gellius, who cited the remark as from Caesar's lost grammatical treatise *De Analogia*.

date of the present work I have published nothing, with my name, which could by any possibility have come before the board of anonymous criticism. Even the three or four poems, printed with the works of a friend,[3] as far as they were censured at all, were charged with the same or similar defects, though I am persuaded not with equal justice: with an EXCESS OF ORNAMENT, in addition to STRAINED AND ELABORATE DICTION. (*Vide the criticisms on the* "Ancient Mariner," *in the Monthly and Critical Reviews of the first volume of the Lyrical Ballads.*) May I be permitted to add, that, even at the early period of my juvenile poems, I saw and admitted the superiority of an austerer, and more natural style, with an insight not less clear, than I at present possess. My judgement was stronger, than were my powers of realizing its dictates; and the faults of my language, though indeed partly owing to a wrong choice of subjects, and the desire of giving a poetic colouring to abstract and metaphysical truths, in which a new world then seemed to open upon me, did yet, in part likewise, originate in unfeigned diffidence of my own comparative talent.— During several years of my youth and early manhood, I reverenced those, who had reintroduced the manly simplicity of the Grecian, and of our own elder poets, with such enthusiasm, as made the hope seem presumptuous of writing successfully in the same style. Perhaps a similar process has happened to others; but my earliest poems were marked by an ease and simplicity, which I have studied, perhaps with inferior success, to impress on my later compositions.

At school I enjoyed the inestimable advantage of a very sensible, though at the same time, a very severe master. He* early moulded my taste to the preference of Demosthenes to Cicero, of Homer and Theocritus to Virgil, and again of Virgil to Ovid. He habituated me to compare Lucretius, (in such extracts as I then read) Terence, and above all the chaster poems of Catullus, not only with the Roman poets of the, so called, silver and brazen ages; but with even those of the Augustan era: and on grounds of plain sense and universal logic to see and assert the superiority of the former, in the truth and nativeness, both of their thoughts and diction. At the same time that we were studying the Greek Tragic Poets, he made us read Shakspeare and Milton as lessons: and they were the

* The Rev. James Bowyer, many years Head Master of the Grammar-School, Christ's Hospital.[4]

3 Refers to "The Rime of the Ancient Mariner," "The Foster-Mother's Tale," "The Nightingale," and "The Dungeon," Coleridge's contributions to the *Lyrical Ballads* (1798).
4 See the account of Bowyer in Lamb's essay "Christ's Hospital Five-and-Thirty Years Ago."

lessons too, which required most time and trouble to *bring up*, so as to escape his censure. I learnt from him, that Poetry, even that of the loftiest, and, seemingly, that of the wildest odes, had a logic of its own, as severe as that of science; and more difficult, because more subtle, more complex, and dependent on more, and more fugitive causes. In the truly great poets, he would say, there is a reason assignable, not only for every word, but for the position of every word; and I well remember, that availing himself of the synonimes to the Homer of Didymus,[5] he made us attempt to show, with regard to each, *why* it would not have answered the same purpose; and *wherein* consisted the peculiar fitness of the word in the original text.

In our own English compositions (at least for the last three years of our school education) he showed no mercy to phrase, metaphor, or image, unsupported by a sound sense, or where the same sense might have been conveyed with equal force and dignity in plainer words. Lute, harp, and lyre, muse, muses, and inspirations, Pegasus, Parnassus, and Hipocrene, were all an abomination to him. In fancy I can almost hear him now, exclaiming "*Harp? Harp? Lyre? Pen and ink, boy, you mean! Muse, boy, Muse? Your Nurse's daughter, you mean! Pierian spring?[6] Oh aye! the cloister-pump, I suppose!*" Nay certain introductions, similes, and examples, were placed by name on a list of interdiction. Among the similes, there was, I remember, that of the Manchineel fruit,[7] as suiting equally well with too many subjects; in which however it yielded the palm at once to the example of Alexander and Clytus,[8] which was equally good and apt, whatever might be the theme. Was it ambition? Alexander and Clytus!—Flattery? Alexander and Clytus!—Anger? Drunkenness? Pride? Friendship? Ingratitude? Late repentance? Still, still Alexander and Clytus! At length, the praises of agriculture having been exemplified in the sagacious observation, that had Alexander been holding the plough, he would not have run his friend Clytus through with a spear, this tried, and serviceable old friend was banished by public edict in secula seculorum. I have sometimes ventured to think, that a list of this kind, or an index expurgatorius of certain well known and ever returning phrases, both introductory, and transitional, including a large assortment of modest egotisms, and flattering illeisms, &c. &c. might be hung up in our law-courts, and both houses of parliament, with great advantage to the public, as an important saving of national time, an incalculable relief to his Majesty's ministers, but above all, as insuring the thanks of country attornies, and their clients, who have private bills to carry through the house.

Be this as it may, there was one custom of our master's, which I cannot pass over in silence, because I think it imitable and worthy of imitation. He would often permit our theme exercises, under some pretext of want of time, to accumulate, till each lad had four or five to be looked over. Then placing the whole number *abreast* on his desk, he would ask the writer, why this or that sentence might not have found as appropriate a place under this or that other thesis: and if no satisfying answer could be returned, and two faults of the same kind were found in one exercise, the irrevocable verdict followed, the exercise was torn up, and another on the same subject to be produced, in addition to the tasks of the day. The reader will, I trust, excuse this tribute of recollection to a man, whose severities, even now, not seldom furnish the dreams, by which the blind fancy would fain interpret to the mind the painful sensations of distempered sleep; but neither lessen nor dim the deep sense of my moral and intellectual obligations. He sent us to the University excellent Latin and Greek scholars, and tolerable Hebraists. Yet our classical knowledge was the least of the good gifts, which we derived from his zealous and conscientious tutorage. He is now gone to his final reward, full of years, and full of honors, even of those honors, which were dearest to his heart, as gratefully bestowed by that school, and still binding him to the interests of that school, in which he had been himself educated, and to which during his whole life he was a dedicated thing.

From causes, which this is not the place to investigate, no models of past times, however perfect, can have the same vivid effect on the youthful mind, as the productions of contemporary genius. The Discipline, my mind had undergone, "Ne falleretur rotundo sono et versuum cursu, concinnis et floribus; sed ut inspiceret quidnam subesset, quæ sedes, quod firmamentum, quis fundus verbis; an figuræ essent mera ornatura et orationis fucus; vel sanguinis e materiæ ipsius corde effluentis rubor quidam nativus et in-

---

5 Didymus Chalcenterus (*c.* 63 B.C.–A.D. 10) was an Alexandrian-Roman scholar and grammarian, whose treatise on the text of Homer had collected, compared, and evaluated the variant readings of earlier editors.

6 Synonymous with poetic inspiration, from a fountain in the Pierian mountains in Macedonia, supposed birthplace of the Muses.

7 The Manchineel was a West Indian tree that produced a poisonous sap and fruit, and whose shade was thought to bring death to all who lay beneath it.

8 Clytus was a Macedonian warrior, who once saved Alexander the Great's life in battle and became his closest friend. At a drinking party, Clytus criticized the arrogance and decadence of Alexander's behavior as triumphant ruler, for which Alexander slew him. He subsequently repented of his hasty action and had Clytus buried with full military honors.

calescentia genuina;"[9] removed all obstacles to the appreciation of excellence in style without diminishing my delight. That I was thus prepared for the perusal of Mr. Bowles's sonnets and earlier poems, at once increased *their* influence, and *my* enthusiasm. The great works of past ages seem to a young man things of another race, in respect to which his faculties must remain passive and submiss, even as to the stars and mountains. But the writings of a contemporary, perhaps not many years elder than himself, surrounded by the same circumstances, and disciplined by the same manners, possess a *reality* for him, and inspire an actual friendship as of a man for a man. His very admiration is the wind which fans and feeds his hope. The poems themselves assume the properties of flesh and blood. To recite, to extol, to contend for them is but the payment of a debt due to one, who exists to receive it.

There are indeed modes of teaching which have produced, and are producing, youths of a very different stamp; modes of teaching, in comparison with which we have been called on to despise our great public schools, and universities

> "in whose halls are hung
> Armoury of the invincible knights of old"—[10]

modes, by which children are to be metamorphosed into prodigies. And prodigies with a vengeance have I known thus produced! Prodigies of self-conceit, shallowness, arrogance, and infidelity! Instead of storing the memory, during the period when the memory is the predominant faculty, with facts for the after exercise of the judgement; and instead of awakening by the noblest models the fond and unmixed LOVE and ADMIRATION, which is the natural and graceful temper of early youth; *these* nurselings of improved pedagogy are taught to dispute and decide; to suspect all, but their own and their lecturer's wisdom; and to hold nothing sacred from their contempt, but their own contemptible arrogance: boy-graduates in all the technicals, and in all the dirty passions and impudence of anonymous criticism. To such dispositions alone can the admonition of Pliny be requisite, "Neque enim debet operibus ejus obesse, quod vivit. An si inter eos, quos nunquam vidimus, floruisset, non solum libros ejus, verum etiam imagines conquireremus,

ejusdem nunc honor præsentis, et gratia quasi satietate languescet? At hoc pravum, malignumque est, non admirari hominem admiratione dignissimum, quia videre, complecti, nec laudare tantum, verum etiam amare contingit." *Plin. Epist. Lib. I.*[11]

I had just entered on my seventeenth year, when the sonnets of Mr. Bowles,[12] twenty in number, and just then published in a quarto pamphlet, were first made known and presented to me, by a schoolfellow who had quitted us for the University, and who, during the whole time that he was in our first form (or in our school language a GRECIAN)[13] had been my patron and protector. I refer to Dr. Middleton, the truly learned, and every way excellent Bishop of Calcutta:

> "Qui laudibus amplis
> Ingenium celebrare meum, calamumque solebat,
> Calcar agens animo validum. Non omnia terræ
> Obruta! Vivit amor, vivit dolor! Ora negatur
> Dulcia conspicere; at flere et meminisse* relictum est."
> *Petr. Ep. Lib. I. Ep. I.*[14]

It was a double pleasure to me, and still remains a tender recollection, that I should have received from a friend so revered the first knowledge of a poet, by whose works, year after year, I was so enthusiastically delighted and inspired. My earliest acquaintances will not have forgotten the undisciplined eagerness and impetuous zeal, with which I laboured to make pro-

* I am most happy to have the necessity of informing the reader, that since this passage was written, the report of Dr. Middleton's death on his voyage to India has been proved erroneous. He lives and long may he live; for I dare prophesy, that with his life only will his exertions for the temporal and spiritual welfare of his fellow men be limited.

[11] "Neque . . . contingit.": "Nor be it any prejudice to his merit that he is a contemporary writer. Had he flourished in some distant age, not only his works, but the very pictures and statues of him would have been passionately inquired after; and shall we then, from a sort of satiety, and merely because he is present among us, suffer his talents to languish and fade away unhonoured and unadmired? It is surely a very perverse and envious disposition, to look with indifference upon a man worthy of the highest approbation, for no other reason but because we have it in our power to see him, and to converse familiarly with him, and not only to give him our applause, but to receive him into our friendship." From Epistle I of *Epistolae* of Pliny the Younger (b. A.D. 61) (Melmoth-Hutchinson translation, Loeb Classical Library, Harvard University Press).

[12] See "Introduction to the Sonnets," paragraph three, and footnote 2, p. 123.

[13] Refers to the most distinguished class of students at Christ's Hospital, specially prepared for university education. On this and Dr. Middleton, see Lamb's essay "Christ's Hospital Five-and-Thirty Years Ago."

[14] "Who was accustomed to honor my genius and my pen with ample praises, offering a powerful incentive to my spirit. All things are not buried in the earth! Love lives, sorrow lives! It is denied to see sweet faces; but to weep and to remember is left to us." Epistola Prima ("Barbabo Sulmonensi"), ll. 12–16, of Petrarch's *Epistolae Metricae*.

[9] "Ne falleretur . . . genuina": "Let him not be deceived with elegant sounds and the quick flow of verses, with elegancies and flowers; but let him examine whatever be beneath, what are the foundations, supports, and grounds of words; if the figures be mere ornaments and disguises of speech; or if it be the native redness of the blood flowing from the matter itself and genuine feelings."

[10] From Wordsworth's sonnet "It is not to be thought of that the Flood" (1807), ll. 9–10.

selytes, not only of my companions, but of all with whom I conversed, of whatever rank, and in whatever place. As my school finances did not permit me to purchase copies, I made, within less than a year and a half, more than forty transcriptions, as the best presents I could offer to those, who had in any way won my regard. And with almost equal delight did I receive the three or four following publications of the same author.

Though I have seen and known enough of mankind to be well aware, that I shall perhaps stand alone in my creed, and that it will be well, if I subject myself to no worse charge than that of singularity; I am not therefore deterred from avowing, that I regard, and ever have regarded the obligations of intellect among the most sacred of the claims of gratitude. A valuable thought, or a particular train of thoughts, gives me additional pleasure, when I can safely refer and attribute it to the conversation or correspondence of another. My obligations to Mr. Bowles were indeed important, and for radical good. At a very premature age, even before my fifteenth year, I had bewildered myself in metaphysics, and in theological controversy. Nothing else pleased me. History, and particular facts, lost all interest in my mind. Poetry (though for a schoolboy of that age, I was above par in English versification, and had already produced two or three compositions which, I may venture to say, without reference to my age, were somewhat above mediocrity, and which had gained me more credit, than the sound, good sense of my old master was at all pleased with) poetry itself, yea, novels and romances, became insipid to me. In my friendless wanderings on our *leave-days,** (for I was an orphan, and had scarce any connections in London) highly was I delighted, if any passenger, especially if he were drest in black, would enter into conversation with me. For I soon found the means of directing it to my favorite subjects

Of providence, fore-knowledge, will, and fate,
Fix'd fate, free will, fore-knowledge absolute,
And found no end in wandering mazes lost.[15]

This preposterous pursuit was, beyond doubt, injurious, both to my natural powers, and to the progress of my education. It would perhaps have been destructive, had it been continued; but from this I was auspiciously withdrawn, partly indeed by an accidental

introduction to an amiable family,[16] chiefly however, by the genial influence of a style of poetry, so tender and yet so manly, so natural and real, and yet so dignified, and harmonious, as the sonnets, &c. of Mr. Bowles! Well were it for me perhaps, had I never relapsed into the same mental disease; if I had continued to pluck the flower and reap the harvest from the cultivated surface, instead of delving in the unwholesome quicksilver mines of metaphysic depths. But if in after time I have sought a refuge from bodily pain and mismanaged sensibility in abstruse researches, which exercised the strength and subtlety of the understanding without awakening the feelings of the heart; still there was a long and blessed interval, during which my natural faculties were allowed to expand, and my original tendencies to develope themselves: my fancy, and the love of nature, and the sense of beauty in forms and sounds.

The second advantage, which I owe to my early perusal, and admiration of these poems (to which let me add, though known to me at a somewhat later period, the Lewsdon Hill of Mr. CROW)[17] bears more immediately on my present subject. Among those with whom I conversed, there were, of course, very many who had formed their taste, and their notions of poetry, from the writings of Mr. Pope and his followers: or to speak more generally, in that school of French poetry, condensed and invigorated by English understanding, which had predominated from the last century. I was not blind to the merits of this school, yet as from inexperience of the world, and consequent want of sympathy with the general subjects of these poems, they gave me little pleasure, I doubtless undervalued the *kind*, and with the presumption of youth withheld from its masters the legitimate name of poets. I saw, that the excellence of this kind consisted in just and acute observations on men and manners in an artificial state of society, as its matter and substance: and in the logic of wit, conveyed in smooth and strong epigrammatic couplets, as its *form*. Even when the subject was addressed to the fancy, or the intellect, as in the Rape of the Lock, or the Essay on Man; nay, when it was a consecutive narration, as in that astonishing product of matchless talent and ingenuity, Pope's Translation of the Iliad; still a *point* was looked for at the end of each second line, and the whole was as it were a sorites, or, if I may exchange a logical for a grammatical metaphor, a *conjunction disjunctive*, of

---

* The Christ's Hospital phrase, not for holidays altogether, but for those on which the boys are permitted to go beyond the precincts of the school.

[15] *Paradise Lost*, II, 559–61.

[16] The family of a school friend Tom Evans. Coleridge fell desperately in love with the eldest sister, Mary.
[17] *Lewesdon Hill* (1788) was the title of a meditative descriptive poem by William Crowe (1745–1829). See C. G. Martin, "Coleridge and Crowe's 'Lewesdon Hill'," *Modern Language Review*, LXII (1967), 400–406.

epigrams.[18] Meantime the matter and diction seemed to me characterized not so much by poetic thoughts, as by thoughts *translated* into the language of poetry. On this last point, I had occasion to render my own thoughts gradually more and more plain to myself, by frequent amicable disputes concerning Darwin's BOTANIC GARDEN,[19] which, for some years, was greatly extolled, not only by the *reading* public in general, but even by those, whose genius and natural robustness of understanding enabled them afterwards to act foremost in dissipating these "painted mists" that occasionally rise from the marshes at the foot of Parnassus. During my first Cambridge vacation, I assisted a friend in a contribution for a literary society in Devonshire: and in this I remember to have compared Darwin's work to the Russian palace of ice, glittering, cold and transitory. In the same essay too, I assigned sundry reasons, chiefly drawn from a comparison of passages in the Latin poets with the original Greek, from which they were borrowed, for the preference of Collins' odes to those of Gray; and of the simile in Shakspeare

> "How like a younker or a prodigal,
>   The skarfed bark puts from her native bay
>   Hugg'd and embraced by the strumpet wind!
> How like the prodigal doth she return,
>   With over-weather'd ribs and ragged sails,
>   Lean, rent, and beggar'd by the strumpet wind!"

to the imitation in the Bard;

> "Fair laughs the morn, and soft the zephyr blows
>   While proudly riding o'er the azure realm
>   In gallant trim the gilded vessel goes,
>   YOUTH at the prow and PLEASURE at the helm,
> Regardless of the sweeping whirlwind's sway,
> That hush'd in grim repose, expects it's evening prey." [20]

(In which, by the bye, the words "realm" and "sway" are rhymes dearly purchased.) I preferred the original on the ground, that in the imitation it depended wholly on the compositor's putting, or not putting a *small Capital*, both in this, and in many other passages of the same poet, whether the words should be personifications, or mere abstractions. I mention this, because,

in referring various lines in Gray to their original in Shakspeare and Milton; and in the clear perception how completely all the propriety was lost in the transfer; I was, at that early period, led to a conjecture, which, many years afterwards was recalled to me from the same thought having been started in conversation, but far more ably, and developed more fully, by Mr. WORDSWORTH; namely, that this style of poetry, which I have characterised above, as translations of prose thoughts into poetic language, had been kept up by, if it did not wholly arise from, the custom of writing Latin verses, and the great importance attached to these exercises, in our public schools. Whatever might have been the case in the fifteenth century, when the use of the Latin tongue was so general among learned men, that Erasmus is said to have forgotten his native language; yet in the present day it is not to be supposed, that a youth can *think* in Latin, or that he can have any other reliance on the force or fitness of his phrases, but the authority of the author from whence he has adopted them. Consequently he must first prepare his thoughts, and then pick out, from Virgil, Horace, Ovid, or perhaps more compendiously from his* Gradus, halves and quarters of lines, in which to embody them.

I never object to a certain degree of disputatiousness in a young man from the age of seventeen to that of four or five and twenty, provided I find him always arguing on one side of the question. The controversies, occasioned by my unfeigned zeal for the honor of a favorite contemporary, then known to me only by his works, were of great advantage in the formation and establishment of my taste and critical opinions. In my defence of the lines running into each other, instead of closing at each couplet; and of natural language, neither bookish, nor vulgar, neither redolent of the

---

* In the Nutricia of Politian there occurs this line:

> "Pura coloratos interstrepit unda lapillos."

Casting my eye on a University prize-poem, I met this line,

> "Lactea purpureos interstrepit unda lapillos."

Now look out in the Gradus for *Purus*, and you may find as the first synonime, *lacteus*; for *coloratus*, and the first synonime is *purpureus*. I mention this by way of elucidating one of the most ordinary processes in the *ferrumination* of these centos.[21]

---

[18] Sorites is a term in formal logic for a connected series of propositions or syllogisms. A conjunction disjunctive is a conjunction such as "but" or "yet" that joins sentences or clauses together grammatically while separating them in meaning.

[19] Erasmus Darwin (1731–1802), physician and scientist, was the grandfather of Charles Darwin. *The Botanic Garden* (1789–1791) was an elaborate allegorical treatment, in heroic couplets, of the properties of plants and other natural phenomena.

[20] *The Merchant of Venice*, II, vi, 14–19; Gray's *The Bard*, ll. 71–76.

[21] *Gradus ad Parnassum* [Steps towards Parnassus] was a thesaurus providing synonyms, epithets, and phrases to aid students in the composition of Latin verses. Angelo Ambrogini (Poliziano) (1454–1494) was one of the most distinguished Renaissance classical scholars, and a Latin and Italian poet of distinction. "Pura . . . lapillos.": "The pure [stainless] wave resounds among the colored pebbles." The synonyms are white as milk (*lactea*) for pure (*pura*), and purple (*purpureos*) for colored (*coloratos*). The line cited by Coleridge does not occur in Politian's *Nutricia*, but in *Rusticus* (1483), l. 14. The phrase "*ferrumination* of these centos" means the binding together of these verbal patches.

lamp, nor of the kennel, such as *I will remember thee*; instead of the same thought tricked up in the rag-fair finery of,

———Thy image on her wing
Before my FANCY's eye shall MEMORY bring,

I had continually to adduce the metre and diction of the Greek Poets from Homer to Theocritus inclusive; and still more of our elder English poets from Chaucer to Milton. Nor was this all. But as it was my constant reply to authorities brought against me from later poets of great name, that no authority could avail in opposition to TRUTH, NATURE, LOGIC, and the LAWS of UNIVERSAL GRAMMAR; actuated too by my former passion for metaphysical investigations; I labored at a solid foundation, on which permanently to ground my opinions, in the component faculties of the human mind itself, and their comparative dignity and importance. According to the faculty of source, from which the pleasure given by any poem or passage was derived, I estimated the merit of such poem or passage. As the result of all my reading and meditation, I abstracted two critical aphorisms, deeming them to comprise the conditions and criteria of poetic style; first, that not the poem which we have *read*, but that to which we *return*, with the greatest pleasure, possesses the genuine power, and claims the name of *essential poetry*. Second, that whatever lines can be translated into other words of the same language, without diminution of their significance, either in sense, or association, or in any worthy feeling, are so far vicious in their diction. Be it however observed, that I excluded from the list of worthy feelings, the pleasure derived from mere novelty, in the reader, and the desire of exciting wonderment at his powers in the author. Oftentimes since then, in pursuing French tragedies, I have fancied two marks of admiration at the end of each line, as hieroglyphics of the author's own admiration at his own cleverness. Our genuine admiration of a great poet is a continuous *under-current* of feeling; it is everywhere present, but seldom any where as a separate excitement. I was wont boldly to affirm, that it would be scarcely more difficult to push a stone out from the pyramids with the bare hand, than to alter a word, or the position of a word, in Milton or Shakspeare, (in their most important works at least) without making the author say something else, or something worse, than he does say. One great distinction, I appeared to myself to see plainly, between, even the characteristic faults of our elder poets, and the false beauty of the moderns. In the former, from DONNE to COWLEY, we find the most fantastic out-of-the-way thoughts, but in the most pure and genuine mother English; in the latter, the most obvious

thoughts, in language the most fantastic and arbitrary. Our faulty elder poets sacrificed the passion, and passionate flow of poetry, to the subtleties of intellect, and to the starts of wit; the moderns to the glare and glitter of a perpetual, yet broken and heterogeneous imagery, or rather to an amphibious something, made up, half of image, and half of abstract* meaning. The one sacrified the heart to the head; the other both heart and head to point and drapery.

The reader must make himself acquainted with the general style of composition that was at that time deemed poetry, in order to understand and account for the effect produced on me by the SONNETS, the MONODY at MATLOCK, and the HOPE, of Mr. Bowles; for it is peculiar to original genius to become less and less *striking*, in proportion to its success in improving the taste and judgement of its contemporaries. The poems of WEST [22] indeed had the merit of chaste and manly diction, but they were cold, and, if I may so express it, only *dead-coloured*; while in the best of Warton's [23] there is a stiffness, which too often gives them the appearance of imitations from the Greek. Whatever relation therefore of cause or impulse Percy's collection of Ballads [24] may bear to the most *popular* poems of the present day; yet in the more sustained and elevated style, of the then living poets Bowles and Cowper† were, to the best of my knowledge, the first who combined natural thoughts with natural diction; the first who reconciled the heart with the head.

It is true, as I have before mentioned, that from diffidence in my own powers, I for a short time adopted a laborious and florid diction, which I myself deemed, if not absolutely vicious, yet of very inferior worth.

* I remember a ludicrous instance in the poem of a young tradesman:

"No more will I endure love's pleasing pain,
Or round my *heart's leg* tie his galling chain."

† Cowper's Task was published some time before the Sonnets of Mr. Bowles; but I was not familiar with it till many years afterwards. The vein of Satire which runs through that excellent poem, together with the sombre hue of its religious opinions, would probably, *at that time*, have prevented its laying any strong hold on my affections. The love of nature seems to have led Thomson to a chearful religion; and a gloomy religion to have led Cowper to a love of nature. The one would carry his fellow-men along with him into nature; the other flies to nature from his fellow-men. In chastity of diction, however, and the harmony of blank verse, Cowper leaves Thomson unmeasurably below him; yet still I feel the latter to have been the *born poet*.

[22] Gilbert West (1703–1756) was best known for his imitations of Spenser and translations of Pindar.
[23] See "Introduction to the Sonnets," footnote 3, page 123.
[24] Refers to the widely influential *Reliques of Ancient English Poetry* (1765), prepared by Thomas Percy (1729–1811).

Gradually, however, my practice conformed to my better judgement; and the compositions of my twenty-fourth and twenty-fifth years (*ex. gr.* the shorter blank verse poems, the lines which are now adopted in the introductory part of the VISION in the present collection in Mr. Southey's Joan of Arc, 2nd book, 1st edition, and the Tragedy of REMORSE)[25] are not more below my present ideal in respect of the general tissue of the style, than those of the latest date. Their faults were at least a remnant of the former leaven, and among the many who have done me the honor of putting my poems in the same class with those of my betters, the one or two, who have pretended to bring examples of affected simplicity from my volume, have been able to adduce but one instance, and that out of a copy of verses half ludicrous, half splenetic, which I intended, and had myself characterized, as *sermoni propiora.*[26]

Every reform, however necessary, will by weak minds be carried to an excess, that itself will need re-forming. The reader will excuse me for noticing, that I myself was the first to expose *risu honesto*[27] the three sins of poetry, one or the other of which is the most likely to beset a young writer. So long ago as the publication of the second number of the Monthly Magazine, under the name of NEHEMIAH HIGGINBOTTOM I contributed three sonnets,[28] the first of which had for its object to excite a good-natured laugh at the spirit of *doleful egotism*, and at the recurrence of favorite phrases, with the double defect of being at once trite, and licentious. The second, on low, creeping language and thoughts, under the pretence of *simplicity*. And the third, the phrases of which were borrowed entirely from my own poems, on the indiscriminate use of elaborate and swelling language and imagery. The

reader will find them in the note* below, and will I trust regard them as reprinted for biographical purposes, and not for their poetic merits. So general at

*

SONNET I.

PENSIVE at eve, on the *hard* world I mused,
And *my poor* heart was sad; so at the MOON
I gazed, and sighed, and sighed; for ah how soon
Eve saddens into night! mine eyes perused
With tearful vacancy the *dampy* grass
That wept and glitter'd in the *paly* ray:
And I *did pause me*, on my lonely way
And *mused me*, on the *wretched ones* that pass
O'er the bleak heath of sorrow. But alas!
Most of myself I thought! when it befel,
That the *soothe* spirit of the *breezy* wood
Breath'd in mine ear: 'All this is very well,
But much of ONE thing, is for NO thing good.'
Oh *my poor heart's* INEXPLICABLE SWELL!

SONNET II.

Oh I do love thee, meek SIMPLICITY!
For of thy lays the lulling simpleness
Goes to my heart, and soothes each small distress,
Distress tho' small, yet haply great to me,
'Tis true on Lady Fortune's gentlest pad
I amble on; and yet I know not why
So said I am! but should a friend and I
Frown, pout and part, then I am *very* sad.
And then with sonnets and with sympathy
My dreamy bosom's mystic woes I pall;
Now of my false friend plaining plaintively,
Now raving at mankind in general;
But whether sad or fierce, 'tis simple all,
All very simple, meek SIMPLICITY!

SONNET III.

AND this reft house is that, the which he built,
Lamented Jack! and here his malt he pil'd,
Cautious in vain! those rats, that squeak so wild,
Squeak not unconscious of their father's guilt.
Did he not see her gleaming thro' the glade!
Belike 'twas she, the maiden all forlorn.
What tho' she milk no cow with crumpled horn,
Yet, *aye* she haunts the dale where *erst* she stray'd:
And *aye*, beside her stalks her amorous knight!
Still on his thighs their wonted brogues are worn,
And thro' those brogues, still tatter'd and betorn,
His hindward charms gleam an unearthly white.
Ah! thus thro' broken clouds at night's high Noon
Peeps in fair fragments forth the full-orb'd harvest-moon!

The following anecdote will not be wholly out of place here, and may perhaps amuse the reader. An amateur performer in verse expressed to a common friend, a strong desire to be introduced to me, but hesitated in accepting my friend's immediate offer, on the score that "he was, he must acknowledge the author of a confounded severe epigram on my *ancient mariner*, which had given me great pain." I assured my friend that, if the epigram was a good one, it would only increase my desire to become acquainted with the author, and begg'd to hear it recited: when, to my no less surprise than amusement, it proved to be one I had myself some time before written and inserted in the Morning Post.

---

[25] "The shorter blank verse poems" would be such as "Eolian Harp," "Reflections on having left a Place of Retirement," both composed 1795, published 1796, and "This Lime Tree Bower my Prison," composed 1797, published 1800. "the lines . . . 1st edition" refers to "The Destiny of Nations. A Vision," published in *Sibylline Leaves*, a collection of Coleridge's poems which appeared in the same month (July 1817) as *Biographia Literaria* and to which the *Biographia* was originally intended to be a preface; the lines had first appeared as part of Southey's epic poem of 1796. "The Tragedy of REMORSE" first written in 1797 and then entitled *Osorio*, was performed in London with considerable success in 1813.

[26] The verses referred to were "To a Young Ass its Mother being Tethered near it," first published 1794. *Sermoni propiora*, "things more like ordinary conversation [than poetry]", is from Horace's *Satires*, I, iv, 42. The phrase (in its variant form *sermoni propriora*) was actually attached by Coleridge to "Reflections on Having Left a Place of Retirement" for its publication in the 1797 edition of his poems.

[27] risu honesto: "with a virtuous laugh".

[28] The three sonnets had appeared in Volume IV, no. 24 (November 1797) of the *Monthly Magazine* under the title "Sonnets attempted in the manner of Contemporary Writers."

that time, and so decided was the opinion concerning the characteristic vices of my style, that a celebrated physician (now, alas! no more) speaking of me in other respects with his usual kindness to a gentleman, who was about to meet me at a dinner party, could not however resist giving him a hint not to mention the "*House that Jack built*" in my presence, for "that I was *as sore as a boil* about that sonnet;" he not knowing, that I was myself the author of it.

FROM

CHAPTER IV

*   *   *   *   *

DURING the last year of my residence at Cambridge, I became acquainted with Mr. Wordsworth's first publication entitled "Descriptive Sketches";[1] and seldom, if ever, was the emergence of an original poetic genius above the literary horizon more evidently announced. In the form, style, and manner of the whole poem, and in the structure of the particular lines and periods, there is an harshness and acerbity connected and combined with words and images all a-glow, which might recall those products of the vegetable world, where gorgeous blossoms rise out of the hard and thorny rind and shell, within which the rich fruit was elaborating. The language was not only peculiar and strong, but at times knotty and contorted, as by its own impatient strength; while the novelty and struggling crowd of images acting in conjunction with the difficulties of the style, demanded always a greater closeness of attention, than poetry, (at all events, than descriptive poetry) has a right to claim. It not seldom therefore justified the complaint of obscurity. In the following extract I have sometimes fancied, that I saw an emblem of the poem itself, and of the author's genius as it was then displayed.

"'Tis storm; and hid in mist from hour to hour,
   All day the floods a deepening murmur pour;
   The sky is veiled, and every cheerful sight:
   Dark in the region as with coming night;
   And yet what frequent bursts of overpowering light!

"To the author of the Ancient Mariner.
         Your poem must eternal be,
         Dear sir! it cannot fail,
         For 'tis incomprehensible,
         And without head or tail."[29]

[29] The epigram, published in the *Morning Post*, January 24, 1800, was actually addressed to the poet laureate Henry James Pye and referred to his *Carmen Seculare for the Year 1800*.
[1] "Descriptive Sketches" was published in 1793. Coleridge cites later in this paragraph ll. 332–47 in the version of the extract from the poem published in Wordsworth's *Poems* (1815).

Triumphant on the bosom of the storm,
Glances the fire-clad eagle's wheeling form;
Eastward, in long perspective glittering, shine
The wood-crowned cliffs that o'er the lake recline;
Wide o'er the Alps a hundred streams unfold,
At once to pillars turn'd that flame with gold;
Behind his sail the peasant strives to shun
The West, that burns like one dilated sun,
Where in a mighty crucible expire
The mountains, glowing hot, like coals of fire."

The poetic PSYCHE, in its process to full developement, undergoes as many changes as its Greek namesake, the butterfly.* And it is remarkable how soon genius clears and purifies itself from the faults and errors of its earliest products; faults which, in its earliest compositions, are the more obtrusive and confluent, because as heterogeneous elements, which had only a temporary use, they constitute the very *ferment*, by which themselves are carried off. Or we may compare them to some diseases, which must work on the humours, and be thrown out on the surface, in order to secure the patient from their future recurrence. I was in my twenty-fourth year,[2] when I had the happiness of knowing Mr. Wordsworth personally, and while memory lasts, I shall hardly forget the sudden effect produced on my mind, by his recitation of a manuscript poem,[3] which still remains unpublished, but of which the stanza, and tone of style, were the same as those of the "Female Vagrant," as originally printed in the first volume of the "Lyrical Ballads." There was here no mark of strained thought, or forced diction, no crowd or turbulence of imagery, and, as the poet hath himself well described in his lines "on revisiting the Wye," manly reflection, and human associations had given both variety, and an additional interest to natural objects, which in the passion and appetite of the first love they had seemed to him neither to need or

* The fact, that in Greek Psyche is the common name for the soul, and the butterfly, is thus alluded to in the following stanza from an unpublished poem of the author:

"The butterfly the ancient Grecians made
The soul's fair emblem, and its only name—
But of the soul, escaped the slavish trade
Of mortal life! For in this earthly frame
Our's is the reptile's lot, much toil, much blame,
Manifold motions making little speed,
And to deform and kill the things, whereon we feed."
                                        S.T.C.

[2] Wordsworth and Coleridge had first met in Bristol in August–September 1795, before Coleridge had reached his twenty-third birthday.
[3] *Salisbury Plain*, written 1793–1795, but not published complete until 1842 as the much revised *Guilt and Sorrow*. A portion of it had appeared as "The Female Vagrant" in *Lyrical Ballads* (1798).

permit. The occasional obscurities, which had risen from an imperfect controul over the resources of his native language, had almost wholly disappeared, together with that worse defect of arbitrary and illogical phrases, at once hackneyed, and fantastic, which hold so distinguished a place in the *technique* of ordinary poetry, and will, more or less, alloy the earlier poems of the truest genius, unless the attention has been specifically directed to their worthlessness and incongruity.*
I did not perceive anything particular in the mere style of the poem alluded to during its recitation, except indeed such difference as was not separable from the thought and manner; and the Spenserian stanza, which always, more or less, recalls to the reader's mind Spenser's own style, would doubtless have authorized in my then opinion a more frequent descent to the phrases of ordinary life, than could without an ill effect have been hazarded in the heroic couplet. It was not however the freedom from false taste, whether as to common defects, or to those more properly his own, which made so unusual an impression on my feelings immediately, and subsequently on my judgement. It was the union of deep feeling with profound thought; the fine balance of truth in observing with the imaginative faculty in modifying the objects observed; and above all the original gift of spreading the tone, the *atmosphere*, and with it the depth and height of the ideal world around forms, incidents, and situations, of which, for the common view, custom had bedimmed all the lustre, had dried up the sparkle and the dew drops. "To find no contradiction in the union of old and new; to contemplate the ANCIENT of days and all his works with feelings as fresh, as if all had then sprang forth

at the first creative fiat; characterizes the mind that feels the riddle of the world, and may help to unravel it. To carry on the feelings of childhood into the powers of manhood; to combine the child's sense of wonder and novelty with the appearances, which every day for perhaps forty years had rendered familiar;

'With sun and moon and stars throughout the year,
　　And man and woman;'

this is the character and privilege of genius, and one of the marks which distinguish genius from talents. And therefore is it the prime merit of genius and its most unequivocal mode of manifestation, so to represent familiar objects as to awaken in the minds of others a kindred feeling concerning them and that freshness of sensation which is the constant accompaniment of mental, no less than of bodily, convalescence. Who has not a thousand times seen snow fall on water? Who has not watched it with a new feeling, from the time that he has read Burns' comparison of sensual pleasure

'To snow that falls upon a river
　A moment white—then gone for ever!'

In poems, equally as in philosophic disquisitions, genius produces the strongest impressions of novelty, while it rescues the most admitted truths from the impotence caused by the very circumstance of their universal admission. Truths of all others the most awful and mysterious, yet being at the same time of universal interest, are too often considered as *so* true, that they lose all the life and efficiency of truth, and lie bed-ridden in the dormitory of the soul, side by side with the most despised and exploded errors." THE FRIEND,* p. 76, No. 5.

This excellence, which in all Mr. Wordsworth's writings is more or less predominant, and which constitutes the character of his mind, I no sooner felt, than I sought to understand. Repeated meditations led me first to suspect, (and a more intimate analysis of the human faculties, their appropriate marks, functions, and effects matured my conjecture into full conviction) that fancy and imagination were two distinct and widely different faculties, instead of being, according to the general belief, either two names with

---

* Mr. Wordsworth, even in his two earliest, "the Evening Walk and the Descriptive Sketches," is more free from this latter defect than most of the young poets his contemporaries. It may however be exemplified, together with the harsh and obscure construction, in which he more often offended, in the following lines:—

"Mid stormy vapours ever driving by,
　Where ospreys, cormorants, and herons cry;
　Where hardly given the hopeless waste to cheer,
　Denied the bread of life, the foodful ear,
　Dwindles the pear on autumn's latest spray,
　And *apple sickens* pale in summer's ray;
　Even here content has fixed her smiling reign
　With independence, child of high disdain."

I hope, I need not say, that I have quoted these lines for no other purpose than to make my meaning fully understood. It is to be regretted that Mr. Wordsworth has not republished these two poems entire.[4]

---

* As "The Friend" was printed on stampt sheets, and sent only by the post to a very limited number of subscribers, the author has felt less objection to quote from it, though a work of his own. To the public at large indeed it is the same as a volume in manuscript.[5]

---

[4] Coleridge quotes ll. 317–24 of *Descriptive Sketches*, again in the 1815 version. This poem and Wordsworth's other early publication *An Evening Walk* (1793) were republished in full in Wordsworth's *Miscellaneous Poems* (1820).

[5] The quotation is from the issue of *The Friend* for September 14, 1809. "With sun and moon ... / And man and woman" is from Milton's sonnet to Cyriack Skinner ("Cyriack, this three years' day these eyes, though clear"), ll. 5–6. "To snow ... gone for ever!" is from Burns' "Tam O'Shanter," ll. 61–62.

one meaning, or, at furthest, the lower and higher degree of one and the same power. It is not, I own, easy to conceive a more opposite translation of the Greek *Phantasia*, than the Latin Imaginatio; but it is equally true that in all societies there exists an instinct of growth, a certain collective, unconscious good sense working progressively to desynonymize* those words originally of the same meaning, which the conflux of dialects had supplied to the more homogeneous languages, as the Greek and German: and which the same cause, joined with accidents of translation from original works of different countries, occasion in mixt languages like our own. The first and most important point to be proved is, that two conceptions perfectly distinct are confused under one and the same word, and (this done) to appropriate that word exclusively to one meaning, and the synonyme (should there be one) to the other. But if (as will be often the case in the arts and sciences) no synonyme exists, we must either invent or borrow a word. In the present instance the appropriation has already begun, and been legitimated in the derivative adjective: Milton had a highly *imaginative*, Cowley a very *fanciful* mind. If therefore I should succeed in establishing the actual existences of two faculties generally different, the nomenclature would be at once determined. To the faculty by which I had

---

* This is effected either by giving to the one word a general, and to the other an exclusive use; as "to put on the back" and "to indorse;" or by the actual distinction of meanings as "naturalist," and "physician;" or by difference of relation as "I" and "Me;" (each of which the rustics of our different provinces still use in all the cases singular of the first personal pronoun). Even the mere difference, or corruption, in the *pronunciation* of the same word, if it have become general, will produce a new word with a distinct signification; thus "property" and "propriety;" the latter of which, even in the time of Charles II, was the *written* word for all the senses of both. Thus too "mister" and "master" both hasty pronunciations of the same word "magister," "mistress," and "miss," "if" and "give," &c. &c There is a sort of *minim immortal* among the animalcula infusoria[6] which have not naturally either birth, or death, absolute beginning, or absolute end: for at a certain period a small point appears on its back, which deepens and lengthens till the creature divides into two, and the same process recommences in each of the halves now become integral. This may be a fanciful, but it is by no means a bad emblem of the formation of words, and may facilitate the conception, how immense a nomenclature may be organized from a few simple sounds by rational beings in a social state. For each new application, or excitement of the same sound, will call forth a different sensation, which cannot but affect the pronunciation. The after recollection of the sound, without the same vivid sensation, will modify it still further; till at length all trace of the original likeness is worn away.

---

[6] The phrase "*minim immortal* among the animalcula infusoria" refers to the tiniest but indestructible part of the microscopic forms of animal life found in decaying animal and vegetable matter.

characterized Milton, we should confine the term *imagination*; while the other would be contradistinguished as *fancy*. Now were it once fully ascertained, that this division is no less grounded in nature, than that of delirium from mania, or Otway's

"Lutes, lobsters, seas of milk, and ships of amber,"

from Shakspeare's

"What! have his daughters brought him to this pass!"[7]

or from the preceding apostrophe to the elements; the theory of the fine arts, and of poetry in particular, could not, I thought, but derive some additional and important light. It would in its immediate effects furnish a torch of guidance to the philosophical critic; and ultimately be the poet himself. In energetic minds, truth soon changes by domestication into power; and from directing in the discrimination and appraisal of the product, becomes influencive in the production. To admire on principle, is the only way to imitate without loss of originality.

It has been already hinted, that metaphysics and psychology have long been my hobby-horse. But to have a hobby-horse, and to be vain of it, are so commonly found together, that they pass almost for the same. I trust therefore, that there will be more good humour than contempt, in the smile with which the reader chastises my self-complacency, if I confess myself uncertain, whether the satisfaction from the perception of a truth new to myself may not have been rendered more poignant by the conceit, that it would be equally so to the public. There was a time, certainly, in which I took some little credit to myself, in the belief that I had been the first of my countrymen, who had pointed out the diverse meaning of which the two terms were capable, and analyzed the faculties to which they should be appropriated. Mr. W. Taylor's recent volume of synonimes I have not yet seen†; but

---

† I ought to have added, with the exception of a single sheet which I accidentally met with at the printers. Even from this scanty specimen, I found it impossible to doubt the talent, or not to admire the ingenuity of the author. That his distinctions were for the greater part unsatisfactory to *my* mind, proves nothing against their accuracy; but it may possibly be serviceable to him in case of a second edition, if I take this opoortunity of suggesting the query; whether he may not have been occasionally misled, by having assumed, as to me he appeared to have done, the non-existence of *any* absolute synonimes in our language? Now I cannot but think, that there are many which remain for our posterity to distinguish and appropriate, and which I regard as so much reversionary wealth in our mother-tongue. When two distinct meanings are confounded under one or more words, (and such must be the case, as sure as our knowledge is pro-

---

[7] See *Venice Preserved*, V, ii, 151; and *King Lear*, III, iv, 65.

his specification of the terms in question has been clearly shown to be both insufficient and erroneous by Mr. Wordsworth in the preface added to the late collection of his "Lyrical Ballads and other poems." [9] The explanation which Mr. Wordsworth has himself given, will be found to differ from mine, chiefly perhaps, as our objects are different. It could scarcely indeed happen otherwise, from the advantage I have enjoyed of frequent conversation with him on a subject to which a poem of his own first directed my attention, and my conclusions concerning which, he had made more lucid to myself by many happy instances drawn from the operation of natural objects on the mind. But it was Mr. Wordsworth's purpose to consider the influences of fancy and imagination as they are manifested in poetry, and from the different effects to conclude their diversity in kind; while it is my object to investigate the seminal principle, and then from the kind to deduce the degree. My friend has drawn a masterly sketch of the branches with their *poetic* fruitage. I wish to add the trunk, and even the roots as far as they lift themselves above ground, and are visible to the naked eye of our common consciousness.

Yet even in this attempt I am aware, that I shall be

gressive and of course imperfect) erroneous consequences will be drawn, and what is true in one sense of the word will be affirmed as true in toto. Men of research startled by the consequences, seek in the things themselves (whether in or out of the mind) for a knowledge of the fact, and having discovered the difference, remove the equivocation either by the substitution of a new word, or by the appropriation of one of the two or more words, that had before been used promiscuously. When this distinction has been so naturalized and of such general currency, that the language itself does as it were *think* for us (like the sliding rule which is the mechanic's safe substitute for arithmetical knowledge) we then say, that it is evident to *common sense*. Common sense, therefore, differs in different ages. What was born and christened in the schools passes by degrees into the world at large, and becomes the property of the market and the tea-table. At least I can discover no other meaning of the term, *common sense*, if it is to convey any specific difference from sense and judgment in genere, and where it is not used scholastically for the *universal reason*. Thus in the reign of Charles II. the philosophic world was called to arms by the moral sophisms of Hobbs, and the ablest writers exerted themselves in the detection of an error, which a school-boy would now be able to confute by the mere recollection that *compulsion* and *obligation* conveyed two ideas perfectly disparate, and that what appertained to the one, had been falsely transferred to the other by a mere confusion of terms. [8]

[8] On "Mr. W. Taylor's recent volume of synonimes," see above, Wordsworth's "Preface to Poems" (1815), footnote 9, p. 72. The phrase "the moral sophisms of Hobbs" was apparently a reference to Thomas Hobbes' *A Treatise of Liberty and Necessity* (1654).
[9] That is, the "Preface to *Poems*" (1815).

obliged to draw more largely on the reader's attention, than so immethodical a miscellany can authorize; when in such a work (the *Ecclesiastical Polity*) of such a mind as Hooker's, the judicious author, though no less admirable for the perspicuity than for the port and dignity of his language; and though he wrote for men of learning in a learned age; saw nevertheless occasion to anticipate and guard against "complaints of obscurity," as often as he was about to trace his subject "to the highest well-spring and fountain." Which, (continues he) "because men are not accustomed to, the pains we take are more needful a great deal, than acceptable; and the matters we handle, seem by reason of newness (till the mind grow better acquainted with them) dark and intricate." I would gladly therefore spare both myself and others this labor, if I knew how without it to present an intelligible statement of my poetic creed; not as my *opinions*, which weigh for nothing, but as deductions from established premises conveyed in such a form, as is calculated either to effect a fundamental conviction, or to receive a fundamental confutation. If I may dare once more adopt the words of Hooker, "they, unto whom we shall seem tedious, are in no wise injured by us, because it is in their own hands to spare that labor, which they are not willing to endure." [10] Those at least, let me be permitted to add, who have taken so much pains to render me ridiculous for a perversion of taste, and have supported the charge by attributing strange notions to me on no other authority than their own conjectures, owe it to themselves as well as to me not to refuse their attention to my own statement of the theory, which I *do* acknowledge; or shrink from the trouble of examining the grounds on which I rest it, or the arguments which I offer in its justification.

F R O M

CHAPTER XII

A Chapter of requests and premonitions concerning the perusal or omission of the chapter that follows.

IN THE perusal of philosophical works I have been greatly benefited by a resolve, which, in the antithetic form and with the allowed quaintness of an adage or maxim, I have been accustomed to word thus: "*until you understand a writer's ignorance, presume yourself ignorant of his understanding.*" This *golden rule* of mine

[10] This quotation as well as those cited earlier in the paragraph comes from Richard Hooker's *On the Laws of Ecclesiastical Polity* (1594-1597), Book I, Chapter 1.

does, I own, resemble those of Pythagoras in its obscurity rather than in its depth. If however the reader will permit me to be my own Hierocles,[1] I trust, that he will find its meaning fully explained by the following instances. I have now before me a treatise of a religious fanatic, full of dreams and supernatural *experiences*. I see clearly the writer's grounds, and their hollowness. I have a complete insight into the causes, which through the medium of his body had acted on his mind; and by application of received and ascertained laws I can satisfactorily explain to my own reason all the strange incidents, which the writer records of himself. And this I can do without suspecting him of any intentional falsehood. As when in broad day-light a man tracks the steps of a traveller, who had lost his way in a fog or by a treacherous moonshine, even so, and with the same tranquil sense of certainty, can I follow the traces of this bewildered visionary. I UNDERSTAND HIS IGNORANCE.

On the other hand, I have been re-perusing with the best energies of my mind the Timaeus of PLATO. Whatever I comprehend, impresses me with a reverential sense of the author's genius; but there is a considerable portion of the work, to which I can attach no consistent meaning. In other treatises of the same philosopher intended for the average comprehensions of men, I have been delighted with the masterly good sense, with the perspicuity of the language, and the aptness of the inductions. I recollect likewise, that numerous passages in this author, which I thoroughly comprehend, were formerly no less unintelligible to me, than the passages now in question. It would, I am aware, be quite *fashionable* to dismiss them at once as Platonic Jargon. But this I cannot do with satisfaction to my own mind, because I have sought in vain for causes adequate to the solution of the assumed inconsistency. I have no insight into the possibility of a man so eminently wise using words with such half-meanings to himself, as must perforce pass into no-meaning to his readers. When in addition to the motives thus suggested by my own reason, I bring into distinct remembrance the number and the series of great men, who after long and zealous study of these works had joined in honoring the name of PLATO with epithets, that almost transcend humanity, I feel, that a contemptuous verdict on my part might argue want of modesty, but would hardly be received by the judicious, as evidence of superior penetration. Therefore, utterly baffled in all my attempts to understand the ignorance of Plato, I

CONCLUDE MYSELF IGNORANT OF HIS UNDERSTANDING.

In lieu of the various requests which the anxiety of authorship addresses to the unknown reader, I advance but this one; that he will either pass over the following chapter altogether, or read the whole connectedly. The fairest part of the most beautiful body will appear deformed and monstrous, if dissevered from its place in the organic Whole. Nay, on delicate subjects, where a seemingly trifling difference of more or less may constitute a difference in *kind*, even a *faithful* display of the main and supporting ideas, if yet they are separated from the forms by which they are at once cloathed and modified, may perchance present a skeleton indeed; but a skeleton to alarm and deter. Though I might find numerous precedents, I shall not desire the reader to strip his mind of all prejudices, or to keep all prior systems out of view during his examination of the present. For in truth, such requests appear to me not much unlike the advice given to hypochondriacal patients in Dr. Buchan's domestic medicine;[2] videlicet, to preserve themselves uniformly tranquil and in good spirits. Till I had discovered the art of destroying the memory *a parte post*,[3] without injury to its future operations, and without detriment to the judgement, I should suppress the request as premature; and therefore, however much I may *wish* to be read with an unprejudiced mind, I do not presume to state it as a necessary condition.

The extent of my daring is to suggest one criterion, by which it may be rationally conjectured beforehand, whether or no a reader would lose his time, and perhaps his temper, in the perusal of this, or any other treatise constructed on similar principles. But it would be cruelly misinterpreted, as implying the least disrespect either for the moral or intellectual qualities of the individuals thereby precluded. The criterion is this: if a man receives as fundamental facts, and therefore of course indemonstrable and incapable of further analysis, the general notions of matter, spirit, soul, body, action, passiveness, time, space, cause, and effect, consciousness, perception, memory and habit; if he feels his mind completely at rest concerning all these, and is satisfied, if only he can analyse all other notions into some one or more of these supposed elements with plausible subordination and apt arrangement: to such a mind I would as courteously as

---

[1] Hierocles was a fifth-century Neoplatonist of Alexandria, who wrote an extended commentary on the "Golden Words," a series of moral precepts in verse attributed to Pythagoras.

[2] William Buchan (1729–1805) was the author of *Domestic Medicine; or, the Family Physician* (1769), an enormously popular home-medical book.

[3] *a parte post*: "in a backward direction," that is, from the present to the past.

possible convey the hint, that for him the chapter was not written.

Vir bonus es, doctus, prudens; ast *haud tibi spiro*.[4]

For these terms do in truth *include* all the difficulties, which the human mind can propose for solution. Taking them therefore in mass, and unexamined, it requires only a decent apprenticeship in logic, to draw forth their contents in all forms and colours, as the professors of legerdemain at our village fairs pull out ribbon after ribbon from their mouths. And not more difficult is it to reduce them back again to their different genera. But though this analysis is highly useful in rendering our knowledge more distinct, it does not really add to it. It does not increase, though it gives us a greater mastery over, the wealth which we before possessed. For forensic purposes, for all the established professions of society, this is sufficient. But for philosophy in its highest sense, as the science of ultimate truths, and therefore scientia scientiarum, this mere analysis of terms is preparative only, though as a preparative discipline indispensable.

Still less dare a favorable perusal be anticipated from the proselytes of that compendious philosophy, which talking of mind but thinking of brick and mortar, or other images equally abstracted from body, contrives a theory of spirit by nicknaming matter, and in a few hours can qualify its dullest disciples to explain the omne scibile by reducing all things to impressions, ideas, and sensations.

But it is time to tell the truth; though it requires some courage to avow it in an age and country, in which disquisitions on all subjects, not privileged to adopt technical terms or scientific symbols, must be addressed to the PUBLIC. I say then, that it is neither possible or necessary for all men, or for many, to be PHILOSOPHERS. There is a *philosophic* (and inasmuch as it is actualized by an effort of freedom, an *artificial*) *consciousness*, which lies beneath or (as it were) *behind* the spontaneous consciousness natural to all reflecting beings. As the elder Romans distinguished their northern provinces into Cis-Alpine and Trans-Alpine, so may we divide all the objects of human knowledge into those on this side, and those on the other side of the spontaneous consciousness; citra et trans conscientiam communem. The latter is exclusively the domain of PURE philosophy, which is therefore properly entitled *transcendental*, in order to discriminate it at once, both from mere reflection and *re*-presentation on the one hand, and on the other from those flights of

lawless speculation which abandoned by *all* distinct consciousness, because transgressing the bounds and purposes of our intellectual faculties, are justly condemned, as *transcendent*.* The first range of hills, that

* This distinction between transcendental and transcendent is observed by our elder divines and philosophers, whenever they express themselves *scholastically*. Dr. Johnson indeed has confounded the two words; but his own authorities do not bear him out. Of this celebrated dictionary I will venture to remark once for all, that I should suspect the man of a morose disposition who should speak of it without respect and gratitude as a most instructive and entertaining *book*, and hitherto, unfortunately, an indispensable book; but I confess, that I should be surprized at hearing from a philosophic and thorough scholar any but very qualified praises of it, as a *dictionary*. I am not now alluding to the number of genuine words omitted; for this is (and perhaps to a greater extent) true, as Mr. Wakefield has noticed, of our best Greek Lexicons, and this too after the successive labors of so many giants in learning. I refer at present both to omissions and commissions of a more important nature. What these are, me saltem judice, will be stated at full in THE FRIEND, re-published and completed.

I had never heard of the correspondence between Wakefield and Fox till I saw the account of it this morning (16th September 1815) in the Monthly Review. I was not a little gratified at finding, that Mr. Wakefield had proposed to himself nearly the same plan for a Greek and English Dictionary, which I had formed, and began to execute, now ten years ago. But far, far more grieved am I, that he did not live to compleat it. I cannot but think it a subject of most serious regret, that the same heavy expenditure, which is now employing in the *re-publication* of STEPHANUS augmented, had not been applied to a new Lexicon on a more philosophical plan, with the English, German, and French Synonimes as well as the Latin. In almost every instance the precise *individual* meaning might be given in an English or German word; whereas in Latin we must too often be contented with a mere general and *inclusive* term. How indeed can it be otherwise, when we attempt to render the most copious language of the world, the most admirable for the fineness of its distinctions, into one of the poorest and most vague languages? Especially, when we reflect on the comparative number of the works, still extant, written, while the Greek and Latin were living languages. Were I asked, what I deemed the greatest and most unmixt benefit, which a wealthy individual, or an association of wealthy individuals could bestow on their country and on mankind, I should not hesitate to answer, "a philosophical English dictionary; with the Greek, Latin, German, French, Spanish, and Italian synonimes, and with correspondent indexes." That the learned languages might thereby be acquired, better, in half the time, is but a part, and not the most important part, of the advantages which would accure from such a work. O! if it should be permitted by providence, that without detriment to freedom and independence our government might be enabled to become more than a committee for war and revenue! There was a time, when every thing was to be done by government. Have we not flown off to the contrary extreme?[5]

4 Vir . . . spiro: "You are a good man, learned and prudent; but *I by no means intend this for you*."

5 Gilbert Wakefield (1756–1801) was a classical scholar and political radical. *The Correspondence of Gilbert Wakefield with the Right Hon. C. J. Fox* was published in 1813. Henri Estienne (Stephanus) (1531–1598) was a French printer and classical scholar, whose *Thesaurus Graecae Linguae* (1572) was re-edited and published in London between 1816 and 1826. me saltem judice: at least in my judgment.

encircles the scanty vale of human life, is the horizon for the majority of its inhabitants. On *its* ridges the common sun is born and departs. From *them* the stars rise, and touching *them* they vanish. By the many, even this range, the natural limit and bulwark of the vale, is but imperfectly known. Its higher ascents are too often hidden by mists and clouds from uncultivated swamps, which few have courage or curiosity to penetrate. To the multitude below these vapors appear, now as the dark haunts of terrific agents, on which none may intrude with impunity; and now all *a-glow*, with colors not their own, they are gazed at, as the splendid palaces of happiness and power. But in all ages there have been a few, who measuring and sounding the rivers of the vale at the feet of their furthest inaccessible falls have learned, that the sources must be far higher and far inward; a few, who even in the level streams have detected elements, which neither the vale itself or the surrounding mountains contained or could supply. How and whence to these thoughts, these strong probabilities, the ascertaining vision, the intuitive knowledge, may finally supervene, can be learnt only by the fact. I might oppose to the question the words with which* Plotinus supposes NATURE to answer a similar difficulty. "Should any one interrogate her, how she works, if graciously she vouchsafe to listen and speak, she will reply, it behoves thee not to disquiet me with interrogatories, but to understand in silence even as I am silent, and work without words."

Likewise in the fifth book of the fifth Ennead, speaking of the highest and intuitive knowledge as distinguished from the discursive, or in the language of Wordsworth,

"The vision and the faculty divine;"[7]

* Ennead, iii. 1. 8. c. 3. The force of the Greek συνιέναι is imperfectly expressed by "understand;" our own idiomatic phrase "*to go along with me*" comes nearest to it. The passage, that follows, full of profound sense, appears to me evidently corrupt; and in fact no writer more wants, better deserves, or is less likely to obtain, a new and more correct edition—τί οὖν συνιέναι; ὅτι τὸ γενόμενόν ἐστι θέαμα ἐμόν, σιώπησις (*mallem*, θέαμα, ἐμοῦ σιωπώσης), καὶ φύσει γενόμενον θεώρημα, καί μοι γενομένη ἐκ θεωρίας τῆς ὡδὶ τὴν φύσιν ἔχειν φιλοθεάμονα ὑπάρχει. (*mallem*, καὶ μοὶ ἡ γενομένη ἐκ θεωρίας αὐτῆς ὡδὶς) "what then are we to understand? That whatever is produced is an intuition, I silent; and that, which is thus generated, is by its nature a theorem, or form of contemplation; and the birth, which results to me from this contemplation, attains to have a contemplative nature." So Synesius: Ὠδὶς ἱερά, Ἄρρητα γονά. The after comparison of the process of the natura naturans and that of the geometrician is drawn from the very heart of philosophy.[6]

<hr>

[6] More accurately, Coleridge quotes from Plotinus' *Ennead*, III, 8, iv. Synesius (c. 373–c. 414) was a Neoplatonist and bishop of Ptolemais in Lybia. Coleridge quotes from his *Hymns*, iii, 226–227 ("O holy Birth, O unspeakable generation").

[7] *Excursion*, I, 79.

he says: "it is not lawful to enquire from whence it sprang, as if it were a thing subject to place and motion, for it neither approached hither, nor again departs from hence to some other place; but it either appears to us or it does not appear. So that we ought not to pursue it with a view of detecting its secret source, but to watch in quiet till it suddenly shines upon us; preparing ourselves for the blessed spectacle as the eye waits patiently for the rising sun."[8] They and they only can acquire the philosophic imagination, the sacred power of self-intuition, who within themselves can interpret and understand the symbol, that the wings of the air-sylph are forming within the skin of the caterpillar; those only, who feel in their own spirits the same instinct, which impels the chrysalis of the horned fly to leave room in its involucrum for antennæ yet to come. They know and feel, that the *potential* works *in* them, even as the *actual* works on them! In short, all the organs of sense are framed for a corresponding world of sense; and we have it. All the organs of spirit are framed for a correspondent world of spirit: though the latter organs are not developed in all alike. But they exist in all, and their first appearance discloses itself in the *moral* being. How else could it be, that even worldlings, not wholly debased, will contemplate the man of simple and disinterested goodness with contradictory feelings of pity and respect? "Poor man! he is not made for *this* world." Oh! herein they utter a prophecy of universal fulfilment; for man *must* either rise or sink.

It is the essential mark of the true philosopher to rest satisfied with no imperfect light, as long as the impossibility of attaining a fuller knowledge has not been demonstrated. That the common consciousness itself will furnish proofs by its own direction, that it is connected with master-currents below the surface, I shall merely assume as a postulate pro tempore. This having been granted, though but in expectation of the argument, I can safely deduce from it the equal truth of my former assertion, that philosophy cannot be intelligible to all, even of the most learned and cultivated classes. A system, the first principle of which it is to render the mind intuitive of the *spiritual* in man (i.e. of that which lies *on the other side* of our natural consciousness) must needs have a greater obscurity for those, who have never disciplined and strengthened this ulterior consciousness. It must in truth be a land of darkness, a perfect *Anti-Goshen*, for men to whom the noblest treasures of their own being are reported only through the imperfect translation of lifeless and sightless *notions*. Perhaps, in great part, through words which

<hr>

[8] *Ennead*, V, 5, viii.

are but the shadows of notions; even as the notional understanding itself is but the shadowy abstraction of living and actual truth. On the IMMEDIATE, which dwells in every man, and on the original intuition, or absolute affirmation of it, (which is likewise in every man, but does not in every man rise into consciousness) all the *certainty* of our knowledge depends; and this becomes intelligible to no man by the ministry of mere words from without. The medium, by which spirits understand each other, is not the surrounding air; but the *freedom* which they possess in common, as the common ethereal element of their being, the tremulous reciprocations of which propagate themselves even to the inmost of the soul. Where the spirit of a man is not *filled* with the consciousness of freedom (were it only from its restlessness, as of one still struggling in bondage) all spiritual intercourse is interrupted, not only with others, but even with himself. No wonder then, that he remains incomprehensible to himself as well as to others. No wonder, that, in the fearful desert of his consciousness, he wearies himself out with empty words, to which no friendly echo answers, either from his own heart, or the heart of a fellow being; or bewilders himself in the pursuit of *notional* phantoms, the mere refractions from unseen and distant truths through the distorting medium of his own unenlivened and stagnant understanding! To remain unintelligible to such a mind, exclaims Schelling [9] on a like occasion, is honor and a good name before God and man.

The history of philosophy (the same writer observes) contains instances of systems, which for successive generations have remained enigmatic. Such he deems the system of Leibnitz, whom another writer (rashly I think, and invidiously) extols as the *only* philosopher, who was himself deeply convinced of his own doctrines. As hitherto interpreted, however, they have not produced the effect, which Leibnitz himself, in a most instructive passage,[10] describes as the criterion of a true philosophy; namely, that it would at once explain and collect the fragments of truth scattered through systems apparently the most incongruous. The truth, says he, is diffused more widely than is commonly believed; but it is often painted, yet oftener masked, and is sometimes mutilated and sometimes, alas! in close alliance with mischievous errors. The deeper, however, we penetrate into the ground of things, the more truth we discover in the doctrines of the greater number of the philosophical sects. The want of *sub-*

stantial reality in the objects of the senses, according to the sceptics; the harmonies or numbers, the prototypes and ideas, to which the Pythagoreans and Platonists reduced all things; the ONE and ALL of Parmenides and Plotinus, without * Spinozism; the necessary connection of things according to the Stoics, reconcileable with the spontaneity of the other schools; the vital-philosophy of the Cabalists and Hermetists, who assumed the universality of sensation; the substantial forms and entelechies [12] of Aristotle and the schoolmen, together with the mechanical solution of all particular phenomena according to Democritus [13] and the recent philosophers—all these we shall find united in one

* This is happily effected in three lines by SYNESIUS, in his fourth HYMN:

Εν καὶ Πάντα—(taken by itself) is *Spinozism.*
Εν δ' 'Απάντων—a mere *anima Mundi.*
Εν τε πρὸ πάντων—is mechanical Theism.

But unite all three, and the result is the Theism of Saint Paul and Christianity.

Synesius was censured for his doctrine of the Pre-existence of the Soul; but never, that I can find, arraigned or deemed heretical for his Pantheism, tho' neither Giordano Bruno, or Jacob Behmen ever avowed it more broadly.

Μύστας δὲ Νόος,
Τά τε καὶ τὰ λέγει,
Βυθὸν ἄρρητον
'Αμφιχορεύων.
Εὺ τὸ τίκτον ἔφυς,
Σὺ τὸ τικτόμενον·
Σὺ τὸ φωτίζον,
Σὺ τὸ λαμπόμενον·
Σὺ τὸ φαινόμενον,
Σὺ τὸ κρυπτόμενον
'Ιδίαις αὐγαῖς.
"Εν καὶ πάντα,
"Εν καθ' ἑαυτὸ,
Καὶ διὰ πάντων.

Pantheism is therefore not necessarily irreligious or heretical; tho' it may be taught atheistically. Thus Spinoza would agree with Synesius in calling God Φύσις ἐν Νοεροῖς, the *Nature* in Intelligences; but he could not subscribe to the preceding Νοῦς καὶ Νοερός, i.e. Himself Intelligence and intelligent.

In this biographical sketch of my literary life I may be excused, if I mention here, that I had translated the eight Hymns of Synesius from the Greek into English Anacreontics before my 15th year.[11]

---

[9] In *Abhandlungen zur Erläuterung des Idealismus der Wissenschaftslehre* published in *Philosophische Schriften* (1809). From this point on, much of Chapter XII consists of translations or paraphrases from the works of the German philosopher Friedrich Wilhelm Joseph von Schelling (1775–1854).

[10] *Trois Lettres à Mr. Remond de Montmort* (1714), iii.

[11] More accurately, Coleridge quotes first from Synesius' *Hymns*, iii, 180–182: "One and All / and the One of All / and the One before All". The extended quotation comes from *Hymns*, iii, 187–200: "The mind initiated in the mysteries says such and such things, moving in harmony the while around Thy awful abysm. Thou art the Generator, Thou the Generated; Thou the Light that shineth, Thou the Illumined; Thou what is revealed, Thou that which is hidden in Thine own beams" (Augustine Fitzgerald translation, 1930).

[12] The realizations of a potentiality or function.

[13] Democritus was a fifth–century B.C. Greek philosopher, who argued that all things are caused by the purely mechanical motion of atoms.

perspective central point, which shows regularity and a coincidence of all the parts in the very object, which from every other point of view must appear confused and distorted. The spirit of sectarianism has been hitherto our fault, and the cause of our failures. We have imprisoned our own conceptions by the lines, which we have drawn, in order to exclude the conceptions of others. J'ai trouvé que la plupart des sectes ont raison dans une bonne partie de ce qu'elles avancent, mais non pas tant en ce qu'elles nient.[14]

A system, which aims to deduce the memory with all the other functions of intelligence, must of course place its first position from beyond the memory, and anterior to it, otherwise the principle of solution would be itself a part of the problem to be solved. Such a position therefore must, in the first instance be demanded, and the first question will be, by what right is it demanded? On this account I think it expedient to make some preliminary remarks on the introduction of POSTULATES in philosophy. The word postulate is borrowed from the science of mathematics. (See Schell. abhandl. zur Erläuter. des id. der Wissenschaftslehre.) In geometry the primary construction is not demonstrated, but postulated. This first and most simple construction in space is the point in motion, or the line. Whether the point is moved in one and the same direction, or whether its direction is continually changed, remains as yet undetermined. But if the direction of the point have been determined, it is either by a point without it, and then there arises the strait line which incloses no space; or the direction of the point is not determined by a point without it, and then it must flow back again on itself, that is, there arises a cyclical line, which does inclose a space. If the strait line be assumed as the positive, the cyclical is then the negation of the strait. It is a line, which at no point strikes out into the strait, but changes its direction continuously. But if the primary line be conceived as undetermined, and the strait line as determined throughout, then the cyclical is the third compounded of both. It is at once undetermined and determined; undetermined through any point without, and determined through itself. Geometry therefore supplies philosophy with the example of a primary intuition, from which every science that lays claim to *evidence* must take its commencement. The mathematician does not begin with a demonstrable proposition, but with an intuition, a practical idea.

But here an important distinction presents itself. Philosophy is employed on objects of the INNER SENSE, and cannot, like geometry appropriate to every construction a correspondent *outward* intuition. Nevertheless, philosophy, if it is to arrive at evidence, must proceed from the most original construction, and the question then is, what is the most original construction or first productive act for the INNER SENSE. The answer to this question depends on the direction which is given to the INNER SENSE. But in philosophy the INNER SENSE cannot have its direction determined by any outward object. To the original construction of the line, I can be compelled by a line drawn before me on the slate or on sand. The stroke thus drawn is indeed not the line itself, but only the image or picture of the line. It is not from it, that we first learn to know the line; but, on the contrary, we bring this stroke to the original line generated by the act of the imagination; otherwise we could not define it as without breadth or thickness. Still however this stroke is the sensuous image of the original or ideal line, and an efficient mean to excite *every* imagination to the intuition of it.

It is demanded then, whether there be found any means in philosophy to determine the direction of the INNER SENSE, as in mathematics it is determinable by its specific image or outward picture. Now the inner sense has its direction determined for the greater part only by an act of freedom. One man's consciousness extends only to the pleasant or unpleasant sensations caused in him by external impressions; another enlarges his inner sense to a consciousness of forms and quantity; a third in addition to the image is conscious of the conception or notion of the thing; a fourth attains to a notion of his notions—he reflects on his own reflections; and thus we may say without impropriety, that the one possesses more or less inner sense, than the other. This more or less betrays already, that philosophy in its first principles must have a practical or moral, as well as a theoretical or speculative side. This difference in degree does not exist in the mathematics. Socrates in Plato shows, that an ignorant slave may be brought to understand and of himself to solve the most difficult geometrical problem. Socrates drew the figures for the slave in the sand.[15] The disciples of the critical philosophy could likewise (as was indeed actually done by La Forge [16] and some other followers of Des Cartes) represent the origin of our representations in copper-plates; but no one has yet attempted it, and it would be utterly useless. To an Esquimaux or New Zealander our most popular philosophy would be

---

[14] J'ai trouvé . . . nient: "I have discovered that most sects are correct in a good part of what they assert, but not in what they deny." Leibnitz' *Trois Lettres*, i.

[15] See *Meno*, 82–85.
[16] Louis de la Forge wrote notes and provided copper-plate illustrations for Descartes' posthumously published *Les Traitez de l'homme, et de la formation du foetus*.

wholly unintelligible. The sense, the inward organ, for it is not yet born in him. So is there many a one among us, yes, and some who think themselves philosophers too, to whom the philosophic organ is entirely wanting. To such a man, philosophy is a mere play of words and notions, like a theory of music to the deaf, or like the geometry of light to the blind. The connection of the parts and their logical dependencies may be seen and remembered; but the whole is groundless and hollow, unsustained by living contact, unaccompanied with any realizing intuition which exists by and in the act that affirms its existence, which is known, because it is, and is, because it is known. The words of Plotinus, in the assumed person of nature, holds true of the philosophic energy. Τὸ θεωροῦν μον θεώρημα ποιεῖ, ὥσπερ οἱ γεωμέτραι θεωροῦντες γράφουσιν· ἀλλ' ἐμοῦ μὴ γραφούσης, θεωρούσης δὲ, ὑφίστανται αἱ τῶν σωμάτων γραμμαί. With me the act of contemplation makes the thing contemplated, as the geometricians contemplating describe lines correspondent; but I not describing lines, but simply contemplating, the representative forms of things rise up into existence.[17]

The postulate of philosophy and at the same time the test of philosophic capacity, is no other than the heaven-descended KNOW THYSELF! (*E cœlo descendit*, Γνῶθι σεαυτον).[18] And this at once practically and speculatively. For as philosophy is neither a science of the reason or understanding only, nor merely a science of morals, but the science of BEING altogether, its primary ground can be neither merely speculative or merely practical, but both in one. All knowledge rests on the coincidence of an object with a subject. (My readers have been warned in a former chapter that, for their convenience as well as the writer's, the term, subject, is used by me in its scholastic sense as equivalent to mind or sentient being, and as the necessary correlative of object or *quicquid objicitur menti*.)[19] For we can *know* that only which is true: and the truth is universally placed in the coincidence of the thought with the thing, of the representation with the object represented.

Now the sum of all that is merely OBJECTIVE, we will henceforth call NATURE, confining the term to its passive and material sense, as comprising all the phænomena by which its existence is made known to us. On the other hand the sum of all that is SUBJECTIVE, we may comprehend in the name of the SELF or INTELLIGENCE. Both conceptions are in

necessary antithesis. Intelligence is conceived of as exclusively representative, nature as exclusively represented; the one as conscious, the other as without consciousness. Now in all acts of positive knowledge there is required a reciprocal concurrence of both, namely of the conscious being, and of that which is in itself unconscious. Our problem is to explain this concurrence, its possibility and its necessity.

During the act of knowledge itself, the objective and subjective are so instantly united, that we cannot determine to which of the two the priority belongs. There is here no first, and no second; both are coinstantaneous and one. While I am attempting to explain this intimate coalition, I must suppose it dissolved. I must necessarily set out from the one, to which therefore I give hypothetical antecedence, in order to arrive at the other. But as there are but two factors or elements in the problem, subject and object, and as it is left indeterminate from which of them I should commence, there are two cases equally possible.

1. EITHER THE OBJECTIVE IS TAKEN AS THE FIRST, AND THEN WE HAVE TO ACCOUNT FOR THE SUPERVENTION OF THE SUBJECTIVE, WHICH COALESCES WITH IT.

The notion of the subjective is not contained in the notion of the objective. On the contrary they mutually exclude each other. The subjective therefore must supervene to the objective. The conception of nature does not apparently involve the co-presence of an intelligence making an ideal duplicate of it, i.e. representing it. This desk for instance would (according to our natural notions) be, though there should exist no sentient being to look at it. This then is the problem of natural philosophy. It assumes the objective or unconscious nature as the first, and has therefore to explain how intelligence can supervene to it, or how itself can grow into intelligence. If it should appear, that all enlightened naturalists without having distinctly proposed the problem to themselves have yet constantly moved in the line of its solution, it must afford a strong presumption that the problem itself is founded in nature. For if all knowledge has as it were two poles reciprocally required and presupposed, all sciences must proceed from the one or the other, and must tend toward the opposite as far as the equatorial point in which both are reconciled and become identical. The necessary tendence therefore of all natural philosophy is from nature to intelligence; and this, and no other is the true ground and occasion of the instinctive striving to introduce theory into our views of natural phænomena. The highest perfection of natural philosophy would consist in the perfect spiritualization of all the laws of nature into laws of intuition and

----

[17] Coleridge quotes and translates *Ennead*, III, 8, iv.

[18] A favorite Coleridge quotation, from Juvenal's *Satires*, xi, 27. "From heaven it descends, Know Thyself." See the concluding passage from *The Statesman's Manual*, "C."

[19] *quicquid objicitur menti:* "Whatever is presented to the mind."

intellect. The phænomena (*the material*) must wholly disappear, and the laws alone (*the formal*) must remain. Thence it comes, that in nature itself the more the principle of law breaks forth, the more does the *husk* drop off, the phænomena themselves become more spiritual and at length cease altogether in our consciousness. The optical phænomena are but a geometry, the lines of which are drawn by light, and the materiality of this light itself has already become matter of doubt. In the appearances of magnetism all trace of matter is lost, and of the phænomena of gravitation, which not a few among the most illustrious Newtonians have declared no otherwise comprehensible than as an immediate spiritual influence, there remains nothing but its law, the execution of which on a vast scale is the mechanism of the heavenly motions. The theory of natural philosophy would then be completed, when all nature was demonstrated to be identical in essence with that, which in its highest known power exists in man as intelligence and self-consciousness; when the heavens and the earth shall declare not only the power of their maker, but the glory and the presence of their God, even as he appeared to the great prophet during the vision of the mount in the skirts of his divinity.

This may suffice to show, that even natural science, which commences with the material phænomenon as the reality and substance of things existing, does yet by the necessity of theorising unconsciously, and as it were instinctively, end in nature as an intelligence; and by this tendency the science of nature becomes finally natural philosophy, the one of the two poles of fundamental science.

2. OR THE SUBJECTIVE IS TAKEN AS THE FIRST, AND THE PROBLEM THEN IS, HOW THERE SUPERVENES TO IT A COINCIDENT OBJECTIVE.

In the pursuit of these sciences, our success in each depends on an austere and faithful adherence to its own principles with a careful separation and exclusion of those, which appertain to the opposite science. As the natural philosopher, who directs his views to the objective, avoids above all things the intermixture of the subjective in his knowledge, as for instance, arbitrary suppositions or rather suffictions, occult qualities, spiritual agents, and the substitution of final for efficient causes; so on the other hand, the transcendental or intelligential philosopher is equally anxious to preclude all interpolation of the objective into the subjective principles of his science, as for instance the assumption of impresses or configurations in the brain, correspondent to miniature pictures on the retina painted by rays of light from supposed originals, which are not the immediate and real objects of vision, but deductions from it for the purposes of explanation.

This purification of the mind is effected by an absolute and scientific scepticism to which the mind voluntarily determines itself for the specific purpose of future certainty. Des Cartes who (in his meditations) himself first, at least of the moderns, gave a beautiful example of this voluntary doubt, this self-determined indetermination, happily expresses its utter difference from the scepticism of vanity or irreligion: Nec tamen in eo scepticos imitabar, qui dubitant tantum ut dubitent, et præter incertitudinem ipsam nihil quærunt. Nam contra totus in eo eram ut aliquid certi reperirem. DES CARTES, *de Methodo*.[20] Nor is it less distinct in its motives and final aim, than in its proper objects, which are not as in ordinary scepticism the prejudices of education and circumstance, but those original and innate prejudices which nature herself has planted in all men, and which to all but the philosopher are the first principles of knowledge, and the final test of truth.

Now these essential prejudices are all reducible to the one fundamental presumption, THAT THERE EXIST THINGS WITHOUT US. As this on the one hand originates, neither in grounds nor arguments, and yet on the other hand remains proof against all attempts to remove it by grounds or arguments (*naturam furca expellas tamen usque redibit*);[21] on the one hand lays claim to IMMEDIATE certainty as a position at once indemonstrable and irresistible, and yet on the other hand, inasmuch as it refers to something essentially different from ourselves, nay even in opposition to ourselves, leaves it inconceivable how it could possibly become a part of our immediate consciousness; (in other words how that, which ex hypothesi is and continues to be extrinsic and alien to our being, should become a modification of our being) the philosopher therefore compels himself to treat this faith as nothing more than a prejudice, innate indeed and connatural, but still a prejudice.

The other position, which not only claims but necessitates the admission of its immediate certainty, equally for the scientific reason of the philosopher as for the common sense of mankind at large, namely, I AM, cannot so properly be intitled a prejudice. It is groundless indeed; but then in the very idea it precludes all ground, and separated from the immediate consciousness loses its whole sense and import. It is groundless; but only because it is itself the ground of all other certainty. Now the apparent contradiction, that the former position, namely, the existence of things with-

---

[20] Nec tamen ... reperirem: "Nor yet in this did I imitate the sceptics, who doubt as much as they may doubt, and desire nothing beyond uncertainty. But on the contrary always in my doubting I was seeking certainty." *Discourse on Method*, III.

[21] naturam ... redibit: "You may drive out nature with a fork, yet still she will return." Horace's *Epistles*, I, x, 24.

out us, which from its nature cannot be immediately certain should be received as blindly and as independently of all grounds as the existence of our own being, the transcendental philosopher can solve only by the supposition, that the former is unconsciously involved in the latter; that it is not only coherent but identical, and one and the same thing with our own immediate self-consciousness. To demonstrate this identity is the office and object of his philosophy.

If it be said, that this is Idealism, let it be remembered that it is only so far idealism, as it is at the same time, and on that very account, the truest and most binding realism. For wherein does the realism of mankind properly consist? In the assertion that there exists a something without them, what, or how, or where they know not, which occasions the objects of their perception? Oh no! This is neither connatural nor universal. It is what a few have taught and learned in the schools, and which the many repeat without asking themselves concerning their own meaning. The realism common to all mankind is far elder and lies infinitely deeper than this hypothetical explanation of the origin of our perceptions, an explanation skimmed from the mere surface of mechanical philosophy. It is the table itself, which the man of common sense believes himself to see, not the phantom of a table, from which he may argumentatively deduce the reality of a table, which he does not see. If to destroy the reality of all, that we actually behold, be idealism, what can be more egregiously so, than the system of modern metaphysics, which banishes us to a land of shadows, surrounds us with apparitions, and distinguishes truth from illusion only by the majority of those who dream the same dream? "*I* asserted that the world was mad," exclaimed poor Lee,[22] "and the world said, that I was mad, and confound them, they outvoted me."

It is to the true and original realism, that I would direct the attention. This believes and requires neither more nor less, than the object which it beholds or presents to itself, is the real and very object. In this sense, however much we may strive against it, we are all collectively born idealists, and therefore and only therefore are we at the same time realists. But of this the philosophers of the schools know nothing, or despise the faith as the prejudice of the ignorant vulgar, because they live and move in a crowd of phrases and notions from which human nature has long ago vanished. Oh, ye that reverence yourselves, and walk humbly with the divinity in your own hearts, ye are worthy of a better philosophy! Let the dead bury the dead, but do you preserve your human nature, the

depth of which was never yet fathomed by a philosophy made up of notions and mere logical entities.

In the third treatise of my *Logosophia*,[23] announced at the end of this volume, I shall give (deo volente) the demonstrations and constructions of the Dynamic Philosophy scientifically arranged. It is, according to my conviction, no other than the system of Pythagoras and of Plato revived and purified from impure mixtures. Doctrina per tot manus tradita tandem in VAPPAM desiit.[24] The science of arithmetic furnishes instances, that a rule may be useful in practical application, and for the particular purpose may be sufficiently authenticated by the result, before it has itself been fully demonstrated. It is enough, if only it be rendered intelligible. This will, I trust, have been effected in the following Theses for those of my readers, who are willing to accompany me through the following Chapter, in which the results will be applied to the deduction of the imagination, and with it the principles of production and of genial criticism in the fine arts.

THESIS I.

Truth is correlative to being. Knowledge without a correspondent reality is no knowledge; if we know, there must be somewhat known by us. To know is in its very essence a verb active.

THESIS II.

All truth is either mediate, that is, derived from some other truth or truths; or immediate and original. The latter is absolute, and its formula A. A.; the former is of dependent or conditional certainty, and represented in the formula B. A. The certainty, which adheres in A, is attributable to B.

SCHOLIUM. A chain without a staple, from which all the links derived their stability, or a series without a first, has been not inaptly allegorized, as a string of blind men, each holding the skirt of the man before him, reaching far out of sight, but all moving without the least deviation in one strait line. It would be naturally taken for granted, that there was a guide at the head of the file: what if it were answered, No! Sir, the men are without number, and infinite blindness supplies the place of sight?

Equally *inconceivable* is a cycle of equal truths without a common and central principle, which prescribes

---

[22] Nathaniel Lee (*c.* 1653–1692) was a Restoration playwright, who was confined in a madhouse from 1683 to 1689.

[23] Referring to Coleridge's long-promised but never completed major philosophic work. See the later reference to "the principal Labour of my Life since Manhood" in *Aids to Reflection*, p. 265.

[24] Doctrina . . . desiit: "Doctrine passed through so many hands finally ends up as stale wine."

to each its proper sphere in the system of science. That the absurdity does not so immediately strike us, that it does not seem equally *unimaginable*, is owing to a surreptitious act of the imagination, which, instinctively and without our noticing the same, not only fills up the intervening spaces, and contemplates the *cycle* (of B. C. D. E. F. &c.) as a continuous *circle* (A.) giving to all collectively the unity of their common orbit; but likewise supplies by a sort of *subintelligitur* the one central power, which renders the movement harmonious and cyclical.

THESIS III.

We are to seek therefore for some absolute truth capable of communicating to other positions a certainty, which it has not itself borrowed; a truth self-grounded, unconditional and known by its own light. In short, we have to find a somewhat which *is*, simply because it *is*. In order to be such, it must be one which is its own predicate, so far at least that all other nominal predicates must be modes and repetitions of itself. Its existence too must be such, as to preclude the possibility of requiring a cause or antecedent without an absurdity.

THESIS IV.

That there can be but one such principle, may be proved a priori; for were there two or more, each must refer to some other, by which its equality is affirmed; consequently neither would be self-established, as the hypothesis demands. And a posteriori, it will be proved by the principle itself when it is discovered, as involving universal antecedents in its very conception.

SCHOLIUM. If we affirm of a board that it is blue, the predicate (blue) is accidental, and not implied in the subject, board. If we affirm of a circle that it is equi-radial, the predicate indeed is implied in the definition of the subject; but the existence of the subject itself is contingent, and supposes both a cause and a percipient. The same reasoning will apply to the indefinite number of supposed indemonstrable truths exempted from the prophane approach of philosophic investigation by the amiable Beattie,[25] and other less eloquent and not more profound inaugurators of common sense on the throne of philosophy; a fruitless attempt, were it only that it is the two-fold function

of philosophy to reconcile reason with common sense, and to elevate common sense into reason.

THESIS V.

Such a principle cannot be any THING or OBJECT. Each thing is what it is in consequence of some other thing. An infinite, independent * *thing*, is no less a contradiction, than an infinite circle or a sideless triangle. Besides a thing is that, which is capable of being an object of which itself is not the sole percipient. But an object is inconceivable without a subject as its antithesis. Omne perceptum percipientem supponit.[26]

But neither can the principle be found in a subject as a subject, contra-distinguished from an object: for unicuique percipienti aliquid objicitur perceptum.[27] It is to be found therefore neither in object nor subject taken separately, and consequently, as no other third is conceivable, it must be found in that which is neither subject nor object exclusively, but which is the identity of both.

THESIS VI.

This principle, and so characterised, manifests itself in the SUM or I AM; which I shall hereafter indiscriminately express by the words spirit, self, and self-consciousness. In this, and in this alone, object and subject, being and knowing are identical, each involving and supposing the other. In other words, it is a subject which becomes a subject by the act of constructing itself objectively to itself; but which never is an object except for itself, and only so far as by the very same act it becomes a subject. It may be described therefore as a perpetual self-duplication of one and the same power into object and subject, which presuppose each other, and can exist only as antitheses.

SCHOLIUM. If a man be asked how he *knows* that he is? he can only answer, sum quia sum. But if (the absoluteness of this certainty having been admitted) he be again asked, how he, the individual person, came to be, then in relation to the ground of his *existence*, not to the ground of his *knowledge* of that existence, he might reply, sum quia deus est, or still more philosophically, sum quia in deo sum.

But if we elevate our conception to the absolute self, the great eternal I AM, then the principle of being, and

---

* The impossibility of an absolute thing (substantia unica) as neither genus, species, nor individuum: as well as its utter unfitness for the fundamental position of a philosophic system will be demonstrated in the critique on Spinozism in the fifth treatise of my Logosophia.

---

[26] Omne perceptum ... supponit: "Every thing perceived presupposes the act of perception."
[27] unicuique ... perceptum: "To every one who perceives something is presented as perceived."

---

[25] James Beattie (1735–1803) was professor of moral philosophy at Marischal College, Aberdeen, and the author of the popular poem *The Minstrel* (1771–1774). Coleridge here refers to his *An Essay on the Nature and Immutability of Truth* (1770), which sought to answer the complex doubts and arguments of "Sophists" and "Sceptics" by appealing to "Common Sense" as the "fixed and invariable standard" of truth.

of knowledge, of idea, and of reality; the ground of existence, and the ground of the knowledge of existence are absolutely identical, Sum quia sum;* I am, because I affirm myself to be; I affirm myself to be, because I am.

THESIS VII.

If then I know myself only through myself, it is contradictory to require any other predicate of self, but that of self-consciousness. Only in the self-consciousness of a spirit is there the required identity of object and of representation; for herein consists the essence of a spirit, that it is self-representative. If therefore this be the one only immediate truth, in the certainty of which the reality of our collective knowledge is grounded, it must follow that the spirit in all the objects which it views, views only itself. If this could be proved, the immediate reality of all intuitive knowledge would be assured. It has been shown, that a spirit is that, which is its own object, yet not originally an object, but an absolute subject for which all, itself included, may

* It is most worthy of notice, that in the first revelation of himself, not confined to individuals; indeed in the very first revelation of his absolute being, Jehovah at the same time revealed the fundamental truth of all philosophy, which must either commence with the absolute, or have no fixed commencement; i.e., cease to be philosophy. I cannot but express my regret, that in the equivocal use of the word *that*, for *in that*, or *because*, our admirable version has rendered the passage susceptible of a degraded interpretation in the mind of common readers or hearers, as if it were a mere reproof to an impertinent question, I am what I am, which might be equally affirmed of himself by any existent being.

The Cartesian *Cogito, ergo sum* is objectionable, because either the *Cogito* is used extra Gradum, and then it is involved in the *sum* and is tautological, or it is taken as a particular mode or dignity, and then it is subordinated to the *sum* as the species to the genus, or rather as a particular modification to the subject modified; and not pre-ordinated as the arguments seem to require. For *Cogito* is *Sum Cogitans.* This is clear by the inevidence of the converse. *Cogitat ergo est* is true, because it is a mere application of the logical rule: *Quicquid in genere est, est et in species. Est (cogitans), ergo est.* It is a cherry tree; therefore it is a tree. But, *est ergo cogitat*, is illogical: for quod est in specie, non *necessario* in genere est. It may be true. I hold it to be true, that *quicquid vere est, est per veram sui affirmationem*; but it is a derivative, not an immediate truth. Here then we have, by anticipation the distinction between the conditional finite I (which as known in distinct consciousness by occasion of experience is called by Kant's followers the empirical I) and the absolute I AM, and likewise the dependence or rather the inherence of the former in the latter; in whom "we live, and move, and have our being," as St. Paul divinely asserts, differing widely from the Theists of the mechanic school (as Sir J. Newton, Locke, &c.) who must say from *whom* we *had* our being, and with it life and the powers of life.[28]

<hr />

[28] The reference to St. Paul is from Acts, xvii, 28.

become an object. It must therefore be an ACT; for every object is, as an *object*, dead, fixed, incapable in itself of any action, and necessarily finite. Again the spirit (originally the identity of object and subject) must in some sense dissolve this identity, in order to be conscious of it: fit alter et idem. But this implies an act, and it follows therefore that intelligence or self-consciousness is impossible, except by and in a will. The self-conscious spirit therefore is a will; and freedom must be assumed as a *ground* of philosophy, and can never be deduced from it.

THESIS VIII.

Whatever in its origin is objective, is likewise as such necessarily finite. Therefore, since the spirit is not originally an object, and as the subject exists in antithesis to an object, the spirit cannot originally be finite. But neither can it be a subject without becoming an object, and as it is originally the identity of both, it can be conceived neither as infinite nor finite exclusively, but as the most original union of both. In the existence, in the reconciling, and the recurrence of this contradiction consists the process and mystery of production and life.

THESIS IX.

This principium commune essendi et cognoscendi, as subsisting in a WILL, or primary ACT of self-duplication, is the mediate or indirect principle of every science; but it is the immediate and direct principle of the ultimate science alone, i.e. of transcendental philosophy alone. For it must be remembered, that all these Theses refer solely to one of the two Polar Sciences, namely, to that which commences with and rigidly confines itself within the subjective, leaving the objective (as far as it is exclusively objective) to natural philosophy, which is its opposite pole. In its very idea therefore as a systematic knowledge of our collective KNOWING, (scientia scientiæ) it involves the necessity of some one highest principle of knowing, as at once the source and accompanying form in all particular acts of intellect and perception. This, it has been shown, can be found only in the act and evolution of self-consciousness. We are not investigating an absolute principium essendi; for then, I admit, many valid objections might be started against our theory; but an absolute principium cognoscendi. The result of both the sciences, or their equatorial point, would be the principle of a total and undivided philosophy, as for prudential reasons, I have chosen to anticipate in the Scholium to Thesis VI. and the note subjoined. In other words, philosophy would pass into religion, and religion become inclusive of philosophy. We begin with the I KNOW MYSELF, in order to end with the absolute I AM. We proceed from the SELF, in order to lose and find all self in GOD.

THESIS X.

The transcendental philosopher does not enquire, what ultimate ground of our knowledge there may lie out of our knowing, but what is the last in our knowing itself, beyond which *we* cannot pass. The principle of our knowing is sought within the sphere of our knowing. It must be something therefore, which can itself be known. It is asserted only, that the act of self-consciousness is for *us* the source and principle of all *our* possible knowledge. Whether abstracted from us there exists any thing higher and beyond this primary self-knowing, which is for us the form of all our knowing, must be decided by the result.

That the self-consciousness is the fixt point, to which for *us* all is morticed and annexed, needs no further proof. But that the self-consciousness may be the modification of a higher form of being, perhaps of a higher consciousness, and this again of a yet higher, and so on in an infinite regressus; in short, that self-consciousness may be itself something explicable into something, which must lie beyond the possibility of our knowledge, because the whole synthesis of our intelligence is first formed in and through the self-consciousness, does not at all concern us as transcendental philosophers. For to us self-consciousness is not a kind of *being*, but a kind of *knowing*, and that too the highest and farthest that exists for *us*. It may however be shown, and has in part already been shown in pages 186–187, that even when the Objective is assumed as the first, we yet can never pass beyond the principle of self-consciousness. Should we attempt it, we must be driven back from ground to ground, each of which would cease to be a Ground the moment we pressed on it. We must be whirl'd down the gulf of an infinite series. But this would make our reason baffle the end and purpose of all reason, namely, unity and system. Or we must break off the series arbitrarily, and affirm an absolute something that is in and of itself at once cause and effect (*causa sui*), subject and object, or rather the absolute identity of both. But as this is inconceivable, except in a self-consciousness, it follows, that even as natural philosophers we must arrive at the same principle from which as transcendental philosophers we set out; that is, in a self-consciousness in which the principium essendi does not stand to the principium cognoscendi in the relation of cause to effect, but both the one and the other are co-inherent and identical. Thus the true system of natural philosophy places the sole reality of things in an ABSOLUTE, which is at once causa sui et

effectus, πατὴρ αὐτοπάτωρ, υἱὸς ἑαυτοῦ[29]—in the absolute identity of subject and object, which it calls nature, and which in its highest power is nothing else but self-conscious will or intelligence. In this sense the position of Malbranche,[30] that we see all things in God, is a strict philosophical truth; and equally true is the assertion of Hobbes, of Hartley, and of their masters in ancient Greece, that all real knowledge supposes a prior sensation. For sensation itself is but vision nascent, not the cause of intelligence, but intelligence itself revealed as an earlier power in the process of self-construction.

> Μάκαρ, ἵλαθί μοι·!
> Πάτερ, ἵλαθί μοι
> Εἰ παρὰ κόσμον,
> Εἰ παρὰ μοῖραν
> Τῶν σῶν ἔθιγον![31]

Bearing then this in mind, that intelligence is a self-developement, not a quality supervening to a substance, we may abstract from all *degree*, and for the purpose of philosophic construction reduce it to *kind*, under the idea of an indestructible power with two opposite and counteracting forces, which by a metaphor borrowed from astronomy, we may call the centrifugal and centripetal forces. The intelligence in the one tends to *objectize* itself, and in the other to *know* itself in the object. It will be hereafter my business to construct by a series of intuitions the progressive schemes, that must follow from such a power with such forces, till I arrive at the fulness of the *human* intelligence. For my present purpose, I *assume* such a power as my principle, in order to deduce from it a faculty, the generation, agency, and application of which form the contents of the ensuing chapter.

*   *   *   *   *

I shall now proceed to the nature and genesis of the imagination; but I must first take leave to notice, that after a more accurate perusal of Mr. Wordsworth's remarks on the imagination, in his preface to the new edition of his poems, I find that my conclusions are not so consentient with his as I confess, I had taken for granted. In an article contributed by me to Mr. Southey's Omniana,[32] on the soul and its organs of

---

[29] πατὴρ . . . ἑαυτοῦ: "father self-engendered, son of himself."

[30] Nicole Malbranche (1638–1715) was a French Cartesian philosopher. Coleridge refers to his *De la Recherche de la Vérité* (1674), III, ii, 6.

[31] Synesius, *Hymns*, iii, 113–117. "Be full of goodness unto me, Blessed One, be full of goodness unto me, Father, if beyond what is ordered, if beyond what is destined, I touch upon that which is Thine."

[32] *Omniana* (1812) was a collection of short essays and comments on various subjects by Coleridge and Southey. The article referred to is No. 174, in Volume II, 13–14.

sense, are the following sentences. "These (the human faculties) I would arrange under the different senses and powers; as the eye, the ear, the touch, &c.; the imitative power, voluntary and automatic; the imagination, or shaping and modifying power; the fancy, or the aggregative and associative power; the understanding, or the regulative, substantiating and realizing power; the speculative reason, — vis theoretica et scientifica, or the power by which we produce, or aim to produce unity, necessity, and universality in all our knowledge by means of principles a priori;* the will, or practical reason; the faculty of choice (*Germanice*, Willkühr) and (distinct both from the moral will and the choice) the *sensation* of volition, which I have found reason to include under the head of single and double touch." To this, as far as it relates to the subject in question, namely the words (*the aggregative and associative power*) Mr. Wordsworth's "only objection is that the definition is too general. To aggregate and to associate, to evoke and to combine, belong as well to the imagination as to the fancy." [33] I reply, that if by the power of evoking and combining, Mr. W. means the same as, and no more than, I meant by the aggregative and associative, I continue to deny, that it belongs at all to the imagination; and I am disposed to conjecture, that he has mistaken the co-presence of fancy with imagination for the operation of the latter singly. A man may work with two very different tools at the same moment; each has its share in the work, but the work effected by each is distinct and different. But it will probably appear in the next Chapter, that deeming it necessary to go back much further than Mr. Wordsworth's subject required or permitted, I have attached a meaning to both fancy and imagination, which he had not in view, at least while he was writing that preface. He will judge. Would to Heaven, I might meet with many such readers. I will conclude with the words of Bishop Jeremy Taylor: he to whom all things are one, who draweth all things to one, and seeth all things in one, may enjoy true peace and rest of spirit. (*J. Taylor's* VIA PACIS).[34]

* This phrase, *a priori*, is in common most grossly misunderstood, and an absurdity burthened on it, which it does not deserve! By knowledge, *a priori*, we do not mean, that we can know anything previously to experience, which would be a contradiction in terms; but that having once known it by occasion of experience (i.e. something acting upon us from without) we then know, that it must have pre-existed, or the experience itself would have been impossible. By experience only I know, that I have eyes; but then my reason convinces me, that I must have had eyes in order to the experience.

---

[33] See Wordsworth's "Preface to *Poems*" (1815), p. 75.
[34] Coleridge quotes from "Sunday," the First Decad. 8, of *Via Pacis*, a section from Taylor's *The Golden Grove; or, a Manual of Daily Prayers and Litanies* (1655).

FROM
CHAPTER XIII

On the imagination, or esemplastic[1] power

*   *   *   *   *

THE IMAGINATION then I consider either as primary, or secondary. The primary IMAGINATION I hold to be the living Power and prime Agent of all human Perception, and as a repetition in the finite mind of the eternal act of creation in the infinite I AM. The secondary I consider as an echo of the former, co-existing with the conscious will, yet still as identical with the primary in the *kind* of its agency, and differing only in *degree*, and in the *mode* of its operation. It dissolves, diffuses, dissipates, in order to re-create; or where this process is rendered impossible, yet still at all events it struggles to idealize and to unify. It is essentially *vital*, even as all objects (*as* objects) are essentially fixed and dead.

FANCY, on the contrary, has no other counters to play with, but fixities and definites. The Fancy is indeed no other than a mode of Memory emancipated from the order of time and space; and blended with, and modified by that empirical phenomenon of the will, which we express by the word CHOICE. But equally with the ordinary memory it must receive all its materials ready made from the law of association. . . .

CHAPTER XIV

Occasion of the Lyrical Ballads, and the objects originally proposed—Preface to the second edition—The ensuing controversy, its causes and acrimony—Philosophic definitions of a poem and poetry with scholia.

DURING the first year that Mr. Wordsworth and I were neighbours, our conversations turned frequently on the two cardinal points of poetry, the power of exciting the sympathy of the reader by a faithful adherence to the truth of nature, and the power of giving the interest of novelty by the modifying colours of imagination. The sudden charm, which accidents of light and shade, which moon-light or sun-set diffused over a known and familiar landscape, appeared to represent the practicability of combining both. These are the poetry of nature. The thought suggested itself (to which of us I do not recollect) that a series of poems might be composed of two sorts. In the one, the incidents and agents were to be, in part at least, supernatural; and the excellence aimed at was to consist in the interesting of the affections by the dramatic truth

---

[1] To shape into one.

of such emotions, as would naturally accompany such situations, supposing them real. And real in *this* sense they have been to every human being who, from whatever source of delusion, has at any time believed himself under supernatural agency. For the second class, subjects were to be chosen from ordinary life; the characters and incidents were to be such, as will be found in every village and its vicinity, where there is a meditative and feeling mind to seek after them, or to notice them, when they present themselves.

In this idea originated the plan of the "Lyrical Ballads;" in which it was agreed, that my endeavours should be directed to persons and characters supernatural, or at least romantic; yet so as to transfer from our inward nature a human interest and a semblance of truth sufficient to procure for these shadows of imagination that willing suspension of disbelief for the moment, which constitutes poetic faith. Mr. Wordsworth, on the other hand, was to propose to himself as his object, to give the charm of novelty to things of every day, and to excite a feeling analogous to the supernatural, by awakening the mind's attention from the lethargy of custom, and directing it to the loveliness and the wonders of the world before us; an inexhaustible treasure, but for which in consequence of the film of familiarity and selfish solicitude we have eyes, yet see not, ears that hear not, and hearts that neither feel nor understand.

With this view I wrote the "Ancient Mariner," and was preparing among other poems, the "Dark Ladie,"[1] and the "Christabel," in which I should have more nearly realized my ideal, than I had done in my first attempt. But Mr. Wordsworth's industry had proved so much more successful, and the number of his poems so much greater, that my compositions, instead of forming a balance, appeared rather an interpolation of heterogeneous matter. Mr. Wordsworth added two or three poems written in his own character,[2] in the impassioned, lofty, and sustained diction, which is characteristic of his genius. In this form the "Lyrical Ballads" were published; and were presented by him, as an *experiment*, whether subjects, which from their nature rejected the usual ornaments and extra-colloquial style of poems in general, might not be so managed in the language of ordinary life as to produce the pleasureable interest, which it is the peculiar business of poetry to impart. To the second edition he added a preface of considerable length; in which not-

withstanding some passages of apparently a contrary import, he was understood to contend for the extension of this style to poetry of all kinds, and to reject as vicious and indefensible all phrases and forms of style that were not included in what he (unfortunately, I think, adopting an equivocal expression) called the language of *real* life. From this preface, prefixed to poems in which it was impossible to deny the presence of original genius, however mistaken its direction might be deemed, arose the whole long continued controversy. For from the conjunction of perceived power with supposed heresy I explain the inveteracy and in some instances, I grieve to say, the acrimonious passions, with which the controversy has been conducted by the assailants.

Had Mr. Wordsworth's poems been the silly, the childish things, which they were for a long time described as being; had they been really distinguished from the compositions of other poets merely by meanness of language and inanity of thought; had they indeed contained nothing more than what is found in the parodies and pretended imitations of them; they must have sunk at once, a dead weight, into the slough of oblivion, and have dragged the preface along with them. But year after year increased the number of Mr. Wordsworth's admirers. They were found too not in the lower classes of the reading public, but chiefly among young men of strong sensibility and meditative minds; and their admiration (inflamed perhaps in some degree by opposition) was distinguished by its intensity, I might almost say, by its *religious* fervour. These facts, and the intellectual energy of the author, which was more or less consciously felt, where it was outwardly and even boisterously denied, meeting with sentiments of aversion to his opinions, and of alarm at their consequences, produced an eddy of criticism, which would of itself have borne up the poems by the violence, with which it whirled them round and round. With many parts of this preface in the sense attributed to them and which the words undoubtedly seem to authorise, I never concurred; but on the contrary objected to them as erroneous in principle, and as contradictory (in appearance at least) both to other parts of the same preface, and to the author's own practice in the greater number of the poems themselves. Mr. Wordsworth in his recent collection[3] has, I find, degraded this prefatory disquisition to the end of his second volume, to be read or not at the reader's choice. But he has not, as far as I can discover, announced any change in his poetic creed. All all events, considering it as the source of a controversy, in which I have been

---

[1] The "Ballad of the Dark Ladie" was first published as "A Fragment" in the collected edition of Coleridge's poems in 1834. "Introduction to the Tale of the Dark Ladie" had appeared in the *Morning Post* in 1799, with a shorter version entitled "Love" in the 1800 edition of *Lyrical Ballads*.
[2] Most notably "Tintern Abbey."

---

[3] The two-volume edition of *Poems* of 1815.

honored more, than I deserve, by the frequent conjunction of my name with his, I think it expedient to
declare once for all, in what points I coincide with his
opinions, and in what points I altogether differ. But in
order to render myself intelligible I must previously,
in as few words as possible, explain my ideas, first, of a
POEM; and secondly, of POETRY itself, in *kind*, and in
essence.

The office of philosophical *disquisition* consists in
just *distinction*; while it is the priviledge of the philosopher to preserve himself constantly aware, that distinction is not division. In order to obtain adequate
notions of any truth, we must intellectually separate its
distinguishable parts; and this is the technical *process*
of philosophy. But having so done, we must then
restore them in our conceptions to the unity, in which
they actually co-exist; and this is the *result* of philosophy. A poem contains the same elements as a prose
composition; the difference therefore must consist in a
different combination of them, in consequence of a
different object proposed. According to the difference
of the object will be the difference of the combination.
It is possible, that the object may be merely to facilitate
the recollection of any given facts or observations by
artificial arrangement; and the composition will be a
poem, merely because it is distinguished from prose by
metre, or by rhyme, or by both conjointly. In this, the
lowest sense, a man might attribute the name of a
poem to the well known enumeration of the days in the
several months:

> "Thirty days hath September,
> April, June, and November, &c."

and others of the same class and purpose. And as a
particular pleasure is found in anticipating the recurrence of sounds and quantities, all compositions that
have this charm superadded, whatever be their contents, *may* be entitled poems.

So much for the superficial *form*. A difference of
object and contents supplies an additional ground of
distinction. The immediate purpose may be the communication of truths; either of truth absolute and
demonstrable, as in works of science; or of facts experienced and recorded, as in history. Pleasure, and
that of the highest and most permanent kind, may
result from the *attainment* of the end; but it is not itself
the immediate end. In other works the communication
of pleasure may be the immediate purpose; and though
truth, either moral or intellectual, ought to be the
ultimate end, yet this will distinguish the character of
the author, not the class to which the work belongs.
Blest indeed is that state of society, in which the immediate purpose would be baffled by the perversion of
the proper ultimate end; in which no charm of diction

or imagery could exempt the Bathyllus even of an
Anacreon, or the Alexis of Virgil, from disgust and
aversion![4]

But the communication of pleasure may be the immediate object of a work not metrically composed; and
that object may have been in a high degree attained, as
in novels and romances. Would then the mere super-
addition of metre, with or without rhyme, entitle *these*
to the name of poems? The answer is, that nothing can
permanently please, which does not contain in itself
the reason why it is so, and not otherwise. If metre be
superadded, all other parts must be made consonant
with it. They must be such, as to justify the perpetual
and distinct attention to each part, which an exact
correspondent recurrence of accent and sound are
calculated to excite. The final definition then, so deduced, may be thus worded. A poem is that species of
composition, which is opposed to works of science, by
proposing for its *immediate* object pleasure, not truth;
and from all other species (having *this* object in common with it) it is discriminated by proposing to itself
such delight from the *whole*, as is compatible with a
distinct gratification from each component *part*.

Controversy is not seldom excited in consequence of
the disputants attaching each a different meaning to
the same word; and in few instances has this been more
striking, than in disputes concerning the present subject. If a man chooses to call every composition a poem,
which is rhyme, or measure, or both, I must leave his
opinion uncontroverted. The distinction is at least
competent to characterize the writer's intention. If it
were subjoined, that the whole is likewise entertaining
or affecting, as a tale, or as a series of interesting reflections, I of course admit this as another fit ingredient
of a poem, and an additional merit. But if the definition
sought for be that of a *legitimate* poem, I answer, it
must be one, the parts of which mutually support and
explain each other; all in their proportion harmonizing
with, and supporting the purpose and known influences
of metrical arrangement. The philosophic critics of all
ages coincide with the ultimate judgement of all
countries, in equally denying the praises of a just poem,
on the one hand, to a series of striking lines or distichs,
each of which absorbing the whole attention of the
reader to itself disjoins it from its context, and makes
it a separate whole, instead of an harmonizing part;
and on the other hand, to an unsustained composition,

---

4 Bathyllus (in various odes by Anacreon) and Alexis (in
Virgil's Second Eclogue) were handsome youths, objects of
homosexual attraction. Coleridge's point is that in a healthy
society, the immediate purpose of giving pleasure through diction
and imagery would be frustrated by the reader's sense of the
moral unsoundness of the ultimate end, a celebration of homosexual love.

from which the reader collects rapidly the general result unattracted by the component parts. The reader should be carried forward, not merely or chiefly by the mechanical impulse of curiosity, or by a restless desire to arrive at the final solution; but by the pleasureable activity of mind excited by the attractions of the journey itself. Like the motion of a serpent, which the Egyptians made the emblem of intellectual power; or like the path of sound through the air; at every step he pauses and half recedes, and from the retrogressive movement collects the force which again carries him onward. *Precipitandus est liber spiritus*, says Petronius Arbiter[5] most happily. The epithet, *liber*, here balances the preceding verb; and it is not easy to conceive more meaning condensed in fewer words.

But if this should be admitted as a satisfactory character of a poem, we have still to seek for a definition of poetry. The writings of PLATO, and Bishop TAYLOR, and the Theoria Sacra of BURNET,[6] furnish undeniable proofs that poetry of the highest kind may exist without metre, and even without the contra-distinguishing objects of a poem. The first chapter of Isaiah (indeed a very large proportion of the whole book) is poetry in the most emphatic sense; yet it would be not less irrational than strange to assert, that pleasure, and not truth, was the immediate object of the prophet. In short, whatever *specific* import we attach to the word, poetry, there will be found involved in it, as a necessary consequence, that a poem of any length neither can be, or ought to be, all poetry. Yet if an harmonious whole is to be produced, the remaining parts must be preserved *in keeping* with the poetry; and this can be no otherwise effected than by such a studied selection and artificial arrangement, as will partake of *one*, though not a *peculiar*, property of poetry. And this again can be no other than the property of exciting a more continuous and equal attention, than the language of prose aims at, whether colloquial or written.

My own conclusions on the nature of poetry, in the strictest use of the word, have been in part anticipated in the preceding disquisition on the fancy and imagination. What is poetry? is so nearly the same question with, what is a poet? that the answer to the one is involved in the solution of the other. For it is a distinction resulting from the poetic genius itself, which sustains and modifies the images, thoughts, and emotions of the poet's own mind. The poet, described in *ideal* perfection, brings the whole soul of man into activity, with the subordination of its faculties to each other, according to their relative worth and dignity. He diffuses a tone, and spirit of unity, that blends, and (as it were) *fuses*, each into each, by that synthetic and magical power, to which we have exclusively appropriated the name of imagination. This power, first put in action by the will and understanding, and retained under their irremissive, though gentle and unnoticed, controul (*laxis effertur habenis*)[7] reveals itself in the balance or reconciliation of opposite or discordant qualities: of sameness, with difference; of the general, with the concrete; the idea, with the image; the individual, with the representative; the sense of novelty and freshness, with old and familiar objects; a more than usual state of emotion, with more than usual order; judgement ever awake and steady self-possession, with enthusiasm and feeling profound or vehement; and while it blends and harmonizes the natural and the artificial, still subordinates art to nature; the manner to the matter; and our admiration of the poet to our sympathy with the poetry. "Doubtless," as Sir John Davies[8] observes of the soul (and his words may with slight alteration be applied, and even more appropriately to the poetic IMAGINATION.)

"Doubtless this could not be, but that she turns
Bodies to spirit by sublimation strange,
As fire converts to fire the things it burns,
As we our food into our nature change.

From their gross matter she abstracts their forms,
And draws a kind of quintessence from things;
Which to her proper nature she transforms
To bear them light, on her celestial wings.

Thus does she, when from individual states
She doth abstract the universal kinds;
Which then re-clothed in divers names and fates
Steal access through our senses to our minds."

Finally, GOOD SENSE is the BODY of poetic genius, FANCY its DRAPERY, MOTION its LIFE, and IMAGINATION the SOUL that is every where, and in each; and forms all into one graceful and intelligent whole.

---

5 *Precipitandus . . . spiritus:* "The *free* spirit must be hurried onward." Petronius' *Satyricon,* l. 118.

6 Jeremy Taylor (1613–1667), an Anglican divine, was the author of "Holy Living" and "Holy Dying" and other prose works much admired by the Romantics. *Telluris Theoria Sacra* (1681–1689) was a richly imaginative account of the formation of the earth by Thomas Burnet (c. 1635–1715). Coleridge had proposed translating Burnet's work into blank verse in 1795–1796.

7 *laxis effertur habenis:* "It is propelled with loosened reins." See Virgil's *Georgics,* II, 364.

8 Coleridge quotes from "Of the Soule of Man, and the immortalitie thereof," stanzas 91–93, in *Nosce Teipsum* (1599) by Sir John Davies (c. 1569–1626).

CHAPTER XV

The specific symptoms of poetic power elucidated in a critical analysis of Shakspeare's Venus and Adonis, and Lucrece.

IN THE application of these principles to purposes of practical criticism as employed in the appraisal of works more or less imperfect, I have endeavoured to discover what the qualities in a poem are, which may be deemed promises and specific symptoms of poetic power, as distinguished from general talent determined to poetic composition by accidental motives, by an act of the will, rather than by the inspiration of a genial and productive nature. In this investigation, I could not, I thought, do better, than keep before me the earliest work of the greatest genius, that perhaps human nature has yet produced, our *myriad-minded* * Shakspeare. I mean the "Venus and Adonis," and the "Lucrece;" works which give at once strong promises of the strength, and yet obvious proofs of the immaturity, of his genius. From these I abstracted the following marks, as characteristics of original poetic genius in general.

1. In the "Venus and Adonis," the first and most obvious excellence is the perfect sweetness of the versification; its adaptation to the subject; and the power displayed in varying the march of the words without passing into a loftier and more majestic rhythm, than was demanded by the thoughts, or permitted by the propriety of preserving a sense of melody predominant. The delight in richness and sweetness of sound, even to a faulty excess, if it be evidently original, and not the result of an easily imitable mechanism, I regard as a highly favorable promise in the compositions of a young man. "The man that hath not music in his soul" [1] can indeed never be a genuine poet. Imagery (even taken from nature, much more when transplanted from books, as travels, voyages, and works of natural history); affecting incidents; just thoughts; interesting personal or domestic feelings; and with these the art of their combination or intertexture in the form of a poem; may all by incessant effort be acquired as a trade, by a man of talents and much reading, who, as I once before observed, has mistaken an intense desire of poetic reputation for a natural poetic genius; the love of the arbitrary end for a possession of the peculiar means. But the sense of

musical delight, with the power of producing it, is a gift of imagination; and this together with the power of reducing multitude into unity of effect, and modifying a series of thoughts by some one predominant thought or feeling, may be cultivated and improved, but can never be learnt. It is in these that "Poeta nascitur non fit." [2]

2. A second promise of genius is the choice of subjects very remote from the private interests and circumstances of the writer himself. At least I have found, that where the subject is taken immediately from the author's personal sensations and experiences, the excellence of a particular poem is but an equivocal mark, and often a fallacious pledge, of genuine poetic power. We may perhaps remember the tale of the statuary, who had acquired considerable reputation for the legs of his goddesses, though the rest of the statue accorded but indifferently with ideal beauty; till his wife elated by her husband's praises, modestly acknowledged, that she herself had been his constant model. In the Venus and Adonis, this proof of poetic power exists even to excess. It is throughout as if a superior spirit more intuitive, more intimately conscious, even than the characters themselves, not only of every outward look and act, but of the flux and reflux of the mind in all its subtlest thoughts and feelings, were placing the whole before our view; himself meanwhile unparticipating in the passions, and actuated only by that pleasurable excitement, which had resulted from the energetic fervor of his own spirit in so vividly exhibiting, what it had so accurately and profoundly contemplated. I think, I should have conjectured from these poems, that even then the great instinct, which impelled the poet to the drama, was secretly working in him, prompting him by a series and never broken chain of imagery, always vivid and because unbroken, often minute; by the highest effort of the picturesque in words, of which words are capable, higher perhaps than was ever realized by any other poet, even Dante not excepted; to provide a substitute for that visual language, that constant intervention and running comment by tone, look and gesture, which in his dramatic works he was entitled to expect from the players. His "Venus and Adonis" seem at once the characters themselves, and the whole representation of those characters by the most consummate actors. You seem to be *told* nothing, but to see and hear every thing. Hence it is, that from the perpetual activity of attention required on the part of the reader; from the rapid flow, the quick change, and the playful nature of the thoughts and images; and above all from the alienation, and, if I

---

* Ἀνὴρ μυριονοῦς, a phrase which I have borrowed from a Greek monk, who applies it to a Patriarch of Constantinople. I might have said, that I have *reclaimed*, rather than borrowed it: for it seems to belong to Shakspeare, de jure singulari, et ex privilegio naturae.

[1] *Merchant of Venice*, V, i, 83.

[2] Poeta ... fit: "A poet is born, not made."

may hazard such an expression, the utter *aloofness* of the poet's own feelings, from those of which he is at once the painter and the analyst; that though the very subject cannot but detract from the pleasure of a delicate mind, yet never was poem less dangerous on a moral account. Instead of doing as Ariosto, and as, still more offensively, Wieland[3] has done, instead of degrading and deforming passion into appetite, the trials of love into the struggles of concupiscence; Shakspeare has here represented the animal impulse itself, so as to preclude all sympathy with it, by dissipating the reader's notice among the thousand outward images, and now beautiful, now fanciful circumstances, which form its dresses and its scenery; or by diverting our attention from the main subject by those frequent witty or profound reflections, which the poet's ever active mind has deduced from, or connected with, the imagery and the incidents. The reader is forced into too much action to sympathize with the merely passive of our nature. As little can a mind thus roused and awakened be brooded on by mean and indistinct emotion, as the low, lazy mist can creep upon the surface of a lake, while a strong gale is driving it onward in waves and billows.

3. It has been before observed, that images however beautiful, though faithfully copied from nature, and as accurately represented in words, do not of themselves characterize the poet. They become proofs of original genius only as far as they are modified by a predominant passion; or by associated thoughts or images awakened by that passion; or when they have the effect of reducing multitude to unity, or succession to an instant; or lastly, when a human and intellectual life is transferred to them from the poet's own spirit,

"Which shoots its being through earth, sea, and air."[4]

In the two following lines for instance, there is nothing objectionable, nothing which would preclude them from forming, in their proper place, part of a descriptive poem:

"Behold yon row of pines, that shorn and bow'd
Bend from the sea-blast, seen at twilight eve."

But with the small alteration of rhythm, the same words would be equally in their place in a book of topography, or in a descriptive tour. The same image will rise into a semblance of poetry if thus conveyed:

"Yon row of bleak and visionary pines,
By twilight-glimpse discerned, mark! how they flee
From the fierce sea-blast, all their tresses wild
Streaming before them."

I have given this as an illustration, by no means as an instance, of that particular excellence which I had in view, and in which Shakspeare even in his earliest, as in his latest works, surpasses all other poets. It is by this, that he still gives a dignity and a passion to the objects which he presents. Unaided by any previous excitement, they burst upon us at once in life and in power.

"Full many a glorious morning have I seen
Flatter the mountain tops with sovereign eye."
                              Shakspeare's Sonnet 33rd.

"Not mine own fears, nor the prophetic soul
Of the wide world dreaming on things to come—
* * * * * * * * * * * * * *
* * * * * * * * * * * * * *
The mortal moon hath her eclipse endur'd,
And the sad augurs mock their own presage;
Incertainties now crown themselves assur'd,
And Peace proclaims olives of endless age.
Now with the drops of this most balmy time
My Love looks fresh: and DEATH to me subscribes!
Since spite of him, I'll live in this poor rhyme,
While he insults o'er dull and speechless tribes.
And thou in this shalt find thy monument,
When tyrant's crests, and tombs of brass are spent.
                              Sonnet 107.

As of higher worth, so doubtless still more characteristic of poetic genius does the imagery become, when it moulds and colors itself to the circumstances, passion, or character, present and foremost in the mind. For unrivalled instances of this excellence, the reader's own memory will refer him to the LEAR, OTHELLO, in short to which not of the "*great, ever living, dead man's*" dramatic works? Inopem me copia fecit.[5] How true it is to nature, he has himself finely expressed in the instance of love in Sonnet 98.

"From you have I been absent in the spring,
When proud pied April drest in all its trim
Hath put a spirit of youth in every thing;
That heavy Saturn laugh'd and leap'd with him.
Yet nor the lays of birds, nor the sweet smell
Of different flowers in odour and in hue,
Could make me any summer's story tell,
Or from their proud lap pluck them, where they grew:
Nor did I wonder at the lilies white,
Nor praise the deep vermillion in the rose;

---

3 Christoph Martin Wieland (1733–1813) was an influential German poet and romance writer. Coleridge refers to Wieland's most popular work *Oberon* (1780).

4 Coleridge's "France: an Ode" (1798), l. 103.

---

5 Inopem . . . fecit: "The very abundance of my riches [of examples of this excellence] beggars me." Ovid's *Metamorphoses*, III, 466.

They were, tho' sweet, but figures of delight,
Drawn after you, you pattern of all those.
Yet seem'd it winter still, and you away,
As with your shadow I with these did play!

Scarcely less sure, or if a less valuable, not less indispensable mark

Γονίμου μέν Ποιητου ——
—— οϛιϛ ρημα γενναιον λακοι,[6]

will the imagery supply, when, with more than the power of the painter, the poet gives us the liveliest image of succession with the feeling of simultaneousness!

With this he breaketh from the sweet embrace
Of those fair arms, that held him to her heart,
And homeward through the dark lawns runs apace:
Look how a bright star shooteth from the sky!
So glides he through the night from Venus' eye.[7]

4. The last character I shall mention, which would prove indeed but little, except as taken conjointly with the former; yet without which the former could scarce exist in a high degree, and (even if this were possible) would give promises only of transitory flashes and a meteoric power; is DEPTH, and ENERGY of THOUGHT. No man was ever yet a great poet, without being at the same time a profound philosopher. For poetry is the blossom and the fragrancy of all human knowledge, human thoughts, human passions, emotions, language. In Shakspeare's *poems*, the creative power, and the intellectual energy wrestle as in a war embrace. Each in its excess of strength seems to threaten the extinction of the other. At length, in the DRAMA they were reconciled, and fought each with its shield before the breast of the other. Or like two rapid streams, that at their first meeting within narrow and rocky banks mutually strive to repel each other, and intermix reluctantly and in tumult; but soon finding a wider channel and more yielding shores blend, and dilate, and flow on in one current and with one voice. The Venus and Adonis did not perhaps allow the display of the deeper passions. But the story of Lucretia seems to favor, and even demand their intensest workings. And yet we find in *Shakspeare's* management of the tale neither pathos, nor any other *dramatic* quality. There is the same minute and faithful imagery as in the former poem, in the same vivid colours, inspirited by the same im-

petuous vigour of thought, and diverging and contracting with the same activity of the assimilative and of the modifying faculties; and with a yet larger display, a yet wider range of knowledge and reflection; and lastly, with the same perfect dominion, often *domination*, over the whole world of language. What then shall we say? even this; that Shakspeare, no mere child of nature; no automaton of genius; no passive vehicle of inspiration possessed by the spirit, not possessing it; first studied patiently, meditated deeply, understood minutely, till knowledge become habitual and intuitive wedded itself to his habitual feelings, and at length gave birth to that stupendous power, by which he stands alone, with no equal or second in his own class; to that power, which seated him on one of the two glory-smitten summits of the poetic mountain, with Milton as his compeer not rival. While the former darts himself forth and passes into all the forms of human character and passion, the one Proteus of the fire and the flood; the other attracts all forms and things to himself, into the unity of his own IDEAL. All things and modes of action shape themselves anew in the being of MILTON; while SHAKSPEARE becomes all things, yet for ever remaining himself. O what great men hast thou not produced, England! my country! truly indeed—

Must *we* be free or die, who speak the tongue,
Which SHAKSPEARE spake; the faith and morals hold,
Which MILTON held. In every thing we are sprung
Of earth's first blood, have titles manifold![8]

Wordsworth.

CHAPTER XVII

Examination of the tenets peculiar to Mr. Wordsworth—Rustic life (above all, low and rustic life) especially unfavorable to the formation of a human diction—The best parts of language the product of philosophers, not clowns or shepherds—Poetry essentially ideal and generic—The language of Milton as much the language of real *life, yea, incomparably more so than that of the cottager.*

As FAR then as Mr. Wordsworth in his preface contended, and most ably contended, for a reformation in our poetic diction, as far as he has evinced the truth of passion, and the *dramatic* propriety of those figures and metaphors in the original poets, which stript of their justifying reasons, and converted into mere artifices of connection or ornament, constitute the characteristic falsity in the poetic style of the moderns; and as far as he has, with equal acuteness and clearness, pointed out

---

[6] "Search where you will, you'll never find a true / Creative genius, uttering startling things." Aristophanes' *The Frogs*, ll. 96–97 (Rogers translation, Loeb Classical Library, Harvard University Press).

[7] *Venus and Adonis*, ll. 811–13, 815–16.

[8] The sonnet "It is not to be thought of that the Flood" (1803), ll. 11–14.

the process in which this change was effected, and the resemblances between that state into which the reader's mind is thrown by the pleasureable confusion of thought from an unaccustomed train of words and images; and that state which is induced by the natural language of empassioned feeling; he undertook a useful task, and deserves all praise, both for the attempt and for the execution. The provocations to this remonstrance in behalf of truth and nature were still of perpetual recurrence before and after the publication of this preface. I cannot likewise but add, that the comparison of such poems of merit, as have been given to the public within the last ten or twelve years, with the majority of those produced previously to the appearance of that preface, leave no doubt on my mind, that Mr. Wordsworth is fully justified in believing his efforts to have been by no means ineffectual. Not only in the verses of those who have professed their admiration of his genius, but even of those who have distinguished themselves by hostility to his theory, and depreciation of his writings, are the impressions of his principles plainly visible. It is possible, that with these principles others may have been blended, which are not equally evident; and some which are unsteady and subvertible from the narrowness or imperfection of their basis. But it is more than possible, that these errors of defect or exaggeration, by kindling and feeding the controversy, may have conduced not only to the wider propagation of the accompanying truths, but that by their frequent presentation to the mind in an excited state, they may have won for them a more permanent and practical result. A man will borrow a part from his opponent the more easily, if he feels himself justified in continuing to reject a part. While there remain important points in which he can still feel himself in the right, in which he still finds firm footing for continued resistance, he will gradually adopt those opinions, which were the least remote from his own convictions, as not less congruous with his own theory, than with that which he reprobates. In like manner with a kind of instinctive prudence, he will abandon by little and little his weakest posts, till at length he seems to forget that they had ever belonged to him, or affects to consider them at most as accidental and "petty annexments," [1] the removal of which leaves the citadel unhurt and unendangered.

My own differences from certain supposed parts of Mr. Wordsworth's theory ground themselves on the assumption, that his words had been rightly interpreted, as purporting that the proper diction for poetry in general consists altogether in a language taken, with due exceptions, from the mouths of men in real life, a language which actually constitutes the natural conversation of men under the influence of natural feelings. My objection is, first, that in *any* sense this rule is applicable only to *certain* classes of poetry; secondly, that even to these classes it is not applicable, except in such a sense, as hath never by any one (as far as I know or have read) been denied or doubted; and lastly, that as far as, and in that degree in which it is *practicable*, yet as a *rule* it is useless, if not injurious, and therefore either need not, or ought not to be practised. The poet informs his reader, that he had generally chosen *low and rustic* life; but not *as* low and rustic, or in order to repeat that pleasure of doubtful moral effect, which persons of elevated rank and of superior refinement oftentimes derive from a happy *imitation* of the rude unpolished manners and discourse of their inferiors. For the pleasure so derived may be traced to three exciting causes. The first is the naturalness, in *fact*, of the things represented. The second is the apparent naturalness of the *representation*, as raised and qualified by an imperceptible infusion of the author's own knowledge and talent, which infusion does, indeed, constitute it an *imitation* as distinguished from a mere *copy*. The third cause may be found in the reader's conscious feeling of his superiority awakened by the contrast presented to him; even as for the same purpose the kings and great barons of yore retained, sometimes *actual* clowns and fools, but more frequently shrewd and witty fellows in that *character*. These, however, were not Mr. Wordsworth's objects. *He* chose low and rustic life, "because in that condition the essential passions of the heart find a better soil, in which they can attain their maturity, are less under restraint, and speak a plainer and more emphatic language; because in that condition of life our elementary feelings co-exist in a state of greater simplicity, and consequently may be more accurately contemplated, and more forcibly communicated; because the manners of rural life germinate from those elementary feelings; and from the necessary character of rural occupations are more easily comprehended, and are more durable; and lastly, because in that condition the passions of men are incorporated with the beautiful and permanent forms of nature."

Now it is clear to me, that in the most interesting of the poems, in which the author is more or less dramatic, as the "Brothers," "Michael," "Ruth," the "Mad Mother," &c. the persons introduced are by no means taken *from low or rustic life* in the common acceptation of those words; and it is not less clear, that the sentiments and language, as far as they can be conceived to have been really transferred from the minds and conversation of such persons, are attributable to causes

[1] See *Hamlet*, III, iii, 21.

and circumstances not necessarily connected with "their occupations and abode." The thoughts, feelings, language, and manners of the shepherd-farmers in the vales of Cumberland and Westmoreland, as far as they are actually adopted in those poems, may be accounted for from causes, which will and do produce the same results in *every* state of life, whether in town or country. As the two principal I rank that INDEPENDENCE, which raises a man above servitude, or daily toil for the profit of others, yet not above the necessity of industry and a frugal simplicity of domestic life; and the accompanying unambitious, but solid and religious EDUCATION, which has rendered few books familiar, but the bible, and the liturgy or hymn book. To this latter cause, indeed, which is so far *accidental*, that it is the blessing of particular countries and a particular age, not the product of particular places or employments, the poet owes the show of probability, that his personages might really feel, think, and talk with any tolerable resemblance to his representation. It is an excellent remark of Dr. Henry More's (Enthusiasmus triumphatus, Sec. XXXV)[2] that "a man of confined education, but of good parts, by constant reading of the bible will naturally form a more winning and commanding rhetoric than those that are learned; the intermixture of tongues and of artificial phrases debasing *their* style."

It is, moreover, to be considered that to the formation of healthy feelings, and a reflecting mind, *negations* involve impediments not less formidable, than sophistication and vicious intermixture. I am convinced, that for the human soul to prosper in rustic life, a certain vantage-ground is pre-requisite. It is not every man, that is likely to be improved by a country life or by country labours. Education, or original sensibility, or both, must pre-exist, if the changes, forms, and incidents of nature are to prove a sufficient stimulant. And where these are not sufficient, the mind contracts and hardens by want of stimulants; and the man becomes selfish, sensual, gross, and hard-hearted. Let the management of the POOR LAWS in Liverpool, Manchester, or Bristol be compared with the ordinary dispensation of the poor rates in agricultural villages, where the *farmers* are the overseers and guardians of the poor. If my own experience have not been particularly unfortunate, as well as that of the many respectable country clergymen with whom I have conversed on the subject, the result would engender more than scepticism concerning the desirable influences of low and rustic life in and for itself. Whatever may be concluded on the other side, from the

stronger local attachments and enterprizing spirit of the Swiss, and other mountaineers, applies to a particular mode of pastoral life, under forms of property, that permit and beget manners truly republican, not to rustic life in general, or to the absence of artificial cultivation. On the contrary the mountaineers, whose manners have been so often eulogized, are in general better educated and greater readers than men of equal rank elsewhere. But where this is not the case, as among the peasantry of North Wales, the ancient mountains, with all their terrors and all their glories, are pictures to the blind, and music to the deaf.

I should not have entered so much into detail upon this passage, but here seems to be the point, to which all the lines of difference converge as to their source and centre. (I mean, as far as, and in whatever respect, my poetic creed *does* differ from the doctrines promulged in this preface.) I adopt with full faith the principle of Aristotle, that poetry as poetry is essentially * *ideal*, that it avoids and excludes all *accident*; that its apparent individualities of rank, character, or occupation must be *representative* of a class; and that the *persons* of poetry must be clothed with *generic*

* Say not that I am recommending abstractions, for these class-characteristics which constitute the instructiveness of a character, are so modified and particularized in each person of the Shaksperian Drama, that life itself does not excite more distinctly the sense of individuality which belongs to real existence. Paradoxical as it may sound, one of the essential properties of Geometry is not less essential to dramatic excellence; and Aristotle has accordingly required of the poet an involution of the universal in the individual. The chief differences are, that in Geometry it is the universal truth, which is uppermost in the consciousness; in poetry the individual form, in which the truth is clothed. With the ancients, and not less with the elder dramatists of England and France, both comedy and tragedy were considered as kinds of poetry. They neither sought in comedy to make us laugh merely; much less to make us laugh by wry faces, accidents of jargon, *slang* phrases for the day, or the clothing of common-place morals in metaphors drawn from the shops or mechanic occupations of their characters. Nor did they condescend in tragedy to wheedle away the applause of the spectators, by representing before them fac-similies of their own mean selves in all their existing meanness, or to work on their sluggish sympathies by a pathos not a whit more respectable than the maudlin tears of drunkenness. Their tragic scenes were meant to *affect* us indeed; but yet within the bounds of pleasure, and in union with the activity both of our understanding and imagination. They wished to transport the mind to a sense of its possible greatness, and to implant the germs of that greatness, during the temporary oblivion of the worthless "things we are," and of the peculiar state in which each man *happens* to be, suspending our individual recollections and lulling them to sleep amid the music of nobler thoughts. FRIEND, Pages 251, 252.[3]

―――――――――――――――――――

[2] Dr. Henry More (1614–1687) was a leading Cambridge platonist. *Enthusiasmus Triumphatus* was published in 1656.

[3] Coleridge quotes from *The Friend*, No. 16 (December 7, 1809). The words "things we are" are from *The Rape of Lucrece*, l. 149. For the references to Aristotle both in the footnote and the text, see *Poetics*, ix.

attributes, with the *common* attributes of the class; not with such as one gifted individual might *possibly* possess, but such as from his situation it is most probable before-hand, that he *would* possess. If my premises are right, and my deductions legitimate, it follows that there can be no *poetic* medium between the swains of Theocritus and those of an imaginary golden age.

The characters of the vicar and the shepherd-mariner in the poem of the "BROTHERS," those of the shepherd of Green-head Gill in the "MICHAEL", have all the verisimilitude and representative quality, that the purposes of poetry can require. They are persons of a known and abiding class, and their manners and sentiments the natural product of circumstances common to the class. Take "MICHAEL" for instance:

An old man stout of heart, and strong of limb;
His bodily frame had been from youth to age
Of an unusual strength: his mind was keen,
Intense and frugal, apt for all affairs,
And in his shepherd's calling he was prompt
And watchful more than ordinary men.
Hence he had learnt the meaning of all winds,
Of blasts of every tone, and oftentimes
When others heeded not, he heard the South
Make subterraneous music, like the noise
Of bagpipers on distant highland hills.
The shepherd, at such warning, of his flock
Bethought him, and he to himself would say,
The winds are now devising work for me!
And truly at all times the storm, that drives
The traveller to a shelter, summon'd him
Up to the mountains. He had been alone
Amid the heart of many thousand mists,
That came to him and left him on the heights.
So liv'd he, till his eightieth year was pass'd.
And grossly that man errs, who should suppose
That the green vallies, and the streams and rocks,
Were things indifferent to the shepherd's thoughts.
Fields, where with chearful spirits he had breath'd
The common air; the hills, which he so oft
Had climb'd with vigorous steps; which had impress'd
So many incidents upon his mind
Of hardship, skill or courage, joy or fear;
Which like a book preserved the memory
Of the dumb animals, whom he had sav'd,
Had fed or shelter'd, linking to such acts,
So grateful in themselves, the certainty
Of honorable gains; these fields, these hills
Which were his living being, even more
Than his own blood—what could they less? had laid
Strong hold on his affections, were to him
A pleasurable feeling of blind love,
The pleasure which there is in life itself.[4]

On the other hand, in the poems which are pitched at a lower note, as the "HARRY GILL," "IDIOT BOY," &c. the *feelings* are those of human nature in general; though the poet has judiciously laid the *scene* in the country, in order to place *himself* in the vicinity of interesting images, without the necessity of ascribing a sentimental perception of their beauty to the persons of his drama. In the "Idiot Boy," indeed, the mother's character is not so much a real and native product of a "situation where the essential passions of the heart find a better soil, in which they can attain their maturity and speak a plainer and more emphatic language," as it is an impersonation of an instinct abandoned by judgement. Hence the two following charges seem to me not wholly groundless: at least, they are the only plausible objections, which I have heard to that fine poem. The one is, that the author has not, in the poem itself, taken sufficient care to preclude from the reader's fancy the disgusting images of *ordinary, morbid idiocy*, which yet it was by no means his intention to represent. He has even by the "burr, burr, burr," uncounteracted by any preceding description of the boy's beauty, assisted in recalling them. The other is, that the idiocy of the *boy* is so evenly balanced by the folly of the *mother*, as to present to the general reader rather a laughable burlesque on the blindness of anile dotage, than an analytic display of maternal affection in its ordinary workings.

In the "Thorn," the poet himself acknowledges in a note the necessity of an introductory poem, in which he should have pourtrayed the character of the person from whom the words of the poem are supposed to proceed: a superstitious man moderately imaginative, of slow faculties and deep feelings, "a captain of a small trading vessel, for example, who being past the middle age of life, had retired upon an annuity, or small independent income, to some village or country town of which he was not a native, or in which he had not been accustomed to live. Such men having nothing to do become credulous and talkative from indolence." But in a poem, still more in a lyric poem (and the NURSE in Shakspeare's Romeo and Juliet[5] alone prevents me from extending the remark even to dramatic *poetry*, if indeed the Nurse itself can be deemed altogether a case in point) it is not possible to imitate truly a dull and garrulous discourser, without repeating the effects of dulness and garrulity. However this may be, I dare assert, that the parts (and these form the far larger portion of the whole) which might as well or still better have proceeded from the poet's own imagination, and have been spoken in his own character,

4 Ll. 42–77.

5 See "Seventh Lecture" (1811), pp. 127–135.

are those which have given, and which will continue to give universal delight; and that the passages exclusively appropriate to the supposed narrator, such as the last couplet of the third stanza;* the seven last lines of the tenth;† and the five following stanzas, with the excep-

*   "I've measured it from side to side;
       'Tis three feet long, and two feet wide."[6]

†   'Nay, rack your brain—'tis all in vain,
      I'll tell you every thing I know;
      But to the Thorn, and to the Pond
      Which is a little step beyond,
      I wish that you would go:
      Perhaps, when you are at the place,
      You something of her tale may trace.

      I'll give you the best help I can:
      Before you up the mountain go,
      Up to the dreary mountain-top,
      I'll tell you all I know.

      'Tis now some two-and-twenty years
      Since she (her name is Martha Ray)
      Gave, with a maiden's true good will,
      Her company to Stephen Hill;
      And she was blithe and gay.
      And she was happy, happy still
      Whene'er she thought of Stephen Hill.

      And they had fix'd the wedding-day,
      The morning that must wed them both;
      But Stephen to another maid
      Had sworn another oath;
      And with this other maid to church
      Unthinking Stephen went—
      Poor Martha! on that woeful day
      A pang of pitiless dismay
      Into her soul was sent;
      A fire was kindled in her breast,
      Which might not burn itself to rest.

      They say, full six months after this,
      While yet the summer leaves were green,
      She to the mountain-top would go,
      And there was often seen.
      'Tis said, a child was in her womb,
      As now to any eye was plain;
      She was with child, and she was mad;
      Yet often she was sober sad
      From her exceeding pain.
      Oh me! ten thousand times I'd rather
      That he had died, that cruel father!

    *   *   *   *   *   *   *
    *   *   *   *   *   *   *
    *   *   *   *   *   *   *
    *   *   *   *   *   *   *

      Last Christmas when we talked of this,
      Old farmer Simpson did maintain,
      That in her womb the infant wrought
      About its mother's heart, and brought
      Her senses back again:
      And when at last her time drew near,
      Her looks were calm, her senses clear.

tion of the four admirable lines at the commencement of the fourteenth are felt by many unprejudiced and unsophisticated hearts, as sudden and unpleasant sinkings from the height to which the poet had previously lifted them, and to which he again re-elevates both himself and his reader.

If then I am compelled to doubt the theory, by which the choice of *characters* was to be directed, not only *a priori*, from grounds of reason, but both from the few instances in which the poet himself *need* be supposed to have been governed by it, and from the comparative inferiority of those instances; still more must I hesitate in my assent to the sentence which immediately follows the former citation; and which I can neither admit as particular fact, or as general rule. "The language too of these men is adopted (purified indeed from what appears to be its real defects, from all lasting and rational causes of dislike or disgust) because such men hourly communicate with the best objects from which the best part of language is originally derived; and because, from their rank in society, and the sameness and narrow circle of their intercourse, being less under the action of social vanity, they convey their feelings and notions in simple and unelaborated expressions." To this I reply; that a rustic's language, purified from all provincialism and grossness, and so far re-constructed as to be made consistent with the rules of grammar (which are in essence no other than the laws of universal logic, applied to psychological materials) will not differ from the language of any other man of common-sense, however learned or refined he may be, except as far as the notions, which the rustic has to convey, are fewer and more indiscriminate. This will become still clearer, if we add the consideration (equally important though less obvious) that the rustic, from the more imperfect developement of his faculties, and from the lower state of their cultivation, aims almost solely to convey *insulated facts*, either

---

      No more I know, I wish I did,
      And I would tell it all to you;
      For what became of this poor child
      There's none that ever knew:
      And if a child was born or no,
      There's no one that could ever tell;
      And if 'twas born alive or dead,
      There's no one knows, as I have said;
      But some remember well,
      That Martha Ray about this time
      Would up the mountain often climb.[7]

[6] This original version of ll. 32–33 was replaced in the 1820 and all succeeding editions of Wordsworth's poetry by: "Though but of compass small, and bare / To thirsty suns and parching air."

[7] The first eleven lines here cited, the most garrulous of the original version, were omitted in the 1820 and all subsequent editions of Wordsworth's poetry. The rest of the lines cited were subjected to some revision, presumably in the light of Coleridge's criticisms.

those of his scanty experience or his traditional belief; while the educated man chiefly seeks to discover and express those *connections* of things, or those relative *bearings* of fact to fact, from which some more or less general law is deducible. For *facts* are valuable to a wise man, chiefly as they lead to the discovery of the indwelling *law*, which is the true *being* of things, the sole solution of their modes of existence, and in the knowledge of which consists our dignity and our power.

As little can I agree with the assertion, that from the objects with which the rustic hourly communicates, the best part of language is formed. For first, if to communicate with an object implies such an acquaintance with it, as renders it capable of being discriminately reflected on; the distinct knowledge of an uneducated rustic would furnish a very scanty vocabulary. The few things, and modes of action, requisite for his bodily conveniences, would alone be individualized; while all the rest of nature would be expressed by a small number of confused, general terms. Secondly, I deny that the words and combinations of words derived from the objects, with which the rustic is familiar, whether with distinct or confused knowledge, can be justly said to form the *best* part of language. It is more than probable, that many classes of the brute creation possess discriminating sounds, by which they can convey to each other notices of such objects as concern their food, shelter, or safety. Yet we hesitate to call the aggregate of such sounds a language, otherwise than metaphorically. The best part of human language, properly so called, is derived from reflection on the acts of the mind itself. It is formed by a voluntary appropriation of fixed symbols to internal acts, to processes and results of imagination, the greater part of which have no place in the consciousness of uneducated man; though in civilized society, by imitation and passive remembrance of what they hear from their religious instructors and other superiors, the most uneducated share in the harvest which they neither sowed or reaped. If the history of the phrases in hourly currency among our peasants were traced, a person not previously aware of the fact would be surprized at finding so large a number, which three or four centuries ago were the exclusive property of the universities and the schools; and at the commencement of the Reformation had been transferred from the school to the pulpit, and thus gradually passed into common life. The extreme difficulty, and often the impossibility, of finding words for the simplest moral and intellectual processes in the languages of uncivilized tribes has proved perhaps the weightiest obstacle to the progress of our most zealous and adroit missionaries. Yet these tribes are surrounded by the same nature, as our peasants are; but in still more impressive forms; and they are, moreover, obliged to *particularize* many more of them. When therefore Mr. Wordsworth adds, "accordingly such a language" (meaning, as before, the language of rustic life purified from provincialism) "arising out of repeated experience and regular feelings is a more permanent, and a far more philosophical language, than that which is frequently substituted for it by poets, who think they are conferring honor upon themselves and their art in proportion as they indulge in arbitrary and capricious habits of expression;" it may be answered, that the language, which he has in view, can be attributed to rustics with no greater right, than the style of Hooker or Bacon to Tom Brown or Sir Roger L'Estrange.[8] Doubtless, if what is peculiar to each were omitted in each, the result must needs be the same. Further, that the poet, who uses an illogical diction, or a style fitted to excite only the low and changeable pleasure of wonder by means of groundless novelty, substitutes a language of *folly* and *vanity*, not for that of the *rustic*, but for that of *good sense* and *natural feeling*.

Here let me be permitted to remind the reader, that the positions, which I controvert, are contained in the sentences—"*a selection of the* REAL *language of men;*" —"*the language of these men* (i.e. men in low and rustic life) *I propose to myself to imitate, and as far as possible, to adopt the very language of men.*" "*Between the language of prose and that of metrical composition, there neither is, nor can be any essential difference.*" It is against these exclusively, that my opposition is directed.

I object, in the very first instance, to an equivocation in the use of the word "real." Every man's language varies, according to the extent of his knowledge, the activity of his faculties, and the depth or quickness of his feelings. Every man's language has, first, its *individualities*; secondly, the common properties of the *class* to which he belongs; and thirdly, words and phrases of *universal* use. The language of Hooker, Bacon, Bishop Taylor, and Burke, differ from the common language of the learned class only by the superior number and novelty of the thoughts and relations which they had to convey. The language of Algernon Sidney[9] differs not at all from that, which every well educated gentleman would wish to write, and (with due allowances for the undeliberateness, and less connected train, of thinking natural and proper to

8 Tom Brown (1663–1704) was a scurrilous London satirist. Sir Roger L'Estrange (1616–1704) was a Tory pamphleteer and translator. Both are cited as essentially "vulgar" writers in contrast to the nobler writers and stylists Bacon and Hooker.
9 Algernon Sidney (1622–1683) was a republican statesman and the author of *Discourses concerning Government* (1698).

conversation) such as he would wish to talk. Neither one or the other differ half as much from the general language of cultivated society, as the language of Mr. Wordsworth's homeliest composition differs from that of a common peasant. For "real" therefore, we must substitute *ordinary*, or *lingua communis*. And this, we have proved, is no more to be found in the phraseology of low and rustic life, than in that of any other class. Omit the peculiarities of each, and the result of course must be common to all. And assuredly the omissions and changes to be made in the language of rustics, before it could be transferred to any species of poem, except the drama or other professed imitation, are at least as numerous and weighty, as would be required in adapting to the same purpose the ordinary language of tradesmen and manufacturers. Not to mention, that the language so highly extolled by Mr. Wordsworth varies in every county, nay in every village, according to the accidental character of the clergyman, the existence or non-existence of schools; or even, perhaps, as the exciseman, publican, or barber happen to be, or not to be, zealous politicians, and readers of the weekly newspaper *pro bono publico*. Anterior to cultivation the lingua communis of every country, as Dante has well observed,[10] exists every where in parts, and no where as a whole.

Neither is the case rendered at all more tenable by the addition of the words, "*in a state of excitement.*" For the nature of a man's words, when he is strongly affected by joy, grief, or anger, must necessarily depend on the number and quality of the general truths, conceptions and images, and of the words expressing them, with which his mind had been previously stored. For the property of passion is not to *create*; but to set in increased activity. At least, whatever new connections of thoughts or images, or (which is equally, if not more than equally, the appropriate effect of strong excitement) whatever generalizations of truth or experience, the heat of passion may produce; yet the terms of their conveyance must have pre-existed in his former conversations, and are only collected and crowded together by the unusual stimulation. It is indeed very possible to adopt in a poem the unmeaning repetitions, habitual phrases, and other blank counters, which an unfurnished or confused understanding interposes at short intervals, in order to keep hold of his subject which is still slipping from him, and to give him time for recollection; or in mere aid of vacancy, as in the scanty companies of a country stage the same player pops backwards and forwards, in order to prevent the appearance of empty spaces, in the procession of

Macbeth, or Henry VIIIth. But what assistance to the poet, or ornament to the poem, these can supply, I am at a loss to conjecture. Nothing assuredly can differ either in origin or in mode more widely from the *apparent* tautologies of intense and turbulent feeling, in which the passion is greater and of longer endurance, than to be exhausted or satisfied by a single representation of the image or incident exciting it. Such repetitions I admit to be a beauty of the highest kind; as illustrated by Mr. Wordsworth himself from the song of Deborah. "*At her feet he bowed, he fell, he lay down; at her feet he bowed, he fell; where he bowed, there he fell down dead.*"[11]

CHAPTER XVIII

Language of metrical composition, why and wherein essentially different from that of prose—Origin and elements of metre—Its necessary consequences, and the conditions thereby imposed on the metrical writer in the choice of his diction.

I CONCLUDE therefore, that the attempt is impracticable; and that, were it not impracticable, it would still be useless. For the very power of making the selection implies the previous possession of the language selected. Or where can the poet have lived? And by what rules could he direct his choice, which would not have enabled him to select and arrange his words by the light of his own judgement? We do not adopt the language of a class by the mere adoption of such words exclusively, as that class would use, or at least understand; but likewise by following the *order*, in which the words of such men are wont to succeed each other. Now this order, in the intercourse of uneducated men, is distinguished from the diction of their superiors in knowledge and power, by the greater *disjunction* and *separation* in the component parts of that, whatever it be, which they wish to communicate. There is a want of that prospectiveness of mind, that *surview*, which enables a man to foresee the whole of what he is to convey, appertaining to any one point; and by this means so to subordinate and arrange the different parts according to their relative importance, as to convey it at once, and as an organized whole.

Now I will take the first stanza, on which I have chanced to open, in the Lyrical Ballads. It is one the most simple and the least peculiar in its language.

---

[10] In *De Vulgari Eloquentia*, Chapter XVI.

[11] Judges, v, 27. The passage is cited by Wordsworth in his note to "The Thorn" in the 1800 edition of *Lyrical Ballads*, as an example of "repetition and apparent tautology [which] are frequent beauties of the highest kind."

"In distant countries I have been,
  And yet I have not often seen
A healthy man, a man full grown,
  Weep in the public road alone.
But such a one, on English ground,
  And in the broad highway I met;
Along the broad highway he came,
  His cheeks with tears were wet.
Sturdy he seem'd, though he was sad,
  And in his arms a lamb he had."[1]

The words here are doubtless such as are current in all ranks of life; and of course not less so, in the hamlet and cottage, than in the shop, manufactory, college, or palace. But is this the *order*, in which the rustic would have placed the words? I am grievously deceived, if the following less *compact* mode of commencing the same tale be not a far more faithful copy. "I have been in a many parts far and near, and I don't know that I ever saw before a man crying by himself in the public road; a grown man I mean, that was neither sick nor hurt," &c. &c. But when I turn to the following stanza in "The Thorn:"

"At all times of the day and night
  This wretched woman thither goes,
And she is known to every star
  And every wind that blows:
And there beside the thorn she sits,
  When the blue day-light's in the skies;
And when the whirlwind's on the hill,
  Or frosty air is keen and still;
And to herself she cries,
  Oh misery! Oh misery!
  Oh woe is me! Oh misery!"[2]

And compare this with the language of ordinary men; or with that which I can conceive at all likely to proceed, in *real* life, from *such* a narrator, as is supposed in the note to the poem; compare it either in the succession of the images or of the sentences, I am reminded of the sublime prayer and hymn of praise,[3] which MILTON, in opposition to an established liturgy, presents as a fair *specimen* of common extemporary devotion, and such as we might expect to hear from every self-inspired minister of a conventicle! And I reflect with delight, how little a mere theory, though of his own workmanship, interferes with the processes of genuine imagination in a man of true poetic genius, who possesses, as Mr. Wordsworth, if ever man did, most assuredly does possess,

---

[1] "The Last of the Flock" (1798), ll. 1–10.
[2] Ll. 67–77.
[3] See *Paradise Lost*, V, 153–208.

"THE VISION AND THE FACULTY DIVINE."[4]

One point then alone remains, but that the most important; its examination having been, indeed, my chief inducement for the preceding inquisition. "*There neither is or can be any essential difference between the language of prose and metrical composition.*" Such is Mr. Wordsworth's assertion. Now prose itself, at least, in all argumentative and consecutive works differs, and ought to differ, from the language of conversation; even as* reading ought to differ from talking. Unless therefore the difference denied be that of the mere *words*, as materials common to all styles of writing, and not of the *style* itself in the universally admitted sense of the term, it might be naturally presumed that there must exist a still greater between the ordonnance of poetic composition and that of prose, than is expected to distinguish prose from ordinary conversation.

There are not, indeed, examples wanting in the history of literature, of apparent paradoxes that have summoned the public wonder as new and startling

---

* It is no less an error in teachers, than a torment to the poor children, to enforce the necessity of reading as they would talk. In order to cure them of *singing* as it is called; that is, of too great a difference. The child is made to repeat the words with his eyes from off the book; and then indeed, his tones resemble talking, as far as his fears, tears and trembling will permit. But as soon as the eye is again directed to the printed page, the spell begins anew; for an instinctive sense tells the child's feelings, that to utter its own momentary thoughts, and to recite the written thoughts of another, as of another, and a far wiser than himself, are two widely different things; and as the two acts are accompanied with widely different feelings, so must they justify different modes of enunciation. Joseph Lancaster, among his other sophistications of the excellent Dr. Bell's invaluable system, cures this fault of *singing*, by hanging fetters and chains on the child, to the music of which, one of his school fellows who walks before, dolefully chaunts out the child's last speech and confession, birth, parentage, and education. And this soul-benumbing ignominy, this unholy and heart-hardening burlesque on the last fearful infliction of outraged law, in pronouncing the sentence to which the stern and familiarized judge not seldom bursts into tears, has been extolled as a happy and ingenious method of remedying—what? and how?—why, one extreme in order to introduce another, scarce less distant from good sense, and certainly likely to have worse moral effects, by enforcing a semblance of petulant ease and self-sufficiency, in repression, and possible after-perversion of the natural feelings. I have to beg Dr. Bell's pardon for this connection of the two names, but he knows that contrast is no less powerful a cause of association than likeness.[5]

---

[4] *Excursion*, I, 79.
[5] Joseph Lancaster (1778–1838) and Andrew Bell (1753–1832) were rival educational innovators, both advocating a system of mutual instruction (the so-called "Madras System" introduced by Bell in 1797), in which the students themselves would serve as teachers or monitors to those below them in age and ability. In 1808, Coleridge had delivered a lecture in support of Bell and in opposition to Lancaster.

truths, but which on examination have shrunk into tame and harmless *truisms*; as the eyes of a cat, seen in the dark, have been mistaken for flames of fire. But Mr. Wordsworth is among the last men, to whom a delusion of this kind would be attributed by any one, who had enjoyed the slightest opportunity of understanding his mind and character. Where an objection has been anticipated by such an author as natural, his answer to it must needs be interpreted in some sense which either is, or has been, or is capable of being controverted. My object then must be to discover some other meaning for the term "*essential difference*" in this place, exclusive of the indistinction and community of the words themselves. For whether there ought to exist a class of words in the English, in any degree resembling the poetic dialect of the Greek and Italian, is a question of very subordinate importance. The number of such words would be small indeed, in our language; and even in the Italian and Greek, they consist not so much of different words, as of slight differences in the *forms* of declining and conjugating the same words; forms, doubtless, which having been, at some period more or less remote, the common grammatic flexions of some tribe or province, had been accidentally appropriated to poetry by the general admiration of certain master intellects, the first established lights of inspiration, to whom that dialect happened to be native.

Essence, in its primary signification, means the principle of *individuation*, the inmost principle of the *possibility* of any thing, *as* that particular thing. It is equivalent to the *idea* of a thing, whenever we use the word idea, with philosophic precision. Existence, on the other hand, is distinguished from essence, by the superinduction of *reality*. Thus we speak of the essence, and essential properties of a circle; but we do not therefore assert, that any thing, which really *exists*, is mathematically circular. Thus too, without any tautology we contend for the *existence* of the Supreme Being; that is, for a reality correspondent to the idea. There is, next, a *secondary* use of the word essence, in which it signifies the point or ground of contra-distinction between two modifications of the same substance or subject. Thus we should be allowed to say, that the style of architecture of Westminster Abbey is *essentially* different from that of Saint Paul, even though both had been built with blocks cut into the same form, and from the same quarry. Only in this latter sense of the term must it have been *denied* by Mr. Wordsworth (for in this sense alone is it *affirmed* by the general opinion) that the language of poetry (i.e., the formal construction, or architecture, of the words and phrases) is *essentially* different from that of

prose. Now the burthen of the proof lies with the oppugner, not with the supporters of the common belief. Mr. Wordsworth, in consequence, assigns as the proof of his position, "that not only the language of a large portion of every good poem, even of the most elevated character, must necessarily, except with reference to the metre, in no respect differ from that of good prose; but likewise that some of the most interesting parts of the best poems will be found to be strictly the language of prose, when prose is well written. The truth of this assertion might be demonstrated by innumerable passages from almost all the poetical writings even of Milton himself." He then quotes Gray's sonnet—

> "In vain to me the smiling mornings shine,
>   And reddening Phœbus lifts his golden fire;
>   The birds in vain their amorous descant join,
>   Or cheerful fields resume their green attire;
>   These ears alas! for other notes repine;
>   *A different object do these eyes require*;
>   *My lonely anguish melts no heart but mine*,
>   *And in my breast the imperfect joys expire!*
>   Yet morning smiles the busy race to cheer,
>   And new born pleasure brings to happier men:
>   The fields to all their wonted tributes bear,
>   To warm their little loves the birds complain.
>   *I fruitless mourn to him that cannot hear*,
>   *And weep the more because I weep in vain.*"

and adds the following remark:—"It will easily be perceived, that the only part of this Sonnet which is of any value, is the lines printed in italics. It is equally obvious, that except in the rhyme, and in the use of the single word 'fruitless' for fruitlessly, which is so far a defect, the language of these lines does in no respect differ from that of prose."

An idealist defending his system by the fact, that when asleep we often believe ourselves awake, was well answered by his plain neighbour, "Ah, but when awake to we ever believe ourselves asleep?"—Things identical must be convertible. The preceding passage seems to rest on a similar sophism. For the question is not, whether there may not occur in prose an order of words, which would be equally proper in a poem; nor whether there are not beautiful lines and sentences of frequent occurrence in good poems, which would be equally becoming as well as beautiful in good prose; for neither the one or the other has ever been either denied or doubted by any one. The true question must be, whether there are not modes of expression, a *construction*, and an *order* of sentences, which are in their fit and natural place in a serious prose composition, but would be disproportionate and heterogeneous in metrical poetry; and, vice versa, whether in the language of a serious poem there may not be an arrangement both of words and sentences, and a use and selection of (what are called) *figures of speech*, both as to their kind, their frequency, and their occasions, which on a subject of equal weight would be vicious and alien in correct and manly prose. I contend, that in both cases this unfitness of each for the place of the other frequently will and ought to exist.

And first from the *origin* of metre. This I would trace to the balance in the mind effected by that spontaneous effort which strives to hold in check the workings of passion. It might be easily explained likewise in what manner this salutary antagonism is assisted by the very state, which it counteracts; and how this balance of antagonists became organized into *metre* (in the usual acceptation of that term) by a supervening act of the will and judgement, consciously and for the foreseen purpose of pleasure. Assuming these principles, as the data of our argument, we deduce from them two legitimate conditions, which the critic is entitled to expect in every metrical work. First, that as the *elements* of metre owe their existence to a state of increased excitement, so the metre itself should be accompanied by the natural language of excitement. Secondly, that as these elements are formed into metre *artificially*, by a *voluntary* act, with the design and for the purpose of blending *delight* with emotion, so the traces of present *volition* should throughout the metrical language be proportionally discernible. Now these two conditions must be reconciled and co-present. There must be not only a partnership, but a union; an interpenetration of passion and of will, of *spontaneous* impulse and of *voluntary* purpose. Again, this union can be manifested only in a frequency of forms and figures of speech (originally the offspring of passion, but now the adopted children of power) greater, than would be desired or endured, where the emotion is not voluntarily encouraged, and kept up for the sake of that pleasure, which such emotion so tempered and mastered by the will is found capable of communicating. It not only dictates, but of itself tends to produce, a more frequent employment, of picturesque and vivifying language, than would be natural in any other case, in which there did not exist, as there does in the present, a previous and well understood, though tacit, *compact* between the poet and his reader, that the latter is entitled to expect, and the former bound to supply this species and degree of pleasurable excitement. We may in some measure apply to this union the answer of POLIXENES, in the Winter's Tale, to PERDITA's neglect of the streaked gilly-flowers, because she had heard it said,

"There is an art which in their piedness shares
"With great creating nature.
       Pol: Say there be:
"Yet nature is made better by no mean,
"But nature makes that mean. So ev'n that art,
"Which you say adds to nature, is an art,
"That nature makes! You see, sweet maid, we marry
"*A gentler scyon to the wildest stock:*
"And make conceive a bark of ruder kind
"By bud of nobler race. This is an art,
"Which does mend nature—change it rather; but
"The art itself is nature." [6]

Secondly, I argue from the EFFECTS of metre. As far as metre acts in and for itself, it tends to increase the vivacity and susceptibility both of the general feelings and of the attention. This effect it produces by the continued excitement of surprize, and by the quick reciprocations of curiosity still gratified and still re-excited, which are too slight indeed to be at any one moment objects of distinct consciousness, yet become considerable in their aggregate influence. As a medicated atmosphere, or as wine during animated conversation; they act powerfully, though themselves unnoticed. Where, therefore, correspondent food and appropriate matter are not provided for the attention and feelings thus roused, there must needs be a disappointment felt; like that of leaping in the dark from the last step of a stair-case, when we had prepared our muscles for a leap of three or four.

The discussion on the powers of metre in the preface is highly ingenious and touches at all points on truth. But I cannot find any statement of its powers considered abstractly and separately. On the contrary Mr. Wordsworth seems always to estimate metre by the powers, which it exerts during (and, as I think, in *consequence of*) its combination with other elements of poetry. Thus the previous difficulty is left unanswered, *what* the elements are, with which it must be combined in order to produce its own effects to any pleasureable purpose. Double and tri-syllable rhymes, indeed, form a lower species of wit, and attended to exclusively for their own sake may become a source of momentary amusement; as in poor Smart's distich to the Welch 'Squire who had promised him a hare:

"Tell me thou son of great Cadwallader!
  Hast sent the hare? or hast thou swallow'd her?" [7]

But for any *poetic* purposes, metre resembles (if the aptness of the simile may excuse its meanness) yeast, worthless or disagreeable by itself, but giving vivacity

---

[6] IV, iv, 87–97.
[7] Christopher Smart's "To the Rev. Mr. P[owel]l" (1752), ll. 13–14.

and spirit to the liquor with which it is proportionally combined.

The reference to the "Children in the Wood" by no means satisfies my judgement. We all willingly throw ourselves back for awhile into the feelings of our childhood. This ballad, therefore, we read under such recollections of our own childish feelings, as would equally endear to us poems, which Mr. Wordsworth himself would regard as faulty in the opposite extreme of gaudy and technical ornament. Before the invention of printing, and in a still greater degree, before the introduction of writing, metre, especially *alliterative* metre, (whether alliterative at the beginning of the words, as in "Pierce Plouman," or at the end as in rhymes) possessed an independent value as assisting the recollection, and consequently the preservation, of *any* series of truths or incidents. But I am not convinced by the collation of facts, that the "*Children in the Wood*" owes either its preservation, or its popularity, to its metrical form. Mr. Marshal's repository[8] affords a number of tales in prose inferior in pathos and general merit, some of as old a date, and many as widely popular. TOM HICKATHRIFT, JACK THE GIANT-KILLER, GOODY TWO-SHOES, and LITTLE RED RIDING-HOOD are formidable rivals. And that they have continued in prose, cannot be fairly explained by the assumption, that the comparative meanness of their thoughts and images precluded even the humblest forms of metre. The scene of GOODY TWO-SHOES in the church[9] is perfectly susceptible of metrical narration; and among the Θαύματα θαυμασότατα[10] even of the present age, I do not recollect a more astonishing image than that of the "*whole rookery, that flew out of the giant's beard*" scared by the tremendous voice, with which this monster answered the challenge of the heroic TOM HICKATHRIFT![11]

If from these we turn to compositions universally, and independently of all early associations, beloved and admired; would the MARIA, THE MONK, or THE POOR MAN'S ASS of STERNE,[12] be read with

more delight, or have a better chance of immortality, had they without any change in the diction been composed in rhyme, than in their present state? If I am not grossly mistaken, the general reply would be in the negative. Nay, I will confess, that in Mr. Wordsworth's own volumes the ANECDOTE FOR FATHERS, SIMON LEE, ALICE FELL, THE BEGGARS, AND THE SAILOR'S MOTHER, notwithstanding the beauties which are to be found in each of them where the poet interposes the music of his own thoughts, would have been more delightful to me in prose, told and managed, as by Mr. Wordsworth they would have been, in a moral essay, or pedestrian tour.

Metre in itself is simply a stimulant of the attention, and therefore excites the question: Why is the attention to be thus stimulated? Now the question cannot be answered by the pleasure of the metre itself: for this we have shown to be *conditional*, and dependent on the appropriateness of the thoughts and expressions, to which the metrical form is superadded. Neither can I conceive any other answer that can be rationally given, short of this: I write in metre, because I am about to use a language different from that of prose. Besides, where the language is not such, how interesting soever the reflections are, that are capable of being drawn by a philosophic mind from the thoughts or incidents of the poem, the metre itself must often become feeble Take the three last stanzas of the SAILOR'S MOTHER, for instance. If I could for a moment abstract from the effect produced on the author's feelings, as a man, by the incident at the time of its real occurrence, I would dare appeal to his own judgement, whether in the *metre* itself he found a sufficient reason for *their* being written *metrically*?

"And thus continuing, she said
  I had a son, who many a day
  Sailed on the seas; but he is dead;
  In Denmark he was cast away:
  And I have travelled far as Hull, to see
  What clothes he might have left, or other property.

The bird and cage, they both were his;
  'Twas my son's bird; and neat and trim
  He kept it; many voyages
  This singing bird hath gone with him;
  When last he sailed he left the bird behind;
  As it might be, perhaps, from bodings of his mind.

He to a fellow-lodger's care
  Had left it, to be watched and fed,
  Till he came back again; and there
  I found it when my son was dead;
  And now, God help me for my little wit!
  I trail it with me, Sir! he took so much delight in it."[13]

[8] John Marshall was a leading publisher of children's books in 1780's and 1790's. In 1799 he began publication of *The Children's Magazine; or Monthly Repository of Instruction and Delight*, to which Coleridge may be referring.

[9] Refers to Part I, Chapter vii, of the very popular *Goody Two-Shoes* (1765), the edifying story of an impoverished orphan girl, whose industry, exceptional character, and religious faith enables her to become the most valued member of her community.

[10] Θαύματα θαυμασότατα: "most marvellous marvels."

[11] TOM HICKATHRIFT refers to the tale of a laborer's son "endowed with such prodigious strength that he was able to kill a giant with the axle-tree and wheel of a wagon" (*Oxford Companion to English Literature*).

[12] Stories in Sterne's *Sentimental Journey* (1768).

[13] (1807), ll. 19–36.

If disproportioning the emphasis we read these stanzas so as to make the rhymes perceptible, even *tri-syllable* rhymes could scarcely produce an equal sense of oddity and strangeness, as we feel here in finding *rhymes at all* in sentences so exclusively colloquial. I would further ask whether, but for that visionary state, into which the figure of the woman and the susceptibility of his own genius had placed the poet's imagination (a state, which spreads its influence and coloring over all, that co-exists with the exciting cause, and in which

"The simplest, and the most familiar things
    Gain a strange power of spreading awe around* them")

I would ask the poet whether he would not have felt an abrupt down-fall in these verses from the preceding stanza?

"The ancient spirit is not dead;
    Old times, thought I, are breathing there!
    Proud was I, that my country bred
    Such strength, a dignity so fair!
    She begged an alms, like one in poor estate;
    I looked at her again, nor did my pride abate." [15]

It must not be omitted, and is besides worthy of notice, that those stanzas furnish the only fair instance that I have been able to discover in all Mr. Wordsworth's writings, of an *actual* adoption, or true imitation, of the *real* and *very* language of *low and rustic life*, freed from provincialisms.

Thirdly, I deduce the position from all the causes elsewhere assigned, which render metre the proper form of poetry, and poetry imperfect and defective without metre. Metre therefore having been connected with *poetry* most often and by a peculiar fitness, whatever else is combined with *metre* must, though it be not itself *essentially* poetic, have nevertheless some property in common with poetry, as an intermedium of affinity, a sort (if I may dare borrow a well-known phrase from technical chemistry) of

* Altered from the description of Night-Mair in the Remorse.

"Oh Heaven! 'twas frightful! Now run-down and stared at,
    By hideous shapes that cannot be remembered;
    Now seeing nothing and imaging nothing;
    But only being afraid—stifled with fear!
    While every goodly or familiar form
    Had a strange power of spreading terror round me."

N.B. Though Shakspeare has for his own *all-justifying* purposes introduced the Night-*Mare* with her own foals, yet Mair means a Sister or perhaps a Hag. [14]

[14] Coleridge quotes from his tragedy *Remorse*, IV, i, 68–72. For the reference to Shakespeare, see *King Lear*, III, iv, 126.
[15] Ll. 7–12.

mordaunt [16] between it and the superadded metre. Now poetry, Mr. Wordsworth truly affirms, does always imply PASSION; which word must be here understood in its most general sense, as an excited state of the feelings and faculties. And as every passion has its proper pulse, so will it likewise have its characteristic modes of expression. But where there exists that degree of genius and talent which entitles a writer to aim at the honors of a poet, the very *act* of poetic composition *itself* is, and is *allowed* to imply and to produce, an unusual state of excitement, which of course justifies and demands a correspondent difference of language, as truly, though not perhaps in as marked a degree, as the excitement of love, fear, rage, or jealousy. The vividness of the descriptions or declamations in DONNE, or DRYDEN, is as much and as often derived from the force and fervour of the describer, as from the reflections, forms or incidents which constitute their subject and materials. The wheels take fire from the mere rapidity of their motion. To what extent, and under what modifications, this may be admitted to act, I shall attempt to define in an after remark on Mr. Wordsworth's reply to this objection, or rather on his objection to this reply, as already anticipated in his preface.

Fourthly, and as intimately connected with this, if not the same argument in a more general form, I adduce the high spiritual instinct of the human being impelling us to seek unity by harmonious adjustment, and thus establishing the principle, that *all* the parts of an organized whole must be assimilated to the more *important* and *essential* parts. This and the preceding arguments may be strengthened by the reflection, that the composition of a poem is among the *imitative* arts; and that imitation, as opposed to copying, consists either in the interfusion of the SAME throughout the radically DIFFERENT, or of the different throughout a base radically the same.

Lastly, I appeal to the practice of the best poets, of all countries and in all ages, as *authorizing* the opinion, (*deduced* from all the foregoing) that in every import of the word ESSENTIAL, which would not here involve a mere truism, there may be, is, and ought to be, an *essential* difference between the language of prose and of metrical composition.

In Mr. Wordsworth's criticism of GRAY'S Sonnet, the reader's sympathy with his praise or blame of the different parts is taken for granted rather perhaps too easily. He has not, at least, attempted to win or compel it by argumentative analysis. In *my* conception at least, the lines rejected as of no value do, with the

[16] "A substance used for fixing colouring matters of stuffs" (*Oxford English Dictionary*).

exception of the two first, differ as much and as little from the language of common life, as those which he has printed in italics as possessing genuine excellence. Of the five lines thus honorably distinguished, two of them differ from prose even more widely, than the lines which either precede or follow, in the *position* of the words.

> "*A different object do these eyes require*;
> My lonely anguish melts no heart but mine;
> *And in my breast the imperfect joys expire.*"

But were it otherwise, what would this prove, but a truth, of which no man ever doubted? Videlicet, that there are sentences, which would be equally in their place both in verse and prose. Assuredly it does not prove the point, which alone requires proof; namely, that there are not passages, which would suit the one, and not suit the other. The first line of this sonnet is distinguished from the ordinary language of men by the epithet to morning. (For we will set aside, at present, the consideration, that the particular word "*smiling*" is hackneyed, and (as it involves a sort of personification) not quite congruous with the common and material attribute of *shining*.) And, doubtless, this adjunction of epithets for the purpose of additional description, where no particular attention is demanded for the quality of the thing, would be noticed as giving a poetic cast to a man's conversation. Should the sportman exclaim, "*come boys! the rosy morning calls you up*," he will be supposed to have some song in his head. But no one suspects this, when he says, "A wet morning shall not confine us to our beds." This then is either a defect in poetry, or it is not. Whoever should decide in the *affirmative*, I would request him to re-peruse any one poem, of any confessedly great poet from Homer to Milton, or from Eschylus to Shakspeare; and to strike out (in thought I mean) every instance of this kind. If the number of these fancied erasures did not startle him; or if he continued to deem the work improved by their total omission; he must advance reasons of no ordinary strength and evidence, reasons grounded in the essence of human nature. Otherwise I should not hesitate to consider him as a man not so much *proof against* all authority, as *dead to* it.

The second line,

> "And reddening Phœbus lifts his golden fire."

has indeed almost as many faults as words. But then it is a bad line, not because the language is distinct from that of prose; but because it conveys incongruous images, because it confounds the cause and the effect, the real *thing* with the personified *representative* of the thing; in short, because it differs from the language of

GOOD SENSE! That the "Phœbus" is hackneyed, and a school-boy image, is an *accidental* fault, dependent on the age in which the author wrote, and not deduced from the nature of the thing. That it is part of an exploded mythology, is an objection more deeply grounded. Yet when the torch of ancient learning was re-kindled, so cheering were its beams, that our eldest poets, cut off by Christianity from all *accredited* machinery, and deprived of all *acknowledged* guardians and symbols of the great objects of nature, were naturally induced to adopt, as a *poetic* language, those fabulous personages, those forms of the* supernatural in nature, which had given them such dear delight in the poems of their great masters. Nay, even at this day what scholar of genial taste will not so far sympathize with them, as to read with pleasure in PETRARCH, CHAUCER, or SPENSER, what he would perhaps condemn as puerile in a modern poet?

I remember no poet, whose writings would safelier stand the test of Mr. Wordsworth's theory, than SPENSER. Yet will Mr. Wordsworth say, that the style of the following stanzas is either undistinguished from prose, and the language of ordinary life? Or that it is vicious, and that the stanzas are *blots* in the Faery Queen?

> "By this the northern waggoner had set
> His sevenfold teme behind the stedfast starre,
> That was in ocean waves yet never wet,
> But firm is fixt and sendeth light from farre
> To all that in the wild deep wandering are.
> And chearful chanticleer with his note shrill
> Had warned once that Phœbus's fiery carre
> In haste was climbing up the easterne hill,
> Full envious that night so long his room did fill."
>
> *Book I. Can. 2. St. 1.*

> "At last the golden orientall gate
> Of greatest heaven gan to open fayre,
> And Phœbus fresh as brydegrome to his mate,
> Came dauncing forth, shaking his deawie hayre,
> And hurl'd his glist'ring beams through gloomy ayre;
> Which when the wakeful elfe perceived, streightway
> He started up, and did him selfe prepayre
> In sun-bright armes, and battailous array;
> For with that pagan proud he combat will that day."
>
> *B. I. Can. 5, St. 2.*

On the contrary to how many passages, both in hymn books and in blank verse poems, could I (were it not invidious) direct the reader's attention, the style

---

* But still more by the mechanical system of philosophy which has needlessly infected our theological opinions, and teaching us to consider the world in its relation to God, as of a building to its mason leaves the idea of omnipresence a mere abstract notion in the state-room of our reason.

of which is most *unpoetic, because,* and only because, it is the style of *prose?* He will not suppose me capable of having in my mind such verses, as

> "I put my hat upon my head
> And walk'd into the Strand;
> And there I met another man,
> Whose hat was in his hand."

To such specimens it would indeed be a fair and full reply, that these lines are not bad, because they are *unpoetic;* but because they are empty of all sense and feeling; and that it were an idle attempt to prove that an ape is not a Newton, when it is evident that he is not a man. But the sense shall be good and weighty, the language correct and dignified, the subject interesting and treated with feeling; and yet the style shall, notwithstanding all these merits, be justly blameable as *prosaic,* and solely because the words and the order of the words would find their appropriate place in prose, but are not suitable to *metrical* composition. The "Civil Wars" of Daniel is an instructive, and even interesting work; but take the following stanzas (and from the hundred instances which abound I might probably have selected others far more striking):

> "And to the end we may with better ease
> Discern the true discourse, vouchsafe to shew
> What were the times foregoing near to these,
> That these we may with better profit know.
> Tell how the world fell into this disease;
> And how so great distemperature did grow;
> So shall we see with what degrees it came;
> How things at full do soon wax out of frame."

> "Ten kings had from the Norman conqu'ror reign'd
> With intermixt and variable fate,
> When England to her greatest height attain'd
> Of power, dominion, glory, wealth, and state;
> After it had with much ado sustain'd
> The violence of princes with debate
> For titles, and the often mutinies
> Of nobles for their ancient liberties."

> "For first the Norman, conqu'ring all by might,
> By might was forced to keep what he had got;
> Mixing our customs and the form of right
> With foreign constitutions, he had brought;
> Mastering the mighty, humbling the poorer wight,
> By all severest means that could be wrought;
> And making the succession doubtful rent
> His new-got state and left it turbulent."
>
> *B. I. St. VII. VIII. & IX.*

Will it be contended on the one side, that these lines are mean and senseless? Or on the other, that they are not prosaic, and for *that* reason unpoetic? This poet's well-merited epithet is that of the "*well-languaged*

Daniel;"[17] but likewise and by the consent of his contemporaries no less than of all succeeding critics, the "prosaic Daniel."[18] Yet those, who thus designate this wise and amiable writer from the frequent in-correspondency of his diction to his metre in the majority of his compositions, not only deem them valuable and interesting on other accounts; but willingly admit, that there are to be found throughout his poems, and especially in his *Epistles* and in his *Hymen's Triumph,* many and exquisite specimens of that style which, as the *neutral ground* of prose and verse, is common to both. A fine and almost faultless extract, eminent as for other beauties, so for its perfection in this species of diction, may be seen in LAMB's Dramatic Specimens,[19] &c. a work of various interest from the nature of the selections themselves (all from the plays of Shakspeare's contemporaries) and deriving a high additional value from the notes, which are full of just and original criticism, expressed with all the freshness of originality.

Among the possible effects of practical adherence to a theory, that aims to *identify* the style of prose and verse (if it does not indeed claim for the latter a yet nearer resemblance to the average style of men in the vivâ voce intercourse of real life) we might anticipate the following as not the least likely to occur. It will happen, as I have indeed before observed, that the metre itself, the sole acknowledged difference, will occasionally become metre to the eye only. The existence of *prosaisms,* and that they detract from the merit of a poem, *must* at length be conceded, when a number of successive lines can be rendered, even to the most delicate ear, unrecognizable as verse, or as having even been intended for verse, by simply transcribing them as prose: when if the poem be in blank verse, this can be effected without any alteration, or at most by merely restoring one or two words to their proper places, from which they had been* transplanted for

* As the ingenious gentleman under the influence of the Tragic Muse contrived to dislocate, "I wish you a good morning, Sir! Thank you, Sir, and I wish you the same," into two blank-verse heroics:—

> To you a morning good, good Sir! I wish.
> You, Sir! I thank: to you the same wish I.

In those parts of Mr. Wordsworth's works which I have thoroughly studied, I find fewer instances in which this would be practicable than I have met in many poems, where an approximation of prose has been sedulously and on system guarded

17 Applied to Daniel in William Browne's *Britannia's Pastorals* (1613–1616), II, ii.
18 See Drayton's "To my most dearly loved friend, Henry Reynolds, Esquire, Of poets and poesy" (1627), ll. 123–28.
19 Refers to Charles Lamb's *Specimens of English Dramatic Poets* (1808), which quotes three passages from Daniel's *Hymen's Triumph. A Pastoral Tragi-Comedy* (1615).

no assignable cause or reason but that of the author's convenience; but if it be in rhyme, by the mere exchange of the final word of each line for some other of the same meaning, equally appropriate, dignified and euphonic.

The answer or objection in the preface to the anticipated remark "that metre paves the way to other distinctions," is contained in the following words. "The distinction of rhyme and metre is voluntary and uniform, and not like that produced by (what is called) poetic diction, arbitrary and subject to infinite caprices upon which no calculation whatever can be made. In the one case the reader is utterly at the mercy of the poet respecting what imagery or diction he may choose to connect with the passion." But is this a *poet*, of whom a poet is speaking? No surely! rather of a fool or madman: or at best of a vain or ignorant phantast! And might not Brains so wild and so deficient make just the same havock with rhymes and metres, as they are supposed to effect with modes and figures of speech? How is the reader at the *mercy* of such men? If he continue to read their nonsense, is it not his own fault? The ultimate end of criticism is much more to establish the principles of writing, than to furnish *rules* how to pass judgement on what has been written by others; if indeed it were possible that the two could be separated. But if it be asked, by what principles the poet is to regulate his own style, if he do not adhere closely to the sort and order of words which he hears

against. Indeed excepting the stanzas already quoted from the *Sailor's Mother*, I can recollect but one instance: viz. a short passage of four or five lines in THE BROTHERS, that model of English pastoral, which I never yet read with unclouded eye. —"James, pointing to its summit, over which they had all purposed to return together, informed them that he would wait for them there. They parted, and his comrades passed that way some two hours after, but they did not find him at the appointed place, *a circumstance of which they took no heed:* but one of them going by chance into the house, which at this time was James's house, learnt *there*, that nobody had seen him all that day." The only change which had been made is in the position of the little word *there* in two instances, the position in the original being clearly such as is not adopted in ordinary conversation. The other words printed in *italics* were so marked because, though good and genuine English, they are not the phraseology of common conversation either in the word put in apposition, or in the connection by the genitive pronoun. Men in general would have said, "but that was a circumstance they paid no attention to, or took no notice of," and the language is, on the theory of the preface, justified only by the narrator's being the *Vicar*. Yet if any ear *could* suspect, that these sentences were ever printed as metre, on those very words alone could the suspicion have been grounded.[20]

[20] Coleridge refers to "The Brothers" (1800), ll. 380–89 in the 1800 version. The passage was significantly revised in the 1820 edition.

in the market, wake, high-road, or plough-field? I reply; by principles, the ignorance or neglect of which would convict him of being no *poet*, but a silly or presumptuous usurper of the name! By the principles of grammar, logic, psychology! In one word by such a knowledge of the facts, material and spiritual, that most appertain to his art, as if it have been governed and applied by *good sense*, and rendered instinctive by habit, becomes the representative and reward of our past conscious reasonings, insights, and conclusions, and acquires the name of TASTE. By what *rule* that does not leave the reader at the poet's mercy, and the poet at his own, is the latter to distinguish between the language suitable to *suppressed*, and the language, which is characteristic of *indulged*, anger? Or between that of rage and that of jealousy? Is it obtained by wandering about in search of angry or jealous people in uncultivated society, in order to copy their words? Or not far rather by the power of imagination proceeding upon the *all in each* of human nature? By *meditation*, rather than by *observation*? And by the latter in consequence only of the former? As eyes, for which the former has pre-determined their field of vision, and to which, as to *its* organ, it communicates a microscopic power? There is not, I firmly believe, a man now living, who has from his own inward experience a clearer intuition, than Mr. Wordsworth himself, that the last mentioned are the true sources of *genial* discrimination. Through the same process and by the same creative agency will the poet distinguish the degree and kind of the excitement produced by the very act of poetic composition. As intuitively will he know, what differences of style it at once inspires and justifies; what intermixture of conscious volition is natural to that state; and in what instances such figures and colors of speech degenerate into mere creatures of an arbitrary purpose, cold technical artifices of ornament or connection. For even as truth is its own light and evidence, discovering at once itself and falsehood, so is it the prerogative of poetic genius to distinguish by parental instinct its proper offspring from the changelings, which the gnomes of vanity or the fairies of fashion may have laid in its cradle or called by its names. Could a rule be given from *without*, poetry would cease to be poetry, and sink into a mechanical art. It would be μορφωσις, not ποιησις.[21] The *rules* of the IMAGINATION are themselves the very powers of growth and production. The *words*, to which they are reducible, present only the outlines and external appearance of the fruit. A deceptive counterfeit of the superficial form and colors may be elaborat-

[21] μορφωσις ... ποιησις: "shaping, not creating."

ed; but the marble peach feels cold and heavy, and *children* only put it to their mouths. We find no difficulty in admitting as excellent, and the legitimate language of poetic fervor self-impassioned, DONNE's apostrophe to the Sun in the second stanza of his "Progress of the Soul."[22]

"Thee, eye of heaven! this great soul envies not:
By thy male force is all, we have, begot.
In the first East thou now beginn'st to shine,
Suck'st early balm and island spices there;
And wilt anon in thy loose-rein'd career
At Tagus, Po, Seine, Thames, and Danow dine,
And see at night this western world of mine:
Yet hast thou not more nations seen, than she,
Who before thee one day began to be,
And, thy frail light being quenched, shall long, long out-
live thee!"

Or the next stanza but one:

"Great destiny, the commissary of God,
That has marked out a path and period
For ev'ry thing! Who, where we offspring took,
Our ways and ends see'st at one instant: thou
Knot of all causes! Thou, whose changeless brow
Ne'er smiles or frowns! O vouchsafe thou to look,
And shew my story in thy eternal book, &c."

As little difficulty do we find in excluding from the honors of unaffected warmth and elevation the madness prepense of Pseudo-poesy, or the startling *hysteric* of weakness over-exerting itself, which bursts on the unprepared reader in sundry odes and apostrophes to abstract terms. Such are the Odes to Jealousy, to Hope, to Oblivion, and the like in Dodsley's collection[23] and the magazines of that day, which seldom fail to remind me of an Oxford copy of verses on the two SUTTONS,[24] commencing with

"INOCULATION, heavenly maid! descend!"

It is not to be denied that men of undoubted talents, and even poets of true, though not of first-rate, genius, have from a mistaken theory deluded both themselves and others in the opposite extreme. I once read to a company of sensible and well-educated women the introductory period of Cowley's preface to his "*Pin-*

daric Odes, written in imitation of the style and manner of the odes of Pindar."[25] "If (says Cowley) a man should undertake to translate Pindar, word for word, it would be thought that one madman had translated another; as may appear, when he, that understands not the original, reads the verbal traduction of him into Latin prose, than which nothing seems more raving." I then proceeded with his own free version of the second Olympic composed for the charitable purpose of *rationalizing* the Theban Eagle.

"Queen of all harmonious things,
Dancing words and speaking strings,
What God, what hero, wilt thou sing?
What happy man to equal glories bring?
Begin, begin thy noble choice,
And let the hills around reflect the image of thy voice.
Pisa does to Jove belong,
Jove and Pisa claim thy song.
The fair first-fruits of war, th' Olympic games,
Alcides offer'd up to Jove;
Alcides too thy strings may move!
But oh! what man to join with these can worthy prove?
Join Theron boldly to their sacred names;
Theron the next honor claims;
Theron to no man gives place;
Is first in Pisa's and in Virtue's race;
Theron there, and he alone,
Ev'n his own swift forefathers has outgone."

One of the company exclaimed, with the full assent of the rest, that if the original were madder than this, it must be incurably mad. I then translated the odes from the Greek, and as nearly as possible, word for word; and the impression was, that in the general movement of the periods, in the form of the connections and transitions, and in the sober majesty of lofty sense, it appeared to them to approach more nearly, than any other poetry they had heard, to the style of our bible in the prophetic books. The first strophe will suffice as a specimen:

"Ye harp-controuling hymns! (or) ye hymns the
sovereigns of harps!
What God? what Hero?
What Man shall we celebrate?
Truly Pisa indeed is of Jove,
But the Olympiad (or the Olympic games) did Hercules
establish,
The first-fruits of the spoils of war.
But Theron for the four-horsed car,
That bore victory to him,
It behoves us now to voice aloud:

---

22 "The Progresse of the Soule, Infinitati Sacrum, 16 August 1601," an unfinished poem, of which Coleridge quotes ll. 11–20, 31–40.
23 *Collection of Poems, by Several Hands* (1748), the leading anthology of eighteenth-century poetry very frequently reprinted throughout the century, prepared by Robert Dodsley (1703–64), editor and publisher.
24 Refers to "Beneficial Effects of Inoculation," the Oxford Prize Poem of 1772, by William Lipscomb. Daniel and Robert Sutton (fl. 1765) were provincial doctors, who greatly improved the process of inoculation (George Sampson).

---

25 "Pindarique Odes" were published in Cowley's *Poems* (1656). Coleridge later quotes the first stanza of "the second Olympic."

The Just, the Hospitable,
The Bulwark of Agrigentum,
Of renowned fathers
The Flower, even him
Who preserves his native city erect and safe."

But are such rhetorical caprices condemnable only for their deviation from the language of real life? and are they by no other means to be precluded, but by the rejection of all distinctions between prose and verse, save that of metre? Surely good sense, and a moderate insight into the constitution of the human mind, would be amply sufficient to prove, that such language and such combinations are the native produce neither of the fancy nor of the imagination; that their operation consists in the excitement of surprize by the juxta-position and *apparent* reconciliation of widely different or incompatible things. As when, for instance, the hills are made to reflect the image of a *voice*. Surely, no unusual taste is requisite to see clearly, that this compulsory juxta-position is not produced by the presentation of impressive or delightful forms to the inward vision, nor by any sympathy with the modifying powers with which the genius of the poet had united and inspirited all the objects of his thought; that it is therefore a species of *wit*, a pure work of the *will*, and implies a leisure and self-possession both of thought and of feeling, incompatible with the steady fervour of a mind possessed and filled with the grandeur of its subject. To sum up the whole in one sentence. When a poem, or a part of a poem, shall be adduced, which is evidently vicious in the figures and contexture of its style, yet for the condemnation of which no reason can be assigned, except that it differs from the style in which men actually converse, then, and not till then, can I hold this theory to be either plausible, or practicable, or capable of furnishing either rule, guidance, or precaution, that might not, more easily and more safely, as well as more naturally, have been deduced in the author's own mind from considerations of grammar, logic, and the truth and nature of things, confirmed by the authority of works, whose fame is, not of ONE country, nor of ONE age.

CHAPTER XIX

Continuation—Concerning the real object which, it is probable, Mr. Wordsworth had before him, in his critical preface—Elucidation and application of this—The neutral style, or that common to Prose and Poetry, exemplified by specimens from Chaucer, Herbert, &c.

I T MIGHT appear from some passages in the former part of Mr. Wordsworth's preface, that he meant to confine his theory of style, and the necessity of a close accordance with the actual language of men, to those particular subjects from low and rustic life, which by way of experiment he had purposed to naturalize as a new species in our English poetry. But from the train of argument that follows; from the reference to Milton; and from the spirit of his critique on Gray's sonnet; those sentences appear to have been rather courtesies of modesty, than actual limitations of his system. Yet so groundless does this system appear on a close examination; and so strange and * over-whelming in its consequences, that I cannot, and I do not, believe that the poet did ever himself adopt it in the unqualified sense, in which his expressions have been understood by others, and which indeed according to all the common laws of interpretation they seem to bear. What then did he mean? I apprehend, that in the clear perception, not unaccompanied with disgust or contempt, of the gaudy affectations of a style which passed too current with too many for poetic diction, (though in truth it had as little pretensions to poetry, as to logic or common sense) he narrowed his view for the time; and feeling a justifiable preference for the language of nature, and of good-sense, even in its humblest and least ornamented forms, he suffered himself to express, in terms at once too large and too exclusive, his predilection for a style the most remote possible from the false and showy splendor which he wished to explode. It is possible, that this predilection, at first merely comparative, deviated for a time into direct partiality. But the real object, which he had in view, was, I doubt not, a species of excellence which had been long before most happily characterized by the judicious and amiable GARVE, whose works are so justly beloved and esteemed by the Germans, in his remarks on GELLERT (see Sammlung Einiger Abhandlungen von Christian Garve)[2] from which the

* I had in my mind the striking but untranslatable epithet, which the celebrated Mendelssohn[1] applied to the great founder of the Critical Philosophy "*Der alleszermalmende* KANT," i.e. the all-becrushing, or rather the *all-to-nothing-crushing* KANT. In the facility and force of compound epithets, the German from the number of its cases and inflections approaches to the Greek: that language so

"Bless'd in the happy marriage of sweet words."

It is in the woeful harshness of its sounds alone that the German need shrink from the comparison.

[1] Moses Mendelssohn (1729–1786) was the leading Jewish philosopher of his time and the grandfather of the composer Felix Mendelssohn.
[2] Christian Garve (1742–1798) was a German philosopher. Coleridge quotes from his *Vermischte Anmerkungen über Gellerts Moral, dessen Schriften überhaupt und Charakter. Sammlung einiger Abhandlungen aus der neuen Bibliothek der schönen Wissenschaften und der freyen Kunste (1799)* (See *The Notebooks of Samuel Taylor*

following is literally translated. "The talent, that is required in order to make excellent verses, is perhaps greater than the philosopher is ready to admit, or would find it in his power to acquire: the talent to seek only the apt expression of the thought, and yet to find at the same time with it the rhyme and the metre. Gellert possessed this happy gift, if ever any one of our poets possessed it; and nothing perhaps contributed more to the great and universal impression which his fables made on their first publication, or conduces more to their continued popularity. It was a strange and curious phenomenon, and such as in Germany had been previously unheard of, to read verses in which every thing was expressed, just as one would wish to talk, and yet all dignified, attractive, and interesting; and all at the same time perfectly correct as to the measure of the syllables and the rhyme. It is certain, that poetry when it has attained this excellence makes a far greater impression than prose. So much so indeed, that even the gratification which the very rhymes afford, becomes then no longer a contemptible or trifling gratification."

However novel this phenomenon may have been in Germany at the time of Gellert, it is by no means new nor yet of recent existence in our language. Spite of the licentiousness with which Spenser occasionally compels the orthography of his words into a subservience to his rhymes, the whole Fairy Queen is an almost continued instance of this beauty. Waller's song "Go, lovely Rose, &c." is doubtless familiar to most of my readers; but if I had happened to have had by me the Poems of COTTON, more but far less deservedly celebrated as the author of the Virgil travestied, I should have indulged myself, and I think have gratified many who are not acquainted with his serious works, by selecting some admirable specimens of this style. There are not a few poems in that volume,[3] replete with every excellence of thought, image, and passion, which we expect or desire in the poetry of the milder muse; and yet so worded, that the reader sees no one reason either in the selection or the order of the words, why he might not have said the very same in an appropriate conversation, and cannot con-

ceive how indeed he could have expressed such thoughts otherwise, without loss or injury to his meaning.

But in truth our language is, and from the first dawn of poetry ever has been, particularly rich in compositions distinguished by this excellence. The final e, which is now mute, in Chaucer's age was either sounded or dropt indifferently. We ourselves still use either *beloved* or *belov'd* according as the rhyme, or measure, or the purpose of more or less solemnity may require. Let the reader then only adopt the pronunciation of the poet and of the court, at which he lived, both with respect to the final e and to the accentuation of the last syllable: I would then venture to ask, what even in the colloquial language of elegant and unaffected women (who are the peculiar mistresses of "pure English and undefiled,")[4] what could we hear more natural, or seemingly more unstudied, than the following stanzas from Chaucer's Troilus and Creseide.

"And after this forth to the gate he went,
    Ther as Creseide out rode a full gode paas:
And up and doun there made he many a wente,
    And to himselfe ful oft he said, Alas!
    Fro hennis rode my blisse and my solas:
As woudè blisful God now for his joie,
I might her sene agen come in to Troie!

And to the yondir hill I gan her guide,
    Alas! and there I toke of her my leave:
And yond I saw her to her fathir ride;
    For sorrow of which mine hearte shall to-cleve;
    And hithir home I came when it was eve;
And here I dwel; out-cast from allè joie,
And shall, til I maic sene her efte in Troie.

And of himself imagined he ofte
    To ben defaitid, pale and waxen lesse
Than he was wonte, and that men saidin softe,
    What may it be? who can the sothè guess,
    Why Troilus hath al this heviness?
And al this n' as but his melancholie,
That he had of himselfe suche fantasie.

Another time imaginin he would
    That every wight, that past him by the wey
Had of him routhe, and that they saien should,
    I am right sorry, Troilus will die!
    And thus he drove a daie yet forth or twey
As ye have herde: suche life gan he to lede
As he that strode betwixin hope and drede:

    For which him likid in his songis shewe
Th' encheson of his wo as he best might,
    And made a songe of wordis but a fewe,
    Somwhat his woefull hertè for to light,
    And when he was from every mann'is sight
With softè voice he of his lady dere,
    That absent was, gan sing as ye may hear:

Coleridge, ed. Coburn, I [Notes], 1702). Christian Gellert (1715–1769) was a professor of philosophy at Leipzig and popular poet of fables (1746–1748) and "spiritual songs" (1757). According to Professor Coburn, "the passage is not literally translated"; "'just as one would wish to talk'... introduces an element of idealisation into the plain naturalism of Garve's statement."

3 Charles Cotton (1630–1687) was the author of *Scarronides: or, Virgile Travestie* (1664–1665), which was a burlesque of Books I and IV of the *Aeneid*. His lyric poems, much admired by the Romantics, had first appeared in the posthumously published volume *Poems on Several Occasions* (1689). For examples of his verses, see Wordsworth's "Preface to *Poems*" (1815), pp. 70–77, and Lamb's "New Year's Eve," p. 365.

4 See *Faerie Queene*, IV, ii, 32.

* * * * * * * *

This song when he thus songin had, full soon
He fell agen into his sighis olde:
And every night, as was his wonte to done,
He stodè the bright monnè to beholde
And all his sorrowe to the moone he tolde,
And said: I wis, when thou art hornid newe,
I shall be glad, if al the world be trewe!"[5]

Another exquisite master of this species of style, where the scholar and the poet supplies the material, but the perfect well-bred gentleman the expressions and the arrangement, is George Herbert. As from the nature of the subject, and the too frequent quaintness of the thoughts, his "Temple; or Sacred Poems and Private Ejaculations" are comparatively but little known, I shall extract two poems. The first is a Sonnet, equally admirable for the weight, number, and expression of the thoughts, and for the simple dignity of the language. (Unless indeed a fastidious taste should object to the latter half of the sixth line.) The second is a poem of greater length, which I have chosen not only for the present purpose, but likewise as a striking example and illustration of an assertion hazarded in a former page of these sketches: namely, that the characteristic fault of our elder poets is the reverse of that, which distinguishes too many of our more recent versifiers; the one conveying the most fantastic thoughts in the most correct and natural language; the other in the most fantastic language conveying the most trivial thoughts. The latter is a riddle of words; the former an enigma of thoughts. The one reminds me of an odd passage in Drayton's IDEAS:

SONNET IX.

As other men, so I myself do muse,
Why in this sort I wrest invention so;
And why these *giddy metaphors* I use,
Leaving the path the greater part do go?
I will resolve you: *I am lunatic!*

The other recalls a still odder passage in the "SYNA-GOGUE: *or the Shadow of the Temple*,"[6] a connected series of poems in imitation of Herbert's "TEMPLE," and in some editions annexed to it.

O how my mind
Is gravell'd!
Not a thought,
That I can find,
But's ravell'd
All to nought!

⸺⸺⸺⸺⸺⸺⸺⸺⸺

5 V, 603–637, 645–51.
6 Coleridge quotes from "Confusion" in Christopher Harvey's *Synagogue* (1640).

Short ends of threds,
And narrow shreds
Of lists;
Knot's snarled ruffs,
Loose broken tufts
Of twists;
Are my torn meditations ragged cloathing,
Which wound and woven shape a sute for nothing:
One while I think, and then I am in pain
To think how to unthink that thought again!

Immediately after these burlesque passages, I cannot proceed to the extracts promised, without changing the ludicrous tone of feeling by the interposition of the three following stanzas of Herbert's.

VIRTUE.

Sweet day so cool, so calm, so bright,
The bridal of the earth and sky:
The dew shall weep thy fall to night,
For thou must dye!

Sweet rose, whose hue angry and brave
Bids the rash gazer wipe his eye:
Thy root is ever in its grave,
And thou must dye!

Sweet spring, full of sweet days and roses,
A nest, where sweets compacted lie:
My musick shews, ye have your closes,
And all must dye!

THE BOSOM SIN:

A SONNET BY GEORGE HERBERT.

Lord, with what care hast thou begirt us round!
Parents first season us; then schoolmasters
Deliver us to laws; they send us bound
To rules of reason, holy messengers,
Pulpits and Sundays, sorrow dogging sin,
Afflictions sorted, anguish of all sizes,
Fine nets and stratagems to catch us in,
Bibles laid open, millions of surprizes;
Blessings before hand, ties of gratefulness,
The sound of glory ringing in our ears:
Without, our shame; within, our consciences;
Angels and grace, eternal hopes and fears!
Yet all these fences, and their whole array
One cunning BOSOM-SIN blows quite away.

LOVE UNKNOWN.

Dear friend, sit down, the tale is long and sad:
And in my faintings, I presume, your love
Will more comply than help. A Lord I had,
And have, of whom some grounds, which may improve,
I hold for two lives, and both lives in me.
To him I brought a dish of fruit one day
And in the middle placed my HEART. But he
(I sigh to say)

Lookt on a servant who did know his eye,
Better than you knew me, or (which is one)
Than I myself. The servant instantly,
Quitting the fruit, seiz'd on my *heart* alone,
And threw it in a font, wherein did fall
A stream of blood, which issued from the side
Of a great rock: I well remember all,
And have good cause: there it was dipt and dy'd,
And washt, and wrung! the very wringing yet
Enforceth tears. *Your heart was foul, I fear.*
Indeed 'tis true. I did and do commit
Many a fault, more than my lease will bear;
Yet still ask'd pardon, and was not deny'd.
But you shall hear. After my heart was well,
And clean and fair, as I one eventide,
                                        (I sigh to tell)
Walkt by myself abroad, I saw a large
And spacious furnance flaming, and thereon
A boiling caldron, round about whose verge
Was in great letters set AFFLICTION.
The greatness shew'd the owner. So I went
To fetch a sacrifice out of my fold,
Thinking with that, which I did thus present,
To warm his love, which, I did fear, grew cold.
But as my heart did tender it, the man
Who was to take it from me, slipt his hand,
And threw my *heart* into the scalding pan;
My heart that brought it (do you understand?)
The *offerer's* heart. *Your heart was hard, I fear.*
Indeed 'tis true. I found a callous matter
Began to spread and to expatiate these:
But with a richer drug than scalding water
I bath'd it often, ev'n with holy blood,
Which at a board, while many drank bare wine,
A friend did steal into my cup for good,
Ev'n taken inwardly, and most divine
To supple hardnesses. But at the length
Out of the caldron getting, soon I fled
Unto my house, where to repair the strength
Which I had lost, I hasted to my bed;
But when I thought to sleep out all these faults,
                                        (I sigh to speak)
I found that some had stuff'd the bed with thoughts,
I would say *thorns.* Dear, could my heart not break,
When with my pleasures even my rest was gone?
Full well I understood who had been there:
For I had given the key to none but one:
It must be he. *Your heart was dull, I fear.*
Indeed a slack and sleepy state of mind
Did oft possess me; so that when I pray'd,
Though my lips went, my heart did stay behind.
But all my scores were by another paid,
Who took my guilt upon him. *Truly, friend;*
For ought I hear, your master shows to you
More favour than you wot of. Mark the end!
The font did only what was old renew:
The caldron suppled what was grown too hard:
The thorns did quicken what was grown too dull:
All did but strive to mend what you had marr'd.

Wherefore be cheer'd, and praise him to the full
Each day, each hour, each moment of the week,
Who fain would have you be new, tender, quick!

CHAPTER XX

The former subject continued.

I HAVE no fear in declaring my conviction, that the excellence defined and exemplified in the preceding Chapter is not the characteristic excellence of Mr. Wordsworth's style; because I can add with equal sincerity, that it is precluded by higher powers. The praise of uniform adherence to genuine, logical English is undoubtedly his; nay, laying the main emphasis on the word *uniform* I will dare add that, of all contemporary poets, it is *his alone.* For in a less absolute sense of the word, I should certainly include MR. BOWLES, LORD BYRON, and, as to all his later writings, MR. SOUTHEY, the exceptions in their works being so few and unimportant. But of the specific excellence described in the quotation from Garve, I appear to find more, and more undoubted specimens in the works of others; for instance, among the minor poems of Mr. Thomas Moore, and of our illustrious Laureate.[1] To me it will always remain a singular and noticeable fact; that a theory which would establish this *lingua communis*, not only as the best, but as the only commendable style, should have proceeded from a poet, whose diction, next to that of Shakspeare and Milton, appears to me of all others the most *individualized* and characteristic. And let it be remembered too, that I am now interpreting the controverted passages of Mr. W.'s critical preface by the purpose and object, which he may be supposed to have intended, rather than by the sense which the words themselves must convey, if they are taken without this allowance.

A person of any taste, who had but studied three or four of Shakspeare's principal plays, would without the name affixed scarcely fail to recognize as Shakspeare's, a quotation from any other play, though but of a few lines. A similar peculiarity, though in a less degree, attends Mr. Wordsworth's style, whenever he speaks in his own person; or whenever, though under a feigned name, it is clear that he himself is still speaking, as in the different dramatis personæ of the "RECLUSE."[2] Even in the other poems in which he

---

[1] Robert Southey.
[2] That is, the various characters in *The Excursion*, originally conceived as the second part of a three-part "philosophical poem, containing views of Man, Nature, and Society; and to be entitled, The Recluse."

purposes to be most dramatic, there are few in which it does not occasionally burst forth. The reader might often address the poet in his own words with reference to the persons introduced:

"It seems as I retrace the ballad line by line
  That but half of it is theirs, and the better half is thine." [3]

Who, having been previously acquainted with any considerable portion of Mr. Wordsworth's publications, and having studied them with a full feeling of the author's genius, would not at once claim as Wordsworthian the little poem on the rainbow?

"The child is father of the man, &c." [4]

Or in the "Lucy Gray"?

"No mate, no comrade Lucy knew;
  She dwelt on a wide moor;
  The sweetest thing that ever grew
  Beside a human door." [5]

Or in the "Idle Shepherd-boys"?

"Along the river's stony marge
  The sand-lark chaunts a joyous song;
  The thrush is busy in the wood,
  And carols loud and strong.
  A thousand lambs are on the rock
  All newly born! both earth and sky
  Keep jubilee, and more than all,
  Those boys with their green coronal,
  They never hear the cry,
  That plaintive cry which up the hill
  Comes from the depth of Dungeon Gill." [6]

Need I mention the exquisite description of the Sea Loch in the "Blind Highland Boy." [7] Who but a poet tells a tale in such language to the little ones by the fire-side as—

"Yet had he many a restless dream
  Both when he heard the eagle's scream,
  And when he heard the torrents roar,
  And heard the water beat the shore
        Near where their cottage stood.

Beside a lake their cottage stood,
  Not small like our's a peaceful flood;
  But one of mighty size, and strange
  That rough or smooth is full or change
        And stirring in its bed.

For to this lake by night and day,
  The greater sea-water finds its way
  Through long, long windings of the hills,
  And drinks up all the pretty rills;
        And rivers large and strong:

Then hurries back the road it came—
  Returns on errand still the same;
  This did it when the earth was new;
  And this for evermore will do,
        As long as earth shall last.

And with the coming of the tide,
  Come boats and ships that sweetly ride,
  Between the woods and lofty rocks;
  And to the shepherd with their flocks
        Bring tales of distant lands."

I might quote almost the whole of his "RUTH," but take the following stanzas:

"But as you have before been told,
  This stripling, sportive gay and bold,
  And with his dancing crest,
  So beautiful, through savage lands
  Had roam'd about with vagrant bands
        Of Indians in the West.

The wind, the tempest roaring high,
  The tumult of a tropic sky,
  Might well be dangerous food
  For him, a youth to whom was given
  So much of earth, so much of heaven,
        And such impetuous blood.

Whatever in those climes he found
  Irregular in sight or sound,
  Did to his mind impart
  A kindred impulse; seem'd allied
  To his own powers, and justified
        The workings of his heart.

Nor less to feed voluptuous thought
  The beauteous forms of nature wrought,
  Fair trees and lovely flowers;
  The breezes their own langour lent,
  The stars had feelings, which they sent
        Into those magic bowers.

Yet in his worst pursuits, I ween,
  That sometimes there did intervene
  Pure hopes of high intent:
  For passions, link'd to forms so fair
  And stately, needs must have their share
        Of noble sentiment." [8]

But from Mr. Wordsworth's more elevated compositions, which already form three-fourths of his

---

3 See "The Pet-Lamb" (1800), ll. 63–64.
4 "My heart leaps up when I behold" (1807), l. 7.
5 (1800), ll. 5–8.
6 (1800), ll. 23–33.
7 (1807), ll. 46–70.

8 (1800), ll. 109–138.

works; and will, I trust, constitute hereafter a still larger proportion;—from these, whether in rhyme or blank-verse, it would be difficult and almost superfluous to select instances of a diction peculiarly his own, of a style which cannot be imitated without its being at once recognized, as originating in Mr. Wordsworth. It would not be easy to open on any one of his loftier strains, that does not contain examples of this; and more in proportion as the lines are more excellent, and most like the author. For those, who may happen to have been less familiar with his writings, I will give three specimens taken with little choice. The first from the lines on the "BOY OF WINANDER-MERE,"[9]—who

> "Blew mimic hootings to the silent owls,
>   That they might answer him. And they would shout,
> Across the water vale and shout again
> With long halloos, and screams, and echoes loud
> Redoubled and redoubled, concourse wild
> Of mirth and jocund din. And when it chanc'd,
> That pauses of deep silence mock'd his skill,
> *Then sometimes in that silence, while he hung*
> *Listening, a gentle shock of mild surprize*
> *Has carried far into his heart the voice*
> *Of mountain torrents; or the visible scene**

* Mr. Wordsworth's having judiciously adopted "*concourse wild*" [l. 15] in this passage for "*a wild scene*" as it stood in the former edition, encourages me to hazard a remark, which I certainly should not have made in the works of a poet less austerely accurate in the use of words, than he is, to his own great honor. It respects the propriety of the word, "*scene*," even in the sentence in which it is retained. DRYDEN, and he only in his more careless verses, was the first as far as my researches have discovered, who for the convenience of rhyme used this word in the vague sense, which has been since too current even in our best writers, and which (unfortunately, I think) is given as its first explanation in Dr. Johnson's Dictionary, and therefore would be taken by an incautious reader as its proper sense. In Shakspeare and Milton the word is never used without some clear reference, proper or metaphorical, to the theatre. Thus Milton:

> "Cedar and pine, and fir and branching palm
>   A Sylvan *scene*; and as the ranks ascend
> Shade above shade, a woody *theatre*
> Of stateliest view."

I object to any extension of its meaning because the word is already more equivocal than might be wished; inasmuch as in the limited use, which I recommend, it may still signify two different things; namely, the scenery, and the characters and actions presented on the stage during the presence of particular scenes. It can therefore be preserved from *obscurity* only by keeping the original signification full in the mind. Thus Milton again,

> "Prepare thou for another scene."[10]

[9] "There was a Boy" (1800), from which Coleridge quotes ll. 10-12, 14-25.
[10] The change from "a wild scene" to "concourse wild" occurred in the 1805 edition of *Lyrical Ballads*. Dr. Johnson cites

> *Would enter unawares into his mind*
> *With all its solemn imagery, its rocks,*
> *Its woods, and that uncertain heaven, received*
> *Into the bosom of the steady lake.*"

The second shall be that noble imitation of Drayton† (if it was not rather a coincidence) in the "JOANNA."

> "When I had gazed perhaps two minutes' space,
> Joanna, looking in my eyes, beheld
> That ravishment of mine, and laugh'd aloud.
> The rock, like something starting from a sleep,
> Took up the lady's voice, and laugh'd again!
> That ancient woman seated on *Helm-crag*
> Was ready with her cavern! *Hammar-scar*,
> And the tall steep of SILVER-HOW sent forth
> A noise of laughter: southern LOUGHRIGG heard,
> And FAIRFIELD answered with a mountain tone.
> HELVELLYN far into the clear blue sky
> Carried the lady's voice!—old SKIDDAW blew
> His speaking trumpet!—back out of the clouds
> From GLARAMARA southward came the voice:
> And KIRKSTONE tossed it from his misty head!"[11]

The third which is in rhyme I take from the "Song at the feast of Brougham Castle, upon the restoration of Lord Clifford the shepherd to the estates of his ancestors."

> "Now another day is come,
>   Fitter hope, and nobler doom:
> He hath thrown aside his crook,
> And hath buried deep his book;

† Which COPLAND scarce had spoke, but quickly every hill
Upon her verge that stands, the neighbouring vallies fill;
HELVILLON from his height, it through the mountains threw.
From whom as soon again, the sound DUNBALRASE drew,
From whose stone-trophied herd, it on the WENDROSS went,
Which, tow'rds the sea again, resounded it to DENT.
That BROADWATER, therewith within her banks astound,
In sailing to the sea told it to EGREMOUND,
Whose buildings, walks and streets, with echoes loud and long
Did mightily commend old COPLAND for her song!
DRAYTON'S POLYOLBION: *Song* XXX.

passages from Dryden's translations of Lucretius, Virgil, and Boccaccio in illustration of the *second* meaning of "scene" as "the general appearance of any action; the whole contexture of objects; a series; a regular disposition." He cites the passage from Milton: "Cedar and pine . . . stateliest view" (*Paradise Lost*, IV, 139-42), in illustration of the *first* meaning of "scene" as "the stage; theatre of dramatick poetry." "Prepare thou for another scene" is from *Paradise Lost*, XI, 637.
[11] "To Joanna" (1800), ll. 51-65.

Armour rusting in the halls
On the blood of Clifford calls;
Quell the Scot, exclaims the lance!
Bear me to the heart of France
Is the longing of the shield—
Tell thy name, thou trembling field!
Field of death, where'er thou be,
Groan thou with our victory!
Happy day, and mighty hour,
When our shepherd, in his power,
Mailed and horsed with lance and sword,
To his ancestors restored,
Like a re-appearing star,
Like a glory from afar,
First shall head the flock of war!"
    Alas! the fervent harper did not know,
That for a tranquil soul the lay was framed,
Who, long compelled in humble walks to go
Was softened into feeling, soothed, and tamed.
Love had he found in huts where poor men lie:
His daily teachers had been woods and rills,
The silence that is in the starry sky,
The sleep that is among the lonely hills." [12]

The words themselves in the foregoing extracts, are, no doubt, sufficiently common for the greater part. (But in what poem are they not so? if we except a few misadventurous attempts to translate the arts and sciences into verse?) In the "Excursion" the number of polysyllabic (or what the common people call, *dictionary*) words is more than usually great. And so must it needs be, in proportion to the number and variety of an author's conceptions, and his solicitude to express them with precision. But are those words *in those places* commonly employed in real life to express the same thought or outward thing? Are they the style used in the ordinary intercourse of spoken words? No! nor are the modes of connections: and still less the breaks and transitions. Would any but a poet—at least could any one without being conscious that he had expressed himself with noticeable vivacity —have described a bird singing loud by, "The thrush is *busy* in the wood?" Or have spoken of boys with a string of club-moss round their rusty hats, as the boys *"with their green coronal?"* Or have translated a beautiful May-day into *"Both earth and sky keep jubilee?"* Or have brought all the different marks and circumstances of a sea-loch before the mind, as the actions of a living and acting power? Or have represented the reflection of the sky in the water, as *"That uncertain heaven received into the bosom of the steady lake?"* Even the grammatical construction is not unfrequently peculiar; as "The wind, the tempest roaring high, the tumult of a tropic sky, might well be

----

[12] (1807), ll. 138–64.

dangerous food to him, a youth to whom was given, &c." There is a peculiarity in the frequent use of the ἀσυναρτητὸν (i.e., the omission of the connective particle before the last of several words, or several sentences used grammatically as single words, all being in the same case and governing or governed by the same verb) and not less in the construction of words by apposition (*to him, a youth*). In short, were there excluded from Mr. Wordsworth's poetic compositions all, that a literal adherence to the theory of his preface *would* exclude, two-thirds at least of the marked beauties of his poetry must be erased. For a far greater number of lines would be sacrificed, than in any other recent poet; because the pleasure received from Wordsworth's poems being less derived either from excitement of curiosity or the rapid flow of narration, the *striking* passages form a larger proportion of their value. I do not adduce it as a fair criterion of comparative excellence, nor do I even think it such; but merely as matter of fact. I affirm, that from no contemporary writer could so many lines be quoted, without reference to the poem in which they are found, for their own independent weight or beauty. From the sphere of my own experience I can bring to my recollection three persons of no every-day powers and acquirements, who had read the poems of others with more and more unallayed pleasure, and had thought more highly of their authors, as poets; who yet have confessed to me, that from no modern work had so many passages started up anew in their minds at different times and as different occasions had awakened a meditative mood.

F R O M

CHAPTER XXII

The characteristic defects of Wordsworth's poetry, with the principles from which the judgement, that they are defects, is deduced—Their proportion to the beauties—For the greatest part characteristic of his theory only.

IF MR. WORDSWORTH have set forth principles of poetry which his arguments are insufficient to support, let him and those who have adopted his sentiments be set right by the confutation of those arguments, and by the substitution of more philosophical principles. And still let the due credit be given to the portion and importance of the truths, which are blended with his theory: truths, the too exclusive attention to which had occasioned its errors, by tempting him to carry those truths beyond their proper limits. If his mistaken theory have at all influenced his poetic compositions, let the effects be pointed out, and the instances given

But let it likewise be shewn, how far the influence has acted; whether diffusively, or only by starts; whether the number and importance of the poems and passages thus infected be great or trifling compared with the sound portion; and lastly, whether they are inwoven into the texture of his works, or are loose and separable. The result of such a trial would evince beyond a doubt, what it is high time to announce decisively and aloud, that the *supposed* characteristics of Mr. Wordsworth's poetry, whether admired or reprobated; whether they are simplicity or simpleness; faithful adherence to essential nature, or wilful selections from human nature of its meanest forms and under the least attractive associations; are as little the *real* characteristics of his poetry at large, as of his genius and the constitution of his mind.

In a comparatively small number of poems, he chose to try an experiment; and this experiment we will suppose to have failed. Yet even in these poems it is impossible not to perceive, that the natural *tendency* of the poet's mind is to great objects and elevated conceptions. The poem intitled "Fidelity" is for the greater part written in language, as unraised and naked as any perhaps in the two volumes. Yet take the following stanza and compare it with the preceding stanzas of the same poem.

> "There sometimes does a leaping fish
>   Send through the tarn a lonely cheer;
>   The crags repeat the Raven's croak
>   In symphony austere;
>   Thither the rainbow comes—the cloud,
>   And mists that spread the flying shroud;
>   And sun-beams; and the sounding blast,
>   That if it could would hurry past,
>   But that enormous barrier binds it fast." [1]

Or compare the four last lines of the concluding stanza with the former half:

> "Yet proof was plain that since the day
>   On which the traveller thus had died,
>   The dog had watch'd about the spot,
>   Or by his master's side:
>   *How nourish'd there for such long time*
>   *He knows who gave that love sublime,*
>   *And gave that strength of feeling great*
>   *Above all human estimate.*"

Can any candid and intelligent mind hesitate in determining, which of these best represents the tendency and native character of the poet's genius? Will he not decide that the one was written because the poet *would*

so write, and the other because he could not so entirely repress the force and grandeur of his mind, but that he must in some part or other of *every* composition write otherwise? In short, that his only disease is the being out of his element; like the swan, that having amused himself, for a while, with crushing the weeds on the river's bank, soon returns to his own majestic movements on its reflecting and sustaining surface. Let it be observed, that I am here supposing the imagined judge, to whom I appeal, to have already decided against the poet's theory, as far as it is different from the principles of the art, generally acknowledged.

I cannot here enter into a detailed examination of Mr. Wordsworth's works; but I will attempt to give the main results of my own judgement, after an acquaintance of many years, and repeated perusals. And though, to appreciate the defects of a great mind it is necessary to understand previously its characteristic excellences, yet I have already expressed myself with sufficient fulness, to preclude most of the ill effects that might arise from my pursuing a contrary arrangement. I will therefore commence with what I deem the prominent *defects* of his poems hitherto published.

The first *characteristic, though only occasional* defect, which I appear to myself to find in these poems is the INCONSTANCY of the *style*. Under this name I refer to the sudden and unprepared transitions from lines or sentences of peculiar felicity (at all events striking and original) to a style, not only unimpassioned but undistinguished. He sinks too often and too abruptly to that style, which I should place in the second division of language, dividing it into the three species: *first*, that which is peculiar to poetry; *second*, that which is only proper in prose; and *third*, the neutral or common to both. There have been works, such as Cowley's essay on Cromwell,[2] in which prose and verse are intermixed (not as in the Consolation of Boetius, or the Argenis of Barclay,[3] by the insertion of poems supposed to have been spoken or composed on occasions previously related in prose, but) the poet passing from one to the other as the nature of the thoughts or his own feelings dictated. Yet this mode of composition does not satisfy a cultivated taste. There is something unpleasant in the being thus obliged to alternate states of feeling so dissimilar, and this too in a species of writing, the pleasure from which is in part derived from the preparation and previous expectation of the reader. A portion of that awkwardness is felt which hangs upon the introduction of songs in our modern comic operas; and to prevent

---

[1] Ll. 25–33.

[2] Abraham Cowley's *A Vision, concerning his late pretended Highness, Cromwell the Wicked* (1661).
[3] *Argenis* (1621) was a very popular Latin romance by John Barclay (1582–1621), poet and satirist.

which the judicious Metastasio [4] (as to whose exquisite *taste* there can be no hesitation, whatever doubts may be entertained as to his *poetic genius*) uniformly placed the ARIA at the end of the scene, at the same time that he almost always raises and impassions the style of the recitative immediately preceding. Even in real life, the difference is great and evident between words used as the *arbitrary marks* of thought, our smooth market-coin of intercourse with the image and superscription worn out by currency; and those which convey pictures either borrowed from *one* outward object to enliven and particularize some *other*; or used allegorically to body forth the inward state of the person speaking; or such as are at least the exponents of his peculiar turn and unusual extent of faculty. So much so indeed, that in the social circles of private life we often find a striking use of the latter put a stop to the general flow of conversation, and by the excitement arising from concentered attention produce a sort of damp and interruption for some minutes after. But in the perusal of works of literary *art*, we *prepare* ourselves for such language; and the business of the writer, like that of a painter whose subject requires unusual splendor and prominence, is so to raise the lower and neutral tints, that what in a different style would be the *commanding* colors, are here used as the means of that gentle *degradation* requisite in order to produce the effect of a *whole*. Where this is not atchieved in a poem, the metre merely reminds the reader of his claims in order to disappoint them; and where this defect occurs frequently, his feelings are alternately startled by anticlimax and hyperclimax.

I refer the reader to the exquisite stanzas cited for another purpose from the blind Highland Boy; and then annex as being in my opinion instances of this *disharmony* in style the two following:

"And one, the rarest, was a shell,
    Which he, poor child, had studied well:
    The shell of a green turtle, thin
    And hollow;—you might sit therein,
        It was so wide, and deep."

"Our Highland Boy oft visited
    The house which held this prize, and led
    By choice or chance did thither come
    One day, when no one was at home,
        And found the door unbarred." [5]

Or page 172, vol. I.

"'Tis gone forgotten, *let me do
    My best*. There was a smile or two—
    I can remember them, I see
    The smiles worth all the world to me.
    Dear Baby, I must lay thee down:
    Thou troublest me with strange alarms!
    Smiles hast thou, sweet ones of thine own;
    I cannot keep thee in my arms,
    For they confound me: *as it is*,
    I have forgot those smiles of his!" [6]

Or page 269, vol. I.

"Thou has a nest, for thy love and thy rest,
    And though little troubled with sloth
    Drunken lark! thou would'st be loth
    To be such a traveller as I.
        Happy, happy liver
    *With a soul as strong as a mountain river
    Pouring out praise to th' Almighty giver!*
    Joy and jollity be with us both,
    Hearing thee or else some other,
        As merry a brother
    I on the earth will go plodding on
    By myself chearfully till the day is done." [7]

The incongruity, which I appear to find in this passage, is that of the two noble lines in italics with the preceding and following. So vol. II, page 30.

"Close by a pond, upon the further side
    He stood alone; a minute's space I guess,
    I watch'd him, he continuing motionless;
    To the pool's further margin then I drew;
    He being all the while before me full in view." [8]

Compare this with the repetition of the same image, in the next stanza but two.

"And still as I drew near with gentle pace,
    Beside the little pond or moorish flood
    Motionless as a cloud the old man stood;
    That heareth not the loud winds as they call
    And moveth altogether, if it move at all."

Or lastly, the second of the three following stanzas, compared both with the first and the third.

---

4 Pietro Trapassi (1698–1782), the greatest and most celebrated author of Italian *opera seria* librettos, and a major Italian lyric poet.
5 Coleridge quotes from stanzas introduced in the 1815 version of the poem. The first of the stanzas cited was considerably revised for the 1820 edition of Wordsworth's poems. For "the exquisite stanzas cited for another purpose," see Chapter XX.

6 "The Emigrant Mother" (1807), ll. 55–64. The offending italicized words were revised in the 1820 edition.
7 The concluding passage of "To a Sky-Lark" (1807). The last four lines were revised for the 1827 edition of Wordsworth's poems.
8 "Resolution and Independence" (1807). Coleridge quotes from the ninth stanza of the 1815 version. The entire stanza was dropped in the 1820 edition. Coleridge next quotes ll. 74–77, 113–31.

"My former thoughts returned, the fear that kills;
   And hope that is unwilling to be fed;
   Cold, pain, and labour, and all fleshly ills;
   And mighty poets in their misery dead.
   But now, perplex'd by what the old man has said,
   My question eagerly did I renew,
   'How is it that you live, and what is it you do?'

He with a smile did then his tale repeat;
   And said, that, gathering leeches far and wide
   He travelled; stirring thus about his feet
   The waters of the ponds where they abide.
'Once I could meet with them on every side,
'But they have dwindled long by slow decay;
'Yet still I persevere, and find them where I may.'

While he was talking thus, the lonely place,
   The old man's shape, and speech, all troubled me;
   In my mind's eye I seemed to see him pace
   About the weary moors continually,
   Wandering about alone and silently."

Indeed this fine poem is *especially* characteristic of the author. There is scarce a defect or excellence in his writings of which it would not present a specimen. But it would be unjust not to repeat that this defect is only occasional. From a careful reperusal of the two volumes of poems, I doubt whether the objectionable passages would amount in the whole to one hundred lines; not the eighth part of the number of pages. In the EXCURSION the feeling of incongruity is seldom excited by the diction of any passage considered in itself, but by the sudden superiority of some other passage forming the context.

The second defect I could generalize with tolerable accuracy, if the reader will pardon an uncouth and new coined word. There is, I should say, not seldom a *matter-of-factness* in certain poems. This may be divided into, *first*, a laborious minuteness and fidelity in the representation of objects, and their positions, as they appeared to the poet himself; *secondly*, the insertion of accidental circumstances, in order to the full explanation of his living characters, their dispositions and actions; which circumstances might be necessary to establish the probability of a statement in real life, where nothing is taken for granted by the hearer, but appear superfluous in poetry, where the reader is willing to believe for his own sake. To this *accidentality*, I object, as contravening the essence of poetry, which Aristotle pronounces to be σπουδαιότατον καὶ φιλοσοφικώτατον γενὸς,[9] the most intense, weighty and philosophical product of human art; adding, as the *reason*, that it is the most catholic and abstract. The

following passage from Davenant's prefatory letter to Hobbs[10] well expresses this truth. "When I considered the actions which I meant to describe (those inferring the persons) I was again persuaded rather to choose those of a former age, than the present; and in a century so far removed as might preserve me from their improper examinations, who know not the requisites of a poem, nor how much pleasure they lose (and even the pleasures of heroic poesy are not unprofitable) who take away the liberty of a poet, and fetter his feet in the shackles of an historian. For why should a poet doubt in story to mend the intrigues of fortune by more delightful conveyances of probable fictions, because austere historians have entered into bond to truth? An obligation, which were in poets as foolish and unnecessary, as is the bondage of false martyrs, who lie in chains for a mistaken opinion. *But by this I would imply, that truth, narrative and past is the idol of historians (who worship a dead thing) and truth operative, and by effects continually alive, is the mistress of poets, who hath not her existence in matter, but in reason.*"

For this minute accuracy in the painting of local imagery, the lines in the EXCURSION, p. 96, 97, and 98,[11] may be taken, if not as a striking instance yet as an illustration of my meaning. It must be some strong motive (as, for instance, that the description was necessary to the intelligibility of the tale) which could induce me to describe in a number of verses what a draftsman could present to the eye with incomparably greater satisfaction by half a dozen strokes of his pencil, or the painter with as many touches of his brush. Such descriptions too often occasion in the mind of a reader, who is determined to understand his author, a feeling of labor, not very dissimilar to that, with which he would construct a diagram, line by line, for a long geometrical proposition. It seems to be like taking the pieces of a dissected map out of its box. We first look at one part, and then at another, then join and dove-tail them; and when the successive acts of attention have been completed, there is a retrogressive effort of mind to behold it as a whole. The Poet should paint to the imagination, not to the fancy; and I know no happier case to exemplify the distinction between these two faculties. Master-pieces of the former mode of poetic painting abound in the writings of Milton, ex. gr.

   "The fig tree, not that kind for fruit renown'd,
   "But such as at this day to Indians known
   "In Malabar or Decan, spreads her arms
   "Branching so broad and long, that in the ground

---

9 σπουδαιότατομ ... γενὸς: "more philosophic and serious than history." See Wordsworth's "Preface to *Lyrical Ballads*," footnote 6, p. 51.

10 "The Authour's Preface to his much honour'd Friend Mr. Hobs," *Gondibert* (1651), an epic of chivalrous romance by William Davenant (1606–1668).
11 See *The Excursion*, III, 12–76.

"*The bended twigs take root, and daughters grow*
"*About the mother-tree, a pillar'd shade*
"*High over-arched, and* ECHOING WALKS BETWEEN;
"*There oft the Indian Herdsman shunning heat*
"*Shelters in cool, and tends his pasturing herds*
"*At loop holes cut through thickest shade.*"
                              MILTON, P. L. 9, 1100.

This is *creation* rather than *painting*, or if painting, yet such, and with such co-presence of the whole picture flash'd at once upon the eye, as the sun paints in a camera obscura. But the poet must likewise understand and command what Bacon calls the *vestigia communia* of the senses, the latency of all in each, and more especially as by a magical *penna duplex*,[12] the excitement of vision by sound and the exponents of sound. Thus, "THE ECHOING WALKS BETWEEN," may be almost said to reverse the fable in tradition of the head of Memnon, in the Egyptian statue.[13] Such may be deservedly entitled the *creative words* in the world of imagination.

The second division respects an apparent minute adherence to *matter-of-fact* in character and incidents; *a biographical* attention to probability, and an *anxiety* of explanation and retrospect. Under this head I shall deliver, with no feigned diffidence, the results of my best reflection on the great point of controversy between Mr. Wordsworth, and his objectors; namely, on THE CHOICE OF HIS CHARACTERS. I have already declared, and, I trust justified, my utter dissent from the mode of argument which his critics have hitherto employed. To *their* question, why did you chuse such a character, or a character from such a rank of life? the Poet might in my opinion fairly retort: why, with the conception of my character did you make wilful choice of mean or ludicrous associations not furnished by me, but supplied from your own sickly and fastidious feelings? How was it, indeed, probable, that such arguments could have any weight with an author, whose plan, whose guiding principle, and main object it was to attack and subdue that state of association, which leads us to place the chief value on those things on which man DIFFERS from man, and to forget or disregard the high dignities, which belong to HUMAN NATURE, the sense and the feeling, which *may* be, and *ought* to be, found in *all* ranks? The feelings with which, as christians, we contemplate a mixed congregation rising or kneeling before their common maker: Mr. Wordsworth would have us entertain at *all* times

as men, and as readers; and by the excitement of this lofty, yet prideless impartiality in *poetry*, he might hope to have encouraged its continuance in *real life*. The praise of good men be his! In real life, and, I trust, even in my imagination, I honor a virtuous and wise man, without reference to the presence or absence of artificial advantages. Whether in the person of an armed baron, a laurel'd bard, &c. or of an old pedlar, or still older leech-gatherer, the same qualities of head and heart must claim the same reverence. And even in poetry I am not conscious, that I have ever suffered my feelings to be disturbed or offended by any thoughts or images, which the poet himself has not presented.

But yet I object nevertheless, and for the following reasons. First, because the object in view, as an *immediate* object, belongs to the moral philosopher, and would be pursued, not only more appropriately, but in my opinion with far greater probability of success, in sermons or moral essays, than in an elevated poem. It seems, indeed, to destroy the main fundamental distinction, not only between a *poem* and *prose*, but even between philosophy and works of fiction, inasmuch as it proposes *truth* for its immediate object, instead of *pleasure*. Now till the blessed time shall come, when truth itself shall be pleasure, and both shall be so united, as to be distinguishable in words only, not in feeling, it will remain the poet's office to proceed upon that state of association, which actually exists as *general;* instead of attempting first to *make* it what it ought to be, and then to let the pleasure follow. But here is unfortunately a small *Hysteron-Proteron*.[14] For the communication of pleasure is the introductory means by which alone the poet must expect to moralize his readers. Secondly: though I were to admit, for a moment, *this* argument to be groundless: yet how is the moral effect to be produced, by merely attaching the name of some low profession to powers which are *least* likely, and to qualities which are assuredly not *more* likely, to be found in it? The poet, speaking in his own person, may at once delight and improve us by sentiments, which teach us the independence of goodness, of wisdom, and even of genius, on the favors of fortune. And having made a due reverence before the throne of Antonine, he may bow with equal awe before Epictetus among his fellow-slaves[15]—

—————"and rejoice
In the plain presence of his dignity."[16]

---

[12] *vestigia communia*: "the common marks," a shared nature. *Penna duplex* "double arrow."

[13] A gigantic statue that supposedly gave forth a musical sound when struck by the morning sun; hence, an example of a sight producing a sound. (See De Quincey's "The Affliction of Childhood," footnote 11.)

[14] A term from classical logic and rhetoric, referring to placing first what should occur last.

[15] Antonine Marcus Aurelius (A.D. 121–180) was a Roman emperor and stoic philosopher. Epictetus was a first-century stoic philosopher who was born a slave.

[16] *Excursion*, I, 75–76. Coleridge next cites the succeeding lines 77–80, 86–93.

Who is not at once delighted and improved, when the POET Wordsworth himself exclaims,

"O many are the poets that are sown
    By Nature; men endowed with highest gifts,
    The vision and the faculty divine,
    Yet wanting the accomplishment of verse,
    Nor having e'er, as life advanced, been led
    By circumstance to take unto the height
    The measure of themselves, these favor'd beings,
    All but a scatter'd few, live out their time
    Husbanding that which they possess within,
    And go to the grave unthought of. Strongest minds
    Are often those of whom the noisy world
    Hears least."
                              EXCURSION, B. I.

To use a colloquial phrase, such sentiments, in such language, do one's heart good; though I for my part, have not the fullest faith in the *truth* of the observation. On the contrary I believe the instances to be exceedingly rare; and should feel almost as strong an objection to introduce such a character in a poetic fiction, as a pair of black swans on a lake, in a fancy-landscape. When I think how many, and how much better books, than Homer, or even than Herodotus, Pindar or Eschylus, could have read, are in the power of almost every man, in a country where almost every man is instructed to read and write; and how restless, how difficultly hidden, the powers of genius are; and yet find even in situations the most favorable, according to Mr. Wordsworth, for the formation of a pure and poetic language; in situations which ensure familiarity with the grandest objects of the imagination; but *one* BURNS, among the shepherds of *Scotland*, and not a single poet of humble life among those of *English* lakes and mountains; I conclude, that POETIC GENIUS is not only a very delicate but a very rare plant.

But be this as it may, the feelings with which,

"I think of CHATTERTON, the marvellous boy,
    The sleepless soul, that perish'd in his pride:
    Of BURNS, that walk'd in glory and in joy
    Behind his plough upon the mountain-side"—[17]

are widely different from those with which I should read a *poem*, where the author, having occasion for the character of a poet and a philosopher in the fable of his narration, had chosen to make him a *chimney-sweeper;* and then, in order to remove all doubts on the subject, had *invented* an account of his birth, parentage and education, with all the strange and fortunate accidents which had concurred in making him at once poet, philosopher, and sweep! Nothing, but biography, can

justify this. If it be admissible even in a *Novel*, it must be one in the manner of De Foe's, that were meant to pass for histories, not in the manner of Fielding's: in the life of Moll Flanders, or Colonel Jack, not in a Tom Jones or even a Joseph Andrews. Much less then can it be legitimately introduced in a *poem*, the characters of which, amid the strongest individualization, must still remain representative. The precepts of Horace,[18] on this point, are grounded on the nature both of poetry and of the human mind. They are not more peremptory, than wise and prudent. For in the first place a deviation from them perplexes the reader's feelings, and all the circumstances which are feigned in order to make such accidents less improbable, divide and disquiet his faith, rather than aid and support it. Spite of all attempts, the fiction *will* appear, and unfortunately not as *fictitious* but as *false*. The reader not only *knows*, that the sentiments and language are the poet's own, and his own too in his *artificial* character, *as poet;* but by the fruitless endeavours to make him think the contrary, he is not even suffered to *forget* it. The effect is similar to that produced by an epic poet, when the fable and the characters are *derived* from Scripture history, as in the *Messiah* of *Klopstock*, or in *Cumberland's Calvary:*[19] and not merely *suggested* by it as in the Paradise Lost of Milton. That *illusion*, contradistinguished from *delusion*, that *negative* faith, which simply permits the images presented to work by their own force, without either denial or affirmation of their real existence by the judgment, is rendered impossible by their immediate neighbourhood to words and facts of known and absolute truth. A faith, which transcends even historic belief, must absolutely *put out* this mere poetic Analogon of faith, as the summer sun is said to extinguish our household fires, when it shines full upon them. What would otherwise have been yielded to as pleasing fiction, is repelled as revolting falsehood. The effect produced in this latter case by the solemn belief of the reader, is in a less degree brought about in the instances, to which I have been objecting, by the baffled attempts of the author to *make* him believe.

Add to all the foregoing the seeming uselessness both of the project and of the anecdotes from which it is to derive support. Is there one word for instance, attributed to the pedlar in the EXCURSION, characteristic

---

17 "Resolution and Independence," ll. 43–46.

18 Various passages in *Ars Poetica* have been suggested (ll. 112–27, 309–322, 338–40), all demanding that the language and other personal endowments given to a character be consistent with and appropriate to the age, occupation, social position, etc., of that character.

19 The *Messiah* of *Klopstock* was a biblical epic (1748–1773) by the German poet Friedrich Klopstock (1724–1803). Richard Cumberland (1732–1811), better known as a dramatist, published his biblical epic in 1792.

of a *pedlar*? One sentiment, that might not more plausibly, even without the aid of any previous explanation, have proceeded from any wise and beneficent old man, of a rank or profession in which the language of learning and refinement are natural and to be expected? Need the rank have been at all particularized, where nothing follows which the knowledge of that rank is to explain or illustrate? When on the contrary this information renders the man's language, feelings, sentiments, and information a riddle, which must itself be solved by episodes of anecdote? Finally when this, and this alone, could have induced a genuine *poet* to inweave in a poem of the loftiest style, and on subjects the loftiest and of most universal interest, such minute matters of fact, (not unlike those furnished for the obituary of a magazine by the friends of some obscure *ornament of society lately deceased* in some obscure town) as

> "Among the hills of Athol he was born.
> There on a small hereditary farm,
> An unproductive slip of rugged ground,
> His Father dwelt; and died in poverty:
> While he, whose lowly fortune I retrace,
> The youngest of three sons, was yet a babe,
> A little one—unconscious of their loss,
> But 'ere he had outgrown his infant days
> His widowed mother, for a second mate,
> Espoused the teacher of the Village School;
> Who on her offspring zealously bestowed
> Needful instruction."

> "From his sixth year, the Boy of whom I speak,
> In summer, tended cattle on the hills;
> But through the inclement and the perilous days
> Of long-continuing winter, he repaired
> To his step-father's school."—&c.[20]

For all the admirable passages interposed in this narration, might, with trifling alterations, have been far more appropriately, and with far greater verisimilitude, told of a poet in the character of a poet; and without incurring another defect which I shall now mention, and a sufficient illustration of which will have been here anticipated.

Third; an undue predilection for the *dramatic* form in certain poems, from which one or other of two evils result. Either the thoughts and diction are different from that of the poet, and then there arises an incongruity of style; or they are the same and indistinguishable, and then it presents a species of ventriloquism,

where two are represented as talking, while in truth one man only speaks.

The fourth class of defects is closely connected with the former; but yet are such as arise likewise from an intensity of feeling disproportionate to *such* knowledge and value of the objects described, as can be fairly anticipated of men in general, even of the most cultivated classes; and with which therefore few only, and those few particularly circumstanced, can be supposed to sympathize: In this class, I comprize occasional prolixity, repetition, and an eddying instead of progression of thought. As instances, see page 27, 28, and 62 of the Poems, Vol. I.[21] and the first eighty lines of the Sixth Book of the Excursion.

Fifth and last; thoughts and images too great for the subject. This is an approximation to what might be called *mental* bombast, as distinguished from verbal: for, as in the latter there is a disproportion of the expressions to the thoughts so in this there is a disproportion of thought to the circumstance and occasion. This, by the bye, is a fault of which none but a man of genius is capable. It is the awkwardness and strength of Hercules with the distaff of Omphale.[22]

It is a well known fact, that bright colours in motion both make and leave the strongest impressions on the eye. Nothing is more likely too, than that a vivid image or visual spectrum, thus originated, may become the link of association in recalling the feelings and images that had accompanied the original impression. But if we describe this in such lines, as

> "They flash upon that inward eye,
> Which is the bliss of solitude!"

in what words shall we describe the joy of retrospection, when the images and virtuous actions of a whole well-spent life, pass before that conscience which is indeed the *inward* eye: which is indeed "*the bliss of solitude?*" Assuredly we seem to sink most abruptly, not to say burlesquely, and almost as in a *medley* from this couplet to—

> "And then my heart with pleasure fills,
> And dances with the *daffodils*." Vol. I. p. 320.

The second instance is from Vol. II. page 12, where the poet having gone out for a day's tour of pleasure, meets early in the morning with a knot of *gypsies*, who have pitched their blanket-tents and straw-beds, to-

---

[20] Passage from Book I of the 1814 version of *The Excursion*. The lines were revised for the 1827 edition, dropping all reference to his father's death and his mother's remarriage.

[21] Refers to the fourth through thirteenth stanzas of "Anecdote for Fathers" (1798), and "Song at the Feast of Brougham Castle" (1807), ll. 78–101.

[22] Hercules became a slave to Queen Omphale, who forced the mighty hero to dress as a woman and engage in the feminine activity of spinning.

gether with their children and asses, in some field by the road-side. At the close of the day on his return our tourist found them in the same place. "Twelve hours," says he,

"Twelve hours, twelve bounteous hours, are gone while I
    Have been a traveller under open sky,
    Much witnessing of change and cheer,
    Yet as I left I find them here!"[23]

Whereat the poet, without seeming to reflect that the poor tawny wanderers might probably have been tramping for weeks together through road and lane, over moor and mountain, and consequently must have been right glad to rest themselves, their children and cattle, for one whole day; and overlooking the obvious truth, that such repose might be quite as necessary for *them*, as a walk of the same continuance was pleasing or healthful for the more fortunate poet; expresses his indignation in a series of lines, the diction and imagery of which would have been rather above, than below the mark, had they been applied to the immense empire of China improgressive for thirty centuries:

"The weary SUN betook himself to rest,
    —Then issued VESPER from the fulgent west,
    Outshining, like a visible God,
    The glorious path in which he trod!
    And now ascending, after one dark hour,
    And one night's diminution of her power,
    Behold the mighty MOON! this way
    She looks, as if at them—but they
    Regard not her:—oh, better wrong and strife,
    Better vain deeds or evil than such life!
    The silent HEAVENS have goings on:
    The STARS have tasks!—but *these* have none!"

The last instance of this defect, (for I know no other than these already cited) is from the Ode, page 351. Vol. II. where, speaking of a child, "a six year's darling of a pigmy size," he thus addresses him:

"Thou best philosopher who yet dost keep
    Thy heritage! Thou eye among the blind,
    That, deaf and silent, read'st the eternal deep,
    Haunted for ever by the Eternal Mind—
    Mighty Prophet! Seer blest!
    On whom those truths do rest,
    Which we are toiling all our lives to find!
    Thou, over whom thy immortality
    Broods like the day, a master o'er the slave,
    A presence that is not to be put by!"[24]

---

[23] "Gipsies" (1807). Coleridge quotes here ll. 9–12, and later the concluding ll. 13–24, from the 1815 text of the poem, which were revised and expanded in the 1820 edition.
[24] "Intimations Ode" (1807), ll. 111–17, 119–21.

Now here, not to stop at the daring spirit of metaphor which connects the epithets "deaf and silent," with the apostrophized *eye:* or (if we are to refer it to the preceding word, philosopher) the faulty and equivocal syntax of the passage; and without examining the propriety of making a "master *brood* o'er a slave," or the *day* brood *at all;* we will merely ask, what does all this mean? In what sense is a child of that age a *philosopher?* In what sense does he *read* "the eternal deep?" In what sense is he declared to be "*for ever haunted*" by the Supreme Being? or so inspired as to deserve the splendid titles of a *mighty prophet,* a *blessed seer?* By reflection? by knowledge? by conscious intuition? or by *any* form or modification of consciousness? These would be tidings indeed; but such as would pre-suppose an immediate revelation to the inspired communicator, and require miracles to authenticate his inspiration. Children at this age give us no such information of themselves; and at what time were we dipt in the Lethe, which has produced such utter oblivion of a state so godlike? There are many of us that still possess some remembrances, more or less distinct, respecting themselves at six years old; pity that the worthless straws only should float, while treasures, compared with which all the mines of Golconda and Mexico were but straws, should be absorbed by some unknown gulf into some unknown abyss.

But if this be too wild and exorbitant to be suspected as having been the poet's meaning; if these mysterious gifts, faculties, and operations, are *not* accompanied with consciousness; who *else* is conscious of them? or how can it be called the child, if it be no part of the child's conscious being? For aught I know, the thinking Spirit within me may be *substantially* one with the principle of life, and of vital operation. For aught I know, it may be employed as a secondary agent in the marvellous organization and organic movements of my body. But, surely, it would be strange language to say, that *I* construct my *heart!* or that *I* propel the finer influences through my *nerves!* or that *I* compress my brain, and draw the curtains of sleep round my own eyes! SPINOZA and BEHMEN were on different systems both Pantheists; and among the ancients there were philosophers, teachers of the EN KAI ΠΑΝ,[25] who not only taught, that God was All, but that this All constituted God. Yet not even these would confound the *part, as* a part, with the Whole, *as* the whole. Nay, in no system is the distinction between the individual and God, between the Modification, and the one only Substance, more sharply drawn, than in that of

---

[25] EN KAI ΠΑΝ: "the one and the all."

SPINOZA. JACOBI indeed relates of LESSING, that after a conversation with him at the house of the poet, GLEIM (the Tyrtæus and Anacreon of the German Parnassus) in which conversation L. had avowed privately to Jacobi his reluctance to admit any *personal* existence of the Supreme Being, or the *possibility* of personality except in a finite Intellect, and while they were sitting at table, a shower of rain came on unexpectedly. Gleim expressed his regret at the circumstance, because they had meant to drink their wine in the garden: upon which Lessing in one of his half-earnest, half-joking moods, nodded to Jacobi, and said, "It is *I*, perhaps, that am doing *that*," i.e. *raining!* and J. answered, "or perhaps I;" Gleim contented himself with staring at them both, without asking for any explanation.[26]

So with regard to this passage. In what sense can the magnificent attributes, above quoted, be appropriated to a *child*, which would not make them equally suitable to a *bee*, or a *dog*, or *a field of corn;* or even to a ship, or to the wind and waves that propel it? The omnipresent Spirit works equally in *them*, as in the child; and the child is equally unconscious of it as they. It cannot surely be, that the four lines, immediately following, are to contain the explanation?

> "To whom the grave
> Is but a lonely bed without the sense or sight
> Of day or the warm light,
> A place of thought where we in waiting lie." [27]

Surely, it cannot be that this wonder-rousing apostrophe is but a comment on the little poem of "We are Seven?" that the whole meaning of the passage is reducible to the assertion, that a *child*, who by the bye at six years old would have been better instructed in most christian families, has no other notion of death than that of lying in a dark, cold place? And still, I hope, not as *in a place of thought!* not the frightful notion of lying *awake* in his grave! The analogy between death and sleep is too simple, too natural, to render so horrid a belief possible for children; even had they not been in the habit, as all christian children are, of hearing the latter term used to express the former. But if the child's belief be only, that "he is not dead, but sleepeth:"[28] wherein does it differ from that of his

---

[26] Friedrich Heinrich Jacobi (1743–1819), was a German philosopher. The incident is recorded in his *Ueber die Lehre des Spinoza, in Briefen an Herrn Moses Mendelssohn* (1785). Johann Wilhelm Gleim (1719–1803) was a German poet. He resembled the Greek poet Tyrtaeus in his writing of poems about national military victories; in a contrary vein, he translated the lighter verses of Anacreon.

[27] Lines omitted from "Intimations Ode" after 1815.

[28] Matthew, ix, 24.

father and mother, or any other adult and instructed person? To form an idea of a thing's becoming nothing; or of nothing becoming a thing; is impossible to all finite beings alike, of whatever age, and however educated or uneducated. Thus it is with splendid paradoxes in general. If the words are taken in the common sense, they convey an absurdity; and if, in contempt of dictionaries and custom, they are so interpreted as to avoid the absurdity, the meaning dwindles into some bald truism. Thus you must at once understand the words *contrary* to their common import, in order to arrive at any *sense; and according* to their common import, if you are to receive from them any feeling of *sublimity* or *admiration.*

Though the instances of this defect in Mr. Wordsworth's poems are so few, that for themselves it would have been scarcely just to attract the reader's attention toward them; yet I have dwelt on it, and perhaps the more for this very reason. For being so very few, they cannot sensibly detract from the reputation of an author, who is even characterized by the number of profound truths in his writings, which will stand the severest analysis; and yet few as they are, they are exactly those passages which his *blind* admirers would be most likely, and best able, to imitate. But WORDS-WORTH, where he is indeed Wordsworth, may be mimicked by Copyists, he may be plundered by Plagiarists; but he cannot be imitated, except by those who are not born to be imitators. For without his depth of feeling and his imaginative power his *Sense* would want its vital warmth and peculiarity; and without his strong sense, his *mysticism* would become *sickly*— mere fog, and dimness!

To these defects which, as appears by the extracts, are only occasional, I may oppose with far less fear of encountering the dissent of any candid and intelligent reader, the following (for the most part correspondent) excellencies. First, an austere purity of language both grammatically and logically; in short a perfect appropriateness of the words to the meaning. Of how high value I deem this, and how particularly estimable I hold the example at the present day, has been already stated: and in part too the reasons on which I ground both the moral and intellectual importance of habituating ourselves to a strict accuracy of expression. It is noticeable, how limited an acquaintance with the master-pieces of art will suffice to form a correct and even a sensitive taste, where none but master-pieces have been seen and admired: while on the other hand, the most correct notions, and the widest acquaintance with the works of excellence of all ages and countries, will not perfectly secure us against the contagious familiarity with the far more numerous offspring of tastelessness or of a perverted taste. If this be the case, as it notoriously is, with the arts of music and painting, much more difficult will it be, to avoid the infection of multiplied and daily examples in the practice of an art, which uses words, and words only, as its instruments. In poetry, in which every line, every phrase, may pass the ordeal of deliberation and deliberate choice, it is possible, and barely possible, to attain that ultimatum which I have ventured to propose as the infallible test of a blameless style; namely, its *untranslatableness* in words of the same language without injury to the meaning. Be it observed, however, that I include in the *meaning* of a word not only its correspondent object, but likewise all the associations which it recalls. For language is framed to convey not the object alone, but likewise the character, mood and intentions of the person who is representing it. In poetry it *is* practicable to preserve the diction uncorrupted by the affectations and misappropriations, which promiscuous authorship, and reading not promiscuous only because it is disproportionally most conversant with the compositions of the day, have rendered general. Yet even to the poet, composing in his own province, it is an arduous work: and as the result and pledge of a watchful good sense, of fine and luminous distinction, and of complete self-possession, may justly claim all the honor which belongs to an attainment equally difficult and valuable, and the more valuable for being rare. It is at *all* times the proper food of the understanding; but in an age of corrupt eloquence it is both food and antidote.

In prose I doubt whether it be even possible to preserve our style wholly unalloyed by the vicious phraseology which meets us every where, from the sermon to the newspaper, from the harangue of the legislator to the speech from the convivial chair, announcing a *toast* or sentiment. Our chains rattle, even while we are complaining of them. The poems of Boetius rise high in our estimation when we compare them with those of his contemporaries, as Sidonius Apollinaris, &c.[29] They might even be referred to a purer age, but that the prose, in which they are set, as jewels in a crown of lead or iron, betrays the true age of the writer. Much however may be effected by education. I believe not only from grounds of reason, but from having in great measure assured myself of the fact by actual though limited experience, that to a youth led from his first boyhood to investigate the meaning of every word and the reason of its choice and position, Logic presents itself as an old acquaintance under new names.

On some future occasion, more especially demanding such disquisition, I shall attempt to prove the close connection between veracity and habits of mental accuracy; the beneficial after-effects of verbal precision in the preclusion of fanaticism, which masters the feelings more especially by indistinct watch-words; and to display the advantages which language alone, at least which language with incomparably greater ease and certainty than any other means, presents to the instructor of impressing modes of intellectual energy so constantly, so imperceptibly, and as it were by such elements and atoms, as to secure in due time the formation of a second nature. When we reflect, that the cultivation of the judgment is a positive command of the moral law, since the reason can give the *principle* alone, and the conscience bears witness only to the *motive*, while the application and effects must depend on the judgment: when we consider, that the greater part of our success and comfort in life depends on distinguishing the similar from the same, that which is peculiar in each thing from that which it has in common with others, so as still to select the most probable, instead of the merely possible or positively unfit, we shall learn to value earnestly and with a practical seriousness a mean, already prepared for us by nature and society, of teaching the young mind to think well and wisely by the same unremembered process and with the same never forgotten results, as those by which it is taught to speak and converse. Now how much warmer the interest is, how much more genial the feelings of reality and practicability, and thence how much stronger the impulses to imitation are, which a *contemporary* writer, and especially a contemporary *poet*, excites in youth and commencing manhood, has been treated of in the earlier pages of these sketches.[30] I have only to add, that all the praise which is due to the exertion of such influence for a purpose so important, joined with that which must be claimed for the infrequency of the same excellence in the same perfection, belongs in full right to Mr. WORDSWORTH. I am far however from denying that we have poets whose *general* style possesses the same excellence, as Mr. Moore, Lord Byron, Mr. Bowles, and in all his later and more important works our laurel-honoring Laureate. But there are none, in whose works I do not appear to myself to find *more* exceptions, than in those of Wordsworth. Quotations or specimens would here be wholly out of place, and must be left for the critic who doubts and would invalidate the justice of this eulogy so applied.

The second characteristic excellence of Mr. W's works is: a correspondent weight and sanity of the

---

[29] Sidonius Apollinaris (*c.* 430–487) was a bishop of Clermont and writer of panegyrics on the Roman emperors and various other poems.

[30] See Chapter I, pp. 171–73.

Thoughts and Sentiments,—won, not from books; but —from the poet's own meditative observation. They are *fresh* and have the dew upon them. His muse, at least when in her strength of wing, and when she hovers aloft in her proper element,

> Makes audible a linked lay of truth,
> Of truth profound a sweet continuous lay,
> Not learnt, but native, her own natural notes!
>   S. T. C.[31]

Even throughout his smaller poems there is scarcely one, which is not rendered valuable by some just and original reflection.

See page 25, vol. 2nd:[32] or the two following passages in one of his humblest compositions.

> "O Reader! had you in your mind
>   Such stores as silent thought can bring,
> O gentle Reader! you would find
>   A tale in every thing."

and

> "I have heard of hearts unkind, kind deeds
>   With coldness still returning:
> Alas! the gratitude of men
>   Has oftener left *me* mourning."

or in a still higher strain the six beautiful quatrains, page 134.

> "Thus fares it still in our decay:
>   And yet the wiser mind
> Mourns less for what age takes away
>   That what it leaves behind.
>
> The Blackbird in the summer trees,
>   The Lark upon the hill,
> Let loose their carols when they please,
>   Are quiet when they will.
>
> With nature never do *they* wage
>   A foolish strife; they see
> A happy youth, and their old age
>   Is beautiful and free!
>
> But we are pressed by heavy laws;
>   And often, glad no more,
> We wear a face of joy, because
>   We have been glad of yore."

If there is one, who need bemoan
His kindred laid in earth,
The household hearts that were his own,
It is the man of mirth.

My days, my Friend, are almost gone,
My life has been approved,
And many love me; but by none
Am I enough beloved."

or the sonnet on Buonaparte, page 202, vol. 2;[33] or finally (for a volume would scarce suffice to exhaust the instances,) the last stanza of the poem on the withered Celandine, vol. 2, p. 312.

> "To be a prodigal's favorite—then, worse truth,
>   A miser's pensioner—behold our lot!
> Oh man! that from thy fair and shining youth
>   Age might but take the things, youth needed not."

Both in respect of this and of the former excellence, Mr. Wordsworth strikingly resembles Samuel Daniel, one of the golden writers of our golden Elizabethan age, now most causelessly neglected: Samuel Daniel, whose diction bears no mark of time, no distinction of age, which has been, and as long as our language shall last, will be so far the language of the to-day and for ever, as that it is more intelligible to us, than the transitory fashions of our own particular age. A similar praise is due to his sentiments. No frequency of perusal can deprive them of their freshness. For though they are brought into the full day-light of every reader's comprehension; yet are they drawn up from depths which few in any age are priviledged to visit, into which few in any age have courage or inclination to descend. If Mr. Wordsworth is not equally with Daniel alike intelligible to all readers of average understanding in all passages of his works, the comparative difficulty does not arise from the greater impurity of the ore, but from the nature and uses of the metal. A poem is not necessarily obscure, because it does not aim to be popular. It is enough, if a work be perspicuous to those for whom it is written, and,

> "Fit audience find, though few."[34]

To the "Ode on the intimation of immortality from recollections of early childhood" the poet might have prefixed the lines which Dante addresses to one of his own Canzoni—

> "Canzon, io credo, che saranno radi
>   Che tua ragione intendan bene:
> Tanto lor sei faticoso ed alto."

---

[31] "To William Wordsworth, composed on the night after his recitation of a poem on the Growth of an individual Mind," ll. 58–60. The poem was composed in 1807 and first published in *Sibylline Leaves* (1817).

[32] Refers to "Star-Gazers" (1807), ll. 9–24. The "two following passages" are from "Simon Lee" (1798), ll. 65–68, 93–96; and the "six beautiful quatrains" are from "The Fountain" (1800), ll. 33–56.

[33] "I grieved for Buonaparté, with a vain" (1802). Coleridge next cites "The Small Celandine" (1807), ll. 21–24.

[34] *Paradise Lost*, VII, 31. The passage from Dante next cited is from *Il Convivio*, II, canzone prima, ll. 53–55.

"O lyric song, there will be few, think I,
Who may thy import understand aright:
Thou art for *them* so arduous and so high!"

But the ode was intended for such readers only as
had been accustomed to watch the flux and reflux of
their inmost nature, to venture at times into the twilight realms of consciousness, and to feel a deep interest
in modes of inmost being, to which they know that the
attributes of time and space are inapplicable and alien,
but which yet can not be conveyed, save in symbols of
time and space. For such readers the sense is sufficiently plain, and they will be as little disposed to
charge Mr. Wordsworth with believing the platonic
pre-existence in the ordinary interpretation of the
words, as I am to believe, that Plato himself ever
meant or taught it.

Πολλα ὅι ὑπ' αγκῶ
—νος ὠκέα βέλη
Ἐʹνδον εντὶ φαρέτρας
Φωνᾶντα συνετõισιν· ες
Δὲ τὸ παν ερμηνέως
Χατίζει. Σοφὸς ὁ πολ-
—λα ἔιδως φυᾷ·
Μαθόντες δὲ, λάβροι
Παγγλωσσία, κόρακες ὥς
Αἴκραντα γαρύετὸν
Διὸς πρὸς ὄρνιχα θεῖον.[35]

Third (and wherein he soars far above Daniel) the
sinewy strength and originality of single lines and
paragraphs: the frequent curiosa felicitas[36] of his diction, of which I need not here give specimens, having
anticipated them in a preceding page. This beauty, and
as eminently characteristic of Wordsworth's poetry,
his rudest assailants have felt themselves compelled to
acknowledge and admire.

Fourth; the perfect truth of nature in his images and
descriptions as taken immediately from nature, and
proving a long and genial intimacy with the very spirit
which gives the physiognomic expression to all the
works of nature. Like a green field reflected in a calm
and perfectly transparent lake, the image is distinguished from the reality only by its greater softness and
lustre. Like the moisture or the polish on a pebble,
genius neither distorts nor false-colours its objects; but

on the contrary brings out many a vein and many a tint,
which escape the eye of common observation, thus
raising to the rank of gems, what had been often kicked
away by the hurrying foot of the traveller on the dusty
high road of custom.

Let me refer to the whole description of skating,
vol. I, page 44 to 47, especially to the lines

"So through the darkness and the cold we flew,
And not a voice was idle: with the din
Meanwhile the precipices rang aloud;
The leafless trees and every icy crag
Tinkled like iron; while the distant hills
Into the tumult sent an alien sound
Of melancholy, not unnoticed, while the stars
Eastward were sparkling clear, and in the west
The orange sky of evening died away."[37]

Or to the poem on the green linnet, vol. I. p. 244.
What can be more accurate yet more lovely than the
two concluding stanzas?

"Upon yon tuft of hazel trees,
That twinkle to the gusty breeze,
Behold him perched in ecstacies,
Yet seeming still to hover,
There! where the flutter of his wings
Upon his back and body flings
Shadows and sunny glimmerings
That cover him all over.

While thus before my eyes he gleams,
A brother of the leaves he seems;
When in a moment forth he teems
His little song in gushes:
As if it pleased him to disdain
And mock the form when he did feign
While he was dancing with the train
Of leaves among the bushes."

Or the description of the blue-cap, and of the noon-
tide silence, p. 284; or the poem to the cuckoo, p. 299;
or, lastly, though I might multiply the references to ten
times the number, to the poem so completely Wordsworth's commencing

"Three years she grew in sun and shower," &c.

Fifth: a meditative pathos, a union of deep and
subtle thought with sensibility; a sympathy with man
as man; the sympathy indeed of a contemplator, rather

---

35 Pindar's Olympian Ode, II, 149–59: "Full many a swift
arrow have I beneath mine arm, within my quiver, many an
arrow that is vocal to the wise; but for the crowd they need
interpreters. The true poet is he who knoweth much by gift of
nature, but they that have only learnt the lore of song, and are
turbulent and intemperate of tongue, like a pair of crows,
chatter in vain against the godlike bird of Zeus." (John Sandys
translation, Loeb Classical Library, Harvard University Press.)
36 curiosa felicitas: "studied felicity." Petronius, *Satyricon*,
l. 118.

37 An excerpt from the then unpublished *Prelude* (I, 438–46),
which appeared in the 1815 edition as "Influence of Natural
Objects in calling forth and strengthening the Imagination in
Boyhood and early Youth." Coleridge next quotes "The Green
Linnet" (1807), ll. 25–40; and then refers to "The Kitten and the
Falling Leaves" (1807), ll. 63–88, "To the Cuckoo" (1807), and
the Lucy poem "Three years she grew. . ." (1800).

than a fellow-sufferer or co-mate, (spectator, haud particeps)[38] but of a contemplator, from whose view no difference of rank conceals the sameness of the nature; no injuries of wind or weather, of toil, or even of ignorance, wholly disguise the human face divine. The superscription and the image of the Creator still remain legible to *him* under the dark lines, with which guilt or calamity had cancelled or cross-barred it. Here the man and the poet lose and find themselves in each other, the one as glorified, the latter as substantiated. In this mild and philosophic pathos, Wordsworth appears to me without a compeer. Such he *is:* so he *writes.* See vol. I. page 134 to 136,[39] or that most affecting composition, the "Affliction of Margaret——of——," page 165 to 168, which no mother, and if I may judge by my own experience, no parent can read without a tear. Or turn to that genuine lyric, in the former edition, entitled, the "Mad Mother,"[40] page 174 to 178, of which I can not refrain from quoting two of the stanzas, both of them for their pathos, and the former for the fine transition in the two concluding lines of the stanza, so expressive of that deranged state, in which from the increased sensibility the sufferer's attention is abruptly drawn off by every trifle, and in the same instant plucked back again by the one despotic thought, and bringing home with it, by the blending, *fusing* power of Imagination and Passion, the alien object to which it had been so abruptly diverted, no longer an alien but an ally and an inmate.

> "Suck, little babe, oh suck again!
> It cools my blood; it cools my brain:
> Thy lips, I feel them, baby! they
> Draw from my heart the pain away.
> Oh! press me with thy little hand;
> It loosens something at my chest;
> About that tight and deadly band
> I feel thy little fingers prest.
> The breeze I see is in the tree!
> It comes to cool my babe and me."

> "Thy father cares not for my breast,
> 'Tis thine, sweet baby, there to rest,
> 'Tis all thine own!—and, if it's hue,
> Be changed, that was so fair to view,
> 'Tis fair enough for thee, my dove!
> My beauty, little child, is flown,
> But thou wilt live with me in love,
> And what if my poor cheek be brown?
> 'Tis well for me, thou can'st not see
> How pale and wan it else would be."

Last, and pre-eminently I challenge for this poet the gift of IMAGINATION in the highest and strictest sense of the word. In the play of *Fancy,* Wordsworth, to my feelings, is not always graceful, and sometimes *recondite.* The *likeness* is occasionally too strange, or demands too peculiar a point of view, or is such as appears the creature of predetermined research, rather than spontaneous presentation. Indeed his fancy seldom displays itself, as mere and unmodified fancy. But in imaginative power, he stands nearest of all modern writers to Shakspeare and Milton; and yet in a kind perfectly unborrowed and his own. To employ his own words, which are at once an instance and an illustration, he does indeed to all thoughts and to all objects—

> "——————add the gleam,
> The light that never was on sea or land,
> The consecration, and the poet's dream."[41]

I shall select a few examples as most obviously manifesting this faculty; but if I should ever be fortunate enough to render my analysis of imagination, its origin and characters thoroughly intelligible to the reader, he will scarcely open on a page of this poet's works without recognizing, more or less, the presence and the influences of this faculty.

From the poem on the Yew Trees, vol. I. page 303, 304.

> "But worthier still of note
> Are those fraternal four of Borrowdale,
> Joined in one solemn and capacious grove;
> Huge trunks!—and each particular trunk a growth
> Of intertwisted fibres serpentine
> Up-coiling, and inveterately convolved,—
> Not uninformed with phantasy, and looks
> That threaten the prophane;—a pillared shade,
> Upon whose grassless floor of red-brown hue,
> By sheddings from the pinal umbrage tinged
> Perennially—beneath whose sable roof
> Of boughs, as if for festal purpose decked
> With unrejoicing berries, ghostly shapes
> May meet at noontide—FEAR and trembling HOPE,
> SILENCE and FORESIGHT—DEATH, the skeleton,
> And TIME, the shadow—there to celebrate,
> As in a natural temple scattered o'er
> With altars undisturbed of mossy stone,
> United worship; or in mute repose
> To lie, and listen to the mountain flood
> Murmuring from Glaramara's inmost caves."[42]

The effect of the old man's figure in the poem of Resignation and Independence, vol. II. page 33.

---

[38] spectator, haud particeps: "A beholder, not a sharer."
[39] Refers to "'Tis said, that some have died for love" (1800).
[40] So entitled in *Lyrical Ballads* (1798); in 1815 and thereafter, entitled "Her Eyes are Wild." Coleridge quotes ll. 31–40, 61–70.

[41] "Elegiac Stanzas, Suggested by a Picture of Peele Castle" (1807), ll. 14–16.
[42] "Yew Trees" (1815), ll. 13–33.

"While he was talking thus, the lonely place,
    The old man's shape, and speech, all troubled me:
In my mind's eye I seemed to see him pace
    About the weary moors continually,
    Wandering about alone and silently."

Or the 8th, 9th, 19th, 26th, 31st, and 33d, in the collection of miscellaneous sonnets [43]—the sonnet on the subjugation of Switzerland, page 210, or the last ode from which I especially select the two following stanzas or paragraphs, page 349 to 350.

"Our birth is but a sleep and a forgetting:
    The soul that rises with us, our life's star
    Hath had elsewhere its setting,
        And cometh from afar.
    Not in entire forgetfulness,
    And not in utter nakedness,
    But trailing clouds of glory do we come
    From God who is our home:
Heaven lies about us in our infancy!
Shades of the prison-house begin to close
        Upon the growing boy;
But he beholds the light, and whence it flows,
        He sees it in his joy!
The youth who daily further from the east
Must travel, still is nature's priest,
        And by the vision splendid
        Is on his way attended;
At length the man perceives it die away,
And fade into the light of common day."

And page 352 to 354 of the same ode.

"O joy that in our embers
    Is something that doth live,
    That nature yet remembers
    What was so fugitive!
The thought of our past years in me doth breed
Perpetual benedictions: not indeed
    For that which is most worthy to be blest;
    Delight and liberty, the simple creed
    Of childhood, whether busy or at rest,
    With new-fledged hope still fluttering in his breast:—
    Not for these I raise
    The song of thanks and praise;
    But for those obstinate questionings
    Of sense and outward things,
    Fallings from us, vanishings;
    Blank misgivings of a creature
    Moving about in worlds not realized,
    High instincts, before which our mortal nature
    Did tremble like a guilty thing surprised!

◇◇◇◇◇◇◇◇◇◇◇◇◇◇◇◇◇◇◇◇◇◇◇◇◇◇◇◇◇◇◇◇

[43] Refers, respectively, to: "Where lies the Land to which yon Ship must go?", "Even as a dragon's eye that feels the stress," "To the River Duddon," "Composed upon Westminster Bridge," "Methought I saw the footsteps of a throne," "It is a beauteous evening, calm and free." The sonnet on the subjugation of Switzerland next referred to is "Two Voices are there; one is of the Sea" (1807).

But for those first affections,
Those shadowy recollections,
    Which, be they what they may,
Are yet the fountain light of all our day,
Are yet a master light of all our seeing;
Uphold us—cherish—and have power to make
Our noisy years seem moments in the being
Of the eternal silence; truths that wake
        To perish never:
Which neither listlessness, nor mad endeavour
Nor man nor boy
Nor all that is at enmity with joy
Can utterly abolish or destroy!
Hence, in a season of calm weather,
    Though inland far we be,
Our souls have sight of that immortal sea
    Which brought us hither,
    Can in a moment travel thither—
And see the children sport upon the shore,
And hear the mighty waters rolling evermore."

And since it would be unfair to conclude with an extract, which though highly characteristic must yet from the nature of the thoughts and the subject be interesting, or perhaps intelligible, to but a limited number of readers; I will add from the poet's last published work a passage equally Wordsworthian; of the beauty of which, and of the imaginative power displayed therein, there can be but one opinion, and one feeling. See White Doe, page 5.

Fast the church-yard fills;—anon
Look again and they are gone;
The cluster round the porch, and the folk
Who sate in the shade of the prior's oak!
And scarcely have they disappear'd
Ere the prelusive hymn is heard:—
With one consent the people rejoice,
Filling the church with a lofty voice!
They sing a service which they feel
For 'tis the sun-rise of their zeal
And faith and hope are in their prime
In great Eliza's golden time.
A moment ends the fervent din
And all is hushed without and within;
For though the priest more tranquilly
Recites the holy liturgy,
The only voice which you can hear
Is the river murmuring near.
When soft!—the dusky trees between
And down the path through the open green,
Where is no living thing to be seen;
And through yon gateway, where is found,
Beneath the arch with ivy bound,
Free entrance to the church-yard ground;
And right across the verdant sod
Towards the very house of God;

Comes gliding in with lovely gleam,
Comes gliding in serene and slow,
Soft and silent as a dream,
A solitary doe!
White she is as lily of June,
And beauteous as the silver moon
When out of sight the clouds are driven
And she is left alone in heaven!
Or like a ship some gentle day
In sunshine sailing far away—
A glittering ship that hath the plain
Of ocean for her own domain.

* * * * * * * * * *

What harmonious pensive changes
Wait upon her as she ranges
Round and round this pile of state
Overthrown and desolate!
Now a step or two her way
Is through space of open day,
Where the enamoured sunny light
Brightens her that was so bright:
Now doth a delicate shadow fall,
Falls upon her like a breath
From some lofty arch or Wall,
As she passes underneath.[44]

The following analogy will, I am apprehensive, appear dim and fantastic, but in reading Bartram's Travels[45] I could not help transcribing the following lines as a sort of allegory, or connected simile and metaphor of Wordsworth's intellect and genius.—"The soil is a deep, rich, dark mould, on a deep stra-"tum of tenacious clay; and that on a foundation of "rocks, which often break through both strata, lifting "their back above the surface. The trees which chiefly "grow here are the gigantic, black oak; magnolia mag-"nifloria; fraximus excelsior; platane; and a few "stately tulip trees." What Mr. Wordsworth *will* produce, it is not for me to prophecy: but I could pronounce with the liveliest convictions what he is capable of producing. It is the FIRST GENUINE PHILOSOPHIC POEM.[46]

*   *   *   *   *

[1817]

THE FRIEND

Written "to found true PRINCIPLES, to oppose false PRINCIPLES, in Criticism, Legislation, Philosophy, Morals, and International Law," The Friend was originally

---

44 *The White Doe of Rylstone* (1815), Canto I, 31–66, 79–90.
45 William Bartram (1739–1823) was the author of *Travels through North and South Carolina* (1791), from which Coleridge quotes p. 36. This was a favorite book of Coleridge's and has been identified as one of the sources for *Kubla Kahn*.
46 Refers to the projected *Recluse*. See Chapter XX, footnote 2, p. 217.

---

published as a periodical, June 1809–March 1810. *The issues were collected in book form in 1812. The 1818 version, described by its author as "rather a rifacciamento [re-making] than a new edition," contained a more orderly arrangement and distribution of materials, considerable revision, and many additions, including the entire Section the Second ("On the Grounds of Morals and Religion, and the Discipline of the Mind Requisite for a True Understanding of the Same"), which Coleridge regarded as among the most valuable of all his writings. "Essays on the Principles of Method" comprise Chapters IV through XI of Section the Second. They are a reworking of material originally published as "General Introduction; or, Preliminary Treatise on Method" for* Encyclopedia Metropolitana *(1818).*

A masterful edition of The Friend, *including both 1809–1810 and 1818 texts, has been prepared by Barbara E. Rooke, as Volume IV (1969) of* The Collected Works of Samuel Taylor Coleridge.

FROM

THE FRIEND

SECTION THE SECOND,

"Essays on the Principles of Method"

ESSAY IV

Ὁ δὲ δίκαιον ἐστι ποιεῖν, ἄκουε πῶς χρὴ ἔχειν ἐμὲ καὶ σὲ πρὸς ἀλλήλους. Εἰ μὲν ὅλως φιλοσοφίας καταπεφρόνηκας, ἔᾶν καίρειν εἰ δὲ παρ' ἑτέρου ἀκήκοας ἢ αὐτὸς βελτίονα εὕρηκας τῶν παρ' ἐμοὶ, ἐκεῖνα τίμα. εἰ δ' ἄρα τὰ παρ' ἡμῶν σοὶ ἀρέσκει, τιμητέον καὶ ἐμὲ μάλιστα.
ΠΛΑΤΩΝ·ΔΙΩΝ: ἐριστ· δευτερα.

(*Translation.*)—Hear then what are the terms on which you and I ought to stand toward each other. If you hold philosophy altogether in contempt, bid it farewell. Or if you have heard from any other person, or have yourself found out a better than mine, then give honor to that, which ever it be. But if the doctrine taught in these our works please you, then it is but just that you should honor me too in the same proportion.
Plato's 2d Letter to Dion.

WHAT IS that which first strikes us, and strikes us at once, in a man of education? And which, among educated men, so instantly distinguishes the man of superior mind, that (as was observed with eminent propriety of the late Edmund Burke) "we cannot stand under the same arch-way during a shower of rain, *without finding him out?*"[1] Not the weight or novelty of his remarks; not any unusual interest of facts communicated by him; for we may suppose both the one and the other precluded by the shortness of our intercourse, and the triviality of the subjects. The difference will be impressed and felt, though the conversation should be confined to the state of the

---

1 See Boswell's *Life of Johnson*, entry for May 15, 1784.

weather or the pavement. Still less will it arise from any peculiarity in his words and phrases. For if he be, as we now assume, a *well*-educated man as well as a man of superior powers, he will not fail to follow the golden rule of Julius Cæsar, *Insolens verbum, tanquam scopulum, evitare*.[2] Unless where new things necessitate new terms, he will avoid an unusual word as a rock. It must have been among the earliest lessons of his youth, that the breach of this precept, at all times hazardous, becomes ridiculous in the topics of ordinary conversation. There remains but one other point of distinction possible; and this must be, and in fact is, the true cause of the impression made on us. It is the unpremeditated and evidently habitual *arrangement* of his words, grounded on the habit of foreseeing, in each integral part, or (more plainly) in every sentence, the whole that he then intends to communicate. However irregular and desultory his talk, there is *method* in the fragments.

Listen, on the other hand, to an ignorant man, though perhaps shrewd and able in his particular calling; whether he be describing or relating. We immediately perceive, that his memory alone is called into action; and that the objects and events recur in the narration in the same order, and with the same accompaniments, however accidental or impertinent, as they had first occurred to the narrator. The necessity of taking breath, the efforts of recollection, and the abrupt rectification of its failures, produce all his pauses; and with exception of the "*and then,*" the "*and there,*" and the still less significant, "*and so,*" they constitute likewise all his connections.

Our discussion, however, is confined to Method as employed in the formation of the understanding, and in the constructions of science and literature. It would indeed be superfluous to attempt a proof of its importance in the business and economy of active or domestic life. From the cotter's hearth or the workshop of the artisan, to the palace or the arsenal, the first merit, that which admits neither substitute nor equivalent, is, that *every thing is in its place.* Where this charm is wanting, every other merit either loses its name, or becomes an additional ground of accusation and regret. Of one, by whom it is eminently possessed, we say proverbially, he is like clock-work. The resemblance extends beyond the point of regularity, and yet falls short of the truth. Both do, indeed, at once divide and announce the silent and otherwise indistinguishable lapse of time. But the man of methodical industry and honorable pursuits, does more: he realizes its ideal divisions, and gives a character and individuality to its moments. If the idle are described as killing time, he may be justly

said to call it into life and moral being, while he makes it the distinct object not only of the consciousness, but of the conscience. He organizes the hours, and gives them a soul: and that, the very essence of which is to fleet away, and evermore *to have been*, he takes up into his own permanence, and communicates to it the imperishableness of a spiritual nature. Of the good and faithful servant, whose energies, thus directed, are thus methodized, it is less truly affirmed, that He lives in time, than that Time lives in him. His days, months, and years, as the stops and punctual marks in the records of duties performed, will survive the wreck of worlds, and remain extant when time itself shall be no more.

But as the importance of Method in the duties of social life is incomparably greater, so are its practical elements proportionably obvious, and such as relate to the will far more than to the understanding. Henceforward, therefore, we contemplate its bearings on the latter.

The difference between the products of a well-disciplined and those of an uncultivated understanding, in relation to what we will now venture to call the *Science of Method*, is often and admirably exhibited by our great Dramatist. We scarcely need refer our readers to the Clown's evidence, in the first scene of the second act of "Measure for Measure," or the Nurse in "Romeo and Juliet." But not to leave the position, without an instance to illustrate it, we will take the "easy-yielding" Mrs. Quickley's relation of the circumstances of Sir John Falstaff's debt to her.

FALSTAFF. What is the gross sum that I owe thee?
Mrs. QUICKLEY. Marry, if thou wert an honest man, thyself and the money too. Thou didst swear to me upon a parcel-gilt goblet, sitting in my dolphin chamber, at the round table, by a sea-coal fire, on Wednesday in Whitsun week, when the prince broke thy head for likening his father to a singing-man in Windsor—thou didst swear to me then, as I was washing thy wound, to marry me and make me my lady thy wife. Canst thou deny it? Did not goodwife Keech, the butcher's wife, come in then and call me gossip Quickley?—coming into borrow a mess of vinegar: telling us she had a good dish of prawns—whereby thou didst desire to eat some—whereby I told thee they were ill for a green wound, &c. &c. &c.
Henry IV. 1st. pt. act ii. sc. 1.[3]

And this, be it observed, is so far from being carried beyond the bounds of a fair imitation, that "the poor soul's" thoughts and sentences are more closely interlinked than the truth of nature would have required, but that the connections and sequence, which the

---

[2] See *Biographia Literaria*, Chapter I, footnote 2, p. 170.

[3] More accurately, *of Henry the Fourth*, Part II, II, i, 91–107.

habit of Method can alone give, have in this instance a
substitute in the fusion of passion. For the absence of
Method, which characterizes the uneducated, is occasioned by an habitual submission of the understanding
to mere events and images as such, and independent of
any power in the mind to classify or appropriate them.
The general accompaniments of time and place are the
only relations which persons of this class appear to
regard in their statements. As this constitutes *their*
leading feature, the contrary excellence, as distinguishing the well-educated man, must be referred to
the contrary habit. METHOD, therefore, becomes
natural to the mind which has been accustomed to contemplate not *things* only, or for their own sake alone,
but likewise and chiefly the *relations* of things, either
their relations to each other, or to the observer, or to
the state and apprehension of the hearers. To enu-
merate and analyze these relations, with the conditions
under which alone they are discoverable, is to teach the
science of Method.

The enviable results of this science, when knowledge has been ripened into those habits which at once
secure and evince its possession, can scarcely be exhibited more forcibly as well as more pleasingly, than
by contrasting with the former extract from Shakspeare
the narration given by Hamlet to Horatio of the occurrences during his proposed transportation to England,
and the events that interrupted his voyage.

HAM. Sir, in my heart there was a kind of fighting
That would not let me sleep: methought I lay
Worse than the mutines in the bilboes. Rashly,
And prais'd be rashness for it—*Let us know*,
Our indiscretion sometimes serves us well,
When our deep plots do fail: and that should teach us,
There's a divinity that shapes our ends,
Rough-hew them how we will.
   HOR. That is most certain.
   HAM. Up from my cabin,
My sea-gown scarf'd about me, in the dark
Grop'd I to find out them; had my desire;
Finger'd their pocket; and, in fine, withdrew
To my own room again: making so bold,
My fears forgetting manners, to unseal
Their grand commission; where *I* found, Horatio,
A royal knavery—an exact command,
Larded with many several sorts of reasons,
Importing Denmark's health, and England's too,
With, ho! such bugs and goblins in *my* life,
That on the supervize, no leisure bated,
No, not to stay the grinding of the axe,
My head should be struck off!
   HOR. Is't possible?
   HAM. Here's the commission.—Read it at more leisure.
                                        Act v. sc. 2.[4]

---

4 Ll. 4–26. Coleridge next quotes the succeeding lines 31–62.

Here the events, with the circumstances of time and
place, are all stated with equal compression and rapidity, not one introduced which could have been omitted
without injury to the intelligibility of the whole process.
If any tendency is discoverable, as far as the mere facts
are in question, it is the tendency to omission: and,
accordingly, the reader will observe, that the attention
of the narrator is called back to one material circumstance, which he was hurrying by, by a direct question
from the friend to whom the story is communicated,
"HOW WAS THIS SEALED?" But by a trait which is
indeed peculiarly characteristic of Hamlet's mind,
ever disposed to generalize, and meditative to excess
(but which, with due abatement and reduction, is distinctive of every powerful and methodizing intellect),
all the digressions and enlargements consist of reflections, truths, and principles of general and permanent
interest, either directly expressed or disguised in
playful satire.

————I sat me down;
Devis'd a new commission; wrote it fair.
I once did hold it, as our statists do,
A baseness to write fair, and laboured much
How to forget that learning; but, sir, now
It did me yeoman's service. Wilt thou know
The effect of what I wrote?
   HOR. Aye, good my lord.
   HAM. An earnest conjuration from the king,
As England was his faithful tributary;
As love between them, like the palm, might flourish;
As peace should still her wheaten garland wear,
And many such like As's of great charge—
That on the view and knowing of these contents
He should the bearers put to sudden death,
No shriving time allowed.
   HOR. How was this sealed?
   HAM. Why, even in that was heaven ordinant.
I had my father's signet in my purse,
Which was the model of that Danish seal:
Folded the writ up in the form of the other;
Subscribed it; gave't the impression; placed it safely,
The changeling never known. Now, the next day
Was our sea-fight; and what to this was sequent,
Thou knowest already.
   HOR. So Guildenstern and Rosencrantz go to't?
   HAM. Why, man, they did make love to this employ-
        ment.
They are not near my conscience: their defeat
Doth by their own insinuation grow.
'Tis dangerous when the baser nature comes
Between the pass and fell incensed points
Of mighty opposites.

It would, perhaps, be sufficient to remark of the
preceding passage, in connection with the humorous
specimen of narration,

"Fermenting o'er with frothy circumstance,"

in Henry IV.; that if overlooking the different value of the *matter* in each, we considered the *form* alone, we should find both *immethodical;* Hamlet from the excess, Mrs. Quickley from the want, of reflection and generalization; and that Method, therefore, must result from the due mean or balance between our passive impressions and the mind's own re-action on the same. (Whether this re-action do not suppose or imply a primary act positively *originating* in the mind itself, and prior to the object in order of nature, though co-instantaneous in its manifestation, will be hereafter discussed.) But we had a further purpose in thus contrasting these extracts from our "myriad-minded Bard," (μυριονῦς ἀνηρ.) We wished to bring forward, each for itself, these two elements of Method, or (to adopt an arithmetical term) its two main *factors*.

Instances of the want of generalization are of no rare occurrence in real life: and the narrations of Shakspeare's Hostess and the Tapster,[5] differ from those of the ignorant and unthinking in general, by their superior humor, the poet's own gift and infusion, not by their want of Method, which is not greater than we often meet with in that class, of which they are the dramatic representatives. Instances of the opposite fault, arising from the excess of generalization and reflection in minds of the opposite class, will, like the minds themselves, occur less frequently in the course of our own personal experience. Yet they will not have been wanting to our readers, nor will they have passed unobserved, though the great poet himself (ὁ τὴν ἑαυτοῦ ψυχὴν ὥσει ὑλὴν τίνα ἀσώματον μορφᾶις ποικιλᾶις μορφώσας*) has more conveniently supplied the illustrations. To complete, therefore, the purpose aforementioned, that of presenting each of the two components as separately as possible, we chose an instance in which, by the surplus of its own activity, Hamlet's mind disturbs the arrangement, of which that very activity had been the cause and impulse.

Thus exuberance of mind, on the one hand, interferes with the *forms* of Method; but sterility of mind, on the other, wanting the spring and impulse to mental action, is wholly destructive of Method itself. For in attending too exclusively to the relations which the past or passing events and objects bear to general truth, and the moods of his own Thought, the most intelligent man is sometimes in danger of overlooking that other relation, in which they are likewise to be placed to the apprehension and sympathies of his hearers. His discourse appears like soliloquy intermixed with dialogue. But the uneducated and unreflecting talker overlooks *all* mental relations, both logical and psychological; and consequently precludes all Method, that is not purely accidental. Hence the nearer the things and incidents in time and place, the more distant, disjointed, and impertinent to each other, and to any common purpose, will they appear in his narration: and this from the want of a *staple*, or *starting-post*, in the narrator himself; from the absence of *the leading Thought*, which, borrowing a phrase from the nomenclature of legislation, we may not inaptly call the INITIATIVE. On the contrary, where the habit of Method is present and effective, things the most remote and diverse in time, place, and outward circumstance, are brought into mental contiguity and succession, the more striking as the less expected. But while we would impress the necessity of this habit, the illustrations adduced give proof that in undue preponderance, and when the prerogative of the mind is stretched into despotism, the discourse may degenerate into the grotesque or the fantastical.

With what a profound insight into the constitution of the human soul is this exhibited to us in the character of the Prince of Denmark, where flying from the sense of reality, and seeking a reprieve from the pressure of its duties, in that ideal activity, the overbalance of which, with the consequent indisposition to action, is his disease, he compels the reluctant good sense of the high yet healthful-minded Horatio, to follow him in his wayward meditation amid the graves? "*To what base uses we may return, Horatio! Why may not imagination trace the noble dust of Alexander, till he find it stopping a bung-hole?* HOR. *It were to consider too curiously to consider so.* HAM. *No, faith, not a jot; but to follow him thither with modesty enough and likelihood to lead it. As thus: Alexander died, Alexander was buried, Alexander returneth to dust—the dust is earth; of earth we make loam: and why of that loam, whereto he was converted, might they not stop a beer-barrel?*

> *Imperial Cæsar, dead and turn'd to clay,*
> *Might stop a hole to keep the wind away!*"[7]

But let it not escape our recollection, that when the objects thus connected are proportionate to the connecting energy, relatively to the real, or at least to the desirable sympathies of mankind; it is from the same character that we derive the genial method in the

---

* TRANSLATION.—He that moulded his own soul, as some incorporeal material, into various forms. THEMISTIUS.[6]

5 Pompey in *Measure for Measure*. Coleridge had earlier referred to Pompey "the Clown's evidence" in II, i, 91ff.

6 Themistius (A.D. 317–c. 387), philosopher and statesman of Constantinople, author of *Paraphrases on Aristotle*.

7 V, i, 223–37.

famous soliloquy, "*To be? or not to be?*" which, admired as it is, and has been, has yet received only the first-fruits of the admiration due to it.

We have seen that from the confluence of innumerable impressions in each moment of time the mere passive memory must needs tend to confusion—a rule, the seeming exceptions to which (the thunder-bursts in Lear, for instance) are really confirmations of its truth. For, in many instances, the predominance of some mighty Passion takes the place of the guiding Thought, and the result presents the method of Nature, rather than the habit of the Individual. For Thought, Imagination (and we may add, Passion), are, in their very essence, the first, connective, the latter co-adunative [8]: and it has been shown, that if the excess lead to Method misapplied, and to connections of the moment, the absence, or marked deficiency, either precludes Method altogether, both form and substance: or (as the following extract will exemplify) retains the outward form only.

> *My liege and madam! to expostulate*
> *What majesty should be, what duty is,*
> *Why day is day, night night, and time is time,*
> *Were nothing but to waste night, day and time.*
> *Therefore—since brevity is the soul of wit,*
> *And tediousness the limbs and outward flourishes,*
> *I will be brief. Your noble son is mad:*
> *Mad call I it—for to define true madness,*
> *What is't, but to be nothing else but mad!*
> *But let that go.*
>   QUEEN. *More matter with less art.*
> POL.
> *Madam! I swear, I use no art at all.*
> *That he is mad, tis true: tis true, tis pity:*
> *And pity tis, tis true (a foolish figure!*
> *But farewell it, for I will use no art.)*
> *Mad let us grant him then: and now remains,*
> *That we find out the cause of this effect,*
> *Or rather say the cause of this defect:*
> *For this effect defective comes by cause.*
> *Thus it remains, and the remainder thus*
> *Perpend!*
>
> Hamlet, act ii. scene 2.[9]

Does not the irresistible sense of the ludicrous in this flourish of the soul-surviving body of old Polonius's intellect, not less than in the endless confirmations and most undeniable matters of fact, of Tapster Pompey or "the hostess of the tavern" prove to our feelings, even before the word is found which presents the truth to our understandings, that confusion and formality are but the opposite poles of the same null-point?

---

[8] Combining or uniting into one.
[9] Ll. 86–105.

It is Shakspeare's peculiar excellence, that throughout the whole of his splendid picture gallery (the reader will excuse the confest inadequacy of this metaphor), we find individuality every where, mere portrait no where. In all his various characters, we still feel ourselves communing with the same human nature, which is every where present as the vegetable sap in the branches, sprays, leaves, buds, blossoms, and fruits, their shapes, tastes, and odours. Speaking of the effect, i.e. his works themselves, we may define the excellence of *their* method as consisting in that just proportion, that union and interpenetration of the universal and the particular, which must ever pervade all works of decided genius and true science. For Method implies a *progressive transition*, and it is the meaning of the word in the original language. The Greek Μεθοδος, is literally *a way*, or *path of Transit*. Thus we extol the Elements of Euclid, or Socrates' discourse with the slave in the Menon,[10] as *methodical*, a term which no one who holds himself bound to think or speak correctly, would apply to the alphabetical order or arrangement of a common dictionary. But as, without continuous transition, there can be no Method, so without a pre-conception there can be no transition with continuity. The term, Method, cannot therefore, otherwise than by abuse, be applied to a mere dead arrangement, containing in itself no principle of progression.

ESSAY V

> *Scientiis idem quod plantis. Si plantâ aliquâ uti in animo habeas, de radice quid fiat, nil refert: si vero transferre cupias in aliud solum, tutius est radicibus uti quam surculis. Sic traditio, quæ nunc in usu est, exhibet plane tanquam truncos (pulchros illos quidem) scientiarum; sed tamen absque radicibus fabro lignario certe commodos, at plantatori inutiles. Quod si, disciplinæ ut crescant, tibi cordi sit, de truncis minus sis solicitus: ad id curam adhibe, ut radices illæsæ, etiam cum aliquantulo terræ adhærentis, extrahantur: dummodo hoc pacto et scientiam propriam revisere, vetigia que cognitionis tuæ remetiri possis; et eam sic transplantare in animum alienum, sicut crevit in tuo.*
>
> BACO de Augment. Scient. l. vi. c. ii.

(*Translation.*)—It is with sciences as with trees. If it be your purpose to make some particular *use* of the tree, you need not concern yourself about the roots. But if you wish to transfer it into another soil, it is then safer to employ the roots, than the scyons. Thus the mode of teaching most common at present exhibits clearly enough the trunks, as it were, of the sciences,

---

[10] Coleridge refers to a passage in Plato's *Meno*, 82–85, in which Socrates asks one of Meno's attendants a series of logically connected questions and thus leads him to affirm a number of geometrical truths that he at first could not answer.

and those too of handsome growth; but nevertheless, without the roots, valuable and convenient as they undoubtedly are to the carpenter, they are useless to the planter. But if you have at heart the advancement of education, as that which proposes to itself the general discipline of the mind for its end and aim, be less anxious concerning the trunks, and let it be your care, that the roots should be extracted entire, even though a small portion of the soil should adhere to them: so that at all events you may be able, by this means, both to review your own scientific acquirements, re-measuring as it were the steps of your knowledge for your own satisfaction, and at the same time to transplant it into the minds of others, just as it grew in your own.

It has been observed, in a preceding page, that the RELATIONS of objects are prime *materials* of Method, and that the contemplation of relations is the indispensible condition of thinking methodically. It becomes necessary therefore to add, that there are two kinds of relation, in which objects of mind may be contemplated. The first is that of LAW, which, in its absolute perfection, is conceivable only of the Supreme Being, whose creative IDEA not only appoints to each thing its *position*, but in that position, and in consequence of that position, gives it its qualities, yea, it gives its very existence, as *that particular* thing. Yet in whatever science the relation of the parts to each other and to the whole is predetermined by a truth originating in the *mind*, and not abstracted or generalized from observation of the parts, there we affirm the presence of a *law*, if we are speaking of the physical sciences, as of Astronomy for instance; or the presence of fundamental *ideas*, if our discourse be upon those sciences, the truths of which, as truths absolute, not merely have an independent *origin* in the mind, but continue to exist in and for the mind alone. Such, for instance, is Geometry, and such are the ideas of a perfect circle, of asymptots,[1] &c.

We have thus assigned the first place in the science of Method to LAW; and first of the first, to *Law*, as the absolute *kind* which comprehending in itself the substance of every possible degree precludes from its conception all degree, not by generalization but by its own plenitude. As such, therefore, and as the sufficient cause of the reality correspondent thereto, we contemplate it as exclusively an attribute of the Supreme Being, inseparable from the idea of God: adding, however, that from the contemplation of law in this, its

only perfect form, must be derived all true insight into all other grounds and principles necessary to Method, as the science common to all sciences, which in each τυγχάνει ὂν ἄλλο αὐτῆς τῆς ἐπισήμης.[2] Alienated from this (intuition shall we call it? or stedfast faith?) ingenious men may produce schemes, conducive to the peculiar purposes of particular sciences, but no scientific system.

But though we cannot enter on the proof of this assertion, we dare not remain exposed to the suspicion of having obtruded a mere private opinion, as a fundamental truth. Our authorities are such that our only difficulty is occasioned by their number. The following extract from Aristocles (preserved with other interesting fragments of the same writer by Eusebius) is as explicit as peremptory. Ἐφιλοσοφησε μὲν Πλάτων, εἰ καὶ τὶς ἄλλος τῶν πώποτε, γνησίως καὶ τελέιως· ἠξιοῦ δὲ μὴ δύνασθαι τὰ ἀνθρώπινα κατιδεῖν ἥμας, εἰ μὴ τὰ θεῖα πρότερον ὀφθείη. EUSEB. Præp. Evan. xi. 3.* And Plato himself in his De republicâ, happily still extant, evidently alludes to the same doctrine. For personating Socrates in the discussion of a most important problem, namely, whether political justice is or is not the same as private honesty, after many inductions, and much analytic reasoning, he breaks off with these words—εὖ γ' ἴσθι, ὦ Γλαύκων, ὡς ἡ ἔμη δοξα, ΑΚΡΙΒΩΣ ΜΕΝ ΤΟΥΤΟ 'ΕΚ ΤΟΙΟΥΤΩΝ ΜΕΘΟΔΩΝ, ΟΙΑΙΣ ΝΥΝ ΕΝ ΤΟΙΣ ΛΟΓΟΙΣ ΧΡΩΜΕΘΑ, ΟΥ ΜΗΠΟΤΕ ΛΑΒΩΜΕΝ· ΑΛΛΑ ΓΑΡ ΜΑΚΡΟΤΕΡΑ ΚΑΙ ΠΛΕΙΩΝ ΟΔΟΣ Η ΕΠΙ ΤΟΥΤΟ ΑΓΟΥΣΑ†—not however, he adds, precluding the former (the analytic, and inductive, to wit) which have their place likewise, in which (but as subordinate to the other) they are both

---

[1] Lines which approach nearer and nearer to a given curve, but do not meet it within a finite distance. In marginal comments on this paragraph in several copies of *The Friend*, Coleridge urged the substitution of the word "Theorems" ("the intelligible Products of mental Contemplation, that are Objects *in, from,* and *for* the mind exclusively") for the word "*ideas.*" See Rooke's edition, I, 459, footnote 2.

* (*Translation*)—Plato, who philosophized legitimately and perfectively, if ever any man did in any age, held it for an axiom, that it is not possible for us to have an insight into things human (i.e. *the nature and relations of man, and the objects presented by nature for his investigation*), without a previous contemplation (or intellectual vision) of things divine: that is, of truths that are to be affirmed concerning the absolute, as far as they can be made known to us.[3]

† (*Translation*)—But know well, O Glaucon, as my firm persuasion, that by such methods, as we have hitherto used in this inquisition, we can never attain to a satisfactory insight: for it is a longer and ampler way that conducts to this.—PLATO *De republicâ,* iv.[4]

[2] τυγχάνει . . . ἐπιστήμη: "may prove to be something more than the mere aggregate of the knowledge in any particular science." Plato's *Charmides,* 166.

[3] Aristocles of Messene, a peripatetic philosopher of the third century, wrote a history of Greek philosophy. A fragment, "De Platonica philosophia," from which Coleridge quotes, is preserved in *Evangelica Preparatio,* XI, iii, by Eusebius Pamphili (c. 260–c. 340), a voluminous writer of Christian apologetics and ecclesiastical history.

[4] Coleridge quotes Book IV, section 435.

useful and requisite. If any doubt could be entertained as to the purport of these words, it would be removed by the fact stated by Aristotle in his Ethics,[5] that Plato had discussed the problem, whether in order to scientific ends we must set out from principles, or ascend towards them: in other words, whether the synthetic or analytic be the right method. But as no such question is directly discussed in the published works of the great master, Aristotle must either have received it orally from Plato himself, or have found it in the αγραφα δογματα,[6] the private text books or manuals constructed by his select disciples, and intelligible to these only who like themselves had been entrusted with the esoteric (interior or unveiled) doctrines of Platonism. Comparing this therefore with the writings, which he held it safe or not profane to make public, we may safely conclude, that Plato considered the investigation of truth *a posteriori* as that which is employed in explaining the *results* of a more scientific process to those, for whom the knowledge of the results was alone requisite and sufficient; or in preparing the mind for legitimate method, by exposing the insufficiency or self-contradictions of the proofs and results obtained by the contrary process. Hence therefore the earnestness with which the genuine Platonists opposed the doctrine (that all demonstration consisted of identical propositions) advanced by Stilpo, and maintained by the Megaric school, who denied the synthesis and as Hume and others in recent times, held geometry itself to be merely analytical.[7]

The grand problem, the solution of which forms, according to Plato, the final object and distinctive character of philosophy, is this: *for all that exists conditionally* (i.e. the existence of which is inconceivable except under the condition of its dependency on some other as its antecedent) *to find a ground that is unconditional and absolute, and thereby to reduce the aggregate of human knowledge to a system.* For the relation common to all being known, the appropriate orbit of each becomes discoverable, together with its peculiar relations to its concentrics in the common sphere of subordination. Thus the centrality of the sun having been established, and the law of the distances of the planets from the sun having been determined, we possess the means of calculating the distance of each from the other. But as all objects of sense are in continual flux,

⬦⬦⬦⬦⬦⬦⬦⬦⬦⬦⬦⬦⬦⬦⬦⬦⬦⬦⬦⬦⬦⬦⬦⬦⬦⬦⬦⬦

5 See *Nicomachean Ethics*, I, iv, 5.

6 αγραφα δογματα: "unwritten dogmas," most private revelations.

7 Coleridge refers to sophists, who deny the ability of the mind to reach a true synthesis, or the discovery of a common essence or vital principle of life in diverse objects. Stilpo was a contemporary of Aristotle and follower of Euclid, the founder of the school of philosophy at Megara, Greece.

and as the notices of them by the senses must, as far as they are true notices, change with them, while scientific principles (or laws) are no otherwise principles of science than as they are permanent and always the same, the latter were appropriated to the pure reason, either as its products or as *implanted in it. And now the remarkable fact forces itself on our attention, viz. that the material world is found to obey the same laws as had been deduced independently from the reason: and that the masses act by a force, which cannot be conceived to result from the component parts, known or imaginable. In the phænomena of magnetism, electricity, galvanism, and in chemistry generally, the mind is led instinctively, as it were, to regard the working powers as conducted, transmitted, or accumulated by the sensible bodies, and not as inherent. This fact has, at all times, been the strong hold alike of the materialists and of the spiritualists, equally solvable by the two contrary hypotheses, and fairly solved by neither. In the clear and masterly† review of the elder

* Which of these two doctrines was Plato's own opinion, it is hard to say. In many passages of his works, the latter (i.e. the doctrine of innate, or rather of connate, ideas) *seems* to be it; but from the character and avowed purpose of these works, as addressed to a promiscuous public, and therefore preparatory and for the discipline of the mind rather than directly doctrinal, it is not improbable that Plato chose it as the more popular representation, and as belonging to the poetic drapery of his Philosophemeta.

† I can conceive no better remedy for the overweening self-complacency of modern philosophy, than the annulment of its pretended originality. The attempt has been made by Dutens, but he failed in it by flying to the opposite extreme. When he should have confined himself to the philosophies, he extended his attack to the sciences and even to the main discoveries of later times: and thus instead of vindicating the ancients, he became the calumniator of the moderns: as far at least as detraction is calumny. It is my intention to give a course of lectures in the course of the present season, comprizing the origin, and progress, the fates and fortunes of philosophy, from Pythagoras to Lock, with the lives and succession of the philosophers in each sect: tracing the progress of speculative science chiefly in relation to the gradual development of the human mind, but without omitting the favorable or inauspicious influence of circumstances and the accidents of individual genius. The main divisions will be, 1. From Thales and Pythagoras to the appearance of the Sophists. 2. And of Socrates. The character and effects of Socrates's life and doctrines, illustrated in the instances of Xenophon, as his most faithful representative, and of Antisthenes or the Cynic sect as the one partial view of his philosophy, and of Aristippus or the Cyrenaic sect as the other and opposite extreme. 3. Plato, and Platonism. 4. Aristotle and the Peripatetic school. 5. Zeno, and Stoicism, Epicurus and Epicurianism, with the effects of these in the Roman republic and empire. 6. The rise of the Eclectic or Alexandrian philosophy, the attempt to set up a pseudo-Platonic Polytheism against Christianity, the degradation of philosophy itself into mysticism and magic, and its final disappearance, as philosophy, under Justinian. 7. The resumption of the Aristotelian philosophy in the thirteenth century, and the successive re-appear-

philosophies, which must be ranked among the most splendid proofs of judgment no less than of genius, and more expressly in the critique on the atomic or corpuscular doctrine of Democritus and his followers, as the one extreme, and that of the pure rationalism of Zeno and the Eleatic school as the other, Plato has proved incontrovertibly, that in both alike the basis is too narrow to support the superstructure; that the grounds of both are false or disputable; and that, if these were conceded, yet neither the one nor the other is adequate to the solution of the problem: viz. what is the ground of the coincidence between reason and experience? Or between the laws of matter and the ideas of the pure intellect? The only answer which Plato deemed the question capable of receiving, compels the reason to pass out of itself and seek the ground of this agreement in a supersensual essence, which being at once the *ideal* of the reason and the cause of the material world, is the pre-establisher of the harmony in and between both. Religion therefore is the ultimate aim of philosophy, in consequence of which philosophy itself becomes the supplement of the sciences, both as the convergence of all to the common end, namely, wisdom; and as supplying the copula, which modified in each in the comprehension of its parts to one whole, is in its principles common to all, as integral parts of one system. And this is METHOD, itself a distinct science, the immediate offspring of philosophy, and the link or *mordant* [9] by which philosophy becomes scientific and the sciences philosophical.

ESSAY VI

Ἀπάντων ζητοῦντες λόγον ἐξωθεν, ἀναιροῦσι λόγον.
THEOPH. *in Met.* [1]

Seeking the reason of all things from without, they preclude reason.

THE SECOND relation is that of THEORY, in which the existing forms and qualities of objects, discovered by observation or experiment, suggest a given arrangement of many under one point of view: and this not merely or principally in order to facilitate the remembrance, recollection, or communication of the same; but for the purposes of understanding, and in most instances of controlling, them. In other words, all THEORY supposes the general idea of cause and effect. The scientific arts of Medicine, Chemistry, and of Physiology in general, are examples of a method hitherto founded on this second sort of relation.

Between these two lies the Method in the FINE ARTS, which belongs indeed to this second or external relation, because the effect and position of the parts is always more or less influenced by the knowledge and experience of their previous qualities; but which nevertheless constitute a link connecting the second form of relation with the first. For in all, that truly merits the name of *Poetry* in its most comprehensive sense, there is a necessary predominance of the Ideas (i.e. of that which originates in the artist himself), and a comparative indifference of the materials. A true musical taste is soon dissatisfied with the Harmonica, or any similar instrument of glass or steel, because the *body* of the sound (as the Italians phrase it), or that effect which is derived from the *materials*, encroaches too far on the effect from the *proportions* of the notes, or that which is *given* to Music by the mind. To prove the high value as well as the superior dignity of the first relation; and to evince, that on this alone a *perfect* Method can be grounded, and that the Methods attainable by the second are at best but approximations to the first, or tentative exercises in the hope of discovering it, form the first object of the present disquisition.

These truths we have (as the most pleasing and popular mode of introducing the subject) hitherto illustrated from Shakspeare. But the same truths, namely the necessity of a mental Initiative to all Method, as well as a careful attention to the conduct of the mind in the exercise of Method itself, may be equally, and here perhaps more characteristically, proved from the most familiar of the SCIENCES. We may draw our elucidation even from those which are at present fashionable among us: from BOTANY or from CHEMISTRY. In the lowest attempt at a methodical arrangement of the former science, that of artificial classification for the preparatory purpose of a nomenclature, some *antecedent* must have been contributed by the mind itself; some *purpose* must be in view; or some question at least must have been proposed to nature, grounded, as all questions are, upon *some* idea of the answer. As for instance, the assumption,

"That two great sexes animate the world." [2]

---

ance of the different sects from the restoration of literature to our own times. S. T. C. [8]

[8] Coleridge refers to Louis Dutens' *Recherches sur l'origine des découvertes attribuées aux modernes* (1766), whose subtitle in the English translation of 1769 indicates the argument of the work: "Wherein it is demonstrated, That our most celebrated Philosophers have, for most part, taken what they advance from the WORKS OF THE ANCIENTS AND That many important Truths in Religion were known to THE PAGAN SAGES." Coleridge's "course of lectures" on the history of philosophy were delivered in London, December 1818–March 1819.

[9] A substance that cements or fixes one thing to another. See *Biographia Literaria*, Chapter XVIII, footnote 16, p. 209.

[1] Theophrastus, *Metaphysics*, VIII, 26.

[2] *Paradise Lost*, VIII, 151.

For no man can confidently conceive a fact to be *universally* true who does not with equal confidence anticipate its *necessity*, and who does not believe that necessity to be demonstrable by an insight into its nature, whenever and wherever such insight can be obtained. We acknowledge, we reverence the obligations of Botany to Linnæus,[3] who, adopting from Bartholinus and others the sexuality of plants, grounded thereon a scheme of classific and distinctive marks, by which one man's experience may be communicated to others, and the objects safely reasoned on while absent, and recognized as soon as and wherever they are met with. He invented a universal character for the language of Botany chargeable with no greater imperfections than are to be found in the alphabets of every particular language. As for the study of the ancients, so of the works of nature, an accidence [4] and a dictionary are the first and indispensible requisites: and to the illustrious Swede, Botany is indebted for both. But neither was the central idea of vegetation itself, by the light of which we might have seen the collateral relations of the vegetable to the inorganic and to the animal world; nor the constitutive nature and inner necessity of sex itself, revealed to Linnæus.* Hence, as in all

---

* The word Nature has been used in two senses, viz. actively and passively; energetic (= forma formans), and material (= forma formata). In the first (the sense in which the word is used in the text) it signifies the inward principle of whatever is requisite for the reality of a thing, as *existent:* while the *essence*, or essential property, signifies the inner principle of all that appertains to the *possibility* of a thing. Hence, in accurate language, we say the *essence* of a mathematical circle or other geometrical figure, not the *nature:* because in the conception of forms purely geometrical there is no expression or implication of their real existence. In the second, or material sense, of the word Nature, we mean by it the sum total of all things, as far as they are objects of our senses, and consequently of possible experience—the aggregate of phænomena, whether existing for our outward senses, or for our inner sense. The doctrine concerning material nature would therefore (the word Physiology being both ambiguous in itself, and already otherwise appropriated) be more properly entitled Phænomenology, distinguished into its two grand divisions, Somatology [5] and Psychology. The doctrine concerning energetic nature is comprised in the science of DYNAMICS: the union of which with Phænomenology, and the alliance of both with the sciences of the Possible, or of the Conceivable, viz. Logic and Mathematics, constitute NATURAL PHILOSOPHY.

Having thus explained the term Nature, we now more especially entreat the reader's attention to the sense, in which here, and every where through this Essay, we use the word IDEA. We assert, that the very impulse to universalize any

◇◇◇◇◇◇◇◇◇◇◇◇◇◇◇◇◇◇◇◇◇◇◇◇◇◇◇◇◇◇◇◇

3 Carl von Linné (1707–1778), the distinguished Swedish botanist, divided plants into two groups: sexual (Phanerogamous or flowering), containing stamens and pistils; and asexual (Cryptogamous or flowerless).

4 Grammar book.

5 Somatology is the science of the properties of bodies.

---

other cases where the master-light is missing, so in this: the reflective mind avoids Scylla only to lose itself on Charybdis. If we adhere to the general notion of sex, as abstracted from the more obvious modes and forms in which the sexual relation manifests itself, we soon meet with whole classes of plants to which it is found inapplicable. If arbitrarily, we give it indefinite extension, it is dissipated into the barren truism, that all specific products suppose specific *means* of production. Thus a growth and a birth are distinguished by the mere verbal definition, that the latter is a whole in itself, the former not: and when we would apply even this to nature, we are baffled by objects (the flower polypus, &c. &c.) in which each is the other. All that can be done by the most patient and active industry, by the widest and most continuous researches; all that the amplest survey of the vegetable realm, brought under immediate contemplation by the most stupendous collections of species and varieties, can suggest; all that minutest dissection and exactest chemical analysis, can unfold; all that varied experiment and the position of plants and of their component parts in every conceivable relation to light, heat, (and whatever else we distinguish as imponderable substances) to earth, air, water, separate and in all proportions—in short all that chemical agents and re-agents can disclose or adduce;—all these have been brought, as conscripts, into the field, with the completest accoutrement, in the best discipline, under the ablest commanders. Yet after all that was

---

phænomenon involves the prior assumption of some efficient law in nature, which in a thousand different forms is evermore one and the same; entire in each, yet comprehending all; and incapable of being abstracted or generalized from any number of phænomena, because it is itself pre-supposed in each and all as their common ground and condition: and because every definition of a genus is the adequate definition of the lowest species alone, while the efficient law must contain the ground of all in all. It is *attributed*, never *derived*. The utmost we ever venture to say is, that the falling of an apple *suggested* the law of gravitation to Sir I. Newton. Now a law and an idea are correlative terms, and differ only as object and subject, as being and truth.

Such is the doctrine of the Novum Organum of Lord Bacon, agreeing (as we shall more largely show in the text) in all essential points with the true doctrine of Plato, the apparent differences being for the greater part occasioned by the Grecian sage having applied his principles chiefly to the investigation of the mind, and the method of evolving its powers, and the English philosopher to the development of nature. That our great countryman speaks too often detractingly of the divine philosopher must be explained, partly by the tone given to thinking minds by the Reformation, the founders and fathers of which saw in the Aristotelians, or schoolmen, the antagonists of Protestantism, and in the Italian Platonists the despisers and secret enemies of Christianity itself; and partly, by his having formed his notions of Plato's doctrines from the absurdities and phantasms of his misinterpreters rather than from an unprejudiced study of the original works.

effected by Linnæus himself, not to mention the labours of Cæsalpinus, Ray, Gesner, Tournefort,[6] and the other heroes who preceded the general adoption of the sexual system, as the basis of artificial arrangement —after all the successive toils and enterprizes of HEDWIG, JUSSIEU, MIRBEL, SMITH, KNIGHT, ELLIS,[7] &c. &c.—what is BOTANY at this present hour? Little more than an enormous nomenclature; a huge catalogue, *bien arrangè*, yearly and monthly augmented, in various editions, each with its own scheme of technical memory and its own conveniences of reference! A dictionary in which (to carry on the metaphor) an Ainsworth arranges the contents by the initials; a Walker by the endings; a Scapula by the radicals; and a Cominius by the similarity of the uses and purposes![8] The terms system, method, science, are mere improprieties of courtesy, when applied to a mass enlarging by endless appositions, but without a nerve that oscillates, or a pulse that throbs, in sign of *growth* or inward sympathy. The innocent amusement, the healthful occupation, the ornamental accomplishment of *amateurs* (most honorable indeed and deserving of all praise as a preventive substitute for the stall, the kennel, and the subscription-room), it has yet to expect the devotion and energies of the philosopher.

So long back as the first appearance of Dr. Darwin's Phytonomia,[9] the writer, then in earliest manhood, presumed to hazard the opinion, that the physiological botanists were hunting in a false direction; and sought for analogy where they should have looked for antithesis. He saw, or thought he saw, that the harmony between the vegetable and animal world, was not a harmony of resemblance, but of contrast; and their relation to each other that of corresponding opposites. They seemed to him (whose mind had been formed by observation, unaided, but at the same time unenthralled, by partial experiment) as two streams from the same fountain indeed, but flowing the one due west, and the other direct east; and that consequently, the resemblance would be as the proximity, greatest in the first and rudimental products of vegetable and animal organization. Whereas, according to the received notion, the highest and most perfect vegetable, and the lowest and rudest animal forms, ought to have seemed the links of the two systems, which is contrary to fact. Since that time, the same idea has dawned in the minds of philosophers capable of demonstrating its objective truth by induction of facts in an unbroken series of correspondences in nature. From these men, or from minds enkindled by their labours, we hope hereafter to receive it, or rather the yet higher idea to which it refers us, matured into *laws* of organic nature; and thence to have one other splendid proof, that with the knowledge of LAW alone dwell Power and Prophecy, decisive Experiment, and, lastly, a scientific method, that dissipating with its earliest rays the gnomes of hypothesis and the mists of theory may, within a single generation, open out on the philosophic Seer discoveries that had baffled the gigantic, but blind and guideless industry of ages.

Such, too, is the case with the assumed indecomponible substances of the LABORATORY. They are the symbols of elementary powers, and the exponents of a law, which, as the root of all these powers, the chemical philosopher, whatever his theory may be, is instinctively labouring to extract. This instinct, again, is itself but the form, in which the idea, the mental Correlative of the law, first announces its incipient germination in his own mind: and hence proceeds the striving after unity of principle through all the diversity of forms, with a feeling resembling that which accompanies our endeavors to recollect a forgotten name; when we seem at once to have and not to have it; which the memory feels but cannot find. Thus, as "the lunatic, the lover, and the poet," [10] suggest each other to Shakspeare's Theseus, as soon as his thoughts present him the ONE FORM, of which they are but varieties; so water and flame, the diamond, the charcoal, and the mantling champagne, with its ebullient sparkles, are convoked and fraternized by the theory of the chemist. This is, in truth, the first charm of chemistry, and the secret of the almost universal interest excited by its discoveries. The serious complacency which is afforded by the sense of truth, utility, permanence, and progression,

---

[6] Andrea Cesalpino (1519–1603) was an Italian scientist and philosopher. John Ray (1627–1705) was an English naturalist. Konrad von Gesner (1516–1565) was a Swiss-German scientist and zoologist. The preceding, along with Joseph Pitton de Tournefort (1656–1708), made important contributions to botanical classification.

[7] Johann Hedwig (1730–1799) was a German botanist. Antoine Laurent de Jussieu (1748–1836) and Charles Francois Brisseau de Mirbel (1776–1854) were French botanists. Sir James Edward Smith (1759–1828) was a botanist and founder of the English Linnean Society. Thomas Andrew Knight (1759–1838) was president of the English Horticultural Society. John Ellis (c. 1710–1776) was an English naturalist. All were discoverers and describers of new botanical species, supplementing or correcting Linneaus.

[8] Robert Ainsworth (1660–1743) was the compiler of a famous alphabetically arranged Latin-English dictionary, *Thesaurus Linguae Latinae* (1736). John Walker (1732–1807) was the compiler of *A Dictionary of the English Language, answering at once the purposes of Rhyming, Spelling, and Pronouncing* (1775). Johann Scapula (f. 1580) was known for his Greek-Latin lexicon. Johann Amos Comenius (1592–1671), a Czech educator, was the author of language texts in which sentences containing useful information were arranged in parallel columns of the vernacular and the language to be learned.

[9] Coleridge has confused the titles of two of Erasmus Darwin's works: *Zoonomia* (1794–1796) and *Phytologia* (1800).

[10] *Midsummer Night's Dream*, V, i, 7.

blends with and ennobles the exhilirating surprize and the pleasurable sting of curiosity, which accompany the propounding and the solving of an Enigma. It is the sense of a principle of connection given by the mind, and sanctioned by the correspondency of nature. Hence the strong hold which in all ages chemistry has had on the imagination. If in SHAKSPEARE we find nature idealized into poetry, through the creative power of a profound yet observant meditation, so through the meditative observation of a DAVY, a WOOLLASTON, or a HATCHETT;[11]

> ———"By some connatural force,
> Powerful at greatest distance to unite
> With secret amity things of like kind,"[12]

we find poetry, as it were, substantiated and realized in nature: yea, nature itself disclosed to us, GEMINAM *istam naturam, quæ fit et facit, et creat et creatur,*[13] as at once the poet and the poem!

ESSAY X

Πολυμαθιη νοον ου διδασκει· ειναι γαρ ἐν το σοφον, επιϛασθαι γνωμην ἥτε εγκυβερνησε ι παντα δια παντων.

(*Translation.*)—The effective education of the reason is not to be supplied by multifarious acquirements: for there is but one knowledge that merits to be called wisdom, a knowledge that is one with a law which shall govern all in and through all.

HERAC. *apud Diogenem Laert.* ix. § 1.[1]

HISTORICAL AND ILLUSTRATIVE.

THERE is still preserved in the Royal Observatory at Richmond the model of a bridge, constructed by the late justly celebrated Mr. Atwood[2] (at that time, however, in the decline of life), in the confidence, that he had explained the wonderful properties of the arch as resulting from compound action of simple wedges, or of the rectilinear solids of which the material arch was composed: and of which supposed discovery, his model was to exhibit ocular proof. Accordingly, he took a

sufficient number of wedges of brass highly polished. Arranging these at first on a skeleton arch of wood, he then removed this scaffolding or support; and the bridge not only stood firm, without any cement between the squares; but he could take away any given portion of them, as a third or a half, and appending a correspondent weight, at either side, the remaining part stood as before. Our venerable sovereign, who is known to have had a particular interest and pleasure in all works and discoveries of mechanic science or ingenuity, looked at it for awhile stedfastly, and, as his manner was, with quick and broken expressions of praise and courteous approbation, in the form of answers to his own questions. At length turning to the constructor, he said, "But, Mr. Atwood, you have *presumed* the figure. You have put the *arch* first in this wooden *skeleton*. Can you build a bridge of the same wedges in any other figure? A strait bridge, or with two lines touching at the apex? If not, is it not evident, that the bits of brass derive their continuance in the present position from the property of the arch, and not the arch from the property of the wedge?" The objection was fatal; the justice of the remark not to be resisted; and we have ever deemed it a forcible illustration of the Aristotelian axiom, with respect to all just reasoning, that the whole is of necessity prior to its parts; nor can we conceive a more apt illustration of the scientific principles we have already laid down.

All method supposes a union of *several* things to a common end, either by disposition, as in the works of man; or by convergence, as in the operations and products of nature. That we acknowledge a *method,* even in the latter, results from the religious instinct which bids us "find tongues in trees; books in the running streams; sermons in stones: and good (*that is, some useful end answering to some good purpose*) in every thing."[3] In a self-conscious and thence reflecting being, no instinct can exist, without engendering the belief of an object corresponding to it, either present or future, real or capable of being realized: much less the instinct, in which humanity itself is grounded: that by which, in every act of conscious perception, we at once identify our being with that of the world without us, and yet place ourselves in contra-distinction to that world. Least of all can this mysterious pre-disposition exist without evolving a belief that the productive power, which is in nature as nature, is essentially one (i.e. of one kind) with the intelligence, which is in the human mind above nature: however disfigured this belief may become, by accidental forms or accompaniments, and though like heat in the thawing of ice, it

---

[11] Sir Humphry Davy (1778–1829) was one of the leading scientists of his day and a close friend of Coleridge. William Hyde Woollaston (1766–1828) was an English scientist. Charles Hatchett (*c.* 1765–1847) was an English chemist.

[12] *Paradise Lost*, X, 246–48.

[13] Geminam . . . creatur: "TWIN nature itself, which is made and is making, which both creates and is created."

[1] Diogenes Laertius, *Lives of Eminent Philosophers*, Book IX, Chapter 1 ("Heraclitus").

[2] George Atwood (1746–1807) was a mathematician and the author of *Dissertation on the Construction and Properties of Arches* (1801, supplement 1804).

[3] *As You Like It*, II, i, 16–17.

may appear only in its effects. So universally has this conviction leavened the very substance of all discourse, that there is no language on earth in which a man can abjure it as a prejudice, without employing terms and conjunctions that suppose its reality, with a feeling very different from that which accompanies a figurative or metaphorical use of words. In all aggregates of construction therefore, which we contemplate as wholes, whether as integral parts or as a system, we assume an intention, as the initiative, of which the end is the correlative.

Hence proceeds the introduction of final causes in the works of nature equally as in those of man. Hence their *assumption*, as constitutive and explanatory by the mass of mankind; and the employment of the *presumption*, as an auxiliary and regulative principle, by the enlightened naturalist, whose office it is to seek, discover, and investigate the *efficient* causes. Without denying, that to resolve the efficient into the final may be the ultimate aim of philosophy, he, of good right, resists the substitution of the latter for the former, as premature, presumptuous, and preclusive of all science; well aware, that those sciences have been most progressive, in which this confusion has been either precluded by the nature of the science itself, as in pure mathematics, or avoided by the good sense of its cultivator. Yet even he admits a teleological ground in physics and physiology: that is, the presumption of a something *analogous* to the causality of the human will, by which, without assigning to nature, as nature, a conscious purpose, he may yet distinguish her agency from a blind and lifeless mechanism. Even he admits its use, and, in many instances, its necessity, as a regulative principle; as a ground of anticipation, for the guidance of his judgment and for the direction of his observation and experiment: briefly in all that preparatory process, which the French language so happily expresses by *s'orienter*, i.e. to find out the east for one's self. When the naturalist contemplates the structure of a bird, for instance, the hollow cavity of the bones, the position of the wings for motion, and of the tail for steering its course, &c., he knows indeed that there must be a correspondent mechanism, as the *nexus effectivus*.[4] But he knows, likewise, that this will no more explain the particular existence of the bird, than the principles of cohesion, &c. could inform him why of two buildings one is a palace, and the other a church. Nay, it must not be overlooked, that the assumption of the nexus effectivus itself originates in the mind, as one of the laws under which alone it can reduce the manifold of the impression from without into unity, and

thus contemplate it as one thing; and could never (as hath been clearly proved by Mr. Hume)[5] have been derived from outward experience, in which it is indeed presupposed, as a necessary condition. *Notio nexûs causalis non oritur, sed supponitur, a sensibus.*[6] Between the purpose and the end the component parts are included, and thence receive their position and character as means, i.e. parts contemplated as parts. It is in this sense, we will affirm, that the parts, as means to an end, derive their position, and therein their qualities (or character)—nay, we dare add, their very existence—as particular things—from the antecedent method, or self-organizing PURPOSE; upon which therefore we have dwelt so long.

We are aware, that it is with our cognitions as with our children. There is a period in which the method of nature is working for them; a period of aimless activity and unregulated accumulation, during which it is enough if we can preserve them in health and *out of harm's way*. Again, there is a period of orderliness, of circumspection, of discipline, in which we purify, separate, define, select, arrange, and settle the nomenclature of communication. There is also a period of dawning and twilight, a period of anticipation, affording trials of strength. And all these, both in the growth of the sciences and in the mind of a rightly-educated individual, will precede the attainment of a scientific METHOD. But, notwithstanding this, unless the importance of the latter be felt and acknowledged, unless its attainment be looked forward to and from the very beginning prepared for, there is little hope and small chance that any education will be conducted aright; or will ever prove in reality worth the name.

Much labor, much wealth may have been expended, yet the final result will too probably warrant the sarcasm of the Scythian traveller: "Væ! quantum nihili!"[7] and draw from a wise man the earnest recommendation of a full draught from Lethe, as the first and indispensible preparative for the waters of the true Helicon. Alas! how many examples are now present to our memory, of young men the most anxiously and expensively be-schoolmastered, be-tutored, be-lectured, any thing but *educated;* who have received arms and ammunition, instead of skill, strength, and courage; varnished rather than polished; perilously over-civilized, and most pitiably uncultivated! And all

---

4 nexus effectivus: "effective tie," jointly operative factor of the separate parts or functions.

5 See Hume's *Philosophical Essays Concerning Human Understanding* (1748), Essay VII ("Of the Idea of Power or Necessary Connexion").

6 Notio . . . a sensibus: "The idea of a causal nexus does not have its origin in outward sensations but is applied to them."

7 Vae! nihili! "Ah, so much for nothing!" The Latin translation of a remark by the Scythian Anacharis in criticism of the Greek zeal for athletic prowess, in Lucian's *Anacharis, or Athletics,* 13.

from inattention to the method dictated by nature herself, to the simple truth, that as the forms in all organized existence, so must all true and living knowledge proceed from within; that it may be trained, supported, fed, excited, but can never be infused or impressed.

Look back on the history of the Sciences. Review the Method in which Providence has brought the more favored portion of mankind to the present state of Arts and Sciences. Lord Bacon has justly remarked *Antiquitas temporis juventus mundi et Scientiæ* [8]—Antiquity of time is the youth of the world and of Science. In the childhood of the human race, its education commenced with the cultivation of the moral sense; the object proposed being such as the mind only could apprehend, and the principle of obedience being placed in the will. The appeal in both was made to the inward man. "Through faith we understand that the worlds were framed by the word of God; so that things which were seen were not made of things which do appear." [9] (*The solution of Phænomena can never be derived from Phænomena*). Upon this ground, the writer of the epistle to the Hebrews (chap. xi.) is not less philosophical than eloquent. The aim, the method throughout was, in the first place, to awaken, to cultivate, and to mature the truly *human* in human nature, in and through itself, or as independently as possible of the notices derived from sense, and of the motives that had reference to the sensations; till the time should arrive when the senses themselves might be allowed to present symbols and attestations of truths, learnt previously from deeper and inner sources. Thus the first period of the education of our race was evidently assigned to the cultivation of humanity itself; or of that in man, which of all known embodied creatures he alone possesses, the pure reason, as designed to regulate the will. And by what method was this done? First, by the excitement of the idea of their Creator as a spirit, of an *idea* which they were strictly forbidden to realize to themselves under any *image;* and, secondly, by the injunction of obedience to the will of a super-sensual Being. Nor did the method stop here. For, unless we are equally to contradict Moses and the New Testament, in compliment to the paradox of a *Warburton,* [10] the *rewards* of their

obedience were placed at a distance. For the time present *they* equally with *us* were to "*endure,* AS SEEING HIM WHO IS INVISIBLE." [11] Their bodies they were taught to consider as fleshly tents, which as pilgrims they were bound to pitch, wherever the invisible Director of their route should appoint, however barren or thorny the spot might appear. "Few and evil have the days of the years of my life been," says the aged Israel. But that life was but "his pilgrimage;" [12] and he "trusted in the *promises.*"

Thus were the very first lessons in the Divine School assigned to the cultivation of the reason and of the will: or rather of both as united in Faith. The common and ultimate object of the will and of the reason was purely *spiritual,* and to be present in the mind of the disciple— μόνον ἐν Ἰδέᾳ, μηδαμῆ ἐιδωλικῶς, *i.e.* in the idea alone, and never as an image or imagination. The *means* too, by which the idea was to be excited, as well as the *symbols* by which it was to be communicated, were to be, as far as possible, *intellectual.*

Those, on the contrary, who wilfully chose a mode opposite to this method, who determined to shape their convictions and deduce their knowledge from without, by exclusive observation of outward and sensible things as the only realities, became, it appears, rapidly *civilized!* They built cities, invented musical instruments, were artificers in brass and in iron, and refined on the means of sensual gratification, and the conveniences of courtly intercourse. They became the great masters of the AGREEABLE, which fraternized readily with cruelty and rapacity: these being, indeed, but alternate moods of the same sensual selfishness. Thus, both before and after the flood, the vicious of mankind receded from all true cultivation, as they hurried towards civilization. Finally, as it was not in their power to make themselves wholly beasts, or to remain without a semblance of religion; and yet continuing faithful to their original maxim, and determined to receive nothing as true, but what they derived, or believed themselves to derive from their senses, or (in modern phrase) what they could prove *a posteriori,*— they became idolaters of the Heavens and the material elements. From the harmony of operation they concluded a certain unity of nature and design, but were incapable of finding in the facts any proof of a unity of person. They did not, in this respect, pretend to *find* what they must themselves have first assumed. Having thrown away the clusters, which had grown in the vineyard of revelation, they could not—as later reasoners, by being born in a Christian country, have been enabled to do—hang the grapes on thorns, and then

---

[8] Somewhat freely altered from a remark in Bacon's *The Advancement of Learning,* Book I.

[9] Hebrews, xi, 3.

[10] William Warburton (1698–1779) was an Anglican divine. His *Divine Legation of Moses* (1737–1741) had developed the "paradoxical" argument that "the inculcating the Doctrine of a future state of rewards and punishments, is necessary to the well being of civil society"; that no such doctrine was to be found in the "Mosaic Dispensation"; and that therefore "the law of Moses is of Divine Origin." That is, the very integrity and survival of the Jewish people and religion of the Old Testament despite this omission proves God's "extraordinary providence" in directing them.

[11] Hebrews xi, 27.

[12] Genesis, xlvii, 9.

pluck them as the native growth of the bushes. But the men of *sense*, of the patriarchal times, neglecting reason and having rejected faith, adopted what the facts seemed to involve and the most obvious analogies to suggest. They acknowledged a whole *bee-hive* of natural Gods; but while they were employed in building a temple* consecrated to the material Heavens, it pleased divine wisdom to send on them *a confusion of lip*, accompanied with the usual embitterment of controversy, where all parties are in the wrong, and the grounds of quarrel are equally plausible on all sides. As the modes of error are endless, the hundred forms of Polytheism had each its groupe of partizans who, hostile or alienated, henceforward formed separate tribes kept aloof from each other by their ambitious leaders. Hence arose, in the course of a few centuries, the diversity of languages, which has sometimes been confounded with the miraculous event that was indeed its first and principal, though remote, cause.

Following next, and as the representative of the youth and approaching manhood of the human intellect, we have ancient Greece, from Orpheus, Linus, Musæus, and the other mythological bards, or perhaps the brotherhoods impersonated under those names, to the time when the republics lost their independence, and their learned men sunk into copyists and commentators of the works of their forefathers. That we

* We are far from being Hutchinsonians, nor have we found much to respect in the twelve volumes of Hutchinson's works, either as biblical comment or natural philosophy: though we give him credit for orthodoxy and good intentions. But his interpretation of the first nine verses of Genesis xi. seems not only rational in itself, and consistent with after accounts of the sacred historian, but proved to be the literal sense of the Hebrew text. His explanation of the cherubim is pleasing and plausible: we dare not say more. Those who would wish to learn the most important points of the Hutchinsonian doctrine in the most favorable form, and in the shortest possible space, we can refer to Duncan Forbes's Letter to a Bishop. If our own judgment did not withhold our assent, we should never be *ashamed* of a conviction held, professed, and advocated by so good, and wise a man, as Duncan Forbes.[13]

13 The Hutchinsonians were a group of writers following the work of John Hutchinson (1674–1737), who sought to counter the challenges to Christianity offered by "modern science." They argued that the Hebrew texts had been mistranslated and that the scriptures contained a thoroughly accurate natural philosophy and logical system. Hutchinson's *Philosophical and Theological Works* were published in twelve volumes in 1748–1749. His *New Account of the Confusion of Tongues* (1731) interpreted God's "confounding of languages" at Babel as the creation of different "lips" or expressions of belief in God rather than different "tongues" or native languages, in order to prevent a single expression of false worship represented by the Temple of Babel as an altar to the Sun. Duncan Forbes (1685–1747) was a distinguished Scottish jurist and political figure, whose *Letter to a Bishop, concerning some important Discoveries in Philosophy and Theology* was published in 1732.

include these as educated under a distinct providential, though not miraculous, dispensation, will surprise no one, who reflects that in whatever has a permanent operation on the destinies and intellectual condition of mankind at large—that in all which has been manifestly employed as a co-agent in the mightiest revolution of the moral world, the propagation of the Gospel; and in the intellectual progress of mankind, the restoration of Philosophy, Science, and the ingenuous Arts—it were irreligion not to acknowledge the hand of divine Providence. The periods, too, join on to each other. The earliest Greeks took up the religious and lyrical poetry of the Hebrews; and the schools of the Prophets were, however partially and imperfectly, represented by the mysteries, derived through the corrupt channel of the Phœnicians. With these secret schools of physiological theology the mythical poets were doubtless in connection: and it was these schools, which prevented Polytheism from producing all its natural barbarizing effects. The mysteries and the mythical Hymns and Pæans shaped themselves gradually into epic Poetry and History on the one hand, and into the ethical Tragedy and Philosophy on the other. Under their protection, and that of a youthful liberty secretly controlled by a species of internal Theocracy, the Sciences and the sterner kinds of the Fine Arts; viz. Architecture and Statuary, grew up together: followed, indeed, by Painting, but a statuesque and austerely idealized painting, which did not degenerate into mere copies of the sense, till the process, for which Greece existed, had been completed. Contrast the rapid progress and perfection of all the products, which owe their existence and character to the mind's own acts, intellectual or imaginative, with the rudeness of their application to the investigation of physical laws and phænomena: then contemplate the Greeks (Γραιοι αει παιδες)[14] as representing a portion only of the education of man: and the conclusion is inevitable.

In the education of the mind of the *race*, as in that of the individual, each different age and purpose requires different objects and different means: though all dictated by the same principle, tending toward the same end, and forming consecutive parts of the same method. But if the scale taken be sufficiently large to neutralize or render insignificant the disturbing forces of accident, the degree of success is the best criterion by which to appreciate, both the wisdom of the general principle, and the fitness of the particular objects to the given epoch or period. Now it is a fact, for the greater

14 Γραιοι αει παιδες: "You Greeks are always children." A remark (recorded in Plato's *Timaeus*, 22) by an ancient priest of Sais in Egypt in response to the recounting by the Athenian Solon of the Greek myth of the flood.

part of universal acceptance, and attested as to the remainder by all that is of highest fame and authority, by the great, wise, and good, during a space of at least seventeen centuries—weighed against whom the opinions of a few distinguished individuals, or the fashion of a single age, must be held light in the balance,—that whatever could be educed by the mind out of its own essence, by attention to its own acts and laws of action, or as the products of the same; and whatever likewise could be reflected from material masses transformed as it were into mirrors, the excellence of which is to reveal, in the least possible degree, their own original forms and natures—all these, whether arts or sciences, the ancient Greeks carried to an almost ideal perfection: while in the application of their skill and science to the investigation of the laws of the sensible world, and the qualities and composition of material concretes, chemical, mechanical, or organic, their essays were crude and improsperous, compared with those of the moderns during the early morning of *their* strength, and even at the first re-ascension of the light. But still more striking will the difference appear, if we contrast the physiological schemes and fancies of the Greeks with their own discoveries in the region of the pure intellect, and with their still unrivalled success in the arts of imagination. In the aversion of their great men from any *practical* use of their philosophic discoveries, as in the well-known instance of Archimedes,[15] "the soul of the world" was at work; and the few exceptions were but as a rush of billows driven shoreward by some chance gust before the hour of tide, instantly retracted, and leaving the sands bare and soundless long after the momentary glitter had been lost in evaporation.

The third period, that of the Romans, was devoted to the preparations for preserving, propagating, and realizing the labors of the preceding; to war, empire, law! To this we may refer the defect of all originality in the Latin poets and philosophers, on the one hand, and on the other, the predilection of the Romans for astrology, magic, divination, in all its forms. It was the Roman instinct to appropriate by conquest and to give fixture by legislation. And it was the bewilderment and *prematurity* of the same instinct which restlessly impelled them to materialize the *ideas* of the Greek philosophers, and to render them *practical* by superstitious *uses*.

Thus the Hebrews may be regarded as the fixed mid point of the living line, toward which the Greeks as the

ideal pole, and the Romans as the *material*, were ever approximating; till the co-incidence and final *synthesis* took place in Christianity, of which the Bible is the law, and Christendom the phænomenon. So little confirmation from History, from the process of education planned and conducted by unerring Providence, do those theorists receive, who would at least begin (too, many, alas! both begin and end) with the objects of the senses; as if nature herself had not abundantly performed this part of the task, by continuous, irresistible enforcements of attention to her presence, to the direct beholding, to the apprehension and observation, of the objects that stimulate the senses! as if the cultivation of the mental powers, by methodical exercise of their own forces, were not the securest means of forming the true correspondents to them in the functions of comparison, judgment, and interpretation.

ESSAY XI

Sapimus animo, fruimur animâ: sine animo anima est debilis.

L. Accii Fragmenta.[1]

AS THERE are two wants connatural to man, so are there two main directions of human activity, pervading in modern times the whole civilized world; and constituting and sustaining that nationality which yet it is their tendency, and, more or less, their *effect*, to transcend and to moderate—Trade and Literature. These were they, which, after the dismemberment of the old Roman world, gradually reduced the conquerors and the conquered at once into several nations and a common Christendom. The natural law of increase and the instincts of family may produce tribes, and under rare and peculiar circumstances, settlements and neighbourhoods: and conquest may form empires. But without trade and literature, mutually commingled, there can be no nation; without commerce and science, no bond of nations. As the one hath for its object the wants of the body, real or artificial, the desires for which are for the greater part, nay, as far as respects the *origination* of trade and commerce, *altogether* excited from without; so the other has for its origin, as well as for its object, the wants of the mind, the gratification of which is a natural and necessary condition of *its* growth and sanity. And the man (or the nation, considered according to its predominant character as one man) may be regarded under these circumstances, as acting in two forms of method, in-

---

[15] Archimedes was a third-century B.C. Greek mathematician and inventor, whose disinterest in the practical and material value of his inventions as against the purity of geometrical speculation is recorded in Plutarch's *Life of Marcellus*, xiv–xvii.

[1] "We know by the mind, we derive enjoyment from the soul: without mind the soul is weak." Lucius Accius (b. 170 B.C.), a Roman tragic poet.

separably co-existent, yet producing very different effects according as one or the other obtains the primacy.* As is the rank assigned to each in the theory and practice of the governing classes, and, according to its prevalence in forming the foundation of their public habits and opinions, so will be the outward and inward life of the people at large: such will the nation be. In tracing the epochs, and alternations of their relative sovereignty or subjection, consists the PHILOSOPHY of History. In the power of distinguishing and appreciating their several results consists the historic SENSE. And that under the ascendency of the mental and moral character the *commercial* relations may thrive to the utmost *desirable* point, while the reverse is ruinous to both, and sooner or later effectuates the fall or debasement of the country itself—this is the richest truth obtained for mankind by historic RESEARCH: though unhappily it is the truth, to which a rich and commercial nation listens with most reluctance and receives with least faith. Where the brain and the immediate conductors of its influence remain healthy and vigorous, the defects and diseases of the eye will most often admit either of a cure or a substitute. And so is it with the outward prosperity of a state, where the *well-being* of the people possesses the primatcy in the aims of the governing classes, and in the public feeling. But what avails the perfect state of the eye,

> Tho' clear
> To outward view of blemish or of spot,[2]

where the optic nerve is paralyzed by a pressure on the brain? And even so is it not only with the well-being, but ultimately with the prosperity of a people, where the former is considered (if it be considered at all) as subordinate and secondary to wealth and revenue.

In the pursuits of commerce the man is called into action from without, in order to appropriate the outward world, as far as he can bring it within his reach, to the purposes of his senses and sensual nature. His ultimate end is—appearance and enjoyment. Where on the other hand the nurture and evolution of humanity is the final aim, there will soon be seen a general tendency toward, an earnest seeking after, some ground common to the world and to man, therein to find the one principle of permanence and identity, the rock of strength and refuge, to which the soul may cling amid the fleeting surge-like objects of the senses. Disturbed as by

the obscure quickening of an inward birth; made restless by swarming thoughts, that, like bees when they first miss the queen and mother of the hive, with vain discursion seek each in the other what is the common need of all; man sallies forth into nature—in nature, as in the shadows and reflections of a clear river, to discover the originals of the forms presented to him in his own intellect. Over these shadows, as if they were the substantial powers and presiding spirits of the stream, Narcissus-like, he hangs delighted: till finding nowhere a representative of that free agency which yet is a *fact* of immediate consciousness sanctioned and made fearfully significant by his prophetic *conscience*, he learns at last that what he *seeks* he has *left behind*, and but lengthens the distance as he prolongs the search. Under the tutorage of scientific ANALYSIS, haply first given to him by express revelation (e cœlo descendit, ΓΝΩΘΙ ΣΕΑΥΤΟΝ)[3] he separates the *relations* that are wholly the creatures of his own abstracting and comparing intellect, and at once discovers and recoils from the discovery, that the *reality*, the *objective* truth, of the objects he has been adoring, derives its whole and sole evidence from an obscure sensation, which he is alike unable to resist or to comprehend, which compels him to contemplate as without and independent of himself what yet he could not contemplate at all, were it not a modification of his own being.

> Earth fills her lap with pleasures of her own;
> Yearnings she hath in her own natural kind,
> And, even with something of a Mother's mind,
>   And no unworthy aim,
>   The homely Nurse doth all she can
> To make her Foster-child, her Inmate Man,
>   Forget the glories he hath known,
> And that imperial palace whence he came.
>   *   *   *   *   *   *
>   O joy! that in our embers
>   Is something that doth live,
>   That nature yet remembers
>   What was so fugitive!
> The thought of our past years in me doth breed
> Perpetual benedictions: not indeed
> For that which is most worthy to be blest;
> Delight and liberty, the simple creed
> Of childhood, whether busy or at rest,
> With new-fledged hope still fluttering in his breast:—
>   Not for these I raise
>   The song of thanks and praise;
>   But for those obstinate questionings
>   Of sense and outward things,
>   Fallings from us, vanishings;

* The senses, the memory, and the understanding (i.e. the retentive, reflective, and judicial functions of his mind) being common to both methods.

2 Milton's sonnet XXII ("Cyriack, this three years' day these eyes, though clear"), ll. 1–2.

3 e coelo ... ΣΕΑΥΤΟΝ: "From heaven it descends, KNOW THYSELF." See *Biographia Literaria*, Chapter XII, footnote 18, p. 186.

Blank misgivings of a Creature
Moving about in worlds not realized,
High instincts, before which our mortal Nature
Did tremble like a guilty Thing surprized!
　　But for those first affections,
　　Those shadowy recollections,
　　　　Which, be they what they may,
Are yet the fountain light of all our day,
Are yet a master light of all our seeing;
　　Uphold us—cherish—and have power to make
Our noisy years seem moments in the being
Of the eternal Silence: truths that wake,
　　　　To perish never;
Which neither listlessness, nor mad endeavour,
　　　　Nor Man nor Boy,
Nor all that is at enmity with joy,
Can utterly abolish or destroy!
　　Hence, in a season of calm weather,
　　　　Though inland far we be,
Our Souls have sight of that immortal sea
　　　　Which brought us hither;
　　Can in a moment travel thither—
And see the Children sport upon the shore,
And hear the mighty waters rolling evermore.
　　　　　　　　　　WORDSWORTH.*

Long indeed will man strive to satisfy the inward querist with the phrase, laws of nature. But though the individual may rest content with the seemly metaphor, the race cannot. If a law of nature be a mere generalization, it is included in the above as an act of the mind.

* During my residence in Rome I had the pleasure of reciting this sublime ode to the illustrious Baron Von Humboldt, then the Prussian minister at the papal court, and now at the court of St. James's. By those who knew and honored both the brothers, the talents of the plenipotentiary were held equal to those of the scientific traveller, his judgment superior. I can only say, that I knew few Englishmen, whom I could compare with him in the extensive knowledge and just appreciation of English literature and its various epochs. He listened to the ode with evident delight, and as evidently not without surprise, and at the close of the recitation exclaimed, "And is this the work of a living English poet? I should have attributed it to the age of Elizabeth, not that I recollect any writer, whose style it resembles; but rather with wonder, that so great and original a poet should have escaped my notice."—Often as I repeat passages from it to myself, I recur to the words of DANTE:

Canzon! io credo, che saranno radi
Che tua ragione bene intenderanno:
Tanto lor sei faticoso ed alto.4

4 Karl Wilhelm von Humboldt (1767–1835), a statesman and man of letters, was the Prussian minister to Rome (1801–1808) and to London (1817). His brother Friedrich Heinrich Alexander, Baron von Humboldt (1769–1859), one of the most famous men of his time, was a distinguished naturalist, whose travels in South America (1799–1804) led to theories and discoveries in physical geography. For Coleridge's translation of the quotation from Dante, see Biographia Literaria, Chapter XXII, p. 231 and footnote 34.

But if it be other and more, and yet manifestable only in and to an intelligent spirit, it must in act and substance be itself spiritual: for things utterly heterogeneous can have no intercommunion. In order therefore to the recognition of himself in nature man must first learn to comprehend nature in himself, and its laws in the ground of his own existence. Then only can he reduce Phænomena to Principles—then only will he have achieved the METHOD, the self-unravelling clue, which alone can securely guide him to the conquest of the former—when he has discovered in the basis of their union the necessity of their differences; in the principle of their continuance the solution of their changes. It is the idea of the common centre, of the universal law, by which all power manifests itself in opposite yet interdependent forces (η γαρ ΔΥΑΣ αει παρα Μοναδι καθηται, και νοεραις ασραπτει τομαις)5 that enlightening inquiry, multiplying experiment, and at once inspiring humility and perseverance will lead him to comprehend gradually and progressively the relation of each to the other, of each to all, and of all to each.

Such is the second of the two possible directions in which the activity of man propels itself: and either in one or other of these channels—or in some one of the rivulets which notwithstanding their occasional refluence (and though, as in successive schematisms of Becher, Stahl, and Lavoisier,6 the varying stream may for a time appear to comprehend and inisle some particular department of knowledge which even then it only peninsulates) are yet flowing towards this mid channel, and will ultimately fall into it—all intellectual METHOD has its bed, its bank, and its line of progression. For be it not forgotten, that this discourse is confined to the evolutions and ordonnance of knowledge, as prescribed by the constitution of the human intellect. Whether there be a correspondent reality, whether the Knowing of the Mind has its correlative in the Being of Nature, doubts may be felt. Never to have felt them, would indeed betray an unconscious unbelief, which traced to its extreme roots will be seen grounded in a latent disbelief. How should it not be so? if to conquer these doubts, and out of the confused multiplicity of

5 η γαρ ΔΥΑΣ ... τομαις: "For the Dyad sits by him [Monad], and glitters in intellectual Sections." Zoroaster's Oracles, "Monad, Dyad, Triad," 1. 3. (Translation from "The History of Chaldaick Philosophy" in Thomas Stanley's History of Philosophy, second edition [1687].)
6 Johann Joachim Becher (1635–1682) and Georg Ernst Stahl (1660–1734) were German chemists. It was from suggestions in Becher that Stahl formulated the phlogiston theory of combustion—that in combustion an inflammable element (phlogiston) in all substances was liberated. This theory was supplanted by the oxygen theory of combustion formulated by the French chemist Antoine Laurent Lavoisier (1734–1794).

seeing with which "the films of corruption" bewilder us, and out of the unsubstantial show of existence, which, like the shadow of an eclipse, or the chasms in the sun's atmosphere, are but *negations* of sight, to attain that *singleness of eye*, with which, "*the whole body shall be full of light*," [7] be the purpose, the means, and the end of our probation, the METHOD which is "profitable to all things, and hath the promise in this life and in the life to come!" [8] Imagine the unlettered African, or rude yet musing Indian, poring over an illuminated manuscript of the inspired volume, with the vague yet deep impression that his fates and fortunes are in some unknown manner connected with its contents. Every tint, every group of characters has its several dream. Say that after long and dissatisfying toils, he begins to sort, first the paragraphs that appear to resemble each other, then the lines, the words—nay, that he has at length discovered that the whole is formed by the recurrence and interchanges of a limited number of cyphers, letters, marks, and points, which, however, in the very height and utmost perfection of his attainment, he makes twentifold more numerous than they are, by classing every different form of the same character, intentional or accidental, as a separate element. And the whole is without soul or substance, a talisman of superstition, a mockery of science: or employed perhaps at last to feather the arrows of death, or to shine and flutter amid the plumes of savage vanity. The poor Indian too truly represents the state of learned and systematic ignorance— arrangement guided by the light of no leading idea, mere orderliness without METHOD!

But see! the friendly missionary arrives. He explains to him the nature of written words, translates them for him into his native sounds, and thence into the thoughts of his heart—how many of these thoughts then first evolved into consciousness, which yet the awakening disciple receives, and not as aliens! Henceforward, the book is unsealed for him; the depth is opened out; he communes with the spirit of the volume as a living oracle. The words become transparent, and he sees them as though he saw them not.

We have thus delineated the two great directions of man and society with their several objects and ends. Concerning the conditions and principles of method appertaining to each, we have affirmed (for the facts hitherto adduced have been rather for illustration than for evidence, to make our position distinctly understood rather than to enforce the conviction of its truth) that in both there must be a mental antecedent; but that in the one it may be an image or conception received through the senses, and originating from without, the inspiriting passion or desire being alone the immediate and proper offspring of the mind; while in the other the initiative thought, the intellectual seed, must itself have its birth-place within, whatever excitement from without may be necessary for its germination. Will the soul thus awakened neglect or undervalue the outward and conditional causes of her growth? For rather, might we dare borrow a wild fancy from the Mantuan bard, or the poet of Arno,[9] will it be with her, as if a stem or trunk, suddenly endued with sense and reflection, should contemplate its green shoots, their leafits and budding blossoms, wondered at as then first noticed, but welcomed nevertheless as its own growth: while yet with undiminished gratitude, and a deepened sense of dependency, it would bless the dews and the sunshine from without, deprived of the awakening and fostering excitement of which, its own productivity would have remained for ever hidden from itself, or felt only as the obscure trouble of a baffled instinct.

Hast thou ever raised thy mind to the consideration of EXISTENCE, in and by itself, as the mere act of existing? Hast thou ever said to thyself thoughtfully, IT IS! heedless in that moment, whether it were a man before thee, or a flower, or a grain of sand? Without reference, in short, to this or that particular mode or form of existence? If thou hast indeed attained to this, thou wilt have felt the presence of a mystery, which must have fixed thy spirit in awe and wonder. The very words, There is nothing! or, There was a time, when there was nothing! are self-contradictory. There is that within us which repels the proposition with as full and instantaneous light, as if it bore evidence against the fact in the right of its own eternity.

Not TO BE, then, is impossible: TO BE, incomprehensible. If thou hast mastered this intuition of absolute existence, thou wilt have learnt likewise, that it was this, and no other, which in the earlier ages seized the nobler minds, the elect among men, with a sort of sacred horror. This it was which first caused them to feel within themselves a something ineffably greater than their own individual nature. It was this which, raising them aloft, and projecting them to an ideal distance from themselves, prepared them to become the lights and awakening voices of other men, the founders of law and religion, the educators and foster-gods of mankind. The power, which evolved this idea of BEING, BEING in its essence, BEING limitless, comprehending its own limits in its dilatation, and condensing itself into its own apparent mounds—how shall we

---

[7] Matthew, vi, 22.   [8] I Timothy, iv, 8.   [9] Virgil or Dante.

name it? The idea itself, which like a mighty billow at once overwhelms and bears aloft—what is it? Whence did it come? In vain would we derive it from the organs of sense: for these supply only surfaces, undulations, phantoms! In vain from the instruments of sensation: for these furnish only the chaos, the shapeless elements of sense! And least of all may we hope to find its origin, or sufficient cause, in the moulds and mechanism of the UNDERSTANDING, the whole purport and functions of which consists in individualization, in outlines and *differencings* by quantity, quality and relation. It were wiser to seek substance in shadow, than absolute fulness in mere negation.

We have asked then for its birth-place in all that constitutes our relative individuality, in all that each man calls exclusively himself. It is an alien of which they know not: and for them the question itself is purposeless, and the very words that convey it are as sounds in an unknown language, or as the vision of heaven and earth expanded by the rising sun, which falls but as warmth on the eye-lids of the blind. To no class of phenomena or particulars can it be referred, itself being none: therefore, to no faculty by which these alone are apprehended. As little dare we refer it to any form of abstraction or generalization: for it has neither co-ordinate or analogon! It is absolutely one, and that it IS, and affirms itself TO BE, is its only predicate. And yet this power, nevertheless, is! In eminence of Being it IS! And he for whom it manifests itself in its adequate idea, dare as little arrogate it to himself as his own, can as little appropriate it either totally or by partition, as he can claim ownership in the breathing air, or make an enclosure in the cope of heaven.* He bears witness of it to his own mind, even as he describes life and light: and, with the silence of light, it describes itself and dwells in *us* only as far as we dwell in *it*. The truths, which it manifests are such as it alone can manifest, and in truth it manifests itself. By what name then canst thou call a truth so manifested? Is it not REVELA-TION? Ask thyself whether thou canst attach to that latter word any consistent meaning not included in the idea of the former. And the manifesting power, the source and the correlative of the idea thus manifested—is it not GOD? Either thou knowest it to be GOD, or thou hast called an idol by that awful name! Therefore in the most appropriate, no less than in the highest, sense of the word were the earliest teachers of human-

ity *inspired*. They alone were the true seers of GOD, and therefore prophets of the human race.

Look round you and you behold everywhere an adaptation of means to ends. Meditate on the nature of a Being whose ideas are creative, and consequently more real, more substantial than the things that, at the height of their *creaturely* state, are but their dim reflexes:† and the intuitive conviction will arise that in such a Being there could exist no motive to the creation of a machine for its own sake; that, therefore, the material world must have been made for the sake of man, at once the high-priest and representative of the Creator, as far as he partakes of that reason in which the essences of all things co-exist in all their distinctions yet as one and indivisible. But I speak of man in his idea, and as subsumed in the divine humanity, in whom alone God loved the world.

If then in all inferior things from the grass on the house top to the giant tree of the forest, to the eagle which builds in its summit, and the elephant which browses on its branches, we behold—first, a subjection to universal laws by which each thing belongs to the Whole, as interpenetrated by the powers of the Whole; and, secondly, the intervention of particular laws by which the universal laws are suspended or tempered for the weal and sustenance of each particular class, and by which each species, and each individual of every species, becomes a system in and for itself, a world of its own—if we behold this economy everywhere

---

† If we may not rather resemble them to the resurgent ashes, with which (according to the tales of the later alchemists) the substantial forms of bird and flower made themselves visible,

'Ὡς τὰ κακῆς ὕλης βλαστήματα χρηστὰ καὶ ἐσθλά.

And let me be permitted to add, in especial reference to this passage, a premonition quoted from the same work (Zoroastri Oracula, Francisci Patricii)

῝Α Νοῦς λέγει, τῷ νοοῦντι δή που λέγει.

Of the flower apparitions so solemnly affirmed by Sir K. Digby, Kercher, Helmont, &c. see a full and interesting account in Southey's Omniana, with a probable solution of this chemical marvel.[11]

---

* See pp. 11–19 of the Appendix to the STATESMAN'S MANUAL; and pp. 47–52 of the second LAY-SERMON.[10]

[10] For the relevant section from *The Statesman's Manual*, see Appendix C, pp. 163–66, above. The "second LAY-SERMON" was Coleridge's *"Blessed are ye that sow beside all Waters!" A Lay Sermon* (1817)

[11] The two quotations are from Zoroaster's *Oracles*, which had been collected and translated into Latin by Francesco Patrizi (1529–1597) in 1593. The first is from "Anima, Corpus, Homo," l. 52 ("The Burgeons, even of ill Matter, are profitable good"); the second is from "Mens, Intelligibilia, et Mentalia," l. 41 ("When the Mind speaks, it speaks by Understanding") (translations by Thomas Stanley). An article on "Spectral Flowers" in Coleridge and Southey's *Omniana* (1812), II, 82–103, refers to the pseudo-scientific doctrine of Palingenesia; from the residual salt or ashes of plants and animals hermetically sealed in glass and then heated, the original product could supposedly be reproduced. Kenelm Digby (1603–1665), an English diplomat, miscellaneous author, and eccentric scientist, had argued that he had "reproduced" a crayfish by this process. Athanasius Kircher (1601–1680), a Jesuit mathematician and scientist, "reproduced" plants and flowers. Jean Baptiste van Helmont (1577–1640) was a Belgian scientist with alchemical learnings.

in the irrational creation, shall we not hold it probable that a similar temperament of universal and general laws by an adequate intervention of appropriate agency, will have been effected for the permanent interest of the creature destined to move progressively towards that divine idea which we have learnt to contemplate as the final cause of all creation, and the centre in which all its lines converge?

To discover the mode of intervention requisite for man's development and progression, we must seek then for some general law by the untempered and uncounteracted action of which both would be prevented and endangered. But this we shall find in that law of his understanding and fancy, by which he is impelled to abstract the outward relations of matter and to arrange these phenomena in time and space, under the form of causes and effects. And this was necessary, as being the condition under which alone experience and intellectual growth are possible. But, on the other hand, by the same law he is inevitably tempted to misinterpret a constant precedence into positive causation, and thus to break and scatter the one divine and invisible life of nature into countless idols of the sense; and falling prostrate before lifeless images, the creatures of his own abstraction, is himself sensualized, and becomes a slave to the things of which he was formed to be the conqueror and sovereign. From the fetisch of the imbruted African to the soul-debasing errors of the proud fact-hunting materialist we may trace the various ceremonials of the same idolatry, and shall find selfishness, hate, and servitude as the results. If, therefore, by the over-ruling and suspension of the phantom-cause of this superstition; if by separating effects from their natural antecedents; if by presenting the phenomena of time (as far as is possible) in the absolute forms of eternity; the nursling of experience should, in the early period of his pupilage, be compelled, by a more impressive experience, to seek in the invisible life alone for the true cause and invisible Nexus of the things that are seen, we shall not demand the evidences of *ordinary* experience for that which, if it ever existed, existed as its antithesis and for its counteraction. Was it an appropriate mean to a necessary end? Has it been attested by lovers of truth; has it been believed by lovers of wisdom? Do we see throughout all nature the occasional intervention of particular agencies in counter-check of universal laws? (And of what other definition is a miracle susceptible?) These are the questions: and if to these our answer must be affirmative, then we too will acquiesce in the traditions of humanity, and yielding, as to a high interest of our own being, will discipline ourselves to the reverential and kindly faith, that the guides and teachers of mankind were the hands of power, no less than the voices of inspiration: and little anxious concerning the particular forms and circumstances of each manifestation we will give an historic credence to the historic fact, that men sent by God have come with signs and wonders on the earth.

If it be objected, that in nature, as distinguished from man, this intervention of particular laws is, or with the increase of science will be, resolvable into the universal laws which they had appeared to counterbalance—we will reply: Even so it may be in the case of miracles; but wisdom forbids her children to antedate their knowledge, or to act and feel otherwise, or further than they know. But should that time arrive, the sole difference, that could result from such an enlargement of our view, would be this: that what we now consider as miracles in opposition to ordinary experience, we should then reverence with a yet higher devotion as harmonious parts of one great complex miracle, when the antithesis between experience and belief would itself be taken up into the unity of intuitive reason.

And what purpose of *philosophy* can this acquiescence answer? A gracious purpose, a most valuable end: if it prevent the energies of philosophy from being idly wasted, by removing the opposition without confounding the distinction between philosophy and faith. The philosopher will remain a man in sympathy with his fellow men. The head will not be disjoined from the heart, nor will speculative truth be alienated from practical wisdom. And vainly without the union of both shall we expect an opening of the inward eye to the glorious vision of that existence which admits of no question out of itself, acknowledges no predicate but the I AM IN THAT I AM![12] Θαυμάζοντες φιλοσοφοῦμεν· φιλοσοφήσαντες θαμβοῦμεν. In *wonder* (τῷ θαυμάζειν) says Aristotle, does philosophy begin: and in *astoundment* (τῷ θαμβεῖν) says Plato, does all true philosophy *finish*.[13] As every faculty, with every the minutest organ of our nature, owes its whole reality and comprehensibility to an existence incomprehensible and groundless, because the ground of all comprehension: not without the union of all that is essential in all the functions of our spirit, not without an emotion tranquil from its very intensity, shall we worthily contemplate in the magnitude and integrity of the world that life-ebullient stream which breaks through every momentary embankment, again, indeed, and evermore to embank itself, but within no banks to stagnate or be imprisoned.

But here it behoves us to bear in mind, that all true reality has both its ground and its evidence in the *will*,

---

[12] Exodus, iii, 14.
[13] See Aristotle's *Metaphysics*, 982, Plato's *Theatetus*, 155.

without which as its complement science itself is but an elaborate game of shadows, begins in abstractions and ends in perplexity. For considered merely intellectually, individuality, as individuality, is only conceivable as with and in the Universal and Infinite, neither before or after it. No transition is possible from one to the other, as from the architect to the house, or the watch to its maker. The finite form can neither be laid hold of, nor is it any thing of itself real, but merely an apprehension, a frame-work which the human imagination forms by its own limits, as the foot measures itself on the snow; and the sole truth of which we must again refer to the divine imagination, in virtue of its omniformity; even as thou art capable of beholding the transparent air as little during the absence as during the presence of light, so canst thou behold the finite things as actually existing neither with nor without the substance. Not without, for then the forms cease to be, and are lost in night. Not with it, for it is the light, the substance shining through it, which thou canst alone really see.

The ground-work, therefore, of all true philosophy is the full apprehension of the difference between the contemplation of reason, namely, that intuition of things which arises when we possess ourselves, as one with the whole, which is substantial knowledge, and that which presents itself when transferring reality to the negations of reality, to the ever-varying framework of the uniform life, we think of ourselves as separated beings, and place nature in antithesis to the mind, as object to subject, thing to thought, death to life. This is abstract knowledge, or the science of the mere understanding. By the former, we know that existence is its own predicate, self-affirmation, the one attribute in which all others are contained, not as parts, but as manifestations. It is an eternal and infinite self-rejoicing, self-loving, with a joy unfathomable, with a love all comprehensive. It is absolute; and the absolute is neither singly that which affirms, nor that which is affirmed; but the identity and living copula of both.

On the other hand, the abstract knowledge which belongs to us as finite beings, and which leads to a science of delusion then only, when it would exist for itself instead of being the instrument of the former—instead of being, as it were, a translation of the living word into a dead language, for the purposes of memory, arrangement, and general communication—it is by this abstract knowledge that the understanding distinguishes the affirmed from the affirming. Well if it distinguish without dividing! Well! if by distinction it add clearness to fulness, and prepare for the intellectual re-union of the all in one, in that eternal reason whose

fulness hath no opacity, whose transparency hath no vacuum.[14]

Thus we prefaced our inquiry into the *Science* of Method with a principle deeper than science, more certain than demonstration.[15] For that the *very* ground, saith Aristotle, is groundless or self-grounded, is an identical proposition.[16] From the indemonstrable flows the sap, that circulates through every branch and spray of the demonstration. To this principle we referred the choice of the final object, the control over time—or, to comprize all in one, the METHOD of the will. From this we started (or rather seemed to start: for it still moved before us, as an invisible guardian and guide), and it is this whose re-appearance announces the conclusion of our circuit, and welcomes us at our goal. Yea (saith an enlightened physician), there is but one principle, which alone reconciles the man with him-

⸺⸺⸺⸺⸺⸺⸺⸺⸺⸺⸺⸺⸺⸺⸺⸺⸺⸺⸺⸺⸺⸺

[14] At this point a paragraph was, in Coleridge's words, "unfortunately omitted—it's object being to preclude all suspicion of any leaning towards Pantheism, in any of it's forms." I give the paragraph from the W. G. T. Shedd edition of *The Complete Works of Samuel Taylor Coleridge* (1853):

If we thoughtfully review the three preceding paragraphs, we shall find the conclusion to be;—that the dialectic intellect by the exertion of its own powers exclusively can lead us to a general affirmation of the supreme reality of an absolute being. But here it stops. It is utterly incapable of communicating insight or conviction concerning the existence or possibility of the world, as different from Deity. It finds itself constrained to identify, more truly to confound, the Creator with the aggregate of his creature, and, cutting the knot which it can not untwist, to deny altogether the reality of all finite existence, and then to shelter itself from its own dissatisfaction, its own importunate queries, in the wretched evasion that of nothings, no solution can be required; till pain haply, and anguish, and remorse, with bitter scoff and moody laughter inquires;—Are we then indeed nothings?—till through every organ of sense nature herself asks;—How and whence did this sterile and pertinacious nothing acquire its plural number?—*Unde quaeso, haec nihili in nihila tam protentosa transnihilatio?*—and lastly;—What is the inward mirror, in which these nothings have at least relative existence? The inevitable result of all consequent reasoning, in which the intellect refuses to acknowledge a higher or deeper ground than it can itself supply, and weens to possess within itself the centre of its own system, is—and from Zeno the Eleatic to Spinosa, and from Spinosa to the Schellings, Okens and their adherents, of the present day, ever has been—pantheism under one or other of its modes, the least repulsive of which differs from the rest, not in its consequences, which are one and the same in all, and in all alike are practically atheistic, but only as it may express the striving of the philosopher himself to hide these consequences from his own mind. This, therefore, I repeat, is the final conclusion. All speculative disquisition must begin with postulates, which the conscience alone can at once authorize and substantiate: and from whichever point the reason may start, from the things which are seen to the one invisible, or from the idea of the absolute one to the things that are seen, it will find a chasm, which the moral being only, which the spirit and religion of man alone, can fill up." [*Unde quaeso . . . transnihilatio?* "Whence, I ask, this so portentous transnihilation of nothing into nothings?"]

[15] See "The Relation of LAW," Essay V.
[16] See Aristotle's *Posterior Analytics*, Book I.

self, with others and with the world; which regulates all relations, tempers all passions, and gives power to overcome or support all suffering; and which is not to be shaken by aught earthly, for it belongs not to the earth—namely, the principle of religion, the living and substantial faith "which passeth all *understanding*," [17] as the cloud-piercing rock, which overhangs the strong-hold of which it had been the quarry and remains the foundation. This elevation of the spirit above the semblances of custom and the senses to a world of spirit, this life in the idea, even in the supreme and godlike, which alone merits the name of life, and without which our organic life is but a state of somnambulism; this it is which affords the sole sure anchorage in the storm, and at the same time the substantiating principle of all true wisdom, the satisfactory solution of all the contradictions of human nature, of the whole riddle of the world. This alone belongs to and speaks intelligibly to all alike, the learned and the ignorant, if but the *heart* listens. For alike present in all, it may be awakened, but it cannot be given. But let it not be supposed, that it is a sort of *knowledge*: No! it is a form of BEING, or indeed it is the only knowledge that truly *is*, and all other science is real only as far as it is symbolical of this. The material universe, saith a Greek philosopher, is but one vast complex MYTHOS (i.e. symbolical representation): and mythology the apex and complement of all genuine physiology. But as this principle cannot be implanted by the discipline of logic, so neither can it be excited or evolved by the arts of rhetoric. For it is an immutable truth, that WHAT COMES FROM THE HEART, THAT ALONE GOES TO THE HEART: WHAT PROCEEDS FROM A DIVINE IMPULSE, THAT THE GODLIKE ALONE CAN AWAKEN.

[1818]

LECTURES ON LITERATURE

A course of fourteen lectures delivered January–March 1818, on various topics of literature from the middle ages to the present. The lecture on Cervantes illustrates Coleridge's application of some of the key concepts of his philosophy and aesthetics to the analysis of a major literary work. "On Poesy and Art" is perhaps the finest statement of his theory of art. The text of both lectures is here reproduced from The Literary Remains of Samuel Taylor Coleridge, *ed. Henry Nelson Coleridge (London, 1836).*

---

[17] Philippians, iv. 7.

F R O M

LECTURES ON LITERATURE

FOR THE

LONDON PHILOSOPHICAL SOCIETY

LECTURE VIII
[February 20, 1818]

DON QUIXOTE
CERVANTES

BORN at Madrid, 1547;—Shakspeare, 1564; both put off mortality on the same day, the 23rd of April, 1616,—the one in the sixty-ninth, the other in the fifty-second, year of his life. The resemblance in their physiognomies is striking, but with a predominance of acuteness in Cervantes, and of reflection in Shakspeare, which is the specific difference between the Spanish and English characters of mind.

I. The nature and eminence of Symbolical writing;—

II. Madness, and its different sorts, (considered without pretension to medical science);—

To each of these, or at least to my own notions respecting them, I must devote a few words of explanation, in order to render the after critique on Don Quixote, the master work of Cervantes' and his country's genius easily and throughout intelligible. This is not the least valuable, though it may most often be felt by us both as the heaviest and least entertaining portion of these critical disquisitions: for without it, I must have foregone one at least of the two appropriate objects of a Lecture, that of interesting you during its delivery, and of leaving behind in your minds the germs of afterthought, and the materials for future enjoyment. To have been assured by several of my intelligent auditors that they have reperused Hamlet or Othello with increased satisfaction in consequence of the new points of view in which I had placed those characters—is the highest compliment I could receive or desire; and should the address of this evening open out a new source of pleasure, or enlarge the former in your perusal of Don Quixote, it will compensate for the failure of any personal or temporary object.

I. The Symbolical cannot, perhaps, be better defined in distinction from the Allegorical, than that it is always itself a part of that, of the whole of which it is the representative.—"Here comes a sail,"—(that is, a ship) is a symbolical expression. "Behold our lion!" when we speak of some gallant soldier, is allegorical. Of most importance to our present subject is this point, that the latter (the allegory) cannot be other than spoken consciously;—whereas in the former (the symbol) it is very possible that the general truth represented may be working unconsciously in the writer's mind during the construction of the symbol;—and it proves itself by being produced out of his own mind,—as the Don Quixote out of the perfectly sane mind of Cervantes, and not by outward observation, or historically. The advantage of symbolical writing over allegory is, that it presumes no disjunction of faculties, but simple predominance.

II. Madness may be divided as—

1. hypochondriasis; or, the man is out of his senses.
2. derangement of the understanding; or, the man is out of his wits.
3. loss of reason.
4. frenzy, or derangement of the sensations.

Cervantes's own preface to Don Quixote is a perfect model of the gentle, every where intelligible, irony in the best essays of the Tatler and the Spectator. Equally natural and easy, Cervantes is more spirited than Addison; whilst he blends with the terseness of Swift, an exquisite flow and music of style, and above all, contrasts with the latter by the sweet temper of a superior mind, which saw the follies of mankind, and was even at the moment suffering severely under hard mistreatment; and yet seems every where to have but one thought as the undersong—"Brethren! with all your faults I love you still!"[1]—or as a mother that chides the child she loves, with one hand holds up the rod, and with the other wipes off each tear as it drops!

Don Quixote was neither fettered to the earth by want, nor holden in its embraces by wealth;—of which, with the temperance natural to his country, as a Spaniard, he had both far too little, and somewhat too much, to be under any necessity of thinking about it. His age too, fifty, may be well supposed to prevent his mind from being tempted out of itself by any of the lower passions;—while his habits, as a very early riser and a keen sportsman, were such as kept his spare body in serviceable subjection to his will, and yet by the play of hope that accompanies pursuit, not only permitted, but assisted, his fancy in shaping what it would. Nor must we omit his meagerness and entire featureliness, face and frame, which Cervantes gives us at once: "It is said that his surname was *Quixada* or *Quesada*," &c.—even in this trifle showing an exquisite judgment;—just once insinuating the association of *lantern-jaws* into the reader's mind, yet not retaining

it obtrusively like the names in old farces and in the Pilgrim's Progress,—but taking for the regular appellative one which had the no meaning of a proper name in real life, and which yet was capable of recalling a number of very different, but all pertinent, recollections, as old armour, the precious metals hidden in the ore, &c.[2] Don Quixote's leanness and featureliness are happy exponents of the excess of the formative or imaginative in him, contrasted with Sancho's plump rotundity, and recipiency of external impression.

He has no knowledge of the sciences or scientific arts which give to the meanest portions of matter an intellectual interest, and which enable the mind to decypher in the world of the senses the invisible agency—that alone, of which the world's phenomena are the effects and manifestations,—and thus, as in a mirror, to contemplate its own reflex, its life in the powers, its imagination in the symbolic forms, its moral instincts in the final causes, and its reason in the laws of material nature: but—estranged from all the motives to observation from self-interest—the persons that surround him too few and too familiar to enter into any connection with his thoughts, or to require any adaptation of his conduct to their particular characters or relations to himself—his judgement lies fallow, with nothing to excite, nothing to employ it. Yet,—and here is the point, where genius even of the most perfect kind, allotted but to few in the course of many ages, does not preclude the necessity in part, and in part counterbalance the craving by sanity of judgment, without which genius either cannot be, or cannot at least manifest itself,—the dependency of our nature asks for some confirmation from without, though it be only from the shadows of other men's fictions.

Too uninformed, and with too narrow a sphere of power and opportunity to rise into the scientific artist, or to be himself a patron of art, and with too deep a principle and too much innocence to become a mere projector, Don Quixote has recourse to romances:—

His curiosity and extravagant fondness herein arrived at that pitch, that he sold many acres of arable land to purchase books of knight-errantry, and carried home all he could lay hands on of that kind! C[HAP]. 1.

The more remote these romances were from the language of common life, the more akin on that very account were they to the shapeless dreams and strivings of his own mind;—a mind, which possessed not the highest order of genius which lives in an atmosphere of power over mankind, but that minor kind which, in

[1] See Cowper's *Task*, II, 206.

[2] The name Quixote recalls "quijada" (Spanish: "jaw"), as well as "quijote" (Spanish: "cuisse" or "armor") and "quixo" (Spanish: "ore of silver or gold mines").

its restlessness, seeks for a vivid representative of its own wishes, and substitutes the movements of that objective puppet for an exercise of actual power in and by itself. The more wild and improbable these romances were, the more were they akin to his will, which had been in the habit of acting as an unlimited monarch over the creations of his fancy! Hence observe how the startling of the remaining common sense, like a glimmering before its death, in the notice of the impossible-improbable of Don Belianis, is dismissed by Don Quixote as impertinent:—

He had some doubt as to the dreadful wounds which Don Belianis gave and received: for he imagined, that notwithstanding the most expert surgeons had cured him, his face and whole body must still be full of seams and scars. Nevertheless he commended in his author the concluding his book with a promise of that unfinishable adventure! C. 1.

Hence also his first intention to turn author; but who, with such a restless struggle within him, could content himself with writing in a remote village among apathists and ignorants? During his colloquies with the village priest and the barber surgeon, in which the fervour of critical controversy feeds the passion and gives reality to its object—what more natural than that the mental striving should become an eddy?—madness may perhaps be defined as the circling in a stream which should be progressive and adaptive: Don Quixote grows at length to be a man out of his wits; his understanding is deranged; and hence without the least deviation from the truth of nature, without losing the least trait of personal individuality, he becomes a substantial living allegory, or personification of the reason and the moral sense, divested of the judgment and the understanding. Sancho is the converse. He is the common sense without reason or imagination; and Cervantes not only shows the excellence and power of reason in Don Quixote, but in both him and Sancho the mischiefs resulting from a severance of the two main constituents of sound intellectual and moral action. Put him and his master together, and they form a perfect intellect; but they are separated and without cement; and hence each having a need of the other for its own completeness, each has at times a mastery over the other. For the common sense, although it may see the practical inapplicability of the dictates of the imagination or abstract reason, yet cannot help submitting to them. These two characters possess the world, alternately and interchangeably the cheater and the cheated. To impersonate them, and to combine the permanent with the individual, is one of the highest creations of genius, and has been achieved by Cervantes and Shakspeare, almost alone.

Observations on particular passages,

B. I. c. 1. But not altogether approving of his having broken it to pieces with so much ease, to secure himself from the like danger for the future, he made it over again, fencing it with small bars of iron within, in such a manner, *that he rested satisfied of its strength; and without caring to make a fresh experiment on it, he approved and looked upon it as a most excellent helmet.*

His not trying his improved scull-cap is an exquisite trait of human character, founded on the oppugnancy of the soul in such a state to any disturbance by doubt of its own broodings. Even the long deliberation about his horse's name is full of meaning;—for in these daydreams the greater part of the history passes and is carried on in words, which look forward to other words as what will be said of them.

Ib. Near the place where he lived, there dwelt a very comely country lass, with whom he had formerly been in love; though, as it is supposed, she never knew it, nor troubled herself about it.

The nascent love for the country lass, but without any attempt at utterance, or an opportunity of knowing her, except as the hint—the ὅτι ἔστι [3]—of the inward imagination, is happily conceived in both parts;—first, as confirmative of the shrinking back of the mind on itself, and its dread of having a cherished image destroyed by its own judgment; and secondly, as showing how necessarily love is the passion of novels. Novels are to love as fairy tales to dreams. I never knew but two men of taste and feeling who could not understand why I was delighted with the Arabian Nights' Tales, and they were likewise the only persons in my knowledge who scarcely remembered having ever dreamed. Magic and war—itself a magic—are the day-dreams of childhood; love is the day-dream of youth and early manhood.

C. 2. "Scarcely had ruddy Phoebus spread the golden tresses of his beauteous hair over the face of the wide and spacious earth; and scarcely had the little painted birds, with the sweet and mellifluous harmony of their forked tongues, saluted the approach of rosy Aurora, who, quitting the soft couch of her jealous husband, disclosed herself to mortals through the gates of the Mauchegan horizon; when the renowned Don Quixote," &c.

How happily already is the abstraction from the senses, from observation, and the consequent confusion of the judgment, marked in this description! The knight is describing objects immediate to his senses and sensations without borrowing a single trait

---

3 ὅτι ἔστι : "the fact that it is."

from either. Would it be difficult to find parallel descriptions in Dryden's plays and in those of his successors?

C. 3. The host is here happily conceived as one who from his past life as a sharper, was capable of entering into and humouring the knight, and so perfectly in character, that he precludes a considerable source of improbability in the future narrative, by enforcing upon Don Quixote the necessity of taking money with him.

C. 3. "Ho, there, whoever thou art, rash knight, that approachest to touch the arms of the most valorous adventurer that ever girded sword," &c.

Don Quixote's high eulogiums on himself—"the most valorous adventurer!"—but it is not himself that he has before him, but the idol of his imagination, the imaginary being whom he is acting. And this, that it is entirely a third person, excuses his heart from the otherwise inevitable charge of selfish vanity; and so by madness itself he preserves our esteem, and renders those actions natural by which he, the first person, deserves it.

C. 4. Andres and his master.

The manner in which Don Quixote redressed this wrong, is a picture of the true revolutionary passion in its first honest state, while it is yet only a bewilderment of the understanding. You have a benevolence limitless in its prayers, which are in fact aspirations towards omnipotence; but between it and beneficence the bridge of judgment—that is, of measurement of personal power—intervenes, and must be passed. Otherwise you will be bruised by the leap into the chasm, or be drowned in the revolutionary river, and drag others with you to the same fate.

C. 4. Merchants of Toledo.

When they were come so near as to be seen and heard, Don Quixote raised his voice, and with arrogant air cried out: "Let the whole world stand! if the whole world does not confess that there is not in the whole world a damsel more beautiful, than," &c.

Now mark the presumption which follows the self-complacency of the last act! That was an honest attempt to redress a real wrong; this is an arbitrary determination to enforce a Brissotine[4] or Rousseau's ideal on all his fellow creatures.

Let the whole world stand!

[4] Jacques Pierre Brissot (1754–1793) was a Girondist leader in the early stages of the French Revolution. See "Introductory Address" to *Conciones ad Populum*, p. 115, where Coleridge describes Brissot as "rather a sublime visionary, than a quick-eyed politician. . . ."

'If there had been any experience in proof of the excellence of our code, where would be our superiority in this enlightened age?'

"No! the business is that without seeing her, you believe, confess, affirm, swear, and maintain it; and if not, I challenge you all to battle."

Next see the persecution and fury excited by opposition however moderate! The only words listened to are those, that without their context and their conditionals, and transformed into positive assertions, might give some shadow of excuse for the violence shown! This rich story ends, to the compassion of the men in their senses, in a sound rib-roasting of the idealist by the muleteer, the mob. And happy for thee, poor knight! that the mob were against thee! For had they been with thee, by the change of the moon and of them, thy head would have been off.

C. 5. first part—The idealist recollects the causes that had been accessory to the reverse and attempts to remove them—too late. He is beaten and disgraced.

C. 6. This chapter on Don Quixote's library proves that the author did not wish to destroy the romances, but to cause them to be read as romances—that is, for their merits as poetry.

C. 7. Among other things, Don Quixote told him, he should dispose himself to go with him willingly;—for some time or other such as adventure might present, that an island might be won, in the turn of a hand, and he be left governor thereof.

At length the promises of the imaginative reason begin to act on the plump, sensual, honest common sense accomplice,—but unhappily not in the same person, and without the *copula*[5] of the judgment,—in hopes of the substantial good things, of which the former contemplated only the glory and the colours.

C. 7. Sancho Panza went riding upon his ass, like any patriarch, with his wallet and leathern bottle, and with a vehement desire to find himself governor of the island which his master had promised him.

The first relief from regular labour is so pleasant to poor Sancho!

C. 8. "I no gentleman! I swear by the great God, thou liest, as I am a Christian. Biscainer by land, gentleman by sea, gentleman for the devil, and thou liest: look then if thou hast any thing else to say."

This Biscainer is an excellent image of the prejudices and bigotry provoked by the idealism of a speculator.

[5] copula: "bond or connection."

This story happily detects the trick which our imagination plays in the description of single combats: only change the preconception of the magnificence of the combatants, and all is gone.

B. II. c. 2. "Be pleased, my lord Don Quixote, to bestow upon me the government of that island," &c.

Sancho's eagerness for his government, the nascent lust of actual democracy, or isocracy![6]

C. 2. "But tell me, on your life, have you ever seen a more valorous knight that I, upon the whole face of the known earth? Have you read in story of any other, who has, or ever had, more bravery in assailing, more breath in holding out, more dexterity in wounding, or more address in giving a fall?"—"The truth is," answered Sancho, "that I never read any history at all; for I can neither read nor write; but what I dare affirm is, that I never served a bolder master," &c.

This appeal to Sancho, and Sancho's answer are exquisitely humorous. It is impossible not to think of the French bulletins and proclamations. Remark the necessity under which we are of being sympathized with, fly as high into abstraction as we may, and how constantly the imagination is recalled to the ground of our common humanity! And note a little further on, the knight's easy vaunting of his balsam, and his quietly deferring the making and application of it.

C. 3. The speech before the goatherds:

"Happy times and happy ages," &c.

Note the rhythm of this, and the admirable beauty and wisdom of the thoughts in themselves, but the total want of judgment in Don Quixote's addressing them to such an audience.

B. III. c. 3. Don Quixote's balsam, and the vomiting and consequent relief; an excellent hit at *panacea nostrums*, which cure the patient by his being himself cured of the medicine by revolting nature.

C. 4. "Peace! and have patience; the day will come," &c.

The perpetual promises of the imagination!

Ib. "Your Worship," said Sancho, "would make a better preacher than knight errant!"

Exactly so. This is the true moral.

C. 6. The uncommon beauty of the description in the commencement of this chapter. In truth, the whole of it seems to put all nature in its heights and its humiliations, before us.

Ib. Sancho's story of the goats:

"Make account, he carried them all over," said Don Quixote, "and do not be going and coming in this manner; for at this rate, you will not have done carrying them over in a twelvemonth." "How many are passed already?" said Sancho, &c.

Observe the happy contrast between the all-generalizing mind of the mad knight, and Sancho's all-particularizing memory. How admirable a symbol of the dependence of all *copula* on the higher powers of the mind, with the single exception of the succession in time and the accidental relations of space. Men of mere common sense have no theory or means of making one fact more important or prominent than the rest; if they lose one link, all is lost. Compare Mrs. Quickly and the Tapster.[7] And note also Sancho's good heart, when his master is about to leave him. Don Quixote's conduct upon discovering the fulling-hammers, proves he was meant to be in his senses. Nothing can be better conceived than his fit of passion at Sancho's laughing, and his sophism of self-justification by the courage he had shown.

Sancho is by this time cured, through experience, as far as his own errors are concerned; yet still is he lured on by the unconquerable awe of his master's superiority, even when he is cheating him.

C. 8. The adventure of the Galley-slaves. I think this is the only passage of moment in which Cervantes slips the mask of his hero, and speaks for himself.

C. 9. Don Quixote desired to have it, and bade him take the money, and keep it for himself. Sancho kissed his hands for the favour, &c.

Observe Sancho's eagerness to avail himself of the permission of his master, who, in the war sports of knight-errantry, had, without any selfish dishonesty, overlooked the *meum* and *tuum*. Sancho's selfishness is modified by his involuntary goodness of heart, and Don Quixote's flighty goodness is debased by the involuntary or unconscious selfishness of his vanity and self-applause.

C. 10 Cardenio is the madman of passion, who meets and easily overthrows for the moment the madman of imagination. And note the contagion of madness of any kind, upon Don Quixote's interruption of Cardenio's story.

C. 11. Perhaps the best specimen of Sancho's proverbializing is this:

"And I (Don Q.) say again, they lie, and will lie two hundred times more, all who say, or think her so." "I neither

[6] Equality of power or rule.

[7] See Essay IV of "The Essays on the Principles of Method" in *The Friend*, pp. 235–38.

say, nor think so," answered Sancho; "let those who say it, eat the lie, and swallow it with their bread: whether they were guilty or no, they have given an account to God before now: I come from my vineyard, I know nothing; I am no friend to inquiring into other men's lives; *for* he that buys and lies shall find the lie left in his purse behind; *besides*, naked was I born, and naked I remain; I neither win nor lose; if they were guilty, what is that to me? Many think to find bacon, where there is not so much as a pin to hang it on: *but* who can hedge in the cuckoo? *Especially*, do they spare God himself?"

Ib. "And it is no greater matter, if it be in another hand; for by what I remember, Dulcinea can neither write nor read," &c.

The wonderful twilight of the mind! and mark Cervantes's courage in daring to present it, and trust to a distant posterity for an appreciation of its truth to nature.

P. II. B. III. c. 9. Sancho's account of what he had seen on Clavileno is a counterpart in his style to Don Quixote's adventures in the cave of Montesinos. This last is the only impeachment of the knight's moral character; Cervantes just gives one instance of the veracity failing before the strong cravings of the imagination for something real and external; the picture would not have been complete without this; and yet it is so well managed, that the reader has no unpleasant sense of Don Quixote having told a lie. It is evident that he hardly knows whether it was a dream or not; and goes to the enchanter to inquire the real nature of the adventure.

SUMMARY ON CERVANTES

A Castilian of refined manners; a gentleman, true to religion, and true to honour.

A scholar and a soldier, and fought under the banners of Don John of Austria, at Lepanto,[8] lost his arm and was captured.

Endured slavery not only with fortitude, but with mirth; and by the superiority of nature, mastered and overawed his barbarian owner.[9]

Finally ransomed, he resumed his native destiny, the awful task of achieving fame; and for that reason died poor and a prisoner, while nobles and kings over their goblets of gold gave relish to their pleasures by the charms of his divine genius. He was the inventor of novels for the Spaniards, and in his Persilis and

Sigismunda,[10] the English may find the germ of their Robinson Crusoe.

The world was a drama to him. His own thoughts, in spite of poverty and sickness, perpetuated for him the feelings of youth. He painted only what he knew and had looked into, but he knew and had looked into much indeed; and his imagination was ever at hand to adapt and modify the world of his experience. Of delicious love he fabled, yet with stainless virtue.

LECTURE XIII
[March 10, 1818]
ON POESY OR ART

M AN COMMUNICATES by articulation of sounds, and paramountly by the memory in the ear; nature by the impression of bounds and surfaces on the eye, and through the eye it gives significance and appropriation, and thus the conditions of memory, or the capability of being remembered, to sounds, smells, &c. Now Art, used collectively for painting, sculpture, architecture and music, is the mediatress between, and reconciler of, nature and man. It is, therefore, the power of humanizing nature, of infusing the thoughts and passions of man into every thing which is the object of his contemplation; colour, form, motion and sound are the elements which it combines, and it stamps them into unity in the mould of a moral idea.

The primary art is writing;—primary, if we regard the purpose abstracted from the different modes of realizing it, those steps of progression of which the instances are still visible in the lower degrees of civilization. First, there is mere gesticulation; then rosaries or *wampun*; then picture-language; then hieroglyphics, and finally alphabetic letters. These all consist of a translation of man into nature, of a substitution of the visible for the audible.

The so called music of savage tribes as little deserves the name of art for the understanding as the ear warrants it for music. Its lowest state is a mere expression of passion by sounds which the passion itself necessitates;—the highest amounts to no more than a voluntary reproduction of these sounds in the absence of the occasioning causes, so as to give the pleasure of contrast,—for example, by the various outcries of battle in the song of security and triumph. Poetry also is purely human; for all its materials are from the mind, and all its products are for the mind. But it is the apotheosis of the former state, in which by excitement of the associative power passion itself imitates order,

8 Don John of Austria (1547–1578) was the leader of the forces of the Holy League against the Turkish fleet at the battle of Lepanto, October 7, 1571, a decisive victory ending the threat to Christian Europe.

9 While returning to Spain from military service in 1575, Cervantes was captured by the Moors and held prisoner in Algiers until 1580.

10 Cervantes' final work, an adventure story, published 1617.

and the order resulting produces a pleasurable passion, and thus it elevates the mind by making its feelings the object of its reflexion. So likewise, whilst it recalls the sights and sounds that had accompanied the occasions of the original passions, poetry impregnates them with an interest not their own by means of the passions, and yet tempers the passion by the calming power which all distinct images exert on the human soul. In this way poetry is the preparation for art, inasmuch as it avails itself of the forms of nature to recall, to express, and to modify the thoughts and feelings of the mind. Still, however, poetry can only act through the intervention of articulate speech, which is so peculiarly human, that in all languages it constitutes the ordinary phrase by which man and nature are contradistinguished. It is the original force of the word "brute," and even "mute," and "dumb" do not convey the absence of sound, but the absence of articulated sounds.

As soon as the human mind is intelligibly addressed by an outward image exclusively of articulate speech, so soon does art commence. But please to observe that I have laid particular stress on the words "human mind,"—meaning to exclude thereby all results common to man and all other sentient creatures, and consequently confining myself to the effect produced by the congruity of the animal impression with the reflective powers of the mind; so that not the thing presented, but that which is re-presented by the thing shall be the source of the pleasure. In this sense nature itself is to a religious observer the art of God; and for the same cause art itself might be defined as of a middle quality between a thought and a thing, or as I said before, the union and reconciliation of that which is nature with that which is exclusively human. It is the figured language of thought, and is distinguished from nature by the unity of all the parts in one thought or idea. Hence nature itself would give us the impression of a work of art if we could see the thought which is present at once in the whole and in every part; and a work of art will be just in proportion as it adequately conveys the thought, and rich in proportion to the variety of parts which it holds in unity.

If, therefore, the term "mute" be taken as opposed not to sound but to articulate speech, the old definition of painting will in fact be the true and best definition of the Fine Arts in general, that is, *muta poesis*, mute poesy, and so of course poesy.[1] And, as all languages perfect themselves by a gradual process of desynony-

---

[1] "Poetry is inarticulate painting, and painting is inarticulate poetry." The statement is found in Plutarch's *Moralia*, 346, and is there attributed to Simonides of Ceos (*c.* 556–467 B.C.). In this passage, as indeed throughout much of the essay, Coleridge is copying or closely paraphrasing Friedrich Schelling's *Oration Concerning the Relation of the Plastic Arts to Nature* (1807).

mizing words originally equivalent, I have cherished the wish to use the word "poesy" as the generic or common term, and to distinguish that species of poesy which is not *muta poesis* by its usual name "poetry;" while of all the other species which collectively form the Fine Arts, there would remain this as the common definition,—that they all, like poetry, are to express intellectual purposes, thoughts, conceptions, and sentiments which have their origin in the human mind,— not, however, as poetry does, by means of articulate speech, but as nature or the divine art does, by form, colour, magnitude, proportion, or by sound, that is, silently or musically.

Well! it may be said—but who has ever thought otherwise? We all know that art is the imitatress of nature. And, doubtless, the truths which I hope to convey would be barren truisms, if all men meant the same by the words "imitate" and "nature." But it would be flattering mankind at large, to presume that such is the fact. First, to imitate. The impression on the wax is not an imitation, but a copy, of the seal; the seal itself is an imitation. But, further, in order to form a philosophic conception, we must seek for the kind, as the heat in ice, invisible light, &c. whilst, for practical purposes, we must have reference to the degree. It is sufficient that philosophically we understand that in all imitation two elements must coexist, and not only coexist, but must be perceived as coexisting. These two constituent elements are likeness and unlikeness, or sameness and difference, and in all genuine creations of art there must be a union of these disparates. The artist may take his point of view where he pleases, provided that the desired effect be perceptibly produced,—that there be likeness in the difference, difference in the likeness, and a reconcilement of both in one. If there be likeness to nature without any check of difference, the result is disgusting, and the more complete the delusion, the more loathsome the effect. Why are such simulations of nature, as wax-work figures of men and women, so disagreeable? Because, not finding the motion and the life which we expected, we are shocked as by a falsehood, every circumstance of detail, which before induced us to be interested, making the distance from truth more palpable. You set out with a supposed reality and are disappointed and disgusted with the deception; whilst, in respect to a work of genuine imitation, you begin with an acknowledged total difference, and then every touch of nature gives you the pleasure of an approximation to truth. The fundamental principle of all this is undoubtedly the horror of falsehood and the love of truth inherent in the human breast. The Greek tragic dance rested on these principles, and I can deeply sympathize in imagination with the Greeks in this favourite part of their theatrical exhibitions, when I call to mind the pleasure I felt in beholding the combat of the Horatii and Curiatti [2] most exquisitely danced in Italy to the music of Cimarosa.

Secondly, as to nature. We must imitate nature! yes, but what in nature,—all and every thing? No, the beautiful in nature. And what then is the beautiful? What is beauty? It is, in the abstract, the unity of the manifold, the coalescence of the diverse; in the concrete, it is the union of the shapely (*formosum*) with the vital. In the dead organic it depends on regularity of form, the first and lowest species of which is the triangle with all its modifications, as in crystals, architecture, &c.; in the living organic it is not mere regularity of form, which would produce a sense of formality; neither is it subservient to any thing beside itself. It may be present in a disagreeable object, in which the proportion of the parts constitutes a whole; it does not arise from association, as the agreeable does, but sometimes lies in the rupture of association; it is not different to different individuals and nations, as has been said, nor is it connected with the ideas of the good, or the fit, or the useful. The sense of beauty is intuitive, and beauty itself is all that inspires pleasure without, and aloof from, and even contrarily to, interest.

If the artist copies the mere nature, the *natura naturata*, what idle rivalry? If he proceeeds only from a given form, which is supposed to answer to the notion of beauty, what an emptiness, what an unreality there always is in his productions, as in Cipriani's pictures! Believe me, you must master the essence, the *natura naturans*, which presupposes a bond between nature in the higher sense and the soul of man. [3]

The wisdom in nature is distinguished from that in man by the co-instantaneity of the plan and the execution; the thought and the product are one, or are given at once; but there is no reflex act, and hence there is no moral responsibility. In man there is reflexion, freedom, and choice; he is, therefore, the head of the visible creation. In the objects of nature are presented, as in a mirror, all the possible elements, steps, and processes of intellect antecedent to consciousness, and therefore to the full development of the intelligential act; and man's mind is the very focus of all the rays of intellect which are scattered throughout the images of nature. Now so to place these images, totalized, and fitted to the limits of the human mind, as to elicit from, and to superinduce upon, the forms themselves the moral reflexions to which they approximate, to make the external internal, the internal external, to make nature thought, and thought nature,—this is the mystery of genius in the Fine Arts. Dare I add that the genius must act on the feeling, that body is but a striving to become mind,—that it is mind in its essence!

In every work of art there is a reconcilement of the external with the internal; the conscious is so impressed on the unconscious as to appear in it; as compare mere letters inscribed on a tomb with figures themselves constituting the tomb. He who combines the two is the man of genius; and for that reason he must partake of both. Hence there is in genius itself an unconscious activity; nay, that is the genius in the man of genius. And this is the true exposition of the rule that the artist must first eloign [4] himself from nature in order to return to her with full effect. Why this? Because if he were to begin by mere painful copying, he would produce masks only, not forms breathing life. He must out of his own mind create forms according to the severe laws of the intellect, in order to generate in himself that co-ordination of freedom and law, that involution of obedience in the prescript, and of the prescript in the impulse to obey, which assimilates him to nature, and enables him to understand her. He merely absents himself for a season from her, that his own spirit, which has the same ground with nature, may learn her unspoken language in its main radicals, before he approaches to her endless compositions of them. Yes, not to acquire cold notions—lifeless technical rules—but living and lifeproducing ideas, which shall contain their own evidence, the certainty that they are essentially one with the germinal causes in nature—his consciousness being the focus and mirror of both,—for this does the artist for a time abandon the external real in order to return to it with a complete sympathy with its internal and actual. For of all we see, hear, feel and touch the substance is and must be in ourselves; and therefore there is no alternative in reason between the dreary (and thank heaven! almost impossible) belief that every thing around us is but a phantom, or that the life which is in us is in them likewise; and that to

---

[2] Referring to the Roman legend of the two sets of three brothers born of twin sisters on the same day. The long-standing conflict for supremacy between the ancient cities of Rome and Alba Longa was settled by combat between the Horatii (Rome) and the Curiatii (Alba Longa).

[3] In this paragraph, Coleridge distinguishes between three ways of achieving the beautiful in the imitation of nature, of which he rejects the first two: (1) the hopeless attempt to exactly copy and thus reproduce the actual natural product (*natura naturata*); (2) an imitation based on an abstract conception of beauty, such as "the many seen as one," or some form of "classical beauty;" (3) working as one with the *natura naturans*, the creative spirit or power controlling the coming-into-being of the natural product. Giovanni Battista Cipriani (1727–1785) was a mediocre Italian painter, who achieved considerable success in England after 1755 as a decorative artist.

[4] Remove.

know is to resemble, when we speak of objects out of ourselves, even as within ourselves to learn is, according to Plato, only to recollect;—the only effective answer to which, that I have been fortunate to meet with, is that which Pope has consecrated for future use in the line—

　　And coxcombs vanquish Berkeley with a grin![5]

The artist must imitate that which is within the thing, that which is active through form and figure, and discourses to us by symbols—the *Natur-geist*, or spirit of nature, as we unconsciously imitate those whom we love; for so only can he hope to produce any work truly natural in the object and truly human in the effect. The idea which puts the form together cannot itself be the form. It is above form, and is its essence, the universal in the individual, or the individuality itself,—the glance and the exponent of the indwelling power.

Each thing that lives has its moment of self-exposition, and so has each period of each thing, if we remove the disturbing forces of accident. To do this is the business of ideal art, whether in images of childhood, youth, or age, in man or in woman. Hence a good portrait is the abstract of the personal; it is not the likeness for actual comparison, but for recollection. This explains why the likeness of a very good portrait is not always recognized; because some persons never abstract, and amongst these are especially to be numbered the near relations and friends of the subject, in consequence of the constant pressure and check exercised on their minds by the actual presence of the original. And each thing that only appears to live has also its possible position of relation to life, as nature herself testifies, who, where she cannot be, prophecies her being in the crystallized metal, or the inhaling plant.

The charm, the indispensable requisite, of sculpture is unity of effect. But painting rests in a material remoter from nature, and its compass is therefore greater. Light and shade give external, as well internal, being even with all its accidents, whilst sculpture is confined to the latter.[6] And here I may observe that the subjects chosen for works of art, whether in sculpture or painting, should be such as really are capable of being expressed and conveyed within the limits of those arts. Moreover they ought to be such as will affect the spectator by their truth, their beauty, or their sublimity, and therefore they may be addressed to the judgment, the senses, or the reason. The peculiarity of the impression which they may make, may be derived either from colour and form, or from proportion and fitness, or from the excitement of the moral feelings; or all these may be combined. Such works as do combine these sources of effect must have the preference in dignity.

Imitation of the antique may be too exclusive, and may produce an injurious effect on modern sculpture; —1st, generally, because such an imitation cannot fail to have a tendency to keep the attention fixed on externals rather than on the thought within;—2ndly, because, accordingly, it leads the artist to rest satisfied with that which is always imperfect, namely, bodily form, and circumscribes his views of mental expression to the ideas of power and grandeur only;—3rdly, because it induces an effort to combine together two incongruous things, that is to say, modern feelings in antique forms;—4thly, because it speaks in a language, as it were, learned and dead, the tones of which, being unfamiliar, leave the common spectator cold and unimpressed;—and lastly, because it necessarily causes a neglect of thoughts, emotions and images of profounder interest and more exalted dignity, as motherly, sisterly, and brotherly love, piety, devotion, the divine become human,—the Virgin, the Apostle, the Christ. The artist's principle in the statue of a great man should be the illustration of departed merit; and I cannot but think that a skilful adoption of modern habiliments would, in many instances, give a variety and force of effect which a bigotted adherence to Greek or Roman costume precludes. It is, I believe, from artists finding Greek models unfit for several important modern purposes, that we see so many allegorical figures on monuments and elsewhere. Painting was, as it were, a new art, and being unshackled by old models it chose its own subjects, and took an eagle's flight. And a new field seems opened for modern sculpture in the symbolical expression of the ends of life, as in Guy's monument, Chantrey's children in Worcester Cathedral, &c.[7]

Architecture exhibits the greatest extent of the difference from nature which may exist in works of art.

---

[5] John Brown's *An Essay on Satire; occasion'd by the Death of Mr. Pope* (1745), l. 210.

[6] Schelling had elaborated and explained the point as follows: "... [painting] represents not by bodily things, but by light and shade, by an immaterial, and in a certain sense intellectual means; it offers its works, too, by no means as the things themselves, and wishes them to be looked upon expressly as pictures; it therefore lays not that stress upon the material, in and for itself, that sculpture does; and appears, from this cause, when elevating the material above the spirit, to sink deeper below itself than, in a like case, sculpture does: on the other hand, it appears, with the greater propriety, to give an evident preponderance to the spirit." (Translation by A. Johnson, *The Philosophy of Art; an Oration on the Relation between the Plastic Arts and Nature. By F. W. J. von Schelling* [London: John Chapman, 1845])

---

[7] "Guy's monument" refers to a statue of Thomas Guy (*c.* 1645–1742), founder of Guy's Hospital in London. Francis Chantrey (1781–1841) was the leading English sculptor of his time. Coleridge refers to one of his most celebrated works, a group of sleeping children in Lichfield (not Worcester) Cathedral.

It involves all the powers of design, and is sculpture and painting inclusively. It shews the greatness of man, and should at the same time teach him humility.

Music is the most entirely human of the fine arts, and has the fewest *analoga* in nature. Its first delightfulness is simple accordance with the ear; but it is an associated thing, and recalls the deep emotions of the past with an intellectual sense of proportion. Every human feeling is greater and larger than the exciting causes,—a proof, I think, that man is designed for a higher state of existence; and this is deeply implied in music in which there is always something more and beyond the immediate expression.

With regard to works in all the branches of the fine arts, I may remark that the pleasure arising from novelty must of course be allowed its due place and weight. This pleasure consists in the identity of two opposite elements, that is to say—sameness and variety. If in the midst of the variety there be not some fixed object for the attention, the unceasing succession of the variety will prevent the mind from observing the difference of the individual objects; and the only thing remaining will be the succession, which will then produce precisely the same effect as sameness. This we experience when we let the trees or hedges pass before the fixed eye during a rapid movement in a carriage, or on the other hand, when we suffer a file of soliders or ranks of men in procession to go on before us without resting the eye on any one in particular. In order to derive pleasure from the occupation of the mind, the principle of unity must always be present, so that in the midst of the multeity the centripetal force be never suspended, nor the sense be fatigued by the predominance of the centrifugal force. This unity in multeity I have elsewhere stated as the principle of beauty.[8] It is equally the source of pleasure in variety, and in fact a higher term including both. What is the seclusive or distinguishing term between them?

Remember that there is a difference between form as proceeding, and shape as superinduced;—the latter is either the death or the imprisonment of the thing;— the former is its self-witnessing and self-effected sphere of agency.[9] Art would or should be the abridgment of nature. Now the fulness of nature is without character, as water is purest when without taste, smell,

or colour; but this is the highest, the apex only,—it is not the whole. The object of art is to give the whole *ad hominem*;[10] hence each step of nature hath its ideal, and hence the possibility of a climax up to the perfect form of a harmonized chaos.

To the idea of life victory or strife is necessary; as virtue consists not simply in the absence of vices, but in the overcoming of them. So it is in beauty. The sight of what is subordinated and conquered heightens the strength and the pleasure; and this should be exhibited by the artist either inclusively in his figure, or else out of it and beside it to act by way of supplement and contrast. And with a view to this, remark the seeming identity of body and mind in infants, and thence the loveliness of the former; the commencing separation in boyhood, and the struggle of equilibrium in youth: thence onward the body is first simply indifferent; then demanding the translucency of the mind not to be worse than indifferent; and finally all that presents the body as body becoming almost of an excremental nature.

[1836]

AIDS TO REFLECTION

Coleridge's major religious work had its genesis in his suggestion to the publisher John Murray in 1822 for a volume of "Beauties" or extracts from the works of Robert Leighton (1611–1684), Archbishop of Glasgow and one of the most saintly and admired of the Anglican divines. Leighton's writings had consisted of sermons, scriptural commentaries, and other religious works; the most notable was "A Practical Commentary upon the first Epistle General of St. Peter," of which Coleridge had once recorded: "Next to the inspired Scriptures,—yea, and as the vibration of that once struck hour remaining on the air, stands Leighton's Commentary . . ." As published in 1825, Aids to Reflection retained the form of a series of aphorisms, drawn from Leighton, other Anglican divines,

---

[8] See *Essays on the Principles of Genial Criticism*, Essay Third.

[9] Schelling had explained the point as follows: "Form would indeed be restrictive of the being or essence if it were present independent of it; but it exists by and through the essence; and how could that feel itself restricted by that which it creates? It might indeed be injured by form which was forced upon it, but never by that which flows from itself; much rather must it rest content in this, and therein recognise its self-sufficing and self-included nature." (Johnson translation)

[10] Schelling writes: "Winckelmann compared beauty to water drawn from the bosom of the spring, which the less taste it had, the purer it was esteemed. It is true that the highest beauty is characterless; but is so, as we say of the universe, that it has no determinate dimension, neither length, breadth, nor depth, because it contains all in a like infinity; or that the art of creative nature is formless, because it is subjected to no form" (Johnson translation). That is, the highest point in the representation of the beauty of the fullness of nature would be nature beyond all limits of space and time, beyond representation in a particular form, hence infinite. But this apex is not the whole, since it excludes representation in a particular form. The object of art is to present the whole in particular images relevant to man, the climax of creation, who combines soul and body, spirit and nature. For Schelling, the "highest and most fully developed" form was the human form: "for, as it is not granted to art to embrace the immeasurable whole, and as in all other creatures merely figurations, but in man alone full and entire being, without fault appears, it is not only allowed, but called upon to behold all nature in man."

and Coleridge himself, with extended commentaries. The whole work was arranged in an ascending order: from "Prudential Aphorisms" to "Moral and Religious Aphorisms" to "Aphorisms on that which is indeed Spiritual Religion" (here reproduced in part, from the 1825 text). In the preface, Coleridge listed the fourfold object of the work: "1. to direct the reader's attention to the value of the science of words, their use and abuse, and the incalculable advantages attached to the habit of using them appropriately, and with a distinct knowledge of their primary, derivative, and metaphorical senses . . . 2. To establish the distinct characters of prudence, morality, and religion . . . 3. To substantiate and set forth at large the momentous distinction between reason and understanding . . . 4. To exhibit a full and consistent scheme of the Christian Dispensation, and more largely of all the peculiar doctrines of the Christian Faith. . . ."

FROM

AIDS TO REFLECTION

IN THE

FORMATION OF A MANLY CHARACTER

ON THE

SEVERAL GROUNDS OF

PRUDENCE, MORALITY, AND RELIGION:

ILLUSTRATED BY

SELECT PASSAGES

FROM OUR ELDER DIVINES,

ESPECIALLY FROM

ARCHBISHOP LEIGHTON

FROM

APHORISMS

ON THAT

WHICH IS INDEED SPIRITUAL RELIGION

In the selection of the Extracts that form the remainder of this Volume and of the Comments affixed, the Editor had the following Objects principally in view. First, to exhibit the true and scriptural meaning and intent of several Articles of Faith, that are rightly classed among the Mysteries and peculiar Doctrines of Christianity. Secondly, to show the perfect rationality of these Doctrines, and their freedom from all just Objection when examined by their proper Organ, the Reason and Conscience of Man. Lastly, to exhibit from the Works of Leighton, who perhaps of all our learned protestant Theologians best deserves the title of a Spiritual Divine, an instructive and affecting picture of the contemplations, reflections, conflicts, consolations

and monitory experiences of a philosophic and richly-gifted mind, amply stored with all the knowledge that Books and long intercourse with men of the most discordant characters can give, under the convictions, impressions, and habits of a Spiritual Religion.

To obviate a possible disappointment in any of my Readers, who may chance to be engaged in theological studies, it may be well to notice, that in vindicating the peculiar tenets of our Faith, I have not entered on the Doctrine of the Trinity, or the still profounder Mystery of the Origin of Moral Evil—and this for the reasons following: 1. These Doctrines are not (strictly speaking) subjects of *Reflection*, in the proper sense of this word: and both of them demand a power and persistency of Abstraction, and a previous discipline in the highest forms of human thought, which it would be unwise, if not presumptuous, to expect from any, who require "*Aids* to Reflection," or would be likely to seek them in the present Work. 2. In my intercourse with men of various ranks and ages, I have found the far larger number of serious and inquiring Persons little if at all disquieted by doubts respecting Articles of Faith, that are simply above their comprehension. It is only where the Belief required of them jars with their *moral* feelings; where a Doctrine in the sense, in which they have been taught to receive it, appears to contradict their clear notions of Right and Wrong, or to be at variance with the divine Attributes of Goodness and Justice; that these men are surprised, perplexed, and alas! not seldom offended and alienated. Such are the Doctrines of Arbitrary Election and Reprobation; the Sentence to everlasting Torment by an eternal and necessitating Decree; vicarious Atonement, and the necessity of the Abasement, Agony, and ignominious Death of a most holy and meritorious Person, to appease the Wrath of God. Now it is more especially for such Persons, unwilling Sceptics, who believing earnestly ask help for their unbelief, that this Volume was compiled, and the Comments written: and therefore, to the Scripture Doctrines, *intended* by the abovementioned, my principal attention has been directed.

But lastly, the whole Scheme of the Christian Faith, including *all* the Articles of Belief common to the Greek and Latin, the Roman and the Protestant Church, with the threefold proof, that it is *ideally, morally,* and *historically* true, will be found exhibited and vindicated in a proportionally larger Work, the principal Labour of my Life since Manhood, and which I am now preparing for the Press under the title, Assertion of Religion,[1] as

[1] Refers to the new title of the major work, now more obviously theological in concern, which Coleridge first publicly described in 1814 as "a large volume on the LOGOS, or the communicative intelligence in nature and man, together with, and as preliminary to, a Commentary on the Gospel of St. John." (See the reference in

necessarily *involving* Revelation; and of Christianity, as the only Revelation of permanent and universal validity.

APHORISM I.   LEIGHTON.[2]

Where, if not in Christ, is the Power that can persuade a Sinner to return, that can *bring home a Heart to God?*

Common mercies of God, though they have a leading faculty to repentance, (Rom. ii. 4.) yet, the rebellious heart will not be led by them. The judgments of God, public or personal, though they ought to drive us to God, yet the heart, unchanged, runs the further from God. Do we not see it by ourselves and other sinners about us? They look not at all towards Him who smites, much less do they return; or if any more serious thoughts of returning arise upon the surprise of an affliction, how soon vanish they, either the stroke abating, or the heart, by time, growing hard and senseless under it! Leave Christ out, I say, and all other means work not this way; neither the works nor the word of God sounding daily in his ear, *Return, return.* Let the noise of the rod speak it too, and both join together to make the cry the louder, *yet the wicked will do wickedly,* Dan. xii. 10.

COMMENT

By the phrase "in Christ," I mean all the supernatural Aids vouchsafed and conditionally promised in the Christian Dispensation: and among them the Spirit of Truth, which the world cannot receive, were it only that the knowledge of *spiritual* Truth is of necessity immediate and *intuitive:* and the World or Natural Man possesses no higher intuitions than those of the pure *Sense*, which are the subjects of *Mathematical* Science. But *Aids*, observe! Therefore, not *by* the Will of man alone; but neither *without* the Will. The doctrine of modern Calvinism, as layed down by Jonathan Edwards and the late Dr. Williams,[3] which represents a Will absolutely passive, clay in the hands of a Potter, destroys all Will, takes away its essence and definition, as effectually as in saying—This Circle is square—I should deny the figure to be a Circle at all. It was in

strict consistency therefore, that these Writers supported the Necessitarian Scheme, and made the relation of Cause and Effect the Law of the Universe, subjecting to its mechanism the moral World no less than the material or physical. It follows, that all is Nature. Thus, though few Writers use the term Spirit more frequently, they in effect deny its existence, and evacuate the term of all its proper meaning. With such a system not the Wit of Man nor all the Theodices ever framed by human ingenuity before and since the attempt of the celebrated Leibnitz,[4] can reconcile the Sense of Responsibility, nor the fact of the difference *in kind* between REGRET and REMORSE. The same compulsion of Consequence drove the Fathers of Modern (or Pseudo-) Calvinism to the origination of Holiness in Power, of Justice in Right of Property, and whatever other outrages on the common sense and moral feelings of Mankind they have sought to cover, under the fair name of *Sovereign Grace.*

I will not take on me to defend sundry harsh and inconvenient Expressions in the Works of Calvin. Phrases equally strong and Assertions not less rash and startling are no rarities in the Writings of Luther: for Catachresis[5] was the favourite Figure of Speech in that age. But let not the opinions of either on this most fundamental Subject be confounded with the New-England System, now entitled Calvinistic. The fact is simply this. Luther considered the Pretensions to Free-will *boastful*, and better suited to the budge Doctors of the Stoic Fur, than to the Preachers of the Gospel, whose great Theme is the Redemption of the Will from Slavery; the restoration of the Will to perfect Freedom being the *end* and consummation of the redemptive Process, and the same with the entrance of the Soul into Glory, *i.e.* its union with Christ: "GLORY" (John xvii. 5.) being one of the names of the Spiritual Messiah. Prospectively to this we are to understand the words of our Lord, At that day ye shall know that I am in my Father, and ye in me, John xiv. 20: the freedom of a finite will being possible under this condition only, that it has become one with the will of God. Now as the difference of a captive and enslaved Will, and *no* Will at all, such is the difference between the *Lutheranism* of Calvin and the Calvinism of Jonathan Edwards.

APHORISM II.   LEIGHTON.[6]

There is nothing in religion farther out of Nature's reach, and more remote from the natural man's liking

---

Biographia Literaria, Chapter XII, p. 188.) It is elsewhere referred to as *Logosophia* and *Opus Maximum*. The work was never completed and published.

[2] Slightly altered from "A Practical Commentary upon the First Epistle General of St. Peter," commentary on chapter iii, verse 18. (The edition of Leighton's writings which Coleridge used in preparing *Aids to Reflection* was: *The Whole Works of Robert Leighton . . .*, 4 volumes, London, 1820. For this quotation, see II, 120–21.)

[3] Jonathan Edwards (1703–1758) was a New England Puritan philosopher and theologian. Edward Williams (1750–1813) was the author of *A Defense of Modern Calvinism* (1812) and *An Essay on the Equity of Divine Government* (1813).

---

[4] Refers to Leibnitz's *Essais de Théodicée sur la bonté de Dieu* (1710).

[5] The application of a term to a thing to which it does not properly belong, but which is somewhat like it.

[6] Drawn, with additions by Coleridge, from "A Practical Commentary upon the first Epistle General of St. Peter," commentary on chapter i, verse 2 (*The Whole Works of Robert Leighton*, I, 11, 19).

and believing, than the doctrine of Redemption by a Saviour, and by a crucified Saviour. It is comparatively easy to persuade men of the necessity of an amendment of conduct; it is more difficult to make them see the necessity of Repentance in the *Gospel* sense, the necessity of a change in the *principle* of action; but to convince men of the necessity of the Death of Christ is the most difficult of all. And yet the first is but varnish and white-wash without the second; and the second but a barren notion without the last. Alas! of those who admit the doctrine in words, how large a number evade it in fact, and empty it of all its substance and efficacy, making the effect the efficient cause, or attributing their election to Salvation to a supposed Foresight of their Faith, Obedience. But it is most vain to imagine a faith in such and such men, which, being foreseen by God, determined him to elect them for salvation: were it only that nothing at all is *future*, or can have this imagined *futurition*, but *as* it is decreed, and *because* it is decreed by God so to be.

COMMENT.

No impartial person, competently acquainted with the History of the Reformation, and the works of the earlier protestant Divines at home and abroad, even to the close of Elizabeth's reign, will deny that the Doctrines of Calvin on Redemption and the natural state of fallen Man, are in all essential points the same as those of Luther, Zuinglius,[7] and the first reformers collectively. These Doctrines have, however, since the re-establishment of the Episcopal Church at the return of the second Charles, been as generally * exchanged

* At a period, in which Doctors Marsh and Wordsworth have, by the Zealots on one side, been charged with popish principles on account of their *Anti-bibliolatry*, and the sturdy Adherents of the doctrines common to Luther and Calvin, and the literal interpreters of the Articles and Homilies, are (I wish I could say, *altogether* without any fault of their own) regarded by the Clergy generally as virtual Schismatics, Dividers *of*, through not *from*, the Church, it is serving the cause of charity to assist in circulating the following instructive passage from the Life of Bishop Hackett respecting the disputes between the Augustinians, or Lutherocalvinistic Divines and the Grotians of his Age: in which controversy (says the Biographer) he, Hackett, "was ever very moderate."

"But having been bred under Bishop Davenant and Dr. Ward in Cambridge, he was addicted to their sentiments. Archbishop Usher would say, that Davenant understood those controversies better than ever any man since St. Augustin. But he (Bishop Hackett) used to say, that he was *sure* he had *three* excellent men of his mind in this controversy, I. *Padre Paulo* (Father Paul) whose Letter is extant to Heinsius, *anno* 1604. 2. *Thomas Aquinas*. 3. *St. Augustin*. But besides and above them all, he believed in his Conscience that St. Paul was of the same mind likewise. Yet at the same time he would profess, that he disliked no Arminians, but

7 Ulrich Zwingli (1484–1531) was a Swiss religious reformer.

for what is commonly entitled Arminianism, but which, taken as a complete and explicit Scheme of Belief, it would be both historically and theologically more accurate to call *Grotianism*,[9] or Christianity according to Grotius. The change was not, we may readily believe, effected without a struggle. In the Romish Church this latitudinarian System, patronized by the Jesuits, was manfully resisted by Jansenius, Arnauld, and Pascal;[10] in our own Church by the Bishops Davenant, Sanderson, Hall, and the Archbishops Usher[11] and Leighton: and in the latter half of the

such as revile and defame every one who is *not so:* and he would often commend Arminius himself for his excellent Wit and Parts, but only tax his want of reading and knowledge in Antiquity. And he ever held, it was the foolishest thing in the world to say the Arminians were *popishly* inclined, when so many Dominicans and Jansenists were rigid followers of Augustin in these points: and no less foolish to say that the *Anti-arminians* were Puritans or Presbyterians when *Ward*, and *Davenant*, and Prideaux, and Brownrig, those stout Champions for Episcopy, were decided Anti-Arminians: while Arminius himself was ever a Presbyterian. There he greatly commended the moderation of our Church, which extended equal Communion to both."[8]

8 Coleridge quotes somewhat inexactly from "An Account of the Life and Death of the Author" by Thomas Plume, prefacing *A Century of Sermons upon Several Remarkable Subjects: Preached by . . . John Hacket* (1675). John Hacket (1592–1670) was bishop of Coventry and Lichfield. Herbert Marsh (1757–1839) was bishop of Peterborough, who in various writings had forwarded a more scientific and critical study of the Bible. Coleridge may be referring to Marsh's opposition to the founding of a Bible Society in Cambridge (1811–1813), on the grounds that the Bible should not be circulated apart from the Anglican liturgy. Christopher Wordsworth (1774–1846) was the brother of the poet, an ecclesiastical scholar, and the master of Trinity College, Cambridge. John Prideaux (1578–1650) was bishop of Worcester. Ralph Brownrig (1592–1659) was bishop of Exeter with strongly Calvinist beliefs.

9 Arminianism was the enormously influential theological position first advanced by Jacobus Arminius (1560–1609), Dutch theologian, who opposed the Calvinist doctrine of election and predestination by arguing for the free response of the human will to God's love and in general for the accommodation of human reason with religious faith. Grotianism refers to the theological doctrines of Hugo Grotius (1583–1645), the famous Dutch jurist and statesman, a pupil of Arminius at the University of Leyden. Grotius had defended Christianity, far beyond the position of Arminius, on secular and rational grounds in his influential *De Veritate Religionis Christianae* (1627). Coleridge saw Grotius as the predecessor of Paley and other "natural theologians" of the eighteenth and early nineteenth centuries.

10 Cornelius Jansen (1585–1638), a Catholic reformer and bishop of Ypres, formulated the theological doctrine of Jansenism, which followed Augustinian principles of man's helplessness and total dependence on the gift of God's grace, somewhat similar to Calvinism, and which urged the necessity of a stricter, more spiritual experience of religion against the "logical," "casuistical" presentation of doctrine and discipline by the Jesuits. Antoine Arnauld (1612–1694), one of the most prominent Jansenist spokesmen, was expelled from the theological faculty at the Sorbonne for his writings against the Jesuits. Pascal's *Provincial Letters* (1656–1657), provoked by Arnauld's expulsion, were a popular attack on Jesuitical doctrines and a vigorous statement of Jansenist principles.

11 John Davenant (1576–1641) was bishop of Salisbury. Robert Sanderson (1587–1663) was bishop of Lincoln. Joseph Hall (1574–1656) was bishop of Norwich. James Usher (1581–1656) was Angli-

preceding Aphorism the Reader has a *specimen* of the *reasonings* by which Leighton strove to invalidate or counterpoise the *reasonings* of the Innovators.

Passages of this sort are, however, of rare occurrence in Leighton's works. Happily for thousands, he was more usefully employed in making his Readers feel, that the Doctrines in question, *scripturally treated, and taken as co-organized parts of a great organic whole,* need no such reasonings. And better still would it have been, had he left them altogether for those, who severally detaching the great Features of Revelation from the living Context of Scripture, do by that very act destroy their life and purpose. And then, like the Eyes of the Aranea prodigiosa,* they become clouded microscopes, to exaggerate and distort all the other parts and proportions. No offence then will be occasioned, I trust, by the frank avowal that I have given to the preceding passage a place among the Spiritual Aphorisms for the sake of the Comment: the following Remark having been the first marginal Note I had pencilled on Leighton's Pages, and thus (remotely, at least), the occasion of the present Work.

Leighton, I observed, throughout his inestimable Work, avoids all metaphysical views of Election, relatively to God, and confines himself to the Doctrine in its relation to Man: and in that sense too, in which every Christian may judge who strives to be sincere with his own heart. The following may, I think, be taken as a safe and useful Rule in religious inquiries. Ideas, that derive their origin and substance from the *Moral* Being, and to the reception of which as true *objectively* (*i.e.* as corresponding to a *reality* out of the human mind) we are determined by a *practical* interest exclusively, may not, like theoretical or speculative Positions, be pressed onward into all their possible *logical* consequences. The Law of Conscience, and not the Canons of discursive Reasoning, must decide in such cases. At least, the latter has no validity, which the single *Veto* of the former is not sufficient to nullify. The most pious conclusion is here the most legitimate.

It is too seldom considered, though most worthy of consideration, how far even those Ideas or Theories of pure Speculation, that bear the same name with the Objects of Religious Faith, are indeed the same. Out of the principles necessarily presumed in all discursive Thinking, and which being, in the first place, *universal,*

* The gigantic Indian spider. See Baker's Microscopic Experiments.[12]

◇◇◇◇◇◇◇◇◇◇◇◇◇◇◇◇◇◇◇◇◇◇◇◇◇◇◇◇◇◇◇◇◇◇

can Primate of Ireland. They are cited here, with Leighton, as representatives of the moderate Calvinist persuasion in the Anglican Church.
[12] Refers to *Employment for the Microscope* (1753), pp. 413–14 by Henry Baker (1698–1774), a poet and naturalist.

and secondly, antecedent to every particular exercise of the Understanding, are therefore referred to the Reason, the human Mind (wherever its powers are sufficiently developed, and its attention strongly directed to speculative or theoretical inquiries,) forms certain Essences, to which for its own purposes it gives a sort of notional *Subsistence.* Hence they are called *Entia rationalia:* the conversion of which into *Entia realia,* or real Objects, by aid of the Imagination, has in all times been the fruitful Stock of empty Theories, and mischievous Superstitions, of surreptitious Premises and extravagant Conclusions. For as these substantiated Notions were in many instances expressed by the same terms, as the objects of religious Faith; as in most instances they were applied, though deceptively, to the explanation of real experiences; and lastly, from the gratifications, which the pride and ambition of man received from the supposed extension of his Knowledge and Insight; it was too easily forgotten or overlooked, that the stablest and most indispensable of these notional Beings were but the necessary *forms* of Thinking, taken abstractedly: and that like the breadthless Lines, depthless Surfaces, and perfect Circles of Geometry, they subsist wholly and solely in and for the Mind, that contemplates them. Where the evidence of the Senses fails us, and beyond the precincts of sensible experience, there is no *Reality* attributable to any Notion, but what is given to it by Revelation, or the Law of Conscience, or the necessary interests of Morality.

Take an instance;

It is the office, and as it were, the instinct of Reason to bring a unity into all our conceptions and several knowledges. On this all system depends: and without this we could reflect connectedly neither on nature or our own minds. Now this is possible only on the assumption or hypothesis of a ONE as the ground and cause of the Universe, and which in all succession and through all changes is the subject neither of Time or Change. The ONE must be contemplated as Eternal and Immutable.

Well! the Idea, which is the basis of Religion, commanded by the Conscience and required by Morality, contains the same truths, or at least Truths that can be expressed in no other terms; but this Idea presents itself to our mind with additional Attributes, and these too not formed by mere Abstraction and Negation—with the Attributes of Holiness, Providence, Love, Justice, and Mercy. It comprehends, moreover, the independent (*extra-mundane*) existence and personality of the supreme ONE, as our Creator, Lord, and Judge.

The hypothesis of a *one* Ground and Principle of the Universe (necessary as an *hypothesis;* but having only a *logical* and *conditional* necessity) is thus raised into the

Idea of the LIVING GOD, the supreme Object of our Faith, Love, Fear, and Adoration. Religion and Morality do indeed constrain us to declare him Eternal and Immutable. But if from the Eternity of the Supreme Being a Reasoner should deduce the impossibility of a Creation; or conclude with Aristotle, that the Creation was co-eternal; or, like the later Platonists, should turn Creation into *Emanation*, and make the universe proceed from Deity, as the Sunbeams from the Solar Orb;—or if from the divine Immutability he should infer, that all Prayer and Supplication must be vain and superstitious: then however evident and logically necessary such conclusions may appear, it is scarcely worth our while to examine, whether they are so or not. The Positions themselves *must* be false. For were they true, the Idea would lose the sole ground of its *reality*. It would be no longer the Idea intended by the Believer in *his* premise—in the Premise, with which alone Religion and Morality are concerned. The very subject of the discussion would be changed. It would no longer be the GOD, in whom we *believe;* but a stoical FATE, or the superessential ONE of Plotinus, to whom neither Intelligence, or Self-consciousness, or Life, or even *Being* dare be attributed; or lastly, the World itself, the indivisible one and only substance (*substantia una et unica*) of Spinoza, of which all Phænomena, all particular and individual Things, Lives, Minds, Thoughts, and Actions are but modifications.

Let the Believer never be alarmed by Objections wholly speculative, however plausible on speculative grounds such objections may appear, if he can but satisfy himself, that the *Result* is repugnant to the dictates of Conscience, and irreconcilable with the interests of Morality. For to baffle the Objector we have only to demand of him, by what right and under what authority he converts a Thought into a Substance, or asserts the existence of a real somewhat corresponding to a Notion not derived from the experience of his Senses. It will be of no purpose for him to answer, that it is a *legitimate* Notion. The *Notion* may have its mould in the understanding; but its realization must be the work of the FANCY.

A reflecting Reader will easily apply these remarks to the subject of Election, one of the stumbling stones in the ordinary conceptions of the Christian Faith, to which the Infidel points in scorn, and which far better men pass by in silent perplexity. Yet surely, from mistaken conceptions of the Doctrine. I suppose the person, with whom I am arguing, already so far a Believer, as to have convinced himself, both that a state of enduring Bliss is attainable under certain conditions; and that these conditions consist in his compliance with the directions given and rules prescribed in the Christian Scriptures. These rules he likewise admits to be such, that, by the very law and constitution of the human mind, a full and faithful compliance with them cannot but have *consequences*, of some sort or other. But these *consequences* are moreover distinctly described, enumerated, and promised in the same Scriptures, in which the Conditions are recorded; and though some of them may be apparent to God only, yet the greater number are of such a nature that they cannot exist unknown to the Individual, in and for whom they exist. As little possible is it, that he should find these consequences in himself, and not find in them the sure marks and the safe pledges, that he is at the time in the right road to the Life promised under these conditions. Now I dare assert, that no such man, however fervent his charity, and however deep his humility, may be, can peruse the records of History with a reflecting spirit, or "look round the world" [13] with an observant eye, and not find himself compelled to admit, that *all* men are *not* on the right Road. He cannot help judging, that even in Christian countries Many, a fearful Many! have not their faces turned toward it.

This then is mere matter of fact. Now comes the question. Shall the Believer, who thus hopes on the appointed *grounds* of Hope, attribute this distinction exclusively to his own resolves and strivings? or if not exclusively, yet primarily and principally? Shall he refer the first movements and preparations to his own Will and Understanding, and bottom his claim to the Promises on his own comparative excellence? If not, if no man dare take this honour to himself, to whom shall he assign it, if not to that Being in whom the Promise originated and on whom its Fulfilment depends? If he stop here, who shall blame him? By what argument shall his reasoning be invalidated, that might not be urged with equal force against any essential difference between Obedient and Disobedient, Christian and Worldling? that would not imply that both *sorts* alike are, in the sight of God, the Sons of God by adoption? If he stop here, I say, who shall drive him from his position? For thus far he is practically concerned—this the Conscience requires, this the highest interests of Morality demand. It is a question of Facts, of the Will and the Deed, to argue against which on the abstract notions and possibilities of the speculative Reason is as unreasonable, as an attempt to decide a question of Colours by pure Geometry, or to unsettle the classes and specific characters of Natural History by the Doctrine of Fluxions.

But if the Self-examinant will abandon this position, and exchange the safe circle of Religion and practical Reason for the shifting Sand-wastes and *Mirages* of

---

[13] See Dryden's translation of Juvenal's *Satires*, X, 1.

Speculative Theology; if instead of seeking after the *marks* of Election in himself he undertakes to determine the ground and origin, the possibility and mode of Election itself *in relation to God;*—in this case, and whether he does it for the satisfaction of curiosity, or from the ambition of answering those, who would call God himself to account, why and by what right certain Souls were born in Africa instead of England ? or why (seeing that it is against all reason and goodness to choose a worse when being omnipotent he could have created a better) God did not create Beasts Men, and Men Angels ? or why God created any men but with pre-knowledge of their obedience, and why he left any occasion for Election ?—in this case, I say, we can only regret, that the Inquirer had not been better instructed in the nature, the bounds, the true purposes and proper objects of his intellectual faculties, and that he had not previously asked himself, by what appropriate Sense, or Organ of Knowledge, he hoped to secure an insight into a Nature which was neither an Object of his Senses, nor a part of his Self-consciousness! and so leave him to ward off shadowy Spears with the shadow of a Shield, and to retaliate the nonsense of Blasphemy with the Abracadabra of Presumption. He that will fly without wings must fly in his dreams: and till he awakes, will not find out, that to fly in a dream is but to dream of flying.

Thus then the Doctrine of Election is in itself a necessary inference from an undeniable fact—necessary at least for all who hold that the best of men are what they are through the grace of God. In relation to the Believer it is a *Hope*, which if it spring out of Christian Principles, be examined by the tests and nourished by the means prescribed in Scripture, will become a *lively*, an *assured* Hope, but which cannot in this life pass into *knowledge*, much less certainty of fore-knowledge. The contrary belief does indeed make the article of Election both tool and parcel of a mad and mischievous fanaticism. But with what force and clearness does not the Apostle confute, disclaim, and prohibit the pretence, treating it as a downright contradiction in terms! See Romans, viii. 24.

But though I hold the doctrine handled as Leighton handles it (that is practically, morally, *humanly*) rational, safe, and of essential importance, I see many*

reasons resulting from the peculiar circumstances, under which St. Paul preached and wrote, why a discreet Minister of the Gospel should avoid the frequent use of the *term*, and express the *meaning* in other words perfectly equivalent and equally scriptural: lest in *saying* truth he might convey error.

Had my purpose been confined to one particular Tenet, an apology might be required for so long a Comment. But the Reader will, I trust, have already perceived, that my Object has been to establish a general Rule of interpretation and vindication applicable to *all* doctrinal Tenets, and especially to the (so called) Mysteries of the Christian Faith: to provide a *Safety-lamp* for religious inquirers. Now this I find in the principle, that all Revealed Truths are to be judged of by us, as far as they are possible subjects of human Conception, or grounds of Practice, or in some way connected with our moral and spiritual Interests. In order to have a reason *for* forming a judgment on any given article, we must be sure that we possess a Reason, by and according to which a judgment may be formed. Now in respect of all Truths, to which a *real* independent existence is assigned, and which yet are not contained in, or to be imagined under, any form of Space or Time, it is strictly demonstrable, that the human Reason, considered abstractly as the source of positive *Science* and theoretical *Insight*, is *not* such a Reason. At the utmost, it has only a *negative* voice. In other words, nothing can be allowed as true for the human Mind, which directly contradicts this Reason. But even here, before we admit the existence of any such contradiction, we must be careful to ascertain, that there is no equivocation in play, that two different subjects are not confounded under one and the same word. A striking instance of this has been adduced in the difference between the notional ONE of the Ontologists, and the Idea of the Living God.[14]

But if not the abstract or speculative Reason, and yet a Reason there must be in order to a rational Belief—then it must be the *Practical* Reason of Man, comprehending the Will, the Conscience, the Moral Being with its inseparable Interests and Affections—that Reason, namely, which is the Organ of *Wisdom*, and (as

---

* *Exempli gratia:* at the date of St. Paul's Epistles the (Roman) World may be resembled to a Mass in the Furnace in the first moment of fusion, here a speck and there a spot of the melted Metal shining pure and brilliant amid the scum and dross. To have received the *name* of Christian was a privilege, a high and distinguishing factor. No wonder therefore, that in St. Paul's writings the words, Elect and Election, often, nay, most often mean the same as *eccalūmeni*, ecclesia, i.e., those who have been *called out* of the World: and it is a dangerous perversion of the Apostle's word to interpret it in the sense, in which it was used by

our Lord, viz. in *opposition to the Called*. (Many are *called* but few *chosen*). In St. Paul's sense and at that time the Believers collectively formed a small and select number; and every Christian, real or nominal, was one of the Elect. Add too, that this ambiguity is increased by the accidental circumstance, that the *kyriak*, Ædes *Dominicae*, Lord's House, *Kirk*; and Ecclesia, the sum total of the Eccalūmeni, *evocati*, *Called-out*; are both rendered by the same word Church.

14 See pp. 268–69.

far as Man is concerned) the Source of living and actual Truths.

From these premises we may further deduce, that every doctrine is to be interpreted in reference to those, to whom it has been revealed, or who have or have had the means of knowing or hearing the same. For instance: the Doctrine that there is no name under Heaven, by which a man can be saved, but the name of Jesus. If the word here rendered *Name*, may be understood (as it well may, and as in other texts it must be) as meaning the Power, or originating Cause, I see no objection on the part of the Practical Reason to our belief of the declaration in its whole extent. It is true universally or not true at all. If there be any redemptive Power not contained in the Power of Jesus, then Jesus is not *the* Redeemer: not the Redeemer of the *World*, not the Jesus (i.e. Saviour) of Man*kind*. But if with Tertullian [15] and Augustin we make the Text assert the condemnation and misery of all who are not Christians by Baptism and explicit Belief in the Revelation of the New Covenant—then I say, the doctrine is true *to all intents and purposes*. It is true, in every respect, in which any practical, moral, or spiritual Interest or End can be connected with its truth. It is true in respect to every man who has had, or who might have had, the Gospel preached to him. It is true and obligatory for every Christian Community and for every individual Believer, wherever the opportunity is afforded of spreading the *Light* of the Gospel and making *known* the name of the only Saviour and Redeemer. For even though the uninformed Heathens should *not* perish, the *guilt* of their Perishing will attach to those who not only had no certainty of their safety, but who were commanded to *act* on the supposition of the contrary. But if, on the other hand, a theological Dogmatist should attempt to persuade me, that this Text was intended to give us an historical knowledge of God's future Actions and Dealings—and for the gratification of our Curiosity to inform us, that Socrates and Phocion, [16] together with all the Savages in the untravelled Woods and Wilds of Africa and America, will be sent to keep company with the Devil and his Angels in everlasting Torments—I should remind him, that the purpose of Scripture was to teach us our duty, not to enable us to sit in judgment on the souls of our fellow creatures.

One other instance will, I trust, prevent all misconception of my meaning. I am clearly convinced, that

the scriptural and only true * Idea of God will, in its development, be found to involve the Idea of the Trinity. But I am likewise convinced, that previous to the promulgation of the Gospel the Doctrine had no claim on the Faith of Mankind: though it might have been a legitimate Contemplation for a speculative philosopher, a Theorem in Metaphysics valid in the Schools.

I form a certain notion in my mind, and say: this is what *I* understand by the term, God. From books and conversation I find, that the Learned generally connect the same notion with the same word. I then apply the Rules, laid down by the Masters of Logic, for the involution and evolution of Terms, and prove (to as many as agree with me in my premises) that the Notion, God, involves the Notion, Trinity. I now pass out of the Schools, and enter into discourse with some friend or neighbour, unversed in the *formal* sciences, unused to the processes of Abstraction, neither Logician or Metaphysician; but sensible and singleminded, "an Israelite indeed," trusting in "the Lord God of his Fathers, even the God of Abraham, of Isaac, and of Jacob." [17] If I speak of God to *him*, what will *he* understand me to be speaking of? What does he mean, and suppose me to mean, by the word? An Accident or Product of the reasoning faculty, or an Abstraction which the human Mind makes by reflecting on its own thoughts and forms of thinking? No. By God he understands me to mean an existing and self-subsisting reality,† a real and personal Being—even the *Person*,

* Or (I might have added) *any* Idea which does not either identify the Creator with the Creation; or else represent the Supreme Being as a mere impersonal LAW or *Ordo ordinans*, differing from the Law of Gravitation only by its *universality*.

† I have elsewhere remarked on the assistance which those that labour after distinct conceptions would receive from the re-introduction of the terms *objective* and *subjective*, *objective and subjective reality*, &c. as substitutes for *real* and *notional*, and to the exclusion of the false antithesis between *real* and *ideal*. For the Student in that noblest of the Sciences, the Scire teipsum, the advantage would be especially great.[a] The few sentences that follow, in illustration of the terms here advocated, will not, I trust, be a waste of the Reader's Time.

The celebrated Euler having demonstrated certain properties of Arches, adds: "All experience is in contradiction to this; but this is no reason for doubting its truth." The words *sound* paradoxical; but mean no more than this—that the mathematical

[a] See the "*Selection from Mr. Coleridge's Literary Correspondence*" in Blackwood's Ed. Magazine, for October 1821, Letter ii. p. 244–253, which, however, should any of my Readers take the trouble of consulting, he must be content with such parts as he finds intelligible at the first perusal. For from defects in the MS., and without any fault on the part of the Editor, too large a portion is so printed that the man must be equally bold and fortunate in his conjectural readings who can make out any meaning at all.

<hr>

[15] Tertullian (*c.* 155–*c.* 222), with Augustine, the greatest of the early Church fathers.
[16] Socrates and Phocion are here cited as examples of virtuous pagans. Phocion, a fourth-century B.C. Athenian general and statesman, was known for his high integrity of character. (Like Socrates, he was unjustly condemned to death by the Athenian court.)

[17] See John, i, 47, and Exodus, xiii, 15.

the I AM, who sent Moses to his Forefathers in Egypt. Of the actual existence of this divine Person he has the same historical assurance as of theirs; confirmed indeed by the Book of Nature, as soon and as far as that stronger and better Light has taught him to read and construe it—confirmed by it, I say, but not derived

from it. Now by what right can I require this Man (and of such men the great majority of serious Believers consisted, previous to the Light of the Gospel) to receive a *Notion* of mine, wholly alien from his habits of thinking, because it may be logically deduced from another Notion, with which he was almost as little

---

properties of Figure and Space are not less certainly the properties of Figure and Space because they can never be perfectly realized in wood, stone, or iron. Now this assertion of Euler's might be expressed at once, briefly and simply, by saying, that the properties in question are *subjectively* true, though not objectively—or that the Mathematical Arch possessed a *subjective reality*, though incapable of being realized *objectively*.

In like manner if I had to express my conviction, that Space was not itself a *Thing*, but a *mode* or *form* of perceiving, or the inward ground and condition in the Percipient, in consequence of which Things are seen as outward and co-existing, I convey this at once by the words, Space is *subjective*, or Space is real in and for the *Subject* alone.

If I am asked, why not say in and for the *mind*, which every one would understand? I reply: we know indeed, that all minds are Subjects; but are by no means certain, that all Subjects are Minds. For a Mind is a Subject that knows itself, or a Subject that is its own Object. The inward principle of Growth and individual Form in every Seed and Plant is a *Subject*, and without any exertion of poetic privilege Poets may speak of the *Soul* of the Flower. But the man would be a Dreamer, who otherwise than poetically should speak of Roses and Lilies as *self-conscious* Subjects. Lastly, by the assistance of the terms, Object and Subject, thus used as correspondent Opposites, or as Negative and Positive in Physics (ex. gr. Neg. and Pos. Electricity) we may arrive at the distinct import and proper use of the strangely misused word, Idea. And as the Forms or Logic are all borrowed from Geometry (Ratiocinatio *discursiva* formas suas sive canonas recipit ab *intuitu*), I may be permitted so to elucidate my present meaning. Every Line may be, and by the ancient Geometricians *was*, considered as a point *produced*, the two extremes being its poles, while the Point itself remains in, or is at least represented by, the mid-point, the Indifference of the two poles or correlative opposites. Logically applied, the two extremes or poles are named Thesis and Antithesis: thus in the line

$$\overset{\text{I}}{\underset{}{\text{T}\!\!-\!\!-\!\!-\!\!-\!\!-\!\!-\!\!-\!\!-\!\!\text{A}}}$$

we have T = Thesis, A = Antithesis, and I = Punctum Indifferens sive *Amphotericum*, which latter is to be conceived as *both* in as far as it may be *either* of the two former. Observe: not both at the same time in the same relation: for this would be the *Identity* = of T and A, not the *Indifference*. But so, that relatively to A I is equal to T, and relatively to T it becomes = A. Thus in chemistry Sulphuretted Hydrogen is an Acid relatively to the more powerful Alkalis, and an Alkali relatively to a powerful Acid. Yet one other remark, and I pass to the question. In order to render the constructions of pure Mathematics applicable to Philosophy, the Pythagoreans, I imagine, represented the Line as *generated*, or, as it were, radiated, by a Point not contained in the Line but independent, and (in the language of that School) transcendent to all production, which it caused but did not partake in. *Facit, non patitur*. This was the Punctum invisibile, et presuppositum: and in this way the Pythagoreans guarded against the error of Pantheism, into which the later schools fell. The assumption of this Point I call the logical PROTHESIS. We have now therefore four Relations of Thought expressed: *viz.* 1. Prothesis, or the Identity of T and A, which is neither, because in it, as the trans-

cendent of both, both are contained and exist as one. Taken *absolutely*, this finds its application in the Supreme Being alone, the Pythagorean TETRACYTS; the INEFFABLE NAME, to which no Image dare be attached; the Point, which has no (real) Opposite or Counter-point, &c. But *relatively* taken and inadequately, the germinal power of every seed might be generalized under the relation of Identity. 2. Thesis or Position. 3. Antithesis, or Opposition. 4. Indifference. (To which when we add the Synthesis or Composition, in its several forms of Equilibrium, as in quiescent Electricity; of Neutralization, as of Oxygen and Hydrogen in Water; and of Predominance, as of Hydrogen and Carbon with Hydrogen predominant, in pure Alcohol, or of Carbon and Hydrogen, with the comparative predominance of the Carbon, in Oil; we complete the five most general Forms or Preconceptions of Constructive Logic).

And now for the Answer to the Question, What is an IDEA; if it mean neither an Impression on the Senses, nor a definite Conception, nor an abstract Notion? (And if it does mean either of these, the word is superfluous: and while it remains undetermined which of these is meant by the word, or whether it is not *which you please*, it is worse than superfluous. See the STATESMAN'S MANUAL, Appendix, *ad finem*). But supposing the word to have a meaning of its own, what does it mean? What is an IDEA? In answer to this I commence with the *absolutely* Real, as the PROTHESIS; the *subjectively* Real as the THESIS; the *objectively* Real as the ANTITHESIS: and I affirm, that Idea is the INDIFFERENCE of the two—so namely, that if it be conceived as in the Subject, the Idea is an Object, and possesses Objective Truth; but if in an Object, it is then a Subject, and is necessarily thought of as exercising the powers of a Subject. Thus an IDEA conceived as subsisting in an Object becomes a LAW; and a Law contemplated *subjectively* (in the mind) is an Idea.

In the third and last Section of my "Elements of Discourse;" in which (after having in the two former sections treated of the Common or Syllogistic Logic—the science of legitimate *Conclusions*; and the Critical Logic, or the Criteria of Truth and Falsehood in all *Premises*) I have given at full my scheme of Constructive Reasoning, or "Logic as the Organ of Philosophy," in the same sense as the Mathematics are the Organ of Science; the Reader will find proofs of the Utility of this Scheme, including the five-fold Division above-stated, and numerous examples of its application. Nor is it only in Theology that its importance will be felt, but equally, nay in a greater degree, as an instrument of Discovery and universal Method in Physics, Physiology, and Statistics. As this third Section does not pretend to the forensic and comparatively popular character and utility of the parts preceding, one of the Objects of the present Note is to obtain the opinions of judicious friends respecting the expedience of publishing it, in the same form, indeed, and as an Annexment to the "Elements of Discourse," yet so as that each may be purchased separately.[18]

---

[18] Leonhard Euler (1707–1783) was a Swiss mathematician and astronomer. The "Elements of Discourse" was a projected work on logic, intended as introductory to *Assertion of Religion*.

acquainted, and not at all concerned? Grant for a moment, that the latter (i.e. the Notion, with which I first set out) as soon as it is combined with the assurance of a corresponding Reality becomes identical with the true and effective Idea of God! Grant, that in thus *realizing* the Notion I am warranted by Revelation, the Law of Conscience, and the interests and necessities of my Moral Being! Yet by what authority, by what inducement, am I entitled to attach the same reality to a second Notion, a Notion drawn from a Notion? It is evident, that if I have the same Right, it must be on the same grounds. Revelation must have assured it, my Conscience required it—or in some way or other I must have an *interest* in this belief. It must *concern* me, as a moral and responsible Being. Now these grounds were first given in the Redemption of Mankind by Christ, the Saviour and Mediator: and by the utter incompatibility of these offices with a mere Creature. On the doctrine of Redemption depends the *Faith*, the *Duty*, of believing in the Divinity of our Lord. And this again is the strongest Ground for the reality of that Idea, in which alone this Divinity can be received without breach of the faith in the unity of the Godhead. But such is the Idea of the Trinity. Strong as the motives are that induce me to defer the full discussion of this great Article of the Christian Creed, I cannot withstand the request of several Divines, whose situation and extensive services entitle them to the utmost deference, that I should so far deviate from my first intention as at least to indicate the point on which I stand, and to prevent the misconception of my purpose: as if I held the doctrine of the Trinity for a truth which Men could be called on to believe by mere force of reasoning, independently of any positive *Revelation*. In short, it had been reported in certain circles, that I considered this doctrine as a demonstrable part of the Religion of Nature. Now though it might be sufficient to say, that I regard the very phrase "*Revealed* Religion" as a pleonasm,[19] inasmuch as a religion not revealed is, in my judgment, no religion at all; I have no objection to announce more particularly and distinctly what I do and what I do not maintain on this point: provided that in the following paragraph, with this view inserted, the reader will look for nothing more than a plain *statement* of my Opinions. The grounds on which they rest, and the arguments by which they are to be vindicated, are for another place.

I hold then, it is true, that all the (so called) Demonstrations of a God either prove too little, as that from the Order and apparent Purpose in Nature; or too much, *viz.* that the World is itself God; or they clan-

destinely involve the conclusion in the Premises, passing off the mere analysis or explication of an Assertion for the Proof of it,—a species of logical legerdemain not unlike that of the Jugglers at a Fair, who putting into their mouths what seems to be a walnut, draw out a score yards of Ribbon. On this Sophism rest the pretended "Demonstrations of a God" grounded on the Postulate of a First Cause. And lastly, in all these Demonstrations the Authors presuppose the Idea or Conception of a God without being able to authenticate it, i.e. to give an account whence they obtained it. For it is clear, that the Proof first mentioned and the most natural and convincing of all (the Cosmological I mean or that from the Order of Nature) presupposes the Ontological—i.e. the proof of a God from the necessity and necessary *Objectivity* of the Idea. *If* the latter can assure us of a God as an existing Reality, the former will go far to prove his Power, Wisdom, and Benevolence. All this I hold. But I also hold, that this Truth, the hardest to demonstrate, is the one which of all others least needs to be demonstrated; that though there may be no conclusive demonstrations of a good, wise, living and personal God, there are so many convincing reasons for it, within and without—a grain of sand sufficing, and a whole universe at hand to echo the decision!—that for every mind not devoid of all reason, and desperately conscience-proof, the Truth which it is the least possible to prove, it is little less than impossible not to believe! only indeed just so much short of impossible, as to leave some room for the will and the moral election, and thereby to keep it a truth of Religion, and the possible subject of a Commandment.*

On this account I do not demand of a *Deist*, that he should adopt the doctrine of the Trinity. For he might

---

* In a letter to a Friend on the mathematical Atheists of the French Revolution, La Lande and others, or rather on a young man of distinguished abilities, but an avowed and proselyting Partizan of their Tenets, I concluded with these words: "The man who will believe nothing but by force of demonstrative evidence (even though it is strictly demonstrable that the demonstrability required would countervene all the purposes of the Truth in question, all that render the belief of the same desirable or obligatory) is not in a state of mind to be reasoned with on any subject. But if he further denies the *fact* of the Law of Conscience, and the essential difference between Right and Wrong, I confess, he puzzles me. I cannot without gross inconsistency appeal to his Conscience and Moral Sense, or I should admonish him that, as an honest man, he ought to *advertise* himself, with a Cavete omnes! Scelus sum. And as an honest man myself, I dare not advise him on prudential grounds to keep his opinions secret, lest I should make myself his accomplice, and *be helping him on with a Wrap-rascal.*"[20]

---

[19] Redundancy.

[20] Cavete . . . sum.: "Let all beware! I am a scoundrel." Wrap-rascal was a loose overcoat; here it means a knave's disguise.

very well be justified in replying, that he rejected the doctrine, *not* because it could not be *demonstrated*, nor yet on the score of any incomprehensibilities and seeming contradictions that might be objected to it, as knowing that these might be, and in fact had been, urged with equal force against a personal God under any form capable of Love and Veneration; *but* because he had not the same theoretical necessity, the same interests and instincts of Reason for the one hypothesis as for the other. It is not enough, the Deist might justly say, that there is no cogent reason why I should *not* believe the Trinity: you must show me some cogent reason why I *should*.

But the case is quite different with a Christian, who accepts the Scriptures as the Word of God, yet refuses his assent to the plainest declarations of these Scriptures, and explains away the most express texts into metaphor and hyperbole, *because* the literal and obvious interpretation is (according to *his* notions) absurd and contrary to reason. *He* is bound to show, that it is so in any sense, not equally applicable to the texts asserting the Being, Infinity, and Personality of God the Father, the Eternal and Omnipresent ONE, who *created* the Heaven and the Earth. And the more is he bound to do this, and the greater is my right to demand it of him, because the doctrine of Redemption from Sin supplies the Christian with motives and reasons for the divinity of the Redeemer far more *concerning* and coercive *subjectively*, i.e. in the economy of his own Soul, than are all the inducements that can influence the Deist *objectively*, i.e. in the interpretation of Nature.

Do I then utterly exclude the speculative Reason from Theology? No! It is its office and rightful privilege to determine on the *negative* truth of whatever we are required to believe. The Doctrine must not *contradict* any universal principle: for this would be a doctrine that contradicted itself. Or Philosophy? No. It may be and has been the servant and pioneer of Faith by convincing the mind, that a Doctrine is cogitable, that the soul can present the *Idea* to itself; and that *if* we determine to contemplate, or *think* of, the subject at all, so and in no other form can this be effected. So far are both Logic and Philosophy to be received and trusted. But the *duty*, and in some cases and for some persons even the *right*, of thinking on subjects beyond the bounds of sensible experience; the grounds of the *real* truth; the *Life*, the *Substance*, the *Hope*, the *Love*, in one word, the *Faith*, these are Derivatives from the practical, moral, and spiritual Nature and Being of Man.

APHORISM III.

That Religion is designed to improve the nature and faculties of Man, in order to the right governing of our actions, to the securing the peace and progress, external

and internal, of Individuals and of Communities, and lastly, to the rendering us capable of a more perfect state, entitled the kingdom of God, to which the present Life is *probationary*—this is a Truth, which all who have truth only in view, will receive on its own evidence. If such then be the main end of Religion altogether (the improvement namely of our nature and faculties), it is plain, that every Part of Religion is to be judged by its relation to this main end. And since the Christian Scheme is Religion in its most perfect and effective Form, a revealed Religion, and therefore, in a *special* sense proceeding from that Being who made us and knows what we are, of course therefore adapted to the needs and capabilities of Human Nature; nothing can be a part of this holy faith that is not duly proportioned to this end.—*Extracted with slight alterations from Burnet's Preface to* Vol. ii. *of the Hist. of the Reformation.*[21]

COMMENT.

This Aphorism should be borne in mind, whenever a theological *Resolve* is proposed to us as an article of Faith. Take, for instance, the Determinations passed at the Synod of Dort,[22] concerning the Absolute Decrees of God in connexion with his Omniscience and Foreknowledge. Or take the Decision in the Council of Trent[23] on the Difference between the two kinds of Transubstantiation, the one in which both the Substance and the Accidents are changed, the same matter remaining—as in the conversion of Water to Wine at Cana; the other, in which the Matter and the Substance are changed, the Accidents remaining unaltered, as in the Eucharist—this latter being Transubstantiation *par eminence!* Or rather take the still more tremendous Dogma, that it is indispensable to a saving Faith carefully to distinguish the one kind from the other, and to believe both, and to believe the necessity of believing both in order to Salvation! For each or either of these *extra-scriptural* Articles of Faith the preceding Aphorism supplies a safe criterion. Will the belief tend to the improvement of any of my moral or intellectual faculties? But before I can be convinced that a Faculty will be *improved*, I must be assured that it *exists*. On all

<hr>

[21] *The History of the Reformation of the Church of England* (1679–1714), by Gilbert Burnet (1643–1715). Volume II was published in 1681.

[22] The Synod of Dort was held in 1618–1619 to settle the dispute between the Calvinist and Arminian parties in the Dutch church. The Calvinist forces expelled the Arminians and drew up a canon of strict beliefs, which became the theological basis of the Dutch Reformed Church.

[23] The Council of Trent was held in 1545–1563 to deal with the reform of ecclesiastical abuses, doctrinal definition, and in general to reassess the Catholic Church following the Protestant revolution.

these dark sayings, therefore, of Dort or Trent, it is quite sufficient to ask, by what *faculty*, *organ*, or *inlet* of knowledge we are to assure ourselves, that the words *mean* any thing, or correspond to any object out of our own mind or even in it: unless indeed the mere craving and striving to think *on*, after all the materials for thinking have been exhausted, can be called an *object*. When a number of trust-worthy Persons assure me, that a portion of Fluid which they saw to be Water, by some change in the Fluid itself or in their Senses, suddenly acquired the Colour, Taste, Smell, and exhilarating property of Wine, I perfectly understand what they tell me, and likewise by what faculties they might have come to the knowledge of the Fact. But if any one of the number not satisfied with my acquiescence in the Fact, should insist on my believing, that the *Matter* remained the same, the Substance and the Accidents having been removed in order to make way for a different Substance with different Accidents, I must entreat his permission to wait till I can discover in myself any faculty, by which there can be presented to me a Matter distinguishable from Accidents, and a Substance that is different from both. It is true, I have a faculty of articulation; but I do not see that it can be *improved* by my using it for the formation of words without meaning, or at best, for the utterance of Thoughts, that mean only the act of so thinking, or of trying so to think. But the end of Religion is the improvement of our Nature and Faculties. Ergo, &c. Q. E. D. I sum up the whole in one great practical Maxim. The Object of *religious* Contemplation, and of a truly Spiritual Faith, is THE WAYS OF GOD TO MAN. Of the Workings of the Godhead, God himself has told us, My Ways are not as your Ways, nor my Thoughts as your Thoughts.[24]

* * * * *

APHORISM VII. EDITOR.

The Being and Providence of One Living God, Holy, Gracious, Merciful, the Creator and Preserver of all things, and a Father of the Righteous; the Moral Law in its [1] utmost height, breadth, and purity; a State of Retribution after Death; the [2] Resurrection of the Dead; and a Day of Judgment—all these were known and received by the Jewish People, as established Articles of the National Faith, at or before the Proclaiming of Christ by the Baptist. They are the ground-work of Christianity, and essentials in the Christian Faith, but not its characteristic and peculiar Doctrines: except indeed as they are confirmed, enlivened, realized and brought home to the *whole Being* of Man, Head, Heart, and Spirit, by the truths and influences of the Gospel.

[24] Isaiah, lv, 8.

Peculiar to Christianity are:

I. The belief that a Means of Salvation has been effected and provided for the Human Race by the incarnation of the Son of God in the person of Jesus Christ; and that his Life on earth, his Sufferings, Death, and Resurrection are not only proofs and manifestations, but likewise essential and effective parts of the great redemptive Act, whereby also the Obstacle from the corruption of our Nature is rendered no longer insurmountable.

II. The belief in the possible appropriation of this benefit by Repentance and Faith, including the Aids that render an effective Faith and Repentance themselves possible.

III. The belief in the reception (by as many as "shall be Heirs of Salvation") of a living and spiritual Principle, a Seed of Life capable of surviving this natural life, and of existing in a divine and immortal State.

IV. The belief in the awakening of the Spirit in them that truly believe, and in the communion of the Spirit, thus awakened, with the Holy Spirit.

V. The belief in the accompanying and consequent gifts, graces, comforts, and privileges of the Spirit, which acting primarily on the heart and will cannot but manifest themselves in suitable works of Love and Obedience, i.e. in right acts with right affections, from right principles.

Further, as Christians, we are taught, that these WORKS are the appointed signs and evidences of our FAITH; and that, under limitation of the power, the means, and the opportunities afforded us individually, they are the rule and measure, by which we are bound and enabled to judge, of *what* spirit we are: and all these together with the doctrine of the Fathers re-proclaimed in the everlasting Gospel, we receive in the full assurance, that God beholds and will finally judge us with a merciful consideration of our infirmities, a gracious acceptance of our sincere though imperfect strivings, a forgiveness of our defects through the mediation, and a completion of our deficiencies by the perfect righteousness, of the Man Christ Jesus, even the Word that was in the beginning with God, and who, being God, became Man for the redemption of Mankind.

COMMENT.

I earnestly entreat the Reader to pause awhile, and to join with me in reflecting on the preceding Aphorism. It has been my aim throughout this work to enforce two points: 1. That MORALITY arising out of the Reason and Conscience of Men, and PRUDENCE, which in like manner flows out of the Understanding and the natural Wants and Desires of the Individual, are two distinct things; 2. That Morality with Prudence as its instrument has, considered abstractedly, not only a value but a *worth* in itself. Now the question is (and it is a question which every man must answer for himself) From what you know of yourself; of your own Heart and Strength; and from what History and personal Experience have led you to conclude of mankind generally; dare you *trust* to it? Dare *you* trust to it? To *it*, and to it alone? If so, well! It is at your own risk. I judge you not. Before Him, who cannot be mocked, you stand or fall. But if not, if you have had too good reason to know, that your heart is deceitful and your strength weakness: if you are disposed to exclaim with Paul—the Law indeed is holy, just, good, spiritual; but I am carnal, sold under sin: for that which I do, I allow not; and what I would, that do I not![25]—in this case, there is a Voice that says, Come unto *me:* and I will give you rest.[26] This is the Voice of Christ: and the Conditions, under which the promise was given by him, are that you believe *in* him, and believe his words. And he has further assured you, that *if* you do so, you will obey him. You are, in short, to embrace the *Christian* Faith as your Religion—those Truths which St. Paul believed *after* his conversion, and not those only which he believed no less undoubtingly while he was persecuting Christ, and an enemy of the Christian Religion. With what consistency could I offer you this volume as Aids to Reflection if I did not call on you to ascertain in the first instance what these truths are? But these I could not lay before you without first enumerating certain other points of belief, which though truths, indispensable truths, and truths comprehended or rather presupposed in the Christian Scheme, are yet not *these* Truths. (1 John v. 17.)

While doing this, I was aware that the Positions, in the first paragraph of the preceding Aphorism, to which the numerical *marks* are affixed, will startle some of my Readers. Let the following sentences serve for the notes corresponding to the marks:

1 Be you holy: even as God is holy.—What more does he require of thee, O man! than to do justice, love mercy, and walk humbly with the Lord thy God?[27] To these summary passages from Moses and the Prophets (the first exhibiting the closed, the second the expanded, Hand of the Moral Law) I might add the Authorities of Grotius and other more orthodox and not less learned Divines, for the opinion, that the Lord's Prayer was a *selection*, and the famous Passage [The Hour is now coming, John v. 28, 29.] a *citation* by our Lord from the Liturgy of the Jewish Church. But it will be sufficient to remind the reader, that the apparent difference between the prominent *moral* truths of the Old and those of the New Testament results from the

latter having been written in Greek; while the conversations recorded by the Evangelists took place in Hebrew or Syro-chaldaic. Hence it happened that where our Lord cited the original text, his Biographers substituted the Septuagint Version,[28] while our English Version is in *both* instances immediate and literal—in the Old Testament from the Hebrew Original, in the New Testament from the freer Greek Translation. Thus in the Text, Love your Neighbour as yourself, *Neighbour* in our New, and *Stranger* in our Old Testament represent one and the same Hebrew work. The text, "I give you a new commandment,"[29] has no connexion with the present subject.

2 There is a current mistake on this point likewise, though this article of the Jewish Belief is not only asserted by St. Paul, but is elsewhere spoken of as common to the Twelve Tribes. The mistake consists in supposing the Pharisees to have been a distinct *Sect*, and in strangely over-rating the number of the Sadducees. The former were distinguished not by holding, as matters of religious belief, articles different from the Jewish Church at large; but by their pretences to a more rigid orthodoxy, a more scrupulous performance. They were, in short (if I may dare use a phrase which I dislike as profane and denounce as uncharitable), the *Evangelicals* and strict *Professors* of the Day. The latter, the Sadducees, whose opinions much more nearly resembled those of the *Stoics* than the Epicureans (a remark that will appear paradoxical to those only who have abstracted their notions of the Stoic Philosophy from Epictetus, Mark Antonine, and certain brilliant inconsistencies of Seneca), were a handful of rich men, *romanized* Jews, not more numerous than Infidels among us, and held by the People at large in at least equal abhorrence. Their great argument was: that the Belief of a future State of rewards and punishments injured or destroyed the purity of the Moral Law for the more enlightened Classes, and weakened the influence of the Laws of the Land for the People, the vulgar Multitude.

————

I will now suppose the Reader to have thoughtfully re-perused the Paragraph containing the Tenets peculiar to Christianity, and if he have his religious principles yet to form, I should expect to overhear a troubled Murmur: How can I comprehend this? How is this to be proved? To the first question I should answer: Christianity is not a Theory, or a Speculation; but a *Life*. Not a *Philosophy* of Life, but a Life and a living Process. To the second: TRY IT. It has been eighteen hundred Years in existence: and has one

---

25 Romans, vii, 14–15.   26 Matthew, xi, 28.
27 Micah, vi, 8.

28 The Alexandrian (Greek) version of the Old Testament.
29 John, xiii, 34.

Individual left a record, like the following? "I tried it; and it did not answer. I made the experiment faithfully according to the directions; and the result has been, a conviction of my own credulity." Have you, in your own experience, met with any one in whose words you could place full confidence, and who has seriously affirmed, "I have given Christianity a fair trial. I was aware, that its promises were made only *conditionally*. But my heart bears me witness, that I have to the utmost of my power complied with these conditions. Both outwardly and in the discipline of my inward acts and affection, I have performed the duties which it enjoins, and I have used the means, which it prescribes. Yet my Assurance of its truth has received no increase. Its promises have not been fulfilled: and I repent me of my delusion!" If neither your own experience nor the History of almost two thousand years has presented a single testimony to this purport; and if you have read and heard of many who have lived and died bearing witness to the contrary: and if you have yourself met with some *one*, in whom on any other point you would place unqualified trust, who has on his own experience made report to you, that "he is faithful who promised, and what he promised he has proved himself able to perform:" [30] is it bigotry, if I fear that the Unbelief, which prejudges and prevents the experiment, has its source elsewhere than in the uncorrupted judgement; that not the strong free Mind, but the enslaved Will, is the true original Infidel in this instance? It would not be the first time, that a treacherous Bosom-Sin had suborned the Understandings of men to bear false witness against its avowed Enemy, the right though unreceived Owner of the House, who had long *warned it out*, and waited only for its ejection to enter and take possession of the same.

I have elsewhere in the present Work, though more at large in the "Elements of Discourse" which, God permitting, will follow it, explained the difference between the Understanding and the Reason, by Reason meaning exclusively the speculative or scientific Power so called, the Nous or Mens of the Ancients. And wider still is the distinction between the Understanding and the Spiritual Mind. But no Gift of God does or can contradict any other Gift, except by misuse of misdirection. Most readily therefore do I admit, that there can be no contrariety between Revelation and the Understanding; unless you call the fact, that the Skin, though sensible of the warmth of the Sun, can convey no notion of its figure, or its joyous light, or of the colours, it impresses on the clouds, a contrariety between the Skin and the Eye; or infer that the cutaneous and the optic nerves *contradict* each other.

But we have grounds to believe, that there are yet other Rays or Effluences from the Sun, which neither Feeling nor Sight can apprehend, but which are to be inferred from the effects. And were it even so with regard to the Spiritual Sun, how would this contradict the Understanding or the Reason? It is a sufficient proof of the contrary, that the Mysteries in question are not *in the direction* of the Understanding or the (speculative) Reason. They do not move on the same line or plane with them, and therefore cannot contradict them. But besides this, in the Mystery that most immediately concerns the Believer, that of the birth into a new and spiritual life, the common sense and experience of mankind come in aid of their faith. The analogous facts, which we know to be true, not only facilitate the apprehension of the facts promised to us, and expressed by the same words in conjunction with a distinctive epithet; but being confessedly not less incomprehensible, the certain *knowledge* of the one disposes us to the *belief* of the other. It removes at least all objections to the truth of the doctrine derived from the mysteriousness of its subject. The Life, we seek after, is a mystery; but so both in itself and in its origin is the Life we have. In order to meet this question, however, with minds duly prepared, there are two preliminary enquiries to be decided; the first respecting the *purport*, the second respecting the *language* of the Gospel.

First then of the *purport*, viz. what the Gospel does *not*, and what it *does* profess to be. The Gospel is not a system of Theology, nor a Syntagma [31] of theoretical propositions and conclusions for the enlargement of speculative knowledge, ethical or metaphysical. But it is a History, a series of Facts and Events related or announced. These do indeed, involve, or rather I should say they at the same time *are*, most important doctrinal Truths; but still *Facts* and Declaration of *Facts*.

Secondly of the *language*. This is a wide subject. But the point, to which I chiefly advert, is the necessity of thoroughly understanding the distinction between *analogous*, and *metaphorical* language. *Analogies* are used in aid of *Conviction: Metaphors*, as means of *Illustration*. The language is analogous, wherever a thing, power, or principle in a higher dignity is expressed by the same thing, power, or principle in a lower but more known form. Such, for instance, is the language of John iii. 6. *That which is born of the Flesh, is Flesh; that which is born of the Spirit, is Spirit.* The latter half of the verse contains the act *asserted;* the former half the *analogous* fact, by which it is rendered intelligible. If any man choose to call this *metaphorical*

---

[30] See Hebrews, x, 23; and Romans, iv, 21.

[31] A systematically arranged treatise.

or figurative, I ask him whether with Hobbs and Bolingbroke [32] he applies the same rule to the moral attributes of the Deity? Whether he regards the divine Justice, for instance, as a *metaphorical* term, a mere figure of speech? If he disclaims this, then I answer, neither do I regard the words, *born again*, or *spiritual life*, as figures or metaphors. I have only to add, that these analogies are the material, or (to speak chemically) the *base*, of Symbols and symbolical expressions; the nature of which as always *tau*tegorical (i.e. expressing the *same* subject but with a *difference*) in contra-distinction from metaphors and similitudes, that are always *alle*gorical (i.e. expressing a *different* subject but with a resemblance) will be found explained at large in the STATESMAN'S MANUAL, p. 35–38. [33]

Of *metaphorical* language, on the other hand, let the following be taken as instance and illustration. I am speaking, we will suppose, of an Act, which in its own nature, and as a producing and efficient cause, is transcendent; but which produces sundry *effects*, each of which is the same in kind with an effect produced by a Cause well known and of ordinary occurrence. Now when I characterize or designate this transcendent Act, in exclusive reference to these its *effects*, by a succession of names borrowed from their ordinary causes; not for the purpose of rendering the Act itself, or the manner of the Agency, conceivable, but in order to show the nature and magnitude of the Benefits received from it, and thus to excite the due admiration, gratitude, and love in the Receivers;—in this case I should be rightly described as speaking *metaphorically*. And in this case to confound *the similarity* in respect of the effects relatively to the Recipients with *an identity* in respect of the causes or modes of causation relatively to the transcendent Act or the Divine Agent, is a confusion of metaphor with analogy, and of figurative with literal; and has been and continues to be a fruitful source of superstition or enthusiasm in Believers, and of objections and prejudices to Infidels and Sceptics. But each of these points is worthy of a separate consideration: and apt occasions will be found of reverting to them severally in the following Aphorisms or the comments thereto attached.

APHORISM VIII.   LEIGHTON. [34]

FAITH elevates the soul not only above Sense and sensible things, but above Reason itself. As Reason corrects the errors which Sense might occasion, so supernatural Faith corrects the errors of natural Reason judging according to Sense.

COMMENT.

The Editor's remarks on this aphorism from Archbishop Leighton cannot be better introduced, or their purport more distinctly announced, than by the following sentence from Harrington, with no other change than was necessary to make the words express without aid of the context what from the context it is evident was the Writer's meaning. "The definition and proper character of Man—that, namely, which should contradistinguish him from the Animals—is to be taken from his Reason rather than from his Understanding: in regard that in other creatures there may be something of Understanding but there is nothing of Reason." [35] See the FRIEND, vol. i. p. 263—277: and the APPENDIX (Note C.) to the STATESMAN'S MANUAL.

Sir Thomas Brown, in his Religio Medici, [36] complains, that there are not impossibilities enough in Religion for his active faith; and adopts by choice and in free preference such interpretations of certain texts and declarations of Holy Writ, as place them in irreconcilable contradiction to the demonstrations of science and the experience of mankind, because (says he) "I love to lose myself in a mystery, and 'tis my solitary recreation to pose my apprehension with those involved enigmas and riddles of the Trinity and Incarnation"— and because he delights (as thinking it no vulgar part of faith) to believe a thing not only above but contrary to Reason, and against the evidence of our proper senses. For the worthy knight could answer all the objections of the Devil and Reason (!!) "with the odd resolution he had learnt of Tertullian: Certum est quia impossibile est. It is certainly true because it is quite impossible!" Now this I call ULTRA-FIDIANISM. *

* There is this advantage in the occasional use of a newly minted term or title expressing the doctrinal schemes of particular sects or parties, that it avoids the inconvenience that presses on either side, whether we adopt the name which the Party has taken up to express its peculiar tenets by, or that by which the same Party is designated by its opponents. If we take the latter, it most often happens that either the persons are invidiously aimed at in the designation of the principles, or that the name implies some consequence or occasional accompaniment of the principles denied by the parties themselves, as applicable to them collectively. On the other hand, convinced as I am, that current apellations are never wholly indifferent or inert; and that, when employed to express the characteristic Belief or Object of a *religious* confederacy, they exert on the Many a great and constant, though insensible, influence; I cannot but fear that in adopting the former I may be sacrificing the interests of Truth beyond what the duties

[32] Henry St. John, First Viscount Bolingbroke (1678–1751) was a statesman, deistic philosopher, and friend of Pope.

[33] See pp. 161–62.

[34] From "A Practical Commentary upon the First Epistle General of St. Peter," commentary on chapter i, verse 8 (*The Whole Works of Robert Leighton*, I, 71).

[35] Freely altered from #27 of *Aphorisms Political* (1659), by James Harrington (1611–1677).

[36] *Religio Medici*, I, 9.

Again, there is a scheme constructed on the principle of retaining the social sympathies, that attend on the

name of Believer, at the least possible expenditure of Belief—a scheme of picking and choosing Scripture

of courtesy can demand or justify. In a tract published in the year 1816, I have stated my objections to the word *Unitarians*: as a name which in its proper sense can belong only to the Maintainers of the Truth impugned by the persons, who have chosen it as their designation. "For *Unity* or Unition, and indistinguishable *Unicity* or Sameness, are incompatible terms. We never speak of the Unity of Attraction, or the Unity of Repulsion; but of the Unity of Attraction *and* Repulsion in each corpuscle. Indeed, the essential diversity of the conceptions, Unity and Sameness, was among the elementary principles of the old Logicians: and Leibnitz in his critique on Wissowatius has ably exposed the sophisms grounded on the confusion of the two terms. But in the exclusive sense, in which the name, Unitarian, is appropriated by the Sect, and in which they mean it to be understood, it is a presumptuous Boast and an uncharitable calumny. No one of the Churches to which they on this article of the Christian Faith stand opposed, Greek or Latin, ever adopted the term, Trini—or Tri-uni-tarians as their ordinary and proper name: and had it been otherwise, yet Unity is assuredly no logical Opposite to Tri-unity, which expressly includes it. The triple Alliance is a fortiori Alliance. The true designation of their characteristic Tenet, and which would simply and inoffensively express a fact admitted on all sides, is Psilanthropism or the assertion of the *mere* humanity of Christ."

I dare not hesitate to avow my regret, that any scheme of doctrines or tenets should be the subject of penal law: though I can easily conceive, that any scheme, however excellent in itself, may be propagated, and however false or injurious, may be assailed, in a manner and by means that would make the Advocate or Assailant justly punishable. But then it is the *manner*, the *means*, that constitute the *crime*. The merit or demerit of the Opinions themselves depends on their originating and determining causes, which may differ in every different Believer, and are certainly known to Him alone, who commanded us: Judge not, lest ye be judged. At all events, in the present state of the Law I do not see where we can begin, or where we can stop, without inconsistency and consequent hardship. Judging by all that *we* can pretend to know or are entitled to infer, who among us will take on himself to deny that the late Dr. Priestley was a good and benevolent man, as sincere in his love, as he was intrepid and indefatigable in his pursuit, of Truth? Now let us construct three parallel tables, the first containing the Articles of Belief, moral and theological, maintained by the venerable Hooker, as the representative of the Established Church, each article being distinctly lined and numbered; the second the Tenets and Persuasions of Lord Herbert, as the representative of the platonizing Deists; and the third, those of Dr. Priestley. Let the points, in which the second and third agree with or differ from the first, be considered as to the comparative number modified by the comparative weight and importance of the several points—and let any competent and upright Man be appointed the Arbiter, to decide according to his best judgment, without any reference to the truth of the opinions, which of the two differed from the first the most widely! I say this, well aware that it would be abundantly more prudent to leave it unsaid. But I say it in the conviction, that the liberality in the adoption of admitted *misnomers* in the naming of doctrinal systems, if only they have been negatively legalized, is but an equivocal proof of liberality towards the *persons* who dissent from us. On the contrary, I more than suspect that the former liberality does in too many men arise from a latent pre-disposition to transfer their reprobation and intolerance from the Doctrines to the Doctors, from the Belief to the

Believers. Indecency, Abuse, Scoffing on subjects dear and aweful to a multitude of our fellow-citizens, Appeals to the vanity, appetites, and malignant passions of ignorant and incompetent judges—these are flagrant overt-acts, condemned by the Law written in the heart of every honest man, Jew, Turk, and Christian. These are points respecting which the humblest honest man feels it his duty to hold himself infallible, and dares not hesitate in giving utterance to the verdict of his conscience, in the Jury-box as fearlessly as by his fireside. It is far otherwise with respect to matters of faith and inward conviction: and with respect to *these* I say—Tolerate no Belief, that you judge false and of injurious tendency: and arraign no Believer. The Man is more and other than his Belief: and God only knows, how small or how large a part of him the Belief in question may be, for good or for evil. Resist every false doctrine: and call no man heretic. The false doctrine does not necessarily make the man a heretic; but an evil heart can make any doctrine heretical.

Actuated by these principles, I have objected to a false and deceptive designation in the case of one System. Persuaded, that the doctrines, enumerated on p. 275, are not only *essential* to the Christian Religion, but those which contra-distinguish the religion as *Christian*, I merely *repeat* this persuasion in another form, when I assert, that (in *my* sense of the word, Christian) Unitarianism is not Christianity. But do I say, that those, who call themselves Unitarians, are not Christians? God forbid! I would not think, much less promulgate, a judgment at once so presumptuous and so uncharitable. Let a friendly antagonist retort on *my* scheme of faith, in the like manner: I shall respect him all the more for his consistency as a reasoner, and not confide the less in his kindness towards me as his Neighbour and Fellow-christian. This latter and most endearing name I scarcely know how to withold even from my friend, HYMAN HURWITZ, as often as I read what every Reverer of Holy Writ and of the English Bible ought to read, his admirable VINDICIAE HEBRAICAE! It has trembled on the verge, as it were, of my lips, every time I have conversed with that pious, learned, strong-minded, and single-hearted Jew, an Israelite indeed and without guile—

Cujus cura sequi naturam, legibus uti,
    Et mentem vitiis, ora negare dolis;
Virtutes opibus, verum praeponere falso,
    Nil vacuum sensu dicere, nil facere.
Post obitum vivam secum, secum requiescam,
    Nec fiat melior sors mea sorte suâ!
        From a poem of Hildebert on his Master,
            the persecuted Berengarius.

Under the same feelings I conclude this *Aid to Reflection* by applying the principle to another misnomer not less inappropriate and far more influential. Of those, whom I have found most reason to respect and value, many have been members of the Church of Rome: and certainly I did not honour those the least, who scrupled even in common parlance to call our Church a reformed Church. A similar scruple would not, methinks, disgrace a Protestant, as to the use of the words, Catholic or Roman Catholic; and if (tacitly at least, and in thought) he remembered that the Romish anti-catholic Church would more truly express the fact.—*Romish*, to mark that the corruptions in discipline, doctrine, and practice do, for the far larger part, owe both their origin and perpetuation to the Romish *Court*, and the local tribunals of the *City* of Rome; and neither are or ever have been *Catholic*, i.e. universal, throughout the Roman *Empire*, or even in

texts for the support of doctrines that had been learned beforehand from the higher oracle of Common Sense; which, as applied to the truths of Religion, means the popular part of the philosophy in fashion. Of course, the scheme differs at different times and in different Individuals in the number of articles excluded; but it

the whole Latin or Western Church—and *Anti*-catholic, because no other Church acts on so narrow and excommunicative a principle, or is characterized by such a jealous spirit of monopoly. Instead of a Catholic (universal) spirit it may be truly described as a spirit of Particularism counterfeiting Catholicity by a *negative* totality, and heretical self-circumscription—in the first instance cutting off, and since then cutting herself off from, all the other members of Christ's Body. For the rest, I think as that man of true catholic spirit and apostolic zeal, Richard Baxter, thought; and my readers will thank me for conveying my reflections in his own words, in the following golden passage from his Life, "faithfully published from his own original MSS. by Matthew Silvester, 1696."

"My censures of the Papists do much differ from what they were at first. I then thought, that their errors in the *doctrines of faith* were their most dangerous mistakes. But now I am assured that their misexpressions and misunderstanding us, with our mistakings of them and inconvenient expressing of our own opinions, have made the difference in most points appear much greater than it is; and that in some it is next to none at all. But the great and unreconcilable differences lie in their Church Tyranny; in the usurpations of their Hierarchy, and Priesthood, under the name of spiritual authority exercising a temporal Lordship; in their corruptions and abasement of God's Worship, but above all in their systematic befriending of Ignorance and Vice.

"At first I thought that Mr. Perkins well proved, that a Papist cannot go beyond a reprobate; but now I doubt not that God hath many sanctified ones among them who have received the true doctrine of Christianity so practically that their contradictory errors prevail not against them, to hinder their love of God and their salvation: but that their errors are like a conquerable dose of poison which a healthful nature doth overcome. *And I can never believe that a man may not be saved by that religion, which doth but bring him to the true Love of God and to a heavenly mind and life: nor that God will ever cast a Soul into hell, that truly loveth him.* Also at first it would disgrace any doctrine with me if I did hear it called popery and anti-christian; but I have long learned to be more impartial, and to know that Satan can use even the names of Popery and Anti-christ, to bring a truth into suspicion and discredit."—Baxter's Life, part I. p. 131.[37]

37 "The tract published in the year 1816" was actually the second Lay Sermon, *"Blessed are ye that sow beside all Waters"* (1817), from which Coleridge quotes, adding some new material. Joseph Priestley was a leading exponent of Unitarianism. Edward Herbert (1583–1648), a poet and philosopher, was popularly regarded as the "Father of Deism." Hyman Hurwitz (1770–1844) was a Polish-born Jew, who directed a private academy for Jews in Highgate. His *Vindiciae Hebraicae, being a Defense of the Hebrew Scriptures as a Vehicle of Revealed Religion* was published in 1820. Hildebert (c. 1055–1133) was Archbishop of Tours and the author of letters and poems of considerable popularity. Berengarius (d. 1088) was a medieval theologian, whose highly independent views on the Eucharist brought him into continual conflict with ecclesiastical authorities, resulting in several trials for heresy and imprisonment. *Reliquiae Baxterianae: Or, Mr. Richard Baxter's Narrative of the most Memorable Passages of his Life and Times* (1696) was the record of Richard Baxter (1615–1691), a presbyterian divine.

may always be recognized by this permanent character, that its object is to draw religion down to the Believer's intellect, instead of raising his intellect up to religion. And this extreme I call MINIMIFIDIANISM.

Now if there be one Preventive of both these extremes more efficacious than another, and preliminary to all the rest, it is the being made fully aware of the diversity of Reason and Understanding. And this is the more expedient, because though there is no want of authorities ancient and modern for the distinction of the faculties and the distinct appropriation of the terms, yet our best writers too often confound the one with the other. Even Lord Bacon himself, who in his Novum Organum has so incomparably set forth the nature of the difference, and the unfitness of the latter faculty for the objects of the former, does nevertheless in sundry places use the term Reason where he means the Understanding, and sometimes, though less frequently, Understanding for Reason. In consequence of thus confounding the two terms, or rather of wasting both words for the expression of one and the same faculty, he left himself no appropriate term for the other and higher gift of Reason, and was thus under the necessity of adopting fantastic and mystical phrases, ex. gr. the dry light (lumen siccum), the lucific vision, &c., meaning thereby nothing more than Reason in contradistinction from the Understanding. Thus too in the preceding Aphorism, by Reason Leighton means the human Understanding, the explanation annexed to it being (by a noticeable coincidence) word for word the very definition which the Founder of the Critical Philosophy [38] gives of the Understanding—namely, "the Faculty judging according to Sense."

On the contrary, Reason is the Power of universal and necessary Convictions, the Source and Substance of Truths above Sense, and having their evidence in themselves. Its presence is always marked by the *necessity* of the position affirmed: this necessity being *conditional*, when a truth of Reason is applied to Facts of Experience or to the rules and maxims of the Understanding, but *absolute*, when the subject matter is itself the growth or offspring of the Reason. Hence arises a distinction in the Reason itself, derived from the different mode of applying it, and from the objects to which it is directed: according as we consider one and the same gift, now as the ground of formal principles, and now as the origin of *Ideas*. Contemplated distinctively in reference to *formal* (or abstract) truth, it is the *speculative* Reason; but in reference to *actual* (or moral) truth, as the fountain of ideas and the *Light* of the Conscience, we name it the *practical* Reason. Whenever

38 Kant.

by Self-subjection to this universal Light, the Will of the Individual, the *particular* Will, has become a Will of Reason, the man is regenerate: and Reason is then the *Spirit* of the regenerated man, whereby the Person is capable of a quickening intercommunion with the Divine Spirit. And herein consists the mystery of Redemption, that this has been rendered possible for us. "And so it is written: the first man Adam was made a living soul, the last Adam a quickening Spirit." (1 Cor. xv. 45.) We need only compare the passages in the writings of the Apostles Paul and John concerning the *Spirit* and Spiritual Gifts, with those in the Proverbs and in the Wisdom of Solomon respecting *Reason*, to be convinced that the terms are synonymous. In this at once most comprehensive and most appropriate acceptation of the word, Reason is pre-eminently spiritual, and a Spirit, even *our* Spirit, through an effluence of the same grace by which we are privileged to say Our Father!

On the other hand, the Judgements of the Understanding are binding only in relation to the objects of our Senses, which we *reflect* under the forms of the Understanding. It is, as Leighton rightly defines it, "the Faculty judging according to Sense." Hence we add the epithet *human*, without tautology: and speak of the *human* Understanding, in disjunction from that of Beings higher or lower than man. But there is, in this sense, no *human* Reason. There neither is nor can be but one Reason, one and the same: even the Light that lighteth every man's individual Understanding (*Discursus*) and thus maketh it a reasonable Understanding, *Discourse of Reason*—"one only, yet manifold; it goeth through all understanding, and remaining in itself regenerateth all other powers." (Wisdom of Solomon c. viii.) The same Writer calls it likewise "an influence from the *Glory of the Almighty*," this being one of the names of the Messiah, as the Logos, or co-eternal Filial Word. And most noticeable for its coincidence is a fragment of Heraclitus, as I have indeed already noticed elsewhere, "To discourse rationally it behoves us to derive strength from that which is common to all men: for all human Understandings are nourished by the one DIVINE WORD."

Beasts, we have said, partake of Understanding. If any man deny this, there is a ready way of settling the question. Let him give a careful perusal to Hüber's two small volumes, on Bees and on Ants (especially the latter), and to Kirby and Spence's Introduction to Entomology:[39] and one or other of two things must follow. He will either change his opinion as irreconcilable with the facts: or he must deny the facts, which yet I cannot suppose, inasmuch as the denial would be tantamount to the no less extravagant than uncharitable assertion, that Hüber, and the several eminent Naturalists, French and English, Swiss, German, and Italian, by whom Hüber's observations and experiments have been repeated and confirmed, had all conspired to impose a series of falsehoods and fairy-tales on the world. I see no way at least, by which he can get out of this dilemma, but by over-leaping the admitted Rules and Fences of all legitimate Discussion, and either transferring to the word, Understanding, the definition already appropriated to Reason, or defining Understanding *in genere* by the *specific* and *accessional* perfections which the *human* Understanding derives from its co-existence with Reason and Free-will in the same individual person; in plainer words, from its being exercised by a self-conscious and responsible Creature. And after all the supporter of Harrington's position would have a right to ask him, by what other name he would designate the faculty in the instances referred to? If it be not Understanding, what is it?

In no former part of this volume has the Editor felt the same anxiety to obtain a patient Attention. For he does not hesitate to avow, that on his success in establishing the validity and importance of the distinction between Reason and Understanding, he rests his hopes of carrying the Reader along with him through all that is to follow. Let the Student but clearly see and comprehend the diversity in the things themselves, the expediency of a correspondent distinction and appropriation of the *words* will follow of itself. Turn back for a moment to the Aphorism, and having reperused the first paragraph of this Comment thereon, regard the two following narratives as the illustration. I do not say proof: for I take these from a multitude of facts equally striking for the one only purpose of placing my *meaning* out of all doubt.

I. Huber put a dozen Humble-bees under a Bell-glass along with a comb of about ten silken cocoons so unequal in height as not to be capable of standing steadily. To remedy this two or three of the Humble-bees got upon the comb, stretched themselves over its edge, and with their heads downwards fixed their fore-feet on the table on which the comb stood, and so with their hind feet kept the comb from falling. When these were weary, others took their places. In this constrained

---

39 "Hüber's two small volumes" actually refers to works by two famous French naturalists, François Huber (1750–1831), author of *Nouvelles Observations sur les abeilles* (1792), and his son Pierre Huber (1777–1840), author of *Recherches sur les moeurs des fourmis*

indigénes (1810). Coleridge quotes later from the English translation of Pierre Huber's work, *The Natural History of Ants* (1820). The *Introduction to Entomology* was a voluminous work published between 1815 and 1826, by William Kirby (1759–1850) and William Spence (1783–1860).

and painful posture, fresh bees relieving their comrades at intervals, and each working in its turn, did
these affectionate little insects support the comb for
nearly three days: at the end of which they had prepared sufficient wax to build pillars with. But these
pillars having accidentally got displaced, the bees had
recourse again to the same manœuvre (or rather
pedœuvre), till Huber pitying their hard case, &c.

II. "I shall at present describe the operations of a
single ant that I observed sufficiently long to satisfy
my curiosity.

"One rainy day, I observed a Labourer digging the
ground near the aperture which gave entrance to the
ant-hill. It placed in a heap the several fragments it had
scraped up, and formed them into small pellets, which
it deposited here and there upon the nest. It returned
constantly to the same place, and appeared to have a
marked design, for it laboured with ardour and perseverance. I remarked a slight furrow, excavated in the
ground in a straight line, representing the plan of a
path or gallery. The Labourer, the whole of whose
movements fell under my immediate observation, gave
it greater depth and breadth, and cleared out its
borders: and I saw at length, in which I could not be
deceived, that it had the intention of establishing an
avenue which was to lead from one of the stories to the
under-ground chambers. This path, which was about
two or three inches in length, and formed by a single
ant, was opened above and bordered on each side by a
buttress of earth; its concavity en forme de gouttiere
was of the most perfect regularity, for the architect had
not left an atom too much. The work of this ant was so
well followed and understood, that I could almost to
a certainty guess its next proceeding, and the very
fragment it was about to remove. At the side of the
opening where this path terminated, was a second opening to which it was necessary to arrive by some road.
The same ant engaged in and executed alone this undertaking. It furrowed out and opened another path,
parallel to the first, leaving between each a little wall of
three or four lines in height. Those ants who lay the
foundation of a wall, a chamber, or gallery, from working separately occasion now and then a want of coincidence in the parts of the same or different objects.
Such examples are of no unfrequent occurrence, but
they by no means embarrass them. What follows
proves that the workman, on discovering his error,
knew how to rectify it. A wall had been erected with the
view of sustaining a vaulted ceiling, still incomplete,
that had been projected from the wall of the opposite
chamber. The workman who began constructing it,
had given it too little elevation to meet the opposite
partition upon which it was to rest. Has it been con-

tinued on the original plan, it must infallibly have
met the wall at about one half of its height, and this
it was necessary to avoid. This state of things very
forcibly claimed my attention, when one of the ants
arriving at the place, and visiting the works, appeared
to be struck by the difficulty which presented itself;
but this it as soon obviated, by taking down the
ceiling and raising the wall upon which it reposed. It
then in my presence, constructed a new ceiling with
the fragments of the former one."—*Huber's Natural
Hist. of Ants*, p. 38–41.

Now I assert, that the faculty manifested in the acts
here narrated does not differ *in kind* from Understanding, and that it *does* so differ from Reason. What I
conceive the former to be, physiologically considered,
will be shown hereafter. In this place I take the Understanding as it exists in *Men*, and in exclusive reference to its *intelligential* functions; and it is in this sense
of the word that I am to prove the necessity of contra-
distinguishing it from Reason.

Premising then, that two or more Subjects having
the same essential characters are said to fall under the
same General Definition, I lay it down, as a self-evident
truth (it is, in fact, an identical proposition), that
whatever subjects fall under one and the same General
Definition are of one and the same kind: consequently,
that which does *not* fall under this definition, must
differ in kind from each and all of those that *do*.
Difference in degree does indeed suppose sameness in
kind: and difference in kind precludes distinction from
differences of degree. *Heterogenea non comparari, ergo
nec distingui*, possunt.[40] The inattention to this Rule
gives rise to the numerous Sophisms comprised by
Aristotle under the head of Μεταβασις εις αλλο γενος,
i.e. Transition into a new kind, or the falsely applying
to X what had been truly asserted of A, and might have
been true of X, had it differed from A in its degree only.
The sophistry consists in the omission to notice what
not being noticed will be supposed not to exist; and
where the silence respecting the difference in kind is
tantamount to an assertion that the difference is merely
in degree. But the fraud is especially gross, where the
heterogeneous subject, thus clandestinely *slipt in*, is·
in its own nature insusceptible of degree: such as, for
instance, Certainty or Circularity, contrasted with
Strength, or Magnitude.

To apply these remarks for our present purpose, we
have only to describe Understanding and Reason, each
by its characteristic qualities. The comparison will
show the difference.

---

[40] *Heterogenea non* ... possunt: "Things different in kind
cannot be compared, and therefore cannot be distinguished."

UNDERSTANDING

1. Understanding is discursive.

2. The Understanding in all its judgments refers to some other Faculty as its ultimate Authority.

3. Understanding is the Faculty of *Reflection*.

REASON.

1. Reason is fixed.

2. The Reason in all its decisions appeals to itself, as the ground and *substance* of their truth. (*Hebrews*, vi. v. 13.)

3. Reason of Contemplation. Reason indeed is far nearer to SENSE than to Understanding: for Reason (says our great HOOKER) is a direct Aspect of Truth, an inward Beholding, having a similar relation to the Intelligible or Spiritual, as SENSE has to the Material or Phenomenal.

The Result is: that neither falls under the definition of the other. They differ *in kind:* and had my object been confined to the establishment of this fact, the preceding Columns would have superseded all further disquisition. But I have ever in view the especial interests of my youthful Readers, whose reflective *power* is to be cultivated, as well as their particular reflections to be called forth and guided. Now the main chance of their *reflecting* on religious subjects *aright*, and of their attaining to the *contemplation* of spiritual truths *at all*, rests on their insight into the *nature* of this disparity still more than on their conviction of its existence. I now, therefore, proceed to a brief analysis of the Understanding, in elucidation of the definitions already given.

The Understanding then (considered exclusively as an organ of human intelligence), is the Faculty by which we reflect and generalize. Take, for instance, any Object consisting of many parts, a House or a Group of Houses: and if it be contemplated, as a Whole, *i.e.* (as many constituting a One), it forms what in the technical language of Psychology is called a *total impression*. Among the various component parts of this we direct our attention especially to such as we recollect to have noticed in other total impressions. They, by a voluntary Act we withhold our attention from all the rest to reflect exclusively on these; and these we henceforward use as *common characters*, by virtue of which the several Objects are referred to one and the same sort.* Thus,

* According as we attend more or less to the differences, the *Sort* becomes, of course, more or less comprehensive. Hence there arises for the systematic Naturalist the necessity of sub-dividing

the whole Process may be reduced to three acts, all depending on and supposing a previous impression on the Senses: first, the appropriation of our Attention; 2. (and in order to the continuance of the first) Abstraction, or the voluntary withholding of the Attention; and 3. Generalization. And these are the proper Functions of the Understanding: and the power of so doing is what we mean when we say we possess Understanding, or are created with the Faculty of Understanding.

[It is obvious, that the third Function includes the act of comparing one object with another. In a note (for, not to interrupt the argument, I avail myself of this most useful contrivance), I have shown, that the act of comparing supposes in the comparing Faculty certain inherent Forms, that is, Modes of reflecting not referable to the Objects reflected on, but pre-determined by the Constitution and (as it were) mechanism of the Understanding itself. And under some one or other of these Forms,† the Resemblances and Differ-

the Sorts into Orders, Classes, Families, &c.: all which, however, resolve themselves for the mere Logician into the conception of Genus and Species, *i.e.* the comprehending and the comprehended.

† Were it not so, how could the first comparison have been possible? It would involve the absurdity of measuring a thing by itself. But if we fix on some one thing, the length of our own foot, or of our hand and arm from the elbow joint, it is evident that in *order* to do this we must have the conception of Measure. Now these antecedent and most general Conceptions are what is meant by the *constituent* forms of the Understanding: we call them *constituent* because they are not *acquired* by the Understanding, but are implied in its constitution. As rationally might a Circle be said to acquire a centre and circumference, as the Understanding to acquire these its inherent *forms*, or ways of conceiving. This is what Leibnitz meant, when to the old adage of the Peripatetics, Nihil in intellectu quod non prius in Sensu (There is nothing in the Understanding not derived from the Senses, or—There is nothing *conceived* that was not previously *perceived*); he replied —praeter intellectum ipsum (except the Understanding itself).

And here let me remark for once and all: whoever would *reflect* to any purpose—whoever is in earnest in his pursuit of Self-knowledge, and of one of the principal means to this, an insight into the meaning of the words he uses, and the different meanings properly or improperly conveyed by one and the same word, according as it is used in the Schools or the Market, according as the *kind* or a high *degree* is intended (ex. gr. Heat, Weight, &c. as employed scientifically, compared with the same word used popularly)—whoever, I say, seriously proposes this as his Object, must so far overcome his dislike of pedantry, and his dread of being sneered at as a Pedant, as not to quarrel with an uncouth word or phrase, till he is quite sure that some other and more familiar would not only have expressed the *precise* meaning with equal clearness, but have been as likely to draw his attention to *this* meaning exclusively. The ordinary language of a Philosopher in conversation or popular writings, compared with the language he uses in strict reasoning, is as his Watch compared with the Chronometer in his Observatory. He sets the former by the Town-clock, or even, perhaps, by the Dutch clock in his kitchen, not because he believes it right, but because his neighbour's and

ences must be subsumed in order to be conceivable, and à fortiori therefore in order to be comparable. The Senses do not compare, but merely furnish the materials for comparison. But this the Reader will find explained in the Note; and will now cast his eye back to the sentence immediately preceding this parenthesis.]

his Cook go by it. To afford the reader an opportunity for exercising the forbearance here recommended, I turn back to the phrase, "most general Conceptions," and observe, that in strict and severe propriety of language I should have said *generalific* or *generific* rather than general, the Concipiencies or Conceptive Acts rather than conceptions.

It is an old Complaint, that a Man of Genius no sooner appears, but the Host of Dunces are up in arms to repel the invading Alien. This observation would have made more converts to its truth, I suspect, had it been worded more dispassionately, and with a less contemptuous antithesis. For "Dunces" let us substitute "the Many" or the "τουτος κοσμος" (*this world*) of the Apostle, and we shall perhaps find no great difficulty in accounting for the fact. To arrive at the *root*, indeed, and last Ground of the problem, it would be necessary to investigate the nature and effects of the sense of Difference on the human mind where it is not held in check by Reason and Reflection. We need not go to the savage tribes of North America, or the yet ruder Natives of the Indian Isles, to learn, how slight a degree of Difference will, in uncultured minds, call up a sense of Diversity, an inward perplexity and contradiction, as if the Strangers were and yet were not of the same *kind* with themselves. Who has not had occasion to observe the effect which the gesticulations and nasal tones of a Frenchman produce on our own Vulgar? Here we may see the origin and primary import of our "*Unkindness*." It is a sense of *Un*kind, and not the mere negation but the positive Opposite of the sense of *kind*. Alienation, aggravated now by fear, now by contempt, and not seldom by a mixture of both, aversion, hatred, enmity, are so many successive shapes of its growth and metamorphosis. In application to the present case, it is sufficient to say, that Pindar's remark on sweet Music holds equally true of Genius: as many as are not delighted by it are disturbed, perplexed, irritated. The Beholder either recognizes it as a projected Form of his own Being, that moves before him with a Glory round its head, or recoils from it as from a Spectre. But this speculation would lead us too far; we must be content with having referred to it as the ultimate ground of the fact, and pass to the more obvious and proximate causes. And as the first, I would rank the Person's *not* understanding what yet he expects to understand, and as if he had a *right* to do so. An original Mathematical Work, or any other that requires peculiar and (so to say) technical marks and symbols, will excite no uneasy feelings—not in the mind of a competent Reader, for he understands it; and not with others, because they neither expect nor are expected to understand it. The second place we may assign to the *Mis*understanding, which is almost sure to follow in cases where the incompetent person, finding no outward marks (Diagrams, arbitrary signs, and the like) to inform him at first sight, that the Subject is one which he does not pretend to understand, and to be ignorant of which does not detract from his estimation as a man of abilities generally, *will* attach some meaning to what he hears or reads; and as he is out of humour with the Author, it will most often be such a meaning as he can quarrel with and exhibit in a ridiculous or offensive point of view.

But above all, the whole World almost of Minds, as far as regards intellectual efforts, may be divided into two classes of the Busy-indolent and Lazy-indolent. To both alike all Thinking is

Now when a person speaking to us of any particular Object or Appearance refers it by means of some common character to a known class (which he does in giving it a Name), we say, that we understand him; *i.e.* we understand his words. The Name of a thing, in the original sense of the word, Name (*Nomen*, Νουμενον,

painful, and all attempts to rouse them to think, whether in the re-examination of their existing Convictions, or for the reception of new light, are irritating. "It *may* all be very deep and clever; but really one ought to be quite sure of it before one wrenches one's brain to find out what it is. I take up a Book as a Companion, with whom I can have an easy cheerful chit-chat on what we both know beforehand, or else matters of fact. In our leisure hours we have a right to relaxation and amusement."

Well! but in their *studious* hours, when their Bow is to be bent, when they are *apud Musas*, or amidst the Muses? Alas! it is just the same! The same craving for *amusement*, *i.e.* to be away from the Muses! for relaxation, *i.e.* the unbending of a Bow which in fact had never been strung! There are two ways of obtaining their applause. The first is: Enable them to reconcile in one and the same occupation the love of Sloth and the hatred of Vacancy! Gratify indolence, and yet save them from *Ennui*—in plain English, from themselves! For, spite of their antipathy to *dry* reading, the keeping company with themselves is, after all, the insufferable annoyance: and the true secret of their dislike to a work of Thought and Inquiry lies in its tendency to make them acquainted with their own permanent Being. The other road to their favour is, to introduce to them their own thoughts and predilections, tricked out in the *fine* language, in which it would gratify their vanity to express them in their own conversation, and with which they can imagine themselves *showing off*: and this (as has been elsewhere remarked)[41] is the characteristic difference between the second-rate Writers of the last two or three generations, and the same class under Elizabeth and the Stuarts. In the latter we find the most far-fetched and singular thoughts in the simplest and most native language; in the former, the most obvious and common-place thoughts in the most far-fetched and motley language. But lastly, and as the sine quâ non of their patronage, a sufficient arc must be left for the Reader's mind to *oscillate* in—freedom of choice,

To make the shifting cloud be what you please,

save only where the attraction of Curiosity determines the line of Motion. The Attention must not be fastened down: and this every work of Genius, not simply narrative, must do before it can be justly appreciated.

In former times a *popular* work meant one that adapted the *results* of studious Meditation or scientific Research to the capacity of the People, presenting in the Concrete, by instances and examples, what had been ascertained in the Abstract and by discovery of the Law. *Now*, on the other hand, that is a popular Work which gives back to the People their own errors and prejudices, and flatters the Many by creating them, under the title of the PUBLIC, into a supreme and inappellable Tribunal of intellectual Excellence. P.S. In a continuous work, the frequent insertion and length of Notes would need an Apology: in a book of Aphorisms and detached Comments none is necessary, it being understood beforehand, that the Sauce and the Garnish are to occupy the greater part of the Dish. S.T.C.

---

41 In *Biographia Literaria*, Chapter I, p. 175. The quotation below, "To make . . . what you please," is from Coleridge's sonnet "Fancy in Nubibus" (1818), l. 3.

τò *intelligibile, id quod intelligitur*) expresses that which is *understood* in an appearance, that which we place (or make to *stand*) *under* it, as the condition of its real existence, and in proof that it is not an accident of the Senses, or Affection of the Individual, not a phantom or *Apparition, i.e.* an Appearance that is *only* an Appearance. (See Gen. ii. 19. 20. Thus too, in Psalm xx. v. 1. and in fifty other places of the Bible, the identity of nomen with numen, *i.e.* invisible power and presence, the *nomen substantivum* of all real Objects, and the ground of their reality, independent of the Affections of Sense in the Percipient). In like manner, in a connected succession of Names, as the Speaker passes from one to the other, we say that we understand his *discourse* (*i.e. discursio* intellectûs, *discursus,* from discurso or discurro, to *course* or pass rapidly from one thing to another). Thus, in all instances, it is words, names, or, if images, yet images used as words or names, that are the alone subjects of Understanding. In no instance do we understand a thing in itself; but only the name to which it is referred. Sometimes indeed, when several classes are recalled conjointly, we identify the words with the Object—though by courtesy of idiom rather than in strict propriety of language. Thus, we may say that we *understand* a Rainbow, when recalling successively the several Names for the several sorts of Colours, we know that they are to be applied to one and the same Phænomenon, at once distinctly and simultaneously; but even in common parlance we should not say this of a single colour. No one would say he understands Red or Blue. He *sees* the Colour, and had seen it before in a vast number and variety of objects; and he understands the *word* red, as referring his fancy or memory to this his collective experience.

If this be so, and so it most assuredly is—if the proper functions of the understanding be that of generalizing the notices received from the Senses in order to the construction of *Names;* of referring particular notices (*i.e.* impressions or sensations) to their proper Name; and, vice versâ, names to their correspondent class or kind of Notices—then it follows of necessity, that the understanding is truly and accurately defined in the words of Leighton and Kant, a Faculty judging according to Sense.

Now whether in defining the speculative Reason (*i.e.* the Reason considered abstractedly as an *intellective* Power) we call it "the source of necessary and universal Principles, according to which the Notices of the Senses are either affirmed or denied;" or describe it as "the Power by which we are enabled to draw from particular and contingent Appearances universal and necessary conclusions ": * it is equally evident that the two defini-

* Take a familiar illustration. My Sight and Touch convey to me a certain impression, to which my Understanding applies its

tions differ in their essential characters, and consequently (by Axiom, p. 282) the Subjects differ in *kind.* Q.E.D.

preconceptions (*conceptus antecedentes et generalissimi*) of Quantity and Relation, and thus refers it to the Class and Name of three-cornered Bodies—We will suppose it the Iron of a Turf-spade. It compares the sides, and finds that any two measured as one are greater than the third; and according to a law of the imagination, there arises a presumption that in all other Bodies of the same figure (*i.e.* three-cornered and equilateral) the same proportion exists. After this, the senses have been directed successively to a number of three-cornered bodies of *unequal* sides—and in these too the same proportion has been found without exception till at length it becomes a fact of *experience,* that in *all* Triangles hitherto seen the two sides are greater than the third: and there will exist no ground or analogy for anticipating an exception to a Rule, generalized from so vast a number of particular instances. So far and no farther could the Understanding carry us: and as far as this "the faculty, judging according to sense," conducts many of the *inferior* animals, if not in the same, yet in instances analogous and fully equivalent.

The Reason supersedes the whole process; and on the first conception presented by the Understanding in consequence of the first sight of a tri-angular Figure, of whatever sort it might chance to be, it affirms with an assurance incapable of future increase, with a perfect *certainty,* that in all possible Triangles any two of the inclosing Lines *will* and *must* be greater than the third. In short, Understanding in its highest form of Experience remains commensurate with the experimental notices of the senses, from which it is generalized. Reason, on the other hand, either pre-determines Experience, or avails itself of a past Experience to supersede its necessity in all future time; and affirms truths which no Sense could perceive, nor Experiment verify, nor Experience confirm.

Yea, this is the test and character of a truth so affirmed, that in its own proper form it is *inconceivable*. For to *conceive* is a function of the Understanding, which can be exercised only on subjects subordinate thereto. And yet to the forms of the Understanding all truth must be reduced, that is to be fixed as an object of reflection, and to be rendered *expressible*. And here we have a second test and sign of a truth so affirmed, that it can come forth out of the moulds of the Understanding only in the disguise of two contradictory conceptions, each of which is partially true, and the conjunction of both conceptions becomes the representative or *expression* (= *exponent*) of a truth *beyond* conception and inexpressible. Examples. Before Abraham *was,* I *am.*—God is a Circle whose centre is every where and circumference no where.—The Soul is all in every part.

If this appear extravagant, it is an extravagance which no man can indeed learn from another, but which (were this possible) I might have learnt from Plato, Kepler, and Bacon; from Luther, Hooker, Pascal, Leibnitz, and Fenelon. But in this last paragraph I have, I see, unwittingly overstepped my purpose, according to which we were to take Reason as a simply intellectual power. Yet even as such, and with all the disadvantage of a technical and arbitrary Abstraction, it has been made evident—1. that there is an *Intuition* or immediate Beholding, accompanied by a conviction of the necessity and universality of the truth so beheld not derived from the Senses, which Intuition, when it is *construed* by *pure* Sense, gives birth to the Science of Mathematics, and when applied to Objects supersensuous or spiritual is the Organ of Theology and Philosophy; and 2. that there is likewise a reflective and discursive Faculty, or *mediate* Apprehension which, taken by itself and uninfluenced by the former, depends on the Senses

The dependence of the Understanding on the representations of the Senses, and its consequent posteriority thereto, as contrasted with the independence and antecedency of Reason, are strikingly exemplified in the Ptolemaic System (that truly wonderful product and highest boast of the Faculty, judging according to the Senses!) compared with the Newtonian, as the Offspring of a yet higher Power, arranging, correcting, and annulling the representations of the Senses according to its own inherent Laws and constitutive Ideas.

APHORISM IX   EDITOR.

In Wonder all Philosophy began: in Wonder it ends: and Admiration fills up the interspace. But the first Wonder is the Offspring of Ignorance: the last is the Parent of Adoration. The First is the birth-throe of our knowledge: the Last is its euthanasy and apotheosis.

*   *   *   *   *

[1825]

---

for the Materials on which it is exercised, and is contained within the Sphere of the Senses. And this Faculty it is, which in generalizing the Notices of the Senses constitutes Sensible Experience, and gives rise to Maxims and Rules which may become more and more *general*, but can never be raised into universal Verities, or beget a consciousness of absolute Certainty; though they may be sufficient to extinguish all doubt. (Putting Revelation out of view, take our first Progenitor in the 50th or 100th year of his existence. His Experience would probably have freed him from all doubt, as the Sun sunk in the Horizon that it would re-appear the next morning. But compare this state of Assurance with that which the same Man would have had of the 37th Proposition of Euclid, supposing him like Pythagoras to have discovered the *Demonstration*). Now is it expedient, I ask, or conformable to the laws and purposes of Language, to call two so altogether disparate Subjects by one and the same name? Or, having two names in our language, should we call each of the two diverse subjects by both —*i.e.* by either name, as caprice might dictate? If not, then as we have the two words, Reason and Understanding (as indeed what Language of cultivated Man has not?) what should prevent us from appropriating the former to the Power distinctive of Humanity? We need only place the derivatives from the two terms in opposition (*ex. gr.* "A and B are both rational Beings; but there is no comparison between them in point of intelligence," or "She always concludes *rationally*, though not a Woman of much *Understanding*") to see, that we cannot reverse the order—*i.e.* call the higher Gift Understanding, and the lower Reason. What *should* prevent us? I asked. Alas! that which *has* prevented us—the cause of this confusion in the terms—is only too obvious: viz. inattention to the momentous distinction in the *things*, and (generally) to the duty and habit recommended in the Vth Intro-

ductory Aphorism of this Volume. But the cause of this, and of all its lamentable Effects and Subcauses, "false doctrine, blindness of Heart and contempt of the Word," is best declared by the philosophic Apostle: "they did not *like* to retain God in their knowledge," (Rom. i. 28), and though they could not extinguish "the Light that lighteth every man," and which "shone in the Darkness;" yet because the Darkness could not *comprehend* the Light, they refused to bear witness of the Light, and worshipped, instead, the shaping Mist, which the Light had drawn upward from *the Ground* (*i.e.* from the mere Animal nature and instinct), and which that Light alone had made visible (*i.e.* by superinducing on the animal instinct the principle of Self-consciousness).[42]

---

[42] "The 37th Proposition of Euclid" is more accurately the 47th proposition: "In right-angle triangles, the square of the hypotenuse is equal to the sum of the squares of the other two sides." "The Vth Introductory Aphorism" of *Aids to Reflection* reads: "As a fruit-tree is more valuable than any one of its fruits singly, or even than all its fruits of a single season, so the noblest object of reflection is the mind itself, by which we reflect: And as the blossoms, the green and the ripe fruit of an orange-tree are more beautiful to behold when on the tree and seen as one with it, than the same growth detached and seen successively, after their importation into another country and different clime; so it is with the manifold objects of reflection, when they are considered principally in reference to the reflective power, and as part and parcel of the same. No object, of whatever value our passions may represent it, but becomes foreign to us as soon as it is altogether unconnected with our intellectual, moral, and spiritual life. To be ours, it must be referred to the mind, either as motive, or consequence, or symptom."

Robert Southey

1774 – 1843

OUTLINE OF EVENTS

1774   Born August 12, at Bristol, second of nine children and eldest surviving son of Robert (1745—1792), shopkeeper, and Margaret (Hill) Southey (1752-1802). Spends part of his early years with his aunt in Bath, attends different schools, and begins to write poetry in a variety of forms (epics, epistles, etc.).

1788–92   Attends Westminster School, London; develops unorthodox religious opinions and becomes exponent of French Revolution. Publishes article against flogging in the Westminster paper *The Flagellant*, resulting in his expulsion from the school and denial of admission to Christ Church College, Oxford.

1793–94   In residence at Balliol College, Oxford. Writes revolutionary poem *Joan of Arc* (published 1796). Refuses to take Anglican orders and enters period of uncertainty about his future career. June 1794, meets Coleridge and develops idea of emigrating to America and forming a community of idealistic young men and their wives ("Pantisocracy") on the banks of the Susquehanna. August, becomes engaged to Edith Fricker (another Pantisocratic exponent, Robert Lovell, had earlier married Mary Fricker). The drama by Southey and Coleridge, *The Fall of Robespierre,* and *Poems by Robert Lovell and Robert Southey* published. Writes radical drama *Wat Tyler* (see under 1817).

1795   January, meets Charles Lamb in London. March–April, delivers historical lectures in Bristol (partly written by Coleridge); growing alienation from Coleridge and abandonment of Pantisocracy. September, meets Wordsworth. November, secretly marries Edith Fricker. December, departs for Portugal with his uncle, who is Anglican chaplain at Oporto.

1796   May, returns to England after travels in Spain and Portugal; partial reconciliation with Coleridge. Begins contributing to *Monthly Magazine*.

1797   February, begins study of law in London. *Letters Written During a Short Residence in Spain and Portugal* and *Poems by Robert Southey* published. Begins to contribute reviews to *The Critical Review*.

1798   Begins to contribute verses to *The Morning Post*.

1799   Edits and contributes to *Annual Anthology* (including poems by Lamb, Coleridge, and other friends). Period of ill health.

1800   April, continuing illness causes Southey and Edith to leave for Portugal, where he begins to prepare a history of Portugal.

1801   Epic poem *Thalaba the Destroyer* published. June, returns to England. August, first visits Lake District. October, in Dublin briefly as secretary to the Chancellor of the Exchequer for Ireland.

1802   August, daughter Margaret born, first of the Southeys' eight children.

1803   Begins to contribute reviews (of poetry, travel literature, memoirs, etc.) to *The Annual Review* (until 1809). September, takes up lifelong residence at Greta Hall, Keswick, sharing house with the Coleridge family. The translation *Amadis of Gaul* and edition of *The Works of Thomas Chatterton* published.

1805   April, epic poem *Madoc* published; meets Sir Walter Scott.

1807   Translation of the Portuguese romance *Palmerin of England*, editions of *Specimens of later English Poets* and *The Remains of Henry Kirke White*, and the satirical *Letters from England by Don Manuel Alvarez Espriella* published. November, meets De Quincey; receives government pension through his school friend Charles W. W. Wynn, under-secretary for the Home Department.

1808   March, meets Walter Savage Landor, beginning an important literary friendship. *Chronicle of the Cid* published.

1809   Begins long period of contributions to the conservative *Quarterly Review*, reflecting the change in Southey's political thought; begins to write the historical section of *Edinburgh Annual Register* (until 1813).

1810   Epic poem *The Curse of Kehama* and first volume of *History of Brazil* published.

1811   December, meets Shelley at Keswick.

1812   *Omniana*, collection of short notes and commentaries by Southey and Coleridge, published.

1813   September, appointed Poet Laureate; meets Byron in London. *Life of Nelson* published.

1814   Epic poem *Roderick, the Last of the Goths* published.

1815   September–October, visits Waterloo and Low Countries; writes *A Poet's Pilgrimage to Waterloo* (published 1816).

1816   April, death of his favorite son Herbert. Begins to write major essays on political conditions in England for *Quarterly Review; Lay of the Laureate* published.

1817   Unauthorized publication of his early radical work *Wat Tyler* causes much embarrassment and many political attacks; he replies in his *Letter to William Smith, Esq., M.P.*

1819   Final volume of *History of Brazil* published.

1820   *Life of Wesley* published and attacked by Nonconformists. June, receives honorary degree from Oxford; first meets Caroline Bowles, later to become his second wife.

1821   *A Vision of Judgment*, a tribute on the death of George III, published.

1823   First volume of *History of the Peninsular War* published.

1824   *The Book of the Church*, an ecclesiastical history of England, published and attacked by Catholics.

1825–26 Visits Low Countries. Is offered seat in parliament but declines.

1829   *Sir Thomas More: or, Colloquies on the Progress and Prospects of Society* published.

1830–43 Final years marked by sadness over deaths of his children and friends, the insanity of his wife Edith, and fears of the political changes in England.

1832   *Essays Moral and Political* (a collection of *Quarterly Review* articles) and final volume of *History of Peninsular War* published.

1834   First two volumes of the miscellaneous work *The Doctor* (including the story of the three bears) published. Mrs. Southey placed in asylum.

1835   Is offered baronetcy by Prime Minister Peel, but declines. His government pension is increased. Multivolumed edition of the *Works of William Cowper* begins to be published.

1837   November, death of Mrs. Southey. Begins publication of the revised edition of his poems.

1839   June, marries Caroline Bowles. Suffers from declining health and mental debility.

1843   Dies, March 21 at Keswick.

SELECTED BIBLIOGRAPHY

BIOGRAPHY

HALLER, WILLIAM, *The Early Life of Robert Southey, 1774–1803*, Columbia University Studies in English and Comparative Literature, New York: Columbia University Press, 1917.

SIMMONS, JACK, *Southey*, London: Collins, 1945.

SOUTHEY, C. C. (ed.), *The Life and Correspondence of Robert Southey*, 6 vols., London: Longman, Brown, Green, and Longmans, 1849–1850.

EDITIONS OF SOUTHEY'S PROSE

CABRAL, ADOLFO (ed.), *Robert Southey: Journals of a Residence in Portugal 1800–1801 and a Visit to France 1838*, Oxford: Clarendon Press, 1960.

CALLENDER, GEOFFREY (ed.), *Life of Nelson*, London: J. M. Dent and Sons, 1922.

FITZGERALD, MAURICE H. (ed.), *Robert Southey: Life of Wesley*, 2 vols., London: Humphrey Milford, 1925.

SIMMONS, JACK (ed.), *Letters from England by Robert Southey*, London: Cresset Press, 1951.

ZEITLIN, JACOB (ed.), *Select Prose of Robert Southey*, New York: The Macmillan Company, 1916.

SCHOLARSHIP AND CRITICISM

BRINTON, CRANE, *The Political Ideas of the English Romanticists*, London: Oxford University Press, 1926.

CARNALL, GEOFFREY, *Robert Southey and his Age: the Development of a Conservative Mind*, Oxford: Clarendon Press, 1960.

COBBAN, ALFRED, *Edmund Burke and the Revolt against the Eighteenth Century*, London: G. Allen and Unwin, 1929.

GRAHAM, WALTER, "Robert Southey as Tory Reviewer," *Philological Quarterly*, II (1923), 97–111.

HALLER, WILLIAM, "Southey's Later Radicalism," *PMLA*, XXXVII (1922), 281–92.

RAIMOND, JEAN, *Robert Southey: L'homme et son temps; L'oeuvre; Le Role*, Paris: Didier, 1968.

THE LIFE OF NELSON

Robert Southey was one of the most prolific and versatile prose-writers of the early nineteenth century, his productions including massive historical studies, eloquent biographies, travel literature, translations of major continental masterpieces, important journalistic essays on the political and social concerns of the day, and innumerable literary reviews. "His prose is perfect," Byron wrote; and the statement is indicative of the almost universal admiration of Southey as the finest prose stylist of the day. Even William Hazlitt, who regularly hurled abuse and ridicule upon Southey's political opinions, declared that his prose style "can scarcely be too much praised. . . . He is the best and most natural prose-writer of any poet of the day." Clarity and simplicity were the qualities of his style most frequently cited. ". . . [Y]ou read page after page," Coleridge recorded, "understanding the author perfectly, without once taking notice of the medium of the communication; it is as if he had been speaking to you all the while." The most enduring of all Southey's prose writings is The Life of Nelson, which first appeared in 1813 and went through six editions in his lifetime. Here reproduced from the revised edition of 1830 is a selection from the final chapter on the Battle of Trafalgar and death of Nelson on October 21, 1805. The patriotic fervor of Southey and his high moral regard for the character of Nelson achieve genuine eloquence and power, and avoid fulsomeness, through the objectivity of perspective produced by the wealth of detail and historical fact.

FROM

THE LIFE OF NELSON

CHAPTER IX

*   *   *   *   *

SOON after daylight, Nelson came upon deck. The 21st of October was a festival in his family, because on that day his uncle, Capt. Suckling, in the Dreadnought, with two other line of battle ships, had beaten off a French squadron of four sail of the line, and three frigates. Nelson, with that sort of superstition from which few persons are entirely exempt, had more than once expressed his persuasion that this was to be the day of his battle also; and he was well pleased at seeing his prediction about to be verified. The wind was now from the west, light breezes, with a long heavy swell. Signal was made to bear down upon the

enemy in two lines; and the fleet set all sail. Collingwood,[1] in the Royal Sovereign, led the lee line of
thirteen ships; the Victory[2] led the weather line of
fourteen. Having seen that all was as it should be,
Nelson retired to his cabin, and wrote the following
prayer:

"May the great God, whom I worship, grant to
my country, and for the benefit of Europe in general,
a great and glorious victory, and may no misconduct
in any one tarnish it; and may humanity after victory
be the predominant feature in the British fleet! For
myself individually, I commit my life to Him that
made me; and may his blessing alight on my endeavours
for serving my country faithfully! To Him I resign
myself, and the just cause which is entrusted to me to
defend. Amen, Amen, Amen." . . .

Blackwood[3] went on board the Victory about six.
He found him in good spirits, but very calm; not in
that exhilaration which he had felt upon entering into
battle at Aboukir and Copenhagen: he knew that his
own life would be particularly aimed at, and seems to
have looked for death with almost as sure an expectation as for victory. His whole attention was fixed upon
the enemy. They tacked to the northward, and formed
their line on the larboard tack; thus bringing the
shoals of Trafalgar and St. Pedro under the lee of the
British, and keeping the port of Cadiz open for themselves. This was judiciously done: and Nelson, aware
of all the advantages which it gave them, made signal
to prepare to anchor.

Villeneuve[4] was a skilful seaman; worthy of serving
a better master, and a better cause. His plan of defence
was as well conceived, and as original, as the plan of
attack. He formed the fleet in a double line; every
alternate ship being about a cable's length to windward
of her second ahead and astern. Nelson, certain of a
triumphant issue to the day, asked Blackwood what
he should consider as a victory. That officer answered,
that, considering the handsome way in which battle
was offered by the enemy, their apparent determination for a fair trial of strength, and the situation of the
land, he thought it would be a glorious result if
fourteen were captured. He replied: "I shall not be
satisfied with less than twenty." Soon afterwards he
asked him, if he did not think there was a signal

wanting. Capt. Blackwood made answer, that he
thought the whole fleet seemed very clearly to understand what they were about. These words were
scarcely spoken before that signal was made, which
will be remembered as long as the language, or even
the memory of England, shall endure;—Nelson's
last signal:—"ENGLAND EXPECTS EVERY MAN
TO DO HIS DUTY!" It was received throughout the
fleet with a shout of answering acclamation, made
sublime by the spirit which it breathed, and the
feeling which it expressed. "Now," said Lord Nelson,
"I can do no more. We must trust to the great Disposer
of all events, and the justice of our cause. I thank God
for this great opportunity of doing my duty."

He wore that day, as usual, his admiral's frock coat,
bearing on the left breast four stars, of the different
orders with which he was invested. Ornaments which
rendered him so conspicuous a mark for the enemy,
were beheld with ominous apprehensions by his
officers. It was known that there were riflemen on
board the French ships; and it could not be doubted
but that his life would be particularly aimed at. They
communicated their fears to each other; and the
surgeon, Mr. Beatty,* spoke to the chaplain, Dr.
Scott, and to Mr. Scott, the public secretary, desiring
that some person would entreat him to change his
dress, or cover the stars: but they knew that such a
request would highly displease him. "In honour I
gained them," he had said, when such a thing had been
hinted to him formerly, "and in honour I will die with
them." Mr. Beatty, however, would not have been
deterred by any fear of exciting his displeasure, from
speaking to him himself upon a subject, in which the
weal of England, as well as the life of Nelson, was
concerned,—but he was ordered from the deck before
he could find an opportunity. This was a point upon
which Nelson's officers knew that it was hopeless to
remonstrate or reason with him; but both Blackwood,
and his own captain, Hardy, represented to him how
advantageous to the fleet it would be for him to keep
out of action as long as possible; and he consented at
last to let the Leviathan and the Téméraire, which
were sailing abreast of the Victory, be ordered to pass
ahead. Yet even here the last infirmity of this noble
mind was indulged, for these ships could not pass
ahead if the Victory continued to carry all her sail;
and so far was Nelson from shortening sail, that it was
evident he took pleasure in pressing on, and rendering
it impossible for them to obey his own orders. A
long swell was setting into the bay of Cadiz: our

---

[1] Cuthbert Collingwood (1750–1810). For his part in the
battle of Trafalgar, he was raised to the peerage as Baron Collingwood and succeeded Nelson as commander-in-chief of British
naval forces.

[2] Nelson's flagship.

[3] Sir Henry Blackwood (1770–1832) was a captain in the British
navy at the time of Trafalgar. He later rose to the rank of vice-
admiral.

[4] Pierre-Charles-Silvestre de Villeneuve (1763–1806) was the
commander of the French fleet at Trafalgar.

---

* In this part of the work I have chiefly been indebted to this
gentleman's Narrative of Lord Nelson's Death—a document as
interesting as it is authentic.

ships, crowding all sail, moved majestically before it, with light winds from the south-west. The sun shone on the sails of the enemy; and their well formed line, with their numerous three-deckers, made an appearance which any other assailants would have thought formidable;—but the British sailors only admired the beauty and the splendour of the spectacle; and, in full confidence of winning what they saw, remarked to each other, what a fine sight yonder ships would make at Spithead![5]

The French admiral, from the Bucentaure, beheld the new manner in which his enemy was advancing—Nelson and Collingwood each leading his line; and, pointing them out to his officers, he is said to have exclaimed, that such conduct could not fail to be successful. Yet Villeneuve had made his own dispositions with the utmost skill, and the fleets under his command waited for the attack with perfect coolness. Ten minutes before twelve they opened their fire. Eight or nine of the ships immediately ahead of the Victory, and across her bows, fired single guns at her, to ascertain whether she was yet within their range. As soon as Nelson perceived that their shot passed over him, he desired Blackwood, and Capt. Prowse, of the Sirius, to repair to their respective frigates; and, on their way, to tell all the captains of the line of battle ships that he depended on their exertions; and that, if by the prescribed mode of attack they found it impracticable to get into action immediately, they might adopt whatever they thought best, provided it led them quickly and closely alongside an enemy. As they were standing on the front of the poop, Blackwood took him by the hand, saying, he hoped soon to return and find him in possession of twenty prizes. He replied, "God bless you, Blackwood: I shall never see you again."

Nelson's column was steered about two points more to the north than Collingwood's, in order to cut off the enemy's escape into Cadiz: the lee line, therefore, was first engaged. "See," cried Nelson, pointing to the Royal Sovereign, as she steered right for the centre of the enemy's line, cut through it astern of the Santa Anna, three-decker, and engaged her at the muzzle of her guns on the starboard side: "see how that noble fellow, Collingwood, carries his ship into action!" Collingwood, delighted at being first in the heat of the fire, and knowing the feelings of his commander and old friend, turned to his captain, and exclaimed: "Rotherham, what would Nelson give to be here!" Both these brave officers, perhaps, at this moment thought of Nelson with gratitude, for a circumstance which had occurred on the preceding day. Admiral Collingwood, with some of the captains, having gone on board the Victory, to receive instructions, Nelson inquired of him, where his captain was? and was told, in reply, that they were not upon good terms with each other. "Terms!" said Nelson;—"good terms with each other!" Immediately he sent a boat for Captain Rotherham; led him, as soon as he arrived, to Collingwood, and saying,—"Look; yonder are the enemy!" bade them shake hands like Englishmen.

The enemy continued to fire a gun at a time at the Victory, till they saw that a shot had passed through her main-top-gallant sail; then they opened their broadsides, aiming chiefly at her rigging, in the hope of disabling her before she could close with them. Nelson, as usual, had hoisted several flags, lest one should be shot away. The enemy showed no colours till late in the action, when they began to feel the necessity of having them to strike.[6] For this reason, the Santissima Trinidad, Nelson's old acquaintance, as he used to call her, was distinguishable only by her four decks; and to the bow of this opponent he ordered the Victory to be steered. Meantime an incessant raking fire was kept up upon the Victory. The admiral's secretary was one of the first who fell; he was killed by a cannon shot while conversing with Hardy. Capt. Adair of the marines, with the help of a sailor, endeavoured to remove the body from Nelson's sight, who had a great regard for Mr. Scott: but he anxiously asked: "Is that poor Scott that's gone?" and being informed that it was indeed so, exclaimed: "Poor fellow!" Presently a double-headed shot struck a party of marines, who were drawn up on the poop and killed eight of them: upon which, Nelson immediately desired Capt. Adair to disperse his men round the ship, that they might not suffer so much from being together. A few minutes afterwards a shot struck the fore brace bits on the quarter deck, and passed between Nelson and Hardy, a splinter from the bit tearing off Hardy's buckle and bruising his foot. Both stopped, and looked anxiously at each other, each supposed the other to be wounded. Nelson then smiled, and said, "This is too warm work, Hardy, to last long."

The Victory had not yet returned a single gun; fifty of her men had been by this time killed or wounded and her main-top-mast, with all her studding sails and her booms, shot away. Nelson declared, that, in all his battles, he had seen nothing which surpassed the cool courage of his crew on this occasion. At four

---

5 Spithead was the main anchorage of the British fleet between the Isle of Wight and the mainland of England; it was also the site of naval reviews in the celebration of major victories.

6 Lower, as a sign of surrender.

minutes after twelve, she opened her fire from both sides of her deck. It was not possible to break the enemy's line without running on board one of their ships: Hardy informed him of this, and asked him which he would prefer. Nelson replied: "Take your choice, Hardy, it does not signify much." The master was ordered to put the helm to port, and the Victory ran on board the Redoutable, just as her tiller ropes were shot away. The French ship received her with a broadside; then instantly let down her lower deck ports, for fear of being boarded through them, and never afterwards fired a great gun during the action. Her tops, like those of all the enemy's ships, were filled with riflemen. Nelson never placed musketry in his tops; he had a strong dislike to the practice; not merely because it endangers setting fire to the sails, but also because it is a murderous sort of warfare, by which individuals may suffer, and a commander now and then be picked off, but which never can decide the fate of a general engagement.

Capt. Harvey, in the Téméraire, fell on board the Redoutable on the other side. Another enemy was in like manner on board the Téméraire: so that these four ships formed as compact a tier as if they had been moored together, their heads lying all the same way. The lieutenants of the Victory, seeing this, depressed their guns of the middle and lower decks, and fired with a diminished charge, lest the shot should pass through, and injure the Téméraire. And because there was danger that the Redoutable might take fire from the lower-deck guns, the muzzles of which touched her side when they were run out, the fire-man of each gun stood ready with a bucket of water; which, as soon as the gun was discharged, he dashed into the hole made by the shot. An incessant fire was kept up from the Victory from both sides; her larboard guns playing upon the Bucentaure and the huge Santissima Trinidad.

It had been part of Nelson's prayer, that the British fleet might be distinguished by humanity in the victory which he expected. Setting an example himself, he twice gave orders to cease firing upon the Redoutable, supposing that she had struck, because her great guns were silent; for, as she carried no flag, there was no means of instantly ascertaining the fact. From this ship, which he had thus twice spared, he received his death. A ball fired from her mizen-top, which, in the then situation of the two vessels, was not more than fifteen yards from that part of the deck where he was standing, struck the epaulette on his left shoulder, about a quarter after one, just in the heat of action. He fell upon his face, on the spot which was covered with his poor secretary's blood. Hardy, who was a few steps from him, turning round, saw three men raising him up.—"They have done for me at last, Hardy," said he.—"I hope not," cried Hardy.—"Yes!" he replied; "my back-bone is shot through." Yet even now, not for a moment losing his presence of mind, he observed, as they were carrying him down the ladder, that the tiller ropes, which had been shot away, were not yet replaced, and ordered that new ones should be rove immediately:—then, that he might not be seen by the crew, he took out his handkerchief, and covered his face and his stars.—Had he but concealed these badges of honour from the enemy, England, perhaps, would not have had cause to receive with sorrow the news of the battle of Trafalgar. The cockpit was crowded with wounded and dying men; over whose bodies he was with some difficulty conveyed, and laid upon a pallet in the midshipmen's birth. It was soon perceived, upon examination, that the wound was mortal. This, however, was concealed from all, except Capt. Hardy, the chaplain, and the medical attendants. He himself being certain, from the sensation in his back, and the gush of blood he felt momently within his breast, that no human care could avail him, insisted that the surgeon should leave him, and attend to those to whom he might be useful; "For," said he, "you can do nothing for me."—All that could be done was to fan him with paper, and frequently to give him lemonade to alleviate his intense thirst. He was in great pain, and expressed much anxiety for the event of the action, which now began to declare itself. As often as a ship struck, the crew of the Victory hurraed; and at every hurra, a visible expression of joy gleamed in the eyes, and marked the countenance of the dying hero. But he became impatient to see Capt. Hardy; and as that officer, though often sent for, could not leave the deck, Nelson feared that some fatal cause prevented him, and repeatedly cried: "Will no one bring Hardy to me? He must be killed! He is surely dead!" —An hour and ten minutes elapsed from the time when Nelson received his wound, before Hardy could come to him. They shook hands in silence; Hardy in vain struggling to suppress the feelings of that most painful and yet sublimest moment. "Well Hardy," said Nelson, "how goes the day with us?"—"Very well," replied Hardy; "ten ships have struck, but five of the van have tacked, and show an intention to bear down upon the Victory. I have called two or three of our fresh ships round, and have no doubt of giving them a drubbing."—"I hope," said Nelson, "none of our ships have struck?" Hardy answered, "There was no fear of that." Then, and not till then, Nelson spoke of himself. "I am a dead man, Hardy," said he: "I am going fast:—it will be all over with me soon. Come nearer to me. Let my dear Lady Hamilton have my hair, and all other things belonging to me." Hardy observed, that he hoped Mr. Beatty could yet hold out some prospect of life. "Oh, no!" he replied: "it is impossible. My back is shot through. Beatty will tell you so." Capt. Hardy then, once more, shook hands with him; and, with a heart almost bursting, hastened upon deck.

By this time all feeling below the breast was gone; and Nelson, having made the surgeon ascertain this, said to him: "You know I am gone, I know it. I feel something rising in my breast,"—putting his hand on his left side,—"which tells me so." And upon Beatty's inquiring whether his pain was very great? he replied, "So great, that he wished he was dead. Yet," said he, in a lower voice, "one would like to live a little longer too!" And after a few minutes, in the same under tone, he added; "What would become of poor Lady Hamilton, if she knew my situation!" Next to his country she occupied his thoughts. Capt. Hardy, some fifty minutes after he had left the cockpit, returned; and, again taking the hand of his dying friend and commander, congratulated him on having gained a complete victory. How many of the enemy were taken he did not know, as it was impossible to perceive them distinctly: but fourteen or fifteen at least. "That's well," cried Nelson, "but I bargained for twenty." And then, in a stronger voice, he said: "Anchor, Hardy; anchor." Hardy, upon this, hinted that Admiral Collingwood would take upon himself the direction of affairs. "Not while I live, Hardy," said the dying Nelson, ineffectually endeavouring to raise himself from the bed: "Do you anchor." His previous order for preparing to anchor had shown how clearly he foresaw the necessity of this. Presently, calling Hardy back, he said to him in a low voice, "Don't throw me overboard:" and he desired that he might be buried by his parents, unless it should please the king to order otherwise. Then reverting to private feelings: "Take care of my dear Lady Hamilton, Hardy: take care of poor Lady Hamilton.—Kiss me, Hardy," said he. Hardy knelt down and kissed his cheek: and Nelson said, "Now I am satisfied. Thank God, I have done my duty." Hardy stood over him in silence for a moment or two, then knelt again, and kissed his forehead. "Who is that?" said Nelson; and being informed he replied, "God bless you, Hardy." And Hardy then left him—for ever.

Nelson now desired to be turned upon his right side, and said: "I wish I had not left the deck; for I shall soon be gone." Death was, indeed, rapidly approaching. He said to the chaplain: "Doctor, I have *not* been a *great* sinner:" and after a short pause, "Remember that I leave Lady Hamilton and my daughter Horatia as a legacy to my country." His articulation now became difficult; but he was distinctly heard to say,

"Thank God, I have done my duty." These words he repeatedly pronounced; and they were the last words which he uttered. He expired at thirty minutes after four,—three hours and a quarter after he had received his wound.

Within a quarter of an hour after Nelson was wounded, above fifty of the Victory's men fell by the enemy's musketry. They, however, on their part were not idle; and it was not long before there were only two Frenchmen left alive in the mizen-top of the Redoutable. One of them was the man who had given the fatal wound: he did not live to boast of what he had done. An old quarter-master had seen him fire; and easily recognised him, because he wore a glazed cocked hat and a white frock. This quarter-master and two midshipmen, Mr. Collingwood and Mr. Pollard, were the only persons left in the Victory's poop;—the two midshipmen kept firing at the top, and he supplied them with cartridges. One of the Frenchmen, attempting to make his escape down the rigging, was shot by Mr. Pollard, and fell on the poop. But the old quarter-master, as he cried out, "That's he—that's he," and pointed at the other, who was coming forward to fire again, received a shot in his mouth, and fell dead. Both the midshipmen then fired at the same time, and the fellow dropped in the top. When they took possession of the prize, they went into the mizen-top, and found him dead; with one ball through his head, and another through his breast.

The Redoutable struck within twenty minutes after the fatal shot had been fired from her. During that time she had been twice on fire,—in her fore-chains and in her fore-castle. The French, as they had done in other battles, made use, in this, of fire-balls, and other combustibles; implements of destruction, which other nations, from a sense of honour and humanity, have laid aside; which add to the sufferings of the wounded, without determining the issue of the combat: which none but the cruel would employ, and which never can be successful against the brave. Once they succeeded in setting fire, from the Redoutable, to some ropes and canvass on the Victory's booms. The cry ran through the ship, and reached the cockpit: but even this dreadful cry produced no confusion: the men displayed that perfect self-possession in danger by which English seamen are characterised; they extinguished the flames on board their own ship, and then hastened to extinguish them in the enemy, by throwing buckets of water from the gangway. When the Redoutable had struck, it was not practicable to board her from the Victory; for, though the two ships touched, the upper works of both fell in so much, that there was a great space between their gangways; and she could not be boarded from the lower or middle decks, because her ports were down. Some of our men went to Lieutenant Quilliam, and offered to swim under her bows, and get up there; but it was thought unfit to hazard brave lives in this manner.

What our men would have done from gallantry, some of the crew of the Santissima Trinidad did to save themselves. Unable to stand the tremendous fire of the Victory, whose larboard guns played against this great four decker, and not knowing how else to escape them, nor where else to betake themselves for protection, many of them leapt overboard, and swam to the Victory; and were actually helped up her sides by the English during the action. The Spaniards began the battle with less vivacity than their unworthy allies, but they continued it with greater firmness. The Argonauta and Bahama were defended till they had each lost about four hundred men: the St. Juan Nepomuceno lost three hundred and fifty. Often as the superiority of British courage has been proved against France upon the seas, it was never more conspicuous than in this decisive conflict. Five of our ships were engaged muzzle to muzzle with five of the French. In all five, the Frenchmen lowered their lower-deck ports, and deserted their guns; while our men continued deliberately to load and fire, till they had made the victory secure.

Once, amidst his sufferings, Nelson had expressed a wish that he were dead; but immediately the spirit subdued the pains of death, and he wished to live a little longer;—doubtless that he might hear the completion of the victory which he had seen so gloriously begun. That consolation—that joy—that triumph, was afforded him. He lived to know that the victory was decisive; and the last guns which were fired at the flying enemy were heard, a minute or two before he expired. The ships which were thus flying were four of the enemy's van, all French, under Rear-Admiral Dumanoir. They had borne no part in the action; and now, when they were seeking safety in flight, they fired not only into the Victory and Royal Sovereign as they passed, but poured their broadsides into the Spanish captured ships; and they were seen to back their top-sails, for the purpose of firing with more precision. The indignation of the Spaniards at this detestable cruelty from their allies, for whom they had fought so bravely, and so profusely bled, may well be conceived. It was such, that when, two days after the action, seven of the ships which had escaped into Cadiz came out, in hopes of retaking some of the disabled prizes, the prisoners, in the Argonauta, in a body, offered their services to the British prize-master, to man the guns against any of the French ships: saying, that if a Spanish ship came alongside, they would quietly go below; but they requested that they might be allowed to fight the French, in resentment for the murderous usage which they had suffered at their hands. Such was their earnestness, and such the implicit confidence which could be placed in Spanish honour, that the offer was accepted, and they were actually stationed at the lower deck guns. Dumanoir and his squadron were not more fortunate than the fleet from whose destruction they fled: they fell in with Sir Richard Strachan, who was cruising for the Rochefort squadron, and were all taken. In the better days of France, if such a crime could then have been committed, it would have received an exemplary punishment from the French government: under Buonaparte, it was sure of impunity, and, perhaps, might be thought deserving of reward. But, if the Spanish court had been independent, it would have become us to have delivered Dumanoir and his captains up to Spain, that they might have been brought to trial, and hanged in sight of the remains of the Spanish fleet.

The total British loss in the battle of Trafalgar amounted to one thousand five hundred and eighty-seven. Twenty of the enemy struck; but it was not possible* to anchor the fleet, as Nelson had enjoined;—a gale came on from the south-west; some of the prizes went down, some went on shore; one effected its escape into Cadiz; others were destroyed; four only were saved, and those by the greatest exertions. The wounded Spaniards were sent ashore, an assurance being given that they should not serve till regularly exchanged; and the Spaniards, with a generous feeling, which would not, perhaps, have been found in any other people, offered the use of their hospitals for our wounded, pledging the honour of Spain that they should be carefully attended there. When the storm, after the action, drove some of the prizes upon the coast, they declared that the English, who were thus thrown into their hands, should not be considered as prisoners of war; and the Spanish soldiers gave up their own beds to their shipwrecked enemies. The Spanish vice-admiral, Alava, died of his wounds. Villeneuve was sent to England, and permitted to return to France. The French govern-

---

* In the former editions it was said that unhappily the fleet did not anchor: implying an opinion that Nelson's orders ought to have been followed by his successor. From the recently published Memoirs and Correspondence of Lord Collingwood, it appears that this was not practicable, and that if it had, and had been done, the consequences, from the state of the weather (which Nelson could not foresee), would, in all likelihood, have been more disastrous than they were.

Having thus referred to Lord Collingwood's life, I may be allowed to say, that the publication of that volume is indeed a national good;—it ought to be in every officer's cabin, and in every statesman's cabinet.

ment say that he destroyed himself on the way to Paris, dreading the consequences of a court-martial: but there is every reason to believe that the tyrant, who never acknowledged the loss of the battle of Trafalgar, added Villeneuve to the numerous victims of his murderous policy.

It is almost superfluous to add, that all the honours which a grateful country could bestow, were heaped upon the memory of Nelson. His brother was made an earl, with a grant of £6000 a year; £10,000 were voted to each of his sisters: and £100,000 for the purchase of an estate. A public funeral was decreed, and a public monument. Statues and monuments also were voted by most of our principal cities. The leaden coffin, in which he was brought home, was cut in pieces, which were distributed as relics of Saint Nelson,—so the gunner of the Victory called them;—and when, at his interment, his flag was about to be lowered into the grave, the sailors, who assisted at the ceremony, with one accord rent it in pieces, that each might preserve a fragment while he lived.

The death of Nelson was felt in England as something more than a public calamity: men started at the intelligence, and turned pale; as if they had heard of the loss of a dear friend. An object of our admiration and affection, of our pride and of our hopes, was suddenly taken from us; and it seemed as if we had never, till then, known how deeply we loved and reverenced him. What the country had lost in its great naval hero—the greatest of our own, and of all former times, was scarcely taken into the account of grief. So perfectly, indeed, had he performed his part, that the maritime war, after the battle of Trafalgar, was considered at an end: the fleets of the enemy were not merely defeated, but destroyed: new navies must be built, and a new race of seamen reared for them, before the possibility of their invading our shores could again be contemplated. It was not, therefore, from any selfish reflection upon the magnitude of our loss that we mourned for him: the general sorrow was of a higher character. The people of England grieved that funeral ceremonies, and public monuments, and posthumous rewards, were all which they could now bestow upon him, whom the king, the legislature, and the nation, would have alike delighted to honour; whom every tongue would have blessed; whose presence in every village through which he might have passed, would have wakened the church bells, have given school-boys a holiday, have drawn children from their sports to gaze upon him, and "old men from the chimney corner," to look upon Nelson ere they died. The victory of Trafalgar was celebrated, indeed, with the usual forms of rejoicing, but they were without joy; for such already was the glory of the British navy, through Nelson's surpassing genius, that it scarcely seemed to receive any addition from the most signal victory that ever was achieved upon the seas: and the destruction of this mighty fleet, by which all the maritime schemes of France were totally frustrated, hardly appeared to add to our security or strength; for, while Nelson was living, to watch the combined squadrons of the enemy, we felt ourselves as secure as now, when they were no longer in existence.

There was reason to suppose, from the appearances upon opening the body, that, in the course of nature, he might have attained, like his father, to a good old age. Yet he cannot be said to have fallen prematurely whose work was done; nor ought he to be lamented, who died so full of honours, and at the height of human fame. The most triumphant death is that of the martyr; the most awful that of the martyred patriot; the most splendid that of the hero in the hour of victory: and if the chariot and the horses of fire had been vouchsafed for Nelson's translation, he could scarcely have departed in a brighter blaze of glory. He has left us, not indeed his mantle of inspiration, but a name and an example, which are at this hour inspiring thousands of the youth of England: a name which is our pride, and an example which will continue to be our shield and our strength. Thus it is that the spirits of the great and the wise continue to live and to act after them; verifying, in this sense, the language of the old mythologist:

Τοι μεν δαιμονες εισι, Διος μεγαλε δια βελας
Εσθλοι, επιχθονιοι, φυλακες θνητων ανθρωπων.[7]

[1813]   [1830]

SIR THOMAS MORE: OR, COLLOQUIES

When in January 1820, Southey began the composition of the Colloquies, *he sent to his friend John Rickman the following description of the proposed work:*

I have just finished the introduction to such a book as is wanted—a full statement of the existing diseases of society, with a view of the consequences etc. You know how much this has been in my thoughts, and I think I have chosen a good form for rendering it more effectual and more attractive than if it appeared as a direct political essay. The plan was suggested by Boethius, which however nobody would discover, and the form is dialogue between the writer and Sir Thomas More . . . He lived in the age of the restoration of letters; of the discovery of printing, and of the Reformation: other great changes too had taken place. In tracing the consequences of these things as far

---

7 Hesiod's *Works and Days*, ll. 122–23: "they are called pure spirits dwelling on the earth, and are kindly, delivering from harm, and guardians of mortal men" (Hugh G. Evelyn-White translation, Loeb Classical Library, Harvard University Press).

as they have hitherto gone, and drawing the parallel between that age and this, a great many home truths may be brought into full view. I take for my motto, three words from St. Bernard, Respice [look back], aspice [look upon the present], prospice, [look forward]! and upon this text I hope to preach a stirring sermon.

According to the preface to Colloquies *as published in 1829, the work had its origins in a dream of November 1817, following the death of Princess Charlotte Augusta, daughter of the Prince Regent and presumptive heiress to the British throne. In contrast to the scandalous behavior of other members of the royal family, the character of the Princess was marked by notable gentleness and propriety; and her death was regarded by the British population as a national calamity. The event sent Southey's thoughts back to a similar event in the early sixteenth century, the death in 1502 of the eldest son of Henry VII, Prince Arthur, which made his brother Henry (King Henry VIII) heir apparent to the throne. Both the scientific advances and the religious and political turbulences of the time of Henry VIII became for Southey an analogue to the situation in England following Waterloo. In the dream, Sir Thomas More visited the author (appearing in the* Colloquies *as "Montesinos", Spanish for "a dweller in the mountains" [of the Lake District]) to discuss the similarities between the "grand climacterics of the world" in which each lived. The fifteen* Colloquies, *which take place in Southey's study at Keswick and in the surrounding landscapes of the Lake District, cover a wide range of topics from the value of paper money to the establishment of a religious order of women to care for the poor; they constitute, in Southey's words, "the sum of my opinions" along with the volume of* Moral and Political Essays *(1832). The text of the* Colloquies *here reproduced is that of the first edition.*

Sir Thomas More: or, Colloquies *is perhaps best known for inspiring a famous review essay in the* Edinburgh Review *(January, 1830) by Thomas B. Macaulay; the Whig historian rejected both Southey's alarm over the "prospects" of modern civilization and the religious basis of the solutions proposed. For a discussion of Southey's work and Macaulay's attack, see Martin Jarrett-Kerr, "Southey's Colloquies,"* Nineteenth Century, *CXXXII (1942), 181–87.*

FROM

SIR THOMAS MORE:
or,
Colloquies on the Progress and Prospects of Society

FROM
COLLOQUY I.
INTRODUCTION.

*　　*　　*　　*　　*

SIR THOMAS MORE.

I NEITHER come to discover secret things nor hidden treasures; but to discourse with you concerning these

portentous and monster-breeding times; for it is your lot, as it was mine, to live during one of the grand climacterics of the world. And I come to you, rather than to any other person, because you have been led to meditate upon the corresponding changes whereby your age and mine are distinguished; and, because, notwithstanding many discrepancies and some dispathies between us, (speaking of myself as I was, and as you know me,) there are certain points of sympathy and resemblance which bring us into contact, and enable us at once to understand each other.

MONTESINOS.

Et in Utopiâ ego.[1]

SIR THOMAS MORE.

You apprehend me. We have both speculated in the joy and freedom of our youth upon the possible improvement of society; and both in like manner have lived to dread with reason the effects of that restless spirit, which, like the Titaness Mutability described by your immortal master[2] insults Heaven and disturbs the earth. By comparing the great operating causes in the age of the Reformation, and in this age of revolutions, going back to the former age, looking at things as I then beheld them, perceiving wherein I judged rightly, and wherein I erred, and tracing the progress of those causes which are now developing their whole tremendous power, you will derive instruction, which you are a fit person to receive and communicate; for without being solicitous concerning present effect, you are contented to cast your bread upon the waters. You are now acquainted with me and my intention. Tomorrow you will see me again; and I shall continue to visit you occasionally as opportunity may serve. Meantime say nothing of what has passed, . . . not even to your wife. She might not like the thoughts of a ghostly visitor; and the reputation of conversing with the dead might be almost as inconvenient as that of dealing with the Devil. For the present then, farewell! I will never startle you with too sudden an apparition; but you may learn to behold my disappearance without alarm.

I was not able to behold it without emotion, although he had thus prepared me: for the sentence was no sooner completed than he was gone. Instead of rising from the chair, he vanished from it. I know not to what the instantaneous disappearance can be likened. Not to the dissolution of a rainbow, because the

---

[1] *Et . . . ego:* "I too have dwelt in Utopia."
[2] A reference to the "Mutabilitie" Cantos of Spenser's *Faerie Queene.*

colours of the rainbow fade gradually till they are lost; not to the flash of cannon, or to lightning, for these things are gone as soon as they are come, and it is known that the instant of their appearance must be that of their departure; not to a bubble upon the water, for you see it burst; not to the sudden extinction of a light, for that is either succeeded by darkness, or leaves a different hue upon the surrounding objects. In the same indivisible point of time when I beheld the distinct, individual and, to all sense of sight, substantial form, . . . the living, moving, reasonable image, . . . in that self-same instant it was gone, as if exemplifying the difference between *to be* and *not to be*. It was no dream, of this I was well assured: realities are never mistaken for dreams, though dreams may be mistaken for realities. Moreover I had long been accustomed in sleep to question my perceptions with a wakeful faculty of reason, and to detect their fallacy. But, as well may be supposed, my thoughts that night, sleeping as well as waking, were filled with this extraordinary interview; and when I arose the next morning, it was not till I had called to mind every circumstance of time and place that I was convinced the apparition was real, and that I might again expect it.

COLLOQUY II.

THE IMPROVEMENT OF THE WORLD.

On the following evening, when my spiritual visitor entered the room, that volume of Dr. Wordsworth's Ecclesiastical Biography,[1] which contains his life, was lying on the table beside me. "I perceive," said he, glancing at the book, "you have been gathering all you can concerning me from my good gossiping chronicler, who tells you that I loved milk and fruit and eggs, preferred beef to young meats, and brown bread to white; was fond of seeing strange birds and beasts, and kept an ape, a fox, a weasel, and a ferret."

I am not one of those fastidious readers, I replied, who quarrel with a writer for telling them too much. But these things were worth telling: they show that you retained a youthful palate as well as a youthful heart; and I like you the better both for your diet and your menagerie. The old biographer, indeed, with the best intentions, has been far from understanding the character which he desired to honour. He seems, however, to have been a faithful reporter, and has

done as well as his capacity permitted. I observe that he gives you credit for "a deep foresight and judgement of the times," and for speaking in a prophetic spirit of the evils which soon afterwards were "full heavily felt."

There could be little need for a spirit of prophecy, Sir Thomas made answer, to foresee troubles which were the sure effect of the causes then in operation, and which were actually close at hand. When the rain is gathering from the south or west, and those flowers and herbs which serve as natural hygrometers,[2] close their leaves, men have no occasion to consult the stars for what the clouds and the earth are telling them . . . You were thinking of Prince Arthur when I introduced myself yesterday, as if musing upon the great events which seem to have received their bias from the apparent accident of his premature death.

MONTESINOS.

I had fallen into one of those idle reveries in which we speculate upon what might have been. Lord Bacon describes him as "very studious, and learned beyond his years, and beyond the custom of great princes." As this indicates a calm and thoughtful mind, it seems to show that he inherited the Tudor character. His brother[3] took after the Plantagenets; but it was not of their nobler qualities that he partook. He had the popular manners of his grandfather, Edward IV., and, like him, was lustful, cruel, and unfeeling.

SIR THOMAS MORE.

The blood of the Plantagenets, as your friends the Spaniards would say, was a strong blood. That temper of mind which (in some of his predecessors) thought so little of fratricide, might perhaps have involved him in the guilt of a parricidal war, if his father had not been fortunate enough to escape such an affliction by a timely death. We might otherwise be allowed to wish that the life of Henry VII. had been prolonged to a good old age. For if ever there was a prince who could so have directed the Reformation as to have averted the evils wherewith that tremendous event was accompanied, and yet to have secured its advantages, he was the man. Cool, wary, farsighted, rapacious, politic, and religious, . . or superstitious if you will, (for his religion had its root rather in fear than in hope,) he was peculiarly adapted for such a crisis both by his good and evil qualities. For the sake of increasing his treasures and his power, he would have promoted the Reformation; but his cautious temper, his sagacity,

---

[1] Publication of 1810 by Christopher Wordsworth (1774–1846), brother of the poet and master of Trinity College, Cambridge.

[2] Instruments for measuring the humidity of the air.
[3] Henry VIII.

and his fear of divine justice would have taught him where to stop.

MONTESINOS.

A generation of politic sovereigns succeeded to the race of warlike ones, just in that age of society when policy became of more importance in their station than military talents. Ferdinand of Spain, Joam II. whom the Portugueze called the Perfect Prince, Louis XI. and Henry VII. were all of this class. Their individual characters were sufficiently distinct; but the circumstances of their situation stampt them with a marked resemblance, and they were of a metal to take and retain the strong, sharp impress of the age.

SIR THOMAS MORE.

The age required such characters; and it is worthy of notice how surely in the order of Providence such men as are wanted are raised up. One generation of these Princes sufficed. In Spain, indeed, there was an exception; for Ferdinand had two successors who pursued the same course of conduct. In the other kingdoms the character ceased with the necessity for it. Crimes enough were committed by succeeding sovereigns, but they were no longer the acts of systematic and reflecting policy. This too is worthy of remark, that the sovereigns whom you have named, and who scrupled at no means for securing themselves on the throne, for enlarging their dominions and consolidating their power, were each severally made to feel the vanity of human ambition, being punished either in or by the children who were to reap the advantage of their crimes. "Verily there is a God that judgeth the earth!"

MONTESINOS.

An excellent friend of mine, one of the wisest, best, and happiest men whom I have ever known, delights in this manner to trace the moral order of Providence through the revolutions of the world; and in his historical writings keeps it in view as the pole-star of his course. I wish he were present, that he might have the satisfaction of hearing his favourite opinion confirmed by one from the dead.

SIR THOMAS MORE.

His opinion requires no other confirmation than what he finds for it in observation and scripture, and in his own calm judgement. I should differ little from that friend of yours concerning the past; but his hopes for the future appear to me like early buds which are in danger of March winds. He believes the world to be in a rapid state of sure improvement; and in the ferment which exists every where he beholds only a purifying process; not considering that there is an acetous as well as a vinous fermentation; and that in the one case the liquor may be spilt, in the other it must be spoilt.

MONTESINOS.

Surely you would not rob us of our hopes for the human race! If I apprehended that your discourse tended to this end, I should suspect you, notwithstanding your appearance, and be ready to exclaim, Avaunt, Tempter! For there is no opinion from which I should so hardly be driven, and so reluctantly part, as the belief that the world will continue to improve, even as it has hitherto continually been improving; and that the progress of knowledge and the diffusion of Christianity will bring about at last, when men become Christians in reality, as well as in name, something like that Utopian state of which philosophers have loved to dream, ... like that millennium in which Saints as well as enthusiasts have trusted.

SIR THOMAS MORE.

Do you hold that this consummation must of necessity come to pass; or that it depends in any degree upon the course of events, that is to say, upon human actions? The former of these propositions you would be as unwilling to admit as your friend Wesley, or the old Welshman Pelagius[4] himself. The latter leaves you little other foundation for your opinion than a desire, which, from its very benevolence, is the more likely to be delusive ... You are in a dilemma.

MONTESINOS.

Not so, Sir Thomas. Impossible as it may be for us to reconcile the free will of man with the foreknowledge of God, I nevertheless believe in both with the most full conviction. When the human mind plunges into time and space in its speculations, it adventures beyond its sphere; no wonder, therefore, that its powers fail, and it is lost. But that my will is free, I know feelingly: it is proved to me by my conscience. And that God provideth all things, I know by his own word, and by that instinct which he hath implanted in me to assure me of his being. My answer to your question then is this: I believe that the happy consummation which I desire is appointed, and must come to pass; but that when it is to come depends upon the obedience of man to the will of God, that is, upon human actions.

---

[4] A fifth-century proponent of the doctrine, condemned as heretical, which emphasized the essential goodness of human nature and the authority of the will, over a necessary reliance on divine grace.

SIR THOMAS MORE.

You hold then that the human race will one day attain the utmost degree of general virtue, and thereby general happiness, of which humanity is capable. Upon what do you found this belief?

MONTESINOS.

The opinion is stated more broadly than I should chuse to advance it. But this is ever the manner of argumentative discourse: the opponent endeavours to draw from you conclusions which you are not prepared to defend, and which perhaps you have never before acknowledged even to yourself. I will put the proposition in a less disputable form. A happier condition of society is possible than that in which any nation is existing at this time, or has at any time existed. The sum both of moral and physical evil may be greatly diminished by good laws, good institutions, and good governments. Moral evil cannot indeed be removed, unless the nature of man were changed; and that renovation is only to be effected in individuals, and in them only by the special grace of God. Physical evil must always, to a certain degree, be inseparable from mortality. But both are so much within the reach of human institutions that a state of society is conceivable almost as superior to that of England in these days, as that itself is superior to the condition of the tattooed Britons, or of the Northern Pirates from whom we are descended. Surely this belief rests upon a reasonable foundation, and is supported by that general improvement (always going on if it be regarded upon the great scale) to which all history bears witness.

SIR THOMAS MORE.

I dispute not this: but to render it a reasonable ground of immediate hope, the predominance of good principles must be supposed. Do you believe that good or evil principles predominate at this time?

MONTESINOS.

If I were to judge by that expression of popular opinion which the press pretends to convey, I should reply without hesitation that never in any other known age of the world have such pernicious principles been so prevalent.

Qua terra patet, fera regnat Erinnys;
In facinus jurasse putes.[5]

◇◇◇◇◇◇◇◇◇◇◇◇◇◇◇◇◇◇◇◇◇◇◇◇◇◇◇◇◇◇◇◇◇

5 *Qua . . . putes*: "Wherever the earth lies open before you, the wild Furies rule; you would think they had sworn an oath to commit crimes."

SIR THOMAS MORE.

Is there not a danger that these principles may bear down every thing before them? and is not that danger obvious, .. palpable, .. imminent? Is there a considerate man who can look at the signs of the times without apprehension, or a scoundrel connected with what is called the public press, who does not speculate upon them, and join with the anarchists as the strongest party? Deceive not yourself by the fallacious notion that truth is mightier than falsehood, and that good must prevail over evil! Good principles enable men to suffer, rather than to act. Think how the dog, fond and faithful creature as he is, from being the most docile and obedient of all animals, is made the most dangerous, if he becomes mad; so men acquire a frightful and not less monstrous power when they are in a state of moral insanity, and break loose from their social and religious obligations. Remember too how rapidly the plague of diseased opinions is communicated, and that if it once gain head, it is as difficult to be stopt as a conflagration or a flood. The prevailing opinions of this age go to the destruction of every thing which has hitherto been held sacred. They tend to arm the poor against the rich; the many against the few: worse than this, .. for it will also be a war of hope and enterprize against timidity, of youth against age.

MONTESINOS.

Sir Ghost, you are almost as dreadful an alarmist as our Cumberland cow, who is believed to have lately uttered this prophecy, delivering it with oracular propriety in verse:

Two winters, a wet spring,
A bloody summer, and no king.

SIR THOMAS MORE.

That prophecy speaks the wishes of the man, whoever he may have been, by whom it was invented: and you who talk of the progress of knowledge, and the improvement of society, and upon that improvement build your hope of its progressive melioration, you know that even so gross and palpable an imposture as this is swallowed by many of the vulgar, and contributes in its sphere to the mischief which it was designed to promote. I admit that such an improved condition of society as you contemplate is possible, and that it ought always to be kept in view: but the error of supposing it too near, of fancying that there is a short road to it, is, of all the errors of these times, the most pernicious, because it seduces the young and generous, and betrays them imperceptibly into an alliance with whatever is flagitious and de-testable. The fact is undeniable that the worst prin-ciples in religion, in morals, and in politics, are at this time more prevalent than they ever were known to be in any former age. You need not be told in what manner revolutions in opinion bring about the fate of empires; and upon this ground you ought to regard the state of the world, both at home and abroad, with fear, rather than with hope.

MONTESINOS.

When I have followed such speculations as may allowably be indulged, respecting what is hidden in the darkness of time and of eternity, I have sometimes thought that the moral and physical order of the world may be so appointed as to coincide; and that the revolutions of this planet may correspond with the condition of its inhabitants; so that the convulsions and changes whereto it is destined should occur, when the existing race of men had either become so corrupt, as to be unworthy of the place which they hold in the universe, or were so truly regenerate by the will and word of God, as to be qualified for a higher station in it. Our globe may have gone through many such revolu-tions. We know the history of the last; the measure of its wickedness was then filled up. For the future we are taught to expect a happier consummation.

SIR THOMAS MORE.

It is important that you should distinctly understand the nature and extent of your expectations on that head. Is it upon the Apocalypse that you rest them?

MONTESINOS.

If you had not forbidden me to expect from this intercourse any communication which might come with the authority of revealed knowledge, I should ask in reply, whether that dark book is indeed to be received for authentic scripture? My hopes are derived from the Prophets and the Evangelists. Believing in them with a calm and settled faith, with that consent of the will and heart and understanding which constitutes religious belief, I find in them the clear annunciation of that kingdom of God upon earth, for the coming of which Christ himself has taught and commanded us to pray.

SIR THOMAS MORE.

Remember that the Evangelists, in predicting that kingdom, announce a dreadful Advent! And that, according to the received opinion of the Church, wars, persecutions and calamities of every kind, the triumph of evil, and the coming of Antichrist are to be looked for, before the promises made by the Prophets shall

be fulfilled. Consider this also, that the speedy fulfil-ment of those promises has been the ruling fancy of the most dangerous of all madmen, from John of Leyden and his frantic followers, down to the Saints of Cromwell's army, Venner and his Fifth-Monarchy men, the fanatics of the Cevennes, and the blockheads of your own days, who beheld with complacency the crimes of the French Revolutionists, and the progress of Buonaparte towards the subjugation of Europe, as events tending to bring about the prophecies; and, under the same besotted persuasion, are ready at this time to co-operate with the miscreants who trade in blasphemy and treason! But you who neither seek to deceive others nor yourself, . . you who are neither insane nor insincere, . . you surely do not expect that the Millennium is to be brought about by the triumph of what are called liberal opinions; nor by enabling the whole of the lower classes to read the incentives to vice, impiety and rebellion, which are prepared for them by an unlicensed press; nor by Sunday Schools, and Religious Tract Societies; nor by the portentous bibliolatry of the age! And if you adhere to the letter of the Scriptures, methinks the thought of that consummation for which you look, might serve rather for consolation under the prospect of impending evils, than for a hope upon which the mind can rest in security with a calm and contented delight.

MONTESINOS.

To this I must reply, that the fulfilment of those calamitous events predicted in the Gospels may safely be referred,* as it usually is, and by the best biblical scholars, to the destruction of Jerusalem. Concerning the visions of the Apocalypse, sublime as they are, I speak with less hesitation, and dismiss them from my thoughts, as more congenial to the fanatics of whom you have spoken than to me. And for the coming of Antichrist, it is no longer a received opinion in these days, whatever it may have been in yours. Your reasoning applies to the enthusiastic Millenarians who discover the number of the Beast, and calculate the year when a Vial is to be poured out, with as much precision as the day and hour of an eclipse. But it leaves my hope unshaken and untouched. I know that the world has improved; I see that it is improving; and I believe that it will continue to improve in natural and certain progress. Good and evil principles are widely at work: a crisis is evidently approaching; it may be dreadful, but I can have no doubts concerning

---

* Matthew xxiv. Luke xxi. There is no difficulty in the passage, if we bear in mind that two questions were asked by the disciples; that our Lord answered both, and that they, according to their Jewish prepossessions, supposed a connection between them in point of time.

the result. Black and ominous as the aspects may appear, I regard them without dismay. The common exclamation of the poor and helpless, when they feel themselves oppressed, conveys to my mind the sum of the surest and safest philosophy. I say with them, "God is above," and trust Him for the event.

SIR THOMAS MORE.

God is above, . . but the devil is below. Evil principles are, in their nature, more active than good. The harvest is precarious, and must be prepared with labour, and cost, and care; weeds spring up of themselves, and flourish and seed whatever may be the season. Disease, vice, folly and madness are contagious; while health and understanding are incommunicable, and wisdom and virtue hardly to be communicated! . . . We have come however to some conclusion in our discourse. Your notion of the improvement of the world has appeared to be a mere speculation, altogether inapplicable in practice; and as dangerous to weak heads and heated imaginations as it is congenial to benevolent hearts. Perhaps that improvement is neither so general, nor so certain as you suppose. Perhaps, even in this country there may be more knowledge than there was in former times, and less wisdom, . . more wealth and less happiness, . . . more display and less virtue. This must be the subject of future conversation. I will only remind you now, that the French had persuaded themselves this was the most enlightened age of the world, and they the most enlightened people in it, . . the politest, the most amiable, the most humane of nations, . . and that a new era of philosophy, philanthropy and peace was about to commence under their auspices, . . when they were upon the eve of a revolution which, for its complicated monstrosities, absurdities and horrors, is more disgraceful to human nature than any other series of events in history. Chew the cud upon this, and farewell!

COLLOQUY III.

THE DRUIDICAL STONES.—VISITATIONS OF PESTILENCE.

INCLINATION would lead me to hibernate during half the year in this uncomfortable climate of Great Britain, where few men who have tasted the enjoyments of a better would willingly take up their abode, if it were not for the habits, and still more for the ties and duties which root us to our native soil. I envy the Turks for their sedentary constitutions, which seem no more to require exercise than an oyster does, or a toad in a stone. In this respect, I am by disposition

as true a Turk as the Grand Seignior himself; and approach much nearer to one in the habit of inaction, than any person of my acquaintance. Willing however as I should be to believe, that any thing which is habitually necessary for a sound body, would be unerringly indicated by an habitual disposition for it, and that if exercise were as needful as food for the preservation of the animal economy, the desire of motion would recur not less regularly than hunger and thirst, it is a theory which will not bear the test; and this I know by experience.

On a grey sober day, therefore, and in a tone of mind quite accordant with the season, I went out unwillingly to take the air, though if taking physic would have answered the same purpose, the dose would have been preferred as the shortest, and for that reason the least unpleasant remedy. Even on such occasions as this, it is desirable to propose to oneself some object for the satisfaction of accomplishing it, and to set out with the intention of reaching some fixed point, though it should be nothing better than a mile-stone, or a directing post. So I walked to the Circle of Stones upon the Penrith road, because there is a long hill upon the way which would give the muscles some work to perform; and because the sight of this rude monument which has stood during so many centuries, and is likely, if left to itself, to outlast any edifice that man could have erected, gives me always a feeling, which, however often it may be repeated, loses nothing of its force.

The circle is of the rudest kind, consisting of single stones, unhewn and chosen without any regard to shape or magnitude, being of all sizes, from seven or eight feet in height, to three or four. The circle however is complete, and is thirty-three paces in diameter. Concerning this, like all similar monuments in Great Britain, the popular superstition prevails, that no two persons can number the stones alike, and that no person will ever find a second counting confirm the first. My children have often disappointed their natural inclination to believe this wonder, by putting it to the test and disproving it. The number of the stones which compose the circle, is thirty-eight, and besides these there are ten which form three sides of a little square within, on the eastern side, three stones of the circle itself forming the fourth; this being evidently the place where the Druids who presided had their station; or where the more sacred and important part of the rites and ceremonies (whatever they may have been) were performed. All this is as perfect at this day, as when the Cambrian Bards, according to the custom of their ancient order, described by my old acquaintance, the living members of the Chair of Glamorgan, met there for the last time,

On the green turf and under the blue sky,
Their heads in reverence bare, and bare of foot.

The site also precisely accords with the description which Edward Williams and William Owen[1] give of the situation required for such meeting places:

————————a high hill top,
Nor bowered with trees, nor broken by the plough:
Remote from human dwellings and the stir
Of human life, and open to the breath
And to the eye of Heaven.

The high hill is now inclosed and cultivated; and a clump of larches has been planted within the circle, for the purpose of protecting an oak in the centre, the owner of the field having wished to rear one there with a commendable feeling, because that tree was held sacred by the Druids, and therefore, he supposed, might be appropriately placed there. The whole plantation however has been so miserably storm-stricken that the poor stunted trees are not even worth the trouble of cutting them down for fuel, and so they continue to disfigure the spot. In all other respects this impressive monument of former times is carefully preserved; the soil within the inclosure is not broken, a path from the road is left, and in latter times a stepping-stile has been placed to accommodate Lakers with an easier access, than by striding over the gate beside it.

The spot itself is the most commanding which could be chosen in this part of the country, without climbing a mountain. Derwent-water and the Vale of Keswick are not seen from it, only the mountains which inclose them on the south and west. Lattrigg and the huge side of Skiddaw are on the north; to the east is the open country toward Penrith, expanding from the Vale of St. John's, and extending for many miles, with Mell-fell in the distance, where it rises alone like a huge tumulus on the right, and Blencathra on the left, rent into deep ravines. On the south-east is the range of Helvellin, from its termination at Wanthwaite Crags to its loftiest summits, and to Dunmailrais. The lower range of Nathdale-fells lies nearer, in a parallel line with Helvellin; and the dale itself, with its little streamlet immediately below. The heights above Leatheswater, with the Borrowdale mountains complete the panorama.

While I was musing upon the days of the Bards and Druids, and thinking that Llywarc Hen[2] himself had probably stood within this very circle at a time when its history was known, and the rites for which it was

erected still in use, I saw a person approaching, and started a little at perceiving that it was my new acquaintance from the world of spirits. I am come, said he, to join company with you in your walk: you may as well converse with a Ghost, as stand dreaming of the dead. I dare say you have been wishing that these stones could speak and tell their tale: or that some record were sculptured upon them, though it were as unintelligible as the hieroglyphics, or as an Ogham inscription.[3]

My ghostly friend, I replied, they tell me something to the purport of our last discourse. Here upon ground where the Druids have certainly held their assemblies, and where, not improbably, human sacrifices have been offered up, you will find it difficult to maintain that the improvement of the world has not been unequivocal, and very great.

SIR THOMAS MORE.

Make the most of your vantage ground! My position is, that this improvement is not general; that while some parts of the earth are progressive in civilization, others have been retrograde; and that even where improvement appears the greatest, it is partial. For example; with all the meliorations which have taken place in England, since these stones were set up, (and you will not suppose that I who laid down my life for a religious principle, would undervalue the most important of all advantages,) ... do you believe that they have extended to all classes? Look at the question well. Consider your fellow-countrymen, both in their physical and intellectual relations; and tell me whether a large portion of the community are in a happier or more hopeful condition at this time, than their forefathers were when Cæsar set foot upon the island?

MONTESINOS.

If it be your aim to prove that the savage state is preferable to the social, I am perhaps the very last person upon whom any arguments to that end could produce the slightest effect. That notion never for a moment deluded me: not even in the ignorance and presumptuousness of youth, when first I perused Rousseau, and was unwilling to feel that a writer whose passionate eloquence I felt and admired so truly, could be erroneous in any of his opinions. But now, in the evening of life, when I know upon what foundation my principles rest, and when the direction

---

[1] Edward Williams (1762–1833) and William Owen (Pughe) (1759–1835) were antiquarian writers.
[2] A legendary Welsh bard of the fifth century.

[3] Referring to the stone inscriptions found in Ireland and Britain, written in the Ogam alphabet used by the Celtic people.

of one peculiar course of study has made it necessary for me to learn every thing which books could teach concerning savage life, the proposition appears to me one of the most untenable that ever was advanced by a perverse or a paradoxical intellect.

SIR THOMAS MORE.

I advanced no such paradox, and you have answered me too hastily. The Britons were not savages when the Romans invaded and improved them. They were already far advanced in the barbarous stage of society, having the use of metals, domestic cattle, wheeled carriages, and money, a settled government, and a regular priesthood, who were connected with their fellow Druids on the continent, and who were not ignorant of letters. . . . Understand me! I admit that improvements of the utmost value have been made, in the most important concerns: but I deny that the melioration has been general; and insist, on the contrary, that a considerable portion of the people are in a state, which, as relates to their physical condition, is greatly worsened, and, as touching their intellectual nature, is assuredly not improved. Look, for example, at the great mass of your populace in town and country, . . a tremendous proportion of the whole community! Are their bodily wants better, or more easily supplied? Are they subject to fewer calamities? Are they happier in childhood, youth and manhood, and more comfortably or carefully provided for in old age, than when the land was uninclosed, and half covered with woods? With regard to their moral and intellectual capacity, you well know how little of the light of knowledge and of revelation has reached them. They are still in darkness, and in the shadow of death!

MONTESINOS.

I perceive your drift; and perceive also that when we understand each other, there is likely to be little difference between us. And I beseech you, do not suppose that I am disputing for the sake of disputation; with that pernicious habit I was never infected, and I have seen too many mournful proofs of its perilous consequences. Toward any person it is injudicious and offensive; toward you it would be irreverent. Your position is undeniable. Were society to be stationary at its present point, the bulk of the people would, on the whole, have lost rather than gained by the alterations which have taken place during the last thousand years. Yet this must be remembered, that in common with all ranks they are exempted from those dreadful visitations of war, pestilence, and famine, by which these kingdoms were so frequently afflicted of old.

The countenance of my companion changed upon this, to an expression of judicial severity which struck me with awe. Exempted from these visitations! he exclaimed; Mortal man! creature of a day, what art thou, that thou shouldst presume upon any such exemption? Is it from a trust in your own deserts, or a reliance upon the forbearance and long-suffering of the Almighty, that this vain confidence arises?

I was silent.

My friend, he resumed, in a milder tone, but with a melancholy manner, your own individual health and happiness are scarcely more precarious than this fancied security. By the mercy of God, twice during the short space of your life, England has been spared from the horrors of invasion, which might with ease have been effected during the American war, when the enemy's fleet swept the channel, and insulted your very ports, and which was more than once seriously intended during the late long contest. The invaders would indeed have found their graves in that soil which they came to subdue: but before they could have been overcome, the atrocious threat of Buonaparte's General might have been in great part realized, that though he could not answer for effecting the conquest of England, he would engage to destroy its prosperity for a century to come. You have been spared from that chastisement. You have escaped also from the imminent danger of peace with a military Tyrant, which would inevitably have led to invasion, when he should have been ready to undertake and accomplish that great object of his ambition, and you must have been least prepared and least able to resist him. But if the seeds of civil war should at this time be quickening among you, ... if your soil is every where sown with the dragon's teeth, and the fatal crop be at this hour ready to spring up, . . the impending evil will be an hundred fold more terrible than those which have been averted; and you will have cause to perceive and acknowledge, that the wrath has been suspended only that it may fall the heavier!

May God avert this also! I exclaimed.

As for famine, he pursued, that curse will always follow in the train of war: and even now the public tranquillity of England is fearfully dependent upon the seasons. And touching pestilence, you fancy yourselves secure, because the plague has not appeared among you for the last hundred and fifty years; a portion of time, which long as it may seem when compared with the brief term of mortal existence, is as nothing in the physical history of the globe. The importation of that scourge is as possible now as it was in former times: and were it once imported, do you suppose it would rage with less violence among the crowded population of your metropolis, than it did before the Fire, or that it would not reach parts of the country which were never infected in any former visitation? On the contrary, its ravages would be more general and more tremendous, for it would inevitably be carried every where. Your provincial cities have doubled and trebled in size; and in London itself, great part of the population is as much crowded now as it was then, and the space which is covered with houses is increased at least fourfold. What if the sweating-sickness, emphatically called the English disease, were to show itself again? Can any cause be assigned why it is not as likely to break out in the nineteenth century as in the fifteenth? What if your manufactures, according to the ominous opinion which your greatest physiologist has expressed, were to generate for you new physical plagues, as they have already produced a moral pestilence unknown to all preceding ages? What if the small-pox, which you vainly believed to be subdued, should have assumed a new and more formidable character; and (as there seems no trifling grounds for apprehending) instead of being protected by vaccination from its danger, you should ascertain that inoculation itself affords no certain security? . . . Visitations of this kind are in the order of nature and of Providence. Physically considered, the likelihood of their recurrence becomes every year more probable than the last; and looking to the moral government of the world, was there ever a time when the sins of this kingdom called more cryingly for chastisement?

MONTESINOS.

Μάντι κᾱκῶν![4]

SIR THOMAS MORE.

I denounce no judgements. But I am reminding you that there is as much cause for the prayer in your Litany against plague, pestilence, and famine, as for that which intreats God to deliver you from all sedition, privy conspiracy and rebellion; from all false doctrine, heresy and schism. In this, as in all things, it behoves the Christian to live in a humble and grateful sense of his continual dependence upon the Almighty, . . . not to rest in a presumptuous confidence upon the improved state of human knowledge, or the altered course of natural visitations.

---

[4] Μάντι κᾱκῶν!: "O prophet of evil!"

MONTESINOS.

Oh how wholesome it is to receive instruction with a willing and a humble mind! In attending to your discourse I feel myself in the healthy state of a pupil, when, without one hostile or contrarient prepossession, he listens to a teacher in whom he has entire confidence. And I feel also how much better it is that the authority of elder and wiser intellects should pass even for more than it is worth, than that it should be undervalued as in these days, and set at nought. When any person boasts that he is

Nullius addictus jurare in verba magistri,[5]

the reason of that boast may easily be perceived; it is because he thinks, like Jupiter, that it would be disparaging his own all-wiseness to swear by any thing but himself. But wisdom will as little enter into a proud, or a conceited mind as into a malicious one. In this sense also it may be said, that he who humbleth himself shall be exalted.

SIR THOMAS MORE.

It is not implicit assent that I require, but reasonable conviction after calm and sufficient consideration. David was permitted to chuse between the three severest dispensations of God's displeasure, and he made choice of pestilence as the least dreadful. Ought a reflecting and religious man to be surprized, if some such punishment were dispensed to this country, not less in mercy than in judgement, as the means of averting a more terrible and abiding scourge? An endemic malady, as destructive as the plague, has naturalized itself among your American brethren, and in Spain. You have hitherto escaped it, speaking with reference to secondary causes, merely because it has not yet been imported. But any season may bring it to your own shores; or at any hour it may appear among you home-bred.

MONTESINOS.

We should have little reason then to boast of our improvements in the science of medicine; for our practitioners at Gibraltar found themselves as unable to stop its progress, or mitigate its symptoms, as the most ignorant empirics in the peninsula.

SIR THOMAS MORE.

You were at one time near enough that pestilence to feel as if you were within its reach?

---

[5] *Nullius . . . magistri:* "bound to swear on the words of no authority."

MONTESINOS.

It was in 1800, the year when it first appeared in Andalusia. That summer I fell in at Cintra with a young German, on the way from his own country to his brothers at Cadiz, where they were established as merchants. Many days had not elapsed after his arrival in that city when a ship which was consigned to their firm brought with it the infection; and the first news which reached us of our poor acquaintance was that the yellow fever had broken out in his brother's house, and that he, they, and the greater part of the household were dead. There was every reason to fear that the pestilence would extend into Portugal, both governments being, as usual, slow in providing any measures of precaution, and those measures being nugatory when taken. I was at Faro in the ensuing spring, at the house of Mr. Lempriere, the British Consul. Enquiring of him upon the subject, the old man lifted up his hands, and replied in a passionate manner which I shall never forget, "O Sir, we escaped by the mercy of God, .. only by the mercy of God!" The Governor of Algarve, even when the danger was known and acknowledged, would not venture to prohibit the communication with Spain till he received orders from Lisbon; and then the prohibition was so enforced as to be useless. The crew of a boat from the infected province were seized and marched through the country to Tavira: they were then sent to perform quarantine upon a little insulated ground, and the guards who were set over them, lived with them, and were regularly relieved. When such were the precautionary measures, well indeed might it be said, that Portugal escaped only by the mercy of God! I have often reflected upon the little effect which this imminent danger appeared to produce upon those persons with whom I associated. The young, with that hilarity which belongs to thoughtless youth, used to converse about the places whither they should retire, and the course of life and expedients to which they should be driven in case it were necessary for them to fly from Lisbon. A few elder and more considerate persons said little upon the subject, but that little denoted a deep sense of the danger, and more anxiety than they thought proper to express. The great majority seemed to be altogether unconcerned; neither their business, nor their amusements were interrupted; they feasted, they danced, they met at the card-table as usual; and the plague (for so it was called at that time, before its nature was clearly understood) was as regular a topic of conversation, as the news brought by the last packet.

SIR THOMAS MORE.

And, what was your own state of mind?

MONTESINOS.

Very much what it has long been with regard to the moral pestilence of this unhappy age, and the condition of this country more especially. I saw the danger in its whole extent, and relied on the mercy of God.

SIR THOMAS MORE.

In all cases that is the surest reliance: but when human means are available, it becomes a Mahommedan rather than a Christian to rely upon Providence or Fate alone, and make no effort for his own preservation. Individuals never fall into this error among you, drink as deeply as they may of fatalism; that narcotic will sometimes paralyse the moral sense, but it leaves the faculty of worldly prudence unimpaired. Far otherwise is it with your government; for such are the notions of liberty in England, that evils of every kind, physical, moral, and political, are allowed their free range. As relates to infectious diseases, for example, this kingdom is now in a less civilized state than it was in my days, three centuries ago, when the leper was separated from general society; and when, although the science of medicine was at once barbarous and phantastical, the existence of pest-houses showed at least some approaches towards a medical police.

MONTESINOS.

They order these things better in Utopia.

SIR THOMAS MORE.

In this, as well as in some other points upon which we shall touch hereafter, the difference between you and the Utopians is as great as between the existing generation and the race by whom yonder circle was set up. With regard to diseases and remedies in general, the real state of the case may be consolatory, but it is not comfortable. Great and certain progress has been made in chirurgery; and if the improvements in the other branch of medical science have not been so certain and so great, it is because the physician works in the dark, and has to deal with what is hidden and mysterious. But the evils for which these sciences are the palliatives, have increased in a proportion that heavily overweighs the benefit of improved therapeutics. For as the intercourse between nations has become greater, the evils of one have been communicated to another. Pigs, Spanish dollars, and Norway rats are not the only commodities and incommodities which have performed the circumnavigation, and are to be found wherever European ships have touched. Diseases also find their way from one part of the inhabited globe to another, wherever it is possible for them to exist. The most formidable endemic or contagious maladies in your nosology are not indigenous;

and as far as regards health therefore, the ancient Britons, with no other remedies than their fields and woods afforded them, and no other medical practitioners than their deceitful priests, were in a better condition than their descendants, with all the instruction which is derived from Sydenham and Heberden and Hunter,[6] and with all the powers which chemistry has put into their hands.

MONTESINOS.

You have well said that there is nothing comfortable in this view of the case: but what is there consolatory in it?

SIR THOMAS MORE.

The consolation is upon your principle of expectant hope. Whenever improved morals, wiser habits, more practical religion, and more efficient institutions shall have diminished the moral and material causes of disease, a thoroughly scientific practice, the result of long experience and accumulated observations, will then exist, to remedy all that is within the power of human art, and to alleviate what is irremediable. To existing individuals this consolation is something like the satisfaction you might feel in learning that a fine estate was entailed upon your family at the expiration of a lease of ninety-nine years from the present time. But I had forgotten to whom I am talking. A poet always look onward to some such distant inheritance. His hopes are usually *in nubibus*,[7] and his expectations in the *paulo post futurum*[8] tense.

MONTESINOS.

His state is the more gracious then, because his enjoyment is always to come. It is however a real satisfaction to me, that there is some sunshine in your prospect.

SIR THOMAS MORE.

More in mine than in yours, because I command a wider horizon; but I see also the storms which are blackening, and may close over the sky. Our discourse began concerning that portion of the community who form the base of the pyramid; we have unawares taken a more general view, but it has not led us out of the way. Returning to the most numerous class of society, it is apparent that in the particular point of which we have been conversing, their condition is greatly worsened: they remain liable to the same indigenous diseases as

their forefathers, and are exposed moreover to all which have been imported. Nor will the estimate of their condition be improved upon farther inquiry. They are worse fed than when they were hunters, fishers, and herdsmen; their clothing and habitations are little better, and, in comparison with those of the higher classes, immeasurably worse. Except in the immediate vicinity of the collieries, they suffer more from cold than when the woods and turbaries were open. They are less religious than in the days of the Romish faith; and if we consider them in relation to their immediate superiors, we shall find reason to confess that the independence which has been gained since the total decay of the feudal system, has been dearly purchased by the loss of kindly feelings and ennobling attachments. They are less contented, and in no respect more happy. . . . That look implies hesitation of judgement, and an unwillingness to be convinced. Consider the point; go to your books and your thoughts; and when next we meet, you will feel little inclination to dispute the irrefragable statement.

F R O M

COLLOQUY VII.

PART II.

MANUFACTURING SYSTEM.—NATIONAL WEALTH.

BY THIS time we had reached the bank above Applethwaite. The last question of my companion was one to which I could make no reply, and as he neither talked for triumph, nor I endeavoured to elude the force of his argument, we remained awhile in silence, looking upon the assemblage of dwellings below. Here, and in the adjoining hamlet of Millbeck, the effects of manufactures and of agriculture may be seen and compared. The old cottages are such as the poet and the painter equally delight in beholding. Substantially built of the native stone without mortar, dirtied with no white-lime, and their long low roofs covered with slate, if they had been raised by the magic of some indigenous Amphion's music, the materials could not have adjusted themselves more beautifully in accord with the surrounding scene; and time has still farther harmonized them with weather stains, lichens and moss, short grasses and short fern, and stone plants of various kinds. The ornamented chimnies, round or square, less adorned than those which, like little turrets, crest the houses of the Portugueze peasantry, and yet not less happily suited to their place; the hedge of clipt box beneath the windows, the rose bushes beside the door, the little patch of flower ground with its tall holyocks in front, the garden beside, the bee-hives, and the orchard with its bank of daffodils and snow-

---

[6] Thomas Sydenham (1642–1689), William Heberden (1710–1801), and John Hunter (1728–1793), leading English physicians and medical discoverers.

[7] *in nubibus:* "in the clouds."

[8] *paulo post futurum:* "little bit after the future."

drops, (the earliest and the profusest in these parts,) indicate in the owners some portion of ease and leisure, some regard to neatness and comfort, some sense of natural and innocent and healthful enjoyment. The new cottages of the manufacturers, are . . . upon the manufacturing pattern . . . naked, and in a row.

How is it, said I, that every thing which is connected with manufactures, presents such features of unqualified deformity? From the largest of Mammon's temples down to the poorest hovel in which his helotry are stalled, the edifices have all one character. Time cannot mellow them; Nature will neither clothe nor conceal them; and they remain always as offensive to the eye as to the mind!

We had proceeded a little way along the terrace, to that spot which commands the finest view of Derwentwater and of the vale of Keswick. How well, said Sir Thomas, has yonder dwelling been placed! pointing to one immediately below us; how happily is it sheltered from the north and east, how humbly and contentedly it appears to rest, and how deep a shade does it enjoy in summer, under those sycamores which have now lost their leaves! If we past the door I should expect to hear the humming of the spinning-wheel; and if I looked into the economy of the household, to find it little different from what I was accustomed to see in my youth.

MONTESINOS.

You would find a Bible and a Prayer Book, instead of a Crucifix and a Rosary; cloth coats instead of leathern jerkins upon the men and boys, and cotton in the place of woollen for the women, when they are in their better dress. The Reformation seems almost to have abolished the use of fish among this class of the community; they have contracted, I know not how, some obstinate prejudice against a kind of food at once wholesome and delicate, and every where to be obtained cheaply and in abundance, were the demand for it as general as it ought to be. Most of the pot-herbs and sallads which Tusser[1] enumerates, have disappeared from the cottager's garden, and even their names are no longer in remembrance. The potatoe has supplanted them. Greater change has been introduced by the now universal use of tea in these kingdoms, a beverage from which more, and more various good

has been derived without any admixture of adventitious evil, than from any other which has ever been devised by human ingenuity. Except as to this difference in their appearance and in their diet, you would find the peasantry little changed in their habits of life and less improved. The Reformation has done *them* no good: and nothing has grown up in the decay of the feudal system, to repay them for the kindly attachments which existed under it. They are neither happier nor wiser in their sphere; but they have the easy opportunity of getting out of it, and the possibility of emerging above it. The adventurous youth may seek his fortune in the United States, or in our own colonies. The industrious may work his way up in trade. And of those who pass their pitiable childhood as part of the machinery in a cotton mill, (for the cotton is now the staple trade of Great Britain,) perhaps one in a thousand, by good conduct and good fortune, obtains an employment in the business, which places him in a respectable station; and one in a myriad becomes a master manufacturer himself, and founds a family who take their place among the monied aristocracy of the land. There is a continual creation of wealth; and in the lottery which this produces, some of the prizes fall to their lot.

SIR THOMAS MORE.

And it is because of the creation of that wealth, that your government considers the prosperity of its manufactures as of so much importance to the state?

MONTESINOS.

For this, and for the still more important object of giving employment to a large part of our great and rapidly increasing population.

SIR THOMAS MORE.

But this sort of employment tends to accelerate that increase, by forcing it even so as to leave a large surplus, after supplying the lavish consumption of health and life which the manufacturing system requires. For among persons so trained up, moral restraint is not to be looked for, and there is little prudential restraint; the fear of the lean wolf is not before their eyes. In proportion, therefore, as the object is effected in one generation, it becomes more difficult in every succeeding one, and yet more necessary. But leaving for the present that consideration, let us examine the consequences of a continual creation of wealth, which, as it is a new thing in the world, must necessarily produce new results. What if it should prove that the wealth which is thus produced is no more an indication of public prosperity, than the size of one whose limbs are swollen with dropsy, is a symptom of health and vigour?

---

[1] Thomas Tusser (c. 1524–1580) was the author of the very popular *Hundreth Good Pointes of Husbandry* (1557), later expanded to *Five Hundreth Pointes of Good Husbandry united to as many of Good Huswifery* (1570), works in verse containing practical hints on agricultural and rural domestic economy.

MONTESINOS.

You are leading me toward the region of metaphysical politics, and as I am not owl-eyed, I can follow no farther than the daylight penetrates into that land of fogs and darkness.

*   *   *   *   *

SIR THOMAS MORE.

Can a nation be too rich?

MONTESINOS.

I am sure individuals can; and have often said that, rather than have been born and bred to a great fortune, I should deem it better for myself always to live precariously, and die poor at last.

SIR THOMAS MORE.

But for a nation?

MONTESINOS.

I cannot answer that question without distinguishing between a people and a state. A state cannot have more wealth at its command than may be employed for the general good, a liberal expenditure in national works being one of the surest means for promoting national prosperity, and the benefit being still more evident of an expenditure directed to the purposes of national improvement. But a people may be too rich; because it is the tendency of the commercial, and more especially of the manufacturing system, to collect wealth rather than to diffuse it. Where wealth is successfully employed in any of the speculations of trade, its increase is in proportion to its amount; great capitalists become like pikes in a fish-pond, who devour the weaker fish; and it is but too certain that the poverty of one part of the people seems to increase in the same ratio as the riches of another. There are examples of this in history. In Portugal, when the high tide of wealth flowed in from the conquests in Africa and the East, the effect of that great influx was not more visible in the augmented splendour of the Court, and the luxury of the higher ranks, than in the distress of the people.

SIR THOMAS MORE.

The prodigality of Henry's courtiers, for which the funds were supplied by sacrilege, was producing the same effect when I was removed from the sight of evils which I had vainly endeavoured to withstand.

MONTESINOS.

In these cases the consequences were so immediate and direct that there could be no doubt concerning the cause. But different causes are in operation at this time, and they are likely to be more permanent and more pernicious. Commerce and manufactures, nearly as they are connected, differ widely in their effects upon society. The former, it cannot be denied, has produced enormous evils when it has been associated with schemes of conquest and usurpation; but this is no natural association; its natural operations are wholly beneficial, binding nations to nations, and man to man. How opposite the manufacturing system is in its tendency, must be manifest to all who see things as they are, and not through the delusive medium of their own theories and prepossessions.

SIR THOMAS MORE.

The desire of gain is common to them both.

MONTESINOS.

A distinction must be made between this and the love of lucre. The pursuit of independence .. of that degree of wealth without which the comforts and respectabilities of life are not to be procured, .. the ambition even of obtaining enough to command those luxuries which may innocently and commendably be enjoyed, must be allowed to be beneficial both to the individuals who are thus stimulated to exertion, and to the community which is affected by their exertions. This is inseparable from commerce; in fact it is the main spring of that social order which is established among us. In this, indeed, as in all other desires, self-watchfulness is necessary, and the restraint of a higher principle: and in the mercantile profession there is much to qualify it and keep it within due bounds. We are not accustomed to class that profession among the liberal ones; and yet it ought to be classed among the most liberal, as being that which, when properly and wisely exercised, requires the most general knowledge, and affords the fairest opportunities for acquiring and enlarging it. There is nothing in its practice which tends to contract the mind, to sophisticate the understanding, or to corrupt the feelings.

SIR THOMAS MORE.

It is from those merchants who were "as Princes," that Princes themselves have derived assistance, states strength, and statesmen information, the arts their best patronage, and literature not unfrequently its best encouragement. Did you know more of the merchants of Tyre, it would appear that in that age no other power or influence upon the face of the earth was so beneficially exercised as theirs. Italy, Germany, and the Low Countries, had such merchants in my days. The Moors had them, before the Portugueze, by the conquest of Ceuta, by the destruction of their little commercial states along the coast of Eastern Africa, where every petty chieftain (like Alcinous) was a merchant, by their seizure of Malacca and Ormuz, and the system of destructive warfare which they carried on in the Indian and Red Seas, cut the roots of Mahommedan power, and unhappily of Mahommedan civilization. You have such merchants now.

MONTESINOS.

Many such. The evil in that profession is, that men are tempted by the hope of great prizes to undue risks; the spirit of enterprize is allowed to pass the bounds of prudence and of principle, and then the merchant becomes in fact a gamester. Examples of this become more frequent as the habits of life become more emulously expensive. But the ordinary and natural consequences of commerce are every way beneficial; they are humanizing, civilizing, liberalizing; if it be for the purpose of gain that it compasses sea and land, it carries with it industry, activity, and improvement: these are its effects abroad, while it brings wealth to us at home. Whereas the immediate and home effect of the manufacturing system, carried on as it now is upon the great scale, is to produce physical and moral evil, in proportion to the wealth which it creates. Here is our danger, our sore and spreading evil . . . here, I had almost said, is

the harm
That never shall recover healthfulness! *

At such a price national prosperity would be dearly purchased, even if any prosperity which is so purchased were, or could be, stable. Alas! wherefore is it that communities and individuals so seldom keep the even line, though it appears to be plain and straight before them!

SIR THOMAS MORE.

Because they walk sometimes in mist and darkness, and sometimes giddily and precipitately when the way is clear. But the way is not always plain, nor, when plain, is it always easy. Both men and nations are liable to evils which are the consequence, not of their own errors, but of their position, . . of circumstances in which they find themselves, and over which they have had no control.

MONTESINOS.

"For he that once hath missed the right way,
    The further he doth go, the further he doth stray." †

* Lord Surrey.
† Faery Queen.²

² See *Faerie Queene*, I, ix, 43.

SIR THOMAS MORE.

Society has its critical periods, and its climacterics; no change, no developement can take place at such seasons without inducing some peculiar and accompanying danger; and at all seasons it is liable to its influenzas and its plagues. This is one of its grand climacterics. A new principle, . . a *novum organum* has been introduced, . . the most powerful that has ever yet been wielded by man. If it was first *Mitrum* ³ that governed the world, and then *Nitrum*, both have had their day, . . gunpowder as well as the triple crown. Steam will govern the world next, . . and shake it too before its empire is established.

F R O M

COLLOQUY XV.

CONCLUSION—DANGERS OF SOCIETY— HOPES OF SOCIETY.

*   *   *   *   *

SIR THOMAS MORE.

THE WILL is revealed; but the plan is hidden. Let man dutifully obey that will, and the perfection of society and of human nature will be the result of such obedience; but upon obedience they depend. Blessings and curses are set before you, . . for nations as for individuals, . . yea, for the human race.

Flatter not yourself with delusive expectations! The end may be according to your hope; . . whether it will be so, (which God grant!) is as inscrutable for Angels as for men. But to descry that great struggles are yet to come is within reach of human foresight, . . that great tribulations must needs accompany them, . . and that these may be . . . you know not how near at hand!

Throughout what is called the Christian world there will be a contest between Impiety and Religion; the former every where is gathering strength, and wherever it breaks loose the foundations of human society will be shaken. Do not suppose that you are safe from this danger because you are blest with a pure creed, a reformed ritual, and a tolerant Church! Even here the standard of Impiety has been set up; and the drummers who beat the march of intellect through your streets, lanes, and market-places, are enlisted under it.

The struggle between Popery and Protestanism is renewed. And let no man deceive himself by a vain reliance upon the increased knowledge, or improved humanity of the times! Wickedness is ever the same;

³ *Mitrum* ("mitre") is an elaborate headdress, a symbol of ecclesiastical authority (the Pope's mitre is a "triple crown"). *Nitrum* ("saltpeter") is an ingredient in gunpowder.

and you never were in so much danger from moral weakness.

Co-existent with these struggles is that between the feudal system of society as variously modified throughout Europe, and the levelling principle of democracy. That principle is actively and indefatiguably at work in these kingdom, allying itself as occasion may serve with Popery or with Dissent, with Atheism or with Fanaticism, with Profligacy or with Hypocrisy, ready confederates, each having its own sinister views, but all acting to one straight forward end. Your rulers meantime seem to be trying that experiment with the British Constitution which Mithridates is said to have tried upon his own; they suffer poison to be administered in daily doses, as if they expected that by such a course the public mind would at length be rendered poison-proof!

The first of these struggles will affect all Christendom; the third may once again shake the monarchies of Europe. The second will be felt widely; but nowhere with more violence than in Ireland, that unhappy country, wherein your Government, after the most impolitic measures into which weakness was ever deluded, or pusillanimity intimidated, seems to have abdicated its functions, contenting itself with the semblance of an authority which it has wanted either wisdom or courage to exert.

There is a fourth danger, the growth of your manufacturing system; and this is peculiarly your own. You have a great and increasing population, exposed at all times by the fluctuations of trade to suffer the severest privations in the midst of a rich and luxurious society, under little or no restraint from religious principle, and if not absolutely disaffected to the institutions of the country, certainly not attached to them: a class of men aware of their numbers and of their strength; experienced in all the details of combination; improvident when they are in the receipt of good wages, yet feeling themselves injured when those wages, during some failure of demand, are so lowered as no longer to afford the means of comfortable subsistence; and directing against the Government and the laws of the country their resentment and indignation for the evils which have been brought upon them by competition and the spirit of rivalry in trade. They have among them intelligent heads and daring minds; and you have already seen how perilously they may be wrought upon by seditious journalists and seditious orators, in a time of distress.

On what do you rely for security against these dangers? On public opinion? You might as well calculate upon the constancy of wind and weather in this uncertain climate. On the progress of knowledge? it is such knowledge as serves only to facilitate the course of delusion. On the laws? the law which should be like a sword in a strong hand, is weak as a bulrush if it be feebly administered in time of danger. On the people? they are divided. On the Parliament? every faction will be fully and formidably represented there. On the Government? if suffers itself to be insulted and defied at home, and abroad it has shown itself incapable of maintaining the relations of peace and amity with its allies, so far has it been divested of power by the usurpation of the press. It is at peace with Spain, and it is at peace with Turkey; and although no government was ever more desirous of acting with good faith, its subjects are openly assisting the Greeks with men and money against the one, and the Spanish Americans against the other. Athens, in the most turbulent times of its democracy, was not more effectually domineered over by its demagogues than you are by the press, . . a press which is not only without restraint, but without responsibility; and in the management of which those men will always have most power who have least probity, and have most completely divested themselves of all sense of honour, and all regard for truth.

The root of all your evils is in the sinfulness of the nation. The principle of duty is weakened among you; that of moral obligation is loosened; that of religious obedience is destroyed. Look at the worldliness of all classes, . . the greediness of the rich, . . the misery of the poor, . . . and the appalling depravity which is* spreading among the lower classes through town and country; . . a depravity which proceeds unchecked because of the total want of discipline, and for which there is no other corrective than what may be supplied by fanaticism, which is itself an evil.

If there be nothing exaggerated in this representation, you must acknowledge that though the human race, considered upon the great scale, should be proceeding toward the perfectibility for which it may be designed, the present aspects in these kingdoms are nevertheless rather for evil than for good . . . Sum you up now upon the hopeful side.

MONTESINOS.

First, then, I rest in a humble but firm reliance upon that Providence which sometimes in its mercy educes from the errors of men a happier issue than could ever have been attained by their wisdom;—that Providence which has delivered this nation from so many and such imminent dangers heretofore.

* The Report of the Committee for inquiring into the cause of the increase of Commitments and Convictions in London and Middlesex, states, that notwithstanding all we hear of schools and the progress of education, juvenile depravity was never so unlimited in degree, or so desperate in character.

Looking, then, to human causes, there is hope to be derived from the humanizing effects of literature, which has now first begun to act upon all ranks. Good principles are indeed used as the stalking horse under cover of which pernicious designs may be advanced; but the better seeds are thus disseminated and fructify after the ill design has failed.

The cruelties of the old criminal law have been abrogated. Debtors are no longer indiscriminately punished by indefinite imprisonment. The iniquity of the slave trade has been acknowledged, and put an end to, so far as the power of this country extends; and although slavery is still tolerated, and must be so for awhile, measures have been taken for alleviating it while it continues, and preparing the way for its gradual and safe removal. These are good works of the Government. And when I look upon the conduct of that Government in all its foreign relations, though there may be some things to disapprove, and some sins of omission to regret, it has been, on the whole, so disinterested, so magnanimous, so just, that this reflection gives me a reasonable, and a religious ground of hope. And the reliance is strengthened when I call to mind that missionaries from Great Britain are at this hour employed in spreading the glad tidings of the Gospel far and wide among heathen nations.

Descending from these wider views to the details of society, there too I perceive ground, if not for confidence, at least for hope. There is a general desire throughout the higher ranks for bettering the condition of the poor, a subject to which the Government also has directed its patient attention: minute inquiries have been made into their existing state, and the increase of pauperism and of crimes. In no other country have the wounds of the commonwealth been so carefully probed. By means of colonization, of an improved parochial order, and of a more efficient police, the further increase of these evils may be prevented; while, by education, by providing means of religious instruction for all, by Saving-Banks, and perhaps by the establishment of Owenite communities[1] among themselves, the labouring classes will have their comforts enlarged, and their well-being secured, if they are not wanting to themselves in prudence and good conduct. A beginning has been made, .. an impulse given: it may be hoped . . . almost, I will say, it may be expected . . . that in a few generations this whole class will be placed within the reach of moral and intellectual gratifications, whereby they may be rendered healthier, happier, better in all respects, an improvement which will be not more beneficial to them as individuals, than to the whole body of the commonweal.

The diffusion of literature, though it has rendered the acquirement of general knowledge impossible, and tends inevitably to diminish the number of sound scholars, while it increases the multitude of sciolists, carries with it a beneficial influence to the lower classes. Our booksellers already perceive that it is their interest to provide cheap publications for a wide public, instead of looking to the rich alone as their customers. There is reason to expect that, in proportion as this is done, .. in proportion as the common people are supplied with wholesome entertainment, (and wholesome it is, if it be only harmless) they will be less liable to be acted upon by fanaticism and sedition.

You have not exaggerated the influence of the newspaper press, nor the profligacy of some of those persons by whom this unrestrained and irresponsible power is exercised. Nevertheless it has done and is doing great and essential good. The greatest evils in society proceed from the abuse of power; and this, though abundantly manifested in the newspapers themselves, they prevent in other quarters. No man engaged in public life could venture now upon such transactions as no one, in their station, half a century ago, would have been ashamed of. There is an end of that scandalous jobbing which at that time existed in every department of the state, and in every branch of the public service; and a check is imposed upon any scandalous and unfit promotion, civil or ecclesiastical. By whatever persons the government may be administered, they are now well aware that they must do nothing which will not bear daylight and strict investigation. The magistrates also are closely observed by this self-constituted censorship; and the inferior officers cannot escape exposure for any perversion of justice, or undue exercise of authority. Public nuisances are abated by the same means, and public grievances which the legislature might else overlook, are forced upon its attention. Thus, in ordinary times, the utility of this branch of the press is so great, that one of the worst evils to be apprehended from the abuse of its power at all times, and the wicked purposes to which it is directed in dangerous ones, is the ultimate loss of a liberty, which is essential to the public good, but which when it passes into licentiousness, and effects the overthrow of a state, perishes in the ruin it has brought on.

In the fine arts, as well as in literature, a levelling principle is going on, fatal perhaps to excellence, but favourable to mediocrity. Such facilities are afforded to imitative talent, that whatever is imitable will be imitated. Genius will often be suppressed by this, and

---

[1] Cooperative ("socialistic") industrial communities along the lines of Robert Owen's model factory and community of New Lanark in Scotland.

when it exerts itself, will find it far more difficult to obtain notice than in former times. There is the evil here that ingenious persons are seduced into a profession which is already crowded with unfortunate adventurers; but, on the other hand, there is a great increase of individual and domestic enjoyment. Accomplishments which were almost exclusively professional in the last age, are now to be found in every family within a certain rank of life. Wherever there is a disposition for the art of design, it is cultivated and in consequence of the general proficiency in this most useful of the fine arts, travellers represent to our view the manners and scenery of the countries which they visit, as well by the pencil as the pen. By means of two fortunate discoveries in the art of engraving, these graphic representations are brought within the reach of whole classes who were formerly precluded by the expense of such things from these sources of gratification and instruction. Artists and engravers of great name are now, like authors and booksellers, induced to employ themselves for this lower and wider sphere of purchasers. In all this I see the cause as well as the effect of a progressive refinement, which must be beneficial in many ways. This very diffusion of cheap books and cheap prints may, in its natural consequences, operate rather to diminish than to increase the number of adventurers in literature and in the arts. For though at first it will create employment for greater numbers, yet in another generation imitative talent will become so common, that neither parents nor possessors will mistake it for an indication of extraordinary genius, and many will thus be saved from a ruinous delusion. More pictures will be painted but fewer exhibited, .. more poetry written, but less published: and in both arts, talents which might else have been carried to an overstocked and unprofitable market, will be cultivated for their own sakes, and for the gratification of private circles, becoming thus a source of sure enjoyment, and indirectly of moral good. Scientific pursuits will, in like manner, be extended, and pursuits which partake of science, and afford pleasures within the reach of humble life.

Here, then, is good in progress which will hold on its course, and the growth of which will only be suspended, not destroyed, during any of those political convulsions which may too probably be apprehended; .. too probably, I say, because when you call upon me to consider the sinfulness of this nation, my heart fails. There can be no health, no soundness in the state, till Government shall regard the moral improvement of the people as its first great duty. The same remedy is required for the rich and for the poor. Religion ought to be so blended with the whole course of instruction, that its doctrines and precepts should indeed "drop

as the rain, and distil as the dew, as the small rain upon the tender herb, and as the showers upon the grass;"[2].. the young plants would then imbibe it, and the heart and intellect assimilate it with their growth. We are, in a great degree, what our institutions make us. Gracious God! were those institutions adapted to Thy will and word, .. were we but broken in from childhood to Thy easy yoke, .. were we but carefully instructed to believe and obey, .. in that obedience and belief we hould surely find our temporal welfare and our eternal happiness!

Here, indeed, I tremble at the prospect! Could I look beyond the clouds and the darkness which close upon it, I should then think that there may come a time when that scheme for a perpetual peace among the states of Christendom which Henri IV.[3] formed, and which has been so ably digested by the Abbé St. Pierre, will no longer be regarded as the speculation of a visionary. The Holy Alliance,[4] imperfect and unstable as it is, is in itself a recognition of the principle. At this day it would be practicable, if one part of Europe were as well prepared for it as the other; but this cannot be, till good shall have triumphed over evil in the struggles which are brooding, or shall have obtained such a predominance as to allay the conflict of opinions before it breaks into open war.

God in his mercy grant that it be so! If I looked to secondary causes alone, my fears would preponderate. But I conclude as I began, in firm reliance upon Him who is the beginning and the end. Our sins are manifold; our danger is great; but His mercy is infinite.

SIR THOMAS MORE.

Rest there in full faith. I leave you to your dreams; draw from them what comfort you can. And now, my friend, farewell!

The look which he fixed on me, as he disappeared, was compassionate and thoughtful; it impressed me with a sad feeling, as if I were not to see him again till we should meet in the world of spirits.

[1829]

---

[2] Cf. Job, xxxvi, 27–28.

[3] Referring to Henri IV (1553–1610), King of France, to whom has been attributed the idea of a "Christian republic," a confederation of fifteen European states directed by a general council of deputies.

[4] The Holy Alliance was signed on September 26, 1815, by Russia, Austria, and Prussia, with France later joining. It was an organization for the collective security of Europe, originating in the somewhat visionary idea of Czar Alexander of Russia for a Christian union of peace and love among all the European powers.

Walter Savage Landor

1775–1864

OUTLINE OF EVENTS

1775 Born January 30 at Warwick, son of a provincial doctor.

1783 Enters Rugby School, where he proves an exceptional classical scholar and begins writing poetry.

1791 Removed from Rugby, under threat of expulsion, for his "rebelliousness."

1793 Takes up residence at Trinity College, Oxford, where he becomes "notorious as a mad Jacobin."

1794 June, "rusticated" for "firing off a gun in the quadrangle [of his college] in the time of prayers;" serious quarrel with his father; December, takes up residence in London.

1795 *The Poems of Walter Savage Landor* published. Spends much of next three years in Wales.

1798 The epic poem *Gebir* published.

1802 *Poetry by the Author of Gebir* published. Summer, visits Paris, sees Napoleon, and becomes disenchanted with the French Revolution.

1803 Latin version of *Gebir* published. At father's death receives a considerable fortune.

1806 *Simonidea*, a collection of English and Latin poems, published.

1808 Meets Southey and commences an enduring friendship. August–October, in Spain, where he provides financial aid to the Spanish and leads a troop against the French.

1811 Marries Julia Thuillier.

1812 The tragedy *Count Julian* published.

1813–14 Brought to financial ruin through his expenditures and the mismanagement of his estate of Llanthony Abbey, Monmouthshire, purchased in 1808. Leaves England May 28, 1814, to escape his creditors. In September 1814, separates from his wife at Jersey and moves to Tours.

1815 February, reunited with his wife. Fall, the Landors proceed to Italy and settle at Como.

1818 March, son Arnold Savage born. September, Landors leave Como and settle in Pisa.

1820 March, daughter Julia born. June, *Idyllia Heroica Decem* published at Pisa.

1821 Landors move to Florence, where son Walter Savage is born (November 1822).

1824 First two volumes of *Imaginary Conversations* published.

1825 Meets Hazlitt and Leigh Hunt. August, son Charles Savage born.

1828 Additional volume of *Imaginary Conversations* published.

1829 Two further volumes of *Imaginary Conversations* published. Takes up residence at Villa Gherardesca, near Fiesole.

1832 May–November, visits England, where he meets Wordsworth, Coleridge, and Lamb.

1834 *Citation and Examination of Wil. Shakspeare ... before the Worshipful Sir Thomas Lucy, Knight, touching deer-stealing* published.

1835   Separates from wife and returns to England.

1836   *Pericles and Aspasia* and *Letters of a Conservative* published. Meets Robert Browning, Elizabeth Barrett, and John Forster (Landor's future editor and biographer). July–October, in Germany in a futile attempt to reclaim his children.

1837   *The Pentameron and Pentalogia* published.

1839   Dramas *Andrea of Hungary* and *Giovanna of Naples* published.

1840   Drama *Fra Rupert* published. Friendship with Dickens whose second son (b. 1841) is christened Walter Landor Dickens.

1846   *The Works of Walter Savage Landor* published.

1847   Collected Latin works, *Poemata et Inscriptiones*, published; *Hellenics* published.

1853   Appears as the character Lawrence Boythorn in Dickens' *Bleak House*. *Imaginary Conversations of Greeks and Romans* and *Last Fruit off an Old Tree* published.

1858   July 16, flees England to escape legal action for "libelous" epigrams in his *Dry Sticks, Fagoted by the Late W. S. Landor*. August, returns to his villa at Fiesole; disgrace and scandal connected with trial lead to illness and debility.

1859   *Mr. Landor's Remarks on a Suit Preferred Against Him* published as an attempted vindication. July, leaves Villa Gherardesca and is cared for by the Brownings. New edition of *Hellenics* published.

1863   *Heroic Idyls* published.

1864   Dies, September 17, in Florence.

SELECTED BIBLIOGRAPHY

BIOGRAPHY

ELWIN, MALCOLM, *Landor: A Replevin*, London: Macdonald, 1958.
SUPER, R. H., *Walter Savage Landor: A Biography*, New York: New York University Press, 1954.

EDITIONS

CRUMP, C. G. (ed.), *Selected Works of Walter Savage Landor*, 10 vols., London: J. M. Dent and Company, 1891–1893.
FORSTER, JOHN (ed.), *The Works and Life of Walter Savage Landor*, 8 vols., London: Chapman and Hall, 1876.
PROUDFIT, CHARLES L. (ed.), *Selected Imaginary Conversations of Literary Men and Statesmen*, Lincoln, Neb.: University of Nebraska Press, 1969.
WELBY, T. EARLE and STEPHEN WHEELER (eds.), *The Complete Works of Walter Savage Landor*, 16 vols., London: Chapman and Hall, 1927–1936.

SCHOLARSHIP AND CRITICISM

DE SELINCOURT, ERNEST, "Landor's Prose," in *Wordsworthian and other Studies*, Oxford: Clarendon Press, 1947.
FLASDIECK, HERMANN M., "Walter Savage Landor und seine 'Imaginary Conversations,'" *Englische Studien*, LVIII (1924), 390–431.
HAZLITT, WILLIAM, review of the first two volumes of *Imaginary Conversations*, *Edinburgh Review*, XL (1824), 67–92.
VITOUX, PIERRE, *L'Œuvre de Walter Savage Landor*, Paris: Presses Universitaires de France, 1964.
WILLIAMS, STANLEY T., "Walter Savage Landor as a Critic of Literature," *PMLA*, XXXVIII (1923), 906–928.

IMAGINARY CONVERSATIONS

*The most popular and enduring of Landor's literary achievements,
Imaginary Conversations were largely written and published
between 1821 and 1829. The speakers of the "Conversations"
include statesmen, philosophers, and literary figures from ancient
Greece through Landor's own times. Some of the compositions,
such as "Marcellus and Hannibal," "Tiberius and Vipsania,"
and "Peter the Great and Alexis," are genuinely and powerfully
dramatic; others, such as "Southey and Porson," are more discursive and provide Landor the opportunity to voice his own
literary and political opinions. The text here followed is that of*
The Works and Life of Walter Savage Landor *(London,
1876), in eight volumes, prepared by John Forster, Landor's
biographer and editor.*

FROM

IMAGINARY
CONVERSATIONS

FROM

SOUTHEY AND PORSON[1]

Porson. I SUSPECT, Mr. Southey, you are angry with
me for the freedom with which I have spoken of your
poetry and Wordsworth's.

Southey. What could have induced you to imagine
it, Mr. Professor? You have indeed bent your eyes
upon me, since we have been together, with somewhat
of fierceness and defiance; I presume you fancied me
to be a commentator. You wrong me, in your belief
that any opinion on my poetical works hath molested
me; but you afford me more than compensation in
supposing me acutely sensible of injustice done to
Wordsworth. If we must converse on these topics,
we will converse on him. What man ever existed who
spent a more inoffensive life, or adorned it with
nobler studies?

Porson. None; and they who attack him with
virulence are men of as little morality as reflection.
I have demonstrated that one of them, he who wrote
the *Pursuits of Literature*,[2] could not construe a Greek
sentence or scan a verse; and I have fallen on the very
Index from which he drew out his forlorn hope on the
parade. This is incomparably the most impudent

fellow I have met with in the course of my reading,
which has lain, you know, in a province where impudence is no rarity. I am sorry to say that we critics
who write for the learned, have sometimes set a bad
example to our younger brothers, the critics who
write for the public: but if they were considerate and
prudent, they would find out that a deficiency in
weight and authority might in some measure be
compensated by deference and decorum. Not to
mention the refuse of the literary world, the sweeping
of booksellers' shops, the dust thrown up by them in a
corner to blow by pinches on new publications; not to
tread upon or disturb this filth, the greatest of our
critics now living are only great comparatively. They
betray their inconsiderateness when they look dis-
dainfully on the humbler in acquirements and intellect. A little wit, or, as that is not always at hand, a
little impudence instead of it, throws its rampant
briar over dry lacunes: a drop of oil, sweet or rancid,
covers a great quantity of poor broth. Instead of
anything in this way, I would seriously recommend to
the employer of our critics, young and old, that he
oblige them to pursue a course of study such as this:
that under the superintendence of some respectable
student from the university, they first read and examine the contents of the book; a thing greatly more
useful in criticism that is generally thought; secondly,
that they carefully write them down, number them,
and range them under their several heads; thirdly,
that they mark every beautiful, every faulty, every
ambiguous, every uncommon expression. Which being
completed, that they inquire what author, ancient or
modern, has treated the same subject; that they compare them, first in smaller, afterward in larger portions, noting every defect in precision and its causes,
every excellence and its nature; that they graduate
these, fixing *plus* and *minus*, and designating them
more accurately and discriminately by means of
colours, stronger or paler. For instance, purple might
express grandeur and majesty of thought; scarlet,
vigour of expression; pink, liveliness; green, elegant
and equable composition: these however and others,
as might best attract their notice and serve their
memory. The same process may be used where
authors have not written on the same subject, when
those who have are wanting, or have touched it but
incidentally. Thus Addison and Fontenelle, not very
like, may be compared in the graces of style, in the
number and degree of just thoughts and lively fancies:
thus the dialogues of Cicero with those of Plato, his
ethics with those of Aristoteles, his orations with those
of Demosthenes. It matters not if one be found superior to the other in this thing, and inferior in that; the
exercise is taken; the qualities of two authors are

---

[1] Richard Porson (1759–1808) was Regius Professor of Greek
at Cambridge University and one of the most distinguished
classical scholars of his time. "Southey and Porson" was the
first of the "Conversations" to be published, appearing in *The
London Magazine* for July 1823, prior to its appearance in the first
volume of *Imaginary Conversations* (1824).

[2] A reference to Thomas James Mathias (c. 1754–1835), whose
satirical poem first appeared, anonymously, in 1794.

explored and understood, and their distances laid down, as geographers speak, from accurate survey. The *plus* and *minus* of good and bad and ordinary, will have something of a scale to rest upon; and after a time the degrees of the higher parts in intellectual dynamics may be more nearly attained, though never quite exactly.

Southey. Nothing is easier than to mark and number the striking parts of Homer: it is little more difficult to demonstrate why they are so: the same thing may then be done in Milton: these pieces in each poet may afterward be collated and summed up. Every man will be capable or incapable of it in proportion as his mind is poetical: few indeed will ever write anything on the subject worth reading; but they will acquire strength and practice. The critic of the trade will gain a more certain livelihood and a more reputable one than before, and no great matter will be spent upon his education.

Porson. Which however must be entered on in an opposite way from the statuary's: the latter begins with dirt and ends with marble; the former begins with marble and ends with dirt. This, nevertheless, he may so manage as neither to be ridiculed nor starved.

Southey. For my own part, I should be well contented with that share of reputation which might come meted out and delivered to me after the analytical and close comparison you propose. Its accomplishment can hardly be expected in an age when everything must be done quickly. To run with oars and sails, was formerly the expression of orators for velocity: it would now express slowness. Our hats, our shoes, our whole habiliments, are made at one stroke; our fortunes the same, and the same our criticisms. Under my fellow-labourers in this vineyard, many vines have bled and few have blossomed. The proprietors seem to keep their stock as agriculturists keep lean sheep, to profit by their hoof and ordure.

Porson. You were speaking this moment of the changes among us. Dwarfs are in fashion still; but they are the dwarfs of literature. These little zanies are incited to the assemblies of the gay world, and admitted to the dinners of the political. Limbs of the law, paralysed and laid up professionally, enter into association with printers, and take retaining fees from some authors, to harangue against others out of any brief before them.

Southey. And they meet with encouragement and success! We stigmatise any lie but a malignant one, and we repel any attack but against fame, virtue, and genius. Fond of trying experiments on poison, we find that the strongest may be extracted from blood; and this itself is rejected as unworthy of our labora-

tory, unless it be drawn from a generous and a capacious heart.

Porson. No other country hath ever been so abundant in speculation as ours; but it would be incredible if we did not see it, that ten or fifteen men, of the humblest attainments, gain a comfortable livelihood by periodical attacks on its best writers. Adverse as I have declared myself to the style and manner of Wordsworth, I never thought that all his reviewers put together could compose anything equal to the worst paragraph in his volumes. I have spoken vehemently against him, and mildly against them; because he could do better, they never could. The same people would treat me with as little reverence as they treat him with, if anything I write were popular, or would become so. It is by fixing on such works that they are carried with them into the doorway. The porter of Cleopatra would not have admitted the asps if they had not been under the figs. Show me, if you can, Mr. Southey, a temperate, accurate, solid expression, of any English work whatever, in any English review.

Southey. Not having at hand so many numbers as it would be requisite to turn over, I must decline the challenge.

Porson. I have observed the same man extol in private, the very book on whose ruin he dined the day before.

Southey. His judgment then may be ambiguous, but you must not deny him the merit of gratitude. If you blame the poor and vicious for abusing the solaces of poverty and vice, how much more should you censure those who administer to them the means of such indulgence.

Porson. The publications which excite the most bustle and biting from these fellows, are always the best, as the fruit on which the flies gather is the ripest. Periodical critics were never so plentiful as they now are. There is hardly a young author who does not make his first attempt in some review; showing his teeth, hanging by his tail, pleased and pleasing by the volubility of his chatter, and doing his best to get a penny for his exhibitor and a nut for his own pouch, by the facetiousness of the tricks he performs upon our heads and shoulders. From all I can recollect of what I noticed when I turned over such matters, a wellsized and useful volume might be compiled and published annually, containing the incorrect expressions, and omitting the opinions, of our booksellers' boys, the reviewers. Looking the other day by accident at two pages of *judgments*, recommendatory of new publications, I found, face to face, the following words, from not the worst of the species. *Scattering so considerable a degree of interest over the contemplation, &c. . . . The dazzling glitter of intellect, &c.* Now in what manner can we *scatter a degree?* unless it be one of those degrees which are scattered at Edinburgh and Glasgow. Such an expression as *dazzling glitter* may often be applied to fancy, but never to intellect. These gentlemen might do somewhat better, if they would read us for the sake of improvement, and not for the sake of showing off a somewhat light familiarity, which never can appertain to them. The time however, I am inclined to believe, is not far distant, when the fashionable will be as much ashamed of purchasing such wayside publications, as the learned would be of reading them. Come, let us away from these criers of cat's-meat and dog's-meat, who excite so many yelpings and mewings as they pass: the vicinity is none of the sweetest.

You will do me the favour, Mr. Southey, not to mention to those who may be kept under the regimen, what I have been proposing here for the benefit of literature: since, although in the street and at college I have had quarrels, lighter or graver, with most other conditions, I have avoided both conflict and contact with writers for reviews and almanacks. Once indeed, I confess it, I was very near falling as low: words passed between me and the more favoured man of letters, who announces to the world the *works and days* of Newmarket, the competitors at its games, their horses, their equisons and colours, and the attendant votaries of that goddess who readily leaves Paphos or Amathus for this annual celebration.

Those who have failed as painters turn picture-cleaners, those who have failed as writers turn reviewers. Orator Henley[3] taught in the last century, that the readiest-made shoes are boots cut down: there are those who abundantly teach us now, that the readiest-made critics are cut-down poets. Their assurance is however by no means diminished from their ill success.

Southey. Puffy fingers have pelted me long enough with snowballs, and I should not wonder if some of them reached the skirts of my greatcoat; but I never turned round to look.

Porson. The little man who followed you in the *Critical Review*, and whose pretensions widen every smile his imbecility excited, would, I am persuaded, if Homer were living, pat him in a fatherly way upon the cheek, and tell him that, by moderating his fire and contracting his prolixity, the public might ere long expect something from him worth reading. I had visited a friend in *King's Road* when he entered.

"Have you seen the Review?" cried he. "Worse than ever! I am resolved to insert a paragraph in the papers, declaring that I had no concern in the last number."

"Is it so very bad?" said I quietly.

"Infamous! detestable!" exclaimed he.

"Sit down then: nobody will believe you:" was my answer.

Since that morning he has discovered that I drink harder than usual, that my faculties are wearing fast away, that once indeed I had some Greek in my head, but . . . he then claps the forefinger to the side of his nose, turns his eye slowly upward, and looks compassionately and calmly.

Southey. Come, Mr. Porson, grant him his merits: no critic is better contrived to make any work a monthly one, no writer more dexterous in giving a finishing touch.

Porson. Let him take his due and be gone: now to the rest. The plagiary has a greater latitude of choice than we: and if he brings home a parsnip or turnip-top, when he could as easily have pocketted a nectarine or a pine-apple, he must be a blockhead. I never heard the name of the *pursuer of literature*, who has little more merit in having stolen, than he would have had if he had never stolen at all; and I have forgotten that other man's,[4] who evinced his fitness to be the censor of our age, by a translation of the most naked and impure satires of antiquity, those of Juvenal, which owe their preservation to the partiality of the friars. I shall entertain an unfavourable opinion of him if he has translated them well: pray has he?

Southey. Indeed I do not know. I read poets for their poetry, and to extract that nutriment of the intellect and of the heart which poetry should contain. I never listen to the swans of the cesspool, and must declare that nothing is heavier to me than rottenness and corruption.

Porson. You are right, sir, perfectly right. A translator of Juvenal would open a public drain to look for a needle, and may miss it. My nose is not easily offended; but I must have something to fill my belly. Come, we will lay aside the scrip of the transpositor and the pouch of the pursuer, in reserve for the days of unleavened bread: and again, if you please, to the lakes and mountains. Now we are both in better humour, I must bring you to a confession that in your friend Wordsworth there is occasionally a little trash.

Southey. A haunch of venison would be trash to a Brahmin, a bottle of burgundy to the xerif of Mecca.

---

3 John Henley (1692–1756) was a famous and eccentric London preacher.

4 William Gifford (see section on Reviewers, p. 804) had published a translation of Juvenal in 1802.

Porson. I will not be anticipated by you. Trash, I confess, is no proof that nothing good can lie above it and about it. The roughest and least manageable soil surrounds gold and diamonds. Homer and Dante and Shakespeare and Milton have each many hundred lines worth little; lines without force, without feeling, without fancy; in short, without beauty of any kind. But it is the character of modern poetry, as it is of modern arms and equipments, to be more uniformly trim and polished. The ancients in both had more strength and splendour; they had also more inequality and rudeness.

Southey. We are guided by precept, by habit, by taste, by constitution. Hitherto our sentiments on poetry have been delivered down to us from authority; and if it can be demonstrated, as I think it may be, that the authority is inadequate, and that the dictates are often inapplicable and often misinterpreted, you will allow me to remove the cause out of court. Every man can see what is very bad in a poem, almost every one can see what is very good; but you, Mr. Porson, who have turned over all the volumes of all the commentators, will inform me whether I am right or wrong in asserting, that no critic hath yet appeared who hath been able to fix or to discern the exact degrees of excellence above a certain point.

Porson. None.

Southey. The reason is, because the eyes of no one have been upon a level with it. Supposing, for the sake of argument, the contest of Hesiod and Homer to have taken place: the judges, who decided in favour of the worse, and he indeed in the poetry has little merit, may have been elegant, wise, and conscientious men. Their decision was in favour of that to the species of which they had been the most accustomed. Corinna[5] was preferred to Pindar no fewer than five times; and the best judges in Greece gave her the preference; yet whatever were her powers, and beyond a question they were extraordinary, we may assure ourselves that she stood many degrees below Pindar. Nothing is more absurd than the report that the judges were prepossessed by her beauty. Plutarch tells us that she was much older than her competitor, who consulted her judgment in his earlier odes. Now, granting their first competition to have been when Pindar was twenty years old, and that the others were in the years succeeding, her beauty must have been somewhat on the decline; for in Greece there are few women who retain the graces, none who retain the bloom of youth, beyond the twenty-third year. Her

---

[5] Corinna was a Greek poetess (*c.* 500 B.C.), who bested Pindar in several poetic contests.

countenance, I doubt not, was expressive: but expression, although it gives beauty to men, makes women pay dearly for its stamp, and pay soon. Nature seems, in protection to their loveliness, to have ordered that they who are our superiors in quickness and sensibility, should be little disposed to laborious thought or to long excursions in the labyrinths of fancy. We may be convinced that the verdict of the judges was biassed by nothing else than their habitudes of thinking: we may be convinced too that, living in an age when poetry was cultivated highly, and selected from the most acute and the most dispassionate, they were subject to no greater errors of opinion than are the learned messmates of our English colleges.

Porson. You are more liberal in your largesses to the fair Greeks than a friend of mine was, who resided in Athens to acquire the language. He assured me that beauty there was in bud at thirteen, in full blossom at fifteen, losing a leaf or two every day at seventeen, trembling on the thorn at nineteen, and under the tree at twenty.

Returning, Mr. Southey, to the difficulty, or rather to the rarity, of an accurate and just survey of poetical and other literary works, I do not see why we should not borrow an idea from geometricians and astronomers, why we should not have our triangles and quadrants, why, in short, we should not measure out writings by small portions at a time, and compare the brighter parts of two authors page by page. The minor beauties, the complection and contexture, may be considered at last, and more at large. Daring geniusses, ensigns and undergraduates, members of Anacreontic and Pindaric clubs, will scoff at me. Painters who can draw nothing correctly, hold Raffael in contempt, and appeal to the sublimity of Michael-Angelo and the splendour of Titian: ignorant that these great men were great by science first, and employed in painting the means I propose for criticism. Venus and the damned submitted to the same squaring.

Such a method would be useful to critics in general, and even the wisest and most impartial would be much improved by it; although few, either by these means or any, are likely to be quite correct or quite unanimous on the merits of any two authors whatsoever.

Southey. Those who are learners would be teachers; while those who have learnt much would procure them at any price. It is only when we have mounted high, that we are sensible of wanting a hand.

Porson. On the subject of poetry in particular, there are some questions not yet sufficiently discussed: I will propose two. First, admitting that in the tragedies of Sophocles there was (which I believe) twice as much of good poetry as in the Iliad, does it follow that he was as admirable a poet as Homer?

Southey. No, indeed: so much I do attribute to the conception and formation of a novel and vast design, and so wide is the difference I see between the completion of one very great, and the perfection of many smaller. Would even these have existed without Homer? I think not.

Porson. My next question is, whether a poet is to be judged from the quantity of his bad poetry, or from the quality of his best?

Southey. I should certainly say from the latter: because it must be in poetry as in sculpture and painting; he who arrives at a high degree of excellence in these arts, will have made more models, more sketches and designs, than he who has reached but a lower; and the conservation of them, whether by accident or by choice, can injure and affect in no manner his more perfect and elaborate works. A drop of sealing-wax, falling by chance or negligence, may efface a fine impression: but what is well done in poetry is never to be effaced by what is ill done afterward. Even the bad poetry of a good poet hath something in it which renders it more valuable, to a judge of these matters, than what passes for much better, and what in many essential points is truly so. I will however keep to the argument, not having lost sight of my illustration in alluding to design and sketches. Many men would leave themselves penniless to purchase an early and rude drawing by Raffael; some arabesque, some nose upon a gryphon or gryphon upon a nose; and never would inquire whether the painter had kept it in his portfolio or had cast it away. The same persons, and others whom we call much wiser, exclaim loudly against any literary sketch unworthy of a leaf among the productions of its author. No ideas are so trivial, so incorrect, so incoherent, but they may have entered the idle fancy, and have taken a higher place than they ought in the warm imagination, of the best poets. We find in Dante, as you just now remarked, a prodigious quantity of them; and indeed not a few in Virgil, grave as he is and stately. Infantine and petty there is hardly anything in the Iliad, but the dull and drowthy stop us unexpectedly now and then. The boundaries of mind lie beyond these writers, although their splendour lets us see nothing on the farther side. In so wide and untrodden a creation as that of Shakespeare's, can we wonder or complain that sometimes we are bewildered and entangled in the exuberance of fertility? Dry-brained men upon the Continent, the trifling wits of the theatre, accurate however and expert calculators, tell us that his beauties are balanced by his faults. The poetical opposition, puffing for popularity, cry cheerily against them, *his faults are balanced by his beauties;* when, in reality, all the faults that ever were committed in poetry would be but as air to earth, if we could weight them against one single thought or image, such as almost every scene exhibits in every drama of this unrivalled genius. Do you hear me with patience?

Porson. With more; although at Cambridge we rather discourse on Bacon, for we know him better. He was immeasurably a less wise man than Shakespeare, and not a wiser writer: for he knew his fellow-man only as he saw him in the street and in the court, which indeed is but a dirtier street and a narrower: Shakespeare, who also knew him there, knew him everywhere else, both as he was and as he might be.

Southey. There is as great a difference between Shakespeare and Bacon as between an American forest and a London timber-yard. In the timber-yard the materials are sawed and squared and set across: in the forest we have the natural form of the tree, all its growth, all its branches, all its leaves, all the mosses that grow about it, all the birds and insects that inhabit it; now deep shadows absorbing the whole wilderness; now bright bursting glades, with exuberant grass and flowers and fruitage; now untroubled skies; now terrific thunderstorms; everywhere multiformity, everywhere immensity.

Porson. If after this ramble in the heat you are not thirsty, I would ask another question. What is the reason why, when not only the glory of great kings and statesmen, but even of great philosophers, is much enhanced by two or three good apophthegms, that of a great poet is lowered by them, even if he should invest them with good verse? For certainly the dignity of a great poet is thought to be lowered by the writing of epigrams.

Southey. As you said of Wordsworth, the great poet could accomplish better things; the others could not. People in this apparent act of injustice do real justice, without intending or knowing it. All writers have afforded some information, or have excited some sentiment or idea, somewhere. This alone should exempt the humblest of them from revilings, unless it appear that he hath misapplied his powers through insolence or malice. In that case, whatever sentence may be passed upon him, I consider it no honour to be the executioner. What must we think of those who travel far and wide that, before they go to rest they may burst into the arbour of a recluse, whose weakest thoughts are benevolence, whose worst are purity? On his poetry I shall say nothing, unless you lead me to it, wishing you however to examine it analytically and severely.

Porson. There are folks who, when they read my criticism, say, "*I do not think so.*" It is because they do not think so, that I write. Men entertain some opinions which it is indeed our duty to confirm, but many also which it is expedient to eradicate, and more which it is important to correct. They read less willingly what may improve their understanding and enlarge their capacity, than what corroborates their prejudices and establishes their prepossessions. I never bear malice toward those who try to reduce me to their own dimensions. A narrow mind cannot be enlarged, nor can a capacious one be contracted. Are we angry with a phial for not being a flask? or do we wonder that the skin of an elephant sits unwieldily on a squirrel?

Southey. Great men will always pay deference to greater: little men will not: because the little are fractious; and the weaker they are, the more obstinate and crooked.

Porson. To proceed on our inquiry. I will not deny that to compositions of a new kind, like Wordsworth's, we come without scales and weights, and without the means of making an assay.

Southey. Mr. Porson, it does not appear to me that anything more is necessary in the first instance, than to interrogate our hearts in what manner they have been affected. If the ear is satisfied; if at one moment a tumult is aroused in the breast, and tranquillised at another, with a perfect consciousness of equal power exerted in both cases; if we rise up from the perusal of the work with a strong excitement to thought, to imagination, to sensibility; above all, if we sat down with some propensities toward evil and walk away with much stronger toward good, in the midst of a world which we never had entered and of which we never had dreamed before, shall we perversely put on again the *old man* of criticism, and dissemble that we have been conducted by a most beneficent and most potent genius? Nothing proves to me so manifestly in what a pestiferous condition are its lazarettos, as when I observe how little hath been objected against those who have substituted words for things, and how much against those who have reinstated things for words.

Porson. I find, however, much to censure in our modern poets; I mean those who have written since Milton. But praise is due to such as threw aside the French models. Percy was the first: then came the Wartons, and then Cowper; more diversified in his poetry and more classical than any since.

Southey. I wonder you admire an author so near your own times, indeed contemporary.

Porson. There is reason for wonder. Men in general do so in regard both to liberty and poetry.

Southey. I know not whether the Gauls had this latter gift before they assaulted the temple of Apollo at Delphi; certainly from that time downward the god hath owed them a grudge, and hath been as unrelenting as he was with the dogs and mules before Troy. The succeeding race, nevertheless, has tightened and gilded and gallantly tagged the drum of tragic declamation. Surely not Cowper nor any other is farther from it than Wordsworth.

Porson. But his drum is damp; and his tags are none the better for being of hemp, with the broken stalks in.

Southey. Let Wordsworth prove to the world that there may be animation without blood and broken bones, and tenderness remote from the stews. Some will doubt it; for even things the most evident are often but little perceived and strangely estimated. Swift ridiculed the music of Handel and the generalship of Marlborough, Pope the perspicacity and the scholarship of Bentley, Gray the abilities of Shaftesbury and the eloquence of Rousseau. Shakespeare hardly found those who would collect his tragedies; Milton was read from godliness; Virgil was antiquated and rustic; Cicero Asiatic.[6] What a rabble has persecuted my friend! An elephant is born to be consumed by ants in the midst of his unapproachable solitudes: Wordsworth is the prey of Jeffrey. Why repine? Let us rather amuse ourselves with allegories, and recollect that God in the creation left his noblest creature at the mercy of a serpent.

Porson. In our authors of the present day I would recommend principally, to reduce the expenditure of words to the means of support, and to be severe in style without the appearance of severity. But this advice is more easily given than taken. Your friend is verbose; not indeed without something for his words to rest upon, but from a resolution to gratify and indulge his capacity. He pursues his thoughts too far; and considers more how he may show them entirely than how he may show them advantageously. Good men may utter whatever comes uppermost, good poets may not. It is better, but it is also more difficult, to make a selection of thoughts than to accumulate them. He who has a splendid sideboard, should have an iron chest with a double lock upon it, and should hold in reserve a greater part than he displays.

I know not why two poets so utterly dissimilar as your author and Coleridge should be constantly mentioned together. In the one I find diffuseness, monotony, not indistinctness, but uninteresting expanse, and such figures, and such colouring as Morland's;[7] in the other, bright colours without form, sublimely void. In his prose he talks like a madman when he calls Saint Paul's Epistle to the Ephesians "the sublimest composition of man."

Southey. This indeed he hath spoken, but he has

---

6 Stylistically florid and extravagant.
7 George Morland (1763–1804) was an English genre painter.

not yet published it in his writings: it will appear in his *Table Talk*, perhaps.

Porson. Such table-talk may be expected to come forth very late in the evening, when the wine and candles are out, and the body lies horizontally underneath. He believes he is a believer; but why does he believe that the Scriptures are best reverenced by bearing false witness to them? Is it an act of piety to play the little child in the *go-cart* of Religion, or to beslaver the pretty dress he has just put on,

> Porrigens teneras manus
> Matris e gremio suæ
> Semihiante labello.[8]

Pardon a quotation: I hate it: I wonder how it escaped me.

Wordsworth goes out of his way to be attacked: he picks up a piece of dirt, throws it on the carpet in the midst of the company, and cries *This is a better man than any of you.* He does indeed mould the base material into what form he chooses; but why not rather invite us to contemplate it than challenge us to condemn it? Here surely is false taste.

Southey. The principal and the most general accusation against him is, that the vehicle of his thoughts is unequal to them. Now did ever the judges at the Olympic games say, "We would have awarded to you the meed of victory, if your chariot had been equal to your horses: it is true they have won; but the people is displeased at a car neither new nor richly gilt, and without a gryphon or sphynx engraved on the axle"? You admire simplicity in Euripides; you censure it in Wordsworth; believe me, sir, it arises in neither from penury of thought, which seldom has produced it, but from the strength of temperance, and at the suggestion of principle. Some of his critics are sincere in their censure, and are neither invidious nor unlearned; but their optics have been exercised on other objects, altogether dissimilar, and they are (permit me an expression not the worse for daily use) entirely out of their element. His very clearness puzzles and perplexes them, and they imagine that straightness is distortion, as children on seeing a wand dipped in limpid and still water. Clear writers, like clear fountains, do not seem so deep as they are: the turbid look the most profound.

Porson. Fleas know not whether they are upon the body of a giant or upon one of ordinary size, and bite both indiscriminately.

---

[8] Porrigens . . . labello: "stretching his baby hands from his mother's lap with lips half-parted." Catullus' "Collis O Heliconii," ll. 213–14, 216 (F. W. Cornish translation, Loeb Classical Library, Harvard University Press).

Southey. Our critics are onion-eaters by the Pyramids of Poetry. They sprawl along the sands, without an idea how high and wonderful are the edifices above, whose base is solid as the earth itself, and whose summits are visible over a hundred ages.

Ignorance has not been single-handed the enemy of Wordsworth; but Petulance and Malignity have accompanied her, and have been unremittent in their attacks. Small poets, small critics, lawyers who have much time on their hands and hanging heavily, come forward unfeed against him; such is the spirit of patriotism, rushing everywhere for the public good. Most of these have tried their fortune at some little lottery-office of literature, and, receiving a blank, have chewed upon it harshly and wryly. We, like jackdaws, are amicable creatures while we are together in the dust; but let any gain a battlement or steeple, and behold! the rest fly about him at once, and beat him down.

Take up a poem of Wordsworth's and read it; I would rather say, read them all; and, knowing that a mind like yours must grasp closely what comes within it, I will then appeal to you whether any poet of our country, since Milton, hath exerted greater powers with less strain and less of ostentation. I would however, by his permission, lay before you for this purpose a poem which is yet unpublished and incomplete.

Porson. Pity, with such abilities, he does not imitate the ancients somewhat more.

Southey. Whom did they imitate? If his genius is equal to theirs he has no need of a guide. He also will be an ancient; and the very counterparts of those who now decry him, will extol him a thousand years hence in malignity to the moderns. The ancients have always been opposed to them; just as, at routs and dances, elderly beauties to younger. It would be wise to contract the scene of action, and to decide the business in both cases by couples.

*   *   *   *   *

Porson. I ought not to have interrupted you so long, in your attempt to prove Wordsworth shall I say the rival or the resembler of the ancients?

Southey. Such excursions are not unseasonable in such discussions, and lay in a store of good humour for them. Your narrative has amused me exceedingly. As you call upon me to return with you to the point we set out from, I hope I may assert without a charge of paradox, that whatever is good in poetry is common to all good poets, however wide may be the diversity of manner. Nothing can be more dissimilar than the three Greek tragedians: but would you prefer the closest and best copier of Homer to the worst (whichever he be) among them? Let us avoid what is indifferent or doubtful, and embrace what is good, whether we see it in another or not; and if we have contracted any peculiarity while our muscles and bones were softer, let us hope finally to outgrow it. Our feelings and modes of thinking forbid and exclude a very frequent imitation of the old classics, not to mention our manners, which have a nearer connection than is generally known to exist with the higher poetry. When the occasion permitted it, Wordsworth has not declined to treat a subject as an ancient poet of equal vigour would have treated it. Let me repeat to you his *Laodamia*.[9]

Porson. After your animated recital of this classic poem, I begin to think more highly of you both. It is pleasant to find two poets living as brothers, and particularly when the palm lies between them, with hardly a third in sight. Those who have ascended to the summit of the mountain, sit quietly and familiarly side by side; it is only those who are climbing with briers about their legs, that kick and scramble. Yours is a temper found less frequently in our country than in others. The French poets indeed must stick together to keep themselves warm. By employing courteous expressions mutually, they indulge their vanity rather than their benevolence, and bring the spirit of contest into action gaily and safely. Among the Romans we find Virgil, Horace, and several of their contemporaries, intimately united and profuse of reciprocal praise. Ovid, Cicero, and Pliny are authors the least addicted to censure, and the most ready to offer their testimony in favour of abilities in Greek or countryman. These are the three Romans, the least amiable of nations, and (one excepted) the least sincere, with whom I should have liked best to spend an evening.

Southey. Ennius and old Cato,[10] I am afraid, would have run away with your first affections.

Porson. Old Cato! he, like a wafer, must have been well wetted to be good for anything. Such gentlemen as old Cato we meet every day in St. Mary Axe, and wholesomer wine than his wherever there are sloes and turnips. Ennius could converse without ignorance about Scipio, and without jealousy about Homer.

Southey. And I think he would not have disdained to nod his head on reading *Laodamia*.

Porson. You have recited a most spirited thing indeed: and now to give you a proof that I have been attentive, I will remark two passages that offend me. In the first stanza,

> With sacrifice before the rising morn
> *Performed*, my slaughtered lord *have I required;*
> And in thick darkness, amid shades forlorn,
> Him of the infernal Gods *have I desired*.[11]

I do not see the necessity of *Performed*, which is dull and cumbersome. The second line and the fourth terminate too much alike, and express to a tittle the same meaning: *have I required* and *have I desired* are worse than prosaic; beside which there are four words together of equal length in each.

Southey. I have seen a couplet oftener than once in which every word of the second verse corresponds in measure to every one above it.

Porson. The Scotch have a scabby and a frost-bitten ear for harmony, both in verse and prose: and I remember in *Douglas*[12] two such as you describe.

> This is the place . . the centre of the grove,
> Here stands the oak . . the monarch of the wood.

After this whiff of vapour I must refresh myself with a draught of pure poetry, at the bottom of which is the flake of tartar I wish away.

> He spake of love, such love as spirits feel
> In worlds whose course is equable and pure;
> No fears to beat away, no strife to heal,
> The past unsighed for, and the future sure;
> Spake, as a witness, of a second birth
> For all that is most perfect upon earth.

How unseasonable is the allusion to *witness* and *second birth!* which things, however holy and venerable in themselves, come stinking and reeking to us from the conventicle. I desire to find Laodamia in the silent and gloomy mansion of her beloved Protesilaus; not elbowed by the godly butchers in Tottenham-court Road, nor smelling devoutly of ratafia[13] among the sugar-bakers' wives at Blackfriars.

Mythologies should be kept distinct: the fire-place of one should never be subject to the smoke of another. The gods of different countries, when they come together unexpectedly, are jealous gods, and, as our old women say, *turn the house out of windows.*

Southey. A current of rich and bright thoughts runs through the poem. Pindar himself would not on that subject have braced one to more vigour, nor Euripides have breathed into it more tenderness and

---

[9] Wordsworth's poem of classical subject, first published in 1815.

[10] Quintus Ennius (239–170 B.C.) was an early Roman poet. Marcus Porcius Cato (234–149 B.C.), known as "Cato the Censor," was an early Roman prose writer.

[11] Porson quotes here ll. 1–4, and later, ll. 97–102. In subsequent editions of the poem, Wordsworth changed the passages in light of the objections and suggestions presented here.

[12] Popular tragedy by John Home, first presented in 1756.

[13] A fruit liquor served with cake or used as a flavoring.

passion. The first part of the stanza you have just now quoted might have been heard with shouts of rapture in the regions it describes.

Porson. I am not insensible to the warmly chaste morality which is the soul of it, nor indifferent to the benefits that literature on many occasions has derived from Christianity. But poetry is a luxury to which, if she tolerates and permits it, she accepts no invitation: she beats down your gates and citadels, levels your high places, and eradicates your groves. For which reason I dwell more willingly with those authors who cannot mix and confound the manners they represent. The hope that we may rescue at Herculaneum a great number of them, hath, I firmly believe, kept me alive. Reasonably may the best be imagined to exist in a library of some thousands. It will be recorded to the infamy of the kings and princes now reigning, or rather of those whose feet put into motion their rocking-horses, that they never have made a common cause in behalf of learning, but, on the contrary, have made a common cause against it. The Earth opened her bosom before them, conjuring them to receive again, while it was possible, the glories of their species; and they turned their backs. They pretended that it is not their business or their duty to interfere in the internal affairs of other nations. This is not an internal affair of any: it interests all; it belongs to all: and these scrupulous men have no scruple to interfere in giving their countenance and assistance when a province is to be invaded or a people to be enslaved.

Southey. To neglect what is recoverable in the authors of antiquity, is like rowing away from a crew that is making its escape from shipwreck.

Porson. The most contemptible of the Medicean family did more for the advancement of letters than the whole body of existing potentates. If their delicacy is shocked or alarmed at the idea of a proposal to send scientific and learned men to Naples, let them send a brace of pointers as internuncios, and the property is their own. Twenty scholars in seven years might retrieve the worst losses we experience from the bigotry of popes and califs. I do not intend to assert that every Herculanean manuscript might within that period be unfolded; but the three first legible sentences might be; which is quite sufficient to inform the intelligent reader whether a farther attempt on the scroll would repay his trouble. There are fewer than thirty Greek authors worth inquiring for; they exist beyond doubt, and beyond doubt they may, by attention, patience, and skill, be brought to light.

Southey. You and I, Mr. Porson, are truly and sincerely concerned in the loss of such treasures: but how often have we heard much louder lamentations than ours, from gentlemen who, if they were brought again to light, would never cast their eyes over them, even in the bookseller's window. I have been present at homilies on the corruption and incredulity of the age, and principally on the violation of the sabbath, from sleek clergymen, canons of cathedrals, who were at the gaming-table the two first hours of that very day; and I have listened to others on the loss of the classics, from men who never took the trouble to turn over half that is remaining to us of Cicero and Livius.

Porson. The Greek language is almost unknown out of England and northern Germany: in the rest of the world, exclusive of Greece, I doubt whether fifty scholars ever read one page of it without a version.

Southey. Give fifteen to Italy, twelve to the Netherlands, as many to France; the remainder will hardly be collected in Sweden, Denmark, Russia, Austria. In regard to Spain and Portugal, we might as well look for them among the Moors and Negroes.

Porson. You are too prodigal to Italy and France. Matthiæ,[14] in his preface to the Greek grammar, speaks of Germany, of England, of Holland; not a word of France; the country of Stephanus, Budæus, and the Scaligers.[15] Latterly we have seen only Villoison and Larcher[16] fairly escape from the barbarous ignorance around them. Catholic nations in general seem as averse to the Greek language as to the Greek ritual.

Southey. The knowledge of books written in our own is extending daily.

Porson. Although the knowledge too of Greek is extending in England, I doubt whether it is to be found in such large masses as formerly. Schools and universities, like rills and torrents, roll down some grains of it every season; but the lumps have been long stored up in cabinets. I delight in the diffusion of learning; yet, I must confess it, I am most gratified and transported at finding a large quantity of it in one place: just as I would rather have a solid pat of butter at breakfast than a splash of grease upon the table-cloth that covers half of it. Do not attempt to defend the idle and inconsiderate knaves who manage our affairs for us; or defend them on some other ground. Prove, if you please, that they have, one after another, been incessantly occupied in rendering us more moral, more prosperous, more free; but abstain, sir, from any

[14] August Heinrich Matthiae (1769–1835) was a German classical scholar, whose Greek Grammar, first published in 1807, went through many editions and was translated into English in 1818.

[15] Henri Estienne (Stephanus) (1531–1598), Guillaume Budé (1467–1540), J. C. Scaliger (1484–1558), and J. J. Scaliger (1540–1609) were leading French classical scholars of the sixteenth century.

[16] Jean-Baptiste-Gaspard Villoison (1750–1805) and Pierre Henri Larcher (1726–1812) were leading French classical scholars of the eighteenth century.

allusion to their solicitude on the improvement of our literary condition. With a smaller sum that is annually expended on the appointment of some silly and impertinent young envoy, we might restore all or nearly all those writers of immortal name, whose disappearance has been the regret of Genius for four entire centuries. In my opinion a few thousand pounds laid out on such an undertaking, would be laid out as creditably as on a Persian carpet or a Turkish tent; as creditably as on a collar of rubies and a ball-dress of Brussels lace for our Lady in the manger, or as on gilding for the adoration of princesses and their capuchins, the posteriors and anteriors of Saint Januarius.[17]

[July 1823]								[1876]

MARCELLUS AND HANNIBAL

Marcus Claudius Marcellus was a Roman Consul and general during the second Punic War. Landor here describes the imaginary encounter between the two distinguished opponents near Venusia in 208 B.C., after Marcellus had been fatally wounded by Numidian soldiers under Hannibal.

MARCELLUS AND HANNIBAL

Hannibal. COULD a Numidian horseman ride no faster? Marcellus! ho! Marcellus! He moves not ... he is dead. Did he not stir his fingers? Stand wide, soldiers .. wide, forty paces .. give him air .. bring water .. halt! Gather those broad leaves, and all the rest, growing under the brushwood .. unbrace his armour. Loose the helmet first .. his breast rises. I fancied his eyes were fixed on me .. they have rolled back again. Who presumed to touch my shoulder? This horse? It was surely the horse of Marcellus! Let no man mount him. Ha! ha! the Romans too sink into luxury: here is gold about the charger.

Gaulish Chieftain. Execrable thief! The golden chain of our king under a beast's grinders! The vengeance of the gods hath overtaken the impure ...

Hannibal. We will talk about vengeance when we have entered Rome, and about purity among the priests, if they will hear us. Sound for the surgeon. That arrow may be extracted from the side, deep as it is ... The conqueror of Syracuse lies before me ... Send a vessel off to Carthage. Say Hannibal is at the gates of Rome ... Marcellus, who stood alone between us, fallen. Brave man! I would rejoice and can not ... How awfully serene a countenance! Such as we hear are in the islands of the Blessed. And how glorious a form and stature! Such too was theirs! They also once lay thus upon the earth wet with their blood .. few other enter there. And what plain armour!

Gaulish Chieftain. My party slew him .. indeed I think I slew him myself. I claim the chain: it belongs to my king: the glory of Gaul requires it. Never will she endure to see another take it: rather would she lose her last man. We swear! we swear!

Hannibal. My friend, the glory of Marcellus did not require him to wear it. When he suspended the arms of your brave king in the temple, he thought such a trinket unworthy of himself and of Jupiter. The shield he battered down, the breast-plate he pierced with his sword, these he showed to the people and to the gods; hardly his wife and little children saw this, ere his horse wore it.

Gaulish Chieftain. Hear me, O Hannibal!

Hannibal. What! when Marcellus lies before me? when his life may perhaps be recalled? when I may lead him in triumph to Carthage? when Italy, Sicily, Greece, Asia, wait to obey me? Content thee! I will give thee mine own bridle, worth ten such.

Gaulish Chieftain. For myself?

Hannibal. For thyself.

Gaulish Chieftain. And these rubies and emeralds and that scarlet ..

Hannibal. Yes, yes.

Gaulish Chieftain. O glorious Hannibal! unconquerable hero! O my happy country! to have such an ally and defender. I swear eternal gratitude .. yes, gratitude, love, devotion, beyond eternity.

Hannibal. In all treaties we fix the time: I could hardly ask a longer. Go back to thy station .. I would see what the surgeon is about, and hear what he thinks. The life of Marcellus! the triumph of Hannibal! what else has the world in it? only Rome and Carthage: these follow.

Surgeon. Hardly an hour of life is left.

Marcellus. I must die then! The gods be praised! The commander of a Roman army is no captive.

Hannibal (*to the Surgeon*). Could not he bear a sea-voyage? Extract the arrow.

Surgeon. He expires that moment.

Marcellus. It pains me: extract it.

Hannibal. Marcellus, I see no expression of pain on your countenance, and never will I consent to hasten the death of an enemy in my power. Since your recovery is hopeless, you say truly you are no captive.

(*To the Surgeon.*) Is there nothing, man, that can assuage the mortal pain? for, suppress the signs of it

---

[17] Patron saint of Naples, martyred in 304. His head and two vials of his blood, which is said to miraculously liquefy three times a year, are preserved in the cathedral at Naples.

as he may, he must feel it. Is there nothing to alleviate and allay it?

Marcellus. Hannibal, give me thy hand .. thou hast found it and brought it me, compassion.

(*To the Surgeon.*) Go, friend; others want thy aid; several fell around me.

Hannibal. Recommend to your country, O Marcellus, while time permits it, reconciliation and peace with me, informing the Senate of my superiority in force, and the impossibility of resistance. The tablet is ready: let me take off this ring .. try to write, to sign it at least. O! what satisfaction I feel at seeing you able to rest upon the elbow, and even to smile!

Marcellus. Within an hour or less, with how severe a brow would Minos[1] say to me, "Marcellus, is this thy writing?"

Rome loses one man: she hath lost many such, and she still hath many left.

Hannibal. Afraid as you are of falsehood, say you this? I confess in shame the ferocity of my countrymen. Unfortunately too the nearer posts are occupied by Gauls, infinitely more cruel. The Numidians are so in revenge; the Gauls both in revenge and in sport. My presence is required at a distance, and I apprehend the barbarity of one or other, learning, as they must do, your refusal to execute my wishes for the common good, and feeling that by this refusal you deprive them of their country, after so long an absence.

Marcellus. Hannibal, thou art not dying.

Hannibal. What then? What mean you?

Marcellus. That thou mayest, and very justly, have many things yet to apprehend: I can have none. The barbarity of thy soldiers is nothing to me: mine would not dare be cruel. Hannibal is forced to be absent; and his authority goes away with his horse. On this turf lies defaced the semblance of a general; but Marcellus is yet the regulator of his army. Dost thou abdicate a power conferred on thee by thy nation? Or wouldst thou acknowledge it to have become, by thy own sole fault, less plenary than thy adversary's?

I have spoken too much: let me rest: this mantle oppresses me.

Hannibal. I placed my mantle on your head when the helmet was first removed, and while you were lying in the sun. Let me fold it under, and then replace the ring.

Marcellus. Take it, Hannibal. It was given me by a poor woman who flew to me at Syracuse, and who covered it with her hair, torn off in desperation that she had no other gift to offer. Little thought I that her gift and her words should be mine. How suddenly may

the most powerful be in the situation of the most helpless! Let that ring and the mantle under my head be the exchange of guests at parting. The time may come, Hannibal, when thou (and the gods alone know whether as conqueror or conquered) mayest sit under the roof of my children, and in either case it shall serve thee. In thy adverse fortune, they will remember on whose pillow their father breathed his last; in thy prosperous (heaven grant it may shine upon thee in some other country) it will rejoice thee to protect them. We feel ourselves the most exempt from affliction when we relieve it, although we are then the most conscious that it may befall us.

There is one thing here which is not at the disposal of either.

Hannibal. What?

Marcellus. This body.

Hannibal. Whither would you be lifted? Men are ready.

Marcellus. I meant not so. My strength is failing. I seem to hear rather what is within than what is without. My sight and my other senses are in confusion. I would have said, This body, when a few bubbles of air shall have left it, is no more worthy of thy notice than of mine; but thy glory will not let thee refuse it to the piety of my family.

Hannibal. You would ask something else. I perceive an inquietude not visible till now.

Marcellus. Duty and Death make us think of home sometimes.

Hannibal. Thitherward the thoughts of the conqueror and of the conquered fly together.

Marcellus. Hast thou any prisoners from my escort?

Hannibal. A few dying lie about .. and let them lie .. they are Tuscans. The remainder I saw at a distance, flying, and but one brave man among them .. he appeared a Roman .. a youth who turned back, though wounded. They surrounded and dragged him away, spurring his horse with their swords. These Etrurians measure their courage carefully, and tack it well together before they put it on, but throw it off again with lordly ease.

Marcellus, why think about them? or does aught else disquiet your thoughts?

Marcellus. I have suppressed it long enough. My son .. my beloved son!

Hannibal. Where is he? Can it be? Was he with you?

Marcellus. He would have shared my fate .. and has not. Gods of my country! beneficent throughout life to me, in death surpassingly beneficent, I render you, for the last time, thanks.

---

[1] Supreme judge of Hades.

[1828]   [1876]

326] WALTER SAVAGE LANDOR

TIBERIUS AND VIPSANIA*

Tiberius. VIPSANIA, my Vipsania, whither art thou walking?

Vipsania. Whom do I see? my Tiberius?

Tiberius. Ah! no, no, no! but thou seest the father of thy little Drusus. Press him to thy heart the more closely for this meeting, and give him . .

Vipsania. Tiberius! the altars, the gods, the destinies, are between us . . I will take it from this hand; thus, thus shall he receive it.

Tiberius. Raise up thy face, my beloved! I must not shed tears. Augustus! Livia! ye shall not extort them from me. Vipsania! I may kiss thy head . . for I have saved it. Thou sayest nothing. I have wronged thee; ay?

Vipsania. Ambition does not see the earth she treads on: the rock and the herbage are of one substance to her. Let me excuse you to my heart, O Tiberius. It has many wants; this is the first and greatest.

Tiberius. My ambition, I swear by the immortal gods, placed not the bar of severance between us. A stronger hand, the hand that composes Rome and sways the world . . .

Vipsania. . . . Overawed Tiberius. I know it; Augustus willed and commanded it.

Tiberius. And overawed Tiberius! Power bent, Death terrified, a Nero! What is our race, that any should look down on us and spurn us! Augustus, my benefactor, I have wronged thee! Livia, my mother, this one cruel deed was thine! To reign forsooth is a lovely thing! O womanly appetite! Who would have been before me, though the palace of Cæsar cracked and split with emperors, while I, sitting in idleness on a cliff of Rhodes, eyed the sun as he swang his golden censer athwart the heavens, or his image as it over-

strode the sea.† I have it before me; and though it seems falling on me, I can smile at it; just as I did from my little favourite skiff, painted round with the marriage of Thetis, when the sailors drew their long shaggy hair across their eyes, many a stadium away from it, to mitigate its effulgence.

These too were happy days: days of happiness like these I could recall and look back upon with unaching brow.

O land of Greece! Tiberius blesses thee, bidding thee rejoice and flourish.

Why can not one hour, Vipsania, beauteous and light as we have led, return?

Vipsania. Tiberius! is it to me that you were speaking? I would not interrupt you; but I thought I heard my name as you walked away and looked up toward the East. So silent!

Tiberius. Who dared to call thee? Thou wert mine before the gods . . do they deny it? Was it my fault . .

Vipsania. Since we are separated, and for ever, O Tiberius, let us think no more on the cause of it. Let neither of us believe that the other was to blame: so shall separation be less painful.

Tiberius. O mother! and did I not tell thee what she was? patient in injury, proud in innocence, serene in grief!

Vipsania. Did you say that too? but I think it was so: I had felt little. One vast wave has washed away the impression of smaller from my memory. Could Livia, could your mother, could she who was so kind to me . .

Tiberius. The wife of Cæsar did it. But hear me now, hear me: be calm as I am. No weaknesses are such as those of a mother who loves her only son immoderately; and none are so easily worked upon from without. Who knows what impulses she received? She is very, very kind; but she regards me only; and that which at her bidding is to encompass and adorn me. All the weak look after power, protectress of weakness. Thou art a woman, O Vipsania! is there nothing in thee to excuse my mother? So good she ever was to me! so loving!

---

* Vipsania, the daugher of Agrippa, was divorced from Tiberius by Augustus and Livia, in order that he might marry Julia, and hold the empire by inheritance. He retained such an affection for her, and showed it so intensely when he once met her afterward, that every precaution was taken lest they should meet again.

There can be no doubt that the Claudii were deranged in intellect. Those of them who succeeded to the empire were by nature no worse than several of their race in the times of the republic. Appius Claudius, Appius Coecus, Publius, Appia, and after these the enemy of Cicero, exhibited as ungovernable a temper as the imperial ones, some breaking forth into tyranny and lust, others into contempt of, and imprecations against, their country. Tiberius was meditative, morose, suspicious. In the pupil of Seneca were dispositions the opposite to these, with many talents, and some good qualities. They could not disappear on a sudden without one of those shocks under which had been engulfed almost every member of the family.

† The Colossus was thrown down by an earthquake during the war between Antiochus and Ptolemy, who sent the Rhodians three thousand talents for the restoration of it. Again in the time of Vespasian, "Coae Veneris, item *Colossi* refectorem congiario magnâque mercede donavit." *Suetonius in Vesp.* The first residence of Tiberius in Rhodes was when he returned from his Armenian expedition, the last was after his divorce from Vipsania and his marriage with Julia.[1]

◇◇◇◇◇◇◇◇◇◇◇◇◇◇◇◇◇◇◇◇◇◇◇◇◇◇◇◇◇◇

[1] Coae Veneris . . . donavit: "he gave a noble gratuity to the restorer of the Coan of Venus, and to another artist who repaired the Colossus." Landor quotes from Suetonius' Life of Vespasian.

Vipsania. I quite forgive her: be tranquil, O Tiberius!

Tiberius. Never can I know peace . . never can I pardon . . anyone. Threaten me with thy exile, thy separation, thy seclusion! remind me that another climate might endanger thy health! . . There death met me and turned me round. Threaten me to take our son from us! our one boy! our helpless little one! him whom we made cry because we kissed him both together. Rememberest thou? or dost thou not hear? turning thus away from me!

Vipsania. I hear; I hear. O cease, my sweet Tiberius! Stamp not upon that stone: my heart lies under it.

Tiberius. Ay, there again death, and more than death, stood before me. O she maddened me, my mother did, she maddened me . . she threw me to where I am at one breath. The gods can not replace me where I was, nor atone to me, nor console me, nor restore my senses. To whom can I fly? to whom can I open my heart? to whom speak plainly?* There was upon the earth a man I could converse with, and fear nothing: there was a woman too I could love, and fear nothing. What a soldier, what a Roman, was thy father, O my young bride! How could those who never saw him have discoursed so rightly upon virtue!

Vipsania. These words cool my breast like pressing his urn against it. He was brave: shall Tiberius want courage?

Tiberius. My enemies scorn me. I am a garland dropped from a triumphal car, and taken up and looked on for the place I occupied: and tossed away and laughed at. Senators! laugh, laugh! Your merits may be yet rewarded . . be of good cheer! Counsel me, in your wisdom, what services I can render you, conscript fathers!

Vipsania. This seems mockery: Tiberius did not smile so, once.

Tiberius. They had not then congratulated me.

Vipsania. On what?

Tiberius. And it was not because she was beautiful, as they thought her, and virtuous as I know she is, but because the flowers on the altar were to be tied together by my heart-string. On this they congratulated me. Their day will come. Their sons and daughters are what I would wish them to be: worthy to succeed them.

Vipsania. Where is that quietude, that resignation, that sanctity, that heart of true tenderness?

---

* The regret of Tiberius at the death of Agrippa may be imagined to arise from a cause of which at this moment he was unconscious. If Agrippa had lived, Julia, who was his wife, could not have been Tiberius's, nor would he and Vipsania have been separated.

Tiberius. Where is my love? my love?

Vipsania. Cry not thus aloud, Tiberius! there is an echo in the place. Soldiers and slaves may burst in upon us.

Tiberius. And see my tears? There is no echo, Vipsania! why alarm and shake me so? We are too high here for the echoes: the city is below us. Methinks it trembles and totters: would it did! from the marble quays of the Tiber to this rock. There is a strange buzz and murmur in my brain; but I should listen so intensely, I should hear the rattle of its roofs, and shout with joy.

Vipsania. Calm, O my life! calm this horrible transport.

Tiberius. Spake I so loud? Did I indeed then send my voice after a lost sound, to bring it back; and thou fanciedest it an echo? Wilt not thou laugh with me, as thou wert wont to do, at such an error? What was I saying to thee, my tender love, when I commanded . . I know not whom . . to stand back, on pain of death? Why starest thou on me in such agony? Have I hurt thy fingers, child? I loose them; now let me look! Thou turnest thine eyes away from me. Oh! oh! I hear my crime! Immortal gods! I cursed then audibly, and before the sun, my mother!

[1828]   [1876]

PETER THE GREAT AND ALEXIS

Peter the Great's continued suspicions of his son's political loyalty and his attempts to control his son's life led Alexis (1690–1718) to flee to Vienna in 1716, where he was protected by the Holy Roman Emperor Charles VI. In February 1718, he returned to Russia under a promise of pardon and reconciliation; he died July 7, 1718, probably as a result of repeated torture.

PETER THE GREAT AND ALEXIS

Peter. AND SO, after flying from thy father's house, thou hast returned again from Vienna. After this affront in the face of Europe, thou darest to appear before me?

Alexis. My emperor and father! I am brought before your majesty, not at my own desire.

Peter. I believe it well.

Alexis. I would not anger you.

Peter. What hope hadst thou, rebel, in thy flight to Vienna?

Alexis. The hope of peace and privacy; the hope of security; and above all things, of never more offending you.

Peter. That hope thou hast accomplished.

Thou imaginedst then that my brother of Austria would maintain thee at his court . . speak!

Alexis. No, sir! I imagined that he would have afforded me a place of refuge.

Peter. Didst thou then take money with thee?

Alexis. A few gold pieces.

Peter. How many?

Alexis. About sixty.

Peter. He would have given thee promises for half the money; but the double of it does not purchase a house: ignorant wretch!

Alexis. I knew as much as that; although my birth did not appear to destine me to purchase a house anywhere; and hitherto your liberality, my father, hath supplied my wants of every kind.

Peter. Not of wisdom, not of duty, not of spirit, not of courage, not of ambition. I have educated thee among my guards and horses, among my drums and trumpets, among my flags and masts. When thou wert a child, and couldst hardly walk, I have taken thee into the arsenal, though children should not enter, according to regulations; I have there rolled cannon-balls before thee over iron plates; and I have shown thee bright new arms, bayonets and sabres; and I have pricked the back of my hands until the blood came out in many places; and I have made thee lick it; and I have then done the same to thine. Afterward, from thy tenth year, I have mixed gunpowder in thy grog; I have peppered thy peaches; I have poured bilge-water (with a little good wholesome tar in it) upon thy melons; I have brought out girls to mock thee and cocker thee, and talk like mariners, to make thee braver. Nothing would do. Nay, recollect thee! I have myself led thee forth to the window when fellows were hanged and shot; and I have shown thee every day the halves and quarters of bodies; and I have sent an orderly or chamberlain for the heads; and I have pulled the cap up from over the eyes; and I have made thee, in spite of thee, look steadfastly upon them; incorrigible coward!

And now another word with thee about thy scandalous flight from the palace; in time of quiet too! To the point! did my brother of Austria invite thee? Did he, or did he not?

Alexis. May I answer without doing an injury or disservice to his Imperial Majesty?

Peter. Thou mayest. What injury canst thou or any one do, by the tongue, to such as he is?

Alexis. At the moment, no; he did not. Nor indeed can I assert that he at any time invited me: but he said he pitied me.

Peter. About what? hold thy tongue: let that pass. Princes never pity but when they would make traitors: then their hearts grow tenderer than tripe. He pitied thee, kind soul, when he would throw thee at thy father's head; but finding thy father too strong for him, he now commiserates the parent, laments the son's rashness and disobedience, and would not make God angry for the world. At first, however, there must have been some overture on his part; otherwise thou art too shame-faced for intrusion. Come . . thou hast never had wit enough to lie . . tell me the truth, the whole truth.

Alexis. He said that, if ever I wanted an asylum, his court was open to me.

Peter. Open! so is the tavern; but folks pay for what they get there. Open truly! and didst thou find it so?

Alexis. He received me kindly.

Peter. I see he did.

Alexis. Derision, O my father, is not the fate I merit.

Peter. True, true! it was not intended.

Alexis. Kind father! punish me then as you will.

Peter. Villain! wouldst thou kiss my hand too? Art thou ignorant that the Austrian threw thee away from him, with the same indifference as he would the outermost leaf of a sandy sunburnt lettuce?

Alexis. Alas! I am not ignorant of this.

Peter. He dismissed thee at my order. If I had demanded from him his daughter, to be the bedfellow of a Kalmuc,[1] he would have given her, and praised God.

Alexis. O father! is his baseness my crime?

Peter. No; thine is greater. Thy intention, I know, is to subvert the institutions it has been the labour of my lifetime to establish. Thou hast never rejoiced at my victories.

Alexis. I have rejoiced at your happiness and your safety.

Peter. Liar! coward! traitor! when the Polanders and Swedes fell before me, didst thou from thy soul congratulate me? Didst thou get drunk at home or abroad, or praise the Lord of Hosts and saint Nicolas?[2] Wert thou not silent and civil and low-spirited?

Alexis. I lamented the irretrievable loss of human life; I lamented that the bravest and noblest were swept away the first; that the gentlest and most domestic were the earliest mourners: that frugality was supplanted by intemperance; that order was succeeded by confusion; and that your majesty was destroying the glorious plans you alone were capable of devising.

Peter. I destroy them! how? Of what plans art thou speaking?

---

[1] A Tartar.
[2] Patron saint of Russia.

Alexis. Of civilising the Muscovites. The Polanders in part were civilised: the Swedes more than any other nation on the continent; and so excellently versed were they in military science, and so courageous, that every man you killed cost you seven or eight.

Peter. Thou liest; nor six. And civilised forsooth! Why, the robes of the metropolitan, him at Upsal, are not worth three ducats, between Jew and Livornese.[3] I have no notion that Poland and Sweden shall be the only countries that produce great princes. What right have they to such as Gustavus and Sobieski? Europe ought to look to this, before discontent becomes general, and the people does to us what we have the privilege of doing to the people. I am wasting my words: there is no arguing with positive fools like thee. So thou wouldst have desired me to let the Polanders and Swedes lie still and quiet! Two such powerful nations!

Alexis. For that reason and others I would have gladly seen them rest, until our own people had increased in numbers and prosperity.

Peter. And thus thou disputest my right, before my face, to the exercise of the supreme power.

Alexis. Sir! God forbid!

Peter. God forbid indeed! What care such villains as thou art what God forbids! He forbids the son to be disobedient to the father: he forbids .. he forbids .. twenty things. I do not wish, and will not have, a successor who dreams of dead people.

Alexis. My father! I have dreamt of none such.

Peter. Thou hast; and hast talked about them .. Scythians I think they call 'em. Now who told thee, Mr. Professor, that the Scythians were a happier people than we are; that they were inoffensive; that they were free; that they wandered with their carts from pasture to pasture, from river to river: that they traded with good faith; that they fought with good courage; that they injured none, invaded none, and feared none? At this rate I have effected nothing. The great founder of Rome, I heard in Holland, slew his brother for despiting the weakness of his walls: and shall the founder of this better place spare a degenerate son, who prefers a vagabond life to a civilised one, a cart to a city, a Scythian to a Muscovite? Have I not shaved my people, and breeched them? Have I not formed them into regular armies, with bands of music and havresacs? Are bows better than cannon? shepherds than dragoons, mare's milk than brandy, raw steaks than broiled? Thine are tenets that strike at the root of politeness and sound government. Every prince in Europe is interested in rooting them out by fire and

sword. There is no other way with false doctrines: breath against breath does little.

Alexis. Sire, I never have attempted to disseminate my opinions.

Peter. How couldst thou? the seed would fall only on granite. Those, however, who caught it brought it to me.

Alexis. Never have I undervalued civilisation: on the contrary, I regretted whatever impeded it. In my opinion, the evils that have been attributed to it, sprang from its imperfections and voids; and no nation has yet acquired it more than very scantily.

Peter. How so? give me thy reasons; thy fancies rather; for reason thou hast none.

Alexis. When I find the first of men, in rank and genius, hating one another, and becoming slanderers and liars in order to lower and vilify an opponent; when I hear the God of mercy invoked to massacres, and thanked for furthering what he reprobates and condemns; I look back in vain on any barbarous people for worse barbarism. I have expressed my admiration of our forefathers, who, not being Christians, were yet more virtuous than those who are; more temperate, more just, more sincere, more chaste, more peaceable.

Peter. Malignant atheist!

Alexis. Indeed, my father, were I malignant I must be an atheist; for malignity is contrary to the command, and inconsistent with the belief, of God.

Peter. Am I Czar of Muscovy, and hear discourses on reason and religion! from my own son too! No, by the Holy Trinity! thou art no son of mine. If thou touchest my knee again, I crack thy knuckles with this tobacco-stopper: I wish it were a sledge-hammer for thy sake. Off, sycophant! Off, run-away slave!

Alexis. Father! father! my heart is broken! If I have offended, forgive me!

Peter. The state requires thy signal punishment.

Alexis. If the state requires it, be it so: but let my father's anger cease!

Peter. The world shall judge between us. I will brand thee with infamy.

Alexis. Until now, O father! I never had a proper sense of glory. Hear me, O Czar! let not a thing so vile as I am stand between you and the world! Let none accuse you!

Peter. Accuse me! rebel! Accuse me! traitor!

Alexis. Let none speak ill of you, O my father! The public voice shakes the palace; the public voice penetrates the grave; it precedes the chariot of Almighty God, and is heard at the judgment-seat.

Peter. Let it go to the devil! I will have none of it here in Petersburgh. Our church says nothing about

---

3 Leghorn (Livorno), Italy, was a major banking center.

it; our laws forbid it. As for thee, unnatural brute, I have no more to do with thee neither!

Ho there! chancellor! What! come at last! Wert napping, or counting thy ducats?

Chancellor. Your majesty's will and pleasure!

Peter. Is the senate assembled in that room?

Chancellor. Every member, sire.

Peter. Conduct this youth with thee, and let them judge him: thou understandest me.

Chancellor. Your majesty's commands are the breath of our nostrils.

Peter. If these rascals are remiss, I will try my new cargo of Livonian hemp upon 'em.

Chancellor (returning). Sire! sire!

Peter. Speak, fellow! Surely they have not condemned him to death, without giving themselves time to read the accusation, that thou comest back so quickly.

Chancellor. No, sire! Nor has either been done.

Peter. Then thy head quits thy shoulders.

Chancellor. O sire!

Peter. Curse thy silly *sires!* what art thou about?

Chancellor. Alas! he fell.

Peter. Tie him up to thy chair then. Cowardly beast! what made him fall?

Chancellor. The hand of Death; the name of father.

Peter. Thou puzzlest me; prythee speak plainlier.

Chancellor. We told him that his crime was proven and manifest; that his life was forfeited.

Peter. So far, well enough.

Chancellor. He smiled.

Peter. He did! did he! Impudence shall do him little good. Who could have expected it from that smock-face! Go on: what then?

Chancellor. He said calmly, but not without sighing twice or thrice, "Lead me to the scaffold: I am weary of life: nobody loves me." I condoled with him, and wept upon his hand, holding the paper against my bosom. He took the corner of it between his fingers, and said, "Read me this paper: read my death-warrant. Your silence and tears have signified it; yet the law has its forms. Do not keep me in suspense. My father says, too truly, I am not courageous: but the death that leads me to my God shall never terrify me."

Peter. I have seen these white-livered knaves die resolutely: I have seen them quietly fierce like white ferrets, with their watery eyes and tiny teeth. You read it?

Chancellor. In part, sire! When we heard your majesty's name, accusing him of treason and attempts at rebellion and parricide, he fell speechless. We raised him up: he was motionless: he was dead!

Peter. Inconsiderate and barbarous varlet as thou art, dost thou recite this ill accident to a father! And to one who has not dined! Bring me a glass of brandy.

Chancellor. And it please your majesty, might I call a . . a . .

Peter. Away, and bring it: scamper! All equally and alike shall obey and serve me.

Harkye! bring the bottle with it: I must cool myself . . and . . harkye! a rasher of bacon on thy life! and some pickled sturgeon, and some krout and caviar, and good strong cheese.

[1828]   [1876]

Charles Lamb

1775–1834

OUTLINE OF EVENTS

1775   Born February 10 in London at the Temple of the Inns of Court. Father, John, servant and clerk for one of the governors of the Inner Temple; mother, Elizabeth (Field); brother John (b. 1763), sister Mary (b. 1764).

1782–89   Attends Christ's Hospital; forms close friendship with fellow-student Coleridge.

1791–92   Clerk at the South-Sea House.

1792–95   Begins employment at East India House. Falls desperately in love with "Alice W———n," leading to severe melancholy and brief commitment to an asylum.

1796   Publishes four sonnets in Coleridge's *Poems on Various Subjects*. September 22, his sister fatally stabs their mother in attack of insanity.

1797   Assumes legal responsibility for Mary. Contributes additional poems to second edition of Coleridge's *Poems*. July, visits Coleridge at Nether Stowey and meets William and Dorothy Wordsworth.

1798   *Blank Verse* [of Lamb and Charles Lloyd] and the novel *Rosamund Gray* published.

1799   Father dies.

1802   Play *John Woodvil* published. August, with Mary visits Coleridge at Keswick and tours Lake District.

1805   *The King and Queen of Hearts* published, first of a number of works for children that he was to write.

1806   December 10, farce *Mr. H.* fails disastrously in single performance at Drury Lane Theatre.

1807   *Tales from Shakespear* (in collaboration with Mary) published.

1808   *Specimens of English Dramatic Poets, who lived about the Time of Shakspeare* published.

1811   Contributes essays on Hogarth and Shakespeare and other prose to Leigh Hunt's *Reflector*.

1812–20   Contributes essays and poems to various periodicals, including Hunt's *Examiner*.

1818   *The Works of Charles Lamb* published.

1819   Proposes to the actress Fanny Kelly but is rejected.

1820   August, contributes first Elia Essay to *London Magazine*.

1821   Brother John dies.

1823   First collection of Elia Essays published.

1825   March, retires from East India House.

1830   *Album Verses and other Poems* published.

1833   *Last Essays of Elia* published.

1834   Dies December 27 at Edmonton, London suburb.

1847   Mary dies.

SELECTED BIBLIOGRAPHY

BIOGRAPHY

LUCAS, E. V., *The Life of Charles Lamb*, 2 vols., London: Methuen and Company, 1905.

EDITIONS OF LAMB'S PROSE

HUTCHINSON, THOMAS (ed.), *The Works of Charles and Mary Lamb*, 2 vols., London: Oxford University Press, 1924.

LUCAS, E. V. (ed.), *The Works of Charles and Mary Lamb*, 7 vols., London: Methuen and Company, 1903–1905.

TILLYARD, E. M. W. (ed.), *Lamb's Criticism*, Cambridge, Eng.: Cambridge University Press, 1923.

LAMB'S CRITICISM

ADES, JOHN I., "Charles Lamb, Shakespeare, and Early Nineteenth-Century Theater," *Publications of the Modern Language Association*, LXXXV (1970), 514–26.

BARNET, SYLVAN, "Charles Lamb's Contribution to the Theory of Dramatic Illusion," *Publications of the Modern Language Association*, LXIX (1954), 1150–59.

FRÉCHET, RENÉ, "Lamb's 'Artificial Comedy,'" *Review of English Literature*, V (1964), 27–41.

HENDERSON, ARNOLD, "Some Constants of Charles Lamb's Criticism," *Studies in Romanticism*, VII (1968), 104–16.

HOUGHTON, WALTER E., "Lamb's Criticism of Restoration Comedy," *English Literary History*, X (1943), 61–72.

WELLEK, RENÉ, *The History of Modern Criticism: 1750–1950*, II (*The Romantic Age*), New Haven, Conn.: Yale University Press, 1955.

THE ELIA ESSAYS

BARNETT, GEORGE L., *Charles Lamb: The Evolution of Elia*, Bloomington, Indiana: Indiana University Press, 1964.

FUKUDA, TSUTOMU, *A Study of Charles Lamb's Essays of Elia*, Tokyo: Hokuseido, 1964.

HAVEN, RICHARD, "The Romantic Art of Charles Lamb," *English Literary History*, XXX (1963), 137–46.

MULCAHY, DANIEL J., "Charles Lamb: The Antithetical Manner in the Two Planes," *Studies in English Literature*, III (1963), 517–42.

REIMAN, DONALD H., "Thematic Unity in Lamb's Familiar Essays," *Journal of English and Germanic Philology*, LXIV (1965), 470–78.

SCOGGINS, JAMES, "Images of Eden in the Essays of Elia," *Journal of English and Germanic Philology*, LXXI (1972), 198–210.

THE WORKS OF CHARLES LAMB

The Works of Charles Lamb, *published in two volumes in 1818, represent Lamb's literary production before the writing of his masterworks, the Elia Essays of the 1820's. The compositions brought together in 1818, some dating back to the start of Lamb's literary career in the 1790's, include poetry, literary criticism, the novel* Rosamund Gray, *and the plays* John Woodvil *and* Mr. H. *Of these the most important are the essays on Shakespeare and Hogarth, which had originally appeared in Leigh Hunt's* Reflector *in 1811. The critical principles contained in these early essays are not only consistent with such later formulations as "Stage Illusion" (1825) and "Barrenness of the Imaginative Faculty in the Productions of Modern Art" (1833), but provide a basis in literary theory for the art of the great familiar essays written "under the phantom cloud of Elia."*

The structure of Lamb's literary criticism may be best revealed through a series of polarities: author vs. actor, tragedy vs. comedy, internal ("poetical") vs. external "(pictorial") representation. In discussing tragedy or other examples of high art (Shakespeare's plays, Cervantes' Don Quixote, Hogarth's engravings, or Titian's paintings), Lamb's focus is on the moral imagination of the author or artist; in discussing comedy, the focus is on the performing skills of the actor. The representations of high art are successful to the extent that they fulfil the elevated conceptions of the imagination by revealing the "internal life," the moral or spiritual significance, of characters and events. Such representations must necessarily be "symbolic" or "poetical," rather than "realistic" or "pictorial"; they seek to appeal to the reader's or observer's imagination, which would be inhibited by any primary emphasis on the external particularities of the characters or events portrayed. Comedy, on the other hand, does represent human life in its external particularities and with all its debilitating imperfections and restrictions of time and space. The skill of the actor is revealed partly in sustaining that reality, especially in his relations with the other characters on stage; but simultaneously in indicating to the audience that this is only a performance, and that what seem of such momentous concern to the other actors and ordinarily to the audience, the painful limitations of daily life, may be viewed with comic detachment. The goals of comedy and tragedy are finally coordinate for Lamb (he was strongly attracted to works of art, whether in literature or painting, which combined both modes): comedy suspends temporarily the restrictions of human existence that we may be able to bear them more courageously; high art penetrates beyond these restrictions to those ultimate sources of courage and strength in the mind and heart of man.

F R O M

THE WORKS OF CHARLES LAMB

ON THE GENIUS AND CHARACTER OF HOGARTH

Like the later essay "On the Barrenness of the Imaginative Faculty," the essay on Hogarth is of particular interest as an example of Romantic art criticism, the "re-creation in words of the impressions the writer had experienced in a non-verbal medium." G. Robert Stange has written of the importance of Lamb and Hazlitt in the development of nineteenth-century art criticism and as predecessors of Ruskin and Pater: "In their modest but genial exercises in criticism they do not use prose as a mere vehicle of distinct ideas, but as an unabashedly expressive language. In their time it was unusual to write at length about a single work of art, and almost unprecedented to find the meaning of the work in the impression that its formal aspects made on a sensitive observer. Lamb and Hazlitt can be said to have made later art criticism possible by challenging traditional ideas about the relations between painting and literature, and thereby extending the possibilities of prose expression" ("Art Criticism as a Prose Genre," in The Art of Victorian Prose, *ed. George Levine and William Madden [New York: Oxford University Press, 1968], p. 42).*

F R O M

ON THE GENIUS & CHARACTER OF HOGARTH;

WITH SOME REMARKS ON A PASSAGE IN THE WRITINGS OF THE LATE MR. BARRY

ONE of the earliest and noblest enjoyments I had when a boy was in the contemplation of those capital prints by Hogarth, the *Harlot's* and *Rake's Progresses*, which, along with some others, hung upon the walls of a great hall in an old-fashioned house in ———shire,[1] and seemed the solitary tenants (with myself) of that antiquated and life-deserted apartment.

Recollection of the manner in which those prints used to affect me, has often made me wonder, when I have heard Hogarth described as a mere comic painter, as one whose chief ambition was to *raise a laugh*. To deny that there are throughout the prints which I have mentioned circumstances introduced of a laughable tendency, would be to run counter to the common notions of mankind; but to suppose that in their *ruling character* they appeal chiefly to the risible faculty, and not first and foremost to the very heart of man, its best and most serious feelings, would be to mistake no less grossly their aim and purpose. A set of severer Satires (for they are not so much Comedies, which they have been likened to, as they are strong and masculine Satires) less mingled with any thing of mere fun, were never written upon paper, or graven upon copper. They resemble Juvenal, or the satiric touches in Timon of Athens.

I was pleased with the reply of a gentleman, who being asked which book he esteemed most in his library, answered,—"Shakspeare:" being asked which he esteemed next best, replied,—"Hogarth." His graphic representations are indeed books: they have

---

[1] The "old-fashioned house" is Blakesware in Hertfordshire, where Lamb's maternal grandmother Mrs. Mary Field lived as servant and eventually as housekeeper until her death in 1792. Lamb refers to the same residence, a vivid memory of childhood, in "Dream Children" and "Blakesmoor in H———shire."

the teeming, fruitful, suggestive meaning of *words*. Other pictures we look at,—his prints we read.

In pursuance of this parallel, I have sometimes entertained myself with comparing the *Timon of Athens* of Shakspeare (which I have just mentioned) and Hogarth's *Rake's Progress* together. The story, the moral, in both is nearly the same. The wild course of riot and extravagance, ending in the one with driving the Prodigal from the society of men into the solitude of the deserts, and in the other with conducting the Rake through his several stages of dissipation into the still more complete desolations of the madhouse, in the play and in the picture are described with almost equal force and nature. The levee of the Rake, which forms the subject of the second plate in the series, is almost a transcript of Timon's levee in the opening scene of that play. We find a dedicating poet, and other similar characters, in both.

The concluding scene in the *Rake's Progress* is perhaps superior to the last scenes of *Timon*. If we seek for something of kindred excellence in poetry, it must be in the scenes of Lear's beginning madness, where the King and the Fool and the Tom-o'-Bedlam conspire to produce such a medley of mirth checked by misery, and misery rebuked by mirth; where the society of those "strange bed-fellows"[2] which misfortunes have brought Lear acquainted with, so finely sets forth the destitute state of the monarch, while the lunatic bans of the one, and the disjointed sayings and wild but pregnant allusions of the other, so wonderfully sympathize with that confusion, which they seem to assist in the production of, in the senses of that "child-changed father."[3]

In the scene in Bedlam, which terminates the *Rake's Progress*, we find the same assortment of the ludicrous with the terrible. Here is desperate madness, the overturning of originally strong thinking faculties, at which we shudder, as we contemplate the duration and pressure of affliction which it must have asked to destroy such a building;—and here is the gradual hurtless lapse into idiocy, of faculties, which at their best of times never having been strong, we look upon the consummation of their decay with no more of pity than is consistent with a smile. The mad taylor, the poor driveller that has gone out of his wits (and truly he appears to have had no great journey to go to get past their confines) for the love of *Charming Betty Careless*,[4]—these half-laughable, scarce-pitiable objects take off from the horror which the principal figure would of itself raise, at the same time that they

assist the feeling of the scene by contributing to the general notion of its subject:—

> Madness, thou chaos of the brain,
> What art, that pleasure giv'st, and pain?
> Tyranny of Fancy's reign!
> Mechanic Fancy, that can build
> Vast labyrinths and mazes wild,
> With rule disjointed, shapeless measure,
> Fill'd with horror, fill'd with pleasure!
> Shapes of horror, that would even
> Cast doubts of mercy upon heaven.
> Shapes of pleasure, that, but seen,
> Would split the shaking sides of spleen.*

Is it carrying the spirit of comparison to excess to remark, that in the poor kneeling weeping female, who accompanies her seducer in his sad decay, there is something analogous to Kent, or Caius, as he delights rather to be called,[5] in *Lear*,—the noblest pattern of virtue which even Shakspeare has conceived,—who follows his royal master in banishment, that had pronounced *his* banishment, and forgetful at once of his wrongs and dignities, taking on himself the disguise of a menial, retains his fidelity to the figure, his loyalty to the carcass, the shadow, the shell and empty husk of Lear?

In the perusal of a book, or of a picture, much of the impression which we receive depends upon the habit of mind which we bring with us to such perusal. The same circumstance may make one person laugh, which shall render another very serious; or in the same person the first impression may be corrected by afterthought. The misemployed incongruous characters at the *Harlot's Funeral*, on a superficial inspection, provoke to laughter; but when we have sacrificed the first emotion to levity, a very different frame of mind succeeds, or the painter has lost half his purpose. I never look at that wonderful assemblage of depraved beings, who, without a grain of reverence or pity in their perverted minds, are performing the sacred exteriors of duty to the relics of their departed partner in folly, but I am as much moved to sympathy from the very want of it in them, as I should be by the finest representation of a virtuous death-bed surrounded by real mourners, pious children, weeping friends,—perhaps more by the very contrast. What reflexions does it not awake, of the dreadful heartless state in which the creature (a female too) must have lived, who in death wants the accompaniment of one genuine tear. That wretch who is removing the lid of

---

[2] *Tempest*, II, ii, 42.
[3] *King Lear*, IV, vii, 17.
[4] A London prostitute.

* Lines inscribed under the plate.

[5] See *King Lear*, V, iii, 283.

the coffin to gaze upon the corpse with a face which indicates a perfect negation of all goodness or womanhood—the hypocrite parson and his demure partner—all the fiendish group—to a thoughtful mind present a moral emblem more affecting than if the poor friendless carcass had been depicted as thrown out to the woods, where wolves had assisted at its obsequies, itself furnishing forth its own funeral banquet.

It is easy to laugh at such incongruities as are met together in this picture,—incongruous objects being of the very essence of laughter,—but surely the laugh is far different in its kind from that thoughtless species to which we are moved by mere farce and grotesque. We laugh when Ferdinand Count Fathom, at the first sight of the white cliffs of Britain, feels his heart yearn with filial fondness towards the land of his progenitors, which he is coming to fleece and plunder,[6]—we smile at the exquisite irony of the passage,—but if we are not led on by such passages to some more salutary feeling than laughter, we are very negligent perusers of them in book or picture.

It is the fashion with those who cry up the great Historical School in this country, at the head of which Sir Joshua Reynolds is placed, to exclude Hogarth from that school, as an artist of an inferior and vulgar class. Those persons seem to me to confound the painting of subjects in common or vulgar life with the being a vulgar artist. The quantity of thought which Hogarth crowds into every picture, would alone *unvulgarize* every subject which he might choose. Let us take the lowest of his subjects, the print called *Gin Lane*.[7] Here is plenty of poverty and low stuff to disgust upon a superficial view; and accordingly, a cold spectator feels himself immediately disgusted and repelled. I have seen many turn away from it, not being able to bear it. The same persons would perhaps have looked with great complacency upon Poussin's celebrated picture of the *Plague at Athens*.* Disease and Death and bewildering Terror, in *Athenian garments* are endurable, and come, as the delicate critics express it, within the "limits of pleasurable sensation." But the scenes of their own St. Giles's, delineated by their own countryman, are too shocking to think of. Yet if we could abstract our

* At the late Mr. Hope's in Cavendish-square.[8]

6 See Chapter XXVII of Smollett's novel *The Adventures of Ferdinand Count Fathom* (1753).

7 An engraving made in 1751 of Gin Lane, a street in the London slum of St. Giles. The work was intended to show the degenerate effects of gin as against the "virtues" of beer-drinking in the companion engraving *Beer Street*.

8 Henry Hope (1736–1811) was a banker and merchant. The painting is no longer attributed to Nicolas Poussin (1595–1665), distinguished French painter of landscapes and subjects of classical and scriptural history.

minds from the fascinating colours of the picture, and forget the coarse execution (in some respects) of the print, intended as it was to be a cheap plate, accessible to the poorer sort of people, for whose instruction it was done, I think we could have no hesitation in conferring the palm of superior genius upon Hogarth, comparing this work of his with Poussin's picture. There is more of imagination in it—that power which draws all things to one,—which makes things animate and inanimate, beings with their attributes, subjects and their accessaries, take one colour, and serve to one effect. Every thing in the print, to use a vulgar expression, *tells*. Every part is full of "strange images of death."[9] It is perfectly amazing and astounding to look at. Not only the two prominent figures, the woman and the half-dead man, which are as terrible as any thing which Michael Angelo every drew, but every thing else in the print contributes to bewilder and stupefy,—the very houses, as I heard a friend of mine express it, tumbling all about in various directions, seem drunk—seem absolutely reeling from the effect of that diabolical spirit of phrenzy which goes forth over the whole composition.—To shew the poetical and almost prophetical conception in the artist, one little circumstance may serve. Not content with the dying and dead figures, which he has strewed in profusion over the proper scene of the action, he shews you what (of a kindred nature) is passing beyond it. Close by the shell,[10] in which, by direction of the parish beadle, a man is depositing his wife, is an old wall, which, partaking of the universal decay around it, is tumbling to pieces. Through a gap in this wall are seen three figures, which appear to make a part in some funeral procession which is passing by on the other side of the wall, out of the sphere of the composition. This extending of the interest beyond the bounds of the subject could only have been conceived by a great genius. Shakspeare, in his description of the painting of the Trojan War, in his *Tarquin and Lucrece*, has introduced a similar device, where the painter made a part stand for the whole:—

> For such imaginary work was there,
> Conceit deceitful, so compact, so kind,
> That for Achilles' image stood his spear,
> Grip'd in an armed hand; himself behind
> Was left unseen, save to the eye of mind:
> A hand, a foot, a face, a leg, a head,
> Stood for the whole to be imagined.[11]

This he well calls *imaginary work*, where the spectator must meet the artist in his conceptions half way;

9 *Macbeth*, I, iii, 97.
10 Coffin.
11 *The Rape of Lucrece*, ll. 1422–28.

and it is peculiar to the confidence of high genius alone to trust so much to spectators or readers. Lesser artists shew every thing distinct and full, as they require an object to be made out to themselves before they can comprehend it.

When I think of the power displayed in this (I will not hesitate to say) sublime print, it seems to me the extreme narrowness of system alone, and of that rage for classification, by which, in matters of taste at least, we are perpetually perplexing instead of arranging our ideas, that would make us concede to the work of Poussin above-mentioned, and deny to this of Hogarth, the name of a grand serious composition.

We are for ever deceiving ourselves with names and theories. We call one man a great historical painter, because he has taken for his subjects kings or great men, or transactions over which time has thrown a grandeur. We term another the painter of common life, and set him down in our minds for an artist of an inferior class, without reflecting whether the quantity of thought shewn by the latter may not much more than level the distinction which their mere choice of subjects may seem to place between them; or whether, in fact, from that very common life a great artist may not extract as deep an interest as another man from that which we are pleased to call history.

I entertain the highest respect for the talents and virtues of Reynolds, but I do not like that his reputation should overshadow and stifle the merits of such a man as Hogarth, nor that to mere names and classifications we should be content to sacrifice one of the greatest ornaments of England.

I would ask the most enthusiastic admirer of Reynolds, whether in the countenances of his *Staring* and *Grinning Despair*, which he has given us for the faces of Ugolino and dying Beaufort,[12] there be any thing comparable to the expression which Hogarth has put into the face of his broken-down rake in the last plate but one of the *Rake's Progress*,* where a letter from the manager is brought to him to say that his play "will not do?" Here all is easy, natural, undistorted, but withal what a mass of woe is here accumulated!—the long history of a mis-spent life is compressed into the countenance as plainly as the

series of plates before had told it; here is no attempt at Gorgonian[14] looks which are to freeze the beholder, no grinning at the antique bedposts, no face-making, or consciousness of the presence of spectators in or out of the picture, but grief kept to a man's self, a face retiring from notice with the shame which great anguish sometimes brings with it,—a final leave taken of hope,—the coming on of vacancy and stupefaction, —a beginning alienation of mind looking like tranquillity. Here is matter for the mind of the beholder to feed on for the hour together,—matter to feed and fertilize the mind. It is too real to admit one thought about the power of the artist who did it.—When we compare the expression in subjects which so fairly admit of comparison, and find the superiority so clearly to remain with Hogarth, shall the mere contemptible difference of the scene of it being laid in the one case in our Fleet or King's Bench Prison, and in the other in the State Prison of Pisa, or the bed-room of a cardinal,—or that the subject of the one has never been authenticated, and the other is matter of history, —so weight down the real points of the comparison, as to induce us to rank the artist who has chosen the one scene or subject (though confessedly inferior in that which constitutes the soul of his art) in a class from which we exclude the better genius (who has happened to make choice of the other) with something like disgrace?*

* Sir Joshua Reynolds, somewhere in his lectures, speaks of the *presumption* of Hogarth in attempting the grand style in painting, by which he means his choice of certain Scripture subjects. Hogarth's excursions into Holy Land were not very numerous, but what he had left us in this kind have at least this merit, that they have expression of *some sort or other* in them,— the *Child Moses before Pharaoh's Daughter*, for instance: which is more than can be said of Sir Joshua Reynolds's *Repose in Egypt*, painted for Macklin's Bible, where for a Madona he has substituted a sleepy, insensible, unmotherly girl, one so little worthy to have been selected as the Mother of the Saviour, that she seems to have neither heart nor feeling to entitle her to become a mother at all. But indeed the race of Virgin Mary painters seems to have been cut up, root and branch, at the Reformation. Our artists are too good Protestants to give life to that admirable commixture of maternal tenderness with reverential awe and wonder approaching to worship, with which the Virgin Mothers of L. da Vinci and Raphael (themselves by their divine countenances inviting men to worship) contemplate the union of the two natures in the person of their Heaven-born Infant.[15]

---

* The first perhaps in all Hogarth for serious expression. That which comes next to it, I think is the jaded morning countenance of the debauchée in the second plate of the *Marriage Alamode*, which lectures on the vanity of pleasure as audibly as any thing in Ecclesiastes.[13]

[12] Lamb refers to Reynolds' paintings: Ugolino and his Children, exhibited in 1773; and the Death of Cardinal Beaufort, exhibited in 1789.
[13] *Marriage a la Mode* was another famous series of Hogarth engravings, issued in 1745.

[14] Hideous and threatening, from the mythological Gorgons, female faces with serpents on their heads instead of hair, the sight of which produced death.
[15] For the remark on Hogarth's "presumption," see Reynolds' Fourteenth Discourse. *The Child Moses before Pharaoh's Daughter* was a Hogarth painting of 1746. Reynolds's painting *Repose in Egypt* was exhibited in 1788; an engraving of it served as the frontispiece for the New Testament volume of Thomas Macklin's *The Holy Bible Embellished with Engravings, from Pictures and Designs by the most eminent English Artists* (1800–1816).

The Boys under Demoniacal Possession of Raphael and Dominichino,[16] by what law of classification are we bound to assign them to belong to the great style in painting, and to degrade into an inferior class the Rake of Hogarth when he is the Madman in the Bedlam scene? I am sure he is far more impressive than either. It is a face which no one that has seen can easily forget. There is the stretch of human suffering to the utmost endurance, severe bodily pain brought on by strong mental agony, the frightful obstinate laugh of madness,—yet all so unforced and natural, that those who never were witness to madness in real life, think they see nothing but what is familiar to them in this face. Here are no tricks of distortion, nothing but the natural face of agony. This is high tragic painting, and we might as well deny to Shakspeare the honours of a great tragedian, because he has interwoven scenes of mirth with the serious business of his plays, as refuse to Hogarth the same praise for the two concluding scenes of the *Rake's Progress*, because of the Comic Lunatics,* which he has thrown into the one, or the Alchymist that he has introduced in the other, who is paddling in the coals of his furnace, keeping alive the flames of vain hope within the very walls of the prison to which the vanity has conducted him, which have taught the darker lesson of extinguished hope to the desponding figure who is the principal person of the scene.

It is the force of these kindly admixtures, which assimilates the scenes of Hogarth and of Shakspeare to the drama of real life, where no such thing as pure tragedy is to be found; but merriment and infelicity, ponderous crime and feather-light vanity, like twiformed births, disagreeing complexions of one intertexture, perpetually unite to shew forth motley spectacles to the world. Then it is that the poet or painter shews his art, when in the selection of these comic adjuncts he chooses such circumstances as shall relieve, contrast with, or fall into, without forming a violent opposition to, his principal object. Who sees

not that the Grave-digger in *Hamlet*, the Fool in *Lear*, have a kind of correspondency to, and fall in with, the subjects which they seem to interrupt, while the comic stuff in *Venice Preserved*, and the doggerel nonsense of the Cook and his poisoning associates in the *Rollo* of Beaumont and Fletcher,[18] are pure, irrelevant, impertinent discords,—as bad as the quarrelling dog and cat under the table of the *Lord and the Disciples at Emmaus* of Titian?

Not to tire the reader with perpetual reference to prints which he may not be fortunate enough to possess, it may be sufficient to remark, that the same tragic cast of expression and incident, blended in some instances with a greater alloy of comedy, characterizes his other great work, the *Marriage Alamode*, as well as those less elaborate exertions of his genius, the prints called *Industry* and *Idleness*, the *Distrest Poet*,[19] &c. forming, with the *Harlot's* and *Rake's Progresses*, the most considerable if not the largest class of his productions,—enough surely to rescue Hogarth from the imputation of being a mere buffoon, or one whose general aim was only to *shake the sides*.

There remains a very numerous class of his performances, the object of which must be confessed to be principally comic. But in all of them will be found something to distinguish them from the droll productions of Bunbury[20] and others. They have this difference, that we do not merely laugh at, we are led into long trains of reflection by them. In this respect they resemble the characters of Chaucer's *Pilgrims*, which have strokes of humour in them enough to designate them for the most part as comic, but our strongest feeling still is wonder at the comprehensiveness of genius which could crowd, as poet and painter have done, into one small canvas so many diverse yet co-operating materials.

The faces of Hogarth have not a mere momentary interest, as in caricatures, or those grotesque physiognomies which we sometimes catch a glance of in the street, and, struck with their whimsicality, wish for a pencil and the power to sketch them down; and forget them again as rapidly,—but they are permanent abiding ideas. Not the sports of nature, but her necessary eternal classes. We feel that we cannot part with any of them, lest a link should be broken.

> * There are of madmen, as there are of tame,
> All humor'd not alike. We have here some
> So apish and fantastic, play with a feather;
> And though 'twould grieve a soul to see God's image
> So blemish'd and defac'd, yet do they act
> Such antick and such pretty lunacies,
> That, spite of sorrow, they will make you smile.
> Others again we have, like angry lions,
> Fierce as wild bulls, untameable as flies.
>
> *Honest Whore.*[17]

---

[16] Referring to figures in Raphael's Transfiguration and Domenichino's St. Nil exorcising the Devil out of the Body of the Son of Polyeucte.

[17] See Thomas Dekker's *The Honest Whore, Part 1* (1604), V, ii.

---

[18] See *The Bloody Brother, or Rollo, Duke of Normandy* (c. 1625–1630), II, ii. The play is now attributed to the multiple authorship of Fletcher, Massinger, Jonson, and George Chapman.

[19] *Industry* and *Idleness* were engravings of 1747 "shewing the Advantages attending Industry and the miserable Effects of Idleness, in the different Fortunes of two APPRENTICES." *Distrest Poet* was an engraving of 1736, satirizing inept poetic talent.

[20] Henry William Bunbury (1750–1811) was an "amateur artist and caricaturist" (*Dictionary of National Biography*).

It is worthy of observation, that he has seldom drawn a mean or insignificant countenance*. Hogarth's mind was eminently reflective; and, as it has been well observed of Shakspeare, that he has transfused his own poetical character into the persons of his drama (they are all more or less *poets*) Hogarth has impressed a *thinking character* upon the persons of his canvas. This remark must not be taken universally. The exquisite idiotism of the little gentleman in the bag and sword beating his drum in the print of the *Enraged Musician*,[22] would of itself rise up against so sweeping an assertion. But I think it will be found to be true of the generality of his countenances. The knife-grinder and Jew flute-player in the plate just mentioned may serve as instances instead of a thousand. They have intense thinking faces, though the purpose to which they are subservient by no means required it; but indeed it seems as if it was painful to Hogarth to contemplate mere vacancy or insignificance.

This reflection of the artist's own intellect from the faces of his characters, is one reason why the works of Hogarth, so much more than those of any other artist are objects of meditation. Our intellectual natures love the mirror which gives them back their own likenesses. The mental eye will not bend long with delight upon vacancy.

Another line of eternal separation between Hogarth and the common painters of droll or burlesque subjects, with whom he is often confounded, is the sense of beauty, which in the most unpromising subjects seems never wholly to have deserted him. "Hogarth himself," says Mr. Coleridge,† from whom I have borrowed this observation, speaking of a scene which took place at Ratzeburg, "never drew a more ludicrous distortion, both of attitude and physiognomy, than this effect occasioned: nor was there wanting

beside it one of those beautiful female faces which the same Hogarth, *in whom the satirist never extinguished that love of beauty which belonged to him as a poet*, so often and so gladly introduces as the central figure in a crowd of humourous deformities, which figure (such is the power of true genius) neither acts nor is meant to act as a contrast; but diffuses through all, and over each of the group, a spirit of reconciliation and human kindness; and even when the attention is no longer consciously directed to the cause of this feeling, still blends its tenderness with our laughter: and *thus prevents the instructive merriment at the whims of nature, or the foibles or humours of our fellow-men, from degenerating into the heart-poison of contempt or hatred*." To the beautiful females in Hogarth, which Mr. C. has pointed out, might be added, the frequent introduction of children (which Hogarth seems to have taken a particular delight in) into his pieces. They have a singular effect in giving tranquillity and a portion of their own innocence to the subject. The baby riding in its mother's lap in the *March to Finchley*,[24] (its careless innocent face placed directly behind the intriguing time-furrowed countenance of the treason-plotting French priest) perfectly sobers the whole of that tumultuous scene. The boy mourner winding up his top with so much unpretending insensibility in the plate of the *Harlot's Funeral*, (the only thing in that assembly that is not a hypocrite) quiets and soothes the mind that has been disturbed at the sight of so much depraved man and woman kind.[25]

*   *   *   *   *

I say not that all the ridiculous subjects of Hogarth have necessarily something in them to make us like them; some are indifferent to us, some in their natures repulsive, and only made interesting by the wonderful skill and truth to nature in the painter; but I contend that there is in most of them that sprinkling of the better nature, which, like holy water, chases away and disperses the contagion of the bad. They have this in them besides, that they bring us acquainted with the every-day human face,—they

---

* If there are any of that description, they are in his *Strolling Players*, a print which has been cried up by Lord Orford as the richest of his productions, and it may be, for what I know, in the mere lumber, the properties, and dead furniture of the scene, but in living character and expression it is (for Hogarth) lamentably poor and wanting; it is perhaps the only one of his performances at which we have a right to feel disgusted.[21]

† *The Friend*, No. XVI.[23]

[21] *Strolling Players*, an engraving of 1738, depicted the enormously cluttered scene of actresses preparing for a performance in a provincial barn. Lord Orford was Horace Walpole (1717–1797), the famous letter writer as well as art critic and collector. Walpole's praise of the Strolling Players occurs in his *Anecdotes of Painting in England*, IV (1780).

[22] An engraving of 1741, in which the practice of a professional musician is disrupted by a wild concatenation of noises from the street below.

[23] The passage occurs in the issue of December 7, 1809, of Coleridge's periodical.

[24] An engraving of 1750 depicting the disorderly march of soldiers to protect the northern approach to London against the supposed attack of "Bonnie Prince Charlie" in the rebellion of 1745.

[25] In the remainder of the essay here omitted with the exception of the final paragraph, Lamb first quotes, and then replies to, the criticism of Hogarth by James Barry (1741–1806), Irish-born painter of grandiose historical canvases and professor of painting at the Royal Academy. Barry praised Hogarth's "admirable fund of invention" and acknowledged the serious moral intention of his satire, but concluded: "Life is short; and the little leisure of it is much better laid out upon that species of art which is employed about the amiable and the admirable" than in pursuing "Hogarth's method of exposing meanness, deformity, and vice . . ."

give us skill to detect those gradations of sense and virtue (which escape the careless or fastidious observer) in the countenances of the world about us; and prevent that disgust at common life, that *tædium quotidianarum formarum*,[26] which an unrestricted passion for ideal forms and beauties is in danger of producing. In this, as in many other things, they are analogous to the best novels of Smollett or Fielding.

[April–September 1811]   [1818]

ON THE
TRAGEDIES OF SHAKSPEARE,

CONSIDERED WITH REFERENCE TO
THEIR FITNESS FOR
STAGE REPRESENTATION

Taking a turn the other day in the Abbey,[1] I was struck with the affected attitude of a figure, which I do not remember to have seen before, and which upon examination proved to be a whole-length of the celebrated Mr. Garrick. Though I would not go so far with some good catholics abroad as to shut players altogether out of consecrated ground, yet I own I was not a little scandalized at the introduction of theatrical airs and gestures into a place set apart to remind us of the saddest realities. Going nearer, I found inscribed under this harlequin figure the following lines:—

> To paint fair Nature, by divine command,
> Her magic pencil in his glowing hand,
> A Shakspeare rose; then, to expand his fame
> Wide o'er this breathing world, a Garrick came.
> Though sunk in death the forms the Poet drew,
> The Actor's genius bade them breathe anew;
> Though, like the bard himself, in night they lay,
> Immortal Garrick call'd them back to day:
> And till Eternity with pow'r sublime
> Shall mark the mortal hour of hoary Time,
> Shakspeare and Garrick like twin-stars shall shine,
> And earth irradiate with a beam divine.

It would be an insult to my readers' understandings to attempt any thing like a criticism of this farrago[2] of false thoughts and nonsense. But the reflection it led me into was a kind of wonder, how, from the days of the actor here celebrated to our own, it should have been the fashion to compliment every performer in his turn, that has had the luck to please the town in any of the great characters of Shakspeare, with the

notion of possessing a *mind congenial with the poet's*: how people should come thus unaccountably to confound the power of originating poetical images and conceptions with the faculty of being able to read or recite the same when put into words;* or what connection that absolute mastery over the heart and soul of man, which a great dramatic poet possesses, has with those low tricks upon the eye and ear, which a player by observing a few general effects, which some common passion, as grief, anger, &c. usually has upon the gestures and exterior, can so easily compass. To know the internal working and movements of a great mind, of an Othello or a Hamlet for instance, the *when* and the *why* and the *how far* they should be moved; to what pitch a passion is becoming; to give the reins and to pull in the curb exactly at the moment when the drawing in or the slackening is most graceful; seems to demand a reach of intellect of a vastly different extent from that which is employed upon the bare imitation of the signs of these passions in the countenance or gesture, which signs are usually observed to be most lively and emphatic in the weaker sort of minds, and which signs can after all but indicate some passion, as I said before, anger, or grief, generally; but of the motives and grounds of the passion, wherein it differs from the same passion in low and vulgar natures, of these the actor can give no more idea by his face or gesture than the eye (without a metaphor) can speak, or the muscles utter intelligible sounds. But such is the instantaneous nature of the impressions which we take in at the eye and ear at a playhouse, compared with the slow apprehension oftentimes of the understanding in reading, that we are apt not only to sink the play-writer in the consideration which we pay to the actor, but even to identify in our minds in a perverse manner, the actor with the character which he represents. It is difficult for a frequent playgoer to disembarrass the idea of Hamlet from the person and voice of Mr. K. We speak of Lady Macbeth, while we are in reality thinking of Mrs. S.[3] Nor is this confusion incidental alone to unlettered persons, who, not possessing the advantage of reading, are necessarily dependent upon the stage-player for all the pleasure which they can

---

* It is observable that we fall into this confusion only in *dramatic* recitations. We never dream that the gentleman who reads Lucretius in public with great applause, is therefore a great poet and philosopher; nor do we find that Tom Davies, the bookseller, who is recorded to have recited the Paradise Lost better than any man in England in his day (though I cannot help thinking there must be some mistake in this tradition) was therefore, by his intimate friends, set upon a level with Milton.

---

[26] *taedium . . . formarum:* "loathing of every-day beauties", a variation of a passage in Terence's comedy *The Eunuch*, Act II.
[1] Westminster Abbey.
[2] Jumble.

[3] Lamb refers to the celebrated actors John Philip Kemble (1757–1823) and his sister Sarah Siddons (1755–1831).

receive from the drama, and to whom the very idea of *what an author is* cannot be made comprehensible without some pain and perplexity of mind: the error is one from which persons otherwise not meanly lettered, find it almost impossible to extricate themselves.

Never let me be so ungrateful as to forget the very high degree of satisfaction which I received some years back from seeing for the first time a tragedy of Shakspeare performed, in which those two great performers sustained the principal parts. It seemed to embody and realize conceptions which had hitherto assumed no distinct shape. But dearly do we pay all our life after for this juvenile pleasure, this sense of distinctness. When the novelty is past, we find to our cost that instead of realizing an idea, we have only materialized and brought down a fine vision to the standard of flesh and blood. We have let go a dream, in quest of an unattainable substance.

How cruelly this operates upon the mind, to have its free conceptions thus crampt and pressed down to the measure of a strait-lacing actuality, may be judged from that delightful sensation of freshness, with which we turn to those plays of Shakspeare which have escaped being performed, and to those passages in the acting plays of the same writer which have happily been left out in the performance. How far the very custom of hearing any thing *spouted*, withers and blows upon a fine passage, may be seen in those speeches from Henry the Fifth, &c. which are current in the mouths of school-boys from their being to be found in *Enfield Speakers*,[4] and such kind of books. I confess myself utterly unable to appreciate that celebrated soliloquy in Hamlet, beginning "To be or not to be," or to tell whether it be good, bad, or indifferent, it has been so handled and pawed about by declamatory boys and men, and torn so inhumanly from its living place and principle of continuity in the play, till it is become to me a perfect dead member.

It may seem a paradox, but I cannot help being of opinion that the plays of Shakspeare are less calculated for performance on a stage, than those of almost any other dramatist whatever. Their distinguishing excellence is a reason that they should be so. There is so much in them, which comes not under the province of acting, with which eye, and tone, and gesture, have nothing to do.

The glory of the scenic art is to personate passion, and the turns of passion; and the more coarse and palpable the passion is, the more hold upon the eyes and ears of the spectators the performer obviously possesses. For this reason, scolding scenes, scenes where two persons talk themselves into a fit of fury, and then in a surprising manner talk themselves out of it again, have always been the most popular upon our stage. And the reason is plain, because the spectators are here most palpably appealed to, they are the proper judges in this war of words, they are the legitimate ring that should be formed round such "intellectual prize-fighters." Talking is the direct object of the imitation here. But in all the best dramas, and in Shakspeare above all, how obvious it is, that the form of *speaking*, whether it be in soliloquy or dialogue, is only a medium, and often a highly artificial one, for putting the reader or spectator into possession of that knowledge of the inner structure and workings of mind in a character, which he could otherwise never have arrived at *in that form of composition* by any gift short of intuition. We do here as we do with novels written in the *epistolary form*. How many improprieties, perfect solecisms in letter-writing, do we put up with in Clarissa[5] and other books, for the sake of the delight which that form upon the whole gives us.

But the practice of stage representation reduces every thing to a controversy of elocution. Every character, from the boisterous blasphemings of Bajazet[6] to the shrinking timidity of womanhood, must play the orator. The love-dialogues of Romeo and Juliet, those silver-sweet sounds of lovers' tongues by night; the more intimate and sacred sweetness of nuptial colloquy between an Othello or a Posthumus[7] with their married wives, all those delicacies which are so delightful in the reading, as when we read of those youthful dalliances in Paradise—

———————As beseem'd
Fair couple link'd in happy nuptial league,
Alone:[8]

by the inherent fault of stage representation, how are these things sullied and turned from their very nature by being exposed to a large assembly; when such speeches as Imogen addresses to her lord, come drawling out of the mouth of a hired actress, whose courtship, though nominally addressed to the personated Posthumus, is manifestly aimed at the spectators, who are to judge of her endearments and her returns of love.

4 *The Speaker: or, Miscellaneous Pieces, selected from the Best English Writers* (1774) was a popular collection of elocutionary pieces for young students, prepared by William Enfield (1741–1797).

5 Samuel Richardson's epistolary novel *Clarissa Harlowe* (1747–1748).
6 Emperor of the Turks in Marlowe's *Tamburlaine the Great*.
7 Husband of Imogen in Shakespeare's *Cymbeline*.
8 *Paradise Lost*, IV, 338–40.

The character of Hamlet is perhaps that by which, since the days of Betterton,[9] a succession of popular performers have had the greatest ambition to distinguish themselves. The length of the part may be one of their reasons. But for the character itself, we find it in a play, and therefore we judge it a fit subject of dramatic representation. The play itself abounds in maxims and reflexions beyond any other, and therefore we consider it as a proper vehicle for conveying moral instruction. But Hamlet himself—what does he suffer meanwhile by being dragged forth as the public schoolmaster, to give lectures to the crowd! Why, nine parts in ten of what Hamlet does, are transactions between himself and his moral sense, they are the effusions of his solitary musings, which he retires to holes and corners and the most sequestered parts of the palace to pour forth; or rather, they are the silent meditations with which his bosom is bursting, reduced to *words* for the sake of the reader, who must else remain ignorant of what is passing there. These profound sorrows, these light-and-noise-abhorring ruminations, which the tongue scarce dares utter to deaf walls and chambers, how can they be represented by a gesticulating actor, who comes and mouths them out before an audience, making four hundred people his confidants at once. I say not that it is the fault of the actor so to do; he must pronounce them *ore rotundo*,[10] he must accompany them with his eye, he must insinuate them into his auditory by some trick of eye, tone, or gesture, or he fails. *He must be thinking all the while of his appearance, because he knows that all the while the spectators are judging of it.* And this is the way to represent the shy, negligent, retiring Hamlet.

It is true that there is no other mode of conveying a vast quantity of thought and feeling to a great portion of the audience, who otherwise would never earn it for themselves by reading, and the intellectual acquisition gained this way may, for aught I know, be inestimable; but I am not arguing that Hamlet should not be acted, but how much Hamlet is made another thing by being acted. I have heard much of the wonders which Garrick performed in this part; but as I never saw him, I must have leave to doubt whether the representation of such a character came within the province of his art. Those who tell me of him, speak of his eye, of the magic of his eye, and of his commanding voice: physical properties, vastly desirable in an actor, and without which he can never insinuate meaning into an auditory,—but what have they to do

with Hamlet? what have they to do with intellect? In fact, the things aimed at in theatrical representation, are to arrest the spectator's eye upon the form and the gesture, and so to gain a more favourable hearing to what is spoken: it is not what the character is, but how he looks; not what he says, but how he speaks it. I see no reason to think that if the play of Hamlet were written over again by some such writer as Banks or Lillo,[11] retaining the process of the story, but totally omitting all the poetry of it, all the divine features of Shakspeare, his stupendous intellect; and only taking care to give us enough of passionate dialogue, which Banks or Lillo were never at a loss to furnish; I see not how the effect could be much different upon an audience, nor how the actor has it in his power to represent Shakspeare to us differently from his representation of Banks or Lillo. Hamlet would still be a youthful accomplished prince, and must be gracefully personated; he might be puzzled in his mind, wavering in his conduct, seemingly cruel to Ophelia, he might see a ghost, and start at it, and address it kindly when he found it to be his father; all this in the poorest and most homely language of the servilest creeper after nature that every consulted the palate of an audience; without troubling Shakspeare for the matter: and I see not but there would be room for all the power which an actor has, to display itself. All the passions and changes of passion might remain: for those are much less difficult to write or act than is thought, it is a trick easy to be attained, it is but rising or falling a note or two in the voice, a whisper with a significant forboding look to announce its approach, and so contagious the counterfeit appearance of any emotion is, that let the words be what they will, the look and tone shall carry it off and make it pass for deep skill in the passions.

It is common for people to talk of Shakspeare's plays being *so natural*; that every body can understand him. They are natural indeed, they are grounded deep in nature, so deep that the depth of them lies out of the reach of most of us. You shall hear the same persons say that George Barnwell is very natural, and Othello is very natural, that they are both very deep; and to them they are the same kind of thing. At the one they sit and shed tears, because a good sort of young man is tempted by a naughty woman to commit *a trifling peccadillo*, the murder of an uncle or

9 Thomas Betterton (1635?–1710), actor and dramatist.
10 *ore rotundo*: "in well-rounded phrases." Horace's *Ars Poetica*, l. 323.

11 John Banks was a Restoration dramatist, whose seven plays are notable chiefly for their melodramatic and pathetic effects. George Lillo (1693-1739) was the author of *The London Merchant: The History of George Barnwell* (1731), the most famous and influential of the domestic and sentimental dramas of the eighteenth century.

so,* that is all, and so comes to an untimely end, which is *so moving*; and at the other, because a black-amoor in a fit of jealousy kills his innocent white wife: and the odds are that ninety-nine out of a hundred would willingly behold the same catastrophe happen to both the heroes, and have thought the rope more due to Othello than to Barnwell. For of the texture of Othello's mind, the inward construction marvelously laid open with all its strengths and weaknesses, its heroic confidences and its human misgivings, its agonies of hate springing from the depths of love, they see no more than the spectators at a cheaper rate, who pay their pennies a-piece to look through the man's telescope in Leicester-fields, see into the inward plot and topography of the moon. Some dim thing or other they see, they see an actor personating a passion, of grief, or anger, for instance, and they recognize it as a copy of the usual external effects of such passions; or at least as being true to *that symbol of the emotion which passes current at the theatre for it*, for it is often no more than that: but of the grounds of the passion, its correspondence to a great or heroic nature, which is the only worthy object of tragedy,— that common auditors know any thing of this, or can have any notions dinned into them by the mere strength of an actor's lúngs,—that apprehensions foreign to them should be thus infused into them by storm, I can neither believe, nor understand how it can be possible.

We talk of Shakspeare's admirable observation of life, when we should feel, that not from a petty inquisition into those cheap and every-day characters which surrounded him, as they surround us, but from his own mind, which was, to borrow a phrase of Ben Jonson's, the very "sphere of humanity," he fetched those images of virtue and of knowledge, of which every one of us recognizing a part, think we comprehend in our natures the whole; and often-times mistake the powers which he positively creates in us, for nothing more than indigenous faculties of

---

* If this note could hope to meet the eye of any of the Managers, I would entreat and beg of them, in the name of both the Galleries, that this insult upon the morality of the common people of London should cease to be eternally repeated in the holiday weeks. Why are the 'Prentices of this famous and well-governed city, instead of an amusement, to be treated over and over again with a nauseous sermon of George Barnwell? Why *at the end of their vistoes* are we to place the *gallows*? Were I an uncle, I should not much like a nephew of mine to have such an example placed before his eyes. It is really making uncle-murder too trivial to exhibit it as done upon such slight motives; —it is attributing too much to such characters as Millwood;— it is putting things into the heads of good young men, which they would never otherwise have dreamed of. Uncles that think any thing of their lives, should fairly petition the Chamberlain against it.

our own minds, which only waited the application of corresponding virtues in him to return a full and clear echo of the same.

To return to Hamlet.—Among the distinguishing features of that wonderful character, one of the most interesting (yet painful) is that soreness of mind which makes him treat the intrusions of Polonius with harshness, and that asperity which he puts on in his interviews with Ophelia. These tokens of an unhinged mind (if they be not mixed in the latter case with a profound artifice of love, to alienate Ophelia by affected discourtesies, so to prepare her mind for the breaking off of that loving intercourse, which can no longer find a place amidst business so serious as that which he has to do) are parts of his character, which to reconcile with our admiration of Hamlet, the most patient consideration of his situation is no more than necessary; they are what we *forgive afterwards*, and explain by the whole of his character, but *at the time* they are harsh and unpleasant. Yet such is the actor's necessity of giving strong blows to the audience, that I have never seen a player in this character, who did not exaggerate and strain to the utmost these am-biguous features,—these temporary deformities in the character. They make him express a vulgar scorn at Polonius which utterly degrades his gentility, and which no explanation can render palatable; they make him shew contemᵽ , and curl up the nose at Ophelia's father,—contempt in its very grossest and most hateful form; but they get applause by it: it is natural, people say; that is, the words are scornful, and the actor expresses scorn, and that they can judge of: but why so much scorn, and of that sort, they never think of asking.

So to Ophelia.—All the Hamlets that I have ever seen, rant and rave at her as if she had committed some great crime, and the audience are highly pleased, because the words of the part are satirical, and they are enforced by the strongest expression of satirical indignation of which the face and voice are capable. But then, whether Hamlet is likely to have put on such brutal appearances to a lady whom he loved so dearly, is never thought on. The truth is, that in all such deep affections as had subsisted between Hamlet and Ophelia, there is a stock of *supererogatory love*, (if I may venture to use the expression) which in any great grief of heart, especially where that which preys upon the mind cannot be communicated, confers a kind of indulgence upon the grieved party to express itself, even to its heart's dearest object, in the lan-guage of a temporary alienation; but it is not aliena-tion, it is a distraction purely, and so it always makes itself to be felt by that object: it is not anger, but grief assuming the appearance of anger,—love awkwardly counterfeiting hate, as sweet countenances when they try to frown: but such sternness and fierce disgust as Hamlet is made to shew, is no counterfeit, but the real face of absolute aversion,—of irreconcileable alienation. It may be said he puts on the madman; but then he should only so far put on this counterfeit lunacy as his own real distraction will give him leave; that is, incompletely, imperfectly; not in that confirmed, practised way, like a master of his art, or as Dame Quickly would say, "like one of those harlotry players."[12]

I mean no disrespect to any actor, but the sort of pleasure which Shakspeare's plays give in the acting seems to me not at all to differ from that which the audience receive from those of other writers; and, *they being in themselves essentially so different from all others*, I must conclude that there is something in the nature of acting which levels all distinctions. And in fact, who does not speak indifferently of the Gamester and of Macbeth as fine stage performances, and praise the Mrs. Beverley in the same way as the Lady Macbeth of Mrs. S.? Belvidera, and Calista, and Isabella, and Euphrasia, are they less liked than Imogen, or than Juliet, or than Desdemona?[13] Are they not spoken of and remembered in the same way? Is not the female performer as great (as they call it) in one as in the other? Did not Garrick shine, and was he not ambitious of shining in every drawling tragedy that his wretched day produced,— the productions of the Hills and the Murphys and the Browns,[14]—and shall he have that honour to dwell in our minds for ever as an inseparable concomitant with Shakspeare? A kindred mind! O who can read that affecting sonnet of Shakspeare which alludes to his profession as a player:—

> Oh for my sake do you with Fortune chide,
> The guilty goddess of my harmless deeds,
> That did not better for my life provide
> Than public means which public custom breeds—
> Thence comes it that my name receives a brand;
> And almost thence my nature is subdued
> To what it works in, like the dyer's hand——

Or that other confession:—

> Alas! 'tis true, I have gone here and there,
> And made myself a motly to thy view,
> Gor'd mine own thoughts, sold cheap what is most dear—[15]

Who can read these instances of jealous self-watchfulness in our sweet Shakspeare, and dream of any congeniality between him and one that, by every tradition of him, appears to have been as mere a player as ever existed; to have had his mind tainted with the lowest players' vices,—envy and jealousy, and miserable cravings after applause; one who in the exercise of his profession was jealous even of the women-performers that stood in his way; a manager full of managerial tricks and stratagems and finesse: that any resemblance should be dreamed of between him and Shakspeare,—Shakspeare who, in the plenitude and consciousness of his own powers, could with that noble modesty, which we can neither imitate nor appreciate, express himself thus of his own sense of his own defects:—

> Wishing me like to one more rich in hope,
> Featur'd like him, like him with friends possest;
> Desiring *this man's art, and that man's scope.*[16]

I am almost disposed to deny to Garrick the merit of being an admirer of Shakspeare. A true lover of his excellencies he certainly was not; for would any true lover of them have admitted into his matchless scenes such ribald trash as Tate and Cibber, and the rest of them, that

> With their darkness durst affront his light,

have foisted into the acting plays of Shakspeare?[17] I believe it impossible that he could have had a proper reverence for Shakspeare, and have condescended to go through that interpolated scene in Richard the Third, in which Richard tries to break his wife's heart by telling her he loves another woman, and says, "if she survives this she is immortal." Yet I doubt not he delivered this vulgar stuff with as much anxiety of emphasis as any of the genuine parts: and for acting, it is as well calculated as any. But we have

---

[12] *Henry the Fourth*, Part I, II, iv, 436–37.
[13] Lamb is referring to the two repertoires in which Garrick and Mrs. Siddons achieved resounding popularity and success: Shakespearean tragedies, and Restoration and eighteenth-century heroic and domestic tragedies. Garrick had created the role of Beverley in *The Gamester* (1753) by Edward Moore. Mrs. Siddons later appeared as Mrs Beverley, Belvidera in Thomas Otway's *Venice Preserved*, Calista in Nicholas Rowe's *The Fair Penitent*, Isabella in the Garrick adaptation of Thomas Southerne's *The Fatal Marriage*, and Euphrasia in Arthur Murphy's *The Grecian Daughter*.
[14] Aaron Hill (1685–1750), Arthur Murphy (1727–1805), and John ("Estimate") Brown (1715–1766).

[15] Lamb first quotes Sonnet 111, ll. 1–7, then Sonnet 110, ll. 1–3.
[16] Sonnet 29, ll. 5–7.
[17] Lamb refers to eighteenth-century "adapters" of Shakespeare. Nahum Tate (1652–1715) made notorious adaptations of a number of Shakespeare's plays, including the contrivance of a happy ending for *King Lear*; Tate's adaptation remained the acting text of the play well into the nineteenth century. Colley Cibber (1671–1757) made an adaptation of *Richard III* in 1700, which remained the acting version until 1821. "With . . . light" *Paradise Lost*, I, 391.

seen the part of Richard lately produce great fame to an actor by his manner of playing it, and it lets us into the secret of acting, and of popular judgments of Shakspeare derived from acting. Not one of the spectators who have witnessed Mr. C's[18] exertions in that part, but has come away with a proper conviction that Richard is a very wicked man, and kills little children in their beds, with something like the pleasure which the giants and ogres in children's books are represented to have taken in that practice; moreover, that he is very close and shrewd and devilish cunning, for you could see that by his eye.

But is in fact this the impression we have in reading the Richard of Shakspeare? Do we feel any thing like disgust, as we do at the butcher-like representation of him that passes for him on the stage? A horror at his crimes blends with the effect which we feel, but how is it qualified, how is it carried off, by the rich intellect which he displays, his resources, his wit, his buoyant spirits, his vast knowledge and insight into characters, the poetry of his part—not an atom of all which is made perceivable in Mr. C.'s way of acting it. Nothing but his crimes, his actions, is visible; they are prominent and staring; the murderer stands out, but where is the lofty genius, the man of vast capacity,—the profound, the witty, accomplished Richard?

The truth is, the Characters of Shakspeare are so much the objects of meditation rather than of interest or curiosity as to their actions, that while we are reading any of his great criminal characters,—Macbeth, Richard, even Iago,—we think not so much of the crimes which they commit, as of the ambition, the aspiring spirit, the intellectual activity, which prompts them to overleap those moral fences. Barnwell is a wretched murderer; there is a certain fitness between his neck and the rope; he is the legitimate heir to the gallows; nobody who thinks at all can think of any alleviating circumstances in his case to make him a fit object of mercy. Or to take an instance from the higher tragedy, what else but a mere assassin is Glenalvon![19] Do we think of any thing but of the crime which he commits, and the rack which he deserves? That is all which we really think about him. Whereas in corresponding characters in Shakspeare so little do the actions comparatively affect us, that while the impulses, the inner mind in all its perverted greatness, solely seems real and is exclusively attended to, the crime is comparatively nothing. But when we see these things represented, the acts which they do are comparatively every thing, their impulses nothing. The

state of sublime emotion into which we are elevated by those images of night and horror which Macbeth is made to utter, that solemn prelude with which he entertains the time till the bell shall strike which is to call him to murder Duncan,—when we no longer read it in a book, when we have given up that vantage-ground of abstraction which reading possesses over seeing, and come to see a man in his bodily shape before our eyes actually preparing to commit a murder, if the acting be true and impressive, as I have witnessed it in Mr. K.'s performance of that part, the painful anxiety about the act, the natural longing to prevent it while it yet seems unperpetrated, the too close pressing semblance of reality, give a pain and an uneasiness which totally destroy all the delight which the words in the book convey, where the deed doing never presses upon us with the painful sense of presence: it rather seems to belong to history,—to something past and inevitable, if it has any thing to do with time at all. The sublime images, the poetry alone, is that which is present to our minds in the reading.

So to see Lear acted,—to see an old man tottering about the stage with a walking-stick, turned out of doors by his daughters in a rainy night, has nothing in it but what is painful and disgusting. We want to take him into shelter and relieve him. That is all the feeling which the acting of Lear ever produced in me. But the Lear of Shakspeare cannot be acted. The contemptible machinery by which they mimic the storm which he goes out in, is not more inadequate to represent the horrors of the real elements, than any actor can be to represent Lear: they might more easily propose to personate the Satan of Milton upon a stage, or one of Michael Angelo's terrible figures. The greatness of Lear is not in corporal dimension, but in intellectual: the explosions of his passion are terrible as a volcano: they are storms turning up and disclosing to the bottom that sea, his mind, with all its vast riches. It is his mind which is laid bare. This case of flesh and blood seems too insignificant to be thought on; even as he himself neglects it. On the stage we see nothing but corporal infirmities and weakness, the impotence of rage; while we read it, we see not Lear, but we are Lear,—we are in his mind, we are sustained by a grandeur which baffles the malice of daughters and storms; in the aberrations of his reason, we discover a mighty irregular power of reasoning, immethodized from the ordinary purposes of life, but exerting its powers, as the wind blows where it listeth, at will upon the corruptions and abuses of mankind. What have looks, or tones, to do with that sublime identification of his age with that of the *heavens themselves*, when in his reproaches to them for conniving at the injustice of his children, he reminds them that "they themselves are

[18] George Frederick Cooke (1756–1811).
[19] The villain in *Douglas* (1756), a popular tragedy by John Home.

old." [20] What gesture shall we appropriate to this? What has the voice or the eye to do with such things? But the play is beyond all art, as the tamperings with it shew: it is too hard and stony; it must have love-scenes, and a happy ending. It is not enough that Cordelia is a daughter, she must shine as a lover too. Tate has put his hook in the nostrils of this Leviathan, for Garrick and his followers, the showmen of the scene, to draw the mighty beast about more easily. A happy ending!—as if the living martyrdom that Lear had gone through,— the flaying of his feelings alive, did not make a fair dismissal from the stage of life the only decorous thing for him. If he is to live and be happy after, if he could sustain this world's burden after, why all this pudder and preparation,—why torment us with all this unnecessary sympathy? As if the childish pleasure of getting his gilt robes and sceptre again could tempt him to act over again his misused station,—as if at his years, and with his experience, any thing was left but to die.

Lear is essentially impossible to be represented on a stage. But how many dramatic personages are there in Shakspeare, which though more tractable and feasible (if 1 may so speak) than Lear, yet from some circumstance, some adjunct to their character, are improper to be shewn to our bodily eye. Othello for instance. Nothing can be more soothing, more flattering to the nobler parts of our natures, than to read of a young Venetian lady of highest extraction, through the force of love and from a sense of merit in him whom she loved, laying aside every consideration of kindred, and country, and colour, and wedding with a *coal-black Moor*—(for such he is represented, in the imperfect state of knowledge respecting foreign countries in those days, compared with our own, or in compliance with popular notions, though the Moors are now well enough known to be by many shades less unworthy of a white woman's fancy)—it is the perfect triumph of virtue over accidents, of the imagination over the senses. She sees Othello's colour in his mind. But upon the stage, when the imagination is no longer the ruling faculty, but we are left to our poor unassisted senses, I appeal to every one that has seen Othello played, whether he did not, on the contrary, sink Othello's mind in his colour; whether he did not find something extremely revolting in the courtship and wedded caresses of Othello and Desdemona; and whether the actual sight of the thing did not over-weigh all that beautiful compromise which we make in reading;— and the reason it should do so is obvious, because there is just so much reality presented to our senses as to

give a perception of disagreement, with not enough of belief in the internal motives,—all that which is unseen,—to overpower and reconcile the first and obvious prejudices.* What we see upon a stage is body and bodily action; what we are conscious of in reading is almost exclusively the mind, and its movements: and this I think may sufficiently account for the very different sort of delight with which the same play so often affects us in the reading and seeing.

It requires little reflection to perceive, that if those characters in Shakspeare which are within the precincts of nature, have yet something in them which appeals too exclusively to the imagination, to admit of their being made objects to the senses without suffering a change and a diminution,—that still stronger the objection must lie against representing another line of characters, which Shakspeare has introduced to give a wildness and supernatural elevation to his scenes, as if to remove them still farther from that assimilation to common life in which their excellence is vulgarly supposed to consist. When we read the incantations of those terrible beings the Witches in Macbeth, though some of the ingredients of their hellish composition savour of the grotesque, yet is the effect upon us other than the most serious and appalling that can be imagined? Do we not feel spell-bound as Macbeth was? Can any mirth accompany a sense of their presence? We might as well laugh under a consciousness of the principle of Evil himself being truly and really present with us. But attempt to bring these beings on to a stage, and you turn them instantly into so many old women, that men and children are to laugh at. Contrary to the old saying, that "seeing is believing," the sight actually destroys the faith: and the mirth in which we indulge at their expense, when we see these creatures upon a stage, seems to be a sort of indemnification which we make to ourselves for the terror which they put us in when reading made them an object of belief,—when we surrendered up our reason to the poet, as children to their nurses and their elders; and we laugh at our fears, as children who thought they saw something in the dark, triumph when the bringing in of a candle discovers the vanity of their fears. For

---

* The error of supposing that because Othello's colour does not offend us in the reading, it should also not offend us in the seeing, is just such a fallacy as supposing that an Adam and Eve in a picture shall affect us just as they do in the poem. But in the poem we for a while have Paradisaical senses given us, which vanish when we see a man and his wife without clothes in the picture. The painters themselves feel this, as is apparent by the aukward shifts they have recourse to, to make them look not quite naked; by a sort of prophetic anachronism, antedating the invention of fig-leaves. So in the reading of the play, we see with Desdemona's eyes; in the seeing of it, we are forced to look with our own.

---

[20] See *King Lear*, II, iv, 194.

this exposure of supernatural agents upon a stage is truly bringing in a candle to expose their own delusiveness. It is the solitary taper and the book that generates a faith in these terrors: a ghost by chandelier light, and in good company, deceives no spectators,—a ghost that can be measured by the eye, and his human dimensions made out at leisure. The sight of a well-lighted house, and a well-dressed audience, shall arm the most nervous child against any apprehensions: as Tom Brown says of the impenetrable skin of Achilles with his impenetrable armour over it, "Bully Dawson would have fought the devil with such advantages."[21]

Much has been said, and deservedly, in reprobation of the vile mixture which Dryden has thrown into the Tempest:[22] doubtless without some such vicious alloy, the impure ears of that age would never have sate out to hear so much innocence of love as is contained in the sweet courtship of Ferdinand and Miranda. But is the Tempest of Shakspeare at all a subject for stage representation? It is one thing to read of an enchanter, and to believe the wondrous tale while we are reading it; but to have a conjuror brought before us in his conjuring-gown, with his spirits about him, which none but himself and some hundred of favoured spectators before the curtain are supposed to see, involves such a quantity of the *hateful incredible*, that all our reverence for the author cannot hinder us from perceiving such gross attempts upon the senses to be in the highest degree childish and inefficient. Spirits and fairies cannot be represented, they cannot even be painted,—they can only be believed. But the elaborate and anxious provision of scenery, which the luxury of the age demands, in these cases works a quite contrary effect to what is intended. That which in comedy, or plays of familiar life, adds so much to the life of the imitation, in plays which appeal to the higher faculties, positively destroys the illusion which it is introduced to aid. A parlour or a drawing-room,—a library opening into a garden,—a garden with an alcove in it,—a street, or the piazza of Covent-garden, does well enough in a scene; we are content to give as much credit to it as it demands; or rather, we think little about it,—it is little more than reading at the top of a page, "Scene, a Garden;" we do not imagine ourselves there, but we readily admit the imitation of familiar objects. But to think by the help of painted trees and caverns, which we know to be painted, to transport our minds to

Prospero, and his island and his lonely cell;* or by the aid of a fiddle dexterously thrown in, in an interval of speaking, to make us believe that we hear those supernatural noises of which the isle was full:—the Orrery Lecturer at the Haymarket might as well hope, by his musical glasses cleverly stationed out of sight behind his apparatus, to make us believe that we do indeed hear the chrystal spheres ring out that chime, which if it were to inwrap our fancy long, Milton thinks,

Time would run back and fetch the age of gold,
And speckled vanity
Would sicken soon and die,
And leprous Sin would melt from earthly mould;
Yea Hell itself would pass away,
And leave its dolorous mansions to the peering day.[23]

The Garden of Eden, with our first parents in it, is not more impossible to be shewn on a stage, than the Enchanted Isle, with its no less interesting and innocent first settlers.

The subject of Scenery is closely connected with that of the Dresses, which are so anxiously attended to on our stage. I remember the last time I saw Macbeth played, the discrepancy I felt at the changes of garment which he varied,—the shiftings and re-shiftings, like a Romish priest at mass. The luxury of stage-improvements, and the importunity of the public eye, require this. The coronation robe of the Scottish monarch was fairly a counterpart to that which our King wears when he goes to the Parliament-house,—just so full and cumbersome, and set out with ermine and pearls. And if things must be represented, I see not what to find fault with in this. But in reading, what robe are we conscious of? Some dim images of royalty—a crown and sceptre, may float before our eyes, but who shall describe the fashion of it? Do we see in our mind's eye what Webb or any other robe-maker could pattern? This is the inevitable consequence of imitating every thing, to make all things natural. Whereas the reading of a tragedy is a fine abstraction. It presents to the fancy just so much of external appearances as to make us feel that we are among flesh and blood, while by far the greater and better part of our imagination is employed upon the thoughts and internal machinery of the character. But in acting, scenery, dress, the most contemptible things, call upon us to judge of their naturalness.

* It will be said these things are done in pictures. But pictures and scenes are very different things. Painting is a world of itself, but in scene-painting there is the attempt to deceive; and there is the discordancy, never to be got over, between painted scenes and real people.

[21] Thomas Brown (1663–1704) was a scurrilous London satirist and miscellaneous writer. Bully Dawson was a disreputable and blustering character on the London scene in the late seventeenth century.
[22] An adaptation of Shakespeare's play produced in 1667, by Dryden in collaboration with Sir William Davenant.

[23] "Hymn on the Morning of Christ's Nativity," ll. 135–40.

Perhaps it would be no bad similitude, to liken the pleasure which we take in seeing one of these fine plays acted, compared with that quiet delight which we find in the reading of it, to the different feelings with which a reviewer, and a man that is not a reviewer, reads a fine poem. The accursed critical habit,—the being called upon to judge and pronounce, must make it quite a different thing to the former. In seeing these plays acted, we are affected just as judges. When Hamlet compares the two pictures of Gertrude's first and second husband, who wants to see the pictures? But in the acting, a miniature must be lugged out; which we know not to be the picture, but only to shew how finely a miniature may be represented. This shewing of every thing, levels all things: it makes tricks, bows, and curtesies, of importance. Mrs. S. never got more fame by any thing than by the manner in which she dismisses the guests in the banquet-scene in Macbeth; it is as much remembered as any of her thrilling tones or impressive looks. But does such a trifle as this enter into the imaginations of the readers of that wild and wonderful scene? Does not the mind dismiss the feasters as rapidly as it can? Does it care about the gracefulness of the doing it? But by acting, and judging of acting, all these non-essentials are raised into an importance, injurious to the main interest of the play.

I have confined my observations to the tragic parts of Shakspeare. It would be no very difficult task to extend the enquiry to his comedies; and to shew why Falstaff, Shallow, Sir Hugh Evans,[24] and the rest, are equally incompatible with stage representation. The length to which this Essay has run, will make it, I am afraid, sufficiently distasteful to the Amateurs of the Theatre, without going any deeper into the subject at present.

[October–December 1811]   [1818]

ESSAYS OF ELIA

Among the most beloved and admired of all the varieties of Romantic prose, Lamb's Elia Essays began with the publication of "Recollections of the South Sea House" in the London Maga-zine, *August 1820. Like those to follow, the initial Elia Essay was a journey in memory, in this case back to the place of Lamb's employment in 1791. The South Sea House has its identity in terms of its more glorious past; similarly, the employees of 1791, by their dedication to family tradition or the stirring events of past history, win for themselves a personality and identity that rescues them from the irrelevance of their actual labors. However, the primary focus of the essay is not on the recovery of the House or its employees of "forty years ago," but on the transformation or*

[24] Characters in *The Merry Wives of Windsor.*

change in perspective of the reader. The essay begins with the "Reader" already cast in relation to the past, but at this point only in mercenary terms as "a lean annuitant." Initially the "Reader" stands outside the building and responds to it in terms of its external appearance and physical location: "a melancholy looking, handsome, brick and stone edifice, to the left—where Threadneedle-street abuts upon Bishopsgate." However, by the end of the opening paragraph his eye has been led within "to view a grave court, with cloisters, and pillars," and he is now asked to respond to it as an object of tragic grandeur, "a desolation some-thing like Balclutha's." It should be noted that by the fifth paragraph, the transformation has so far progressed that Elia is now willing to present the building to his reader no longer as a dead physical object; it is now addressed as alive and as a source of "delight" and "reverence," which wins for it the reader's sym-pathies over the surrounding establishments "with their impor-tant faces, as it were, insulting thee, their* poor neighbour *out of business . . ."*

The Essays to follow were to play rich variations on the sub-ject matter and rhetoric of the opening paragraphs of this initial Elia Essay. Through the power of his own memory ("New Year's Eve," "Blakesmoor in H——shire"), or the agency of "Bridget Elia" ("Old China," "Mackery End in Hertfordshire") or "G. D." ("Oxford in the Vacation"), Elia leads the reader away from the restrictions of a present reality into the dignity, innocence, and hope of the past. By recovering these past ener-gies, both Elia and the reader may face the limited present more courageously. This summoning of the past has its obvious the-matic counterparts in the poetry of Wordsworth and Coleridge; what deserves equal notice is Lamb's rhetorical skill in effecting radical changes in perspective in his readers, equal to the trans-formations achieved in the finest Romantic lyrics.

The Elia Essays are here reproduced from their versions in the two collections: Elia: Essays . . . *(1823) and* Last Essays of Elia *(1833). They had originally appeared in the pages of the* London Magazine *and other periodicals between 1820 and 1833.*

FROM

ESSAYS OF ELIA

PREFACE.

BY A FRIEND OF THE LATE ELIA.[1]

THIS POOR gentleman, who for some months past had been in a declining way, hath at length paid his final tribute to nature.

To say truth, it is time he were gone. The humour of the thing, if there was ever much in it, was pretty well exhausted; and a two years' and a half existence has been a tolerable duration for a phantom.[2]

[1] Elia is the pseudonym adopted by Lamb in 1820, under which he wrote his most famous essays. He derived the name from that of a fellow clerk at the South-Sea House.
[2] The first Elia essay, in its original title "Recollections of the South Sea House," had appeared in the *London Magazine*, August 1820; the "Preface" [to the 1833 *Last Essays of Elia*] has been first published in the issue of January 1823, as "A Character of the Late Elia, by a Friend."

I am now at liberty to confess, that much which I have heard objected to my late friend's writings was well-founded. Crude they are, I grant you—a sort of unlicked, incondite [3] things—villainously pranked in an affected array of antique modes and phrases. They had not been *his*, if they had been other than such; and better it is, that a writer should be natural in a self-pleasing quaintness, than to affect a naturalness (so called) that should be strange to him. Egotistical they have been pronounced by some who did not know, that what he tells us, as of himself, was often true only (historically) of another; as in a former Essay [4] (to save many instances)—where under the *first person* (his favourite figure) he shadows forth the forlorn estate of a country-boy placed at a London school, far from his friends and connections—in direct opposition to his own early history. If it be egotism to imply and twine with his own identity the griefs and affections of another—making himself many, or reducing many unto himself—then is the skilful novelist, who all along brings in his hero, or heroine, speaking of themselves, the greatest egotist of all; who yet has never, therefore, been accused of that narrowness. And how shall the intenser dramatist escape being faulty, who doubtless, under cover of passion uttered by another, oftentimes gives blameless vent to his most inward feelings, and expresses his own story modestly?

My late friend was in many respects a singular character. Those who did not like him, hated him; and some, who once liked him, afterwards became his bitterest haters. The truth is, he gave himself too little concern what he uttered, and in whose presence. He observed neither time nor place, and would e'en out with what came uppermost. With the severe religionist he would pass for a free-thinker; while the other faction set him down for a bigot, or persuaded themselves that he belied his sentiments. Few understood him; and I am not certain that at all times he quite understood himself. He too much affected that dangerous figure—irony. He sowed doubtful speeches, and reaped plain, unequivocal hatred.—He would interrupt the gravest discussion with some light jest; and yet, perhaps, not quite irrelevant in ears that could understand it. Your long and much talkers hated him. The informal habit of his mind, joined to an inveterate impediment of speech, forbade him to be an orator; and he seemed determined that no one else should play that part when he was present. He was *petit* and ordinary in his person and appearance. I have seen him sometimes in what is called good company, but where he has been a stranger,

sit silent, and be suspected for an odd fellow; till some unlucky occasion provoking it, he would stutter out some senseless pun (not altogether senseless perhaps, if rightly taken), which has stamped his character for the evening. It was hit or miss with him; but nine times out of ten, he contrived by this device to send away a whole company his enemies. His conceptions rose kindlier than his utterance, and his happiest *impromptus* had the appearance of effort. He has been accused of trying to be witty, when in truth he was but struggling to give his poor thoughts articulation. He chose his companions for some individuality of character which they manifested.—Hence, not many persons of science, and few professed *literati*, were of his councils. They were, for the most part, persons of an uncertain fortune; and, as to such people commonly nothing is more obnoxious than a gentleman of settled (though moderate) income, he passed with most of them for a great miser. To my knowledge this was a mistake. His *intimados*, to confess a truth, were in the world's eye a ragged regiment. He found them floating on the surface of society; and the colour, or something else, in the weed pleased him. The burrs stuck to him—but they were good and loving burrs for all that. He never greatly cared for the society of what are called good people. If any of these were scandalised (and offences were sure to arise), he could not help it. When he has been remonstrated with for not making more concessions to the feelings of good people, he would retort by asking, what one point did these good people ever concede to him? He was temperate in his meals and diversions, but always kept a little on this side of abstemiousness. Only in the use of the Indian weed he might be thought a little excessive. He took it, he would say, as a solvent of speech. Marry—as the friendly vapour ascended, how his prattle would curl up sometimes with it! the ligaments, which tongue-tied him, were loosened, and the stammerer proceeded a statist! [5]

I do not know whether I ought to bemoan or rejoice that my old friend is departed. His jests were beginning to grow obsolete, and his stories to be found out. He felt the approaches of age; and while he pretended to cling to life, you saw how slender were the ties left to bind him. Discoursing with him latterly on this subject, he expressed himself with a pettishness, which I thought unworthy of him. In our walks about his suburban retreat (as he called it) at Shacklewell, [6] some children belonging to a school of industry had met us, and

---

3 Unpolished, ill-constructed.
4 "Christ's Hospital Five and Thirty Years Ago," which appeared in the *London Magazine*, November 1820.

5 Statesman, here meant as a man of oratorical skills. The reference to the "impediment of speech" was biographically true of Lamb.
6 In Lamb's time, a suburb north of London and popular residence for retired and pensioned Londoners.

bowed and curtseyed, as he thought, in an especial manner to *him*. "They take me for a visiting governor," he muttered earnestly. He had a horror, which he carried to a foible, of looking like anything important and parochial. He thought that he approached nearer to that stamp daily. He had a general aversion from being treated like a grave or respectable character, and kept a wary eye upon the advances of age that should so entitle him. He herded always, while it was possible, with people younger than himself. He did not conform to the march of time, but was dragged along in the procession. His manners lagged behind his years. He was too much of the boy-man. The *toga virilis*[7] never sate gracefully on his shoulders. The impressions of infancy had burnt into him, and he resented the impertinence of manhood. These were weaknesses; but such as they were, they are a key to explicate some of his writings.

[January 1823]   [1833]

THE SOUTH-SEA HOUSE[1]

Reader, in thy passage from the Bank—where thou hast been receiving thy half-yearly dividends (supposing thou art a lean annuitant like myself)—to the Flower Pot,[2] to secure a place for Dalston, or Shacklewell, or some other thy suburban retreat northerly,—didst thou never observe a melancholy looking, handsome, brick and stone edifice, to the left—where Threadneedle-street abuts upon Bishopsgate? I dare say thou hast often admired its magnificent portals ever gaping wide, and disclosing to view a grave court, with cloisters, and pillars, with few or no traces of goers-in or comers-out—a desolation something like Balclutha's.*

This was once a house of trade,—a centre of busy

* I passed by the walls of Balclutha, and they were desolate —OSSIAN.[3]

7 *toga virilis:* "the garb of manhood." Lamb refers to a Roman family ceremony of the initiation of the male child into adult society, symbolized by his donning the adult toga for the first time.
1 The headquarters of the South-Sea Company founded in 1711 to direct the highly prosperous British trade with South America and the Pacific islands. The Company was at the center of one of England's most sensational financial scandals, the South-Sea Bubble of 1720–21; through shady manipulations, the stock shares of the Company reached enormous heights and were sold off to the advantage of the directors of the Company and various government ministers. The subsequent sudden and disastrous drop in the shares brought ruin to many and precipitated a government crisis.
2 The inn from which the coaches for the north left (E. V. Lucas).
3 Lamb quotes, somewhat inaccurately, from *Carthon* (1760), one of the supposed epics by an ancient Gaelic bard Ossian, "discovered" and "translated" by James Macpherson.

interests. The throng of merchants was here—the quick pulse of gain—and here some forms of business are still kept up, though the soul be long since fled. Here are still to be seen stately porticos; imposing staircases; offices roomy as the state apartments in palaces—deserted, or thinly peopled with a few straggling clerks; the still more sacred interiors of court and committee rooms, with venerable faces of beadles, door-keepers—directors seated in form on solemn days (to proclaim a dead dividend,) at long worm-eaten tables, that have been mahogany, with tarnished gilt-leather coverings, supporting massy silver inkstands long since dry;—the oaken wainscots hung with pictures of deceased governors and sub-governors, of queen Anne, and the two first monarchs of the Brunswick dynasty;[4]—huge charts, which subsequent discoveries have antiquated;—dusty maps of Mexico, dim as dreams,—and soundings of the Bay of Panama!—The long passages hung with buckets, appended, in idle row, to walls, whose substance might defy any, short of the last, conflagration:—with vast ranges of cellarage under all, where dollars and pieces of eight once lay, an "unsunned heap,"[5] for Mammon to have solaced his solitary heart withal,—long since dissipated, or scattered into air at the blast of the breaking of that famous BUBBLE.——

Such is the SOUTH-SEA HOUSE. At least, such it was forty years ago, when I knew it,—a magnificent relic! What alterations may have been made in it since, I have had no opportunities of verifying. Time, I take for granted, has not freshened it. No wind has resuscitated the face of the sleeping waters. A thicker crust by this time stagnates upon it. The moths, that were then battening upon its obsolete ledgers and day-books, have rested from their depredations, but other light generations have succeeded, making fine fretwork among their single and double entries. Layers of dust have accumulated (a superfoetation[6] of dirt!) upon the old layers, that seldom used to be disturbed, save by some curious finger, now and then, inquisitive to explore the mode of book-keeping in Queen Anne's reign; or, with less hallowed curiosity, seeking to unveil some of the mysteries of that tremendous HOAX, whose extent the petty peculators of our day look back upon with the same expression of incredulous admiration, and hopeless ambition of rivalry, as would become the puny face of modern conspiracy contemplating the Titan size of Vaux's superhuman plot.[7]

4 George I (1714–1727), and George II (1727–1760).
5 Milton's *Comus*, l. 398.   6 Superabundant addition.
7 A reference to the famous Gunpowder Plot of 1605, a conspiracy by various Catholics, including Guy Fawkes (Vaux) (1570–1606), to destroy the King and the Houses of Parliament.

Peace to the manes of the BUBBLE! Silence and destitution are upon thy walls, proud house, for a memorial!

Situated as thou art, in the very heart of stirring and living commerce,—amid the fret and fever of speculation—with the Bank, and the 'Change, and the India-house about thee, in the hey-day of present prosperity, with their important faces, as it were, insulting thee, their *poor neighbour out of business*—to the idle and merely contemplative,—to such as me, old house! there is a charm in thy quiet:—a cessation—a coolness from business—an indolence almost cloistral—which is delightful! With what reverence have I paced thy great bare rooms and courts at eventide! They spoke of the past:—the shade of some dead accountant, with visionary pen in ear, would flit by me, stiff as in life. Living accounts and accountants puzzle me. I have no skill in figuring. But thy great dead tomes, which scarce three degenerate clerks of the present day could lift from their enshrining shelves—with their old fantastic flourishes, and decorative rubric interlacings—their sums in triple columniations,[8] set down with formal superfluity of cyphers—with pious sentences at the beginning, without which our religious ancestors never ventured to open a book of business, or bill of lading—the costly vellum covers of some of them almost persuading us that we are got into some *better library*,—are very agreeable and edifying spectacles. I can look upon these defunct dragons with complacency. Thy heavy odd-shaped ivory-handled penknives (our ancestors had every thing on a larger scale than we have hearts for) are as good as any thing from Herculaneum.[9] The pounce-boxes [10] of our days have gone retrograde.

The very clerks which I remember in the South-Sea House—I speak of forty years back—had an air very different from those in the public offices that I have had to do with since. They partook of the genius of the place!

They were mostly (for the establishment did not admit of superfluous salaries) bachelors. Generally (for they had not much to do) persons of a curious and speculative turn of mind. Old-fashioned, for a reason mentioned before. Humorists, for they were of all descriptions; and, not having been brought together in early life (which has a tendency to assimilate the members of corporate bodies to each other), but, for the most part, placed in this house in ripe or middle age, they necessarily carried into it their separate

habits and oddities, unqualified, if I may so speak, as into a common stock. Hence they formed a sort of Noah's ark. Odd fishes. A lay-monastery. Domestic retainers in a great house, kept more for show than use. Yet pleasant fellows, full of chat—and not a few among them had arrived at considerable proficiency on the German flute.

The cashier at that time was one Evans, a Cambro-Briton.[11] He had something of the choleric complexion of his countrymen stamped on his visage, but was a worthy sensible man at bottom. He wore his hair, to the last, powdered and frizzed out, in the fashion which I remember to have seen in caricatures of what were termed, in my young days, *Maccaronies*.[12] He was the last of that race of beaux. Melancholy as a gib-cat[13] over his counter all the forenoon, I think I see him, making up his cash (as they call it) with tremulous fingers, as if he feared every one about him was a defaulter; in his hypochondry ready to imagine himself one; haunted, at least, with the idea of the possibility of his becoming one: his tristful visage clearing up a little over his roast neck of veal at Anderton's at two (where his picture still hangs, taken a little before his death by desire of the master of the coffee-house, which he had frequented for the last five-and-twenty years), but not attaining the meridian of its animation till evening brought on the hour of tea and visiting. The simultaneous sound of his well-known rap at the door with the stroke of the clock announcing six, was a topic of never-failing mirth in the families which this dear old bachelor gladdened with his presence. Then was his *forte*, his glorified hour! How would he chirp, and expand, over a muffin! How would he dilate into secret history! His countryman, Pennant himself, in particular could not be more eloquent than he in relation to old and new London [14]—the site of old theatres, churches, streets gone to decay—where Rosamond's pond stood—the Mulberry-gardens—and the Conduit in Cheap—with many a pleasant anecdote, derived from paternal tradition, of those grotesque figures which Hogarth has immortalized in his picture of *Noon*,—the worthy descendants of those heroic confessors, who, flying to this country, from the wrath of Louis the Fourteenth and his dragoons, kept alive the flame of pure religion in the sheltering ob-

---

[8] Arrangements in columns.

[9] An ancient Italian city, near Pompeii, destroyed by the eruption of Vesuvius in A.D. 79. Lamb refers to the excavations carried out in the eighteenth century.

[10] Containing a fine powder used to dry fresh ink.

[11] A Welshman.

[12] Term applied to rather affected and foppish young men of the eighteenth century, who aped continental fashions in dress and deportment.

[13] Castrated cat.

[14] Thomas Pennant (1726–1798) was a famous naturalist and antiquarian, who, beginning in 1771, published a long series of works on his travels and historical investigations of various parts of the British isles. His study of London appeared in 1790.

scurities of Hog-lane, and the vicinity of the Seven Dials![15]

Deputy, under Evans, was Thomas Tame. He had the air and stoop of a nobleman. You would have taken him for one, had you met him in one of the passages leading to Westminster-hall.[16] By stoop, I mean that gentle bending of the body forwards, which, in great men, must be supposed to be the effect of an habitual condescending attention to the applications of their inferiors. While he held you in converse, you felt strained to the height in the colloquy. The conference over, you were at leisure to smile at the comparative insignificance of the pretensions which had just awed you. His intellect was of the shallowest order. It did not reach to a saw or a proverb. His mind was in its original state of white paper.[17] A sucking babe might have posed him. What was it then? Was he rich? Alas, no! Thomas Tame was very poor. Both he and his wife looked outwardly gentlefolks, when I fear all was not well at all times within. She had a neat meagre person, which it was evident she had not sinned in over-pampering; but in its veins was noble blood. She traced her descent, by some labyrinth of relationship, which I never thoroughly understood,—much less can explain with any heraldic certainty at this time of day,—to the illustrious, but unfortunate house of Derwentwater.[18] This was the secret of Thomas's stoop. This was the thought—the sentiment—the bright solitary star of your lives,—ye mild and happy pair,—which cheered you in the night of intellect, and in the obscurity of your station! This was to you instead of riches, instead of rank, instead of glittering attainments: and it was worth them all together. You insulted none with it; but, while you wore it as a piece of defensive armour only, no insult likewise could reach you through it. *Decus et solamen.*[19]

Of quite another stamp was the then accountant, John Tipp. He neither pretended to high blood, nor in good truth cared one fig about the matter. He "thought an accountant the greatest character in the world, and himself the greatest accountant in it."[20] Yet John was not without his hobby. The fiddle relieved his vacant hours. He sang, certainly, with other notes than to the Orphean lyre. He did, indeed, scream and scrape most abominably. His fine suite of official rooms in Thread-needle-street, which, without any thing very substantial appended to them, were enough to enlarge a man's notions of himself that lived in them, (I know not who is the occupier of them now) resounded fortnightly to the notes of a concert of "sweet breasts," as our ancestors would have called them, culled from club-rooms and orchestras—chorus singers—first and second violincellos—double basses—and clarinets—who ate his cold mutton, and drank his punch, and praised his ear. He sat like Lord Midas among them. But at the desk Tipp was quite another sort of creature. Thence all ideas, that were purely ornamental, were banished. You could not speak of any thing romantic without rebuke. Politics were excluded. A newspaper was though too refined and abstracted. The whole duty of man consisted in writing off dividend warrants. The striking of the annual balance in the company's books (which, perhaps, differed from the balance of last year in the sum of 25*l.*1*s.*6*d.*) occupied his days and nights for a month previous. Not that Tipp was blind to the deadness of *things* (as they call them in the city) in his beloved house, or did not sigh for a return of the old stirring days when South Sea hopes were young—(he was indeed equal to the wielding of any the most intricate accounts of the most flourishing company in these or those days):— but to a genuine accountant the difference of proceeds is as nothing. The fractional farthing is as dear to his heart as the thousands which stand before it. He is the true actor, who, whether his part be a prince or a peasant, must act it with like intensity. With Tipp form was every thing. His life was formal. His actions seemed ruled with a ruler. His pen was not less erring than his heart. He made the best executor in the world: he was plagued with incessant executorships accordingly, which excited his spleen and soothed his vanity in equal ratios. He would swear (for Tipp swore) at the little orphans, whose rights he would guard with a tenacity like the grasp of the dying hand, that commended their interests to his protection. With all this there was about him a sort of timidity—(his few enemies used to give it a worse name)—a something which, in reverence to the dead, we will place, if you please, a little on this side of the heroic. Nature certainly had been pleased to endow John Tipp with a sufficient measure of the principle of self-preservation. There is a cowardice which we do not despise, because

[15] Hogarth's painting of 1736 represented the congregation leaving the French Chapel in Hog Lane. The "heroic confessors" were the Huguenots, who fled to England following the revocation of their civil and religious liberties in 1685 and the subsequent persecutions carried out by the French King.

[16] Westminster-hall adjoined the Houses of Parliament, and was the site of the chief law courts.

[17] An image from the English empirical philosopher John Locke, used to illustrate the original blankness of the mind before sensory experience supplied the impressions from which ideas are derived.

[18] Earl of Derwentwater was the title of the Radcliffes, an English Catholic family. James Radcliffe, the last official holder of the title, was beheaded for his participation in the Catholic Pretender's attempt to win the English throne in 1715.

[19] *Decus et solamen:* "honor and consolation." See *Aeneid*, X, 858–59.

[20] Modelled on a remark by Parson Adams, in Book III, Chapter 5, of Fielding's *Joseph Andrews* (1742).

it has nothing base or treacherous in its elements; it
betrays itself, not you: it is mere temperament; the
absence of the romantic and the enterprising; it sees a
lion in the way, and will not, with Fortinbras, "greatly
find quarrel in a straw,"[21] when some supposed honour
is at stake. Tipp never mounted the box of a stage-
coach in his life; or leaned against the rails of a balcony;
or walked upon the ridge of a parapet; or looked down
a precipice; or let off a gun; or went upon a water-
party; or would willingly let you go if he could have
helped it: neither was it recorded of him, that for
lucre, or for intimidation, he ever forsook friend or
principle.

Whom next shall we summon from the dusty dead,
in whom common qualities become uncommon? Can
I forget thee, Henry Man,[22] the wit, the polished man
of letters, the *author*, of the South Sea House? who
never enteredst thy office in a morning, or quittedst it
in mid-day—(what didst *thou* in an office?)—without
some quirk that left a sting! Thy gibes and thy jokes
are now extinct, or survive but in two forgotten volumes,
which I had the good fortune to rescue from a stall in
Barbican, not three days ago, and found thee terse,
fresh, epigrammatic, as alive. Thy wit is a little gone
by in these fastidious days—thy topics are staled by the
"new-born gauds"[23] of the time:—but great thou
used to be in Public Ledgers, and in Chronicles, upon
Chatham, and Shelburne, and Rockingham, and Howe,
and Burgoyne, and Clinton, and the war which ended
in the tearing from Great Britain her rebellious colonies,—and Keppel, and Wilkes, and Sawbridge, and
Bull, and Dunning, and Pratt, and Richmond,—and
such small politics.——[24]

A little less facetious, and a great deal more ob-
streperous, was fine rattling, rattleheaded Plumer. He
was descended,—not in a right line, reader, (for his

lineal pretensions, like his personal, favoured a little of
the sinister bend) from the Plumers of Hertfordshire.
So tradition gave him out; and certain family features
not a little sanctioned the opinion. Certainly old
Walter Plumer (his reputed author) had been a rake in
his days, and visited much in Italy, and had seen the
world. He was uncle, bachelor-uncle, to the fine old
whig still living, who has represented the county in so
many successive parliaments, and has a fine old mansion near Ware. Walter flourished in George the
Second's days, and was the same who was summoned
before the House of Commons about a business of
franks, with the old Duchess of Marlborough. You may
read of it in Johnson's Life of Cave.[25] Cave come off
cleverly in that business. It is certain our Plumer did
nothing to discountenance the rumour. He rather
seemed pleased whenever it was, with all gentleness,
insinuated. But, besides his family pretensions, Plumer
was an engaging fellow, and sang gloriously.——

Not so sweetly sang Plumer as thou sangest, mild,
child-like, pastoral M——; a flute's breathing less
divinely whispering than thy Arcadian melodies, when,
in tones worthy of Arden, thou didst chant that song
sung by Amiens to the banished Duke, which proclaims the winter wind more lenient than for a man to
be ungrateful.[26] Thy sire was old surly M——, the
unapproachable churchwarden of Bishopsgate. He
knew not what he did, when he begat thee, like spring,
gentle offspring of blustering winter:—only unfortunate in thy ending, which should have been mild,
conciliatory, swan-like.——

Much remains to sing. Many fantastic shapes rise up,
but they must be mine in private:—already I have
fooled the reader to the top of his bent; else could I
omit that strange creature Woollett, who existed in
trying the question, and *bought litigations*?—and still
stranger, inimitable, solemn Hepworth, from whose
gravity Newton might have deduced the law of gravitation. How profoundly would he nib a pen—with
what deliberation would he wet a wafer!——

But it is time to close—night's wheels are rattling
fast over me—it is proper to have done with this solemn
mockery.

Reader, what if I have been playing with thee all this
while—peradventure the very *names*, which I have
summoned up before thee, are fantastic—insubstan-

---

[21] *Hamlet*, IV, iv, 55.

[22] Henry Man (1747–1799). His *Miscellaneous Works, in Verse
and Prose* were published in two volumes in 1802.

[23] Shakespeare's *Troilus and Cressida*, III, iii, 176.

[24] Man contributed political essays and letters critical of the
conduct of the American War to the *Morning Chronicle*. William
Pitt, first Earl of Chatham (1708–1778), William Petty, Lord
Shelburne (1737–1805), Charles Watson-Wentworth, second
Marquis of Rockingham (1730–1782) were leading politicians and
statesmen of their time, and supporters of the American colonies
against the repressive measures of the King and his ministers.
William Howe (1729–1814), John Burgoyne (1722–1792), and
Sir Henry Clinton (c. 1738–1795) were commanders of the
British forces in America during the Revolution. Augustus
Keppel (1725–1786) was an admiral and popular hero. John
Wilkes (1727–1797), member of parliament, was a famous contro-
versialist and political agitator. His imprisonment in the Tower
for remarks made against the King in his journal *North Briton*
(1763) was reversed by Charles Pratt (1714–1794), lord chancellor
at the time. John Sawbridge (c. 1732–1795) was Lord Mayor of
London and a supporter of Wilkes.

[25] Edward Cave (1691–1754) was clerk of the franks, the
privilege of sending letters post free enjoyed by members of
parliament and other dignitaries. The signature on the envelope
constituted the frank. Cave was zealous in protecting the privilege from such abuses as the one mentioned here, in which Plumer
had given the Duchess some of his franks.

[26] See *As You Like It*, II, vii, 174–90.

tial—like Henry Pimpernel, and old John Naps of Greece:[27]——

Be satisfied that something answering to them has had a being. Their importance is from the past.

[August 1820]   [1823]

OXFORD IN THE VACATION

CASTING a preparatory glance at the bottom of this article—as the wary connoisseur in prints, with cursory eye (which, while it reads, seems as though it read not,) never fails to consult the *quis sculpsit*[1] in the corner, before he pronounces some rare piece to be a Vivares, or a Woollet[2]—methinks I hear you exclaim, Reader, *Who is Elia?*

Because in my last I tried to divert thee with some half-forgotten humours of some old clerks defunct, in an old house of business, long since gone to decay, doubtless you have already set me down in your mind as one of the self-same college—a votary of the desk—a notched and cropt scrivener—one that sucks his sustenance, as certain sick people are said to do, through a quill.

Well, I do agnize[3] something of the sort. I confess that it is my humour, my fancy—in the forepart of the day, when the mind of your man of letters requires some relaxation—(and none better than such as at first sight seems most abhorrent from his beloved studies)—to while away some good hours of my time in the contemplation of indigos, cottons, raw silks, piece-goods, flowered or otherwise. In the first place * * * * * * * and then it sends you home with such increased appetite to your books * * * * * * * * * not to say, that your outside sheets, and waste wrappers of foolscap, do receive into them, most kindly and naturally, the impression of sonnets, epigrams, *essays*—so that the very parings of a counting-house are, in some sort, the settings up of an author. The enfranchised quill, that has plodded all the morning among the cart-rucks[4] of figures and cyphers, frisks and curvets so at its ease over the flowery carpet-ground of a midnight dissertation.—It feels its promotion.* * * * So that you see, upon the whole,

the literary dignity of *Elia* is very little, if at all, compromised in the condescension.

Not that, in my anxious detail of the many commodities incidental to the life of a public office, I would be thought blind to certain flaws, which a cunning carper might be able to pick in this Joseph's vest. And here I must have leave, in the fulness of my soul, to regret the abolition, and doing-away-with altogether, of those consolatory interstices, and sprinklings of freedom, through the four seasons,—the *red-letter days*, now become, to all intents and purposes, *dead-letter days*.[5] There was Paul, and Stephen, and Barnabas—

Andrew and John, men famous in old times[6]

—we were used to keep all their days holy, as long back as I was at school at Christ's. I remember their effigies, by the same token, in the old *Basket* Prayer Book.[7] There hung Peter in his uneasy posture——holy Bartlemy in the troublesome act of flaying, after the famous Marsyas by Spagnoletti.[8] ——I honoured them all, and could almost have wept the defalcation of Iscariot[9]—so much did we love to keep holy memories sacred:—only methought I a little grudged at the coalition of the better *Jude* with Simon[10]—clubbing (as it were) their sanctities together, to make up one poor gaudy-day between them—as an economy unworthy of the dispensation.

These were bright visitations in the scholar's and a clerk's life—"far off their coming shone."[11]—I was as good as an almanac in those days, I could have told you such a saint's-day falls out next week, or the week after. Peradventure the Epiphany, by some periodical infelicity, would, once in six years, merge in a Sabbath. Now am I little better than one of the profane. Let me not be thought to arraign the wisdom of my civil superiors, who have judged the further observation of these holy tides to be papistical, superstitious. Only in a custom of such long standing, methinks, if their Holinesses the Bishops had, in decency, been first

---

[27] Henry Pimpernel and John Naps of Greece are mentioned in the induction to *Taming of the Shrew* as the names of men "which never were nor no man ever saw" (ii, 95–98).

[1] *quis sculpsit*: Latin phrase ("who engraves") appearing after the name of the engraver.

[2] Francois Vivares (1709–1780) and William Woollett (1735–1785) were the leading landscape engravers in England in the late eighteenth century.

[3] Acknowledge.

[4] Deep, deliberate markings or indentations, like ruts made by the wheels of a cart.

[5] By 1820, the year "Oxford in the Vacation" was published, the number of holidays in Lamb's office at the East India House had been reduced to five (E. V. Lucas).

[6] Cf. *Paradise Regained*, II, 7.

[7] John Baskett (d. 1742) and his descendants held the royal patent for the printing of the Bible and the Book of Common Prayer from 1709 to 1769.

[8] St. Peter is thought to have been crucified upside down, St. Bartholomew to have been flayed alive. Jose de Ribera Spagnoletto (1591–1652), a Spanish-Neapolitan artist, painted a picture of Apollo flaying Marsyas.

[9] That is, Judas's defection from Christ.

[10] St. Judas (Jude Thaddaeus), to be distinguished from Judas Iscariot, was also one of the twelve apostles. His feast day is celebrated jointly with that of St. Simon on October 28.

[11] See *Paradise Lost*, VI, 768.

sounded——but I am wading out of my depths. I am not the man to decide the limits of civil and ecclesiastical authority——I am plain Elia—no Selden, nor Archbishop Usher[12]—though at present in the thick of their books, here in the heart of learning, under the shadow of the mighty Bodley.[13]

I can here play the gentleman, enact the student. To such a one as myself, who has been defrauded in his young years of the sweet food of academic institution, nowhere is so pleasant, to while away a few idle weeks at, as one or other of the Universities. Their vacation, too, at this time of the year, falls in so pat with *ours*. Here I can take my walks unmolested, and fancy myself of what degree of standing I please. I seem admitted *ad eundem*.[14] I fetch up past opportunities. I can rise at the chapel-bell, and dream that it rings for *me*. In moods of humility I can be a Sizar, or a Servitor. When the peacock vein rises, I strut a Gentleman Commoner.[15] In graver moments, I proceed Master of Arts. Indeed I do not think I am much unlike that respectable character. I have seen your dim-eyed vergers, and bed-makers in spectacles, drop a bow or curtsy, as I pass, wisely mistaking me for something of the sort. I go about in black, which favours the notion. Only in Christ Church reverend quadrangle, I can be content to pass for nothing short of a Seraphic Doctor.

The walks at these times are so much óne's own,— the tall trees of Christ's, the groves of Magdalen! The halls deserted, and with open doors, inviting one to slip in unperceived, and pay a devoir to some Founder, or noble or royal Benefactress (that should have been ours) whose portrait seems to smile upon their overlooked beadsman, and to adopt me for their own. Then, to take a peep in by the way at the butteries, and sculleries, redolent of antique hospitality: the immense caves of kitchens, kitchen fire-places, cordial recesses; ovens whose first pies were baked four centuries ago; and spits which have cooked for Chaucer! Not the meanest minister among the dishes but is hallowed to me through his imagination, and the Cook goes forth a Manciple.[16]

Antiquity! thou wondrous charm, what art thou? that, being nothing, art every thing! When thou *wert*, thou wert not antiquity—then thou wert nothing, but hadst a remoter *antiquity*, as thou called'st it, to look back to with blind veneration; thou thyself being to thyself flat, jejune, *modern*! What mystery lurks in this retroversion? or what half Januses * are we, that cannot look forward with the same idolatry with which we for ever revert! The mighty future is as nothing, being every thing! The past is every thing, being nothing!

What were thy *dark ages*? Surely the sun rose as brightly then as now, and man got him to his work in the morning. Why is it that we can never hear mention of them without an accompanying feeling, as though a palpable obscure had dimmed the face of things, and that our ancestors wandered to and fro groping!

Above all thy rarities, old Oxenford, what do most arride[18] and solace me, are thy repositories of mouldering learning, thy shelves——

What a place to be in is an old library! It seems as though all the souls of all the writers, that have bequeathed their labors to these Bodleians, were reposing here, as in some dormitory, or middle state. I do not want to handle, to profane the leaves, their winding-sheets. I could as soon dislodge a shade. I seem to inhale learning, walking amid their foliage; and the odour of their old moth-scented coverings is fragrant as the first bloom of those sciential apples which grew amid the happy orchard.

Still less have I curiosity to disturb the elder repose of MSS. Those *variae lectiones*,[19] so tempting to the more erudite palates, do but disturb and unsettle my faith. I am no Herculanean raker.[20] The credit of the three witnesses might have slept unimpeached for me. I leave these curiosities to Porson, and to G. D.[21]——, whom, by the way, I found busy as a moth over some rotten archive, rummaged out of some seldom-explored press, in a nook at Oriel. With long poring, he is grown almost into a book. He stood as passive as one by the side of the old shelves. I longed to newcoat him in

* Januses of one face.—Sir Thomas Browne.[17]

[12] John Selden was a persistent opponent of abuses of power and privilege by crown, parliament, or clergy. James Ussher (1581–1656), Anglican Primate of Ireland and ecclesiastical historian, was famous for his defense of the history and traditions of the Anglican Church.

[13] The Bodleian Library at Oxford, founded by Sir Thomas Bodley (1545–1613).

[14] *ad eundem*: "to the same."

[15] Sizars and Servitors were students who worked at college in return for a reduction in fees. Gentlemen Commoners were a class of students who enjoyed special privileges of dress and dining, and exemption from certain academic duties, by the payment of higher fees.

[16] A Manciple is the steward or caterer of the college. Both a cook and a manciple were among the pilgrims in Chaucer's *Canterbury Tales*.

[17] The phrase appears in Browne's *Christian Morals*, III, xxii, first published in 1716.

[18] Delight.

[19] Variant readings in the manuscripts of a text.

[20] Lamb refers to a large collection of papyri of classical philosophers found in the excavations at Herculaneum.

[21] "The three witnesses" refers to a much disputed passage in the First Epistle of John, v, 7. Richard Porson (1759–1808), distinguished scholar and editor of Greek texts, proved the spuriousness of this passage in *Letters to Travis* (1790). G.[eorge] D.[yer] (1755–1841) was an eccentric friend of Lamb's and miscellaneous writer. Lamb has transferred his researches from Cambridge to Oxford; Dyer had published a history of Cambridge in 1814, and in 1824 was to appear his study of *The Privileges of the University and Colleges of Cambridge*.

Russia, and assign him his place. He might have mustered for a tall Scapula.[22]

D. is assiduous in his visits to these seats of learning. No inconsiderable portion of his moderate fortune, I apprehend, is consumed in journeys between them and Clifford's-inn [23]——where, like a dove on the asp's nest, he has long taken up his unconscious abode, amid an incongruous assembly of attorneys, attorneys' clerks, apparitors, promoters, vermin of the law, among whom he sits, "in calm and sinless peace." [24] The fangs of the law pierce him not—the winds of litigation blow over his humble chambers—the hard sheriff's officer moves his hat as he passes—legal nor illegal discourtesy touches him—none thinks of offering violence or injustice to him—you would as soon "strike an abstract idea."

D. has been engaged, he tells me, through a course of laborious years, in an investigation into all curious matter connected with the two Universities; and has lately lit upon a MS. collection of charters, relative to C——, by which he hopes to settle some disputed points—particularly that long controversy between them as to priority of foundation. The ardor with which he engages in these liberal pursuits, I am afraid, has not met with all the encouragement it deserved, either here, or at C——. Your caputs, and heads of colleges, care less than any body else about these questions.— Contented to suck the milky fountains of their Alma Maters, without inquiring into the venerable gentle-women's years, they rather hold such curiosities to be impertinent—unreverend. They have their good glebe lands *in manu*,[25] and care not much to rake into the title-deeds. I gather at least so much from other sources, for D. is not a man to complain.

D. started like an unbroke heifer, when I interrupted him. *A priori* it was not very probable that we should have met at Oriel. But D. would have done the same, had I accosted him on the sudden in his own walks in Clifford's-inn, or in the Temple. In addition to a provoking shortsightedness (the effect of late studies and watchings at the midnight oil) D. is the most absent of men. He made a call the other morning at our friend M.'s in Bedford-square; and, finding nobody at home, was ushered into the hall, where, asking for pen and ink, with great exactitude of purpose he enters me his name in the book—which ordinarily

lies about in such places, to record the failures of the untimely or unfortunate visitor—and takes his leave with many ceremonies, and professions of regret. Some two or three hours after, his walking destinies returned him into the same neighbourhood again, and again the quiet image of the fire-side circle at M.'s—— Mrs. M. presiding at it like a Queen Lar,[26] with pretty A. S. at her side——striking irresistibly on his fancy, he makes another call (forgetting that they were "certainly not to return from the country before that day week") and disappointed a second time, inquires for pen and paper as before: again the book is brought, and in the line just above that in which he is about to print his second name (his re-script)—his first name (scarce dry) looks out upon him like another Sosia,[27] or as if a man should suddenly encounter his own duplicate!—The effect may be conceived. D. made many a good resolution against any such lapses in future. I hope he will not keep them too rigorously.

For with G. D.—to be absent from the body, is sometimes (not to speak it profanely) to be present with the Lord. At the very time when, personally encountering thee, he passes on with no recognition——or, being stopped, starts like a thing surprised—at that moment, reader, he is on Mount Tabor—or Parnassus—or co-sphered with Plato—or, with Harrington, framing "immortal commonwealths." [28]—devising some plan of amelioration to thy country, or thy species—peradventure meditating some individual kindness or courtesy, to be done to *thee thyself*, the returning consciousness of which made him to start so guiltily at thy obtruded personal presence.

D. is delightful any where, but he is at the best in such places as these. He cares not much for Bath. He is out of his element at Buxton, at Scarborough, or Harrowgate. The Cam and the Isis [29] are to him "better than all the waters of Damascus." [30] On the Muses' hill he is happy, and good, as one of the Shepherds on the Delectable Mountains; and when he goes about with you to show you the halls and colleges, you think you have with you the Interpreter at the House Beautiful. [31]

[October 1820]   [1823]

---

26 Roman household diety.

27 A servant whose identity is assumed by the god Mercury, in the comedy *Amphitryon* by the Roman dramatist Plautus. One of various comic complications in the play involves Sosia's confrontation with himself (Mercury in disguise).

28 James Harrington (1611–1677) wrote the political romance *The Commonwealth of Oceana* (1656), which describes an ideal government.

29 The four towns mentioned are popular English spas. Cam and Isis are rivers at Cambridge and Oxford, respectively.

30 Cf. II Kings, v, 12.

31 Like the Shepherds mentioned earlier, the Interpreter at the House Beautiful is a character in Bunyan's *Pilgrim's Progress*.

---

22 The phrase "in Russia" refers to Russia leather, an elegant binding for books. A "tall Scapula" is a folio edition of Johann Scapula's Greek lexicon.

23 A residence for lawyers and students of law, belonging to the Inner Temple.

24 *Paradise Regained*, IV, 425.

25 The "glebe lands" were income-producing property for holders of religious offices, in the assignment of the heads of colleges; *in manu*: in actual possession or power.

CHRIST'S HOSPITAL

In the course of this essay Lamb draws upon his own experiences at Christ's Hospital as well as those of his fellow-student Coleridge. For a detailed account of the people and events at Christ's that find their way into the essay, see Edmund Blunden, "Elia and Christ's Hospital," Essays and Studies by Members of the English Association, XXII (1937), 37–60.

CHRIST'S HOSPITAL

FIVE AND THIRTY YEARS AGO

IN Mr. Lamb's "Works," published a year or two since, I find a magnificent eulogy on my old school,[*] such as it was, or now appears to him to have been, between the years 1782 and 1789. It happens, very oddly, that my own standing at Christ's was nearly corresponding with his; and, with all gratitude to him for his enthusiasm for the cloisters, I think he has contrived to bring together whatever can be said in praise of them, dropping all the other side of the argument most ingeniously.

I remember L. at school; and can well recollect that he had some peculiar advantages, which I and others of his schoolfellows had not. His friends lived in town, and were near at hand; and he had the privilege of going to see them, almost as often as he wished, through some invidious distinction, which was denied to us. The present worthy sub-treasurer to the Inner Temple[2] can explain how that happened. He had his tea and hot rolls in a morning, while we were battening upon our quarter of a penny loaf—our *crug*[3]—moistened with attenuated small beer, in wooden piggins, smacking of the pitched leathern jack[4] it was poured from. Our Monday's milk porritch, blue and tasteless, and the pease soup of Saturday, coarse and choking, were enriched for him with a slice of "extraordinary bread and butter," from the hot-loaf of the Temple. The Wednesday's mess of millet,[5] somewhat less repugnant—(we had three banyan[6] to four meat days in the week)—was endeared to his palate with a lump of double-refined, and a smack of ginger (to make it go down the more glibly) or the fragrant cinnamon. In

* Recollections of Christ's Hospital.[1]

[1] Lamb refers to his essay originally published in the *Gentleman's Magazine*, June 1813, and later collected in *The Works of Charles Lamb* (1818). "Recollections" was an essentially praiseful account of Christ's Hospital written in answer to various charges levelled against the school and leading to a Chancery Court investigation in 1811.
[2] Randal Norris (d. 1827), a long-time friend and associate of the Lamb family.
[3] Slang word at Christ's Hospital for bread.
[4] Piggins were small drinking pails or vessels. A pitched leathern jack was a leather pitcher covered on the outside with tar.
[5] A cereal.   [6] Meatless.

lieu of our *half-pickled* Sundays, or *quite fresh* boiled beef on Thursdays (strong as *caro equina*),[7] with detestable marigolds floating in the pail to poison the broth—our scanty mutton crags[8] on Fridays—and rather more savoury, but grudging, portions of the same flesh, rotten-roasted or rare, on the Tuesdays (the only dish which excited our appetites, and disappointed our stomachs, in almost equal proportion)— he had his hot plate of roast veal, or the more tempting griskin[9] (exotics unknown to our palates), cooked in the paternal kitchen (a great thing), and brought him daily by his maid or aunt! I remember the good old relative (in whom love forbade pride) squatting down upon some odd stone in a by-nook of the cloisters, disclosing the viands (of higher regale than those cates which the ravens ministered to the Tishbite),[10] and the contending passions of L. at the unfolding. There was love for the bringer; shame for the thing brought, and the manner of its bringing; sympathy for those who were too many to share in it; and, at top of all, hunger (eldest, strongest of the passions!) predominant, breaking down the stony fences of shame, and awkwardness, and a troubling over-consciousness.

I was a poor friendless boy. My parents, and those who should care for me, were far away. Those few acquaintances of theirs, which they could reckon upon as being kind to me in the great city, after a little forced notice, which they had the grace to take of me on my first arrival in town, soon grew tired of my holiday visits. They seemed to them to recur too often, though I thought them few enough; and, one after another, they all failed me, and I felt myself alone among six hundred playmates.

O the cruelty of separating a poor lad from his early homestead! The yearnings which I used to have towards it in those unfledged years! How, in my dreams, would my native town (far in the west) come back, with its church, and trees, and faces! How I would wake weeping, and in the anguish of my heart exclaim upon sweet Calne in Wiltshire![11]

To this late hour of my life, I trace impressions left by the recollection of those friendless holidays. The long warm days of summer never return but they bring with them a gloom from the haunting memory of those *whole-day-leaves*, when, by some strange arrangement, we were turned out, for the live-long day, upon our own hands, whether we had friends to go to, or none. I remember those bathing-excursions to the

[7] Caro equina: "horsemeat."   [8] Necks.
[9] Lean pork or beef chops or steaks.
[10] See I Kings, xvii, 1–6.
[11] Although at this point in the essay Lamb is clearly thinking of Coleridge's experiences at Christ's Hospital, he disguises his true childhood home Ottery St. Mary in Devonshire.

New-River, which L. recalls with such relish, better, I think, than he can—for he was a home-seeking lad, and did not much care for such water-pastimes:— How merrily we would sally forth into the fields; and strip under the first warmth of the sun; and wanton like young dace [12] in the streams; getting us appetites for noon, which those of us that were pennyless (our scanty morning crust long since exhausted) had not the means of allaying—while the cattle, and the birds, and the fishes, were at feed about us, and we had nothing to satisfy our cravings—the very beauty of the day, and the exercise of the pastime, and the sense of liberty, setting a keener edge upon them!—How faint and languid, finally, we would return, towards night-fall, to our desired morsel, half-rejoicing, half-reluctant, that the hours of our uneasy liberty had expired!

It was worse in the days of winter, to go prowling about the streets objectless—shivering at cold windows of print-shops, to extract a little amusement; or haply, as a last resort, in the hopes of a little novelty, to pay a fifty-times repeated visit (where our individual faces should be as well known to the warden as those of his own charges) to the Lions in the Tower [13]—to whose levée, by courtesy immemorial, we had a prescriptive title to admission.

L.'s governor [14] (so we called the patron who presented us to the foundation) lived in a manner under his paternal roof. Any complaint which he had to make was sure of being attended to. This was understood at Christ's, and was an effectual screen to him against the severity of masters, or worse tyranny of the monitors. The oppressions of these young brutes are heart-sickening to call to recollection. I have been called out of my bed, and *waked for the purpose*, in the coldest winter nights—and this not once, but night after night—in my shirt, to receive the discipline of a leathern thong, with eleven other sufferers, because it pleased my callow overseer, when there has been any talking heard after we were gone to bed, to make the six last beds in the dormitory, where the youngest children of us slept, answerable for an offence they neither dared to commit, nor had the power to hinder. —The same execrable tyranny drove the younger part of us from the fires, when our feet were perishing with snow; and, under the cruellest penalties, forbad the indulgence of a drink of water, when we lay in sleep-

less summer nights, fevered with the season, and the day's sports.

There was one H——, who, I learned in after days, was seen expiating some maturer offence in the hulks. [15] (Do I flatter myself in fancying that this might be the planter of that name, who suffered—at Nevis, I think, or St. Kits,—some few years since? My friend Tobin [16] was the benevolent instrument of bringing him to the gallows.) This petty Nero actually branded a boy, who had offended him, with a red hot iron; and nearly starved forty of us, with exacting contributions, to the one half of our bread, to pamper a young ass, which, incredible as it may seem, with the connivance of the nurse's daughter (a young flame of his) he had contrived to smuggle in, and keep upon the leads of the *wards*, as they called our dormitories. This game went on for better than a week, till the foolish beast, not able to fare well but he must cry roast meat— happier than Caligula's minion, [17] could he have kept his own counsel—but, foolisher, alas! than any of his species in the fables—waxing fat, and kicking, in the fulness of bread, one unlucky minute would needs proclaim his good fortune to the world below; and, laying out his simple throat, blew such a ram's horn blast, as (toppling down the walls of his own Jericho) set concealment any longer at defiance. The client was dismissed, with certain attentions, to Smithfield; [18] but I never understood that the patron underwent any censure on the occasion. This was in the stewardship of L.'s admired Perry. [19]

Under the same *facile* administration, can L. have forgotten the cool impunity with which the nurses used to carry away openly, in open platters, for their own tables, one out of two of every hot joint, which the careful matron had been seeing scrupulously weighed out for our dinners? These things were daily practised in that magnificent apartment, which L. (grown connoisseur since, we presume) praises so highly for the grand paintings "by Verrio and others," with which it is "hung round and adorned." [20] But the sight of sleek well-fed blue-coat boys [21] in pictures

---

[12] Small fresh-water fish.
[13] The Tower of London housed a famous menagerie of lions.
[14] Samuel Salt (d. 1792), one of the directors ("Benchers") of the Inner Temple. Lamb's father served as clerk and servant to Salt, who had helped arrange Lamb's nomination to Christ's Hospital.

[15] Old ships used as prisons.
[16] James Webbe Tobin (d. 1814) was a London friend of Lamb's, who went to live in Nevis in the British West Indies in 1809.
[17] Caligula was a cruel and eccentric Roman emperor (A.D. 37–41). Among other signs of his "madness," he was alleged to have raised his favorite horse to the post of Roman consul.
[18] Center of the cattle trade and the meat markets in London.
[19] John Perry, steward at Christ's Hospital 1761–1785.
[20] Lamb quotes his earlier essay "Recollections." Antonio Verrio (c. 1639–1707) was an Italian painter employed by the English court, best known for his elaborate ceiling and wall paintings.
[21] Familiar name for students at Christ's Hospital, derived from their distinctively colored uniform.

was, at that time, I believe, little consolatory to him, or us, the living ones, who saw the better part of our provisions carried away before our faces by harpies;[22] and ourselves reduced (with the Trojan in the hall of Dido)

> To feed our mind with idle portraiture.[23]

L. has recorded the repugnance of the school to *gags*, or the fat of fresh beef boiled; and sets it down to some superstition. But these unctuous morsels are never grateful to young palates (children are universally fat-haters), and in strong, coarse, boiled meats, *unsalted*, are detestable. A *gag-eater* in our time was equivalent to a *goul*,[24] and held in equal detestation. —— suffered under the imputation.

> ——'Twas said,
> He ate strange flesh.[25]

He was observed, after dinner, carefully to gather up the remnants left at his table (not many, nor very choice fragments, you may credit me)—and, in an especial manner, these disreputable morsels, which he would convey away, and secretly stow in the settle that stood at his bed-side. None saw when he ate them. It was rumoured that he privately devoured them in the night. He was watched, but no traces of such midnight practices were discoverable. Some reported, that, on leave-days, he had been seen to carry out of the bounds a large blue check handkerchief, full of something. This then must be the accursed thing. Conjecture next was at work to imagine how he could dispose of it. Some said he sold it to the beggars. This belief generally prevailed. He went about moping. None spake to him. No one would play with him. He was excommunicated; put out of the pale of the school. He was too powerful a boy to be beaten, but he underwent every mode of that negative punishment, which is more grievous than many stripes. Still he persevered. At length he was observed by two of his school-fellows, who were determined to get at the secret, and had traced him one leave-day for that purpose, to enter a large worn-out building, such as there exist specimens of in Chancery-lane, which are let out to various scales of pauperism, with open door, and a common staircase. After him they silently slunk in, and followed by stealth up four flights, and saw him

tap at a poor wicket, which was opened by an aged woman, meanly clad. Suspicion was now ripened into certainty. The informers had secured their victim. They had him in their toils. Accusation was formally preferred, and retribution most signal was looked for. Mr. Hathaway, the then steward (for this happened a little after my time), with that patient sagacity which tempered all his conduct, determined to investigate the matter, before he proceeded to sentence. The result was, that the supposed mendicants, the receivers or purchasers of the mysterious scraps, turned out to be the parents of ——, an honest couple come to decay,—whom this seasonable supply had, in all probability, saved from mendicancy; and that this young stork, at the expense of his own good name, had all this while been only feeding the old birds!—The governors on this occasion, much to their honour, voted a present relief to the family of ——, and presented him with a silver medal. The lesson which the steward read upon RASH JUDGMENT, on the occasion of publicly delivering the medal to ——, I believe, would not be lost upon his auditory.—I had left school then, but I well remember ——. He was a tall, shambling youth, with a cast in his eye, not at all calculated to conciliate hostile prejudices. I have since seen him carrying a baker's basket. I think I heard he did not do quite so well by himself as he had done by the old folks.

I was a hypochondriac lad; and the sight of a boy in fetters, upon the day of my first putting on the blue clothes, was not exactly fitted to assuage the natural terrors of initiation. I was of tender years, barely turned of seven; and had only read of such things in books, or seen them but in dreams. I was told he had *run away*. This was the punishment for the first offence.—As a novice I was soon after taken to see the dungeons. These were little, square, Bedlam cells,[26] where a boy could just lie at his length upon straw and a blanket—a mattress, I think, was afterwards substituted—with a peep of light, let in askance, from a prison-orifice at top, barely enough to read by. Here the poor boy was locked in by himself all day, without sight of any but the porter who brought him his bread and water—who *might not speak to him*;—or of the beadle, who came twice a week to call him out to receive his periodical chastisement, which was almost welcome, because it separated him for a brief interval from solitude:—and here he was shut up by himself *of nights*, out of the reach of any sound, to suffer whatever horrors the weak nerves, and superstition incident to his time of life, might subject him

---

[22] See *Aeneid*, III, 219–28.
[23] Lamb refers to another scene in the *Aeneid* (I, 441–93), where Aeneas tearfully "feeds his mind" with the sight of painted representations of the Trojan war upon a temple at Carthage.
[24] Ghoul or vampire.
[25] *Anthony and Cleopatra*, I, iv, 67.

[26] As at the London asylum Bethlem (Bedlam) Hospital.

to.* This was the penalty for the second offence.— Wouldest thou like, reader, to see what became of him in the next degree?

The culprit, who had been a third time an offender, and whose expulsion was at this time deemed irreversible, was brought forth, as at some solemn *auto da fe*,[28] arrayed in uncouth and most appalling attire, all trace of his late "watchet weeds"[29] carefully effaced, he was exposed in a jacket, resembling those which London lamplighters formerly delighted in, with a cap of the same. The effect of this divestiture was such as the ingenious devisers of it could have anticipated. With his pale and frightened features, it was as if some of those disfigurements in Dante had seized upon him. In this disguisement he was brought into the hall (*L.'s favourite state-room*), where awaited him the whole number of his school-fellows, whose joint lessons and sports he was thenceforth to share no more; the awful presence of the steward, to be seen for the last time; of the executioner beadle, clad in his state robe for the occasion; and of two faces more, of direr import, because never but in these extremities visible. These were governors; two of whom, by choice, or charter, were always accustomed to officiate at these *Ultima Supplicia*;[30] not to mitigate (so at least we understood it), but to enforce the uttermost stripe. Old Bamber Gascoigne, and Peter Aubert, I remember, were colleagues on one occasion, when the beadle turning rather pale, a glass of brandy was ordered to prepare him for the mysteries. The scourging was, after the old Roman fashion, long and stately. The lictor[31] accompanied the criminal quite round the hall. We were generally too faint with attending to the previous disgusting circumstances, to make accurate report with our eyes of the degree of corporal suffering inflicted. Report, of course, gave out the back knotty and livid. After scourging, he was made over, in his *San Benito*,[32] to his friends, if he had any (but commonly such poor runagates were friendless), or to his parish officer, who, to enhance the effect of the scene, had his station allotted to him on the outside of the hall gate.

These solemn pageantries were not played off so often as to spoil the general mirth of the community. We had plenty of exercise and recreation *after* school hours; and, for myself, I must confess, that I was never happier, than *in* them. The Upper and the Lower Grammar Schools were held in the same room; and an imaginary line only divided their bounds. Their character was as different as that of the inhabitants on the two sides of the Pyrenees. The Rev. James Boyer[33] was the Upper Master; but the Rev. Matthew Field[34] presided over that portion of the apartment, of which I had the good fortune to be a member. We lived a life as careless as birds. We talked and did just what we pleased, and nobody molested us. We carried an accidence,[35] or a grammar, for form; but, for any trouble it gave us, we might take two years in getting through the verbs deponent,[36] and another two in forgetting all that we had learned about them. There was now and then the formality of saying a lesson, but if you had not learned it, a brush across the shoulders (just enough to disturb a fly) was the sole remonstrance. Field never used the rod; and in truth he wielded the cane with no great good will—holding it "like a dancer."[37] It looked in his hands rather like an emblem than an instrument of authority; and an emblem, too, he was ashamed of. He was a good easy man, that did not care to ruffle his own peace, nor perhaps set any great consideration upon the value of juvenile time. He came among us, now and then, but often staid away whole days from us; and when he came, it made no difference to us—he had his private room to retire to, the short time he staid, to be out of the sound of our noise. Our mirth and uproar went on. We had classics of our own, without being beholden to "insolent Greece or haughty Rome,"[38] that passed current among us—Peter Wilkins—the Adventures of the Hon. Capt. Robert Boyle—the Fortunate Blue Coat Boy[39]—and the like. Or we cultivated a turn for

* One or two instances of lunacy, or attempted suicide, accordingly, at length convinced the governors of the impolicy of this part of the sentence, and the midnight torture to the spirits was dispensed with.—This fancy of dungeons for children was a sprout of Howard's brain; for which (saving the reverence due to Holy Paul) methinks, I could willingly spit upon his statue.[27]

27 John Howard (*c.* 1726–1790) was a leading prison reformer and philanthropist. His statue was in St. Paul's Cathedral.
28 *auto da fé*: the judging and sentencing of heretics in the Spanish Inquisition.
29 William Collins' "The Manners. An Ode" (1747), l. 68. "Watchet" means light blue in color.
30 "Extreme punishments."
31 In Roman law, the executioner of the sentences on criminals.
32 The garment worn by the accused and confessed heretic at the Inquisition.

33 Rev. James Boyer (1736–1814).
34 Rev. Matthew Field (d. 1796) was the Under Grammar master.
35 Rudimentary Latin grammar dealing with the "accidents" or inflections of words.
36 Term in Latin grammar applied to verbs passive in form but active in meaning.
37 *Anthony and Cleopatra*, III, xi, 36.
38 Ben Jonson's verses prefacing the First Folio of Shakespeare, "To the memory of my beloved author, Mr. William Shakespeare," l. 39.
39 Narratives suited to the taste of juvenile readers: Richard Paltock's *The Life and Adventures of Peter Wilkins* (1751), the record of exotic experiences among a race of winged men; *The*

mechanic and scientific operations; making little sun-dials of paper; or weaving those ingenious paren-theses, called *cat-cradles*; or making dry peas to dance upon the end of a tin pipe; or studying the art military over that laudable game "French and English," and a hundred other such devices to pass away the time—mixing the useful with the agreeable—as would have made the souls of Rousseau and John Locke[40] chuckle to have seen us.

Matthew Field belonged to that class of modest divines who affect to mix in equal proportion the *gentleman*, the *scholar*, and the *Christian*; but, I know not how, the first ingredient is generally found to be the predominating dose in the composition. He was engaged in gay parties, or with his courtly bow at some episcopal levée, when he should have been attending upon us. He had for many years the classical charge of a hundred children, during the four or five first years of their education; and his very highest form seldom proceeded further than two or three of the introductory fables of Phædrus.[41] How things were suffered to go on thus, I cannot guess. Boyer, who was the proper person to have remedied these abuses, always affected, perhaps felt, a delicacy in interfering in a province not strictly his own. I have not been without my suspicions, that he was not altogether displeased at the contrast we presented to his end of the school. We were a sort of Helots[42] to his young Spartans. He would sometimes, with ironic deference, send to borrow a rod of the Under Master, and then, with Sardonic grin, observe to one of his upper boys, "how neat and fresh the twigs looked." While his pale students were battering their brains over Xenophon and Plato, with a silence as deep as that enjoined by the Samite,[43] we were enjoying ourselves at our ease in our little Goshen.[44] We saw a little into the secrets

of his discipline, and the prospect did but the more reconcile us to our lot. His thunders rolled innocuous for us; his storms came near, but never touched us; contrary to Gideon's miracle, while all around were drenched, our fleece was dry.* His boys turned out the better scholars; we, I suspect, have the advantage in temper. His pupils cannot speak of him without something of terror allaying their gratitude; the re-membrance of Field comes back with all the soothing images of indolence, and summer slumbers, and work like play, and innocent idleness, and Elysian exemp-tions, and life itself a "playing holiday."[46]

Though sufficiently removed from the jurisdiction of Boyer, we were near enough (as I have said) to understand a little of his system. We occasionally heard sounds of the *Ululantes*,[47] and caught glances of Tartarus. B. was a rabid pedant. His English style was crampt to barbarism. His Easter anthems (for his duty obliged him to those periodical flights) were grating as scrannel pipes.†—He would laugh, ay, and heartily, but then it must be at Flaccus's quibble about *Rex* —— or at the *tristis severitas in vultu*, or *inspicere in patinas*, of Terence[49]—thin jests, which at their first broaching could hardly have had *vis*[50] enough to move a Roman muscle.—He had two wigs, both pedantic, but of differing omen. The one serene, smiling, fresh powdered, betokening a mild day. The other, an old discoloured, unkempt, angry caxon,[51] denoting fre-quent and bloody execution. Woe to the school, when he made his morning appearance in his *passy*, or *pas-*

* Cowley.[45]

† In this and every thing B. was the antipodes of his co-adjutor. While the former was digging his brains for crude an-thems, worth a pig-nut, F. would be recreating his gentlemanly fancy in the more flowery walks of the Muses. A little dramatic effusion of his, under the name of Vertumnus and Pomona, is not yet forgotten by the chroniclers of that sort of literature. It was accepted by Garrick, but the town did not give it their sanction.—B. used to say of it, in a way of half-compliment, half-irony, that it was *too classical for representation*.[48]

Voyages and Adventures of Captain Robert Boyle (1726), variously attributed to Daniel Defoe, William Rufus Chetwood (d. 1766), and Benjamin Victor (d. 1778), the story of a British orphan boy, whose resourcefulness enables him to rise to the command of a ship and see his way safely through a number of threatening situ-ations; *The Fortunate Blue-Coat Boy, or Memoirs of the Life and Happy Adventures of Mr. Benjamin Templeman; by an Orphano-trophian* [one brought up in an orphanage or hospital] (1760), the tale of a youth who, while still a student at Christ's Hospital, marries a lady of great wealth.

40 Lamb refers to their tracts on education: Rousseau's *Émile* (1762), Locke's *Thoughts Concerning the Education of Children* (1693).

41 First-century Roman writer, whose verse translation of Aesop's fables was a standard text for elementary students of Latin.

42 Inferior slave class in ancient Sparta.

43 The Greek philosopher Pythagoras of Samos demanded a five-year probationary period of silence from his students before admitting them as his intimate associates.

44 That part of Egypt allotted to the Hebrews and preserved from the various plagues which afflicted the country. See Exodus, viii–x.

45 Lamb refers to Abraham Cowley's poem "The Complaint" (1663), stanza 4, based on Judges, vi, 36–40: Gideon asks God to work the following miracle as a sign that Israel is to be saved—a fleece left overnight on the ground will be covered with dew while the surrounding earth remains dry.

46 *Henry the Fourth*, Part I, I, ii, 227.

47 "Those howling and shrieking in pain."

48 For the reference to "scrannel pipes," see Milton's *Lycidas*, l. 124. Field's *Vertumnus and Pomona* was performed in 1782, but hooted off the stage after one performance.

49 See Horace's *Satires*, I, vii, 34–35, for the feeble pun on the word *Rex*. tristis severitas in vultu: "somber truthfulness in his face," is said of a bold liar in Terence's comedy *The Lady of Andros*, Act V. [*tamquam in speculum*] *inspicere in patinas*: "to look into the dishes as in a looking-glass," are the words of advice of a servant to those below him in the kitchen, parodying in the advice of his master to his son "to observe men as in a looking-glass," in Terence's *The Brothers*, Act III.

50 *vis*: "force."

51 An old-fashioned wig.

sionate wig. No comet expounded surer.—J. B. had a heavy hand. I have known him double his knotty fist at a poor trembling child (the maternal milk hardly dry upon its lips) with a "Sirrah, do you presume to set your wits at me?"—Nothing was more common than to see him make a head-long entry into the school-room, from his inner recess, or library, and, with turbulent eye, singling out a lad, roar out, "Od's my life, Sirrah," (his favourite adjuration) "I have a great mind to whip you,"—then, with as sudden a retracting impulse, fling back into his lair—and, after a cooling lapse of some minutes (during which all but the culprit had totally forgotten the context) drive headlong out again, piecing out his imperfect sense, as if it had been some Devil's Litany, with the expletory yell—"*and I* WILL *too*."—In his gentler moods, when the *rabidus furor*[52] was assuaged, he had resort to an ingenious method, peculiar, for what I have heard, to himself, of whipping the boy, and reading the Debates, at the same time; a paragraph and a lash between; which in those times, when parliamentary oratory was most at a height and flourishing in these realms, was not calculated to impress the patient with a veneration for the diffuser graces of rhetoric.

Once, and but once, the uplifted rod was known to fall ineffectual from his hand—when droll squinting W—— having been caught putting the inside of the master's desk to a use for which the architect had clearly not designed it, to justify himself, with great simplicity averred, that *he did not know that the thing had been forewarned*. This exquisite irrecognition of any law antecedent to the *oral* or *declaratory*, struck so irresistibly upon the fancy of all who heard it (the pedagogue himself not excepted) that remission was unavoidable.

L. has given credit to B.'s great merits as an instructor. Coleridge, in his literary life,[53] has pronounced a more intelligible and ample encomium on them. The author of the Country Spectator doubts not to compare him with the ablest teachers of antiquity.[54] Perhaps we cannot dismiss him better than with the pious ejaculation of C.—when he heard that his old master was on his death-bed—"Poor J. B.!—may all his faults be forgiven; and may he be wafted to bliss by little cherub boys, all head and wings, with no *bottoms* to reproach his sublunary infirmities."

Under him were many good and sound scholars bred.—First Grecian[55] of my time was Lancelot Pepys Stevens, kindest of boys and men, since Co-grammar-master (and inseparable companion) with Dr. T——e.[56] What an edifying spectacle did this brace of friends present to those who remembered the anti-socialities of their predecessors!—You never met the one by chance in the street without a wonder, which was quickly dissipated by the almost immediate sub-appearance of the other. Generally arm in arm, these kindly coadjutors lightened for each other the toilsome duties of their profession, and when, in advanced age, one found it convenient to retire, the other was not long in discovering that it suited him to lay down the fasces[57] also. Oh, it is pleasant, as it is rare, to find the same arm linked in yours at forty, which at thirteen helped it to turn over the *Cicero De Amicitia*,[58] or some tale of Antique Friendship, which the young heart even then was burning to anticipate! —Co-Grecian with S. was Th——,[59] who has since executed with ability various diplomatic functions at the Northern courts. Th—— was a tall, dark, saturnine youth, sparing of speech, with raven locks.— Thomas Fanshaw Middleton followed him (now Bishop of Calcutta) a scholar and a gentleman in his teens. He has the reputation of an excellent critic; and is author (besides the Country Spectator) of a Treatise on the Greek Article, against Sharpe.[60]—M. is said to bare his mitre high in India, where the *regni novitas*[61] (I dare say) sufficiently justifies the bearing. A humility quite as primitive as that of Jewel or Hooker[62] might not be exactly fitted to impress the

---

[52] *rabidus furor*: "violent raging."

[53] Coleridge's *Biographia Literaria*, Chapter I. See pp. 170–71.

[54] Thomas Fanshaw Middleton (see footnote 60) edited the weekly periodical *The Country Spectator* at Gainsborough in 1792–1793. The issue of April 30, 1793, had compared Boyer to three famous teachers of classical Greece, Gorgias of Leontini, Prodicus of Ceos, and Hippias of Elis.

[55] The top class of students at Christ's Hospital, all of whom were destined for university educations and careers in the Anglican church. Perhaps because of his stammer, Lamb remained a Deputy Grecian.

[56] Lancelot Pepys Stevens [Stephens] (1766–1833) was a student at Christ's Hospital 1774–1784, succeeded Field as Under Grammar master in 1796, and held the post until 1817. Arthur William Trollope (1768–1827) was a student at Christ's Hospital 1775–1787, succeeded Boyer in his post in 1799, and remained Upper Grammar master until 1826.

[57] The symbol of authority carried by the lictor in Roman courts.

[58] Cicero's essay "On Friendship."

[59] Sir Edward Thornton (1766–1852), a student at Christ's Hospital 1773–1785, was a British diplomat. Between 1807 and 1815, Thornton served at various Scandinavian courts, seeking to unite the northern countries and Russia against Napoleon.

[60] Thomas Fanshaw Middleton (1769–1822) was appointed the first Bishop of Calcutta (in effect, the Anglican primate for all of India) in 1814 and held the post until his death. Middleton's *The Doctrine of the Greek Article applied to the Criticism and the Illustration of the New Testament* (1808) was one of a number of contributions to a theological controversy inspired by the publication of *Remarks on the Uses of the Definitive Article in the Greek Text of the New Testament* (1798), by Granville Sharp (1735–1813).

[61] *regni novitas*: "the newness of his reign." *Aeneid*, I, 563.

[62] John Jewel (1522–1571) was Bishop of Salisbury and leading Anglican apologist during the reign of Elizabeth. Richard Hooker

minds of those Anglo-Asiatic diocesans with a reverence for home institutions, and the church which those fathers watered. The manners of M. at school, though firm, were mild, and unassuming.—Next to M. (if not senior to him) was Richards,[63] author of the Aboriginal Britons, the most spirited of the Oxford Prize Poems; a pale, studious Grecian.—Then followed poor S——, ill-fated M——![64] of these the Muse is silent.

> Finding some of Edward's race
> Unhappy, pass their annals by.[65]

Come back into memory, like as thou wert in the day-spring of thy fancies, with hope like a fiery column before thee—the dark pillar not yet turned—Samuel Taylor Coleridge—Logician, Metaphysician, Bard!—How have I seen the casual passer through the Cloisters stand still, intranced with admiration (while he weighed the disproportion between the *speech* and the *garb* of the young Mirandula),[66] to hear thee unfold, in thy deep and sweet intonations, the mysteries of Jamblichus, or Plotinus (for even in those years thou waxedst not pale at such philosophic draughts), or reciting Homer in his Greek, or Pindar—— while the walls of the old Grey Friars[67] re-echoed to the accents of the *inspired charity-boy!*—Many were the "wit-combats" (to dally awhile with the words of old Fuller)[68] between him and C. V. Le G——,[69] "which two I behold like a Spanish great gallion, and an English man of war; Master Coleridge, like the former, was built far higher in learning, solid, but slow in his performances. C. V. L., with the English man of war, lesser in bulk, but lighter in sailing, could turn with all times, tack about, and take advantage of all winds, by the quickness of his wit and invention."

Nor shalt thou, their compeer, be quickly forgotten, Allen,[70] with the cordial smile, and still more cordial laugh, with which thou wert wont to make the old Cloisters shake, in thy cognition of some poignant jest of theirs; or the anticipation of some more material, and, peradventure, practical one, of thine own. Extinct are those smiles, with that beautiful countenance, with which (for thou wert the *Nireus formosus*[71] of the school), in the days of thy maturer waggery, thou didst disarm the wrath of infuriated town-damsel, who, incensed by provoking pinch, turning tigress-like round, suddenly converted to thy angel-look, exchanged the half-formed terrible "*bl*——," for a gentler greeting—"*bless thy handsome face!*"

Next follow two, who ought to be now alive, and the friends of Elia—the junior Le G—— and F——;[72] who impelled, the former by a roving temper, the latter by too quick a sense of neglect—ill capable of enduring the slights poor Sizars are sometimes subject to in our seats of learning—exchanged their Alma Mater for the camp; perishing, one by climate, and one on the plains of Salamanca:—Le G——, sanguine, volatile, sweet-natured; F——, dogged, faithful, anticipative of insult, warm-hearted, with something of the old Roman height about him.

Fine, frank-hearted Fr——, the present master of Hertford, with Marmaduke T——,[73] mildest of Missionaries—and both my good friends still—close the catalogue of Grecians in my time.

[November 1820]   [1823]

NEW YEAR'S EVE

EVERY man hath two birth-days: two days, at least, in every year, which set him upon revolving the lapse of time, as it affects his mortal duration. The one is that which in an especial manner he termeth *his*. In the gradual desuetude[1] of old observances, this custom

---

(c. 1554–1600) was an Anglican clergyman and theologian, author of *Laws of Ecclesiastical Polity* (1594–1597). For evidence of the unpretentiousness of Hooker's conduct toward his parishioners and in all matters of religion, see Walton's *Life of Mr. Richard Hooker* (1675).

[63] George Richards (1767–1837) was a student at Christ's Hospital 1776–1785, clergyman, and minor poet. *Aboriginal Britons* was the prize poem at Oxford in 1791.

[64] Henry Scott, Senior Grecian of 1789, died in Bedlam asylum. John Maunde had been expelled from Christ's Hospital in 1789 (Blunden).

[65] Matthew Prior's *Carmen Seculare* (1700), ll. 104–105.

[66] Pico della Mirandula (1463–1494) was a Renaissance humanist and proponent of Neoplatonic philosophy which had been formulated and developed by Plotinus (A.D. 204–270) and Jamblichus (c. A.D. 250–c. 330).

[67] Christ's Hospital had been a Franciscan monastery until the dissolution of the religious orders in England in the sixteenth century.

[68] In this passage Lamb copies the description of the "wit-combats" between Ben Jonson and Shakespeare in the section "Worthies of Warwickshire" in Thomas Fuller's *The History of the Worthies of England* (1662).

[69] Charles Valentine LeGrice (1773–1858) was a student at Christ's Hospital 1781–1792.

[70] Robert Allen (1772–1805) was a Senior Grecian of 1792.

[71] *Nireus formosus:* "beautiful Nireus." In the *Iliad* (II, 673–74), Nireus is described as the most handsome of all the Greeks who fought at Troy, with the exception of "perfect" Achilles.

[72] Samuel LeGrice was a student at Christ's Hospital 1783–1794. Samuel Favell was a Senior Grecian of 1795. Both of them abandoned their university careers to join the army. LeGrice died in the West Indies, Favell in battle in Spain in 1812.

[73] Frederick William Franklin (d. 1836), was a student at Christ's Hospital 1783–1793; he held the mastership of the Grammar School at Hertford, a branch of Christ's, from 1801 to 1827. Marmaduke Thompson (1776–1851) was a Senior Grecian of 1796, later serving as Chaplain for the East India Company in Madras.

[1] Passing into a state of disuse.

of solemnizing our proper birth-day hath nearly passed away, or is left to children, who reflect nothing at all about the matter, nor understand any thing in it beyond cake and orange. But the birth of a New Year is of an interest too wide to be pretermitted [2] by king or cobbler. No one ever regarded the First of January with indifference. It is that from which all date their time, and count upon what is left. It is the nativity of our common Adam.

Of all sound of all bells—(bells, the music nighest bordering upon heaven)—most solemn and touching is the peal which rings out the Old Year. I never hear it without a gathering-up of my mind to a concentration of all the images that have been diffused over the past twelvemonth; all I have done or suffered, performed or neglected—in that regretted time. I begin to know its worth, as when a person dies. It takes a personal colour; nor was it a poetical flight in a·contemporary, when he exclaimed

I saw the skirts of the departing Year.[3]

It is no more than what in sober sadness every one of us seems to be conscious of, in what awful leave-taking. I am sure I felt it, and all felt it with me, last night; though some of my companions affected rather to manifest an exhilaration at the birth of the coming year, than any very tender regrets for the decease of its predecessor. But I am none of those who—

Welcome the coming, speed the parting guest.[4]

I am naturally, beforehand, shy of novelties; new books, new faces, new years,—from some mental twist which makes it difficult in me to face the prospective. I have almost ceased to hope; and am sanguine only in the prospects of other (former) years. I plunge into foregone visions and conclusions. I encounter pell-mell with past disappointments. I am armour-proof against old discouragements. I forgive, or overcome in fancy, old adversaries. I play over again *for love*, as the gamesters phrase it, games, for which I once paid so dear. I would scarce now have any of those untoward accidents and events of my life reversed. I would no more alter them than the incidents of some well-contrived novel. Methinks, it is better that I should have pined away seven of my goldenest years, when I was thrall to the fair hair, and fairer eyes, of Alice W——n, than that so passionate a love-adventure should be lost. It was better that our family should have missed that legacy, which old Dorrell

cheated us of, than that I should have at this moment two thousand pounds *in banco*, and be without the idea of that specious old rogue.

In a degree beneath manhood, it is my infirmity to look back upon those early days. Do I advance a paradox, when I say, that, skipping over the intervention of forty years, a man may have leave to love *himself*, without the imputation of self-love?

If I know aught of myself, no one whose mind is introspective—and mine is painfully so—can have a less respect for his present identity, than I have for the man Elia. I know him to be light, and vain, and humorsome; a notorious ***; addicted to ****: averse from counsel, neither taking it, nor offering it; —*** besides; a stammering buffoon; what you will; lay it on, and spare not; I subscribe to it all, and much more, than thou canst be willing to lay at his door—— but for the child Elia—that "other me," there, in the back-ground—I must take leave to cherish the remembrance of that young master—with as little reference, I protest, to this stupid changeling of five-and-forty, as if it had been a child of some other house, and not of my parents. I can cry over its patient small-pox at five, and rougher medicaments. I can lay its poor fevered head upon the sick pillow at Christ's, and wake with it in surprise at the gentle posture of maternal tenderness hanging over it, that unknown had watched its sleep. I know how it shrank from any the least colour of falsehood.—God help thee, Elia, how art thou changed! Thou are sophisticated.—I know how honest, how courageous (for a weakling) it was—how religious, how imaginative, how hopeful! From what have I not fallen, if the child I remember was indeed myself,—and not some dissembling guardian, presenting a false identity, to give the rule to my unpractised steps, and regulate the tone of my moral being!

That I am fond of indulging, beyond a hope of sympathy, in such retrospection, may be the symptom of some sickly idiosyncrasy. Or is it owing to another cause; simply, that being without wife or family, I have not learned to project myself enough out of myself; and having no offspring of my own to dally with, I turn back upon memory, and adopt my own early idea, as my heir and favorite? If these speculations seems fantastical to thee, reader—(a busy man, perchance), if I tread out of the way of thy sympathy, and ·am singularly-conceited only, I retire, impenetrable to ridicule, under the phantom cloud of Elia.

The elders, with whom I was brought up, were of a character not likely to let slip the sacred observance of any old institution; and the ringing out of the Old Year was kept by them with circumstances of peculiar ceremony.—In those days the sound of those midnight

---

2 Ignored.
3 Coleridge's "Ode to the Departing Year" (1796), l. 8.
4 Pope's translation of the *Odyssey*, XV, 84.

chimes, though it seemed to raise hilarity in all around me, never failed to bring a train of pensive imagery into my fancy. Yet I then scarce conceived what it meant, or thought of it as a reckoning that concerned me. Not childhood alone, but the young man till thirty, never feels practically that he is mortal. He knows it indeed, and, if need were, he could preach a homily on the fragility of life; but he brings it not home to himself, any more than in a hot June we can appropriate to our imagination the freezing days of December. But now, shall I confess a truth?—I feel these audits but too powerfully. I begin to count the probabilities of my duration, and to grudge at the expenditure of moments and shortest periods, like miser's farthings. In proportion as the years both lessen and shorten, I set more count upon their periods, and would fain lay my ineffectual finger upon the spoke of the great wheel. I am not content to pass away "like a weaver's shuttle." [5] These metaphors solace me not, nor sweeten the unpalatable draught of mortality. I care not to be carried with the tide, that smoothly bears human life to eternity; and reluct [6] at the inevitable course of destiny. I am in love with this green earth; the face of town and country; the unspeakable rural solitudes, and the sweet security of streets. I would set up my tabernacle here. I am content to stand still at the age to which I am arrived; I, and my friends: to be no younger, no richer, no handsomer. I do not want to be weaned by age; or drop, like mellow fruit, as they say, into the grave.—Any alteration, on this earth of mine, in diet or in lodging, puzzles and discomposes me. My household-gods plant a terrible fixed foot, and are not rooted up without blood. They do not willingly seek Lavinian shores. [7] A new state of being staggers me.

Sun, and sky, and breeze, and solitary walks, and summer holidays, and the greenness of fields, and the delicious juices of meats and fishes, and society, and the cheerful glass, and candle-light, and fire-side conversations, and innocent vanities, and jests, and *irony itself*—do these things go out with life?

Can a ghost laugh, or shake his gaunt sides, when you are pleasant with him?

And you, my midnight darlings, my Folios! must I part with the intense delight of having you (huge armfuls) in my embraces? Must knowledge come to me, if it come at all, by some awkward experiment of intuition, and no longer by this familiar process of reading?

Shall I enjoy friendships there, wanting the smiling indications which point me to them here,—the recognisable face—the "sweet assurance of a look" [8]—?

In winter this intolerable disinclination to dying—to give it its mildest name—does more especially haunt and beset me. In a genial August noon, beneath a sweltering sky, death is almost problematic. At those times do such poor snakes as myself enjoy an immortality. Then we expand and burgeon. Then are we as strong again, as valiant again, as wise again, and a great deal taller. The blast that nips and shrinks me, puts me in thoughts of death. All things allied to the insubstantial, wait upon that master feeling; cold, numbness, dreams, perplexity; moonlight itself, with its shadowy and spectral appearances,—that cold ghost of the sun, or Phoebus' sickly sister, like that innutritious one denounced in the Canticles: [9]—I am none of her minions—I hold with the Persian. [10]

Whatsoever thwarts, or puts me out of my way, brings death into my mind. All partial evils, like humours, run into that capital plague-sore.—I have heard some profess an indifference to life. Such hail the end of their existence as a port of refuge; and speak of the grave as of some soft arms, in which they may slumber as on a pillow. Some have wooed death——but out upon thee, I say, thou foul, ugly phantom! I detest, abhor, execrate, and (with Friar John) give thee to six-score thousand devils, [11] as in no instance to be excused or tolerated, but shunned as a universal viper; to be branded, proscribed, and spoken evil of! In no way can I be brought to digest thee, thou thin, melancholy *Privation*, or more frightful and confounding *Positive!*

Those antidotes, prescribed against the fear of thee, are altogether frigid and insulting, like thyself. For what satisfaction hath a man, that he shall "lie down with kings and emperors in death," [12] who in his lifetime never greatly coveted the society of such bedfellows?—or, forsooth, that "so shall the fairest face appear?" [13]—why, to comfort me, must Alice W——n [14] be a goblin? More than all, I conceive disgust at those impertinent and misbecoming familiarities, inscribed upon your ordinary tombstones. Every

---

[5] Cf. Job, vii, 6.   [6] Revolt.
[7] A reference to Virgil's *Aeneid*, in which the hero Aeneas seeks a new home and kingdom in Italy, following the destruction of Troy. He achieves his goal by marriage with Lavinia, daughter of King Latinus of Italy.

[8] Adapted from "An Elegy, or Friends passion for his Astrophill [Sir Philip Sidney]," ll. 103–104, by Matthew Roydon, a contemporary and friend of Sidney and Spenser.
[9] See Song of Solomon, viii, 8.
[10] Sun-worshipper.
[11] Friar John was an earthy and warlike monk in Rabelais' *Gargantua*, who dispatches his enemies in battle with the curse "I deliver thee to all the Devils in hell!"
[12] See Job, iii, 13–14.
[13] The ballad "William and Margaret," l. 9, by David Mallet (c. 1705–1765).
[14] The pseudonym for an early love of Lamb's. See "Dream Children" and "Blakesmoor in H——shire" for other references.

dead man must take upon himself to be lecturing me with his odious truism, that "such as he now is, I must shortly be." Not so shortly, friend, perhaps, as thou imaginest. In the meantime I am alive. I move about. I am worth twenty of thee. Know thy betters! Thy New Years' Days are past. I survive, a jolly candidate for 1821. Another cup of wine—and while that turncoat bell, that just now mournfully chanted the obsequies of 1820 departed, with changed notes lustily rings in a successor, let us attune to its peal the song made on a like occasion, by hearty, cheerful Mr. Cotton.[15]—

THE NEW YEAR

Hark, the cock crows, and yon bright star
Tells us, the day himself's not far;
And see where, breaking from the night,
He gilds the western hills with light.
With him old Janus doth appear,
Peeping into the future year,
With such a look as seems to say,
The prospect is not good that way.
Thus do we rise ill sights to see,
And 'gainst ourselves to prophesy;
When the prophetic fear of things
A more tormenting mischief brings,
More full of soul tormenting gall,
Than direst mischiefs can befall.
But stay! but stay! methinks my sight,
Better inform'd by clearer light,
Discerns sereneness in that brow,
That all contracted seem'd but now.
His revers'd face may show distaste,
And frown upon the ills are past;
But that which this way looks is clear,
And smiles upon the New-born Year.
He looks too from a place so high,
The Year lies open to his eye;
And all the moments open are
To the exact discoverer.
Yet more and more he smiles upon
The happy revolution.
Why should we then suspect or fear
The influences of a year,
So smiles upon us the first morn,
And speaks us good so soon as born?
Plague on't! the last was ill enough,
This cannot but make better proof;
Or, at the worst, as we brush'd through
The last, why so we may this too;

And then the next in reason shou'd
Be superexcellently good:
For the worst ills (we daily see)
Have no more perpetuity,
Than the best fortunes that do fall;
Which also bring us wherewithal
Longer their being to support,
Than those do of the other sort:
And who has one good year in three,
And yet repines at destiny,
Appears ungrateful in the case,
And merits not the good he has.
Then let us welcome the New Guest
With lusty brimmers of the best;
Mirth always should Good Fortune meet,
And renders e'en Disaster sweet:
And though the Princess turn her back,
Let us but line ourselves with sack,
We better shall by far hold out,
Till the next Year she face about.

How say you, reader—do not these verses smack of the rough magnanimity of the old English vein? Do they not fortify like a cordial; enlarging the heart, and productive of sweet blood, and generous spirits, in the concoction? Where be those puling fears of death, just now expressed or affected?—Passed like a cloud—absorbed in the purging sunlight of clear poetry—clean washed away by a wave of genuine Helicon,[16] your only Spa for these hypochondries—And now another cup of the generous! and a merry New Year, and many of them, to you all, my masters!

[January 1821]   [1823]

MACKERY END, IN HERTFORDSHIRE

Bridget Elia[1] has been my housekeeper for many a long year. I have obligations to Bridget, extending beyond the period of memory. We house together, old bachelor and maid, in a sort of double singleness; with such tolerable comfort, upon the whole, that I, for one, find in myself no sort of disposition to go out upon the mountains, with the rash king's offspring, to bewail my celibacy.[2]—We agree pretty well in our tastes and habits—yet so, as "with a difference."[3]

---

15 Charles Cotton (1630–1687) was a poet, translator of Montaigne's *Essays*, and contributor to Walton's *Complete Angler*.

16 The mythological home of the Muses on mount Parnassus in Greece. The mountain and its streams are synonymous with poetic inspiration.
1 In the Elia essays, Lamb disguises his sister Mary as cousin Bridget.
2 See Judges, xi, 30–38.   3 *Hamlet*, IV, v, 183.

We are generally in harmony, with occasional bicker-ings—as it should be among near relations. Our sympathies are rather understood, than expressed; and once, upon my dissembling a tone in my voice more kind than ordinary, my cousin burst into tears, and complained that I was altered. We are both great readers in different directions. While I am hanging over (for the thousandth time) some passage in old Burton, or one of his strange contemporaries, she is abstracted in some modern tale or adventure, whereof our common reading-table is daily fed with assiduously fresh supplies. Narrative teazes me. I have little concern in the progress of events. She must have a story—well, ill, or indifferently told—so there be life stirring in it, and plenty of good or evil accidents. The fluctuations of fortune in fiction—and almost in real life—have ceased to interest, or operate but dully upon me. Out-of-the-way humours and opinions—heads with some diverting twist in them—the oddities of authorship please me most. My cousin has a native disrelish of any thing that sounds odd or bizarre. Nothing goes down with her that is quaint, irregular, or out of the road of common sympathy. She "holds Nature more clever."[4] I can pardon her blindness to the beautiful obliquities of the Religio Medici; but she must apologise to me for certain disrespectful insinuations, which she has been pleased to throw out latterly, touching the intellectuals of a dear favourite of mine, of the last century but one—the thrice noble, chaste, and virtuous,—but again somewhat fantastical and original-brain'd, generous Margaret Newcastle.[5]

It has been the lot of my cousin, oftener perhaps than I could have wished, to have had for her associates and mine, free-thinkers—leaders, and disciples, of novel philosophies and systems; but she neither wrangles with, nor accepts, their opinions. That which was good and venerable to her, when a child, retains its authority over her mind still. She never juggles or plays tricks with her understanding.

We are both of us inclined to be a little too positive; and I have observed the result of our disputes to be almost uniformly this—that in matters of fact, dates, and circumstances, it turns out, that I was in the right, and my cousin in the wrong. But where we have differed upon moral points; upon something proper to be done, or let alone; whatever heat of opposition, or steadiness of conviction, I set out with, I am sure

always, in the long run, to be brought over to her way of thinking.

I must touch upon the foibles of my kinswoman with a gentle hand, for Bridget does not like to be told of her faults. She hath an awkward trick (to say no worse of it) of reading in company: at which times she will answer *yes* or *no* to a question, without fully understanding its purport—which is provoking, and derogatory in the highest degree to the dignity of the putter of the said question. Her presence of mind is equal to the most pressing trials of life, but will sometimes desert her upon trifling occasions. When the purpose requires it, and is a thing of moment, she can speak to it greatly; but in matters which are not stuff of the conscience, she hath been known sometimes to let slip a word less seasonably.

Her education in youth was not much attended to; and she happily missed all that train of female garniture, which passeth by the name of accomplishments. She was tumbled early, by accident or design, into a spacious closet of good old English reading, without much selection or prohibition, and browsed at will upon that fair and wholesome pasturage. Had I twenty girls, they should be brought up exactly in this fashion. I know not whether their chance in wedlock might not be diminished by it; but I can answer for it, that it makes (if the worst come to the worst) most incomparable old maids.

In a season of distress, she is the truest comforter; but in the teazing accidents and minor perplexities, which do not call out the *will* to meet them, she sometimes maketh matters worse by an excess of participation. If she does not always divide your trouble, upon the pleasanter occasions of life she is sure always to treble your satisfaction. She is excellent to be at a play with, or upon a visit: but best, when she goes a journey with you.

We made an excursion together a few summers since, into Hertfordshire, to beat up the quarters of some of our less-known relations in that fine corn country.

The oldest thing I remember is Mackery End; or Mackarel End, as it is spelt, perhaps more properly, in some old maps of Hertfordshire; a farm-house,—delightfully situated within a gentle walk from Wheat-hampstead. I can just remember having been there, on a visit to a great-aunt, when I was a child, under the care of Bridget; who, as I have said, is older than myself by some ten years. I wish that I could throw into a heap the remainder of our joint existences, that we might share them in equal division. But that is impossible. The house was at that time in the occupation of a substantial yeoman, who had married my grand-mother's sister. His name was Gladman. My grand-

---

4 From the verses "Epitaph of Bye-Words" attributed to John Gay.

5 Margaret Cavendish, Duchess of Newcastle (*c.* 1624–1674) was the author of various works in poetry and prose, often embodying eccentric philosophic and scientific speculations.

mother was a Bruton, married to a Field. The Gladmans and the Brutons are still flourishing in that part of the county, but the Fields are almost extinct. More than forty years had elapsed since the visit I speak of; and, for the greater portion of that period, we had lost sight of the other two branches also. Who or what sort of persons inherited Mackery End—kindred or strange folk—we were afraid almost to conjecture, but determined some day to explore.

By somewhat a circuitous route, taking the noble park at Luton in our way from Saint Alban's, we arrived at the spot of our anxious curiosity about noon. The sight of the old farm-house, though every trace of it was effaced from my recollection, affected me with a pleasure which I had not experienced for many a year. For though *I* had forgotten it, *we* had never forgotten being there together, and we had been talking about Mackery End all our lives, till memory on my part became mocked with a phantom of itself, and I thought I knew the aspect of a place, which, when present, O how unlike it was to *that*, which I had conjured up so many times instead of it!

Still the air breathed balmily about it; the season was in the "heart of June,"[6] and I could say with the poet,

> But thou, that didst appear so fair
> To fond imagination,
> Dost rival in the light of day
> Her delicate creation![7]

Bridget's was more a waking bliss than mine, for she easily remembered her old acquaintance again—some altered features, of course, a little grudged at. At first, indeed, she was ready to disbelieve for joy; but the scene soon re-confirmed itself in her affections—and she traversed every out-post of the old mansion, to the wood-house, the orchard, the place where the pigeon-house had stood (house and birds were alike flown)—with a breathless impatience of recognition, which was more pardonable perhaps than decorous at the age of fifty odd. But Bridget in some things is behind her years.

The only thing left was to get into the house—and that was a difficulty which to me singly would have been insurmountable; for I am terribly shy in making myself known to strangers and out-of-date kinsfolk. Love, stronger than scruple, winged my cousin in without me; but she soon returned with a creature that might have sat to a sculptor for the image of Welcome.

It was the youngest of the Gladmans; who, by marriage with a Bruton, had become mistress of the old mansion. A comely brood are the Brutons. Six of them, females, were noted as the handsomest young women in the county. But this adopted Bruton, in my mind, was better than they all—more comely. She was born too late to have remembered me. She just recollected in early life to have had her cousin Bridget once pointed out to her, climbing a style. But the name of kindred, and of cousinship, was enough. Those slender ties, that prove slight as gossamer in the rending atmosphere of a metropolis, bind faster, as we found it, in hearty, homely, loving Hertfordshire. In five minutes we were as thoroughly acquainted as if we had been born and bred up together; were familiar, even to the calling each other by our Christian names. So Christians should call one another. To have seen Bridget, and her—it was like the meeting of the two scriptural 'cousins![8] There was a grace and dignity, an amplitude of form and stature, answering to her mind, in this farmer's wife, which would have shined in a palace—or so we thought it. We were made welcome by husband and wife equally—we, and our friend that was with us.—I had almost forgotten him—but B. F. will not so soon forget that meeting, if peradventure he shall read this on the far distant shores where the Kangaroo haunts.[9] The fatted calf was made ready, or rather was already so, as if in anticipation of our coming; and, after an appropriate glass of native wine, never let me forget with what honest pride this hospitable cousin made us proceed to Wheathampstead, to introduce us (as some new-found rarity) to her mother and sister Gladmans, who did indeed know something more of us, at a time when she almost knew nothing.—With what corresponding kindness we were received by them also—how Bridget's memory, exalted by the occasion, warmed into a thousand half-obliterated recollections of things and persons, to my utter astonishment, and her own—and to the astoundment of B. F. who sat by, almost the only thing that was not a cousin there,—old effaced images of more than half-forgotten names and circumstances still crowding back upon her, as words written in lemon come out upon exposure to a friendly warmth, —when I forget all this, then may my country cousins forget me; and Bridget no more remember, that in the days of weakling infancy I was her tender charge—as I have been her care in foolish manhood since—in those

[6] Ben Jonson's "Epithalamion; or, a Song: Celebrating the Nuptials of that Noble Gentleman, Mr. Hierome Weston . . ." (1641), l. 16.

[7] Wordsworth's "Yarrow Visited" (1815), ll. 41–44.

[8] A reference to the visit of the Virgin Mary to her cousin Elizabeth following the annunciation. See Luke, i, 39–45.

[9] Barron Field (1786–1846) was a minor literary figure and lawyer. From 1816 to 1824 Field served as judge of the Supreme Court in Australia. E. V. Lucas conjectures that the Lambs' visit to Mackery End with Barron Field occurred in 1815.

pretty pastoral walks, long ago, about Mackery End, in Hertfordshire.

[July 1821]   [1823]

IMPERFECT SYMPATHIES

I am of a constitution so general, that it consorts and sympathizeth with all things, I have no antipathy, or rather idiosyncracy in any thing. Those national repugnancies do not touch me, nor do I behold with prejudice the French, Italian, Spaniard, or Dutch.
Religio Medici.[1]

THAT the author of the Religio Medici, mounted upon the airy stilts of abstraction, conversant about notional and conjectural essences; in whose categories of Being the possible took the upper hand of the actual; should have overlooked the impertinent individualities of such poor concretions as mankind, is not much to be admired. It is rather to be wondered at, that in the genus of animals he should have condescended to distinguish that species at all. For myself—earth-bound and fettered to the scene of my activities,—

Standing on earth, not rapt above the sky,[2]

I confess that I do feel the differences of mankind, national or individual, to an unhealthy excess. I can look with no indifferent eye upon things or persons. Whatever is, is to me a matter of taste or distaste; or when once it becomes indifferent, it begins to be disrelishing. I am, in plainer words, a bundle of prejudices—made up of likings and dislikings—the veriest thrall to sympathies, apathies, antipathies. In a certain sense, I hope it may be said of me that I am a lover of my species. I can feel for all indifferently, but I cannot feel towards all equally. The more purely-English word that expresses sympathy, will better explain my meaning. I can be a friend to a worthy man, who upon another account cannot be my mate or *fellow*. I cannot *like* all people alike.*

* I would be understood as confining myself to the subject of *imperfect sympathies*. To nations or classes of men there can be no direct *antipathy*. There may be individuals born and constellated so opposite to another individual nature, that the same sphere cannot hold them. I have met with my moral antipodes, and can believe the story of two persons meeting (who never saw one another before in their lives) and instantly fighting.

——We by proof find there should be
'Twixt man and man such an antipathy,
That though he can show no just reason why
For any former wrong or injury,

I have been trying all my life to like Scotchmen, and am obliged to desist from the experiment in despair. They cannot like me—and in truth, I never knew one of that nation who attempted to do it. There is something more plain and ingenuous in their mode of proceeding. We know one another at first sight. There is an order of imperfect intellects (under which mine must be content to rank) which in its constitution is essentially anti-Caledonian.[4] The owners of the sort of faculties I allude to, have minds rather suggestive than comprehensive. They have no pretences to much clearness or precision in their ideas, or in their manner of expressing them. Their intellectual wardrobe (to confess fairly) has few whole pieces in it. They are content with fragments and scattered pieces of Truth. She presents no full front to them—a feature or side-face at the most. Hints and glimpses, germs and crude essays at a system, is the utmost they pretend to. They beat up a little game peradventure—and leave it to knottier heads, more robust constitutions, to run it down. The light that lights them is not steady and polar, but mutable and shifting: waxing, and again waning. Their conversation is accordingly. They will throw out a random word in or out of season, and be content to let it pass for what it is worth. They cannot speak always as if they were upon their oath—but must be understood, speaking or writing, with some abatement. They seldom wait to mature a proposition, but e'en bring it to market in the green ear. They delight to impart their defective discoveries as they arise, without waiting for their full developement. They are no systematizers, and would but err more by attempting it. Their minds, as I said before, are suggestive merely. The brain of a true Caledonian (if I am not mistaken) is constituted upon quite a different plan. His Minerva is born in panoply.[5] You are never

---

Can neither find a blemish in his fame,
Nor aught in face or feature justly blame,
Can challenge or accuse him of no evil,
Yet notwithstanding hates him as a devil.

The lines are from old Heywood's "Hierarchie of Angels," and he subjoins a curious story in confirmation, of a Spaniard who attempted to assassinate a King Ferdinand of Spain, and being put to the rack could give no other reason for the deed but an inveterate antipathy which he had taken to the first sight of the King.

——The cause which to that act compell'd him
Was, he ne'er loved him since he first beheld him.[3]

---

[3] Lamb quotes from Book IV ("Dominations") of *Hierarchie of the Blessed Angells* (1635), an elaborate theological poem by Thomas Heywood (1573–1641), poet and dramatist.
[4] Caledonia is the Latin name for Scotland.
[5] That is, the products of his mind arrive fully formed and defined; from the myth of Minerva, who sprang fully developed and armed from the brain of Zeus.

---

[1] Lamb quotes from the Second Part, Section 1, of Sir Thomas Browne's *Religio Medici*.
[2] *Paradise Lost*, VII, 23.

admitted to see his ideas in their growth—if, indeed, they do grow, and are not rather put together upon principles of clock-work. You never catch his mind in an undress. He never hints or suggests anything, but unlades his stock of ideas in perfect order and completeness. He brings his total wealth into company, and gravely unpacks it. His riches are always about him. He never stoops to catch a glittering something in your presence to share it with you, before he quite knows whether it be true touch or not. You cannot cry *halves* to any thing that he finds. He does not find, but bring. You never witness his first apprehension of a thing. His understanding is always at its meridian—you never see the first dawn, the early streaks.—He has no falterings of self-suspicion. Surmises, guesses, misgivings, half-intuitions, semi-consciousnesses, partial illuminations, dim instincts, embryo conceptions, have no place in his brain, or vocabulary. The twilight of dubiety never falls upon him. Is he orthodox—he has no doubts. Is he an infidel—he has none either. Between the affirmative and the negative there is no border-land with him. You cannot hover with him upon the confines of truth, or wander in the maze of a probable argument. He always keeps the path. You cannot make excursions with him—for he sets you right. His taste never fluctuates. His morality never abates. He cannot compromise, or understand middle actions. There can be but a right and a wrong. His conversation is as a book. His affirmations have the sanctity of an oath. You must speak upon the square [6] with him. He stops a metaphor like a suspected person in an enemy's country. "A healthy book!"—said one of his countrymen to me, who had ventured to give that appellation to John Buncle,[7]—"Did I catch rightly what you said? I have heard of a man in health, and of a healthy state of body, but I do not see how that epithet can be properly applied to a book." Above all, you must beware of indirect expressions before a Caledonian. Clap an extinguisher upon your irony, if you are unhappily blest with a vein of it. Remember you are upon your oath. I have a print of a graceful female after Leonardo da Vinci, which I was showing off to Mr. * * * *. After he had examined it minutely, I ventured to ask him how he liked MY BEAUTY (a foolish name it goes by among my friends) —when he very gravely assured me, that "he had considerable respect for my character and talents" (so he was pleased to say), "but had not given himself much thought about the degree of my personal pretensions." The misconception staggered me, but did

not seem much to disconcert him.—Persons of this nation are particularly fond of affirming a truth—which nobody doubts. They do not so properly affirm, as annunciate it. They do indeed appear to have such a love of truth (as if, like virtue, it were valuable for itself) that all truth becomes equally valuable, whether the proposition that contains it be new or old, disputed, or such as is impossible to become a subject of disputation. I was present not long since at a party of North Britons, where a son of Burns was expected; and happened to drop a silly expression (in my South British way), that I wished it were the father instead of the son—when four of them started up at once to inform me, that "that was impossible, because he was dead." An impracticable wish, it seems, was more than they could conceive. Swift has hit off this part of their character, namely their love of truth, in his biting way, but with an illiberality that necessarily confines the passage to the margin.* The tediousness of these people is certainly provoking. I wonder if they ever tire one another!—In my early life I had a passionate fondness for the poetry of Burns. I have sometimes foolishly hoped to ingratiate myself with his countrymen by expressing it. But I have always found that a true Scot resents your admiration of his compatriot, even more than he would your contempt of him. The latter he imputes to your "imperfect acquaintance with many of the words which he uses;" and the same objection makes it a presumption in you to suppose that you can admire him.—Thomson[9] they seem to have forgotten. Smollett they have neither forgotten nor forgiven for his delineation of Rory and his companion, upon their first introduction to our metropolis.—Speak of Smollett as a great genius, and they will retort upon you Hume's History compared with *his* Continuation of it. What if the historian had continued Humphrey Clinker?[10]

I have, in the abstract, no disrespect for Jews. They

* There are some people who think they sufficiently acquit themselves, and entertain their company, with relating facts of no consequence, not at all out of the road of such common incidents as happen every day; and this I have observed more frequently among the Scots than any other nation, who are very careful not to omit the minutest circumstances of time or place; which kind of discourse, if it were not a little relieved by the uncouth terms and phrases, as well as accent and gesture peculiar to that country, would be hardly tolerable.—*Hints towards an Essay on Conversation.*[8]

6 Without indirection.
7 Long eccentric novel published between 1756 and 1770, by Thomas Amory.

8 Lamb quotes the final paragraph of Swift's essay, first published in 1763.
9 James Thomson (1700–1748), poet of *The Seasons* and *The Castle of Indolence*, left his native Scotland at age 25 to live the rest of his life in England.
10 Tobias Smollett (1721–1771) was born and educated in Scotland but lived the rest of his life abroad or in England. His first novel *Roderick Random* (1748) records the travels and adventures of a picaresque Scotch hero Roderick [Rory] and

are a piece of stubborn antiquity, compared with which Stonehenge is in its nonage. They date beyond the pyramids. But I should not care to be in habits of familiar intercourse with any of that nation. I confess that I have not the nerves to enter their synagogues. Old prejudices cling about me. I cannot shake off the story of Hugh of Lincoln.[11] Centuries of injury, contempt, and hate, on the one side,—of cloaked revenge, dissimulation, and hate, on the other, between our and their fathers, must and ought, to affect the blood of the children. I cannot believe it can run clear and kindly yet; or that a few fine words, such as candour, liberality, the light of a nineteenth century, can close up the breaches of so deadly a disunion. A Hebrew is nowhere congenial to me. He is least distasteful on 'Change— for the mercantile spirit levels all distinctions, as all are beauties in the dark. I boldly confess that I do not relish the approximation of Jew and Christian, which has become so fashionable. The reciprocal endearments have, to me, something hypocritical and unnatural in them. I do not like to see the Church and Synagogue kissing and congeeing[12] in awkward postures of an affected civility. If *they* are converted, why do they not come over to us altogether? Why keep up a form of separation, when the life of it is fled? If they can sit with us at table, why do they keck[13] at our cookery? I do not understand these half convertites. Jews christianizing—Christians judaizing —puzzle me. I like fish or flesh. A moderate Jew is a more confounding piece of anomaly than a wet Quaker.[14] The spirit of the synagogue is essentially *separative*. B——[15] would have been more in keeping if he had abided by the faith of his forefathers. There is a fine scorn in his face, which nature meant to be of ——Christians.—The Hebrew spirit is strong in him, in spite of his proselytism. He cannot conquer the Shibboleth.[16] How it breaks out, when he sings, "The

Children of Israel passed through the Red Sea!"[17] The auditors, for the moment, are as Egyptians to him, and he rides over our necks in triumph. There is no mistaking him.—B——has a strong expression of sense in his countenance, and it is confirmed by his singing. The foundation of his vocal excellence is sense. He sings with understanding, as Kemble delivered dialogue. He would sing the Commandments, and give an appropriate character to each prohibition. His nation, in general, have not oversensible countenances. How should they?—but you seldom see a silly expression among them. Gain, and the pursuit of gain, sharpen a man's visage. I never heard of an idiot being born among them.—Some admire the Jewish female-physiognomy. I admire it— but with trembling. Jael[18] had those full dark inscrutable eyes.

In the Negro countenance you will often meet with strong traits of benignity. I have felt yearnings of tenderness towards some of these faces—or rather masks—that have looked out kindly upon one in casual encounters in the streets and highways. I love what Fuller beautifully calls—these "images of God cut in ebony."[19] But I should not like to associate with them, to share my meals and my good-nights with them— because they are black.

I love Quaker ways, and Quaker worship. I venerate the Quaker principles. It does me good for the rest of the day when I meet any of their people in my path. When I am ruffled or disturbed by any occurrence, the sight, or quiet voice of a Quaker, acts upon me as a ventilator, lightening the air, and taking off a load from the bosom. But I cannot like the Quakers (as Desdemona would say) "to live with them."[20] I am all over sophisticated—with humours, fancies, craving hourly sympathy. I must have books, pictures, theatres, chitchat, scandal, jokes, ambiguities, and a thousand whimwhams, which their simpler taste can do without. I should starve at their primitive banquet. My appetites are too high for the salads which (according to Evelyn) Eve dressed for the angel, my gusto too excited

> To sit a guest with Daniel at his pulse.[21]

The indirect answers which Quakers are often

---

his school-fellow Strap. Within forty-eight hours of their arrival in London, the gullible young men are "jeered, reproached, buffeted, pissed upon, and at last stripped of money" by a series of wily Londoners (see Chapters XIII–XIV). The Scottish philosopher David Hume's *History of England*, published between 1754 and 1761, traced events *from the Invasion of Julius Caesar to the Revolution of 1688*. Smollett's *The History of England Designed as a Continuation of Hume* brought events down to the reign of George III. *Humphry Clinker* (1771) was Smollett's final and most famous novel.

[11] The popular legend of a young boy brutally tortured and murdered by a Jew at Lincoln in 1255. See Chaucer's "Prioress's Tale."

[12] Bowing in courtesy.   [13] Reject with loathing.

[14] The Quaker religion rejects baptism by water.

[15] John Braham (*c.* 1774–1856) was a popular tenor of the London operatic stage.

[16] A distinctive or ingrained mark; originally the Hebrew word whose correct pronunciation was used to distinguish the true men of Gilead under Jephthah from their enemies the Ephraimites. See Judges, xii, 4–6.

[17] From Handel's oratorio *Israel in Egypt*.

[18] Jael, the wife of Heber the Kenite, offered welcome and hospitality to Sisera, captain of the Canaanite army, then slew him in his sleep. See Judges, iv, 17–22.

[19] Thomas Fuller's *The Holy State and the Profane State* (1642), II, Chapter 20.

[20] *Othello*, I, iii, 249.

[21] John Evelyn (1620–1706) was a writer, translator, and famous diarist. Lamb refers to his *Acetaria. A Discourse of Sallets* (1669). "To sit . . . pulse" is from *Paradise Regained*, II, 278.

found to return to a question put to them may be explained, I think, without the vulgar assumption, that they are more given to evasion and equivocating than other people. They naturally look to their words more carefully, and are more cautious of committing themselves. They have a peculiar character to keep up on this head. They stand in a manner upon their veracity. A Quaker is by law exempted from taking an oath. The custom of resorting to an oath in extreme cases, sanctified as it is by all religious antiquity, is apt (it must be confessed) to introduce into the laxer sort of minds the notion of two kinds of truth—the one applicable to the solemn affairs of justice, and the other to the common proceedings of daily intercourse. As truth bound upon the conscience by an oath can be but truth, so in the common affirmations of the shop and the market-place a latitude is expected, and conceded upon questions wanting this solemn covenant. Something less than truth satisfies. It is common to hear a person say, "You do not expect me to speak as if I were upon my oath." Hence a great deal of incorrectness and inadvertency, short of falsehood, creeps into ordinary conversation; and a kind of secondary or laic-truth is tolerated, where clergy-truth—oath-truth, by the nature of the circumstances, is not required. A Quaker knows none of this distinction. His simple affirmation being received, upon the most sacred occasions, without any further test, stamps a value upon the words which he is to use upon the most indifferent topics of life. He looks to them, naturally, with more severity. You can have of him no more than his word. He knows, if he is caught tripping in a casual expression, he forfeits, for himself, at least, his claim to the invidious exemption. He knows that his syllables are weighed—and how far a consciousness of this particular watchfulness, exerted against a person, has a tendency to produce indirect answers, and a diverting of the question by honest means, might be illustrated, and the practice justified, by a more sacred example than is proper to be adduced upon this occasion. The admirable presence of mind, which is notorious in Quakers upon all contingencies, might be traced to this imposed self-watchfulness—if it did not seem rather an humble and secular scion of that old stock of religious constancy, which never bent or faltered, in the Primitive Friends, or gave way to the winds of persecution, to the violence of judge or accuser, under trials and racking examinations. "You will never be the wiser, if I sit here answering your questions till midnight," said one of those upright Justicers to Penn,[22] who had been putting law-cases with a

---

[22] William Penn (1644–1718), the Quaker leader, was frequently brought to trial in England for his religious activities.

puzzling subtlety. "Thereafter as the answers may be," retorted the Quaker. The astonishing composure of this people is sometimes ludicrously displayed in lighter instances.—I was travelling in a stage-coach with three male Quakers, buttoned up in the straitest non-conformity of their sect. We stopped to bait at Andover, where a meal, partly tea apparatus, partly supper, was set before us. My friends confined themselves to the tea-table. I in my way took supper. When the landlady brought in the bill, the eldest of my companions discovered that she had charged for both meals. This was resisted. Mine hostess was very clamorous and positive. Some mild arguments were used on the part of the Quakers, for which the heated mind of the good lady seemed by no means a fit recipient. The guard came in with his usual peremptory notice. The Quakers pulled out their money, and formally tendered it—so much for tea—I, in humble imitation, tendering mine—for the supper which I had taken. She would not relax in her demand. So they all three quietly put up their silver, as did myself, and marched out of the room, the eldest and gravest going first, with myself closing up the rear, who thought I could not do better than follow the example of such grave and warrantable personages. We got in. The steps went up. The coach drove off. The murmurs of mine hostess, not very indistinctly or ambiguously pronounced, became after a time inaudible—and now my conscience, which the whimsical scene had for a while suspended, beginning to give some twitches, I waited, in the hope that some justification would be offered by these serious persons for the seeming injustice of their conduct. To my great surprise not a syllable was dropped on the subject. They sat as mute as at a meeting. At length the eldest of them broke silence, by inquiring of his next neighbour, "Hast thou heard how indigos go at the India House?" and the question operated as a soporific on my moral feeling as far as Exeter.

[August 1821]   [1823]

WITCHES, AND OTHER NIGHT-FEARS

WE ARE too hasty when we set down our ancestors in the gross for fools, for the monstrous inconsistencies (as they seem to us) involved in their creed of witchcraft. In the relations of this visible world we find them to have been as rational, and shrewd to detect an historic anomaly, as ourselves. But when once the invisible world was supposed to be open, and the lawless agency of bad spirits assumed, what measures of probability, of decency, of fitness, or proportion—

of that which distinguishes the likely from the palpable absurd—could they have to guide them in the rejection or admission of any particular testimony?—That maidens pined away, wasting inwardly as their waxen images consumed before a fire—that corn was lodged,[1] and cattle lamed—that whirlwinds uptore in diabolic revelry the oaks of the forest—or that spits and kettles only danced a fearful-innocent vagary about some rustic's kitchen when no wind was stirring—were all equally probable where no law of agency was understood. That the prince of the powers of darkness, passing by the flower and pomp of the earth, should lay preposterous siege to the weak fantasy of indigent eld—has neither likelihood nor unlikelihood *à priori* to us, who have no measure to guess at his policy, or standard to estimate what rate those anile[2] souls may fetch in the devil's market. Nor, when the wicked are expressly symbolized by a goat, was it to be wondered at so much, that *he* should come sometimes in that body, and assert his metaphor.—That the intercourse was opened at all between both worlds was perhaps the mistake—but that once assumed, I see no reason for disbelieving one attested story of this nature more than another on the score of absurdity. There is no law to judge of the lawless, or canon by which a dream may be criticised.

I have sometimes thought that I could not have existed in the days of received witchcraft; that I could not have slept in a village where one of those reputed hags dwelt. Our ancestors were bolder or more obtuse. Amidst the universal belief that these wretches were in league with the author of all evil, holding hell tributary to their muttering, no simple Justice of the Peace seems to have scrupled issuing, or silly Headborough[3] serving, a warrant upon them—as if they should subpoena Satan!—Prospero in his boat, with his books and wand about him, suffers himself to be conveyed away at the mercy of his enemies to an unknown island.[4] He might have raised a storm or two, we think, on the passage. His acquiescence is in exact analogy to the non-resistance of witches to the constituted powers.—What stops the Fiend in Spenser from tearing Guyon to pieces—or who had made it a condition of his prey, that Guyon must take assay of the glorious bait[5]—we have no guess. We do not know the laws of that country.

From my childhood I was extremely inquisitive about witches and witch-stories. My maid, and more

legendary aunt, supplied me with good store. But I shall mention the accident which directed my curiosity originally into this channel. In my father's book-closet, the History of the Bible, by Stackhouse,[6] occupied a distinguished station. The pictures with which it abounds—one of the ark, in particular, and another of Solomon's temple, delineated with all the fidelity of ocular admeasurement, as if the artist had been upon the spot—attracted my childish attention. There was a picture, too, of the Witch raising up Samuel,[7] which I wish that I had never seen. We shall come to that hereafter. Stackhouse is in two huge tomes—and there was a pleasure in removing folios of that magnitude, which, with infinite straining, was as much as I could manage, from the situation which they occupied upon an upper shelf. I have not met with the work from that time to this, but I remember it consisted of Old Testament stories, orderly set down, with the *objection* appended to each story, and the *solution* of the objection regularly tacked to that. The *objection* was a summary of whatever difficulties had been opposed to the credibility of the history, by the shrewdness of ancient or modern infidelity, drawn up with an almost complimentary excess of candour. The *solution* was brief, modest, and satisfactory. The bane and antidote were both before you. To doubts so put, and so quashed, there seemed to be an end for ever. The dragon lay dead, for the foot of the veriest babe to trample on. But—like as was rather feared than realised from that slain monster in Spenser[8]—from the womb of those crushed errors young dragonets would creep, exceeding the prowess of so tender a Saint George as myself to vanquish. The habit of expecting objections to every passage, set me upon starting more objections, for the glory of finding a solution of my own for them. I became staggered and perplexed, a sceptic in long-coats.[9] The pretty Bible stories which I had read, or heard read in church, lost their purity and sincerity of impression, and were turned into so many historic or chronologic theses to be defended against whatever impugners. I was not to disbelieve them, but—the next thing to that—I was to be quite sure that some one or other would or had disbelieved them. Next to making a child an infidel, is the letting him know that there are infidels at all. Credulity is the man's weakness, but the child's strength. O, how ugly sound scriptural doubts from the mouth of a babe and a suckling!—I should have lost myself in these mazes, and have pined

---

[1] Beaten flat to the ground.
[2] Old-womanish, imbecile.
[3] The parish officer.
[4] See *The Tempest*, I, ii, 144–51.
[5] *Faerie Queene*, II, vii, 63–64.

[6] Thomas Stackhouse's *New History of the Holy Bible from the Beginning of the World to the Establishment of Christianity* (1737).
[7] I Samuel, xxviii.
[8] *Faerie Queene*, I, xii, 9–10.
[9] The garments of an infant.

away, I think, with such unfit sustenance as these husks afforded, but for a fortunate piece of ill-fortune, which about this time befel me. Turning over the picture of the ark with too much haste, I unhappily made a breach in its ingenious fabric—driving my inconsiderate fingers right through the two larger quadrupeds—the elephant and the camel—that stare (as well they might) out of the two last windows next the steerage in that unique piece of naval architecture. Stackhouse was henceforth locked up, and became an interdicted treasure. With the book, the *objections* and *solutions* gradually cleared out of my head, and have seldom returned since in any force to trouble me.— But there was one impression which I had imbibed from Stackhouse, which no lock or bar could shut out, and which was destined to try my childish nerves rather more seriously.—That detestable picture!

I was dreadfully alive to nervous terrors. The night-time, solitude, and the dark, were my hell. The sufferings I endured in this nature would justify the expression. I never laid my head on my pillow, I suppose, from the fourth to the seventh or eighth year of my life—so far as memory serves in things so long ago—without an assurance, which realized its own prophecy, of seeing some frightful spectre. Be old Stackhouse then acquitted in part, if I say, that to this picture of the Witch raising up Samuel—(O that old man covered with a mantle!) I owe—not my midnight terrors, the hell of my infancy—but the shape and manner of their visitation. It was he who dressed up for me a hag that nightly sate upon my pillow—a sure bed-fellow, when my aunt or my maid was far from me. All day long, while the book was permitted me, I dreamed waking over his delineation, and at night (if I may use so bold an expression) awoke into sleep, and found the vision true. I durst not, even in the day-light, once enter the chamber where I slept, without my face turned to the window, aversely from the bed where my witch-ridden pillow was.—Parents do not know what they do when they leave tender babes alone to go to sleep in the dark. The feeling about for a friendly arm—the hoping for a familiar voice—when they wake screaming—and find none to soothe them—what a terrible shaking it is to their poor nerves! The keeping them up till midnight, through candle-light and the unwholesome hours, as they are called,—would, I am satisfied, in a medical point of view, prove the better caution.—That detestable picture, as I have said, gave the fashion to my dreams—if dreams they were—for the scene of them was invariably the room in which I lay. Had I never met with the picture, the fears would have come self-pictured in some shape or other—

> Headless bear, black man, or ape— [10]

but, as it was, my imaginations took that form.—It is not book, or picture, or the stories of foolish servants, which create these terrors in children. They can at most but give them a direction. Dear little T. H. [11] who of all children has been brought up with the most scrupulous exclusion of every taint of superstition— who was never allowed to hear of goblin or apparition, or scarcely to be told of bad men, or to read or hear of any distressing story—finds all this world of fear, from which he has been so rigidly excluded *ab extra*, in his own "thick-coming fancies;" [12] and from his little midnight pillow, this nurse-child of optimism will start at shapes, unborrowed of tradition, in sweats to which the reveries of the cell-damned murderer are tranquillity.

Gorgons, and Hydras, and Chimæras—dire stories of Celæno and the Harpies [13]—may reproduce themselves in the brain of superstition—but they were there before. They are transcripts, types—the archetypes are in us, and eternal. How else should the recital of that, which we know in a waking sense to be false, come to affect us at all?—or

> ———Names, whose sense we see not,
> Fray us with things that be not? [14]

Is it that we naturally conceive terror from such objects, considered in their capacity of being able to inflict upon us bodily injury?—O, least of all! These terrors are of older standing. They date beyond body—or, without the body, they would have been the same. All the cruel, tormenting, defined devils in Dante— tearing, mangling, choking, stifling, scorching demons —are they one half so fearful to the spirit of a man, as the simple idea of a spirit unembodied following him—

> Like one that on a lonesome road
> Doth walk in fear and dread,
> And having once turn'd round, walks on,
> And turns no more his head;
> Because he knows a frightful fiend
> Doth close behind him tread. *

* Mr. Coleridge's Ancient Mariner. [15]

[10] From prefatory verses "The Author's Abstract of Melancholy: A Dialogue," to Robert Burton's *The Anatomy of Melancholy*.
[11] Thornton Hunt (1810-1873) was the eldest son of Leigh Hunt.
[12] *Macbeth*, V, iii, 38.
[13] "Gorgons, Hydras. and Chimæras dire" is a quotation from *Paradise Lost*, II, 628. For the "stories of Celæno and the Harpies," see *Aeneid*, III, 219-66.
[14] Spenser's *Epithalamion*, ll. 343-44.   [15] Ll. 446-51.

That the kind of fear here treated of is purely spiritual—that it is strong in proportion as it is objectless upon earth—that it predominates in the period of sinless infancy—are difficulties, the solution of which might afford some probable insight into our ante-mundane condition, and a peep at least into the shadow-land of pre-existence.

My night-fancies have long ceased to be afflictive. I confess an occasional night-mare; but I do not, as in early youth, keep a stud[16] of them. Fiendish faces, with the extinguished taper, will come and look at me; but I know them for mockeries, even while I cannot elude their presence, and I fight and grapple with them. For the credit of my imagination, I am almost ashamed to say how tame and prosaic my dreams are grown. They are never romantic, seldom even rural. They are of architecture and of buildings—cities abroad, which I have never seen and hardly have hoped to see. I have traversed, for the seeming length of a natural day, Rome, Amsterdam, Paris, Lisbon—their churches, palaces, squares, market-places, shops, suburbs, ruins, with an inexpressible sense of delight—a map-like distinctness of trace, and a day-light vividness of vision, that was all but being awake.—I have formerly travelled among the Westmoreland fells[17]—my highest Alps,—but they are objects too mighty for the grasp of my dreaming recognition; and I have again and again awoke with ineffectual struggles of the inner eye, to make out a shape in any way whatever, of Helvellyn. Methought I was in that country, but the mountains were gone. The poverty of my dreams mortifies me. There is Coleridge, at his will can conjure up icy domes, and pleasure-houses for Kubla Khan, and Abyssinian maids, and songs of Abara, and caverns,

Where Alph, the sacred river, runs,[18]

to solace his night solitudes—when I cannot muster a fiddle. Barry Cornwall has his tritons and his nereids gamboling before him in nocturnal visions, and proclaiming sons born to Neptune—when my stretch of imaginative activity can hardly, in the night season, raise up the ghost of a fish-wife. To set my failures in somewhat a mortifying light—it was after reading the noble Dream of this poet,[19] that my fancy ran strong

upon these marine spectra; and the poor plastic power, such as it is, within me set to work, to humour my folly in a sort of dream that very night. Methought I was upon the ocean billows at some sea nuptials, riding and mounted high, with the customary train sounding their conchs before me, (I myself, you may be sure, the *leading god*,) and jollily we went careering over the main, till just where Ino Leucothea[20] should have greeted me (I think it was Ino) with a white embrace, the billows gradually subsiding, fell from a sea-roughness to a sea-calm, and thence to a river-motion, and that river (as happens in the familiarization of dreams) was no other than the gentle Thames, which landed me in the wafture of a placid wave or two, alone, safe and inglorious, somewhere at the foot of Lambeth palace.[21]

The degree of the soul's creativeness in sleep might furnish no whimsical criterion of the quantum of poetical faculty resident in the same soul waking. An old gentleman, a friend of mine, and a humourist, used to carry this notion so far, that when he saw any stripling of his acquaintance ambitious of becoming a poet, his first question would be,—"Young man, what sort of dreams have you?" I have so much faith in my old friend's theory, that when I feel that idle vein returning upon me, I presently subside into my proper element of prose, remembering those eluding nereids, and that inauspicious inland landing.

[October 1821]   [1823]

DREAM-CHILDREN; A REVERIE

CHILDREN love to listen to stories about their elders, when *they* were children; to stretch their imagination to the conception of a traditionary great-uncle, or grandame, whom they never saw. It was in this spirit that my little ones crept about me the other evening to hear about their great-grandmother Field, who lived in a great house in Norfolk (a hundred times bigger than that in which they and papa lived) which had been the scene—so at least it was generally believed in that part of the country—of the tragic incidents which they had lately become familiar with from the ballad of the Children in the Wood. Certain it is that the whole story of the children and their cruel uncle was to be seen fairly carved out in wood upon the chimney-piece of the great hall, the whole story

---

[16] A collection or breed.

[17] Charles and Mary Lamb had paid a visit to the Lake District in 1802, during which they crossed the mountain Helvellyn.

[18] *Kubla Kahn*, l. 3.

[19] Barry Cornwall [Bryan Waller Procter] (1787–1874) was a poet and dramatist. "A Dream" was published in *Dramatic Scenes and other Poems* (1819). The dreamer imagines he is on the ocean and has the power to summon from the depths both real and mythological figures of the past. The boisterous celebration of the birth of Neptune's son concludes the poem and dissolves the dream.

[20] In Greek mythology, the daughter of Cadmus who threw herself into the sea in order to escape the threats of her maddened husband. She was transformed into a goddess of the sea and the benevolent protectress of ships and sailors.

[21] The residence of the Archbishop of Canterbury on the banks of the Thames in London.

down to the Robin Redbreasts,[1] till a foolish rich person pulled it down to set up a marble one of modern invention in its stead, with no story upon it. Here Alice put out one of her dear mother's looks, too tender to be called upbraiding. Then I went on to say, how religious and how good their great-grandmother Field was, how beloved and respected by every body, though she was not indeed the mistress of this great house, but had only the charge of it (and yet in some respects she might be said to be the mistress of it too) committed to her by the owner, who preferred living in a newer and more fashionable mansion which he had purchased somewhere in the adjoining county; but still she lived in it in a manner as if it had been her own, and kept up the dignity of the great house in a sort while she lived, which afterwards came to decay, and was nearly pulled down, and all its old ornaments stripped and carried away to the owner's other house, where they were set up, and looked as awkward as if some one were to carry away the old tombs they had seen lately at the Abbey, and stick them up in Lady C.'s tawdry gilt drawing-room. Here John smiled, as much as to say, "that would be foolish indeed." And then I told how, when she came to die, her funeral was attended by a concourse of all the poor, and some of the gentry too, of the neighbourhood for many miles round, to show their respect for her memory, because she had been such a good and religious woman; so good indeed that she knew all the Psaltery by heart, ay, and a great part of the Testament besides. Here little Alice spread her hands. Then I told what a tall, upright, graceful person their great-grandmother Field once was; and how in her youth she was esteemed the best dancer—here Alice's little right foot played an involuntary movement, till, upon my looking grave, it desisted—the best dancer, I was saying, in the county, till a cruel disease, called a cancer, came, and bowed her down with pain; but it could never bend her good spirits, or make them stoop, but they were still upright, because she was so good and religious. Then I told how she was used to sleep by herself in a lone chamber of the great lone house; and how she believed that an apparition of two infants was to be seen at midnight gliding up and down the great staircase near where she slept, but she said "those innocents would do her no harm"; and how frightened I used to be, though in those days I had my maid to sleep with me, because I was never half so good or religious as she—and yet I never saw the infants. Here

John expanded all his eye-brows and tried to look courageous. Then I told how good she was to all her grand-children, having us to the great-house in the holydays, where I in particular used to spend many hours by myself, in gazing upon the old busts of the Twelve Caesars, that had been Emperors of Rome, till the old marble heads would seem to live again, or I to be turned into marble with them; how I never could be tired with roaming about that huge mansion, with its vast empty rooms, with their worn-out hangings, fluttering tapestry, and carved oaken pannels, with the gilding almost rubbed out—sometimes in the spacious old-fashioned gardens, which I had almost to myself, unless when now and then a solitary gardening man would cross me—and how the nectarines and peaches hung upon the walls, without my ever offering to pluck them, because they were forbidden fruit, unless now and then,—and because I had more pleasure in strolling about among the old melancholy-looking yew trees, or the firs, and picking up the red berries, and the fir apples, which were good for nothing but to look at—or in lying about upon the fresh grass, with all the fine garden smells around me—or basking in the orangery, till I could almost fancy myself ripening too along with the oranges and the limes in that grateful warmth—or in watching the dace that darted to and fro in the fish-pond, at the bottom of the garden, with here and there a great sulky pike hanging midway down the water in silent state, as if it mocked at their impertinent friskings,—I had more pleasure in these busy-idle diversions than in all the sweet flavours of peaches, nectarines, oranges, and such like common baits of children. Here John slyly deposited back upon the plate a bunch of grapes, which, not unobserved by Alice, he had meditated dividing with her, and both seemed willing to relinquish them for the present as irrelevant. Then in somewhat a more heightened tone, I told how, though their grandmother Field loved all her grand-children, yet in an especial manner she might be said to love their uncle, John L——,[2] because he was so handsome and spirited a youth, and a king to the rest of us; and, instead of moping about in solitary corners, like some of us, he would mount the most mettlesome horse he could get, when but an imp no bigger than themselves, and make it carry him half over the county in a morning, and join the hunters when there were any out—and yet he loved the old great house and gardens too, but had too much spirit to be always pent up within their boundaries—and how their uncle grew up to man's estate as brave as he was handsome, to the

---

[1] "Children in the Wood" was a popular ballad of two orphaned children, whose guardian uncle conspires to kill them in order to obtain their inheritance. They escape death at the hands of hired assassins, but become lost and die in a forest, where a robin covers their bodies with leaves.

[2] John Lamb (James Elia later in this essay) was Charles's older brother, who died in the fall of 1821.

admiration of every body, but of their great-grand-mother Field most especially; and how he used to carry me upon his back when I was a lame-footed boy—for he was a good bit older than me—many a mile when I could not walk for pain;—and how in after life he became lame-footed too, and I did not always (I fear) make allowances enough for him when he was impatient, and in pain, nor remember suffici-ently how considerate he had been to me when I was lame-footed; and how when he died, though he had not been dead an hour, it seemed as if he had died a great while ago, such a distance there is betwixt life and death; and how I bore his death as I thought pretty well at first, but afterwards it haunted and haunted me; and though I did not cry or take it to heart as some do, and as I think he would have done if I had died, yet I missed him all day long, and knew not till then how much I had loved him. I missed his kind-ness, and I missed his crossness, and wished him to be alive again, to be quarrelling with him (for we quarreled sometimes), rather than not have him again, and was as uneasy without him, as he their poor uncle must have been when the doctor took off his limb. Here the children fell a crying, and asked if their little mourning which they had on was not for uncle John, and they looked up, and prayed me not to go on about their uncle, but to tell them some stories about their pretty dead mother. Then I told how for seven long years, in hope sometimes, sometimes in despair, yet persisting ever, I courted the fair Alice W——n;[3] and, as much as children could understand, I explained to them what coyness, and difficulty, and denial meant in maidens—when suddenly, turning to Alice, the soul of the first Alice looked out at her eyes with such a reality of re-presentment, that I became in doubt which of them stood there before me, or whose that bright hair was; and while I stood gazing, both the children gradually grew fainter to my view, receding, and still receding till nothing at last but two mournful features were seen in the uttermost distance, which, without speech, strangely impressed upon me the effects of speech; "We are not of Alice, nor of thee, nor are we children at all. The children of Alice call Bartrum father. We are nothing; less than nothing, and dreams. We are only what might have been, and must wait upon the tedious shores of Lethe millions of ages before we have existence, and a name"[4]—and immediately awaking, I found myself quietly seated

in my bachelor arm-chair, where I had fallen asleep, with the faithful Bridget unchanged by my side—but John L. (or James Elia) was gone for ever.

[January 1822]   [1823]

ON THE ARTIFICIAL COMEDY

Perhaps none of Lamb's writings has provoked so much com-mentary and controversy as this essay. In 1841, Thomas Macaulay offered the following "Victorian" objection:

In the name of art, as well as in the name of virtue, we protest against the principle that the world of pure comedy is one into which no moral enters. If comedy be an imitation, under what-ever conventions, of real life, how is it possible that it can have no reference to the great rule which directs life, and to feelings which are called forth by every incident of life? ... But it is not the fact that the world of these dramatists is a world into which no moral enters. Morality constantly enters into that world, a sound morality, and an unsound morality; the sound morality to be insulted, derided, associated with everything mean and hateful; the unsound morality to be set off to every advantage, and inculcated by all methods, direct and indirect.

For more recent objections (on other grounds) to Lamb's interpre-tation of Restoration comedy, see Leo Hughes, A Century of English Farce *(Princeton: Princeton University Press, 1956), p. 237; and "Restoration Theatre," Stratford-upon-Avon Stud-ies VI (1965), 15, 185. In addition to the various explanations and defenses of Lamb's essay listed in the bibliography, see Stuart Tave's* The Amiable Humorist *(Chicago: University of Chi-cago Press, 1960), pp. 198–201. Tave examines the essay in terms of the evolving comic theory of the eighteenth and early nineteenth centuries and concludes that Lamb's reading of Restoration comedy as presenting "another and magical world, as a respite that lends power to daily life, if only by making it more bearable," will appear "less odd when it is seen in this historical context." Ex-amples of a similar view of comedy are cited from writers as diverse as Gray, Sterne, and Hazlitt.*

It is worth considering that Lamb's essay may be read less as an explicit statement of critical opinion than, like the other Elia Essays, as a dramatic experience for the reader. The pompous "we" of the first paragraph, who are gratified only by highly "virtuous" theatre mirroring our own restricted and negative lives, are gradu-ally led by the playful Elia to enter into the "amoral" world of Restoration comedy. By the end of the sixth paragraph, "we" are able to look back on the strenuously moralistic drama and recognize its essential hypocrisy, its easy gratification of our consciences: "Oh who ... would forego the true scenic delight—the escape from life—the oblivion of consequences ... to sit instead at one of our modern plays—to have his coward conscience (that forsooth must not be left for a moment) stimulated with perpetual appeals—dulled rather, and blunted, as a faculty without repose must be—and his moral vanity pampered with images of notional justice, notional beneficence, lives saved without the spectators' risk, and fortunes given away that cost the author nothing?" Lamb's essay has become "A School for Scandal" for the reader, the exposure of our own limited morality and the opportunity for a fresher and more truthful response to existence.

---

3 See "New Year's Eve," footnote 14, p. 364.
4 Lethe was the river of forgetfulness in the underworld. As described in Book VI of Virgil's *Aeneid*, the souls of the dead must wait a thousand years before drinking the waters of Lethe, which banish all knowledge of the past; they may then return to existence and a new identity.

ON THE ARTIFICIAL COMEDY
OF THE LAST CENTURY

THE ARTIFICIAL Comedy, or Comedy of manners, is quite extinct on our stage. Congreve and Farquhar show their heads once in seven years only, to be exploded and put down instantly. The times cannot bear them. Is it for a few wild speeches, an occasional license of dialogue? I think not altogether. The business of their dramatic characters will not stand the moral test. We screw every thing up to that. Idle gallantry in a fiction, a dream, the passing pageant of an evening, startles us in the same way as the alarming indications of profligacy in a son or ward in real life should startle a parent or guardian. We have no such middle emotions as dramatic interests left. We see a stage libertine playing his loose pranks of two hours' duration, and of no after consequence, with the severe eyes which inspect real vices with their bearings upon two worlds. We are spectators to a plot or intrigue (not reducible in life to the point of strict morality) and take it all for truth. We substitute a real for a dramatic person, and judge him accordingly. We try him in our courts, from which there is no appeal to the *dramatis personæ*, his peers. We have been spoiled with—not sentimental comedy [1]—but a tyrant far more pernicious to our pleasures which has succeeded to it, the exclusive and all devouring drama of common life; [2] where the moral point is every thing; where, instead of the fictitious half-believed personages of the stage (the phantoms of old comedy) we recognize ourselves, our brothers, aunts, kinsfolk, allies, patrons, enemies, —the same as in life,—with an interest in what is going on so hearty and substantial, that we cannot afford our moral judgment, in its deepest and most vital results, to compromise or slumber for a moment. What is *there* transacting, by no modification is made to affect us in any other manner than the same events or characters would do in our relationships of life. We carry our fire-side concerns to the theatre with us. We do not go thither, like our ancestors, to escape from the pressure of reality, so much as to confirm our experience of it; to make assurance double, and take a bond of fate. We must live our toilsome lives twice over, as it was the mournful privilege of Ulysses to

descend twice to the shades. All that neutral ground of character, which stood between vice and virtue; or which in fact was indifferent to neither, where neither properly was called in question; that happy breathing-place from the burthen of a perpetual moral questioning—the sanctuary and quiet Alsatia of hunted casuistry [3]—is broken up and disfranchised, as injurious to the interests of society. The privileges of the place are taken away by law. We dare not dally with images, or names, of wrong. We bark like foolish dogs at shadows. We dread infection from the scenic representation of disorder; and fear a painted pustule. [4] In our anxiety that our morality should not take cold, we wrap it up in a great blanket surtout [5] of precaution against the breeze and sunshine.

I confess for myself that (with no great delinquencies to answer for) I am glad for a season to take an airing beyond the diocese of the strict conscience, —not to live always in the precincts of the law-courts, —but now and then, for a dream-while or so, to imagine a world with no meddling restrictions—to get into recesses, whither the hunter cannot follow me—

> ——Secret shades
> Of woody Ida's inmost grove,
> While yet there was no fear of Jove— [6]

I come back to my cage and my restraint the fresher and more healthy for it. I wear my shackles more contentedly for having respired the breath of an imaginary freedom. I do not know how it is with others, but I feel the better always for the perusal of one of Congreve's—nay, why should I not add even of Wycherley's [7]—comedies. I am the gayer at least for it; and I could never connect those sports of a witty fancy in any shape with any result to be drawn from them to imitation in real life. They are a world of themselves almost as much as fairyland. Take one of their characters, male or female (with few exceptions they are alike), and place it in a modern play, and my virtuous indignation shall rise against the profligate wretch as warmly as the Catos [8] of the pit could desire; because in a modern play I am to judge of the right and the wrong. The standard of *police* is the measure of *political justice*. The atmosphere will blight it, it

---

[1] Sentimental comedy was an eighteenth-century response to the supposed immorality of the Restoration "comedy of manners." In sentimental comedy "the virtues of private life are exhibited, rather than the vices exposed, and the distresses rather than the faults of mankind make our interest in the piece" (Oliver Goldsmith).

[2] The "drama of common life" probably refers to the highly moralistic, humanitarian dramas that came into vogue in the 1790's. Thomas Holcroft (1745–1809) and Mrs. Elizabeth Inchbald (1753–1821) were influential practitioners.

[3] Alsatia was a London district, which until 1697 was a sanctuary for debtors and lawbreakers. Casuistry is a preoccupation with fine, often ingenious questions of moral conduct.

[4] Sign of smallpox infection.

[5] Overcoat.

[6] Milton's "Il Penseroso," ll. 28–30.

[7] William Wycherley (1640–1716) was, perhaps, the most licentious of the Restoration writers of comedy.

[8] Marcus Porcius Cato (234–149 B.C.) held the post of Censor, or supervisor of public morals, in Rome; the name is synonymous with rigorous opposition to immorality and luxury.

cannot live here. It has got into a moral world, where it has no business, from which it must needs fall head-long; as dizzy, and incapable of making a stand, as a Swedenborgian bad spirit that has wandered unawares into the sphere of one of his Good Men, or Angels.[9] But in its own world do we feel the creature is so very bad?—The Fainalls and the Mirabels, the Dorimants and the Lady Touchwoods,[10] in their own sphere, do not offend my moral sense; in fact they do not appeal to it at all. They seem engaged in their proper element. They break through no laws, or conscientious re-straints. They know of none. They have got out of Christendom into the land—what shall I call it?—of cuckoldry—the Utopia of gallantry, where pleasure is duty, and the manners perfect freedom. It is altogether a speculative scene of things, which has no reference whatever to the world that is. No good person can be justly offended as a spectator, because no good person suffers on the stage. Judged morally, every character in these plays—the few exceptions only are *mistakes*— is alike essentially vain and worthless. The great art of Congreve is especially shown in this, that he has en-tirely excluded from his scenes,—some little generosi-ties in the part of Angelica[11] perhaps excepted,—not only any thing like a faultless character, but any pre-tensions to goodness or good feelings whatsoever. Whether he did this designedly, or instinctively, the effect is as happy, as the design (if design) was bold. I used to wonder at the strange power which his Way of the World is particular possesses of interesting you all along in the pursuits of characters, for whom you absolutely care nothing—for you neither hate nor love his personages—and I think it is owing to this very indifference for any, that you endure the whole. He has spread a privation of moral light, I will call it, rather than by the ugly name of palpable darkness, over his creations; and his shadows flit before you without distinction or preference. Had he introduced a good character, a single gush of moral feeling, a revulsion of the judgment to actual life and actual duties, the im-pertinent Goshen would have only lighted to the dis-covery of deformities, which now are none, because we think them none.

Translated into real life, the characters of his, and his friend Wycherley's dramas, are profligates and strumpets,—the business of their brief existence, the undivided pursuit of lawless gallantry. No other spring of action, or possible motive of conduct, is recognised;

principles which, universally acted upon, must reduce this frame of things to a chaos. But we do them wrong in so translating them. No such effects are produced in *their* world. When we are among them, we are amongst a chaotic people. We are not to judge them by our usages. No reverend institutions are insulted by their proceedings,—for they have none among them. No peace of families is violated,—for no family ties exist among them. No purity of the marriage bed is stained, —for none is supposed to have a being. No deep affec-tions are disquieted,—no holy wedlock bands are snapped asunder,—for affection's depth and wedded faith are not of the growth of that soil. There is neither right nor wrong,—gratitude or its opposite,—claim or duty,—paternity or sonship. Of what consequence is it to virtue, or how is she at all concerned about it, whether Sir Simon, or Dapperwit, steal away Miss Martha; or who is the father of Lord Froth's, or Sir Paul Pliant's children.[12]

The whole is a passing pageant, where we should sit as unconcerned at the issues, for life or death, as at a battle of frogs and mice.[13] But, like Don Quixote, we take part against the puppets,[14] and quite as im-pertinently. We dare not contemplate an Atlantis,[15] a scheme, out of which our coxcombical moral sense is for a little transitory ease excluded. We have not the courage to imagine a state of things for which there is neither reward nor punishment. We cling to the pain-ful necessities of shame and blame. We would indict our very dreams.

Amidst the mortifying circumstances attendant upon growing old, it is something to have seen the School for Scandal in its glory. The comedy grew out of Congreve and Wycherley, but gathered some allays of the sentimental comedy which followed theirs. It is impossible that it should be now *acted*, though it con-tinues, at long intervals, to be announced in the bills. Its hero, when Palmer played it at least, was Joseph Surface.[16] When I remember the gay boldness, the graceful solemn plausibility, the measured step, the insinuating voice—to express it in a word—the down-right *acted* villany of the part, so different from the

---

[9] A reference to the vision of heaven and hell presented in the writings of Emanuel Swedenborg (1688–1772), a Swedish scientist and mystic.

[10] Characters in various Restoration comedies, notable for their amorous intrigues.

[11] The heroine of *Love for Love* (1695).

[12] Sir Simon, Dapperwit, and Miss Martha were characters in Wycherley's *Love in a Wood* (1671). Lord Froth and Sir Paul Pliant were characters in Congreve's *Double Dealer* (1694).

[13] A reference to the *Batrachomyomachia*, a mock-heroic Greek poem in the style of Homeric battle scenes, but with frogs and mice as the opposing forces.

[14] See *Don Quixote*, Part II, Chapter 26, in which the Don takes the actions and figures in a puppet show for reality, and attacks and destroys the villainous characters.

[15] A fabulous island, the site of an ideal society described in Plato's *Critias*.

[16] John Palmer (c. 1742–1798), created the role of Joseph Sur-face the scheming hypocrite, who contrasts sharply with his spontaneous, good-natured brother Charles.

pressure of conscious actual wickedness,—the hypo-critical assumption of hypocrisy,—which made Jack so deservedly a favourite in that character, I must needs conclude the present generation of playgoers more virtuous than myself, or more dense. I freely confess that he divided the palm with me with his better brother; that, in fact, I liked him quite as well. Not but there are passages,—like that, for instance, where Joseph is made to refuse a pittance to a poor relation,—incongruities which Sheridan was forced upon by the attempt to join the artificial with the sentimental comedy, either of which must destroy the other—but over these obstructions Jack's manner floated him so lightly, that a refusal from him no more shocked you, than the easy compliance of Charles gave you in reality any pleasure; you got over the paltry question as quickly as you could, to get back into the regions of pure comedy, where no cold moral reigns. The highly artificial manner of Palmer in this charac-ter counteracted every disagreeable impression which you might have received from the contrast, supposing them real, between the two brothers. You did not believe in Joseph with the same faith with which you believed in Charles. The latter was a pleasant reality, the former a no less pleasant poetical foil to it. The comedy, I have said, is incongruous; a mixture of Congreve with sentimental incompatibilities: the gaiety upon the whole is buoyant; but it required the consummate art of Palmer to reconcile the discordant elements.

A player with Jack's talents, if we had one now, would not dare to do the part in the same manner. He would instinctively avoid every turn which might tend to unrealise, and so to make the character fascinating. He must take his cue from his spectators, who would expect a bad man and a good man as rigidly opposed to each other as the death-beds of those geniuses are contrasted in the prints, which I am sorry to say have disappeared from the windows of my old friend Car-rington Bowles, of St. Paul's Church-yard memory—(an exhibition as venerable as the adjacent cathedral, and almost coeval) of the bad and good man at the hour of death; where the ghastly apprehensions of the for-mer,—and truly the grim phantom with his reality of a toasting fork is not to be despised,—so finely con-trast with the meek complacent kissing of the rod,—taking it in like honey and butter,—with which the latter submits to the scythe of the gentle bleeder, Time, who wields his lancet with the apprehensive finger of a popular young ladies' surgeon. What flesh, like loving grass, would not covet to meet half-way the stroke of such a delicate mower?—John Palmer was twice an actor in this exquisite part. He was playing to you all the while that he was playing upon Sir Peter

and his lady. You had the first intimation of a senti-ment before it was on his lips. His altered voice was meant to you, and you were to suppose that his fictitious co-flutterers on the stage perceived nothing at all of it. What was it to you if that half-reality, the husband, was over-reached by the puppetry—or the thin thing (Lady Teazle's reputation) was persuaded it was dying of a plethory? [17] The fortunes of Othello and Desdemona were not concerned in it. Poor Jack has past from the stage in good time, that he did not live to this our age of seriousness. The pleasant old Teazle *King*,[18] too, is gone in good time. His manner would scarce have past current in our day. We must love or hate—acquit or condemn—censure or pity—exert our detestable coxcombry of moral judgment upon every thing. Joseph Surface, to go down now, must be a downright revolting villain—no compromise—his first appearance must shock and give horror—his specious plausibilities, which the pleasurable faculties of our fathers welcomed with such hearty greetings, knowing that no harm (dramatic harm even) could come, or was meant to come to them, must in-spire a cold and killing aversion. Charles (the real canting person of the scene—for the hypocrisy of Joseph has its ulterior legitimate ends, but his brother's professions of a good heart centre in down-right self-satisfaction) must be *loved*, and Joseph *hated*. To balance one disagreeable reality with an-other, Sir Peter Teazle must be no longer the comic idea of a fretful old bachelor bridegroom, whose teasings (while King acted it) were evidently as much played off at you, as they were meant to concern any body on the stage,—he must be a real person, capable in law of sustaining an injury—a person towards whom duties are to be acknowledged—the genuine crim-con antagonist[19] of the villanous seducer Joseph. To realise him more, his sufferings under his unfortunate match must have the downright pungency of life—must (or should) make you not mirthful but uncom-fortable, just as the same predicament would move you in a neighbour or old friend. The delicious scenes which give the play its name and zest, must affect you in the same serious manner as if you heard the reputa-tion of a dear female friend attacked in your real presence. Crabtree, and Sir Benjamin—those poor snakes that live but in the sunshine of your mirth—

---

[17] Overabundance, excess. Lamb is recalling the seductive argument of Joseph to Lady Teazle that her reputation has been subject to suspicion and gossip precisely because she is so per-sistently virtuous and circumspect in her conduct. See Act IV, iii.
[18] Thomas King (1730–1805) played Sir Peter in the first production of *School for Scandal*.
[19] The wounded party in a case of adultery ("criminal con-versation").

must be ripened by this hot-bed process of realization into asps or amphisbaenas;[20] and Mrs. Candour—O! frightful! become a hooded serpent. Oh who that remembers Parsons and Dodd—the wasp and butterfly of the School for Scandal—in those two characters; and charming natural Miss Pope,[21] the perfect gentlewoman as distinguished from the fine lady of comedy, in this latter part—would forego the true scenic delight—the escape from life—the oblivion of consequences—the holiday barring out of the pedant Reflection—those Saturnalia[22] of two or three brief hours, well won from the world—to sit instead at one of our modern plays—to have his coward conscience (that forsooth must not be left for a moment) stimulated with perpetual appeals—dulled rather, and blunted, as a faculty without repose must be—and his moral vanity pampered with images of notional justice, notional beneficence, lives saved without the spectators' risk, and fortunes given away that cost the author nothing?

No piece, was, perhaps, ever so completely cast in all its parts as this *manager's comedy*.[23] Miss Farren had succeeded to Mrs. Abington in Lady Teazle; and Smith,[24] the original Charles, had retired, when I first saw it. The rest of the characters, with very slight exceptions, remained. I remember it was then the fashion to cry down John Kemble, who took the part of Charles after Smith; but, I thought, very unjustly. Smith, I fancy, was more airy, and took the eye with a certain gaiety of person. He brought with him no sombre recollections of tragedy. He had not to expiate the fault of having pleased beforehand in lofty declamation. He had no sins of Hamlet or of Richard to atone for. His failure in these parts was a passport to success in one of so opposite a tendency. But, as far as I could judge, the weighty sense of Kemble made up for more personal incapacity than he had to answer for. His harshest tones in this part came steeped and dulcified in good humour. He made his defects a grace. His exact declamatory manner, as he managed it, only served to convey the points of his dialogue with more precision. It seemed to head the shafts to carry them deeper. Not one of his sparkling sentences was lost. I remember minutely how he delivered each in succession, and cannot by any effort imagine how any of them could be altered for the better. No man could

deliver brilliant dialogue—the dialogue of Congreve or of Wycherley—because none understood it—half so well as John Kemble. His Valentine, in Love for Love, was, to my recollection, faultless. He flagged sometimes in the intervals of tragic passion. He would slumber over the level parts of an heroic character. His Macbeth has been known to nod. But he always seemed to me to be particularly alive to pointed and witty dialogue. The relaxing levities of tragedy have not been touched by any since him—the playful courtbred spirit in which he condescended to the players in Hamlet—the sportive relief which he threw into the darker shades of Richard—disappeared with him. He had his sluggish moods, his torpors—but they were the halting-stones and resting-places of his tragedy—politic savings, and fetches of the breath—husbandry of the lungs, where nature pointed him to be an economist—rather, I think, than errors of the judgment. They were, at worst, less painful than the eternal tormenting unappeasable vigilance, the "lidless dragon eyes,"[25] of present fashionable tragedy.

[April 1822]   [1823]

OLD CHINA

I HAVE an almost feminine partiality for old china. When I go to see any great house, I inquire for the china-closet, and next for the picture gallery. I cannot defend the order of preference, but by saying, that we have all some taste or other, of too ancient a date to admit of our remembering distinctly that it was an acquired one. I can call to mind the first play, and the first exhibition, that I was taken to; but I am not conscious of a time when china jars and saucers were introduced into my imagination.

I had no repugnance then—why should I now have? —to those little, lawless, azure-tinctured grotesques, that under the notion of men and women, float about, uncircumscribed by any element, in that world before perspective—a china tea-cup.

I like to see my old friends—whom distance cannot diminish—figuring up in the air (so they appear to our optics), yet on *terra firma* still—for so we must in courtesy interpret that speck of deeper blue, which the decorous artist, to prevent absurdity, has made to spring up beneath their sandals.

I love the men with women's faces, and the women, if possible, with still more womanish expressions.

Here is a young and courtly Mandarin, handing tea to a lady from a salver—two miles off. See how distance

---

[20] Fabulous snakes with a head at both ends.
[21] William Parsons (1736–1795), James William Dodd (*c.* 1740–1796), and Jane Pope (1742–1818).
[22] Periods of unrestrained revelry and license.
[23] Sheridan was manager of Drury Lane Theatre when *The School for Scandal* was first produced in May 1777.
[24] Elizabeth Farren (*c.* 1759–1829), afterwards the Countess of Derby; Frances Abington (1737–1815); and William ("Gentleman") Smith (*c.* 1730–1819).

[25] Coleridge's "Ode to the Departing Year", l. 145.

seems to set off respect! And here the same lady, or another—for likeness is identity on tea-cups—is stepping into a little fairy boat, moored on the hither side of this calm garden river, with a dainty mincing foot, which in a right angle of incidence (as angles go in our world) must infallibly land her in the midst of a flowery mead—a furlong off on the other side of the same strange stream!

Farther on—if far or near can be predicated of their world—see horses, trees, pagodas, dancing the hays![1]

Here—a cow and rabbit couchant,[2] and co-extensive—so objects show, seen through the lucid atmosphere of fine Cathay.

I was pointing out to my cousin last evening, over our Hyson,[3] (which we are old fashioned enough to drink unmixed still of an afternoon) some of these *speciosa miracula*[4] upon a set of extraordinary old blue china (a recent purchase) which we were now for the first time using; and could not help remarking, how favourable circumstances had been to us of late years, that we could afford to please the eye sometimes with trifles of this sort—when a passing sentiment seemed to over-shade the brows of my companion. I am quick at detecting these summer clouds in Bridget.

"I wish the good old times would come again," she said, "when we were not quite so rich. I do not mean, that I want to be poor; but there was a middle state;"—so she was pleased to ramble on,—"in which I am sure we were a great deal happier. A purchase is but a purchase, now that you have money enough and to spare. Formerly it used to be a triumph. When we coveted a cheap luxury (and, O! how much ado I had to get you to consent in those times!) we were used to have a debate two or three days before, and to weigh the *for* and *against*, and think what we might spare it out of, and what saving we could hit upon, that should be an equivalent. A thing was worth buying then, when we felt the money that we paid for it.

"Do you remember the brown suit, which you made to hang upon you, till all your friends cried shame upon you, it grew so thread-bare—and all because of that folio Beaumont and Fletcher,[5] which you dragged home late at night from Barker's in Covent-garden? Do you remember how we eyed it for weeks before we could make up our minds to the purchase, and had not come to a determination till it

was near ten o'clock of the Saturday night, when you set off from Islington, fearing you should be too late—and when the old bookseller with some grumbling opened his shop, and by the twinkling taper (for he was setting bedwards) lighted out the relic from his dusty treasures—and when you lugged it home, wishing it were twice as cumbersome—and when you presented it to me—and when we were exploring the perfectness of it (*collating* you called it)—and while I was repairing some of the loose leaves with paste, which your impatience would not suffer to be left till day-break—was there no pleasure in being a poor man? or can those neat black clothes which you wear now, and are so careful to keep brushed, since we have become rich and finical, give you half the honest vanity, with which you flaunted it about in that over-worn suit—your old corbeau[6]—for four or five weeks longer than you should have done, to pacify your conscience for the mighty sum of fifteen—or sixteen shillings was it?—a great affair we thought it then—which you had lavished on the old folio. Now you can afford to buy any book that pleases you, but I do not see that you ever bring me home any nice old purchases now.

"When you came home with twenty apologies for laying out a less number of shillings upon that print after Lionardo, which we christened the 'Lady Blanch;' when you looked at the purchase, and thought of the money—and thought of the money, and looked again at the picture—was there no pleasure in being a poor man? Now, you have nothing to do but to walk into Colnaghi's, and buy a wilderness of Lionardos. Yet do you?

"Then, do you remember our pleasant walks to Enfield, and Potter's Bar, and Waltham, when we had a holyday—holydays, and all other fun, are gone, now we are rich—and the little hand-basket in which I used to deposit our day's fare of savory cold lamb and salad—and how you would pry about at noon-tide for some decent house, where we might go in, and produce our store—only paying for the ale that you must call for—and speculate upon the looks of the landlady, and whether she was likely to allow us a table-cloth—and wish for such another honest hostess, as Izaak Walton has described many a one on the pleasant banks of the Lea, when he went a fishing—and sometimes they would prove obliging enough, and sometimes they would look grudgingly upon us—but we had cheerful looks still for one another, and would eat our plain food savorily, scarcely grudging Piscator[7]

---

[1] A country dance akin to a reel.
[2] An heraldic term, indicating an animal lying down but with head raised.
[3] A species of green tea.
[4] *speciosa miracula*: "beautiful wonders." Horace's *Ars Poetica*, l. 144.
[5] That is, the collected comedies and tragedies of the Jacobean playwrights Francis Beaumont and John Fletcher, which Lamb owned in the 1679 folio edition.

[6] A dark green color verging on black.
[7] Piscator (Latin, "fisherman") was the central character and main speaker in the dialogues that compose Walton's *Complete Angler*.

his Trout Hall? Now, when we go out a day's pleasuring, which is seldom moreover, we *ride* part of the way—and go into a fine inn, and order the best of dinners, never debating the expense—which, after all, never has half the relish of those chance country snaps, when we were at the mercy of uncertain usage, and a precarious welcome.

"You are too proud to see a play anywhere now but in the pit. Do you remember where it was we used to sit, when we saw the battle of Hexham, and the surrender of Calais, and Bannister and Mrs. Bland in the Children in the Wood [8]—when we squeezed out our shillings a-piece to sit three or four times in a season in the one-shilling gallery—where you felt all the time that you ought not to have brought me—and more strongly I felt obligation to you for having brought me —and the pleasure was the better for a little shame— and when the curtain drew up, what cared we for our place in the house, or what mattered it where we were sitting, when our thoughts were with Rosalind in Arden, or with Viola at the Court of Illyria? You used to say, that the gallery was the best place of all for enjoying a play socially—that the relish of such exhibitions must be in proportion to the infrequency of going—that the company we met there, not being in general readers of plays, were obliged to attend the more, and did attend, to what was going on, on the stage—because a word lost would have been a chasm, which it was impossible for them to fill up. With such reflections we consoled our pride then—and I appeal to you, whether, as a woman, I met generally with less attention and accommodation, than I have done since in more expensive situations in the house? The getting in indeed, and the crowding up those inconvenient staircases, was bad enough—but there was still a law of civility to women recognized to quite as great an extent as we ever found in the other passages—and how a little difficulty overcome heightened the snug seat, and the play, afterwards! Now we can only pay our money, and walk in. You cannot see, you say, in the galleries now. I am sure we saw, and heard too, well enough then—but sight, and all, I think, is gone with our poverty.

"There was pleasure in eating strawberries, before they became quite common—in the first dish of peas, while they were yet dear—to have them for a nice supper, a treat. What treat can we have now? If we were to treat ourselves now—that is, to have dainties a little above our means, it would be selfish and wicked.

---

[8] *The Battle of Hexham* (1789) and *The Surrender of Calais* (1791) were musical dramas by George Colman, the younger. *Children in the Wood* (1793) was a popular musical drama by Thomas Morton.

It is the very little more that we allow ourselves beyond what the actual poor can get at, that makes what I call a treat—when two people living together, as we have done, now and then indulge themselves in a cheap luxury, which both like; while each apologises, and is willing to take both halves of the blame to his single share. I see no harm in people making much of themselves in that sense of the word. It may give them a hint how to make much of others. But now—what I mean by the word—we never do make much of ourselves. None but the poor can do it. I do not mean the veriest poor of all, but persons as we were, just above poverty.

"I know what you were going to say, that it is mighty pleasant at the end of the year to make all meet —and much ado we used to have every Thirty-first night of December to account for our exceedings— many a long face did you make over your puzzled accounts, and in contriving to make it out how we had spent so much—or that we had not spent so much— or that it was impossible we should spend so much next year—and still we found our slender capital decreasing—but then, betwixt ways, and projects, and compromises of one sort of another, and talk of curtailing this charge, and doing without that for the future—and the hope that youth brings, and laughing spirits (in which you were never poor till now,) we pocketed up our loss, and in conclusion, with 'lusty brimmers' (as you used to quote it out of *hearty cheerful Mr. Cotton*, as you called him), we used to welcome in the 'coming guest.' Now we have no reckoning at all at the end of the old year—no flattering promises about the new year doing better for us."

Bridget is so sparing of her speech on most occasions, that when she gets into a rhetorical vein, I am careful how to interrupt it. I could not help, however, smiling at the phantom of wealth which her dear imagination had conjured up out of a clear income of poor --- hundred pounds a year. "It is true we were happier when we were poorer, but we were also younger, my cousin. I am afraid we must put up with the excess, for if we were to shake the superflux into the sea, we should not much mend ourselves. That we had much to struggle with, as we grew up together, we have reason to be most thankful. It strengthened, and knit our compact closer. We could never have been what we have been to each other, if we had always had the sufficiency which you now complain of. The resisting power—those natural dilations of the youthful spirit, which circumstances cannot straiten— with us are long since passed away. Competence to age is supplementary youth; a sorry supplement indeed, but I fear the best that is to be had. We must ride, where we formerly walked: live better, and lie softer—and shall be wise to do so—than we had means to do in those good old days you speak of. Yet could those days return—could you and I once more walk our thirty miles a-day—could Bannister and Mrs. Bland again be young, and you and I be young to see them—could the good old one shilling gallery days return—they are dreams, my cousin, now—but could you and I at this moment, instead of this quiet argument, by our well-carpeted fire-side, sitting on this luxurious sofa—we once more struggling up those inconvenient stair-cases, pushed about, and squeezed, and elbowed by the poorest rabble of poor gallery scramblers—could I once more hear those anxious shrieks of yours—and the delicious *Thank God, we are safe*, which always followed when the topmost stair, conquered, let in the first light of the whole cheerful theatre down beneath us—I know not the fathom line that ever touched a descent so deep as I would be willing to bury more wealth in than Croesus [9] had, or the great Jew R——[10] is supposed to have, to purchase it. And now do just look at that merry little Chinese waiter holding an umbrella, big enough for a bedtester, over the head of that pretty insipid half-Madona-ish chit of a lady in that very blue summer house."

[March 1823]   [1833]

BLAKESMOOR IN H——SHIRE

I DO NOT know a pleasure more affecting than to range at will over the deserted apartments of some fine old family mansion. The traces of extinct grandeur admit of a better passion than envy: and contemplations on the great and good, whom we fancy in succession to have been its inhabitants, weave for us illusions, incompatible with the bustle of modern occupancy, and vanities of foolish present aristocracy. The same difference of feeling, I think, attends us between entering an empty and a crowded church. In the latter it is chance but some present human frailty —an act of inattention on the part of some of the auditory—or a trait of affectation, or worse, vain-glory, on that of the preacher—puts us by our best thoughts, disharmonising the place and the occasion. But would'st thou know the beauty of holiness?—go alone on some week-day, borrowing the keys of good Master Sexton, traverse the cool aisles of some country church: think of the piety that has kneeled there—the

congregations, old and young, that have found consolation there—the meek pastor—the docile parishioner. With no disturbing emotions, no cross conflicting comparisons, drink in the tranquillity of the place, till thou thyself become as fixed and motionless as the marble effigies that kneel and weep around thee.

Journeying northward lately, I could not resist going some few miles out of my road to look upon the remains of an old great house with which I had been impressed in this way in infancy.[1] I was apprised that the owner of it had lately pulled it down; still I had a vague notion that it could not all have perished, that so much solidity with magnificence could not have been crushed all at once into the mere dust and rubbish which I found it.

The work of ruin had proceeded with a swift hand indeed, and the demolition of a few weeks had reduced it to—an antiquity.

I was astonished at the indistinction of everything. Where had stood the great gates? What bounded the court-yard? Whereabout did the out-houses commence? a few bricks only lay as representatives of that which was so stately and so spacious.

Death does not shrink up his human victim at this rate. The burnt ashes of a man weigh more in their proportion.

Had I seen these brick-and-mortar knaves at their process of destruction, at the plucking of every pannel I should have felt the varlets at my heart. I should have cried out to them to spare a plank at least out of the cheerful store-room, in whose hot window-seat I used to sit and read Cowley,[2] with the grass-plat before, and the hum and flappings of that one solitary wasp that ever haunted it about me—it is in mine ears now, as oft as summer returns; or a pannel of the yellow room.

Why, every plank and pannel of that house for me had magic in it. The tapestried bed-rooms—tapestry so much better than painting—not adorning merely, but peopling the wainscots—at which childhood ever and anon would steal a look, shifting its coverlid (replaced as quickly) to exercise its tender courage in a momentary eye-encounter with those stern bright visages, staring reciprocally—all Ovid on the walls, in colours vivider than his descriptions. Actaeon in mid sprout, with the unappeasable prudery of Diana; and the still more provoking, and almost culinary coolness of Dan Phoebus, eel-fashion, deliberately divesting of Marsyas.[3]

---

9 King of Lydia (560–546 B.C.), proverbial for enormous wealth.

10 Nathan Meyer Rothschild (1777–1836) was the founder of the London branch of the House of Rothschild, leading financial institution in Europe.

1 See "On the Genius and Character of Hogarth," footnote 1, p. 333.

2 Abraham Cowley (1618–1667), the poet and essayist.

3 Lamb refers to the Latin poet Publius Ovidius Naso (43 B.C.– A.D. 17), whose most famous work *Metamorphoses* was a series of mythological tales involving the transformations of characters:

Then, that haunted room—in which old Mrs. Battle died—whereinto I have crept, but always in the day-time, with a passion of fear; and a sneaking curiosity, terror-tainted, to hold communication with the past. —*How shall they build it up again?*

It was an old deserted place, yet not so long deserted but that traces of the splendour of past inmates were everywhere apparent. Its furniture was still standing —even to the tarnished gilt leather battledores,[4] and crumbling feathers of shuttlecocks in the nursery, which told that children had once played there. But I was a lonely child, and had the range at will of every apartment, knew every nook and corner, wondered and worshipped everywhere.

The solitude of childhood is not so much the mother of thought, as it is the feeder of love, and silence, and admiration. So strange a passion for the place possessed me in those years, that, though there lay—I shame to say how few roods distant from the mansion—half hid by trees, what I judged some romantic lake, such was the spell which bound me to the house, and such my carefulness not to pass its strict and proper precincts, that the idle waters lay unexplored for me; and not till late in life, curiosity prevailing over elder devotion, I found, to my aston-ishment, a pretty brawling brook had been the Lacus Incognitus[5] of my infancy. Variegated views, exten-sive prospects—and those at no great distance from the house—I was told of such—what were they to me, being out of the boundaries of my Eden?—So far from a wish to roam, I would have drawn, methought, still closer the fences of my chosen prison; and have been hemmed in by a yet securer cincture of those excluding garden walls. I could have exclaimed with that garden-loving poet[6]—

> Bind me, ye woodbines, in your twines;
> Curl me about, ye gadding vines;
> And oh so close your circles lace,
> That I may never leave this place;
> But, lest your fetters prove too weak,
> Ere I your silken bondage break,
> Do you, O brambles, chain me too,
> And courteous briars, nail me through.

I was here as in a lonely temple. Snug firesides— the low-built roof—parlours ten feet by ten—frugal boards, and all the homeliness of home—these were the condition of my birth—the wholesome soil which I was planted in.[7] Yet, without impeachment to their tenderest lessons, I am not sorry to have had glances of something beyond; and to have taken, if but a peep, in childhood, at the contrasting accidents of a great fortune.

To have the feeling of gentility, it is not necessary to have been born gentle. The pride of ancestry may be had on cheaper terms than to be obliged to an im-portunate race of ancestors; and the coatless antiquary in his unemblazoned cell, revolving the long line of a Mowbray's or De Clifford's pedigree, at those sound-ing names may warm himself into as gay a vanity as those who do inherit them. The claims of birth are ideal merely, and what herald shall go about to strip me of an idea? Is it trenchant to their swords? can it be hacked off as a spur can? or torn away like a tarnished garter?

What, else, were the families of the great to us? what pleasure should we take in their tedious genealogies, or their capitulatory[8] brass monuments? What to us the uninterrupted current of their bloods, if our own did not answer within us to a cognate and correspond-ent elevation?

Or wherefore, else, O tattered and diminished 'Scutcheon that hung upon the time-worn walls of thy princely stairs, BLAKESMOOR! have I in childhood so oft stood poring upon thy mystic characters— thy emblematic supporters, with their prophetic "Re-surgam"[9]—till, every dreg of peasantry purging off, I received into myself Very Gentility? Thou were first in my morning eyes; and of nights, hast detained my steps from bedward, till it was but a step from gazing at thee to dreaming on thee.

This is the only true gentry by adoption; the veri-table change of blood, and not, as empirics have fabled, by transfusion.

Who it was by dying that had earned the splendid trophy, I know not, I inquired not; but its fading rags, and colours cobweb-stained, told that its subject was of two centuries back.

And what if my ancestor at that date was some Damoetas—feeding flocks, not his own, upon the hills of Lincoln—did I in less earnest vindicate to myself the family trappings of this once proud Ægon?[10]—

Actaeon was changed into a stag and destroyed by his own hunt-ing dogs, for daring to observe Diana bathing; Marsyas was flayed alive by Apollo (Phoebus) for challenging the god in song, then changed into a river.

[4] Small rackets used in a game with shuttlecocks.

[5] Lacus Incognitus: "unknown lake."

[6] Andrew Marvell. Lamb quotes from "Upon Appleton House," stanza LXXVII.

[7] The "here" is "Blakesmoor." The "snug firesides" and following refer to Lamb's birthplace and childhood residence in London at the Inner Temple of the Inns of Court.

[8] Presenting a summary of great deeds.

[9] Resurgam: "I shall rise again."

[10] In Virgil's Third Eclogue, Damoetas tended the flock of Ægon, while the latter courted the shepherdess Neaera. The reference to Lincoln is to the Lamb family origins in Lincolnshire.

repaying by a backward triumph the insults he might possibly have heaped in his life-time upon my poor pastoral progenitor.

If it were presumption so to speculate, the present owners of the mansion had least reason to complain. They had long forsaken the old house of their fathers for a newer trifle; and I was left to appropriate to myself what images I could pick up, to raise my fancy, or to soothe my vanity.

I was the true descendant of those old W——s;[11] and not the present family of that name, who had fled the old waste places.

Mine was the gallery of good old family portraits, which as I have gone over, giving them in fancy my own family name, one—and then another—would seem to smile, reaching forward from the canvas, to recognize the new relationship; while the rest looked grave, as it seemed, at the vacancy in their dwelling, and thoughts of fled posterity.

That Beauty with the cool blue pastoral drapery, and a lamb—that hung next the great bay window— with the bright yellow H——shire hair, and eye of watchet blue[12]—so like my Alice![13]—I am persuaded she was a true Elia—Mildred Elia, I take it.

Mine, too, BLAKESMOOR, was thy noble Marble Hall, with its mosaic pavements, and its Twelve Caesars—stately busts in marble—ranged round: of whose countenances, young reader of faces as I was, the frowning beauty of Nero, I remember, had most of my wonder; but the mild Galba[14] had my love. There they stood in the coldness of death, yet freshness of immortality.

Mine too, thy lofty Justice Hall, with its one chair of authority, high-backed and wickered, once the terror of luckless poacher, or self-forgetful maiden— so common since, that bats have roosted in it.

Mine too—whose else?—thy costly fruit-garden, with its sun-baked southern wall; the ampler pleasure-garden, rising backwards from the house in triple terraces, with flower-pots now of palest lead, save that a speck here and there, saved from the elements, bespake their pristine state to have been gilt and glittering; the verdant quarters backwarder still; and, stretching still beyond, in old formality, thy firry wilderness, the haunt of the squirrel, and the daylong murmuring woodpigeon, with that antique image in the centre, God or Goddess I wist not; but child of Athens or old Rome paid never a sincerer worship to Pan or to Sylvanus[15] in their native groves, than I to that fragmental mystery.

Was it for this, that I kissed my childish hands too fervently in your idol worship, walks and windings of BLAKESMOOR! for this, or what sin of mine, has the plough passed over your pleasant places? I sometimes think that as men, when they die, do not die all, so of their extinguished habitations there may be a hope—a germ to be revivified.

[September 1824]   [1833]

THE SUPERANNUATED MAN

See George Williamson's "The Equation of the Essay," *Sewanee Review, XXXV (1927), 73–77, which compares* *Lamb's letters to various correspondents regarding his retirement* *with the fuller "intimacy" achieved in the "impersonality" of* *the essay.*

THE SUPERANNUATED MAN

Sera tamen respexit
Libertas.   VIRGIL.

A Clerk I was in London gay.   O'KEEFE.[1]

IF PERADVENTURE, Reader, it has been thy lot to waste the golden years of thy life—thy shining youth —in the irksome confinement of an office; to have thy prison days prolonged through middle age down to decrepitude and silver hairs, without hope of release or respite; to have lived to forget that there are such things as holidays, or to remember them but as the prerogatives of childhood; then, and then only, will you be able to appreciate my deliverance.

It is now six and thirty years since I took my seat at the desk in Mincing-lane.[2] Melancholy was the transition at fourteen from the abundant playtime, and the frequently-intervening vacations of school days, to the eight, nine, and sometimes ten hours' a-day attendance at the counting-house. But time partially reconciles us

---

11 Lamb's pseudonym for the Plumer family, who owned Blakesware.

12 Light or sky blue.

13 See "New Year's Eve," footnote 14, p. 364.

14 Roman emperor (A.D. 68–69) following the death of Nero.

15 Mythological gods of the woods and pastoral life.

1 Sera . . . Libertas: "Though late in doing so Liberty looked kindly [on me]," Virgil's First Eclogue, l. 28. "A Clerk I was in London gay" was a song from the third act of the comic opera *Inkle and Yarico* (1787) by George Colman the younger (1762–1836), not the work of John O'Keefe (1747–1833), another popular writer of comedies.

2 Lamb retired from the East India House in March 1825; thirty-six years earlier would actually mark his departure from Christ's Hospital, not his employment as a clerk, which did not begin until 1791 (South-Sea House) and 1792 (East India House). Mincing-lane was a street in the heart of the business and financial district of London. The East India House was actually located in neighboring Leadenhall Street. Throughout the essay, as in this instance, Lamb disguises the exact details of his employment.

to anything. I gradually became content—doggedly contented, as wild animals in cages.

It is true I had my Sundays to myself; but Sundays, admirable as the institution of them is for purposes of worship, are for that very reason the very worst adapted for days of unbending and recreation. In particular, there is a gloom for me attendant upon a city Sunday; a weight in the air. I miss the cheerful cries of London, the music, and the ballad-singers—the buzz and stirring murmur of the streets. Those eternal bells depress me. The closed shops repel me. Prints, pictures, all the glittering and endless succession of knacks and gewgaws, and ostentatiously displayed wares of tradesmen, which make a week-day saunter through the less busy parts of the metropolis so delightful—are shut out. No book-stalls deliciously to idle over—no busy faces to recreate the idle man who contemplates them ever passing by—the very face of business a charm by contrast to his temporary relaxation from it. Nothing to be seen but unhappy countenances—or half-happy at best—of emancipated 'prentices and little tradesfolks, with here and there a servant maid that has got leave to go out, who, slaving all the week, with the habit has lost almost the capacity of enjoying a free hour; and livelily expressing the hollowness of a day's pleasuring. The very strollers in the fields on that day look anything but comfortable.

But besides Sundays I had a day at Easter, and a day at Christmas, with a full week in the summer to go and air myself in my native fields of Hertfordshire. This last was a great indulgence; and the prospect of its recurrence, I believe, alone kept me up through the year, and made my durance tolerable. But when the week came round, did the glittering phantom of the distance keep touch with me? or rather was it not a series of seven uneasy days, spent in restless pursuit of pleasure, and a wearisome anxiety to find out how to make the most of them? Where was the quiet, where the promised rest? Before I had a taste of it, it was vanished. I was at the desk again, counting upon the fifty-one tedious weeks that must intervene before such another snatch would come. Still the prospect of its coming threw something of an illumination upon the darker side of my captivity. Without it, as I have said, I could scarcely have sustained my thraldom.

Independently of the rigours of attendance, I have ever been haunted with a sense (perhaps a mere caprice) of incapacity for business. This, during my latter years, had increased to such a degree, that it was visible in all the lines of my countenance. My health and my good spirits flagged. I had perpetually a dread of some crisis, to which I should be found unequal. Besides my daylight servitude, I served over again all night in my sleep, and would awake with terrors of imaginary false entries, errors in my accounts, and the like. I was fifty years of age, and no prospect of emancipation presented itself. I had grown to my desk, as it were; and the wood had entered into my soul.

My fellows in the office would sometimes rally me upon the trouble legible in my countenance; but I did not know that it had raised the suspicions of any of my employers, when, on the 5th of last month, a day ever to be remembered by me, L——, the junior partner in the firm, calling me on one side, directly taxed me with my bad looks, and frankly inquired the cause of them. So taxed, I honestly made confession of my infirmity, and added that I was afraid I should eventually be obliged to resign his service. He spoke some words of course to hearten me, and there the matter rested. A whole week I remained labouring under the impression that I had acted imprudently in my disclosure; that I had foolishly given a handle against myself, and had been anticipating my own dismissal. A week passed in this manner, the most anxious one, I verily believe, in my whole life, when on the evening of the 12th of April, just as I was about quitting my desk to go home (it might be about eight o'clock) I received an awful summons to attend the presence of the whole assembled firm in the formidable back parlour. I thought, now my time is surely come, I have done for myself, I am going to be told that they have no longer occasion for me. L——, I could see, smiled at the terror I was in, which was a little relief to me,—when to my utter astonishment B——, the eldest partner, began a formal harangue to me on the length of my services, my very meritorious conduct during the whole of the time (the deuce, thought I, how did he find out that? I protest I never had the confidence to think as much). He went on to descant [3] on the expediency of retiring at a certain time of life (how my heart panted!) and asking me a few questions as to the amount of my own property, of which I have a little, ended with a proposal, to which his three partners nodded a grave assent, that I should accept from the house, which I had served so well, a pension for life to the amount of two-thirds of my accustomed salary—a magnificent offer! I do not know what I answered between surprise and gratitude, but it was understood that I accepted their proposal, and I was told that I was free from that hour to leave their service. I stammered out a bow, and at just ten minutes after eight I went home—for ever. This noble benefit—gratitude forbids me to conceal their names—I owe to the kindness of the most munificent firm in the world—the house of Boldero, Merryweather, Bosanquet, and Lacy.

<hr/>

[3] To comment or discourse at large.

Esto perpetua! [4]

For the first day or two I felt stunned, overwhelmed. I could only apprehend my felicity; I was too confused to taste it sincerely. I wandered about, thinking I was happy, and knowing that I was not. I was in the condition of a prisoner in the old Bastile, suddenly let loose after a forty years' confinement. I could scarce trust myself with myself. It was like passing out of Time into Eternity—for it is a sort of Eternity for a man to have all his Time to himself. It seemed to me that I had more time on my hands than I could ever manage. From a poor man, poor in Time, I was suddenly lifted up into a vast revenue; I could see no end of my possessions; I wanted some steward, or judicious bailiff, to manage my estates in Time for me. And here let me caution persons grown old in active business, not lightly, nor without weighing their own resources, to forego their customary employment all at once; for there may be danger in it. I feel it by myself, but I know that my resources are sufficient; and now that those first giddy raptures have subsided, I have a quiet home-feeling of the blessedness of my condition. I am in no hurry. Having all holidays, I am as though I had none. If Time hung heavy upon me, I could walk it away; but I do *not* walk all day long, as I used to do in those old transient holidays, thirty miles a day, to make the most of them. If Time were troublesome, I could read it away; but I do *not* read in that violent measure, with which, having no Time my own but candlelight Time, I used to weary out my head and eyesight in by-gone winters. I walk, read or scribble (as now) just when the fit seizes me. I no longer hunt after pleasure; I let it come to me. I am like the man

> —That's born and has his years come to him,
> In some green desart. [5]

"Years," you will say! "what is this superannuated simpleton calculating upon ? He has already told us, he is past fifty."

I have indeed lived nominally fifty years, but deduct out of them the hours which I have lived to other people, and not to myself, and you will find me still a young fellow. For *that* is the only true Time, which a man can properly call his own, that which he has all to himself; the rest, though in some sense he may be said to live it, is other people's time, not his. The remnant of my poor days, long or short, is at least multiplied for me threefold. My ten next years, if I stretch so far, will be as long as any preceding thirty. 'Tis a fair rule-of-three sum.

Among the strange fantasies which beset me at the commencement of my freedom, and of which all traces are not yet gone, one was, that a vast tract of time had intervened since I quitted the Counting House. I could not conceive of it as an affair of yesterday. The partners, and the clerks, with whom I had for so many years, and for so many hours in each day of the year, been closely associated—being suddenly removed from them—they seemed as dead to me. There is a fine passage, which may serve to illustrate this fancy, in a Tragedy by Sir Robert Howard, speaking of a friend's death:

> —'T was but just now he went away;
> I have not since had time to shed a tear;
> And yet the distance does the same appear
> As if he had been a thousand years from me.
> Time takes no measure in Eternity. [6]

To dissipate this awkward feeling, I have been fain to go among them once or twice since; to visit my old desk-fellows—my co-brethren of the quill—that I had left below in the state militant. [7] Not all the kindness with which they received me could quite restore to me that pleasant familiarity, which I had heretofore enjoyed among them. We cracked some of our old jokes, but methought they went off but faintly. My old desk; the peg where I hung my hat, were appropriated to another. I knew it must be, but I could not take it kindly. D——l take me, if I did not feel some remorse—beast, if I had not,—at quitting my old compeers, the faithful partners of my toils for six and thirty years, that soothed for me with their jokes and conundrums the ruggedness of my professional road. Had it been so rugged then after all ? or was I a coward simply ? Well, it is too late to repent; and I also know, that these suggestions are a common fallacy of the mind on such occasions. But my heart smote me. I had violently broken the bands betwixt us. It was at least not courteous. I shall be some time before I get quite reconciled to the separation. Farewell, old cronies, yet not for long, for again and again I will come among ye, if I shall have your leave. Farewell, Ch——, dry, sarcastic, and friendly! Do——, mild, slow to move, and gentlemanly! Pl——, officious to do, and to volunteer, good services!—and thou, thou dreary pile, fit mansion

---

[4] *Esto perpetua!*: "May it be forever!"
[5] Thomas Middleton's play *The Mayor of Queenborough* (c. 1619), I, i, 133–34.

[6] *The Vestal Virgin: Or, the Roman Ladies*, Act V, a tragedy by Sir Robert Howard (1626–1698), first performed in 1664.
[7] Lamb here makes humorous secular use of the orthodox Christian notion of "the church triumphant" (the souls in heaven) and "the church militant" (the souls still struggling on earth).

for a Gresham or a Whittington of old,[8] stately House of Merchants; with thy labyrinthine passages, and light-excluding, pent-up offices, where candles for one half the year supplied the place of the sun's light; unhealthy contributor to my weal, stern fosterer of my living, farewell! In thee remain, and not in the obscure collection of some wandering bookseller, my "works!" There let them rest, as I do from my labours, piled on thy massy shelves, more MSS. in folio than ever Aquinas[9] left, and full as useful! My mantle I bequeath among ye.

A fortnight has passed since the date of my first communication. At that period I was approaching to tranquillity, but had not reached it. I boasted of a calm indeed, but it was comparative only. Something of the first flutter was left; an unsettling sense of novelty; the dazzle to weak eyes of unaccustomed light. I missed my old chains, forsooth, as if they had been some necessary part of my apparel. I was a poor Carthusian, from strict cellular discipline suddenly by some revolution returned upon the world.[10] I am now as if I had never been other than my own master. It is natural for me to go where I please, to do what I please. I find myself at eleven o'clock in the day in Bond-Street, and it seems to me that I have been sauntering there at that very hour for years past. I digress into Soho, to explore a book-stall. Methinks I have been thirty years a collector. There is nothing strange nor new in it. I find myself before a fine picture in the morning. Was it ever otherwise? What is become of Fish-street Hill? Where is Fenchurch-street?[11] Stones of old Mincing-lane which I have worn with my daily pilgrimage for six and thirty years, to the footsteps of what toil-worn clerk are your everlasting flints now vocal? I indent the gayer flags of Pall Mall.[12] It is Change time, and I am strangely among the Elgin marbles.[13] It was no hyperbole when I ventured to compare the change in my condition to a passing into another world. Time stands still in a manner to me. I

have lost all distinction of season. I do not know the day of the week, or of the month. Each day used to be individually felt by me in its reference to the foreign post days; in its distance from, or propinquity to, the next Sunday. I had my Wednesday feelings, my Saturday nights' sensations. The genius of each day was upon me distinctly during the whole of it, affecting my appetite, spirits, &c. The phantom of the next day, with the dreary five to follow, sate as a load upon my poor Sabbath recreations. What charm has washed that Ethiop white? What is gone of Black Monday? All days are the same. Sunday itself—that unfortunate failure of a holyday, as it too often proved, what with my sense of its fugitiveness, and over-care to get the greatest quantity of pleasure out of it—is melted down into a week day. I can spare to go to church now, without grudging the huge cantle[14] which it used to seem to cut out of the holyday. I have Time for every thing. I can visit a sick friend. I can interrupt the man of much occupation when he is busiest. I can insult over him with an invitation to take a day's pleasure with me to Windsor this fine May-morning. It is Lucretian pleasure[15] to behold the poor drudges, whom I have left behind in the world, carking and caring; like horses in a mill, drudging on in the same eternal round—and what is it all for? A man can never have too much Time to himself, nor too little to do. Had I a little son, I would christen him NOTHING-TO-DO; he should do nothing. Man, I verily believe, is out of his element as long as he is operative. I am altogether for the life contemplative. Will no kindly earthquake come and swallow up those accursed cotton mills? Take me that lumber of a desk there, and bowl it down

As low as to the fiends.[16]

I am no longer * * * * * *, clerk to the Firm of &c. I am Retired Leisure. I am to be met with in trim gardens.[17] I am already come to be known by my vacant face and careless gesture, perambulating at no fixed pace, nor with any settled purpose. I walk about; not to and from. They tell me, a certain *cum dignitate*[18] air, that has been buried so long with my other good parts, has begun to shoot forth in my person. I grow into gentility perceptibly. When I take up a newspaper, it is to read the state of the opera. *Opus operatum*

---

[8] Sir Thomas Gresham (1519–1579) was a merchant and financier, founder of the Royal Exchange. Richard Whittington (d. 1423) was a successful merchant and Lord Mayor of London; his life provided the basis for the popular legend of "Dick Whittington."

[9] St. Thomas Aquinas (1225–1274), the medieval theologian.

[10] The Carthusians were a religious order founded in 1084 by St. Bruno and known for an especially severe and disciplined existence. In 1792, the monks had been expelled from their monastery the Grande Chartreuse by the armies of the French Revolution.

[11] Like Mincing-lane, sites in the financial and business section of London.

[12] A fashionable thoroughfare in the most elegant section of London.

[13] Sculptures from the Parthenon in Athens, brought to England in 1802–1804 by Lord Elgin (1766–1841) and located in the British Museum in 1816.

[14] Segment.

[15] In the opening lines of Book II of *De Rerum Natura*, Lucretius cites various examples of the pleasure received from knowing one's self free from the labors and perils experienced by others, especially the "pitiable" struggle for worldly power and riches as the keys to contentment.

[16] *Hamlet*, II, ii, 519.

[17] See *Il Penseroso*, ll. 49–50.

[18] *cum dignitate*: "dignified."

est.[19] I have done all that I came into this world to do. I have worked task work, and have the rest of the day to myself.

[May 1825]   [1833]

STAGE ILLUSION

A PLAY is said to be well or ill acted in proportion to the scenical illusion produced. Whether such illusion can in any case be perfect, is not the question. The nearest approach to it, we are told, is, when the actor appears wholly unconscious of the presence of spectators. In tragedy—in all which is to affect the feelings—this undivided attention to his stage business, seems indispensable. Yet it is, in fact, dispensed with every day by our cleverest tragedians; and while these references to an audience, in the shape of rant or sentiment, are not too frequent or palpable, a sufficient quantity of illusion for the purposes of dramatic interest may be said to be produced in spite of them. But, tragedy apart, it may be inquired whether, in certain characters in comedy, especially those which are a little extravagant, or which involve some notion repugnant to the moral sense, it is not a proof of the highest skill in the comedian when, without absolutely appealing to an audience, he keeps up a tacit understanding with them; and makes them, unconsciously to themselves, a party in the scene. The utmost nicety is required in the mode of doing this; but we speak only of the great artists in the profession.

The most mortifying infirmity in human nature, to feel in ourselves, or to contemplate in another, is, perhaps, cowardice. To see a coward *done to the life* upon a stage would produce anything but mirth. Yet we most of us remember Jack Bannister's cowards. Could any thing be more agreeable, more pleasant? We loved the rogues. How was this effected but by the exquisite art of the actor in a perpetual sub-insinuation to us, the spectators, even in the extremity of the shaking fit, that he was not half such a coward as we took him for? We saw all the common symptoms of the malady upon him; the quivering lip, the cowering knees, the teeth chattering; and could have sworn "that man was frightened." But we forgot all the whole—or kept it almost a secret to ourselves—that he never once lost his self-possession; that he let out by a thousand droll looks and gestures—meant at *us*, and not at all supposed to be visible to his fellows in the scene, that his confidence in his own resources had

never once deserted him. Was this a genuine picture of a coward? or not rather a likeness, which the clever artist contrived to palm upon us instead of an original; while we secretly connived at the delusion for the purpose of greater pleasure, than a more genuine counterfeiting of the imbecility, helplessness, and utter self-desertion, which we know to be concomitants of cowardice in real life, could have given us?

Why are misers so hateful in the world, and so endurable on the stage, but because the skilful actor, by a sort of sub-reference, rather than direct appeal to us, disarms the character of a great deal of its odiousness, by seeming to engage *our* compassion for the insecure tenure by which he holds his money bags and parchments? By this subtle vent half of the hatefulness of the character—the self-closeness with which in real life it coils itself up from the sympathies of men—evaporates. The miser becomes sympathetic; *i.e.* is no genuine miser. Here again a diverting likeness is substituted for a very disagreeable reality.

Spleen, irritability—the pitiable infirmities of old men, which produce only pain to behold in the realities, counterfeited upon a stage, divert not altogether for the comic appendages to them, but in part from an inner conviction that they are *being acted* before us; that a likeness only is going on, and not the thing itself. They please by being done under the life, or beside it; not *to the life*. When Gatty[1] acts an old man, is he angry indeed? or only a pleasant counterfeit, just enough of a likeness to recognise, without pressing upon us the uneasy sense of reality?

Comedians, paradoxical as it may seem, may be too natural. It was the case with a late actor. Nothing could be more earnest or true than the manner of Mr. Emery;[2] this told excellently in his Tyke, and characters of a tragic cast. But when he carried the same rigid exclusiveness of attention to the stage business, and wilful blindness and oblivion of everything before the curtain into his comedy, it produced a harsh and dissonant effect. He was out of keeping with the rest of the *Personae Dramatis*. There was as little link between him and them as betwixt himself and the audience. He was a third estate, dry, repulsive, and unsocial to all. Individually considered, his execution was masterly. But comedy is not this unbending thing; for this reason, that the same degree of credibility is not required of it as to serious scenes. The degrees of credibility demanded to the two things may be illustrated by the different sort of truth which we expect when a man

---

[19] *Opus operatum est:* "The work is performed." This is a punning reference to the end of Lamb's employment and the performance of the opera.

[1] Henry Gattie (1774–1844), whose reputation was based on his characterizations of old-men.

[2] John Emery (1777–1822), whose greatest role was the kind-hearted and long-suffering servant Tyke in Thomas Morton's sentimental comedy *The School of Reform* (1805).

tells us a mournful or a merry story. If we suspect the former of falsehood in any one tittle, we reject it altogether. Our tears refuse to flow at a suspected imposition. But the teller of a mirthful tale has latitude allowed him. We are content with less than absolute truth. 'Tis the same with dramatic illusion. We confess we love in comedy to see an audience naturalised behind the scenes, taken in into the interest of the drama, welcomed as by-standers however. There is something ungracious in a comic actor holding himself aloof from all participation or concern with those who are come to be diverted by him. Macbeth must see the dagger, and no ear but his own be told of it; but an old fool in farce may think he *sees something*, and by conscious words and looks express it, as plainly as he can speak, to pit, box, and gallery. When an impertinent in tragedy, an Osric,[3] for instance, breaks in upon the serious passions of the scene, we approve of the contempt with which he is treated. But when the pleasant impertinent of comedy, in a piece purely meant to give delight, and raise mirth out of whimsical perplexities, worries the studious man with taking up his leisure, or making his house his home, the same sort of contempt expressed (however *natural*) would destroy the balance of delight in the spectators. To make the intrusion comic, the actor who plays the annoyed man must a little desert nature; he must, in short, be thinking of the audience, and express only so much dissatisfaction and peevishness as is consistent with the pleasure of comedy. In other words, his perplexity must seem half put on. If he repel the intruder with the sober set face of a man in earnest, and more especially if he deliver his expostulations in a tone which in the world must necessarily provoke a duel; his real-life manner will destroy the whimsical and purely dramatic existence of the other character (which to render it comic demands an antagonist comicality on the part of the character opposed to it), and convert what was meant for mirth, rather than belief, into a downright piece of impertinence indeed, which would raise no diversion in us, but rather stir pain, to see inflicted in earnest upon any unworthy person. A very judicious actor (in most of his parts) seems to have fallen into an error of this sort in his playing with Mr. Wrench in the farce of *Free and Easy*.[4]

Many instances would be tedious; these may suffice to show that comic acting at least does not always demand from the performer that strict abstraction from all reference to an audience, which is exacted of it; but that in some cases a sort of compromise may

take place, and all the purposes of dramatic delight be attained by a judicious understanding, not too openly announced, between the ladies and gentlemen—on both sides of the curtain.

[August 1825]   [1833]

SANITY OF TRUE GENIUS

So FAR from the position holding true, that great wit (or genius in our modern way of speaking), has a necessary alliance with insanity, the greatest wits, on the contrary, will ever be found to be the sanest writers. It is impossible for the mind to conceive of a mad Shakspeare. The greatness of wit, by which the poetic talent is here chiefly to be understood, manifests itself in the admirable balance of all the faculties. Madness is the disproportionate straining or excess of any one of them. "So strong a wit," says Cowley, speaking of a poetical friend,

> "——did Nature to him frame,
> As all things but his judgment overcame,
> His judgment like the heavenly moon did show,
> Tempering that mighty sea below."[1]

The ground of the mistake is, that men, finding in the raptures of the higher poetry a condition of exaltation, to which they have no parallel in their own experience, besides the spurious resemblance of it in dreams and fevers, impute a state of dreaminess and fever to the poet. But the true poet dreams being awake. He is not possessed by his subject, but has dominion over it. In the groves of Eden he walks familiar as in his native paths. He ascends the empyrean heaven, and is not intoxicated. He treads the burning marl without dismay; he wins his flight without self-loss through realms of chaos "and old night."[2] Or if, abandoning himself to that severer chaos of a "human mind untuned," he is content awhile to be mad with Lear, or to hate mankind (a sort of madness) with Timon, neither is that madness, nor this misanthropy, so unchecked, but that, —never letting the reins of reason wholly go, while most he seems to do so,—he has his better genius still whispering at his ear, with the good servant Kent suggesting saner counsels, or with the honest steward Flavius recommending kindlier resolutions. Where he seems most to recede from humanity, he will be found the truest to it. From beyond the scope of Nature if he summon possible existences, he subjugates them to the law of her consistency. He is beautifully loyal to that sovereign directress, even when he appears most to

---

[3] Foppish courtier in *Hamlet*. See Act V, ii.
[4] Benjamin Wrench (1778–1843) in the musical farce *Free and Easy* (1816) by Samuel James Arnold.

---

[1] "On the Death of Mr. William Hervey," stanza 13.
[2] See *Paradise Lost*, I, 296, 543.

betray and desert her. His ideal tribes submit to policy; his very monsters are tamed to his hand, even as that wild seabrood, shepherded by Proteus.[3] He tames, and he clothes them with attributes of flesh and blood, till they wonder at themselves, like Indian Islanders forced to submit to European vesture. Caliban, the Witches, are as true to the laws of their own nature (ours with a difference), as Othello, Hamlet, and Macbeth. Herein the great and the little wits are differenced; that if the latter wander ever so little from nature or actual existence, they lose themselves, and their readers. Their phantoms are lawless; their visions nightmares. They do not create, which implies shaping and consistency. Their imaginations are not active— for to be active is to call something into act and form— but passive, as men in sick dreams. For the super-natural, or something super-added to what we know of nature, they give you the plainly non-natural. And if this were all, and that these mental hallucinations were discoverable only in the treatment of subjects out of nature, or transcending it, the judgment might with some plea be pardoned if it ran riot, and a little wantonized: but even in the describing of real and every day life, that which is before their eyes, one of these lesser wits shall more deviate from nature—show more of that inconsequence, which has a natural alliance with frenzy,—than a great genius in his "mad-dest fits,"[4] as Withers somewhere calls them. We appeal to any one that is acquainted with the common run of Lane's novels,[5] as they existed some twenty or thirty years back,—those scanty intellectual viands of the whole female reading public, till a happier genius arose,[6] and expelled for ever the innutritious phantoms, —whether he has not found his brain more "betossed," his memory more puzzled, his sense of when and where more confounded, among the improbable events, the incoherent incidents, the inconsistent characters, or no-characters, of some third-rate love intrigue—where the persons shall be a Lord Glendamour and a Miss Rivers, and the scene only alternate between Bath and Bond-Street—a more bewildering dreaminess induced upon him, than he has felt wandering over all the fairy grounds of Spenser. In the productions we refer to, nothing but names and places is familiar; the persons are neither of this world nor of any other conceivable one; an endless string of activities without purpose, of

purposes destitute of motive:—we meet phantoms in our known walks; *fantasques* only christened.[7] In the poet we have names which announce fiction; and we have absolutely no place at all, for the things and persons of the Fairy Queen prate not of their "where-about." But in their inner nature, and the law of their speech and actions, we are at home and upon ac-quainted ground. The one turns life into a dream; the other to the wildest dreams gives the sobrieties of every day occurrences. By what subtile art of tracing the mental processes it is effected, we are not philosophers enough to explain, but in that wonderful episode of the cave of Mammon, in which the Money God appears first in the lowest form of a miser, is then a worker of metals, and becomes the god of all the treasures of the world; and has a daughter, Ambition, before whom all the world kneels for favours—with the Hesperian fruit, the waters of Tantalus, with Pilate washing his hands vainly, but not impertinently, in the same stream —that we should be at one moment in the cave of an old hoarder of treasures, at the next at the forge of the Cyclops, in a palace and yet in hell,[8] all at once, with the shifting mutations of the most rambling dream, and our judgment yet all the time awake, and neither able nor willing to detect the fallacy,—is a proof of that hidden sanity which still guides the poet in his widest seeming-aberrations.

It is not enough to say that the whole episode is a copy of the mind's conceptions in sleep; it is, in some sort—but what a copy! Let the most romantic of us, that has been entertained all night with the spectacle of some wild and magnificent vision, recombine it in the morning, and try it by his waking judgment. That which appeared so shifting, and yet so coherent, while that faculty was passive, when it comes under cool examination, shall appear so reasonless and so un-linked, that we are ashamed to have been so deluded; and to have taken, though but in sleep, a monster for a god. But the transitions in this episode are every whit as violent as in the most extravagant dream, and yet the waking judgment ratifies them.

[May 1826]   [1833]

F R O M

BARRENNESS OF THE IMAGINATIVE FACULTY IN THE PRODUCTIONS OF MODERN ART

H OGARTH excepted, can we produce any one painter within the last fifty years, or since the humour of ex-

---

[3] A sea-god in Greek mythology.
[4] The phrase occurs in *The Shepherd's Hunting* (1615), Fourth Eclogue, l. 409, by George Wither (1588–1667).
[5] William Lane (*c.* 1745–1814) was a London publisher and founder of the Minerva Press, under whose imprint from 1790 to 1820 appeared countless sentimental and melodramatic novels, largely calculated for the susceptible female reader.
[6] Lamb refers to Sir Walter Scott, whose Waverley novels began to appear in 1814.

[7] Fantastic and improbable figures made to pass for real by simply being given Christian names.
[8] Sequence of events described in *The Faerie Queen*, II, vii.

hibiting began, that has treated a story *imaginatively?* By this we mean, upon whom his subject has so acted, that it has seemed to direct *him*—not to be arranged by him? Any upon whom its leading or collateral points have impressed themselves so tyrannically, that he dared not treat it otherwise, lest he should falsify a revelation? Any that has imparted to his compositions, not merely so much truth as is enough to convey a story with clearness, but that individualising property, which should keep the subject so treated distinct in feature from every other subject, however similar, and to common apprehensions almost identical; so as that we might say, this and this part could have found an appropriate place in no other picture in the world but this? Is there anything in modern art—we will not demand that it should be equal—but in any way analogous to what Titian has effected, in that wonderful bringing together of two times in the "Ariadne,"[1] in the National Gallery? Precipitous, with his reeling Satyr rout about him, re-peopling and re-illuming suddenly the waste places, drunk with a new fury beyond the grape, Bacchus, born in fire, fire-like flings himself at the Cretan. This is the time present. With this telling of the story an artist, and no ordinary one, might remain richly proud. Guido,[2] in his harmonious version of it, saw no further. But from the depths of the imaginative spirit Titian has recalled past time, and laid it contributory with the present to one simultaneous effect. With the desert all ringing with the mad cymbals of his followers, made lucid with the presence and new offers of a god,—as if unconscious of Bacchus, or but idly casting her eyes as upon some unconcerning pageant—her soul undistracted from Theseus— Ariadne is still pacing the solitary shore, in as much heart-silence, and in almost the same local solitude, with which she awoke at day-break to catch the forlorn last glances of the sail that bore away the Athenian.

Here are two points miraculously co-uniting; fierce society, with the feeling of solitude still absolute; noon-day revelations, with the accidents of the dull grey dawn unquenched and lingering; the *present* Bacchus, with the *past* Ariadne; two stories, with double Time; separate, and harmonising. Had the artist made the woman one shade less indifferent to the God; still more, had she expressed a rapture at his advent, where would have been the story of the mighty desolation of the heart previous? merged in the insipid accident of a

flattering offer met with a welcome acceptance. The broken heart for Theseus was not lightly to be pieced up by a God.

We have before us a fine rough print, from a picture by Raphael in the Vatican. It is the Presentation of the new-born Eve to Adam by the Almighty. A fairer mother of mankind we might imagine, and a goodlier sire perhaps of men since born. But these are matters subordinate to the conception of the *situation*, displayed in this extraordinary production. A tolerably modern artist would have been satisfied with tempering certain raptures of connubial anticipation, with a suitable acknowledgment to the Giver of the blessing, in the countenance of the first bridegroom; something like the divided attention of the child (Adam was here a child man) between the given toy, and the mother who had just blest it with the bauble. This is the obvious, the first-sight view, the superficial. An artist of a higher grade, considering the awful presence they were in, would have taken care to subtract something from the expression of the more human passion, and to heighten the more spiritual one. This would be as much as an exhibition-goer, from the opening of Somerset House[3] to last year's show, has been encouraged to look for. It is obvious to hint at a lower expression, yet in a picture, that for respects of drawing and colouring, might be deemed not wholly inadmissible within these art-fostering walls, in which the raptures should be as ninety-nine, the gratitude as one, or perhaps Zero! By neither the one passion nor the other has Raphael expounded the situation of Adam. Singly upon his brow sits the absorbing sense of wonder at the created miracle. The *moment* is seized by the intuitive artist, perhaps not self-conscious of his art, in which neither of the conflicting emotions—a moment how abstracted—have had time to spring up or to battle for indecorous mastery.—We have seen a landscape of a justly admired neoteric,[4] in which he aimed at delineating a fiction, one of the most severely beautiful in antiquity—the gardens of the Hesperides. To do Mr. —— justice, he had painted a laudable orchard, with fitting seclusion, and a veritable dragon (of which a Polypheme by Poussin is somehow a facsimile for the situation), looking over into the world shut out backwards, so that none but a "still-climbing Hercules" could hope to catch a peep at the admired Ternary of Recluses.[5] No conventual porter could

---

[1] Ariadne, daughter of Minos, king of Crete, had fled from her homeland with her Athenian lover Theseus, after he had slain the Minotaur. The subject of Titian's painting refers to her subsequent abandonment by Theseus on the island of Naxos, where she is then wooed and won by Bacchus.

[2] Guido Reni (1575–1642) was an Italian painter of religious and mythological subjects.

[3] The Royal Academy of Art held its exhibitions at Somerset House in London from 1780 to 1837. Lamb is thus criticizing the approved, academic painting of his day.

[4] A person of modern times and new ideas. Lamb may be referring to J. M. W. Turner (1775–1851), whose painting of the Garden of the Hesperides was exhibited in 1806.

[5] In Greek mythology, the Hesperides were three sisters who guarded the golden apples presented to Juno upon her marriage

keep his keys better than this custos with the "lidless eyes." [6] He not only sees that none *do* intrude into that privacy, but, as clear as daylight, that none but *Hercules aut Diabolus* [7] by any manner of means *can*. So far all is well. We have absolute solitude here or nowhere. *Ab extra* the damsels are snug enough. But here the artist's courage seems to have failed him. He began to pity his pretty charge, and, to comfort the irksomeness, has peopled their solitude with a bevy of fair attendants, maids of honour, or ladies of the bedchamber, according to the approved etiquette at a court of the nineteenth century; giving to the whole scene the air of a *fête champêtre*, if we will but excuse the absence of the gentlemen. This is well, and Watteauish. [8] But what is become of the solitary mystery —the

> Daughters three,
> That sing around the golden tree? [9]

This is not the way in which Poussin would have treated this subject.

The paintings, or rather the stupendous architectural designs of a modern artist, [10] have been urged as objections to the theory of our motto. They are of a character, we confess, to stagger it. His towered structures are of the highest order of the material sublime. Whether they were dreams, or transcripts of some elder workmanship—Assyrian ruins old—restored by this mighty artist, they satisfy our most stretched and craving conceptions of the glories of the antique world. It is a pity that they were ever peopled. On that side, the imagination of the artist halts, and appears defective. Let us examine the point of the story in the "Belshazzar's Feast." We will introduce it by an apposite anecdote.

The court historians of the day record, that at the first dinner given by the late King (then Prince Regent) at the Pavilion, [11] the following characteristic frolic was played off. The guests were select and admiring; the banquet profuse and admirable; the lights lustrous

and oriental; the eye was perfectly dazzled with the display of plate, among which the great gold saltcellar, brought from the regalia in the Tower for this especial purpose, itself a tower! stood conspicuous for its magnitude. And now the Rev. * * * * the then admired court Chaplain, was proceeding with the grace, when, at a signal given, the lights were suddenly overcast, and a huge transparency [12] was discovered, in which glittered in golden letters—

"BRIGHTON—EARTHQUAKE— SWALLOW-UP-ALIVE!"

Imagine the confusion of the guests; the Georges and garters, [13] jewels, bracelets, moulted upon the occasion! The fans dropt, and picked up the next morning by the sly court pages! Mrs. Fitz-what's-her-name fainting, and the Countess of * * * * holding the smelling bottle, till the good humoured Prince caused harmony to be restored by calling in fresh candles, and declaring that the whole was nothing but a pantomime *hoax*, got up by the ingenious Mr. Farley, of Covent Garden, from hints that his Royal Highness himself had furnished! Then imagine the infinite applause that followed, the mutual rallyings, the declarations that "they were not much frightened," of the assembled galaxy.

The point of time in the picture exactly answers to the appearance of the transparency in the anecdote. The huddle, the flutter, the bustle, the escape, the alarm, and the mock alarm; the prettinesses heightened by consternation; the courtier's fear which was flattery, and the lady's which was affectation; all that we may conceive to have taken place in a mob of Brighton courtiers, sympathising with the well-acted surprise of their sovereign; all this, and no more, is exhibited by the well-dressed lords and ladies in the Hall of Belus. [14] Just this sort of consternation we have seen among a flock of disquieted wild geese at the report only of a gun having gone off!

But is this vulgar fright, this mere animal anxiety for the preservation of their persons,—such as we have witnessed at a theatre, when a slight alarm of fire has been given—an adequate exponent of a supernatural terror? the way in which the finger of God, writing judgments, would have been met by the withered conscience? There is a human fear, and a divine fear. The one is disturbed, restless, and bent upon escape. The other is bowed down, effortless, passive. When the spirit appeared before Eliphaz in the visions of the

---

with Zeus. The Hesperides were assisted by the dragon Ladon. The final labor of Hercules was the slaying of the dragon and stealing some of the apples. Polypheme, the Cyclops, was the subject of a landscape by Nicolas Poussin.

6 Coleridge's "Ode to the Departing Year," l. 145.

7 *Hercules aut Diabolus:* "Hercules or the Devil," variation of an old maxim of conviction.

8 Referring to a rural or outdoor festivity or entertainment, which was a frequent subject of painting by Jean Antoine Watteau (1684–1721).

9 Milton's *Comus*, ll. 982–83.

10 John Martin (1789–1854) was a painter of enormous melodramatic canvases on Biblical subjects. "Belshazzar's Feast" was exhibited in 1821.

11 Lamb refers to George IV and his elegant residence, the Royal Pavilion, at Brighton.

12 A screen made of some translucent substance, illuminated from behind by a light.

13 A George is the name given to the jewel that forms part of the insignia of the Order of the Garter, the badge of the highest order of English knighthood.

14 Belshazzar.

night, and the hair of his flesh stood up, was it in the thoughts of the Temanite to ring the bell of his chamber, or to call up the servants? [15] But let us see in the text what there is to justify all this huddle of vulgar consternation.

From the words of Daniel it appears that Belshazzar had made a great feast to a thousand of his lords, and drank wine before the thousand. The golden and silver vessels are gorgeously enumerated, with the princes, the king's concubines, and his wives. Then follows—

"In the same hour came forth fingers of a man's hand, and wrote over against the candlestick upon the plaster of the wall of the king's palace; and the *king* saw the part of the hand that wrote. Then the *king's* countenance was changed, and his thoughts troubled him, so that the joints of his loins were loosened, and his knees smote one against another."

This is the plain text. By no hint can it be otherwise inferred, but that the appearance was solely confined to the fancy of Belshazzar, that his single brain was troubled. Not a word is spoken of its being seen by any one else there present, not even by the queen herself, who merely undertakes for the interpretation of the phenomenon, as related to her, doubtless, by her husband. The lords are simply said to be astonished; *i.e.* at the trouble and the change of countenance in their sovereign. Even the prophet does not appear to have seen the scroll, which the king saw. He recalls it only, as Joseph did the Dream to the King of Egypt. "Then was the part of the hand sent from him [the Lord], and this writing was written." He speaks of the phantasm as past.

Then what becomes of this needless multiplication of the miracle? this message to a royal conscience, singly expressed—for it was said, "thy kingdom is divided,"—simultaneously impressed upon the fancies of a thousand courtiers, who were implied in it neither directly nor grammatically?

But admitting the artist's own version of the story, and that the sight was seen also by the thousand courtiers—let it have been visible to all Babylon—as the knees of Belshazzar were shaken, and his countenance troubled, even so would the knees of every man in Babylon, and their countenances, as of an individual man, been troubled; bowed, bent down, so would they have remained, stupor-fixed, with no thought of struggling with the inevitable judgment.

Not all that is optically possible to be seen, is to be shown in every picture. The eye delightedly dwells upon the brilliant individualities in a "Marriage at Cana," by Veronese,[16] or Titian, to the very texture and colour of the wedding garments, the ring glittering upon the bride's fingers, the metal and fashion of the wine pots; for at such seasons there is leisure and luxury to be curious. But in a "day of judgment," or in a "day of lesser horrors, yet divine," as at the impious feast of Belshazzar, the eye should see, as the actual eye of an agent or patient in the immediate scene would see, only in masses and indistinction. Not only the female attire and jewelry exposed to the critical eye of the fashion, as minutely as the dresses in a lady's magazine, in the criticised picture,—but perhaps the curiosities of anatomical science, and studied diversities of posture in the falling angels and sinners of Michael Angelo,— have no business in their great subjects. There was no leisure of them.

By a wise falsification, the great masters of painting got at their true conclusions; by not showing the actual appearances, that is, all that was to be seen at any given moment by an indifferent eye, but only what the eye might be supposed to see in the doing or suffering of some portentous action. Suppose the moment of the swallowing up of Pompeii. There they were to be seen —houses, columns, architectural proportions, differences of public and private buildings, men and women at their standing occupations, the diversified thousand postures, attitudes, dresses, in some confusion truly, but physically they were visible. But what eye saw them at that eclipsing moment, which reduces confusion to a kind of unity, and when the senses are upturned from their proprieties, when sight and hearing are a feeling only? A thousand years have passed, and we are at leisure to contemplate the weaver fixed standing at his shuttle, the baker at his oven, and to turn over with antiquarian coolness the pots and pans of Pompeii.

*   *   *   *   *

Artists again err in the confounding of *poetic* with *pictorial subjects.* In the latter, the exterior accidents are nearly everything, the unseen qualities as nothing. Othello's colour—the infirmities and corpulence of a Sir John Falstaff—do they haunt us perpetually in the reading? or are they obtruded upon our conceptions one time for ninety-nine that we are lost in admiration at the respective moral or intellectual attributes of the character? But in a picture Othello is *always* a Black-amoor; and the other only Plump Jack. Deeply corporealised, and enchained hopelessly in the grovelling fetters of externality, must be the mind, to which, in its better moments, the image of the high-souled, high-intelligenced Quixote—the errant Star of Knight-

---

[15] An event recorded by Eliphaz, one of Job's comforters. See Job, iv, 11-15.

[16] Paolo Veronese (1528-1588), Venetian painter.

hood, made more tender by eclipse—has never presented itself, divested from the unhallowed accompaniment of a Sancho, or a rabblement at the heels of Rosinante.[17] That man has read his book by halves; he has laughed, mistaking his author's purport, which was —tears. The artist that pictures Quixote (and it is in this degrading point that he is every season held up at our Exhibitions) in the shallow hope of exciting mirth, would have joined the rabble at the heels of his starved steed. We wish not to see *that* counterfeited, which we would not have wished to see in the reality. Conscious of the heroic inside of the noble Quixote, who, on hearing that his withered person was passing, would have stepped over his threshold to gaze upon his forlorn habiliments, and the "strange bed-fellows which misery brings a man acquainted with?"[18] Shade of Cervantes! who in thy Second Part could put into the mouth of thy Quixote those high aspirations of a super-chivalrous gallantry, where he replies to one of the shepherdesses, apprehensive that he would spoil their pretty net-works, and inviting him to be a guest with them, in accents like these: "Truly, fairest Lady, Actaeon was not more astonished when he saw Diana bathing herself at the fountain, than I have seen in beholding your beauty: I commend the manner of your pastime, and thank you for your kind offers; and, if I may serve you, so I may be sure you will be obeyed, you may command me: for my profession is this, To shew myself thankful, and a doer of good to all sorts of people, especially of the rank that your person shows you to be; and if those nets, as they take up but a little piece of ground, should take up the whole world, I would seek out new worlds to pass through, rather than break them: and (he adds,) that you may give credit to this my exaggeration, behold at least he that promiseth you this, is Don Quixote de la Mancha, if haply this name hath come to your hearing." Illustrious Romancer! were the "fine frenzies,"[19] which possessed the brain of thy own Quixote, a fit subject, as in this Second Part, to be exposed to the jeers of Duennas and Serving Men? to be monstered, and shown up at the heartless banquets of great men? Was that pitiable infirmity, which in thy First Part misleads him, *always from within*, into half-ludicrous, but more than half-compassionable and admirable errors, not infliction enough from heaven, that men by studied artifices must devise and practise upon the humour, to inflame where they should soothe it? Why, Goneril would have blushed to practise upon the abdicated king at this rate, and the she-wolf Regan not have

endured to play the pranks upon his fled wits, which thou hast made thy Quixote suffer in Duchesses' halls, and at the hands of that unworthy nobleman.*

In the First Adventures, even, it needed all the art of the most consummate artist in the Book way that the world hath yet seen, to keep up in the mind of the reader the heroic attributes of the character without relaxing; so as absolutely that they shall suffer no alloy from the debasing fellowship of the clown. If it ever obtrudes itself as a disharmony, are we inclined to laugh; or not, rather to indulge a contrary emotion?— Cervantes, stung, perchance, by the relish with which *his* Reading Public had received the fooleries of the man, more to their palates than the generosities of the master, in the sequel let his pen run riot, lost the harmony and the balance, and sacrificed a great idea to the taste of his contemporaries. We know that in the present day the Knight has fewer admirers than the Squire. Anticipating, what did actually happen to him —as afterwards it did to his scarce inferior follower, the Author of "Guzman de Alfarache"—that some less knowing hand would prevent him by a spurious Second Part:[21] and judging, that it would be easier for his competitor to outbid him in the comicalities, than in the *romance*, of his work, he abandoned his Knight, and his fairly set up the Squire for his Hero. For what else has he unsealed the eyes of Sancho; and instead of that twilight state of semi-insanity—the madness at second-hand—the contagion, caught from a stronger mind infected—that war between native cunning, and hereditary deference, with which he has hitherto accompanied his master—two for a pair almost—does he substitute a downright Knave, with open eyes, for his own ends only following a confessed Madman; and offering at one time to lay, if not actually laying, hands upon him! From the moment that Sancho loses his reverence, Don Quixote is become a—treatable lunatic. Our artists handle him accordingly.

[January–February 1833]   [1833]

---

* Yet from this Second Part, our cried-up pictures are mostly selected; waiting-women with beards, &c.[20]

◇◇

[20] Lamb refers to a long series of episodes in the Second Part of *Don Quixote*, in which the Don is elegantly entertained by a Duke and Duchess. His hosts lead him to believe that he is indeed a great chivalric figure, but all the time they are mocking him and playing on him a number of embarrassing and cruel tricks.
[21] The great popularity of the first part of *Don Quixote* (1605) gave rise to a spurious second part in 1614; Cervantes published the true second part in 1615. *Guzman de Alfarache* was a picaresque novel by Mateo Aleman (1547–1614), published in 1599. The spurious second part appeared in 1602, the true version in 1604.

---

[17] Don Quixote's emaciated and awkward horse.
[18] See *The Tempest*, II, ii, 41–42.
[19] See *A Midsummer Night's Dream*, V, i, 12.

William Hazlitt

1778–1830

OUTLINE OF EVENTS

1778   Born April 10, at Maidstone, Kent. Father, William (b. 1737), a Unitarian minister; mother, Grace (Loftus) (b. 1746); brother, John (b. 1767); sister, Margaret (b. 1770).

1780–83   In Ireland, where father has congregation.

1783–87   In America; father is instrumental in founding the first Unitarian church in Boston.

1787   Family resides at Wem, Shropshire.

1793–95   Studies at the Unitarian New College at Hackney, where prominent religious and political dissenters (including Joseph Priestley) composed the faculty.

1796   Abandons study for the ministry and begins period of intensive independent study of "modern philosophy" (leading eventually to the *Essay* of 1805), and reading in literature and politics.

1798   January, meets Coleridge. Late spring, at Nether Stowey to see Coleridge, and meets Wordsworth (see "My First Acquaintance with Poets").

1800–02   Following instruction under his brother in London, becomes itinerant portrait-painter. In October 1802, goes to Paris to study and make copies of paintings in the Louvre.

1803   February, returns from Paris; meets Charles Lamb (whose portrait he paints the following year). Summer and fall with Wordsworth and Coleridge in Lake District; creates a scandal for his supposed assaults on country women.

1805   *Essay on the Principles of Human Action* published.

1806   *Free Thoughts on Public Affairs* published.

1807   Three works published: *An Abridgment of the Light of Nature Pursued, by Abraham Tucker; The Eloquence of the British Senate; A Reply to the Essay on Population, by the Rev. T. R. Malthus.*

1808   May, marries Sarah Stoddart and lives at Winterslow, Wiltshire.

1809   *A New and Improved Grammar of the English Tongue* published.

1811   September, son William is born.

1812   January–April, lectures in London on the history of English philosophy. Begins journalistic career as parliamentary reporter for *Morning Chronicle*.

1814   Begins writing for *Champion, Edinburgh Review*, and Leigh Hunt's *Examiner*.

1816   *Memoirs of the Late Thomas Holcroft* published.

1817   *Round Table* and *Characters of Shakespear's Plays* published.

1818   *Lectures on the English Poets* (delivered January–March) and *View of the English Stage* published.

1819   *Lectures on the English Comic Writers* (delivered November 1818–January 1819), *A Letter to William Gifford*, and *Political Essays* published. Separated from his wife.

1820   *Lectures on the Dramatic Literature of the Age of Elizabeth* (delivered November–December 1819) published. Begins writing drama criticism and "Table-Talks" for *London Magazine*. July, death of Father. Meets Sarah Walker.

1821   *Table-Talk, or Original Essays* published.

1822   Goes to Scotland to arrange divorce, but is subsequently rejected by Sarah Walker. June, second volume of *Table-Talk* published.

1823   *Characteristics: In the Manner of Rochefoucault's Maxims* and *Liber Amoris* (record of the disastrous infatuation with Sarah Walker) published. Contributes "My First Acquaintance with Poets" and other essays to Leigh Hunt's *Liberal*.

1824   *Sketches of the Principal Picture-Galleries in England* and *Select British Poets or, New Elegant Extracts from Chaucer to the Present Time, with Critical Remarks* published. Marries Mrs. Isabella Bridgwater and begins tour of continent.

1825   *Spirit of the Age* published.

1826   *Plain Speaker* (collection of familiar essays) and *Notes of a Journey through France and Italy* published. Begins residence in Paris to write *Life of Napoleon*.

1827   Separated from his second wife.

1828   First two volumes of *Life of Napoleon* published. Summer, in Paris for additional work on the biography.

1830   Final volumes of *Life of Napoleon* and *Conversations of James Northcote, Esq., R.A.*, published. September 18, dies in London.

SELECTED BIBLIOGRAPHY

BIOGRAPHY

BAKER, HERSCHEL, *William Hazlitt*, Cambridge, Mass.: Harvard University Press, 1962.
HOWE, P. P., *The Life of William Hazlitt*, London: Hamish Hamilton, 1947 [first edition 1922].
WARDLE, RALPH M., *Hazlitt*, Lincoln, Neb.: University of Nebraska Press, 1971.

EDITIONS OF HAZLITT'S PROSE

HAZLITT, WILLIAM, *An Essay on the Principles of Human Action* (1805), A Facsimile Reproduction with an introduction by John R. Nabholtz, Gainesville, Florida: Scholars' Facsimiles and Reprints, 1969.
HOWE, P. P. (ed.), *The Complete Works of William Hazlitt,* 21 vols., London: J. M. Dent and Sons, Ltd., 1930–1934.

HAZLITT'S AESTHETICS AND LITERARY THEORY

ALBRECHT, W. P., *Hazlitt and the Creative Imagination*, Lawrence, Kan.: University of Kansas Press, 1965.
BULLITT, JOHN M., "Hazlitt and the Romantic Conception of the Imagination," *Philological Quarterly*, XXIV (1945), 343–61.
O'HARA, J. D., "Hazlitt and the Functions of the Imagination," *Publications of the Modern Language Association*, LXXXI (1966), 552–62.
PARK, ROY, *Hazlitt and the Spirit of the Age: Abstraction and Critical Theory*, Oxford: Clarendon Press, 1971.
SCHNEIDER, ELISABETH, *The Aesthetics of William Hazlitt: a Study of the Philosophical Basis of his Criticism*, Philadelphia: University of Pennsylvania Press, 1933.

HAZLITT'S POLITICAL THOUGHT

BRINTON, CRANE, *The Political Ideas of the English Romanticists*, London: Oxford University Press, 1926.

THE PRINCIPLES OF HUMAN ACTION

An Essay on the Principles of Human Action was Hazlitt's first published work, and to the end of his life he regarded it as his most important achievement. Its significance did not lie in its anticipation of any of the stylistic variety and power that were to inform such later masterpieces as Lectures on the English Poets *(1818),* Table-Talk *(1821–1822), or* The Spirit of the Age *(1825); as the author himself admitted, the* Essay *was a "dry, tough, metaphysical* choke-pear." *Nor could Hazlitt have valued the work for its contemporary influence or reputation; its publication in 1805 drew little notice, and apart from Keats's enthusiastic reading of it in 1817 and a praiseful footnote reference in Coleridge's* Lay Sermon *"Blessed are ye that sow beside all Waters" of the same year, it remained virtually unknown during its author's lifetime. The* Essay *was important to Hazlitt for its exposition of a "metaphysical discovery" concerning the creative and sympathetic powers of the mind, a "discovery" which he saw as rescuing the mind from the chains of selfishness, sensation, and habit in which it had been imprisoned by the "materialistic philosophy" of the eighteenth century.*

Hazlitt bases his argument for "disinterested benevolence" on three faculties of the mind: memory, consciousness, and imagination, which concern themselves, respectively, with events of the past, present, and future. Hazlitt agrees with his eighteenth-century opponents that in regard to past and present, man is a creature of self-concern, the subject of sensations that act in mechanical ways; and that personal identity is established in these terms. However, future events, by the very fact that they are future, cannot be known by immediate sensation; our relation to them cannot, therefore, be established in terms of mechanical self-interest or exclusive personal identity. The future exists as an idea of the imagination, that faculty which creates and projects objects of future good or evil. These ideas of the imagination call out in us corresponding desires for, or aversion to, the good or evil projected. The central point of Hazlitt's "discovery" is that it is the good or evil that provokes in us feelings of desire or aversion, not our sense of self-interest. Objects "are not converted into good and evil," he argues, "by being impressed on our minds, but they affect our minds in a certain manner because they are essentially good or evil." There must be some object of good, or there would be no feelings of desire aroused, and no motive for action. If love of self were our exclusive principle of operation, we would remain forever fixed, robot-like, on our past and present sensations.

In Hazlitt's argument, the love of self does not precede, but follows from, our love of the good; we silently transfer our love of the good and our happiness in the experience of it to ourselves as the persons benefited by it. However, precisely because it is the good that draws us and not self-interest, as we become aware of the good existing for and benefiting others, the same feelings of happiness will be aroused at another's possession of the good and the same transfer of love from the object to the person will occur. In these terms, Hazlitt declares: "The imagination, by means of which alone I can anticipate future objects, or be interested in them, must carry me out of myself into the feelings of others by one and the same process by which I am thrown forward as it were into my future being and interested in it. I could not love myself, if I were not capable of loving others. Self-love, used in this sense, is in its fundamental principle the same with disinterested benevolence."

Hazlitt's defense of the creative and morally sympathetic powers of the mind, so strenuously set forth in the Essay *of 1805, was to inform virtually everything he wrote until his death twenty-five years later. The major premise of his aesthetics and literary criticism was the artist's ability to move beyond his own limited identity into sympathetic union with the object of his contemplation. In these terms, Hazlitt was to praise Shakespeare's Protean*

ability "only to think of any thing in order to become that thing, with all the circumstances belonging to it;" and to criticize contemporary poets, Wordsworth and Byron most notably, for their self-centered aversion to "outward fact." His political writings were directed against those dogmas and institutions which rivet man to his economic and social environment and thus inhibit the flowering of individual consciousness and sympathetic union between classes, nations, and races. His famous personal essays, such as "On Going a Journey" and "A Farewell to Essay-Writing," are brilliant demonstrations of the imaginative ordering of memories and present sensations in terms of both personal and broadly human aspirations.

The text of the Essay *here reproduced is that of the 1805 edition, with emendation of the punctuation at various points from "a new Edition, considerably improved . . . from marginal corrections in the Author's copy," brought out by Hazlitt's son in 1835.*

F R O M

AN ESSAY ON THE PRINCIPLES OF HUMAN ACTION: Being an Argument in Favour of the Natural Disinterestedness of the Human Mind

IT IS the design of the following Essay to shew that the human mind is naturally disinterested, or that it is naturally interested in the welfare of others in the same way, and from the same direct motives, by which we are impelled to the pursuit of our own interest.

The objects in which the mind is interested may be either past or present, or future. These last alone can be the objects of rational or voluntary pursuit; for neither the past nor present can be altered for the better, or worse by any efforts of the will. It is only from the interest excited in him by future objects that man becomes a moral agent, or is denominated selfish, or the contrary, according to the manner in which he is affected by what relates to his own *future* interest, or that of others. I propose then to shew that the mind is naturally interested in its own welfare in a peculiar mechanical manner, only as far as relates to its past or present impressions. I have an interest in my own actual feelings or impressions by means of consciousness, and in my past feelings by means of memory, which I cannot have in the past, or present feelings of others, because these faculties can only be exerted upon those things which immediately and properly affect myself. As an affair of sensation, or memory, I can feel no interest in any thing but what relates to myself in the strictest sense. But this distinction does not apply to future objects, or to those impressions, which determine my voluntary actions. I have not the same sort of exclusive, or mechanical self-interest in my future being or welfare, because I have no distinct faculty giving me a direct present interest in my future sensations, and none at all in those of others. The imagination, by means of which alone I can anticipate future objects, or be interested in them, must carry me out of myself into the feelings of others by one and the same process by which I am thrown forward as it were into my future being, and interested in it. I could not love myself, if I were not capable of loving others. Self-love, used in this sense, is in its fundamental principle the same with disinterested benevolence.

Those who have maintained the doctrine of the natural selfishness of the human mind have always taken it for granted as a self-evident principle that *a man must love himself*, or that it is not less absurd to ask why a man should be interested in his own personal welfare, than it would be to ask why a man in a state of actual enjoyment or suffering likes what gives him pleasure, and dislikes what gives him pain. They say, that no such necessity, nor any positive reason whatever can be conceived to exist for my promoting the welfare of another, since I cannot possibly feel the pleasures, or pains which another feels without first becoming that other, that our interests must be as necessarily distinct as we ourselves are, that the good which I do to another, in itself and for its own sake can be nothing to me. *Good* is a term relative only to the being who enjoys it. The good which he does not feel must be matter of perfect indifference to him. How can I be required to make a painful exertion, or sacrifice a present convenience to serve another, if I am to be nothing the better for it? I waste my powers out of myself without sharing in the effects which they produce. Whereas when I sacrifice my present ease or convenience, for the sake of a greater good to myself at a future period, the same being who suffers afterwards enjoys, both the loss and the gain are mine, I am upon the whole a gainer in real enjoyment, and am therefore justified to myself: I act with a view to an end in which I have a real, substantial interest. The human soul, continue some of these writers, naturally thirsts after happiness; it either enjoys, or seeks to enjoy. It constantly reaches forward towards the possession of happiness, it strives to draw it to itself, and to be absorbed in it. But as the mind cannot enjoy any good but what it possesses within itself, neither can it seek to produce any good but what it can enjoy: it is just as idle to suppose that the love of happiness or good should prompt any being to give up his own

interest for the sake of another, as it would be to attempt to allay violent thirst by giving water to another to drink.

Now I can conceive that a man must be necessarily interested in his own actual feelings, whatever these may be merely because he feels them. He cannot help receiving pain from what gives him pain, or pleasure from what gives him pleasure. But I cannot conceive how he can have the same necessary, absolute interest in whatever relates to himself, or in his own pleasures and pains, generally speaking, whether he feels them or not. This kind of reasoning, which in itself is all along founded in a mere play of words, could not have gained the assent of thinking men but for the force with which the idea of self habitually clings to the mind of every man, binding it as with a spell, deadening its discriminating powers, and spreading the confused associations which belong only to past and present impressions over the whole of our imaginary existence. It therefore becomes difficult to separate ideas which have been thus knit together by custom, or "by a long tract of time, by the use of language, and want of reflection." If it were possible for a man's particular successive interests to be all bound up in one general feeling of self-interest as they are all comprehended under the same word, *self*, or if a man on the rack really felt no more than he must have done from the apprehension of the same punishment a year before, there would be some foundation for this reasoning, which supposes the mind to have the same absolute interest in its own feelings both past, present, and to come. I say the sophism here employed consists in comparing the motives by which we are interested in the welfare of others with the mechanical impulses of self-love, as if because we are mechanically affected by the actual impression of objects on our senses in a manner in which we cannot be affected by the feelings of others, all our feelings with respect to ourselves must be of the same kind, and we could feel no interest in any thing but what was excited in the same way. It is plain we are not interested in our general, remote welfare in the same manner, or by the same necessity that we are affected by the actual sense of pleasure, or pain. We have no instinctive secret sympathy with our future sensations by which we are attracted either consciously or unconsciously to our greatest good; we are for the most part indifferent to it, ignorant of it. We certainly do not know, and we very often care as little what is to happen to ourselves in future: it has no more effect upon us in any way, than if it were never to happen. Were it not for this shortsightedness and insensibility, where would be the use, or what would become of the rules of personal prudence?

It will be said, I know, that this is foreign to the purpose; for that whether he feels it or not, every man *has* a real interest in his own welfare which he cannot have in that of another person. First, this is to shift the ground of the argument; for it requires to be made out how a man can be said to have an interest in what he does not feel. There is not evidently the same contradiction in supposing him not to be particularly interested in feelings which he has not, as there is in supposing him not to be interested in his actual, sensible pleasures and pains. Secondly, I shall very readily grant that *to have* and *to feel* an interest in any thing are not always convertible terms, that is, an interest may attach or belong to an individual in some way or other though he does not feel it at the time. My having a *real* interest in any object may refer to the matter of fact that such an object will sometime or other exist: now the reality of its existence does not certainly depend on my feeling an interest in it previously. Neither is the reality of another's pleasures, or pains affected by my not feeling such an interest in them as I ought to do. The feelings of others are evidently as real, or as much matters of fact in themselves as my own feelings can ever be. This distinction between that which is true and what has merely an imaginary existence, or none at all, does not therefore so far apply to the question, if by a real interest be meant that which relates to a real object, for it is supposed at first that this object does not excite any immediate or real interest in the mind. Another difference that may be insisted on is this, that I *shall have* a real sensible interest in my own future feelings which I cannot possibly have in those of others. I must therefore as the same individual have the same necessary interest in them at present. This may either proceed on the supposition of the absolute, metaphysical identity of my individual being, so that whatever can be affirmed of that principle at any time must be strictly and logically true of it at all times, which is a wild and absurd notion; or it may refer to some other less strict connection between my present and future self, in consequence of which I am considered as the same being, the different events and impressions of my life constituting one regular succession of conscious feelings. In this sense, the saying that *I have* a general interest in whatever concerns my future welfare in fact amounts to no more than affirming, that *I shall have* an interest in that welfare, or that I am nominally and in certain other respects the same being who will hereafter have a real interest in it. The reason why we are so ready to attribute a real identity of interests to the same person is, that we have an indistinct idea of extended consciousness, and a community of feelings as essential to the same thinking being; so that whatever interests me at one time must interest me, or be

capable of interesting me, at other times. Now this continued consciousness only serves to connect my past with my present impressions. It only acts retrospectively. I have not previously the same sympathy with my future being that I have with my past being, nor consequently the same natural or necessary interest in my future welfare that I have in my past. Lastly, it may be said, that there is something in the very *idea* of pleasure or pain as affecting myself which naturally excites a lively, unavoidable interest in my mind. I cannot conceive how the mere idea of self can produce any such effect as is here described, unless we imagine that self-love literally consists in the love of self, or in a proper attachment to our own persons instead of referring to the feelings of desire and aversion, hope, and fear, &c. excited in us by those things which either do, or may immediately affect ourselves. In consequence of the impression of many such objects on the thinking being, we shall come no doubt to connect a sense of self-interest with this very being, with the motions of our blood, and with life itself, and shall by degrees transfer the emotions of interest excited by particular positive feelings to the idea of our own interest generally speaking. This however must be the work of time, the gradual result of habit, and reflection, and cannot be the natural reason why a man pursues his own welfare, or is interested in his own feelings. I think therefore that in the first instance the idea of personal pleasure or pain can only affect the mind as a distinct idea of that which is in itself the object of desire, or aversion, and that the idea of self is nothing more than the first and most distinct idea we have of a being capable of receiving pleasure and pain. It will be the business of the greatest part of the following essay to make out these several points more distinctly.

*   *   *   *   *

To suppose that the mind is originally determined in its choice of good and rejection of evil solely by a regard to self is to suppose a state of *indifference* to both, which would make the existence of such a feeling as self-interest utterly impossible. If there were not something in the very notion of good, or evil which naturally made the one an object of immediate desire and the other of aversion, it is not easy to conceive how the mind should ever come to feel an interest in the prospect of obtaining the one or avoiding the other. It is great folly to think of deducing our desire of happiness and fear of pain from a principle of self-love, instead of deducing self-love itself from our natural desire of happiness and fear of pain. This sort of attachment to self could signify nothing more than a foolish complacency in our own idea, an idle dotage, and idolatry of our own abstract being; it must leave the mind indifferent to every thing else, and could not have any connection with the motives to action, unless some one should choose to make it the foundation of a new theory of the love of life and fear of death. So long as the individual exists, and remains entire, this principle is satisfied. As to the manner in which it exists, by what objects it shall be affected, whether it shall prefer one mode of being to another, all this is left undetermined. If then by self-love be meant a desire of one mode of being and aversion to another, or a desire of our own well-being, what is it that is to constitute this well-being? It is plain there must be something in the nature of the objects themselves which of itself determines the mind to consider them as desirable or the contrary previously to any reference of them to ourselves. They are not converted into good and evil by being impressed on our minds, but they affect our minds in a certain manner because they are essentially good or evil. How shall we reconcile this with supposing that the nature of those objects or their effect on the mind is entirely changed by their being referred to this or that person? I repeat it that self-interest implies certain objects and feelings for the mind to be interested in: to suppose that it can exist separately from all such objects, or that our attachment to certain objects is solely deduced from, and regulated by our attachment to self is plain, palpable nonsense.

Take the example of a child that has been burnt by the fire, and consequently conceives a dread of it. This dread we will say does not consist simply in the apprehension of the pain itself abstractedly considered, but together with this apprehension of pain he connects the idea (though not a very distinct one) of himself as about to feel it. Let us consider in what way the intervention of this idea can be supposed to cause or increase his dread of the pain itself. In the first place then it is evident that the fire actually burns the child, not because he is thinking of himself, or of its burning him, but because it is the nature of fire to burn and of the child's hand to feel pain, and his dislike of the pain while it actually exists is the immediate, necessary and physical consequence of the *sense* of pain, not an indirect and reflex result of the child's love to himself, or after-consideration that pain is an evil as it affects himself. Again I apprehend that after the actual pain has ceased, it continues to be thought of and is afterwards recollected as pain, or in other words, the feeling or sense of pain leaves a correspondent impression in the memory which adheres to the recollection of the object, and makes the child involuntarily shrink from it by the same sort of necessity, that is from the nature

of the human mind and the recollected impression, and not from his referring it historically to his own past existence. In like manner I conceive that this idea of pain when combined by the imagination with other circumstances and transferred to the child's future being will still retain its original tendency to give pain, and that the recurrence of the same painful sensation is necessarily regarded with terror and aversion by the child, not from its being conceived of in connection with his own idea, but because it is conceived of as pain.* It should also be remembered as the constant principle of all our reasonings, that the impression which the child has of himself as the subject of future pain is never any thing more than an idea of imagination, and that he cannot possibly by any kind of anticipation feel that pain as a real sensation a single moment before it exists. How then are we to account for his supposed exclusive attachment to this ideal self so as to make that the real source of the dislike and dread which the apprehension of any particular pain to be inflicted on himself causes in the mind? There are two ways in which this may at first sight appear to be satisfactorily made out. The first is from the notion of personal identity: this has been already considered,[1] and will be again considered by and by. The other is something as follows. The child having been burnt by the fire and only knowing what the pain of a burn is from his recollecting to have felt it himself, as soon as he finds himself in danger of it again, has a very vivid recollection of the pain it formerly gave him excited in his mind; and by a kind of sudden transposition substituting this idea in the place of his immediate apprehension, in thinking of the danger to which he is exposed he confounds the pain he is to feel with that which he has already actually felt, and in reality shrinks from the latter. I mean that the child strongly *recollects* that particular sort of pain as it has affected himself, and as it is not possible for him to have a recollection of its effect on any one else, he only regards it as an evil in future in connection with the same idea, or as affecting himself, and is entirely indifferent to it as it is supposed to affect any one else. Or in other words he remembers being burnt himself

* This account is loose enough. I shall endeavour to give a better, as to the manner in which ideas may be supposed to be connected with volition, at the end of this essay. In the mean time I wish the reader to be apprized, that I do not use the word *imagination* as contradistinguished from or opposed to reason, or the faculty by which we reflect upon and compare our ideas, but as opposed to sensation, or memory. It has been shewn above that by the word *idea* is not meant a merely abstract idea.

[1] See the fifth paragraph of the *Essay*, pp. 400–401.

as an actual sensation, but he does not remember the actual sensations of any one but himself: therefore being able to trace back his present feelings to his past impressions, and struck with the extreme faintness of the one compared with the other, he gives way to his immediate apprehensions and imaginary fears only as he is conscious of, and dreads, the possibility of their returning into the same state of actual sensation again.

I do not deny that some such illusion of the imagination as I have here attempted to describe begins to take place very soon in the mind, and continues to acquire strength ever after from various causes. What I would contend for (and this is all that my argument requires) is that it is and can be nothing more than an illusion of the imagination, strengthening a difference in subordinate, indirect, collateral circumstances into an essential difference of kind. The objection would indeed hold good if it were true that the child's imaginary sympathy with the danger of another must be derived as it were in a kind of direct line from that other's actual sense of past pain, or its immediate communication to his own senses, which is absurd. It is not supposed that the child can ever have felt the actual pains of another as his own actual pains, or that his sympathy with others is a real continuation and result of this original organic sympathy in the same way that his dread of personal pain is to be deduced from his previous consciousness of it. His sympathy with others is necessarily the result of his own past experience: if he had never felt any thing himself, he could not possibly feel for others. I do not know that any light would be thrown upon the argument by entering into a particular analysis of the faculty of imagination; nor shall I pretend to determine at what time this faculty acquires sufficient strength to enable the child to take a distinct interest in the feelings of others. I shall content myself with observing that this faculty is absolutely necessary to the child's having any apprehension or concern either about his own future interest, or that of others; that but for this faculty of multiplying, varying, extending, combining, and comparing his original passive impressions he must be utterly blind to the future and indifferent to it, insensible to every thing beyond the present moment, altogether incapable of hope, or fear, or exertion of any kind, unable to avoid or remove the most painful impressions, or to wish for or even think of their removal, to withdraw his hand out of the fire, or to move his lips to quench the most burning thirst; that without this faculty of conceiving of things which have not been impressed on his senses and of inferring like things from like, he must remain totally destitute of foresight, of self-motion, or a sense of self-interest,

the passive instrument of undreaded pain and unsought-for pleasure, suffering and enjoying without resistance and without desire just so long as the different outward objects continued to act upon his senses, in a state of more than idiot imbecility; and that with this faculty enabling him to throw himself forward into the future, to anticipate unreal events and to be affected by his own imaginary interest, he must necessarily be capable in a greater or less degree of entering into the feelings and interests of others and of being influenced by them. The child (by the time that his perceptions and actions begin to take any thing of a consistent form so that they can be made the subject of reasoning) being supposed to know from experience what the pain of a burn is, and seeing himself in danger a second time is immediately filled with terror, and strives either by suddenly drawing back his hand, catching hold of something, or by his cries for assistance to avoid the danger to which he is exposed. Here then his memory and senses present him with nothing more than certain external objects in themselves indifferent, and the recollection of extreme pain formerly connected with the same or similar objects. If he had no other faculties than these, he must stop here. He would see and feel his own body moved rapidly towards the fire, but his apprehensions would not outrun its actual motion: he would not think of his nearer approach to the fire as a consequence of the force with which he was carried along, nor dream of falling into the fire till he found it actually burning him. Even if it were possible for him to foresee the consequence, it would not be an object of dread to him; because without a reasoning imagination he would not and could not connect with the painted flame before him the idea of violent pain which the same kind of object had formerly given him by its actual contact. But in fact he *imagines* his continued approach to the fire till he falls into it; by his imagination he attributes to the fire a power to burn, he conceives of an ideal self endued with a power to feel, and by the force of imagination solely, anticipates a repetition of the same sense of pain which he before felt. If then he considers this pain, which is but an ideal sensation impressed on an ideal being, as an object of real, present, necessary and irresistible interest to him, and, knowing that it cannot be avoided but by an immediate exertion of voluntary power, makes a sudden and eager effort to avoid it by the first means he can think of, why are we to suppose that the apprehension of the same pain to be inflicted on another whom he must believe to be endued with the same feelings, and with whose feelings he must be capable of sympathizing in the same manner as with his own imaginary feelings, may not affect him with the same sort of interest, the same sort of terror, and impel him to the same exertions for his relief?*

Because, it is said, in his own case there is a natural deception, by which he confounds his future being with his past being, and the idea of a future imaginary pain with the recollection of a past conscious pain. At any rate, this must be unconsciously: if the sense of present danger acts so powerfully on his mind as to bring back the recollection of a past sensation, and set that before him in the place of the real object of his fear, so that, while he is endeavouring to avoid an immediate danger, he is in fact thinking only of past suffering without his perceiving this confusion of ideas, surely the same thing must take place in a less degree with respect to others. If it be thought necessary for him, before he can seek his own future interest, to confound it with his past interest by the violent transition of an immediate apprehension into the stronger recollection of an actual impression, then I say that by the same sort of substitution he will identify his own interest with that of others, whenever a like obvious danger recals forcibly to his mind his former situation and feelings, the lenses of memory being applied in the one case to excite his sympathy and in the other to excite personal fear, the objects of both being in themselves equally imaginary and according to this hypothesis both perfectly indifferent. But I should contend that the assumption here made that the direct and proper influence of the imagination is insufficient to account for the effects of personal fear, or of no force at all in itself is without any foundation. For there is no reason to be shewn why the ideas of the imagination should not be efficient, operative, as well as those of memory, of which they are essentially compounded. Their substance is the same. They are of one flesh and blood. The same vital spirit animates them both. To suppose that the imagination does not exert a direct influence over human actions is to reject the plain inference from the most undoubted facts without any motive for so doing from the nature and reason of things. This notion could not

have gained ground as an article of philosophical faith but from a perverse restriction of the use of the word *idea* to abstract ideas, or external forms, as if the essential quality in the feelings of pleasure, or pain, must entirely evaporate in passing through the imagination; and, again, from associating the word *imagination* with merely fictitious situations and events, that is, such as never will have a real existence, and as it is supposed never will, and which consequently do not admit of action.† Besides, though it is certain that the imagination is strengthened in its operation by the indirect assistance of our other faculties, yet as it is this faculty which must be the immediate spring and guide to action (unless we attribute to it an inherent, independent power over the will so as to make it bend to every change of circumstances or probability of advantage, and a power at the same time of controuling the blind impulses of associated mechanical feelings and of making them subservient to the accomplishment of some particular purpose, or in words without a power of willing a given *end* for itself, and of employing the means immediately necessary to the production of that end, because they are perceived to be so), there could be neither volition, nor action, neither rational fear nor steady pursuit of any object, neither wisdom nor folly, generosity nor selfishness: all would be left to the accidental concurrence of some mechanical impulse with the immediate desire to obtain some very simple object: in no other case can either accident or habit be supposed likely to carry any rational purpose into effect. To return however to what I have said above in answer to this objection, it is evident that all persons are more inclined to compassionate those pains and calamities in others by which they have been affected themselves, which proves that the operation of that principle, even supposing it to be the true one, is not confined to selfish objects. Our sympathy is always directly excited in proportion to our knowledge of the pain, and of the disposition and feelings of the sufferer. Thus with respect to ourselves we are little affected by the apprehension of physical pain which we have never felt and therefore can know little of; and we have still less sympathy with others in this case. Our incredulity and insensibility with respect to what others frequently suffer from the tooth-ache and other incidental disorders must have been remarked by every one, and are even ludicrous from the excess to which they are carried. Give what account you will of it, the effect is the same:—our self-love and sympathy depend upon

---

* I take it for granted that the only way to establish the selfish hypothesis is by shewing that our own interest is in reality brought home to the mind as a motive to action by some means or other by which that of others cannot possibly affect it. This is unavoidable, unless we ascribe a particular genius of selfishness to each individual which never suffers his affections to wander from himself for a moment; or shall we suppose that a man's attachment to himself is because he has a long nose or a short one, because his hair is black or red, or from an unaccountable fancy for his own name, for all these make a part of the individual, and must be deemed very weighty reasons by those who think it self-evident that a man must love himself because he is himself?

† See the last note but one.[2]

◇—◇—◇—◇—◇—◇—◇—◇—◇—◇—◇—◇—◇—◇—◇—◇—◇—◇—◇

[2] Referring to Hazlitt's footnote, p. 402.

the same causes, and constantly bear a determinate proportion to each other, at least in the same individual. The same knowledge of any pain, which increases our dread of it, makes us more ready to feel for others who are exposed to it. When a boy I had my arm put out of joint, and I feel a kind of nervous twitching in it to this day whenever I see any one with his arm bound up in consequence of a similar accident. This part of my subject has been so well detailed by Smith[3] and others that it is needless to insist on it farther. There are certain disorders which have a disgusting appearance, that shock and force attention by their novelty; but they do not properly excite our sympathy, or compassion, as they would do if we had ever been subject to them ourselves. Children seem to sympathize more naturally with the outward signs of passion in others without inquiring into the particular causes by which it is excited, whether it is that their ideas of pain are more gross and simple, and therefore more uniform and more easily substituted for each other, or that grown up persons, having a greater number of ideas and being oftener able to sympathize with others from knowing what they feel, habitually make this knowledge the foundation of their sympathy.* In general it seems that those physical evils,

* The general clue to that ænigma, the character of the French, seems to be that their feelings are very imperfectly modified by the objects exciting them. That is, the difference between the several degrees and kinds of feeling in them does not correspond, as much as it does in most other people, with the different degrees and kinds of power in the external objects. They want neither feeling nor ideas in the abstract; but there seems to be no connection in their minds between the one and the other. Consequently their feelings want compass and variety, and whatever else must depend on the "building up of our feelings through the imagination." The feelings of a Frenchman seem to be all one feeling. The moment any thing produces a change in him, he is thrown completely out of his character, he is quite beside himself. This is perhaps in a great measure owing to their quickness of perception. They do not give the object time to be *thoroughly* impressed on their minds, their feelings are roused at the first notice of its approach, and if I may so express myself, fairly run away from the object instead of grappling with it. The least stimulus is sufficient to excite them and more is superfluous, for they do not wait for the whole impression, or stop to inquire what degree or kind it is of. There is not resistance enough in the matter to receive those sharp incisions, those deep, marked, and strongly rooted impressions, the traces of which

[3] Adam Smith (1723–1790), in his *Theory of Moral Sentiments* (1759), had similarly argued for the central role of the imagination in the development of our "moral sentiments": "It is the impressions of our own senses only, not those of [a man whom we observe in pain], which our imaginations copy. By the imagination we place ourselves in his situation, we conceive ourselves enduring all the same torments, we enter as it were into his body, and become in some measure the same person with him, and thence form some idea of his sensations, and even feel something which, though weaker in degree, is not altogether unlike them" (Section I, Chapter I).

which we have actually experienced, and which from their nature must produce nearly the same effect upon

——————

remain for ever. From whatever cause it proceeds, the sensitive principle in them does not seem to be susceptible of the same modification and variety of action as it does in others; and certainly the outward forms of things do not adhere to, nor wind themselves round their feelings in the same manner. For any thing that appears to the contrary, objects might be supposed to have no direct communication with the internal sense of pleasure or pain, but to act upon it through some intermediate, very confined organ, capable of transmitting little more than the simple impulse. But the same thing will follow, if we suppose the principle itself to be this very organ, that is, to want comprehensiveness, elasticity, and plastic force. (It is difficult to express this in English: but the French have a word, *ressort*, which expresses it exactly. This is possibly owing to their feeling the want of it; as there is no word in any other language to answer to the English word, *comfort*, I suppose, because the English are the most uncomfortable. of all people.) It will rather follow from what has been here said than be inconsistent with it, that the French must be more sensible of minute impressions and slight shades of difference in their feelings than others, because having, as is here supposed, less real variety, a narrower range of feeling, they will attend more to the differences contained within that narrow circle, and so produce an artificial variety. In short their feelings are very easily set in motion and by slight causes, but they do not go the whole length of the impression, nor are they capable of combining a great variety of complicated actions to correspond with the distinct characters and complex forms of things. Hence they have no such things as poetry. This however must not be misunderstood. I mean then that I never met with any thing in French that produces the same kind of feeling in the mind as the following passage.[4] If there is any thing that belongs even to the same class with it, I am ready to give the point up.

> *Antony. Eros*, thou yet behold'st me.
> *Eros.* Ay, noble Lord.
> *Ant.* Sometimes we see a cloud that's Dragonish,
> A vapour sometimes like a Bear, or Lion,
> A tower'd Citadel, a pendant Rock,
> A forked Mountain, or blue Promontory
> With Trees upon't, that nod unto the World
> And mock our Eyes with Air. Thou hast seen these Signs,
> They are black Vesper's Pageants.
> *Eros.* Ay, my Lord.
> *Ant.* That which is now a Horse, even with a Thought
> The rack dislimns, and makes it indistinct
> As Water is in Water.
> *Eros.* It does, my Lord.
> *Ant.* My good Knave, *Eros*, now thy Captain is
> Even such a body, &c.

It is remarkable that the French, who are a lively people and fond of shew and striking images, should be able to read and hear with such delight their own dramatic pieces, which abound in nothing but general maxims, and vague declamation, never embodying any thing, and which would appear quite tedious to an English audience, who are generally considered as a dry, dull, plodding people, much more likely to be satisfied with formal descriptions and grave reflections. This appears to me to come to the same thing that I have said before, namely, that it is characteristic of the French that their feelings let go their hold of things

[4] *Antony and Cleopatra*, IV, xiv, 1–13.

every one, must excite a more immediate and natural sympathy than those which depend on sentiment or moral causes. It is however neither so complete nor durable, as these last being the creatures of imagination appeal more strongly to our sympathy, which is itself an act of the imagination, than mere physical evils can ever do, whether they relate to ourselves or others. Our sympathy with physical evil is also a more unpleasant feeling, and therefore submitted to with more reluctance. So that it is necessary to take another circumstance into the account in judging of the quantity of our sympathy besides the two above mentioned, namely, the nature of the pain or its fitness to excite our sympathy. This makes no difference in the question.

To say that the child recollects the pain of being burnt only in connection with his own idea, and can therefore conceive of it as an evil only with respect to himself, is in effect to deny the existence of any such

---

almost as soon as the first impression is made. Except sensible impressions therefore (which have on that account more force, and carry them away without opposition while they last) all their feelings are general; and being general, not being marked by any strong distinctions, nor built on any deep foundation of inveterate associations, one thing serves to excite them as well as another, the name of the general class to which any feeling belongs, the words *pleasure, charming, delicious,* &c., convey just the same meaning, and excite the same kind of emotion in the mind of a Frenchman, and at the same time do it more readily than the most forcible description of real feelings, and objects. The English on the contrary are not so easily moved with words, because being in the habit of retaining individual images and of brooding over the feelings connected with them, the mere names of general classes, or (which is the same thing) vague and unmeaning descriptions or sentiments must appear perfectly indifferent to them. Hence the French are all delighted with Racine, the English (I mean some of them) admire Shakespeare. Rousseau is the only French writer I am acquainted with (though he by the bye was not exactly a Frenchman) who from the depth of his feelings, without many distinct images, produces the same kind of interest in the mind that is excited by the events and recollections of our own lives. If he had not true genius, he had at least something which was a very good substitute for it. The French generalise perpetually, but seldom comprehensively: they make an infinite number of observations, but have never discovered any great principle. They immediately perceive the analogy between a number of facts of the same class, and make a general inference, which is done the more easily, the fewer particulars you trouble them with; it is in a good measure the art of forgetting. The difficult part of philosophy is, when a number of particular observations and contradictory facts have been stated, to reconcile them together by finding out some other distinct view of the subject, or collateral circumstance, applicable to all the different facts or appearances, which is the true principle from which, when combined with particular circumstances, they are all derived. Opposite appearances are always immediately incompatible with each other, and cannot be deduced from the same immediate cause, but must be accounted for from a combination of different causes, the discovery of which is an affair of comprehension, and not of mere abstraction.

power as the imagination. By the same power of mind which enables him to conceive of a past sensation as about to be re-excited in the same being, namely, himself, he must be capable of transferring the same idea of pain to a different person. He *creates* the object, he pushes his ideas beyond the bounds of his memory and senses in the first instance, and he does no more in the second. If his mind were merely passive in the operation, he would not be busy in anticipating a new impression, but would still be dreaming of the old one. It is of the very nature of the imagination to change the order in which things have been impressed on the senses, and to connect the same properties with different objects, and different properties with the same objects; to combine our original impressions in all possible forms, and to modify these impressions themselves to a very great degree. Man without this would not be a rational agent: he would be below the dullest and most stupid brute. It must therefore be proved in some other way that the human mind cannot conceive of or be interested in the pleasure or pains of others because it has never felt them.

*　　*　　*　　*　　*

[1805]

THE ROUND TABLE

Hazlitt's career as a journalist began in 1812 with his appointment as a parliamentary reporter for the Morning Chronicle. *In the succeeding years, he was to become one of the busiest and most prominent of British journalists, contributing theater and art criticism, book reviews, informal essays, and political articles to a variety of periodicals. The first prophecy of his later distinction as a familiar essayist came with a series of "Common-Places," which he began to contribute to the Morning Chronicle in September 1813; these consisted of short, informal examinations of received opinions, or in Hazlitt's words, "[the exposure of] certain vulgar errors, which have crept into our reasonings on men and manners." The series was continued in the* Examiner, *to which Hazlitt began contributing in 1814. When in 1815 he became a full-time member of Leigh Hunt's staff, he wrote similar essays for the "Round Table" column on a regular basis through January 1817.*

In 1819, Hazlitt thus described the informal essays contributed to the "Round Table", and his remarks are equally applicable to the earlier "Common-Places" and to the longer familiar essays of the 1820's, his major contribution to the variety of Romantic prose:

> *My object in writing [them] was to set down such observations as had occurred to me from time to time on different subjects, and as appeared to be any ways worth preserving. I wished to make a sort of* Liber Veritatis, *a set of studies from human life. As my object was not to flatter, neither was it to offend or contradict others, but to state my own feelings or opinions such as they really were, but more particularly of course when this had not been done before, and where I thought I could*

throw any new light upon a subject . . . I wrote to the public with the same sincerity and want of disguise as if I had been making a register of my private thoughts; and this has been construed by some into a breach of decorum . . . As to my style, I thought little about it. I used only the word which seemed to me to signify the idea I wanted to convey, and I did not rest till I had got it. In seeking for truth, I sometimes found beauty.

The Round Table, published in two volumes in 1817, is richly representative of Hazlitt's early journalism. It brought together forty essays by Hazlitt (and twelve by Leigh Hunt) on a variety of subjects (theatrical reviews, commentaries on art and literature, as well as the informal essays "Common-Places" and "Round Table"), largely but not exclusively drawn from the pages of the Examiner. *Of Hazlitt's contributions, twenty-two were properly drawn from the "Round Table" columns of the* Examiner *(here represented by "On Gusto"); "On the Love of the Country" (one of the "Common-Places") and the review of Wordsworth's* Excursion *came from other columns of Leigh Hunt's journal; still others, such as "Why the Arts are not Progressive?," had first appeared in the* Morning Chronicle *and the* Champion. *The text of these essays here reproduced is from the 1817 collection.*

F R O M

THE ROUND TABLE

ON THE LOVE OF THE COUNTRY
TO THE EDITOR OF THE ROUND TABLE.

S IR,—I do not know that any one has ever explained satisfactorily the true source of our attachment to natural objects, or of that soothing emotion which the sight of the country hardly ever fails to infuse into the mind. Some persons have ascribed this feeling to the natural beauty of the objects themselves, others to the freedom from care, the silence and tranquillity which scenes of retirement afford— others to the healthy and innocent employments of a country life—others to the simplicity of country manners—and others to different causes; but none to the right one. All these causes may, I believe, have a share in producing this feeling; but there is another more general principle, which has been left untouched, and which I shall here explain, endeavouring to be as little sentimental as the subject will admit.

Rousseau, in his Confessions,[1] (the most valuable of all his works,) relates, that when he took possession of his room at Annecy, at the house of his beloved mistress and friend, he found that he could see "a little spot of green" from his window, which endeared his situation the more to him, because, he says, it was the first time he had had this object constantly before him since he left Boissy, the place where he was at school when a child.* Some such feeling as that here described will be found lurking at the bottom of all our attachments of this sort. Were it not for the recollections habitually associated with them, natural objects could not interest the mind in the manner they do. No doubt, the sky is beautiful; the clouds sail majestically along its bosom; the sun is cheering; there is something exquisitely graceful in the manner in which a plant or tree puts forth its branches; the motion with which they bend and tremble in the evening breeze is soft and lovely; there is music in the babbling of a brook; the view from the top of a mountain is full of grandeur; nor can we behold the ocean with indifference. Or, as the Minstrel sweetly sings—

"Oh how can'st thou renounce the boundless store
Of charms which Nature to her votary yields!
The warbling woodland, the resounding shore,
The pomp of groves, and garniture of fields;
All that the genial ray of morning gilds,
And all that echoes to the song of even,
All that the mountain's sheltering bosom shields,
And all the dread magnificence of heaven,
Oh how can'st thou renounce, and hope to be forgiven!"[2]

It is not, however, the beautiful and magnificent alone that we admire in Nature; the most insignificant and rudest objects are often found connected with the strongest emotions; we become attached to the most common and familiar images as to the face of a friend whom we have long known, and from whom we have received many benefits. It is because natural objects have been associated with the sports of our childhood, with air and exercise, with our feelings in solitude, when the mind takes the strongest hold of things, and clings with the fondest interest to whatever strikes its attention; with change of place, the pursuit of new scenes, and thoughts of distant friends; it is because they have surrounded us in almost all situations, in joy and in sorrow, in pleasure and in pain; because they have been one chief source and nourishment of our feelings, and a part of our being, that we love them as we do ourselves.

There is, generally speaking, the same foundation for our love of Nature as for all our habitual attach-

* Pope also declares that he had a particular regard for an old post which stood in the court-yard before the house where he was brought up.

[1] See Book III of the *Confessions* for the incident of Rousseau's taking up residence at the house of his patroness and mistress Madame de Warens.

[2] James Beattie's *The Minstrel* (1771), I, ix.

ments, namely, association of ideas. But this is not all. That which distinguishes this attachment from others is the transferable nature of our feelings with respect to physical objects; the associations connected with any one object extending to the whole class. My having been attached to any particular person does not make me feel the same attachment to the next person I may chance to meet; but, if I have once associated strong feelings of delight with the objects of natural scenery, the tie becomes indissoluble, and I shall ever after feel the same attachment to other objects of the same sort. I remember when I was abroad,[3] the trees, and grass, and wet leaves, rustling in the walks of the Thuilleries, seemed to be as much English, to be as much the same trees and grass, that I had always been used to, as the sun shining over my head was the same sun which I saw in England; the faces only were foreign to me. Whence comes this difference? It arises from our always imperceptibly connecting the idea of the individual with man, and only the idea of the class with natural objects. In the one case, the external appearance or physical structure is the least thing to be attended to; in the other, it is every thing. The springs that move the human form, and make it friendly or adverse to me, lie hid within it. There is an infinity of motives, passions, and ideas, contained in that narrow compass, of which I know nothing, and in which I have no share. Each individual is a world to himself, governed by a thousand contradictory and wayward impulses. I can, therefore, make no inference from one individual to another; nor can my habitual sentiments, with respect to any individual, extend beyond himself to others. But it is otherwise with respect to Nature. There is neither hypocrisy, caprice, nor mental reservation in her favours. Our intercourse with her is not liable to accident or change, interruption or disappointment. She smiles on us still the same. Thus, to give an obvious instance, if I have once enjoyed the cool shade of a tree, and been lulled into a deep repose by the sound of a brook running at its feet, I am sure that wherever I can find a tree and a brook, I can enjoy the same pleasure again. Hence, when I imagine these objects, I can easily form a mystic personification of the friendly power that inhabits them, Dryad or Naiad, offering its cool fountain or its tempting shade. Hence the origin of the Grecian mythology. All objects of the same kind being the same, not only in their appearance, but in their practical uses, we habitually confound them together under the same general idea; and, whatever

fondness we may have conceived for one, is immediately placed to the common account. The most opposite kinds and remote trains of feeling gradually go to enrich the same sentiment; and in our love of Nature, there is all the force of individual attachment, combined with the most airy abstraction. It is this circumstance which gives that refinement, expansion, and wild interest to feelings of this sort, when strongly excited, which every one must have experienced who is a true lover of Nature. The sight of the setting sun does not affect me so much from the beauty of the object itself, from the glory kindled through the glowing skies, the rich broken columns of light, or the dying streaks of day, as that it indistinctly recals to me numberless thoughts and feelings with which, through many a year and season, I have watched his bright descent in the warm summer evenings, or beheld him struggling to cast a "farewel sweet"[4] through the thick clouds of winter. I love to see the trees first covered with leaves in the spring, the primroses peeping out from some sheltered bank, and the innocent lambs running races on the soft green turf; because, at that birth-time of Nature, I have always felt sweet hopes and happy wishes—which have not been fulfilled! The dry reeds rustling on the side of a stream,—the woods swept by the loud blast,—the dark massy foliage of autumn,—the grey trunks and naked branches of the trees in winter, —the sequestered copse and wide extended heath,— the warm sunny showers, and December snows,— have all charms for me; there is no object, however trifling or rude, that has not, in some mood or other, found the way to my heart; and I might say, in the words of the poet,

> "To me the meanest flower that blows can give
> Thoughts that do often lie too deep for tears."

Thus Nature is a kind of universal home, and every object it presents to us an old acquaintance with unaltered looks.

> ——"Nature did ne'er betray
> The heart that lov'd her, but through all the years
> Of this our life, it is her privilege
> To lead from joy to joy."[5]

For there is that consent and mutual harmony among all her works, one undivided spirit pervading them throughout, that, if we have once knit ourselves in hearty fellowship to any of them, they will never afterwards appear as strangers to us, but, which ever

---

[3] Referring to Hazlitt's visit to Paris in 1802–1803 in order to study and copy paintings at the Louvre.

[4] *Paradise Lost*, II, 492.
[5] Hazlitt quotes, respectively, from Wordsworth's "Intimations Ode," ll. 203–204, and "Tintern Abbey," ll. 122–125.

way we turn, we shall find a secret power to have gone out before us, moulding them into such shapes as fancy loves, informing them with life and sympathy, bidding them put on their festive looks and gayest attire at our approach, and to pour all their sweets and choicest treasures at our feet. For him, then, who has well acquainted himself with Nature's works, she wears always one face, and speaks the same well-known language, striking on the heart, amidst unquiet thoughts and the tumult of the world, like the music of one's native tongue heard in some far off country.

We do not connect the same feelings with the works of art as with those of nature, because we refer them to man, and associate with them the separate interests and passions which we know belong to those who are the authors or possessors of them. Nevertheless, there are some such objects, as a cottage, or a village church, which excite in us the same sensations as the sight of nature, and which are, indeed, almost always included in descriptions of natural scenery.

> "Or from the mountain's sides
> View wilds and swelling floods,
> And hamlets brown, and dim-discover'd spires,
> And hear their simple bell." 6

Which is in part, no doubt, because they are surrounded with natural objects, and, in a populous country, inseparable from them; and also because the human interest they excite relates to manners and feelings which are simple, common, such as all can enter into, and which, therefore, always produce a pleasing effect upon the mind.

[November 1814]   [1817]

ON GUSTO

Gusto in art is power or passion defining any object.—It is not difficult to explain this term in what relates to expression (of which it may be said to be the highest degree) as in what relates to things without expression, to the natural appearances of objects, as mere colour or form. In one sense, however, there is hardly any object entirely devoid of expression, without some character of power belonging to it, some precise association with pleasure or pain: and it is in giving this truth of character from the truth of feeling, whether in the highest or the lowest degree, but always in the highest degree of which the subject is capable, that gusto consists.

There is a gusto in the colouring of Titian. Not only

do his heads seem to think—his bodies seem to feel. This is what the Italians mean by the *morbidezza*[1] of his flesh-colour. It seems sensitive and alive all over; not merely to have the look and texture of flesh, but the feeling in itself. For example, the limbs of his female figures have a luxurious softness and delicacy, which appears conscious of the pleasure of the beholder. As the objects themselves in nature would produce an impression on the sense, distinct from every other object, and having something divine in it, which the heart owns and the imagination consecrates, the objects in the picture preserve the same impression, absolute, unimpaired, stamped with all the truth of passion, the pride of the eye, and the charm of beauty. Rubens makes his flesh-colour like flowers; Albano's[2] is like ivory; Titian's is like flesh, and like nothing else. It is as different from that of other painters, as the skin is from a piece of white or red drapery thrown over it. The blood circulates here and there, and blue veins just appear, the rest is distinguished throughout only by that sort of tingling sensation to the eye, which the body feels within itself. This is gusto.—Vandyke's flesh-colour, though it has great truth and purity, wants gusto. It has not the internal character, the living principle in it. It is a smooth surface, not a warm, moving mass. It is painted without passion, with indifference. The hand only has been concerned. The impression slides off from the eye, and does not, like the tones of Titian's pencil, leave a sting behind it in the mind of the spectator. The eye does not acquire a taste or appetite for what it sees. In a word, gusto in painting is where the impression made on one sense excites by affinity those of another.

Michael Angelo's forms are full of gusto. They every where obtrude the sense of power upon the eye. His limbs convey an idea of muscular strength, of moral grandeur, and even of intellectual dignity: they are firm, commanding, broad, and massy, capable of executing with ease the determined purposes of the will. His faces have no other expression than his figures, conscious power and capacity. They appear only to think what they shall do, and to know that they can do it. This is what is meant by saying that his style is hard and masculine. It is the reverse of Correggio's,[3] which is effeminate. That is, the gusto of Michael Angelo consists in expressing energy of will without proportionable sensibility, Correggio's in expressing exquisite sensibility without

---

6 William Collins' "Ode to Evening" (1746), ll. 35–38.

1 *morbidezza:* "a softness inviting one to touch."
2 Francesco Albano (1578–1660) was an Italian painter of religious and mythological subjects.
3 The paintings of Antonio Allegri da Correggio (1494–1534) are notable for their charm and tender gracefulness.

energy of will. In Correggio's faces as well as figures we see neither bones nor muscles, but then what a soul is there, full of sweetness and of grace—pure, playful, soft, angelical! There is sentiment enough in a hand painted by Correggio to set up a school of history painters. Whenever we look at the hands of Correggio's women or of Raphael's, we always wish to touch them.

Again, Titian's landscapes have a prodigious gusto, both in the colouring and forms. We shall never forget one that we saw many years ago in the Orleans Gallery[4] of Acteon hunting. It had a brown, mellow, autumnal look. The sky was of the colour of stone. The winds seemed to sing through the rustling branches of the trees, and already you might hear the twanging of bows resound through the tangled mazes of the wood. Mr. West,[5] we understand, has this landscape. He will know if this description of it is just. The landscape back-ground of the St Peter Martyr[6] is another well known instance of the power of this great painter to give a romantic interest and an appropriate character to the objects of his pencil, where every circumstance adds to the effect of the scene,—the bold trunks of the tall forest trees, the trailing ground plants, with that cold convent spire rising in the distance, amidst the blue sapphire mountains and the golden sky.

Rubens has a great deal of gusto in his Fauns and Satyrs, and in all that expresses motion, but in nothing else. Rembrandt has it in every thing; every thing in his pictures has a tangible character. If he puts a diamond in the ear of a Burgomaster's wife, it is of the first water; and his furs and stuffs are proof against a Russian winter. Raphael's gusto was only in expression; he had no idea of the character of any thing but the human form. The dryness and poverty of his style in other respects is a phenomenon in the art. His trees are like sprigs of grass stuck in a book of botanical specimens. Was is that Raphael never had time to go beyond the walls of Rome? That he was always in the streets, at church, or in the bath? He was not one of the Society of Arcadians.*

* Raphael not only could not paint a landscape; he could not paint people in a landscape. He could not have painted the heads

Claude's landscapes,[7] perfect as they are, want gusto. This is not easy to explain. They are perfect abstractions of the visible images of things; they speak the visible language of nature truly. They resemble a mirror or a microscope. To the eye only they are more perfect than any other landscapes that ever were or will be painted; they give more of nature, as cognizable by one sense alone; but they lay an equal stress on all visible impressions; they do not interpret one sense by another; they do not distinguish the character of different objects as we are taught, and can only be taught, to distinguish them by their effect on the different senses. That is, his eye wanted imagination: it did not strongly sympathize with his other faculties. He saw the atmosphere, but he did not feel it. He painted the trunk of a tree or a rock in the foreground as smooth—with as complete an abstraction of the gross, tangible impression, as any other part of the picture; his trees are perfectly beautiful, but quite immoveable; they have a look of enchantment. In short, his landscapes are unequalled imitations of nature, released from its subjection to the elements,—as if all objects were become a delightful fairy vision, and the eye had rarefied and refined away the other senses.

The gusto in the Greek statues is of a very singular kind. The sense of perfect form nearly occupies the whole mind, and hardly suffers it to dwell on any other feeling. It seems enough for them *to be*, without acting or suffering. Their forms are ideal, spiritual. Their beauty is power. By their beauty they are raised above the frailties of pain or passion; by their beauty they are deified.

The infinite quantity of dramatic invention in Shakspeare takes from his gusto. The power he delights to show is not intense, but discursive. He never insists on any thing as much as he might, except a quibble. Milton has great gusto. He repeats his blows twice; grapples with and exhausts his subject. His imagination has a double relish of its objects, an inveterate attachment to the things he describes, and to the words describing them.

---

or the figures, or even the dresses of the St Peter Martyr. His figures have always an *in-door* look, that is, a set, determined, voluntary, dramatic character, arising from their own passions, or a watchfulness of those of others, and want that wild uncertainty of expression, which is connected with the accidents of nature and the changes of the elements. He has nothing *romantic* about him.

---

4 The Orleans Gallery was a celebrated exhibition of Italian paintings, from the collection of the Duc d'Orleans, shown in London in 1798–1799. Hazlitt had attended the exhibition, which he regarded as the formative influence on his taste in painting thereafter.
5 Benjamin West (1738–1820) was an American-born historical painter, who became one of the leading painters in England after 1763 and president of the Royal Academy.
6 A famous altarpiece painted by Titian in 1528–1530, depicting the murder of Peter, a thirteenth-century Dominican friar and preacher against the Manichean heretics.

7 Claude Lorraine (1600–1682) was a distinguished French painter of classical landscapes.

————"Or where Chineses drive
With sails and wind their *cany* waggons *light*."

* * * * * * * * * *

"Wild above rule or art, *enormous* bliss." [8]

There is a gusto in Pope's compliments, in Dryden's satires, and Prior's tales; [9] and among prose-writers, Boccacio and Rabelais [10] had the most of it. We will only mention one other work which appears to us to be full of gusto, and that is the *Beggar's Opera*. [11] If it is not, we are altogether mistaken in our notions on this delicate subject.

[May 1816]   [1817]

OBSERVATIONS ON
MR. WORDSWORTH'S POEM
THE EXCURSION

THE POEM of the *Excursion* resembles that part of the country in which the scene is laid. It has the same vastness and magnificence, with the same nakedness and confusion. It has the same overwhelming, oppressive power. It excites or recals the same sensations which those who have traversed that wonderful scenery must have felt. We are surrounded with the constant sense and superstitious awe of the collective power of matter, of the gigantic and eternal forms of nature, on which, from the beginning of time, the hand of man has made no impression. Here are no dotted lines, no hedge-row beauties, no box-tree borders, no gravel walks, no square mechanic inclosures; all is left loose and irregular in the rude chaos of aboriginal nature. The boundaries of hill and valley are the poet's only geography, where we wander with him incessantly over deep beds of moss and waving fern, amidst the troops of red-deer and wild animals. Such is the severe simplicity of Mr Wordsworth's taste, that we doubt whether he would not reject a druidical temple, or time-hallowed ruin as too modern and artificial for his purpose. He only familiarizes himself or his readers with a stone, covered with lichens, which has slept in the same spot of ground from the creation of the world, or with the rocky fissure between two mountains caused by thunder, or with a cavern scooped out by the sea. His mind is, as it were, coëval with the primary

forms of things; his imagination holds immediately from nature, and "owes no allegiance" but "to the elements." [1]

The *Excursion* may be considered as a philosophical pastoral poem,—as a scholastic romance. It is less a poem on the country, than on the love of the country. It is not so much a description of natural objects, as of the feelings associated with them; not an account of the manners of rural life, but the result of the poet's reflections on it. He does not present the reader with a lively succession of images or incidents, but paints the outgoings of his own heart, the shapings of his own fancy. He may be said to create his own materials; his thoughts are his real subject. His understanding broods over that which is "without form and void," and "makes it pregnant." [2] He sees all things in himself. He hardly ever avails himself of remarkable objects or situations, but, in general, rejects them as interfering with the workings of his own mind, as disturbing the smooth, deep, majestic current of his own feelings. Thus his descriptions of natural scenery are not brought home distinctly to the naked eye by forms and circumstances, but every object is seen through the medium of innumerable recollections, is clothed with the haze of imagination like a glittering vapour, is obscured with the excess of glory, [3] has the shadowy brightness of a waking dream. The image is lost in the sentiment, as sound in the multiplication of echoes.

> "And visions, as prophetic eyes avow,
> Hang on each leaf, and cling to every bough." [4]

In describing human nature, Mr Wordsworth equally shuns the common 'vantage-grounds of popular story, of striking incident, or fatal catastrophe, as cheap and vulgar modes of producing an effect. He scans the human race as the naturalist measures the earth's zone, without attending to the picturesque points of view, the abrupt inequalities of surface. He contemplates the passions and habits of men, not in their extremes, but in their first elements; their follies and vices, not at their height, with all their embossed evils upon their heads, but as lurking in embryo,—the seeds of the disorder inwoven with our very constitution. He only sympathises with those

---

8 *Paradise Lost*, III, 438–39; V, 297.
9 Hazlitt refers to "Idle Tales," a group of bawdy poems by Matthew Prior (1664–1721).
10 Giovanni Boccaccio (*c.* 1313–1375) was the author of the famous collection of bawdy tales *The Decameron*. François Rabelais (1494–1553) was the author of the lusty satire *Gargantua and Pantagruel* (1532).
11 John Gay's popular comic opera.

1 Cf. Browne's *Religio Medici*, Part II, Section 11: "There is surely a piece of Divinity in us, something that was before the Elements, and owes no homage unto the Sun."
2 See Genesis, i, 2 and *Paradise Lost*, I, 21–22.
3 Cf. *Paradise Lost*, I, 593–94.
4 Verses presumably by Thomas Gray contained in a letter from the poet to Horace Walpole dated "September, 1737" in William Mason's *Memoirs of the Life and Writings of Mr. Gray* (1775). See *Horace Walpole's Correspondence*, ed. W. S. Lewis et al., XIII (New Haven: Yale University Press, 1948), 105–107.

simple forms of feeling, which mingle at once with his own identity, or with the stream of general humanity. To him the great and the small are the same; the near and the remote; what appears, and what only is. The general and the permanent, like the Platonic ideas, are his only realities. All accidental varieties and individual contrasts are lost in an endless continuity of feeling; like drops of water in the ocean-stream! An intense intellectual egotism swallows up every thing. Even the dialogues introduced in the present volume are soliloquies of the same character, taking different views of the subject. The recluse, the pastor, and the pedlar, are three persons in one poet. We ourselves disapprove of these "interlocutions between Lucius and Caius" as impertinent babbling, where there is no dramatic distinction of character. But the evident scope and tendency of Mr Wordsworth's mind is the reverse of dramatic. It resists all change of character, all variety of scenery, all the bustle, machinery, and pantomime of the stage, or of real life,—whatever might relieve, or relax, or change the direction of its own activity, jealous of all competition. The power of his mind preys upon itself. It is as if there were nothing but himself and the universe. He lives in the busy solitude of his own heart; in the deep silence of thought. His imagination lends life and feeling only to "the bare trees and mountains bare";[5] peoples the viewless tracts of air, and converses with the silent clouds!

We could have wished that our author had given to his work the form of a didactic poem altogether, with only occasional digressions or allusions to particular instances. But he has chosen to encumber himself with a load of narrative and description, which sometimes hinders the progress and effect of the general reasoning, and which, instead of being inwoven with the text, would have come in better in plain prose as notes at the end of the volume. Mr Wordsworth, indeed, says finely, and perhaps as truly as finely:

> —"Exchange the shepherd's frock of native grey
> For robes with regal purple tinged; convert
> The crook into a sceptre; give the pomp
> Of circumstance; and here the tragic Muse
> Shall find apt subjects for her highest art.
> Amid the groves, beneath the shadowy hills,
> The generations are prepared; the pangs,
> The internal pangs, are ready; the dread strife
> Of poor humanity's afflicted will
> Struggling in vain with ruthless destiny."[6]

But he immediately declines availing himself of these resources of the rustic moralist: for the priest, who officiates as "the sad historian of the pensive plain"[7] says in reply:

> "Our system is not fashioned to preclude
> That sympathy which you for others ask:
> And I could tell, not travelling for my theme
> Beyond the limits of these humble graves,
> Of strange disasters; but I pass them by,
> Loth to disturb what Heaven hath hushed to peace."[8]

There is, in fact, in Mr Wordsworth's mind an evident repugnance to admit anything that tells for itself, without the interpretation of the poet,—a fastidious antipathy to immediate effect,—a systematic unwillingness to share the palm with his subject. Where, however, he has a subject presented to him, "such as the meeting soul may pierce,"[9] and to which he does not grudge to lend the aid of his fine genius, his powers of description and fancy seem to be little inferior to those of his classical predecessor, Akenside.[10] Among several others which we might select we give the following passage, describing the religion of ancient Greece:

> "In that fair clime, the lonely herdsman, stretch'd
> On the soft grass through half a summer's day,
> With music lulled his indolent repose:
> And in some fit of weariness, if he,
> When his own breath was silent, chanced to hear
> A distant strain, far sweeter than the sounds
> Which his poor skill could make, his fancy fetch'd,
> Even from the blazing chariot of the sun,
> A beardless youth, who touched a golden lute,
> And filled the illumined groves with ravishment.
> The nightly hunter, lifting up his eyes
> Towards the crescent moon, with grateful heart
> Called on the lovely wanderer, who bestowed
> That timely light, to share his joyous sport:
> And hence, a beaming Goddess with her Nymphs
> Across the lawn and through the darksome grove,
> (Nor unaccompanied with tuneful notes
> By echo multiplied from rock or cave),
> Swept in the storm of chase, as moon and stars
> Glance rapidly along the clouded heavens,
> When winds are blowing strong. The traveller slaked
> His thirst from rill, or gushing fount, and thanked
> The Naiad. Sun beams, upon distant hills
> Gliding apace, with shadows in their train,
> Might, with small help from fancy, be transformed
> Into fleet Oreads, sporting visibly.

---

5 Wordsworth's "Lines written at a small distance from my House [to my Sister]" (1798), l. 7.
6 *Excursion*, VI, 548–57, a favorite quotation of Hazlitt's.
7 Goldsmith's *Deserted Village*, l. 136.
8 VI, 567–72.
9 Milton's *l'Allegro*, l. 138.
10 Mark Akenside (1721–1790) was the author of *The Pleasures of Imagination*, first published in 1744; like *The Excursion*, it was a long philosophic poem in blank verse.

The zephyrs fanning as they passed their wings
Lacked not for love fair objects, whom they wooed
With gentle whisper. Withered boughs grotesque,
Stripped of their leaves and twigs by hoary age,
From depth of shaggy covert peeping forth
In the low vale, or on steep mountain side:
And sometimes intermixed with stirring horns
Of the live deer, or goat's depending beard;
These were the lurking satyrs, a wild brood
Of gamesome Deities! or Pan himself,
The simple shepherd's awe-inspiring God." [11]

The foregoing is one of a succession of splendid passages equally enriched with philosophy and poetry, tracing the fictions of Eastern mythology to the immediate intercourse of the imagination with Nature, and to the habitual propensity of the human mind to endow the outward forms of being with life and conscious motion. With this expansive and animating principle, Mr Wordsworth has forcibly, but somewhat severely, contrasted the cold, narrow, lifeless spirit of modern philosophy:—

"How, shall our great discoverers obtain
From sense and reason less than these obtained,
Though far misled? Shall men for whom our age
Unbaffled powers of vision hath prepared,
To explore the world without and world within,
Be joyless as the blind? Ambitious souls—
Whom earth at this late season hath produced
To regulate the moving spheres, and weigh
The planets in the hollow of their hand;
And they who rather dive than soar, whose pains
Have solved the elements, or analysed
The thinking principle—shall they in fact
Prove a degraded race? And what avails
Renown, if their presumption make them such?
Inquire of ancient wisdom; go, demand
Of mighty nature, if 'twas ever meant
That we should pry far off, yet be unraised;
That we should pore, and dwindle as we pore,
Viewing all objects unremittingly
In disconnection dead and spiritless;
And still dividing and dividing still
Break down all grandeur, still unsatisfied
With the perverse attempt, while littleness
May yet become more little; waging thus
An impious warfare with the very life
Of our own souls! And if indeed there be
An all-pervading spirit, upon whom
Our dark foundations rest, could he design,
That this magnificent effect of power,
The earth we tread, the sky which we behold
By day, and all the pomp which night reveals,
That these—and that superior mystery,

Our vital frame, so fearfully devised,
And the dread soul within it—should exist
Only to be examined, pondered, searched,
Probed, vexed, and criticised—to be prized
No more than as a mirror that reflects
To proud Self-love her own intelligence?" [12]

From the chemists and metaphysicians our author turns to the laughing sage of France, Voltaire. "Poor gentleman, it fares no better with him, for he's a wit." [13] We cannot, however, agree with Mr Wordsworth that *Candide* is *dull*. It is, if our author pleases, "the production of a scoffer's pen," [14] or it is any thing but dull. It may not be proper in a grave, discreet, orthodox, promising young divine, who studies his opinions in the contraction or distension of his patron's brow, to allow any merit to a work like *Candide*; but we conceive that it would have been more manly in Mr Wordsworth, nor do we think it would have hurt the cause he espouses, if he had blotted out the epithet, after it had peevishly escaped him. Whatsoever savours of a little, narrow, inquisitorial spirit, does not sit well on a poet and a man of genius. The prejudices of a philosopher are not natural. There is a frankness and sincerity of opinion, which is a paramount obligation in all questions of intellect, though it may not govern the decisions of the spiritual courts, who may, however, be safely left to take care of their own interests. There is a plain directness and simplicity of understanding, which is the only security against the evils of levity, on the one hand, or of hypocrisy, on the other. A speculative bigot is a solecism in the intellectual world. We can assure Mr Wordsworth, that we should not have bestowed so much serious consideration on a single voluntary perversion of language, but that our respect for his character makes us jealous of his smallest faults!

With regard to his general phillippic against the contractedness and egotism of philosophical pursuits, we only object to its not being carried further. We shall not affirm with Rousseau (his authority would perhaps have little weight with Mr Wordsworth)— *Tout homme reflechi est mechant;* [15] but we conceive that the same reasoning which Mr Wordsworth applies so eloquently and justly to the natural philosopher and metaphysician may be extended to the moralist, the divine, the politician, the orator, the

---

[11] IV, 851–87.

[12] IV, 941–92 (with omissions).
[13] Said by Mrs. Crossbite of the fop Dapperwit, in Wycherley's comedy *Love in a Wood* (1671), III, i.
[14] II, 484.
[15] *Tout . . . mechant:* "Every reflective man is depraved." Cf. "l'homme qui médite est un animal dépravé" in Rousseau's *Sur l'origine de l'inégalité parmi les hommes* (1755), Part I.

artist, and even the poet. And why so? Because wherever an intense activity is given to any one faculty, it necessarily prevents the due and natural exercise of others. Hence all those professions or pursuits, where the mind is exclusively occupied with the ideas of things as they exist in the imagination or understanding, as they call for the exercise of intellectual activity, and not as they are connected with practical good or evil, must check the genial expansion of the moral sentiments and social affections; must lead to a cold and dry abstraction, as they are found to suspend the animal functions, and relax the bodily frame. Hence the complaint of the want of natural sensibility and constitutional warmth of attachment in those persons who have been devoted to the pursuit of any art or science,—or their restless morbidity of temperament, and indifference to every thing that does not furnish an occasion for the display of their mental superiority, and the gratification of their vanity. The philosophical poet himself, perhaps, owes some of his love of nature to the opportunity it affords him of analyzing his own feelings, and contemplating his own powers,—of making every object about him a whole length mirror to reflect his favourite thoughts, and of looking down on the frailties of others in undisturbed leisure, and from a more dignified height.

One of the most interesting parts of this work is that in which the author treats of the French Revolution, and of the feelings connected with it, in ingenuous minds, in its commencement and its progress. The *solitary*,* who, by domestic calamities and disappointments, had been cut off from society, and almost from himself, gives the following account of the manner in which he was roused from his melancholy: . . .[16]

In the application of these memorable lines, we should, perhaps, differ a little from Mr Wordsworth; nor can we indulge with him in the fond conclusion afterwards hinted at, that one day *our* triumph, the triumph of humanity and liberty, may be complete. For this purpose, we think several things necessary which are impossible. It is a consummation which cannot happen till the nature of things is changed, till the many become as united as the *one*, till romantic generosity shall be as common as gross selfishness, till reason shall have acquired the obstinate blindness of prejudice, till the love of power and of change shall no longer goad man on to restless action, till passion

* This word is not English.

and will, hope and fear, love and hatred, and the objects proper to excite them, that is, alternate good and evil, shall no longer sway the bosoms and businesses of men. All things move, not in progress, but in a ceaseless round; our strength lies in our weakness; our virtues are built on our vices; our faculties are as limited as our being; nor can we lift man above his nature more than above the earth he treads. But though we cannot weave over again the airy, unsubstantial dream, which reason and experience have dispelled,

"What though the radiance, which was once so bright,
   Be now for ever taken from our sight,
   Though nothing can bring back the hour
   Of glory in the grass, of splendour in the flower:"—[17]

yet we will never cease, nor be prevented from returning on the wings of imagination to that bright dream of our youth; that glad dawn of the day-star of liberty; that spring-time of the world, in which the hopes and expectations of the human race seemed opening in the same gay career with our own; when France called her children to partake her equal blessings beneath her laughing skies; when the stranger was met in all her villages with dance and festive songs, in celebration of a new and golden era; and when, to the retired and contemplative student, the prospects of human happiness and glory were seen ascending like the steps of Jacob's ladder, in bright and never-ending succession. The dawn of that day was suddenly overcast; that season of hope is past; it is fled with the other dreams of our youth, which we cannot recal, but has left behind it traces, which are not to be effaced by Birth-day and Thanksgiving odes, or the chaunting of *Te Deums* [18] in all the churches of Christendom. To those hopes eternal regrets are due; to those who maliciously and wilfully blasted them, in the fear that they might be accomplished, we feel no less what we owe—hatred and scorn as lasting!

[August 21, 28, 1814]   [1817]

WHY THE ARTS ARE NOT PROGRESSIVE?—A FRAGMENT

IT IS often made a subject of complaint and surprise, that the arts in this country, and in modern times, have

---

[16] Quoted here are III, 706–79 (with omissions), and IV, 260–73, 296–309.

[17] "Intimations Ode," ll. 176–79, another favorite passage of Hazlitt's, with a characteristic misquotation of the final line.
[18] The chantings of *Te Deums* were traditional ceremonies of national rejoicing, in this case inspired by the defeats of the Napoleonic armies. The Birth-day odes were tributes to the monarch composed annually by the poet laureate.

not kept pace with the general progress of society and civilization in other respects, and it has been proposed to remedy the deficiency by more carefully availing ourselves of the advantages which time and circumstances have placed within our reach, but which we have hitherto neglected, the study of the antique, the formation of academies, and the distribution of prizes.

First, the complaint itself, that the arts do not attain that progressive degree of perfection which might reasonably be expected from them, proceeds on a false notion, for the analogy appealed to in support of the regular advances of art to higher degrees of excellence, totally fails; it applies to science, not to art.—Secondly, the expedients proposed to remedy the evil by adventitious means are only calculated to confirm it. The arts hold immediate communication with nature, and are only derived from that source. When that original impulse no longer exists, when the inspiration of genius is fled, all the attempts to recal it are no better than the tricks of galvanism to restore the dead to life.[1] The arts may be said to resemble Antæus[2] in his struggle with Hercules, who was strangled when he was raised above the ground, and only revived and recovered his strength when he touched his mother earth.

Nothing is more contrary to the fact than the supposition that in what we understand by the *fine arts*, as painting and poetry, relative perfection is only the result of repeated efforts, and that what has been once well done constantly leads to something better. What is mechanical, reducible to rule, or capable of demonstration, is progressive, and admits of gradual improvement: what is not mechanical or definite, but depends on genius, taste, and feeling, very soon becomes stationary or retrograde, and loses more than it gains by transfusion. The contrary opinion is, indeed, a common error, which has grown up, like many others, from transferring an analogy of one kind to something quite distinct, without thinking of the difference in the nature of the things, or attending to the difference of the results. For most persons, finding what wonderful advances have been made in biblical criticism, in chemistry, in mechanics, in geometry, astronomy, etc. —*i.e.* in things depending on mere inquiry and experiment, or on absolute demonstration, have been led hastily to conclude, that there was a general tendency in the efforts of the human intellect to improve by repetition, and in all other arts and institutions to grow

perfect and mature by time. We look back upon the theological creed of our ancestors, and their discoveries in natural philosophy, with a smile of pity; science, and the arts connected with it, have all had their infancy, their youth, and manhood, and seem to have in them no principle of limitation or decay; and, inquiring no farther about the matter, we infer, in the height of our self-congratulation, and in the intoxication of our pride, that the same progress has been, and will continue to be, made in all other things which are the work of man. The fact, however, stares us so plainly in the face, that one would think the smallest reflection must suggest the truth, and overturn our sanguine theories. The greatest poets, the ablest orators, the best painters, and the finest sculptors that the world ever saw, appeared soon after the birth of these arts, and lived in a state of society, which was, in other respects, comparatively barbarous. Those arts, which depend on individual genius and incommunicable power, have always leaped at once from infancy to manhood, from the first rude dawn of invention to their meridian height and dazzling lustre, and have in general declined ever after. This is the peculiar distinction and privilege of each, of science and of art; of the one, never to attain its utmost summit of perfection, and of the other, to arrive at it almost at once. Homer, Chaucer, Spenser, Shakspeare, Dante, and Ariosto, (Milton alone was of a later age, and not the worse for it,) Raphael, Titian, Michael Angelo, Correggio, Cervantes, and Boccaccio —all lived near the beginning of their arts—perfected, and all but created them. These giant sons of genius stand, indeed, upon the earth, but they tower above their fellows, and the long line of their successors does not interpose anything to obstruct their view, or lessen their brightness. In strength and stature they are unrivalled, in grace and beauty they have never been surpassed. In after-ages, and more refined periods, (as they are called,) great men have arisen one by one, as it were by throes and at intervals: though in general the best of these cultivated and artificial minds were of an inferior order, as Tasso and Pope among poets, Guido and Vandyke among painters. But in the earliest stages of the arts, when the first mechanical difficulties had been got over, and the language as it were acquired, they rose by clusters and in constellations, never to rise again.

The arts of painting and poetry are conversant with the world of thought within us, and with the world of sense without us—with what we know, and see, and feel intimately. They flow from the sacred shrine of our own breasts, and are kindled at the living lamp of nature. The pulse of the passions assuredly beat as high, the depths and soundings of the human heart were as well understood three thousand years ago, as

---

[1] That is, by producing a current between the supposed "electricity" in muscles and attached metal plates; named for Luigi Galvani (1737–1798), who published his theory of "animal electricity" in 1791.

[2] Antæus was a giant wrestler, son of Poseidon and Gaea (sea and earth), of invincible strength as long as he was in contact with the earth.

they are at present; the face of nature and "the human face divine,"[3] shone as bright then as they have ever done. It is this light, reflected by true genius on art, that marks out its path before it, and sheds a glory round the Muses' feet, like that which "circled Una's angel face,

> "And made a sunshine in the shady place."[4]

Nature is the soul of art. There is a strength in the imagination that reposes entirely on nature, which nothing else can supply. There is in the old poets and painters a vigour and grasp of mind, a full possession of their subject, a confidence and firm faith, a sublime simplicity, an elevation of thought, proportioned to their depth of feeling, an increasing force and impetus, which moves, penetrates, and kindles all that comes in contact with it, which seems, not theirs, but given to them. It is this reliance on the power of nature which has produced those masterpieces by the Prince of Painters,[5] in which expression is all in all, where one spirit—that of truth—pervades every part, brings down heaven to earth, mingles cardinals and popes with angels and apostles, and yet blends and harmonises the whole by the true touches and intense feeling of what is beautiful and grand in nature. It was the same trust in nature that enabled Chaucer to describe the patient sorrow of Griselda; or the delight of that young beauty in the Flower and the Leaf,[6] shrouded in her bower, and listening, in the morning of the year, to the singing of the nightingale, while her joy rises with the rising song, and gushes out afresh at every pause, and is borne along with the full tide of pleasure, and still increases and repeats and prolongs itself, and knows no ebb. It is thus that Boccaccio, in the divine story of the Hawk,[7] has represented Frederigo Alberigi steadily contemplating his favourite Falcon (the wreck and remnant of his fortune,) and glad to see how fat and fair a bird she is, thinking what a dainty repast she would make for his Mistress, who had deigned to visit him in his low cell. So Isabella mourns over her pot of Basile, and never asks for any thing but that. So Lear calls out for

his poor fool, and invokes the heavens, for they are old like him. So Titian impressed on the countenance of that young Neapolitan nobleman in the Louvre,[8] a look that never passed away. So Nicolas Poussin describes some shepherds wandering out in a morning of the spring, and coming to a tomb with this inscription, "I ALSO WAS AN ARCADIAN."[9]

In general, it must happen in the first stages of the Arts, that as none but those who had a natural genius for them would attempt to practise them, so none but those who had a natural taste for them would pretend to judge of or criticise them. This must be an incalculable advantage to the man of true genius, for it is no other than the privilege of being tried by his peers. In an age when connoisseurship had not become a fashion; when religion, war, and intrigue, occupied the time and thoughts of the great, only those minds of superior refinement would be led to notice the works of art, who had a real sense of their excellence; and in giving way to the powerful bent of his own genius, the painter was most likely to consult the taste of his judges. He had not to deal with pretenders to taste, through vanity, affectation, and idleness. He had to appeal to the higher faculties of the soul; to that deep and innate sensibility to truth and beauty, which required only a proper object to have its enthusiasm excited; and to that independent strength of mind, which, in the midst of ignorance and barbarism, hailed and fostered genius, wherever it met with it. Titian was patronised by Charles v., Count Castiglione[10] was the friend of Raphael. These were true patrons, and true critics; and as there were no others, (for the world, in general, merely looked on and wondered,) there can be little doubt, that such a period of dearth of factitious patronage would be the most favourable to the full developement of the greatest talents, and the attainment of the highest excellence.

The diffusion of taste is not the same thing as the improvement of taste; but it is only the former of these objects that is promoted by public institutions and other artificial means. The number of candidates for fame, and of pretenders to criticism, is thus increased beyond all proportion, while the quantity of genius and feeling remains the same; with this difference, that the man of genius is lost in the crowd of competitors, who would never have become such but from encouragement and example; and that the opinion of those few persons whom nature intended for judges, is drowned

---

[3] *Paradise Lost*, III, 44.   [4] *Faerie Queene*, I, iii, 4.
[5] Raphael.
[6] Griselda was the heroine of "The Clerk's Tale." "The Flower and the Leaf" is an allegorical poem no longer attributed to Chaucer.
[7] The "story of the Hawk" occurs in the Ninth Novel of the fifth Day of Boccaccio's *Decameron*. Frederigo spent all his fortune, except for a small farm and a beloved falcon, in courting a lady, who rejected him for another. Years later, the lady (now a widow) comes to him intending to ask for the falcon as the only thing that gives pleasure and comfort to her dying son. Not knowing her intention, Frederigo kills the falcon in order to provide meat for a banquet in honor of the lady on her visit to his humble dwelling. The story of Isabella and the pot of Basil, mentioned next, occurs in the Fifth Novel of the fourth Day.

[8] Titian's Young Man with a Glove, which Hazlitt copied during his visit to Paris in 1802–1803.
[9] Hazlitt refers to "The Shepherds of Arcady," a famous canvas also in the Louvre.
[10] Count Castiglione (1478–1529) was an Italian diplomat and author of *The Courtier* (1528).

in the noisy suffrages of shallow smatterers in taste. The principle of universal suffrage, however applicable to matters of government, which concern the common feelings and common interests of society, is by no means applicable to matters of taste, which can only be decided upon by the most refined understandings. The highest efforts of genius, in every walk of art, can never be properly understood by the generality of mankind: There are numberless beauties and truths which lie far beyond their comprehension. It is only as refinement and sublimity are blended with other qualities of a more obvious and grosser nature, that they pass current with the world. Taste is the highest degree of sensibility or the impression made on the most cultivated and sensible of minds, as genius is the result of the highest powers both of feeling and invention. It may be objected, that the public taste is capable of gradual improvement, because, in the end, the public do justice to works of the greatest merit. This is a mistake. The reputation ultimately, and often slowly affixed to works of genius, is stamped upon them by authority, not by popular consent or the common sense of the world. We imagine that the admiration of the works of celebrated men has become common, because the admiration of their names has become so. But does not every ignorant connoisseur pretend the same veneration, and talk with the same vapid assurance of Michael Angelo, though he has never seen even a copy of any of his pictures, as if he had studied them accurately,—merely because Sir Joshua Reynolds has praised him? Is Milton more popular now than when the Paradise Lost was first published? Or does he not rather owe his reputation to the judgment of a few persons in every successive period, accumulating in his favour, and overpowering by its weight the public indifference? Why is Shakspeare popular? Not from his refinement of character or sentiment, so much as from his power of telling a story—the variety and invention—the tragic catastrophe and broad farce of his plays? Spenser is not yet understood. Does not Boccaccio pass to this day for a writer of ribaldry, because his jests and lascivious tales were all that caught the vulgar ear, while the story of the Falcon is forgotten!

[January 11, 15;   [1817]
September 11, 1814]

LECTURES ON THE ENGLISH POETS

The series of eight lectures, surveying English poetry from Chaucer to "the Living Poets," was delivered at the Surrey Institution in London, January–March 1818, and published in May of that year. The text here followed is that of the second edition of 1819.

LECTURES ON THE ENGLISH POETS

LECTURE I.

INTRODUCTORY—ON POETRY IN GENERAL.

THE BEST general notion which I can give of poetry is, that it is the natural impression of any object or event, by its vividness exciting an involuntary movement of imagination and passion, and producing, by sympathy, a certain modulation of the voice, or sounds, expressing it.

In treating of poetry, I shall speak first of the subject-matter of it, next of the forms of expression to which it gives birth, and afterwards of its connection with harmony of sound.

Poetry is the language of the imagination and the passions. It relates to whatever gives immediate pleasure or pain to the human mind. It comes home to the bosoms and businesses of men; for nothing but what so comes home to them in the most general and intelligible shape, can be a subject for poetry. Poetry is the universal language which the heart holds with nature and itself. He who has a contempt for poetry, cannot have much respect for himself, or for any thing else. It is not a mere frivolous accomplishment, (as some persons have been led to imagine) the trifling amusement of a few idle readers or leisure hours—it has been the study and delight of mankind in all ages. Many people suppose that poetry is something to be found only in books, contained in lines of ten syllables, with like endings; but wherever there is a sense of beauty, or power, or harmony, as in the motion of a wave of the sea, in the growth of a flower that "spreads its sweet leaves to the air, and dedicates its beauty to the sun," [1]—*there* is poetry, in its birth. If history is a grave study, poetry may be said to be a graver: its materials lie deeper, and are spread wider. History treats, for the most part, of the cumbrous and unwieldy masses of things, the empty cases in which the affairs of the world are packed, under the heads of intrigue or war, in different states, and from century to century: but there is no thought or feeling that can have entered into the mind of man, which he would be eager to communicate to others, or which they would listen to with delight, that is not a fit subject for poetry. It is not a branch of authorship: it is "the stuff of which our

---

[1] *Romeo and Juliet*, I, i, 159–60.

life is made." [2] The rest is "mere oblivion," a dead letter: for all that is worth remembering in life, is the poetry of it. Fear is poetry, hope is poetry, love is poetry, hatred is poetry; contempt, jealousy, remorse, admiration, wonder, pity, despair, or madness, are all poetry. Poetry is that fine particle within us, that expands, rarefies, refines, raises our whole being: without it "man's life is poor as beast's." [3] Man is a poetical animal: and those of us who do not study the principles of poetry, act upon them all our lives, like Moliere's *Bourgeois Gentilhomme*, who had always spoken prose without knowing it. [4] The child is a poet in fact, when he first plays at hide-and-seek, or repeats the story of Jack the Giant-killer; the shepherd-boy is a poet, when he first crowns his mistress with a garland of flowers; the countryman, when he stops to look at the rainbow; the city-apprentice, when he gazes after the Lord-Mayor's show; [5] the miser, when he hugs his gold; the courtier, who builds his hopes upon a smile; the savage, who paints his idol with blood; the slave, who worships a tyrant, or the tyrant, who fancies himself a god;—the vain, the ambitious, the proud, the choleric man, the hero and the coward, the beggar and the king, the rich and the poor, the young and the old, all live in a world of their own making; and the poet does no more than describe what all the others think and act. If his art is folly and madness, it is folly and madness at second hand. "There is warrant for it." [6] Poets alone have not "such seething brains, such shaping fantasies, that apprehend more than cooler reason" can.

"The lunatic, the lover, and the poet
  Are of imagination all compact.
  One sees more devils than vast hell can hold;
  The madman. While the lover, all as frantic,
  Sees Helen's beauty in a brow of Egypt.
  The poet's eye in a fine frenzy rolling,
  Doth glance from heav'n to earth, from earth to heav'n;
  And as imagination bodies forth
  The forms of things unknown, the poet's pen
  Turns them to shape, and gives to airy nothing
  A local habitation and a name.
  Such tricks hath strong imagination." [7]

If poetry is a dream, the business of life is much the same. If it is a fiction, made up of what we wish things to be, and fancy that they are, because we wish them

so, there is no other nor better reality. Ariosto has described the loves of Angelica and Medoro: [8] but was not Medoro, who carved the name of his mistress on the barks of trees, as much enamoured of her charms as he? Homer has celebrated the anger of Achilles: but was not the hero as mad as the poet? Plato banished the poets from his Commonwealth, [9] lest their descriptions of the natural man should spoil his mathematical man, who was to be without passions and affections, who was neither to laugh nor weep, to feel sorrow nor anger, to be cast down nor elated by any thing. This was a chimera, however, which never existed but in the brain of the inventor; and Homer's poetical world has outlived Plato's philosophical Republic.

Poetry then is an imitation of nature, but the imagination and the passions are a part of man's nature. We shape things according to our wishes and fancies, without poetry; but poetry is the most emphatical language that can be found for those creations of the mind "which ecstacy is very cunning in." [10] Neither a mere description of natural objects, nor a mere delineation of natural feelings, however distinct or forcible, constitutes the ultimate end and aim of poetry, without the heightenings of the imagination. The light of poetry is not only a direct but also a reflected light, that while it shews us the object, throws a sparkling radiance on all around it: the flame of the passions, communicated to the imagination, reveals to us, as with a flash of lightning, the inmost recesses of thought, and penetrates our whole being. Poetry represents forms chiefly as they suggest other forms; feelings, as they suggest forms or other feelings. Poetry puts a spirit of life and motion into the universe. It describes the flowing, not the fixed. It does not define the limits of sense, or analyze the distinctions of the understanding, but signifies the excess of the imagination beyond the actual or ordinary impression of any object or feeling. The poetical impression of any object is that uneasy, exquisite sense of beauty or power that cannot be contained within itself; that is impatient of all limit; that (as flame bends to flame) strives to link itself to some other image of kindred beauty or grandeur; to enshrine itself, as it were, in the highest forms of fancy, and to relieve the aching sense of pleasure by expressing it in the boldest manner, and by the most striking examples of the same quality in other instances. Poetry, according to Lord Bacon, for this reason, "has something divine in it, because it raises the mind and hurries it into sublimity, by conforming the shows of things to the desires of the soul,

---

[2] Cf. *Tempest*, IV, i, 156–57. The next quotation occurs in *As You Like It*, II, vii, 165.
[3] *King Lear*, II, iv, 270.
[4] See Act II, scene vi.
[5] An elaborate street pageant held annually in London on November 9th, in celebration of the inauguration of the Lord Mayor.
[6] Cf. *Macbeth*, II, iii, 151 and *Richard the Third*, I, iv, 112.
[7] *A Midsummer Night's Dream*, V, i, 4–18.

[8] Young lovers in Ariosto's epic *Orlando Furioso*.
[9] See *Republic*, Book X.
[10] *Hamlet*, III, iv, 138–39.

instead of subjecting the soul to external things, as reason and history do." [11] It is strictly the language of the imagination; and the imagination is that faculty which represents objects, not as they are in themselves, but as they are moulded by other thoughts and feelings, into an infinite variety of shapes and combinations of power. This language is not the less true to nature, because it is false in point of fact; but so much the more true and natural, if it conveys the impression which the object under the influence of passion makes on the mind. Let an object, for instance, be presented to the senses in a state of agitation or fear—and the imagination will distort or magnify the object, and convert it into the likeness of whatever is most proper to encourage the fear. "Our eyes are made the fools" [12] of our other faculties. This is the universal law of the imagination,

> "That if it would but apprehend some joy,
> It comprehends some bringer of that joy:
> Or in the night imagining some fear,
> How easy is each bush suppos'd a bear!"

When Iachimo says of Imogen,

> "——The flame o' th' taper
> Bows toward her, and would under-peep her lids
> To see the enclosed lights"—

this passionate interpretation of the motion of the flame to accord with the speaker's own feelings, is true poetry. The lover, equally with the poet, speaks of the auburn tresses of his mistress as locks of shining gold, because the least tinge of yellow in the hair has, from novelty and a sense of personal beauty, a more lustrous effect to the imagination than the purest gold. We compare a man of gigantic stature to a tower: not that he is any thing like so large, but because the excess of his size beyond what we are accustomed to expect, or the usual size of things of the same class, produces by contrast a greater feeling of magnitude and ponderous strength than another object of ten times the same dimensions. The intensity of the feeling makes up for the disproportion of the objects. Things are equal to the imagination, which have the power of affecting the mind with an equal degree of terror, admiration, delight, or love. When Lear calls upon the heavens to avenge his cause, "for they are old like him," [13] there is nothing extravagant or impious in this sublime identification of his age with theirs; for there is no other image which

could do justice to the agonising sense of his wrongs and his despair!

Poetry is the high-wrought enthusiasm of fancy and feeling. As in describing natural objects, it impregnates sensible impressions with the forms of fancy, so it describes the feelings of pleasure or pain, by blending them with the strongest movements of passion, and the most striking forms of nature. Tragic poetry, which is the most impassioned species of it, strives to carry on the feeling to the utmost point of sublimity or pathos, by all the force of comparison or contrast; loses the sense of present suffering in the imaginary exaggeration of it; exhausts the terror or pity by an unlimited indulgence of it; grapples with impossibilities in its desperate impatience of restraint; throws us back upon the past, forward into the future; brings every moment of our being or object of nature in startling review before us; and in the rapid whirl of events, lifts us from the depths of woe to the highest contemplations on human life. When Lear says of Edgar, "Nothing but his unkind daughters could have brought him to this;" [14] what a bewildered amazement, what a wrench of the imagination, that cannot be brought to conceive of any other cause of misery than that which has bowed it down, and absorbs all other sorrow in its own! His sorrow, like a flood, supplies the sources of all other sorrow. Again, when he exclaims in the mad scene, "The little dogs and all, Tray, Blanche, and Sweetheart, see, they bark at me!" it is passion lending occasion to imagination to make every creature in league against him, conjuring up ingratitude and insult in their least looked-for and most galling shapes, searching every thread and fibre of his heart, and finding out the last remaining image of respect or attachment in the bottom of his breast, only to torture and kill it! In like manner, the "So I am" of Cordelia, gushes from her heart like a torrent of tears, relieving it of a weight of love and of supposed ingratitude, which had pressed upon it for years. What a fine return of the passion upon itself is that in Othello—with what a mingled agony of regret and despair he clings to the last traces of departed happiness—when he exclaims,

> "——Oh now, for ever
> Farewel the tranquil mind. Farewel content;
> Farewel the plumed troops and the big war,
> That make ambition virtue! Oh farewel!
> Farewel the neighing steed, and the shrill trump,
> The spirit-stirring drum, th' ear-piercing fife,
> The royal banner, and all quality,
> Pride, pomp, and circumstance of glorious war:

---

[11] Cf. Bacon's *The Advancement of Learning*, II, iv, 2.
[12] *Macbeth*, II, i, 44. The next two quotations are, respectively, from *A Midsummer Night's Dream*, V, i, 19–22 and *Cymbeline*, II, ii, 19–21.
[13] See *King Lear*, II, iv, 194.

[14] *King Lear*, III, iv, 72–73. The next two quotations are from III, vi, 65–66, and IV, vii, 70.

And O you mortal engines, whose rude throats
Th' immortal Jove's dread clamours counterfeit,
Farewel! Othello's occupation's gone!"[15]

How his passion lashes itself up and swells and rages
like a tide in its sounding course, when in answer to the
doubts expressed of his returning love, he says,

"Never, Iago. Like to the Pontic sea,
Whose icy current and compulsive course
Ne'er feels retiring ebb, but keeps due on
To the Propontic and the Hellespont:
Even so my bloody thoughts, with violent pace,
Shall ne'er look back, ne'er ebb to humble love,
Till that a capable and wide revenge
Swallow them up."—

The climax of his expostulation afterwards with
Desdemona is at that line,

"But there where I had garner'd up my heart,
To be discarded thence!"—

One mode in which the dramatic exhibition of
passion excites our sympathy without raising our disgust is, that in proportion as it sharpens the edge of
calamity and disappointment, it strengthens the desire
of good. It enhances our consciousness of the blessing,
by making us sensible of the magnitude of the loss.
The storm of passion lays bare and shews us the rich
depths of the human soul: the whole of our existence,
the sum total of our passions and pursuits, of that
which we desire and that which we dread, is brought
before us by contrast; the action and re-action are
equal; the keenness of immediate suffering only gives
us a more intense aspiration after, and a more intimate
participation with the antagonist world of good; makes
us drink deeper of the cup of human life; tugs at the
heart-strings; loosens the pressure about them; and
calls the springs of thought and feeling into play with
tenfold force.

Impassioned poetry is an emanation of the moral and
intellectual part of our nature, as well as of the sensitive
—of the desire to know, the will to act, and the power
to feel; and ought to appeal to these different parts of
our constitution, in order to be perfect. The domestic
or prose tragedy, which is thought to be the most
natural, is in this sense the least so, because it appeals
almost exclusively to one of these faculties, our
sensibility. The tragedies of Moore and Lillo,[16] for

---

[15] *Othello*, III, iii, 347–57. The next two quotations are from
III, iii, 453–60 and IV, ii, 57, 60.
[16] Edward Moore (1712–1757) and George Lillo (1693–1739)
were the authors, respectively, of *The Gamester* (1753) and *The
London Merchant* (1731), two of the most successful examples of
eighteenth-century "domestic tragedy," dealing with contemporary middle-class Londoners in sentimental and melodramatic plots.

this reason, however affecting at the time, oppress and
lie like a dead weight upon the mind, a load of misery
which it is unable to throw off: the tragedy of Shakspeare, which is true poetry, stirs our inmost affections;
abstracts evil from itself by combining it with all the
forms of imagination, and with the deepest workings
of the heart, and rouses the whole man within us.

The pleasure, however, derived from tragic poetry,
is not any thing peculiar to it as poetry, as a fictitious
and fanciful thing. It is not an anomaly of the imagination. It has its source and ground-work in the common
love of strong excitement. As Mr. Burke observes,[17]
people flock to see a tragedy; but if there were a public
execution in the next street, the theatre would very
soon be empty. It is not then the difference between
fiction and reality that solves the difficulty. Children
are satisfied with the stories of ghosts and witches in
plain prose: nor do the hawkers of full, true, and particular accounts of murders and executions about the
streets, find it necessary to have them turned into
penny ballads, before they can dispose of these interesting and authentic documents. The grave politician
drives a thriving trade of abuse and calumnies poured
out against those whom he makes his enemies for no
other end than that he may live by them. The popular
preacher makes less frequent mention of heaven than
of hell. Oaths and nicknames are only a more vulgar
sort of poetry or rhetoric. We are as fond of indulging
our violent passions as of reading a description of those
of others. We are as prone to make a torment of our
fears, as to luxuriate in our hopes of good. If it be
asked, Why we do so? the best answer will be, Because
we cannot help it. The sense of power is as strong a
principle in the mind as the love of pleasure. Objects
of terror and pity exercise the same despotic control
over it as those of love or beauty. It is as natural to hate
as to love, to despise as to admire, to express our hatred
or contempt, as our love or admiration.

"Masterless passion sways us to the mood
Of what it likes or loathes."[18]

Not that we like what we loathe; but we like to
indulge our hatred and scorn of it; to dwell upon it, to
exasperate our idea of it by every refinement of ingenuity and extravagance of illustration; to make it a
bugbear to ourselves, to point it out to others in all the
splendour of deformity, to embody it to the senses, to
stigmatise it by name, to grapple with it in thought, in
action, to sharpen our intellect, to arm our will against
it, to know the worst we have to contend with, and to

---

[17] See *A Philosophical Enquiry into . . . the Sublime and Beautiful*
(1757), Part I, Section xv.
[18] *The Merchant of Venice*, IV, i, 51–52.

contend with it to the utmost. Poetry is only the highest eloquence of passion, the most vivid form of expression that can be given to our conception of any thing, whether pleasurable or painful, mean or dignified, delightful or distressing. It is the perfect coincidence of the image and the words with the feeling we have, and of which we cannot get rid in any other way, that gives an instant "satisfaction to the thought." [19] This is equally the origin of wit and fancy, of comedy and tragedy, of the sublime and pathetic. When Pope says of the Lord Mayor's shew,—

> "Now night descending, the proud scene is o'er,
> But lives in Settle's numbers one day more!"

—when Collins makes Danger, "with limbs of giant mould,"

> ——"Throw him on the steep
> Of some loose hanging rock asleep:"

when Lear calls out in extreme anguish,

> "Ingratitude, thou marble-hearted fiend,
> How much more hideous shew'st in a child
> Than the sea-monster!"

—the passion of contempt in the one case, of terror in the other, and of indignation in the last, is perfectly satisfied. We see the thing ourselves, and show it to others as we feel it to exist, and as, in spite of ourselves, we are compelled to think of it. The imagination, by thus embodying them and turning them to shape, gives an obvious relief to the indistinct and importunate cravings of the will.—We do not wish the thing to be so; but we wish it to appear such as it is. For knowledge is conscious power; and the mind is no longer, in this case, the dupe, though it may be the victim of vice or folly.

Poetry is in all its shapes the language of the imagination and the passions, of fancy and will. Nothing, therefore, can be more absurd than the outcry which has been sometimes raised by frigid and pedantic critics, for reducing the language of poetry to the standard of common sense and reason: for the end and use of poetry, "both at the first and now, was and is to hold the mirror up to nature," [20] seen through the medium of passion and imagination, not divested of that medium by means of literal truth or abstract reason. The painter of history might as well be required to represent the face of a person who has just trod upon a serpent with the still-life expression of a common portrait, as the poet to describe the most striking and vivid impressions which things can be supposed to make upon the mind, in the language of common conversation. Let who will strip nature of the colours and the shapes of fancy, the poet is not bound to do so; the impressions of common sense and strong imagination, that is, of passion and indifference, cannot be the same, and they must have a separate language to do justice to either. Objects must strike differently upon the mind, independently of what they are in themselves, as long as we have a different interest in them, as we see them in a different point of view, nearer or at a greater distance (morally or physically speaking) from novelty, from old acquaintance, from our ignorance of them, from our fear of their consequences, from contrast, from unexpected likeness. We can no more take away the faculty of the imagination, than we can see all objects without light or shade. Some things must dazzle us by their preternatural light; others must hold us in suspense, and tempt our curiosity to explore their obscurity. Those who would dispel these various illusions, to give us their drab-coloured creation in their stead, are not very wise. Let the naturalist, if he will, catch the glow-worm, carry it home with him in a box, and find it next morning nothing but a little grey worm; let the poet or the lover of poetry visit it at evening, when beneath the scented hawthorn and the crescent moon it has built itself a palace of emerald light. This is also one part of nature, one appearance which the glow-worm presents, and that not the least interesting; so poetry is one part of the history of the human mind, though it is neither science nor philosophy. It cannot be concealed, however, that the progress of knowledge and refinement has a tendency to circumscribe the limits of the imagination, and to clip the wings of poetry. The province of the imagination is principally visionary, the unknown and undefined: the understanding restores things to their natural boundaries, and strips them of their fanciful pretensions. Hence the history of religious and poetical enthusiasm is much the same; and both have received a sensible shock from the progress of experimental philosophy. It is the undefined and uncommon that gives birth and scope to the imagination; we can only fancy what we do not know. As in looking into the mazes of a tangled wood we fill them with what shapes we please, with ravenous beasts, with caverns vast, and drear enchantments, so in our ignorance of the world about us, we make gods or devils of the first object we see, and set no bounds to the wilful suggestions of our hopes and fears.

---

[19] *Othello*, III, iii, 97. The next three quotations are, respectively, from *The Dunciad*, I, 89–90; William Collins' "Ode to Fear" (1746), ll. 10, 14–15; and *King Lear*, I, iv, 281–83.

[20] *Hamlet*, III, ii, 23–25.

"And visions, as poetic eyes avow,
Hang on each leaf and cling to every bough." [21]

There can never be another Jacob's dream. [22] Since that time, the heavens have gone farther off, and grown astronomical. They have become averse to the imagination, nor will they return to us on the squares of the distances, or on Doctor Chalmers's Discourses. [23] Rembrandt's picture brings the matter nearer to us.— It is not only the progress of mechanical knowledge, but the necessary advances of civilization that are unfavourable to the spirit of poetry. We not only stand in less awe of the preternatural world, but we can calculate more surely, and look with more indifference, upon the regular routine of this. The heroes of the fabulous ages rid the world of monsters and giants. At present we are less exposed to the vicissitudes of good or evil, to the incursions of wild beasts or "bandit fierce," [24] or to the unmitigated fury of the elements. The time has been that "our fell of hair would at a dismal treatise rouse and stir as life were in it." But the police spoils all; and we now hardly so much as dream of a midnight murder. Macbeth is only tolerated in this country for the sake of the music; and in the United States of America, where the philosophical principles of government are carried still farther in theory and practice, we find that the Beggar's Opera is hooted from the stage. [25] Society, by degrees, is constructed into a machine that carries us safely and insipidly from one end of life to the other, in a very comfortable prose style.

"Obscurity her curtain round them drew,
And siren Sloth a dull quietus sung." [26]

The remarks which have been here made, would, in some measure, lead to a solution of the question of the comparative merits of painting and poetry. I do not mean to give any preference, but it should seem that the argument which has been sometimes set up, that painting must affect the imagination more strongly, because it represents the image more distinctly, is not well founded. We may assume without much temerity, that poetry is more poetical than painting. When artists or connoisseurs talk on stilts about the poetry of painting, they shew that they know little about poetry, and have little love for the art. Painting gives the object itself; poetry what it implies. Painting embodies what a thing contains in itself: poetry suggests what exists out of it, in any manner connected with it. But this last is the proper province of the imagination. Again, as it relates to passion, painting gives the event, poetry the progress of events: but it is during the progress, in the interval of expectation and suspense, while our hopes and fears are strained to the highest pitch of breathless agony, that the pinch of the interest lies.

"Between the acting of a dreadful thing
And the first motion, all the interim is
Like a phantasma or a hideous dream.
The mortal instruments are then in council;
And the state of man suffers an insurrection." [27]

But by the time that the picture is painted, all is over. Faces are the best part of a picture; but even faces are not what we chiefly remember in what interests us most.—But it may be asked then, Is there any thing better than Claude Lorraine's landscapes, than Titian's portraits, than Raphael's cartoons, or the Greek statues? Of the two first I shall say nothing, as they are evidently picturesque, rather than imaginative. Raphael's cartoons are certainly the finest comments that ever were made on the Scriptures. Would their effect be the same if we were not acquainted with the text? But the New Testament existed before the cartoons. There is one subject of which there is no cartoon, Christ washing the feet of the disciples the night before his death. But that chapter does not need a commentary! It is for want of some such resting place for the imagination that the Greek statues are little else than specious forms. They are marble to the touch and to the heart. They have not an informing principle within them. In their faultless excellence they appear sufficient to themselves. By their beauty they are raised above the frailties of passion or suffering. By their beauty they are deified. But they are not objects of religious faith to us, and their forms are a satire upon common humanity. They seem to have no sympathy with us, and not to want our admiration.

Poetry in its matter and form is natural imagery or feeling, combined with passion and fancy. In its mode

---

[21] See above, "Observations on Mr. Wordsworth's Poem the Excursion," footnote 4, p. 411.

[22] See Genesis, xxviii, 11–12, and Hazlitt's discussion of the poetry of the Bible later in this lecture.

[23] Hazlitt refers to Thomas Chalmers' *A Series of Discourses on the Christian Revelation viewed in connection with the Modern Astronomy* (1817). The purpose of the *Discourses* was to refute those "Free-thinkers" who had questioned, on the basis of astronomical discoveries, whether such a "paltry" planet as earth "could ever have been the object of such high and distinguished attentions as Christianity has assigned to it."

[24] Milton's *Comus*, l. 426. The next quotation occurs in *Macbeth*, V, v, 11–13.

[25] Hazlitt refers to a disastrous production of Gay's comic opera in New York, October 1817.

[26] From "To the Honourable and Reverend F. C." by Sneyd Davies (1709–1769), published in Robert Dodsley's *A Collection of Poems by Several Hands* (1775).

[27] *Julius Caesar*, II, i, 63–69.

of conveyance, it combines the ordinary use of language, with musical expression. There is a question of long standing, in what the essence of poetry consists; or what it is that determines why one set of ideas should be expressed in prose, another in verse. Milton has told us his idea of poetry in a single line—

> "Thoughts that voluntary move
> Harmonious numbers." [28]

As there are certain sounds that excite certain movements, and the song and dance go together, so there are, no doubt, certain thoughts that lead to certain tones of voice, or modulations of sound, and change "the words of Mercury into the songs of Apollo." [29] There is a striking instance of this adaptation of the movement of sound and rhythm to the subject, in Spenser's description of the Satyrs accompanying Una to the cave of Sylvanus.

> "So from the ground she fearless doth arise
>   And walketh forth without suspect of crime.
> They, all as glad as birds of joyous prime,
>   Thence lead her forth, about her dancing round,
> Shouting and singing all a shepherd's rhyme;
>   And with green branches strewing all the ground,
> Do worship her as queen with olive garland crown'd.
>
> And all the way their merry pipes they sound,
>   That all the woods and doubled echoes ring;
> And with their horned feet do wear the ground,
>   Leaping like wanton kids in pleasant spring;
> So towards old Sylvanus they her bring,
>   Who with the noise awaked, cometh out."
>   *Faery Queen*, b. i. c. vi.

On the contrary, there is nothing either musical or natural in the ordinary construction of language. It is a thing altogether arbitrary and conventional. Neither in the sounds themselves, which are the voluntary signs of certain ideas, nor in their grammatical arrangements in common speech, is there any principle of natural imitation, or correspondence to the individual ideas, or to the tone of feeling with which they are conveyed to others. The jerks, the breaks, the inequalities, and harshnesses of prose, are fatal to the flow of a poetical imagination, as a jolting road or a stumbling horse disturbs the reverie of an absent man. But poetry makes these odds all even. It is the music of language, answering to the music of the mind, untying as it were "the secret soul of harmony." [30] Wherever any object takes such a hold of the mind as to make us dwell upon it, and brood over it, melting the heart in

tenderness, or kindling it to a sentiment of enthusiasm;—wherever a movement of imagination or passion is impressed on the mind, by which it seeks to prolong and repeat the emotion, to bring all other objects into accord with it, and to give the same movement of harmony, sustained and continuous, or gradually varied according to the occasion, to the sounds that express it—this is poetry. The musical in sound is the sustained and continuous; the musical in thought is the sustained and continuous also. There is a near connection between music and deep-rooted passion. Mad people sing. As often as articulation passes naturally into intonation, there poetry begins. Where one idea gives a tone and colour to others, where one feeling melts others into it, there can be no reason why the same principle should not be extended to the sounds by which the voice utters these emotions of the soul, and blends syllables and lines into each other. It is to supply the inherent defect of harmony in the customary mechanism of language, to make the sound an echo to the sense, when the sense becomes a sort of echo to itself—to mingle the tide of verse, "the golden cadences of poetry," [31] with the tide of feeling, flowing and murmuring as it flows—in short, to take the language of the imagination from off the ground, and enable it to spread its wings where it may indulge its own impulses—

> "Sailing with supreme dominion
> Through the azure deep of air—"

without being stopped, or fretted, or diverted with the abruptnesses and petty obstacles, and discordant flats and sharps of prose, that poetry was invented. It is to common language, what springs are to a carriage, or wings to feet. In ordinary speech we arrive at a certain harmony by the modulations of voice: in poetry the same thing is done systematically by a regular collocation of syllables. It has been well observed, that every one who declaims warmly, or grows intent upon a subject, rises into a sort of blank verse or measured prose. The merchant, as described in Chaucer, went on his way "sounding always the increase of his winning." [32] Every prose-writer has more or less of rhythmical adaptation, except poets, who, when deprived of the regular mechanism of verse, seem to have no principle of modulation left in their writings.

An excuse might be made for rhyme in the same manner. It is but fair that the ear should linger on the sounds that delight it, or avail itself of the same

---

[28] *Paradise Lost*, III, 37–38.
[29] *Love's Labour's Lost*, V, ii, 940–41.
[30] Cf. Milton's *l'Allegro*, l. 144.

[31] *Love's Labour's Lost*, IV, ii, 126–27. The next quotation occurs in Gray's *The Progress of Poesy*, ll. 116–17.
[32] Prologue to *The Canterbury Tales*, l. 275.

brilliant coincidence and unexpected recurrence of syllables, that have been displayed in the invention and collocation of images. It is allowed that rhyme assists the memory; and a man of wit and shrewdness has been heard to say, that the only four good lines of poetry are the well-known ones which tell the number of days in the months of the year.

> "Thirty days hath September," &c.

But if the jingle of names assists the memory, may it not also quicken the fancy? and there are other things worth having at our fingers' ends, besides the contents of the almanac.—Pope's versification is tiresome, from its excessive sweetness and uniformity. Shakspeare's blank verse is the perfection of dramatic dialogue.

All is not poetry that passes for such: nor does verse make the whole difference between poetry and prose. The Iliad does not cease to be poetry in a literal translation; and Addison's Campaign has been very properly denominated a Gazette in rhyme.[33] Common prose differs from poetry, as treating for the most part either of such trite, familiar, and irksome matters of fact, as convey no extraordinary impulse to the imagination, or else of such difficult and laborious processes of the understanding, as do not admit of the wayward or violent movements either of the imagination or the passions.

I will mention three works which come as near to poetry as possible without absolutely being so, namely, the Pilgrim's Progress, Robinson Crusoe, and the Tales of Boccaccio. Chaucer and Dryden have translated some of the last into English rhyme, but the essence and the power of poetry was there before. That which lifts the spirit above the earth, which draws the soul out of itself with indescribable longings, is poetry in kind, and generally fit to become so in name, by being "married to immortal verse."[34] If it is of the essence of poetry to strike and fix the imagination, whether we will or no, to make the eye of childhood glisten with the starting tear, to be never thought of afterwards with indifference, John Bunyan and Daniel Defoe may be permitted to pass for poets in their way. The mixture of fancy and reality in the Pilgrim's Progress was never equalled in any allegory. His pilgrims walk above the earth, and yet are on it. What zeal, what beauty, what truth of fiction! What deep feeling in the description of Christian's swimming across the water at last, and in the picture of the Shining

Ones within the gates, with wings at their backs and garlands on their heads, who are to wipe all tears from his eyes! The writer's genius, though not "dipped in dews of Castalie,"[35] was baptised with the Holy Spirit and with fire. The prints in this book are no small part of it. If the confinement of Philoctetes in the island of Lemnos was a subject for the most beautiful of all the Greek tragedies,[36] what shall we say to Robinson Crusoe in his? Take the speech of the Greek hero on leaving his cave, beautiful as it is, and compare it with the reflections of the English adventurer in his solitary place of confinement. The thoughts of home, and of all from which he is for ever cut off, swell and press against his bosom, as the heaving ocean rolls its ceaseless tide against the rocky shore, and the very beatings of his heart become audible in the eternal silence that surrounds him. Thus he says,

> "As I walked about, either in my hunting, or for viewing the country, the anguish of my soul at my condition would break out upon me on a sudden, and my very heart would die within me to think of the woods, the mountains, the deserts I was in; and how I was a prisoner, locked up with the eternal bars and bolts of the ocean, in an uninhabited wilderness, without redemption. In the midst of the greatest composures of my mind, this would break upon me like a storm, and make me wring my hands, and weep like a child. Sometimes it would take me in the middle of my work, and I would immediately sit down and sigh, and look upon the ground for an hour or two together, and this was still worse to me, for if I could burst into tears or vent myself in words, it would go off, and the grief having exhausted itself would abate." P. 50.

The story of his adventures would not make a poem like the Odyssey, it is true; but the relator had the true genius of a poet. It has been made a question whether Richardson's romances are poetry; and the answer perhaps is, that they are not poetry, because they are not romance. The interest is worked up to an inconceivable height; but it is by an infinite number of little things, by incessant labour and calls upon the attention, by a repetition of blows that have no rebound in them. The sympathy excited is not a voluntary contribution, but a tax. Nothing is unforced and spontaneous. There is a want of elasticity and motion. The story does not "give an echo to the seat where love is throned."[37] The heart does not answer of itself like a chord in music. The fancy does not run on before the writer with breathless expectation, but is dragged along with an infinite number of pins and wheels, like those

---

[33] The Campaign (1705) by Joseph Addison was a celebration of the military victories by the Duke of Marlborough. Joseph Warton had referred to the poem as "a Gazette in rhyme" in his Essay on the Writings and Genius of Pope (1756), p. 30.
[34] l'Allegro, l. 137.

[35] Spenser's "The Ruines of Time," l. 431.
[36] Sophocles' Philoctetes. The speech next referred to may be ll. 255–315 or 1452–1469.
[37] Twelfth Night, II, iv, 21–22.

with which the Lilliputians dragged Gulliver pinioned to the royal palace.—Sir Charles Grandison is a coxcomb. What sort of a figure would he cut translated into an epic poem, by the side of Achilles? Clarissa, the divine Clarissa, is too interesting by half. She is interesting in her ruffles, in her gloves, her samplers, her aunts and uncles—she is interesting in all that is uninteresting. Such things, however intensely they may be brought home to us, are not conductors to the imagination. There is infinite truth and feeling in Richardson; but it is extracted from a *caput mortuum* [38] of circumstances: it does not evaporate of itself. His poetical genius is like Ariel confined in a pine-tree, [39] and requires an artificial process to let it out. Shakspeare says—[40]

> "Our posey is as a gum
> Which issues whence 'tis nourished, our gentle flame
> Provokes itself, and like the current flies
> Each bound it chafes." *

I shall conclude this general account with some remarks on four of the principal works of poetry in the world, at different periods of history—Homer, the Bible, Dante, and let me add, Ossian. In Homer, the principle of action or life is predominant; in the Bible, the principle of faith and the idea of Providence; Dante is a personification of blind will; and in Ossian we see the decay of life, and the lag end of the world. Homer's poetry is the heroic: it is full of life and action: it is bright as the day, strong as a river. In the vigour of his intellect, he grapples with all the objects of nature, and enters into all the relations of social life. He saw many countries, and the manners of many men; and he has brought them all together in his poem. He describes his heroes going to battle with a prodigality of life, arising from an exuberance of animal spirits: we see

* Burke's writings are not poetry, notwithstanding the vividness of the fancy, because the subject matter is abstruse and dry, not natural, but artificial. The difference between poetry and eloquence is, that the one is the eloquence of the imagination, and the other of the understanding. Eloquence tries to persuade the will, and convince the reason: poetry produced its effect by instantaneous sympathy. Nothing is a subject for poetry that admits of a dispute. Poets are in general bad prose-writers, because their images, though fine in themselves, are not to the purpose, and do not carry on the argument. The French poetry wants the forms of the imagination. It is didactic more than dramatic. And some of our own poetry which has been most admired, is only poetry in the rhyme, and in the studied use of poetic diction.

◇◇◇◇◇◇◇◇◇◇◇◇◇◇◇◇◇◇◇◇◇◇◇◇◇◇◇◇◇◇◇◇

[38] *caput mortuum:* rubbish (literally, "dead head"); an alchemical term used to designate the worthless residue left after exhaustive distillation or sublimation.
[39] See *Tempest*, I, ii, 269–84.
[40] In *Timon of Athens*, I, i, 21–25.

them before us, their number, and their order of battle, poured out upon the plain "all plumed like estriches, like eagles newly bathed, wanton as goats, wild as young bulls, youthful as May, and gorgeous as the sun at midsummer," [41] covered with glittering armour, with dust and blood; while the gods quaff their nectar in golden cups, or mingle in the fray; and the old men assembled on the walls of Troy rise up with reverence as Helen passes by them. The multitude of things in Homer is wonderful; their splendour, their truth, their force, and variety. His poetry is, like his religion, the poetry of number and form: he describes the bodies as well as the souls of men.

The poetry of the Bible is that of imagination and of faith: it is abstract and disembodied: it is not the poetry of form, but of power; not of multitude, but of immensity. It does not divide into many, but aggrandizes into one. Its ideas of nature are like its ideas of God. It is not the poetry of social life, but of solitude: each man seems alone in the world, with the original forms of nature, the rocks, the earth, and the sky. It is not the poetry of action or heroic enterprise, but of faith in a supreme Providence, and resignation to the power that governs the universe. As the idea of God was removed farther from humanity, and a scattered polytheism, it became more profound and intense, it became more universal, for the Infinite is present to every thing: "If we fly into the uttermost parts of the earth, it is there also; if we turn to the east or the west, we cannot escape from it." [42] Man is thus aggrandised in the image of his Maker. The history of the patriarchs is of this kind; they are founders of a chosen race of people, the inheritors of the earth; they exist in the generations which are to come after them. Their poetry, like their religious creed, is vast, unformed, obscure, and infinite; a vision is upon it—an invisible hand is suspended over it. The spirit of the Christian religion consists in the glory hereafter to be revealed; but in the Hebrew dispensation, Providence took an immediate share in the affairs of this life. Jacob's dream arose out of this intimate communion between heaven and earth: it was this that let down, in the sight of the youthful patriarch, a golden ladder from the sky to the earth, with angels ascending and descending upon it, and shed a light upon the lonely place, which can never pass away. The story of Ruth, again, is as if all the depth of natural affection in the human race was involved in her breast. There are descriptions in the book of Job more prodigal of imagery, more intense in passion, than any thing in Homer, as that of the state of his prosperity, and of the vision that came upon him

◇◇◇◇◇◇◇◇◇◇◇◇◇◇◇◇◇◇◇◇◇◇◇◇◇◇◇◇◇◇◇◇

[41] *Henry the Fourth*, Part I, IV, i, 98–102.
[42] Cf. Psalms, cxxxix, 9–11.

by night. The metaphors in the Old Testament are more boldly figurative. Things were collected more into masses, and gave a greater *momentum* to the imagination.

Dante was the father of modern poetry, and he may therefore claim a place in this connection. His poem is the first great step from Gothic darkness and barbarism; and the struggle of thought in it to burst the thraldom in which the human mind had been so long held, is felt in every page. He stood bewildered, not appalled, on that dark shore which separates the ancient and the modern world; and saw the glories of antiquity dawning through the abyss of time, while revelation opened its passage to the other world. He was lost in wonder at what had been done before him, and he dared to emulate it. Dante seems to have been indebted to the Bible for the gloomy tone of his mind, as well as for the prophetic fury which exalts and kindles his poetry; but he is utterly unlike Homer. His genius is not a sparkling flame, but the sullen heat of a furnace. He is power, passion, self-will personified. In all that relates to the descriptive or fanciful part of poetry, he bears no comparison to many who had gone before, or who have come after him; but there is a gloomy abstraction in his conceptions, which lies like a dead weight upon the mind; a benumbing stupor, a breathless awe, from the intensity of the impression; a terrible obscurity, like that which oppresses us in dreams; an identity of interest, which moulds every object to its own purposes, and clothes all things with the passions and imaginations of the human soul,—that make amends for all other deficiencies. The immediate objects he presents to the mind are not much in themselves, they want grandeur, beauty, and order; but they become every thing by the force of the character he impresses upon them. His mind lends its own power to the objects which it contemplates, instead of borrowing it from them. He takes advantage even of the nakedness and dreary vacuity of his subject. His imagination peoples the shades of death, and broods over the silent air. He is the severest of all writers, the most hard and impenetrable, the most opposite to the flowery and glittering; who relies most on his own power, and the sense of it in others, and who leaves most room to the imagination of his readers. Dante's only object is to interest; and he interests by exciting our sympathy with the emotion by which he is himself possessed. He does not place before us the objects by which that emotion has been excited; but he seizes on the attention, by shewing us the effect they produce on his feelings; and his poetry accordingly gives the same thrilling and overwhelming sensation, which is caught by gazing on the face of a person who has seen some object of horror. The improbability of the events, the

abruptness and monotony in the Inferno, are excessive: but the interest never flags, from the intense earnestness of the author's mind. Dante's great power is in combining internal feelings with external objects. Thus the gate of hell, on which that withering inscription is written,[43] seems to be endowed with speech and consciousness, and to utter its dread warning, not without a sense of mortal woes. This author habitually unites the absolutely local and individual with the greatest wildness and mysticism. In the midst of the obscure and shadowy regions of the lower world, a tomb suddenly rises up with this inscription, "I am the tomb of Pope Anastasius the Sixth:" and half the personages whom he has crowded into the Inferno are his own acquaintance. All this, perhaps, tends to heighten the effect by the bold intermixture of realities, and the appeal, as it were, to the individual knowledge and experience of the reader. He affords few subjects for picture. There is, indeed, one gigantic one, that of Count Ugolino, of which Michael Angelo made a bas-relief, and which Sir Joshua Reynolds ought not to have painted.[44]

Another writer whom I shall mention last, and whom I cannot persuade myself to think a mere modern in the groundwork, is Ossian. He is a feeling and a name that can never be destroyed in the minds of his readers. As Homer is the first vigour and lustihed, Ossian is the decay and old age of poetry. He lives only in the recollection and regret of the past. There is one impression which he conveys more entirely than all other poets, namely, the sense of privation, the loss of all things, of friends, of good name, of country—he is even without God in the world. He converses only with the spirits of the departed; with the motionless and silent clouds. The cold moonlight sheds its faint lustre on his head; the fox peeps out of the ruined tower; the thistle shakes its beard to the passing gale; and the strings of his harp seem, as the hand of age, as the tale of other times, passes over them, to sigh and rustle like the dry reeds in the winter's wind! The feeling of cheerless desolation, of the loss of the pith and sap of existence, of the annihilation of the substance, and the clinging to the shadow of all things as in a mock-embrace, is here perfect. In this way, the lamentation of Selma for the loss of Salgar[45] is the finest of all. If it were indeed possible to shew that this writer was

---

[43] See *Inferno*, Canto III. The inscription is "Abandon all hope, ye who enter here!" For the subsequent reference to "the tomb of Pope Anastasius the Sixth," see Canto XI, 6–9.

[44] Count Ugolino numbered among the traitors in *Inferno*, Canto XXXIII. Sir Joshua Reynolds' painting of Ugolino and his Children was exhibited in 1773.

[45] More accurately, the lamentation of Colma, in *The Songs of Selma* (1760). The next quotation is from the concluding paragraph of the same Ossianic work.

nothing, it would only be another instance of mutability, another blank made, another void left in the heart, another confirmation of that feeling which makes him so often complain, "Roll on, ye dark brown years, ye bring no joy on your wing to Ossian!"

[1818]   [1819]

FROM
LECTURE III.
ON SHAKSPEARE AND MILTON. [1]

*   *   *   *   *

THE FOUR greatest names in English poetry, are almost the four first we come to—Chaucer, Spenser, Shakspeare, and Milton. There are no others that can really be put in competition with these. The two last have had justice done them by the voice of common fame. Their names are blazoned in the very firmament of reputation; while the two first, (though "the fault has been more in their stars than in themselves that they are underlings")[2] either never emerged far above the horizon, or were too soon involved in the obscurity of time. The three first of these are excluded from Dr. Johnson's Lives of the Poets (Shakspeare indeed is so from the dramatic form of his compositions): and the fourth, Milton, is admitted with a reluctant and churlish welcome.

In comparing these four writers together, it might be said that Chaucer excels as the poet of manners, or of real life; Spenser, as the poet of romance; Shakspeare, as the poet of nature (in the largest use of the term); and Milton, as the poet of morality. Chaucer most frequently describes things as they are; Spenser, as we wish them to be; Shakspeare, as they would be; and Milton as they ought to be. As poets, and as great poets, imagination, that is, the power of feigning things according to nature, was common to them all: but the principle, or moving power, to which this faculty was most subservient in Chaucer, was habit, or inveterate prejudice; in Spenser, novelty, and the love of the marvellous; in Shakspeare, it was the force of passion, combined with every variety of possible circumstances; and in Milton, only with the highest. The characteristic of Chaucer is intensity; of Spenser, remoteness; of Milton, elevation; of Shakspeare, every

thing.—It has been said by some critic, that Shakspeare was distinguished from the other dramatic writers of his day only by his wit; that they had all his other qualities but that; that one writer had as much sense, another as much fancy, another as much knowledge of character, another the same depth of passion, and another as great a power of language. This statement is not true; nor is the inference from it well-founded, even if it were. This person does not seem to have been aware that, upon his own shewing, the great distinction of Shakspeare's genius was its virtually including the genius of all the great men of his age, and not its differing from them in one accidental particular. But to have done with such minute and literal trifling.

The striking peculiarity of Shakspeare's mind was its generic quality, its power of communication with all other minds—so that it contained a universe of thought and feeling within itself, and had no one peculiar bias, or exclusive excellence more than another. He was just like any other man, but that he was like all other men. He was the least of an egotist that it was possible to be. He was nothing in himself; but he was all that others were, or that they could become. He not only had in himself the germs of every faculty and feeling, but he could follow them by anticipation, intuitively, into all their conceivable ramifications, through every change of fortune or conflict of passion, or turn of thought. He had "a mind reflecting ages past,"[3] and present:—all the people that ever lived are there. There was no respect of persons with him. His genius shone equally on the evil and on the good, on the wise and the foolish, the monarch and the beggar: "All corners of the earth, kings, queens, and states, maids, matrons, nay, the secrets of the grave,"[4] are hardly hid from his searching glance. He was like the genius of humanity, changing places with all of us at pleasure, and playing with our purposes as with his own. He turned the globe round for his amusement, and surveyed the generations of men, and the individuals as they passed, with their different concerns, passions, follies, vices, virtues, actions, and motives—as well those that they knew, as those which they did not know, or acknowledge to themselves. The dreams of childhood, the ravings of despair, were the toys of his fancy. Airy beings waited at his call, and came at his bidding. Harmless fairies "nodded to him, and did him curtesies:"[5] and the night-hag bestrode the blast at the command of "his so potent art." The world of spirits

---

[1] The first two paragraphs of the essay, which reproduce sections of "Why the Arts are not Progressive?—A Fragment," are omitted.
[2] *Julius Caesar*, I, ii, 140–41.

[3] From prefatory verses to the second folio of Shakespeare's works, 1632.
[4] *Cymbeline*, III, iv, 39–40.
[5] *A Midsummer Night's Dream*, III, i, 177. The next quotation occurs in *Tempest*, V, i, 50.

lay open to him, like the world of real men and women: and there is the same truth in his delineations of the one as of the other; for if the preternatural characters he describes could be supposed to exist, they would speak, and feel, and act, as he makes them. He had only to think of any thing in order to become that thing, with all the circumstances belonging to it. When he conceived of a character, whether real or imaginary, he not only entered into all its thoughts and feelings, but seemed instantly, and as if by touching a secret spring, to be surrounded with all the same objects, "subject to the same skyey influences,"[6] the same local, outward and unforeseen accidents which would occur in reality. Thus the character of Caliban not only stands before us with a language and manners of its own, but the scenery and situation of the enchanted island he inhabits, the traditions of the place, its strange noises, its hidden recesses, "his frequent haunts and ancient neighbourhood,"[7] are given with a miraculous truth of nature, and with all the familiarity of an old recollection. The whole "coheres semblably together" in time, place, and circumstance. In reading this author, you do not merely learn what his characters say,—you see their persons. By something expressed or understood, you are at no loss to decypher their peculiar physiognomy, the meaning of a look, the grouping, the bye-play, as we might see it on the stage. A word, an epithet paints a whole scene, or throws us back whole years in the history of the person represented. So (as it has been ingeniously remarked)[8] when Prospero describes himself as left alone in the boat with his daughter, the epithet which he applies to her, "Me and thy *crying* self," flings the imagination instantly back from the grown woman to the helpless condition of infancy, and places the first and most trying scene of his misfortunes before us, with all that he must have suffered in the interval. How well the silent anguish of Macduff is conveyed to the reader, by the friendly expostulation of Malcolm—"What! man, ne'er pull your hat upon your brows!"[9] Again, Hamlet, in the scene with Rosencrans and Guildenstern, somewhat abruptly concludes his fine soliloquy on life by saying, "Man delights not me, nor woman neither, though by your smiling you seem to say so." Which is explained by their answer—"My lord, we had no such stuff in our thoughts. But we smiled to think, if you delight not in man, what lenten entertainment the players shall

receive from you, whom we met on the way:"—as if while Hamlet was making this speech, his two old schoolfellows from Wittenberg had been really standing by, and he had seen them smiling by stealth, at the idea of the players crossing their minds. It is not "a combination and a form" of words, a set speech or two, a preconcerted theory of a character, that will do this: but all the persons concerned must have been present in the poet's imagination, as at a kind of rehearsal; and whatever would have passed through their minds on the occasion, and have been observed by others, passed through his, and is made known to the reader.—I may add in passing, that Shakspeare always gives the best directions for the costume and carriage of his heroes. Thus to take on example, Ophelia gives the following account of Hamlet: and as Ophelia had seen Hamlet, I should think her word ought to be taken against that of any modern authority....[10] How after this airy, fantastic idea of irregular grace and bewildered melancholy any one can play Hamlet, as we have seen it played, with strut, and stare, and antic right-angled sharp-pointed gestures, it is difficult to say, unless it be that Hamlet is not bound, by the prompter's cue, to study the part of Ophelia. The account of Ophelia's death begins thus:

> "There is a willow hanging o'er a brook,
> That shows its hoary leaves in the glassy stream."—

Now this is an instance of the same unconscious power of mind which is as true to nature as itself. The leaves of the willow are, in fact, white underneath, and it is this part of them which would appear "hoary" in the reflection in the brook. The same sort of intuitive power, the same faculty of bringing every object in nature, whether present or absent, before the mind's eye, is observable in the speech of Cleopatra, when conjecturing what were the employments of Antony in his absence:—"He's speaking now or murmuring, where's my serpent of old Nile?"[11] How fine to make Cleopatra have this consciousness of her own character, and to make her feel that it is this for which Antony is in love with her! She says, after the battle of Actium, when Antony has resolved to risk another fight, "It is my birth-day; I had thought to have held it poor: but since my lord is Antony again, I will be Cleopatra." What other poet would have thought of such a casual resource of the imagination, or would have dared to avail himself of it? The thing happens in the play as it might have happened in fact.—That which, perhaps,

---

[6] See *Measure for Measure*, III, i, 9.

[7] Cf. *Comus*, l. 314. For the next quotation, cf. *Henry the Fourth*, Part II, V, i, 72–73.

[8] By Coleridge. See his Ninth Lecture (December 16, 1811) of "A Course of Lectures on Shakespear and Milton," p. 140.

[9] *Macbeth*, IV, iii, 208. The next three quotations are from *Hamlet*, II, ii, 322–25, 327–30; III, iv, 60.

[10] Hazlitt here quotes II, i, 77–100. The next quotation occurs at IV, vii, 168–69.

[11] *Antony and Cleopatra*, I, v, 24–25. The next quotation occurs at III, xiii, 185–87.

more than any thing else distinguishes the dramatic productions of Shakspeare from all others, is this wonderful truth and individuality of conception. Each of his characters is as much itself, and as absolutely independent of the rest, as well as of the author, as if they were living persons, not fictions of the mind. The poet may be said, for the time, to identify himself with the character he wishes to represent, and to pass from one to another, like the same soul successively animating different bodies. By an art like that of the ventriloquist, he throws his imagination out of himself, and makes every word appear to proceed from the mouth of the person in whose name it is given. His plays alone are properly expressions of the passions, not descriptions of them. His characters are real beings of flesh and blood; they speak like men, not like authors. One might suppose that he had stood by at the time, and overheard what passed. As in our dreams we hold conversations with ourselves, make remarks, or communicate intelligence, and have no idea of the answer which we shall receive, and which we ourselves make, till we hear it: so the dialogues in Shakspeare are carried on without any consciousness of what is to follow, without any appearance of preparation or premeditation. The gusts of passion come and go like sounds of music borne on the wind. Nothing is made out by formal inference and analogy, by climax and antithesis: all comes, or seems to come, immediately from nature. Each object and circumstance exists in his mind, as it would have existed in reality: each several train of thought and feeling goes on of itself, without confusion or effort. In the world of his imagination, every thing has a life, a place, and being of its own!

Chaucer's characters are sufficiently distinct from one another, but they are too little varied in themselves, too much like identical propositions. They are consistent, but uniform; we get no new idea of them from first to last; they are not placed in different lights, nor are their subordinate *traits* brought out in new situations; they are like portraits or physiognomical studies, with the distinguishing features marked with inconceivable truth and precision, but that preserve the same unaltered air and attitude. Shakspeare's are historical figures, equally true and correct, but put into action, where every nerve and muscle is displayed in the struggle with others, with all the effect of collision and contrast, with every variety of light and shade. Chaucer's characters are narrative, Shakspeare's dramatic, Milton's epic. That is, Chaucer told only as much of his story as he pleased, as was required for a particular purpose. He answered for his characters himself. In Shakspeare they are introduced upon the stage, are liable to be asked all sorts of questions, and are forced to answer for themselves. In Chaucer we perceive a fixed essence of character. In Shakspeare there is a continual composition and decomposition of its elements, a fermentation of every particle in the whole mass, by its alternate affinity or antipathy to other principles which are brought in contact with it. Till the experiment is tried, we do not know the result, the turn which the character will take in its new circumstances. Milton took only a few simple principles of character, and raised them to the utmost conceivable grandeur, and refined them from every base alloy. His imagination, "nigh sphered in Heaven," [12] claimed kindred only with what he saw from that height, and could raise to the same elevation with itself. He sat retired and kept his state alone, "playing with wisdom;" while Shakspeare mingled with the crowd, and played the host, "to make society the sweeter welcome."

The passion in Shakspeare is of the same nature as his delineation of character. It is not some one habitual feeling or sentiment preying upon itself, growing out of itself, and moulding every thing to itself; it is passion modified by passion, by all the other feelings to which the individual is liable, and to which others are liable with him; subject to all the fluctuations of caprice and accident; calling into play all the resources of the understanding and all the energies of the will; irritated by obstacles or yielding to them; rising from small beginnings to its utmost height; now drunk with hope, now stung to madness, now sunk in despair, now blown to air with a breath, now raging like a torrent. The human soul is made the sport of fortune, the prey of adversity: it is stretched on the wheel of destiny, in restless ecstacy. The passions are in a state of projection. Years are melted down to moments, and every instant teems with fate. We know the results, we see the process. Thus after Iago has been boasting to himself of the effect of his poisonous suggestions on the mind of Othello, "which, with a little act upon the blood, will work like mines of sulphur," he adds—

"Look where he comes! not poppy, nor mandragora,
    Nor all the drowsy syrups of the East,
    Shall ever medicine thee to that sweet sleep
    Which thou ow'dst yesterday."—[13]

And he enters at this moment, like the crested serpent, crowned with his wrongs and raging for revenge! The whole depends upon the turn of a thought. A word, a look, blows the spark of jealousy into a flame; and the explosion is immediate and terrible as a volcano. The dialogues in Lear, in Macbeth, that between Brutus

---

[12] William Collins' "Ode on the Poetical Character" (1746), l. 66. For the next two quotations, see *Paradise Lost*, VII, 10; *Macbeth*, III, i, 42–43.
[13] *Othello*, III, iii, 328–33.

and Cassius, and nearly all those in Shakspeare, where the interest is wrought up to its highest pitch, afford examples of this dramatic fluctuation of passion. The interest in Chaucer is quite different; it is like the course of a river, strong, and full, and increasing. In Shakspeare, on the contrary, it is like the sea, agitated this way and that, and loud-lashed by furious storms; while in the still pauses of the blast, we distinguish only the cries of despair, or the silence of death! Milton, on the other hand, takes the imaginative part of passion—that which remains after the event, which the mind reposes on when all is over, which looks upon circumstances from the remotest elevation of thought and fancy, and abstracts them from the world of action to that of contemplation. The objects of dramatic poetry affect us by sympathy, by their nearness to ourselves, as they take us by surprise, or force us upon action, "while rage with rage doth sympathise:" [14] the objects of epic poetry affect us through the medium of the imagination, by magnitude and distance, by their permanence and universality. The one fill us with terror and pity, the other with admiration and delight. There are certain objects that strike the imagination, and inspire awe in the very idea of them, independently of any dramatic interest, that is, of any connection with the vicissitudes of human life. For instance, we cannot think of the pyramids of Egypt, of a Gothic ruin, or an old Roman encampment, without a certain emotion, a sense of power and sublimity coming over the mind. The heavenly bodies that hang over our heads wherever we go, and "in their untroubled element shall shine when we are laid in dust, and all our cares forgotten," [15] affect us in the same way. Thus Satan's address to the Sun has an epic, not a dramatic interest; for though the second person in the dialogue makes no answer and feels no concern, yet the eye of that vast luminary is upon him, like the eye of heaven, and seems conscious of what he says, like an universal presence. Dramatic poetry and epic, in their perfection, indeed, approximate to and strengthen one another. Dramatic poetry borrows aid from the dignity of persons and things, as the heroic does from human passion, but in theory they are distinct.—When Richard II. calls for the looking-glass to contemplate his faded majesty in it, and bursts into that affecting exclamation: "Oh, that I were a mockery-king of snow, to melt away before the sun of Bolingbroke," [16] we have here the utmost force of human passion, combined with the ideas of regal

splendour and fallen power. When Milton says of Satan:

> "——His form had not yet lost
> All her original brightness, nor appear'd
> Less than archangel ruin'd, and th' excess
> Of glory obscur'd;"—

the mixture of beauty, of grandeur, and pathos, from the sense of irreparable loss, of never-ending, unavailing regret, is perfect.

The great fault of a modern school of poetry is, that it is an experiment to reduce poetry to a mere effusion of natural sensibility; or what is worse, to divest it both of imaginary splendour and human passion, to surround the meanest objects with the morbid feelings and devouring egotism of the writers' own minds. Milton and Shakspeare did not so understand poetry. They gave a more liberal interpretation both to nature and art. They did not do all they could to get rid of the one and the other, to fill up the dreary void with the Moods of their own Minds. [17] They owe their power over the human mind to their having had a deeper sense than others of what was grand in the objects of nature, or affecting in the events of human life. But to the men I speak of there is nothing interesting, nothing heroical, but themselves. To them the fall of gods or of great men is the same. They do not enter into the feeling. They cannot understand the terms. They are even debarred from the last poor, paltry consolation of an unmanly triumph over fallen greatness; for their minds reject, with a convulsive effort and intolerable loathing, the very idea that there ever was, or was thought to be, any thing superior to themselves. All that has ever excited the attention or admiration of the world, they look upon with the most perfect indifference; and they are surprised to find that the world repays their indifference with scorn. "With what measure they mete, it has been meted to them again." [18]

Shakspeare's imagination is of the same plastic kind as his conception of character or passion. "It glances from heaven to earth, from earth to heaven." [19] Its movement is rapid and devious. It unites the most opposite extremes; or, as Puck says, in boasting of his own feats, "puts a girdle round about the earth in forty minutes." He seems always hurrying from his subject, even while describing it; but the stroke, like the lightning's, is sure as it is sudden. He takes the widest possible range, but from that very range he has

---

[14] *Troilus and Cressida*, I, iii, 52.
[15] See Wordsworth's *Excursion*, VI, 763–66. "Satan's address to the Sun" next mentioned occurs in *Paradise Lost*, IV, 32–113.
[16] *Richard the Second*, IV, i, 260–62. The next quotation occurs in *Paradise Lost*, I, 591–94.

[17] Hazlitt refers to "Moods of my own Mind," the section title of a group of poems in Wordsworth's *Poems in Two Volumes* (1807).
[18] Luke, vi, 38.
[19] *A Midsummer Night's Dream*, V, i, 13. The next quotation occurs at II, i, 175.

his choice of the greatest variety and aptitude of materials. He brings together images the most alike, but placed at the greatest distance from each other; that is, found in circumstances of the greatest dissimilitude. From the remoteness of his combinations, and the celerity with which they are effected, they coalesce the more indissolubly together. The more the thoughts are strangers to each other, and the longer they have been kept asunder, the more intimate does their union seem to become. Their felicity is equal to their force. Their likeness is made more dazzling by their novelty. They startle, and take the fancy prisoner in the same instant. I will mention one or two which are very striking, and not much known, out of Troilus and Cressida. Æneas says to Agamemnon,

"I ask that I may waken reverence,
    And on the cheek be ready with a blush
    Modest as morning, when she coldly eyes
    The youthful Phœbus."[20]

Ulysses urging Achilles to shew himself in the field, says—

"No man is the lord of any thing,
    Till he communicate his parts to others:
    Nor doth he of himself know them for aught,
    Till he behold them formed in the applause,
    Where they're extended! which like an arch reverberates
    The voice again, or like a gate of steel,
    Fronting the sun, receives and renders back
    Its figure and its heat."

Patroclus gives the indolent warrior the same advice.

"Rouse yourself; and the weak wanton Cupid
    Shall from your neck unloose his amorous fold,
    And like a dew-drop from the lion's mane
    Be shook to air."

Shakspeare's language and versification are like the rest of him. He has a magic power over words: they come winged at his bidding; and seem to know their places. They are struck out at a heat, on the spur of the occasion, and have all the truth and vividness which arise from an actual impression of the objects. His epithets and single phrases are like sparkles, thrown off from an imagination, fired by the whirling rapidity of its own motion. His language is hieroglyphical. It translates thoughts into visible images. It abounds in sudden transitions and elliptical expressions. This is the source of his mixed metaphors, which are only abbreviated forms of speech. These, however, give no pain from long custom. They have, in fact, become

idioms in the language. They are the building, and not the scaffolding to thought. We take the meaning and effect of a well-known passage entire, and no more stop to scan and spell out the particular words and phrases, than the syllables of which they are composed. In trying to recollect any other author, one sometimes stumbles, in case of failure, on a word as good. In Shakspeare, any other word but the true one, is sure to be wrong. If any body, for instance, could not recollect the words of the following description,

"——Light thickens,
    And the crow makes wing to the rooky wood,"[21]

he would be greatly at a loss to substitute others for them equally expressive of the feeling. These remarks, however, are strictly applicable only to the impassioned parts of Shakspeare's language, which flowed from the warmth and originality of his imagination, and were his own. The language used for prose conversation and ordinary business is sometimes technical, and involved in the affectation of the time. Compare, for example, Othello's apology to the senate, relating "his whole course of love,"[22] with some of the preceding parts relating to his appointment, and the official dispatches from Cyprus. In this respect, "the business of the state does him offence."—His versification is no less powerful, sweet, and varied. It has every occasional excellence, of sullen intricacy, crabbed and perplexed, or of the smoothest and loftiest expansion—from the ease and familiarity of measured conversation to the lyrical sounds

"——Of ditties highly penned,
    Sung by a fair queen in a summer's bower,
    With ravishing division to her lute."[23]

It is the only blank verse in the language, except Milton's, that for itself is readable. It is not stately and uniformly swelling like his, but varied and broken by the inequalities of the ground it has to pass over in its uncertain course,

"And so by many winding nooks it strays,
    With willing sport to the wild ocean."

It remains to speak of the faults of Shakspeare. They are not so many or so great as they have been represented; what there are, are chiefly owing to the following causes:—The universality of his genius was, perhaps, a disadvantage to his single works; the variety of his resources, sometimes diverting him from apply-

---

[20] *Troilus and Cressida*, I, iii, 227–30. The next two quotations occur at III, iii, 115–21 and 222–25.

[21] *Macbeth*, III, ii, 50–51.
[22] I, iii, 91. The next quotation occurs at IV, ii, 166.
[23] *Henry the Fourth*, Part I, III, i, 208–10. The next quotation occurs in *Two Gentlemen of Verona*, II, vii, 31–32.

ing them to the most effectual purposes. He might be said to combine the powers of Æschylus and Aristophanes, of Dante and Rabelais, in his own mind. If he had been only half what he was, he would perhaps have appeared greater. The natural ease and indifference of his temper made him sometimes less scrupulous than he might have been. He is relaxed and careless in critical places; he is in earnest throughout only in Timon, Macbeth, and Lear. Again, he had no models of acknowledged excellence constantly in view to stimulate his efforts, and by all that appears, no love of fame. He wrote for the "great vulgar and the small,"[24] in his time, not for posterity. If Queen Elizabeth and the maids of honour laughed heartily at his worst jokes, and the catcalls in the gallery were silent at his best passages, he went home satisfied, and slept the next night well. He did not trouble himself about Voltaire's criticisms.[25] He was willing to take advantage of the ignorance of the age in many things; and if his plays pleased others, not to quarrel with them himself. His very facility of production would make him set less value on his own excellences, and not care to distinguish nicely between what he did well or ill. His blunders in chronology and geography do not amount to above half a dozen, and they are offences against chronology and geography, not against poetry. As to the unities, he was right in setting them at defiance. He was fonder of puns than became so great a man. His barbarisms were those of his age. His genius was his own. He had no objection to float down with the stream of common taste and opinion: he rose above it by his own buoyancy, and an impulse which he could not keep under, in spite of himself or others, and "his delights did shew most dolphin-like."[26]

He had an equal genius for comedy and tragedy; and his tragedies are better than his comedies, because tragedy is better than comedy. His female characters, which have been found fault with as insipid, are the finest in the world. Lastly, Shakspeare was the least of a coxcomb of any one that ever lived, and much of a gentleman.

Shakspeare discovers in his writings little religious enthusiasm, and an indifference to personal reputation; he had none of the bigotry of his age, and his political prejudices were not very strong. In these respects, as well as in every other, he formed a direct contrast to

Milton. Milton's works are a perpetual invocation to the Muses; a hymn to Fame. He had his thoughts constantly fixed on the contemplation of the Hebrew theocracy, and of a perfect commonwealth; and he seized the pen with a hand just warm from the touch of the ark of faith. His religious zeal infused its character into his imagination; so that he devotes himself with the same sense of duty to the cultivation of his genius, as he did to the exercise of virtue, or the good of his country. The spirit of the poet, the patriot, and the prophet, vied with each other in his breast. His mind appears to have held equal communion with the inspired writers, and with the bards and sages of ancient Greece and Rome;—

> "Blind Thamyris, and blind Mæonides,
>   And Tiresias, and Phineus, prophets old."[27]

He had a high standard, with which he was always comparing himself, nothing short of which could satisfy his jealous ambition. He thought of nobler forms and nobler things than those he found about him. He lived apart, in the solitude of his own thoughts, carefully excluding from his mind whatever might distract its purposes, or alloy its purity, or damp its zeal. "With darkness and with dangers compassed round,"[28] he had the mighty models of antiquity always present to his thoughts, and determined to raise a monument of equal height and glory, "piling up every stone of lustre from the brook," for the delight and wonder of posterity. He had girded himself up, and as it were, sanctified his genius to this service from his youth. "For after," he says, "I had from my first years, by the ceaseless diligence and care of my father, been exercised to the tongues, and some sciences as my age could suffer, by sundry masters and teachers, it was found that whether aught was imposed upon me by them, or betaken to of my own choice, the style by certain vital signs it had, was likely to live; but much latelier, in the private academies of Italy, perceiving that some trifles which I had in memory, composed at under twenty or thereabout, met with acceptance above what was looked for; I began thus far to assent both to them and divers of my friends here at home, and not less to an inward prompting which now grew daily upon me, that by labour and intense study (which I take to be my portion in this life), joined with the strong propensity of nature, I might perhaps leave something so written to after-times as they should not willingly let it die. The accomplishment of these intentions, which have lived within me ever since I could conceive myself any thing

---

[24] Line 2 of Abraham Cowley's translation of Horace's Ode "Odi profanum" in *Verses lately written upon several Occasions* (1663).
[25] In various works Voltaire had criticized Shakespeare for not observing the classical unities, for mixing comedy and tragedy, for portraying scenes of violence, and in general for submitting his genius to the "barbarous" standards of his audience.
[26] *Antony and Cleopatra*, V, ii, 88–89.

[27] *Paradise Lost*, III, 35–36.
[28] *Paradise Lost*, VII, 27. The next quotation occurs at XI, 324–25.

worth to my country, lies not but in a power above man's to promise; but that none hath by more studious ways endeavoured, and with more unwearied spirit that none shall, that I dare almost aver of myself, as far as life and free leisure will extend. Neither do I think it shame to covenant with any knowing reader, that for some few years yet, I may go on trust with him toward the payment of what I am now indebted, as being a work not to be raised from the heat of youth or the vapours of wine; like that which flows at waste from the pen of some vulgar amourist, or the trencher fury of a rhyming parasite, nor to be obtained by the invocation of Dame Memory and her Siren daughters, but by devout prayer to that eternal spirit who can enrich with all utterance and knowledge, and sends out his Seraphim with the hallowed fire of his altar, to touch and purify the lips of whom he pleases: to this must be added industrious and select reading, steady observation, and insight into all seemly and generous arts and affairs. Although it nothing content me to have disclosed thus much beforehand; but that I trust hereby to make it manifest with what small willingness I endure to interrupt the pursuit of no less hopes than these, and leave a calm and pleasing solitariness, fed with cheerful and confident thoughts, to embark in a troubled sea of noises and hoarse disputes, put from beholding the bright countenance of truth in the quiet and still air of delightful studies." [29]

So that of Spenser:

"The noble heart that harbours virtuous thought,
    And is with child of glorious great intent,
Can never rest until it forth have brought
    The eternal brood of glory excellent."

Milton, therefore, did not write from casual impulse, but after a severe examination of his own strength, and with a resolution to leave nothing undone which it was in his power to do. He always labours, and almost always succeeds. He strives hard to say the finest things in the world, and he does say them. He adorns and dignifies his subject to the utmost: he surrounds it with every possible association of beauty or grandeur, whether moral, intellectual, or physical. He refines on his descriptions of beauty; loading sweets on sweets, till the sense aches at them; and raises his images of terror to a gigantic elevation, that "makes Ossa like a wart." [30] In Milton, there is always an appearance of effort: in Shakspeare, scarcely any.

Milton has borrowed more than any other writer, and exhausted every source of imitation, sacred or profane; yet he is perfectly distinct from every other writer. He is a writer of centos, [31] and yet in originality scarcely inferior to Homer. The power of his mind is stamped on every line. The fervour of his imagination melts down and renders malleable, as in a furnace, the most contradictory materials. In reading his works, we feel ourselves under the influence of a mighty intellect, that the nearer it approaches to others, becomes more distinct from them. The quantity of art in him shews the strength of his genius: the weight of his intellectual obligations would have oppressed any other writer. Milton's learning has the effect of intuition. He describes objects, of which he could only have read in books, with the vividness of actual observation. His imagination has the force of nature. He makes words tell as pictures.

"Him followed Rimmon, whose delightful seat
    Was fair Damascus, on the fertile banks
    Of Abbana and Pharphar, lucid streams." [32]

The word *lucid* here gives to the idea all the sparkling effect of the most perfect landscape.

And again:

"As when a vulture on Imaus bred,
    Whose snowy ridge the roving Tartar bounds,
    Dislodging from a region scarce of prey,
    To gorge the flesh of lambs and yeanling kids
    On hills where flocks are fed, flies towards the springs
    Of Ganges or Hydaspes, Indian streams;
    But in his way lights on the barren plains
    Of Sericana, where Chineses drive
    With sails and wind their cany waggons light."

If Milton had taken a journey for the express purpose, he could not have described this scenery and mode of life better. Such passages are like demonstrations of natural history. Instances might be multiplied without end.

We might be tempted to suppose that the vividness with which he describes visible objects, was owing to their having acquired an unusual degree of strength in his mind, after the privation of his sight; but we find the same palpableness and truth in the descriptions which occur in his early poems. In Lycidas he speaks of "the great vision of the guarded mount," [33] with that preternatural weight of impression with which it

[29] Hazlitt runs together several passages from the Preface to Book II of Milton's *The Reason of Church Government urged against Prelaty* (1641). The next quotation is from *Faerie Queene*, I, v, 1.
[30] *Hamlet*, V, i, 306.

[31] Compositions formed by patching together borrowings from other writers.
[32] *Paradise Lost*, I, 467–69. The next quotation occurs at III, 431–39.
[33] Line 161. The next quotations are from *Paradise Lost*, I, 204; and *Il Penseroso*, ll. 68–70.

would present itself suddenly to "the pilot of some small night-foundered skiff;" and the lines in the Penseroso, describing the wandering moon,

> "Riding near her highest noon,
>   Like one that had been led astray
>   Through the heaven's wide pathless way,"

are as if he had gazed himself blind in looking at her. There is also the same depth of impression in his descriptions of the objects of all the different senses, whether colours, or sounds, or smells—the same absorption of his mind in whatever engaged his attention at the time. It has been indeed objected to Milton, by a common perversity of criticism, that his ideas were musical rather than picturesque, as if because they were in the highest degree musical, they must be (to keep the sage critical balance even, and to allow no one man to possess two qualities at the same time) proportionably deficient in other respects. But Milton's poetry is not cast in any such narrow, common-place mould; it is not so barren of resources. His worship of the Muse was not so simple or confined. A sound arises "like a steam of rich distilled perfumes;" [34] we hear the pealing organ, but the incense on the altars is also there, and the statues of the gods are ranged around! The ear indeed predominates over the eye, because it is more immediately affected, and because the language of music blends more immediately with, and forms a more natural accompaniment to, the variable and indefinite associations of ideas conveyed by words. But where the associations of the imagination are not the principal thing, the individual object is given by Milton with equal force and beauty. The strongest and best proof of this, as a characteristic power of his mind, is, that the persons of Adam and Eve, of Satan, &c. are always accompanied, in our imagination, with the grandeur of the naked figure; they convey to us the ideas of sculpture. As an instance, take the following: . . . [35]

The figures introduced here have all the elegance and precision of a Greek statue; glossy and impurpled, tinged with golden light, and musical as the strings of Memnon's harp! [36]

Again, nothing can be more magnificent than the portrait of Beelzebub:

> "With Atlantean shoulders fit to bear
>   The weight of mightiest monarchies:" [37]

Or the comparison of Satan, as he "lay floating many a rood," to "that sea beast,"

> "Leviathan, which God of all his works
>   Created hugest that swim the ocean-stream!"

What a force of imagination is there in this last expression! What an idea it conveys of the size of that hugest of created beings, as if it shrunk up the ocean to a stream, and took up the sea in its nostrils as a very little thing! Force of style is one of Milton's greatest excellences. Hence, perhaps, he stimulates us more in the reading, and less afterwards. The way to defend Milton against all impugners, is to take down the book and read it.

Milton's blank verse is the only blank verse in the language (except Shakspeare's) that deserves the name of verse. Dr. Johnson, who had modelled his ideas of versification on the regular sing-song of Pope, condemns the Paradise Lost as harsh and unequal. [38] I shall not pretend to say that this is not sometimes the case; for where a degree of excellence beyond the mechanical rules of art is attempted, the poet must sometimes fail. But I imagine that there are more perfect examples in Milton of musical expression, or of an adaptation of the sound and movement of the verse to the meaning of the passage, than in all our other writers, whether of rhyme or blank verse, put together, (with the exception already mentioned). Spenser is the most harmonious of our poets, as Dryden is the most sounding and varied of our rhymists. But in neither is there any thing like the same ear for music, the same power of approximating the varieties of poetical to those of musical rhythm, as there is in our great epic poet. The sound of his lines is moulded into the expression of the sentiment, almost of the very image. They rise or fall, pause or hurry rapidly on, with exquisite art, but without the least trick or affectation, as the occasion seems to require. . . .

Dr. Johnson and Pope would have converted his vaulting Pegasus into a rocking-horse. Read any other blank verse but Milton's,—Thomson's, Young's, Cowper's, Wordsworth's,—and it will be found, from the want of the same insight into "the hidden soul of harmony," to be mere lumbering prose.

To proceed to a consideration of the merits of Paradise Lost, in the most essential point of view, I mean as to the poetry of character and passion. I shall

---

34 *Comus*, l. 556.
35 Hazlitt here quotes *Paradise Lost*, III, 621–44, descriptive of the Archangel Uriel and Satan disguised as an angel.
36 A reference to a colossal Egyptian statue to the mythological Memnon, king of the Ethiopians. When the rays of the sun struck the statue, it was alleged to give forth a harp-like sound. See De Quincey's *Suspiria de Profundis*. Part I. "The Affliction of Childhood," footnote 11, p. 604.

37 *Paradise Lost*, II, 306–307. The next quotation occurs at I, 196, 200–202.
38 See Johnson's "Life of Milton" in *The Lives of the Poets*.

say nothing of the fable, or of other technical objections or excellences; but I shall try to explain at once the foundation of the interest belonging to the poem. I am ready to give up the dialogues in Heaven, where, as Pope justly observes, "God the Father turns a school-divine;"[39] nor do I consider the battle of the angels as the climax of sublimity, or the most successful effort of Milton's pen. In a word, the interest of the poem arises from the daring ambition and fierce passions of Satan, and from the account of the paradisaical happiness, and the loss of it by our first parents. Three-fourths of the work are taken up with these characters, and all that relates to them is unmixed sublimity and beauty. The two first books alone are like two massy pillars of solid gold.

Satan is the most heroic subject that was ever chosen for a poem; and the execution is as perfect as the design is lofty. He was the first of created beings, who, for endeavouring to be equal with the highest, and to divide the empire of heaven with the Almighty, was hurled down to hell. His aim was no less than the throne of the universe; his means, myriads of angelic armies bright, the third part of the heavens, whom he lured after him with his countenance, and who durst defy the Omnipotent in arms. His ambition was the greatest, and his punishment was the greatest; but not so his despair, for his fortitude was as great as his sufferings. His strength of mind was matchless as his strength of body; the vastness of his designs did not surpass the firm, inflexible determination with which he submitted to his irreversible doom, and final loss of all hope. His power of action and of suffering was equal. He was the greatest power that was ever overthrown, with the strongest will left to resist or to endure. He was baffled, not confounded. He stood like a tower; or

"——As when Heaven's fire
Hath scathed the forest oaks or mountain pines."[40]

He was still surrounded with hosts of rebel angels, armed warriors, who own him as their sovereign leader, and with whose fate he sympathises as he views them round, far as the eye can reach; though he keeps aloof from them in his own mind, and holds supreme counsel only with his own breast. An outcast from Heaven, Hell trembles beneath his feet, Sin and Death are at his heels, and mankind are his easy prey.

"All is not lost; th' unconquerable will,
And study of revenge, immortal hate,
And courage never to submit or yield,
And what else is not to be overcome,"[41]

are still his. The sense of his punishment seems lost in the magnitude of it; the fierceness of tormenting flames is qualified and made innoxious by the greater fierceness of his pride; the loss of infinite happiness to himself is compensated in thought, by the power of inflicting infinite misery on others. Yet Satan is not the principle of malignity, or of the abstract love of evil—but of the abstract love of power, of pride, of self-will personified, to which last principle all other good and evil, and even his own, are subordinate. From this principle he never once flinches. His love of power and contempt for suffering are never once relaxed from the highest pitch of intensity. His thoughts burn like a hell within him; but the power of thought holds dominion in his mind over every other consideration. The consciousness of a determined purpose, of "that intellectual being, those thoughts that wander through eternity," though accompanied with endless pain, he prefers to nonentity, to "being swallowed up and lost in the wide womb of uncreated night."[42] He expresses the sum and substance of all ambition in one line. "Fallen cherub, to be weak is miserable, doing or suffering!" After such a conflict as his, and such a defeat, to retreat in order, to rally, to make terms, to exist at all, is something; but he does more than this—he founds a new empire in hell, and from it conquers this new world, whither he bends his undaunted flight, forcing his way through nether and surrounding fires. The poet has not in all this given us a mere shadowy outline; the strength is equal to the magnitude of the conception. The Achilles of Homer is not more distinct; the Titans were not more vast; Prometheus chained to his rock was not a more terrific example of suffering and of crime. Wherever the figure of Satan is introduced, whether he walks or flies, "rising aloft incumbent on the dusky air,"[43] it is illustrated with the most striking and appropriate images: so that we see it always before us, gigantic, irregular, portentous, uneasy, and disturbed—but dazzling in its faded splendour, the clouded ruins of a god. The deformity of Satan is only in the depravity of his will; he has no bodily deformity to excite our loathing or disgust. The horns and tail are not there, poor emblems of the unbending, unconquered spirit, of the writhing agonies within. Milton was too magnanimous and open an antagonist to support his argument by the bye-tricks of a hump and cloven foot; to bring into the fair field of controversy the good old catholic prejudices of which Tasso and Dante have availed themselves, and which the mystic German critics would restore. He relied on the justice of his cause, and did not scruple to

---

39 Pope's "The First Epistle of the Second Book of Horace" (1737), l. 102.
40 *Paradise Lost*, I, 612–13.   41 I, 106–109.

42 II, 147–50. The next quotation occurs at I, 157–58.
43 I, 226.

give the devil his due. Some persons may think that he has carried his liberality too far, and injured the cause he professed to espouse by making him the chief person in his poem. Considering the nature of his subject, he would be equally in danger of running into this fault, from his faith in religion, and his love of rebellion; and perhaps each of these motives had its full share in determining the choice of his subject.

Not only the figure of Satan, but his speeches in council, his soliloquies, his address to Eve, his share in the war in heaven, or in the fall of man, shew the same decided superiority of character. . . .

The whole of the speeches and debates in Pandemonium are well worthy of the place and the occasion —with Gods for speakers, and angels and archangels for hearers. There is a decided manly tone in the arguments and sentiments, an eloquent dogmatism, as if each person spoke from thorough conviction; an excellence which Milton probably borrowed from his spirit of partisanship, or else his spirit of partisanship from the natural firmness and vigour of his mind. In this respect Milton resembles Dante, (the only modern writer with whom he has any thing in common) and it is remarkable that Dante, as well as Milton, was a political partisan. That approximation to the severity of impassioned prose which has been made an objection to Milton's poetry, and which is chiefly to be met with in these bitter invectives, is one of its great excellences. The author might here turn his philippics against Salmasius [44] to good account. The rout in Heaven is like the fall of some mighty structure, nodding to its base, "with hideous ruin and combustion down." [45] But, perhaps, of all the passages in Paradise Lost, the description of the employments of the angels during the absence of Satan, some of whom "retreated in a silent valley, sing with notes angelical to many a harp their own heroic deeds and hapless fall by doom of battle," is the most perfect example of mingled pathos and sublimity.—What proves the truth of this noble picture in every part, and that the frequent complaint of want of interest in it is the fault of the reader, not of the poet, is that when any interest of a practical kind take a shape that can be at all turned into this, (and there is little doubt that Milton had some such in his eye in writing it,) each party converts it to its own purposes, feels the absolute identity of these abstracted and high speculations; and that, in fact, a noted political writer of the present day [46] has

exhausted nearly the whole account of Satan in the Paradise Lost, by applying it to a character whom he considered as after the devil, (though I do not know whether he would make even that exception) the greatest enemy of the human race. This may serve to shew that Milton's Satan is not a very insipid personage.

Of Adam and Eve it has been said, that the ordinary reader can feel little interest in them, because they have none of the passions, pursuits, or even relations of human life, except that of man and wife, the least interesting of all others, if not to the parties concerned, at least to the by-standers. The preference has on this account been given to Homer, who, it is said, has left very vivid and infinitely diversified pictures of all the passions and affections, public and private, incident to human nature—the relations of son, of brother, parent, friend, citizen, and many others. Longinus preferred the Iliad to the Odyssey, on account of the greater number of battles it contains; [47] but I can neither agree to his criticism, nor assent to the present objection. It is true, there is little action in this part of Milton's poem; but there is much repose, and more enjoyment. There are none of the every-day occurrences, contentions, disputes, wars, fightings, feuds, jealousies, trades, professions, liveries, and common handicrafts of life, "no kind of traffic; letters are not known; no use of service, of riches, poverty, contract, succession, bourne, bound of land, tilth, vineyard none; no occupation, no treason, felony, sword, pike, knife, gun, nor need of any engine." [48] So much the better; thank Heaven, all these were yet to come. But still the die was cast, and in them our doom was sealed. In them

"The generations were prepared; the pangs,
The internal pangs, were ready, the dread strife
Of poor humanity's afflicted will,
Struggling in vain with ruthless destiny."

In their first false step we trace all our future woe, with loss of Eden. But there was a short and precious interval between, like the first blush of morning before the day is overcast with tempest, the dawn of the world, the birth of nature from "the unapparent deep," [49] with its first dews and freshness on its cheek, breathing odours. Theirs was the first delicious taste of life, and on them depended all that was to come of it. In them hung trembling all our hopes and fears. They were as yet alone in the world, in the eye of nature, wondering at their new being, full of enjoyment and enraptured with one another, with the voice of their Maker walking

---

[44] Milton's *Defensio pro Populo Anglicano* (1651), was a reply to *Defensio Regia pro Carolo I* (1649) by Claudius Salmasius (1588–1653).

[45] I, 46. The next quotation occurs at II, 547–50.

[46] P. P. Howe suggests John Stoddart, Hazlitt's brother-in-law, who was editor of the London newspaper *The Times*.

[47] See *On the Sublime*, Section IX.

[48] See *Tempest*, II, i, 148–61. The next quotation is from Wordsworth's *Excursion*, VI, 554–57.

[49] *Paradise Lost*, VII, 103.

in the garden, and ministering angels attendant on their steps, winged messengers from heaven like rosy clouds descending in their sight. Nature played around them her virgin fancies wild; and spread for them a repast where no crude surfeit reigned. Was there nothing in this scene, which God and nature alone witnessed, to interest a modern critic? What need was there of action, where the heart was full of bliss and innocence without it! They had nothing to do but feel their own happiness, and "know to know no more."[50] "They toiled not, neither did they spin; yet Solomon in all his glory was not arrayed like one of these." All things seem to acquire fresh sweetness, and to be clothed with fresh beauty in their sight. They tasted as it were for themselves and us, of all that there ever was pure in human bliss. "In them the burthen of the mystery, the heavy and the weary weight of all this unintelligible world, is lightened."[51] They stood awhile perfect, but they afterwards fell, and were driven out of Paradise, tasting the first fruits of bitterness as they had done of bliss. But their pangs were such as a pure spirit might feel at the sight— their tears "such as angels weep."[52] The pathos is of that mild contemplative kind which arises from regret for the loss of unspeakable happiness, and resignation to inevitable fate. There is none of the fierceness of intemperate passion, none of the agony of mind and turbulence of action, which is the result of the habitual struggles of the will with circumstances, irritated by repeated disappointment, and constantly setting its desires most eagerly on that which there is an impossibility of attaining. This would have destroyed the beauty of the whole picture. They had received their unlooked-for happiness as a free gift from their Creator's hands, and they submitted to its loss, not without sorrow, but without impious and stubborn repining.

> "In either hand the hast'ning angel caught
> Our ling'ring parents, and to th' eastern gate
> Led them direct, and down the cliff as fast
> To the subjected plain; then disappear'd.
> They looking back, all th' eastern side beheld
> Of Paradise, so late their happy seat,
> Wav'd over by that flaming brand, the gate
> With dreadful faces throng'd, and fiery arms:
> Some natural tears they dropt, but wip'd them soon;
> The world was all before them, where to choose
> Their place of rest, and Providence their guide."

[1818]   [1819]

⋄⋄

[50] Cowper's "Truth" (1782), l. 327. The next quotation occurs in Matthew, vi, 28–29.

[51] See Wordsworth's "Tintern Abbey," ll. 38–41.

[52] *Paradise Lost*, I, 620. The next quotation is the concluding lines of the poem, XII, 637–47.

LECTURE IV.

ON DRYDEN AND POPE.

DRYDEN and Pope are the great masters of the artificial style of poetry in our language, as the poets of whom I have already treated, Chaucer, Spenser, Shakspeare, and Milton, were of the natural; and though this artificial style is generally and very justly acknowledged to be inferior to the other, yet those who stand at the head of that class, ought, perhaps, to rank higher than those who occupy an inferior place in a superior class. They have a clear and independent claim upon our gratitude, as having produced a kind and degree of excellence which existed equally nowhere else. What has been done well by some later writers of the highest style of poetry, is included in, and obscured by a greater degree of power and genius in those before them: what has been done best by poets of an entirely distinct turn of mind, stands by itself, and tells for its whole amount. Young, for instance, Gray, or Akenside, only follow in the train of Milton and Shakspeare: Pope and Dryden walk by their side, though of an unequal stature, and are entitled to a first place in the lists of fame. This seems to be not only the reason of the thing, but the common sense of mankind, who, without any regular process of reflection, judge of the merit of a work, not more by its inherent and absolute worth, than by its originality and capacity of gratifying a different faculty of the mind, or a different class of readers; for it should be recollected, that there may be readers (as well as poets) not of the highest class, though very good sort of people, and not altogether to be despised.

The question, whether Pope was a poet, has hardly yet been settled, and is hardly worth settling; for if he was not a great poet, he must have been a great prose-writer, that is, he was a great writer of some sort. He was a man of exquisite faculties, and of the most refined taste; and as he chose verse (the most obvious distinction of poetry) as the vehicle to express his ideas, he has generally passed for a poet, and a good one. If, indeed, by a great poet, we mean one who gives the utmost grandeur to our conceptions of nature, or the utmost force to the passions of the heart, Pope was not in this sense a great poet; for the bent, the characteristic power of his mind, lay the clean contrary way; namely, in representing things as they appear to the indifferent observer, stripped of prejudice and passion, as in his Critical Essays; or in representing them in the most contemptible and insignificant point of view, as in his

Satires; or in clothing the little with mock-dignity, as in his poems of Fancy; or in adorning the trivial incidents and familiar relations of life with the utmost elegance of expression, and all the flattering illusions of friendship or self-love, as in his Epistles. He was not then distinguished as a poet of lofty enthusiasm, of strong imagination, with a passionate sense of the beauties of nature, or a deep insight into the workings of the heart; but he was a wit, and a critic, a man of sense, of observation, and the world, with a keen relish for the elegances of art, or of nature when embellished by art, a quick tact for propriety of thought and manners as established by the forms and customs of society, a refined sympathy with the sentiments and habitudes of human life, as he felt them within the little circle of his family and friends. He was, in a word, the poet, not of nature, but of art; and the distinction between the two, as well as I can make it out, is this—The poet of nature is one who, from the elements of beauty, of power, and of passion in his own breast, sympathises with whatever is beautiful, and grand, and impassioned in nature, in its simple majesty, in its immediate appeal to the senses, to the thoughts and hearts of all men; so that the poet of nature, by the truth, and depth, and harmony of his mind, may be said to hold communion with the very soul of nature; to be identified with and to foreknow and to record the feelings of all men at all times and places, as they are liable to the same impressions; and to exert the same power over the minds of his readers, that nature does. He sees things in their eternal beauty, for he sees them as they are; he feels them in their universal interest, for he feels them as they affect the first principles of his and our common nature. Such was Homer, such was Shakspeare, whose works will last as long as nature, because they are a copy of the indestructible forms and everlasting impulses of nature, welling out from the bosom as from a perennial spring, or stamped upon the senses by the hand of their maker. The power of the imagination in them, is the representative power of all nature. It has its centre in the human soul, and makes the circuit of the universe.

Pope was not assuredly a poet of this class, or in the first rank of it. He saw nature only dressed by art; he judged of beauty by fashion; he sought for truth in the opinions of the world; he judged of the feelings of others by his own. The capacious soul of Shakspeare had an intuitive and mighty sympathy with whatever could enter into the heart of man in all possible circumstances: Pope had an exact knowledge of all that he himself loved or hated, wished or wanted. Milton has winged his daring flight from heaven to earth, through Chaos and old Night. Pope's Muse never wandered with safety, but from his library to his grotto, or from his grotto into his library back again. His mind dwelt with greater pleasure on his own garden, than on the garden of Eden; he could describe the faultless whole-length mirror that reflected his own person, better than the smooth surface of the lake that reflects the face of heaven—a piece of cut glass or a pair of paste buckles with more brilliance and effect, than a thousand dew-drops glittering in the sun. He would be more delighted with a patent lamp, than with "the pale reflex of Cynthia's brow,"[1] that fills the skies with its soft silent lustre, that trembles through the cottage window, and cheers the watchful mariner on the lonely wave. In short, he was the poet of personality and of polished life. That which was nearest to him, was the greatest; the fashion of the day bore sway in his mind over the immutable laws of nature. He preferred the artificial to the natural in external objects, because he had a stronger fellow-feeling with the self-love of the maker or proprietor of a gewgaw, than admiration of that which was interesting to all mankind. He preferred the artificial to the natural in passion, because the involuntary and uncalculating impulses of the one hurried him away with a force and vehemence with which he could not grapple; while he could trifle with the conventional and superficial modifications of mere sentiment at will, laugh at or admire, put them on or off like a masquerade-dress, make much or little of them, indulge them for a longer or a shorter time, as he pleased; and because while they amused his fancy and exercised his ingenuity, they never once disturbed his vanity, his levity, or indifference. His mind was the antithesis of strength and grandeur; its power was the power of indifference. He had none of the enthusiasm of poetry; he was in poetry what the sceptic is in religion.

It cannot be denied, that his chief excellence lay more in diminishing, than in aggrandizing objects; in checking, not in encouraging our enthusiasm; in sneering at the extravagances of fancy or passion, instead of giving a loose to them; in describing a row of pins and needles, rather than the embattled spears of Greeks and Trojans; in penning a lampoon or a compliment, and in praising Martha Blount.[2]

Shakspeare says,

---

[1] *Romeo and Juliet*, III, v, 20.
[2] Martha Blount (1690–1762) was a lifelong friend of Pope, to whom he addressed his moral essay "Of the Characters of Women" and several "Epistles."

"——In Fortune's ray and brightness
The herd hath more annoyance by the brize
Than by the tyger: but when the splitting wind
Makes flexible the knees of knotted oaks,
And flies fled under shade, why then
The thing of courage,
As roused with rage, with rage doth sympathise;
And with an accent tuned in the self-same key,
Replies to chiding Fortune." [3]

There is none of this rough work in Pope. His Muse was on a peace-establishment,[4] and grew somewhat effeminate by long ease and indulgence. He lived in the smiles of fortune, and basked in the favour of the great. In his smooth and polished verse we meet with no prodigies of nature, but with miracles of wit; the thunders of his pen are whispered flatteries; its forked lightnings pointed sarcasms; for "the gnarled oak," he gives us "the soft myrtle:" [5] for rocks, and seas, and mountains, artificial grass-plats, gravel-walks, and tinkling rills; for earthquakes and tempests, the breaking of a flower-pot, or the fall of a china jar; for the tug and war of the elements, or the deadly strife of the passions, we have

"Calm contemplation and poetic ease." [6]

Yet within this retired and narrow circle how much, and that how exquisite, was contained! What discrimination, what wit, what delicacy, what fancy, what lurking spleen, what elegance of thought, what pampered refinement of sentiment! It is like looking at the world through a microscope, where every thing assumes a new character and a new consequence, where things are seen in their minutest circumstances and slightest shades of difference; where the little becomes gigantic, the deformed beautiful, and the beautiful deformed. The wrong end of the magnifier is, to be sure, held to every thing, but still the exhibition is highly curious, and we know not whether to be most pleased or surprised. Such, at least, is the best account I am able to give of this extraordinary man, without doing injustice to him or others.

*   *   *   *   *

It should appear, in tracing the history of our literature, that poetry had, at the period of which we are speaking, in general declined, by successive gradations, from the poetry of imagination, in the time of Elizabeth, to the poetry of fancy (to adopt a modern distinction) in the time of Charles I.; and again from the poetry of fancy to that of wit, as in the reigns of Charles II. and Queen Anne. It degenerated into the poetry of mere common places, both in style and thought, in the succeeding reigns: as in the latter part of the last century, it was transformed, by means of the French Revolution, into the poetry of paradox.[7]

*   *   *   *   *

[1818]   [1819]

PREFACE TO POLITICAL ESSAYS

Political Essays was a selection of Hazlitt's political journalism originally published between 1813 and 1818 in the Examiner, Morning Chronicle, *and other newspapers and periodicals, but including also selections from his early works* Free Thoughts on Public Affairs *(1806),* The Eloquence of the British Senate *(1807), and* A Reply to Malthus *(1807). A savage indictment of the policies at home and abroad of the British government in the Napoleonic and post-Napoleonic years, the volume was appropriately dedicated to John Hunt, who along with his brother Leigh had been imprisoned from 1813 to 1815 for publishing a "libel" on the Prince Regent; equally appropriately, the volume was brought out by the radical bookseller William Hone, who also had been tried (but acquitted) for seditious publications in 1817. The volume appeared in August 1819, the same month as the "Peterloo Massacre," the event regarded as both the symbol and the culmination of political conditions in England following Waterloo; on August 16, cavalry charged into a large crowd gathered in political protest near Manchester, resulting in the death of eleven persons and the wounding of hundreds.*

F R O M

PREFACE TO
POLITICAL ESSAYS

I AM NO politician, and still less can I be said to be a party-man: but I have a hatred of tyranny, and a con-

---

3 *Troilus and Cressida*, I, iii, 47–54.
4 The reduced condition of the standing army in time of peace.
5 *Measure for Measure*, II, ii, 116–17.
6 Thomson's *Autumn*, l. 1277.

---

7 "The poetry of paradox" was the phrase Hazlitt applied to Wordsworth and other contemporary poets, paradox here meaning "extravagant speculative opinions, abstracted from all existing customs, prejudices and institutions." In the concluding lecture of the series "On the Living Poets," Hazlitt had written:

> The paradox they set out with was, that all things are by nature equally fit subjects for poetry; or that if there is any preference to be given, those that are the meanest and most unpromising are the best, as they leave the greatest scope for the unbounded stores of thought and fancy in the writer's own mind.

Hazlitt traced this development in poetry to the writers' revolutionary reaction against the hackneyed expression and subject matter of the *common-place* poetry of the successors to Pope in the late eighteenth century. To the paradoxical poet's egotistical insistence on "having it all proceed from his own power and originality of mind," Hazlitt throughout his criticism opposed Shakespeare's *imaginative* identification with and representation of objects and characters.

tempt for its tools; and this feeling I have expressed as often and as strongly as I could. I cannot sit quietly down under the claims of barefaced power, and I have tried to expose the little arts of sophistry by which they are defended. I have no mind to have my person made a property of, nor my understanding made a dupe of. I deny that liberty and slavery are convertible terms, that right and wrong, truth and falsehood, plenty and famine, the comforts or wretchedness of a people, are matters of perfect indifference. That is all I know of the matter; but on these points I am likely to remain incorrigible, in spite of any arguments that I have seen used to the contrary. It needs no sagacity to discover that two and two make four; but to persist in maintaining this obvious position, if all the fashion, authority, hypocrisy, and venality of mankind were arrayed against it, would require a considerable effort of personal courage, and would soon leave a man in a very formidable minority. Again, I am no believer in the doctrine of *divine right*, either as it regards the Stuarts or the Bourbons; nor can I bring myself to approve of the enormous waste of blood and treasure wilfully incurred by a family that supplanted the one in this country to restore the others in France. It is to my mind a piece of sheer impudence. The question between natural liberty and hereditary slavery, whether men are born free or slaves, whether kings are the servants of the people, or the people the property of kings (whatever we may think of it in the abstract, or debate about it in the schools)—in this country, in Old England, and under the succession of the House of Hanover, is not a question of theory, but has been long since decided by certain facts and feelings, to call which in question would be equally inconsistent with proper respect to the people, or common decency towards the throne. An English subject cannot call this principle in question without renouncing his country; an English prince cannot call it in question without disclaiming his title to the crown, which was placed by our ancestors on the head of his ancestors, on no other ground and for no other possible purpose than to vindicate this sacred principle in their own persons, and to hold it out as an example to posterity and to the world. An Elector of Hanover, called over here to be made king of England, in contempt and to the exclusion of the claims of the old, hereditary possessors and pretenders to the throne, on any other plea except that of his being the chosen representative and appointed guardian of the rights and liberties of the people (the consequent pledge and guarantee of the rights and liberties of other nations) would indeed be a solecism more absurd and contemptible than any to be found in history. What! Send for a petty Elector of a petty foreign state to reign over us from respect to *his*

right to the throne of these realms, in defiance of the legitimate heir to the crown, and "in contempt of the choice of the people!" [1] Oh monstrous fiction! Miss Flora Mac Ivor would not have heard of such a thing: the author of Waverley has well answered Mr. Burke's "Appeal from the New to the Old Whigs."* Let not our respect for our ancestors, who fought and bled for their own freedom, and to aid (not to stifle) the cause of freedom in other nations, suffer us to believe this poor ideot calumny of them. Let not our shame at having been inveigled into crusades and Holy Alliances against the freedom of mankind, suffer us to be made the dupes of it ourselves, in thought, in word, or deed. The question of genuine liberty or of naked slavery, if put in words, should be answered by Eng-

---

* Mr. Burke pretends in this Jesuitical Appeal, that a nation has a right to insist upon and revert to old establishments and prescriptive privileges, but not to lay claim to new ones; in a word, to change its governors, if refractory, but not its form of government, however bad. Thus he says we had a right to cashier James II., because he wished to alter the laws and religion as they were then established. By what right did we emancipate ourselves from popery and arbitrary power a century before? He defends his consistency in advocating the American Revolution, though the rebels, in getting rid of the reigning branch of the Royal Family, did not send for the next of kin to rule over them "in contempt of their choice," but prevented all such equivocations by passing at once from a viceroyalty to a republic. He also extols the Polish Revolution as a monument of wisdom and virtue (I suppose because it had not succeeded), though this also was a total and absolute change in the frame and principles of the government, to which the people were in this case bound by no feudal tenure or divine right. But he insists that the French Revolution was stark-naught, because the people here did the same thing, passed from slavery to liberty, from an arbitrary to a constitutional government, to which they had, it seems, no prescriptive right, and therefore, according to the appellant, no right at all. Oh nice professor of humanity! We had a right to turn off James II. because he broke a compact with the people. The French had no right to turn off Louis XVI. because he broke no compact with them, for he had none to break; in other words, because he was an arbitrary despot, tied to no laws, and they a herd of slaves, and therefore they were bound, by every law divine and human, always to remain so, in perpetuity and by the grace of God! Oh unanswerable logician! [2]

◇◇◇◇◇◇◇◇◇◇◇◇◇◇◇◇◇◇◇◇◇◇◇◇◇◇

[1] See Burke's *Reflections on the Revolution in France* (1790): ". . . the king of Great Britain is at this day king by a fixed rule of succession, according to the laws of his country; . . . he holds his crown in contempt of the choice of the Revolution Society . . ." Burke's point is that King William may have been brought to the throne in 1688 by Parliamentary action; but his *right* to the crown resided in his title to succession.
[2] In "An Appeal from the New to the Old Whigs" (1791), Burke argued that by opposing the principles of the French Revolution in his *Reflections*, which had won for him the charge of political apostasy by the Whig party, he was in fact the spokesman for the principles of the true Whig philosophy, under which the revolution of 1688 had been carried out and justified. Miss Flora Mac Ivor was the ardent supporter of the Stuart cause in Scott's *Waverley* (1814), a story of the uprising of 1745 in favor of the Stuart Pretender "Bonnie Prince Charlie."

lishmen with scorn: if put in any other shape than words, it must be answered in a different way, unless they would lose the name of Englishmen! An Englishman has no distinguishing virtue but honesty: he has and can have no privilege or advantage over other nations but liberty. If he is not free, he is the worst of slaves, for he is nothing else. If he feels that he has wrongs and dare not say so, he is the meanest of hypocrites; for it is certain that he cannot be contented under them.—This was once a free, a proud, and a happy country, when under a constitutional monarchy and a Whig king, it had just broken the chains of tyranny that were prepared for it, and successfully set at defiance the menaces of an hereditary pretender; when the monarch still felt what he owed to himself and the people, and in the opposite claims which were set up to it, saw the real tenure on which he held his crown; when civil and religious liberty were the watchwords by which good men and true subjects were known to one another, not by the cant of legitimacy; when the reigning sovereign stood between you and the polluted touch of a bigot and a despot who stood ready to seize upon you and yours as his lawful prey; when liberty and loyalty went hand in hand, and the Tory principles of passive obedience and non-resistance were more unfashionable at court than in the country; when to uphold the authority of the throne, it was not thought necessary to undermine the privileges or break the spirit of the nation; when an Englishman felt that his name was another name for independence, "the envy of less happier lands,"[3] when it was his pride to be born, and his wish that other nations might become free; before a sophist and an apostate had dared to tell him that he had no share, no merit, no free agency, in the glorious Revolution of 1688, and that he was bound to lend a helping hand to crush all others, that implied a right in the people to chuse their own form of government; before he was become sworn brother to the Pope, familiar to the Holy Inquisition, an encourager of the massacres of his Protestant brethren, a patron of the Bourbons, and jailor to the liberties of mankind! Ah, John Bull! John Bull! thou art not what thou wert in the days of thy friend, Arbuthnot![4] Thou wert an honest fellow then: now thou art turned bully and coward.

This is the only politics I know; the only patriotism I feel. The question with me is, whether I and all mankind are born slaves or free. That is the one thing necessary to know and to make good: the rest is *flocci,*

nauci, nihili, pili.[5] Secure this point, and all is safe: lose this, and all is lost. There are people who cannot understand a principle; nor perceive how a cause can be connected with an individual, even in spite of himself, nor how the salvation of mankind can be bound up with the success of one man. It is in vain that I address to them what follows.—"One fate attends the altar and the throne."[6] So sings Mr. Southey. I say, that one fate attends the people and the assertor of the people's rights against those who say they have no rights, that they are their property, their goods, their chattels, the live-stock on the estate of Legitimacy. This is what kings at present tell us with their swords, and poets with their pens. He who tells me this deprives me not only of the right, but of the very heart and will to be free, takes the breath out of the body of liberty, and leaves it a dead and helpless corse, destroys "at one fell swoop"[7] the dearest hopes, and blasts the fairest prospects of mankind through all ages and nations, sanctifies slavery, binds it as a spell on the understanding, and makes freedom a mockery, and the name a bye-word. The poor wretch immured in the dungeons of the Inquisition may breathe a sigh to liberty, may repeat its name, may think of it as a blessing, if not to himself, to others; but the wretch imprisoned in the dungeon of Legitimacy, the very tomb of freedom, that "painted sepulchre, white without, but full of ravening and all uncleanness within,"[8] must not even think of it, must not so much as dream of it, but as a thing forbid: it is a profanation to his lips, an impiety to his thoughts; his very imagination is enthralled, and he can only look forward to the never-ending flight of future years, and see the same gloomy prospect of abject wretchedness and hopeless desolation spread out for himself and his species. They who bow to thrones and hate mankind may here feast their eyes with blight, mildew, the blue pestilence and glittering poison of slavery, "bogs, dens, and shades of death—a universe of death."[9] This is that true moral atheism, the equal blasphemy against God and man, the sin against the Holy Ghost, that lowest deep of debasement and despair to which there is no lower deep. He who saves me from this conclusion, who makes a mock of this doctrine, and sets at nought its power, is to me not less than the God of my idolatry, for he has left one drop of comfort in my soul. The plague-spot has not tainted me quite; I am not leprous all over, the lie of Legitimacy does not fix its mortal

---

3 *Richard the Second*, II, i, 49.

4 John Arbuthnot (1667–1735) had introduced the personification of the British character in the political satire *The History of John Bull* (1712).

5 That is, the rest means nothing. The Latin words are synonyms for worthlessness and trifles.

6 Southey's *Carmen Nuptiale. The Lay of the Laureate* (1816), stanza 51.

7 *Macbeth*, IV, iii, 219.   8 See Matthew, xxiii, 27.

9 *Paradise Lost*, II, 621–22.

sting in my inmost soul, nor, like an ugly spider, entangle me in its slimy folds; but is kept off from me, and broods on its own poison. He who did this for me, and for the rest of the world, and who alone could do it, was Buonaparte. He withstood the inroads of this new Jaggernaut, this foul Blatant Beast,[10] as it strode forward to its prey over the bodies and minds of a whole people, and put a ring in its nostrils, breathing flame and blood, and led it in triumph, and played with its crowns and sceptres, and wore them in its stead, and tamed its crested pride, and made it a laughing-stock and a mockery to the nations. He, one man, did this, and as long as he did this, (how, or for what end, is nothing to the magnitude of this mighty question) he saved the human race from the last ignominy, and that foul stain that had so long been intended, and was at last, in an evil hour and by evil hands, inflicted on it. He put his foot upon the neck of kings, who would have put their yoke upon the necks of the people: he scattered before him with fiery execution, millions of hired slaves, who came at the bidding of their masters to deny the right of others to be free. The monument of greatness and of glory he erected, was raised on ground forfeited again and again to humanity—it reared its majestic front on the ruins of the shattered hopes and broken faith of the common enemies of mankind. If he could not secure the freedom, peace, and happiness of his country, he made her a terror to those who by sowing civil dissension and exciting foreign wars, would not let her enjoy those blessings. They who had trampled upon Liberty could not at least triumph in her shame and her despair, but themselves became objects of pity and derision. Their determination to persist in extremity of wrong only brought on themselves repeated defeat, disaster, and dismay: the accumulated aggressions their infuriated pride and disappointed malice meditated against others, returned in just and aggravated punishment upon themselves: they heaped coals of fire upon their own heads; they drank deep and long, in gall and bitterness, of the poisoned chalice they had prepared for others: the destruction with which they had threatened a people daring to call itself free, hung suspended over their heads, like a precipice, ready to fall upon and crush them. "Awhile they stood abashed,"[11] abstracted from their evil purposes, and felt how awful freedom is, its power how dreadful. Shrunk from the boasted pomp of royal state into

their littleness as men, defeated of their revenge, baulked of their prey, their schemes stripped of their bloated pride, and with nothing left but the deformity of their malice, not daring to utter a syllable or move a finger, the lords of the earth, who had looked upon men as of an inferior species, born for their use, and devoted to be their slaves, turned an imploring eye to the people, and with coward hearts and hollow tongues invoked the name of Liberty, thus to get the people once more within their unhallowed gripe, and to stifle the name of Liberty for ever. I never joined the vile and treacherous cry of spurious humanity in favour of those who have from the beginning of time, and will to the end of it, make a butt of humanity, and its distresses their sport. I knew that shameful was this new alliance between kings and people; fatal this pretended league: that "never can true reconcilement grow where wounds of deadly hate have pierced so deep." I was right in this respect. I knew my friends from my foes. So did Lord Castlereagh: so did not Benjamin Constant.[12] Did any of the Princes of Europe ever regard Buonaparte as any thing more than the child and champion of Jacobinism? Why then should I: for on that point I bow to their judgments as infallible. Passion speaks truer than reason. If Buonaparte was a conqueror, he conquered the grand conspiracy of kings against the abstract right of the human race to be free; and I, as a man, could not be indifferent which side to take. If he was ambitious, his greatness was not founded on the unconditional, avowed surrender of the rights of human nature. But with him, the state of man rose exalted too. If he was arbitrary and a tyrant, first, France as a country was in a state of military blockade, on garrison-duty, and not to be defended by mere paper bullets of the brain; secondly, but chief, he was not, nor he could not become, a tyrant by right divine. Tyranny in him was not sacred: it was not eternal: it was not instinctively bound in league of amity with other tyrannies; it was not sanctioned by all the laws of religion and morality. There was an end of it with the individual: there was an end of it with the temporary causes, which gave it birth, and of which it was only the too necessary reaction. But there are persons of that low and inordinate appetite for servility, that they cannot be satisfied with any thing short of that sort of tyranny that has lasted for ever,

---

[10] Jaggernaut was a Hindu god; his worshippers were hurled and crushed beneath the wheels of his triumphant cart. Blatant Beast is a many-tongued monster in *The Faerie Queene*, Book VI, who afflicts all men through venomous untruthfulness.

[11] Cf. *Paradise Lost*, IV, 846. The next quotation is from the same book of *Paradise Lost*, ll. 98–99.

---

[12] Benjamin Constant (1767–1830) was a French writer and politician, noted for his political "inconsistency." After being strongly anti-Napoleonic, Constant supported Napoleon on his return to power in 1814; with the restoration of Louis XVII following Waterloo, Constant left France in exile for several years. In contrast, Robert Stewart, Viscount Castlereagh (1769–1822), British Foreign Secretary from 1812, was "consistent" in his repressive and anti-democratic policies.

and is likely to last for ever; that is strengthened and made desperate by the superstitions and prejudices of ages; that is enshrined in traditions, in laws, in usages, in the outward symbols of power, in the very idioms of language; that has struck its roots into the human heart, and clung round the human understanding like a nightshade; that overawes the imagination, and disarms the will to resist it, by the very enormity of the evil; that is cemented with gold and blood; guarded by reverence, guarded by power; linked in endless succession to the principle by which life is transmitted to the generations of tyrants and slaves, and destroying liberty with the first breath of life; that is absolute, unceasing, unerring, fatal, unutterable, abominable, monstrous. These true devotees of superstition and despotism cried out Liberty and Humanity in their desperate phrenzy at Buonaparte's sudden elevation and incredible successes against their favourite idol, "that Harlot old, the same that is, that was, and is to be," [13] but we have heard no more of their triumph of Liberty and their *douce humanité*, since they clapped down the hatches upon us again, like wretches in a slave-ship who have had their chains struck off and pardon promised them to fight the common enemy; and the poor Reformers who were taken in to join the cry, because they are as fastidious in their love of liberty as their opponents are inveterate in their devotion to despotism, continue in vain to reproach them with their temporary professions, woeful grimaces, and vows made in pain, which ease has recanted; but to these reproaches the legitimate professors of Liberty and Humanity do not even deign to return the answer of a smile at their credulity and folly. Those who did not see this result at the time were, I think, weak; those who do not acknowledge it now are, I am sure, hypocrites.—To this pass have we been brought by the joint endeavours of Tories, Whigs, and Reformers; and as they have all had a hand in it, I shall here endeavour to ascribe to each their share of merit in this goodly piece of work. It is, perhaps, a delicate point, but it is of no inconsiderable importance, that the friends of Freedom should know the strength of their enemies, and their own weakness as well; for

> ——"At this day,
> When a Tartarean darkness overspreads
> The groaning nations; when the impious rule,
> By will or by established ordinance,
> Their own dire agents, and constrain the good
> To acts which they abhor; though I bewail
> This triumph, yet the pity of my heart
> Prevents me not from owning that the law
> By which mankind now suffers, is most just.

[13] Southey's *Carmen Nuptiale*, stanza 52.

> For by superior energies; more strict
> Affiance to each other; faith more firm
> In their unhallowed principles; the bad
> Have fairly earned a victory o'er the weak,
> The vacillating, inconsistent good." [14]

. . . Tory sticks to Tory: Whig sticks to Whig: the Reformer sticks neither to himself nor to any body else. It is no wonder he comes to the ground with all his schemes and castle-building. A house divided against itself cannot stand. It is a pity, but it cannot be helped. A Reformer is necessarily and naturally a Marplot, [15] for the foregoing and the following reasons. First, he does not very well know what he would be at. Secondly, if he did, he does not care very much about it. Thirdly, he is governed habitually by a spirit of contradiction, and is always wise beyond what is practicable. He is a bad tool to work with; a part of a machine that never fits its place; he cannot be trained to discipline, for he follows his own idle humours, or drilled into an obedience to orders, for the first principle of his mind is the supremacy of conscience, and the independent right of private judgment. A man to be a Reformer must be more influenced by imagination and reason than by received opinions or sensible impressions. With him ideas bear sway over things; the possible is of more value than the real; that which is not, is better than that which is. He is by the supposition a speculative (and somewhat fantastical) character; but there is no end of possible speculations, of imaginary questions, and nice distinctions; or if there were, he would not willingly come to it; he would still prefer living in the world of his own ideas, be for raising some new objection, and starting some new chimera, and never be satisfied with any plan that he found he could realise. Bring him to a fixed point, and his occupation would be gone. A Reformer never is—but always to be blest, [16] in the accomplishment of his airy hopes and shifting schemes of progressive perfectibility. Let him have the plaything of his fancy, and he will spoil it, like the child that makes a hole in its drum: set some brilliant illusion before his streaming eyes, and he will lay violent hands upon it, like little wanton boys that play with air-bubbles. Give him one thing, and he asks for another; like the dog in the fable, he loses the substance for the shadow: offer him a great good, and he will not stretch out his hand to take it, unless it were the greatest possible good. And then who is to determine what is the greatest possible good? Among a thousand pragmatical speculators, there will be a thousand opinions on

[14] Wordsworth's *Excursion*, IV, 296–309.
[15] A blundering busybody.
[16] A variation of the statement in Pope's *Essay on Man*, I, 96.

this subject; and the more they differ, the less will they be inclined to give way or compromise the matter. With each of these, his self-opinion is the first thing to be attended to; his understanding must be satisfied in the first place, or he will not budge an inch; he cannot for the world give up a principle to a party. He would rather have slavery than liberty, unless it is a liberty precisely after his own fashion; he would sooner have the Bourbons than Buonaparte; for he truly is for a Republic, and if he cannot have that, is indifferent about the rest. . . .

. . . A Tory is one who is governed by sense and habit alone. He considers not what is possible, but what is real; he gives might the preference over right. He cries Long Life to the conqueror, and is ever strong upon the stronger side—the side of corruption and prerogative. He says what others say; he does as he is prompted by his own advantage. He knows on which side his bread is buttered, and that St. Peter is well at Rome. He is for going with Sancho to Camacho's wedding, and not for wandering with Don Quixote in the desert, after the mad lover.[17] Strait is the gate and narrow is the way that leadeth to Reform, but broad is the way that leadeth to Corruption, and multitudes there are that walk therein. The Tory is sure to be in the thickest of them. His principle is to follow the leader; and this is the infallible rule to have numbers and success on your side, to be on the side of success and numbers. Power is the rock of his salvation; priestcraft is the second article of his implicit creed. He does not trouble himself to inquire which is the best form of government—but he knows that the reigning monarch is "the best of kings." He does not, like a fool, contest for modes of faith; but like a wise man, swears by that which is by law established. He has no principles himself, nor does he profess to have any, but will cut your throat for differing with any of his bigotted dogmas, or for objecting to any act of power that he supposes necessary to his interest. He will take his Bible-oath that black is white, and that whatever is, is right, if it is for his convenience. He is for having a slice in the loan, a share in a borough, a situation in the church or state, or for standing well with those who have. He is not for empty speculations, but for full pockets. He is for having plenty of beef and pudding, a good coat to his back, a good house over his head, and for cutting a respectable figure in the world. He is *Epicuri de grege porcus* [18]—not a man but a beast. He is styed in his prejudices—he wallows

in the mire of his senses—he cannot get beyond the trough of his sordid appetites, whether it is of gold or wood. Truth and falsehood are, to him, something to buy and sell; principle and conscience, something to eat and drink. He tramples on the plea of Humanity, and lives, like a caterpillar, on the decay of public good. Beast as he is, he knows that the King is the fountain of honour, that there are good things to be had in the Church, treats the cloth with respect, bows to a magistrate, lies to the tax-gatherer, nicknames the Reformers, and "blesses the Regent and the Duke of York." He treads the primrose path of preferment; "when a great wheel goes up a hill, holds fast by it, and when it rolls down, lets it go." [19] He is not an enthusiast, a Utopian philosopher or a Theophilanthropist, [20] but a man of business and the world, who minds the main chance, does as other people do, and takes his wife's advice to get on in the world, and set up a coach for her to ride in, as fast as possible. This fellow is in the right, and "wiser in his generation than the children of the light." [21] The "servile slaves" of wealth and power have a considerable advantage over the independent and the free. How much easier is it to smell out a job than to hit upon a scheme for the good of mankind! How much safer is it to be the tool of the oppressor than the advocate of the oppressed! How much more fashionable to fall in with the opinion of the world, to bow the knee to Baal, [22] than to seek for obscure and obnoxious truth! How strong are the ties that bind men together for their own advantage, compared with those that bind them to the good of their country or of their kind! For as the Reformer has no guide to his conclusions but speculative reason, which is a source not of unanimity or certainty, but of endless doubt and disagreement, so he has no ground of attachment to them but a speculative interest, which is too often liable to be warped by sinister motives, and is a flimsy barrier against the whole weight of worldly and practical interests opposed to it. He either tires and grows lukewarm after the first gloss of novelty is over, and is thrown into the hands of the adverse party, or to keep alive an interest in it, he makes it the stalking-horse of his ambition, of his personal enmity, of his conceit or love of gossipping; as we have seen. An opinion backed by power and prejudice, rivetted and mortised to the throne, is of more force and validity than all the abstract reason in the world, without power and prejudice. A cause centred in an individual, which is

---

[17] See *Don Quixote*, Part 2, III, xix–xxi.
[18] *Epicuri . . . porcus* (Horace's *Epistles*, I, iv, 16): "a hog from the herd of Epicurus;" that is, one totally given over to his own comforts and pleasures.

[19] See *King Lear*, II, iv, 72–73.
[20] "Friend of God and man," member of a deistic sect founded in Paris in 1796.
[21] Luke, xvi, 8.			[22] Heathen or false god.

strengthened by all the ties of passion and self-interest, as in the case of a king against a whole people, is more likely to prevail than that of a scattered multitude, who have only a common and divided interest to hold them together, and "screw their courage to the sticking-place," [23] against an influence, that is never distracted or dissipated; that neither slumbers nor sleeps; that is never lulled into security, nor tamed by adversity; that is intoxicated with the insolence of success, and infuriated with the rage of disappointment; that eyes its one sole object of personal aggrandisement, moves unremittingly to it, and carries after it millions of its slaves and train-bearers. Can you persuade a king to hear reason, to submit his pretensions to the tribunal of the people, to give up the most absurd and mischievous of his prerogatives? No: he is always true to himself, he grasps at power and hugs it close, as it is exorbitant or invidious, or likely to be torn from him; and his followers stick to him, and never boggle at any lengths they are forced to go, because they know what they have to trust to in the good faith of kings to themselves and one another. Power then is fixed and immoveable, for this reason, because it is lodged in an individual who is driven to madness by the undisputed possession, or apprehended loss of it; his self-will is the key-stone that supports the tottering arch of corruption, steadfast as it leans on him:—liberty is vacillating, transient, and hunted through the world, because it is entrusted to the breasts of many, who care little about it, and quarrel in the execution of their trust. Too many cooks spoil the broth. The principle of tyranny is in fact identified with a man's pride and the servility of others in the highest degree; the principle of liberty abstracts him from himself, and has to contend in its feeble course with all his own passions, prejudices, interests, and those of the world and of his own party; the cavils of Reformers, the threats of Tories, and the sneers of Whigs.* . . .

* There is none of this perplexity and jarring of different objects in the tools of power. Their jealousies, heart-burnings, love of precedence, or scruples of conscience, are made subservient to the great cause in which they are embarked; they leave the amicable division of the spoil to the powers that be; all angry disputes are hushed in the presence of the throne, and the corrosive, fretful particles of human nature fly off, and are softened by the influence of a court atmosphere. Courtiers hang together like a swarm of bees about a honeycomb. Not so the Reformers; for they have no honey-comb to attract them. It has been said that Reformers are often indifferent characters. The reason is, that the ties which bind most men to their duties—habit, example, regard to appearances—are relaxed in them; and other and better principles are, as yet, weak and unconfirmed.

[23] *Macbeth*, I, vii, 60.

. . . A Whig is properly what is called a Trimmer—that is, a coward to both sides of a question, who dare not be a knave nor an honest man, but is a sort of whiffling, shuffling, cunning, silly, contemptible, unmeaning negation of the two. He is a poor purblind creature, who halts between two opinions, and complains that he cannot get any two people to think alike. He is a cloak for corruption, and a mar-plot to freedom. He will neither do any thing himself, nor let any one else do it. He is on bad terms with the Government, and not on good ones with the people. He is an impertinence and a contradiction in the state. If he has a casting weight, for fear of overdoing the mark, he throws it into the wrong scale. He is a person of equally feeble understanding and passions. He has some notion of what is right, just enough to hinder him from pursuing his own interest: he has selfish and worldly prudence enough, not to let him embark in any bold or decided measure for the advancement of truth and justice. He is afraid of his own conscience, which will not let him lend his unqualified support to arbitrary measures; he stands in awe of the opinion of the world, which will not let him express his opposition to those measures with warmth and effect. His politics are a strange mixture of cross-purposes. He is wedded to forms and appearances, impeded by every petty obstacle and pretext of difficulty, more tenacious of the means than the end—anxious to secure all suffrages, by which he secures none—hampered not only by the ties of friendship to his actual associates, but to all those that he thinks may become so; and unwilling to offer arguments to convince the reason of his opponents lest he should offend their prejudices, by shewing them how much they are in the wrong; "letting I dare not wait upon I would, like the poor cat in the adage;" [24] stickling for the letter of the Constitution, with the affectation of a prude, and abandoning its principles with the effrontery of a prostitute to any shabby Coalition he can patch up with its deadly enemies. This is very pitiful work; and, I believe, the public with me are tolerably sick of the character. At the same time, he hurls up his cap with a foolish face of wonder and incredulity at the restoration of the Bourbons, and affects to chuckle with secret satisfaction over the last act of the Revolution, which reduced him to perfect insignificance. We need not wonder at the results, when it comes to the push between parties so differently constituted and unequally matched. We have seen what those results are. . . .

[1819]

[24] *Macbeth*, I, vii, 44–45.

TABLE-TALK

Hazlitt's longer familiar essays "Table-Talks" began in the
London Magazine *in June 1820, with an essay "On the Quali-*
fications Necessary to Success in Life." Twelve more, on subjects
as diverse as "On the Pleasure of Painting" and "On the Present
State of Parliamentary Eloquence," appeared in subsequent issues
of the London Magazine *through December 1821, after which*
the series was transferred to the New Monthly Magazine. *The*
first volume of Table-Talk *appeared in 1821, with a second*
volume the following year. So prodigious was Hazlitt's produc-
tion in this congenial genre in the space of two years that only
seven of the thirty-three "Table-Talks" in the two volumes were
reprints of essays previously published in the periodicals. Hazlitt's
total production of the longer familiar essay in the 1820's fills
several of the closely printed volumes of P. P. Howe's edition of
the complete works.

For a discussion of the "Style and Structure" of Hazlitt's
essays, see Chapter VII of W. P. Albrecht's Hazlitt and the
Creative Imagination (*Lawrence, Kan.: University of Kansas*
Press, 1965). Though not dealing specifically with the Table-
Talk essays, W. K. Wimsatt, Jr. has valuable comments on
Hazlitt's style in The Prose Style of Samuel Johnson, *Yale*
Studies in English, Volume XCIV (New Haven, Conn.: Yale
University Press, 1941). See also the earlier study by Zilpha E.
Chandler, An Analysis of the Stylistic Technique of Addison,
Johnson, Hazlitt, and Pater, *University of Iowa Humanistic*
Studies, Volume IV (Iowa City, Iowa: University of Iowa Press,
1928).

The text of the Table-Talk *essays here reproduced is from the*
edition of 1824, with the exception of "On Going a Journey"
reproduced from a Paris edition of 1825.

F R O M

TABLE-TALK

F R O M

ON GENIUS AND COMMON SENSE

WE HEAR it maintained by people of more gravity
than understanding, that genius and taste are strictly
reducible to rules, and that there is a rule for every
thing. So far is it from being true that the finest breath
of fancy is a definable thing, that the plainest common
sense is only what Mr. Locke would have called a
mixed mode,[1] subject to a particular sort of acquired
and undefinable tact. It is asked, "If you do not know
the rule by which a thing is done, how can you be sure
of doing it a second time?" And the answer is, "If

---

[1] In his *Essay Concerning Human Understanding* (1690), II, xxii,
Locke had used the term "mixed mode" to refer to such complex
and abstract ideas as "obligation," "drunkenness," "a lie," which
have no existence as such outside the mind, but are the result of
the act of the mind in combining together into one conception a
number of "simple ideas" or particular impressions of "different
kinds."

you do not know the muscles by the help of which you
walk, how is it you do not fall down at every step you
take?" In art, in taste, in life, in speech, you decide
from feeling, and not from reason; that is, from the
impression of a number of things on the mind, which
impression is true and well-founded, though you may
not be able to analyse or account for it in the several
particulars. In a gesture you use, in a look you see, in
a tone you hear, you judge of the expression, propriety,
and meaning from habit, not from reason or rules;
that is to say, from innumerable instances of like
gestures, looks, and tones, in innumerable other circumstances, variously modified, which are too many
and too refined to be all distinctly recollected, but
which do not therefore operate the less powerfully
upon the mind and eye of taste. Shall we say that these
impressions (the immediate stamp of nature) do not
operate in a given manner till they are classified and
reduced to rules, or is not the rule itself grounded upon
the truth and certainty of that natural operation? How
then can the distinction of the understanding as to the
manner in which they operate be necessary to their
producing their due and uniform effect upon the
mind? If certain effects did not regularly arise out of
certain causes in mind as well as matter, there could
be no rule given for them: nature does not follow the
rule, but suggests it. Reason is the interpreter and
critic of nature and genius, not their lawgiver and
judge. He must be a poor creature indeed whose
practical convictions do not in almost all cases outrun
his deliberate understanding, or who does not feel and
know much more then he can give a reason for.—
Hence the distinction between eloquence and wisdom,
between ingenuity and common sense. A man may be
dextrous and able in explaining the grounds of his
opinions, and yet may be a mere sophist, because he
only sees one half of a subject. Another may feel the
whole weight of a question, nothing relating to it may
be lost upon him, and yet he may be able to give no
account of the manner in which it affects him, or to
drag his reasons from their silent lurking-places. This
last will be a wise man, though neither a logician nor
rhetorician. Goldsmith was a fool to Dr. Johnson in
argument; that is, in assigning the specific grounds of
his opinions: Dr. Johnson was a fool to Goldsmith in
the fine tact, the airy, intuitive faculty with which he
skimmed the surface of things, and unconsciously
formed his opinions. Common sense is the just result
of the sum-total of such unconscious impressions in
the ordinary occurrences of life, as they are treasured
up in the memory, and called out by the occasion.
Genius and taste depend much upon the same principle exercised on loftier ground and in more unusual
combinations.

*   *   *   *   *

I shall here try to go more at large into this subject, and to give such instances and illustrations of it as occur to me.

One of the persons who had rendered themselves obnoxious to Government, and been included in a charge for high treason in the year 1794, had retired soon after into Wales to write an epic poem and enjoy the luxuries of a rural life.[2] In his peregrinations through that beautiful scenery, he had arrived one fine morning at the inn at Llangollen, in the romantic valley of that name. He had ordered his breakfast, and was sitting at the window in all the dalliance of expectation, when a face passed of which he took no notice at the instant—but when his breakfast was brought in presently after, he found his appetite for it gone, the day had lost its freshness in his eye, he was uneasy and spiritless; and without any cause that he could discover, a total change had taken place in his feelings. While he was trying to account for this odd circumstance, the same face passed again—it was the face of Taylor the spy; and he was no longer at a loss to explain the difficulty. He had before caught only a transient glimpse, a passing side-view of the face; but though this was not sufficient to awaken a distinct idea in his memory, his feelings, quicker and surer, had taken the alarm; a string had been touched that gave a jar to his whole frame, and would not let him rest, though he could not at all tell what was the matter with him. To the flitting, shadowy, half-distinguished profile that had glided by his window was linked unconsciously and mysteriously, but inseparably, the impression of the trains that had been laid for him by this person;—in this brief moment, in this dim, illegible short-hand of the mind he had just escaped the speeches of the Attorney and Solicitor-General over again; the gaunt figure of Mr. Pitt[3] glared by him; the walls of a prison enclosed him; and he felt the hands of the executioner near him, without knowing it till the tremor and disorder of his nerves gave information to his reasoning faculties that all was not well within. That is, the same state of mind was recalled by one circumstance in the series of association that had been produced by the whole set of circumstances at the time, though the manner in which this was done was not immediately perceptible. In other words, the feeling of pleasure or pain, of good or evil, is revived,

and acts instantaneously upon the mind, before we have time to recollect the precise objects which had originally given birth to it.* The incident here mentioned was merely, then, one case of what the learned understand by the *association of ideas*: but all that is meant by feeling or common sense is nothing but the different cases of the association of ideas, more or less true to the impression of the original circumstances, as reason begins with the more formal developement of those circumstances, or pretends to account for the different cases of the association of ideas. But it does not follow that the dumb and silent pleading of the former (though sometimes, nay often mistaken) is less true than that of its babbling interpreter, or that we are never to trust its dictates without consulting the express authority of reason. Both are imperfect, both are useful in their way, and therefore both are best together, to correct or to confirm one another. It does not appear that in the singular instance above mentioned, the sudden impression on the mind was superstition or fancy, though it might have been thought so, had it not been proved by the event to have a real physical and moral cause. Had not the same face returned again, the doubt would never have been properly cleared up, but would have remained a puzzle ever after, or perhaps have been soon forgot.—By the law of association, as laid down by physiologists, any impression in a series can recal any other impression in that series without going through the whole in order: so that the mind drops the intermediate links, and passes on rapidly and by stealth to the more striking effects of pleasure or pain which have naturally taken the strongest hold of it. By doing this habitually and skilfully with respect to the various impressions and circumstances with which our experience makes us acquainted, it forms a series of unpremeditated conclusions on almost all subjects that can be brought

---

* Sentiment has the same source as that here pointed out. Thus the *Ranz des Vaches*, which has such an effect on the minds of the Swiss peasantry, when its well-known sound is heard, does not merely recal to them the idea of their country, but has associated with it a thousand nameless ideas, numberless touches of private affection, of early hope, romantic adventure, and national pride, all which rush in (with mingled currents) to swell the tide of fond remembrance, and make them languish or die for home. What a fine instrument the human heart is! Who shall touch it? Who shall fathom it? Who shall "sound it from its lowest note to the top of its compass?" Who shall put his hand among the strings, and explain their wayward music? The heart alone, when touched by sympathy, trembles and responds to their hidden meaning![4]

---

[2] John Thelwall (1764–1834) was a political radical and vigorous opponent of the crown. He was arrested on a charge of sedition in May 1794, but was acquitted in the famous "Hardy Trials" of October–November 1794.

[3] William Pitt was prime minister at the time of the "Hardy Trials" and was actively responsible for the arrest and imprisonment of Thelwall and other "seditionists" in that celebrated case.

[4] *Ranz des Vaches* "the air of the cows," a melody played to call the cattle in Switzerland. Its ability to stir the hearts of Swiss soldiers serving in foreign lands was proverbial in Hazlitt's time. For "sound . . . compass," see *Hamlet*, III, ii, 383–84.

before it, as just as they are of ready application to human life; and common sense is the name of this body of unassuming but practical wisdom. Common sense, however, is an impartial, instinctive result of truth and nature, and will therefore bear the test and abide the scrutiny of the most severe and patient reasoning. It is indeed incomplete without it. By ingrafting reason on feeling, we "make assurance double sure."[5]

> " 'Tis the last key-stone that makes up the arch—
> Then stands it a triumphal mark! Then men
> Observe the strength, the height, the why and when
> It was erected: and still walking under,
> Meet some new matter to look up, and wonder."[6]

But reason, not employed to interpret nature, and to improve and perfect common sense and experience, is, for the most part, a building without a foundation.— The criticism exercised by reason then on common sense may be as severe as it pleases, but it must be as patient as it is severe. Hasty, dogmatical, self-satisfied reason is worse than idle fancy, or bigotted prejudice. It is systematic, ostentatious in error, closes up the avenues of knowledge, and "shuts the gates of wisdom on mankind."[7] It is not enough to show that there is no reason for a thing, that we do not see the reason of it: if the common feeling, if the involuntary prejudice sets in strong in favour of it, if, in spite of all we can do, there is a lurking suspicion on the side of our first impressions, we must try again, and believe that truth is mightier than we. So, in offering a definition of any subject, if we feel a misgiving that there is any fact or circumstance omitted, but of which we have only a vague apprehension, like a name we cannot recollect, we must ask for more time, and not cut the matter short by an arrogant assumption of the point in dispute. Common sense thus acts as a check-weight on sophistry, and suspends our rash and superficial judgments. On the other hand, if not only no reason can be given for a thing, but every reason is clear against it, and we can account from ignorance, from authority, from interest, from different causes, for the prevalence of an opinion or sentiment, then we have a right to conclude that we have mistaken a prejudice for an instinct, or have confounded a false and partial impression with the fair and unavoidable inference from general observation. Mr. Burke said that we ought not to reject every prejudice, but should separate the husk of prejudice from the truth it encloses, and so try to

get at the kernel within; and thus far he was right. But he was wrong in insisting that we are to cherish our prejudices, "because they are prejudices:" for if they are all well-founded, there is no occasion to inquire into their origin or use; and he who sets out to philosophise upon them, or make the separation Mr. Burke talks of in this spirit and with this previous determination, will be very likely to mistake a maggot or a rotten canker for the precious kernel of truth, as was indeed the case with our political sophist.

There is nothing more distinct than common sense and vulgar opinion. Common sense is only a judge of things that fall under common observation, or immediately come home to the business and bosoms of men. This is of the very essence of its principle, the basis of its pretensions. It rests upon the simple process of feeling, it anchors in experience. It is not, nor it cannot be, the test of abstract, speculative opinions. But half the opinions and prejudices of mankind, those which they hold in the most unqualified approbation and which have been instilled into them under the strongest sanctions, are of this latter kind, that is, opinions, not which they have ever thought, known, or felt one tittle about, but which they have taken up on trust from others, which have been palmed on their understandings by fraud or force, and which they continue to hold at the peril of life, limb, property, and character, with as little warrant from common sense in the first instance as appeal to reason in the last. The *ultima ratio regum*[8] proceeds upon a very different plea. Common sense is neither priest-craft nor state-policy. Yet "there's the rub that makes absurdity of so long life;"[9] and, at the same time, gives the sceptical philosophers the advantage over us. Till nature has fair play allowed it, and is not adulterated by political and polemical quacks (as it so often has been), it is impossible to appeal to it as a defence against the errors and extravagances of mere reason. If we talk of common sense, we are twitted with vulgar prejudice, and asked how we distinguish the one from the other: but common and received opinion is indeed "a compost heap" of crude notions, got together by the pride and passions of individuals, and reason is itself the thrall or manumitted slave of the same lordly and besotted masters, dragging its servile chain, or committing all sorts of Saturnalian[10] licences, the moment it feels itself freed from it.—If ten millions of Englishmen are furious in thinking themselves right in making war upon thirty millions of Frenchmen,

---

[5] *Macbeth*, IV, i, 83.
[6] See "Epistle to Sir Edward Sacvile," ll. 136–42, in Ben Jonson's *Under-Woods* (1640).
[7] Cf. Gray's *Elegy*, l. 68.

[8] *ultima ratio regum*: the logic or "final argument" of kings; that is, threat of force and violence.
[9] See *Hamlet*, III, i, 65, 68–69.
[10] Unrestrainedly riotous or dissolute.

and if the last are equally bent upon thinking the others always in the wrong, though it is a common and national prejudice, both opinions cannot be the dictate of good sense: but it may be the infatuated policy of one or both governments to keep their subjects always at variance. If a few centuries ago all Europe believed in the infallibility of the Pope, this was not an opinion derived from the proper exercise or erroneous direction of the common sense of the people: common sense had nothing to do with it—they believed whatever their priests told them. England at present is divided into Whigs and Tories, Churchmen and Dissenters: both parties have numbers on their side; but common sense and party-spirit are two different things. Sects and heresies are upheld partly by sympathy, and partly by the love of contradiction: if there was nobody of a different way of thinking, they would fall to pieces of themselves. If a whole court say the same thing, this is no proof that they think it, but that the individual at the head of the court has said it: if a mob agree for a while in shouting the same watch-word, this is not to me an example of the *sensus communis*; they only repeat what they have heard repeated by others. If indeed a large proportion of the people are in want of food, of clothing, of shelter, if they are sick, miserable, scorned, oppressed, and if each feeling it in himself, they all say so with one voice and one heart, and lift up their hands to second their appeal, this I should say was but the dictate of common sense, the cry of nature. But to wave this part of the argument, which it is needless to push farther, I believe that the best way to instruct mankind is not by pointing out to them their mutual errors, but by teaching them to think rightly on indifferent matters, where they will listen with patience in order to be amused, and where they do not consider a definition or a syllogism as the greatest injury you can offer them.

There is no rule for expression. It is got at solely by *feeling*, that is, on the principle of the association of ideas, and by transferring what has been found to hold good in one case (with the necessary modifications) to others. A certain look has been remarked strongly indicative of a certain passion or trait of character, and we attach the same meaning to it or are affected in the same pleasurable or painful manner by it, where it exists in a less degree, though we can define neither the look itself nor the modification of it. Having got the general clue, the exact result may be left to the imagination to vary, to extenuate or aggravate it according to circumstances. In the admirable profile of Oliver Cromwell after ——, the drooping eye-lids, as if drawing a veil over the fixed, penetrating glance, the nostrils somewhat distended, and lips compressed

so as hardly to let the breath escape him, denote the character of the man for high-reaching policy and deep designs as plainly as they can be written. How is it that we decipher this expression in the face? First, by feeling it: and how is it that we feel it? Not by pre-established rules, but by the instinct of analogy, by the principle of association, which is subtle and sure in proportion as it is variable and indefinite. A circumstance, apparently of no value, shall alter the whole interpretation to be put upon an expression or action; and it shall alter it thus powerfully because in proportion to its very insignificance it shews a strong general principle at work that extends in its ramifications to the smallest things. This in fact will make all the difference between minuteness and subtlety or refinement; for a small or trivial effect may in given circumstances imply the operation of a great power. Stillness may be the result of a blow too powerful to be resisted; silence may be imposed by feelings too agonising for utterance. The minute, the trifling and insipid, is that which is little in itself, in its causes and its consequences: the subtle and refined is that which is slight and evanescent at first sight, but which mounts up to a mighty sum in the end, which is an essential part of an important whole, which has consequences greater than itself, and where more is meant than meets the eye or ear. We complain sometimes of littleness in a Dutch picture, where there are a vast number of distinct parts and objects, each small in itself, and leading to nothing else. A sky of Claude's cannot fall under this censure, where one imperceptible gradation is as it were the scale to another, where the broad arch of heaven is piled up of endlessly intermediate gold and azure tints, and where an infinite number of minute, scarce noticed particulars blend and melt into universal harmony. The subtlety in Shakespear, of which there is an immense deal every where scattered up and down, is always the instrument of passion, the vehicle of character. The action of a man pulling his hat over his forehead is indifferent enough in itself, and, generally speaking, may mean any thing or nothing: but in the circumstances in which Macduff is placed, it is neither insignificant nor equivocal.

"What! man, ne'er pull your hat upon your brows," &c.

It admits but of one interpretation or inference, that which follows it:—

"Give sorrow words: the grief that does not speak, Whispers the o'er-fraught heart, and bids it break." [11]

The passage in the same play, in which Duncan and his attendants are introduced commenting on the

---

[11] *Macbeth*, IV, iii, 209–210.

beauty and situation of Macbeth's castle, though familiar in itself, has been often praised for the striking contrast it presents to the scenes which follow.[12]— The same look in different circumstances may convey a totally different expression. Thus the eye turned round to look at you without turning the head indicates generally slyness or suspicion: but if this is combined with large expanded eye-lids or fixed eye-brows, as we see it in Titian's pictures, it will denote calm contemplation or piercing sagacity, without any thing of meanness or fear of being observed. In other cases, it may imply merely indolent enticing voluptuousness, as in Lely's[13] portraits of women. The langour and weakness of the eye-lids gives the amorous turn to the expression. How should there be a rule for all this beforehand, seeing it depends on circumstances every varying, and scarce discernible but by their effect on the mind? Rules are applicable to abstractions, but expression is concrete and individual. We know the meaning of certain looks, and we feel how they modify one another in conjunction. But we cannot have a separate rule to judge of all their combinations in different degrees and circumstances, without foreseeing all those combinations, which is impossible: or if we did foresee them, we should only be where we are, that is, we could only make the rule as we now judge without it, from imagination and the feeling of the moment. The absurdity of reducing expression to a preconcerted system was perhaps never more evidently shewn than in a picture of the Judgment of Solomon by so great a man as N. Poussin,[14] which I once heard admired for the skill and discrimination of the artist in making all the women, who are ranged on one side, in the greatest alarm at the sentence of the judge, while all the men on the opposite side see through the design of it. Nature does not go to work or cast things in a regular mould in this sort of way. I once heard a person remark of another—"He has an eye like a vicious horse." This was a fair analogy. We all, I believe, have noticed the look of an horse's eye, just before he is going to bite or kick. But will any one, therefore, describe to me exactly what that look is? It was the same acute observer that said of a self-sufficient prating music-master—"He talks on all subjects *at sight*"—which expressed the man at once by an allusion to his profession. The coincidence was indeed perfect. Nothing else could compare to the easy assurance with which this gentleman would volunteer

an explanation of things of which he was most ignorant; but the *nonchalance* with which a musician sits down to a harpsichord to play a piece he has never seen before. My physiognomical friend would not have hit on this mode of illustration without knowing the profession of the subject of his criticism; but having this hint given him, it instantly suggested itself to his "sure trailing."[15] The manner of the speaker was evident; and the association of the music-master sitting down to play at sight, lurking in his mind, was immediately called out by the strength of his impression of the character. The feeling of character, and the felicity of invention in explaining it, were nearly allied to each other. The first was so wrought up and running over, that the transition to the last was easy and unavoidable. When Mr. Kean was so much praised for the action of Richard in his last struggle with his triumphant antagonist, where he stands, after his sword is wrested from him, with his hands stretched out, "as if his will could not be disarmed, and the very phantoms of his despair had a withering power," he said that he borrowed it from seeing the last efforts of Painter in his fight with Oliver.[16] This assuredly did not lessen the merit of it. Thus it ever is with the man of real genius. He has the feeling of truth already shrined in his own breast, and his eye is still bent on nature to see how she expresses herself. When we thoroughly understand the subject, it is easy to translate from one language into another. Raphael, in muffling up the figure of Elymas the Sorcerer[17] in his garments, appears to have extended the idea of blindness even to his clothes. Was this design? Probably not; but merely the feeling of analogy thoughtlessly suggesting this device, which being so suggested was retained and carried on, because it flattered or fell in with the original feeling. The tide of passion, when strong, overflows and gradually insinuates itself into all nooks and corners of the mind. Invention (of the best kind) I therefore do not think so distinct a thing from feeling, as some are apt to imagine. The springs of pure feeling will rise and fill

---

12 See Act I, scene vi.

13 Sir Peter Lely (1618–80) was a famous Dutch-English portrait painter, who specialized in the elegant women of the court circles around Charles II.

14 Nicholas Poussin (1595–1665) was a famous French painter of classical landscapes and historical subjects.

---

15 Cf. *Hamlet*, II, ii, 47.

16 Edmund Kean (1787–1833) was a leading actor of the London stage. His performance of Richard III was considered unrivaled in his time. Hazlitt quotes from his own review of Kean's first London performance of Richard III on February 12, 1814. Edward Painter (1784–1852) and Tom Oliver (1789–1864) were boxers; Hazlitt refers to the match of May 17, 1814, in which Oliver bested Painter.

17 The subject of one of Raphael's famous Cartoons, a series of colored drawings of scenes from the Acts of the Apostles to serve as models for tapestries for the Sistine Chapel at the Vatican. The Cartoon to which Hazlitt refers depicts the appearance of Paul and Barnabas before the Roman governor of Cyprus to present the Christian faith. A magician Elymas attempts to thwart their success and is striken with blindness. See Acts, xiii, 6–12.

the moulds of fancy that are fit to receive it. There are some striking coincidences of colour in well-composed pictures, as in a straggling weed in the foreground streaked with blue or red to answer to a blue or red drapery, to the tone of the flesh or an opening in the sky:—not that this was intended, or done by rule (for then it would presently become affected and ridiculous), but the eye being imbued with a certain colour, repeats and varies it from a natural sense of harmony, a secret craving and appetite for beauty, which in the same manner soothes and gratifies the eye of taste, though the cause is not understood. *Tact, finesse,* is nothing but the being completely aware of the feeling belonging to certain situations, passions, &c. and the being consequently sensible to their slightest indications or movements in others. One of the most remarkable instances of this sort of faculty is the following story, told of Lord Shaftesbury,[18] the grandfather of the author of the Characteristics. He had been to dine with Lady Clarendon and her daughter, who was at that time privately married to the Duke of York (afterwards James II.)[19] and as he returned home with another nobleman who had accompanied him, he suddenly turned to him, and said, "Depend upon it, the Duke has married Hyde's daughter." His companion could not comprehend what he meant; but on explaining himself, he said, "Her mother behaved to her with an attention and a marked respect that it is impossible to account for in any other way; and I am sure of it." His conjecture shortly afterwards proved to be the truth. This was carrying the prophetic spirit of common sense as far as it could go.—

[1821]   [1824]

THE SAME SUBJECT CONTINUED

GENIUS or originality is, for the most part, *some strong quality in the mind, answering to and bringing out some new and striking quality in nature.*

Imagination is, more properly, the power of carrying on a given feeling into other situations, which must be done best according to the hold which the feeling itself has taken of the mind.* In new and un-

* I do not here speak of the figurative or fanciful exercise of the imagination, which consists in finding out some striking object or image to illustrate another.

18 Anthony Ashley Cooper, first Earl of Shaftesbury (1621–1683).
19 In September, 1660, the future king had secretly married Anne Hyde (1637–1671), daughter of Edward Hyde, first Earl of Clarendon (1609–1674), a leading statesman of his time and author of the famous *History of the Rebellion* (1702–1704). The marriage was publicly acknowledged in December 1660.

known combinations, the impression must act by sympathy, and not by rule; but there can be no sympathy, where there is no passion, no original interest. The personal interest may in some cases oppress and circumscribe the imaginative faculty, as in the instance of Rousseau: but in general the strength and consistency of the imagination will be in proportion to the strength and depth of feeling; and it is rarely that a man even of lofty genius will be able to do more than carry on his own feelings and character, or some prominent and ruling passion, into fictitious and uncommon situations. Milton has by allusion embodied a great part of his political and personal history in the chief characters and incidents of Paradise Lost. He has, no doubt, wonderfully adapted and heightened them, but the elements are the same; you trace the bias and opinions of the man in the creations of the poet. Shakespear (almost alone) seems to have been a man of genius, raised above the definition of genius. "Born universal heir to all humanity," he was "as one, in suffering all who suffered nothing;"[1] with a perfect sympathy with all things, yet alike indifferent to all: who did not tamper with nature or warp her to his own purposes; who "knew all qualities with a learned spirit,"[2] instead of judging of them by his own predilections; and was rather "a pipe for the Muse's finger to play what stop she pleased,"[3] than anxious to set up any character or pretensions of his own. His genius consisted in the faculty of transforming himself at will into whatever he chose: his originality was the power of seeing every object from the exact point of view in which others would see it. He was the Proteus[4] of human intellect. Genius in ordinary is a more obstinate and less versatile thing. It is sufficiently exclusive and self-willed, quaint and peculiar. It does some one thing by virtue of doing nothing else: it excels in some one pursuit by being blind to all excellence but its own. It is just the reverse of the cameleon; for it does not borrow, but lend its colours to all about it: or like the glow-worm, discloses a little circle of gorgeous light in the twilight of obscurity, in the night of intellect, that surrounds it. So did Rembrandt. If ever there was a man of genius, he was one, in the proper sense of the term. He lived in and revealed to others a world of his own, and might be said to have invented a new view of nature. He did not discover things *out of* nature, in fiction or fairy land, or make a voyage to the moon "to descry new lands, rivers, or mountains in

1 *Hamlet*, III, ii, 71.
2 *Othello*, III, iii, 259.
3 See *Hamlet*, III, ii, 75–76.
4 In Greek mythology, a sea-god capable of assuming many shapes.

her spotty globe," [5] but saw things *in* nature that every one had missed before him, and gave others eyes to see them with. This is the test and triumph of originality, not to shew us what has never been, and what we may therefore very easily never have dreamt of, but to point out to us what is before our eyes and under our feet, though we have had no suspicion of its existence, for want of sufficient strength of intuition, or determined grasp of mind to seize and retain it. Rembrandt's conquests were not over the *ideal*, but the real. He did not contrive a new story or character, but we nearly owe to him a fifth part of painting, the knowledge of *chiaroscuro* [6]—a distinct power and element in art and nature. He had a steadiness, a firm keeping of mind and eye, that first stood the shock of "fierce extremes" [7] in light and shade, or reconciled the greatest obscurity and the greatest brilliancy into perfect harmony; and he therefore was the first to hazard this appearance upon canvas, and give full effect to what he saw and delighted in. He was led to adopt this style of broad and startling contrast from its congeniality to his own feelings: his mind grappled with that which afforded the best exercise to its master-powers: he was bold in act, because he was urged on by a strong native impulse. Originality is then nothing but nature and feeling working in the mind. A man does not affect to be original: he is so, because he cannot help it, and often without knowing it. This extraordinary artist indeed might be said to have had a particular organ for colour. His eye seemed to come in contact with it as a feeling, to lay hold of it as a substance, rather than to contemplate it as a visual object. The texture of his landscapes is "of the earth, earthy" [8]—his clouds are humid, heavy, slow; his shadows are "darkness that may be felt," [9] a "palpable obscure;" [10] his lights are lumps of liquid splendour! There is something more in this than can be accounted for from design or accident: Rembrandt was not a man made up of two or three rules and directions for acquiring genius.

I am afraid I shall hardly write so satisfactory a character of Mr. Wordsworth, though he, too, like Rembrandt, has a faculty of making something out of nothing, that is, out of himself, by the medium through which he sees and with which he clothes the barrenest subject. Mr. Wordsworth is the last man to "look abroad into universality," [11] if that alone constituted

genius: he looks at home into himself, and is "content with riches fineless." He would in the other case be "poor as winter," [12] if he had nothing but general capacity to trust to. He is the greatest, that is, the most original poet of the present day, only because he is the greatest egotist. He is "self-involved, not dark." [13] He sits in the centre of his own being, and there "enjoys bright day." [14] He does not waste a thought on others. Whatever does not relate exclusively and wholly to himself, is foreign to his views. He contemplates a whole-length figure of himself, he looks along the unbroken lines of his personal identity. He thrusts aside all other objects, all other interests with scorn and impatience, that he may repose on his own being, that he may dig out the treasures of thought contained in it, that he may unfold the precious stores of a mind for ever brooding over itself. His genius is the effect of his individual character. He stamps that character, that deep individual interest, on whatever he meets. The object is nothing but as it furnishes food for internal meditation, for old associations. If there had been no other being in the universe, Mr. Wordsworth's poetry would have been just what it is. If there had been neither love nor friendship, neither ambition nor pleasure nor business in the world, the author of the Lyrical Ballads need not have been greatly changed from what he is—might still have "kept the noiseless tenour of his way," [15] retired in the sanctuary of his own heart, hallowing the Sabbath of his own thoughts. With the passions, the pursuits, and imaginations of other men, he does not profess to sympathise, but "finds tongues in the trees, books in the running brooks, sermons in stones, and good in every thing." [16] With a mind averse from outward objects, but ever intent upon its own workings, he hangs a weight of thought and feeling upon every trifling circumstance connected with his past history. The note of the cuckoo sounds in his ear like the voice of other years; the daisy spreads its leaves in the rays of boyish delight, that stream from his thoughtful eyes; the rainbow lifts its proud arch in heaven but to mark his progress from infancy to manhood; an old thorn is buried, bowed down under the mass of associations he has wound about it; and to him, as he himself beautifully says,

——"The meanest flow'r that blows can give
Thoughts that do often lie too deep for tears." [17]

---

[5] *Paradise Lost*, I, 290–91.
[6] The treatment of light and shade in a painting.
[7] *Paradise Lost*, II, 599.
[8] I Corinthians, xv, 47.   [9] Exodus, x, 21.
[10] *Paradise Lost*, II, 406.
[11] From Francis Bacon's *Advancement of Learning* (1605), Book I.

[12] See *Othello*, III, iii, 172–73.
[13] James Thomson's *The Castle of Indolence* (1748), stanza 57.
[14] Milton's *Comus*, l. 382.
[15] Gray's *Elegy*, l. 76.
[16] *As You Like It*, II, i, 16–17.
[17] "Ode: Intimations of Immortality from Recollections of Early Childhood" (1807), ll. 203–204.

It is this power of habitual sentiment, or of transferring the interest of our conscious existence to whatever gently solicits attention, and is a link in the chain of association, without rousing our passions or hurting our pride, that is the striking feature in Mr. Wordsworth's mind and poetry. Others have felt and shown this power before, as Withers,[18] Burns, &c. but none have felt it so intensely and absolutely as to lend to it the voice of inspiration, as to make it the foundation of a new style and school in poetry. His strength, as it so often happens, arises from the excess of his weakness. But he has opened a new avenue to the human heart, has explored another secret haunt and nook of nature, "sacred to verse, and sure of everlasting fame." Compared with his lines, Lord Byron's stanzas are but exaggerated commonplace, and Walter Scott's poetry (not his prose) old wives' fables.* There is no one in whom I have been more disappointed than in the writer here spoken of, nor with whom I am more disposed on certain points to quarrel: but the love of truth and justice which obliges me to do this, will not suffer me to blench his merits. Do what he can, he cannot help being an original-minded man. His poetry is not servile. While the cuckoo returns in the spring, while the daisy looks bright in the sun, while the rainbow lifts its head above the storm—

> "Yet I'll remember thee, Glencairn,
> And all that thou hast done for me!"[19]

Sir Joshua Reynolds, in endeavouring to show that there is no such thing as proper originality, a spirit emanating from the mind of the artist and shining through his works, has traced Raphael through a number of figures which he has borrowed from Masaccio and others.[20] This is a bad calculation. If Raphael had only borrowed those figures from others, would he, even in Sir Joshua's sense, have been entitled to the praise of originality? Plagiarism, I presume, in so far as it is plagiarism, is not originality. Salvator[21] is considered by many as a great genius. He was what they call an irregular genius. My notion of genius is not exactly the same as theirs. It has also been made a

question whether there is not more genius in Rembrandt's *Three Trees*[22] than in all Claude Lorraine's landscapes? I do not know how that may be: but it was enough for Claude to have been a perfect landscape-painter.

Capacity is not the same thing as genius. Capacity may be described to relate to the quantity of knowledge, however acquired; genius to its quality and the mode of acquiring it. Capacity is a power over given ideas or combinations of ideas; genius is the power over those which are not given, and for which no obvious or precise rule can be laid down. Or capacity is power of any sort: genius is power of a different sort from what has yet been shown. A retentive memory, a clear understanding is capacity, but it is not genius. The admirable Crichton[23] was a person of prodigious capacity; but there is no proof (that I know) that he had an atom of genius. His verses that remain are dull and sterile. He could learn all that was known of any subject: he could do any thing if others could show him the way to do it. This was very wonderful: but that is all you can say of it. It requires a good capacity to play well at chess: but, after all, it is a game of skill, and not of genius. Know what you will of it, the understanding still moves in certain tracks in which others have trod before it, quicker or slower, with more or less comprehension and presence of mind. The greatest skill strikes out nothing for itself, from its own peculiar resources; the nature of the game is a thing determinate and fixed: there is no royal or poetical road to check-mate your adversary. There is no place for genius but in the indefinite and unknown. The discovery of the binomial theorem was an effort of genius; but there was none shown in Jedediah Buxton's[24] being able to multiply 9 figures by 9 in his head. If he could have multiplied 90 figures by 90 instead of 9, it would have been equally useless toil and trouble.† He is a man of capacity who possesses

* Mr. Wordsworth himself should not say this, and yet I am not sure he would not.

† The only good thing I ever heard come of this man's singular faculty of memory was the following. A gentleman was mentioning his having been sent up to London from the place where he lived to see Garrick act. When he went back into the country, he was asked what he thought of the player and the play. "Oh!" he said, "he did not know: he had only seen a little man strut about the stage, and repeat 7956 words." We all laughed at this, but a person in one corner of the room, holding one hand to his forehead, and seeming mightily delighted, called out, "Ay, indeed! And pray, was he found to be correct?" This was the supererogation of literal matter-of-fact curiosity. Jedediah Bux-

[18] George Wither (1588–1667) was a miscellaneous poet and pamphleteer. Hazlitt probably refers here to Wither's pastoral *The Shepherd's Hunting* (1615).

[19] Burns's "Lament for James, Earl of Glencairn," ll. 79–80.

[20] See Reynolds' *Discourses* VI and XII. Tomaso Guidi (Masaccio) (1401–c. 1428) was a Florentine painter, whose frescoes in the Church of the Carmine in Florence influenced Raphael, Michelangelo and other painters of the time.

[21] Salvator Rosa (1615–73) was a Neapolitan landscape painter of great reputation in eighteenth-century England.

[22] Rembrandt's most famous landscape, an etching of 1643.

[23] James Crichton (c. 1560–1582) was a young Scotsman who achieved a legendary reputation for his phenomenal memory, wide learning, and great oratorical skills.

[24] Jedediah Buxton (1707–1772) was an illiterate Derbyshire farm-worker who possessed extraordinary arithmetical skills.

considerable intellectual riches: he is a man of genius who finds out a vein of new ore. Originality is the seeing nature differently from others, and yet as it is in itself. It is not singularity or affectation, but the discovery of new and valuable truth. All the world do not see the whole meaning of any object they have been looking at. Habit blinds them to some things: short-sightedness to others. Every mind is not a gauge and measure of truth. Nature has her surface and her dark recesses. She is deep, obscure, and infinite. It is only minds on whom she makes her fullest impressions that can penetrate her shrine or unveil her *Holy of Holies*. It is only those whom she has filled with her spirit that have the boldness or the power to reveal her mysteries to others. But nature has a thousand aspects, and one man can only draw out one of them. Whoever does this, is a man of genius. One displays her force, another her refinement, one her power of harmony, another her suddenness of contrast, one her beauty of form, another her splendour of colour. Each does that for which he is best fitted by his particular genius, that is to say, by some quality of mind into which the quality of the object sinks deepest, where it finds the most cordial welcome, is perceived to its utmost extent, and where again it forces its way out from the fulness with which it has taken possession of the mind of the student. The imagination gives out what it has first absorbed by congeniality of temperament, what it has attracted and moulded into itself by elective affinity, as the loadstone draws and impregnates iron. A little originality is more esteemed and sought for than the greatest acquired talent, because it throws a new light upon things, and is peculiar to the individual. The other is common; and may be had for the asking, to any amount.

The value of any work is to be judged of by the quantity of originality contained in it. A very little of this will go a great way. If Goldsmith had never written any thing but the two or three first chapters of the Vicar of Wakefield, or the character of a Village-Schoolmaster,[26] they would have stamped him a man of genius. The Editors of Encyclopedias are not usually reckoned the first literary characters of the age. The works, of which they have the management, contain a great deal of knowledge, like chests or warehouses, but the goods are not their own. We should as soon think

of admiring the shelves of a library; but the shelves of a library are useful and respectable. I was once applied to, in a delicate emergency, to write an article on a difficult subject for an Encyclopedia, and was advised to take time and give it a systematic and scientific form, to avail myself of all the knowledge that was to be obtained on the subject, and arrange it with clearness and method. I made answer that as to the first, I had taken time to do all that I ever pretended to do, as I had thought incessantly on different matters for twenty years of my life;[*] that I had no particular knowledge of the subject in question, and had no head for arrangement; and that the utmost I could do in such a case would be, when a systematic and scientific article was prepared, to write marginal notes upon it, to insert a remark or illustration of my own (not to be found in former Encyclopedias) or to suggest a better definition than had been offered in the text. There are two sorts of writing. The first is compilation; and consists in collecting and stating all that is already known of any question in the best possible manner, for the benefit of the uninformed reader. An author of this class is a very learned amanuensis of other people's thoughts. The second sort proceeds on an entirely different principle. Instead of bringing down the account of knowledge to the point at which it has already arrived, it professes to start from that point on the strength of the writer's individual reflections; and supposing the reader in possession of what is already known, supplies deficiencies, fills up certain blanks, and quits the beaten road in search of new tracts of observation or sources of feeling. It is in vain to object to this last style that it is disjointed, disproportioned, and irregular. It is merely a set of additions and corrections to other men's works, or to the common stock of human knowledge, printed separately. You might as well expect a continued chain of reasoning in the notes to a book. It skips all the trite, intermediate, level common-places of the subject, and only stops at the difficult passages of the human mind, or touches on some striking point that has been overlooked in previous editions. A view of a subject, to be connected and regular, cannot be all new. A writer will always be liable to be charged either with paradox or commonplace, either with dullness or affectation. But we have no right to demand from any one more than he pretends to. There is indeed a medium in all things, but to unite opposite excellencies, is a task ordinarily too hard for mortality. He who succeeds in what he aims at, or who takes the lead in any one mode or path of excellence, may think himself very well off. It would

---

ton's counting the number of words was idle enough; but here was a fellow who wanted some one to count them over again to see if he was correct.

"The force of *dulness* could not farther go!"[25]

[25] See Dryden's "Lines Printed Under the Engraved Portrait of Milton" (1688).
[26] See "The Deserted Village," ll. 193–216.

[*] Sir Joshua Reynolds being asked how long it had taken him to do a certain picture, made answer, "All his life."

not be fair to complain of the style of an Encyclopedia as dull, as wanting volatile salt; nor of the style of an Essay because it is too light and sparkling, because it is not a *caput mortuum*.[27] So it is rather an odd objection to a work that it is made up entirely of "brilliant passages"—at least it is a fault that can be found with few works, and the book might be pardoned for its singularity. The censure might indeed seem like adroit flattery, if it were not passed on an author whom any objection is sufficient to render unpopular and ridiculous. I grant it is best to unite solidity with show, general information with particular ingenuity. This is the pattern of a perfect style: but I myself do not pretend to be a perfect writer. In fine, we do not banish light French wines from our tables, or refuse to taste sparkling Champagne when we can get it, because it has not the body of Old Port. Besides, I do not know that dulness is strength, or that an observation is slight, because it is striking. Mediocrity, insipidity, want of character is the great fault. *Mediocribus esse poetis non Dii, non homines, non concessêre columnae*.[28] Neither is this privilege allowed to prose-writers in our time, any more than to poets formerly.

It is not then acuteness of organs or extent of capacity that constitutes rare genius or produces the most exquisite models of art, but an intense sympathy with some one beauty or distinguishing characteristic in nature. Irritability alone, or the interest taken in certain things, may supply the place of genius in weak and otherwise ordinary minds. As there are certain instruments fitted to perform certain kinds of labour, there are certain minds so framed as to produce certain *chef-d'oeuvres* in art and literature, which is surely the best use they can be put to. If a man had all sorts of instruments in his shop and wanted one, he would rather have that one than be supplied with a double set of all the others. If he had them all twice over, he could only do what he can do as it is, whereas without that one he perhaps cannot finish any one work he has in hand. So if a man can do one thing better than any body else, the value of this one thing is what he must stand or fall by, and his being able to do a hundred other things merely *as well* as any body else, would not alter the sentence or add to his respectability; on the contrary, his being able to do so many other things well would probably interfere with and incumber him

in the execution of the only thing that others cannot do as well as he, and so far be a draw-back and a disadvantage. More people in fact fail from a multiplicity of talents and pretensions than from an absolute poverty of resources. I have given instances of this elsewhere. Perhaps Shakespear's tragedies would in some respects have been better, if he had never written comedies at all; and in that case, his comedies might well have been spared, though they might have cost us some regret. Racine, it is said, might have rivalled Moliere in comedy; but he gave up the cultivation of his comic talents to devote himself wholly to the tragic Muse. If, as the French tell us, he in consequence attained to the perfection of tragic composition, this was better than writing comedies as well as Moliere and tragedies as well as Crebillon.[29] Yet I count those persons fools who think it a pity Hogarth did not succeed better in serious subjects. The division of labour is an excellent principle in taste as well as in mechanics. Without this, I find from Adam Smith, we could not have a pin made to the degree of perfection it is.[30] We do not, on any rational scheme of criticism, inquire into the variety of a man's excellences, or the number of his works, or his facility of production. Venice Preserved is sufficient for Otway's fame. I hate all those nonsensical stories about Lopez de Vega and his writing a play in a morning before breakfast.[31] He had time enough to do it after. If a man leaves behind him any work which is a model in its kind, we have no right to ask whether he could do any thing else, or how he did it, or how long he was about it. All that talent which is not necessary to the actual quantity of exccllence existing in the world, loses its object, is so much waste talent or *talent to let*. I heard a sensible man say he should like to do some one thing better than all the rest of the world, and in every thing else to be like all the rest of the world. Why should a man do more than his part? The rest is vanity and vexation of spirit.[32] We look with jealous and grudging eyes at all those qualifications which are not essential; first, because they are superfluous, and next, because we suspect they will be prejudicial. Why does Mr. Kean play all those harlequin tricks of singing, dancing, fencing, &c.? They say, "It is for his benefit."[33] It is not for

[27] Alchemical terms: a volatile salt (as distinguished from a "fixed salt") was one subject to rapid conversion into a gaseous or vaporous state, hence, anything of a light and lively character; *caput mortuum* ("dead head") was the worthless residue left after exhaustive distillation or sublimation, hence, anything of a lifeless character.

[28] *Mediocribus . . . columnae:* "Neither Gods, nor men, nor booksellers have allowed poets to be mediocre." Horace's *Ars Poetica*, ll. 372–73.

[29] Prosper Jolyot de Crebillon (1674–1762) was a leading French tragedian of the eighteenth century.

[30] Hazlitt refers to Adam Smith's *The Wealth of Nations* (1776), Book I, Chapter i.

[31] Lope Felix de Vega (1562–1635), the father of Spanish drama, was the author of more than 500 plays.

[32] Ecclesiastes, i, 14.

[33] Hazlitt refers to the "benefit" (a theatrical presentation, the proceeds of which are given to the leading actor) of June 12, 1820, in which Kean followed his performance in *Venice Preserved* with a farce and a demonstration of his skill in singing, dancing, and impersonation.

his reputation. Garrick indeed shone equally in comedy and tragedy. But he was first, not second-rate in both. There is not a greater impertinence than to ask, if a man is clever out of his profession. I have heard of people trying to cross-examine Mrs. Siddons. I would as soon try to entrap one of the Elgin Marbles [34] into an argument. Good nature and common sense are required from all people: but one proud distinction is enough for any one individual to possess or to aspire to!

[1821]   [1824]

ON GOING A JOURNEY

ONE OF the pleasantest things in the world is going a journey; but I like to go by myself. I can enjoy society in a room; but out of doors, nature is company enough for me. I am then never less alone than when alone.

> "The fields his study, nature was his book." [1]

I cannot see the wit of walking and talking at the same time. When I am in the country, I wish to vegetate like the country. I am not for criticising hedge-rows and black cattle. I go out of town in order to forget the town and all that is in it. There are those who for this purpose go to watering-places, and carry the metropolis with them. I like more elbow-room, and fewer incumbrances. I like solitude, when I give myself up to it, for the sake of solitude; nor do I ask for

> ——"a friend in my retreat,
> Whom I may whisper solitude is sweet." [2]

The soul of a journey is liberty; perfect liberty, to think, feel, do just as one pleases. We go a journey chiefly to be free of all impediments and of all inconveniences; to leave ourselves behind, much more to get rid of others. It is because I want a little breathing-space to muse on indifferent matters, where Contemplation

> "May plume her feathers and let grow her wings,
> That in the various bustle of resort
> Where all too ruffled, and sometimes impair'd," [3]

that I absent myself from the town for a while, without feeling at a loss the moment I am left by myself.

Instead of a friend in a post-chaise or in a tilbury, to exchange good things with, and vary the same stale topics over again, for once let me have a truce with impertinence. Give me the clear blue sky over my head, and the green turf beneath my feet, a winding road before me, and a three hours' march to dinner—and then to thinking! It is hard if I cannot start some game on these lone heaths. I laugh, I run, I leap, I sing for joy. From the point of yonder rolling cloud, I plunge into my past being, and revel there, as the sun-burnt Indian plunges headlong into the wave that wafts him to his native shore. Then long-forgotten things, like "sunken wrack and sumless treasuries," [4] burst upon my eager sight, and I begin to feel, think, and be myself again. Instead of an awkward silence, broken by attempts at wit or dull common-places, mine is that undisturbed silence of the heart which alone is perfect eloquence. No one likes puns, alliterations, antitheses, argument, and analysis better than I do; but I sometimes had rather be without them. "Leave, oh, leave me to my repose!" [5] I have just now other business in hand, which would seem idle to you, but is with me "the very stuff of the conscience." [6] Is not this wild rose sweet without a comment? Does not this daisy leap to my heart, set in its coat of emerald? Yet if I were to explain to you the circumstance that has so endeared it to me, you would only smile. Had I not better then keep it to myself, and let it serve me to brood over, from here to yonder craggy point, and from thence onward to the far-distant horizon? I should be but bad company all that way, and therefore prefer being alone. I have heard it said that you may, when the moody fit comes on, walk or ride on by yourself, and indulge your reveries. But this looks like a breach of manners, a neglect of others, and you are thinking all the time that you ought to rejoin your party. "Out upon such half-faced fellowship," [7] say I. I like to be either entirely to myself, or entirely at the disposal of others; to talk or be silent, to walk or sit still, to be sociable or solitary. I was pleased with an observation of Mr. Cobbett's, that "he thought it a bad French custom to drink our wine with our meals, and that an Englishman ought to do only one thing at a time." So I cannot talk and think, or indulge in melancholy musing and lively conversation by fits and starts. "Let me have a companion of my way," says Sterne, "were it but to remark how the shadows lengthen as the sun goes down." It is beautifully said: but in my opinion, this continual comparing of notes interferes with the in-

---

34 A famous collection of Greek sculpture brought to England by Lord Elgin (1766–1841), purchased for the nation by act of Parliament in 1816, and located in the British Museum.

1 "Spring," l. 32, *The Farmer's Boy* (1800), by Robert Bloomfield.

2 Cowper's "Retirement" (1782), ll. 741–42.

3 Milton's *Comus*, ll. 378–80.

---

4 *Henry the Fifth*, I, ii, 165.

5 Refrain in Gray's "The Descent of Odin" (1768).

6 *Othello*, I, ii, 2.

7 *Henry the Fourth*, Part I, I, iii, 208.

voluntary impression of things upon the mind, and hurts the sentiment. If you only hint what you feel in a kind of dumb show, it is insipid: if you have to explain it, it is making a toil of a pleasure. You cannot read the book of nature, without being perpetually put to the trouble of translating it for the benefit of others. I am for the synthetical method on a journey, in preference to the analytical. I am content to lay in a stock of ideas then, and to examine and anatomise them afterwards. I want to see my vague notions float like the down of the thistle before the breeze, and not to have them entangled in the briars and thorns of controversy. For once, I like to have it all my own way; and this is impossible, unless you are alone, or in such company as I do not covet. I have no objection to argue a point with any one for twenty miles of measured road, but not for pleasure. If you remark the scent of a bean-field crossing the road, perhaps your fellow-traveller has no smell. If you point to a distant object, perhaps he is short-sighted, and has to take out his glass to look at it. There is a feeling in the air, a tone in the colour of a cloud which hits your fancy, but the effect of which you are unprepared to account for. There is then no sympathy, but an uneasy craving after it, and a dissatisfaction which pursues you on the way, and in the end probably produces ill humour. Now I never quarrel with myself, and take all my own conclusions for granted till I find it necessary to defend them against objections. It is not merely that you may not be of accord on the objects and circumstances that present themselves before you—they may recall a number of ideas, and lead to associations too delicate and refined to be possibly communicated to others. Yet these I love to cherish, and sometimes still fondly clutch them, when I can escape from the throng to do so. To give way to our feelings before company, seems extravagance or affectation; on the other hand, to have to unravel this mystery of our being at every turn, and to make others take an equal interest in it (otherwise the end is not answered) is a task to which few are competent. We must "give it an understanding, but no tongue." [8] My old friend Coleridge, however, could do both. He could go on in the most delightful explanatory way over hill and dale, a summer's day, and convert a landscape into a didactic poem or a Pindaric ode. "He talked far above singing." [9] If I could so clothe my ideas in sounding and flowing words, I might perhaps wish to have some one with me to admire the swelling theme; or I could be more content, were it possible for me still to hear his echoing voice in the woods of All-

Foxden. [10] They had "that fine madness in them which our first poets had;" [11] and if they could have been caught by some rare instrument, would have breathed such strains as the following:

> ——"Here be woods as green
> As any, air likewise as fresh and sweet
> As when smooth Zephyrus plays on the fleet
> Face of the curled stream, with flow'rs as many
> As the young spring gives, and as choice as any;
> Here be all new delights, cool streams, and wells,
> Arbours o'ergrown with woodbine, caves and dells;
> Choose where thou wilt, while I sit by and sing,
> Or gather rushes to make many a ring
> For thy long fingers; tell thee tales of love,
> How the pale Phoebe, hunting in a grove,
> First saw the boy Endymion, from whose eyes
> She took eternal fire that never dies;
> How she convey'd him softly in a sleep,
> His temples bound with poppy, to the steep
> Head of old Latmos, where she stoops each night,
> Gilding the mountain with her brother's light,
> To kiss her sweetest."——
>   FAITHFUL SHEPHERDESS [12]

Had I words and images at command like these, I would attempt to wake the thoughts that lie slumbering on golden ridges in the evening clouds: but at the sight of nature my fancy, poor as it is, droops and closes up its leaves, like flowers at sunset. I can make nothing out on the spot:—I must have time to collect myself.

In general, a good thing spoils out-of-door prospects: it should be reserved for Table-talk. L——[13] is for this reason, I take it, the worst company in the world out of doors; because he is the best within. I grant, there is one subject on which it is pleasant to talk on a journey; and that is, what one shall have for supper when we get to our inn at night. The open air improves this sort of conversation or friendly altercation, by setting a keener edge on appetite. Every mile of the road heightens the flavour of the viands we expect at the end of it. How fine it is to enter some old town, walled and turreted, just at the approach of night-fall, or to come to some straggling village, with the lights streaming through the surrounding gloom; and then after inquiring for the best entertainment that the place affords, to "take one's ease at one's inn!" [14] These eventful moments in our lives are in fact too precious, too full of solid, heart-felt happiness to be

---

[8] *Hamlet*, I, ii, 250.
[9] See Beaumont and Fletcher's tragic-comedy *Philaster*, V, v.
[10] Wordsworth and Coleridge wrote *Lyrical Ballads* (1798) at Alfoxden in Somersetshire. See "My First Acquaintance with Poets," p. 469 ff.
[11] Cf. "Elegy to my Most Dearely-loved Friend Henery Reynolds Esquire" (1627), ll. 109–110, by Michael Drayton.
[12] A pastoral play by John Fletcher.
[13] Charles Lamb.
[14] See *Henry the Fourth*, Part I, III, iii, 93.

frittered and dribbled away in imperfect sympathy. I would have them all to myself, and drain them to the last drop: they will do to talk of or to write about afterwards. What a delicate speculation it is, after drinking whole goblets of tea,

"The cups that cheer, but not inebriate,"[15]

and letting the fumes ascend into the brain, to sit considering what we shall have for supper—eggs and a rasher, a rabbit smothered in onions, or an excellent veal-cutlet! Sancho in such a situation once fixed upon cow-heel; and his choice, though he could not help it, is not to be disparaged. Then, in the intervals of pictured scenery and Shandean contemplation,[16] to catch the preparation and the stir in the kitchen—*Procul, O procul este profani!*[17] These hours are sacred to silence and to musing, to be treasured up in the memory, and to feed the source of smiling thoughts hereafter. I would not waste them in idle talk; or if I must have the integrity of fancy broken in upon, I would rather it were by a stranger than a friend. A stranger takes his hue and character from the time and place; he is a part of the furniture and costume of an inn. If he is a Quaker, or from the West Riding of Yorkshire, so much the better. I do not even try to sympathise with him, and he *breaks no squares.*[18] I associate nothing with my travelling companion but present objects and passing events. In his ignorance of me and my affairs, I in a manner forget myself. But a friend reminds one of other things, rips up old grievances, and destroys the abstraction of the scene. He comes in ungraciously between us and our imaginary character. Something is dropped in the course of conversation that gives a hint of your profession and pursuits; or from having some one with you that knows the less sublime portions of your history, it seems that other people do. You are no longer a citizen of the world: but your "unhoused free condition is put into circumscription and confine."[19] The *incognito* of an inn is one of its striking privileges—"lord of one's-self, uncumber'd with a name."[20] Oh! it is great to shake off the trammels of the world and of public opinion—to lose our importunate, tormenting, everlasting personal identity in the elements of nature, and become the creature of the moment, clear of all ties—to hold to the universe only by a dish of sweet-breads, and to owe nothing but the score of the evening—and no longer seeking for applause and meeting with contempt, to be known by no other title than the *Gentleman in the parlour!* One may take one's choice of all characters in this romantic state of uncertainty as to one's real pretensions, and become indefinitely respectable and negatively right-worshipful. We baffle prejudice and disappoint conjecture; and from being so to others, begin to be objects of curiosity and wonder even to ourselves. We are no more those hackneyed commonplaces that we appear in the world: an inn restores us to the level of nature, and quits scores with society! I have certainly spent some enviable hours at inns—sometimes when I have been left entirely to myself, and have tried to solve some metaphysical problem, as once at Witham-Common, where I found out the proof that likeness is not a case of the association of ideas—at other times, when there have been pictures in the room, as at St. Neot's[21] (I think it was) where I first met with Gribelin's engravings of the Cartoons,[22] into which I entered at once; and at a little inn on the borders of Wales, where there happened to be hanging some of Westall's drawings,[23] which I compared triumphantly (for a theory that I had, not for the admired artist) with the figure of a girl who had ferried me over the Severn,[24] standing up in the boat between me and the fading twilight—at other times I might mention luxuriating in books with a peculiar interest in this way, as I remember sitting up half the night to read Paul and Virginia,[25] which I picked up at an inn at Bridgewater, after being drenched in the rain all day; and at the same place I got through two volumes of Madame D'Arblay's Camilla.[26] It was on the tenth of April, 1798, that I sat down to a volume of the New Eloise, at the inn at Llangollen,[27] over a bottle of sherry and a cold chicken. The letter I chose was St. Preux's description of his feelings as he first caught a glimpse from the heights of the Jura of the Pays de Vaud, which I had brought with me as a *bonne bouche*[28]

---

[15] Cowper's *The Task*, IV, 39–40.

[16] Referring to the apparently random and bizarre speculations and associations of ideas that define the main characters in Sterne's *Tristram Shandy.*

[17] *Procul . . . profani!*: "O ye profane, be far, far away!" Virgil's *Aeneid*, VI, 258.

[18] Makes no difference.

[19] *Othello*, I, ii, 26–27.

[20] Dryden's "To my Honour'd Kinsman, John Driden" (1700) l. 18.

[21] A town in Huntingdonshire.

[22] Simon Gribelin (1661–1733) was a French-English engraver, who prepared a popular set of engravings of Raphael's Cartoons.

[23] Richard Westall (1765–1838) was an English painter of historical and rural subjects.

[24] Major river in Wales and western England.

[25] *Paul and Virginia*, a sentimental novel, was published in 1786, by Bernardin de St. Pierre (1737–1814).

[26] Frances (Fanny) Burney (Madame D'Arblay) (1752–1840), daughter of Dr. Charles and sister of Admiral James, was a popular English novelist. *Camilla, or a Picture of Youth*, was published in 1796.

[27] *New Eloise*, Rousseau's most famous novel, was published in 1761. The setting of the novel is a village at the foot of the Alps. Llangollen was a town in Wales.

[28] *bonne bouche*: a tidbit or sweetmeat taken after a meal, which leaves a pleasant taste in one's mouth.

to crown the evening with. It was my birth-day, and I had for the first time come from a place in the neighborhood to visit this delightful spot. The road to Llangollen turns off between Chirk and Wrexham; and on passing a certain point, you come all at once upon the valley, which opens like an amphitheatre, broad, barren hills rising in majestic state on either side, with "green upland swells that echo to the bleat of flocks"[29] below, and the river Dee babbling over its stony bed in the midst of them. The valley at this time "glittered green with sunny showers," and a budding ash-tree dipped its tender branches in the chiding stream. How proud, how glad I was to walk along the high road that commanded the delicious prospect, repeating the lines which I have just quoted from Mr. Coleridge's poems! But besides the prospect which opened beneath my feet, another also opened to my inward sight, a heavenly vision, on which were written, in letters large as Hope could make them, these four words, LIBERTY, GENIUS, LOVE, VIRTUE; which have since faded into the light of common day, or mock my idle gaze.

"The beautiful is vanished, and returns not."[30]

Still I would return some time or other to this enchanted spot; but I would return to it alone. What other self could I find to share that influx of thoughts, of regret, and delight, the traces of which I could hardly conjure up to myself, so much have they been broken and defaced! I could stand on some tall rock, and overlook the precipice of years that separates me from what I then was. I was at that time going shortly to visit the poet whom I have above named. Where is he now? Not only I myself have changed—the world, which was then new to me, has become old and incorrigible. Yet will I turn to thee in thought, O sylvan Dee, as then thou wert in joy, in youth and gladness; and thou shalt always be to me the river of Paradise, where I will drink of the waters of life freely!

There is hardly any thing that shews the shortsightedness or capriciousness of the imagination more than travelling does. With change of place we change our ideas, nay, our opinions and feelings. We can by an effort indeed transport ourselves to old and long-forgotten scenes, and then the picture of the mind revives again;[31] but we forget those that we have just left. It seems that we can think but of one place at a time. The canvas of the fancy has only a certain extent, and if we paint one set of objects upon it, they immediately efface every other. We cannot enlarge our conceptions; we only shift our point of view. The landscape bares its bosom to the enraptured eye; we take our fill of it; and seem as if we could form no other image of beauty or grandeur. We pass on, and think no more of it: the horizon that shuts it from our sight also blots it from our memory, like a dream. In travelling through a wild barren country, I can form no idea of a woody and cultivated one. It appears to me that all the world must be barren, like what I see of it. In the country we forget the town, and in town we despise the country. "Beyond Hyde Park," says Sir Fopling Flutter, "all is a desert."[32] All that part of the map that we do not see before us is a blank. The world in our conceit of it is not much bigger than a nutshell. It is not one prospect expanded into another, county joined to county, kingdom to kingdom, lands to seas, making an image voluminous and vast;—the mind can form no larger idea of space than the eye can take in at a single glance. The rest is a name written on a map, a calculation of arithmetic. For instance, what is the true signification of that immense mass of territory and population, known by the name of China to us? An inch of paste-board on a wooden globe, of no more account than a China orange! Things near us are seen of the size of life: things at a distance are diminished to the size of the understanding. We measure the universe by ourselves, and even comprehend the texture of our own being only piece-meal. In this way, however, we remember an infinity of things and places. The mind is like a mechanical instrument that plays a great variety of tunes, but it must play them in succession. One idea recalls another, but it at the same time excludes all others. In trying to renew old recollections, we cannot as it were unfold the whole web of our existence; we must pick out the single threads. So in coming to a place where we have formerly lived and with which we have intimate associations, every one must have found that the feeling grows more vivid the nearer we approach the spot, from the mere anticipation of the actual impression: we remember circumstances, feelings, persons, faces, names, that we had not thought of for years; but for the time all the rest of the world is forgotten!—To return to the question I have quitted above.

I have no objection to go to see ruins, aqueducts, pictures, in company with a friend or a party, but rather the contrary, for the former reason reversed.

---

[29] See Coleridge's "Ode to the Departing Year" (1796), ll. 125–26.

[30] The phrase "into the light of common day" is from Wordsworth's "Intimations Ode", l. 77. "The beautiful is vanished and returns not" occurs in Coleridge's *The Death of Wallenstein*, V, i, 68.

[31] See Wordsworth's "Tintern Abbey," l. 61.

[32] See George Etherege's comedy *The Man of Mode or Sir Fopling Flutter* (1676), V, ii. The line is spoken by the heroine, Harriet.

They are intelligible matters, and will bear talking about. The sentiment here is not tacit, but communicable and overt. Salisbury Plain is barren of criticism; but Stonehenge will bear a discussion antiquarian, picturesque, and philosophical. In setting out on a party of pleasure, the first consideration always is where we shall go: in taking a solitary ramble, the question is what we shall meet with by the way. The mind then is "its own place;"[33] nor are we anxious to arrive at the end of our journey. I can myself do the honours indifferently well to works of art and curiosity. I once took a party to Oxford with no mean *éclat*—shewed them that seat of the Muses at a distance,

"With glistering spires and pinnacles adorn'd—"[34]

descanted on the learned air that breathes from the grassy quadrangles and stone-walls of halls and colleges—was at home in the Bodleian; and at Blenheim quite superseded the powdered Cicerone[35] that attended us, and that pointed in vain with his wand to common-place beauties in matchless pictures.—As another exception to the above reasoning, I should not feel confident in venturing on a journey in a foreign country without a companion. I should want at intervals to hear the sound of my own language. There is an involuntary antipathy in the mind of an Englishman to foreign manners and notions, that requires the assistance of social sympathy to carry it off. As the distance from home increases, this relief, which was at first a luxury, becomes a passion and an appetite. A person would almost feel stifled to find himself in the deserts of Arabia without friends and countrymen: there must be allowed to be something in the view of Athens or old Rome, that claims the utterance of speech; and I own that the Pyramids are too mighty for any single contemplation. In such situations, so opposite to all one's ordinary train of ideas, one seems a species by one's-self, a limb torn off from society, unless one can meet with instant fellowship and support.—Yet I did not feel this want or craving very pressing once, when I first set my foot on the laughing shores of France. Calais was peopled with novelty and delight. The confused, busy murmur of the place was like oil and wine poured into my ears; not did the mariners' hymn, which was sung from the top of an old crazy vessel in the harbour, as the sun went down, send an alien sound into my soul. I breathed the air of general humanity. I walked over "the vine-covered hills and

gay regions of France," erect and satisfied; for the image of man was not cast down and chained to the foot of arbitrary thrones. I was at no loss for language, for that of all the great schools of painting was open to me.[36] The whole is vanished like a shade. Pictures, heroes, glory, freedom, all are fled: nothing remains but the Bourbons and the French people!—There is undoubtedly a sensation in travelling into foreign parts that is to be had nowhere else: but it is more pleasing at the time than lasting. It is too remote from our habitual associations to be a common topic of discourse or reference; and, like a dream or another state of existence, does not piece into our daily modes of life. It is an animated but a momentary hallucination. It demands an effort to exchange our actual for our ideal identity; and to feel the pulse of our old transports revive very keenly, we must "jump" all our present comforts and connexions. Our romantic and itinerant character is not to be domesticated. Dr. Johnson remarked how little foreign travel added to the facilities of conversation in those who had been abroad.[37] In fact, the time we have spent there is both delightful and in one sense instructive; but it appears to be cut out of our substantial, downright existence, and never to join kindly on to it. We are not the same, but another, and perhaps more enviable individual, all the time we are out of our own country. We are lost to ourselves, as well as to our friends. So the poet somewhat quaintly sings,

"Out of my country and myself I go."

Those who wish to forget painful thoughts, do well to absent themselves for a while from the ties and objects that recall them: but we can be said only to fulfil our destiny in the place that gave us birth. I should on this account like well enough to spend the whole of my life in travelling abroad, if I could any where borrow another life to spend afterwards at home!

[January 1822]   [1825]

ON FAMILIAR STYLE

IT IS not easy to write a familiar style. Many people mistake a familiar for a vulgar style, and suppose that to write without affectation is to write at random. On the contrary, there is nothing that requires more precision, and, if I may so say, purity of expression, than

---

33 *Paradise Lost*, I, 254.
34 *Paradise Lost*, III, 550.
35 The Bodleian is the major library at Oxford. Blenheim Palace is the residence of the Duke of Marlborough, near Oxford. Cicerone is a guide.

36 The passages refer to Hazlitt's visit to France in 1802–1803, in order to make copies of paintings in the Louvre. The phrase "the vine-covered hills and gay regions of France" is from the "Song written for the purpose of being recited on the anniversary of the 14th August, 1791," by William Roscoe (P. P. Howe).
37 See Boswell's *Life of Johnson*, entry for May 13, 1778.

the style I am speaking of. It utterly rejects not only all unmeaning pomp, but all low, cant phrases, and loose, unconnected, *slipshod* allusions. It is not to take the first word that offers, but the best word in common use; it is not to throw words together in any combinations we please, but to follow and avail ourselves of the true idiom of the language. To write a genuine familiar or truly English style, is to write as any one would speak in common conversation, who had a thorough command and choice of words, or who could discourse with ease, force, and perspicuity, setting aside all pedantic and oratorical flourishes. Or to give another illustration, to write naturally is the same thing in regard to common conversation, as to read naturally is in regard to common speech. It does not follow that it is an easy thing to give the true accent and inflection to the words you utter, because you do not attempt to rise above the level of ordinary life and colloquial speaking. You do not assume indeed the solemnity of the pulpit, or the tone of stage-declamation: neither are you at liberty to gabble on at a venture, without emphasis or discretion, or to resort to vulgar dialect or clownish pronunciation. You must steer a middle course. You are tied down to a given and appropriate articulation, which is determined by the habitual associations between sense and sound, and which you can only hit by entering into the author's meaning, as you must find the proper words and style to express yourself by fixing your thoughts on the subject you have to write about. Any one may mouth out a passage with a theatrical cadence, or get upon stilts to tell his thoughts: but to write or speak with propriety and simplicity is a more difficult task. Thus it is easy to affect a pompous style, to use a word twice as big as the thing you want to express: it is not so easy to pitch upon the very word that exactly fits it. Out of eight or ten words equally common, equally intelligible, with nearly equal pretensions, it is a matter of some nicety and discrimination to pick out the very one, the preferableness of which is scarcely perceptible, but decisive. The reason why I object to Dr. Johnson's style is, that there is no discrimination, no selection, no variety in it. He uses none but "tall, opaque words," taken from the "first row of the rubric:"—words with the greatest number of syllables, or Latin phrases with merely English terminations. If a fine style depended on this sort of arbitrary pretension, it would be fair to judge of an author's elegance by the measurement of his words, and the substitution of foreign circumlocutions (with no precise associations) for the mother-tongue.* How

simple it is to be dignified without ease, to be pompous without meaning! Surely, it is but a mechanical rule for avoiding what is low to be always pedantic and affected. It is clear you cannot use a vulgar English word, if you never use a common English word at all. A fine tact is shewn in adhering to those which are perfectly common, and yet never falling into any expressions which are debased by disgusting circumstances, or which owe their signification and point to technical or professional allusions. A truly natural or familiar style can never be quaint or vulgar, for this reason, that it is of universal force and applicability, and that quaintness and vulgarity arise out of the immediate connection of certain words with coarse and disagreeable, or with confined ideas. The last form what we understand by *cant* or *slang* phrases.—To give an example of what is not very clear in the general statement. I should say that the phrase *To cut with a knife*, or *To cut a piece of wood*, is perfectly free from vulgarity, because it is perfectly common: but *to cut an acquaintance* is not quite unexceptionable, because it is not perfectly common or intelligible, and has hardly yet escaped out of the limits of slang phraseology. I should hardly therefore use the word in this sense without putting it in italics as a license of expression, to be received *cum grano salis*.[1] All provincial or byephrases come under the same mark of reprobation—all such as the writer transfers to the page from his fireside or a particular *coterie*, or that he invents for his own sole use and convenience. I conceive that words are like money, not the worse for being common, but that it is the stamp of custom alone that gives them circulation or value. I am fastidious in this respect, and would almost as soon coin the currency of the realm as counterfeit the King's English. I never invented or gave a new and unauthorised meaning to any word but one single one (the term *impersonal* applied to feelings)[2] and that was in an abstruse metaphysical discussion to express a very difficult distinction. I have been (I know) loudly accused of revelling in vulgarisms and broken English. I cannot speak to that point: but so far I plead guilty to the determined use of acknowledged idioms and common elliptical expressions. I am not sure that the critics in question know the one from the other, that is, can distinguish any medium between formal pedantry and the most barbarous solecism.[3] As an author, I endeavour to employ plain words and popular modes of construction, as were I a chapman[4] and dealer, I should common weights and measures.

---

* I have heard of such a thing as an author, who makes it a rule never to admit a monosyllable into his vapid verse. Yet the charm and sweetness of Marlow's lines depended often on their being made up almost entirely of monosyllables.

[1] *cum grano salis:* "with a grain of salt".
[2] Hazlitt refers to a passage, not included in the selection above, from *An Essay on the Principles of Human Action.*
[3] Mistake in the use of language.
[4] An itinerant merchant or trader.

The proper force of words lies not in the words themselves, but in their application. A word may be a fine-sounding word, of an unusual length, and very imposing from its learning and novelty, and yet in the connection in which it is introduced, may be quite pointless and irrelevant. It is not pomp or pretension, but the adaptation of the expression to the idea that clenches a writer's meaning:—as it is not the size or glossiness of the materials, but their being fitted each to its place, that gives strength to the arch; or as the pegs and nails are as necessary to the support of the building as the larger timbers, and more so than the mere shewy, unsubstantial ornaments. I hate any thing that occupies more space than it is worth. I hate to see a load of band-boxes go along the street, and I hate to see a parcel of big words without any thing in them. A person who does not deliberately dispose of all his thoughts alike in cumbrous draperies and flimsy disguises, may strike out twenty varieties of familiar every-day language, each coming somewhat nearer to the feeling he wants to convey, and at last not hit upon that particular and only one, which may be said to be identical with the exact impression in his mind. This would seem to shew that Mr. Cobbett is hardly right in saying that the first word that occurs is always the best.[5] It may be a very good one; and yet a better may present itself on re-flection or from time to time. It should be suggested naturally, however, and spontaneously, from a fresh and lively conception of the subject. We seldom suc-ceed by trying at improvement, or by merely sub-stituting one word for another that we are not satisfied with, as we cannot recollect the name of a place or person by merely plaguing ourselves about it. We wander farther from the point by persisting in a wrong scent; but it starts up accidentally in the memory when we least expected it, by touching some link in the chain of previous association.

There are those who hoard up and make a cautious display of nothing but rich and rare phraseology;— ancient medals, obscure coins, and Spanish pieces of eight. They are very curious to inspect; but I myself would neither offer nor take them in the course of exchange. A sprinkling of archaisms is not amiss; but a tissue of obsolete expressions is more fit *for keep than wear*. I do not say I would not use any phrase that had been brought into fashion before the middle or the end of the last century; but I should be shy of using any that had not been employed by any approved author during the whole of that time. Words, like clothes, get old-fashioned, or mean and ridiculous, when they have

been for some time laid aside. Mr. Lamb is the only imitator of old English style I can read with pleasure; and he is so thoroughly imbued with the spirit of his authors, that the idea of imitation is almost done away. There is an inward unction, a marrowy vein both in the thought and feeling, an intuition, deep and lively, of his subject, that carries off any quaintness or awkward-ness arising from an antiquated style and dress. The matter is completely his own, though the manner is assumed. Perhaps his ideas are altogether so marked and individual, as to require their point and pungency to be neutralised by the affectation of a singular but traditional form of conveyance. Tricked out in the pre-vailing costume, they would probably seem more startling and out of the way. The old English authors, Burton, Fuller, Coryate,[6] Sir Thomas Brown, are a kind of mediators between us and the more eccentric and whimsical modern, reconciling us to his peculiar-ities. I do not however know how far this is the case or not, till he condescends to write like one of us. I must confess that what I like best of his papers under the signature of Elia (still I do not presume, amidst such excellence, to decide what is most excellent) is the account of *Mrs. Battle's Opinions on Whist*, which is also the most free from obsolete allusions and turns of expression—

"A well of native English undefiled."[7]

To those acquainted with his admired prototypes, these Essays of the ingenious and highly gifted author have the same sort of charm and relish, that Erasmus's Colloquies[8] or a fine piece of modern Latin have to the classical scholar. Certainly, I do not know any bor-rowed pencil that has more power or felicity of execu-tion than the one of which I have here been speaking.

It is as easy to write a gaudy style without ideas, as it is to spread a pallet of shewy colours, or to smear in a flaunting transparency.[9] "What do you read?"— "Words, words, words."—"What is the matter?"— "*Nothing*," it might be answered.[10] The florid style is the reverse of the familiar. The last is employed as an unvarnished medium to convey ideas; the first is resorted to as a spangled veil to conceal the want of them. When there is nothing to be set down but words, it costs little to have them fine. Look through the

---

5 Hazlitt refers to William Cobbett's *Grammar of the English Language* (1818), letter XXIII.

6 Thomas Coryate (*c.* 1577–1617) was a famous traveller and author of *Coryats Crudities* (1611).
7 *Faerie Queene*, IV, ii, 32.
8 Erasmus' *Colloquia*, first published in 1519, were a series of witty Latin dialogues or conversations on social and religious questions, intended as a textbook for students of Latin style.
9 A screen made of some translucent substance to which figures, letters, or colors are applied, illuminated from behind by a light.
10 See *Hamlet*, II, ii, 193–95.

dictionary, and cull out a *florilegium*, rival the *tulip-pomania*.[11] *Rouge* high enough, and never mind the natural complexion. The vulgar, who are not in the secret, will admire the look of preternatural health and vigour; and the fashionable, who regard only appearances, will be delighted with the imposition. Keep to your sounding generalities, your tinkling phrases, and all will be well. Swell out an unmeaning truism to a perfect tympany of style. A thought, a distinction is the rock on which all this brittle cargo of verbiage splits at once. Such writers have merely *verbal* imaginations, that retain nothing but words. Or their puny thoughts have dragon-wings, all green and gold. They soar far above the vulgar failing of the *Sermo humi obrepens*[12]— their most ordinary speech is never short of an hyperbole, splendid, imposing, vague, incomprehensible, magniloquent, a cento[13] of sounding common-places. If some of us, whose "ambition is more lowly," pry a little too narrowly into nooks and corners to pick up a number of "unconsidered trifles,"[14] they never once direct their eyes or lift their hands to seize on any but the most gorgeous, tarnished, threadbare patch-work set of phrases, the left-off finery of poetic extravagance, transmitted down through successive generations of barren pretenders. If they criticise actors and actresses, a huddled phantasmagoria[15] of feathers, spangles, floods of light, and oceans of sound float before their morbid sense, which they paint in the style of Ancient Pistol.[16] Not a glimpse can you get of the merits or defects of the performers: they are hidden in a profusion of barbarous epithets and wilful rhodomontade.[17] Our hypercritics are not thinking of these little fantoccini[18] beings—

"That strut and fret their hour upon the stage"—[19]

but of tall phantoms of words, abstractions, *genera* and *species*, sweeping clauses, periods that unite the Poles, forced alliterations, astounding antitheses—

"And on their pens *Fustian* sits plumed."[20]

---

[11] *florilegium:* literally, a collection of flowers; by extension, an anthology or collection of fancy or flowery words. *tulippomania:* a craze for tulips, originally applied to seventeenth-century Dutchmen.
[12] *Sermo humi obrepens:* "language crawling on the ground." Cf. Horace's *Epistles,* II, i, 250–51.
[13] Verbal patchword.
[14] *Winter's Tale,* IV, iii, 26.
[15] A constantly shifting scene of differing and illusory shapes.
[16] One of Falstaff's associates in *Merry Wives of Windsor, Henry IV,* and *Henry V,* and his standard-bearer (Ancient), whose speech is persistently overblown and rhetorical.
[17] Inflated language of boasting.
[18] Puppet-like.
[19] *Macbeth,* V, v, 25.
[20] Cf. *Paradise Lost,* IV, 988–89. Fustian: high-sounding but empty language.

If they describe kings and queens, it is an Eastern pageant. The Coronation at either House is nothing to it. We get at four repeated images—a curtain, a throne, a sceptre, and a foot-stool. These are with them the wardrobe of a lofty imagination; and they turn their servile strains to servile uses. Do we read a description of pictures? It is not a reflection of tones and hues which "nature's own sweet and cunning hand laid on,"[21] but piles of precious stones, rubies, pearls, emeralds, Golconda's mines,[22] and all the blazonry of art. Such persons are in fact besotted with words, and their brains are turned with the glittering, but empty and sterile phantoms of things. Personifications, capital letters, seas of sunbeams, visions of glory, shining inscriptions, the figures of a transparency, Britannia with her shield, or Hope leaning on an anchor, make up their stock in trade. They may be considered as *hieroglyphical* writers. Images stand out in their minds isolated and important merely in themselves, without any ground-work of feeling—there is no context in their imaginations. Words affect them in the same way, by the mere sound, that is, by their possible, not by their actual application to the subject in hand. They are fascinated by first appearances, and have no sense of consequences. Nothing more is meant by them than meets the ear: they understand or feel nothing more than meets their eye. The web and texture of the universe, and of the heart of man, is a mystery to them: they have no faculty that strikes a chord in unison with it. They cannot get beyond the daubings of fancy, the varnish of sentiment. Objects are not linked to feelings, words to things, but images revolve in splendid mockery, words represent themselves in their strange rhapsodies. The categories of such a mind are pride and ignorance—pride in outside show, to which they sacrifice every thing, and ignorance of the true worth and hidden structure both of words and things. With a sovereign contempt for what is familiar and natural, they are the slaves of vulgar affectation—of a routine of high-flown phrases. Scorning to imitate realities, they are unable to invent any thing, to strike out one original idea. They are not copyists of nature, it is true: but they are the poorest of all plagiarists, the plagiarists of words. All is far-fetched, dear-bought, artificial, oriental in subject and allusion: all is mechanical, conventional, vapid, formal, pedantic in style and execution. They startle and confound the understanding of the reader, by the remoteness and obscurity of their illustrations: they soothe the ear by the monotony of the same everlasting round

---

[21] *Twelfth Night,* I, v, 258.
[22] A source of diamonds in India.

of circuitous metaphors. They are the *mock-school* in poetry and prose. They flounder about between fustian in expression, and bathos in sentiment. They tantalise the fancy, but never reach the head nor touch the heart. Their Temple of Fame is like a shadowy structure raised by Dulness to Vanity,[23] or like Cowper's description of the Empress of Russia's palace of ice, as "worthless as in shew 'twas glittering"—

"It smiled, and it was cold!"[24]

[1822]   [1824]

[END OF SELECTIONS FROM TABLE TALK]

MY FIRST ACQUAINTANCE
WITH POETS[1]

My FATHER was a Dissenting Minister at W——m in Shropshire; and in the year 1798 (the figures that compose that date are to me like the "dreaded name of Demogorgon")[2] Mr. Coleridge came to Shrewsbury, to succeed Mr. Rowe in the spiritual charge of a Unitarian Congregation there. He did not come till late on the Saturday afternoon before he was to preach; and Mr. Rowe, who himself went down to the coach in a state of anxiety and expectation, to look for the arrival of his successor, could find no one at all answering the description but a round-faced man in a short black coat (like a shooting-jacket) which hardly seemed to have been made for him, but who seemed to be talking at a great rate to his fellow-passengers. Mr. Rowe had scarce returned to give an account of his disappointment, when the round-faced man in black entered, and dissipated all doubts on the subject, by beginning to talk. He did not cease while he staid; nor has he since, that I know of. He held the good town of Shrewsbury in delightful suspense for three weeks that he remained there, "fluttering the *proud Salopians* like an eagle in a dove-cote;"[3] and the Welsh moun-

tains that skirt the horizon with their tempestuous confusion, agree to have heard no such mystic sounds since the days of

"High-born Hoel's harp or soft Llewellyn's lay!"

As we passed along between W——m and Shrewsbury, and I eyed their blue tops seen through the wintry branches, or the red rustling leaves of the sturdy oak-trees by the roadside, a sound was in my ears as of a Siren's song; I was stunned, startled with it, as from deep sleep; but I had no notion then that I should ever be able to express my admiration to others in motley imagery or quaint allusion, till the light of his genius shone into my soul, like the sun's rays glittering in the puddles of the road. I was at that time dumb, inarticulate, helpless, like a worm by the way-side, crushed, bleeding, lifeless; but now, bursting from the deadly bands that "bound them,

"With Styx nine times round them,"[4]

my ideas float on winged words, and as they expand their plumes, catch the golden light of other years. My soul has indeed remained in its original bondage, dark, obscure, with longings infinite and unsatisfied; my heart, shut up in the prison-house of this rude clay, has never found, nor will it ever find, a heart to speak to; but that my understanding also did not remain dumb and brutish, or at length found a language to express itself, I owe to Coleridge. But this is not to my purpose.

My father lived ten miles from Shrewsbury, and was in the habit of exchanging visits with Mr. Rowe, and with Mr. Jenkins of Whitchurch (nine miles farther on) according to the custom of Dissenting Ministers in each other's neighbourhood. A line of communication is thus established, by which the flame of civil and religious liberty is kept alive, and nourishes its smouldering fire unquenchable, like the fires in the Agamemnon of Æschylus, placed at different stations, that waited for ten long years to announce with their blazing pyramids the destruction of Troy. Coleridge had agreed to come over to see my father, according to the courtesy of the country, as Mr. Rowe's probable successor; but in the mean time I had gone to hear him preach the Sunday after his arrival. A poet and a philosopher getting up into a Unitarian pulpit to preach the Gospel, was a romance in these degenerate days, a sort of revival of the primitive spirit of Christianity, which was not to be resisted.

It was in January, 1798, that I rose one morning before day-light, to walk ten miles in the mud, and

[23] Hazlitt refers to two poems by Alexander Pope: *The Temple of Fame* (1715), a dream-vision (based on Chaucer), in which the poet is transported to the temple enshrining the heroes of human history and literature; and the *Dunciad* (1728–1743), Pope's great satire on the intellectual mediocrity and corruption of his age, which involves the coronation of the poetaster Colley Cibber in the Temple of Dullness.

[24] See *The Task* (1785), V, 173–76.

[1] This famous autobiographical essay was published in Volume III (April 1823) of Leigh Hunt's *The Liberal;* it was never republished in Hazlitt's lifetime.

[2] *Paradise Lost*, II, 964–65.

[3] See *Coriolanus*, V, vi, 114–15. *Salopians* are natives of Shropshire. The next quotation is from Gray's *The Bard*, l. 28. Hoel and Llewellyn were famous and beloved Welsh princes and bards of the twelfth and thirteenth centuries.

[4] Pope's "Ode on St. Cecilia's Day," ll. 90–91.

went to hear this celebrated person preach. Never, the longest day I have to live, shall I have such another walk as this cold, raw, comfortless one, in the winter of the year 1798.—*Il y a des impressions que ni le tems ni les circonstances peuvent effacer. Dusse-je vivre des siècles entiers, le doux tems de ma jeunesse ne peut renaitre pour moi, ni s'effacer jamais dans ma mémoire.*[5] When I got there, the organ was playing the 100th psalm, and, when it was done, Mr. Coleridge rose and gave out his text, "And he went up into the mountain to pray, HIMSELF, ALONE."[6] As he gave out this text, his voice "rose like a steam of rich distilled perfumes,"[7] and when he came to the two last words, which he pronounced loud, deep, and distinct, it seemed to me, who was then young, as if the sounds had echoed from the bottom of the human heart, and as if that prayer might have floated in solemn silence through the universe. The idea of St. John came into mind, "of one crying in the wilderness, who had his loins girt about, and whose food was locusts and wild honey."[8] The preacher then launched into his subject, like an eagle dallying with the wind. The sermon was upon peace and war; upon church and state—not their alliance, but their separation—on the spirit of the world and the spirit of Christianity, not as the same, but as opposed to one another. He talked of those who had "inscribed the cross of Christ on banners dripping with human gore." He made a poetical and pastoral excursion,—and to shew the fatal effects of war, drew a striking contrast between the simple shepherd boy, driving his team afield, or sitting under the hawthorn, piping to his flock, "as though he should never be old,"[9] and the same poor country-lad, crimped, kidnapped, brought into town, made drunk at an alehouse, turned into a wretched drummer-boy, with his hair sticking on end with powder and pomatum, a long cue at his back, and tricked out in the loathsome finery of the profession of blood.

"Such were the notes our once-lov'd poet sung."[10]

And for myself, I could not have been more delighted if I had heard the music of the spheres. Poetry and Philosophy had met together, Truth and Genius had embraced, under the eye and with the sanction of Religion. This was even beyond my hopes. I returned

home well satisfied. The sun that was still labouring pale and wan through the sky, obscured by thick mists, seemed an emblem of the *good cause*; and the cold dank drops of dew that hung half melted on the beard of the thistle, had something genial and refreshing in them; for there was a spirit of hope and youth in all nature, that turned every thing into good. The face of nature had not then the brand of JUS DIVINUM on it:

"Like to that sanguine flower inscrib'd with woe."[11]

On the Tuesday following, the half-inspired speaker came. I was called down into the room where he was, and went half-hoping, half-afraid. He received me very graciously, and I listened for a long time without uttering a word. I did not suffer in his opinion by my silence. "For those two hours," he afterwards was pleased to say, "he was conversing with W. H.'s forehead!" His appearance was different from what I had anticipated from seeing him before. At a distance, and in the dim light of the chapel, there was to me a strange wildness in his aspect, a dusky obscurity, and I thought him pitted with the small-pox. His complexion was at that time clear, and even bright—

"As are the children of yon azure sheen."[12]

His forehead was broad and high, light as if built of ivory, with large projecting eyebrows, and his eyes rolling beneath them like a sea with darkened lustre. "A certain tender bloom his face o'erspread," a purple tinge as we see it in the pale thoughtful complexions of the Spanish portrait-painters, Murillo and Velasquez. His mouth was gross, voluptuous, open, eloquent; his chin good-humoured and round; but his nose, the rudder of the face, the index of the will, was small, feeble, nothing—like what he has done. It might seem that the genius of his face as from a height surveyed and projected him (with sufficient capacity and huge aspiration) into the world unknown of thought and imagination, with nothing to support or guide his veering purpose, as if Columbus had launched his adventurous course for the New World in a scallop without oars or compass. So at least I comment on it after the event. Coleridge in his person was rather above the common size, inclining to the corpulent, or like Lord Hamlet, "somewhat fat and pursy."[13] His hair (now, alas! grey) was then black and glossy as the raven's, and fell in smooth masses over his forehead.

---

[5] *Il y a ... memoire:* "There are some impressions which neither time nor circumstance can efface. Were I to live entire centuries, the sweet time of my youth could not return for me, nor ever be effaced from my memory." From Rousseau's *Confessions*, Book VII.

[6] John, vi, 15.   [7] *Comus*, l. 556.

[8] Matthew, iii, 3–4.

[9] Sidney's *Arcadia*, Book I, Chapter 2.

[10] Pope's "Epistle to Robert Earl of Oxford, and Earl Mortimer," l. 1.

---

[11] Jus divinum: "divine right." The quotation is from *Lycidas*, l. 106, referring to the hyacinth, whose petals were said to be marked by Apollo *ai, ai* (woe, woe) in memory of the youth Hyacinthus accidentally slain by the god.

[12] Thomson's *Castle of Indolence*, II, xxxiii. The next quotation is from I, lvii.

[13] Cf. *Hamlet*, III, iv, 153.

This long pendulous hair is peculiar to enthusiasts, to those whose minds tend heavenward; and is traditionally inseparable (though of a different colour) from the pictures of Christ. It ought to belong, as a character, to all who preach *Christ crucified*, and Coleridge was at that time one of those!

It was curious to observe the contrast between him and my father, who was a veteran in the cause, and then declining into the vale of years. He had been a poor Irish lad, carefully brought up by his parents, and sent to the University of Glasgow (where he studied under Adam Smith) to prepare him for his future destination. It was his mother's proudest wish to see her son a Dissenting Minister. So if we look back to past generations (as far as eye can reach) we see the same hopes, fears, wishes, followed by the same disappointments, throbbing in the human heart; and so we may see them (if we look forward) rising up for ever, and disappearing, like vapourish bubbles, in the human breast! After being tossed about from congregation to congregation in the heats of the Unitarian controversy, and squabbles about the American war, he had been relegated to an obscure village, where he was to spend the last thirty years of his life, far from the only converse that he loved, the talk about disputed texts of Scripture and the cause of civil and religious liberty. Here he passed his days, repining but resigned, in the study of the Bible, and the perusal of the Commentators,—huge folios, not easily got through, one of which would outlast a winter! Why did he pore on these from morn to night (with the exception of a walk in the fields or a turn in the garden to gather brocoli-plants or kidney-beans of his own rearing, with no small degree of pride and pleasure)?—Here were "no figures nor no fantasies,"[14]—neither poetry nor philosophy—nothing to dazzle, nothing to excite modern curiosity; but to his lack-lustre eyes there appeared, within the pages of the ponderous, unwieldy, neglected tomes, the sacred name of JEHOVAH in Hebrew capitals: pressed down by the weight of the style, worn to the last fading thinness of the understanding, there were glimpses, glimmering notions of the patriarchal wanderings, with palm-trees hovering in the horizon, and processions of camels at the distance of three thousand years; there was Moses with the Burning Bush, the number of the Twelve Tribes, types, shadows, glosses on the law and the prophets; there were discussions (dull enough) on the age of Methuselah, a mighty speculation! there were outlines, rude guesses at the shape of Noah's Ark and of the riches of Solomon's Temple; questions as to the date

of the creation, predictions of the end of all things; the great lapses of time, the strange mutations of the globe were unfolded with the voluminous leaf, as it turned over; and though the soul might slumber with an hieroglyphic veil of inscrutable mysteries drawn over it, yet it was in a slumber ill-exchanged for all the sharpened realities of sense, wit, fancy, or reason. My father's life was comparatively a dream; but it was a dream of infinity and eternity, of death, the resurrection, and a judgment to come!

No two individuals were ever more unlike than were the host and his guest. A poet was to my father a sort of nondescript: yet whatever added grace to the Unitarian cause was to him welcome. He could hardly have been more surprised or pleased, if our visitor had worn wings. Indeed, his thoughts had wings; and as the silken sounds rustled round our little wainscoted parlour, my father threw back his spectacles over his forehead, his white hairs mixing with its sanguine hue; and a smile of delight beamed across his rugged cordial face, to think that Truth had found a new ally in Fancy!* Besides, Coleridge seemed to take considerable notice of me, and that of itself was enough. He talked very familiarly, but agreeably, and glanced over a variety of subjects. At dinner-time he grew more animated, and dilated in a very edifying manner on Mary Wolstonecraft and Mackintosh.[15] The last, he said, he considered (on my father's speaking of his *Vindiciæ Gallicæ* as a capital performance) as a clever scholastic man—a master of the topics,—or as the ready warehouseman of letters, who knew exactly where to lay his hand on what he wanted, though the goods were not his own. He thought him no match for Burke, either in style or matter. Burke was a metaphysician, Mackintosh a mere logician. Burke was an orator (almost a poet) who reasoned in figures, because he had an eye for nature: Mackintosh, on the other hand, was a rhetorician, who had only an eye to common-places. On this I ventured to say that I had always entertained a great opinion of Burke, and that (as far as I could find) the speaking of him with contempt might be made the test of a vulgar democratical mind. This was the first observation I ever made to Coleridge, and

* My father was one of those who mistook his talent after all. He used to be very much dissatisfied that I preferred his Letters to his Sermons. The last were forced and dry: the first came naturally from him. For ease, half-plays on words, and a supine, monkish, indolent pleasantry, I have never seen them equalled.

[14] *Julius Caesar*, II, i, 231.

[15] Mary Wolstonecraft (1759–1797) was the wife of William Godwin and author of *Vindication of the Rights of Women* (1792). Sir James Mackintosh (1765–1832) was an important political figure and the author of *Vindiciae Gallicae* (1791), a defense of the French Revolution in reply to Burke's *Reflections*.

he said it was a very just and striking one. I remember the leg of Welsh mutton and the turnips on the table that day had the finest flavour imaginable. Coleridge added that Mackintosh and Tom. Wedgwood [16] (of whom, however, he spoke highly) had expressed a very indifferent opinion of his friend Mr. Wordsworth, on which he remarked to them—"He strides on so far before you, that he dwindles in the distance!" Godwin had once boasted to him of having carried on an argument with Mackintosh for three hours with dubious success; Coleridge told him—"If there had been a man of genius in the room, he would have settled the question in five minutes." He asked me if I had ever seen Mary Wolstonecraft, and I said, I had once for a few moments, and that she seemed to me to turn off Godwin's objections to something she advanced with quite a playful, easy air. He replied, that "this was only one instance of the ascendancy which people of imagination exercised over those of mere intellect." He did not rate Godwin very high* (this was caprice or prejudice, real or affected) but he had a great idea of Mrs. Wolstonecraft's powers of conversation, none at all of her talent for book-making. We talked a little about Holcroft. [17] He had been asked if he was not much struck *with* him, and he said, he thought himself in more danger of being struck *by* him. I complained that he would not let me get on at all, for he required a definition of every the commonest word, exclaiming, "What do you mean by a *sensation*, Sir? What do you mean by an *idea*?" This, Coleridge said, was barricadoing the road to truth:—it was setting up a turnpike-gate at every step we took. I forgot a great number of things, many more than I remember; but the day passed off pleasantly, and the next morning Mr. Coleridge was to return to Shrewsbury. When I came down to breakfast, I found that he had just received a letter from his friend, T. Wedgwood, making him an offer of £150. a-year if he chose to wave his present pursuit, and devote himself entirely to the study of poetry and philosophy. Coleridge seemed to make up his mind to close with this proposal in the act of tying on one of his shoes. It threw an additional damp on his departure. It took the wayward enthusiast quite from us to cast

him into Deva's winding vales, [18] or by the shores of old romance. Instead of living at ten miles distance, of being the pastor of a Dissenting congregation at Shrewsbury, he was henceforth to inhabit the Hill of Parnassus, to be a Shepherd on the Delectable Mountains. Alas! I knew not the way thither, and felt very little gratitude for Mr. Wedgwood's bounty. I was presently relieved from this dilemma; for Mr. Coleridge, asking for a pen and ink, and going to a table to write something on a bit of card, advanced towards me with undulating step, and giving me the precious document, said that that was his address, *Mr. Coleridge, Nether-Stowey, Somersetshire*; and that he should be glad to see me there in a few weeks' time, and, if I chose, would come half-way to meet me. I was not less surprised than the shepherd-boy (this simile is to be found in Cassandra) [19] when he sees a thunder-bolt fall close at his feet. I stammered out my acknowledgments and acceptance of this offer (I thought Mr. Wedgwood's annuity a trifle to it) as well as I could; and this mighty business being settled, the poet-preacher took leave, and I accompanied him six miles on the road. It was a fine morning in the middle of winter, and he talked the whole way. The scholar in Chaucer is described as going

——"Sounding on his way." [20]

So Coleridge went on his. In digressing, in dilating, in passing from subject to subject, he appeared to me to float in air, to slide on ice. He told me in confidence (going along) that he should have preached two sermons before he accepted the situation at Shrewsbury, one on Infant Baptism, the other on the Lord's Supper, shewing that he could not administer either, which would have effectually disqualified him for the object in view. I observed that he continually crossed me on the way by shifting from one side of the foot-path to the other. This struck me as an odd movement; but I did not at that time connect it with any instability of purpose or involuntary change of principle, as I have done since. He seemed unable to keep on in a strait line. He spoke slightingly of Hume (whose Essay on Miracles he said was stolen from an objection started in one of South's Sermons—*Credat Judæus Apella!*). [21] I was not

---

* He complained in particular of the presumption of his attempting to establish the future immortality of man, "without" (as he said) "knowing what Death was or what Life was"—and the tone in which he pronounced these two words seemed to convey a complete image of both.

---

[16] Thomas Wedgwood (1771–1805) was the son of the famous potter Josiah Wedgwood and an early admirer and supporter of Coleridge.

[17] Thomas Holcroft (1745–1805) was a playwright and political radical.

[18] Referring to the river Dee, which flows between England and Wales. Hazlitt is probably recalling Milton's *Lycidas*, l. 55, in which "Deva" is described as one of the haunts of the Muses.

[19] A popular romance published between 1642 and 1650, by La Calprenède, Gaultier de Coste, and frequently translated into English. The simile occurs in Part II, Book 5.

[20] Cf. Prologue to *Canterbury Tales*, l. 307, and Wordsworth's *Excursion*, III, 701.

[21] Robert South (1634–1716) was a popular Anglican preacher. His Sermons were collected in six volumes between 1679 and 1715. *Credat Judaeus Apella!*: "Let the Jew Apella believe it!" Horace's *Satires*, I, v, 101. According to popular Roman belief, the Jews were superstitious enough to believe anything.

very much pleased at this account of Hume, for I had just been reading, with infinite relish, that completest of all metaphysical *choke-pears*,[22] his *Treatise on Human Nature*, to which the *Essays*, in point of scholastic subtlety and close reasoning, are mere elegant trifling, light summer-reading. Coleridge even denied the excellence of Hume's general style, which I think betrayed a want of taste or candour. He however made me amends by the manner in which he spoke of Berkeley. He dwelt particularly on his *Essay on Vision* as a masterpiece of analytical reasoning. So it undoubtedly is. He was exceedingly angry with Dr. Johnson for striking the stone with his foot, in allusion to this author's Theory of Matter and Spirit, and saying, "Thus I confute him, Sir."[23] Coleridge drew a parallel (I don't know how he brought about the connection) between Bishop Berkeley and Tom Paine. He said the one was an instance of a subtle, the other of an acute mind, than which no two things could be more distinct. The one was a shop-boy's quality, the other the characteristic of a philosopher. He considered Bishop Butler[24] as a true philosopher, a profound and conscientious thinker, a genuine reader of nature and of his own mind. He did not speak of his *Analogy*, but of his *Sermons at the Rolls' Chapel*, of which I had never heard. Coleridge somehow always contrived to prefer the *unknown* to the *known*. In this instance he was right. The *Analogy* is a tissue of sophistry, of wiredrawn, theological special-pleading; the *Sermons* (with the Preface to them) are in a fine vein of deep, matured reflection, a candid appeal to our observation of human nature, without pedantry and without bias. I told Coleridge I had written a few remarks, and was sometimes foolish enough to believe that I had made a discovery on the same subject (the *Natural Disinterestedness of the Human Mind*)—and I tried to explain my view of it to Coleridge, who listened with great willingness, but I did not succeed in making myself understood. I sat down to the task shortly afterwards for the twentieth time, got new pens and paper, determined to make clear work of it, wrote a few meagre sentences in the skeleton-style of a mathematical demonstration, stopped half-way down the second page; and, after trying in vain to pump up any words, images, notions, apprehensions, facts, or observations, from that gulph of abstraction in which I had plunged myself for four or five years preceding, gave up the attempt as labour in vain, and shed tears of helpless despondency on the blank unfinished paper. I can write fast enough now. Am I better than I was then? Oh no! One truth discovered, one pang of regret at not being able to express it, is better than all the fluency and flippancy in the world. Would that I could go back to what I then was! Why can we not revive past times as we can revisit old places? If I had the quaint Muse of Sir Philip Sidney to assist me, I would write a *Sonnet to the Road between W——m and Shrewsbury*, and immortalise every step of it by some fond enigmatical conceit. I would swear that the very milestones had ears, and that Harmer-hill stooped with all its pines, to listen to a poet, as he passed! I remember but one other topic of discourse in this walk. He mentioned Paley,[25] praised the naturalness and clearness of his style, but condemned his sentiments, thought him a mere time-serving casuist, and said that "the fact of his work on Moral and Political Philosophy being made a text-book in our Universities was a disgrace to the national character." We parted at the six-mile stone; and I returned homeward pensive but much pleased. I had met with unexpected notice from a person, whom I believed to have been prejudiced against me. "Kind and affable to me had been his condescension, and should be honoured ever with suitable regard."[26] He was the first poet I had known, and he certainly answered to that inspired name. I had heard a great deal of his powers of conversation, and was not disappointed. In fact, I never met with any thing at all like them, either before or since. I could easily credit the accounts which were circulated of his holding forth to a large party of ladies and gentlemen, an evening or two before, on the Berkeleian Theory, when he made the whole material universe look like a transparency of fine words; and another story (which I believe he has somewhere told himself) of his being asked to a party at Birmingham, of his smoking tobacco and going to sleep after dinner on a sofa, where the company found him to their no small surprise, which was increased to wonder when he started up of a sudden, and rubbing his eyes, looked about him, and launched into a three-hours' description of the third heaven, of which he had had a dream, very different from Mr. Southey's Vision of Judgment, and also from that other Vision of Judgment, which Mr. Murray, the Secretary of the

---

[22] Objects unpalatable and hard to "swallow," here referring to the difficulty in comprehending the complexities of Hume's argument.

[23] Berkeley's *Essay towards a New Theory of Vision* was published in 1709, his *Theory of Vision* in 1733. For the reference to Dr. Johnson, see Boswell's *Life of Johnson*, entry for August 6, 1763.

[24] Joseph Butler (1692–1752) was a preacher and moralist, whose *Fifteen Sermons* (1726) and *The Analogy of Religion* (1736) were influential religious texts into the nineteenth century.

[25] William Paley (1743–1805) was a popular theologian and philosopher. His *Moral and Political Philosophy* (1785) was an exposition of Christian doctrine in utilitarian terms.

[26] *Paradise Lost*, VIII, 648–50.

Bridge-street Junto, has taken into his especial keeping![27]

On my way back, I had a sound in my ears, it was the voice of Fancy: I had a light before me, it was the face of Poetry. The one still lingers there, the other has not quitted my side! Coleridge in truth met me half-way on the ground of philosophy, or I should not have been won over to his imaginative creed. I had an uneasy, pleasurable sensation all the time, till I was to visit him. During those months the chill breath of winter gave me a welcoming; the vernal air was balm and inspiration to me. The golden sun-sets, the silver star of evening, lighted me on my way to new hopes and prospects. *I was to visit Coleridge in the Spring.* This circumstance was never absent from my thoughts, and mingled with all my feelings. I wrote to him at the time proposed, and received an answer postponing my intended visit for a week or two, but very cordially urging me to complete my promise then. This delay did not damp, but rather increase my ardour. In the mean time, I went to Llangollen Vale,[28] by way of initiating myself in the mysteries of natural scenery; and I must say I was enchanted with it. I had been reading Coleridge's description of England, in his fine *Ode on the Departing Year*, and I applied it, *con amore*, to the objects before me. That valley was to me (in a manner) the cradle of a new existence: in the river that winds through it, my spirit was baptised in the waters of Helicon!

I returned home, and soon after set out on my journey with unworn heart and untried feet. My way lay through Worcester and Gloucester, and by Upton, where I thought of Tom Jones and the adventure of the muff.[29] I remember getting completely wet through one day, and stopping at an inn (I think it was at Tewkesbury) where I sat up all night to read Paul and Virginia. Sweet were the showers in early youth that drenched my body, and sweet the drops of pity that fell upon the books I read! I recollect a remark of Coleridge's upon this very book, that nothing could shew the gross indelicacy of French manners and the entire corruption of their imagination more strongly than the behaviour of the heroine in the last fatal scene, who turns away from a person on board the sinking vessel, that offers to save her life, because he has thrown off his clothes to assist him in swimming. Was this a time to think of such a circumstance? I once hinted to Wordsworth, as we were sailing in his boat on Grasmere lake, that I thought he had borrowed the idea of his *Poems on the Naming of Places*[30] from the local inscriptions of the same kind in Paul and Virginia. He did not own the obligation, and stated some distinction without a difference, in defence of his claim to originality. Any the slightest variation would be sufficient for this purpose in his mind; for whatever *he* added or omitted would inevitably be worth all that any one else had done, and contain the marrow of the sentiment.—I was still two days before the time fixed for my arrival, for I had taken care to set out early enough. I stopped these two days at Bridgewater, and when I was tired of sauntering on the banks of its muddy river, returned to the inn, and read Camilla. So have I loitered my life away, reading books, looking at pictures, going to plays, hearing, thinking, writing on what pleased me best. I have wanted only one thing to make me happy; but wanting that, have wanted every thing![31]

I arrived, and was well received. The country about Nether Stowey is beautiful, green and hilly, and near the sea-shore. I saw it but the other day, after an interval of twenty years, from a hill near Taunton. How was the map of my life spread out before me, as the map of the country lay at my feet! In the afternoon, Coleridge took me over to All-Foxden, a romantic old family-mansion of the St. Aubins, where Wordsworth lived. It was then in the possession of a friend of the poet's, who gave him the free use of it. Somehow that period (the time just after the French Revolution) was not a time when *nothing was given for nothing*. The mind opened, and a softness might be perceived coming over the heart of individuals, beneath "the scales that fence" our self-interest. Wordsworth himself was from home, but his sister kept house, and set before us a frugal repast; and we had free access to her brother's poems, the *Lyrical Ballads*, which were still in manuscript, or in the form of *Sybilline Leaves*.[32] I dipped into a few of these with great satisfaction, and with the faith of a novice. I slept that night in an old room with blue hangings, and covered with the round-faced family-portraits of the age of George I. and II. and

[27] Charles Murray, an officer of the Constitutional Association for opposing Disloyal and Seditious Principles ("the Bridge-Street Gang"), had brought charges against John Hunt for publishing Byron's *Vision of Judgment* (1822) as a "gross, impious, and slanderous" libel on the memory of George III. Byron's *Vision* was a parody of Southey's fulsome poem of the same title published in 1821 in honor of the death of the monarch.

[28] See "On Going a Journey," pp. 458–59, for another account of the events mentioned here and in the next paragraph.

[29] See *Tom Jones*, Book X, Chapters 5 and 6.

[30] *Poems on the Naming of Places*, a group of poems first appearing in the 1800 edition of *Lyrical Ballads*.

[31] Possibly a reference to his recent disastrous infatuation for Sarah Walker, or to the defeat of his political hopes at Waterloo.

[32] Scattered jottings or fragments; a reference to the prophecies of the Sibyl written on leaves, which were accordingly easily dispersed (*Aeneid*, VI, 74–75). Coleridge so entitled a collection of his poems in 1817.

from the wooded declivity of the adjoining park that overlooked my window, at the dawn of day, could

——"hear the loud stag speak."[33]

In the outset of life (and particularly at this time I felt it so) our imagination has a body to it. We are in a state between sleeping and waking, and have indistinct but glorious glimpses of strange shapes, and there is always something to come better than what we see. As in our dreams the fulness of the blood gives warmth and reality to the coinage of the brain, so in youth our ideas are clothed, and fed, and pampered with our good spirits; we breathe thick with thoughtless happiness, the weight of future years presses on the strong pulses of the heart, and we repose with undisturbed faith in truth and good. As we advance, we exhaust our fund of enjoyment and of hope. We are no longer wrapped in *lamb's-wool*, lulled in Elysium. As we taste the pleasures of life, their spirit evaporates, the sense palls; and nothing is left but the phantoms, the lifeless shadows of what *has been*!

That morning, as soon as breakfast was over, we strolled out into the park, and seating ourselves on the trunk of an old ash-tree that stretched along the ground, Coleridge read aloud with a sonorous and musical voice, the ballad of *Betty Foy*.[34] I was not critically or sceptically inclined. I saw touches of truth and nature, and took the rest for granted. But in the *Thorn*, the *Mad Mother*, and the *Complaint of a Poor Indian Woman*, I felt that deeper power and pathos which have been since acknowledged,

"In spite of pride, in erring reason's spite,"[35]

as the characteristics of this author; and the sense of a new style and a new spirit in poetry came over me. It had to me something of the effect that arises from the turning up of the fresh soil, or of the first welcome breath of Spring,

"While yet the trembling year is unconfirmed."[36]

Coleridge and myself walked back to Stowey that evening, and his voice sounded high

"Of Providence, foreknowledge, will, and fate,
Fix'd fate, free-will, foreknowledge absolute,"[37]

as we passed through echoing grove, by fairy stream or waterfall, gleaming in the summer moonlight! He lamented that Wordsworth was not prone enough to

belief in the traditional superstitions of the place, and that there was a something corporeal, a *matter-of-fact-ness*, a clinging to the palpable, or often to the petty, in his poetry,[38] in consequence. His genius was not a spirit that descended to him through the air; it sprung out of the ground like a flower, or unfolded itself from a green spray, on which the gold-finch sang. He said, however (if I remember right) that this objection must be confined to his descriptive pieces, that his philosophic poetry had a grand and comprehensive spirit in it, so that his soul seemed to inhabit the universe like a palace, and to discover truth by intuition, rather than by deduction. The next day Wordsworth arrived from Bristol at Coleridge's cottage. I think I see him now. He answered in some degree to his friend's description of him, but was more gaunt and Don Quixote-like. He was quaintly dressed (according to the *costume* of that unconstrained period) in a brown fustian jacket and striped pantaloons. There was something of a roll, a lounge in his gait, not unlike his own Peter Bell. There was a severe, worn pressure of thought about his temples, a fire in his eye (as if he saw something in objects more than the outward appearance) an intense high narrow forehead, a Roman nose, cheeks furrowed by strong purpose and feeling, and a convulsive inclination to laughter about the mouth, a good deal at variance with the solemn, stately expression of the rest of his face. Chantry's bust[39] wants the marking traits; but he was teazed into making it regular and heavy: Haydon's head of him, introduced into the *Entrance of Christ into Jerusalem*,[40] is the most like his drooping weight of thought and expression. He sat down and talked very naturally and freely, with a mixture of clear gushing accents in his voice, a deep guttural intonation, and a strong tincture of the northern *burr*, like the crust on wine. He instantly began to make havoc of the half of a Cheshire cheese on the table, and said trimphantly that "his marriage with experience had not been so unproductive as Mr. Southey's in teaching him a knowledge of the good things of this life." He had been to see the *Castle Spectre* by Monk Lewis,[41] while at Bristol, and described it very well. He said "it fitted the taste of the audience like a glove." This *ad captandum*[42]

---

[33] Ben Jonson's "To Sir Robert Wroth," l. 22, in *The Forrest* (1616).
[34] "The Idiot Boy," published in *Lyrical Ballads* (1798).
[35] Pope's *Essay on Man*, I, 293.
[36] Thomson's "Spring," l. 18.
[37] *Paradise Lost*, II, 559–60.

[38] See *Biographia Literaria*, Chapter XXII, above, pp. 223–24.
[39] Refers to Sir Francis Chantrey (1781–1841), whose bust of Wordsworth was exhibited in 1821.
[40] A grandiose painting exhibited in 1820, in which a number of Haydon's contemporaries, including Keats and Hazlitt as well as Wordsworth, are represented. (The painting is now in St. Gregory Seminary, Cincinnati.)
[41] Gothic play, first presented in London in 1797, by Matthew Lewis (1775–1818), author of the sensational novel *The Monk* (1796).
[42] *ad captandum*: "for capturing [the attention of the audience]."

merit was however by no means a recommendation of it, according to the severe principles of the new school, which reject rather than court popular effect. Wordsworth, looking out of the low, latticed window, said "How beautifully the sun sets on that yellow bank!" I thought within myself, "With what eyes these poets see nature!" and ever after, when I saw the sun-set stream upon the objects facing it, conceived I had made a discovery, or thanked Mr. Wordsworth for having made one for me! We went over to All-Foxden again the day following, and Wordsworth read us the story of Peter Bell in the open air; and the comment made upon it by his face and voice was very different from that of some later critics![43] Whatever might be thought of the poem, "his face was as a book where men might read strange matters,"[44] and he announced the fate of his hero in prophetic tones. There is a *chaunt* in the recitation both of Coleridge and Wordsworth, which acts as a spell upon the hearer, and disarms the judgment. Perhaps they have deceived themselves by making habitual use of this ambiguous accompaniment. Coleridge's manner is more full, animated, and varied; Wordsworth's more equable, sustained, and internal. The one might be termed more *dramatic*, the other more *lyrical*. Coleridge has told me that he himself liked to compose in walking over uneven ground, or breaking through the straggling branches of a copsewood; whereas Wordsworth always wrote (if he could) walking up and down a strait gravel-walk, or in some spot where the continuity of his verse met with no collateral interruption. Returning that same evening, I got into a metaphysical argument with Wordsworth, while Coleridge was explaining the different notes of the nightingale to his sister, in which we neither of us succeeded in making ourselves perfectly clear and intelligible. Thus I passed three weeks at Nether Stowey and in the neighbourhood, generally devoting the afternoons to a delightful chat in an arbour made of bark by the poet's friend Tom Poole,[45] sitting under two fine elm-trees, and listening to the bees humming round us, while we quaffed our *flip*.[46] It was agreed, among other things, that we should make a jaunt down the Bristol-Channel, as far as Linton. We set off together on foot, Coleridge, John Chester, and I. This Chester was a native of Nether Stowey, one of those who were attracted to Coleridge's discourse as flies are to honey, or bees in swarming-time to the sound of a brass pan. He "followed in the chace, like a dog who hunts, not like one that made up the cry."[47] He had on a brown cloth coat, boots, and corduroy breeches, was low in stature, bow-legged, had a drag in his walk like a drover, which he assisted by a hazel switch, and kept on a sort of trot by the side of Coleridge, like a running footman by a state coach, that he might not lose a syllable or sound, that fell from Coleridge's lips. He told me his private opinion, that Coleridge was a wonderful man. He scarcely opened his lips, much less offered an opinion the whole way: yet of the three, had I to chuse during that journey, I would be John Chester. He afterwards followed Coleridge into Germany, where the Kantean philosophers were puzzled how to bring him under any of their categories. When he sat down at table with his idol, John's felicity was complete; Sir Walter Scott's, or Mr. Blackwood's, when they sat down at the same table with the King, was not more so.[48] We passed Dunster on our right, a small town between the brow of a hill and the sea. I remember eyeing it wistfully as it lay below us: contrasted with the woody scene around, it looked as clear, as pure, as *embrowned* and ideal as any landscape I have seen since, of Gaspar Poussin's[49] or Domenichino's. We had a long day's march—(our feet kept time to the echoes of Coleridge's tongue)—through Minehead and by the Blue Anchor, and on to Linton, which we did not reach till near midnight, and where we had some difficulty in making a lodgment. We however knocked the people of the house up at last, and we were repaid for our apprehensions and fatigue by some excellent rashers of fried bacon and eggs. The view in coming along had been splendid. We walked for miles and miles on dark brown heaths overlooking the channel, with the Welsh hills beyond, and at times descended into little sheltered valleys close by the sea-side, with a smuggler's face scowling by us, and then had to ascend conical hills with a path winding up through a coppice to a barren top, like a monk's shaven crown, from one of which I pointed out to Coleridge's notice the bare masts of a vessel on the very edge of the horizon and within the red-orbed disk of the setting sun, like his own spectre-ship in the *Ancient Mariner*. At Linton the character of the sea-coast becomes more marked and rugged. There is a place called the *Valley of Rocks* (I suspect this was

---

43 When Wordsworth finally published *Peter Bell* in 1819, it was hostilely reviewed and provoked a number of parodies and burlesques including Shelley's "Peter Bell the Third."

44 *Macbeth*, I, v, 63–64.

45 Tom Poole (1765–1837), a tanner and farmer, was one of Coleridge's most devoted friends and admirers. Poole was largely responsible for Coleridge's removal to Nether Stowey in 1796, where they were next-door neighbors.

46 A hot punch of beer and spirits.

47 *Othello*, II, iii, 369–70.

48 Refers to the visit of George IV to Scotland in 1822, at which Scott presided as master of ceremonies. William Blackwood (1776–1834) was Edinburgh publisher of the Tory *Blackwood's Magazine*.

49 Gaspar Dughet (1615–1675) was a French-Italian landscape painter, brother-in-law to Nicholas Poussin.

only the poetical name for it) bedded among precipices overhanging the sea, with rocky caverns beneath, into which the waves dash, and where the sea-gull for ever wheels its screaming flight. On the tops of these are huge stones thrown transverse, as if an earthquake had tossed them there, and behind these is a fretwork of perpendicular rocks, something like the *Giant's Causeway*. A thunder-storm came on while we were at the inn, and Coleridge was running out bareheaded to enjoy the commotion of the elements in the *Valley of Rocks*, but as if in spite, the clouds only muttered a few angry sounds, and let fall a few refreshing drops. Coleridge told me that he and Wordsworth were to have made this place the scene of a prose-tale, which was to have been in the manner of, but far superior to, the *Death of Abel*,[50] but they had relinquished the design. In the morning of the second day, we breakfasted luxuriously in an old-fashioned parlour, on tea, toast, eggs, and honey, in the very sight of the bee-hives from which it had been taken, and a garden full of thyme and wild flowers that had produced it. On this occasion Coleridge spoke of Virgil's Georgics, but not well. I do not think he had much feeling for the classical or elegant. It was in this room that we found a little worn-out copy of the *Seasons*, lying in a window-seat, on which Coleridge exclaimed, "*That* is true fame!" He said Thomson was a great poet, rather than a good one; his style was as meretricious as his thoughts were natural. He spoke of Cowper as the best modern poet. He said the *Lyrical Ballads* were an experiment about to be tried by him and Wordsworth, to see how far the public taste would endure poetry written in a more natural and simple style than had hitherto been attempted; totally discarding the artifices of poetical diction, and making use only of such words as had probably been common in the most ordinary language since the days of Henry II. Some comparison was introduced between Shakespear and Milton. He said "he hardly knew which to prefer. Shakespear seemed to him a mere stripling in the art; he was as tall and as strong, with infinitely more activity than Milton, but he never appeared to have come to man's estate; or if he had, he would not have been a man, but a monster." He spoke with contempt of Gray, and with intolerance of Pope. He did not like the versification of the latter. He observed that "the ears of these couplet-writers might be charged with having short memories, that could not retain the harmony of whole passages." He

thought little of Junius as a writer; he had a dislike of Dr. Johnson; and a much higher opinion of Burke as an orator and politician, than of Fox or Pitt. He however thought him very inferior in richness of style and imagery to some of our elder prose-writers, particularly Jeremy Taylor. He liked Richardson, but not Fielding; nor could I get him to enter into the merits of *Caleb Williams*.* In short, he was profound and discriminating with respect to those authors whom he liked, and where he gave his judgment fair play; capricious, perverse, and prejudiced in his antipathies and distastes. We loitered on the "ribbed sea-sands,"[52] in such talk as this, a whole morning, and I recollect met with a curious sea-weed, of which John Chester told us the country name! A fisherman gave Coleridge an account of a boy that had been drowned the day before, and that they had tried to save him at the risk of their own lives. He said "he did not know how it was that they ventured, but, Sir, we have a *nature* towards one another." This expression, Coleridge remarked to me, was a fine illustration of that theory of disinterestedness which I (in common with Butler) had adopted. I broached to him an argument of mine to prove that *likeness* was not mere association of ideas. I said that the mark in the sand put one in mind of a man's foot, not because it was part of a former impression of a man's foot (for it was quite new) but because it was like the shape of a man's foot. He assented to the justness of this distinction (which I have explained at length elsewhere,[53] for the benefit of the curious) and John Chester listened; not from any interest in the subject, but because he was astonished that I should be able to suggest any thing to Coleridge that he did not already know. We returned on the third morning, and Coleridge remarked the silent cottage-smoke curling up the valleys where, a few evenings before, we had seen the lights gleaming through the dark.

---

* He had no idea of pictures, of Claude or Raphael, and at this time I had as little as he. He sometimes gives a striking account at present of the Cartoons at Pisa, by Buffamalco and others; of one in particular, where Death is seen in the air brandishing his scythe, and the great and the mighty of the earth shudder at his approach, while the beggars and the wretched kneel to him as their deliverer. He would of course understand so broad and fine a moral as this at any time.[51]

---

50 The prose-tale referred to is "The Wanderings of Cain," first published by Coleridge in 1828. *The Death of Abel* was a very popular biblical epic of 1758 by the Swiss author Solomon Gessner (1730–1788); it was written in a form of "poetic" prose. See Leigh Hunt's "An Answer to the Question What is Poetry?", footnote 35, p. 547.

51 The Cartoons at Pisa were the famous frescoes of the Campo Santo cemetery by various artists. Buonamico Cristofani ("Buffalmacco") was a Florentine painter of the fourteenth century. The attribution of the frescoes to him is now debatable. Coleridge saw the frescoes during his visit to Italy in 1806, and praised them in his Philosophical Lectures delivered in London in 1819. *Caleb Williams* was a novel of 1794 by William Godwin.

52 *Ancient Mariner*, l. 227.

53 In "Remarks on the Systems of Hartley and Helvetius" appended to *Essay on the Principles of Human Action*.

In a day or two after we arrived at Stowey, we set out, I on my return home, and he for Germany. It was a Sunday morning, and he was to preach that day for Dr. Toulmin of Taunton. I asked him if he had prepared any thing for the occasion? He said he had not even thought of the text, but should as soon as we parted. I did not go to hear him,—this was a fault,—but we met in the evening at Bridgewater. The next day we had a long day's walk to Bristol, and sat down, I recollect, by a well-side on the road, to cool ourselves and satisfy our thirst, when Coleridge repeated to me some descriptive lines from his tragedy of Remorse; which I must say became his mouth and that occasion better than they, some years after, did Mr. Elliston's and the Drury-lane boards,[54]—

"Oh memory! shield me from the world's poor strife,
And give those scenes thine everlasting life."

I saw no more of him for a year or two, during which period he had been wandering in the Hartz Forest in Germany; and his return was cometary, meteorous, unlike his setting out. It was not till some time after that I knew his friends Lamb and Southey. The last always appears to me (as I first saw him) with a common-place book under his arm, and the first with a *bon-mot* in his mouth. It was at Godwin's that I met him with Holcroft and Coleridge, where they were disputing fiercely which was the best—*Man as he was, or man as he is to be.* "Give me," says Lamb, "man as he is *not* to be." This saying was the beginning of a friendship between us, which I believe still continues. —Enough of this for the present.

"But there is matter for another rhyme,
And I to this may add a second tale."[55]

[April 1823]

FROM

A REVIEW: SHELLEY'S *POSTHUMOUS POEMS*[1]

MR SHELLEY'S style is to poetry what astrology is to natural science—a passionate dream, a straining after impossibilities, a record of fond conjectures, a confused embodying of vague abstractions,—a fever of the soul, thirsting and craving after what it cannot have, indulging its love of power and novelty at the expense of truth and nature, associating ideas by contraries, and wasting great powers by their application to unattainable objects.

Poetry, we grant, creates a world of its own; but it creates it out of existing materials. Mr. Shelley is the maker of his own poetry—out of nothing. Not that he is deficient in the true sources of strength and beauty, if he had given himself fair play (the volume before us, as well as his other productions, contains many proofs to the contrary): But, in him, fancy, will, caprice, predominated over and absorbed the natural influences of things; and he had no respect for any poetry that did not strain the intellect as well as fire the imagination—and was not sublimed into a high spirit of metaphysical philosophy. Instead of giving a language to thought, or lending the heart a tongue, he utters dark sayings, and deals in allegories and riddles. His Muse offers her services to clothe shadowy doubts and inscrutable difficulties in a robe of glittering words, and to turn nature into a brilliant paradox. We thank him—but we must be excused. Where we see the dazzling beacon-lights streaming over the darkness of the abyss, we dread the quicksands and the rocks below. Mr Shelley's mind was of "too fiery a quality"[2] to repose (for any continuance) on the probable or the true—it soared "beyond the visible diurnal sphere,"[3] to the strange, the improbable, and the impossible. He mistook the nature of the poet's calling, which should be guided by involuntary, not by voluntary impulses. He shook off, as an heroic and praiseworthy act, the trammels of sense, custom, and sympathy, and became the creature of his own will. He was "all air," disdaining the bars and ties of mortal mould. He ransacked his brain for incongruities, and believed in whatever was incredible. Almost all is effort, almost all is extravagant, almost all is quaint, incomprehensible, and abortive, from aiming to be more than it is. Epithets are applied, because they do not fit: subjects are chosen, because they are repulsive: the colours of his style, for their gaudy, changeful, startling effect, resemble the display of fire-works in the dark, and, like them, have neither durability, nor keeping, nor discriminate form. Yet Mr Shelley, with all his faults, was a man of genius; and we lament that uncontrollable violence of temperament which gave it a forced and false direction. He has single thoughts of great depth and force, single images of rare beauty, detached passages of extreme tenderness; and, in his

---

54 Coleridge's tragedy *Remorse* was written at Nether Stowey in 1797 and then entitled *Osorio*; it was presented in London to considerable success in 1813. Robert W. Elliston (1774-1831), one of the leading actors of the London stage, played the role of Don Alvar.

55 Wordsworth's "Hart-leap Well," ll. 95-96.

1 Hazlitt's review appeared in *The Edinburgh Review*, XL (July 1824).

2 See *King Lear*, II, iv, 93.

3 See *Paradise Lost*, VII, 22.

smaller pieces, where he has attempted little, he has done most. If some casual and interesting idea touched his feelings or struck his fancy, he expressed it in pleasing and unaffected verse: but give him a larger subject, and time to reflect, and he was sure to get entangled in a system. The fumes of vanity rolled volumes of smoke, mixed with sparkles of fire, from the cloudy tabernacle of his thought. The success of his writings is therefore in general in the inverse ratio of the extent of his undertakings; inasmuch as his desire to teach, his ambition to excel, as soon as it was brought into play, encroached upon, and outstripped his powers of execution.

Mr Shelley was a remarkable man. His person was a type and shadow of his genius. His complexion, fair, golden, freckled, seemed transparent with an inward light, and his spirit within him

> ——"so divinely wrought,
> That you might almost say his body thought."[4]

He reminded those who saw him of some of Ovid's fables. His form, graceful and slender, drooped like a flower in the breeze. But he was crushed beneath the weight of thought which he aspired to bear, and was withered in the lightning-glare of a ruthless philosophy! He mistook the nature of his own faculties and feelings—the lowly children of the valley, by which the skylark makes its bed, and the bee murmurs, for the proud cedar or the mountain-pine, in which the eagle builds its eyry, "and dallies with the wind, and scorns the sun."[5]—He wished to make of idle verse and idler prose the frame-work of the universe, and to bind all possible existence in the visionary chain of intellectual beauty—

> "More subtle web Arachne cannot spin,
> Nor the fine nets, which oft we woven see
> Of scorched dew, do not in th' air more lightly flee."[6]

Perhaps some lurking sense of his own deficiencies in the lofty walk which he attempted, irritated his impatience and his desires; and urged him on, with winged hopes, to atone for past failures, by more arduous efforts, and more unavailing struggles.

With all his faults, Mr Shelley was an honest man. His unbelief and his presumption were parts of a disease, which was not combined in him either with indifference to human happiness, or contempt for human infirmities. There was neither selfishness nor malice at the bottom of his illusions. He was sincere in

all his professions; and he practised what he preached —to his own sufficient cost. He followed up the letter and the spirit of his theoretical principles in his own person, and was ready to share both the benefit and the penalty with others. He thought and acted logically, and was what he professed to be, a sincere lover of truth, of nature, and of human kind. To all the rage of paradox, he united an unaccountable candour and severity of reasoning: in spite of an aristocratic education, he retained in his manners the simplicity of a primitive apostle. An Epicurean in his sentiments, he lived with the frugality and abstemiousness of an ascetick. His fault was, that he had no deference for the opinions of others, too little sympathy with their feelings (which he thought he had a right to sacrifice, as well as his own, to a grand ethical experiment)— and trusted too implicitly to the light of his own mind, and to the warmth of his own impulses. He was indeed the most striking example we remember of the two extremes described by Lord Bacon as the great impediments to human improvement, the love of Novelty, and the love of Antiquity.

"The first of these (impediments) is an extreme affection of two extremities, the one Antiquity, the other Novelty; wherein it seemeth the children of time do take after the nature and malice of the father. For as he devoureth his children, so one of them seeketh to devour and suppress the other; while Antiquity envieth there should be new additions, and Novelty cannot be content to add, but it may deface. Surely the advice of the Prophet is the true direction in this matter: *Stand upon the old ways, and see which is the right and good way, and walk therein.* Antiquity deserveth that reverence, that men should make a stand thereupon, and discover what is the best way; but when the discovery is well taken, then to take progression. And to speak truly, *Antiquitas seculi Juventas mundi.* These times are the ancient times, when the world is ancient, and not those which we count ancient, *ordine retrogrado*, by a computation backwards from ourselves." (Advancement of Learning, Book I. p. 46.)—

Such is the text: and Mr Shelley's writings are a splendid commentary on one half of it. Considered in this point of view, his career may not be uninstructive even to those whom it most offended; and might be held up as a beacon and warning no less to the bigot than the sciolist. We wish to speak of the errors of a man of genius with tenderness. His nature was kind, and his sentiments noble; but in him the rage of free inquiry and private judgment amounted to a species of madness. Whatever was new, untried, unheard of, unauthorized, exerted a kind of fascination over his mind. The examples of the world, the opinion of others, instead of acting as a check upon him, served but to impel him forward with double velocity in his

---

4 Donne's *Of the Progresse of the Soule. The Second Anniversarie*, ll. 245–46.
5 *Richard the Third*, I, iii, 265.
6 *Faerie Queene*, II, xii, 77.

wild and hazardous career. Spurning the world of realities, he rushed into the world of nonentities and contingencies, like air into a *vacuum*. If a thing was old and established, this was with him a certain proof of its having no solid foundation to rest upon: if it was new, it was good and right. Every paradox was to him a self-evident truth; every prejudice an undoubted absurdity. The weight of authority, the sanction of ages, the common consent of mankind, were vouchers only for ignorance, error, and imposture. Whatever shocked the feelings of others, conciliated his regard; whatever was light, extravagant, and vain, was to him a proportionable relief from the dulness and stupidity of established opinions. The worst of it however was, that he thus gave great encouragement to those who believe in all received absurdities, and are wedded to all existing abuses: his extravagance seeming to sanction their grossness and selfishness, as theirs were a full justification of his folly and eccentricity. The two extremes in this way often meet, jostle,—and confirm one another. The infirmities of age are a foil to the presumption of youth; and "there the antics sit,"[7] mocking one another—the ape Sophistry pointing with reckless scorn at "palsied eld,"[8] and the bed-rid hag, Legitimacy, rattling her chains, counting her beads, dipping her hands in blood, and blessing herself from all change and from every appeal to common sense and reason! Opinion thus alternates in a round of contradictions: the impatience or obstinacy of the human mind takes part with, and flies off to one or other of the two extremes "of affection" and leaves a horrid gap, a blank sense and feeling in the middle, which seems never likely to be filled up, without a total change in our mode of proceeding. The martello-towers[9] with which we are to repress, if we cannot destroy, the systems of fraud and oppression should not be castles in the air, or clouds in the verge of the horizon, but the enormous and accumulated pile of abuses which have arisen out of their own continuance. The principles of sound morality, liberty and humanity, are not to be found only in a few recent writers, who have discovered the secret of the greatest happiness to the greatest numbers, but are truths as old as the creation. To be convinced of the existence of wrong, we should read history rather than poetry: the levers with which we must work out our regeneration are not the cobwebs of the brain, but the warm, palpitating fibres of the human heart. It is the collision of pas-

sions and interests, the petulance of party-spirit, and the perversities of self-will and self-opinion that have been the great obstacles to social improvement—not stupidity or ignorance; and the caricaturing one side of the question and shocking the most pardonable prejudices on the other, is not the way to allay hearts or produce unanimity. By flying to the extremes of scepticism, we make others shrink back, and shut themselves up in the strongholds of bigotry and superstition—by mixing up doubtful or offensive matters with salutary and demonstrable truths, we bring the whole into question, fly-blow the cause, risk the principle, and give a handle and a pretext to the enemy to treat all philosophy and all reform as a compost of crude, chaotic, and monstrous absurdities. We thus arm the virtues as well as the vices of the community against us; we trifle with their understandings, and exasperate their self-love; we give to superstition and injustice all their old security and sanctity, as if they were the only alternatives of impiety and profligacy, and league the natural with the selfish prejudices of mankind in hostile array against us. To this consummation, it must be confessed that too many of Mr Shelley's productions pointedly tend. He makes no account of the opinions of others, or the consequences of any of his own; but proceeds—tasking his reason to the utmost to account for every thing, and discarding every thing as mystery and error for which he cannot account by an effort of mere intelligence—measuring man, providence, nature, and even his own heart, by the limits of the understanding—now hallowing high mysteries, now desecrating pure sentiments, according as they fall in with or exceeded those limits; and exalting and purifying, with Promethean heat, whatever he does not confound and debase.

Mr Shelley died, it seems, with a volume of Mr Keats's poetry grasped with one hand in his bosom! These are two out of four poets, patriots and friends,[10] who have visited Italy within a few years, both of whom have been soon hurried to a more distant shore. Keats died young; and "yet his infelicity had years too many." A canker had blighted the tender bloom that o'erspread a face in which youth and genius strove with beauty. The shaft was sped—venal, vulgar, venomous, that drove him from his country, with sickness and penury for companions, and followed him to his grave. And yet there are those who could trample on the faded flower—men to whom breaking hearts are a subject of merriment—who laugh loud over the silent urn of Genius, and play out their game of

---

[7] *Richard the Second*, III, ii, 162.

[8] *Measure for Measure*, III, i, 36.

[9] Symbols of invincible strength and defense, named from the fortress at Cape Martella in Corsica under repeated attack by the British naval forces in 1794.

---

[10] The other two were, of course, Byron and Leigh Hunt. The next quotation is from *The Duchess of Malfi*, IV, ii.

venality and infamy with the crumbling bones of their victims! To this band of immortals a third [11] has since been added!—a mightier genius, a haughtier spirit, whose stubborn impatience and Achilles-like pride only Death could quell. Greece, Italy, the world, have lost their poet-hero; and his death has spread a wider gloom, and been recorded with a deeper awe, than has waited on the obsequies of any of the many great who have died in our remembrance. Even detraction has been silent at his tomb; and the more generous of his enemies have fallen into the rank of his mourners. But he set like the sun in his glory; and his orb was greatest and brightest at the last; for his memory is now consecrated no less by freedom than genius. He probably fell a martyr to his zeal against tyrants. He attached himself to the cause of Greece, and dying, clung to it with a convulsive grasp, and has thus gained a niche in her history; for whatever *she* claims as hers is immortal, even in decay, as the marble sculptures on the columns of her fallen temples!

*   *   *   *   *

[July 1824]

THE SPIRIT OF THE AGE

Hazlitt's major masterpiece began as a series of five articles in the New Monthly Magazine *in 1824. In its three editions of 1825,* The Spirit of the Age *surveyed twenty-five of the leading figures of the early nineteenth century: creative writers (Coleridge, Wordsworth, Byron, Scott, Southey, Lamb, Thomas Moore, Leigh Hunt, Thomas Campbell, Crabbe, Washington Irving), politicians (Horne Tooke, Sir James Mackintosh, George Canning, Henry Brougham, Sir Francis Burdett, Lord Eldon, William Cobbett, William Wilberforce), social and political philosophers (Bentham, Godwin, Malthus), literary critics (Jeffrey and Gifford), and the preacher Edward Irving. Herschel Baker has said of the collection:*

> *If in some unimaginable holocaust all the other literary arti-facts of early nineteenth-century England were destroyed, it would help us gauge our loss, for hardly any other book de-lineates with such precision and perception the contour of the age . . . Hazlitt chose to write on men who, important in and for themselves, were also emblematic of the time.*

Although the title phrase is used with little consistency of meaning throughout the essays, there is one constant theme in Hazlitt's treatment of his diverse subjects: a widespread failure or misuse of the sympathetic and ethical imaginative in creating (or criticizing) the new poetry of the age, or in dealing with the social and political upheavals of the French Revolution and its aftermath. Artists like Wordsworth and Byron turned away from a Shakespearean identification with character and event to focus on the "moods" and "egotisms" of their own personalities. Philos-ophers like Bentham and Godwin inevitably failed in their goals

---

[11] Byron, who died April 19, 1824 at Missolonghi in Greece.

of reform by ignoring the stubborn weaknesses (and strengths) of men in favor of abstract conceptions of perfectability. Mr. Gifford was unable to keep pace "with the whirling, eccentric motion, the rapid, perhaps extravagant combinations of modern literature" by his reliance on "mechanic rules" at the expense of fresh and inde-pendent response. Even a political leader of such obvious talent as Sir James Mackintosh could not deal effectively with the condi-tions of the time: "to persons of this class of mind things must be translated into words, visible images into abstract propositions to meet their refined apprehensions, and they have no more to say to a matter-of-fact staring them in the face without a label in its mouth, than they would to a hippopotamus!" The essay on Coleridge sounds the sad chord of regret over the wasted energies of prodigious talents in confronting the challenges of a new era in human experience.

The text of the essays here reproduced is from the "second English edition" of 1825.

F R O M

THE SPIRIT OF THE AGE

JEREMY BENTHAM[1]

MR. BENTHAM is one of those persons who verify the old adage, that "A prophet has most honour, out of his own country." [2] His reputation lies at the cir-cumference; and the lights of his understanding are reflected, with increasing lustre, on the other side of the globe. His name is little known in England, better in Europe, best of all in the plains of Chili and the mines of Mexico. He has offered constitutions for the New World, and legislated for future times. The people of Westminster, where he lives, hardly dream of such a person; but the Siberian savage has re-ceived cold comfort from his lunar aspect, and may say to him with Caliban—"I know thee, and thy dog and thy bush!" [3] The tawny Indian may hold out the hand of fellowship to him across the GREAT PACIFIC. We believe that the Empress Catherine [4] corresponded with him; and we know that the Emperor Alexander [5] called upon him, and presented him with his miniature in a gold snuffbox, which the

---

[1] Jeremy Bentham (1748–1832) was one of the leading social and political reformers of his age; exponent of the philosophy of Utilitarianism, which viewed man as a creature subject to pleasures and pains, desiring to maximize his pleasures and avoid pains. According to Bentham, all social legislation and political activity, as well as all individual moral behavior, should conform to the "principles of utility," the securing of "the greatest happiness of the greatest number."

[2] Cf. Matthew, xiii, 57.

[3] Cf. *The Tempest*, II, ii, 143–44.

[4] Catherine the Great, Empress of Russia.

[5] Alexander I was Emperor of Russia from 1801 to 1825.

philosopher, to his eternal honour, returned. Mr. Hobhouse is a greater man at the hustings, Lord Rolle at Plymouth Dock;[6] but Mr. Bentham would carry it hollow, on the score of popularity, at Paris[7] or Pegu. The reason is, that our author's influence is purely intellectual. He has devoted his life to the pursuit of abstract and general truths, and to those studies—

"That waft a *thought* from Indus to the Pole"—[8]

and has never mixed himself up with personal intrigues or party politics. He once, indeed, stuck up a hand-bill to say that he (Jeremy Bentham) being of sound mind, was of opinion that Sir Samuel Romilly[9] was the most proper person to represent Westminster; but this was the whim of the moment. Otherwise, his reasonings, if true at all, are true every where alike: his speculations concern humanity at large, and are not confined to the hundred or the bills of morality.[10] It is in moral as in physical magnitude. The little is seen best near: the great appears in its proper dimensions, only from a more commanding point of view, and gains strength with time, and elevation from distance!

Mr. Bentham is very much among philosophers what La Fontaine[11] was among poets:—in general habits and in all but his professional pursuits, he is a mere child. He has lived for the last forty years in a house in Westminster, overlooking the Park, like an anchoret in his cell, reducing law to a system, and the mind of man to a machine. He scarcely ever goes out, and sees very little company. The favoured few, who have the privilege of the *entrée*, are always admitted one by one. He does not like to have witnesses to his conversation. He talks a great deal, and listens to nothing but facts. When any one calls upon him, he invites them to take a turn round his garden with him (Mr. Bentham is an economist of his time, and sets apart this portion of it to air and exercise)—and there

you may see the lively old man, his mind still buoyant with thought and with the prospect of futurity, in eager conversation with some Opposition Member, some expatriated Patriot, or Transatlantic Adventurer, urging the extinction of Close Boroughs,[12] or planning a code of laws for some "lone island in the watery waste,"[13] his walk almost amounting to a run, his tongue keeping pace with it in shrill, cluttering accents, negligent of his person, his dress, and his manner, intent only on his grand theme of UTILITY—or pausing, perhaps, for want of breath and with lack-lustre eye to point out to the stranger a stone in the wall at the end of his garden (overarched by two beautiful cotton-trees) *Inscribed to the Prince of Poets*, which marks the house where Milton formerly lived. To show how little the refinements of taste or fancy enter into our author's system, he proposed at one time to cut down these beautiful trees, to convert the garden where he had breathed the air of Truth and Heaven for near half a century into a paltry *Chrestomathic School*,[14] and to make Milton's house (the cradle of Paradise Lost) a thoroughfare, like a three-stalled stable, for the idle rabble of Westminster to pass backwards and forwards to it with their cloven hoofs. Let us not, however, be getting on too fast—Milton himself taught school! There is something not altogether dissimilar between Mr. Bentham's appearance, and the portraits of Milton, the same silvery tone, a few dishevelled hairs, a peevish, yet puritanical expression, an irritable temperament corrected by habit and discipline. Or in modern times, he is something between Franklin and Charles Fox, with the comfortable double-chin and sleek thriving look of the one, and the quivering lip, the restless eye, and animated acuteness of the other. His eye is quick and lively; but it glances not from object to object, but from thought to thought. He is evidently a man occupied with some train of fine and inward association. He regards the people about him no more than the flies of a summer. He meditates the coming age. He hears and sees only what suits his purpose, or some "foregone conclusion;"[15] and looks out for facts and passing occurrences in order to put them into his logical machinery and grind them into the dust and powder of some subtle theory, as the

---

6 John Cam Hobhouse (1786–1869) Byron's closest friend was member of Parliament from 1820 to 1833. John Rolle (1750–1842) was a member of Parliament for Devonshire from 1780 to 1796, subsequently a member of the House of Lords as Baron Rolle of Stevenstone. Plymouth Dock was in Devonshire.

7 Between 1789 and 1793, Bentham addressed a number of publications on matters of political reform to the French National Assembly, and in 1792 was awarded honorary French citizenship.

8 Cf. Pope's *Eloisa to Abelard*, l. 58.

9 Sir Samuel Romilly (1757–1818) was a leading spokesman for the reform of English criminal law and a member of Parliament from 1806 until his death by suicide.

10 That is, his concerns were not restricted to his immediate vicinity. The hundred: "a subdivision of a county or shire, having its own court" (*Oxford English Dictionary*). The bills of mortality were originally a published list of deaths and births in and around London; by extension, the area itself.

11 Jean de La Fontaine (1621–1695).

12 Parliamentary districts completely in the purchase or control of one person, not open to contest or competition.

13 Cf. Pope's *Essay on Man*, I, 106.

14 Hazlitt refers to Bentham's plan in 1815 to set up a model school "for the use of the middling and higher ranks of life," with a curriculum emphasizing the natural and physical sciences rather than the traditional study of the classics and theology. *Chrestomathic*: Greek, "conducive to useful learning."

15 *Othello*, III, iii, 428.

miller looks out for grist to his mill! Add to this physiognomical sketch the minor points of costume, the open shirt-collar, the single-breasted coat, the old-fashioned half-boots and ribbed stockings; and you will find in Mr. Bentham's general appearance a singular mixture of boyish simplicity and of the venerableness of age. In a word, our celebrated jurist presents a striking illustration of the difference between the *philosophical* and the *regal* look; that is, between the merely abstracted and the merely personal. There is a lack-adaisical *bonhommie* about his whole aspect, none of the fierceness of pride or power; an unconscious neglect of his own person, instead of a stately assumption of superiority; a good-humoured, placid intelligence, instead of a lynx-eyed watchfulness, as if it wished to make others its prey, or was afraid they might turn and rend him; he is a beneficent spirit, prying into the universe, not lording it over it; a thoughtful spectator of the scenes of life, or ruminator on the fate of mankind, not a painted pageant, a stupid idol set up on its pedestal of pride for men to fall down and worship with idiot fear and wonder at the thing themselves have made, and which, without that fear and wonder, would in itself be nothing!

Mr. Bentham, perhaps, over-rates the importance of his own theories. He has been heard to say (without any appearance of pride or affectation) that "he should like to live the remaining years of his life, a year at a time at the end of the next six or eight centuries, to see the effect which his writings would by that time have had upon the world." Alas! his name will hardly live so long! Nor do we think, in point of fact, that Mr. Bentham has given any new or decided impulse to the human mind. He cannot be looked upon in the light of a discoverer in legislation or morals. He has not struck out any great leading principle or parent-truth, from which a number of others might be deduced; nor has he enriched the common and established stock of intelligence with original observations, like pearls thrown into wine. One truth discovered is immortal, and entitles its author to be so: for, like a new substance in nature, it cannot be destroyed. But Mr. Bentham's *forte* is arrangement; and the form of truth, though not its essence, varies with time and circumstance. He has methodised, collated, and condensed all the materials prepared to his hand on the subjects of which he treats, in a masterly and scientific manner; but we should find a difficulty in adducing from his different works (however elaborate or closely reasoned) any new element of thought, or even a new fact or illustration. His writings are, therefore, chiefly valuable as *books of reference*, as bringing down the account of intellectual inquiry to the present period,

and disposing the results in a compendious, connected and tangible shape; but books of reference are chiefly serviceable for facilitating the acquisition of knowledge, and are constantly liable to be superseded and to grow out of fashion with its progress, as the scaffolding is thrown down as soon as the building is completed. Mr. Bentham is not the first writer (by a great many) who has assumed the principle of UTILITY as the foundation of just laws, and of all moral and political reasoning:—his merit is, that he has applied this principle more closely and literally; that he has brought all the objections and arguments, more distinctly labelled and ticketted, under this one head, and made a more constant and explicit reference to it at every step of his progress, than any other writer. Perhaps the weak side of his conclusions also is, that he has carried this single view of his subject too far, and not made sufficient allowance for the varieties of human nature, and the caprices and irregularities of the human will. "He has not allowed for the *wind*." [16] It is not that you can be said to see his favourite doctrine of Utility glittering every where through his system, like a vein of rich, shining ore (that is not the nature of the material)—but it might be plausibly objected that he had struck the whole mass of fancy, prejudice, passion, sense, whim, with his petrific, leaden mace, that he had "bound volatile Hermes," [17] and reduced the theory and practice of human life to a *caput mortuum* of reason, and dull, plodding, technical calculation. The gentleman is himself a capital logician; and he has been led by this circumstance to consider man as a logical animal. We fear this view of the matter will hardly hold water. If we attend to the *moral* man the constitution of his mind will scarcely be found to be built up of pure reason and a regard to consequences: if we consider the *criminal* man (with whom the legislator has chiefly to do) it will be found to be still less so.

Every pleasure, says Mr. Bentham, is equally a good, and is to be taken into the account as such in a moral estimate, whether it be the pleasure of sense or of conscience, whether it arise from the exercise of virtue or the perpetration of crime. We are afraid the human mind does not readily come into this doctrine, this *ultima ratio philosophorum*, [18] interpreted according to the letter. Our moral sentiments are made up of sympathies and antipathies, of sense and imagination, of understanding and prejudice. The soul, by reason of its weakness, is an aggregating and exclusive

[16] Cf. Scott's *Ivanhoe*, Chapter XIII.
[17] *Paradise Lost*, III, 602–603.
[18] *Ultima . . . philosophorum*: "Ultimate argument of philosophers".

principle; it clings obstinately to some things, and violently rejects others. And it must do so, in a great measure, or it would act contrary to its own nature. It needs helps and stages in its progress, and "all appliances and means to boot,"[19] which can raise it to a partial conformity to truth and good (the utmost it is capable of) and bring it into a tolerable harmony with the universe. By aiming at too much, by dismissing collateral aids, by extending itself to the farthest verge of the conceivable and possible, it loses its elasticity and vigour, its impulse and its direction. The moralist can no more do without the 'vantage ground of habit, without the levers of the understanding, than the mechanist can discard the use of wheels and pulleys, and perform every thing by simple motion. If the mind of man were competent to comprehend the whole of truth and good, and act upon it at once, and independently of all other considerations, Mr. Bentham's plan would be a feasible one, and *the truth, the whole truth, and nothing but the truth* would be the best possible ground to place morality upon. But it is not so. In ascertaining the rules of moral conduct, we must have regard not merely to the nature of the object, but to the capacity of the agent, and to his fitness for apprehending or attaining it. Pleasure is that which is so in itself: good is that which approves itself as such on reflection, or the idea of which is a source of satisfaction. All pleasure is not, therefore (morally speaking) equally a good; for all pleasure does not equally bear reflecting on. There are some tastes that are sweet in the mouth and bitter in the belly; and there is a similar contradiction and anomaly in the mind and heart of man. Again, what would become of the *Posthaec meminisse juvabit* of the poet,[20] if a principle of fluctuation and reaction is not inherent in the very constitution of our nature, or if all moral truth is a mere literal truism? We are not, then, so much to inquire what certain things are abstractedly or in themselves, as how they affect the mind, and to approve or condemn them accordingly. The same object seen near strikes us more powerfully than at a distance: things thrown into masses give a greater blow to the imagination than when scattered and divided into their component parts. A number of mole-hills do not make a mountain, though a mountain is actually made up of atoms: so moral truth must present itself under a certain aspect and from a certain point of view, in order to produce its full and proper effect upon the mind. The laws of the affections are as necessary as those of optics. A calculation of consequences is no more equivalent to a sentiment, than a *seriatim* enumeration of square yards or feet touches the fancy like the sight of the Alps or Andes.

To give an instance or two of what we mean. Those who on pure cosmopolite principles, or on the ground of abstract humanity affect an extraordinary regard for the Turks and Tartars, have been accused of neglecting their duties to their friends and next-door neighbours. Well, then, what is the state of the question here? One human being is, no doubt, as much worth in himself, independently of the circumstances of time or place, as another; but he is not of so much value to us and our affections. Could our imagination take wing (with our speculative faculties) to the other side of the globe or to the ends of the universe, could our eyes behold whatever our reason teaches us to be possible, could our hands reach as far as our thoughts or wishes, we might then busy ourselves to advantage with the Hottentots, or hold intimate converse with the inhabitants of the Moon; but being as we are, our feelings evaporate in so large a space—we must draw the circle of our affections and duties somewhat closer—the heart hovers and fixes nearer home. It is true, the bands of private, or of local and natural affection are often, nay in general, too tightly strained, so as frequently to do harm instead of good: but the present question is whether we can, with safety and effect, be wholly emancipated from them? Whether we should shake them off at pleasure and without mercy, as the only bar to the triumph of truth and justice? Or whether benevolence, constructed upon a logical scale, would not be merely *nominal*, whether duty, raised to too lofty a pitch of refinement, might not sink into callous indifference or hollow selfishness? Again, is it not to exact too high a strain from humanity, to ask us to qualify the degree of abhorrence we feel against a murderer by taking into our cool consideration the pleasure he may have in committing the deed, and in the prospect of gratifying his avarice or his revenge? We are hardly so formed as to sympathise at the same moment with the assassin and his victim. The degree of pleasure the former may feel, instead of extenuating, aggravates his guilt, and shows the depth of his malignity. Now the mind revolts against this by mere natural antipathy, if it is itself well-disposed; or the slow process of reason would afford but a feeble resistance to violence and wrong. The will, which is necessary to give consistency and promptness to our good intentions, cannot extend so much candour and courtesy to the antagonist principle of evil: virtue, to be sincere and practical, cannot be divested entirely of the blindness and impetuosity of passion! It has been made a plea (half jest, half earnest) for the

---

[19] *Henry the Fourth*, Part II, III, 1, 29.
[20] *Posthaec meminisse juvabit*: "it will delight us someday to have remembered these things." *Aeneid*, I, 203.

horrors of war, that they promote trade and manufactures. It has been said, as a set-off for the atrocities practised upon the negro slaves in the West Indies, that without their blood and sweat, so many millions of people could not have sugar to sweeten their tea. Fires and murders have been argued to be beneficial, as they serve to fill the newspapers, and for a subject to talk of—this is a sort of sophistry that it might be difficult to disprove on the bare scheme of contingent utility; but on the ground that we have stated, it must pass for mere irony. What the proportion between the good and the evil will really be found in any of the supposed cases, may be a question to the understanding; but to the imagination and the heart, that is, to the natural feelings of mankind, it admits of none!

Mr. Bentham, in adjusting the provisions of a penal code, lays too little stress on the co-operation of the natural prejudices of mankind, and the habitual feelings of that class of persons for whom they are more particularly designed. Legislators (we mean writers on legislation) are philosophers, and governed by their reason: criminals, for whose controul laws are made, are a set of desperadoes, governed only by their passions. What wonder that so little progress has been made towards a mutual understanding between the two parties! They are quite a different species, and speak a different language, and are sadly at a loss for a common interpreter between them. Perhaps the Ordinary of Newgate[21] bids as fair for this office as any one. What should Mr. Bentham, sitting at ease in his arm-chair, composing his mind before he begins 'to write by a prelude on the organ, and looking out at a beautiful prospect when he is at a loss for an idea, know of the principles of action of rogues, outlaws, and vagabonds? No more than Montaigne of the motions of his cat![22] If sanguine and tender-hearted philanthropists have set on foot an inquiry into the barbarity and the defects of penal laws, the practical improvements have been mostly suggested by reformed cut-throats, turnkeys, and thief-takers. What even can the Honourable House, who when the Speaker has pronounced the well-known, wished-for sound "That this house do now adjourn," retire, after voting a royal crusade or a loan of millions, to lie on down, and feed on plate in spacious palaces, know of

what passes in the hearts of wretches in garrets and night-cellars, petty pilferers and marauders, who cut throats and pick pockets with their own hands? The thing is impossible. The laws of the country are, therefore, ineffectual and abortive, because they are made by the rich for the poor, by the wise for the ignorant, by the respectable and exalted in station for the very scum and refuse of the community. If Newgate would resolve itself into a committee of the whole Press-yard, with Jack Ketch at its head, aided by confidential persons from the county prisons or the Hulks,[23] and would make a clear breast, some *data* might be found out to proceed upon; but as it is, the *criminal mind* of the country is a book sealed, no one has been able to penetrate to the inside! Mr. Bentham, in his attempts to revise and amend our criminal jurisprudence, proceeds entirely on his favourite principle of Utility. Convince highwaymen and house breakers that it will be for their interest to reform, and they will reform and lead honest lives; according to Mr. Bentham. He says, "All men act from calculation, even madmen reason."[24] And, in our opinion, he might as well carry this maxim to Bedlam or St. Luke's,[25] and apply it to the inhabitants, as think to coerce or overawe the inmates of a goal, or those whose practices make them candidates for that distinction, by the mere dry, detailed convictions of the understanding. Criminals are not to be influenced by reason; for it is of the very essence of crime to disregard consequences both to ourselves and others. You may as well preach philosophy to a drunken man, or to the dead, as to those who are under the instigation of any mischievous passion. A man is a drunkard, and you tell him he ought to be sober; he is debauched, and you ask him to reform; he is idle, and you recommend industry to him as his wisest course; he gambles, and you remind him that he may be ruined by this foible; he has lost his character, and you advise him to get into some reputable service or lucrative situation; vice becomes a habit with him, and you request him to rouse himself and shake it off; he is starving, and you warn him that if he breaks the law, he will be hanged. None of this reasoning reaches the mark it aims at. The culprit, who violates and suffers the vengeance of the laws, is not the dupe of ignor-

---

[21] Ordinary of Newgate: the Chaplain of Newgate prison.

[22] See Montaigne's essay "Apology for Raimond de Sebonde." In attacking man's "presumptuous" belief that because animals do not possess human faculties they are necessarily stupid, Montaigne declares: "When I play with my cat, who knows whether I do not make her more sport than she makes me? we mutually divert one another with our monkey-tricks: if I have my hour to begin or to refuse, she also has hers."

[23] Press-yard: "name of a yard or court of old Newgate Prison . . . from which . . . capitally convicted prisoners started for the place of execution" (*Oxford English Dictionary*). Jack Ketch, that is, a hangman; from a notorious seventeenth-century executioner John Ketch. The Hulks were ships used as prisons.

[24] From *An Introduction to the Principles of Morals and Legislation* (1789), the work in which Bentham first formulated the "principles of utility."

[25] London insane asylums.

ance, but the slave of passion, the victim of habit or necessity. To argue with strong passion, with inveterate habit, with desperate circumstances, is to talk to the winds. Clownish ignorance may indeed be dispelled, and taught better; but it is seldom that a criminal is not aware of the consequences of his act, or has not made up his mind to the alternative. They are, in general, *too knowing by half*. You tell a person of this stamp what is his interest; he says he does not care about his interest, or the world and he differ on that particular. But there is one point on which he must agree with them, namely, what *they* think of his conduct, and that is the only hold you have of him. A man may be callous and indifferent to what happens to himself; but he is never indifferent to public opinion, or proof against open scorn and infamy. Shame, then, not fear, is the sheet-anchor [26] of the law. He who is not afraid of being pointed at as a *thief*, will not mind a month's hard labour. He who is prepared to take the life of another, is already reckless of his own. But every one makes a sorry figure in the pillory; and the being launched from the New Drop [27] lowers a man in his own opinion. The lawless and violent spirit, who is hurried by head-strong self-will to break the laws, does not like to have the ground of pride and obstinacy struck from under his feet. This is what gives the *swells* of the metropolis such a dread of the *tread-mill*,[28]—it makes them ridiculous. It must be confessed, that this very circumstance renders the reform of criminals nearly hopeless. It is the apprehension of being stigmatized by public opinion, the fear of what will be thought and said of them, that deters men from the violation of the laws, while their character remains unimpeached; but honour once lost, all is lost. The man can never be himself again! A citizen is like a soldier, a part of a machine, who submits to certain hardships, privations, and dangers, not for his own ease, pleasure, profit, or even conscience, but— *for shame*. What is it that keeps the machine together in either case? Not punishment or discipline, but sympathy. The soldier mounts the breach or stands in the trenches, the peasant hedges and ditches, or the mechanic plies his ceaseless task, because the one will not be called a *coward*, the other a *rogue*: but let the one turn deserter and the other vagabond, and there is an end of him. The grinding law of necessity, which is no other than a name, a breath, loses its force; he is no longer sustained by the good opinion of others, and

he drops out of his place in society, a useless cog! Mr. Bentham takes a culprit, and puts him into what he calls a *Panopticon*, that is, a sort of circular prison, with open cells, like a glass bee-hive. He sits in the middle, and sees all the other does. He gives him work to do, and lectures him if he does not do it. He takes liquor from him, and society, and liberty; but he feeds and clothes him, and keeps him out of mischief; and when he has convinced him, by force and reason together, that this life is for his good, he turns him out upon the world a reformed man, and as confident of the success of his handy-work, as the shoemaker of that which he has just taken off the last, or the Parisian barber in Sterne, of the buckle of his wig. "Dip it in the ocean," said the perruquier, "and it will stand!" [29] But we doubt the durability of our projector's patchwork. Will our convert to the great principle of Utility work when he is from under Mr. Bentham's eye, because he was forced to work when under it? Will he keep sober, because he has been kept from liquor so long? Will he not return to loose company, because he has had the pleasure of sitting vis-à-vis with a philosopher of late? Will he not steal, now that his hands are untied? Will he not take the road, now that it is free to him? Will he not call his benefactor all the names he can set his tongue to, the moment his back is turned? All this is more than to be feared. The charm of criminal life, like that of savage life, consists in liberty, in hardship, in danger, and in the contempt of death, in one word, in extraordinary excitement; and he who has tasted of it, will no more return to regular habits of life, than a man will take to water after drinking brandy, or than a wild beast will give over hunting its prey. Miracles never cease, to be sure; but they are not to be had wholesale, or *to order*. Mr. Owen,[30] who is another of these proprietors and patentees of reform, has lately got an American savage with him, whom he carries about in great triumph and complacency, as an antithesis to his *New View of Society*, and as winding up his reasoning to what it mainly wanted, an epigrammatic point. Does the benevolent visionary of the Lanark cotton-mills really think this *natural man* will act as a foil to his *artificial man*? Does he for a moment imagine that his *Address to the higher and middle classes*, with all its advantages of fiction, makes any thing like so interesting a romance as *Hunter's Captivity among the North*

---

[26] A large anchor for use in emergencies.

[27] In Hazlitt's day, the name of the trap-door on which the condemned man stood for his hanging.

[28] A revolving cylinder on which the prisoner was placed for the purpose of doing exhausting but useless hard labour.

---

[29] See "The Wig. Paris," in Laurence Sterne's *A Sentimental Journey* (1768).

[30] Robert Owen (1771–1858) was a social reformer and humanitarian. *A New View of Society*, first published in 1813, was Owen's major statement on the reform of English industrial society, based on the "ideal community" he had established for his employees at the New Lanark (Scotland) textile mills.

American Indians?[31] Has he any thing to show, in all the apparatus of New Lanark and its desolate monotony, to excite the thrill of imagination like the blankets made of wreaths of snow under which the wild wood-rovers bury themselves for weeks in winter? Or the skin of a leopard, which our hardy adventurer slew, and which served him for great coat and bedding? Or the rattle-snake that he found by his side as a bed-fellow? Or his rolling himself into a ball to escape from him? Or his suddenly placing himself against a tree to avoid being trampled to death by the herd of wild buffaloes, that came rushing on like the sound of thunder? Or his account of the huge spiders that prey on blue-bottles and gilded flies in green pathless forests; or of the great Pacific Ocean, that the natives look upon as the gulf that parts time from eternity, and that is to waft them to the spirits of their fathers? After all this, Mr. Hunter must find Mr. Owen and his parallelograms trite and flat, and will, we suspect, take an opportunity to escape from them!

Mr. Bentham's method of reasoning, though comprehensive and exact, labours under the defect of most systems—it is too *topical*. It includes every thing; but it includes every thing alike. It is rather like an inventory, than a valuation of different arguments. Every possible suggestion finds a place, so that the mind is distracted as much as enlightened by this perplexing accuracy. The exceptions seem as important as the rule. By attending to the minute, we overlook the great; and in summing up an account, it will not do merely to insist on the number of items without considering their amount. Our author's page presents a very nicely dove-tailed mosaic pavement of legal common-places. We slip and slide over its even surface without being arrested any where. Or his view of the human mind resembles a map, rather than a picture: the outline, the disposition is correct, but it wants colouring and relief. There is a technicality of manner, which renders his writings of more value to the professional inquirer than to the general reader. Again, his style is unpopular, not to say unintelligible. He writes a language of his own, that *darkens knowledge*. His works have been translated into French—they ought to be translated into English. People wonder that Mr. Bentham has not been prosecuted for the boldness and severity of some of his invectives. He might wrap up high treason in one of his inextricable periods, and it would never find its way into Westminster-Hall.[32] He is a kind of Manuscript author—he writes a cipher-hand, which the vulgar have no key to. The construction of his sentences is a curious frame-work with pegs and hooks to hang his thoughts upon, for his own use and guidance, but almost out of the reach of every body else. It is a barbarous philosophical jargon, with all the repetitions, parentheses, formalities, uncouth nomenclature and verbiage of law-Latin; and what makes it worse, it is not mere verbiage, but has a great deal of acuteness and meaning in it, which you would be glad to pick out if you could. In short, Mr. Bentham writes as if he was allowed but a single sentence to express his whole view of a subject in, and as if, should he omit a single circumstance or step of the argument, it would be lost to the world for ever, like an estate by a flaw in the title-deeds. This is over-rating the importance of our own discoveries, and mistaking the nature and object of language altogether. Mr. Bentham has *acquired* this disability—it is not natural to him. His admirable little work *On Usury*, published forty years ago, is clear, easy, and vigorous. But Mr. Bentham has shut himself up since then "in nook monastic,"[33] conversing only with followers of his own, or with "men of Ind,"[34] and has endeavoured to overlay his natural humour, sense, spirit, and style, with the dust and cobwebs of an obscure solitude. The best of it is, he thinks his present mode of expressing himself perfect, and that whatever may be objected to his law or logic, no one can find the least fault with the purity, simplicity, and perspicuity of his style.

Mr. Bentham, in private life, is an amiable and exemplary character. He is a little romantic, or so; and has dissipated part of a handsome fortune in practical speculations. He lends an ear to plausible projectors, and, if he cannot prove them to be wrong in their premises or their conclusions, thinks himself bound *in reason* to stake his money on the venture. Strict logicians are licensed visionaries. Mr. Bentham is half-brother to the late Mr. Speaker Abbott—*Proh pudor!** He was educated at Eton, and still takes our novices to task about a passage in Homer, or a metre in Virgil. He was afterwards at the University, and he has described the scruples of an ingenuous youthful mind about subscribing the articles, in a passage in his *Church-of-Englandism*,[36] which smacks of truth and

* Now Lord Colchester.[35]

---

[31] A popular narrative published in 1823, by John Dunn Hunter (1798–1827), American "frontiersman".

[32] A building adjoining the House of Parliament; in Hazlitt's day, the site of the law courts.

[33] *As You Like It*, III, ii, 440–41.

[34] *Tempest*, II, ii, 61.

[35] Charles Abbot (1757–1829) was a Tory politician and Speaker of the House of Commons from 1802 to 1817. *Proh pudor!*: "O Shame!"

[36] All university students of the time were required to assent ("subscribe") to the Thirty-nine Articles, a summary of Anglican religious belief. *Church of Englandism and its Cathechism Examined* was published in 1818.

honour both, and does one good to read it in an age, when "to be honest" (or not to laugh at the very idea of honesty) "is to be one man picked out of ten thousand!" 37 Mr. Bentham relieves his mind sometimes, after the fatigue of study, by playing on a fine old organ, and has a relish for Hogarth's prints. He turns wooden utensils in a lathe for exercise, and fancies he can turn men in the same manner. He has no great fondness for poetry, and can hardly extract a moral out of Shakspeare. His house is warmed and lighted by steam. He is one of those who prefer the artificial to the natural in most things, and think the mind of man omnipotent. He has a great contempt for out-of-door prospects, for green fields and trees, and is for referring every thing to Utility. There is a little narrowness in this; for if all the sources of satisfaction are taken away, what is to become of utility itself? It is, indeed, the great fault of this able and extraordinary man, that he has concentrated his faculties and feelings too entirely on one subject and pursuit, and has not "looked enough abroad into universality."*

[January 1824]   [1825]

MR. COLERIDGE

THE PRESENT is an age of talkers, and not of doers; and the reason is, that the world is growing old. We are so far advanced in the Arts and Sciences, that we live in retrospect, and dote on past achievements. The accumulation of knowledge has been so great, that we are lost in wonder at the height it has reached, instead of attempting to climb or add to it; while the variety of objects distracts and dazzles the looker-on. What *niche* remains unoccupied? What path untried? What is the use of doing any thing, unless we could do better than all those who have gone before us? What hope is there of this? We are like those who have been to see some noble monument of art, who are content to admire without thinking of rivalling it; or like guests after a feast, who praise the hospitality of the donor "and thank the bounteous Pan" 1—perhaps carrying away some trifling fragments; or like the spectators of a mighty battle, who still hear its sound afar off, and the clashing of armour and the neighing of the war-horse and the shout of victory is in their ears, like the rushing of innumerable waters!

* Lord Bacon's Advancement of Learning.

37 *Hamlet*, II, ii, 178–79.
  1 Cf. Milton's *Comus*, l. 176.

Mr. Coleridge has "a mind reflecting ages past:" 2 his voice is like the echo of the congregated roar of the "dark rearward and abyss" 3 of thought. He who has seen a mouldering tower by the side of a crystal lake, hid by the mist, but glittering in the wave below, may conceive the dim, gleaming, uncertain intelligence of his eye: he who has marked the evening clouds uprolled (a world of vapours), has seen the picture of his mind, unearthly, unsubstantial, with gorgeous tints and ever-varying forms—

"That which was now a horse, even with a thought
The rack dislimns, and makes it indistinct
As water is in water." 4

Our author's mind is (as he himself might express it) *tangential*. There is no subject on which he has not touched, none of which he has rested. With an understanding fertile, subtle, expansive, "quick, forgetive, apprehensive," 5 beyond all living precedent, few traces of it will perhaps remain. He lends himself to all impressions alike; he gives up his mind and liberty of thought to none. He is a general lover of art and science, and wedded to no one in particular. He pursues knowledge as a mistress, with outstretched hands and winged speed; but as he is about to embrace her, his Daphne turns—alas! not to a laurel! 6 Hardly a speculation has been left on record from the earliest time, but it is loosely folded up in Mr. Coleridge's memory, like a rich, but somewhat tattered piece of tapestry. We might add (with more seeming than real extravagance), that scarce a thought can pass through the mind of man, but its sound has at some time or other passed over his head with rustling pinions. On whatever question or author you speak, he is prepared to take up the theme with advantage—from Peter Abelard down to Thomas Moore, from the subtlest metaphysics to the politics of the *Courier*. 7 There is no man of genius, in whose praise he descants, but the critic seems to stand above the author, and "what in him is weak, to strengthen, what is low, to raise and support:" 8 nor is there any work of genius that does not come out of his hands like an illuminated Missal, sparkling even in its defects. If Mr. Coleridge had not been the most impressive talker of his age, he would

2 From laudatory verses prefacing the Second Folio of Shakespeare's Works, 1632.
3 Cf. *The Tempest*, I, ii, 50.
4 *Anthony and Cleopatra*, IV, xiv, 9–11.
5 *Henry the Fourth*, Part II, IV, iii, 106.
6 A reference to the myth of the nymph Daphne, who is changed into a laurel tree to escape the embraces of the amorous Apollo.
7 *Courier* was a London newspaper to which Coleridge contributed irregularly over a number of years.
8 Cf. *Paradise Lost*, I, 22–23.

probably have been the finest writer; but he lays down his pen to make sure of an auditor, and mortages the admiration of posterity for the stare of an idler. If he had not been a poet, he would have been a powerful logician; if he had not dipped his wing in the Unitarian controversy, he might have soared to the very summit of fancy. But in writing verse, he is trying to subject the Muse to *transcendental* theories: in his abstract reasoning, he misses his way by strewing it with flowers. All that he has done of moment, he had done twenty years ago: since then, he may be said to have lived on the sound of his own voice. Mr. Coleridge is too rich in intellectual wealth, to need to task himself to any drudgery: he has only to draw the sliders of his imagination, and a thousand subjects expand before him, startling him with their brilliancy, or losing themselves in endless obscurity—

> "And by the force of blear illusion,
> They draw him on to his confusion." [9]

What is the little he could add to the stock, compared with the countless stores that lie about him, that he should stoop to pick up a name, or to polish an idle fancy? He walks abroad in the majesty of an universal understanding, eyeing the "rich strond," [10] or golden sky above him, and "goes sounding on his way," in eloquent accents, uncompelled and free!

Persons of the greatest capacity are often those, who for this reason do the least; for surveying themselves from the highest point of view, amidst the infinite variety of the universe, their own share in it seems trifling, and scarce worth a thought, and they prefer the contemplation of all that is, or has been, or can be, to the making a coil [11] about doing what, when done, is no better than vanity. It is hard to concentrate all our attention and efforts on one pursuit, except from ignorance of others; and without this concentration of our faculties, no great progress can be made in any one thing. It is not merely that the mind is not capable of the effort; it does not think the effort worth making. Action is one; but thought is manifold. He whose restless eye glances through the wide compass of nature and art, will not consent to have "his own nothings monstered:" [12] but he must do this, before he can give his whole soul to them. The mind, after "letting contemplation have its fill," or

> "Sailing with supreme dominion
> Through the azure deep of air," [13]

sinks down on the ground, breathless, exhausted, powerless, inactive; or if it must have some vent to its feelings, seeks the most easy and obvious; is soothed by friendly flattery, lulled by the murmur of immediate applause, thinks as it were aloud, and babbles in its dreams! A scholar (so to speak) is a more disinterested and abstracted character than a mere author. The first looks at the numberless volumes of a library, and says, "All these are mine:" the other points to a single volume (perhaps it may be an immortal one) and says, "My name is written on the back of it." This is a puny and groveling ambition, beneath the lofty amplitude of Mr. Coleridge's mind. No, he revolves in his wayward soul, or utters to the passing wind, or discourses to his own shadow, things mightier and more various!—Let us draw the curtain, and unlock the shrine.

Learning rocked him in his cradle, and, while yet a child,

> "He lisped in numbers, for the numbers came." [14]

At sixteen he wrote his *Ode on Chatterton*, and he still reverts to that period with delight, not so much as it relates to himself (for that string of his own early promise of fame rather jars than otherwise) but as exemplifying the youth of a poet. Mr. Coleridge talks of himself, without being an egotist, for in him the individual is always merged in the abstract and general. He distinguished himself at school and at the University by his knowledge of the classics, and gained several prizes for Greek epigrams. How many men are there (great scholars, celebrated names in literature) who having done the same thing in their youth, have no other idea all the rest of their lives but of this achievement, of a fellowship and dinner, and who, installed in academic honours, would look down on our author as a mere strolling bard! At Christ's Hospital, [15] where he was brought up, he was the idol of those among his school fellows, who mingled with their bookish studies the music of thought and of humanity; and he was usually attended round the cloisters by a group of these (inspiring and inspired) whose hearts, even then, burnt within them as he talked, and where the sounds yet linger to mock ELIA on his way, still turning pensive to the past! One of the finest and rarest parts of Mr. Coleridge's conversation, is when he expatiates on the Greek tragedians (not that he is not well acquainted, when he pleases, with the epic poets, or the philosophers, or

---

[9] See *Macbeth*, III, v, 28–29.
[10] *Faerie Queene*, III, iv, 34.   [11] Fuss.
[12] *Coriolanus*, II, ii, 81.
[13] See John Dyer's *Grongar Hill* (1726), l. 26, and Gray's "Progress of Poesy," ll. 116–117.

[14] Pope's *Epistle to Dr. Arbuthnot*, l. 128.
[15] The London grammar school that Coleridge attended from 1782 to 1791. Charles Lamb was a fellow student.

orators, or historians of antiquity)—on the subtle reasonings and melting pathos of Euripides, on the harmonious gracefulness of Sophocles, tuning his love-laboured song, like sweetest warblings from a sacred grove; on the high-wrought trumpet-tongued eloquence of Æschylus, whose Prometheus, above all, is like an Ode to Fate, and a pleading with Providence, his thoughts being let loose as his body is chained on his solitary rock, and his afflicted will (the emblem of mortality)

"Struggling in vain with ruthless destiny."[16]

As the impassioned critic speaks and rises in his theme, you would think you heard the voice of the Man hated by the Gods, contending with the wild winds as they roar, and his eye glitters with the spirit of Antiquity! Next he was engaged with Hartley's tribes of mind, "etherial braid, thought-woven,"—and he busied himself for a year or two with vibrations and vibratiuncles and the great law of association that binds all things in its mystic chain, and the doctrine of Necessity (the mild teacher of Charity) and the Millennium,[17] anticipative of a life to come—and he plunged deep into the controversy on Matter and Spirit, and, as an escape from Dr. Priestley's Materialism,[18] where he felt himself imprisoned by the logician's spell, like Ariel in the cloven pine-tree,[19] he became suddenly enamoured of Bishop Berkeley's fairy-world,* and used in all companies to build the universe, like a brave poetical fiction, of fine words— and he was deep-read in Malebranche, and in

* Mr. Coleridge named his eldest son (the writer of some beautiful Sonnets) after Hartley, and the second after Berkeley. The third was called Derwent, after the river of that name. Nothing can be more characteristic of his mind than this circumstance. All his ideas indeed are like a river, flowing on for ever, and still murmuring as it flows, discharging its waters and still replenished—

"And so by many winding nooks it strays,
With willing sport to the wild ocean!"[20]

[16] Wordsworth's Excursion, VI, 557.
[17] David Hartley (1705–1757) was the author of the influential Observations on Man (1749). The first volume explained the operation of the mind and the development of human thought by the association of ideas and by vibrations in the brain from the sensible impressions of external objects. The second volume discussed matters of religion and morality.
[18] In various writings, Joseph Priestley (1733–1804) advanced the "atheistic" doctrine that man's soul was merely an activity or property of his material nature.
[19] See The Tempest, I, ii, 269–93.
[20] George Berkeley (1685–1753) was a clergyman and idealistic philosopher, who argued that spirit and mind were the only sources of reality. "And so . . . ocean" Two Gentlemen of Verona, II, vii, 31–32.

Cudworth's Intellectual System[21] (a huge pile of learning, unwieldy, enormous) and in Lord Brook's hieroglyphic theories, and in Bishop Butler's Sermons, and in the Duchess of Newcastle's fantastic folios, and in Clarke and South and Tillotson,[22] and all the fine thinkers and masculine reasoners of that age—and Leibnitz's Pre-established Harmony[23] reared its arch above his head, like the rainbow in the cloud, covenanting with the hopes of man—and then he fell plump, ten thousand fathoms down (but his wings saved him harmless) into the hortus siccus of Dissent,[24] where he pared religion down to the standard of reason and stripped faith of mystery, and preached Christ crucified and the Unity of the Godhead, and so dwelt for a while in the spirit with John Huss and Jerome of Prague and Socinus and old John Zisca,[25] and ran through Neal's History of the Puritans and Calamy's Non-Conformists' Memorial,[26] having like thoughts and passions with them—but then Spinoza[27] became his God, and he took up the vast chain of being in his hand, and the round world became the centre and the soul of all things in some shadowy sense, forlorn of meaning, and around him he beheld the living traces and the sky-pointing proportions of the mighty Pan—but poetry redeemed him from this spectral philosophy, and he bathed his heart in beauty, and gazed at the golden light of heaven, and drank of

[21] Nicolas Malebranche (1638–1715) was a French philosopher and follower of Descartes. Ralph Cudworth (1617–1688) was an English philosopher and theologian, one of the Cambridge Platonists.
[22] The works of the poet and dramatist Fulke Greville, first Baron Brooke (1554–1628) were notable for their stylistic and philosophic complexity. Joseph Butler (1692–1752) was a preacher and moralist, whose Fifteen Sermons (1726) anticipated Hazlitt's own discovery of the "Natural Disinterestedness of the Human Mind" (see "My First Acquaintance with Poets," p. 468). Margaret Cavendish, Duchess of Newcastle (c. 1624–1674), was the author of various works in poetry and prose, often embodying eccentric philosophic and scientific speculations. Samuel Clarke (1675–1729), Robert South (1634–1716), and John Tillotson (1630–1694) were leading theologians and preachers.
[23] Referring to the highly optimistic philosophic doctrines of Gottfried Wilhelm Leibnitz (1646–1716).
[24] The phrase is from Burke's Reflections on the Revolution in France, referring to the Unitarian political and religious Dissenters of the late eighteenth century. On Coleridge's Unitarian engagement, see "My First Acquaintance with Poets."
[25] John Huss (c. 1369–1415), Jerome of Prague (d. 1416), Lelio Francesco Maria Sozini (1525–1562) or Fausto Paolo Sozzini (1539–1604) were early religious reformers and dissenters from Roman Catholicism. John Zisca (d. 1424) was military leader of the Hussite armies in Bohemia.
[26] Daniel Neal (1678–1743) and Edmund Calamy (1671–1732) were dissenting ministers and leading historians of the non-conformist movement.
[27] Benedictus de Spinoza (1632–1677) was the Dutch philosopher, who advanced the "pantheistic" doctrine of the unity and co-existence of God, nature, and the mind as "one infinite substance."

the spirit of the universe, and wandered at eve by fairy-stream or fountain,

> ———— When he saw nought but beauty,
> When he heard the voice of that Almighty One
> In breeze that blew, or wave that murmured "—[28]

and wedded with truth in Plato's shade, and in the writings of Proclus and Plotinus [29] saw the ideas of things in the eternal mind, and unfolded all mysteries with the Schoolmen and fathomed the depths of Duns Scotus and Thomas Aquinas, [30] and entered the third heaven with Jacob Behmen, and walked hand in hand with Swedenborg [31] through the pavilions of the New Jerusalem, and sung his faith in the promise and in the word in his *Religious Musings* [32]—and lowering himself from that dizzy height, poised himself on Milton's wings, and spread out his thoughts in charity with the glad prose of Jeremy Taylor, and wept over Bowles's Sonnets, [33] and studied Cowper's blank verse, and betook himself to Thomson's Castle of Indolence, and sported with the wits of Charles the Second's days and of Queen Anne, and relished Swift's style and that of the John Bull (Arbuthnot's we mean, not Mr. Croker's), [34] and dallied with the British Essayists and Novelists, and knew all qualities of more modern writers with a learned spirit, Johnson, and Goldsmith, and Junius, and Burke, and Godwin, and the Sorrows of Werter, [35] and Jean Jacques Rousseau, and Voltaire, and Marivaux, and Crebillon, [36] and thousands more—now "laughed with Rabelais in his easy chair" [37] or pointed to Hogarth, or afterwards dwelt on Claude's classic scenes or spoke with rapture of Raphael, and compared the women at Rome to figures that had walked out of his pictures, or visited the Oratory at Pisa, and described the works of Giotto and Ghirlandaio [38] and Massaccio, and gave the moral of the picture of the Triumph of Death, [39] where the beggars and the wretched invoke his dreadful dart, but the rich and mighty of the earth quail and shrink before it; and in that land of siren sights and sounds, saw a dance of peasant girls, and was charmed with lutes and gondolas,—or wandered into Germany and lost himself in the labyrinths of the Hartz Forest and of the Kantean philosophy, and amongst the cabalistic names of Fichtè and Schelling and Lessing, [40] and God knows who—this was long after, but all the former while, he had nerved his heart and filled his eyes with tears, as he hailed the rising orb of liberty, since quenched in darkness and in blood, and had kindled his affections at the blaze of the French Revolution, and sang for joy when the towers of the Bastile and the proud places of the insolent and the oppressor fell, and would have floated his bark, freighted with fondest fancies, across the Atlantic wave with Southey and others to seek for peace and freedom—

> "In Philharmonia's undivided dale!" [41]

Alas! "Frailty, thy name is *Genius*!" [42]—What is become of all this mighty heap of hope, of thought, of learning, and humanity? It has ended in swallowing doses of oblivion and in writing paragraphs in the *Courier*.—Such, and so little is the mind of man!

It is not to be supposed that Mr. Coleridge could keep on at the rate he set off; he could not realize all he knew or thought, and less could not fix his desultory ambition; other stimulants supplied the place, and kept up the intoxicating dream, the fever and the madness of his early impressions. Liberty (the philosopher's and the poet's bride) had fallen a victim, meanwhile, to the murderous practices of the hag, Legitimacy. Proscribed by court-hirelings, too

---

[28] Coleridge's tragedy *Remorse* (1813), IV, ii, 101–103.

[29] Proclus (c. 410–485), and Plotinus (204–270) were leading formulators of neo-Platonic philosophy.

[30] Duns Scotus (c. 1265–c. 1308) and St. Thomas Aquinas (c. 1225–1274) were leading spokesmen for the Scholastic philosophy of the middle ages.

[31] Jacob Behmen (1575–1624) was a German religious mystic and writer. Emanuel Swedenborg (1688–1772) was a Swedish scientist and mystic.

[32] A "desultory poem" by Coleridge, published in 1796.

[33] Jeremy Taylor (1613–1667) was a clergyman and writer of works on religions and morality; a famous model of English prose style. For the sonnets of Bowles, see "Introduction to the Sonnets," p. 123, and *Biographia Literaria*, Chapter I, pp. 172–75.

[34] John Arbuthnot's political satire *The History of John Bull* (1712) had introduced the famous characterization of the British personality. John Wilson Croker (1780–1857), Tory politician and journalist, was erroneously thought to have been the editor of *John Bull*, a virulently anti-Whig newspaper first published in 1820.

[35] Goethe's famous sentimental novel, first published in 1774.

[36] Pierre Carlet de Chamblain de Marivaux (1688–1763) was a popular French writer of sentimental novels and plays. Prosper Jolyot de Crébillon (1674–1762) was a leading French tragedian of the eighteenth century.

[37] See Pope's *Dunciad*, I, 22.

[38] Giotto (c. 1266–1337) was a famous painter of religious frescoes and architect, early master of the Florentine school. Domenico Ghirlandaio (c. 1449–1494) was a Florentine painter and the master of Michelangelo. On Massaccio, see, the second of Hazlitt's essays "On Genius and Common Sense," footnote 20, p. 453.

[39] See "My First Acquaintance with Poets," Hazlitt's footnote, p. 472.

[40] Hazlitt refers to the German idealistic philosophers, Johann Gottlieb Fichte (1762–1814) and Friedrich Wilhelm Joseph von Schelling (1775–1854); and the famous critic and dramatist Gotthold Ephraim Lessing (1729–1781).

[41] Hazlitt quotes from Coleridge's poem "To the Rev. W. J. Hort" (1796), referring to Pantisocracy, an idealistic plan devised by Coleridge and Southey in 1794 for emigrating to Pennsylvania and forming a "communistic" settlement on the banks of the Susquehanna.

[42] Cf. *Hamlet*, I, ii, 146.

romantic for the herd of vulgar politicians, our enthusiast stood at bay, and at last turned on the pivot of
a subtle casuistry to the *unclean side*: but his discursive
reason would not let him trammel himself into a poet-
laureate or stamp-distributor,[43] and he stopped, ere
he had quite passed that well-known "bourne from
whence no traveller returns"[44]—and so has sunk into
torpid, uneasy repose, tantalized by useless resources,
haunted by vain imaginings, his lips idly moving, but
his heart for ever still, or, as the shattered chords
vibrate of themselves, making melancholy music to
the ear of memory! Such is the fate of genius in an
age, when in the unequal contest with sovereign
wrong, every man is ground to powder who is not
either a born slave, or who does not willingly and at
once offer up the yearnings of humanity and the dictates of reason as a welcome sacrifice to besotted prejudice and loathsome power.

Of all Mr. Coleridge's productions, the *Ancient
Mariner* is the only one that we could with confidence
put into any person's hands, on whom we wished to
impress a favourable idea of his extraordinary powers.
Let whatever other objections be made to it, it is unquestionably a work of genius—of wild, irregular,
overwhelming imagination, and has that rich, varied
movement in the verse, which gives a distant idea of
the lofty or changeful tones of Mr. Coleridge's voice.
In the *Christabel*, there is one splendid passage on
divided friendship.[45] The *Translation of Schiller's
Wallenstein* is also a masterly production in its kind,
faithful and spirited. Among his smaller pieces there
are occasional bursts of pathos and fancy, equal to
what we might expect from him; but these form the
exception, and not the rule. Such, for instance, is his
affecting Sonnet to the author of the Robbers.

"Schiller! that hour I would have wish'd to die,
    If through the shudd'ring midnight I had sent
    From the dark dungeon of the tower time-rent,
    That fearful voice, a famish'd father's cry—
    That in no after-moment aught less vast
    Might stamp me mortal! A triumphant shout
    Black horror scream'd, and all her goblin rout
From the more with'ring scene diminish'd pass'd.
    Ah! Bard tremendous in sublimity!
    Could I behold thee in thy loftier mood,

Wand'ring at eve, with finely frenzied eye,
    Beneath some vast old tempest-swinging wood!
    Awhile, with mute awe gazing, I would brood,
Then weep aloud in a wild ecstasy."

His Tragedy, entitled *Remorse*, is full of beautiful and
striking passages, but it does not place the author in
the first rank of dramatic writers. But if Mr. Coleridge's works do not place him in that rank, they injure instead of conveying a just idea of the man, for he
himself is certainly in the first class of general intellect.

If our author's poetry is inferior to his conversation,
his prose is utterly abortive. Hardly a gleam is to be
found in it of the brilliancy and richness of those
stores of thought and language that he pours out incessantly, when they are lost like drops of water in the
ground. The principal work, in which he has attempted to embody his general views of things, is the
FRIEND, of which, though it contains some noble
passages and fine trains of thought, prolixity and obscurity are the most frequent characteristics.

No two persons can be conceived more opposite in
character or genius than the subject of the present and
of the previous sketch. Mr. Godwin with less natural
capacity, and with fewer acquired advantages, by concentrating his mind on some given object, and doing
what he had to do with all his might, has accomplished
much, and will leave more than one monument of a
powerful intellect behind him; Mr. Coleridge, by dissipating his, and dallying with every subject by turns,
has done little or nothing to justify to the world or to
posterity, the high opinion which all who have ever
heard him converse, or known him intimately, with
one accord entertain of him. Mr. Godwin's faculties
have kept at home, and plied their task in the workshop of the brain, diligently and effectually: Mr.
Coleridge's have gossiped away their time, and gadded
about from house to house, as if life's business were to
melt the hours in listless talk. Mr. Godwin is intent
on a subject, only as it concerns himself and his reputation; he works it out as a matter of duty, and dis-
cards from his mind whatever does not forward his
main object as impertinent and vain. Mr. Coleridge,
on the other hand, delights in nothing but episodes
and digressions, neglects whatever he undertakes to
perform, and can act only on spontaneous impulses,
without object or method. "He cannot be constrained by mastery."[46] While he should be occupied
with a given pursuit, he is thinking of a thousand
other things; a thousand tastes, a thousand objects

---

[43] Referring to Southey and Wordsworth, who renounced
the revolutionary principles of their early years and became
supporters of the policies of the British government against the
French. In 1813, Southey was named laureate, and Wordsworth
was appointed Distributor of Stamps for the County of Westmoreland.
[44] *Hamlet*, III, i, 79–80.
[45] See ll. 408–426.

[46] Cf. Wordsworth's *Excursion*, VI, 163–64.

tempt him, and distract his mind, which keeps open house, and entertains all comers; and after being fatigued and amused with morning calls from idle visitors, finds the day consumed and its business unconcluded. Mr. Godwin, on the contrary, is somewhat exclusive and unsocial in his habits of mind, entertains no company but what he gives his whole time and attention to, and wisely writes over the doors of his understanding, his fancy, and his senses—"No admittance except on business." He has none of that fastidious refinement and false delicacy, which might lead him to balance between the endless variety of modern attainments. He does not throw away his life (nor a single half-hour of it) in adjusting the claims of different accomplishments, and in choosing between them or making himself master of them all. He sets about his task, (whatever it may be) and goes through it with spirit and fortitude. He has the happiness to think an author the greatest character in the world, and himself the greatest author in it. Mr. Coleridge, in writing an harmonious stanza, would stop to consider whether there was not more grace and beauty in a *Pas de trois*, and would not proceed till he had resolved this question by a chain of metaphysical reasoning without end. Not so Mr. Godwin. That is best to him, which he can do best. He does not waste himself in vain aspirations and effeminate sympathies. He is blind, deaf, insensible to all but the trump of Fame. Plays, operas, painting, music, ballrooms, wealth, fashion, titles, lords, ladies, touch him not—all these are no more to him than to the magician in his cell, and he writes on to the end of the chapter, through good report and evil report. *Pingo in eternitatem*[47]—is his motto. He neither envies nor admires what others are, but is contented to be what he is, and strives to do the utmost he can. Mr. Coleridge has flirted with the Muses as with a set of mistresses: Mr. Godwin has been married twice, to Reason and to Fancy,[48] and has to boast no short-lived progeny by each. So to speak, he has *valves* belonging to his mind, to regulate the quantity of gas admitted into it, so that like the bare, unsightly, but well-compacted steamvessel, it cuts its liquid way, and arrives at its promised end: while Mr. Coleridge's bark, "taught with the little nautilus to sail," the sport of every breath, dancing to every wave,

"Youth at its prow, and Pleasure at its helm,"[49]

flutters its gaudy pennons in the air, glitters in the sun, but we wait in vain to hear of its arrival in the destined harbour. Mr. Godwin, with less variety and vividness, with less subtlety and susceptibility both of thought and feeling, has had firmer nerves, a more determined purpose, a more comprehensive grasp of his subject, and the results are as we find them. Each has met with his reward: for justice has, after all, been done to the pretensions of each; and we must, in all cases, use means to ends!

It was a misfortune to any man of talent to be born in the latter end of the last century. Genius stopped the way of Legitimacy, and therefore it was to be abated, crushed, or set aside as a nuisance. The spirit of the monarchy was at variance with the spirit of the age. The flame of liberty, the light of intellect was to be extinguished with the sword—or with slander, whose edge is sharper than the sword. The war between power and reason was carried on by the first of these abroad—by the last at home. No quarter was given (then or now) by the Government-critics, the authorised censors of the press, to those who followed the dictates of independence, who listened to the voice of the tempter, Fancy. Instead of gathering fruits and flowers, immortal fruits and amaranthine flowers, they soon found themselves beset not only by a host of prejudices, but assailed by all the engines of power, by nicknames, by lies, by all the arts of malice, interest, and hypocrisy, without a possibility of their defending themselves from the "pelting of the pitiless storm,"[50] that poured down upon them from the strong-holds of corruption and authority. The philosophers, the dry abstract reasoners, submitted to this reverse pretty well, and armed themselves with patience "as with triple steel,"[51] to bear discomfiture, persecution, and disgrace. But the poets, the creatures of sympathy, could not stand the frowns both of king and people. They did not like to be shut out when places and pensions, when the critic's praises, and the laurel-wreath were about to be distributed. They did not stomach being *sent to Coventry*,[52] and Mr. Coleridge sounded a retreat for them by the help of casuistry and a musical voice—"His words were hollow, but they pleased the ear"[53] of his friends of the Lake School, who turned back disgusted and panic-struck from the dry desert of unpopularity, like Hassan the camel-driver,

---

[47] *Pingo in eternitatem*: "I paint for eternity," a remark attributed to the Greek painter Zeuxis.
[48] Hazlitt refers to Godwin's intellectual career as philosopher and novelist. In private life, Godwin had been married twice: to Mary Wollstonecraft, author of the *Vindication of the Rights of Woman* (1792), and mother of Shelley's wife Mary; and to Mrs. Mary Clairmont.

[49] Gray's "The Bard", l. 74.
[50] *King Lear*, III, iv, 29.
[51] *Paradise Lost*, II, 569.
[52] Proverbial expression for social disgrace.
[53] Cf. *Paradise Lost*, II, 112–117.

"And curs'd the hour, and curs'd the luckless day,
    When first from Schiraz' walls they bent their way." [54]

They are safely inclosed there, but Mr. Coleridge did not enter with them; pitching his tent upon the barren-waste without, and having no abiding city nor place of refuge!

[1825]

F R O M

SIR WALTER SCOTT

SIR WALTER SCOTT is undoubtedly the most popular writer of the age—the "lord of the ascendant" [1] for the time being. He is just half what the human intellect is capable of being: if you take the universe, and divide it into two parts, he knows all that it *has been*; all that it *is to be* is nothing to him. His is a mind brooding over antiquity—scorning "the present ignorant time." [2] He is "laudator temporis acti" [3]—a "*prophesier* of things past." The old world is to him a crowded map; the new one a dull, hateful blank. He dotes on all well-authenticated superstitions; he shudders at the shadow of innovation. His retentiveness of memory, his accumulated weight of interested prejudice or romantic association have overlaid his other faculties. The cells of his memory are vast, various, full even to bursting with life and motion; his speculative understanding is empty, flaccid, poor, and dead. His mind receives and treasures up every thing brought to it by tradition or custom—it does not project itself beyond this into the world unknown, but mechanically shrinks back as from the edge of a precipice. The land of pure reason is to his apprehension like *Van Dieman's Land*; [4]—barren, miserable, distant, a place of exile, the dreary abode of savages, convicts, and adventurers. Sir Walter would make a bad hand of a description of the *Millennium*, unless he could lay the scene in Scotland five hundred years ago, and then he would want facts and worm-eaten parchments to support his drooping style. Our historical novelist firmly thinks that nothing *is* but what *has been*—that the moral world stands still, as the ma-

terial one was supposed to do of old—and that we can never get beyond the point where we actually are without utter destruction, though every thing changes and will change from what it was three hundred years ago to what it is now,—from what it is now to all that the bigoted admirer of the good old times most dreads and hates!

It is long since we read, and long since we thought of our author's poetry. It would probably have gone out of date with the immediate occasion, even if he himself had not contrived to banish it from our recollection. It is not to be denied that it had great merit, both of an obvious and intrinsic kind. It abounded in vivid descriptions, in spirited action, in smooth and flowing versification. But it wanted *character*. It was "poetry of no mark or likelihood." [5] It slid out of the mind as soon as read, like a river; and would have been forgotten, but that the public curiosity was fed with ever new supplies from the same teeming liquid source. It is not every man that can write six quarto volumes in verse, [6] that are caught up with avidity, even by fastidious judges. But what a difference between *their* popularity and that of the Scotch Novels! It is true, the public read and admired the *Lay of the Last Minstrel*, *Marmion*, and so on, and each individual was contented to read and admire because the public did so: but with regard to the prose-works of the same (supposed) author, it is quite *another-guess* [7] sort of thing. Here every one stands forward to applaud on his own ground, would be thought to go before the public opinion, is eager to extol his favourite characters louder, to understand them better than every body else, and has his own scale of comparative excellence for each work, supported by nothing but his own enthusiastic and fearless convictions. It must be amusing to the *Author of Waverley* to hear his readers and admirers (and are not these the same thing?*) quarrelling which of his novels is the best, opposing character to character, quoting passage against passage, striving to surpass each other in the

* No! For we met with a young lady who kept a circulating library and a milliner's shop, in a watering-place in the country, who, when we inquired for the *Scotch Novels*, spoke indifferently about them, said they were "so dry she could hardly get through them," and recommended us to read *Agnes*. [8] We never thought of it before; but we would venture to lay a wager that there are many other young ladies in the same situation, and who think "Old Mortality" "dry."

---

54 William Collins' Second Persian Ecologue, "Hassan; or, the Camel Driver" (1742).
1 Term from astrology, referring to the dominant or controlling planet.
2 Cf. *Macbeth*, I, v, 58.
3 laudator temporis acti: "a praiser of past events." Horace's *Ars Poetica*, l. 173.
4 Until 1853, the name of Tasmania, from Antonio van Dieman, governor general of the Dutch East Indies at the time of discovery (1642).

---

5 Cf. *Henry the Fourth*, Part I, III, ii, 45.
6 *The Lay of the Last Minstrel* (1805), *Marmion* (1808), *The Lady of the Lake* (1810), *The Vision of Don Roderick* (1811), *Rokeby* (1813), *The Lord of the Isles* (1815).
7 Archaic expression meaning "of another kind."
8 *Agnes, or the Triumph of Principle*, anonymous novel of 1822.

extravagance of their encomiums, and yet unable to
settle the precedence, or to do the author's writings
justice—so various, so equal, so transcendant are their
merits! His volumes of poetry were received as
fashionable and well-dressed acquaintances: we are
ready to tear the others in pieces as old friends. There
was something meretricious in Sir Walter's ballad-
rhymes; and like those who keep opera *figurantes*,[9] we
were willing to have our admiration shared, and our
taste confirmed by the town: but the Novels are like
the betrothed of our hearts, bone of our bone, and
flesh of our flesh, and we are jealous that any one
should be as much delighted or as thoroughly acquainted with their beauties as ourselves. For which
of his poetical heroines would the reader break a lance
so soon as for Jeanie Deans? What *Lady of the Lake*
can compare with the beautiful Rebecca?[10] We believe the late Mr. John Scott went to his death-bed
(though a painful and premature one) with some degree of satisfaction, inasmuch as he had penned the
most elaborate panegyric on the *Scotch Novels* that had
as yet appeared![11]—The *Epics* are not poems, so much
as metrical romances. There is a glittering veil of
verse thrown over the features of nature and of old
romance. The deep incisions into character are
"skinned and filmed over"[12]—the details are lost or
shaped into flimsy and insipid decorum; and the truth
of feeling and of circumstance is translated into a
tinkling sound, a tinsel *common-place*. It must be
owned, there is a power in true poetry that lifts the
mind from the ground of reality to a higher sphere,
that penetrates the inert, scattered, incoherent materials presented to it, and by a force and inspiration
of its own, melts and moulds them into sublimity and
beauty. But Sir Walter (we contend, under correction)
has not this creative impulse, this plastic power, this
capacity of reacting on his first impressions. He is a
learned, a literal, a *matter-of-fact* expounder of truth
or fable:* he does not soar above and look down upon
his subject, imparting his own lofty views and feelings
to his descriptions of nature—he relies upon it, is
raised by it, is one with it, or he is nothing. A poet is

* Just as Cobbett is a matter-of-fact reasoner.[13]

〰〰〰〰〰〰〰〰〰〰〰〰〰〰〰〰〰〰

9 Dancers.
10 Jeanie Deans and Rebecca were the heroines, respectively,
of *The Heart of Midlothian* (1818) and *Ivanhoe* (1819).
11 John Scott (1783–1821) was founder and editor of the
London Magazine, whose first issue (January 1820) contained a
praiseful essay on "The Author of the Scotch Novels." John
Scott was fatally injured in a duel, the result of a dispute between
himself and John Lockhart, editor of *Blackwood's Magazine*.
12 Cf. *Hamlet*, III, iv, 147.
13 William Cobbett (1762–1835) the political controversalist
and editor of *Cobbett's Weekly Register*.

essentially a *maker*; that is, he must atone for what he
loses in individuality and local resemblance by the
energies and resources of his own mind. The writer of
whom we speak is deficient in these last. He has either
not the faculty or not the will to impregnate his subject by an effort of pure invention. The execution also
is much upon a par with the more ephemeral effusions of the press. It is light, agreeable, effeminate,
diffuse. Sir Walter's Muse is a *Modern Antique*. The
smooth, glossy texture of his verse contrasts happily
with the quaint, uncouth, rugged materials of which
it is composed; and takes away any appearance of
heaviness or harshness from the body of local traditions and obsolete costume. We see grim knights and
iron armour; but then they are woven in silk with a
careless, delicate hand, and have the softness of
flowers. The poet's figures might be compared to old
tapestries copied on the finest velvet:—they are not
like Raphael's *Cartoons*, but they are very like Mr.
Westall's drawings,[14] which accompany, and are intended to illustrate them. This facility and grace of
execution is the more remarkable, as a story goes that
not long before the appearance of the *Lay of the Last
Minstrel* Sir Walter (then Mr.) Scott, having, in the
company of a friend, to cross the Firth of Forth in a
ferry-boat, they proposed to beguile the time by writing a number of verses on a given subject, and that at
the end of an hour's hard study, they found they had
produced only six lines between them. "It is plain,"
said the unconscious author to his fellow-labourer,
"that you and I need never think of getting our living
by writing poetry!" In a year or so after this, he set to
work, and poured out quarto upon quarto, as if they
had been drops of water. As to the rest, and compared
with true and great poets, our Scottish Minstrel is but
"a metre ballad-monger."[15] We would rather have
written one song of Burns, or a single passage in Lord
Byron's *Heaven and Earth*, or one of Wordsworth's
"fancies and good-nights,"[16] than all his epics. What
is he to Spenser, over whose immortal, ever-amiable
verse beauty hovers and trembles, and who has shed
the purple light of Fancy, from his ambrosial wings,
over all nature? What is there of the might of Milton,
whose head is canopied in the blue serene, and who
takes us to sit with him there? What is there (in his
ambling rhymes) of the deep pathos of Chaucer? Or
of the o'er-informing power of Shakespear, whose eye,

〰〰〰〰〰〰〰〰〰〰〰〰〰〰〰〰〰〰

14 Richard Westall (1765–1836) provided illustrations for
editions of *Lay of the Last Minstrel, Marmion, Lord of the Isles*, and
Lady of the Lake.
15 *Henry the Fourth*, Part I, III, i, 130.
16 *Heaven and Earth*, a "mystery" drama of 1823. The quotation "fancies and good-nights," meaning light lyrics, is from
Henry the Fourth, Part II, III, ii, 342.

watching alike the minutest traces of characters and the strongest movements of passion, "glances from heaven to earth, from earth to heaven," [17] and with the lambent flame of genius, playing round each object, lights up the universe in a robe of its own radiance? Sir Walter has no voluntary power of combination: all his associations (as we said before) are those of habit or of tradition. He is a mere narrative and descriptive poet, garrulous of the old time. The definition of his poetry is a pleasing superficiality.

Not so of his NOVELS AND ROMANCES. There we turn over a new leaf—another and the same—the same in matter, but in form, in power how different! The author of Waverley has got rid of the tagging of rhymes, the eking out of syllables, the supplying of epithets, the colours of style, the grouping of his characters, and the regular march of events, and comes to the point at once, and strikes at the heart of his subject, without dismay and without disguise. His poetry was a lady's waiting-maid, dressed out in cast-off finery; his prose is a beautiful, rustic nymph, that, like Dorothea in Don Quixote,[18] when she is surprised with dishevelled tresses bathing her naked feet in the brook, looks round her, abashed at the admiration her charms have excited! The grand secret of the author's success in these latter productions is that he has completely got rid of the trammels of authorship; and torn off at one rent (as Lord Peter got rid of so many yards of lace in the *Tale of a Tub*)[19] all the ornaments of fine writing and worn-out sentimentality. All is fresh, as from the hand of nature: by going a century or two back and laying the scene in a remote and uncultivated district, all becomes new and startling in the present advanced period.—Highland manners, characters, scenery, superstitions, Northern dialect and costume, the wars, the religion, and politics of the sixteenth and seventeenth centuries, give a charming and wholesome relief to the fastidious refinement and "over-laboured lassitude"[20] of modern readers, like the effect of plunging a nervous valetudinarian into a cold-bath. The *Scotch Novels*, for this reason, are not so much admired in Scotland as in England. The contrast, the transition is less striking. From the top of the Calton-Hill, the inhabitants of "Auld Reekie"[21] can descry, or fancy they descry the peaks of Ben Lomond and the waving outline of Rob

Roy's country: we who live at the southern extremity of the island can only catch a glimpse of the billowy scene in the descriptions of the Author of Waverley. The mountain air is most bracing to our languid nerves, and it is brought us in ship-loads from the neighbourhood of Abbot's-Ford.[22] There is another circumstance to be taken into the account. In Edinburgh there is a little opposition and something of the spirit of cabal between the partisans of works proceeding from Mr. Constable's and Mr. Blackwood's shops.[23] Mr. Constable gives the highest prices; but being the Whig bookseller, it is grudged that he should do so. An attempt is therefore made to transfer a certain share of popularity to the second-rate Scotch novels, "the embryo fry, the little airy of *ricketty* children," issuing through Mr. Blackwood's shop-door.[24] This operates a diversion which does not affect us here. The Author of Waverley wears the palm of legendary lore alone. Sir Walter may, indeed, surfeit us: his imitators make us sick! It may be asked, it has been asked, "Have we no materials for romance in England? Must we look to Scotland for a supply of whatever is original and striking in this kind?" And we answer—"Yes!" Every foot of soil is with us worked up: nearly every movement of the social machine is calculable. We have no room left for violent catastrophes; for grotesque quaintnesses; for wizard spells. The last skirts of ignorance and barbarism are seen hovering (in Sir Walter's pages) over the Border. We have, it is true, gipsies in this country as well as at the Cairn of Derncleugh:[25] but they live under clipped hedges, and repose in camp-beds, and do not perch on crags, like eagles, or take shelter, like sea-mews, in basaltic subterranean caverns. We have heaths with rude heaps of stone upon them: but no existing superstition converts them into the Geese of Mickelstane-Moor, or sees a Black Dwarf groping among them. We have sects in religion: but the only thing sublime or ridiculous in that way is Mr. Irving, the Caledonian preacher, who "comes like a satyr staring from the woods, and yet speaks like an orator!"[26] We had a Parson Adams not quite a hundred years ago—a Sir Roger de Coverley rather more

---

[17] *Midsummer Night's Dream*, V, i, 13.

[18] See Part I, Chapter XXVIII.

[19] In Section VI of Swift's satire, where it is actually Martin [Luther] and Jack [Calvin] who remove the trimmings [Roman Catholic ceremonies] from their coats [the original doctrines of Christianity].

[20] From Burke's *Reflections on the French Revolution*.

[21] "Old Smoky," nickname for Edinburgh.

[22] The elaborate "medieval" castle and country estate that Scott had built on the banks of the Tweed.

[23] Archibald Constable (1774–1827) and William Blackwood (1776–1834) were leading and rival publishers in Edinburgh.

[24] Blackwood published *The Black Dwarf* and *Old Mortality* in 1816.

[25] See *Guy Mannering*, Chapters XXVI and XLVI for the Kaim [camp or hillock] of Derncleugh, a ruined tower occupied by Meg Merrilies.

[26] Edward Irving (1792–1834) was a thunderous and theatrical Scotch preacher, whose sermons in London created a sensation. The quotation is from Horace's *Ars Poetica*, ll. 281–82.

than a hundred![27] Even Sir Walter is ordinarily obliged to pitch his angle (strong as the hook is) a hundred miles to the North of the "Modern Athens"[28] or a century back. His last work,* indeed, is mystical, is romantic in nothing but the title-page. Instead of "a holy-water sprinkle dipped in dew,"[30] he has given us a fashionable watering-place—and we see what he has made of it. He must not come down from his fastnesses in traditional barbarism and native rusticity: the level, the littleness, the frippery of modern civilization will undo him as it has undone us!

Sir Walter has found out (oh, rare discovery) that facts are better than fiction; that there is no romance like the romance of real life; and that if we can but arrive at what men feel, do, and say in striking and singular situations, the result will be "more lively, audible, and full of vent,"[31] than the fine-spun cobwebs of the brain. With reverence be it spoken, he is like the man who having to imitate the squeaking of a pig upon the stage, brought the animal under his coat with him. Our author has conjured up the actual people he has to deal with, or as much as he could get of them, in "their habits as they lived."[32] He has ransacked old chronicles, and poured the contents upon his page; he has squeezed out musty records; he has consulted wayfaring pilgrims, bed-rid sibyls; he has invoked the spirits of the air; he has conversed with the living and the dead, and let them tell their story their own way; and by borrowing of others, has enriched his own genius with everlasting variety, truth, and freedom. He has taken his materials from the original, authentic sources, in large concrete masses, and not tampered with or too much frittered them away. He is only the amanuensis of truth and history. It is impossible to say how fine his writings in consequence are, unless we could describe how fine nature is. All that portion of the history of his country that he has touched upon (wide as the scope is) the manners, the personages, the events, the scenery, lives over again in his volumes. Nothing is wanting—the illusion is complete. There is a hurtling in the air, a trampling of feet upon the ground, as these perfect representations of human character or fanciful belief come thronging back upon our imaginations. . . .[33]

* St. Ronan's Well.[29]

〰〰〰〰〰〰〰〰〰〰〰〰〰〰〰〰〰〰〰

[27] Parson Adams in Fielding's *Joseph Andrews* (1742); Sir Roger de Coverley in the *Spectator Papers* (1711–1712).
[28] Edinburgh.
[29] Novel published in 1824.
[30] *Faerie Queene*, III, xii, 13.
[31] See *Coriolanus*, IV, v, 237–38.
[32] See *Hamlet*, III, iv, 135.
[33] Here omitted a long paragraph listing some of Hazlitt's favorite characters and events in the Waverley Novels.

The political bearing of the *Scotch Novels* has been a considerable recommendation to them. They are a relief to the mind, rarefied as it has been with modern philosophy, and heated with ultra-radicalism. At a time also, when we bid fair to revive the principles of the Stuarts, it is interesting to bring us acquainted with their persons and misfortunes. The candour of Sir Walter's historic pen levels our bristling prejudices on this score, and sees fair play between Roundheads and Cavaliers, between Protestant and Papist. He is a writer reconciling all the diversities of human nature to the reader. He does not enter into the distinctions of hostile sects or parties, but treats of the strength or the infirmity of the human mind, of the virtues or vices of the human breast, as they are to be found blended in the whole race of mankind. Nothing can show more handsomely or be more gallantly executed. There was a talk at one time that our author was about to take Guy Faux for the subject of one of his novels, in order to put a more liberal and humane construction on the Gunpowder Plot than our "No Popery" prejudices have hitherto permitted. Sir Walter is a professed *clarifier* of the age from the vulgar and still lurking old-English antipathy to Popery and Slavery. Through some odd process of *servile* logic, it should seem, that in restoring the claims of the Stuarts by the courtesy of romance, the House of Brunswick are more firmly seated in point of fact, and the Bourbons, by collateral reasoning, become legitimate! In any other point of view, we cannot possibly conceive how Sir Walter imagines "he has done something to revive the declining spirit of loyalty" by these novels. His loyalty is founded on *would-be* treason: he props the actual throne by the shadow of rebellion. Does he really think of making us enamoured of the "good old times" by the faithful and harrowing portraits he has drawn of them? Would he carry us back to the early stages of barbarism, of clanship, of the feudal system as "a consummation devoutly to be wished?"[34] Is he infatuated enough, or does he so dote and drivel over his own slothful and self-willed prejudices, as to believe that he will make a single convert to the beauty of Legitimacy, that is, of lawless power and savage bigotry, when he himself is obliged to apologise for the horrors he describes, and even render his descriptions credible to the modern reader by referring to the authentic history of these delectable times?† He is in-

† "And here we cannot but think it necessary to offer some better proof than the incidents of an idle tale, to vindicate the melancholy representation of manners which has been just laid before the reader. It is grievous to think that those valiant Barons, to whose stand against the crown the liberties of England

〰〰〰〰〰〰〰〰〰〰〰〰〰〰〰〰〰〰〰

[34] *Hamlet*, III, i, 63–64.

deed so besotted as to the moral of his own story, that he has even the blindness to go out of his way to have a fling at *flints* and *dungs* 36 (the contemptible ingredients, as he would have us believe, of a modern rabble) at the very time when he is describing a mob of the twelfth century—a mob (one should think) after the writer's own heart, without one particle of modern philosophy or revolutionary politics in their composition, who were to a man, to a hair, just what priests, and kings, and nobles *let* them be, and who were collected to witness (a spectacle proper to the times) the burning of the lovely Rebecca at a stake for a sorceress, because she was a Jewess, beautiful and innocent, and the consequent victim of insane bigotry and unbridled profligacy. And it is at this moment (when the heart is kindled and bursting with indignation at the revolting abuses of self-constituted power) that Sir Walter *stops the press* to have a sneer at the people, and to put a spoke (as he thinks) in the wheel of upstart innovation! This is what he "calls backing his friends" 37—it is thus he administers charms and philtres to our love of Legitimacy, makes us conceive a horror of all reform, civil, political, or religious, and would fain put down the *Spirit of the Age*. The author of Waverley might just as well get up and make a speech at a dinner at Edinburgh, abusing Mr. Mac-Adam for his improvements in the roads, on the

ground that they were nearly *impassable* in many places "sixty years since;" 38 or object to Mr. Peel's *Police-Bill*, by insisting that Hounslow-Heath was formerly a scene of greater interest and terror to highwaymen and travellers, and cut a greater figure in the Newgate Calendar than it does at present.39—Oh! Wickliff, Luther, Hampden, Sidney, Somers,40 mistaken Whigs, and thoughtless Reformers in religion and politics, and all ye, whether poets or philosophers, heroes or sages, inventors of arts or sciences, patriots, benefactors of the human race, enlighteners and civilisers of the world, who have (so far) reduced opinion to reason, and power to law, who are the cause that we no longer burn witches and heretics at slow fires, that the thumb-screws are no longer applied by ghastly, smiling judges, to extort confession of imputed crimes from sufferers for conscience sake; that men are no longer strung up like acorns on trees without judge or jury, or hunted like wild beasts through thickets and glens, who have abated the cruelty of priests, the pride of nobles, the divinity of kings in former times; to whom we owe it, that we no longer wear round our necks the collar of Gurth the swineherd, and of Wamba the jester; 41 that the castles of great lords are no longer the dens of banditti, from whence they issue with fire and sword, to lay waste the land; that we no longer expire in loathsome dungeons without knowing the cause, or have our right hands struck off for raising them in self-defence against wanton insult; that we can sleep without fear of being burnt in our beds, or travel without making our wills; that no Amy Robsarts are thrown down trap-doors by Richard Varneys with impunity, that no Red Reiver of Westburn-Flat sets fire to peaceful cottages;42 that no Claverhouse signs cold-blooded death-warrants in sport; that we have no Tristan the Hermit, or Petit-

---

were indebted for their existence, should themselves have been such dreadful oppressors, and capable of excesses, contrary not only to the laws of England, but to those of nature and humanity. But alas! we have only to extract from the industrious Henry one of those numerous passages which he has collected from contemporary historians, to prove that fiction itself can hardly reach the dark reality of the horrors of the period.

"The description given by the author of the Saxon Chronicle of the cruelties exercised in the reign of King Stephen by the great barons and lords of castles, who were all Normans, affords a strong proof of the excesses of which they were capable when their passions were inflamed. 'They grievously oppressed the poor people by building castles; and when they were built, they filled them with wicked men or rather devils, who seized both men and women who they imagined had any money, threw them into prison, and put them to more cruel tortures than the martyrs ever endured. They suffocated some in mud, and suspended others by the feet, or the head, or the thumbs, kindling fires below them. They squeezed the heads of some with knotted cords till they pierced their brains, while they threw others into dungeons swarming with serpents, snakes, and toads.' But it would be cruel to put the reader to the pain of perusing the remainder of the description."—*Henry's Hist.* edit. 1805, vol. vii. p. 346.35

35 Hazlitt is quoting a passage from *Ivanhoe*, Chapter XXIII.
36 Slang of the tailor trade, referring to independent-minded journeymen tailors (*flints*) who refused to submit to their master's terms, in contrast to the more slavish and compliant *dungs*. Hazlitt refers to a passage in *Ivanhoe*, Chapter XLIII.
37 *Henry the Fourth*, Part I, II, iv, 166.

38 John McAdam (1756–1836) was the famous road-builder. "Sixty years since" was the subtitle of *Waverley*.
39 Police-Bill refers to The Peace Preservation Act of 1814, the first step in the creation of a national police force, the Royal Irish Constabulary or "Peelers." Hazlitt may be referring also to various actions taken by Robert Peel on becoming Home Secretary in 1822, to strengthen the police force of Metropolitan London. Newgate Calendar was the published account of prisoners in Newgate Jail.
40 Famous opponents of arbitrary royal power. John Hampden (1594–1643), leader of the resistance to Charles the First's imposition of ship-money, met his death in battle against the royalist forces. Algernon Sidney (1622–1683), leader of republican forces in the Civil War, was executed for his supposed part in a plot against the life of Charles the Second. John Somers (1651–1716), lord chancellor of England, was instrumental in framing the Act of Settlement, which brought William of Orange to the throne and assured parliamentary control of the government.
41 Characters in *Ivanhoe*.
42 Amy Robsart and Richard Varney were characters in *Kenilworth* (1821). Red Reiver of Westburn-Flat was in *The Black Dwarf*.

Andrè,[43] crawling near us, like spiders, and making our flesh creep, and our hearts sicken within us at every moment of our lives—ye who have produced this change in the face of nature and society, return to earth once more, and beg pardon of Sir Walter and his patrons, who sigh at not being able to undo all that you have done! Leaving this question, there are two other remarks which we wished to make on the Novels. The one was, to express our admiration of the good-nature of the mottos, in which the author has taken occasion to remember and quote almost every living author (whether illustrious or obscure) but himself—an indirect argument in favour of the general opinion as to the source from which they spring—and the other was, to hint our astonishment at the innumerable and incessant instances of bad and slovenly English in them, more, we believe, than in any other works now printed. We should think the writer could not possibly read the manuscript after he has once written it, or overlook the press.

If there were a writer, who "born for the universe"—

"—— Narrow'd his mind,
And to party gave up what was meant for mankind—"[44]

who, from the height of his genius looking abroad into nature, and scanning the recesses of the human heart, "winked and shut his apprehension up" to every thought or purpose that tended to the future good of mankind—who, raised by affluence, the reward of successful industry, and by the voice of fame above the want of any but the most honourable patronage, stooped to the unworthy arts of adulation, and abetted the views of the great with the pettifogging feelings of the meanest dependant on office—who, having secured the admiration of the public (with the probable reversion of immortality), showed no respect for himself, for that genius that had raised him to distinction, for that nature which he trampled under foot—who, amiable, frank, friendly, manly in private life, was seized with the dotage of age and the fury of a woman, the instant politics were concerned—who reserved all his candour and comprehensiveness of view for history, and vented his littleness, pique, resentment, bigotry, and intolerance on his contemporaries—who took the wrong side, and defended it by unfair means—who, the moment his own interest or the prejudices of others interfered, seemed to forget all that was due to the pride of intellect, to the sense of manhood—who,

praised, admired by men of all parties alike, repaid the public liberality by striking a secret and envenomed blow at the reputation of every one who was not the ready tool of power—who strewed the slime of rankling malice and mercenary scorn over the bud and promise of genius, because it was not fostered in the hot-bed of corruption, or warped by the trammels of servility—who supported the worst abuses of authority in the worst spirit—who joined a gang of desperadoes to spread calumny, contempt, infamy, wherever they were merited by honesty or talent on a different side—who officiously undertook to decide public questions by private insinuations, to prop the throne by nicknames, and the altar by lies—who being (by common consent), the finest, the most humane and accomplished writer of his age, associated himself with and encouraged the lowest panders of a venal press; deluging, nauseating the public mind with the offal and garbage of Billingsgate[45] abuse and vulgar *slang*; showing no remorse, no relenting or compassion towards the victims of this nefarious and organized system of party-proscription, carried on under the mask of literary criticism and fair discussion, insulting the misfortunes of some, and trampling on the early grave of others—

"Who would not grieve if such a man there be?
Who would not weep if Atticus were he?"[46]

But we believe there is no other age or country of the world (but ours), in which such genius could have been so degraded!

[April 1824]   [1825]

LORD BYRON

LORD BYRON and Sir Walter Scott are among writers now living* the two, who would carry away a majority of suffrages as the greatest geniuses of the age. The former would, perhaps, obtain the preference with the fine gentlemen and ladies (squeamishness apart)—the latter with the critics and the vulgar. We shall treat of them in the same connection, partly on account of their distinguished pre-eminence, and partly because they afford a complete contrast to each other. In their poetry, in their prose, in their politics, and in their tempers, no two men can be more unlike.

* This Essay was written just before Lord Byron's death.

---

43 Characters in *Quentin Durward* (1823).
44 Goldsmith's *Retaliation* (1774), ll. 31–32. The next quotation occurs in the Prologue, l. 17, of John Marston's play *Antonio's Revenge* (c. 1599).

45 The London fish-market. The bad language of the fish-wives was proverbial.
46 Pope's *Epistle to Dr. Arbuthnot*, ll. 213–14. The entire last paragraph of Hazlitt's essay is based on an elaborate period in Pope's poem, ll. 193–214.

If Sir Walter Scott may be thought by some to have been

"Born universal heir to all humanity,"

it is plain Lord Byron can set up no such pretension. He is, in a striking degree, the creature of his own will. He holds no communion with his kind; but stands alone, without mate or fellow—

"As if a man were author of himself,
And owned no other kin." ¹

He is like a solitary peak, all access to which is cut off not more by elevation than distance. He is seated on a lofty eminence, "cloud-capt," ² or reflecting the last rays of setting suns; and in his poetical moods, reminds us of the fabled Titans, retired to a ridgy steep, playing on their Pan's-pipes, and taking up ordinary men and things in their hands with haughty indifference. He raises his subject to himself, or tramples on it; he neither stoops to, nor loses himself in it. He exists not by sympathy, but by antipathy. He scorns all things, even himself. Nature must come to him to sit for her picture—he does not go to her. She must consult his time, his convenience, and his humour; and wear a *sombre* or a fantastic garb, or his Lordship turns his back upon her. There is no ease, no unaffected simplicity of manner, no "golden mean." All is strained, or petulant in the extreme. His thoughts are sphered and crystalline; his style "prouder than when blue Iris bends;" ³ his spirit fiery, impatient, wayward, indefatigable. Instead of taking his impressions from without, in entire and almost unimpaired masses, he moulds them according to his own temperament, and heats the materials of his imagination in the furnace of his passions.—Lord Byron's verse glows like a flame, consuming every thing in its way; Sir Walter Scott's glides like a river, clear, gentle, harmless. The poetry of the first scorches, that of the last scarcely warms. The light of the one proceeds from an internal source, ensanguined, sullen, fixed; the other reflects the hues of Heaven, or the face of nature, glancing vivid and various. The productions of the Northern Bard have the rust and the freshness of antiquity about them; those of the Noble Poet cease to startle from their extreme ambition of novelty, both in style and matter. Sir Walter's rhymes are "silly sooth"—

"And dally with the innocence of thought,
Like the old age"—⁴

his Lordship's Muse spurns *the olden time*, and affects all the supercilious airs of a modern fine lady and an upstart. The object of the one writer is to restore us to truth and nature: the other chiefly thinks how he shall display his own power, or vent his spleen, or astonish the reader either by starting new subjects and trains of speculation, or by expressing old ones in a more striking and emphatic manner than they have been expressed before. He cares little what it is he says, so that he can say it differently from others. This may account for the charges of plagiarism which have been repeatedly brought against the Noble Poet—if he can borrow an image or sentiment from another, and heighten it by an epithet or an allusion of greater force and beauty than is to be found in the original passage, he thinks he shows his superiority of execution in this in a more marked manner than if the first suggestion had been his own. It is not the value of the observation itself he is solicitous about; but he wishes to shine by contrast—even nature only serves as a foil to set off his style. He therefore takes the thoughts of others (whether contemporaries or not) out of their mouths, and is content to make them his own, to set his stamp upon them, by imparting to them a more meretricious gloss, a higher relief, a greater loftiness of tone, and a characteristic inveteracy of purpose. Even in those collateral ornaments of modern style, slovenliness, abruptness, and eccentricity (as well as in terseness and significance), Lord Byron, when he pleases, defies competition and surpasses all his contemporaries. Whatever he does, he must do in a more decided and daring manner than any one else—he lounges with extravagance, and yawns so as to alarm the reader! Self-will, passion, the love of singularity, a disdain of himself and of others (with a conscious sense that this is among the ways and means of procuring admiration) are the proper categories of his mind: he is a lordly writer, is above his own reputation, and condescends to the Muses with a scornful grace!

Lord Byron, who in his politics is a *liberal*, in his genius is haughty and aristocratic: Walter Scott, who is an aristocrat in principle, is popular in his writings, and is (as it were) equally *servile* to nature and to opinion. The genius of Sir Walter is essentially imitative, or "denotes a foregone conclusion:" ⁵ that of Lord Byron is self-dependent; or at least requires no aid, is governed by no law, but the impulses of its own will. We confess, however much we may admire independence of feeling and erectness of spirit in general or practical questions, yet in works of genius we prefer him who bows to the authority of nature, who appeals

---

¹ *Coriolanus*, V, iii, 36–37.   ² *Tempest*, IV, i, 152.
³ *Troilus and Cressida*, I, iii, 380.
⁴ *Twelfth Night*, II, iv, 47–49.

⁵ *Othello*, III, iii, 428.

to actual objects, to mouldering superstitions, to history, observation, and tradition, before him who only consults the pragmatical and restless workings of his own breast, and gives them out as oracles to the world. We like a writer (whether poet or prose-writer) who takes in (or is willing to take in) the range of half the universe in feeling, character, description, much better than we do one who obstinately and invariably shuts himself up in the Bastile of his own ruling passions. In short, we had rather be Sir Walter Scott (meaning thereby the Author of Waverley) than Lord Byron, a hundred times over. And for the reason just given, namely, that he casts his descriptions in the mould of nature, ever-varying, never tiresome, always interesting and always instructive, instead of casting them constantly in the mould of his own individual impressions. He gives us man as he is, or as he was, in almost every variety of situation, action, and feeling. Lord Byron makes man after his own image, woman after his own heart; the one is a capricious tyrant, the other a yielding slave; he gives us the misanthrope and the voluptuary by turns; and with these two characters, burning or melting in their own fires, he makes out everlasting centos of himself. He hangs the cloud, the film of his existence over all outward things—sits in the centre of his thoughts, and enjoys dark night, bright day, the glitter and the gloom "in cell monastic"[6]—we see the mournful pall, the crucifix, the death's heads, the faded chaplet of flowers, the gleaming tapers, the agonized brow of genius, the wasted form of beauty—but we are still imprisoned in a dungeon, a curtain intercepts our view, we do not breathe freely the air of nature or of our own thoughts—the other admired author draws aside the curtain, and the veil of egotism is rent, and he shows us the crowd of living men and women, the endless groups, the landscape back-ground, the cloud and the rainbow, and enriches our imaginations and relieves one passion by another, and expands and lightens reflection, and takes away that tightness at the breast which arises from thinking or wishing to think that there is nothing in the world out of a man's self!—In this point of view, the Author of Waverley is one of the greatest teachers of morality that ever lived, by emancipating the mind from petty, narrow, and bigotted prejudices: Lord Byron is the greatest pamperer of those prejudices, by seeming to think there is nothing else worth encouraging but the seeds or the full luxuriant growth of dogmatism and self-conceit. In reading the *Scotch Novels*, we never think about the author, except from a feeling of curiosity respecting our unknown benefactor: in

reading Lord Byron's works, he himself is never absent from our minds. The colouring of Lord Byron's style, however rich and dipped in Tyrian dyes, is nevertheless opaque, is in itself an object of delight and wonder: Sir Walter Scott's is perfectly transparent. In studying the one, you seem to gaze at the figures cut in stained glass, which exclude the view beyond, and where the pure light of Heaven is only a means of setting off the gorgeousness of art: in reading the other, you look through a noble window at the clear and varied landscape without. Or to sum up the distinction in one word, Sir Walter Scott is the most *dramatic* writer now living; and Lord Byron is the least so. It would be difficult to imagine that the Author of Waverley is in the smallest degree a pedant; as it would be hard to persuade ourselves that the author of Childe Harold and Don Juan is not a coxcomb, though a provoking and sublime one. In this decided preference given to Sir Walter Scott over Lord Byron, we distinctly include the prose-works of the former; for we do not think his poetry alone by any means entitles him to that precedence. Sir Walter in his poetry, though pleasing and natural, is a comparative trifler: it is in his anonymous productions that he has shown himself for what he is!—

Intensity is the great and prominent distinction of Lord Byron's writings. He seldom gets beyond force of style, nor has he produced any regular work or masterly whole. He does not prepare any plan beforehand, nor revise and retouch what he has written with polished accuracy. His only object seems to be to stimulate himself and his readers for the moment—to keep both alive, to drive away *ennui*, to substitute a feverish and irritable state of excitement for listless indolence or even calm enjoyment. For this purpose he pitches on any subject at random without much thought or delicacy—he is only impatient to begin—and takes care to adorn and enrich it as he proceeds with "thoughts that breathe and words that burn."[7] He composes (as he himself has said) whether he is in the bath, in his study, or on horseback—he writes as habitually as others talk or think—and whether we have the inspiration of the Muse or not, we always find the spirit of the man of genius breathing from his verse. He grapples with his subject, and moves, penetrates, and animates it by the electric force of his own feelings. He is often monotonous, extravagant, offensive; but he is never dull, or tedious, but when he writes prose. Lord Byron does not exhibit a new view of nature, or raise insignificant objects into importance by the romantic associations with which he surrounds

---

[6] See *Comus*, l. 382 ("May sit i'the centre, and enjoy bright day"). For "in cell monastic" see *As You Like It*, III, ii, 441–42.

[7] Gray's *The Progress of Poesy*, l. 110.

them; but generally (at least) takes common-place thoughts and events, and endeavours to express them in stronger and statelier language than others. His poetry stands like a Martello tower [8] by the side of his subject. He does not, like Mr. Wordsworth, lift poetry from the ground, or create a sentiment out of nothing. He does not describe a daisy or a periwinkle, but the cedar or the cypress: not "poor men's cottages, but princes' palaces." [9] His *Childe Harold* contains a lofty and impassioned review of the great events of history, of the mighty objects left as wrecks of time, but he dwells chiefly on what is familiar to the mind of every school-boy; has brought out few new traits of feeling or thought; and has done no more than justice to the reader's preconceptions by the sustained force and brilliancy of his style and imagery.

Lord Byron's earlier productions, *Lara*, the *Corsair*, &c. were wild and gloomy romances, put into rapid and shining verse. They discover the madness of poetry, together with the inspiration: sullen, moody, capricious, fierce, inexorable, gloating on beauty, thirsting for revenge, hurrying from the extremes of pleasure to pain, but with nothing permanent, nothing healthy or natural. The gaudy decorations and the morbid sentiments remind one of flowers strewed over the face of death! In his *Childe Harold* (as has been just observed) he assumes a lofty and philosophic tone, and "reasons high of providence, fore-knowledge, will, and fate." [10] He takes the highest points in the history of the world, and comments on them from a more commanding eminence: he shows us the crumbling monuments of time, he invokes the great names, the mighty spirit of antiquity. The universe is changed into a stately mausoleum:—in solemn measures he chaunts a hymn to fame. Lord Byron has strength and elevation enough to fill up the moulds of our classical and time-hallowed recollections, and to rekindle the earliest aspirations of the mind after greatness and true glory with a pen of fire. The names of Tasso, of Ariosto, of Dante, of Cincinnatus, of Cæsar, of Scipio, lose nothing of their pomp or their lustre in his hands, and when he begins and continues a strain of panegyric on such subjects, we indeed sit down with him to a banquet of rich praise, brooding over imperishable glories,

"Till Contemplation has her fill." [11]

Lord Byron seems to cast himself indignantly from "this bank and shoal of time," [12] or the frail tottering bark that bears up modern reputation, into the huge sea of ancient renown, and to revel there with untired, outspread plume. Even this in him is spleen—his contempt of his contemporaries makes him turn back to the lustrous past, or project himself forward to the dim future!—Lord Byron's tragedies, Faliero,* Sardanapalus, &c. are not equal to his other works. They want the essence of the drama. They abound in speeches and descriptions, such as he himself might make either to himself or others, lolling on his couch of a morning, but do not carry the reader out of the poet's mind to the scenes and events recorded. They have neither action, character, nor interest, but are a sort of *gossamer* tragedies, spun out, and glittering, and spreading a flimsy veil over the face of nature. Yet he spins them on. Of all that he has done in this way the *Heaven and Earth* (the same subject as Mr. Moore's *Loves of the Angels*) is the best. [14] We prefer it even to *Manfred*. *Manfred* is merely himself, with a fancy-drapery on: but in the dramatic fragment published in the *Liberal*, the space between Heaven and Earth, the stage on which his characters have to pass to and fro, seems to fill his Lordship's imagination; and the Deluge, which he has so finely described, may be said to have drowned all his own idle humours.

We must say we think little of our author's turn for satire. His "English Bards and Scotch Reviewers" is dogmatical and insolent, but without refinement or point. He calls people names, and tries to transfix a character with an epithet, which does not stick, because it has no other foundation than his own petulance and spite; or he endeavours to degrade by alluding to some circumstance of external situation. He says of Mr. Wordsworth's poetry, that "it is his aversion." [15] That may be: but whose fault is it? This is the satire of a lord, who is accustomed to have all

* "Don Juan was my Moscow, and Faliero
My Leipsic, and my Mont St. Jean seems Cain."
Don Juan, Canto XI. [13]

---

[8] See Hazlitt's review of Shelley's *Posthumous Poems*, p. 475, footnote 9. The point of the reference here would be that Byron's poetic treatment completely overshadows and overwhelms the subject.
[9] *The Merchant of Venice*, I, ii, 15.
[10] *Paradise Lost*, II, 558–59.
[11] John Dyer's poem *Grongar Hill* (1726), l. 26.

[12] *Macbeth*, I, vii, 6.
[13] Moscow and Leipsic were famous defeats for the French armies. Mont St. Jean (Waterloo) was the final and decisive defeat. Leslie Marchand has explained the reference: "Byron felt that the outcry against *Cain* [including charges of blasphemy and threat of prosecution of the publisher] made it his Waterloo with the British public."
[14] *Heaven and Earth* was a theological "mystery" drama published in Leigh Hunt's *Liberal* in 1823; Thomas Moore's *Loves of the Angels* appeared the same year. Both works drew on the biblical legend (Genesis, vi) of the wicked love of the fallen angels for mortal women, which stirred God's wrath and brought on the punishment of the Deluge. Byron's poem ends with the rising of the waters and the appearance of the ark.
[15] *Don Juan*, III, xciv.

his whims or dislikes taken for gospel, and who cannot be at the pains to do more than signify his contempt or displeasure. If a great man meets with a rebuff which he does not like, he turns on his heel, and this passes for a repartee. The Noble Author says of a celebrated barrister and critic, that he was "born in a garret sixteen stories high."[16] The insinuation is not true; or if it were, it is low. The allusion degrades the person who makes, not him to whom it is applied. This is also the satire of a person of birth and quality, who measures all merit by external rank, that is, by his own standard. So his Lordship, in a "Letter to the Editor of My Grandmother's Review,"[17] addresses him fifty times as "*my dear Robarts;*" nor is there any other wit in the article. This is surely a mere assumption of superiority from his Lordship's rank, and is the sort of *quizzing* he might use to a person who came to hire himself as a valet to him at *Long's*[18]—the waiters might laugh, the public will not. In like manner, in the controversy about Pope,[19] he claps Mr. Bowles on the back with a coarse facetious familiarity, as if he were his chaplain whom he had invited to dine with him, or was about to present to a benefice. The reverend divine might submit to the obligation, but he has no occasion to subscribe to the jest. If it is a jest that Mr. Bowles should be a parson, and Lord Byron a peer, the world knew this before; there was no need to write a pamphlet to prove it.

The *Don Juan* indeed has great power; but its power is owing to the force of the serious writing, and to the oddity of the contrast between that and the flashy passages with which it is interlarded. From the sublime to the ridiculous there is but one step. You laugh and are surprised that any one should turn round and *travestie* himself: the drollery is in the utter discontinuity of ideas and feelings. He makes virtue serve as a foil to vice; *dandyism* is (for want of any other) a variety of genius. A classical intoxication is followed by the splashing of soda-water, by frothy effusions of ordinary bile. After the lightning and the hurricane, we are introduced to the interior of the cabin and the contents of wash-hand basins. The solemn hero of tragedy plays *Scrub*[20] in the farce. This is "very tolerable and not to be endured." The Noble Lord is almost the only writer who has prostituted his

talents in this way. He hallows in order to desecrate; takes a pleasure in defacing the images of beauty his hands have wrought; and raises our hopes and our belief in goodness to Heaven only to dash them to the earth again, and break them in pieces the more effectually from the very height they have fallen. Our enthusiasm for genius or virtue is thus turned into a jest by the very person who has kindled it, and who thus fatally quenches the sparks of both. It is not that Lord Byron is sometimes serious and sometimes trifling, sometimes profligate, and sometimes moral—but when he is most serious and most moral, he is only preparing to mortify the unsuspecting reader by putting a pitiful *hoax* upon him. This is a most unaccountable anomaly. It is as if the eagle were to build its eyry in a common sewer, or the owl were seen soaring to the mid-day sun. Such a sight might make one laugh, but one would not wish or expect it to occur more than once!*

In fact, Lord Byron is the spoiled child of fame as well as fortune. He has taken a surfeit of popularity, and is not contented to delight, unless he can shock the public. He would force them to admire in spite of decency and common sense—he would have them read what they would read in no one but himself, or he would not give a rush for their applause. He is to be "a chartered libertine,"[21] from whom insults are favours, whose contempt is to be a new incentive to admiration. His Lordship is hard to please: he is equally averse to notice or neglect, enraged at censure and scorning praise. He tries the patience of the town to the very utmost, and when they show signs of weariness or disgust, threatens to *discard* them. He says he will write on, whether he is read or not. He would never write another page, if it were not to court popular applause, or to affect a superiority over it. In this respect also, Lord Byron presents a striking contrast to Sir Walter Scott. The latter takes what part of the public favour falls to his share, without grumbling (to be sure he has no reason to complain); the former is always quarrelling with the world about his *modicum* of applause, the *spolia opima*[22] of vanity, and ungraciously throwing the offerings of incense heaped on his shrine back in the faces of his admirers. Again, there is no taint in the writings of the Author of Waverley, all is fair and natural and *above-board*: he never outrages the public mind. He introduces no

[16] *English Bards and Scotch Reviewers*, ll. 481–82, referring to Francis Jeffrey.
[17] Published in the *Liberal* in 1822, the "Letter" was a facetious essay (signed as by "Wortley Clutterbuck") addressed to William Roberts (1767–1849), editor of the conservative *British Review*.
[18] A fashionable London restaurant.
[19] See Byron's *Letter to* **** ******, p. 665.
[20] A servant in Farquhar's *The Beaux Stratagem*. The next quotation occurs in *Much Ado about Nothing*, III, iii, 37–38.

* This censure applies to the first Cantos of DON JUAN much more than to the last. It has been called a TRISTRAM SHANDY in rhyme: it is rather a poem written about itself.

[21] *Henry the Fifth*, I, i, 48.
[22] *spolia opima*: "the honorable spoils."

anomalous character: broaches no staggering opinion. If he goes back to old prejudices and superstitions as a relief to the modern reader, while Lord Byron floats on swelling paradoxes—

"Like proud seas under him;"[23]

if the one defers too much to the spirit of antiquity, the other panders to the spirit of the age, goes to the very edge of extreme and licentious speculation, and breaks his neck over it. Grossness and levity are the playthings of his pen. It is a ludicrous circumstance that he should have dedicated his *Cain* to the worthy Baronet! Did the latter ever acknowledge the obligation? We are not nice, not very nice; but we do not particularly approve those subjects that shine chiefly from their rottenness: nor do we wish to see the Muses drest out in the flounces of a false or questionable philosophy, like *Portia* and *Nerissa* in the garb of Doctors of Law. We like metaphysics as well as Lord Byron; but not to see them making flowery speeches, nor dancing a measure in the fetters of verse. We have as good as hinted, that his Lordship's poetry consists mostly of a tissue of superb common-places; even his paradoxes are *common-place*. They are familiar in the schools: they are only new and striking in his dramas and stanzas, by being out of place. In a word, we think that poetry moves best within the circle of nature and received opinion: speculative theory and subtle casuistry are forbidden ground to it. But Lord Byron often wanders into this ground wantonly, wilfully, and unwarrantably. The only apology we can conceive for the spirit of some of Lord Byron's writings, is the spirit of some of those opposed to him. They would provoke a man to write any thing. "Farthest from them is best."[24] The extravagance and license of the one seems a proper antidote to the bigotry and narrowness of the other. The first *Vision of Judgment* was a set-off to the second, though

"None but itself could be its parallel."[25]

Perhaps the chief cause of most of Lord Byron's errors is, that he is that anomaly in letters and in society, a Noble Poet. It is a double privilege, almost too much for humanity. He has all the pride of birth and genius. The strength of his imagination leads him to indulge in fantastic opinions; the elevation of his rank sets censure at defiance. He becomes a pampered egotist. He has a seat in the House of Lords, a niche in the Temple of Fame. Every-day mortals, opinions, things are not good enough for him to touch or think of. A mere nobleman is, in his estimation, but "the tenth transmitter of a foolish face:"[26] a mere man of genius is no better than a worm. His Muse is also a lady of quality. The people are not polite enough for him; the Court not sufficiently intellectual. He hates the one and despises the other. By hating and despising others, he does not learn to be satisfied with himself. A fastidious man soon grows querulous and splenetic. If there is nobody but ourselves to come up to our idea of fancied perfection, we easily get tired of our idol. When a man is tired of what he is, by a natural perversity he sets up for what he is not. If he is a poet, he pretends to be a metaphysician: if he is a patrician in rank and feeling, he would fain be one of the people. His ruling motive is not the love of the people, but of distinction; not of truth, but of singularity. He patronizes men of letters out of vanity, and deserts them from caprice, or from the advice of friends. He embarks in an obnoxious publication to provoke censure, and leaves it to shift for itself for fear of scandal. We do not like Sir Walter's gratuitous servility: we like Lord Byron's preposterous *liberalism* little better. He may affect the principles of equality, but he resumes his privilege of peerage, upon occasion. His Lordship has made great offers of service to the Greeks—money and horses. He is at present in Cephalonia, waiting the event!

*　　*　　*　　*　　*

We had written thus far when news came of the death of Lord Byron, and put an end at once to a strain of somewhat peevish invective, which was intended to meet his eye, not to insult his memory. Had we known that we were writing his epitaph, we must have done it with a different feeling. As it is, we think it better and more like himself, to let what we had written stand, than to take up our leaden shafts, and try to melt them into "tears of sensibility," or mould them into dull praise, and an affected show of candour. We were not silent during the author's life-time, either for his reproof or encouragement (such as we could give, and *he* did not disdain to accept) nor can we now turn undertakers' men to fix the glittering plate upon his coffin, or fall into the procession of popular woe.— Death cancels every thing but truth; and strips a man of every thing but genius and virtue. It is a sort of natural canonization. It makes the meanest of us

---

[23] *The Two Noble Kinsmen*, II, ii, 23, by John Fletcher in probable collaboration with Shakespeare.

[24] *Paradise Lost*, I, 247.

[25] Southey's *Vision of Judgment* (1821) was a solemn tribute on the death of George III. Byron's *Vision* of the following year was an irreverent parody. The quotation is from the play *Double Falsehood* (1727), III, i, prepared by Lewis Theobald as "Written Originally by W. Shakespeare."

[26] Richard Savage's poem *The Bastard* (1728), l. 8.

sacred—it installs the poet in his immortality, and lifts him to the skies. Death is the great assayer of the sterling ore of talent. At his touch the drossy particles fall off, the irritable, the personal, the gross, and mingle with the dust—the finer and more ethereal part mounts with the winged spirit to watch over our latest memory, and protect our bones from insult. We consign the least worthy qualities to oblivion, and cherish the nobler and imperishable nature with double pride and fondness. Nothing could show the real superiority of genius in a more striking point of view than the idle contests and the public indifference about the place of Lord Byron's interment, whether in Westminster Abbey or his own family-vault. A king must have a coronation—a nobleman a funeral-procession.—The man is nothing without the pageant. The poet's cemetery is the human mind, in which he sows the seeds of never-ending thought—his monument is to be found in his works:

> "Nothing can cover his high fame but Heaven;
> No pyramids set off his memory,
> But the eternal substance of his greatness." 27

Lord Byron is dead: he also died a martyr to his zeal in the cause of freedom, for the last, best hopes of man. Let that be his excuse and his epitaph!

[1825]

[END OF SELECTIONS FROM THE SPIRIT OF THE AGE]

A FAREWELL TO ESSAY-WRITING

"This life is best, if quiet life is best." 1

Food, warmth, sleep, and a book; these are all I at present ask—the *ultima thule* 2 of my wandering desires. Do you not then wish for

> "A friend in your retreat,
> Whom you may whisper, solitude is sweet?" 3

Expected, well enough:—gone, still better. Such attractions are strengthened by distance. Nor a mistress? "Beautiful mask! I know thee!" When I can judge of the heart from the face, of the thoughts from the lips, I may again trust myself. Instead of these, give me the robin red-breast, pecking the crumbs at the door, or warbling on the leafless spray, the same glancing form that has followed me wherever I have been, and "done its spiriting gently"; 4 or the rich

notes of the thrush that startle the ear of winter, and seem to have drunk up the full draught of joy from the very sense of contrast. To these I adhere and am faithful, for they are true to me; and, dear in themselves, are dearer for the sake of what is departed, leading me back (by the hand) to that dreaming world, in the innocence of which they sat and made sweet music, waking the promise of future years, and answered by the eager throbbings of my own breast. But now "the credulous hope of mutual minds is o'er," 5 and I turn back from the world that has deceived me, to nature that lent it a false beauty, and that keeps up the illusion of the past. As I quaff my libations of tea in a morning, I love to watch the clouds sailing from the west, and fancy that "the spring comes slowly up this way." 6 In this hope, while "fields are dank and ways are mire," 7 I follow the same direction to a neighbouring wood, where, having gained the dry, level greensward, I can see my way for a mile before me, closed in on each side by copse-wood, and ending in a point of light more or less brilliant, as the day is bright or cloudy. What a walk is this to me! I have no need of book or companion—the days, the hours, the thoughts of my youth are at my side, and blend with the air that fans my cheek. Here I can saunter for hours, bending my eye forward, stopping and turning to look back, thinking to strike off into some less trodden path, yet hesitating to quit the one I am in, afraid to snap the brittle threads of memory. I remark the shining trunks and slender branches of the birch-trees, waving in the idle breeze; or a pheasant springs up on whirring wing; or I recall the spot where I once found a wood-pigeon at the foot of a tree, weltering in its gore, and think how many seasons have flown since "it left its little life in air." Dates, names, faces come back—to what purpose? Or why think of them now? Or rather, why not think of them oftener? We walk through life, as through a narrow path, with a thin curtain drawn around it; behind are ranged rich portraits, airy harps are strung—yet we will not stretch forth our hands and lift aside the veil, to catch glimpses of the one, or sweep the chords of the other. As in a theatre, when the old-fashioned green curtain drew up, groups of figures, fantastic dresses, laughing faces, rich banquets, stately columns, gleaming vistas appeared beyond; so we have only at any time to "peep through the blanket of the past," 8 to possess ourselves at once of all that has regaled our senses, that is stored up in

---

27 Beaumont and Fletcher's *The False One* (1619), II, i.
1 *Cymbeline*, III, iii, 29–30.
2 *ultima thule*: the final point or ultimate achievement.
3 Cowper's "Retirement" (1782), ll. 741–42.
4 *The Tempest*, I, ii, 298.

5 Byron's *Don Juan*, I, ccxvi.
6 Coleridge's *Christabel*, l. 22.
7 Milton's Sonnet XX (To Mr. Lawrence), l. 2.
8 Cf. *Macbeth*, I, v, 54.

our memory, that has struck our fancy, that has pierced our hearts:—yet to all this we are indifferent, insensible, and seem intent only on the present vexation, the future disappointment. If there is a Titian hanging up in the room with me, I scarcely regard it: how then should I be expected to strain the mental eye so far, or to throw down, by the magic spells of the will, the stone-walls that enclose it in the Louvre? There is one head there, of which I have often thought, when looking at it, that nothing should ever disturb me again, and I would become the character it represents—such perfect calmness and self-possession reigns in it! Why do I not hang an image of this in some dusky corner of my brain, and turn an eye upon it ever and anon, as I have need of some such talisman to calm my troubled thoughts? The attempt is fruitless, if not natural; or, like that of the French, to hang garlands on the grave, and to conjure back the dead by miniature-pictures of them while living! It is only some actual coincidence, or local association that tends, without violence, to "open all the cells where memory slept."⁹ I can easily, by stooping over the long-sprent grass and clay-cold clod, recall the tufts of primroses, or purple hyacinths, that formerly grew on the same spot, and cover the bushes with leaves and singing-birds, as they were eighteen summers ago;¹⁰ or prolonging my walk and hearing the sighing gale rustle through a tall, strait wood at the end of it, can fancy that I distinguish the cry of hounds, and the fatal group issuing from it, as in the tale of Theodore and Honoria.¹¹ A moaning gust of wind aids the belief; I look once more to see whether the trees before me answer to the idea of the horror-stricken grove, and an air-built city towers over their grey tops.

> "Of all the cities in Romanian lands,
> The chief and most renown'd Ravenna stands."¹²

I return home resolved to read the entire poem through, and, after dinner, drawing my chair to the fire, and holding a small print close to my eyes, launch into the full tide of Dryden's couplets (a stream of sound), comparing his didactic and descriptive pomp with the simple pathos and picturesque truth of Boccacio's story, and tasting with a pleasure, which none but an habitual reader can feel, some quaint examples of pronunciation in this accomplished versifier.

> "Which when Honoria view'd,
> The fresh *impulse* her former fright renew'd."
> *Theodore and Honoria.*¹³

> "And made th'*insult*, which in his grief appears,
> The means to mourn thee with my pious tears."
> *Sigismonda and Guiscardo.*¹⁴

These trifling instances of the wavering and unsettled state of the language give double effect to the firm and stately march of the verse, and make me dwell with a sort of tender interest on the difficulties and doubts of an earlier period of literature. They pronounced words then in a manner which we should laugh at now; and they wrote verse in a manner which we can do anything but laugh at. The pride of a new acquisition seems to give fresh confidence to it; to impel the rolling syllables through the moulds provided for them, and to overflow the envious bounds of rhyme into time-honoured triplets. I am much pleased with Leigh Hunt's mention¹⁵ of Moore's involuntary admiration of Dryden's free, unshackled verse, and of his repeating *con amore*, and with an Irish spirit and accent, the fine lines—

> "Let honour and preferment go for gold,
> But glorious beauty isn't to be sold!"¹⁶

What sometimes surprises me in looking back to the past, is, with the exception already stated, to find myself so little changed in the time. The same images and trains of thought stick by me: I have the same tastes, likings, sentiments, and wishes that I had then. One great ground of confidence and support has, indeed, been struck from under my feet; but I have made it up to myself by proportionable pertinacity of opinion. The success of the great cause, to which I had vowed myself, was to me more than all the world: I had a strength in its strength, a resource which I knew not of, till it failed me for the second time.

> "Fall'n was Glenartny's stately tree!
> Oh! ne'er to see Lord Ronald more!"¹⁷

---

⁹ Cowper's *Task*, VI, 11–12.

¹⁰ This essay was written at Winterslow, Wiltshire, where Hazlitt's first wife owned property. He first lived there following his marriage in 1808, and it remained a rural retreat until the end of his life.

¹¹ A tale from Boccaccio's *Decameron*, translated by Dryden in his *Fables Ancient and Modern* (1700). The tale involves the horrifying appearance in a dense thicket of a pair of lovers from hell, who live out their eternity with the maiden being pursued and hideously attacked by the suitor and his hounds.

¹² The opening lines of Dryden's translation.

¹³ Ll. 342–43.

¹⁴ Ll. 668–69 of another tale from Boccaccio translated by Dryden.

¹⁵ In *Lord Byron and Some of his Contemporaries* (1828), an ill-tempered account of Byron, with essays on Shelley, Keats, Coleridge, and other contemporaries. An essay critical of Hazlitt's character was written for the volume, but withdrawn before publication.

¹⁶ Dryden's Epilogue to Nathaniel Lee's tragedy *Mithridates, King of Pontus* (1678), ll. 16–17.

¹⁷ From Scott's ballad "Glenfinlas" (1801).

It was not till I saw the axe laid to the root, that I found the full extent of what I had to lose and suffer. But my conviction of the right was only established by the triumph of the wrong; and my earliest hopes will be my last regrets. One source of this unbendingness (which some may call obstinacy,) is that, though living much alone, I have never worshipped the Echo. I see plainly enough that black is not white, that the grass is green, that kings are not their subjects; and, in such self-evident cases, do not think it necessary to collate my opinions with the received prejudices. In subtler questions, and matters that admit of doubt, as I do not impose my opinion on others without a reason, so I will not give up mine to them without a better reason; and a person calling me names, or giving himself airs of authority, does not convince me of his having taken more pains to find out the truth than I have, but the contrary. Mr. Gifford [18] once said, that "while I was sitting over my gin and tobacco-pipes, I fancied myself a Leibnitz." He did not so much as know that I had ever read a metaphysical book:—was I therefore, out of complaisance or deference to him, to forget whether I had or not? I am rather disappointed, both on my own account and his, that Mr. Hunt has missed the opportunity of explaining the character of a friend, as clearly as he might have done. He is puzzled to reconcile the shyness of my pretensions, with the inveteracy and sturdiness of my principles. I should have thought they were nearly the same thing. Both from disposition and habit, I can *assume* nothing in word, look, or manner. I cannot steal a march upon public opinion in any way. My standing upright, speaking loud, entering a room gracefully, proves nothing; therefore I neglect these ordinary means of recommending myself to the good graces and admiration of strangers (and, as it appears, even of philosophers and friends). Why? Because I have other resources, or, at least, am absorbed in other studies and pursuits. Suppose this absorption to be extreme, and even morbid, that I have brooded over an idea till it has become a kind of substance in my brain, that I have reasons for a thing which I have found out with much labour and pains, and to which I can scarcely do justice without the utmost violence of exertion, (and that only to a few persons,)—is this the reason for my playing off my out-of-the way notions in all companies, wearing a prim and self-complacent air, as if I were "the admired of all observers?" [19] or is it not rather an argument, (together with a want of animal spirits,) why I should retire into

myself, and perhaps acquire a nervous and uneasy look, from a consciousness of the disproportion between the interest and conviction I feel on certain subjects, and my ability to communicate what weighs upon my own mind to others? If my ideas, which I do not avouch, but suppose, lie below the surface, why am I to be always attempting to dazzle superficial people with them, or smiling, delighted, at my own want of success?

What I have here stated is only the excess of the common and well-known English and scholastic character. I am neither a buffoon, a fop, nor a Frenchman, which Mr. Hunt would have me to be. He finds it odd that I am a close reasoner and a loose dresser. I have been (among other follies) a hard liver as well as a hard thinker; and the consequences of that will not allow me to dress as I please. People in real life are not like players on a stage, who put on a certain look or *costume*, merely for effect. I am aware, indeed, that the gay and airy pen of the author does not seriously probe the errors or misfortunes of his friends—he only glances at their seeming peculiarities, so as to make them odd and ridiculous; for which forbearance few of them will thank him. Why does he assert that I was vain of my hair when it was black, and am equally vain of it now it is grey, when this is true in neither case? This transposition of motives makes me almost doubt whether Lord Byron was thinking so much of the rings on his fingers as his biographer was. These sorts of criticisms should be left to women. I am made to wear a little hat, stuck on the top of my head, the wrong way. Nay, I commonly wear a large slouching hat over my eyebrows; and it ever I had another, I must have twisted it about in any shape to get rid of the annoyance. This probably tickled Mr. Hunt's fancy, and retains possession of it, to the exclusion of the obvious truism, that I naturally wear "a melancholy hat."

I am charged with using strange gestures and contortions of features in argument, in order to "look energetic." One would rather suppose that the heat of the argument produced the extravagance of the gestures, as I am said to be calm at other times. It is like saying that a man in a passion clenches his teeth, not because he is, but in order to seem, angry. Why should everything be construed into air and affectation? With Hamlet, I may say, "I know not seems." [20]

Again, my old friend and pleasant "Companion" remarks it, as an anomaly in my character, that I crawl about the Fives-Court like a cripple till I get the racket in my hand, when I start up as if I was pos-

---

[18] William Gifford (1756–1826), the editor of *The Quarterly Review*. See section on REVIEWERS, p. 785.
[19] Cf. *Hamlet*, III, i, 162.

[20] *Hamlet*, I, ii, 76.

sessed with a devil. I have then a motive for exertion; I lie by for difficulties and extreme cases. *Aut Caesar aut nullus.*[21] I have no notion of doing nothing with an air of importance, nor should I ever take a liking to the game of battledoor and shuttlecock.—I have only seen by accident a page of the unpublished Manuscript relating to the present subject, which I dare say is, on the whole, friendly and just, and which has been suppressed as being too favourable, considering certain prejudices against me.

In matters of taste and feeling, one proof that my conclusions have not been quite shallow or hasty, is the circumstance of their having been lasting. I have the same favourite books, pictures, passages, that I ever had: I may therefore presume that they will last me my life—nay, I may indulge a hope that my thoughts will survive me. This continuity of impression is the only thing on which I pride myself. Even L——,[22] whose relish of certain things is as keen and earnest as possible, takes a surfeit of admiration, and I should be afraid to ask about his select authors or particular friends, after a lapse of ten years. As to myself, any one knows where to have me. What I have once made up my mind to, I abide by to the end of the chapter. One cause of my independence of opinion is, I believe, the liberty I give to others, or the very diffidence and distrust of making converts. I should be an excellent man on a jury: I might say little, but should starve "the other eleven obstinate fellows" out. I remember Mr. Godwin writing to Mr. Wordsworth, that "his tragedy of Antonio could not fail of success." It was damned past all redemption.[23] I said to Mr. Wordsworth that I thought this a natural consequence; for how could any one have a dramatic turn of mind who judged entirely of others from himself? Mr. Godwin might be convinced of the excellence of his work; but how could he know that others would be convinced of it, unless by supposing that they were as wise as himself, and as infallible critics of dramatic poetry—so many Aristotles sitting in judgment on Euripides! This shows why pride is connected with shyness and reserve; for the really proud have not so high an opinion of the generality as to suppose that they can understand them, or that there is any common measure between them. So Dryden exclaims of his opponents with bitter disdain—

"Nor can I think what thoughts they can conceive."[24]

I have not sought to make partisans, still less did I dream of making enemies; and have therefore kept my opinions myself, whether they were currently adopted or not. To get others to come into our ways of thinking, we must go over to theirs; and it is necessary to follow, in order to lead. At the time I lived here formerly, I had no suspicion that I should ever become a voluminous writer; yet I had just the same confidence in my feelings before I had ventured to air them in public as I have now. Neither the outcry *for* or *against* moves me a jot: I do not say that the one is not more agreeable than the other.

Not far from the spot where I write, I first read Chaucer's *Flower and Leaf*[25], and was charmed with that young beauty, shrouded in her bower, and listening with ever-fresh delight to the repeated song of the nightingale close by her—the impression of the scene, the vernal landscape, the cool of the morning, the gushing notes of the songstress,

"And ayen, methought she sung close by mine ear,"

is as vivid as if it had been of yesterday; and nothing can persuade me that that is not a fine poem. I do not find this impression conveyed in Dryden's version, and therefore nothing can persuade me that that is as fine. I used to walk out at this time with Mr. and Miss L——[26] of an evening, to look at the Claude Lorraine skies over our heads, melting from azure into purple and gold, and to gather mushrooms, that sprung up at our feet, to throw into our hashed mutton at supper. I was at that time an enthusiastic admirer of Claude, and could dwell for ever on one or two of the finest prints from him hung round my little room; the fleecy flocks, the bending trees, the winding streams, the groves, the nodding temples, the air-wove hills, and distant sunny vales; and tried to translate them into their lovely living hues. People then told me that Wilson[27] was much superior to Claude. I did not believe them. Their pictures have since been seen together at the British Institution,[28] and all the world have come into my opinion. I have not, on that account, given it up. I will not compare our hashed mutton with Amelia's;[29] but it put us in mind of it, and led to a discussion, sharply seasoned and well sustained, till midnight, the result of which appeared

---

[21] *Aut . . . nullus*: "Either Caesar or no one."
[22] Lamb.
[23] Godwin's *Antonio* was produced in London in 1800.
[24] Dryden's *Hind and the Panther*, I, 315.

[25] The *Flower and Leaf* is an allegorical poem no longer attributed to Chaucer.
[26] Charles and Mary Lamb.
[27] Richard Wilson (*c.* 1713–1782) was an English landscape-painter.
[28] The British Institution was founded in 1805–1806 for the encouragement of the Fine Arts in England.
[29] Hazlitt refers to an affecting scene in Book X, Chapter v, of Fielding's novel *Amelia* (1751); in which the long-suffering heroine delays her dinner and finally eats alone, while her husband drinks and gambles at a tavern.

some years after in the Edinburgh Review.[30] Have I a better opinion of those criticisms on that account, or should I therefore maintain them with greater vehemence and tenaciousness? Oh no! Both rather with less, now that they are before the public, and it is for them to make their election.

It is in looking back to such scenes that I draw my best consolation for the future. Later impressions come and go, and serve to fill up the intervals; but these are my standing resource, my true classics. If I have had few real pleasures or advantages, my ideas, from their sinewy texture, have been to me in the nature of realities; and if I should not be able to add to the stock, I can live by husbanding the interest. As to my speculations, there is little to admire in them but my admiration of others; and whether they have an echo in time to come or not, I have learnt to set a grateful value on the past, and am content to wind up the account of what is personal only to myself and the immediate circle of objects in which I have moved, with an act of easy oblivion,

"And curtain close such scene from every future view."[31]

[March 1828]

---

[30] Referring to Hazlitt's essay "Standard Novels and Romances," published in February 1815.

[31] William Collins' "Ode on the Poetical Character" (1746), l. 76.

Leigh Hunt

1784–1859

OUTLINE OF EVENTS

1784   Born October 19 at Southgate, north of London, fifth son of colonial-American family. Father, Isaac Hunt, clergyman, born in Barbados, West Indies, escaped from imprisonment in Philadelphia in 1776 for his support of England in the American Revolution.

1791–99   Educated at Christ's Hospital, London.

1801   *Juvenilia, or a collection of poems written between the ages of twelve and sixteen* published.

1805   Dramatic critic for *The News*, liberal weekly published by brother John (b. 1775). Accepts employment in office of Minister of War (until 1808).

1808   January 3, *The Examiner* begins publication, with Leigh Hunt as editor-in-chief and John Hunt as publisher. The Hunts threatened with government prosecution for libel for an *Examiner* article on "Military Depravity," but not brought to trial. *Critical Essays on the Performers of the London Theatre* published.

1809   July 3, marries Marianne Kent.

1810   February 24, Hunts brought to trial on charge of libel for an *Examiner* article critical of George III, but charge withdrawn. Leigh Hunt edits *The Reflector, a Quarterly Magazine* (October 1810–December 1811).

1811   February 22, the Hunts brought to trial for reprinting in *The Examiner* an article criticizing the severe punishments used in the army; acquitted.

1812   December 9, the Hunts brought to trial for an *Examiner* article "The Prince on Saint Patrick's Day"; sentenced February 3, 1813, to two years in jail and fined £500.

1814   *The Feast of the Poets* published.

1815   February 3, released from prison. *The Descent of Liberty, a Mask* published.

1816   *The Story of Rimini* published.

1818   *Foliage, or Poems original and translated* published.

1819   *The Poetical Works of Leigh Hunt*, 3 vols., published. Begins to edit the weekly *Indicator* (October 13, 1819–March 21, 1821).

1820   *Amyntas, a Tale of the Woods from the Italian of Torquato Tasso* published, with dedication to John Keats.

1821   *The Months, descriptive of the successive beauties of the year* published. At the urging of Byron and Shelley, decides to move to Italy; ceases editorship of *The Examiner*.

1822   May 13, 1822, sails with his family for Italy and eventually settles at Pisa. Begins editing *The Liberal* (October 1822–July 1823).

1823   October, settles near Florence.

1825   *Bacchus in Tuscany, a Dithyramic Poem, from the Italian of Francesco Redi* published. October, returns to London.

1828   Edits *The Companion* (January 9–July 23). *Lord Byron and some of his Contemporaries* published.

1830   Edits *Chat of the Week* (June 5–August 28) and *The Tatler, a Daily Journal of Literature and the Stage* (September 4, 1830–February 13, 1832).

1832   *Christianism; or Belief and Unbelief Reconciled* and the novel *Sir Ralph Esher, or a Gentleman of the Court of Charles II* published. Friendship with Thomas Carlyle.

1834   Edits *Leigh Hunt's London Journal* (April 2, 1834–December 31, 1835).

1837   July, appointed editor-in-chief of *The Monthly Repository* (through April, 1838).

1840   February 7, *A Legend of Florence* produced with success at Covent Garden, London. Edits *The Dramatic Works of Wycherley, Congreve, Vanbrugh and Farquhar* and *The Dramatic Works of Richard Brinsley Sheridan*. *The Seer* (a selection of Hunt's essays) published.

1844   *Imagination and Fancy* published.

1846   *Stories from the Italian poets* and *Wit and Humour* published.

1847   Granted government pension. *A Jar of Honey from Mount Hybla* and *Men, Women and Books* (a selection of his essays) published.

1848   *The Town; its memorable Characters and Events* published.

1850   *The Autobiography of Leigh Hunt* published. Edits *Leigh Hunt's Journal, a Miscellany* (December 1850–March 1851). Begins to contribute to Charles Dickens' journal *Household Words*.

1853   Appears as the character "Harold Skimpole" in *Bleak House*.

1855   *The Old Court Suburb; or Memories of Kensington, regal, critical and anecdotal* published.

1857   January 26, death of wife.

1859   August 28, dies in the London suburb of Putney.

SELECTED BIBLIOGRAPHY

BIOGRAPHY

BLUNDEN, EDMUND, *Leigh Hunt and His Circle*, New York: Harper and Brothers, 1930.
LANDRÉ, LOUIS, *Leigh Hunt (1784–1859): Contribution à l'histoire du Romanticisme anglais*, Paris: Société d'Édition, "Les Belles Lettres," Vol. I ["l'Auteur"] (1935).

EDITIONS OF HUNT'S PROSE

BLUNDEN, EDMUND, *Leigh Hunt's "Examiner" Examined*, London: Cobden-Sanderson, 1928. [Part II contains a selection of Hunt's literary reviews.]
COOK, ALBERT S. (ed.), *Leigh Hunt: An Answer to the Question "What is Poetry?" including Remarks on Versification*, Boston: Ginn and Company, 1893.
HOUTCHENS, LAWRENCE HUSTON and CAROLYN WASHBURN HOUTCHENS (eds.), *Leigh Hunt's Dramatic Criticism, 1808–1831*, New York: Columbia University Press, 1949; *Leigh Hunt's Literary Criticism*, New York: Columbia University Press, 1956; *Leigh Hunt's Political and Occasional Essays*, New York: Columbia University Press, 1962.

JOHNSON, R. BRIMLEY (ed.), *Prefaces by Leigh Hunt, mainly to his Periodicals*, London: Frank Hollings, 1927; *Shelley–Leigh Hunt: How Friendship made History . . .* , London: Ingpen and Grant, 1928. [A selection of Hunt's political columns from *The Examiner* appears in the latter volume.]

MORPURGO, J. E. (ed.), *The Autobiography of Leigh Hunt*, London: Cresset Press, 1949.

HUNT AS ESSAYIST, CRITIC, AND MAN OF LETTERS

LANDRÉ, op. cit., Vol. II ["l'Oeuvre"] (1936).

LAW, MARIE HAMILTON, *The English Familiar Essay in the Early Nineteenth Century*, a dissertation . . . presented to the Graduate School of the University of Pennsylvania, published, Philadelphia, 1934.

MARSHALL, WILLIAM H., *Byron, Shelley, Hunt and the Liberal*, Philadelphia: University of Pennsylvania Press, 1960.

WATSON, MELVIN R., "The *Spectator* Tradition and the Development of the Familiar Essay," *Journal of English Literary History*, XIII (1946), 189–215.

THE EXAMINER

The Examiner, *a weekly Sunday newspaper, began publication on January 3, 1808, with John Hunt as publisher, Robert Hunt as art critic, and Leigh Hunt as editor-in-chief supplying the political columns and the literary and theatrical reviews. In his* Autobiography *many years later, Leigh Hunt recalled the "main objects" of* The Examiner *as: "to assist in producing Reform in Parliament, liberality of opinion in general (especially freedom from superstition), and a fusion of literary taste into all subjects whatsoever." The services of* The Examiner *to literature are well known: it was in the pages of Hunt's newspaper that, among other things, Keats's poems were first published and Hazlitt revealed his distinctive literary voice and style; Hunt's reviews of the second generation of Romantic poets were both enthusiastic and discerning, and remain today critically valuable. However, it was as a political journal that* The Examiner *achieved its initial reputation and notoriety in its own time.*

The avowed policy of The Examiner *was one of political independence: however, the domestic and foreign policies of the Tory government soon led the paper to become a voice of political opposition and a strong advocate of reform. "Zeal for the public good," rather than a specific political affiliation or ideology, fashioned Hunt's opinions. As the political columns here reproduced testify, it was the incompetence and corruption of government leaders and the absence of "philosophy" and "morality" in fashioning policy which he attacked both in the English government and in the courts of Europe; at home, he sought a remedy not through republican revolution, but by parliamentary reform. Hunt's "zeal for the public good" led to prosecution for libel or threats of prosecution in four of the initial five years of publication. The last of the charges of libel, caused by the article "The Prince on St. Patrick's Day" of March 22, 1812, resulted in a famous trial and conviction, a two-year jail sentence, and fine.*

The opposition to the Prince Regent (Prince of Wales), which exploded in the "libelous" editorial, had a considerable background. The Prince had early aligned himself with the Whigs against his father's Tory government and had supported reformist and liberal positions. However, as Hunt had pointed out in "A Letter of Strong Advice" (Examiner, *August 21, 1808), the Prince's political authority was seriously jeopardized by the conduct of his private life; he enjoyed a scandalous reputation for his financial extravagance and his dissolute and libertine behavior, including an early affair with the actress Mary Robinson, a long relationship and secret marriage to a Mrs. Fitzherbert, and unconscionable cruelty towards his wife, Princess Caroline. In his "Letter," Hunt had urged: "Dismiss therefore from your presence those idle and dissipated men, who would reduce you to a level with themselves. Patronise the arts for themselves, rather than their professors; admire a good singer, but never condescend to talk with a common prostitute. . . . Turn away with contempt from those ever-grinning minions, who doat on all you say and all you do, . . . who call your worst errors the foibles of a generous heart. The first instance of generosity you could give to the public would be to sacrifice these dastards to your country; the second to commence economy; the third to take home your Royal Consort."*

Much to the dismay and disgust of those who continued to see him as a hoped-for avenue of political change, on becoming Regent in 1811 the Prince retained the Tory government, re-appointed his discredited brother the Duke of York as commander-in-chief of the Army, and failed to act on his earlier political positions, including support for the Irish in their religious and political struggles with England. In an editorial of March 8, 1812, Hunt had declared himself unable to find a single trace of "nobleness, uprightness, patriotism, philosophy, and magnanimity" in the Regent. Two weeks later, "The Prince on St. Patrick's Day" climaxed Hunt's indignation and produced one of the major events in the journalistic history of the period.

The politics of The Examiner *have been studied in George Dumas Stout's* The Political History of Leigh Hunt's Examiner, *Washington University [St. Louis] Studies in Language and Literature, No. 19 (1949); and in Carl Woodring's introduction "Leigh Hunt as Political Essayist" to the Houtchens' edition of Leigh Hunt's Political and Occasional Essays (1962). The importance of* The Examiner *as a literary journal has been described by Edmund Blunden in his* Leigh Hunt's "Examiner" Examined *(1928).*

FROM

THE EXAMINER

FROM

NEW FEATURES OF THE WAR

ONE OF the natural effects of war is the increase of human prejudice. The violent passions always mislead the understanding, and nations at war with each other forget the causes and consequences of their dispute to indulge in petty abuse and in a mean hatred of their enemies individually as well as generally. European warfare has at length become a warfare of words as well as actions, and the intervals of the cannon are filled with a thousand vollies of invective. In short, the Battle of the Books is revived in all its terror, and when England and France cannot fight with guns, they attack each other like little boys with clappers of paper.

It is miserable to see the eagerness with which the various editors seize upon every royal and official paper to crush it with the grasp of inveteracy. They overthrow one argument after another with the flattest contradiction: if they meet with a reasoning evidently unfounded, they call upon all Europe to listen with horror, and if they meet with a reasoning evidently true, they acknowledge their conviction by nothing but a more obstinate rage or a more malicious and constrained ridicule. Thus the criticism of politics has become void of every feeling of gentlemanly candour: the writers forget, that in making their rivals altogether foolish and contemptible, they lessen the difficulty and degrade the dignity of their own rivalry; their system of attack and defence has lost all its grace because it has lost all its calmness, and one would think that they never looked at their enemies but through the cannon-smoke, which renders every object black and disgusting.

Perhaps I am guilty of prejudice, when I think that the French are not so renowned as formerly for that universal gallantry, which threw a grace over all their actions national as well as domestic; but I would even wish to be guilty of a prejudice, when I cannot help thinking that with the usual contagion of bad example the English have caught from their neighbours that illiberality and pettiness of proceeding which has given to modern warfare so wretched and malicious an aspect. The times are certainly different from those, when the two enemies were eager to afford each other every little comfort characteristic of a generous hostility: the times are different from those, when by a kind of romantic feeling half amiable and half ludicrous, the officers of the English and French guards, at the battle of Fontenoy,[1] pulled off their hats to each other and mutually insisted on receiving the first fire. If this was ridiculous, it was not diabolical. But in these matters the French appear to me to have no longer a character to lose. The EMPEROR by his pride and his violence, by his contemptible arrests of the visitors of his kingdom, by his infinitely contemptible arrests of helpless and terrified females, and by his tyrannical violations of the fire-sides of other countries, has broken that invisible bond which connected the most hostile nations by the involuntary feelings of human nature. This behaviour however was new to the English; it met with their execration. Alas, it has since met with their imitation! What will posterity say of my country, of England, the philosophic and the manly; of England in which the old age of liberty, like the saint banished to his island, has been driven to its last retreat, when it hears that we have made war with the very sick, with the very hospitals of our enemies, with human beings fainting under disease and death. The prohibition of the exportation of bark[2] to France has been defended upon the plea that France is reduced to the situation of a garrison town, from which every supply, down to the common necessaries of life, may be cut off. But this is very false reasoning. A garrison town may be thus deprived, because it is supposed that it will sooner yield, because the town is aware of these deprivations, and because it consents to them according to the usages of war. But of what effect is the deprivation of the necessaries of sick men among the general population of the country but to irritate those who are healthy? Of what effect is this war with helpless men but to rouse the indignation of their friends and countrymen against so barbarous an enemy? There has been one argument produced for it, which ought to make every generous mind recoil. The sick and the dying, it is said, will be roused by their wants to make a last effort and to execrate the French EMPEROR who is the author of their miseries. What an ignorance of human nature does this reasoning exhibit? The want of bark in the French hospitals is to make men execrate their own country rather than their enemies! The want of bark in the French hospitals is to create revolt against the man, who has aggrandized and therefore flattered his country, and who by his artful representations has rendered England hateful in its eyes! And grant that it would create revolt, is this the proceeding of a great and generous enemy? Must we, instead of fighting nobly and fairly with a fellow-creature, exercise some diabolical art

---

[1] Major military engagement between English and French forces during the War of the Austrian Succession, 1745.

[2] The bark of the cinchona tree (the source of quinine), ground into powder and taken to reduce fever.

which in the midst of his sufferings shall make him turn his own hand against himself? Gracious God! Shall we withhold the last reviving draught from the parched lips of women and infants burning with fever? Shall we fight with the wives and children of our enemies, with diseased old age, with the innocent sufferings of babes, and the despair of mothers? I am sick of my country when it acts so inhumanly. . . .

[February 28, 1808]

DELIVERANCE OF EUROPE

What the Deliverance of Europe Means.—Characteristic Touches of its Monarchs.—The Editor's Professions of Independence.

THERE are people who talk of the downfall of BONA-PARTE and the deliverance of Europe as if the two circumstances were indisputably the same. They seem to imagine that when he is overthrown, a kind of millenium will arise on earth; that things, in returning to their old channel, will flow with a delicious peace and purity; that every man in short will be free and every nation happy. These men forget that the overthrow of one tyrant is not the destruction of all, and that governments have in general much more to fear from themselves than their enemies.

I have no inclination whatever to lament the degeneracy of the times, which are in some respects much better than any preceding age, but I think there never was a less portion of *philosophy* in our political writers than at present. They look upon the circumstances and changes of the world with so partial an eye, that they account for every event upon the most petty causes of party: their minds are so nearsighted, that they can behold but a few minute objects at once, and in poring over little dates and disturbances they are unable to look abroad upon the world, to seek for the changes of things in the vast revolutions of the human mind, and to discover that one nation has generally reduced itself to an humiliated state, before another can trample on its freedom. These are the politicians, who unable to look or to move out of their little sphere, are so tenacious of the prejudices of their circle, of the privileges of their mental dungeon: the least attempt to lighten their darkness renders them irritable, and makes them shut their eyes with an impatient weakness that cannot bear the light. These are the patriots, who confound national prejudices with patriotism; who cannot bear to hear an enemy praised; who attribute all the misfortunes of their country to its external enemies or to a mere existing party; who think every war necessary,

provided the French are its objects; who call any stupid and selfish ally *magnanimous*; and who in their zeal to forget what are called little corruptions in their government and to exaggerate every corruption in another, are always flattering the vices of the state and literally killing their country with kindness.

On the other hand, there are politicians who take quite a different though quite as narrow a view of the subject, and though they are not slow to retort the charge of ignorance and corruption upon the opposite party, attribute the principal humiliation of Europe to the sole genius of the FRENCH EMPEROR. These men, who are of a more enthusiastic turn of mind, are also more inconsistent than their opponents, for while the latter are blind to their country's errors and therefore have the excuse of ignorance on their side, the former inveigh against the folly and corruption of the government without seeing that the real talents of our neighbour naturally decrease in value proportionably to the folly and corruption of his competitors; they will have all his opponents to be fools, and yet he must shew consummate wisdom in defeating them; and they are guilty of an enormity against reason and against their professed love of freedom, in railing against the best existing constitution in Europe, however corrupted it may have become, while *at the same time* they are wishing success to a man who would exterminate liberty from the face of the earth.

All this prejudice arises from the want of a little philosophy, from the want of a love of truth on truth's account, and from a vanity which few men will acknowledge even to their own hearts, that of maintaining an old opinion at all events. Wherever there have been violent political disputes, they have proved that the truth has nothing to do with extremes: its force is truly centripetal; and the moral as well as the natural philosopher may say, that whatever is stable and accordant with the true harmony of things tends directly to a centre.

The misfortunes of Europe are originally owing neither to the errors of party in this single country nor to the talents, great as they are, of the French Emperor. They are owing to the corruptions of the several states, and to various political tyrannies similar in their origin to that now exercised by BONAPARTE, though weakened by age and rendered contemptible by sloth and ignorance. The tyranny of France will come to the very same end, when the talents and freshness of the French Revolution shall be corrupted by the gradual influence of court and party interest, when tyrants shall have become stupid and contemptible, and the people not possess one intoxicating cause of self-glory to keep them in spirits and hinder them from thinking. Europe therefore must be delivered, not only from the

French Emperor, but from itself, not by the death of one tyrant, but by the purification of many bad and tyrannical governments. It always seems to me, that Providence has placed us in an age of wretched kings in order to give a lasting lesson to slavish minds and to shew the nothingness of mere royalty. The only mystery is, how any common reasoner can wonder at the successes of a man of talent when the opponents are so supremely weak, how he can wonder at the thraldom of the Continent when its princes are bound in their own ignorance and its nations in their own tyranny.

I forget what facetious nobleman it was, who, bold enough in common but bashful in the senate, laid a wager that he would make a speech in the House of Lords, and upon the strength of two or three bottles made that memorable and pithy oration against impeachers, which consisted of producing an example and then saying: "And you see, my Lords, what became of him." But it produced a great sensation, as the French say, for it consisted of the best logic in the world, the logic of fact. I think I may fairly exercise the same mode of reasoning upon the subject of the present "*noble race of potentates.*" I have only to fancy myself replying to the speech of a Noble Lord, now living, who in a manner little to be expected either from his talents or way of thinking reprobated the little respect which has been shewn by some of the public papers to the existing Princes of Europe.

In the first place, my Lords, there is the Emperor of AUSTRIA,[1] who ought still to have been Emperor of Germany if his common sense had permitted him.— This Prince, my lords, could never divest himself of the military prepossessions of his house; so he directed his army in person though he was some hundred miles off, and waged war against the French with a closet-faction instead of a field-officer; and your Lordships see what has become of the Emperor of AUSTRIA.

Then there is the Emperor of RUSSIA,[2] my Lords, a very magnanimous prince—that is to say, when he was on our side. This great man is weak enough to be ruled by every Ambassador that can reach him, especially after having received a beating from the said Ambassador's master: he once presented the novel sight of a despot fighting for the liberties of Europe, but his natural dulness was too powerful for him and he is now fighting against them—and your Lordships see what has become of the Emperor of RUSSIA.

Then, again my Lords, there is the King of PRUSSIA,[3] a very amiable man, except that he has attempted to cheat both friends and foes and is a little given to prevarication. The King of PRUSSIA, my Lords, is the petty tyrant of a worn-out state who wished to beat the tyrant of a young one, and your Lordships very well know what has become of the King of PRUSSIA.

Fourthly, my Lords, there is the King of DENMARK,[4] who it must be confessed—but if your Lordships please, I'll drop the King of DENMARK.

Well, my Lords, then there is the POPE of ROME,[5] who anointed BONAPARTE with holy oil, and after being his slave till this very moment suddenly began to question his master, and your Lordships know what has become of the POPE of ROME.

Then, my Lords, there were the States of Holland and of Venice, consisting of a hundred little tyrants, my Lords; I need not say any thing of them, but will conclude with King CHARLES of Spain, a very stupid and worthless old gentleman, and his son King FERDINAND,[6] whom I will not teach to despise his father by calling him any better. These two personages, my Lords, are manifestly the most stupid, corrupt, and cowardly princes in Europe, and I believe your Lordships pretty well know what has become of King CHARLES and King FERDINAND.

In short, to drop my oration, if the deliverance of Europe means the destruction of all tyranny, that is, not only BONAPARTE'S tyranny, but the whole pandemonium of corrupt courts, interests, and factions, I coincide with all my soul in the honest ardour of those who cry so loudly for it: but if it merely means the restoration of *the noble race of Potentates*, with all their suite mental and bodily, if it means the restoration of corrupt courts, of senseless and profligate princes, and

[1] Francis I (1768–1835) was Emperor of Austria and last ruler of the Holy Roman Empire from 1792 until 1806, when the Confederation of the Rhine (a union of German states protected by Napoleon) ended the Empire and its rule over German territories.

[2] Alexander I (1777–1825), who made peace with England in 1801 and initially opposed Napoleon, but in 1807 entered into alliance with him in his European conquests.

[3] Frederick William III (1770–1840), ineffective and vacillating ruler. By the Peace of Tilsit (July 9, 1807), following the military defeat of Prussia, Frederick lost half his territory and agreed to an enormous indemnity to Napoleon and military occupation of his remaining territories.

[4] Frederick VI (1768–1839), who became king in March 1808. In 1807, in order to prevent the Danish fleet from falling into the hands of Napoleon, a British fleet had sailed to Denmark, offered alliance with England, and guaranteed the security of Danish territories. As crown prince, Frederick refused the British offer, leading to the bombardment and surrender of Copenhagen and the capture of the entire Danish fleet.

[5] Pius VII (1740–1823) consecrated Napoleon as emperor in 1804. In 1808, Rome was occupied by French troops, following the degeneration of relations between the papacy and Napoleon.

[6] King Charles of Spain (1748–1819), Spanish monarch from 1788 to 1808, had allowed his government to be directed by his minister Manuel de Godoy, who aligned Spain with France and authorized French occupation of Spanish territories. Following an insurrection, his son Ferdinand assumed the throne in March 1808, only to yield it back to his father at Napoleon's insistence. The crown then passed into the complete power of Napoleon, and Ferdinand became a French prisoner.

of prejudices that do nothing for the people but render their slavery sacred, I really think that Europe is already delivered as much as ever she can be, or to borrow a phrase from the ladies, that she is already as well as can be expected.

I foresaw, when I adopted my political motto,[7] that my professions of independence would raise not only mistrust but malevolence, and that he who is of no party, is by turns caressed and abused by all parties. The event has proved as I expected. People cannot imagine how an Editor can be neither Pittite nor Foxite, and as if they had not had enough of Pittites and Foxites already, are determined he shall be one or the other whenever they please. If I praise consistency and rail at place-hunters, then the Foxites shake their heads at me: if I dislike war and remonstrate against new alliances, then the Pittites shake theirs. I was a very good Windhamite till I differed with General WHITELOCKE;[8] an excellent Burdettite till I mentioned the words "credulous young man;"[9] and a very promising Wilberforcite till I laughed at the Methodists. It is infinitely amusing, but piteous too, to see the regard which all party men have to relative instead of positive opinion: a Foxite will rejoice, not that you wish to have no placemen in parliament, or in other words to have nothing but the constitution, but that you like Mr. Fox and hate the Pittites: a Pittite on the other hand will rejoice, not that you know any thing about Mr. PITT, but that you like him at all events and hate the Foxites. If I must give my creed, it is simply this—The truth, the whole truth, and nothing but the truth; the constitution, the whole constitution, and *nothing but the constitution.* I can admire the talents of an illustrious scoundrel without applauding his ambition, and lament the errors of the state without wishing to live under any other: in short, I will flatter neither my country nor its enemies, and the distinction which

I make between the corruptions of the British constitution and the corruptions of the French, is precisely the same which I make between the errors of a good man and the vices of a profligate.

[September 11, 1808]

FRANCE AND ENGLAND

THE present age, however it may affect our interests, is unquestionably a brilliant period in the history of the world. Great as it has been in arms, it promises, at the return of peace, equal greatness in arts; and to survive such an age—to be handed down in despite of its conquerors to posterity, when all the little great, the PERCEVALS[1] and the weak princes, have been silently swept away, is a thought almost sufficient to inspire the soul of mediocrity itself. I mean not to pay homage to the renown of mere conquest or to the vices of conquerors; NAPOLEON in his gusts of passion, CÆSAR in his brothel, and ALEXANDER in his drunkenness, are equally as contemptible, as in their indifference of bloodshed they are detestable: ambition so degraded and unfeeling is but the keeper of a huge charnelhouse; and when the poet talked of it as

The glorious fault of angels and of gods,[2]

he should have added, that it converted those angels and gods into devils. But ALEXANDER the friend of ARISTOTLE, CÆSAR the cultivator of literature and the overcomer of difficulty, and NAPOLEON the patron of arts and annihilator of corrupt monarchies, are worthy of accompanying the poet and the philosopher to immortality; and it must be allowed, with all the weakness of mankind in admiring their destroyers, that posterity will not place a conqueror in the rank of great men, unless he exhibit some great quality of the mind, beyond a brutal inflexibility. TIMOUR and JENGHIS[3] are considered but as lucky and frightful barbarians: CHARLES the 12th,[4] with all his contempt of danger and wonderful successes, has obtained no title but that of a splendid madman; and the overthrowers of Rome itself are remembered only as the lightning from heaven, which comes to flash, to execute, and to vanish.

---

7 "Party is the madness of many for the gain of a few." Hunt originally attributed the statement to Swift. It occurs in Pope's "Thoughts on Various Subjects" (see William Lisle Bowles, ed., *The Works of Alexander Pope* [1806], VI, 405).

8 William Windham (1750–1810) was secretary of war under William Pitt from 1794 to 1801, and again under Lord Grenville's administration (1806–1807), during which he began plans for a South American campaign against the Spanish. General Whitelocke (1757–1833), lieutenant-general of the British army, was court-marshalled in March 1808, for the incompetence of his direction of the attack on Buenos Aires, leading to an ignominious surrender to the Spanish forces.

9 Sir Francis Burdett (1770–1844) was a popular Whig politician and vigorous exponent of reform. James Paull (1770–1808) stood for parliament from Westminster in 1806 and 1807, with the presumed support of Burdett, who did not wish to stand for a contested seat. In the 1807 contest, Burdett's failure to chair a dinner in Paull's support led to a duel, the removal of Paull from the contest, and an election victory for Burdett. Paull committed suicide on April 15, 1808.

---

1 Spencer Perceval (1762–1812), Tory prime minister from 1809 to 1812.

2 Pope's "Elegy to the Memory of an Unfortunate Lady," l. 14.

3 Tamerlane (1336–1405), the Mongol despot and invader of Russia, India, and Asia Minor. Genghis Kahn (1167–1227), the Mongolian despot and invader of lands from China to Russia.

4 Charles the 12th (1682–1718), ambitious soldier-king of Sweden.

The first great features, which will engage the attention of posterity in looking back to our time, are the empire of NAPOLEON and the facilities or obstructions he experienced in obtaining it. The former will naturally remind them of the Roman; the latter will awaken very different reflections, in which we have a peculiar interest. The Roman empire, during the ages of its genuine strength, was bounded by the Atlantic on the West, the river Euphrates on the East, the Rhine and Danube on the North, and the desarts of Barbary on the South. To the possession of this empire, besides all the facilities it will give to unbounded conquest from the state of the modern world, is BONAPARTE rapidly hastening. On the North indeed he is beyond it; on the West he will be complete master in three months; on the East he is already inclosing Turkey with Poland and his new Illyrian provinces; and the South, containing the states of Barbary, only waits for the settled master of the European Continent to yield at the first attack. Add to these, his influence in remoter Asia and over the whole civilized north of the Continent, and the Romans themselves might admire a conqueror who, in surpassing them in ambition, has reason also to surpass them in hope. Whether his successors will be able to keep his acquisitions, is another question: many natural causes, particularly the barbarism of the surrounding nations, operated both as a check and a protection to the empire inherited by AUGUSTUS: his successors quietly obtained or fought with each other for the whole dominion; and the strength of the empire was not dissipated by those independent divisions, which lost the conquests of ALEXANDER and of CHARLEMAGNE. The *causes* of French empire are the most interesting subject, for they involve every effect which a nation like ours has reason to fear. These are very different from the causes of Roman conquest, and should make Europe blush for her civilization. Barbarism, with its vices and its virtues, was the only formidable obstacle through which the Romans had to cut their way to dominion, and while their civilization and discipline rendered them irresistible to the vices of barbarism, they met with enough of its virtues to give dignity to their prowess. How direct has been the reverse with the enemies of France! Equal to her in civilization, originally superior in discipline, with their long reputation to sustain, and at last their very independence to preserve, they have nevertheless displayed all the weakness of barbarism without making a single use of experience. Some of the very countries which the Romans conquered with difficulty from their savage possessors, have fallen, in the height of their civilization, at the first attack. Such are the German countries west of the

Danube; the most renowned provinces of Spain; and the wretched nation of Portugal, once celebrated by the title of the warlike Lusitania.[5] Yet even these are not sunk lower than Rome herself, the mistress of them all. Perhaps the bitterest satire that can be cast on this once all-powerful city, is the feeling which hinders a writer from indulging in declamations on her fate:— pity itself has become common-place on the subject.*

Ask a Contractor the cause of these changes, and he will answer "The ambition of BONAPARTE;" ask a Courtier, he will say "The ambition of BONAPARTE;" ask a Minister, and he will still say "The ambition of BONAPARTE;" ask a King, and he will impatiently say "Nothing *but* the ambition of BONAPARTE;"— but ask an impartial observer, and he will say "The corruption of Courts." The ambition of BONAPARTE sprang out of the facilities that presented themselves to such a man; but the corruption of Courts was at its height when he was a child, and is the sole, putrid and deadly fountain of all the bloodshed that has deluged the Continent. Had BONAPARTE left Spain to herself, she would soon have committed suicide from nervous exhaustion; her limbs could no longer have borne their own feelings; and where the King was an idiot, and his first Minister [6] an ignorant favourite living upon that idiotcy, what was to be expected for a Court already worn out with debauchery—or from a people already ruined by that Court? God forbid I should defend his atrocious as well as contemptible arts against the Span-

* Yet one may well stop, in the midst of one's contempt, to admire the native artifices by which Italy managed so long to maintain the form of dominion when the reality had been lost for ages. First, it obtained empire by the perfection of the military art; when it lost this, it assumed and gained a dominion over the minds of mankind by superstition; the Pope, from becoming the Caesar of the religious world and conquering all sorts of barbarians by the force of terror, became in time the arbiter of the temporal Caesars; and it may be said that the very corpse of Roman power still sat on the throne of the Vatican, ruling almost as mightily, when it could do nothing, as when it enjoyed its glorious faculties. When this ghostly power began to be disputed, Italy still reigned the mistress of arts, as she had been of arms: no longer the forceful conqueror, she yet subdued the nations with her song; her laws of harmony won the implicit obedience of the artist as well as musician; and RAPHAEL and MICHAEL ANGELO are to this day the acknowledged princes of painting. Nay, when the sovereign arts have at last divided their residence among various countries, and nothing but the name of Rome survives, Fortune, as if she still lingered from very habit near her former residence, has selected from a little Italian island, directly opposite her beloved city, a new Favourite to work her imperial will, and subdue the nations.

<hr />

5 Ancient name of the central-western part of the Iberian peninsula, whose people fought vigorously against Roman invasion in the second century B.C.
6 Manuel de Godoy.

ish monarchy; he should have left it to JOVELLANOS[7] and its other enlightened men to see what they could do for its regeneration; but whenever BONAPARTE'S ambition is mentioned in terms of abhorrence, it is but an etiquette due to such monarchs as CHARLES of Spain, and FERDINAND of Naples,[8] &c. &c. that court-corruption should have the precedence in our detestation. In fact, had this corruption not existed, or had it even existed but to half its extent, it would have required a miracle from heaven to account for the elevation and triumphs of this extraordinary man.

Posterity then will know where to look for the true causes of these wars; and it will most assuredly brand them with infamy. But shall our enemy, thus brightening his fame by contrast, be handed down to future ages at the expense of England herself? To England, posterity will look either as the consummator or eclipser of this man's glory; and shall we continue to add to his beams by assisting his course over countries where he dissipates in an instant every thin cloud of opposition, and bursts forth in the full heat of meridian triumph?—To England posterity will look; and shall we, confessedly the most moral nation in Europe, with the example of a thousand illustrious forefathers to inspire us, consent to creep on in petty corruptions at home, and petty intrigues abroad, and petty compromises with our hopes and fears, till at last we grow sufficiently corrupt and timid to become the prey of our rival? The apathy of this nation, in suffering the present despicable Ministry to rule a moment longer without petitioning the KING for their removal, is the worst sign for its independence that has appeared for years. The business of Walcheren[9] is the common theme of execration; yet we ourselves, we, the people, who suffer from these fooleries and fatalities, do nothing towards their prevention; we seem to think there is no such thing as the right of petitioning the Throne, that Ministers cannot be removed, and that if a pug-dog were to be Premier, it would be the sole business of our lives to wait on the snarling and craving puppy like the vilest of slaves. England wants a man of a great mind at its helm; it wants, not a man who will do nothing but cram his conscience with places, and then go to church to sleep off or to pray off the surfeit, but a man, truly highminded; a man above all place and above all *politics*, as they are called; a man with one avowed principle and object of action, *this* an inflexible integrity, and *that* a preservation of his country; a man, in short, as full of disdain as the great CHATHAM[10] for those vermin and bloodsuckers the Jobbers, and as deaf as our *enemy* to the importunities of his friends for this *little* office and that *small* department; for how is he who cannot withstand the soft voice and cringing of his friends, or his uncle's friends, or his wife's brother's nephew's friends, to stem the progress of a great conqueror? Common sense laughs us to scorn, if we think so for an instant. "Well," say we, "but who is such a man? Where is he? How is he to be made Minister?" So saying, we sit down and have no more to say, except when the Income-tax-gatherer knocks at our door, and then we cry out, "Ah, this is a terrible evil;" or except when BONAPARTE'S invasion of us is mentioned, and then we exclaim, "Ah, perhaps he *may* come indeed." But the time is past for these gapings and groanings, so unworthy of Englishmen; and unless we get rid of our apathy, we shall soon get rid of more guineas and more fine armies. It was well observed the other day, that an individual has no right to plead his inability to do any thing *as* an individual: individuals compose bodies, and bodies do every thing: a body obtained for us our Magna Charta; a body settled the Bill of Rights; and a body, animating other bodies, may restore to us all our blessings by procuring REFORM. If we trust to our insular situation or to our navy, we trust to a certain extent very justly; but as worms can eat through the hardest wood, so corruption can render the best arms of no avail. On such a land indeed, and with such a navy, pure political *honesty* would be to us a wall of adamant; and this, I firmly believe, is as little to be obtained without REFORM, as Reform is without individual exertion. Whatever be our fate, to this age posterity will look as to the last rivalry of character between England and France. If we go on as at present, and value neither our character with our children's children nor *their* happiness, then France decidedly wins the palm in the greatest contest she ever fought with us;—but if we reform and rouse all our faculties, driving Corruption from the land as we would the most fatal of the enemy's spies, then shall our comparative glory shine upon posterity, like the sun compared

---

7 Gaspar Melchor de Jovellanos (1744–1811), a Spanish author and statesman of great honesty and integrity, had opposed the policies of Manuel de Godoy and suffered imprisonment from 1801 to 1808. He became a leader of the popular movement against the French.

8 Ferdinand IV (1751–1825), dictatorial ruler and stern opponent of republican principles.

9 In 1809, England had sent an expedition to capture Antwerp and destroy Napoleon's naval power. The mission was ineptly executed and ended disastrously, producing a government crisis, the resignations of the minster of war and foreign secretary, and the formation of a new cabinet under Spencer Perceval. Walcheren was one of several large islands controlling the water route to Antwerp, where 4,000 British soldiers perished of fever and pestilence.

---

10 William Pitt, Lord Chatham (1708–1778).

with a comet, and history will still say, "France is a
nation of brilliant eccentricity; but England is one
illustrious family of freemen and philosophers."

[November 19, 1809]

THE PRINCE ON
ST. PATRICK'S DAY

THE PRINCE REGENT is still in every body's mouth,
and unless he is as insensible to biting as to bantering,
a delicious time he has of it in that remorseless ubiquity! If a person takes in a newspaper, the first thing he
does, when he looks at it, is to give the old groan and
say, "Well,—what of the PRINCE REGENT now!" If
he goes out after breakfast, the first friend he meets is
sure to begin talking about the PRINCE REGENT;—
and the two always separate with a shrug. He who is
lounging along the street, will take your arm and turn
back with you to expatiate on the PRINCE REGENT;
and he in a hurry, who is skimming the other side of
the way, halloes out as he goes, "Fine doings these, of
the PRINCE REGENT!" You can scarcely pass by two
people walking together, but you shall hear the words
"PRINCE REGENT;"—"if the PRINCE REGENT has
done that, he must be—," or such as "the PRINCE
REGENT and Lord YAR—:"[1]—the rest escapes in the
distance. At dinner the PRINCE REGENT quite eclipses
the goose or the calf's-head: the tea-table, of course,
rings of the PRINCE REGENT: if the company goes to
the theatre to see the *Hypocrite*, or the new farce of
Turn Out, they cannot help thinking of the PRINCE
REGENT; and as Dean SWIFT extracted philosophical meditation from a Broomstick,[2] so it would not be
surprising if any serious person in going to bed should
find in his very nightcap something to remind him of
the merits of the PRINCE REGENT. In short, there is
no other subject but one that can at all pretend to a
place in the attention of our countrymen, and that is
their old topic the weather; their whole sympathies are
at present divided between the PRINCE REGENT and
the barometer;—

Nocte pluit totâ: redeunt spectacula manè;—
Divisum imperium cum JOVE CAESAR habet.
                                        VIRGIL.

[1] Frances Charles Seymour-Conway (1777–1842), Earl of
Yarmouth, was a close companion of the Regent and in 1812 had
been appointed Vice-Chamberlain of the Prince's Household.
Like the Regent, Yarmouth was notorious for his extravagant
life-style.
[2] Swift's parody *A Meditation upon a Broomstick* (1710).

All night the weeping tempests blow;
All day our state surpasseth shew;—
Doubtless a blessed empire share
The PRINCE OF WALES and PRINCE OF AIR.

But the Ministerial Journalists, and other creatures
of Government, will tell you, that there is nothing in
all this; or rather they will insist that it is to be taken in
a good sense, and that the universal talk respecting the
PRINCE REGENT is highly to his advantage: for it is
to be remarked, that these gentlemen have a pleasant
way of proving to us that we have neither eyes nor ears;
and would willingly persuade us in time, that to call a
man an idiot or a profligate is subscribing to his wisdom
and virtue;—a logic, by the bye, which enables us to
discover how it is they turn their own reputation to
account, and contrive to have so good an opinion of
themselves. Thus whenever they perceive an obnoxious
sensation excited among the people by particular
measures, they always affect to confine it to the organs
by which it is expressed, and to cry out against what
they are pleased to term "a few factious individuals,"
who are represented as a crafty set of fellows, that get
their living by contradicting and disgusting every body
else!—How such a trade can be thriving, we are not
informed: it is certainly a very different one from their
own, which however it may disgust other people, succeeds by echoing and flattering the opinions of men in
power. It is in vain that you refer them to human nature
and to the opinions that are naturally created by profligate rulers; they are not acquainted with human
nature, and still less with any such rulers:—it is in vain
that you refer them to companies in which impartial
and independent men are accustomed to meet;—they
know no such companies:—it is in vain that you refer
them to popular meetings, to common-halls, and to
political dinners;—they call the popular meetings unpopular, and can bring counter-dinners and common-
halls of their own. Be it so then;—let us compound
with them, and agree to consider all direct political
meetings as party assemblages, particularly those of the
Reformists, who, whatever room they may occupy on
the occasion, and whatever advocates they may possess
from one end of the kingdom to the other, shall be
nothing but a few factious individuals, as contemptible
for their numbers and public effect as for their bad
writing and worse principles. Nay, let us even resort on
this occasion to persons, who having but one great
political object, unconnected with the abstract merits
of party, persisted for so many years in expressing an
ardent and hopeful attachment to the PRINCE RE-
GENT, and in positively shutting their eyes to such
parts of his character as might have shaken their
dependence upon him, looking only to his succession

in the government as the day of their country's happiness, and caring not who should surround his throne provided he would only be true to his own word. An assembly of such persons,—such at least was their composition for the much greater part,—met the other day at the Freemasons' Tavern to celebrate the Irish Anniversary of Saint Patrick; and I shall proceed to extract from the *Morning Chronicle* such passages of what passed on the occasion as apply to his ROYAL HIGHNESS, in order that the Reader may see at once what is now thought of him, not by Whigs or Pittites, or any other party of the state, but by the fondest and most trusting of his fellow-subjects,—by those whose hearts have danced at his name,—who have caught from it inspiration to their poetry, patience to their afflictions, and hope to their patriotism.—

"The Anniversary of this day—a day always precious in the estimation of an Irishman, was celebrated yesterday at the Freemasons' Tavern, by a numerous and highly respectable assemblage of individuals. The Marquis of LANSDOWNE presided at the Meeting, supported by the Marquis of DOWNSHIRE, the Earl of MOIRA, Mr. SHERIDAN, the LORD MAYOR, Mr. Sheriff HEYGATE, &c. &c. When the cloth was removed, *Non nobis Domine* was sung, after which the Marquis of LANSDOWNE, premising that the Meeting was assembled for purposes of charity rather than of party or political feeling, gave the Health of the King, which was drunk with enthusiastic and rapturous applause. This was followed by *God save the King*, and then the Noble Marquis gave 'The Health of the Prince Regent,' which was drunk with partial applause and *loud and reiterated hisses*. The next toast, which called forth great and continued applause, lasting nearly five minutes, was 'The Navy and Army.'"

The interests of the Charity were then considered, and after a procession of the children (a sight worth all the gaudiness and hollow flourish of military and courtly pomps) a very handsome collection was made from the persons present. Upon this, the toasts were resumed; and "Lord MOIRA's health being drank with loud and reiterated cheering," his Lordship made a speech in which *not a word was uttered of the Regent.*— Here let the reader pause a moment, and consider what a quantity of meaning must be wrapped up in the silence of such a man with regard to his old companion and PRINCE. Lord MOIRA universally bears the character of a man who is generous to a fault; he is even said to be almost unacquainted with the language of denial or rebuke, and if this part of his character has been injurious to him, it has at least, with his past and his present experience, helped him to a thorough knowledge of the PRINCE's character. Yet this nobleman, so generous, so kindly affectioned, so well ex-

perienced,—even he has nothing to say in favour of his old acquaintance. The PRINCE has had obligations from him, and therefore his Lordship feels himself bound in gentlemanly feeling to say nothing in his disparagement; and in spite of the additional tenderness which that very circumstance would give him for the better side of his ROYAL HIGHNESS's character, he feels himself bound in honesty to say nothing in his praise,—not a word—not a syllable!—No more need be observed on this point.—His Lordship concluded with proposing the health of the Marquis of LANSDOWNE, who upon receiving the applauses of the company expressed himself "deeply sensible of such an honour, coming from men whose national character it was to be generously warm in their praise, but not more generously warm than faithfully sincere." This elegant compliment was justly received, and told more perhaps than every body imagined; for those who are "faithfully sincere" in their praise are apt to be equally so in their censure, and thus the hisses bestowed were put on an equal footing of sincerity with the applauses. The healths of the Vice-Presidents was then given, and after a short speech from Lord MOUNTJOY, and much *anticipating* clamour with "Mr. SHERIDAN's health," "Mr. SHERIDAN *at length* arose, and in a low tone of voice returned his thanks for the honourable notice by which so large a meeting of his countrymen thought proper to distinguish him. (*Applauses.*) He had ever been proud of Ireland, and hoped that his country might never have cause to be ashamed of him. (*Applauses.*) Ireland never forgot those who did all they could do, however little that might be, in behalf of her best interests. All allusion to politics had been industriously deprecated by their Noble Chairman.—He was aware that charity was the immediate object of their meeting; but standing as he did before an assembly of his countrymen, he could not affect to disguise his conviction that at the present crisis Ireland involved in itself every consideration dear to the best interests of the empire. (*Hear, hear!*) It was, therefore, that he was most anxious that nothing should transpire in that meeting calculated to injure those great objects, or to visit with undeserved censure the conduct of persons whose love to Ireland was as cordial and zealous as it ever had been. He confessed frankly that knowing as he did the unaltered and unalterable sentiments of an ILLUSTRIOUS PERSONAGE towards Ireland, he could not conceal from the meeting that he had felt considerably shocked at the *sulky coldness* and *surly discontent* with which they had on that evening drank the health of the PRINCE REGENT. (Here we were sorry to observe that Mr. S. was interrupted by *no very equivocal* symptoms of disapprobation)—When silence was somewhat restored, Mr. SHERIDAN said, that he *knew the Prince Regent well*—(*hisses*)—he knew his *principles*—(*hisses*,)—they would at least, he hoped, give him credit for believing that he knew them, when he said he did.—(*Applause.*)—He repeated, that he knew well the principles of the PRINCE REGENT, and that so well satisfied was he that they were all that Ireland could wish, that he (Mr. SHERIDAN) hoped, that as he had lived up to them, so he might die in the principles of the PRINCE REGENT—(*hisses and applauses.*)—He should be sorry personally to have merited their disapprobation (*general applause*, with cries of "Change the subject and speak out.")—He could only assure them, that the PRINCE REGENT remained unchangeably true to those principles. (*Here the clamours became so loud and general that we could collect nothing more.*)"

Although the company however refused to give a quiet hearing to Mr. SHERIDAN while he talked in this manner, yet the moment he sat down, they rose up, it seems, and as a mark that they were not personally offended, gave him a general clap:—the *Chronicle* says, it was "to mark their peculiar respect and esteem for him;" and as the rest of the above report is taken from that paper, it is fit that this encomiastic assertion should accompany it; but however the reporter might chuse to interpret the applause, there appears to be no reason for giving it a livelier construction than the one before-mentioned. We know well enough what the Irish think of Mr SHERIDAN. They believe he has been, and is, their friend; and on that account their gratitude will always endeavour to regard him as complacently as possible, and to separate what his masters can do from what he himself cannot:—it even prevents them perhaps from discerning the harm which a man of his lax turn of thinking, in countenancing the loose principles of another, may have done to the cause which he hoped to assist:—but they are not blind to his defects in general any more than the English, and after the terrible example that has been furnished us of the bad effects of those principles, "peculiar respect and esteem" are words not to be prostituted to every occasion of convivial good temper: it is too late to let a contingent and partial goodwill exaggerate in this manner, and throw away the panegyrics that belong to first-rate worthiness.

But to return to the immediate subject. Here is an assembly of Irishmen, respectable for their rank and benevolence, and desirous for years of thinking well of the PRINCE of WALES, absolutely loading with contempt the very mention of his "principles," and shutting their ears against a repetition of the word,—so great is their disdain and their indignation. Principles! How are we to judge of principles but by conduct? And what, in the name of common sense, does Mr. SHERI-

DAN mean by saying that the PRINCE adheres to his principles? Was it a principle then in his ROYAL HIGHNESS not to adhere to his professions and promises? And is it in keeping to such a principle, that Mr. SHERIDAN informs us and "the public in general" that he means to live and die in the principles of his Master? What did Lord MOIRA, the Marquis LANSDOWNE, or the Duke of DEVONSHIRE, say to these praises? Did they anticipate or echo them? No: *they kept a dead silence*; and for this conscientiousness they are reproved by the ministerial papers, which pathetically tell us how good his ROYAL HIGHNESS had been to the Charity, and what a shame it was to mingle political feelings with the object of such a meeting! Political candour, they mean: had it been political flattery, they would not have cared what had been said of the PRINCE REGENT, nor how many foreign questions had been discussed. It might have been proper in the meeting, had it been possible, to distinguish between the PRINCE of WALES as a subscriber to the Irish Charity and the PRINCE REGENT as a clencher of Irish chains; but when the health of such a Personage is proposed to such a meeting, political considerations are notoriously supposed to be implied in the manner of its reception, and had the reception been favourable, the ministerialists would have been as eager to take advantage of it as they now are to take umbrage. So much for the inevitable disclosure of truth, in one way or another; and thus has the very first utterance of the public opinion, vivâ voce, been loud and unequivocal in rebuke of the PRINCE REGENT.

It is impossible however, before the present article is closed, to resist an observation or two on the saddest of these Ministerial papers. Our readers are aware that the *Morning Post*, above all its rivals, has a faculty of carrying its nonsense to a pitch, that becomes amusing in spite of itself, and affords a relief to one's feelings in the very excess of its inflictions. Its paper of Thursday last, in answer to a real or pretended correspondent, contained the following paragraph:—"The publication of the Article of a Friend, relative to the ungenerous, unmanly conduct, displayed at a late public meeting, though evidently well meant, would only serve to give consequence to a set of worthless beings, whose imbecile efforts are best treated with sovereign contempt." *Worthless beings* and *sovereign contempt!* Who would not suppose that some lofty and exemplary character was here speaking of a set of informers and profligates? One, at any rate, whose notice was an honour, and whose silent disdain would keep the noisiest of us in obscurity? Yet this is the paper, notorious above all others, in the annals of perfidy, scandal, imbecility, and indecency,—the paper which has gone directly from one side to another, which has levied contributions upon this very PRINCE, which has become a bye-word for its cant and bad writing, and which has rioted in a doggrel, an adulation, and a ribaldry, that none but the most prostituted pens would consent to use,—the paper, in short, of the STUARTS, the BENJAFIELDS, the BYRNES, and the ROSA MATILDAS![3] And this delicious compound is to "give consequence" to a Society, consisting of the most respectable Irishmen in London, with rank and talent at their head!—Help us, benevolent Compositors, to some mark or other,—some significant and comprehensive index,—that shall denote a laugh of an hour's duration!—If any one of our readers should not be so well acquainted as another with the taste and principles of this bewitching *Post*, he may be curious to see what notions of praise and political justice are entertained by the persons whose contempt is so overwhelming. He shall have a specimen; and when he is reading it, let him lament, in the midst of his laughter, that a paper, capable of such sickening adulation, should have the power of finding its way to the table of an English Prince, and of helping to endanger the country by polluting the sources of its government. The same page, which contained the specimen of contempt above-mentioned, contained also a set of wretched common-place lines in French, Italian, Spanish, and English, *literally* addressing the PRINCE REGENT in the following terms, among others:—"You are the *glory of the People*— You are the *Protector of the Arts*—You are the *Mecænas of the Age*—Wherever you appear, you *conquer all hearts*, wipe away tears, excite *desire and love*, and win *beauty* towards you—You breathe *eloquence*—You inspire the Graces—You are an *Adonis in loveliness!* Thus gifted,"—it proceeds in English,

"Thus gifted with each grace of mind,
"Born to delight and bless mankind,
"Wisdom, with Pleasure in her train,
"Great Prince! shall signalize thy reign:—
"To Honour, Virtue, Truth, allied—
"The Nation's safeguard and its pride;
"With Monarchs of immortal fame
"Shall bright Renown enrol thy Name."

What person, unacquainted with the true state of the case, would imagine, in reading these astounding eulogies, that this *Glory of the People* was the subject of millions of shrugs and reproaches! That this *Protector of the Arts* had named a wretched Foreigner his Historical Painter in disparagement or in ignorance of the merits of his own countrymen! That this *Mecænas of the Age* patronized not a single deserving writer! That this *Breather of Eloquence* could not say a few decent, extempore words,—if we are to judge at least from what he said to his regiment on its embarkation for Portugal! That this *Conqueror of Hearts* was the disappointer of hopes! That this *Exciter of Desire* (bravo, Messieurs of the *Post*!) this *Adonis in Loveliness*, was a corpulent gentleman of fifty! In short, that this *delightful, blissful, wise, pleasurable, honourable, virtuous, true*, and *immortal* PRINCE, was a violator of his word, a libertine over head and ears in debt and disgrace, a despiser of domestic ties, the companion of gamblers and demireps, a man who has just closed half a century without one single claim on the gratitude of his country or the respect of posterity!

These are hard truths; but are they *not* truths? And have we not suffered enough;—are we not now suffering bitterly,—from the disgusting flatteries, of which the above is a repetition? The ministers may talk of the shocking boldness of the press, and may throw out their wretched warnings about interviews between Mr. PERCEVAL and Sir VICARY GIBBS;[4] but let us inform them, that such vices as have just been enumerated are shocking to all Englishmen who have a just sense of the state of Europe; and that he is a bolder man, who, in times like the present, dares to afford reason for the description. Would to GOD, the *Examiner* could ascertain that difficult, and perhaps undiscoverable point, which enables a public writer to keep clear of an appearance of the love of scandal while he is hunting out the vices of those in power! Then should one paper, at least, in this metropolis help to rescue the nation from the charge of silently encouraging what it must publicly rue; and the SARDANAPALUS[5] who is now afraid of none but informers, be taught to shake, in the midst of his minions, in the very drunkenness of his heart, at the voice of honesty. But if this be impossible, still there is one benefit which truth may derive from adulation,—one benefit, which is favourable to the former in proportion to the grossness of the latter, and of which none of his flatterers seem to be aware,—the opportunity of contradicting its assertions. Let us never for-

---

3 Daniel Stuart (1766–1846) was proprietor and editor of *The Morning Post*, 1795–1803. Mr. Benjafield was part owner of the paper in 1783 and acting editor in 1788; he was accused of having removed certain articles critical of the Prince of Wales in return for the payment of an annuity. Nicholas Byrne succeeded Stuart as editor in 1803. "Rosa Matilda" was the pseudonym of Charlotte Dacre, wife of Nicholas Byrne, and writer of novels and of effusive poems appearing in *The Morning Post*.

4 That is, between the Tory prime minister and his attorney general. Sir Vicary Gibbs (1751–1820) was attorney general from 1807 to 1812; he carried out an aggressive policy of prosecution for libel against the English press, including the actions against the Hunts in 1808, 1809, and 1810.

5 Sardanapalus, 7th-century B.C. king of Assyria, proverbial for a corrupt and effeminate tyrant.

get this advantage, which adulation cannot help giving us; and let such of our readers, as are inclined to deal insincerely with the Great from a false notion of policy and of knowledge of the world, take warning from what they now see of the miserable effects of courtly disguise, paltering, and profligacy. Flattery in any shape is unworthy a man and a gentleman: but political flattery is almost a request to be made slaves. If we would have the Great to be what they ought, we must find some means or other to speak of them as they are.

[March 22, 1812]

YOUNG POETS

IN SITTING down to this subject, we happen to be restricted by time to a much shorter notice than we could wish: but we mean to take it up again shortly. Many of our readers however have perhaps observed for themselves, that there has been a new school of poetry rising of late, which promises to extinguish the French one that has prevailed among us since the time of Charles the 2d. It began with something excessive, like most revolutions, but this gradually wore away; and an evident aspiration after real nature and original fancy remained, which called to mind the finer times of the English Muse. In fact it is wrong to call it a new school, and still more so to represent it as one of innovation, its only object being to restore the same love of Nature, and of *thinking* instead of mere *talking*, which formerly rendered us real poets, and not merely versifying wits, and bead-rollers of couplets.

We were delighted to see the departure of the old school acknowledged in the number of the *Edinburgh Review* just published,—a candour the more generous and spirited, inasmuch as that work has hitherto been the greatest surviving ornament of the same school in prose and criticism, as it is now destined, we trust, to be still the leader in the new.

We also felt the same delight at the third canto of Lord Byron's *Childe Harold*, in which, to our conceptions at least, he has fairly renounced a certain leaven of the French style, and taken his place where we always said he would be found,—among the poets who have a real feeling for numbers, and who go directly to Nature for inspiration. But more of this poem in our next.*

* By the way, we are authorised to mention, that the person in Cheapside who announces some new publications by his Lordship, and says he has given five hundred guineas for them, has no warrant whatsoever for so stating. We are sorry to hurt the man's sale, as far as some other booksellers are concerned, who are just as money-getting and impudent in different ways; but truth must be told of one, as it will also be told of others.—

The object of the present article is merely to notice three young writers, who appear to us to promise a considerable addition of strength to the new school. Of the first who came before us, we have, it is true, yet seen only one or two specimens, and these were no sooner sent us than we unfortunately mislaid them; but we shall procure what he has published, and if the rest answer to what we have seen, we shall have no hesitation in announcing him for a very striking and original thinker. His name is PERCY BYSSHE SHELLEY, and he is the author of a poetical work entitled *Alastor, or the Spirit of Solitude*.

The next with whose name we became acquainted, was JOHN HENRY REYNOLDS,[2] author of a tale called *Safie*, written, we believe, in imitation of Lord Byron, and more lately of a small set of poems published by Taylor and Hessey, the principal of which is called the *Naiad*. It opens thus:—

> The gold sun went into the west,
> And soft airs sang him to his rest;
> And yellow leaves all loose and dry,
> Play'd on the branches listlessly:
> The sky wax'd palely blue, and high
> A cloud seem'd touch'd upon the sky—
> A spot of cloud,—blue, thin, and still,
> And silence bask'd on vale and hill.
>   'Twas autumn-tide,—the eve was sweet,
>   As mortal eye hath e'er beholden;
>   The grass look'd warm with sunny heat,—
>   Perchance some fairy's glowing feet
>   Had lightly touch'd—and left it golden:
> A flower or two were shining yet;
> The star of the daisy had not yet set,—
> It shone from the turf to greet the air,
> Which tenderly came breathing there:
> And in a brook which lov'd to fret
>   O'er yellow sand and pebble blue,
>   The lily of the silvery hue
> All freshly dwelt, with white leaves wet.
> Away the sparkling water play'd,
>   Through bending grass, and blessed flower;
>   Light, and delight seem'd all its dower:

(Since writing this note, we find the business noticed in Chancery, and some of the *verses* quoted, which will certainly satisfy the public that the Noble Poet was not the author.) [1]

◇◇◇◇◇◇◇◇◇◇◇◇◇◇◇◇◇◇◇◇◇◇◇◇◇◇◇◇◇◇◇◇◇

[1] Hunt refers to the spurious works *Lord Byron's Farewell to England, with Three Others Poems*, and *Lord Byron's Pilgrimage to the Holy Land*, published by James Johnston. Byron's publisher John Murray filed suit, the case was argued in the Court of Chancery on November 28, 1816, and an injunction against Johnston was obtained.

[2] More accurately, John Hamilton Reynolds (1794–1852), minor poet and writer, friend of Keats. His *Safie, An Eastern Tale* was published in 1814; *The Naiad, a Tale; with other Poems* appeared in 1816. See p. 752.

Away in merriment it stray'd,—
  Singing, and bearing, hour after hour,
Pale, lovely splendour to the shade.

We shall give another extract or two in a future number. The author's style is too artificial, though he is evidently an admirer of Mr. Wordsworth. Like all young poets too, properly so called, his love of detail is too overwrought and indiscriminate: but still he is a young poet, and only wants a still closer attention to things as opposed to the seduction of words, to realize all that he promises. His nature seems very true and amiable.

The last of these young aspirants whom we have met with, and who promise to help the new school to revive Nature and

"To put a spirit of youth in every thing,"—

is, we believe, the youngest of them all, and just of age. His name is JOHN KEATS. He has not yet published any thing except in a newspaper; but a set of his manuscripts was handed us the other day, and fairly surprised us with the truth of their ambition, and ardent grappling with Nature. In the following Sonnet there is one incorrect rhyme, which might be easily altered, but which shall serve in the mean time as a peace-offering to the rhyming critics. The rest of the composition, with the exception of a little vagueness in calling the regions of poetry "the realms of gold," we do not hesitate to pronounce excellent, especially the last six lines. The word *swims* is complete; and the whole conclusion is equally powerful and quiet:—

ON FIRST LOOKING INTO CHAPMAN'S HOMER.

MUCH have I travel'd in the realms of Gold,
  And many goodly States and Kingdoms seen;
  Round many western Islands have I been,
Which Bards in fealty to Apollo hold;
But of one wide expanse had I been told,
  That deep-brow'd Homer ruled as his demesne;
  Yet could I never judge what men could mean,
Till I heard CHAPMAN speak out loud and bold.
Then felt I like some watcher of the skies,
  When a new planet swims into his ken;
Or like stout CORTEZ, when with eagle eyes
  He stared at the Pacific,—and all his men
Looked at each other with a wild surmise,—
  Silent, upon a peak in Darien.

Oct. 1816.   JOHN KEATS.

We have spoken with the less scruple of these poetical promises, because we really are not in the habit of lavishing praises and announcements, and because we have no fear of any pettier vanity on the part of young men, who promise to understand human nature so well.

[December 1, 1816]

REVIEW: *POEMS BY JOHN KEATS*

THIS is the production of the young writer, whom we had the pleasure of announcing to the public a short time since, and several of whose Sonnets have appeared meanwhile in the *Examiner* with the signature of J. K.[1] From these and stronger evidences in the book itself, the readers will conclude that the author and his critic are personal friends; and they are so,—made however, in the first instance, by nothing but his poetry, and at no greater distance of time than the announcement above-mentioned. We had published one of his Sonnets in our paper, without knowing more of him than any other anonymous correspondent; but at the period in question, a friend brought us one morning some copies of verses, which he said were from the pen of a youth. We had not been led, generally speaking, by a good deal of experience in these matters, to expect pleasure from introductions of the kind, so much as pain; but we had not read more than a dozen lines, when we recognized "a young poet indeed."

It is no longer a new observation, that poetry has of late years undergone a very great change, or rather, to speak properly, poetry has undergone no change, but something which was not poetry has made way for the return of something which is. The school which existed till lately since the restoration of Charles the 2d, was rather a school of wit and ethics in verse, than any thing else; nor was the verse, with the exception of Dryden's, of the best order. The authors, it is true, are to be held in great honour. Great wit there certainly was, excellent satire, excellent sense, pithy sayings; and Pope distilled as much real poetry as could be got from the drawing-room world in which the art then lived,—from the flowers and luxuries of artificial life,—into that exquisite little toilet-bottle of essence, the *Rape of the Lock*. But there was little imagination, of a higher order, no intense feeling of nature, no sentiment, no real music or variety. Even the writers who gave evidences meanwhile of a truer poetical faculty, Gray, Thomson, Akenside, and Collins himself, were content with a great deal of second-hand workmanship, and with false styles made up of other languages and a certain kind of inverted cant. It has been thought that Cowper was the first poet who re-opened the true way to nature and a natural style; but we hold this to be a

---

[1] In addition to the sonnet "On First Looking into Chapman's Homer" printed in the article on "Young Poets," six other sonnets by Keats had appeared in various issues of *The Examiner* by this date: "To Solitude" (May 5, 1816); "To Kosciusko" (February 16, 1817); "After dark vapours" (February 23, 1817); "To Haydon" ["Haydon! forgive me that I cannot speak"] and "On Seeing the Elgin Marbles" (March 9, 1817); "Written on a Blank Space at the end of Chaucer's Tale of 'The Floure and the Lefe'"(March 16, 1817).

mistake, arising merely from certain negations on the part of that amiable but by no means powerful writer. Cowper's style is for the most part as inverted and artificial as that of the others; and we look upon him to have been by nature not so great a poet as Pope: but Pope, from certain infirmities on his part, was thrown into the society of the world, and thus had to get what he could out of an artificial sphere:—Cowper, from other and more distressing infirmities, (which by the way the wretched superstition that undertook to heal, only burnt in upon him) was confined to a still smaller though more natural sphere, and in truth did not much with it, though quite as much perhaps as was to be expected from an organization too sore almost to come in contact with any thing.

It was the Lake Poets in our opinion (however grudgingly we say it, on some accounts) that were the first to revive a true taste for nature; and like most Revolutionists, especially of the case which they have since turned out to be, they went to an extreme, calculated rather at first to make the readers of poetry disgusted with originality and adhere with contempt and resentment to their magazine common-places. This had a bad effect also in the way of re-action; and none of those writers have ever since been able to free themselves from certain stubborn affectations, which having been ignorantly confounded by others with the better part of them, have been retained by their self-love with a still less pardonable want of wisdom. The greater part indeed of the poetry of Mr. Southey, a weak man in all respects, is really made up of little else. Mr. Coleridge still trifles with his poetical as he has done with his metaphysical talent. Mr. Lamb, in our opinion, has a more real tact of humanity, a modester, Shakspearean wisdom, than any of them; and had he written more, might have delivered the school victoriously from all its defects. But it is Mr. Wordsworth who has advanced it the most, and who in spite of some morbidities as well as mistaken theories in other respects, has opened upon us a fund of thinking and imagination, that ranks him as the successor of the true and abundant poets of the older time. Poetry, like Plenty, should be represented with a cornucopia, but it should be a real one; not swelled out and insidiously *optimized* at the top, like Mr. Southey's stale strawberry baskets, but fine and full to the depth, like a heap from the vintage. Yet from the time of Milton till lately, scarcely a tree had been planted that could be called a poet's own. People got shoots from France, that ended in nothing but a little barren wood, from which they made flutes for young gentlemen and fan-sticks for ladies. The rich and enchanted ground of real poetry, fertile with all that English succulence could produce, bright with all that Italian sunshine could lend, and haunted with

exquisite humanities, had become invisible to mortal eyes like the garden of Eden:—

"And from that time those Graces were not found."

These Graces, however, are re-appearing; and one of the greatest evidences is the little volume before us; for the work is not one of mere imitation, or a compilation of ingenious and promising things that merely announce better, and that after all might only help to keep up a bad system; but here is a young poet giving himself up to his own impressions, and revelling in real poetry for its own sake. He has had his advantages, because others have cleared the way into those happy bowers; but it shews the strength of his natural tendency, that he has not been turned aside by the lingering enticements of a former system, and by the self-love which interests others in enforcing them. We do not, of course, mean to say, that Mr. Keats has as much talent as he will have ten years hence, or that there are no imitations in his book, or that he does not make mistakes common to inexperience;—the reverse is inevitable at his time of life. In proportion to our ideas, or impressions of the images of things, must be our acquaintance with the things themselves. But our author has all the sensitiveness of temperament requisite to receive these impressions; and wherever he has turned hitherto, he has evidently felt them deeply.

The very faults indeed of Mr. Keats arise from a passion for beauties, and a young impatience to vindicate them; and as we have mentioned these, we shall refer to them at once. They may be comprised in two;—first, a tendency to notice every thing too indiscriminately and without an eye to natural proportion and effect; and second, a sense of the proper variety of versification without a due consideration of its principles.

The former error is visible in several parts of the book, but chiefly though mixed with great beauties in the Epistles, and more between pages 28 and 47, where are collected the author's earliest pieces, some of which, we think, might have been omitted, especially the string of magistrate-interrogatories about a shell and a copy of verses.[2] See also (p. 61) a comparison of wine poured out in heaven to the appearance of a falling star, and (p. 62) the sight of far-seen fountains in the same region to "silver streaks across a dolphin's fin."[3] It was by thus giving way to every idea that came across him, that Marino,[4] a man of real poetical fancy, but no judgment, corrupted the poetry of Italy; a catastrophe,

---

[2] Referring to the poem "On Receiving a Curious Shell and a Copy of Verses, from the same Ladies."
[3] The Epistle "To my Brother George," ll. 39–42 and 47–50.
[4] Giovanni Battista Marino (1569–1625) was a Neapolitan writer of verses abounding in extravagant conceits.

which however we by no means anticipate from our author, who with regard to this point is much more deficient in age than in good taste. We shall presently have to notice passages of a reverse nature, and these are by far the most numerous. But we warn him against a fault, which is the more tempting to a young writer of genius, inasmuch as it involves something so opposite to the contented common-place and vague generalities of the late school of poetry. There is a superabundance of detail, which, though not so wanting, of course, in power of perception, is as faulty and unseasonable sometimes as common-place. It depends upon circumstances, whether we are to consider ourselves near enough, as it were, to the subject we are describing to grow microscopical upon it. A person basking in a landscape for instance, and a person riding through it, are in two very different situations for the exercise of their eyesight; and even where the license is most allowable, care must be taken not to give to small things and great, to nice detail and to general feeling, the same proportion of effect. Errors of this kind in poetry answer to a want of perspective in painting, and of a due distribution of light and shade. To give an excessive instance in the former art, there was Denner,[5] who copied faces to a nicety amounting to a horrible want of it, like Brobdignagian visages encountered by Gulliver; and who, according to the facetious Peter Pindar,

Made a bird's beak appear at twenty mile.[6]

And the same kind of specimen is afforded in poetry by Darwin,[7] a writer now almost forgotten and deservedly, but who did good in his time by making unconscious caricatures of all the poetical faults in vogue, and flattering himself that the sum total went to the account of his original genius. Darwin would describe a dragon-fly and a lion in the same terms of proportion. You did not know which he would have scrambled from the sooner. His pictures were like the two-penny sheets which the little boys buy, and in which you see J Jackdaw and K King, both of the same dimensions.

Mr. Keats's other fault, the one in his versification, arises from a similar cause,—that of contradicting over-zealously the fault on the opposite side. It is this which provokes him now and then into mere roughnesses and discords for their own sake, not for that of variety and

contrasted harmony. We can manage, by substituting a greater feeling for a smaller, a line like the following:—

I shall roll on the grass with two-fold ease;—[8]

but by no contrivance of any sort can we prevent this from jumping out of the heroic measure into mere rhythmicality,—

How many bards gild the lapses of time!

We come now however to the beauties; and the reader will easily perceive that they not only outnumber the faults a hundred fold, but that they are of a nature decidedly opposed to what is false and inharmonious. Their characteristics indeed are a fine ear, a fancy and imagination at will, and an intense feeling of external beauty in its most natural and least expressible simplicity.

We shall give some specimens of the last beauty first, and conclude with a noble extract or two that will show the second, as well as the powers of our young poet in general. The harmony of his verses will appear throughout.

The first poem consists of a piece of luxury in a rural spot, ending with an allusion to the story of Endymion and to the origin of other lovely tales of mythology, on the ground suggested by Mr. Wordsworth in a beautiful passage of his *Excursion*.[9] Here, and in the other largest poem, which closes the book, Mr. Keats is seen to his best advantage, and displays all that fertile power of association and imagery which constitutes the abstract poetical faculty as distinguished from every other. He wants age for a greater knowledge of humanity, but evidences of this also bud forth here and there.—To come however to our specimens:—

The first page of the book presents us with a fancy, founded, as all beautiful fancies are, on a strong sense of what really exists or occurs. He is speaking of

A gentle Air in Solitude.
There crept
A little noiseless noise among the leaves,
Born of the very sigh that silence heaves.

---

5 Balthasar Denner (1685–1749), German painter and portrait miniaturist, who worked in England with great success from 1721 to 1728.

6 Ode VII ("Peter groweth ironically facetious") of *More Lyric Odes to the Royal Academicians* (1783), by John Wolcot (1738–1819), who wrote satirical verses under the pseudonym "Peter Pindar."

7 Erasmus Darwin (1731–1802). See Coleridge's *Biographia Literaria*, Chapter I, p. 174.

8 "Epistle to Charles Cowden Clarke," l. 79. The next quotation is the title and first line of the fourth sonnet in the 1817 volume.

9 The "first poem" is "I Stood Tiptoe upon a little hill." (The 1817 volume closed with the "other largest poem," "Sleep and Poetry.") The passage from *The Excursion* to which Hunt refers is IV, 718–62, 847–87, where Wordsworth had traced the origin of Greek myths to the poet's delight in the objects of nature. In "I stood Tiptoe" (ll. 125–204), Keats had similarly explained the stories of Psyche and Cupid, Pan, Narcissus, and Endymion.

Young Trees.
There too should be
The frequent chequer of a youngling tree,
That with a score of light green brethren shoots
From the quaint mossiness of aged roots:
Round which is heard a spring-head of clear waters.[10]

Any body who has seen a throng of young beeches, furnishing those natural clumpy seats at the root, must recognise the truth and grace of this description. The remainder of this part of the poem, especially from—

Open afresh your round of starry folds,
Ye ardent marigolds!—[11]

down to the bottom of page 5, affords an exquisite proof of close observation of nature as well as the most luxuriant fancy.

The Moon.
Lifting her silver rim
Above a cloud, and with a gradual swim
Coming into the blue with all her light.

Fir Trees.
Fir trees grow around,
Aye dropping their hard fruit upon the ground.

This last line is in the taste of the Greek simplicity.

A Starry Sky.
The dark silent blue
With all its diamonds trembling through and through.

Sound of a Pipe.
And some are hearing eagerly the wild
Thrilling liquidity of dewy piping.

The *Specimen of an Induction to a Poem*, and the fragment of the Poem itself entitled *Calidore*, contain some very natural touches on the human side of things; as when speaking of a lady who is anxiously looking out on the top of a tower for her defender, he describes her as one

Who cannot feel for cold her tender feet:[12]

and when Calidore has fallen into a fit of amorous abstraction, he says that

——The kind voice of good Sir Clerimond
Came to his ear, as something from beyond
His present being.

The Epistles, the Sonnets, and indeed the whole of the book, contain strong evidences of warm and social feelings, but particularly the Epistle to Charles Cowden Clarke, and the Sonnet to his own Brothers, in which the "faint cracklings" of the coal-fire are said to be

Like whispers of the household gods that keep
A gentle empire o'er fraternal souls.[13]

The Epistle to Mr. Clarke is very amiable as well as poetical, and equally honourable to both parties,—to the young writer who can be so grateful towards his teacher, and to the teacher who had the sense to perceive his genius, and the qualities to call forth his affection. It consists chiefly of recollections of what his friend had pointed out to him in poetry and in general taste: and the lover of Spenser will readily judge of his preceptor's qualifications, even from a single triplet, in which he is described, with a deep feeling of simplicity, as one

Who had beheld Belphœbe in a brook,
And lovely Una in a leafy nook,
And Archimago leaning o'er his book.

The Epistle thus concludes:—

Picture of Companionship.
But many days have past—
Since I have walked with you through shady lanes,
That freshly terminate in open plains,
And revell'd in a chat that ceased not,
When at night-fall among your books we got;
No, nor when supper came,—nor after that,—
Nor when reluctantly I took my hat;
No, nor till cordially you shook my hand
Midway between our homes:—your accents bland
Still sounded in my ears, when I no more
Could hear your footsteps touch the gravelly floor.
Sometimes I lost them, and then found again,
You changed the footpath for the grassy plain.
In those still moments I have wished you joys
That well you know to honour:—"Life's very toys
With him," said I, "will take a pleasant charm;
It cannot be that ought will work him harm."[14]

And we can only add, without any disrespect to the graver warmth of our young poet, that if Ought at-

---

[10] "I Stood Tiptoe", ll. 10–12, 37–41.

[11] "I Stood Tiptoe," ll. 47–48. The next group of quotations are, respectively, from: "I Stood Tiptoe," ll. 113–15; "Calidore. A Fragment," ll. 40–41; "To my Brother George," ll. 57–58; and "Sleep and Poetry," ll. 370–71.

[12] "Specimen of an Induction to a Poem," l. 14. The next quotation is from "Calidore. A Fragment," ll. 99–101.

[13] Sonnet "To my Brothers," ll. 3–4.

[14] Epistle "To Charles Cowden Clarke," ll. 35–37, 109, 115–30. Charles Cowden Clarke (1787–1877) was assistant to his father Dr. John Clarke, schoolmaster of Enfield Academy, which Keats attended 1803–1811. Following his departure, Keats maintained a close friendship with the son, borrowing books and discussing literature. It was a reading of Chapman's translation of Homer with Charles in October 1816, which inspired the famous sonnet.

tempted it, Ought would find he had stout work to do with more than one person.

The following passage in one of the Sonnets passes, with great happiness, from the mention of physical associations to mental; and concludes with a feeling which must have struck many a contemplative mind, that has found the sea-shore like a border, as it were, of existence. He is speaking of

The Ocean.

The Ocean with its vastness, its blue green,
Its ships, its rocks, its caves,—its hopes, its fears,—
Its voice mysterious, which whoso hears
Must think on what will be, and what has been.[15]

We have read somewhere the remark of a traveller, who said that when he was walking alone at night-time on the sea-shore, he felt conscious of the earth, not as the common every day sphere it seems, but as one of the planets, rolling round with him in the mightiness of space. The same feeling is common to imaginations that are not in need of similar local excitements.

The best poem is certainly the last and longest, entitled *Sleep and Poetry*. It originated in sleeping in a room adorned with busts and pictures, and is a striking specimen of the restlessness of the young poetical appetite, obtaining its food by the very desire of it, and glancing for fit subjects of creation "from earth to heaven." [16] Nor do we like it the less for an impatient, and as it may be thought by some, irreverend assault upon the late French school of criticism and monotony, which has held poetry chained long enough to render it somewhat indignant when it has got free.

The following ardent passage is highly imaginative:—

An Aspiration after Poetry.

O Poesy! for thee I grasp my pen
That am not yet a glorious denizen
Of thy wide heaven; yet, to my ardent prayer,
Yield from thy sanctuary some clear air,
Smoothed for intoxication by the breath
Of flowering bays, that I may die a death
Of luxury, and my young spirit follow
The morning sun-beams to the great Apollo
Like a fresh sacrifice; or, if I can bear
The o'erwhelming sweets, 'twill bring to me the fair
Visions of all places: a bowery nook
Will be elysium—an eternal book
Whence I may copy many a lovely saying
About the leaves and flowers—about the playing
Of nymphs in woods and fountains; and the shade
Keeping a silence round a sleeping maid;

And many a verse from so strange influence
That we must ever wonder how and whence
It came. Also imaginings will hover
Round my fire-side, and haply there discover
Vistas of solemn beauty, where I'd wander
In happy silence, like the clear meander
Through its lone vales: and where I found a spot
Of awfuller shade, or an enchanted grot,
Or a green hill o'erspread with chequered dress
Of flowers, and fearful from its loveliness,
Write on my tablets all that was permitted,
All that was for our human senses fitted.
Then the events of this wide world I'd seize
Like a strong giant, and my spirit tease
Till at it shoulders it should proudly see
Wings to find out an immortality.[17]

Mr. Keats takes an opportunity, though with very different feelings towards the school than he has exhibited towards the one above-mentioned, to object to the morbidity that taints the productions of the Lake Poets. They might answer perhaps, generally, that they chuse to grapple with what is unavoidable, rather than pretend to be blind to it; but the more smiling Muse may reply, that half of the evils alluded to are produced by brooding over them; and that it is much better to strike at as many *causes* of the rest as possible, than to pretend to be satisfied with them in the midst of the most evident dissatisfaction.

Happy Poetry Preferred.

These things are doubtless: yet in truth we've had
Strange thunders from the potency of song;
Mingled indeed with what is sweet and strong,
From majesty: but in clear truth the themes
Are ugly clubs, the Poets Polyphemes
Disturbing the grand sea. A drainless shower
Of light is poesy; 'tis the supreme of power:
'Tis might half slumb'ring on its own right arm.
The very archings of her eye-lids charm
A thousand willing agents to obey.
And still she governs with the mildest sway:
But strength alone though of the Muses born
Is like a fallen angel: trees uptorn,
Darkness, and worms, and shrouds, and sepulchres
Delight it; for it feeds upon the burrs
And thorns of life; forgetting the great end
Of poesy, that it should be a friend
To soothe the cares, and lift the thoughts of man.

We conclude with the beginning of the paragraph which follows this passage, and which contains an idea of as lovely and powerful a nature in embodying an abstraction, as we ever remember to have seen put into words:—

---

[15] Sonnet "To my Brother George," ll. 5–8.
[16] The room "adorned with busts and pictures" was at Hunt's own cottage at Hampstead Heath. The quotation "from earth to heaven" is from *Midsummer Night's Dream*, V, i, 13.

[17] Ll. 53–84. Hunt subsequently quotes ll. 230–51.

Yet I rejoice: a myrtle fairer than
E'er grew in Paphos, from the bitter weeds
Lifts its sweet head into the air, *and feeds*
A silent space with ever sprouting green.

Upon the whole, Mr. Keats's book cannot be better described than in a couplet written by Milton when he too was young, and in which he evidently alludes to himself. It is a little luxuriant heap of

Such sights as youthful poets dream
On summer eves by haunted stream.[18]

[June 1–July 13, 1817]

F R O M

REVIEW:
SHELLEY'S *THE REVOLT OF ISLAM*[1]

*   *   *   *   *

MR. SHELLEY is of opinion with many others that the world is a very beautiful one externally, but wants a good deal of mending with respect to its mind and habits; and for this purpose he would quash as many cold and selfish passions as possible, and rouse up the gentle element of Love, till it set our earth rolling more harmoniously. The answer made to a writer, who sets out with endeavours like these, is that he is idly aiming at perfection; but Mr. Shelley has no such aim, neither have nine hundred and ninety-nine out of a thousand of the persons who have ever been taunted with it. Such a charge, in truth, is only the first answer which egotism makes to any one who thinks he can go beyond its own ideas of the possible. If this however be done away, the next answer is, that you are attempting something wild and romantic,—that you will get disliked for it as well as lose your trouble,—and that you had better coquet, or rather play the prude, with things as they are. The worldly sceptic smiles, and says "Hah!"—the dull rogues wonder, or laugh out;—the disappointed egotist gives you a sneering admonition, having made up his mind about all these things because he and his friends could not alter them; the hypocrite affects to be shocked; the bigot anticipates the punishment that awaits you for daring to say that God's creation is not a vile world, nor his creatures bound to be miserable;—and even the more amiable compromiser

with superstition expresses alarm for you,—does not know what you may be hazarding, though he believes nevertheless that God is all good and just,—refers you to the fate of Adam, to shew you that because he introduced the knowledge of evil, you must not attempt to do it away again,—and finally, advises you to comfort yourself with *faith*, and to secure a life in the next world because *this* is a bad business, and *that*, of course, you may find a worse. It seems forgotten all this while, that Jesus Christ himself recommended Love as the great law that was to supersede others; and recommended it too to an extreme, which has been held impracticable. How far it has been found impracticable, in consequence of his doctrines having been mixed up with contradictions and threatening dogmas, and with a system of after-life which contradicts all its principles, may be left to the consideration. Will theologians never discover, that men, in order to be good and just to each other, must either think well of a Divine Being, really and not pretendingly, or not think of him at all? That they must worship Goodness and a total absence of the revengeful and malignant passions, if not Omnipotence? or else that they must act upon this quality for themselves, and agree with a devout and amiable Pagan, that "it were better men should say there was no such being as Plutarch, than that there was one Plutarch who eat his own children?" Instead of the alarms about searches after happiness being wise and salutary, when the world is confessedly discordant, they would seem, if we believed in such things, the most fatal and ingenious invention of an enemy of mankind. But it is only so much begging of the question, fatal indeed as far as it goes, and refusing in the strangest manner to look after good, because there is a necessity for it. And as to the Eastern apologue of Adam and Eve (for so many Christians as well as others have thought it), it would be merely shocking to humanity and to a sense of justice in any other light; but it is, in fact, a very deep though not wisely managed allegory, deprecating the folly of mankind in losing their simplicity and enjoyment, and in taking to those very mistakes about vice and virtue, which it is the object of such authors as the one before us to do away again. Faith! It is the very object they have in view; not indeed faiths in endless terrors and contradictions, but "a faith and hope," as Mr. Shelley says, "in something good,"—that faith in the power of men to be kinder and happier, which other faiths take so much pains, and professed pains, to render unbelievable even while they recommend it! "Have faith," says the theologian, "and bear your wretchedness, and escape the wrath to come." "*Have* faith," says the philosopher, "and begin to be happier now, and do not attribute odious qualities to any one."

---

[18] *l'Allegro*, ll. 129–30.
[1] Hunt's three-part review appeared in *The Examiner* between February 1 and March 1, 1818. Here reproduced is the final installment, with the omission of the opening introductory paragraph.

People get into more inconsistencies in opposing the hopes and efforts of a philosophical enthusiasm than on any other subject. They say "use your reason, instead of your expectations;" and yet this is the reverse of what they do in their own beliefs. They say, take care how you contradict custom;—yet Milton, whom they admire, set about ridiculing it, and paying his addresses to another woman in his wife's life-time, till the latter treated him better. They say it is impossible the world should alter; and yet it has often altered. They say it is impossible, at any rate, it should mend; yet people are no longer burnt at the stake. They say, but it is too old to alter to any great purpose of happiness,—that all its experience goes to the contrary; and yet they talk at other times of the brief life and short-sighted knowledge of man, and of the nothingness of "a thousand years." The experience of a man and an ephemeris are in fact just on a par in all that regards the impossibility of change. But one man,—they say—what can one man do? Let a glorious living person answer,—let Clarkson[2] answer; who sitting down in his youth by a road-side, thought upon the horrors of the Slave Trade, and vowed he would dedicate his life to endeavour at overthrowing it. He was laughed at; he was violently opposed; he was called presumptuous and even irreligious; he was thought out of his senses; he made a noble sacrifice of his own health and strength; and he has *lived* to see the Slave Trade, aye, even the slavery of the descendants of the "cursed" Ham, made a Felony.

We have taken up so much room in noticing these objections, that we have left ourselves none for entering into a further account of Mr. Shelley's views than he himself has given; and we have missed any more quotations at last. But we are sure that he will be much better pleased to see obstructions cleared away from the progress of such opinions as his, than the most minute account given of them in particular. It may be briefly repeated, that they are at war with injustice, violence, and selfishness of every species, however disguised;—that they represent, in a very striking light, the folly and misery of systems, either practical or theoretical, which go upon penal and resentful grounds, and add "pain to pain;" and that they would have men, instead of worshipping tyrannies and terrors of any sort, worship goodness and gladness, diminish the vices and sorrows made by custom only, encourage the virtues and enjoyments which mutual benevolence may realize; and in short, make the best and utmost of this world, as well as hope for another.

The beauties of the poem consist in depth of senti-ment, in grandeur of imagery, and a versification remarkably sweet, various, and noble, like the placid playing of a great organ. If the author's genius reminds us of any other poets, it is of two very opposite ones, Lucretius and Dante. The former he resembles in the Dædalian part of it, in the boldness of his speculations, and in his love of virtue, of external nature, and of love itself. It is his gloomier or more imaginative passages that sometimes remind us of Dante. The sort of supernatural architecture in which he delights has in particular the grandeur as well as obscurity of that great genius, to whom however he presents this remarkable and instructive contrast, that superstition and pain and injustice go hand in hand even in the pleasantest parts of Dante, like the three Furies, while philosophy, pleasure, and justice, smile through the most painful passages of our author, like the three Graces.

Mr. Shelley's defects as a poet are obscurity, inartificial and yet not natural economy, violation of costume, and too great a sameness and gratuitousness of image and metaphor, and of image and metaphor too drawn from the elements, particularly the sea. The book is full of humanity; and yet it certainly does not go the best way to work of appealing to it, because it does not appeal to it through the medium of its common knowledges. It is for this reason that we must say something, which we would willingly leave unsaid, both from admiration of Mr. Shelley's genius and love of his benevolence; and this is, that the work cannot possibly become popular. It may set others thinking and writing, and we have no doubt will do so; and those who can understand and relish it, will relish it exceedingly; but the author must forget his metaphysics and seasides a little more in his future works, and give full effect to that nice knowledge of men and things which he otherwise really possesses to an extraordinary degree. We have no doubt he is destined to be one of the leading spirits of his age, and indeed has already fallen into his place as such; but however resolute as to his object, he will only be doing it justice to take the most effectual means in his power to forward it.

We have only to observe in conclusion, as another hint to the hopeless, that although the art of printing is not new, yet the Press in any great and true sense of the word is a modern engine in the comparison, and the changeful times of society have never yet been accompanied with so mighty a one. *Books* did what was done before; they have now a million times the range and power; and the Press, which has got hold of Superstition and given it some irrecoverable wounds already, will, we hope and believe, finally draw it in altogether, and crush it as a steam-engine would a great serpent.

[2] Thomas Clarkson (1760–1846), leading abolitionist.

[March 1, 1818]

REVIEW:
BYRON'S DON JUAN,
CANTOS I AND II

SOME persons consider this the finest work of Lord Byron,—or at least that in which he displays most power. It is at all events the most extraordinary that he has yet published. His other poems, with the exception of that amusing satire—*Beppo*, are written for the most part with one sustained serious feeling throughout,—either of pathos, or grandeur, or passion, or all united. But *Don Juan* contains specimens of all the author's modes of writing, which are mingled together and push one another about in a strange way. The ground-work (if we may so speak of a stile) is the satirical and humourous; but you are sometimes surprised and moved by a touching piece of human nature, and again startled and pained by the sudden transition from loveliness or grandeur to ridicule or the mock-heroic. The delicious and deep descriptions of love, and youth, and hope, came upon us like the "young beams" of the sun breaking through the morning dew, and the terrific pictures of the misery of man and his most appalling sensations, like awful flashes of lightning;—but when the author reverses this change, he trifles too much with our feelings, and occasionally goes on, turning to ridicule or hopelessness all the fine ideas he has excited, with a recklessness that becomes extremely unpleasant and mortifying. What, for instance, can be more beautiful and at the same time true to nature than where,—just after a very anti-pathetic description of the confusion of *Julia* at her husband's sudden appearance, and her contrivances and lovers' falsehoods to elude his search for the beloved youth, he says (speaking of their alarm at the expected return of the old gentleman)—

> Julia did not speak,
> But pressed her bloodless lip to Juan's cheek.
>
> He turn's his lip to hers, and with his hand
>   Call'd back the tangles of her wandering hair;
> Even then their love they could not all command,
>   And half forgot their danger and despair.[1]

What more calculated to "harrow up one's soul" than the following stanzas, which come in the very midst of some careless jests on the abstract ludicrousness of the wretched shifts of starving sailors in a becalmed boat, surrounded by a boundless prospect of the ocean? The Italics are our own.

> The seventh day, and no wind—the burning sun
>   Blister'd and scorch'd; and, stagnant on the sea,
> They lay like carcases! and hope was none,

---

[1] Canto I, clxix–clxx.

> Save in the breeze which came not: *savagely*
> *They glared upon each other*—all was done,
>   Water, and wine, and food,—and you might see
> The *longings of the cannibal arise*,
> (*Although they spoke not*) in their *wolfish* eyes.
>
> At length one whispered his companion, who
>   Whispered another, and thus it went round,
> And then into a *hoarser murmur* grew,
>   An ominous and wild and desperate sound;
> And when his comrade's thought each sufferer knew,
>   'Twas but his own, suppress'd till now, he found:
> And *out they spoke* of lots for flesh and blood,
> And who should die to be his fellows' food.[2]

Then, immediately following this awful passage, comes an affected delicacy at the tearing up of *Julia's* letter to *Juan* to make the lots ("materials which must shock the muse"), and a *sang froid* account of the division of the body: shortly after follow some terrific lines relating the dreadful consequences of this gorging of human flesh; and a little farther on there is a laughable description of *Juan's* dislike to feed on "poor Pedrillo," and his preference for "chewing a piece of bamboo and some lead," the stanza ending with the irresistible fact, that

> At length they caught two boobies and a noddy,
> And then they left off eating the dead body.

It is not difficult to account for this heterogeneous mixture,—for the bard has furnished us with the key to his own mind. His early hopes were blighted, and his disappointment vents itself in satirizing absurdities which rouse his indignation; and indeed a good deal of bitterness may be found at the bottom of much of this satire. But his genius is not naturally satirical; he breaks out therefore into those frequent veins of passion and true feeling of which we have just given specimens, and goes on with them till his memory is no longer able to bear the images conjured up by his fine genius; and it is to get rid of such painful and "thick-coming" recollections, that he dashes away and relieves himself by getting into another train of ideas, however incongruous or violently contrasted with the former. This solution will, we think, be borne out by the following affecting description of the poet's feelings. Observe in particular the remarkable parenthesis after the first line, whose pregnant meaning seems to have compelled him to take refuge in a lighter and more humourous idea:—

> But now at thirty years my hair is grey—
>   (I wonder what it will be like at forty?

---

[2] Canto II, lxxii–lxxiii. The next quotation is from stanza lxxxii.

I thought of a peruke the other day)—
　My heart is not much greener; and, in short, I
Have squandered my whole summer while 'twas May,
　And feel no more the spirit to retort; I
Have spent my life, both interest and principal,
And deem not, what I deem'd, my soul invincible.

No more—no more—Oh! never more on me
　The freshness of the heart can fall like dew,
Which out of all the lovely things we see
　Extracts emotions beautiful and new,
Hived in our bosoms like the bag o' the bee:
　Think'st thou the honey with those objects grew?
Alas! 'twas not in them, but in thy power
To double even the sweetness of a flower.

No more—no more—Oh! never more, my heart,
　Canst thou be my sole world—my universe!
Once all in all, but now a thing apart
　Thou canst not be my blessing or my curse.[3]

Here is some evidence that the poet is not without the milk of human kindness, and to our minds there is much more in the rest of the volume. His bent is not, as we have said, satirical, nor is he naturally disposed to be ill-natured with respect to the faults and vices of his fellow-creatures. There is an evident struggle throughout these two cantos in the feelings of the writer, and it is very fine to see him, as he gets on, growing more interested in his fiction, and pouring out at the conclusion in a much less interrupted strain of rich and deep beauty. We might fill many pages with extracts of the highest order, but we can do little more than name a few. They all relate to the exquisite description of the fostering attention of the young "island virgin" to the shipwrecked *Juan*, and of the growing love between the "wave-worn" youth and his lovely preserver. When he wakes from his first sleep after being thrown by the waves on the coast, he sees a beautiful face hanging over him:—

'Twas bending close o'er his, and the small mouth
　Seem'd almost prying into his for breath;
And chafing him, the soft warm hand of youth
　Recall'd his answering spirits back from death.
*　*　*　*　*　*　*　*　*
　　　　　　The fair arm
Raised higher the faint head o'er which it hung;
　And her transparent cheek, all pure and warm,
Pillow'd his death-like forehead.[4]

She visits him every morning, and her attendant provides his nourishment. The second morning she enters the cave where he lies with silent steps, and sees

3 Canto I, ccxiii–ccxv.
4 Canto II, cxiii–cxiv. The succeeding quotations, all refering to Juan and Haidee, are from stanzas cxliii, cxlvii, clxxxviii, cxcii, cciv.

That like an infant Juan sweetly slept;
　And then she stopp'd, and *stood as if in awe*,
(*For sleep is awful*)　*　*　*　*　*
*　*　*　*　then o'er him, still as death,
Bent with hush'd lips, that drank his scarce-drawn breath.

He had been severely handled by hunger and fatigue:—

　　　On his thin worn cheek
　A purple hectic played like dying day
On the snow-tops of distant hills; the streak
　Of sufferance yet upon his forehead lay.

Juan soon recovers, and wanders with his love along the shore one evening. They turn into a cave and rest in each others arms:—

They were alone, but not alone as they
　Who shut in chambers think it loneliness;
The silent ocean and the starlight bay,
　The twilight glow, which momently grew less,
The *voiceless sands*, and dropping caves, that lay
　Around them, made them to each other press,
As if there were no life beneath the sky
Save theirs, and that their life *could never die.*

After "deep and burning moments," *Juan* sinks to sleep in her arms. What divine *truth* is there in the following description of the pleasure of watching a beloved object:—

For there it lies so tranquil, so beloved,
　All that it hath of life with us is living;
So gentle, stirless, *helpless*, and unmoved,
　And *all unconscious of the joy 'tis giving*:
All it hath felt, inflicted, pass'd and proved,
　Hush'd into depths beyond the watcher's diving;
There lies the thing we love with all its errors
And all its charms, *like death without its terrors.*

These passages are well wound up by a stanza full of delicacy and chaste passion:—

And now 'twas done—on the lone shore were plighted
　Their hearts; the stars, their nuptial torches, *shed*
Beauty upon the beautiful they lighted:
　Ocean their witness, and the cave their bed,
By their own feelings hallowed and united,
　Their priest was Solitude, and they were wed;
And they were happy; for to their young eyes
Each was an angel, and earth paradise.

Don Juan is accused of being an "immoral" work, which we cannot at all discover. We suppose that this charge more particularly alludes to the first canto. Let us see then on what foundation it rests. The son of a Spanish patrician, educated in the most prudish manner by a licentious, yet affectedly virtuous mother, falls in love with the young wife of an old man. She returns his affection, and their passion being favoured by opportunity, she gives way to her natural feelings, and is unfaithful to her marriage vows, the example (observe) being set her by this very husband's intrigues with *Juan's* mother. Now Lord Byron speaks lightly of the effect of any scruples of conscience upon her, and of her infidelity; and this, it is said, has tendency to corrupt the minds of "us youth," and to make us *think* lightly of breaking the matrimonial contract. But if to do this be immoral, we can only say that Nature is immoral. Lord Byron does no more than relate the consequences of certain absurdities. If he speaks slightingly of the ties between a girl and a husband old enough for her father, it is because the ties themselves *are* slight. He does not ridicule the bonds of marriage generally, or where they are formed as they should be: he merely shows the folly and wickedness of setting forms and opinions against nature. If stupid and selfish parents will make up matches between persons whom difference of age or disposition disqualifies for mutual affection, they must take the consequences:—but we do not think it fair that a poet should be exclaimed against as a promoter of nuptial infidelity because he tells them what those consequences are. In this particular case, too, the author does not omit some painful consequences to those who have sinned according to "nature's law." *Julia*, the victim of selfishness and "damned custom," is shut up in a convent, where no consolation remains to her but the remembrance of her entire and hapless love; but even that was perhaps pleasanter to her than living in the constant irksomeness of feigning an affection she could not feel.

There are a set of prudish and very suspicious moralists who endeavour to make vice appear to inexperienced eyes much more hateful than it really is. They would correct Nature:—and they always overreach themselves. Nature has made vice to a certain degree pleasurable, though its painful consequences outweigh its present gratification. Now the said prudes, in their lectures and sermons and moral discourses (for they are chiefly priests) are constantly declaiming on the *deformity* of vice, and its almost total want of attraction. The consequence is, that when they are found to have deceived (as they always are) and immoral indulgence is discovered to be not without its charms,—the minds of young persons are apt to confound their true with their false maxims, and to think the threats of future pain and repentance mere fables invented to deter them from their rightful enjoyments. Which then, we would ask, are the immoral writings,—those which, by misrepresenting the laws of nature, lead to false views of morality and consequent licentiousness? —or those, which ridicule and point out the effects of absurd contradictions of human feelings and passions,

and help to bring about a reformation of such practises.

Of the story in the second canto it is unnecessary to say much, for these remarks will apply to both. We suppose there has been some sermonizing on the description of the delight arising from the "illicit intercourse" of *Juan* and *Haidee*. People who talk in this way can perceive no distinctions. It certainly is not to be inculcated, that every handsome young man and woman will find their account in giving way to all their impulses, because the very violent breaking through the habits and forms of society would create a great deal of unhappiness, both to the individuals, and to others. But what is there to blame in a beautiful and affectionate girl who gives way to a passion for a young shipwrecked human creature, bound to her by gratitude as well as love? She exacts no promises, says the bard, because she fears no inconstancy. Her father had exposed her to the first temptation that comes across her, because he had not provided against it by allowing her to know more of mankind. And does she not receive, as well as bestow, more real pleasure (for that is the question) in the enjoyment of a first and deep passion, than in becoming the wife of some brother in iniquity to whom her pirating father would have trucked her for lucre?

The fact is, at the bottom of all these questions, that many things are made vicious, which are not so by nature; and many things mad virtuous, which are only so by calling and agreement: and it is on the horns of this self-created dilemma, that society is continually writhing and getting desperate.

We must not conclude without informing our readers of the Poet's intention of continuing the story of *Don Juan* through twelve or (perhaps) twenty-four cantos, of which these two are the first. The following is the poetical table of contents:—

> My poem's epic, and is meant to be
>   Divided in twelve books; each book containing
> With love and war, a heavy gale at sea,
>   A list of ships and captains, and kings reigning;
> New characters; the episodes are three;
>   A panorama view of hell's in training,
> After the stile of Virgil and of Homer,
> So that my name of epic's no misnomer.[5]

And he adds, with a hit at the "moral" conclusion of hell-fire,—that "comfortable creed" (as he elsewhere stiles it) of some Christians—

> I've got new mythological machinery,
> And very handsome supernatural scenery.

[October 31, 1819]

5 Canto I, cc.

THE ROUND TABLE

ON WASHERWOMEN

As Hazlitt explains in the "Advertisement" to the two-volume collection of Round Table *essays, "Mr. Hunt, as the Editor [of* The Examiner], *was to take the characteristic or dramatic part of the work on himself. I undertook to furnish occasional Essays and Criticisms ... But our plan had been no sooner arranged and entered upon, than Buonaparte landed at Frejus [in March 1815, on his return from Elba], et voila la Table Ronde dissoûte. Our little congress was broken up as well as the great one; Politics called off the attention of the Editor from the Belles Lettres; and the task of continuing the work fell chiefly upon the person who was least able to give life and spirit to the original design." Twelve contributions by Hunt appear in the edition of 1817, ranging from an essay on Chaucer to a two-part essay "On the Night-Mare." The "characteristic" essay "On Washerwomen," which first appeared in* The Examiner *on September 15, 1816, has proved the most popular of Hunt's contributions.*

ON WASHERWOMEN

Writers, we think, might oftener indulge themselves in direct picture-making, that is to say, in detached sketches of men and things, which should be to *manners*, what those of Theophrastus are to *character*.

Painters do not always think it necessary to paint epics, or to fill a room with a series of pictures on one subject. They deal sometimes in single figures and groups; and often exhibit a profounder feeling in these little concentrations of their art, than in subjects of a more numerous description. Their *gusto*, perhaps, is less likely to be lost on that very account. They are no longer Sultans in a seraglio, but lovers with a favourite mistress, retired and absorbed. A Madonna of Corregio's, the Bath of Michael Angelo, the Standard of Leonardo da Vinci,[1] Titian's Mistress, and other single subjects or groups of the great masters, are acknowledged to be among their greatest performances, some of them their greatest of all.

It is the same with music. Overtures, which are supposed to make allusion to the whole progress of the story they precede, are not always the best productions of the master; still less are chorusses, and quintetts, and other pieces involving a multiplicity of actors. The

overture to Mozart's *Magic Flute* (*Zauberflutc*) is worthy of the title of the piece; it is truly enchanting; but what are so intense, in their way, as the duet of the two lovers, *Ah Perdonna*,—or the laughing trio in *Cosi Fan Tutte*,—or that passionate serenade in Don Giovanni, *Dëh vieni alla finistra*, which breathes the very soul of refined sensuality! The gallant is before you, with his mandolin and his cap and feather, taking place of the nightingale for that amorous hour; and you feel that the sounds must inevitably draw his mistress to the window. Their intenseness even renders them pathetic; and his heart seems in earnest, because his senses are.

We do not mean to say, that, in proportion as the work is large and the subject numerous, the merit may not be the greater if all is good. Raphael's Sacrament is a greater work than his Adam and Eve; but his Transfiguration would still have been the finest picture in the world, had the second group in the foreground been away; nay, the latter is supposed, and, we think, with justice, to injure its effect. We only say that there are times, when the numerousness may scatter the individual gusto;—that the greatest possible feeling may be proved without it;—and, above all, returning to our more immediate subject, that writers, like painters, may sometimes have leisure for excellent detached pieces, when they want it for larger productions. Here, then, is an opportunity for them. Let them, in their intervals of history, or, if they want time for it, give us portraits of humanity. People lament that Sappho did not write more: but, at any rate, her two odes are worth twenty epics like Tryphiodorus.[2]

But, in portraits of this kind, writing will also have a great advantage; and may avoid what seems to be an inevitable stumbling-block in paintings of a similar description. Between the matter-of-fact works of the Dutch artists, and the subtle compositions of Hogarth, there seems to be a medium reserved only for the pen. The writer only can tell you all he means,—can let you into his whole mind and intention. The moral insinuations of the painter are, on the one hand, apt to be lost for want of distinctness, or tempted, on the other, by their visible nature, to put on too gross a shape. If he leaves his meanings to be imagined, he may unfortunately speak to unimaginate spectators, and generally does; if he wishes to explain himself so as not to be mistaken, he will paint a set of comments upon his own incidents and characters, rather than let them tell for themselves. Hogarth himself, for instance, who never does anything without a sentiment or a moral, is too apt to perk them both in your face, and to be over-

---

[1] Hazlitt refers to companion paintings of incidents from the Florentine–Pisan wars, commissioned in 1504. Michelangelo's The Battle of Cascina shows Florentine soldiers surprised by the enemy while bathing; Da Vinci's The Battle of Anghiari survives in the often copied central portion representing a group of horsemen fighting for the standard. Both are examples of what Hunt calls "detached pieces" or "groups," selected portions of larger actions.

[2] A Fifth-century Egyptian poet, author of a poetic account of the Trojan War, *The Taking of Ilios*.

redundant in his combinations. His persons, in many instances, seem too much taken away from their proper indifference to effect, and to be made too much of conscious agents and joint contributors. He "o'er-informs his tenements." [3] His very goods and chattels are didactic. He makes a capital remark of a cow's horn, and brings up a piece of cannon in aid of a satire on vanity.* It is the writer only who, without hurting the most delicate propriety of the representation, can leave no doubt of all his intentions,—who can insinuate his object in two or three words, to the dullest conception, and, in conversing with the most foreign minds, take away all the awkwardness of interpretation. What painting gains in universality to the eye, it loses by an infinite proportion in power of suggestion to the understanding.

There is something of the sort of sketches we are recommending in Sterne: but Sterne had a general connected object before him, of which the parts apparently detached were still connecting links: and while he also is apt to overdo his subject like Hogarth, is infinitely less various and powerful. The greatest master of detached portrait is Steele: but his pictures too form a sort of link in a chain. Perhaps the completest specimen of what we mean in the English language is Shenstone's *School-Mistress*, by far his best production, and a most natural, quiet, and touching old dame.—But what? Are we leaving out *Chaucer?* Alas, we thought to be doing something a little original, and find it all existing already, and in unrivalled perfection, in his portraits of the Canterbury Pilgrims! We can only dilate, and vary upon his principle.

But we are making a very important preface to what may turn out a very trifling subject; and must request the reader not to be startled at the homely specimen we are about to give him, after all this gravity of recommendation. Not that we would apologise for homeliness, as homeliness. The beauty of this unlimited power of suggestion in writing is, that you may take up the driest and most common-place of all possible subjects, and strike a light out of it to warm your intellect and your heart by. The fastidious habits of polished life generally incline us to reject, as incapable of interesting us, whatever does not present itself in

a graceful shape of its own, and a ready-made suit of ornaments. But some of the plainest weeds become beautiful under the microscope. It is the benevolent provision of nature, that in proportion as you feel the necessity of extracting interest from common things, you are enabled to do so;—and the very least that this familiarity with homeliness will do for us is to render our artificial delicacy less liable to annoyance, and to teach us how to grasp the nettles till they obey us.

The reader sees that we are Wordsworthians enough not to confine our tastes to the received elegancies of society; and, in one respect, we go farther than Mr Wordsworth, for, though as fond, perhaps, of the country as he, we can manage to please ourselves in the very thick of cities, and even find there as much reason to do justice to Providence, as he does in the haunts of sportsmen, and anglers, and all-devouring insects.

To think, for instance, of that laborious and inelegant class of the community,—*Washerwomen*, and of all the hot, disagreeable, dabbing, smoking, splashing, kitcheny, cold-dining, anti-company-receiving associations, to which they give rise.—What can be more annoying to any tasteful lady or gentleman, at their first waking in the morning, than when that dreadful thump at the door comes, announcing the tub-tumbling viragoes, with their brawny arms and brawling voices? We must confess, for our own parts, that our taste, in the abstract, is not for washerwomen; we prefer Dryads and Naiads, and the figures that resemble them;—

> "Fair forms, that glance amid the green of woods,
>   Or from the waters give their sidelong shapes
>   Half swelling."

Yet, we have lain awake sometimes in a street in town, after this first confounded rap, and pleased ourselves with reflecting how equally the pains and enjoyments of this world are dealt out, and what a pleasure there is in the mere contemplation of any set of one's fellow-creatures and their humours, when our knowledge has acquired humility enough to look at them steadily.

The reader knows the knock which we mean. It comes like a lump of lead, and instantly wakes the maid, whose business it is to get up, though she pretends not to hear it. Another knock is inevitable, and it comes, and then another; but still Betty does not stir, or stirs only to put herself in a still snugger posture, knowing very well that they must knock again. "How, 'drat that Betty," says one of the washerwomen; "she hears as well as we do, but the deuce a bit will she move till we give her another;" and at the word another, down goes the knocker again. "It's very odd," says the master of the house, mumbling from under the bed-clothes,

---

* See the cannon going off in the turbulent portrait of a General-Officer: and the cow's head coming just over that of a citizen who is walking with his wife.[4]

3 See Dryden's *Absalom and Achitophel*, l. 158.
4 For the second of the works referred to in the footnote, see Hogarth's print of "Evening," 1738. The cow's horns appearing over the citizen's head make the obvious point that he is a cuckold.

"that Betty does not get up to let the people in; I've heard that knocker three times."—"Oh," returns the mistress, "she's as lazy as she's high,"—and off goes the chamber-bell;—by which time Molly, who begins to lose her sympathy with her fellow-servant in impatience of what is going on, gives her one or two conclusive digs in the side; when the other gets up, and rubbing her eyes and mumbling, and hastening and shrugging herself down stairs, opens the door with—"Lard, Mrs Watson, I hope you haven't been standing here long?"—"Standing here long! Mrs Betty! Oh don't tell me; people might stand starving their legs off, before you'd put a finger out of bed."— "Oh don't say so, Mrs Watson; I'm sure I always rises at the first knock; and there—you'll find every thing comfortable below, with a nice hock of ham, which I made John leave for you." At this the washerwomen leave their mumbling, and shuffle down stairs, hoping to see Mrs Betty early at breakfast. Here, after warming themselves at the copper, taking a mutual pinch of snuff, and getting things ready for the wash, they take a snack at the promised hock; for people of this profession have always their appetite at hand, and every interval of labour is invariably cheered by the prospect of *having something* at the end of it. "Well," says Mrs Watson, finishing the last cut, "some people thinks themselves mighty generous for leaving one what little they can't eat; but, howsomever, it's better than nothing."—"Ah," says Mrs Jones, who is a minor genius, "one must take what one can get now-a-days; but Squire Hervey's for my money."—"Squire Hervey!" rejoins Mrs Watson, "what's that the great what's-his-name as lives yonder?"—"Aye," returns Mrs Jones, "him as has a niece and nevvy, as they say eats him out of house and land;"—and here commences the history of all the last week of the whole neighbourhood round, which continues amidst the dipping of splashing fists, the rumbling of suds, and the creaking of wringings out, till an hour or two are elapsed; and then for another snack and a pinch of snuff, till the resumption of another hour's labour or so brings round the time for first breakfast. Then, having had nothing to signify since five, they sit down at half-past six in the wash-house, to take their own meal before the servants meet at the general one. This is the chief moment of enjoyment. They have just laboured enough to make the tea and bread and butter welcome, are at an interesting point of the conversation, (for there they contrive to leave off on purpose,) and so down they sit, fatigued and happy, with their red elbows and white corrugated fingers, to a tub turned upside down, and a dish of good christian souchong, fit for a body to drink.

We could dwell a good deal upon this point of time, but we have already, we fear, ran out our limits; and shall only admonish the fastidious reader, who thinks he has all the taste and means of enjoyment to himself, how he looks with scorn upon two persons, who are perhaps at this moment the happiest couple of human beings in the street,—who have discharged their duty, have earned their enjoyment, and have health and spirits to relish it to the full. A washerwoman's cup of tea may vie with the first drawn cork at a bon-vivant's table, and the complacent opening of her snuff-box with that of the most triumphant politician over a scheme of partition. We say nothing of the continuation of their labours, of the scandal they resume, or the complaints they pour forth, when they first set off again in the indolence of a satisfied appetite, at the quantity of work which the mistress of the house, above all other mistresses, is sure to heap upon them. Scandal and complaint, in these instances, do not hurt the complacency of our reflections; they are in their proper sphere; and are nothing but a part, as it were, of the day's work, and are so much vent to the animal spirits. Even the unpleasant day which the work causes up stairs in some houses,—the visitors which it excludes, and the leg of mutton which it hinders from roasting, are only so much enjoyment kept back and contracted, in order to be made keener the rest of the week. Beauty itself is indebted to it, and draws from that steaming out-house and splashing tub the well-fitting robe that gives out its figure, and the snowy cap that contrasts its curls and its complexion. In short, whenever we hear a washerwoman at her foaming work, or see her plodding towards us with her jolly warm face, her mob cap, her black stockings, clattering pattens, and tub at arm's length resting on her hip-joint, we look upon her as a living lesson to us to make the most both of time and comfort, and as a sort of allegorical union of pain and pleasure, a little too much, perhaps, in the style of Rubens.

[September 15, 1816]   [1817]

F R O M

FOLIAGE[1]

F R O M

PREFACE
INCLUDING
CURSORY OBSERVATIONS ON POETRY AND CHEERFULNESS

THE downfall of the French school of poetry has of late been increasing in rapidity; its cold and artificial compositions have given way, like so many fantastic figures of snow; and imagination breathes again in a more green and genial time. An attachment to the school undoubtedly survives in some quarters; but those who defend it as a superior one of *poetry*, merely shew that they have no real perception of that art; and the other critics, who are either loth to give it up from a natural self-love, or not magnanimous enough to own the conviction they feel, are in danger of being left behind by the public whom they would lead.

This has undoubtedly been owing, in the first instance, to the political convulsions of the world, which shook up the minds of men, and rendered them too active and speculative to be satisfied with their common-places. A second cause was the revived inclination for our older and great school of poetry, chiefly produced, I have no doubt, by the commentators on Shakspeare, though they were certainly not aware what fine countries they were laying open. The third, and not the least, was the accession of a new school of poetry itself, of which Wordsworth has justly the reputation of being the most prominent ornament, but whose inner priest of the temple perhaps was Coleridge,—a man who has been the real oracle of the time in more than one respect, and who ought to have been the greatest visible person in it, instead of a hopeless and dreary sophist. Between these two for natural powers, and superior to both in what renders wisdom amiable and useful, which is social sentiment, I should place Charles Lamb, a single one of whose speculations upon humanity, unostentatiously scattered about in comments and magazines, is worth all the half-way-house gabbling of critics on the establishment.

The consequence of this re-awakening of the poetical faculty is not, as some imagine, a *contempt* for Pope and the other chief writers of the French school. It justly appreciates their wit, terseness, and acuteness; but it can neither confound their monotony with a fine music, nor recognize the real spirit of poetry in their town habits, their narrow sphere of imagination, their knowledge of manners rather than natures, and their gross mistake about what they called classical, which was Horace and the Latin breeding, instead of the elementary inspiration of Greece.* The notions about poetry can no longer be controuled, like the fashions, by a coterie of town gentlemen. People have ceased to believe that wit and verse are the great essentials of the art; much less cant phrases, and lines cut in two; or that any given John Tomkins, Esq. upon the strength of his stock of Johnson's Poets, can sit down, and draw upon our admiration in the usual formulas, as he would upon his banker for money.

A sensativeness to the beauty of the external world, to the unsophisticated impulses of our nature, and above all, imagination, or the power to see, with verisimilitude, what others do not,—these are the properties of poetry; and in proportion as the enjoyer applies them according to his experience, to his sense of good, and especially his natural disposition, he turns what he possesses of them to account. This is a secret which I saw very early; and I attribute to the knowledge of it whatever popularity I may have obtained, whether in verse or prose. The three living poets, who may chiefly be said to have characters of their own, have found their advantage in it, especially Byron and Moore, experience being the principal ground on which the former goes, and natural disposition the latter. The remaining one, Wordsworth, whose ground is morals,

* It is curious to see how circumstances influence every thing. It may appear a joke if not a paradox. to say that Pope would have been a better poet, had he had a stouter pair of legs; yet this nevertheless I believe to be very true. Not that delicacy of organization is incompatible with the poetical temperament; perhaps it is necessary to its reception of vivid impressions; but health and a proper strength are other matters; and Pope, whom I consider a much greater poet by nature than he became from circumstances, was shut up by his bodily infirmities within a small and artificial sphere of life. He saw little or nothing of nature and natural manners. When he went out, he rode, and he was even carried into his boat in a sedan-chair. Thus he is always commonplace in passion and description, *except* where he was personally touched by the living, or drew from his own grotto by the Thames or his youthful recollections of Windsor Park. One of the most pathetic passages he ever wrote, as well as best pieces of description, (for most of the beauties of Abelard and Eloisa are in the original Latin letters), is a few lines which he enclosed in a letter to Lady Mary Montague, comparing a *lover* in a *grotto* to a *bleeding stag.*[2]

---

[1] A collection of verses by Hunt, divided into: "Greenwoods" (original poems) and "Evergreens" (translations from Greek and Latin poets); published 1818.

[2] Referring to Pope's verses "To Mr. Gay, who wrote him a congratulatory Letter on his finishing his house" ["Ah friend, tis true—this truth you lovers know—"], dating from around 1720.

has not succeeded so well as either in one sense of the word; but taking every thing into consideration, the novelty of his poetical system, and the very unattractive and in my opinion mistaken nature of his moral one, he has succeeded still more; and is generally felt among his own profession to be at the head of it. Among the poets who were bred up in the French school, Moore, who is a real musician also, has lately given a valuable proof of his approbation of a different system of verse in the new-modelled heroic numbers of his Lalla Rookh;[3] and my noble friend, Lord Byron, who waits as little for his own genius to be admired, before he admires that of others, does justice, I know, to the new school, though his charity inclines him to say what he can for a falling one.[4]

An unattractive creed, however the hypocritical or envious may affect to confound the chearful tendencies of our nature with vicious ones, or the melancholy may be led really to do so, is an argument against itself. Shall we never have done with begging the question against enjoyment, and denying or doubting the earthly possibility of the only end of virtue itself, with a dreary wilfulness that prevents our obtaining it? The fatality goes even farther; for let them say what they please to the contrary, they who are most doubtful of earth, are far from being the most satisfied with regard to heaven. Even when they think they have got at their security in the latter respect, it is through the medium of opinions which make humanity shudder; and this, except with the most brutal selfishness, comes round to the same thing. The depreciators of this world,— the involuntary blasphemers of Nature's goodness,— have tried melancholy and partial systems enough, and talked enough of their own humility. It is high time for them, and for all of us, to look after health and sociality; and to believe, that although we cannot alter the world with an ipse dixit, we need not become desponding, or mistake a disappointed egotism for humility. We should consider ourselves as what we really are,— creatures made to enjoy more than we know, to know infinitely nevertheless in proportion as we enjoy kindly, and finally, to put our own shoulders to the wheel and get out of the mud upon the green sward again, like the waggoner whom Jupiter admonishes in the fable. But we persist in being unhealthy, body and mind, and taking our jaundice for wisdom; and then because we persist, we say we must persist on. We admire the happiness, and sometimes the better wisdom of children; and yet we imitate the worst of their nonsense—"I can't—because I can't."

For my part, though the world as I found it, and the circumstances that connected me with its habits, have formerly given me my portion of sorrow, some of it of no ordinary kind, my creed, I confess, is not only hopeful, but cheerful; and I would pick the best parts out of other creeds too, sure that I was right in what I believed or chose to fancy, in proportion as I did honour to the beauty of nature, and spread cheerfulness and a sense of justice among my fellow-creatures. It was in this spirit, though with a more serious aspect, that I wrote the Story of Rimini,[5] the moral of which is not as some would wish it to be,—unjust, and bigoted, and unhappy, sacrificing virtue under pretence of supporting it;—but tolerant and reconciling, recommending men's minds to the consideration of *first* causes in misfortune, and to see the danger of confounding forms with justice, of setting authorized selfishness above the most natural impulses, and making guilt by mistaking innocence.

It is in the same spirit, though more obviously, that I put forth the present work. I do not write, I confess, for the sake of a moral only, nor even for that purpose principally:—I write to enjoy myself; but I have learnt in the course of it to write for others also; and my poetical tendencies luckily fall in with my moral theories. The main features of the book are a love of sociality, of the country, and of the fine imagination of the Greeks. I need not inform any reader acquainted with real poetry, that a delight in rural luxury has ever been a constituent part of the very business of poets as well as one of the very best things which they have recommended, as counteractions to the more sordid tendencies of cities. But I may as well insinuate, that the luxuries which poets recommend, and which are thought so beautiful on paper, are much more within the reach of every one, and much more beautiful in reality, than people's fondness for considering all poetry as fiction would imply. The poets only do with their imaginations what all might do with their practice,—live at as cheap, natural, easy, and truly pleasurable a rate as possible; for it is not industry, but a defeat of the ends of it, and a mere want of ideas, to work and trouble themselves so much as most of our countrymen do; neither is it taste, but an ostentatious want of it, that is expensive; and the French in some of these matters are better practical poets than we are; for they refuse to get more than is reasonable, or than leaves fair play for enjoyment; and they spend their afternoons in dancing under the trees or in-doors, or attending the theatres, where they see imitations of the

---

3 *Lalla Rookh, an Oriental Romance*, published 1817.
4 Referring to Byron's life-long admiration for, and defense of, Pope's genius.

5 Hunt's most famous poem, published 1816, a sentimentalized version of the story of Paolo and Francesca found in Dante's *Inferno*, Canto V.

Golden Age in dances more poetical. The fashionable world among us see a great deal farther into these things, from the mere absence of this yellow atmosphere of money-getting; and it is curious to observe, how they come round, through all their refinements, to place their best entertainment in music and dancing, which are two of the most natural and pastoral of pleasures.

As little need be said in order to deprecate the notion of effeminacy in pleasures of this kind. The French, whatever may be their defects in some matters, are at any rate not deficient in courage; and the age of Shakspeare was at once the most wise and lively, the most dancing, rural, and manly period of our English history. It is a confusion of ideas to think that these are the luxuries which announce the downfall of nations. It is bad taste of all sorts, and not good, which belongs to such a period of disease and imbecility;—gaudiness, gross intemperance, submission to ignorant tyranny, frivolous disputation,—a forsaking of real art and nature, not a love of them. The swords, with which Harmodius and Aristogeiton slew the Grecian tyrant,[6] were braided with myrtle.

The principal original poem in this collection[7] is founded on that beautiful mythology, which it is not one of the least merits of the new school to be restoring to its proper estimation. It was one of the frigid mistakes of the French school of wit and satire, who pretended nevertheless to a great taste in ancient poetry, to see nothing but school-boy inexperience in making use of the gods and goddesses; or what is worse, to use them themselves, with the customary bad compliment at the bottom of their gallantry, as a set of toys for the ladies. The goddesses in their hands, compared with the Grecian ones, cut much about the same figure, as the perking shepherds and shepherdesses did on their mantle-pieces, compared with Theocritus. It was the mistake of men deficient in sentiment, and in a feeling for natural beauty. Yet Quinault, whom Boileau so much ridiculed,[8] might have taught him better; and so might a common French ballet; though it appears to be the highest pitch of mythological taste to which his lively countrymen have arrived. They are a nation quick to see the superficial part of grace, but too easily satisfied perhaps to go deeper, unless the late revolution and their encreased intimacy with other countries have begun, as is probable, to render their

sprightly egotism a little more thoughtful. Boileau ridiculed Quinault, and was insensible to his merits; but our English wits, which was worse, ridiculed Boileau and fell into his faults; and to complete this chaos of mythological mistake, Johnson could justly ridicule Prior[9] for his comparisons of Chloe to Venus and *all that*, and yet take pains, in his criticisms on Milton, to shew that he had no taste for Venus in all her beauty. Certainly, with every due sense of its merit in other respect, it was a very "periwig-pated" age in all that regarded poetry, from Waller down to the Doctor inclusive; and their heads were not the better even for the periwigs themselves. A bad and shapeless costume is one of the instinctive artifices, by which dullness can authorize or suppress what associations it pleases.

Shakspeare, and the rest of our great school of poetry, saw farther into the beauty of the Greek mythology. Spenser, Ben Jonson, Beaumont and Fletcher, evidently sparkled up, and had their most graceful perceptions upon them, whenever they turned to the fair forms and leafy luxuries of ancient imagination. Shakspeare, in particular, though he did not write so much about them as Spenser and Fletcher, was in this as in every thing else, a remarkable specimen of the very finest poetical instinct; for though not a scholar, he needed nothing more than the description given by scholars, good or indifferent, in order to pierce back at once into all the recesses of the original country. They told him where they had been, and he was there in an instant, though not in the track of their footing;—

> Battendo l'ali verso l'aurea fronde—PETR.[10]
> Beating his wings towards the golden bough.

The truth is, he felt the Grecian mythology not as a set of school-boy common-places which it was thought manly to give up, but as something which it requires more than mere scholarship to understand,—as the elevation of the external world and of accomplished humanity to the highest pitch of the graceful, and as embodied essences of all the grand and lovely qualities of nature. His description of Proserpine and her flowers in the Winter's Tale,[11] of the characteristic beauties of some of the gods in Hamlet, and that single couplet in the Tempest,

> You Nymphs called Naiads, of the wandering brooks,
> With your sedged crowns and *ever harmless looks*,

---

[6] The Athenian youths Harmodius and Aristogeiton slew Hipparchus at the Panathenaic festival in 514 B.C.

[7] "The Nymphs."

[8] Philippe Quinault (1635–1688), French dramatist and librettist, who was "ridiculed" in the third of the *Satires* (1666) by Nicolas Boileau-Despréaux (1636–1711), a French poet and influential neoclassical critic.

[9] See Johnson's life of Prior in *Lives of the Poets*.

[10] Petrarch's sonnet, "Po, ben puo' tu portartene la scorza," l. 7.

[11] IV, iv, 116–27. The next references are to *Hamlet*, III, iv, 55–59; and *Tempest*, IV, i, 128–29.

are in the deepest taste of antiquity, and shew that all great poets look at themselves and the fine world about them in the same clear and ever-living fountains.

The taste lingered a little, though become too Ovidian, with Cowley, who with all the conceits of the inferior Italian school then succeeding to that of Petrarch and Tasso, had nevertheless quite poetry enough as well as amiableness to relish

> The golden fruit that worthy is
> Of Galatea's purple kiss:—[12]

but Milton, the last of our greater poets, was the last to maintain the dignity and beauty of natural and ancient taste;—the Hesperian gardens were shut;—and in strange company with "the mountain-nymph sweet Liberty," [13] in came the Dragon Phantom Calvinism, whose breath even affected him for a while;—

> And in he came, with his eyes of flame,
> The fiend to fetch the dead;
> And all the place with his presence glowed,
> Like a fiery furnace red.
> *Southey's Witch of Berkeley.*[14]

Milton, when he was young and happy, wrote Grecian mythology in his Lycidas and Comus; and hung, as it were, in the ears of antiquity those two exquisite jewels, the Pensieroso and L'Allegro. In his old age, there is good reason to suspect that he was, at any rate, not bigoted; and in the meantime, allusions to romance and to Greek mythology, which he never could prevail on himself to give up, are the most refreshing things in his Paradise Lost and Regained, next to the bridal happiness of poor Adam and Eve. They are not merely drops in the desert;—they are escapes from every heart-withering horror, which Eastern storms and tyranny could generate together. The light shed by Apollo's bow to the Argonauts, when they were benighted, is trivial refreshment to them.*

*　　　*　　　*　　　*　　　*

* See this and other beautiful imaginations, particularly the passage of the same God by the sea-shore, and the apparition of Sthenelus, in the Argonautics of Apollonius Rhodius, whom Virgil thought better of than the critics,—which is just as it should be.[15]

12 Cowley's poem "The Garden," stanza x.
13 *l'Allegro*, l. 36.
14 "The Old Woman of Berkeley, a ballad" (1799), ll. 163–66.
15 Hunt refers to *Argonautica*, an Homeric-style epic on the expedition of the Argonauts by Apollonius of Rhodes, poet of the late third and early second centuries B.C. The "passage of the same God by the sea-shore, and the apparition of Sthenelus" occur in Book II, 669–85, 911–30. A number of passages in Book IV of Virgil's *Aeneid* were based on the *Argonautica*.

It has been well said by a German critic,[16] that "the Greeks invented the poetry of gladness." But it is very ill advised by the same German, that we should imitate their poetry of a different complexion;—I mean the spirit of their tragic drama, in which they have contrived to concentrate all that was fiery and unjust in their mythology. It is Ætna among the fields of Sicily. M. Schlegel, with a great deal of talent, not uninstructed perhaps by an eminent German scholar of our own, has also, like the Knight of the Rueful Countenance before mentioned, a sickly imagination. He loves to get into the void atmosphere out of the pale of sunlight, and to sit staring through the darkness, upon fancied "Gorgons, Hydras, and Chimeras dire." [17] M. Schlegel, I am afraid, owes a sort of grudge to cheerfulness, because he thinks it possessed by the French; yet he can enjoy Aristophanes, especially where the sceptic Euripides is cut up; and the glad poetry he speaks of, as well as Shakspeare whom he so well appreciates, might have relieved his philosophy from any responsibility on that score. The best excuse for his melancholy vagaries is his fondness for whatever he writes upon, always excepting, however, the French and Euripides, with whom he seems to agree in nothing but sneering at women. But be this as it may, he fairly doats upon the shocking plots and catastrophes of the Greek tragedy, and wishes to make out that the tragic spirit of Shakspeare owes its grandeur to the same use of the idea of destiny,—a position certainly not made out by facts, and wholly incompatible with the universality as well as cheerfulness of the poet's philosophy.† Shakspeare may or may not have believed in

† It is a striking instance of the exquisite good sense of Butler, which shared the palm with his wit, that notwithstanding his great book-learning and the unpoetical nature of his class of poetry, both of which might be supposed to give him a leaning to the prejudices of the French school, he would not hear of servile adherence to rules, much less of imitating the gratuitous horrors of Greek tragedy. Among his Posthumous Works, which ought to be more known (they are luckily in Chalmers's Poets) is a set of verses upon "Critics who judge of modern plays precisely by the rules of the ancients." There is as warm a feeling of Shakspeare and Fletcher in them, as if he had written imagination all his life instead of satire; and as to M. Schlegel's pet sphinx Destiny, he cuts a series of exquisite jokes against the system, by which some god or daemon

> Chances to have piques
> Against an ancient family of Greeks,
> That other men may tremble and take warning
> How such a fatal progeny they're born in.[18]

16 August Wilhelm Schlegel. The remark cited occurs in the first of his *Lectures on Dramatic Art and Literature* (1809–1811). See Ninth Lecture, footnote 9, p. 137, of Coleridge's *A Course of Lectures on Shakespear and Milton.*
17 *Paradise Lost*, II, 628.
18 Hunt quotes ll. 31–34 of Samuel Butler's poem. *The Works of the English Poets from Chaucer to Cowper* (1810) in 21 volumes

destiny; I believe he did, just about as much as he believed in the contrary. But whatever he might have thought of its use in a play or so, as connected with popular superstition, he knew well, that utility of some sort or other, though not the mere mechanical idea of it, was the only test of truth within the limits of the human understanding; and therefore he would extract from the idea of destiny all that was necessary for human charity or kindness, being certain that so far he was realizing something with it: but beyond that, he would anticipate the inevitable ignorance to which the rest of the question would lead him; and much more would he refuse to look at the question diseasedly; and because there is evil mixed with good, blaspheme the obvious beauty of nature, and have chimney-corner fears about "a great Sphinx who will eat you up, if you do not discover her secret." The body of the German people, though it had a good shake given it by the French revolution, and produced some sprightly children in Wieland [19] and others, does not seem to have recovered yet from the nightmares of its old eating and drinking habits, and its sedentary school-divinity. But I am forgetting the object of this part of my conclusion.—All I meant to say was, that one melancholy vein in their poetry was necessary perhaps for the lively Greeks in order to keep sentiment alive among them, and prevent their happiness from running into mere levity; but with us of the north, the vicissitudes of climate supply this wholesome counteraction quite enough; we should be sufficiently admonished by "the skyey influences," [20] even if we made the most (which we certainly do not) of our green fields and our firesides; and he, in my opinion, wishes his countrymen most good, who would see fair play between their real wants and a cheerful leisure.

[1818]

FROM

A "NOW."

DESCRIPTIVE OF A HOT DAY.[1]

Now the rosy- (and lazy-) fingered Aurora, issuing from her saffron house, calls up the moist vapours to

surround her, and goes veiled with them as long as she can; till Phœbus, coming forth in his power, looks every thing out of the sky, and holds sharp uninterrupted empire from his throne of beams. Now the mower begins to make his sweeping cuts more slowly, and resorts oftener to the beer. Now the carter sleeps a-top of his load of hay, or plods with double slouch of shoulder, looking out with eyes winking under his shading hat, and with a hitch upward of one side of his mouth. Now the little girl at her grandmother's cottage-door watches the coaches that go by, with her hand held up over her sunny forehead. Now labourers look well resting in their white shirts at the doors of rural alehouses. Now an elm is fine there, with a seat under it; and horses drink out of the trough, stretching their yearning necks with loosened collars; and the traveller calls for his glass of ale, having been without one for more than ten minutes; and his horse stands wincing at the flies, giving sharp shivers of his skin, and moving to and fro his ineffectual docked tail; and now Miss Betty Wilson, the host's daughter, comes streaming forth in a flowered gown and ear-rings, carrying with four of her beautiful fingers the foaming glass, for which, after the traveller has drank it, she receives with an indifferent eye, looking another way, the lawful twopence. Now grasshoppers "fry," as Dryden says.[2] Now cattle stand in water, and ducks are envied. Now boots and shoes, and trees by the road side, are thick with dust; and dogs, rolling in it, after issuing out of the water, into which they have been thrown to fetch sticks, come scattering horror among the legs of the spectators. Now a fellow who finds he has three miles further to go in a pair of tight shoes, is in a pretty situation. Now rooms with the sun upon them become intolerable; and the apothecary's apprentice, with a bitterness beyond aloes,[3] thinks of the pond he used to bathe in at school. Now men with powdered heads (especially if thick) envy those that are unpowdered, and stop to wipe them up hill, with countenances that seem to expostulate with destiny. Now boys assemble round the village pump with a ladle to it, and delight to make a forbidden splash and get wet through the shoes. Now also they make suckers of leather, and bathe all day long in rivers and ponds, and make mighty fishings for "tittle-bats."[4] Now the bee, as he hums along, seems to be talking heavily of the heat. Now doors and brick-walls are burning to the hand; and a

---

was prepared by Alexander Chalmers (1759–1835), voluminous writer and editor.

[19] Christoph Martin Wieland (1733–1813), German poet and romance writer.

[20] *Measure for Measure*, III, i, 9.

[1] First published in the *Indicator*, June 28, 1820; subsequently collected and revised in *The Indicator and The Companion: A Miscellany for the Fields and the Fireside*, 1834. The latter text is here reproduced.

---

[2] See Dryden's translation of Virgil's second Pastoral, ll. 13–14.

[3] A bitter purgative from the juice of the aloe plant.

[4] The childish name for sticklebacks, small, spiny-finned fishes.

walled lane, with dust and broken bottles in it, near a brick-field, is a thing not to be thought of. Now a green lane, on the contrary, thickset with hedge-row elms, and having the noise of a brook "rumbling in pebble-stone,"[5] is one of the pleasantest things in the world.

Now, in town, gossips talk more than ever to one another, in rooms, in door-ways, and out of window, always beginning the conversation with saying that the heat is overpowering. Now blinds are let down, and doors thrown open, and flannel waistcoats left off, and cold meat preferred to hot, and wonder expressed why tea continues so refreshing, and people delight to sliver lettuces into bowls, and apprentices water door-ways with tin-canisters that lay several atoms of dust. Now the water-cart, jumbling along the middle of the street, and jolting the showers out of its box of water, really does something. Now fruiterers' shops and dairies look pleasant, and ices are the only things to those who can get them. Now ladies loiter in baths; and people make presents of flowers; and wine is put into ice; and the after-dinner lounger recreates his head with applications of perfumed water out of long-necked bottles. Now the lounger, who cannot resist riding his new horse, feels his boots burn him. Now buck-skins are not the lawn of Cos.[6] Now jockies, walking in great coats to lose flesh, curse inwardly. Now five fat people in a stage-coach, hate the sixth fat one who is coming in, and think he has no right to be so large. Now clerks in offices do nothing but drink soda-water and spruce-beer, and read the newspaper. Now the old clothesman drops his solitary cry more deeply into the areas on the hot and forsaken side of the street; and bakers look vicious; and cooks are aggravated: and the steam of a tavern-kitchen catches hold of us like the breath of Tartarus. Now delicate skins are beset with gnats: and boys make their sleeping companion start up, with playing a burning-glass on his hand; and blacksmiths are super-carbonated; and cobblers in their stalls almost feel a wish to be transplanted; and butter is too easy to spread; and the dragoons wonder whether the Romans liked their helmets; and old ladies, with their lappets unpinned, walk along in a state of dilapidation; and the servant-maids are afraid they look vulgarly hot; and the author, who has a plate of strawberries brought him, finds that he has come to the end of his writing. . . .

[June 28, 1820]   [1834]

◇◇◇◇◇◇◇◇◇◇◇◇◇◇◇◇◇◇◇◇◇◇◇◇◇◇◇◇◇◇

5 Spenser's "Virgil's Gnat," l. 163.
6 The fine cloth of Cos, a Greek island famous from early times for its cotton and silk manufacture.

FROM

IMAGINATION AND FANCY

AN ANSWER TO THE QUESTION
WHAT IS POETRY?

The essay appeared as the introduction to Imagination and Fancy (1844), *a volume of selections from the works of English poets from Spenser to Keats. The "educational" purpose of the entire volume is indicated in Hunt's prefatory remark: " The object of the book is threefold;—to present the public with some of the finest passages in English poetry, so marked and commented;—to furnish such an account, in an Essay, of the nature and requirements of poetry, as may enable readers in general to give an answer on these points to themselves and others; —and to show, throughout the greater part of the volume, what sort of poetry is to be considered as poetry of the most poetical kind, or such as exhibits the imagination and fancy in a state of predominance, undisputed by interests of another sort." For detailed analysis of the essay, see Alba H. Warren, Jr.,* English Poetic Theory, 1825–1865 *(New York: Octagon Books, 1966) [first published 1950], Chapter VI; and Clarence Dewitt Thorpe, "Leigh Hunt as Man of Letters," which appeared as the introduction to the Houtchens' edition of* Leigh Hunt's Literary Criticism *(1956).*

Hunt's definitions and discussion of imagination and fancy and of poetry in general are a composite of the familiar tenets of Romantic literary criticism; they will be found, often expressed with greater theoretical sophistication, in the critical writing of Wordsworth, Coleridge, and Hazlitt. However, as Thorpe points out, it was the geniality and enthusiasm of Hunt's writing both in the essay of 1844 and throughout his lifetime, which helped to popularize these tenets and make them familiar. Amy Lowell's tribute to Hunt, which Thorpe recalls in his essay, is a just statement of Hunt's important contribution to the literary life of the nineteenth century: " Hunt was not a great creator certainly, but he was a great introducer . . . I can never forget that it was his Imagination and Fancy *which first taught me what poetry was. There is no better text-book for the appreciation of poetry than that volume. He had what I may call a touch-stone mind; he knew instinctively what was good and never feared to proclaim it."*

FROM

AN ANSWER TO THE QUESTION
WHAT IS POETRY?

INCLUDING
REMARKS ON VERSIFICATION

POETRY, strictly and artistically so called, that is to say, considered not merely as poetic feeling, which is more or less shared by all the world, but as the operation of that feeling, such as we see it in the poet's book, is the utterance of a passion for truth, beauty, and power, embodying and illustrating its conceptions by imagination and fancy, and modulating its language on the principle of variety in uniformity. Its means are whatever the universe contains; and its ends, pleasure and exaltation. Poetry stands between nature and convention, keeping alive among us the enjoyment of the external and the spiritual world: it has constituted the most enduring fame of nations; and, next to Love and Beauty, which are its parents, is the greatest proof to man of the pleasure to be found in all things, and of the probable riches of infinitude.

Poetry is a passion,* because it seeks the deepest impressions; and because it must undergo, in order to convey, them.

It is a passion for truth, because without truth the impression would be false or defective.

It is a passion for beauty, because its office is to exalt and refine by means of pleasure, and because beauty is nothing but the loveliest form of pleasure.

It is a passion for power, because power is impression triumphant, whether over the poet, as desired by himself, or over the reader, as affected by the poet.

It embodies and illustrates its impressions by imagination, or images of the objects of which it treats, and other images brought in to throw light on those objects, in order that it may enjoy and impart the feeling of their truth in its utmost conviction and affluence.

It illustrates them by fancy, which is a lighter play of imagination, or the feeling of analogy coming short of seriousness, in order that it may laugh with what it loves, and show how it can decorate it with fairy ornament.

It modulates what it utters, because in running the whole round of beauty it must needs include beauty of sound; and because, in the height of its enjoyment, it must show the perfection of its triumph, and make difficulty itself become part of its facility and joy.

And lastly, Poetry shapes this modulation into uniformity for its outline, and variety for its parts, because it thus realizes the last idea of beauty itself, which includes the charm of diversity within the flowing round of habit and ease.

Poetry is imaginative passion. The quickest and subtlest test of the possession of its essence is in expression; the variety of things to be expressed shows the amount of its resources; and the continuity of the song completes the evidence of its strength and greatness. He who has thought, feeling, expression, imagination, action, character, and continuity, all in the largest amount and highest degree, is the greatest poet.

Poetry includes whatsoever of painting can be made visible to the mind's eye, and whatsoever of music can be conveyed by sound and proportion without singing or instrumentation. But it far surpasses those divine arts in suggestiveness, range, and intellectual wealth;—the first, in expression of thought, combination of images, and the triumph over space and time; the second, in all that can be done by speech, apart from the tones and modulations of pure sound. Painting and music, however, include all those portions of the gift of poetry that can be expressed and heightened by the visible and melodious. Painting, in a certain apparent manner, is things themselves; music, in a certain audible manner, is their very emotion and grace. Music and painting are proud to be related to poetry, and poetry loves and is proud of them.

Poetry begins where matter of fact or of science ceases to be merely such, and to exhibit a further truth; that is to say, the connexion it has with the world of emotion, and its power to produce imaginative pleasure. Inquiring of a gardener, for instance, what flower it is we see yonder, he answers, "a lily." This is matter of fact. The botanist pronounces it to be of the order of "Hexandria Monogynia." This is matter of science. It is the "lady" of the garden, says Spenser;[1] and here we begin to have a poetical sense of its fairness and grace. It is

> The plant and flower of *light*,

says Ben Jonson; and poetry then shows us the beauty of the flower in all its mystery and splendour.

If it be asked, how we know perceptions like these to be true, the answer is, by the fact of their existence,—by the consent and delight of poetic readers. And as feeling is the earliest teacher, and perception the only final proof, of things the most demonstrable by science, so the remotest imaginations of the poets may often be found to have the closest connexion with matter of fact; perhaps might always be so, if the subtlety of our perceptions were a match for the causes of them. Consider this image of Ben Jonson's—of a lily being the flower of light. Light, undecomposed, is white; and as the lily is white, and light is white, and whiteness itself is nothing *but* light, the two things, so far, are not merely similar, but identical. A poet might add, by an analogy drawn from the connexion of light and colour, that there is a "golden dawn" issuing out of the white lily, in the rich yellow of the stamens. I have no desire to push this similarity farther than it may be worth. Enough has been stated to show that, in poetical as in other analogies, "the same feet of Nature," as Bacon says, may be seen "treading in different paths;"[2] and

---

* *Passio*, suffering in a good sense,—ardent subjection of one's-self to emotion.

[1] *Faerie Queene*, II, vi, 16. The next quotation is from Jonson's "To the immortal memory and friendship of that noble pair Sir Lucius Cary and Sir H. Morison," l. 72.
[2] Bacon's *Advancement of Learning*, Book II.

that the most scornful, that is to say, dullest disciple of fact, should be cautious how he betrays the shallowness of his philosophy by discerning no poetry in its depths.

But the poet is far from dealing only with these subtle and analogical truths. Truth of every kind belongs to him, provided it can bud into any kind of beauty, or is capable of being illustrated and impressed by the poetic faculty. Nay, the simplest truth is often so beautiful and impressive of itself, that one of the greatest proofs of his genius consists in his leaving it to stand alone, illustrated by nothing but the light of its own tears or smiles, its own wonder, might, or playfulness. Hence the complete effect of many a simple passage in our old English ballads and romances, and of the passionate sincerity in general of the greatest early poets, such as Homer and Chaucer, who flourished before the existence of a "literary world," and were not perplexed by a heap of notions and opinions, or by doubts how emotions ought to be expressed. The greatest of their successors never write equally to the purpose, except when they can dismiss every thing from their minds but the like simple truth. In the beautiful poem of "Sir Eger, Sir Graham, and Sir Gray-Steel" (see it in Ellis's Specimens, or Laing's Early Metrical Tales),[3] a knight thinks himself disgraced in the eyes of his mistress:—

> Sir Eger said, "If it be so,
> Then wot I well I must forego
> Love-liking, and manhood, all clean!"
> *The water rush'd out of his een!*

Sir Gray-Steel is killed:—

Gray-Steel into his death thus thraws (throes?)
He *walters* (welters,—throws himself about) *and the grass up draws;*

> *   *   *   *   *

> *A little while then lay he still*
> *(Friends that him saw, liked full ill)*
> *And bled into his armour bright.*

The abode of Chaucer's *Reve*, or Steward, in the Canterbury Tales, is painted in two lines, which nobody ever wished longer:—

> His wonning (dwelling) was full fair upon an heath,
> With greeny trees yshadowed was his place.[4]

Every one knows the words of Lear, "most *matter-of-fact*, most melancholy."[5]

> Pray do not mock me;
> I am a very foolish fond old man
> Fourscore and upwards:
> Not an hour more, nor less; and to deal plainly
> I fear I am not in my perfect mind.

It is thus, by exquisite pertinence, melody, and the implied power of writing with exuberance, if need be, that beauty and truth become identical in poetry, and that pleasure, or at the very worst, a balm in our tears, is drawn out of pain.

It is a great and rare thing, and shows a lovely imagination, when the poet can write a commentary, as it were, of his own, on such sufficing passages of nature, and be thanked for the addition. There is an instance of this kind in Warner, an old Elizabethan poet, than which I know nothing sweeter in the world. He is speaking of Fair Rosamond, and of a blow given her by Queen Eleanor.

> With that she dash'd her on the lips,
> *So dyed double red:*
> *Hard was the heart that gave the blow,*
> *Soft were those lips that bled.*[6]

There are different kinds and degrees of imagination, some of them necessary to the formation of every true poet, and all of them possessed by the greatest. Perhaps they may be enumerated as follows:—First, that which presents to the mind any object or circumstance in every-day life; as when we imagine a man holding a sword, or looking out of a window;—Second, that which presents real, but not every-day circumstances; as King Alfred tending the loaves,[7] or Sir Philip Sidney giving up the water to the dying soldier;—Third, that which combines character and events directly imitated from real life, with imitative realities of its own invention; as the probable parts of the histories of Priam and Macbeth, or what may be called natural fiction as distinguished from supernatural;—Fourth, that which conjures up things and events not to be found in nature; as Homer's gods, and Shakspeare's witches,

---

3 "Sir Eger, Sir Graham, and Sir Gray-Steel" was a popular Scotch ballad. The passages quoted, ll. 773-76, 1611-1612, 1615-1617, are found in the complete text of the ballad published in David Laing's *Early Metrical Tales* (1826), pp. 27 and 55; and are also cited in an analysis of the poem in George Ellis' *Specimens of Early English Metrical Romances* (1805), pp. 315 and 331.

4 Prologue to *Canterbury Tales*, ll. 606-607.

5 See Milton's *Il Penseroso*, l. 62. The next quotation is from *King Lear*, IV, vii, 59-63.

6 *Albion's England* (1592), VIII, xli. The popular versified history of England was by William Warner (*c.* 1558-1609).

7 Hunt refers to a legendary incident in which Alfred, disguised as a poor serf in order to hide from the Danish occupiers of England, was asked to look after the baking of some loaves of bread by a peasant's wife. When the loaves were burnt, the woman reviled the king. The incident of Sir Philip Sidney next mentioned is recorded in Fulke Greville's *Life of the Renowned Sir Philip Sidney* (1652); it occurred when Sidney was himself dying of wounds received in battle against the Spanish army at Zutphen in the Netherlands.

enchanted horses and spears, Ariosto's hippogriff,[8] &c.;—Fifth, that which, in order to illustrate or aggravate one image, introduces another; sometimes in simile, as when Homer compares Apollo descending in his wrath at noon-day to the coming of night-time:[9] sometimes in metaphor, or simile comprised in a word, as in Milton's "motes that *people* the sunbeams;" sometimes in concentrating into a word the main history of any person or thing, past or even future, as in the "starry Galileo" of Byron, and that ghastly foregone conclusion of the epithet "murdered" applied to the yet living victim in Keats's story from Boccaccio,—

> So the two brothers and their *murder'd* man
> Rode towards fair Florence;—

sometimes in the attribution of a certain representative quality which makes one circumstance stand for others; as in Milton's grey-fly winding its "*sultry horn*," which epithet contains the heat of a summer's day;—Sixth, that which reverses this process, and makes a variety of circumstances take colour from one, like nature seen with jaundiced or glad eyes, or under the influence of storm or sunshine; as when in Lycidas, or the Greek pastoral poets, the flowers and the flocks are made to sympathize with a man's death; or, in the Italian poet, the river flowing by the sleeping Angelica seems talking of love—

> Parea che l' erba le fiorisse intorno,
> *E d' amor ragionasse quella riva!*—
>   *Orlando Innamorato*, Canto iii.[10]

or in the voluptuous homage paid to the sleeping Imogen by the very light in the chamber and the reaction of her own beauty upon itself; or in the "witch element" of the tragedy of Macbeth and the May-day night of Faust;—Seventh, and last, that which by a single expression, apparently of the vaguest kind, not only meets but surpasses in its effect the extremest force of the most particular description; as in that exquisite passage of Coleridge's Christabel, where the unsuspecting object of the witch's malignity is bidden to go to bed:—

> Quoth Christabel, So let it be!
> And as the lady bade, did she.
> Her gentle limbs did she undress,
> *And lay down in her loveliness;*—[11]

a perfect verse surely, both for feeling and music. The very smoothness and gentleness of the limbs is in the series of the letter *l*'s.

I am aware of nothing of the kind surpassing that most lovely inclusion of physical beauty in moral, neither can I call to mind any instances of the imagination that turns accompaniments into accessories, superior to those I have alluded to. Of the class of comparison, one of the most touching (many a tear must it have drawn from parents and lovers) is in a stanza which has been copied into the "Friar of Orders Grey,"[12] out of Beaumont and Fletcher:—

> Weep no more, lady, weep no more,
>   Thy sorrow is in vain;
> *For violets pluck'd the sweetest showers*
>   *Will ne'er make grow again.*

And Shakspeare and Milton abound in the very grandest; such as Antony's likening his changing fortunes to the cloud-rack; Lear's appeal to the old age of the heavens; Satan's appearance in the horizon, like a fleet "hanging in the clouds;" and the comparisons of him with the comet and the eclipse. Nor unworthy of this glorious company, for its extraordinary combination of delicacy and vastness, is that enchanting one of Shelley's in the Adonais:—

> Life, like a dome of many-coloured glass,
> Stains the white radiance of eternity.

I multiply these particulars in order to impress upon the reader's mind the great importance of imagination in all its phases, as a constituent part of the highest poetic faculty.

The happiest instance I remember of imaginative metaphor, is Shakspeare's moonlight "sleeping" on a bank;[13] but half his poetry may be said to be made up of it, metaphor indeed being the common coin of discourse. Of imaginary creatures, none out of the pale of mythology and the East, are equal, perhaps, in point of invention, to Shakspeare's Ariel and Caliban;

---

8 *Orlando Furioso*, IV, i–xiv.
9 See *Iliad*, I, 47. The succeeding examples of the fifth "kind and degree of imagination" are, respectively: *Il Penseroso*, l. 8; Byron's *Childe Harold's Pilgrimage*, IV, liv; Keats's "Isabella; or the Pot of Basil," ll. 209–210; and *Lycidas*, l. 28.
10 *Orlando Innamorato* (1495), I, iii. The romantic epic, the model and inspiration for Ariosto, was by the Italian poet Matteo Maria Boiardo (1434–1494). The succeeding examples of the sixth "kind and degree of imagination" are, respectively: *Cymbeline*, II, ii, 19–23; and the Walpurgis night scene in Goethe's *Faust*, Part I.

11 I, 235–38.
12 "Friar of Orders Grey" was published in Percy's *Reliques* (1765). The passage cited (ll. 45–48 in Percy's text) is drawn from the tragic-comedy *The Queen of Corinth*, III, ii, 1–4, of uncertain authorship but attributed to Beaumont and Fletcher and published in the 1647 edition of their works. The succeeding examples are, respectively: *Antony and Cleopatra*, IV, xiv, 1–14; *King Lear*, II, iv, 192–95; *Paradise Lost*, II, 636–37, 707–711, and I, 597–99; and Shelley's *Adonais*, ll. 462–63.
13 *Merchant of Venice*, V, i, 54.

though poetry may grudge to prose the discovery of a Winged Woman, especially such as she has been described by her inventor in the story of Peter Wilkins; [14] and in point of treatment, the Mammon and Jealousy of Spenser, some of the monsters in Dante, particularly his Nimrod, his interchangements of creatures into one another, and (if I am not presumptuous in anticipating what I think will be the verdict of posterity) the Witch in Coleridge's Christabel, may rank even with the creations of Shakspeare. It may be doubted, indeed, whether Shakspeare had bile and nightmare enough in him to have thought of such detestable horrors as those of the interchanging adversaries (now serpent, now man), or even of the huge, half-blockish enormity of Nimrod,—in Scripture, the "mighty hunter" [15] and builder of the tower of Babel,—in Dante, a tower of a man in his own person, standing with some of his brother giants up to the middle in a pit in hell, blowing a horn to which a thunderclap is a whisper, and hallooing after Dante and his guide in the jargon of a lost tongue! The transformations are too odious to quote: but of the towering giant we cannot refuse ourselves the "fearful joy" [16] of a specimen. It was twilight, Dante tells us, and he and his guide Virgil were silently pacing through one of the dreariest regions of hell, when the sound of a tremendous horn made him turn all his attention to the spot from which it came. He there discovered through the dusk, what seemed to be the towers of a city. Those are no towers, said his guide; they are giants, standing up to the middle in one of these circular pits. . . .

I look'd again; and as the eye makes out,
By little and little, what the mist conceal'd
In which, till clearing up, the sky was steep'd;
So, looming through the gross and darksome air,
As we drew nigh, those mighty bulks grew plain,
And error quitted me, and terror join'd:
For in like manner as all round its height
Montereggione crowns itself with towers,
So tower'd above the circuit of that pit,
Though but half out of it, and half within,
The horrible giants that fought Jove, and still
Are threaten'd when he thunders. As we near'd
The foremost, I discern'd his mighty face,
His shoulders, breast, and more than half his trunk,
With both the arms down hanging by the sides.
His face appear'd to me, in length and breadth,
Huge as St. Peter's pinnacle at Rome,
And of a like proportion all his bones.

He open'd, as we went, his dreadful mouth,
Fit for no sweeter psalmody; and shouted
After us, in the words of some strange tongue,
Ràfel ma-èe amech zabèe almee!—
"Dull wretch!" my leader cried, "keep to thine horn,
And so vent better whatsoever rage
Or other passion stuff thee. Feel thy throat
And find the chain upon thee, thou confusion!
Lo! what a hoop is clench'd about thy gorge."
Then turning to myself, he said, "His howl
Is its own mockery. This is Nimrod, he
Through whose ill thought it was that humankind
Were tongue-confounded. Pass him, and say nought:
For as he speaketh language known of none,
So none can speak save jargon to himself." [17]

Assuredly it could not have been easy to find a fiction so uncouthly terrible as this in the hypochondria of Hamlet. Even his father had evidently seen no such ghost in the other world. All his phantoms were in the world he had left. Timon, Lear, Richard, Brutus, Prospero, Macbeth himself, none of Shakspeare's men had, in fact, any thought but of the earth they lived on, whatever supernatural fancy crossed them. The thing fancied was still a thing of this world, "in its habit as it lived," [18] or no remoter acquaintance than a witch or a fairy. Its lowest depths (unless Dante suggested them) were the cellars under the stage. Caliban himself is a cross-breed between a witch and a clown. No offence to Shakspeare; who was not bound to be the greatest of healthy poets, and to have every morbid inspiration besides. What he might have done, had he set his wits to compete with Dante, I know not: all I know is, that in the infernal line he did nothing like him; and it is not to be wished he had. It is far better that, as a higher, more universal, and more beneficent variety of the genus Poet, he should have been the happier man he was, and left us the plump cheeks on his monument, instead of the carking visage of the great, but over-serious, and comparatively one-sided Florentine. Even the imagination of Spenser, whom we take to have been a "nervous gentleman" compared with Shakspeare, was visited with no such dreams as Dante. Or, if it was, he did not choose to make himself thinner (as Dante says *he* did) with dwelling upon them. He had twenty visions of nymphs and bowers, to one of the mud of Tartarus. Chaucer, for all he was "a man of this world" as well as the poets' world, and as great, perhaps a greater enemy of oppression than Dante, besides being one of the profoundest masters

[14] Referring to *The Life and Adventures of Peter Wilkins* (1751), by Richard Paltock. See Lamb's "Christ's Hospital Five-and-Thirty Years Ago," footnote 39, p. 359.
[15] Genesis, x, 9.
[16] Gray's "Ode on a Distant Prospect of Eton College," l. 40.

[17] *Inferno*, XXXI, 34–80. Before his translation, Hunt quotes the Italian verses, here omitted. In the remainder of this reprint of the essay, I have also omitted the original Italian or Greek texts that Hunt quotes before his translations.
[18] *Hamlet*, III, iv, 135.

of pathos that ever lived, had not the heart to conclude the story of the famished father and his children, as finished by the inexorable anti-Pisan.[19] But enough of Dante in this place. Hobbes, in order to daunt the reader from objecting to his friend Davenant's want of invention, says of these fabulous creations in general, in his letter prefixed to the poem of Gondibert, that "impenetrable armours, enchanted castles, invulnerable bodies, iron men, flying horses, and a thousand other such things, are easily feigned by them that dare."[20] These are girds at Spenser and Ariosto. But, with leave of Hobbes (who translated Homer as if on purpose to show what execrable verses could be written by a philosopher), enchanted castles and flying horses are not easily feigned, as Ariosto and Spenser feigned them; and that just makes all the difference. For proof, see the accounts of Spenser's enchanted castle in Book the Third, Canto Twelfth, of the Fairy Queen; and let the reader of Italian open the Orlando Furioso at its first introduction of the Hippogriff (Canto iii. st. 4),[21] where Bradamante, coming to an inn, hears a great noise, and sees all the people looking up at something in the air; upon which, looking up herself, she sees a knight in shining armour riding towards the sunset upon a creature with variegated wings, and then dipping and disappearing among the hills. Chaucer's steed of brass, that was

So horsly and so quick of eye,[22]

is copied from the life. You might pat him and feel his brazen muscles. Hobbes, in objecting to what he thought childish, made a childish mistake. His criticism is just such as a boy might pique himself upon, who was educated on mechanical principles, and thought he had outgrown his Goody Two-shoes. With a wonderful dimness of discernment in poetic matters, considering his acuteness in others, he fancies he has settled the question by pronouncing such creations "impossible!" To the brazier they are impossible, no doubt; but not to the poet. Their possibility, if the poet wills it, is to be conceded; the problem is, the creature being given, how to square its actions with probability, according to the nature assumed of it. Hobbes did not see, that the skill and beauty of these fictions lay in bringing them within those very regions of truth and likelihood in which he thought they could not exist. Hence the serpent Python of Chaucer,

Sleeping against the sun upon a day,[23]

when Apollo slew him. Hence the chariot-drawing dolphins of Spenser, softly swimming along the shore lest they should hurt themselves against the stones and gravel. Hence Shakspeare's Ariel, living under blossoms, and riding at evening on the bat; and his domestic namesake in the "Rape of the Lock" (the imagination of the drawing-room) saving a lady's petticoat from the coffee with his plumes, and directing atoms of snuff into a coxcomb's nose. In the "Orlando Furioso" (Canto xv. st. 65) is a wild story of a cannibal necromancer, who laughs at being cut to pieces, coming together again like quicksilver, and picking up his head when it is cut off, sometimes by the hair, sometimes by the nose! This, which would be purely childish and ridiculous in the hands of an inferior poet, becomes interesting, nay grand, in Ariosto's, from the beauties of his style, and its conditional truth to nature. The monster has a fated hair on his head,—a single hair,—which must be taken from it before he can be killed. Decapitation itself is of no consequence, without that proviso. The Paladin Astolfo, who has fought this phenomenon on horseback, and succeeded in getting the head and galloping off with it, is therefore still at a loss what to be at. How is he to discover such a needle in such a bottle of hay? The trunk is spurring after him to recover it, and he seeks for some evidence of the hair in vain. At length he bethinks him of scalping the head. He does so; and the moment the operation arrives at the place of the hair, *the face of the head becomes pale, the eyes turn in their sockets*, and the lifeless pursuer tumbles from his horse. . . .

> Then grew the visage pale, and deadly wet;
> The eyes turn'd in their sockets, drearily;
> And all things show'd the villain's sun was set.
> His trunk that was in chace, fell from its horse,
> And giving the last shudder, was a corse.

It is thus, and thus only, by making Nature his companion wherever he goes, even in the most supernatural region, that the poet, in the words of a very instructive phrase, takes the world along with him. It is true, he must not (as the Platonists would say) humanize weakly or mistakenly in that region; otherwise he runs the chance of forgetting to be true to the supernatural itself, and so betraying a want of imagination from that quarter. His nymphs will have no

---

[19] See Chaucer's "The Monk's Tale," section De Hugelino Comte de Pize; and Dante's *Inferno*, XXXIII.

[20] "The Answer of Mr. Hobbes to Sir Will. Davenant's Preface before Gondibert" (1651), p. 59.

[21] More accurately, Canto IV. See footnote 8, p. 540.

[22] "The Squire's Tale," l. 194.

[23] "The Manciple's Tale," l. 6. The succeeding examples that Hunt cites of bringing "[these fictions] within those very regions of truth and likelihood" are, respectively: *Faerie Queene*, III, iv, 33–34; *Tempest*, V, i, 91–94; and *Rape of the Lock*, III, 114–16, and V, 81–86.

taste of their woods and waters; his gods and goddesses be only so many fair or frowning ladies and gentlemen, such as we see in ordinary paintings; he will be in no danger of having his angels likened to a sort of wild-fowl, as Rembrandt has made them in his Jacob's Dream. His Bacchuses will never remind us, like Titian's, of the force and fury, as well as of the graces, of wine. His Jupiter will reduce no females to ashes; his fairies be nothing fantastical; his gnomes not "of the earth, earthy." [24] And this again will be wanting to Nature; for it will be wanting to the supernatural, as Nature would have made it, working in a supernatural direction. Nevertheless, the poet, even for imagination's sake, must not become a bigot to imaginative truth, dragging it down into the region of the mechanical and the limited, and losing sight of its paramount privilege, which is to make beauty, in a human sense, the lady and queen of the universe. He would gain nothing by making his ocean-nymphs mere fishy creatures, upon the plea that such only could live in the water: his wood-nymphs with faces of knotted oak; his angels without breath and song, because no lungs could exist between the earth's atmosphere and the empyrean. The Grecian tendency in this respect is safer than the Gothic; nay, more imaginative; for it enables us to imagine *beyond* imagination, and to bring all things healthily round to their only present final ground of sympathy,—the human. When we go to heaven, we may idealize in a superhuman mode, and have altogether different notions of the beautiful; but till then we must be content with the loveliest capabilities of earth. The sea-nymphs of Greece were still beautiful women, though they lived in the water. The gills and fins of the ocean's natural inhabitants were confined to their lowest semi-human attendants; or if Triton himself was not quite human, it was because he represented the fiercer part of the vitality of the seas, as they did the fairer.

To conclude this part of my subject, I will quote from the greatest of all narrative writers two passages; —one exemplifying the imagination which brings supernatural things to bear on earthly, without confounding them; the other, that which paints events and circumstances after real life. The first is where Achilles, who has long absented himself from the conflict between his countrymen and the Trojans, has had a message from heaven bidding him reappear in the enemy's sight, standing outside the camp-wall upon the trench, but doing nothing more; that is to say, taking no part in the fight. He is simply to be seen. The two armies down by the sea-side are contending which

shall possess the body of Patroclus; and the mere sight of the dreadful Grecian chief—supernaturally indeed impressed upon them, in order that nothing may be wanting to the full effect of his courage and conduct upon courageous men—is to determine the question. We are to imagine a slope of ground towards the sea, in order to elevate the trench; the camp is solitary; the battle ("a dreadful roar of men," as Homer calls it) is raging on the sea-shore; and the goddess Iris has just delivered her message, and disappeared. . . .

But up Achilles rose, the lov'd of heaven;
And Pallas on his mighty shoulders cast
The shield of Jove; and round about his head
She put the glory of a golden mist,
From which there burnt a fiery-flaming light.
And as, when smoke goes heaven-ward from a town,
In some far island which its foes besiege,
Who all day long with dreadful martialness
Have pour'd from their own town; soon as the sun
Has set, thick lifted fires are visible,
Which, rushing upward, make a light in the sky,
And let the neighbours know, who may perhaps
Bring help across the sea; so from the head
Of great Achilles went up an effulgence.

Upon the trench he stood, without the wall,
But mix'd not with the Greeks, for he rever'd
His mother's word; and so, thus standing there,
He shouted; and Minerva, to his shout,
Added a dreadful cry; and there arose
Among the Trojans an unspeakable tumult.
And as the clear voice of a trumpet, blown
Against a town by spirit-withering foes,
So sprang the clear voice of Æacides.
And when they heard the brazen cry, their hearts
All leap'd within them; and the proud-maned horses
Ran with the chariots round, for they foresaw
Calamity; and the charioteers were smitten,
When they beheld the ever-active fire
Upon the dreadful head of the great-minded one
Burning; for bright-eyed Pallas made it burn.
Thrice o'er the trench divine Achilles shouted;
And thrice the Trojans and their great allies
Roll'd back; and twelve of all their noblest men
Then perish'd, crush'd by their own arms and chariots. [25]

Of course there is no further question about the body of Patroclus. It is drawn out of the press, and received by the awful hero with tears.

The other passage is where Priam, kneeling before Achilles, and imploring him to give up the dead body of Hector, reminds him of his own father; who, what-

---

[24] I Corinthians, xv, 47.

[25] *Iliad*, XVIII, 203–231. The "other passage" from the *Iliad*, which Hunt discusses and translates in the next paragraph, is from XXIV, 468–516.

ever (says the poor old king) may be his troubles with
his enemies, has the blessing of knowing that his son is
still alive, and may daily hope to see him return.
Achilles, in accordance with the strength and noble
honesty of the passions in those times, weeps aloud
himself at this appeal, feeling, says Homer, "desire"
for his father in his very "limbs." He joins in grief
with the venerable sufferer, and can no longer withstand the look of "his grey head and his grey *chin*."
Observe the exquisite introduction of this last word. It
paints the touching fact of the chin's being imploringly
thrown upward by the kneeling old man, and the very
motion of his beard as he speaks. . . .

So saying, Mercury vanished up to heaven:
And Priam then alighted from his chariot,
Leaving Idœus with it, who remain'd
Holding the mules and horses; and the old man
Went straight in doors, where the belov'd of Jove
Achilles sat, and found him. In the room
Were others, but apart; and two alone,
The hero Automedon, and Alcimus,
A branch of Mars, stood by him. They had been
At meals, and had not yet remov'd the board.
Great Priam came, without seeing him,
And kneeling down, he clasp'd Achilles' knees,
And kiss'd those terrible, homicidal hands,
Which had deprived him of so many sons.
And as a man who is press'd heavily
For having slain another, flies away
To foreign lands, and comes into the house
Of some great man, and is beheld with wonder,
So did Achilles wonder to see Priam;
And the rest wonder'd, looking at each other.
But Priam, praying to him, spoke these words:—
"God-like Achilles, think of thine own father!
To the same age have we both come, the same
Weak pass; and though the neighbouring chiefs may vex
Him also, and his borders find no help,
Yet when he hears that thou art still alive,
He gladdens inwardly, and daily hopes
To see his dear son coming back from Troy.
But I, bereav'd old Priam! I had once
Brave sons in Troy, and now I cannot say
That one is left me. Fifty children had I,
When the Greeks came; nineteen were of one womb;
The rest my women bore me in my house.
The knees of many of these fierce Mars has loosen'd;
And he who had no peer, Troy's prop and theirs,
Him hast thou kill'd now, fighting for his country,
Hector; and for his sake am I come here
To ransom him, bringing a countless ransom.
But thou, Achilles, fear the gods, and think
Of thine own father, and have mercy on me:
For I am much more wretched, and have borne
What never mortal bore, I think, on earth,
To lift unto my lips the hand of him
Who slew my boys."

He ceased; and there arose
Sharp longing in Achilles for his father;
And taking Priam by the hand, he gently
Put him away; for both shed tears to think
Of other times; the one, most bitter ones
For Hector, and with wilful wretchedness
Lay right before Achilles: and the other,
For his own father now, and now his friend;
And the whole house might hear them as they moan'd.
But when divine Achilles had refresh'd
His soul with tears, and sharp desire had left
His heart and limbs, he got up from his throne,
And rais'd the old man by the hand, and took
Pity on his grey head and his grey chin.

O lovely and immortal privilege of genius! that can
stretch its hand out of the wastes of time, thousands
of years back, and touch our eyelids with tears. In
these passages there is not a word which a man of the
most matter-of-fact understanding might not have
written, *if he had thought of it*. But in poetry, feeling
and imagination are necessary to the perception and
presentation even of matters of fact. They, and they
only, see what is proper to be told, and what to be kept
back; what is pertinent, affecting, and essential. Without feeling, there is a want of delicacy and distinction;
without imagination, there is no true embodiment. In
poets, even good of their kind, but without a genius for
narration, the action would have been encumbered or
diverted with ingenious mistakes. The over-contem-
plative would have given us too many remarks; the
over-lyrical, a style too much carried away; the over-
fanciful, conceits and too many similes; the unimaginative, the facts without the feeling, and not even those.
We should have been told nothing of the "grey chin,"
of the house hearing them as they moaned, or of
Achilles gently putting the old man aside; much less
of that yearning for his father, which made the hero
tremble in every limb. Writers without the greatest
passion and power do not feel in this way, nor are
capable of expressing the feeling; though there is
enough sensibility and imagination all over the world
to enable mankind to be moved by it, when the poet
strikes his truth into their hearts.

The reverse of imagination is exhibited in pure absence of ideas, in commonplaces, and, above all, in
conventional metaphor, or such images and their
phraseology as have become the common property of
discourse and writing. Addison's Cato is full of them.

Passion unpitied and successless love
Plant daggers in my breast.

I've sounded my Numidians, man by man,
And find them *ripe for a revolt.*

The virtuous Marcia *towers above her sex.*[26]

Of the same kind is his "courting the yoke"—"distracting my very heart"—"calling up all" one's "father" in one's soul—"working every nerve"—"copying a bright example;" in short, the whole play, relieved now and then with a smart sentence or turn of words. The following is a pregnant example of plagiarism and weak writing. It is from another tragedy of Addison's time,—the Mariamne of Fenton:—[27]

> Mariamne, *with superior charms,*
> *Triumphs o'er reason:* in her look she *bears*
> A paradise of ever-blooming sweets;
> Fair as the first idea beauty *prints*
> In the young lover's soul; a winning grace
> Guides every gesture, and obsequious love
> *Attends* on all her steps.

"Triumphing o'er reason" is an old acquaintance of every body's. "Paradise in her look" is from the Italian poets through Dryden.[28] "Fair as the first idea," &c. is from Milton, spoilt;—"winning grace" and "steps" from Milton and Tibullus, both spoilt. Whenever beauties are stolen by such a writer, they are sure to be spoilt: just as when a great writer borrows, he improves.

To come now to Fancy,—she is a younger sister of Imagination, without the other's weight of thought and feeling. Imagination indeed, purely so called, is all feeling; the feeling of the subtlest and most affecting analogies; the perception of sympathies in the natures of things, or in their popular attributes. Fancy is a sporting with their resemblance, real or supposed, and with airy and fantastical creations.

> —Rouse yourself; and the weak wanton Cupid
> Shall from your neck unloose his amorous fold,
> *And, like a dew-drop from the lion's mane,*
> *Be shook to air.*
> *Troilus and Cressida*, Act iii. sc. 3.

That is imagination;—the strong mind sympathizing with the strong beast, and the weak love identified with the weak dew-drop.

> Oh!—and I forsooth
> In love! I that have been love's whip!
> *A very beadle to a humorous sigh!*—
> A domineering pedant o'er the boy,—

This whimpled, whining, purblind, wayward boy,
This senior-junior, giant-dwarf, Dan Cupid,
Regent of love-rhymes, lord of folded arms,
The anointed sovereign of sighs and groans, &c.
Love's Labour Lost, Act iii. sc. 1.

That is fancy;—a combination of images not in their nature connected, or brought together by the feeling, but by the will and pleasure; and having just enough hold of analogy to betray it into the hands of its smiling subjector.

> Silent icicles
> *Quietly shining to the quiet moon.*
> Coleridge's *Frost at Midnight.*

That, again, is imagination;—analogical sympathy; and exquisite of its kind it is.

> "You are now sailed *into the north of my lady's opinion;* where you will hang *like an icicle on a Dutchman's beard,* unless you do redeem it by some laudable attempt."
> *Twelfth Night*, Act iii. sc. 2.

And that is fancy;—one image capriciously suggested by another, and but half connected with the subject of discourse; nay, half opposed to it; for in the gaiety of the speaker's animal spirits, the "Dutchman's beard" is made to represent the lady!

Imagination belongs to Tragedy, or the serious muse; Fancy to the comic. Macbeth, Lear, Paradise Lost, the poem of Dante, are full of imagination: the Midsummer Night's Dream and the Rape of the Lock, of fancy: Romeo and Juliet, the Tempest, the Fairy Queen, and the Orlando Furioso, of both. The terms were formerly identical, or used as such; and neither is the best that might be found. The term Imagination is too confined: often too material. It presents too invariably the idea of a solid body;—of "images" in the sense of the plaster-cast cry about the streets. Fancy, on the other hand, while it means nothing but a spiritual image or apparition (Φαντασμα, appearance, *phantom*), has rarely that freedom from visibility which is one of the highest privileges of imagination. Viola, in Twelfth Night, speaking of some beautiful music, says:—

> It gives a very echo to the seat,
> Where Love is throned.[29]

In this charming thought, fancy and imagination are combined; yet the fancy, the assumption of Love's sitting on a throne, is the image of a solid body; while the imagination, the sense of sympathy between the passion of love and impassioned music, presents us no

---

[26] From Act I, scenes, i, iii, and iv, respectively, of Addison's tragedy. The succeeding quotations are all from Act I, scene i.
[27] A popular tragedy first produced in 1723, by Elijah Fenton (1683–1730). The passage quoted occurs in Act I, scene ii.
[28] See *Absalom and Achitophel*, l. 30. The succeeding references are to *Paradise Lost*, VII, 556–57, and VIII, 61, 488; and Tibullus' *Elegies*, IV, ii, 7–8.

[29] II, iv, 21–22.

image at all. Some new term is wanting to express the more spiritual sympathies of what is called Imagination.

One of the teachers of Imagination is Melancholy; and like Melancholy, as Albert Durer has painted her, she looks out among the stars, and is busied with spiritual affinities and the mysteries of the universe. Fancy turns her sister's wizard instruments into toys. She takes a telescope in her hand, and puts a mimic star on her forehead, and sallies forth as an emblem of astronomy. Her tendency is to the child-like and sportive. She chases butterflies, while her sister takes flight with angels. She is the genius of fairies, of gallantries, of fashions; of whatever is quaint and light, showy and capricious; of the poetical part of wit. She adds wings and feelings to the images of wit; and delights as much to people nature with smiling ideal sympathies, as wit does to bring antipathies together, and make them strike light on absurdity. Fancy, however, is not incapable of sympathy with Imagination. She is often found in her company; always, in the case of the greatest poets; often in that of less, though with them she is the greater favourite. Spenser has great imagination and fancy too, but more of the latter; Milton both also, the very greatest, but with imagination predominant; Chaucer, the strongest imagination of real life, beyond any writers but Homer, Dante, and Shakspeare, and in comic painting inferior to none; Pope has hardly any imagination, but he has a great deal of fancy; Coleridge little fancy, but imagination exquisite. Shakspeare alone, of all poets that ever lived, enjoyed the regard of both in equal perfection. A whole fairy poem of his writing will be found in the present volume.[30] See also his famous description of Queen Mab and her equipage, in Romeo and Juliet:—

> Her waggon-spokes made of long spinners' legs;
> The cover, of the wings of grasshoppers:
> Her traces of the smallest spider's web;
> Her collars of the moonshine's watery beams, &c.

That is Fancy, in its playful creativeness. As a small but pretty rival specimen, less known, take the description of a fairy palace from Drayton's Nymphidia:—

> This palace standeth in the air,
> By necromancy placèd there,
> That it no tempest needs to fear,
>   Which way soe'er it blow it:

> And somewhat southward tow'rd the noon,
> Whence lies a way up to the moon,
> And thence the Fairy can as soon
>   Pass to the earth below it.
> The walls of spiders' legs are made,
> Well morticèd and finely laid:
> He was the master of his trade,
>   It curiously that builded:
> *The windows of the eyes of cats:*

(because they see best at night)

> And for the roof instead of slats
> Is cover'd with the skins of bats
>   *With moonshine that are gilded.*[31]

Here also is a fairy bed, very delicate, from the same poet's Muse's Elysium.

> Of leaves of roses, *white and red,*
> Shall be the covering of the bed;
> The curtains, vallens, tester all,
> Shall be the flower imperial;
> And for the fringe it all along
> *With azure hare-bells shall be hung.*
> *Of lilies shall the pillows be*
> *With down stuft of the butterfly.*

Of fancy, so full of gusto as to border on imagination, Sir John Suckling, in his "Ballad on a Wedding," has given some of the most playful and charming specimens in the language. They glance like twinkles of the eye, or cherries bedewed:

> *Her feet beneath her petticoat,*
> *Like little mice stole in and out,*
>   *As if they fear'd the light:*
> But oh! she dances such a way!
> *No sun upon an Easter day*
> Is half so fine a sight.[32]

It is very daring, and has a sort of playful grandeur, to compare a lady's dancing with the sun. But as the sun has it all to himself in the heavens, so she, in the blaze of her beauty, on earth. This is imagination fairly displacing fancy. The following has enchanted every body:—

> Her lips were red, *and one was thin*
> *Compared with that was next her chin,*
>   *Some bee had stung it newly.*

Every reader has stolen a kiss at that lip, gay or grave.

With regard to the principle of Variety in Uniform-

---

[30] "The Quarrel of Oberon and Titania. A Fairy Drama," drawn from *Midsummer-night's Dream.* The succeeding quotation is from *Romeo and Juliet,* I, iv, 59–62.

[31] Ll. 33–48, of Drayton's fairy romance, published 1627. The next quotation is from his *Muses' Elysium* (1630), "the eight Nymphall," ll. 119–26.

[32] Ll. 43–48, of Suckling's ballad published 1646. Hunt next quotes ll. 62–64.

ity by which verse ought to be modulated, and one-ness of impression diversely produced, it has been contended by some, that Poetry need not be written in verse at all; that prose is as good a medium, provided poetry be conveyed through it; and that to think other-wise is to confound letter with spirit, or form with essence. But the opinion is a prosaical mistake. Fitness and unfitness for *song*, or metrical excitement, just make all the difference between a poetical and pro-saical subject; and the reason why verse is necessary to the form of poetry is, that the perfection of poetical spirit demands it;—that the circle of its enthusiasm, beauty and power, is incomplete without it. I do not mean to say that a poet can never show himself a poet in prose; but that, being one, his desire and necessity will be write in verse; and that, if he were unable to do so, he would not, and could not, deserve his title. Verse to the true poet is no clog. It is idly called a trammel and a difficulty. It is a help. It springs from the same enthusiasm as the rest of his impulses, and is necessary to their satisfaction and effect. Verse is no more a clog than the condition of rushing upward is a clog to fire, or than the roundness and order of the globe we live on is a clog to the freedom and variety that abound within its sphere. Verse is no dominator over the poet, except inasmuch as the bond is reciprocal, and the poet dominates over the verse. They are lovers, playfully challenging each other's rule, and delighted equally to rule and obey. Verse is the final proof to the poet that his mastery over his art is complete. It is the shutting up of his powers in "*measureful* content;" [33] the answer of form to his spirit; of strength and ease to his guid-ance. It is the willing action, the proud and fiery hap-piness, of the winged steed on whose back he has vaulted,

To witch the world with wondrous horsemanship.

Verse, in short, is that finishing, and rounding, and "tuneful planetting" of the poet's creations, which is produced of necessity by the smooth tendencies of their energy or inward working, and the harmonious dance into which they are attracted round the orb of the beautiful. Poetry, in its complete sympathy with beauty, must, of necessity, leave no sense of the beauti-ful, and no power over its forms, unmanifested; and verse flows as inevitably from this condition of its in-tegrity, as other laws of proportion do from any other kind of embodiment of beauty (say that of the human figure), however free and various the movements may

be that play within their limits. What great poet ever wrote his poems in prose? or where is a good prose poem, of any length, to be found? The poetry of the Bible is understood to be in verse, in the original. Mr. Hazlitt has said a good word for those prose enlarge-ments of some fine old song, which are known by the name of Ossian; [34] and in passages they deserve what he said; but he judiciously abstained from saying any-thing about the form. Is Gesner's Death of Abel a poem? or Hervey's Meditations? [35] The Pilgrim's Pro-gress has been called one; and, undoubtedly, Bunyan had a genius which tended to make him a poet, and one of no mean order: and yet it was of as ungenerous and low a sort as was compatible with so lofty an affinity; and this is the reason why it stopped where it did. He had a craving after the beautiful, but not enough of it in himself to echo to its music. On the other hand, the possession of the beautiful will not be suffi-cient without force to utter it. The author of Tele-machus [36] had a soul full of beauty and tenderness. He was not a man who, if he had had a wife and children, would have run away from them, as Bunyan's hero did, to get a place by himself in heaven. He was "a little lower than the angels," [37] like our own Bishop Jewells and Berkeleys; and yet he was no poet. He was too delicately, not to say feebly, absorbed in his devotions, to join in the energies of the seraphic choir.

Every poet, then, is a versifier; every fine poet an excellent one; and he is the best whose verse exhibits the greatest amount of strength, sweetness, straight-forwardness, unsuperfluousness, *variety*, and *one-ness;* —one-ness, that is to say, consistency, in the general impression, metrical and moral; and variety, or every pertinent diversity of tone and rhythm, in the process.

*   *   *   *   *

[1844]

---

33 See *Macbeth*, II, i, 17. The next quotation is from *Henry the Fourth*, Part I, IV, i, 110.

34 See Hazlitt's "On Poetry in General," pp. 426–27.

35 Solomon Gessner (1730–1788) was a Swiss author, whose biblical epic *Der Tod Abels* (1758) enjoyed great popularity and was widely translated. Like Gessner's other works, *The Death of Abel* was written in a form of "poetic" prose; his English trans-lator Mrs. Mary Collyer had described his style as "a middle species between verse and prose," "a kind of loose poetry, un-shackled by the tagging of rhymes, or counting of syllables." James Hervey (1714–1758) was the author of *Meditations and Contemplations* (1748), a very popular devotional work written in a highly inflated prose style.

36 Fénelon (1651–1715). His quasi epic and moralizing novel *Télémaque* was published in 1699.

37 In the Scriptures (Psalms, viii, 5; Hebrews, ii, 7, 9), the phrase is used to describe man in his highest state as originally created by God and "crowned with glory and honour." Hunt applies the phrase to men of such great talent and notably humane character as the French churchman Fénelon and his English coun-terparts: John Jewel (1522–1571), bishop of Salisbury, and George Berkeley (1685–1753), the philosopher and bishop of Cloyne.

Thomas De Quincey

1785–1859

OUTLINE OF EVENTS

1785   Born August 15, at Manchester, son of merchant Thomas Quincey. (Prefix "De" added to family name sometime after father's death.)

1792   Death of beloved sister Elizabeth.

1793   Death of father. Begins education under one of his guardians, Rev. Samuel Hall.

1796   Family moves to Bath where Thomas enters Bath Grammar School and proves a brilliant and precocious scholar.

1799   Transferred to Winkfield (Wiltshire) Grammar School.

1800   Wins third prize in a London competition for translations of Horace's Ode "Integer Vitae" (Leigh Hunt wins first prize). Summer, travels to Ireland as companion to young Lord Westport, enroute visiting London for first time; November, enrolled in Manchester Grammar School.

1802   July, "elopes" from Manchester Grammar School, travels in Wales and resides in London (until March 1803).

1803   Initiates correspondence with Wordsworth. December, enters Worcester College, Oxford.

1804   Takes opium for first time.

1805   Meets Charles Lamb in London.

1807   July, meets Coleridge at Bridgwater (Somersetshire) and anonymously offers him gift of £300. November, meets Wordsworth at Grasmere.

1808   May, leaves Oxford without taking degree. November, settles with Wordsworth family in Grasmere.

1809   February, moves to London to supervise publication of Wordsworth's *Convention of Cintra*. Fall, takes up long-term residence at Dove Cottage, Grasmere.

1813   "Now then it was . . . that I became a regular and confirmed (no longer an intermitting) opium eater."

1817   February, marries Margaret Simpson (their son William born in 1816).

1818–19   Edits *Westmorland Gazette*.

1821   Begins to contribute to *London Magazine* (until 1825).

1822   *Confessions* appear in book form.

1826   Begins to contribute to *Blackwood's Magazine* (until 1849).

[549]

1830   De Quincey family settles in Edinburgh where they undergo years of severe financial distress, with Thomas in frequent hiding from creditors.

1832   The novel *Klosterheim* published.

1833   Begins to contribute to *Tait's Magazine* (until 1851).

1835–38   Contributes articles on Goethe, Pope, Schiller, and Shakespeare to *Encyclopedia Britannica*.

1837   Wife Margaret dies, leaving De Quincey to care for the six surviving children.

1841–43   In Glasgow to escape creditors; serious illness; June 1843, rejoins family at Lasswade (near Edinburgh).

1844   *The Logic of Political Economy* published.

1846   Financial situation eased through inheritance on death of his mother. December, returns to Glasgow to write for *North British Daily Mail* and *Tait's Magazine*, remaining until November 1847.

1847–54   Resides at Lasswade.

1850   Begins to contribute to *Hogg's Weekly Instructor* (until 1853).

1851–59   *De Quincey's Writings*, American edition of collected works, published.

1853–60   *Selections Grave and Gay*, De Quincey's own edition of his works, published.

1854–59   Resides in Edinburgh.

1859   December 8, dies.

SELECTED BIBLIOGRAPHY

BIOGRAPHY

EATON, HORACE AINSWORTH, *Thomas De Quincey*, New York: Oxford University Press, 1936.

JORDAN, JOHN E., *De Quincey to Wordsworth: A Biography of a Relationship*, Berkeley–Los Angeles: University of California Press, 1962.

SACKVILLE-WEST, EDWARD, *A Flame in Sunlight: The Life and Work of Thomas De Quincey*, London: Cassell and Company, 1936.

EDITIONS OF DE QUINCEY'S PROSE

BURWICK, FREDERICK (ed.), *Selected Essays on Rhetoric by Thomas De Quincey*, Carbondale and Edwardsville, Ill.: Southern Illinois University Press, 1967.

De Quincey's Writings, 24 vols., Boston: Ticknor, Reed, and Fields, 1851–1859 [the first collected edition, reprinting the essays from their original magazine texts].

DE QUINCEY, THOMAS, *Selections Grave and Gay, from Writings Published and Unpublished*, 14 vols., Edinburgh: James Hogg, 1853–1860. [De Quincey's own collection of his works, with revisions of the original texts].

ELWIN, MALCOLM (ed.), *Confessions of an English Opium-eater, in both revised and original texts . . .*, London: Macdonald, 1956.

JAPP, ALEXANDER H. (ed.), *The Posthumous Works of Thomas De Quincey*, 2 vols., London: William Heinemann, 1891–1893.

MASSON, DAVID (ed.), *The Collected Writings of Thomas De Quincey*, 14 vols., Edinburgh: Adam and Charles Black, 1889–1890 [the "standard" edition, with introductions and annotations to the selections].

TAVE, STUART, *New Essays by De Quincey: His Contributions to the Edinburgh Saturday Post and the Edinburgh Evening Post 1827–1828*, Princeton, N. J.: Princeton University Press, 1966.

CRITICISM AND SCHOLARSHIP

BAUDELAIRE, CHARLES, *Les Paradis Artificiels*, Paris, 1860 [translations and commentary on the *Confessions* and *Suspiria*].

GOLDMAN, ALBERT, *The Mine and the Mint: Sources for the Writings of Thomas De Quincey*, Carbondale, Ill.: Southern Illinois University Press, 1965.

JACK, IAN, *English Literature 1815–1832* [Volume X of *Oxford History of English Literature*], Oxford: Clarendon Press, 1963.

JORDAN, JOHN E., *Thomas De Quincey Literary Critic*, Berkeley and Los Angeles: University of California Press, 1952.

LEECH, CLIFFORD, "De Quincey as Literary Critic," *Review of English Literature*, II (1961), 38–48.

POULET, GEORGES, "Timelessness and Romanticism," *Journal of the History of Ideas*, XV (1954), 3–22.

PROCTOR, SIGMUND K., *Thomas De Quincey's Theory of Literature*, New York: Octagon Books, 1966 [first published 1943].

WOOLF, VIRGINIA, "De Quincey's Autobiography," *The Common Reader: Second Series*, New York: Harcourt, Brace and Company, 1932.

CONFESSIONS OF AN ENGLISH OPIUM-EATER

Originally published in The London Magazine *in September–October 1821, the* Confessions *first appeared in book form in 1822. De Quincey prepared a much-expanded version as volume V of his collected works* Selections Grave and Gay *in 1856, but wrote that "greatly I doubt whether many readers will not prefer it in its original fragmentary state to its present full-blown development." The 1822 text is here followed, omitting the "Appendix."*

De Quincey's long career as a journalist and man of letters began with the Confessions, *which proved an immediate success and which has remained the most famous and popular of his works. This initial publication influenced much of his later writing; his greatest masterpiece* Suspiria de Profundis *is an elaboration of the power of dreams under the influence of opium and a deepened analysis of the materials of the dreams from De Quincey's traumatic early history. On the subject of opium and its relation to dreams and literary expression, see: Meyer Howard Abrams,* The Milk of Paradise *(Cambridge, Mass.: Harvard University Press, 1934), and Elisabeth Schneider,* Coleridge, Opium, and "Kubla Kahn" *(Chicago, Ill.: University of Chicago, 1953). Although not restricted to the* Confessions, *chapter II of J. Hillis Miller's* The Disappearance of God: Five Nineteenth Century Writers *(Cambridge, Mass.: Harvard University Press, 1963) is an illuminating introduction to any study of De Quincey's thought and writing.*

FROM
CONFESSIONS
OF AN
ENGLISH OPIUM-EATER

TO THE READER.

I HERE present you, courteous reader, with the record of a remarkable period in my life: according to my application of it, I trust that it will prove, not merely an interesting record, but, in a considerable degree, useful and instructive. In *that* hope it is, that I have drawn it up: and *that* must be my apology for breaking through that delicate and honourable reserve, which, for the most part, restrains us from the public exposure of our own errors and infirmities. Nothing, indeed, is more revolting to English feelings, than the spectacle of a human being obtruding on our notice his moral ulcers or scars, and tearing away that "decent drapery," which time, or indulgence to human frailty, may have drawn over them: accordingly, the greater part of *our* confessions (that is, spontaneous and extra-judicial confessions) proceed from demireps, adventurers, or swindlers: and for any such acts of gratuitous self-humiliation from those who can be supposed in sympathy with the decent and self-respecting part of society, we must look to French literature, or to that part of the German, which is tainted with the spurious and defective sensibility of the French. All this I feel so forcibly, and so nervously am I alive to reproach of this tendency, that I have for many months hesitated about the propriety of allowing this, or any part of my narrative, to come before the public eye, until after my death (when, for many reasons, the whole will be published): and it is not without an anxious review of the reasons for and against this step, that I have, at last, concluded on taking it.

Guilt and misery shrink, by a natural instinct, from public notice: they court privacy and solitude: and, even in their choice of a grave, will sometimes sequester themselves from the general population of the church-yard, as if declining to claim fellowship with the great family of man, and wishing (in the affecting language of Mr. Wordsworth)

—humbly to express
A penitential loneliness.[1]

It is well, upon the whole, and for the interest of us all, that it should be so: nor would I willingly, in my own person, manifest a disregard of such salutary feeling; nor in act or word do any thing to weaken them. But, on the one hand, as my self-accusation does not amount to a confession of guilt, so, on the other, it is possible that, if it *did*, the benefit resulting to others, from the record of an experience purchased at so heavy a price, might compensate, by a vast over-balance, for any violence done to the feelings I have noticed, and justify a breach of the general rule. In-firmity and misery do not, of necessity, imply guilt. They approach, or recede from, the shades of that dark alliance, in proportion to the probable motives and prospects of the offender, and the palliations, known or secret, of the offence: in proportion as the temptations to it were potent from the first, and the resistance to it, in act or in effort, was earnest to the last. For my own part, without breach of truth or modesty, I may affirm, that my life has been, on the whole, the life of a philosopher: from my birth I was made an intellectual creature: and intellectual in the highest sense my pursuits and pleasures have been, even from my school-boy days. If opium-eating be a sensual pleasure, and if I am bound to confess that I have indulged in it to an excess, not yet *recorded** of

any other man, it is no less true, that I have struggled against this fascinating enthralment with a religious zeal, and have, at length, accomplished what I never yet heard attributed to any other man—have un-twisted, almost to its final links, the accursed chain which fettered me. Such a self-conquest may reasonably be set off in counterbalance to any kind or degree of self-indulgence. Not to insist, that in my case, the self-conquest was unquestionable, the self-indulgence open to doubts of casuistry, according as that name shall be extended to acts aiming at the bare relief of pain, or shall be restricted to such as aim at the excitement of positive pleasure.

Guilt, therefore, I do not acknowledge: and, if I did, it is possible that I might still resolve on the present act of confession, in consideration of the service which I may therefore render to the whole class of opium-eaters. But who are they? Reader, I am sorry to say, a very numerous class indeed. Of this I became convinced some years ago, by computing, at that time, the number of those in one small class of English society (the class of men distinguished for talents, or of eminent station), who were known to me, directly or indirectly, as opium-eaters; such, for instance, as the eloquent and benevolent ——,[3] the late dean of ——; Lord ——; Mr. ——, the philosopher; a late under-secretary of state (who described to me the sensation which first drove him to the use of opium, in the very same words as the dean of ——, viz. "that he felt as though rats were gnawing and abrading the coats of his stomach"); Mr. ——; and many others, hardly less known, whom it would be tedious to mention. Now, if one class, comparatively so limited, could furnish so many scores of cases (and *that* within the knowledge of one single inquirer), it was a natural inference, that the entire population of England would furnish a proportionable number. The soundness of this inference, however, I doubted, until some facts became known to me, which satisfied me that it was not incorrect. I will mention two: 1. Three respectable London druggists, in widely remote quarters of London, from whom I happened lately to be purchas-ing small quantities of opium, assured me, that the number of *amateur* opium-eaters (as I may term them) was, at this time, immense; and that the difficulty of distinguishing these persons, to whom habit had rendered opium necessary, from such as were purchas-

---

* "Not yet *recorded*," I say: for there is one celebrated man of the present day who, if all be true which is reported of him, has greatly exceeded me in quantity.[2]

[1] *The White Doe of Rylstone*, I, 176–77.
[2] Referring to Coleridge.

[3] The 1856 edition fills in the blanks as follows: "the eloquent and benevolent William Wilberforce; the late Dean of Carlisle, Dr. Isaac Milner; the first Lord Erskine; . . . a late under-secretary of state (viz., Mr. Addington, brother to the first Lord Sidmouth . . .); Samuel Taylor Coleridge. . . ." Of "Mr. ——, the philos-opher," De Quincey recorded in a footnote: "Who is Mr. Dash, the philosopher? Really I have forgot."

ing it with a view to suicide, occasioned them daily trouble and disputes. This evidence respected London only. But, 2. (which will possibly surprise the reader more,) some years ago, on passing through Manchester, I was informed by several cotton-manufacturers, that their work-people were rapidly getting into the practice of opium-eating; so much so, that on a Saturday afternoon the counters of the druggists were strewed with pills of one, two, or three grains, in preparation for the known demand of the evening. The immediate occasion of this practice was the lowness of wages, which, at that time, would not allow them to indulge in ale or spirits: and, wages rising, it may be thought that this practice would cease: but, as I do not readily believe that any man, having once tasted the divine luxuries of opium, will afterwards descend to the gross and mortal enjoyments of alcohol, I take it for granted

That those eat now, who never ate before;
And those who always ate, now eat the more.[4]

Indeed the fascinating powers of opium are admitted, even by medical writers, who are its greatest enemies: thus, for instance, Awsiter, apothecary to Greenwich-hospital, in his "Essay on the Effects of Opium," (published in the year 1763), when attempting to explain, why Mead[5] had not been sufficiently explicit on the properties, counteragents, &c. of this drug, expresses himself in the following mysterious terms, (φωναντα συνετοισι)[6] "perhaps he thought the subject of too delicate a nature to be made common; and as many people might then indiscriminately use it, it would take from that necessary fear and caution, which should prevent their experiencing the extensive power of this drug: *for there are many properties in it, if universally known, that would habituate the use, and make it more in request with us than the Turks themselves*: the result of which knowledge," he adds, "must prove a general misfortune." In the necessity of this conclusion I do not altogether concur: but upon that point I shall have occasion to speak at the close of my confessions, where I shall present the reader with the *moral* of my narrative.

FROM

PART I

PRELIMINARY CONFESSIONS

These preliminary confessions, or introductory narrative of the youthful adventures which laid the foundation of the writer's habit of opium-eating in after-life, it has been judged proper to premise, for three several reasons:

1. As forestalling that question, and giving it a satisfactory answer, which else would painfully obtrude itself in the course of the Opium-Confessions— "How came any reasonable being to subject himself to such a yoke of misery, voluntarily to incur a captivity so servile, and knowingly to fetter himself with such a sevenfold chain?"—a question which, if not somewhere plausibly resolved, could hardly fail, by the indignation which it would be apt to raise as against an act of wanton folly, to interfere with that degree of sympathy which is necessary in any case to an author's purposes.

2. As furnishing a key to some parts of that tremendous scenery which afterwards peopled the dreams of the opium-eater.

3. As creating some previous interest of a personal sort in the confessing subject, apart from the matter of the confessions, which cannot fail to render the confessions themselves more interesting. If a man "whose talk is of oxen,"[1] should become an opium-eater, the probability is, that (if he is not too dull to dream at all) —he will dream about oxen: whereas, in the case before him, the reader will find that the opium-eater boasteth himself to be a philosopher; and accordingly, that the phantasmagoria of *his* dreams (waking or sleeping, day-dreams or night-dreams) is suitable to one who in that character,

Humani nihil a se alienum putat.[2]

For amongst the conditions which he deems indispensable to the sustaining of any claim to the title of philosopher, is not merely the possession of a superb intellect in its *analytic* functions (in which part of the pretension, however, England can for some generations show but a few claimants; at least, he is not aware of any known candidate for this honour, who can be styled emphatically a *subtle thinker*, with the exception of *Samuel Taylor Coleridge*, and in a narrower department of thought, with the recent illustrious

---

[4] A parody of the refrain from "The Vigil of Venus," a translation of the Latin *Pervigilium Veneris*, by Thomas Parnell (1679–1718).

[5] Richard Mead (1673–1574), one of the leading physicians of the period.

[6] φωναντα συνετοισι: "Vocal [known only] to the wise." Pindar's *Olympian Odes*, II, 85.

---

[1] See Ecclesiasticus, xxxviii, 25.

[2] Humani ... putat: "thinks nothing human foreign to him." Terence's Latin comedy *Heuton Timoroumenos* [*The Self-Tormentor*], I, i, 25.

exception* of *David Ricardo*)³—but also such a consti-tution of the *moral* faculties, as shall give him an inner eye and power of intuition for the vision and the mysteries of our human nature: *that* constitution of faculties, in short, which (amongst all the generations of men that from the beginning of time have deployed into life, as it were, upon this planet) our English poets have possessed in the highest degree,—and Scottish† professors in the lowest.

I have often been asked, how I first came to be a regular opium-eater; and have suffered, very unjustly, in the opinion of my acquaintance, from being reputed to have brought upon myself all the sufferings which I shall have to record, by a long course of indulgence in this practice purely for the sake of creating an artificial state of pleasurable excitement. This, however, is a misrepresentation of my case. True it is, that for nearly ten years I did occasionally take opium, for the sake of the exquisite pleasure it gave me: but, so long as I took it with this view, I was effectually protected from all material bad consequences, by the necessity of interposing long intervals between the several acts of indulgence, in order to renew the pleasurable sensa-tions. It was not for the purpose of creating pleasure, but of mitigating pain in the severest degree, that I first began to use opium as an article of daily diet. In the twenty-eighth year of my age, a most painful affection

* A third exception might perhaps have been added: and my reason for not adding that exception is chiefly because it was only in his juvenile efforts that the writer [William Hazlitt] whom I allude to addressed himself to philosophical themes; his riper powers having been all dedicated (on very excusable and very intelligible grounds, under the present direction of the popular mind in England) to criticism and the fine arts. This reason apart, however, I doubt whether he is not rather to be considered an acute thinker than a subtle one. It is, besides, a great drawback on his mastery over philosophical subjects, that he has obviously not had the advantage of a regular scholastic education: he has not read Plato in his youth (which most likely was only his misfortune); but neither had he read Kant in his manhood (which is his fault).

† I disclaim any allusion to *existing* professors, of whom indeed I know only one.⁴

◇◇◇◇◇◇◇◇◇◇◇◇◇◇◇◇◇◇◇◇◇◇◇◇◇◇◇

3 David Ricardo (1772–1823) was the author of the famous *Principles of Political Economy and Taxation* (1817). In a section from "The Pains of Opium" here omitted, De Quincey describes the electric effect a reading of Ricardo had on him in the midst of his "intellectual torpor" from opium in 1818, rousing him to compose "a Prolegomena to all future Systems of Political Economy." The work was not completed for publication at the time. However, De Quincey did contribute essays on Ricardo and on Political Economy to *The London Magazine* in 1824; and in 1844 appeared his *Logic of Political Economy*.
4 Referring to John Wilson (1785–1854), elected professor of moral philosophy at Edinburgh in 1820, now better known as the reviewer and journalist "Christopher North" of *Blackwood's Magazine*. Wilson and De Quincey had been friends since meeting at Grasmere in 1808–1809.

of the stomach, which I had first experienced about ten years before, attacked me in great strength. This affection had originally been caused by extremities of hunger, suffered in my boyish days. During the season of hope and redundant happiness which succeeded (that is, from eighteen to twenty-four) it had slum-bered: for the three following years it had revived at intervals: and now, under unfavourable circumstances, from depression of spirits, it attacked me with a violence that yielded to no remedies but opium. As the youthful sufferings, which first produced this de-rangement of the stomach, were interesting in them-selves, and in the circumstances that attended them, I shall here briefly retrace them.

My father died when I was about seven years old, and left me to the care of four guardians. I was sent to various schools, great and small; and was very early distinguished for my classical attainments, especially for my knowledge of Greek. At thirteen, I wrote Greek with ease; and at fifteen my command of that language was so great, that I not only composed Greek verses in lyric metres, but could converse in Greek fluently, and without embarrassment—an accom-plishment which I have not since met with in any scholar of my times, and which, in my case, was owing to the practice of daily reading off the newspapers into the best Greek I could furnish *extempore:* for the necessity of ransacking my memory and invention, for all sorts and combinations of periphrastic expressions, as equivalents for modern ideas, images, relations of things, &c. gave me a compass of diction which would never have been called out by a dull translation of moral essays, &c. "That boy," said one of my masters, pointing the attention of a stranger to me, "that boy could harangue an Athenian mob, better than you or I could address an English one." He who honoured me with this eulogy, was a scholar, "and a ripe and good one:"⁵ and, of all my tutors, was the only one whom I loved or reverenced. Unfortunately for me (and, as I afterwards learned, to this worthy man's great indignation), I was transferred to the care, first of a blockhead, who was in a perpetual panic, lest I should expose his ignorance; and finally, to that of a respectable scholar, at the head of a great school on an ancient foundation.⁶ This man had been appointed to his situation by —— College, Oxford; and was a sound, well-built scholar, but (like most men, whom I have known from that college) coarse, clumsy, and inelegant. A miserable contrast he presented, in my

◇◇◇◇◇◇◇◇◇◇◇◇◇◇◇◇◇◇◇◇◇◇◇◇◇◇◇

5 *Henry the Eighth*, IV, ii, 51. De Quincey refers to Mr. Morgan of the Bath Grammar School.
6 Referring to Mr. Charles Lawson, headmaster of the Manchester Grammar School.

eyes, to the Etonian brilliancy of my favourite master: and, besides, he could not disguise from my hourly notice, the poverty and meagreness of his understanding. It is a bad thing for a boy to be, and to know himself, far beyond his tutors, whether in knowledge or in power of mind. This was the case, so far as regarded knowledge at least, not with myself only: for the two boys, who jointly with myself composed the first form, were better Grecians than the head-master, though not more elegant scholars, nor at all more accustomed to sacrifice to the graces. When I first entered, I remember that we read Sophocles; and it was a constant matter of triumph to us, the learned triumvirate of the first form, to see our "Archididascalus"[7] (as he loved to be called) conning our lesson before we went up, and laying a regular train, with lexicon and grammar, for blowing up and blasting (as it were) any difficulties he found in the choruses; whilst *we* never condescended to open our books until the moment of going up, and were generally employed in writing epigrams upon his wig, or some such important matter. My two class-fellows were poor, and dependent for their future prospects at the university, on the recommendation of the headmaster: but I, who had a small patrimonial property, the income of which was sufficient to support me at college, wished to be sent thither immediately. I made earnest representations on the subject to my guardians, but all to no purpose. One, who was more reasonable, and had more knowledge of the world than the rest, lived at a distance: two of the other three resigned all their authority into the hands of the fourth; and this fourth with whom I had to negociate, was a worthy man, in his way, but haughty, obstinate, and intolerant of all opposition to his will. After a certain number of letters and personal interviews, I found that I had nothing to hope for, not even a compromise of the matter, from my guardian: unconditional submission was what he demanded: and I prepared myself, therefore, for other measures. Summer was now coming on with hasty steps, and my seventeenth birthday was fast approaching; after which day I had sworn within myself, that I would no longer be numbered amongst school-boys. Money being what I chiefly wanted, I wrote to a woman of high rank, who, though young herself, had known me from a child, and had latterly treated me with great distinction, requesting that she would "lend" me five guineas. For upwards of a week no answer came; and I was beginning to despond, when, at length, a servant put into my hands a double letter, with a coronet on the seal. The letter was kind and

obliging: the fair writer was on the sea-coast, and in that way the delay had arisen: she enclosed double of what I had asked, and good-naturedly hinted, that if I should *never* repay her, it would not absolutely ruin her. Now then, I was prepared for my scheme: ten guineas, added to about two which I had remaining from my pocket money, seemed to me sufficient for an indefinite length of time: and at that happy age, if no *definite* boundary can be assigned to one's power, the spirit of hope and pleasure makes it virtually infinite.

It is a just remark of Dr. Johnson's[8] (and what cannot often be said of his remarks, it is a very feeling one), that we never do any thing consciously for the last time (of things, that is, which we have long been in the habit of doing) without sadness of heart. This truth I felt deeply, when I came to leave ——, a place which I did not love, and where I had not been happy. On the evening before I left —— for ever, I grieved when the ancient and lofty school-room resounded with the evening service, performed for the last time in my hearing; and at night, when the muster-roll of names was called over, and mine (as usual) was called first, I stepped forward, and, passing the head master, who was standing by, I bowed to him, and looked earnestly in his face, thinking to myself, "He is old and infirm, and in this world I shall not see him again." I was right: I never *did* see him again, nor ever shall. He looked at me complacently, smiled good-naturedly, returned my salutation (or rather, my valediction), and we parted (though he knew it not) for ever. I could not reverence him intellectually: but he had been uniformly kind to me, and had allowed me many indulgences: and I grieved at the thought of the mortification I should inflict upon him.

The morning came, which was to launch me into the world, and from which my whole succeeding life has, in many important points, taken its colouring. I lodged in the head master's house, and had been allowed, from my first entrance, the indulgence of a private room, which I used both as a sleeping-room and as a study. At half after three I rose, and gazed with deep emotion at the ancient towers of ——, "drest in earliest light," and beginning to crimson with the radiant lustre of a cloudless July morning. I was firm and immovable in my purpose: but yet agitated by anticipation of uncertain danger and troubles; and, if I could have foreseen the hurricane, and perfect hailstorm of affliction which soon fell upon me, well might I have been agitated. To this agitation the deep peace of the morning presented an affecting contrast, and in some degree a medicine. The silence was more pro-

---

7 Chief ("Arch") schoolteacher.

8 See *The Idler*, No. 103 (April 5, 1760).

found than that of midnight: and to me the silence of a
summer morning is more touching than all other
silence, because, the light being broad and strong, as
that of noon-day at other seasons of the year, it seems to
differ from perfect day, chiefly because man is not yet
abroad; and thus, the peace of nature, and of the innocent creatures of God, seems to be secure and deep,
only so long as the presence of man, and his restless
and unquiet spirit, are not there to trouble its sanctity.
I dressed myself, took my hat and gloves, and lingered
a little in the room. For the last year and a half this room
had been my "pensive citadel:"⁹ here I had read and
studied through all the hours of night: and, though
true it was, that for the latter part of this time I, who
was framed for love and gentle affections, had lost my
gaiety and happiness, during the strife and fever of
contention with my guardian; yet, on the other hand,
as a boy, so passionately fond of books, and dedicated
to intellectual pursuits, I could not fail to have enjoyed
many happy hours in the midst of general dejection.
I wept as I looked round on the chair, hearth, writing-
table, and other familiar objects, knowing too certainly,
that I looked upon them for the last time. Whilst I
write this, it is eighteen years ago: and yet, at this
moment, I see distinctly as if it were yesterday, the
lineaments and expression of the object on which I
fixed my parting gaze: it was a picture of the lovely
——, which hung over the mantle-piece; the eyes and
mouth of which were so beautiful, and the whole
countenance so radiant with benignity, and divine
tranquillity, that I had a thousand times laid down my
pen, or my book, to gather consolation from it, as a
devotee from his patron saint. Whilst I was yet gazing
upon it, the deep tones of —— clock proclaimed that
it was four o'clock. I went up to the picture, kissed it,
and then gently walked out, and closed the door for
ever!

*   *   *   *   *10

Soon after this, I contrived, by means which I must
omit for want of room, to transfer myself to London.
And now began the latter and fiercer stage of my long
sufferings; without using a disproportionate expression
I might say, of my agony. For I now suffered, for upwards of sixteen weeks, the physical anguish of hunger
in various degrees of intensity; but as bitter, perhaps,
as ever any human being can have suffered who has

survived it. I would not needlessly harass my reader's
feelings by a detail of all that I endured: for extremities
such as these, under any circumstances of heaviest
misconduct or guilt, cannot be contemplated, even in
description, without a rueful pity that is painful to the
natural goodness of the human heart. Let it suffice, at
least on this occasion, to say, that a few fragments of
bread from the breakfast-table of one individual (who
supposed me to be ill, but did not know of my being
in utter want), and these at uncertain intervals, constituted my whole support. During the former part of
my sufferings (that is, generally in Wales, and always
for the first two months in London) I was houseless,
and very seldom slept under a roof. To this constant
exposure to the open air I ascribe it mainly, that I did
not sink under my torments. Latterly, however, when
colder and more inclement weather came on, and when,
from the length of my sufferings, I had begun to sink
into a more languishing condition, it was, no doubt,
fortunate for me, that the same person to whose
breakfast-table I had access, allowed me to sleep in a
large unoccupied house, of which he was tenant. Unoccupied, I call it, for there was no household or establishment in it; nor any furniture, indeed, except a table,
and a few chairs. But I found, on taking possession of
my new quarters, that the house already contained one
single inmate, a poor friendless child, apparently ten
years old; but she seemed hunger-bitten; and sufferings of that sort often make children look older than
they are. From this forlorn child I learned, that she
had slept and lived there alone, for some time before I
came: and great joy the poor creature expressed, when
she found that I was, in future, to be her companion
through the hours of darkness. The house was large;
and, from the want of furniture, the noise of the rats
made a prodigious echoing on the spacious staircase
and hall; and, amidst the real fleshly ills of cold, and, I
fear, hunger, the forsaken child had found leisure to
suffer still more (it appeared) from the self-created one
of ghosts. I promised her protection against all ghosts
whatsoever: but, alas! I could offer her no other
assistance. We lay upon the floor, with a bundle of
cursed law papers for a pillow: but with no other covering than a sort of large horseman's cloak: afterwards,
however, we discovered, in a garret, an old sofa-cover,
a small piece of rug, and some fragments of other
articles, which added a little to our warmth. The poor
child crept close to me for warmth, and for security
against her ghostly enemies. When I was not more
than usually ill, I took her into my arms, so that, in
general, she was tolerably warm, and often slept when
I could not: for, during the last two months of my
sufferings, I slept much in the day-time, and was apt to
fall into transient dozings at all hours. But my sleep

---

⁹ Wordsworth's sonnet "Nuns fret not . . ." (1807), l. 3.
¹⁰ In four paragraphs here omitted, De Quincey describes his
adventures in Wales before proceeding to London. He had
originally intended to depart Manchester for Westmorland in the
hope of meeting Wordsworth, of whose poetry he was an
enthusiastic admirer.

distressed me more than my watching: for, besides the tumultuousness of my dreams (which were only not so awful as those which I shall have to describe hereafter as produced by opium), my sleep was never more than what is called *dog-sleep*; so that I could hear myself moaning, and was often, as it seemed to me, wakened suddenly by my own voice; and, about this time, a hideous sensation began to haunt me as soon as I fell into a slumber, which has since returned upon me, at different periods of my life, viz. a sort of twitching (I know not where, but apparently about the region of the stomach), which compelled me violently to throw out my feet for the sake of relieving it. This sensation coming on as soon as I began to sleep, and the effort to relieve it constantly awaking me, at length I slept only from exhaustion; and from increasing weakness (as I said before) I was constantly falling asleep, and constantly awaking. Meantime, the master of the house sometimes came in upon us suddenly, and very early, sometimes not till ten o'clock, sometimes not at all. He was in constant fear of bailiffs: improving on the plan of Cromwell,[11] every night he slept in a different quarter of London; and I observed that he never failed to examine, through a private window, the appearance of those who knocked at the door, before he would allow it to be opened. He breakfasted alone: indeed, his tea equipage would hardly have admitted of his hazarding an invitation to a second person—any more than the quantity of esculent *matériel*, which, for the most part, was little more than a roll, or a few biscuits, which he had bought on his road from the place where he had slept. Or, if he *had* asked a party, as I once learnedly and facetiously observed to him— the several members of it must have *stood* in the relation to each other (not *sat* in any relation whatever) of succession, as the metaphysicians have it, and not of co-existence; in the relation of the parts of time, and not of the parts of space. During his breakfast, I generally contrived a reason for lounging in; and, with an air of as much indifference as I could assume, took up such fragments as he had left—sometimes, indeed, there were none at all. In doing this, I committed no robbery except upon the man himself, who was thus obliged (I believe) now and then to send out at noon for an extra biscuit; for, as to the poor child, *she* was never admitted into his study (if I may give that name to his chief depository of parchments, law writings,

&c.); that room was to her the Blue-beard room of the house, being regularly locked on his departure to dinner, about six o'clock, which usually was his final departure for the night. Whether this child were an illegitimate daughter of Mr. ——, or only a servant, I could not ascertain; she did not herself know; but certainly she was treated altogether as a menial servant. No sooner did Mr. —— make his appearance, than she went below stairs, brushed his shoes, coat, &c.; and, except when she was summoned to run an errand, she never emerged from the dismal Tartarus of the kitchens, &c. to the upper air, until my welcome knock at night called up her little trembling footsteps to the front door. Of her life during the day-time, however, I knew little but what I gathered from her own account at night; for, as soon as the hours of business commenced, I saw that my absence would be acceptable; and, in general, therefore, I went off, and sat in the parks, or elsewhere, until night-fall.

But who, and what, meantime, was the master of the house himself? Reader, he was one of those anomalous practitioners in lower departments of the law, who— what shall I say?—who, on prudential reasons, or from necessity, deny themselves all indulgence in the luxury of too delicate a conscience: (a periphrasis which might be abridged considerably, but *that* I leave to the reader's taste:) in many walks of life, a conscience is a more expensive encumbrance, than a wife or a carriage; and just as people talk of "laying down"[12] their carriages, so I supposed my friend, Mr. —— had "laid down" his conscience for a time; meaning, doubtless, to resume it as soon as he could afford it. The inner economy of such a man's daily life would present a most strange picture, if I could allow myself to amuse the reader at his expense. Even with my limited opportunities for observing what went on, I saw many scenes of London intrigues, and complex chicanery, "cycle and epicycle, orb in orb,"[13] at which I sometimes smile to this day—and at which I smiled then, in spite of my misery. My situation, however, at that time, gave me little experience, in my own person, of any qualities in Mr. ——'s character but such as did him honour; and of his whole strange composition, I must forget every thing but that towards me he was obliging, and, to the extent of his power, generous.

That power was not, indeed, very extensive; however, in common with the rats, I sat rent free; and, as Dr. Johnson has recorded,[14] that he never but once

[11] As reported in Clarendon's *History of the Rebellion*, Chapter XV, Cromwell's fear of assassination led him to lodge rarely "two nights together in one chamber, but [he] had many furnished and prepared, to which his own key conveyed him and those he would have with him, when he had a mind to go to bed ...".

[12] Relinquishing.
[13] *Paradise Lost*, VIII, 84.
[14] The remark is reported in Mrs. Piozzi's *Anecdotes of the late Samuel Johnson* (1786), pp. 102–103.

in his life had as much wall-fruit as he could eat, so let me be grateful, that on that single occasion I had as large a choice of apartments in a London mansion as I could possibly desire. Except the Blue-beard room, which the poor child believed to be haunted, all others, from the attics to the cellars, were at our service; "the world was all before us;"[15] and we pitched our tent for the night in any spot we chose. This house I have already described as a large one; it stands in a conspicuous situation, and in a well-known part of London. Many of my readers will have passed it, I doubt not, within a few hours of reading this. For myself, I never fail to visit it when business draws me to London; about ten o'clock, this very night, August 15, 1821, being my birth-day,—I turned aside from my evening walk, down Oxford-street, purposely to take a glance at it: it is now occupied by a respectable family; and, by the lights in the front drawing-room, I observed a domestic party, assembled perhaps at tea, and apparently cheerful and gay. Marvellous contrast in my eyes to the darkness—cold—silence—and desolation of that same house eighteen years ago, when its nightly occupants were one famishing scholar, and a neglected child.—Her, by the bye, in after years, I vainly endeavoured to trace. Apart from her situation, she was not what would be called an interesting child: she was neither pretty, nor quick in understanding, nor remarkably pleasing in manners. But, thank God! even in those years I needed not the embellishments of novel-accessaries to conciliate my affections; plain human nature, in its humblest and most homely apparel, was enough for me: and I loved the child because she was my partner in wretchedness. If she is now living, she is probably a mother, with children of her own; but, as I have said, I could never trace her.

This I regret, but another person there was at that time, whom I have since sought to trace with far deeper earnestness, and with far deeper sorrow at my failure. This person was a young woman, and one of that unhappy class who subsist upon the wages of prostitution. I feel no shame, nor have any reason to feel it, in avowing, that I was then on familiar and friendly terms with many women in that unfortunate condition. The reader needs neither smile at this avowal, nor frown. For, not to remind my classical readers of the old Latin proverb—"*Sine Cerere*,"[16] &c., it may well be supposed that in the existing state of my purse, my connexion with such women could not have been an impure one. But the truth is, that

at no time of my life have I been a person to hold myself polluted by the touch or approach of any creature that wore a human shape: on the contrary, from my very earliest youth it has been my pride to converse familiarly, *more Socratico*,[17] with all human beings, man, woman, and child, that chance might fling in my way: a practice which is friendly to the knowledge of human nature, to good feelings, and to that frankness of address which becomes a man who would be thought a philosopher. For a philosopher should not see with the eyes of the poor limitary creature, calling himself a man of the world, and filled with narrow and self-regarding prejudices of birth and education, but should look upon himself as a catholic creature, and as standing in an equal relation to high and low—to educated and uneducated, to the guilty and the innocent. Being myself at that time of necessity a peripatetic, or a walker of the street, I naturally fell in more frequently with those female peripatetics who are technically called street-walkers. Many of these women had occasionally taken my part against watchmen who wished to drive me off the steps of houses where I was sitting. But one amongst them, the one on whose account I have at all introduced this subject—yet no! let me not class thee, oh noble-minded Ann——, with that order of women; let me find, if it be possible, some gentler name to designate the condition of her to whose bounty and compassion, ministering to my necessities when all the world had forsaken me, I owe it that I am at this time alive.—For many weeks I had walked at nights with this poor friendless girl up and down Oxford-street, or had rested with her on steps and under the shelter of porticos. She could not be so old as myself: she told me, indeed, that she had not completed her sixteenth year. By such questions as my interest about her prompted, I had gradually drawn forth her simple history. Hers was a case of ordinary occurrence (as I have since had reason to think), and one in which, if London beneficence had better adapted its arrangements to meet it, the power of the law might oftener be interposed to protect, and to avenge. But the stream of London charity flows in a channel which, though deep and mighty, is yet noiseless and underground; not obvious or readily accessible to poor houseless wanderers: and it cannot be denied that the outside air and frame-work of London society is harsh, cruel, and repulsive. In any case, however, I saw that part of her injuries might easily have been redressed; and I urged her often and earnestly to lay her complaint before a magistrate: friendless as she was, I assured her that

[15] *Paradise Lost*, XII, 646.
[16] "Sine Cerere et Libero friget Venus" ("Without Ceres and Bacchus [food and drink] Venus is a-chill"). The proverb is quoted in Terence's *Eunuchus*, IV, v, 5.

[17] *more Socratico*: "in the manner of Socrates."

she would meet with immediate attention; and that English justice, which was no respecter of persons, would speedily and amply avenge her on the brutal ruffian who had plundered her little property. She promised me often that she would; but she delayed taking the steps I pointed out from time to time: for she was timid and dejected to a degree which showed how deeply sorrow had taken hold of her young heart: and perhaps she thought justly that the most upright judge, and the most righteous tribunals, could do nothing to repair her heaviest wrongs. Something, however, would perhaps have been done: for it had been settled between us at length, but unhappily on the very last time but one that I was ever to see her, that in a day or two we should go together before a magistrate, and that I should speak on her behalf. This little service it was destined, however, that I should never realise. Meantime, that which she rendered to me, and which was greater than I could ever have repaid her, was this:—One night, when we were pacing slowly along Oxford-street, and after a day when I had felt more than usually ill and faint, I requested her to turn off with me into Soho-square: thither we went; and we sat down on the steps of a house, which, to this hour, I never pass without a pang of grief, and an inner act of homage to the spirit of that unhappy girl, in memory of the noble action which she there performed. Suddenly, as we sat, I grew much worse: I had been leaning my head against her bosom; and all at once I sank from her arms and fell backwards on the steps. From the sensations I then had, I felt an inner conviction of the liveliest kind that without some powerful and reviving stimulus, I should either have died on the spot—or should at least have sunk to a point of exhaustion from which all re-ascent under my friendless circumstances would soon have become hopeless. Then it was, at this crisis of my fate, that my poor orphan companion—who had herself met with little but injuries in this world—stretched out a saving hand to me. Uttering a cry of terror, but without a moment's delay, she ran off into Oxford-street, and in less time than could be imagined, returned to me with a glass of port wine and spices, that acted upon my empty stomach (which at that time would have rejected all solid food) with an instantaneous power of restoration: and for this glass the generous girl without a murmur paid out of her own humble purse at a time—be it remembered!—when she had scarcely wherewithal to purchase the bare necessaries of life, and when she could have no reason to expect that I should ever be able to reimburse her.——Oh! youthful benefactress! how often in succeeding years, standing in solitary places, and thinking of thee with grief of heart and perfect love, how often have I wished

that, as in ancient times the curse of a father was believed to have a supernatural power, and to pursue its object with a fatal necessity of self-fulfilment,— even so the benediction of a heart oppressed with gratitude, might have a like prerogative; might have power given to it from above to chase—to haunt—to way-lay—to overtake—to pursue thee into the central darkness of a London brothel, or (if it were possible) into the darkness of the grave—there to awaken thee with an authentic message of peace and forgiveness, and of final reconciliation!

I do not often weep: for not only do my thoughts on subjects connected with the chief interests of man daily, nay hourly, descend a thousand fathoms "too deep for tears;" [18] not only does the sternness of my habits of thought present an antagonism to the feelings which prompt tears—wanting of necessity to those who, being protected usually by their levity from any tendency to meditative sorrow, would by that same levity be made incapable of resisting it on any casual access of such feelings:—but also, I believe that all minds which have contemplated such objects as deeply as I have done, must, for their own protection from utter despondency, have early encouraged and cherished some tranquillizing belief as to the future balances and the hieroglyphic meanings of human sufferings. On these accounts, I am cheerful to this hour; and, as I have said, I do not often weep. Yet some feelings, though not deeper or more passionate, are more tender than others; and often, when I walk at this time in Oxford-street by dreamy lamp-light, and hear those airs played on a barrel-organ which years ago solaced me and my dear companion (as I must always call her), I shed tears, and muse with myself at the mysterious dispensation which so suddenly and so critically separated us for ever. How it happened, the reader will understand from what remains of this introductory narration.

Soon after the period of the last incident I have recorded, I met, in Albemarle-street, a gentleman of his late majesty's household. This gentleman had received hospitalities, on different occasions, from my family: and he challenged me upon the strength of my family likeness. I did not attempt any disguise: I answered his questions ingenuously,—and, on his pledging his word of honour that he would not betray me to my guardians, I gave him an address to my friend the attorney's. The next day I received from him a 10l. Bank-note. The letter enclosing it was delivered with other letters of business to the attorney; but, though his look and manner informed me that he

---

[18] Wordsworth's "Intimations Ode," l. 203.

suspected its contents, he gave it up to me honourably and without demur.

This present, from the particular service to which it was applied, leads me naturally to speak of the purpose which had allured me up to London, and which I had been (to use a forensic word) *soliciting* from the first day of my arrival in London, to that of my final departure.

In so mighty a world as London, it will surprise my readers that I should not have found some means of staving off the last extremities of penury: and it will strike them that two resources at least must have been open to me,—viz. either to seek assistance from the friends of my family, or to turn my youthful talents and attainments into some channel of pecuniary emolument. As to the first course, I may observe, generally, that what I dreaded beyond all other evils was the chance of being reclaimed by my guardians; not doubting that whatever power the law gave them would have been enforced against me to the utmost; that is, to the extremity of forcibly restoring me to the school which I had quitted: a restoration which as it would in my eyes have been a dishonour, even if submitted to voluntarily, could not fail, when extorted from me in contempt and defiance of my known wishes and efforts, to have been a humiliation worse to me than death, and which would indeed have terminated in death. I was, therefore, shy enough of applying for assistance even in those quarters where I was sure of receiving it—at the risk of furnishing my guardians with any clue for recovering me. But, as to London in particular, though, doubtless, my father had in his life-time had many friends there, yet (as ten years had passed since his death) I remembered few of them even by name: and never having seen London before, except once for a few hours, I knew not the address of even those few. To this mode of gaining help, there-fore, in part the difficulty, but much more the paramount fear which I have mentioned, habitually indisposed me. In regard to the other mode, I now feel half inclined to join my reader in wondering that I should have overlooked it. As a corrector of Greek proofs (if in no other way), I might doubtless have gained enough for my slender wants. Such an office as this I could have discharged with an exemplary and punctual accuracy that would soon have gained me the confidence of my employers. But it must not be forgotten that, even for such an office as this, it was necessary that I should first of all have an introduction to some respectable publisher: and this I had no means of obtaining. To say the truth, however, it had never once occurred to me to think of literary labours as a source of profit. No mode sufficiently speedy of obtaining money had ever occurred to me, but that

of borrowing it on the strength of my future claims and expectations. This mode I sought by every avenue to compass, and amongst other persons I applied to a Jew named D——.[*]

To this Jew, and to other advertising money-lenders (some of whom were, I believe, also Jews), I had intro-duced myself with an account of my expectations; which account, on examining my father's will, at Doctor's Commons, they had ascertained to be correct. The person there mentioned as the second son of ——, was found to have all the claims (or more than all) that I had stated: but one question still remained, which the faces of the Jews pretty significantly suggested,—was *I* that person? This doubt had never occurred to me as a possible one: I had rather feared, whenever my Jewish friends scrutinized me keenly, that I might be too well known to be that person—and that some scheme might be passing in their minds for entrapping me, and selling me to my guardians. It was strange to me to find my own self, *materialiter* considered (so I expressed it, for I doted on logical accuracy of distinc-tions), accused, or at least suspected, of counterfeiting my own self, *formaliter* considered. However, to satisfy their scruples, I took the only course in my power. Whilst I was in Wales, I had received various letters from young friends: these I produced: for I carried them constantly in my pocket—being, indeed, by this time, almost the only relics of my personal incum-

---

[*] To this same Jew, by the way, some eighteen months afterwards, I applied again on the same business; and, dating at that time from a respectable college, I was fortunate enough to gain his serious attention to my proposals. My necessities had not arisen from any extravagance, or youthful levities (these my habits and the nature of my pleasures raised me far above), but simply from the vindictive malice of my guardian, who, when he found himself no longer able to prevent me from going to the university, had, as a parting token of his good nature, refused to sign an order for granting me a shilling beyond the allowance made to me at school—viz. 100*l.* per annum. Upon this sum it was, in my time, barely possible to have lived at college; and not possible to a man who, though above the paltry affection of ostentatious disregard for money, and without any expensive tastes, confided, nevertheless, rather too much in servants, and did not delight in the petty details of minute economy. I soon, therefore, became embarrassed: and at length, after a most voluminous negotiation with the Jew (some parts of which, if I had leisure to rehearse them, would greatly amuse my readers), I was put in possession of the sum I asked for—on the "regular" terms of paying the Jew seventeen and a half per cent., by way of annuity, on all the money furnished; Israel, on his part, graciously resuming no more than about ninety guineas of the said money, on account of an attorney's bill (for what services, to whom rendered, and when, whether at the siege of Jerusalem—at the building of the Second Temple—or on some earlier occasion, I have not yet been able to discover). How many perches this bill measured I really forget: but I still keep it in a cabinet of natural curiosities; and sometime or other, I believe, I shall present it to the British Museum.

brances (excepting the clothes I wore) which I had not in one way or other disposed of. Most of these letters were from the Earl of ——,[19] who was at that time my chief (or rather only) confidential friend. These letters were dated from Eton. I had also some from the Marquess of ——, his father, who, though absorbed in agricultural pursuits, yet having been an Etonian himself, and as good a scholar as a nobleman needs to be—still retained an affection for classical studies, and for youthful scholars. He had, accordingly, from the time that I was fifteen, corresponded with me; sometimes upon the great improvements which he had made, or was meditating, in the counties of M— and Sl— since I had been there; sometimes upon the merits of a Latin poet; at other times suggesting subjects to me, on which he wished me to write verses.

On reading the letters, one of my Jewish friends agreed to furnish two or three hundred pounds on my personal security—provided I could persuade the young Earl, who was, by the way, not older than myself, to guarantee the payment on our coming of age: the Jew's final object being, as I now suppose, not the trifling profit he could expect to make by me, but the prospect of establishing a connexion with my noble friend, whose immense expectations were well known to him. In pursuance of this proposal on the part of the Jew, about eight or nine days after I had received the 10l., I prepared to go down to Eton. Nearly 3l. of the money I had given to my money-lending friend, on his alleging that the stamps must be bought, in order that the writings might be preparing whilst I was away from London. I thought in my heart that he was lying; but I did not wish to give him any excuse for charging his own delays upon me. A smaller sum I had given to my friend the attorney (who was connected with the money-lenders as their lawyer), to which, indeed, he was entitled for his unfurnished lodgings. About fifteen shillings I had employed in re-establishing (though in a very humble way) my dress. Of the remainder I gave one quarter to Ann, meaning on my return to have divided with her whatever might remain. These arrangements made,—soon after six o'clock, on a dark winter evening, I set off, accompanied by Ann, towards Piccadilly; for it was my intention to go down as far as Salt-hill on the Bath or Bristol mail. Our course lay through a part of the town which has now all disappeared, so that I can no longer retrace its ancient boundaries: Swallow-street, I think it was called. Having time enough before us, however, we bore away to the left until we came into Golden-square: there, near the corner of Sherrard-street, we

sat down; not wishing to part in the tumult and blaze of Piccadilly. I had told her of my plans some time before: and I now assured her again that she should share in my good fortune, if I met with any; and that I would never forsake her, as soon as I had power to protect her. This I fully intended, as much from inclination as from a sense of duty: for, setting aside gratitude, which in any case must have made me her debtor for life, I loved her as affectionately as if she had been my sister: and at this moment, with seven-fold tenderness, from pity at witnessing her extreme dejection. I had, apparently, most reason for dejection, because I was leaving the saviour of my life: yet I, considering the shock my health had received, was cheerful and full of hope. She, on the contrary, who was parting with one who had little means of serving her, except by kindness and brotherly treatment, was overcome by sorrow; so that, when I kissed her at our final farewell, she put her arms about my neck, and wept without speaking a word. I hoped to return in a week at farthest, and I agreed with her that on the fifth night from that, and every night afterwards, she should wait for me at six o'clock, near the bottom of Great Titchfield-street, which had been our customary haven, as it were, of rendezvous, to prevent our missing each other in the great Mediterranean of Oxford-street. This, and other measures of precaution I took: one only I forgot. She had either never told me, or (as a matter of no great interest) I had forgotten, her sur-name. It is a general practice, indeed, with girls of humble rank in her unhappy condition, not (as novel-reading women of higher pretensions) to style them-selves—*Miss Douglass, Miss Montague*, &c. but simply by their Christian names, *Mary, Jane, Frances*, &c. Her surname, as the surest means of tracing her hereafter, I ought now to have inquired: but the truth is, having no reason to think that our meeting could, in consequence of a short interruption, be more difficult or uncertain than it had been for so many weeks, I had scarcely for a moment adverted to it as necessary, or placed it amongst my memoranda against this parting interview: and, my final anxieties being spent in com-forting her with hopes, and in pressing upon her the necessity of getting some medicines for a violent cough and hoarseness with which she was troubled, I wholly forgot it until it was too late to recal her.[20]

*   *   *   *   *

Recomforted by this promise, which was not quite equal to the best, but far above the worst that I had

---

[19] Referring to the Earl of Altamont, formerly Lord Westport, with whom De Quincey had traveled to Ireland in 1800.

[20] Here are omitted four paragraphs describing De Quincey's journey to Eton, where he finds his friend absent, but another acquaintance, the Earl of Desart, gives security for a loan.

pictured to myself as possible, I returned in a Windsor coach to London three days after I had quitted it. And now I come to the end of my story:—the Jews did not approve of Lord D——'s terms; whether they would in the end have acceded to them, and were only seeking time for making due inquires, I know not; but many delays were made—time passed on—the small fragment of my Bank-note had just melted away; and before any conclusion could have been put to the business, I must have relapsed into my former state of wretchedness. Suddenly, however, at this crisis, an opening was made, almost by accident, for reconciliation with my friends. I quitted London, in haste, for a remote part of England: after some time, I proceeded to the university; and it was not until many months had passed away, that I had it in my power again to revisit the ground which had become so interesting to me, and to this day remains so, as the chief scene of my youthful sufferings.

Meantime, what had become of poor Ann? For her I have reserved my concluding words: according to our agreement, I sought her daily, and waited for her every night, so long as I staid in London, at the corner of Titchfield-street. I inquired for her of every one who was likely to know her; and, during the last hours of my stay in London, I put into activity every means of tracing her that my knowledge of London suggested, and the limited extent of my power made possible. The street where she had lodged I knew, but not the house; and I remembered at last some account which she had given me of ill treatment from her landlord, which made it probable that she had quitted those lodgings before we parted. She had few acquaintance; most people, besides, thought that the earnestness of my inquiries arose from motives which moved their laughter, or their slight regard; and others, thinking I was in chase of a girl who had robbed me of some trifles, were naturally and excusably indisposed to give me any clue to her, if, indeed, they had any to give. Finally, as my despairing resource, on the day I left London I put into the hands of the only person who (I was sure) must know Ann by sight, from having been in company with us once or twice, an address to —— in ——shire, at that time the residence of my family. But, to this hour, I have never heard a syllable about her. This, amongst such troubles as most men meet with in this life, has been my heaviest affliction.— If she lived, doubtless we must have been sometimes in search of each other, at the very same moment, through the mighty labyrinths of London; perhaps even within a few feet of each other—a barrier no wider in a London street, often amounting in the end to a separation for eternity! During some years, I hoped that she *did* live; and I suppose that, in the

literal and unrhetorical use of the word *myriad*, I may say that on my different visits to London, I have looked into many, many myriads of female faces, in the hope of meeting her. I should know her again amongst a thousand, if I saw her for a moment; for, though not handsome, she had a sweet expression of countenance, and a peculiar and graceful carriage of the head.—I sought her, I have said, in hope. So it was for years; but now I should fear to see her; and her cough, which grieved me when I parted with her, is now my consolation. I now wish to see her no longer; but think of her, more gladly, as one long since laid in the grave; in the grave, I would hope, of a Magdalen; taken away, before injuries and cruelty had blotted out and transfigured her ingenuous nature, or the brutalities of ruffians had completed the ruin they had begun.

[September 1821]   [1822]

PART II

SO THEN, Oxford-street, stony-hearted stepmother! thou that listenest to the sighs of orphans, and drinkest the tears of children, at length I was dismissed from thee: the time was come at last that I no more should pace in anguish thy never-ending terraces; no more should dream, and wake in captivity to the pangs of hunger. Successors, too many, to myself and Ann, have, doubtless, since trodden in our footsteps,— inheritors of our calamities: other orphans than Ann have sighed: tears have been shed by other children: and thou, Oxford-street, hast since, doubtless, echoed to the groans of innumerable hearts. For myself, however, the storm which I had outlived seemed to have been the pledge of a long fair-weather; the premature sufferings which I had paid down, to have been accepted as a ransom for many years to come, as a price of long immunity from sorrow: and if again I walked in London, a solitary and contemplative man (as oftentimes I did), I walked for the most part in serenity and peace of mind. And, although it is true that the calamities of my noviciate in London had struck root so deeply in my bodily constitution that afterwards they shot up and flourished afresh, and grew into a noxious umbrage that has overshadowed and darkened my latter years, yet these second assaults of suffering were met with a fortitude more confirmed, with the resources of a maturer intellect, and with alleviations from sympathising affection—how deep and tender!

Thus, however, with whatsoever alleviations, years that were far asunder were bound together by subtle links of suffering derived from a common root. And herein I notice an instance of the short-sightedness of human desires, that oftentimes on moonlight nights, during my first mournful abode in London, my consolation was (if such it could be thought) to gaze from Oxford-street up every avenue in succession which pierces through the heart of Marylebone to the fields and the woods; and *that*, said I, travelling with my eyes up the long vistas which lay part in light and part in shade, "*that* is the road to the north, and therefore to ———,[1] and if I had the wings of a dove, *that* way I would fly for comfort."[2] Thus I said, and thus I wished, in my blindness; yet, even in that very northern region it was, even in that very valley, nay, in that very house to which my erroneous wishes pointed, that this second birth of my sufferings began; and that they again threatened to besiege the citadel of life and hope. There it was, that for years I was persecuted by visions as ugly, and as ghastly phantoms as ever haunted the couch of an Orestes: and in this unhappier than he, that sleep, which comes to all as a respite and a restoration, and to him especially, as a blessed* balm for his wounded heart and his haunted brain, visited me as my bitterest scourge. Thus blind was I in my desires; yet, if a veil interposes between the dimsightedness of man and his future calamities, the same veil hides from him their alleviations; and a grief which had not been feared is met by consolations which had not been hoped. I, therefore, who participated, as it were, in the troubles of Orestes (excepting only in his agitated conscience), participated no less in all his supports: my Eumenides, like his, were at my bed-feet, and stared in upon me through the curtains: but, watching by my pillow, or defrauding herself of sleep to bear me company through the heavy watches of the night, sat my Electra: for thou, beloved M.,[4] dear companion of my later years, thou wast my Electra! and neither in nobility of mind nor in long-suffering affection, wouldst permit that a Grecian sister should excel an English wife. For thou thoughtest not much to stoop to humble offices of kindness, and to servile† ministrations of tenderest affection;—to wipe away for years the unwholesome dews upon the forehead, or to refresh the lips when parched and baked with fever; nor, even when thy own peaceful slumbers had by long sympathy become infected with the

---

* Φιλον ὑπου θελγητρον ἐπικουρον νοσου.[3]

† ἠδυ δουλευμα. *Eurip. Orest.*[5]

◇◆◇◆◇◆◇◆◇◆◇◆◇◆◇◆◇◆◇◆◇◆◇

[1] Referring to Wordsworth, then living at Dove Cottage in Grasmere, where De Quincey had taken up long-term residence in 1809. See "Preliminary Confessions," footnote 10, p. 556.

[2] See Psalms, lv, 6.

[3] De Quincey cites Euripides' *Orestes*, l. 211, "dear spell of sleep, assuager of disease." (Arthur S. Way translation, Loeb Classical Library, Harvard University Press).

[4] Margaret Simpson, whom De Quincey had married in 1817.

[5] L. 221 ("sweet service").

---

spectacle of my dread contest with phantoms and shadowy enemies that oftentimes bade me "sleep no more!"[6]—not even then, didst thou utter a complaint or any murmur, nor withdraw thy angelic smiles, nor shrink from thy service of love more than Electra did of old. For she too, though she was a Grecian woman, and the daughter of the king‡ of men, yet wept sometimes, and hid her face§ in her robe.

But these troubles are past: and thou wilt read these records of a period so dolorous to us both as the legend of some hideous dream that can return no more. Meantime, I am again in London: and again I pace the terraces of Oxford-street by night: and oftentimes, when I am oppressed by anxieties that demand all my philosophy and the comfort of thy presence to support, and yet remember that I am separated from thee by three hundred miles, and the length of three dreary months,—I look up the streets that run northwards from Oxford-street, upon moonlight nights, and recollect my youthful ejaculation of anguish;—and remembering that thou art sitting alone in that same valley, and mistress of that very house to which my heart turned in its blindness nineteen years ago, I think that, though blind indeed, and scattered to the winds of late, the promptings of my heart may yet have had reference to a remoter time, and may be justified if read in another meaning:—and, if I could allow myself to descend again to the impotent wishes of childhood, I should again say to myself, as I look to the north, "Oh, that I had the wings of a dove—" and with how just a confidence in thy good and gracious nature might I add the other half of my early ejaculation—"And *that* way I would fly for comfort."

F R O M

THE PLEASURES OF OPIUM

I<small>T IS</small> so long since I first took opium, that if it had been a trifling incident in my life, I might have for-

---

‡ ἀναξἀνδρων ᾽Αγαμεμνων.[7]

§ ὀμμα θεισ ἐισω πεπλων. The scholar will know that throughout this passage I refer to the early scenes of the Orestes; one of the most beautiful exhibitions of the domestic affection which even the dramas of Euripides can furnish. To the English reader, it may be necessary to say, that the situation at the opening of the drama is that of a brother attended only by his sister during the demoniacal possession of a suffering conscience (or, in the mythology of the play, haunted by the furies), and in circumstances of immediate danger from enemies, and of desertion or cold regard from nominal friends.[8]

◇◆◇◆◇◆◇◆◇◆◇◆◇◆◇◆◇◆◇◆◇◆◇

[6] *Macbeth*, II, ii, 35.

[7] "King of men Agamemnon," an epithet from the *Iliad*.

[8] The Greek phrase, "muffling o'er thine head," occurs at l. 280 of Euripides' tragedy.

gotten its date: but cardinal events are not to be forgotten; and from circumstances connected with it, I remember that it must be referred to the autumn of 1804. During that season I was in London, having come thither for the first time since my entrance at college. And my introduction to opium arose in the following way. From an early age I had been accustomed to wash my head in cold water at least once a day: being suddenly seized with tooth-ache, I attributed it to some relaxation caused by an accidental intermission of that practice; jumped out of bed; plunged my head into a basin of cold water; and with hair thus wetted went to sleep. The next morning, as I need hardly say, I awoke with excruciating rheumatic pains of the head and face, from which I had hardly any respite for about twenty days. On the twenty-first day, I think it was, and on a Sunday, that I went out into the streets; rather to run away, if possible, from my torments, than with any distinct purpose. By accident I met a college acquaintance who recommended opium. Opium! dread agent of unimaginable pleasure and pain! I had heard of it as I had of manna or of ambrosia, but no further: how unmeaning a sound was it at that time! what solemn chords does it now strike upon my heart! what heart-quaking vibrations of sad and happy remembrances! Reverting for a moment to these, I feel a mystic importance attached to the minutest circumstances connected with the place and the time, and the man (if man he was) that first laid open to me the Paradise of Opium-eaters. It was a Sunday afternoon, wet and cheerless: and a duller spectacle this earth of ours has not to show than a rainy Sunday in London. My road homewards lay through Oxford-street; and near "the *stately* Pantheon,"[1] (as Mr. Wordsworth has obligingly called it) I saw a druggist's shop. The druggist, unconscious minister of celestial pleasures!—as if in sympathy with the rainy Sunday, looked dull and stupid, just as any mortal druggist might be expected to look on a Sunday: and, when I asked for the tincture of opium, he gave it to me as any other man might do: and furthermore, out of my shilling, returned me what seemed to be real copper halfpence, taken out of a real wooden drawer. Nevertheless, in spite of such indications of humanity, he has ever since existed in my mind as the beatific vision of an immortal druggist, sent down to earth on a special mission to myself. And it confirms me in this way of considering him that, when I next came up to London, I sought him near the stately Pantheon, and found him not: and thus to me, who knew not his name (if indeed he had one) he seemed rather to have vanished from Oxford-street than to have removed in any bodily

◇◇◇◇◇◇◇◇◇◇◇◇◇◇◇◇◇◇◇◇◇◇◇◇◇◇◇◇◇◇

[1] Wordsworth's "Power of Music" (1807), l. 3.

fashion. The reader may choose to think of him as, possibly, no more than a sublunary druggist: it may be so: but my faith is better: I believe him to have evanesced,* or evaporated. So unwillingly would I connect any mortal remembrances with that hour, and place, and creature, that first brought me acquainted with the celestial drug.

Arrived at my lodgings, it may be supposed that I lost not a moment in taking the quantity prescribed. I was necessarily ignorant of the whole art and mystery of opium-taking: and, what I took, I took under every disadvantage. But I took it:—and in an hour, oh! heavens! what a revulsion! what an upheaving, from its lowest depths, of the inner spirit! what an apocalypse of the world within me! That my pains had vanished, was now a trifle in my eyes:—this negative effect was swallowed up in the immensity of those positive effects which had opened before me—in the abyss of divine enjoyment thus suddenly revealed. Here was a panacea —a φαρμακον νηπενθες[3] for all human woes: here was the secret of happiness, about which philosophers had disputed for so many ages, at once discovered: happiness might now be bought for a penny, and carried in the waistcoat pocket: portable ecstasies might be had corked up in a pint bottle: and peace of mind could be sent down in gallons by the mail coach. But, if I talk in this way, the reader will think I am laughing: and I can assure him, that nobody will laugh long who deals much with opium: its pleasures even are of a grave and solemn complexion; and in his happiest state, the opium-eater cannot present himself in the character of *l'Allegro*: even then, he speaks and thinks as becomes *Il Penseroso*. Nevertheless, I have a very reprehensible way of jesting at times in the midst of my own misery: and, unless when I am checked by some more powerful feelings, I am afraid I shall be guilty of this indecent practice even in these annals of suffering or enjoyment. The reader must allow a little to my infirm nature in this respect: and

* *Evanesced*:—this way of going off the stage of life appears to have been well known in the 17th century, but at that time to have been considered a peculiar privilege of blood-royal, and by no means to be allowed to druggists. For about the year 1686, a poet of rather ominous name (and who, by the by, did ample justice to his name), viz. Mr. *Flat-man*, in speaking of the death of Charles II. expresses his surprise that any prince should commit so absurd an act as dying; because, says he,

Kings should disdain to die, and only *disappear*.

They should *abscond*, that is, into the other world.[2]

◇◇◇◇◇◇◇◇◇◇◇◇◇◇◇◇◇◇◇◇◇◇◇◇◇◇◇◇◇◇

[2] De Quincey gives a free rendering of lines in the first stanza of an ode "On the much lamented Death of our late Sovereign Lord King Charles II. of Blessed Memory" (1685) by Thomas Flatman (1635–1688).

[3] φαρμακον νηπενθες: "a drug to quiet all pain and strife." *Odyssey*, IV, 220–21.

with a few indulgences of that sort, I shall endeavour to be as grave, if not drowsy, as fits a theme like opium, so anti-mercurial as it really is, and so drowsy as it is falsely reputed.

And, first, one word with respect to its bodily effects: for upon all that has been hitherto written on the subject of opium, whether by travellers in Turkey (who may plead their privilege of lying as an old immemorial right), or by professors of medicine, writing *ex cathedrâ*,—I have but one emphatic criticism to pronounce—Lies! lies! lies! I remember once, in passing a bookstall, to have caught these words from a page of some satiric author:—"By this time I became convinced that the London newspapers spoke truth at least twice a week, viz. on Tuesday and Saturday, and might safely be depended upon for —— the list of bankrupts." In like manner, I do by no means deny that some truths have been delivered to the world in regard to opium: thus it has been repeatedly affirmed by the learned, that opium is a dusky brown in colour; and this, take notice, I grant: secondly, that it is rather dear; which also I grant: for in my time, East-India opium has been three guineas a pound, and Turkey eight: and, thirdly, that if you eat a good deal of it, most probably you must—do what is particularly disagreeable to any man of regular habits, viz. die.* These weighty propositions are, all and singular, true: I cannot gainsay them: and truth ever was, and will be, commendable. But in these three theorems, I believe we have exhausted the stock of knowledge as yet accumulated by man on the subject of opium. And therefore, worthy doctors, as there seems to be room for further discoveries, stand aside, and allow me to come forward and lecture on this matter.

First, then, it is not so much affirmed as taken for granted, by all who ever mention opium, formally or incidentally, that it does, or can, produce intoxication. Now, reader, assure yourself, *meo periculo*,[5] that no quantity of opium ever did, or could intoxicate. As to the tincture of opium (commonly called laudanum)[6] *that* might certainly intoxicate if a man could bear to

take enough of it; but why? because it contains so much proof spirit, and not because it contains so much opium. But crude opium, I affirm peremptorily, is incapable of producing any state of body at all resembling that which is produced by alcohol: and not in *degree* only incapable, but even in *kind*: it is not in the quantity of its effects merely, but in the quality, that it differs altogether. The pleasure given by wine is always mounting, and tending to a crisis, after which it declines: that from opium, when once generated, is stationary for eight or ten hours: the first, to borrow a technical distinction from medicine, is a case of acute—the second, of chronic pleasure: the one is a flame, the other a steady and equable glow. But the main distinction lies in this, that whereas wine disorders the mental faculties, opium, on the contrary (if taken in a proper manner), introduces amongst them the most exquisite order, legislation, and harmony. Wine robs a man of his self-possession: opium greatly invigorates it. Wine unsettles and clouds the judgment, and gives a preternatural brightness, and a vivid exaltation to the contempts and the admirations, the loves and the hatreds, of the drinker: opium, on the contrary, communicates serenity and equipoise to all the faculties, active or passive: and with respect to the temper and moral feelings in general, it gives simply that sort of vital warmth which is approved by the judgment, and which would probably always accompany a bodily constitution of primeval or antediluvian health. Thus, for instance, opium, like wine, gives an expansion to the heart and the benevolent affections: but then, with this remarkable difference, that in the sudden development of kind-heartedness which accompanies inebriation, there is always more or less of a maudlin character, which exposes it to the contempt of the by-stander. Men shake hands, swear eternal friendship, and shed tears—no mortal knows why: and the sensual creature is clearly uppermost. But the expansion of the benigner feelings, incident to opium, is no febrile access, but a healthy restoration to that state which the mind would naturally recover upon the removal of any deep-seated irritation of pain that had disturbed and quarrelled with the impulses of a heart originally just and good. True it is, that even wine, up to a certain point, and with certain men, rather tends to exalt and to steady the intellect: I myself, who have never been a great wine-drinker, used to find that half a dozen glasses of wine advantageously affected the faculties—brightened and intensified the consciousness—and gave to the mind a feeling of being "ponderibus librata suis:"[7] and certainly it is most absurdly

---

* Of this, however, the learned appear latterly to have doubted: for in a pirated edition of Buchan's *Domestic Medicine*, which I once saw in the hands of a farmer's wife who was studying it for the benefit of her health, the doctor was made to say—"Be particularly careful never to take above five-and-twenty *ounces* of laudanum at once;" the true reading being probably five and twenty *drops*, which are held equal to about one grain of crude opium.[4]

[4] Buchan's *Domestic Medicine; or the Family Physician* (1769) was an enormously successful home-remedy and medical work by William Buchan (1729–1805).
[5] *meo periculo*: "at my own risk."
[6] That is, opium drops in alcoholic solution, the standard pain-killer or "aspirin" of the time.

[7] "ponderibus librata suis": "poised by her own weight." Ovid's *Metamorphosis*, I, 13.

said, in popular language, of any man, that he is *disguised* in liquor: for, on the contrary, most men are disguised by sobriety; and it is when they are drinking (as some old gentleman says in Athenæus),[8] that men ἑαυτοὺς ἐμφανίζουσιν οἵτινες εἰσίν—display themselves in their true complexion of character; which surely is not disguising themselves. But still, wine constantly leads a man to the brink of absurdity and extravagance; and, beyond a certain point, it is sure to volatilize and to disperse the intellectual energies: whereas opium always seems to compose what had been agitated, and to concentrate what had been distracted. In short, to sum up all in one word, a man who is inebriated, or tending to inebriation, is, and feels that he is, in a condition which calls up into supremacy the merely human, too often the brutal, part of his nature: but the opium-eater (I speak of him who is not suffering from any disease, or other remote effects of opium,) feels that the diviner part of his nature is paramount; that is, the moral affections are in a state of cloudless serenity; and over all is the great light of the majestic intellect.

* * * * *

With respect to the torpor supposed to follow, or rather (if we were to credit the numerous pictures of Turkish opium-eaters) to accompany the practice of opium-eating, I deny that also. Certainly, opium is classed under the head of narcotics; and some such effect it may produce in the end: but the primary effects of opium are always, and in the highest degree, to excite and stimulate the system: this first stage of its action always lasted with me, during my noviciate, for upwards of eight hours; so that it must be the fault of the opium-eater himself if he does not so time his exhibition of the dose (to speak medically) as that the whole weight of its narcotic influence may descend upon his sleep. Turkish opium-eaters, it seems, are absurd enough to sit, like so many equestrian statues, on logs of wood as stupid as themselves. But that the reader may judge of the degree in which opium is likely to stupify the faculties of an Englishman, I shall (by way of treating the question illustratively, rather than argumentatively) describe the way in which I myself often passed an opium evening in London, during the period between 1804 and 1812. It will be seen, that at least opium did not move me to seek solitude, and much less to seek inactivity, or the torpid state of self-involution ascribed to the Turks. I give this account at the risk of being pronounced a crazy enthusiast or visionary: but I regard *that* little: I must desire my reader to bear in mind, that I was a hard student, and at severe studies for all the rest of my time: and certainly I had a right occasionally to relaxations as well as other people: these, however, I allowed myself but seldom.

The late Duke of ——[9] used to say, "Next Friday, by the blessing of Heaven, I purpose to be drunk:" and in like manner I used to fix beforehand how often, within a given time, and when, I would commit a debauch of opium. This was seldom more than once in three weeks: for at that time I could not have ventured to call every day (as I did afterwards) for "*a glass of laudanum negus, warm, and without sugar.*" No: as I have said, I seldom drank laudanum, at that time, more than once in three weeks: this was usually on a Tuesday or a Saturday night; my reason for which was this. In those days Grassini[10] sang at the Opera: and her voice was delightful to me beyond all that I had ever heard. I know not what may be the state of the Opera-house now, having never been within its walls for seven or eight years, but at that time it was by much the most pleasant place of public resort in London for passing an evening. Five shillings admitted one to the gallery, which was subject to far less annoyance than the pit of the theatres: the orchestra was distinguished by its sweet and melodious grandeur from all English orchestras, the composition of which, I confess, is not acceptable to my ear, from the predominance of the clangorous instruments, and the absolute tyranny of the violin. The choruses were divine to hear: and when Grassini appeared in some interlude, as she often did, and poured forth her passionate soul as Andromache, at the tomb of Hector, &c. I question whether any Turk, of all that ever entered the paradise of opium-eaters, can have had half the pleasure I had. But, indeed, I honour the Barbarians too much by supposing them capable of any pleasures approaching to the intellectual ones of an Englishman. For music is an intellectual or a sensual pleasure, according to the temperament of him who hears it. And, by the by, with the exception of the fine extravaganza on that subject in Twelfth Night,[11] I do not recollect more than one thing said adequately on the subject of music in

---

[8] Late second to early third century author of *Deipnosophistae* (*the Sophists at Dinner*), a miscellaneous work, set in the frame of a Roman dinner attended by learned men, including elaborate discussions of cookery, banquets, and other topics.

[9] Norfolk. The identification was provided in the 1856 edition of the *Confessions.*

[10] Josephina Grassini (1773–1850), popular Italian contralto, who sang in London 1804–1806.

[11] See *Twelfth Night*, I, i, 1–7.

all literature: it is a passage in the *Religio Medici** of Sir T. Brown; and, though chiefly remarkable for its sublimity, has also a philosophic value, inasmuch as it points to the true theory of musical effects. The mistake of most people is to suppose that it is by the ear they communicate with music, and, therefore, that they are purely passive to its effects. But this is not so: it is by the reaction of the mind upon the notices of the ear, (the *matter* coming by the senses, the *form* from the mind,) that the pleasure is constructed: and therefore it is that people of equally good ear differ so much in this point from one another. Now opium, by greatly increasing the activity of the mind generally, increases, of necessity, that particular mode of its activity by which we are able to construct out of the raw material of organic sound an elaborate intellectual pleasure. But, says a friend, a succession of musical sounds is to me like a collection of Arabic characters: I can attach no ideas to them. Ideas! my good sir? there is no occasion for them: all that class of ideas, which can be available in such a case, has a language of representative feelings. But this is a subject foreign to my present purposes: it is sufficient to say, that a chorus, &c. of elaborate harmony, displayed before me, as in a piece of arras work, the whole of my past life—not as if recalled by an act of memory, but as if present and incarnated in the music: no longer painful to dwell upon: but the detail of its incidents removed, or blended in some hazy abstraction; and its passions exalted, spiritualized, and sublimed. All this was to be had for five shillings. And over and above the music of the stage and the orchestra, I had all around me, in the intervals of the performance, the music of the Italian language talked by Italian women: for the gallery was usually crowded with Italians: and I listened with a pleasure such as that with which Weld the traveller [13] lay and listened, in Canada, to the sweet laughter of Indian women; for the less you understand of a language, the more sensible you are to the melody or harshness of its sounds: for such a purpose, therefore, it was an advantage to me that I was a poor Italian scholar, reading it but little, and not speaking it at all, nor understanding a tenth part of what I heard spoken.

* I have not the book at this moment to consult: but I think the passage begins—"And even that tavern music, which makes one man merry, another mad, in me strikes a deep fit of devotion," &c.[12]

⬥⬥⬥⬥⬥⬥⬥⬥⬥⬥⬥⬥⬥⬥⬥⬥⬥⬥⬥⬥⬥⬥⬥⬥⬥⬥⬥⬥⬥⬥

[12] The passage occurs in *Religio Medici*, II, 9.
[13] Isaac Weld (1774–1856), Irish topographer and author of *Travels through the States of North America and the Provinces of Upper and Lower Canada* (1799). De Quincey refers to a passage on pp. 411–12.

These were my Opera pleasures: but another pleasure I had which, as it could be had only on a Saturday night, occasionally struggled with my love of the Opera; for, at that time, Tuesday and Saturday were the regular Opera nights. On this subject I am afraid I shall be rather obscure, but, I can assure the reader, not at all more so than Marinus in his life of Proclus,[14] or many other biographers and auto-biographers of fair reputation. This pleasure, I have said, was to be had only on a Saturday night. What then was Saturday night to me more than any other night? I had no labours that I rested from; no wages to receive: what needed I to care for Saturday night, more than as it was a summons to hear Grassini? True, most logical reader: what you say is unanswerable. And yet so it was and is, that, whereas different men throw their feelings into different channels, and most are apt to show their interest in the concerns of the poor, chiefly by sympathy, expressed in some shape or other, with their distresses and sorrows, I, at that time, was disposed to express my interest by sympathising with their pleasures. The pains of poverty I had lately seen too much of; more than I wished to remember: but the pleasures of the poor, their consolations of spirit, and their reposes from bodily toil, can never become oppressive to contemplate. Now Saturday night is the season for the chief, regular, and periodic return of rest to the poor: in this point the most hostile sects unite, and acknowledge a common link of brotherhood: almost all Christendom rests from its labours. It is a rest introductory to another rest: and divided by a whole day and two nights from the renewal of toil. On this account I feel always, on a Saturday night, as though I also were released from some yoke of labour, had some wages to receive, and some luxury of repose to enjoy. For the sake, therefore, of witnessing, upon as large a scale as possible, a spectacle with which my sympathy was so entire, I used often, on Saturday nights, after I had taken opium, to wander forth, without much regarding the direction or the distance, to all the markets, and other parts of London, to which the poor resort on a Saturday night, for laying out their wages. Many a family party, consisting of a man, his wife, and sometimes one or two of his children, have I listened to, as they stood consulting on their ways and means, or the strength of their exchequer, or the price of household articles. Gradually I became familiar with their wishes, their difficulties, and their opinions. Sometimes there might be heard murmurs of discontent: but far oftener expressions on the

⬥⬥⬥⬥⬥⬥⬥⬥⬥⬥⬥⬥⬥⬥⬥⬥⬥⬥⬥⬥⬥⬥⬥⬥⬥⬥⬥⬥⬥⬥

[14] Proclus (c. 410–485), the Neoplatonic philosopher, whose life was written by his pupil Marinus.

countenance, or uttered in words, of patience, hope, and tranquillity. And taken generally, I must say, that, in this point at least, the poor are far more philosophic than the rich—that they show a more ready and cheerful submission to what they consider as irremediable evils, or irreparable losses. Whenever I saw occasion, or could do it without appearing to be intrusive, I joined their parties; and gave my opinion upon the matter in discussion, which, if not always judicious, was always received indulgently. If wages were a little higher, or expected to be so, or the quartern loaf a little lower, or it was reported that onions and butter were expected to fall, I was glad: yet, if the contrary were true, I drew from opium some means of consoling myself. For opium (like the bee, that extracts its materials indiscriminately from roses and from the soot of chimneys) can overrule all feelings into a compliance with the master key. Some of these rambles led me to great distances: for an opium-eater is too happy to observe the motion of time. And sometimes in my attempts to steer homewards, upon nautical principles, by fixing my eye on the pole-star, and seeking ambitiously for a north-west passage, instead of circumnavigating all the capes and headlands I had doubled in my outward voyage, I came suddenly upon such knotty problems of alleys, such enigmatical entries, and such sphinx's riddles of streets without thoroughfares, as must, I conceive, baffle the audacity of porters, and confound the intellects of hackney-coachmen. I could almost have believed, at times, that I must be the first discoverer of some of these *terræ incognitæ*,[15] and doubted, whether they had yet been laid down in the modern charts of London. For all this, however, I paid a heavy price in distant years, when the human face tyrannized over my dreams, and the perplexities of my steps in London came back and haunted my sleep, with the feeling of perplexities moral or intellectual, that brought confusion to the reason, or anguish and remorse to the conscience.

Thus I have shown that opium does not, of necessity, produce inactivity or torpor; but that, on the contrary, it often led me into markets and theatres. Yet, in candour, I will admit that markets and theatres are not the appropriate haunts of the opium-eater, when in the divinest state incident to his enjoyment. In that state, crowds become an oppression to him; music even, too sensual and gross. He naturally seeks solitude and silence, as indispensable conditions of those trances, or profoundest reveries, which are the crown and consummation of what opium can do for human

nature. I, whose disease it was to meditate too much, and to observe too little, and who, upon my first entrance at college, was nearly falling into a deep melancholy, from brooding too much on the sufferings which I had witnessed in London, was sufficiently aware of the tendencies of my own thoughts to do all I could to counteract them.—I was, indeed, like a person who, according to the old legend, had entered the cave of Trophonius[16]: and the remedies I sought were to force myself into society, and to keep my understanding in continual activity upon matters of science. But for these remedies, I should certainly have become hypochondriacally melancholy. In after years, however, when my cheerfulness was more fully re-established, I yielded to my natural inclination for a solitary life. And, at that time, I often fell into these reveries upon taking opium; and more than once it has happened to me, on a summer night, when I have been at an open window, in a room from which I could overlook the sea at a mile below me, and could command a view of the great town of L——,[17] at about the same distance, that I have sat, from sun-set to sun-rise, motionless, and without wishing to move.

I shall be charged with mysticism, Behmenism,[18] quietism, &c. but *that* shall not alarm me. Sir H. Vane, the younger,[19] was one of our wisest men: and let my readers see if he, in his philosophical works, be half as unmystical as I am.—I say, then, that it has often struck me that the scene itself was somewhat typical of what took place in such a reverie. The town of L—— represented the earth, with its sorrows and its graves left behind, yet not out of sight, nor wholly forgotten. The ocean, in everlasting but gentle agitation, and brooded over by a dove-like calm, might not unfitly typify the mind and the mood which then swayed it. For it seemed to me as if then first I stood at a distance, and aloof from the uproar of life; as if the tumult, the fever, and the strife, were suspended; a respite granted from the secret burthens of the heart; a sabbath of repose; a resting from human labours. Here were the hopes which blossom in the paths of life, reconciled with the peace which is in the grave; motions of the intellect as unwearied as the heavens, yet for all anxieties a halcyon calm: a tranquillity that seemed no product of inertia, but as if resulting from mighty and equal antagonisms; infinite activities, infinite repose.

---

[15] *terræ incognitæ*: "unknown lands."

[16] The site of an oracle in Boeotia; by legend, those who entered the cave and consulted the oracle never again smiled.

[17] Liverpool.

[18] Referring to Jacob Behmen (1575–1624), the German mystic.

[19] Sir H. Vane, the younger (1613–1662), statesman and political figure of the Commonwealth period, executed following the Restoration; he was the author of *The Retired Man's Meditations* (1655) and *Of Love of God and Union with God* (1664).

Oh! just, subtle, and mighty opium! that to the hearts of poor and rich alike, for the wounds that will never heal, and for "the pangs that tempt the spirit to rebel,"[20] bringest an assuaging balm; eloquent opium! that with thy potent rhetoric stealest away the purposes of wrath; and to the guilty man, for one night givest back the hopes of his youth, and hands washed pure from blood; and the the proud man, a brief oblivion for

> Wrongs unredress'd, and insults unavenged:

that summonest to the chancery of dreams, for the triumphs of suffering innocence, false witnesses; and confoundest perjury; and dost reverse the sentences of unrighteous judges:—thou buildest upon the bosom of darkness, out of the fantastic imagery of the brain, cities and temples, beyond the art of Phidias and Praxiteles—beyond the splendour of Babylon and Hekatómpylos[21]: and "from the anarchy of dreaming sleep,"[22] callest into sunny light the faces of long-buried beauties, and the blessed household countenances, cleansed from the "dishonours of the grave." Thou only givest these gifts to man; and thou has the keys of Paradise, oh, just, subtle, and mighty opium!

FROM

INTRODUCTION TO THE PAINS OF OPIUM

*   *   *   *   *

THIS then, let me repeat, I postulate—that, at the time I began to take opium daily, I could not have done otherwise.[1] Whether, indeed, afterwards I might not have succeeded in breaking off the habit, even when it seemed to me that all efforts would be unavailing, and whether many of the innumerable efforts which I *did* make might not have been carried much further, and my gradual re-conquests of ground lost might not have been followed up much more energetically—these are questions which I must decline. Perhaps I might make out a case of palliation; but, shall I speak ingenuously? I confess it, as a besetting infirmity of mine, that I am too much of an Eudæmonist:[2] I hanker too much after a state of happiness, both for myself and others: I cannot face misery, whether my own or not, with an eye of sufficient firmness: and am little capable of encountering present pain for the sake of any reversionary benefit. On some other matters, I can agree with the gentlemen in the cotton-trade* at Manchester in affecting the Stoic philosophy: but not in this. Here I take the liberty of an Eclectic philosopher, and I look out for some courteous and considerate sect that will condescend more to the infirm condition of an opium-eater; that are "sweet men," as Chaucer says, "to give absolution,"[4] and will show some conscience in the penances they inflict, and the efforts of abstinence they exact, from poor sinners like myself. An inhuman moralist I can no more endure in my nervous state than opium that has not been boiled. At any rate, he, who summons me to send out a large freight of self-denial and mortification upon any cruising voyage of moral improvement, must make it clear to my understanding that the concern is a hopeful one. At my time of life (six and thirty years of age) it cannot be supposed that I have much energy to spare: in fact, I find it all little enough for the intellectual labours I have on my hands: and, therefore, let no man expect to frighten me by a few hard words into embarking any part of it upon desperate adventures of morality.

Whether desperate or not, however, the issue of the struggle in 1813 was what I have mentioned; and from this date, the reader is to consider me as a regular and confirmed opium-eater, of whom to ask whether on any particular day he had or not had taken opium, would be to ask whether his lungs had performed respiration, or the heart fulfilled its functions.—You understand now, reader, what I am: and you are by this time aware, that no old gentleman, "with a snow-white beard," will have any chance of persuading me to surrender "the little golden receptacle of the pernici-

---

[20] Wordsworth's *White Doe of Rylstone*, "Dedication," l. 36. The next quotation is from *The Excursion*, III, 374.

[21] The "hundred-gated" city of Thebes in Egypt.

[22] *Excursion*, IV, 87.

[1] In the long opening paragraph here omitted, De Quincey transports the reader from London, 1804, when he first took opium, to Grasmere, 1813. In the intervening years he had been "only a *dilettante* eater of opium." However, in 1813 he experienced "a most appalling irritation of the stomach, in all respects the same that which had caused me so much suffering in youth" (see "Preliminary Confessions," p. 557). De Quincey suggests the illness may have been brought on by his suffering of body and mind from "a most melancholy event," the death in June 1812, of Wordsworth's daughter Catherine, much beloved by De Quincey. The present chapter carries the reader through the first period of addiction, ending in the "happiest year" 1816–1817, to be followed by the nightmarish "Pains of Opium."

---

* A handsome news-room, of which I was very politely made free in passing through Manchester by several gentlemen of that place, is called, I think, *The Porch*: whence I, who am a stranger in Manchester, inferred that the subscribers meant to profess themselves followers of Zeno. But I have since been assured that this is a mistake.[3]

---

[2] One who regards happiness as the chief end to be attained.

[3] Zeno was the fourth-century B.C. founder of Stoic philosophy, so named from the Stoa (porch) at Athens where he taught.

[4] See *Canterbury Tales*, "Prologue," ll. 221–24.

ous drug."[5] No: I give notice to all, whether moralists or surgeons, that, whatever be their pretensions and skill in their respective lines of practice, they must not hope for any countenance from me, if they think to begin by any savage proposition for a Lent or Ramadan of abstinence from opium. This then being all fully understood between us, we shall in future sail before the wind. Now then, reader, from 1813, where all this time we have been sitting down and loitering —rise up, if you please, and walk forward about three years more. Now draw up the curtain, and you shall see me in a new character.

If any man, poor or rich, were to say that he would tell us what had been the happiest day in his life, and the why, and the wherefore, I suppose that we should all cry out—Hear him! Hear him!—As to the happiest *day*, that must be very difficult for any wise man to name: because any event, that could occupy so distinguished a place in a man's retrospect of his life, or be entitled to have shed a special felicity on any one day, ought to be of such an enduring character, as that (accidents apart) it should have continued to shed the same felicity, or one not distinguishably less, on many years together. To the happiest *lustrum*,[6] however, or even to the happiest *year*, it may be allowed to any man to point without discountenance from wisdom. This year, in my case, reader, was the one which we have now reached; though it stood, I confess, as a parenthesis between years of a gloomier character. It was a year of brilliant water (to speak after the manner of jewellers), set as it were, and insulated, in the gloom and cloudy melancholy of opium. Strange as it may sound, I had a little before this time descended suddenly, and without any considerable effort, from 320 grains of opium (i.e. eight* thousand drops of laudanum) per day, to forty grains, or one eighth part. Instantaneously, and as if by magic, the cloud of profoundest melancholy which rested upon my brain,

* I here reckon twenty-five drops of laudanum as equivalent to one grain of opium, which, I believe, is the common estimate. However, as both may be considered variable quantities (the crude opium varying much in strength, and the tincture still more), I suppose that no infinitesimal accuracy can be had in such a calculation. Teaspoons vary as much in size as opium in strength. Small ones hold about 100 drops: so that 8,000 drops are about eighty times a teaspoonful. The reader sees how much I kept within Dr. Buchan's indulgent allowance.

◇◇◇◇◇◇◇◇◇◇◇◇◇◇◇◇◇◇◇◇◇◇◇◇◇◇

[5] De Quincey here quotes from the novel *Anastasius, or Memoirs of a Greek written in the close of the Eighteenth Century*, published anonymously in 1819, by Thomas Hope. In a footnote to a passage in "The Pleasures of Opium" here omitted, De Quincey describes the "grievous misrepresentations" of the effects of opium presented in the novel by an old gentleman, who succeeds in scaring Anastasius out of his supply of opium.

[6] *lustrum*: a period of five years.

like some black vapours that I have seen roll away from the summits of mountains, drew off in one day (νυχθημερον)[7]; passed off with its murky banners as simultaneously as a ship that has been stranded, and is floated off by a spring tide—

That moveth altogether, if it move at all.[8]

Now, then, I was again happy: I now took only 1000 drops of laudanum per day: and what was that? A latter spring had come to close up the season of youth: my brain performed its functions as healthily as ever before: I read Kant again; and again I understood him, or fancied that I did. Again my feelings of pleasure expanded themselves to all around me: and if any man from Oxford or Cambridge, or from neither, had been announced to me in my unpretending cottage, I should have welcomed him with as sumptuous a reception as so poor a man could offer. Whatever else was wanting to a wise man's happiness,—of laudanum I would have given him as much as he wished, and in a golden cup. And, by the way, now that I speak of giving laudanum away, I remember, about this time, a little incident, which I mention, because, trifling as it was, the reader will soon meet it again in my dreams, which it influenced more fearfully than could be imagined. One day a Malay knocked at my door. What business a Malay could have to transact amongst English mountains, I cannot conjecture: but possibly he was on his road to a sea-port about forty miles distant.

The servant who opened the door to him was a young girl born and bred amongst the mountains, who had never seen an Asiatic dress of any sort: his turban, therefore, confounded her not a little: and, as it turned out, that his attainments in English were exactly of the same extent as hers in the Malay, there seemed to be an impassable gulf fixed between all communication of ideas, if either party had happened to possess any. In this dilemma, the girl, recollecting the reputed learning of her master (and, doubtless, giving me credit for a knowledge of all the languages of the earth, besides, perhaps, a few of the lunar ones), came and gave me to understand that there was a sort of demon below, whom she clearly imagined that my art could exorcise from the house. I did not immediately go down: but, when I did, the group which presented itself, arranged as it was by accident, though not very elaborate, took hold of my fancy and my eye in a way that none of the statuesque attitudes exhibited in the ballets at the Opera House, though so ostentatiously

◇◇◇◇◇◇◇◇◇◇◇◇◇◇◇◇◇◇◇◇◇◇◇◇◇◇

[7] νυχθημερον: that is, twenty-four hours ("a day and a night").

[8] Wordsworth's "Resolution and Independence," l. 77.

complex, had ever done. In a cottage kitchen, but panelled on the wall with dark wood that from age and rubbing resembled oak, and looking more like a rustic hall of entrance than a kitchen, stood the Malay—his turban and loose trowsers of dingy white relieved upon the dark panelling: he had placed himself nearer to the girl than she seemed to relish; though her native spirit of mountain intrepidity contended with the feeling of simple awe which her countenance expressed as she gazed upon the tiger-cat before her. And a more striking picture there could not be imagined, than the beautiful English face of the girl, and its exquisite fairness, together with her erect and independent attitude, contrasted with the sallow and bilious skin of the Malay, enamelled or veneered with mahogany, by marine air, his small, fierce, restless eyes, thin lips, slavish gestures and adorations. Half-hidden by the ferocious looking Malay, was a little child from a neighbouring cottage who had crept in after him, and was now in the act of reverting its head, and gazing upwards at the turban and the fiery eyes beneath it, whilst with one hand he caught at the dress of the young woman for protection. My knowledge of the Oriental tongues is not remarkably extensive, being indeed confined to two words—the Arabic word for barley, and the Turkish for opium (madjoon), which I have learnt from Anastasius. And, as I had neither a Malay dictionary, nor even Adelung's *Mithridates*,⁹ which might have helped me to a few words, I addressed him in some lines from the Iliad; considering that, of such languages as I possessed, Greek, in point of longitude, came geographically nearest to an Oriental one. He worshipped me in a most devout manner, and replied in what I suppose was Malay. In this way I saved my reputation with my neighbours: for the Malay had no means of betraying the secret. He lay down upon the floor for about an hour, and then pursued his journey. On his departure, I presented him with a piece of opium. To him, as an Orientalist, I concluded that opium must be familiar: and the expression of his face convinced me that it was. Nevertheless, I was struck with some little consternation when I saw him suddenly raise his hand to his mouth, and (in the schoolboy phrase) bolt the whole, divided into three pieces, at one mouthful. The quantity was enough to kill three dragoons and their horses: and I felt some alarm for the poor creature: but what could be done? I had given him the opium in compassion for his solitary life, on recollecting that if he had travelled on foot from London, it must be nearly three weeks since he could have exchanged a thought with any human being. I could not think of violating the laws of hospitality, by having him seized and drenched with an emetic, and thus frightening him into a notion that we were going to sacrifice him to some English idol. No: there was clearly no help for it:—he took his leave: and for some days I felt anxious: but as I never heard of any Malay being found dead, I became convinced that he was used * to opium: and that I must have done him the service I designed, by giving him one night of respite from the pains of wandering.

This incident I have digressed to mention, because this Malay (partly from the picturesque exhibition he assisted to frame, partly from the anxiety I connected with his image for some days) fastened afterwards upon my dreams, and brought other Malays with him worse than himself, that ran "a-muck"† at me, and led me into a world of troubles.—But to quit this episode, and to return to my intercalary year of happiness. I have said already, that on a subject so important to us all as happiness, we should listen with pleasure to any man's experience or experiments, even though he were but a plough-boy, who cannot be supposed to have ploughed very deep into such an intractable soil as that of human pains and pleasures, or to have conducted his researches upon any very enlightened principles. But I, who have taken happiness, both in a solid and a liquid shape, both boiled and unboiled, both East India and Turkey—who have conducted my experiments upon this interesting subject with a sort of galvanic battery—and have, for the general benefit of the world, inoculated myself, as it were, with the poison of 8000 drops of laudanum per day (just, for the same reason, as a French surgeon inoculated himself lately with cancer—an English one, twenty years ago, with plague—and a third, I know not of what nation, with hydrophobia),—*I* (it will be admitted) must surely know what happiness is, if any-

---

* This, however, is not a necessary conclusion: the varieties of effect produced by opium on different constitutions are infinite. A London magistrate (Harriott's *Struggles through Life*, vol. iii. p. 391, third edition), has recorded that, on the first occasion of his trying laudanum for the gout, he took *forty* drops, the next night *sixty*, and on the fifth night *eighty*, without any effect whatever: and this at an advanced age. I have an anecdote from a country surgeon, however, which sinks Mr. Harriott's case into a trifle; and in my projected medical treatise on opium, which I will publish, provided the College of Surgeons will pay me for enlightening their benighted understandings upon this subject, I will relate it: but it is far too good a story to be published gratis.

† See the common accounts in any Eastern traveller or voyager of the frantic excesses committed by Malays who have taken opium, or are reduced to desperation by ill luck at gambling.

---

⁹ Johann Christoph Adelung (1732–1806) was a distinguished German grammarian and philologist. The first volume of his *Mithridates, oder allgemaine Sprachenkunde* (1806–1817) dealt with Asiatic languages.

body does. And, therefore, I will here lay down an analysis of happiness; and as the most interesting mode of communicating it, I will give it, not didactically, but wrapt up and involved in a picture of one evening, as I spent every evening during the intercalary year when laudanum, though taken daily, was to me no more than the elixir of pleasure. This done, I shall quit the subject of happiness altogether, and pass to a very different one—the *pains of opium.*

Let there be a cottage, standing in a valley, 18 miles from any town—no spacious valley, but about two miles long, by three quarters of a mile in average width; the benefit of which provision is, that all the families resident within its circuit will compose, as it were, one larger household personally familiar to your eye, and more or less interesting to your affections. Let the mountains be real mountains, between 3 and 4000 feet high; and the cottage, a real cottage; not (as a witty author has it) [10] "a cottage with a double coach-house:" let it be, in fact (for I must abide by the actual scene), a white cottage, embowered with flowering shrubs, so chosen as to unfold a succession of flowers upon the walls, and clustering round the windows through all the months of spring, summer, and autumn—beginning, in fact, with May roses, and ending with jasmine. Let it, however, *not* be spring, nor summer, nor autumn—but winter, in his sternest shape. This is a most important point in the science of happiness. And I am surprised to see people overlook it, and think it matter of congratulation that winter is going; or, if coming, is not likely to be a severe one. On the contrary, I put up a petition annually, for as much snow, hail, frost, or storm, of one kind or other, as the skies can possibly afford us. Surely every body is aware of the divine pleasures which attend a winter fire-side: candles at four o'clock, warm hearth-rugs, tea, a fair tea-maker, shutters closed, curtains flowing in ample draperies on the floor, whilst the wind and rain are raging audibly without,

> And at the doors and windows seem to call,
> As heav'n and earth they would together mell;
> Yet the least entrance find they none at all;
> Whence sweeter grows our rest secure in massy hall.
> *Castle of Indolence.* [11]

All these are items in the description of a winter evening, which must surely be familiar to every body born in a high latitude. And it is evident, that most of these delicacies, like ice-cream, require a very low temperature of the atmosphere to produce them: they are fruits which cannot be ripened without weather stormy or inclement, in some way or other. I am not "*particular,*" as people say, whether it be snow, or black frost, or wind so strong, that (as Mr. ——[12] says) "you may lean your back against it like a post." I can put up even with rain, provided it rains cats and dogs: but something of the sort I must have: and, if I have it not, I think myself in a manner ill-used: for why am I called on to pay heavily for winter, in coals, and candles, and various privations that will occur even to gentlemen, if I am not to have the article good of its kind? No: a Canadian winter for my money: or a Russian one, where every man is but a co-proprietor with the north wind in the fee-simple of his own ears. Indeed, so great an epicure am I in this matter, that I cannot relish a winter night fully if it be much past St. Thomas's day; [13] and have degenerated into disgusting tendencies to vernal appearances: no: it must be divided by a thick wall of dark nights from all return of light and sunshine.—From the latter weeks of October to Christmas-eve, therefore, is the period during which happiness is in season, which, in my judgment, enters the room with the tea-tray: for tea, though ridiculed by those who are naturally of coarse nerves, or are become so from wine-drinking, and are not susceptible of influence from so refined a stimulant, will always be the favourite beverage of the intellectual: and, for my part, I would have joined Dr. Johnson in a *bellum internecinum* against Jonas Hanway; [14] or any other impious person, who should presume to disparage it.—But here, to save myself the trouble of too much verbal description, I will introduce a painter; and give him directions for the rest of the picture. Painters do not like white cottages, unless a good deal weather-stained: but as the reader now understands that it is a winter night, his services will not be required, except for the inside of the house.

Paint me, then, a room seventeen feet by twelve, and not more than seven and a half feet high. This, reader, is somewhat ambitiously styled, in my family, the drawing-room: but, being contrived "a double debt to pay," [15] it is also, and more justly, termed the

---

[10] De Quincey refers to a popular satiric poem "The Devil's Thoughts," joint production of Coleridge and Southey, first published in *The Morning Post,* September 6, 1799.

[11] James Thomson's poem, I, stanza xliii.

[12] Thomas Clarkson (1760–1846), the famous abolitionist. The identification is provided in the 1856 edition of *The Confessions.*

[13] December 21.

[14] See Boswell's *Life of Johnson,* entry for 1756. Johnson had written a review defending tea against a "violent attack upon that elegant and popular beverage" in *Essay on Tea* (1756) by Jonas Hanway (1712–1786). Hanway wrote "an angry answer," to which Johnson replied: "the only instance," Boswell reports, "in the whole course of his life, when he condescended to oppose any thing that was written against him." *bellum internecinum:* "deadly war."

[15] *The Deserted Village,* l. 229.

library; for it happens that books are the only article of property in which I am richer than my neighbours. Of these, I have about five thousand, collected gradually since my eighteenth year. Therefore, painter, put as many as you can into this room. Make it populous with books: and, furthermore, paint me a good fire; and furniture, plain and modest, befitting the unpretending cottage of a scholar. And, near the fire, paint me a tea-table; and (as it is clear that no creature can come to see one such a stormy night,) place only two cups and saucers on the tea-tray: and, if you know how to paint such a thing symbolically, or otherwise, paint me an eternal tea-pot—eternal *à parte ante*, and *à parte post*;[16] for I usually drink tea from eight o'clock at night to four o'clock in the morning. And, as it is very unpleasant to make tea, or to pour it out for oneself, paint me a lovely young woman, sitting at the table. Paint her arms like Aurora's, and her smiles like Hebe's:—But no, dear M., not even in jest let me insinuate that thy power to illuminate my cottage rests upon a tenure so perishable as mere personal beauty; or that the witchcraft of angelic smiles lies within the empire of any earthly pencil. Pass, then, my good painter, to something more within its power: and the next article brought forward should naturally be myself—a picture of the Opium-eater, with his "little golden receptacle of the pernicious drug," lying beside him on the table. As to the opium, I have no objection to see a picture of *that*, though I would rather see the original: you may paint it, if you choose; but I apprize you, that no "little" receptacle would, even in 1816, answer *my* purpose, who was at a distance from the "stately Pantheon," and all druggists (mortal or otherwise). No: you may as well paint the real receptacle, which was not of gold, but of glass, and as much like a wine-decanter as possible. Into this you may put a quart of ruby-coloured laudanum: that, and a book of German metaphysics placed by its side, will sufficiently attest my being in the neighbourhood; but, as to myself,—there I demur. I admit that, naturally, I ought to occupy the foreground of the picture; that being the hero of the piece, or (if you choose) the criminal at the bar, my body should be had into court. This seems reasonable: but why should I confess, on this point, to a painter? or why confess at all? If the public (into whose private ear I am confidentially whispering my confessions, and not into any painter's) should chance to have framed some agreeable picture for itself, of the Opium-eater's exterior,—should have ascribed to him, romantically, an

elegant person, or a handsome face, why should I barbarously tear from it so pleasing a delusion—pleasing both to the public and to me? No: paint me, if at all, according to your own fancy: and, as a painter's fancy should teem with beautiful creations, I cannot fail, in that way, to be a gainer. And now, reader, we have run through all the ten categories of my condition, as it stood about 1816–17: up to the middle of which latter year I judge myself to have been a happy man: and the elements of that happiness I have endeavoured to place before you, in the above sketch of the interior of a scholar's library, in a cottage among the mountains, on a stormy winter evening.

But now farewell—a long farewell to happiness—winter or summer! farewell to smiles and laughter! farewell to peace of mind! farewell to hope and to tranquil dreams, and to the blessed consolations of sleep! for more than three years and a half I am summoned away from these: I am now arrived at an Iliad of woes: for I have now to record

FROM

THE PAINS OF OPIUM

*   *   *   *   *

I NOW pass to what is the main subject of these latter confessions, to the history and journal of what took place in my dreams; for these were the immediate and proximate cause of my acutest suffering.

The first notice I had of any important change going on in this part of my physical economy, was from the re-awakening of a state of eye generally incident to childhood, or exalted states of irritability. I know not whether my reader is aware that many children, perhaps most, have a power of painting, as it were, upon the darkness, all sorts of phantoms; in some, that power is simply a mechanic affection of the eye; others have a voluntary, or a semi-voluntary power to dismiss or to summon them; or, as a child once said to me when I questioned him on this matter, "I can tell them to go, and they go; but sometimes they come, when I don't tell them to come." Whereupon I told him that he had almost as unlimited a command over apparitions, as a Roman centurion over his soldiers.—In the middle of 1817, I think it was, that this faculty became positively distressing to me: at night, when I lay awake in bed, vast processions passed along in mournful pomp; friezes of never-ending stories, that to my feelings were as sad and solemn as if they were stories drawn from times before Œdipus or Priam—before Tyre—before Memphis. And, at the same time, a corresponding change took place in my dreams; a theatre seemed

---

[16] *à parte ante*, and *à parte post*: "from the part before, and from the part after"; thus, eternal in having no beginning and no ending.

suddenly opened and lighted up within my brain, which presented nightly spectacles of more than earthly splendour. And the four following facts may be mentioned, as noticeable at this time:

1. That, as the creative state of the eye increased, a sympathy seemed to arise between the waking and the dreaming states of the brain in one point—that whatsoever I happened to call up and to trace by a voluntary act upon the darkness was very apt to transfer itself to my dreams; so that I feared to exercise this faculty; for, as Midas turned all things to gold, that yet baffled his hopes and defrauded his human desires, so whatsoever things capable of being visually represented I did but think of in the darkness, immediately shaped themselves into phantoms of the eye; and, by a process apparently no less inevitable, when thus once traced in faint and visionary colours, like writings in sympathetic ink, they were drawn out by the fierce chemistry of my dreams, into insufferable splendour that fretted my heart.

2. For this, and all other changes in my dreams, were accompanied by deep-seated anxiety and gloomy melancholy, such as are wholly incommunicable by words. I seemed every night to descend, not metaphorically, but literally to descend, into chasms and sunless abysses, depths below depths, from which it seemed hopeless that I could ever reascend. Nor did I, by waking, feel that I *had* reascended. This I do not dwell upon; because the state of gloom which attended these gorgeous spectacles, amounting at least to utter darkness, as of some suicidal despondency, cannot be approached by words.

3. The sense of space, and in the end, the sense of time, were both powerfully affected. Buildings, landscapes, &c. were exhibited in proportions so vast as the bodily eye is not fitted to receive. Space swelled, and was amplified to an extent of unutterable infinity. This, however, did not disturb me so much as the vast expansion of time; I sometimes seemed to have lived for 70 or 100 years in one night; nay, sometimes had feelings representative of a millennium passed in that time, or, however, of a duration far beyond the limits of any human experience.

4. The minutest incidents of childhood, or forgotten scenes of later years, were often revived: I could not be said to recollect them; for if I had been told of them when waking, I should not have been able to acknowledge them as parts of my past experience. But placed as they were before me, in dreams like intuitions, and clothed in all their evanescent circumstances and accompanying feelings, I *recognised* them instantaneously. I was once told by a near relative of mine, that having in her childhood fallen into a river, and being on the very verge of death but for

the critical assistance which reached her, she saw in a moment her whole life, in its minutest incidents, arrayed before her simultaneously as in a mirror; and she had a faculty developed as suddenly for comprehending the whole and every part. This, from some opium experiences of mine, I can believe; I have, indeed, seen the same thing asserted twice in modern books, and accompanied by a remark which I am convinced is true; viz. that the dread book of account, which the Scriptures speak of,[1] is, in fact, the mind itself of each individual. Of this, at least, I feel assured, that there is no such thing as *forgetting* possible to the mind; a thousand accidents may, and will interpose a veil between our present consciousness and the secret inscriptions on the mind; accidents of the same sort will also rend away this veil; but alike, whether veiled or unveiled, the inscription remains for ever; just as the stars seem to withdraw before the common light of day, whereas, in fact, we all know that it is the light which is drawn over them as a veil—and that they are waiting to be revealed, when the obscuring daylight shall have withdrawn.

Having noticed these four facts as memorably distinguishing my dreams from those of health, I shall now cite a case illustrative of the first fact; and shall then cite any others that I remember, either in their chronological order, or any other that may give them more effect as pictures to the reader.

I had been in youth, and even since, for occasional amusement, a great reader of Livy, whom, I confess, that I prefer, both for style and matter, to any other of the Roman historians; and I had often felt as most solemn and appalling sounds, and most emphatically representative of the majesty of the Roman people, the two words so often occurring in Livy—*Consul Romanus;* especially when the consul is introduced in his military character. I mean to say, that the words king—sultan—regent, &c. or any other titles of those who embody in their own persons the collective majesty of a great people, had less power over my reverential feelings. I had also, though no great reader of history, made myself minutely and critically familiar with one period of English history, viz. the period of the Parliamentary War, having been attracted by the moral grandeur of some who figured in that day, and by the many interesting memoirs which survive those unquiet times. Both these parts of my lighter reading, having furnished me often with matter of reflection, now furnished me with matter for my dreams. Often I used to see, after painting upon the blank darkness a sort of rehearsal whilst waking, a crowd of ladies, and

[1] See Revelation, xx, 12–15.

perhaps a festival, and dances. And I heard it said, or I said to myself, "These are English ladies from the unhappy times of Charles I. These are the wives and the daughters of those who met in peace, and sat at the same tables, and were allied by marriage or by blood; and yet, after a certain day in August, 1642,[2] never smiled upon each other again, nor met but in the field of battle; and at Marston Moor, at Newbury, or at Naseby, cut asunder all ties of love by the cruel sabre, and washed away in blood the memory of ancient friendship."—The ladies danced, and looked as lovely as the court of George IV. Yet I knew, even in my dream, that they had been in the grave for nearly two centuries.—This pageant would suddenly dissolve: and, at a clapping of hands, would be heard the heart-quaking sound of *Consul Romanus;* and immediately came "sweeping by,"[3] in gorgeous paludaments, Paulus or Marius,[4] girt round by a company of centurions, with the crimson tunic* hoisted on a spear, and followed by the *alalagmos*† of the Roman legions.

Many years ago, when I was looking over Piranesi's[5] Antiquities of Rome, Mr. Coleridge, who was standing by, described to me a set of plates by that artist, called his *Dreams,* and which record the scenery of his own visions during the delirium of a fever. Some of them (I describe only from memory of Mr. Coleridge's account) represented vast Gothic halls: on the floor of which stood all sorts of engines and machinery, wheels, cables, pulleys, levers, catapults, &c. &c. expressive of enormous power put forth, and resistance overcome. Creeping along the sides of the walls, you perceived a staircase; and upon it, groping his way upwards, was Piranesi himself: follow the stairs a little further, and you perceive it come to a sudden abrupt termination, without any balustrade, and allowing no step onwards to him who had reached the extremity, except into the depths below. Whatever is to become of poor Piranesi, you suppose, at least, that his labours

must in some way terminate here. But raise your eyes, and behold a second flight of stairs still higher: on which again Piranesi is perceived, but this time standing on the very brink of the abyss. Again elevate your eye, and a still more aerial flight of stairs is beheld: and again is poor Piranesi busy on his aspiring labours: and so on, until the unfinished stairs and Piranesi both are lost in the upper gloom of the hall.— With the same power of endless growth and self-reproduction did my architecture proceed in dreams. In the early stage of my malady, the splendours of my dreams were indeed chiefly architectural: and I beheld such pomp of cities and palaces as was never yet beheld by the waking eye, unless in the clouds. From a great modern poet I cite part of a passage which describes, as an appearance actually beheld in the clouds, what in many of its circumstances I saw frequently in sleep:

> The appearance, instantaneously disclosed,
> Was of a mighty city—boldly say
> A wilderness of building, sinking far
> And self-withdrawn into a wondrous depth,
> Far sinking into splendour—without end!
> Fabric it seem'd of diamond, and of gold,
> With alabaster domes, and silver spires,
> And blazing terrace upon terrace, high
> Uplifted; here, serene pavilions bright
> In avenues disposed; there towers begirt
> With battlements that on their restless fronts
> Bore stars—illumination of all gems!
> By earthly nature had the effect been wrought
> Upon the dark materials of the storm
> Now pacified: on them, and on the coves,
> And mountain-steeps and summits, whereunto
> The vapours had receded,—taking there
> Their station under a cerulean sky, &c, &c.[6]

The sublime circumstance—"battlements that on their *restless* fronts bore stars,"—might have been copied from my architectural dreams, for it often occurred.—We hear it reported of Dryden, and of Fuseli[7] in modern times, that they thought proper to eat raw meat for the sake of obtaining splendid dreams: how much better for such a purpose to have eaten opium, which yet I do not remember that any poet is recorded to have done, except the dramatist Shadwell:[8] and in ancient days, Homer is, I think, rightly reputed to have known the virtues of opium.

To my architecture succeeded dreams of lakes—and silvery expanses of water:—these haunted me so

---

* The signal which announced a day of battle. [1856 edition.]
† A word expressing collectively the gathering of the Roman war-cries—*Alála, alála!* [1856 edition.]

2 On August 22, 1642, Charles I raised the royal standard at Nottingham and thus formally began the Civil War. Marston Moor (July 1644), Newbury (October 1644), and Naseby (June 1645) were all decisive victories by Parliamentary forces over the Royalists.
3 *Il Penseroso,* l. 98.
4 Lucius Aemilius Paulus (*c.* 229–160 B.C.), successfully completed the Macedonian war and won a magnificent Roman triumph. Gaius Marius (155–86 B.C.), Roman general and consul, was similarly honored in 101 B.C. for his decisive defeat of the Cimbri and Teutones.
5 Giambattista Piranesi (1720–1778), the Italian architect and engraver.

6 *Excursion,* II, 834–851.
7 Henry Fuseli (1741–1825), Anglo-Swiss artist, professor of painting at the English Royal Academy.
8 Thomas Shadwell (*c.* 1642–1692), the playwright and poet, object of satire in Dryden's *Mac Flecknoe.*

much, that I feared (though possibly it will appear ludicrous to a medical man) that some dropsical state or tendency of the brain might thus be making itself (to use a metaphysical word) *objective;* and the sentient organ *project* itself as its own object.—For two months I suffered greatly in my head—a part of my bodily structure which had hitherto been so clear from all touch or taint of weakness (physically, I mean), that I used to say of it, as the last Lord Orford [9] said of his stomach, that it seemed likely to survive the rest of my person.—Till now I had never felt a headache even, or any the slightest pain, except rheumatic pains caused by my own folly. However, I got over this attack, though it must have been verging on something very dangerous.

The waters now changed their character,—from translucent lakes, shining like mirrors, they now became seas and oceans. And now came a tremendous change, which, unfolding itself slowly like a scroll, through many months, promised an abiding torment; and, in fact, it never left me until the winding up of my case. Hitherto the human face had mixed often in my dreams, but not despotically, nor with any special power of tormenting. But now that which I have called the tyranny of the human face began to unfold itself. Perhaps some part of my London life might be answerable for this. Be that as it may, now it was that upon the rocking waters of the ocean the human face began to appear: the sea appeared paved with innumerable faces, upturned to the heavens: faces, imploring, wrathful, despairing, surged upwards by thousands, by myriads, by generations, by centuries: —my agitation was infinite,—my mind tossed—and surged with the ocean.

May, 1818.

The Malay has been a fearful enemy for months. I have been every night, through his means, transported into Asiatic scenes. I know not whether others share in my feelings on this point; but I have often thought that if I were compelled to forego England, and to live in China, and among Chinese manners and modes of life and scenery, I should go mad. The causes of my horror lie deep; and some of them must be common to others. Southern Asia, in general, is the seat of awful images and associations. As the cradle of the human race, it would alone have a dim and reverential feeling connected with it. But there are other reasons. No man can pretend that the wild, barbarous, and capricious superstitions of Africa, or of savage tribes elsewhere, affect him in the way that he is affected by the

ancient, monumental, cruel, and elaborate religions of Indostan, &c. The mere antiquity of Asiatic things, of their institutions, histories, modes of faith, &c. is so impressive, that to me the vast age of the race and name overpowers the sense of youth in the individual. A young Chinese seems to me an antediluvian man renewed. Even Englishmen, though not bred in any knowledge of such institutions, cannot but shudder at the mystic sublimity of *castes* that have flowed apart, and refused to mix, through such immemorial tracts of time; nor can any man fail to be awed by the names of the Ganges, or the Euphrates. It contributes much to these feelings, that southern Asia is, and has been for thousands of years, the part of the earth most swarming with human life; the great *officina gentium*.[10] Man is a weed in those regions. The vast empires also, into which the enormous population of Asia has always been cast, give a further sublimity to the feelings associated with all Oriental names or images. In China, over and above what it has in common with the rest of southern Asia, I am terrified by the modes of life, by the manners, and the barrier of utter abhorrence, and want of sympathy, placed between us by feelings deeper than I can analyze. I could sooner live with lunatics, or brute animals. All this, and much more than I can say, or have time to say, the reader must enter into before he can comprehend the unimaginable horror which these dreams of Oriental imagery, and mythological tortures, impressed upon me. Under the connecting feelings of tropical heat and vertical sunlights, I brought together all creatures, birds, beasts, reptiles, all trees and plants, usages and appearances, that are found in all tropical regions, and assembled them together in China or Indostan. From kindred feelings, I soon brought Egypt and all her goods under the same law. I was stared at, hooted at, grinned at, chattered at, by monkeys, by paroquets, by cockatoos. I ran into pagodas: and was fixed, for centuries, at the summit, or in secret rooms; I was the idol; I was the priest; I was worshipped; I was sacrificed. I fled from the wrath of Brama through all the forests of Asia: Vishnu hated me: Seeva laid wait for me. I came suddenly upon Ibis and Osiris: I had done a deed, they said, which the ibis and the crocodile trembled at.[11] I was buried, for a thousand years, in stone coffins, with mummies and sphinxes, in narrow chambers at the heart of eternal pyramids. I was kissed, with cancerous kisses, by crocodiles; and laid, confounded

---

9 Horace Walpole.

10 *officina gentium*: "manufactory of populations".

11 In Hindu theology, Brahma the Creator, Vishnu the Maintainer, and Siva the Destroyer, represent the divine Triad. Isis and Osiris were deities of ancient Egypt, identified respectively with the moon and the sun. The ibis and the crocodile were the sacred bird and beast of Egypt.

with all unutterable slimy things, amongst reeds and Nilotic mud.

I thus give the reader some slight abstraction of my Oriental dreams, which always filled me with such amazement at the monstrous scenery, that horror seemed absorbed, for a while, in sheer astonishment. Sooner or later, came a reflux of feeling that swallowed up the astonishment, and left me, not so much in terror, as in hatred and abomination of what I saw. Over every form, and threat, and punishment, and dim sightless incarceration, brooded a sense of eternity and infinity that drove me into an oppression as of madness. Into these dreams only, it was, with one or two slight exceptions, that any circumstances of physical horror entered. All before had been moral and spiritual terrors. But here the main agents were ugly birds, or snakes, or crocodiles; especially the last. The cursed crocodile became to me the object of more horror than almost all the rest. I was compelled to live with him; and (as was always the case almost in my dreams) for centuries. I escaped sometimes, and found myself in Chinese houses, with cane tables, &c. All the feet of the tables, sofas, &c. soon became instinct with life: the abominable head of the crocodile, and his leering eyes, looked out at me, multiplied into a thousand repetitions: and I stood loathing and fascinated. And so often did this hideous reptile haunt my dreams, that many times the very same dream was broken up in the very same way: I heard gentle voices speaking to me (I hear every thing when I am sleeping); and instantly I awoke: it was broad noon; and my children were standing, hand in hand, at my bed-side; come to show me their coloured shoes, or new frocks, or to let me see them dressed for going out. I protest that so awful was the transition from the damned crocodile, and the other unutterable monsters and abortions of my dreams, to the sight of innocent *human* natures and of infancy, that, in the mighty and sudden revulsion of mind, I wept, and could not forbear it, as I kissed their faces.

June, 1819.

I have had occasion to remark, at various periods of my life, that the deaths of those whom we love, and indeed the contemplation of death generally, is (*cæteris paribus*)[12] more affecting in summer than in any other season of the year. And the reasons are these three, I think: first, that the visible heavens in summer appear far higher, more distant, and (if such a solecism may be excused) more infinite; the clouds, by which chiefly the eye expounds the distance of the blue pavilion stretched over our heads, are in summer more voluminous, massed, and accumulated in far grander and more towering piles: secondly, the light and the appearances of the declining and the setting sun are much more fitted to be types and characters of the Infinite: and, thirdly, (which is the main reason) the exuberant and riotous prodigality of life naturally forces the mind more powerfully upon the antagonist thought of death, and the wintry sterility of the grave. For it may be observed, generally, that wherever two thoughts stand related to each other by a law of antagonism, and exist, as it were, by mutual repulsion, they are apt to suggest each other. On these accounts it is that I find it impossible to banish the thought of death when I am walking alone in the endless days of summer; and any particular death, if not more affecting, at least haunts my mind more obstinately and besiegingly in that season. Perhaps this cause, and a slight incident which I omit, might have been the immediate occasions of the following dream; to which, however, a predisposition must always have existed in my mind; but having been once roused, it never left me, and split into a thousand fantastic varieties, which often suddenly reunited, and composed again the original dream.

I thought that it was a Sunday morning in May, that it was Easter Sunday, and as yet very early in the morning. I was standing, as it seemed to me, at the door of my own cottage. Right before me lay the very scene which could really be commanded from that situation, but exalted, as was usual, and solemnized by the power of dreams. There were the same mountains, and the same lovely valley at their feet; but the mountains were raised to more than Alpine height, and there was interspace far larger between them of meadows and forest lawns; the hedges were rich with white roses; and no living creature was to be seen, excepting that in the green churchyard there were cattle tranquilly reposing upon the verdant graves, and particularly round about the grave of a child whom I had tenderly loved, just as I had really beheld them, a little before sun-rise in the same summer, when that child died. I gazed upon the well-known scene, and I said aloud (as I thought) to myself, "It yet wants much of sun-rise; and it is Easter Sunday; and that is the day on which they celebrate the first-fruits of resurrection. I will walk abroad; old griefs shall be forgotten to-day; for the air is cool and still, and the hills are high, and stretch away to heaven; and the forest-glades are as quiet as the churchyard; and, with the dew, I can wash the fever from my forehead, and then I shall be unhappy no longer." And I turned, as if to open my garden gate; and immediately I saw upon the left a scene far different; but which yet the

---

[12] *cæteris paribus*: "other things being equal."

power of dreams had reconciled into harmony with the other. The scene was an Oriental one; and there also it was Easter Sunday, and very early in the morning. And at a vast distance were visible, as a stain upon the horizon, the domes and cupolas of a great city—an image or faint abstraction, caught perhaps in childhood from some picture of Jerusalem. And not a bow-shot from me, upon a stone, and shaded by Judean palms, there sat a woman; and I looked; and it was—Ann! She fixed her eyes upon me earnestly; and I said to her at length: "So then I have found you at last." I waited: but she answered me not a word. Her face was the same as when I saw it last, and yet again how different! Seventeen years ago, when the lamp-light fell upon her face, as for the last time I kissed her lips (lips, Ann, that to me were not polluted), her eyes were streaming with tears: the tears were now wiped away; she seemed more beautiful than she was at that time, but in all other points the same, and not older. Her looks were tranquil, but with unusual solemnity of expression; and I now gazed upon her with some awe, but suddenly her countenance grew dim, and, turning to the mountains I perceived vapours rolling between us; in a moment, all had vanished; thick darkness came on; and, in the twinkling of an eye, I was far away from mountains, and by lamp-light in Oxford-street, walking again with Ann—just as we walked seventeen years before, when we were both children.

As a final specimen, I cite one of a different character, from 1820.

The dream commenced with a music which now I often heard in dreams—a music of preparation and of awakening suspense; a music like the opening of the Coronation Anthem, and which, like *that*, gave the feeling of a vast march—of infinite cavalcades filing off —and the tread of innumerable armies. The morning was come of a mighty day—a day of crisis and of final hope for human nature, then suffering some mysterious eclipse, and labouring in some dread extremity. Somewhere, I knew not where—somehow, I knew not how—by some beings, I knew not whom—a battle, a strife, an agony, was conducting,—was evolving like a great drama, or piece of music; with which my sympathy was the more insupportable from my confusion as to its place, its cause, its nature, and its possible issue. I, as is usual in dreams (where, of necessity, we make ourselves central to every movement), had the power, and yet had not the power, to decide it. I had the power, if I could raise myself, to will it; and yet again had not the power, for the weight of twenty Atlantics was upon me, or the oppression of inexpiable guilt. "Deeper than ever plummet sound-

ed," [13] I lay inactive. Then, like a chorus, the passion deepened. Some greater interest was at stake; some mightier cause than ever yet the sword had pleaded, or trumpet had proclaimed. Then came sudden alarms: hurryings to and fro: trepidations of innumerable fugitives, I knew not whether from the good cause or the bad: darkness and lights: tempest and human faces: and at last, with the sense that all was lost, female forms, and the features that were worth all the world to me, and but a moment allowed, —and clasped hands, and heart-breaking partings, and then—everlasting farewells! and with a sigh, such as the caves of hell sighed when the incestuous mother uttered the abhorred name of death,[14] the sound was reverberated—everlasting farewells! and again, and yet again reverberated—everlasting farewells!

And I awoke in struggles, and cried aloud—"I will sleep no more!"

But I am now called upon to wind up a narrative which has already extended to an unreasonable length. Within more spacious limits, the materials which I have used might have been better unfolded; and much which I have not used might have been added with effect. Perhaps, however, enough has been given. It now remains that I should say something of the way in which this conflict of horrors was finally brought to its crisis. The reader is already aware (from a passage near the beginning of the introduction to the first part) that the opium-eater has, in some way or other, "unwound, almost to its final links, the accursed chain which bound him." By what means? To have narrated this, according to the original intention, would have far exceeded the space which can now be allowed. It is fortunate, as such a cogent reason exists for abridging it, that I should, on a maturer view of the case, have been exceedingly unwilling to injure, by any such unaffected details, the impression of the history itself, as an appeal to the prudence and the conscience of the yet unconfirmed opium-eater— or even (though a very inferior consideration) to injure its effect as a composition. The interest of the judicious reader will not attach itself chiefly to the subject of the fascinating spells, but to the fascinating power. Not the opium-eater, but the opium, is the true hero of the tale; and the legitimate centre on which the interest revolves. The object was to display the marvellous agency of opium, whether for pleasure or for pain: if that is done, the action of the piece has closed.

However, as some people, in spite of all laws to the

---

13 *The Tempest*, III, iii, 101.
14 See *Paradise Lost*, II, 787–89.

contrary, will persist in asking what became of the opium-eater, and in what state he now is, I answer for him thus: The reader is aware that opium had long ceased to found its empire on spells of pleasure; it was solely by the tortures connected with the attempt to abjure it, that it kept its hold. Yet, as other tortures, no less it may be thought, attended the non-abjuration of such a tyrant, a choice only of evils was left; and *that* might as well have been adopted, which, however terrific in itself, held out a prospect of final restoration to happiness. This appears true; but good logic gave the author no strength to act upon it. However, a crisis arrived for the author's life, and a crisis for other objects still dearer to him—and which will always be far dearer to him than his life, even now that it is again a happy one.—I saw that I must die if I continued the opium: I determined, therefore, if that should be required, to die in throwing it off. How much I was at that time taking I cannot say; for the opium which I used had been purchased for me by a friend who afterwards refused to let me pay him; so that I could not ascertain even what quantity I had used within the year. I apprehend, however, that I took it very irregularly: and that I varied from about fifty or sixty grains, to 150 a-day. My first task was to reduce it to forty, to thirty, and, as fast as I could, to twelve grains.

I triumphed: but think not, reader, that therefore my sufferings were ended; nor think of me as of one sitting in a *dejected* state. Think of me as of one, even when four months had passed, still agitated, writhing, throbbing, palpitating, shattered; and much, perhaps, in the situation of him who has been racked, as I collect the torments of that state from the affecting account of them left by the most innocent sufferer * (of the times of James I.). Meantime, I derived no benefit from any medicine, except one prescribed to me by an Edinburgh surgeon of great eminence, viz. ammoniated tincture of Valerian. Medical account, therefore, of my emancipation I have not much to give: and even that little, as managed by a man so ignorant of medicine as myself, would probably tend only to mislead. At all events, it would be misplaced in this situation. The moral of the narrative is addressed to the opium-eater; and therefore, of necessity, limited

in its application. If he is taught to fear and tremble, enough has been effected. But he may say, that the issue of my case is at least a proof that opium, after a seventeen years' use, and an eight years' abuse of its powers, may still be renounced: and that *he* may chance to bring to the task greater energy than I did, or that with a stronger constitution than mine he may obtain the same results with less. This may be true: I would not presume to measure the efforts of other men by my own: I heartily wish him more energy: I wish the same success. Nevertheless, I had motives external to myself which he may unfortunately want: and these supplied me with conscientious supports which mere personal interests might fail to supply to a mind debilitated by opium.

Jeremy Taylor conjectures that it may be as painful to be born as to die:[16] I think it probable: and, during the whole period of diminishing the opium, I had the torments of a man passing out of one mode of existence into another. The issue was not death, but a sort of physical regeneration: and I may add, that ever since, at intervals, I have had a restoration of more than youthful spirits, though under the pressure of difficulties, which, in a less happy state of mind, I should have called misfortunes.

One memorial of my former condition still remains: my dreams are not yet perfectly calm: the dread swell and agitation of the storm have not wholly subsided: the legions that encamped in them are drawing off, but not all departed: my sleep is still tumultuous and, like the gates of Paradise to our first parents when looking back from afar, it is still (in the tremendous line of Milton)—

With dreadful faces throng'd and fiery arms.[17]

[October 1821]   [1822]

* William Lithgow: his book (*Travels*, &c.) is ill and pedantically written: but the account of his own sufferings on the rack at Malaga is overpoweringly affecting.[15]

◇◇◇◇◇◇◇◇◇◇◇◇◇◇◇◇◇◇◇◇◇◇◇◇◇◇◇◇◇◇◇

[15] William Lithgow (1582–c. 1645), traveler and adventurer, was arrested in 1620 by the Spanish authorities as a spy and subjected to inhuman tortures. His book is *The Totall Discourse, of the Rare Adventures, and painefull Peregrinations of long nineteene years travayles* (1632).

ON THE KNOCKING AT THE GATE IN MACBETH

De Quincey's writings on literature and aesthetics were many and varied, ranging from critical and biographical essays on contemporary writers through more general but original studies of "Style" and "Rhetoric." Perhaps his most famous piece of literary criticism came very early in his journalistic career. "On the Knocking at the Gate in Macbeth" appeared in the London Magazine *in October 1823, as part of a series* Notes from the Pocket-Book of a Late Opium-Eater. *It is here published from the original text, with the omission of the short, final paragraph, a "Nota Bene" to the reader.*

◇◇◇◇◇◇◇◇◇◇◇◇◇◇◇◇◇◇◇◇◇◇◇◇◇◇◇◇◇◇◇

[16] In the 1856 edition, De Quincey corrected this to Francis Bacon, referring to his essay "Of Death."
[17] *Paradise Lost*, XII, 644.

In his study Thomas De Quincey Literary Critic *(1952),
John E. Jordan has said of the essay, that it reveals "the pattern
of his psychological criticism, a pattern wrought by the cooperation
of the dreamer, with his emotional tension and feeling for the
supernatural, and the logician with his analytical power and
common-sense analogies. Four steps were necessary in the
evolution and presentation of that interpretation: a feeling of the
effect, an awareness and a localization of that feeling, an analysis
of the causative principle involved in its production, and finally,
a descriptive recapturing of the effect for the benefit of the reader."*

ON THE
KNOCKING AT THE GATE
IN MACBETH

FROM my boyish days I had always felt a great perplexity on one point in Macbeth: it was this: the
knocking at the gate,[1] which succeeds to the murder
of Duncan, produced to my feelings an effect for
which I never could account: the effect was—that it
reflected back upon the murder a peculiar awfulness
and a depth of solemnity: yet, however obstinately I
endeavoured with my understanding to comprehend
this, for many years I never could see *why* it should
produce such an effect.—

Here I pause for one moment to exhort the reader
never to pay any attention to his understanding when
it stands in opposition to any other faculty of his
mind. The mere understanding, however useful and
indispensable, is the meanest faculty in the human
mind and the most to be distrusted: and yet the great
majority of people trust to nothing else; which may
do for ordinary life, but not for philosophic purposes.
Of this, out of ten thousand instances that I might
produce, I will cite one. Ask of any person whatsoever,
who is not previously prepared for the demand by a
knowledge of perspective, to draw in the rudest way
the commonest appearance which depends upon the
laws of that science—as for instances, to represent the
effect of two walls standing at right angles to each
other, or the appearance of the houses on each side of
a street, as seen by a person looking down the street
from one extremity. Now in all cases, unless the person has happened to observe in pictures how it is that
artists produce these effects, he will be utterly unable
to make the smallest approximation to it. Yet why?—
For he has actually seen the effect every day of his life.
The reason is—that he allows his understanding to
overrule his eyes. His understanding, which includes
no intuitive knowledge of the laws of vision, can
furnish him with no reason why a line which is known
and can be proved to be a horizontal line, should not

appear a horizontal line: a line, that made any angle
with the perpendicular less than a right angle, would
seem to him to indicate that his houses were all
tumbling down together. Accordingly he makes the
line of his houses a horizontal line, and fails of course
to produce the effect demanded. Here then is one
instance out of many, in which not only the understanding is allowed to overrule the eyes, but where the
understanding is positively allowed to obliterate the
eyes as it were: for not only does the man believe
the evidence of his understanding in opposition to
that of his eyes, but (which is monstrous!) the idiot
is not aware that his eyes ever gave such evidence. He
does not know that he has seen (and therefore *quoad*[2]
his consciousness has *not* seen) that which he *has* seen
every day of his life. But, to return from this digression,—my understanding could furnish no reason why
the knocking at the gate in Macbeth should produce
any effect direct or reflected: in fact, my understanding said positively that it could *not* produce any effect.
But I knew better: I felt that it did: and I waited and
clung to the problem until further knowledge should
enable me to solve it.—At length, in 1812, Mr. Williams made his *début* on the stage of Ratcliffe Highway, and executed those unparalleled murders which
have procured for him such a brilliant and undying
reputation.[3] On which murders, by the way, I must
observe, that in one respect they have had an ill effect,
by making the connoisseur in murder very fastidious
in his taste, and dissatisfied with any thing that has
been since done in that line. All other murders look
pale by the deep crimson of his: and, as an amateur
once said to me in a querulous tone, "There has been
absolutely nothing *doing* since his time, or nothing
that's worth speaking of." But this is wrong: for it is
unreasonable to expect all men to be great artists, and
born with the genius of Mr. Williams.—Now it will be
remembered that in the first of these murders (that of
the Marrs) the same incident (of a knocking at the
door soon after the work of extermination was complete) did actually occur which the genius of Shakspeare had invented: and all good judges and the most
eminent dilettanti acknowledged the felicity of Shakspeare's suggestion as soon as it was actually realized.
Here then was a fresh proof that I had been right in
relying on my own feeling in opposition to my understanding; and again I set myself to study the problem:

---

[1] See *Macbeth*, II, ii–iii.

[2] *quoad*: "with respect to."
[3] John Williams, a seaman, had committed famous multiple
murders in London in 1811. The murderer and his deeds long
fascinated and haunted De Quincey (see "On Murder Considered
as one of the Fine Arts"). In 1854, he published a brilliantly
suspenseful account of the murders in Volume IV of his *Selections
Grave and Gay*.

at length I solved it to my own satisfaction; and my solution is this. Murder in ordinary cases, where the sympathy is wholly directed to the case of the murdered person, is an incident of coarse and vulgar horror; and for this reason—that it flings the interest exclusively upon the natural but ignoble instinct by which we cleave to life; an instinct which, as being indispensable to the primal law of self-preservation, is the same in kind (though different in degree) amongst all living creatures; this instinct therefore, because it annihilates all distinctions, and degrades the greatest of men to the level of "the poor beetle that we tread on,"[4] exhibits human nature in its most abject and humiliating attitude. Such an attitude would little suit the purposes of the poet. What then must he do? He must throw the interest on the murderer: our sympathy must be with *him;* (of course I mean a sympathy of comprehension, a sympathy by which we enter into his feelings, and are made to understand them,—not a sympathy* of pity or approbation:) in the murdered person all strife of thought, all flux and reflux of passion and of purpose, are crushed by one overwhelming panic: the fear of instant death smites him "with its petrific mace."[5] But in the murderer, such a murderer as a poet will condescend to, there must be raging some great storm of passion,— jealousy, ambition, vengeance, hatred,—which will create a hell within him; and into this hell we are to look. In Macbeth, for the sake of gratifying his own enormous and teeming faculty of creation, Shakspeare has introduced two murderers: and, as usual in his hands, they are remarkably discriminated: but, though in Macbeth the strife of mind is greater than in his wife, the tiger spirit not so awake, and his feelings caught chiefly by contagion from her,—yet, as both were finally involved in the guilt of murder, the murderous mind of necessity is finally to be presumed in both. This was to be expressed; and on its own account, as well as to make it a more proportionable antagonist to the unoffending nature of their victim, "the gracious Duncan," and adequately to expound

* It seems almost ludicrous to guard and explain my use of a word in a situation where it should naturally explain itself. But it has become necessary to do so, in consequence of the unscholarlike use of the word sympathy, at present so general, by which, instead of taking it in its proper sense, as the act of reproducing in our minds the feelings of another, whether for hatred, indignation, love, pity, or approbation, it is made a mere synonyme of the word *pity;* and hence, instead of saying, "sympathy *with* another," many writers adopt the monstrous barbarism of "sympathy *for* another."

[4] *Measure for Measure,* III, i, 79.
[5] *Paradise Lost,* X, 294.

"the deep damnation of his taking off,"[6] this was to be expressed with peculiar energy. We were to be made to feel that the human nature, *i.e.* the divine nature of love and mercy, spread through the hearts of all creatures, and seldom utterly withdrawn from man,—was gone, vanished, extinct; and that the fiendish nature had taken its place. And, as this effect is marvellously accomplished in the dialogues and soliloquies themselves, so it is finally consummated by the expedient under consideration; and it is to this that I now solicit the reader's attention. If the reader has ever witnessed a wife, daughter, or sister, in a fainting fit, he may chance to have observed that the most affecting moment in such a spectacle, is *that* in which a sigh and a stirring announce the recommencement of suspended life. Or, if the reader has ever been present in a vast metropolis on the day when some great national idol was carried in funeral pomp to his grave, and chancing to walk near to the course through which it passed, has felt powerfully, in the silence and desertion of the streets and in the stagnation of ordinary business, the deep interest which at that moment was possessing the heart of man,—if all at once he should hear the death-like stillness broken up by the sound of wheels rattling away from the scene, and making known that the transitory vision was dissolved, he will be aware that at no moment was his sense of the complete suspension and pause in ordinary human concerns so full and affecting as at that moment when the suspension ceases, and the goings-on of human life are suddenly resumed. All action in any direction is best expounded, measured, and made apprehensible, by reaction. Now apply this to the case in Macbeth. Here, as I have said, the retiring of the human heart and the entrance of the fiendish heart was to be expressed and made sensible. Another world has stepped in; and the murderers are taken out of the region of human things, human purposes, human desires. They are transfigured: Lady Macbeth is "unsexed;"[7] Macbeth has forgot that he was born of woman; both are conformed to the image of devils; and the world of devils is suddenly revealed. But how shall this be conveyed and made palpable? In order that a new world may step in, this world must for a time disappear. The murderers, and the murder, must be insulated—cut off by an immeasurable gulph from the ordinary tide and succession of human affairs —locked up and sequestered in some deep recess: we must be made sensible that the world of ordinary life is suddenly arrested—laid asleep—tranced—racked

[6] III, i, 66; I, vii, 20.
[7] See I, v, 42.

into a dread armistice: time must be annihilated; relation to things without abolished; and all must pass self-withdrawn into a deep syncope[8] and suspension of earthly passion. Hence it is that when the deed is done—when the work of darkness is perfect, then the world of darkness passes away like a pageantry in the clouds: the knocking at the gate is heard; and it makes known audibly that the reaction has commenced: the human has made its reflux upon the fiendish: the pulses of life are beginning to beat again: and the re-establishment of the goings-on of the world in which we live, first makes us profoundly sensible of the awful parenthesis that had suspended them.

Oh! mighty poet!—Thy works are not as those of other men, simply and merely great works of art; but are also like the phenomena of nature, like the sun and the sea, the stars and the flowers,—like frost and snow, rain and dew, hail-storm and thunder, which are to be studied with entire submission of our own faculties, and in the perfect faith that in them there can be no too much or too little, nothing useless or inert— but that, the further we press in our discoveries, the more we shall see proofs of design and self-supporting arrangement where the careless eye had seen nothing but accident!

* * * * *

[October 1823]

ON MURDER, CONSIDERED AS ONE OF THE
FINE ARTS

This masterpiece of macabre humor was first published in Blackwood's Magazine, *February 1827. (A shorter supplementary piece in the same vein appeared in November 1839.) In revised form, the essay appeared in Volume IV* [Miscellanies] *of* Selections Grave and Gay, *1854, which text is here followed.*

ON MURDER,
CONSIDERED AS ONE OF THE
FINE ARTS.

ADVERTISEMENT OF A MAN MORBIDLY
VIRTUOUS.

MOST of us, who read books, have probably heard of a Society for the Promotion of Vice, of the Hell-Fire Club, founded in the last century by Sir Francis Dashwood, &c. At Brighton I think it was, that a Society was formed for the Suppression of Virtue. That society was itself suppressed; but I am sorry to

say that another exists in London, of a character still more atrocious. In tendency, it may be denominated a Society for the Encouragement of Murder; but, according to their own delicate εὐφημισμὸς,[1] it is styled, The Society of Connoisseurs in Murder. They profess to be curious in homicide; amateurs and dilettanti in the various modes of carnage; and, in short, Murder-Fanciers. Every fresh atrocity of that class which the police annals of Europe bring up, they meet and criticise as they would a picture, statue, or other work of art. But I need not trouble myself with any attempt to describe the spirit of their proceedings, as the reader will collect *that* much better from one of the Monthly Lectures read before the society last year. This has fallen into my hands accidentally, in spite of all the vigilance exercised to keep their transactions from the public eye. The publication of it will alarm them; and my purpose is, that it should. For I would much rather put them down quietly, by an appeal to public opinion, than by such an exposure of names as would follow an appeal to Bow Street;[2] which last appeal, however, if this should fail, I must really resort to. For my intense virtue will not put up with such things in a Christian land. Even in a heathen land, the toleration of murder, —viz., in the dreadful shows of the amphitheatre— was felt by a Christian writer to be the most crying reproach of the public morals. This writer was Lactantius;[3] and with his words, as singularly applicable to the present occasion, I shall conclude:— "Quid tam horribile," says he, "tam tetrum, quam hominis trucidatio? Ideo severissimis legibus vita nostra munitur; ideo bella execrabilia sunt. Invenit tamen consuetudo quatenus homicidium sine bello ac sine legibus faciat: et hoc sibi voluptas quod scelus vindicavit. Quod si interesse homicidio sceleris conscientia est,—et eidem facinori spectator obstrictus est cui et admissor; ergo et in his gladiatorum cædibus non minus cruore profunditur qui spectat, quam ille qui facit: nec potest esse immunis à sanguine qui voluit effundi; aut videri non interfecisse, qui interfectori et favit et prœmium postulavit." "What is so dreadful," says Lactantius, "what so dismal and revolting, as the murder of a human creature? Therefore it is, that life for us is protected by laws the most rigorous: therefore it is, that wars are objects of execration. And yet the traditional usage of Rome has devised a mode of authorising murder apart from war, and in defiance of law; and the demands of taste (voluptas) are now become the same as those of aban-

---

[8] Loss of consciousness.

[1] εὐφημισμὸς: "euphemism."
[2] The London Police Court.
[3] Lucius Caecilius Firmianus (*c.* 250–*c.* 330).

doned guilt." Let the Society of Gentlemen Amateurs consider this; and let me call their especial attention to the last sentence, which is so weighty, that I shall attempt to convey it in English: "Now, if merely to be present at a murder fastens on a man the character of an accomplice; if barely to be a spectator involves us in one common guilt with the perpetrator, it follows, of necessity, that, in these murders of the amphitheatre, the hand which inflicts the fatal blow is not more deeply imbrued in blood than his who passively looks on; neither can *he* be clear of blood who has countenanced its shedding; nor that man seem other than a participator in murder, who gives his applause to the murderer, and calls for prizes on his behalf." The "*præmia postulavit*" I have not yet heard charged upon the Gentlemen Amateurs of London, though undoubtedly their proceedings tend to that; but the "*interfectori favit*" is implied in the very title of this association, and expressed in every line of the lecture which follows.   X. Y. Z.

LECTURE.

Gentlemen,—I have had the honour to be appointed by your committee to the trying task of reading the Williams' Lecture on Murder, considered as one of the Fine Arts; a task which might be easy enough three or four centuries ago, when the art was little understood, and few great models had been exhibited; but in this age, when masterpieces of excellence have been executed by professional men, it must be evident, that in the style of criticism applied to them, the public will look for something of a corresponding improvement. Practice and theory must advance *pari passu*.[1] People begin to see that something more goes to the composition of a fine murder than two blockheads to kill and be killed—a knife—a purse—and a dark lane. Design, gentlemen, grouping, light and shade, poetry, sentiment, are now deemed indispensable to attempts of this nature. Mr Williams has exalted the ideal of murder to all of us; and to me, therefore, in particular, has deepened the arduousness of my task. Like Æschylus or Milton in poetry, like Michael Angelo in painting, he has carried his art to a point of colossal sublimity; and, as Mr Wordsworth observes, has in a manner "created the taste by which he is to be enjoyed."[2] To sketch the history of the art, and to examine its principles critically, now remains as a duty for the connoisseur, and for judges of quite another stamp from his Majesty's Judges of Assize.

Before I begin, let me say a word or two to certain prigs, who affect to speak of our society as if it were in some degree immoral in its tendency. Immoral! Jupiter protect me, gentlemen, what is it that people mean? I am for morality, and always shall be, and for virtue, and all that; and I do affirm, and always shall (let what will come of it), that murder is an improper line of conduct, highly improper; and I do not stick to assert, that any man who deals in murder, must have very incorrect ways of thinking, and truly inaccurate principles; and so far from aiding and abetting him by pointing out his victim's hiding-place, as a great moralist* of Germany declared it to be every good man's duty to do, I would subscribe one shilling and sixpence to have him apprehended, which is more by eighteenpence than the most eminent moralists have hitherto subscribed for that purpose. But what then? Everything in this world has two handles. Murder, for instance, may be laid hold of by its moral handle (as it generally is in the pulpit, and at the Old Bailey);[3] and *that*, I confess, is its weak side; or it may also be treated *æsthetically*, as the Germans call it— that is, in relation to good taste.

To illustrate this, I will urge the authority of three eminent persons; viz., S. T. Coleridge, Aristotle, and Mr Howship the surgeon. To begin with S. T. C. One night, many years ago, I was drinking tea with him in Berners Street (which, by the way, for a short street, has been uncommonly fruitful in men of genius). Others were there besides myself; and, amidst some carnal considerations of tea and toast, we were all imbibing a dissertation on Plotinus from the Attic lips of S. T. C. Suddenly a cry arose of, "*Fire—fire!*" upon which all of us, master and disciples, Plato and οἱ περὶ τον Πλάτωνα,[4] rushed out, eager for the spectacle. The fire was in Oxford Street, at a pianoforte-maker's; and, as it promised to be a conflagration of merit, I was sorry that my engagements forced me away from Mr Coleridge's party, before matters had come to a crisis. Some days after, meeting with my Platonic host, I reminded him of the case, and begged to know how that very promising exhibition had terminated. "Oh, sir," said he, "it turned out so ill that we damned

* Kant—who carried his demands of unconditional veracity to so extravagant a length as to affirm, that, if a man were to see an innocent person escape from a murderer, it would be his duty, on being questioned by the murderer, to tell the truth, and to point out the retreat of the innocent person, under any certainty of causing murder. Lest this doctrine should be supposed to have escaped him in any heat of dispute, on being taxed with it by a celebrated French writer, he solemnly re-affirmed it, with his reasons.

---

[1] *pari passu*: "with an equal pace."
[2] See Wordsworth's "Essay, Supplementary to the Preface" (1815), p. 87.

[3] The central criminal court of London.
[4] οἱ . . . Πλάτωνα: "those around Plato," his disciples.

it unanimously." Now, does any man suppose that Mr Coleridge—who, for all he is too fat to be a person of active virtue, is undoubtedly a worthy Christian—that this good S. T. C., I say, was an incendiary, or capable of wishing any ill to the poor man and his pianofortes (many of them, doubtless, with the additional keys)? On the contrary, I know him to be that sort of man, that I durst stake my life upon it, he would have worked an engine in a case of necessity, although rather of the fattest for such fiery trials of his virtue. But how stood the case? Virtue was in no request. On the arrival of the fire engines, morality had devolved wholly on the insurance office. This being the case, he had a right to gratify his taste. He has left his tea. Was he to have nothing in return?

I contend that the most virtuous man, under the premises stated, was entitled to make a luxury of the fire, and to hiss it, as he would any other performance that raised expectations in the public mind which afterwards it disappointed. Again, to cite another great authority, what says the Stagirite? He (in the Fifth Book, I think it is, of his Metaphysics) describes what he calls κλεπτὴν τέλειον—i.e., a perfect thief;[5] and, as to Mr Howship, in a work of his on Indigestion, he makes no scruple to talk with admiration of a certain ulcer which he had seen, and which he styles "a beautiful ulcer." Now, will any man pretend, that, abstractedly considered, a thief could appear to Aristotle a perfect character, or that Mr Howship could be enamoured of an ulcer? Aristotle, it is well known, was himself so very moral a character, that, not content with writing his Nichomachéan Ethics, in one volume octavo, he also wrote another system, called *Magna Moralia*, or Big Ethics. Now, it is impossible that a man who composes any ethics at all, big or little, should admire a thief *per se*; and as to Mr Howship, it is well known that he makes war upon all ulcers, and, without suffering himself to be seduced by their charms, endeavours to banish them from the County of Middlesex. But the truth is, that, however objectionable *per se*, yet, relatively to others of their class, both a thief and an ulcer may have infinite degrees of merit. They are both imperfections, it is true; but, to be imperfect being their essence, the very greatness of their imperfection becomes their perfection. *Spartam nactus es, hanc exorna.*[6] A thief like Autolycus or the once famous George Barrington,[7] and a grim phagedænic ulcer,

superbly defined, and running regularly through all its natural stages, may no less justly be regarded as ideals after *their* kind, than the most faultless moss-rose amongst flowers, in its progress from bud to "bright consummate flower;"[8] or, amongst human flowers, the most magnificent young female, apparelled in the pomp of womanhood. And thus not only the ideal of an inkstand may be imagined (as Mr Coleridge illustrated in his celebrated correspondence with Mr Blackwood), in which, by the way, there is not so much, because an inkstand is a laudable sort of thing, and a valuable member of society; but even imperfection itself may have its ideal or perfect state.

Really, gentlemen, I beg pardon for so much philosophy at one time; and now let me apply it. When a murder is in the paulo-post-futurum tense—not done, not even (according to modern purism) *being* done, but only going to be done—and a rumour of it comes to our ears, by all means let us treat it morally. But suppose it over and done, and that you can say of it, Τετέλεσται, It is finished, or (in that adamantine molossus of Medea) εἴργασται, Done it is: it is a *fait accompli;* suppose the poor murdered man to be out of his pain, and the rascal that did it off like a shot, nobody knows whither; suppose, lastly, that we have done our best, by putting out our legs, to trip up the fellow in his flight, but all to no purpose—"abiit, evasit, excessit, erupit,"[9] &c.—why, then, I say, what's the use of any more virtue? Enough has been given to morality; now comes the turn of Taste and the Fine Arts. A sad thing it was, no doubt, very sad; but *we* can't mend it. Therefore let us make the best of a bad matter; and, as it is impossible to hammer anything out of it for moral purposes, let us treat it æsthetically, and see if it will turn to account in that way. Such is the logic of a sensible man, and what follows? We dry up our tears, and have the satisfaction, perhaps, to discover that a transaction, which, morally considered, was shocking, and without a leg to stand upon, when tried by principles of Taste, turns out to be a very meritorious performance. Thus all the world is pleased; the old proverb is justified, that it is an ill wind which blows nobody good; the amateur, from looking bilious and sulky, by too close an attention to virtue, begins to pick up his crumbs; and general hilarity prevails. Virtue has had her day; and henceforward, *Virtù*, so nearly the same thing as to differ only by a single letter (which surely is not worth haggling or higgling about)—*Virtù*, I repeat, and

---

5 Aristotle's *Metaphysics*, V, xvi, 2–3.
6 *Spartam . . . exorna:* "You've won Sparta, now adorn her." In comparison to Athens, Sparta was a plain and artistically undeveloped city. In context, the sense of the quotation would seem to be, "Imperfect Sparta is yours, make the best of a bad matter."
7 Autolycus was the thieving rogue in *The Winter's Tale*. George Barrington (b. 1755) was a celebrated pickpocket.

---

8 *Paradise Lost*, V, 481.
9 "abiit . . . erupit": "he left, he withdrew, he escaped, he broke violently away." Cicero's *Second Oration Against Catiline*, l. 1.

Connoisseurship, have leave to provide for themselves. Upon this principle, gentlemen, I propose to guide your studies, from Cain to Mr Thurtell.[10] Through this great gallery of murder, therefore, together let us wander hand in hand, in delighted admiration; while I endeavour to point your attention to the objects of profitable criticism.

The first murder is familiar to you all. As the inventor of murder, and the father of the art, Cain must have been a man of first-rate genius. All the Cains were men of genius. Tubal Cain invented tubes, I think, or some such thing. But, whatever might be the originality and genius of the artist, every art was then in its infancy, and the works turned out from each several *studio*, must be criticised with a recollection of that fact. Even Tubal's work would probably be little approved at this day in Sheffield; and therefore of Cain (Cain senior, I mean) it is no disparagement to say, that his performance was but so-so. Milton, however, is supposed to have thought differently. By his way of relating the case, it should seem to have been rather a pet murder with him, for he retouches it with an apparent anxiety for its picturesque effect:—

> "Whereat he inly raged; and, as they talk'd,
> Smote him into the midriff with a stone
> That beat out life: he fell; and, deadly pale,
> Groan'd out his soul *with gushing blood effused.*"
> *Par. Lost*, B. xi.[11]

Upon this, Richardson the painter,[12] who had an eye for effect, remarks as follows, in his "Notes on Paradise Lost," p. 497:—"It has been thought," says he, "that Cain beat (as the common saying is) the breath out of his brother's body with a great stone; Milton gives in to this, with the addition, however, of a large wound." In this place it was a judicious addition; for the rudeness of the weapon, unless raised and enriched by a warm, sanguinary colouring, has too much of the naked air of the savage school; as if the deed were perpetrated by a Polypheme without science, premeditation, or anything but a mutton bone. However, I am chiefly pleased with the improvement, as it implies that Milton was an amateur. As to Shakspere, there never was a better; witness his description of the murdered Duncan, Banquo, &c.; and above all, witness

his incomparable miniature, in "Henry VI.," of the murdered Gloucester.*

The foundation of the art having been once laid, it is pitiable to see how it slumbered without improvement for ages. In fact, I shall now be obliged to leap over all murders, sacred and profane, as utterly unworthy of notice, until long after the Christian era. Greece, even

---

* The passage occurs in the *second* part (act 3) of "Henry VI.," and is doubly remarkable—first, for its critical fidelity to nature, were the description meant only for *poetic* effect; but, secondly, for the *judicial* value impressed upon it when offered (as here it *is* offered) in silent corroboration legally of a dreadful whisper, all at once arising, that foul play had been dealing with a great prince, clothed with an official state character. It is the Duke of Gloucester, faithful guardian and loving uncle of the simple and imbecile king, who has been found dead in his bed. How shall this event be interpreted? Had he died under some natural visitation of Providence, or by violence from his enemies? The two court factions read the circumstantial indications of the case into opposite constructions. The affectionate and afflicted young king, whose position almost pledges him to neutrality, cannot, nevertheless, disguise his overwhelming suspicions of hellish conspiracy in the background. Upon this, a leader of the opposite faction endeavours to break the force of this royal frankness, countersigned and echoed most impressively by Lord Warwick. "What *instance*," he asks—meaning by *instance* not example or illustration, as thoughtless commentators have constantly supposed, but in the common scholastic sense—what *instantia*, what pressure of argument, what urgent plea, can Lord Warwick put forward in support of his "dreadful oath"—an oath, namely, that, as surely as he hopes for the life eternal, so surely

> "I do believe that violent hands were laid
> Upon the life of this thrice faméd duke."

Ostensibly the challenge is to Warwick, but substantially it is meant for the king. And the reply of Warwick, the argument on which he builds, lies in a solemn array of all the changes worked in the duke's features by death, as irreconcileable with any other hypothesis than that this death had been a violent one. What argument have I that Gloucester died under the hands of murderers? Why the following roll-call of awful changes, affecting head, face, nostrils, eyes, hands, &c., which do not belong indifferently to *any* mode of death, but exclusively to a death by violence:—

> "But see, his face is black and full of blood;
> His eyeballs farther out than when he lived,
> Staring full ghastly, like a strangled man;
> His hair uprear'd, his nostrils stretch'd with struggling;
> His hands abroad display'd, as one that grasp'd
> And tugg'd for life, and was by strength subdued.
> Look on the sheets:—his hair, you see, is sticking;
> His well-proportion'd beard made rough and rugged,
> Like to the summer's corn by tempest lodged.
> It cannot be but he was murder'd here;
> The least of all these signs were probable."

As the logic of the case, let us not for a moment forget, that, to be of any value, the signs and indications pleaded must be sternly *diagnostic*. The discrimination sought for is between death that is natural, and death that is violent. All indications, therefore, that belong equally and indifferently to either, are equivocal, useless, and alien from the very purpose of the signs here registered by Shakspere.

---

[10] John Thurtell (1794–1824) committed the "Dreadful Murder of Mr. William Weare," on October 24, 1823.

[11] Ll. 444–47.

[12] Jonathan Richardson (1665–1745) was a portrait painter and author of *Explanatory Notes and Remarks on Milton's Paradise Lost* (1734).

in the age of Pericles, produced no murder, or at least none is recorded, of the slightest merit; and Rome had too little originality of genius in any of the arts to succeed where her model failed her.* In fact, the Latin language sinks under the very idea of murder. "The man was murdered;"—how will this sound in Latin? *Interfectus est, interemptus est*—which simply expresses a homicide; and hence the Christian Latinity of the middle ages was obliged to introduce a new word, such as the feebleness of classic conceptions never ascended to. *Murdratus est*, says the sublimer dialect of Gothic ages. Meantime, the Jewish school of murder kept alive whatever was yet known in the art, and gradually transferred it to the Western World. Indeed, the Jewish school was always respectable, even in its medieval stages, as the case of Hugh of Lincoln shows, which was honoured with the approbation of Chaucer, on occasion of another performance from the same school, which, in his Canterbury Tales, he puts into the mouth of the Lady Abbess.

Recurring, however, for one moment, to classical antiquity, I cannot but think that Catiline, Clodius, and some of that coterie, would have made first-rate artists; and it is on all accounts to be regretted, that the priggism of Cicero robbed his country of the only chance she had for distinction in this line. As the *subject* of a murder, no person could have answered better than himself. Oh Gemini! how he would have howled with panic, if he had heard Cethegus [13] under his bed. It would have been truly diverting to have listened to him; and satisfied I am, gentlemen, that he would have preferred the *utile* of creeping into a closet, or even into a *cloaca*, [14] to the *honestum* of facing the bold artist.

To come now to the dark ages—(by which we that speak with precision mean, *par excellence*, the tenth

century as a meridian line, and the two centuries immediately before and after, full midnight being from A.D. 888 to A.D. 1111)—these ages ought naturally to be favourable to the art of murder, as they were to church architecture, to stained glass, &c.; and, accordingly, about the latter end of this period, there arose a great character in our art, I mean the Old Man of the Mountains. [15] He was a shining light, indeed, and I need not tell you, that the very word "assassin" is deduced from him. So keen an amateur was he, that on one occasion, when his own life was attempted by a favourite assassin, he was so much pleased with the talent shown, that, notwithstanding the failure of the artist, he created him a duke upon the spot, with remainder to the female line, and settled a pension on him for three lives. Assassination is a branch of the art which demands a separate notice; and it is possible that I may devote an entire lecture to it. Meantime, I shall only observe how odd it is, that this branch of the art has flourished by intermitting fits. It never rains, but it pours. Our own age can boast of some fine specimens, such, for instance, as Bellingham's affair with the prime minister Perceval, the Duc de Berri's case at the Parisian Opera House, [16] the Maréchal Bessieres' case at Avignon; and about two and a half centuries ago, there was a most brilliant constellation of murders in this class. I need hardly say, that I allude especially to those seven splendid works—the assassinations of William I., of Orange; of the three French Henries, viz.—Henri, Duke of Guise, that had a fancy for the throne of France; of Henri III., last prince in the line of Valois, who then occupied that throne; and finally of Henri IV., his brother-in-law, who succeeded to that throne as first prince in the line of Bourbon; not eighteen years later came the 5th on the roll, viz., that of our Duke of Buckingham (which you will find excellently described in the letters published by Sir Henry Ellis, of the British Museum), 6thly of Gustavus Adolphus, and 7thly of Wallenstein. [17] What a glorious

---

* At the time of writing this, I held the common opinion upon that subject. Mere inconsideration it was that led to so erroneous a judgment. Since then, on closer reflection, I have seen ample reason to retract it: satisfied I now am, that the Romans, in every art which allowed to them any parity of advantages, had merits as racy, native, and characteristic, as the best of the Greeks. Elsewhere I shall plead this cause circumstantially, with the hope of converting the reader. In the meantime, I was anxious to lodge my protest against this ancient error; an error which commenced in the time-serving sycophancy of Virgil the court-poet. With the base purpose of gratifying Augustus in his vindictive spite against Cicero, and by way of introducing, therefore, the little clause, *orabunt Causas melius* as applying to all Athenian against all Roman orators, Virgil did not scruple to sacrifice by wholesale the just pretensions of his compatriots collectively.

[13] Gaius Cornelius Cethegus was an associate of Catiline, and the man who was personally to undertake the murder of Cicero in the conspiracy of 63 B.C.
[14] *cloaca*: "sewer."

[15] The usual English translation of *Sheik-al-Jabal*, the title of the supreme ruler of a fanatical sect active between the eleventh and thirteenth centuries in Persia and Syria. Their practice of secretly murdering their enemies brought the word "assassin" into currency, a corruption of "Hashish," which the chosen murderers were fed before being sent out on their assignments.
[16] Spencer Perceval (1762–1812) was the British prime minister murdered in the lobby of the House of Commons on May 11, 1812, by John Bellingham, whom Perceval had refused to aid in a matter involving Bellingham's arrest for bankruptcy. Charles-Ferdinand de Bourbon, Duc de Berri (1778–1820), was murdered on February 13, 1820, on leaving the Paris Opera House.
[17] George Villiers, first Duke of Buckingham (1592–1628), a favorite of Charles I, was murdered August 23, 1628. Sir Henry Ellis (1777–1869), principal librarian of the British Museum, began publication in 1824 of *Original Letters illustrative of English History*. Gustavus Adolphus (1594–1632), king of Sweden from 1611, died in the Battle of Lützen (November 16, 1632), while

Pleiad of murders! And it increases one's admiration—that this bright constellation of artistic displays, comprehending 3 Majesties, 3 Serene Highnesses, and 1 Excellency, all lay within so narrow a field of time as between A.D. 1588 and 1635. The King of Sweden's assassination, by the by, is doubted by many writers, Harte amongst others; but they are wrong. He was murdered; and I consider his murder unique in its excellence; for he was murdered at noon-day, and on the field of battle—a feature of original conception, which occurs in no other work of art that I remember. To conceive the idea of a secret murder on private account, as enclosed within a little parenthesis on a vast stage of public battle-carnage, is like Hamlet's subtle device of a tragedy within a tragedy. Indeed, all of these assassinations may be studied with profit by the advanced connoisseur. They are all of them *exemplaria* model murders, pattern murders, of which one may say,—

"Nocturnâ versate manu, versate diurná;"[18]

especially *nocturnâ*.

In these assassinations of princes and statesmen, there is nothing to excite our wonder; important changes often depend on their deaths; and, from the eminence on which they stand, they are peculiarly exposed to the aim of every artist who happens to be possessed by the craving for scenical effect. But there is another class of assassinations, which has prevailed from an early period of the seventeenth century, that really *does* surprise me; I mean the assassination of philosophers. For, gentlemen, it is a fact, that every philosopher of eminence for the two last centuries has either been murdered, or, at the least, been very near it; insomuch, that if a man calls himself a philosopher, and never had his life attempted, rest assured there is nothing in him; and against Locke's philosophy in particular, I think it an unanswerable objection (if we needed any), that, although he carried his throat about with him in this world for seventy-two years, no man ever condescended to cut it. As these cases of philosophers are not much known, and are generally good and well composed in their circumstances, I shall here read an excursus on that subject, chiefly by way of showing my own learning.

The first great philosopher of the seventeenth century (if we except Bacon and Galileo) was Des Cartes;

and if ever one could say of a man that he was all *but* murdered—murdered within an inch—one must say it of him. The case was this, as reported by Baillet[19] in his "Vie De M. Des Cartes," tom. I. p. 102–3. In the year 1621, when Des Cartes might be about twenty-six years old, he was touring about as usual (for he was as restless as a hyena); and, coming to the Elbe, either at Gluckstadt or at Hamburgh, he took shipping for East Friezland. What he could want in East Friezland no man has ever discovered; and perhaps he took this into consideration himself; for, on reaching Embden, he resolved to sail instantly for *West* Friezland; and being very impatient of delay, he hired a bark, with a few mariners to navigate it. No sooner had he got out to sea, than he made a pleasing discovery, viz., that he had shut himself up in a den of murderers. His crew, says M. Baillet, he soon found out to be "des scélérats"[20]—not *amateurs*, gentlemen, as we are, but professional men—the height of whose ambition at that moment was to cut his individual throat. But the story is too pleasing to be abridged; I shall give it, therefore, accurately, from the French of his biographer: "M. Des Cartes had no company but that of his servant, with whom he was conversing in French. The sailors, who took him for a foreign merchant, rather than a cavalier, concluded that he must have money about him. Accordingly, they came to a resolution by no means advantageous to his purse. There is this difference, however, between sea-robbers and the robbers in forests, that the latter may, without hazard, spare the lives of their victims; whereas the others cannot put a passenger on shore in such a case without running the risk of being apprehended. The crew of M. Des Cartes arranged their measures with a view to evade any danger of that sort. They observed that he was a stranger from a distance, without acquaintance in the country, and that nobody would take any trouble to inquire about him, in case he should never come to hand (*quand il viendroit à manquer*)." Think, gentlemen, of these Friezland dogs discussing a philosopher as if he were a puncheon of rum consigned to some ship-broker. "His temper, they remarked, was very mild and patient; and, judging from the gentleness of his deportment, and the courtesy with which he treated themselves, that he could be nothing more than some green young man, without station or root in the world, they concluded that they should have all the easier task in disposing of his life. They made no scruple to discuss the whole matter in his presence, as not supposing that he understood any other language

<hr>

leading his forces against those of Albrecht Eusebius Wenzel von Wallenstein (1583–1634), an ambitious Czech-born soldier and statesman during the Thirty Years' War. Wallenstein was murdered February 25, 1634.

[18] "Nocturnâ . . . diurná": "Turn them over in your hand [meditate upon them], by night and by day." Horace's *Ars Poetica*, l. 269.

[19] Adrien Baillet (1649–1706), whose life of Descartes was published in 1691.

[20] "des scélérats": "villainous criminals".

than that in which he conversed with his servant; and the amount of their deliberation was—to murder him, then to throw him into the sea, and to divide his spoils."

Excuse my laughing, gentlemen; but the fact is, I always *do* laugh when I think of this case—two things about it seem so droll. One is, the horrid panic or "funk" (as the men of Eton call it) in which Des Cartes must have found himself, upon hearing this regular drama sketched for his own death—funeral—succession and administration to his effects. But another thing which seems to me still more funny about this affair is, that if these Friezland hounds had been "game," we should have no Cartesian philosophy; and how we could have done without *that*, considering the world of books it has produced, I leave to any respectable trunk-maker to declare.

However, to go on: spite of his enormous funk, Des Cartes showed fight, and by that means awed these Anti-Cartesian rascals. "Finding," says M. Baillet, "that the matter was no joke, M. Des Cartes leaped upon his feet in a trice, assumed a stern countenance that these cravens had never looked for, and, addressing them in their own language, threatened to run them through on the spot if they dared to give him any insult." Certainly, gentlemen, this would have been an honour far above the merits of such inconsiderable rascals—to be spitted like larks upon a Cartesian sword; and therefore I am glad M. Des Cartes did not rob the gallows by executing his threat, especially as he could not possibly have brought his vessel to port, after he had murdered his crew; so that he must have continued to cruise for ever in the Zuyder Zee, and would probably have been mistaken by sailors for the *Flying Dutchman*, homeward bound. "The spirit which M. Des Cartes manifested," says his biographer, "had the effect of magic on these wretches. The suddenness of their consternation struck their minds with a confusion which blinded them to their advantage, and they conveyed him to his destination as peaceably as he could desire."

Possibly, gentlemen, you may fancy that, on the model of Cæsar's address to his poor ferryman—"*Cæsarem vehis et fortunas ejus*"[21]—M. Des Cartes needed only to have said, "Dogs, you cannot cut my throat, for you carry Des Cartes and his philosophy," and might safely have defied them to do their worst. A German emperor had the same notion, when, being cautioned to keep out of the way of a cannonading, he replied, "Tut! man. Did you ever hear of a cannon-ball

that killed an emperor?"* As to an emperor I cannot say, but a less thing has sufficed to smash a philosopher; and the next great philosopher of Europe undoubtedly *was* murdered. This was Spinosa.

I know very well the common opinion about him is, that he died in his bed. Perhaps he did, but he was murdered for all that; and this I shall prove by a book published at Brussels in the year 1731, entitled "La Vie de Spinosa, par M. Jean Colerus," with many additions, from a MS. life, by one of his friends. Spinosa died on the 21st February, 1677, being then little more than forty-four years old. This, of itself, looks suspicious; and M. Jean admits, that a certain expression in the MS. life of him would warrant the conclusion, "que sa mort n' a pas été tout-à-fait naturelle."[22] Living in a damp country, and a sailor's country, like Holland, he may be thought to have indulged a good deal in grog, especially in punch,† which was then newly discovered. Undoubtedly he might have done so; but the fact is, that he did not. M. Jean calls him "extrêmement sobre en son boire et en son manger."[23] And though some wild stories were afloat about his using the juice of mandragora (p. 140) and opium (p. 144), yet neither of these articles is found in his druggist's bill. Living, therefore, with such sobriety, how was it possible that he should die a natural death at forty-four? Hear his biographer's account:—"Sunday morning, the 21st of February, before it was church time, Spinosa came down stairs, and conversed with the master and mistress of the house." At this time, therefore, perhaps ten o'clock on Sunday morning, you see that Spinosa was alive, and pretty well. But it seems "he had summoned from Amsterdam a certain physician, whom," says the biographer, "I shall not otherwise point out to notice

---

* This same argument has been employed at least once too often: some centuries back a dauphin of France, when admonished of his risk from small-pox, made the same demand as the emperor—"Had any gentleman heard of a dauphin killed by small-pox?" No; not any gentleman *had* heard of such a case. And yet, for all that, this dauphin died of that same small-pox.

† "June 1, 1675.—Drinke part of three boules of punch (a liquor very strainge to me)," says the Rev. Mr Henry Teonge, in his Diary published by C. Knight. In a note on this passage, a reference is made to Fryer's Travels to the East Indies, 1672, who speaks of "that enervating liquor called *paunch* (which is Hindostanee for five), from five ingredients." Made thus, it seems the medical men called it diapente; if with four only, diatessaron. No doubt, it was this evangelical name that recommended it to the Rev. Mr Teonge.

---

21 "*Cæsarem . . . ejus*": "You carry Caesar and his fortunes."

22 "que sa mort . . . naturelle": "that his death was not altogether natural."

23 "extrêmement . . . manger": "extremely moderate in drinking and eating."

than by these two letters, L. M." This L. M. had directed the people of the house to purchase "an ancient cock," and to have him boiled forthwith, in order that Spinosa might take some broth about noon; which in fact he did; and ate some of the *old cock* with a good appetite, after the landlord and his wife had returned from church.

"In the afternoon, L. M. staid alone with Spinosa, the people of the house having returned to church; on coming out from which, they learned, with much surprise, that Spinosa had died about three o'clock, in the presence of L. M., who took his departure for Amsterdam that same evening, by the night-boat, without paying the least attention to the deceased," and probably without paying very much attention to the payment of his own little account. "No doubt he was the readier to dispense with these duties, as he had possessed himself of a ducatoon,[24] and a small quantity of silver, together with a silver-hafted knife, and had absconded with his pillage." Here you see, gentlemen, the murder is plain, and the manner of it. It was L. M. who murdered Spinosa for his money. Poor Spinosa was an invalid, meagre and weak: as no blood was observed, L. M. no doubt threw him down, and smothered him with pillows—the poor man being already half suffocated by his infernal dinner. After masticating that "ancient cock," which I take to mean a cock of the preceding century, in what condition could the poor invalid find himself for a stand-up fight with L. M.? But who was L. M.? It surely never could be Lindley Murray,[25] for I saw him at York in 1825; and, besides, I do not think he would do such a thing—at least, not to a brother grammarian: for you know, gentlemen, that Spinosa wrote a very respectable Hebrew grammar.

Hobbes—but why, or on what principle, I never could understand—was not murdered. This was a capital oversight of the professional men in the seventeenth century; because in every light he was a fine subject for murder, except, indeed, that he was lean and skinny; for I can prove that he had money, and (what is very funny) he had no right to make the least resistance; since, according to himself, irresistible power creates the very highest species of right, so that it is rebellion of the blackest dye to refuse to be murdered, when a competent force appears to murder you. However, gentlemen, though he was not murdered, I am happy to assure you that (by his own

account) he was three times very near being murdered, which is consolatory. The first time was in the spring of 1640, when he pretends to have circulated a little MS. on the king's behalf against the Parliament; he never could produce this MS., by the by; but he says, that, "Had not His Majesty dissolved the Parliament" (in May), "it had brought him into danger of his life." Dissolving the Parliament, however, was of no use; for in November of the same year the Long Parliament assembled, and Hobbes, a second time fearing he should be murdered, ran away to France. This looks like the madness of John Dennis,[26] who thought that Louis XIV. would never make peace with Queen Anne, unless he (Dennis to wit) were given up to French vengeance; and actually ran away from the sea-coast under that belief. In France, Hobbes managed to take care of his throat pretty well for ten years; but at the end of that time, by way of paying court to Cromwell, he published his "Leviathan." The old coward now began to "funk" horribly for the third time; he fancied the swords of the cavaliers were constantly at his throat, recollecting how they had served the Parliament ambassadors at the Hague and Madrid. "Tum," says he, in his dog-Latin life of himself,

"Tum venit in mentem mihi Dorislaus et Ascham;
Tanquam proscripto terror ubique aderat."[27]

And accordingly he ran home to England. Now, certainly, it is very true that a man deserved a cudgelling for writing "Leviathan;" and two or three cudgellings for writing a pentameter ending so villanously as "terror ubique aderat!" But no man ever thought him worthy of anything beyond cudgelling. And, in fact, the whole story is a bounce[28] of his own. For, in a most abusive letter which he wrote "to a learned person" (meaning Wallis the mathematician), he gives quite another account of the matter, and says (p. 8), he ran home "because he would not trust his safety with the French clergy;" insinuating that he was likely to be murdered for his religion, which would have been a high joke indeed—Tom's being brought to the stake for religion.

Bounce or not bounce, however, certain it is that Hobbes, to the end of his life, feared that somebody

---

[24] "A silver coin formerly current in Italian and some other European states" (*Oxford English Dictionary*).

[25] Lindley Murray (1745–1826), author of *English Grammar*, first published in 1795, which became the standard textbook in English and American schools.

[26] John Dennis (1657–1734), the playwright and critic.

[27] "Tum . . . aderat": "Then I began on this to Ruminate / On *Dorislaus*, and on *Ascham*'s Fate, / And stood amazed, like a poor Exile, / Encompassed with Terrour all the while" (English translation, published 1680, of *Thomae Hobbesii Malmesburiensis Vita. Authore Seipso* [1679]). Masson identifies Isaac Dorislaus and Anthony Ascham as envoys from the English Commonwealth to Holland and Spain, respectively; they were both assassinated abroad by exiled English Royalists.

[28] A boastful falsehood.

would murder him. This is proved by the story I am going to tell you: it is not from a manuscript, but (as Mr Coleridge says) it is as good as manuscript; for it comes from a book now entirely forgotten, viz., "The Creed of Mr Hobbes Examined: in a Conference between him and a Student in Divinity" (published about ten years before Hobbes's death). The book is anonymous, but it was written by Tennison,[29] the same who, about thirty years after, succeeded Tillotson as Archbishop of Canterbury. The introductory anecdote is as follows:—"A certain divine" (no doubt Tennison himself) "took an annual tour of one month to different parts of the island." In one of these excursions (1670), he visited the Peak in Derbyshire, partly in consequence of Hobbes's description of it. Being in that neighbourhood, he could not but pay a visit to Buxton; and at the very moment of his arrival, he was fortunate enough to find a party of gentlemen dismounting at the inn-door, amongst whom was a long thin fellow, who turned out to be no less a person than Mr Hobbes, who probably had ridden over from Chatsworth.* Meeting so great a lion, a tourist, in search of the picturesque, could do no less than present himself in the character of bore. And luckily for this scheme, two of Mr Hobbes's companions were suddenly summoned away by express; so that, for the rest of his stay at Buxton, he had Leviathan entirely to himself, and had the honour of bowsing with him in the evening. Hobbes, it seems, at first showed a good deal of stiffness, for he was shy of divines; but this wore off, and he became very sociable and funny, and they agreed to go into the bath together. How Tennison could venture to gambol in the same water with Leviathan, I cannot explain; but so it was: they frolicked about like two dolphins, though Hobbes must have been as old as the hills; and "in those intervals wherein they abstained from swimming and plunging themselves" (i.e., diving), "they discoursed of many things relating to the baths of the Ancients, and the Origine of Springs. When they had in this manner passed away an hour, they stepped out of the bath; and, having dried and cloathed themselves, they sate down in expectation of such a supper as the place

* Chatsworth was then, as now, the superb seat of the Cavendishes in their highest branch—in those days Earl, at present Duke, of Devonshire. It is to the honour of this family that, through two generations, they gave an asylum to Hobbes. It is noticeable that Hobbes was born in the year of the Spanish Armada, i.e., in 1588: such, at least, is my belief. And, therefore, at this meeting with Tennison in 1670, he must have been about 82 years old.

[29] Thomas Tenison (1636–1715), who became Archbishop of Canterbury in 1695. His *Creed of Mr. Hobbes Examined* was published in 1670.

afforded; designing to refresh themselves like the *Deipnosophistæ*,[30] and rather to reason than to drink profoundly. But in this innocent intention they were interrupted by the disturbance arising from a little quarrel, in which some of the ruder people in the house were for a short time engaged. At this Mr Hobbes seemed much concerned, though he was at some distance from the persons." And why was he concerned, gentlemen? No doubt, you fancy, from some benign and disinterested love of peace, worthy of an old man and a philosopher. But listen—"For awhile he was not composed, but related it once or twice as to himself, with a low and careful, *i.e.*, anxious, tone, how Sextus Roscius was murthered after supper by the Balneæ Palatinæ. Of such general extent is that remark of Cicero, in relation to Epicurus the Atheist, of whom he observed, that he of all men dreaded most those things which he contemned—Death and the Gods." Merely because it was supper time, and in the neighbourhood of a bath, Mr Hobbes must have the fate of Sextus Roscius. He must be mur*th*ered, because Sextus Roscius was mur*th*ered. What logic was there in this, unless to a man who was always dreaming of murder? Here was Leviathan, no longer afraid of the daggers of English cavaliers or French clergy, but "frightened from his propriety" by a row in an ale house between some honest clod-hoppers of Derbyshire, whom his own gaunt scarecrow of a person, that belonged to quite another century, would have frightened out of their wits.

Malebranche, it will give you pleasure to hear, was murdered. The man who murdered him is well known: it was Bishop Berkeley. The story is familiar, though hitherto not put in a proper light. Berkeley, when a young man, went to Paris, and called on Père Malebranche. He found him in his cell cooking. Cooks have ever been a *genus irritabile*;[31] authors still more so: Malebranche was both: a dispute arose; the old father, warm already, became warmer; culinary and metaphysical irritations united to derange his liver: he took to his bed, and died. Such is the common version of the story: "So the whole ear of Denmark is abused."[32] The fact is, that the matter was hushed up, out of consideration for Berkeley, who (as Pope justly observes) had "every virtue under heaven:"[33] else it was well known that Berkeley, feeling himself nettled by the waspishness of the old Frenchman, squared at him; a *turn-up* was the consequence: Malebranche was

[30] *Deipnosophistæ*: "The Sophists at Dinner." See "The Pleasures of Opium," footnote 8, p. 566.
[31] *genus irritabile*: "an irritable race." Horace's *Epistles*, II, ii, 102.
[32] *Hamlet*, I, v, 36.
[33] Pope's *Epilogue to the Satires*, II, 73.

floored in the first round; the conceit was wholly taken out of him; and he would perhaps have given in; but Berkeley's blood was now up, and he insisted on the old Frenchman's retracting his doctrine of Occasional Causes. The vanity of the man was too great for this; and he fell a sacrifice to the impetuosity of Irish youth, combined with his own absurd obstinacy.

Leibnitz, being every way superior to Malebranche, one might, *a fortiori*, have counted on *his* being murdered; which, however, was not the case. I believe he was nettled at this neglect, and felt himself insulted by the security in which he passed his days. In no other way can I explain his conduct at the latter end of his life, when he chose to grow very avaricious, and to hoard up large sums of gold, which he kept in his own house. This was at Vienna, where he died; and letters are still in existence, describing the immeasurable anxiety which he entertained for his throat. Still his ambition, for being *attempted* at least, was so great, that he would not forego the danger. A late English pedagogue, of Birmingham manufacture—viz., Dr Parr [34]—took a more selfish course under the same circumstance. He had amassed a considerable quantity of gold and silver plate, which was for some time deposited in his bedroom at his parsonage house, Hatton. But growing every day more afraid of being murdered, which he knew that he could not stand (and to which, indeed, he never had the slightest pretensions), he transferred the whole to the Hatton blacksmith; conceiving, no doubt, that the murder of a blacksmith would fall more lightly on the *salus reipublicæ*,[35] than that of a pedagogue. But I have heard this greatly disputed; and it seems now generally agreed, that one good horse-shoe is worth about two and a quarter Spital sermons.*

As Leibnitz, though not murdered, may be said to have died, partly of the fear that he should be murdered, and partly of vexation that he was not, Kant, on the other hand—who manifested no ambition in that way—had a narrower escape from a murderer than any man we read of, except Des Cartes. So absurdly does fortune throw about her favours! The case is

told, I think, in an anonymous life of this very great man. For health's sake, Kant imposed upon himself, at one time, a walk of six miles every day along a highroad. This fact becoming known to a man who had his private reasons for committing murder, at the third milestone from Königsberg, he waited for his "intended," who came up to time as duly as a mail-coach.

But for an accident, Kant was a dead man. This accident lay in the scrupulous, or what Mrs Quickly would have called the *peevish*, morality of the murderer. An old professor, he fancied, might be laden with sins. Not so a young child. On this consideration, he turned away from Kant at the critical moment, and soon after murdered a child of five years old. Such is the German account of the matter; but my opinion is, that the murderer was an amateur, who felt how little would be gained to the cause of good taste by murdering an old, arid, and adust metaphysician; there was no room for display, as the man could not possibly look more like a mummy when dead, than he had done alive.

Thus, gentlemen, I have traced the connection between philosophy and our art, until insensibly I find that I have wandered into our own era. This I shall not take any pains to characterise apart from that which preceded it, for, in fact, they have no distinct character. The seventeenth and eighteenth centuries, together with so much of the nineteenth as we have yet seen, jointly compose the Augustan age of murder. The finest work of the seventeenth century is, unquestionably, the murder of Sir Edmondbury Godfrey,[36] which has my entire approbation. In the grand feature of *mystery*, which in some shape or other ought to colour every judicious attempt at murder, it is excellent; for the mystery is not yet dispersed. The attempt to fasten the murder upon the Papists, which would injure it as much as some well-known Correggios have been injured by the professional picture-cleaners, or would even ruin it by translating it into the spurious class of mere political or partisan murders, thoroughly wanting in the murderous *animus*, I exhort the society to discountenance. In fact, this notion is altogether baseless, and arose in pure Protestant fanaticism. Sir Edmondbury had not distinguished himself amongst the London magistrates by any severity against the

---

* Dr Parr's chief public appearances as an author, after his original appearance in the famous Latin preface to Bellendĕnus (don't say Bellendēnus), occurred in certain Sermons at periodic intervals, delivered on behalf of some hospital (I really forget what) which retained for its official designation the old word *Spital*; and thus it happened that the Sermons themselves were generally known by the Title of *Spital* Sermons.

<><><><><><><><><><><><><><><><><><><>

34 Samuel Parr (1747–1825), clergyman, schoolteacher, and miscellaneous author.
35 *salus reipublicæ*: "the welfare of the state."

<><><><><><><><><><><><><><><><><><><>

36 Sir Edmondbury Godfrey (1621–1678) was the justice of the peace for Westminster, who in September 1678 had officially reported Titus Oates's allegations of a plot to assassinate Charles II and restore Catholicism in England by force. In the following month, at the height of public alarm over Oates's revelations, Godfrey was found dead under mysterious circumstances. The murder of "the Protestant Martyr" was immediately attributed to the work of Catholics.

Papists, or in favouring the attempts of zealots to enforce the penal laws against individuals. He had not armed against himself the animosities of any religious sect whatever. And as to the droppings of wax lights upon the dress of the corpse when first discovered in a ditch, from which it was inferred at the time that the priests attached to the Popish Queen's Chapel had been concerned in the murder, either these were mere fraudulent artifices devised by those who wished to fix the suspicion upon the Papists, or else the whole allegation—wax-droppings, and the suggested cause of the droppings—might be a bounce or fib of Bishop Burnet; who, as the Duchess of Portsmouth used to say, was the one great master of fibbing and romancing in the seventeenth century. At the same time, it must be observed that the quantity of murder was not great in Sir Edmondbury's century, at least amongst our own artists; which, perhaps, is attributable to the want of enlightened patronage. *Sint Mæcenates, non deerunt, Flacce, Marones.*[37] Consulting Grant's "Observations on the Bills of Mortality" (4th edition, Oxford, 1665), I find, that, out of 229,250, who died in London during one period of twenty years in the seventeenth century, not more than eighty-six were murdered; that is, about four three-tenths per annum. A small number this, gentlemen, to found an academy upon; and certainly, where the quantity is so small, we have a right to expect that the quality should be first-rate. Perhaps it was; yet still I am of opinion that the best artist in this century was not equal to the best in that which followed. For instance, however praiseworthy the case of Sir Edmondbury Godfrey may be (and nobody can be more sensible of its merits than I am), still, I cannot consent to place it on a level with that of Mrs Ruscombe of Bristol, either as to originality of design, or boldness and breadth of style. This good lady's murder took place early in the reign of George III.—a reign which was notoriously favourable to the arts generally. She lived in College Green, with a single maidservant, neither of them having any pretension to the notice of history but what they derived from the great artist whose workmanship I am recording. One fine morning, when all Bristol was alive and in motion, some suspicion arising, the neighbours forced an entrance into the house, and found Mrs Ruscombe murdered in her bedroom, and the servant murdered on the stairs: this was at noon; and, not more than two hours before, both mistress and servant had been seen alive. To the best of my remembrance, this was in 1764; upwards of sixty years, therefore, have now elapsed, and yet the artist is still undiscovered. The

suspicions of posterity have settled upon two pretenders—a baker and a chimney-sweeper. But posterity is wrong; no unpractised artist could have conceived so bold an idea as that of a noonday murder in the heart of a great city. It was no obscure baker, gentlemen, or anonymous chimney-sweeper, be assured, that executed this work. I know who it was. (*Here there was a general buzz, which at length broke out into open applause; upon which the lecturer blushed, and went on with much earnestness.*) For heaven's sake, gentlemen, do not mistake me; it was not I that did it. I have not the vanity to think myself equal to any such achievement; be assured that you greatly overrate my poor talents; Mrs Ruscombe's affair was far beyond my slender abilities. But I came to know who the artist was, from a celebrated surgeon who assisted at his dissection. This gentleman had a private museum in the way of his profession, one corner of which was occupied by a cast from a man of remarkably fine proportions.

"That," said the surgeon, "is a cast from the celebrated Lancashire highwayman, who concealed his profession for some time from his neighbours, by drawing woollen stockings over his horse's legs, and in that way muffling the clatter which he must else have made in riding up a flagged alley that led to his stable. At the time of his execution for highway robbery, I was studying under Cruickshank:[38] and the man's figure was so uncommonly fine, that no money or exertion was spared to get into possession of him with the least possible delay. By the connivance of the under-sheriff, he was cut down within the legal time, and instantly put into a chaise-and-four; so that, when he reached Cruickshank's, he was positively not dead. Mr ——, a young student at that time, had the honour of giving him the *coup de grace*, and finishing the sentence of the law." This remarkable anecdote, which seemed to imply that all the gentlemen in the dissecting-room were amateurs of our class, struck me a good deal; and I was repeating it one day to a Lancashire lady, who thereupon informed me, that she had herself lived in the neighbourhood of that highwayman, and well remembered two circumstances, which combined, in the opinion of all his neighbours, to fix upon him the credit of Mrs Ruscombe's affair. One was, the fact of his absence for a whole fortnight at the period of that murder; the other, that, within a very little time after, the neighbourhood of this highwayman was deluged with dollars: now, Mrs Ruscombe was known to have hoarded about two thousand of that coin. Be the artist, however, who he might, the affair remains a durable monument of his

---

[37] *Sint . . . Marones*: "Let these be Maecenases [wealthy patrons], Horace, and Virgils will not be lacking."

[38] William Cumberland Cruickshank (1745–1800), famous teacher of anatomy.

genius; for such was the impression of awe, and the sense of power left behind, by the strength of conception manifested in this murder, that no tenant (as I was told in 1810) had been found up to that time for Mrs Ruscombe's house.

But, whilst I thus eulogise the Ruscombian case, let me not be supposed to overlook the many other specimens of extraordinary merit spread over the face of this century. Such cases, indeed, as that of Miss Bland, or of Captain Donnellan, and Sir Theophilus Boughton, shall never have any countenance from me. Fie on these dealers in poison, say I: can they not keep to the old honest way of cutting throats, without introducing such abominable innovations from Italy? I consider all these poisoning cases, compared with the legitimate style, as no better than waxwork by the side of sculpture, or a lithographic print by the side of a fine Volpato.[39] But, dismissing these, there remain many excellent works of art in a pure style, such as nobody need be ashamed to own; and this every candid connoisseur will admit. *Candid*, observe, I say; for great allowances must be made in these cases; no artist can ever be sure of carrying through his own fine preconception. Awkward disturbances will arise; people will not submit to have their throats cut quietly; they will run, they will kick, they will bite; and whilst the portrait painter often has to complain of too much torpor in his subject, the artist in our line is generally embarrassed by too much animation. At the same time, however disagreeable to the artist, this tendency in murder to excite and irritate the subject is certainly one of its advantages to the world in general, which we ought not to overlook, since it favours the development of latent talent. Jeremy Taylor notices with admiration the extraordinary leaps which people will take under the influence of fear. There was a striking instance of this in the recent case of the M'Keans:[40] the boy cleared a height, such as he will never clear again to his dying day. Talents also of the most brilliant description for thumping, and, indeed, for all the gymnastic exercises, have sometimes been developed by the panic which accompanies our artists; talents else buried and hid under a bushel, to the possessors, as much as to their friends. I remember an interesting illustration of this fact, in a case which I learned in Germany.

Riding one day in the neighbourhood of Munich, I overtook a distinguished amateur of our society, whose name, for obvious reasons, I shall conceal. This gentleman informed me that, finding himself wearied

with the frigid pleasures (such as he esteemed them) of mere amateurship, he had quitted England for the Continent—meaning to practise a little professionally. For this purpose he resorted to Germany, conceiving the police in that part of Europe to be more heavy and drowsy than elsewhere. His *debut* as a practitioner took place at Mannheim; and, knowing me to be a brother amateur, he freely communicated the whole of his maiden adventure. "Opposite to my lodging," said he, "lived a baker: he was somewhat of a miser, and lived quite alone. Whether it were his great expanse of chalky face, or what else, I know not, but the fact was, I 'fancied' him, and resolved to commence business upon his throat, which, by the way, he always carried bare—a fashion which is very irritating to my desires. Precisely at eight o'clock in the evening, I observed that he regularly shut up his windows. One night I watched him when thus engaged—bolted in after him—locked the door—and, addressing him with great suavity, acquainted him with the nature of my errand; at the same time advising him to make no resistance, which would be mutually unpleasant. So saying, I drew out my tools; and was proceeding to operate. But at this spectacle the baker, who seemed to have been struck by catalepsy at my first announcement, awoke into tremendous agitation. 'I will *not* be murdered!' he shrieked aloud; 'what for will I' (meaning *shall* I) 'lose my precious throat?'—'What for?' said I; 'if for no other reason, for this—that you put alum into your bread. But no matter, alum or no alum (for I was resolved to forestall any argument on that point), know that I am a virtuoso in the art of murder—am desirous of improving myself in its details—and am enamoured of your vast surface of throat, to which I am determined to be a customer.'—'Is it so?' said he, 'but I'll find you a customer in another line;' and so saying, he threw himself into a boxing attitude. The very idea of his boxing struck me as ludicrous. It is true, a London baker had distinguished himself in the ring, and became known to fame under the title of the Master of the Rolls; but he was young and unspoiled: whereas, this man was a monstrous feather-bed in person, fifty years old, and totally out of condition. Spite of all this, however, and contending against me, who am a master in the art, he made so desperate a defence, that many times I feared he might turn the tables upon me; and that I, an amateur, might be murdered by a rascally baker. What a situation! Minds of sensibility will sympathise with my anxiety. How severe it was, you may understand by this, that for the first thirteen rounds the baker positively had the advantage. Round the 14th, I received a blow on the right eye, which closed it up; in the end, I believe, this was my salvation; for the anger it roused in me was so

---

39 Giovanni Volpato (1733–1803) was an Italian engraver.
40 Alexander and Michael Mackean, murderers of 1826.

great, that, in the next, and every one of the three following rounds, I floored the baker.

"Round 19th. The baker came up piping, and manifestly the worse for wear. His geometrical exploits in the four last rounds had done him no good. However, he showed some skill in stopping a message which I was sending to his cadaverous mug; in delivering which, my foot slipped, and I went down.

"Round 20th. Surveying the baker, I became ashamed of having been so much bothered by a shapeless mass of dough; and I went in fiercely, and administered some severe punishment. A rally took place—both went down—baker undermost—ten to three on amateur.

"Round 21st. The baker jumped up with surprising agility; indeed, he managed his pins capitally, and fought wonderfully, considering that he was drenched in perspiration; but the shine was now taken out of him, and his game was the mere effect of panic. It was now clear that he could not last much longer. In the course of this round we tried the weaving system, in which I had greatly the advantage, and hit him repeatedly on the conk.[41] My reason for this was, that his conk was covered with carbuncles; and I thought I should vex him by taking such liberties with his conk, which in fact I did.

"The three next rounds, the master of the rolls staggered about like a cow on the ice. Seeing how matters stood, in round 24th I whispered something into his ear, which sent him down like a shot. It was nothing more than my private opinion of the value of his throat at an annuity office. This little confidential whisper affected him greatly; the very perspiration was frozen on his face, and for the next two rounds I had it all my own way. And when I called *time* for the 27th round, he lay like a log on the floor."

After which, said I to the amateur, "It may be presumed that you accomplished your purpose." "You are right," said he, mildly, "I did; and a great satisfaction, you know, it was to my mind, for by this means I killed two birds with one stone;" meaning that he had both thumped the baker and murdered him. Now, for the life of me, I could not see *that*; for, on the contrary, to my mind it appeared that he had taken two stones to kill one bird, having been obliged to take the conceit out of him first with his fist, and then with his tools. But no matter for his logic. The moral of his story was good, for it showed what an astonishing stimulus to latent talent is contained in any reasonable prospect of being murdered. A pursy, unwieldy, half cataleptic baker of Mannheim had absolutely fought seven-and-twenty rounds with an

◇◇◇◇◇◇◇◇◇◇◇◇◇◇◇◇◇◇◇◇◇◇◇◇◇◇◇◇◇◇◇◇◇◇◇◇◇◇

41 Slang word for nose.

accomplished English boxer, merely upon this inspiration; so greatly was natural genius exalted and sublimed by the genial presence of his murderer.

Really, gentlemen, when one hears of such things as these, it becomes a duty, perhaps, a little to soften that extreme asperity with which most men speak of murder. To hear people talk, you would suppose that all the disadvantages and inconveniences were on the side of being murdered, and that there were none at all in *not* being murdered. But considerate men think otherwise. "Certainly," says Jeremy Taylor, "it is a less temporal evil to fall by the rudeness of a sword than the violence of a fever: and the axe" (to which he might have added the ship-carpenter's mallet and the crowbar), "a much less affliction than a strangury." Very true; the bishop talks like a wise man and an amateur, as I am sure he was; and another great philosopher, Marcus Aurelius, was equally above the vulgar prejudices on this subject. He declares it to be one of "the noblest functions of reason to know whether it is time to walk out of the world or not." (Book iii., Collers' Translation.) No sort of knowledge being rarer than this, surely *that* man must be a most philanthropic character, who undertakes to instruct people in this branch of knowledge gratis, and at no little hazard to himself. All this, however, I throw out only in the way of speculation to future moralists; declaring in the meantime my own private conviction, that very few men commit murder upon philanthropic or patriotic principles, and repeating what I have already said once at least—that, as to the majority of murderers, they are very incorrect characters.

With respect to the Williams' murders, the sublimest and most entire in their excellence that ever were committed, I shall not allow myself to speak incidentally. Nothing less than an entire lecture, or even an entire course of lectures, would suffice to expound their merits. But one curious fact connected with his case I shall mention, because it seems to imply that the blaze of his genius absolutely dazzled the eye of criminal justice. You all remember, I doubt not, that the instruments with which he executed his first great work (the murder of the Marrs) were a ship-carpenter's mallet and a knife. Now, the mallet belonged to an old Swede, one John Peterson, and bore his initials. This instrument Williams left behind him in Marr's house, and it fell into the hands of the magistrates. But, gentlemen, it is a fact that the publication of this circumstance of the initials led immediately to the apprehension of Williams, and, if made earlier, would have prevented his second great work (the murder of the Williamsons), which took place precisely twelve days after. Yet the magistrates kept back this fact from the public for the entire twelve days, and until that second work was accomplished. That finished, they published it, apparently feeling that Williams had now done enough for his fame, and that his glory was at length placed beyond the reach of accident.

As to Mr Thurtell's case, I know not what to say. Naturally, I have every disposition to think highly of my predecessor in the chair of this society; and I acknowledge that his lectures were unexceptionable. But, speaking ingenuously, I do really think that his principal performance, as an artist, has been much overrated. I admit, that at first I was carried away by the general enthusiasm. On the morning when the murder was made known in London, there was the fullest meeting of amateurs that I have ever known since the days of Williams; old bedridden connoisseurs, who had got into a peevish way of sneering and complaining "that there was nothing doing," now hobbled down to our club-room: such hilarity, such benign expression of general satisfaction, I have rarely witnessed. On every side you saw people shaking hands, congratulating each other, and forming dinner parties for the evening; and nothing was to be heard but triumphant challenges of—"Well, will *this* do?" "Is *this* the right thing?" "Are you satisfied at last?" But, in the middle of the row, I remember, we all grew silent, on hearing the old cynical amateur L. S—— stumping along with his wooden leg; he entered the room with his usual scowl; and, as he advanced, he continued to growl and stutter the whole way—"Mere plagiarism—base plagiarism from hints that I threw out! Besides, his style is as harsh as Albert Durer, and as coarse as Fuseli." Many thought that this was mere jealousy, and general waspishness; but I confess that, when the first glow of enthusiasm had subsided, I have found most judicious critics to agree that there was something *falsetto* in the style of Thurtell. The fact is, he was a member of our society, which naturally gave a friendly bias to our judgments; and his person was universally familiar to the "fancy," which gave him, with the whole London public, a temporary popularity, that his pretensions are not capable of supporting; for *opinionum commenta delet dies, naturæ judicia confirmat.*[42] There was, however, an unfinished design of Thurtell's for the murder of a man with a pair of dumb-bells, which I admired greatly; it was a mere outline, that he never filled in; but to my mind it seemed every way superior to his chief work. I remember that there was great regret expressed by some amateurs that this sketch should have been left in an unfinished state: but there I cannot agree with

them; for the fragments and first bold outlines of original artists have often a felicity about them which is apt to vanish in the management of the details.

The case of the M'Keans I consider far beyond the vaunted performance of Thurtell—indeed, above all praise; and bearing that relation, in fact, to the immortal works of Williams, which the "Æneid" bears to the "Iliad."

But it is now time that I should say a few words about the principles of murder, not with a view to regulate your practice, but your judgment: as to old women, and the mob of newspaper readers, they are pleased with anything, provided it is bloody enough. But the mind of sensibility requires something more. *First*, then, let us speak of the kind of person who is adapted to the purpose of the murderer; *secondly*, of the place where; *thirdly*, of the time when, and other little circumstances.

As to the person, I suppose it is evident that he ought to be a good man; because, if he were not, he might himself, by possibility, be contemplating murder at the very time; and such "diamond-cut-diamond" tussles, though pleasant enough where nothing better is stirring, are really not what a critic can allow himself to call murders. I could mention some people (I name no names) who have been murdered by other people in a dark lane; and so far all seemed correct enough; but, on looking farther into the matter, the public have become aware that the murdered party was himself, at the moment, planning to rob his murderer, at the least, and possibly to murder him, if he had been strong enough. Whenever that is the case, or may be thought to be the case, farewell to all the genuine effects of the art. For the final purpose of murder, considered as a fine art, is precisely the same as that of tragedy, in Aristotle's account of it; viz., "to cleanse the heart by means of pity and terror." Now, terror there may be, but how can there be any pity for one tiger destroyed by another tiger?

It is also evident that the person selected ought not to be a public character. For instance, no judicious artist would have attempted to murder Abraham Newland.* For the case was this: everybody read so

* Abraham Newland is not utterly forgotten. But when this was written, his name had not ceased to ring in British ears, as the most familiar and most significant that perhaps has ever existed. It was the name which appeared on the face of all Bank of England notes, great or small; and had been, for more than a quarter of a century (especially through the whole career of the French Revolution), a short-hand expression for paper money in its safest form.[43]

---

[42] *opinionum . . . confirmat*: "Time effaces the fictions of opinion, but confirms the judgments of nature."

[43] Abraham Newland (1730–1807) was chief Cashier of the Bank of England.

much about Abraham Newland, and so few people ever saw him, that to the general belief he was a mere abstract idea. And I remember, that once, when I happened to mention that I had dined at a coffee-house in company with Abraham Newland, everybody looked scornfully at me, as though I had pretended to have played at billiards with Prester John,[44] or to have had an affair of honour with the Pope. And, by the way, the Pope would be a very improper person to murder: for he has such a virtual ubiquity as the father of Christendom, and, like the cuckoo, is so often heard but never seen, that I suspect most people regard *him* also as an abstract idea. Where, indeed, a public man is in the habit of giving dinners, "with every delicacy of the season," the case is very different: every person is satisfied that *he* is no abstract idea; and, therefore, there can be no impropriety in murdering him; only that his murder will fall into the class of assassinations, which I have not yet treated.

Thirdly. The subject chosen ought to be in good health: for it is absolutely barbarous to murder a sick person, who is usually quite unable to bear it. On this principle, no tailor ought to be chosen who is above twenty-five, for after that age he is sure to be dyspeptic. Or at least, if a man will hunt in that warren, he will of course think it his duty, on the old established equation, to murder some multiple of 9—say 18, 27, or 36. And here, in this benign attention to the comfort of sick people, you will observe the usual effect of a fine art to soften and refine the feelings. The world in general, gentlemen, are very bloody-minded; and all they want in a murder is a copious effusion of blood; gaudy display in this point is enough for *them*. But the enlightened connoisseur is more refined in his taste; and from our art, as from all the other liberal arts when thoroughly mastered, the result is, to humanise the heart; so true is it, that

> "Ingenuas didicisse fideliter artes,
> Emollit mores, nec sinit esse feros."[45]

A philosophical friend, well known for his philanthropy and general benignity, suggests that the subject chosen ought also to have a family of young children wholly dependent on his exertions, by way of deepening the pathos. And, undoubtedly, this is a judicious caution. Yet I would not insist too keenly on such a condition. Severe good taste unquestionably suggests it; but still, where the man was otherwise unobjection-

able in point of morals and health, I would not look with too curious a jealousy to a restriction which might have the effect of narrowing the artist's sphere.

So much for the person. As to the time, the place, and the tools, I have many things to say, which at present I have no room for. The good sense of the practitioner has usually directed him to night and privacy. Yet there have not been wanting cases where this rule was departed from with excellent effect. In respect to time, Mrs Ruscombe's case is a beautiful exception, which I have already noticed; and in respect both to time and place, there is a fine exception in the annals of Edinburgh (year 1805), familiar to every child in Edinburgh, but which has unaccountably been defrauded of its due portion of fame amongst English amateurs. The case I mean is that of a porter to one of the banks, who was murdered, whilst carrying a bag of money, in broad daylight, on turning out of the High Street, one of the most public streets in Europe; and the murderer is to this hour undiscovered.

> "Sed fugit interea, fugit irreparabile tempus,
> Singula dum capti circumvectamur amore."[46]

And now, gentlemen, in conclusion, let me again solemnly disclaim all pretensions on my own part to the character of a professional man. I never attempted any murder in my life, except in the year 1801, upon the body of a tomcat; and *that* turned out differently from my intention. My purpose, I own, was downright murder. "Semper ego auditor tantum?" said I, "nunquamne reponam?"[47] And I went down-stairs in search of Tom at one o'clock on a dark night, with the "animus," and no doubt with the fiendish looks, of a murderer. But when I found him, he was in the act of plundering the pantry of bread and other things. Now this gave a new turn to the affair; for the time being one of general scarcity, when even Christians were reduced to the use of potato-bread, rice-bread, and all sorts of things, it was downright treason in a tom-cat to be wasting good wheaten-bread in the way he was doing. It instantly became a patriotic duty to put him to death; and, as I raised aloft and shook the glittering steel, I fancied myself rising, like Brutus, effulgent from a crowd of patriots, and, as I stabbed him, I

---

[44] A mythical Christian monarch in Asia, of enormous wealth and power.

[45] "Ingenuas . . . feros": "Note too that a faithful study of the liberal arts humanizes character and permits it not to be cruel." Ovid's *Ex Ponto*, II, ix, 47–48 (Wheeler translation, Loeb Classical Library, Harvard University Press).

[46] "Sed . . . amore": "But time meanwhile is flying, flying beyond recall, while we, charmed with the love of our theme, linger around each detail." Virgil's *Georgics*, III, 284–85 (H. Rushton Fairclough translation, Loeb Classical Library, Harvard University Press).

[47] "Semper . . . reponam": "Must I be always merely a passive pupil [in the art of murder], never a performer?" Juvenal's *First Satire*, l. 1.

"Call'd aloud on Tully's name,
And bade the father of his country hail!"[48]

Since then, what wandering thoughts I may have had of attempting the life of an ancient ewe, of a superannuated hen, and such "small deer," are locked up in the secrets of my own breast; but, for the higher departments of the art, I confess myself to be utterly unfit. My ambition does not rise so high. No, gentlemen, in the words of Horace,

"Fungar vice cotis, acutum
Reddere quæ ferrum valet, exsors ipsa secandi."[49]

[February 1827]   [1854]

SUSPIRIA DE PROFUNDIS

Described by De Quincey as "modes of impassioned prose ranging under no precedents that I am aware of in any literature," Suspiria de Profundis ("Sighs from the Depths") were published in Blackwood's Magazine in four installments between March and July 1845. As the note at the end of "Levana and Our Ladies of Sorrow" would indicate, the 1845 publication by no means constituted the complete projected work. The English Mail-Coach (1849) was conceived as part of the larger work; and still other portions were meant to constitute "a crowning grace" in the fifth or Confessions volume of Selections Grave and Gay, as "a succession of some twenty or twenty-five dreams and noon-day visions, which had arisen under the latter stages of opium influence." Of these only "The Daughter of Lebanon" was published in the 1856 volume, others having been mislaid or accidentally destroyed. (In his edition of The Posthumous Works of Thomas De Quincey [1891–1893], Alexander H. Japp published four other sections of Suspiria which have survived.) Apart from the interpolation of some passages into Volume I [Autobiographic Sketches] of Selections Grave and Gay, the Suspiria of 1845, which text is here followed, were never reprinted in De Quincey's lifetime.

"The master-idea of the Suspiria," Japp has written, "is the power which lies in suffering, in agony unuttered and unutterable, to develop the intellect and the spirit of man; to open these to the ineffable conceptions of the infinite, and to some discernment, otherwise impossible, of the beneficent might that lies in pain and sorrow . . . Prose-poems, as they have been called, they are deeply philosophical, presenting under the guise of phantasy the profoundest laws of the working of the human spirit in its most terrible disciplines, and asserting for the darkest phenomena of human life some compensating elements as awakeners of hope and fear and awe. The sense of a great pariah world is ever present with him—a world of outcasts and of innocents bearing the burden of vicarious woes; and thus it is that his title is justified— Suspiria de Profundis: 'Sighs from the Depths.'"

FROM

SUSPIRIA DE PROFUNDIS:
BEING A SEQUEL TO THE
CONFESSIONS OF AN ENGLISH OPIUM-EATER.

INTRODUCTORY NOTICE.

IN 1821, as a contribution to a periodical work—in 1822, as a separate volume—appeared the "Confessions of an English Opium-Eater." The object of that work was to reveal something of the grandeur which belongs *potentially* to human dreams. Whatever may be the number of those in whom this faculty of dreaming splendidly can be supposed to lurk, there are not perhaps very many in whom it is developed. He whose talk is of oxen, will probably dream of oxen: and the condition of human life, which yokes so vast a majority to a daily experience incompatible with much elevation of thought, oftentimes neutralizes the tone of grandeur in the reproductive faculty of dreaming, even for those whose minds are populous with solemn imagery. Habitually to dream magnificently, a man must have a constitutional determination to reverie. This in the first place; and even this, where it exists strongly, is too much liable to disturbance from the gathering agitation of our present English life. Already, in this year 1845, what by the procession through fifty years of mighty revolutions amongst the kingdoms of the earth, what by the continual development of vast physical agencies—steam in all its applications, light getting under harness as a slave for man,* powers from heaven descending upon education and accelerations of the press, powers from hell (as it might seem, but these also celestial) coming round upon artillery and the forces of destruction—the eye of the calmest observer is troubled; the brain is haunted as if by some jealousy of ghostly beings moving amongst us; and it becomes too evident that, unless this colossal pace of advance can be retarded, (a thing not to be expected,) or, which is happily more probable, can be met by counterforces of corresponding magnitude, forces in the direction of religion or profound philosophy, that shall radiate centrifugally against this storm of life so perilously centripetal towards the vortex of the merely

---

* Daguerreotype, &c.[1]

human, left to itself the natural tendency of so chaotic a tumult must be to evil; for some minds to lunacy, for others to a reagency [2] of fleshly torpor. How much this fierce condition of eternal hurry, upon an arena too exclusively human in its interests, is likely to defeat the grandeur which is latent in all men, may be seen in the ordinary effect from living too constantly in varied company. The word *dissipation*, in one of its uses, expresses that effect; the action of thought and feeling is too much dissipated and squandered. To reconcentrate them into meditative habits, a necessity is felt by all observing persons for sometimes retiring from crowds. No man ever will unfold the capacities of his own intellect who does not at least chequer his life with solitude. How much solitude, so much power. Or, if not true in that rigour of expression, to this formula undoubtedly it is that the wise rule of life must approximate.

Among the powers in man which suffer by this too intense life of the *social* instincts, none suffers more than the power of dreaming. Let no man think this a trifle. The machinery for dreaming planted in the human brain was not planted for nothing. That faculty, in alliance with the mystery of darkness, is the one great tube through which man communicates with the shadowy. And the dreaming organ, in connexion with the heart, the eye, and the ear, compose the magnificent apparatus which forces the infinite into the chambers of a human brain, and throws dark reflections from eternities below all life upon the mirrors of the sleeping mind.

But if this faculty suffers from the decay of solitude, which is becoming a visionary idea in England, on the other hand, it is certain that some merely physical agencies can and do assist the faculty of dreaming almost preternaturally. Amongst these is intense exercise; to some extent at least, and for some persons: but beyond all others is opium, which indeed seems to possess a *specific* power in that direction; not merely for exalting the colours of dream-scenery, but for deepening its shadows; and, above all, for strengthening the sense of its fearful *realities*.

The *Opium Confessions* were written with some slight secondary purpose of exposing this specific power of opium upon the faculty of dreaming, but much more with the purpose of displaying the faculty itself; and the outline of the work travelled in this course. Supposing a reader acquainted with the true object of the Confessions as here stated, viz. the revelation of dreaming, to have put this question:—

"But how came you to dream more splendidly than others?"

The answer would have been:—"Because (*præmissis præmittendis*) [3] I took excessive quantities of opium."

Secondly, suppose him to say, "But how came you to take opium in this excess?"

The answer to *that* would be, "Because some early events in my life had left a weakness in one organ which required (or seemed to require) that stimulant."

Then, because the opium dreams could not always have been understood without a knowledge of these events, it became necessary to relate them. Now, these two questions and answers exhibit the *law* of the work, *i.e.* the principle which determined its form, but precisely in the inverse or regressive order. The work itself opened with the narration of my early adventures. These, in the natural order of succession, led to the opium as a resource for healing their consequences; and the opium as naturally led to the dreams. But in the synthetic order of presenting the facts, what stood last in the succession of development, stood first in the order of my purposes.

At the close of this little work, the reader was instructed to believe—and *truly* instructed—that I had mastered the tyranny of opium. The fact is, that *twice* I mastered it, and by efforts even more prodigious, in the second of these cases, than in the first. But one error I committed in both. I did not connect with the abstinence from opium—so trying to the fortitude under *any* circumstances—that enormity of exercise which (as I have since learned) is the one sole resource for making it endurable. I overlooked, in those days, the one *sine quâ non* for making the triumph permanent. Twice I sank—twice I rose again. A third time I sank; partly from the cause mentioned, (the oversight as to exercise,) partly from other causes, on which it avails not now to trouble the reader. I could moralize if I chose; and perhaps *he* will moralize whether I choose it or not. But, in the mean time, neither of us is acquainted properly with the circumstances of the case; I, from natural bias of judgment, not altogether acquainted; and he (with his permission) not at all.

During this third prostration before the dark idol, and after some years, new and monstrous phenomena began slowly to arise. For a time, these were neglected as accidents, or palliated by such remedies as I knew of. But when I could no longer conceal from myself that these dreadful symptoms were moving forward for ever, by a pace steadily, solemnly, and equably increasing, I endeavoured, with some feeling of panic, for a third time to retrace my steps. But I had not reversed my motions for many weeks, before I became profoundly aware that this was impossible. Or, in the

---

[2] Reaction.

[3] (*præmissis præmittendis*): "passing over those things which may reasonably be omitted."

imagery of my dreams, which translated every thing into their own language, I saw through vast avenues of gloom those towering gates of ingress which hitherto had always seemed to stand open, now at last barred against my retreat, and hung with funeral crape.

As applicable to this tremendous situation, (the situation of one escaping by some refluent current from the maelstrom roaring for him in the distance, who finds suddenly that this current is but an eddy, wheeling round upon the same maelstrom,) I have since remembered a striking incident in a modern novel. A lady abbess of a convent, herself suspected of Protestant leanings, and in that way already disarmed of all effectual power, finds one of her own nuns (whom she knows to be innocent) accused of an offence leading to the most terrific of punishments. The nun will be immured alive if she is found guilty; and there is no chance that she will not—for the evidence against her is strong—unless something were made known that cannot be made known; and the judges are hostile. All follows in the order of the reader's fears. The witnesses depose; the evidence is without effectual contradiction; the conviction is declared; the judgment is delivered; nothing remains but to see execution done. At this crisis the abbess, alarmed too late for effectual interposition, considers with herself that, according to the regular forms, there will be one single night open during which the prisoner cannot be withdrawn from her own separate jurisdiction. This one night, therefore, she will use, at any hazard to herself, for the salvation of her friend. At midnight, when all is hushed in the convent, the lady traverses the passages which lead to the cells of prisoners. She bears a master-key under her professional habit. As this will open every door in every corridor,—already, by anticipation, she feels the luxury of holding her emancipated friend within her arms. Suddenly she has reached the door; she descries a dusky object; she raises her lamp; and, ranged within the recess of the entrance, she beholds the funeral banner of the Holy Office, and the black robes of its inexorable officials.

I apprehend that, in a situation such as this, supposing it a real one, the lady abbess would not start, would not show any marks externally of consternation or horror. The case was beyond *that*. The sentiment which attends the sudden revelation that *all is lost!* silently is gathered up into the heart; it is too deep for gestures or for words; and no part of it passes to the outside. Were the ruin conditional, or were it in any point doubtful, it would be natural to utter ejaculations, and to seek sympathy. But where the ruin is understood to be absolute, where sympathy cannot be consolation, and counsel cannot be hope, this is otherwise. The voice perishes; the gestures are frozen; and

the spirit of man flies back upon its own centre. I, at least, upon seeing those awful gates closed and hung with draperies of woe, as for a death already past, spoke not, nor started, nor groaned. One profound sigh ascended from my heart, and I was silent for days.

It is the record of this third, or final stage of opium, as one differing in something more than degree from the others, that I am now undertaking. But a scruple arises as to the true interpretation of these final symptoms. I have elsewhere explained, that it was no particular purpose of mine, and *why* it was no particular purpose, to warn other opium-eaters. Still, as some few persons may use the record in that way, it becomes a matter of interest to ascertain how far it is likely, that, even with the same excesses, other opium-eaters could fall into the same condition. I do not mean to lay a stress upon any supposed idiosyncrasy in myself. Possibly every man has an idiosyncrasy. In some things, undoubtedly, he has. For no man ever yet resembled another man so far, as not to differ from him in features innumerable of his inner nature. But what I point to are not peculiarities of temperament or of organization, so much as peculiar circumstances and incidents through which my own separate experience had revolved. Some of these were of a nature to alter the whole economy of my mind. Great convulsions, from whatever cause, from conscience, from fear, from grief, from struggles of the will, sometimes, in passing away themselves, do not carry off the changes which they have worked. *All* the agitations of this magnitude which a man may have threaded in his life, he neither ought to report, nor *could* report. But one which affected my childhood is a privileged exception. It is privileged as a proper communication for a stranger's ear; because, though relating to a man's proper self, it is a self so far removed from his present self as to wound no feelings of delicacy or just reserve. It is privileged also as a proper subject for the sympathy of the narrator. An adult sympathizes with himself in childhood because he *is* the same, and because (being the same) yet he is *not* the same. He acknowledges the deep, mysterious identity between himself, as adult and as infant, for the ground of his sympathy; and yet, with this general agreement, and necessity of agreement, he feels the differences between his two selves as the main quickeners of his sympathy. He pities the infirmities, as they arise to light in his young forerunner, which now perhaps he does not share; he looks indulgently upon errors of the understanding, or limitations of view which now he has long survived; and sometimes, also, he honours in the infant that rectitude of will which, under *some* temptations, he may since have felt it so difficult to maintain.

The particular case to which I refer in my own childhood, was one of intolerable grief; a trial, in fact, more severe than many people at *any* age are called upon to stand. The relation in which the case stands to my latter opium experiences, is this:—Those vast clouds of gloomy grandeur which overhung my dreams at all stages of opium, but which grew into the darkest of miseries in the last, and that haunting of the human face, which latterly towered into a curse—were they not partly derived from this childish experience? It is certain that, from the essential solitude in which my childhood was passed; from the depth of my sensibility; from the exaltation of this by the resistance of an intellect too prematurely developed, it resulted that the terrific grief which I passed through, drove a shaft for me into the worlds of death and darkness which never again closed, and through which it might be said that I ascended and descended at will, according to the temper of my spirits. Some of the phenomena developed, in my dream-scenery, undoubtedly, do but repeat the experiences of childhood; and others seem likely to have been growths and fructifications from seeds at that time sown.

The reasons, therefore, for prefixing some account of a "passage" in childhood, to this record of a dreadful visitation from opium excess, are—1st, That, in colouring, it harmonizes with that record, and, therefore, is related to it at least in point of feeling; 2dly, That possibly it was in part the origin of some features in that record, and so far is related to it in logic; 3dly, That, the final assault of opium being of a nature to challenge the attention of medical men, it is important to clear away all doubts and scruples which can gather about the roots of such a malady. Was it opium, or was it opium in combination with something else, that raised these storms?

Some cynical reader will object—that for this last purpose it would have been sufficient to state the fact, without rehearsing *in extenso* the particulars of that case in childhood. But the reader of more kindness (for a surly reader is always a bad critic) will also have more discernment; and he will perceive that it is not for the mere facts that the case is reported, but because these facts move through a wilderness of natural thoughts or feelings; some in the child who suffers; some in the man who reports; but all so far interesting as they relate to solemn objects. Meantime, the objection of the sullen critic reminds me of a scene sometimes beheld at the English lakes. Figure to yourself an energetic tourist, who protests every where that he comes only to see the lakes. He has no business whatever; he is not searching for any recreant indorser of a bill, but simply in search of the picturesque. Yet this man adjures every landlord, "by the virtue of his oath," to tell him, and as he hopes for peace in this world to tell him truly, which is the *nearest* road to Keswick. Next, he applies to the postilions—the Westmoreland postilions always fly down hills at full stretch without locking—but nevertheless, in the full career of their fiery race, our picturesque man lets down the glasses, pulls up four horses and two postilions, at the risk of six necks and twenty legs, adjuring them to reveal whether they are taking the *shortest* road. Finally, he descries my unworthy self upon the road; and, instantly stopping his flying equipage, he demands of me (as one whom he believes to be a scholar and a man of honour) whether there is not, in the possibility of things, a *shorter* cut to Keswick. Now, the answer which rises to the lips of landlord, two postilions, and myself, is this—"Most excellent stranger, as you come to the lakes simply to see their loveliness, might it not be as well to ask after the most beautiful road, rather than the shortest? Because, if abstract shortness, if τὸ brevity[4] is your object, then the shortest of all possible tours would seem, with submission—never to have left London." On the same principle, I tell my critic that the whole course of this narrative resembles, and was meant to resemble, a *caduceus*[5] wreathed about with meandering ornaments, or the shaft of a tree's stem hung round and surmounted with some vagrant parasitical plant. The mere medical subject of the opium answers to the dry withered pole, which shoots all the rings of the flowering plants and seems to do so by some dexterity of its own; whereas, in fact, the plant and its tendrils have curled round the sullen cylinder by mere luxuriance of *theirs*. Just as in Cheapside, if you look right and left, the streets so narrow, that lead off at right angles, seem quarried and blasted out of some Babylonian brick kiln; bored, not raised artificially by the builder's hand. But, if you enquire of the worthy men who live in that neighbourhood, you will find it unanimously deposed—that not the streets were quarried out of the bricks, but, on the contrary, (most ridiculous as it seems,) that the bricks have supervened upon the streets.

The streets did not intrude amongst the bricks, but those cursed bricks came to imprison the streets. So, also, the ugly pole—hop pole, vine pole, espalier, no matter what—is there only for support. Not the flowers are for the pole, but the pole is for the flowers. Upon the same analogy view me, as one (in the words

---

4 τὸ brevity: "quintessential brevity."
5 The winged, serpent-twined staff of Mercury.

of a true and most impassioned poet*) "*viridantem floribus hastas*"—making verdant, and gay with the life of flowers, murderous spears and halberts—things that express death in their origin, (being made from dead substances that once had lived in forests,) things that express ruin in their use. The true object in my "Opium Confessions" is not the naked physiological theme—on the contrary, *that* is the ugly pole, the murderous spear, the halbert—but those wandering musical variations upon the theme—those parasitical thoughts, feelings, digressions, which climb up with bells and blossoms round about the arid stock; ramble away from it at times with perhaps too rank a luxuriance; but at the same time, by the eternal interest attached to the *subjects* of these digressions, no matter what were the execution, spread a glory over incidents that for themselves would be—less than nothing.

FROM

PART I.
THE AFFLICTION OF CHILDHOOD.

*   *   *   *   *

THE earliest incidents in my life which affected me so deeply as to be remembered at this day, were two, and both before I could have completed my second year, viz. a remarkable dream of terrific grandeur about a favourite nurse, which is interesting for a reason to be noticed hereafter; and secondly, the fact of having connected a profound sense of pathos with the re-appearance, very early in spring, of some crocuses. This I mention as inexplicable, for such annual resurrections of plants and flowers affect us only as memorials, or suggestions of a higher change, and therefore in connexion with the idea of death; but of death I could, at that time, have had no experience whatever.

This, however, I was speedily to acquire. My two eldest sisters—eldest of three *then* living, and also elder than myself—were summoned to an early death. The first who died was Jane¹—about a year older than myself. She was three and a half, I two and a half, *plus* or *minus* some trifle that I do not recollect. But death was then scarcely intelligible to me, and I could not so properly be said to suffer sorrow as a sad perplexity. . . .

So passed away from earth one out of those sisters that made up my nursery playmates; and so did my

* Valerius Flaccus.⁶

⁶ Gaius Valerius Flaccus (*c.* A.D. 40–90), author of the Latin epic *Argonautica*. De Quincey quotes from VI, 136.
¹ Jane died March 18, 1790. She was actually about a year *younger* than Thomas, having been born September 18, 1786.

acquaintance (if such it could be called) commence with mortality. Yet, in fact, I knew little more of mortality than that Jane had disappeared. She had gone away; but, perhaps, she would come back. Happy interval of heaven-born ignorance! Gracious immunity of infancy from sorrow disproportioned to its strength! I was sad for Jane's absence. But still in my heart I trusted that she would come again. Summer and winter came again—crocuses and roses; why not little Jane?

Thus easily was healed, then, the first wound in my infant heart. Not so the second. For thou, dear, noble Elizabeth, around whose ample brow, as often as thy sweet countenance rises upon the darkness, I fancy a tiara of light or a gleaming *aureola*² in token of thy premature intellectual grandeur—thou whose head, for its superb developments, was the astonishment of science*—thou next, but after an interval of happy years, thou also wert summoned away from our nursery;⁴ and the night which, for me, gathered upon that event, ran after my steps far into life; and perhaps at this day I resemble little for good or for ill that which else I should have been. Pillar of fire, that didst go before me to guide and to quicken—pillar of darkness,⁵ when thy countenance was turned away to God, that didst too truly shed the shadow of death over my young

* Her medical attendants were Dr Percival, a well-known literary physician, who had been a correspondent of Condorcet, D'Alembert, &c., and Mr Charles White,³ a very distinguished surgeon. It was he who pronounced her head to be the finest in its structure and development of any that he had ever seen—an assertion which, to my own knowledge, he repeated in after years, and with enthusiasm. That he had some acquaintance with the subject may be presumed from this, that he wrote and published a work on the human skull, supported by many measurements which he had made of heads selected from all varieties of the human species. Meantime, as I would be loth that any trait of what might seem vanity should creep into this record, I will candidly admit that she died of hydrocephalus; and it has been often supposed that the premature expansion of the intellect in cases of that class, is altogether morbid—forced on, in fact, by the mere stimulation of the disease. I would, however, suggest, as a possibility, the very inverse order of relation between the disease and the intellectual manifestations. Not the disease may always have caused the preternatural growth of the intellect, but, on the contrary, this growth coming on spontaneously, and outrunning the capacities of the physical structure, may have caused the disease.

² In the interpolation of this passage into *Autobiographic Sketches*, De Quincey provided the footnote: "The *aureola* is the name given in the 'Legends of the Christian Saints' to that golden diadem or circlet of supernatural light (that *glory*, as it is commonly called in English) which, amongst the great masters of painting in Italy, surrounded the heads of Christ and of distinguished saints."
³ Dr. Thomas Percival (1740–1804); Charles White (1728–1813).
⁴ Elizabeth Quincey died June 2, 1792.
⁵ See Exodus, xiii, 21–22; xiv, 19–20.

heart—in what scales should I weigh thee? Was the blessing greater from thy heavenly presence, or the blight which followed thy departure? Can a man weigh off and value the glories of dawn against the darkness of hurricane? Or, if he could, how is it that, when a memorable love has been followed by a memorable bereavement, even suppose that God would replace the sufferer in a point of time anterior to the entire experience, and offer to cancel the woe, but so that the sweet face which had caused the woe should also be obliterated—vehemently would every man shrink from the exchange! In the *Paradise Lost*, this strong instinct of man—to prefer the heavenly, mixed and polluted with the earthly, to a level experience offering neither one nor the other—is divinely commemorated. What worlds of pathos are in that speech of Adam's—"If God should make another Eve," &c.—that is, if God should replace him in his primitive state, and should condescend to bring again a second Eve, one that would listen to no temptation—still that original partner of his earliest solitude—

> "Creature in whom excell'd
> Whatever can to sight or thought be form'd,
> Holy, divine, good, amiable, or sweet"—

even now, when she appeared in league with an eternity of woe, and ministering to his ruin, could not be displaced for him by any better or happier Eve. "Loss of thee!" he exclaims in this anguish of trial—

> "Loss of thee
> Would never from my heart; no, no, I feel
> The link of nature draw me; flesh of flesh,
> Bone of my bone thou art; and from thy state
> Mine never shall be parted, bliss or woe."*

* Amongst the oversights in the *Paradise Lost*, some of which have not yet been perceived, it is certainly *one*—that, by placing in such overpowering light of pathos the sublime sacrifice of Adam to his love for his frail companion, he has too much lowered the guilt of his disobedience to God. All that Milton can say afterwards, does not, and cannot, obscure the beauty of that action: reviewing it calmly, we condemn—but taking the impassioned station of Adam at the moment of temptation, we approve in our hearts. This was certainly an oversight; but it was one very difficult to redress. I remember, amongst the many exquisite thoughts of John Paul, (Richter,) one which strikes me as peculiarly touching upon this subject. He suggests—not as any grave theological comment, but as the wandering fancy of a poetic heart—that, had Adam conquered the anguish of separation as a pure sacrifice of obedience to God, his reward would have been the pardon and reconciliation of Eve, together with her restoration to innocence.[6]

6 The quotations from *Paradise Lost* are from IX, 897–99, 911–16.

But what was it that drew my heart, by gravitation so strong, to my sister? Could a child, little above six years of age, place any special value upon her intellectual forwardness? Serene and capacious as her mind appeared to me upon after review, was *that* a charm for stealing away the heart of an infant? Oh, no! I think of it *now* with interest, because it lends, in a stranger's ear, some justification to the excess of my fondness. But then it was lost upon me; or, if not lost, was but dimly perceived. Hadst thou been an idiot, my sister, not the less I must have loved thee—having that capacious heart overflowing, even as mine overflowed, with tenderness, and stung, even as mine was stung, by the necessity of being loved. This it was which crowned thee with beauty—

> "Love, the holy sense,
> Best gift of God, in thee was most intense."[7]

That lamp lighted in Paradise was kindled for me which shone so steadily in thee; and never but to thee only, never again since thy departure, *durst* I utter the feelings which possessed me. For I was the shiest of children; and a natural sense of personal dignity held me back at all stages of life, from exposing the least ray of feelings which I was not encouraged *wholly* to reveal.

It would be painful, and it is needless, to pursue the course of that sickness which carried off my leader and companion. She (according to my recollection at this moment) was just as much above eight years as I above six. And perhaps this natural precedency in authority of judgment, and the tender humility with which she declined to assert it, had been amongst the fascinations of her presence. It was upon a Sunday evening, or so people fancied, that the spark of fatal fire fell upon that train of predispositions to a brain-complaint which had hitherto slumbered within her. She had been permitted to drink tea at the house of a labouring man, the father of an old female servant. The sun had set when she returned in the company of this servant through meadows reeking with exhalations after a fervent day. From that time she sickened. Happily a child in such circumstances feels no anxieties. Looking upon medical men as people whose natural commission it is to heal diseases, since it is their natural function to profess it, knowing them only as *ex-officio* privileged to make war upon pain and sickness—I never had a misgiving about the result. I grieved indeed that my sister should lie in bed: I grieved still more sometimes to hear her moan. But all this appeared to me no more than a night of trouble on which the dawn would soon arise. Oh!

7 See Wordsworth's "Tribute to the Memory of the Same Dog" (1807), ll. 27–28.

moment of darkness and delirium, when a nurse awakened me from that delusion, and launched God's thunderbolt at my heart in the assurance that my sister *must* die. Rightly it is said of utter, utter misery, that it "cannot be *remembered*."* Itself, as a remembrable thing, is swallowed up in its own chaos. Mere anarchy and confusion of mind fell upon me. Deaf and blind I was, as I reeled under the revelation. I wish not to recal the circumstances of that time, when *my* agony was at its height, and hers in another sense was approaching. Enough to say—that all was soon over; and the morning of that day had at last arrived which looked down upon her innocent face, sleeping the sleep from which there is no awaking, and upon me sorrowing the sorrow for which there is no consolation.

On the day after my sister's death, whilst the sweet temple of her brain was yet unviolated by human scrutiny, I formed my own scheme for seeing her once more. Not for the world would I have made this known, nor have suffered a witness to accompany me. I had never heard of feelings that take the name of "sentimental," nor dreamed of such a possibility. But grief even in a child hates the light, and shrinks from human eyes. The house was large; there were two staircases; and by one of these I knew that about noon, when all would be quiet, I could steal up into her chamber. I imagine that it was exactly high noon when I reached the chamber door; it was locked; but the key was not taken away. Entering, I closed the door so softly, that, although it opened upon a hall which ascended through all the stories, no echo ran along the silent walls. Then turning round, I sought my sister's face. But the bed had been moved; and the back was now turned. Nothing met my eyes but one large window wide open, through which the sun of midsummer at noonday was showering down torrents of splendour. The weather was dry, the sky was cloudless, the blue depths seemed to express types of infinity; and it was not possible for eye to behold or for heart to conceive any symbols more pathetic of life and the glory of life.

Let me pause for one instant in approaching a remembrance so affecting and revolutionary for my own mind, and one which (if any earthly remembrance) will survive for me in the hour of death,—to remind some readers, and to inform others, that in the original *Opium Confessions* I endeavoured to explain the reason† why death, *cæteris paribus*, is more profoundly affecting in summer than in other parts of the year; so far at least as it is liable to any modification at all from accidents of scenery or season. The reason, as I there suggested,[9] lies in the antagonism between the tropical redundancy of life in summer and the dark sterilities of the grave. The summer we see, the grave we haunt with our thoughts; the glory is around us, the darkness is within us. And, the two coming into collision, each exalts the other into stronger relief. But in my case there was even a subtler reason why the summer had this intense power of vivifying the spectacle or the thoughts of death. And, recollecting it, often I have been struck with the important truth—that far more of our deepest thoughts and feelings pass to us through perplexed combinations of *concrete* objects, pass to us as *involutes* (if I may coin that word) in compound experiences incapable of being disentangled, than ever reach us *directly*, and in their own abstract shapes. It had happened that amongst our nursery collection of books was the Bible illustrated with many pictures. And in long dark evenings, as my three sisters with myself sate by the firelight round the *guard*[10] of our nursery, no book was so much in request amongst us. It ruled us and swayed us as mysteriously as music. One young nurse, whom we all loved, before any candle was lighted, would often strain her eyes to read it for us; and sometimes, according to her simple powers, would endeavour to explain what we found obscure. We, the children, were all constitutionally touched with pensiveness; the fitful gloom and sudden lambencies of the room by firelight, suited our evening state of feelings; and they suited also the divine revelations of power and mysterious beauty which awed us. Above all, the story of a just man,—man and yet *not* man, real above all things and yet shadowy above all things, who had suffered the passion of death in Palestine, slept upon our minds like early dawn upon the waters. The nurse knew and explained to us the chief differences in Oriental climates; and all these differences (as it happens) express themselves in the great varieties of summer. The cloudless sunlights of Syria—those seemed to argue everlasting summer; the disciples plucking the ears of corn—that *must* be summer; but, above all, the very name of Palm Sunday, (a festival in the English church,) troubled me

† Some readers will question the *fact*, and seek no reason. But did they ever suffer grief at *any* season of the year?

---

9 See "The Pains of Opium," p. 577.
10 In *Autobiographic Sketches*, De Quincey provided the footnote: "I know not whether the word is a local one in this sense. What I mean is a sort of fender, four or five feet high, which locks up the fire from too near an approach on the part of children."

---

*   "I stood in unimaginable trance
And agony, which cannot be remember'd."
—*Speech of Alhadra in Coleridge's Remorse.*[8]

8 De Quincey cites IV, iii, 78–79, of Coleridge's tragedy of 1813.

like an anthem. "Sunday!" what was *that*? That was
the day of peace which masqued another peace deeper
than the heart of man can comprehend. "Palms!"—
what were they? *That* was an equivocal word: palms,
in the sense of trophies, expressed the pomps of life:
palms, as a product of nature, expressed the pomps of
summer. Yet still even this explanation does not suffice:
it was not merely by the peace and by the summer, by
the deep sound of rest below all rest, and of ascending
glory,—that I had been haunted. It was also because
Jerusalem stood near to those deep images both in time
and in place. The great event of Jerusalem was at hand
when Palm Sunday came; and the scene of that Sunday
was near in place to Jerusalem. Yet what then was
Jerusalem? Did I fancy it to be the *omphalos* (navel) of
the earth? That pretension had once been made for
Jerusalem, and once for Delphi; and both pretensions
had become ridiculous, as the figure of the planet became known. Yes; but if not of the earth, for earth's
tenant Jerusalem was the *omphalos* of mortality. Yet
how? there on the contrary it was, as we infants understood, that mortality had been trampled under foot.
True; but for that very reason there it was that mortality had opened its very gloomiest crater. There it
was indeed that the human had risen on wings from
the grave; but for that reason there also it was that the
divine had been swallowed up by the abyss: the lesser
star could not rise, before the greater would submit to
eclipse. Summer, therefore, had connected itself with
death not merely as a mode of antagonism, but also
through intricate relations to Scriptural scenery and
events.

Out of this digression, which was almost necessary
for the purpose of showing how inextricably my feelings and images of death were entangled with those of
summer, I return to the bedchamber of my sister.
From the gorgeous sunlight I turned round to the
corpse. There lay the sweet childish figure, there the
angel face: and, as people usually fancy, it was said in
the house that no features had suffered any change.
Had they not? The forehead indeed, the serene and
noble forehead, *that* might be the same; but the frozen
eyelids, the darkness that seemed to steal from beneath
them, the marble lips, the stiffening hands, laid palm
to palm, as if repeating the supplications of closing
anguish, could these be mistaken for life? Had it been
so, wherefore did I not spring to those heavenly lips
with tears and never-ending kisses? But so it was *not*.
I stood checked for a moment; awe, not fear, fell upon
me; and, whilst I stood, a solemn wind began to blow—
the most mournful that ear ever heard. Mournful! that
is saying nothing. It was a wind that had swept the
fields of mortality for a hundred centuries. Many times
since, upon a summer day, when the sun is about the

hottest, I have remarked the same wind arising and
uttering the same hollow, solemn, Memnonian,[11] but
saintly swell: it is in this world the one sole *audible*
symbol of eternity. And three times in my life I have
happened to hear the same sound in the same circumstances, viz. when standing between an open window
and a dead body on a summer day.

Instantly, when my ear caught this vast Æolian
intonation, when my eye filled with the golden fulness
of life, the pomps and glory of the heavens outside, and
turning when it settled upon the frost which overspread
my sister's face, instantly a trance fell upon me. A vault
seemed to open in the zenith of the far blue sky, a shaft
which ran up for ever. I in spirit rose as if on billows
that also ran up the shaft for ever; and the billows
seemed to pursue the throne of God; but *that* also ran
before us and fled away continually. The flight and the
pursuit seemed to go on for ever and ever. Frost,
gathering frost, some Sarsar[12] wind of death, seemed
to repel me; I slept—for how long I cannot say; slowly
I recovered my self-possession, and found myself
standing, as before, close to my sister's bed.

Oh* flight of the solitary child to the solitary God—
flight from the ruined corpse to the throne that could
not be ruined!—how rich wert thou in truth for after
years. Rapture of grief, that, being too mighty for a
child to sustain, foundest a happy oblivion in a heaven-
born sleep, and within that sleep didst conceal a dream,
whose meanings in after years, when slowly I deciphered, suddenly there flashed upon me new light;
and even by the grief of a child, as I will show you

* Φυγὴ μονου ὗρος μονον:—Plotinus.[13]

~~~~~~

[11] In *Autobiographic Sketches*, De Quincey provided an extended footnote, which reads in part: "For the sake of many
readers, whose hearts may go along earnestly with a record of
infant sorrow, but whose course of life has not allowed them much
leisure for study, I pause to explain—that the head of Memnon
[from a grand Egyptian statue] . . . is represented on the authority of ancient traditions to have uttered at sunrise, or soon after,
as the sun's rays had accumulated heat enough to rarify the air
within certain cavities in the bust, a solemn and dirge-like series
of intonations; the simple explanation being, in its general outline, this—that sonorous currents of air were produced by causing
chambers of cold and heavy air to press upon other collections of
air, warmed, and therefore rarified, and therefore yielding readily
to the pressure of heavier air. Currents being thus established, by
artificial arrangements of tubes, a certain succession of notes
could be concerted and sustained . . . [N]obody will doubt that
the current of blood pouring through the tubes of the human
frame will utter to the learned ear . . . an elaborate gamut or
compass of music . . . as faithfully as the cavities within this
ancient Memnonian bust reported this mighty event of sunrise to
the rejoicing world of light and life—or, again, under the sad
passion of the dying day, uttered the sweet requiem that belonged
to its departure."
[12] Arabic word for the wind of death. See Southey's *Thalaba
the Destroyer* (1801), I, 476–77.
[13] "the flight of the only to the only."

reader hereafter, were confounded the falsehoods of philosophers.*

In the *Opium Confessions* I touched a little upon the extraordinary power connected with opium (after long use) of amplifying the dimensions of time. Space also it amplifies by degrees that are sometimes terrific. But time it is upon which the exalting and multiplying power of opium chiefly spends its operation. Time becomes infinitely elastic, stretching out to such immeasurable and vanishing termini, that it seems ridiculous to compute the sense of it on waking by expressions commensurate to human life. As in starry fields one computes by diameters of the earth's orbit, or of Jupiter's, so in valuing the *virtual* time lived during some dreams, the measurement by generations is ridiculous—by millennia is ridiculous: by æons, I should say, if æons were more determinate, would be also ridiculous. On this single occasion, however, in my life, the very inverse phenomenon occurred. But why speak of it in connexion with opium? Could a child of six years old have been under that influence? No, but simply because it so exactly reversed the operation of opium. Instead of a short interval expanding into a vast one, upon this occasion a long one had contracted into a minute. I have reason to believe that a *very* long one had elapsed during this wandering or suspension of my perfect mind. When I returned to myself, there was a foot (or I fancied so) on the stairs. I was alarmed. For I believed that, if any body should detect me, means would be taken to prevent my coming again. Hastily, therefore, I kissed the lips that I should kiss no more, and slunk like a guilty thing with stealthy steps from the room. Thus perished the vision, loveliest amongst all the shows which earth has revealed to me; thus mutilated was the parting which should have lasted for ever; thus tainted with fear was the farewell sacred to love and grief, to perfect love and perfect grief.

Oh, Ahasuerus, everlasting Jew!† fable or not a fable, thou when first starting on thy endless pilgrimage of woe, thou when first flying through the gates of Jerusalem, and vainly yearning to leave the pursuing curse behind thee, couldst not more certainly have read thy doom of sorrow in the misgivings of thy troubled brain that I when passing for ever from my sister's room. The worm was at my heart: and, confining myself to that stage of life, I may say—the worm that could not die. For if, when standing upon the threshold of manhood, I had ceased to feel its perpetual gnawings, *that* was because a vast expansion of intellect, it was because new hopes, new necessities, and the frenzy of youthful blood, had translated me into a new creature. Man is doubtless *one* by some subtle *nexus* that we cannot perceive, extending from the new-born infant to the superannuated dotard: but as regards many affections and passions incident to his nature at different stages, he is *not* one; the unity of man in this respect is coextensive only with the particular stage to which the passion belongs. Some passions, as that of sexual love, are celestial by one half of their origin, animal and earthy by the other half. These will not survive their own appropriate stage. But love, which is *altogether* holy, like that between two children, will revisit undoubtedly by glimpses the silence and the darkness of old age: and I repeat my belief—that, unless bodily torment should forbid it, that final experience in my sister's bedroom, or some other in which her innocence was concerned, will rise again for me to illuminate the hour of death. . . .

Then came the funeral. I, as a point of decorum, was carried thither. I was put into a carriage with some gentlemen whom I did not know. They were kind to me; but naturally they talked of things disconnected with the occasion, and their conversation was a torment. At the church, I was told to hold a white handkerchief to my eyes. Empty hypocrisy! What need had *he* of masques or mockeries, whose heart died within him at every word that was uttered? During that part of the service which passed within the church, I made an effort to attend, but I sank back continually into my own solitary darkness, and I heard little consciously, except some fugitive strains from the sublime chapter of St Paul, which in England is always read at burials.[15] And here I notice a profound error of our present illustrious Laureate. When I heard those dreadful words—for dreadful they were to me—"It is sown in corruption, it is raised in incorruption; it is sown in dishonour, it is raised in glory;" such was the recoil of my feelings, that I could even have shrieked out a protesting—"Oh, no, no!" if I had not been restrained by the publicity of the occasion. In after years, reflecting upon this revolt of my feelings, which, being the voice of nature in a child, must be as true as any mere *opinion* of a child might probably be false, I saw at once the unsoundness of a passage in *The Excursion*.[16] The

* The thoughts referred to will be given in final notes; as at this point they seemed too much to interrupt the course of the narrative.[14]

† "Everlasting Jew!"—*der ewige Jude*—which is the common German expression for "The Wandering Jew," and sublimer even than our own.

14 The "final notes" were never written.

15 In *Autobiographic Sketches*, De Quincey provided the footnote: "First Epistle to Corinthians, chap. xv., beginning at verse 20."

16 *The Excursion* IV, 153–61.

book is not here, but the substance I remember perfectly. Mr Wordsworth argues, that if it were not for the unsteady faith which people fix upon the beatific condition after death of those whom they deplore, nobody could be found so selfish, as even secretly to wish for the restoration to earth of a beloved object. A mother, for instance, could never dream of yearning for her child, and secretly calling it back by her silent aspirations from the arms of God, if she were but reconciled to the belief that really it *was* in those arms. But this I utterly deny. To take my own case, when I heard those dreadful words of St Paul applied to my sister—viz. that she should be raised a spiritual body— nobody can suppose that selfishness, or any other feeling than that of agonizing love, caused the rebellion of my heart against them. I knew already that she was to come again in beauty and power. I did not now learn this for the first time. And that thought, doubtless, made my sorrow sublimer; but also it made it deeper. For here lay the sting of it, viz. in the fatal words— "We shall be *changed*." How was the unity of my interest in her to be preserved, if she were to be altered, and no longer to reflect in her sweet countenance the traces that were sculptured on my heart? Let a magician ask any woman whether she will permit him to improve her child, to raise it even from deformity to perfect beauty, if that must be done at the cost of its identity, and there is no loving mother but would reject his proposal with horror. Or, to take a case that has actually happened, if a mother were robbed of her child at two years old by gipsies, and the same child were restored to her at twenty, a fine young man, but divided by a sleep as it were of death from all remembrances that could restore the broken links of their once-tender connexion, would she not feel her grief unhealed, and her heart defrauded? Undoubtedly she would. All of us ask not of God for a better thing than that we have lost; we ask for the same, even with its faults and its frailties. It is true that the sorrowing person will also be changed eventually, but that must be by death. And a prospect so remote as that, and so alien from our present nature, cannot console us in an affliction which is not remote but present—which is not spiritual but human.

Lastly came the magnificent service which the English church performs at the side of the grave. There is exposed once again, and for the last time, the coffin. All eyes survey the record of name, of sex, of age, and the day of departure from earth—records how useless! and dropped into darkness as if messages addressed to worms. Almost at the very last comes the symbolic ritual, tearing and shattering the heart with volleying discharges, peal after peal, from the final artillery of woe. The coffin is lowered into its home; it has dis-

appeared from the eye. The sacristan stands ready with his shovel of earth and stones. The priest's voice is heard once more—*earth to earth*, and the dread rattle ascends from the lid of the coffin; *ashes to ashes*, and again the killing sound is heard; *dust to dust*, and the farewell volley announces that the grave—the coffin— the face are sealed up for ever and ever.

*   *   *   *   *

Interesting it is to observe how certainly all deep feelings agree in this, that they seek for solitude, and are nursed by solitude. Deep grief, deep love, how naturally do these ally themselves with religious feeling; and all three, love, grief, religion, are haunters of solitary places. Love, grief, the passion of reverie, or the mystery of devotion—what were these without solitude? All day long, when it was not impossible for me to do so, I sought the most silent and sequestered nooks in the grounds about the house, or in the neighbouring fields. The awful stillness occasionally of summer noons, when no winds were abroad, the appealing silence of grey or misty afternoons—these were fascinations as of witchcraft. Into the woods or the desert air I gazed as if some comfort lay hid in *them*. I wearied the heavens with my inquest of beseeching looks. I tormented the blue depths with obstinate scrutiny, sweeping them with my eyes and searching them for ever after one angelic face that might perhaps have permission to reveal itself for a moment. The faculty of shaping images in the distance out of slight elements, and grouping them after the yearnings of the heart, aided by a slight defect in my eyes, grew upon me at this time. And I recal at the present moment one instance of that sort, which may show how merely shadows, or a gleam of brightness, or nothing at all, could furnish a sufficient basis for this creative faculty. On Sunday mornings I was always taken to church: it was a church on the old and natural model of England, having aisles, galleries, organ, all things ancient and venerable, and the proportions majestic. Here, whilst the congregation knelt through the long Litany, as often as we came to that passage, so beautiful amongst many that are so, where God is supplicated on behalf of "all sick persons and young children," and that he would "show his pity upon all prisoners and captives" —I wept in secret, and raising my streaming eyes to the windows of the galleries, saw, on days when the sun was shining, a spectacle as affecting as ever prophet can have beheld. The sides of the windows were rich with storied glass; through the deep purples and crimsons streamed the golden light; emblazonries of heavenly illumination mingling with the earthly emblazonries of what is grandest in man. There were the apostles that had trampled upon earth, and the glories of earth, out of celestial love to man. There were the martyrs that had borne witness to the truth through flames, through torments, and through armies of fierce insulting faces. There were the saints who, under intolerable pangs, had glorified God by meek submission to his will. And all the time, whilst this tumult of sublime memorials held on as the deep chords from an accompaniment in the bass, I saw through the wide central field of the window, where the glass was uncoloured, white fleecy clouds sailing over the azure depths of the sky; were it but a fragment or a hint of such a cloud, immediately under the flash of my sorrow-haunted eye, it grew and shaped itself into a vision of beds with white lawny curtains; and in the beds lay sick children, dying children, that were tossing in anguish, and weeping clamorously for death. God, for some mysterious reason, could not suddenly release them from their pain; but he suffered the beds, as it seemed, to rise slowly through the clouds; slowly the beds ascended into the chambers of the air; slowly, also, his arms descended from the heavens, that he and his young children whom in Judea, once and for ever, he had blessed, though they *must* pass slowly through the dreadful chasm of separation, might yet meet the sooner. These visions were self-sustained. These visions needed not that any sound should speak to me, or music mould my feelings. The hint from the Litany, the fragment from the clouds, those and the storied windows were sufficient. But not the less the blare of the tumultuous organ wrought its own separate creations. And oftentimes in anthems, when the mighty instrument threw its vast columns of sound, fierce yet melodious, over the voices of the choir—when it rose high in arches, as might seem, surmounting and over-riding the strife of the vocal parts, and gathering by strong coercion the total storm into unity—sometimes I seemed to walk triumphantly upon those clouds which so recently I had looked up to as mementos of prostrate sorrow, and even as ministers of sorrow in its creations; yes, sometimes under the transfigurations of music I felt * of grief itself as a fiery chariot for mounting victoriously above the causes of grief.

* * * * *

* The reader must not forget, in reading this and other passages, that, though a child's feelings are spoken of, it is not the child who speaks. *I* decipher what the child only felt in cipher. And so far is this distinction or this explanation from pointing to any thing metaphysical or doubtful, that a man must be grossly unobservant who is not aware of what I am here noticing, not as a peculiarity of this child or that, but as a necessity of all children. Whatsoever in a man's mind blossoms and expands to his own consciousness in mature life, must have pre-existed in germ during his infancy. I, for instance, did not, as a child, *consciously* read in my own deep feeling these ideas. No, not at all; nor was it possible for a child to do so. I the child had

God speaks to children also in dreams, and by the oracles that lurk in darkness. But in solitude, above all things, when made vocal by the truths and services of a national church, God holds "communion undisturbed" [17] with children. Solitude, though silent as light, is, like light, the mightiest of agencies; for solitude is essential to man. All men come into this world *alone*—all leave it *alone*. Even a little child has a dread, whispering consciousness, that if he should be summoned to travel into God's presence, no gentle nurse will be allowed to lead him by the hand, nor mother to carry him in her arms, nor little sister to share his trepidations. King and priest, warrior and maiden, philosopher and child, all must walk those mighty galleries alone. The solitude, therefore, which in this world appals or fascinates a child's heart, is but the echo of a far deeper solitude through which already he has passed, and of another solitude deeper still, through which he *has* to pass: reflex of one solitude—prefiguration of another.

Oh, burthen of solitude, that cleavest to man through every stage of his being—in his birth, which *has* been—in his life, which *is*—in his death, which *shall* be—mighty and essential solitude! that wast, and art, and art to be;—thou broodest, like the spirit of God moving upon the surface of the deeps, over every heart that sleeps in the nurseries of Christendom. Like the vast laboratory of the air, which, seeming to be nothing, or less than the shadow of a shade, hides within itself the principles of all things, solitude for a child is the Agrippa's mirror [18] of the unseen universe. Deep is the solitude in life of millions upon millions who, with hearts welling forth love, have none to love them. Deep is the solitude of those who, with secret griefs, have none to pity them. Deep is the solitude of those who, fighting with doubts or darkness, have none to counsel them. But deeper than the deepest of these solitudes is that which broods over childhood, bringing before it at intervals the final solitude which watches for it, and is waiting for it within the gates of death. Reader, I tell you a truth, and hereafter I will convince you of this truth, that for a Grecian child solitude was nothing, but for a Christian child it has become the power of God and the mystery of God. Oh, mighty and

the feelings, I the man decipher them. In the child lay the handwriting mysterious to him; in me the interpretation and the comment.

[17] *Excursion*, IV, 86.
[18] Heinrich Cornelius Agrippa (1486–1535), German writer and physician, was an advocate of occult and magical studies. Thomas Nashe's *The Unfortunate Traveller* (1594) describes Agrippa's magic mirror, in which past or distant people and events were called into life.

essential solitude, that wast, and art, and art to be—
thou, kindling under the torch of Christian revelations,
art now transfigured for ever, and hast passed from a
blank negation into a secret hieroglyphic from God,
shadowing in the hearts of infancy the very dimmest of
his truths!

[March 1845]

*   *   *   *   *19

Here pause, reader! Imagine yourself seated in
some cloud-scaling swing, oscillating under the impulse of lunatic hands; for the strength of lunacy may
belong to human dreams, the fearful caprice of lunacy,
and the malice of lunacy, whilst the *victim* of those
dreams may be all the more certainly removed from
lunacy; even as a bridge gathers cohesion and strength
from the increasing resistance into which it is forced by
increasing pressure. Seated in such a swing, fast as you
reach the lowest point of depression, may you rely on
racing up to a starry altitude of corresponding ascent.
Ups and downs you will see, heights and depths, in our
fiery course together, such as will sometimes tempt you
to look shyly and suspiciously at me, your guide, and
the ruler of the oscillations. Here, at the point where I
have called a halt, the reader has reached the lowest
depth in my nursery afflictions. From that point,
according to the principles of *art* which govern the
movement of these Confessions, I had meant to launch
him upwards through the whole arch of ascending
visions which seemed requisite to balance the sweep
downwards, so recently described in his course. But
accidents of the press have made it impossible to
accomplish this purpose in the present month's
journal. There is reason to regret that the advantages of
position, which were essential to the full effect of passages planned for equipoise and mutual resistance,
have thus been lost. Meantime, upon the principle of
the mariner who rigs a *jury*-mast in default of his
regular spars, I find my resource in a sort of "jury"
peroration—not sufficient in the way of a balance by its
proportions, but sufficient to indicate the *quality* of the
balance which I had contemplated. He who has *really*
read the preceding parts of these present Confessions,
will be aware that a stricter scrutiny of the past, such
as was natural after the whole economy of the dreaming
faculty had been convulsed beyond all precedents on
record, led me to the conviction that not one agency,
but two agencies, had co-operated to the tremendous
result. The nursery experience had been the ally and
the natural coefficient of the opium. For that reason it
was that the nursery experience has been narrated.

<hr/>

¹⁹ Here follows the conclusion of the second installment of
Suspiria.

Logically, it bears the very same relation to the convulsions of the dreaming faculty as the opium. The
idealizing tendency existed in the dream-theatre of my
childhood; but the preternatural strength of its action
and colouring was first developed after the confluence
of the *two* causes. The reader must suppose me at
Oxford: twelve years and a half are gone by; I am in
the glory of youthful happiness; but I have now first
tampered with opium; and now first the agitations of
my childhood reopened in strength, now first they
swept in upon the brain with power and the grandeur
of recovered life, under the separate and the concurring
inspirations of opium.

Once again, after twelve years' interval, the nursery
of my childhood expanded before me—my sister was
moaning in bed—I was beginning to be restless with
fears not intelligible to myself. Once again the nurse,
but now dilated to colossal proportions, stood as upon
some Grecian stage with her uplifted hand, and like the
superb Medea standing alone with her children in the
nursery at Corinth,* smote me senseless to the ground.
Again, I was in the chamber with my sister's corpse—
again the pomps of life rose up in silence, the glory of
summer, the frost of death. Dream formed itself
mysteriously within dream; within these Oxford
dreams remoulded itself continually the trance in my
sister's chamber,—the blue heavens, the everlasting
vault, the soaring billows, the throne steeped in the
thought (but not the sight) of "Him that sate thereon;"
the flight, the pursuit, the irrecoverable steps of my
return to earth. Once more the funeral procession
gathered; the priest in his white surplice stood waiting
with a book in his hand by the side of an open grave,
the sacristan with his shovel; the coffin sank; the *dust
to dust* descended. Again I was in the church on a
heavenly Sunday morning. The golden sunlight of God
slept amongst the heads of his apostles, his martyrs, his
saints; the fragment from the litany—the fragment
from the clouds—awoke again the lawny beds that
went up to scale the heavens—awoke again the shadowy
arms that moved downwards to meet them. Once
again, arose the swell of the anthem—the burst of the
Hallelujah chorus—the storm—the trampling movement of the choral passion—the agitation of my own
trembling sympathy—the tumult of the choir—the
wrath of the organ. Once more I, that wallowed,
became he that rose up to the clouds. And now in
Oxford, all was bound up into unity; the first state and
the last were melted into each other as in some sunny
glorifying haze. For high above my own station,
hovered a gleaming host of heavenly beings, surrounding the pillows of the dying children. And such beings

<hr/>

* Euripides.

sympathize equally with sorrow that grovels and with sorrow that soars. Such beings pity alike the children that are languishing in death, and the children that live only to languish in tears.

[April 1845]

THE PALIMPSEST.

YOU know perhaps, masculine reader, better than I can tell you, what is a *Palimpsest*. Possibly you have one in your own library. But yet, for the sake of others who may *not* know, or may have forgotten, suffer me to explain it here: lest any female reader, who honours these papers with her notice, should tax me with explaining it once too seldom; which would be worse to bear than a simultaneous complaint from twelve proud men, that I had explained it three times too often. You therefore, fair reader, understand that for *your* accommodation exclusively, I explain the meaning of this word. It is Greek; and our sex enjoys the office and privilege of standing counsel to yours, in all questions of Greek. We are, under favour, perpetual and hereditary dragomans [1] to you. So that if, by accident, you know the meaning of a Greek word, yet by courtesy to us, your counsel learned in that matter, you will always seem *not* to know it.

A palimpsest, then, is a membrane or roll cleansed of its manuscript by reiterated successions.

What was the reason that the Greeks and the Romans had not the advantage of printed books? The answer will be, from ninety-nine persons in a hundred —Because the mystery of printing was not then discovered. But this is altogether a mistake. The secret of printing must have been discovered many thousands of times before it was used, or *could* be used. The inventive powers of man are divine; and also his stupidity is divine—as Cowper so playfully illustrates in the slow development of the *sofa* through successive generations of immortal dulness. It took centuries of blockheads to raise a joint stool into a chair; and it required something like a miracle of genius, in the estimate of elder generations, to reveal the possibility of lengthening a chair into a *chaise-longue*, or a sofa. [2] Yes, these were inventions that cost mighty throes of intellectual power. But still, as respects printing, and admirable as is the stupidity of man, it was really not quite equal to the task of evading an object which stared him in the face with so broad a gaze. It did not

require an Athenian intellect to read the main secret of printing in many scores of processes which the ordinary uses of life were *daily* repeating. To say nothing of analogous artifices amongst various mechanic artisans, all that is essential in printing must have been known to every nation that struck coins and medals. Not, therefore, any want of a printing art— that is, of an art for multiplying impressions—but the want of a cheap material for *receiving* such impressions, was the obstacle to an introduction of printed books even as early as Pisistratus.[3] The ancients *did* apply printing to records of silver and gold; to marble and many other substances cheaper than gold and silver, they did *not*, since each monument required a *separate* effort of inscription. Simply this defect it was of a cheap material for receiving impresses, which froze in its very fountains the early resources of printing.

Some twenty years ago, this view of the case was luminously expounded by Dr Whately,[4] the present archbishop of Dublin, and with the merit, I believe, of having first suggested it. Since then, this theory has received indirect confirmation. Now, out of that original scarcity affecting all materials proper for durable books, which continued up to times comparatively modern, grew the opening for palimpsests. Naturally, when once a roll of parchment or of vellum had done its office, by propagating through a series of generations what once had possessed an interest for *them*, but which, under changes of opinion or of taste, had faded to their feelings or had become obsolete for their understandings, the whole *membrana* or vellum skin, the twofold product of human skill, costly material, and costly freight of thought, which it carried, drooped in value concurrently—supposing that each were inalienably associated to the other. Once it had been the impress of a human mind which stamped its value upon the vellum; the vellum, though costly, had contributed but a secondary element of value to the total result. At length, however, this relation between the vehicle and its freight has gradually been undermined. The vellum, from having been the setting of the jewel, has risen at length to be the jewel itself; and the burden of thought, from having given the chief value to the vellum, has now become the chief obstacle to its value; nay, has totally extinguished its value, unless it can be dissociated from the connexion. Yet, if this unlinking *can* be effected, then—fast as the inscription upon the membrane is sinking into rubbish—the membrane itself is reviving in its separate importance; and, from

---

[1] Interpreters, originally of the Arabic, Turkish, or Persian tongues.
[2] See *The Task*, I, 1–88.

[3] Pisistratus (*c.* 605–*c.* 528 B.C.), ruler of Athens from 546 to his death and a notable supporter of art and literature.
[4] Richard Whately (1787–1863), Anglican theologian and writer, was appointed Archbishop of Dublin in 1831.

bearing a ministerial value, the vellum has come at last to absorb the whole value.

Hence the importance for our ancestors that the separation *should* be effected. Hence it arose in the middle ages, as a considerable object for chemistry, to discharge the writing from the roll, and thus to make it available for a new succession of thoughts. The soil, if cleansed from what once had been hot-house plants, but now were held to be weeds, would be ready to receive a fresh and more appropriate crop. In that object the monkish chemists succeeded; but after a fashion which seems almost incredible; incredible not as regards the extent of their success, but as regards the delicacy of restraints under which it moved; so equally adjusted was their success to the immediate interests of that period, and to the reversionary interests of our own. They did the thing; but not so radically as to prevent us, their posterity, from *un*doing it. They expelled the writing sufficiently to leave a field for the new manuscript, and yet not sufficiently to make the traces of the elder manuscript irrecoverable for us. Could magic, could Hermes Trismegistus,[5] have done more? What would you think, fair reader, of a problem such as this—to write a book which should be sense for your own generation, nonsense for the next, should revive into sense for the next after that, but again became nonsense for the fourth; and so on by alternate successions, sinking into night or blazing into day, like the Sicilian river Arethusa, and the English river Mole[6] —or like the undulating motions of a flattened stone which children cause to skim the breast of a river, now diving below the water, now grazing its surface, sinking heavily into darkness, rising buoyantly into light, through a long vista of alternations? Such a problem, you say, is impossible. But really it is a problem not harder apparently than—to bid a generation kill, but so that a subsequent generation may call back into life; bury, but so that posterity may command to rise again. Yet *that* was what the rude chemistry of past ages effected when coming into combination with the reaction from the more refined chemistry of our own. Had *they* been better chemists, had *we* been worse—the mixed result, viz. that, dying for *them*, the flower should revive for *us*, could not have been effected. They did the thing proposed to them: they did it effectually; for they founded upon it all that was wanted: and yet ineffectually, since we unravelled their work; effacing all above which they had superscribed; restoring all below which they had effaced.

Here, for instance, is a parchment which contained some Grecian tragedy, the Agamemnon of Æschylus, or the Phœnissæ of Euripides. This had possessed a value almost inappreciable in the eyes of accomplished scholars, continually growing rarer through generations. But four centuries are gone by since the destruction of the Western Empire. Christianity, with towering grandeurs of another class, has founded a different empire; and some bigoted yet perhaps holy monk has washed away (as he persuades himself) the heathen's tragedy, replacing it with a monastic legend; which legend is disfigured with fables in its incidents, and yet, in a higher sense, is true, because interwoven with Christian morals and with the sublimest of Christian revelations. Three, four, five, centuries more find man still devout as ever; but the language has become obsolete, and even for Christian devotion a new era has arisen, throwing it into the channel of crusading zeal or of chivalrous enthusiasm. The *membrana* is wanted now for a knightly romance—for "my Cid," or Cœur de Lion; for Sir Tristrem, or Lybæus Disconus.[7] In this way, by means of the imperfect chemistry known to the mediæval period, the same roll has served as a conservatory for three separate generations of flowers and fruits, all perfectly different, and yet all specially adapted to the wants of the successive possessors. The Greek tragedy, the monkish legend, the knightly romance, each has ruled its own period. One harvest after another has been gathered into the garners of man through ages far apart. And the same hydraulic machinery has distributed, through the same marble fountains, water, milk, or wine, according to the habits and training of the generations that came to quench their thirst.

Such were the achievements of rude monastic chemistry. But the more elaborate chemistry of our own days has reversed all these motions of our simple ancestors, with results in every stage that to *them* would have realized the most fantastic amongst the promises of thaumaturgy. Insolent vaunt of Paracelsus,[8] that he would restore the original rose or violet out of the ashes settling from its combustion—*that* is now rivalled in this modern achievement. The traces of each successive handwriting, regularly effaced, as had been imagined, have, in the inverse order, been regularly called back: the footsteps of the game pursued, wolf or stag, in each several chase, have been unlinked, and hunted back through all their doubles; and, as the chorus of the

---

5 "The thrice-greatest Hermes," honorific title of the Egyptian god Thoth, supposed inventor of writing, the author or inspiration of all the "Hermetic" books of ancient religion and learning.

6 In Surrey.

7 Lybæus Disconus was a popular Arthurian romance in English verse, dating from before 1340.

8 Paracelsus (*c.* 1490–1541), famous German physician and alchemist. On the pseudo-scientific doctrine of Palingenesia here referred to, see Coleridge's "Essay on Method" XI, footnote 11, p. 252.

Athenian stage unwove through the antistrophe every step that had been mystically woven through the strophe, so, by our modern conjurations of science, secrets of ages remote from each other have been exorcised* from the accumulated shadows of centuries. Chemistry, a witch as potent as the Erictho of Lucan, (*Pharsalia*, lib. vi. or vii.,)[9] has extorted by her torments, from the dust and ashes of forgotten centuries, the secrets of a life extinct for the general eye, but still glowing in the embers. Even the fable of the Phœnix—that secular bird, who propagated his solitary existence, and his solitary births, along the line of centuries, through eternal relays of funeral mists—is but a type of what we have done with Palimpsests. We have backed up on each Phœnix in the long *regressus*, and forced him to expose his ancestral Phœnix, sleeping in the ashes below his own ashes. Our good old forefathers would have been aghast at our sorceries; and, if they speculated on the propriety of burning Dr Faustus, *us* they would have burned by acclamation. Trial there would have been none; and they could no otherwise have satisfied their horror of the brazen profligacy marking our modern magic, than by ploughing up the houses of all who had been parties to it, and sowing the ground with salt.[10]

Fancy not, reader, that this tumult of images, illustrative or allusive, moves under any impulse or purpose of mirth. It is but the coruscation of a restless understanding, often made ten times more so by irritation of the nerves, such as you will first learn to comprehend (its *how* and its *why*) some stage or two ahead. The image, the memorial, the record, which for me is derived from a palimpsest, as to one great fact in our human being, and which immediately I will show you, is but too repellent of laughter; or, even if laughter *had* been possible, it would have been such laughter as oftentimes is thrown off from the fields of ocean†—

laughter that hides, or that seems to evade mustering tumult; foam-bells that weave garlands of phosphoric radiance for one moment round the eddies of gleaming abysses; mimicries of earth-born flowers that for the eye raise phantoms of gaiety, as oftentimes for the ear they raise echoes of fugitive laughter, mixing with the ravings and choir-voices of an angry sea.

What else than a natural and mighty palimpsest is the human brain? Such a palimpsest is my brain; such a palimpsest, O reader! is yours. Everlasting layers of ideas, images, feelings, have fallen upon your brain softly as light. Each succession has seemed to bury all that went before. And yet in reality not one has been extinguished. And if, in the vellum palimpsest, lying amongst the other *diplomata*[12] of human archives or libraries, there is any thing fantastic or which moves to laughter, as oftentimes there is in the grotesque collisions of those successive themes, having no natural connexion, which by pure accident have consecutively occupied the roll, yet, in our own heaven-created palimpsest, the deep memorial palimpsest of the brain, there are not and cannot be such incoherencies. The fleeting accidents of a man's life, and its external shows, may indeed be irrelate[13] and incongruous; but the organizing principles which fuse into harmony, and gather about fixed predetermined centres, whatever heterogeneous elements life may have accumulated from without, will not permit the grandeur of human unity greatly to be violated, or its ultimate repose to be troubled in the retrospect from dying moments, or from other great convulsions.

Such a convulsion is the struggle of gradual suffocation, as in drowning; and, in the original Opium Confessions, I mentioned a case of that nature communicated to me by a lady from her own childish experience. The lady is still living, though now of unusually great age; and I may mention—that amongst her faults never was numbered any levity of principle, or carelessness of the most scrupulous veracity; but, on the contrary, such faults as arise from austerity, too harsh perhaps, and gloomy—indulgent neither to others nor herself. And, at the time of relating this incident, when already very old, she had become religious to asceticism. According to my present belief, she had completed her ninth year, when playing by the side of a solitary brook, she fell into one of its deepest pools. Eventually, but after what lapse of time nobody

---

* Some readers may be apt to suppose, from all English experience, that the word *exorcise* means properly banishment to the shades. Not so. Citation *from* the shades, or sometimes the torturing coercion of mystic adjurations, is more truly the primary sense.

† Many readers will recall, though at the moment of writing my own thoughts did *not* recall, the well-known passage in the Prometheus—

ὥοντιων τε κυμᾰτων
Ἀνηρίθμον γελασμα.

"Oh multitudinous laughter of the ocean billows!" It is not

clear whether Æschylus contemplated the laughter as addressing the ear or the eye.[11]

---

9 Erictho, a Thessalian witch of extraordinary power, is described in Book VI, 507ff., of the *Pharsalia*, Latin epic poem by Marcus Annaeus Lucan (A.D. 39–65). Through drugs and spells, Erictho restores a ghost to its unburied corpse, forces it to prophesy, and then kills the corpse again.
10 An act of exorcism.

11 De Quincey quotes ll. 89–90 of *Prometheus Bound*.
12 Historical or literary documents.
13 Unrelated.

ever knew, she was saved from death by a farmer, who, riding in some distant lane, had seen her rise to the surface; but not until she had descended within the abyss of death, and looked into its secrets, as far, perhaps, as ever human eye *can* have looked that had permission to return. At a certain stage of this descent, a blow seemed to strike her—phosphoric radiance sprang forth from her eyeballs; and immediately a mighty theatre expanded within her brain. In a moment, in the twinkling of an eye, every act—every design of her past life lived again—arraying themselves not as a succession, but as parts of a coexistence. Such a light fell upon the whole path of her life backwards into the shades of infancy, as the light perhaps which wrapt the destined apostle on his road to Damascus. Yet that light blinded for a season; but hers poured celestial vision upon the brain, so that her consciousness became omnipresent at one moment to every feature in the infinite review.

This anecdote was treated sceptically at the time by some critics. But besides that it has since been confirmed by other experiences essentially the same, reported by other parties in the same circumstances who had never heard of each other; the true point for astonishment is not the *simultaneity* of arrangement under which the past events of life—though in fact successive—had formed their dread line of revelation. This was but a secondary phenomenon; the deeper lay in the resurrection itself, and the possibility of resurrection, for what had so long slept in the dust. A pall, deep as oblivion, had been thrown by life over every trace of these experiences; and yet suddenly, at a silent command, at the signal of a blazing rocket sent up from the brain, the pall draws up, and the whole depths of the theatre are exposed. Here was the greater mystery: now this mystery is liable to no doubt; for it is repeated, and ten thousand times repeated by opium, for those who are its martyrs.

Yes, reader, countless are the mysterious handwritings of grief or joy which have inscribed themselves successively upon the palimpsest of your brain; and, like the annual leaves of aboriginal forests, or the undissolving snows on the Himalaya, or light falling upon light, the endless strata have covered up each other in forgetfulness. But by the hour of death, but by fever, but by the searchings of opium, all these can revive in strength. They are not dead, but sleeping. In the illustration imagined by myself, from the case of some individual palimpsest, the Grecian tragedy had seemed to be displaced, but was *not* displaced, by the monkish legend; and the monkish legend had seemed to be displaced, but was *not* displaced, by the knightly romance. In some potent convulsion of the system, all wheels back into its earliest elementary stage. The bewildering

romance, light tarnished with darkness, the semi-fabulous legend, truth celestial mixed with human falsehoods, these fade even of themselves as life advances. The romance has perished that the young man adored. The legend has gone that deluded the boy. But the deep deep tragedies of infancy, as when the child's hands were unlinked for ever from his mother's neck, or his lips for ever from his sister's kisses, these remain lurking below all, and these lurk to the last. Alchemy there is none of passion or disease that can scorch away these immortal impresses. And the dream which closed the preceding section, together with the succeeding dreams of this, (which may be viewed as in the nature of choruses winding up the overture contained in Part I.,) are but illustrations of this truth, such as every man probably will meet experimentally who passes through similar convulsions of dreaming or delirium from any similar or equal disturbance in his nature.*

LEVANA AND OUR LADIES OF SORROW.

OFTENTIMES at Oxford I saw Levana in my dreams. I knew her by her Roman symbols. Who is Levana? Reader, that do not pretend to have leisure for very much scholarship, you will not be angry with me for telling you. Levana was the Roman goddess that performed for the new-born infant the earliest office of ennobling kindness—typical, by its mode, of that grandeur which belongs to man every where, and of that benignity in powers invisible, which even in Pagan worlds sometimes descends to sustain it. At the very moment of birth, just as the infant tasted for the first time the atmosphere of our troubled planet, it was laid on the ground. *That* might bear different interpretations. But immediately, lest so grand a creature should grovel there for more than one instant, either the paternal hand, as proxy for the goddess Levana, or some near kinsman, as proxy for the father, raised it upright, bade it look erect as the king of all this world, and presented its forehead to the stars, saying, perhaps, in his heart—"Behold what is greater than yourselves!" This symbolic act represented the function of

---

* This, it may be said, requires a corresponding duration of experiences; but, as an argument for this mysterious power lurking in our nature, I may remind the reader of one phenomenon open to the notice of every body, viz. the tendency of very aged persons to throw back and concentrate the light of their memory upon scenes of early childhood, as to which they recall many traces that had faded even to *themselves* in middle life, whilst they often forget altogether the whole intermediate stages of their experience. This shows that naturally, and without violent agencies, the human brain is by tendency a palimpsest.

Levana. And that mysterious lady, who never revealed her face, (except to me in dreams,) but always acted by delegation, had her name from the Latin verb (as still it is the Italian verb) *levare*, to raise aloft.

This is the explanation of Levana. And hence it has arisen that some people have understood by Levana the tutelary power that controls the education of the nursery. She, that would not suffer at his birth even a prefigurative or mimic degradation for her awful ward, far less could be supposed to suffer the real degradation attaching to the non-development of his powers. She therefore watches over human education. Now, the word *edŭco*, with the penultimate short, was derived (by a process often exemplified in the crystallization of languages) from the word *edūco*, with the penultimate long. Whatsoever *educes* or developes—*educates*. By the education of Levana, therefore, is meant—not the poor machinery that moves by spelling-books and grammars, but that mighty system of central forces hidden in the deep bosom of human life, which by passion, by strife, by temptation, by the energies of resistance, works for ever upon children—resting not day or night, any more than the mighty wheel of day and night themselves, whose moments, like restless spokes, are glimmering* for ever as they revolve.

If, then, *these* are the ministries by which Levana works, how profoundly must she reverence the agencies of grief! But you, reader! think—that children generally are not liable to grief such as mine. There are two senses in the word *generally*—the sense of Euclid where it means *universally*, (or in the whole extent of the *genus*,) and a foolish sense of this world where it means *usually*. Now I am far from saying that children universally are capable of grief like mine. But there are more than you ever heard of, who die of grief in this island of ours. I will tell you a common case. The rules of Eton require that a boy on the *foundation* [2] should be

---

* As I have never allowed myself to covet any man's ox nor his ass, nor any thing that is his, still less would it become a philosopher to covet other people's images, or metaphors. Here, therefore, I restore to Mr Wordsworth this fine image of the revolving wheel, and the glimmering spokes, as applied by him to the flying successions of day and night.[1] I borrowed it for one moment in order to point my own sentence; which being done, the reader is witness that I now pay it back instantly by a note made for that sole purpose. On the same principle I often borrow their seals from young ladies—when closing my letters. Because there is sure to be some tender sentiment upon them about "memory," or "hope," or "roses," or "reunion:" and my correspondent must be a sad brute who is not touched by the eloquence of the seal, even if his taste is so bad that he remains deaf to mine.

---

[1] Referring to Wordsworth's sonnet "If these brief Records, by the Muses' art" (1827), ll. 9–11.
[2] "Said of the members of an endowed college" (*Oxford English Dictionary*).

there twelve years: he is superannuated at eighteen, consequently he must come at six. Children torn away from mothers and sisters at that age not unfrequently die. I speak of what I know. The complaint is not entered by the registrar as grief; but *that* it is. Grief of that sort, and at that age, has killed more than ever have been counted amongst its martyrs.

Therefore it is that Levana often communes with the powers that shake man's heart: therefore it is that she doats upon grief. "These ladies," said I softly to myself, on seeing the ministers with whom Levana was conversing, "these are the Sorrows; and they are three in number, as the *Graces* are three, who dress man's life with beauty; the *Parcæ* are three, who weave the dark arras of man's life in their mysterious loom always with colours sad in part, sometimes angry with tragic crimson and black; the *Furies* are three, who visit with retributions called from the other side of the grave offences that walk upon this; and once even the *Muses* were but three, who fit the harp, the trumpet, or the lute, to the great burdens of man's impassioned creations. These are the Sorrows, all three of whom I know." The last words I say *now;* but in Oxford I said —"one of whom I know, and the others too surely I *shall* know." For already, in my fervent youth, I saw (dimly relieved upon the dark background of my dreams) the imperfect lineaments of the awful sisters. These sisters—by what name shall we call them?

If I say simply—"The Sorrows," there will be a chance of mistaking the term; it might be understood of individual sorrow—separate cases of sorrow,— whereas I want a term expressing the mighty abstractions that incarnate themselves in all individual sufferings of man's heart; and I wish to have these abstractions presented as impersonations, that is, as clothed with human attributes of life, and with functions pointing to flesh. Let us call them, therefore, *Our Ladies of Sorrow*. I know them thoroughly, and have walked in all their kingdoms. Three sisters they are, of one mysterious household; and their paths are wide apart; but of their dominion there is no end. Them I saw often conversing with Levana, and sometimes about myself. Do they talk, then? Oh, no! Mighty phantoms like these disdain the infirmities of language. They may utter voices through the organs of man when they dwell in human hearts, but amongst themselves is no voice nor sound—eternal silence reigns in *their* kingdoms. *They* spoke not as they talked with Levana. *They* whispered not. *They* sang not. Though oftentimes methought they *might* have sung; for I upon earth had heard their mysteries oftentimes deciphered by harp and timbrel, by dulcimer and organ. Like God, whose servants they are, they utter their pleasure, not by sounds that perish, or by words that go astray, but by signs in heaven—by changes on earth—by pulses in secret rivers—heraldries painted on darkness—and hieroglyphics written on the tablets of the brain. *They* wheeled in mazes; *I* spelled the steps. *They* telegraphed from afar; *I* read the signals. *They* conspired together; and on the mirrors of darkness *my* eye traced the plots. *Theirs* were the symbols,—*mine* are the words.

What is it the sisters are? What is it that they do? Let me describe their form, and their presence; if form it were that still fluctuated in its outline; or presence it were that for ever advanced to the front, or for ever receded amongst shades.

The eldest of the three is named *Mater Lachrymarum*, Our Lady of Tears. She it is that night and day raves and moans, calling for vanished faces. She stood in Rama, when a voice was heard of lamentation— Rachel weeping for her children, and refusing to be comforted.[3] She it was that stood in Bethlehem on the night when Herod's sword swept its nurseries of Innocents, and the little feet were stiffened for ever, which, heard at times as they tottered along floors overhead, woke pulses of love in household hearts that were not unmarked in heaven.[4]

Here eyes are sweet and subtle, wild and sleepy by turns; oftentimes rising to the clouds; oftentimes challenging the heavens. She wears a diadem round her head. And I knew by childish memories that she could go abroad upon the winds, when she heard the sobbing of litanies or the thundering of organs, and when she beheld the mustering of summer clouds. This sister, the elder, it is that carries keys more than Papal at her girdle, which open every cottage and every palace. She, to my knowledge, sate all last summer by the bedside of the blind beggar, him that so often and so gladly I talked with, whose pious daughter, eight years old, with the sunny countenance, resisted the temptations of play and village mirth to travel all day long on dusty roads with her afflicted father. For this did God send her a great reward. In the spring-time of the year, and whilst yet her own spring was budding, he recalled her to himself. But her blind father mourns for ever over *her;* still he dreams at midnight that the little guiding hand is locked within his own; and still he wakens to a darkness that is *now* within a second and a deeper darkness. This *Mater Lachrymarum* also has been sitting all this winter of 1844–5 within the bedchamber of the Czar,[5] bringing before his eyes a daughter (not less pious) that vanished to God not less suddenly, and left behind her a darkness not less profound. By the power

of her keys it is that Our Lady of Tears glides a ghostly intruder into the chambers of sleepless men, sleepless women, sleepless children, from Ganges to the Nile, from Nile to Mississippi. And her, because she is the first-born of her house, and has the widest empire, let us honour with the title of "Madonna."

The second sister is called *Mater Suspiriorum*, Our Lady of Sighs. She never scales the clouds, nor walks abroad upon the winds. She wears no diadem. And her eyes, if they were ever seen, would be neither sweet nor subtle; no man could read their story; they would be found filled with perishing dreams, and with wrecks of forgotten delirium. But she raises not her eyes; her head, on which sits a dilapidated turban, droops for ever; for ever fastens on the dust. She weeps not. She groans not. But she sighs inaudibly at intervals. Her sister, Madonna, is oftentimes stormy and frantic; raging in the highest against heaven; and demanding back her darlings. But Our Lady of Sighs never clamours, never defies, dreams not of rebellious aspirations. She is humble to abjectness. Hers is the meekness that belongs to the hopeless. Murmur she may, but it is in her sleep. Whisper she may, but it is to herself in the twilight. Mutter she does at times, but it is in solitary places that are desolate as she is desolate, in ruined cities, and when the sun has gone down to his rest. This sister is the visitor of the Pariah, of the Jew, of the bondsman to the oar in Mediterranean galleys, of the English criminal in Norfolk island,[6] blotted out from the books of remembrance in sweet far-off England, of the baffled penitent reverting his eye for ever upon a solitary grave, which to him seems the altar overthrown of some past and bloody sacrifice, on which altar no oblations can now be availing, whether towards pardon that he might implore, or towards reparation that he might attempt. Every slave that at noonday looks up to the tropical sun with timid reproach, as he points with one hand to the earth, our general mother, but for *him* a stepmother, as he points with the other hand to the Bible, our general teacher, but against *him* sealed and sequestered;*—every woman sitting in darkness, without love to shelter her head, or hope to illumine her solitude, because the heaven-born instincts kindling in her nature germs of holy affections, which God implanted in her womanly bosom, having been stifled by social necessities, now burn sullenly to waste, like

* This, the reader will be aware, applies chiefly to the cotton and tobacco States of North America; but not to them only: on which account I have not scrupled to figure the sun, which looks down upon slavery, as *tropical*—no matter if strictly within the tropics or simply so near to them as to produce a similar climate.

---

3 Jeremiah, xxxi, 15.
4 Matthew, ii, 16–18.
5 Czar Nicholas I, emperor of Russia 1825–1855. His youngest daughter Alexandra had died on July 29, 1844.

6 South Pacific island, east of Australia; for a number of years it served as a penal settlement.

sepulchral lamps amongst the ancients;—every nun defrauded of her unreturning May-time by wicked kinsmen, whom God will judge;—every captive in every dungeon;—all that are betrayed, and all that are rejected; outcasts by traditionary law, and children of *hereditary* disgrace—all these walk with "Our Lady of Sighs." She also carries a key; but she needs it little. For her kingdom is chiefly amongst the tents of Shem,[7] and the houseless vagrant of every clime. Yet in the very highest ranks of man she finds chapels of her own; and even in glorious England there are some that, to the world, carry their heads as proudly as the reindeer, who yet secretly have received her mark upon their foreheads.

But the third sister, who is also the youngest—! Hush! whisper, whilst we talk of *her!* Her kingdom is not large, or else no flesh should live; but within that kingdom all power is hers. Her head, turreted like that of Cybèle,[8] rises almost beyond the reach of sight. She droops not; and her eyes rising so high, *might* be hidden by distance. But, being what they are, they cannot be hidden; through the treble veil of crape which she wears, the fierce light of a blazing misery, that rests not for matins or for vespers—for noon of day or noon of night—for ebbing or for flowing tide—may be read from the very ground. She is the defier of God. She also is the mother of lunacies, and the suggestress of suicides. Deep lie the roots of her power; but narrow is the nation that she rules. For she can approach only those in whom a profound nature has been upheaved by central convulsions; in whom the heart trembles and the brain rocks under conspiracies of tempest from without and tempest from within. Madonna moves with uncertain steps, fast or slow, but still with tragic grace. Our Lady of Sighs creeps timidly and stealthily. But this youngest sister moves with incalculable motions, bounding, and with a tiger's leaps. She carries no key; for, though coming rarely amongst men, she storms all doors at which she is permitted to enter at all. And *her* name is *Mater Tenebrarum*—Our Lady of Darkness.

These were the *Semnai Theai*, or Sublime Goddesses*—these were the *Eumenides*, or Gracious Ladies, (so called by antiquity in shuddering propitia-

tion)[9]—of my Oxford dreams. MADONNA spoke. She spoke by her mysterious hand. Touching my head, she beckoned to Our Lady of Sighs; and *what* she spoke, translated out of the signs which (except in dreams) no man reads, was this:—

"Lo! here is he, whom in childhood I dedicated to my altars. This is he that once I made my darling. Him I led astray, him I beguiled, and from heaven I stole away his young heart to mine. Through me did he become idolatrous; and through me it was, by languishing desires, that he worshipped the worm, and prayed to the wormy grave. Holy was the grave to him; lovely was its darkness; saintly its corruption. Him, this young idolater, I have seasoned for thee, dear gentle Sister of Sighs! Do thou take him now to *thy* heart, and season him for our dreadful sister. And thou"—turning to the *Mater Tenebrarum*, she said—"wicked sister, that temptest and hatest, do thou take him from *her*. See that thy sceptre lie heavy on his head. Suffer not woman and her tenderness to sit near him in his darkness. Banish the frailties of hope—wither the relentings of love—scorch the fountains of tears: curse him as only thou canst curse. So shall he be accomplished in the furnace—so shall he see the things that ought *not* to be seen—sights that are abominable, and secrets that are unutterable. So shall he read elder truths, sad truths, grand truths, fearful truths. So shall he rise again *before* he dies. And so shall our commission be accomplished which from God we had—to plague his heart until we had unfolded the capacities of his spirit."†

† The reader, who wishes at all to understand the course of these Confessions, ought not to pass over this dream-legend. There is no great wonder that a vision, which occupied my waking thoughts in those years, should re-appear in my dreams. It was in fact a legend recurring in sleep, most of which I had myself silently written or sculptured in my daylight reveries. But its importance to the present Confessions is this—that it rehearses or prefigures their course. The FIRST part belongs to Madonna. The THIRD belongs to the "Mater Suspiriorum," and will be entitled *The Pariah Worlds*. The FOURTH, which terminates the work, belongs to the "Mater Tenebrarum," and will be entitled *The Kingdom of Darkness*. As to the SECOND, it is an interpolation requisite to the effect of the others; and will be explained in its proper place.[10]

* The word σεμνός is usually rendered *venerable* in dictionaries; not a very flattering epithet for females. But by weighing a number of passages in which the word is used pointedly, I am disposed to think that it comes nearest to our idea of the *sublime*; as near as a Greek word *could* come.

7 See Genesis, ix, 27. The phrase is here used to suggest a nomadic existence.
8 In Greek mythology, the great mother of the gods, represented with her head crowned.

9 *Eumenides*: literally "the well-minded Ones," more familiarly known as the Furies.
10 The "SECOND part" was published in July 1845, as the final installment of the *Suspiria* in *Blackwood's Magazine*. It resembles the earlier "Affliction of Childhood" in being largely an autobiographical narrative, in this case of De Quincey's experiences from the death of his sister through his early days in London. It retraces some of the ground of the "Preliminary Confessions;" however, the emphasis is more specifically on how the events "furnished or exposed the germs of later experiences in worlds more shadowy."

THE APPARITION OF THE BROCKEN.

ASCEND with me on this dazzling Whitsunday the Brocken [1] of North Germany. The dawn opened in cloudless beauty; it is a dawn of bridal June; but, as the hours advance, her youngest sister April, that sometimes cares little for racing across both frontiers of May, frets the bridal lady's sunny temper with sallies of wheeling and careering showers—flying and pursuing, opening and closing, hiding and restoring. On such a morning, and reaching the summits of the forest-mountain about sunrise, we shall have one chance the more for seeing the famous Spectre of the Brocken.*

* This very striking phenomenon has been continually described by writers, both German and English, for the last fifty years. Many readers, however, will not have met with these descriptions: and on *their* account I add a few words in explanation; referring them for the best scientific comment on the case to Sir David Brewster's "Natural Magic." [2] The spectre takes the shape of a human figure, or, if the visitors are more than one, then the spectres multiply; they arrange themselves on the blue ground of the sky, or the dark ground of any clouds that may be in the right quarter, or perhaps they are strongly relieved against a curtain of rock, at a distance of some miles, and always exhibiting gigantic proportions. At first, from the distance and the colossal size, every spectator supposes the appearance to be quite independent of himself. But very soon he is surprised to observe his own motions and gestures mimicked; and wakens to the conviction that the phantom is but a dilated reflection of himself. This Titan amongst the apparitions of earth is exceedingly capricious, vanishing abruptly for reasons best known to himself, and more coy in coming forward than the Lady Echo of Ovid. One reason why he is seen so seldom must be ascribed to the concurrence of conditions under which only the phenomenon can be manifested: the sun must be near to the horizon, (which of itself implies a time of day inconvenient to a person starting from a station as distant as Elbingerode;) the spectator must have his back to the sun; and the air must contain some vapour—but *partially* distributed. Coleridge ascended the Brocken on the Whitsunday of 1799, with a party of English students from Goettingen, but failed to see the phantom; afterwards in England (and under the same conditions) he saw a much rarer phenomenon, which he described in the following eight lines. I give them from a corrected copy: (the apostrophe in the beginning must be understood as addressed to an ideal conception):—

> 'And art thou nothing? Such thou art as when
> The woodman winding westward up the glen
> At wintry dawn, when o'er the sheep-track's maze
> The viewless snow-mist weaves a glist'ning haze,
> Sees full before him, gliding without tread,
> An image with a glory round its head:
> This shade he worships for its golden hues,
> And *makes* (not knowing) that which he pursues.'

[1] The highest mountain in northern Germany, and the source of many superstitions.
[2] *Letters on Natural Magic addressed to Sir Walter Scott, Bart.* (1832), of which pages 128–31 give an account of the Spectre of the Brocken. The verses quoted later in De Quincey's footnote are from Coleridge's "Constancy to an Ideal Object" (1828), ll. 25–32.

Who and what is he? He is a solitary apparition, in the sense of loving solitude; else he is not always solitary in his personal manifestations, but on proper occasions has been known to unmask a strength quite sufficient to alarm those who had been insulting him.

Now, in order to test the nature of this mysterious apparition, we will try two or three experiments upon him. What we fear, and with some reason, is, that as he lived so many ages with foul Pagan sorcerers, and witnessed so many centuries of dark idolatries, his heart may have been corrupted; and that even now his faith may be wavering or impure. We will try.

Make the sign of the cross, and observe whether he repeats it, (as, on Whitsunday,† he surely ought to do.) Look! he *does* repeat it; but the driving showers perplex the images, and *that*, perhaps, it is which gives him the air of one who acts reluctantly or evasively. Now, again, the sun shines more brightly, and the showers have swept off like squadrons of cavalry to the rear. We will try him again.

Pluck an anemone, one of these many anemones which once was called the sorcerer's flower,‡ and bore a part perhaps in his horrid ritual of fear; carry it to that stone which mimics the outline of a heathen altar, and once was called the sorcerer's altar;‡ then, bending your knee, and raising your right hand to God, say, —"Father, which art in heaven—this lovely anemone, that once glorified the worship of fear, has travelled back into thy fold; this altar, which once reeked with bloody rites to Cortho, [3] has long been rebaptized into thy holy service. The darkness is gone—the cruelty is gone which the darkness bred; the moans have passed away which the victims uttered; the cloud has vanished which once sate continually upon their graves—cloud of protestation that ascended for ever to thy throne from the tears of the defenceless, and the anger of the just. And lo! I thy servant, with this dark phantom, whom, for one hour on this thy festival of Pentecost, I make *my* servant, render thee united worship in this thy recovered temple."

† It is singular, and perhaps owing to the temperature and weather likely to prevail in that early part of summer, that more appearances of the spectre have been witnessed on Whitsunday than on any other day.
‡ These are names still clinging to the anemone of the Brocken, and to an altar-shaped fragment of granite near one of the summits; and it is not doubted that they both connect themselves through links of ancient tradition with the gloomy realities of Paganism, when the whole Hartz and the Brocken formed for a very long time the last asylum to a ferocious but perishing idolatry.

[3] A pagan idol "whom the Saxons worshipped on the summit of the Brocken" (Brewster, p. 128).

Look, now! the apparition plucks an anemone, and places it on an altar; he also bends his knee, he also raises his right hand to God. Dumb he is; but sometimes the dumb serve God acceptably. Yet still it occurs to you, that perhaps on this high festival of the Christian Church, he may be overruled by supernatural influence into confession of his homage, having so often been made to bow and bend his knee at murderous rites. In a service of religion he may be timid. Let us try him, therefore, with an earthly passion, where he will have no bias either from favour or from fear.

If, then, once in childhood you suffered an affliction that was ineffable; if once, when powerless to face such an enemy, you were summoned to fight with the tiger that couches within the separations of the grave; in that case, after the example of Judæa (on the Roman coins) —sitting under her palm-tree to weep, but sitting with with her head veiled—do you also veil your head. Many years are passed away since then; and you were a little ignorant thing at that time, hardly above six years old; or perhaps (if you durst tell all the truth) not quite so much. But your heart was deeper than the Danube; and, as was your love, so was your grief. Many years are gone since that darkness settled on your head; many summers, many winters; yet still its shadows wheel round upon you at intervals, like these April showers upon this glory of bridal June. Therefore now, on this dovelike morning of Pentecost, do you veil your head like Judæa in memory of that transcendant woe, and in testimony that, indeed, it surpassed all utterance of words. Immediately you see that the apparition of the Brocken veils *his* head, after the model of Judæa weeping under her palm-tree, as if he also had a human heart, and that *he* also, in childhood, having suffered an affliction which was ineffable, wished by these mute symbols to breathe a sigh towards heaven in memory of that affliction, and by way of record, though many a year after, that it was indeed unutterable by words.

This trial is decisive. You are now satisfied that the apparition is but a reflex of yourself; and, in uttering your secret feelings to *him*, you make this phantom the dark symbolic mirror for reflecting to the daylight what else must be hidden for ever.

Such a relation does the Dark Interpreter, whom immediately the reader will learn to know as an intruder into my dreams, bear to my own mind. He is originally a mere reflex of my inner nature. But as the apparition of the Brocken sometimes is disturbed by storms or by driving showers, so as to dissemble his real origin, in like manner the Interpreter sometimes swerves out of my orbit, and mixes a little with alien natures. I do not always know him in these cases as my

own parhelion.[4] What he says, generally is but that which *I* have said in daylight, and in meditation deep enough to sculpture itself on my heart. But sometimes, as his face alters, his words alter; and they do not always seem such as I have used, or *could* use. No man can account for all things that occur in dreams. Generally I believe this—that he is a faithful representative of myself; but he also is at times subject to the action of the god *Phantasus*, who rules in dreams.

Hailstone choruses* besides, and storms, enter my dreams. Hailstones and fire that run along the ground, sleet and blinding hurricanes, revelations of glory insufferable pursued by volleying darkness—these are powers able to disturb any features that originally were but shadow, and to send drifting the anchors of any vessel that rides upon deeps so treacherous as those of dreams. Understand, however, the Interpreter to bear generally the office of a tragic chorus at Athens. The Greek chorus is perhaps not quite understood by critics, any more than the Dark Interpreter by myself. But the leading function of both must be supposed this —not to tell you any thing absolutely new, *that* was done by the actors in the drama; but to recall you to your own lurking thoughts—hidden for the moment or imperfectly developed, and to place before you, in immediate connexion with groups vanishing too quickly for any effort of meditation on your own part, such commentaries, prophetic or looking back, pointing the moral or deciphering the mystery, justifying Providence, or mitigating the fierceness of anguish, as would or might have occurred to your own meditative heart—had only time been allowed for its motions.

The Interpreter is anchored and stationary in my dreams; but great storms and driving mists cause him to fluctuate uncertainly, or even to retire altogether, like his gloomy counterpart the shy Phantom of the Brocken—and to assume new features or strange features, as in dreams always there is a power not contented with reproduction, but which absolutely creates or transforms. This dark being the reader will see again in a further stage of my opium experience; and I warn him that he will not always be found sitting inside my dreams, but at times outside, and in open daylight.

---

* I need not tell any lover of Handel that his oratorio of "Israel in Egypt" contains a chorus familiarly known by this name. The words are—"And he gave them hailstones for rain; fire, mingled with the hail, ran along upon the ground."

<><><><><><><><><><><><><><><><><><><><>

4 Fainter image or reflection of one's self.

FINALE TO PART I.
SAVANNAH-LA-MAR.

GOD smote Savannah-la-Mar,[1] and in one night, by earthquake, removed her, with all her towers standing and population sleeping, from the steadfast foundations of the shore to the coral floors of ocean. And God said—"Pompeii did I bury and conceal from men through seventeen centuries: this city I will bury, but not conceal. She shall be a monument to men of my mysterious anger; set in azure light through generations to come: for I will enshrine her in a crystal dome of my tropic seas." This city, therefore, like a mighty galleon with all her apparel mounted, streamers flying, and tackling perfect, seems floating along the noiseless depths of ocean: and oftentimes in glassy calms, through the translucid atmosphere of water that now stretches like an air-woven awning above the silent encampment, mariners from every clime look down into her courts and terraces, count her gates, and number the spires of her churches. She is one ample cemetery, and *has* been for many a year; but in the mighty calms that brood for weeks over tropic latitudes, she fascinates the eye with a *Fata-Morgana* revelation,[2] as of human life still subsisting in submarine asylums sacred from the storms that torment our upper air.

Thither, lured by the loveliness of cerulean depths, by the peace of human dwellings privileged from molestation, by the gleam of marble altars sleeping in everlasting sanctity, oftentimes in dreams did I and the dark Interpreter cleave the watery veil that divided us from her streets. We looked into the belfries, where the pendulous bells were waiting in vain for the summons which should awaken their marriage peals; together we touched the mighty organ keys, that sang no *jubilates* for the ear of Heaven—that sang no requiems for the ear of human sorrow; together we searched the silent nurseries, where the children were all asleep, and *had* been asleep through five generations. "They are waiting for the heavenly dawn," whispered the Interpreter to himself; "and, when *that* comes, the bells and the organs will utter a *jubilate* repeated by the echoes of Paradise." Then, turning to me, he said—"This is sad: this is piteous: but less would not have sufficed for the purposes of God. Look here: put into a Roman clepsydra [3] one hundred drops of water; let these run out as the sands in an hourglass; every drop measuring the hundredth part of a second, so that each shall represent but the three-hundred-and-sixty-thousandth part of an hour. Now, count the drops as they race along; and, when the fiftieth of the hundred is passing, behold! forty-nine are not, because already they have perished; and fifty are not, because they are yet to come. You see, therefore, how narrow, how incalculably narrow, is the true and actual present. Of that time which we call the present, hardly a hundredth part but belongs either to a past which has fled, or to a future which is still on the wing. It has perished, or it is not born. It was, or it is not. Yet even this approximation to the truth is *infinitely* false. For again subdivide that solitary drop, which only was found to represent the present, into a lower series of similar fractions, and the actual present which you arrest measures now but the thirty-sixth millionth of an hour; and so by infinite declensions the true and very present, in which only we live and enjoy, will vanish into a mote of a mote, distinguishable only by a heavenly vision. Therefore the present, which only man possesses, offers less capacity for his footing than the slenderest film that ever spider twisted from her womb. Therefore, also, even this incalculable shadow from the narrowest pencil of moonlight, is more transitory than geometry can measure, or thought of angel can overtake. The time which *is*, contracts into a mathematic point; and even that point perishes a thousand times before we can utter its birth. All is finite in the present; and even that finite is infinite in its velocity of flight towards death. But in God there is nothing finite; but in God there is nothing transitory; but in God there *can* be nothing that tends to death. Therefore, it follows—that for God there can be no present. The future is the present of God; and to the future it is that he sacrifices the human present. Therefore it is that he works by earthquake. Therefore it is that he works by grief. Oh, deep is the ploughing of earthquake! Oh, deep," [and his voice swelled like a *sanctus* rising from the choir of a cathedral,]—"oh, deep is the ploughing of grief! But oftentimes less would not suffice for the agriculture of God. Upon a night of earthquake he builds a thousand years of pleasant habitations for man. Upon the sorrow of an infant, he raises oftentimes from human intellects glorious vintages that could not else have been. Less than these fierce ploughshares would not have stirred the stubborn soil. The one is needed for earth, our planet—for earth itself as the dwelling-place of man. But the other is needed yet oftener for God's mightiest

---

[1] A coastal town in Jamaica, destroyed by fire and earthquake on October 3, 1780.
[2] De Quincey refers to the phenomenon called *Fata-Morgana* or *Castles of the Fairy Morgana*, an optical illusion occurring in the straits of Messina between Sicily and Italy. Under certain atmospheric conditions, the objects on the shore appear to exist in and move along the surface of the water.

---

[3] An instrument used to measure time by the discharge of water.

instrument; yes," [and he looked solemnly at myself,] "is needed for the mysterious children of the earth!"

END OF PART I.

[June 1845]

THE ENGLISH MAIL-COACH

Originally published in Blackwood's Magazine, *October–December 1849,* The English Mail-Coach *was revised for its inclusion in Volume IV [Miscellanies] of* Selections Grave and Gay, *1854. The "Explanatory Notice" was added at that time. The revised text is here followed. See Robert Hopkins' essay "De Quincey on War and the Pastoral Design of* The English Mail-Coach" *(Studies in Romanticism, VI [1967], 129–51) for a discussion of the essay as "a meaningful, coherent, imaginative prose work written by a conservative first-generation Romantic trying to sum up the profound significances, historical and cultural, of the Napoleonic Wars for himself and for the Victorian era." Calvin S. Brown, Jr. (Musical Quarterly, XXIV [1938], 341–50) presents a serious study of "The Musical Structure of De Quincey's* Dream-Fugue" *as variations on "a group of ideas: speed, urgency, and a girl in danger of sudden death."*

THE ENGLISH MAIL-COACH.

EXPLANATORY NOTICE.

THIS little paper, according to my original intention, formed part of the "Suspiria de Profundis," from which, for a momentary purpose, I did not scruple to detach it, and to publish it apart, as sufficiently intelligible even when dislocated from its place in a larger whole. To my surprise, however, one or two critics, not carelessly in conversation, but deliberately in print, professed their inability to apprehend the meaning of the whole, or to follow the links of the connection between its several parts. I am myself as little able to understand where the difficulty lies, or to detect any lurking obscurity, as those critics found themselves to unravel my logic. Possibly I may not be an indifferent and neutral judge in such a case. I will therefore sketch a brief abstract of the little paper according to my own original design, and then leave the reader to judge how far this design is kept in sight through the actual execution.

Thirty-seven years ago, or rather more, accident made me, in the dead of night, and of a night memorably solemn, the solitary witness to an appalling scene, which threatened instant death in a shape the most terrific to two young people, whom I had no means of assisting, except in so far as I was able to give them a most hurried warning of their danger; but even *that* not until they stood within the very shadow of the catastrophe, being divided from the most frightful of deaths by scarcely more, if more at all, than seventy seconds.

Such was the scene, such in its outline, from which the whole of this paper radiates as a natural expansion. This scene is circumstantially narrated in Section the Second, entitled, "The Vision of Sudden Death."

But a movement of horror, and of spontaneous recoil from this dreadful scene, naturally carried the whole of that scene, raised and idealised, into my dreams, and very soon into a rolling succession of dreams. The actual scene, as looked down upon from the box of the mail, was transformed into a dream, as tumultuous and changing as a musical fugue. This troubled dream is circumstantially reported in Section the Third, entitled, "Dream-Fugue upon the Theme of Sudden Death." What I had beheld from my seat upon the mail; the scenical strife of action and passion, of anguish and fear, as I had there witnessed them moving in ghostly silence; this duel between life and death narrowing itself to a point of such exquisite evanescence as the collision neared; all these elements of the scene blended, under the law of association, with the previous and permanent features of distinction investing the mail itself: which features at that time lay—1st, in velocity unprecedented; 2dly, in the power and beauty of the horses; 3dly, in the official connection with the government of a great nation; and, 4thly, in the function, almost a consecrated function, of publishing and diffusing through the land the great political events, and especially the great battles during a conflict of unparalleled grandeur. These honorary distinctions are all described circumstantially in the FIRST or introductory section ("The Glory of Motion"). The three first were distinctions maintained at all times; but the fourth and grandest belonged exclusively to the war with Napoleon; and this it was which most naturally introduced Waterloo into the dream. Waterloo, I understood, was the particular feature of the "Dream-Fugue" which my censors were least able to account for. Yet surely Waterloo, which, in common with every other great battle, it had been our special privilege to publish over all the land, most naturally entered the Dream under the license of our privilege. If not—if there be anything amiss—let the Dream be responsible. The Dream is a law to itself: and as well quarrel with a rainbow for showing, or for *not* showing, a secondary arch. So far as I know, every element in the shifting movements of the Dream derived itself either primarily from the incidents of the actual scene, or from secondary features associated with the mail. For example, the cathedral aisle derived itself from the mimic combination of features which grouped themselves together at the point of approaching collision—viz., an arrow-like section of the road, six hundred yards long, under the solemn lights described, with lofty trees meeting overhead in arches. The guard's horn, again—a humble instrument in itself—was yet glorified as the organ of publication for so many great national events. And the incident of the Dying Trumpeter, who rises from a marble bas-relief, and carries a marble trumpet to his marble lips for the purpose of warning the female infant, was doubtless secretly suggested by my own imperfect effort to seize the guard's horn, and to blow a warning blast. But the Dream knows best; and the Dream, I say again, is the responsible party.

SECTION THE FIRST.
THE GLORY OF MOTION.

SOME twenty or more years before I matriculated at Oxford, Mr Palmer,[1] at that time M.P. for Bath, had accomplished two things, very hard to do on our little planet, the Earth, however cheap they may be held by eccentric people in comets—he had invented mail-coaches, and he had married the daughter * of a duke. He was, therefore, just twice as great a man as Galileo, who did certainly invent (or, which is the same thing,† discover) the satellites of Jupiter, those very next things extant to mail-coaches in the two capital pretensions of speed and keeping time, but, on the other hand, who did *not* marry the daughter of a duke.

These mail-coaches, as organised by Mr Palmer, are entitled to a circumstantial notice from myself, having had so large a share in developing the anarchies of my subsequent dreams; an agency which they accomplished, 1st, through velocity, at that time unprecedented—for they first revealed the glory of motion; 2dly, through grand effects for the eye between lamp-light and the darkness upon solitary roads; 3dly, through animal beauty and power so often displayed in the class of horses selected for this mail service; 4thly, through the conscious presence of a central intellect, that, in the midst of vast distances‡—of storms, of darkness, of danger—overruled all obstacles into one steady co-operation to a national result. For my own feeling, this post-office service spoke as by some mighty orchestra, where a thousand instruments, all disregarding each other, and so far in danger of discord, yet all obedient as slaves to the supreme *baton* of some great leader, terminate in a perfection of harmony like that of heart, brain, and lungs, in a healthy animal organisation. But, finally, that particular element in this whole combination which most impressed myself, and through which it is that to this hour Mr Palmer's mail-coach system tyrannises over my dreams by terror and terrific beauty, lay in the awful *political*

* Lady Madeline Gordon.

† Thus, in the calendar of the Church Festivals, the discovery of the true cross (by Helen, the mother of Constantine) is recorded (and one might think—with the express consciousness of sarcasm) as the *Invention* of the Cross.

‡ One case was familiar to mail-coach travellers, where two mails in opposite directions, north and south, starting at the same minute from points six hundred miles apart, met almost constantly at a particular bridge which bisected the total distance.

[1] John Palmer (1742–1818), a theatrical proprietor in Bristol, had proposed the inauguration of mail-coaches, which first went into service in 1784 between London and Bristol and were soon extended between major cities throughout England and Scotland. Palmer was comptroller-general of the post office from 1786 to 1792 and was first elected to Parliament from Bristol in 1801.

mission which at that time it fulfilled. The mail-coach it was that distributed over the face of the land, like the opening of apocalyptic vials,[2] the heart-shaking news of Trafalgar, of Salamanca, of Vittoria,[3] of Waterloo. These were the harvest that, in the grandeur of their reaping, redeemed the tears and blood in which they had been sown. Neither was the meanest peasant so much below the grandeur and the sorrow of the times as to confound battles such as these, which were gradually moulding the destinies of Christendom, with the vulgar conflicts of ordinary warfare, so often no more than gladiatorial trials of national prowess. The victories of England in this stupendous contest rose of themselves as natural *Te Deums* to heaven; and it was felt by the thoughtful that such victories, at such a crisis of general prostration, were not more beneficial to ourselves than finally to France, our enemy, and to the nations of all western or central Europe, through whose pusillanimity it was that the French domination had prospered.

The mail-coach, as the national organ for publishing these mighty events thus diffusively influential, became itself a spiritualised and glorified object to an impassioned heart; and naturally, in the Oxford of that day, *all* hearts were impassioned, as being all (or nearly all) in *early* manhood. In most universities there is one single college; in Oxford there were five-and-twenty, all of which were peopled by young men, the *élite* of their own generation; not boys, but men; none under eighteen. In some of these many colleges, the custom permitted the student to keep what are called "short terms;" that is, the four terms of Michaelmas, Lent, Easter, and Act,[4] were kept by a residence, in the aggregate, of ninety-one days, or thirteen weeks. Under this interrupted residence, it was possible that a student might have a reason for going down to his home four times in the year. This made eight journeys to and fro. But, as these homes lay dispersed through all the shires of the island, and most of us disdained all coaches except his majesty's mail, no city out of London could pretend to so extensive a connection with Mr Palmer's establishment as Oxford. Three mails, at the least, I remember as passing every day through Oxford, and benefiting by my personal patronage—viz., the Worcester, the Gloucester, and the Holyhead mail. Naturally, therefore, it became a point of some interest with us, whose journeys revolved every six weeks on an average, to look a little into the

[2] See Revelation, xvi.

[3] Trafalgar was the site of the victory of October 21, 1805, by Lord Nelson over the combined French and Spanish fleets. Salamanca and Vittoria were victories by Wellington in the Peninsular War, of July 1812, and June 1813, respectively.

[4] The summer term, so called from the Act or public defense of a thesis by the degree candidate.

executive details of the system. With some of these Mr Palmer had no concern; they rested upon bye-laws enacted by posting-houses for their own benefit, and upon other bye-laws, equally stern, enacted by the inside passengers for the illustration of their own haughty exclusiveness. These last were of a nature to rouse our scorn, from which the transition was not very long to systematic mutiny. Up to this time, say 1804, or 1805 (the year of Trafalgar), it had been the fixed assumption of the four inside people (as an old tradition of all public carriages derived from the reign of Charles II.), that they, the illustrious quaternion, constituted a porcelain variety of the human race, whose dignity would have been compromised by exchanging one word of civility with the three miserable delf-ware outsides. Even to have kicked an outsider, might have been held to attaint the foot concerned in that operation; so that, perhaps, it would have required an act of Parliament to restore its purity of blood. What words, then, could express the horror, and the sense of treason, in that case, which *had* happened, where all three outsides (the trinity of Pariahs) made a vain attempt to sit down at the same breakfast-table or dinner-table with the consecrated four? I myself witnessed such an attempt; and on that occasion a benevolent old gentleman endeavoured to soothe his three holy associates, by suggesting that, if the outsides were indicted for this criminal attempt at the next assizes, the court would regard it as a case of lunacy, or *delirium tremens*, rather than of treason. England owes much of her grandeur to the depth of the aristocratic element in her social composition, when pulling against her strong democracy. I am not the man to laugh at it. But sometimes, undoubtedly, it expressed itself in comic shapes. The course taken with the infatuated outsiders, in the particular attempt which I have noticed, was that the waiter, beckoning them away from the privileged *salle-à-manger*, sang out, "This way, my good men," and then enticed these good men away to the kitchen. But that plan had not always answered. Sometimes, though rarely, cases occurred where the intruders, being stronger than usual, or more vicious than usual, resolutely refused to budge, and so far carried their point, as to have a separate table arranged for themselves in a corner of the general room. Yet, if an Indian screen could be found ample enough to plant them out from the very eyes of the high table, or *dais*, it then became possible to assume as a fiction of law—that the three delf fellows, after all, were not present. They could be ignored by the porcelain men, under the maxim, that objects not appearing, and not existing, are governed by the same logical construction.*

Such being, at that time, the usages of mail-coaches, what was to be done by us of young Oxford? We, the most aristocratic of people, who were addicted to the practice of looking down superciliously even upon the insides themselves as often very questionable characters—were we, by voluntarily going outside, to court indignities? If our dress and bearing sheltered us, generally, from the suspicion of being "raff" (the name at that period for "snobs"†) we really *were* such constructively, by the place we assumed. If we did not submit to the deep shadow of eclipse, we entered at least the skirts of its penumbra. And the analogy of theatres was valid against us, where no man can complain of the annoyances incident to the pit or gallery, having his instant remedy in paying the higher price of the boxes. But the soundness of this analogy we disputed. In the case of the theatre, it cannot be pretended that the inferior situations have any separate attractions, unless the pit may be supposed to have an advantage for the purposes of the critic or the dramatic reporter. But the critic or reporter is a rarity. For most people, the sole benefit is in the price. Now, on the contrary, the outside of the mail had its own incommunicable advantages. These we could not forego. The higher price we would willingly have paid, but not the price connected with the condition of riding inside; which condition we pronounced insufferable. The air, the freedom of prospect, the proximity to the horses, the elevation of seat—these were what we required; but, above all, the certain anticipation of purchasing occasional opportunities of driving.

Such was the difficulty which pressed us; and under the coercion of this difficulty, we instituted a searching inquiry into the true quality and valuation of the different apartments about the mail. We conducted this inquiry on metaphysical principles; and it was ascertained satisfactorily, that the roof of the coach, which by some weak men had been called the attics, and by some the garrets, was in reality the drawing-room; in which drawing-room the box was the chief ottoman or sofa; whilst it appeared that the *inside*, which had been traditionally regarded as the only room tenantable by gentlemen, was, in fact, the coal-cellar in disguise.

Great wits jump.[5] The very same idea had not long before struck the celestial intellect of China. Amongst the presents carried out by our first embassy to that

† "*Snobs*," and its antithesis, "*nobs*," arose among the internal factions of shoemakers perhaps ten years later. Possibly enough, the terms may have existed much earlier; but they were then first made known, picturesquely and effectively, by a trial at some assizes which happened to fix the public attention.

---

* *De non apparentibus*, &c.

5 Coincide, agree completely.

country was a state-coach. It had been specially selected as a personal gift by George III.; but the exact mode of using it was an intense mystery to Pekin. The ambassador, indeed (Lord Macartney),[6] had made some imperfect explanations upon this point; but, as his excellency communicated these in a diplomatic whisper, at the very moment of his departure, the celestial intellect was very feebly illuminated, and it became necessary to call a cabinet council on the grand state question, "Where was the Emperor to sit?" The hammer-cloth[7] happened to be unusually gorgeous; and partly on that consideration, but partly also because the box offered the most elevated seat, was nearest to the moon, and undeniably went foremost, it was resolved by acclamation that the box was the imperial throne, and for the scoundrel who drove, he might sit where he could find a perch. The horses, therefore, being harnessed, solemnly his imperial majesty ascended his new English throne under a flourish of trumpets, having the first lord of the treasury on his right hand, and the chief jester on his left. Pekin gloried in the spectacle; and in the whole flowery people, constructively present by representation, there was but one discontented person, and *that* was the coachman. This mutinous individual audaciously shouted, "Where am *I* to sit?" But the privy council, incensed by his disloyalty, unanimously opened the door, and kicked him into the inside. He had all the inside places to himself; but such is the rapacity of ambition, that he was still dissatisfied. "I say," he cried out in an extempore petition, addressed to the emperor through the window—"I say, how am I to catch hold of the reins?"—"Anyhow," was the imperial answer; "don't trouble *me*, man, in my glory. How catch the reins? Why, through the windows, through the keyholes—*any*how." Finally this contumacious coachman lengthened the check-strings into a sort of jury-reins,[8] communicating with the horses; with these he drove as steadily as Pekin had any right to expect. The emperor returned after the briefest of circuits; he descended in great pomp from his throne, with the severest resolution never to remount it. A public thanksgiving was ordered for his majesty's happy escape from the disease of broken neck; and the state-coach was dedicated thenceforward as a votive offering to the god Fo, Fo—whom the learned more accurately called Fi, Fi.

A revolution of this same Chinese character did young Oxford of that era effect in the constitution of mail-coach society. It was a perfect French revolution; and we had good reason to say, *ça ira*.[9] In fact, it soon became *too* popular. The "public"—a well known character, particularly disagreeable, though slightly respectable, and notorious for affecting the chief seats in synagogues—had at first loudly opposed this revolution; but when the opposition showed itself to be ineffectual, our disagreeable friend went into it with headlong zeal. At first it was a sort of race between us; and, as the public is usually from thirty to fifty years old, naturally we of young Oxford, that averaged about twenty, had the advantage. Then the public took to bribing, giving fees to horse-keepers, &c., who hired out their persons as warming-pans on the box-seat. *That*, you know, was shocking to all moral sensibilities. Come to bribery, said we, and there is an end to all morality, Aristotle's, Zeno's, Cicero's, or anybody's. And, besides, of what use was it? For *we* bribed also. And as our bribes to those of the public were as five shillings to sixpence, here again young Oxford had the advantage. But the contest was ruinous to the principles of the stables connected with the mails. This whole corporation was constantly bribed, rebribed, and often sur-rebribed; a mail-coach yard was like the hustings in a contested election; and a horse-keeper, ostler, or helper, was held by the philosophical at that time to be the most corrupt character in the nation.

There was an impression upon the public mind, natural enough from the continually augmenting velocity of the mail, but quite erroneous, that an outside seat on this class of carriages was a post of danger. On the contrary, I maintained that, if a man had become nervous from some gipsy prediction in his childhood, allocating to a particular moon now approaching some unknown danger, and he should inquire earnestly, "Whither can I fly for shelter? Is a prison the safest retreat? or a lunatic hospital? or the British Museum?" I should have replied, "Oh, no; I'll tell you what to do. Take lodgings for the next forty days on the box of his majesty's mail. Nobody can touch you there. If it is by bills at ninety days after date that you are made unhappy—if noters and protesters[10] are the sort of wretches whose astrological shadows darken the house of life[11]—then note you what I vehemently

[6] George Macartney (1737–1806), diplomat and colonial governor, was appointed head of an embassy to China in 1792.
[7] "A cloth covering the driver's seat or 'box' in a state or family coach" (*Oxford English Dictionary*).
[8] Temporary or substitute reins; from the naval term *jury-mast*, a temporary mast put up in place of one broken or carried away.

[9] Popular refrain of a French Revolutionary song, variously translated as: "it will go on," "we will succeed," "that will certainly happen."
[10] Those who formally declare the nonpayment or nonacceptance of a bill; preliminary step in legal action against debtors.
[11] Astrological term referring to one of the twelve divisions or "houses" of the heavens corresponding to the signs of the

protest—viz., that no matter though the sheriff and under-sheriff in every county should be running after you with his *posse*, touch a hair of your head he cannot whilst you keep house, and have your legal domicile on the box of the mail. It is felony to stop the mail; even the sheriff cannot do that. And an *extra* touch of the whip to the leaders (no great matter if it grazes the sheriff) at any time guarantees your safety." In fact, a bedroom in a quiet house seems a safe enough retreat, yet it is liable to its own notorious nuisances—to robbers by night, to rats, to fire. But the mail laughs at these terrors. To robbers, the answer is packed up and ready for delivery in the barrel of the guard's blunder-buss. Rats again!—there *are* none about mail-coaches, any more than snakes in Von Troil's Iceland;* except, indeed, now and then a parliamentary rat,[13] who always hides his shame in what I have shown to be the "coal cellar." And as to fire, I never knew but one in a mail-coach, which was in the Exeter mail, and caused by an obstinate sailor bound to Devonport. Jack, making light of the law and the law-giver that had set their faces against his offence, insisted on taking up a forbidden seat† in the rear of the roof, from which he

* The allusion is to a well-known chapter in Von Troil's work, entitled, "Concerning the Snakes of Iceland." The entire chapter consists of these six words—" *There are no snakes in Iceland.*"[12]

† The very sternest code of rules was enforced upon the mails by the Post-office. Throughout England, only three outsides were allowed, of whom one was to sit on the box, and the other two immediately behind the box; none, under any pretext, to come near the guard; an indispensable caution; since else, under the guise of passenger, a robber might by any one of a thousand advantages—which sometimes are created, but always are favoured, by the animation of frank social intercourse—have disarmed the guard. Beyond the Scottish border, the regulation was so far relaxed as to allow of *four* outsides, but not relaxed at all as to the mode of placing them. One, as before, was seated on the box, and the other three on the front of the roof, with a determinate and ample separation from the little insulated chair of the guard. This relaxation was conceded by way of compensating to Scotland her disadvantages in point of population. England, by the superior density of her population, might always count upon a large fund of profits in the fractional trips of chance passengers riding for short distances of two or three stages. In Scotland, this chance counted for much less. And therefore, to make good the deficiency, Scotland was allowed a compensatory profit upon one *extra* passenger.

❖❖❖❖❖❖❖❖❖❖❖❖❖❖❖❖❖❖❖❖❖❖❖❖❖❖❖

zodiac. One's fortune is determined by the particular predominance or conjunction of planets inhabiting the "houses" at the time of birth.

[12] Uno von Troil (1746–1803) was archbishop of Upsala; his *Letters on Iceland* was published in an English translation in 1780. No such chapter or remark on snakes occurs in the work. De Quincey is apparently thinking of an entry in Boswell's *Life of Johnson*, for April 13, 1778, regarding Niels Horrebov's *The Natural History of Iceland* (1758).

[13] One who deserts his party.

could exchange his own yarns with those of the guard. No greater offence was then known to mail-coaches; it was treason, it was *læsa majestas*,[14] it was by tendency arson; and the ashes of Jack's pipe, falling amongst the straw of the hinder boot containing the mail-bags, raised a flame which (aided by the wind of our motion) threatened a revolution in the republic of letters. Yet even this left the sanctity of the box unviolated. In dignified repose, the coachman and myself sat on, resting with benign composure upon our knowledge that the fire would have to burn its way through four inside passengers before it could reach ourselves. I remarked to the coachman, with a quotation from Virgil's "Æneid" really too hackneyed—

"Jam proximus ardet
Ucalegon."[15]

But, recollecting that the Virgilian part of the coachman's education might have been neglected, I interpreted so far as to say, that perhaps at that moment the flames were catching hold of our worthy brother and inside passenger, Ucalegon. The coachman made no answer, which is my own way when a stranger addresses me either in Syriac or in Coptic, but by his faint sceptical smile he seemed to insinuate that he knew better; for that Ucalegon, as it happened, was not in the way-bill,[16] and therefore could not have been booked.

No dignity is perfect which does not at some point ally itself with the mysterious. The connection of the mail with the state and the executive government—a connection obvious, but yet not strictly defined—gave to the whole mail establishment an official grandeur which did us service on the roads, and invested us with seasonable terrors. Not the less impressive were those terrors, because their legal limits were imperfectly ascertained. Look at those turnpike gates; with what deferential hurry, with what an obedient start, they fly open at our approach! Look at that long line of carts and carters ahead, audaciously usurping the very crest of the road. Ah! traitors, they do not hear us as yet; but, as soon as the dreadful blast of our horn reaches them with proclamation of our approach, see with what frenzy of trepidation they fly to their horses' heads, and deprecate our wrath by the precipitation of their crane-neck quarterings.[17] Treason they feel to be their crime; each individual carter feels himself

❖❖❖❖❖❖❖❖❖❖❖❖❖❖❖❖❖❖❖❖❖❖❖❖❖❖❖

[14] *læsa majestas*: offense against his majesty; high treason.

[15] *Aeneid*, II, 311–12. "Jam . . . Ucalegon": "Now [the house of] Ucalegon nearby blazes," on the night of the capture and destruction of Troy by the Greeks.

[16] The list of passengers booked for seats in a stage-coach.

[17] See "The Vision of Sudden Death," De Quincey's footnote, p. 636.

under the ban of confiscation and attainder; his blood is attainted through six generations; and nothing is wanting but the headsman and his axe, the block and the saw-dust, to close up the vista of his horrors. What! shall it be within benefit of clergy to delay the king's message on the high road?—to interrupt the great respirations, ebb and flood, *systole* and *diastole*, of the national intercourse?—to endanger the safety of tidings, running day and night between all nations and languages? Or can it be fancied, amongst the weakest of men, that the bodies of the criminals will be given up to their widows for Christian burial? Now the doubts which were raised as to our powers did more to wrap them in terror, by wrapping them in uncertainty, than could have been effected by the sharpest definitions of the law from the Quarter Sessions.[18] We, on our parts (we, the collective mail, I mean), did our utmost to exalt the idea of our privileges by the insolence with which we wielded them. Whether this insolence rested upon law that gave it a sanction, or upon conscious power that haughtily dispensed with that sanction, equally it spoke from a potential station; and the agent, in each particular insolence of the moment, was viewed reverentially, as one having authority.

Sometimes after breakfast his majesty's mail would become frisky; and in its difficult wheelings amongst the intricacies of early markets, it would upset an apple-cart, a cart loaded with eggs, &c. Huge was the affliction and dismay, awful was the smash. I, as far as possible, endeavoured in such a case to represent the conscience and moral sensibilities of the mail; and, when wildernesses of eggs were lying poached under our horses' hoofs, then would I stretch forth my hands in sorrow, saying (in words too celebrated at that time, from the false echoes* of Marengo), "Ah! wherefore have we not time to weep over you?" which was evidently impossible, since, in fact, we had not time to

laugh over them. Tied to post-office allowance, in some cases of fifty minutes for eleven miles, could the royal mail pretend to undertake the offices of sympathy and condolence? Could it be expected to provide tears for the accidents of the road? If even it seemed to trample on humanity, it did so, I felt, in discharge of its own more peremptory duties.

Upholding the morality of the mail, *à fortiori* I upheld its rights; as a matter of duty, I stretched to the uttermost its privilege of imperial precedency, and astonished weak minds by the feudal powers which I hinted to be lurking constructively in the charters of this proud establishment. Once I remember being on the box of the Holyhead mail, between Shrewsbury and Oswestry, when a tawdry thing from Birmingham, some "Tallyho" or "Highflyer," all flaunting with green and gold, came up alongside of us. What a contrast to our royal simplicity of form and colour in this plebeian wretch! The single ornament on our dark ground of chocolate colour was the mighty shield of the imperial arms, but emblazoned in proportions as modest as a signet-ring bears to a seal of office. Even this was displayed only on a single pannel, whispering, rather than proclaiming, our relations to the mighty state; whilst the beast from Birmingham, our green-and-gold friend from false, fleeting, perjured Brummagem,[20] had as much writing and painting on its sprawling flanks as would have puzzled a decipherer from the tombs of Luxor.[21] For some time this Birmingham machine ran along by our side—a piece of familiarity that already of itself seemed to me sufficiently jacobinical. But all at once a movement of the horses announced a desperate intention of leaving us behind. "Do you see *that*?" I said to the coachman. —"I see," was his short answer. He was wide awake, yet he waited longer than seemed prudent; for the horses of our audacious opponent had a disagreeable air of freshness and power. But his motive was loyal; his wish was, that the Birmingham conceit should be full-blown before he froze it. When *that* seemed right, he unloosed, or, to speak by a stronger word, he *sprang*, his known resources: he slipped our royal horses like cheetahs, or hunting-leopards, after the affrighted game. How they could retain such a reserve of fiery power after the work they had accomplished, seemed hard to explain. But on our side, besides the physical superiority, was a tower of moral strength, namely, the king's name, "which they upon the adverse faction wanted."[22] Passing them without an effort, as it seemed, we threw them into the rear with so lengthen-

---

* Yes, false! for the words ascribed to Napoleon, as breathed to the memory of Desaix, never were uttered at all. They stand in the same category of theatrical fictions as the cry of the foundering line-of-battle ship Vengeur, as the vaunt of General Cambronne at Waterloo, "*La Garde meurt, mais ne se rend pas,*" or as the repartees of Talleyrand.[19]

[18] "A court of limited criminal and civil jurisdiction and of appeal, held quarterly by the justices of the peace in the counties" (*Oxford English Dictionary*).

[19] Louis-Charles-Antoine Desaix de Veygoux (1768–1800) was a French general who died at the battle of Marengo, June 14, 1800, in which the Napoleonic armies defeated the Austrians. "The cry of the Vengeur" refers to the famous naval victory, "The Battle of the First of June [1794]," by Lord Howe over the French fleet, in which six French vessels were taken and the Vengeur was sunk before all of its crew could be rescued; allegedly the sailors on board sent up the shout "Vive la République" as they went to their deaths. "The vaunt of General Cambronne" was "The Guard dies, but never surrenders."

[20] Vulgar name for Birmingham.
[21] The site of a magnificent ancient temple at Thebes, Egypt.
[22] *Richard the Third*, V, iii, 13.

ing an interval between us, as proved in itself the bitterest mockery of their presumption; whilst our guard blew back a shattering blast of triumph, that was really too painfully full of derision.

I mention this little incident for its connection with what followed. A Welsh rustic, sitting behind me, asked if I had not felt my heart burn within me during the progress of the race? I said, with philosophic calmness, *No*; because we were not racing with a mail, so that no glory could be gained. In fact, it was sufficiently mortifying that such a Birmingham thing should dare to challenge us. The Welshman replied, that he didn't see *that*; for that a cat might look at a king, and a Brummagem coach might lawfully race the Holyhead mail. "*Race* us, if you like," I replied, "though even *that* has an air of sedition, but not *beat* us. This would have been treason; and for its own sake I am glad that the 'Tallyho' was disappointed." So dissatisfied did the Welshman seem with this opinion, that at last I was obliged to tell him a very fine story from one of our elder dramatists—viz., that once, in some far oriental kingdom, when the sultan of all the land, with his princes, ladies, and chief omrahs, were flying their falcons, a hawk suddenly flew at a majestic eagle; and in defiance of the eagle's natural advantages, in contempt also of the eagle's traditional royalty, and before the whole assembled field of astonished spectators from Agra and Lahore, killed the eagle on the spot. Amazement seized the sultan at the unequal contest, and burning admiration for its unparalleled result. He commanded that the hawk should be brought before him; he caressed the bird with enthusiasm; and he ordered that, for the commemoration of his matchless courage, a diadem of gold and rubies should be solemnly placed on the hawk's head; but then that, immediately after this solemn coronation, the bird should be led off to execution, as the most valiant indeed of traitors, but not the less a traitor, as having dared to rise rebelliously against his liege lord and anointed sovereign, the eagle. "Now," said I to the Welshman, "to you and me, as men of refined sensibilities, how painful it would have been that this poor Brummagem brute, the 'Tallyho,' in the impossible case of a victory over us, should have been crowned with Birmingham tinsel, with paste diamonds, and Roman pearls, and then led off to instant execution." The Welshman doubted if that could be warranted by law. And when I hinted at the 6th of Edward Longshanks, chap. 18,[23] for regulating the precedency of coaches, as being probably the statute relied on for the capital punishment of such offences, he replied drily, that if the attempt to pass a mail really were treasonable, it was a pity that the "Tallyho" appeared to have so imperfect an acquaintance with law.

The modern modes of travelling cannot compare with the old mail-coach system in grandeur and power. They boast of more velocity, not, however, as a consciousness, but as a fact of our lifeless knowledge, resting upon *alien* evidence; as, for instance, because somebody *says* that we have gone fifty miles in the hour, though we are far from feeling it as a personal experience, or upon the evidence of a result, as that actually we find ourselves in York four hours after leaving London. Apart from such an assertion, or such a result, I myself am little aware of the pace. But, seated on the old mail-coach, we needed no evidence out of ourselves to indicate the velocity. On this system the word was, *Non magna loquimur*, as upon railways, but *vivimus*. Yes, "magna *vivimus*;" we do not make verbal ostentation of our grandeurs, we realise our grandeurs in act, and in the very experience of life. The vital experience of the glad animal sensibilities made doubts impossible on the question of our speed; we heard our speed, we saw it, we felt it as a thrilling; and this speed was not the product of blind insensate agencies, that had no sympathy to give, but was incarnated in the fiery eyeballs of the noblest amongst brutes, in his dilated nostril, spasmodic muscles, and thunder-beating hoofs. The sensibility of the horse, uttering itself in the maniac light of his eye, might be the last vibration of such a movement; the glory of Salamanca might be the first. But the intervening links that connected them, that spread the earthquake of battle into the eyeball of the horse, were the heart of man and its electric thrillings—kindling in the rapture of the fiery strife, and then propagating its own tumults by contagious shouts and gestures to the heart of his servant the horse.

But now, on the new system of travelling, iron tubes and boilers have disconnected man's heart from the ministers of his locomotion. Nile[24] nor Trafalgar has power to raise an extra bubble in a steam-kettle. The galvanic cycle is broken up for ever; man's imperial nature no longer sends itself forward through the electric sensibility of the horse; the inter-agencies are gone in the mode of communication between the horse and his master, out of which grew so many aspects of sublimity under accidents of mists that hid, or sudden blazes that revealed, of mobs that agitated, or midnight

[23] Referring to Edward I, King of England 1272–1307, known as the "English Justinian" for his legal reforms. Apparently this is a joke on De Quincey's part; the "6th of Edward Longshanks" would be the Statute of Gloucester, 1278, which has only 15 chapters.

[24] The Battle of the Nile, August 1, 1798, at Aboukir, in which the British ships under Nelson dealt a devastating blow to the French fleet.

solitudes that awed. Tidings, fitted to convulse all nations, must henceforwards travel by culinary process; and the trumpet that once announced from afar the laurelled mail, heart-shaking, when heard screaming on the wind, and proclaiming itself through the darkness to every village or solitary house on its route, has now given way for ever to the pot-wallopings of the boiler.

Thus have perished multiform openings for public expressions of interest, scenical yet natural, in great national tidings; for revelations of faces and groups that could not offer themselves amongst the fluctuating mobs of a railway station. The gatherings of gazers about a laurelled mail had one centre, and acknowledged one sole interest. But the crowds attending at a railway station have as little unity as running water, and own as many centres as there are separate carriages in the train.

How else, for example, than as a constant watcher for the dawn, and for the London mail that in summer months entered about daybreak amongst the lawny thickets of Marlborough forest, couldst thou, sweet Fanny of the Bath road, have become the glorified inmate of my dreams? Yet Fanny, as the loveliest young woman for face and person that perhaps in my whole life I have beheld, merited the station which even now, from a distance of forty years, she holds in my dreams; yes, though by links of natural association she brings along with her a troop of dreadful creatures, fabulous and not fabulous, that are more abominable to the heart, than Fanny and the dawn are delightful.

Miss Fanny of the Bath road, strictly speaking, lived at a mile's distance from that road; but came so continually to meet the mail, that I on my frequent transits rarely missed her, and naturally connected her image with the great thoroughfare where only I had ever seen her. Why she came so punctually, I do not exactly know; but I believe with some burden of commissions to be executed in Bath, which had gathered to her own residence as a central rendezvous for converging them. The mail-coachman who drove the Bath mail, and wore the royal livery,* happened to be Fanny's grandfather. A good man he was, that loved his beautiful granddaughter; and, loving her wisely, was vigilant over her deportment in any case where young Oxford

---

* The general impression was, that the royal livery belonged of right to the mail-coachmen as their professional dress. But this was an error. To the guard it *did* belong, I believe, and was obviously essential as an official warrant, and as a means of instant identification for his person, in the discharge of his important public duties. But the coachman, and especially if his place in the series did not connect him immediately with London and the General Post-office, obtained the scarlet coat only as an honorary distinction after long (or, if not long, trying and special) service.

might happen to be concerned. Did my vanity then suggest that I myself, individually, could fall within the line of his terrors? Certainly not, as regarded any physical pretensions that I could plead; for Fanny (as a chance passenger from her own neighbourhood once told me) counted in her train a hundred and ninety-nine professed admirers, if not open aspirants to her favour; and probably not one of the whole brigade but excelled myself in personal advantages. Ulysses even, with the unfair advantage of his accursed bow, could hardly have undertaken that amount of suitors. So the danger might have seemed slight—only that woman is universally aristocratic; it is amongst her nobilities of heart that she *is* so. Now, the aristocratic distinctions in my favour might easily with Miss Fanny have compensated my physical deficiencies. Did I then make love to Fanny? Why, yes; about as much love as one *could* make whilst the mail was changing horses—a process which, ten years later, did not occupy above eighty seconds; but *then*—viz., about Waterloo—it occupied five times eighty. Now, four hundred seconds offer a field quite ample enough for whispering into a young woman's ear a great deal of truth, and (by way of parenthesis) some trifle of falsehood. Grandpapa did right, therefore, to watch me. And yet, as happens too often to the grandpapas of earth, in a contest with the admirers of granddaughters, how vainly would he have watched me had I meditated any evil whispers to Fanny! She, it is my belief, would have protected herself against any man's evil suggestions. But he, as the result showed, could not have intercepted the opportunities for such suggestions. Yet, why not? Was he not active? Was he not blooming? Blooming he was as Fanny herself.

"Say, all our praises why should lords——"[25]

Stop, that's not the line.

"Say, all our roses why should girls engross?"

The coachman showed rosy blossoms on his face deeper even than his granddaughter's—*his* being drawn from the ale cask, Fanny's from the fountains of the dawn. But, in spite of his blooming face, some infirmities he had; and one particularly in which he too much resembled a crocodile. This lay in a monstrous inaptitude for turning round. The crocodile, I presume, owes that inaptitude to the absurd *length* of his back; but in our grandpapa it arose rather from the absurd *breadth* of his back, combined, possibly, with some growing stiffness in his legs. Now, upon this crocodile infirmity of his I planted a human advantage

---

[25] Pope's *Moral Essays*, Epistle III (to Allen, Lord Bathurst), l. 249.

for tendering my homage to Miss Fanny. In defiance of all his honourable vigilance, no sooner had he presented to us his mighty Jovian back (what a field for displaying to mankind his royal scarlet!), whilst inspecting professionally the buckles, the straps, and the silvery turrets * of his harness, than I raised Miss Fanny's hand to my lips, and, by the mixed tenderness and respectfulness of my manner, caused her easily to understand how happy it would make me to rank upon her list as No. 10 or 12, in which case a few casualties amongst her lovers (and observe, they *hanged* liberally in those days) might have promoted me speedily to the top of the tree; as, on the other hand, with how much loyalty of submission I acquiesced by anticipation in her award, supposing that she should plant me in the very rear-ward of her favour, as No. 199+1. Most truly I loved this beautiful and ingenuous girl; and had it not been for the Bath mail, timing all courtships by post-office allowance, heaven only knows what might have come of it. People talk of being over head and ears in love; now, the mail was the cause that I sank only over ears in love, which, you know, still left a trifle of brain to overlook the whole conduct of the affair.

Ah, reader! when I look back upon those days, it seems to me that all things change—all things perish. "Perish the roses and the palms of kings:" perish even the crowns and trophies of Waterloo: thunder and lightning are not the thunder and lightning which I remember. Roses are degenerating. The Fannies of our island—though this I say with reluctance—are not visibly improving; and the Bath road is notoriously superannuated. Crocodiles, you will say, are stationary. Mr Waterton tells me that the crocodile does *not* change; that a cayman, in fact, or an alligator, is just as good for riding upon as he was in the time of the Pharaohs. *That* may be; but the reason is, that the crocodile does not live fast—he is a slow coach. I believe it is generally understood among naturalists, that the crocodile is a blockhead. It is my own impression that the Pharaohs were also blockheads. Now, as the Pharaohs and the crocodile domineered over Egyptian society, this accounts for a singular mistake that prevailed through innumerable generations on the Nile. The crocodile made the ridiculous blunder of supposing man to be meant chiefly for his own eating. Man, taking a different view of the subject, naturally

met that mistake by another: he viewed the crocodile as a thing sometimes to worship, but always to run away from. And this continued until Mr Waterton† changed the relations between the animals. The mode of escaping from the reptile he showed to be, not by running away, but by leaping on its back, booted and spurred. The two animals had misunderstood each other. The use of the crocodile has now been cleared up—viz., to be ridden; and the final cause of man is, that he may improve the health of the crocodile by riding him a fox-hunting before breakfast. And it is pretty certain that any crocodile, who has been regularly hunted through the season, and is master of the weight he carries, will take a six-barred gate now as well as ever he would have done in the infancy of the pyramids.

If, therefore, the crocodile does *not* change, all things else undeniably *do*: even the shadow of the pyramids grows less. And often the restoration in vision of Fanny and the Bath road, makes me too pathetically sensible of that truth. Out of the darkness, if I happen to call back the image of Fanny, up rises suddenly from a gulf of forty years a rose in June; or, if I think for an instant of the rose in June, up rises the heavenly face of Fanny. One after the other, like the antiphonies in the choral service, rise Fanny and the rose in June, then back again the rose in June and Fanny. Then come both together, as in a chorus—roses and Fannies, Fannies and roses, without end, thick as blossoms in paradise. Then comes a venerable crocodile, in a royal livery of scarlet and gold, with sixteen capes; and the crocodile is driving four-in-hand from the box of the Bath mail. And suddenly we upon the mail are pulled up by a mighty dial, sculptured with the hours, that mingle with the heavens and the heavenly host. Then all at once we are arrived at Marlborough forest, amongst the lovely households‡ of the

---

* As one who loves and venerates Chaucer for his unrivalled merits of tenderness, of picturesque characterisation, and of narrative skill, I noticed with great pleasure that the word *torrettes* is used by him to designate the little devices through which the reins are made to pass. This same word, in the same exact sense, I heard uniformly used by many scores of illustrious mail-coachmen, to whose confidential friendship I had the honour of being admitted in my younger days.

† Had the reader lived through the last generation, he would not need to be told that some thirty or thirty-five years back, Mr Waterton, a distinguished country gentleman of ancient family in Northumberland, publicly mounted and rode in top-boots a savage old crocodile, that was restive and very impertinent, but all to no purpose. The crocodile jibbed and tried to kick, but vainly. He was no more able to throw the Squire, than Sinbad was to throw the old scoundrel who used his back without paying for it, until he discovered a mode (slightly immoral, perhaps, though some think not) of murdering the old fraudulent jockey, and so circuitously of unhorsing him.[26]

‡ Roe-deer do not congregate in herds like the fallow or the red deer, but by separate families, parents and children; which feature of approximation to the sanctity of human hearths, added to their comparatively miniature and graceful proportions,

[26] Charles Waterton (1782–1865) was a naturalist and the author of the popular *Wanderings in South America, the North-West of the United States and the Antilles* ... (1825).

roe-deer; the deer and their fawns retire into the dewy thickets; the thickets are rich with roses; once again the roses call up the sweet countenance of Fanny; and she, being the granddaughter of a crocodile, awakens a dreadful host of semi-legendary animals—griffins, dragons, basilisks, sphinxes—till at length the whole vision of fighting images crowds into one towering armorial shield, a vast emblazonry of human charities and human loveliness that have perished, but quartered heraldically with unutterable and demoniac natures, whilst over all rises, as a surmounting crest, one fair female hand, with the forefinger pointing, in sweet, sorrowful admonition, upwards to heaven, where is sculptured the eternal writing which proclaims the frailty of earth and her children.

GOING DOWN WITH VICTORY.

But the grandest chapter of our experience, within the whole mail-coach service, was on those occasions when we went down from London with the news of victory. A period of about ten years stretched from Trafalgar to Waterloo; the second and third years of which period (1806 and 1807) were comparatively sterile; but the other nine (from 1805 to 1815 inclusively) furnished a long succession of victories; the least of which, in such a contest of Titans, had an inappreciable value of position—partly for its absolute interference with the plans of our enemy, but still more from its keeping alive through central Europe the sense of a deep-seated vulnerability in France. Even to tease the coasts of our enemy, to mortify them by continual blockades, to insult them by capturing if it were but a baubling schooner under the eyes of their arrogant armies, repeated from time to time a sullen proclamation of power lodged in one quarter to which the hopes of Christendom turned in secret. How much more loudly must this proclamation have spoken in the audacity * of having bearded the *élite* of

their troops, and having beaten them in pitched battles! Five years of life it was worth paying down for the privilege of an outside place on a mail-coach, when carrying down the first tidings of any such event. And it is to be noted that, from our insular situation, and the multitude of our frigates disposable for the rapid transmission of intelligence, rarely did any unauthorised rumour steal away a prelibation from the first aroma of the regular despatches. The government news was generally the earliest news.

From eight P.M., to fifteen or twenty minutes later, imagine the mails assembled on parade in Lombard Street, where, at that time,† and not in St Martin's-le-Grand, was seated the General Post-office. In what exact strength we mustered I do not remember; but, from the length of each separate *attelage*, [2] we filled the street, though a long one, and though we were drawn up in double file. On *any* night the spectacle was beautiful. The absolute perfection of all the appointments about the carriages and the harness, their strength, their brilliant cleanliness, their beautiful simplicity—but, more than all, the royal magnificence of the horses—were what might first have fixed the attention. Every carriage, on every morning in the year, was taken down to an official inspector for examination—wheels, axles, linchpins, pole, glasses, lamps, were all critically probed and tested. Every part of every carriage had been cleaned, every horse had been groomed, with as much rigour as if they belonged to a private gentleman; and that part of the spectacle offered itself always. But the night before us is a night of victory; and, behold! to the ordinary display, what a heart-shaking addition!—horses, men, carriages, all are dressed in laurels and flowers, oak-leaves and ribbons. The guards, as being officially his Majesty's servants, and of the coachmen such as are within the privilege of the post-office, wear the royal liveries of course; and as it is summer (for all the *land* victories

---

conciliate to them an interest of peculiar tenderness, supposing even that this beautiful creature is less characteristically impressed with the grandeurs of savage and forest life.

* Such the French accounted it; and it has struck me that Soult would not have been so popular in London, at the period of her present Majesty's coronation, or in Manchester, on occasion of his visit to that town, if they had been aware of the insolence with which he spoke of us in notes written at intervals from the field of Waterloo. As though it had been mere felony in our army to look a French one in the face, he said in more notes than one, dated from two to four P.M. on the field of Waterloo, "Here are the English—we have them; they are caught *en flagrant delit*." Yet no man should have known us better; no man had drunk deeper from the cup of humiliation than Soult had in 1809, when ejected by us with headlong violence from Oporto, and pursued through a long line of wrecks to the frontier of Spain; sub-

sequently at Albuera, in the bloodiest of recorded battles, to say nothing of Toulouse, he should have learned our pretensions.[1]

† I speak of the era previous to Waterloo.

[1] Nicolas Jean De Dieu Soult (1769–1851) was marshal of France and one of the leading French generals in the Peninsular War. Soult captured Oporto in March 1809, but was forced to abandon it two months later. The battle of Albuera (May 16, 1811) produced around 15,000 combined casualties, but ended with the retreat of Soult before the allied Portuguese-Spanish-British forces. The Battle of Toulouse (April 10, 1814), the last major battle of the war, ended with Soult's retreat and the capture of the city by Wellington. In 1838, Soult had attended Victoria's coronation as ambassador extraordinary. *En flagrant delit:* "in the very act."

[2] *attelage:* complete equipage, team of horses and coach together.

were naturally won in summer), they wear, on this fine evening, these liveries exposed to view, without any covering of upper coats. Such a costume, and the elaborate arrangement of the laurels in their hats, dilate their hearts, by giving to them openly a personal connection with the great news, in which already they have the general interest of patriotism. That great national sentiment surmounts and quells all sense of ordinary distinctions. Those passengers who happen to be gentlemen are now hardly to be distinguished as such except by dress; for the usual reserve of their manner in speaking to the attendants has on this night melted away. One heart, one pride, one glory, connects every man by the transcendent bond of his national blood. The spectators, who are numerous beyond precedent, express their sympathy with these fervent feelings by continual hurrahs. Every moment are shouted aloud by the post-office servants, and summoned to draw up, the great ancestral names of cities known to history through a thousand years—Lincoln, Winchester, Portsmouth, Gloucester, Oxford, Bristol, Manchester, York, Newcastle, Edinburgh, Glasgow, Perth, Stirling, Aberdeen—expressing the grandeur of the empire by the antiquity of its towns, and the grandeur of the mail establishment by the diffusive radiation of its separate missions. Every moment you hear the thunder of lids locked down upon the mail-bags. That sound to each individual mail is the signal for drawing off, which process is the finest part of the entire spectacle. Then come the horses into play. Horses! can these be horses that bound off with the action and gestures of leopards? What stir!—what sea-like ferment!—what a thundering of wheels!—what a trampling of hoofs!—what a sounding of trumpets!—what farewell cheers—what redoubling peals of brotherly congratulation, connecting the name of the particular mail—"Liverpool for ever!"—with the name of the particular victory—"Badajoz [3] for ever!" or Salamanca for ever!" The half-slumbering consciousness that, all night long, and all the next day—perhaps for even a longer period—many of these mails, like fire racing along a train of gunpowder, will be kindling at every instant new successions of burning joy, has an obscure effect of multiplying the victory itself, by multiplying to the imagination into infinity the stages of its progressive diffusion. A fiery arrow seems to be let loose, which from that moment is destined to travel, without intermission, westwards for

◇◇◇◇◇◇◇◇◇◇◇◇◇◇◇◇◇◇◇◇◇◇◇◇◇◇◇◇◇◇◇◇

3 Badajoz and Salamanca were major reversals for the French and decisive victories for Wellington. Badajoz was captured after a long siege on April 7, 1812; Salamanca, on July 22, 1812.

three hundred * miles—northwards for six hundred; and the sympathy of our Lombard Street friends at parting is exalted a hundredfold by a sort of visionary sympathy with the yet slumbering sympathies which in so vast a succession we are going to awake.

Liberated from the embarrassments of the city, and issuing into the broad uncrowded avenues of the northern suburbs, we soon begin to enter upon our natural pace of ten miles an hour. In the broad light of the summer evening, the sun, perhaps, only just at the point of setting, we are seen from every storey of every house. Heads of every age crowd to the windows—young and old understand the language of our victorious symbols—and rolling volleys of sympathising cheers run along us, behind us, and before us. The beggar, rearing himself against the wall, forgets his lameness—real or assumed—thinks not of his whining trade, but stands erect, with bold exulting smiles, as we pass him. The victory has healed him, and says, Be thou whole! Women and children, from garrets alike and cellars, through infinite London, look down or look up with loving eyes upon our gay ribbons and our

* Of necessity, this scale of measurement, to an American, if he happens to be a thoughtless man, must sound ludicrous. Accordingly, I remember a case in which an American writer indulges himself in the luxury of a little fibbing, by ascribing to an Englishman a pompous account of the Thames, constructed entirely upon American ideas of grandeur, and concluding in something like these terms:—"And, sir, arriving at London, this mighty father of rivers attains a breadth of at least two furlongs, having, in its winding course, traversed the astonishing distance of one hundred and seventy miles." And this the candid American thinks it fair to contrast with the scale of the Mississippi. Now, it is hardly worth while to answer a pure fiction gravely, else one might say that no Englishman out of Bedlam ever thought of looking in an island for the rivers of a continent; nor, consequently, could have thought of looking for the peculiar grandeur of the Thames in the length of its course, or in the extent of soil which it drains; yet, if he had been so absurd, the American might have recollected that a river, not to be compared with the Thames even as to volume of water—viz., the Tiber—has contrived to make itself heard of in this world for twenty-five centuries to an extent not reached as yet by any river, however corpulent, of his own land. The glory of the Thames is measured by the destiny of the population to which it ministers, by the commerce which it supports, by the grandeur of the empire in which, though far from the largest, it is the most influential stream. Upon some such scale, and not by a transfer of Columbian standards, is the course of our English mails to be valued. The American may fancy the effect of his own valuations to our English ears, by supposing the case of a Siberian glorifying his country in these terms: "These wretches, sir, in France and England, cannot march half a mile in any direction without finding a house where food can be had and lodging; whereas, such is the noble desolation of our magnificent country, that in many a direction for a thousand miles, I will engage that a dog shall not find shelter from a snow-storm, nor a wren find an apology for breakfast."

martial laurels; sometimes kiss their hands; sometimes hang out, as signals of affection, pocket-handkerchiefs, aprons, dusters, anything that, by catching the summer breezes, will express an aerial jubilation. On the London side of Barnet,[4] to which we draw near within a few minutes after nine, observe that private carriage which is approaching us. The weather being so warm, the glasses are all down; and one may read, as on the stage of a theatre, everything that goes on within. It contains three ladies—one likely to be "mamma," and two of seventeen or eighteen, who are probably her daughters. What lovely animation, what beautiful unpremeditated pantomime, explaining to us every syllable that passes, in these ingenuous girls! By the sudden start and raising of the hands, on first discovering our laurelled equipage!—by the sudden movement and appeal to the elder lady from both of them—and by the heightened colour on their animated countenances, we can almost hear them saying, "See, see! Look at their laurels! Oh, mamma! there has been a great battle in Spain; and it has been a great victory." In a moment we are on the point of passing them. We passengers—I on the box, and the two on the roof behind me—raise our hats to the ladies; the coachman makes his professional salute with the whip; the guard even, though punctilious on the matter of his dignity as an officer under the crown, touches his hat. The ladies move to us, in return, with a winning graciousness of gesture; all smile on each side in a way that nobody could misunderstand, and that nothing short of a grand national sympathy could so instantaneously prompt. Will these ladies say that we are nothing to *them*? Oh, no; they will not say *that*. They cannot deny—they do not deny—that for this night they are our sisters; gentle or simple, scholar or illiterate servant, for twelve hours to come, we on the outside have the honour to be their brothers. Those poor women, again, who stop to gaze upon us with delight at the entrance of Barnet, and seem, by their air of weariness, to be returning from labour—do you mean to say that they are washerwomen and charwomen? Oh, my poor friend, you are quite mistaken. I assure you they stand in a far higher rank; for this one night they feel themselves by birth-right to be daughters of England, and answer to no humbler title.

Every joy, however, even rapturous joy—such is the sad law of earth—may carry with it grief, or fear of grief, to some. Three miles beyond Barnet, we see approaching us another private carriage, nearly repeating the circumstances of the former case. Here, also, the glasses are all down—here, also, is an elderly

lady seated; but the two daughters are missing; for the single young person sitting by the lady's side, seems to be an attendant—so I judge from her dress, and her air of respectful reserve. The lady is in mourning; and her countenance expresses sorrow. At first she does not look up; so that I believe she is not aware of our approach, until she hears the measured beating of our horses' hoofs. Then she raises her eyes to settle them painfully on our triumphal equipage. Our decorations explain the case to her at once; but she beholds them with apparent anxiety, or even with terror. Some time before this, I, finding it difficult to hit a flying mark, when embarrassed by the coachman's person and reins intervening, had given to the guard a "Courier" evening paper, containing the gazette,[5] for the next carriage that might pass. Accordingly he tossed it in, so folded that the huge capitals expressing some such legend as—GLORIOUS VICTORY, might catch the eye at once. To see the paper, however, at all, interpreted as it was by our ensigns of triumph, explained everything; and, if the guard were right in thinking the lady to have received it with a gesture of horror, it could not be doubtful that she had suffered some deep personal affliction in connection with this Spanish war.

Here, now, was the case of one who, having formerly suffered, might, erroneously perhaps, be distressing herself with anticipations of another similar suffering. That same night, and hardly three hours later, occurred the reverse case. A poor woman, who too probably would find herself, in a day or two, to have suffered the heaviest of afflictions by the battle, blindly allowed herself to express an exultation so unmeasured in the news and its details, as gave to her the appearance which amongst Celtic Highlanders is called *fey*.[6] This was at some little town where we changed horses an hour or two after midnight. Some fair or wake had kept the people up out of their beds, and had occasioned a partial illumination of the stalls and booths, presenting an unusual but very impressive effect. We saw many lights moving about as we drew near; and perhaps the most striking scene on the whole route was our reception at this place. The flashing of torches and the beautiful radiance of blue lights (technically, Bengal lights)[7] upon the heads of our horses; the fine effect of such a showery and ghostly illumination falling upon our flowers and glittering laurels;* whilst

---

* I must observe, that the colour of *green* suffers almost a spiritual change and exaltation under the effect of Bengal lights.

---

[4] Market town in Hertfordshire, ten miles north of London.

[5] The official account of current events.
[6] "Fated" or doomed to die; in this case, said of one who exhibits such unusual and unnaturally high emotion.
[7] "A kind of firework producing a steady and vivid blue-coloured light, used for signals" (*Oxford English Dictionary*).

all around ourselves, that formed a centre of light, the darkness gathered on the rear and flanks in massy blackness; these optical splendours, together with the prodigious enthusiasm of the people, composed a picture at once scenical and affecting, theatrical and holy. As we staid for three or four minutes, I alighted; and immediately from a dismantled stall in the street, where no doubt she had been presiding through the earlier part of the night, advanced eagerly a middle-aged woman. The sight of my newspaper it was that had drawn her attention upon myself. The victory which we were carrying down to the provinces on *this* occasion, was the imperfect one of Talavera—imperfect for its results, such was the virtual treachery of the Spanish general, Cuesta,[8] but not imperfect in its ever-memorable heroism. I told her the main outline of the battle. The agitation of her enthusiasm had been so conspicuous when listening, and when first applying for information, that I could not but ask her if she had not some relative in the Peninsular army. Oh, yes; her only son was there. In what regiment? He was a trooper in the 23d Dragoons. My heart sank within me as she made that answer. This sublime regiment, which an Englishman should never mention without raising his hat to their memory, had made the most memorable and effective charge recorded in military annals. They leaped their horses—*over* a trench where they could, *into* it, and with the result of death or mutilation when they could *not*. What proportion cleared the trench is nowhere stated. Those who *did*, closed up and went down upon the enemy with such divinity of fervour (I use the word *divinity* by design: the inspiration of God must have prompted this movement to those whom even then He was calling to His presence), that two results followed. As regarded the enemy, this 23d Dragoons, not, I believe, originally three hundred and fifty strong, paralysed a French column, six thousand strong, then ascended the hill, and fixed the gaze of the whole French army. As regarded themselves, the 23d were supposed at first to have been barely not annihilated; but eventually, I believe, about one in four survived. And this, then, was the regiment—a regiment already for some hours glorified and hallowed to the ear of all London, as lying stretched, by a large majority, upon one bloody

aceldama[9]—in which the young trooper served whose mother was now talking in a spirit of such joyous enthusiasm. Did I tell her the truth? Had I the heart to break up her dreams? No. To-morrow, said I to myself—to-morrow, or the next day, will publish the worst. For one night more, wherefore should she not sleep in peace? After to-morrow, the chances are too many that peace will forsake her pillow. This brief respite, then, let her owe to *my* gift and *my* forbearance. But, if I told her not of the bloody price that had been paid, not, therefore, was I silent on the contributions from her son's regiment to that day's service and glory. I showed her not the funeral banners under which the noble regiment was sleeping. I lifted not the over-shadowing laurels from the bloody trench in which horse and rider lay mangled together. But I told her how these dear children of England, officers and privates, had leaped their horses over all obstacles as gaily as hunters to the morning's chase. I told her how they rode their horses into the mists of death (saying to myself, but not saying to *her*), and laid down their young lives for thee, O mother England! as willingly—poured out their noble blood as cheerfully—as ever, after a long day's sport, when infants, they had rested their wearied heads upon their mother's knees, or had sunk to sleep in her arms. Strange it is, yet true, that she seemed to have no fears for her son's safety, even after this knowledge that the 23d Dragoons had been memorably engaged; but so much was she enraptured by the knowledge that *his* regiment, and therefore that *he*, had rendered conspicuous service in the dreadful conflict—a service which had actually made them, within the last twelve hours, the foremost topic of conversation in London—so absolutely was fear swallowed up in joy—that, in the mere simplicity of her fervent nature, the poor woman threw her arms round my neck, as she thought of her son, and gave to *me* the kiss which secretly was meant for *him*.

[October 1849]   [1854]

SECTION THE SECOND.
THE VISION OF SUDDEN DEATH.

WHAT IS to be taken as the predominant opinion of man, reflective and philosophic, upon SUDDEN DEATH? It is remarkable that, in different conditions of society, sudden death has been variously regarded as the consummation of an earthly career most fervently to be desired, or, again, as that consummation which is

---

8 The battle of Talavera occurred on July 27 and 28, 1809. Following the battle, from which the French finally retreated, General Gregorio García de la Cuesta (1741–1811) failed to care for the wounded British soldiers entrusted to him, led his forces away from the positions they were to continue to protect, and left Wellesley unaided to encounter additional French troops. Wellesley was forced to abandon Talavera. As a result of his heroism at Talavera, Wellesley was created Viscount Wellington in September 1809.

---

9 Field of slaughter and butchery; from the name given to the field purchased with the blood money of Judas.

with most horror to be deprecated. Cæsar the Dictator, at his last dinner party (*cæna*), on the very evening before his assassination, when the minutes of his earthly career were numbered, being asked what death, in *his* judgment, might be pronounced the most eligible, replied, "That which should be most sudden." [1] On the other hand, the divine Litany of our English Church, when breathing forth supplications, as if in some representative character for the whole human race prostrate before God, places such a death in the very van of horrors:—"From lightning and tempest; from plague, pestilence, and famine; from battle and murder, and from SUDDEN DEATH—*Good Lord, deliver us.*" Sudden death is here made to crown the climax in a grand ascent of calamities; it is ranked among the last of curses; and yet, by the noblest of Romans, it was ranked as the first of blessings. In that difference, most readers will see little more than the essential difference between Christianity and Paganism. But this, on consideration, I doubt. The Christian Church may be right in its estimate of sudden death; and it is a natural feeling, though after all it may also be an infirm one, to wish for a quiet dismissal from life—as that which *seems* most reconcilable with meditation, with penitential retrospects, and with the humilities of farewell prayer. There does not, however, occur to me any direct scriptural warrant for this earnest petition of the English Litany, unless under a special construction of the word "sudden." It seems a petition—indulged rather and conceded to human infirmity, than exacted from human piety. It is not so much a doctrine built upon the eternities of the Christian system, as a plausible opinion built upon special varieties of physical temperament. Let that, however, be as it may, two remarks suggest themselves as prudent restraints upon a doctrine, which else *may* wander, and *has* wandered, into an uncharitable superstition. The first is this: that many people are likely to exaggerate the horror of a sudden death, from the disposition to lay a false stress upon words or acts, simply because by an accident they have become *final* words or acts. If a man dies, for instance, by some sudden death when he happens to be intoxicated, such a death is falsely regarded with peculiar horror; as though the intoxication were suddenly exalted into a blasphemy. But *that* is unphilosophic. The man was, or he was not, *habitually* a drunkard. If not, if his intoxication were a solitary accident, there can be no reason for allowing special emphasis to this act, simply because through misfortune it became his final act. Nor, on the other hand, if it were no accident, but one

of his *habitual* transgressions, will it be the more habitual or the more a transgression, because some sudden calamity, surprising him, has caused this habitual trangression to be also a final one. Could the man have had any reason even dimly to foresee his own sudden death, there would have been a new feature in his act of intemperance—a feature of presumption and irreverence, as in one that, having known himself drawing near to the presence of God, should have suited his demeanour to an expectation so awful. But this is no part of the case supposed. And the only new element in the man's act is not any element of special immorality, but simply of special misfortune.

The other remark has reference to the meaning of the word *sudden*. Very possibly Cæsar and the Christian Church do not differ in the way supposed; that is, do not differ by any difference of doctrine as between Pagan and Christian views of the moral temper appropriate to death, but perhaps they are contemplating different cases. Both contemplate a violent death, a Βιαθανατος [2]—death that is Βιαιος, or, in other words, death that is brought about, not by internal and spontaneous change, but by active force having its origin from without. In this meaning the two authorities agree. Thus far they are in harmony. But the difference is, that the Roman by the word "sudden" means *unlingering;* whereas the Christian Litany by "sudden death" means a death *without warning,* consequently without any available summons to religious preparation. The poor mutineer, who kneels down to gather into his heart the bullets from twelve firelocks of his pitying comrades, dies by a most sudden death in Cæsar's sense; one shock, one mighty spasm, one (possibly *not* one) groan, and all is over. But, in the sense of the Litany, the mutineer's death is far from sudden; his offence originally, his imprisonment, his trial, the interval between his sentence and its execution, having all furnished him with separate warnings of his fate—having all summoned him to meet it with solemn preparation.

Here at once, in this sharp verbal distinction, we comprehend the faithful earnestness with which a holy Christian Church pleads on behalf of her poor departing children, that God would vouchsafe to them the last great privilege and distinction possible on a death-bed—viz., the opportunity of untroubled preparation for facing this mighty trial. Sudden death, as a mere variety in the modes of dying, where death in some shape is inevitable, proposes a question of choice which, equally in the Roman and the Christian sense, will be variously answered according to each man's

---

[1] The incident is recorded in Suetonius' *Life of Julius Caesar,* 87.

[2] The word is possibly derived from the title of Donne's treatise on suicide *Biathanatos.*

variety of temperament. Meantime, one aspect of sudden death there is, one modification, upon which no doubt can arise, that of all martyrdoms it is the most agitating—viz., where it surprises a man under circumstances which offer (or which seem to offer) some hurrying, flying, inappreciably minute chance of evading it. Sudden as the danger which it affronts, must be any effort by which such an evasion can be accomplished. Even *that*, even the sickening necessity for hurrying in extremity where all hurry seems destined to be vain, even that anguish is liable to a hideous exasperation in one particular case—viz., where the appeal is made not exclusively to the instinct of self-preservation, but to the conscience, on behalf of some other life besides your own, accidentally thrown upon *your* protection. To fail, to collapse in a service merely your own, might seem comparatively venial; though, in fact, it is far from venial. But to fail in a case where Providence has suddenly thrown into your hands the final interests of another—a fellow-creature shuddering between the gates of life and death; this, to a man of apprehensive conscience, would mingle the misery of an atrocious criminality with the misery of a bloody calamity. You are called upon, by the case supposed, possibly to die; but to die at the very moment when, by any even partial failure, or effeminate collapse of your energies, you will be self-denounced as a murderer. You had but the twinkling of an eye for your effort, and that effort might have been unavailing; but to have risen to the level of such an effort, would have rescued you, though not from dying, yet from dying as a traitor to your final and farewell duty.

The situation here contemplated exposes a dreadful ulcer, lurking far down in the depths of human nature. It is not that men generally are summoned to face such awful trials. But potentially, and in shadowy outline, such a trial is moving subterraneously in perhaps all men's natures. Upon the secret mirror of our dreams such a trial is darkly projected, perhaps, to every one of us. That dream, so familiar to childhood, of meeting a lion, and, through languishing prostration in hope and the energies of hope, that constant sequel of lying down before the lion, publishes the secret frailty of human nature—reveals its deep-seated falsehood to itself—records its abysmal treachery. Perhaps not one of us escapes that dream; perhaps, as by some sorrowful doom of man, that dream repeats for every one of us, through every generation, the original temptation in Eden. Every one of us, in this dream, has a bait offered to the infirm places of his own individual will; once again a snare is presented for tempting him into captivity to a luxury of ruin; once again, as in aboriginal Paradise, the man falls by his own choice; again, by

infinite iteration, the ancient earth groans to Heaven, through her secret caves, over the weakness of her child: "Nature, from her seat, sighing through all her works," again "gives signs of wo that all is lost;" [3] and again the counter sigh is repeated to the sorrowing heavens for the endless rebellion against God. It is not without probability that in the world of dreams every one of us ratifies for himself the original transgression. In dreams, perhaps under some secret conflict of the midnight sleeper, lighted up to the consciousness at the time, but darkened to the memory as soon as all is finished, each several child of our mysterious race completes for himself the treason of the aboriginal fall.

* * * * *

The incident, so memorable in itself by its features of horror, and so scenical by its grouping for the eye, which furnished the text for this reverie upon *Sudden Death*, occurred to myself in the dead of night, as a solitary spectator, when seated on the box of the Manchester and Glasgow mail, in the second or third summer after Waterloo. I find it necessary to relate the circumstances, because they are such as could not have occurred unless under a singular combination of accidents. In those days, the oblique and lateral communications with many rural post-offices were so arranged, either through necessity or through defect of system, as to make it requisite for the main northwestern mail (*i.e.*, the *down* mail), on reaching Manchester, to halt for a number of hours; how many, I do not remember; six or seven, I think; but the result was, that, in the ordinary course, the mail recommenced its journey northwards about midnight. Wearied with the long detention at a gloomy hotel, I walked out about eleven o'clock at night for the sake of fresh air; meaning to fall in with the mail and resume my seat at the post-office. The night, however, being yet dark, as the moon had scarcely risen, and the streets being at that hour empty, so as to offer no opportunities for asking the road, I lost my way; and did not reach the post-office until it was considerably past midnight; but, to my great relief (as it was important for me to be in Westmoreland by the morning), I saw in the huge saucer eyes of the mail, blazing through the gloom, an evidence that my chance was not yet lost. Past the time it was; but, by some rare accident, the mail was not even yet ready to start. I ascended to my seat on the box, where my cloak was still lying as it had lain at the Bridgewater Arms. I had left it there in imitation of a nautical discoverer, who leaves a bit of bunting on the shore of his discovery, by way of warning off the

3 *Paradise Lost*, IX, 782–84.

ground the whole human race, and notifying to the Christian and the heathen worlds, with his best compliments, that he has hoisted his pocket-handkerchief once and for ever upon that virgin soil; thenceforward claiming the *jus dominii*[4] to the top of the atmosphere above it, and also the right of driving shafts to the centre of the earth below it; so that all people found after this warning, either aloft in upper chambers of the atmosphere, or groping in subterraneous shafts, or squatting audaciously on the surface of the soil, will be treated as trespassers—kicked, that is to say, or decapitated, as circumstances may suggest, by their very faithful servant, the owner of the said pocket-handkerchief. In the present case, it is probable that my cloak might not have been respected, and the *jus gentium*[5] might have been cruelly violated in my person—for, in the dark, people commit deeds of darkness, gas being a great ally of morality—but it so happened that, on this night, there was no other outside passenger; and thus the crime, which else was but too probable, missed fire for want of a criminal.

Having mounted the box, I took a small quantity of laudanum, having already travelled two hundred and fifty miles—viz., from a point seventy miles beyond London. In the taking of laudanum there was nothing extraordinary. But by accident it drew upon me the special attention of my assessor on the box, the coachman. And in *that* also there was nothing extraordinary. But by accident, and with great delight, it drew my own attention to the fact that this coachman was a monster in point of bulk, and that he had but one eye. In fact, he had been foretold by Virgil as

"Monstrum horrendum, informe, ingens cui lumen ademptum."[6]

He answered to the conditions in every one of the items:—1. a monster he was; 2. dreadful; 3. shapeless; 4. huge; 5. who had lost an eye. But why should *that* delight me? Had he been one of the Calendars in the "Arabian Nights,"[7] and had paid down his eye as the price of his criminal curiosity, what right had *I* to exult in his misfortune? I did *not* exult: I delighted in no man's punishment, though it were even merited. But these personal distinctions (Nos. 1, 2, 3, 4, 5) identified in an instant an old friend of mine, whom I had known in the south for some years as the most masterly of

mail-coachmen. He was the man in all Europe that could (if *any* could) have driven six-in-hand full gallop over *Al Sirat*—that dreadful bridge of Mahomet, with no side battlements, and of *extra* room not enough for a razor's edge—leading right across the bottomless gulf.[8] Under this eminent man, whom in Greek I cognominated Cyclops *diphrélates* (Cyclops the charioteer), I, and others known to me, studied the diphrelatic art. Excuse, reader, a word too elegant to be pedantic. As a pupil, though I paid extra fees, it is to be lamented that I did not stand high in his esteem. It showed his dogged honesty (though, observe, not his discernment), that he could not see my merits. Let us excuse his absurdity in this particular, by remembering his want of an eye. Doubtless *that* made him blind to my merits. In the art of conversation, however, he admitted that I had the whip-hand of him. On this present occasion, great joy was at our meeting. But what was Cyclops doing here? Had the medical men recommended northern air, or how? I collected, from such explanations as he volunteered, that he had an interest at stake in•some suit-at-law now pending at Lancaster; so that probably he had got himself transferred to this station, for the purpose of connecting with his professional pursuits an instant readiness for the calls of his lawsuit.

Meantime, what are we stopping for? Surely we have now waited long enough. Oh, this procrastinating mail, and this procrastinating post-office! Can't they take a lesson upon the subject from *me?* Some people have called *me* procrastinating. Yet you are witness, reader, that I was here kept waiting for the post-office. Will the post-office lay its hand on its heart, in its moments of sobriety, and assert that ever it waited for me? What are they about? The guard tells me that there is a large extra accumulation of foreign mails this night, owing to irregularities caused by war, by wind, by weather, in the packet service, which as yet does not benefit at all by steam. For an *extra* hour, it seems, the post-office has been engaged in threshing out the pure wheaten correspondence of Glasgow, and winnowing it from the chaff of all baser intermediate towns. But at last all is finished. Sound your horn, guard. Manchester, good-by; we've lost an hour by your criminal conduct at the post-office: which, however, though I do not mean to part with a serviceable ground of complaint, and one which really *is* such for the horses, to me secretly is an advantage, since it compels us to look

---

4 *jus dominii*: the law of eminent domain.
5 *jus gentium*: "the law of nations."
6 *Aeneid*, III, 658. "Monstrum ... ademptum": "a horrid monster, deformed, huge, whose eye had been taken out" (referring to Polyphemus the Cyclops).
7 The Calendars were Mahometan monks, all blinded in the right eye. Their stories cover the twenty-eighth through sixty-third nights.

8 In Mahometan theology, *Al-Sirat* is the bridge of judgment "which is laid over the midst of hell, and is finer than a hair, and sharper than the edge of a sword" (James Hastings' *Encyclopedia of Religion and Ethics* [1951], II, 852). The good may easily cross and enter Paradise; the wicked lose their footing and plunge into the abyss.

sharply for this lost hour amongst the next eight or nine, and to recover it (if we can) at the rate of one mile extra per hour. Off we are at last, and at eleven miles an hour; and for the moment I detect no changes in the energy or in the skill of Cyclops.

From Manchester to Kendal, which virtually (though not in law) is the capital of Westmoreland, there were at this time seven stages of eleven miles each. The first five of these, counting from Manchester, terminate in Lancaster, which is therefore fifty-five miles north of Manchester, and the same distance exactly from Liverpool. The first three stages terminate in Preston (called, by way of distinction from other towns of that name, *proud* Preston), at which place it is that the separate roads from Liverpool and from Manchester to the north become confluent.* Within these first three stages lay the foundation, the progress, and termination of our night's adventure. During the first stage, I found out that Cyclops was mortal: he was liable to the shocking affection of sleep—a thing which previously I had never suspected. If a man indulges in the vicious habit of sleeping, all the skill in aurigation⁹ of Apollo himself, with the horses of Aurora to execute his notions, avail him nothing. "Oh, Cyclops!" I exclaimed, "thou art mortal. My friend, thou snorest." Through the first eleven miles, however, this infirmity—which I grieve to say that he shared with the whole Pagan Pantheon—betrayed itself only by brief snatches. On waking up, he made an apology for himself, which, instead of mending matters, laid open a gloomy vista of coming disasters. The summer assizes, he reminded me, were now going on at Lancaster: in consequence of which, for three nights and three days, he had not lain down in a bed. During the day, he was waiting for his own summons as a witness on the trial in which he was interested; or else, lest he should be missing at the critical moment, was drinking with the other witnesses, under the pastoral surveillance of the attorneys. During the night, or that part of it which at sea would form the middle watch, he was driving. This explanation certainly accounted for his drowsiness, but in a way which made it much more alarming; since now, after several days' resistance to this infirmity, at length he was

steadily giving way. Throughout the second stage he grew more and more drowsy. In the second mile of the third stage, he surrendered himself finally and without a struggle to his perilous temptation. All his past resistance had but deepened the weight of this final oppression. Seven atmospheres of sleep rested upon him; and to consummate the case, our worthy guard, after singing "Love amongst the Roses" for perhaps thirty times, without invitation, and without applause, had in revenge moodily resigned himself to slumber—not so deep, doubtless, as the coachman's, but deep enough for mischief. And thus at last, about ten miles from Preston, it came about that I found myself left in charge of his Majesty's London and Glasgow mail, then running at the least twelve miles an hour.

What made this negligence less criminal than else it must have been thought, was the condition of the roads at night during the assizes. At that time, all the law business of populous Liverpool, and also of populous Manchester, with its vast cincture of populous rural districts, was called up by ancient usage to the tribunal of Lilliputian Lancaster. To break up this old traditional usage required, 1. a conflict with powerful established interests; 2. a large system of new arrangements; and 3. a new parliamentary statute. But as yet this change was merely in contemplation. As things were at present, twice in the year† so vast a body of business rolled northwards, from the southern quarter of the county, that for a fortnight at least it occupied the severe exertions of two judges in its despatch. The consequence of this was, that every horse available for such a service, along the whole line of road, was exhausted in carrying down the multitudes of people who were parties to the different suits. By sunset, therefore, it usually happened that, through utter exhaustion amongst men and horses, the road sank into profound silence. Except the exhaustion in the vast adjacent county of York from a contested election, no such silence succeeding to no such fiery uproar was ever witnessed in England.

On this occasion, the usual silence and solitude prevailed along the road. Not a hoof nor a wheel was to be heard. And to strengthen this false luxurious confidence in the noiseless roads, it happened also that the night was one of peculiar solemnity and peace. For my own part, though slightly alive to the possibilities of peril, I had so far yielded to the influence of the mighty calm as to sink into a profound reverie. The month was August, in the middle of which lay my own birth-day—a festival to every thoughtful man sug-

---

* Suppose a capital Y (the Pythagorean letter): Lancaster is at the foot of this letter; Liverpool at the top of the *right* branch; Manchester at the top of the *left*; proud Preston at the centre, where the two branches unite. It is thirty-three miles along either of the two branches; it is twenty-two miles along the stem—viz., from Preston in the middle, to Lancaster at the root. There's a lesson in geography for the reader.

⁹ The art of driving a chariot or coach.

† There were at that time only two assizes even in the most populous counties—viz., the Lent Assizes, and the Summer Assizes.

gesting solemn and often sigh-born* thoughts. The county was my own native county—upon which, in its southern section, more than upon any equal area known to man past or present, had descended the original curse of labour in its heaviest form, not mastering the bodies only of men as of slaves, or criminals in mines, but working through the fiery will. Upon no equal space of earth was, or ever had been, the same energy of human power put forth daily. At this particular season also of the assizes, that dreadful hurricane of flight and pursuit, as it might have seemed to a stranger, which swept to and from Lancaster all day long, hunting the county up and down, and regularly subsiding back into silence about sunset, could not fail (when united with this permanent distinction of Lancashire as the very metropolis and citadel of labour) to point the thoughts pathetically upon that counter vision of rest, of saintly repose from strife and sorrow, towards which, as to their secret haven, the profounder aspirations of man's heart are in solitude continually travelling. Obliquely upon our left we are nearing the sea, which also must, under the present circumstances, be repeating the general state of halycon repose. The sea, the atmosphere, the light, bore each an orchestral part in this universal lull. Moonlight, and the first timid tremblings of the dawn, were by this time blending; and the blendings were brought into a still more exquisite state of unity by a slight silvery mist, motionless and dreamy, that covered the woods and fields, but with a veil of equable transparency. Except the feet of our own horses, which, running on a sandy margin of the road, made but little disturbance, there was no sound abroad. In the clouds, and on the earth, prevailed the same majestic peace; and in spite of all that the villain of a schoolmaster has done for the ruin of our sublimer thoughts, which are the thoughts of our infancy, we still believe in no such nonsense as a limited atmosphere. Whatever we may swear with our false feigning lips, in our faithful hearts we still believe, and must for ever believe, in fields of air traversing the total gulf between earth and the central heavens. Still, in the confidence of children that tread without fear *every* chamber in their father's house, and to whom no door is closed, we, in that Sabbatic vision which sometimes is revealed for an hour upon nights like this, ascend with easy steps from the sorrow-stricken fields of earth, upwards to the sandals of God.

* I owe the suggestion of this word to an obscure remembrance of a beautiful phrase in "Giraldus Cambrensis"—viz., *suspiriosae cogitationes.* [10]

◇◇◇◇◇◇◇◇◇◇◇◇◇◇◇◇◇◇◇◇◇◇◇◇

[10] Giraldus de Barri (*c.* 1146–*c.* 1220) was an ecclesiastical figure and historian of Wales.

Suddenly, from thoughts like these, I was awakened to a sullen sound, as of some motion on the distant road. It stole upon the air for a moment; I listened in awe; but then it died away. Once roused, however, I could not but observe with alarm the quickened motion of our horses. Ten years' experience had made my eye learned in the valuing of motion; and I saw that we were now running thirteen miles an hour. I pretend to no presence of mind. On the contrary, my fear is, that I am miserably and shamefully deficient in that quality as regards action. The palsy of doubt and distraction hangs like some guilty weight of dark unfathomed remembrances upon my energies, when the signal is flying for *action*. But, on the other hand, this accursed gift I have, as regards *thought*, that in the first step towards the possibility of a misfortune, I see its total evolution; in the radix of the series I see too certainly and too instantly its entire expansion; in the first syllable of the dreadful sentence, I read already the last. It was not that I feared for ourselves. *Us*, our bulk and impetus charmed against peril in any collision. And I had ridden through too many hundreds of perils that were frightful to approach, that were matter of laughter to look back upon, the first face of which was horror—the parting face a jest, for any anxiety to rest upon *our* interests. The mail was not built, I felt assured, nor bespoke, that could betray *me* who trusted to its protection. But any carriage that we could meet would be frail and light in comparison of ourselves. And I remarked this ominous accident of our situation. We were on the wrong side of the road. But then, it may be said, the other party, if other there was, might also be on the wrong side; and two wrongs might make a right. *That* was not likely. The same motive which had drawn *us* to the right-hand side of the road—viz., the luxury of the soft beaten sand, as contrasted with the paved centre—would prove attractive to others. The two adverse carriages would therefore, to a certainty, be travelling on the same side; and from this side, as not being ours in law, the crossing over to the other would, of course, be looked for from *us*.† Our lamps, still lighted, would give the impression of vigilance on our part. And every creature that met us, would rely upon *us* for quartering.‡ All this, and if the separate links of the anticipation had been a thousand times more, I saw, not discursively, or by effort, or by

† It is true that, according to the law of the case as established by legal precedents, all carriages were required to give way before Royal equipages, and therefore before the mail as one of them. But this only increased the danger, as being a regulation very imperfectly made known, very unequally enforced, and therefore often embarrassing the movements on both sides.

‡ This is the technical word, and, I presume, derived from the French *cartayer*, to evade a rut or any obstacle.

succession, but by one flash of horrid simultaneous intuition.

Under this steady though rapid anticipation of the evil which *might* be gathering ahead, ah! what a sullen mystery of fear, what a sigh of wo, was that which stole upon the air, as again the far-off sound of a wheel was heard! A whisper it was—a whisper from, perhaps, four miles off—secretly announcing a ruin that, being foreseen, was not the less inevitable; that, being known, was not, therefore, healed. What could be done—who was it that could do it—to check the storm-flight of these maniacal horses? Could I not seize the reins from the grasp of the slumbering coachman? You, reader, think that it would have been in *your* power to do so. And I quarrel not with your estimate of yourself. But, from the way in which the coachman's hand was viced between his upper and lower thigh, this was impossible. Easy, was it? See, then, that bronze equestrian statue. The cruel rider has kept the bit in his horse's mouth for two centuries. Unbridle him, for a minute, if you please, and wash his mouth with water. Easy, was it? Unhorse me, then, that imperial rider; knock me those marble feet from those marble stirrups of Charlemagne.

The sounds ahead strengthened, and were now too clearly the sounds of wheels. Who and what could it be? Was it industry in a taxed cart? Was it youthful gaiety in a gig? Was it sorrow that loitered, or joy that raced? For as yet the snatches of sound were too intermitting, from distance, to decipher the character of the motion. Whoever were the travellers, something must be done to warn them. Upon the other party rests the active responsibility, but upon *us*—and, wo is me! that *us* was reduced to my frail opium-shattered self—rests the responsibility of warning. Yet, how should this be accomplished? Might I not sound the guard's horn? Already, on the first thought, I was making my way over the roof to the guard's seat. But this, from the accident which I have mentioned, of the foreign mails' being piled upon the roof, was a difficult and even dangerous attempt to one cramped by nearly three hundred miles of outside travelling. And, fortunately, before I had lost much time in the attempt, our frantic horses swept round an angle of the road, which opened upon us that final stage where the collision must be accomplished, and the catastrophe sealed. All was apparently finished. The court was sitting; the case was heard; the judge had finished; and only the verdict was yet in arrear.

Before us lay an avenue, straight as an arrow, six hundred years, perhaps, in length; and the umbrageous trees, which rose in a regular line from either side, meeting high overhead, gave to it the character of a cathedral aisle. These trees lent a deeper solemnity to the early light; but there was still light enough to perceive, at the further end of this Gothic aisle, a frail reedy gig, in which were seated a young man, and by his side a young lady. Ah, young sir! what are you about? If it is requisite that you should whisper your communications to this young lady—though really I see nobody, at an hour and on a road so solitary, likely to overhear you—is it therefore requisite that you should carry your lips forward to hers? The little carriage is creeping on at one mile an hour; and the parties within it being thus tenderly engaged, are naturally bending down their heads. Between them and eternity, to all human calculation, there is but a minute and a-half. Oh heavens! what is it that I shall do? Speaking or acting, what help can I offer? Strange it is, and to a mere auditor of the tale might seem laughable, that I should need a suggestion from the "Iliad" to prompt the sole resource that remained. Yet so it was. Suddenly I remembered the shout of Achilles,[11] and its effect. But could I pretend to shout like the son of Peleus, aided by Pallas? No: but then I needed not the shout that should alarm all Asia militant; such a shout would suffice as might carry terror into the hearts of two thoughtless young people, and one gig-horse. I shouted—and the young man heard me not. A second time I shouted—and now he heard me, for now he raised his head.

Here, then, all had been done that, by me, *could* be done: more on *my* part was not possible. Mine had been the first step; the second was for the young man; the third was for God. If, said I, this stranger is a brave man, and if, indeed, he loves the young girl at his side—or, loving her not, if he feels the obligation, pressing upon every man worthy to be called a man, of doing his utmost for a woman confided to his protection—he will, at least, make some effort to save her. If *that* fails, he will not perish the more, or by a death more cruel, for having made it; and he will die as a brave man should, with his face to the danger, and with his arm about the woman that he sought in vain to save. But, if he makes no effort, shrinking, without a struggle, from his duty, he himself will not the less certainly perish for this baseness of poltroonery. He will die no less: and why not? Wherefore should we grieve that there is one craven less in the world? No; *let* him perish, without a pitying thought of ours wasted upon him; and, in that case, all our grief will be reserved for the fate of the helpless girl who now, upon the least shadow of failure in *him*, must, by the fiercest of translations—must, without time for a prayer—must,

---

[11] See *Iliad*, XVIII, 217–29. The shout of Achilles, on re-entering the battle following the death of his friend Patroclus, struck terror in the hearts of the Trojans.

within seventy seconds, stand before the judgment-seat of God.

But craven he was not: sudden had been the call upon him, and sudden was his answer to the call. He saw, he heard, he comprehended, the ruin that was coming down: already its gloomy shadow darkened above him; and already he was measuring his strength to deal with it. Ah! what a vulgar thing does courage seem, when we see nations buying it and selling it for a shilling a-day: ah! what a sublime thing does courage seem, when some fearful summons on the great deeps of life carries a man, as if running before a hurricane, up to the giddy crest of some tumultuous crisis, from which lie two courses, and a voice says to him audibly, "One way lies hope; take the other, and mourn for ever!" How grand a triumph, if, even then, amidst the raving of all around him, and the frenzy of the danger, the man is able to confront his situation—is able to retire for a moment into solitude with God, and to seek his counsel from *Him!*

For seven seconds, it might be, of his seventy, the stranger settled his countenance stedfastly upon us, as if to search and value every element in the conflict before him. For five seconds more of his seventy he sat immovably, like one that mused on some great purpose. For five more, perhaps, he sat with eyes upraised, like one that prayed in sorrow, under some extremity of doubt, for light that should guide him to the better choice. Then suddenly he rose; stood upright; and by a powerful strain upon the reins, raising his horse's fore-feet from the ground, he slewed him round on the pivot of his hind-legs, so as to plant the little equipage in a position nearly at right angles to ours. Thus far his condition was not improved; except as a first step had been taken towards the possibility of a second. If no more were done, nothing was done; for the little carriage still occupied the very centre of our path, though in an altered direction. Yet even now it may not be too late: fifteen of the seventy seconds may still be unexhausted; and one almighty bound may avail to clear the ground. Hurry, then, hurry! for the flying moments—*they* hurry! Oh, hurry, hurry, my brave young man! for the cruel hoofs of our horses—*they* also hurry! Fast are the flying moments, faster are the hoofs of our horses. But fear not for *him*, if human energy can suffice; faithful was he that drove to his terrific duty; faithful was the horse to *his* command. One blow, one impulse given with voice and hand, by the stranger, one rush from the horse, one bound as if in the act of rising to a fence, landed the docile creature's fore-feet upon the crown or arching centre of the road. The larger half of the little equipage had then cleared our over-towering shadow: *that* was evident even to my own agitated sight. But it mattered little

that one wreck should float off in safety, if upon the wreck that perishered were embarked the human freightage. The rear part of the carriage—was *that* certainly beyond the line of absolute ruin? What power could answer the question? Glance of eye, thought of man, wing of angel, which of these had speed enough to sweep between the question and the answer, and divide the one from the other? Light does not tread upon the steps of light more indivisibly, than did our all-conquering arrival upon the escaping efforts of the gig. *That* must the young man have felt too plainly. His back was now turned to us; not by sight could he any longer communicate with the peril; but by the dreadful rattle of our harness, too truly had his ear been instructed—that all was finished as regarded any further effort of *his*. Already in resignation he had rested from his struggle; and perhaps in his heart he was whispering, "Father, which art in heaven, do Thou finish above what I on earth have attempted." Faster than ever mill-race we ran past them in our inexorable flight. Oh, raving of hurricanes that must have sounded in their young ears at the moment of our transit! Even in that moment the thunder of collision spoke aloud. Either with the swingle-bar,[12] or with the haunch of our near leader, we had struck the offwheel of the little gig, which stood rather obliquely, and not quite so far advanced, as to be accurately parallel with the near-wheel. The blow, from the fury of our passage, resounded terrifically. I rose in horror, to gaze upon the ruins we might have caused. From my elevated station I looked down, and looked back upon the scene, which in a moment told its own tale, and wrote all its records on my heart for ever.

Here was the map of the passion that now had finished. The horse was planted immovably, with his fore-feet upon the paved crest of the central road. He of the whole party might be supposed untouched by the passion of death. The little cany carriage—partly, perhaps, from the violent torsion of the wheels in its recent movement, partly from the thundering blow we had given to it—as if it sympathised with human horror, was all alive with tremblings and shiverings. The young man trembled not, nor shivered. He sat like a rock. But *his* was the steadiness of agitation frozen into rest by horror. As yet he dared not to look round; for he knew that, if anything remained to do, by him it could no longer be done. And as yet he knew not for certain if their safety were accomplished. But the lady—

But the lady——! Oh, heavens! will that spectacle

---

[12] The swinging cross-bar of a carriage, to the ends of which the traces of the harness were fastened.

ever depart from my dreams, as she rose and sank upon her seat, sank and rose, threw up her arms wildly to heaven, clutched at some visionary object in the air, fainting, praying, raving, despairing? Figure to yourself, reader, the elements of the case; suffer me to recall before your mind the circumstances of that unparalleled situation. From the silence and deep peace of this saintly summer night—from the pathetic blending of this sweet moonlight, dawnlight, dreamlight—from the manly tenderness of this flattering, whispering, murmuring love—suddenly as from the woods and fields—suddenly as from the chambers of the air opening in revelation—suddenly as from the ground yawning at her feet, leaped upon her, with the flashing of cataracts, Death the crowned phantom, with all the equipage of his terrors, and the tiger roar of his voice.

The moments were numbered; the strife was finished; the vision was closed. In the twinkling of an eye, our flying horses had carried us to the termination of the umbrageous aisle; at right angles we wheeled into our former direction; the turn of the road carried the scene out of my eyes in an instant, and swept it into my dreams for ever.

SECTION THE THIRD.
DREAM-FUGUE.
FOUNDED ON THE
PRECEDING THEME OF SUDDEN DEATH.

> "Whence the sound
> Of instruments, that made melodious chime,
> Was heard, of harp and organ; and who moved
> Their stops and chords, was seen; his volant touch
> Instinct through all proportions, low and high,
> Fled and pursued transverse the resonant fugue."
>
> *Par. Lost, B. XI.*[1]

Tumultuosissimamente.[2]

PASSION of sudden death! that once in youth I read and interpreted by the shadows of thy averted signs!*— rapture of panic taking the shape (which amongst tombs in churches I have seen) of woman bursting her

---

* I read the course and changes of the lady's agony in the succession of her involuntary gestures; but it must be remembered that I read all this from the rear, never once catching the lady's full face, and even her profile imperfectly.

---

[1] Ll. 558–63.
[2] *Tumultuosissimamente*: "in the most tumultuous manner;" the "musical" notation for the "performance" of the "Dream-fugue."

sepulchral bonds—of woman's Ionic form[3] bending forward from the ruins of her grave with arching foot, with eyes upraised, with clasped adoring hands— waiting, watching, trembling, praying for the trumpet's call to rise from dust for ever! Ah, vision too fearful of shuddering humanity on the brink of almighty abysses!—vision that didst start back, that didst reel away, like a shrivelling scroll from before the wrath of fire racing on the wings of the wind! Epilepsy so brief of horror, wherefore is it that thou canst not die? Passing so suddenly into darkness, wherefore is it that still thou sheddest thy sad funeral blights upon the gorgeous mosaics of dreams? Fragment of music too passionate, heard once, and heard no more, what aileth thee, that thy deep rolling chords come up at intervals through all the worlds of sleep, and after forty years, have lost no element of horror?

I.

Lo, it is summer—almighty summer! The everlasting gates of life and summer are thrown open wide; and on the ocean, tranquil and verdant as a savannah, the unknown lady from the dreadful vision and I myself are floating—she upon a fairy pinnace, and I upon an English three-decker. Both of us are wooing gales of festal happiness within the domain of our common country, within that ancient watery park, within that pathless chase of ocean, where England takes her pleasure as a huntress through winter and summer, from the rising to the setting sun. Ah, what a wilderness of floral beauty was hidden, or was suddenly revealed, upon the tropic islands through which the pinnace moved! And upon her deck what a bevy of human flowers—young women how lovely, young men how noble, that were dancing together, and slowly drifting towards *us* amidst music and incense, amidst blossoms from forests and gorgeous corymbi[4] from vintages, amidst natural carolling, and the echoes of sweet girlish laughter. Slowly the pinnace nears us, gaily she hails us, and silently she disappears beneath the shadow of our mighty bows. But then, as at some signal from heaven, the music, and the carols, and the sweet echoing of girlish laughter—all are hushed. What evil has smitten the pinnace, meeting or overtaking her? Did ruin to our friends couch within our own dreadful shadow? Was our shadow the shadow of death? I looked over the bow for an answer, and, behold! the pinnace was dismantled; the revel and the revellers were found no more; the glory of the vintage

---

[3] According to Vitruvius' *De Architectura*, IV, i, the Doric column was founded on the proportions of a man's body, the Ionic on the proportions of a woman's body.
[4] Clusters of grapes.

was dust; and the forests with their beauty were left without a witness upon the seas. "But where"—and I turned to our crew—"where are the lovely women that danced beneath the awning of flowers and clustering corymbi? Whither have fled the noble young men that danced with *them*?" Answer there was none. But suddenly the man at the mast-head, whose countenance darkened with alarm, cried out, "Sail on the weather beam! Down she comes upon us: in seventy seconds she also will founder."

II.

I looked to the weather side, and the summer had departed. The sea was rocking, and shaken with gathering wrath. Upon its surface sat mighty mists, which grouped themselves into arches and long cathedral aisles. Down one of these, with the fiery pace of a quarrel[5] from a crossbow, ran a frigate right athwart our course. "Are they mad?" some voice exclaimed from our deck. "Do they woo their ruin?" But in a moment, as she was close upon us, some impulse of a heady current or local vortex gave a wheeling bias to her course, and off she forged without a shock. As she ran past us, high aloft amongst the shrouds stood the lady of the pinnace. The deeps opened ahead in malice to receive her, towering surges of foam ran after her, the billows were fierce to catch her. But far away she was borne into desert spaces of the sea: whilst still by sight I followed her, as she ran before the howling gale, chased by angry sea-birds and by maddening billows; still I saw her, as at the moment when she ran past us, standing amongst the shrouds, with her white draperies streaming before the wind. There she stood, with hair dishevelled, one hand clutched amongst the tackling—rising, sinking, fluttering, trembling, praying—there for leagues I saw her as she stood, raising at intervals one hand to heaven, amidst the fiery crests of the pursuing waves and the raving of the storm; until at last, upon a sound from afar of malicious laughter and mockery, all was hidden for ever in driving showers; and afterwards, but when I know not, nor how,

III.

Sweet funeral bells from some incalculable distance, wailing over the dead that die before the dawn, awakened me as I slept in a boat moored to some familiar shore. The morning twilight even then was breaking; and, by the dusky revelations which it spread, I saw a girl, adorned with a garland of white roses about her head for some great festival, running

---

[5] "A short, heavy, square-headed arrow" (*Oxford English Dictionary*).

along the solitary strand in extremity of haste. Her running was the running of panic; and often she looked back as to some dreadful enemy in the rear. But when I leaped ashore, and followed on her steps to warn her of a peril in front, alas! from me she fled as from another peril, and vainly I shouted to her of quicksands that lay ahead. Faster and faster she ran; round a promontory of rocks she wheeled out of sight; in an instant I also wheeled round it, but only to see the treacherous sands gathering above her head. Already her person was buried; only the fair young head and the diadem of white roses around it were still visible to the pitying heavens; and, last of all, was visible one white marble arm. I saw by the early twilight this fair young head, as it was sinking down to darkness—saw this marble arm, as it rose above her head and her treacherous grave, tossing, faltering, rising, clutching, as at some false deceiving hand stretched out from the clouds—saw this marble arm uttering her dying hope, and then uttering her dying despair. The head, the diadem, the arm—these all had sunk; at last over these also the cruel quicksand had closed; and no memorial of the fair young girl remained on earth, except my own solitary tears, and the funeral bells from the desert seas, that, rising again more softly, sang a requiem over the grave of the buried child, and over her blighted dawn.

I sat, and wept in secret the tears that men have ever given to the memory of those that died before the dawn, and by the treachery of earth, our mother. But suddenly the tears and funeral bells were hushed by a shout as of many nations, and by a roar as from some great king's artillery, advancing rapidly along the valleys, and heard afar by echoes from the mountains. "Hush!" I said, as I bent my ear earthwards to listen—"hush!—this either is the very anarchy of strife, or else"—and then I listened more profoundly, and whispered as I raised my head—"or else, oh heavens! it is *victory* that is final, victory that swallows up all strife."

IV.

Immediately, in trance, I was carried over land and sea to some distant kingdom, and placed upon a triumphal car, amongst companions crowned with laurel. The darkness of gathering midnight, brooding over all the land, hid from us the mighty crowds that were weaving restlessly about ourselves as a centre: we heard them, but saw them not. Tidings had arrived, within an hour, of a grandeur that measured itself against centuries; too full of pathos they were, too full of joy, to utter themselves by other language than by tears, by restless anthems, and *Te Deums* reverberated from the choirs and orchestras of earth. These tidings we that sat upon the laurelled car had it for our privilege to publish amongst all nations. And already, by signs audible through the darkness, by snortings and tramplings, our angry horses, that knew no fear of fleshly weariness, upbraided us with delay. Wherefore *was* it that we delayed? We waited for a secret word, that should bear witness to the hope of nations, as now accomplished for ever. At midnight the secret word arrived; which word was—Waterloo and Recovered Christendom! The dreadful word shone by its own light; before us it went; high above our leaders' heads it rode, and spread a golden light over the paths which we traversed. Every city, at the presence of the secret word, threw open its gates. The rivers were conscious as we crossed. All the forests, as we ran along their margins, shivered in homage to the secret word. And the darkness comprehended it.

Two hours after midnight we approached a mighty Minster. Its gates, which rose to the clouds, were closed. But when the dreadful word, that rode before us, reached them with its golden light, silently they moved back upon their hinges; and at a flying gallop our equipage entered the grand aisle of the cathedral. Headlong was our pace; and at every altar, in the little chapels and oratories to the right hand and left of our course, the lamps, dying or sickening, kindled anew in sympathy with the secret word that was flying past. Forty leagues we might have run in the cathedral, and as yet no strength of morning light had reached us, when before us we saw the aerial galleries of organ and choir. Every pinnacle of the fretwork, every station of advantage amongst the traceries, was crested by white-robed choristers, that sang deliverance; that wept no more tears, as once their fathers had wept; but at intervals that sang together to the generations, saying,

"Chant the deliverer's praise in every tongue,"

and receiving answers from afar,

"Such as once in heaven and earth were sung."

And of their chanting was no end; of our headlong pace was neither pause nor slackening.

Thus, as we ran like torrents—thus, as we swept with bridal rapture over the Campo Santo * of the cathedral

---

* It is probable that most of my readers will be acquainted with the history of the Campo Santo (or cemetery) at Pisa, composed of earth brought from Jerusalem from a bed of sanctity, as the highest prize which the noble piety of crusaders could ask or imagine. To readers who are unacquainted with England, or who (being English) are yet unacquainted with the cathedral cities of England, it may be right to mention that the graves within-side the cathedrals often form a flat pavement over which carriages and horses *might* run; and perhaps a boyish remembrance of one particular cathedral, across which I had

graves—suddenly we became aware of a vast necropolis rising upon the far-off horizon—a city of sepulchres, built within the saintly cathedral for the warrior dead that rested from their feuds on earth. Of purple granite was the necropolis; yet, in the first minute, it lay like a purple stain upon the horizon, so mighty was the distance. In the second minute it trembled through many changes, growing into terraces and towers of wondrous altitude, so mighty was the pace. In the third minute already, with our dreadful gallop, we were entering its suburbs. Vast sarcophagi rose on every side, having towers and turrets that, upon the limits of the central aisle, strode forward with haughty intrusion, that ran back with mighty shadows into answering recesses. Every sarcophagus showed many bas-reliefs—bas-reliefs of battles and of battle-fields; battles from forgotten ages—battles from yesterday—battle-fields that, long since, nature had healed and reconciled to herself with the sweet oblivion of flowers—battle-fields that were yet angry and crimson with carnage. Where the terraces ran, there did *we* run; where the towers curved, there did *we* curve. With the flight of swallows our horses swept round every angle. Like rivers in flood, wheeling round headlands—like hurricanes that ride into the secrets of forests—faster than ever light unwove the mazes of darkness, our flying equipage carried earthly passions, kindled warrior instincts, amongst the dust that lay around us—dust oftentimes of our noble fathers that had slept in God from Créci [6] to Trafalgar. And now had we reached the last sarcophagus, now were we abreast of the last bas-relief, already had we recovered the arrow-like flight of the illimitable central aisle, when coming up this aisle to meet us we beheld afar off a female child, that rode in a carriage as frail as flowers. The mists, which went before her, hid the fawns that drew her, but could not hide the shells and tropic flowers with which she played—but could not hide the lovely smiles by which she uttered her trust in the mighty cathedral, and in the cherubim that looked down upon her from the mighty shafts of its pillars. Face to face she was meeting us; face to face she rode, as if danger there were none. "Oh, baby!" I exclaimed, "shalt thou be the ransom for Waterloo? Must we, that carry tidings of great joy to every people, be messengers of ruin to thee!" In horror I

---

seen passengers walk and burdens carried, as about two centuries back they were through the middle of St Paul's in London, may have assisted my dream.

6 Town in northern France, scene of one of England's most famous military victories, August 26, 1346, when the armies under Edward III defeated the forces of King Philip of France. Usually spelled Crécy.

rose at the thought; but then also, in horror at the thought, rose one that was sculptured on a bas-relief—a Dying Trumpeter. Solemnly from the field of battle he rose to his feet; and, unslinging his stony trumpet, carried it, in his dying anguish, to his stony lips—sounding once, and yet once again; proclamation that, in *thy* ears, oh baby! spoke from the battlements of death. Immediately deep shadows fell between us, and aboriginal silence. The choir had ceased to sing. The hoofs of our horses, the dreadful rattle of our harness, the groaning of our wheels, alarmed the graves no more. By horror the bas-relief had been unlocked unto life. By horror we, that were so full of life, we men and our horses, with their fiery fore-legs rising in mid air to their everlasting gallop, were frozen to a bas-relief. Then a third time the trumpet sounded; the seals were taken off all pulses; life, and the frenzy of life, tore into their channels again; again the choir burst forth in sunny grandeur, as from the muffling of storms and darkness; again the thunderings of our horses carried temptation into the graves. One cry burst from our lips, as the clouds, drawing off from the aisle, showed it empty before us—"Whither has the infant fled?—is the young child caught up to God?" Lo! afar off, in a vast recess, rose three mighty windows to the clouds; and on a level with their summits, at height insuperable to man, rose an altar of purest alabaster. On its eastern face was trembling a crimson glory. A glory was it from the reddening dawn that now streamed *through* the windows? Was it from the crimson robes of the martyrs painted *on* the windows? Was it from the bloody bas-reliefs of earth? There, suddenly, within that crimson radiance, rose the apparition of a woman's head, and then of a woman's figure. The child it was—grown up to woman's height. Clinging to the horns of the altar, voiceless she stood—sinking, rising, raving, despairing; and behind the volume of incense, that, night and day, streamed upwards from the altar, dimly was seen the fiery font, and the shadow of that dreadful being who should have baptized her with the baptism of death. But by her side was kneeling her better angel, that hid his face with wings; that wept and pleaded for *her;* that prayed when *she* could *not;* that fought with Heaven by tears for *her* deliverance; which also, as he raised his immortal countenance from his wings, I saw, by the glory in his eye, that from Heaven he had won at last.

v.

Then was completed the passion of the mighty fugue. The golden tubes of the organs, which as yet had but muttered at intervals—gleaming amongst clouds and surges of incense—threw up, as from fountains unfathomable, columns of heart-shattering

music. Choir and anti-choir were filling fast with unknown voices. Thou also, Dying Trumpeter!—with thy love that was victorious, and thy anguish that was finishing—didst enter the tumult; trumpet and echo—farewell love, and farewell anguish—rang through the dreadful *sanctus*. Oh, darkness of the grave! that from the crimson altar and from the fiery font wert visited and searched by the effulgence in the angel's eye—were these indeed thy children? Pomps of life, that, from the burials of centuries, rose again to the voice of perfect joy, did ye indeed mingle with the festivals of Death? Lo! as I looked back for seventy leagues through the mighty cathedral, I saw the quick and the dead that sang together to God, together that sang to the generations of man. All the hosts of jubilation, like armies that ride in pursuit, moved with one step. Us, that, with laurelled heads, were passing from the cathedral, they overtook, and, as with a garment, they wrapped us round with thunders greater than our own. As brothers we moved together; to the dawn that advanced—to the stars that fled; rendering thanks to God in the highest—that, having hid His face through one generation behind thick clouds of War, once again was ascending—from the Campo Santo of Waterloo was ascending—in the visions of Peace; rendering thanks for thee, young girl! whom, having overshadowed with His ineffable passion of death, suddenly did God relent; suffered thy angel to turn aside His arm; and even in thee, sister unknown! shown to me for a moment only to be hidden for ever, found an occasion to glorify His goodness. A thousand times, amongst the phantoms of sleep, have I seen thee entering the gates of the golden dawn—with the secret word riding before thee—with the armies of the grave behind thee; seen thee sinking, rising, raving, despairing; a thousand times in the worlds of sleep have seen thee followed by God's angel through storms; through desert seas; through the darkness of quicksands; through dreams, and the dreadful revelations that are in dreams—only that at the last, with one sling of His victorious arm, He might snatch thee back from ruin, and might emblazon in thy deliverance the endless resurrections of His love!

[December 1849]   [1854]

ALEXANDER POPE

This famous piece of literary criticism had first appeared as part of a long review of William Roscoe's edition of The Works of Alexander Pope, *in the* North British Review, *August, 1848. The review was revised as the essay "Alexander Pope" in Volume IX* [Leaders in Literature] *in* Selections Grave and Gay, *published in 1858. The latter text is here followed. For* discussion, see John W. Bilsland, "On De Quincey's Theory of Literary Power," University of Toronto Quarterly, XXVI, No. 4 (July, 1957), 469–80.

FROM

ALEXANDER POPE

["THE LITERATURE OF KNOWLEDGE AND THE LITERATURE OF POWER"]

*   *   *   *   *

WHAT is it that we mean by *literature*? Popularly, and amongst the thoughtless, it is held to include everything that is printed in a book. Little logic is required to disturb *that* definition; the most thoughtless person is easily made aware, that in the idea of *literature*, one essential element is,—some relation to a general and common interest of man, so that, what applies only to a local, or professional, or merely personal interest, even though presenting itself in the shape of a book, will not belong to literature. So far the definition is easily narrowed; and it is as easily expanded. For not only is much that takes a station in books not literature; but inversely, much that really *is* literature never reaches a station in books. The weekly sermons of Christendom, that vast pulpit literature which acts so extensively upon the popular mind—to warn, to uphold, to renew, to comfort, to alarm, does not attain the sanctuary of libraries in the ten-thousandth part of its extent. The drama again, as for instance, the finest of Shakspeare's plays in England, and all leading Athenian plays in the noontide of the Attic stage, operated as a literature on the public mind, and were (according to the strictest letter of that term) *published* through the audiences that witnessed * their representation some time before they were published as things to be read; and they were published in this scenical mode of publication with much more effect than they could have had as books, during ages of costly copying, or of costly printing.

Books, therefore, do not suggest an idea co-extensive and interchangeable with the idea of literature; since much literature, scenic, forensic, or didactic (as from lecturers and public orators), may never come into books; and much that *does* come into books, may connect itself with no literary interest.† But a far more important correction, applicable to the common vague idea of literature, is to be sought—not so much in a better definition of literature, as in a sharper distinction of the two functions which it fulfils. In that great social organ, which, collectively, we call literature, there may be distinguished two separate offices that may blend and often *do* so, but capable, severally, of a severe insulation, and naturally fitted for reciprocal repulsion. There is, first, the literature of *knowledge*; and, secondly, the literature of *power*. The function of the first is—to *teach*; the function of the second is—to *move*: the first is a rudder; the second, an oar or a sail. The first speaks to the *mere* discursive understanding; the second speaks ultimately, it may happen, to the higher understanding or reason, but always *through* affections of pleasure and sympathy. Remotely, it may travel towards an object seated in what Lord Bacon calls *dry* light;[1] but, proximately, it does and must operate, else it ceases to be a literature of *power*, on and through that *humid* light which clothes itself in the mists and glittering *iris*[2] of human passions, desires, and genial emotions. Men have so little reflected on the higher functions of literature, as to find it a paradox if one should describe it as a mean or subordinate purpose of books to give information. But this is a paradox only in the sense which makes it honourable to be paradoxical. Whenever we talk in ordinary language of seeking information or gaining knowledge, we understand the words as connected with something of absolute novelty. But it is the grandeur of all truth, which *can* occupy a very high place in human interests, that it is never absolutely novel to the meanest of minds: it exists eternally by way of germ or latent principle in the lowest as in the highest, needing to be developed, but never to be planted. To be capable of transplantation is the immediate criterion of a truth that ranges on a lower scale. Besides which, there is a rarer thing than truth; namely, *power*, or deep sympathy with truth. What is the effect, for instance, upon society, of children? By the pity, by the tenderness, and by the peculiar modes of admiration, which connect themselves with the helplessness, with the innocence, and with the simplicity of children, not only are the primal affec-

---

* Charles I., for example, when Prince of Wales, and many others in his father's court, gained their known familiarity with Shakspeare—not through the original quartos, so slenderly diffused, nor through the first folio of 1623, but through the court representations of his chief dramas at Whitehall.

† What are called *The Blue Books*, by which title are understood the folio Reports issued every session of Parliament by committees of the two Houses, and stitched into blue covers,— though often sneered at by the ignorant as so much waste paper, will be acknowledged gratefully by those who have used them diligently, as the main wellheads of all accurate information as to the Great Britain of this day. As an immense depository of faithful (*and not superannuated*) statistics, they are indispensable to the honest student. But no man would therefore class the *Blue Books* as literature.

◇◇◇◇◇◇◇◇◇◇◇◇◇◇◇◇◇◇◇◇◇◇◇◇◇◇◇◇

[1] See his essay "Of Friendship," which cites Heraclitus.
[2] "A rainbow-like or iridescent appearance" (*Oxford English Dictionary*).

tions strengthened and continually renewed, but the qualities which are dearest in the sight of heaven—the frailty, for instance, which appeals to forbearance; the innocence which symbolizes the heavenly, and the simplicity which is most alien from the worldly, are kept up in perpetual remembrance, and their ideals are continually refreshed. A purpose of the same nature is answered by the higher literature, viz., the literature of power. What do you learn from "Paradise Lost"? Nothing at all. What do you learn from a cookery-book? Something new—something that you did not know before, in every paragraph. But would you therefore put the wretched cookery-book on a higher level of estimation than the divine poem? What you owe to Milton is not any knowledge, of which a million separate items are still but a million of advancing steps on the same earthly level; what you owe, is *power*, that is, exercise and expansion to your own latent capacity of sympathy with the infinite, where every pulse and each separate influx is a step upwards— a step ascending as upon a Jacob's ladder from earth to mysterious altitudes above the earth. *All* the steps of knowledge, from first to last, carry you further on the same plane, but could never raise you one foot above your ancient level of earth: whereas, the very *first* step in power is a flight—is an ascending movement into another element where earth is forgotten.

Were it not that human sensibilities are ventilated and continually called out into exercise by the great phenomena of infancy, or of real life as it moves through chance and change, or of literature as it recombines these elements in the mimicries of poetry, romance, &c., it is certain that, like any animal power or muscular energy falling into disuse, all such sensibilities would gradually drop and dwindle. It is in relation to these great *moral* capacities of man that the literature of power, as contradistinguished from that of knowledge, lives and has its field of action. It is concerned with what is highest in man; for the Scriptures themselves never condescended to deal by suggestion or co-operation, with the mere discursive understanding: when speaking of man in his intellectual capacity, the Scriptures speak not of the understanding, but of "*the understanding heart*," [3]—making the heart, *i.e.*, the great *intuitive* (or non-discursive) organ, to be the interchangeable formula for man in his highest state of capacity for the infinite. Tragedy, romance, fairy tale, or epopee,[4] all alike restore to man's mind the ideals of justice, of hope, of truth, of mercy, of retribution, which else (left to the support of daily life in its

realities) would languish for want of sufficient illustration. What is meant, for instance, by *poetic justice?*—It does not mean a justice that differs by its object from the ordinary justice of human jurisprudence; for then it must be confessedly a very bad kind of justice; but it means a justice that differs from common forensic justice by the degree in which it *attains* its object, a justice that is more omnipotent over its own ends, as dealing—not with the refractory elements of earthly life—but with the elements of its own creation, and with materials flexible to its own purest preconceptions. It is certain that, were it not for the literature of power, these ideals would often remain amongst us as mere arid notional forms; whereas, by the creative forces of man put forth in literature, they gain a vernal life of restoration, and germinate into vital activities. The commonest novel, by moving in alliance with human fears and hopes, with human instincts of wrong and right, sustains and quickens those affections. Calling them into action, it rescues them from torpor. And hence the pre-eminency over all authors that merely *teach*, of the meanest that *moves;* or that teaches, if at all, indirectly *by* moving. The very highest work that has ever existed in the literature of knowledge, is but a *provisional* work: a book upon trial and sufferance, and *quamdiu bene se gesserit.*[5] Let its teaching be even partially revised, let it be but expanded, nay, even let its teaching be but placed in a better order, and instantly it is superseded. Whereas the feeblest works in the literature of power, surviving at all, survive as finished and unalterable amongst men. For instance, the *Principia* of Sir Isaac Newton was a book *militant* on earth from the first. In all stages of its progress it would have to fight for its existence: 1st, as regards absolute truth; 2dly, when that combat was over, as regards its form or mode of presenting the truth. And as soon as a La Place,[6] or anybody else, builds higher upon the foundations laid by this book, effectually he throws it out of the sunshine into decay and darkness; by weapons won from this book he superannuates and destroys this book, so that soon the name of Newton remains, as a mere *nominis umbra*,[7] but his book, as a living power, has transmigrated into other forms. Now, on the contrary, the Iliad, the Prometheus of Æschylus,—the Othello or King Lear, —the Hamlet or Macbeth,—and the Paradise Lost, are not militant but triumphant for ever as long as the languages exist in which they speak or can be taught to

---

3 See I Kings, iii, 9–12.
4 Epic poem.

5 *quamdiu bene se gesserit:* "as long as it shall conduct itself properly."
6 Pierre Simon Laplace (1749–1827), scientist and astronomer, called "the Newton of France," was the author of *Traité de Mécanique céleste* (1799–1825).
7 *nominis umbra:* "shadow of a name."

speak. They never *can* transmigrate into new incarnations. To reproduce *these* in new forms, or variations, even if in some things they should be improved, would be to plagiarize. A good steam-engine is properly superseded by a better. But one lovely pastoral valley is not superseded by another, nor a statue of Praxiteles by a statue of Michael Angelo. These things are separated not by imparity, but by disparity. They are not thought of as unequal under the same standard, but as different in *kind*, and if otherwise equal, as equal under a different standard. Human works of immortal beauty and works of nature in one respect stand on the same footing; they never absolutely repeat each other; never approach so near as not to differ; and they differ not as better and worse, or simply by more and less: they differ by undecipherable and incommunicable differences, that cannot be caught by mimicries, that cannot be reflected in the mirror of copies, that cannot become ponderable in the scales of vulgar comparison.

Applying these principles to Pope, as a representative of fine literature in general, we would wish to remark the claim which he has, or which any equal writer has, to the attention and jealous winnowing of those critics, in particular, who watch over public morals. Clergymen, and all the organs of public criticism put in motion by clergymen, are more especially concerned in the just appreciation of such writers, if the two canons are remembered, which we have endeavoured to illustrate, viz., that all works in this class, as opposed to those in the literature of knowledge, 1st, work by far deeper agencies; and, 2dly, are more permanent; in the strictest sense they are κτήματα ἐς ἀεί:[8] and what evil they do, or what good they do, is commensurate with the national language, sometimes long after the nation has departed. At this hour, five hundred years since their creation, the tales of Chaucer,* never equalled on this earth for their tenderness, and for life of picturesqueness, are read familiarly by many in the charming language of their natal day, and by others in the modernizations of Dryden, of Pope, and Wordsworth. At this hour, one thousand eight hundred years since their creation, the Pagan tales of Ovid, never equalled on this earth for the gaiety of their movement and the capricious graces of their narrative, are read by all Christendom. This man's people and their monuments are dust; but

he is alive: he has survived them, as he told us that he had it in his commission to do, by a thousand years; "and *shall* a thousand more."

All the literature of knowledge builds only ground-nests, that are swept away by floods, or confounded by the plough; but the literature of power builds nests in aërial altitudes of temples sacred from violation, or of forests inaccessible to fraud. *This* is a great prerogative of the *power* literature; and it is a greater which lies in the mode of its influence. The *knowledge* literature, like the fashion of this world, passeth away. An Encyclopædia is its abstract; and, in this respect, it may be taken for its speaking symbol—that, before one generation has passed, an Encyclopædia is superannuated; for it speaks through the dead memory and unimpassioned understanding, which have not the repose of higher faculties, but are continually enlarging and varying their phylacteries. But all literature, properly so called—literature κατ᾽ ἐξοχην,[9] for the very same reason that it is so much more durable than the literature of knowledge, is (and by the very same proportion it is) more intense and electrically searching in its impressions. The directions in which the tragedy of this planet has trained our human feelings to play, and the combinations into which the poetry of this planet has thrown our human passions of love and hatred, of admiration and contempt, exercise a power bad or good over human life, that cannot be contemplated, when stretching through many generations, without a sentiment allied to awe.† And of this let every one be assured—that he owes to the impassioned books which he has read, many a thousand more of emotions than he can consciously trace back to them. Dim by their origination, these emotions yet arise in him, and mould him through life like forgotten incidents of his childhood.

[August 1848]   [1858]

---

* The Canterbury Tales were not made public until 1380 or thereabouts; but the composition must have cost thirty or more years; not to mention that the work had probably been finished for some years before it was divulged.

---

8 κτήματα ἐς ἀεί: "lasting possessions."

† The reason why the broad distinctions between the two literatures of power and knowledge so little fix the attention, lies in the fact, that a vast proportion of books—history, biography, travels, miscellaneous essays, &c., lying in a middle zone, confound these distinctions by interblending them. All that we call "amusement" or "entertainment," is a diluted form of the power belonging to passion, and also a mixed form; and where threads of direct *instruction* intermingle in the texture with these threads of *power*, this absorption of the duality into one representative *nuance* neutralizes the separate perception of either. Fused into a *tertium quid*, or neutral state, they disappear to the popular eye as the repelling forces, which, in fact, they are.

---

9 κατ᾽ ἐξοχην: "eminent literature."

CHARLES LAMB

The essay first appeared in the North British Review, *November 1848, as a review of* Final Memorials of Charles Lamb, *a collection of Lamb's letters "with sketches of some of his Companions" prepared by Thomas Noon Talfourd (1795– 1854), long-time friend of Lamb's, a jurist and man of letters. Like many of De Quincey's essays, "Charles Lamb" is somewhat miscellaneous in its subject matter and procedure; it is a combination of biographical narrative, personal reminiscence, and literary theory and criticism, even including a provocative analysis of William Hazlitt. Framing and shaping the entire essay, however, is De Quincey's profound sympathy with the pariah-like figures of Charles and Mary Lamb. The essay is here published, omitting the biographical sections, from the text that appeared in* Leaders in Literature *(1858).*

F R O M

CHARLES LAMB

IT SOUNDS paradoxical, but is not so in a bad sense, to say, that in every literature of large compass some authors will be found to rest much of the interest which surrounds them on their essential *non*-popularity. They are good for the very reason that they are not in conformity to the current taste. They interest because to the world they are *not* interesting. They attract by means of their repulsion. Not as though it could separately furnish a reason for loving a book, that the majority of men had found it repulsive. *Prima facie*, it must suggest some presumption *against* a book, that it has failed to gain public attention. To have roused hostility indeed, to have kindled a feud against its own principles or its temper, may happen to be a good sign. *That* argues power. Hatred may be promising. The deepest revolutions of mind sometimes begin in hatred. But simply to have left a reader unimpressed, is in itself a neutral result, from which the inference is doubtful. Yet even *that*, even simple failure to impress, may happen at times to be a result from positive powers in a writer, from special originalities, such as rarely reflect themselves in the mirror of the ordinary understanding. It seems little to be perceived, how much the great scriptural* idea of the *worldly* and the *unworldly* is found to emerge in literature as well as in life. In reality, the very same combinations of moral qualities, infinitely varied, which compose the harsh physiognomy of what we call worldliness in the living groups of life, must unavoidably present themselves in books. A library

---

* "*Scriptural*" we call it, because this element of thought, so indispensable to a profound philosophy of morals, is not simply *more* used in Scripture than elsewhere, but is so exclusively significant or intelligible amidst the correlative ideas of Scripture, as to be absolutely insusceptible of translation into classical Greek or classical Latin.

divides into sections of worldly and unworldly, even as a crowd of men divides into that same majority and minority. The world has an instinct for recognising its own; and recoils from certain qualities when exemplified in books, with the same disgust or defective sympathy as would have governed it in real life. From qualities, for instance, of childlike simplicity, of shy profundity, or of inspired self-communion, the world does and must turn away its face towards grosser, bolder, more determined, or more intelligible expressions of character and intellect; and not otherwise in literature, nor at all less in literature, than it does in the realities of life.

Charles Lamb, if any ever *was*, is amongst the class here contemplated; he, if any ever *has*, ranks amongst writers whose works are destined to be for ever unpopular, and yet for ever interesting; interesting, moreover, by means of those very qualities which guarantee their non-popularity. The same qualities which will be found forbidding to the world and the thoughtless, which will be found insipid to many even amongst robust and powerful minds, are exactly those which will continue to command a select audience in every generation. The prose essays, under the signature of *Elia*, form the most delightful section amongst Lamb's works. They traverse a peculiar field of observation, sequestered from general interest; and they are composed in a spirit too delicate and unobtrusive to catch the ear of the noisy crowd, clamouring for strong sensations. But this retiring delicacy itself, the pensiveness chequered by gleams of the fanciful, and the humour that is touched with cross lights of pathos, together with the picturesque quaintness of the objects casually described, whether men, or things, or usages, and, in the rear of all this, the constant recurrence to ancient recollections and to decaying forms of household life, as things retiring before the tumult of new and revolutionary generations; these traits in combination communicate to the papers a grace and strength of originality which nothing in any literature approaches, whether for degree or kind of excellence, except the most felicitious papers of Addison, such as those on Sir Roger de Coverley, and some others in the same vein of composition. They resemble Addison's papers also in the diction, which is natural and idiomatic, even to carelessness. They are equally faithful to the truth of nature; and in this only they differ remarkably—that the sketches of Elia reflect the stamp and impress of the writer's own character, whereas in all those of Addison the personal peculiarities of the delineator (though known to the reader from the beginning through the account of the club) are nearly quiescent. Now and then they are recalled into a momentary notice, but they do not act, or at all modify his pictures of Sir Roger or Will Wimble. *They* are slightly and amiably eccentric; but the Spectator himself, in describing them, takes the station of an ordinary observer.

Everywhere, indeed, in the writings of Lamb, and not merely in his *Elia*, the character of the writer co-operates in an under current to the effect of the thing written. To understand, in the fullest sense, either the gaiety or the tenderness of a particular passage, you must have some insight into the particular bias of the writer's mind, whether native and original, or impressed gradually by the accidents of situation; whether simply developed out of predispositions by the action of life, or violently scorched into the constitution by some fierce fever of calamity. There is in modern literature a whole class of writers, though not a large one, standing within the same category; some marked originality of character in the writer becomes a co-efficient with what he says to a common result; you must sympathize with this *personality* in the author before you can appreciate the most significant parts of his views. In most books the writer figures as a mere abstraction, without sex or age or local station, whom the reader banishes from his thoughts. What is written seems to proceed from a blank intellect, not from a man clothed with fleshly peculiarities and differences. These peculiarities and differences neither do, nor (generally speaking) *could* intermingle with the texture of the thoughts, so as to modify their force or their direction. In such books, and they form the vast majority, there is nothing to be found or to be looked for beyond the direct objective. (*Sit venia verbo!*)[1] But, in a small section of books, the objective in the thought becomes confluent with the subjective in the thinker—the two forces unite for a joint product; and fully to enjoy the product, or fully to apprehend either element, both must be known. It is singular, and worth inquiring into, for the reason that the Greek and Roman literature had no such books. Timon of Athens, or Diogenes, one may conceive qualified for this mode of authorship, had journalism existed to rouse them in those days; their "articles" would no doubt have been fearfully caustic. But, as *they* failed to produce anything, and Lucian in an after age is scarcely characteristic enough for the purpose, perhaps we may pronounce Rabelais and Montaigne the earliest of writers in the class described. In the century following *theirs*, came Sir Thomas Browne, and immediately after *him* La Fontaine. Then came Swift, Sterne, with others less distinguished; in Germany, Hippel, the friend of Kant, Harmann, the obscure;

and the greatest of the whole body—John Paul Fr. Richter.[2] In *him*, from the strength and determinateness of his nature, as well as from the great extent of his writing, the philosophy of this interaction between the author as a human agency and his theme as an intellectual re-agency, might best be studied. From *him* might be derived the largest number of cases, illustrating boldly this absorption of the universal into the concrete—of the pure intellect into the human nature of the author. But nowhere could illustrations be found more interesting—shy, delicate, evanescent—shy as lightning, delicate and evanescent as the coloured pencillings on a frosty night from the northern lights, than in the better parts of Lamb.

To appreciate Lamb, therefore, it is requisite that his character and temperament should be understood in their coyest and most wayward features. A capital defect it would be if these could not be gathered silently from Lamb's works themselves. It would be a fatal mode of dependency upon an alien and separable accident if they needed an external commentary. But they do *not*. The syllables lurk up and down the writings of Lamb which decipher his eccentric nature. His character lies there dispersed in anagram; and to any attentive reader the regathering and restoration of the total word from its scattered parts is inevitable without an effort. Still it is always a satisfaction in knowing a result, to know also its *why* and *how*; and in so far as every character is likely to be modified by the particular experience, sad or joyous, through which the life has travelled, it is a good contribution towards the knowledge of that resulting character as a whole to have a sketch of that particular experience. What trials did it impose? What energies did it task? What temptations did it unfold? These calls upon the moral powers, which in music so stormy, many a life is doomed to hear, how were they faced? The character in a capital degree moulds oftentimes the life, but the life *always* in a subordinate degree moulds the character. And the character being in this case of Lamb so much of a key to the writings, it becomes important that the life should be traced, however briefly, as a key to the character.

That is *one* reason for detaining the reader with some slight record of Lamb's career. Such a record by preference and of right belongs to a case where the intellectual display, which is the sole ground of any public interest at all in the man, has been intensely modified

---

[1] *Sit venia verbo!*: Pardon me for saying so.

[2] Theodor Gottlieb von Hippel (1741–1796), German satirist and humorist; like Richter, his works strongly resemble Sterne's. Jean Paul Richter (1763–1825) was a leading German writer and a favorite of De Quincey, who had published translations of his works in the *London Magazine* between 1821 and 1824.

by the *humanities* and moral *personalities* distinguishing the subject. We read a Physiology, and need no information as to the life and conversation of its author; a meditative poem becomes far better understood by the light of such information; but a work of genial and at the same time eccentric sentiment, wandering upon untrodden paths, is barely intelligible without it. There is a good reason for arresting judgment on the writer, that the court may receive evidence on the life of the man. But there is another reason, and, in any other place, a better; which reason lies in the extraordinary value of the life considered separately for itself. Logically, it is not allowable to say that *here;* and, considering the principal purpose of this paper, any possible *independent* value of the life must rank as a better reason for reporting it. Since, in a case where the original object is professedly to estimate the writings of a man, whatever promises to further that object must, merely by that tendency, have, in relation to that place, a momentary advantage which it would lose if valued upon a more abstract scale. Liberated from this casual office of throwing light upon a book— raised to its grander station of a solemn deposition to the moral capacities of man in conflict with calamity— viewed as a return made into the chanceries of heaven— upon an issue directed from that court to try the amount of power lodged in a poor desolate pair of human creatures for facing the very anarchy of storms—this obscure life of the two Lambs, brother and sister (for the two lives were one life), rises into a grandeur that is not paralleled once in a generation.

Rich, indeed, in moral instruction was the life of Charles Lamb; and perhaps in one chief result it offers to the thoughtful observer a lesson of consolation that is awful, and of hope that ought to be immortal, viz., in the record which it furnishes, that by meekness of submission, and by earnest conflict with evil, in the spirit of cheerfulness, it is possible ultimately to disarm or to blunt the very heaviest of curses—even the curse of lunacy. Had it been whispered, in hours of infancy, to Lamb, by the angel who stood by his cradle—"Thou, and the sister that walks by ten years before thee, shall be through life, each to each, the solitary fountain of comfort; and except it be from this fountain of mutual love, except it be as brother and sister, ye shall not taste the cup of peace on earth!"— here, if there was sorrow in reversion, there was also consolation.

But what funeral swamps would have instantly ingulfed this consolation, had some meddling fiend prolonged the revelation, and, holding up the curtain from the sad future a little longer, had said scornfully— "Peace on earth! Peace for you two, Charles and Mary Lamb! What peace is possible under the curse which even now is gathering against your heads? Is there peace on earth for the lunatic—peace for the parenticide—peace for the girl that, without warning, and without time granted for a penitential cry to Heaven, sends her mother to the last audit?" And then, without treachery, speaking bare truth, this prophet of wo might have added—"Thou also, thyself, Charles Lamb, thou in thy proper person, shalt enter the skirts of this dreadful hail-storm; even thou shalt taste the secrets of lunacy, and enter as a captive its house of bondage;* whilst over thy sister the accursed scorpion shall hang suspended through life, like Death hanging over the beds of hospitals, striking at times, but more often threatening to strike; or withdrawing its instant menaces only to lay bare her mind more bitterly to the persecutions of a haunted memory!" Considering the nature of the calamity, in the first place; considering, in the second place, its life-long duration; and, in the last place, considering the quality of the resistance by which it was met, and under what circumstances of humble resources in money or friends—we have come to the deliberate judgment, that the whole range of history scarcely presents a more affecting spectacle of perpetual sorrow, humiliation, or conflict, and that was supported to the end (that is, through forty years) with more resignation, or with more absolute victory.

*   *   *   *   *

The account given of Lamb's friends, of those whom he endeavoured to love because he admired them, or to esteem intellectually because he loved them personally, is too much coloured for general acquiescence by Sergeant (since Mr. Justice) Talfourd's own early prepossessions. It is natural that an intellectual man like the Sergeant, personally made known in youth to people, whom from childhood he had regarded as powers in the ideal world, and in some instances as representing the eternities of human speculation, since their names had perhaps dawned upon his mind in concurrence with the very earliest suggestion of topics which they had treated, should overrate their intrinsic grandeur. Hazlitt accordingly is styled "The great thinker." But had he even been such potentially, there was an absolute bar to his achievement of that station in act and consummation. No man *can* be a great thinker in our days upon large and elaborate questions without being also a great student. To think profoundly, it is indispensable that a man should have read down to his own starting-point, and have read as a collating student to the particular stage at which he himself takes up the subject. At this moment, for

---

* Lamb was himself confined for six weeks at one period of his life in a lunatic asylum.

instance, how could geology be treated otherwise than childishly by one who should rely upon the encyclopædias of 1800? or comparative physiology by the most ingenious of men unacquainted with Marshall Hall,[3] and with the apocalyptic glimpses of secrets unfolding under the hands of Professor Owen?[4] In such a condition of undisciplined thinking, the ablest man thinks to no purpose. He lingers upon parts of the inquiry that have lost the importance which once they had, under imperfect charts of the subject; he wastes his strength upon problems that have become obsolete; he loses his way in paths that are not in the line of direction upon which the improved speculation is moving; or he gives narrow conjectural solutions of difficulties that have long since received sure and comprehensive ones. It is as if a man should in these days attempt to colonize, and yet, through inertia or through ignorance, should leave behind him all modern resources of chemistry, of chemical agriculture, or of steam-power. Hazlitt had read nothing. Unacquainted with Grecian philosophy, with Scholastic philosophy, and with the recomposition of these philosophies in the looms of Germany during the last seventy and odd years, trusting merely to the untrained instincts of keen mother-wit—whence should Hazlitt have had the materials for great thinking? It is through the collation of many abortive voyages to polar regions that a man gains his first chance of entering the polar basin, or of running ahead on the true line of approach to it. The very reason for Hazlitt's defect in eloquence as a lecturer, is sufficient also as a reason why he could not have been a comprehensive thinker. "He was not eloquent," says the Sergeant, "in the true sense of the term." But why? Because it seems "his thoughts were too weighty to be moved along by the shallow stream of feeling which an evening's excitement can rouse,"—an explanation which leaves us in doubt whether Hazlitt forfeited his chance of eloquence by accommodating himself to this evening's excitement, or by gloomily resisting it. Our own explanation is different, Hazlitt was not eloquent, because he was discontinuous. No man can be eloquent whose thoughts are abrupt, insulated, capricious, and (to borrow an impressive word from Coleridge) non-sequacious. Eloquence resides not in separate or fractional ideas, but in the relations of manifold ideas, and in the mode of their evolution from each other. It is not indeed

---

3 Marshall Hall (1790–1857) was a leading English doctor and physiologist who made important discoveries on the circulation of the blood and on the nervous system.

4 Richard Owen (1804–1892) was a naturalist and leading comparative anatomist of his time. In 1836, Owen was appointed the first Hunterian Professor of Comparative Anatomy and Physiology at the Royal College of Surgeons.

enough that the ideas should be many, and their relations coherent; the main condition lies in the *key* of the evolution, in the *law* of the succession. The elements are nothing without the atmosphere that moulds, and the dynamic forces that combine. Now Hazlitt's brilliancy is seen chiefly in separate splinterings of phrase or image which throw upon the eye a vitreous scintillation for a moment, but spread no deep suffusions of colour, and distribute no masses of mighty shadow. A flash, a solitary flash, and all is gone. Rhetoric, according to its quality, stands in many degrees of relation to the permanencies of truth; and all rhetoric, like all flesh, is partly unreal, and the glory of both is fleeting. Even the mighty rhetoric of Sir Thomas Browne, or Jeremy Taylor, to whom only it has been granted to open the trumpet-stop on that great organ of passion, oftentimes leaves behind it the sense of sadness which belongs to beautiful apparitions starting out of darkness upon the morbid eye, only to be reclaimed by darkness in the instant of their birth, or which belongs to pageantries in the clouds. But if all rhetoric is a mode of pyrotechny, and all pyrotechnics are by necessity fugitive, yet even in these frail pomps, there are many degrees of frailty. Some fireworks require an hour's duration for the expansion of their glory; others, as if formed from fulminating powder, expire in the very act of birth. Precisely on that scale of duration and of power stand the glitterings of rhetoric that are not worked into the texture, but washed on from the outside. Hazlitt's thoughts were of the same fractured and discontinuous order as his illustrative images—seldom or never self-diffusive; and *that* is a sufficient argument that he had never cultivated philosophic thinking.

Not, however, to conceal any part of the truth, we are bound to acknowledge that Lamb thought otherwise on this point, manifesting what seemed to us an extravagant admiration of Hazlitt, and perhaps even in part for that very glitter which we are denouncing—at least he did so in conversation with ourselves. But, on the other hand, as this conversation travelled a little into the tone of a disputation, and *our* frost on this point might seem to justify some undue fervour by way of balance, it is very possible that Lamb did not speak his absolute and most dispassionate judgment. And yet again, if he *did*, may we, with all reverence for Lamb's exquisite genius, have permission to say—that his own constitution of intellect sinned by this very habit of discontinuity. It was a habit of mind not unlikely to be cherished by his habits of life. Amongst these habits was the excess of his social kindness. He scorned so much to deny his company and his redundant hospitality to any man who manifested a wish for either by calling upon him that he almost seemed to think it a criminality in himself if, by accident, he really *was* from home on your visit, rather than by possibility a negligence in you, that had not forewarned him of your intention. What was the consequence? All his life, from this and other causes, he must have read in the spirit of one liable to sudden interruption; like a dragoon, in fact, reading with one foot in the stirrup, when expecting momentarily a summons to mount for action. In such situations, reading by snatches, and by intervals of precarious leisure, people form inevitably the habit of seeking and unduly valuing condensations of the meaning, where in reality the truth suffers by this short-hand exhibition; or else they demand too vivid illustrations of the meaning. Lord Chesterfield, so brilliant a man by nature, already therefore making a morbid estimate of brilliancy, and so hurried throughout his life as a public man, read under this double coercion for craving instantaneous effects. At one period, his only time for reading was in the morning, whilst under the hands of his hairdresser, who, in that age, or even thirty years later, was an artist that, more even than a tailor, ministered to respectability. Compelled to take the hastiest of flying shots at his author, naturally Lord Chesterfield demanded a very conspicuous mark to fire at. But the author could not, in so brief a space, be always sure to crowd any very prominent objects on the eye, unless by being audaciously oracular and peremptory as regarded the sentiment, or flashy in excess as regarded its expression. "Come now, my friend," was Lord Chesterfield's morning adjuration to his author; "come now, cut it short—don't prose—don't hum and haw." The author had doubtless no ambition to enter his name on the honourable and ancient roll of gentlemen prosers; probably he conceived himself not at all tainted with the asthmatic infirmity of humming and hawing; but, as to "cutting it short," how could he be sure of meeting his lordship's expectations in that point, unless by dismissing all the limitations that might be requisite to fit the idea for use, or the adjuncts that might be requisite to integrate its truth, or the final consequences that might involve some deep *arrière pensée*.[5] To be lawfully and usefully brilliant, after this rapid fashion, a man must come forward as a refresher of old truths, when *his* suppressions are supplied by the reader's memory; not as an expounder of new truths, where oftentimes a dislocated fraction of the true is not less dangerous than the false itself.

To read therefore habitually, by hurried instalments, has this bad tendency—that it is likely to found a taste for modes of composition too artificially irritating, and

to disturb the equilibrium of the judgment in relation to the colourings of style. Lamb, however, whose constitution of mind was even ideally sound in reference to the natural, the simple, the genuine, might seem of all men least liable to a taint in this direction. And undoubtedly he *was* so, as regarded those modes of beauty which nature had specially qualified him for apprehending. Else, and in relation to other modes of beauty, where his sense of the true, and of its distinction from the spurious, had been an acquired sense, it is impossible for us to hide from ourselves—that not through habits only, not through stress of injurious accidents only, but by original structure and temperament of mind, Lamb had a bias towards those very defects on which rested the startling characteristics of style which we have been noticing. He himself, we fear, not bribed by indulgent feelings to another, not moved by friendship, but by native tendency, shrank from the continuous, from the sustained, from the elaborate.

The elaborate, indeed, without which much truth and beauty must perish in germ, was by name the object of his invectives. The instances are many, in his own beautiful essays, where he literally collapses, literally sinks away from openings suddenly offering themselves to flights of pathos or solemnity in direct prosecution of his own theme. On any such summons, where an ascending impulse, and an untired pinion were required, he *refuses* himself (to use military language) invariably. The least observing reader of *Elia* cannot have failed to notice that the most felicitous passages always accomplish their circuit in a few sentences. The gyration within which his sentiment wheels, no matter of what kind it may be, is always the shortest possible. It does not prolong itself—it does not repeat itself—it does not propagate itself. But, in fact, other features in Lamb's mind would have argued this feature by analogy, had we by accident been left unaware of it directly. It is not by chance, or without a deep ground in his nature, *common* to all his qualities, both affirmative and negative, that Lamb had an insensibility to music more absolute than can have been often shared by any human creature, or perhaps than was ever before acknowledged so candidly. The sense of music—as a pleasurable sense, or as any sense at all other than of certain unmeaning and impertinent differences in respect to high and low, sharp or flat— was utterly obliterated as with a sponge by nature herself from Lamb's organization. It was a corollary, from the same large *substratum* in his nature, that Lamb had no sense of the rhythmical in prose composition. Rhythmus, or pomp of cadence, or sonorous ascent of clauses, in the structure of sentences, were effects of art as much thrown away upon *him* as the voice of the

---

5 *arrière pensée*: mental reservation.

charmer upon the deaf adder. We ourselves, occupying the very station of polar opposition to that of Lamb, being as morbidly, perhaps, in the one excess as he in the other, naturally detected this omission in Lamb's nature at an early stage of our acquaintance. Not the fabled Regulus,[6] with his eyelids torn away, and his uncurtained eye-balls exposed to the noon-tide glare of a Carthaginian sun, could have shrieked with more anguish of recoil from torture than we from certain sentences and periods in which Lamb perceived no fault at all. *Pomp*, in our apprehension, was an idea of two categories; the pompous might be spurious, but it might also be genuine. It is well to love the simple—*we* love it; nor is there any opposition at all between *that* and the very glory of pomp. But, as we once put the case to Lamb, if, as a musician, as the leader of a mighty orchestra, you had this theme offered to you—"Belshazzar the king gave a great feast to a thousand of his lords"—or this, "And on a certain day, Marcus Cicero stood up, and in a set speech rendered solemn thanks to Caius Cæsar for Quintus Ligarius pardoned, and for Marcus Marcellus restored"—surely no man would deny that, in such a case, simplicity, though in a passive sense not lawfully absent, must stand aside as totally insufficient for the *positive* part. Simplicity might guide, even here, but could not furnish the power; a rudder it might be, but not an oar or a sail. This Lamb was ready to allow; as an intellectual *quiddity*, he recognised pomp in the character of a privileged thing; he was obliged to do so; for take away from great ceremonial festivals, such as the solemn rendering of thanks, the celebration of national anniversaries, the commemoration of public benefactors, &c., the element of pomp, and you take away their very meaning and life; but, whilst allowing a place for it in the rubric of the logician, it is certain that, *sensuously*, Lamb would not have sympathized with it, nor have *felt* its justification in any concrete instance. We find a difficulty in pursuing this subject, without greatly exceeding the just limits. We pause, therefore, and add only this one suggestion as partly explanatory of the case. Lamb had the Dramatic intellect and taste, perhaps in perfection; of the Epic, he had none at all. Here, as happens sometimes to men of genius preternaturally endowed in one direction, he might be considered as almost starved. A favourite of nature, so eminent in some directions, by what right could he complain that her bounties were not indiscriminate? From this defect in his nature it arose, that, except by

culture and by reflection, Lamb had no genial appreciation of Milton. The solemn planetary wheelings of the Paradise Lost were not to his taste. What he *did* comprehend, were the motions like those of lightning, the fierce angular coruscations of that wild agency which comes forward so vividly in the sudden περιπέτεια,[7] in the revolutionary catastrophe, and in the tumultuous conflicts, through persons or through situations, of the tragic drama.

*   *   *   *   *

Of Lamb's writings, some were confessedly failures, and some were so memorably beautiful as to be uniques in their class. The character of Lamb it is, and the life-struggle of Lamb, that must fix the attention of many, even amongst those wanting in sensibility to his intellectual merits. This character and this struggle, as we have already observed, impress many traces of themselves upon Lamb's writings. Even in that view, therefore, they have a ministerial value; but separately, for themselves, they have an independent value of the highest order. Upon this point we gladly adopt the eloquent words of Sergeant Talfourd:—

"The sweetness of Lamb's character, breathed through his writings, was felt even by strangers; but its heroic aspect was unguessed even by many of his friends. Let them now consider it, and ask if the annals of self-sacrifice can show anything in human action and endurance more lovely than its self-devotion exhibits? It was not merely that he saw, through the ensanguined cloud of misfortune which had fallen upon his family, the unstained excellence of his sister, whose madness had caused it; that he was ready to take her to his own home with reverential affection, and cherish her through life; and he gave up, for *her* sake, all meaner and more selfish love, and all the hopes which youth blends with the passion which disturbs and ennobles it; not even that he did all this cheerfully, without pluming himself upon his brotherly nobleness as a virtue, or seeking to repay himself (as some uneasy martyrs do) by small instalments of long repining; but that he carried the spirit of the hour in which he first knew and took his course to his last. So far from thinking that his sacrifice of youth and love to his sister gave him a license to follow his own caprice at the expense of her feelings, even in the lightest matters, he always wrote and spoke of her as his wiser self, his generous benefactress, of whose protecting care he was scarcely worthy."

---

[6] Marcus Atilius Regulus, third-century B.C. Roman general and consul, a leader in the Punic wars. He was supposedly tortured to death by the Carthaginians following his defeat and capture.

---

[7] "Peripeteia," the reversal of intention by which the action of the play veers round to the opposite of what the character anticipates.

It must be remembered also, which the Sergeant does not overlook, that Lamb's efforts for the becoming support of his sister lasted through a period of forty years. Twelve years before his death, the munificence of the India House, by granting him a liberal retiring allowance, had placed his own support under shelter from accidents of any kind. But this died with himself; and he could not venture to suppose that, in the event of his own death, the India House would grant to his sister the same allowance as by custom is granted to a wife. This, however, they did; but Lamb not venturing to calculate upon such nobility of patronage, had applied himself through life to the saving of a provision for his sister under any accident to himself. And this he did with a persevering prudence, but little known in the literary class, amongst a continued tenor of generosities, often so princely as to be scarcely known in any class. . . .

Charles Lamb is gone; his life was a continued struggle in the service of love the purest, and within a sphere visited by little of contemporary applause. Even his intellectual displays won but a narrow sympathy at any time, and in his earlier period were saluted with positive derision and contumely on the few occasions when they were not oppressed by entire neglect. But slowly all things right themselves. All merit, which is founded in truth, and is strong enough, reaches by sweet exhalations in the end a higher sensory; reaches higher organs of discernment, lodged in a selecter audience. But the original obtuseness or vulgarity of feeling that thwarted all just estimation of Lamb in life, will continue to thwart its popular diffusion. There are even some that continue to regard him with the old hostility, and the old unmitigated scorn. And we, therefore, standing by the side of Lamb's grave, seemed to hear, on one side (but in abated tones), strains of the ancient malice—"This man, that thought himself to be somebody, is dead—is buried—is forgotten!" and, on the other side, seemed to hear ascending as with the solemnity of a saintly requiem— "This man, that thought himself to be nobody, is dead—is buried; his life has been searched; and his memory is hallowed for ever!"

[November 1848]   [1858]

Thomas Love Peacock

1785–1866

OUTLINE OF EVENTS

1785   Born October 18 at Weymouth, Dorsetshire, only son of the London merchant Samuel (d. 1788 ?) and Sarah (Love) (1754–1833). Moves at an early age to Chertsey, Surrey, in the region of the Thames where he is to live most of his life.

1791–99   Attends school at Englefield Green, where he proves a precocious student and begins writing verses.

1800   Employed as clerk in a London merchant house. Wins prize in a magazine competition for his poem in heroic couplets "Is History or Biography the more improving Study?"

1804   The farcical poem *The Monks of St. Mark* published.

1805   *Palmyra and other Poems* published.

1806   Walking tour of Scotland.

1808–09   Serves as under-secretary on board H.M.S. *Venerable*.

1810   *Genius of the Thames* published.

1812   *The Philosophy of Melancholy* published. October, meets Shelley, beginning a long and important literary association and friendship.

1813   Travels with Shelley and Harriet to Lake District and Edinburgh. Begins writing epic poem *Ahrimanes* (abandoned 1815).

1816   Novel *Headlong Hall* published.

1817   Novel *Melincourt* published.

1818   Novel *Nightmare Abbey*, including satiric pictures of Byron as "Mr. Cypress" and Shelley as "Scythrop," and poem *Rhododaphne* published.

1819   Begins employment at East India Company.

1820   November, *Four Ages of Poetry* published. Marries Jane Gryffydh, whom he had first met in 1809 in Wales.

1822   Romance *Maid Marian* published.

1822–25   Becomes acquainted with John Stuart Mill (whose father is fellow-employee at East India House) and Jeremy Bentham.

1827   Reviews Thomas Moore's novel *Epicurean* in *Westminster Review* (further reviews in 1830).

1829   Novel *Misfortunes of Elphin* published. Begins career as music critic in the *Globe* (later filling same role in the *Examiner*).

1831   Novel *Crotchet Castle* published.

1836   Appointed to important post of Examiner at East India House.

1849   Daughter Mary marries George Meredith.

1851   Death of wife.

1856   Retires from East India House.

1858–62   Peacock's *Memoirs of Percy Bysshe Shelley* appear in *Fraser's Magazine*.

1861   Final novel, *Gryll Grange*, published.

1862   Final literary work, *Gl'Ingannati*, prose translation of the Italian comedy that was the source for *Twelfth Night*, published.

1866   Dies, January 23, at Lower Halliford.

SELECTED BIBLIOGRAPHY

BIOGRAPHY

BRETT-SMITH, H. F. B., "Biographical Introduction" to Halliford Edition (see *Editions* below), I, xii–ccxii.

VAN DOREN, CARL, *The Life of Thomas Love Peacock*, London-New York: J. M. Dent and Sons, Ltd., and E. P. Dutton and Co., 1911.

EDITIONS

BRETT-SMITH, H. F. B. (ed.), *Peacock's Four Ages of Poetry, Shelley's Defence of Poetry, Browning's Essay on Shelley*, Percy Reprints No. 3, Oxford: Basil Blackwell, 1921.

—— and C. E. JONES (eds.), *The Works of Thomas Love Peacock*, the Halliford Edition, 10 vols., London: Constable and Co., Ltd., 1924–1934.

CAMERON, KENNETH NEILL (ed.), *Shelley and his Circle 1773–1822* (see under *Editions* in Shelley bibliography) [contains letters and manuscripts of Peacock, with detailed commentaries].

JORDAN, JOHN E. (ed.), *A Defence of Poetry: Percy Bysshe Shelley, The Four Ages of Poetry: Thomas Love Peacock*, The Library of Liberal Arts, Indianapolis, Ind.: Bobbs-Merrill Company, 1965.

SCHOLARSHIP AND CRITICISM

DAWSON, CARL, *His Fine Wit: A Study of Thomas Love Peacock*, London: Routledge and Kegan Paul, 1970.

MAYOUX, JEAN-JACQUES, *Un Épicurien Anglais: Thomas Love Peacock*, Paris: Nizet et Bastard, 1933.

MILLS, HOWARD, *Peacock: His Circle and His Age*, Cambridge, Eng.: Cambridge University Press, 1969.

THE FOUR AGES OF POETRY

The reading of his friend Peacock's essay in January 1821 aroused in Shelley "a sacred rage," and led to the composition of an eloquent and impassioned answer, A Defence of Poetry. *The note of playfulness and irony in* The Four Ages of Poetry *has prevented most readers from taking the work quite so seriously. The essay has been called "the most sustained account in English of the conflict between poetry and science as it stood in the era of the romantic poets" (W. K. Wimsatt, Jr.); yet the tone suggests it was perhaps conceived much more as a* jeu d'esprit *than as a meaningful statement of aesthetic theory and literary history. M. H. Abrams, who relates the "parodic" quality of the essay to the informing tone and procedure of Peacock's many other writings, has concluded: "It is idle to inquire about the exact boundaries between the serious and the playful in this witty essay. Peacock cannot be pinned down" (The Mirror and the Lamp, p. 126). Whatever may have been his precise intentions, it should be noted that Peacock's theory about the decline of imagination with the advance of scientific intellect and his objections to the "egotism" of Wordsworth's poetry were not eccentric notions; they had been expressed also in the essays and lectures of Hazlitt, and through Hazlitt had exerted a significant influence on the thought and poetry of Keats. For further discussion of the essay, see: William K. Wimsatt, Jr. and Cleanth Brooks (eds.), Literary Criticism: A Short History (New York: Alfred A. Knopf, 1957), pp. 416–18; Howard Mills, Peacock: His Circle and his Age (1969), pp. 39–47; Carl Dawson, His Fine Wit: A Study of Thomas Love Peacock (1970), pp. 78–110.*

The Four Ages of Poetry *had been published in* Ollier's Literary Miscellany, I *(November 1820). The text is here reproduced from the edition by H. F. B. Brett-Smith, Peacock's* Four Ages of Poetry, Shelley's Defence of Poetry, Browning's Essay on Shelley, *second edition (Oxford: Basil Blackwell, 1923).*

THE FOUR AGES OF POETRY

Qui inter hæc nutriuntur non magis sapere possunt,
quam bene olere qui in culinâ habitant. PETRONIUS.[1]

POETRY, like the world, may be said to have four ages, but in a different order: the first age of poetry being the age of iron; the second, of gold; the third, of silver; and the fourth, of brass.

The first, or iron age of poetry, is that in which rude bards celebrate in rough numbers the exploits of ruder chiefs, in days when every man is a warrior, and when the great practical maxim of every form of society, "to keep what we have and to catch what we can," is not yet disguised under names of justice and forms of law, but is the naked motto of the naked sword, which is the only judge and jury in every question of *meum* and *tuum*. In these days, the only three trades flourishing (besides that of priest which flourishes always) are

those of king, thief, and beggar: the beggar being for the most part a king deject, and the thief a king expectant. The first question asked of a stranger is, whether he is a beggar or a thief*: the stranger, in reply, usually assumes the first, and awaits a convenient opportunity to prove his claim to the second appellation.

The natural desire of every man to engross to himself as much power and property as he can acquire by any of the means which might makes right, is accompanied by the no less natural desire of making known to as many people as possible the extent to which he has been a winner in this universal game. The successful warrior becomes a chief; the successful chief becomes a king: his next want is an organ to disseminate the fame of his achievements and the extent of his possessions; and this organ he finds in a bard, who is always ready to celebrate the strength of his arm, being first duly inspired by that of his liquor. This is the origin of poetry, which, like all other trades, takes its rise in the demand for the commodity, and flourishes in proportion to the extent of the market.

Poetry is thus in its origin panegyrical. The first rude songs of all nations appear to be a sort of brief historical notices, in a strain of tumid hyperbole, of the exploits and possessions of a few pre-eminent individuals. They tell us how many battles such an one has fought, how many helmets he has cleft, how many breastplates he has pierced, how many widows he has made, how much land he has appropriated, how many houses he has demolished for other people, what a large one he has built for himself, how much gold he has stowed away in it, and how liberally and plentifully he pays, feeds, and intoxicates the divine and immortal bards, the sons of Jupiter, but for whose everlasting songs the names of heroes would perish.

This is the first stage of poetry before the invention of written letters. The numerical modulation is at once useful as a help to memory, and pleasant to the ears of uncultured men, who are easily caught by sound: and from the exceeding flexibility of the yet unformed language, the poet does no violence to his ideas in subjecting them to the fetters of number. The savage indeed lisps in numbers,[2] and all rude and uncivilized people express themselves in the manner which we call poetical.

The scenery by which he is surrounded, and the superstitions which are the creed of his age, form the poet's mind. Rocks, mountains, seas, unsubdued forests, unnavigable rivers, surround him with forms of power and mystery, which ignorance and fear have

---

[1] Petronius' *Satyricon*, 2: "People who are fed on this diet can no more be sensible than people who live in the kitchen can be savoury" (Michael Heseltine translation, Loeb Classical Library, Harvard University Press).

* See the Odyssey, passim: and Thucydides, I. 5.

---

[2] See Pope's *Epistle to Dr. Arbuthnot*, l. 128.

peopled with spirits, under multifarious names of gods, goddesses, nymphs, genii, and dæmons. Of all these personages marvellous tales are in existence: the nymphs are not indifferent to handsome young men, and the gentlemen-genii are much troubled and very troublesome with a propensity to be rude to pretty maidens: the bard therefore finds no difficulty in tracing the genealogy of his chief to any of the deities in his neighbourhood with whom the said chief may be most desirous of claiming relationship.

In this pursuit, as in all others, some of course will attain a very marked pre-eminence; and these will be held in high honour, like Demodocus in the Odyssey, and will be consequently inflated with boundless vanity, like Thamyris in the Iliad.[3] Poets are as yet the only historians and chroniclers of their time, and the sole depositories of all the knowledge of their age; and though this knowledge is rather a crude congeries of traditional phantasies than a collection of useful truths, yet, such as it is, they have it to themselves. They are observing and thinking, while others are robbing and fighting: and though their object be nothing more than to secure a share of the spoil, yet they accomplish this end by intellectual, not by physical, power: their success excites emulation to the attainment of intellectual eminence: thus they sharpen their own wits and awaken those of others, at the same time that they gratify vanity and amuse curiosity. A skilful display of the little knowledge they have gains them credit for the possession of much more which they have not. Their familiarity with the secret history of gods and genii obtains for them, without much difficulty, the reputation of inspiration; thus they are not only historians but theologians, moralists, and legislators: delivering their oracles *ex cathedrâ*, and being indeed often themselves (as Orpheus and Amphion) regarded as portions and emanations of divinity: building cities with a song, and leading brutes with a symphony; which are only metaphors for the faculty of leading multitudes by the nose.

The golden age of poetry finds its materials in the age of iron. This age begins when poetry begins to be retrospective; when something like a more extended system of civil polity is established; when personal strength and courage avail less to the aggrandizing of their possessor and to the making and marring of kings and kingdoms, and are checked by organized bodies, social institutions, and hereditary successions. Men also live more in the light of truth and within the interchange of observation; and thus perceive that the agency of gods and genii is not so frequent among themselves as, to judge from the songs and legends of the past time, it was among their ancestors. From these two circumstances, really diminished personal power, and apparently diminished familiarity with gods and genii, they very easily and naturally deduce two conclusions: 1st, That men are degenerated, and 2nd, That they are less in favour with the gods. The people of the petty states and colonies, which have now acquired stability and form, which owed their origin and first prosperity to the talents and courage of a single chief, magnify their founder through the mists of distance and tradition, and perceive him achieving wonders with a god or goddess always at his elbow. They find his name and his exploits thus magnified and accompanied in their traditionary songs, which are their only memorials. All that is said of him is in this character. There is nothing to contradict it. The man and his exploits and his tutelary deities are mixed and blended in one invariable association. The marvellous too is very much like a snowball: it grows as it rolls downward, till the little nucleus of truth which began its descent from the summit is hidden in the accumulation of superinduced hyperbole.

When tradition, thus adorned and exaggerated, has surrounded the founders of families and states with so much adventitious power and magnificence, there is no praise which a living poet can, without fear of being kicked for clumsy flattery, address to a living chief, that will not still leave the impression that the latter is not so great a man as his ancestors. The man must in this case be praised through his ancestors. Their greatness must be established, and he must be shown to be their worthy descendant. All the people of a state are interested in the founder of their state. All states that have harmonized into a common form of society, are interested in their respective founders. All men are interested in their ancestors. All men love to look back into the days that are past. In these circumstances traditional national poetry is reconstructed and brought like chaos into order and form. The interest is more universal: understanding is enlarged: passion still has scope and play: character is still various and strong: nature is still unsubdued and existing in all her beauty and magnificence, and men are not yet excluded from her observation by the magnitude of cities or the daily confinement of civic life: poetry is more an art: it requires greater skill in numbers, greater command of language, more extensive and various knowledge, and greater comprehensiveness of mind. It still exists without rivals in any other department of literature; and even the arts, painting and sculpture

---

3 Demodocus was the "lord of song," a minstrel at the court of King Alcinous (see *Odyssey*, VIII). Thamyris was a Thracian minstrel who boasted that he could surpass even the Muses in song; in anger, they took from him his gifts of song and story (see *Iliad*, II, 594–600).

certainly, and music probably, are comparatively rude and imperfect. The whole field of intellect is its own. It has no rivals in history, nor in philosophy, nor in science. It is cultivated by the greatest intellects of the age, and listened to by all the rest. This is the age of Homer, the golden age of poetry. Poetry has now attained its perfection: it has attained the point which it cannot pass: genius therefore seeks new forms for the treatment of the same subjects: hence the lyric poetry of Pindar and Alcæus, and the tragic poetry of Æschylus and Sophocles. The favour of kings, the honour of the Olympic crown, the applause of present multitudes, all that can feed vanity and stimulate rivalry, await the successful cultivator of this art, till its forms become exhausted, and new rivals arise around it in new fields of literature, which gradually acquire more influence as, with the progress of reason and civilization, facts become more interesting than fiction: indeed the maturity of poetry may be considered the infancy of history. The transition from Homer to Herodotus is scarcely more remarkable than that from Herodotus to Thucydides: in the gradual dereliction of fabulous incident and ornamented language, Herodotus is as much a poet in relation to Thucydides as Homer is in relation to Herodotus. The history of Herodotus is half a poem: it was written while the whole field of literature yet belonged to the Muses, and the nine books of which it was composed were therefore of right, as well as of courtesy, superinscribed with their nine names.

Speculations, too, and disputes, on the nature of man and of mind; on moral duties and on good and evil; on the animate and inanimate components of the visible world; begin to share attention with the eggs of Leda and the horns of Io,[4] and to draw off from poetry a portion of its once undivided audience.

Then comes the silver age, or the poetry of civilized life. This poetry is of two kinds, imitative and original. The imitative consists in recasting, and giving an exquisite polish to, the poetry of the age of gold: of this Virgil is the most obvious and striking example. The original is chiefly comic, didactic, or satiric: as in Menander, Aristophanes, Horace, and Juvenal. The poetry of this age is characterized by an exquisite and fastidious selection of words, and a laboured and somewhat monotonous harmony of expression: but its monotony consists in this, that experience having exhausted all the varieties of modulation, the civilized

poetry selects the most beautiful, and prefers the repetition of these to ranging through the variety of all. But the best expression being that into which the idea naturally falls, it requires the utmost labour and care so to reconcile the inflexibility of civilized language and the laboured polish of versification with the idea intended to be expressed, that sense may not appear to be sacrificed to sound. Hence numerous efforts and rare success.

This state of poetry is however a step towards its extinction. Feeling and passion are best painted in, and roused by, ornamental and figurative language; but the reason and the understanding are best addressed in the simplest and most unvarnished phrase. Pure reason and dispassionate truth would be perfectly ridiculous in verse, as we may judge by versifying one of Euclid's demonstrations. This will be found true of all dispassionate reasoning whatever, and all reasoning that requires comprehensive views and enlarged combinations. It is only the more tangible points of morality, those which command assent at once, those which have a mirror in every mind, and in which the severity of reason is warmed and rendered palatable by being mixed up with feeling and imagination, that are applicable even to what is called moral poetry: and as the sciences of morals and of mind advance towards perfection, as they become more enlarged and comprehensive in their views, as reason gains the ascendancy in them over imagination and feeling, poetry can no longer accompany them in their progress, but drops into the background, and leaves them to advance alone.

Thus the empire of thought is withdrawn from poetry, as the empire of facts had been before. In respect of the latter, the poet of the age of iron celebrates the achievements of his contemporaries; the poet of the age of gold celebrates the heroes of the age of iron; the poet of the age of silver re-casts the poems of the age of gold: we may here see how very slight a ray of historical truth is sufficient to dissipate all the illusions of poetry. We know no more of the men than of the gods of the Iliad; no more of Achilles than we do of Thetis;[5] no more of Hector and Andromache than we do of Vulcan and Venus: these belong altogether to poetry; history has no share in them: but Virgil knew better than to write an epic about Cæsar; he left him to Livy; and travelled out of the confines of truth and history into the old regions of poetry and fiction.

Good sense and elegant learning, conveyed in polished and somewhat monotonous verse, are the perfection of the original and imitative poetry of civilized life. Its range is limited, and when exhausted, nothing

---

4 Peacock refers to the amorous exploits of Zeus. In the form of a swan, the god had made love to Leda, who produced the children Castor and Pollux, and Helen and Clytemnestra. Zeus changed Io into a heifer in order to conceal her from the suspicions of his wife Hera.

---

5 A sea-nymph and goddess-mother of Achilles.

remains but the *crambe repetita*[6] of common-place, which at length becomes thoroughly wearisome, even to the most indefatigable readers of the newest new nothings.

It is now evident that poetry must either cease to be cultivated, or strike into a new path. The poets of the age of gold have been imitated and repeated till no new imitation will attract notice: the limited range of ethical and didactic poetry is exhausted: the associations of daily life in an advanced state of society are of very dry, methodical, unpoetical matters-of-fact: but there is always a multitude of listless idlers, yawning for amusement, and gaping for novelty: and the poet makes it his glory to be foremost among their purveyors.

Then comes the age of brass, which, by rejecting the polish and the learning of the age of silver, and taking a retrograde stride to the barbarisms and crude traditions of the age of iron, professes to return to nature and revive the age of gold. This is the second childhood of poetry. To the comprehensive energy of the Homeric Muse, which, by giving at once the grand outline of things, presented to the mind a vivid picture in one or two verses, inimitable alike in simplicity and magnificence, is substituted a verbose and minutely-detailed description of thoughts, passions, actions, persons, and things, in that loose rambling style of verse, which any one may write, *stans pede in uno*,[7] at the rate of two hundred lines in an hour. To this age may be referred all the poets who flourished in the decline of the Roman Empire. The best specimen of it, though not the most generally known, is the Dionysiaca of Nonnus,[8] which contains many passages of exceeding beauty in the midst of masses of amplification and repetition.

The iron age of classical poetry may be called the bardic; the golden, the Homeric; the silver, the Virgilian; and the brass, the Nonnic.

Modern poetry has also its four ages: but " it wears its rue with a difference." [9]

To the age of brass in the ancient world succeeded the dark ages, in which the light of the Gospel began to spread over Europe, and in which, by a mysterious and inscrutable dispensation, the darkness thickened with the progress of the light. The tribes that overran the Roman Empire brought back the days of barbarism, but with this difference, that there were many books in the world, many places in which they were preserved, and occasionally some one by whom they were read, who indeed (if he escaped being burned *pour l'amour de Dieu*,) generally lived an object of mysterious fear, with the reputation of magician, alchymist, and astrologer. The emerging of the nations of Europe from this superinduced barbarism, and their settling into new forms of polity, was accompanied, as the first ages of Greece had been, with a wild spirit of adventure, which, co-operating with new manners and new superstitions, raised up a fresh crop of chimæras, not less fruitful, though far less beautiful, than those of Greece. The semi-deification of women by the maxims of the age of chivalry, combining with these new fables, produced the romance of the middle ages. The founders of the new line of heroes took the place of the demi-gods of Grecian poetry. Charlemagne and his Paladins, Arthur and his knights of the round table, the heroes of the iron age of chivalrous poetry, were seen through the same magnifying mist of distance, and their exploits were celebrated with even more extravagant hyperbole. These legends, combined with the exaggerated love that pervades the songs of the troubadours, the reputation of magic that attached to learned men, the infant wonders of natural philosophy, the crazy fanaticism of the crusades, the power and privileges of the great feudal chiefs, and the holy mysteries of monks and nuns, formed a state of society in which no two laymen could meet without fighting, and in which the three staple ingredients of lover, prize-fighter, and fanatic, that composed the basis of the character of every true man, were mixed up and diversified, in different individuals and classes, with so many distinctive excellencies, and under such an infinite motley . variety of costume, as gave the range of a most extensive and picturesque field to the two great constituents of poetry, love and battle.

From these ingredients of the iron age of modern poetry, dispersed in the rhymes of minstrels and the songs of the troubadours, arose the golden age, in which the scattered materials were harmonized and blended about the time of the revival of learning; but with this peculiar difference, that Greek and Roman literature pervaded all the poetry of the golden age of modern poetry, and hence resulted a heterogeneous compound of all ages and nations in one picture; an infinite licence, which gave to the poet the free range of the whole field of imagination and memory. This was carried very far by Ariosto, but farthest of all by Shakespeare and his contemporaries, who used time and locality merely because they could not do without them, because every action must have its when and where: but they made no scruple of deposing a Roman Emperor by an Italian Count, and sending him off in the disguise of a French pilgrim to be shot with a

---

6 *crambe repetita*: cabbage warmed up or served again.
7 *stans pede in uno*: "standing on one foot."
8 Late fourth to early fifth century author of the Greek epic *Dionysiaca*. See the reference in Shelley's *Defence of Poetry*, p. 733.
9 See *Hamlet*, IV, v, 184.

blunderbuss by an English archer. This makes the old English drama very picturesque, at any rate, in the variety of costume, and very diversified in action and character; though it is a picture of nothing that ever was seen on earth except a Venetian carnival.

The greatest of English poets, Milton, may be said to stand alone between the ages of gold and silver, combining the excellencies of both; for with all the energy, and power, and freshness of the first, he united all the studied and elaborate magnificence of the second.

The silver age succeeded; beginning with Dryden, coming to perfection with Pope, and ending with Goldsmith, Collins, and Gray.

Cowper divested verse of its exquisite polish; he thought in metre, but paid more attention to his thoughts than his verse. It would be difficult to draw the boundary of prose and blank verse between his letters and his poetry.

The silver age was the reign of authority; but authority now began to be shaken, not only in poetry but in the whole sphere of its dominion. The contemporaries of Gray and Cowper were deep and elaborate thinkers. The subtle scepticism of Hume, the solemn irony of Gibbon, the daring paradoxes of Rousseau, and the biting ridicule of Voltaire, directed the energies of four extraordinary minds to shake every portion of the reign of authority. Enquiry was roused, the activity of intellect was excited, and poetry came in for its share of the general result. The changes had been rung on lovely maid and sylvan shade, summer heat and green retreat, waving trees and sighing breeze, gentle swains and amorous pains, by versifiers who took them on trust, as meaning something very soft and tender, without much caring what: but with this general activity of intellect came a necessity for even poets to appear to know something of what they professed to talk of. Thomson and Cowper looked at the trees and hills which so many ingenious gentlemen had rhymed about so long without looking at them at all, and the effect of the operation on poetry was like the discovery of a new world. Painting shared the influence, and the principles of picturesque beauty were explored by adventurous essayists with indefatigable pertinacity.[10] The success which attended these experiments, and

the pleasure which resulted from them, had the usual effect of all new enthusiasms, that of turning the heads of a few unfortunate persons, the patriarchs of the age of brass, who, mistaking the prominent novelty for the all-important totality, seem to have ratiocinated much in the following manner: "Poetical genius is the finest of all things, and we feel that we have more of it than any one ever had. The way to bring it to perfection is to cultivate poetical impressions exclusively. Poetical impressions can be received only among natural scenes: for all that is artificial is anti-poetical. Society is artificial, therefore we will live out of society. The mountains are natural, therefore we will live in the mountains. There we shall be shining models of purity and virtue, passing the whole day in the innocent and amiable occupation of going up and down hill, receiving poetical impressions, and communicating them in immortal verse to admiring generations." To some such perversion of intellect we owe that egregious confraternity of rhymesters, known by the name of the Lake Poets; who certainly did receive and communicate to the world some of the most extraordinary poetical impressions that ever were heard of, and ripened into models of public virtue, too splendid to need illustration. They wrote verses on a new principle; saw rocks and rivers in a new light; and remaining studiously ignorant of history, society, and human nature, cultivated the phantasy only at the expence of the memory and the reason; and contrived, though they had retreated from the world for the express purpose of seeing nature as she was, to see her only as she was not, converting the land they lived in into a sort of fairy-land, which they peopled with mysticisms and chimæras. This gave what is called a new tone to poetry, and conjured up a herd of desperate imitators, who have brought the age of brass prematurely to its dotage.

The descriptive poetry of the present day has been called by its cultivators a return to nature. Nothing is more impertinent than this pretension. Poetry cannot travel out of the regions of its birth, the uncultivated lands of semi-civilized men. Mr. Wordsworth, the great leader of the returners to nature, cannot describe a scene under his own eyes without putting into it the shadow of a Danish boy or the living ghost of Lucy Gray, or some similar phantastical parturition of the moods of his own mind.[11]

In the origin and perfection of poetry, all the associations of life were composed of poetical materials. With us it is decidedly the reverse. We know too that there

---

[10] Peacock refers to the vogue of landscape painting and sketching and of "picturesque" travel literature in the late eighteenth century; and to the heated controversy over the definition of "picturesque" and the relevance of the principles of painting to landscape design, involving William Gilpin (*Three Essays: on Picturesque Beauty, on Picturesque Travel, and on Sketching Landscape* [1792]), Uvedale Price (*Essay on the Picturesque* [1794]), Richard Payne Knight (*The Landscape* [1794] and *Analytical Inquiry into the Principles of Taste* [1805]), and Humphry Repton (*Sketches and Hints on Landscape Gardening* [1795] and *Inquiry into the Changes of Taste in Landscape Gardening* [1806]).

---

[11] "Moods of my own Mind" was the title of a group of verses in Wordsworth's collection *Poems in Two Volumes* (1807).

are no Dryads in Hyde-park nor Naiads in the Regent's-canal. But barbaric manners and supernatural interventions are essential to poetry. Either in the scene, or in the time, or in both, it must be remote from our ordinary perceptions. While the historian and the philosopher are advancing in, and accelerating, the progress of knowledge, the poet is wallowing in the rubbish of departed ignorance, and raking up the ashes of dead savages to find gewgaws and rattles for the grown babies of the age. Mr. Scott digs up the poachers and cattle-stealers of the ancient border. Lord Byron cruizes for thieves and pirates on the shores of the Morea and among the Greek Islands. Mr. Southey wades through ponderous volumes of travels and old chronicles, from which he carefully selects all that is false, useless, and absurd, as being essentially poetical; and when he has a commonplace book full of monstrosities, strings them into an epic. Mr. Wordsworth picks up village legends from old women and sextons; and Mr. Coleridge, to the valuable information acquired from similar sources, superadds the dreams of crazy theologians and the mysticisms of German metaphysics, and favours the world with visions in verse, in which the quadruple elements of sexton, old woman, Jeremy Taylor, and Emanuel Kant, are harmonized into a delicious poetical compound. Mr. Moore presents us with a Persian, and Mr. Campbell with a Pennsylvanian tale,[12] both formed on the same principle as Mr. Southey's epics, by extracting from a perfunctory and desultory perusal of a collection of voyages and travels, all that useful investigation would not seek for and that common sense would reject.

These disjointed relics of tradition and fragments of second-hand observation, being woven into a tissue of verse, constructed on what Mr. Coleridge calls a new principle (that is, no principle at all), compose a modern-antique compound of frippery and barbarism, in which the puling sentimentality of the present time is grafted on the misrepresented ruggedness of the past into a heterogeneous congeries of unamalgamating manners, sufficient to impose on the common readers of poetry, over whose understandings the poet of this class possesses that commanding advantage, which, in all circumstances and conditions of life, a man who knows something, however little, always possesses over one who knows nothing.

A poet in our times is a semi-barbarian in a civilized community. He lives in the days that are past. His ideas, thoughts, feelings, associations, are all with barbarous manners, obsolete customs, and exploded superstitions. The march of his intellect is like that of a crab, backward. The brighter the light diffused around him by the progress of reason, the thicker is the darkness of antiquated barbarism, in which he buries himself like a mole, to throw up the barren hillocks of his Cimmerian labours. The philosophic mental tranquillity which looks round with an equal eye on all external things, collects a store of ideas, discriminates their relative value, assigns to all their proper place, and from the materials of useful knowledge thus collected, appreciated, and arranged, forms new combinations that impress the stamp of their power and utility on the real business of life, is diametrically the reverse of that frame of mind which poetry inspires, or from which poetry can emanate. The highest inspirations of poetry are resolvable into three ingredients: the rant of unregulated passion, the whining of exaggerated feeling, and the cant of factitious sentiment: and can therefore serve only to ripen a splendid lunatic like Alexander, a puling driveller like Werter,[13] or a morbid dreamer like Wordsworth. It can never make a philosopher, nor a statesman, nor in any class of life an useful or rational man. It cannot claim the slightest share in any one of the comforts and utilities of life of which we have witnessed so many and so rapid advances. But though not useful, it may be said it is highly ornamental, and deserves to be cultivated for the pleasure it yields. Even if this be granted, it does not follow that a writer of poetry in the present state of society is not a waster of his own time, and a robber of that of others. Poetry is not one of those arts which, like painting, require repetition and multiplication, in order to be diffused among society. There are more good poems already existing than are sufficient to employ that portion of life which any mere reader and recipient of poetical impressions should devote to them, and these having been produced in poetical times, are far superior in all the characteristics of poetry to the artificial reconstructions of a few morbid ascetics in unpoetical times. To read the promiscuous rubbish of the present time to the exclusion of the select treasures of the past, is to substitute the worse for the better variety of the same mode of enjoyment.

But in whatever degree poetry is cultivated, it must necessarily be to the neglect of some branch of useful study: and it is a lamentable spectacle to see minds, capable of better things, running to seed in the specious indolence of these empty aimless mockeries of intellectual exertion. Poetry was the mental rattle that

---

[12] Referring to Moore's *Lalla Rookh* (1817) and Campbell's *Gertrude of Wyoming* (1809).

[13] The sensitive and artistically inclined hero of Goethe's sentimental novel *The Sorrows of Young Werther* (1774), who eventually commits suicide in despair over losing the woman he loves.

awakened the attention of intellect in the infancy of civil society: but for the maturity of mind to make a serious business of the playthings of its childhood, is as absurd as for a full-grown man to rub his gums with coral, and cry to be charmed to sleep by the jingle of silver bells.

As to that small portion of our contemporary poetry, which is neither descriptive, nor narrative, nor dramatic, and which, for want of a better name, may be called ethical, the most distinguished portion of it, consisting merely of querulous, egotistical rhapsodies, to express the writer's high dissatisfaction with the world and every thing in it, serves only to confirm what has been said of the semi-barbarous character of poets, who from singing dithyrambics and "Io Triumphe," while society was savage, grow rabid, and out of their element, as it becomes polished and enlightened.

Now when we consider that it is not the thinking and studious, and scientific and philosophical part of the community, not to those whose minds are bent on the pursuit and promotion of permanently useful ends and aims, that poets must address their minstrelsy, but to that much larger portion of the reading public, whose minds are not awakened to the desire of valuable knowledge, and who are indifferent to any thing beyond being charmed, moved, excited, affected, and exalted: charmed by harmony, moved by sentiment, excited by passion, affected by pathos, and exalted by sublimity: harmony, which is language on the rack of Procrustes; sentiment, which is canting egotism in the mask of refined feeling; passion, which is the commotion of a weak and selfish mind; pathos, which is the whining of an unmanly spirit; and sublimity, which is the inflation of an empty head: when we consider that the great and permanent interests of human society become more and more the main spring of intellectual pursuit; that in proportion as they become so, the subordinacy of the ornamental to the useful will be more and more

seen and acknowledged; and that therefore the progress of useful art and science, and of moral and political knowledge, will continue more and more to withdraw attention from frivolous and unconducive, to solid and conducive studies: that therefore the poetical audience will not only continually diminish in the proportion of its number to that of the rest of the reading public, but will also sink lower and lower in the comparison of intellectual acquirement: when we consider that the poet must still please his audience, and must therefore continue to sink to their level, while the rest of the community is rising above it: we may easily conceive that the day is not distant, when the degraded state of every species of poetry will be as generally recognized as that of dramatic poetry has long been: and this not from any decrease either of intellectual power, or intellectual acquisition, but because intellectual power and intellectual acquisition have turned themselves into other and better channels, and have abandoned the cultivation and the fate of poetry to the degenerate fry of modern rhymesters, and their olympic judges, the magazine critics, who continue to debate and promulgate oracles about poetry, as if it were still what it was in the Homeric age, the all-in-all of intellectual progression, and as if there were no such things in existence as mathematicians, astronomers, chemists, moralists, metaphysicians, historians, politicians, and political economists, who have built into the upper air of intelligence a pyramid, from the summit of which they see the modern Parnassus far beneath them, and, knowing how small a place it occupies in the comprehensiveness of their prospect, smile at the little ambition and the circumscribed perceptions with which the drivellers and mountebanks upon it are contending for the poetical palm and the critical chair.

[November 1820] [1923]

George Gordon, Lord Byron

1788 – 1824

OUTLINE OF EVENTS

1788   Born January 22, in London; father, John ("Mad Jack") (1756–1791); mother, Catherine (Gordon) (1765–1811). Father had been previously married to Baroness Conyers, who had given birth to Byron's half sister, Augusta (1783–1851).

1789–98 Grows up in Aberdeen.

1791   Death of father in France, perhaps by suicide.

1798   Becomes sixth Lord Byron, inheriting family property of Rochdale (Lancashire) and Newstead Abbey, near Nottingham.

1801–05 Attends Harrow, where he is befriended by headmaster, Dr. Drury, and begins writing verses. Falls in love with his cousin Mary Chaworth of Annesley Hall (near Newstead Abbey).

1804   Begins correspondence with Augusta, who has been brought up by her mother's family.

1805   Fall, enters Trinity College, Cambridge, where he lives undisciplined and extravagant existence and is in residence for only sporadic periods in initial three years. Forms romantic attachment to John Edleston, Trinity Chapel choirboy.

1806   First volume of poems *Fugitive Pieces* privately printed, but Byron has copies destroyed because of charges of immorality.

1807   *Poems on Various Occasions* privately printed. *Hours of Idleness* published. Initiates lifelong friendship with John Cam Hobhouse. July, publishes review of Wordsworth's *Poems in Two Volumes* in the London magazine *Monthly Literary Recreations*. August, Augusta marries Col. George Leigh.

1808   January, an offensively condescending review of *Hours of Idleness* published in *Edinburgh Review*. July, receives M.A. from Cambridge.

1809   March 13, takes seat in House of Lords. *English Bards and Scotch Reviewers* published. July 2, sails with Hobhouse for Portugal and tour through Spain, Malta, Albania, and Greece. Begins to write *Childe Harold's Pilgrimage*. December 25, arrives in Athens.

1810   Lives in Athens and travels through Turkey and Greece. May 3, swims the Hellespont.

1811   July, arrives back in England. Death of mother. Meets Thomas Moore, Samuel Rogers, and Thomas Campbell.

1812   February 27, delivers first speech in House of Lords against Tory-sponsored Frame-work Bill. March, *Childe Harold's Pilgrimage*, I and II, published and proves instant success ("I awoke one morning and found myself famous"). Becomes celebrity in London society, where he has affair with Lady Caroline Lamb and meets his future wife, Anne Isabella Milbanke. April 21, speaks in House of Lords in favor of Catholic Emancipation.

[663]

1813   Visits Leigh Hunt in jail. Begins intimacy with Augusta. June, first of Oriental tales *The Giaour* published. December, *The Bride of Abydos* published.

1814   February, *The Corsair* published (10,000 copies sold on first day). August, *Lara* published; engagement to Miss Milbanke.

1815   January 2, marries Miss Milbanke and settles in London. April, *Hebrew Melodies* published. December 10, daughter Augusta Ada born.

1816   January 15, out of fear of her husband's "insanity" and following long period of abuse and insult, Lady Byron leaves London; rumors of incest now widespread. April, legal separation of the Byrons and departure for continent where Byron settles in Geneva with the Shelleys and Claire Clairmont, Mary Godwin's stepsister; writes *Childe Harold's Pilgrimage*, III, and *The Prisoner of Chillon* (published later in year). October, moves to Italy and settles in Venice, where he engages in life of dissipation; begins to compose *Manfred* (published 1817).

1817   January 12, Allegra, daughter of Byron and Claire, born. Travels to Florence and Rome in spring. Composes *Childe Harold's Pilgrimage*, IV, and *Beppo* (both published 1818).

1818   Begins to compose *Don Juan* (first two cantos published 1819).

1819   Becomes *cavalier servente* to Teresa, Countess Guiccoli of Ravenna, where Byron settles in December and gradually becomes involved with the Carboneria, political revolutionary movement. Writes *Letter to my Grandmother's Review* (published in Leigh Hunt's *Liberal*, 1822), in answer to review of *Don Juan* in the *British Review*.

1820   March, writes *Some Observations upon an Article in Blackwood's Magazine* (first published 1833), a defense of his character and an attack on the Lake Poets with a corresponding expression of admiration for Pope. July, Teresa is separated from her husband.

1821   *Letter to **** *******, the plays *Cain, Marino Faliero, The Two Foscari, Sardanapalus*, and further cantos of *Don Juan* published. October, leaves Ravenna for Pisa, where Teresa lives in exile with her father and brother.

1822   April, death of Allegra. July, arrival of the Leigh Hunt family and death of Shelley. Fall, moves to Genoa. October, *Vision of Judgment* published in the first number of Leigh Hunt's *The Liberal*.

1823   Further cantos of *Don Juan* published. July, sails to Greece in support of cause of independence; settles at Missolonghi, where he provides funds for military operations and supervises training and supplying of troops.

1824   April 19, dies of fever at Missolonghi.

SELECTED BIBLIOGRAPHY

BIOGRAPHY

MARCHAND, LESLIE A., *Byron: A Biography*, 3 vols., New York: Alfred A. Knopf, 1957.
———— *Byron: A Portrait*, New York: Alfred A. Knopf, 1970.

EDITIONS

CAMERON, KENNETH NEILL (ed.), *Shelley and his Circle 1773–1822* (see under *Editions* in Shelley Selected Bibliography) [contains letters and manuscripts of Byron, with detailed commentaries].
LOVELL, ERNEST J., JR. (ed.), *His Very Self and Voice: Collected Conversations of Lord Byron*, New York: Macmillan Publishing Co., Inc., 1954.

PROTHERO, ROWLAND E. (ed.), *The Works of Lord Byron: Letters and Journals*, 6 vols., London: John Murray, 1898–1901.

QUENNELL, PETER (ed.), *Byron: A Self-Portrait*, 2 vols., London: John Murray, 1950.

SCHOLARSHIP AND CRITICISM

ARNOLD, MATTHEW, "Byron," *Essays in Criticism*, Second Series, London: Macmillan, 1888.

BOSTETTER, EDWARD E., *The Romantic Ventriloquists*, Seattle: University of Washington Press, 1963.

CALVERT, WILLIAM J., *Byron: Romantic Paradox*, Chapel Hill: University of North Carolina Press, 1935.

ELIOT, T. S., "Byron," *On Poetry and Poets*, London: Faber and Faber, 1957 [first published 1937].

GLECKNER, ROBERT F., *Byron and the Ruins of Paradise*, Baltimore, Md.: Johns Hopkins Press, 1967.

GOODE, CLEMENT TYSON, *Byron as Critic*, Weimar: R. Wagner Sohn, 1923.

KNIGHT, G. WILSON, *Lord Byron, Christian Virtues*, London: Routledge and Kegan Paul, 1952.

LOVELL, ERNEST J., JR., *Byron: The Record of a Quest. Studies in a Poet's Concept and Treatment of Nature*, Austin: University of Texas Press, 1949.

MACAULAY, THOMAS B., review of Thomas Moore's *Letters and Journals of Lord Byron*, *Edinburgh Review*, LIII (1831), 544–72.

MARJARUM, EDWARD WAYNE, *Byron as Skeptic and Believer*, Princeton Studies in English, No. 16, Princeton, N.J.: Princeton University Press, 1938.

RAYMOND, DORA NEILL, *The Political Career of Lord Byron*, New York: Henry Holt and Company, 1924.

RUSSELL, BERTRAM, "Byron," *A History of Western Philosophy*, New York: Simon and Schuster, 1945.

WOODRING, CARL, *Politics in English Romantic Poetry*, Cambridge, Mass.: Harvard University Press, 1970.

LETTER TO **** ****** [JOHN MURRAY]

Byron's lifelong admiration for Pope and for "Augustan" standards of literary taste and judgment are given vigorous statement in his Letter of 1821, a lively contribution to one of the minor "battles of the books" in the early nineteenth century. The controversy had a considerable background. William Lisle Bowles, whose Sonnets (1789) had been such a significant influence on Coleridge (see Biographia Literaria, Chapter I), had published a ten-volume edition of The Works of Alexander Pope in 1806. In the chapter "General Observations on the Character of Pope" in the first volume, Bowles had been critical of the personal and moral character of the poet, especially "his predominant and insatiable love of praise" and "the strange mixture of indecent, and sometimes profane, levity, which his conduct and language often exhibited." Moreover, in his "Concluding Observations on the Poetical Character of Pope" in the final volume, Bowles had argued that although "none ever was his superior" in "powers of execution," Pope's choice of subject matter from artificial life and manners necessarily denied him a position among the first rank of poets. Bowles's standard of literary judgment was explicitly stated in the opening words of the "Concluding Observations:"

I presume it will readily be granted, that "all images drawn from what is beautiful or sublime in the works of NATURE, *are more beautiful and sublime than any images drawn from* ART;" *and that they are therefore, per se, more poetical.*

In like manner, those Passions *of the human heart, which belong to Nature in general, are* per se, *more adapted to the higher species of Poetry, than those which are derived from incidental and transient* MANNERS.

In his introductory "Essay on English Poetry" to Specimens of the British Poets *(1819), Thomas Campbell had argued against Bowles's standards and his assessment of Pope: "I would beg leave to observe, in the first place, that the faculty by which a poet luminously describes objects of art, is essentially the same faculty, which enables him to be a faithful describer of simple nature; in the second place, that nature and art are to a greater degree relative terms in poetical description than is generally recollected; and, thirdly, that artificial objects and manners are of so much importance in fiction, as to make the exquisite description of them no less characteristic of genius than the description of simple physical appearances.... Nature, in the wide and proper sense of the word, means life in all its circumstances— nature moral as well as external. As the subject of inspired fiction, nature includes artificial forms and manners."*

To this, Bowles replied in his Invariable Principles of Poetry *(1819), thus inaugurating a war of pamphlets that was to last until 1825. Byron had criticized Bowles's attack on Pope in* English Bards and Scotch Reviewers *(1809) and was drawn into the controversy a decade later "by the frequent recurrence of my name in the pamphlets." His Letter to **** ****** [John Murray] was published in March 1821, and went through three editions in that year. He also wrote a second* letter *"Observations on Observations,"* which was not published until *1832.*

For a history of the pamphlet war over Pope, see Jacob Johan van Rennes, Bowles, Byron and the Pope-Controversy (*Amsterdam: H. J. Paris, 1927*). Byron's Letter is here reproduced from the text of the second edition.

FROM

LETTER TO **** ****** [John Murray], ON THE REV. W. L. BOWLES' STRICTURES ON THE LIFE AND WRITINGS OF POPE

*   *   *   *   *

THE TRUTH is, that in these days the grand *"primum mobile"* of England is *cant;* cant political, cant poetical, cant religious, cant moral; but always cant, multiplied through all the varieties of life. It is the fashion, and while it lasts will be too powerful for those who can only exist by taking the tone of the time. I say *cant,* because it is a thing of words, without the smallest influence upon human actions; the English being no wiser, no better, and much poorer, and more divided amongst themselves, as well as far less moral, than they were before the prevalence of this verbal decorum. This hysterical horror of poor Pope's not very well ascertained, and never fully proved amours, (for even Cibber[1] owns that he prevented the somewhat perilous adventure in which Pope was embarking), sounds very virtuous in a controversial pamphlet; but all men of the world who know what life is, or at least what it was to them in their youth, must laugh at such a ludicrous foundation of the charge of "a libertine sort of love;" while the more serious will look upon those who bring forward such charges upon an insulated fact, as fanatics or hypocrites, perhaps both. The two are sometimes compounded in a happy mixture.

*   *   *   *   *

I now come to Mr. Bowles's "invariable principles of poetry." These Mr. Bowles and some of his correspondents pronounce "unanswerable;" and they are "unanswered," at least by Campbell, who seems to have been astounded by the title. The sultan of the time being offered to ally himself to a king of France, because "he hated the word league;" which proves that the Padishan understood French. Mr. Campbell has no need of my alliance, nor shall I presume to offer it; but I do hate that word *"invariable."* What is there of *human,* be it poetry, philosophy, wit, wis-

dom, science, power, glory, mind, matter, life, or death, which is *"invariable?"* Of course I put things divine out of the question. Of all arrogant baptisms of a book, this title to a pamphlet appears the most complacently conceited. It is Mr. Campbell's part to answer the contents of this performance, and especially to vindicate his own "Ship,"[2] which Mr. Bowles most triumphantly proclaims to have struck to his very first fire.

> "Quoth he, there was a *Ship;*
> Now let me go, thou grey-haired loon,
> Or my staff shall make thee skip."[3]

It is no affair of mine, but having once begun (certainly not by my own wish, but called upon by the frequent recurrence to my name in the pamphlets), I am like an Irishman in a "row," "anybody's customer." I shall therefore say a word or two on the "Ship."

Mr. Bowles asserts that Campbell's "Ship of the Line" derives all its poetry not from *"art,"* but from *"nature."* "Take away the waves, the winds, the sun, &c. &c. *one* will become a stripe of blue bunting; and the other a piece of coarse canvas on three tall poles." Very true; take away the "waves," "the winds," and there will be no ship at all, not only for poetical, but for any other purpose; and take away "the sun," and we must read Mr. Bowles's pamphlet by candle-light. But the "poetry" of the "Ship" does *not* depend on "the waves," &c.; on the contrary, the "Ship of the Line" confers its own poetry upon the waters, and heightens *theirs.* I do not deny, that the "waves and winds," and above all "the sun," are highly poetical; we know it to our cost, by the many descriptions of them in verse: but if the waves bore only the foam upon their bosoms, if the winds wafted only the sea-weed to the shore, if the sun shone neither upon pyramids, nor fleets, nor fortresses, would its beams be equally poetical? I think not: the poetry is at least reciprocal. Take away "the Ship of the Line" "swinging round" the "calm water," and the calm water becomes a somewhat monotonous thing to look at, particularly if not transparently *clear;* witness the thousands who pass by without looking on it at all. What was it attracted the thousands to the launch? they might have seen the poetical "calm water" at Wapping, or in the "London Dock," or in the Paddington Canal, or in a horse-pond, or in a slop-basin, or in any other vase. They might have heard the

---

[1] Colley Cibber (1671–1757).

[2] Campbell had offered the launching of a ship of the line as another example "of the sublime objects of artificial life."

[3] See Coleridge's "Rime of the Ancient Mariner," ll. 10–12 in the reading of the 1798 edition of *Lyrical Ballads.*

poetical winds howling through the chinks of a pigsty, or the garret window; they might have seen the sun shining on a footman's livery, or on a brass warming-pan; but could the "calm water," or the "wind," or the "sun," make all, or any of these "poetical?" I think not. Mr. Bowles admits "the Ship" to be poetical, but only from those accessaries: now if they *confer* poetry so as to make one thing poetical, they would make other things poetical; the more so, as Mr. Bowles calls a "ship of the line" without them, that is to say, its "masts and sails and streamers," "blue bunting," and "coarse canvas," and "tall poles." So they are; and porcelain is clay, and man is dust, and flesh is grass, and yet the two latter at least are the subjects of much poesy.

Did Mr. Bowles ever gaze upon the sea? I presume that he has, at least upon a sea-piece. Did any painter ever paint the sea *only*, without the addition of a ship, boat, wreck, or some such adjunct? Is the sea itself a more attractive, a more moral, a more poetical object, with or without a vessel, breaking its vast but fatiguing monotony? Is a storm more poetical without a ship? or, in the poem of the Shipwreck,[4] is it the storm or the ship which most interests? both *much* undoubtedly; but without the vessel, what should we care for the tempest? It would sink into mere descriptive poetry, which in itself was never esteemed a high order of that art.

I look upon myself as entitled to talk of naval matters, at least to poets:—with the exception of Walter Scott, Moore, and Southey, perhaps, who have been voyagers, I have *swam* more miles than all the rest of them together now living ever *sailed*, and have lived for months and months on shipboard; and, during the whole period of my life abroad, have scarcely ever passed a month out of sight of the ocean: besides being brought up from two years till ten on the brink of it. I recollect, when anchored off Cape Sigeum in 1810, in an English frigate, a violent squall coming on at sunset, so violent as to make us imagine that the ship would part cable, or drive from her anchorage. Mr. Hobhouse and myself, and some officers, had been up the Dardanelles to Abydos, and were just returned in time. The aspect of a storm in the Archipelago is as poetical as need be, the sea being particularly short, dashing, and dangerous, and the navigation intricate and broken by the isles and currents. Cape Sigeum, the tumuli of the Troad, Lemnos, Tenedos, all added to the associations of the time. But what seemed the most "*poetical*" of all at the moment, were the numbers (about two hundred)

of Greek and Turkish craft, which were obliged to "cut and run" before the wind, from their unsafe anchorage, some for Tenedos, some for other isles, some for the main, and some it might be for eternity. The sight of these little scudding vessels, darting over the foam in the twilight, now appearing and now disappearing between the waves in the cloud of night, with their peculiarly *white* sails, (the Levant sails not being of "*coarse canvas*," but of white cotton), skimming along as quickly, but less safely than the sea-mews which hovered over them; their evident distress, their reduction to fluttering specks in the distance, their crowded succession, their *littleness*, as contending with the giant element, which made our stout forty-four's *teak* timbers, (she was built in India), creak again; their aspect and their motion, all struck me as something far more "poetical" than the mere broad, brawling, shipless sea, and the sullen winds, could possibly have been without them.

The Euxine is a noble sea to look upon, and the port of Constantinople the most beautiful of harbours, and yet I cannot but think that the twenty sail of the line, some of one hundred and forty guns, rendered it more "poetical" by day in the sun, and by night perhaps still more, for the Turks illuminate their vessels of war in a manner the most picturesque, and yet all this is *artificial*. As for the Euxine, I stood upon the Symplegades—I stood by the broken altar still exposed to the winds upon one of them—I felt all the "*poetry*" of the situation, as I repeated the first lines of Medea;[5] but would not that "poetry" have been heightened by the *Argo*? It was so even by the appearance of any merchant vessel arriving from Odessa. But Mr. Bowles says, "why bring your ship off the stocks?" for no reason that I know, except that ships are built to be launched. The water, &c. undoubtedly HEIGHTENS the poetical associations, but it does not *make* them; and the ship amply repays the obligation: they aid each other; the water is more poetical with the ship—the ship less so without the water. But even a ship, laid up in dock, is a grand and a poetical sight. Even an old boat, keel upwards, wrecked upon the barren sand, is a "poetical" object; (and Wordsworth, who made a poem about a washing-tub and a blind boy, may tell you so as well as I),[6] whilst a long extent of sand and unbroken water, without the boat, would be as like dull prose as any pamphlet lately published.

---

4 Popular poem of 1762 by William Falconer (1732–1769), describing the wreck of a ship on the coast of Greece.

5 "Ah! would to Heaven the good ship Argo ne'er had sped its course to the Colchian land through the misty blue Symplegades . . ." (E. P. Coleridge translation of Euripides' tragedy).

6 Byron refers to Wordsworth's poem "The Blind Highland Boy" (1807).

What makes the poetry in the image of the "*marble waste of Tadmor*," of Grainger's "Ode to Solitude," so much admired by Johnson?[7] It is the "*marble*," or the "*waste*," the *artificial* or the *natural* object? The "*waste*" is like all other *wastes;* but the "*marble*" of Palmyra makes the poetry of the passage as of the place.

The beautiful but barren Hymettus, the whole coast of Attica, her hills and mountains, Pentelicus, Anchesmus, Philopappus, &c. &c., are in themselves poetical, and would be so if the name of Athens, of Athenians, and her very ruins, were swept from the earth. But am I to be told that the "nature" of Attica would be *more* poetical without the "art" of the Acropolis? of the Temple of Theseus? and of the still all Greek and glorious monuments of her exquisitely artificial genius? Ask the traveller what strikes him as most poetical, the Parthenon, or the rock on which it stands? The COLUMNS of Cape Colonna, or the Cape itself? The rocks at the foot of it, or the recollection that Falconer's *ship* was bulged upon them? There are a thousand rocks and capes, far more picturesque than those of the Acropolis and Cape Sunium in themselves; what are they to a thousand scenes in the wilder parts of Greece, of Asia Minor, Switzerland, or even of Cintra in Portugal, or to many scenes of Italy, and the Sierras of Spain? But it is the "*art*," the columns, the temples, the wrecked vessel, which give them their antique and their modern poetry, and not the spots themselves. Without them, the *spots* of earth would be unnoticed and unknown; buried, like Babylon and Nineveh, in indistinct confusion, without poetry, as without existence; but to whatever spot of earth these ruins were transported, if they were *capable* of transportation, like the obelisk and the sphinx, and the Memnon's head, *there* they would still exist in the perfection of their beauty, and in the pride of their poetry. I opposed, and will ever oppose, the robbery of ruins from Athens, to instruct the English in sculpture; but why did I do so? The *ruins* are as poetical in Piccadilly as they were in the Parthenon; but the Parthenon and its rock are less so without them. Such is the poetry of art.

Mr. Bowles contends again that the pyramids of Egypt are poetical, because of "the association with boundless deserts," and that a "pyramid of the same dimensions" would not be sublime in "Lincoln's Inn Fields:" not *so* poetical certainly; but take away the "pyramids," and what is the "*desert?*" Take away Stone-henge from Salisbury plain, and it is nothing more than Hounslow heath, or any other uninclosed down. It appears to me that St. Peter's, the Coliseum, the Pantheon, the Palatine, the Apollo, the Laocoon, the Venus di Medicis, the Hercules, the dying Gladiator, the Moses of Michael Angelo, and all the higher works of Canova,[8] (I have already spoken of those of ancient Greece, still extant in that country, or transported to England), are as *poetical* as Mont Blanc or Mount Ætna, perhaps still more so, as they are direct manifestations of mind, and *presuppose* poetry in their very conception; and have moreover, as being such, a something of actual life, which cannot belong to any part of inanimate nature, unless we adopt the system of Spinosa, that the world is the Deity. There can be nothing more poetical in its aspect than the city of Venice: does this depend upon the sea, or the canals?—

"The dirt and sea-weed whence proud Venice rose?"[9]

Is it the canal which runs between the palace and the prison, or the "Bridge of Sighs," which connects them, that render it poetical? Is it the "Canal' Grande," or the Rialto which arches it, the churches which tower over it, the palaces which line, and the gondolas which glide over the waters, that render this city more poetical than Rome itself? Mr. Bowles will say perhaps, that the Rialto is but marble, the palaces and churches only stone, and the gondolas a "coarse" black cloth, thrown over some planks of carved wood, with a shining bit of fantastically formed iron at the prow, "*without*" the water. And I tell him that without these, the water would be nothing but a clay-coloured ditch, and whoever says the contrary, deserves to be at the bottom of that, where Pope's heroes are embraced by the mud nymphs.[10] There would be nothing to make the canal of Venice more poetical than that of Paddington, were it not for the artificial adjuncts above-mentioned, although it is a perfectly natural canal, formed by the sea, and the innumerable islands which constitute the site of this extraordinary city.

The very Cloacae of Tarquin at Rome are as poetical as Richmond Hill;[11] many will think more

---

7 See Boswell's *Life of Johnson*, entry for September 23, 1777. The phrase "Tadmor's marble wastes" occurs in l. 9 of James Grainger's poem, first published in the 1755 edition of Richard Dodsley's *A Collection of Poems. By Several Hands.* Tadmor is the original Arabic name for the once magnificent city of Palmyra in Syria.

8 Antonio Canova (1757–1822) was a leading Italian neoclassic sculptor.

9 Pope's *Essay on Man*, IV, 292.

10 See *Dunciad*, II, 331–46.

11 The Cloacae were the great sewers constructed by Tarquinius Priscus (616–578 B.C.), legendary king of ancient Rome. Richmond Hill (in Richmond Park, near London) was a famous and fashionable prospect-point for viewing the Thames and the surrounding landscape.

so: take away Rome, and leave the Tibur and the seven hills, in the nature of Evander's time.[12] Let Mr. Bowles, or Mr. Wordsworth, or Mr. Southey, or any of the other "naturals," make a poem upon them, and then see which is most poetical, their production, or the commonest guide-book, which tells you the road from St. Peter's to the Coliseum, and informs you what you will see by the way. The ground interests in Virgil, because it *will* be *Rome*, and not because it is Evander's rural domain.

Mr. Bowles then proceeds to press Homer into his service, in answer to a remark of Mr. Campbell's, that "Homer was a great describer of works of art." Mr. Bowles contends that all his great power, even in this, depends upon their connexion with nature. The "shield of Achilles derives its poetical interest from the subjects described on it." And from what does the *spear* of Achilles derive its interest? and the helmet and the mail worn by Patroclus, and the celestial armour, and the very brazen greaves of the well-booted Greeks? Is it solely from the legs, and the back, and the breast, and the human body, which they enclose? In that case, it would have been more poetical to have made them fight naked; and Gulley and Gregson, as being nearer to a state of nature, are more poetical boxing in a pair of drawers than Hector and Achilles in radiant armour, and with heroic weapons.[13]

Instead of the clash of helmets, and the rushing of chariots, and the whizzing of spears, and the glancing of swords, and the cleaving of shields, and the piercing of breastplates, why not represent the Greeks and Trojans like two savage tribes, tugging and tearing, and kicking, and biting, and gnashing, foaming, grinning, and gouging, in all the poetry of martial nature, unincumbered with gross, prosaic, artificial arms, an equal superfluity to the natural warrior, and his natural poet. Is there anything unpoetical in Ulysses striking the horses of Rhesus with *his bow*, (having forgotten his thong),[14] or would Mr. Bowles have had him kick them with his foot, or smack them with his hand, as being more unsophisticated?

In Gray's Elegy, is there an image more striking than his "shapeless sculpture?"[15] Of sculpture in general, it may be observed, that it is more poetical than nature itself, inasmuch as it represents and bodies forth that ideal beauty and sublimity which is never to be found in actual nature. This at least is the general opinion. But, always excepting the Venus di Medicis, I differ from that opinion, at least as far as regards female beauty; for the head of Lady Charlemont,[16] (when I first saw her nine years ago), seemed to possess all that sculpture could require for its ideal. I recollect seeing something of the same kind in the head of an Albanian girl, who was actually employed in mending a road in the mountains, and in some Greek, and one or two Italian, faces. But of *sublimity*, I have never seen any thing in human nature at all to approach the expression of sculpture, either in the Apollo, the Moses, or other of the sterner works of ancient or modern art.

Let us examine a little further this "babble of green fields"[17] and of bare nature in general as superior to artificial imagery, for the poetical purposes of the fine arts. In landscape painting, the great artist does not give you a literal copy of a country, but he invents and composes one. Nature, in her actual aspect, does not furnish him with such existing scenes as he requires. Even where he presents you with some famous city, or celebrated scene from mountain or other nature, it must be taken from some particular point of view, and with such light, and shade, and distance, &c. as serve not only to heighten its beauties, but to shadow its deformities. The poetry of Nature alone, *exactly* as she appears, is not sufficient to bear him out. The very sky of his painting is not the *portrait* of the sky of Nature; it is a composition of different *skies*, observed at different times, and not the whole copied from any *particular* day. And why? Because Nature is not lavish of her beauties; they are widely scattered, and occasionally displayed, to be selected with care, and gathered with difficulty.

Of sculpture I have just spoken. It is the great scope of the sculptor to heighten Nature into heroic beauty, *i. e.* in plain English, to surpass his model. When Canova forms a statue, he takes a limb from one, a hand from another, a feature from a third, and a shape, it may be, from a fourth, probably at the same time improving upon all, as the Greek of old did in embodying his Venus.

Ask a portrait painter to describe his agonies in accommodating the faces with which Nature and his sitters have crowded his painting-room to the principles of his art: with the exception of perhaps ten faces in as many millions, there is not one which he

---

[12] See *Aeneid*, VIII. The ally of Aeneas in Italy, Evander had been exiled from his kingdom of Arcadia and had occupied the land that was to become the city of Rome.

[13] John Gulley (1783–1863) and Bob Gregson (1778–1824), "the Lancashire giant," had met in two remarkable matches in 1807–08.

[14] See *Iliad*, X, 500–501.

[15] L. 79.

[16] Anne Bermingham (d. 1876), wife of the second Earl of Charlemont, and one of "the Blues," pretentiously literary ladies in London society.

[17] *Henry the Fifth*, II, iii, 17.

can venture to give without shading much and adding more. Nature, exactly, simply, barely Nature, will make no great artist of any kind, and least of all a poet—the most artificial, perhaps, of all artists in his very essence. With regard to natural imagery, the poets are obliged to take some of their best illustrations from *art*. You say that a "fountain is as clear or clearer than *glass*," to express its beauty—

"O fons Bandusiæ, splendidior vitro!"[18]

In the speech of Mark Antony, the body of Cæsar is displayed, but so also is his *mantle*:

"You all do know this *mantle*," &c.

———　———

"Look! in this place ran Cassius' *dagger* through."[19]

If the poet had said that Cassius had run his *fist* through the rent of the mantle, it would have had more of Mr. Bowles's "nature" to help it; but the artificial *dagger* is more poetical than any natural *hand* without it. In the sublime of sacred poetry, "Who is this that cometh from Edom? with *dyed garments* from Bozrah?"[20] Would "the comer" be poetical without his "*dyed garments?*" which strike and startle the spectator, and identify the approaching object.

The mother of Sisera is represented listening for the "*wheels of his chariot.*"[21] Solomon, in his Song, compares the nose of his beloved to "a tower,"[22] which to us appears an eastern exaggeration. If he had said, that her stature was like that of a "tower's," it would have been as poetical as if he had compared her to a tree.

"The virtuous Marcia *towers* above her sex"[23]

is an instance of an artificial image to express a *moral* superiority. But Solomon, it is probable, did not compare his beloved's nose to a "tower" on account of its length, but of its symmetry; and making allowance for eastern hyperbole, and the difficulty of finding a discreet image for a female nose in nature, it is perhaps as good a figure as any other.

Art is *not* inferior to nature for poetical purposes. What makes a regiment of soldiers a more noble object of view than the same mass of mob? Their arms, their dresses, their banners, and the *art* and artificial symmetry of their position and movements. A Highlander's plaid, a Mussulman's turban, and a Roman toga, are more poetical than the tattooed or untattooed buttocks of a New Sandwich savage, although they were described by William Wordsworth himself like the "idiot in his glory."

I have seen as many mountains as most men, and more fleets than the generality of landsmen; and to my mind, a large convoy with a few sail of the line to conduct them, is as noble and as poetical a prospect as all that inanimate nature can produce. I prefer the "mast of some great ammiral," with all its tackle, to the Scotch fir or the alpine tannen; and think that *more* poetry *has been* made out of it. In what does the infinite superiority of "Falconer's Shipwreck" over all other shipwrecks consist? In his admirable application of the terms of his art; in a poet-sailor's description of the sailor's fate. These *very terms*, by his application, make the strength and reality of his poem. Why? because he was a poet, and in the hands of a poet *art* will not be found less ornamental than nature. It is precisely in general nature, and in stepping out of his element, that Falconer fails; where he digresses to speak of ancient Greece, and "such branches of learning."

In Dyer's Grongar Hill,[24] upon which his fame rests, the very appearance of nature herself is moralized into an artificial image:

"Thus is nature's *vesture* wrought,
　　To instruct our wandering thought;
Thus she *dresses green and gay*,
　　To disperse our cares away."

And here also we have the telescope; the misuse of which, from Milton, has rendered Mr. Bowles so triumphant over Mr. Campbell:

"So we mistake the future's face,
　　Eyed through Hope's deluding *glass*."

And here a word en passant to Mr. Campbell:

"As yon summits, soft and fair,
　　Clad in colours of the air,
Which to those who journey near
　　Barren, brown, and rough appear,
Still we tread the same coarse way—
　　The present's still a cloudy day."

Is not this the original of the far-famed—

"'Tis distance lends enchantment to the view,
　　And robes the mountain in its azure hue?"[25]

[18] Horace's *Odes*, III, xiii, 1.
[19] *Julius Cæsar*, III, ii, 174, 178.
[20] Isaiah, lxiii, 1.　　　[21] Judges, v, 28.
[22] The Song of Solomon, vii, 4.
[23] Addison's tragedy, *Cato*, I, iv.

[24] *Grongar Hill* was a popular loco-descriptive poem of 1726, by John Dyer (1699–1757). Byron quotes ll. 99–102, 121–22, 123–28.
[25] Thomas Campbell's *The Pleasures of Hope* (1799), I, 7–8.

To return once more to the sea. Let any one look on the long wall of Malamocco,[26] which curbs the Adriatic, and pronounce between the sea and its master. Surely that Roman work, (I mean *Roman* in conception and performance), which says to the ocean, "thus far shalt thou come, and no further,"[27] and is obeyed, is not less sublime and poetical than the angry waves which vainly break beneath it.

Mr. Bowles makes the chief part of a ship's poesy depend upon the "*wind :*" then why is a ship under sail more poetical than a hog in a high wind? The hog is all nature, the ship is all art, "coarse canvas," "blue bunting," and "tall poles;" both are violently acted upon by the wind, tossed here and there, to and fro, and yet nothing but excess of hunger could make me look upon the pig as the more poetical of the two, and then only in the shape of a griskin.

Will Mr. Bowles tell us that the poetry of an aqueduct consists in the *water* which it conveys? Let him look on that of Justinian, on those of Rome, Constantinople, Lisbon, and Elvas, or even at the remains of that in Attica.

We are asked, "what makes the venerable towers of Westminster Abbey more poetical, as objects, than the tower for the manufactory of patent shot, surrounded by the same scenery?" I will answer—the *architecture.* Turn Westminster Abbey, or Saint Paul's, into a powder magazine, their poetry, as objects, remains the same; the Parthenon was actually converted into one by the Turks, during Morosini's[28] Venetian siege, and part of it destroyed in consequence. Cromwell's dragoons stalled their steeds in Worcester cathedral; was it less poetical as an object than before? Ask a foreigner of his approach to London, what strikes him as the most poetical of the towers before him: he will point out Saint Paul's and Westminster Abbey, without, perhaps, knowing the names or associations of either, and pass over the "tower for patent shot," not that for any thing he knows to the contrary, it might not be the mausoleum of a monarch, or a Waterloo column, or a Trafalgar monument, but because its architecture is obviously inferior.

To the question, "whether the description of a game of cards be as poetical, supposing the execution of the artists equal, as a description of a walk in a forest?" it may be answered, that the *materials* are certainly not equal; but that "the *artist,*" who has rendered the "game of cards poetical," is *by far the greater* of the two. But all this "ordering" of poets is purely arbitrary on the part of Mr. Bowles. There may or may not be, in fact, different "orders" of poetry, but the poet is always ranked according to his execution, and not according to his branch of the art.

Tragedy is one of the highest presumed orders. Hughes has written a tragedy, and a very successful one; Fenton[29] another; and Pope none. Did any man, however,—will even Mr. Bowles himself, rank Hughes and Fenton as poets above *Pope?* Was even Addison, (the author of Cato), or Rowe, (one of the higher order of dramatists as far as success goes), or Young, or even Otway and Southerne,[30] ever raised for a moment to the same rank with Pope in the estimation of the reader or the critic, before his death or since? If Mr. Bowles will contend for classifications of this kind, let him recollect that descriptive poetry has been ranked as among the lowest branches of the art, and description as a mere ornament, but which should never form "the subject" of a poem. The Italians, with the most poetical language, and the most fastidious taste in Europe, possess now five *great* poets, they say, Dante, Petrarch, Ariosto, Tasso, and lastly Alfieri; and whom do they esteem one of the highest of these, and some of them the very highest? Petrarch the *sonneteer:* it is true that some of his Canzoni are *not less* esteemed, but *not* more; who ever dreams of his Latin Africa?[31]

Were Petrarch to be ranked according to the "order" of his compositions, where would the best of sonnets place him? with Dante and the others? no; but, as I have before said, the poet who *executes* best, is the highest, whatever his department, and will ever be so rated in the world's esteem.

Had Gray written nothing but his Elegy, high as he stands, I am not sure that he would not stand higher; it is the corner-stone of his glory: without it, his odes would be insufficient for his fame. The depreciation of Pope is partly founded upon a false idea of the dignity of his order of poetry, to which he has partly contributed by the ingenuous boast,

---

[26] In the Venetian lagoon.

[27] Job, xxxviii, 11.

[28] Francesco Morosini (1618–1694) was the famous commander-in-chief of the Venetian navy during the wars with the Turkish Empire.

[29] John Hughes was the author of the popular tragedy *The Siege of Damascus* (1720). Elizah Fenton was the author of *Mariamne* (1723).

[30] Nicholas Rowe (1674–1718) was the author of *The Fair Penitent* (1703), *Jane Shore* (1715), and other tragedies. Edward Young (1683–1765) wrote the poem *Night Thoughts* (1742–1746) and two plays *Busiris* (1719) and *The Revenge* (1721). Thomas Otway (1652–1685) was the author of the eminent Restoration tragedy *Venice Preserved* (1682) and other plays. Thomas Southerne (1660–1746) was the author of the tragedies *The Fatal Marriage* (1694) and *Oroonoko* (1696).

[31] Referring to Petrarch's epic poem on the Second Punic War.

"That not in fancy's maze he wandered long,
    But *stoop'd* to truth, and moralized his song." [32]

He should have written "rose to truth." In my mind the highest of all poetry is ethical poetry, as the highest of all earthly objects must be moral truth. Religion does not make a part of my subject; it is something beyond human powers, and has failed in all human hands except Milton's and Dante's, and even Dante's powers are involved in his delineation of human passions, though in supernatural circumstances. What made Socrates the greatest of men? His moral truth—his ethics. What proved Jesus Christ the Son of God hardly less than his miracles? His moral precepts. And if ethics have made a philosopher the first of men, and have not been disdained as an adjunct to his Gospel by the Deity himself, are we to be told that ethical poetry, or didactic poetry, or by whatever name you term it, whose object is to make men better and wiser, is not the *very first order* of poetry; and are we to be told this too by one of the priesthood? It requires more mind, more wisdom, more power, than all the "forests" that ever were "walked" for their "description," and all the epics that ever were founded upon fields of battle. The Georgics are indisputably, and, I believe, *undisputedly* even a finer poem than the Æneid. Virgil knew this; he did not order *them* to be burnt. [33]

"The proper study of mankind is man."

It is the fashion of the day to lay great stress upon what they call "imagination" and "invention," the two commonest of qualities: an Irish peasant with a little whiskey in his head will imagine and invent more than would furnish forth a modern poem. If Lucretius had not been spoiled by the Epicurean system, we should have had a far superior poem to any now in existence. As mere poetry, it is the first of Latin poems. What then has ruined it? His ethics. Pope has not this defect; his moral is as pure as his poetry is glorious.

*   *   *   *   *

The attempt of the poetical populace of the present day to obtain an ostracism against Pope is as easily accounted for as the Athenians' shell against Aristides; they are tired of hearing him always called "the

Just." [34] They are also fighting for life; for if he maintains his station, they will reach their own by falling. They have raised a mosque by the side of a Grecian temple of the purest architecture; and, more barbarous than the barbarians from whose practice I have borrowed the figure, they are not contented with their own grotesque edifice, unless they destroy the prior and purely beautiful fabric which preceded, and which shames them and theirs for ever and ever. I shall be told that amongst those I *have* been (or it may be, still *am*) conspicuous—true, and I am ashamed of it. I *have* been amongst the builders of this Babel, attended by a confusion of tongues, but *never* amongst the envious destroyers of the classic temple of our predecessor. I have loved and honoured the fame and name of that illustrious and unrivalled man, far more than my own paltry renown, and the trashy jingle of the crowd of "Schools" and upstarts, who pretend to rival, or even surpass him. Sooner than a single leaf should be torn from his laurel, it were better that all which these men, and that I, as one of their set, have ever written, should

"Line trunks, clothe spice, or, fluttering in a row,
    Befringe the rails of Bedlam, or Soho!" [35]

There are those who will believe this, and those who will not. You, sir, know how far I am sincere, and whether my opinion, not only in the short work intended for publication, and in private letters which can never be published, has or has not been the same. I look upon this as the declining age of English poetry; no regard for others, no selfish feeling, can prevent me from seeing this, and expressing the truth. There can be no worse sign for the taste of the times than the depreciation of Pope. It would be better to receive for proof Mr. Cobbett's rough but strong attack upon Shakspeare and Milton, than to allow this smooth and "candid" undermining of the reputation of the most *perfect* of our poets, and the purest of our moralists. Of his power in the *passions*, in description, in the mock heroic, I leave others to descant. I take him on his strong ground, as an *ethical* poet: in the former none excel; in the mock heroic and the ethical, none

---

[32] "Epistle to Dr. Arbuthnot," ll. 340–41.

[33] A reference to Virgil's supposed order at the time of his death for the destruction of the manuscript of the *Aeneid*, which he considered incomplete and unsatisfactory. The poetic quotation which follows is from Pope's *Essay on Man*, II, 2.

[34] The reference is explained by a passage in Plutarch's Life of Aristides, Athenian statesman (c. 530–468 B.C.) of remarkable honesty and integrity. His political opponents first spread the rumor that Aristides intended to assume all power, then started a move for ostracism by having each citizen write on a piece of pottery (a shell) the name of the man they wished to see banished. An illiterate citizen, who did not recognize Aristides, came up to him and asked him to write "Aristides" on his shell. When the statesman asked why that name was to be written, the citizen replied that he was "tired of hearing him always called 'the Just.'"

[35] Pope's "The First Epistle to the Second Book of Horace" (1737), ll. 418–19.

equal him; and in my mind, the latter is the highest of all poetry, because it does that in *verse*, which the greatest of men have wished to accomplish in prose. If the essence of poetry must be a *lie*, throw it to the dogs, or banish it from your republic, as Plato would have done. He who can reconcile poetry with truth and wisdom, is the only true "*poet*" in its real sense, "the maker," "the *creator*"—why must this mean the "liar," the "feigner," the "tale teller?" A man may make and create better things than these.

I shall not presume to say that Pope is as high a poet as Shakspeare and Milton, though his enemy, Warton,[36] places him immediately under them. I would not more say this than I would assert in the mosque (once Saint Sophia's), that Socrates was a greater man than Mahomet. But if I say that he is very near them, it is no more than has been asserted of Burns, who is supposed

"To rival all but Shakspeare's name below."

I say nothing against this opinion. But of what "*order*," according to the poetical aristocracy, are Burns's poems? There are his *opus magnum*, "Tam O'Shanter," a *tale*, the Cotter's Saturday Night, a descriptive sketch; some others in the same style; the rest are songs. So much for the *rank* of his *productions;* the *rank* of *Burns* is the very first of his art. Of Pope I have expressed my opinion elsewhere, as also of the effect which the present attempts at poetry have had upon our literature. If any great national or natural convulsion could or should overwhelm your country in such sort, as to sweep Great Britain from the kingdoms of the earth, and leave only that, after all the most living of human things, a *dead language*, to be studied and read, and imitated by the wise of future and far generations, upon foreign shores; if your literature should become the learning of mankind, divested of party cabals, temporary fashions, and national pride and prejudice; an Englishman, anxious that the posterity of strangers should know that there had been such a thing as a British Epic and Tragedy, might wish for the preservation of Shakspeare and Milton; but the surviving world would snatch Pope from the wreck, and let the rest sink with the people. He is the moral poet of all civilization; and as such, let us hope that he will one day be the national poet of mankind. He is the only poet that never shocks; the only poet whose *faultlessness* has been made his reproach. Cast your eye over his productions; consider their extent, and contemplate their variety:—pastoral,

passion, mock-heroic, translation, satire, ethics,—all excellent, and often perfect. If his great charm be his *melody*, how comes it that foreigners adore him even in their diluted translations? But I have made this letter too long. Give my compliments to Mr. Bowles.

Yours ever, very truly,
BYRON.

To
John Murray, Esq.

[1821]

DETACHED THOUGHTS

"Detached Thoughts" was a series of observations that Byron wrote beginning in Ravenna on October 15, 1821; he had reached No. 119 by the end of the year, and a final "thought" was added in May 1822. The series was taken to England in June by his friend Lord Clare for his publisher John Murray and was intended to be supplementary to his "Memoirs" written earlier. With the destruction of the "Memoirs" following his death, "Detached Thoughts" has become an important record of Byron's reflections on some of the major events of his life and a fascinating index of his literary, political, and philosophical opinions. The series was not published complete before its appearance in Volume V (1900) of the Rowland E. Prothero edition, The Works of Lord Byron: Letters and Journals, 6 vols. (London: John Murray, 1898–1901), which text is here followed.

FROM

DETACHED THOUGHTS

Oct^r· 15th· 1821.

I HAVE been thinking over the other day on the various comparisons, good or evil, which I have seen published of myself in different journals English and foreign. This was suggested to me by accidentally turning over a foreign one lately; for I have made it a rule latterly never to *search* for anything of the kind, but not to avoid the perusal if presented by Chance.

To begin then—I have seen myself compared personally or poetically, in English, French, *German* (*as* interpreted to me), Italian, and Portuguese, within these nine years, to Rousseau—Göethe—Young—Aretino—Timon of Athens—"An Alabaster Vase lighted up within"—Satan—Shakespeare—Buonaparte—Tiberius—Aeschylus—Sophocles—Euripides—Harlequin—The Clown—Sternhold and Hopkins—to the Phantasmagoria—to Henry the 8th—to Chenies—to Mirabeau—to young R. Dallas (the Schoolboy)—to Michel Angelo—to Raphael—to a *petit maître*—to Diogenes—to Childe Harold—to Lara—to the Count in Beppo—to Milton—to Pope—to Dryden—to Burns—to Savage—to Chatterton—to "oft have I

---

[36] Joseph Warton's *Essay on the Genius and Writings of Pope* (1756–1782) concluded its assessment of the poet by placing him "*next to Milton, and just above Dryden.*"

heard of thee my Lord Biron" in Shakespeare [1]—to Churchill the poet—to Kean the Actor—to Alfieri, etc., etc., etc. The likeness to Alfieri was asserted very seriously by an Italian, who had known him in his younger days: it of course related merely to our apparent personal dispositions. He did not assert it to *me* (for we were not then good friends), but in society.

The Object of so many contradictory comparisons must probably be like something different from them all; but what *that* is, is more than *I* know, or any body else.

My Mother, before I was twenty, would have it that I was like Rousseau, and Madame de Staël used to say so too in 1813, and the *Edin*[h]. *Review* has something of the sort in its critique on the 4th Canto of *Ch*[e]. Ha[d].[2] I can't see any point of resemblance: he wrote prose, I verse: he was of the people, I of the Aristocracy: he was a philosopher, I am none: he published his first work at forty, I mine at eighteen: his first essay brought him universal applause, mine the contrary: he married his housekeeper, I could not keep house with my wife: he thought all the world in a plot against *him*, my little world seems to think *me* in a plot against it, if I may judge by their abuse in print and coterie: he liked Botany, I like flowers, and herbs, and trees, but know nothing of their pedigrees: he wrote Music, I limit my knowledge of it to what I catch by *Ear*—I never could learn any thing by *study*, not even a language, it was all by rote and ear and memory: he had a bad memory, I *had* at least an excellent one (ask Hodgson the poet,[3] a good judge, for he has an astonishing one): he wrote with hesitation and care, I with rapidity and rarely with pains: *he* could never ride nor swim "nor was cunning of fence," *I* am an excellent swimmer, a decent though not at all a dashing rider (having staved in a rib at eighteen in the course of scampering), and was sufficient of fence—particularly of the Highland broadsword; not a bad boxer when I could keep my temper, which was difficult, but which I strove to do ever since I knocked down Mr. Purling and put his knee-pan out (with the gloves on) in Angelo's and Jackson's rooms in 1806 during the sparring; and I was besides a very fair cricketer—one of the Harrow Eleven when we play[ed] against Eton in 1805. Besides, Rousseau's way of life, his country, his manners, his whole character, were so very different, that I am at a

loss to conceive how such a comparison could have arisen, as it has done three several times, and all in rather a remarkable manner. I forgot to say, that *he* was also short-sighted, and that hitherto my eyes have been the contrary to such a degree, that, in the largest theatre of Bologna, I distinguished and read some busts and inscriptions painted near the stage, from a box so distant, and so *darkly* lighted, that none of the company (composed of young and very bright-eyed people—some of them in the same box) could make out a letter, and thought it was a trick, though I had never been in that theatre before.

Altogether, I think myself justified in thinking the comparison not well founded. I don't say this out of pique, for Rousseau was a great man, and the thing if true were flattering enough; but I have no idea of being pleased with a chimera.

10.

Sheridan's liking for me (whether he was not mystifying me I do not know; but Lady C[e]. L. and others told me he said the same both before and after he knew me) was founded upon *English Bards and S. Reviewers*. He told me that he did not care about poetry (or about mine—at least, any but *that* poem of mine), but he was sure, from *that* and other symptoms, I should make an Orator, if I would but take to speaking, and grow a parliament man. He never ceased harping upon this to me, to the last; and I remembered my old tutor Dr. Drury[4] had the same notion when I was a *boy*: but it never was my turn of inclination to try. I spoke once or twice as all young peers do, as a kind of introduction into public life; but dissipation, shyness, haughty and reserved opinions, together with the short time I lived in England—after my majority (only about five years in all)—prevented me from resuming the experiment. As far as it went, it was not discouraging—particularly my *first* speech[5] (I spoke three or four times in all); but just after it my poem of *C*[e]. *H*[d]. was published, and nobody ever thought about my *prose* afterwards: nor indeed did I; it became to me a secondary and neglected object, though I sometimes wonder to myself *if* I should have succeeded?

11.

The Impression of Parliament upon me was that its members are not formidable as *Speakers*, but very much so as an *audience*; because in so numerous a

---

[1] *Love's Labours Lost*, V, ii, 850.
[2] Byron refers to the review of 1818 by John Wilson reproduced in the section on Reviewers, pp. 796–804.
[3] Francis Hodgson (1781–1852), friend of Byron from 1807, was a tutor at Cambridge and later an Anglican clergyman who attempted to convert Byron to religious orthodoxy. He was the author of a translation of Juvenal (1807) and several collections of poems, and had served as critic and "corrector" of Byron's poetry.

---

[4] Headmaster at Harrow.
[5] On February 27, 1812, during the debate in the House of Lords on the Tory-sponsored Frame-work Bill. Byron spoke in opposition to the Bill, which was aimed at stopping the riots and destruction caused by weavers thrown out of work by the introduction of machinery.

body there may be little Eloquence (after all there were but *two* thorough Orators in all Antiquity, and I suspect still *fewer* in modern times), but must be a leaven of thought and good sense sufficient to make them *know* what is right, though they can't express it nobly.

13.

Whenever an American requests to see me (which is *not* infrequently), I comply: 1stly, because I respect a people who acquired their freedom by firmness without excess; and 2ndly, because these trans-atlantic visits, "few and far between," make me feel as if talking with Posterity from the other side of the Styx. In a century or two, the new English and Spanish Atlantides will be the masters of the old Countries in all probability, as Greece and Europe overcame their Mother Asia in the older, or earlier ages as they are called.

34.

... What a strange thing is life and man? Were I to present myself at the door of the house, where my daughter now is, the door would be shut in my face, unless (as is not impossible) I knocked down the porter; and if I had gone in that year (and perhaps now) to Drontheim (the furthest town in Norway), or into Holstein, I should have been received with open arms into the mansions of Strangers and foreigners, attached to me by no tie but that of mind and rumour.

As far as *Fame* goes, I have had my share: it has indeed been leavened by other human contingencies, and this in a greater degree than has occurred to most literary men of a *decent* rank in life; but on the whole I take it that such equipoise is the condition of humanity.

I doubt sometimes whether, after all, a quiet and unagitated life would have suited me: yet I sometimes long for it. My earliest dreams (as most boys' dreams are) were martial; but a little later they were all for *love* and retirement, till the hopeless attachment to M. C.[6] began, and continued (though sedulously concealed) *very* early in my teens; and so upwards for a time. *This* threw me out again "alone on a wide, wide sea."[7]

In the year 1804, I recollect meeting my Sister at General Harcourt's in Portland Place. I was then *one* thing, and *as* she had always till then found me. When we met again in 1805 (she told me since), that my temper and disposition were so completely altered, that I was hardly to be recognized. I was not then

---

[6] Mary Anne Chaworth, a distant cousin of Byron's, of Annesley Hall (near Newstead Abbey). Her marriage to John Musters in 1805 was one of the major emotional crises of Byron's life.
[7] *Rime of the Ancient Mariner*, l. 233.

sensible of the change, but I can believe it, and account for it.

51.

It is singular how soon we lose the impression of what ceases to be *constantly* before us. A year impairs, a lustre obliterates. There is little distinct left without an *effort* of memory: *then* indeed the lights are rekindled for a moment; but who can be sure that Imagination is not the torch-bearer? Let any man try at the end of *ten* years to bring before him the features, or the mind, or the sayings, or the habits, of his best friend, or his *greatest* man (I mean his favourite—his Buonaparte, his this, that or 'tother), and he will be surprized at the extreme confusion of his ideas. I speak confidently on this point, having always past for one who had a good, aye, an excellent memory. I except indeed our recollections of Womankind: there is no forgetting *them* (and be d—d to them) any more than any other remarkable Era, such as "the revolution," or "the plague," or "the Invasion," or "the Comet," or "the War" of such and such an Epoch—being the favourite dates of Mankind, who have so many *blessings* in their lot, that they never make their Calendars from them, being too common. For instance, you see "the great drought," "the Thames frozen over," "the Seven years war broke out," the E. or F. or S. "Revolution commenced," "The Lisbon Earthquake," "the Lima Earthquake," "The Earthquake of Calabria," the "Plague of London," "Ditto of Constantinople," "the Sweating Sickness," "The Yellow fever of Philadelphia," etc., etc., etc.; but you don't see "the abundant harvest," "the fine Summer," "the long peace," "the wealthy speculation," the "wreckless voyage," recorded so emphatically? By the way, there has been a *thirty years war*, and a *Seventy years war*: was there ever a *Seventy or a thirty years Peace?* Or was there ever even a *day's Universal* peace, except perhaps in China, where they have found out the miserable happiness of a stationary and unwarlike mediocrity? And is all this, because Nature is niggard or savage? or Mankind ungrateful? Let philosophers decide. I am none.

60.

No man would live his life over again, is an old and true saying, which all can resolve for themselves. At the same time, there are probably *moments* in most men's lives, which they would live over the rest of life to *regain?* Else, why do we live at all? Because Hope recurs to Memory, both false; but—but—but—but—and this *but* drags on till—What? I do not know, and who does? "He that died o' Wednesday." By the way, there is a poor devil to be shot tomorrow here

(Ravenna) for murder. He hath eaten half a Turkey for his dinner, besides fruit and pudding; and he refuses to confess! Shall I go to see him exhale? No. And why? Because it is to take place at *Nine*. Now, could I *save* him, or a fly even from the same catastrophe, I would out-match years; but as I cannot, I will not get up earlier to see another man shot, than I would to run the same risk in person. Besides, I have seen more men than one die that death (and other deaths) before to-day.

It is not cruelty which actuates mankind, but excitement, on such occasions; at least, I suppose so. It is detestable to *take* life in that way, unless it be to preserve two lives.

66.

One of my notions, different from those of my cotemporaries, is, that the present is not a high age of English Poetry: there are *more* poets (soi-disant) than ever there were, and proportionally *less* poetry.

This *thesis* I have maintained for some years, but, strange to say, it meeteth not with favour from my brethren of the Shell. Even Moore shakes his head, and firmly believes that it is the grand Era of British Poesy.

72.

When I first went up to College, it was a new and a heavy hearted scene for me. Firstly, I so much disliked leaving Harrow, that, though it was time (I being seventeen), it broke my very rest for the last quarter with counting the days that remained. I always *hated* Harrow till the last year and half, but then I liked it. Secondly, I wished to go to Oxford and not to Cambridge. Thirdly, I was so completely alone in this new world, that it half broke my Spirits. My companions were not unsocial, but the contrary—lively, hospitable, of rank, and fortune, and gay far beyond my gaiety. I mingled with, and dined and supped, etc., with them; but, I know not how, it was one of the deadliest and heaviest feelings of my life to feel that I was no longer a boy. From that moment I began to grow old in my own esteem; and in my esteem age is not estimable. I took my gradations in the vices with great promptitude, but they were not to my taste; for my early passions, though violent in the extreme, were concentrated, and hated division or spreading abroad. I could have left or lost the world with or for that which I loved; but, though my temperament was naturally burning, I could not share in the common place libertinism of the place and time without disgust. And yet this very disgust, and my heart thrown back upon itself, threw me into excesses perhaps more fatal than those from which I shrunk, as fixing upon one (at a time) the

passions, which, spread amongst many, would have hurt only myself.

73.

People have wondered at the Melancholy which runs through my writings. Others have wondered at my personal gaiety; but I recollect once, after an hour, in which I had been sincerely and particularly gay, and rather brilliant, in company, my wife replying to me when I said (upon her remarking my high spirits) "and "yet, Bell, I have been called and mis-called Melan- "choly—you must have seen how falsely, fre- "quently." "No, B.," (she answered) "it is not so: at "*heart* you are the most melancholy of mankind, and "often when apparently gayest."

74.

If I could explain at length the *real* causes which have contributed to increase this perhaps *natural* temperament of mine, this Melancholy which hath made me a bye-word, nobody would wonder; but this is impossible without doing much mischief. I do not know what other men's lives have been, but I cannot conceive anything more strange than some of the earlier parts of mine. I have written my memoirs, but omitted *all* the really *consequential* and *important* parts, from deference to the dead, to the living, and to those who must be both.

75.

I sometimes think that I should have written the *whole* as a *lesson*, but it might have proved a *lesson* to be *learnt* rather than *avoided*; for passion is a whirlpool, which is not to be viewed nearly without attraction from its Vortex.

76.

I must not go on with these reflections, or I shall be letting out some secret or other to paralyze posterity.

79.

My first dash into poetry was as early as 1800. It was the ebullition of a passion for my first Cousin Margaret Parker (daughter and grand-daughter of the two Admirals Parker), one of the most beautiful of evanescent beings. I have long forgotten the verses, but it would be difficult for me to forget her. Her dark eyes! her long eye-lashes! her completely Greek cast of face and figure! I was then about twelve—She rather older, perhaps a year. She died about a year or two afterwards, in consequence of a fall which injured her spine and induced consumption. Her Sister, Augusta (by some thought still more beautiful), died of the same malady; and it was indeed in attending her that

Margaret met with the accident, which occasioned her own death. My Sister told me that, when she went to see her shortly before her death, upon accidentally mentioning my name, Margaret coloured through the paleness of mortality to the eyes, to the great astonishment of my Sister, who (residing with her Grandmother, Lady Holderness) saw at that time but little of me for family reasons, knew nothing of our attachment, nor could conceive why my name should affect her at such a time. I knew nothing of her illness (being at Harrow and in the country), till she was gone.

Some years after, I made an attempt at an Elegy.[8] A very dull one. I do not recollect scarcely any thing equal to the *transparent* beauty of my cousin, or to the sweetness of her temper, during the short period of our intimacy. She looked as if she had been made out of a rainbow—all beauty and peace.

My passion had its usual effects upon me: I could not sleep, could not eat; I could not rest; and although I had reason to know that she loved me, it was the torture of my life to think of the time which must elapse before we could meet again—being usually about *twelve hours* of separation! But I was a fool then, and am not much wiser now.

80.

My passions were developed very early—so early, that few would believe me, if I were to state the period, and the facts which accompanied it. Perhaps this was one of the reasons which caused the anticipated melancholy of my thoughts—having anticipated life.

My earlier poems are the thoughts of one at least ten years older than the age at which they were written: I don't mean for their solidity, but their Experience. The two first Cantos of C^e. H^d. were completed at twenty two, and they are written as if by a man older than I shall probably ever be.

82.

Upon Parnassus, going to the fountain of Delphi (Castri), in 1809, I saw a flight of twelve Eagles (Hobhouse says they are Vultures—at least in conversation), and I seized the Omen. On the day before, I composed the lines to Parnassus (in Childe Harold), and, on beholding the birds, had a hope that Apollo had accepted my homage. I have at least had the name and fame of a Poet during the poetical period of life (from twenty to thirty): whether it will last is another matter; but I *have been* a votary of the Deity and the place, and am grateful for what he has done in my behalf, leaving the future in his hands as I left the past.

83.

Like Sylla, I have always believed that all things depend upon Fortune, and nothing upon ourselves. I am not aware of any one thought or action worthy of being called good to myself or others, which is not to be attributed to the Good Goddess, Fortune!

87.

Till I was eighteen years old (odd as it may seem), I had never read a review. But, while at Harrow, my general information was so great on modern topics, as to induce a suspicion that I could only collect so much information from *reviews*, because I was never *seen* reading, but always idle and in mischief, or at play. The truth is that I read eating, read in bed, read when no one else reads; and had read all sorts of reading since I was five years old, and yet never *met* with a review, which is the only reason that I know of why I should not have read them. But it is true; for I remember when Hunter and Curzon, in 1804, told me this opinion at Harrow, I made them laugh by my ludicrous astonishment in asking them, "*what is* a review?" To be sure, they were then less common. In three years more, I was better acquainted with that same, but the first I ever read was in 1806–7.

88.

At School, I was (as I have said) remarked for the extent and readiness of my *general* information; but in all other respects idle; capable of great sudden exertions (such as thirty or forty Greek Hexameters—of course with such prosody as it pleased God), but of few continuous drudgeries. My qualities were much more oratorical and martial, than poetical; and Dr. D., my grand patron (our head-master), had a great notion that I should turn out an Orator, from my fluency, my turbulence, my voice, my copiousness of declamation, and my action. I remember that my first declamation astonished him into some unwonted (for he was economical of such), and sudden compliments, before the declaimers at our first rehearsal. My first Harrow verses (that is, English as exercises), a translation of a chorus from the Prometheus of Aeschylus, were received by him but cooly: no one had the least notion that I should subside into poesy.

91.

My School friendships were with *me passions* (for I was always violent), but I do not know that there is one which has endured (to be sure, some have been cut short by death) till now. That with Lord Clare[9] began

---

8 "On the Death of a Young Lady," first published in *Fugitive Pieces* (1806).

9 John Fitzgibbon (1792–1851), who became Earl of Clare in 1802.

one of the earliest and lasted longest, being only interrupted by distance, that I know of. I never hear the word "*Clare*" without a beating of the heart even *now*, and I write it with the feelings of 1803–4–5 ad infinitum.

95.

If I had to live over again, I do not know what I would change in my life, unless it were *for not to have lived at all.* All history and experience, and the rest, teaches us that the good and evil are pretty equally balanced in this existence, and that what is most to be desired is an easy passage out of it.

What can it give us but *years?* and those have little of good but their ending.

96.

Of the Immortality of the Soul, it appears to me that there can be little doubt, if we attend for a moment to the action of Mind. It is in perpetual activity. I used to doubt of it, but reflection has taught me better. It acts also so very independent of body: in dreams for instance incoherently and madly, I grant you; but still it is *Mind*, and much more *Mind* than when we are awake. Now, that *this* should not act *separately*, as well as jointly, who can pronounce? The Stoics, Epictetus and Marcus Aurelius, call the present state "a Soul which drags a Carcase:" a heavy chain, to be sure; but all chains, being material, may be shaken off.

How far our future life will be individual, or, rather, how far it will at all resemble our *present* existence, is another question; but that the *Mind* is *eternal*, seems as probable as that the body is not so. Of course, I have ventured upon the question without recurring to Revelation, which, however, is at least as rational a solution of it as any other.

A *material* resurrection seems strange, and even absurd, except for purposes of punishment; and all punishment, which is to *revenge* rather than *correct*, must be *morally wrong.* And *when* the *World is at an end*, what moral or warning purpose *can* eternal tortures answer? Human passions have probably disfigured the divine doctrines here, but the whole thing is inscrutable. It is useless to tell me *not* to reason, but to *believe.* You might as well tell a man not to wake but *sleep.* And then to *bully* with torments! and all that! I cannot help thinking that the *menace* of Hell makes as many devils, as the severe penal codes of inhuman humanity make villains.

Man is born *passionate* of body, but with an innate though secret tendency to the Love of Good in his Mainspring of Mind. But God help us all! It is at present a sad jar of atoms.

97.

Matter is eternal, always changing, but reproduced, and, as far as we can comprehend Eternity, Eternal; and why not *Mind?* Why should not the Mind act with and upon the Universe? as portions of it act upon and with the congregated dust called Mankind? See, how one man acts upon himself and others, or upon multitudes? The same Agency, in a higher and purer degree, may act upon the Stars, etc., ad infinitum.

98.

I have often been inclined to Materialism in philosophy but could never bear its introduction into *Christianity*, which appears to me essentially founded upon the *Soul.* For this reason, Priestley's Christian Materialism [10] always struck me as deadly. Believe the resurrection of the body, if you will, but *not without a Soul.* The devil's in it, if, after having had a Soul (as surely the *Mind*, or whatever you call it, *is*) in this world, we must part with it in the next, even for an Immortal Materiality. I own my partiality for *Spirit.*

99.

I am always most religious upon a sun-shiny day; as if there was some association between an internal approach to greater light and purity, and the kindler of this dark lanthorn of our external existence.

100.

The Night is also a religious concern; and even more so, when I viewed the Moon and Stars through Herschell's [11] telescope, and saw that they were worlds.

101.

If, according to some speculations, you could prove the World many thousand years older than the Mosaic Chronology, or if you could knock up Adam and Eve and the Apple and Serpent, still what is to be put up in their stead? or how is the difficulty removed? Things must have had a beginning, and what matters it *when* or *how?*

I sometimes think that *Man* may be the relic of some higher material being, wrecked in a former world, and degenerated in the hardships and struggle through Chaos into Conformity—or something like it; as we see Laplanders, Esquimaux, etc., inferior in the present state, as the Elements become more inexorable.

---

[10] Joseph Priestley (1733–1804), the English scientist. Byron refers to his philosophic writings, which had argued for the existence of the soul as part of the body.
[11] Sir William Herschel (1738–1822), the distinguished astronomer and inventor of improved telescopes.

But even then this higher pre-Adamite supppstitious Creation must have had an Origin and a *Creator*; for a *Creator* is a more natural imagination than a fortuitous concourse of atoms. All things remount to a fountain, though they may flow to an Ocean.

102.

What a strange thing is the propagation of life! A bubble of Seed * * * might (for aught we know) have formed a Caesar or a Buonaparte: there is nothing remarkable recorded of their Sires, that I know of.

103.

Lord Kames [12] has said (if I misquote not), "that a "power to call up agreeable ideas at will would be "something greater for mortals than all the boons of a "fairy tale."

I have found increasing upon me (without sufficient cause at times) the depression of Spirits (with few intervals), which I have some reason to believe constitutional or inherited.

104.

Plutarch says, in his life of Lysander, that Aristotle observes, "that in general great Geniuses are of a "melancholy turn, and instances Socrates, Plato, and "Hercules (or Heracleitus), as examples, and Lysan-"der, though not *while* young, yet as inclined to it when "approaching towards age." Whether I am a Genius or not, I have been called such by my friends as well as enemies, and in more countries and languages than one, and also within a no very long period of existence. Of my Genius, I can say nothing, but of my melancholy, that it is "increasing and ought to be diminished"—but how?

105.

I take it that most men are so at bottom, but that it is only remarked in the remarkable. The Duchesse de Broglie, [13] in reply to a remark of mine on the errors of clever people, said, "that they were not *worse* than "others, only being more in view, more noted, "especially in all that could reduce them to the rest, "or raise the rest to them." In 1816, this was.

106.

In fact (I suppose that), if the follies of fools were all set down like those of the wise, the wise (who seem at

present only a better sort of fools), would appear almost intelligent.

112.

There is nothing left for Mankind but a Republic, and I think that there are hopes of such. The two Americas (South and North) have it; Spain and Portugal approach it; all thirst for it. Oh Washington!

113.

Pisa, Novr. 5th. 1821.

"There is a strange coincidence sometimes in the little things of this world, Sancho," says Sterne in a letter (if I mistake not); and so I have often found it.

Page 128, article 91, of this collection of scattered things, I had alluded to my friend Lord Clare in terms such as my feelings suggested. About a week or two afterwards, I met him on the road between Imola and Bologna, after not having met for seven or eight years. He was abroad in 1814, and came home just as I set out in 1816.

This meeting annihilated for a moment all the years between the present time and the days of *Harrow*. It was a new and inexplicable feeling, like rising from the grave, to me. Clare, too, was much agitated—*more* in appearance than even myself; for I could feel his heart beat to his fingers' ends, unless, indeed, it was the pulse of my own which made me think so. He told me that I should find a note from him, left at Bologna. I did. We were obliged to part for our different journeys —he for Rome, I for Pisa; but with the promise to meet again in Spring. We were but five minutes together, and in the public road; but I hardly recollect an hour of my existence which could be weighed against them. He had heard that I was coming on, and had left his letter for me at B., because the people with whom he was travelling could not wait longer.

Of all I have ever known, he has always been the least altered in every thing from the excellent qualities and kind affections which attached me to him so strongly at School. I should hardly have thought it possible for Society (or the World as it is called), to leave a being with so little of the leaven of bad passions. I do not speak from personal experience only, but from all I have ever heard of him from others during absence and distance.

116.

I have lately been reading Fielding over again. They talk of Radicalism, Jacobinism, etc., in England (I am told), but they should turn over the pages of "Jonathan Wild the Great." The inequality of conditions, and the littleness of the great, were never set forth in stronger terms; and his contempt for Conquerors and the like is such, that, had he lived *now*, he would have been denounced in "the Courier"[14] as the grand Mouth-piece and Factionary of the revolutionists. And yet I never recollect to have heard this turn of Fielding's mind noticed, though it is obvious in every page.

119.

My daughter Ada, on her recent birthday the other day (the 10th· of December 1821), completed her sixth year. Since she was a Month old, or rather better, I have not seen her. But I hear that she is a fine child, with a violent temper.

I have been thinking of an odd circumstance. My daughter, my wife, my half sister, my mother, my sister's mother, my natural daughter, and myself, are or were all *only* children. My sister's Mother (Lady Conyers) had only my half *sister* by that second marriage (herself too an only child), and my father had only me (an only child) by his second marriage with my Mother (an only child too). Such a complication of *only* children, all tending to *one family*, is singular enough, and looks like fatality almost. But the fiercest Animals have the rarest numbers in their litters, as Lions, tigers, and even Elephants which are mild in comparison.

[1900]

---

[14] The conservative London newspaper.

Percy Bysshe Shelley

1792–1822

OUTLINE OF EVENTS

1792   Born August 4, at the family estate of Field Place, near Horsham, Sussex; father, Timothy; mother, Elizabeth (Pilford); sisters: Elizabeth (b. 1794), Hellen (b. 1796, died within four months), Mary (b. 1797), Hellen (b. 1799), Margaret (b. 1801); brother, John (b. 1806).

1802–04   At Syon House Academy, Isleworth (near London), where lecturer Adam Walker inspires Shelley's lifelong fascination with science; avid reading of tales of terror and Gothic romances.

1804–10   At Eton College, where he performs scientific experiments and wins a reputation as "Mad Shelley" and "Shelley the atheist"; reads with enthusiasm Southey's epic poems *Thalaba the Destroyer* and *The Curse of Kehama*; writes the Gothic romance *Zastrozzi* and *Original Poetry by Victor and Cazire* (both published in 1810). October 1810, enters University College, Oxford; reads Godwin's *Political Justice* and works of Hume and Locke; forms friendship with Thomas Jefferson Hogg. November–December, the poems *Posthumous Fragments of Margaret Nicholson* and the second Gothic romance *St. Irvyne* published.

1811   January, meets Harriet Westbrook. February, *The Necessity of Atheism* published. March 25, Shelley and Hogg expelled from the University, initiating for Shelley a long period of dispute with and alienation from his family. Meets Leigh Hunt in London. August, marries Harriet Westbrook in Edinburgh. November, settles at Keswick in the Lake District (until February 1812) and meets Southey.

1812   Initiates correspondence with Godwin. February–April, in Ireland in support of the cause of Irish nationalism, publishing the pamphlets *Address to the Irish People*, *Proposals for an Association . . .*, and *A Declaration of Rights*. Lives in Wales and Devon, where he writes *Letter to Lord Ellenborough* (significant appeal for freedom of the press) and begins first major poem *Queen Mab*. Fall, in London, where he meets Godwin and his daughter Mary (1797–1851) and Thomas Love Peacock.

1813   Becomes exponent of vegetarianism. May–June, *Queen Mab* published. June, daughter Eliza Ianthe born (d. 1876).

1814   *A Refutation of Deism* published. June, final visit to Field Place. June, Mary Godwin and Shelley declare their love for each other, and in July elope to continent, traveling through France, Switzerland, and the Rhineland to Holland. September, return to England. November, son Charles born (d. 1826).

1815   January, death of grandfather leaves Shelley financially secure for rest of life. February, Mary's first child is born and dies within a few days.

1816   January, son William born to Mary. February, *Alastor* published. May–August, in Switzerland in close association with Byron. November, Harriet commits suicide. December 1, "Hymn to Intellectual Beauty" published in *The Examiner* (see Leigh Hunt's "Young Poets," pp. 518–19). December 30, marries Mary Godwin.

1817   March, publishes pamphlet *A Proposal for Putting Reform to the Vote Throughout the Kingdom*. September, daughter Clara born. Writes *An Address to the People on the Death of Princess Charlotte* and *Laon and Cythna* (revised as *The Revolt of Islam* and published in January 1818).

1818   March, the Shelleys leave for Italy. September, death of Clara at Venice. Writes *Julian and Maddalo*, "Lines written among the Euganean Hills" and first act of *Prometheus Unbound*.

1819   June, death of son William. August, completes *Cenci* (published 1820). September, *The Mask of Anarchy* composed in response to "Peterloo Massacre." November, composition of *A Philosophical View of Reform* begun and birth of son Percy Florence (d. 1889). Writes "Ode to the West Wind" and "Peter Bell the Third."

1820   January, Shelleys settle in Pisa. Writes "Sensitive Plant," "To a Skylark," *The Witch of Atlas*, and other poems.

1821   February, writes *Epipsychidion* and begins *A Defence of Poetry*. *Adonais*, inspired by death of Keats, published in July. Fall, completes *Hellas*.

1822   Composes *The Triumph of Life*. July 8, drowns in storm while sailing from Leghorn to Spezia in his boat *Don Juan*.

SELECTED BIBLIOGRAPHY

BIOGRAPHY

WHITE, NEWMAN IVEY, *Shelley*, 2 vols., New York: Alfred A. Knopf, 1940.
——— *Portrait of Shelley*, New York: Alfred A. Knopf, 1945. [One-volume condensation of the larger study.]

EDITIONS

BRETT-SMITH, H. F. (ed.), *Peacock's Four Ages of Poetry, Shelley's Defence of Poetry, Browning's Essay on Shelley*, The Percy Reprints, Boston: Houghton Mifflin Company, 1921.
CAMERON, KENNETH NEILL (ed.), *Shelley and his Circle 1773-1822*, Cambridge, Mass.: Harvard University Press, 1961-. [Four volumes thus far published.]
CLARK, DAVID LEE (ed.), *Shelley's Prose, or The Trumpet of a Prophecy*, corrected edition, Albuquerque: University of New Mexico Press, 1966.
INGPEN, ROGER, and WALTER E. PECK (eds.), *The Complete Works of Percy Bysshe Shelley*, the Julian Edition, 10 vols., London-New York: Ernest Benn Limited and Charles Scribner's Sons, 1926-1930.
SHAWCROSS, JOHN (ed.), *Shelley's Literary and Philosophical Criticism*, London: Henry Frowde, 1909.

SHELLEY'S POLITICAL, MORAL, AND PHILOSOPHIC THOUGHT

BARNARD, ELLSWORTH, *Shelley's Religion*, New York: Russell and Russell, 1964. [First published 1937.]
CAMERON, KENNETH NEILL, "Shelley and the Reformers," *ELH*, XII (1945), 62-85.
——— *The Young Shelley: Genesis of a Radical*, New York: Macmillan Publishing Co., Inc., 1950.
GRABO, CARL, *The Magic Plant: The Growth of Shelley's Thought*, Chapel Hill: University of North Carolina Press, 1936.
GUINN, JOHN POLLARD, *Shelley's Political Thought*, the Hague, Netherlands: Mouton and Company, 1969.
HUGHES, A. M. D., *The Nascent Mind of Shelley*, Oxford: Clarendon Press, 1947.
McNIECE, GERALD, *Shelley and the Revolutionary Idea*, Cambridge, Mass.: Harvard University Press, 1969.

PULOS, C. E., *The Deep Truth: A Study of Shelley's Scepticism*, Lincoln: University of Nebraska Press, 1954.

WALKER, A. STANLEY, "Peterloo, Shelley and Reform," *PMLA*, XL (1925), 128–64.

SHELLEY'S LITERARY CRITICISM

ABRAMS, M. H., "Shelley and Romantic Platonism," *The Mirror and the Lamp*, New York: Oxford University Press, 1953, pp. 126–32.

BRADLEY, A. C., "Shelley's View of Poetry," *Oxford Lectures on Poetry*, London: The Macmillan Company, 1909, pp. 151–74.

McELDERRY, B. R., JR., "Common Elements in Wordsworth's 'Preface' and Shelley's *Defence of Poetry*," *Modern Language Quarterly*, V (1944), 175–81.

SLOTE, MELVIN T., *Shelley: His Theory of Poetry*, New York: Russell and Russell, 1964. [First published 1927.]

VERKOREN, LUCAS, *A Study of Shelley's Defence of Poetry* ..., Amsterdam: D. Mijs, 1937.

WASSERMAN, EARL R., "Shelley's Last Poetics: A Reconsideration," in *From Sensibility to Romanticism*, ed. F. W. Hilles and Harold Bloom, New York: Oxford University Press, 1965, pp. 487–511.

THE NECESSITY OF ATHEISM

Shelley's lifelong attack on the established dogmas of Christianity had its genesis with his readings at Eton in the materialism of Lucretius and the skeptical treatment of religious belief in Pliny's Natural History. *It was supported at Oxford by the study of Locke's empiricism and especially Hume's* Essay on Miracles, *the two most evident influences on* The Necessity of Atheism, *which was the joint product of Shelley and his Oxford friend Thomas Jefferson Hogg. The purpose in publishing the pamphlet was, in the words of the advertisement (signed "Thro' deficiency of proof, an* ATHEIST"), *to draw out answers and objections from "those of his readers who may discover any deficiency in his reasoning, or may be in possession of proofs which his mind could never obtain...." The results of the publication in February 1811, are now legendary. "In about twenty minutes [after the pamphlet had been placed in the window of an Oxford bookseller] a fellow of New College, the Reverend John Walker, strolling past the shop, was smitten with the alarming title,* The Necessity of Atheism. *He entered, examined the book, and straightway took counsel with the proprietors. All agreed that the copies should be burned. They were collected then and there, carried into the back kitchen, and burned in the presence of the Reverend Mr. Walker" (Newman Ivey White,* Portrait of Shelley [*New York: Alfred A. Knopf, 1945*], p. 50). *On March 25, Shelley and Hogg were expelled from the University. For discussion of the pamphlet, see Kenneth Neill Cameron,* The Young Shelley: Genesis of a Radical (*New York: Macmillan, 1950*), *a detailed study of the evolution of Shelley's moral and political thought through the publication of* A Refutation of Deism.*

The text of The Necessity of Atheism *and of all of Shelley's prose here reproduced is that of "The Julian Edition,"* The Complete Works of Percy Bysshe Shelley, *ed. Roger Ingpen and Walter E. Peck, 10 vols. (London–New York: Ernest Benn Ltd. and Charles Scribner's Sons, 1926–1930).*

THE NECESSITY OF ATHEISM

A CLOSE examination of the validity of the proofs adduced to support any proposition, has ever been allowed to be the only sure way of attaining truth, upon the advantages of which it is unnecessary to descant; our knowledge of the existence of a Deity is a subject of such importance that it cannot be too minutely investigated; in consequence of this conviction, we proceed briefly and impartially to examine the proofs which have been adduced. It is necessary first to consider the nature of Belief.

When a proposition is offered to the mind, it perceives the agreement or disagreement of the ideas of which it is composed. A perception of their agreement is termed belief, many obstacles frequently prevent this perception from being immediate, these the mind attempts to remove in order that the perception may be distinct. The mind is active in the investigation, in order to perfect the state of perception which is passive; the investigation being confused with the perception has induced many falsely to imagine that the mind is active in belief, that belief is an act of volition, in consequence of which it may be regulated by the mind; pursuing, continuing this mistake they have attached a degree of criminality to disbelief of which in its nature it is incapable; it is equally so of merit.

The strength of belief like that of every other passion is in proportion to the degrees of excitement.

The degrees of excitement are three.

The senses are the sources of all knowledge to the mind, consequently their evidence claims the strongest assent.

The decision of the mind founded upon our own experience derived from these sources, claims the next degree.

The experience of others which addresses itself to the former one, occupies the lowest degree.—

Consequently no testimony can be admitted which is contrary to reason, reason is founded on the evidence of our senses.

Every proof may be referred to one of these three divisions; we are naturally led to consider what arguments we receive from each of them to convince us of the existence of a Deity.

1st. The evidence of the senses.—If the Deity should appear to us, if he should convince our senses of his existence; this revelation would necessarily command belief;—Those to whom the Deity has thus appeared, have the strongest possible conviction of his existence.

Reason claims the 2nd. place, it is urged that man knows that whatever is, must either have had a beginning or existed from all eternity, he also knows that whatever is not eternal must have had a cause.— Where this is applied to the existence of the universe, it is necessary to prove that it was created, until that is clearly demonstrated, we may reasonably suppose that it has endured from all eternity.—In a case where two propositions are diametrically opposite, the mind believes that which is less incomprehensible, it is easier to suppose that the Universe has existed from all eternity, than to conceive a being capable of creating it; if the mind sinks beneath the weight of one, is it an alleviation to increase the intolerability of the burden? —The other argument which is founded upon a man's knowledge of his own existence, stands thus. . . . A man knows not only he now is, but that there was a time when he did not exist, consequently there must have been a cause.`. . . But what does this prove? we can only infer from effects causes exactly adequate to those effects; . . . But there certainly is a generative power which is effected by particular instruments; we cannot prove that it is inherent in these instruments, nor is the contrary hypothesis capable of demonstration; we admit that the generative power is incomprehensible, but to suppose that the same effect is produced by an eternal, omniscient, Almighty Being, leaves the cause in the obscurity, but renders it more incomprehensible.

The 3rd. and last degree of assent is claimed by Testimony . . . it is required that it should not be contrary to reason. . . . The testimony that the Deity convinces the senses of men of his existence can only

be admitted by us, if our mind considers it less probable that these men should have been deceived, than that the Deity should have appeared to them . . . our reason can never admit the testimony of men, who not only declare that they were eye-witnesses of miracles but that the Deity was irrational, for he commanded that he should be believed, he proposed the highest rewards for faith, eternal punishments for disbelief . . . we can only command voluntary actions, belief is not an act of volition, the mind is even passive, from this it is evident that we have not sufficient testimony, or rather that testimony is insufficient to prove the being of a God, we have before shewn that it cannot be deduced from reason, . . . they who have been convinced by the evidence of the senses, they only can believe it.

From this it is evident that having no proofs from any of the three sources of conviction: the mind *cannot* believe the existence of a God, it is also evident that as belief is a passion of the mind, no degree of criminality can be attached to disbelief, they only are reprehensible who willingly neglect to remove the false medium thro' which their mind views the subject.

It is almost unnecessary to observe, that the general knowledge of the deficiency of such proof, cannot be prejudicial to society: Truth has always been found to promote the best interests of mankind. . . . Every reflecting mind must allow that there is no proof of the existence of a Deity.—Q.E.D.

[1811]   [1928]

A REFUTATION OF DEISM

The work was published privately and anonymously in 1814. For discussion, consult Kenneth Neill Cameron, The Young Shelley: Genesis of a Radical, *pp. 274–87; and C. E. Pulos,* The Deep Truth: A Study of Shelley's Scepticism (Lincoln, Neb.: University of Nebraska Press, 1954), *pp. 89–104.*

A REFUTATION OF DEISM

PREFACE

THE object of the following Dialogue is to prove that the system of Deism is untenable. It is attempted to shew that there is no alternative between Atheism and Christianity; that the evidences of the Being of a God are to be deduced from no other principles than those of Divine Revelation.

The Author endeavours to shew how much the cause of natural and revealed Religion has suffered from the mode of defence adopted by Theosophistical Christians. How far he will accomplish what he proposed to himself, in the composition of this Dialogue, the world will finally determine.

The mode of printing this little work may appear too expensive, either for its merits or its length. However inimical this practice confessedly is, to the general diffusion of knowledge, yet it was adopted in this instance with a view of excluding the multitude from the abuse of a mode of reasoning, liable to misconstruction on account of its novelty.

EUSEBES

O THEOSOPHUS, I have long regretted and observed the strange infatuation which has blinded your understanding. It is not without acute uneasiness that I have beheld the progress of your audacious scepticism trample on the most venerable institutions of our forefathers, until it has rejected the salvation which the only begotten Son of God deigned to proffer in person to a guilty and unbelieving world. To this excess then has the pride of the human understanding at length arrived? To measure itself with Omniscience! To scan the intentions of Inscrutability!

You can have reflected but superficially on this awful and important subject. The love of paradox, an affectation of singularity, or the pride of reason has seduced you to the barren and gloomy paths of infidelity. Surely you have hardened yourself against the truth with a spirit of coldness and cavil.

Have you been wholly inattentive to the accumulated evidence which the Deity has been pleased to attach to the revelation of his will? The antient books in which the advent of the Messiah was predicted, the miracles by which its truth has been so conspicuously confirmed, the martyrs who have undergone every variety of torment in attestation of its veracity? You seem to require mathematical demonstration in a case which admits of no more than strong moral probability. Surely the merit of that faith which we are required to repose in our Redeemer would be thus entirely done away. Where is the difficulty of according credit to that which is perfectly plain and evident? How is he entitled to a recompense who believes what he cannot disbelieve?

When there is satisfactory evidence that the witnesses of the Christian miracles passed their lives in labours, dangers and sufferings, and consented severally to be racked, burned and strangled, in testimony of the truth of their account, will it be asserted that they were actuated by a disinterested desire of deceiving others? That they were hypocrites for no end but to teach the purest doctrine that ever enlightened the world, and martyrs without any prospect of emolument or fame? The sophist who gravely advances an opinion thus absurd, certainly sins with gratuitous and indefensible pertinacity.

The history of Christianity is itself the most indisputable proof of those miracles by which its origin was sanctioned to the world. It is itself one great miracle. A few humble men established it in the face of an opposing universe. In less than fifty years an astonishing multitude was converted, as Suetonius,*— Pliny,† Tacitus,‡ and Lucian attest; and shortly

---

* *Judaei, impulsore Chresto, turbantes, facile comprimuntur.*—Suet. *in Tib.*
Affecti suppliciis Christiani, genus hominum superstitionis novae et maleficae.—Id. *in Neron.* [1]

† *Multi omnis aetatis utriusque sexus etiam; neque enim civitates tantum, sed vicos etiam et agros superstitionis istius contagio pervagata est.*—Plin. *Epist.* [2]

‡ *Ergo abolendo rumori Nero subdidit reos et quaesitissimis poenis adfecit, quos, suo flagitio invisos, vulgus 'Christianos' appellabat. Auctor nominis ejus Christus, Tiberio imperitanti, per procuratorem Pontium Pilatum supplicio adfectus erat. Repressaque in praesens exitiabilis superstitio rursus erumpebat, non modo per Judaeam, originem ejus mali, sed per urbem etiam, quò cuncta, undique atrocia aut pudenda, confluunt concelebranturque. Igitur primo correpti, qui fatebantur; deinde indicio eorum multitudo ingens haud perinde in crimine incendii, quam odio humani generis convicti sunt, et pereuntibus addita ludibria, ut, ferarum tergis contecti, laniatu canum interirent, aut crucibus affixi, aut flammandi, atque ubi defecisset dies, in usum nocturni luminis urerentur. Hortos suos ei spectaculo Nero obtulerat, et Circense ludibrium edebat, habitu aurigae permixtus plebi, vel curriculo insistens. Unde quanquam adversus sontes, et novissima exempla meritos, miseratio oriebatur, tanquam non utilitate publicâ, sed in saevitiam unius absumerentur.*—Tacitus, *Annal.* L. xv., Sect. xlv. [3]

---

[1] *Judaei . . . comprimuntur*: Shelley would seem to be thinking of a passage in Suetonius's Life of Claudius, 25, rather than in the Life of Tiberius: "Since the Jews constantly made disturbances at the instigation of Christ, he expelled them from Rome." *Affecti . . . maleficae*: "Punishment was afflicted on the Christians, a class of men given to a new and mischievous superstition." Suetonius's Life of Nero, 16 (J. C. Rolfe translation, Loeb Classical Library, Harvard University Press).

[2] "For a great many individuals of every age and class, both men and women, are being brought to trial, and this is likely to continue. It is not only the towns, but villages and rural districts too which are infected through contact with this wretched cult." —Pliny's *Letters*, X (to Trajan), xcvi, 9 (Betty Radice translation, Loeb Classical Library, Harvard University Press).

[3] "Therefore, to scotch the rumour, Nero substituted as culprits, and punished with the utmost refinements of cruelty, a class of men, loathed for their vices, whom the crowd styled Christians. Christus, the founder of the name, had undergone the death penalty in the reign of Tiberius, by sentence of the procurator Pontius Pilatus, and the pernicious superstition was checked for a moment, only to break out once more, not merely in Judaea, the home of the disease, but in the capital itself, were all things horrible or shameful in the world collect and find a vogue. First, then, the

afterwards thousands who had boldly overturned the altars, slain the priests and burned the temples of Paganism, were loud in demanding the recompense of martyrdom from the hands of the infuriated Heathens. Not until three centuries after the coming of the Messiah did his holy religion incorporate itself with the institutions of the Roman Empire, and derive support from the visible arm of fleshly strength. Thus long without any assistance but that of its Omnipotent author, Christianity prevailed in defiance of incredible persecutions, and drew fresh vigour from circumstances the most desperate and unpromising. By what process of sophistry can a rational being persuade himself to reject a religion, the original propagation of which is an event wholly unparalleled in the sphere of human experience?

The morality of the Christian religion is as original and sublime, as its miracles and mysteries are unlike all other portents. A patient acquiescence in injuries and violence; a passive submission to the will of sovereigns; a disregard of those ties by which the feelings of humanity have ever been bound to this unimportant world; humility and faith, are doctrines neither similar nor comparable to those of any other system.* Friendship, patriotism and magnanimity; the heart that is quick in sensibility, the hand that is inflexible in execution; genius, learning and courage, are qualities which have engaged the admiration of mankind, but which we are taught by Christianity to consider as splendid and delusive vices.

I know not why a Theist should feel himself more inclined to distrust the historians of Jesus Christ, than those of Alexander the Great. What do the tidings of redemption contain which render them peculiarly obnoxious to discredit? It will not be disputed that a revelation of the Divine will is a benefit to mankind.†

* See the *Internal Evidence of Christianity*; see also Paley's Evidences, Vol. II, p. 27.[4]

† Paley's Evidences, Vol. I., p. 3.

confessed members of the sect were arrested; next, on their disclosures, vast numbers were convicted, not so much on the count of arson as for hatred of the human race. And derision accompanied their end: they were covered with wild beasts' skins and torn to death by dogs; or they were fastened on crosses, and, when daylight failed were burned to serve as lamps by night. Nero had offered his Gardens for the spectacle, and gave an exhibition in his Circus, mixing with the crowd in the habit of a charioteer, or mounted on his car. Hence, in spite of a guilt which had earned the most exemplary punishment, there arose a sentiment of pity, due to the impression that they were being sacrificed not for the welfare of the state but to the ferocity of a single man." Tacitus' *Annals*, XV, xliv (John Jackson translation, Loeb Classical Library, Harvard University Press).

[4] Referring to Soame Jenyns' *View of the Internal Evidence of the Christian Religion* (1776); and to William Paley's *A View of the Evidences of Christianity* (1794).

It will not be asserted that even under the Christian revelation, we have too clear a solution of the vast enigma of the Universe, too satisfactory a justification of the attributes of God. When we call to mind the profound ignorance in which, with the exception of the Jews, the philosophers of antiquity were plunged; when we recollect that men eminent for dazzling talents and fallacious virtues, Epicurus, Democritus, Pliny, Lucretius, Euripides,‡ and innumerable others,

‡ *Imperfectae vero in homine naturae praecipua solatia ne Deum quidem posse omnia. Namque nec sibi potest mortem consciscere, si velit, quod homini dedit optimum in tantis vitae poenis; nec mortales aeternitate donare, aut revocare defunctos; nec facere ut qui vixit non vixerit, qui honores gessit non gesserit, nullumque habere in praeteritum jus praeterquam oblivionis, atque ut facetis quoque argumentis societas haec cum Deo copuletur ut bis dena viginti non sint, et multa similer efficere non posse. Per quae, declaratur haud dubiè, naturae potentiam id quoque esse, quod Deum vocamus.*—Plin. *Nat. Hist. Cap. de Deo.*

Φησιν τις, ειναι δητ' εν ουρανῳ Θεοῦς;
Ουκ εισιν, ουκ εισ'. ει τις ανθρωπων λεγει,
Μη τῳ παλαιῳ μωρος ων χρησθω λογῳ·
Σκεψασθε δ' αυτα, μη' πι τοις εμοις λογοις
Γνωμην εχοντες. Φημ' εγω, τυραννιδα
Κτεινειν τε πολλους, κτηματων τ' αποστερειν,
Ορκουατε παραβαινοντας εκπορθειν πολεις.
Και ταυτα δρωντες μαλλον εισ' ενδαιμονες
Των ευσεβουντων ηαυχη καθ' ημεραν.
Πολειστε μικρας οιδα τιμουσας Θεους,
Αι μειζονων κλυουσι δυσσεβεστερων
Λογχης αριθμῳ πλειονος κρατουμεναι.
Οιμαι δ' αν υμας, ει τις αργος ων Θεοις
Ευχοιτο, και μη χειρι συλλεγοι βιον.***

Euripides, *Belerophon*, Frag. xxv.

*Hunc igitur terrorem animi, tenebrasque necesse est
Non radii solis, neque lucida tela diei
Discutient, sed naturae species ratioque:
Principium hinc cujus nobis exordia sumet,*
NULLAM REM NIHILO GIGNI DIVINITUS UNQUAM.
Luc. *der Rer. Nat. Lib.* I.[5]—

[5] *Imperfectae . . . vocamus:* "But the chief consolations for nature's imperfection in the case of man are that not even for God are all things possible—for he cannot, even if he wishes, commit suicide, the supreme boon that he has bestowed on man among all the penalties of life, nor bestow eternity on mortals or recall the deceased, nor cause a man that has lived not to have lived, or one that has held high office not to have held it—and that he has no power over what is past save to forget it, and (to link our fellowship with God by means of frivolous arguments as well) that he cannot cause twice ten not to be twenty or do many things on similar lines: which facts unquestionably demonstrate the power of nature, and prove that it is this that we mean by the word 'God.'" —Pliny's *Natural History*, II, v, 27 (H. Rackham translation, Loeb Classical Library, Harvard University Press).

Translation of the Euripides fragment: "Does any one say that there are surely gods in heaven? There are not, there are not, if a man speaks sensibly and without reliance on the old myths. Consider it yourselves and form an opinion not on my word. I say that a tyranny kills many men and deprives them of their possessions; and men transgressing their oaths sack cities, and doing these things they are much happier than those who are reverent in peace day by day. And I know that small cities honor gods, which cities

dared publicly to avow their faith in Atheism with impunity, and that the Theists, Anaxagoras, Pythagoras and Plato, vainly endeavoured by that human reason, which is truly incommensurate to so vast a purpose, to establish among philosophers the belief in one Almighty God, the creator and preserver of the world; when we recollect that the multitude were grossly and ridiculously idolatrous, and that the magistrates, if not Atheists, regarded the being of a God in the light of an abstruse and uninteresting speculation;* when we add to these considerations a remembrance of the wars and the oppressions, which about the time of the advent of the Messiah, desolated the human race, is it not more credible that the Deity actually interposed to check the rapid progress of human deterioration, than that he permitted a specious and pestilent imposture to seduce mankind into the labyrinth of a deadlier superstition? Surely the Deity has not created man immortal, and left him for ever in ignorance of his glorious destination. If the Christian Religion is false, I see not upon what foundation our belief in a moral governor of the universe, or our hopes of immortality can rest.

Thus when the plain reason of the case, and the suffrage of the civilized world conspire with the more indisputable suggestions of faith, to render impregnable that system which has been so vainly and so wantonly assailed. Suppose, however, it were admitted that the conclusions of human reason and the lessons of worldly virtue should be found, in the detail, incongruous with Divine Revelation, by the dictates of which would it become us to abide? Not by that which errs whenever it is employed, but by that which is incapable of error: not by the ephemeral systems of vain philosophy, but by the word of God, which shall endure for ever.

Reflect, O Theosophus, that if the religion you reject be true, you are justly excluded from the benefits which result from a belief in its efficiency to salvation. Be not regardless, therefore, I entreat you, of the curses so emphatically heaped upon infidels by the

* See Cicero *de Natura Deorum*.

◇◇◇◇◇◇◇◇◇◇◇◇◇◇◇◇◇◇◇◇◇◇◇◇◇◇◇◇◇◇◇◇◇◇◇◇

obey greater cities and less reverend ones [because the smaller cities are] overpowered by the number of greater armaments. I think that you, if any one should passively pray to the gods and not gather his life in his own hand—."

Hunc . . . UNQUAM:

"This terror, then, this darkness of the mind,
Not sunrise with its flaring spokes of light,
Nor glittering arrows of morning can disperse,
But only Nature's aspect and her law,
Which, teaching us, hath this exordium:
'*Nothing from nothing ever yet was born.*'"—

Lucretius' *De Rerum Naturae*, I, 146–50 (William Ellery Leonard translation).

inspired organs of the will of God: the fire which is never quenched, the worm that never dies. I dare not think that the God in whom I trust for salvation would terrify his creatures with menaces of punishment, which he does not intend to inflict. The ingratitude of incredulity is, perhaps, the only sin to which the Almighty cannot extend his mercy without compromising his justice. How can the human heart endure, without despair, the mere conception of so tremendous an alternative? Return, I entreat you, to that tower of strength which securely overlooks the chaos of the conflicting opinions of men. Return to that God who is your creator and preserver, by whom alone you are defended from the ceaseless wiles of your eternal enemy. Are human institutions so faultless that the principle upon which they are founded may strive with the voice of God? Know that faith is superior to reason, in as much as the creature is surpassed by the Creator; and that whensoever they are incompatible, the suggestions of the latter, not those of the former, are to be questioned.

Permit me to exhibit in their genuine deformity the errors which are seducing you to destruction. State to me, with candour the train of sophisms by which the evil spirit has deluded your understanding. Confess the secret motives of your disbelief; suffer me to administer a remedy to your intellectual disease. I fear not the contagion of such revolting sentiments: I fear only lest patience should desert me before you have finished the detail of your presumptuous credulity.

THEOSOPHUS

I am not only prepared to confess, but to vindicate my sentiments. I cannot refrain, however, from premising, that in this controversy I labour under a disadvantage from which you are exempt. You believe that incredulity is immoral, and regard him as an object of suspicion and distrust whose creed is incongruous with your own. But truth is the perception of the agreement or disagreement of ideas. I can no more conceive that a man who perceives the disagreement of any ideas, should be persuaded of their agreement, than that he should overcome a physical impossibility. The reasonableness or the folly of the articles of our creed is therefore no legitimate object of merit or demerit; our opinions depend not on the will, but on the understanding.

If I am in error (and the wisest of us may not presume to deem himself secure from all illusion) that error is the consequence of the prejudices by which I am prevented, of the ignorance by which I am incapacitated from forming a correct estimation of the subject. Remove those prejudices, dispel that ignorance, make truth apparent, and fear not the obstacles that remain to be encountered. But do not repeat to me those terrible and frequent curses, by whose intolerance and cruelty I have so often been disgusted in the perusal of your sacred books. Do not tell me that the All-Merciful will punish me for the conclusions of that reason by which he has thought fit to distinguish me from the beasts that perish. Above all, refrain from urging considerations drawn from reason, to degrade that which you are thereby compelled to acknowledge as the ultimate arbiter of the dispute. Answer my objections as I engage to answer your assertions, point by point, word by word.

You believe that the only and ever-present God begot a Son whom he sent to reform the world, and to propitiate its sins; you believe that a book, called the Bible, contains a true account of this event, together with an infinity of miracles and prophecies which preceded it from the creation of the world. Your opinion that these circumstances really happened appears to me, from some considerations which I will proceed to state, destitute of rational foundation.

To expose all the inconsistency, immorality and false pretensions which I perceive in the Bible, demands a minuteness of criticism at least as voluminous as itself. I shall confine myself, therefore, to the confronting of your tenets with those primitive and general principles which are the basis of all moral reasoning.

In creating the Universe, God certainly proposed to himself the happiness of his creatures. It is just, therefore, to conclude that he left no means unemployed, which did not involve an impossibility to accomplish this design. In fixing a residence for this image of his own Majesty, he was doubtless careful that every occasion of detriment, every opportunity of evil should be removed. He was aware of the extent of his powers, he foresaw the consequences of his conduct, and doubtless modelled his being consentaneously with the world of which he was to be the inhabitant, and the circumstances which were destined to surround him.

The account given by the Bible has but a faint concordance with the surmises of reason concerning this event.

According to this book, God created Satan, who instigated by the impulses of his nature contended with the Omnipotent for the throne of Heaven. After a contest, for the empire, in which God was victorious, Satan was thrust into a pit of burning sulphur. On man's creation God placed within his reach a tree whose fruit he forbade him to taste, on pain of death; permitting Satan at the same time, to employ all his artifice to persuade this innocent and wondering creature to transgress the fatal prohibition.

The first man yielded to this temptation; and to satisfy Divine Justice the whole of his posterity must have been eternally burned in hell, if God had not sent his only Son on earth, to save those few whose salvation had been foreseen and determined before the creation of the world.

God is here represented as creating man with certain passions and powers, surrounding him with certain circumstances, and then condemning him to everlasting torments because he acted as omniscience had foreseen, and was such as omnipotence had made him. For to assert that the Creator is the author of all good, and the creature the author of all evil, is to assert that one man makes a straight line and a crooked one, and that another makes the incongruity.*

Barbarous and uncivilized nations have uniformly adored, under various names, a God of which themselves were the model; revengeful, blood-thirsty, grovelling and capricious. The idol of a savage is a demon that delights in carnage. The steam of slaughter, the dissonance of groans, the flames of a desolated land, are the offerings which he deems acceptable, and his innumerable votaries throughout the world have made it a point of duty to worship him to his taste.† The Phenicians, the Druids and the Mexicans have immolated hundreds at the shrines of their divinity, and the high and holy name of God has been in all ages the watch word of the most unsparing massacres, the sanction of the most atrocious perfidies.

But I appeal to your candour, O Eusebes, if there exist a record of such grovelling absurdities and enormities so atrocious, a picture of the Deity so characteristic of a demon as that which the sacred writings of the Jews contain. I demand of you, whether as a conscientious Theist you can reconcile the conduct which is attributed to the God of the Jews with your conceptions of the purity and benevolence of the divine nature.

The loathsome and minute obscenities to which the inspired writers perpetually descend, the filthy observances which God is described as personally instituting,‡ the total disregard of truth and contempt of the

---

* Hobbes.
† See Preface to Le Bon Sens.[6]
‡ See Hosea, chap. i., chap. ix. Ezekiel, chap. iv., chap. xvi., chap. xxiii. Henyë, speaking of the opinions entertained of the Jews by antient poets and philosophers, says:—*Meminit quidem superstitionis Judaicae Horatius, verum ut eam risu exploderet.—Heyn. ad Virg. Poll. in Arq.*[7]

---

[6] Referring to Baron d'Holbach's *Le Bon-Sens* (1772).
[7] Christian Gottlieb Heyne (1729–1812) was a German classical scholar. *Meminit ... exploderet*: "Horace indeed makes mention of the Jewish superstition, but only that he might expel it with a laugh."

first principles of morality, manifested on the most public occasions by the chosen favourites of Heaven, might corrupt, were they not so flagitious as to disgust.

When the chief of this obscure and brutal horde of assassins asserts that the God of the Universe was enclosed in a box of shittim wood,* "two feet long and three feet wide,"† and brought home in a new cart, I smile at the impertinence of so shallow an imposture. But it is blasphemy of a more hideous and unexampled nature to maintain that the Almighty God expressly commanded Moses to invade an unoffending nation, and on account of the difference of their worship utterly to destroy every human being it contained, to murder every infant and unarmed man in cold blood, to massacre the captives, to rip up the matrons, and to retain the maidens alone for concubinage and violation.‡ At the very time that philosophers of the most

* I. Sam. chap. v., 8.
† Wordsworth's Lyrical Ballads.[8]
‡ When Moses stood in the gate of the court and said— Who is on the Lord's side? Let him come unto me. And all the sons of Levi gathered themselves together unto him. *Thus saith the Lord God of Israel*, put every man his sword by his side, and go in and out from gate to gate throughout the camp, *and slay every man his brother, and every man his companion, and every man his neighbour*. And the children of Levi did according to the word of Moses, and there fell of the people on that day twenty three thousand men.—*Exodus*, chap. xxxii., 26.

And they warred against the Midianites, as the Lord commanded Moses, and they slew all the males; and the children of Israel took all the women of Midian captives, and their little ones, and took the spoil of all their cattle, and all their flocks, and all their goods. And they burned all their huts wherein they dwelt and all their goodly castles with fire. And Moses and Eleazar the priest, and all the princes of the congregation came forth to meet them without the camp. And Moses was wroth with the officers of the post, with the captains over hundreds and captains over thousands that came from the battle. And Moses said unto them—*Have ye saved all the women alive?*—Behold these caused the children of Israel through the counsel of Balaam to commit trespass against the Lord in the matter of Peor, and there was a plague among the congregation of the Lord. *Now therefore kill every male among the little ones, and kill every woman that hath known man by lying with him. And all the women-children that have not known a man by lying with him*, KEEP ALIVE FOR YOURSELVES.—*Numbers* xxxi.

And we utterly destroyed them, as we did unto Sihon king of Heshbon utterly destroying the men, women and children of every city.—*Deut.* iii., 6.

And they utterly destroyed all that was in the city both man and woman, young and old, and ox and sheep and ass with the edge of the sword.—*Joshua*.

So Joshua fought against Debir, and utterly destroyed all the souls that were therein, he left none remaining, but utterly destroyed all that breathed, as the *Lord God of Israel commanded*.—*Joshua*, chap. x.

And David gathered all the people together, and went to

8 See "The Thorn," ll. 32–33 in the 1798 text of *Lyrical Ballads*.

enterprising benevolence were founding in Greece those institutions which have rendered it the wonder and luminary of the world, am I required to believe that the weak and wicked king of an obscure and barbarous nation, a murderer, a traitor and a tyrant was the man after God's own heart? A wretch, at the thought of whose unparalleled enormities the sternest soul must sicken in dismay! An unnatural monster who sawed his fellow beings in sunder, harrowed them to fragments under harrows of iron, chopped them to pieces with axes and burned them in brick-kilns, because they bowed before a different, and less bloody idol than his own. It is surely no perverse conclusion of an infatuated understanding that the God of the Jews is not the benevolent author of this beautiful world.

The conduct of the Deity in the promulgation of the Gospel, appears not to the eye of reason more compatible with His immutability and omnipotence than the history of his actions under the law accords with his benevolence.

You assert that the human race merited eternal reprobation because their common father had transgressed the divine command, and that the crucifixion of the Son of God was the only sacrifice of sufficient efficacy to satisfy eternal justice. But it is no less inconsistent with justice and subversive of morality that millions should be responsible for a crime which they had no share in committing; than that, if they had really committed it, the crucifixion of an innocent being could absolve them from moral turpitude. *Ferretne ulla civitas latorem istiusmodi legis, ut condemnaretur filius, aut nepos, si pater aut avus deliquisset?*[9] Certainly this is a mode of legislation peculiar to a state of savageness and anarchy; this is the irrefragable logic of tyranny and imposture.

The supposition that God has ever supernaturally revealed his will to man at any other period than the original creation of the human race, necessarily involves a compromise of his benevolence. It assumes that he withheld from mankind a benefit which it was in his power to confer. That he suffered his creatures to remain in ignorance of truths essential to their happiness and salvation. That during the lapse of innumerable ages every individual of the human race

Rabbah, and took it. And he brought forth the people therein, and *put them under saws, and under harrows of iron, and made them pass through the brick kiln. This did he also unto all the children of Ammon.—II. Sam.* xii., 29.

9 *Ferretne . . . deliquisset?*: "Would any state put up with the proposer of a law of the sort you speak of, namely, that a son or grandson be condemned if a father or a grandfather had committed a crime?"

had perished without redemption from an universal stain which the Deity at length descended in person to erase. That the good and wise of all ages, involved in one common fate with the ignorant and wicked, have been tainted by involuntary and inevitable error which torments infinite in duration may not avail to expiate.

In vain will you assure me with amiable inconsistency that the mercy of God will be extended to the virtuous, and that the vicious will alone be punished. The foundation of the Christian Religion is manifestly compromised by a concession of this nature. A subterfuge thus palpable plainly annihilates the necessity of the incarnation of God for the redemption of the human race, and represents the descent of the Messiah as a gratuitous display of Deity, solely adapted to perplex, to terrify and to embroil mankind.

It is sufficiently evident that an omniscient being never conceived the design of reforming the world by Christianity. Omniscience would surely have foreseen the inefficacy of that system, which experience demonstrates not only to have been utterly impotent in restraining, but to have been most active in exhaling the malevolent propensities of men. During the period which elapsed between the removal of the seat of empire to Constantinople in 328, and its capture by the Turks in 1453, what salutary influence did Christianity exercise upon that world which it was intended to enlighten? Never before was Europe the theatre of such ceaseless and sanguinary wars; never were the people so brutalized by ignorance and debased by slavery.

I will admit that one prediction of Jesus Christ has been indisputably fulfilled. *I come not to bring peace upon earth, but a sword.*[10] Christianity indeed has equalled Judaism in the atrocities, and exceeded it in the extent of its desolation. Eleven millions of men, women and children have been killed in battle, butchered in their sleep, burned to death at public festivals of sacrifice, poisoned, tortured, assassinated and pillaged in the spirit of the Religion of Peace, and for the glory of the most merciful God.

In vain will you tell me that these terrible effects flow not from Christianity, but from the abuse of it. No such excuse will avail to palliate the enormities of a religion pretended to be divine. A limited intelligence is only so far responsible for the effects of its agency as it foresaw, or might have foreseen them; but Omniscience is manifestly chargeable with all the consequences of its conduct. Christianity itself declares that the worth of the tree is to be determined by the quality of its fruit. The extermination of infidels; the

mutual persecutions of hostile sects; the midnight massacres and slow burning of thousands because their creed contained either more or less than the orthodox standard, of which Christianity has been the immediate occasion; and the invariable opposition which philosophy has ever encountered from the spirit of revealed religion, plainly show that a very slight portion of sagacity was sufficient to have estimated at its true value the advantages of that belief to which some Theists are unaccountably attached.

You lay great stress upon the originality of the Christian system of morals. If this claim be just, either your religion must be false, or the Deity has willed that opposite modes of conduct should be pursued by mankind at different times, under the same circumstances; which is absurd.

The doctrine of acquiescing in the most insolent despotism; of praying for and loving our enemies; of faith and humility, appears to fix the perfection of the human character in that abjectness and credulity which priests and tyrants of all ages have found sufficiently convenient for their purposes. It is evident that a whole nation of Christians (could such an anomaly maintain itself a day) would become, like cattle, the property of the first occupier. It is evident that ten highwaymen would suffice to subjugate the world if it were composed of slaves who dared not to resist oppression.

The apathy to love and friendship, recommended by your creed, would, if attainable, not be less pernicious. This enthusiasm of anti-social misanthropy if it were an actual rule of conduct, and not the speculation of a few interested persons, would speedily annihilate the human race. A total abstinence from sexual intercourse is not perhaps enjoined, but is strenuously recommended,* and was actually practised to a frightful extent by the primitive Christians.†

The penalties inflict by that monster Constantine, the first Christian Emperor, on the pleasures of unlicenced love, are so iniquitously severe, that no modern legislator could have affixed them to the most atrocious crimes.‡ This cold-blooded and hypocritical ruffian cut his son's throat, strangled his wife, murdered his father-in-law and his brother-in-law, and maintained at his court a set of blood-thirsty and bigoted Christian Priests, one of whom was sufficient to excite the one half of the world to massacre the other.

---

10 Matthew, x, 34.

* Now concerning the things whereof ye wrote to me. It is good for a man not to touch a woman.

I say, therefore, to the unmarried and widows, it is good for them if they abide even as I; but if they cannot contain, let them marry; it is better to marry than burn.—*I. Corinthians*, chap. vii.

† See Gibbon's "Decline and Fall," vol. ii., p. 210.

‡ See Gibbon's "Decline and Fall," vol. ii., p. 269.

I am willing to admit that some few axioms of morality, which Christianity has borrowed from the philosophers of Greece and India, dictate, in an unconnected state, rules of conduct worthy of regard; but the purest and most elevated lessons of morality must remain nugatory, the most probable inducements to virtue must fail of their effect, so long as the slightest weight is attached to that dogma which is the vital essence of revealed religion.

Belief is set up as the criterion of merit or demerit; a man is to be judged not by the purity of his intentions but by the orthodoxy of his creed; an assent to certain propositions, is to outweigh in the balance of Christianity the most generous and elevated virtue.

But the intensity of belief, like that of every other passion, is precisely proportioned to the degrees of excitement. A graduated scale, on which should be marked the capabilities of propositions to approach to the test of the senses, would be a just measure of the belief which ought to be attached to them: and but for the influence of prejudice or ignorance this invariably *is* the measure of belief. That is believed which is apprehended to be true, nor can the mind by any exertion avoid attaching credit to an opinion attended with overwhelming evidence. Belief is not an act of volition, nor can it be regulated by the mind: it is manifestly incapable therefore of either merit or criminality. The system which assumes a false criterion of moral virtue, must be as pernicious as it is absurd. Above all, it cannot be divine, as it is impossible that the Creator of the human mind should be ignorant of its primary powers.

The degree of evidence afforded by miracles and prophecies in favour of the Christian Religion is lastly to be considered.

Evidence of a more imposing and irresistible nature is required in proportion to the remoteness of any event from the sphere of our experience. Every case of miracles is a contest of opposite improbabilities, whether it is more contrary to experience that a miracle should be true, or that the story on which it is supported should be false: whether the immutable laws of this harmonious world should have undergone violation, or that some obscure Greeks and Jews should have conspired to fabricate a tale of wonder.

The actual appearance of a departed spirit would be a circumstance truly unusual and portentous; but the accumulated testimony of twelve old women that a spirit had appeared is neither unprecedented nor miraculous.

It seems less credible that the God whose immensity is uncircumscribed by space, should have committed adultery with a carpenter's wife, than that some bold knaves or insane dupes had deceived the credulous multitude.* We have perpetual and mournful experience of the latter: the former is yet under dispute. History affords us innumerable examples of the possibility of the one: Philosophy has in all ages protested against the probability of the other.

Every superstition can produce its dupes, its miracles and its mysteries; each is prepared to justify its peculiar tenets by an equal assemblage of portents, prophecies and martyrdoms.

Prophecies, however circumstantial, are liable to the same objection as direct miracles: it is more agreeable to experience that the historical evidence of the prediction really having preceded the event pretended to be foretold should be false, or that a lucky conjuncture of events should have justified the conjecture of the prophet, than that Gold should communicate to a man the discernment of future events.† I defy you to produce more than one instance of prophecy in the Bible, wherein the inspired writer speaks so as to be understood, wherein his prediction has not been so unintelligible and obscure as to have been itself the subject of controversy among Christians.

That one prediction which I except is certainly most explicit and circumstantial. It is the only one of this nature which the Bible contains. Jesus himself here predicts his own arrival in the clouds to consummate a period of supernatural desolation, before the generation which he addressed should pass away.‡ Eighteen hundred years have past, and no such event is pretended to have happened. This single plain prophecy, thus conspicuously false, may serve as a criterion of those which are more vague and indirect, and which apply in an hundred senses to a hundred things.

Either the pretended predictions in the Bible were meant to be understood, or they were not. If they were, why is there any dispute concerning them: if they were not, wherefore were they written at all? But the God of Christianity spoke to mankind in parables,

* See Paley's Evidences. Vol. i. chap. I.

† See the Controversy of Bishop Watson and Thomas Paine.—Paine's Criticism on the xixth chapter of Isaiah.[11]

‡ Immediately after the tribulation of these days, shall the sun be darkened and the moon shall not give her light, and the stars shall fall from Heaven, and the powers of the heavens shall be shaken; and then shall appear the sign of the son of man in Heaven: and then shall all the tribes of the Earth mourn, and they shall see the son of man coming in the clouds of Heaven with power and great Glory; and he shall send his Angel with a great sound of a trumpet, and they shall gather together his elect from the four winds, from one end of Heaven to the other. *Verily I say unto you: This generation shall not pass, until all these things be fulfilled.*—*Matt.* chap. xxiv.

11 Richard Watson (1737–1816), Bishop of Llandaff, wrote *Apology for the Bible* (1796) in answer to the second part of Paine's *Age of Reason* (1795).

that seeing they might not see, and hearing they might not understand.

The Gospels contain internal evidence that they were not written by eye-witnesses of the event which they pretend to record. The Gospel of St. Matthew was plainly not written until some time after the taking of Jerusalem, that is, at least forty years after the execution of Jesus Christ: for he makes Jesus say *that upon you may come all the righteous blood shed upon the earth, from the blood of righteous Abel unto the blood of Zacharias son of Barachias whom ye slew between the altar and the temple.** Now Zacharias son of Barachias was assassinated between the altar and the temple by a faction of zealots, during the siege of Jerusalem.†

You assert that the design of the instances of supernatural interposition which the Gospel records was to convince mankind that Jesus Christ was truly the expected Redeemer. But it is as impossible that any human sophistry should frustrate the manifestation of Omnipotence, as that Omniscience should fail to select the most efficient means of accomplishing its design. Eighteen centuries have passed and the tenth part of the human race have a blind and mechanical belief in that Redeemer, without a complete reliance on the merits of whom, their lot is fixed in everlasting misery: surely if the Christian system be thus dreadfully important its Omnipotent author would have rendered it incapable of those abuses from which it has never been exempt, and to which it is subject in common with all human institutions, he would not have left it a matter of ceaseless cavil or complete indifference to the immense majority of mankind. Surely some more conspicuous evidences of its authenticity would have been afforded than driving out devils, drowning pigs, curing blind men, animating a dead body, and turning water into wine. Some theatre worthier of the transcendent event, than Judea, would have been chosen, some historians more adapted by their accomplishments and their genius to record the incarnation of the immutable God. The humane society restores drowned persons; every empiric can cure every disease; drowning pigs is no very difficult matter, and driving out devils was far from being an original or an unusual occupation in Judea. Do not recite these stale absurdities as proofs of the Divine origin of Christianity.

If the Almighty has spoken, would not the Universe have been convinced? If he had judged the knowledge of his will to have been more important than any other

* See Matthew, chap. xxiii, v. 35.
† Josephus.[12]

◇◇◇

[12] Flavius Josephus (A.D. 38–93), historian of the Jews.

science to mankind, would he not have rendered it more evident and more clear?

Now, O Eusebes, have I enumerated the general grounds of my disbelief of the Christian Religion.—I could have collated its Sacred Writings with the Brahminical record of the early ages of the world, and identified its institutions with the antient worship of the Sun. I might have entered into an elaborate comparison of the innumerable discordances which exist between the inspired historians of the same event. Enough however has been said to vindicate me from the charge of groundless and infatuated scepticism. I trust therefore to your candour for the consideration, and to your logic for the refutation, of my arguments.

EUSEBES

I will not dissemble, O Theosophus, the difficulty of solving your general objections to Christianity, on the grounds of human reason. I did not assist at the councils of the Almighty when he determined to extend his mercy to mankind, nor can I venture to affirm that it exceeded the limits of his power to have afforded a more conspicuous or universal manifestation of his will.

But this is a difficulty which attends Christianity in common with the belief in the being and attributes of God. This whole scheme of things might have been, according to our partial conceptions, infinitely more admirable and perfect. Poisons, earthquakes, disease, war, famine and venomous serpents; slavery and persecution are the consequences of certain causes, which according to human judgment might well have been dispensed with an arranging of the economy of the globe.

Is this the reasoning which the Theist will choose to employ? Will he impose limitations on that Deity whom he professes to regard with so profound a veneration? Will he place his God between the horns of a logical dilemma which shall restrict the fulness either of his power or his bounty?

Certainly he will prefer to resign his objections to Christianity, than pursue the reasoning upon which they are found, to the dreadful conclusions of cold and dreary Atheism.

I confess, that Christianity appears not unattended with difficulty to the understanding which approaches it with a determination to judge its mysteries by reason. I will even confess that the discourse, which you have just delivered, ought to unsettle any candid mind engaged in a similar attempt. The children of this world are wiser in their generation than the children of light.

But if I succeed in convincing you that reason conducts to conclusions destructive of morality, happiness, and the hope of futurity, and inconsistent with the very existence of human society, I trust that you will no longer confide in a director so dangerous and faithless.

I require you to declare, O Theosophus, whether you would embrace Christianity or Atheism, if no other systems of belief shall be found to stand the touchstone of enquiry.

THEOSOPHUS

I do not hesitate to prefer the Christian system, or indeed any system of religion, however rude and gross, to Atheism.—Here we truly sympathise; nor do I blame, however I may feel inclined to pity, the man who in his zeal to escape this gloomy faith, should plunge into the most abject superstition.

The Atheist is a monster among men. Inducements, which are Omnipotent over the conduct of others, are impotent for him. His private judgment is his criterion of right and wrong. He dreads no judge but his own conscience, he fears no hell but the loss of his self esteem. He is not to be restrained by punishments, for death is divested of its terror, and whatever enters into his heart, to conceive, that will he not scruple to execute. *Iste non timet omnia providentem et cogitantem, et animadvertentem, et omnia ad se pertinere putantem, curiosum et plenum negotii Deum.*[13]

This dark and terrible doctrine was surely the abortion of some blind speculator's brain: some strange and hideous perversion of intellect, some portentous distortion of reason. There can surely be no metaphysician sufficiently bigotted to his own system to look upon this harmonious world, and dispute the necessity of intelligence; to contemplate the design and deny the designer; to enjoy the spectacle of this beautiful Universe and not feel himself instinctively persuaded to gratitude and adoration. What arguments of the slightest plausibility can be adduced to support a doctrine rejected alike by the instinct of the savage and the reason of the sage?

I readily engage, with you, to reject reason as a faithless guide, if you can demonstrate that it conducts to Atheism. So little however do I mistrust the dictates of reason, concerning a supreme Being, that I promise, in the event of your success, to subscribe the wildest and most monstrous creed which you can devise. I will call credulity, faith; reason, impiety; the dictates of the understanding shall be the temptations of the Devil, and the wildest dreams of the imagination, the infallible inspirations of Grace.

EUSEBES

Let me request you then to state, concisely, the grounds of your belief in the being of God. In my reply I shall endeavour to controvert your reasoning, and shall hold myself acquitted by my zeal for the Christian religion, of the blasphemies which I must utter in the progress of my discourse.

THEOSOPHUS

I will readily state the grounds of my belief in the being of a God. You can only have remained ignorant of the obvious proofs of this important truth, from a superstitious reliance upon the evidence afforded by a revealed religion. The reasoning lies within an extremely narrow compass: *quicquid enim nos vel meliores vel beatiores facturum est, aut in aperto, aut in proximo posuit natura.*[14]

From every design we justly infer a designer. If we examine the structure of a watch, we shall readily confess the existence of a watch-maker. No work of man could possibly have existed from all eternity. From the contemplation of any product of human art, we conclude that there was an artificer who arranged its several parts. In like manner, from the marks of design and contrivance exhibited in the Universe, we are necessitated to infer a designer, a contriver. If the parts of the Universe have been designed, contrived and adapted, the existence of a God is manifest.

But design is sufficiently apparent. The wonderful adaptation of substances which act to those which are acted upon; of the eye to light, and of light to the eye; of the ear to sound, and of sound to the ear; of every object of sensation to the sense which it impresses prove that neither blind chance, nor undistinguishing necessity has brought them into being. The adaptation of certain animals to certain climates, the relations borne to each other by animals and vegetables, and by different tribes of animals; the relation lastly, between man and the circumstances of his external situation are so many demonstrations of Deity.

All is order, design and harmony, so far as we can descry the tendency of things, and every new enlargement of our views, every new display of the material world, affords a new illustration of the power, the wisdom and the benevolence of God.

The existence of God has never been the topic of popular dispute. There is a tendency to devotion, a thirst for reliance on supernatural aid inherent in the human mind. Scarcely any people, however barbarous,

---

[13] *Iste . . . Deum:* "Such a man does not fear a god who foresees and arranges everything and notices everything and considers that everything is his business, a god who is full of care and full of work."

[14] *quicquid . . . natura:* "All that tends to make us better and happier has been placed either in plain sight or near by." Seneca's *De Beneficiis,* VII, i, 6 (John W. Basore translation, Loeb Classical Library, Harvard University Press).

have been discovered, who do not acknowledge with reverence and awe the supernatural causes of the natural effects which they experience. They worship, it is true, the vilest and most inanimate substances, but they firmly confide in the holiness and power of these symbols, and thus own their connexion with what they can neither see nor perceive.

If there is motion in the Universe, there is a God.* The power of beginning motion is no less an attribute of mind than sensation or thought. Wherever motion exists it is evident that mind has operated. The phenomena of the Universe indicate the agency of powers which cannot belong to inert matter.

Every thing which begins to exist must have a cause: every combination, conspiring to an end, implies intelligence.

EUSEBES

Design must be proved before a designer can be inferred. The matter in controversy is the existence of design in the Universe, and it is not permitted to assume the contested premises and thence infer the matter in dispute. Insidiously to employ the words contrivance, design and adaptation before these circumstances are made apparent in the Universe, thence justly inferring a contriver, is a popular sophism against which it behoves us to be watchful.

To assert that motion is an attribute of mind, that matter is inert, that every combination is the result of intelligence is also an assumption of the matter in dispute.

Why do we admit design in any machine of human contrivance? Simply, because innumerable instances of machines having been contrived by human art are present to our mind, because we are acquainted with persons who could construct such machines; but if, having no previous knowledge of any artificial contrivance, we had accidentally found a watch upon the ground, we should have been justified in concluding that it was a thing of Nature, that it was a combination of matter with whose cause we were unacquainted, and that any attempt to account for the origin of its existence would be equally presumptuous and unsatisfactory.

The analogy which you attempt to establish between the contrivances of human art, and the various existences of the Universe, is inadmissible. We attribute these effects to human intelligence, because we know before hand that human intelligence is capable of producing them. Take away this knowledge,

*See Dugald Stewart's Outlines of Moral Philosophy, and Paley's Natural Theology.

and the grounds of our reasoning will be destroyed. Our entire ignorance, therefore, of the Divine Nature leaves this analogy defective in its most essential point of comparison.

What consideration remains to be urged in support of the creation of the Universe by a supreme Being? Its admirable fitness for the production of certain effects, that wonderful consent of all its parts, that universal harmony by whose changeless laws innumerable systems of worlds perform their stated revolutions, and the blood is driven through the veins of the minutest animalcule that sports in the corruption of an insect's lymph: on this account did the Universe require an intelligent Creator, because it exists producing invariable effects, and inasmuch as it is admirably organised for the production of these effects, so the more did it require a creative intelligence.

Thus have we arrived at the substance of your assertion, "That whatever exists, producing certain effects, stands in need of a Creator, and the more conspicuous is its fitness for the production of these effects, the more certain will be our conclusion that it would not have existed from eternity, but must have derived its origin from an intelligent creator."

In what respect then do these arguments apply to the Universe, and not apply to God? From the fitness of the Universe to its end you infer the necessity of an intelligent Creator. But if the fitness of the Universe, to produce certain effects, be thus conspicuous and evident, how much more exquisite fitness to his end must exist in the Author of this Universe? If we find great difficulty from its admirable arrangement, in conceiving that the Universe has existed from all eternity, and to resolve this difficulty suppose a Creator, how much more clearly must we perceive the necessity of this very Creator's creation whose perfections comprehend an arrangement far more accurate and just.

The belief of an infinity of creative and created Gods, each more eminently requiring an intelligent author of his being than the foregoing, is a direct consequence of the premises which you have stated. The assumption that the Universe is a design, leads to a conclusion that there are infinity of creative and created Gods, which is absurd. It is impossible indeed to prescribe limits to learned error, when Philosophy relinquishes experience and feeling for speculation.

Until it is clearly proved that the Universe was created, we may reasonably suppose that it has endured from all eternity. In a case where two propositions are diametrically opposite, the mind believes that which is less incomprehensible: it is easier to suppose that the Universe has existed from all eternity, than to conceive an eternal being capable of creating it. If the mind sinks beneath the weight of one, is it an alleviation to encrease the intolerability of the burthen?

A man knows, not only that he now is, but that there was a time when he did not exist; consequently there must have been a cause. But we can only infer, from effects, causes exactly adequate to those effects. There certainly is a generative power which is effected by particular instruments; we cannot prove that it is inherent in these instruments, nor is the contrary hypothesis capable of demonstration. We admit that the generative power is incomprehensible, but to suppose that the same effects are produced by an eternal Omnipotent and Omniscient Being, leaves the cause in the same obscurity, but renders it more incomprehensible.

We can only infer from effects causes exactly adequate to those effects. An infinite number of effects demand an infinite number of causes, nor is the philosopher justified in supposing a greater connection or unity in the latter, than is perceptible in the former. The same energy cannot be at once the cause of the serpent and the sheep; of the blight by which the harvest is destroyed, and the sunshine by which it is matured; of the ferocious propensities by which man becomes a victim to himself, and of the accurate judgment by which his institutions are improved. The spirit of our accurate and exact philosophy is outraged by conclusions which contradict each other so glaringly.

The greatest, equally with the smallest motions of the Universe, are subjected to the rigid necessity of inevitable laws. These laws are the unknown causes of the known effects perceivable in the Universe. Their effects are the boundaries of our knowledge, their names the expressions of our ignorance. To suppose some existence beyond, or above them, is to invent a second and superfluous hypothesis to account for what has already been accounted for by the laws of motion and the properties of matter. I admit that the nature of these laws is incomprehensible, but the hypothesis of a Deity adds a gratuitous difficulty, which so far from alleviating those which it is adduced to explain, requires new hypotheses for the elucidation of its own inherent contradictions.

The laws of attraction and repulsion, desire and aversion, suffice to account for every phenomenon of the moral and physical world. A precise knowledge of the properties of any object, is alone requisite to determine its manner of action. Let the mathematician be acquainted with the weight and volume of a cannon ball, together with the degree of velocity and inclination with which it is impelled, and he will accurately delineate the course it must describe, and determine the force with which it will strike an object at a given distance. Let the influencing motive, present to the mind of any person be given, and the knowledge of his consequent conduct will result. Let the bulk and velocity of a comet be discovered, and the astronomer, by the accurate estimation of the equal and contrary actions of the centripetal and centrifugal forces, will justly predict the period of its return.

The anomalous motions of the heavenly bodies, their unequal velocities and frequent aberrations, are corrected by that gravitation by which they are caused. The illustrious Laplace,[15] has shewn, that the approach of the Moon to the Earth, and the Earth to the Sun, is only a secular equation of a very long period, which has its maximum and minimum. The system of the Universe then is upheld solely by physical powers. The necessity of matter is the ruler of the world. It is vain philosophy which supposes more causes than are exactly adequate to explain the phenomena of things. *Hypotheses non fingo : quicquid enim ex phænomenis non deducitur, hypothesis vocanda est ; et hypotheses vel metaphysicæ, vel physicæ, vel qualitatum occultarum, seu mechanicæ, in philosophiâ locum non habent.*[16]

You assert that the construction of the animal machine, the fitness of certain animals to certain situations, the connexion between the organs of perception and that which is perceived; the relation between every thing which exists, and that which tends to preserve it in its existence, imply design. It is manifest that if the eye could not see, nor the stomach digest, the human frame could not preserve its present mode of existence. It is equally certain, however, that the elements of its composition, if they did not exist in one form, must exist in another; and that the combinations which they would form, must so long as they endured, derive support for their peculiar mode of being from their fitness to the circumstances of their situation.

It by no means follows, that because a being exists, performing certain functions, he was fitted by another being to the performance of these functions. So rash a conclusion would conduct, as I have before shewn, to an absurdity; and it becomes infinitely more unwarrantable from the consideration that the known laws of matter and motion, suffice to unravel, even in the present imperfect state of moral and physical science, the majority of those difficulties which the hypothesis of a Deity was invented to explain.

Doubtless no disposition of inert matter, or matter

15 Pierre Simon de Laplace (1749–1827), French astronomer and mathematician.

16 *Hypotheses . . . non habent*: "I do not make up hypotheses; for whatever is not deduced from phenomena must be called an hypothesis, and hypotheses, whether they are metaphysical or physical or concern hidden qualities or the mechanical, have no place in philosophy."

deprived of qualities, could ever have composed an animal, a tree, or even a stone. But matter deprived of qualities, is an abstraction, concerning which it is impossible to form an idea. Matter, such as we behold it, is not inert. It is infinitely active and subtile. Light, electricity and magnetism are fluids not surpassed by thought itself in tenuity and activity; like thought they are sometimes the cause and sometimes the effect of motion; and, distinct as they are from every other class of substances, with which we are acquainted, seem to possess equal claims with thought to the unmeaning distinction of immateriality.

The laws of motion and the properties of matter suffice to account for every phenomenon, or combination of phenomena exhibited in the Universe. That certain animals exist in certain climates, results from the consentaneity of their frames to the circumstances of their situation: let these circumstances be altered to a sufficient degree, and the elements of their composition, must exist in some new combination no less resulting than the former from those inevitable laws by which the Universe is governed.

It is the necessary consequence of the organization of man, that his stomach should digest his food: it inevitably results also from his gluttonous and unnatural appetite for the flesh of animals that his frame be diseased and his vigour impaired; but in neither of these cases is adaptation of means to end to be perceived. Unnatural diet, and the habits consequent upon its use are the means, and every complication of frightful disease is the end, but to assert that these means were adapted to this end by the Creator of the world, or that human caprice can avail to traverse the precautions of Omnipotence, is absurd. These are the consequences of the properties of organized matter; and it is a strange perversion of the understanding to argue that a certain sheep was created to be butchered and devoured by a certain individual of the human species, when the conformation of the latter, as is manifest to the most superficial student of comparative anatomy classes him with those animals who feed on fruits and vegetables.*

* See Cuvier, *Leçons d' Anat. Comp.* tom. iii. p. 169, 373, 448, 465, 480. Rees's *Cyclopaeăia*, Art. Man.

Ουκ αιδεισθε τους ἡμερους καρπους ἁιματι και φονω μιγνυοντες; αλλα δρακοντας αγριους καλειτε, και παρδαλεις και λεοντας, αυτοι δε μιαιφονειτε εις ωμοτητα καταλιποντες εκεινοις ουδεν. Εκεινοις μεν ὁ φονος τροφη, ὑμιν δε οψον εστιν.
Ὅτι γαρ ουκ εστιν ανθρωπω κατα φυσιν το σαρκοφαγεν, πρωτον μεν απο των σωματων δηλουται της κατασκευης. Ουδενι γαρ εοικε το ανθρωπου σωμα των απο σαρκοφαγια γεγονοτων. ου γρυποτης χειλους, ουκ οξυτης ονυχος, ου τραχυτης οδοντων προσεστιν, ου κοιλιας ευτονια και πνευματος θερμοτος τρεψαι και κατεργασασθαι το βαρυ και κρεωδες. Αλλ' αυτοθεν ἡ φυσις τη λειοτητι των οδοντων, και τη σμικροτητι του σωματος, και τη

The means by which the existence of an animal is sustained, requires a designer in no greater degree than the existence itself of the animal. If it exists, there must be means to support its existence. In a world where *omne mutatur nihil interit*,[18] no organized being can exist without a continual separation of that substance which is incessantly exhausted, nor can this separation take place otherwise, than by the invariable laws which result from the relations of matter. We are incapacitated only by our ignorance from referring every phenomenon, however unusual, minute or complex, to the laws of motion and the properties of matter; and it is an egregious offence against the first principles of reason, to suppose an immaterial creator of the world, *in quo omnia moventur sed sine mutuâ passione;*[19] which is equally a superfluous hypothesis in the mechanical philosophy of Newton, and a useless excrescence on the inductive logic of Bacon.

What then is this harmony, this order which you maintain to have required for its establishment, what it needs not for its maintenance, the agency of a supernatural intelligence? Inasmuch as the Order visible in the Universe requires one cause, so does the disorder whose operation is not less clearly apparent, demand another. Order and disorder are no more than modifications of our own perceptions of the relations which

μαλακοτητι της λγωσσης, και τη ρπος πεψιν αμβλυτητι του πνευματος, εξομνυται την σαρκοφαγιαν. Ει δε λεγεις πεφυκεναι σεαυτον επι τοιαυτην εδωδην, ὁ βουλει φαγειν, πρωτον αυτος αποκτεινον αλλ' αυτος δια σεαυτου, μη χρησαμενος κοπιδι. μηδε τυμπανω τινι, μηδε πελεκει· αλλα ὡς λυκοι και αρκτοι και λεοντες αυτοι ὡς εσθιουσι φονευουσιν, ανελε δηγματι βουν, η σωματι συν, η αρνα η λαγωον διαρρηξον, και φαγε προσπεσων ετι ζωντος, ὡς εκεινα· Πλουτ. περι Σαρκοφαγ. Λογ. β.[17]

[17] Shelley quotes two passages (994B, 995A–B) from Plutarch's first essay "On the Eating of Flesh" in *Moralia*: "Are you not ashamed to mingle domestic crops with blood and gore? You call serpents and panthers and lions savage, but you yourselves, by your own foul slaughters, leave them no room to outdo you in cruelty; for their slaughter is their living, yours is a mere appetizer.

"For that man is not naturally carnivorous is, in the first place, obvious from the structure of his body. A man's frame is in no way similar to those creatures who were made for flesh-eating: he has no hooked beak or sharp nails or jagged teeth, no strong stomach or warmth of vital fluids able to digest and assimilate a heavy diet of flesh. It is from this very fact, the evenness of our teeth, the smallness of our mouths, the softness of our tongues, our possession of vital fluids too inert to digest meat that Nature disavows our eating of flesh. If you declare that you are naturally designed for such a diet, then first kill for yourself what you want to eat. Do it, however, only through your own resources, unaided by cleaver or cudgel or any kind of axe. Rather, just as wolves and bears and lions themselves slay what they eat, so you are to fell an ox with your fangs or a boar with your jaws, or tear a lamb or hare in bits" (Harold Cherniss and William C. Helmbold translation, Loeb Classical Library, Harvard University Press).

[18] *omne . . . interit:* "everything changes but nothing perishes."
[19] *in quo . . . passione:* "in whom all things are moved but without being affected by each other."

subsist between ourselves and external objects, and if we are justified in inferring the operation of a benevolent power from the advantages attendant on the former, the evils of the latter bear equal testimony to the activity of a malignant principle, no less pertinacious in inducing evil out of good, than the other is unremitting in procuring good from evil.

If we permit our imagination to traverse the obscure regions of possibility, we may doubtless imagine, according to the complexion of our minds, that disorder may have a relative tendency to unmingled good, or order be relatively replete with exquisite and subtile evil. To neither of these conclusions, which are equally presumptuous and unfounded, will it become the philosopher to assent. Order and disorder are expressions denoting our perceptions of what is injurious or beneficial to ourselves, or to the beings in whose welfare we are compelled to sympathize by the similarity of their conformation to our own.*

A beautiful antelope panting under the fangs of a tiger, a defenceless ox, groaning beneath the butcher's axe, is a spectacle which instantly awakens compassion in a virtuous and unvitiated breast. Many there are, however, sufficiently hardened to the rebukes of justice and the precepts of humanity, as to regard the deliberate butchery of thousands of their species, as a theme of exultation and a source of honour, and to consider any failure in these remorseless enterprises as a defect in the system of things. The criteria of order and disorder are as various as those beings from whose opinions and feelings they result.

Populous cities are destroyed by earthquakes, and desolated by pestilence. Ambition is every where devoting its millions to incalculable calamity. Superstition, in a thousand shapes, is employed in brutalizing and degrading the human species, and fitting it to endure without a murmur the oppression of its innumerable tyrants. All this is abstractedly neither good nor evil because good and evil are words employed to designate that peculiar state of our own perceptions, resulting from the encounter of any object calculated to produce pleasure or pain. Exclude the idea of relation, and the words good and evil are deprived of import.

Earthquakes are injurious to the cities which they destroy, beneficial to those whose commerce was injured by their prosperity, and indifferent to others which are too remote to be affected by their influence. Famine is good to the corn-merchant, evil to the poor, and indifferent to those whose fortunes can at all times command a superfluity. Ambition is evil to the restless bosom it inhabits, to the innumerable victims who are dragged by its ruthless thirst for infamy, to expire in every variety of anguish, to the inhabitants of the country it depopulates, and to the human race whose improvement it retards; it is indifferent with regard to the system of the Universe, and is good only to the vultures and the jackalls that track the conqueror's career, and to the worms who feast in security on the desolation of his progress. It is manifest that we cannot reason with respect to the universal system from that which only exists in relation to our own perceptions.

You allege some considerations in favour of a Deity from the universality of a belief in his existence.

The superstitions of the savage, and the religion of civilized Europe appear to you to conspire to prove a first cause. I maintain that it is from the evidence of revelation alone that this belief derives the slightest countenance.

That credulity should be gross in proportion to the ignorance of the mind which it enslaves, is in strict consistency with the principles of human nature. The idiot, the child and the savage, agree in attributing their own passions and propensities† to the inanimate substances by which they are either benefited or injured. The former become Gods and the latter Demons; hence prayers and sacrifices, by the means of which the rude Theologian imagines that he may confirm the benevolence of the one, or mitigate the malignity of the other. He has averted the wrath of a powerful enemy by supplications and submission; he has secured the assistance of his neighbour by offerings; he has felt his own anger subside before the entreaties of a vanquished foe, and has cherished gratitude for the kindness of another. Therefore does he believe that the elements will listen to his vows. He is capable of love and hatred towards his fellow beings, and is variously impelled by those principles to benefit or injure them. The source of his error is sufficiently obvious. When the winds, the waves and the atmosphere, act in such a manner as to thwart or forward his designs, he attributes to them the same propensities of whose existence within himself he is conscious when he is instigated by benefits to kindness, or by injuries to revenge. The bigot of the woods can form no conception of beings possessed of properties differing from his own: it requires, indeed, a mind considerably tinctured with science, and enlarged by cultivation to contemplate itself, not as the centre and model of the Universe, but as one of the infinitely various multitude of beings of which it is actually composed.

There is no attribute of God which is not either borrowed from the passions and powers of the human mind, or which is not a negation. Omniscience, Omnipotence, Omnipresence, Infinity, Immutability, In-

* See Godwin's *Political Justice*, Vol. i. p. 449.

† See Southey's *History of Brazil*, p. 255.

comprehensibility, and Immateriality, are all words which designate properties and powers, peculiar to organised beings, with the addition of negations, by which the idea of limitation is excluded.*

That the frequency of a belief in God (for it is not Universal) should be any argument in its favour, none to whom the innumerable mistakes of men are familiar, will assert. It is among men of genius and science that Atheism alone is found, but among these alone is cherished an hostility to those errors, with which the illiterate and vulgar are infected.

How small is the proportion of those who really believe in God, to the thousands who are prevented by their occupations from ever bestowing a serious thought upon the subject, and the millions who worship butterflies, bones, feathers, monkeys, calabashes and serpents. The word God, like other abstractions, signifies the agreement of certain propositions, rather than the presence of any idea. If we found our belief in the existence of God on the universal consent of mankind, we are duped by the most palpable of sophisms. The word God cannot mean at the same time an ape, a snake, a bone, a calabash, a Trinity, and a Unity. Nor can that belief be accounted universal against which men of powerful intellect and spotless virtue have in every age protested. *Non pudet igitur physicum, id est speculatorem venatoremque naturæ, ex animis consuetudine imbutis petere testimonium veritatis?* [21]

Hume has shewn, to the satisfaction of all philosophers, that the only idea which we can form of causation is derivable from the constant conjunction of objects, and the consequent inference of one from the other. We denominate that phenomenon the cause of another which we observe with the fewest exceptions to precede its occurrence. Hence it would be inadmissible to deduce the being of a God from the existence of the Universe; even if this mode of reasoning did not conduct to the monstrous conclusion of an infinity of creative and created Gods, each more eminently requiring a Creator than its predecessor.

If Power† be an attribute of existing substance,

substance could not have derived its origin from power. One thing cannot be at the same time the cause and the effect of another.—The word power expresses the capability of any thing to be or act. The human mind never hesitates to annex the idea of power to any object of its experience. To deny that power is the attribute of being, is to deny that being can be. If power be an attribute of substance, the hypothesis of a God is a superfluous and unwarrantable assumption.

Intelligence is that attribute of the Deity, which you hold to be most apparent in the Universe. Intelligence is only known to us as a mode of animal being. We cannot conceive intelligence distinct from sensation and perception, which are attributes to organized bodies. To assert that God is intelligent, is to assert that he has ideas; and Locke has proved that ideas result from sensation. Sensation can exist only in an organized body, an organized body is necessarily limited both in extent and operation. The God of the rational Theosophist is a vast and wise animal.

You have laid it down as a maxim that the power of beginning motion is an attribute of mind as much as thought and sensation.

Mind cannot create, it can only perceive. Mind is the recipient of impressions made on the organs of sense, and without the action of external objects we should not only be deprived of all knowledge of the existence of mind, but totally incapable of the knowledge of any thing. It is evident therefore that mind deserves to be considered as the effect, rather than the cause of motion. The ideas which suggest themselves too are prompted by the circumstances of our situation, these are the elements of thought, and from the various combinations of these our feelings, opinions and volitions, inevitably result.

That which is infinite necessarily includes that which is finite. The distinction therefore between the Universe, and that by which the Universe is upheld, is manifestly erroneous. To devise the word God, that you may express a certain portion of the universal system, can answer no good purpose in philosophy: In the language of reason, the words God and Universe are synonymous. *Omnia enim per Dei potentiam facta sunt: imo, quia naturæ potentia nulla est nisi ipsa Dei potentia, certum est nos eatenus Dei potentiam non intelligere quatenus causas naturales ignoramus; adeoque stultè ad eandem Dei potentiam recurritur, quando rei alicujus, causam naturalem, hoc est, ipsam Dei potentiam ignoramus.*‡

---

* See *Le Système de la Nature*: this book is one of the most eloquent vindications of Atheism.[20]

† For a very profound disquisition on this subject, see Sir William Drummond's *Academical Questions*, chap. i, p. 1.[22]

‡ Spinosa, *Tract. Theologico—Pol.*, chap. i. p. 14.[23]

[20] Referring to Baron d'Holbach's influential work of 1770.

[21] *Non pudet . . . veritatis?*: "Is a physicist, therefore, that is, a contemplator and hunter of nature, not ashamed to seek the testimony of truth from spirits drenched with habit?"

[22] Referring to a treatise of philosophic scepticism published in 1805, by Sir William Drummond (*c.* 1770–1828). See Shelley's other praiseful reference to the work in the fragment "On Life." On the importance of Drummond's work in the evolution of Shelley's thought, consult the study by C. E. Pulos mentioned in the headnote, p. 684.

[23] *Omnia . . . ignoramus*: "For everything is made through the power of God; in fact, since the power of nature is nothing but the

Thus, from the principles of that reason to which you so rashly appealed as the ultimate arbiter of our dispute, have I shewn that the popular arguments in favour of the being of a God are totally destitute of colour. I have shewn the absurdity of attributing intelligence to the cause of those effects which we perceive in the Universe, and the fallacy which lurks in the argument from design. I have shewn that order is no more than a peculiar manner of contemplating the operation of necessary agents, that mind is the effect, not the cause of motion, that power is the attribute, not the origin of Being. I have proved that we can have no evidence of the existence of a God from the principles of reason.

You will have observed, from the zeal with which I have urged arguments so revolting to my genuine sentiments, and conducted to a conclusion in direct contradiction to that faith which every good man must eternally preserve, how little I am inclined to sympathise with those of my religion who have pretended to prove the existence of God by the unassisted light of reason. I confess that the necessity of a revelation has been compromised by treacherous friends to Christianity, who have maintained that the sublime mysteries of the being of a God and the immortality of the soul are discoverable from other sources than itself.

I have proved, that on the principles of that philosophy to which Epicurus, Lord Bacon, Newton, Locke and Hume were addicted, the existence of God is a chimera.

The Christian Religion then, alone, affords indisputable assurance that the world was created by the power, and is preserved by the Providence of an Almighty God, who, in justice has appointed a future life for the punishment of the vicious and the remuneration of the virtuous.

Now, O Theosophus, I call upon you to decide between Atheism and Christianity; to declare whether you will pursue your principles to the destruction of the bonds of civilized society, or wear the easy yoke of that Religion which proclaims "peace upon earth, good-will to all men."

THEOSOPHUS

I am not prepared at present, I confess, to reply clearly to your unexpected arguments. I assure you that no considerations, however specious, should seduce me to deny the existence of my Creator.

I am willing to promise that if, after mature deliberation, the arguments which you have advanced in favour of Atheism should appear incontrovertible, I will endeavour to adopt so much of the Christian scheme as is consistent with my persuasion of the goodness, unity and majesty of God.

[1814]   [1929]

ON LIFE[1]

LIFE AND the world, or whatever we call that which we are and feel, is an astonishing thing. The mist of familiarity obscures from us the wonder of our being. We are struck with admiration at some of its transient modifications, but it is itself the great miracle. What are changes of empires, the wreck of dynasties, with the opinions which supported them; what is the birth and the extinction of religious and of political systems, to life? What are the revolutions of the globe which we inhabit, and the operations of the elements of which it is composed, compared with life? What is the universe of stars, and suns, of which this inhabited earth is one, and their motions, and their destiny, compared with life? Life, the great miracle, we admire not, because it is so miraculous. It is well that we are thus shielded by the familiarity of what is at once so certain and so unfathomable, from an astonishment which would otherwise absorb and overawe the functions of that which is its object.

If any artist, I do not say had executed, but had merely conceived in his mind the system of the sun, and the stars, and planets, they not existing, and had painted to us in words, or upon canvas, the spectacle now afforded by the nightly cope of heaven, and illustrated it by the wisdom of astronomy, great would be our admiration. Or had he imagined the scenery of this earth, the mountains, the seas, and the rivers; the grass, and the flowers, and the variety of the forms and masses of the leaves of the woods, and the colours which attend the setting and the rising sun, and the hues of the atmosphere, turbid or serene, these things not before existing, truly we should have been astonished, and it would not have been a vain boast to have said of such a man, "Non merita nome di creatore, sennon Iddio ed il Poeta."[2] But now these things are looked on with little wonder, and to be conscious of them with intense delight is esteemed to

power of God itself, it is certain that we do not understand the power of God to the extent that we are ignorant of natural causes; so stupidly is recourse had to that same power of God when we are ignorant of the natural cause of some thing, that is, of the power of God itself."

[1] The date of composition of this fragment is uncertain, but probably 1812–1814. It was first published in 1832.
[2] "Non merita . . . Poeta." "No one deserves the name of Creator, except God and the Poet." In *A Defence of Poetry* (see p. 736), Shelley cites Tasso as the author of this remark.

be the distinguishing mark of a refined and extraordinary person. The multitude of men care not for them. It is thus with Life—that which includes all.

What is life? Thoughts and feelings arise, with or without our will, and we employ words to express them. We are born, and our birth is unremembered, and our infancy remembered but in fragments; we live on, and in living we lose the apprehension of life. How vain is it to think that words can penetrate the mystery of our being! Rightly used they may make evident our ignorance to ourselves, and this is much. For what are we? When do we come? and whither do we go? Is birth the commencement, is death the conclusion of our being? What is birth and death?

The most refined abstractions of logic conduct to a view of life, which, though startling to the apprehension, is, in fact, that which the habitual sense of its repeated combinations has extinguished in us. It strips, as it were, the painted curtain from this scene of things. I confess that I am one of those who am unable to refuse my assent to the conclusions of those philosophers who assert that nothing exists but as it is perceived.

It is a decision against which all our persuasions struggle, and we must be long convicted before we can be convinced that the solid universe of external things is "such stuff as dreams are made of."[3] The shocking absurdities of the popular philosophy of mind and matter, its fatal consequences in morals, and their violent dogmatism concerning the source of all things, had early conducted me to materialism. This materialism is a seducing system to young and superficial minds. It allows its disciples to talk, and dispenses them from thinking. But I was discontented with such a view of things as it afforded; man is a being of high aspirations, "looking both before and after,"[4] whose "thoughts wander through eternity,"[5] disclaiming alliance with transience and decay; incapable of imagining to himself annihilation; existing but in the future and the past; being, not what he is, but what he has been and shall be. Whatever may be his true and final destination, there is a spirit within him at enmity with nothingness and dissolution. This is the character of all life and being. Each is at once the centre and the circumference; the point to which all things are referred, and the line in which all things are contained. Such contemplations as these, materialism and the popular philosophy of mind and matter alike forbid; they are only consistent with the intellectual system.

It is absurd to enter into a long recapitulation of arguments sufficiently familiar to those inquiring minds, whom alone a writer on abstruse subjects can be conceived to address. Perhaps the most clear and vigorous statement of the intellectual system is to be found in Sir William Drummond's Academical Questions.[6] After such an exposition, it would be idle to translate into other words what could only lose its energy and fitness by the change. Examined point by point, and word by word, the most discriminating intellects have been able to discern no train of thoughts in the process of reasoning, which does not conduct inevitably to the conclusion which has been stated.

What follows from the admission? It establishes no new truth, it gives us no additional insight into our hidden nature, neither its action nor itself. Philosophy, impatient as it may be to build, has much work yet remaining, as pioneer for the overgrowth of ages. It makes one step towards this object; it destroys error, and the roots of error. It leaves, what is too often the duty of the reformer in political and ethical questions to leave, a vacancy. It reduces the mind to that freedom in which it would have acted, but for the misuse of words and signs, the instruments of its own creation. By signs, I would be understood in a wide sense, including what is properly meant by the term, and what I peculiarly mean. In this latter sense, almost all familiar objects are signs, standing, not for themselves, but for others, in their capacity of suggesting one thought which shall lead to a train of thoughts. Our whole life is thus an education of error.

Let us recollect our sensations as children. What a distinct and intense apprehension had we of the world and of ourselves! Many of the circumstances of social life were then important to us which are now no longer so. But that is not the point of comparison on which I mean to insist. We less habitually distinguished all that we saw and felt, from ourselves. They seemed as it were to constitute one mass. There are some persons who, in this respect, are always children. Those who are subject to the state called reverie, feel as if their nature were dissolved into the surrounding universe, or as if the surrounding universe were absorbed into their being. They are conscious of no distinction. And these are states which precede, or accompany, or follow an unusually intense and vivid apprehension of life. As men grow up this power commonly decays and they become mechanical and habitual agents. Thus feelings and then reasonings are the combined result of a multitude of entangled thoughts, and of a series of what are called impressions, planted by reiteration.

---

[3] *The Tempest*, IV, i, 156–57.
[4] *Hamlet*, IV, iv, 37.   [5] *Paradise Lost*, II, 148.

[6] See *A Refutation of Deism*, footnote 22, p. 698.

The view of life presented by the most refined deductions of the intellectual philosophy, is that of unity. Nothing exists but as it is perceived. The difference is merely nominal between those two classes of thought, which are vulgarly distinguished by the names of ideas and of external objects. Pursuing the same thread of reasoning, the existence of distinct individual minds, similar to that which is employed in now questioning its own nature, is likewise found to be a delusion. The words *I, you, they*, are not signs of any actual difference subsisting between the assemblage of thoughts thus indicated, but are merely marks employed to denote the different modifications of the one mind.

Let it not be supposed that this doctrine conducts to the monstrous presumption that I, the person who now write and think, am that one mind. I am but a portion of it. The words *I* and *you*, and *they* are grammatical devices invented simply for arrangement, and totally devoid of the intense and exclusive sense usually attached to them. It is difficult to find terms adequate to express so subtle a conception as that to which the Intellectual Philosophy has conducted us. We are on that verge where words abandon us, and what wonder if we grow dizzy to look down the dark abyss of how little we know.

The relations of *things* remain unchanged, by whatever system. By the word *things* is to be understood any object of thought, that is, any thought upon which any other thought is employed, with an apprehension of distinction. The relations of these remain unchanged; and such is the material of our knowledge.

What is the cause of life? that is, how was it produced, or what agencies distinct from life have acted or act upon life? All recorded generations of mankind have wearily busied themselves in inventing answers to this question; and the result has been,—Religion. Yet, that the basis of all things cannot be, as the popular philosophy alleges, mind, is sufficiently evident. Mind, as far as we have any experience of its properties, and beyond that experience how vain is argument! cannot create, it can only perceive. It is said also to be the cause. But cause is only a word expressing a certain state of the human mind with regard to the manner in which two thoughts are apprehended to be related to each other. If any one desires to know how unsatisfactorily the popular philosophy employs itself upon this great question, they need only impartially reflect upon the manner in which thoughts develop themselves in their minds. It is infinitely improbable that the cause of mind, that is, of existence, is similar to mind.

[1832]   [1929]

ON LOVE[1]

WHAT is love? Ask him who lives, what is life? ask him who adores, what is God?

I know not the internal constitution of other men, nor even thine, whom I now address. I see that in some external attributes they resemble me, but when, misled by that appearance, I have thought to appeal to something in common, and unburthen my inmost soul to them, I have found my language misunderstood, like one in a distant and savage land. The more opportunities they have afforded me for experience, the wider has appeared the interval between us, and to a greater distance have the points of sympathy been withdrawn. With a spirit ill fitted to sustain such proof, trembling and feeble through its tenderness, I have everywhere sought sympathy, and have found only repulse and disappointment.

Thou demandest what is love? It is that powerful attraction towards all that we conceive, or fear, or hope beyond ourselves, when we find within our own thoughts the chasm of an insufficient void, and seek to awaken in all things that are, a community with what we experience within ourselves. If we reason, we would be understood; if we imagine, we would that the airy children of our brain were born anew within another's; if we feel, we would that another's nerves should vibrate to our own, that the beams of their eyes should kindle at once and mix and melt into our own, that lips of motionless ice should not reply to lips quivering and burning with the heart's best blood. This is Love. This is the bond and the sanction which connects not only man with man, but with every thing which exists. We are born into the world, and there is something within us which, from the instant that we live, more and more thirsts after its likeness. It is probably in correspondence with this law that the infant drains milk from the bosom of its mother; this propensity develops itself with the development of our nature. We dimly see within our intellectual nature a miniature as it were of our entire self, yet deprived of all that we condemn or despise, the ideal prototype of every thing excellent or lovely that we are capable of conceiving as belonging to the nature of man. Not only the portrait of our external being, but an assemblage of the minutest particles of which our nature is composed*; a mirror whose surface reflects only the forms of purity and brightness; a soul within our soul that describes a circle around its proper para-

* These words are ineffectual and metaphorical. Most words are so—No help!

[1] The date of composition of this fragment is uncertain, but probably 1815–1819. It was first published in 1829.

dise, which pain, and sorrow, and evil dare not over-leap. To this we eagerly refer all sensations, thirsting that they should resemble or correspond with it. The discovery of its antitype; the meeting with an understanding capable of clearly estimating our own; an imagination which should enter into and seize upon the subtle and delicate peculiarities which we have delighted to cherish and unfold in secret; with a frame whose nerves, like the chords of two exquisite lyres, strung to the accompaniment of one delightful voice, vibrate with the vibrations of our own; and of a combination of all these in such proportion as the type within demands; this is the invisible and unattainable point to which Love tends; and to attain which, it urges forth the powers of man to arrest the faintest shadow of that, without the possession of which there is no rest nor respite to the heart over which it rules. Hence in solitude, or in that deserted state when we are surrounded by human beings, and yet they sympathise not with us, we love the flowers, the grass, and the waters, and the sky. In the motion of the very leaves of spring, in the blue air, there is then found a secret correspondence with our heart. There is eloquence in the tongueless wind, and a melody in the flowing brooks and the rustling of the reeds beside them, which by their inconceivable relation to something within the soul, awaken the spirits to a dance of breathless rapture, and bring tears of mysterious tenderness to the eyes, like the enthusiasm of patriotic success, or the voice of one beloved singing to you alone. Sterne says that, if he were in a desert, he would love some cypress. So soon as this want or power is dead, man becomes the living sepulchre of himself, and what yet survives is the mere husk of what once he was.

[1829]   [1929]

A PHILOSOPHICAL VIEW OF REFORM

Shelley's most important political essay was composed 1819–1820 but never completed, and survives in a manuscript with many cancellations and omissions. It was first published in 1920.

When Shelley received word in Italy of the "Peterloo Massacre" (see Chapter III, footnote 1, p. 721), he wrote to his London publisher Charles Ollier: ". . . the torrent of my indignation has not yet done boiling in my veins. I wait anxiously to hear how the Country will express its sense of this bloody murderous oppression of its destroyers." Shelley immediately gave expression to his "indignation" in the powerful verses of The Mask of Anarchy. A Philosophical View of Reform, *which he began to write in November of that year, was also a product of that "indignation;" however, in contrast to the Mask, whose passionate tone caused Leigh Hunt to defer its publication in* The Examiner *at the time, the prose treatise was moderate in tone and "philosophical" in its procedure. "I intend it to be an*

instructive and readable book," Shelley declared, "appealing from the passions to the reason of men." The first Chapter views the disturbances of the time and the goals of reform in the light of the long historical struggle for freedom since the dissolution of the Roman Empire. In the second Chapter, Shelley analyzes the more immediate economic and social causes of the disturbances and calls for change. Chapter III spells out the nature of the change, which is not to be the precipitous and violent overthrow of the established government. Instead, in keeping with the informing premise of much of his greatest poetry, Shelley sees the need for the moral regeneration and preparation of a debilitated population for the full exercise of freedom; and he accordingly emphasizes the instructive role of a minority of enlightened patriots, and counsels a program of gradual but steady elimination and correction of abuses.

In Politics in English Romantic Poetry *(Cambridge, Mass.: Harvard University Press, 1970), pp. 307–10, Carl Woodring argues that the "proposals for incremental process" in Shelley's prose treatise find "symbolic expression" in* Prometheus Unbound.

A PHILOSOPHICAL VIEW OF REFORM

CHAPTER I

INTRODUCTION

FROM the dissolution of the Roman Empire, that vast and successful scheme for the enslaving [of] the most civilized portion of mankind, to the epoch of the present year, have succeeded a series of schemes, on a smaller scale, operating to the same effect. Names borrowed from the life; and opinions of Jesus Christ were employed as symbols of domination and imposture; and a system of liberty and equality (for such was the system preached by that great Reformer) was perverted to support oppression.—Not his doctrines, for they are too simple and direct to be susceptible of such perversion—but the mere names. Such was the origin of the Catholic Church, which together with the several dynasties then beginning to consolidate themselves in Europe, means, being interpreted, a plan according to which the cunning and selfish few have employed the fears and hopes of the ignorant many to the establishment of their own power and the destruction of the real interests of all.

The Republics and municipal Governments of Italy opposed for some time a systematic and effectual resistance to the all-surrounding tyranny. The Lombard League defeated the armies of the despot in open field, and until Florence was betrayed to those flattered traitors [and] polished tyrants, the Medici, Freedom had one citadel wherein it could find refuge from a world which was its enemy. Florence long balanced, divided, and weakened the strength of the Empire and the Popedom. To this cause, if to any thing, was due the undisputed superiority of Italy in literature and the arts over all its contemporary nations, that union of energy and of beauty which distinguish[es] from all other poets the writings of Dante, that restlessness of fervid power which expressed itself in painting and sculpture, and in daring architectural forms, and from which, and conjointly from the creations of Athens, its predecessor and its image, Raphael and Michel Angelo drew the inspiration which created those forms and colours now the astonishment of the world. The father of our own literature, Chaucer, wrought from the simple and powerful language of a nursling of this Republic the basis of our own literature. And thus we owe, among other causes, the exact condition belonging to [our own] intellectual existence to the generous disdain of submission which burned in the bosoms of men who filled a distant generation and inhabited another land.

When this resistance was overpowered (as what resistance to fraud and [tyranny] has not been overpowered?) another was even then maturing. The progress of philosophy and civilization which ended in that imperfect emancipation of mankind from the yoke of priests and kings called the Reformation, had already commenced. Exasperated by their long sufferings, inflamed by the spark of that superstition from the flames of which they were emerging, the poor rose against their natural enemies, the rich, and repaid with bloody interest the tyranny of ages. One of the signs of the times was that the oppressed peasantry rose like the negro slaves of West Indian Plantations, and murdered their tyrants when they were unaware. For so dear is power that the tyrants themselves neither then, nor now, nor ever, left or leave a path to freedom but through their own blood. The contest then waged under the names of religion which have seldom been any more [than] the popular and visible symbols which express the degree of power in some shape or other asserted by one party and disclaimed by the other, ended; and the result, though partial and imperfect, is perhaps the most animating that the philanthropist can contemplate in the history of man. The Republic of Holland, which has been so long an armoury of the arrows of learning by which superstition has been wounded even to death, was established by this contest. What though the name of Republic—and by whom but by conscience stricken tyrants could it be extinguished—is no more? The Republics of Switzerland derived from this event their consolidation and their union. From England then first began to pass away the stain of conquest. The exposition of a certain portion of religious imposture

drew with it an enquiry into political imposture, and was attended with an extraordinary exertion of the energies of intellectual power. Shakespeare and Lord Bacon and the great writers of the age of Elizabeth and James the 1st were at once the effects of the new spirit in men's minds, and the causes of its more complete developement. By rapid gradation the nation was conducted to the temporary abolition of aristocracy and episcopacy, and [to] the mighty example which, "in teaching nations how to live," England afforded to the world—of bringing to public justice one of those chiefs [1] of a conspiracy of privileged murderers and robbers whose impunity has been the consecration of crime.

After the selfish passions and compromising interests of men had enlisted themselves to produce and establish the Restoration of Charles the 2nd the unequal combat was renewed under the reign of his successor, and that compromise between the unextinguishable spirit of Liberty, and the ever watchful spirit of fraud and tyranny, called the Revolution, had place. On this occasion monarchy and aristocracy and episcopacy were at once established and limited by law. Unfortunately they lost no more in extent of power than they gained in security of possession. Meanwhile those by whom they were established acknowledged and declared that the will of the People was the source from which these powers, in this instance, derived the right to subsist. A man has no right to be a King or a Lord or a Bishop but so long as it is for the benefit of the People and so long as the People judge that it is for their benefit that he should impersonate that character. The solemn establishment of this maxim as the basis of our constitutional law, more than any beneficial and energetic application of it to the circumstances of this æra of its promulgation, was the fruit of that vaunted event. Correlative with this series of events in England was the commencement of a new epoch in the history of the progress of civilization and society.

That superstition which has disguised itself under the name of the religion of Jesus subsisted under all its forms, even where it had been separated from those things especially considered as abuses by the multitude, in the shape of intolerant and oppressive hierarchies. Catholics massacred Protestants and Protestants proscribed Catholics, and extermination was the sanction of each faith within the limits of the power of its professors. The New Testament is in everyone's hand, and the few who ever read it with the simple sincerity of an unbiassed judgement may perceive how

---

[1] Charles I, who was brought to trial and executed in January 1649.

distinct from the opinions of any of those professing themselves establishers were the doctrines and the actions of Jesus Christ. At the period of the Reformation this test was applied, and this judgement formed of the then existing hierarchy, and the same compromise was then made between the spirit of truth and the spirit of imposture after [the] struggle which ploughed up the area of the human mind, as was made in the particular instance of England between the spirit of freedom and the spirit of tyranny at that event called the Revolution. In both instances the maxims so solemnly recorded remain as trophies of our difficult and incomplete victory, planted in the enemies' land. *The will of the People to change their government is an acknowledged right in the Constitution of England.* The protesting against religious dogmas which present themselves to his mind as false is the inalienable prerogative of every human being.—

The new epoch was marked by the commencement of deeper enquiries into the forms of human nature than are compatible with an unreserved belief in any of those popular mistakes upon which popular systems of faith with respect to the cause and agencies of the universe, with all their superstructure of political and religious tyranny, are built. Lord Bacon, Spinoza, Hobbes, Bayle, Montaigne, regulated the reasoning powers, criticized the past history, exposed the errors by illustrating their causes and their connexion, and anatomized the inmost nature of social man. Then, with a less interval of time than of genius, followed [Locke] and the philosophers of his exact and intelligible but superficial school. Their illustrations of some of the minor consequences of the doctrines established by the sublime genius of their predecessors were correct, popular, simple and energetic. Above all, they indicated inferences the most incompatible with the popular religions and the established governments of Europe. [Philosophy went forth into the inchanted forest of the demons of worldly power, as the pioneer of the over-growth of ages.] Berkeley and Hume, [and] Hartley [at a] later age, following the traces of these inductions, have clearly established the certainty of our ignorance with respect to those obscure questions which under the name of religious truths have been the watchwords of contention and the symbols of unjust power ever since they were distorted by the narrow passions of the immediate followers of Jesus from that meaning to which philosophers are even now restoring them. A crowd of writers in France seized upon the most popular portions of the new philosophy which conducted to inferences at war with the dreadful oppressions under which the country groaned, made familiar to mankind the fals[e]hood of their religious mediators and political

oppressors. Considered as philosophers their error seems to have consisted chiefly of a limitedness of view; they told the truth, but not the whole truth. This might have arisen from the terrible sufferings of their countrymen inviting them rather to apply a portion of what had already been discovered to their immediate relief, than to pursue one interest, the abstractions of thought, as the great philosophers who preceded them had done, for the sake of a future and more universal advantage. Whilst that philosophy which, burying itself in the obscure part of our nature, regards the truth and fals[e]hood of dogmas relating to the cause of the universe, and the nature and manner of man's relation with it, was thus stripping Power of its darkest mask, Political Philosophy, or that which considers the relations of man as a social being, was assuming a precise form. This philosophy indeed sprang from and maintained a connexion with that other as its parent. What would Swift and Bolingbroke and Sidney and Locke and Montesquieu, or even Rousseau, not to speak of political philosophers of our own age, Godwin and Bentham, have been but for Lord Bacon, Montaigne and Spinoza, and the other great luminaries of the preceding epoch? Something excellent and eminent, no doubt, the least of these would have been, but something different from and inferior to what they are. A series of these writers illustrated with more or less success the principles of human nature as applied to man in political society. A thirst for accommodating the existing forms according to which mankind are found divided to those rules of freedom and equality which are thus discovered as being the elementary principles according to which the happiness resulting from the social union ought to be produced and distributed, was kindled by these inquiries. Contemporary with this condition of the intellect all the powers of man seemed, though in most cases under forms highly inauspicious, to develop themselves with uncommon energy. The mechanical sciences attained to a degree of perfection which, though obscurely foreseen by Lord Bacon, it had been accounted madness to have prophesied in a preceding age. Commerce was pursued with a perpetually increasing vigour, and the same area of the Earth was perpetually compelled to furnish more and more subsistence. The means and sources of knowledge were thus increased together with knowledge itself, and the instruments of knowledge. The benefit of this increase of the powers of man became, in consequence of the inartificial forms into which society came to be distributed, an instrument of his additional evil. The capabilities of happiness were increased, and applied to the augmentation of misery. Modern society is thus a[n] engine assumed to be for useful purposes, whose force is by a system of subtle mechanism augmented to the highest pitch, but which, instead of grinding corn or raising water acts against itself and is perpetually wearing away or breaking to pieces the wheels of which it is composed. The result of the labours of the political philosophers has been the establishment of the principle of Utility as the substance, and liberty and equality as the forms according to which the concerns of human life ought to be administered. By this test the various institutions regulating political society have been tried, and as the undigested growth of the private passions, errors, and interests of barbarians and oppressors have been condemned. And many new theories, more or less perfect, but all superior to the mass of evil which they would supplant, have been given to the world.

The system of government in the United States of America was the first practical illustration of the new philosophy. Sufficiently remote, it will be confessed, from the accuracy of ideal excellence is that representative system which will soon cover the extent of that vast Continent. But it is scarcely less remote from the insolent and contaminating tyrannies under which, with some limitation of these terms as regards England, Europe groaned at the period of the successful rebellion of America. America holds forth the victorious example of an immensely populous, and as far as the external arts of life are concerned, a highly civilized community administered according to republican forms. It has no king, that is it has no officer to whom wealth and from whom corruption flows. It has no hereditary oligarchy, that is it acknowledges no order of men privileged to cheat and insult the rest of the members of the state, and who inherit a right of legislating and judging which the principles of human nature compel them to exercise to their own profit and to the detriment of those not included within their peculiar class. It has no established Church, that is it has no system of opinions respecting the abstrusest questions which can be topics of human thought, founded in an age of error and fanaticism, and opposed by law to all other opinions, defended by prosecutions, and sanctioned by enormous bounties given to idle priests and forced thro' the unwilling hands of those who have an interest in the cultivation and improvement of the soil. It has no false representation, whose consequences are captivity, confiscation, infamy and ruin, but a true representation. The will of the many is represented by the few in the assemblies of legislation and by the officers of the executive entrusted with the administration of the executive power almost as directly as the will of one person can be represented by the will of

another. [This is not the place for dilating upon the inexpressible advantages (if such advantages require any manifestation) of a self-governing Society, or one which approaches in the degree of the Republic of the United States.] Lastly, it has an institution by which it is honourably distinguished from all other governments which ever existed. It constitutionally acknowledges the progress of human improvement, and is framed under the limitation of the probability of more simple views of political science being rendered applicable to human life. There is a law by which the constitution is reserved for revision every ten years. Every other set of men who have assumed the office of legislation, and framing institutions for future ages, with far less right to such an assumption than the founders of the American Republic assumed that their work was the wisest and the best that could possibly have been produced: these illustrious men looked upon the past history of their species and saw that it was the history of his mistakes, and his sufferings arising from his mistakes; they observed the superiority of their own work to all the works which had preceded it, and they judged it probable that other political institutions would be discovered bearing the same relation to those which they had established which they bear to those which have preceded them. They provided therefore for the application of these contingent discoveries to the social state without the violence and misery attendant upon such change in less modest and more imperfect governments. The United States, as we would have expected from theoretical deduction, affords an example, compared with the old governments of Europe and Asia, of a free, happy, and strong people. Nor let it be said that they owe their superiority rather to the situation than to their government. Give them a king, and let that king waste in luxury, riot and bribery the same sum which now serves for the entire expenses of their government. Give them an aristocracy, and let that aristocracy legislate for the people. Give them a priesthood, and let them bribe with a tenth of the produce of the soil a certain set of men to say a certain set of words. Pledge the larger part of them by financial subterfuges to pay the half of their property or earnings to another portion, and let the proportion of those who enjoy the fruits of the toil of others without toiling themselves be three instead of one. Give them a Court of Chancery and let the property, the liberty and the interest in the dearest concerns of life, the exercise of the most sacred rights of a social being depend upon the will of one of the most servile creature[s] of that kingly and oligarchical and priestly power to which every man, in proportion as he is of an enquiring and philosophical mind and of a sincere and honourable disposition is a natural, a necessary enemy. Give them, as you must if you give them these things, a great standing army to cut down the people if they murmur. If any American should see these words, his blood would run cold at the imagination of such a change. He well knows that the prosperity and happiness of the United States if subjected to such institutions [would] be no more.

The just and successful Revolt of America corresponded with a state of public opinion in Europe of which it was the first result. The French Revolution was the second. The oppressors of mankind had enjoyed (O that we could say suffered) a long and undisturbed reign in France, and to the pining famine, the shelterless destitution of the inhabitants of that country had been added and heaped up insult harder to endure than misery. For the feudal system (the immediate causes and conditions of its institution having become obliterated) had degenerated into an instrument not only of oppression but of contumely, and both were unsparingly inflicted. Blind in the possession of strength, drunken as with the intoxication of ancestral greatness, the rulers perceived not that increase of knowledge in their subjects which made its exercise insecure. They called soldiers to hew down the people when their power was already past. The tyrants were, as usual, the aggressors. Then the oppressed, having been rendered brutal, ignorant, servile and bloody by long slavery, having had the intellectual thirst, excited in them by the progress of civilization, satiated from fountains of literature poisoned by the spirit and the form of monarchy, arose and took a dreadful revenge on their oppressors. Their desire to wreak revenge, to this extent, in itself a mistake, a crime, a calamity, arose from the same source as their other miseries and errors, and affords an additional proof of the necessity of that long-delayed change which it accompanied and disgraced. If a just and necessary revolution could have been accomplished with as little expense of happiness and order in a country governed by despotic as [in] one governed by free laws, equal liberty and justice would lose their chief recommendations and tyranny be divested of its most revolting attributes. Tyranny entrenches itself within the existing interests of the most refined citizens of a nation and says 'If you dare trample upon these, be free.' Though this terrible condition shall not be evaded, the world is no longer in a temper to decline the challenge.

The French were what their literature is (excluding Montaigne and Rousseau, and some few leaders of the . . .) weak, superficial, vain, with little imagination, and with passions as well as judgements cleaving to the external form of things. Not that [they] are organically different from the inhabitants of the nations who have become . . . or rather not that their organical differences, whatever they may amount to, incapacitate them from arriving at the exercise of the highest powers to be attained by man. Their institutions made them what they were. Slavery and superstition, contumely and the tame endurance of contumely, and the habits engendered from generation to generation out of this transmitted inheritance of wrong, created this thing which has extinguished what has been called the likeness of God in man. The Revolution in France overthrew the hierarchy, the aristocracy and the monarchy, and the whole of that peculiarly insolent and oppressive system on which they were based. But as it only partially extinguished those passions which are the spirit of these forms a reaction took place which has restored in a certain limited degree the old system. In a degree, indeed, exceedingly limited, and stript of all its antient terrors. The hope of the Monarchy of France, with his teeth drawn and his claws pared, was its maintaining the formal likeness of most imperfect and insecure dominion. The usurpation of Bonaparte and then the Restoration of the Bourbons were the shapes in which this reaction clothed itself, and the heart of every lover of liberty was struck as with palsy by the succession of these events. But reversing the proverbial expression of Shakespeare,[2] it may be the good which the Revolutionists did lives after them, their ills are interred with their bones. But the military project of government of the great tyrant having failed, and there being even no attempt—and, if there were any attempt, there being not the remotest possibility of re-establishing the enormous system of tyranny abolished by the Revolution, France is, as it were, regenerated. Its legislative assemblies are in a certain limited degree representations of the popular will, and the executive power is hemmed in by jealous laws. France occupies in this respect the same situation as was occupied by England at the restoration of Charles the 2nd. It has undergone a revolution (unlike in the violence and calamities which attended it, because unlike in the abuses which it was excited to put down) which may be paralleled with that in our own country which ended in the death of Charles the 1st. The authors of both Revolutions proposed a greater and more glorious object than the degraded passions of their countrymen permitted them to attain. But in both cases abuses were abolished which never since have dared to show their face. There remains in the natural order of human things that the

---

[2] *Julius Caesar*, III, ii, 80–81.

tyranny and perfidy of the reigns of Charles the 2nd and James the 2nd (for these were less the result of the disposition of particular men than the vices which would have been engendered in any but an extraordinary man by the natural necessities of their situation) perhaps under a milder form and within a shorter period should produce the institution of a Government in France which may bear the same relation to the state of political knowledge existing at the present day, as the Revolution under William the 3rd bore to the state of political knowledge existing at that period.

Germany, which is, among the great nations of Europe, one of the latest civilized, with the exception of Russia, is rising with the fervour of a vigorous youth to the assertion of those rights for which it has that desire arising from knowledge, the surest pledge of victory. The deep passion and the bold and Æschylean vigour of the imagery of their poetry; the enthusiasm, however distorted, of their religious sentiments; the flexibility and comprehensiveness of their language which is a many-sided mirror of every changing thought, their severe, bold and liberal spirit of criticism, their subtle and deep philosophy however erroneous and illogical mingling fervid intuitions into truth with obscure error (for the period of just distinction is yet to come) and their taste and power in the plastic arts, prove that they are a great People. And every great people either has been or is or will be free. The panic-stricken tyrants of that country promised to their subjects that their governments should be administered according to republican forms, they retaining merely the right of hereditary chief magistracy in their families. This promise, made in danger, the oppressors dream that they can break in security. And everything in consequence wears in Germany the aspect of rapidly maturing revolution.

In Spain and in the dependencies of Spain good and evil in the forms of Despair and Tyranny are struggling foot to foot. That great people have been delivered bound hand and foot to be trampled upon and insulted by a traitorous and sanguinary tyrant, a wretch who makes credible all that might have been doubted in the history of Nero, Christiern, Muley Ismael or Ezzelin[3]—the persons who have thus delivered them were that hypocritical knot of conspiring tyrants, who proceeded upon the credit they gained by putting down the only tyrant among them who was not a hypocrite, to undertake the administration of those *arrondissements* of consecrated injustice and violence which they deliver to those who the nearest resemble them under the name of the 'kingdoms of the earth'—This action signed a sentence of death, confiscation, exile or captivity against every philosopher and patriot in Spain. The tyrant Ferdinand,[4] he whose name is changed into a proverb of execration, found natural allies in all the priests and a few of the most dishonourable military chiefs of that devoted country. And the consequences of military despotism and the black, stagnant, venomous hatred which priests in common with eunuchs seek every opportunity to wreak upon the portion of mankind exempt from their own unmanly disqualifications is slavery. And what is slavery—in its mildest form hideous, and, so long as one amiable or great attribute survives in its victims, rankling and intolerable, but in its darkest shape [as] it now exhibits itself in Spain it is the presence of all and more than all the evils for the sake of an exemption from which mankind submit to the mighty calamity of government. It is a system of insecurity of property, and of person, of prostration of conscience and understanding, of famine heaped upon the greater number and contumely heaped upon all, defended by unspeakable tortures employed not merely as punishments but as precautions, by want, death and captivity, and the application to political purposes of the execrated and enormous instruments of religious cruelty. Those men of understanding, integrity, and courage who rescued their country from one tyrant are exiled from it by his successor and his enemy and their legitimate king. Tyrants, however they may squabble among themselves, have common friends and foes. The taxes are levied at the point of the sword. Armed insurgents occupy all the defensible mountains of the country. The dungeons are peopled thickly, and persons of every sex and age have the fibres of their frame torn by subtle torments. Boiling water (such is an article in the last news from Spain) is poured upon the legs of a noble Spanish Lady newly delivered, slowly and cautiously that she may confess what she knows of a conspiracy against the tyrant, and she dies, as constant as the slave Epicharis,[5] imprecating curses upon her torturers and passionately calling upon her children. These events, in the present condition of the understanding and sentiment of mankind, are the rapidly passing shadows, which forerun successful insurrection, the ominous comets of our republican

---

3 Christian II (1481–1559) was a tyrannical and cruel King of Denmark, Norway, and Sweden. Muley Ismael, Emperor of Morocco (1672–1727), was called "the Bloodthirsty." Eccelino da Romano (1194–1259) was a Ghibelline leader of notorious cruelty.

4 Ferdinand VII, King of Spain. His dictatorial practices in the years following his restoration to the throne in 1814 led to a revolt in 1820.

5 See Tacitus, *Annals*, XV, lvii.

poet perplexing great monarchs with fear of change.[6] Spain, having passed through an ordeal severe in proportion to the wrongs and errors which it is kindled to erase must of necessity be renovated. [The country which] produced Calderon and Cervantes, what else did it but breathe, thro the tumult of the despotism and superstition which invested them, the prophecy of a glorious consummation?

The independents of South America are as it were already free. Great Republics are about to consolidate themselves in a portion of the globe sufficiently vast and fertile to nourish more human beings than at present occupy, with the exception perhaps of China, the remainder of the inhabited earth—— Some indefinite arrears of misery and blood remain to be paid to the Moloch of oppression. These, to the last drop and groan it will implacably exact. But not the less are [they] inevitably enfranchised. The Great Monarchies of Asia cannot, let us confidently hope, remain unshaken by the earthquake which shatters to dust the 'mountainous strongholds' of the tyrants of the western world.

Revolutions in the political and religious state of the Indian peninsula seem to be accomplishing, and it cannot be doubted but the zeal of the missionaries of what is called the Christian faith will produce beneficial innovation there, even by the application of dogmas and forms of what is here an outworn incumbrance. The Indians have been enslaved and cramped in the most severe and paralysing forms which were ever devised by man; some of this new enthusiasm ought to be kindled among them to consume it and leave them free, and even if the doctrines of Jesus do not penetrate through the darkness of that which those who profess to be his followers call Christianity, there will yet be a number of social forms modelled upon those European feelings from which it has taken its colour substituted to those according to which they are at present cramped, and from which, when the time for complete emancipation shall arrive, their disengagement may be less difficult, and under which their progress to it may be the less imperceptibly slow. Many native Indians have acquired, it is said, a competent knowledge in the arts and philosophy of Europe, and Locke and Hume and Rousseau are familiarly talked of in Brahminical society. But the thing to be sought is that they should, as they would if they were free, attain to a system of arts and literature of their own.—Of Persia we know little, but that it has been the theatre of sanguinary contests for power, and that it is now at Peace. The Persians appear to be from organization a beautiful refined and impassioned people and would probably soon be infected by the contagion of good. The Jews, that wonderful people which has preserved so long the symbols of their union may reassume their ancestral seats, and——The Turkish Empire is in its last stage of ruin, and it cannot be doubted but that the time is approaching when the deserts of Asia Minor and of Greece will be colonized by the overflowing population of countries less enslaved and debased, and that the climate and the scenery which was the birthplace of all that is wise and beautiful will not remain for ever the spoil of wild beasts and unlettered Tartars.—In Syria and Arabia the spirit of human intellect has roused a sect of people called Wahabees, who maintain the Unity of God, and the equality of man, and their enthusiasm must go on 'conquering and to conquer' even if it must be repressed in its present shape.—Egypt having but a nominal dependence upon Constantinople is under the government of Ottoman Bey,* a person of enlightened views who is introducing European literature and arts, and is thus beginning that change which Time, the great innovator, will accomplish in that degraded country; [and] by the same means its sublime enduring monuments may excite lofty emotions in the hearts of the posterity of those who now contemplate them without admiration.—

Lastly, in the West Indian islands, first from the disinterested yet necessarily cautious measures of the English Nation, and then from the infection of the spirit of Liberty in France, the deepest stain upon civilized man is fading away. Two nations of free negroes are already established; one, in pernicious mockery of the usurpation over France, an empire, the other a republic;—both animating yet terrific spectacles to those who inherit around them the degradation of slavery and the peril of dominion.

Such is a slight sketch of the general condition of the human race to which they have been conducted after the obliteration of the Greek republics by the successful external tyranny of Rome,— its internal liberty having been first abolished,—and by those miseries and superstitions consequent upon this event, which compelled the human race to begin anew its difficult and obscure career of producing, according to the forms of society, the greatest portion of good.

Meanwhile England, the particular object for the

---

[6] See *Paradise Lost*, I, 597–98.

* This person sent his Nephew to Lucca to study European learning, & when his Nephew asked with reference to some branch of study at enmity with Mahometanism whether he was permitted to engage in it, he replied, "You are at liberty to do anything which will not injure another."

sake of which these general considerations have been stated on the present occasion, has arrived, like the nations which surround it, at a crisis in its destiny. The literature of England, an energetic development of which has ever followed or preceded a great and free development of the national will, has arisen, as it were, from a new birth. In spite of that low-thoughted envy which would undervalue, thro a fear of comparison with its own insignificance, the eminence of contemporary merit, it is *felt by the British* [that] ours is in intellectual achievements a *memorable age*, and we live among such philosophers and poets as surpass beyond comparison any who have appeared in our nation since its last struggle for liberty. For the most unfailing herald, or companion, or follower, of an universal employment of the sentiments of a nation to the production of beneficial change is poetry, meaning by poetry an intense and impassioned power of communicating intense and impassioned impressions respecting man and nature. The persons in whom this power takes its abode may often, as far as regards many portions of their nature, have little tendency [to] the spirit of good of which it is the minister. But although they may deny and abjure, they are yet compelled to serve that which is seated on the throne of their own soul. And whatever systems they may [have] professed by support, they actually advance the interests of Liberty. It is impossible to read the productions of our most celebrated writers, whatever may be their system relating to thought or expression, without being startled by the electric life which there is in their words. They measure the circumference or sound the depths of human nature with a comprehensive and all-penetrating spirit at which they are themselves perhaps most sincerely astonished, for it [is] less their own spirit than the spirit of their age. They are the priests of an unapprehended inspiration, the mirrors of gigantic shadows which futurity casts upon the present; the words which express what they conceive not; the trumpet which sings to battle and feels not what it inspires; the influence which is moved not but moves. Poets and philosophers are the unacknowledged legislators of the world.[7]

But, omitting these more abstracted considerations, has there not been and is there not in England a desire of change arising from the profound sentiment of the exceeding inefficiency of the existing institutions to provide for the physical and intellectual happiness of the people? It is proposed in this work (1) to state and examine the present condition of this desire, (2)

to elucidate its causes and its object, (3) to then show the practicability and utility, nay the necessity of change, (4) to examine the state of parties as regards it, and (5) to state the probable, the possible, and the desirable mode in which it should be accomplished.

CHAPTER II

ON THE SENTIMENT OF THE NECESSITY OF CHANGE

Two circumstances arrest the attention of those who turn their regard to the present political condition of the English nation—first, that there is an almost universal sentiment of the approach of some change to be wrought in the institutions of the government, and secondly, the necessity and desirableness of such a change. From the first of these propositions, it being matter of fact, no person addressing the public can dissent. The latter, from a general belief in which the former flows and on which it depends, is matter of opinion, but [one] which to the mind of all, excepting those interested in maintaining the contrary is a doctrine so clearly established that even they, admitting that great abuses exist, are compelled to impugn it by insisting upon the specious topic, that popular violence, by which they alone could be remedied, would be more injurious than the continuance of these abuses. But as those who argue thus derive for the most part great advantage and convenience from the continuance of these abuses, their estimation of the mischiefs of uprisings [&] popular violence as compared with the mischiefs of tyrannical and fraudulent forms of government are likely, from the known principles of human nature, to be exaggerated. Such an estimate comes too with a worse grace from them, who if they would, in opposition to their own unjust advantage, take the lead in reform, might spare the nation from the inconveniences of the temporary dominion of the poor, who by means of that degraded condition which their insurrection would be designed to ameliorate, are sufficiently incapable of discerning their own genuine and permanent advantage, tho surely less incapable than those whose interests consist in proposing to themselves an object perfectly opposite [to] and wholly incompatible with that advantage. All public functionaries who are overpaid either in money or in power for their public services, beginning with the person invested with the royal authority, and ending with the turnkey who extorts his last shilling from his starving prisoner. All members of the House of Lords who tremble lest the annihilation of their

---

[7] Most of this paragraph appeared again as the concluding paragraph of *A Defence of Poetry*. See pp. 737–38.

borough interest might not involve the risk of their hereditary legislative power, and of those distinctions which considered in a pecuniary point of view are injurious to those beyond the pale of their caste in proportion as they are beneficial to those within. An immense majority of the assembly called the house of Commons, who would be reduced, if they desired to administer public business, to consult the interest of their electors and conform themselves. The functionaries who know that their claims to several millions yearly of the produce of the soil for the service of certain dogmas, which if necessary other men would enforce as effectually for as many thousands, would undergo a very severe examination [in the event of a general Reform]. These persons propose to us the dilemma of submitting to a despotism which is notoriously gathering like an avalanche year by year; or taking the risk of something which it must be confessed bears the aspect of revolution. To this alternative we are reduced by the selfishness of those who taunt us with it. And the history of the world teaches us not to hesitate an instant in the decision, if indeed the power of decision be not already past——

The establishment of King William III on the throne of England has already been referred to as a compromise between liberty and despotism. The Parliament of which that event was the act had ceased to be in an emphatic sense, a representation of the people. The Long Parliament, questionless, was the organ of the will of all classes of people in England since it effected the complete revolution in a tyranny consecrated by time. But since its meeting and since its dissolution a great change had taken place in England. Feudal manners and institutions having become obliterated, monopolies and patents having been abolished, property and personal liberty having been rendered secure, the nation advanced rapidly towards the acquirement of the elements of national prosperity. Population increased, a greater number of hands were employed in the labours of agriculture and commerce, towns arose where villages had been, and the proportion borne by those whose labour produces the materials of subsistence and enjoyment to those who claim for themselves a superfluity of these materials began to increase indefinitely. A fourth class therefore appeared in the nation, the unrepresented multitude. Nor was it so much that villages which sent no members to Parliament became great cities, and that towns which had been considerable enough to send members dwindled from local circumstances into villages. This cause no doubt contributed to the general effect of rendering the Commons' House a less complete representation of the people. Yet had this been all, though it had ceased to be a legal and actual it might still have been a virtual Representation of the People. But the nation universally became multiplied into a denomination which had no constitutional presence in the state. This denomination had not existed before, or had existed only to a degree in which its interests were sensibly interwoven with that of those who enjoyed a constitutional presence. Thus, the proportion borne by the Englishmen who possessed [the] faculty of suffrage to those who were excluded from that faculty at the several periods of 1641 and 1688 had changed by the operation of these causes from 1 to 8 to 1 to 20. The rapid and effectual progress by which it changed from 1 to 20 to one to many hundreds in the interval between 1688 and 1819 is a process, to those familiar with the history of the political economy of that period, which is rendered by these principles sufficiently intelligible. The number therefore of those who have influence on the government, even if numerically the same as at the former period, was relatively different. And a sufficiently just measure is afforded of the degree in which a country is enslaved or free, by the consideration of the relative number of individuals who are admitted to the exercise of political rights. Meanwhile another cause was operating of a deeper and more extensive nature. The *class* who compose the Lords must, by the advantage of their situation as the great landed proprietors, possess a considerable influence over nomination to the Commons. This influence, from an original imperfection in the equal distribution of suffrage, was always enormous, but it is only since it has been combined with the cause before stated that it has appeared to be fraught with consequences incompatible with public liberty. In 1641 this influence was almost wholly [inoperative to] pervert the counsels of the nation from its own advantage. But at that epoch the enormous tyranny of the agents of the royal power weighed equally upon all denominations of men, and united all counsels to extinguish it; add to which, the nation was, as stated before, in a very considerable degree fairly represented in Parliament. [The] common danger which was the bond of union between the aristocracy and the people having been destroyed, the former systematized their influence through the permanence of hereditary right, whilst the latter were losing power by the inflexibility of the institutions which forbade a just accommodation to their numerical increase. After the operations of these causes had commenced, the accession of William the III placed a seal upon forty years of Revolution.——

The government of this country at the period of 1688 was regal, tempered by aristocracy, for what conditions of democracy attach to an assembly one portion of which [was] imperfectly nominated by less than a twentieth part of the people, and another perfectly nominated by the nobles? For the nobility, having by the assistance of the people imposed close limitations upon the royal power, finding that power to be its natural ally and the people (for the people from the increase of their numbers acquired greater and more important rights whilst the organ through which those rights might be asserted grew feebler in proportion to the increase of the cause of those rights and of their importance) its natural enemy, made the Crown the mask and pretence of their own authority. At this period began that despotism of the oligarchy of party, and under colour of administering the executive power lodged in the king, represented in truth the interests of the rich. When it is said by political reasoners, speaking of the interval between 1688 and the present time, that the royal power progressively increased, they use an expression which suggests a very imperfect and partial idea. The power which has increased is that entrusted with the administration of affairs, composed of men responsible to the aristocratic assemblies, or to the reigning party in those assemblies, which represents those orders of the nation which are privileged, and will retain power as long as it pleases them and must be divested of power as soon as it ceases to please them. The power which has increased therefore is the [pow]er of the rich. The name and office of king is merely the mask of this power, and is a kind of stalking-horse used to conceal these 'catchers of men,' whilst they lay their nets. Monarchy is only the string which ties the robber's bundle. Though less contumelious and abhorrent from the dignity of human nature than an absolute monarchy, an oligarchy of this nature exacts more of suffering from the people because it reigns both by the opinion generated by imposture, and the force which that opinion places within its grasp.

At the epoch adverted to, the device of public credit was first systematically applied as an instrument of government. It was employed at the accession of William III less as a resource for meeting the financial exigencies of the state than as a bond to connect those in the possession of property with those who had, by taking advantage of an accident of party, acceded to power. In the interval elapsed since that period it has accurately fulfilled the intention of its establishment, and has continued to add strength to the government even until the present crisis. Now this device is one of those execrable contrivances of misrule which overbalance the materials of common advantage produced by the progress of civilization, and increase

the number of those who are idle in proportion to those who work, while it increases, through the factitious wants of those indolent, privileged persons, the quantity of work to be done. The rich, no longer being able to rule by force, have invented this scheme that they may rule by fraud.—

The most despotic governments of antiquity were strangers to this invention, which is a compendious method of extorting from the people far more than praetorian guards, and arbitrary tribunals, and excise officers created judges in the last resort, could ever wring. Neither the Persian monarchy nor the Roman empire, where the will of one person was acknowledged as unappealable law, ever extorted a twentieth part the proportion now extorted from the property and labour of the inhabitants of Great Britain. The precious metals have been from the earliest records of civilization employed as the signs of labour and the titles to an unequal distribution of its produce. The [Government of] a country is necessarily entrusted with the affixing to certain portions of these metals a stamp, by which to mark their genuineness; no other is considered as current coin, nor can be a legal tender. The reason of this is that no alloyed coin should pass current, and thereby depreciate the genuine, and by augmenting the price of the articles which are the produce of labour defraud the holders of that which is genuine of the advantages legally belonging to them. If the Government itself abuses the trust reposed in it to debase the coin, in order that it may derive advantage from the unlimited multiplication of the mark entitling the holder to command the labour and property of others, the gradations by which it sinks, as labour rises, to the level of their comparative values, produces public confusion and misery. The foreign exchange meanwhile instructs the Government how temporary was its resource. This mode of making the distribution of the sign of labour, a source of private aggrandisement at the expense of public confusion and loss, was not wholly unknown to the nations of antiquity.

But the modern scheme of public credit is a far subtler and more complicated contrivance of misrule. All great transactions of personal property in England are managed by signs and that is by the authority of the possessor expressed upon paper, thus representing in a compendious form his right to so much gold, which represents his right to so much labour. A man may write on a piece of paper what he pleases; he may say he is worth a thousand when he is not worth a hundred pounds. If he can make others believe this, he has credit for the sum to which his name is attached. And so long as this credit lasts, he can enjoy all the advantages which would arise out of the actual possession of the sum he is believed to possess. He can lend two hundred to this man and three to that other, and his bills, among those who believe that he possesses this sum, pass like money. Of course in the same proportion as bills of this sort, beyond the actual goods or gold and silver possessed by the drawer, pass current, they defraud those who have gold and silver and goods of the advantages legally attached to the possession of them, and they defraud the labourer and artizan of the advantage attached to increasing the nominal price of labour, and such a participation in them as their industry *might* command, whilst they render wages fluctuating and add to the toil of the cultivator and manufacturer.

The existing government of England in substituting a currency of paper [for] one of gold has had no need to depreciate the currency by alloying the coin of the country; they have merely fabricated pieces of paper on which they promise to pay a certain sum. The holders of these papers came for payment in some representation of property universally exchangeable. They then declared that the persons who held the office for that payment could not be forced by law to pay. They declared subsequently that these pieces of paper were the legal coin of the country. Of this nature are all such transactions of companies and banks as consist in the circulation of promissory notes to a greater amount than the actual property possessed by those whose names they bear. They have the effect of augmenting the prices of provision, and of benefiting at the expense of the community the speculators in this traffic.—One of the vaunted effects of this system is to increase the national industry. That is, to increase the labours of the poor and those luxuries of the rich which they supply. To make a manufacturer work 16 hours where he only worked 8. To turn children into lifeless and bloodless machines at an age when otherwise they would be at play before the cottage doors of their parents. To augment indefinitely the proportion of those who enjoy the profit of the labour of others, as compared with those who exercise this labour. To screw effi[?ciency]. . . .

The consequences of this transaction have been the establishment of a new aristocracy, which has its basis in fraud as the old one has its basis in force. The hereditary land-owners in England derived their title from royal grants—they are fiefs bestowed by conquerors, or church-lands, or they have been bought by bankers & merchants from those persons. Now bankers & merchants are persons whose . . . Since usage has consecrated the distinction of the word aristocracy from its primitive meaning . . . . Let me be assumed to employ the word aristocracy in that ordinary sense which signifies that class of persons who possess a right to the produce of the labour of others, without dedicating to the common service any labour in return.—This class of persons, whose existence is a prodigious anomaly in the social system, has ever constituted an inseparable portion of it, and there has never been an approach in practice towards any plan of political society modelled on equal justice, at least in the complicated mechanism of modern life. Mankind seem to acquiesce, as in a necessary condition of the imbecility of their own will and reason, in the existence of an aristocracy. With reference to this imbecility, it has doubtless been the instrument of great social advantage, although that advantage would have been greater which might have been produced according to the forms of a just distribution of the goods and evils of life. The object therefore of all enlightened legislation, and administration, is to enclose within the narrowest practicable limits this order of drones. The effect of the financial impostures of the modern rulers of England has been to increase the numbers of the drones. Instead of one aristocracy, the condition [to] which, in the present state of human affairs, the friends of justice and liberty are willing to subscribe as to an inevitable evil, they have supplied us with two aristocracies. The one, consisting [of] great land proprietors, and merchants who receive and interchange the produce of this country with the produce of other countries: in this, because all other great communities have as yet acquiesced in it, we acquiesce. Connected with the members of [it] is a certain generosity and refinement of manners and opinion which, although neither philosophy nor virtue, has been that acknowledged substitute for them, which at least is a religion which makes respected those venerable names. The other is an aristocracy of attornies and excisemen and directors and government pensioners, usurers, stock jobbers, country bankers, with their dependents and descendants. These are a set of pelting wretches in whose employment there is nothing to exercise, even to their distortion, the more majestic faculties of the soul. Though at the bottom it is all trick, there is something frank and magnificent in the chivalrous disdain of infamy connected with a gentleman. There is something to which—until you see through the base fals[e]hood upon which all inequality is founded—it is difficult for the imagination to refuse its respect, in the faithful and direct dealings of the substantial merchant. But in the habits and lives of this new aristocracy created out of an increase [in] the public calamities, and whose existence must be determined by their termination, there is nothing to qualify our disapprobation. They eat and drink and sleep, and in the intervals of those things performed with most ridiculous ceremony and accompaniments they cringe and lie. They poison the literature of the age in which they live by requiring either the antitype or their own mediocrity in books, or such stupid and distorted and inharmonious idealisms as alone have the power to stir their torpid imaginations. Their hopes and fears are of the narrowest description. Their domestic affections are feeble, and they have no others. They think of any commerce with their species but as a means, never as an end, and as a means to the basest forms of personal advantage.

If this aristocracy had arisen from a false and depreciated currency to the exclusion of the other, its existence would have been a moral calamity and disgrace, but it would not have constituted an oppression. But the hereditary aristocracy who held the political administration of affairs took the measures which created this other for purposes peculiarly its own. Those measures were so contrived as in no manner to diminish the wealth and power of the contrivers. The lord does not spare himself one luxury, but the peasant and artizan are assured of many needful things. To support the system of social order according to its supposed unavoidable constitution, those from whose labour all those external accommodations which distinguish a civilized being from a savage arise, worked, before the institution of this double aristocracy, eight hours. And of these only the healthy were compelled to labour, the efforts of the old, the sick and the immature being dispensed with, and they maintained by the labour of the sane, for such is the plain English of the poor-rates. That labour procured a competent share of the decencies of life, and society seemed to extend the benefits of its institution even to its most unvalued instruments. Although deprived of those resources of sentiment and knowledge which might have been their lot could the wisdom of the institutions of social forms have established a system of strict justice, yet they earned by their labour a competency in those external materials of life which, and not the loss of moral and intellectual excellence, is supposed to be the legitimate object of the desires and murmurs of the poor. Since the institution of this double aristocracy, however, they have often worked not ten but twenty hours a day. Not that all the poor have rigidly worked twenty hours, but that the worth of the labour of twenty hours now, in food and clothing, is equivalent to the worth of ten hours then. And because twenty hours' labour cannot, from the nature of the human frame, be exacted from those who before performed ten, the aged and the sickly are compelled either to work or starve. Children who were exempted from labour are put in requisition, and the vigorous promise

of the coming generation blighted by premature exertion. For fourteen hours' labour, which they do perform, they receive—no matter in what nominal amount—the price of seven. They eat less bread, wear worse clothes, are more ignorant, immoral, miserable and desperate. This then is the condition of the lowest and the largest class, from whose labour the whole materials of life are wrought, of which the others are only the receivers or the consumers. They are more superstitious, for misery on earth begets a diseased expectation and panic-stricken faith in miseries beyond the grave. "God," they argue, "rules this world as well as that; and assuredly since his nature is immutable, and his powerful will unchangeable, he rules them by the same laws." The gleams of hope which speak of Paradise seem like the flames in Milton's hell only to make darkness visible, and all things take [their] colour from what surrounds them. They become revengeful . . .

But the condition of all classes of society, excepting those within the privileged pale, is singularly unprosperous, and even they experience the reaction of their own short-sighted tyranny in all those sufferings and deprivations which are not of a distinctly physical nature, in the loss of dignity, simplicity, and energy, and in the possession of all those qualities which distinguish a slavedriver from a proprietor. Right government being an institution for the purpose of securing such a moderate degree of happiness to men as has been experimentally practicable, the sure character of misgovernment is misery, and first discontent and, if that be despised, then insurrection, as the legitimate expression of that misery. The public ought to demand happiness; the labouring classes, when they cannot get food for their labour, are impelled to take it by force. Laws and assemblies and courts of justice and delegated powers placed in balance or in opposition are the means and the form, but public happiness is the substance and the end of political institution. Whenever this is attainted in a nation, not from external force, but from the internal arrangement and divisions of the common burthens of defence and maintenance, then there is oppression. And then arises an alternative between Reform, & the institution of a military Despotism, or a Revolution in which these two parties, one striving after ill-digested systems of democracy, and the other clinging to the outworn abuses of power, leave the few who aspire to more than the former and who would overthrow the latter at whatever expense, to wait until that modified advantage which results from this conflict produces a small portion of that social improvement which, with the temperance and the toleration which both regard as a crime, might have resulted from the occasion which they let pass in a far more signal manner.

The propositions which are the consequences or the corollaries, to which the preceding reasoning seems to have conducted us are:—

—That the majority [of] the people of England are destitute and miserable, ill-clothed, ill-fed, ill-educated.

—That they know this, and that they are impatient to procure a reform of the cause of their abject and wretched state.

—That the cause of this peculiar misery is the unequal distribution which, under the form of the national debt, has been surreptitiously made of the products of their labour and the products of the labour of their ancestors; for all property is the produce of labour.

—That the cause of that cause is a defect in the government.

—That if they knew nothing of their condition, but believed that all they endured and all [they] were deprived of arose from the unavoidable condition of human life, this belief being an error, and [one] the endurance of [which] enforces an injustice, every enlightened and honourable person, whatever may be the imagined interest of his peculiar class, ought to excite them to the discovery of the true state of the case, and to the temperate but irresistible vindication of their rights.

It is better that they should be instructed in the whole truth, that they should see the clear grounds of their rights, the objects to which they ought to tend; and be impressed with the first persuasion, that patience and reason and endurance, and a calm yet invisible progress . . .

A Reform in England is most just and necessary. What ought to be that reform?

A writer of the present day[1] (a priest of course, for his doctrines are those of a eunuch and of a tyrant) has stated that the evils of the poor arise from an excess of population, and that after they have been stript naked by the tax-gatherer and reduced to bread and tea and fourteen hours of hard labour by their masters, and after the frost has bitten their defenceless limbs, and the cramp has wrung like a disease within their bones, and hunger and the suppressed revenge of hunger has stamped the ferocity of want like the mark of Cain upon their countenance, that the last tie by which Nature holds them to benignant earth whose plenty is garnered up in the strongholds of their tyrants, is to be divided; that the single alleviation of their sufferings and their scorns, the one thing which made it impossible to degrade them below the beasts, which amid all their crimes and miseries yet separated a cynical and unmanly contamination, an anti-social cruelty, from all the soothing, elevating and harmonious gentleness of the sexual intercourse and the humanizing charities of domestic life which are its appendages,—that this is to be obliterated. They are required to abstain from marrying under penalty of starvation. And it is threatened to deprive them of that property which is as strictly their birthright as a gentleman's land is his birthright, without giving them any compensation but the insulting advice to conquer, with minds undisciplined in the habits of higher gratification, a propensity which persons of the most consummate wisdom have been unable to resist, and which it is difficult to admire a person for having resisted. The doctrine of this writer is that the principle of population, when under no dominion of moral restraint, [is] outstripping the sustenance produced by the labour of man, and that not in proportion to the number of inhabitants, but operating equally in a thinly peopled community as in one where the population is enormous, being not a prevention but a check. So far a man might have been conducted by a train of reasoning which, though it may be shown to be defective, would argue in the reasoner no selfish and slavish feelings. But he has the hardened insolence to propose as a remedy that the poor should be compelled (for what except compulsion is a threat of the confiscation of those funds which by the institutions of their country had been set apart for their sustenance in sickness or destitution?) to abstain from sexual intercourse, whilst the rich are to be permitted to add as many mouths to consume the products of the labour as they please. [The rights of all men are intrinsically and originally equal and they forgo the assertion of all of them only that they may the more securely enjoy a portion.] If any new disadvantages are found to attach to the condition of social existence, those disadvantages ought not to be borne exclusively by one class of men, nor especially by that class whose ignorance leads them to exaggerate the advantages of sensual enjoyment, whose callous habits render domestic endearments more important to dispose them to resist the suggestions to violence and cruelty by which their situation ever exposes them to be tempted, and all whose other enjoyments are limited and few, whilst their sufferings are various and many. In this sense I cannot imagine how the

---

[1] Thomas Robert Malthus (1766–1834), author of *Essay on the Principle of Population* (1798).

advocates of equality would so readily have conceded that the unlimited operation of the principle of population affects the truth of these theories. On the contrary, the more heavy and certain are the evils of life, the more injustice is there in casting the burden of them exclusively on one order in the community. They seem to have conceded it merely because their opponents have insolently assumed it. Surely it is enough that the rich should possess to the exclusion of the poor all other luxuries and comforts, and wisdom and refinement, the least envied but the most deserving of envy among all their privileges.

What is the Reform that we desire? Before we aspire after theoretical perfection in the amelioration of our political state, it is necessary that we possess those advantages which we have been cheated of, and to which the experience of modern times has proved that nations even under the present [conditions] are susceptible. 1st. We would regain these. 2d. We would establish some form of government which might secure us against such a series of events as have conducted us to a persuasion that the forms according to which it is now administered are inadequate to that purpose.

We would abolish the national debt.

We would disband the standing army.

We would, with every possible regard to the existing interests of the holders, abolish sinecures.

We would, with every possible regard to the existing interests of the holders, abolish tithes, and make all religions, all forms of opinion respecting the origin and government of the Universe, equal in the eye of the law.

We would make justice cheap, certain and speedy, and extend the institution of juries to every possible occasion of jurisprudence.

The national debt was chiefly contracted in two liberticide wars, undertaken by the privileged classes of the country—the first for the ineffectual purpose of tyrannizing over one portion of their subjects, the second, in order to extinguish the resolute spirit of obtaining their rights, in another. The labour which this money represents, and that which is represented by the money wrung for purposes of the same detestable character, out of the people since the commencement of the American war would, if properly employed, have covered our land with monuments of architecture exceeding the sumptuousness and the beauty of Egypt and Athens; it might have made every peasant's cottage, surrounded with its garden, a little paradise of comfort, with every convenience desirable in civilized life; neat tables and chairs, and good beds, and a nice collection of useful books; and our ships manned by sailors well-paid and well-clothed, might have kept watch round this glorious island against the less enlightened nations which assuredly would have envied, until they could have imitated, its prosperity. But the labour which is expressed by these sums has been diverted from these purposes of human happiness to the promotion of slavery, or the attempt at dominion, and a great portion of the sum in question is debt and must be paid. Is it to remain unpaid for ever, an eternal rent-charge upon the sacred soil from which the inhabitants of these islands draw their subsistence? This were to pronounce the perpetual institution of two orders of aristocracy, and men are in a temper to endure one with some reluctance. Is it to be paid now? If so what are the funds, or when and how is it to be paid? The fact is that the national debt is a debt not contracted by the whole nation towards a portion of it, but a debt contracted by the whole mass of the privileged classes towards one particular portion of those classes. If the principal were paid, the whole property of those who possess property must be valued and the public creditor, whose property would have been included in this estimate, satisfied out of the proceeds. It has been said that all the land in the nation is mortgaged for the amount of the national debt. This is a partial statement. Not only all the land in the nation, but all the property of whatever denomination, all the houses and the furniture and goods and every article of merchandise, and the property which is represented by the very money lent by the fund-holder, who is bound to pay a certain portion as debtor whilst he is to receive another certain portion as creditor. The property of the rich is mortgaged: to use the language of the law, let the mortgagee foreclose.—

If the principal of this debt were paid, after such reductions had been made so as to make an equal value, taking corn for the standard, be given as was received, it would be the rich who alone could, as justly they ought to pay it. It would be a mere transfer among persons of property. Such a gentleman must lose a third of his estate, such a citizen a fourth of his money in the funds; the persons who borrowed would have paid, and the juggling and complicated system of paper finance be suddenly at an end. As it is, the interest is chiefly paid by those who had no hand in the borrowing, and who are sufferers in other respects from the consequences of those transactions in which the money was spent.

The payment of the principal of what is called the national debt, which it is pretended is so difficult a problem, is only difficult to those who do not see who is the creditor, and who the debtor, and who the wretched sufferers from whom they both wring the taxes which under the form of interest is given by the [latter] and accepted by the [former]. It is from the labour of those who have no property that all the persons who possess property think to extort the perpetual interest of a debt, the whole of them to the part, which the [former] know they could not persuade the [latter] to pay, but by conspiring with them in an imposture which makes the third class pay what the [second] neither received by their sanction nor spent for their benefit, and what the [first] never lent to them. They would both shift to the labour of the present and of all succeeding generations the payment of the interest of their own debt, from themselves and their posterity, because the payment of the principal would be no more than a compromise and transfer of property between each other, by which the nation would be spared forty four millions a year, which now is paid to maintain in luxury and indolence the public debtors and to protect them from the demand of their creditors upon them, who, being part of the same body, and owing as debtors whilst they possess a claim as creditors, agree to abstain from demanding the principal which they must all unite to pay, for the sake of receiving an enormous interest which is principally wrung out of those who had no concern whatever in the transaction. One of the first acts of a reformed government would undoubtedly be an effectual scheme for compelling these to compromise their debt between themselves.

When I speak of persons of property I mean not every man who possesses any right of property; I mean the rich. Every man whose scope in society has a plebeian and intelligible utility, whose personal exertions are more valuable to him than his capital; every tradesman who is not a monopolist, all surgeons and physicians and those mechanics and editors and literary men and artists, and farmers, all those persons whose profits spring from honourably and honestly exerting their own skill and wisdom or strength in greater abundance than from the employment of money to take advantage of the necessity of the starvation of their fellow-citizens for their profit, are those who pay, as well as those more obviously understood by the labouring classes, the interest of the national debt. It is the interest of all these persons as well as that of the poor to insist upon the payment of the principal.

For this purpose the form ought to be as simple and succinct as possible. The operations deciding who was to pay, at what time, and how much, and to whom, are divested of financial chicanery, problems readily to be determined. The common tribunals may possess a legal jurisdiction to award the proportion due upon the several claim of each.

There are two descriptions of property which, without entering into the subtleties of a more refined moral theory as applicable to the existing forms of society, are entitled to two very different measures of forbearance and regard. And this forbearance and regard have by political institutions usually been accorded in an inverse reason from what is just and natural. Labour, industry, economy, skill, genius, or any similar powers honourably and innocently exerted are the foundations of one description of property, and all true political institutions ought to defend every man in the exercise of his discretion with respect to property so acquired. Of this kind is the principal part of the property enjoyed by those who are but one degree removed from the class which subsists by daily labour. [Yet there are instances of persons in this class who have procured their property by fraudulent and violent means, as there are instances in the other of persons who have acquired their property by innocent or honourable exertion. All political science abounds with limitations and exceptions.] Property thus acquired men leave to their children. Absolute right becomes weakened by descent, first because it is only to avoid the greater evil of arbitrarily interfering with the discretion of any man in matters of property that the great evil of acknowledging any person to have an exclusive right to property who has not created it by his skill or labour is admitted, and secondly because the mode of its having been originally acquired is forgotten, and it is confounded with property acquired in a very different manner; and the principle upon which all property justly rests, after the great principle of the general advantage, becomes thus disregarded and misunderstood. Yet the privilege of disposing of property by will is one necessarily connected with the existing forms of domestic life; and exerted merely by those who have acquired property by industry or who have preserved it by economy, would never produce any great and invidious inequality of fortune. A thousand accidents would perpetually tend to level the accidental elevation, and the signs of property would perpetually recur to those whose deserving skill might attract or whose labour might create it.

But there is another species of property which has its foundation in usurpation, or imposture, or violence, without which, by the nature of things, immense possessions of gold or land could never have been accumulated. Of this nature is the principal part of the property enjoyed by the aristocracy and by the great fundholders, the great majority of whose ancestors never either deserved it by their skill and talents or acquired and created it by their personal labour. It could not be that they deserved it, for if the honourable exertion of the most glorious imperial faculties of our nature had been the criterion of the possession of property, the posterity of Shakespeare, of Milton, of Hampden, or Lor[d Bacon] would be the wealthiest proprietors in England. It could not be that they acquired it by legitimate industry,—for, besides that the real mode of acquisition is matter of history,—no honourable profession or honest trade, nor the hereditary exercise of it, ever in such numerous instances accumulated masses of property so vast as those enjoyed by the ruling orders in England. They were either grants from the feudal sovereigns whose right to what they granted was founded upon conquest or oppression, both a denial of all right; or they were the lands of the antient Catholic clergy which according to the most acknowledged principles of public justice reverted to the nation at their suppression, or they were the products of patents and monopolies, an exercise of sovereignty most pernicious that direct violence to the interests of a commercial nation; or in later times such property has been accumulated by dishonourable cunning and the taking advantage of a fictitious paper currency to obtain an unfair power over labour and the fruits of labour.

Property thus accumulated, being transmitted from father to son, acquires, as property of the more legitimate kind loses, force and sanction, but in a more limited manner. For not only on an examination and recurrence to first principles is it seen to have been founded on a violation of all that to which the latter owes its sacredness, but it is felt in its existence and perpetuation as a public burthen, and known as a rallying point to the ministers of tyranny, having the property of a snowball, gathering as it rolls, and rolling until it bursts. [It] is astonishing that political theorists have not branded [it] as the most pernicious and odious. [Yet] there are three sets of people, one who can place a thing to another in an intelligible light, another who can understand it when so communicated, and a third who can neither discover or understand it.

Labour and skill and the immediate wages of labour and skill is a property of the most sacred and indisputable right, and the foundation of all other property. And the right of a man [to] property in the exertion of his own bodily and mental faculties, or to the produce and free reward from and for that exertion is the most [inalienable of rights]. If however he takes by violence or appropriates to himself through fraudulent cunning, or receives from another property so acquired, his claim to that property is of a far inferior force. We may acquiesce, if we evidently perceive an overbalance of public advantage in submission under this claim; but if any public emergency should arise, at which it might be necessary as at present by a tax on capital to satisfy the claims of a part of the nation by a contribution from such national resources as may with the least injustice be appropriated to that purpose, assuredly it would not be on labour and skill, the foundation of all property, nor on the profits and savings of labour and skill, which are property itself, but on such possessions which can only be called property in a modified sense, as have from their magnitude and their nature an evident origin in violence or imposture.

The national debt, as has been stated, is a debt contracted by the whole of a particular class in the nation towards a portion of that class. It is sufficiently clear that this debt was not contracted for the purpose of the public advantage. Besides there was no authority in the nation competent to a measure of this nature. The usual vindication of national debts is that, [since] they are contracted in an overwhelming measure for the purpose of defence against a common danger, for the vindication of the rights and liberties of posterity, it is just that posterity should bear the burthen of payment. This reasoning is most fallacious. The history of nations presents us with a succession of extraordinary emergencies, and thro' their present imperfect organization their existence is perpetually threatened by new and unexpected combinations and developments of foreign or internal force. Imagine a situation of equal emergency to occur to England as that which the ruling party assume to have occurred as their excuse for burthening the nation with the perpetual payment of £45,000,000 annually. Suppose France, Russia, and America were to enter into a league against England, the first to revenge its injuries, the second to satisfy its ambition, the third to soothe its jealousy. Could the nation bear £90,000,000 of yearly interest? must there be twice as many luxurious and idle persons? must the labourer receive for twenty-eight hours' work what he now receives for fourteen, as he now receives for fourteen what he once received for seven? But this argument . . .

What is meant by a Reform of Parliament? If England were a Republic governed by one assembly; if there were no chamber of hereditary aristocracy which is at once an actual and a virtual representation of all who claim through rank or wealth superiority over their countrymen; if there were no king who is as the rallying point of those whose tendency is at once to [gather] and to confer that power which is consolidated at the expense of the nation, then . . .

The advocates of universal suffrage have reasoned correctly that no individual who is governed can be denied a direct share in the government of his country without supreme injustice. If we pursue the train of reasonings which have conducted to this conclusion, we discover that systems of social order still more incompatible than universal suffrage with any reasonable hope of instant accomplishment appear to be that which should result from a just combination of the elements of social life. I do not understand why those reasoners who propose at any price an immediate appeal to universal suffrage, because it is that which it is injustice to withhold, do not insist, on the same ground, on the immediate abolition, for instance, of monarchy and aristocracy, and the levelling of inordinate wealth, and an agrarian distribution, including the Parks and Chases of the rich, of the uncultivated districts of the country. No doubt the institution of universal suffrage would by necessary consequence *immediately* tend to the *temporary* abolition of these forms; because it is impossible that the people, having attained power, should fail to see, what the demagogues now conceal from them, the legitimate consequence of the doctrines through which they had attained it. A Republic, however just in its principle and glorious in its object, would through violence and sudden change which must attend it, incur a great risk of being as rapid in its decline as in its growth. It is better that they should be instructed in the whole truth; that they should see the clear grounds of their rights, the objects to which they ought to tend; and be impressed with the just persuasion that patience and reason and endurance [are the means of] a calm yet irresistible progress. A civil war, which might be engendered by the passions attending on this mode of reform, would confirm in the mass of the nation those military habits which have been already introduced by our tyrants, and with which liberty is incompatible. From the moment that a man is a soldier, he becomes a slave. He is taught obedience; his will is no longer, which is the most sacred prerogative of man, guided by his own judgement. He is taught to despise human life and human suffering; this is the universal distinction of slaves. He is more degraded than a murderer; he is like the bloody knife which has stabbed and feels not: a murderer we may abhor and despise; a soldier is by profession, beyond abhorrence and below contempt.

CHAPTER III

PROBABLE MEANS

THAT Commons should reform itself, uninfluenced by any fear that the people would, on their refusal, assume to itself that office, seems a contradiction. What need of Reform if it expresses the will and watches over the interests of the public? And if, as is sufficiently evident, it despises that will and neglects that interest, what motives would incite it to institute a reform which the aspect of the times renders indeed sufficiently perilous, but without which there will speedily be no longer anything in England to distinguish it from the basest and most abject community of slaves that ever existed.

One motive . . .

The great principle of Reform consists in every individual of mature age and perfect understanding giving his consent to the institution and the continued existence of the social system, which is instituted for his advantage and for the advantage of others in his situation. As in a great nation this is practically impossible, masses of individuals consent to qualify other individuals, whom they delegate to superintend their concerns. These delegates have constitutional authority to exercise the functions of sovereignty; they unite in the highest degree the legislative and executive functions. A government that is founded on any other basis is a government of fraud or force and ought on the first convenient occasion to be overthrown. The [?] broad principle of political reform is the natural equality of men, not with relation to their property but to their rights. That equality in possessions which Jesus Christ so passionately taught is a moral rather than a political truth and is such as social institutions cannot without mischief inflexibly secure. Morals and politics can only be considered as portions of the same science, with relation to a system of such absolute perfection as Christ and Plato and Rousseau and other reasoners have asserted, and as Godwin has, with irresistible eloquence, systematised and developed. Equality in possessions must be the last result of the utmost refinements of civilization; it is one of the conditions of that system of society, towards which with whatever hope of ultimate success, it is our duty to tend. We may and ought to advert to it as to the elementary principle, as to the goal, unattainable, perhaps, by us, but which, as it were, we revive in our posterity to pursue. We derive tranquillity and courage and grandeur of soul from contemplating an object which is, because we will it, and may be, because we hope and desire it, and must be if succeeding generations of the enlightened sincerely and earnestly seek it. We should with sincere and patient aspi- [? ration] . . .

But our present business is with the difficult and unbending realities of actual life, and when we have drawn inspiration from the great object of our hopes it becomes us with patience and resolution to apply ourselves to accommodating our theories to immediate practice.

That Representative Assembly called the House of Commons ought questionless to be *immediately* nominated by the great mass of the people. The aristocracy and those who unite in their own persons the vast privileges conferred by the possession of inordinate wealth are sufficiently represented by the House of Peers and by the King. Those theorists who admire and would put into action the mechanism of what is called the British Constitution would acquiesce in this view of the question. For if the House of Peers be a permanent representation of the privileged classes, if the regal power be no more than another form, and a form still more jealously to be regarded, of the same representation, whilst the House of Commons be not chosen by the mass of the population, what becomes of that democratic element, upon the presence of which it has been supposed that the waning superiority of England over the surrounding nations has depended?

Any sudden attempt at universal suffrage would produce an immature attempt at a Republic. It [is better] that [an] object so inexpressibly great and sacred should never have been attempted than that it should be attempted and fail. It is no prejudice to the ultimate establishment of the boldest political innovations that we temporize so as, when they shall be accomplished they may be rendered permanent.

Considering the population of Great Britain and Ireland as twenty millions and the representative assembly as five hundred, each member ought to be the expression of the will of 40,000 persons; of these two-thirds would [consist of] women and children and persons under age; the actual number of voters therefore for each member would be 13,333. The whole extent of the empire might be divided into five hundred electoral departments or parishes, and the inhabitants assemble on a certain day to exercise their rights of suffrage.

Mr. Bentham and other writers have urged the admission of females to the right of suffrage; this attempt seems somewhat immature.—Should my opinion be the result of despondency, the writer of these pages would be the last to withhold his vote from any system which might tend to an equal and full development of the capacities of all living beings.

The system of voting by ballot which some reasoners have recommended is attended with obvious inconveniences. [It withdraws the elector from the regard of his country, and] his neighbors, and permits him to conceal the motives of his vote, which, if concealed, cannot but be dishonourable; when, if he had known that he had to render a public account of his conduct, he

would have never permitted them to guide him. There is in this system of voting by ballot and of electing a member of the *Representative Assembly* as a church-warden is elected something too mechanical. The elector and the elected ought to meet one another face to face, and interchange the meanings of actual presence and share some common impulses, and, in a degree, understand each other. There ought to be the common sympathy of the excitements of a popular assembly among the electors themselves. The imagination would thus be strongly excited, and a mass of generous and enlarged and popular sentiments be awakened, which would give the vitality of . . .

That republican boldness of censuring and judging one another, which has indeed [been] exerted in England under the title of 'public opinion,' though perverted from its true uses into an instrument of prejudice and calumny, would then be applied to its genuine purposes. Year by year the people would become more susceptible of assuming forms of government more simple and beneficial.

It is in this publicity of the exercise of sovereignty that the difference between the republics of Greece and the monarchies of Asia consisted. The actions of the times . . .

If the existing government shall compel the Nation to take the task of reform into its own hands, one of the most obvious consequences of such a circumstance would be the abolition of monarchy and aristocracy. Why, it will then be argued, if the subsisting condition of social forms is to be thrown into confusion, should these things be endured? Then why do we now endure them? Is it because we think that an hereditary King is cheaper and wiser than an elected President, or a House of Lords and a Bench of Bishops are institutions modelled by the wisdom of the most refined and civilized periods, beyond which the wit of mortal man can furnish nothing more perfect? In case the subsisting Government should compel the people to revolt to establish a representative assembly in defiance of them, and to assume in that assembly an attitude of resistance and defence, this question would probably be answered in a very summary manner.—No friend of mankind and of his country can desire that such a crisis should suddenly arrive; but still less, once having arrived, can he hesitate under what banner to array his person and his power. At the peace, the people would have been contented with strict economy and severe retrenchment, and some direct and intelligible plan for producing that equilibrium between the capitalists and the landholders which is delusively styled the payment of the national debt: had this system been adopted, they probably would have refrained from exacting Parliamentary Reform, the

only secure guarantee that it would have been pursued.
—Two years ago it might still have been possible to
have commenced a system of gradual reform. The
people were then insulted, tempted and betrayed, and
the petitions of a million of men rejected with disdain.
Now they are more miserable, more hopeless, more
impatient of their misery. Above all, they have become
more universally aware of the true sources of their
misery. It is possible that the period of conciliation
is past, and that after having played with the confidence
and cheated the expectations of the people, their
passions will be too little under discipline to allow
them to wait the slow, gradual and certain operation of
such a Reform as we can imagine the constituted
authorities to concede.

Upon the issue of this question depends the species
of reform which a philosophical mind should regard
with approbation. If Reform shall be begun by the
existing government, let us be contented with a
limited *beginning*, with any whatsoever opening; let
the rotten boroughs be disfranchised and their rights
transferred to the unrepresented cities and districts of
the Nation; it is no matter how slow, gradual and
cautious be the change; we shall demand more and
more with firmness and moderation, never anticipating
but never deferring the moment of successful opposition, so that the people may become habituated [to]
exercising the functions of sovereignty, in proportion
as they acquire the possession of it. If reform could
begin from within the Houses of Parliament, as
constituted at present, it appears to me that what is
called moderate reform, that is a suffrage whose
qualification should be the possession of a certain small
property, and triennial parliaments, would be principles—a system in which for the sake of obtaining
without bloodshed or confusion ulterior improvements
of a more important character, all reformers ought to
acquiesce. Not that such are first principles, or that they
would produce a system of perfect social institutions or
one approaching to [such]. But nothing is more idle
than to reject a limited benefit because we cannot
without great sacrifices obtain an unlimited one. We
might thus reject a Representative Republic, if it were
obtainable, on the plea that the imagination of man
can conceive of something more absolutely perfect.
Towards whatsoever we regard as perfect, undoubtedly
it is no less our duty than it is our nature to press
forward; this is the generous enthusiasm which
accomplishes not indeed the consummation after
which it aspires, but one which approaches it in a
degree far nearer than if the whole powers had not been
developed by a delusion.—It is in politics rather than
in religion that faith is meritorious.—

If the Houses of Parliament obstinately and per-

petually refuse to concede any reform to the people,
my vote is for universal suffrage and equal representation. My vote is——but, it is asked, how shall this be
accomplished, in defiance of and in opposition to the
constituted authorities of the Nation, they who possess
whether with or without its consent the command of a
standing army and of a legion of spies and police
officers, and hold all the strings of that complicated
mechanism with which the hopes and fears of men are
moved like puppets? They would disperse any assembly really chosen by the people, they would shoot and
hew down any multitude, without regard to sex or age,
as the Jews did the Canaanites, which might be collected in its defence; they would calumniate, imprison,
starve, ruin and expatriate every person who wrote or
acted, or thought, or might be suspected to think
against them; misery and extermination would fill the
country from one end to another . . . ?

This question I would answer by another.

Will you endure to pay the half of your earnings to
maintain in luxury and idleness the confederation of
your tyrants as the reward of a successful conspiracy to
defraud and oppress you? Will you make your tame
cowardice and the branding record of it the everlasting
inheritance of your posterity? Not only this; will you
render by your torpid endurance this condition of
things as permanent as the system of castes in India,
by which the same horrible injustice is perpetrated
under another form?

Assuredly no Englishmen by whom these propositions are understood will answer in the affirmative;
and the opposite side of the alternative remains.—

When the majority in any nation arrive at a conviction
that it is their duty and their interest to divest the
minority of a power employed to their disadvantage;
and the minority are sufficiently mistaken as to believe
that their superiority is tenable, a struggle must ensue.

If the majority are enlightened, united, impelled by
a uniform enthusiasm and animated by a distinct and
powerful apprehension of their object,—and full
confidence in their undoubted power—the struggle is
merely nominal. The minority perceive the approaches
of the development of an irresistible force, by the
influence of the public opinion of their weakness, on
those political forms of which no government but an
absolute despotism is devoid. They divest themselves
of their usurped distinctions; the public tranquillity is
not disturbed by the revolution——

But these conditions may only be imperfectly
fulfilled by the state of a people grossly oppressed and
impotent to cast off the load. Their enthusiasm may
have been subdued by the killing weight of toil and
suffering; they may be panic-stricken and disunited
by their oppressors, and the demagogues; the influence

of fraud may have been sufficient to weaken the union of classes which compose them by suggesting jealousies, and the position of the conspirators, although it is to be forced by repeated assaults, may be tenable until the siege can be vigorously urged. The true patriot will endeavor to enlighten and to unite the nation and animate it with enthusiasm and confidence. For this purpose he will be indefatigable in promulgating political truth. He will endeavor to rally round one standard the divided friends of liberty, and make them forget the subordinate objects with regard to which they differ by appealing to that respecting which they are all agreed. He will promote such open confederations among men of principle and spirit as may tend to make their intentions and their efforts converge to a common centre. He will discourage all secret associations, which have a tendency, by making national will develop itself in a partial and premature manner, to cause tumult and confusion. He will urge the necessity of exciting the people frequently to exercise their right of assembling, in such limited numbers as that all present may be actual parties to the proceedings of the day. Lastly, if circumstances had collected a more considerable number as at Manchester on the memorable 16th of August,[1] if the tyrants command their troops to fire upon them or cut them down unless they disperse, he will exhort them peaceably to risque the danger, and to expect without resistance the onset of the cavalry, and wait with folded arms the event of the fire of the artillery and receive with unshrinking bosoms the bayonets of the charging battalions. Men are every day persuaded to incur greater perils for a less manifest advantage. And this, not because active resistance is not justifiable when all other means shall have failed, but because in this instance temperance and courage would produce greater advantages than the most decisive victory. In the first place, the soldiers are men and Englishmen, and it is not to be believed that they would massacre an unresisting multitude of their countrymen drawn up in unarmed array before

---

[1] Shelley refers to the "Peterloo Massacre" of August 16, 1819, when 50,000 to 60,000 people had assembled in political protest at St. Peter's Field, Manchester. In order to arrest the radical reformer and mob orator Henry Hunt, soldiers charged into the crowd, causing the death of eleven persons and wounding hundreds. The event had repercussions far beyond the actual loss of life. It was seen by many as presaging violent popular revolution, and it brought into being the Tory government's "Six Acts," severe restrictions on the exercise of civil liberties. For details of the event and its importance for Shelley, see A. Stanley Walker, "Peterloo, Shelley and Reform," *PMLA*, XL (1925), 128–64. Walker calls the assemblage at Manchester "perhaps the most important of all meetings held in England in the interests of democracy between the gathering of Stephen Langton and his barons at Runnymede in 1215 and the passing of the Reform Bill of 1832."

them, and bearing in their looks the calm, deliberate resolution to perish rather than abandon the assertion of their rights. In the confusion of flight the ideas of the soldier become confused, and he massacres those who fly from him by the instinct of his trade. In the struggle of conflict and resistance he is irritated by a sense of his own danger, he is flattered by an apprehension of his magnanimity in incurring it, he considers the blood of his countrymen at once the price of his valour, the pledge of his security. He applauds himself by reflecting that these base and dishonourable motives will gain him credit among his comrades and his officers who are animated by the same as if they were something the same. But if he should observe neither resistance nor flight he would be reduced to impotence and indecision. Thus far, his ideas were governed by the same law as those of a dog who chases a flock of sheep to the corner of a field, and keeps aloof when they make the firm parade of resistance.—But the soldier is a man and an Englishman. This unexpected reception would probably throw him back upon a recollection of the true nature of the measures of which he was made the instrument, and the enemy might be converted into the ally.

The patriot will be foremost to publish the boldest truths in the most fearless manner, yet without the slightest tincture of personal malignity. He would encourage all others to the same efforts and assist them to the utmost of his power with the resources both of his intellect and fortune. He would call upon them to despise imprisonment and persecution and lose no opportunity of bringing public opinion and the power of the tyrants into circumstances of perpetual contest and opposition.—

All might however be ineffectual to produce so uniform an impulse of the national will as to preclude a further struggle. The strongest argument, perhaps, for the necessity of Reform, is the inoperative and unconscious abjectness to which the purposes of a considerable mass of the people are reduced. They neither know nor care.—They are sinking into a resemblance with the Hindoos and the Chinese, who were once men as they are. Unless the cause which renders them passive subjects instead of active citizens be removed, they will sink with accelerated gradations into that barbaric and unnatural civilization which destroys all the differences among men. It is in vain to exhort us to wait until all men shall desire Freedom whose real interest will consist in its establishment. It is in vain to hope to enlighten them whilst their tyrants employ the utmost artifices of all their complicated engine to perpetuate the infection of every species of fanaticism and error from generation to generation. The advocates of Reform ought indeed to leave no effort unexerted, and they ought to be indefatigable in exciting all men to examine.—

But if they wait until those neutral politicians, a class whose opinions represent the actions of this class, are persuaded that so soon [as] effectual reform is necessary, the occasion will have passed or will never arrive, and the people will have exhausted their strength in ineffectual expectation and will have sunk into incurable supineness. It was principally the [effect of] a similar quietism that the populous and extensive nations of Asia have fallen into their existing decrepitude; and that anarchy, insecurity, ignorance and barbarism, the symptoms of the confirmed disease of monarchy, have reduced nations of the most delicate physical and intellectual organization and under the most fortunate climates of the globe to a blank in the history of man. The manufacturers to a man are persuaded of the necessity of reform; an immense majority of the inhabitants of London. . . .

The reasoners who incline to the opinion that it is not sufficient that the innovators should produce a majority in the nation, but that we ought to expect such an unanimity as would preclude anything amounting to a serious dispute, are prompted to this view of the question by the dread of anarchy and massacre. Infinite and inestimable calamities belong to oppression, but the most fatal of them all is that mine of unexploded mischief which it has practiced beneath the foundations of society, and with which, "pernicious to one touch"[2] it threatens to involve the ruin of the entire building together with its own. But delay merely renders these mischiefs more tremendous, not the less inevitable. For the utmost may now be the crisis of the social disease [which] is rendered thus periodical, chronic and incurable.

The savage brutality of the populace is proportioned to the arbitrary character of their government, and tumults and insurrections soon, as in Constantinople, become consistent with the permanence of the causing evil, of which they might have been the critical determination.

The public opinion in England ought first to [be] excited to action, and the durability of those forms within which the oppressors intrench themselves brought perpetually to the test of its operation. No law or institution can last if this opinion be distinctly pronounced against it. For this purpose government ought to be defied, in cases of questionable result, to prosecute for political libel. All questions relating to the jurisdiction of magistrates and courts of law respecting which any doubt could be raised ought to be agitated

_____

[2] *Paradise Lost*, VI, 520.

with indefatigable pertinacity. Some two or three of the popular leaders have shown the best spirit in this respect; they only want system and co-operation. The taxgatherer ought to be compelled in every practicable instance to distrain, whilst the right to impose taxes, as was the case in the beginning of the resistance to the tyranny of Charles the 1st is formally contested by an overwhelming multitude of defendants before the courts of common law. Confound the subtlety of lawyers with the subtlety of the law. All of the nation would thus be excited to develop itself, and to declare whether it acquiesced in the existing forms of government.—The manner in which all questions of this nature might be decided would develop the occasions, and afford a prognostic as to the success, of more decisive measures. Simultaneously with this active and vigilant system of opposition, means ought to be taken of solemnly conveying the sense of large bodies and various denominations of the people in a manner the most explicit to the existing depositaries of power. Petitions, couched in the actual language of the petitioners, and emanating from distinct assemblies, ought to load the tables of the House of Commons. The poets, philosophers and artists ought to remonstrate, and the memorials entitled their petitions might shew the diversit[y] [of] convictions they entertain of the inevitable connection between national prosperity and freedom, and the cultivation of the imagination and the cultivation of scientific truth, and the profound development of moral and metaphysical enquiry. Suppose these memorials to be severally written by Godwin, Hazlitt, Bentham and Hunt, they would be worthy of the age and of the cause; these, radiant and irresistible like the meridian sun would strike all but the eagles who dared to gaze upon its beams, with blindness and confusion. These appeals of solemn and emphatic argument from those who have already a predestined existence among posterity, would appal the enemies of mankind by their echoes from every corner of the world in which the majestic literature of England is cultivated; it would be like a voice from beyond the dead of those who will live in the memories of men, when they must be forgotten; it would be Eternity warning Time.

Let us hope that at this stage of the progress of Reform, the oppressors would feel their impotence and reluctantly and imperfectly concede some limited portion of the rights of the people, and disgorge some morsels of their undigested prey. In this case, the people ought to be exhorted by everything ultimately dear to them to pause until by the exercise of those rights which they have regained they become fitted to demand more. It is better that we gain what we demand by a process of negotiation which would occupy twenty years, than that by communicating a sudden shock to the interests of those who are the depositaries and dependents of power we should incur the calamity which their revenge might inflict upon us by giving the signal of civil war.—If, after all, they consider the chance of personal ruin, and the infamy of figuring on the page of history as the promoters of civil war preferable to resigning any portion how small soever of their usurped authority, we are to recollect that we possess a right beyond remonstrance. It has been acknowledged by the most approved writers on the English constitution, which is in this instance merely [a] declaration of the superior decisions of eternal justice, that we possess a right of resistance. The claim of the [reigning] family is founded upon a memorable exertion of this solemnly recorded right.

The last resort of resistance is undoubtedly insurrection.—The right of insurrection is derived from the employment of armed force to counteract the will of the nation. Let the government disband the standing army, and the purpose of resistance would be sufficiently fulfilled by the incessant agitation of the points of dispute before the courts of common law, and by an unwarlike display of the irresistible number and union of the people.

Before we enter into a consideration of the measures which might terminate in civil war, let us for a moment consider the nature and the consequences of war. This is the alternative which the unprincipled cunning of the tyrants has presented to us, from which we must not sh[rink]. There is secret sympathy between Destruction and Power, between Monarchy and War; and the long experience of the history of all recorded time teaches us with what success they have played into each other's hands. War is a kind of superstition; the pageantry of arms and badges corrupts the imagination of men. How far more appropriate would be the symbols of an inconsolable grief—muffled drums, and melancholy music, and arms reversed, and the livery of sorrow rather than of blood. When men mourn at funerals for what do they mourn in comparison with the calamities which they hasten with all circumstance of festivity to suffer and to inflict! Visit in imagination the scene of a field of battle or a city taken by assault, collect into one group the groans and the distortions of the innumerable dying, the inconsolable grief and horror of their surviving friends, the hellish exultation, and unnatural drunkenness of destruction of the conquerors, the burning of the harvests and the obliteration of the traces of cultivation—To this, in civil war, is to be added the sudden disruption of the bonds of social life, and 'father against son.'

If there had never been war, there could never have been tyranny in the world; tyrants take advantage of the mechanical organization of armies to establish and defend their encroachments. It is thus that the mighty advantages of the French Revolution have been almost compensated by a succession of tyrants (for demagogues, oligarchies, usurpers and legitimate kings are merely varieties of the same class) from Robespierre to Louis 18. War, waged from whatever motive, extinguishes the sentiment of reason and justice in the mind. The motive is forgotten, or only adverted to in a mechanical and habitual manner. A sentiment of confidence in brute force and in a contempt of death and danger is considered as the highest virtue, when in truth, and however indispensable, they are merely the means and the instruments, highly capable of being perverted to destroy the cause they were assumed to promote. It is a foppery the most intolerable to an amiable and philosophical mind.—It is like what some reasoners have observed of religious faith; no false and indirect motive to action can subsist in the mind without weakening the effect of those which are genuine and true. The person who thinks it virtuous to believe, will think a less degree of virtue attaches to good actions than if he had considered it as indifferent. The person who has been accustomed to subdue men by force will be less inclined to the trouble of convincing or persuading them.

These brief considerations suffice to show that the true friend of mankind and of his country would hesitate before he recommended measures which tend to bring down so heavy a calamity as war—

I imagine however that before the English Nation shall arrive at that point of moral and political degradation now occupied by the Chinese, it will be necessary to appeal to an exertion of physical strength. If the madness of parties admits no other mode of determining the question at issue, . . .

When the people shall have obtained, by whatever means, the victory over their oppressors and when persons appointed by them shall have taken their seats in the Representative Assembly of the nation, and assumed the control of public affairs according to constitutional rules, there will remain the great task of accommodating all that can be preserved of antient forms with the improvements of the knowledge of a more enlightened age, in legislation, jurisprudence, government and religious and academical institution. The settlement of the national debt is on the principles before elucidated merely circumstance of form, and however necessary and important is an affair of mere arithmetical proportions readily determined; nor can I see how those who, being deprived of their unjust advantages, will probably inwardly murmur, can oppose one word of open expostulation to a measure of such inescapable justice.

There is one thing, which certain vulgar agitators endeavour to flatter the most uneducated part of the people by assiduously proposing, which they ought not to do nor to require; and that is Retribution. Men having been injured, desire to injure in return. This is falsely called an universal law of human nature; it is a law from which many are exempt, and all in proportion to their virtue and cultivation. The savage is more revengeful than the civilized man, the ignorant and uneducated than the person of a refined and cultivated intellect; the generous and . . .

[1920]   [1930]

A DEFENCE OF POETRY

Written in 1821 as an answer to Peacock's The Four Ages of Poetry, *Shelley's* Defence *was not published until 1840. Only Part I of a projected three-part essay was ever written. Although the essay has won almost universal admiration for its eloquence and rhetorical power, there have been much discussion and considerable reservation about the clarity and consistency of its argument. For contrasting analyses, see the titles by M. H. Abrams and Earl R. Wasserman in the Selected Bibliography.*

A DEFENCE OF POETRY

PART I

ACCORDING to one mode of regarding those two classes of mental action, which are called reason and imagination, the former may be considered as mind contemplating the relations borne by one thought to another, however produced; and the latter, as mind acting upon those thoughts so as to colour them with its own light, and composing from them, as from elements, other thoughts, each containing within itself the principle of its own integrity. The one is the τὸ ποιεῖν, or the principle of synthesis, and has for its objects those forms which are common to universal nature and existence itself; the other is the τὸ λογίζειν, or principle of analysis, and its action regards the relations of things, simply as relations; considering thoughts, not in their integral unity, but as the algebraical representations which conduct to certain general results. Reason is the enumeration of quantities already known; imagination is the perception of the value of those quantities, both separately and as a whole. Reason respects the differences, and imagination the similitudes of things. Reason is to imagination as the instrument to the agent, as the body to the spirit, as the shadow to the substance.

Poetry, in a general sense, may be defined to be "the expression of the imagination": and poetry is connate with the origin of man. Man is an instrument over which a series of external and internal impressions are driven, like the alternations of an ever-changing wind over an Æolian lyre, which move it by their motion to ever-changing melody. But there is a principle within the human being, and perhaps within all sentient beings, which acts otherwise than in the lyre, and produces not melody, alone, but harmony, by an internal adjustment of the sounds or motions thus excited to the impressions which excite them. It is as if the lyre could accommodate its chords to the motions of that which strikes them, in a determined proportion of sound; even as the musician can accommodate his voice to the sound of the lyre. A child at play by itself will express its delight by its voice and motions; and every inflexion of tone and every gesture will bear exact relation to a corresponding antitype in the pleasurable impressions which awakened it; it will be the reflected image of that impression; and as the lyre trembles and sounds after the wind has died away, so the child seeks, by prolonging in its voice and motions the duration of the effect, to prolong also a consciousness of the cause. In relation to the objects which delight a child, these expressions are, what poetry is to higher objects. The savage (for the savage is to ages what the child is to years) expresses the emotions produced in him by surrounding objects in a similar manner; and language and gesture, together with plastic or pictorial imitation, become the image of the combined effect of those objects, and of his apprehension of them. Man in society, with all his passions and his pleasures, next becomes the object of the passions and pleasures of man; an additional class of emotions produces an augmented treasure of expressions; and language, gesture, and the imitative arts, become at once the representation and the medium, the pencil and the picture, the chisel and the statue, the chord and the harmony. The social sympathies, or those laws from which, as from its elements, society results, begin to develop themselves from the moment that two human beings coexist; the future is contained within the present, as the plant within the seed; and equality, diversity, unity, contrast, mutual dependence, become the principles alone capable of affording the motives according to which the will of a social being is determined to action, inasmuch as he is social; and constitute pleasure in sensation, virtue in sentiment, beauty in art, truth in reasoning, and love in the intercourse of kind. Hence men, even in the infancy of society, observe a certain order in their words and actions, distinct from that of the objects and the impressions represented by them, all expression being subject to the laws of that from which it proceeds. But let us dismiss those more general considerations which might involve an inquiry into the principles of society itself, and restrict our view to the manner in which the imagination is expressed upon its forms.

In the youth of the world, men dance and sing and imitate natural objects, observing in these actions, as in all others, a certain rhythm or order. And, although all men observe a similar, they observe not the same order, in the motions of the dance, in the melody of the song, in the combinations of language, in the series of their imitations of natural objects. For there is a certain order or rhythm belonging to each of these classes of mimetic representation, from which the hearer and the spectator receive an intenser and purer pleasure than from any other: the sense of an approximation to this order has been called taste by modern writers. Every man in the infancy of art, observes an order which approximates more or less closely to that from which this highest delight results: but the diversity is not sufficiently marked, as that its gradations should be sensible, except in those instances where the predominance of this faculty of approximation to the beautiful (for so we may be permitted to name the relation between this highest pleasure and its cause) is very great. Those in whom it exists in excess are poets, in the most universal sense of the word; and the pleasure resulting from the manner in which they express the influence of society or nature upon their own minds, communicates itself to others, and gathers a sort of reduplication from that community. Their language is vitally metaphorical; that is, it marks the before unapprehended relations of things and perpetuates their apprehension, until the words which represent them, become, through time, signs for portions or classes of thoughts instead of pictures of integral thoughts; and then if no new poets should arise to create afresh the associations which have been thus disorganised, language will be dead to all the nobler purposes of human intercourse. These similitudes or relations are finely said by Lord Bacon to be "the same footsteps of nature impressed upon the various subjects of the world" *—and he considers the faculty which perceives them as the storehouse of axioms common to all knowledge. In the infancy of society every author is necessarily a poet, because language itself is poetry; and to be a poet is to apprehend the true and the beautiful, in a word, the good which exists in the relation, subsisting, first between existence and perception, and secondly between perception and expression. Every original language near to its source is in itself the chaos of a cyclic poem: the copiousness

* *De Augment. Scient.*, cap. I, lib. iii.

of lexicography and the distinctions of grammar are the works of a later age, and are merely the catalogue and the form of the creations of poetry.

But poets, or those who imagine and express this indestructible order, are not only the authors of language and of music, of the dance and architecture, and statuary, and painting; they are the institutors of laws, and the founders of civil society, and the inventors of the arts of life, and the teachers, who draw into a certain propinquity with the beautiful and the true, that partial apprehension of the agencies of the invisible world which is called religion. Hence all original religions are allegorical, or susceptible of allegory, and, like Janus, have a double face of false and true. Poets, according to the circumstances of the age and nation in which they appeared, were called, in the earlier epochs of the world, legislators, or prophets: a poet essentially comprises and unites both these characters. For he not only beholds intensely the present as it is, and discovers those laws according to which present things ought to be ordered, but he beholds the future in the present, and his thoughts are the germs of the flower and the fruit of latest time. Not that I assert poets to be prophets in the gross sense of the word, or that they can foretell the form as surely as they foreknow the spirit of events: such is the pretence of superstition, which would make poetry an attribute of prophecy, rather than prophecy an attribute of poetry. A poet participates in the eternal, the infinite, and the one; as far as relates to his conceptions, time and place and number are not. The grammatical forms which express the moods of time, and the difference of persons, and the distinction of place, are convertible with respect to the highest poetry without injuring it as poetry; and the choruses of Æschylus, and the book of Job, and Dante's Paradise, would afford, more than any other writings, examples of this fact, if the limits of this essay did not forbid citation. The creations of sculpture, painting, and music, are illustrations still more decisive.

Language, colour, form, and religious and civil habits of action, are all the instruments and materials of poetry; they may be called poetry by that figure of speech which considers the effect as a synonyme of the cause. But poetry in a more restricted sense expresses those arrangements of language, and especially metrical language, which are created by that imperial faculty, whose throne is curtained within the invisible nature of man. And this springs from the nature itself of language, which is a more direct representation of the actions and passions of our internal being, and is susceptible of more various and delicate combinations, than colour, form, or motion, and is more plastic and obedient to the control of that faculty of which it is the creation. For language is arbitrarily produced by the imagination, and has relation to thoughts alone; but all other materials, instruments, and conditions of art, have relations among each other, which limit and interpose between conception and expression. The former is as a mirror which reflects, the latter as a cloud which enfeebles, the light of which both are mediums of communication. Hence the fame of sculptors, painters, and musicians, although the intrinsic powers of the great masters of these arts may yield in no degree to that of those who have employed language as the hieroglyphic of their thoughts, has never equalled that of poets in the restricted sense of the term; as two performers of equal skill will produce unequal effects from a guitar and a harp. The fame of legislators and founders of religions, so long as their institutions last, alone seems to exceed that of poets in the restricted sense; but it can scarcely be a question, whether, if we deduct the celebrity which their flattery of the gross opinions of the vulgar usually conciliates, together with that which belonged to them in their higher character of poets, any excess will remain.

We have thus circumscribed the meaning of the word Poetry within the limits of that art which is the most familiar and the most perfect expression of the faculty itself. It is necessary, however, to make the circle still narrower, and to determine the distincton between measured and unmeasured language; for the popular division into prose and verse is inadmissible in accurate philosophy.

Sounds as well as thoughts have relation both between each other and towards that which they represent, and a perception of the order of those relations has always been found connected with a perception of the order of those relations of thoughts. Hence the language of poets has ever affected a certain uniform and harmonious recurrence of sound, without which it were not poetry, and which is scarcely less indispensable to the communication of its action, than the words themselves, without reference to that peculiar order. Hence the vanity of translation; it were as wise to cast a violet into a crucible that you might discover the formal principle of its colour and odour, as seek to transfuse from one language into another the creations of a poet. The plant must spring again from its seed, or it will bear no flower—and this is the burthen of the curse of Babel.

An observation of the regular mode of the recurrence of this harmony in the language of poetical minds, together with its relation to music, produced metre, or a certain system of traditional forms of harmony of language. Yet it is by no means essential that a poet should accommodate his language to this traditional form, so that the harmony, which is its spirit, be observed. The practice is indeed convenient and popular, and to be preferred, especially in such composition as includes much form and action: but every great poet must inevitably innovate upon the example of his predecessors in the exact structure of his peculiar versification. The distinction between poets and prose writers is a vulgar error. The distinction between philosophers and poets has been anticipated. Plato was essentially a poet—the truth and splendour of his imagery, and the melody of his language, is the most intense that it is possible to conceive. He rejected the measure of the epic, dramatic, and lyrical forms, because he sought to kindle a harmony in thoughts divested of shape and action, and he forbore to invent any regular plan of rhythm which should include, under determinate forms, the varied pauses of his style. Cicero sought to imitate the cadence of his periods, but with little success. Lord Bacon was a poet.* His language has a sweet and majestic rhythm, which satisfies the sense, no less than the almost superhuman wisdom of his philosophy satisfies the intellect; it is a strain which distends, and then bursts the circumference of the hearer's mind, and pours itself forth together with it into the universal element with which it has perpetual sympathy. All the authors of revolutions in opinion are not only necessarily poets as they are inventors, nor even as their words unveil the permanent analogy of things by images which participate in the life of truth; but as their periods are harmonious and rhythmical, and contain in themselves the elements of verse; being the echo of the eternal music. Nor are those supreme poets, who have employed traditional forms of rhythm on account of the form and action of their subjects, less capable of perceiving and teaching the truth of things, than those who have omitted that form. Shakspeare, Dante, and Milton (to confine ourselves to modern writers) are philosophers of the very loftiest power.

A poem is the image of life expressed in its eternal truth. There is this difference between a story and a poem, that a story is a catalogue of detached facts, which have no other bond of connexion than time, place, circumstance, cause and effect; the other is the creation of actions according to the unchangeable forms of human nature, as existing in the mind of the creator, which is itself the image of all other minds. The one is partial, and applies only to a definite period of time, and a certain combination of events which can never again recur; the other is universal, and contains within itself the germ of a relation to whatever motives or actions have place in the possible varieties

---

* See the *Filium Labyrinthi* and the *Essay on Death* particularly.

of human nature. Time, which destroys the beauty and the use of the story of particular facts, stript' of the poetry which should invest them, augments that of Poetry, and for ever develops new and wonderful applications of the eternal truth which it contains. Hence epitomes have been called the moths of just history; they eat out the poetry of it. The story of particular facts is as a mirror which obscures and distorts that which should be beautiful: Poetry is a mirror which makes beautiful that which is distorted.

The parts of a composition may be poetical, without the composition as a whole being a poem. A single sentence may be considered as a whole, though it be found in a series of unassimilated portions; a single word even may be a spark of inextinguishable thought. And thus all the great historians, Herodotus, Plutarch, Livy, were poets; and although the plan of these writers, especially that of Livy, restrained them from developing this faculty in its highest degree, they make copious and ample amends for their subjection, by filling all the interstices of their subjects with living images.

Having determined what is poetry, and who are poets, let us proceed to estimate its effects upon society.

Poetry is ever accompanied with pleasure: all spirits on which it falls open themselves to receive the wisdom which is mingled with its delight. In the infancy of the world, neither poets themselves nor their auditors are fully aware of the excellence of poetry: for it acts in a divine and unapprehended manner, beyond and above consciousness; and it is reserved for future generations to contemplate and measure the mighty cause and effect in all the strength and splendour of their union. Even in modern times, no living poet ever arrived at the fulness of his fame; the jury which sits in judgment upon a poet, belonging as he does to all time, must be composed of his peers: it must be impanneled by Time from the selectest of the wise of many generations. A Poet is a nightingale, who sits in darkness and sings to cheer its own solitude with sweet sounds; his auditors are as men entranced by the melody of an unseen musician, who feel that they are moved and softened, yet know not whence or why. The poems of Homer and his contemporaries were the delight of infant Greece; they were the elements of that social system which is the column upon which all succeeding civilization has reposed. Homer embodied the ideal perfection of his age in human character; nor can we doubt that those who read his verses were awakened to an ambition of becoming like to Achilles, Hector, and Ulysses: the truth and beauty of friendship, patriotism, and persevering devotion to an object, were unveiled to the depths in these im-

mortal creations: the sentiments of the auditors must have been refined and enlarged by a sympathy with such great and lovely impersonations, until from admiring they imitated, and from imitation they identified themselves with the objects of their admiration. Nor let it be objected, that these characters are remote from moral perfection, and that they can by no means be considered as edifying patterns for general imitation. Every epoch, under names more or less specious, has deified its peculiar errors; Revenge is the naked Idol of the worship of a semi-barbarous age; and Self-deceit is the veiled Image of unknown evil, before which luxury and satiety lie prostrate. But a poet considers the vices of his contemporaries as the temporary dress in which his creations must be arrayed, and which cover without concealing the eternal proportions of their beauty. An epic or dramatic personage is understood to wear them around his soul, as he may the antient armour or the modern uniform around his body; whilst it is easy to conceive a dress more graceful than either. The beauty of the internal nature cannot be so far concealed by its accidental vesture, but that the spirit of its form shall communicate itself to the very disguise, and indicate the shape it hides from the manner in which it is worn. A majestic form and graceful motions will express themselves through the most barbarous and tasteless costume. Few poets of the highest class have chosen to exhibit the beauty of their conceptions in its naked truth and splendour; and it is doubtful whether the alloy of costume, habit, &c., be not necessary to temper this planetary music for mortal ears.

The whole objection, however, of the immorality of poetry rests upon a misconception of the manner in which poetry acts to produce the moral improvement of man. Ethical science arranges the elements which poetry has created, and propounds schemes and proposes examples of civil and domestic life: nor is it for want of admirable doctrines that men hate, and despise, and censure, and deceive, and subjugate one another. But Poetry acts in another and diviner manner. It awakens and enlarges the mind itself by rendering it the receptacle of a thousand unapprehended combinations of thought. Poetry lifts the veil from the hidden beauty of the world, and makes familiar objects be as if they were not familiar; it reproduces all that it represents, and the impersonations clothed in its Elysian light stand thenceforward in the minds of those who have once contemplated them, as memorials of that gentle and exalted content which extends itself over all thoughts and actions with which it coexists. The great secret of morals is love; or a going out of our own nature, and an identification of ourselves with the beautiful which exists in thought, action, or person, not our own. A man, to be greatly good, must imagine intensely and comprehensively; he must put himself in the place of another and of many others; the pains and pleasures of his species must become his own. The great instrument of moral good is the imagination; and poetry administers to the effect by acting upon the cause. Poetry enlarges the circumference of the imagination by replenishing it with thoughts of ever new delight, which have the power of attracting and assimilating to their own nature all other thoughts, and which form new intervals and interstices whose void for ever craves fresh food. Poetry strengthens that faculty which is the organ of the moral nature of man, in the same manner as exercise strengthens a limb. A Poet therefore would do ill to embody his own conceptions of right and wrong, which are usually those of his place and time, in his poetical creations, which participate in neither. By this assumption of the inferior office of interpreting the effect, in which perhaps after all he might acquit himself but imperfectly, he would resign the glory in a participation in the cause. There was little danger that Homer, or any of the eternal Poets, should have so far misunderstood themselves as to have abdicated this throne of their widest dominion. Those in whom the poetical faculty, though great, is less intense, as Euripides, Lucan, Tasso, Spenser, have frequently affected a moral aim, and the effect of their poetry is diminished in exact proportion to the degree in which they compel us to advert to this purpose.

Homer and the cyclic poets were followed at a certain interval by the dramatic and lyrical Poets of Athens, who flourished contemporaneously with all that is most perfect in the kindred expressions of the poetical faculty; architecture, painting, music, the dance, sculpture, philosophy, and we may add, the forms of civil life. For although the scheme of Athenian society was deformed by many imperfections which the poetry existing in Chivalry and Christianity have erased from the habits and institutions of modern Europe; yet never at any other period has so much energy, beauty, and virtue, been developed; never was blind strength and stubborn form so disciplined and rendered subject to the will of man, or that will less repugnant to the dictates of the beautiful and the true, as during the century which preceded the death of Socrates. Of no other epoch in the history of our species have we records and fragments stamped so visibly with the image of the divinity in man. But it is Poetry alone, in form, in action, or in language, which has rendered this epoch memorable above all others, and the storehouse of examples to everlasting time. For written poetry existed at that epoch simultaneously

with the other arts, and it is an idle enquiry to demand which gave and which received the light, which all, as from a common focus, have scattered over the darkest periods of succeeding age. We know no more of cause and effect than a constant conjunction of events: Poetry is ever found to coexist with whatever other arts contribute to the happiness and perfection of man. I appeal to what has already been established to distinguish between the cause and the effect.

It was at the period here adverted to, that the Drama had its birth; and however a succeeding writer may have equalled or surpassed those few great specimens of the Athenian drama which have been preserved to us, it is indisputable that the art itself never was understood or practised according to the true philosophy of it, as at Athens. For the Athenians employed language, action, music, painting, the dance, and religious institutions, to produce a common effect in the representation of the loftiest idealisms of passion and of power; each division in the art was made perfect in its kind by artists of the most consummate skill, and was disciplined into a beautiful proportion and unity one towards another. On the modern stage a few only of the elements capable of expressing the image of the poet's conception are employed at once. We have tragedy without music and dancing; and music and dancing without the high impersonations of which they are the fit accompaniment, and both without religion and solemnity; religious institution has indeed been usually banished from the stage. Our system of divesting the actor's face of a mask, on which the many expressions appropriated to his dramatic character might be moulded into one permanent and unchanging expression, is favourable only to a partial and inharmonious effect; it is fit for nothing but a monologue, where all the attention may be directed to some great master of ideal mimicry. The modern practice of blending comedy with tragedy, though liable to great abuse in point of practice, is undoubtedly an extension of the dramatic circle; but the comedy should be as in King Lear, universal, ideal, and sublime. It is perhaps the intervention of this principle which determines the balance in favour of King Lear against the Œdipus Tyrannus or the Agamemnon, or, if you will the trilogies with which they are connected; unless the intense power of the choral poetry, especially that of the latter, should be considered as restoring the equilibrium. King Lear, if it can sustain this comparison, may be judged to be the most perfect specimen of the dramatic art existing in the world; in spite of the narrow conditions to which the poet was subjected by the ignorance of the philosophy of the drama which has prevailed in modern Europe.

Calderon,[1] in his religious Autos, has attempted to fulfil some of the high conditions of dramatic representation neglected by Shakspeare; such as the establishing a relation between the drama and religion, and the accommodating them to music and dancing; but he omits the observation of conditions still more important, and more is lost than gained by a substitution of the rigidly-defined and ever-repeated idealisms of a distorted superstition for the living impersonations of the truth of human passion.

But we digress.—The Author of the Four Ages of Poetry has prudently omitted to dispute on the effect of the Drama upon life and manners. For, if I know the Knight by the device of his shield, I have only to inscribe Philoctetes or Agamemnon or Othello upon mine to put to flight the giant sophisms which have enchanted him, as the mirror of intolerable light though on the arm of one of the weakest of the Paladines could blind and scatter whole armies of necromancers and pagans. The connexion of scenic exhibitions with the improvement or corruption of the manners of men, has been universally recognised: in other words, the presence or absence of poetry in its most perfect and universal form, has been found to be connected with good and evil in conduct and habit. The corruption which has been imputed to the drama as an effect, begins, when the poetry employed in its constitution ends: I appeal to the history of manners whether the gradations of the growth of the one and the decline of the other have not corresponded with an exactness equal to any other example of moral cause and effect.

The drama at Athens, or wheresoever else it may have approached to its perfection, coexisted with the moral and intellectual greatness of the age. The tragedies of the Athenian poets are as mirrors in which the spectator beholds himself, under a thin disguise of circumstance, stript of all but that ideal perfection and energy which every one feels to be the internal type of all that he loves, admires, and would become. The imagination is enlarged by a sympathy with pains and passions so mighty, that they distend in their conception the capacity of that by which they are conceived; the good affections are strengthened by pity, indignation, terror and sorrow; and an exalted calm is prolonged from the satiety of this high exercise of them into the tumult of familiar life: even crime is disarmed of half its horror and all its contagion by being represented as the fatal consequence of the unfathomable agencies of nature; error is thus divested of its wilful-

ness; men can no longer cherish it as the creation of their choice. In a drama of the highest order there is little food for censure or hatred; it teaches rather self-knowledge and self-respect. Neither the eye nor the mind can see itself, unless reflected upon that which it resembles. The drama, so long as it continues to express poetry, is as a prismatic and many-sided mirror, which collects the brightest rays of human nature and divides and reproduces them from the simplicity of these elementary forms, and touches them with majesty and beauty, and multiplies all that it reflects, and endows it with the power of propagating its like wherever it may fall.

But in periods of the decay of social life, the drama sympathises with that decay. Tragedy becomes a cold imitation of the form of the great masterpieces of antiquity, divested of all harmonious accompaniment of the kindred arts; and often the very form misunderstood, or a weak attempt to teach certain doctrines, which the writer considers as moral truths; and which are usually no more than specious flatteries of some gross vice or weakness, with which the author, in common with his auditors, are infected. Hence what has been called the classical and domestic drama. Addison's "Cato"[2] is a specimen of the one; and would it were not superfluous to cite examples of the other! To such purposes poetry cannot be made subservient. Poetry is a sword of lightning, ever unsheathed, which consumes the scabbard that would contain it. And thus we observe that all dramatic writings of this nature are unimaginative in a singular degree; they affect sentiment and passion, which, divested of imagination, are other names for caprice and appetite. The period in our own history of the grossest degradation of the drama is the reign of Charles II., when all forms in which poetry had been accustomed to be expressed became hymns to the triumph of kingly power over liberty and virtue. Milton stood alone illuminating an age unworthy of him. At such periods the calculating principle pervades all the forms of dramatic exhibition, and poetry ceases to be expressed upon them. Comedy loses its ideal universality: wit succeeds to humour; we laugh from self complacency and triumph, instead of pleasure; malignity, sarcasm and contempt, succeed to sympathetic merriment; we hardly laugh, but we smile. Obscenity, which is ever blasphemy against the divine beauty in life, becomes, from the very veil which it assumes, more active if less disgusting: it is a monster for which the corruption of society for ever brings forth new food, which it devours in secret.

[1] Pedro Calderón de la Barca (1600–1681) was a Spanish dramatist and poet. His *Autos Sacramentales* were a long series of allegorical and religious plays.

[2] Classical tragedy of 1713.

The drama being that form under which a greater number of modes of expression of poetry are susceptible of being combined than any other, the connexion of poetry and social good is more observable in the drama than in whatever other form. And it is indisputable that the highest perfection of human society has ever corresponded with the highest dramatic excellence; and that the corruption or the extinction of the drama in a nation where it has once flourished, is a mark of a corruption of manners, and an extinction of the energies which sustain the soul of social life. But, as Machiavelli says of political institutions, that life may be preserved and renewed, if men should arise capable of bringing back the drama to its principles. And this is true with respect to poetry in its most extended sense; all language, institution and form, require not only to be produced but to be sustained: the office and character of a poet participates in the divine nature as regards providence, no less than as regards creation.

Civil war, the spoils of Asia, and the fatal predominance first of the Macedonian, and then of the Roman arms, were so many symbols of the extinction or suspension of the creative faculty in Greece. The bucolic writers, who found patronage under the lettered tyrants of Sicily and Egypt, were the latest representatives of its most glorious reign. Their poetry is intensely melodious; like the odour of the tuberose, it overcomes and sickens the spirit with excess of sweetness; whilst the poetry of the preceding age was as a meadow-gale of June, which mingles the fragrance of all the flowers of the field, and adds a quickening and harmonising spirit of its own which endows the sense with a power of sustaining its extreme delight. The bucolic and erotic delicacy in written poetry is correlative with that softness in statuary, music, and the kindred arts, and even in manners and institutions, which distinguished the epoch to which we now refer. Nor is it the poetical faculty itself, or any misapplication of it, to which this want of harmony is to be imputed. An equal sensibility to the influence of the senses and the affections is to be found in the writings of Homer and Sophocles: the former, especially, has clothed sensual and pathetic images with irresistible attractions. Their superiority over these succeeding writers consists in the presence of those thoughts which belong to the inner faculties of our nature, not in the absence of those which are connected with the external: their incomparable perfection consists in an harmony of the union of all. It is not what the erotic writers have, but what they have not, in which their imperfection consists. It is not inasmuch as they were Poets, but inasmuch as they were not Poets, that they can be considered with any

plausibility as connected with the corruption of their age. Had that corruption availed so as to extinguish in them the sensibility to pleasure, passion, and natural scenery, which is imputed to them as an imperfection, the last triumph of evil would have been achieved. For the end of social corruption is to destroy all sensibility to pleasure; and, therefore, it is corruption. It begins at the imagination and the intellect as at the core, and distributes itself thence as a paralysing venom, through the affections into the very appetites, till all become a torpid mass in which sense hardly survives. At the approach of such a period, Poetry ever addresses itself to those faculties which are the last to be destroyed, and its voice is heard, like the footsteps of Astræa,[3] departing from the world. Poetry ever communicates all the pleasure which men are capable of receiving: it is ever still the light of life; the source of whatever of beautiful or generous or true can have place in an evil time. It will readily be confessed that those among the luxurious citizens of Syracuse and Alexandria, who were delighted with the poems of Theocritus, were less cold, cruel, and sensual than the remnant of their tribe. But corruption must have utterly destroyed the fabric of human society before poetry can ever cease. The sacred links of that chain have never been entirely disjoined, which descending through the minds of many men is attached to those great minds, whence as from a magnet the invisible effluence is sent forth, which at once connects, animates and sustains the life of all. It is the faculty which contains within itself the seeds at once of its own and of social renovation. And let us not circumscribe the effects of the bucolic and erotic poetry within the limits of the sensibility of those to whom it was addressed. They may have perceived the beauty of those immortal compositions, simply as fragments and isolated portions: those who are more finely organised, or born in a happier age, may recognise them as episodes to that great poem, which all poets, like the co-operating thoughts of one great mind, have built up since the beginning of the world.

The same revolutions within a narrower sphere had place in antient Rome; but the actions and forms of its social life never seem to have been perfectly saturated with the poetical element. The Romans appear to have considered the Greeks as the selectest treasuries of the selectest forms of manners and of nature, and to have abstained from creating in measured language, sculpture, music, or architecture, any thing which might bear a particular relation to their own condition, whilst it might bear a general one to the universal constitution

---

[3] Astræa was the goddess of justice, who lived among men during the Golden Age. As a result of mankind's later wickedness, she withdrew from the earth and became the constellation Virgo.

of the world. But we judge from partial evidence, and we judge perhaps partially. Ennius, Varro, Pacuvius, and Accius, all great poets, have been lost. Lucretius is in the highest, and Virgil in a very high sense, a creator. The chosen delicacy of the expressions of the latter, are as a mist of light which conceal from us the intense and exceeding truth of his conceptions of nature. Livy is instinct with poetry. Yet Horace, Catullus, Ovid, and generally the other great writers of the Virgilian age, saw man and nature in the mirror of Greece. The institutions also, and the religion of Rome, were less poetical than those of Greece, as the shadow is less vivid than the substance. Hence poetry in Rome, seemed to follow, rather than accompany, the perfection of political and domestic society. The true poetry of Rome lived in its institutions; for whatever of beautiful, true, and majestic, they contained, could have sprung only from the faculty which creates the order in which they consist. The life of Camillus,[4] the death of Regulus;[5] the expectation of the Senators, in their godlike state, of the victorious Gauls; the refusal of the Republic to make peace with Hannibal, after the battle of Cannæ, were not the consequences of a refined calculation of the probable personal advantage to result from such a rhythm and order in the shews of life, to those who were at once the poets and the actors of these immortal dramas. The imagination beholding the beauty of this order, created it out of itself according to its own idea; the consequence was empire, and the reward ever-living fame. These things are not the less poetry, *quia carent vate sacro*.[6] They are the episodes of that cyclic poem written by Time upon the memories of men. The Past, like an inspired rhapsodist, fills the theatre of everlasting generations with their harmony.

At length the antient system of religion and manners had fulfilled the circle of its revolution. And the world would have fallen into utter anarchy and darkness, but that there were found poets among the authors of the Christian and Chivalric systems of manners and religion, who created forms of opinion and action never before conceived; which, copied into the imaginations of men, became as generals to the bewildered armies of their thoughts. It is foreign to the present purpose to touch upon the evil produced by these systems: except that we protest, on the ground of the principles already established, that no portion of it can be imputed to the poetry they contain.

It is probable that the astonishing poetry of Moses, Job, David, Solomon, and Isaiah, had produced a great effect upon the mind of Jesus and his disciples. The scattered fragments preserved to us by the biographers of this extraordinary person, are all instinct with the most vivid poetry. But his doctrines seem to have been quickly distorted. At a certain period after the prevalence of doctrines founded upon those promulgated by him, the three forms into which Plato had distributed the faculties of mind underwent a sort of apotheosis, and became the object of the worship of Europe. Here it is to be confessed that "Light seems to thicken," and

> "The crow makes wing to the rooky wood,
> Good things of day begin to droop and drowse,
> And night's black agents to their preys do rouse."[7]

But mark how beautiful an order has sprung from the dust and blood of this fierce chaos! how the World, as from a resurrection, balancing itself on the golden wings of knowledge and of hope, has reassumed its yet unwearied flight into the Heaven of time. Listen to the music, unheard by outward ears, which is as a ceaseless and invisible wind, nourishing its everlasting course with strength and swiftness.

The poetry in the doctrines of Jesus Christ, and the mythology and institutions of the Celtic conquerors of the Roman empire, outlived the darkness and the convulsions connected with their growth and victory, and blended themselves into a new fabric of manners and opinion. It is an error to impute the ignorance of the dark ages to the Christian doctrines or the predominance of the Celtic nations. Whatever of evil their agencies may have contained sprang from the extinction of the poetical principle, connected with the progress of despotism and superstition. Men, from causes too intricate to be here discussed, had become insensible and selfish: their own will had become feeble, and yet they were its slaves, and thence the slaves of the will of others: lust, fear, avarice, cruelty, and fraud, characterised a race amongst whom no one was to be found capable of *creating* in form, language, or institution. The moral anomalies of such a state of society are not justly to be charged upon any class of events immediately connected with them, and those events are most entitled to our approbation which could dissolve it most expeditiously. It is unfortunate for those who cannot distinguish words from thoughts,

---

[4] Marcus Furius Camillus (4th century B.C.), one of the most admired of Roman heroes, was called "Father of his country and second founder of Rome" for putting down the Gallic invasion.

[5] Marcus Atilius Regulus (3rd century B.C.), Roman general and consul, initially defeated the Carthaginians but was later captured. He was sent to Rome to arrange an exchange of prisoners and make peace, but he urged the Romans not to accept the terms offered by the Carthaginians. He voluntarily returned to Carthage, where he supposedly died from torture.

[6] *quia . . . sacro*: "because they do not have a sacred poet." Horace, *Odes*, IV, ix, 28.

[7] *Macbeth*, III, ii, 50-53.

that many of these anomalies have been incorporated into our popular religion.

It was not until the eleventh century that the effects of the poetry of the Christian and Chivalric systems began to manifest themselves. The principle of equality had been discovered and applied by Plato in his Republic, as the theoretical rule of the mode in which the materials of pleasure and of power produced by the common skill and labour of human beings ought to be distributed among them. The limitations of this rule were asserted by him to be determined only by the sensibility of each, or the utility to result to all. Plato, following the doctrines of Timæus and Pythagoras, taught also a moral and intellectual system of doctrine, comprehending at once the past, the present, and the future condition of man. Jesus Christ divulged the sacred and eternal truths contained in these views to mankind, and Christianity, in its abstract purity, became the exoteric expression of the esoteric doctrines of the poetry and wisdom of antiquity. The incorporation of the Celtic nations with the exhausted population of the south, impressed upon it the figure of the poetry existing in their mythology and institutions. The result was a sum of the action and reaction of all the causes included in it; for it may be assumed as a maxim that no nation or religion can supersede any other without incorporating into itself a portion of that which it supersedes. The abolition of personal and domestic slavery, and the emancipation of women from a great part of the degrading restraints of antiquity, were among the consequences of these events.

The abolition of personal slavery is the basis of the highest political hope that it can enter into the mind of man to conceive. The freedom of women produced the poetry of sexual love. Love became a religion, the idols of whose worship were ever present. It was as if the statues of Apollo and the Muses had been endowed with life and motion, and had walked forth among their worshippers; so that earth became peopled by the inhabitants of a diviner world. The familiar appearance and proceedings of life became wonderful and heavenly; and a paradise was created as out of the wrecks of Eden. And as this creation itself is poetry, so its creators were poets; and language was the instrument of their art: "Galeotto fù il libro, e chi lo scrisse."[8] The Provençal Trouveurs, or inventors, preceded Petrarch, whose verses are as spells, which unseal the inmost enchanted fountains of the delight which is in the grief of love. It is impossible to feel them without becoming a portion of that beauty which we contemplate: it were superfluous to explain

how the gentleness and the elevation of mind connected with these sacred emotions can render men more amiable, and generous and wise, and lift them out of the dull vapours of the little world of self. Dante understood the secret things of love even more than Petrarch. His *Vita Nuova* is an inexhaustible fountain of purity of sentiment and language: it is the idealised history of that period, and those intervals of his life which were dedicated to love. His apotheosis of Beatrice in Paradise, and the gradations of his own love and her loveliness, by which as by steps he feigns himself to have ascended to the throne of the Supreme Cause, is the most glorious imagination of modern poetry. The acutest critics have justly reversed the judgment of the vulgar, and the order of the great acts of the "Divine Drama," in the measure of the admiration which they accord to the Hell, Purgatory, and Paradise. The latter is a perpetual hymn of everlasting Love. Love, which found a worthy poet in Plato alone of all the antients, has been celebrated by a chorus of the greatest writers of the renovated world; and the music has penetrated the caverns of society, and its echoes still drown the dissonance of arms and superstition. At successive intervals, Ariosto, Tasso, Shakspeare, Spenser, Calderon, Rousseau, and the great writers of our own age, have celebrated the dominion of love, planting as it were trophies in the human mind of that sublimest victory over sensuality and force. The true relation borne to each other by the sexes into which human kind is distributed, has become less misunderstood; and if the error which confounded diversity with inequality of the powers of the two sexes has become partially recognised in the opinions and institutions of modern Europe, we owe this great benefit to the worship of which Chivalry was the law, and poets the prophets.

The poetry of Dante may be considered as the bridge thrown over the stream of time, which unites the modern and antient World. The distorted notions of invisible things which Dante and his rival Milton have idealised, are merely the mask and the mantle in which these great poets walk through eternity enveloped and disguised. It is a difficult question to determine how far they were conscious of the distinction which must have subsisted in their minds between their own creeds and that of the people. Dante at least appears to wish to mark the full extent of it by placing Riphæus, whom Virgil calls *justissimus unus*,[9] in Paradise, and observing a most heretical caprice in his distribution of rewards and punishments. And Milton's poem contains within itself a philosophical

8 "Galeotto . . . scrisse": "Galeotto [a pander] was the book, and he who wrote it." *Inferno*, V, 137.

9 *justissimus unus*: "the one most just man" (*Aeneid*, II, 426). Dante placed the Trojan warrior in the circle of the just in *Paradiso*, XX, 67–69.

refutation of that system, of which, by a strange and natural antithesis, it has been a chief popular support. Nothing can exceed the energy and magnificence of the character of Satan as expressed in "Paradise Lost." It is a mistake to suppose that he could ever have been intended for the popular personification of evil. Implacable hate, patient cunning and a sleepless refinement of device to inflict the extremest anguish on an enemy, these things are evil; and, although venial in a slave, are not to be forgiven in a tyrant; although redeemed by much that ennobles his defeat in one subdued, are marked by all that dishonours his conquest in the victor. Milton's Devil as a moral being is as far superior to his God, as One who perseveres in some purpose which he has conceived to be excellent in spite of adversity and torture, is to One who in the cold security of undoubted triumph inflicts the most horrible revenge upon his enemy, not from any mistaken notion of inducing him to repent of a perseverance in enmity, but with the alleged design of exasperating him to deserve new torments. Milton has so far violated the popular creed (if this shall be judged to be a violation) as to have alleged no superiority of moral virtue to his God over his Devil. And this bold neglect of a direct moral purpose is the most decisive proof of the supremacy of Milton's genius. He mingled as it were the elements of human nature as colours upon a single pallet, and arranged them in the composition of his great picture according to the laws of epic truth; that is, according to the laws of that principle by which a series of actions of the external universe and of intelligent and ethical beings is calculated to excite the sympathy of succeeding generations of mankind. The Divina Commedia and Paradise Lost have conferred upon modern mythology a systematic form; and when change and time shall have added one more superstition to the mass of those which have arisen and decayed upon the earth, commentators will be learnedly employed in elucidating the religion of ancestral Europe, only not utterly forgotten because it will have been stamped with the eternity of genius.

Homer was the first and Dante the second epic poet: that is, the second poet, the series of whose creations bore a defined and intelligible relation to the knowledge and sentiment and religion and political conditions of the age in which he lived, and of the ages which followed it: developing itself in correspondence with their development. For Lucretius had limed the wings of his swift spirit in the dregs of the sensible world; and Virgil, with a modesty which ill became his genius, had affected the fame of an imitator, even whilst he created anew all that he copied; and none among the flock of Mock-birds, though their notes were sweet, Apollonius

Rhodius, Quintus Calaber Smyrnetheus, Nonnus, Lucan, Statius, or Claudian,[10] have sought even to fulfil a single condition of epic truth. Milton was the third epic poet. For if the title of epic in its highest sense be refused to the Æneid, still less can it be conceded to the Orlando Furioso, the Gerusalemme Liberata, the Lusiad, or the Fairy Queen.

Dante and Milton were both deeply penetrated with the antient religion of the civilized world; and its spirit exists in their poetry probably in the same proportion as its forms survived in the unreformed worship of modern Europe. The one preceded and the other followed the Reformation at almost equal intervals. Dante was the first religious reformer, and Luther surpassed him rather in the rudeness and acrimony, than in the boldness of his censures of papal usurpation. Dante was the first awakener of entranced Europe; he created a language, in itself music and persuasion, out of a chaos of inharmonious barbarisms. He was the congregator of those great spirits who presided over the resurrection of learning; the Lucifer of that starry flock which in the thirteenth century shone forth from republican Italy, as from a heaven, into the darkness of the benighted world. His very words are instinct with spirit; each is as a spark, a burning atom of inextinguishable thought; and many yet lie covered in the ashes of their birth, and pregnant with a lightning which has yet found no conductor. All high poetry is infinite; it is as the first acorn, which contained all oaks potentially. Veil after veil may be undrawn, and the inmost naked beauty of the meaning never exposed. A great poem is a fountain for ever overflowing with the waters of wisdom and delight; and after one person and one age has exhausted all its divine effluence which their peculiar relations enable them to share, another and yet another succeeds, and new relations are ever developed, the source of an unforeseen and an unconceived delight.

The age immediately succeeding to that of Dante, Petrarch, and Boccaccio, was characterized by a revival of painting, sculpture, music, and architecture. Chaucer caught the sacred inspiration, and the superstructure of English literature is based upon the materials of Italian invention.

But let us not be betrayed from a defence into a critical history of Poetry and its influence on Society.

<hr />

[10] Apollonius Rhodius (3rd century B.C.) was the author of the Greek epic *Argonautica*. Quintus Calber Smyrnetheus (4th century of the Christian era) was the author of the Greek epic *Posthomerica*. Nonnus (late 4th–early 5th century) was the author of the Greek epic *Dionysiaca*. Lucan (1st century) was the author of the Latin epic *Bellum Civile* (or *Pharsalia*). Statius (1st century) was the author of the Latin epic *Thebiad*. Claudian (4th century) was the author of the Latin epic *The Rape of Proserpine*.

Be it enough to have pointed out the effects of poets, in the large and true sense of the word, upon their own and all succeeding times, and to revert to the partial instances cited as illustrations of an opinion the reverse of that attempted to be established by the Author of the Four Ages of Poetry.

But poets have been challenged to resign the civic crown to reasoners and mechanists on another plea. It is admitted that the exercise of the imagination is most delightful, but it is alleged, that that of reason is more useful. Let us examine as the grounds of this distinction, what is here meant by utility. Pleasure or good, in a general sense, is that which the consciousness of a sensitive and intelligent being seeks, and in which, when found, it acquiesces. There are two modes or degrees of pleasure, one durable, universal and permanent; the other transitory and particular. Utility may either express the means of producing the former or the latter. In the former sense, whatever strengthens and purifies the affections, enlarges the imagination, and adds spirit to sense, is useful. But the meaning in which the Author of the Four Ages of Poetry seems to have employed the word utility is the narrower one of banishing the importunity of the wants of our animal nature, the surrounding men with security of life, the dispersing the grosser delusions of superstition, and the conciliating such a degree of mutual forbearance among men as may consist with the motives of personal advantage.

Undoubtedly the promoters of utility, in this limited sense, have their appointed office in society. They follow the footsteps of poets, and copy the sketches of their creations into the book of common life. They make space, and give time. Their exertions are of the highest value, so long as they confine their administration of the concerns of the inferior powers of our nature within the limits due to the superior ones. But whilst the sceptic destroys gross superstitions, let him spare to deface, as some of the French writers have defaced, the eternal truths charactered upon the imaginations of men. Whilst the mechanist abridges, and the political economist combines, labour, let them beware that their speculations, for want of correspondence with those first principles which belong to the imagination, do not tend, as they have in modern England, to exasperate at once the extremes of luxury and want. They have exemplified the saying, "To him that hath, more shall be given; and from him that hath not, the little that he hath shall be taken away." [11] The rich have become richer, and the poor have become poorer; and the vessel of the state is driven between the Scylla and

Charybdis of anarchy and despotism. Such are the effects which must ever flow from an unmitigated exercise of the calculating faculty.

It is difficult to define pleasure in its highest sense; the definition involving a number of apparent paradoxes. For, from an inexplicable defect of harmony in the constitution of human nature, the pain of the inferior is frequently connected with the pleasures of the superior portions of our being. Sorrow, terror, anguish, despair itself, are often the chosen expressions of an approximation to the highest good. Our sympathy in tragic fiction depends on this principle; tragedy delights by affording a shadow of the pleasure which exists in pain. This is the source also of the melancholy which is inseparable from the sweetest melody. The pleasure that is in sorrow is sweeter than the pleasure of pleasure itself. And hence the saying, "It is better to go to the house of mourning, than to the house of mirth." [12] Not that this highest species of pleasure is necessarily linked with pain. The delight of love and friendship, the ecstasy of the admiration of nature, the joy of the perception and still more of the creation of poetry is often wholly unalloyed.

The production and assurance of pleasure in this highest sense is true utility. Those who produce and preserve this pleasure are Poets or poetical philosophers.

The exertions of Locke, Hume, Gibbon, Voltaire, Rousseau,* and their disciples, in favour of oppressed and deluded humanity, are entitled to the gratitude of mankind. Yet it is easy to calculate the degree of moral and intellectual improvement which the world would have exhibited, had they never lived. A little more nonsense would have been talked for a century or two; and perhaps a few more men, women, and children, burnt as heretics. We might not at this moment have been congratulating each other on the abolition of the Inquisition in Spain. [13] But it exceeds all imagination to conceive what would have been the moral condition of the world if neither Dante, Petrarch, Boccaccio, Chaucer, Shakspeare, Calderon, Lord Bacon, nor Milton, had ever existed; if Raphael and Michael Angelo had never been born; if the Hebrew poetry had never been translated; if a revival of the study of Greek literature had never taken place; if no monuments of antient sculpture had been handed down to us; and if the poetry of the religion of the antient world had been

* I follow the classification adopted by the Author of the Four Ages of Poetry; but he [Rousseau] was essentially a Poet. The others, even Voltaire, were mere reasoners.

---

[11] See Matthew, xxv, 29; Mark, iv, 25.

[12] Ecclesiastes, vii, 2.

[13] The Spanish Inquisition had been suppressed in 1808, restored by Ferdinand VII in 1814, then suppressed again in 1820.

extinguished together with its belief. The human mind could never, except by the intervention of these excitements, have been awakened to the invention of the grosser sciences, and that application of analytical reasoning to the aberrations of society, which it is now attempted to exalt over the direct expression of the inventive and creative faculty itself.

We have more moral, political and historical wisdom, than we know how to reduce into practice; we have more scientific and economical knowledge than can be accommodated to the just distribution of the produce which it multiplies. The poetry in these systems of thought, is concealed by the accumulation of facts and calculating processes. There is no want of knowledge respecting what is wisest and best in morals, government, and political economy, or at least, what is wiser and better than what men now practise and endure. But we let "*I dare not* wait upon *I would*, like the poor cat i' the adage." [14] We want the creative faculty to imagine that which we know; we want the generous impulse to act that which we imagine; we want the poetry of life: our calculations have outrun conception; we have eaten more than we can digest. The cultivation of those sciences which have enlarged the limits of the empire of man over the external world, has, for want of the poetical faculty, proportionally circumscribed those of the internal world; and man, having enslaved the elements, remains himself a slave. To what but a cultivation of the mechanical arts in a degree disproportioned to the presence of the creative faculty, which is the basis of all knowledge, is to be attributed the abuse of all invention for abridging and combining labour, to the exasperation of the inequality of mankind? From what other cause has it arisen that these inventions which should have lightened, have added a weight to the curse imposed on Adam? Thus Poetry, and the principle of Self, of which Money is the visible incarnation, are the God and Mammon of the world.

The functions of the poetical faculty are twofold; by one it creates new materials for knowledge, and power and pleasure; by the other it engenders in the mind a desire to reproduce and arrange them according to a certain rhythm and order which may be called the beautiful and the good. The cultivation of poetry is never more to be desired than at periods when, from an excess of the selfish and calculating principle, the accumulation of the materials of external life exceed the quantity of the power of assimilating them to the internal laws of human nature. The body has then become too unwieldy for that which animates it.

Poetry is indeed something divine. It is at once the centre and circumference of knowledge; it is that which comprehends all science, and that to which all science must be referred. It is at the same time the root and blossom of all other systems of thought; it is that from which all spring, and that which adorns all; and that which, if blighted, denies the fruit and the seed, and withholds from the barren world the nourishment and the succession of the scions of the tree of life. It is the perfect and consummate surface and bloom of things; it is as the odour and the colour of the rose to the texture of the elements which compose it, as the form and the splendour of unfaded beauty to the secrets of anatomy and corruption. What were Virtue, Love, Patriotism, Friendship—what were the scenery of this beautiful Universe which we inhabit; what were our consolations on this side of the grave, and what were our aspirations beyond it, if Poetry did not ascend to bring light and fire from those eternal regions where the owl-winged faculty of calculation dare not ever soar? Poetry is not like reasoning, a power to be exerted according to the determination of the will. A man cannot say, "I will compose poetry." The greatest poet even cannot say it: for the mind in creation is as a fading coal, which some invisible influence, like an inconstant wind, awakens to transitory brightness: this power arises from within, like the colour of a flower which fades and changes as it is developed, and the conscious portions of our natures are unprophetic either of its approach or its departure. Could this influence be durable in its original purity and force, it is impossible to predict the greatness of the results; but when composition begins, inspiration is already on the decline, and the most glorious poetry that has ever been communicated to the world is probably a feeble shadow of the original conception of the Poet. I appeal to the great poets of the present day, whether it be not an error to assert that the finest passages of poetry are produced by labour and study. The toil and the delay recommended by critics, can be justly interpreted to mean no more than a careful observation of the inspired moments, and an artificial connexion of the spaces between their suggestions by the intertexture of conventional expressions; a necessity only imposed by the limitedness of the poetical faculty itself. For Milton conceived the Paradise Lost as a whole before he executed it in portions. We have his own authority also for the Muse having "dictated" to him the "unpremeditated song," [15] and let this be an answer to those who would allege the fifty-six various readings of the first line of the Orlando Furioso.

---

[14] *Macbeth*, I, vii, 44–45.

[15] *Paradise Lost*, IX, 24.

Compositions so produced are to poetry what mosaic is to painting. This instinct and intuition of the poetical faculty is still more observable in the plastic and pictorial arts; a great statue or picture grows under the power of the artist as a child in the mother's womb; and the very mind which directs the hands in formation is incapable of accounting to itself for the origin, the gradations, or the media of the process.

Poetry is the record of the best and happiest moments of the happiest and best minds. We are aware of evanescent visitations of thought and feeling sometimes associated with place or person, sometimes regarding our own mind alone, and always arising unforeseen and departing unbidden, but elevating and delightful beyond all expression: so that even in the desire and the regret they leave, there cannot but be pleasure, participating as it does in the nature of its object. It is as it were the interpenetration of a diviner nature through our own; but its footsteps are like those of a wind over a sea, which the coming calm erases, and whose traces remain only, as on the wrinkled sand which paves it. These and corresponding conditions of being are experienced principally by those of the most delicate sensibility and the most enlarged imagination; and the state of mind produced by them is at war with every base desire. The enthusiasm of virtue, love, patriotism, and friendship, is essentially linked with these emotions; and whilst they last, self appears as what it is, an atom to a Universe. Poets are not only subject to these experiences as spirits of the most refined organisation, but they can colour all that they combine with the evanescent hues of this ethereal world; a word, or a trait in the representation of a scene or a passion, will touch the enchanted chord, and reanimate, in those who have ever experienced these emotions, the sleeping, the cold, the buried image of the past. Poetry thus makes immortal all that is best and most beautiful in the world; it arrests the vanishing apparitions which haunt the interlunations of life, and veiling them, or in language or in form, sends them forth among mankind, bearing sweet news of kindred joy to those with whom their sisters abide—abide, because there is no portal of expression from the caverns of the spirit which they inhabit into the universe of things. Poetry redeems from decay the visitations of the divinity in Man.

Poetry turns all things to loveliness; it exalts the beauty of that which is most beautiful, and it adds beauty to that which is most deformed; it marries exultation and horror, grief and pleasure, eternity and change; it subdues to union under its light yoke, all irreconcilable things. It transmutes all that it touches, and every form moving within the radiance of its presence is changed by wondrous sympathy to an incarnation of the spirit which it breathes; its secret alchemy turns to potable gold the poisonous waters which flow from death through life; it strips the veil of familiarity from the world, and lays bare the naked and sleeping beauty, which is the spirit of its forms.

All things exist as they are perceived; at least in relation to the percipient. "The mind is its own place, and of itself can make a Heaven of Hell, a Hell of Heaven." [16] But poetry defeats the curse which binds us to be subjected to the accident of surrounding impressions. And whether it spreads its own figured curtain, or withdraws life's dark veil from before the scene of things, it equally creates for us a being within our being. It makes us the inhabitants of a world to which the familiar world is a chaos. It reproduces the common Universe of which we are portions and percipients, and it purges from our inward sight the film of familiarity which obscures from us the wonder of our being. It compels us to feel that which we perceive, and to imagine that which we know. It creates anew the universe, after it has been annihilated in our minds by the recurrence of impressions blunted by reiteration. It justifies that bold and true word of Tasso: *Non merita nome di creatore, se non Iddio ed il Poeta.* [17]

A poet, as he is the author to others of the highest wisdom, pleasure, virtue and glory, so he ought personally to be the happiest, the best, the wisest, and the most illustrious of men. As to his glory, let Time be challenged to declare whether the fame of any other institutor of human life be comparable to that of a poet. That he is the wisest, the happiest, and the best, inasmuch as he is a poet, is equally incontrovertible: the greatest Poets have been men of the most spotless virtue, of the most consummate prudence, and, if we could look into the interior of their lives, the most fortunate of men: and the exceptions, as they regard those who possessed the imaginative faculty in a high yet inferior degree, will be found on consideration to confirm rather than destroy the rule. Let us for a moment stoop to the arbitration of popular breath, and usurping and uniting in our own persons the incompatible characters of accuser, witness, judge and executioner, let us without trial, testimony, or form, determine that certain motives of those who are "there sitting where we dare not soar," [18] are reprehensible. Let us assume that Homer was a drunkard, that Virgil

---

[16] *Paradise Lost*, I, 254–55.
[17] *Non merita . . . Poeta:* "No one deserves the name of creator, except God and the Poet."
[18] *Paradise Lost*, IV, 829.

was a flatterer, that Horace was a coward, that Tasso was a madman, that Lord Bacon was a peculator, that Raphael was a libertine, that Spenser was a poet laureate. It is inconsistent with this division of our subject to cite living poets, but Posterity has done ample justice to the great names now referred to. Their errors have been weighed and found to have been dust in the balance; if their sins were as scarlet, they are now white as snow: they have been washed in the blood of the mediator and the redeemer, Time. Observe in what a ludicrous chaos the imputations of real or fictitious crime have been confused in the contemporary calumnies against poetry and poets; consider how little is, as it appears—or appears, as it is; look to your own motives, and judge not, lest ye be judged.

Poetry, as has been said, in this respect differs from logic, that it is not subject to the controul of the active powers of the mind, and that its birth and recurrence has no necessary connexion with consciousness or will. It is presumptuous to determine that these are the necessary conditions of all mental causation, when mental effects are experienced insusceptible of being referred to them. The frequent recurrence of the poetical power, it is obvious to suppose, may produce in the mind an habit of order and harmony correlative with its own nature and with its effects upon other minds. But in the intervals of inspiration, and they may be frequent without being durable, a Poet becomes a man, and is abandoned to the sudden reflux of the influences under which others habitually live. But as he is more delicately organized than other men, and sensible to pain and pleasure, both his own and that of others, in a degree unknown to them, he will avoid the one and pursue the other with an ardour proportioned to this difference. And he renders himself obnoxious to calumny, when he neglects to observe the circumstances under which these objects of universal pursuit and flight have disguised themselves in one another's garments.

But there is nothing necessarily evil in this error, and thus cruelty, envy, revenge, avarice, and the passions purely evil, have never formed any portion of the popular imputations on the lives of poets.

I have thought it most favourable to the cause of truth to set down these remarks according to the order in which they were suggested to my mind, by a consideration of the subject itself, instead of following that of the treatise that excited me to make them public. Thus although devoid of the formality of a polemical reply; if the view they contain be just, they will be found to involve a refutation of the doctrines of the Four Ages of Poetry, so far at least as regards the first

division of the subject. I can readily conjecture what should have moved the gall of the learned and intelligent author of that paper; I confess myself, like him, unwilling to be stunned by the Theseids of the hoarse Codri of the day.[19] Bavius and Mævius[20] undoubtedly are, as they ever were, insufferable persons. But it belongs to a philosophical critic to distinguish rather than confound.

The first part of these remarks has related to Poetry in its elements and principles; and it has been shewn, as well as the narrow limits assigned them would permit, that what is called poetry, in a restricted sense, has a common source with all other forms of order and of beauty, according to which the materials of human life are susceptible of being arranged, and which is Poetry in an universal sense.

The second part will have for its object an application of these principles to the present state of the cultivation of Poetry, and a defence of the attempt to idealize the modern forms of manners and opinions, and compel them into a subordination to the imaginative and creative faculty. For the literature of England, an energetic development of which has ever preceded or accompanied a great and free development of the national will, has arisen as it were from a new birth. In spite of the low-thoughted envy which would undervalue contemporary merit, our own will be a memorable age in intellectual achievements, and we live among such philosophers and poets as surpass beyond comparison any who have appeared since the last national struggle for civil and religious liberty. The most unfailing herald, companion, and follower of the awakening of a great people to work a beneficial change in opinion or institution, is Poetry. At such periods there is an accumulation of the power of communicating and receiving intense and impassioned conceptions respecting man and nature. The persons in whom this power resides, may often as far as regards many portions of their nature, have little apparent correspondence with that spirit of good of which they are the ministers. But even whilst they deny and abjure, they are yet compelled to serve, the Power which is seated upon the throne of their own soul. It is impossible to read the compositions of the most celebrated writers of the present day without being startled with the electric life which burns within their words. They measure the circumference and sound the depths of human nature with a comprehensive and all-penetrating spirit, and they are themselves perhaps

<hr />

[19] See Juvenal, *Satires*, I, 1–2.
[20] Like Codrus, contemptible poets. See Virgil's Third Eclogue, l. 90.

the most sincèrely astonished at its manifestations; for it is less their spirit than the spirit of the age. Poets are the hierophants [21] of an unapprehended inspiration; the mirrors of the gigantic shadows which futurity casts upon the present; the words which express what they understand not; the trumpets which sing to battle, and feel not what they inspire; the influence which is moved not, but moves. Poets are the unacknowledged legislators of the world.

[1840]   [1930]

---

[21] Ministers of revelation.

John Keats

1795–1821

OUTLINE OF EVENTS

1795   Born October 31, at London; father, Thomas (b. 1773), manager (and subsequent owner) of his father-in-law's (John Jennings) livery stable; mother, Frances (b. 1775); brothers, George (b. 1797), Thomas (b. 1799), Edward (b. 1801–d. 1802); sister, Frances ("Fanny") (b. 1803).

1803   Enters academy at Enfield under headmaster John Clarke, where he forms close friendship with Charles Cowden Clarke, son of headmaster and his assistant.

1804   April, death of father; June, mother marries William Rawlings; Keats children now cared for by maternal grandmother.

1806   Mother separates from Rawlings, with attendant loss of the family business.

1809   Becomes voracious reader, and wins first prize in competition for translations from French and Latin at Clarke's academy.

1810   March, mother dies; grandmother leaves her estate in trust for Keats children under direction of the London businessmen Richard Abbey and John Sandell.

1811–15   Leaves Enfield Academy and becomes apprentice to the apothecary and surgeon Thomas Hammond. Maintains close relationship with Charles Cowden Clarke, reading literature with him and developing poetic interests.

1814   Writes first poem "Imitation of Spenser." December, Mrs. Jennings dies.

1815   Writes poems throughout year, including "Ode to Apollo," verse epistle "To George Felton Mathew," a fellow poetic aspirant, and sonnet to Leigh Hunt, whose poetry Keats admires and whose political views he shares. October, enters Guy's Hospital for training as apothecary and surgeon.

1816   May, sonnet "To Solitude" published in *The Examiner*. July, passes examination for his medical license and goes to Margate (Kentish coastal resort) for period of poetic composition, remaining until September. October, writes "On First Looking into Chapman's Homer," meets Leigh Hunt, R. B. Haydon, and John Hamilton Reynolds, is encouraged to pursue career as poet, and begins to prepare first collection of poems. December, sonnet "On Chapman's Homer" published in *Examiner* (see Hunt's "Young Poets," pp. 518–19), meets Shelley, and completes first major poem "Sleep and Poetry." Decision to abandon medicine for poetic career made by end of year or early 1817.

1817   March, *Poems* published with dedication to Leigh Hunt. April, goes to Isle of Wight to write a "long poem" (*Endymion*), and begins serious study of Shakespeare. Subsequently moves to Margate and Canterbury and returns to London in June. September, at Oxford with Benjamin Bailey, where he engages in formative readings and discussions in philosophy (including Hazlitt's *Essay on the Principles of Human Action*) and literature (including Milton and Wordsworth). December, meets Wordsworth and publishes theatrical review "Mr. Kean" in *The Champion*.

1818   January–February, attends Hazlitt's Lectures on the English Poets. March–May, at Teignmouth (Devonshire) with his brother Tom, who is seriously ill with turberculosis. April, *Endymion* published. June–August, on walking tour to Lake District and Scotland with Charles Brown. Fall, begins composition of *Hyperion* and meets Fanny Brawne. December 1, brother Tom dies; later that month, Keats and Fanny Brawne acknowledge their love for each other.

1819   Winter–spring, writes "Eve of St. Agnes," "Eve of St. Mark," "La Belle Dame sans Merci," the Odes. April, meets Coleridge. July–August, at Isle of Wight (and later Winchester) for concentrated writing in hope of improving his financial position and prospects for marriage; writes "Lamia," the drama *Otho the Great* (with Brown), and revises *Hyperion* into *Fall of Hyperion*. September, writes "To Autumn." Fall, engagement to Fanny Brawne and increasing illness.

1820   February 3, serious lung hemorrhage. July, volume of poems *Lamia, Isabella, The Eve of St. Agnes, and Other Poems* published. September, sails for Italy in desperate attempt to regain his health.

1821   February 23, dies in Rome.

SELECTED BIBLIOGRAPHY

(with special relevance to Keats's letters)

BIOGRAPHY

BATE, WALTER JACKSON, *John Keats*, Cambridge, Mass.: Harvard University Press, 1963. [Like the Ward biography listed below, Bate's biography is an important critical study, with explication and interpretation of the letters.]

GITTINGS, ROBERT, *John Keats*, London: Heinemann Educational Books, 1968.

WARD, AILEEN, *John Keats; the Making of a Poet*, New York: Viking Press, 1963.

EDITIONS

FORMAN, H. BUXTON (ed.), revised by Maurice Buxton Forman, The Hampstead Edition, *The Poetical Works and other Writings of John Keats*, 8 vols., New York: Charles Scribner's Sons, 1938–1939.

ROLLINS, HYDER EDWARD (ed.), *The Letters of John Keats 1814–1821*, 2 vols., Cambridge, Mass.: Harvard University Press, 1958.

TRILLING, LIONEL (ed.), *The Selected Letters of John Keats*, New York: Farrar, Strauss and Young, Inc., 1951. [The introduction, a valuable critical essay, was republished as "The Poet as Hero: Keats in his Letters" in Trilling's *The Opposing Self* (New York: Viking Press, 1955).]

CRITICISM AND SCHOLARSHIP

BATE, WALTER JACKSON, *Negative Capability; the intuitive approach in Keats*, Cambridge, Mass.: Harvard University Press, 1939.

CALDWELL, JAMES RALSTON, *John Keats' Fancy: The Effect on Keats of the Psychology of his Day*, Ithaca, New York: Cornell University Press, 1945. [See Chapter IV.]

DAVIES, R. T., "Was 'Negative Capability' Enough for Keats? A Re-assessment of the Evidence of the Letters," *Studies in Philology*, LV (1958), 76–85.

ELIOT, T. S., *The Use of Poetry and the Use of Criticism*, Cambridge, Mass.: Harvard University Press, 1933. [Pages 91–94 contain a tribute to the letters of Keats.]

FORD, NEWELL, F., *The Prefigurative Imagination of John Keats: A Study of the Beauty-Truth Identification and its Implications*, Stanford University Publications, Language and Literature, Volume

IX, Number 2, Stanford, Calif.: Stanford University Press, 1951. [Chapter II is a lengthy explication of the letter to Bailey, 22 November 1817.]

GUILHAMET, LEON M., "Keats's 'Negative Capability' and 'Disinterestedness': A Confusion of Ideals," *University of Toronto Quarterly*, XL (1970), 2–14.

PERKINS, DAVID, "Keats's Odes and Letters: Recurrent Diction and Imagery," *Keats-Shelley Journal*, II (1953), 51–60.

THORPE, CLARENCE DEWITT, *The Mind of John Keats*, New York: Oxford University Press, 1926.

MR. KEAN

The first of three theatrical reviews Keats wrote for The Champion *in December 1817–January 1818, in the absence of his friend John Hamilton Reynolds, the regular drama critic. The text is here reproduced from* The Poetical Works and other Writings of John Keats, *Hampstead Edition (1938–39), V, 227–32.*

Edmund Kean (1787–1833) was one of the leading actors of the London stage from his sensational debut as Shylock in 1814. He had been much admired and championed by Hazlitt, whose influence is evident in both the style and thought of Keats's review. Compare the praise of Kean's "intensity" and "gusto" with similar remarks on the nature of art and the character of "Men of Genius" in the letters of November 22 and December 21–27. For discussion of the review, see Bernice Slote, Keats and the Dramatic Principle *(Lincoln, Neb.: University of Nebraska Press, 1958), pp. 89–91.*

MR. KEAN

"IN OUR unimaginative days,"—*Habeas Corpus'd* as we are, out of all wonder, uncertainty and fear;—in these fireside, delicate, gilded days,—these days of sickly safety and comfort, we feel very grateful to Mr. Kean for giving us some excitement by his old passion in one of the old plays. He is a relict of romance;—a Posthumous ray of chivalry, and always seems just arrived from the camp of Charlemagne. In Richard he is his sword's dear cousin; in Hamlet his footing is germain to the platform. In Macbeth his eye laughs siege to scorn; in Othello he is welcome to Cyprus. In Timon he is of the palace—of Athens—of the woods, and is worthy to sleep in a grave "which once a day with its embossed froth, the burbulent surge doth cover."[1] For all these was he greeted with enthusiasm on his reappearance in Richard; for all these, his sickness will ever be a public misfortune. His return was full of power. He is not the man to "bate a jot."[2] On Thurs-

day evening, he acted *Luke* in *Riches*,[3] as far as the stage will admit, to perfection. In the hypocritical self-possession, in the caution, and afterwards the pride, cruelty, and avarice, Luke appears to us a man incapable of imagining to the extreme heinousness of crimes. To him, they are mere magic-lantern horrors. He is at no trouble to deaden his conscience.

Mr. Kean's two characters of this week, comprising as they do, the utmost of quiet and turbulence, invite us to say a few words on his acting in general. We have done this before, but we do it again without remorse. Amid his numerous excellencies, the one which at this moment most weighs upon us, is the elegance, gracefulness, and music of elocution. A melodious passage in poetry is full of pleasures both sensual and spiritual. The spiritual is felt when the very letters and points of charactered language show like the hieroglyphics of beauty;—the mysterious signs of an immortal freemasonry! "A thing to dream of, not to tell!" The sensual life of verse springs warm from the lips of Kean, and to one learned in Shakespearian hieroglyphics,—learned in the spiritual portion of those lines to which Kean adds a sensual grandeur: his tongue must seem to have robbed "the Hybla bees, and left them honeyless."[4] There is an indescribable gusto in his voice, by which we feel that the utterer is thinking of the past and the future, while speaking of the instant. When he says in Othello "put up your bright swords, for the dew will rust them,"[5] we feel that his throat had commanded where swords were as thick as reeds. From eternal risk, he speaks as though his body were unassailable. Again, his exclamation of "blood, blood,

---

[1] *Timon of Athens*, V, i, 220–21.
[2] See *Coriolanus*, II, ii, 144–45.

[3] *Riches, or the Wife and Brother*, an adaptation of Massinger's *City Madam*, by Sir James Bland Burger, first produced in 1810. Keats had attended the performance of December 18 at the Drury Lane Theatre, as well as Kean's "reappearance" in *Richard the Third* on December 15.
[4] *Julius Caesar*, V, i, 34–35.
[5] *Othello*, I, ii, 59. The exclamation "blood, blood, blood!" occurs in III, iii, 451.

blood!" is direful and slaughterous to the deepest degree, the very words appear stained and gory. His nature hangs over them, making a prophetic repast. His
voice is loosed on them, like the wild dog on the savage
relics of an eastern conflict; and we can distinctly hear
it "gorging, and growling o'er carcase and limb." In
Richard, "Be stirring with the lark to-morrow, gentle
Norfolk!"[6] comes from him, as through the morning
atmosphere, towards which he yearns. We could cite
a volume of such immortal scraps, and dote upon them
with our remarks; but as an end must come, we will
content ourselves with a single syllable. It is in those
lines of impatience to the night who, "like a foul and
ugly witch, doth limp so tediously away."[7] Surely this
intense power of anatomizing the passion of every syllable—of taking to himself the wings of verse, is the
mean⟨s⟩ by which he becomes a storm with such fiery
decision; and by which, with a still deeper charm, he
"does his spiriting gently."[8] Other actors are continually thinking of their sum-total effect throughout
a play. Kean delivers himself up to the instant feeling, without a shadow of a thought about any thing
else. He feels his being as deeply as Wordsworth, or
any other of our intellectual monopolists. From all his
comrades he stands alone, reminding us of him, whom
Dante has so finely described in his Hell:

"And sole apart retir'd, the Soldan fierce."[9]

Although so many times he has lost the battle of Bos-
worth Field, we can easily conceive him really expectant of victory, and a different termination of the
piece. Yet we are as moths about a candle in speaking
of this great man. "Great, let us call him, for he conquered us!" We will say no more. Kean! Kean! have
a carefulness of thy health, an in-nursed respect for
thy own genius, a pity for us in these cold and en-
feebling times! Cheer us a little in the failure of our
days! for romance lives but in books. The goblin is
driven from the heath, and the rainbow is robbed of
its mystery![10]

[December 21, 1817]   [1938–39]

---

[6] See *Richard III*, V, iii, 56.
[7] *Henry the Fifth*, IV, chorus, ll. 21–22.
[8] *The Tempest*, I, ii, 298.
[9] Keats quotes from Cary's translation of the *Inferno*, IV, 126,
referring to one of the virtuous pagans, a twelfth-century Sultan
of Egypt and Syria.
[10] Keats was to give a poetic statement of the same idea in
Lamia, II, 229–37.

NOTES ON MILTON'S PARADISE LOST
*Keats's annotations are here reproduced from the Hampstead
Edition, V, 292–305. The italicized lines in the quotations indicate Keats's underlinings. The annotations are thought to date
from 1818. The influence of Paradise Lost is evident in the
versification, "stationing" of characters (see note 17), and some
details of the plot of Hyperion, which Keats was to compose in
the fall of that year.*

NOTES ON MILTON'S PARADISE LOST

1
ON THE POET AND THE POEM

The Genius of Milton, more particularly in respect
to its span in immensity, calculated him, by a sort of
birthright, for such an 'argument' as the paradise lost:
he had an exquisite passion for what is properly, in the
sense of ease and pleasure, poetical Luxury; and with
that it appears to me he would fain have been content,
if he could, so doing, have preserved his self-respect and
feel of duty performed; but there was working in him
as it were that same sort of thing as operates in the great
world to the end of a Prophecy's being accomplish'd:
therefore he devoted himself rather to the Ardours than
the pleasures of Song, solacing himself at intervals with
cups of old wine; and those are with some exceptions
the finest parts of the Poem. With some exceptions—
for the spirit of mounting and adventure can never be
unfruitful or unrewarded: had he not broken through
the clouds which envellope so deliciously the Elysian fields of Verse, and committed himself to the Extreme, we never should have seen Satan as described—

"But his face
Deep Scars of thunder had entrench'd,"[1] &c.

2
ON 'THE ARGUMENT'

There is a greatness which the Paradise Lost possesses over every other Poem—*the Magnitude of Contrast*,
and that is softened by the contrast being ungrotesque
to a degree. Heaven moves on like music throughout.
Hell is also peopled with angels; it also move⟨s⟩ on like
music, not grating and harsh, but like a grand accompaniment in the Base to Heaven.

3
ON THE OPENING

There is always a great charm in the openings of
great Poems, more particularly where the action
begins—that of Dante's Hell. Of Hamlet, the first step

---

[1] I, 600–601.

must be heroic and full of power; and nothing can be more impressive and shaded than the commencement of the action here—'Round he throws his baleful eyes—'

4
BOOK I, LINES 53 TO 75

But his doom
Reserv'd him to more wrath; for now the thought
Both of lost happiness and lasting pain
Torments him: *round he throws his baleful eyes,*
That witness'd huge affliction and dismay
Mix'd with obdurate pride and stedfast hate:
At once, as far as Angel's ken, he views
The dismal situation waste and wild;
A dungeon horrible on all sides round
As one great furnace flamed, yet from those flames
No light, but rather darkness visible
Serv'd only to discover *sights of woe,*
Regions of sorrow, doleful shades, where peace
And rest can never dwell; hope never comes
That comes to all; but torture without end
Still urges, and a fiery deluge, fed
With ever-burning sulphur unconsumed.
Such place eternal Justice had prepared
For those rebellious, here their prison ordain'd
In utter darkness, and their portion set
As far removed from God and light of Heaven,
As from the centre thrice to the utmost pole.
Oh how unlike the place from whence they fell!

One of the most mysterious of semi-speculations is, one would suppose, that of one Mind's imagining into another. Things may be described by a Man's self in parts so as to make a grand whole which that Man himself would scarcely inform to its excess. A Poet can seldom have justice done to his imagination—for men are as distinct in their conceptions of material shadowings as they are in matters of spiritual understanding: it can scarcely be conceived how Milton's Blindness might here aid the magnitude of his conceptions as a bat in a large gothic vault.

5
BOOK I, LINES 318–21

or have ye chosen this place
After the toil of battle to repose
Your wearied virtue, for the ease you find
To slumber here, as in the vales of Heaven?

There is a cool pleasure in the very sound of vale. The english word is of the happiest chance. Milton has put vales in heaven and hell with the very utter affection and yearning of a great Poet. It is a sort of delphic Abstraction—a beautiful thing made more beautiful by being reflected and put in a Mist. The next mention of Vale is one of the most pathetic in the whole range of Poetry.

Others, more mild,
Retreated in a silent Valley &c.
⟨BOOK II, lines 546–7.⟩

How much of the charm is in the Valley!—

6
BOOK I, LINES 527–67

but he, his wonted pride
Soon recollecting, with high words, that bore
Semblance of worth not substance, gently raised
Their fainting courage, and dispell'd their fears.
Then straight commands that at the warlike sound
Of trumpets loud and clarions be uprear'd
His mighty standard: that proud honour claim'd
Azazel as his right, a Cherub tall;
Who forthwith from *the glittering staff unfurl'd*
The imperial ensign, which full high advanced
Shone like a meteor streaming to the wind,
With gems and golden lustre rich emblazed,
Seraphic arms and trophies; all the while
Sonorous metal blowing martial sounds:
At which the universal host up-sent
A shout, that tore Hell's concave, and beyond
Frighted the reign of Chaos and old Night.
All in a moment through the gloom were seen
Ten thousand banners rise into the air
With orient colours waving: with them rose
A forest huge of spears, and thronging helms
Appear'd, and serried shields in thick array
Of depth immeasurable : anon they move
In perfect phalanx to the Dorian mood
Of flutes and soft recorders; such as raised
To height of noblest temper heroes old
Arming to battle, and instead of rage
Deliberate valour breath'd, firm and unmoved
With dread of death to flight or foul retreat;
Nor wanting power to mitigate and swage
With solemn touches, troubled thoughts, and chase
Anguish, and doubt, and fear, and sorrow, and pain,
From mortal or immortal minds. Thus they
Breathing united force with fixed thought
Moved on in silence to soft pipes, that charm'd
Their painful steps o'er the burnt soil; and now
Advanced in view they stand, a horrid front
Of dreadful length and dazzling arms, in guise
Of warriors old with order'd spear and shield,
Awaiting what command their mighty chief
Had to impose.

The light and shade—the sort of black brightness—the ebon diamonding—the ethiop Immortality—the sorrow, the pain, the sad-sweet Melody—the P⟨h⟩alanges of Spirits so depressed as to be 'uplifted beyond hope'[2]—the short mitigation of Misery—the thousand Melancholies and Magnificences of this Page—leaves no room for anything to be said thereon but "*so it is.*"

7
BOOK I, LINES 591–9

his form had not yet lost
All her original brightness, nor appear'd
Less than Arch-Angel ruin'd, and the excess
Of glory obscured; as when the sun new risen
Looks through the horizontal misty air
Shorn of his beams; or from behind the moon
In dim eclipse disastrous twilight sheds
On half the nations, and with fear of change
Perplexes monarchs.

How noble and collected an indignation against Kings, '*and for fear of change perplexes Monarchs*' &c. His very wishing should have had power to pull that feeble animal Charles from his bloody throne. 'The evil days'[3] had come to him; he hit the new System of things a mighty mental blow; the exertion must have had or is yet to have some sequences.

8
BOOK I, LINES 710–30

Anon out of the earth a fabric huge
Rose like an exhalation, with the sound
Of dulcet symphonies and voices sweet,
Built like a temple, where pilasters round
Were set, and Doric pillars overlaid
With golden architrave; nor did there want
Cornice or frieze, with bossy sculptures graven;
The roof was fretted gold. Not Babylon,
Nor great Alcairo such magnificence
Equall'd in all their glories, to inshrine
Belus or Serapis their Gods, or seat
Their kings, when Egypt with Assyria strove
In wealth and luxury. The ascending pile
Stood fix'd her stately height; and straight the doors
Opening their brazen folds, discover, wide
Within, her ample spaces, o'er the smooth
And level pavement: from the arched roof
Pendent by subtle magic many a row
Of starry lamps and blazing cressets, fed
With Naphtha and Asphaltus, yielded light
As from a sky.

What creates the intense pleasure of not knowing? A sense of independence, of power, from the fancy's creating a world of its own by the sense of probabilities. We have read the Arabian Nights and hear there are thousands of those sort of Romances lost—we imagine after

them—but not their realities if we had them nor our fancies in their strength can go further than this Pandemonium—

'Straight the doors opening' &c.
'rose like an exhalation'—

9
BOOK II, LINES 546–61

Others, more mild,
Retreated in a silent valley, sing
With notes angelical to many a harp
Their own heroic deeds and hapless fall
By doom of battle; and complain that Fate
Free Virtue should inthrall to force or chance.
Their song was partial, but the harmony
(What could it less when Spirits immortal sing?)
Suspended Hell, and took with ravishment
The thronging audience. *In discourse more sweet*
(*For eloquence the soul, song charms the sense*)
Others apart sat on a hill retired,
In thoughts more elevate, and reason'd high
Of providence, foreknowledge, will, and fate,
Fixed fate, free will, foreknowledge absolute,
And found no end, in wandering mazes lost.

Milton is godlike in the sublime pathetic. In Demons, fallen Angels, and Monsters the delicacies of passion, living in and from their immortality, is of the most softening and dissolving nature. It is carried to the utmost here—'Others more mild'—nothing can express the sensation one feels at '*Their song was partial*' &c. Examples of this nature are divine to the utmost in other poets—in Caliban '*Sometimes a thousand twangling instruments*'[4] &c. In Theocritus, Polyphemus—and Homer's Hymn to Pan where Mercury is represented as taking his '*homely fac'd*'[5] to heaven. There are numerous other instances in Milton—where Satan's progeny is called his '*daughter dear,*'[6] and where this same Sin, a female, and with a feminine instinct for the showy and martial is in pain lest death should sully his bright arms, '*nor vainly hope to be invulnerable in those bright arms.*' Another instance is '*pensive I sat* alone.' We need not mention '*Tears such as Angels weep.*'

10
BOOK III, LINES I AND 51–9

Hail, holy Light, offspring of Heaven first-born!
*   *   *   *   *
So much the rather thou, celestial Light,

---

[2] II, 7.
[3] See VII, 25.

[4] *The Tempest* III, ii, 146.
[5] Chapman's translation of the Homeric "Hymn to Pan," l. 74. For the reference to Polyphemus, see the eleventh of Theocritus' *Idyls*, the complaint of the Cyclops to his beloved Galatea.
[6] II, 817. The next three quotations occur in II, 811–12; II, 777–78; I, 620.

Shine inward, and the mind through all her powers
Irradiate; there plant eyes, all mist from thence
Purge and disperse, that I may see and tell
Of things invisible to mortal sight.
    Now had the Almighty Father from above,
From the pure empyrean where he sits
High throned above all height, bent down his eye,
His own works and their works at once to view.

The management of this Poem is Apollonian. Satan first '*throws round his baleful eyes,*' the⟨n⟩ awakes his legions, he consults, he sets forward on his voyage—and just as he is getting to the end of it we see the Great God and our first parent, and that same satan all brought in one's vision—we have the invocation to light before we mount to heaven—we breathe more freely—we feel the great Author's consolations coming thick upon him at a time when he complains most—we are getting ripe for diversity—the immediate topic of the Poem opens with a grand Perspective of all concerned.

11
BOOK III, LINES 135–7

Thus while God spake, ambrosial fragrance fill'd
All Heaven, and in the blessed Spirits elect
Sense of new joy ineffable diffused.

Hell is finer than this.

12
BOOK III, LINES 487–9

A violent cross wind from either coast
Blows them transverse, ten thousand leagues awry
Into the devious air.

This part in its sound is unaccountably expressive of the description.

13
BOOK III, LINES 606–17

What wonder then if fields and regions here
Breathe forth Elixir pure, and rivers run
Potable gold, *when with one virtuous touch*
The arch-chemic Sun, so far from us remote,
Produces with terrestrial humour mix'd,
Here in the dark so many precious things
Of colour glorious and effect so rare?
Here matter new to gaze the Devil met
Undazzled, far and wide his eye commands,
For sight no obstacle found here, nor shade,
But all sunshine, *as when his beams at noon*
Culminate from the Equator, . . .

A Spirit's eye.

14
BOOK IV, LINES 1–5

O for that warning voice, which he who saw
The Apocalypse heard cry in Heaven aloud,
Then when the Dragon, put to second rout,
Came furious down to be revenged on men,
"Woe to the inhabitants on earth!"

A friend of mine says this Book has the finest opening of any—the point of time is gigantically critical—the wax is melted, the seal is about to be applied—and Milton breaks out, '*O for that warning voice,*' &c. There is moreover an op⟨p⟩ortunity for a Grandeur of Tenderness—the opportunity is not lost. Nothing can be higher—Nothing so more than delphic.

15
BOOK IV, LINES 268–72

Not that fair field
Of Enna, where Proserpin gathering flowers,
Herself a fairer flower, by gloomy Dis
Was gather'd, which cost Ceres all that pain
To seek her through the world;

There are two specimens of a very extraordinary beauty in the Paradise Lost; they are of a nature as far as I have read, unexampled elsewhere—they are entirely distinct from the brief pathos of Dante—and they are not to be found even in Shakspeare—these are according to the great prerogative of poetry better described in themselves than by a volume. The one is in the fol⟨lowing⟩—'*which cost Ceres all that pain*'—the other is that ending '*Nor could the Muse defend her son*'[7]—they appear exclusively Miltonic without the shadow of another mind ancient or modern.

16
BOOK VI, LINES 58–9

reluctant flames, the sign
Of wrath awaked; . . .

'Reluctant' with its original and modern meaning combined and woven together, with all its shades of signification has a powerful effect.

17
BOOK VII, LINES 420–3

but feather'd soon and fledge
They summ'd their pens, and, soaring the air sublime
With clang despised the ground, under a cloud
In prospect.

Milton in every instance pursues his imagination to the utmost—he is 'sagacious of his Quarry,'[8] he sees

---

[7] VII, 37–38.   [8] X, 281.

Beauty on the wing, pounces upon it and gorges it to the producing his essential verse. "So from the root the springs lighter the green stalk,"[9] &c. But in no instance is this sort of perseverance more exemplified than in what may be called his *stationing or statu⟨a⟩ry.* He is not content with simple description, he must station,— thus here, we not only see how the Birds '*with clang despised the ground,*' but we see them '*under a cloud in prospect.*' So we see Adam '*Fair indeed and tall—under a plantane*'[10]—and so we see Satan '*disfigured—on the Assyrian Mount.*' This last with all its accompaniments, and keeping in mind the Theory of Spirits' eyes and the simile of Gallilio, has a dramatic vastness and solemnity fit and worthy to hold one amazed in the midst of this Paradise Lost—

18
BOOK IX, LINES 41–7

Me, of these
Nor skill'd nor studious, higher argument
Remains, sufficient of itself to raise
That name, unless an age too late, or cold
Climate, or years, damp my intended wing
Depress'd; and much they may, if all be mine,
Not hers who brings it nightly to my ear.

Had not Shakespeare liv'd?

19
BOOK IX, LINES 179–91

So saying, through each thicket, dank or dry,
Like a black mist low creeping, he held on
His midnight search, where soonest he might find
The serpent: *him fast sleeping soon he found*
In labyrinth of many a round self-roll'd,
His head the midst, well stored with subtle wiles.
Not yet in horrid shade or dismal den,
Nor nocent yet; but, on the grassy herb
Fearless, unfear'd, he slept: in at his mouth
The Devil enter'd, and his brutal sense,
In heart or head, possessing, soon inspired
With act intelligential; but his sleep
Disturb'd not, waiting close the approach of morn.

Satan having entered the Serpent, and inform'd his brutal sense—might seem sufficient—but Milton goes on '*but his sleep disturb'd not.*' Whose spirit does not ache at the smothering and confinement—the unwilling stillness—the '*waiting close*'? Whose head is not dizzy at the possible speculations of satan in the serpent prison—no passage of poetry ever can give a greater pain of suffocation.

[1938–1939]

9 V, 479–80.
10 IV, 477–78. The next quotation occurs in IV, 126–27.

The letters of Keats are perhaps the most remarkable ever written by a major literary figure, both for their revelation of an extraordinary human being and for their depth of speculation and insight on the nature and value of the poetic talent. In reading the letters, it is often difficult to separate the report of day-to-day events (a dispute between friends or attendance at a party) from progressive self-definition and aesthetic speculation, for in Keats more than most artists the experiential drama and the development of personality and thought are richly joined. This constant relationship between experience and the evolving understanding of himself and his art is itself illustrative of one of Keats's most mature and resonant speculations, the conception of the world as "The Vale of Soul-making;" only by the "heart's" confrontation with "a world of Circumstances" can the "Intelligence" become a "Soul," that is, achieve "the sense of Identity" (see letter to George and Georgiana Keats, April 21, 1819). The letters here reproduced chronicle one of the most rewarding and heroic of those journeys in the "Vale of Soul-making," from the early courageously ambitious dedication to the highest goals of art through the personal and artistic achievements and discouragements of the succeeding years to the tragically premature death.

The text of the letters is from the edition by Hyder E. Rollins, The Letters of John Keats 1814–1821 (1958). Cancelled words and letters are indicated in shaped brackets (⟨ ⟩); where Keats's misspellings or omissions from haste in writing are likely to cause confusion, the correct reading has been inserted in brackets ([ ]).

LETTERS

Benjamin Robert Haydon (1786–1846), a painter of ambitious and grandiose canvases, had met Keats in October 1816, and strongly encouraged him in his poetic aspirations. In a sonnet written in November 1816, Keats had described Haydon as one of the "Great Spirits now on Earth sojourning;" and in January 1818, he was to hail Haydon's pictures as one of the "three things to rejoice at in this Age" (the other two being Wordsworth's Excursion and Hazlitt's "depth of Taste").

TO B. R. HAYDON
10, 11 May 1817

Margate Saturday Eve

My dear Haydon,

Let Fame, which all hunt after in their Lives,
Live register'd upon our brazen tombs,
And so grace us in the disgrace of death:
When spite of cormorant devouring time
The endeavour of this pre⟨a⟩sent breath may buy
That Honor which shall bate his Scythe's keen edge
And make us heirs of all eternity.[1]

To think that I have no right to couple myself with you in this speech would be death to me so I have e'en

1 *Love's Labour's Lost,* I, i, 1–7.

written it—and I pray God that our brazen Tombs be nigh neighbors. It cannot be long first the endeavor of this present breath will soon be over—and yet it is as well to breathe freely during our sojourn—it is as well if you have not been teased with that Money affair—that bill-pestilence. However I must think that difficulties nerve the Spirit of a Man—they make our Prime Objects a Refuge as well as a Passion. The Trumpet of Fame is as a tower of Strength the ambitious bloweth it and is safe—I suppose by your telling me not to give way to forebodings George[2] has mentioned to you what I have lately said in my Letters to him—truth is I have been in such a state of Mind as to read over my Lines and hate them. I am "one that gathers Samphire dreadful trade"[3] the Cliff of Poesy Towers above me—yet when, Tom who meets with some of Pope's Homer in Plutarch's Lives reads some of those to me they seem like Mice to mine. I read and write about eight hours a day. There is an old saying well begun is half done"—'t is a bad one. I would use instead—Not begun at all 'till half done" so according to that I have not begun my Poem[4] and consequently (a priori) can say nothing about it. Thank God! I do begin arduously where I leave off, notwithstanding occasional depressions: and I hope for the support of a High Power while I clime this little eminence and especially in my Years of more momentous Labor. I remember your saying that you had notions of a good Genius presiding over you—I have of late had the same thought. for things which [I] do half at Random are afterwards confirmed by my judgment in a dozen features of Propriety—Is it too daring to Fancy Shakspeare this Presider? When in the Isle of W⟨h⟩ight I met with a Shakspeare in the Passage of the House at which I lodged—it comes nearer to my idea of him than any I have seen—I was but there a Week yet the old Woman made me take it with me though I went off in a hurry—Do you not think this is ominous of good? I am glad you say every Man of great Views is at times tormented as I am—

Sunday Aft. This Morning I received a letter from George by which it appears that Money Troubles are to follow us up for some time to come perhaps for always—these vexations are a great hindrance to one—they are not like Envy and detraction stimulants to further exertion as being immediately relative and reflected on at the same time with the prime object—

but rather like a nettle leaf or two in your bed. So now I revoke my Promise of finishing my Poem by the Autumn which I should have done had I gone on as I have done—but I cannot write while my spirit is fe⟨a⟩vered in a contrary direction and I am now sure of having plenty of it this Summer—At this moment I am in no enviable Situation—I feel that I am not in a Mood to write any to day; and it appears that the lo⟨o⟩ss of it is the beginning of all sorts of irregularities. I am extremely glad that a time must come when every thing will leave not a wrack behind.[5] You tell me never to despair—I wish it was as easy for me to observe the saying—truth is I have a horrid Morbidity of Temperament which has shown itself at intervals—it is I have no doubt the greatest Enemy and stumbling block I have to fear—I may even say that it is likely to be the cause of my disappointment. How ever every ill has its share of good—this very bane would at any time enable me to look with an obstinate eye on the Devil Himself—ay to be as proud of being the lowest of the human race as Alfred could be in being of the highest. I feel confident I should have been a rebel Angel had the opportunity been mine. I am very sure that you do love me as your own Brother—I have seen it in your continual anxiety for me—and I assure you that your wellfare and fame is and will be a chief pleasure to me all my Life. I know no one but you who can be fully sensible of the turmoil and anxiety, the sacrifice of all what is called comfort the readiness to Measure time by what is done and to die in 6 hours could plans be brought to conclusions.—the looking upon the Sun the Moon the Stars, the Earth and its contents as materials to form greater things—that is to say ethereal things——but here I am talking like a Madman greater things than our Creator himself made!! I wrote to Hunt[6] yesterday—scar[c]ely know what I said in it—I could not talk about Poetry in the way I should have liked for I was not in humor with either his or mine. His self delusions are very lamentable they have inticed him into a Situation which I should be less eager after than that of a galley Slave—what you observe thereon is very true must be in time. Perhaps it is a self delusion to say so—but I think I could not be deceived in the Manner that Hunt is—may I die tomorrow if I am to be. There is no greater Sin after the 7 deadly than to flatter oneself into an idea of being a great Poet—or one of those beings who are privileged to wear out their Lives in the pursuit of Honor—how comfortable a feel it is that such a Crime must bring its heavy Penalty? That if one be a Self-deluder accounts will be balanced? I am glad you are

[2] George Keats (1797–1841), the poet's brother.
[3] *King Lear*, IV, vi, 15.
[4] On April 14, Keats had left London for the Isle of Wight in order to proceed with his projected major poem *Endymion*. Depressed by his lack of progress in composition, he moved before the end of the month to Margate, a resort town on the Kentish coast.

[5] Cf. *The Tempest*, IV, i, 156.
[6] Leigh Hunt.

hard at Work—'t will now soon be done—I long to see Wordsworth's as well as to have mine in: [7] but I would rather not show my face in Town till the end of the Year—if that will be time enough—if not I shall be disappointed if you do not write for me even when you think best—I never quite despair and I read Shakspeare—indeed I shall I think never read any other Book much—Now this might lead me into a long Confab but I desist. I am very near Agreeing with Hazlit that Shakspeare is enough for us—By the by what a tremendous Southean Article his last was [8]—I wish he had left out "grey hairs" It was very gratifying to meet your remarks of the Manuscript [9]—I was reading Anthony and Cleopat[ra] when I got the Paper and there are several Passages applicable to the events you commentate. You say that he arrived by degrees, and not by any single Struggle to the height of his ambition—and that his Life had been as common in particulars as other Mens—Shakspeare makes Enobarb say—Where's Antony Eros—He's walking in the garden—thus: *and spurns the rush that lies* before him, cries fool, Lepidus! [10] In the same scene we find: "let determined things to destiny hold unbewailed their way". Dolabella says of Ant⟨h⟩ony's Messenger

"An argument that he is pluck'd when hither
He sends so poor a pinion of his wing"—Then again,
  Eno—"I see Men's Judgments are
  A parcel of their fortunes; and things outward
  Do draw the inward quality after them,
  To suffer all alike"—The following applies well to
   Bertram
    "Yet he that can endure
  To follow with allegience a fallen Lord,
  Does conquer him that did his Master conquer,
  And earns a place i' the story" [11]

But how differently does Buonap bear his fate from Antony!
'T is good too that the Duke of Wellington has a good Word or so in the Examiner A Man ought to have the Fame he deserves—and I begin to think that detracting from him as well as from Wordsworth is the same thing. I wish he had a little more taste—and did not in that respect "deal in Lieutenantry" [12] You should have heard from me before this—but in the first place I did not like to do so before I had got a little way in the 1st Book and in the next as G. told me you were going to write I delayed till I had hea[r]d from you—Give my Respects the next time you write to the North [13] and also to John Hunt—Remember me to Reynolds [14] and tell him to write, Ay, and when you sent Westward tell your Sister that I mentioned her in this—So now in the Name of Shakespeare Raphael and all our Saints I commend you to the care of heaven!

    Your everlasting friend
    John Keats—

———

Benjamin Bailey (1791–1853), author and clergyman, had met Keats in the spring of 1817 and invited him to Oxford where Bailey was studying for holy orders and where Keats was to compose Book III of Endymion. *Keats's readings and discussion with Bailey in matters of literature, philosophy, and religion were to prove a formative intellectual experience. In later years, Bailey was to become Anglican Archdeacon of Colombo, Ceylon, to prepare a dictionary of the Malayan tongue, and to make a number of translations from Malayan.*

 *This letter is of first importance for the unfolding of Keats's speculations on the character of the artist and the process of the imagination. The first paragraph ends with a description of "Men of Genius" as characterless, a point he was to develop as "Negative Capability" in the letter to his brothers in December 1817. The famous passage in the second paragraph beginning: "I am certain of nothing but of the holiness of the Heart's affections . . ." has been much discussed. Walter Jackson Bate (*John Keats *[1963], pp. 238–39) notes in the passage the interweaving of two premises. "The first is the premise of all objective idealism: what the human mind itself contributes to what it assumes are direct perceptions of the material world—supplementing, channeling, even helping to create them—is not, as the subjective idealist argues, something imposed completely* ab extra, *something invented or read into nature that is not really there. Instead, this cooperating creativity of the mind has, to use a phrase of Coleridge's, 'the same ground with nature': its insights are to this extent a valid and necessary supplement in attaining the reconciliation or union of man and nature that constitutes knowledge.... The second general premise involves the familiar romantic protest on behalf of concreteness and the conviction that the analytic and logical procedures of what Keats calls 'consequitive reasoning' violate the organic process of nature. They abstract from the full concreteness, reduce the living process to static concepts, and substitute an artificial order." In the exclamation "O for a Life of Sensations rather than of Thoughts!" the word "Sensations" should not be read as meaning gross physical responses. Douglas Bush paraphrases the exclamation: "O, for the sensuous, imaginative, and intuitive life of the artist rather than that of analytical reason!"*

———

[7] Referring to Haydon's painting "Christ's Entry into Jerusalem," in which Keats, Wordsworth, and Hazlitt, among others, were represented. The painting was first exhibited in 1820 in London; it now hangs in St. Gregory Seminary, Cincinnati.

[8] The first part of Hazlitt's devastating review of Southey's *A Letter to William Smith* (1817) had appeared in *The Examiner* of May 4 and was continued in the issues of May 11 and 18.

[9] In *The Examiner* issues of April 27 and May 4, Haydon had written a review of the recently published *Manuscrit venu de St. Hélène d'une manière inconnue.* These supposed memoirs of Napolcon, which caused a great stir in both France and England, were actually written by J. F. Lullin de Chateauvieux.

[10] *Anthony and Cleopatra,* III, v, 16–18; the next quotation occurs in III, vi, 84–85.

[11] See III, xii, 3–4; xiii, 31–33, 43–46. By Bertram, Keats means Henri Gratien Bertrand (1773–1844), French military engineer and confident of Napoleon, who shared his exile at St. Helena.

[12] *Anthony and Cleopatra,* III, xi, 39.
[13] Wordsworth.
[14] John Hamilton Reynolds (see p. 752).

Among the many discussions of this letter, see Jack Stillinger's exploration of the confusions between the naturalistic and visionary imagination in this "fascinating and valuable—and also very mixed-up—piece of prose" (The Hoodwinking of Madeline, and other Essays on Keats's Poems [Urbana, Illinois: University of Illinois Press, 1971], pp. 151–57).

TO BENJAMIN BAILEY
22 November 1817

My dear Bailey,

I will get over the first part of this (*un*said) Letter as soon as possible for it relates to the affair of poor Crips[1]—To a Man of your nature, such a Letter as Haydon's must have been extremely cutting—What occasions the greater part of the World's Quarrels? simply this, two Minds meet and do not understand each other time enough to p[r]aevent any shock or surprise at the conduct of either party—As soon as I had known Haydon three days I had got enough of his character not to have been surp[r]ised at such a Letter as he has hurt you with. Nor when I knew it was it a principle with me to drop his acquaintance although with you it would have been an imperious feeling. I wish you knew all that I think about Genius and the Heart—and yet I think you are thoroughly acquainted with my innermost breast in that respect or you could not have known me even thus long and still hold me worthy to be your dear friend. In passing however I must say of one thing that has pressed upon me lately and encreased my Humility and capability of submission and that is this truth—Men of Genius are great as certain ethereal Chemicals operating on the Mass of neutral intellect—by [but] they have not any individuality, any determined Character. I would call the top and head of those who have a proper self Men of Power—

But I am running my head into a Subject which I am certain I could not do justice to under five years s[t]udy and 3 vols octavo—and moreover long to be talking about the Imagination—so my dear Bailey do not think of this unpleasant affair if possible—do not—I defy any ha[r]m to come of it—I defy—I'll shall write to Crips this Week and reque[s]t him to tell me all his

---

[1] Charles Cripps was a young painter whom Haydon had met at Oxford and whom he had offered, with characteristic first enthusiasm, to train in his London studio without charge. Keats and Bailey were attempting to raise funds for Cripps' expenses in London, but at the time of this letter Haydon had apparently turned uncooperative. The phrase "this (*un*said) Letter" has been thus explained: "A mild play upon the lawyerly phrase 'this said letter' which would be Haydon's to Bailey: 'this *un*said letter' Keats's to Bailey" (*The Letters of John Keats*, ed. Maurice Buxton Forman, 4th edition [London: Oxford University Press, 1952], p. 66n).

goings on from time to time by Letter whererever I may be—it will all go on well—so dont because you have suddenly discover'd a Coldness in Haydon suffer yourself to be teased. Do not my dear fellow. O I wish I was as certain of the end of all your troubles as that of your momentary start about the authenticity of the Imagination. I am certain of nothing but of the holiness of the Heart's affections and the truth of Imagination—What the imagination seizes as Beauty must be truth—whether it existed before or not—for I have the same Idea of all our Passions as of Love they are all in their sublime, creative of essential Beauty—In a Word, you may know my favorite Speculation by my first Book and the little song I sent in my last[2]—which is a representation from the fancy of the probable mode of operating in these Matters—The Imagination may be compared to Adam's dream[3]—he awoke and found it truth. I am the more zealous in this affair, because I have never yet been able to perceive how any thing can be known for truth by consequitive reasoning—and yet it must be—Can it be that even the greatest Philosopher ever ⟨when⟩ arrived at his goal without putting aside numerous objections—However it may be, O for a Life of Sensations rather than of Thoughts! It is 'a Vision in the form of Youth' a Shadow of reality to come—and this consideration has further conv[i]nced me for it has come as auxiliary to another favorite Speculation of mine, that we shall enjoy ourselves here after by having what we called happiness on Earth repeated in a finer tone and so repeated—and yet such a fate can only befall those who delight in sensation rather than hunger as you do after Truth—Adam's dream will do here and seems to be a conviction that Imagination and its empyreal reflection is the same as human Life and its spiritual repetition. But as I was saying—the simple imaginative Mind may have its rewards in the repeti[ti]on of its own silent Working coming continually on the spirit with a fine suddenness—to compare great things with small—have you never by being surprised with an old Melody—in a delicious place—by a delicious voice, fe[l]t over again your very speculations and surmises at the time it first operated on your soul—do you not remember forming to yourself the singer's face more beautiful that [than] it was possible and yet with the elevation of the Moment you did not think so—even then you were mounted on the Wings of Imagination so high—that the Prototype must be here after—that delicious face you will see—What a time! I am continually running away from the subject—sure this

---

[2] The Indian Maid's song "O Sorrow" in Canto IV of *Endymion*.

[3] See *Paradise Lost*, VIII, 452–90.

cannot be exactly the case with a complex Mind—one that is imaginative and at the same time careful of its fruits—who would exist partly on sensation partly on thought—to whom it is necessary that years should bring the philosophic Mind [4]—such as one I consider your's and therefore it is necessary to your eternal drink
Happiness that you not only ⟨have⟩ this old Wine of Heaven which I shall call the redigestion of our most ethereal Musings on Earth; but also increase in knowledge and know all things. I am glad to hear you are in a fair Way for Easter—you will soon get through your unpleasant reading and then!—but the world is full of troubles and I have not much reason to think myself pesterd with many—I think Jane or Marianne [5] has a better opinion of me than I deserve—for really and truly I do not think my Brothers illness [6] connected with mine—you know more of the real Cause than they do—nor have I any chance of being rack'd as you have been—you perhaps at one time thought there was such a thing as Worldly Happiness to be arrived at, at certain periods of time marked out—you have of necessity from your disposition been thus led away—I scarcely remember counting upon any Happiness—I look not for it if it be not in the present hour—nothing startles me beyond the Moment. The setting sun will always set me to rights—or if a Sparrow come before my Window I take part in its existence and pick about the Gravel. The first thing that strikes me on hea[r]ing a Misfortune having befalled another is this. 'Well it cannot be helped.—he will have the pleasure of trying the resources of his spirit, and I beg now my dear Bailey that hereafter should you observe any thing cold in me not to but [put] it to the account of heartlessness but abstraction—for I assure you I sometimes feel not the influence of a Passion or Affection during a whole week—and so long this sometimes continues I begin to suspect myself and the genuiness of my feelings at other times—thinking them a few barren Tragedy-tears—My Brother Tom is much improved—he is going to Devonshire—whither I shall follow him—at present I am just arrived at Dorking to change the Scene—change the Air and give me a spur to wind up my Poem, of which there are wanting 500 Lines. I should have been here a day sooner but the Reynoldses persuaded me to spop [stop] in Town to meet your friend Christie—There were Rice and Martin—we talked about Ghosts—I will have some talk with

Taylor and let you know—when please God I come down a[t] Christmas—I will find that Examiner if possible. My best regards to Gleig—My Brothers to you and Mrs Bentley

Your affectionate friend
John Keats—

I want to say much more to you—a few hints will set me going Direct Burford Bridge near dorking

TO GEORGE AND TOM KEATS
21, 27 (?) December 1817

My dear Brothers
I must crave your pardon for not having written ere this & & I saw Kean return to the public in Richard III, & finely he did it, & at the request of Reynolds I went to criticise his Luke in Riches—the critique is in todays champion, which I send you with the Examiner in which you will find very proper lamentation on the obsoletion of christmas Gambols & pastimes: [1] but it was mixed up with so much egotism of that drivelling nature that pleasure is entirely lost. Hone the publisher's trial, you must find very amusing; & as Englishment very ⟨amusing⟩ encouraging—his *Not Guilty* is a thing, which not to have been, would have dulled still more Liberty's Emblazoning—Lord Ellenborough has been paid in his own coin—Wooler & Hone have done us an essential service [2]—I have had two very pleasant evenings with Dilke [3] yesterday & today; & am at this moment just come from him & feel in the humour to go on with this, began in the morning, & from which he came to fetch me. I spent Friday evening with Wells & went the next morning to see *Death on the Pale horse*. [4] It is a

---

4 See Wordsworth's "Intimations Ode," l. 186.
5 Sisters of John Hamilton Reynolds.
6 Tom Keats (1799–1818), who was to die of tuberculosis, now apparently showing first symptoms of poor health. However, consult Robert Gittings' *John Keats* (1968), appendix 3, on this confusing section of the letter.

1 Referring to Hunt's essay "Christmas and other old National Merry-Makings Considered...", which appeared in *The Examiner* issues of December 21 and 28.
2 William Hone (1780–1842), writer and publisher, was tried on December 18, 19, and 20, on three successive charges of "impious and profane libel" for publishing the parodies *The Late John Wilkes's Catechism*, *The Sinecurist's Creed*, and *The Political Litany*. He was acquitted in all three trials. Edward Law, first Baron Ellenborough (1750–1818), Lord Chief Justice, presided at the second and third trials and spoke against Hone. An account of the three trials was contained in *The Examiner* issue of December 21. Thomas Jonathan Wooler (c. 1786–1853), politician and publisher of the Sunday paper *The Black Dwarf*, had been tried in June 1817, for libel against the government and was acquitted.
3 Charles Wentworth Dilke (1789–1864) was a friend of Keats and his brothers, preparer of an edition of *Old English Plays* (1814–1816), and in later years a successful journalist. With Charles Armitage Brown (see footnote 6), Dilke owned the two-family Hampstead residence Wentworth Place (now the Keats House), where both Keats and the Brawne family were to live.
4 Painting exhibited in 1817, by Benjamin West (1738–1820), American-born painter of historical and mythological subjects, the president of the Royal Academy. His painting of Christ Rejected by the Jews, referred to later, had been first exhibited in 1814.

wonderful picture, when West's age is considered; But there is nothing to be intense upon; no women one feels mad to kiss; no face swelling into reality. the excellence of every Art is its intensity, capable of making all disagreeables evaporate, from their being in close relationship with Beauty & Truth—Examine King Lear & you will find this examplified throughout; but in this picture we have unpleasantness without any momentous depth of speculation excited, in which to bury its repulsiveness—The picture is larger than Christ rejected—I dined with Haydon the sunday after you left, & had a very pleasant day, I dined too (for I have been out too much lately) with Horace Smith[5] & met his two Brothers with Hill & Kingston & one Du Bois, they only served to convince me, how superior humour is to wit in respect to enjoyment—These men say things which make one start, without making one feel, they are all alike; their manners are alike; they all know fashionables; they have a mannerism in their very eating & drinking, in their mere handling a Decanter—They talked of Kean & his low company—Would I were with that company instead of yours said I to myself! I know such like acquaintance will never do for me & yet I am going to Reynolds, on wednesday—Brown[6] & Dilke walked with me & back from the Christmas pantomime. I had not a dispute but a disquisition with Dilke, on various subjects; several things dovetailed in my mind, & at once it struck me, what quality went to form a Man of Achievement especially in Literature & which Shakespeare posessed so enormously—I mean *Negative Capability*, that is when man is capable of being in uncertainties, Mysteries, doubts, without any irritable reaching after fact & reason—Coleridge, for instance, would let go by a fine isolated verisimilitude caught from the Penetralium of mystery, from being incapable of remaining content with half knowledge. This pursued through Volumes would perhaps take us no further than this, that with a great poet the sense of Beauty overcomes every other consideration, or rather obliterates all consideration.

Shelley's poem[7] is out & there are words about its being objected too, as much as Queen Mab[8] was.

5 Horace Smith (1779–1849), author, with his brother James, of the popular parodies *Rejected Addresses* (1812).

6 Charles Armitage Brown (1787–1842), friend of Keats from the summer of 1817, author of a very successful comic opera *Narensky* (1814). It was with Brown that Keats was to make a walking tour of the Lake District and Scotland in the summer of 1818; and following the death of Tom in December 1818, Keats was to live in Brown's quarters at Wentworth Place.

7 *Laon and Cythna*, issued in December 1817; because of anticipated objections to its radical theological content and its story of incest, copies were recalled, revisions were made and the work reissued as *The Revolt of Islam* in January 1818.

8 *Queen Mab*, Shelley's first major poem, published in 1813,

Poor Shelley I think he has his Quota of good qualities, in sooth la!! Write soon to your most sincere friend & affectionate Brother

(Signed) John

John Taylor (1781–1864) was, with James Augustus Hessey, the publisher of Endymion *(1818) and Keats's final volume* Lamia, Isabella, The Eve of St. Agnes *and other Poems* (1820).

TO JOHN TAYLOR
30 January 1818

My dear Taylor,   Friday

These Lines, as they now stand, about Happiness have rung in my ears like a 'chime of mending.'[1] see here,

> Behold
> Wherein Lies happiness Pœona? fold—

This appears to me the very contrary of blessed. I hope this will appear to you more eligible.

> Wherein lies Happiness? In that which becks
> Our ready Minds to fellowship divine;
> A fellowship with essence, till we shine
> Full alchymized and free of space. Behold
> The clear Religion of heaven—fold &c—[2]

You must indulge me by putting this in for setting aside the badness of the other, such a preface is necessary to the Subject. The whole thing must I think have appeared to you, who are a consequitive Man, as a thing almost of mere words—but I assure you that when I wrote it, it was a regular stepping of the Imagination towards a Truth. My having written

Argument

that ⟨Passage⟩ will perhaps be of the greatest Service to me of any thing I ever did—It set before me at once the gradations of Happiness even like a kind of Pleasure Thermometer—and is my first Step towards the chief Attempt in the Drama—the playing of different Natures with Joy and Sorrow.

Do me this favor and believe Me, Your sincere friend

John Keats

was revolutionary and "anti-Christian" in its political and religious philosophy.

1 *Troilus and Cressida*, I, iii, 159.

2 *Endymion*, I, 777–81. As the passage continues, Keats lists various degrees of happiness on the "pleasure thermometer," with the intensity of happiness being in relation to the loss of one's own identity and the corresponding absorption in friendship and love with another.

I hope your next Work³ will be of a more general interest—I s[u]ppose you cogitate a little about it now and then.

John Hamilton Reynolds (1794–1852), one of Keats's most beloved friends, was a lawyer, minor poet, and drama critic for The Champion and later The London Magazine. They had met in the fall of 1816. In addition to sending Reynolds some of his most penetrating letters, Keats addressed to him an important verse "Epistle" ("Dear Reynolds, as last night I lay in bed") in March 1818.

TO J. H. REYNOLDS
3 February 1818

Hampstead Tuesday.

My dear Reynolds,

I thank you for your dish of Filberts¹—Would I could get a basket of them by way of desert every day for the sum of two pence—Would we were a sort of ethereal Pigs, & turn'd loose to feed upon spiritual Mast & Acorns—which would be merely being a squirrel & feed upon filberts. for what is a squirrel but an airy pig, or a filbert but a sort of archangelical acorn. About the nuts being worth cracking, all I can say is that where there are a throng of delightful Images ready drawn simplicity is the only thing. the first is the best on account of the first line, and the "arrow—foil'd of its antler'd food"—and moreover (and this is the only ⟨only⟩ word or two I find fault with, the more because I have had so much reason to shun it as a quicksand) the last has "tender and true"—We must cut this, and not be rattlesnaked into any more of the like—It may be said that we ought to read our Contemporaries. that Wordsworth &c should have their due from us. but for the sake of a few fine imaginative or domestic passages, are we to be bullied into a certain Philosophy engendered in the whims of an Egotist—Every man has his speculations, but every man does not brood and peacock over them till he makes a false coinage and deceives himself—Many a man can travel to the very bourne of Heaven, and yet want confidence to put down his halfseeing. Sancho will invent a Journey heavenward as well as any body. We hate poetry that has a palpable design upon us—and if we do not agree, seems to put its hand in its breeches pocket. Poetry should be great & unobtrusive, a thing which enters into one's soul, and does not startle it or amaze it with itself but with its subject.—

---

³ Taylor was the author of various works, published between 1813 and 1818, on the identity of the author of the Junius letters.
¹ Keats's metaphor for some sonnets on Robin Hood which Reynolds had sent him.

How beautiful are the retired flowers! how would they lose their beauty were they to throng into the highway crying out, "admire me I am a violet! dote upon me I am a primrose! Modern poets differ from the Elizabethans in this. Each of the moderns like an Elector of Hanover governs his petty state, & knows how many straws are swept daily from the Causeways in all his dominions & has a continual itching that all the Housewives should have their coppers well scoured: Emperors of vast the antients were ⟨Emperors of large⟩ Provinces, they had only heard of the remote ones and scarcely cared to visit them.—I will cut all this—I will have no more of Wordsworth or Hunt in particular—Why should we be of the tribe of Manasseh, when we can wander with Esau?² why should we kick against the Pricks,³ when we can walk on Roses? Why should we be owls, when we can be Eagles? Why be teased with "nice Eyed wagtails,"⁴ when we have in sight "the Cherub Contemplation"?⁵—Why with Wordsworths "Matthew with a bough of wilding in his hand"⁶ when we can have Jacques "under an oak &c"⁷—The secret of the Bough of Wilding will run through your head faster than I can write it—Old Matthew spoke to him some years ago on some nothing, & because he happens in an Evening Walk to imagine the figure of the old man—he must stamp it down in black & white, and it is henceforth sacred—I don't mean to deny Wordsworth's grandeur & Hunt's merit, but I mean to say we need not be teazed with grandeur & merit—when we can have them uncontaminated & unobtrusive. Let us have the old Poets, & robin Hood Your letter and its sonnets gave me more pleasure than will the 4ᵗʰ Book of Childe Harold⁸ & the whole of any body's life & opinions. In return for your dish of filberts, I have gathered a few Catkins,⁹ I hope they'll look pretty.

To J. H. R. In answer to his Robin Hood Sonnets.

"No those days are gone away &c"—

I hope you will like them they are at least written in the Spirit of Outlawry.—Here are the Mermaid lines

---

² For tribe of Manasseh, Rollins suggests Judges, vi, 15; vii, 23. With the phrase "wander with Esau?" Keats may be thinking of Genesis, xxv, 27, which describes Esau as "a cunning hunter, a man of the field" as against his brother Jacob "a plain man dwelling in tents."
³ Acts, xxvi, 14.
⁴ From the poem "The Nymphs" in Hunt's Foliage (1818).
⁵ "Il Penseroso," l. 54.
⁶ Wordsworth's "The Two April Mornings," ll. 59–60.
⁷ As You Like It, II, i, 31.
⁸ Its forthcoming appearance had been announced; it was published in April 1818.
⁹ Blossoms of the hazel or willow tree, continuing the metaphor introduced with "filberts."

"Souls of Poets dead & gone, &c"—[10]

I will call on you at 4 tomorrow, and we will trudge together for it is not the thing to be a stranger in the Land of Harpsicols[11] I hope also to bring you my 2ᵈ book—In the hope that these Scribblings will be some amusement for you this Evening—I remain copying ⟨still⟩ on the Hill

Yʳ sincere friend and Coscribbler
John Keats.

TO J. H. REYNOLDS
19 February 1818

My dear Reynolds,

I have an idea that a Man might pass a very pleasant life in this manner—let him on any certain day read a certain Page of full Poesy or distilled Prose and let him wander with it, and muse upon it, and reflect from it, and bring home to it, and prophesy upon it, and dream upon it—untill it becomes stale—but when will it do so? Never—When Man has arrived at a certain ripeness in intellect any one grand and spiritual passage serves him as a starting post towards all "the two-and thirty Pallaces" How happy is such a "voyage of conception," what delicious diligent Indolence! A doze upon a Sofa does not hinder it, and a nap upon Clover engenders ethereal finger-pointings —the prattle of a child gives it wings, and the converse of middle age a strength to beat them—a strain of musick conducts to 'an odd angle of the Isle'[1] and when the leaves whisper it puts a 'girdle round the earth.[2]—Nor will this sparing touch of noble Books be any irreverance to their Writers—for perhaps the honors paid by Man to Man are trifles in comparison to the Benefit done by great Works to the 'Spirit and pulse of good'[3] by their mere passive existence. Memory should not be called knowledge—Many have original Minds who do not think it—they are led away by Custom—Now it appears to me that almost any Man may like the Spider spin from his own inwards his own airy Citadel—the points of leaves and twigs on which the Spider begins her work are few and she fills the Air with a beautiful circuiting: man should be content with as few points to tip with the fine Webb of his Soul and wave a tapestry empyrean—full of Symbols for his spiritual eye, of softness for his spiritual touch, of space for his wandering of distinct-

ness for his Luxury—But the Minds of Mortals are so different and bent on such diverse Journeys that it may at first appear impossible for any common taste and fellowship to exist ⟨bettween⟩ between two or three under these suppositions—It is however quite the contrary—Minds would leave each other in contrary directions, traverse each other in Numberless points, and all [at] last greet each other at the Journeys end—A old Man and a child would talk together and the old Man be led on his Path, and the child left thinking—Man should not dispute or assert but whisper results to his neighbour, and thus by every germ of Spirit sucking the Sap from mould ethereal every human might become great, and Humanity instead of being a wide heath of Furse and Briars with here and there a remote Oak or Pine, would become a grand democracy of Forest Trees. It has been an old Comparison for our urging on—the Bee hive—however it seems to me that we should rather be the flower than the Bee—for it is a false notion that more is gained by receiving than giving—no the receiver and the giver are equal in their benefits—The f[l]ower I doubt not receives a fair guerdon from the Bee—its leaves blush deeper in the next spring—and who shall say between Man and Woman which is the most delighted? Now it is more noble to sit like Jove that [than] to fly like Mercury—let us not therefore go hurrying about and collecting honey-bee like, buzzing here and there impatiently from a knowledge of what is to be arrived at: but let us open our leaves like a flower and be passive and receptive—budding patiently under the eye of Apollo and taking hints from every noble insect that favors us with a visit—sap will be given us for Meat and dew for drink—I was led into these thoughts, my dear Reynolds, by the beauty of the morning operating on a sense of Idleness—I have not read any Books—the Morning said I was right— I had no Idea but of the Morning and the Thrush said I was right—seeming to say—

'O thou whose face hath felt the Winter's wind;
    Whose eye has seen the Snow clouds hung in Mist
And the black-elm tops 'mong the freezing Stars
To thee the Spring will be a harvest-time—
O thou whose only book has been the light
Of supreme darkness which thou feddest on
Night after night, when Phœbus was away
To thee the Spring shall be a tripple morn—
O fret not after knowledge—I have none
And yet my song comes native with the warmth
O fret not after knowledge—I have none
And yet the Evening listens—He who saddens
At thought of Idleness cannot be idle,
And he's awake who thinks himself asleep.'

[10] The first lines, respectively, of Keats's "Robin Hood" and "Lines on the Mermaid Tavern," first published in 1820.
[11] Harpsichords. The "2ᵈ book" referred to next would be a copy of the second book of *Endymion*.
[1] *The Tempest*, I, ii, 223.
[2] *Midsummer Night's Dream*, II, i, 175.
[3] Wordsworth's "The Old Cumberland Beggar," l. 77.

Now I am sensible all this is a mere sophistication, however it may neighbour to any truths, to excuse my own indolence—so I will not deceive myself that Man should be equal with jove—but think himself very well off as a sort of scullion-Mercury or even a humble Bee—It is not [no] matter whether I am right or wrong either one way or another, if there is sufficient to lift a little time from your Shoulders.

Your affectionate friend
John Keats—

TO JOHN TAYLOR
27 February 1818

My dear Taylor,

Your alteration strikes me as being a great improvement—the page looks much better. And now I will attend to the Punctuations you speak of—the comma should be at *soberly*, and in the other passage the comma should follow *quiet*.[1] I am extremely indebted to you for this attention and also for your after admonitions—It is a sorry thing for me that any one should have to overcome Prejudices in reading my Verses—that affects me more than any hypercriticism on any particular Passage. In *Endymion* I have most likely but moved into the Go-cart from the leading strings. In Poetry I have a few Axioms, and you will see how far I am from their Centre. 1st I think Poetry should surprise by a fine excess and not by Singularity—it should strike the Reader as a wording of his own highest thoughts, and appear almost a Remembrance—2nd Its touches of Beauty should never be half way therby making the reader breathless instead of content: the rise, the progress, the setting of imagery should like the Sun come natural natural too him—shine over him and set soberly although in magnificence leaving him in the Luxury of twilight—but it is easier to think what Poetry should be than to write it—and this leads me on to another axiom. That if Poetry comes not as naturally as the Leaves to a tree it had better not come at all. However it may be with me I cannot help looking into new countries with 'O for a Muse of fire to ascend!'[2]—If Endymion serves me as a Pioneer perhaps I ought to be content. I have great reason to be content, for thank God I can read and perhaps understand Shakspeare to his depths, and I have I am sure many friends, who, if I fail, will attribute any change in my Life and Temper to Humbleness rather than to Pride—to a cowering under the Wings of great Poets rather

than to a Bitterness that I am not appreciated. I am anxious to get Endymion printed that I may forget it and proceed. I have coppied the 3rd Book and have begun the 4th. On running my Eye over the Proofs—I saw one Mistake I will notice it presently and also any others if there be any—There should be no comma in 'the raft branch down sweeping from a tall Ash top'[3]—I have besides made one or two alteration⟨s⟩ and also altered the 13 Line Page 32 to make sense of it as you will see. I will take care the Printer shall not trip up my Heels—There should be no dash after Dryope in the Line 'Dryope's lone lulling of her child.[4] Remember me to Percy Street.

Your sincere and oblig^d friend
John Keats—
P.S. You shall have a sho[r]t *Preface* in good time—

TO BENJAMIN BAILEY
13 March 1818

My dear Bailey,   Teignmouth[1] Friday

When a poor devil is drowning, it is said he comes thrice to the surface, ere he makes his final sink if however, even at the third rise, he can manage to catch hold of a piece of weed or rock, he stands a fair chance,—as I hope I do now, of being saved. I have sunk twice in our Correspondence, have risen twice and been too idle, or something worse, to extricate myself—I have sunk the third time and just now risen again at this two of the Clock P.M. and saved myself from utter perdition—by beginning this, all drench'd as I am and fresh from the Water—and I would rather endure the present inconvenience of a Wet Jacket, than you should keep a laced one in store for me. Why did I not stop at Oxford in my Way?—How can you ask such a Question? Why did I not promise to do so? Did I not in a Letter to you make a promise to do so? Then how can you be so unreasonable as to ask me why I did not? This is the thing—(for I have been rubbing up my invention; trying several sleights—I first polish'd a cold, felt in it my fingers tried it on the table, but could not pocket it: I tried Chilblains, Rheumatism, Gout, tight Boots, nothing of that sort would do, so this is, as I was going to say, the thing.—I had a Letter from Tom saying how much better he had got, and thinking he had better stop—I went down to prevent his coming up—Will not this do? Turn it which way you like—it is selvaged all round—I have used it these three last

---

[1] Referring to *Endymion*, I, 149 and 247.
[2] See *Henry V*, Prologue, l. 1.

[3] *Endymion*, I, 334–35.
[4] *Endymion*, I, 495.
[1] On the Devonshire coast, where Keats was to remain with his brother Tom from early March until early May.

days to keep out the Abominable Devonshire Weather —by the by you may say what you will of devonshire: the thuth [truth] is, it is a splashy, rainy, misty snowy, foggy, haily floody, muddy, slipshod County—the hills are very beautiful, when you get a sight of 'em—the Primroses are out, but then you are in—the Cliffs are of a fine deep Colour, but then the Clouds are continually vieing with them—The Women like your London People in a sort of negative way—because the native men are the poorest creatures in England—because Government never have thought it worth while to send a recruiting party among them. When I think of Wordswo[r]th's Sonnet 'Vanguard of Liberty! ye Men of Kent!'[2] the degenerated race about me are Pulvis Ipecac. Simplex[3] a strong dose— Were I a Corsair I'd make a descent on the South Coast of Devon, if I did not run the chance of having Cowardice imputed to me: as for the Men they'd run away into the methodist meeting houses, and the Women would be glad of it—Had England been a large devonshire we should not have won the Battle of Waterloo—There are knotted oaks—there are lusty rivulets there are Meadows such as are not—there are vallies of femminine Climate—but there are no thews and Sinews—Moor's Almanack[4] is here a curiosity— A[r]ms Neck and shoulders may at least be⟨e⟩ seen there, and The Ladies read it as some out of the way romance—Such a quelling Power have these thoughts over me, that I fancy the very Air of a deteriorating quality—I fancy the flowers, all precocious, have an Acrasian[5] spell about them—I feel able to beat off the devonshire waves like soap froth—I think it well for the honor of Brittain that Julius Cæsar did not first land in this County—A Devonshirer standing on his native hills is not a distinct object—he does not show against the light—a wolf or two would dispossess him. I like, I love England, I like its strong Men—Give me a "long brown plain" for my Morning so I may meet with some of Edmond Iron side's desendants—Give me a barren mould so I may meet with some shadowing of Alfred in the shape of a Gipsey, a Huntsman or as [a] Shepherd. Scenery is fine—but human nature is finer—The Sward is richer for the tread of a real, nervous, english foot—the eagles nest is finer for the Mountaineer has look'd into it—Are these facts or prejudices? Whatever they are, for them I shall never

be able to relish entirely any devonshire scenery— Homer is very fine, Achilles is fine, Diomed is fine, Shakspeare is fine, Hamlet is fine, Lear is fine, but dwindled englishmen are not fine—Where too the Women are so passable, and have such english names, such as Ophelia, Cordelia &—that they should have such Paramours or rather Imparamours—As for them I cannot, in thought help wishing as did the cruel Emperour,[6] that they had but one head and I might cut it off to deliver them from any horrible Courtesy they may do their undeserving Countrymen—I wonder I meet with no born Monsters—O Devonshire, last night I thought the Moon had dwindled in heaven—I have never had your Sermon[7] from Wordsworth but Mrs Dilke lent it me—You know my ideas about Religion—I do not think myself more in the right than other people and that nothing in this world is proveable. I wish I could enter into all your feelings on the subject merely for one short 10 Minutes and give you a Page or two to your liking. I am sometimes so very sceptical as to think Poetry itself a mere Jack a lanthern to amuse whoever may chance to be struck with its brilliance—As Tradesmen say every thing is worth what it will fetch, so probably every mental pursuit takes its reality and worth from the ardour of the pursuer—being in itself a nothing— Ethereal thing[s] may at least be thus real, divided under three heads—Things real—things semireal— and no things—Things real—such as existences of Sun Moon & Stars and passages of Shakspeare— Things semireal such as Love, the Clouds &c which require a greeting of the Spirit to make them wholly exist—and Nothings which are made Great and dignified by an ardent pursuit—Which by the by stamps the burgundy mark on the bottles of our Minds, insomuch as they are able to "consec[r]ate whate'er they look upon"[8] I have written a Sonnet here of a somewhat collateral nature—so don't imagine it an a propos des bottes.

Four Seasons fill the Measure of the year;
 Four Seasons are there in the mind of Man.
He hath his lusty spring when fancy clear
 Takes in all beauty with an easy span:
He hath his Summer, when luxuriously
 He chews the honied cud of fair spring thoughts,
Till, in his Soul dissolv'd they come to be
 Part of himself. He hath his Autumn ports

---

2 "To the Men of Kent, October, 1803" (1807), l. 1.
3 An emetic medication, hence nauseating (Rollins, citing Sir William Hale-White).
4 Francis Moore (1657–c. 1715) was an astrologer and almanac-maker. His first almanac appeared in 1699.
5 From the enchantress Arcasia of the Bower of Bliss, who seduces men away from heroic and virtuous actions with sensuous indulgence. See *Faerie Queene*, II, xii.

---

6 Caligula. The remark was reported by Suetonius in his *Lives of the Caesars*, Book IV, and was available to Keats in *Spectator* papers 16, 246, and 435.
7 *A Discourse Inscribed to the Memory of Princess Charlotte Augusta* (1817) (Rollins).
8 See Shelley's "Hymn to Intellectual Beauty," ll. 13–14.

And Havens of repose, when his tired wings
  Are folded up, and he content to look
On Mists in idleness: to let fair things
  Pass by unheeded as a threshhold brook.
    He hath his Winter too of pale Misfeature,
    Or else he would forget his mortal nature.

Aye this may be carried—but what am I talking of—it
is an old maxim of mine and of course must be well
known that evey [every] point of thought is the centre
of an intellectual world—the two uppermost thoughts
in a Man's mind are the two poles of his World he
revolves on them and every thing is southward or
northward to him through their means—We take but
three steps from feathers to iron. Now my dear fellow
I must once for all tell you I have not one Idea of the
truth of any of my speculations—I shall never be a
Reasoner because I care not to be in the right, when
retired from bickering and in a proper philosophical
temper—So you must not stare if in any future letter I
endeavour to prove that Appollo as he had a cat gut
string⟨s⟩ to his Lyre used a cats' paw as a Pecten—and
further from said Pecten's reiterated and continual
teasing came the term Hen peck'd. My Brother Tom
desires to be remember'd to you—he has just this
moment had a spitting of blood poor fellow—Remember me to Greig and Whitehed—
                Your affectionate friend
                John Keats—

This truly remarkable letter reveals the central concerns of Keats's mind as he moved beyond the "heart-easing myths" of Endymion *and his early poetry to define the goal of his future poetic career. Bate appropriately makes this the central document for considera- tion in his chapter on "The Emergence of the Modern Poet." At the heart of the letter is Keats's description of the parallel prog- resses of the individual mind and the general "march of intel- lect" through human history.*

The progress of the individual mind is a steady movement away from the "thoughtless" state of childhood, first into "maiden thought," then finally into the "dark corridors" and the bearing of "the burden of the Mystery;" that is, away from a world of innocence and comforting assurances into a confrontation with human suffering and the growth of tragic consciousness. Human history follows a similar pattern, as one "resting place in reasoning" (religious belief or other certainty) after another is supplanted. Thus, Milton's religious beliefs represent the casting off of earlier dogmas; but these beliefs are in turn supplanted by the nakedly humanistic vision, by Wordsworth's "thinking into the human heart." It is at this point, at the birth of the purely secular imagination, that Keats stands, and he questions the nature and possibilities of this new orientation. Among other things, he questions whether Wordsworth truly "martyrs himself to the human heart;" that is, whether the assurances provided by Wordsworth's vision are based on a genuine bearing of the "burden," or are simply another comforting myth thrown up as a "resting place in reasoning."

The response Keats provides to this questioning in his willing- ness to undertake the same journey of exploration, for "until we are sick, we understand not." He also adds the caution that "Wisdom is folly;" one must at all costs avoid resting in any one solution (as he suspects may be the case with Wordsworth), but must repeatedly test any solution by further experience. The great poems of 1818–19, especially Hyperion *and* The Fall of Hyperion, *are the records of that journey of exploration.*

TO J. H. REYNOLDS
3 May 1818

                            Teignmouth May 3ᵈ
My dear Reynolds.
    What I complain of is that I have been in so an
uneasy a state of Mind as not to be fit to write to an
invalid. I cannot write to any length under a dis-guised
feeling. I should have loaded you with an addition of
gloom, which I am sure you do not want. I am now
thank God in a humour to give you a good groats
worth—for Tom, after a Night without a Wink of
sleep, and overburdened with fever, has got up after a
refreshing day sleep and is better than he has been for
a long time; and you I trust have been again round the
Common without any effect but refreshment.—As to
the Matter I hope I can say with Sir Andrew "I have
matter enough in my head"[1] in your favor And now,
in the second place, for I reckon that I have finished
my Imprimis, I am glad you blow up the weather—all
through your letter there is a leaning towards a
climate-curse. and you know what a delicate satisfaction there is in having a vexation anathematized:
one would think there has been growing up for these
last four thousand years, a grandchild Scion of the old
forbidden tree, and that some Modern Eve had just
violated it; and that there was come with double charge,
"Notus and Afer black with thunderous clouds from
Sierra-
⟨Sera⟩leona"[2]—I shall breathe worsted stockings
sooner than I thought for. Tom wants to be in Town—
we will have some such days upon the heath like that of
last summer and why not with the same book: or
what say you to a black Letter Chaucer printed in
1596: aye I've got one huzza! I shall have it bounden
gothique a nice sombre binding—it will go a little
way to unmodernize. And also I see no reason, because
I have been away this last month, why I should not
have a peep at your Spencerian[3]—notwithstanding

---

[1] See *Merry Wives of Windsor*, I, i, 127.
[2] *Paradise Lost*, X, 702–703. The passage refers to one of the "changes on sea and land" that were to characterize the physical universe after the fall of Adam and Eve.
[3] Referring to Reynolds' poem in Spenserian stanzas "The Romance of Youth," first published in his collection *The Gar- den of Florence* (1821).

you speak of your office, in my thought a little too early, for I do not see why a Mind like yours is not capable of harbouring and digesting the whole Mystery of Law as easily as Parson Hugh does Pepins[4]—which did not hinder him from his poetic Canary—Were I to study physic or rather Medicine again,—I feel it would not make the least difference in my Poetry; when the Mind is in its infancy a Bias is ⟨in⟩ in reality a Bias, but when we have acquired more strength, a Bias becomes no Bias. Every department of knowledge we see excellent and calculated towards a great whole. I am so convinced of this, that I am glad at not having given away my medical Books, which I shall again look over to keep alive the little I know thitherwards; and moreover intend through you and Rice to become a sort of Pip-civilian.[5] An extensive knowlege is needful to thinking people—it takes away the heat and fever; and helps, by widening speculation, to ease the Burden of the Mystery:[6] a thing I begin to understand a little, and which weighed upon you in the most gloomy and true sentence in your Letter. The difference of high Sensations with and without knowledge appears to me this—in the latter case we are falling continually ten thousand fathoms deep and being blown up again without wings and with all [the] horror of a bare ⟨Case⟩ shoulderd Creature—in the former case, our shoulders are fledge⟨d⟩, and we go thro' the same air ⟨Fir⟩ and space without fear. This is running onc's rigs on the score of abstracted benefit—when we come to human Life and the affections it is impossible how a parallel of breast and head can be drawn—(you will treading forgive me for thus privately ⟨heading⟩ out [of] my tread depth and take it for treading as schoolboys ⟨head⟩ the water⟨s⟩)—it is impossible to know how far knowlege us will console ⟨as⟩ for the death of a friend and the ill "that flesh is heir to⟨o⟩[7]—With respect to the affections and Poetry you must know by a sympathy my thoughts that way; and I dare say these few lines will be but a ratification: I wrote them on May-day—and intend to finish the ode all in good time.—

Mother of Hermes! and still youthful Maia!
    May I sing to thee

As thou wast hymned on the shores of Baiæ?
    Or may I woo thee
In earlier Sicilian? or thy smiles
Seek as they once were sought, in Grecian isles,
By Bards who died content in pleasant sward,
Leaving great verse unto a little clan?
O give me their old vigour, and unheard,
Save of the quiet Primrose, and the span//
Of Heaven, and few ears// rounded by thee
My song should die away// content as ⟨this⟩ theirs//
Rich in the simple worship of a day.—//

You may be anxious to know for fact to what sentence in your Letter I allude. You say "I fear there is little chance of any thing else in this life." You seem by that to have been going through with a more painful zest and acute ⟨test⟩ the same labyrinth that I have—I have come to the same conclusion thus far. My Branchings out therefrom have been numerous: one of them is the consideration of Wordsworth's genius and as a help, in the manner of gold being the meridian Line of worldly wealth,—how he differs from Milton.— And here I have nothing but surmises, from an uncertainty whether Miltons apparently less anxiety for Humanity proceeds from his seeing further or no than Wordsworth: And whether Wordsworth has in truth epic passion⟨s⟩, and martyrs himself to the human heart, the main region of his song[8]—In regard to his genius alone—we find what he says true as far as we have experienced and we can judge no further but by larger experience—for axioms in philosophy are not axioms until they are proved upon our pulses: We read fine——things but never feel them to thee full until we have gone the same steps as the Author.— I know this is not plain; you will know exactly my meaning when I say, that now I shall relish Hamlet more than I ever have done—Or, better—You are sensible no man can set down Venery as a bestial or joyless thing until he is sick of it and therefore all philosophizing on it would be mere wording. Until we are sick, we understand not;—in fine, as Byron says, "Knowledge is Sorrow";[9] and I go on to say that "Sorrow is Wisdom"—and further for aught we can know for certainty! "Wisdom is folly"—So you see how I have run away from Wordsworth, and Milton; and shall still run away from what was in my head, to observe, that some kind of letters are good squares others handsome ovals, and others some orbicular, others spheroid—and why should there not be

---

4 See *Merry Wives of Windsor*, I, ii, 12.
5 Amateur lawyer (Robert Gittings).
6 Wordsworth's "Tintern Abbey," l. 38.
7 *Hamlet*, III, i, 63.

8 See "Prospectus to *The Recluse*," l. 41, published in the preface to *The Excursion* (1814).
9 *Manfred*, I, i, 10.

another species with two rough edges like a Rat-trap? I hope you will find all my long letters of that species, and all will be well; for by merely touching the spring delicately and etherially, the rough edged will fly immediately into a proper compactness, and thus you may make a good wholesome loaf, with your own leven in it, of my fragments—If you cannot find this said Rat-trap sufficiently tractable—alas for me, it being an impossibility in grain for my ink to stain otherwise: If I scribble long letters I must play my vagaries. I must be too heavy, or too light, for whole pages—I must be quaint and free of Tropes and figures—I must play my draughts as I please, and for my advantage and your erudition, crown a white with a black, or a black with a white, and move into black or white, far and near as I please—I must go from Hazlitt to Patmore,[10] and make Wordsworth and Coleman play at leap-frog—or keep one of them down a whole half holiday at fly the garter[11]—"From Gray to Gay, from Little to Shakespeare"[12]—Also as a long cause requires two or more sittings of the Court, so a long letter will require two or more sittings of the Breech wherefore I shall resume after dinner.—

Have you not seen a Gull, an orc, a sea Mew,[13] or any thing to bring this Line to a proper length, and also fill up this clear part; that like the Gull I may *dip*— I hope, not out of sight—and also, like a Gull, I hope to be lucky in a good sized fish—This crossing a letter is not without its association—for chequer work leads us naturally to a Milkmaid, a Milkmaid to Hogarth Hogarth to Shakespeare Shakespear to Hazlitt— Hazlitt to Shakespeare and thus by merely pulling an apron string we set a pretty peal of Chimes at work— Let them chime on while, with your patience,—I will return to Wordsworth—whether or no he has an extended vision or a circumscribed grandeur— whether is is an eagle in his nest, or on the wing—And to be more explicit and to show you how tall I stand by the giant, I will put down a simile of human life as far as I now perceive it; that is, to the point to which I say we both have arrived at—' Well—I compare human life to a large Mansion of Many Apartments, two of which I can only describe, the doors of the rest being as yet shut upon me—The first we step into we

call the infant or thoughtless Chamber, in which we remain as long as we do not think—We remain there a long while, and notwithstanding the doors of the second Chamber remain wide open, showing a bright appearance, we care not to hasten to it; but are at length imperceptibly impelled by the awakening of the thinking principle—within us—we no sooner get into the second Chamber, which I shall call the Chamber of Maiden-Thought, than we become intoxicated with the light and the atmosphere, we see nothing but pleasant wonders, and think of delaying there for ever in delight: However among the effects this breathing is father of is that tremendous one of heart
sharpening one's vision into the ⟨head⟩ and nature of Man—of convincing ones nerves that the World is full of Misery and Heartbreak, Pain, Sickness and oppression—whereby This Chamber of Maiden Thought becomes gradually darken'd and at the same time on all sides of it many doors are set open—but all dark—all leading to dark passages—We see not the ballance of good and evil. We are in a Mist—*We* are now in that state—We feel the "burden of the Mystery," To this point was Wordsworth come, as far as I can conceive when he wrote 'Tintern Abbey' and it seems to me that his Genius is explorative of those dark Passages. Now if we live, and go on thinking, we too shall explore them. he is a Genius and superior [to] us, in so far as he can, more than we, make discoveries, and shed a light in them—Here I must think Wordsworth is deeper than Milton—though I think it has depended more upon the general and gregarious advance of intellect, than individual greatness of Mind—From the Paradise Lost and the other Works of Milton, I hope it is not too presuming, even between ourselves to say, his Philosophy, human and divine, may be tolerably understood by one not much advanced in years, In his time englishmen were just emancipated from a great superstition—and Men had got hold of certain points and resting places in reasoning which were too newly born to be doubted, and too opposed
much ⟨oppressed⟩ by the Mass of Europe not to be thought etherial and authentically divine—who could gainsay his ideas on virtue, vice, and Chastity in Comus, just at the time of the dismissal of Cod-pieces and a hundred other disgraces? who would not rest satisfied with his hintings at good and evil in the Paradise Lost, when just free from the inquisition and burrning in Smithfield?[14] The Reformation produced such immediate and great⟨s⟩ benefits, that Protestant-

---

[10] Peter George Patmore (1786–1855), journalist and author, intimate friend of Lamb and Hazlitt. P. G. Patmore was the father of Coventry Patmore. The Colèman next mentioned is George Colman the younger (1762–1836), playwright and theatrical manager.

[11] "A game in which the players leap from one side of a 'garter' or line of stones over the back of one of their number" (*Oxford English Dictionary*).

[12] See Pope's *Essay on Man*, IV, 380. "Thomas Little" was the pseudonym for the poet Thomas Moore.

[13] See *Paradise Lost*, XI, 835.

---

[14] In the sixteenth century, a place of execution for heretics just outside the walls of London.

ism was considered under the immediate eye of heaven, and its own remaining Dogmas and superstitions, then, as it were, regenerated, constituted those resting places and seeming sure points of Reasoning—from that I have mentioned, Milton, whatever he may have thought in the sequel, appears to have been content with these by his writings—He did not think into the human heart, as Wordsworth has done—Yet Milton as a Philosop⟨h⟩er, had sure as great powers as Wordsworth—What is then to be inferr'd? O many things—It proves there is really a grand march of intellect—, It proves that a mighty providence subdues the mightiest Minds to the service of the time being, whether it be in human Knowledge or Religion—I have often pitied a Tutor who has to hear "Nomᵉ: Musa"—so often dinn'd into his ears—I hope you may not have the same pain in this scribbling—I may have read these things before, but I never had even a thus dim perception of them; and moreover I like to say my lesson to one who will endure my tediousness for my own sake—After all there is certainly something real in the World—Moore's [15] present to Hazlitt is real—I like that Moore, and am glad ⟨that⟩ I saw him at the Theatre just before I left Town. Tom has spit a leetle blood this afternoon, and that is rather a damper—but I know—the truth is there is something real in the World Your third Chamber of Life shall be a lucky and a gentle one—stored with the wine of love—and the Bread of Friendship—When you see George if he should not have recēd a letter from me tell him he will find one at home most likely—tell Bailey I hope soon to see him—Remember me to all The leaves have been out here, for MONY a day—I have written to George for the first stanzas of my Isabel—I shall have them soon and will copy the whole out for you.

Your affectionate friend
John Keats.

Keats's first report from a walking trip to the Lake District and Scotland undertaken with Charles Armitage Brown. They had set out on June 22 from London in company with George Keats and his bride Georgiana, who were emigrating to America and were to sail from Liverpool.

TO TOM KEATS
25–27 June 1818

Here beginneth my journal, this Thursday, the 25th day of June, Anno Domini 1818. This morning

15 Peter Moore (1753–1828), member of parliament and one of the managers of the Drury Lane Theatre (Louis A. Holman).

we arose at 4, and set off in a Scotch mist; put up once under a tree, and in fine, have walked wet and dry to this place, called in the vulgar tongue Endmoor, 17 miles; we have not been incommoded by our knapsacks; they serve capitally, and we shall go on very well.

June 26—I merely put *pro forma*, for there is no such thing as time and space, which by the way came forcibly upon me on seeing for the first hour the Lake and Mountains of Winander—I cannot describe them—they surpass my expectation—beautiful water—shores and islands green to the marge—mountains all round up to the clouds. We set out from Endmoor this morning, breakfasted at Kendal with a soldier who had been in all the wars for the last seventeen years—then we have walked to Bowne's [Bowness] to dinner—said Bowne's situated on the Lake where we have just dined, and I am writing at this present. I took an oar to one of the islands to take up some trout for dinner, which they keep in porous boxes. I enquired of the waiter for Wordsworth—he said he knew him, and that he had been here a few days ago, canvassing for the Lowthers. What think you of that—Wordsworth versus Brougham!! [1] Sad—sad—sad—and yet the family has been his friend always. What can we say? We are now about seven miles from Rydale, [2] and expect to see him to-morrow. You shall hear all about our visit.

There are many disfigurements to this Lake—not in the way of land or water. No; the two views we have had of it are of the most noble tenderness—they can never fade away—they make one forget the divisions of life; age, youth, poverty and riches; and refine one's sensual vision into a sort of north star which can never cease to be open lidded and stedfast over the wonders of the great Power. The disfigurement I mean is the miasma of London. I do suppose it contaminated with bucks and soldiers, and women of fashion—and hatband ignorance. The border inhabitants are quite out of keeping with the romance about them, from a continual intercourse with London rank and fashion. But why should I grumble? They let me have a prime glass of soda water—O they are as good as their neighbors. But Lord Wordsworth, instead of being in retirement, has himself and his house full in the thick of fashionable visitors quite convenient to be pointed at all the summer long. When we had gone about half this morning, we began to get among the hills and to

1 Henry Brougham (1778–1868), politician and radical reformer, was contesting one of the two seats in Parliament for Westmorland County held by the Tories Lord Lowther and Colonel Henry Lowther.
2 Rydal Mount had been Wordsworth's home from 1813.

see the mountains grow up before us—the other half brought us to Wynandermere, 14 miles to dinner. The weather is capital for the views, but is now rather misty, and we are in doubt whether to walk to Ambleside to tea—it is five miles along the borders of the Lake. Loughrigg will swell up before us all the way—I have an amazing partiality for mountains in the clouds. There is nothing in Devon like this, and Brown says there is nothing in Wales to be compared to it. I must tell you, that in going through Cheshire and Lancashire, I saw the Welsh mountains at a distance. We have passed the two castles, Lancaster and Kendal. 27th—We walked here to Ambleside yesterday along the border of Winandermere all beautiful with wooded shores and Islands—our road was a winding lane, wooded on each side, and green overhead, full of Foxgloves—every now and then a glimpse of the Lake, and all the while Kirkstone and other large hills nestled together in a sort of grey black mist. Ambleside is at the northern extremity of the Lake. We arose this morning at six, because we call it a day of rest, having to call on Wordsworth who lives only two miles hence—before breakfast we went to see the Ambleside water fall. The morning beautiful—the walk easy among the hills. We, I may say, fortunately, missed the direct path, and after wandering a little, found it out by the noise—for, mark you, it is buried in trees, in the bottom of the valley—the stream itself is interesting throughout with "mazy error over pendant shades."[3] Milton meant a smooth river—this is buffetting all the way on a rocky bed ever various—but the waterfall itself, which I came suddenly upon, gave me a pleasant twinge. First we stood a little below the head about half way down the first fall, buried deep in trees, and saw it streaming down two more descents to the depth of near fifty feet—then we went on a jut of rock nearly level with the second fall-head, where the first fall was above us, and the third below our feet still—at the same time we saw that the water was divided by a sort of cataract island on whose other side burst out a glorious stream—then the thunder and the freshness. At the same time the different falls have as different characters; the first darting down the slate-rock like an arrow; the second spreading out like a fan—the third dashed into a mist—and the one on the other side of the rock a sort of mixture of all these. We afterwards moved away a space, and saw nearly the whole more mild, streaming silverly through the trees. What astonishes me more than any thing is the tone, the coloring, the slate, the stone, the moss, the rock-weed; or, if I may so say, the intellect, the countenance

of such places. The space, the magnitude of mountains and waterfalls are well imagined before one sees them; but this countenance or intellectual tone must surpass every imagination and defy any remembrance. I shall learn poetry here and shall henceforth write more than ever, for the abstract endeavor of being able to add a mite to that mass of beauty which is harvested from these grand materials, by the finest spirits, and put into etherial existence for the relish of one's fellows. I cannot think with Hazlitt that these scenes make man appear little. I never forgot my stature so completely[4]—I live in the eye; and my imagination, surpassed, is at rest—We shall see another waterfall near Rydal to which we shall proceed after having put these letters in the post office. I long to be at Carlisle, as I expect there a letter from George and one from you. Let any of my friends see my letters—they may not be interested in descriptions—descriptions are bad at all times—I did not intend to give you any; but how can I help it? I am anxious you should taste a little of our pleasure; it may not be an unpleasant thing, as you have not the fatigue. I am well in health. Direct henceforth to Port Patrick till the 12th July. Content that probably three or four pair of eyes whose owners I am rather partial to will run over these lines I remain; and moreover that I am your affectionate brother John.

Richard Woodhouse (1788–1834) was the legal advisor to Keats's publishers, Taylor & Hessey. A great admirer of Keats, he made meticulous transcripts of all of his unpublished poems and letters he could secure, several of these copies now being the only surviving texts of the works contained in them.

TO RICHARD WOODHOUSE
27 October 1818

My dear Woodhouse,

Your Letter gave me a great satisfaction; more on account of its friendliness, than any relish of that matter in it which is accounted so acceptable in the 'genus irritabile'[1] The best answer I can give you is in a clerklike manner to make some observations on

---

3 See *Paradise Lost*, IV, 239.

4 The remark has particular meaning, since at full growth Keats was just barely over five feet tall. On several occasions he had revealed his sensitivity to his "little stature," especially in the eyes of women.

1 'genus irritabile': "The irritable race [of poets]," (irritable in being anxious for praise and acutely sensitive to criticism). Horace, *Epistles*, II, ii, 102. Keats writes in answer to a letter of October 21, in which Woodhouse urged him to persist in his poetic ambitions despite the hostile review of *Endymion* in the *Quarterly Review* (see pp. 794–96), and hailed him as the poetic hope of the age.

two principle points, which seem to point like indices into the midst of the whole pro and con, about genius, and views and atchievements and ambition and cœtera. 1st As to the poetical Character itself, (I mean that sort of which, if I am any thing, I am a Member; that sort distinguished from the wordsworthian or egotistical sublime; which is a thing per se and stands alone 2) it is not itself—it has no self—it is every thing and nothing—It has no character—it enjoys light and shade; it lives in gusto, be it foul or fair, high or low, rich or poor, mean or elevated—It has as much delight in conceiving an Iago as an Imogen. What shocks the virtuous philosop[h]er, delights the camelion Poet. It does no harm from its relish of the dark side of things any more than from its taste for the bright one; because they both end in speculation. A Poet is the most unpoetical of any thing in existence; because he has no Identity—he is continually in for [informing]—and filling some other Body—The Sun, the Moon, the Sea and Men and Women who are creatures of impulse are poetical and have about them an unchangeable attribute—the poet has none; no identity—he is certainly the most unpoetical of all God's Creatures. If then he has no self, and if I am a Poet, where is the Wonder that I should say I would ⟨right⟩ no more? Might I not at that very instant [have] been cogitating on the Characters of saturn and Ops? 3 It is a wretched thing to confess; but is a very fact that not one word I ever utter can be taken for granted as an opinion growing out of my identical nature—how can it, when I have no nature? When I am in a room with People if I ever am free from speculating on creations of my own brain, then not myself goes home to myself: but the identity of every one in the room begins to [so] to press upon me that, I am in a very little time anhilated—not only among Men; it would be the same in a Nursery of children: I know not whether I make myself wholly understood: I hope enough so to let you see that no dependence is to be placed on what I said that day.

In the second place I will speak of my views, and of the life I purpose to myself—I am ambitious of doing the world some good: if I should be spared that may be the work of maturer years—in the interval I will assay to reach to as high a summit in Poetry as the nerve bestowed upon me will suffer. The faint conceptions I have of Poems to come brings the blood frequently into my forehead—All I hope is that I may not lose all interest in human affairs—that the solitary

indifference I feel for applause even from the finest Spirits, will not blunt any acuteness of vision I may have. I do not think it will—I feel assured I should write from the mere yearning and fondness I have for the Beautiful even if my night's labours should be burnt every morning and no eye ever shine upon them. But even now I am perhaps not speaking from myself; but from some character in whose soul I now live. I am sure however that this next sentence is from myself. I feel your anxiety, good opinion and friendliness in the highest degree, and am

Your's most sincerely
John Keats

F R O M

TO GEORGE AND GEORGIANA KEATS[1]

14, 19 February, 3 (?), 12, 13, 17, 19 March, 15, 16, 21, 30 April, 3 May 1819

*   *   *   *   *

[February 19]
. . . A Man's life of any worth is a continual allegory—and very few eyes can see the Mystery of his life—a life like the scriptures, figurative—which such people can no more make out than they can the hebrew Bible. Lord Byron cuts a figure—but he is not figurative—Shakspeare led a life of Allegory; his works are the comments on it—

*   *   *   *   *

Friday [March] *19*th Yesterday I got a black eye—the first time I took a Cr{icket} bat—Brown who is always one's friend in a disaster {app}lied a lee{ch to} the eyelid, and there is no infla{mm}ation this morning though the ball hit me dir{ectl}y on the sight—'t was a white ball—I am glad it was not a clout—This is the second black eye I have had since leaving school—during all my {scho}ol days I never had one at all—we must e{a}t a peck before we die—This morning I am in a sort of temper indolent and supremely careless: I long after a stanza or two of Thompson's Castle of indolence[2]—My passions are all asleep from my having slumbered till nearly eleven and weakened the animal fibre all over me to a delightful sensation about three degrees on this side of faintness—if I had teeth of pearl and the breath of lillies I should call it languor —but as I am + I must call it Laziness—In this

+ especially as I have a black eye.

2 See Shakespeare's *Troilus and Cressida*, I, ii, 15–16.
3 Characters in *Hyperion*, upon which Keats was working at the time of this letter.

1 They were now living in Louisville, Kentucky.
2 Next to *The Seasons*, the best-known poem by the Scottish poet, James Thomson (1700–1748).

state of effeminacy the fibres of the brain are relaxed in common with the rest of the body, and to such a happy degree that pleasure has no show of enticement and pain no unbearable frown. Neither Poetry, nor Ambition, nor Love have any alertness of countenance as they pass by me: they seem rather like three figures on a greek vase—a Man and two women—whom no one but myself could distinguish in their disguisement. This is the only happiness; and is a rare instance of advantage in the body overpowering the Mind. I have this moment received a note from Haslam[3] in which he expects the death of his Father who has been for some time in a state of insensibility—his mother bears up he says very well—I shall go to town tomorrow to see him. This is the world—thus we cannot expect to give way many hours to pleasure—Circumstances are like Clouds continually gathering and bursting—While we are laughing the seed of some trouble is put into ⟨he⟩ the wide arable land of events—while we are laughing it sprouts is [it] grows and suddenly bears a poison fruit which we must pluck—Even so we have leisure to reason on the misfortunes of our friends; our own touch us too nearly for words. Very few men have ever arrived at a complete disinterestedness of Mind: very few have been influenced by a pure desire of the benefit of others—in the greater part of the Benefactors ⟨of⟩ & to Humanity some meretricious motive has sullied their greatness—some melodramatic scenery has facinated them—From the manner in which I feel Haslam's misfortune I perceive how far I am from any humble standard of disinterestedness—Yet this feeling ought to be carried to its highest pitch, as there is no fear of its ever injuring society—which it would do I fear pushed to an extremity—For in wild nature the Hawk would loose his Breakfast of Robins and the Robin his of Worms The Lion must starve as well as the swallow—The greater part of Men make their way with the same instinctiveness, the same unwandering eye from their purposes, the same animal eagerness as the Hawk—The Hawk wants a Mate, so does the Man —look at them both they set about it and procure on[e] in the same manner—They want both a nest and they both set about one in the same manner—they get their food in the same manner—The noble animal Man for his amusement smokes his pipe—the Hawk balances about the Clouds—that is the only difference of their leisures. This it is that makes the Amusement of Life— to a speculative Mind. I go among the Feilds and catch a glimpse of a stoat or a fieldmouse peeping out of the withered grass—the creature hath a purpose and its eyes are bright with it—I go amongst the buildings

of a city and I see a Man hurrying along—to what? The Creature has a purpose and his eyes are bright with it. But then as Wordsworth says, "we have all one human heart"[4]—there is an ellectric fire in human nature tending to purify—so that among these human creature[s] there is continually some birth of new hero- ism—The pity is that we must wonder at it: as we should at finding a pearl in rubbish—I have no doubt that thousands of people never heard of have had hearts comp[l]etely disinterested: I can remember but two—Socrates and Jesus—their Histories evince it— What I heard a little time ago, Taylor observe with respect to Socrates, may be said of Jesus—That he was so great a⟨s⟩ man that though he transmitted no writing of his own to posterity, we have his Mind and his sayings and his greatness handed to us by others. It is to be lamented that the history of the latter was written and revised by Men interested in the pious frauds of Religion. Yet through all this I see his splen- dour. Even here though I myself am pursueing the same instinctive course as the veriest human animal you can think of—I am however young writing at random—straining at particles of light in the midst of a great darkness—without knowing the bearing of any one assertion of any one opinion. Yet may I not in this be free from sin? May there not be superior beings amused with any graceful, though instinctive attitude my mind my [may] fall into, as I am entertained with the alertness of a Stoat or the anxiety of a Deer? Though a quarrel in the streets is a thing to be hated, the energies displayed in it are fine; the commonest Man shows a grace in his quarrel—By a superior being our reasoning[s] may take the same tone—though er- roneous they may be fine—This is the very thing in which consists poetry; and if so it is not so fine a thing as philosophy—For the same reason that an eagle is not so fine a thing as a truth—Give me this credit— Do you not think I strive—to know myself? Give me this credit—and you will not think that on my own accou[n]t I repeat Milton's lines

> "How charming is divine Philosophy
> Not harsh and crabbed as dull fools suppose
> But musical as is Apollo's lute"—[5]

No—no for myself—feeling grateful as I do to have got into a state of mind to relish them properly— Nothing ever becomes real till it is experienced—Even a Proverb is no proverb to you till your Life has illus- trated it—I am ever affraid that your anxiety for me will lead you to fear for the violence of my tempera- ment continually smothered down: for that reason I

---

3 William Haslam was a young lawyer and generous friend to Keats since 1816.

4 "The Old Cumberland Beggar," l. 153.
5 Comus, ll. 475–77.

did not intend to have sent you the following sonnet—but look over the two last pages and ask yoúrselves whether I have not that in me which will well bear the buffets of the world. It will be the best comment on my sonnet; it will show you that it was written with no Agony but that of ignorance; with no thirst of any thing but knowledge when pushed to the point though the first steps to it were throug[h] my human passions —they went away, and I wrote with my Mind—and perhaps I must confess a little bit of my heart—

Why did I laugh tonight ? No voice will tell:
   No God, no Deamon of severe response
Deigns to reply from heaven or from Hell.—
   Then to my human heart I turn at once—
Heart! thou and I are here sad and alone;
   Say, wherefore did I laugh ? O mortal pain!
O Darkness! Darkness! ever must I moan
   To question Heaven and Hell and Heart in vain!
Why did I laugh ? I know this being's lease
   My fancy to its utmost blisses spreads:
Yet could I on this very midnight cease,
   And the world's gaudy ensigns see in shreds.
Verse, fame and Beauty are intense indeed
But Death intenser—Deaths is Life's high mead."

*   *   *   *   *

[April 15]
. . . Last Sunday I took a Walk towards highgate and in the lane that winds by the side of Lord Mansfield's park I met M[r] Green[6] our Demonstrator at Guy's in conversation with Coleridge—I joined them, after enquiring by a look whether it would be agreeable—I walked with him a[t] his alderman-after dinner pace for near two miles I suppose In those two Miles he broached a thousand things—let me see if I can give you a list—Nightingales, Poetry—on Poetical sensation—Metaphysics—Different genera and species of
                         by
Dreams—Nightmare—a dream accompanied ⟨with⟩ a sense of touch—single and double touch—A dream related—First and second consciousness—the difference explained between will and Volition—so my [many] metaphysicians from a want of smoking the second consciousness—Monsters—the Kraken[7]—Mermaids—southey believes in them—southeys belief too much diluted—A Ghost story—Good morning —I heard his voice as he came towards me—I heard it as he moved away—I had heard it all the interval—

if it may be called so. He was civil enough to ask me to call on him at Highgate Good Night!

*   *   *   *   *

[April 21]
I have been reading lately two very different books Robertson's America and Voltaire's Siecle De Louis xiv[8] It is like walking arm and arm between Pizarro and the great-little Monarch. In How lementabl[e] a case do we see the great body of the people in both instances: in the first, where Men might seem to inherit quiet of Mind from unsophisticated senses; from uncontamination of civilisation; and especially from their being as it were estranged from the mutual helps of Society and its mutual injuries—and thereby more immediately under the Protection of Providence— even there they had mortal pains to bear as bad; or even worse than Baliffs, Debts and Poverties of civilised Life—The whole appears to resolve into this—that Man is originally 'a poor forked creature'[9] subject to the same mischances as the beasts of the forest, destined to hardships and disquietude of some kind or other. If he improves by degrees his bodily accomodations and comforts—at each stage, at each accent there are waiting for him a fresh set of annoyances—he is mortal and there is still a heaven with its Stars abov[e] his head. The most interesting question that can come before us is, How far by the persevering endeavours of a seldom appearing Socrates Mankind may be made happy—I can imagine such happiness carried to an extreme—but what must it end in?— Death—and who could in such a case bear with death— the whole troubles of life which are now frittered away in a series of years, would the[n] be accumulated for the last days of a being who instead of hailing its approach, would leave this world as Eve left Paradise— But in truth I do not at all believe in this sort of perfectibility—the nature of the world will not admit of it—the inhabitants of the world will correspond to itself—Let the fish philosophise the ice away from the Rivers in winter time and they shall be at continual play in the tepid delight of summer. Look at the Poles and at the sands of Africa, Whirlpools and volcanoes— Let men exterminate them and I will say that they may arrive at earthly Happiness—The point at which Man may arrive is as far as the paralel state in inanimate nature and no further—For instance suppose a rose to have sensation, it blooms on a beautiful morning it enjoys itself—but there comes a cold wind, a hot sun—it can not escape it, it cannot destroy its annoy-

---

6 Joseph Henry Green (1791–1863), a surgeon, was Coleridge's close friend and literary executor. In 1813, Green had been appointed Demonstrator of Anatomy at St. Thomas's Hospital, joint medical school with Guy's Hospital where Keats studied.

7 A fabulous sea-monster, supposed to inhabit the North Sea.

8 William Robertson's *The History of America* (1777); Voltaire's *Siècle de Louis XIV* (1751).

9 *King Lear*, III, iv, 112–13.

ances—they are as native to the world as itself: no more can man be happy in spite, the world[l]y elements will prey upon his nature—The common cognomen of this world among the misguided and superstitious is 'a vale of tears' from which we are to be redeemed by a certain arbitary interposition of God and taken to Heaven—What a little circumscribe[d] straightened notion! Call the world if you Please "The vale of Soul-making" Then you will find out the use of the world (I am speaking now in the highest terms for human nature admitting it to be immortal which I will here take for granted for the purpose of showing a thought which has struck me concerning it) I say 'Soul making' Soul as distinguished from an Intelligence—There may be intelligences or sparks of the divinity in millions—but they are not Souls ⟨the⟩ till they acquire identities, till each one is personally itself. I[n]telligences are atoms of perception—they know and they see and they are pure, in short they are God— how then are Souls to be made? How then are these sparks which are God to have identity given them— so as ever to possess a bliss peculiar to each ones individual existence? How, but by the medium of a world like this? This point I sincerely wish to consider because I think it is a grander system of salvation than the chryst⟨e⟩ain religion—or rather it is a system of Spirit-creation—This is effected by three grand materials acting the one upon the other for a series of years—These three Materials are the *Intelligence*—the *human heart* (as distinguished from intelligence or Mind) and the *World* or *Elemental space* suited for the proper action of *Mind and Heart* on each other for the purpose of forming the *Soul* or *Intelligence destined to possess the sense of Identity*. I can scarcely express what I but dimly perceive—and yet I think I perceive it— that you may judge the more clearly I will put it in the most homely form possible—I will call the *world* a School instituted for the purpose of teaching little children to read—I will call the *human heart* the *horn Book* used in that School—and I will call the *Child able to read, the Soul* made from that *school* and its *hornbook*. Do you not see how necessary a World of Pains and troubles is to school an Intelligence and make it a soul? A Place where the heart must feel and suffer in a thousand diverse ways! Not merely is the Heart a Hornbook, It is the Minds Bible, it is the Minds experience, it is the teat from which the Mind or intelligence sucks its identity—As various as the Lives of Men are—so various become their souls, and thus does God make individual beings, Souls, Identical Souls of the sparks of his own essence—This appears to me a faint sketch of a system of Salvation which does not affront our reason and humanity—I am convinced that many difficulties which christians labour under would

vanish before it—There is one wh[i]ch even now Strikes me—the Salvation of Children—In them the Spark or intelligence returns to God without any identity—it having had no time to learn of, and be altered by, the heart—or seat of the human Passions— It is pretty generally suspected that the chr[i]stian scheme has been coppied from the ancient persian and greek Philosophers. Why may they not have made this simple thing even more simple for common apprehension by introducing Mediators and Personages in the same manner as in the hethen mythology abstractions are personified—Seriously I think it probable that this System of Soul-making—may have been the Parent of all the more palpable and personal Schemes of Redemption, among the Zoroastrians the Christians and the Hindoos. For as one part of the human species must have their carved Jupiter; so another part must have the palpable and named Mediator and saviour, their Christ their Oromanes [10] and their Vishnu—If what I have said should not be plain enough, as I fear it may not be, I will but [put] you in the place where I began in this series of thoughts—I mean, I began by seeing how man was formed by circumstances—and what are circumstances?—but touchstones of his heart—? and what are touchstones?—but proovings of his hearrt?—and what are proovings of his heart but fortifiers or alterers of his nature? and what is his altered nature but his soul?—and what was his soul before it came into the world and had These provings and alterations and perfectionings?—An intelligence⟨s⟩—without Identity—and how is this Identity to be made? Through the medium of the Heart? And how is the heart to become this Medium but in a world of Circumstances?—There now I think what with Poetry and Theology you may thank your Stars that my pen is not very long winded—

*		*		*		*		*

Keats met Fanny Brawne (1800–1865) sometime in the summer or fall of 1818. In December of that year they had acknowledged their love for each other, but did not become engaged until October 1819. Keats's continued financial uncertainties and his developing illness prevented their union and produced the greatest frustration and unhappiness of his personal life. For a balanced and touching view of Fanny Brawne and her relationship with Keats, see John Middleton Murry's Keats *(New York: Noonday Press, 1955), pp. 19–81.*

10 In "Sir Charles Morell's" [James Ridley's] *Tales of the Genii* (1764), the search for "the Talisman of Oromanes," an imagined source of perfect happiness, sends a wealthy merchant on a long and fruitless quest. Vishnu was "the Preserver" in Hindu theology.

TO FANNY BRAWNE
1 July 1819

Shanklin,
Isle of Wight, Thursday.

My dearest Lady,

I am glad I had not an opportunity of sending off a Letter which I wrote for you on Tuesday night—'twas too much like one out of Ro[u]sseau's Heloise. I am more reasonable this morning. The morning is the only proper time for me to write to a beautiful Girl whom I love so much: for at night, when the lonely day has closed, and the lonely, silent, unmusical Chamber is waiting to receive me as into a Sepulchre, then believe me my passion gets entirely the sway, then I would not have you see those Rapsodies which I once thought it impossible I should ever give way to, and which I have often laughed at in another, for fear you should [think me] either too unhappy or perhaps a little mad. I am now [1] at a very pleasant Cottage window, looking onto a beautiful hilly country, with a glimpse of the sea; the morning is very fine. I do not know how elastic my spirit might be, what pleasure I might have in living here and breathing and wandering as free as a stag about this beautiful Coast if the remembrance of you did not weigh so upon me. I have never known any unalloy'd Happiness for many days together: the death or sickness of some one has always spoilt my hours—and now when none such troubles oppress me, it is you must confess very hard that another sort of pain should haunt me. Ask yourself my love whether you are not very cruel to have so entrammelled me, so destroyed my freedom. Will you confess this in the Letter you must write immediately and do all you can to console me in it—make it rich as a draught of poppies to intoxicate me—write the softest words and kiss them that I may at least touch my lips where yours have been. For myself I know not how to express my devotion to so fair a form: I want a brighter word than bright, a fairer word than fair. I almost wish we were butterflies and liv'd but three summer days—three such days with you I could fill with more delight than fifty common years could ever contain. But however selfish I may feel, I am sure I could never act selfishly: as I told you a day or two before I left Hampstead, I will never return to London if my Fate does not turn up Pam or at least a Court-card.[2] Though I could centre my Happiness in you, I cannot expect to engross your heart so entirely—indeed if I thought

---

you felt as much for me as I do for you at this moment I do not think I could restrain myself from seeing you again tomorrow for the delight of one embrace. But no—I must live upon hope and Chance. In case of the worst that can happen, I shall still love you—but what hatred shall I have for another! Some lines I read the other day are continually ringing a peal in my ears:

> To see those eyes I prize above mine own
> Dart favors on another—
> And those sweet lips (yielding immortal nectar)
> Be gently press'd by any but myself—
> Think, think Francesca, what a cursed thing
> It were beyond expression![3]

Do write immediately. There is no Post from this Place, so you must address Post Office, Newport, Isle of Wight. I know before night I shall curse myself for having sent you so cold a Letter; yet it is better to do it as much as in my senses as possible. Be as kind as the distance will permit to your

J. Keats.

Present my Compliments to your mother, my love to Margaret and best remembrances to your Brother—if you please so.

TO FANNY BRAWNE
8 July 1819

July 8th

My sweet Girl,

Your Letter gave me more delight, than any thing in the world but yourself could do; indeed I am almost astonished that any absent one should have that luxurious power over my senses which I feel. Even when I am not thinking of you I receive your influence and a tenderer nature steeling upon me. All my thoughts, my unhappiest days and nights have I find not a⟨l⟩t all cured me of my love of Beauty, but made it so intense that I am miserable that you are not with me: or rather breathe in that dull sort of patience that cannot be called Life. I never knew before, what such a love as you have made me feel, was; I did not believe in it; my Fancy was affraid of it, lest it should burn me up. But if you will fully love me, though there may be some fire, 't will not be more than we can bear when moistened and bedewed with Pleasures. You mention 'horrid people' and ask me whether it depend upon them, whether I see you again—Do understand me, my love, in this—I have so much of you in my heart that I must turn Mentor when I see a chance of ha[r]m beffaling

---

[1] He had gone to the Isle of Wight in order to write and thereby improve his desperate financial situation.

[2] In the five-card game of loo, Pam (knave of clubs) was the highest trump. A Court-card was any face card.

[3] See Philip Massinger's *The Duke of Milan* (1623), I, iii.

you. I would never see any thing but Pleasure in your eyes, love on your lips, and Happiness in your steps. I would wish to see you among those amusements suitable to your inclinations and spirits; so that our loves might be a delight in the midst of Pleasures agreeable enough, rather than a resource from vexations and cares—But I doubt much, in case of the worst, whether I shall be philosopher enough to follow my own Lessons: if I saw my resolution give you a pain I could not. Why may I not speak of your Beauty, since without that I could never have lov'd you—I cannot conceive any beginning of such love as I have for you but Beauty. There may be a sort of love for which, without the least sneer at it, I have the highest respect, and can admire it in others: but it has not the richness, the bloom, the full form, the enchantment of love after my own heart. So let me speak of you Beauty, though to my own endangering; if you could be so cruel to me as to try elsewhere its Power. You say you are affraid I shall think you do not love me—in saying this you make me ache the more to be near you. I am at the diligent use of my faculties here, I do not pass a day without sprawling some blank verse or tagging some rhymes; and here I must confess, that, (since I am on that subject,) I love you the more in that I believe you have liked me for my own sake and for nothing else—I have met ⟨wht⟩ with women whom I really think would like to be married to a Poem and to be given away by a Novel. I have seen your Comet,[1] and only wish it was a sign that poor Rice[2] would get well whose illness makes him rather a melancholy companion: and the more so as so to conquer his feelings and hide them from me, with a forc'd Pun. I kiss'd your writing over in the hope you had indulg'd me by leaving a trace of honey—What was your dream? Tell it me and I will tell you the interpretation thereof.

Ever yours my love!
John Keats—

Do not accuse me of delay—we have not here an opportunity of sending letters every day—Write speedily—

F R O M

TO FANNY BRAWNE
25 July 1819

Sunday Night.

My sweet Girl,

I hope you did not blame me much for not obeying your request of a Letter on Saturday: we have had

---

[1] The first comet observed in England since 1811 had appeared July 3, 1819.
[2] James Rice, Jr. (see p. 769).

four in our small room playing at cards night and morning leaving me no undisturb'd opportunity to write. Now Rice and Martin are gone I am at liberty. Brown to my sorrow confirms the account you give of your ill health. You cannot conceive how I ache to be with you: how I would die for one hour——for what is in the world? I say you cannot conceive; it is impossible you should look with such eyes upon me as I have upon you: it cannot be. Forgive me if I wander a little this evening, for I have been all day employ'd in a very abstr[a]ct Poem[1] and I am in deep love with you—two things which must excuse me. I have, believe me, not been an age in letting you take possession of me; the very first week I knew you I wrote myself your vassal; but burnt the Letter as the very next time I saw you I thought you manifested some dislike to me. If you should ever feel for Man at the first sight what I did for you, I am lost. Yet I should not quarrel with you, but hate myself if such a thing were to happen—only I should burst if the thing were not as fine as a Man as you are as a Woman. Perhaps I am too vehement, then fancy me on my knees, especially when I mention a part of you Letter which hurt me; you say speaking of Mr. Severn "but you must be satisfied in knowing that I admired you much more than your friend." My dear love, I cannot believe there ever was or ever could be any thing to admire in me especially as far as sight goes—I cannot be admired, I am not a thing to be admired. You are, I love you; all I can bring you is a swooning admiration of your Beauty. I hold that place among Men which snubnos'd brunettes with meeting eyebrows do among women—they are trash to me—unless I should find one among them with a fire in her heart like the one that burns in mine. You absorb me in spite of myself—you alone: for I look not forward with any pleasure to what is call'd being settled in the world; I tremble at domestic cares—yet for you I would meet them, though if it would leave you the happier I would rather die than do so. I have two luxuries to brood over in my walks, your Loveliness and the hour of my death. O that I could have possession of them both in the same minute. I hate the world: it batters too much the wings of my self-will, and would I could take a sweet poison from your lips to send me out of it. From no others would I take it. I am indeed astonish'd to find myself so careless of all cha[r]ms but yours—remembering as I do the time when even a bit of ribband was a matter of interest with me. What softer words can I find for you after this—what it is I will not read. Nor will I say more here, but in a Postscript answer any thing else you may have men-

---

[1] The Fall of Hyperion.

tioned in your Letter in so many words—for I am distracted with a thousand thoughts. I will imagine you Venus tonight and pray, pray, pray to your star like a Hethen.

Your's ever, fair Star,
John Keats.

*   *   *   *   *

F R O M

TO CHARLES BROWN
23 September 1819

*   *   *   *   *

Do not suffer me to disturb you unpleasantly: I do not mean that you should not suffer me to occupy your thoughts, but to occupy them pleasantly; for, I assure you, I am as far from being unhappy as possible. Imaginary grievances have always been ⟨my⟩ more my torment than real ones. You know this well. Real ones will never have any other effect upon me than to stimulate me to get out of or avoid them. This is easily accounted for. Our imaginary woes are conjured up by our passions, and are fostered by passionate feeling; our real ones come of themselves, and are opposed by an abstract exertion of mind. Real grievances are displacers of passion. The imaginary nail a man down for a sufferer, as on a cross; the real spur him up into an agent. I wish, at one view, you could see my heart towards you. 'Tis only from a high tone of feeling that I can put that word upon paper—out of poetry. I ought to have waited for your answer to my last before I wrote ⟨send⟩ this. I felt, however, compelled to make a rejoinder to your's. I had written to x x x x[1] on the subject of my last,—I scarcely know whether I shall send my letter now. I think he would approve of my plan; it is so evident. Nay, I am convinced, out and out, that by prosing for awhile in periodical works I may maintain myself decently.

*   *   *   *   *

TO FANNY BRAWNE
13 October 1819

25 College Street.

My dearest Girl,

This moment I have set myself to copy some verses out fair. I cannot proceed with any degree of content.

---

[1] When Brown transcribed Keats's letters to him for inclusion in a proposed biography, he replaced most of the personal names with x x x x. Inasmuch as the originals of these letters are not known to exist, the identification of the blanks is a matter of conjecture.

I must write you a line or two and see if that will assist in dismissing you from my Mind for ever so short a time. Upon my Soul I can think of nothing else—The time is passed when I had power to advise and warn you again[s]t the unpromising morning of my Life— My love has made me selfish. I cannot exist without you—I am forgetful of every thing but seeing you again—my Life seems to stop there—I see no further. You have absorb'd me. I have a sensation at the present moment as though I was dissolving—I should be exquisitely miserable without the hope of soon seeing you. I should be affraid to separate myself far from you. My sweet Fanny, will your heart never change? My love, will it? I have no limit now to my love—You note came in just here—I cannot be happier away from you —'T is richer than an Argosy of Pearles. Do not threat me even in jest. I have been astonished that Men could die Martyrs for religion—I have shudder'd at it—I shudder no more—I could be martyr'd for my Religion —Love is my religion—I could die for that—I could die for you. My Creed is Love and you are its only tenet—You have ravish'd me away by a Power I cannot resist; and yet I could resist till I saw you; and even since I have seen you I have endeavoured often "to reason against the reasons of my Love."[1] I can do that no more—the pain would be too great—My Love is selfish—I cannot breathe without you.

Yours for ever
John Keats

TO JOHN TAYLOR
17 November 1819

Wentworth Place
Wednesday,

My dear Taylor,

I have come to a determination not to publish any thing I have now ready written; but for all that to publish a Poem before long and that I hope to make a fine one. As the marvellous is the most enticing and the surest guarantee of harmonious numbers[1] I have been endeavouring to persuade myself to untether Fancy and let her manage for herself—I and myself cannot agree about this at all. Wonders are no wonders to me. I am more at home amongst Men and women. I would rather read Chaucer than Ariosto—The little dramatic skill I may as yet have however badly it might show in a Drama would I think be sufficient for a Poem—I wish to diffuse the colouring of St Agnes eve throughout a Poem in which Character and Sentiment would

---

[1] John Ford's tragedy *'Tis Pity She's a Whore* (1633), I, ii, 222.
[1] See *Paradise Lost*, III, 38.

be the figures to such drapery—Two or three such Poems, if God should spare me, written in the course of the next six years, would be a famous gradus ad Parnassum altissimum—I mean they would nerve me up to the writing of a few fine Plays—my greatest ambition—when I do feel ambitious. I am sorry to say that is very seldom. The subject we have once or twice talked of appears a promising one, The Earl of Leicester's history. I am this morning reading Holingshed's Elisabeth,[2] You had some Books awhile ago, you promised to lend me, illustrative of my Subject. If you can lay hold of them or any others which may be serviceable to me I know you will encourage my low-spirited Muse by sending them—or rather by letting me know when our Errand cart Man shall call with my little Box. I will endeavour to set my self selfishly at work on this Poem that is to be—

> Your sincere friend
> John Keats—

F R O M

TO GEORGIANA KEATS
13, 15, 17, 28 January 1820

*   *   *   *   *

*Saturday Jan*ʸ *15* It is strange that George[1] having to stop so short {a} time in England I should not have seen him for nearly two days—He has been to {H}aslam's and does not encourage me to follow his example—He had given promise to dine with the same party tomorrow, but has sent an excuse which I am glad of as we shall have a pleasant party with us tomorrow. We expect Charles[2] here today—This is a beautiful day; I hope you will not quarrel with it if I call it an american one. The Sun comes upon the snow and makes a prettier candy than we have on twelvth cakes. George is busy this morning in making copies of my verses—He is making now one of an Ode to the nightingale, which is like reading an account of the back [black] hole at Calcutta on an ice bergh. You will say this is a matter of course, I am glad it is, I mean that I should like your Brothers more, the more I know them. I should spend much more time with them if our lives were more run in paralel, but we can talk but on one subject that is you—The more I know of Men the more I know how to value entire liberality in any of them. Thank God there are a great many who will sacrifice their worldly interest for a friend: I wish there were more who would sacrifice their passions. The worst of Men are those whose self interests are their passion—the next those whose passions are their self-interest. Upon the whole I dislike Mankind: whatever people on the other side of the question may advance they cannot deny that they are always surprised at hearing of a good action and never of a bad one. I am glad you have something [to] like in America, Doves—Gertrude of Wyoming and Birkbeck's book[3] should be bound up together like a Brace of Decoy Ducks—One is almost as poetical as the other. Precious miserable people at the Prarie. I have been sitting in the Sun whilest I wrote this till it became quite oppressive, this is very odd for January—The vulcan fire is the true natural heat for Winter: the Sun has nothing to do in winter but to give a "little glooming light much like a Shade"[4]—Our irish servant has piqued me this morning by saying that her Father in Ireland was very much like my Shakspeare only he had more color than the Engraving. You will find on Georges return that I have not been neglecting your affairs. The delay was unfortunate, not faulty;—perhaps by this time you have received my three last letters not one of which had reach'd [you] before George sail'd, I would give two {pe}nce to have been over the world as much as he has—I wish I had money enough to do nothing but travel about for years—Were you now in England I dare say you would be able (setting aside the pleasure you would have in seeing your mother) to suck out more amusemement for Saciety than I am able to do. To me it is all as dull here as Louisville could be. I am tired of the Theatres. Almost all the parties I may chance to fall into I know by heart—I know the different Styles of talk in different places: what subjects will be started how it will proceed, like an acted play, from the first to the last Act—If I go to Hunt's I run my head into many-times heard puns and music. To Haydon's worn out discourses of poetry and painting: the Miss Reynolds I am affraid to speak to for fear of some sickly reiteration of Phrase or Sentiment. When they were at the dance the other night I tried manfully to sit near and talk to them, but to not [no] purpose, and if I had 't would have been to no purpose still—My question or observation must have been an old one, and the rejoinder very antique indeed. At Dilkes I fall foul of Politics. 'T is best to remain aloof from people and like their good parts

---

[2] Raphael Holinshed's *Chronicles* (1577) were the source for Shakespeare's history plays.

[1] George Keats had returned to England in January 1820, in order to obtain funds to relieve his desperate financial situation in America.

[2] Charles Wylie, one of Georgiana's brothers.

[3] *Gertrude of Wyoming* was Thomas Campbell's poem with a Pennsylvania setting, published in 1809. *Letters from Illinois* (1818) was written by Morris Birkbeck (1764–1825), who had formed and publicized a settlement in Illinois where George Keats had originally intended to purchase land and make his American home.

[4] *Faerie Queene*, I, i, 14.

without being eternally troubled with the dull processes of their every day Lives. When once a person has smok'd the vapidness of the routine of Society he must have either self interest or the love of some sort of distinction to keep him in good humour with it. All I can say is that standing at Charing cross and looking east west north and south I can see nothing but dullness—I hope while I am young to live retired in the Country, when I grow in years and have a right to be idle I shall enjoy cities more. If the American Ladies are worse than the English they must be very bad— You say you should like your Emily [5] brought up here. You had better bring her up yourself. You know a good number of english Ladies what encomium could you give of half a dozen of them—the greater part seem to me downright American. I have known more than one Mrs Audubon [6] their affectation of fashion and politeness cannot transcend ours—Look at our Cheapside Trademans sons and daughters—only fit to be taken off by a plague—I hope now soon to come to the time when I shall never be forc'd to walk through the City and hate as I walk—

*   *   *   *   *

TO FANNY BRAWNE
February (?) 1820

My dearest Girl,

According to all appearances I am to be separated from you as much as possible. How I shall be able to bear it, or whether it will not be worse than your presence now and then, I cannot tell. I must be patient, and in the mean time you must think of it as little as possible. Let me not longer detain you from going to Town—there may be no end to this emprisoning of you. Perhaps you had better not come before tomorrow evening: send me however without fail a good night. You know our situation—what hope is there if I should be recoverd ever so soon—my very health with [will] not suffer me to make any great exertion. I am reccommended not even to read poetry much less write it. I wish I had even a little hope. I cannot say forget me— but I would mention that there are impossibilities in the world. No more of this—I am not strong enough to

be weaned—take no notice of it in your good night. Happen what may I shall ever be my dearest Love
Your affectionate
J—K—

James Rice, Jr. (1792–1832), an attorney, met Keats early in 1817 through John Hamilton Reynolds, and became a lasting friend.

F R O M

TO JAMES RICE
14, 16 February 1820

Wentworth Place
Monday Morn.

My dear Rice,

I have not been well enough [1] to make any tolerable rejoinder to your kind Letter. I will as you advise be very chary of my health and spirits. I am sorry to hear of your relapse and hypochondriac symptoms attending it. Let us hope for the best as you say. I shall follow your example in looking to the future good rather than brooding upon present ill. I have not been so worn with lengthen'd illnesses as you have therefore cannot answer you on your own ground with respect to those haunting and deformed thoughts and feelings you speak of. When I have been or supposed myself in health I have had my share of them, especially within this last year. I may say that for 6 Months before I was taken ill I had not passed a tranquil day—Either that gloom overspred me or I was suffering under some passionate feeling, or if I turn'd to versify that acerbated the poison of either sensation. The Beauties of Nature had lost their power over me. How astonishingly (here I must premise that illness as far as I can judge in so short a time has relieved my Mind of a load of deceptive thoughts and images and makes me perceive things in a truer light)—How astonishingly does the chance of leaving the world impress a sense of its natural beauties on us. Like poor Falstaff,[2] though I do not babble, I think of green fields. I muse with the greatest affection on every flower I have known from my infancy—their shapes and coulours as are new to me as if I had just created them with a superhuman fancy— It is because they are connected with the most thoughtless and happiest moments of our Lives—I have seen foreign flowers in hothouses of the most beautiful

---

5 The first child of George and Georgiana, born 1819.
6 George Keats and his wife had met John James Audubon (1785–1851), the famous artist and naturalist, then an unsuccessful merchant, in Henderson, Kentucky. Perhaps as a deliberate swindle, Audubon had persuaded George to place his funds in a Mississippi steamboat venture, resulting in the total loss of the investment.

---

1 On February 3, Keats had suffered a massive lung hemorrhage, which he diagnosed as "my death warrant."
2 Henry the Fifth, II, iii, 17–18.

nature, but I do not care a straw for them. The simple flowers of our sp[r]ing are what I want to see again. . . .

TO FANNY BRAWNE
February (?) 1820

My dear Fanny,

Do not let your mother suppose that you hurt me by writing at night. For some reason or other your last night's note was not so treasureable as former ones. I would fain that you call me *Love* still. To see you happy and in high spirits is a great consolation to me—still let me believe that you are not half so happy as my restoration would make you. I am nervous, I own, and may think myself worse than I really am; if so you must indulge me, and pamper with that sort of tenderness you have manifested towards me in different Letters. My sweet creature when I look back upon the pains and torments I have suffer'd for you from the day I left you to go to the Isle of Wight; the ecstasies in which I have pass'd some days and the miseries in their turn, I wonder the more at the Beauty which has kept up the spell so fervently. When I send this round I shall be in the front parlour watching to see you show yourself for a minute in the garden. How illness stands as a barrier betwixt me and you! Even if I was well—— I must make myself as good a Philosopher as possible. Now I have had opportunities of passing nights anxious and awake I have found other thoughts intrude upon me. "If I should die," said I to myself, "I have left no immortal work behind me—nothing to make my friends proud of my memory—but I have lov'd the principle of beauty in all things, and if I had had time I would have made myself remember'd." Thoughts like these came very feebly whilst I was in health and every pulse beat for you—now you divide with this (may *I* say it?) "last infirmity of noble minds"[1] all my reflection.

God bless you, Love.

J. Keats.

TO FANNY BRAWNE
5 July (?) 1820

Wednesday Morng.

My dearest Girl,

I have been a walk this morning with a book in my hand, but as usual I have been occupied with nothing but you: I wish I could say in an agreeable manner. I am tormented day and night. They talk of my going to Italy. 'Tis certain I shall never recover if I am to be so long separate from you: yet with all this devotion to you I cannot persuade myself into any confidence of you. Past experience connected with the fact of my long separation from you gives me agonies which are scarcely to be talked of. When your mother comes I shall be very sudden and expert in asking her whether you have been to Mrs. Dilke's, for she might say no to make me easy. I am literally worn to death, which seems my only recourse. I cannot forget what has pass'd. What? nothing with a man of the world, but to me deathful. I will get rid of this as much as possible. When you were in the habit of flirting with Brown you would have left off, could your own heart have felt one half the pang mine did. Brown is a good sort of Man—he did not know he was doing me to death by inches. I feel the effect of every one of those hours in my side now; and for that cause, though he has done me many services, though I know his love and friendship for me, though at this moment I should be without pence were it not for his assistance, I will never see or speak to him until we are both old men, if we are to be. I *will* resent my heart having been made a football. You will call this madness. I have heard you say that it was not unpleasant to wait a few years—you have amusements—your mind is away—you have not brooded over one idea as I have, and how should you? You are to me an object intensely desireable—the air I breathe in a room empty of you is unhealthy. I am not the same to you—no—you can wait—you have a thousand activities—you can be happy without me. Any party, any thing to fill up the day has been enough. How have you pass'd this month? Who have you smil'd with? All this may seem savage in me. You do not feel as I do—you do not know what it is to love—one day you may—your time is not come. Ask yourself how many unhappy hours Keats has caused you in Loneliness. For myself I have been a Martyr the whole time, and for this reason I speak; the confession is forc'd from me by the torture. I appeal to you by the blood of that Christ you believe in: Do not write to me if you have done anything this month which it would have pained me to have seen. You may have altered—if you have not—if you still behave in dancing rooms and other societies as I have seen you—I do not want to live—if you have done so I wish this coming night may be my last. I cannot live without you, and not only you but *chaste you; virtuous you.* The Sun rises and sets, the day passes, and you follow the bent of your inclination to a certain extent—you have no conception of the quantity of miserable feeling that passes through me in a day.—Be serious! Love is not a plaything—and again do not write unless you can do it

---

[1] "Lycidas," l. 71.

with a crystal conscience. I would sooner die for want of you than—

Yours for ever
J. Keats.

TO FANNY BRAWNE
August (?) 1820

I do not write this till the last, that no eye may catch it.

My dearest Girl,

I wish you could invent some means to make me at all happy without you. Every hour I am more and more concentrated in you; every thing else tastes like chaff in my Mouth. I feel it almost impossible to go to Italy—the fact is I cannot leave you, and shall never taste one minute's content until it pleases chance to let me live with you for good. But I will not go on at this rate. A person in health as you are can have no conception of the horrors that nerves and a temper like mine go through. What Island do your friends propose retiring to? I should be happy to go with you there alone, but in company I should object to it; the backbitings and jealousies of new colonists who have nothing else to amuse them selves, is unbearable. Mr Dilke came to see me yesterday, and gave me a very great deal more pain than pleasure. I shall never be able any more to endure to [the] society of any of those who used to meet at Elm Cottage and Wentworth Place. The last two years taste like brass upon my Palate. If I cannot live with you I will live alone. I do not think my health will improve much while I am separated from you. For all this I am averse to seeing you—I cannot bear flashes of light and return into my glooms again. I am not so unhappy now as I should be if I had seen you yesterday. To be happy with you seems such an impossibility! it requires a luckier Star than mine! it will never be. I enclose a passage from one of your Letters which I want you to alter a little—I want (if you will have it so) the matter express'd less coldly to me. If my health would bear it, I could write a Poem which I have in my head, which would be a consolation for people in such a situation as mine. I would show some one in Love as I am, with a person living in such Liberty as you do. Shakspeare always sums up matters in the most sovereign manner. Hamlet's heart was full of such Misery as mine is when he said to Ophelia "Go to a Nunnery, go go!"[1] Indeed I should like to give up the matter at once—I should like to die. I am sickened at the brute world which you are smiling with. I hate men

and women more. I see nothing but thorns for the future—wherever I may be next winter in Italy or nowhere Brown will be living near you with his indecencies—I see no prospect of any rest. Suppose me in Rome—well, I should there see you as in a magic glass going to and from town at all hours,———I wish you could infuse a little confidence in human nature into my heart. I cannot muster any—the world is too brutal for me—I am glad there is such a thing as the grave—I am sure I shall never have any rest till I get there At any rate I will indulge myself by never seeing any more Dilke or Brown or any of their Friends. I wish I was either in you a[r]ms full of faith or that a Thunder bolt would strike me.

God bless you—J. K—

TO PERCY BYSSHE SHELLEY
16 August 1820

Hampstead August 16th

My dear Shelley,

I am very much gratified that you, in a foreign country, and with a mind almost over occupied, should write to me in the strain of the Letter beside me. If I do not take advantage of your invitation it will be prevented by a circumstance I have very much at heart to prophesy—There is no doubt that an english winter would put an end to me, and do so in a lingering hateful manner, therefore I must either voyage or journey to Italy as a soldier marches up to a battery. My nerves at present are the worst part of me, yet they feel soothed when I think that come what extreme may, I shall not be destined to remain in one spot long enough to take a hatred of any four particular bed-posts. I am glad you take any pleasure in my poor Poem;[1]—which I would willingly take the trouble to unwrite, if possible, did I care so much as I have done about Reputation. I received a copy of the Cenci, as from yourself from Hunt. There is only one part of it I am judge of; the Poetry, and dramatic effect, which by many spirits now a days is considered the mammon. A modern work it is said must have a purpose, which may be the God—*an artist* must serve Mammon—he must have "self concentration" selfishness perhaps. You I am sure will forgive me for sincerely remarking that you might curb your magnanimity and be more of an artist, and 'load every rift' of your subject with ore.[2] The

---

[1] See *Hamlet*, III, i, 122.

[1] Shelley had written from Pisa on July 27: "I have lately read your Endymion again & ever with a new sense of the treasures it contains, though treasures poured forth with indistinct profusion."
[2] See *Faerie Queene*, II, vii, 28.

thought of such discipline must fall like cold chains upon you, who perhaps never sat with your wings furl'd for six Months together. And is not this extra-ordina[r]y talk for the writer of Endymion? whose mind was like a pack of scattered cards—I am pick'd up and sorted to a pip.[3] My Imagination is a Monastry and I am its Monk—you must explain my metap[cs] [metaphysics] to yourself. I am in expectation of Prometheus every day. Could I have my own wish for its interest effected you would have it still in manuscript—or be but now putting an end to the second act. I remember you[4] advising me not to publish my first-blights, on Hampstead heath—I am returning advice upon your hands. Most of the Poems in the volume I send you[5] have been written above two years, and would never have been publish'd but from a hope of gain; so you see I am inclined enough to take your advice now. I must exp[r]ess once more my deep sense of your kindness, adding my sincere thanks and respects for M[rs] Shelley. In the hope of soon seeing you {I} remain

most sincerely {yours,}
John Keats—

TO CHARLES BROWN
1 November 1820

Naples. Wednesday first in November.
My dear Brown,

Yesterday we were let out of Quarantine, during which my health suffered more from bad air and a stifled cabin than it had done the whole voyage. The fresh air revived me a little, and I hope I am well enough this morning to write to you a short calm letter; —if that can be called one, in which I am afraid to speak of what I would the fainest dwell upon. As I have gone thus far into it, I must go on a little;—perhaps it may relieve the load of WRETCHED-NESS which presses upon me. The persuasion that I shall see her no more will kill me. I cannot q—— (Note)[1] My dear Brown, I should have had her when I was in health, and I should have remained well. I can bear to die—I cannot bear to leave her. Oh, God! God! God! Every thing I have in my trunks that reminds me of her goes through me like a spear. The silk lining she put in my travelling cap scalds my head. My imagination is horribly vivid about her—I see her—I hear her. There is nothing in the world of sufficient interest to divert me from her a moment. This was the case when I was in England; I cannot recollect, without shuddering, the time that I was prisoner at Hunt's, and used to keep my eyes fixed on Hampstead all day. Then there was a good hope of seeing her again—Now!—O that I could be buried near where she lives! I am afraid to write to her—to receive a letter from her —to see her hand writing would break my heart—even to hear of her any how, to see her name written would be more than I can bear. My dear Brown, what am I to do? Where can I look for consolation or ease? If I had any chance of recovery, this passion would kill me. Indeed through the whole of my illness, both at your house and at Kentish Town, this fever has never ceased wearing me out. When you write to me, which you will do immediately, write to Rome (poste restante)— if she is well and happy, put a mark thus +,—if— Remember me to all. I will endeavour to bear my miseries patiently. A person in my state of health should ⟨to⟩ not have such miseries to bear. Write a short note to my sister, saying you have heard from me. Severn[2] is very well. If I were in better health I should urge your coming to Rome. I fear there is no one can give me any comfort. Is there any news of George? O, that something fortunate had ever happened to me or my brothers!—then I might hope,—but despair is forced upon me as a habit. My dear Brown, for my sake, be her advocate for ever. I cannot say a word about Naples; I do not feel at all concerned in the thousand novelties around me. I am afraid to write to her. I should like her to know that I do not forget her. Oh, Brown, I have coals of fire in my breast. It surprised me that the human heart is capable of containing and bearing so much misery. Was I born for this end? God bless her, and her mother, and my sister, and George, and his wife, and you, and all!

Your ever affectionate friend,
John Keats.

Thursday. I was a day too early for the courier. He sets out now. I have been more calm to-day, though in half dread of not continuing so. I said nothing of my health; I know nothing of it; you will hear Severn's

---

[3] That is, in contrast to the undisciplined poetic faculty which produced the immature excesses of *Endymion*, my imagination is now better ordered and more precise in its operation, like a pack of cards arranged in exact order. (Pip was the name given to each of the spots on playing cards.)

[4] In early 1817, before the publication of Keats's first volume in March of that year.

[5] Keats's collection of 1820, a copy of which was found on Shelley's body after his drowning.

[1] "(Note) He could not go on with this sentence, nor even write the word 'quit',—as I suppose. The word WRETCHED-NESS above he himself wrote in large characters"—note supplied by Brown.

[2] Joseph Severn (1793–1879), painter and friend of Keats since 1816. He accompanied the poet to Rome and nursed him throughout the final months of his life. In later years, Severn became British Consul at Rome and was buried beside Keats in the Protestant Cemetery.

account from x x x x x x. I must leave off. You bring my thoughts too near to ——

God bless you!

TO CHARLES BROWN
30 November 1820[1]

Rome. 30 November 1820.

My dear Brown,   to

'Tis the most difficult thing in the world ⟨for⟩ me to write a letter. My stomach continues so bad, that I feel it worse on opening any book,—yet I am much better than I was in Quarantine. Then I am afraid to encounter the proing and conning of any thing interesting to me in England. I have an habitual feeling of my real life having past, and that I am leading a posthumous existence. God knows how it would have been—but it appears to me—however, I will not speak of that subject. I must have been at Bedhampton nearly at the time you were writing to me from Chichester—how unfortunate—and to pass on the river too! There was my star predominant! I cannot answer any thing in your letter, which followed me from Naples to Rome, because I am afraid to look it over again. I am so weak (in mind) that I cannot bear the sight of any hand writing of a friend I love so much as I do you. Yet I ride the little horse,—and, at my worst, even in Quarantine, summoned up more puns, in a sort of desperation, in one week than in any year of my life. There is one thought enough to kill me—I have been well, healthy, alert &c, walking with her—and now—the knowledge of contrast, feeling for light and shade, all that information (primitive sense) necessary for a poem are great enemies to the recovery of the stomach. There, you rogue, I put you to the torture,—but you must bring your philosophy to bear—as I do mine, really—or how should I be able to live? Dr Clarke is very attentive to me; he says, there is very little the matter with my lungs, but my stomach, he says, is very bad. I am well disappointed in hearing good news from George,—for it runs in my head we shall all die young. I have not written to x x x x x yet, which he must think very neglectful; being anxious to send him a good account of my health, I have delayed it from week to week. If I recover, I will do all in my power to correct the mistakes made during sickness; and if I should not, all my faults will be forgiven. I shall write to x x x to-morrow, or next day. I will write to x x x x x in the middle of next week. Severn is very well, though he leads so dull a life with me. Remember me to all friends, and tell x x x x I should not have left London without taking leave of him, but from being so low in body and mind. Write to George as soon as you receive this, and tell him how I am, as far as you can guess;—and also a note to my sister—who walks about my imagination like a ghost—she is so like Tom. I can scarcely bid you good bye even in a letter. I always made an awkward bow.

God bless you!
John Keats.

---

[1] This is the last letter that Keats is known to have written.

The Reviewers

JEFFREY'S REVIEW OF SOUTHEY'S THALABA

As John O. Hayden has indicated in his history of The Romantic Reviewers 1802–1824, *"the early nineteenth century was in fact the heyday of periodical reviewing" with more than sixty periodicals carrying literary reviews. Of these the most significant was the quarterly publication* Edinburgh Review. *Its first number appeared in October 1802, almost exactly four years after the publication of* Lyrical Ballads, *and it was to have as great an influence on its own field of journalism as Wordsworth and Coleridge's volume was to exert on the future course of English poetry. Instead of the perfunctory notice or short hack-work review written to promote the publications of booksellers who financed the journals in the late eighteenth century, the* Edinburgh Review *initiated the policy of the long essay-review limited to those works "that have attained, or deserve, a certain portion of celebrity." As a result of the greater length allowed as well as the generally high caliber of the contributors, the reviews in the* Edinburgh *and the other periodicals that copied its format were often wide-ranging discussions of politics, philosophy, history, or aesthetics. Examples of this creatively open-ended reviewing are represented in the present anthology by De Quincey's poignant study of Charles Lamb written as a review of Talfourd's* Final Memorials, *and the famous passage on "The Literature of Knowledge and the Literature of Power" occurring in an essay-review of an edition of Pope's works. To look to Victorian figures, it is well to remember that Macaulay's most famous essays, such as those on Milton, Southey, and Frederick the Great, all appeared as reviews in the* Edinburgh Review; *and Carlyle's brilliant early assessment of the intellectual tendencies of the age "Characteristics" (*Edinburgh Review, *1831) was ostensibly a review of the now forgotten* Essay on the Origins and Prospects of Man *by Thomas Hope.*

The Edinburgh Review *was founded by four young Scotsmen of liberal-Whig political persuasion, the Reverend Sydney Smith and the three lawyers Francis Jeffrey, Henry Brougham, and Francis Horner. Jeffrey (1773–1850) soon became sole editor and was himself to contribute more than 200 reviews of books in a variety of fields between 1802 and 1848. Among other notable contributors of literary reviews in the early years of publication were Sir Walter Scott (from 1803 to 1808) and William Hazlitt, whose 1824 review of Shelley's* Posthumous Poems *is represented in this anthology. Among reviewers in other fields were Thomas Malthus, Sir James Mackintosh, Macaulay, and Carlyle.*

Jeffrey is perhaps most famous for his critical remarks on Wordsworth, represented here by a section from a review of Southey's Thalaba, *and by the review of* The Excursion *with its memorably damning first sentence (his review of* The White Doe of Rylstone *in 1815 contains an equally memorable opening sentence: "This, we think, has the merit of being the very worst poem we ever saw imprinted in a quarto volume"). As the remarks in the essay on* Thalaba *would indicate, Jeffrey's objection was not to Wordsworth's poetic talents as such, but to controversial principles of poetry announced in the preface to the second edition of* Lyrical Ballads; *indeed, he was to praise the poems for their "strong spirit of originality, of pathos, and natural feelings." It was precisely because such "a great deal of genius and of laudable feeling" was "perverted" by false principles of taste that*

Jeffrey felt it necessary to enter into controversy "with a degree of zeal and animosity," he admitted, "which some might think unreasonable towards authors, to whom so much merit has been conceded." Among the other poets of the age, Jeffrey admired Crabbe, Scott, and Byron, and wrote discerningly on their merits and limitations. It is well to know, that following the vicious and mindless assaults on Keats by the Quarterly Review *and* Blackwood's Magazine, *Jeffrey raised a voice of praise for "a poet of such great power and promise" in a belated review of the* Endymion *and* Lamia *volumes in 1820.*

In the Spirit of the Age, *Hazlitt was to hail Jeffrey for his "great range of knowledge, an equal familiarity with the principles and details of a subject, and a glancing brilliancy and rapidity of style;" and many years later Carlyle declared that "there has no critic appeared among us since who was worth standing beside him." Jeffrey's reviewing voice was often unnecessarily "inquisitorial" and pompous, especially in the early years of the* Edinburgh Review; *but these defects seem less objectionable when compared with the abusive tone of other reviewers of the time (including, one might add, Hazlitt in his not infrequent vindictive moods). Whatever his merits or limitations as a critic, Jeffrey remains of historic importance as the guiding spirit of the periodical that effected a revolution in journalism by establishing literary reviewing as a serious intellectual endeavor.*

Among the works to be consulted on Francis Jeffrey, see: Henry Cockburn, Life of Lord Jeffrey, *2 vols. (Edinburgh: A. and C. Black, 1852) [a list of Jeffrey's articles appears as an appendix to the first volume]; Russell Noyes,* Wordsworth and Jeffrey in Controversy, *Indiana University Publications, Humanities Series, No. 5, Bloomington, Indiana, 1941; and James A. Greig,* Francis Jeffrey and the Edinburgh Review *(Edinburgh: Oliver and Boyd, 1948). Jeffrey brought together his essays as* Contributions to the Edinburgh Review, *4 vols. (London: Longman and Company, 1844); and D. Nichol Smith edited fourteen of his most famous essays in the collection* Jeffrey's Literary Criticism *(London: Henry Frowde, 1910). A detailed history of the early years of the periodical is presented in John Clive's* Scotch Reviewers: The Edinburgh Review, 1802–1815 *(Cambridge, Mass.: Harvard University Press, 1957). On the general history of literary reviewing in the early nineteenth century, two studies are highly recommended: Walter Graham,* English Literary Periodicals *(New York: Thomas Nelson and Sons, 1930); and John O. Hayden,* The Romantic Reviewers 1802–1824 *(Chicago: University of Chicago Press, 1969). Hayden has also assembled a valuable collection of literary reviews* Romantic Bards and British Reviewers *(Lincoln, Nebraska: University of Nebraska Press, 1971), much fuller than the earlier but still useful collection prepared by John Wain,* Contemporary Reviews of Romantic Poetry *(New York: Barnes and Noble, 1953).*

Like most contributions to these early nineteenth-century periodicals, literary reviews were published anonymously. Attributions of authorship for the reviews here reproduced in their original texts are derived from John O. Hayden's The Romantic Reviewers 1802–1824 *and Hill Shine and Helen Chadwick Shine's* The Quarterly Review under Gifford: Identification of Contributors 1809–1824 *(Chapel Hill, N.C.: University of North Carolina Press, 1949).*

Francis Jeffrey

F R O M

REVIEW OF SOUTHEY'S *THALABA*, IN THE *EDINBURGH REVIEW*

ON THE NEW SCHOOL OF POETRY

POETRY has this much, at least, in common with religion, that its standards were fixed long ago, by certain inspired writers, whose authority it is no longer lawful to call in question; and that many profess to be entirely devoted to it, who have no *good works* to produce in support of their pretensions. The catholic poetical church, too, has worked but few miracles since the first ages of its establishment; and has been more prolific, for a long time, of Doctors, than of Saints: it has had its corruptions and reformation also, and has given birth to an infinite variety of heresies and errors, the followers of which have hated and persecuted each other as cordially as other bigots.

The author who is now before us, belongs to a *sect* of poets, that has established itself in this country within these ten or twelve years, and is looked upon, we believe, as one of its chief champions and apostles. The peculiar doctrines of this sect, it would not, perhaps, be very easy to explain; but, that they are *dissenters* from the established systems in poetry and criticism, is admitted, and proved indeed, by the whole tenor of their compositions. Though they lay claim, we believe, to a creed and a revelation of their own, there can be little doubt, that their doctrines are of *German* origin, and have been derived from some of the great modern reformers in that country. Some of their leading principles, indeed, are probably of an earlier date, and seem to have been borrowed from the great apostle of Geneva.[1] As Mr Southey is the first author, of this persuasion, that has yet been brought before us for judgment, we cannot discharge our inquisitorial office conscientiously, without premising a few words upon the nature and tendency of the tenets he has helped to promulgate.

The disciples of this school boast much of its originality, and seem to value themselves very highly, for having broken loose from the bondage of ancient authority, and re-asserted the independence of genius. Originality, however, we are persuaded, is rarer than mere alteration; and a man may change a good master for a bad one, without finding himself at all nearer to independence. That our new poets have abandoned the old models, may certainly be admitted; but we have not been able to discover that they have yet created any models of their own; and are very much inclined to call in question the worthiness of those to which they have transferred their admiration. The productions of this school, we conceive, are so far from being entitled to the praise of originality, that they cannot be better characterised, than by an enumeration of the sources from which their materials have been derived. The greater part of them, we apprehend, will be found to be composed of the following elements: 1. The antisocial principles, and distempered sensibility of Rousseau— his discontent with the present constitution of society —his paradoxical morality, and his perpetual hankerings after some unattainable state of voluptuous virtue and perfection. 2. The simplicity and energy (*horresco referens*)[2] of Kotzebue and Schiller. 3. The homeliness and harshness of some of Cowper's language and versification, interchanged occasionally with the *innocence* of Ambrose Philips, or the quaintness of Quarles and Dr Donne. From the diligent study of these few originals, we have no doubt that an entire art of poetry may be collected, by the assistance of which, the very *gentlest* of our readers may soon be qualified to compose a poem as correctly versified as Thalaba, and to deal out sentiment and description, with all the sweetness of Lamb, and all the magnificence of Coleridge.

The authors, of whom we are now speaking, have, among them, unquestionably, a very considerable portion of poetical talent, and have, consequently, been enabled to seduce many into an admiration of the false taste (as it appears to us) in which most of their productions are composed. They constitute, at present, the most formidable conspiracy that has lately been formed against sound judgement in matters poetical; and are entitled to a larger share of our censorial notice, than could be spared for an individual delinquent. We shall hope for the indulgence of our readers, therefore, in taking this opportunity to inquire a little more particularly into their merits, and to make a few remarks upon those peculiarities which seem to be regarded by their admirers as the surest proofs of their excellence.

Their most distinguishing symbol is undoubtedly an affectation of great simplicity and familiarity of language. They disdain to make use of the common poetical phraseology, or to ennoble their diction by a selection of fine or dignified expressions. There would be too much *art* in this, for that great love of nature with which they are all of them inspired; and their sentiments, they are determined shall be indebted, for their effect, to nothing but their intrinsic tenderness or elevation. There is something very noble and conscientious, we will confess, in this plan of

---

[1] Rousseau.

[2] *horresco referens*: "I shudder even in mentioning it." (*Aeneid*, II, 204.)

composition; but the misfortune is, that there are passages in all poems, that can neither be pathetic nor sublime; and that, on these occasions, a neglect of the embellishments of language is very apt to produce absolute meanness and insipidity. The language of passion, indeed, can scarcely be deficient in elevation; and when an author is wanting in that particular, he may commonly be presumed to have failed in the truth, as well as in the dignity of his expression. The case, however, is extremely different with the subordinate parts of a composition; with the narrative and description, that are necessary to preserve its connexion; and the explanation, that must frequently prepare us for the great scenes and splendid passages. In these, all the requisite ideas may be conveyed, with sufficient clearness, by the meanest and most negligent expressions; and, if magnificence or beauty is ever to be observed in them, it must have been introduced from some other motive than that of adapting the style to the subject. It is in such passages, accordingly, that we are most frequently offended with low and inelegant expressions; and that the language, which was intended to be simple and natural, is found oftenest to degenerate into mere slovenliness and vulgarity. It is in vain, too, to expect that the meanness of those parts may be redeemed by the excellence of others. A poet, who aims at all at sublimity or pathos, is like an actor in a high tragic character, and must sustain his dignity throughout, or become altogether ridiculous. We are apt enough to laugh at the mock-majesty of those whom we know to be but common mortals in private; and cannot permit Hamlet to make use of a single provincial intonation, although it should only be in his conversation with the grave-diggers.

The followers of simplicity are, therefore, at all times in danger of occasional degradation; but the simplicity of this new school seems intended to ensure it. *Their* simplicity does not consist, by any means, in the rejection of glaring or superfluous ornament,—in the substitution of elegance to splendour, or in that refinement of art which seeks concealment in its own perfection. It consists, on the contrary, in a very great degree, in the positive and *bona fide* rejection of art altogether, and in the bold use of those rude and negligent expressions, which would be banished by a little discrimination. One of their own authors, indeed, has very ingenuously set forth, (in a kind of manifesto that preceded one of their most flagrant acts of hostility), that it was their capital object 'to adapt to the uses of poetry, the ordinary language of conversation among the middling and lower orders of the people.'[3] What

advantages are to be gained by the success of this project, we confess ourselves unable to conjecture. The language of the higher and more cultivated orders may fairly be presumed to be better than that of their inferiors: at any rate, it has all those associations in its favour, by means of which, a style can ever appear beautiful or exalted, and is adapted to the purposes of poetry, by having been long consecrated to its use. The language of the vulgar, on the other hand, has all the opposite associations to contend with; and must seem unfit for poetry, (if there were no other reason), merely because it has scarcely ever been employed in it. A great genius may indeed overcome these disadvantages; but we can scarcely conceive that he should court them. We may excuse a certain homeliness of language in the productions of a ploughman or a milkwoman; but we cannot bring ourselves to admire it in an author, who has had occasion to indite odes to his college bell, and inscribe hymns to the Penates.[4]

But the mischief of this new system, is not confined to the depravation of language only; it extends to the sentiments and emotions, and leads to the debasement of all those feelings which poetry is designed to communicate. It is absurd to suppose, that an author should make use of the language of the vulgar, to express the sentiments of the refined. His professed object, in employing that language, is to bring his compositions nearer to the true standard of nature; and his intention to copy the sentiments of the lower orders, is implied in his resolution to make use of their style. Now, the different classes of society have each of them a distinct character, as well as a separate idiom; and the names of the various passions to which they are subject respectively, have a signification that varies essentially, according to the condition of the persons to whom they are applied. The love, or grief, or indignation of an enlightened and refined character, is not only expressed in a different language, but is in itself a different emotion from the love, or grief, or anger of a clown, a tradesman, or a market-wench. The things themselves are radically and obviously distinct; and the representation of them is calculated to convey a very different train of sympathies and sensations to the mind. The question, therefore, comes simply to be—which of them is the most proper object for poetical imitation? It is needless for us to answer a question, which the practice of all the world has long ago decided irrevocably. The poor and vulgar may interest us, in poetry, by their *situation;* but never, we apprehend, by any sentiments that are peculiar to their condition, and still less by any language that is characteristic of it. The truth is, that it is impossible to copy their diction

---

[3] A very inexact quotation-reference to Wordsworth's Preface to *Lyrical Ballads.*

[4] Referring to early poems by Southey.

or their sentiments correctly, in a serious composition; and this, not merely because poverty makes men ridiculous, but because just taste and refined sentiment are rarely to be met with among the uncultivated part of mankind; and a language, fitted for their expression, can still more rarely form any part of their 'ordinary conversation.'

The low-bred heroes, and interesting rustics of poetry, have no sort of affinity to the real vulgar of this world; they are imaginary beings, whose characters and language are in contrast with their situation; and please those who can be pleased with them, by the marvellous, and not by the nature of such a combination. In serious poetry, a man of the middling or lower order *must necessarily* lay aside a great deal of his ordinary language; he must avoid errors in grammar and orthography; and steer clear of the cant of particular professions, and of every impropriety that is ludicrous or disgusting: nay, he must speak in good verse, and observe all the graces in prosody and collocation. After all this, it may not be very easy to say how we are to find him out to be a low man, or what marks can remain of the ordinary language of conversation in the inferior orders of society. If there will be any phrases that are not used in good society, they will appear as blemishes in the composition, no less palpably, than errors in syntax or quantity; and, if there be no such phrases, the style cannot be characteristic of that condition of life, the language of which it professes to have adopted. All approximation to that language, in the same manner, implies a deviation from that purity and precision, which no one, we believe, ever violated spontaneously.

It has been argued, indeed, (for men will argue in support of what they do not venture to practise), that as the middling and lower orders of society constitute by far the greater part of mankind, so, their feelings and expressions should interest more extensively, and may be taken, more fairly than any other, for the standards of what is natural and true. To this, it seems obvious to answer, that the arts that aim at exciting admiration and delight, do not take their models from what is ordinary, but from what is excellent; and that our interest in the representation of any event, does not depend upon our familiarity with the original, but on its intrinsic importance, and the celebrity of the parties it concerns. The sculptor employs his art in delineating the graces of Antinous or Apollo, and not in the representation of those ordinary forms that belong to the crowd of his admirers. When a chieftain perishes in battle, his followers mourn more for him, than for thousands of their equals that may have fallen around him.

After all, it must be admitted, that there is a class of persons (we are afraid they cannot be called *readers*), to whom the representation of vulgar manners, in vulgar language, will afford much entertainment. We are afraid, however, that the ingenious writers who supply the hawkers and ballad-singers, have very nearly monopolized that department, and are probably better qualified to hit the taste of their customers, than Mr Southey, or any of his brethren, can yet pretend to be. To fit them for the higher task of original composition, it would not be amiss if they were to undertake a translation of Pope or Milton into the vulgar tongue, for the benefit of those children of nature.

There is another disagreeable effect of this affected simplicity, which, though of less importance than those which have been already noticed, it may yet be worth while to mention: This is, the extreme difficulty of supporting the same low tone of expression throughout, and the inequality that is consequently introduced into the texture of the composition. To an author of reading and education, it is a style that must always be assumed and unnatural, and one from which he will be perpetually tempted to deviate. He will rise, therefore, every now and then, above the level to which he has professedly degraded himself; and make amends for that transgression, by a fresh effort of descension. His composition, in short, will be like that of a person who is attempting to speak in an obsolete or provincial dialect; he will betray himself by expressions of occasional purity and elegance, and exert himself to efface that impression, by passages of unnatural meanness or absurdity.

In making these strictures on the perverted taste for simplicity, that seems to distinguish our modern school of poetry, we have no particular allusion to Mr Southey, or the production now before us: On the contrary, he appears to us, to be less addicted to this fault than most of his fraternity; and if we were in want of examples to illustrate the preceding observations, we should certainly look for them in the effusions of that poet who commemorates, with so much effect, the chattering of Harry Gill's teeth, tells the tale of the one-eyed huntsman 'who had a cheek like a cherry,' and beautifully warns his studious friend of the risk he ran of 'growing double.'[5]

At the same time, it is impossible to deny that the author of the 'English Eclogues' is liable to a similar censure; and few persons, we believe, will peruse the following verses (taken, almost at random, from the

---

[5] Referring to Wordsworth poems in *Lyrical Ballads*: "Goody Blake and Harry Gill," "Simon Lee the Old Huntsman," and "The Tables Turned."

Thalaba)⁶ without acknowledging that he still continues to deserve it.

> 'At midnight Thalaba started up,
> For he felt that the ring on his finger was moved.
> He called on Allah aloud,
> And he called on the Prophet's name.
> Moath arose in alarm,
> "What ails thee Thalaba?" he cried,
> "Is the Robber of night at hand?"
> "Dost thou not see," the youth exclaimed,
> "A Spirit in the Tent?"
> Moath looked round, and said,
> "The moon-beam shines in the Tent,
> 'I see thee stand in the light,
> 'And thy shadow is black on the ground."
> Thalaba answered not.
> "Spirit!" he cried, "what brings thee here?" &c.

> 'WOMAN.
>
> Go not among the Tombs, Old Man!
> There is a madman there.
>
> OLD MAN.
>
> Will he harm me if I go?
>
> WOMAN.
>
> Not he, poor miserable man!
> But 'tis a wretched sight to see
> His utter wretchedness.
> For all day long he lies on a grave,
> And never is he seen to weep,
> And never is he heard to groan,
> Nor ever at the hour of prayer
> Bends his knee, nor moves his lips.
> I have taken him food for charity,
> And never a word he spake;
> But yet, so ghastly he looked,
> That I have awakened at night,' &c.

Now, this style, we conceive, possesses no one character of excellence; it is feeble, low, and disjointed; without elegance, and without dignity; the offspring, we should imagine, of mere indolence and neglect, or the unhappy fruit of a system that would teach us to undervalue that vigilance and labour which sustained the loftiness of Milton, and gave energy and direction to the pointed and fine propriety of Pope.

The *style* of our modern poets, is that, no doubt, by which they are most easily distinguished: but their genius has also an internal character; and the peculiarities of their taste may be discovered, without the assistance of their diction. Next after great familiarity of language, there is nothing that appears to them so

meritorious as perpetual exaggeration of thought. There must be nothing moderate, natural, or easy, about their sentiments. There must be a 'qu'il mourut,'⁷ and a 'let there be light,' in every line; and all their characters must be in agonies and ecstasies, from their entrance to their exit. To those who are acquainted with their productions, it is needless to speak of the fatigue that is produced by this unceasing summons to admiration, or of the compassion which is excited by the spectacle of these eternal strainings and distortions. Those authors appear to forget, that a whole poem cannot be made up of striking passages; and that the sensations produced by sublimity, are never so powerful and entire, as when they are allowed to subside and revive, in a slow and spontaneous succession. It is delightful, now and then, to meet with a rugged mountain, or a roaring stream; but where there is no sunny slope, nor shaded plain, to relieve them—where all is beetling cliff and yawning abyss, and the landscape presents nothing on every side but prodigies and terrors—the head is apt to grow giddy, and the heart to languish for the repose and security of a less elevated region.

The effect even of genuine sublimity, therefore, is impaired by the injudicious frequency of its exhibition, and the omission of those intervals and breathing-places, at which the mind should be permitted to recover from its perturbation or astonishment: but, where it has been summoned upon a false alarm, and disturbed in the orderly course of its attention, by an impotent attempt at elevation, the consequences are still more disastrous. There is nothing so ridiculous (at least for a poet) as to fail in great attempts. If the reader foresaw the failure, he may receive some degree of mischievous satisfaction from its punctual occurrence; if he did not, he will be vexed and disappointed; and, in both cases, he will very speedily be disgusted and fatigued. It would be going too far, certainly, to maintain, that our modern poets have never succeeded in their persevering endeavours at elevation and emphasis; but it is a melancholy fact, that their successes bear but a small proportion to their miscarriages; and that the reader who has been promised an energetic sentiment, or sublime allusion, must often be contented with a very miserable substitute. Of the many contrivances they employ to give the appearance of uncommon force and animation to a very ordinary conception, the most usual is, to wrap it up in a veil of mysterious and unintelligible language, which flows past with so much solemnity, that it is difficult to be-

---

⁶ Southey's epic *Thalaba the Destroyer* was published in 1801. Jeffrey quotes: III, stanzas 7–8; and VIII, stanza 1.

⁷ 'qu'il mourut': "that he die"; like "let there be light," a grandiloquent utterance.

lieve it conveys nothing of any value. Another device for improving the effect of a cold idea, is, to embody it in a verse of unusual harshness and asperity. Compound words, too, of a portentous sound and conformation, are very useful in giving an air of energy and originality; and a few lines of scripture, written out into verse from the original prose, have been found to have a very happy effect upon those readers to whom they have the recommendation of novelty.

The qualities of style and imagery, however, form but a small part of the characteristics by which a literary faction is to be distinguished. The subject and object of their compositions, and the principles and opinions they are calculated to support, constitute a far more important criterion, and one to which it is usually altogether as easy to refer. Some poets are sufficiently described as the flatterers of greatness and power, and others as the champions of independence. One set of writers is known by its antipathy to decency and religion; another, by its methodistical cant and intolerance. Our new school of poetry has a moral character also; though it may not be possible, perhaps, to delineate it quite so concisely.

A splenetic and idle discontent with the existing institutions of society, seems to be at the bottom of all their serious and peculiar sentiments. Instead of contemplating the wonders and the pleasures which civilization has created for mankind, they are perpetually brooding over the disorders by which its progress has been attended. They are filled with horror and compassion at the sight of poor men spending their blood in the quarrels of princes, and brutifying their sublime capabilities in the drudgery of unremitting labour. For all sorts of vice and profligacy in the lower orders of society, they have the same virtuous horror, and the same tender compassion. While the existence of these offences overpowers them with grief and confusion, they never permit themselves to feel the smallest indignation or dislike towards the offenders. The present vicious constitution of society alone is responsible for all these enormities: the poor sinners are but the helpless victims or instruments of its disorders, and could not possibly have avoided the errors into which they have been betrayed. Though they can bear with crimes, therefore, they cannot reconcile themselves to punishments; and have an unconquerable antipathy to prisons, gibbets, and houses of correction, as engines of oppression, and instruments of atrocious injustice. While the plea of moral necessity is thus artfully brought forward to convert all the excesses of the poor into innocent misfortunes, no sort of indulgence is shown to the offences of the powerful and rich. Their oppressions, and seductions, and debaucheries, are the theme of many an angry verse; and the indignation and ab-

horrence of the reader is relentlessly conjured up against those perturbators of society, and scourges of mankind.

It is not easy to say, whether the fundamental absurdity of this doctrine, or the partiality of its application, be entitled to the severest reprehension. If men are driven to commit crimes, through a certain moral necessity; other men are compelled, by a similar necessity, to hate and despise them for their commission. The indignation of the sufferer is at least as natural as the guilt of him who makes him suffer; and the good order of society would probably be as well preserved, if our sympathies were sometimes called forth in behalf of the former. At all events, the same apology ought certainly to be admitted for the wealthy as for the needy offender. They are subject alike to the overruling influence of necessity, and equally affected by the miserable condition of society. If it be natural for a poor man to murder and rob, in order to make himself comfortable, it is no less natural for a rich man to gormandize and domineer, in order to have the full use of his riches. Wealth is just as valid an excuse for the one class of vices, as indigence is for the other. There are many other peculiarities of false sentiment in the productions of this class of writers, that are sufficiently deserving of commemoration; but we have already exceeded our limits in giving these general indications of their character, and must now hasten back to the consideration of the singular performance which has given occasion to all this discussion.

*　　*　　*　　*　　*

[October 1802]

Francis Jeffrey

FROM

REVIEW OF WORDSWORTH'S
THE EXCURSION,
IN THE *EDINBURGH REVIEW*

THIS will never do. It bears no doubt the stamp of the author's heart and fancy; but unfortunately not half so visibly as that of his peculiar system. His former poems were intended to recommend that system, and to bespeak favour for it by their individual merit;—but this, we suspect, must be recommended by the system —and can only expect to succeed where it has been previously established. It is longer, weaker, and tamer, than any of Mr Wordsworth's other productions; with less boldness of originality, and less even of that extreme simplicity and lowliness of tone which wavered so prettily, in the Lyrical Ballads, between silliness and pathos. We have imitations of Cowper, and even of Milton here, engrafted on the natural drawl of the Lakers—and all diluted into harmony by that profuse and irrepressible wordiness which deluges all the blank verse of this school of poetry, and lubricates and weakens the whole structure of their style.

Though it fairly fills four hundred and twenty good quarto pages, without note, vignette, or any sort of extraneous assistance, it is stated in the title—with something of an imprudent candour—to be but 'a portion' of a larger work; and in the preface, where an attempt is rather unsuccessfully made to explain the whole design, it is still more rashly disclosed, that it is but 'a part of the second part of a *long* and laborious work'—which is to consist of three parts.

What Mr Wordsworth's ideas of length are, we have no means of accurately judging; but we cannot help suspecting that they are liberal, to a degree that will alarm the weakness of most modern readers. As far as we can gather from the preface, the entire poem—or one of them, for we really are not sure whether there is to be one or two—is of a biographical nature; and is to contain the history of the author's mind, and of the origin and progress of his poetical powers, up to the period when they were sufficiently matured to qualify him for the great work on which he has been so long employed. Now, the quarto before us contains an account of one of his youthful rambles in the vales of Cumberland, and occupies precisely the period of three days; so that, by the use of a very powerful *calculus*, some estimate may be formed of the probable extent of the entire biography.

This small specimen, however, and the statements with which it is prefaced, have been sufficient to set our minds at rest in one particular. The case of Mr Wordsworth, we perceive, is now manifestly hopeless; and we give him up as altogether incurable, and beyond the power of criticism. We cannot indeed altogether omit taking precautions now and then against the spreading of the malady;—but for himself, though we shall watch the progress of his symptoms as a matter of professional curiosity and instruction, we really think it right not to harass him any longer with nauseous remedies,—but rather to throw in cordials and lenitives, and wait in patience for the natural termination of the disorder. In order to justify this desertion of our patient, however, it is proper to state why we despair of the success of a more active practice.

A man who has been for twenty years at work on such matter as is now before us, and who comes complacently forward with a whole quarto of it after all the admonitions he has received, cannot reasonably be expected to 'change his hand, or check his pride,' upon the suggestion of far weightier monitors than we can pretend to be. Inveterate habit must now have given a

kind of sanctity to the errors of early taste; and the very powers of which we lament the perversion, have probably become incapable of any other application. The very quantity, too, that he has written, and is at this moment working up for publication upon the old pattern, makes it almost hopeless to look for any change of it. All this is so much capital already sunk in the concern; which must be sacrificed if it be abandoned: and no man likes to give up for lost the time and talent and labour which he has embodied in any permanent production. We were not previously aware of these obstacles to Mr Wordsworth's conversion; and, considering the peculiarities of his former writings merely as the result of certain wanton and capricious experiments on public taste and indulgence, conceived it to be our duty to discourage their repetition by all the means in our power. We now see clearly, however, how the case stands;—and, making up our minds, though with the most sincere pain and reluctance, to consider him as finally lost to the good cause of poetry, shall endeavour to be thankful for the occasional gleams of tenderness and beauty which the natural force of his imagination and affections must still shed over all his productions,—and to which we shall ever turn with delight, in spite of the affectation and mysticism and prolixity, with which they are so abundantly contrasted.

Long habits of seclusion, and an excessive ambition of originality, can alone account for the disproportion which seems to exist between this author's taste and his genius; or for the devotion with which he has sacrificed so many precious gifts at the shrine of those paltry idols which he has set up for himself among his lakes and his mountains. Solitary musings, amidst such scenes, might no doubt be expected to nurse up the mind to the majesty of poetical conception,— (though it is remarkable, that all the greater poets lived, or had lived, in the full current of society):—But the collision of equal minds,—the admonition of prevailing impressions—seems necessary to reduce its redundancies, and repress that tendency to extravagance or puerility, into which the self-indulgence and self-admiration of genius is so apt to be betrayed, when it is allowed to wanton, without awe or restraint, in the triumph and delight of its own intoxication. That its flights should be graceful and glorious in the eyes of men, it seems almost to be necessary that they should be made in the consciousness that men's eyes are to behold them,—and that the inward transport and vigour by which they are inspired, should be tempered by an occasional reference to what will be thought of them by those ultimate dispensers of glory. An habitual and general knowledge of the few settled and permanent maxims, which form the canon of general taste in all large and polished societies—a certain tact, which informs us at once that many things, which we still love and are moved by in secret, must necessarily be despised as childish, or derided as absurd, in all such societies—though it will not stand in the place of genius, seems necessary to the success of its exertions; and though it will never enable any one to produce the higher beauties of art, can alone secure the talent which does produce them, from errors that must render it useless. Those who have most of the talent, however, commonly acquire this knowledge with the greatest facility;—and if Mr Wordsworth, instead of confining himself almost entirely to the society of the dalesmen and cottagers, and little children, who form the subjects of his book, had condescended to mingle a little more with the people that were to read and judge of it, we cannot help thinking, that its texture would have been considerably improved: At least it appears to us to be absolutely impossible, that any one who had lived or mixed familiarly with men of literature and ordinary judgment in poetry, (of course we exclude the coadjutors and disciples of his own school), could ever have fallen into such gross faults, or so long mistaken them for beauties. His first essays we looked upon in a good degree as poetical paradoxes,—maintained experimentally, in order to display talent, and court notoriety;—and so maintained, with no more serious belief in their truth, than is usually generated by an ingenious and animated defence of other paradoxes. But when we find, that he has been for twenty years exclusively employed upon articles of this very fabric, and that he has still enough of raw material on hand to keep him so employed for twenty years to come, we cannot refuse him the justice of believing that he is a sincere convert to his own system, and must ascribe the peculiarities of his composition, not to any transient affectation, or accidental caprice of imagination, but to a settled perversity of taste or understanding, which has been fostered, if not altogether created, by the circumstances to which we have already alluded.

The volume before us, if we were to describe it very shortly, we should characterize as a tissue of moral and devotional ravings, in which innumerable changes are rung upon a few very simple and familiar ideas:—but with such an accompaniment of long words, long sentences, and unwieldy phrases—and such a hubbub of strained raptures and fantastical sublimities, that it is often extremely difficult for the most skilful and attentive student to obtain a glimpse of the author's meaning—and altogether impossible for an ordinary reader to conjecture what he is about. Moral and religious enthusiasm, though undoubtedly poetical emotions, are at the same time but dangerous inspirers of poetry; nothing being so apt to run into interminable dulness or mellifluous extravagance, without giving the unfortunate author the slightest intimation of his danger. His laudable zeal for the efficacy of his preachments, he very naturally mistakes for the ardour of poetical inspiration;—and, while dealing out the high words and glowing phrases which are so readily supplied by themes of this description, can scarcely avoid believing that he is eminently original and impressive: —All sorts of commonplace notions and expressions are sanctified in his eyes, by the sublime ends for which they are employed; and the mystical verbiage of the methodist pulpit is repeated, till the speaker entertains no doubt that he is the elected organ of divine truth and persuasion. But if such be the common hazards of seeking inspiration from those potent fountains, it may easily be conceived what chance Mr Wordsworth had of escaping their enchantment,—with his natural propensities to wordiness, and his unlucky habit of debasing pathos with vulgarity. The fact accordingly is, that in this production he is more obscure than a Pindaric poet of the seventeenth century; and more verbose 'than even himself of yore;' while the wilfulness with which he persists in choosing his examples of intellectual dignity and tenderness exclusively from the lowest ranks of society, will be sufficiently apparent, from the circumstance of his having thought fit to make his chief prolocutor in this poetical dialogue, and chief advocate of Providence and Virtue, *an old Scotch Pedlar*—retired indeed from business—but still rambling about in his former haunts, and gossiping among his old customers, without his pack on his shoulders. The other persons of the drama are, a retired military chaplain, who has grown half an atheist and half a misanthrope—the wife of an unprosperous weaver—a servant girl with her infant—a parish pauper, and one or two other personages of equal rank and dignity.

The character of the work is decidedly didactic; and more than nine tenths of it are occupied with a species of dialogue, or rather a series of long sermons or harangues which pass between the pedlar, the author, the old chaplain, and a worthy vicar, who entertains the whole party at dinner on the last day of their excursion. The incidents which occur in the course of it are as few and trifling as can be imagined;—and those which the different speakers narrate in the course of their discourses, are introduced rather to illustrate their arguments or opinions, than for any interest they are supposed to possess of their own.— The doctrine which the work is intended to enforce, we are by no means certain that we have discovered. In so far as we can collect, however, it seems to be neither more nor less than the old familiar one, that a firm belief in the providence of a wise and beneficent

Being must be our great stay and support under all afflictions and perplexities upon earth—and that there are indications of his power and goodness in all the aspects of the visible universe, whether living or inanimate—every part of which should therefore be regarded with love and reverence, as exponents of those great attributes. We can testify, at least, that these salutary and important truths are inculcated at far greater length, and with more repetitions, than in any ten volumes of sermons that we ever perused. It is also maintained, with equal conciseness and originality, that there is frequently much good sense, as well as much enjoyment, in the humbler conditions of life; and that, in spite of great vices and abuses, there is a reasonable allowance both of happiness and goodness in society at large. If there be any deeper or more recondite doctrines in Mr Wordsworth's book, we must confess that they have escaped us;—and, convinced as we are of the truth and soundness of those to which we have alluded, we cannot help thinking that they might have been better enforced with less parade and prolixity. His effusions on what may be called the physiognomy of external nature, or its moral and theological expression, are eminently fantastic, obscure, and affected.—It is quite time, however, that we should give the reader a more particular account of this singular performance.

It opens with a picture of the author toiling across a bare common in a hot summer day, and reaching at last a ruined hut surrounded with tall trees, where he meets by appointment with a hale old man, with an iron-pointed staff lying beside him. Then follows a retrospective account of their first acquaintance—formed, it seems, when the author was at a village school; and his aged friend occupied 'one room,—the fifth part of a house' in the neighbourhood. After this, we have the history of this reverend person at no small length. He was born, we are happy to find, in Scotland —among the hills of Athol; and his mother, after his father's death, married the parish schoolmaster—so that he was taught his letters betimes: But then, as it is here set forth with much solemnity,

'From his sixth year, the boy, of whom I speak,
In summer, tended cattle on the hills.'

And again, a few pages after, that there may be no risk of mistake as to a point of such essential importance—

'From early childhood, even, as hath been said,
From his *sixth year*, he had been sent abroad,
In summer, to tend herds: Such was his task!'

In the course of this occupation, it is next recorded, that he acquired such a taste for rural scenery and open air, that when he was sent to teach a school in a neigh-

bouring village, he found it 'a misery to him;' and determined to embrace the more romantic occupation of a Pedlar—or, as Mr Wordsworth more musically expresses it,

'A vagrant merchant bent beneath his load;'

—and in the course of his peregrinations had acquired a very large acquaintance, which, after he had given up dealing, he frequently took a summer ramble to visit.

The author, on coming up to this interesting personage, finds him sitting with his eyes half shut;—and, not being quite sure whether he is asleep or awake, stands 'some minutes space' in silence beside him. 'At length,' says he, with his own delightful simplicity—

'At length I hailed him—*seeing that his hat
Was moist* with water-drops, as if the brim
Had newly scooped a running stream!—
———— "'Tis," said I, "a burning day;
My lips are parched with thirst;—but you, I guess,
Have somewhere found relief."'

Upon this, the benevolent old man points him out a well in a corner, to which the author repairs; and, after minutely describing its situation, beyond a broken wall, and between two alders that 'grew in a cold damp nook,' he thus faithfully chronicles the process of his return.

'My thirst I slaked—and from the cheerless spot
Withdrawing, straightway to the shade returned,
Where sate the old man on the cottage bench.'

The Pedlar then gives an account of the last inhabitants of the deserted cottage beside them. These were, a good industrious weaver and his wife and children. They were very happy for a while; till sickness and want of work came upon them; and then the father enlisted as a soldier, and the wife pined in the lonely cottage—growing every year more careless and desponding, as her anxiety and fears for her absent husband, of whom no tidings ever reached her, accumulated. Her children died, and left her cheerless and alone; and at last she died also; and the cottage fell to decay. We must say, that there is very considerable pathos in the telling of this simple story; and that they who can get over the repugnance excited by the triteness of its incidents, and the lowness of its objects, will not fail to be struck with the author's knowledge of the human heart, and the power he possesses of stirring up its deepest and gentlest sympathies. His prolixity, indeed, it is not so easy to get over. This little story fills about twenty-five quarto pages; and abounds, of course, with mawkish sentiment, and details of preposterous minuteness. When the tale is told, the travellers take their staffs, and end their first day's journey, without further adventure, at a little inn. . . .

Besides those more extended passages of interest or beauty, which we have quoted, and omitted to quote, there are scattered up and down the book, and in the midst of its most repulsive portions, a very great number of single lines and images, that sparkle like gems in the desert, and startle us with an intimation of the great poetic powers that lie buried in the rubbish that has been heaped around them. It is difficult to pick up these, after we have once passed them by; but we shall endeavour to light upon one or two. The beneficial effect of intervals of relaxation and pastime on youthful minds, is finely expressed, we think, in a single line, when it is said to be—

'Like vernal ground to Sabbath sunshine left.'[1]

The following image of the bursting forth of a mountain-spring, seems to us also to be conceived with great elegance and beauty.

'And a few steps may bring us to the spot,
Where haply crown'd with flowrets and green herbs;
The Mountain Infant to the Sun comes forth
Like human life from darkness.'—[2]

The ameliorating effects of song and music on the minds which most delight in them, are likewise very poetically expressed.

——'And when the stream
Which overflowed the soul was passed away,
A consciousness remained that it had left,
Deposited upon the silent shore
Of Memory, images and precious thoughts,
That shall not die, and cannot be destroyed.'[3]

Nor is any thing more elegant than the representation of the graceful tranquillity occasionally put on by one of the author's favourites; who, though gay and airy, in general—

'Was graceful, when it pleased him, smooth and still
As the mute Swan that floats adown the stream,
Or on the waters of th' unruffled lake
Anchored her placid beauty. Not a leaf
That flutters on the bough more light than he,
And now a flower that droops in the green shade,
More winningly reserved.'——[4]

Nor are there wanting morsels of a sterner and more majestic beauty; as when, assuming the weightier diction of Cowper, he says, in language which the hearts of all readers of modern history must have responded—

——'Earth is sick,
And Heaven is weary of the hollow words
Which States and Kingdoms utter when they speak
Of Truth and Justice.'[5]

These examples, we perceive, are not very well chosen—but we have not leisure to improve the selection; and, such as they are, they may serve to give the reader a notion of the sort of merit which we meant to illustrate by their citation.—When we look back to them, indeed, and to the other passages which we have now extracted, we feel half inclined to rescind the severe sentence which we passed on the work at the beginning:—But when we look into the work itself, we perceive that it cannot be rescinded. Nobody can be more disposed to do justice to the great powers of Mr Wordsworth than we are; and, from the first time that he came before us, down to the present moment, we have uniformly testified in their favour, and assigned indeed our high sense of their value as the chief ground of the bitterness with which we resented their perversion. That perversion, however, is now far more visible than their original dignity; and while we collect the fragments, it is impossible not to lament the ruins from which we are condemned to pick them. If any one should doubt of the existence of such a perversion, or be disposed to dispute about the instances we have hastily brought forward, we would just beg leave to refer him to the general pla˜ and the characters of the poem now before us.—Why should Mr Wordsworth have made his hero a superannuated Pedlar? What but the most wretched and provoking perversity of taste and judgment, could induce any one to place his chosen advocate of wisdom and virtue in so absurd and fantastic a condition? Did Mr Wordsworth really imagine, that his favourite doctrines were likely to gain any thing in point of effect or authority by being put into the mouth of a person accustomed to higgle about tape, or brass sleeve-buttons? Or is it not plain that, independent of the ridicule and disgust which such a personification must give to many of his readers, its adoption exposes his work throughout to the charge of revolting incongruity, and utter disregard of probability or nature? For, after he has thus wilfully debased his moral teacher by a low occupation, is there one word that he puts into his mouth, or one sentiment of which he makes him the organ, that has the most remote reference to that occupation? Is there any thing in his learned, abstracted, and logical harangues, that savours of the calling that is ascribed to him? Are any of their materials such as a pedlar could possibly have dealt in? Are the manners, the diction, the sentiments, in any, the very smallest degree, accommodated to a

---

[1] VII, 781.　　[2] III, 32–35.
[3] VII, 25–30.　　[4] VI, 292–98.

[5] V, 378–81.

person in that condition ? or are they not eminently and conspicuously such as could not by possibility belong to it? A man who went about selling flannel and pocket-handkerchiefs in this lofty diction, would soon frighten away all his customers; and would infallibly pass either for a madman, or for some learned and affected gentleman, who, in a frolic, had taken up a character which he was peculiarly ill qualified for supporting.

The absurdity in this case, we think, is palpable and glaring; but it is exactly of the same nature with that which infects the whole substance of the work—a puerile ambition of singularity engrafted on an unlucky predilection for truisms; and an affected passion for simplicity and humble life, most awkwardly combined with a taste for mystical refinements, and all the gorgeousness of obscure phraseology. His taste for simplicity is evinced, by sprinkling up and down his interminable declamations, a few descriptions of baby-houses, and of old hats with wet brims; and his amiable partiality for humble life, by assuring us, that a wordy rhetorician, who talks about Thebes, and allegorizes all the heathen mythology, was once a pedlar—and making him break in upon his magnificent orations with two or three awkward notices of something that he had seen when selling winter raiment about the country—or of the changes in the state of society, which had almost annihilated his former calling.

[November 1814]

SCOTT'S REVIEW OF AUSTEN'S EMMA

The periodicals of the early nineteenth century almost invariably took a particular political stance or had "unofficial" connections with political parties, ranging from the conservative "Church and State" Tory publications The British Critic *and* Quarterly Review, *through the Whiggish* Edinburgh Review, *to Leigh Hunt's "radical"* Examiner. *It was, in fact, political considerations that brought into being the second most important periodical of the time,* The Quarterly Review, *whose first number appeared in February 1809. As the reformist-Whig opinions of the* Edinburgh Review *became more explicit and insistent, a group of men of Tory persuasion saw the necessity for a rival voice. In 1807 uncoordinated discussion and planning had begun; among those interested and involved were the publisher John Murray, George Canning (Secretary of Foreign Affairs), his cousin Stratford Canning, Sir Walter Scott, and William Gifford. It was the publication of an article in the* Edinburgh Review *for October 1808, criticizing the upper classes and calling for reform, which brought matters to a head and, in the words of Henry Brougham, "called the* Quarterly Review *into existence in three months."*

William Gifford (1756–1826), who had earlier been the editor of the Anti-Jacobin; or Weekly Examiner (1797–1798), *was appointed first editor of the* Quarterly Review *and retained the position until 1824. Gifford had been born in poverty and worked for a time as a shoemaker's apprentice; on the basis of his literary interests and abilities, he was sent to Oxford. In the 1790's he had published the literary satires* Baviad *and* Maeviad *and was later to prepare editions of the plays of Massinger, Jonson, and Ford. Although he himself contributed only eight reviews, Gifford's "anti-jacobin" prejudices colored much of the material in the* Quarterly; *he was not above editing manuscripts to instill the proper political tone, often of an abusive nature.*

The political position of the Quarterly Review *being what it was, it is no surprise that its columns should have waged persistent attack on the younger "radical" authors such as Hunt, Keats, Hazlitt, and Shelley; the periodical is best known today for such articles as Croker's nasty-minded review of Keats's* Endymion. *However, it should be remembered that the* Quarterly *numbered among its writers some of the most distinguished talents of the time, and many of its reviews are significant literary essays by first-rate minds. Among the reviewers in its early years of publication were the literary figures Scott, Southey, George Ellis, and Charles Lamb (who contributed a review of* The Excursion); *Anglican churchmen such as Reginald Heber, later bishop of Calcutta, and William Rowe Lyall, later dean of Canterbury; Tory politicians and appointees such as George Canning, John Wilson Croker (first secretary of the admiralty), and John Barrow (second secretary of the admiralty).*

Sir Walter Scott was not only a guiding force in the founding of the Quarterly Review, *but also one of its regular reviewers. Poetry (Southey's and Byron's, among others), history, novels, and biography were among the fields he covered. He is represented here by his review of Jane Austen's* Emma, *which is both a mature criticism of that novel and at the same time a significant discussion of the history of the English novel by one of its leading practitioners.*

On the history of the Quarterly Review, *see the relevant sections in Hayden's* Romantic Reviewers *and Graham's* English Literary Periodicals; *as well as Graham's* Tory Criticism in the Quarterly Review 1809–1853 *(New York: Columbia University Press, 1921), and Hill Shine and Helen Chadwick Shine's* The Quarterly Review under Gifford: Identification of Contributions 1809–1824 *(Chapel Hill, N.C.: University of North Carolina Press, 1949). Roy Benjamin Clark has written the biography* William Gifford, Tory Satirist, Critic, and Editor *(New York: Columbia Columbia University Press, 1930). Hazlitt devotes an appropriately destructive chapter to Gifford in* The Spirit of the Age.

Sir Walter Scott

REVIEW OF JANE AUSTEN'S
EMMA,
IN *THE QUARTERLY REVIEW*

THERE are some vices in civilized society so common that they are hardly acknowledged as stains upon the moral character, the propensity to which is nevertheless carefully concealed, even by those who most frequently give way to them; since no man of pleasure would willingly assume the gross epithet of a debauchee or a drunkard. One would almost think that novel-reading fell under this class of frailties, since among the crowds who read little else, it is not common to find an individual of hardihood sufficient to avow his taste for these frivolous studies. A novel, therefore, is frequently 'bread eaten in secret;' and it is not upon

Lydia Languish's [1] toilet alone that Tom Jones and Peregrine Pickle are to be found ambushed behind works of a more grave and instructive character. And hence it has happened, that in no branch of composition, not even in poetry itself, have so many writers, and of such varied talents, exerted their powers. It may perhaps be added, that although the composition of these works admits of being exalted and decorated by the higher exertions of genius; yet such is the universal charm of narrative, that the worst novel ever written will find some gentle reader content to yawn over it, rather than to open the page of the historian, moralist, or poet. We have heard, indeed, of one work of fiction so unutterably stupid, that the proprietor, diverted by the rarity of the incident, offered the book, which consisted of two volumes in duodecimo, handsomely bound, to any person who would declare, upon his honour, that he had read the whole from beginning to end. But although this offer was made to the passengers on board an Indiaman, during a tedious outward-bound voyage, the 'Memoirs of Clegg the Clergyman,' (such was the title of this unhappy composition,) completely baffled the most dull and determined student on board, and bid fair for an exception to the general rule above-mentioned,—when the love of glory prevailed with the boatswain, a man of strong and solid parts, to hazard the attempt, and he actually conquered and carried off the prize!

The judicious reader will see at once that we have been pleading our own cause while stating the universal practice, and preparing him for a display of more general acquaintance with this fascinating department of literature, than at first sight may seem consistent with the graver studies to which we are compelled by duty: but in truth, when we consider how many hours of languor and anxiety, of deserted age and solitary celibacy, of pain even and poverty, are beguiled by the perusal of these light volumes, we cannot austerely condemn the source from which is drawn the alleviation of such a portion of human misery, or consider the regulation of this department as beneath the sober consideration of the critic.

If such apologies may be admitted in judging the labours of ordinary novelists, it becomes doubly the duty of the critic to treat with kindness as well as candour works which, like this before us, proclaim a knowledge of the human heart, with the power and resolution to bring that knowledge to the service of honour and virtue. The author is already known to the public by the two novels announced in her title-page, and both, the last especially, attracted, with justice, an attention from the public far superior to what is

---

[1] The sentimental heroine of Sheridan's *The Rivals*.

granted to the ephemeral productions which supply the regular demand of watering-places and circulating libraries. They belong to a class of fictions which has arisen almost in our own times, and which draws the characters and incidents introduced more immediately from the current of ordinary life than was permitted by the former rules of the novel.

In its first appearance, the novel was the legitimate child of the romance; and though the manners and general turn of the composition were altered so as to suit modern times, the author remained fettered by many peculiarities derived from the original style of romantic fiction. These may be chiefly traced in the conduct of the narrative, and the tone of sentiment attributed to the fictitious personages. On the first point, although

> The talisman and magic wand were broke,
> Knights, dwarfs, and genii vanish'd into smoke,

still the reader expected to peruse a course of adventures of a nature more interesting and extraordinary than those which occur in his own life, or that of his next-door neighbours. The hero no longer defeated armies by his single sword, clove giants to the chine, or gained kingdoms. But he was expected to go through perils by sea and land, to be steeped in poverty, to be tried by temptation, to be exposed to the alternate vicissitudes of adversity and prosperity, and his life was a troubled scene of suffering and achievement. Few novelists, indeed, adventured to deny to the hero his final hour of tranquillity and happiness, though it was the prevailing fashion never to relieve him out of his last and most dreadful distress until the finishing chapters of his history; so that although his prosperity in the record of his life was short, we were bound to believe it was long and uninterrupted when the author had done with him. The heroine was usually condemned to equal hardships and hazards. She was regularly exposed to being forcibly carried off like a Sabine virgin by some frantic admirer. And even if she escaped the terrors of masked ruffians, an insidious ravisher, a cloak wrapped forcibly around her head, and a coach with the blinds up driving she could not conjecture whither, she had still her share of wandering, of poverty, of obloquy, of seclusion, and of imprisonment, and was frequently extended upon a bed of sickness, and reduced to her last shilling before the author condescended to shield her from persecution. In all these dread contingencies the mind of the reader was expected to sympathize, since by incidents so much beyond the bounds of his ordinary experience, his wonder and interest ought at once to be excited. But gradually he became familiar with the land of fiction, the adventures of which he assimilated not with those of real life, but with each other. Let the distress of the hero or heroine be ever so great, the reader reposed an imperturbable confidence in the talents of the author, who, as he had plunged them into distress, would in his own good time, and when things, as Tony Lumkin[2] says, were in a concatenation accordingly, bring his favourites out of all their troubles. Mr. Crabbe has expressed his own and our feelings excellently on this subject.

> For should we grant these beauties all endure
> Severest pangs, they've still the speediest cure;
> Before one charm be wither'd from the face,
> Except the bloom which shall again have place,
> In wedlock ends each wish, in triumph all disgrace.
> And life to come, we fairly may suppose,
> One light bright contrast to these wild dark woes.

In short, the author of novels was, in former times, expected to tread pretty much in the limits between the concentric circles of probability and possibility; and as he was not permitted to transgress the latter, his narrative, to make amends, almost always went beyond the bounds of the former. Now, although it may be urged that the vicissitudes of human life have occasionally led an individual through as many scenes of singular fortune as are represented in the most extravagant of these fictions, still the causes and personages acting on these changes have varied with the progress of the adventurer's fortune, and do not present that combined plot, (the object of every skilful novelist,) in which all the more interesting individuals of the dramatis personæ have their appropriate share in the action and in bringing about the catastrophe. Here, even more than in its various and violent changes of fortune, rests the improbability of the novel. The life of man rolls forth like a stream from the fountain, or it spreads out into tranquillity like a placid or stagnant lake. In the latter case, the individual grows old among the characters with whom he was born, and is contemporary,—shares precisely the sort of weal and woe to which his birth destined him,—moves in the same circle,—and, allowing for the change of seasons, is influenced by, and influences the same class of persons by which he was originally surrounded. The man of mark and of adventure, on the contrary, resembles, in the course of his life, the river whose mid-current and discharge into the ocean are widely removed from each other, as well as from the rocks and wild flowers which its fountains first reflected;

---

2 The rowdy, mischievous son in Goldsmith's *She Stoops to Conquer.* The remark to which Scott refers occurs in Act I, scene ii, and is actually spoken by one of Tony's vulgar drinking companions.

violent changes of time, of place, and of circumstances, hurry him forward from one scene to another, and his adventures will usually be found only connected with each other because they have happened to the same individual. Such a history resembles an ingenious, fictitious narrative, exactly in the degree in which an old dramatic chronicle of the life and death of some distinguished character, where all the various agents appear and disappear as in the page of history, approaches a regular drama, in which every person introduced plays an appropriate part, and every point of the action tends to one common catastrophe.

We return to the second broad line of distinction between the novel, as formerly composed, and real life, —the difference, namely, of the sentiments. The novelist professed to give an imitation of nature, but it was, as the French say, *la belle nature.* Human beings, indeed, were presented, but in the most sentimental mood, and with minds purified by a sensibility which often verged on extravagance. In the serious class of novels, the hero was usually

> 'A knight of love, who never broke a vow.'

And although, in those of a more humorous cast, he was permitted a license, borrowed either from real life or from the libertinism of the drama, still a distinction was demanded even from Peregrine Pickle, or Tom Jones; and the hero, in every folly of which he might be guilty, was studiously vindicated from the charge of infidelity of the heart. The heroine was, of course, still more immaculate; and to have conferred her affections upon any other than the lover to whom the reader had destined her from their first meeting, would have been a crime against sentiment which no author, of moderate prudence, would have hazarded, under the old *régime.*

Here, therefore, we have two essential and important cimcumstances, in which the earlier novels differed from those now in fashion, and were more nearly assimilated to the old romances. And there can be no doubt that, by the studied involution and extrication of the story, by the combination of incidents new, striking, and wonderful beyond the course of ordinary life, the former authors opened that obvious and strong sense of interest which arises from curiosity; as by the pure, elevated, and romantic cast of the sentiment, they conciliated those better propensities of our nature which loves to contemplate the picture of virtue, even when confessedly unable to imitate its excellences.

But strong and powerful as these sources of emotion and interest may be, they are, like all others, capable of being exhausted by habit. The imitators who rushed in crowds upon each path in which the great masters

788] THE REVIEWERS, SCOTT

of the art had successively led the way, produced upon the public mind the usual effect of satiety. The first writer of a new class is, as it were, placed on a pinnacle of excellence, to which, at the earliest glance of a surprized admirer, his ascent seems little less than miraculous. Time and imitation speedily diminish the wonder, and each successive attempt establishes a kind of progressive scale of ascent between the lately deified author, and the reader, who had deemed his excellence inaccessible. The stupidity, the mediocrity, the merit of his imitators, are alike fatal to the first inventor, by shewing how possible it is to exaggerate his faults and to come within a certain point of his beauties.

Materials also (and the man of genius as well as his wretched imitator must work with the same) become stale and familiar. Social life, in our civilized days, affords few instances capable of being painted in the strong dark colours which excite surprize and horror; and robbers, smugglers, bailiffs, caverns, dungeons, and mad-houses, have been all introduced until they ceased to interest. And thus in the novel, as in every style of composition which appeals to the public taste, the more rich and easily worked mines being exhausted, the adventurous author must, if he is desirous of success, have recourse to those which were disdained by his predecessors as unproductive, or avoided as only capable of being turned to profit by great skill and labour.

Accordingly a style of novel has arisen, within the last fifteen or twenty years, differing from the former in the points upon which the interest hinges; neither alarming our credulity nor amusing our imagination by wild variety of incident, or by those pictures of romantic affection and sensibility, which were formerly as certain attributes of fictitious characters as they are of rare occurrence among those who actually live and die. The substitute for these excitements, which had lost much of their poignancy by the repeated and injudicious use of them, was the art of copying from nature as she really exists in the common walks of life, and presenting to the reader, instead of the splendid scenes of an imaginary world, a correct and striking representation of that which is daily taking place around him.

In adventuring upon this task, the author makes obvious sacrifices, and encounters peculiar difficulty. He who paints from *le beau idéal*, if his scenes and sentiments are striking and interesting, is in a great measure exempted from the difficult task of reconciling them with the ordinary probabilities of life: but he who paints a scene of common occurrence, places his composition within that extensive range of criticism which general experience offers to every reader. The resemblance of a statue of Hercules we must take on the

artist's judgment; but every one can criticize that which is presented as the portrait of a friend, or neighbour. Something more than a mere sign-post likeness is also demanded. The portrait must have spirit and character, as well as resemblance; and being deprived of all that, according to Bayes,[3] goes 'to elevate and surprize,' it must make amends by displaying depth of knowledge and dexterity of execution. We, therefore, bestow no mean compliment upon the author of Emma, when we say that, keeping close to common incidents, and to such characters as occupy the ordinary walks of life, she has produced sketches of such spirit and originality, that we never miss the excitation which depends upon a narrative of uncommon events, arising from the consideration of minds, manners, and sentiments, greatly above our own. In this class she stands almost alone; for the scenes of Miss Edgeworth are laid in higher life, varied by more romantic incident, and by her remarkable power of embodying and illustrating national character. But the author of Emma confines herself chiefly to the middling classes of society; her most distinguished characters do not rise greatly above well-bred country gentlemen and ladies; and those which are sketched with most originality and precision, belong to a class rather below that standard. The narrative of all her novels is composed of such common occurrences as may have fallen under the observation of most folks; and her dramatis personæ conduct themselves upon the motives and principles which the readers may recognize as ruling their own and that of most of their acquaintances. The kind of moral, also, which these novels inculcate, applies equally to the paths of common life, as will best appear from a short notice of the author's former works, with a more full abstract of that which we at present have under consideration.

'Sense and Sensibility,' the first of these compositions, contains the history of two sisters. The elder, a young lady of prudence and regulated feelings, becomes gradually attached to a man of an excellent heart and limited talents, who happens unfortunately to be fettered by a rash and ill-assorted engagement. In the younger sister, the influence of sensibility and imagination predominates; and she, as was to be expected, also falls in love, but with more unbridled and wilful passion. Her lover, gifted with all the qualities of exterior polish and vivacity, proves faithless, and marries a woman of large fortune. The interest and merit of the piece depend altogether upon the behaviour of the elder sister, while obliged at once to sustain her own disappointment with fortitude, and to support her

---

3 Character in the satiric comedy *The Rehearsal* (1672) by George Villiers, second Duke of Buckingham.

sister, who abandons herself, with unsuppressed feelings, to the indulgence of grief. The marriage of the unworthy rival at length relieves her own lover from his imprudent engagement, while her sister, turned wise by precept, example, and experience, transfers her affection to a very respectable and somewhat too serious admirer, who had nourished an unsuccessful passion through the three volumes.

In 'Pride and Prejudice' the author presents us with a family of young women, bred up under a foolish and vulgar mother, and a father whose good abilities lay hid under such a load of indolence and insensibility, that he had become contented to make the foibles and follies of his wife and daughters the subject of dry and humorous sarcasm, rather than of admonition, or restraint. This is one of the portraits from ordinary life which shews our author's talents in a very strong point of view. A friend of ours, whom the author never saw or heard of, was at once recognized by his own family as the original of Mr Bennett, and we do not know if he has yet got rid of the nickname. A Mr Collins, too, a formal, conceited, yet servile young sprig of divinity, is drawn with the same force and precision. The story of the piece consists chiefly in the fates of the second sister, to whom a man of high birth, large fortune, but haughty and reserved manners, becomes attached, in spite of the discredit thrown upon the object of his affection by the vulgarity and ill-conduct of her relations. The lady, on the contrary, hurt at the contempt of her connections, which the lover does not even attempt to suppress, and prejudiced against him on other accounts, refuses the hand which he ungraciously offers, and does not perceive that she has done a foolish thing until she accidentally visits a very handsome seat and grounds belonging to her admirer. They chance to meet exactly as her prudence had begun to subdue her prejudice; and after some essential services rendered to her family, the lover becomes encouraged to renew his addresses, and the novel ends happily.

Emma has even less story than either of the preceding novels. Miss Emma Woodhouse, from whom the book takes its name, is the daughter of a gentleman of wealth and consequence residing at his seat in the immediate vicinage of a country village called Highbury. The father, a good-natured, silly valetudinary, abandons the management of his household to Emma, he himself being only occupied by his summer and winter walk, his apothecary, his gruel, and his whist table. The latter is supplied from the neighbouring village of Highbury with precisely the sort of persons who occupy the vacant corners of a regular whist table, when a village is in the neighbourhood, and better cannot be found within the family. We have the smiling and courteous vicar, who nourishes the ambitious hope of obtaining

Miss Woodhouse's hand. We have Mrs. Bates, the wife of a former rector, past every thing but tea and whist; her daughter, Miss Bates, a good-natured, vulgar, and foolish old maid; Mr. Weston, a gentleman of a frank disposition and moderate fortune, in the vicinity, and his wife an amiable and accomplished person, who had been Emma's governess, and is devotedly attached to her. Amongst all these personages, Miss Woodhouse walks forth, the princess paramount, superior to all her companions in wit, beauty, fortune, and accomplishments, doated upon by her father and the Westons, admired, and almost worshipped by the more humble companions of the whist table. The object of most young ladies is, or at least is usually supposed to be, a desirable connection in marriage. But Emma Woodhouse, either anticipating the taste of a later period of life, or, like a good sovereign, preferring the weal of her subjects of Highbury to her own private interest, sets generously about making matches for her friends without thinking of matrimony on her own account. We are informed that she had been eminently successful in the case of Mr. and Miss Weston; and when the novel commences she is exerting her influence in favour of Miss Harriet Smith, a boarding-school girl without family or fortune, very good humoured, very pretty, very silly, and, what suited Miss Woodhouse's purpose best of all, very much disposed to be married.

In these conjugal machinations Emma is frequently interrupted, not only by the cautions of her father, who had a particular objection to any body committing the rash act of matrimony, but also by the sturdy reproof and remonstrances of Mr. Knightley, the elder brother of her sister's husband, a sensible country gentleman of thirty-five, who had known Emma from her cradle, and was the only person who ventured to find fault with her. In spite, however, of his censure and warning, Emma lays a plan of marrying Harriet Smith to the vicar; and though she succeeds perfectly in diverting her simple friend's thoughts from an honest farmer who had made her a very suitable offer, and in flattering her into a passion for Mr. Elton, yet, on the other hand, that conceited divine totally mistakes the nature of the encouragement held out to him, and attributes the favour which he found in Miss Woodhouse's eyes to a lurking affection on her own part. This at length encourages him to a presumptuous declaration of his sentiments; upon receiving a repulse, he looks abroad elsewhere, and enriches the Highbury society by uniting himself to a dashing young woman with as many thousands as are usually called ten, and a corresponding quantity of presumption and ill breeding.

While Emma is thus vainly engaged in forging

wedlock-fetters for others, her friends have views of the same kind upon her, in favour of a son of Mr. Weston by a former marriage, who bears the name, lives under the patronage, and is to inherit the fortune of a rich uncle. Unfortunately Mr. Frank Churchill had already settled his affections on Miss Jane Fairfax, a young lady of reduced fortune; but as this was a concealed affair, Emma, when Mr. Churchill first appears on the stage, has some thoughts of being in love with him herself; speedily, however, recovering from that dangerous propensity, she is disposed to confer him upon her deserted friend Harriet Smith. Harriet has, in the interim, fallen desperately in love with Mr. Knightley, the sturdy, advice-giving bachelor; and, as all the village supposes Frank Churchill and Emma to be attached to each other, there are cross purposes enough (were the novel of a more romantic cast) for cutting half the men's throats and breaking all the women's hearts. But at Highbury Cupid walks decorously, and with good discretion, bearing his torch under a lanthorn, instead of flourishing it around to set the house on fire. All these entanglements bring on only a train of mistakes and embarrassing situations, and dialogues, at balls and parties of pleasure, in which the author displays her peculiar powers of humour and knowledge of human life. The plot is extricated with great simplicity. The aunt of Frank Churchill dies; his uncle, no longer under her baneful influence, consents to his marriage with Jane Fairfax. Mr. Knightley and Emma are led, by this unexpected incident, to discover that they had been in love with each other all along. Mr. Woodhouse's objections to the marriage of his daughter are overpowered by the fears of housebreakers, and the comfort which he hopes to derive from having a stout son-in-law resident in the family; and the facile affections of Harriet Smith are transferred, like a bank bill by indorsation, to her former suitor, the honest farmer, who had obtained a favourable opportunity of renewing his addresses. Such is the simple plan of a story which we peruse with pleasure, if not with deep interest, and which perhaps we might more willingly resume than one of those narratives where the attention is strongly riveted, during the first perusal, by the powerful excitement of curiosity.

The author's knowledge of the world, and the peculiar tact with which she presents characters that the reader cannot fail to recognize, reminds us something of the merits of the Flemish school of painting. The subjects are not often elegant, and certainly never grand; but they are finished up to nature, and with a precision which delights the reader. This is a merit which it is very difficult to illustrate by extracts, because it pervades the whole work, and is not to be comprehended from a single passage. The following is a dialogue between Mr. Woodhouse, and his elder daughter Isabella, who shares his anxiety about health, and has, like her father, a favourite apothecary. The reader must be informed that this lady, with her husband, a sensible, peremptory sort of person, had come to spend a week with her father. . . .[4]

Perhaps the reader may collect from the preceding specimen both the merits and faults of the author. The former consists much in the force of a narrative conducted with much neatness and point, and a quiet yet comic dialogue, in which the characters of the speakers evolve themselves with dramatic effect. The faults, on the contrary, arise from the minute detail which the author's plan comprehends. Characters of folly or simplicity, such as those of old Woodhouse and Miss Bates, are ridiculous when first presented, but if too often brought forward or too long dwelt upon, their prosing is apt to become as tiresome in fiction as in real society. Upon the whole, the turn of this author's novels bears the same relation to that of the sentimental and romantic cast, that cornfields and cottages and meadows bear to the highly adorned grounds of a show mansion, or the rugged sublimities of a mountain landscape. It is neither so captivating as the one, nor so grand as the other, but it affords to those who frequent it a pleasure nearly allied with the experience of their own social habits; and what is of some importance, the youthful wanderer may return from his promenade to the ordinary business of life, without any chance of having his head turned by the recollection of the scene through which he has been wandering.

One word, however, we must say in behalf of that once powerful divinity, Cupid, king of gods and men, who in these times of revolution, has been assailed, even in his own kingdom of romance, by the authors who were formerly his devoted priests. We are quite aware that there are few instances of first attachment being brought to a happy conclusion, and that it seldom can be so in a state of society so highly advanced as to render early marriages among the better class, acts, generally speaking, of imprudence. But the youth of this realm need not at present be taught the doctrine of selfishness. It is by no means their error to give the world or the good things of the world all for love; and before the authors of moral fiction couple Cupid indivisibly with calculating prudence, we would have them reflect, that they may sometimes lend their aid to substitute more mean, more sordid, and more selfish motives of conduct, for the romantic feelings which

---

4 Scott here quotes a passage from Chapter 12, beginning with the paragraph: "While they were thus comfortably occupied" and continuing through the paragraph: "And she talked in this way so long and successfully . . ."

their predecessors perhaps fanned into too powerful a flame. Who is it, that in his youth has felt a virtuous attachment, however romantic or however unfortunate, but can trace back to its influence much that his character may possess of what is honourable, dignified, and disinterested? If he recollects hours wasted in unavailing hope, or saddened by doubt and disappointment; he may also dwell on many which have been snatched from folly or libertinism, and dedicated to studies which might render him worthy of the object of his affection, or pave the way perhaps to that distinction necessary to raise him to an equality with her. Even the habitual indulgence of feelings totally unconnected with ourself and our own immediate interest, softens, graces, and amends the human mind; and after the pain of disappointment is past, those who survive (and by good fortune those are the greater number) are neither less wise nor less worthy members of society for having felt, for a time, the influence of a passion which has been well qualified as the 'tenderest, noblest and best.'

[October 1815]

LOCKHART'S "ON THE COCKNEY SCHOOL OF POETRY"
Like the Quarterly Review, Blackwood's Edinburgh Magazine *was called into being as a Tory answer to the* Edinburgh Review. *Unlike the two leading literary quarterlies, however, Blackwood's was a monthly publication and a magazine rather than a quarterly; it contained not only literary reviews but works of fiction and poetry, reports of scientific and historical research, and a "Monthly Register" of events at home and abroad. In the words of Walter Graham, it was set up as "a more pert and nimble Quarterly." However, in its initial years, Blackwood's went beyond pertness and nimbleness; as Ian Jack has observed, "mischief was an end in itself." The initial issue of October 1817 revealed the beginning of its most famous example of literary "mischief," the series of essays "On the Cockney School of Poetry" by John G. Lockhart. In an age of journalism not noted for its restraint and good manners, the series represented an extreme of scurrilous critical opinion. The fourth essay of the series, appearing in August 1818, was devoted to Keats; it belabored his "Cockney" background, described Endymion as "imperturbable drivelling idiocy," and concluded: ". . . so back to the shop Mr. John, back to 'plasters, pills, and ointment boxes,' &c. But, for Heaven's sake, young Sangrado, be a little more sparing of extenuatives and soporifics in your practice than you have been in your poetry." The venom of Blackwood's early literary attacks led to the death of John Scott, the gifted editor of the London Magazine, in a duel caused by his strong replies to Lockhart's "duplicity" and "scurrility."*

The author of the "Cockney School" essays was John Gibson Lockhart (1794–1854), who was one of the early editors and with John Wilson wrote most of the literary reviews. In 1825 Lockhart became editor of the Quarterly Review and retained the post until 1853. He was the son-in-law of Sir Walter Scott, and prepared the justly praised biography Memoirs of the Life of Sir Walter Scott (1837–1838). Despite its critical irre-

sponsibility, Blackwood's *did attract to its columns in its early years some notable and distinguished writers, among them Sir Walter Scott, Coleridge, De Quincey, and James Hogg ("the Ettrick Shepherd"). And "after a few years of lusty youth," as Graham observes, the magazine adopted a more moderate critical voice and was destined to become one of the major literary magazines of the nineteenth and twentieth centuries.*

John Gibson Lockhart

ARTICLE
IN BLACKWOOD'S MAGAZINE

ON THE COCKNEY SCHOOL
OF POETRY.

No I.

Our talk shall be (a theme we never tire on)
Of Chaucer, Spenser, Shakspeare, Milton, Byron,
(Our England's Dante)—Wordsworth—HUNT, and KEATS,
The Muses' son of promise; and of what feats
He yet may do.
                                    CORNELIUS WEBB.

WHILE the whole critical world is occupied with balancing the merits, whether in theory or in execution, of what is commonly called THE LAKE SCHOOL, it is strange that no one seems to think it at all necessary to say a single word about another new school of poetry which has of late sprung up amongst us. This school has not, I believe, as yet received any name; but if I may be permitted to have the honour of christening it, it may henceforth be referred to by the designation of THE COCKNEY SCHOOL. Its chief Doctor and Professor is Mr Leigh Hunt, a man certainly of some talents, of extravagant pretensions both in wit, poetry, and politics, and withal of exquisitely bad taste, and extremely vulgar modes of thinking and manners in all respects. He is a man of little education. He knows absolutely nothing of Greek, almost nothing of Latin, and his knowledge of Italian literature is confined to a few of the most popular of Petrarch's sonnets, and an imperfect acquaintance with Ariosto, through the medium of Mr Hoole. As to the French poets, he dismisses them in the mass as a set of prim, precise, unnatural pretenders. The truth is, he is in a state of happy ignorance about them and all that they have done. He has never read Zaïre nor Phèdre. To those great German poets who have illuminated the last fifty years with a splendour to which this country has, for a long time, seen nothing comparable, Mr Hunt is an absolute stranger. Of Spanish books he has read Don Quixote (in the translation of Motteux), and some poems of Lope de Vega in the imitations of my Lord Holland. Of all the great critical writers, either of ancient or of modern times, he is utterly ignorant, excepting only Mr Jeffrey among ourselves.

With this stock of knowledge, Mr Hunt presumes to become the founder of a new school of poetry, and throws away entirely the chance which he might have had of gaining some true poetical fame, had he been less lofty in his pretensions. The story of Rimini is not wholly undeserving of praise. It possesses some tolerable passages, which are all quoted in the Edinburgh Reviewer's account of the poem, and not one of which is quoted in the very illiberal attack upon it in the Quarterly. But such is the wretched taste in which the greater part of the work is executed, that most certainly no man who reads it once will ever be able to prevail upon himself to read it again. One feels the same disgust at the idea of opening Rimini, that impresses itself on the mind of a man of fashion, when he is invited to enter, for a second time, the gilded drawing-room of a little mincing boarding-school mistress, who would fain have an *At Home* in her house. Every thing is pretence, affectation, finery, and gaudiness. The beaux are attorneys' apprentices, with chapeau bras and Limerick gloves—fiddlers, harp-teachers, and clerks of genius: the belles are faded fan-twinkling spinsters, prurient vulgar misses from school, and enormous citizens' wives. The company are entertained with lukewarm negus, and the sounds of a paltry piano-forte.

All the great poets of our country have been men of some rank in society, and there is no vulgarity in any of their writings; but Mr Hunt cannot utter a dedication, or even a note, without betraying the *Shibboleth* of low birth and low habits. He is the ideal of a Cockney Poet. He raves perpetually about "green fields," "jaunty streams," and "o'er-arching leafiness," exactly as a Cheapside shop-keeper does about the beauties of his box on the Camberwell road. Mr Hunt is altogether unacquainted with the face of nature in her magnificent scenes; he has never seen any mountain higher than Highgate-hill, nor reclined by any stream more pastoral than the Serpentine River. But he is determined to be a poet eminently rural, and he rings the changes—till one is sick of him, on the beauties of the different "high views" which he has taken of God and nature, in the course of some Sunday dinner parties, at which he has assisted in the neighbourhood of London. His books are indeed not known in the country; his fame as a poet (and I might almost say, as a politician too,) is entirely confined to the young attorneys and embryo-barristers about town. In the opinion of these competent judges, London is the world—and Hunt is a Homer.

Mr Hunt is not disqualified by his ignorance and vulgarity alone, for being the founder of a respectable sect in poetry. He labours under the burden of a sin more deadly than either of these. The two great elements of all dignified poetry, religious feeling, and patriotic feeling, have no place in his writings. His religion is a poor tame dilution of the blasphemies of the *Encyclopædie*—his patriotism a crude, vague, ineffectual, and sour Jacobinism. His works exhibit no reverence either for God or man; neither altar nor throne have any dignity in his eyes. He speaks well of nobody but two or three great dead poets, and in so speaking of them he does well; but, alas! Mr Hunt is no conjurer, τεχνη ου λανθανει.[1] He pretends, indeed, to be an admirer of Spenser and Chaucer, but what he praises in them is never what is most deserving of praise—it is only that which he humbly conceives bears some resemblance to the more perfect productions of Mr Leigh Hunt; and we can always discover, in the midst of his most violent ravings about the Court of Elizabeth, and the days of Sir Philip Sidney, and the Fairy Queen—that the real objects of his admiration are the Coterie of Hampstead and the Editor of the Examiner. When he talks about chivalry and King Arthur, he is always thinking of himself, and "*a small party of friends, who meet once a-week at a Round Table, to discuss the merits of a leg of mutton, and of the subjects upon which we are to write.*"—Mr Leigh Hunt's ideas concerning the sublime, and concerning his own powers, bear a considerable resemblance to those of his friend Bottom, the weaver, on the same subjects; "I will roar, that it shall do any man's heart good to hear me."—"I will roar you an 'twere any nightingale."

The poetry of Mr Hunt is such as might be expected from the personal character and habits of its author. As a vulgar man is perpetually labouring to be genteel—in like manner, the poetry of this man is always on the stretch to be grand. He has been allowed to look for a moment from the antichamber into the saloon, and mistaken the waving of feathers and the painted floor for the *sine qua non's* of elegant society. He would fain be always tripping and waltzing, and is sorry that he cannot be allowed to walk about in the morning with yellow breeches and flesh-coloured silk-stockings. He sticks an artificial rosebud into his button hole in the midst of winter. He wears no neckcloth, and cuts his hair in imitation of the Prints of Petrarch. In his verses he is always desirous of being airy, graceful, easy, courtly, and ITALIAN. If he had the smallest acquaintance with the great demi-gods of Italian poetry, he could never fancy that the style in which he writes,

---

[1] τεχνη . . . λανθανει: You can see his tricks; literally, "his technique does not escape notice."

bears any, even the most remote, resemblance to the severe and simple manner of Dante—the tender stillness of the lover of Laura—or the sprightly and good-natured unconscious elegance of the inimitable Ariosto. He has gone into a strange delusion about himself, and is just as absurd in supposing that he resembles the Italian Poets, as a greater Quack still (Mr Coleridge) is, in imagining that he is a Philosopher after the manner of Kant or Mendelssohn—and that "the eye of Lessing bears a remarkable likeness to MINE," i.e. the eye of Mr Samuel Coleridge.*

The extreme moral depravity of the Cockney School is another thing which is for ever thrusting itself upon the public attention, and convincing every man of sense who looks into their productions, that they who sport such sentiments can never be great poets. How could any man of high original genius ever stoop publicly, at the present day, to dip his fingers in the least of those glittering and rancid obscenities which float on the surface of Mr Hunt's Hippocrene? His poetry resembles that of a man who has kept company with kept-mistresses. His muse talks indelicately like a tea-sipping milliner girl. Some excuse for her there might have been, had she been hurried away by imagination or passion; but with her, indecency seems a disease, she appears to speak unclean things from perfect inanition. Surely they who are connected with Mr Hunt by the tender relations of society, have good reason to complain that his muse should have been so prostituted. In Rimini a deadly wound is aimed at the dearest confidences of domestic bliss. The author has voluntarily chosen—a subject not of simple seduction alone—one in which his mind seems absolutely to gloat over all the details of adultery and incest.

The unhealthy and jaundiced medium through which the Founder of the Cockney School views every thing like moral truth, is apparent, not only from his obscenity, but also from his want of respect for all that numerous class of plain upright men, and unpretending women, in which the real worth and excellence of human society consists. Every man is, according to Mr Hunt, a dull potato-eating blockhead—of no greater value to God or man than any ox or dray-horse—who is not an admirer of Voltaire's *romans*, a worshipper of Lord Holland and Mr Haydon, and a quoter of John Buncle and Chaucer's Flower and Leaf. Every woman is useful only as a breeding machine,

unless she is fond of reading Launcelot of the Lake, in an antique summer-house.

How such an indelicate writer as Mr Hunt can pretend to be an admirer of Mr Wordsworth, is to us a thing altogether inexplicable. One great charm of Wordsworth's noble compositions consists in the dignified purity of thought, and the patriarchal simplicity of feeling, with which they are throughout penetrated and imbued. We can conceive a vicious man admiring with distant awe the spectacle of virtue and purity; but if he does so sincerely, he must also do so with the profoundest feeling of the error of his own ways, and the resolution to amend them. His admiration must be humble and silent, not pert and loquacious. Mr Hunt praises the purity of Wordsworth as if he himself were pure, his dignity as if he also were dignified. He is always like the ball of Dung in the fable, pleasing himself, and amusing bye-standers with his "nos poma natamus."[3] For the person who writes *Rimini*, to admire the Excursion, is just as impossible as it would be for a Chinese polisher of cherry-stones, or a gilder of tea-cups, to burst into tears at the sight of the Theseus or the Torso.

The Founder of the Cockney School would fain claim poetical kindred with Lord Byron and Thomas Moore. Such a connexion would be as unsuitable for them as for William Wordsworth. The days of Mr Moore's follies are long since over; and, as he is a thorough gentleman, he must necessarily entertain the greatest contempt for such an under-bred person as Mr Leigh Hunt. But Lord Byron! How must the haughty spirit of Lara and Harold contemn the subaltern sneaking of our modern tuft-hunter. The insult which he offered to Lord Byron in the dedication of Rimini,—in which he, a paltry cockney newspaper scribbler, had the assurance to address one of the most nobly-born of English Patricians, and one of the first geniuses whom the world ever produced, as "My dear Byron," although it may have been forgotten and despised by the illustrious person whom it most nearly concerned,—excited a feeling of utter loathing and disgust in the public mind, which will always be remembered whenever the name of Leigh Hunt is mentioned. We dare say Mr Hunt has some fine dreams about the true nobility being the nobility of talent, and flatters himself, that with those who

---

* Mr. Wordsworth (meaning, we presume, to pay Mr. Coleridge a compliment,) makes him look very absurdly.

'A noticeable man, with *large grey eyes*.'[2]

[2] Quoting Wordsworth's "Stanzas Written in my Pocket-Copy of Thomson's Castle of Indolence" (1815), l. 39.

[3] In his collection *Contemporary Reviews of Romantic Poetry* (1953), John Wain refers to the account of the fable in Swift's verses "On the Words—Brother Protestants, and Fellow Christians" (1733), in which an inundation of farm land washes down in one flood "Things of heterogeneous Kind." The passage in Swift concludes: "A Ball of new-dropt Horse's Dung, / Mingling with Apples in the Throng, / Said to the Pippin, plump, and prim, / See, Brother, how we Apples swim [*nos poma natamus*]."

acknowledge only that sort of rank, he himself passes for being the *peer* of Byron. He is sadly mistaken. He is as completely a Plebeian in his mind as he is in his rank and station in society. To that highest and unalienable nobility which the great Roman satirist styles "sola atque unica,"[4] we fear his pretensions would be equally unavailing.

The shallow and impotent pretensions, tenets, and attempts, of this man,—and the success with which his influence seems to be extending itself among a pretty numerous, though certainly a very paltry and pitiful, set of readers,—have for the last two or three years been considered by us with the most sickening aversion. The very culpable manner in which his chief poem was reviewed in the Edinburgh Review (we believe it is no secret, at his own impatient and feverish request, by his partner in the Round Table), was matter of concern to more readers than ourselves. The masterly pen which inflicted such signal chastisement on the early licentiousness of Moore, should not have been idle on that occasion. Mr Jeffrey does ill, when he delegates his important functions into such hands as those of Mr Hazlitt. It was chiefly in consequence of that gentleman's allowing Leigh Hunt to pass unpunished through the scene of slaughter, which his execution might so highly have graced, that we came to the resolution of laying before our readers a series of essays on the *Cockney School*—of which here terminates the first.   Z.

[October 1817]

CROKER'S REVIEW OF KEATS'S ENDYMION

John Wilson Croker (1780–1857), born in Ireland, was trained as a lawyer and had a long and quite distinguished career as a Tory politician both in parliament and as first Secretary to the Admiralty. In addition to his many contributions on literary and historical subjects to the Quarterly Review, *Croker's literary career included an edition of Boswell's* Life of Johnson *(1831), which, in turn, was unfairly but vigorously pilloried by Macaulay. For biographical details, see Myron Franklin Brightfield,* John Wilson Croker *(Berkeley, Calif.: University of California Press, 1940).*

J. W. Croker

REVIEW OF KEATS'S *ENDYMION*, IN THE *QUARTERLY REVIEW*

Reviewers have been sometimes accused of not reading the works which they affected to criticise. On the present occasion we shall anticipate the author's complaint, and honestly confess that we have not read his work. Not that we have been wanting in our duty—far from it—indeed, we have made efforts almost as superhuman as the story itself appears to be, to get through it; but with the fullest stretch of our perseverance, we are forced to confess that we have not been able to struggle beyond the first of the four books of which this Poetic Romance consists. We should extremely lament this want of energy, or whatever it may be, on our parts, were it not for one consolation—namely, that we are no better acquainted with the meaning of the book through which we have so painfully toiled, than we are with that of the three which we have not looked into.

It is not that Mr. Keats, (if that be his real name, for we almost doubt that any man in his senses would put his real name to such a rhapsody,) it is not, we say, that the author has not powers of language, rays of fancy, and gleams of genius—he has all these; but he is unhappily a disciple of the new school of what has been somewhere called Cockney poetry; which may be defined to consist of the most incongruous ideas in the most uncouth language.

Of this school, Mr. Leigh Hunt, as we observed in a former Number, aspires to be the hierophant. Our readers will recollect the pleasant recipes for harmonious and sublime poetry which he gave us in his preface to 'Rimini,' and the still more facetious instances of his harmony and sublimity in the verses themselves; and they will recollect above all the contempt of Pope, Johnson, and such like poetasters and pseudo-critics, which so forcibly contrasted itself with Mr. Leigh Hunt's self-complacent approbation of

> ——'all the things itself had wrote,
> Of special merit though of little note.'

This author is a copyist of Mr. Hunt; but he is more unintelligible, almost as rugged, twice as diffuse, and ten times more tiresome and absurd than his prototype, who, though he impudently presumed to seat himself in the chair of criticism, and to measure his own poetry by his own standard, yet generally had a meaning. But Mr. Keats had advanced no dogmas which he was bound to support by examples; his nonsense therefore is quite gratuitous; he writes it for its own sake, and, being bitten by Mr. Leigh Hunt's insane criticism, more than rivals the insanity of his poetry.

Mr. Keats's preface hints that his poem was produced under peculiar circumstances.

'Knowing within myself (he says) the manner in which this Poem has been produced, it is not without a feeling of regret that I make it public.—What manner I mean, will be *quite clear* to the reader, who must soon perceive great

---

[4] *sola atque unica*: "alone and only." Juvenal's Eighth Satire, l. 20. The full Latin sentence translates: "Virtue alone is the only true nobility."

inexperience, immaturity, and every error denoting a feverish attempt, rather than a deed accomplished.'—*Preface*, p. vii.

We humbly beg his pardon, but this does not appear to us to be *quite so clear*—we really do not know what he means—but the next passage is more intelligible.

'The two first books, and indeed the two last, I feel sensible are not of such completion as to warrant their passing the press.'—*Preface*, p. vii.

Thus 'the two first books' are, even in his own judgment, unfit to appear, and 'the last two' are, it seems, in the same condition—and as two and two make four, and as that is the whole number of books, we have a clear and, we believe, a very just estimate of the entire work.

Mr. Keats, however, deprecates criticism on this 'immature and feverish work' in terms which are themselves sufficiently feverish; and we confess that we should have abstained from inflicting upon him any of the tortures of the '*fierce hell*' of criticism, which terrify his imagination, if he had not begged to be spared in order that he might write more; if we had not observed in him a certain degree of talent which deserves to be put in the right way, or which, at least, ought to be warned of the wrong; and, if finally, he had not told us that he is of an age and temper which imperiously require mental discipline.

Of the story we have been able to make out but little; it seems to be mythological, and probably relates to the loves of Diana and Endymion; but of this, as the scope of the work has altogether escaped us, we cannot speak with any degree of certainty; and must therefore content ourselves with giving some instances of its diction and versification:—and here again we are perplexed and puzzled.—At first it appeared to us, that Mr. Keats had been amusing himself and wearying his readers with an immeasurable game at *bouts rimés;*[1] but, if we recollect rightly, it is an indispensable condition at this play, that the rhymes when filled up shall have a meaning; and our author, as we have already hinted, has no meaning. He seems to us to write a line at random, and then he follows not the thought excited by this line, but that suggested by the *rhyme* with which it concludes. There is hardly a complete couplet inclosing a complete idea in the whole book. He wanders from one subject to another, from the association, not of ideas but of sounds, and the work is composed of hemistichs which, it is quite evident, have forced themselves upon the author by the mere force of the catchwords on which they turn.

We shall select, not as the most striking instance,

[1] *bouts rimés*: verses composed to given rhymes.

but as that least liable to suspicion, a passage from the opening of the poem.

⸻'Such the sun, the moon,
Trees old and young, sprouting a shady boon
For simple sheep; and such are daffodils
With the green world they live in; and clear rills
That for themselves a cooling covert make
'Gainst the hot season; the mid forest brake,
Rich with a sprinkling of fair musk-rose blooms:
And such too is the grandeur of the dooms
We have imagined for the mighty dead; &c. &c.'—
pp. 3, 4.

Here it is clear that the word, and not the idea, *moon* produces the simple sheep and their shady *boon*, and that 'the *dooms* of the mighty dead' would never have intruded themselves but for the '*fair musk-rose blooms.*'

Again.

'For 'twas the morn: Apollo's upward fire
Made every eastern cloud a silvery pyre
Of brightness so unsullied, that therein
A melancholy spirit well might win
Oblivion, and melt out his essence fine
Into the winds: rain-scented eglantine
Gave temperate sweets to that well-wooing sun;
The lark was lost in him; cold springs had run
To warm their chilliest bubbles in the grass;
Man's voice was on the mountains; and the mass
Of nature's lives and wonders puls'd tenfold,
To feel this sun-rise and its glories old.'—p. 8.

Here Apollo's *fire* produces a *pyre*, a silvery pyre of clouds *wherein* a spirit might *win* oblivion and melt his essence *fine*, and scented *eglantine* gives sweets to the *sun*, and cold springs had *run* into the *grass*, and then the pulse of the *mass* pulsed *tenfold* to feel the glories *old* of the new-born day, &c.

One example more.

'Be still the unimaginable lodge
For solitary thinkings; such as dodge
Conception to the very bourne of heaven,
Then leave the naked brain: be still the leaven,
That spreading in this dull and clodded earth
Gives it a touch ethereal—a new birth.'—p. 17.

Lodge, doge—heaven, leaven—earth, birth; such, in six words, is the sum and substance of six lines.

We come now to the author's taste in versification. He cannot indeed write a sentence, but perhaps he may be able to spin a line. Let us see. The following are specimens of his prosodial notions of our English heroic metre.

'Dear as the temple's self, so does the moon,
The passion poesy, glories infinite.'—p. 4.

'So plenteously all weed-hidden roots.'—p. 6.

'Of some strange history, potent to send.'—p. 18.

'Before the deep intoxication.'—p. 27.

'Her scarf into a fluttering pavilion.'—p. 33.

'The stubborn canvass for my voyage prepared——.'
                                                    [—p. 39.
'"Endymion! the cave is secreter
Than the isle of Delos. Echo hence shall stir
No sighs but sigh-warm kisses, or light noise
Of thy combing hand, the while it travelling cloys
And trembles through my labyrinthine hair."'—p. 48.

By this time our readers must be pretty well satisfied as to the meaning of his sentences and the structure of his lines: we now present them with some of the new words with which, in imitation of Mr. Leigh Hunt, he adorns our language.

We are told that 'turtles *passion* their voices,' (p. 15); that 'an arbour was *nested*,' (p. 23); and a lady's locks '*gordian*'d up,' (p. 32); and to supply the place of the nouns thus verbalized Mr. Keats, with great fecundity, spawns new ones; such as 'men-slugs and human *serpentry*,' (p. 41); the '*honey-feel* of bliss,' (p. 45); 'wives prepare *needments*,' (p. 13)—and so forth.

Then he has formed new verbs by the process of cutting off their natural tails, the adverbs, and affixing them to their foreheads; thus, 'the wine out-sparkled,' (p. 10); the 'multitude up-followed,' (p. 11); and 'night up-took,' (p. 29). 'The wind up-blows,' (p. 32); and the 'hours are down-sunken,' (p. 36).

But if he sinks some adverbs in the verbs he compensates the language with adverbs and adjectives which he separates from the parent stock. Thus, a lady 'whispers *pantingly* and close,' makes '*hushing* signs,' and steers her skiff into a '*ripply* cove,' (p. 23); a shower falls '*refreshfully*,' (p. 45); and a vulture has a '*spreaded* tail,' (p. 44.)

But enough of Mr. Leigh Hunt and his simple neophyte.—If any one should be bold enough to purchase this 'Poetic Romance,' and so much more patient, than ourselves, as to get beyond the first book, and so much more fortunate as to find a meaning, we entreat him to make us acquainted with his success; we shall then return to the task which we now abandon in despair, and endeavour to make all due amends to Mr. Keats and to our readers.

[April 1818]

WILSON'S REVIEW OF BYRON'S
CHILDE HAROLD'S PILGRIMAGE, CANTO IV

John Wilson (1785–1854), who wrote under the pseudonym "Christopher North," was one of the editors of Blackwood's Magazine *and was responsible (with Lockhart) for most of its* literary reviews in its early years. Friend of Wordsworth, Coleridge, and De Quincey, Wilson was the author of several volumes of verse, and in 1820 became professor of moral philosophy at Edinburgh University. As a literary reviewer in Blackwood's, Wilson has become a by-word for critical capriciousness, praising and damning the successive publications of an author with equal irresponsibility. However, his review of Childe Harold's Pilgrimage, Canto IV, in the Edinburgh Review is a model of the essay-review of the early nineteenth century; it is an intelligent assessment, not only of the characteristics of Byron's genius, but of the literary temper of the age.*

John Wilson

FROM

REVIEW OF BYRON'S
CHILDE HAROLD'S PILGRIMAGE,
CANTO IV,
IN THE *EDINBURGH REVIEW*

THERE are two writers, in modern literature, whose extraordinary power over the minds of men, it may be truly said, has existed less in their works than in themselves,—Rousseau and Lord Byron. They have other points of resemblance. Both are distinguished by the most ardent and vivid delineations of intense conception, and by an intense sensibility of passion, rather than of affection. Both, too, by this double power, have held a dominion over the sympathy of their readers, far beyond the range of those ordinary feelings which are usually excited by the mere efforts of genius. The impression of this interest still accompanies the perusal of their writings. But there is another interest of more lasting, and far stronger power, which the one has possessed, and the other now possesses,—which lies in the continual embodying of the individual character,—it might almost be said, of the very person of the writer. When we speak or think of Rousseau or Byron, we are not conscious of speaking or thinking of an author. We have a vague but empassioned remembrance of men of surpassing genius, eloquence and power,—of prodigious capacity both of misery and happiness. We feel as if we had transiently met such beings in real life, or had known them in the dim and dark communion of a dream. Each of their works presents, in succession, a fresh idea of themselves; and, while the productions of other great men stand out from them, like something they have created, theirs, on the contrary, are images, pictures, busts of their living selves,—clothed, no doubt, at different times in different drapery, and prominent from a different background,—but uniformly impressed with the same form, and mien, and lineaments, and not to be mistaken for the representations of any other of the children of men.

But this view of the subject, though universally felt to be a true one, requires perhaps a little explanation. The personal character of which we have spoken, it should be understood, is not, altogether, that on which the seal of life has been set,—and to which, therefore, moral approval or condemnation is necessarily annexed, as to the language or conduct of actual existence. It is the character, so to speak, which is prior to conduct, and yet open to good and to ill,—the constitution of the being, in body and in soul. Each of those illustrious writers has, in this light, filled his works with expressions of his own character,—has unveiled to the world the secrets of his own being,—the mysteries of the framing of man. They have gone down into those depths which every man may sound for himself, though not for another; and they have made disclosures to the world of what they beheld and knew there—disclosures that have commanded and enforced a profound and universal sympathy, by proving that all mankind, the troubled and the untroubled, the lofty and the low, the strongest and the frailest, are linked together by the bonds of a common but inscrutable nature.

Thus, each of these wayward and richly-gifted spirits has made himself the object of profound interest to the world,—and that too, during periods of society when ample food was everywhere spread abroad for the meditations and passions of men. What love and desire,—what longing and passionate expectation hung upon the voice of Rousseau, the idol of his day!—That spell is broken. We now can regard his works in themselves, in great measure free from all the delusions and illusions that, like the glories of a bright and vapoury atmosphere, were for ever rising up and encircling the image of their wonderful creator. Still is the impression of his works vivid and strong. The charm which cannot pass away is there,—life breathing in dead words,—the pulses of passion,—the thrilling of the frame,—the sweet pleasure stealing from senses touched with ecstasy into sounds which the tongue frames, and the lips utter with delight. All these still are there,—the fresh beauty, the undimmed lustre—the immortal bloom and verdure and fragrance of life. These, light and vision-like as they seem, endure as in marble. But that which made the spirits of men, from one end of Europe to the other, turn to the name of Rousseau,—that idolizing enthusiasm which we can now hardly conceive, was the illusion of one generation, and has not survived to another. And what was the spell of that illusion? Was it merely that bewitching strain of dreaming melancholy which lent to moral declamation the tenderness of romance? Or that fiery impress of burning sensibility which threw over abstract and subtle disquisitions all the colours of a

lover's tale? These undoubtedly—but not these alone. It was that continual impersonation of himself in his writings, by which he was for ever kept brightly present before the eyes of men. There was in him a strange and unsated desire of depicturing himself, throughout all the changes of his being. His wild temper only found ease in tracing out, in laying bare to the universal gaze, the very groundwork, the most secret paths, the darkest coverts of one of the most wayward and unimaginable minds ever framed by nature. From the moment that his first literary success had wedded him to the public, this was his history,—and such his strange, contradictory, divided life. Shy, and shunning the faces of men in his daily walks, yet searching and rending up the inmost recesses of his heart for the inspection of that race which he feared or hated. As a man, turning from the light, as from something unsupportably loathsome, and plunging into the thickest shades. Yet, in that other existence which he held from imagination, living only in the presence of men,—in the full broad glare of the world's eye,—and eagerly, impetuously, passionately, unsparingly seizing on all his own most hidden thoughts—his loneliest moods—his most sacred feelings—which had been cherished for the seclusion in which they sprung—for their own still deep peace—and for their breathings of unbeheld communions,—seizing upon all these, and flinging them out into the open air, that they might feed the curiosity of that eager, idle, frivolous world from which he had fled in misanthropical disgust—that he might array an exhibition to their greedy gaze, —and that he, the morbid and melancholy lover of solitude, might act a conspicuous and applauded part on the crowded theatre of public fame.

It might, on a hasty consideration, seem to us, that such undisguised revelation of feelings and passions, which the becoming pride of human nature, jealous of its own dignity, would, in general, desire to hold in unviolated silence, could produce in the public mind only pity, sorrow, or repugnance. But, in the case of men of real genius, like Rousseau or Byron, it is otherwise. Each of us must have been aware in himself of a singular illusion, by which these disclosures, when read with that tender or high interest which attaches to poetry, seem to have something of the nature of private and confidential communications. They are not felt, while we read, as declarations published to the world, —but almost as secrets whispered to chosen ears. Who is there that feels, for a moment, that the voice which reaches the inmost recesses of his heart is speaking to the careless multitudes around him? Or, if we do so remember, the words seem to pass by others like air, and to find their way to the hearts for whom they were intended,—kindred and sympathizing spirits, who discern and own that secret language, of which the privacy is not violated, though spoken in hearing of the uninitiated,—because it is not understood. There is an unobservcd beauty that smiles on us alone; and the more beautiful to us, because we feel as if chosen out from a crowd of lovers. Something analogous to this is felt in the grandest scenes of Nature and of Art. Let a hundred persons look from a hilltop over some transcendent landscape. Each will select from the widespread glory at his feet, for his more special love and delight, some different glimpse of sunshine,—or solemn grove,—or embowered spire,—or brown-mouldering ruin,—or castellated cloud. During their contemplation, the soul of each man is amidst its own creations, and in the heart of his own solitude;—nor is the depth of that solitude broken, though it lies open to the sunshine, and before the eyes of unnumbered spectators. It is the same in great and impressive scenes of art,—for example, in a theatre. The tenderest tones of acted tragedy reach our hearts with a feeling as if that inmost soul which they disclose revealed itself to us alone. The audience of a theater forms a sublime unity to the actor; but each person sees and feels with the same incommunicated intensity, as if all passed only before his own gifted sight. The publicity which is before our eyes is not acknowledged by our minds; and each heart feels itself to be the sole agitated witness of the pageant of misery.

But there are other reasons why we read with complacency writings which, by the most public declaration of most secret feelings, ought, it might seem, to shock and revolt our sympathy. A great poet may address the whole world in the language of intensest passion, concerning objects of which, rather than speak, face to face, with any one human being on earth, he would perish in his misery. For it is in solitude that he utters what is to be wafted by all the winds of heaven. There are, during his inspiration, present with him only the shadows of men. He is not daunted, or perplexed, or disturbed, or repelled by real living breathing features. He can updraw just as much as he chuses of the curtain that hangs between his own solitude and the world of life. He thus pours his soul out, partly to himself alone,—partly to the ideal abstractions, and impersonated images that float round him at his own conjuration,—and partly to human beings like himself, moving in the dark distance of the every-day world. He confesses himself, not before men, but before the Spirit of Humanity. And he thus fearlessly lays open his heart,—assured that nature never prompted unto genius that which will not triumphantly force its wide way into the human heart. We can thus easily imagine the poet whom, in real life, the countenances and voices of his fellowmen

might silence into shame, or fastidiousness, or timidity, or aversion or disdain,—yet kindling in his solitude into irrepressible passion and enthusiasm towards human nature and all its transitory concerns,—anxiously moulding himself into the object of men's most engrossing and vehement love or aversion,—identifying his own existence with all their strongest and profoundest passions,—claiming kindred with them, not in their virtues alone, but in their darkest vices and most fatal errors;—yet, in the midst of all this, proudly guarding his own prevailing character, so that it shall not merge in the waves of a common nature, but stand 'in shape and gesture proudly eminent,' contemplated with still-increasing interest by the millions that, in spite of themselves, feel and acknowledge its strange and unaccountable ascendency.

The reasons then are obvious, why a writer of very vivid sensibilities may, by impassioned self-delineation, hold a wondrous power over the entranced minds of his readers. But this power is in his living hands; and, like the wand of the magician, it loses its virtue on its master's death. We feel chiefly the influence of such a writer, while he lives—our cotemporary—going with us a fellow-voyager on the stream of life, and from time to time flashing towards us the emanations of his spirit. Our love—our expectation follow the courses of his mind, and, if his life repel us not, the courses of his life. It was the strange madness of Rousseau to pour the blaze of his reputation over the scandals of his life. But this was later in his career; and his name for a long time in Europe was that of an hermit-sage,—a martyr of liberty and virtue,—a persecuted good man loving a race unworthy of him, and suffering alike from their injustice and from the excess of his own spirit. He made a character for himself;—and whatever he had made it, it might have been believed. It was an assumed ideal impersonation of a character of literary and philosophical romance. At last, indeed, he broke up his own spell. But if he could have left the delusion behind him, he could not have left the power;—for the power hangs round the living man: it does not rest upon the grave.

When death removes such a writer from our sight, the magical influence of which we have spoken gradually fades away; and a new generation, free from all personal feelings towards the idol of a former age, may perhaps be wearied with that perpetual self-reference which to them seems merely the querulousness or the folly of unhappy or diseased egoism. It is even probable, that they may perversely withhold a portion of just admiration and delight from him who was once the undisputed sovereign of the soul, and that they may show their surprise at the subjection of their predecessors beneath the tyrannical despotism of genius, by scorning themselves to bow before its power, or acknowledge its legitimacy. It is at least certain, that by the darkness of death such luminaries, if not eclipsed, are shorn of their beams. So much, even in their works of most general interest, derives its beauty and fascination from a vivid feeling, in the reader's mind, of its being a portraiture of one with whom he has formed a kind of strange, wild and disturbed friendship, that they who come after, and have never felt the sorcery of the living man, instead of being kindled up by such pictures into impassioned wonder and delight, may gaze on them with no stronger emotion than curiosity, and even turn from them with indifference. Such must be more or less the fate of all works of genius, however splendid and powerful, of which the chief interest is not in universal truth, so much as in the intensity of individual feeling, and the impersonation of individual character.

It would, indeed, be in most violent contradiction to all we have formerly written of Lord Byron, were we to say that he stands in this predicament. Yet, there is a certain applicability of our observations even to him, as well as to Rousseau, with whom, perhaps too fancifully, we have now associated his nature and his name. Posterity may make fewer allowances for much in himself and his writings, than his contemporaries are willing to do; nor will they, with the same passionate and impetuous zeal, follow the wild voice that too often leads into a haunted wilderness of doubt and darkness. To them, as to us, there will always be something majestic in his misery—something sublime in his despair. But they will not, like us, be withheld from sterner and severer feelings, and from the more frequent visitings of moral condemnation, by that awful commiseration and sympathy which a great poet breathes at will into all hearts, from his living agonies,—nor, by that restless, and watchful, and longing anxiety, to see again and again the princely sufferer rising up with fresh confessions of a still more magnificent sorrow,—nor, by that succession of affecting appeals to the frailties and troubles of our own hearts, which now keeps him vividly, and brightly, in our remembrance, wherever his soul, tempest-like, may have driven him over earth and sea,—nor, above all, by the cheering and lofty hope now felt by them who wish to see genius the inseparable companion of virtue,—that he whose inspiration holds us always in wonder, and so often in delight, may come ere long to breathe a serener atmosphere of thought,—and, after all his wanderings, and all his woes,—with subsided passions, and invigorated intellect, calmly rest at last in the collected majesty of his power.

We are not now writing a formal critique on the genius of Byron, but rather expressing our notions of the relation in which he stands with the lovers of poetry. There is felt to be between him and the public mind, a stronger personal bond than ever linked its movements to any other living poet. And we think that this bond will in future be still more closely rivetted. During the composition of the first cantos of Childe Harold, he had but a confused idea of the character he wished to delineate,—nor did he perhaps very distinctly comprehend the scope and tendencies of his own genius. Two conceptions, distinct from each other, seem therein to be often blended,—one, of ideal human beings, made up of certain troubled powers and passions,—and one, of himself ranging the world of Nature and Man in wonder and delight and agitation, in his capacity of a poet. These conceptions, which frequently jostled and interfered with each other, he has since more distinctly unfolded in separate poems. His troubled imaginary beings,—possessing much of himself, and far more not of himself, he has made into Giaours, Conrads, Laras and Alps,—and his conception of himself has been expanded into Childe Harold, as we now behold him on that splendid pilgrimage. It is not enough to say that the veil is at last thrown off. It is a nobler creature who is before us. The ill-sustained misanthropy, and disdain of the two first Cantos, more faintly glimmer throughout the third, and may be said to disappear wholly from the fourth, which reflects the high and disturbed visions of earthly glory, as a dark swollen tide images the splendours of the sky in portentous colouring, and broken magnificence.

We have admitted, that much of himself is depicted in all his heroes; but when we seem to see the poet shadowed out in all those states of disordered being which such heroes exhibit, we are far from believing that his own mind has gone through those states of disorder, in its own experience of life. We merely conceive of it as having felt within itself the capacity of such disorders, and therefore exhibiting itself before us in possibility. This is not general—it is rare with great poets. Neither Homer, nor Shakspeare, nor Milton, ever so show themselves in the characters which they portray. Their poetical personages have no reference to themselves; but are distinct, independent creatures of their minds, produced in the full freedom of intellectual power. In Byron, there does not seem this freedom of power. There is little appropriation of character to events. Character is first, and all in all. It is dictated—compelled by some force in his own mind necessitating him,—and the events obey. These poems, therefore, with all their beauty and vigour, are not, like Scott's poems, full and complete narrations of some one definite story, containing within itself a picture of human life. They are merely bold, confused, and turbulent exemplifications of certain sweeping energies and irresistible passions. They are fragments of a poet's dark dream of life. The very personages, vividly as they are pictured, are yet felt to be fictitious; and derive their chief power over us from their supposed mysterious connexion with the poet himself, and, it may be added, with each other. The law of his mind is, to embody his own peculiar feelings in the forms of other men. In all his heroes we accordingly recognise—though with infinite modifications, the same great characteristics,—a high and audacious conception of the power of the mind,—an intense sensibility of passion,—an almost boundless capacity of tumultuous emotion,—a haunting admiration of the grandeur of disordered power,—and, above all, a soul-felt, blood-felt delight in beauty,—a beauty which, in his wild creations, is often scared away from the agitated surface of life by stormier passions, but which, like a bird of calm, is for ever returning, on its soft, silvery wings, before the black swell has finally subsided into sunshine and peace.

It seems to us, that this exquisite sense of beauty has of late become still more exquisite in the soul of Byron. Parasina, the most finished of all his poems, is full of it to overflowing;—it breathes from every page of the Prisoner of Chillon;—but it is in Manfred that it riots and revels among the streams and waterfalls, and groves, and mountains, and heavens. Irrelevant and ill-managed as many parts are of that grand drama, there is in the character of Manfred more of the self-might of Byron than in all his previous productions. He has therein brought, with wonderful power, metaphysical conceptions into forms,—and we know of no poem in which the aspect of external nature is throughout lighted up with an expression at once so beautiful, solemn and majestic. It is the poem, next to Childe Harold, which we should give to a foreigner to read, that he might know something of Byron. Shakspeare has given to those abstractions of human life and being, which are truth in the intellect, forms as full, clear, glowing as the idealized forms of visible nature. The very words of Ariel picture to us his beautiful being. In Manfred, we see glorious but immature manifestations of similar power. The poet there creates, with delight, thoughts and feelings and fancies into visible forms, that he may cling and cleave to them, and clasp them in his passion. The beautiful Witch of the Alps seems exhaled from the luminous spray of the Cataract, —as if the poet's eyes, unsated with the beauty of inanimate nature, gave spectral apparitions of loveliness to feed the pure passion of the poet's soul.

We speak of Manfred now, because it seems to us to hold a middle place between the Tales of Byron, and Childe Harold, as far as regards the Poet himself. But

we likewise do so, that we may have an opportunity of saying a few words on the moral of this poem, and a few words on a subject that may scarcely seem to fall under the legitimate province of the critic, but which, in the case of this great writer, forms so profoundly-interesting a part of his poetical character—we mean, his scepticism.

The moral character of Byron's poetry has often been assailed, and we have ourselves admitted that some strong objections might be urged against it. But we think that his mind is now clearing up, like noon-day, after a stormy and disturbed morning;— and when the change which we anticipate has been fully brought about, the moral character of his poetry will be lofty and pure. Over this fine drama, a moral feeling hangs like a sombrous thunder cloud. No other guilt but that so darkly shadowed out could have furnished so dreadful an illustration of the hideous aberrations of human nature, however noble and majestic, when left a prey to its desires, its passions and its imagination. The beauty, at one time so innocently adored, is at last soiled, profaned and violated. Affection, love, guilt, horror, remorse and death come in terrible succession, yet all darkly linked together. We think of Astartè as young, beautiful, innocent—guilty—lost—murdered—buried— judged—pardoned; but still, in her permitted visit to earth, speaking in a voice of sorrow, and with a countenance yet pale with mortal trouble. We had but a glimpse of her in her beauty and innocence; but, at last, she rises up before us in all the mortal silence of a ghost, with fixed, glazed and passionless eyes, revealing death, judgement and eternity. The moral breathes and burns in every word,—in sadness, misery, insanity, desolation and death. The work is 'instinct with spirit,'—and in the agony and distraction, and all its dimly imagined causes, we behold, though broken up, confused and shattered, the elements of a purer existence.

On the other point, namely, the dark and sceptical spirit prevalent through the works of this poet, we shall not now utter all that we feel, but rather direct the notice of our readers to it as a singular phenomenon in the poetry of the age. Whoever has studied the spirit of Greek and Roman literature, must have been struck with the comparative disregard and indifference wherewith the thinking men of these exquisitely polished nations contemplated those subjects of darkness and mystery which afford, at some period or other of his life, so much disquiet—we had almost said so much agony to the mind of every reflecting modern. It is difficult to account for this in any very satisfactory, and we suspect altogether impossible to do so in any strictly logical manner. In reading the works of Plato and his interpreter Cicero, we find the germs of all the doubts and anxieties to which we have alluded, so far as these are connected with the workings of our reason. The singularity is, that those clouds of darkness, which hang over the intellect, do not appear, so far as we can perceive, to have thrown at any time any very alarming shade upon the feelings or temper of the ancient sceptic. We should think a very great deal of this was owing to the brilliancy and activity of his southern fancy. The lighter spirits of antiquity, like the more mercurial of our moderns, sought refuge in mere *gaieté du cœur* and derision. The graver poets and philosophers—and poetry and philosophy were in those days seldom disunited—built up some airy and beautiful system of mysticism, each following his own devices, and suiting the erection to his own peculiarities of hope and inclination; and this being once accomplished, the mind appears to have felt quite satisfied with what it had done, and to have reposed amidst the splendours of its sand-built fantastic edifice, with as much security as if it had been grooved and rivetted into the rock of ages. The mere exercise of ingenuity in devising a system, furnished consolation to its creators or improvers. Lucretius is a striking example of all this; and it may be averred that, down to the time of Claudian, who lived in the 4th century of our era, in no classical writer of antiquity do there occur any traces of what moderns understand by the restlessness and discomfort of uncertainty as to the government of the world, and the future destinies of Man.

There are three only even among the great poets of modern times, who have chosen to depict, in their full shape and vigour, those agonies to which great and meditative intellects are, in the present progress of human history, exposed by the eternal recurrence of a deep and discontented scepticism. But there is only one who has dared to represent himself as the victim of these nameless and undefinable sufferings. Goëthe chose for his doubts and his darkness the terrible disguise of the mysterious Faustus. Schiller, with still greater boldness, planted the same anguish in the restless, haughty and heroic bosom of Wallenstein. But Byron has sought no external symbol in which to embody the inquietudes of his soul. He takes the world and all that it inherit for his arena and his spectators; and his displays himself before their gaze, wrestling unceasingly and ineffectually with the demon that torments him. At times there is something mournful and depressing in his scepticism; but oftener, it is of a high and solemn character, approaching to the very verge of a confiding faith. Whatever the poet may believe, we his readers always feel ourselves too much ennobled and elevated even by his melancholy, not to

be confirmed in our own belief by the very doubts so majestically conceived and uttered. His scepticism, if it ever approaches to a creed, carries with it its refutation in its grandeur. Their is neither philosophy nor religion in those bitter and savage taunts which have been cruelly thrown out, from many quarters, against those moods of mind which are involuntary, and will not pass away;—the shadows and spectres which still haunt his imagination, may once have disturbed our own;—through his gloom there are frequent flashes of illumination;—and the sublime sadness which, to him, is breathed from the mysteries of mortal existence, is always joined with a longing after immortality, and expressed in language that is itself divine.

But it is our duty now to give our readers an analysis of the concluding Canto of Childe Harold; and as it is, in our opinion, the finest of them all, our extracts shall be abundant. The poem which it brings to an end is perhaps the most original in the language, both in conception and execution. It is no more like Beattie's Minstrel than Paradise Lost—though the former production was in the Noble author's mind when first thinking of Childe Harold. A great poet, who gives himself up, free and unconfined, to the impulses of his genius, as Byron has done in the better part of this singular creation, shows to us a spirit as it is sent out from the hands of Nature, to range over the earth and the societies of men. Even Shakspeare himself submits to the shackles of history and society. But here Byron traverses the whole earth, borne along by the whirlwind of his own spirit. Wherever a forest frowns, or a temple glitters—there he is privileged to bend his flight. He may suddenly start up from his solitary dream by the secret fountain of the desert, and descend at once into the tumult of peopled, or the silence of desolated cities. Whatever lives now—has perished heretofore—or may exist hereafter—and that has within it a power to kindle passion, may become the material of his all-embracing song. There are no unities of time or place to fetter him,—and we fly with him from hilltop to hilltop, and from tower to tower, over all the solitude of nature, and all the magnificence of art. When the past pageants of history seem too dim and faded, he can turn to the splendid spectacles that have dignified our own days; and the images of kings and conquerors of old may give place to those yet living in sovereignty or exile. Indeed, much of the power which Harold holds over us is derived from this source. He lives in a sort of sympathy with the public mind—sometimes wholly distinct from it—sometimes acting in opposition to it—sometimes blending with it,—but, at all times,—in all his thoughts and actions having a reference to the public mind. His spirit need not go back into the past,—though it often does so,—to bring the objects of its love back to earth in more beautiful life. The existence he paints is—now. The objects he presents are marked out to him by men's present regards. It is his to speak of all those great political events which have been objects of such passionate sympathy to the nation. And when he does speak of them, he either gives us back our own feelings, raised into powerful poetry, or he endeavours to displace them from our breasts, and to substitute others of his own. In either case, it is a living speaker standing up before us, and ruling our minds. But chiefly he speaks our own feelings, exalted in thought, language, and passion. The whole substance and basis of his poem is, therefore, popular. All the scenes through which he has travelled, were, at the very moment, of strong interest to the public mind, and that interest still hangs over them. His travels were not, at first, the self-impelled act of a mind severing itself in lonely roaming from all participation with the society to which it belonged, but rather obeying the general motion of the mind of that society. The southern regions of Europe have been like a world opening upon us with fresh and novel beauty, and our souls have enjoyed themselves there, of late years, with a sort of romantic pleasure. This fanciful and romantic feeling was common to those who went to see those countries, and to those who remained at home to hear the narrations of the adventurers,—so that all the Italian, Grecian, Peninsular, Ionian and Ottoman feeling which pervades Childe Harold, singularly suited as it is to the genius of Byron, was not first brought upon the English mind by the power of that genius, but was there already in great force and activity.

There can be no limits set to the interest that attaches to a great poet thus going forth, like a spirit, from the heart of a powerful and impassioned people, to range among the objects and events to them most pregnant with passion,—who is, as it were, the representative of our most exalted intellect,—and who often seems to disclose within ourselves that splendour with which he invests our own ordinary conceptions. The consciousness that he is so considered by a great people, must give a kingly power and confidence to a poet. He feels himself entitled, and, as it were, elected to survey the phenomena of the times, and to report upon them in poetry. He is the speculator of the passing might and greatness of his own generation. But though he speaks to the public, at all times, he does not consider them as his judges. He looks upon them as sentient existences that are important to his poetical existence,—but, so that he command their feelings and passions, he cares not for their censure or their praise,—for his fame is more than mere literary fame;

and he aims in poetry, like the fallen chief whose image is so often before him, at universal dominion, we had almost said, universal tyranny, over the minds of men.

*　　*　　*　　*　　*

The Pilgrimage of Childe Harold has now been brought to its close; and of his character there remains nothing more to be laid open to our view. It is impossible to reflect on the years which have elapsed since this mysterious stranger was first introduced to our acquaintance, without feeling that our own spirits have undergone in that time many mighty changes—sorrowful in some it may be, in others happy changes. Neither can we be surprised, knowing as we well do who Childe Harold is, that he also has been changed. He represented himself, from the beginning, as a ruin; and when we first gazed upon him, we saw indeed in abundance the black traces of recent violence and convulsion. The edifice has not been rebuilt; but its hues have been sobered by the passing wings of time, and the calm slow ivy has had leisure to wreathe the soft green of its melancholy among the fragments of the decay. In so far, the Pilgrim has become wiser. He seems to think more of others, and with a greater spirit of humanity. There was something tremendous, and almost fiendish, in the air with which he surveyed the first scenes of his wanderings; and no proof of the strength of genius was ever exhibited so strong and unquestionable, as the sudden and entire possession of the minds of Englishmen by such a being as he then appeared to be. He looked upon a bull-fight, and a field of battle, with no variety of emotion. Brutes and men were, in his eyes, the same blind, stupid victims of the savage lust of power. He seemed to shut his eyes to every thing of that citizenship and patriotism which ennobles the spirit of the soldier, and to delight in scattering the dust and ashes of his derision over all the most sacred resting-places of the soul of man.

Even then, we must allow, the original spirit of the Englishman and the poet broke triumphantly, at times, through the chilling mist in which it had been spontaneously enveloped. In Greece, above all, the contemplation of Athens, Salamis, Marathon, Thermopylæ and Platæa, subdued the prejudices of him who had gazed unmoved upon the recent glories of Trafalgar and Talavera. The nobility of manhood appeared to delight this moody visitant; and he accorded, without reluctance, to the shades of long-departed heroes that reverent homage, which, in the strange mixture of envy and scorn wherewith the contemplative so often regard active men, he had refused to the living, or to the newly dead.

At all times, however, the sympathy and respect of Childe Harold—when these have been excited by any circumstances external to himself—have been given almost exclusively to the intellectual, and refused to the moral greatness of his species. There is certainly less of this in his last Canto. Yet we think that the ruins of Rome might have excited within him not a few glorious recollections, quite apart from those vague lamentations and worshippings of imperial power, which occupy so great a part of the conclusion of his Pilgrimage. The stern purity and simplicity of domestic manners—the devotion of male and female bosoms—the very names of Lucretia, Valeria, and the mother of the Gracchi, have a charm about them at least as enduring as any others, and a thousand times more delightful than all the iron memories of conquerors and consuls.—But the mind must have something to admire—some breathing-place of veneration—some idol, whether of demon or of divinity, before which it is its pride to bow. Byron has chosen too often to be the undoubting adorer of Power. The idea of tyrannic and unquestioned sway seems to be the secret delight of his spirit. He would pretend, indeed, to be a republican,—but his heroes are all stamped with the leaden signet of despotism; and we sometimes see the most cold, secluded, immitigable tyrant of the whole, lurking beneath the 'scallop-shell and sandal-shoon' of the Pilgrim himself.

In every mien and gesture of this dark being, we discover the traces of one that has known the delights, and sympathized with the possessors of intellectual power; but too seldom any vestiges of a mind that delights in the luxuries of quiet virtue, or that could repose itself in the serenity of home. The very possession of purity would sometimes almost seem to degrade, in his eyes, the intellectual greatness with which it has been sometimes allied. He speaks of Pompey with less reverence than Cæsar; and, in spite of many passing visitings of anger and scorn, it is easy to see that, of all contemporary beings, there is ONE[1] only with whom he is willing to acknowledge mental sympathy—one only whom he looks upon with real reverence—one only whose fortunes touch the inmost sanctuaries of his proud soul—and that this one is no other than that powerful, unintelligible, unrivalled spirit, who, had he possessed either private virtue or public moderation, might still have been in a situation to despise the offerings of even such a worshipper as Harold.

But there would be no end of descanting on the character of the Pilgrim, nor of the moral reflections which it awakens. Of the Poet himself, the completion of this wonderful performance inspires us with lofty

---

[1] Napoleon.

and magnificent hopes. It is most assuredly in his power to build up a work that shall endure among the most august fabrics of the genius of England. Indeed, the impression which the collective poetry of our own age makes upon our minds is, that it contains great promise of the future; and that, splendid as many of its achievements have been, some of our living poets seem destined still higher to exalt the imaginative character of their countrymen. When we look back and compare the languid, faint, cold delineations of the very justest and finest subjects of inspiration, in the poetry of the first half of the last century, with the warm, life-flushed and life-breathing pictures of our own, we feel that a great accession has been made to the literature of our day,—an accession not only of delight, but of power. We cannot resist the persuasion, that if literature, in any great degree, impresses and nourishes the character of a people,—then this literature of ours, pregnant as it is with living impressions,—gathered from Nature in all her varieties of awfulness and beauty,—gathered too from those high and dread Passions of men, which our ordinary life scarcely shows, and indeed could scarcely bear, but which, nevertheless, have belonged, and do belong, to our human life,—and held up in the powerful representations of the poets to our consciousness at times, when the deadening pressure of the days that are going by might bereave us of all genial hope and all dignified pride,—we say it is impossible for us to resist the belief that such pregnant, glowing, powerful poetry, must carry influences into the heart of this generation, even like those which are breathed from the heart of Nature herself,—or like those which lofty passions leave behind them in bosoms which they have once possessed. The same spirit of poetical passion which so uniformly marks the works of all our living poets, must exist very widely among those who do not aspire to the name of genius; it must be very widely diffused throughout the age, and, as we think, must very materially influence the reality of life. Yet highly as we estimate the merits of our modern poetry, it is certain, that the age has not yet produced any one great epic or tragic performance. Vivid and just delineations of passion there are in abundance,—but of moments of passions—fragments of representation. The giant grasp of thought, which conceives, and brings into full and perfect life, full and perfect passion—passion pervading alike action and character, through a majestic series of events, and at the same time cast in the mould of grand imagination, —this seems not to be of our age. In the delineation of external nature, which, in a poet's soul, requires rather moral beauty than intellectual strength, this age has excelled. But it has produced no poem gloriously illustrative of the agencies, existences, and events, of the complex life of man. It has no Lear—no Macbeth—no Othello. Some such glory as this Byron may yet live to bring over his own generation. His being has in it all the elements of the highest poetry. And that being he enjoys in all the strength of its prime. We might almost say, that he needs but to exercise his will to construct a great poem. There is, however, much for him to alter in what may be called, his Theory of Imagination respecting Human Life. Some idols of his own setting-up he has himself overthrown. There are yet some others, partly of gold, and partly of clay, which should be dashed against the floor of the sanctuary. We have already spoken of his personal character, as it shines forth in his poetry. This personal character exists in the nature of his imagination, and may therefore be modified—purified—dignified by his own will. His imagination does, to his own eyes, invest him with an unreal character. Purposes, passions, loves, deeds, events, may seem great and paramount in imagination, which have yet no power to constrain to action; and those which perhaps may govern our actions, vanish altogether from our imagination. There is a region—a world—a sphere of being in imagination, which, to our real life, is no more than the world of a dream; yet, long as we are held in it by the transport of our delusion, we live, not in delight only, but in the conscious exaltation of our nature. It is in this world that the spirit of Byron must work a reformation for itself. He knows, far better than we can tell him, what have been the most hallowed objects of love and of passion to the souls of great poets in the most splendid eras of poetry,—and he also knows well, that those objects, if worshipped by him with becoming and steadfast reverence, will repay the worship which they receive, by the more fervent and divine inspiration which they kindle.

[June 1818]

Eaton Stannard Barrett[1]
and
William Gifford

FROM

REVIEW OF HAZLITT'S
LECTURES ON THE ENGLISH POETS,
IN THE *QUARTERLY REVIEW*

MR. HAZLITT seems to have bound himself, in imitation of Hannibal, to wage everlasting war, not,

[1] Eaton Stannard Barrett (1786–1820), was a minor poet and political satirist.

indeed, against Rome, but against accurate reasoning, just observation, and precise or even intelligible language. We have traced him in his two former predatory incursions on taste and common sense. He has now taken the field a third time, and with a more hostile aspect than ever. Had he written on any other subject, we should scarcely have thought of watching his movements. But though his book is dull, his theme is pleasing, and interests in spite of the author. As we read we forget Mr. Hazlitt, to think of those concerning whom he writes. In fact, few works of poetical criticism are so deplorably bad, as not to be perused with some degree of pleasure. The remarks may be trite, or paradoxical, or unintelligible; they may be expressed in a vague and inanimate style: but the mind is occasionally awakened and relieved by the recurrence of extracts, in which the powers of taste and genius are displayed.

This is the case with Mr. Hazlitt's book. We are not aware that it contains a single just observation, which has not been expressed by other writers more briefly, more perspicuously, and more elegantly. The passages which he has quoted are, with one or two exceptions, familiar to all who have the slightest acquaintance with English literature. His remarks on particular quotations are often injudicious; his general reasonings, for the most part, unintelligible. Indeed he seems to think that meaning is a superfluous quality in writing, and that the task of composition is merely an exercise in varying the arrangement of words. In the lately invented optical toy we have a few bits of coloured glass, the images of which are made to present themselves in an endless variety of forms. Mr. Hazlitt's mind appears to be furnished in a similar manner, and to act in a similar way; for its most vigorous operations are limited to throwing a number of pretty picturesque phrases into senseless and fantastic combinations.

Mr. Hazlitt's work may be regarded as consisting of two parts; first, of general reasonings on poetry, under which we include his remarks on the characters of particular poets; secondly, of minute remarks upon the passages which he has quoted. The greater part of the volume belongs to the first of these classes; for though many fine extracts are given, little pains have been employed to bring their latent beauties into view. Looking upon such a task as too humble for his genius, Mr. Hazlitt prefers appearing chiefly in the character of a philosophical reasoner. In this choice he is unfortunate; for his mode of thinking, or rather of using words, is most singularly unphilosophical. Some vague half-formed notion seems to be floating before his mind; instead of seizing the notion itself, he lays hold of a metaphor, or of an idea connected with it by slight associations: this he expresses; but after he has expressed it, he finds that he has not conveyed his meaning; another metaphor is therefore thrown out, the same course is trodden over and over again, and half a dozen combinations of phrases are used in vague endeavours to express what ought to have been said directly and concisely in one. The mischief, thus originating in indistinctness of conception, is increased by the ambition of the writer. Mr. Hazlitt wishes to dazzle: but with no new matter to communicate, without an imagination capable of lending new force to old observations, and without skill to array them in appropriate language, he can only succeed (as Harlequin does with children) by surprizing us with the rapid succession of antic forms in which the same, or nearly the same thought is exhibited. He is ever hovering on the limits between sense and nonsense, and he trusts to the dimness of the twilight which reigns in that region, for concealing the defects of his arguments and increasing the power of his imagery. There is no subject on which it is of more importance that those terms only should be used whose meaning is well fixed, than in treating of the emotions and operations of the mind; but Mr. Hazlitt indulges himself in a rambling inaccuracy of expression, which would not be tolerated even in inquiries, where there was little hazard of error from the vague use of words.

Next to want of precision, the most striking peculiarity of his style is the odd expressions with which it is diversified, from popular poets, especially from Shakspeare. If a trifling thing is to be told, he will not mention it in common language: he must give it, if possible, in words which the bard of Avon has somewhere used. Were the beauty of the applications conspicuous, we might forget, or at least forgive, the deformity produced by the constant stitching in of these patches; unfortunately, however, the phrases thus obtruded upon us seem to be selected, not on account of any intrinsic beauty, but merely because they are fantastic and unlike what would naturally occur to an ordinary writer.

The most important of Mr. Hazlitt's general reasonings are contained in the first lecture. As a specimen of the work we shall extract the commencement, which bears evident marks of elaborate composition, and in which the intellect of the writer, fresh and unfatigued, may be expected to put forth its utmost vigour. He sets out with a definition of poetry.

'The best general notion,' he says, 'which I can give of poetry, is that it is the natural impression of any object or circumstance, by its vividness exciting an involuntary movement of imagination and passion, and producing, by sympathy, a certain modulation of the voice, or sounds, expressing it.'

This is not a definition of poetry—it neither is nor can be a definition of any thing, because it is completely unintelligible. The impression, of which Mr. Hazlitt talks, is an impression producing by sympathy a certain modulation of sounds. The term sympathy has two significations. In a physiological sense it is used to denote the fact, that the disorder of one organ produces disorder in the functions of certain other parts of the system. Does Mr. Hazlitt mean, that the impression produces the modulation of sound essential to poetry, in a mode analogous to that in which diseases of the brain affect the digestive powers? Sympathy, again, in its application to the moral part of our constitution, denotes that law of our nature by which we share in the feelings that agitate the bosoms of our fellow creatures. This signification obviously will not suit Mr. Hazlitt's purpose. His meaning therefore must be left to himself to divine. One thing is clear, that the modulation of verse is the result of great labour, consummate art, and long practice; and that his words, therefore, can admit no interpretation, conformable to truth, till sympathy becomes synonymous with skill and labour.

The passage which immediately follows the definition, and is devoted to the illustration of it, can scarcely be equalled, in the whole compass of English prose, for rapid transitions from idea to idea, while not one gleam of light is thrown upon the subject; for the accumulation of incoherent motions; and for the extravagance of the sentiments, or rather of the combinations of words.

'Poetry is the language of the imagination and the passions. It relates to whatever gives immediate pleasure or pain to the human mind. It comes home to the bosoms and businesses of men; for nothing but what so comes home to them in the most general and intelligible shape can be a subject for poetry. Poetry is the universal language which the heart holds with nature and itself. He who has a contempt for poetry cannot have much respect for himself, or for any thing else. It is not a mere frivolous accomplishment, (as some persons have been led to imagine,) the trifling amusement of a few idle readers or leisure hours— it has been the study and delight of mankind in all ages. Many people suppose that poetry is something to be found only in books, contained in lines of ten syllables, with like endings: but wherever there is a sense of beauty, or power, or harmony, as in the motion of a wave of the sea, in the growth of a flower that "spreads its sweet leaves to the air, and dedicates its beauty to the sun,"—*there* is poetry in its birth. If history is a grave study, poetry may be said to be a graver: its materials lie deeper, and are spread wider. History treats, for the most part, of the cumbrous and unwieldy masses of things, the empty cases in which the affairs of the world are packed, under the heads of intrigue or war, in different states, and from century to century: but there is no thought or feeling that can have entered into the mind of man, which he would be eager to communicate to others, or which they would listen to with delight, that is not a fit subject for poetry. It is not a branch of authorship: it is "the stuff of which our life is made." The rest is "mere oblivion," a dead letter; for all that is worth remembering in life is the poetry of it. Fear is poetry, hope is poetry, love is poetry, hatred is poetry, contempt, jealousy, remorse, admiration, wonder, pity, despair, or madness, are all poetry. Poetry is that fine particle within us, that expands, rarifies, raises our whole being: without it "man's life is poor as beast's." Man is a poetical animal: and those of us who do not study the principles of poetry, act upon them all our lives, like Molière's *Bourgeois Gentilhomme*, who had always spoken prose without knowing it. The child is a poet, in fact, when he first plays at hide-and-seek, or repeats the story of Jack the Giant-killer; the shepherd-boy is a poet when he first crowns his mistress with a garland of flowers; the countryman, when he stops to look at the rainbow; the city-apprentice, when he gazes after the Lord-Mayor's show; the miser, when he hugs his gold; the courtier, who builds his hopes upon a smile; the savage, who paints his idol with blood; the slave, who worships a tyrant, or the tyrant, who fancies himself a god.'—pp. 2—4.

Thus there is nothing which is not poetry, and poetry is every thing. It is a particular kind of language; it is a fine particle which produces certain chemical and mechanical effects; it is the stuff of our lives; it is the important part of business; it is not a thing contained in books; it is fear, hope, jealousy, and twenty other things besides; in short it is the characteristical quality of our nature, for man is a poetical animal, and there is nobody who is not a poet; the miser, the slave, the tyrant, the child playing at hide and seek, the city apprentice—all, in Mr. Hazlitt's eye, are poets. The means, by which he arrives at these extravagant propositions, are sufficiently simple and common: the misapplication of words is the whole of his art. He employs the term poetry in three distinct meanings, and his legerdemain consists in substituting one of these for the other. Sometimes it is the general appellation of a certain class of compositions, as when he says that poetry is graver than history. Secondly, it denotes the talent by which these compositions are produced; and it is in this sense that he calls poetry that fine particle within us, which produces in our being rarefaction, expansion, elevation, and purification. Thirdly, it denotes the subjects of which these compositions treat. It is in this meaning that he uses the term, when he says, that all that is worth remembering in life is the poetry of it; that fear is poetry, that hope is poetry, that love is poetry; and in the very same sense he might assert that fear is sculpture and painting and music, that the crimes of Verres are the eloquence of Cicero, and the poetry of Milton the criticism of Mr. Hazlitt. When he tells us, that though we have never studied the principles of poetry, we have acted upon them all our lives, like the man who talked

prose without knowing it, we suspect that the commonplace allusion at the end of the sentence has tempted him into nonsense at the beginning. The principles of poetry a reader would naturally imagine to be the chief rules of the art; but by that phrase Mr. Hazlitt means the principal subjects of which poetry treats. These are the passions and affections of mankind; we are all under the influence of our passions and affections; that is, in Mr. Hazlitt's new language, we all act on the principles of poetry, and are, in truth, poets. We all exert our muscles and limbs, therefore we are anatomists and surgeons; we have teeth which we employ in chewing, therefore we are dentists; we use our eyes to look at objects, therefore we are oculists; we eat beef and mutton, therefore we are all deeply versed in the sciences of breeding and fattening sheep and oxen. Mr. Hazlitt will forgive us for anticipating these brilliant conclusions, which he no doubt intends to promulgate in a course of lectures at some future day; we claim no merit for announcing them; the praise, we admit, is exclusively his own, for they are merely legitimate inferences from his peculiar mode of abusing English.

As another specimen of his definitions we may take the following. 'Poetry does not define the limits of sense, or analyse the distinctions of the understanding, but signifies the excess of the imagination beyond the actual or ordinary impression of any object or feeling.' Poetry was at the beginning of the book asserted to be an impression; it is now the excess of the imagination beyond an impression: what this excess is we cannot tell, but at least it must be something very unlike an impression. Though the total want of meaning is the weightiest objection to such writing; yet the abuse which it involves of particular words is very remarkable, and will not be overlooked by those who are aware of the inseparable connection between justness of thought and precision of language. What, in strict reasoning, can be meant by the impression of a feeling? How can *actual* and *ordinary* be used as synonymous? Every impression must be an actual impression; and the use of that epithet annihilates the limitations, with which Mr. Hazlitt meant to guard his proposition. In another part of his work he asserts, that 'words are the *voluntary* signs of certain ideas.' By *voluntary* we suppose he means that there is no natural connection between the sign and the thing signified, though this is an acceptation which the term never bore before. In a passage already quoted, he says that 'wherever there is a sense of beauty, or power, or harmony, as in the motion of a wave of the sea, or in the growth of a flower, there is poetry in its birth.' Can the motion of a wave, or the growth of a flower have any sense of beauty, or power, or harmony; or can either form a convenient cradle for newly born poetry? If he meant to place the beauty, and not the sense of beauty, in the wave and the flower, he ought to have expressed himself very differently.

One of the secrets of Mr. Hazlitt's composition is to introduce as many words as possible, which he has at any time seen or heard used in connection with that term which makes, for the moment, the principal figure before his imagination. Is he speaking, for instance, of the heavenly bodies—He recollects that the phrase *square of the distance* often recurs in astronomy, and that in Dr. Chalmers's Discourses a great deal is said about the sun and stars. Dr. Chalmers's Discourses, and the square of the distance, must, therefore, be impressed into his service, without caring whether they are or are not likely to be of the least use. 'There can never be another Jacob's dream. Since that time the heavens have gone farther off and grown astronomical. They have become averse to the imagination; nor will they return to us on the squares of the distances, or in Dr. Chalmers's Discourses.' We really have not a variety of language adequate to do justice to the variety of shapes, in which unmeaning jargon is perpetually coming upon us in this performance. We can therefore only say, what we have said of so many other passages, that we have not the faintest conception of what is meant by *the heavenly bodies returning on the squares of the distances, or in Dr. Chalmers's Discourses.* As to the assertion that there can never be another Jacob's dream, we see no reason why dreams should be scientific; particularly as Mr. Hazlitt's work is a convincing proof, that even the waking thoughts of some men are safe from the encroachments of reason and philosophy.

The passages, which we have quoted hitherto, are all taken from the Lecture on Poetry. But Mr. Hazlitt is a metaphysician; and in his criticisms upon individual poets, loves to soar into general remarks. Thus he tells us, that when a person walks from Oxford Street to Temple Bar, 'every man he meets is a blow to his personal identity.' Much puzzling matter has been written concerning personal identity, but nothing that surpasses this. 'There is nothing more likely to drive a man mad, than the being unable to get rid of the idea of the distinction between right and wrong, and an obstinate constitutional preference of the true to the agreeable.' The loss of all idea of the distinction between right and wrong is the very essence of madness, and not to prefer the true to the agreeable, where they are inconsistent, is folly. Mr. Hazlitt's doctrine therefore is, that the inability to become mad is very likely to drive a man mad.

Mr. Hazlitt is fond of running parallels between great poets; and his parallels have only two faults—the

first, that it is generally impossible to comprehend them—the second, that they are in no degree characteristical of the poets to whom they are applied. 'In Homer the principle of action or life is predominant; in the Bible, the principle of faith and the idea of providence; Dante is a personification of blind will; and in Ossian we see the decay of life, and the lag end of the world.'

The following extract is still more exquisite. 'Chaucer excels as the poet of manners or of real life; Spenser as the poet of romance; Shakspeare as the poet of nature (in the largest use of the term); and Milton, as the poet of morality. Chaucer most frequently describes things as they are; Spenser as we wish them to be; Shakspeare as they would be; and Milton as they ought to be. The characteristic of Chaucer is intensity; of Spenser, remoteness; of Milton, elevation; of Shakspeare, everything.' The whole passage is characteristical of nothing but Mr. Hazlitt.

We occasionally discover a faint semblance of connected thinking in Mr. Hazlitt's pages; but wherever this is the case, his reasoning is for the most part incorrect. He maintains, for instance, that poetical enthusiasm has sustained a check from the progress of experimental philosophy:—a doctrine which may be regarded as a sprout from a principle very popular among certain critics, that the progress of science is unfavourable to the culture of the imagination. It is no doubt true, that the individual who devotes his labour to the investigation of abstract truth, must acquire habits of thought very different from those which the exercise of fancy demands: the cause lies *in the exclusive appropriation of his time to reasoning, and not in the logical accuracy with which he reasons.* But while science is making rapid progress in the hands of some, the arts which depend upon the imagination may be cultivated with equal success by others, whose efforts will be aided, rather than impeded, by the general diffusion of new and valuable truths. We have parted with the systems of Ptolemy and Des Cartes to adopt that of Newton; the dreams of the Alchemists are superseded by the chemistry of Black, of Cavendish, of Lavoisier, of Davy; the subtle disquisitions of the schoolmen have given way to the speculations of Locke and Reid. We do not conceive that poetry has suffered any loss by the change, nor would she be a gainer by the total extirpation of science. Among every people, who are in a state approaching to civilization, systems of doctrines upon certain subjects must exist: they who devote their lives to the study of these systems will not be poets; but they will not be the less likely to be so, because the systems which they study have been erected cautiously on a firm foundation. The progress of true science is favourable to poetical genius in two ways: it supplies an abundant store of new materials for the poet to work upon; and there is a sublimity in its views, far superior to any thing that the framers of fanciful hypotheses can invent, which exalts the genius and trains it to lofty contemplations.

*   *   *   *   *

Upon the whole, the greater part of Mr. Hazlitt's book is either completely unintelligible, or exhibits only faint and dubious glimpses of meaning; and the little portion of it that may be understood is not of so much value, as to excite regret on account of the vacancy of thought which pervades the rest. One advantage of this style of writing is, that Mr. Hazlitt's lectures will always be new to his hearers, whether delivered at the Surrey Institution or elsewhere. They may have been read or they may have been heard before; but they are of that happy texture that leaves not a trace in the mind of either reader or hearer. Connected thought may be retained, but no effort of recollection has any power over an incoherent jumble of gaudy words.

[July 1818]

REVIEW OF BYRON'S DON JUAN, CANTOS I–II
The British Critic, *founded in 1793, was "professedly intended to uphold the tenets of the Established Church and the Tory politics of the ruling government" (Thomas Rees, Reminiscences of Literary London, [London, 1896]. pp. 32–33, quoted in Hayden, p. 44). The author of the review of Don Juan, of which the concluding section is here reproduced, is unknown.*

Anonymous

FROM

REVIEW OF BYRON'S DON JUAN, CANTOS I AND II, IN THE BRITISH CRITIC

*   *   *   *   *

UPON the indecency, and the blasphemy which this volume contains, a very few words will suffice. The adventures which it recounts are of such a nature, and described in such language, as to forbid its entrance within the doors of any modest woman, or decent man. Nor is it a history only, but a manual of profligacy. Its tendency is not only to excite the passions, but to point out the readiest means and method of their indulgence. Vice is here represented not merely in that grosser form which carries with it its own shame, and almost its own destruction, but in that alluring and

sentimental shape, which at once captivates and corrupts. If without knowing the name of the poet, or the history of the work, our opinion had been required of the intention of the canto, we should have answered—that it was a calm and deliberate design to palliate and recommend the crime of adultery, to work up the passions of the young to its commission, and to afford them the most practical hints for its consummation. But it is not, we trust, by the maudlin and meretricious cant of the lascivious Little,[1] nor by the doggrel narrations of his friend and admirer, the author of the poem before us, that the British nation is to be tricked out of that main bulwark of its national strength, its sturdy and unbending morality.

Of the blasphemous sneers, so liberally scattered through the present volume, it is our intention to say but little. He that has no regard for the feelings of human misery, or for the claims of public morality, has not (and we should be sorry if he had) the slightest respect for public religion. The assaults of such a man are true Religion's best defence. Nor is it to be wondered, that the man who can so laboriously inculcate the breach of one commandment, should furnish a parody, *a la* Hone,[2] of all the ten. A parody indeed it is, but so miserable and poor, that it is really difficult to say whether the bad principle, or the bad poetry, most predominates. It certainly has not the sin of recommending itself by its wit.

The beauties of this strange production are very few. The best stanzas in the poem are the following: ... [Canto I, cxxii–cxxiv].

The two first stanzas, though the ideas which they contain are common, have yet a sweetness, and an elegance in their expression, that gives them an air even of originality. In the third there is a lamentable falling off; we have seen many a better one upon the same subject, both in the work of Master George Dallas, aged only thirteen, and of other school-boys equally precocious. In the second canto, there are stanzas descriptive of the sinking of the ship, in which the Noble Lord rises out of the circumambient doggrel. ... [stanzas lii–liii].

We do not affect to say that we can construe, or understand every line of the preceding stanzas; but, in justice to the Noble Lord, we would not let any part of the poem which has the appearance even of beauty pass by, without paying it its due respect. We are the more anxious to present to the reader all that is worthy of his approbation, as we trust that the work itself will

---

[1] "Thomas Little" was the pseudonym of the poet Thomas Moore, whose own "voluptuous verse" and translations of Anacreon "established for Moore the reputation of a licentious poet" (Hayden, p. 217).
[2] On William Hone, see above, p. 750, n. 2.

never be read, but in a Review. The good sense, and the good feeling of the English nation must, and will banish it from their houses. We should have the worst opinion indeed of any man, upon whose family table this volume were to lie exposed.

Reports from without, and evidence from within, fix this composition upon Lord Byron. His name indeed is not upon the title-page; but this is not the first time that his Lordship has played off that piece of coquetry with the public. Should however his Lordship be tempted in reality to disavow it, we shall be among the first to hail the disavowal, and to give it the publicity which it deserves, accompanying it with our sincere apology for having in common with the whole English nation, fixed upon his Lordship the stain of so flippant, dull and disgraceful a publication.

[August 1819]

REVIEW OF SHELLEY'S THE CENCI
The Literary Gazette, *founded in 1817, was an important weekly of conservative, Tory persuasion. The author of the review of* The Cenci *is unknown.*

Anonymous

F R O M

REVIEW OF SHELLEY'S *THE CENCI*, IN *THE LITERARY GAZETTE*

OF ALL the abominations which intellectual perversion, and poetical atheism, have produced in our times, this tragedy appears to us to be the most abominable. We have much doubted whether we ought to notice it; but, as watchmen place a light over the common sewer which has been opened in a way dangerous to passengers, so have we concluded it to be our duty to set up a beacon on this noisome and noxious publication. We have heard of Mr. Shelley's genius; and were it exercised upon any subject not utterly revolting to human nature, we might acknowledge it. But there are topics so disgusting ... and this is one of them; there are themes so vile ... as this is; there are descriptions so abhorrent to mankind ... and this drama is full of them; there are crimes so beastly and demoniac ... in which The Cenci riots and luxuriates, that no feelings can be excited by their obtrusion but those of detestation at the choice, and horror at the elaboration. We protest most solemnly, that when we reached the last page of this play, our minds were so impressed with its odious and infernal character, that we could not believe it to be written

by a mortal being for the gratification of his fellow-creatures on this earth: it seemed to be the production of a fiend, and calculated for the entertainment of devils in hell.

That monsters of wickedness have been seen in the world, is too true; but not to speak of the diseased appetite which would delight to revel in their deeds, we will affirm that depravity so damnable as that of Count Cenci, in the minute portraiture of which Mr. S. takes so much pains, and guilt so atrocious as that which he paints in every one of his dramatic personages, never had either individual or aggregate existence. No; the whole design, and every part of it, is a libel upon humanity; the conception of a brain not only distempered, but familiar with infamous images, and accursed contemplations. What adds to the shocking effect is the perpetual use of the sacred name of God, and incessant appeals to the Saviour of the universe. The foul mixture of religion and blasphemy, and the dreadful association of virtuous principles with incest, parricide, and every deadly sin, form a picture which, "To look upon we dare not."

*　　*　　*　　*　　*

It will readily be felt by our readers why we do not multiply our extracts. In truth there are very few passages which will bear transplanting to a page emulous of being read in decent and social life. The lamentable obliquity of the writer's mind pervades every sentiment, and "corruption mining all within," renders his florid tints and imitations of beauty only the more loathsome. Are loveliness and wisdom incompatible? Mr. Shelley makes one say of Beatrice, that

Men wondered how such loveliness and wisdom
Did not destroy each other!

Cenci's imprecation on his daughter, though an imitation of Lear, and one of a multitude of direct plagiarisms, is absolutely too shocking for perusal; and the dying infidelity of that paragon of parricides, is all we dare to venture to lay before the public.

Whatever comes, my heart shall sink no more.
And yet, I know not why, your words strike chill:
How tedious, false and cold seem all things. I
Have met with much injustice in this world;
No difference has been made by God or man,
Or any power moulding my wretched lot,
'Twixt good or evil as regarded me.
I am cut off from the only world I know,
From light, and life, and love, in youth's sweet prime.
You do well telling me to trust in God,
I hope I do trust in him. In whom else
Can any trust? And yet my heart is cold.

We now most gladly take leave of this work; and sincerely hope, that should we continue our literary pursuits for fifty years, we shall never need again to look into one so stamped with pollution, impiousness, and infamy.

[April 1, 1820]

W. S. Walker[1]

FROM

REVIEW OF SHELLEY'S
PROMETHEUS UNBOUND,
WITH OTHER POEMS,
IN THE *QUARTERLY REVIEW*

A GREAT lawyer of the present day is said to boast of practising three different modes of writing: one which any body can read; another which only himself can read; and a third, which neither he nor any body else can read. So Mr. Shelley may plume himself upon writing in three different styles: one which can be generally understood; another which can be understood only by the author; and a third which is absolutely and intrinsically unintelligible. Whatever his command may be of the first and second of these styles, this volume is a most satisfactory testimonial of his proficiency in the last.

If we might venture to express a general opinion of what far surpasses our comprehension, we should compare the poems contained in this volume to the visions of gay colours mingled with darkness, which often in childhood, when we shut our eyes, seem to revolve at an immense distance around us. In Mr. Shelley's poetry all is brilliance, vacuity, and confusion. We are dazzled by the multitude of words which sound as if they denoted something very grand or splendid: fragments of images pass in crowds before us; but when the procession has gone by, and the tumult of it is over, not a trace of it remains upon the memory. The mind, fatigued and perplexed, is mortified by the consciousness that its labour has not been rewarded by the acquisition of a single distinct conception; the ear, too, is dissatisfied: for the rhythm of the verse is often harsh and unmusical; and both the ear and the understanding are disgusted by new and uncouth words, and by the awkward, and intricate construction of the sentences.

‒‒‒‒‒‒‒‒‒‒‒‒‒‒‒‒‒‒‒‒‒‒‒‒‒‒‒‒‒‒‒‒‒‒‒‒

[1] William Sidney Walker (1795–1846) was a classical scholar at Cambridge and a minor poet. After his death, two volumes of his studies of Shakespeare were published.

The predominating characteristic of Mr. Shelley's poetry, however, is its frequent and total want of meaning. Far be it from us to call for strict reasoning, or the precision of logical deductions, in poetry; but we have a right to demand clear, distinct conceptions. The colouring of the pictures may be brighter or more variegated than that of reality; elements may be combined which do not in fact exist in a state of union; but there must be no confusion in the forms presented to us. Upon a question of mere beauty, there may be a difference of taste. That may be deemed energetic or sublime, which is in fact unnatural or bombastic; and yet there may be much difficulty in making the difference sensible to those who do not preserve an habitual and exclusive intimacy with the best models of composition. But the question of meaning, or no meaning, is a matter of fact on which common sense, with common attention, is adequate to decide; and the decision to which we may come will not be impugned, whatever be the want of taste, or insensibility to poetical excellence, which it may please Mr. Shelley, or any of his coterie, to impute to us. We permit them to assume, that they alone possess all sound taste and all genuine feeling of the beauties of nature and art: still they must grant that it belongs only to the judgment to determine, whether certain passages convey any signification or none; and that, if we are in error ourselves, at least we can mislead nobody else, since the very quotations which we must adduce as examples of nonsense, will, if our charge be not well founded, prove the futility of our accusation at the very time that it is made. If, however, we should completely establish this charge, we look upon the question of Mr. Shelley's poetical merits as at an end; for he who has the trick of writing very showy verses without ideas, or without coherent ideas, can contribute to the instruction of none, and can please only those who have learned to read without having ever learned to think.

The want of meaning in Mr. Shelley's poetry takes different shapes. Sometimes it is impossible to attach any signification to his words; sometimes they hover on the verge between meaning and no meaning, so that a meaning may be obscurely conjectured by the reader, though none is expressed by the writer; and sometimes they convey ideas, which, taken separately, are sufficiently clear, but, when connected, are altogether incongruous. We shall begin with a passage which exhibits in some parts the first species of nonsense, and in others the third.

'Lovely apparitions, dim at first,
   Then radiant, as the mind, arising bright
   From the embrace of beauty, whence the forms
   Of which these are the phantoms, casts on them
   The gathered rays which are reality,

Shall visit us, the immortal progeny
Of painting, sculpture, and rapt poesy,
And arts, tho' unimagined, yet to be.'—p. 105. [2]

The verses are very sonorous; and so many fine words are played off upon us, such as, *painting, sculpture, poesy, phantoms, radiance, the embrace of beauty, immortal progeny,* &c. that a careless reader, influenced by his habit of associating such phrases with lofty or agreeable ideas, may possibly have his fancy tickled into a transient feeling of satisfaction. But let any man try to ascertain what is really said, and he will immediately discover the imposition that has been practised. From beauty, or the embrace of beauty, (we know not which, for ambiguity of phrase is a very frequent companion of nonsense,) certain forms proceed: of these forms there are phantoms; these phantoms are dim; but the mind arises from the embrace of beauty, and casts on them the gathered rays which are reality; they are then baptized by the name of the immortal progeny of the arts, and in that character proceed to visit Prometheus. This *galimatias* [3] (for it goes far beyond simple nonsense) is rivalled by the following description of something that is done by a cloud.

'I am the daughter of earth and water,
 And the nursling of the sky;
I pass through the pores of the oceans and shores,
 I change, but I cannot die.
For after the rain, when with never a stain
 The pavilion of heaven is bare,
And the winds and sunbeams with their convex gleams,
 Build up the blue dome of air,
I silently laugh at my own cenotaph,
 And out of the caverns of rain,
Like a child from the womb, like a ghost from the tomb,
 I arise, and unbuild it again.'—pp. 199, 200. [4]

There is a love-sick lady, who 'dwells under the glaucous caverns of ocean,' and '*wears the shadow of Prometheus' soul*,' without which (she declares) she cannot *go to sleep.* The rest of her story is utterly incomprehensible; we therefore pass on to the *debut* of the Spirit of the earth. . . . [5] We have neither leisure nor room to develope all the absurdities here accumulated, in defiance of common sense, and even of grammar; whirlwind harmony, a solid sphere which is as many thousand spheres, and contains ten thousand orbs or spheres, with intertranspicuous spaces between them, whirling over each other on a thousand sightless (alias invisible) axles; self-destroying swiftness; intelligible words and wild music, kindled by the said sphere, which also grinds a bright brook into an azure mist of elemental subtlety; odour, music, and light, kneaded into one aërial mass, and the sense drowned by it!

'Oh quanta species! et cerebrum non habet.' [6]

One of the personages in the Prometheus is Demogorgon. As he is the only agent in the whole drama, and effects the only change of situation and feeling which befals the other personages; and as he is likewise employed to sing or say divers hymns, we have endeavoured to find some intelligible account of him. The following is the most perspicuous which we have been able to discover:—

 '——A mighty power, which is as darkness,
 Is rising out of earth, and from the sky,
 Is showered like night, and from within the air
 Bursts, *like eclipse which had been gathered up
 Into the pores of sun-light.*'—p. 149. [7]

Love, as might be expected, is made to perform a variety of very extraordinary functions. It fills 'the void annihilation of a sceptred curse' (p. 140); and, not to mention the other purposes to which it is applied, it is in the following lines dissolved in air and sun-light, and then folded round the world.

 '——The impalpable thin air,
 And the all circling sun-light were transformed,
 As if the sense of love dissolved in them,
 Had folded itself round the sphered world.'—p. 116. [8]

Metaphors and similes can scarcely be regarded as ornaments of Mr. Shelley's compositions; for his poetry is in general a mere jumble of words and heterogeneous ideas, connected by slight and accidental associations, among which it is impossible to distinguish the principal object from the accessory. In illustrating the incoherency which prevails in his metaphors, as well as in the other ingredients of his verses, we shall take our first example, not from that great storehouse of the obscure and the unintelligible—the Prometheus, but from the opening of a poem, entitled, 'A Vision of the Sea,' which we have often heard praised as a splendid work of imagination.

 '——The rags of the sail
Are flickering in ribbons within the fierce gale:
From the stark night of vapours the dim rain is driven,
And when lightning is loosed, like a deluge from heaven,

---

2 *Prometheus Unbound*, III, iii, 49–56.
3 *galimatias*: gibberish.
4 "The Cloud," ll. 73–84.
5 Act IV, 236–61 here quoted.

---

6 *Oh quanta . . . habet*: "Oh how splendid an outward appearance! but it has no brain." Phaedrus' *Fables*, I, vii, 2.
7 IV, 510–14.
8 III, iv, 100–104.

She sees the black trunks of the water-spouts spin,
And bend, as if heaven was raining in,
Which they seem'd to sustain with their terrible mass
As if ocean had sunk from beneath them: they pass
To their graves in the deep with an earthquake of sound,
And the waves and the thunders made silent around
Leave the wind to its echo.'—p. 174.

At present we say nothing of the cumbrous and uncouth style of these verses, nor do we ask who this 'she' is, who sees the water-spouts; but the funeral of the water-spouts is curious enough: 'They pass to their graves with an earthquake of sound.' The sound of an earthquake is intelligible, and we suspect that this is what Mr. Shelley meant to say: but an earthquake of sound is as difficult to comprehend as a cannon of sound, or a fiddle of sound. The same vision presents us with a battle between a tiger and a sea-snake; of course we have—

'——The whirl and the splash
As of some hideous engine, whose brazen teeth smash
The thin winds and soft waves into thunder; the screams
And hissings crawl fast o'er the smooth ocean streams,
Each sound like a centipede.'—p. 180.[9]

The comparison of sound to a centipede would be no small addition to a cabinet of poetical monstrosities: but it sinks into tame common-place before the engine, whose brazen teeth pound thin winds and soft waves into thunder.

Sometimes Mr. Shelley's love of the unintelligible yields to his preference for the disgusting and the impious. Thus the bodies of the dead sailors are thrown out of the ship:

'And the sharks and the dog-fish their grave-cloths
    unbound,
And were glutted, like Jews, with this manna rained down
From God on their wilderness.'—p. 177.[10]

Asia turns her soul into an enchanted boat, in which she performs a wonderful voyage: . . .[11]

The following comparison of a poet to a cameleon has no more meaning than the jingling of the bells of a fool's cap, and far less music.

'Poets are on this cold earth,
    As camelions might be,
Hidden from their early birth
    In a cave beneath the sea;
Where light is camelions change:
    Where love is not, poets do:
Fame is love disguised; if few
Find either never think it strange
That poets range.'—p. 186.[12]

---

[9] Lines 144–48.   [10] Lines 56–58.
[11] Act II, 73–94 here quoted.
[12] "An Exhortation," ll. 10–18.

Sometimes to the charms of nonsense those of doggrel are added. This is the conclusion of a song of certain beings, who are called 'Spirits of the human mind:'

'And Earth, Air, and Light,
    And the Spirit of Might,
Which drives round the stars in their fiery flight;
    And Love, Thought, and Breath,
    The powers that quell Death,
Wherever we soar shall assemble beneath.
    And our singing shall build
    In the void's loose field
A world for the Spirit of Wisdom to wield;
    We will take our plan
    From the new world of man,
And our work shall be called the Promethean.'
                                    —p. 130.[13]

Another characteristic trait of Mr. Shelley's poetry is, that in his descriptions he never describes the thing directly, but transfers it to the properties of something which he conceives to resemble it by language which is to be taken partly in a metaphorical meaning, and partly in no meaning at all. The whole of a long poem, in three parts, called 'the Sensitive Plant,' the object of which we cannot discover, is an instance of this. The first part is devoted to the description of the plants. The sensitive plant takes the lead:

'No flower ever trembled and panted with bliss,
    In the garden, the field, or the wilderness,
    Like a doe in the noon-tide with love's sweet want,
    As the companionless sensitive plant.'—p. 157.

Next come the snow-drop and the violet:

'And their breath was mixed with fresh odour, sent
    From the turf, *like the voice and the instrument*.'

The rose, too,

'——Unveiled the depth of her glowing breast,
    Till, fold after fold, *to the fainting air
    The soul of her beauty and love lay bare*.'

The hyacinth is described in terms still more quaint and affected:

'The hyacinth, purple, and white, and blue,
    Which flung from *its bells a sweet peal anew*,
    Of music so delicate, soft, and intense,
    It was felt like an odour within the sense.'

It is worth while to observe the train of thought in this stanza. The bells of the flower occur to the poet's mind; but ought not bells to ring a peal? Accordingly,

---

[13] IV, 147–58.

by a metamorphosis of the odour, the bells of the hyacinth are supposed to do so: the fragrance of the flower is first converted into a peal of music, and then the peal of music is in the last line transformed back into an odour. These are the tricks of a mere poetical harlequin, amusing himself with

'The clock-work tintinnabulum of rhyme.'[14]

In short, it is not too much to affirm, that in the whole volume there is not one original image of nature, one simple expression of human feeling, or one new association of the appearances of the moral with those of the material world.

* * * * *

[October 1821]

---

[14] Cowper's "Table Talk," l. 529.

GENERAL BIBLIOGRAPHY

POLITICAL HISTORY OF THE ENGLISH ROMANTIC PERIOD

> "In times like these, every body almost is, one way or another, a politician . . ."—Leigh Hunt, *The Examiner*, September 30, 1810

On the political history of the period, consult the relevant volumes in the *Oxford History of England*, John Steven Watson's *The Reign of George III, 1760–1815* (Oxford: Clarendon Press, 1960) and E. L. Woodward's *The Age of Reform, 1815–1870*, second edition (Oxford: Clarendon Press, 1962); Arthur Bryant's three volumes, *The Years of Endurance, 1793–1802* (London: Collins, 1942), *The Years of Victory, 1802–1812* (London: Collins, 1944), and *The Age of Elegance, 1812–1822* (London: Collins, 1950); Élie Halévy's two volumes as translated by E. I. Watkin and D. A. Barker, *A History of the English People in 1815* (London: T. Fisher Unwin, 1924) and *A History of the English People 1815–1830* (London: T. Fisher Unwin, 1926). Donald Grove Barnes's *George III and William Pitt, 1783–1806* (Stanford, Calif.–London: Stanford University Press and Oxford University Press, 1939) is very detailed on the seminal decade of the 1790's.

Two works are standard on the political ideas of the Romantics: Crane Brinton's *The Political Ideas of the English Romanticists* (London: Oxford University Press, 1926) and Alfred Cobban's *Edmund Burke and the Revolt Against the Eighteenth Century* (London: G. Allen and Unwin, 1929). More specifically on the literary expression of politics are Carl Woodring's two studies, *Politics and the Poetry of Coleridge* (Madison: University of Wisconsin, 1960), and *Politics in English Romantic Poetry* (Cambridge, Mass.: Harvard University Press, 1970); and M. H. Abrams' essay "Romanticism: The Spirit of the Age," in *Romanticism Reconsidered*, edited by Northrup Frye (New York: Columbia University Press, 1963).

ENGLISH ROMANTIC PROSE STYLE

> ". . . the whole structure of Johnsonian English breaking up from its foundations,—revolution *there* as visible as anywhere else!"—Thomas Carlyle, letter to John Sterling, June 4, 1835

A detailed history of prose style and forms of prose expression in the Romantic period has yet to be written.

Illuminating comments can be found in two essays from *The Art of Victorian Prose*, edited by George Levine and William Madden (New York: Oxford University Press, 1968): Travis R. Merritt's "Taste, Opinion, and Theory in the Rise of Victorian Prose Stylism" and G. Robert Stange's "Art Criticism as a Prose Genre." Frederick Burwick's introduction to *Selected Essays on Rhetoric by Thomas De Quincey* (Carbondale, Ill.: Southern Illinois University Press, 1967) is an excellent discussion of De Quincey's stylistic theories, with important ramifications for Romantic prose in general. Readers may also consult George Saintsbury's *A History of English Prose Rhythm* (London: Macmillan and Co., 1912). "The Familiar Essay," a unique form of Romantic prose expression, has been dealt with in two studies: Marie H. Law's *The English Familiar Essay in the Early Nineteenth Century* (Philadelphia, 1934), and Melvin R. Watson's *Magazine Serials and the Essay Tradition 1746–1820*, Louisiana State University Studies. Humanities Series Number Six (Baton Rouge: Louisiana State University Press, 1956).

GENERAL LITERARY HISTORY OF THE ROMANTIC PERIOD

> "Great and rapid as have been the changes in all that constitutes the moral, political, and productive power of England, not one among the varied features of her character has within the same space of time undergone so thorough a revolution as her Literature"—James Silk Buckingham, *The Athenaeum*, 1828

Two volumes in the *Oxford History of English Literature* cover the period: W. L. Renwick's *English Literature 1789–1815* (Oxford: Clarendon Press, 1963) and Ian Jack's *English Literature 1815–1832* (Oxford: Clarendon Press, 1963). Earlier studies include Oliver Elton's *A Survey of English Literature, 1780–1830*, 2 vols. (London: Longmans, 1912) and Samuel C. Chew's *The Nineteenth Century and After (1789–1939)* in *A Literary History of England*, edited by Albert C. Baugh (New York: Appleton-Century-Crofts, 1948) [revision of Chew by Richard D. Altick for second edition, 1967].

Very helpful surveys of scholarship on the English Romantic prose writers can be found in two volumes prepared by the Modern Language Association of

America: *The English Romantic Poets: A Review of Research and Criticism*, edited by Frank Jordan, third edition (New York: Modern Language Association of America, 1972), and *The English Romantic Poets and Essayists*, edited by Carolyn W. Houtchens and Lawrence H. Houtchens, revised edition (New York: New York University Press, 1966). Since 1965, "The Romantic Movement: A Selective and Critical Bibliography" has appeared annually as a supplement to the September issue of *English Language Notes*; it was previously published in *Journal of English Literary History* (1937–49) and *Philological Quarterly* (1950–1964).

INDEX TO TITLES